D0788968

CONCORDANCE TO *POEMA DE MIO CID*

CONCORDANCE TO

POEMA DE MIO CID

Franklin M. Waltman

THE PENNSYLVANIA STATE
UNIVERSITY PRESS

University Park and London

Library of Congress Cataloging in Publication Data
Waltman, Franklin M 1938-
Concordance to Poema de mío Cid.
Originally presented as part of the author's thesis, Pennsylvania State University.
"Based on the paleographic edition of the poem by Menéndez Pidal."
1. El Cid Campeador — Concordances. I. El Cid Campeador. II. Title.
PQ6385.W3 861'.1 71-161582
ISBN 0-271-00557-2

Library of Congress Catalogue Card Number: 71-161582
International Standard Book Number: 0-271-00557-2

Printed in the United States of America

to Pegge, my very dear friend, for seven years of patience and the wonderful gift, Tracy

PREFACE

Polemics concerning the *Poema de mio Cid* have existed for many years, and the best known of these is the question of unity of authorship. This concordance is the result of an attempt to resolve this question. It was used in a dissertation study entitled *Unity of Authorship in the Poema de mio Cid* at The Pennsylvania State University.

Many critics have expressed opinions — some directly, others indirectly — on the problem of authorship in the poem. Basically the problem centers around whether one person is responsible for the composition of the poem, or whether two or more may have been responsible.

E. C. Hills, in 1929, was apparently the first to suggest that there may be more than one author to the *Poema del Cid.*[1] His findings initiated the polemic which has at least been discussed, if only in passing comment, by most *cidófilos* in any lengthy treatise on the poem.

Hills begins the polemic by expressing some common differences in the two parts of the poem. For purposes of division, lines 1–1820 belong to the first half, and lines 1821–3230 to the second. This division was arbitrarily chosen in order to split the poem into two equal parts. The differences he finds are as follows: the first half is sober and historical; the second is fantastic, less serious, and mostly fictitious. The assonances *á, á-a, á-o* predominate in the first half, while the *ó* assonance predominates in the second part.

He also finds that the epithets "Mio Çid don Rodrigo," "Mio Çid Roy Diaz," and "Mio Çid el de Bivar" appear four times more often in part one, while "Campeador" and "Çid Campeador" appear twice as often in the second part. By studying synonyms, Hills finds the following differences:

	Part One	*Part Two*
respuso	5	5
respondio	0	5
compeçar de	7	1
compeçar a	0	3
exir	28	0
salir	17	46
non	52	21
no	27	41

He then goes on to question the locale for the writing of the poem. He feels that the poem may have been written in a monastery, probably San Pedro de Cardeña. But he does not question it further, since Ramón Menéndez Pidal seemed convinced that it was written in the province of Soria (see Menéndez Pidal's three-volume critical edition; I, 73,74). Hills states:

> This opinion [Menéndez Pidal's] is based on the poet's evident acquaintance with the country around Medina . . . and around San Esteban de Gormaz near which the poet places the tragic episode of the "Afrenta de Corpes." It is clear that Menéndez Pidal's theory of *localización* assumes the unity of the poem; that is to say, that it was written by one and the same man. If it is at all likely that the latter half of the poem, roughly speaking, was written by a second poet, the *localización* of the poem would have to be studied anew.[2]

The critic here seems to suggest that part one was written at San Pedro de Cardeña and the second part near Medina. It is precisely this double *localización* which Menéndez Pidal will present himself some thirty years later, as will be seen further on.

Mack Singleton and Oliver T. Meyers have also proposed that there may be more than one author responsible for the poem.[3,4] It is Menéndez Pidal, however, who, in his excellent treatise on this subject,[5] offers the strongest of possibilities for two poets. His article is based on the assumption that there existed two poets, an early one from San Esteban de Gormaz, and a later one from Medinaceli. He says: ". . . que hubo un poeta de San Esteban bastante antiguo, buen conocedor de los tiempos pasados, el cual poetizaba muy cerca de la realidad histórica; y hubo un poeta de Medina, más tardío, muy extraño a los hechos acaecidos en tiempos del Cid, y que por eso poetizaba más libremente."[6]

The rest of Menéndez Pidal's essay is dedicated to proving his hypothesis of two poets. The greater part of his study is based on historical fact versus imaginative recreation within the poem, assigning those verses which can be proven to the earlier poet, and those containing anything fictitious to the later one.

The many critics who favor only one composer have also presented strong arguments. Américo Castro feels that it is precisely the mythical elements which make the poem an epic; that without these elements, one would have a chronicle.[7] Pedro Salinas feels that *The Cid,* like most other epic poems, relates only a part of the Cid's life.[8] The theme of the poem, the unifying element, is the honor of the Cid: "Si se considera como el tema real de la epopeya, su tema profundo, la honra del Cid, su estructura es sumamente lógica" (p. 42).

Hermenegildo Corbató was the first to refute the theory of Hills.[9] Concentrating on one of the points examined by Hills, Corbató chooses to study the appearances of synonyms in the poem. Hills, it should be remembered, pointed out the differences in the use of such synonyms as *salir* and *exir.* Corbató has studied a group of 49 synonyms to determine if other similar cases could be found.

Following Hills' plan, he divides the poem into two equal parts and also considers the appearance of the synonyms by *cantar.* Comment is made with each pair, or group, of synonyms showing how each disproves Hills' theory. Corbató can find no other examples where one synonym is preferred over another to a great extent.

G. T. Northup, like Salinas, feels that the unity of the poem lies in the Cid's struggle to regain his honor.[10] This event takes place at the Cortes de Toledo. All other events are incidentally treated, and all lead up to the climax of the poem.

Leo Spitzer is one of the first to refute Menéndez Pidal.[11] For Spitzer, the poem is more a work of art and fiction than of history. He disagrees with Menéndez Pidal's theory of a historical poem, blaming the idea on the influence of the Generation of '98. Many of the locations and episodes of the poem are fictitious and lead to the completely unreal *Afrenta de Corpes.*

Jules Horrent does not feel that the three parts existed as autonomous poems, since they are too closely woven together.[12] The poem is a story of how the Cid struggles to overcome his problems and adversaries to become lord of Valencia.

A. D. Deyermond is concerned with the adaptation of *The Singer of Tales,* by Lord, to the Spanish epic.[13] He feels that this may answer the questions of variation found within the poem:

> . . . a more likely explanation is provided by Lord: "One of the reasons also why different singings of the same song by the same man vary most in their endings is that the end of a song is sung less often by the singer" (The Singer of Tales, 17), the reason for this being the impatience of the audience on most occasions" (p. 2).

Deyermond feels that the study of formula, formulaic expression, and theme done by Lord should also be applied to the Spanish epic.

Against this background of varying opinions a study was made through analysis of synonym placement, formulaic expression, tagmemic analysis, and the use of selected verb tenses. The concordance was made to be used as a tool to aid in this study.

Following the scheme of verses as described by Menéndez Pidal, it was shown that there exists no appreciable difference in vocabulary usage in any part of the poem. It is felt that if there were a second poet some fifty years later, as Menéndez Pidal suggests, there would probably be a difference in synonym choice, since this is a period of great change in the language.

In the study of formulaic expressions, suggested by Deyermond, the appearance of at least 26 different formulaic expressions, which are found in all parts of the poem, is the strongest evidence found in support of only one author. The poet is constantly drawing on these expressions for use as half-lines or full lines. A thorough knowledge of the poem would be necessary to enable another poet to make use of all the formulaic expressions in exactly the same form throughout the complete poem, since Lord himself feels that the same singer will change a song somewhat each time that he sings it.

Because the style of epic composition was basically simple, the use of tagmemic analysis is not conclusive in itself. The patterns found, however, do support a one-author theory. The basic subject-predicate and subject-predicate-complement tagmemes, which are abundant in both parts studied, help to affirm this belief.

The study of the use of the future, the imperfect, and the conditional in the dialogue portion of the poem also must be considered important. There was no difference found in the use of any tense studied.

On the basis of the information studied in the concordance listing, it can be concluded that there is but one poet responsible for the composition of the *Poema de mio Cid* in the form in which it exists today. E. C. Hills proposed that his two-part division of the poem showed differences; the first historical and sober, the second fantastic and mostly fictitious. This really is not the case. First, the critic arbitrarily divided the poem into two equal parts without justification for dividing it in this manner. Second, in part one he has ignored the appearance of the dream and the Raquel and Vidas episodes (fantastic events); he accepts the abbot at Cardeña as don Sancho; he believes the battle at Alcocer actually took place; and he accepts events out of the time sequence. Both parts contain fantastic elements; both historical events. Both Jules Horrent and Leo Spitzer have already pointed these out.

Hills finds that the *ó* assonance predominates in the second half. (This also has been pointed out by Oliver T. Meyers.) While this is true, it does not point to a different poet. Lord has shown, in his *The Singer of Tales,* that this also exists in the Yugoslav epics: "One of the reasons also why different singings of the same song by the same man vary most in their endings is that the end of the song is sung less often by the singer."[14] One cannot suppose that this poem was sung every time in its entirety. Those verses in *ó* assonance may have been left out at different singings, sung alone as a separate theme, or simply used to make a change for purposes of variety in order to rest the audience. Lord feels that "it is the length of the song which is most affected by the audience's restlessness" (p. 17). Certainly the poet's ending of each *cantar* supports this theory.

Hills also finds that the epithets "Campeador," "Çid Campeador," and "don Alfonso" appear more in the second half. This is a result of the assonance rhyme, just as "Mio Çid Roy Diaz" and "Mio Çid el de Bivar" appear more in the first part, where the assonances *á, á-a* predominate.

Hills' study of synonyms is also affected by his arbitrary division of the poem. By changing his division, one would change the results. His best example in support of dual-authorship is the use of *exir* 29 times in part one and none in part two, while *salir* appears 17 times in the first part and 46 times in the second. But this is not conclusive proof. In the study of synonyms done following Menéndez Pidal's scheme of verses, it was found that *traer* appears only in those verses attributed to the poet from Medinaceli. This is a similar case, but not conclusive proof of two authors, in view of the fact that no difference was discovered in the study of other synonyms. This was also shown to be true of Hills' theory in the synonym study done by Hermenegildo Corbató.

Mack Singleton's theory that there were two poems cannot be refuted. As was pointed out earlier, there is a strong possibility that the poem was not sung in its entirety. The second half of the poem would, then, by its nature, be different from the first. It is singing of different events. The first part sings of the Cid and the battles he has won; the second sings of different people and events. The poet has sung his praise of the Cid; now he relates events of the people who surround him. But the Cid is relegated to no lesser role in the poem because of this. The Cid's honor, of so much concern to the poet in the first half, is still as important in the second, as was pointed out by Pedro Salinas. The Cid is still important to the poet and the center of interest throughout the entire poem. As a point in proof, it is interesting to note that the concordance shows that the Cid's name appears on the average of once every nine lines in the poem.

Menéndez Pidal's theory for dual-authorship has been partially refuted by Jules Horrent. His theory that the poet from San Esteban de Gormaz is responsible for all that is historical fact, and that the poet from Medinaceli is responsible for all that is not historical fact has been shown to be doubtful in several respects. The study of synonyms helps to refute his theory since no differences were found. Menéndez Pidal's theory that a poet from San Esteban would not be familiar with the region of Medinaceli is based on subjective opinion. The two regions are not far enough apart to preclude one person knowing the environs of both locations.

The purpose of this concordance, then, is to provide a tool for research in other directions which will aid in resolving this and other polemics surrounding the poem. The concordance will also provide students of historical linguistics with the opportunity to study twelfth-century Spanish snytax and morphology in the context of a single verse and/or a particular usage as it appears throughout the poem.

This concordance listing is based on the paleographic edition of the poem by Menéndez Pidal. This edition was chosen, rather than his critical edition, because it represents perfectly the original text of the single manuscript of the poem. Menéndez Pidal's critical edition, upon which most others are based, makes corrections in assonance, syllable count, orthography, and so forth, and for this reason it was unsuitable for a concordance printout. In his paleographic edition, Menéndez Pidal attempts to reproduce exactly the manuscript in its original form, with no divisions into *cantar* nor corrections.

In order to adapt the Spanish orthography to computer usage, some symbols were used for several letters. The Gothic ſ has been converted to the English *S,* and the conjunction ⁊, standard medieval abbreviation for *e* and *et,* is shown by the symbol &. The reader will also find the symbol % used for the Spanish ç and the symbol @ in place of the *ñ.*

The concordance follows the text of the paleographic edition perfectly. No changes were made in the text. These changes were purposely not made in order not to disturb the text in its original form. The listing must therefore be carefully studied to insure that certain words are not excluded from study. The only exception to this is the combining of certain words that were separated, since they seemed to be formed from prepositions. An example is: en grameo > engrameo. The reader will therefore find some words joined with others in the listing which are not accepted in modern Spanish. Examples are: del > de él, ala > a la, amyo > a myo, enel > en el, nol > no le (lo, la), and so forth.

Words beginning with *ç,* represented by *%,* are listed in alphabetical order immediately following the letter *c.* At times the *ç* is not used as expected. The reader therefore might find *cerca* listed under the letter *c* and *%erca* listed under the symbol %. Words containing a symbol within (gra%ia) will follow in normal alphabetical order, %, following *c* and @ following *n.* The symbol *&,* representing *e* and *et,* follows the letter *e.*

Computers are being used with more frequency in the humanities. This concordance was done on an I.B.M. 360 computer at The Pennsylvania State University. The program was developed and adapted to my needs by Dr. George A. Borden of the Department of Speech at The Pennsylvania State University. A system flow chart and an explanation of the program can be found in an article by George A. Borden and James J. Watts.[15] A word is listed once in the first column. Following this, each time the word appears in the poem, the context of the entire verse is shown. Then, the total number of times the word appears in that form in the poem is given. The last four digits of the ten-space prefix will show in which verse(s) the word is found. The asterisk(s) in each verse shows the location of the word being listed.

Sincere appreciation is expressed to Dr. George A. Borden for help provided in adapting the computer program for this concordance. Grateful acknowledgment is also made to Professor H. Tracy Sturcken for his assistance in obtaining research funds for this printout.

FRANKLIN M. WALTMAN

August, 1971

NOTES

1. E. C. Hills, "The Unity of the Poem of the Cid," *Hispania* 12 (1929): 113–18.
2. Hills, p. 117.
3. Mack Singleton, "The Two Techniques of the Poema de Mio Cid: An Interpretative Essay," *Romance Philology* 5 (1951–52): 222–27.

4. Oliver T. Meyers, "Assonance and Tense in the Poema del Cid," *PMLA* 81 (1966): 493–98.
5. Ramón Menéndez Pidal, "Dos poetas en el Cantar de Mio Cid," *Romania* 82 (1961): 145–200.
6. Menéndez Pidal, p. 148.
7. Américo Castro, "Poesía y realidad en el Poema del Cid," *Tierra Firme* 1 (1935): 7–30.
8. Pedro Salinas, "El Cantar de Mio Cid, poema de la honra," in *Ensayos de literatura hispánica* (Madrid: Aquilar, 1961), pp. 27–43.
9. Hermenegildo Corbató, "Sinonimia y unidad del Cid," *Hispanic Review* 9 (1941): 327–47.
10. G. T. Northup, "The Poem of the Cid Viewed as a Novel," *Philological Quarterly* 21 (1942): 17–18.
11. Leo Spitzer, "Sobre el carácter histórico del Cantar de Mio Cid," *Nueva Revista de Filología Hispánica* 2 (1948): 108.
12. Jules Horrent, "Tradition Poétique du 'Cantar de mio Cid' aux XII Siècle," *Cahiers de Civilisation Medievale* 7 (1964): 451–477.
13. A. D. Deyermond, "The Singer of Tales and Mediaeval Spanish Epic," *Bulletin of Hispanic Studies* 42 (1965): 1.
14. Albert B. Lord, *The Singer of Tales* (New York: Atheneum, 1968), p. 17.
15. George A. Borden and James J. Watts, "A Computerized Language Analysis System," *Computers and the Humanities 5* (1971): 129–42.

WORD C# PREFIX CONTEXT

A

84 5ELCID0012 E ENTRANDO * BURGOS OUIERON LA SINIESTRA.
187 5ELCID0025 QUE * MYO %ID RUY DIAZ, QUE NADI NOL DIESSEN POSADA,
198 5ELCID0026 E * QUEL QUE GELA DIESSE SOPIESSE UERA PALABRA,
279 5ELCID0035 LOS DE MYO %ID * ALTAS UOZES LAMAN,
320 5ELCID0040 VNA NI@A DE NUEF A@OS * OIO SE PARAUA:
415 5ELCID0052 LEGO * SANTA MARIA, LUEGO DESCAUALGA,
556 5ELCID0070 FABLO MARTIN ATOLINEZ, ODREDES LO QUE * DICHO:
714 5ELCID0090 QUANDO EN BURGOS ME VEDARON COMPRA & EL REY ME * AYRADO,
836 5ELCID0107 QUE NON ME DESCUBRADES * MOROS NIN A CHRISTIANOS;
839 5ELCID0107 QUE NON ME DESCUBRADES A MOROS NIN * CHRISTIANOS;
1021 5ELCID0131 RESPUSO MARTIN ANTOLINEZ * GUISA DE MENBRADO:
1034 5ELCID0133 PEDIR UOS * POCO POR DEXAR SO AUER EN SALUO.
1049 5ELCID0135 * MENESTER SEYS %IENTOS MARCOS.
1235 5ELCID0159 DON RACHEL & VIDAS * MYO %ID BESARON LE LAS MANOS.
1246 5ELCID0160 MARTIN ANTOLINEZ EL PLEYTO * PARADO,
1319 5ELCID0169 CA AMOUER * MYO %ID ANTE QUE CANTE EL GALLO.
1572 5ELCID0201 EXIDO ES DE BURGOS & ARLAN%ON * PASXADO,
1677 5ELCID0215 LA CARA DEL CAUALLO TORNO * SANTA MARIA,
1824 5ELCID0232 TORNAUAS MARTIN ANTOLINEZ * BURGOS & MYO %ID AAGUIJAR
1837 5ELCID0233 PORA SAN PERO DE CARDENA QUANTO PUDO * ESPOLEAR,
1856 5ELCID0236 QUANDO LEGO * SAN PERO EL BUEN CAMPEADOR;
1885 5ELCID0240 ROGANDO * SAN PERO & AL CRIADOR:
2237 5ELCID0282 PLEGA ADIOS & * SANTA MARIA, QUE AUN CON MIS MANOS CASE ESTAS MIS
2278 5ELCID0286 TANEN LAS CAMPA@AS EN SAN PERO * CLAMOR.
2357 5ELCID0298 TORNOS * SONRISAR; LEGAN LE TODOS, LA MANOL BAN BESAR.
2405 5ELCID0304 PLOGO * MIO %ID, POR QUE CRE%IO EN LA IANTAR,
2442 5ELCID0308 MANDO EL REY * MYO %ID A AGUARDAR,
2445 5ELCID0308 MANDO EL REY A MYO %ID * AGUARDAR,
2513 5ELCID0318 EN SAN PERO * MATINS TANDRA EL BUEN ABBAT,
2538 5ELCID0321 CA EL PLAZO VIENE * %ERCA, MUCHO AUEMOS DE ANDAR.
2569 5ELCID0325 TANEN * MATINES A VNA PRIESSA TAN GRAND;
2571 5ELCID0325 TANEN A MATINES * VNA PRIESSA TAN GRAND;
2581 5ELCID0326 MYO %ID & SU MUGIER * LA EGLESIA UAN.
2654 5ELCID0335 PASTORES TO GLOORIFFICARON, OUIERON DE * LAUDARE,
2679 5ELCID0339 * IONAS, QUANDO CAYO EN LA MAR,
2687 5ELCID0340 SALUEST * DANIEL CON LOS LEONES EN LA MALA CAR%EL,
2705 5ELCID0342 SALUEST * SANTA SUSANNA DEL FALSO CRIMINAL;
2735 5ELCID0346 RESU%ITEST * LAZARO, CA FUE TU VOLUNTAD;
2873 5ELCID0363 E RUEGO * SAN PEYDRO QUE ME AIUDE A ROGAR
2879 5ELCID0363 E RUEGO A SAN PEYDRO QUE ME AIUDE * ROGAR
2917 5ELCID0368 EL %ID * DO@A XIMENA YUA LA ABRA%AR;
2953 5ELCID0372 ADIOS UOS ACOMIENDO, FIJAS, & * LA MUGIER & AL PADRE SPIRITAL;
3057 5ELCID0385 E * TODAS SUS DUENAS QUE CON ELLAS ESTAN;
3126 5ELCID0393 VINO MYO %ID IAZER * SPINAZ DE CAN.
3161 5ELCID0398 DE DIESTRO * LILON LAS TORRES, QUE MOROS LAS HAN;
3224 5ELCID0406 EL ANGEL GABRIEL * EL VINO EN SUE@O:
3261 5ELCID0411 SINAUA LA CARA, * DIOS SE ACOMENDO,
3271 5ELCID0412 MUCHO ERA PAGADO DEL SUE@O QUE * SO@ADO.
3281 5ELCID0414 ES DIA * DE PLAZO, SEPADES QUE NON MAS.
3495 5ELCID0441 PUES QUE * CASTEION SACAREMOS A %ELADA,. . . .
3498 5ELCID0441 PUES QUE A CASTEION SACAREMOS * %ELADA,. . . .
3526 5ELCID0444 LAN%A, CAUALLEROS BUENOS QUE ACONPANE@ * MINAYA.
3594 5ELCID0453 DA QUESTE * CORRO FABLARA TODA ESPA@A.
3740 5ELCID0473 GA@O * CASTEION & EL ORO ELA PLATA.
3755 5ELCID0475 DEXAN LA * MYO %ID, TODO ESTO NON PRE%IA NADA.
3858 5ELCID0488 LOS BRA%OS ABIERTOS RE%IBE * MINAYA:
3915 5ELCID0497 ADIOS LO PROMETO, * AQUEL QUE ESTA EN ALTO:
4029 5ELCID0513 * CADA VNO DELLOS CAEN C MARCHOS DE PLATA,
4039 5ELCID0514 E * LOS PEONES LA MEATAD SIN FALLA;
4049 5ELCID0515 TODA LA QUINTA * MYO %ID FINCAUA.
4104 5ELCID0522 PLOGO * MYO %ID DA QUESTA PRESENTAIA.
4236 5ELCID0539 LO QUE DIXO EL %ID * TODOS LOS OTROS PLAZ.
4334 5ELCID0552 PASSO * BOUIERCA & ATECA QUE ES ADELANT,
4403 5ELCID0561 * TODOS SOS VARONES MANDO FAZER VNA CARCAUA,
4446 5ELCID0566 VENIDO ES * MOROS, EXIDO ES DE CHRISTIANOS;
4480 5ELCID0570 LOS DE ALCO%ER * MYO %ID YAL DAN PARIAS DE GRADO
4567 5ELCID0581 FALIDO * AMYO %ID EL PAN & LA %EUADA.
4577 5ELCID0582 LAS OTRAS * BES LIEUA, VNA TIENCA A DEXADA.
4582 5ELCID0582 LAS OTRAS A BES LIEUA, VNA TIENDA * DEXADA.
4594 5ELCID0584 DEMOS SALTO * EL & FEREMOS GRANT GANA%IA,
4616 5ELCID0586 LA PARIA QUEL * PRESA TORNAR NOS LA HA DOBLADA.
4703 5ELCID0596 MANDO TORNAR LA SE@A, * PRIESSA ESPOLONEAUAN.
4799 5ELCID0608 LAS ESPADAS DESNUDAS, * LA PUERTA SE PARAUAN.
4816 5ELCID0610 MYO %ID GA@O * ALCO%ER, SABENT, POR ESTA MA@A.
4852 5ELCID0614 GRADO * DIOS DEL %IELO & ATODOS LOS SOS SANTOS,
4961 5ELCID0628 QUE * VNO QUE DIZIEN MYO %ID RUY DIAZ DE BIUAR
4990 5ELCID0631 SACOLOS * %ELADA, EL CASTIELLO GANADO A;
4995 5ELCID0631 SACOLOS A %ELADA, EL CASTIELLO GANADO *;
5000 5ELCID0632 SI NON DAS CONSEIO, * TECA & A TERUEL PERDERAS,
5003 5ELCID0632 SI NON DAS CONSEIO, A TECA & * TERUEL PERDERAS,
5110 5ELCID0646 VINIERON * LA NOCH A %ELFA POSAR.
5113 5ELCID0646 VINIERON A LA NOCH * %ELFA POSAR.

WORD C# PREFIX CONTEXT

A (CON'T)

5270 5ELCID0666 MYO %ID CON LOS SOS TORNOS * ACORDAR:
5362 5ELCID0677 DIXO EL CAMPEADOR: * MI GUISA FABLASTES;
5519 5ELCID0695 QUE PRIESSA VA EN LOS MOROS, E TORNARON SE * ARMAR;
5569 5ELCID0701 PORA MYO %ID & ALOS SOS * MANOS LOS TOMAR.
5680 5ELCID0716 ABAXAN LAS LAN%AS * BUESTAS DELOS PENDONES,
5698 5ELCID0719 * GRANDES VOZES LAMA EL QUE EN BUEN ORA NASCO:
5837 5ELCID0738 MARTIN MU@OZ, EL QUE MANDO * MONT MAYOR,
5867 5ELCID0743 ACORREN LA SE@A & * MYO %ID EL CAMPEADOR.
5872 5ELCID0744 * MYNAYA ALBARFANEZ MATARON LE EL CAUALLO,
5887 5ELCID0746 LA LAN%A * QUEBRADA, AL ESPADA METIO MANO,
6036 5ELCID0765 MARTIN ANTOLINEZ VN COLPE DIO * GALUE,
6146 5ELCID0783 QUE * CASTIELLA YRAN BUENOS MANDADOS,
6158 5ELCID0784 QUE MYO %ID RUY DIAZ LID CAMPAL * VEN%IDA.
6167 5ELCID0785 TANTOS MOROS YAZEN MUERTOS QUE POCOS BIUOS * DEXADOS,
6215 5ELCID0792 GRADO * DIOS, A QUEL QUE ESTA EN ALTO,
6217 5ELCID0792 GRADO A DIOS, * QUEL QUE ESTA EN ALTO,
6303 5ELCID0803 GRANT * EL GOZO MYO %ID CON TODOS SOS VASSALOS.
6333 5ELCID0806 DIOS, QUE BIEN PAGO * TODOS SUS VASSALLOS,
6340 5ELCID0807 ALOS PEONES & * LOS ENCAUALGADOS
6371 5ELCID0812 * UUESTRA GUISA PRENDED CON UUESTRA MANO.
6381 5ELCID0813 ENBIAR UOS QUIERO * CASTIELLA CON MANDADO
6395 5ELCID0815 AL REY ALFONSSSO QUE ME * AYRADO
6447 5ELCID0823 LO QUE ROMANE%IERE DALDO * MI MUGIER & A MIS FIJAS,
6451 5ELCID0823 LO QUE ROMANE%IERE DALDO A MI MUGIER & * MIS FIJAS,
6505 5ELCID0830 * NUESTRO AMIGOS BIEN LES PODEDES DEZIR:
6572 5ELCID0839 TODOS LOS DIAS * MYO %ID AGUARDAUAN
6620 5ELCID0845 VENDIDO LES * ALCO%ER POR TRES MILL MARCHOS DE PLATA.
6632 5ELCID0846 MYO %ID RUY DIAZ * ALCOL%ER ES VENIDO;
6639 5ELCID0847 QUE BIEN PAGO * SUS VASSALOS MISMOS
6643 5ELCID0848 * CAUALLEROS & A PEONES FECHOS LOS HA RICOS,
6646 5ELCID0848 A CAUALLEROS & * PEONES FECHOS LOS HA RICOS,
6661 5ELCID0850 QUI * BUEN SE@OR SIRUE, SIEMPRE BIUE EN DELI%IO.
6681 5ELCID0852 MOROS & MORAS TOMARON SE * QUEXAR:
6699 5ELCID0855 QUANDO QUITO * ALCO%ER MYO %ID EL DE BIUAR,
6777 5ELCID0865 NON TEME GERRA, SABET, * NULLA PART.
6787 5ELCID0867 DESI * MOLINA, QUE ES DEL OTRA PART,
6804 5ELCID0869 EN SU MANO TENIE * %ELFA LA DE CANAL.
6820 5ELCID0871 YDO ES * CASTIELLA ALBARFANEZ MINAYA,
6868 5ELCID0878 * UOS, REY ONDRADO, ENBIA ESTA PRESENTAIA;
6906 5ELCID0883 POR ACOGELLO * CABO DE TRES SEMMANAS.
7001 5ELCID0895 GRADO & GRA%IAS, REY, COMMO * SE@OR NATURAL;
7022 5ELCID0898 SI NULLA DUBDA YD * MYO %ID BUSCAR GANAN%IA.
7147 5ELCID0915 QUANDO ESTO FECHO OUO, * CABO DE TRES SEMANAS,
7176 5ELCID0919 QUANDO VIO MYO %ID ASOMAR * MINAYA,
7304 5ELCID0937 E * DERREDOR TODO LO VA PREANDO.
7366 5ELCID0945 PLOGO * MYO %ID, & MUCHO A ALBARFANEZ.
7371 5ELCID0945 PLOGO A MYO %ID, & MUCHO * ALBARFANEZ.
7423 5ELCID0952 DENT CORRE MYO %ID * HUESCA & A MONT ALUAN;
7426 5ELCID0952 DENT CORRE MYO %ID A HUESCA & * MONT ALUAN;
7439 5ELCID0954 FUERON LOS MANDADOS * TODAS PARTES,
7479 5ELCID0959 OUO GRAND PESAR & TOUOS LO * GRAND FONTA.
7546 5ELCID0967 GRANDES SON LOS PODERES & * PRIESSA SEUAN LEGANDO,
7576 5ELCID0971 ALCON%ARON * MYO %ID EN TEUAR & EL PINAR;
7608 5ELCID0974 DI%E DE VNA SIERRA & LEGAUA * VN VAL.
7632 5ELCID0977 DIGADES AL CONDE NON LO TENGA * MAL,
7662 5ELCID0981 SABRA EL SALIDO * QUIEN VINO DESONDRAR.
7681 5ELCID0984 QUE * MENOS DE BATALLA NOS PUEDEN DEN QUITAR.
7691 5ELCID0985 YA CAUALLEROS, * PART FAZED LA GANAN%IA;
7772 5ELCID0995 %IENTO CAUALLEROS DEUEMOS VEN%ER * QUELAS MESNADAS.
7779 5ELCID0996 ANTES QUE ELLOS LEGEN * LA@O, PRESENTEMOS LES LAS LAN%AS;
7879 5ELCID1007 ALOS VNOS FIRIENDO & * LOS OTROS DE ROCANDO.
7885 5ELCID1008 VEN%IDO * ESTA BATALLA EL QUE EN BUEN ORA NASCO;
7898 5ELCID1009 AL CONDE DON REMONT * PRESON LEAN TOMADO;
7904 5ELCID1010 HY GA@O * COLADA QUE MAS VALE DE MILL MARCOS DE PLATA.
7951 5ELCID1016 PLOGO * MYO %ID, CA GRANDES SON LAS GANAN%IAS.
7959 5ELCID1017 * MYO %ID DON RODRIGO GRANT COZINAL ADOBAUAN;
8157 5ELCID1040 AUOS & * OTROS DOS DAR UOS HE DE MANO.
8228 5ELCID1048 COMMO QUE YRA * DE REY & DE TIERRA ES ECHADO.
8309 5ELCID1057 CON ESTOS DOS CAUALLEROS * PRIESSA VA IANTANDO;
8565 5ELCID1088 DEXADO * SARAGO%A & ALAS TIERRAS DUCA,
8573 5ELCID1089 E DEXADO * HUESCA & LAS TIERRAS DE MONT ALUAN.
8601 5ELCID1092 MYO %ID GA@O AXERICA & * ONDA & ALMENAR,
8626 5ELCID1095 EL CON TODO ESTO PRISO * MURUIEDRO.
8725 5ELCID1108 LOS VNOS AXERICA & LOS OTROS * ALUCAD,
8728 5ELCID1119 DESI * ONDA & LOS OTROS A ALMENAR,
8733 5ELCID1119 DESI A ONDA & LOS OTROS * ALMENAR,
8784 5ELCID1117 NON FUE * NUESTRO GRADO NI NOS NON PUDIEMOS MAS,
8793 5ELCID1118 GRADO * DIOS, LO NUESTRO FUE ADELANT.
8815 5ELCID1121 FIRME MIENTRE SON ESTOS * ESCARMENTAR.
8827 5ELCID1123 APAREIADOS ME SED * CAUALLOS & ARMAS;
8860 5ELCID1129 * MI DEDES C CAUALLEROS, QUE NON UOS PIDO MAS,
8903 5ELCID1134 COMMO GELO * DICHO, AL CAMPEADOR MUCHO PLAZE.
9000 5ELCID1145 MAGER LES PESA, OUIERON SE ADAR & * ARANCAR.
9057 5ELCID1153 ENTRAUAN * MURUIEDRO CON ESTAS GANAN%IAS QUE TRAEN GRANDES.

WORD C# PREFIX CONTEXT

A (CON'T)

9114 5ELCID1160 LEGAN * GUIERA & LEGAN AXATIUA,
9248 5ELCID1176 NIN DA COSSEIO PADRE * FIJO, NON FIJO A PADRE,
9252 5ELCID1176 NIN DA COSSEIO PADRE A FIJO, NON FIJO * PADRE,
9256 5ELCID1177 NIN AMIGO * AMIGO NOS PUEDEN CONSOLAR.
9291 5ELCID1181 POR EL REY DE MARRUECOS OUIERON * ENBIAR;
9340 5ELCID1188 * TIERRAS DE CASTIELLA ENBIO SUS MENSSAIES:
9353 5ELCID1189 QUIEN QUIERE PERDER CUETA & VENIR * RRITAD,
9356 5ELCID1190 VINIESSE * MYO %ID QUE A SABOR DE CAUALGAR;
9360 5ELCID1190 VINIESSE A MYO %ID QUE * SABOR DE CAUALGAR;
9366 5ELCID1191 %ERCAR QUIERE * VALEN%IA PORA CHRISTIANOS LA DAR.
9377 5ELCID1192 QUIEN QUIERE YR CCMIGC %ERCAR * VALEN%IA,
9406 5ELCID1196 TORNAUAS * MURUIEDRO, CA EL SE LA A GANADA.
9412 5ELCID1196 TORNAUAS A MURUIEDRO, CA EL SE LA * GANADA.
9439 5ELCID1200 CRE%IENDO UA RIQUEZA * MYO %ID EL DE BIUAR.
9495 5ELCID1207 MAS LE VIENEN * MYO %ID, SABET, QUE NOS LE VAN.
9535 5ELCID1212 QUANDO MYO %ID GA@O * VALEN%IA & ENTRO ENLA %IBDAD.
9761 5ELCID1240 POR AMOR DE REY ALFFCNSSO, QUE DE TIERRA ME * ECHADO,
9950 5ELCID1261 AQUESTOS MYOS VASSALOS QUE CURIAN * VALEN%IA & ANDAN AROBDANDO.
9967 5ELCID1263 MANDO LCS VENIR ALA CORTH & * TODOS LOS IUNTAR,
9998 5ELCID1267 GRADO * DIOS, MYNAYA, & A SANTA MARIA MADRE
10002 5ELCID1267 GRADO A DIOS, MYNAYA, & * SANTA MARIA MADRE
10034 5ELCID1271 ENBIAR UOS QUIERO * CASTIELLA, DO AUEMOS HEREDADES,
10138 5ELCID1284 CIENTO OMNES LE DIO MYO %ID * ALBARFANEZ POR SERUIR LE EN LA CARRERA,
10152 5ELCID1285 E MANDO MILL MARCOS DE PLATA * SAN PERO LEUAR
10271 5ELCID1300 E DAR GELO * ESTE BUEN CHRISTIANO:
10278 5ELCID1301 VOS, QUANDO YDES * CASTIELLA, LEUAREDES BUENOS MANDADOS.
10284 5ELCID1302 PLOGO * ALBARFANEZ DELO QUE DIXO DON RODRIGO.
10357 5ELCID1312 FUERA EL REY * SAN FAGUNT AVN POCO HA,
10364 5ELCID1313 TORNOS * CARRION, Y LO PODRIE FALLAR.
10469 5ELCID1327 GANADA * XERICA & A ONDA POR NOMBRE,
10472 5ELCID1327 GANADA A XERICA & * ONDA PCR NOMBRE,
10477 5ELCID1328 PRISO * ALMENAR & A MURUIEDRO QUE ES MIYOR,
10480 5ELCID1328 PRISO A ALMENAR & * MURUIEDRO QUE ES MIYOR,
10583 5ELCID1341 DE TAN FIERAS GANAN%IAS CCMMO * FECHAS EL CAMPEADOR
10616 5ELCID1345 MAGER PLOGO AL REY, MUCHO PESO * GAR%IORDONEZ:
10625 5ELCID1346 SEMEIA QUE EN TIERRA DE MOROS NON * BIUO OMNE,
10631 5ELCID1347 QUANDO ASSI FAZE * SU GUISA EL %ID CAMPEADOR
10727 5ELCID1358 QUANDO EN CABO DE MI TIERRA * QUESTAS DUE@AS FUEREN,
10758 5ELCID1362 ATODAS LAS ESCUELLAS QUE * EL DIZEN SE@OR
10861 5ELCID1375 NON LA OSARIEMOS * CCMETER NOS ESTA RAZON,
10880 5ELCID1377 NON LO DIZEN * NADI, & FINCO ESTA RAZON.
10945 5ELCID1385 LOS YFFANTES DE CARRION DANDO YUAN CONPA@A * MINAYA ALBARFANEZ:
10959 5ELCID1387 SALUDAD NOS * MYO %ID EL DE BIUAR,
11036 5ELCID1397 ASSI FFAGA * UUESTRAS FIJAS AMAS.
11067 5ELCID1401 POR LEUAROS * VALEN%IA QUE AUEMOS POR HEREDAD.
11103 5ELCID1406 ENVIOLOS * MYO %ID, AVALEN%IA DO ESTA,
11159 5ELCID1411 SEREMOS YO & SU MUGIER & SUS FIJAS QUE EL *
11191 5ELCID1416 HYR SE QUIERE * VALEN%IA A MYO %ID EL DE BIUAR.
11193 5ELCID1416 HYR SE QUIERE A VALEN%IA * MYO %ID EL DE BIUAR.
11204 5ELCID1417 QUE LES TOUIESSE PRO ROGAUAN * ALBARFANEZ;
11216 5ELCID1419 AMINAYA LXV CAUALLEROS * CRE%IDOL HAN,
11252 5ELCID1424 MINAYA * DO@A XIMINA & A SUS FIJAS QUE HA,
11256 5ELCID1424 MINAYA A DO@A XIMINA & * SUS FIJAS QUE HA,
11497 5ELCID1455 PLOGOL DE CORA%ON & TORNOS * ALEGRAR,
11548 5ELCID1463 VAYADES * MOLINA, QUE IAZE MAS ADELANT,
11585 5ELCID1468 ASI COMMO * MY DIXIERON, HY LOS PODREDES FALAR;
11637 5ELCID1475 TRO%IERON * SANTA MARIA & VINIERON ALBERGAR A FRONTAEL,
11643 5ELCID1475 TRO%IERON A SANTA MARIA & VINIERON ALBERGAR * FRONTAEL,
11650 5ELCID1476 E EL OTRO DIA VINIERON * MOLINA POSAR.
11687 5ELCID1481 FABLO MU@O GUSTIOZ, NON SPERO * NADI:
11777 5ELCID1493 POR EL VAL DE ARBUXEDC PIENSSAN * DEPRUNAR.
11812 5ELCID1497 EL VNO FINCO CON ELLOS & EL OTRO TORNO * ALBARFANEZ:
11893 5ELCID1508 EN BUENCS CAUALLOS * PETRALES & A CASCAUELES,
11896 5ELCID1508 EN BUENOS CAUALLOS A PETRALES & * CASCAUELES,
11899 5ELCID1509 E * CUBERTURAS DE %ENDALES, & ESCUDOS ALOS CUELLOS,
11947 5ELCID1514 LUEGO TOMAN ARMAS & TOMANSE * DEPORTAR,
11961 5ELCID1516 DON LEGAN LOS OTROS, * MINAYA ALBARFANEZ SE UAN HOMILAR.
12169 5ELCID1545 VINIERON * MOLINA, LA QUE AUEGALUON MANDAUA.
12206 5ELCID1549 ENTRE EL & ALBARFANEZ HYUAN * VNA COMPA@A.
12211 5ELCID1550 ENTRADOS SON * MOLINA, BUENA & RICA CASA;
12279 5ELCID1559 APRES SON DE VALEN%IA * TRES LEGUAS CONTADAS.
12292 5ELCID1561 DENTRO * VALEN%IA LIEUAN LE EL MANDADO.
12323 5ELCID1565 QUE RE%IBAN * MYANAYA & ALAS DUENAS FIJAS DALGO;
12349 5ELCID1568 AFEUOS TODOS AQUESTOS RE%IBEN * MINAYA
12439 5ELCID1578 RE%EBIDAS LAS DUENAS * VNA GRANT ONDRAN%A,
12552 5ELCID1593 ADELINO * SU MUGIER & A SUS FIJAS AMAS;
12556 5ELCID1593 ADELINO A SU MUGIER & * SUS FIJAS AMAS;
12565 5ELCID1594 QUANDO LO VIO DO@A XIMENA, * PIES SE LE ECHAUA:
12677 5ELCID1609 * TAN GRAND ONDRA ELLAS A VALEN%IA ENTRAUAN.
12682 5ELCID1609 A TAN GRAND ONDRA ELLAS * VALEN%IA ENTRAUAN.
12702 5ELCID1612 OIOS VELIDOS CATAN * TODAS PARTES,
12715 5ELCID1614 E DEL OTRA PARTE * OIO HAN EL MAR,
12800 5ELCID1624 E EL NON GELO GRADE%E SI NON * IHESU CHRISTO.
12829 5ELCID1628 VAN BUSCAR * VALEN%IA A MYO %ID DON RODRIGO.

WORD C# PREFIX CONTEXT

A (CON'T)

12831 5ELCID1628 VAN BUSCAR A VALENZIA * MYO ZID DON RODRIGO.
12844 5ELCID1630 LEGARON * VALENZIA, LA QUE MYO ZID A CONQUISTA,
12850 5ELCID1630 LEGARON A VALENZIA, LA QUE MYO ZID * CONQUISTA,
12862 5ELCID1632 ESTAS NUEUAS * MYO ZID ERAN VENIDAS;
12871 5ELCID1633 GRADO AL CRIADOR & * PADRE ESPIRITAL
12887 5ELCID1635 CON AFAN GANE * VALENZIA, & ELA POR HEREDAD,
12893 5ELCID1636 * MENOS DE MUERT NO LA PUEDO DEXAR;
12905 5ELCID1637 GRADO AL CRIADOR & * SANTA MARIA MADRE,
12993 5ELCID1648 RIQUEZA ES QUE NOS * CREZE MARAUILLOSA & GRAND;
13058 5ELCID1656 CON DIOS * QUESTA LID YO LA HE DE ARRANCAR.
13074 5ELCID1658 * VNA GRAND PRIESSA TANIEN LOS ATAMORES;
13092 5ELCID1660 MIEDO * SU MUGIER & QUIEREL QUEBRAR EL CORAZON,
13105 5ELCID1661 ASSI FFAZIE ALAS DUE@AS & * SUS FIJAS AMAS ADOS:
13138 5ELCID1665 ANTES DESTOS XV DIAS, SI PLOGIERE * CRIADOR,
13261 5ELCID1682 TORNADOS SON * MYO ZID LOS QUE COMIEN SO PAN;
13365 5ELCID1694 PUES ESSO QUEREDES, ZID, * MI MANDADES AL;
13441 5ELCID1704 EL QUE * QUI MURIERE LIDIANDO DE CARA,
13554 5ELCID1717 QUATRO MILL MENOS XXX CON MYO ZID VAN * CABO,
13681 5ELCID1733 TODA ESTA GANANZIA EN SU MANO * RASTADO.
13754 5ELCID1743 CON C CAUALLEROS * VALENZIA ES ENTRADO,
14068 5ELCID1782 QUANDO * MYO ZID CAYERON TANTOS, LOS OTROS BIEN PUEDEN FINCAR PAGADOS.
14087 5ELCID1784 QUE * GANADO MYO ZID CON TODOS SUS VASSALLOS
14159 5ELCID1792 CON AQUESTAS RIQUEZAS TANTAS * VALENZIA SON ENTRADOS.
14349 5ELCID1815 MANDO * PERO VERMUEZ QUE FUESSE CON MYNAYA.
14409 5ELCID1822 TALLES GANANZIAS TRAEN QUE SON * AGUARDAR.
14446 5ELCID1827 LEGAN * VALADOLID, DO EL REY ALFONSSO ESTAUA;
14463 5ELCID1829 QUE MANDASSE REZEBIR * ESTA CONPA@A:
14562 5ELCID1842 FIRIERON SE * TIERRA, DEZENDIERON DELOS CAUALOS,
14595 5ELCID1847 * UOS LAMA POR SE@OR, & TIENES POR UUESTRO VASSALLO,
14621 5ELCID1849 POCOS DIAS HA, REY, QUE VNA LID * ARRANCADO:
14623 5ELCID1850 * AQUEL REY DE MARRUECOS, YUCEFF POR NOMBRADO,
14670 5ELCID1856 GRADESCOLO * MYO ZID QUE TAL DON ME HA ENBIADO;
14689 5ELCID1858 ESTO PLOGO * MUCHOS & BESARON LE LAS MANOS.
14710 5ELCID1860 CON X DE SUS PARIENTES * PARTE DAUAN SALTO:
14844 5ELCID1876 TODAS ESTAS NUEUAS * BIEN ABRAN DE VENIR.
14855 5ELCID1877 BESARON LE LAS MANOS & ENTRARON * POSAR;
14912 5ELCID1885 MERZED UOS PIDIMOS COMMO * REY & SE@OR NATURAL;
14937 5ELCID1888 CASAR QUEREMOS CON ELLAS ASU ONDRA & * NUESTRA PRO.
14981 5ELCID1894 * MYNAYA ALBARFANEZ & A PERO VERMUEZ
14985 5ELCID1894 A MYNAYA ALBARFANEZ & * PERO VERMUEZ
14995 5ELCID1896 * VNA QUADRA ELE LOS APARTO:
15022 5ELCID1899 E DE MI ABRA PERDON; VINIESSEM * VISTAS, SI OUIESSE DENT SABOR.
15082 5ELCID1907 FABLO MYNAYA & PLOGO * PER VERMUEZ:
15101 5ELCID1910 DEZID * RUY DIAZ, EL QUE EN BUEN ORA NASCO,
15112 5ELCID1911 QUEL YRE * VISTAS DO FUERE AGUISADO;
15127 5ELCID1913 ANDAR LE QUIERO * MYO ZID EN TODA PRO.
15175 5ELCID1920 EN POCAS TIERRAS * TALES DOS VARONES.
15263 5ELCID1933 ESTO GRADESCO * CHRISTUS EL MYO SE@OR.
15413 5ELCID1952 POR DAR LE GRAND ONDRA COMMO * REY DE TIERRA.
15501 5ELCID1964 NON LO DETARDAN, * MYO ZID SE TORNAUAN.
15584 5ELCID1976 LO VNO * DEBDAN & LO OTRO PAGAUAN;
15609 5ELCID1979 EL REY DON ALFONSSO * PRIESSA CAUALGAUA,
15647 5ELCID1984 SUELTAN LAS RIENDAS, ALAS VISTAS SEUAN * DELI@ADAS.
15756 5ELCID2000 * AQUESTOS DOS MANDO EL CAMPEADOR QUE CURIEN A VALENZIA
15764 5ELCID2000 A AQUESTOS DOS MANDO EL CAMPEADOR QUE CURIEN * VALENZIA
15898 5ELCID2016 DON LO OUO * OIO EL QUE EN BUEN ORA NASCO,
15914 5ELCID2018 SI NON * ESTOS CAUALLEROS QUE QUERIE DE CORAZON;
15924 5ELCID2009 CON VNOS XV * TIERRAS FIRIO,
15949 5ELCID2022 LAS YERBAS DEL CAMPO * DIENTES LAS TOMO,
15965 5ELCID2024 ASI SABE DAR OMILDANZA * ALFONSSO SO SE@OR.
16063 5ELCID2037 GRADESCOLO * DIOS DEL ZIELO & DESPUES AUOS,
16071 5ELCID2038 E * ESTAS MESNADAS QUE ESTAN A DERREDOR.
16076 5ELCID2038 E A ESTAS MESNADAS QUE ESTAN * DERREDOR.
16099 5ELCID2042 PESO * ALBARDIAZ & A GARCIORDONEZ.
16102 5ELCID2042 PESO A ALBARDIAZ & * GARCIORDONEZ.
16126 5ELCID2045 VALER ME * DIOS DE DIA & DE NOCH.
16342 5ELCID2073 COMETER QUIERO VN RUEGO * MYO ZID EL CAMPEADOR;
16566 5ELCID2099 HYO LAS CASO * UUESTRAS FIJAS CON UUESTRO AMOR,
16651 5ELCID2109 MUCHO UOS LO GRADESCO, COMMO * REY & A SE@OR
16654 5ELCID2109 MUCHO UOS LO GRADESCO, COMMO A REY & * SE@OR
16849 5ELCID2133 DAD MANERO * QUI LAS DE, QUANDO UOS LAS TOMADES;
17071 5ELCID2161 HYREMOS EN PODER DE MYO ZID * VALENZIA LA MAYOR;
17133 5ELCID2168 EA DON FERNANDO & * DON DIEGO AGUARDAR LOS MANDO
17150 5ELCID2170 EN CASA DE MYO ZID NON * DOS MEIORES,
17198 5ELCID2176 QUANDO * ELLA ASSOMARON, LOS GOZOS SON MAYORES.
17211 5ELCID2177 DIXO MYO ZID ADON PERO & * MU@O GUSTIOZ:
17244 5ELCID2181 VERAN ASUS ESPOSAS, * DON ELUIRA & A DONA SOL.
17248 5ELCID2181 VERAN ASUS ESPOSAS, A DON ELUIRA & * DONA SOL.
17255 5ELCID2182 TODOS ESSA NOCH FUERON * SUS POSADAS,
17464 5ELCID2209 TODOS SUS CAUALLEROS * PRIESSA SON IUNTADOS.
17651 5ELCID2233 QUE LAS TOMASSEDES POR MUGIERES * ONDRA & A RECABDO.
17654 5ELCID2233 QUE LAS TOMASSEDES POR MUGIERES A ONDRA & * RECABDO.
17663 5ELCID2235 * MYO ZID & A SU MUGIER VAN BESAR LA MANO.
17667 5ELCID2235 A MYO ZID & * SU MUGIER VAN BESAR LA MANO.

WORD C# PREFIX CONTEXT

A (CON'T)

17684 5ELCID2237 PORA SANTA MARIA * PRIESSA ADELINNANDO;
17704 5ELCID2240 DIOLES BENDICTIONES, LA MISSA * CANTADO.
17759 5ELCID2247 TORNAN SE CON LAS DUE@AS, * VALEN%IA AN ENTRADO;
17868 5ELCID2261 RICOS TORNAN * CASTIELLA LOS QUE ALAS BODAS LEGARON.
17968 5ELCID2274 PLEGA * SANTA MARIA & AL PADRE SANTO
18330 5ELCID2319 AMOS HERMANOS * PART SALIDOS SON:
18345 5ELCID2321 YA EN ESTA BATALLA * ENTRAR ABREMOS NOS;
18371 5ELCID2325 VINO CON ESTAS NUEUAS * MUO %ID RUYDIAZ EL CANPEADOR:
18447 5ELCID2334 HYO DESSEO LIDES, & UOS * CARRION;
18452 5ELCID2335 EN VALEN%IA FOLGAD * TODO UUESTRO SABOR,
18495 5ELCID2341 PLOGO * MYO %ID & ATODOS SOS VASSALLOS;
18688 5ELCID2365 EL DEBDO QUE * CADA VNO A CONPLIR SERA.
18691 5ELCID2365 EL DEBDO QUE A CADA VNO * CONPLIR SERA.
18769 5ELCID2375 PENDON TRAYO * CORCAS & ARMAS DE SE@AL,
18817 5ELCID2381 AFE LOS MOROS * OIO, YD LOS ENSAYAR.
18834 5ELCID2383 EL OBISPO DON IHERONIMO PRISO * ESPOLONADA
18839 5ELCID2384 EYUA LOS FERIR * CABO DEL ALBERGADA.
18862 5ELCID2387 EL ASTIL * QUEBRADO & METIO MANO AL ESPADA.
18920 5ELCID2394 AGUIJO * BAUIECA, EL CAUALLO QUE BIEN ANDA,
18943 5ELCID2397 ABATIO * VIJ & A IIIJ MATAUA.
18946 5ELCID2397 ABATIO A VIJ & * IIIJ MATAUA.
18950 5ELCID2398 PLOGO * DIOS, AQUESTA FUE EL ARRANCADA.
19006 5ELCID2404 TANTO BRA%O CON LORIGA VERIEDES CAER * PART,
19021 5ELCID2406 CAUALLOS SIN DUENOS SALIR * TODAS PARTES.
19135 5ELCID2420 ALCAN%OLO EL %ID ABUCAR * TRES BRACAS DEL MAR,
19171 5ELCID2425 MATO * BUCAR, AL REY DE ALEN MAR,
19180 5ELCID2426 E GANO * TIZON QUE MILL MARCOS DORO VAL.
19279 5ELCID2440 E VIO VENIR ADIEGO & * FERNANDO;
19455 5ELCID2465 TODAS LAS GANAN%IAS * VALEN%IA SON LEGADAS;
19509 5ELCID2472 CON DUCHOS * SAZONES, BUENAS PIELES & BUENOS MANTOS.
19550 5ELCID2477 GRADO * CHRISTUS, QUE DEL MUNDO ES SE@OR,
19576 5ELCID2480 MANDADOS BUENOS YRAN DELLOS * CARRION,
19750 5ELCID2504 QUE PAGUEN AMI O * CUI YO QUIER SABOR.
19899 5ELCID2524 GRADO * SANTA MARIA, MADRE DEL NUESTRO SE@OR DIOS
19928 5ELCID2528 GRADO AL CRIADOR & * UOS, %ID ONDRADO,
20002 5ELCID2538 AMOS SALIERON * PART, VERA MIENTRE SON HERMANOS;
20163 5ELCID2560 QUE PLEGA * DO@A XIMENA & PRIMERO AUOS
20173 5ELCID2561 EA MYNAYA ALBARFANEZ & * QUANTOS AQUI SON:
20187 5ELCID2563 LEUAR LAS HEMOS * NUESTRAS TIERRAS DE CARRION,
20291 5ELCID2575 DAR UOS HE DOS ESPADAS, * COLADA & A TIZON,
20294 5ELCID2575 DAR UOS HE DOS ESPADAS, A COLADA & * TIZON,
20341 5ELCID2581 * MIS FIJAS SIRUADES, QUE UUESTRAS MUGIERES SON;
20373 5ELCID2585 CONPIE%AN * RE%EBIR LO QUE EL %ID MANDO.
20405 5ELCID2589 TODOS PRENDEN ARMAS & CAUALGAN * VIGOR,
20466 5ELCID2598 DEBDO NOS ES * CUNPLIR LO QUE MANDAREDES VOS.
20519 5ELCID2605 HYD * CARRION DO SODES HEREDADAS,
20650 5ELCID2621 VERAS LAS HEREDADES QUE * MIS FIJAS DADAS SON;
20679 5ELCID2625 TORNEMOS NOS, %ID, * VALEN%IA LA MAYOR;
20754 5ELCID2636 SALUDAD * MYO AMIGO EL MORO AVENGALUON:
20761 5ELCID2637 RE%IBA * MYOS YERNOS COMMO EL PUDIER MEIOR;
20773 5ELCID2638 DIL QUE ENBIO MIS FIJAS * TIERRAS DE CARRION,
20913 5ELCID2656 TRO%IERON ARBUXUELO & LEGARON * SALON,
21159 5ELCID2688 CUEMMO DE BUEN SESO * MOLINA SE TORNO.
21173 5ELCID2690 ACOIEN SE * ANDAR DE DIA & DE NOCH;
21199 5ELCID2693 POR LOS MONTES CLAROS AGUIJAN * ESPOLON;
21211 5ELCID2695 ALLI SON CA@OS DO * ELPHA EN%ERRO;
21840 5ELCID2779 ARRENDO EL CAUALLO, * ELLAS ADELINO;
21863 5ELCID2782 ADIOS PLEGA & * SANTA MARIA QUE DENT PRENDAN ELLOS MAL GALARDON
21874 5ELCID2783 VALAS TORNANDO * ELLAS AMAS ADOS;
21973 5ELCID2796 TAN * GRANT DUELO FABLAUA DO@A SOL:
22056 5ELCID2807 CON EL SO MANTO * AMAS LAS CUBRIO,
22101 5ELCID2813 * SANTESTEUAN VINO FELEZ MUNOZ,
22107 5ELCID2814 FALLO * DIEGO TELLEZ EL QUE DE ALBARFANEZ FUE;
22191 5ELCID2826 VAN AQUESTOS MANDADOS * VALEN%IA LA MAYOR;
22198 5ELCID2827 QUANDO GELO DIZEN * MYO %ID EL CAMPEADOR,
22218 5ELCID2830 GRADO * CHRISTUS, QUE DEL MUNDO ES SE@OR,
22256 5ELCID2835 PESO * MYO %ID & ATODA SU CORT, & ALBARFANEZ DALMA & DE CORA%ON.
22301 5ELCID2840 ADUXIESSEN ASSUS FIJAS * VALEN%IA LA MAYOR.
22322 5ELCID2843 VINIERON * SANTESTEUAN DE GORMAZ, VN CASTIELLO TAN FUERT,
22351 5ELCID2847 VARONES DE SANTESTEUAN, * GUISA DE MUY PROS,
22363 5ELCID2849 PRESENTAN * MINAYA ESSA NOCH GRANT ENFFUR%ION;
22390 5ELCID2852 POR AQUESTA ONDRA QUE VOS DIESTES * ESTO QUE NOS CUNTIO;
22431 5ELCID2857 ADELINAN * POSAR PORA FOLGAR ESSA NOCH.
22463 5ELCID2861 EUOS * EL LO GRADID, QUANDO BIUAS SOMOS NOS.
22596 5ELCID2878 OTRO DIA MA@ANA METEN SE * ANDAR,
22606 5ELCID2880 E DE MEDINA * MOLINA EN OTRO DIA VAN;
22620 5ELCID2882 SALIOLOS * RE%EBIR DE BUENA VOLUNTAD,
22650 5ELCID2886 PRIUADO CAUALGA, * RE%EBIR LOS SALE;
22783 5ELCID2903 LIEUES EL MANDADO * CASTIELLA AL REY ALFONSSO;
22881 5ELCID2914 ADUGA MELOS AVISTAS, O AIUNTAS, O * CORTES,
22910 5ELCID2918 CON EL DOS CAUALLEROS QUEL SIRUAN * SO SABOR,
22956 5ELCID2924 E DELAS ASTURIAS BIEN * SAN %ALUADOR,
22971 5ELCID2926 ELLOS CONDES GALLIZANOS * EL TIENEN POR SE@OR.
23015 5ELCID2932 VIOLOS EL REY & CONNOS%IO * MU@O GUSTIOZ;

WORD C# PREFIX CONTEXT

A (CON'T)

23108 5ELCID2944 MAIADAS & DESNUDAS * GRANDE DESONOR,
23140 5ELCID2948 POR ESTO UOS BESA LAS MANOS, COMMO VASSALLO * SE@OR,
23149 5ELCID2949 QUE GELOS LEUEDES AVISTAS, O AIUNTAS, O * CORTES;
23216 5ELCID2957 FIZ LO POR BIEN, QUE FFUESSE * SU PRO.
23284 5ELCID2966 E COMMO DEN DERECHO * MYO %ID EL CAMPEADOR,
23315 5ELCID2970 VENGAM * TOLLEDO, ESTOL DO DE PLAZO.
23347 5ELCID2974 ESPIDIOS MU@O GUSTIOZ, * MYO %ID ES TORNADO.
23374 5ELCID2977 ENBIA SUS CARTAS PORA LEON & * SANTI YAGUO,
23380 5ELCID2978 ALOS PORTOGALESES & * GALIZIANOS,
23397 5ELCID2981 * CABO DE VIJ SEMANAS QUE Y FUESSEN IUNTADOS;
23505 5ELCID2993 QUI LO FER NON QUISIESSE, O NO YR * MI CORT,
23635 5ELCID3010 E CON ELLOS GRAND BANDO QUE ADUXIERON * LA CORT:
23641 5ELCID3011 EBAYR LE CUYDAN * MYO %ID EL CAMPEADOR.
23739 5ELCID3024 QUANDO LOOVO * OIO EL BUEN REY DON ALFFONSSO,
23841 5ELCID3037 E AL CONDE DON ARRICH & * QUANTOS QUE Y SON;
23848 5ELCID3038 DIOS SALUE * NUESTROS AMIGOS & AUOS MAS, SE@OR
23922 5ELCID3047 E YO CON LOS MYOS POSARE * SAN SERUAN:
23959 5ELCID3053 EL REY DON ALFONSSO * TOLLEDO ES ENTRADO,
23979 5ELCID3056 SABOR * DE VELAR ENESSA SANTIDAD,
24202 5ELCID3086 SOBRELLAS VNOS %APATOS QUE * GRANT HUEBRA SON;
24346 5ELCID3104 ALA PUERTA DE FUERA DESCAUALGA * SABOR;
24462 5ELCID3118 SED EN UUESTRO ESCA@O COMMO REY * SE@OR;
24496 5ELCID3123 CATANDO ESTAN * MYO %ID QUANTOS HA EN LA CORT,
24566 5ELCID3131 ESTA TER%ERA * TOLLEDO LA VIN FER OY,
24656 5ELCID3141 QUITAR ME * EL REYNO, PERDERA MIAMOR.
24700 5ELCID3146 MUCHO UOS LO GRADESCO COMMO * REY & A SE@OR,
24703 5ELCID3146 MUCHO UOS LO GRADESCO COMMO A REY & * SE@OR,
24757 5ELCID3153 DILES DOS ESPADAS, * COLADA & A TIZON,
24760 5ELCID3153 DILES DOS ESPADAS, A COLADA & * TIZON,
25047 5ELCID3191 * MARTIN ANTOLINEZ, EL BURGALES DE PRO,
25068 5ELCID3194 PRENDED * COLADA, GANELA DE BUEN SE@OR,
25270 5ELCID3217 ESSORA SALIEN * PARTE YFANTES DE CARRION;
25351 5ELCID3228 * ESTAS PALABRAS FABLO EL REY DON ALFONSSO:
25394 5ELCID3234 ENTERGEN * MYO %ID, EL QUE EN BUEN ORA NA%IO;
25595 5ELCID3259 O EN ALGUNA RAZON? AQUI LO MEIORARE * JUUIZYO DELA CORT.
25599 5ELCID3260 * QUEM DESCUBRIESTES LAS TELAS DEL CORA%ON?
25621 5ELCID3262 CON MUY GRAND ONDRA & AVERES * NOMBRE;
25638 5ELCID3265 * QUE LAS FIRIESTES A %INCHAS & A ESPOLONES?
25642 5ELCID3265 A QUE LAS FIRIESTES * %INCHAS & A ESPOLONES?
25645 5ELCID3265 A QUE LAS FIRIESTES A %INCHAS & * ESPOLONES?
25758 5ELCID3281 GRADO * DIOS QUE %IELO & TIERRA MANDA
25815 5ELCID3288 QUANDO PRIS * CABRA, & AUOS POR LA BARBA,
25908 5ELCID3301 MYO %ID RUY DIAZ * PERO VERMUEZ CATA;
26072 5ELCID3323 FASTA ESTE DIA NOLO DESCUBRI * NADI;
26188 5ELCID3338 EL LEON PREMIO LA CABE%A, * MYO %ID ESPERO,
26210 5ELCID3341 ASOS VASSALOS VIOLOS * DERREDOR;
26274 5ELCID3350 TULO OTORGARAS * GUISA DE TRAYDOR;
26481 5ELCID3379 FUESSE * RIO DOUIRNA LOS MOLINOS PICAR
26517 5ELCID3384 ANTES ALMUERZAS QUE VAYAS * ORA%ION,
26534 5ELCID3387 FALSSO * TODOS & MAS AL CRIADOR.
26614 5ELCID3398 PIDEN SUS FIJAS * MYO %ID EL CAMPEADOR
26631 5ELCID3400 E QUE GELAS DIESSEN * ONDRA & ABENDI%ION,
26789 5ELCID3421 QUE UOS LAS DE AONDRA & * BENCI%ION.
26827 5ELCID3427 * MUCHOS PLAZE DE TOD ESTA CORT,
26851 5ELCID3430 MER%ED UOS PIDO COMMO * REY & A SE@OR,
26854 5ELCID3430 MER%ED UOS PIDO COMMO A REY & * SE@OR,
26920 5ELCID3439 ELLOS LAS PRISIERON * ONDRA & A BENDI%ION;
26923 5ELCID3439 ELLOS LAS PRISIERON A ONDRA & * BENDI%ION;
26937 5ELCID3441 ELLOS LAS HAN DEXADAS * PESAR DE NOS.
27032 5ELCID3453 ASIL CRE%E LA ONDRA * MYO %ID EL CAMPEADOR
27178 5ELCID3474 MAS QUIERO * VALEN%IA QUE TIERRAS DE CARRION.
27212 5ELCID3478 HYO VOS LO SOBRELIEUO COMMO BUEN VASSALLO FAZE * SE@OR,
27293 5ELCID3488 DAQUI UOS LOS ACOMIENDO COMO * REY & A SE@OR.
27296 5ELCID3488 DAQUI UOS LOS ACOMIENDO COMO A REY & * SE@OR.
27309 5ELCID3490 ONDRADOS MELOS ENBIAD * VALEN%IA, POR AMOR DEL CRIADOR
27359 5ELCID3496 ADELINO * EL EL CONDE DON ANRICH & EL CONDE DON REMOND;
27496 5ELCID3512 FUE BESAR LA MANO * SO SE@OR ALFONSSO;
27619 5ELCID3526 BUENOS MANDADOS ME VAYAN * VALEN%IA DE VOS.
27636 5ELCID3528 PRESO AUEMOS EL DEBDO & * PASSAR ES POR NOS;
27711 5ELCID3537 DOS DIAS ATENDIERON * YFANTES DE CARRION.
27762 5ELCID3543 CA GRAND MIEDO OUIERON * ALFONSSO EL DE LEON.
27949 5ELCID3566 ESSI FUERES VEN%IDOS, NON REBTEDES * NOS,
28004 5ELCID3574 BESAMOS VOS LAS MANOS, COMMO * REY & A SE@OR,
28007 5ELCID3574 BESAMOS VOS LAS MANOS, COMMO A REY & * SE@OR,
28071 5ELCID3583 SANTIGUARON LAS SIELAS & CAUALGAN * VIGOR;
28393 5ELCID3626 FERRANGO%ALEZ * PERO VERMUEZ EL ESCUDOL PASSO,
28433 5ELCID3631 QUEBRANTO LA BOCA DEL ESCUDO, * PART GELA ECHO,
28643 5ELCID3657 QUANDO ESTE COLPE * FERIDO COLADA LA PRE%IADA,
28777 5ELCID3675 FIRIO ENEL ESCUDO * DON MUNO GUSTIOZ,
29170 5ELCID3725 * TODOS ALCAN%A ONDRA POR EL QUE EN BUEN ORA NA%IO.

WORD # 1 OCCURS 498 TIMES.
INDEX OF DIVERSIFICATION = 57.52 WITH STANDARD DEVIATION OF 67.86

WORD C# PREFIX CONTEXT

```
AAGUIJAR             1829 5ELCID0232 TORNAUAS MARTIN ANTOLINEZ A BURGOS & MYO %ID ********
         WORD #   2 OCCURS   1 TIMES.

AALFAMA              4328 5ELCID0551 E PASSO *******, LA FOZ AYUSO UA,
         WORD #   3 OCCURS   1 TIMES.

AALTAS              25843 5ELCID3292 ****** VOZES ONDREDES QUE FABLO:
         WORD #   4 OCCURS   1 TIMES.

AAMAS               22671 5ELCID2889 BESANDO LAS *****, TORNOS DE SONRRISAR:
         WORD #   5 OCCURS   1 TIMES.

AAQUEL              19893 5ELCID2523 ****** REY BUCAR, TRAYDOR PROUADO.
         WORD #   6 OCCURS   1 TIMES.

AAQUESTO              872 5ELCID0112 POR EN VINO ******** POR QUE FUE ACUSADO.
         WORD #   7 OCCURS   1 TIMES.

ABASTAD              2054 5ELCID0259 BIEN LAS *******, YO ASSI UOS LO MANDO;
         WORD #   8 OCCURS   1 TIMES.

ABASTADO            17865 5ELCID2260 QUI AUER QUIERE PRENDER BIEN ERA ********;
         WORD #   9 OCCURS   1 TIMES.

ABASTALES             517 5ELCID0066 AMYO %ID & ALOS SUYOS ********* DE PAN & DE UINO;
         WORD #  10 OCCURS   1 TIMES.

ABATIO              18942 5ELCID2397 ****** A VIJ & A IIIJ MATAUA.
         WORD #  11 OCCURS   1 TIMES.

ABAUIECA            12392 5ELCID1573 E ADUXIESSEN LE ********; POCO AUIE QUEL GANARA,
                    12495 5ELCID1585 ENSIELLAN LE ********, CUBERTURAS LE ECHAUAN,
                    13670 5ELCID1732 ALI PRE%IO ******** DELA CABE%A FASTA ACABO.
                    27503 5ELCID3513 MANDASTES ME MOUER ******** EL CORREDOR,
         WORD #  12 OCCURS   4 TIMES.

ABAXAN               5677 5ELCID0716 ****** LAS LAN%AS A BUESTAS DELOS PENDONES,
                    28324 5ELCID3616 ****** LAS LAN%AS ABUELTAS CON LOS PENDONES,
         WORD #  13 OCCURS   2 TIMES.

ABAXO               18916 5ELCID2393 EN BRA%O EL ESCUDO & ***** EL ASTA,
         WORD #  14 OCCURS   1 TIMES.

ABBAT                1863 5ELCID0237 EL ***** DON SANCHO, CHRISTIANO DEL CRIADOR,
                     1912 5ELCID0243 DIOS, QUE ALEGRE FUE EL ***** DON SANCHO
                     1942 5ELCID0246 GRADESCO LO ADIOS, MYO %ID, DIXO EL ***** DON SANCHO;
                     1959 5ELCID0248 DIXO EL %ID:  GRA%IAS, DON *****, & SO UUESTRO PAGADO;
                     2034 5ELCID0256 AQUELLAS UOS ACOMIENDO AUOS, ***** DON SANCHO;
                     2074 5ELCID0261 OTORGADO GELO AUIE EL ***** DE GRADO.
                     2518 5ELCID0318 EN SAN PERO A MATINS TANDRA EL BUEN *****,
                     3041 5ELCID0383 AL ***** DON SANCHO TORNAN DE CASTIGAR,
                     3068 5ELCID0386 BIEN SEPA EL ***** QUE BUEN GALARDON DELLO PRENDRA.
                     3088 5ELCID0389 *****, DEZILDES QUE PRENDAN EL RASTRO & PIESSEN DE ANDAR,
                    10161 5ELCID1286 E QUE LOS DIESSE AL ***** DON SANCHO.
                    11242 5ELCID1422 LOS QUINIENTOS MARCOS DIO MINAYA AL *****,
                    11392 5ELCID1441 GRAND DUELO ES AL PARTIR DEL *****:
                    18828 5ELCID2382 NOS DAQUENT VEREMOS COMMO LIDIA EL *****.
                    29225 5ELCID3732 PER ***** LE ESCRIUIO ENEL MES DE MAYO,
         WORD #  15 OCCURS  15 TIMES.
            INDEX OF DIVERSIFICATION =  1953.43 WITH STANDARD DEVIATION OF  3525.90

ABENDI%ION          26634 5ELCID3400 E QUE GELAS DIESSEN A ONDRA & **********,
         WORD #  16 OCCURS   1 TIMES.

ABENDI%IONES        20183 5ELCID2562 DAD NOS NUESTRAS MUGIERES QUE AUEMOS ************;
         WORD #  17 OCCURS   1 TIMES.

ABENDREMOS          24859 5ELCID3166 BIEN NOS ********** CON EL REY DON ALFONSSO.
         WORD #  18 OCCURS   1 TIMES.

ABIERTA             18074 5ELCID2286 FERRAN GON%ALEZ NON VIO ALLI DOS AL%ASSE, NIN CAMARA ******* NIN
         WORD #  19 OCCURS   1 TIMES.

ABIERTAS               17 5ELCID0003 VIO PUERTAS ******** & V%OS SIN CA@ADOS,
                     3658 5ELCID0461 TODOS SON EXIDOS, LAS PUERTAS DEXADAS AN ********
                     4674 5ELCID0593 ******** DEXAN LAS PUERTAS QUE NINGUNO NON LAS GUARDA.
         WORD #  20 OCCURS   3 TIMES.

ABIERTOS             1587 5ELCID0203 RE%IBIOLO EL %ID ******** AMOS LOS BRA%OS:
                     3856 5ELCID0488 LOS BRA%OS ******** RE%IBE A MINAYA:
         WORD #  21 OCCURS   2 TIMES.

ABILTADOS           14731 5ELCID1862 EN LA ONDRA QUE EL HA NOS SEREMOS *********;
                    23094 5ELCID2942 CUEMO NOS HAN ********* YFANTES DE CARRION:
         WORD #  22 OCCURS   2 TIMES.
```

```
WORD                C#  PREFIX                                   CONTEXT

ABILTAREDES         21489 5ELCID2732 SI NOS FUEREMOS MAIADAS, *********** AUOS,
         WORD #  23 OCCURS   1 TIMES.

ABINO               23339 5ELCID2973 DESTO QUE LES ***** AVN BIEN SERAN ONDRADOS.
                    23875 5ELCID3041 DESTO QUE NOS ***** QUE UOS PESE, SE@OR.
         WORD #  24 OCCURS   2 TIMES.

ABOBASSE            13413 5ELCID1700 NOS DETARDAN DE ******** ESSAS YENTES CHRISTIANAS.
         WORD #  25 OCCURS   1 TIMES.

ABONDADOS            9807 5ELCID1245 LOS QUE EXIERCN DE TIERRA DE RITAD SON *********,
         WORD #  26 OCCURS   1 TIMES.

ABRA                12033 5ELCID1525 EN PAZ O EN GERRA DELC NUESTRO ****;
                    13454 5ELCID1705 PRENDOL YO LOS PECADCS, & DIOS LE **** EL ALMA.
                    14970 5ELCID1892 DEL CASAMIENTC NCN SE SIS **** SABOR;
                    15019 5ELCID1899 E DE MI **** PERDON; VINIESSEM A VISTAS, SI OUIESSE DENT SABOR.
                    15064 5ELCID1905 **** Y ONDRA & CRE%RA EN ONOR,
         WORD #  27 OCCURS   5 TIMES.
            INDEX OF DIVERSIFICATION =    756.75 WITH STANDARD DEVIATION OF    821.62

ABRA%AN             28318 5ELCID3615 ******* LOS ESCUDOS DELANT LOS CORA%ONES,
         WORD #  28 OCCURS   1 TIMES.

ABRA%AR              2922 5ELCID0368 EL %ID A DO@A XIMENA YUA LA *******;
                     7182 5ELCID0920 EL CAUALLO CORRIENDC, UALO ******* SIN FALLA,
                    11978 5ELCID1518 SONRRISANDO SE DELA BCCA, HYUALO *******,
                    22668 5ELCID2888 MYO %ID ASUS FIJAS YUA LAS *******,
         WORD #  29 OCCURS   4 TIMES.

ABRA%AUA            12609 5ELCID1599 ALA MADRE & ALAS FIJAS BIEN LAS ********,
         WORD #  30 OCCURS   1 TIMES.

ABRA%EN             19881 5ELCID2521 BIEN UOS ******* & SIRUAN UCS DE CORA%ON.
         WORD #  31 OCCURS   1 TIMES.

ABRA%O              15165 5ELCID1918 SONRRISOS MYO %ID & BIEN LOS ******:
         WORD #  32 OCCURS   1 TIMES.

ABRA%OLAS           20487 5ELCID2601 ********* MYO %ID & SALUDOLAS AMAS ADOS.
         WORD #  33 OCCURS   1 TIMES.

ABRA%OLOS           27370 5ELCID3497 ********* TAN BIEN & RUEGA LOS DE CORA%ON
         WORD #  34 OCCURS   1 TIMES.

ABRAM               19715 5ELCID2500 QUE ***** DE MI SALTO QUI%AB ALGUNA NOCH
         WORD #  35 OCCURS   1 TIMES.

ABRAN                1801 5ELCID0229 CASTIGAR LOS HE CCMMO ***** AFAR.
                    14846 5ELCID1876 TODAS ESTAS NUEUAS A BIEN ***** DE VENIR.
                    18623 5ELCID2356 QUE OY LOS YFANTES AMI POR AMO NON *****;
                    27904 5ELCID3560 SI BUENAS LAS TENEDES, PRO ***** AUOS;
         WORD #  36 OCCURS   4 TIMES.

ABRE                  308 5ELCID0039 NON SE **** LA PUERTA, CA BIEN ERA %ERRADA.
                     5951 5ELCID0754 OY EN ESTE DIA DE UOS **** GRAND BANDO;
         WORD #  37 OCCURS   2 TIMES.

ABREDES             19911 5ELCID2525 DESTOS NUESTRCS CASAMIENTOS UOS ******* HONOR.
                    21374 5ELCID2717 NON ******* PART EN TIERRAS DE CARRION.
         WORD #  38 OCCURS   2 TIMES.

ABREMOS              3575 5ELCID0450 TERNE YO CASTEION DON ******* GRAND EN PARA.
                     8217 5ELCID1047 ******* ESTA VIDA MIENTRA PLOGIERE AL PADRE SANTO,
                    14755 5ELCID1865 POR ESTO QUE EL FAZE NOS ******* ENBARGO.
                    18347 5ELCID2321 YA EN ESTA BATALLA A ENTRAR ******* NOS;
                    20970 5ELCID2664 TAN EN SALUC LO ******* CCMMO LO DE CARRION;
                    27152 5ELCID3470 NOS ANTES ******* AYR ATIERRAS DE CARRION.
         WORD #  39 OCCURS   6 TIMES.
            INDEX OF DIVERSIFICATION =   4714.40 WITH STANDARD DEVIATION OF   1667.21

ABREN                3636 5ELCID0459 ***** LAS PUERTAS, DE FUERA SALTO DAUAN,
         WORD #  40 OCCURS   1 TIMES.

ABRIA                3870 5ELCID0490 DO YO UOS ENBIAS BIEN ***** TAL ESPERAN%A.
                    16416 5ELCID2082 NON ***** FIJAS DE CASAR, RESPUSO EL CAMPEADOR,
         WORD #  41 OCCURS   2 TIMES.

ABRIE               12413 5ELCID1575 SI SERIE CORREDOR OSSI ***** BUENA PARADA;
         WORD #  42 OCCURS   1 TIMES.

ABRIEDES            17453 5ELCID2208 SABOR ******** DE SER & DE COMER ENEL PALA%IO.
         WORD #  43 OCCURS   1 TIMES.
```

WORD C# PREFIX CONTEXT

ABRIEN 24315 5ELCID3100 ENEL ****** QUE VER QUANTOS QUE Y SON.
WORD # 44 OCCURS 1 TIMES.

ABRIERON 5493 5ELCID0693 ******** LAS PUERTAS, FUERA VN SALTO DAN;
21936 5ELCID2791 ******** LOS OIOS & VIERON AFELEZ MUNOZ.
WORD # 45 OCCURS 2 TIMES.

ABRIESE 273 5ELCID0034 QUE SI NON LA QUEBRANTAS POR FUERCA, QUE NON GELA ******* NADI.
WORD # 46 OCCURS 1 TIMES.

ABRIESSEN 15785 5ELCID2002 LAS PUERTAS DEL ALCA%AR QUE NON SE ********* DE DIA NIN DE NOCH,
WORD # 47 OCCURS 1 TIMES.

ABRIO 2819 5ELCID0356 ***** SOS OIOS, CATO ATODAS PARTES,
WORD # 48 OCCURS 1 TIMES.

ABRIR 351 5ELCID0044 NON UOS OSARIEMOS ***** NON COGER POR NADA;
WORD # 49 OCCURS 1 TIMES.

ABUCAR 19134 5ELCID2420 ALCAN%OLO EL %ID ****** A TRES BRACAS DEL MAR,
19401 5ELCID2458 MATASTES ****** & ARRANCAMOS EL CANPO.
WORD # 50 OCCURS 2 TIMES.

ABUELTA 1872 5ELCID0238 REZAUA LOS MATINES ******* DELOS ALBORES.
4646 5ELCID0589 COIOS SALON AYUSO, CON LOS SOS ******* NADI.
WORD # 51 OCCURS 2 TIMES.

ABUELTAS 28327 5ELCID3616 ABAXAN LAS LAN%AS ******** CON LOS PENDONES,
WORD # 52 OCCURS 1 TIMES.

ACA 5321 5ELCID0672 DE CASTIELLA LA GENTIL EXIDOS SOMOS ***,
8740 5ELCID1110 LOS DE BORRIANA LUEGO VENGAN ***;
10051 5ELCID1273 DESTAS MIS GANAN%IAS, QUE AUEMOS FECHAS ***,
11716 5ELCID1485 QUE VAYADES POR ELLAS, ADUGADES GELAS ***,
12917 5ELCID1638 MIS FIJAS & MI MUGIER QUE LAS TENGO ***;
14261 5ELCID1804 DO SODES, CABOSO? VENID ***, MYNAYA;
17553 5ELCID2221 VENIT ***, ALBARFANEZ, EL QUE YO QUIERO & AMO
19038 5ELCID2409 *** TORNA, BUCAR VENIST DALENT MAR,
19848 5ELCID2517 *** VENID, CUNADOS, QUE MAS VALEMOS POR UOS.
24431 5ELCID3114 EL REY DIXO AL %ID: VENJD *** SER, CAMPEADOR,
24464 5ELCID3119 *** POSARE CON TODOS AQUESTOS MIOS.
WORD # 53 OCCURS 11 TIMES.
INDEX OF DIVERSIFICATION = 1913.30 WITH STANDARD DEVIATION OF 1393.93

ACABA 29213 5ELCID3730 EN ESTE LOGAR SE ***** ESTA RAZON.
WORD # 54 OCCURS 1 TIMES.

ACABADA 2906 5ELCID0366 LA ORA%ION FECHA, LA MISSA ******* LA AN,
WORD # 55 OCCURS 1 TIMES.

ACABADO 13989 5ELCID1771 COMMO LO DIXO EL %ID ASSI LO HAN *******.
25534 5ELCID3252 MAS QUANDO ESTO OUO *******, PENSSARON LUEGO DAL.
WORD # 56 OCCURS 2 TIMES.

ACABAN 26573 5ELCID3392 ASSI COMMO ****** ESTA RAZON,
WORD # 57 OCCURS 1 TIMES.

ACABANDO 17992 5ELCID2276 LAS COPLAS DESTE CANTAR AQUIS VAN ********.
WORD # 58 OCCURS 1 TIMES.

ACABARON 25171 5ELCID3205 HYO FAZIENDO ESTO, ELLOS ******** LO SO;
WORD # 59 OCCURS 1 TIMES.

ACABO 5256 5ELCID0665 ***** DE TRES SEMANAS, LA QUARTA QUERIE ENTRAR,
11019 5ELCID1395 QUANDO ***** LA ORA%ION, ALAS DUE@AS SE TORNO:
13674 5ELCID1732 ALI PRE%IO ABAUIECA DELA CABE%A FASTA *****.
27232 5ELCID3481 ***** DE TRES SEMANAS, EN BEGAS DE CARRION,
28903 5ELCID3691 VEN%UDO ES EL CAMPO, QUANDO ESTO SE *****
WORD # 60 OCCURS 5 TIMES.
INDEX OF DIVERSIFICATION = 5910.75 WITH STANDARD DEVIATION OF 5387.57

ACADA 13938 5ELCID1766 ***** VNA DELLAS DO LES CC MARCOS DE PLATA,
WORD # 61 OCCURS 1 TIMES.

ACAE%IERE 25097 5ELCID3197 SE QUE SI UOS *********, CON ELLA GANAREDES GRAND PREZ & GRAND VALOR.
WORD # 62 OCCURS 1 TIMES.

ACARRION 19306 5ELCID2445 ******** DE UOS YRAN BUENOS MANDADOS,
WORD # 63 OCCURS 1 TIMES.

ACASAR 26500 5ELCID3381 QUIL DARIE CON LOS DE CARRION ******?
WORD # 64 OCCURS 1 TIMES.

ACASTEION 3682 5ELCID0464 EL CAMPEADOR SALIO DE LA %ELADA, CORRIE ********* SIN FALLA.
WORD # 65 OCCURS 1 TIMES.

WORD C# PREFIX CONTEXT

ACASTIELLA 6502 5ELCID0829 HYDES UOS, MYNAYA, ********** LA GENTIL?
17931 5ELCID2269 VENIDOS SON ********** AQUESTOS OSPEDADOS,
WORD # 66 OCCURS 2 TIMES.

ACATAR 2947 5ELCID0371 E EL ALAS NI@AS TORNO LAS ******:
WORD # 67 OCCURS 1 TIMES.

ACAUALLOS 4866 5ELCID0615 YA MEIORAREMOS POSADAS ADUENOS & *********.
20559 5ELCID2610 AGRANDES GUARNJMIENTCS, ********* & ARMAS.
WORD # 68 OCCURS 2 TIMES.

ACAYAZ 21001 5ELCID2669 ******, CURIATE DESTCS, CA ERES MYO SE@OR:
WORD # 69 OCCURS 1 TIMES.

ACOGELLO 6905 5ELCID0883 POR ******** A CABO DE TRES SEMMANAS.
WORD # 70 OCCURS 1 TIMES.

ACOGEN 1042 5ELCID0134 ****** SELE CMNES DE TOCAS PARTES MEGUADOS,
11382 5ELCID1440 MUCHAS YENTES SELE ******, PENSSO DE CAUALGAR,
WORD # 71 OCCURS 2 TIMES.

ACOGIENDO 3199 5ELCID0403 VANSSELE ********* YENTES DE TODAS PARTES.
WORD # 72 OCCURS 1 TIMES.

ACOIAN 3548 5ELCID0447 E BIEN ****** TODAS LAS GANAN%IAS,
WORD # 73 OCCURS 1 TIMES.

ACOIEN 3139 5ELCID0395 GRANDES YENTES SELE ****** ESSA NOCH DE TODAS PARTES.
9432 5ELCID1199 GRANDES YENTES SE LE ****** DELA BUENA CHRISTIANDAD.
21171 5ELCID2690 ****** SE A ANDAR DE DIA & DE NOCH;
WORD # 74 OCCURS 3 TIMES.

ACOMENDO 3264 5ELCID0411 SINAUA LA CARA, A DIOS SE ********,
WORD # 75 OCCURS 1 TIMES.

ACOMIENDO 2032 5ELCID0256 AQUELLAS UOS ********* AUOS, ABBAT DON SANCHO;
2950 5ELCID0372 ADIOS UOS *********, FIJAS, & A LA MUGIER & AL PADRE SPIRITAL;
17013 5ELCID2154 ADIOS UOS *********, DESTAS VISTAS ME PARTO.
27291 5ELCID3488 DAQUI UOS LOS ********* COMO A REY & A SE@OR.
WORD # 76 OCCURS 4 TIMES.

ACONPANE@ 3525 5ELCID0444 LAN%A, CAUALLEROS BUENOS QUE ********* A MINAYA.
WORD # 77 OCCURS 1 TIMES.

ACONPA@ADOS 28133 5ELCID3592 MUY BIEN ***********, CA MUCHOS PARIENTES SON.
WORD # 78 OCCURS 1 TIMES.

ACORDADO 10192 5ELCID1290 BIEN ENTENDIDO ES DE LETRAS & MUCHO ********,
WORD # 79 OCCURS 1 TIMES.

ACORDADOS 17527 5ELCID2217 TODOS LOS DE MYO %ID TAN BIEN SON *********,
17850 5ELCID2258 LOS VASSALLOS DE MIO %ID, ASSI SON *********,
19634 5ELCID2488 ASSI LO FAZEN TODOS, CA ERAN *********.
23999 5ELCID3059 ********* FUERON, QUANDO VINO LA MAN.
28110 5ELCID3589 TODOS TRES SON ********* LOS DEL CAMPEADOR,
WORD # 80 OCCURS 5 TIMES.
INDEX OF DIVERSIFICATION = 2644.75 WITH STANDARD DEVIATION OF 1935.68

ACORDANDO 13514 5ELCID1712 MIO %ID ALOS SOS VASSALOS TAN BIEN LOS *********.
WORD # 81 OCCURS 1 TIMES.

ACORDAR 5271 5ELCID0666 MYO %ID CON LOS SOS TORNOS A *******:
8076 5ELCID1030 FASTA TER%ER DIA NOL PUEDEN *******.
15368 5ELCID1946 ******* UOS YEDES DESPUES ATODO LO MEIOR.
WORD # 82 OCCURS 3 TIMES.

ACORDARON 12467 5ELCID1581 CON QUANTOS QUE EL PUEDE, QUE CON ORAS SE *********,
WORD # 83 OCCURS 1 TIMES.

ACORDAUA 6498 5ELCID0828 MYO %ID RUY DIAZ CON LOS SOS SE ********:
WORD # 84 OCCURS 1 TIMES.

ACORRA 1737 5ELCID0222 EL ME ****** DE NOCH & DE DIA
WORD # 85 OCCURS 1 TIMES.

ACORRADES 11701 5ELCID1483 CO %IENTO CAUALLEROS QUE PRIUADOL *********;
WORD # 86 OCCURS 1 TIMES.

ACORREDES 5627 5ELCID0708 LOS QUE EL DEBDO AUEDES VEREMOS COMMO LA *********.
WORD # 87 OCCURS 1 TIMES.

ACORREN 5863 5ELCID0743 ******* LA SE@A & A MYO %ID EL CAMPEADOR.
5881 5ELCID0745 BIEN LO ******* MESNADAS DE CHRISTIANOS.
WORD # 88 OCCURS 2 TIMES.

```
WORD                 C#  PREFIX                               CONTEXT

ACOSTAR            8976 5ELCID1142 ARANCAR SE LAS ESTACAS & ******* SE ATODAS PARTES LOS TENDALES.
        WORD #  89 OCCURS   1 TIMES.

ACOSTOS            5907 5ELCID0749 ******* AVN AGUAZIL QUE TENIE BUEN CAUALLO,
        WORD #  90 OCCURS   1 TIMES.

ACRIADOR          22987 5ELCID2928 OMILLOS ALOS SANTOS & ROGO ********;
        WORD #  91 OCCURS   1 TIMES.

ACUERDAN          16288 5ELCID2066 TODOS ERAN ALEGRES & ******** EN VNA RAZON:
                  24838 5ELCID3163 APRIESSA LO YUAN TRAYENDO & ******** LA RAZON:
                  25276 5ELCID3218 NON ******** EN CONSSEIO, CA LOS HAUERES GRANDES SON:
                  27827 5ELCID3551 TODOS TRES SE ********, CA SON DE VN SE@OR.
        WORD #  92 OCCURS   4 TIMES.

ACUERDE           15342 5ELCID1942 AFE DIOS DEL %IELLO QUE NOS ******* EN LO MIIOR.
        WORD #  93 OCCURS   1 TIMES.

ACUESTAS           6202 5ELCID0790 ALMOFAR ********, LA ESPADA EN LA MANO.
        WORD #  94 OCCURS   1 TIMES.

ACUSADO             574 5ELCID0073 CA ******* SERE DELO QUE UOS HE SERUIDO,
                    876 5ELCID0112 POR EN VINO AAQUESTO POR QUE FUE *******.
        WORD #  95 OCCURS   2 TIMES.

A%ELADA            4556 5ELCID0579 AGUISA DE MENBRADO, POR SACAR LOS *******.
        WORD #  96 OCCURS   1 TIMES.

A%ERCA             4355 5ELCID0555 ****** CORRE SALON, AGUA NOL PUEDENT VEDAR.
                   8666 5ELCID1101 ****** DE MURUIEDRO TORNAN TIENDAS AFINCAR.
        WORD #  97 OCCURS   2 TIMES.

A%ERTARON         14511 5ELCID1835 LOS YFANTES DE CARRION, SABET, YS *********,
        WORD #  98 OCCURS   1 TIMES.

ADADO              6370 5ELCID0811 DAQUESTA RIQUEZA QUE EL CRIADOR NOS *****
        WORD #  99 OCCURS   1 TIMES.

ADAGARA            5759 5ELCID0727 TANTA ******* FORADAR & PASSAR,
        WORD # 100 OCCURS   1 TIMES.

ADAR               5087 5ELCID0642 POR QUE SEME ENTRO EN MI TIERRA DERECHO ME AURA ****.
                   8998 5ELCID1145 MAGER LES PESA, OUIERON SE **** & A ARANCAR.
                   9521 5ELCID1210 QUANDO VINO EL DEZENO, OUIERON GELA ****.
                  16703 5ELCID2115 CONPE%O MYO %ID **** AQUIEN QUIERE PRENDER SO DON,
                  21513 5ELCID2735 ESSORA LES CONPIE%AN **** LOS YFANTES DE CARRION;
        WORD # 101 OCCURS   5 TIMES.
           INDEX OF DIVERSIFICATION =  4105.50 WITH STANDARD DEVIATION OF  2758.82

ADELANT            2093 5ELCID0263 SE@AS DUE@AS LAS TRAEN & ADUZEN LAS *******.
                   4267 5ELCID0543 TRO%EN LAS ALCARIAS & YUAN *******,
                   4340 5ELCID0552 PASSO A BOUIERCA & ATECA QUE ES *******,
                   4742 5ELCID0601 MYO %ID & ALBARFANEZ ******* AGUIIAUAN;
                   5562 5ELCID0700 LAS AZES DE LOS MOROS YAS MUEUEN *******,
                   7009 5ELCID0896 ESTO FECHES AGORA, AL FEREDES *******.
                   7409 5ELCID0950 DEXAT ESTAS POSADAS & YREMOS *******.
                   8798 5ELCID1118 GRADO A DIOS, LO NUESTRO FUE *******.
                   9040 5ELCID1150 PRISIERON %EBOLA & QUANTO QUE ES Y *******.
                  10020 5ELCID1269 AGORA AUEMOS RIQUIZA, MAS AUREMOS *******.
                  10489 5ELCID1329 ASSI FIZO %EBOLLA & ******* CASTEION,
                  10927 5ELCID1383 DESI ******* PIENSSE DELLAS EL CAMPEADOR.
                  11422 5ELCID1445 TODOS LOS DIAS DEL SIEGLO EN LEUAR LO *******
                  11553 5ELCID1463 VAYADES A MOLINA, QUE IAZE MAS *******,
                  12447 5ELCID1579 EL OBISPO DON IHERONIMO ******* SE ENTRAUA,
                  14557 5ELCID1841 MYNAYA & PER VERMUEZ ******* SON LEGADOS,
                  14786 5ELCID1869 MYO REYNO ******* MEIOR ME PODRA SERUIR.
                  14886 5ELCID1881 LAS NUEUAS DEL %ID MUCHO VAN *******,
                  14900 5ELCID1883 CRE%REMOS EN NUESTRA ONDRA & YREMOS *******.
                  17478 5ELCID2211 CAUALGAN LOS YFFANTES, ******* ADELINAUAN AL PALA%IO,
                  19272 5ELCID2439 AL%O SOS OIOS, ESTEUA ******* CATANDO,
                  19438 5ELCID2463 QUANDO AGORA SON BUENOS, ******* SERAN PRE%IADOS.
                  21298 5ELCID2707 ******* ERAN YDOS LOS DE CRIAZON:
                  22706 5ELCID2893 QUE UOS VEA MEIOR CASADAS DAQUI EN *******.
                  24394 5ELCID3110 E DESI *******, SABET, TODOS LOS OTROS:
                  27489 5ELCID3511 MYO %ID ENEL CAUALLO ******* SE LEGO,
        WORD # 102 OCCURS  26 TIMES.
           INDEX OF DIVERSIFICATION =  1014.84 WITH STANDARD DEVIATION OF   883.17

ADELANTE           5858 5ELCID0742 DESI ********, QUANTOS QUE Y SON,
                  21746 5ELCID2766 MANDARON LE YR ********, MAS DE SU GRADO NON FUE.
        WORD # 103 OCCURS   2 TIMES.
```

```
WORD                C#  PREFIX                         CONTEXT

ADELANTEL          23681 5ELCID3016 ALUAR FANEZ ********* ENBIO,
         WORD # 104 OCCURS   1 TIMES.

ADELI%IO           25785 5ELCID3284 CA DE QUANDO NASCO ******** FUE CRIADA,
         WORD # 105 OCCURS   1 TIMES.

ADELINAN            7559 5ELCID0969 ******** TRAS MYO %ID EL BUENO DE BIUAR,
                   17120 5ELCID2167 ******** PORA VALEN%IA, LA QUE EN BUEN PUNTO GANO.
                   22430 5ELCID2857 ******** A POSAR PORA FOLGAR ESSA NOCH.
         WORD # 106 OCCURS   3 TIMES.

ADELINAUA          12457 5ELCID1580 Y DEXAUA EL CAUALLO, PORA LA CAPIELLA *********;
         WORD # 107 OCCURS   1 TIMES.

ADELINAUAN         17479 5ELCID2211 CAUALGAN LOS YFFANTES, ADELANT ********** AL PALA%IO,
         WORD # 108 OCCURS   1 TIMES.

ADELINECHOS        22637 5ELCID2884 DENT PORA VALEN%IA *********** VAN.
         WORD # 109 OCCURS   1 TIMES.

ADELINNANDO        17686 5ELCID2237 PORA SANTA MARIA A PRIESSA ***********;
         WORD # 110 OCCURS   1 TIMES.

ADELINO              242 5ELCID0031 EL CAMPEADOR ******* ASU POSADA;
                    9463 5ELCID1203 ******* PORA VALEN%IA & SOBRELLAS VA ECHAR,
                   10334 5ELCID1309 ******* PORA CASTIELLA MINAYA ALBARFANEZ.
                   10379 5ELCID1315 CON ESTA PRESENTEIA ******* PORA ALLA;
                   10996 5ELCID1392 ******* PORA SAN PERO, OLAS DUE@AS ESTAN,
                   12551 5ELCID1593 ******* A SU MUGIER & A SUS FIJAS AMAS;
                   12685 5ELCID1610 ******* MYO %ID CON ELLAS AL ALCA%AR,
                   18159 5ELCID2297 EL MANTO TRAE ALCUELLO, & ******* PORA LEON;
                   21842 5ELCID2779 ARRENDO EL CAUALLO, A ELLAS *******;
                   22988 5ELCID2929 ******* PORAL PALA%IO DO ESTAUA LA CORT,
                   27358 5ELCID3496 ******* A EL EL CONDE DON ANRICH & EL CONDE DON REMOND;
         WORD # 111 OCCURS  11 TIMES.
            INDEX OF DIVERSIFICATION =  2710.60 WITH STANDARD DEVIATION OF  2963.03

ADELI@AUA           3705 5ELCID0467 MYO %ID DON RODRIGO ALA PUERTA *********;
         WORD # 112 OCCURS   1 TIMES.

ADELLANT            7730 5ELCID0990 PUES ******** YRAN TRAS NOS, AQUI SEA LA BATALLA;
         WORD # 113 OCCURS   1 TIMES.

ADENTRO            13190 5ELCID1672 POR LAS HUERTAS ******* ESTAN SINES PAUOR.
                   28835 5ELCID3683 METIOL POR LA CARNE ******* LA LAN%A CONEL PENDON,
         WORD # 114 OCCURS   2 TIMES.

ADERECHO           23238 5ELCID2960 AIUDAR LE ********, SIN SALUE EL CRIADOR
                   28017 5ELCID3576 ******** NOS VALED, ANINGUN TUERTO NO.
                   28046 5ELCID3580 TENENDOS ********, POR AMOR DEL CRIADOR
         WORD # 115 OCCURS   3 TIMES.

ADERREDOR          21244 5ELCID2699 ELAS BESTIAS FIERAS QUE ANDAN *********.
                   24363 5ELCID3106 EL VA EN MEDIO, ELOS %IENTO *********.
                   24493 5ELCID3122 LOS %IENTO QUEL AGUARDAN POSAN *********.
                   26525 5ELCID3385 ALOS QUE DAS PAZ, FARTAS LOS *********.
                   28242 5ELCID3605 LIBRAUAN SE DEL CAMPO TODOS *********.
                   28263 5ELCID3608 TODAS LAS YENTES ESCONBRARON *********,
                   28372 5ELCID3622 CUEDAN SE QUE ESSORA CADRAN MUERTOS LOS QUE ESTAN *********.
         WORD # 116 OCCURS   7 TIMES.
            INDEX OF DIVERSIFICATION =  1187.00 WITH STANDARD DEVIATION OF  1293.56

ADESTRANDO         18190 5ELCID2301 E LIEUA LO **********, ENLA RED LE METIO.
         WORD # 117 OCCURS   1 TIMES.

ADEXAR             20948 5ELCID2661 HYA PUES QUE ****** AUEMOS FIJAS DEL CAMPEADOR,
         WORD # 118 OCCURS   1 TIMES.

ADEYNA              9122 5ELCID1161 AVN MAS AYUSSO, ****** LA CASA;
         WORD # 119 OCCURS   1 TIMES.

ADICHO             24176 5ELCID3083 ASSI COMMO LO ******, TODOS ADOBADOS SON.
         WORD # 120 OCCURS   1 TIMES.

ADIEGO             18585 5ELCID2352 CURIES ME ****** & CURIES ME ADON FERNANDO,
                   19277 5ELCID2440 E VIO VENIR ****** & A FERNANDO;
                   19975 5ELCID2534 MAS NON FALLAUAN Y ****** NI AFERRANDO.
         WORD # 121 OCCURS   3 TIMES.

ADIESTRO           21214 5ELCID2696 ******** DEXAN ASANT ESTEUAN, MAS CAE ALUEN;
                   22572 5ELCID2875 TRO%IERON ALCO%EUA, ******** DE SANTESTEUAN DE GORMAZ,
         WORD # 122 OCCURS   2 TIMES.
```

WORD C# PREFIX CONTEXT

ADIOS 1937 5ELCID0246 GRADESCO LO *****, MYO %ID, DIXO EL ABBAT DON SANCHO;
2235 5ELCID0282 PLEGA ***** & A SANTA MARIA, QUE AUN CON MIS MANOS CASE ESTAS MIS
2374 5ELCID0300 YO RUEGO ***** & AL PADRE SPIRITAL,
2948 5ELCID0372 ***** UOS ACOMIENDO, FIJAS, & A LA MUGIER & AL PADRE SPIRITAL:
3912 5ELCID0497 ***** LO PROMETO, A AQUEL QUE ESTA EN ALTO:
7206 5ELCID0924 GRADO ***** & ALAS SUS VERTUDES SANTAS;
15284 5ELCID1936 ***** LO GRADESCO QUE DEL REY HE SU GRA%IA,
17011 5ELCID2154 ***** UOS ACOMIENDO, DESTAS VISTAS ME PARTO.
18777 5ELCID2376 SI PLOGIESSE ***** QUERRIA LAS ENSAYAR,
19383 5ELCID2456 GRADO ***** & AL PADRE QUE ESTA EN ALTO,
20685 5ELCID2626 QUE SI ***** PLOGUIERE & AL PADRE CRIADOR,
20698 5ELCID2628 ***** UOS HACOMENDAMOS, DON ELUIRA & DO@A SOL,
21860 5ELCID2782 ***** PLEGA & A SANTA MARIA QUE DENT PRENDAN ELLOS MAL GALARDON
23824 5ELCID3035 GRADO *****, QUANDO UOS VEO, SE@OR.
27020 5ELCID3452 GRADO ***** DEL %IELO & AQUEL REY DON ALFONSSO,
WORD # 123 OCCURS 15 TIMES.
INDEX OF DIVERSIFICATION = 1790.64 WITH STANDARD DEVIATION OF 2077.67

ADOBADA 12079 5ELCID1531 VAYAMOS POSAR, CA LA %ENA ES *******.
WORD # 124 OCCURS 1 TIMES.

ADOBADAS 11294 5ELCID1429 QUANDO ESTAS DUE@AS ******** LAS HAN,
WORD # 125 OCCURS 1 TIMES.

ADOBADO 13537 5ELCID1715 DE TODAS GUARNIZONES MUY BIEN ES *******.
24338 5ELCID3103 ASSI YUA MYO %ID ******* ALLA CORT.
WORD # 126 OCCURS 2 TIMES.

ADOBADOS 7814 5ELCID1000 TODOS SON ******** QUANDO MYO %ID ESTO OUO FABLADO;
16942 5ELCID2144 TRAYO VOS XX PALAFRES, ESTOS BIEN ********,
17488 5ELCID2212 CON BUENAS VESTIDURAS & FUERTE MIENTRE ********;
24178 5ELCID3083 ASSI COMMO LO ADICHO, TODOS ******** SON.
27300 5ELCID3489 ELLOS SON ******** PORA CUMPLLIR TODO LO SO;
27718 5ELCID3538 MUCHO VIENEN BIEN ******** DE CAUALLOS & DE GUARNIZONES,
WORD # 127 OCCURS 6 TIMES.
INDEX OF DIVERSIFICATION = 3979.80 WITH STANDARD DEVIATION OF 3842.60

ADOBAN 13209 5ELCID1675 ****** SE DE CORA%ON E DAN SALTO DE LA VILLA;
15735 5ELCID1997 ESTOS SE ****** POR YR CON EL CAMPEADOR,
WORD # 128 OCCURS 2 TIMES.

ADOBAR 5401 5ELCID0681 ELDIA & LA NOCHE PIENSSAN SE DE ******.
10131 5ELCID1283 PUES ESTO AN FABLADO, PIENSSAN SE DE ******.
11275 5ELCID1426 EL BUENO DE MINAYA PENSOLAS DE ******
17431 5ELCID2205 PENSSARON DE ****** ESSORA EL PALA%IO,
24326 5ELCID3101 CON AQUESTOS %IENTO QUE ****** MANDO,
WORD # 129 OCCURS 5 TIMES.
INDEX OF DIVERSIFICATION = 4730.25 WITH STANDARD DEVIATION OF 2554.74

ADOBARE 1965 5ELCID0249 YO ******* CON DUCHO PORA MI & PORA MIS VASSALLOS;
WORD # 130 OCCURS 1 TIMES.

ADOBASSEN 16269 5ELCID2064 QUE ********* COZINA PORA QUANTOS QUE YSON;
WORD # 131 OCCURS 1 TIMES.

ADOBAUAN 7966 5ELCID1017 A MYO %ID DON RODRIGO GRANT COZINAL ********;
15514 5ELCID1965 DELLA PART & DELLA PORA LAS VISTAS SE ********;
WORD # 132 OCCURS 2 TIMES.

ADOBES 23310 5ELCID2969 QUE DESTAS VIJ SEMANAS ****** CON SUS VASSALLOS,
WORD # 133 OCCURS 1 TIMES.

ADOBO 15663 5ELCID1986 NON LO DETARDA, PORA LAS VISTAS SE *****;
28759 5ELCID3672 CON ASSUR GONZALEZ COMMO SE *****.
WORD # 134 OCCURS 2 TIMES.

ADON 17208 5ELCID2177 DIXO MYO %ID **** PERO & A MU@O GUSTIOZ:
18589 5ELCID2352 CURIES ME ADIEGO & CURIES ME **** FERNANDO,
22130 5ELCID2817 HYUA RE%EBIR **** ELUIRA & ADON@A SOL;
WORD # 135 OCCURS 3 TIMES.

ADON@A 22133 5ELCID2817 HYUA RE%EBIR ADON ELUIRA & ****** SOL;
WORD # 136 OCCURS 1 TIMES.

ADO@A 3049 5ELCID0384 COMMO SIRUA ***** XIMENA & ALAS FIJAS QUE HA,
WORD # 137 OCCURS 1 TIMES.

ADORAR 2662 5ELCID0336 TRES REYES DE ARABIA TE VINIERON ******,
WORD # 138 OCCURS 1 TIMES.

ADORO 2865 5ELCID0362 ATI ***** & CREO DE TODO VOLUNTAD,
WORD # 139 OCCURS 1 TIMES.

ADOROCA 6783 5ELCID0866 METIO EN PARIA ******* EN ANTES,
WORD # 140 OCCURS 1 TIMES.

```
WORD                C#  PREFIX                    CONTEXT

ADOS              10678 5ELCID1352 POR SU MUGIER DO@A XIMENA & SUS FIJAS AMAS ****:
                  13109 5ELCID1661 ASSI FFAZIE ALAS DUE@AS & A SUS FIJAS AMAS ****:
                  15050 5ELCID1902 SABOR HAN DE CASAR CCN SUS FIJAS AMAS ****.
                  15799 5ELCID2003 DENTRO ES SU MUGIER & SUS FIJAS AMAS ****,
                  17418 5ELCID2203 METIUOS EN SUS MANOS, FIJAS, AMAS ****;
                  18594 5ELCID2353 MYOS YERNOS AMCS ****, LA CCSA QUE MUCHO AMO,
                  19571 5ELCID2479 QUE LIDIARAN CCMIGO EN CAMPO MYOS YERNOS AMOS ****;
                  19783 5ELCID2507 GRANDES SON LCS GOZOS DE SUS YERNOS AMOS ****:
                  19797 5ELCID2509 VALIA DE %INCC MILL MARCCS GANARON AMOS ****;
                  20340 5ELCID2580 CON QUE RIQUEZA ENBIC MICS YERNOS AMOS ****.
                  20478 5ELCID2599 ASSI UOS PEDIMOS MER%ED NOS AMAS ****,
                  20493 5ELCID2601 ABRA%OLAS MYC %ID & SALUDOLAS AMAS ****.
                  21544 5ELCID2738 RONPIEN LAS CAMISAS & LAS CARNES AELLAS AMAS ****;
                  21595 5ELCID2745 CANSSADOS SON DE FERIR ELLOS AMOS ****,
                  21782 5ELCID2770 FASTA QUE VIESSE VENIR SUS PRIMAS AMAS ****
                  21831 5ELCID2777 FALLO SUS PRIMAS AMORTE%IDAS AMAS ****.
                  21877 5ELCID2783 VALAS TORNANDO A ELLAS AMAS ****;
                  22347 5ELCID2846 QUE VINIE MYNAYA POR SUS PRIMAS AMAS ****.
                  23627 5ELCID3009 E DIEGO & FERRANDO Y SON AMOS ****,
                  23871 5ELCID3040 BESA UOS LAS MANOS, & MIS FIJAS AMAS ****,
                  25154 5ELCID3203 QUANDO SACARON DE VALEN%IA MIS FIJAS AMAS ****,
         WORD # 141 OCCURS  21 TIMES.
            INDEX OF DIVERSIFICATION =   722.80 WITH STANDARD DEVIATION OF   717.82

ADTORES              34 5ELCID0005 E SIN FALCONES & SIN ******* MUDADOS.
         WORD # 142 OCCURS   1 TIMES.

ADUCHAS            1143 5ELCID0147 LAS ARCHAS *******, PRENDET SEYES %IENTOS MARCOS.
         WORD # 143 OCCURS   1 TIMES.

ADUENOS            4864 5ELCID0615 YA MEIORAREMOS POSADAS ******* & ACAUALLOS.
         WORD # 144 OCCURS   1 TIMES.

ADUGA             22875 5ELCID2914 ***** MELOS AVISTAS, O AIUNTAS, O A CORTES,
         WORD # 145 OCCURS   1 TIMES.

ADUGADES          11714 5ELCID1485 QUE VAYADES POR ELLAS, ******** GELAS ACA,
         WORD # 146 OCCURS   1 TIMES.

ADUGAMOS           1314 5ELCID0168 YO YRE CON UUSO, QUE ******** LOS MARCOS,
         WORD # 147 OCCURS   1 TIMES.

ADUGO             17296 5ELCID2188 HYERNOS UOS ***** DE QUE AUREMOS ONDRAN%A;
         WORD # 148 OCCURS   1 TIMES.

ADURMJO            3220 5ELCID0405 VN SUENOL PRISO DUL%E, TAN BIEN SE *******.
         WORD # 149 OCCURS   1 TIMES.

ADUX              28193 5ELCID3599 HYO LOS **** ASALUO ATIERRAS DE CARRION:
         WORD # 150 OCCURS   1 TIMES.

ADUXIER            1411 5ELCID0181 SIUOS LA ******* DALLA; SI NON, CONTALDA SOBRE LAS ARCAS. . . .
         WORD # 151 OCCURS   1 TIMES.

ADUXIERA          11225 5ELCID1420 E EL SE TENIE C QUE ******** DALLA;
         WORD # 152 OCCURS   1 TIMES.

ADUXIERON         23634 5ELCID3010 E CON ELLOS GRAND BANDO QUE ********* A LA CORT:
         WORD # 153 OCCURS   1 TIMES.

ADUXIESSEN        12390 5ELCID1573 E ********** LE ABAUIECA; POCO AUIE QUEL GANARA,
                  22298 5ELCID2840 ********** ASSUS FIJAS A VALEN%IA LA MAYOR.
         WORD # 154 OCCURS   2 TIMES.

ADUXIESTES        13925 5ELCID1764 ESTAS DUE@AS QUE **********, QUE UOS SIRUEN TANTO,
         WORD # 155 OCCURS   1 TIMES.

ADUZEN             2091 5ELCID0263 SE@AS DUE@AS LAS TRAEN & ****** LAS ADELANT.
                   7975 5ELCID1019 ****** LE LCS COMERES, DELANT GELOS PARAUAN;
                  13010 5ELCID1650 POR CASAR SON UUESTRAS FIJAS, ****** UOS AXUUAR.
                  28059 5ELCID3582 ****** LES LOS CAUALLOS BUENOS & CORREDORES,
         WORD # 156 OCCURS   4 TIMES.

ADUZID             5074 5ELCID0641 PRENDET MELO AUIDA, ****** MELO DELAND;
                  11595 5ELCID1469 CON GRAND ONDRA ****** MELAS DELANT.
         WORD # 157 OCCURS   2 TIMES.

ADUZIR             1117 5ELCID0144 POR ****** LAS ARCHAS & METER LAS EN UUESTRO SALUO,
                  14745 5ELCID1864 COMMO SI LOS FALASSE MUERTOS ****** SE LOS CAUALLOS,
                  25459 5ELCID3242 VERIEDES ****** TANTO CAUALLO CORREDOR,
         WORD # 158 OCCURS   3 TIMES.
```

WORD C# PREFIX CONTEXT

AEL 14191 5ELCID1796 LO QUE CAYE *** MUCHO ERA SOBEIANO;
17505 5ELCID2215 *** & EASSU MUGIER DELANT SELE OMILLARON,
WORD # 159 OCCURS 2 TIMES.

AELLA 2009 5ELCID0254 ***** & ASUS FIJAS & ASUS DUENAS SIRUADES LAS EST A@O.
25792 5ELCID3285 CA NON ME PRISO ***** FIJO DE MUGIER NADA,
WORD # 160 OCCURS 2 TIMES.

AELLAS 21542 5ELCID2738 RONPIEN LAS CAMISAS & LAS CARNES ****** AMAS ADOS;
WORD # 161 OCCURS 1 TIMES.

AESPOLON 21819 5ELCID2775 VANSSE LOS YFANTES, AGUIJAN ********.
WORD # 162 OCCURS 1 TIMES.

AESSA 8594 5ELCID1091 AORIENT EXE EL SOL, E TORNOS ***** PART.
WORD # 163 OCCURS 1 TIMES.

AESSOS 27386 5ELCID3499 ****** & ALOS OTROS QUE DE BUENA PARTE SON,
WORD # 164 OCCURS 1 TIMES.

AESTAS 10111 5ELCID1281 ****** TIERRAS ESTRANAS QUE NOS PUDIEMOS GANAR.
19919 5ELCID2527 ****** PALABRAS FABLO FERAN GON%ALEZ:
WORD # 165 OCCURS 2 TIMES.

AESTE 10291 5ELCID1303 ***** DON IERONIMO YAL OTORGAN POR OBISPO;
WORD # 166 OCCURS 1 TIMES.

AESTO 24814 5ELCID3160 DIXO EL CONDE DON GAR%IA: ***** NOS FABLEMOS.
26635 5ELCID3401 ***** CALLARON & ASCUCHO TODA LA CORT.
WORD # 167 OCCURS 2 TIMES.

AFAN 12885 5ELCID1635 CON **** GANE A VALEN%IA, & ELA POR HEREDAD,
15278 5ELCID1935 CON GRAND **** GANE LO QUE HE YO;
27453 5ELCID3507 E YR ME QUIERO PORA VALEN%IA, CON **** LA GANE YO.
WORD # 168 OCCURS 3 TIMES.

AFAR 1802 5ELCID0229 CASTIGAR LOS HE COMMO ABRAN ****.
3418 5ELCID0431 MANDADO DE SO SE@OR TODO LO HAN ****.
WORD # 169 OCCURS 2 TIMES.

AFARTO 12951 5ELCID1643 ****** VERAN POR LOS OIOS COMMO SE GANA EL PAN.
27074 5ELCID3459 CA EN ESTA CORT ****** HA PORA VOS,
WORD # 170 OCCURS 2 TIMES.

AFAZER 17544 5ELCID2220 PUES QUE ****** LO AUEMOS, POR QUE LO YMOS TARDANDO?
WORD # 171 OCCURS 1 TIMES.

AFE 10390 5ELCID1317 *** MINAYA LABARFANEZ DO LEGA TAN APUESTO;
12584 5ELCID1597 *** ME AQUI, SE@OR, YO UUESTRAS FIJAS & AMAS,
15336 5ELCID1942 *** DIOS DEL %IELLO QUE NOS ACUERDE EN LO MIIOR.
16872 5ELCID2135 RESPONDIO EL REY: *** AQUI ALBARFANEZ;
16910 5ELCID2140 DIXO ALBARFANEZ: SE@OR, *** QUE ME PLAZ.
17018 5ELCID2155 *** DIOS DEL %IELO, QUE LO PONGA EN BUEN LOGAR
18814 5ELCID2381 *** LOS MOROS A OIO, YO LOS ENSAYAR.
26676 5ELCID3407 *** MIS FIJAS, EN UUESTRAS MANOS SON:
WORD # 172 OCCURS 8 TIMES.
INDEX OF DIVERSIFICATION = 2325.57 WITH STANDARD DEVIATION OF 2642.78

AFEA 13233 5ELCID1677 SACAN LOS DELAS HUERTAS MUCHO **** GUISA,
WORD # 173 OCCURS 1 TIMES.

AFELAS 23126 5ELCID2947 ****** SUS FIJAS EN VALENCIA DOSON.
WORD # 174 OCCURS 1 TIMES.

AFELEZ 21941 5ELCID2791 ABRIERON LOS OIOS & VIERON ****** MUNOZ.
WORD # 175 OCCURS 1 TIMES.

AFELLAS 16465 5ELCID2088 ******* EN UUESTRA MANO DON ELUIRA & DO@A SOL,
WORD # 176 OCCURS 1 TIMES.

AFELLOS 16579 5ELCID2101 ******* EN UUESTRAS MANOS LOS YFANTES DE CARRION,
WORD # 177 OCCURS 1 TIMES.

AFELO 3980 5ELCID0505 TODO LO OTRO ***** EN UUESTRA MANO.
WORD # 178 OCCURS 1 TIMES.

AFELOS 17189 5ELCID2175 ****** EN VALEN%IA, LA QUE MYO %ID GA@O;
WORD # 179 OCCURS 1 TIMES.

AFER 23520 5ELCID2995 HYA LO VIERON QUE ES **** LOS YFANTES DE CARRION,
25453 5ELCID3241 HYA VIERON QUE ES **** LOS YFANTES DE CARRION.
25987 5ELCID3312 POR LO QUE YO OUIER **** POR MI NON MANCARA.
WORD # 180 OCCURS 3 TIMES.

AFERRANDO 19977 5ELCID2534 MAS NON FALLAUAN Y ADIEGO NI *********.
WORD # 181 OCCURS 1 TIMES.

WORD C# PREFIX CONTEXT

AFEUOS
1178 5ELCID0152 ****** LOS ALA TIENDA DEL CAMPEADOR CONTADO;
2077 5ELCID0262 ****** DO@A XIMENA CON SUS FIJAS DO UA LEGANDO;
3763 5ELCID0476 ****** LOS CCIIJ ENEL ALGARA,
9895 5ELCID1255 ****** TODO AQUESTO PUESTO EN BUEN RECABDO.
11305 5ELCID1431 ****** RACHEL & VIDAS ALOS PIES LE CAEN:
11820 5ELCID1499 ****** AQUI PERO VERMUEZ & MU@O GUSTIOZ QUE UOS QUIEREN SIN HART,
12345 5ELCID1568 ****** TODOS AQUESTOS RE%IBEN A MINAYA
17623 5ELCID2230 ****** DELANT MINAYA, AMOS SODES HERMANOS.
18709 5ELCID2368 ****** EL OBISPO DON IHERONIMO MUY BIEN ARMADO,
WORD # 182 OCCURS 9 TIMES.
INDEX OF DIVERSIFICATION = 2190.38 WITH STANDARD DEVIATION OF 2216.85

AFFE
17561 5ELCID2222 **** AMAS MIS FIJAS, METOLAS EN UUESTRA MANO;
22413 5ELCID2855 **** DIOS DELOS %IELOS QUE UOS DE DENT BUEN GALARDON
26576 5ELCID3393 **** DOS CAUALLEROS ENTRARON POR LA CORT;
WORD # 183 OCCURS 3 TIMES.

AFINCA
25300 5ELCID3221 MUCHO NOS ****** EL QUE VALEN%IA GA@O,
WORD # 184 OCCURS 1 TIMES.

AFINCAR
8671 5ELCID1101 A%ERCA DE MURUIEDRO TORNAN TIENDAS *******.
WORD # 185 OCCURS 1 TIMES.

AFITA
4079 5ELCID0518 FABLO CON LOS DE CASTEION, & ENVIO ***** & AGUADELFAGARA,
WORD # 186 OCCURS 1 TIMES.

AFONTADO
20240 5ELCID2569 EL %ID QUE NOS CURIAUA DE ASSI SER ********;
WORD # 187 OCCURS 1 TIMES.

AFUERA
28490 5ELCID3638 POR LA BOCA ****** LA SANGREL SALIO;
WORD # 188 OCCURS 1 TIMES.

AGALUE
6094 5ELCID0774 E ****** NOL COGIERON ALLA;
WORD # 189 OCCURS 1 TIMES.

AGARDANDO
4461 5ELCID0568 ********* SEUA MYO %ID CON TODOS SUS VASSALLOS;
WORD # 190 OCCURS 1 TIMES.

AGENA
10462 5ELCID1326 MAGER EN TIERRA *****, EL BIEN FAZE LO SO;
WORD # 191 OCCURS 1 TIMES.

AGENAS
12944 5ELCID1642 EN ESTAS TIERRAS ****** VERAN LAS MORADAS COMMO SE FAZEN,
WORD # 192 OCCURS 1 TIMES.

AGENO
25503 5ELCID3248 ENPRESTAN LES DELO *****, QUE NON LES CUMPLE LO SUYO.
WORD # 193 OCCURS 1 TIMES.

AGORA
2960 5ELCID0373 ***** NOS PARTIMOS, DIOS SABE EL AIUNTAR.
6142 5ELCID0782 DIZE MYNAYA: ***** SO PAGADO,
6482 5ELCID0827 ***** DAUAN %EUADA, YA LA NOCH ERA ENTRADA,
7006 5ELCID0896 ESTO FECHES *****, AL FEREDES ADELANT.
7516 5ELCID0964 ***** CORREM LAS TIERRAS QUE EN MI ENPARA ESTAN;
7655 5ELCID0980 LO DE ANTES & DE ***** TODOM LO PECHARA;
10015 5ELCID1269 ***** AUEMOS RIQUIZA, MAS AUREMOS ADELANT.
11867 5ELCID1504 TODOS VIENEN EN VNO, ***** LEGARAN.
16147 5ELCID2048 VOS ***** LEGASTES, & NOS VINJEMOS ANOCH;
19435 5ELCID2463 QUANDO ***** SON BUENOS, ADELANT SERAN PRE%IADOS.
19674 5ELCID2494 ANTES FU MINGUADO, ***** RICO SO,
20457 5ELCID2597 ***** NOS ENVIADES ATIERRAS DE CARRION,
21697 5ELCID2758 DE NUESTROS CASAMIENTOS ***** SOMOS VENGADOS;
24671 5ELCID3143 ***** DEMANDE MYO %ID EL CAMPEADOR:
27001 5ELCID3450 ***** BESAREDES SUS MANOS & LAMAR LAS HEDES SE@ORAS,
29084 5ELCID3715 ***** LAS AYAN QUITAS HEREDADES DE CARRION.
WORD # 194 OCCURS 16 TIMES.
INDEX OF DIVERSIFICATION = 1740.60 WITH STANDARD DEVIATION OF 1316.01

AGRAND
10108 5ELCID1280 DE GUISA YRAN POR ELLAS QUE ****** ONDRA VERNAN
12746 5ELCID1618 MYO %ID & SUS COMPANAS TAN ****** SABOR ESTAN.
WORD # 195 OCCURS 2 TIMES.

AGRANDES
20557 5ELCID2610 ******** GUARNJMIENTOS, ACAUALLOS & ARMAS.
WORD # 196 OCCURS 1 TIMES.

AGRANT
21959 5ELCID2794 ****** PRIESSA SERE BUSCADO YO;
22839 5ELCID2909 QUANDO LAS HAN DEXADAS ****** DESONOR,
24399 5ELCID3111 ****** ONDRA LO RE%IBEN AL QUE EN BUEN ORA NA%IO.
WORD # 197 OCCURS 3 TIMES.

AGRIZA
21203 5ELCID2694 ASSINIESTRO DEXAN ****** QUE ALAMOS POBLO,
WORD # 198 OCCURS 1 TIMES.

AGUA
1168 5ELCID0150 NON VIENE ALA PUEENT, CA POR EL **** APASSADO,
2727 5ELCID0345 DEL **** FEZIST VINO & DELA PIEDRA PAN,

```
WORD                    C#  PREFIX                               CONTEXT

AGUA (CON'T)

                   4137 5ELCID0526 E QUE SERIE RETENEDOR, MAS NON YAURIE ****.
                   4358 5ELCID0555 A%ERCA CORRE SALON, **** NOL PUEDENT VEDAR.
                   4387 5ELCID0558 LOS VNOS CONTRA LA SIERRA & LOS OTROS CONTRA LA ****.
                   4402 5ELCID0560 DERREDOR DEL OTERO, BIEN %ERCA DEL ****,
                   5231 5ELCID0661 ALOS DE MYO %ID YA LES TUELLEN EL ****.
                   5273 5ELCID0667 EL **** NOS AN VEDADA, EXIR NOS HA EL PAN,
                   8242 5ELCID1049 ALEGRE ES EL CONDE & PIDIO **** ALAS MANOS,
                   9671 5ELCID1229 MOROS EN ARUEN%O AMIDOS BEUER ****.
                  15430 5ELCID1954 SOBRE TAIO, QUE ES UNA **** CABDAL,
                  21991 5ELCID2798 DANDOS DEL ****, SI UOS VALA EL CRIADOR
                  22014 5ELCID2801 COGIO DEL **** ENEL & ASUS PRIMAS DIO;
         WORD # 199 OCCURS  13 TIMES.
            INDEX OF DIVERSIFICATION =  1736.17 WITH STANDARD DEVIATION OF  2256.60

AGUADELFAGARA      4081 5ELCID0518 FABLO CON LOS DE CASTEION, & ENVIO AFITA & *************,
         WORD # 200 OCCURS   1 TIMES.

AGUARDAN          23000 5ELCID2930 CON EL DOS CAUALLEROS QUEL ******** CUM ASSE@OR.
                  24491 5ELCID3122 LOS %IENTO QUEL ******** POSAN ADERREDOR.
         WORD # 201 OCCURS   2 TIMES.

AGUARDANDO         8320 5ELCID1058 PAGADO ES MYO %ID, QUE LO ESTA **********,
                  12190 5ELCID1547 LAS NOCHES & LOS DIAS LAS DUENAS **********.
         WORD # 202 OCCURS   2 TIMES.

AGUARDAR           2446 5ELCID0308 MANDO EL REY A MYO %ID A ********,
                  11449 5ELCID1449 EL PORTERO CON ELLOS QUE LOS HA DE ********;
                  14410 5ELCID1822 TALLES GANAN%IAS TRAEN QUE SON A ********.
                  17136 5ELCID2168 EA DON FERNANDO & A DON DIEGO ******** LOS MANDO
         WORD # 203 OCCURS   4 TIMES.

AGUARDAUAN         6575 5ELCID0839 TODOS LOS DIAS A MYO %ID **********
         WORD # 204 OCCURS   1 TIMES.

AGUAS              4277 5ELCID0545 PASSARON LAS *****, ENTRARON AL CAMPO DE TORAN%IO,
                  14444 5ELCID1826 PASSANDO VAN LAS SIERRAS & LOS MONTES & LAS *****,
                  15562 5ELCID1973 ALAS ***** DE TAIO, OLAS UISTAS SON APAREIADAS.
                  22087 5ELCID2811 ALAS ***** DE DUERO ELLOS ARRIBADOS SON,
         WORD # 205 OCCURS   4 TIMES.

AGUAZIL            5909 5ELCID0749 ACOSTOS AVN ******* QUE TENIE BUEN CAUALLO,
         WORD # 206 OCCURS   1 TIMES.

AGUDAS            21530 5ELCID2737 CON LAS ESPUELAS ******, DON ELLAS AN MAL SABOR,
         WORD # 207 OCCURS   1 TIMES.

AGUDO             28680 5ELCID3661 VN COLPEL DIO DE LANO, CON LO ***** NOL TOMAUA.
         WORD # 208 OCCURS   1 TIMES.

AGUIIAR              69 5ELCID0010 ALLI PIENSSAN DE *******, ALLI SUELTAN LAS RIENDAS.
         WORD # 209 OCCURS   1 TIMES.

AGUIIAUAN          4743 5ELCID0601 MYO %ID & ALBARFANEZ ADELANT *********;
         WORD # 210 OCCURS   1 TIMES.

AGUIIO              291 5ELCID0037 ****** MYO %ID, ALA PUERTA SE LEGAUA,
         WORD # 211 OCCURS   1 TIMES.

AGUIJAN           15841 5ELCID2009 SALIEN DE VALEN%IA, ******* & ESPOLONAUAN.
                  20838 5ELCID2646 ******* QUANTO PUEDEN YFANTES DE CARRION:
                  21198 5ELCID2693 POR LOS MONTES CLAROS ******* A ESPOLON;
                  21818 5ELCID2775 VANSSE LOS YFANTES, ******* AESPOLON.
         WORD # 212 OCCURS   4 TIMES.

AGUIJAR            1787 5ELCID0227 SUELTAN LAS RIENDAS & PIENSSAN DE *******.
                  19078 5ELCID2413 EL ESPADA TIENES DESNUDA EN LA MANO & VEOT *******;
         WORD # 213 OCCURS   2 TIMES.

AGUIJAUA            413 5ELCID0051 PARTIOS DELA PUERTA, POR BURGOS ********,
                   8470 5ELCID1077 ******** EL CONDE E PENSSAUA DE ANDAR,
         WORD # 214 OCCURS   2 TIMES.

AGUIJAUAN         12161 5ELCID1543 ARBUXUELO ARRIBA PRIUADO *********,
         WORD # 215 OCCURS   1 TIMES.

AGUIJEDES          5475 5ELCID0691 MAS NON ********* CON ELLA, SI YO NON UOS LO MANDAR.
         WORD # 216 OCCURS   1 TIMES.

AGUIJO             6722 5ELCID0858 PASO SALON AYUSO, ****** CABA DELANT,
                   6750 5ELCID0862 ****** MYO %ID, YUAS CABA DELANT,
                  18919 5ELCID2394 ****** A BAUIECA, EL CAUALLO QUE BIEN ANDA,
         WORD # 217 OCCURS   3 TIMES.
```

```
WORD                    C#  PREFIX                              CONTEXT

AGUISA                  800 5ELCID0102 LEGO MARTIN ATOLINEZ ****** DEMENBRADO:
                       4550 5ELCIDC579 ****** CE MENBRADO, PCR SACAR LOS A%ELADA.
                       6345 5ELCID0808 BIEN LO ****** EL QUE EN BUEN ORA NASCO,
                       8403 5ELCID1068 HYA UOS YDES, CONDE, ****** DE MUY FRANCO,
                      1C657 5ELCID1350 FABLAUA MINAYA Y ****** CE VARCN:
                      20303 5ELCID2576 BIEN LC SABEDES UCS QUE LAS GANE ****** DE VARON;
                      24766 5ELCID3154 ESTAS YO LAS GANE ****** CE VARON,
                      27612 5ELCID3525 E MUNO GUSTIOZ, FIRMES SED EN CAMPO ****** DE VARONES;
                      27924 5ELCID3563 HUEBOS VOS ES QUE LIDIECES ****** DE VARONES,
                      28966 5ELCID3700 ****** DE MENBRADOS ANCAN DIAS & NOCHES,
         WORD # 218 CCCURS  10 TIMES.
            INDEX OF DIVERSIFICATICN =  3128.56 WITH STANCARD CEVIATION OF  2754.54

AGUISADO               1C31 5ELCID0132 MYC %ID QUERRA LC QUE SSEA ********;
                       1115 5ELCIDC143 E NOS UCS AIUCAREMCS, QUE ASSI ES ********,
                       1543 5ELCIDC197 MERE%ER NOLC HEDES, CA ESTO ES ********:
                       6551 5ELCIDC836 YA ES ********, MA@ANAS FUE MINAYA,
                       9960 5ELCID1262 ALI DIXO MINAYA: CCNSEIC ES ********.
                      15116 5ELCID1911 QUEL YRE A VISTAS CC FUERE ********;
                      16144 5ELCID2047 DIXO EL REY: NON ES ******** CY:
                      17915 5ELCID2266 GRANT BIEN CIZEN CELLCS, CA SERA ********.
                      18351 5ELCID2322 ESTO ES ******** POR NON VER CARRION,
                      23722 5ELCID3022 BIEN ******** VIENE EL %ID CCN TODOS LOS SOS,
         WORD # 219 OCCURS  10 TIMES.
            INDEX OF DIVERSIFICATICN =  2520.22 WITH STANCARD CEVIATION OF  2221.99

AGUISAMIENTOS         24515 5ELCID3125 EN SOS ************* BIEN SEMEIA VARON.
         WORD # 220 OCCURS   1 TIMES.

AIANTAR               17784 5ELCID2250 ANTES QUE ENTRASSEN ******* TOCOS LOS QUEBRANTARON.
         WORD # 221 OCCURS   1 TIMES.

AIUDA                 19743 5ELCID2503 ELLOS ME DARAN PARIAS CON ***** DEL CRIADOR,
         WORD # 222 OCCURS   1 TIMES.

AIUDAR                 8718 5ELCID1107 VAYAN LCS MANDADCS POR LOS QUE NOS CEUEN ******,
                      23236 5ELCID2960 ****** LE ACERECHO, SIN SALUE EL CRIADOR
         WORD # 223 OCCURS   2 TIMES.

AIUDARA                9101 5ELCID1158 QUE DICS LE ******* & FIZIERA ESTA ARRANCADA.
         WORD # 224 OCCURS   1 TIMES.

AIUDARAN               5070 5ELCIDC640 CON LOS DELA FRONTERA QUE UOS ********,
         WORD # 225 OCCURS   1 TIMES.

AIUDAREMOS             1111 5ELCID0143 E NOS UOS **********, QUE ASSI ES AGUISADO,
         WORD # 226 OCCURS   1 TIMES.

AIUDE                  1734 5ELCID0221 VUESTRA UERTUC ME UALA, GLORICSA, EN MY EXIDA & ME *****,
                       2878 5ELCID0363 E RUEGO A SAN PEYCRO QUE ME ***** A ROGAR
         WORD # 227 OCCURS   2 TIMES.

AIUDOL                 8612 5ELCID1094 ****** EL CRIADOR, EL SE@NOR QUE ES EN %IELO.
         WORD # 228 CCCURS   1 TIMES.

AIUNTA                29110 5ELCID3718 OUIERON SU ****** CCN ALFCNSSO EL DE LEON,
         WORD # 229 OCCURS   1 TIMES.

AIUNTADO               3877 5ELCID0491 ESSO CCN ESTO SEA ********;
         WORD # 230 OCCURS   1 TIMES.

AIUNTAR                2966 5ELCID0373 AGORA NOS PARTIMOS, DIOS SABE EL *******.
                       9203 5ELCID1171 NON OSAN FUERAS EXIR NIN CON EL SE *******;
                      26052 5ELCID3320 PASSE POR TI, CCN EL MORO ME OFF DE *******,
         WORD # 231 OCCURS   3 TIMES.

AIUNTARON              5162 5ELCID0653 GENTES SE ********* SCBEIANAS DE GRANDES
                       7949 5ELCID1015 DE TODAS PARTES LCS SCS SE *********;
         WORD # 232 OCCURS   2 TIMES.

AIUNTAS               22879 5ELCID2914 ADUGA MELOS AVISTAS, C *******, O A CORTES,
                      23147 5ELCID2949 QUE GELCS LEUEDES AVISTAS, O *******, O A CORTES;
         WORD # 233 OCCURS   2 TIMES.

AIUNTAUA              12807 5ELCID1625 AQUEL REY DE MARRUECOS ******** SUS VIRTOS;
         WORD # 234 OCCURS   1 TIMES.

AL                      571 5ELCID0072 ESTA NOCH YGAMOS & UAYMCS NCS ** MATINO,
                        772 5ELCIDC098 PASSO POR BURGOS, ** CASTIELLO ENTRAUA,
                       1188 5ELCIDC153 ASSI CCMMO ENTRARON, ** %IC BESARON LE LAS MANOS.
                       1755 5ELCID0224 MANDO ** UUESTRO ALTAR BUENAS DONAS & RICAS;
                       1889 5ELCID0240 ROGANDO A SAN PERO & ** CRIADOR:
                       1920 5ELCID0244 CON LUMBRES & CCN CANDELAS ** CORAL DIERON SALTO.
                       1929 5ELCID0245 CON TAN GRANT GOZO RE%IBEN ** QUE EN BUEN ORA NASCO.
                       2065 5ELCID0260 POR VN MARCHO QUE DESPENCADES ** MONESTERIO DARE YO QUATRO.
```

WORD C# PREFIX CONTEXT

AL (CON'T)

2190 5ELCIDC276 LEGOLAS ** CROA%ON, CA MUCHO LAS QUERIA.
2269 5ELCIDC285 GRAND IANTAR LE FAZEN ** BUEN CAMPEADOR.
2376 5ELCIDC300 YO RUEGO ADIOS & ** PADRE SPIRITAL,
2594 5ELCID0328 ROGANDO ** CRIADOR QUANTO ELLA MEIOR SABE,
2700 5ELCID0341 SALUEST DENTRO EN ROMA ** SE@OR SAN SABASTIAN,
2828 5ELCID0357 EN TI CROUO ** ORA, POR END ES SALUO DE MAL;
2925 5ELCID0369 DO@A XIMENA ** %ID LA MANOL VA BESAR,
2957 5ELCIDC372 ADIOS UOS ACOMIENDO, FIJAS, & A LA MUGIER & ** PADRE SPIRITAL;
3040 5ELCIDC383 ** ABBAT DON SANCHO TORNAN DE CASTIGAR,
3583 5ELCID0451 SICUETA UOS FUERE ALGUNA ** ALGARA,
3940 5ELCID0500 QUE ENPLEYE LA LAN%A & ** ESPACA META MANO,
3999 5ELCIDC508 ** REY ALFONSSO QUE LEGARIEN SUS COMPA@AS,
4279 5ELCID0545 PASSARON LAS AGUAS, ENTRARON ** CAMPO DE TORAN%IO,
4670 5ELCID0592 ALSABOR DEL PRENDER DELC ** NON PIENSSAN NADA,
4953 5ELCIDC627 ** REY DE VALEN%IA ENBIARON CON MENSAIE,
5175 5ELCID0655 ** BUENO DE MYO %ID EN ALCO%ER LEUAN %ERCAR.
5350 5ELCID0675 EN EL NOBRE DEL CRIADOR, QUE NON PASE POR **:
5484 5ELCID0692 ** %ID BESO LA MANO, LA SE@A UA TOMAR.
5506 5ELCIDC694 VIERON LO LAS AROBDAS DELOS MOROS, ** ALMOFALLA SEUAN TORNAR.
5641 5ELCID0710 RESPUSO PERO VERMUEZ: NON RASTARA POR **.
5889 5ELCIDC746 LA LAN%A A QUEBRACA, ** ESPACA METIO MANO,
5991 5ELCIDC760 ** REY FARIZ IIJ COLPES LE AUIE DADO;
6108 5ELCIDC776 EL CAMPEADOR YUAL EN ** CAZ,
6324 5ELCIDC805 EN LA SU QUINTA ** %ID CAEN C CAUALLOS.
6390 5ELCIDC815 ** REY ALFONSSSO QUE ME A AYRADO
6725 5ELCID0859 ** EXIR DE SALON MUCHO OUO BUENAS AUES.
6826 5ELCIDC872 TREYNTA CAUALLOS ** REY LOS ENPRESENTAUA;
7C07 5ELCIDC896 ESTO FECHES AGORA, ** FEREDES ADELANT.
7415 5ELCIDC951 ESTON%ES SE MUDO EL %ID ** PUERTO DE ALCAT,
7627 5ELCIDC977 DIGADES ** CONDE NON LO TENGA A MAL,
7894 5ELCID1009 ** CONDE DON REMONT A PRESON LEAN TOMADO;
7924 5ELCID1012 PRISO LO ** CONDE, PORA SU TIERRA LO LEUAUA;
8222 5ELCID1047 ABREMOS ESTA VIDA MIENTRA PLOGIERE ** PADRE SANTO,
8662 5ELCID1100 TRASNOCHARON DE NOCH, ** ALUA DELA MAN
8905 5ELCID1134 COMMO GELO A DICHO, ** CAMPEADOR MUCHO PLAZE.
9420 5ELCID1198 ** SABOR DELA GANAN%IA NON LO GUIERE DETARDAR,
10039 5ELCID1272 ** REY ALFONSSO MYO SE@OR NATURAL;
10160 5ELCID1286 E QUE LOS DIESSE ** ABBAT DON SANCHO.
1C612 5ELCID1345 MAGER PLOGO ** REY, MUCHO PESO A GAR%IORDONEZ:
1C641 5ELCID1348 DIXO EL REY REY ** CONDE: DEXAD ESSA RAZON,
1C690 5ELCID1354 E YRIEN PORA VALEN%IA ** BUEN CAMPEADOR.
1C812 5ELCID1369 LOS QUE QUISIEREN YR SEUIR ** CAMPEADOR
11110 5ELCID1407 DEZID ** CANPEADOR, QUE DIOS LE CURIE DE MAL,
11241 5ELCID1422 LOS QUINIENTOS MARCOS DIO MINAYA ** ABBAT,
11389 5ELCID1441 GRAND DUELO ES ** PARTIR DEL ABBAT:
11402 5ELCID1443 POR MI ** CAMPEADOR LAS MANOS LE BESAD
11475 5ELCID1454 ** ORA QUE LO SOPO MYO %ID EL DE BIUAR,
12058 5ELCID1529 SI DIOS ME LEGARE ** %ID ELO VEA CON EL ALMA,
12480 5ELCID1583 RE%IBIR SALIEN LAS DUENAS & ** BUENO DE MINAYA.
12690 5ELCID1610 ADELINO MYO %ID CON ELLAS ** ALCA%AR,
12776 5ELCID1622 PESOL ** REY DE MARRUECOS DE MYO %ID DON RODRIGO:
12868 5ELCID1633 GRADO ** CRIADOR & A PADRE ESPIRITAL
12902 5ELCID1637 GRADO ** CRIADOR & A SANTA MARIA MADRE,
12967 5ELCID1644 SU MUGIER & SUS FIJAS SUBIOLAS ** ALCA%AR,
13017 5ELCID1651 AUOS GRADO, %ID, & ** PADRE SPIRITAL.
13292 5ELCID1685 OYD ME, CAUALLEROS, NON RASTARA POR **;
13368 5ELCID1694 PUES ESSO QUEREDES, %ID, A MI MANDADES **;
13578 5ELCID1721 PLOGO ** CRIADOR & OUIERON LOS DE ARRANCAR.
13590 5ELCID1722 MYO %ID ENPLEO LA LAN%A, ** ESPADA METIO MANO,
13609 5ELCID1725 ** REY YU%EF TRES COLPES LE OUO DADOS,
13737 5ELCID1741 QUANDO ** REY DE MARUECOS ASSI LO AN ARRANCADO,
13789 5ELCID1747 MYO %ID FINCO ANTELLAS, TOUO LA RYENDA ** CAUALLO:
13845 5ELCID1754 ROGAND ** CRIADOR QUE UOS BIUA ALGUNT A@O,
13903 5ELCID1761 EN BUELTA CON EL ENTRARON ** PALA%IO,
14697 5ELCID1859 PESO ** CONDE DON GAR%IA, E MAL ERA YRADO;
14767 5ELCID1867 GRADO ** CRIADOR & AL SE@OR SANT ESIDRO EL DE LEON
14770 5ELCID1867 GRADO AL CRIADOR & ** SE@OR SANT ESIDRO EL DE LEON
14902 5ELCID1884 VINIEN ** REY ALFONSSO CON ESTA PORIDAD:
14952 5ELCID1890 HYO ECHE DE TIERRA ** BUEN CAMPEADOR,
15134 5ELCID1914 ESPIDIENSSE ** REY, CON ESTO TORNADOS SON,
15210 5ELCID1925 DIXO MYO %ID: GRADO ** CRIADOR
15459 5ELCID1959 ** REY ONDRADO DELANT LE ECHARON LAS CARTAS;
16113 5ELCID2043 FABLO MYO %ID & DIXO ESTA RAZON: ESTO GRADESCO ** CRIADOR,
16299 5ELCID2068 ** OTRO DIA MA@ANA, ASSI COMMO SALIO EL SOL,
16315 5ELCID2070 ** SALIR DE LA MISSA TODOS IUNTADOS SON,
16533 5ELCID2095 GRADO & GRA%IAS, CID, COMMO TAN BUENO, & PRIMERO ** CRIADOR,
16572 5ELCID2100 ** CRIADOR PLEGA QUE AYADES ENDE SABOR.
16973 5ELCID2149 PLEGA ** CRIADOR CON TODOS LOS SOS SANTOS, ESTE PLAZER
17096 5ELCID2164 ESTO PLOGO ** REY, & ATODOS LOS SOLTO;
17176 5ELCID2173 QUE ES LARGO DE LENGUA, MAS EN LO ** NON ES TAN PRO.
17262 5ELCID2183 MYO %ID EL CAMPEADOR ** ALCA%AR ENTRAUA;
17289 5ELCID2187 GRADO ** CRIACOR, VENGO, MUGIER ONDRADA
17327 5ELCID2192 GRADO ** CRIADOR & AUOS, %ID, BARBA VELIDA
17361 5ELCID2196 MUGIER DO@A XIMENA, GRADO ** CRIAADOR.

WORD C# PREFIX CONTEXT

AL (CON'T)

17480 5ELCID2211 CAUALGAN LOS YFFANTES, ADELANT ADELINAUAN ** PALA%IO,
17571 5ELCID2223 SABEDES QUE ** REY ASSI GELO HE MANDADO,
17706 5ELCID2241 ** SALIR DELA ECCLEGIA CAUALGARON TAN PRIUADO,
17772 5ELCID2249 E ** OTRO DIA FIZO MYO %ID FINCAR VIJ TABLADOS:
17825 5ELCID2255 EN BESTIAS SINES ** C SON MANCADOS;
17972 5ELCID2274 PLEGA A SANTA MARIA & ** PADRE SANTO
18305 5ELCID2316 QUE LES CRE%E LA GANAN%IA, GRADO ** CRIADOR.
18719 5ELCID2369 PARAUAS DELANT ** CAMPEADOR, SIEMPRE CON LA BUEN AUZE:
18867 5ELCID2387 EL ASTIL A QUEBRADO & METIO MANO ** ESPADA.
19032 5ELCID2408 MYO %ID ** REY BUCAR CAYOL EN ALCAZ:
19063 5ELCID2412 RESPUSO BUCAR ** %ID: CONFONDA DIOS TAL AMISTAD
19173 5ELCID2425 MATO A BUCAR, ** REY DE ALEN MAR,
19313 5ELCID2446 COMMO ** REY BUCAR AVEMOS ARRANCADO.
19342 5ELCID2450 EL ESCUDO TRAE ** CUELLO & TODO ESPADO;
19385 5ELCID2456 GRADO ADIOS & ** PADRE QUE ESTA EN ALTO,
19538 5ELCID2475 DESPUES QUE ESTA BATALLA VEN%IERON & ** REY BUCAR MATO;
19639 5ELCID2489 CAYERON LE EN QUINTA ** %ID SEYX %IENTOS CAUALLOS,
19697 5ELCID2497 ARRANCO LAS LIDES COMMO PLAZE ** CRIADOR,
19925 5ELCID2528 GRADO ** CRIADOR & A UOS, %ID ONDRADO,
20039 5ELCID2543 PIDAMOS NUESTRAS MUGIERES ** %ID CAMPEADOR,
20532 5ELCID2607 ** PADRE & ALA MADRE LAS MANOS LES BESAUAN:
20659 5ELCID2622 CON AQUESTAS NUEUAS VERNAS ** CAMPEADOR.
20688 5ELCID2626 QUE SI ADIOS PLOGUIERE & ** PADRE CRIADOR,
21086 5ELCID2679 ELUEGO LEUARIA SUS FIJAS ** CAMPEADOR LEAL;
21225 5ELCID2697 ENTRADOS SON LOS YFANTES ** ROBREDO DE CORPES,
21383 5ELCID2718 HYRAN AQUESTOS MANDADOS ** %ID CAMPEADOR;
21448 5ELCID2727 ** VNA DIZEN COLADA & AL OTRA TIZON,
21453 5ELCID2727 AL VNA DIZEN COLADA & ** OTRA TIZON,
21566 5ELCID2741 QUAL VENTURA SERIE ESTA, SI PLOGUIESSE ** CRIADOR,
21680 5ELCID2756 QUE EL VNA ** OTRA NOL TORNA RECABDO.
22183 5ELCID2825 DE CUER PESO ESTO ** BUEN REY DON ALFONSSO.
22460 5ELCID2860 ATANTO UOS LO GRADIMOS COMMO SI VIESSEMOS ** CRAIDOR;
22612 5ELCID2881 ** MORO AUENGALUON DE CORA%ON LE PLAZ,
22639 5ELCID2885 ** QUE EN BUEN ORA NASCO LEGAUA EL MENSSAIE;
22691 5ELCID2891 HYO TOME EL CASAMIENTO, MAS NON OSE DEZIR **.
22693 5ELCID2892 PLEGA ** CRIADOR, QUE EN %IELO ESTA,
22721 5ELCID2895 BESARON LAS MANOS LAS FIJAS ** PADRE.
22755 5ELCID2900 ** REY ALFONSSO DE CASTIELLA PENSSO DE ENBIAR;
22785 5ELCID2903 LIEUES EL MANDADO A CASTIELLA ** REY ALFONSSO;
22819 5ELCID2907 QUEL PESE ** BUEN REY DALMA & DE CORA%ON.
22936 5ELCID2922 ** REY EN SAN FAGUNT LO FALLO.
23299 5ELCID2968 DIZID LE ** CAMPEADOR, QUE EN BUEN ORA NASCO,
23467 5ELCID2989 RUEGAN ** REY QUE LOS QUITE DESTA CORT.
23670 5ELCID3015 ** QUINTO DIA VENIDO ES MYO %ID EL CAMPEADOR;
23687 5ELCID3017 QUE BESASSE LAS MANOS ** REY SO SE@OR:
23836 5ELCID3037 E ** CONDE DON ARRICH & A QUANTOS QUE Y SON;
23984 5ELCID3057 ** CRIADOR ROGANDO & FABLANDO EN PORIDAD.
24224 5ELCID3089 ** PUNO BIEN ESTAN, CA EL SELO MANDO;
24282 5ELCID3096 QUE NON LE CONTALASSEN LOS PELOS ** BUEN %ID CANPEADOR;
24368 5ELCID3107 QUANDO LO VIERON ENTRAR ** QUE EN BUEN ORA NA%IO,
24403 5ELCID3111 AGRANT ONDRA LO RE%IBEN ** QUE EN BUEN ORA NA%IO.
24428 5ELCID3114 EL REY DIXO ** %ID: VENJD ACA SER, CAMPEADOR,
24475 5ELCID3120 LO QUE DIXO EL %ID ** REY PLOGO DE CORA%ON.
24688 5ELCID3145 MYO %ID LA MANO BESO ** REY & EN PIE SE LEUANTO;
24974 5ELCID3181 TORNOS ** ESCA@O DON SE LEUANTO;
25123 5ELCID3200 GRADO ** CRIADOR & AUOS, REY SE@OR,
25214 5ELCID3211 QUE ** NO NOS DEMANDASSE, QUE AQUI FINCO LA BOZ. . .
25225 5ELCID3212 SI PLOGUIERE ** REY, ASSI DEZIMOS NOS: DIXO EL REY
25329 5ELCID3225 SI ESSO PLOGIERE ** %ID, NON GELO VEDAMOS NOS;
25494 5ELCID3247 PAGARON LOS YFANTES ** QUE EN BUEN ORA NASCO;
26270 5ELCID3349 QUANDO FUERE LA LID, SI PLOGUIERE ** CRIADOR,
26378 5ELCID3364 SALISTE POR LA PUERTA, METISTET ** CORAL,
26399 5ELCID3367 HYCLLO LIDIARE, NON PASSARA POR **:
26416 5ELCID3370 ** PARTIR DELA LID POR TU BOCA LO DIRAS,
26538 5ELCID3387 FALSSO A TODOS & MAS ** CRIADOR.
26583 5ELCID3394 ** VNO DIZEN OIARRA & AL OTRO YENEGO SIMENEZ,
26588 5ELCID3394 AL VNO DIZEN OIARRA & ** OTRO YENEGO SIMENEZ,
26607 5ELCID3397 BESAN LAS MANOS ** REY CON ALFONSSO,
26659 5ELCID3404 ESTO GRADESCO YO ** CRIADOR,
26730 5ELCID3414 LEUANTOS MYO %ID, ** REY LAS MANOS LE BESO;
26861 5ELCID3431 E QUE NON PESE ESTO ** %ID CAMPEADOR:
27080 5ELCID3460 E QUI ** QUISIESSE SERIE SU OCASION.
27250 5ELCID3483 QUEN NON VINIERE ** PLAZO PIERDA LA RAZON,
27270 5ELCID3486 MYO %ID ** REY LAS MANOS LE BESO & DIXO: PLAZME, SE@OR.
27413 5ELCID3502 LOS CC MARCOS ** REY LOS SOLTO.
27418 5ELCID3503 DELO ** TANTO PRISO QUANT OUO SABOR.
27684 5ELCID3534 FELOS ** PLAZO LOS DEL CAMPEADOR,
27755 5ELCID3542 EL COMETER FUE MALO, QUE LO ** NOS ENPE%O,
27774 5ELCID3544 DE NOCHE BELARON LAS ARMAS & ROGARON ** CRIADOR.
27852 5ELCID3554 ANDIDIERON EN PLEYTO, DIXIERON LO ** REY ALFONSSO,
27886 5ELCID3558 DIXIERON GELO ** REY, MAS NON GELO CONLOYO;
28101 5ELCID3588 HYA SALIERON ** CAMPO DO ERAN LOS MOIONES.
28147 5ELCID3593 EL REY DIOLES FIELES POR DEZIR EL DERECHO & ** NON,
28273 5ELCID3609 MAS DE VJ ASTAS DE LAN%AS QUE NON LEGASSEN ** MOION.

WORD C# PREFIX CONTEXT

AL (CON'T)

```
                    28316 5ELCID3614 CADA VNO DELLCS MIENTES TIENE ** SO.
                    28527 5ELCID3642 EL DEXO LA LANZA & ** ESPACA METIO MANO,
                    28574 5ELCID3648 MARTIN ANTOLINEZ MANO METIO ** ESPADA,
                    28637 5ELCID3656 LO VNO CAYO ENEL CAMPC & LO ** SUSO FINCAUA.
                    28660 5ELCID3659 BOLUIO LA RIENDA ** CAUALLC POR TORNASSE DE CARA;
                    28856 5ELCID3686 ** TIRAR DELA LANZA EN TIERRA LO ECHO,
                    28939 5ELCID3696 VEN%IERON ESTA LID, GRADO ** CRIADOR.
                    29076 5ELCID3714 GRADO ** REY DEL %IELC, MIS FIJAS VENGADAS SON
                    29147 5ELCID3722 VED QUAL CNDRA CRE%E ** QUE EN BUEN ORA NA%IO,
         WORD # 235 CCCURS 185 TIMES.
            INDEX OF DIVERSIFICATION =   154.30 WITH STANDARD DEVIATION OF   151.33

ALA                    74 5ELCID0011 *** EXIDA DE BIUAR CUIERON LA CORNEIA DIESTRA,
                      248 5ELCID0032 ASSI CCMMO LEGO *** PUERTA, FALOLA BIEN %ERRADA,
                      294 5ELCID0037 AGUIIO MYO %ID, *** PUERTA SE LEGAUA,
                     1163 5ELCID0150 NON VIENE *** PUEENT, CA POR EL AGUA APASSADO,
                     1180 5ELCID0152 AFEUOS LOS *** TIENDA DEL CAMPEADOR CONTADO;
                     1792 5ELCID0228 DIXO MARTIN ANTOLINEZ:  VERE *** MUGIER ATODO MYO SOLAZ,
                     1901 5ELCID0242 LAMAUAN *** PUERTA, Y SCPIERON EL MANDADO;
                     2212 5ELCID0279 COMMO *** MI ALMA YC TANTO UOS QUERIA.
                     2303 5ELCID0290 EN AQUES DIA *** PUENT DE ARLA%ON
                     2499 5ELCID0316 *** MA@ANA, QUANDO LOS GALLOS CANTARAN,
                     2775 5ELCID0350 EL VNO ES EN PARAYSO, CA EL OTRO NON ENTRO ***;
                     2817 5ELCID0355 AL%OLAS ARRIBA, LEGOLAS *** FAZ,
                     3192 5ELCID0402 *** FIGERUELA MYO %ID IUA POSAR.
                     3288 5ELCID0415 *** SIERRA DE MIEDES ELLOS YUAN POSAR.
                     3508 5ELCID0442 VOS CON LOS CC YD UOS EN ALGARA; *** VAYA ALBARABAREZ,
                     3590 5ELCID0452 FAZED ME MANDADO MUY PRIUADO *** %AGA;
                     3703 5ELCID0467 MYO %ID DON RODRIGO *** PUERTA ADELI@AUA;
                     3823 5ELCID0483 NON OSA NINGUNO DAR SALTO *** %AGA.
                     4219 5ELCID0537 CRAS *** MA@ANA PENSEMOS DE CAUALGAR,
                     5098 5ELCID0644 ELLOS VINIERON *** NOCH EN SOGORUE POSAR.
                     5238 5ELCID0662 MESNADAS DE MYO %ID EXIR QUERIEN *** BATALLA,
                     5745 5ELCID0725 *** TORNADA QUE FAZEN OTROS TANTOS SON.
                     6050 5ELCID0767 CORTOL EL YELMO, QUE LEGO *** CARNE;
                     6519 5ELCID0832 *** TORNADA, SI NOS FALLAREDES AQUI;
                     7355 5ELCID0943 CON ESTAS GANAN%IAS *** POSADA TORNANDO SEUAN,
                     7399 5ELCID0949 CRAS *** MA@ANA PENSSEMOS DE CAUALGAR,
                     9964 5ELCID1263 MANDO LOS VENIR *** CORTH & A TODOS LOS IUNTAR,
                    10820 5ELCID1370 DE MI SEAN QUITOS & VAYAN *** GRA%IA DEL CRIADOR.
                    10897 5ELCID1379 HYA UOS YDES, MYNAYA?, YD *** GRA%IA DEL CRIADOR
                    11346 5ELCID1435 HYO LO VERE CON EL %ID, SI DIOS ME LIEUA ***.
                    11739 5ELCID1489 *** MA@ANA PIENSSAN DE CAUALGAR;
                    12416 5ELCID1576 *** PUERTA DE VALEN%IA, DO FUESSE EN SO SALUO,
                    12602 5ELCID1599 *** MADRE & ALAS FIJAS BIEN LAS ABRA%AUA,
                    12692 5ELCID1611 *** LAS SUBIE ENEL MAS ALTO LOGAR;
                    13119 5ELCID1663 PRISOS *** BARBA EL BUEN %ID CAMPEADOR:
                    17694 5ELCID2239 *** PUERTA DELA ECLEGIA SEDIELLOS SPERANDO;
                    17713 5ELCID2242 *** GLERA DE VALEN%IA FUERA DIERON SALTO;
                    18576 5ELCID2351 ***, PERO VERMUEZ, EL MYO SOBRINO CARO
                    18644 5ELCID2359 VOS CON LOS UUESTROS FIRME MIENTRE *** %AGA TENGADES;
                    19468 5ELCID2467 QUE *** RA%ION CAYE SEYS %IENTOS MARCOS DE PLATA.
                    19545 5ELCID2476 AL%O LA MANO, *** BARBA SE TOMO:
                    19707 5ELCID2499 *** DENTRO EN MARRUECOS, OLAS MEZQUITAS SON,
                    19811 5ELCID2511 ELLOS CON LOS OTROS VINIERON *** CORT;
                    20535 5ELCID2607 AL PADRE & *** MADRE LAS MANOS LES BESAUAN;
                    20725 5ELCID2631 GRANDES FUERON LOS DUELOS *** DEPARTI%ION.
                    22093 5ELCID2812 *** TORRE DE DON VRRACA ELLE LAS DEXO.
                    22213 5ELCID2829 AL%O LA SU MANO, *** BARBA SE TOMO;
                    22584 5ELCID2877 *** CASA DE BERLANGA POSADA PRESA HAN.
                    22728 5ELCID2896 TENIENDO YUAN ARMAS, ENTRARON SE *** CIBDAD;
                    23409 5ELCID2982 QUI NON VINIESSE *** CORT NON SE TOUIESSE POR SU VASSALLO.
                    23557 5ELCID3000 LEGAUA EL PLAZO, QUERIEN YR *** CORT;
                    23914 5ELCID3046 PENSSAD, SE@OR, DE ENTRAR *** %IBDAD,
                    23940 5ELCID3050 CRAS MA@ANA ENTRARE *** %IBDAD,
                    23944 5ELCID3051 E YRE *** CORT ENANTES DE IANTAR.
                    24142 5ELCID3078 DAQUESTA GUISA QUIERO YR *** CORT,
                    24341 5ELCID3104 *** PUERTA DE FUERA DESCAUALGA A SABOR;
                    24504 5ELCID3124 *** BARBA QUE AUIE LUENGA & PRESA CONEL CORDON;
                    24896 5ELCID3170 CON AQUESTA FABLA TORNARON *** CORT:
                    25008 5ELCID3185 AL%AUA LA MANO, *** BARBA SE TOMO;
                    25606 5ELCID3261 *** SALIDA DE VALEN%IA MIS FIJAS VOS DI YO,
                    25755 5ELCID3280 ESSORA EL CAMPEADOR PRISOS *** BARBA;
                    26197 5ELCID3339 DEXOS LE PRENDER ALCUELO, & *** RED LE METIO.
                    28627 5ELCID3655 RAXOL LOS PELOS DELA CABE%A, BIEN *** CARNE LEGAUA;
                    29069 5ELCID3713 PRISOS *** BARBA RUY DIAZ SO SE@OR;
                    29253 5ELCID3735 *** VNOS PE@OS, QUE BIEN VOS LO DARARAN SOBRELOS.
         WORD # 236 OCCURS  65 TIMES.
            INDEX OF DIVERSIFICATION =   454.92 WITH STANDARD DEVIATION OF   707.14

ALABA               18492 5ELCID2340 ASSI LO OTORGA DON PERO CUEMO SE ***** FERRANDO.
         WORD # 237 OCCURS   1 TIMES.

ALABANDO            21693 5ELCID2757 POR LOS MONTES DO YUAN, ELLOS YUAN SE ********:
         WORD # 238 OCCURS   1 TIMES.
```

```
WORD                C#  PREFIX                                    CONTEXT

ALABANDOS            21725 5ELCID2763 ********* YUAN LOS YFANTES DE CARRION.
          WORD # 239 OCCURS   1 TIMES.

ALABAR               26083 5ELCID3324 DELANT MYO %ID & DELANTE TODOS OVISTE TE DE ******
          WORD # 240 OCCURS   1 TIMES.

ALABARAN             16868 5ELCID2134 NON GELAS DARE YO CON MI MANO, NIN DED NON SE ********.
          WORD # 241 OCCURS   1 TIMES.

ALABAUAN              4565 5ELCID0580 VEYEN LO LOS DE ALCO%ER, DIOS, COMMO SE ********
          WORD # 242 OCCURS   1 TIMES.

ALAMOS               21205 5ELCID2694 ASSINIESTRO DEXAN AGRIZA QUE ****** POBLO,
          WORD # 243 OCCURS   1 TIMES.

ALARIDOS              4780 5ELCID0606 DANDO GRANDES ******** LOS QUE ESTAN EN LA %ELADA,
          WORD # 244 OCCURS   1 TIMES.

ALAS                  2183 5ELCID0275 **** SUS FIJAS ENBRA%O LAS PRENDIA,
                      2943 5ELCID0371 E EL **** NI@AS TORNO LAS ACATAR:
                      3052 5ELCID0384 COMMO SIRUA ADO@A XIMENA & **** FIJAS QUE HA,
                      7208 5ELCID0924 GRADO ADIOS & **** SUS VERTUDES SANTAS;
                      8243 5ELCID1049 ALEGRE ES EL CONDE & PIDIO AGUA **** MANOS,
                      8568 5ELCID1088 DEXADO A SARAGO%A & **** TIERRAS DUCA,
                     11022 5ELCID1395 QUANDO ACABO LA ORA%ION, **** DUE@AS SE TORNO:
                     11262 5ELCID1425 E **** OTRAS DUE@AS QUE LAS SIRUEN DELANT,
                     12240 5ELCID1554 AMYNAYA & **** DUE@AS, DIOS COMMO LAS ONDRAUA
                     12326 5ELCID1565 QUE RE%IBAN A MYANAYA & **** DUENAS FIJAS DALGO;
                     12352 5ELCID1569 E **** DUENAS & ALAS NI@AS & ALAS OTRAS CONPA@AS.
                     12355 5ELCID1569 E ALAS DUENAS & **** NI@AS & ALAS OTRAS CONPA@AS.
                     12358 5ELCID1569 E ALAS DUENAS & ALAS NI@AS & **** OTRAS CONPA@AS.
                     12605 5ELCID1599 ALA MADRE & **** FIJAS BIEN LAS ABRA%AUA,
                     13102 5ELCID1661 ASSI FFAZIE **** DUE@AS & A SUS FIJAS AMAS ADOS:
                     13516 5ELCID1713 DEXAN **** PUERTAS OMNES DE GRANT RECABDO.
                     15561 5ELCID1973 **** AGUAS DE TAIO, OLAS UISTAS SON APAREIADAS.
                     15644 5ELCID1984 SUELTAN LAS RIENDAS, **** VISTAS SEUAN A DELI@ADAS.
                     16754 5ELCID2121 EL REY ALOS YFANTES **** MANOS LES TOMO,
                     16818 5ELCID2129 QUI QUIERE YR COMIGO **** BODAS, O RE%EBIR MI DON,
                     17076 5ELCID2162 SEREMOS **** BODAS DELOS YFANTES DE CARRION
                     17872 5ELCID2261 RICOS TORNAN A CASTIELLA LOS QUE **** BODAS LEGARON.
                     19214 5ELCID2431 **** TIENDAS ERAN LEGADOS, DO ESTAUA
                     20127 5ELCID2555 ASSI LAS ESCARNIREMOS **** FIJAS DEL CAMPEADOR,
                     20893 5ELCID2654 **** FIJAS DEL %ID EL MORO SUS DO@AS DIO,
                     21637 5ELCID2751 E **** AUES DEL MONTE & ALAS BESTIAS DELA FIERA GUISA.
                     21642 5ELCID2751 E ALAS AUES DEL MONTE & **** BESTIAS DELA FIERA GUISA.
                     22086 5ELCID2811 **** AGUAS DE DUERO ELLOS ARRIBADOS SON,
                     23118 5ELCID2946 **** BESTIAS FIERAS & ALAS AUES DEL MONT.
                     23122 5ELCID2946 ALAS BESTIAS FIERAS & **** AUES DEL MONT.
                     25654 5ELCID3267 **** BESTIAS FIERAS & ALAS AUES DEL MONT;
                     25658 5ELCID3267 ALAS BESTIAS FIERAS & **** AUES DEL MONT;
          WORD # 245 OCCURS  32 TIMES.
             INDEX OF DIVERSIFICATION =    756.26 WITH STANDARD DEVIATION OF    937.35

ALBA                 24010 5ELCID3060 MATINES & PRIMA DIXIERON FAZAL ****,
          WORD # 246 OCCURS   1 TIMES.

ALBAFANEZ            26842 5ELCID3429 MYNAYA ********* EN PIE SE LEUANTO;
          WORD # 247 OCCURS   1 TIMES.

ALBAR                 3512 5ELCID0443 E ***** SALUADOREZ SIN FALLA, & GALIN GAR%IA, VNA FARDIDA
                      5840 5ELCID0739 ***** ALBAREZ & ALBAR SALUADOREZ,
                      5843 5ELCID0739 ALBAR ALBAREZ & ***** SALUADOREZ,
                     13254 5ELCID1681 ***** SALUADOREZ PRESO FINCO ALLA.
                     24059 5ELCID3067 E ***** ALBAREZ & ALBAR SALUADOREZ
                     24062 5ELCID3067 E ALBAR ALBAREZ & ***** SALUADOREZ
          WORD # 248 OCCURS   6 TIMES.
             INDEX OF DIVERSIFICATION =   4109.00 WITH STANDARD DEVIATION OF   4812.22

ALBARABAREZ          3510 5ELCID0442 VOS CON LOS CC YD UOS EN ALGARA; ALA VAYA ***********,
          WORD # 249 OCCURS   1 TIMES.

ALBARDIAZ            16100 5ELCID2042 PESO A ********* & A GARCIORDONEZ.
          WORD # 250 OCCURS   1 TIMES.

ALBAREZ               5841 5ELCID0739 ALBAR ******* & ALBAR SALUADOREZ,
                     24060 5ELCID3067 E ALBAR ******* & ALBAR SALUADOREZ
          WORD # 251 OCCURS   2 TIMES.

ALBARFANEZ            3003 5ELCID0378 ATAN GRAND SABOR FABLO MINAYA **********:
                      3080 5ELCID0387 TORNADO ES DON SANCHO, & FABLO **********:
                      3478 5ELCID0438 COMMO LOS CONSEIAUA MINAYA **********:
                      3861 5ELCID0489  VENIDES, **********, UNA FARDIDA LAN%A
```

WORD C# PREFIX CONTEXT

ALBARFANEZ (CON'T)

4741 5ELCID0601 MYO %ID & ********** ADELANT AGUIIAUAN;
4869 5ELCID0616 OYD AMI, ********** & TODOS LOS CAUALLEROS
5816 5ELCID0735 MYNAYA **********, QEU CORITA MANDO,
5874 5ELCID0744 A MYNAYA ********** MATARON LE EL CAUALLO,
5932 5ELCID0752 AMYNAYA ********** YUAL DAR EL CAUALLO:
6116 5ELCID0778 AMYNAYA ********** BIEN LANDA EL CAUALLO,
6417 5ELCID0819 DIXO MYNAYA **********: ESTO FARE YO DE GRADO.
6471 5ELCID0826 MYNAYA ********** DESTO ES PAGADO; POR YR CON EL OMNES SON CONTADOS.
6822 5ELCID0871 YDO ES A CASTIELLA ********** MINAYA,
6995 5ELCID0894 BESO LE LAS MANOS MINAYA **********:
7229 5ELCID0927 QUE MINAYA ********** ASSI ERA LEGADO,
7257 5ELCID0931 QUE ********** PAGO LAS MILL MISSAS,
7284 5ELCID0934 YA **********, BIUADES MUCHOS DIAS . . .
7372 5ELCID0945 PLOGO A MYO %ID, & MUCHO A **********.
8853 5ELCID1127 OYD QUE DIXO MINAYA **********:
8992 5ELCID1144 DEL OTRA PART ENTROLES **********;
9904 5ELCID1256 CON MINAYA ********** EL SEUA CONSEGAR:
10139 5ELCID1284 CIENTO OMNES LE DIO MYO %ID A ********** POR SERUIR LE EN LA CARRERA,
10245 5ELCID1297 OYD, MINAYA **********, POR AQUEL QUE ESTA EN ALTO,
10285 5ELCID1302 PLOGO A ********** DELO QUE DIXO DON RODRIGO.
10338 5ELCID1309 ADELINO PORA CASTIELLA MINAYA **********.
10375 5ELCID1314 ALEGRE FUE DE AQUESTO MINAYA **********,
10796 5ELCID1367 MYNAYA ********** LAS MANOS LE BESO.
10887 5ELCID1378 MINAYA ********** ALBUEN REY SE ESPIDIO.
10947 5ELCID1385 LOS YFFANTES DE CARRION DANDO YUAN CONPA@A A MINAYA **********:
11101 5ELCID1405 DIO TRES CAUALLEROS MYNAYA **********,
11181 5ELCID1414 REMANE%IO EN SAN PERO MINAYA **********.
11205 5ELCID1417 QUE LES TOUIESSE PRO ROGAUAN A **********;
11378 5ELCID1439 HYDO ES PORA SAN PERO MINAYA **********,
11399 5ELCID1442 SI UOS VALA EL CRIADOR, MINAYA **********,
11474 5ELCID1452 FELOS EN MEDINA LAS DUENAS & **********.
11790 5ELCID1495 ENVIO DOS CAUALLEROS MYNAYA ********** QUE SOPIESSE LA VERDAD;
11813 5ELCID1497 EL VNO FINCO CON ELLOS & EL OTRO TORNO A **********:
11923 5ELCID1511 QUE SOPIENSSEN LES OTROS DE QUE SESO ERA **********
11929 5ELCID1512 O CUEMO SALIERA DE CASTIELLA ********** CON ESTAS DUE@AS QUE TRAHE.
11963 5ELCID1516 DON LEGAN LOS OTROS, A MINAYA ********** SE UAN HOMILAR.
11994 5ELCID1520 TAN BUEN DIA CON UUSCO, MINAYA **********
12047 5ELCID1527 SORRISOS DELA BOCA MINAYA **********:
12204 5ELCID1549 ENTRE EL & ********** HYUAN A VNA COMPA@A.
12341 5ELCID1567 CA BIEN SABE QUE ********** TRAHE TODO RECABDO;
13571 5ELCID1719 ALUAR ALUAREZ & ALUAR SALUADOREZ & MINAYA **********
13746 5ELCID1742 DEXO ********** POR SABER TODO RECABDO.
13991 5ELCID1772 MYNAYA ********** FUERA ERA ENEL CAMPO,
14793 5ELCID1870 AUOS, MINAYA **********, & EA PERO VERMUEZ AQUI,
14983 5ELCID1894 A MYNAYA ********** & A PERO VERMUEZ
15695 5ELCID1991 MYNAYA ********** & AQUEL PERO VERMUEZ,
16874 5ELCID2135 RESPONDIO EL REY: AFE AQUI **********;
16908 5ELCID2140 DIXO **********: SE@OR, AFE QUE ME PLAZ.
17554 5ELCID2221 VENIT ACA, **********, EL QUE YO QUIERO & AMO
18657 5ELCID2361 AQUI LEGO MYNAYA **********: OYD, YA %ID, CANPEADOR LEAL
19335 5ELCID2449 MYNAYA ********** ESSORA ES LEGADO,
19825 5ELCID2513 EL BUENO DE **********, CAUALLERO LIDIADOR,
20171 5ELCID2561 EA MYNAYA ********** & A QUANTOS AQUI SON:
20670 5ELCID2624 MINAYA ********** ANTE MYO %ID SE PARO:
22113 5ELCID2814 FALLO A DIEGO TELLEZ EL QUE DE ********** FUE;
22264 5ELCID2835 PESO A MYO %ID & ATODA SU CORT, & ********** DALMA & DE CORA%ON.
22487 5ELCID2863 LORAUAN DELOS OIOS LAS DUE@AS & **********,
24031 5ELCID3063 VOS, MYNAYA **********, EL MYO BRA%O MEIOR,
25249 5ELCID3215 DIXO ********** LEUANTADOS EN PIE EL %ID CAMPEADOR:
27054 5ELCID3456 HYO SO ********** PORA TODEL MEIOR.

WORD # 252 OCCURS 64 TIMES.
INDEX OF DIVERSIFICATION = 380.76 WITH STANDARD DEVIATION OF 455.52

ALBARFFANEZ
99 5ELCID0014 ALBRICIA, ***********, CA ECHADOS SOMOS DE TIERRA
9791 5ELCID1244 CON EL MYNAYA *********** QUE NOS LE PARTE DE SO BRA%O.
11582 5ELCID1467 MY MUGIER & MIS FIJAS CON MYNAYA ***********,
WORD # 253 OCCURS 3 TIMES.

ALBERGADA
6229 5ELCID0794 ESTA ********* LOS DE MYO %ID LUEGO LA AN ROBADA
8395 5ELCID1067 FATA CABO DEL ********* ESCURRIOLOS EL CASTELANO:
18842 5ELCID2384 EYUA LOS FERIR A CABO DEL *********.
WORD # 254 OCCURS 3 TIMES.

ALBERGAR
4297 5ELCID0547 ENTRE FARIZA & %ETINA MYO %ID YUA ********.
11642 5ELCID1475 TRO%IERON A SANTA MARIA & VINIERON ******** A FRONTAEL,
22602 5ELCID2879 AQUAL DIZEN MEDINA YUAN ********,
WORD # 255 OCCURS 3 TIMES.

ALBERGARON
21295 5ELCID2706 COGIDA HAN LA TIENDA DO ********** DE NOCH,
22331 5ELCID2844 HY ********** POR VERDAD VNA NOCH.
WORD # 256 OCCURS 2 TIMES.

ALBORES
1853 5ELCID0235 APRIESSA CANTAN LOS GALLOS & QUIEREN QUEBRAR *******,
1874 5ELCID0238 REZAUA LOS MATINES ABUELTA DELOS *******.

WORD C# PREFIX CONTEXT

ALBORES (CON'T)

```
                     3619 5ELCID0456 YA QUIEBRAN LOS ******* & VINIE LA MA@ANA,
                    27783 5ELCID3545 TROCIDA ES LA NOCHE, YA QUIEBRAN LOS *******.
         WORD # 257 OCCURS    4 TIMES.

ALBRICIA               98 5ELCID0014 ********, ALBARFFANEZ, CA ECHADOS SOMOS DE TIERRA
         WORD # 258 OCCURS    1 TIMES.

ALBUEN              10888 5ELCID1378 MINAYA ALBARFANEZ ****** REY SE ESPIDIO.
                    15062 5ELCID1904 QUE GELO DIGADES ****** CAMPEADOR:
         WORD # 259 OCCURS    2 TIMES.

ALCA%AR              9607 5ELCID1220 QUANDO SU SE@A CABDAL SEDIE EN SOMO DEL *******.
                    12373 5ELCID1571 QUE GUARDASSEN EL ******* & LAS OTRAS TORRES ALTAS
                    12691 5ELCID1610 ADELINO MYO %ID CON ELLAS AL *******,
                    12968 5ELCID1644 SU MUGIER & SUS FIJAS SUBIOLAS AL *******,
                    13030 5ELCID1652 MUGIER, SED EN ESTE PALA%IO, & SI QUISIEREDES EN EL *******;
                    15781 5ELCID2002 LAS PUERTAS DEL ******* QUE NON SE ABRIESSEN DE DIA NIN DE NOCH,
                    15824 5ELCID2007 QUE DEL ******* VNA SALIR NON PUEDE,
                    17263 5ELCID2183 MYO %ID EL CAMPEADOR AL ******* ENTRAUA;
                    17769 5ELCID2248 RICAS FUERON LAS BODAS EN EL ******* ONDRADO,
         WORD # 260 OCCURS    9 TIMES.
            INDEX OF DIVERSIFICATION =  1019.25 WITH STANDARD DEVIATION OF  1158.93

ALCALA               3542 5ELCID0446 FITA AYUSO & POR GUADALFAIARA, FATA ****** LEGEN LAS ALGARAS,
                     3773 5ELCID0477 E SIN DUBDA CORREN; FASTA ****** LEGO LA SE@A DE MINAYA,
         WORD # 261 OCCURS    2 TIMES.

ALCALDES            24600 5ELCID3135 ******** SEAN DESTO EL CONDE DON ANRRICH & EL CONDE DON REMOND
                    24804 5ELCID3169 ATORGAN LOS ********: TOD ESTO ES RAZON.
                    25322 5ELCID3224 DIXIERON LOS ******** QUANDO MANFESTADOS SON:
         WORD # 262 OCCURS    3 TIMES.

ALCAMPEADOR          1105 5ELCID0142 AMOS TRED *********** CON TADO,
         WORD # 263 OCCURS    1 TIMES.

ALCAMPO             27915 5ELCID3562 LEUAD & SALID *******, YFANTES DE CARRION,
         WORD # 264 OCCURS    1 TIMES.

ALCAN%A              5978 5ELCID0758 ALOS QUE ******* VALOS DELIBRANDO.
                     7800 5ELCID0998 VERA REMONT VERENGEL TRAS QUIEN VINO EN *******
                    18963 5ELCID2399 MYO %ID CON LOS SUYOS CAE EN *******;
                    29172 5ELCID3725 A TODOS ******* ONDRA POR EL QUE EN BUEN ORA NA%IO.
         WORD # 265 OCCURS    4 TIMES.

ALCAN%ADO            9884 5ELCID1253 SIL PUDIESSEN PRENDER OFUESSE *********,
         WORD # 266 OCCURS    1 TIMES.

ALCAN%ANDO          19128 5ELCID2419 MAS BAUIECA EL DE MIO %ID ********** LO VA.
         WORD # 267 OCCURS    1 TIMES.

ALCAN%AR             3107 5ELCID0390 CA EN YERMO O EN POBLADO PODER NOS HAN ********.
         WORD # 268 OCCURS    1 TIMES.

ALCAN%AUA            3738 5ELCID0472 QUINZE MOROS MATAUA DELOS QUE *********.
         WORD # 269 OCCURS    1 TIMES.

ALCAN%O             19970 5ELCID2533 QUIEN LIDIARA MEIOR OQUIEN FUERA EN *******;
         WORD # 270 OCCURS    1 TIMES.

ALCAN%OLO           19131 5ELCID2420 ********* EL %ID ABUCAR A TRES BRACAS DEL MAR,
         WORD # 271 OCCURS    1 TIMES.

ALCANDARAS             22 5ELCID0004 ********** UAZIAS SIN PIELLES & SIN MANTOS
         WORD # 272 OCCURS    1 TIMES.

ALCANPEADOR         26022 5ELCID3317 PEDIST LAS FERIDAS PRIMERAS *********** LEAL,
         WORD # 273 OCCURS    1 TIMES.

ALCARGAR             1327 5ELCID0170 ******** DELAS ARCHAS VERIEDES GOZO TANTO:
         WORD # 274 OCCURS    1 TIMES.

ALCARIAS             4264 5ELCID0543 TRO%EN LAS ******** & YUAN ADELANT,
         WORD # 275 OCCURS    1 TIMES.

ALCAT                7418 5ELCID0951 ESTON%ES SE MUDO EL %ID AL PUERTO DE *****,
         WORD # 276 OCCURS    1 TIMES.

ALCAYAZ             11847 5ELCID1502 E EL ******* AUEGALUON CON SUS FUER%AS QUE TRAHE,
         WORD # 277 OCCURS    1 TIMES.

ALCAZ                6084 5ELCID0772 LOS DE MYO %ID FIRIENDO EN *****,
                     6171 5ELCID0786 CA EN ***** SIN DUBDA LES FUERON DANDO.
                     9018 5ELCID1147 DOS REYES DE MOROS MATARON EN ES *****,
                    13247 5ELCID1679 BIEN FATA LAS TIENDAS DURA AQUESTE *****,
```

WORD C# PREFIX CONTEXT

ALCAZ (CON'T)

```
                13643 5ELCID1728 MYO %ID EL DE BIUAR FASTA ALLI LEGO EN *****,
                18999 5ELCID2403 SACAN LCS DELAS TIENDAS, CAEN LOS EN *****;
                19037 5ELCID2408 MYO %ID AL REY BUCAR CAYOL EN *****:
        WORD # 278 OCCURS   7 TIMES.
          INDEX OF DIVERSIFICATION =  2157.83 WITH STANDARD DEVIATION OF  2318.58

ALCOBIELLA       3171 5ELCID0399 PASSO PAR ********** QUE DE CASTIELLA FINES YA;
        WORD # 279 OCCURS   1 TIMES.

ALCO%ER          4343 5ELCID0553 E SOBRE ******* MYO %ID YUA POSAR,
                 4366 5ELCID0556 MOI %ID DON RODRIGO ******* CUECA GANAR.
                 4472 5ELCID0569 EL CASTIELLO DE ******* EN PARIA UA ENTRANDO.
                 4479 5ELCID0570 LOS DE ******* A MYO %ID YAL DAN PARIAS DE GRADO
                 4516 5ELCID0574 QUANDO VIO MYO %ID QUE ******* NON SELE DAUA:
                 4561 5ELCID0580 VEYEN LO LOS DE *******, DICS, COMMO SE ALABAUAN
                 4625 5ELCID0587 SALIERON DE ******* AVNA PRIESSA MUCH ESTRANA.
                 4651 5ELCID0590 DIZEN LOS DE *******:  YA SE NOS VA LA GANA%IA
                 4817 5ELCID0610 MYO %ID GA@O A *******, SABENT, POR ESTA MA@A.
                 4926 5ELCID0623 MYO %ID CON ESTA GANAN%IA EN ******* ESTA;
                 4983 5ELCID0630 VINO POSAR SOBRE *******, EN VN TAN FUERTE LOGAR;
                 5181 5ELCID0655 AL BUENO DE MYO %ID EN ******* LEUAN %ERCAR.
                 6621 5ELCID0845 VENDIDO LES A ******* POR TRES MILL MARCHOS DE PLATA.
                 6700 5ELCID0855 QUANDO QUITO A ******* MYO %ID EL DE BIUAR,
                 6745 5ELCID0861 PESO ALOS DE *******, CA PROLES FAZIE GRANT.
        WORD # 280 OCCURS  15 TIMES.
          INDEX OF DIVERSIFICATION =   170.57 WITH STANDARD DEVIATION OF   369.16

ALCO%EUA        22571 5ELCID2875 TRO%IERON ********, ADIESTRO DE SANTESTEUAN DE GORMAZ,
        WORD # 281 OCCURS   1 TIMES.

ALCOL%ER         6633 5ELCID0846 MYO %ID RUY DIAZ A ******** ES VENIDO;
        WORD # 282 OCCURS   1 TIMES.

ALCON%ARON       7575 5ELCID0971 *********** A MYO %ID EN TEUAR & EL PINAR;
        WORD # 283 OCCURS   1 TIMES.

ALCONDE          7460 5ELCID0957 LEGARON LAS NUEUAS ******* DE BAR%ILONA,
                23832 5ELCID3036 OMILLOM AUOS & ******* DO REMOND
        WORD # 284 OCCURS   2 TIMES.

ALCRIADOR       26975 5ELCID3446 ESTO GRADESCO YO *********,
        WORD # 285 OCCURS   1 TIMES.

ALCUELLO        18157 5ELCID2297 EL MANTO TRAE ********, & ADELINO PORA LEON;
                18184 5ELCID2300 MYO %ID DON RODRIGO ******** LO TOMO,
        WORD # 286 OCCURS   2 TIMES.

ALCUELO         26195 5ELCID3339 DEXOS LE PRENDER *******, & ALA RED LE METIO.
        WORD # 287 OCCURS   1 TIMES.

AL%ADA           4542 5ELCID0577 COIO SALON AYUSO LA SU SE@A ******,
        WORD # 288 OCCURS   1 TIMES.

AL%AN           12727 5ELCID1616 ***** LAS MANOS PORA DIOS ROGAR,
        WORD # 289 OCCURS   1 TIMES.

AL%AR            5757 5ELCID0726 VERIEDES TANTAS LAN%AS PREMER & *****,
        WORD # 290 OCCURS   1 TIMES.

AL%ASSE         18071 5ELCID2286 FERRAN GON%ALEZ NON VIO ALLI DOS *******, NIN CAMARA ABIERTA NIN
        WORD # 291 OCCURS   1 TIMES.

AL%AUA          25005 5ELCID3185 ****** LA MANO, ALA BARBA SE TOMO;
        WORD # 292 OCCURS   1 TIMES.

AL%AUAN         12969 5ELCID1645 ******* LOS OIOS, TIENDAS VIERON FINCADAS:
        WORD # 293 OCCURS   1 TIMES.

AL%ID           25211 5ELCID3210 POR ESSOL DIEMOS SUS ESPADAS ***** CAMPEADOR,
        WORD # 294 OCCURS   1 TIMES.

AL%O             1680 5ELCID0216 **** SU MANO DIESTRA, LA CARA SE SANTIGUA:
                 6712 5ELCID0857 **** SU SE@A, EL CAMPEADOR SE UA,
                10570 5ELCID1340 **** LA MANO DIESTRA, EL REY SE SANTIGO:
                19141 5ELCID2421 ARRIBA **** COLADA, VN GRANT COLPE DADOL HA,
                19268 5ELCID2439 **** SOS OIOS, ESTEUA ADELANT CATANDO,
                19542 5ELCID2476 **** LA MANO, ALA BARBA SE TOMO:
                22209 5ELCID2829 **** LA SU MANO, ALA BARBA SE TOMO;
                27459 5ELCID3508 EL REY **** LA MANO, LA CARA SE SANTIGO;
        WORD # 295 OCCURS   8 TIMES.
          INDEX OF DIVERSIFICATION =  3681.71 WITH STANDARD DEVIATION OF  2986.00

AL%OLAS          2814 5ELCID0355 ******* ARRIBA, LEGOLAS ALA FAZ,
        WORD # 296 OCCURS   1 TIMES.
```

```
WORD                C#  PREFIX                          CONTEXT

ALEGAN              7553 5ELCID0968 GENTES SE LE ****** GRANDES ENTRE MOROS & CHRISTIANOS,
        WORD # 297 OCCURS    1 TIMES.

ALEGANDO            6213 5ELCID0791 VIO LOS SOS COMMCS VAN ********:
                   18528 5ELCID2344 ESTO VAN DIZIENDC & LAS YENTES SE ********,
        WORD # 298 OCCURS    2 TIMES.

ALEGASSES          26033 5ELCID3318 VIST VN MORO, FUSTEL ENSAYAR; ANTES FUXISTE QUE ALTE *********.
        WORD # 299 OCCURS    1 TIMES.

ALEGRANDO           8132 5ELCID1036 QUANDO ESTO OYO EL CONDE, YAS YUA *********:
                   10169 5ELCID1287 EN ESTAS NUEUAS TODOS SEA *********,
        WORD # 300 OCCURS    2 TIMES.

ALEGRAR            11498 5ELCID1455 PLOGOL DE CORA%ON & TORNOS A *******,
        WORD # 301 OCCURS    1 TIMES.

ALEGRAS             9990 5ELCID1266 ******* LE EL CORA%ON & TORNOS ASONRRISAR:
        WORD # 302 OCCURS    1 TIMES.

ALEGRAUAS          13081 5ELCID1659 ********* MIO %ID & DIXO: TAN BUEN DIA ES OY
                   18292 5ELCID2315 ********* EL %ID & TODOS SUS VARONES,
        WORD # 303 OCCURS    2 TIMES.

ALEGRE              1909 5ELCID0243 DIOS, QUE ****** FUE EL ABBAT CON SANCHO
                    7223 5ELCID0926  DIOS, COMMO FUE ****** TODO AQUEL FONSSADO,
                    7252 5ELCID0930  DIOS, COMMO ES ****** LA BAREA VELIDA,
                    8236 5ELCID1049 ****** ES EL CONDE & PIDIO AGUA ALAS MANOS,
                    9090 5ELCID1157 ****** ERA EL %ID & TODAS SUS COMPA@AS,
                    9590 5ELCID1219 ****** ERA EL CAMPEADOR CON TODOS LOS QUE HA,
                   10309 5ELCID1305  DIOS, QUE ****** ERA TODA CHRISTIANISMO,
                   10321 5ELCID1307 ****** FUE MINAYA & SPIDIOS & VINOS.
                   10370 5ELCID1314 ****** FUE DE AQUESTO MINAYA ALBARFANEZ,
                   11084 5ELCID1403 TODO SERIE ******, QUE NON AURIE NINGUN PESAR.
                   12298 5ELCID1562 ****** FUE MYO %ID, QUE NUNQUA MAS NIN TANTO,
                   13173 5ELCID1670 ****** SON LAS DUENAS, PERDIENDO VAN EL PAUOR.
                   13278 5ELCID1684 ****** ES MYO %ID POR QUANTO FECHO HAN:
                   13663 5ELCID1731 MUCHO ERA ****** DELO QUE AN CA%ADO.
                   13719 5ELCID1739 ****** ERA MYO %ID & TODOS SOS VASSALLOS,
                   14230 5ELCID1801 ****** ES DO@A XIMENA & SUS FIJAS AMAS,
                   14474 5ELCID1831 ****** FUE EL REY, NON VIESTES ATANTO,
                   17959 5ELCID2273 ****** ERA EL %ID & TODOS SUS VASSALLOS.
                   19459 5ELCID2466 ****** ES MYO %ID CON TODAS SUS CONPA@AS,
                   20586 5ELCID2614 ****** VA MYO %ID CON TODAS SUS COMPA@AS.
                   27649 5ELCID3530 ****** FUE DAQUESTO EL QUE EN BUEN ORA NA%IO;
                   28998 5ELCID3704 ****** FFUE DAQUESTO MYO %ID EL CAMPEADOR.
        WORD # 304 OCCURS   22 TIMES.
           INDEX OF DIVERSIFICATION =  1288.95 WITH STANDARD DEVIATION OF  1821.62

ALEGRES             7361 5ELCID0944 TODOS SON *******, GANAN%IAS TRAEN GRANDES.
                   12100 5ELCID1535 TODOS FUERON ******* DEL %ERUI%IO QUE TOMARON,
                   14214 5ELCID1799 ******* SON POR VALEN%IA LAS YENTES CHRISTIANAS,
                   15580 5ELCID1975 LOS YFFANTES DE CARRIC MUCHO ******* ANDAN,
                   16286 5ELCID2066 TODOS ERAN ******* & ACUERDAN EN VNA RAZON:
                   17918 5ELCID2267 MUCHO ERAN ******* DIEGO & FERRANDO;
                   19518 5ELCID2473 MUCHOS SON ******* MYO %ID & SUS VASSALLOS,
        WORD # 305 OCCURS    7 TIMES.
           INDEX OF DIVERSIFICATION =  2025.17 WITH STANDARD DEVIATION OF  1405.90

ALEGREYA            6257 5ELCID0797 GRAND ******** VA ENTRE ESSOS CHISTIANOS,
        WORD # 306 OCCURS    1 TIMES.

ALEGRIA             7282 5ELCID0933  DIOS, COMMO FUE EL %ID PAGADO & FIZO GRANT *******
                    9720 5ELCID1236 GRAND ******* ES ENTRE TODOS ESSOS CHRISTIANOS
                   13975 5ELCID1770 GRANT FUE EL ******* QUE FUE POR EL PALA%IO;
        WORD # 307 OCCURS    3 TIMES.

ALEGRIAS           12270 5ELCID1558 CON ESTAS ******** & NUEUAS TAN ONDRADAS
        WORD # 308 OCCURS    1 TIMES.

ALEGROS            19288 5ELCID2442 ******* MYO %ID FERMOSO SONRRISANDO:
                   24998 5ELCID3184 ******* LE TODEL CUERPO, SONRRISOS DE CORA%ON,
        WORD # 309 OCCURS    2 TIMES.

ALEN                7118 5ELCID0911 **** DE TERUEL DON RODRIGO PASSAUA,
                   19176 5ELCID2425 MATO A BUCAR, AL REY DE **** MAR,
        WORD # 310 OCCURS    2 TIMES.

ALENT               9086 5ELCID1156 SONANDO VAN SUS NUEUAS ***** PARTE DEL MAR.
                   12763 5ELCID1620 DEZIR UOS QUIERO NUEUAS DE ***** PARTES DEL MAR,
        WORD # 311 OCCURS    2 TIMES.
```

WORD C# PREFIX CONTEXT

ALEUOSO 26361 5ELCID3362 CALA, *******, BCCA SIN VERCAD
26509 5ELCID3383 CALA, *******, MALO & TRAYDOR
WORD # 312 CCCURS 2 TIMES.

ALFFONSSO 585 5ELCID0074 EN YRA DEL RAY ********* YO SERE METIDO.
9756 5ELCID1240 POR AMCR DE REY *********, QUE DE TIERRA ME A ECHADO,
23745 5ELCID3024 QUANDO LOOVC A OIC EL BUEN REY DON *********,
WORD # 313 CCCURS 3 TIMES.

ALFONDON 7838 5ELCID1003 ******** DELA CUESTA, %ERCA ES DE LA@O,
WORD # 314 CCCURS 1 TIMES.

ALFONSSO 164 5ELCID0022 EL REY DON ******** TANTO AUIE LA GRAND SA@A,
257 5ELCID0033 POR MIEDO DEL REY ********, QUE ASSI LO AUIEN PARADO
3355 5ELCID0423 LA TIERRA DEL REY ******** ESTA NOCH LA PODEMOS QUITAR.
3902 5ELCIDC495 PAGAR SE YA DELLA ******** EL CASTELLANO.
4001 5ELCID0508 AL REY ******** QUE LEGARIEN SUS COMPA@AS,
4151 5ELCID0528 BUSCAR NOS YE EL REY ******** CON TODA SU MESNADA.
4180 5ELCIDC532 %ERCA ES EL REY ******** & BUSCAR NOS VERNA.
4225 5ELCID0538 CON ******** MYO SE@OR NON QUERRIA LIDIAR.
4974 5ELCID0629 AYROLO EL REY ********, DE TIERRA ECHADO LO HA,
10041 5ELCID1272 AL REY ******** MYO SE@CR NATURAL;
10349 5ELCID1311 DEMANDO POR ********, DC LO PODRIE FALLAR.
10389 5ELCID1316 DE MISSA ERA EXIDO ESSORA EL REY ********,
10407 5ELCID1319 ALOS PIES DEL REY ******** CAYO CON GRAND DUELO,
10422 5ELCID1321 MER%ED, SE@OR ********, POR AMOR DEL CRIADOR
14142 5ELCID1790 ENBIAR LA CUIERO ******** EL CASTELLANO,
14343 5ELCID1814 QUE NON DIGA MAL EL REY ******** DEL QUE VALEN%IA MANDA.
14431 5ELCID1825 POR EL REY DCN ******** TCMAN SSE APREGUNTAR.
14451 5ELCID1827 LEGAN A VALADCLID, DO EL REY ******** ESTAUA;
14550 5ELCID1840 EL REY DON ******** SEYSE SANTIGUANDO.
14569 5ELCID1843 ANTEL REY ******** LOS YNOIOS FINCADOS,
14582 5ELCID1845 MER%ED, REY ********, SCDES TAN ONDRADO
14665 5ELCID1855 DIXO EL REY DCN ********: RE%IBOLOS DE GRADO.
14761 5ELCID1866 FABLO EL REY DON ******** & DIXO ESTA RAZON:
14904 5ELCID1884 VINIEN AL REY ******** CCN ESTA PORIDAD:
14991 5ELCID1895 EL REY DON ******** ESSCRA LOS LAMO,
15184 5ELCID1921 COMMO SCN LAS SALUDES DE ******** MYO SENOR.
15220 5ELCID1927 LO QUEL ROGAUA ******** EL CE LEON
15351 5ELCID1943 CON TODC ESTC, AUOS DIXC ********
15398 5ELCID1950 NON ERA MARAUILLA SIQUISIESSE EL REY ********,
15608 5ELCID1979 EL REY DON ******** A PRIESSA CAUALGAUA,
15880 5ELCID2013 DE VN DIA ES LEGADO ANTES EL REY CON ********.
15966 5ELCID2024 ASI SABE DAR CMILDAN%A A ******** SO SE@OR.
15983 5ELCID2026 TAN GRAND PESAR OUO EL REY CCN ********:
16059 5ELCID2036 FABLO MYO %ID & DIXO: MER%ED; YOLO RE%IBO, ******** MYO SE@OR;
16121 5ELCID2044 QUANDO HE LA GRA%IA DE CCN ******** MYO SE@OR;
16514 5ELCID2093 CAMEARON LAS ESPACAS ANTEL REY DON ********.
16519 5ELCID2094 FABLO EL REY DON ******** CCMMO TAN BUEN SE@OR:
16813 5ELCID2128 AQUI LC DIGC ANTE MYC SE@OR EL REY ********:
16925 5ELCID2142 HYA REY DON ********, SE@OR TAN ONDRADO,
16960 5ELCID2147 DIXO EL REY DCN ********: MUCHC ME AUEDES ENBARGADO.
17035 5ELCID2156 HYAS ESPIDIC MYC %ID DE SO SE@OR ********,
17056 5ELCID2159 BEFAR LAS MANCS, ESPECIR SE DE REY ********:
17395 5ELCID2200 PEDIDAS UOS HA & ROGACAS EL MYO SE@OR ********,
17633 5ELCID2231 POR MANO DEL REY ********, QUE AMI LO OUO MANDADO,
22187 5ELCID2825 DE CUER PESC ESTO AL BUEN REY DON ********.
22757 5ELCID2900 AL REY ******** DE CASTIELLA PENSSO DE ENBIAR;
22787 5ELCID2903 LIEUES EL MANDADO A CASTIELLA AL REY ********;
23043 5ELCID2936 MER%ED, REY ********, DE LARGOS REYNOS AUOS DIZEN SE@OR
23365 5ELCID2976 NON LO DETIENE POR NACA ******** EL CASTELLANO,
23567 5ELCID3001 EN LOS PRIMEROS VA EL BUEN REY DON ********,
23958 5ELCID3053 EL REY DON ******** A TCLLECC ES ENTRADO,
24381 5ELCID3108 LEUANTOS EN PIE EL BUEN REY DON ********
24536 5ELCID3127 ESSORA SE LEUO EN PIE EL BUEN REY DON ********;
24864 5ELCID3166 BIEN NCS ABENDREMCS CCN EL REY DON ********.
24902 5ELCID3171 MER%ED, YA REY DON ********, SCDES NUESTRO SE@OR
25358 5ELCID3228 A ESTAS PALABRAS FABLC EL REY DON ********:
25440 5ELCID3239 POR JUUIZIC LC CAMOS ANTEL REY CON ********:
25490 5ELCID3246 SOBRE LCS DOZIENTOS MARCOS QUE TENIE EL REY ********
26233 5ELCID3344 ESTOT LIDIARE AQUI ANTEL REY DON ********
26558 5ELCID3390 DIXO EL REY ********: CALLE YA ESTA RAZON.
26610 5ELCID3397 BESAN LAS MANCS AL REY CCN ********,
26651 5ELCID3403 MER%ED, REY ********, VCS SODES MYO SE@OR
26804 5ELCID3423 BESARON LAS MANOS DEL REY DON ********,
26916 5ELCID3438 HYO LES DI MIS PRIMAS POR MANCACO DEL REY ********,
27027 5ELCID3452 GRADO ADIOS DEL %IELC & AQUEL REY DON ********,
27499 5ELCID3512 FUE BESAR LA MANO A SC SE@OR ********;
27704 5ELCID3536 ELLOS SON ENPCER DEL REY DON ******** EL DE LEON;
27763 5ELCID3543 CA GRAND MIEDC CUIERON A ******** EL DE LEON.
27806 5ELCID3548 DEMAS SOBRE TODOS YES EL REY DON ********,
27854 5ELCID3554 ANDIDIERON EN PLEYTC, CIXIERCN LO AL REY ********,
27994 5ELCID3572 HYUA LOS VER EL REY DCN ********;
28166 5ELCID3595 DO SEDIEN ENEL CAMPO FABLC EL REY DON ********:

WORD C# PREFIX CONTEXT

ALFONSSO (CON'T)

28918 5ELCID3693 MANDO LIBRAR EL CANPO EL BUEN REY DON ********,
29112 5ELCID3718 QUIERON SU AIUNTA CON ******** EL DE LEON,
WORD # 315 OCCURS 74 TIMES.
INDEX OF DIVERSIFICATION = 395.55 WITH STANDARD DEVIATION OF 935.06

ALFONSSSO 6392 5ELCID0815 AL REY ********* QUE ME A AYRADO
WORD # 316 OCCURS 1 TIMES.

ALGARA 3507 5ELCID0442 VOS CON LOS CC YD UOS EN ******; ALA VAYA ALBARABAREZ,
3584 5ELCID0451 SICUETA UOS FUERE ALGUNA AL ******,
3605 5ELCID0454 NONBRADOS SON LOS QUE YRAN ENEL ******,
3767 5ELCID0476 AFEUOS LOS CCIIJ ENEL ******,
WORD # 317 OCCURS 4 TIMES.

ALGARAS 3545 5ELCID0446 FITA AYUSO & POR GUADALFAIARA, FATA ALCALA LEGEN LAS *******,
WORD # 318 OCCURS 1 TIMES.

ALGO 868 5ELCID0111 RETOUO DELLOS QUANTO QUE FUE ****;
962 5ELCID0123 NOS HUEBOS AUEMOS EN TODO DE GANAR ****.
968 5ELCID0124 BIEN LO SABEMOS QUE EL **** GAƏO,
1224 5ELCID0157 ALO QUEM SEMEIA, DE LO MIO AUREDES ****;
1605 5ELCID0205 AUN VEA EL DIA QUE DEMI AYADES ****
2051 5ELCID0258 SIESSA DESPENSSA UOS FALLEZIERE OUOS MENGUARE ****,
6301 5ELCID0802 MANDO MYO ZID AUN QUELES DIESSEN ****.
8095 5ELCID1033 DIXO MYO ZID: COMED, CONDE, ****, CASI NON COMEDES, NON VEREDES
8446 5ELCID1073 DE LO UUESTRO, O DELC MYO LEUAREDES ****.
9922 5ELCID1258 DELOS QUE SON AQUI & COMIGO GANARON ****;
13883 5ELCID1758 LAS DUEƏAS & LAS FIJAS & LA MUGIER QUE VALE ****
14049 5ELCID1779 LOS MOROS DELAS TIERRAS GANADO SEAN Y ****;
14154 5ELCID1791 QUE CROUIESSE SOS NUEUAS DE MYO ZID QUE AUIE ****.
16935 5ELCID2143 DESTAS VISTAS QUE OUIEMOS, DEMY TOMEDES ****.
17010 5ELCID2153 AVN BIUO SEYENDO, DE MI AYADES ****
17985 5ELCID2275 QUES PAGE DES CASAMIENTO MYO ZID O EL QUE LO ****
19239 5ELCID2434 CON DOS ESPADAS QUE EL PREZIAUA ****
19260 5ELCID2438 **** VIE MYO ZID DELO QUE ERA PAGADO,
20229 5ELCID2568 DIXO EL CAMPEADOR: DARUOS HE MYS FIJAS & **** DELO MYO;
WORD # 319 OCCURS 19 TIMES.
INDEX OF DIVERSIFICATION = 1074.61 WITH STANDARD DEVIATION OF 1330.78

ALGUANDRE 2790 5ELCID0352 LONGINOS ERA ZIEGO, QUE NUQUAS VIO *********,
8510 5ELCID1081 VNA DES LEATANZA CA NON LA FIZO *********.
WORD # 320 OCCURS 2 TIMES.

ALGUN 1986 5ELCID0251 SI YO ***** DIA VISGUIER, SERUOS HAN DOBLADOS.
2392 5ELCID0302 EN ANTES QUE YO MUERA, ***** BIEN UOS PUEDA FAR:
18749 5ELCID2372 POR SABOR QUE AUIA DE ***** MORO MATAR;
WORD # 321 OCCURS 3 TIMES.

ALGUNA 3582 5ELCID0451 SICUETA UOS FUERE ****** AL ALGARA,
19720 5ELCID2500 QUE ABRAM DE MI SALTO QUIZAB ****** NOCH
20611 5ELCID2616 QUE ESTOS CASAMIENTOS NON SERIEN SIN ****** TACHA.
22845 5ELCID2910 SI DESONDRA Y CABE ****** CONTRA NOS,
25590 5ELCID3259 O EN ****** RAZON? AQUI LO MEIORARE A JUUIZYO DELA CORT.
WORD # 322 OCCURS 5 TIMES.
INDEX OF DIVERSIFICATION = 5501.00 WITH STANDARD DEVIATION OF 7133.64

ALGUNOS 2254 5ELCID0283 O QUE DE VENTURA & ******* DIAS VIDA,
5337 5ELCID0674 BIEN SOMOS NOS VI ZIENTOS, ******* AY DE MAS;
9934 5ELCID1260 QUE SI ******* FURTARE O MENOS LE FALLAREN, EL AUER ME AURA ATORNAR
24442 5ELCID3116 MAGER QUE ******* PESA, MEIOR SODES QUE NOS.
WORD # 323 OCCURS 4 TIMES.

ALGUNT 13850 5ELCID1754 ROGAND AL CRIADOR QUE UOS BIUA ****** AƏO,
WORD # 324 OCCURS 1 TIMES.

ALI 4504 5ELCID0573 *** YOGO MYO ZID COMPLIDAS XV SEMMANAS.
7090 5ELCID0907 *** SOUO MIO ZID CONPLIDAS XV SEMANAS;
8842 5ELCID1126 *** PAREZRA EL QUE MEREZE LA SOLDADA.
9955 5ELCID1262 *** DIXO MINAYA: CONSEIO ES AGUISADO.
13668 5ELCID1732 *** PREZIO ABAUIECA DELA CABEZA FASTA ACABO.
15494 5ELCID1963 SYO BIUO SO, *** YRE SIN FALLA.
WORD # 325 OCCURS 6 TIMES.
INDEX OF DIVERSIFICATION = 2197.00 WITH STANDARD DEVIATION OF 995.03

ALLA 4935 5ELCID0624 FIZO ENBIAR POR LA TIENDA QUE DEXARA ****.
5055 5ELCID0638 NON LO DETARDEDES, LOS DOS YD PORA ****,
6097 5ELCID0774 E AGALUE NOL COGIERON ****;
7625 5ELCID0976 MYO ZID QUANDO LO OYO, ENBIO PORA ****:
10381 5ELCID1315 CON ESTA PRESENTEIA ADELINO PORA ****;
11044 5ELCID1398 SALUDA UOS MYO ZID **** ONDDE ELLE ESTA;
13258 5ELCID1681 ALBAR SALUADOREZ PRESO FINCO ****.
20315 5ELCID2578 **** ME LEUADES LAS TELAS DEL CORAZON.
22399 5ELCID2853 MUCHO UOS LO GRADEZE, **** DO ESTA, MYO ZID EL CANPEADOR,
22581 5ELCID2876 ODIZEN BADO DE REY, **** YUAN POSAR,
23267 5ELCID2964 QUE **** ME VAYAN CUENDES & YFANZONES,

WORD C# PREFIX CONTEXT

ALLA (CON'T)

```
                 24339 5ELCID3103 ASSI YUA MYO %ID ADOBADO **** CORT.
                 28605 5ELCID3653 **** LEUO EL ALMOFAR, FATA LA COFIA LEGAUA,
         WORD # 326 OCCURS  13 TIMES.
           INDEX OF DIVERSIFICATION =  1971.50 WITH STANDARD DEVIATION OF  1992.68

ALLABANDOS       22173 5ELCID2824 ********** SEYAN LOS YFANTES DE CARRION.
         WORD # 327 OCCURS   1 TIMES.

ALLAS            22159 5ELCID2822 ***** FIJAS DEL %ID DAN LES ESFUER%O.
                 25695 5ELCID3272 VEZOS MYO %ID ***** CORTES PREGONADAS;
         WORD # 328 OCCURS   2 TIMES.

ALLI                66 5ELCID0010 **** PIENSSAN DE AGUIIAR, ALLI SUELTAN LAS RIENDAS.
                    70 5ELCID0010 ALLI PIENSSAN DE AGUIIAR, **** SUELTAN LAS RIENDAS.
                  3986 5ELCID0506 ESTAS GANAN%IAS **** ERAN IUNTADAS.
                  4426 5ELCID0563 QUE SOPIESSEN QUE MYO %ID **** AUIE FINCAN%A.
                  4441 5ELCID0565 QUE EL CAMPEADOR MYO %ID **** AUIE POBLADO,
                  7065 5ELCID0903 ESTANDO ****, MUCHA TIERRA PREAUA,
                  9565 5ELCID1215 TODOS ERAN RICOS QUANTOS QUE **** HA.
                 13640 5ELCID1728 MYO %ID EL DE BIUAR FASTA **** LEGO EN ALCAZ,
                 18069 5ELCID2286 FERRAN GON%ALEZ NON VIO **** DOS AL%ASSE, NIN CAMARA ABIERTA NIN
                 18564 5ELCID2349 POR LA SU VOLUNTAD NON SERIEN **** LEGADOS.
                 21207 5ELCID2695 **** SON CA@OS DO A ELPHA EN%ERRO;
                 21393 5ELCID2720 **** LES TUELLEN LOS MANTOS & LOS PELLI%ONES,
                 22144 5ELCID2819 QUANTO EL MEIOR PUEDE **** LAS ONDRO.
                 22166 5ELCID2823 **** SOUIERON ELLAS FATA QUE SA@AS SON.
                 23649 5ELCID3012 DE TODAS PARTES **** IUNTADOS SON.
                 27323 5ELCID3492 **** SE TOLLIO EL CAPIELO EL %ID CAMPEADOR,
         WORD # 329 OCCURS  16 TIMES.
           INDEX OF DIVERSIFICATION =  1816.13 WITH STANDARD DEVIATION OF  1666.55

ALLONGANDO        9743 5ELCID1238 YAL CRE%E LA BARBA & VALE **********;
         WORD # 330 OCCURS   1 TIMES.

ALMA              2214 5ELCID0279 COMMO ALA MI **** YO TANTO UOS QUERIA.
                  8007 5ELCID1022 ANTES PERDERE EL CUERPO & DEXARE EL ****,
                 12064 5ELCID1529 SI DIOS ME LEGARE AL %ID ELO VEA CON EL ****,
                 12655 5ELCID1605 MY CORA%ON & MI ****,
                 13456 5ELCID1705 PRENDOL YO LOS PECADOS, & DIOS LE ABRA EL ****.
                 14396 5ELCID1820 E SERUIR LO HE SIENPRE MIENTRA QUE OUISSE EL ****.
                 15804 5ELCID2004 EN QUE TIENE SU **** & SU CORA%ON,
                 18934 5ELCID2395 HYUA LOS FERIR DE CORA%ON & DE ****.
                 28656 5ELCID3658 VIO DIEGO GON%ALEZ QUE NO ESCAPARIE CON EL ****;
         WORD # 331 OCCURS   9 TIMES.
           INDEX OF DIVERSIFICATION =  3304.25 WITH STANDARD DEVIATION OF  3180.11

ALMAS              223 5ELCID0028 E AUN DEMAS LOS CUERPOS & LAS *****.
                  3036 5ELCID0382 DIOS QUE NOS DIO LAS *****, CONSEIO NOS DARA.
         WORD # 332 OCCURS   2 TIMES.

ALMENAR           8604 5ELCID1092 MYO %ID GA@O AXERICA & A ONDA & *******,
                  8734 5ELCID1119 DESI A ONDA & LOS OTROS A *******,
                 10478 5ELCID1328 PRISO A ******* & A MURUIEDRO QUE ES MIYOR,
         WORD # 333 OCCURS   3 TIMES.

ALMENOS            505 5ELCID0064 NON LE OSARIEN UENDER ******* DINARADA.
         WORD # 334 OCCURS   1 TIMES.

ALMOFALLA         1425 5ELCID0182 EN MEDIO DEL PALA%IO TENDIERON VN *********,
                  5222 5ELCID0660 MUCHAS SON LAS AROBDAS & GRANDE ES EL *********.
                  5507 5ELCID0694 VIERON LO LAS AROBDAS DELOS MOROS, AL ********* SEUAN TORNAR.
                  8835 5ELCID1124 HYREMOS VER AQUELA SU *********,
                 14541 5ELCID1839 CUEDAN SE QUE ES *********, CA NON VIENEN CON MANDADO;
         WORD # 335 OCCURS   5 TIMES.
           INDEX OF DIVERSIFICATION =  3278.00 WITH STANDARD DEVIATION OF  2245.37

ALMOFAR           6201 5ELCID0790 ******* ACUESTAS, LA ESPADA EN LA MANO.
                 19250 5ELCID2436 LA CARA FRONZIDA & ******* SOLTADO,
                 28608 5ELCID3653 ALLA LEUO EL *******, FATA LA COFIA LEGAUA,
                 28617 5ELCID3654 LA COFIA & EL ******* TODO GELO LEUAUA,
         WORD # 336 OCCURS   4 TIMES.

ALMORZADO        26455 5ELCID3375 VERMEIO VIENE, CA ERA *********;
         WORD # 337 OCCURS   1 TIMES.

ALMUERZAS        26514 5ELCID3384 ANTES ********* QUE VAYAS A ORA%ION,
         WORD # 338 OCCURS   1 TIMES.

ALO               1217 5ELCID0157 *** QUEM SEMEIA, DE LO MIO AUREDES ALGO;
                 25233 5ELCID3213 *** QUE DEMANDA EL %IC CUEL RECUDADES VOS.
         WORD # 339 OCCURS   2 TIMES.

ALOS               515 5ELCID0066 AMYO %ID & **** SUYOS ABASTALES DE PAN & DE UINO;
                  2415 5ELCID0305 PLOGO **** OTROS OMNES TODOS QUANTOS CON EL ESTAN.
```

WORD C# PREFIX CONTEXT

ALOS (CON'T)

```
2562 5ELCID0324 **** MEDIADOS GALLOS PIESSAN DE CAUALGAR.
2741 5ELCID0347 **** IUDIOS TE DEXESTE PRENDER; DO DIZEN MONTE CALUARIE
2840 5ELCID0358 ENEL MONUMENTC RESU%ITEST, FUST **** YNFIERNOS,
4498 5ELCID0572 **** DE CALATAUTH, SABET, MALES PESAUA.
4938 5ELCID0625 MUCHO PESA **** DE TECA & ALOS DE TERUAL NON PLAZE,
4942 5ELCID0625 MUCHO PESA ALCS DE TECA & **** DE TERUAL NON PLAZE,
4948 5ELCID0626 E **** DE CALATAYUTH NON PLAZE.
5223 5ELCID0661 **** DE MYC %ID YA LES TUELLEN EL AGUA.
5567 5ELCID0701 PORA MYO %ID & **** SCS A MANCS LOS TOMAR.
5976 5ELCID0758 **** QUE ALCAN%A VALCS CELIBRANDO.
6289 5ELCID0801 ASOS CASTIELLCS **** MORCS CENTRO LOS AN TORNADOS,
6337 5ELCID0807 **** PEONES & A LOS ENCAUALGADOS
6734 5ELCID0860 PLOGO **** DE TERER & ALCS DE CALATAYUT MAS,
6738 5ELCID0860 PLCGO ALOS DE TERER & **** DE CALATAYUT MAS,
6743 5ELCID0861 PESO **** DE ALCO%ER, CA PROLES FAZIE GRANT.
7084 5ELCID0906 NON PLAZE **** MOROS, FIRME MIENTRE LES PESAUA.
7327 5ELCID0940 PESANDO VA **** DE MON%CN & ALCS DE HUESCA;
7331 5ELCID0940 PESANDO VA ALOS DE MCN%CN & **** DE HUESCA;
7339 5ELCID0941 POR QUE CAN PARIAS PLAZE **** DE SARAGO%A,
7875 5ELCID1007 **** VNCS FIRIENDO & A LOS OTROS DE ROCANDO.
8646 5ELCID1098 PESA **** DE VALEN%IA, SABET, NON LES PLAZE;
9189 5ELCID1170 **** DE VALEN%IA ESCARMENTACOS LOS HAN,
10226 5ELCID1295 **** DIAS DEL SIEGLC NCN LE LCRASSEN CHRISTIANOS.
10403 5ELCID1319 **** PIES DEL REY ALFCNSSO CAYO CON GRAND DUELO,
11309 5ELCID1431 AFEUOS RACHEL & VIDAS **** PIES LE CAEN:
11905 5ELCID1509 E A CUBERTURAS DE %ENDALES, & ESCUDOS **** CUELLOS,
12364 5ELCID1570 MANDO MYO %ID **** QUE HA EN SU CASA
13417 5ELCID1701 **** MEDIADOS GALLCS, ANTES DE LA MA@ANA,
13508 5ELCID1712 MIO %ID **** SOS VASSALCS TAN BIEN LOS ACORDANDO.
13556 5ELCID1718 **** %INQUAENTA MILL VAN LOS FERIR DE GRADO;
14519 5ELCID1837 **** VNCS PLAZE & ALOS CTRCS VA PESANDO.
14523 5ELCID1837 ALOS VNOS PLAZE & **** OTROS VA PESANDO.
15228 5ELCID1928 DE DAR SUS FIJAS **** YFANTES DE CARRION,
15972 5ELCID2025 DE AQUESTA GUISA **** PIES LE CAYO.
16264 5ELCID2063 EL CAMPEADOR **** SOS LC MANDC
16369 5ELCID2076 QUE LAS DEDES POR MUGIERES **** YFANTES DE CARRION.
16559 5ELCID2098 E DOLAS POR VELADAS **** YFANTES DE CARRION.
16752 5ELCID2121 EL REY **** YFANTES ALAS MANOS LES TOMO,
16881 5ELCID2136 PRENDELLAS CON UUESTRAS MANCS & DALDAS **** YFANTES,
17185 5ELCID2174 GRANT ONDRA LES DAN **** YFANTES DE CARRION.
17219 5ELCID2178 DAD LES VN REYAL & **** YFANTES DE CARRION,
17586 5ELCID2225 **** YFANTES DE CARRICN DAC LAS CON UUESTRA MANO,
17616 5ELCID2229 **** YFANTES DE CARRICN MINAYA VA FABLANDO:
17895 5ELCID2264 EA TODAS LAS DUE@AS & **** FIJOS DALGO;
18313 5ELCID2317 MAS, SABED, DE CUER LES PESA **** YFANTES DE CARRION;
18851 5ELCID2386 **** PRIMERCS COLPES DOS MOROS MATAUA DE LA LAN%A.
18985 5ELCID2402 LOS DE MYO %IC **** DE EUCAR DELAS TIENDAS LOS SACAN.
20905 5ELCID2655 BUENOS SE@CS CAUALLOS **** YFANTES DE CARRION.
21012 5ELCID2670 TU MUERT OY COSSEIAR **** YFANTES DE CARRION.
21041 5ELCID2674 DELO QUE EL MCRO DIXO **** YFANTES NON PLAZE:
22983 5ELCID2928 CMILLOS **** SANTOS & RCGC ACRIADOR;
23377 5ELCID2978 **** PCRTOGALESES & A GALIZIANOS,
23383 5ELCID2979 E **** DE CARRICN & AVARONES CASTELLANOS,
26519 5ELCID3385 **** QUE DAS PAZ, FARTAS LCS ADERREDOR.
26837 5ELCID3428 MAS NON PLAZE **** YFANTES DE CARRION.
27388 5ELCID3499 AESSOS & **** OTRCS QUE DE BUENA PARTE SON,
27590 5ELCID3523 EL CAMPEADOR **** QUE HAN LIDIAR TAN BIEN LOS CASTIGO:
27736 5ELCID3540 QUE SI LOS PUDIESSEN APARTAR **** DEL CAMPEADOR,
27909 5ELCID3561 OTRO SI FARAN **** DEL CANPEADOR.
28075 5ELCID3584 LOS ESCUDOS **** CUELLOS QUE BIEN BLOCADOS SON;
28225 5ELCID3603 HYA LES VA PESANDO **** YFANTES DE CARRION.
28300 5ELCID3612 DESI VINIEN LCS DE MYO %ID **** YFANTES DE CARRION,
28308 5ELCID3613 ELLOS YFANTES DE CARRICN **** DE CAMPEADOR;
28951 5ELCID3698 EL REY **** DE MYC %IC DE NOCHE LOS ENBIO,
28985 5ELCID3702 POR MALOS LCS DEXARON **** YFANTES DE CARRION,
WORD # 340 OCCURS 67 TIMES.
INDEX OF DIVERSIFICATICN = 430.36 WITH STANDARD DEVIATION OF 572.44

ALQUE 16503 5ELCID2092 BAN BESAR LAS MANOS ***** EN ORA BUENA NA%IO;
17531 5ELCID2218 ESTAN PARANDO MIENTES ***** EN BUEN ORA NASCO.
23716 5ELCID3021 E YUA RE%EBIR ***** EN BUEN ORA NA%IO.
WORD # 341 OCCURS 3 TIMES.

ALSABOR 4666 5ELCID0592 ******* DEL PRENDER DELO AL NON PIENSSAN NADA,
WORD # 342 OCCURS 1 TIMES.

ALSO 23438 5ELCID2985 HYA LES VA PESANDO **** YFANTES DE CARRION,
28355 5ELCID3620 CADA VNO DELLCS MIENTES TIENE ****;
WORD # 343 OCCURS 2 TIMES.

ALTAR 1757 5ELCID0224 MANDO AL UUESTRO ***** BUENAS DONAS & RICAS;
2592 5ELCID0327 ECHOS DO@A XIMENA EN LOS GRADOS DELANTEL *****,
23977 5ELCID3055 MANDO FAZER CANDELAS & PONER ENEL *****;
WORD # 344 OCCURS 3 TIMES.
```

WORD C# PREFIX CONTEXT

```
ALTAS              280 5ELCID0035 LOS DE MYO %ID A ***** UOZES LAMAN,
                 12378 5ELCID1571 QUE GUARDASSEN EL ALCA%AR & LAS OTRAS TORRES *****
        WORD # 345 OCCURS   2 TIMES.

ALTE             26032 5ELCID3318 VIST VN MORO, FUSTEL ENSAYAR; ANTES FUXISTE QUE **** ALEGASSES.
        WORD # 346 OCCURS   1 TIMES.

ALTER%ER          7310 5ELCID0938 ******** DIA, DON YXC Y ES TORNADO.
                  8754 5ELCID1113 ******** DIA TODOS IUNTADOS SON,
        WORD # 347 OCCURS   2 TIMES.

ALTO                58 5ELCID0008 GRADO ATI, SE@OR PADRE, QUE ESTAS EN ****
                  3920 5ELCID0497 ADIOS LO PROMETO, A AQUEL QUE ESTA EN ****:
                  4838 5ELCID0612 METIOLA EN SOMO EN TODO LO MAS ****.
                  6222 5ELCID0792 GRADO A DIOS, A QUEL QUE ESTA EN ****,
                  6766 5ELCID0864 **** ES EL POYO, MARAUILLOSO & GRANT;
                 10251 5ELCID1297 OYD, MINAYA ALBARFANEZ, POR AQUEL QUE ESTA EN ****,
                 12697 5ELCID1611 ALA LAS SUBIE ENEL MAS **** LOGAR;
                 18512 5ELCID2342 AVN SI DIOS QUISIERE & EL PADRE QUE ESTA EN ****,
                 19390 5ELCID2456 GRADO ADIOS & AL PADRE QUE ESTA EN ****,
                 23075 5ELCID2940 **** FUE EL CASAMIENO CALO QUISIESTES UOS
        WORD # 348 OCCURS  10 TIMES.
           INDEX OF DIVERSIFICATION =  2556.44 WITH STANDARD DEVIATION OF  1781.74

ALTOS            21232 5ELCID2698 LOS MONTES SON *****, LAS RAMAS PUIAN CON LAS NUES,
        WORD # 349 OCCURS   1 TIMES.

ALTRO%IR         21152 5ELCID2687 TENIENDO YUAN ARMAS ******** DE SALON:
        WORD # 350 OCCURS   1 TIMES.

ALUA              8663 5ELCID1100 TRASNOCHARON DE NOCH, AL **** DELA MAN
        WORD # 351 OCCURS   1 TIMES.

ALUAN             7428 5ELCID0952 DENT CORRE MYO %ID A HUESCA & A MONT *****;
                  8580 5ELCID1089 E DEXADO A HUESCA & LAS TIERRAS DE MONT *****.
        WORD # 352 OCCURS   2 TIMES.

ALUAR            13564 5ELCID1719 ***** ALUAREZ & ALUAR SALUADOREZ & MINAYA ALBARFANEZ
                 13567 5ELCID1719 ALUAR ALUAREZ & ***** SALUADOREZ & MINAYA ALBARFANEZ
                 15715 5ELCID1994 ***** ALUAREZ & ALUAR SAUADOREZ,
                 15718 5ELCID1994 ALUAR ALUAREZ & ***** SAUADOREZ,
                 15748 5ELCID1999 ***** SALUADOREZ & GALIND GARCIAZ EL DE ARAGON,
                 23679 5ELCID3016 ***** FANEZ ADELANTEL ENBIO,
        WORD # 353 OCCURS   6 TIMES.
           INDEX OF DIVERSIFICATION =  2022.00 WITH STANDARD DEVIATION OF  3429.76

ALUAREZ          13565 5ELCID1719 ALUAR ******* & ALUAR SALUADOREZ & MINAYA ALBARFANEZ
                 15716 5ELCID1994 ALUAR ******* & ALUAR SAUADOREZ,
        WORD # 354 OCCURS   2 TIMES.

ALUCAD            8726 5ELCID1108 LOS VNOS AXERICA & LOS OTROS A ******,
        WORD # 355 OCCURS   1 TIMES.

ALUCANT           8563 5ELCID1087 POBLADO HA MYO %ID EL PUERTO DE *******,
        WORD # 356 OCCURS   1 TIMES.

ALUEN            21220 5ELCID2696 ADIESTRO DEXAN ASANT ESTEUAN, MAS CAE *****;
        WORD # 357 OCCURS   1 TIMES.

ALUORES           8929 5ELCID1137 CON LOS ******* MYO %ID FERIR LOS VA:
                 13073 5ELCID1657 FINCADAS SON LAS TIENDAS & PARE%EN LOS *******,
        WORD # 358 OCCURS   2 TIMES.

AMAL              4170 5ELCID0530 LO QUE YO DIXIER NON LO TENGADES ****:
                  5017 5ELCID0634 RIBERA DE SALON TODA YRA ****,
                 19451 5ELCID2464 POR BIEN LO DIXO EL %ID, MAS ELLOS LO TOUIERON ****.
        WORD # 359 OCCURS   3 TIMES.

AMANE%IO          9324 5ELCID1186 ******** AMYO %ID EN TIERRAS DE MON REAL.
        WORD # 360 OCCURS   1 TIMES.

AMANOS            7591 5ELCID0972 ASI VIENE ES FOR%ADO QUE EL CONDE ****** SELE CUYDO TOMAR.
        WORD # 361 OCCURS   1 TIMES.

AMARAUILLA       18195 5ELCID2302 ********** LO HAN QUANTOS QUE YSON,
        WORD # 362 OCCURS   1 TIMES.

AMARAUILLAR       8676 5ELCID1102 VIOLO MYO %ID, TOMOS ***********: GRADO ATI, PADRE SPIRITAL
        WORD # 363 OCCURS   1 TIMES.

AMARAULLA        18537 5ELCID2346 ********* LO AUIEN MUCHOS DESSOS CHRISTIANOS,
        WORD # 364 OCCURS   1 TIMES.
```

```
WORD                C#  PREFIX                                CONTEXT

AMAS                   991 5ELCID0127 ESTAS ARCHAS PRENDAMOS LAS ****,
                      6882 5ELCID0879 BESA UOS LOS PIES & LAS MANOS ****,
                     10677 5ELCID1352 POR SU MUGIER DO@A XIMENA & SUS FIJAS **** ADOS:
                     11039 5ELCID1397 ASSI FFAGA A UUESTRAS FIJAS ****.
                     12559 5ELCID1593 ADELINO A SU MUGIER & A SUS FIJAS ****;
                     12592 5ELCID1597 AFE ME AQUI, SE@OR, YO UUESTRAS FIJAS & ****,
                     12648 5ELCID1604 VOS, QUERIDA & ONDRADA MUGIER, & **** MIS FIJAS,
                     13108 5ELCID1661 ASSI FFAZIE ALAS DUE@AS & A SUS FIJAS **** ADOS:
                     13388 5ELCID1697 ODE **** ODEL VNA DIOS NOS VALDRA.
                     14175 5ELCID1794 QUANDO ES FARTO DE LIDIAR CON **** LAS SUS MANOS,
                     14237 5ELCID1801 ALEGRE ES DO@A XIMENA & SUS FIJAS ****,
                     14321 5ELCID1811 POR AMOR DE MI MUGIER & DE MIS FIJAS ****,
                     15049 5ELCID1902 SABOR HAN DE CASAR CON SUS FIJAS **** ADOS.
                     15798 5ELCID2003 DENTRO ES SU MUGIER & SUS FIJAS **** ADOS,
                     16452 5ELCID2086 HYO LAS ENGENDRE **** & CRIASTES LAS UOS
                     17271 5ELCID2184 RE%IBIOLO DO@A XIMENA & SUS FIJAS ****:
                     17319 5ELCID2190 BESARON LE LAS MANOS LA MUGIER & LAS FIJAS ****,
                     17417 5ELCID2203 METIUOS EN SUS MANOS, FIJAS, **** ADOS;
                     17562 5ELCID2222 AFFE **** MIS FIJAS, METOLAS EN UUESTRA MANO;
                     17642 5ELCID2232 DOUOS ESTAS DUE@AS, **** SON FIJAS DALGO,
                     20423 5ELCID2592 **** HERMANAS, DON ELUIRA & DO@A SOL,
                     20477 5ELCID2599 ASSI UOS PEDIMOS MER%ED NOS **** ADOS,
                     20492 5ELCID2601 ABRA%OLAS MYO %ID & SALUDOLAS **** ADOS.
                     20620 5ELCID2617 NOS PUEDE REPENTIR, QUE CASADAS LAS HA ****.
                     20632 5ELCID2619 PRIMO ERES DE MIS FIJAS **** DALMA & DE CORA%ON
                     21320 5ELCID2710 SI NON **** SUS MUGIERES DO@A ELUIRA & DO@A SOL:
                     21543 5ELCID2738 RONPIEN LAS CAMISAS & LAS CARNES AELLAS **** ADOS;
                     21781 5ELCID2770 FASTA QUE VIESSE VENIR SUS PRIMAS **** ADOS
                     21830 5ELCID2777 FALLO SUS PRIMAS AMORTE%IDAS **** ADOS.
                     21876 5ELCID2783 VALAS TORNANDO A ELLAS **** ADOS;
                     22024 5ELCID2802 MUCHO SON LAZRADAS & **** LAS FARTO.
                     22043 5ELCID2805 FATA QUE ESFUER%AN, & **** LAS TOMO
                     22057 5ELCID2807 CON EL SO MANTO A **** LAS CUBRIO,
                     22346 5ELCID2846 QUE VINIE MYNAYA POR SUS PRIMAS **** ADOS.
                     23870 5ELCID3040 BESA UOS LAS MANOS, & MIS FIJAS **** ADOS,
                     24985 5ELCID3182 EN LAS MANOS LAS TIENE & **** LAS CATO;
                     25153 5ELCID3203 QUANDO SACARON DE VALEN%IA MIS FIJAS **** ADOS,
                     28569 5ELCID3647 TALES FUERON LOS COLPES QUE LES QUEBRARON ****.
          WORD # 365 OCCURS  38 TIMES.
              INDEX OF DIVERSIFICATION =   744.35 WITH STANDARD DEVIATION OF  1267.68

AMAUA                12311 5ELCID1563 CA DELO QUE MAS ***** YAL VIENE EL MANDADO.
                     18850 5ELCID2385 POR LA SU VENTURA & DIOS QUEL *****
          WORD # 366 OCCURS   2 TIMES.

AMAYOR               29134 5ELCID3721 ****** ONDRA LAS CASA QUE LO QUE PRIMERO FUE.
          WORD # 367 OCCURS   1 TIMES.

AMEN                 23809 5ELCID3033 ****, DIXO MYO %ID EL CAMPEADOR;
                     29223 5ELCID3731 QUIEN ESCRIUIO ESTE LIBRO DEL DIOS PARAYSO, ****
          WORD # 368 OCCURS   2 TIMES.

AMENOS                7721 5ELCID0989 ****** DE BATALLA NON NOS DEXARIE POR NADA.
                      8704 5ELCID1106 ****** DE LID NOS PARTIRA AQUESTO;
                     25571 5ELCID3257 ****** DE RIEBTOS NO LOS PUEDO DEXAR.
          WORD # 369 OCCURS   3 TIMES.

AMI                   1809 5ELCID0230 SI EL REY MELO QUISIERE TOMAR *** NON MINCHAL.
                      4868 5ELCID0616 OYD ***, ALBARFANEZ & TODOS LOS CAUALLEROS
                     14962 5ELCID1891 EFAZIENDO YO HA EL MAL, & EL *** GRAND PRO,
                     17635 5ELCID2231 POR MANO DEL REY ALFONSSO, QUE *** LO OUO MANDADO,
                     18619 5ELCID2356 QUE OY LOS YFANTES *** POR AMO NON ABRAN;
                     19748 5ELCID2504 QUE PAGUEN *** O A QUI YO QUIER SABOR.
                     23794 5ELCID3031 DELO QUE AUOS PESA *** DUELE EL CORA%ON;
                     25927 5ELCID3304 *** LO DIZEN, ATI DAN LAS OREIADAS.
                     28728 5ELCID3668 ESSORA DIXO EL REY: VENID UOS *** COMPA@A;
          WORD # 370 OCCURS   9 TIMES.
              INDEX OF DIVERSIFICATION =  3363.88 WITH STANDARD DEVIATION OF  2898.78

AMIDOS                 663 5ELCID0084 FER LO HE ******, DE GRADO NON AURIE NADA.
                      9669 5ELCID1229 MOROS EN ARUEN%O ****** BEUER AGUA.
          WORD # 371 OCCURS   2 TIMES.

AMIGO                  604 5ELCID0076 AUN %ERCA OTARDE EL REY QUERER ME HA POR *****;
                      9255 5ELCID1177 NIN ***** A AMIGO NOS PUEDEN CONSOLAR.
                      9257 5ELCID1177 NIN AMIGO A ***** NOS PUEDEN CONSOLAR.
                     11557 5ELCID1464 TIENELA AUEGALUON, MYO ***** ES DE PAZ,
                     11672 5ELCID1479  VENIDES, LOS VASSALLOS DE MYO ***** NATURAL?
                     20756 5ELCID2636 SALUDAD A MYO ***** EL MORO AVENGALUON:
                     26529 5ELCID3386 NON DIZES VERDAD ***** NI HA SE@OR,
          WORD # 372 OCCURS   7 TIMES.
              INDEX OF DIVERSIFICATION =  4319.83 WITH STANDARD DEVIATION OF  4098.10

AMIGOL               12050 5ELCID1528 HY AUEGALUON, ****** SODES SIN FALLA.
          WORD # 373 OCCURS   1 TIMES.
```

WORD C# PREFIX CONTEXT

AMIGOS 809 5ELCID0103 O SODES, RACHEL & VIDAS, LOS MYOS ****** CAROS?
6507 5ELCID0830 A NUESTRO ****** BIEN LES PODECES DEZIR:
23850 5ELCID3038 DIOS SALUE A NUESTROS ****** & AUOS MAS, SE@OR
27664 5ELCID3531 ESPIDIOS DE TODOS LOS QUE SOS ****** SON.
WORD # 374 OCCURS 4 TIMES.

AMINAYA 11213 5ELCID1419 ******* LXV CAUALLEROS A CRE%IDOL HAN,
22357 5ELCID2848 RE%IBEN ******* & ATODOS SUS VARONES,
WORD # 375 OCCURS 2 TIMES.

AMIO 2601 5ELCID0329 QUE **** %ID EL CAMPEADOR QUE DIOS LE CURIAS DE MAL:
WORD # 376 OCCURS 1 TIMES.

AMIS 22249 5ELCID2834 QUE **** FIJAS BIEN LAS CASARE YO
WORD # 377 OCCURS 1 TIMES.

AMISTAD 19068 5ELCID2412 RESPUSO BUCAR AL %ID: CONFONDA DIOS TAL *******
26542 5ELCID3388 EN TU ******* NON QUIERO AVER RA%ION.
WORD # 378 OCCURS 2 TIMES.

AMISTAS 19060 5ELCID2411 SALUDAR NOS HEMOS AMOS, & TAIAREMOS *******.
WORD # 379 OCCURS 1 TIMES.

AMJ 7218 5ELCID0925 MIENTRA UOS VISQUIEREDES, BIEN ME YRA ***, MINAYA
WORD # 380 OCCURS 1 TIMES.

AMO 17560 5ELCID2221 VENIT ACA, ALBARFANEZ, EL QUE YO QUIERO & ***
18599 5ELCID2353 MYOS YERNOS AMOS ADOS, LA COSA QUE MUCHO ***,
18621 5ELCID2356 QUE OY LOS YFANTES AMI POR *** NON ABRAN;
WORD # 381 OCCURS 3 TIMES.

AMOIADAS 7759 5ELCID0993 ELAS SIELLAS CO%ERAS & LAS %INCHAS ********;
WORD # 382 OCCURS 1 TIMES.

AMOR 2171 5ELCID0273 DAND NOS CONSEIO POR **** DE SANTA MARIA
5712 5ELCID0720 FERID LOS, CAUALLEROS, POR **** DE CARIDAD
9753 5ELCID1240 POR **** DE REY ALFFONSSO, QUE DE TIERRA ME A ECHADO,
9821 5ELCID1247 DE QUE SON PAGADOS; EL **** DE MY %ID YA LO YUAN PROUANDO.
10424 5ELCID1321 MER%ED, SE@OR ALFONSSO, POR **** DEL CRIADOR
10458 5ELCID1325 ECHASTES LE DE TIERRA, NON HA LA UUESTRA ****;
14313 5ELCID1811 POR **** DE MI MUGIER & DE MIS FIJAS AMAS,
15205 5ELCID1924 ES PAGADO, & DAUOS SU ****.
15367 5ELCID1945 QUERER UOS YE VER & DAR UOS SU ****,
16003 5ELCID2029 SIESTO NON FECHES, NON AUREDES MY ****.
16021 5ELCID2032 ASSI ESTANDO, DEDES ME UUESTRA ****, QUE LO OYAN QUANTOS AQUI SON.
16043 5ELCID2034 AQUI UOS PERDONO & DOUOS MY ****,
16571 5ELCID2099 HYO LAS CASO A UUESTRAS FIJAS CON UUESTRO ****,
18796 5ELCID2379 SI ESTE **** NON FECHES, YO DEUOS ME QUIERO QUITAR.
20793 5ELCID2640 DESI ESCURRA LAS FASTA MEDINA POR LA MI ****;
20929 5ELCID2658 TOD ESTO LES FIZO EL MORO POR EL **** DEL %ID CAMPEADOR.
21275 5ELCID2703 CON SUS MUGIERES EN BRA%OS DEMUESTRAN LES ****;
21908 5ELCID2787 DESPERTEDES, PRIMAS, POR **** DEL CRIADOR
21947 5ELCID2792 ESFOR%AD UOS, PRIMAS, POR **** DEL CRIADOR
22626 5ELCID2883 POR **** DE MYO %ID RICA CENA LES DA.
23322 5ELCID2971 POR **** DE MYO %ID ESTA CORT YO FAGO.
24574 5ELCID3132 POR EL **** DE MYO %ID EL QUE EN BUEN ORA NA%IO,
24712 5ELCID3147 POR QUANTO ESTA CORT FIZIESTES POR MI ****.
24792 5ELCID3157 COMIGO NON QUISIERON AUER NADA & PERDIERON MI ****;
24843 5ELCID3164 AVN GRAND **** NOS FAZE EL %ID CAMPEADOR,
25543 5ELCID3253 MER%ED, AY REY SE@OR, POR **** DE CARIDAD
27312 5ELCID3490 ONDRADOS MELOS ENBIAD A VALEN%IA, POR **** DEL CRIADOR
27429 5ELCID3504 MER%ED UOS PIDO, REY, POR **** DEL CRIADOR
28048 5ELCID3580 TENENDOS ADERECHO, POR **** DEL CRIADOR
WORD # 383 OCCURS 29 TIMES.
INDEX OF DIVERSIFICATION = 923.18 WITH STANDARD DEVIATION OF 1182.06

AMORAR 7435 5ELCID0953 EN AQUESSA CORRIDA X DIAS OUIERON ******.
WORD # 384 OCCURS 1 TIMES.

AMORES 17953 5ELCID2272 LOS ****** QUELES FAZEN MUCHO ERAN SOBEIANOS.
WORD # 385 OCCURS 1 TIMES.

AMORTE%IDAS 21829 5ELCID2777 FALLO SUS PRIMAS *********** AMAS ADOS.
WORD # 386 OCCURS 1 TIMES.

AMOS 787 5ELCID0100 RACHEL & VIDAS EN VNO ESTAUAN ****,
816 5ELCID0104 EN PORIDAD FLABLAR QUERRIA CON ****.
827 5ELCID0106 RACHEL & VIDAS, **** ME DAT LAS MANOS,
940 5ELCID0120 CON GRAND IURA METED Y LAS FES ****,
1103 5ELCID0142 **** TRED ALCAMPEADOR CON TADO,
1356 5ELCID0173 CA MIENTRA QUE VISQUIESSEN REFECHOS ERAN ****.
1498 5ELCID0191 ENTRE RACHEL & VIDAS APARTE YXIERON ****:
1565 5ELCID0200 GRADO EXIR DELA POSADA & ESPIDIOS DE ****.
1588 5ELCID0203 RE%IBIOLO EL %ID ABIERTOS **** LOS BRA%OS:

WORD C# PREFIX CONTEXT

AMOS (CON'T)

```
2101 5ELCID0264 ANTEL CAMPEADCR DO@A XIMENA FINCO LOS YNOIOS ****,
8295 5ELCID1055 AQUI FEREMOS LA MORADA, NO NOS PARTIREMOS ****.
14579 5ELCID1844 BESAN LA TIERRA & LOS PIES ****:
17626 5ELCID2230 AFEUOS DELANT MINAYA, **** SODES HERMANOS.
17656 5ELCID2234 **** LAS RE%IBEN DAMOR & DE GRADO,
18013 5ELCID2279 CON EL **** SUS YERNOS LOS YFANTES DE CARRION.
18328 5ELCID2319 **** HERMANOS A PART SALIDOS SON:
18484 5ELCID2339 EN VNA CONPA@A TORNADOS SON ****.
18513 5ELCID2343 **** LOS MYOS YERNOS BUENOS SERAN EN CAPO.
18593 5ELCID2353 MYOS YERNOS **** ADOS, LA COSA QUE MUCHO AMO,
19057 5ELCID2411 SALUDAR NOS HEMOS ****, & TAIAREMOS AMISTAS.
19281 5ELCID2441 **** SON FIJOS DEL CONDE DON GO%ALO.
19299 5ELCID2443  VENIDES, MYOS YERNOS, MYOS FIJOS SODES ****
19570 5ELCID2479 QUE LIDIARAN CCMIGO EN CAMPO MYOS YERNOS **** ADOS;
19782 5ELCID2507 GRANDES SON LOS GOZOS DE SUS YERNOS **** ADOS:
19796 5ELCID2509 VALIA DE %INCO MILL MARCOS GANARON **** ADOS;
19999 5ELCID2537 TAN MAL SE CONSSEIARON ESTOS YFFANTES ****.
20000 5ELCID2538 **** SALIERON A PART, VERA MIENTRE SON HERMANOS;
20143 5ELCID2557 CON AQUESTE CONSSEIO **** TORNADOS SON,
20309 5ELCID2577 MIOS FIJOS SODES ****, QUANDO MIS FIJAS VOS DO;
20339 5ELCID2580 CON QUE RIQUEZA ENBIO MIOS YERNOS **** ADOS.
20453 5ELCID2596 DELANT SODES ****, SE@ORA & SE@OR.
20541 5ELCID2608 **** LAS BENDIXIERON & DIERON LES SU GRA%IA.
21594 5ELCID2745 CANSSADOS SON DE FERIR ELLOS **** ADOS,
21597 5ELCID2746 ENSAYANDOS **** QUAL DARA MEIORES COLPES.
23626 5ELCID3009 E DIEGO & FERRANDO Y SON **** ADOS,
26286 5ELCID3352 DAQUESTOS **** AQUI QUEDO LA RAZON.
26435 5ELCID3372 DESTOS **** LA RAZON FINCO.
WORD # 387 OCCURS 37 TIMES.
INDEX OF DIVERSIFICATION = 711.44 WITH STANDARD DEVIATION OF 1533.77

AMOUER 1318 5ELCID0169 CA ****** A MYO %ID ANTE QUE CANTE EL GALLO.
WORD # 388 OCCURS 1 TIMES.

AMY 11674 5ELCID1480 *** NON ME PESA, SABET, MUCHO ME PLAZE
WORD # 389 OCCURS 1 TIMES.

AMYDOS 755 5ELCID0095 YO MAS NON PUEDO & ****** LO FAGO.
WORD # 390 OCCURS 1 TIMES.

AMYNAYA 5931 5ELCID0752 ******* ALBARFANEZ YUAL DAR EL CAUALLO:
6115 5ELCID0778 ******* ALBARFANEZ BIEN LANCA EL CAUALLO,
12238 5ELCID1554 ******* & ALAS DUE@AS, DIOS COMMO LAS ONDRAUA
WORD # 391 OCCURS 3 TIMES.

AMYO 512 5ELCID0066 **** %ID & ALOS SUYOS ABASTALES DE PAN & DE UINO;
1358 5ELCID0174 RACHEL **** %ID LA MANOL BA BESAR:
4568 5ELCID0581 FALIDO A **** %ID EL PAN & LA %EUADA.
9325 5ELCID1186 AMANE%IO **** %ID EN TIERRAS DE MON REAL.
12283 5ELCID1560 **** %ID, EL QUE EN BUEN ORA NASCO,
WORD # 392 OCCURS 5 TIMES.
INDEX OF DIVERSIFICATION = 2941.75 WITH STANDARD DEVIATION OF 1608.26

AN 61 5ELCID0009 ESTO ME ** BUELTO MYOS ENEMIGOS MALOS.
2430 5ELCID0306 LOS VJ DIAS DE PLAZO PASSADOS LOS **,
2432 5ELCID0307 TRES ** POR TRO%IR, %EPADES QUE NON MAS.
2551 5ELCID0322 CUEMO LO MANDO MYO %ID, ASSI LO ** TODOS HA FAR.
2908 5ELCID0366 LA ORA%ION FECHA, LA MISSA ACABADA LA **,
3410 5ELCID0430 VASSALLOS TAN BUENOS POR CORA%ON LO **,
3657 5ELCID0461 TODOS SON EXIDOS, LAS PUERTAS DEXADAS ** ABIERTAS
4317 5ELCID0549 NON LO SABEN LOS MOROS EL ARDIMENT QUE **.
5275 5ELCID0667 EL AGUA NOS ** VEDADA, EXIR NOS HA EL PAN,
6236 5ELCID0794 ESTA ALBERGADA LOS DE MYO %ID LUEGO LA ** ROBADA
6293 5ELCID0801 ASOS CASTIELLOS ALOS MOROS DENTRO LOS ** TORNADOS,
6612 5ELCID0844 ASI LO ** ASMADO & METUDO EN CARTA:
8530 5ELCID1084 DE LA GANAN%IA QUE ** FECHA MARAUILLOSA & GRAND.
8555 5ELCID1086 TAN RICOS SON LOS SOS QUE NON SABEN QUE SE **.
9074 5ELCID1155 MIEDO ** EN VALEN%IA QUE NON SABEN QUESE FAR.
10126 5ELCID1283 PUES ESTO ** FABLADO, PIENSSAN SE DE ADOBAR.
12837 5ELCID1629 ARRIBADO ** LAS NAUES, FUERA ERAN EXIDOS,
12939 5ELCID1641 MIS FIJAS & MI MUGIER VERME ** LIDIAR,
13151 5ELCID1667 DESI ** ASSER DEL OBISPO DON IHERONIMO,
13666 5ELCID1731 MUCHO ERA ALEGRE DELO QUE ** CA%ADO.
13702 5ELCID1736 MESNADAS DE MYO %ID ROBADO ** EL CANPO;
13743 5ELCID1741 QUANDO AL REY DE MARUECOS ASSI LO ** ARRANCADO,
13825 5ELCID1751 QUANDO EN VUESTRA VENIDA TAL GANAN%IA NOS ** DADA.
15308 5ELCID1938 ELLOS SON MUCHO VRGULLOSOS & ** PART EN LA CORT,
17752 5ELCID2246 LOS YFANTES DE CARRION BIEN ** CAUALGADO.
17761 5ELCID2247 TORNAN SE CON LAS DUE@AS, A VALEN%IA ** ENTRADO;
19591 5ELCID2482 SOBEIANAS SON LAS GANAN%IAS QUETODOS ** GANADAS;
21494 5ELCID2733 RETRAER UOS LO ** EN VISTAS O EN CORTES.
21533 5ELCID2737 CON LAS ESPUELAS AGUDAS, DON ELLAS ** MAL SABOR,
21785 5ELCID2771 O QUE ** FECHO LOS YFANTES DE CARRION.
22862 5ELCID2912 MYOS AUERES SE ME ** LEUADO, QUE SOBEIANOS SON;
```

WORD C# PREFIX CONTEXT

AN (CON'T)

```
                23734 5ELCID3023 BUENAS CONPA@AS QUE ASSI ** TAL SE@OR.
                25406 5ELCID3235 QUANDO ELLOS LOS ** APECHAR, NON GELOS QUIERO YO.
                26565 5ELCID3391 LOS QUE ** REBTADO LIDIARAN, SIN SALUE DIOS
                29038 5ELCID3709 DELO QUE ** PRESO MUCHO AN MAL SABOR;
                29041 5ELCID3709 DELO QUE AN PRESO MUCHO ** MAL SABOR;
         WORD # 393 OCCURS  36 TIMES.
           INDEX OF DIVERSIFICATION =   827.00 WITH STANDARD DEVIATION OF   850.11

ANDA            15527 5ELCID1967 E TANTO PALAFRE QUE BIEN ****,
                18926 5ELCID2394 AGUIJO A BAUIECA, EL CAUALLO QUE BIEN ****,
                24080 5ELCID3070 COMIGO YRA MAL ****, QUE ES BIEN SABIDOR.
         WORD # 394 OCCURS   3 TIMES.

ANDAD           20501 5ELCID2603 *****, FIJAS, DAQUI EL CRIADOR VOS VALA
         WORD # 395 OCCURS   1 TIMES.

ANDADA           1408 5ELCID0180 PLAZME, DIXO EL %ID, DAQUI SEA  ******.
         WORD # 396 OCCURS   1 TIMES.

ANDAMOS         16191 5ELCID2054 EN QUANTO PODEMOS ******* EN UUESTRO PRO.
         WORD # 397 OCCURS   1 TIMES.

ANDAN            3698 5ELCID0466 E ESSOS GA@ADOS QUANTOS EN DERREDOR *****.
                 4751 5ELCID0602 TIENEN BUENOS CAUALLOS, SABET, ASU GUISA LES *****;
                 5211 5ELCID0659 E DE NOCH EN BUELTOS ***** EN ARMAS;
                 8201 5ELCID1045 QUE COMIGO ***** LAZRADOS, & NON UOS LO DARE.
                 9953 5ELCID1261 AQUESTOS MYOS VASSALOS QUE CURIAN A VALEN%IA & ***** AROBDANDO.
                14035 5ELCID1778 QUE ***** ARRIADOS & NON HA QUI TOMALOS,
                14411 5ELCID1823 ***** LOS DIAS & LAS NOCHES, & PASSADA HAN LA SIERRA,
                15581 5ELCID1975 LOS YFFANTES DE CARRIC MUCHO ALEGRES *****,
                21243 5ELCID2699 ELAS BESTIAS FIERAS QUE ***** ADERREDOR.
                22320 5ELCID2842 APIRESSA CAUALGAN, LOS DIAS & LAS NOCHES *****;
                22925 5ELCID2920 SALIEN DE VALEN%IA & ***** QUANTO PUEDEN,
                28969 5ELCID3700 AGUISA DE MENBRADOS ***** DIAS & NOCHES,
         WORD # 398 OCCURS  12 TIMES.
           INDEX OF DIVERSIFICATION =  2296.36 WITH STANDARD DEVIATION OF  2087.11

ANDANTES        17047 5ELCID2158 VERIEDES CAUALLEROS, QUE BIEN ******** SON,
         WORD # 399 OCCURS   1 TIMES.

ANDAR            2543 5ELCID0321 CA EL PLAZO VIENE A %ERCA, MUCHO AUEMOS DE *****.
                 3097 5ELCID0389 ABBAT, DEZILDES QUE PRENDAN EL RASTRO & PIESSEN DE *****,
                 3113 5ELCID0391 SOLTARON LAS RIENDAS, PIESSAN DE *****;
                 3384 5ELCID0426 E POR LA LOMA AYUSO PIENSSAN DE *****.
                 4261 5ELCID0542 VANSSE FENARES ARRIBA QUANTO PUEDEN *****,
                 4289 5ELCID0546 POR ESSAS TIERRAS AYUSO QUANTO PUEDEN *****.
                 5095 5ELCID0643 TRES MILL MOROS CAUALGAN & PIENSSAN DE *****,
                 5780 5ELCID0730 TANOS BUENOS CAUALLOS SIN SOS DUENOS *****.
                 7016 5ELCID0897 HYD POR CASTIELLA & DEXEN UOS *****, MINAYA,
                 7574 5ELCID0970 TRES DIAS & DOS NOCHES PENSSARON DE *****,
                 8476 5ELCID1077 AGUIJAUA EL CONDE E PENSSAUA DE *****,
                11635 5ELCID1474 E QUANTO QUE PUEDEN NON FINCAN DE *****.
                14403 5ELCID1821 SALIDOS SON DE VALEN%IA EPIENSSAN DE *****,
                15124 5ELCID1913 ***** LE QUIERO A MYO %ID EN TODA PRO.
                21174 5ELCID2690 ACOIEN SE A ***** DE DIA & DE NOCH;
                22597 5ELCID2878 OTRO DIA MA@ANA METEN SE A *****,
         WORD # 400 OCCURS  16 TIMES.
           INDEX OF DIVERSIFICATION =  1335.93 WITH STANDARD DEVIATION OF  1578.87

ANDARAN         23252 5ELCID2962 ******* MYOS PORTEROS POR TODO MYO REYNO,
         WORD # 401 OCCURS   1 TIMES.

ANDAUA           6186 5ELCID0788 ****** MYO %ID SOBRE SO BUEN CAUALLO,
         WORD # 402 OCCURS   1 TIMES.

ANDAUALAS       10206 5ELCID1292 LAS PROUEZAS DE MYO %ID ********* DEMANDANDO,
         WORD # 403 OCCURS   1 TIMES.

ANDIDIERON       3436 5ELCID0434 *********** DE NOCH, QUE VAGAR NON SE DAN.
                 5139 5ELCID0650 *********** TODOL DIA, QUE VAGAR NON SE DAN,
                 9414 5ELCID1197 *********** LOS PREGONES, SABET, ATODAS PARTES,
                27847 5ELCID3554 *********** EN PLEYTO, DIXIERON LO AL REY ALFONSSO,
                29099 5ELCID3717 *********** EN PLEYTOS LOS DE NAUARRA & DE ARAGON,
         WORD # 404 OCCURS   5 TIMES.
           INDEX OF DIVERSIFICATION =  6414.75 WITH STANDARD DEVIATION OF  8121.40

ANDIDIESSEN     22292 5ELCID2839 DIXOLES FUERTE MIENTRE QUE *********** DE DIA & DE NOCH,
         WORD # 405 OCCURS   1 TIMES.

ANDIDISTE        2713 5ELCID0343 POR TIERRA ********* XXXIJ A@OS, SE@OR SPIRITAL,
         WORD # 406 OCCURS   1 TIMES.

ANDIDO          13624 5ELCID1726 SALIOS LE DE SOL ESPADA, CA MUCHOL ****** EL CAUALLO,
         WORD # 407 OCCURS   1 TIMES.
```

```
WORD                    C#  PREFIX                          CONTEXT

ANGEL              3222 5ELCID0406 EL ***** GABRIEL A EL VINO EN SUE@O:
        WORD # 408 OCCURS    1 TIMES.

ANGOSTA            6545 5ELCID0835 SI NON, ENESTA TIERRA ******* NON PODRIEMOS BIUIR.
                   6564 5ELCID0838 LA TIERRA ES ******* & SOBEIANA DE MALA;
        WORD # 409 OCCURS    2 TIMES.

ANINGUN           28020 5ELCID3576 ADERECHO NOS VALED, ******* TUERTO NO.
        WORD # 410 OCCURS    1 TIMES.

ANOCH               336 5ELCID0042 EL REY LO HA UEDADO, ***** DEL ETRO SU CARTA,
                  16152 5ELCID2048 VOS AGORA LEGASTES, & NOS VINJEMOS *****;
        WORD # 411 OCCURS    2 TIMES.

ANOCHESCA          3421 5ELCID0432 ANTE QUE ********* PIENSSAN DE CAUALGAR;
        WORD # 412 OCCURS    1 TIMES.

ANOS              11817 5ELCID1498 VIRTOS DEL CAMPEADOR **** VIENEN BUSCAR.
                  20713 5ELCID2629 ATALES COSAS FED QUE EN PLAZER CAYA ****.
                  23090 5ELCID2941 HYA UOS SABEDES LA ONDRA QUE ES CUNTIDA ****,
        WORD # 413 OCCURS    3 TIMES.

ANRICH            27364 5ELCID3496 ADELINO A EL EL CONDE DON ****** & EL CONDE DON REMOND;
        WORD # 414 OCCURS    1 TIMES.

ANRRICH           23571 5ELCID3002 EL CONDE DON ******* & EL CONDE DON REMOND;
                  24386 5ELCID3109 E EL CONDE DON ******* & EL CONDE DON REMONT

                  24606 5ELCID3135 ALCALDES SEAN DESTO EL CONDE DON ******* & EL CONDE DON REMOND
        WORD # 415 OCCURS    3 TIMES.

ANSSARERA         20917 5ELCID2657 ODIZEN EL ********* ELLOS POSADOS SON.
                  21166 5ELCID2689 YA MOUIERON DEL ********* LOS YFANTES DE CARRION,
        WORD # 416 OCCURS    2 TIMES.

ANTE               1322 5ELCID0169 CA AMOUER A MYO %ID **** QUE CANTE EL GALLO.
                   2130 5ELCID0269 FEM **** UOS YO & UUESTRAS FFIJAS, YFFANTES SON & DE DIAS CHICAS,
                   3419 5ELCID0432 **** QUE ANOCHESCA PIENSSAN DE CAUALGAR;
                   3952 5ELCID0502 **** RUY DIAZ EL LIDIADOR CONTADO,
                   5521 5ELCID0696 **** ROYDO DE ATAMORES LA TIERRA QUERIE QUEBRAR;
                  10400 5ELCID1318 FINCO SOS YNOIOS **** TODEL PUEBLO,
                  12198 5ELCID1548 E BUEN CAUALLO EN DIESTRO QUE UA **** SUS ARMAS.
                  14821 5ELCID1873 QUE BIEN PARESCADES **** RUY DIAZ MYO %ID;
                  16808 5ELCID2128 AQUI LO DIGO **** MYO SE@OR EL REY ALFONSSO:
                  18170 5ELCID2299 **** MYO %ID LA CABE%A PREMIO & EL ROSTRO FINCO;
                  20072 5ELCID2548 **** QUE NOS RETRAYAN LO QUE CUNTIO DEL LEON.
                  20671 5ELCID2624 MINAYA ALBARFANEZ **** MYO %ID SE PARO:
                  21033 5ELCID2673 ARMAS YUA TENIENDO, PAROS **** LOS YFANTES;
                  21915 5ELCID2788 MIENTRA ES EL DIA, **** QUE ENTRE LA NOCH,
        WORD # 417 OCCURS   14 TIMES.
           INDEX OF DIVERSIFICATION =  1583.08 WITH STANDARD DEVIATION OF  1191.83

ANTEL              2094 5ELCID0264 ***** CAMPEADOR DO@A XIMENA FINCO LOS YNOIOS AMOS,
                  14567 5ELCID1843 ***** REY ALFONSSO LOS YNOIOS FINCADOS,
                  16511 5ELCID2093 CAMEARON LAS ESPADAS ***** REY DON ALFONSSO.
                  20433 5ELCID2593 FINCARON LOS YNOIOS ***** %ID CAMPEADOR:
                  25437 5ELCID3239 POR JUUIZIO LO DAMOS ***** REY DON ALFONSSO:
                  26230 5ELCID3344 ESTOT LIDIARE AQUI ***** REY DON ALFONSSO
        WORD # 418 OCCURS    6 TIMES.
           INDEX OF DIVERSIFICATION =  4826.20 WITH STANDARD DEVIATION OF  4579.75

ANTELLAS          13785 5ELCID1747 MYO %ID FINCO ********, TOUO LA RYENDA AL CAUALLO:
        WORD # 419 OCCURS    1 TIMES.

ANTES               170 5ELCID0023 ***** DELA NOCHE EN BURGOS DEL ENTRO SU CARTA,
                   1277 5ELCID0164 QUE SI ***** LAS CATASSEN QUE FUESSEN PERIURADOS,
                   1812 5ELCID0231 ***** SERE CON UUSCO QUE EL SOL QUIERA RAYAR.
                   2388 5ELCID0302 EN ***** QUE YO MUERA, ALGUN BIEN UOS PUEDA FAR:
                   4600 5ELCID0585 ***** QUEL PRENDAN LOS DE TERUEL, SI NON NON NOS DARAN DENT NADA;
                   6785 5ELCID0866 METIO EN PARIA ADOROCA EN *****,
                   7652 5ELCID0980 LO DE ***** & DE AGORA TODOM LO PECHARA;
                   7775 5ELCID0996 ***** QUE ELLOS LEGEN A LA@O, PRESENTEMOS LES LAS LAN%AS;
                   8000 5ELCID1022 ***** PERDERE EL CUERPO & DEXARE EL ALMA,
                  12085 5ELCID1533 ***** DESTE TE%ER DIA UOS LA DARE DOBLADA.
                  13132 5ELCID1665 ***** DESTOS XV DIAS, SI PLOGIERE A CRIADOR,
                  13420 5ELCID1701 ALOS MEDIADOS GALLOS, ***** DE LA MA@ANA,
                  15876 5ELCID2013 DE VN DIA ES LEGADO ***** EL REY DON ALFONSSO.
                  17781 5ELCID2250 ***** QUE ENTRASSEN AIANTAR TODOS LOS QUEBRANTARON.
                  19671 5ELCID2494 ***** FU MINGUADO, AGORA RICO SO,
                  20131 5ELCID2556 ***** QUE NOS RETRAYAN LO QUE FUE DEL LEON.
                  24015 5ELCID3061 SUELTA FUE LA MISSA ***** QUE SALIESSE EL SOL,
                  26029 5ELCID3318 VIST VN MORO, FUSTEL ENSAYAR; ***** FUXISTE QUE ALTE ALEGASSES.
                  26513 5ELCID3384 ***** ALMUERZAS QUE VAYAS A ORA%ION,
                  26672 5ELCID3406 VOS LAS CASASTES *****, CA YO NON,
```

WORD C# PREFIX CONTEXT

ANTES (CON'T)

```
                    26992 5ELCID3449 ***** LAS AVIEDES PAREIAS PORA EN BRA%OS LAS TENER,
                    27151 5ELCID3470 NOS ***** ABREMOS AYR ATIERRAS DE CARRION.
                    28377 5ELCID3623 PERO VERMUEZ, EL QUE ***** REBTO,
                    28537 5ELCID3644 ***** QUE EL COLPE ESPERASSE DIXO: VEN%UDO SO.
          WORD # 420 OCCURS  24 TIMES.
             INDEX OF DIVERSIFICATION =  1232.35 WITH STANDARD DEVIATION OF  1162.09

ANTOLINEZ             508 5ELCID0065 MARTIN *********, EL BURGALES CONPLIDO,
                      624 5ELCID0079 MARTIN *********, SODES ARDIDA LAN%A
                      759 5ELCID0096 MARTIN ********* NON LO DETARUA,
                     1020 5ELCID0131 RESPUSO MARTIN ********* A GUISA DE MENBRADO:
                     1098 5ELCID0141 DIXO MARTIN *********:  YO CESSO ME PAGO.
                     1149 5ELCID0148 MARTIN ********* CAUALGO PRIUADO
                     1243 5ELCID0160 MARTIN ********* EL PLEYTO A PARADO,
                     1295 5ELCID0166 DIXO MARTIN *********:  CARGEN LAS ARCHAS PRIUADO.
                     1510 5ELCID0193 MARTIN *********, UN BURGALES CONTADO,
                     1593 5ELCID0204  VENIDES, MARTIN *********, EL MIO FIEL VASSALO
                     1790 5ELCID0228 DIXO MARTIN *********:  VERE ALA MUGIER ATODO MYO SOLAZ,
                     1823 5ELCID0232 TORNAUAS MARTIN ********* A BURGOS & MYO %ID AAGUIJAR
                     2321 5ELCID0293 MARTIN ********* CON ELLOS COIO.
                     5821 5ELCID0736 MARTIN *********, EL BURGALES DE PRO,
                     6032 5ELCID0765 MARTIN ********* VN COLPE DIO A GALUE,
                    11522 5ELCID1459 E MARTIN *********, VN BURGALES LEAL,
                    11834 5ELCID1500 E MARTIN *********, EL BURGALES NATURAL,
                    15704 5ELCID1992 MARTIN MUNOZ & MARTIN *********, EL BURGALES DE PRO,
                    22276 5ELCID2837 E MARTIN *********, EL BURGLES DE PRO,
                    24053 5ELCID3066 E MARTIN *********, EL BURGALES DE PRO,
                    25049 5ELCID3191 A MARTIN *********, EL BURGALES DE PRO,
                    25062 5ELCID3193 MARTIN *********, MYO VASSALO DE PRO,
                    26355 5ELCID3361 MARTIN ********* EN PIE SE LEUANTAUA;
                    27600 5ELCID3524 HYA MARTIN *********, & VOS, PERO VERMUEZ,
                    27625 5ELCID3527 DIXO MARTIN *********:  POR QUE LO DEZIDES, SE@OR
                    28554 5ELCID3646 MARTIN ********* & DIEGO GON%ALEZ FIRIERON SE DELAS LAN%AS,
                    28571 5ELCID3648 MARTIN ********* MANO METIO AL ESPADA,
                    28668 5ELCID3660 ESSORA MARTIN ********* RE%IBIOL CON EL ESPADA,
          WORD # 421 OCCURS  28 TIMES.
             INDEX OF DIVERSIFICATION =  1041.96 WITH STANDARD DEVIATION OF  1754.51

ANTOLJNEZ           28717 5ELCID3667 SACOL DEL MOION; MARTIN ********* EN EL CAMPO FINCAUA.
          WORD # 422 OCCURS   1 TIMES.

A@O                   948 5ELCID0121 QUE NON LAS CATEDES EN TODO AQUESTE ***.
                     1017 5ELCID0130 O QUE GANAN%IA NOS DARA POR TODO AQUESTE ***?
                     1265 5ELCID0162 E BIEN GELAS GUARDARIEN FASTA CABO DEL ***;
                     2019 5ELCID0254 AELLA & ASUS FIJAS & ASUS DUENAS SIRUADES LAS EST ***.
                     8461 5ELCID1075 PAGADO UOS HE POR TODO AQUESTE ***;
                    13851 5ELCID1754 ROGAND AL CRIADOR QUE UOS BIUA ALGUNT ***,
          WORD # 423 OCCURS   6 TIMES.
             INDEX OF DIVERSIFICATION =  2579.60 WITH STANDARD DEVIATION OF  3077.69

A@OS                  319 5ELCID0040 VNA NI@A DE NUEF **** A OIO SE PARAUA:
                     2715 5ELCID0343 POR TIERRA ANDIDISTE XXXIJ ****, SE@OR SPIRITAL,
                     9188 5ELCID1169 EN GANAR AQUELAS VILLAS MYO %ID DURO IIJ ****.
                     9217 5ELCID1173 EN CADA VNO DESTOS **** MYO %ID LES TOLIO EL PAN.
                    13897 5ELCID1760 SOMOS EN UUESTRA MER%ED, & BIUADES MUCHOS ****
                    16295 5ELCID2067 PASSADO AUIE IIJ **** NO COMIERAN MEIOR.
                    17951 5ELCID2271 HY MORAN LOS YFANTES BIEN CERCA DE DOS ****,
                    29238 5ELCID3733 EN ERA DE MILL & CCXLV ****.  EN EL ROMANZ
          WORD # 424 OCCURS   8 TIMES.
             INDEX OF DIVERSIFICATION =  4130.29 WITH STANDARD DEVIATION OF  3785.06

AOIO                14527 5ELCID1838 **** LO AUIEN LOS DEL QUE EN BUEN ORA NASCO,
          WORD # 425 OCCURS   1 TIMES.

AONDRA              26787 5ELCID3421 QUE UOS LAS DE ****** & A BENDI%ION.
          WORD # 426 OCCURS   1 TIMES.

AORIENT              8588 5ELCID1091 ******* EXE EL SOL, E TORNOS AESSA PART.
          WORD # 427 OCCURS   1 TIMES.

AOSADAS              3528 5ELCID0445 ******* CORRED, QUE POR MIEDO NON DEXEDES NADA.
                    27188 5ELCID3475 ENESSORA DIXO EL REY: *******, CAMPEADOR.
          WORD # 428 OCCURS   2 TIMES.

APALA%IO            18203 5ELCID2303 ETORNARON SEAL ******** PORA LA CORT.
          WORD # 429 OCCURS   1 TIMES.

APARE%IDOS          26309 5ELCID3355 ESTOS CASAMIENTOS NON FUESSEN **********
          WORD # 430 OCCURS   1 TIMES.

APARE%IST            2644 5ELCID0334 EN BELLEM *********, COMMO FUE TU VELUNTAD;
          WORD # 431 OCCURS   1 TIMES.

APAREIADAS          15568 5ELCID1973 ALAS AGUAS DE TAIO, OLAS UISTAS SON **********.
          WORD # 432 OCCURS   1 TIMES.
```

```
WORD                    C#  PREFIX                          CONTEXT

APAREIADOS           8824 5ELCID1123 ********** ME SED A CAUALLOS & ARMAS;
         WORD # 433 OCCURS    1 TIMES.

APART               28595 5ELCID3651 EL CASCO DE SCMO ***** GELO ECHAUA,
                    28824 5ELCID3682 ***** LE PRISO, QUE NCN CABEL CORA%ON;
         WORD # 434 OCCURS    2 TIMES.

APARTAR             27735 5ELCID3540 QUE SI LOS PUDIESSEN ******* ALOS DEL CAMPEADOR,
         WORD # 435 OCCURS    1 TIMES.

APARTARON             823 5ELCID0105 NON LO DETARCAN, TODCS TRES SE *********.
         WORD # 436 OCCURS    1 TIMES.

APARTE               1496 5ELCID0191 ENTRE RACHEL & VIDAS ****** YXIERON AMOS:
                     6044 5ELCID0766 LAS CARBONCLAS DEL YELMC ECHO GELAS ******,
                    21764 5ELCID2768 DE TODOS LOS CTROS ****** SE SALIO,
                    24819 5ELCID3161 ESSORA SALIEN ****** YFFANTES DE CARRION,
         WORD # 437 OCCURS    4 TIMES.

APARTIR              6313 5ELCID0804 DIO ******* ESTOS DINERCS & ESTOS AUERES LARGOS;
         WORD # 438 OCCURS    1 TIMES.

APARTO              15000 5ELCID1896 A VNA QUADRA ELE LOS ******:
         WORD # 439 OCCURS    1 TIMES.

APASSADO             1169 5ELCID0150 NON VIENE ALA PUEENT, CA POR EL AGUA ********,
         WORD # 440 OCCURS    1 TIMES.

APECHAR             25407 5ELCID3235 QUANDO ELLOS LOS AN *******, NON GELOS QUIERO YO.
         WORD # 441 OCCURS    1 TIMES.

APERO               17139 5ELCID2169 ***** VERMUEZ & MUNO GUSTIOZ,
         WORD # 442 OCCURS    1 TIMES.

APIRESSA            22313 5ELCID2842 ******** CAUALGAN, LOS DIAS & LAS NOCHES ANDAN;
         WORD # 443 OCCURS    1 TIMES.

APOCO               12998 5ELCID1649 ***** QUE VINIESTES, PRESEND UOS QUIEREN DAR:
         WORD # 444 OCCURS    1 TIMES.

APOSTOL              8941 5ELCID1138 ENEL NOMBRE DEL CRIADOR & DEL ******* SANTI YAGUE,
                    13334 5ELCID1690 HYR LOS HEMOS FFERIR ENEL NCMBRE DEL CRIADOR & DEL ******* SANTI
         WORD # 445 OCCURS    2 TIMES.

APRE%IADURA        25444 5ELCID3240 PAGEN LE EN *********** & PRENDALO EL CAMPEADOR.
         WORD # 446 OCCURS    1 TIMES.

APRE%IADURAS       25517 5ELCID3250 ESTAS ************ MYO %ID PRESAS LAS HA,
         WORD # 447 OCCURS    1 TIMES.

APRE%IARON         25479 5ELCID3245 RECIBIOLO MYO %ID COMMO ********** ENLA CORT.
         WORD # 448 OCCURS    1 TIMES.

APREGUNTAR          14434 5ELCID1825 POR EL REY DON ALFONSSO TOMAN SSE **********.
         WORD # 449 OCCURS    1 TIMES.

APRES                9639 5ELCID1225 ***** DELA VERTA OUIERON LA BATALLA,
                    12275 5ELCID1559 ***** SON DE VALEN%IA A TRES LEGUAS CONTADAS.
         WORD # 450 OCCURS    2 TIMES.

APRETAD              7738 5ELCID0991 ******* LOS CAUALLOS, & BISTADES LAS ARMAS.
         WORD # 451 OCCURS    1 TIMES.

APRIESSA              767 5ELCID0097 POR RACHEL & VIDAS ******** DEMANDAUA.
                      779 5ELCID0099 POR RACHEL & VIDAS ******** DEMANDAUA.
                     1846 5ELCID0235 ******** CANTAN LOS GALLOS & QUIEREN QUEBRAR ALBORES,
                     2351 5ELCID0297 ******** CAUALGA, RE%EBIR LOS SALIE,
                     5533 5ELCID0697 VERIEDES ARMAR SE MCRCS, ******** ENTRAR EN AZ.
                     7696 5ELCID0986 ******** UOS GUARNID & METEDOS EN LAS ARMAS.
                    11876 5ELCID1506 ESSO FFUE ******** FECHO, QUE NOS QUIEREN DETARDAR.
                    14483 5ELCID1832 MANDO CAUALGAR ******** TOSCOS SOS FIJOS DALGO,
                    15154 5ELCID1917 ******** CAUALGA, ARE%EBIR LOS SALIO;
                    24328 5ELCID3102 ******** CAUALGA, DE SAN SERUAN SALIO;
                    24833 5ELCID3163 ******** LO YUAN TRAYENDO & ACUERDAN LA RAZON:
         WORD # 452 OCCURS   11 TIMES.
            INDEX OF DIVERSIFICATION =  2405.60 WITH STANDARD DEVIATION OF  2736.92

APUESTO             10396 5ELCID1317 AFE MINAYA LABARFANEZ DO LEGA TAN *******;
                    10419 5ELCID1320 BESAUA LE LAS MANOS & FABLO TAN *******:
         WORD # 453 OCCURS    2 TIMES.

APUNTAR              5408 5ELCID0682 OTRO DIA MA@ANA, EL SOL QUERIE *******,
         WORD # 454 OCCURS    1 TIMES.
```

WORD C# PREFIX CONTEXT

```
APUNTARE          17238 5ELCID2180 QUANDO VINIERE LA MA@ANA, QUE ******** EL SOL,
        WORD # 455 OCCURS   1 TIMES.

APUNTAUA           3630 5ELCID0457 YXIE EL SOL, DIOS, QUE FERMOSO ********
        WORD # 456 OCCURS   1 TIMES.

AQUAL             22598 5ELCID2879 ***** DIZEN MEDINA YUAN ALBERGAR,
        WORD # 457 OCCURS   1 TIMES.

AQUEL              3916 5ELCID0497 ADIOS LO PROMETO, A ***** QUE ESTA EN ALTO:
                   5355 5ELCID0676 VAYAMOS LOS FERIR EN ***** DIA DE CRAS.
                   5588 5ELCID0704 ***** PERO VERMUEZ NON LO PUDO ENDURAR,
                   6025 5ELCID0764 POR ***** COLPE RANCADO ES EL FONSSADO.
                   7039 5ELCID0900 ***** POYO ENEL PRISO POSADA;
                   7225 5ELCID0926  DIOS, COMMO FUE ALEGRE TODO ***** FONSSADO,
                   9616 5ELCID1222 ***** REY DE SEUILLA EL MANDADO LEGAUA,
                   9672 5ELCID1230 ***** REY DE MARRUECOS CON TRES COLPES ESCAPA.
                  10247 5ELCID1297 OYD, MINAYA ALBARFANEZ, POR ***** QUE ESTA EN ALTO,
                  12768 5ELCID1621 DE ***** REY YUCEF QUE EN MARRUECOS ESTA.
                  12803 5ELCID1625 ***** REY DE MARRUECOS AIUNTAUA SUS VIRTOS;
                  14624 5ELCID1850 A ***** REY DE MARRUECOS, YUCEFF POR NOMBRADO,
                  15697 5ELCID1991 MYNAYA ALBARFANEZ & ***** PERO VERMUEZ,
                  16213 5ELCID2057 EN ***** DIA DEL REY SO HUESPED FUE;
                  18364 5ELCID2324 OYO LA PORIDAD ***** MU@O GUSTIOZ,
                  22979 5ELCID2927 ASSI COMMO DESCAUALGA ***** MU@O GUSTIOZ
                  23031 5ELCID2934 DELANT EL REY FINCO LOS YNOIOS ***** MU@O GUSTIOZ,
                  23038 5ELCID2935 BESABA LE LOS PIES ***** MU@O GUSTIOZ;
                  23394 5ELCID2980 QUE CORT FAZIE EN TOLLEDO ***** REY ONDRADO,
                  27024 5ELCID3452 GRADO ADIOS DEL %IELO & ***** REY DON ALFONSSO,
        WORD # 458 OCCURS  20 TIMES.
           INDEX OF DIVERSIFICATION =  1215.21 WITH STANDARD DEVIATION OF  1325.96

AQUELA             5616 5ELCID0707 VO METER LA UUESTRA SE@A EN ****** MAYOR AZ;
                   8833 5ELCID1124 HYREMOS VER ****** SU ALMOFALLA,
        WORD # 459 OCCURS   2 TIMES.

AQUELAS             899 5ELCID0116 ******* NON LAS PUEDE LEUAR, SINON, SER YEN VENTADAS;
                   1250 5ELCID0161 QUE SOBRE ******* ARCHAS DAR LE YEN VJ %IENTOS MARCOS
                   7245 5ELCID0929 E DE SUS COMPA@AS, ******* QUE AUIEN DEXADAS
                   9182 5ELCID1169 EN GANAR ******* VILLAS MYO %ID DURO IIJ A@OS.
        WORD # 460 OCCURS   4 TIMES.

AQUELLAS           2030 5ELCID0256 ******** UOS ACOMIENDO AUOS, ABBAT DON SANCHO;
        WORD # 461 OCCURS   1 TIMES.

AQUELOS            3458 5ELCID0436 MYO %ID SE ECHO EN %ELADA CON ******* QUE EL TRAE.
                  13140 5ELCID1666 ******* ATAMORES AUOS LOS PONDRAN DELANT & VEREDES QUANLES SON,
                  19354 5ELCID2452 ******* QUE GELOS DIERAN NON GELO AUIEN LOGRADO.
        WORD # 462 OCCURS   3 TIMES.

AQUES              2301 5ELCID0290 EN ***** DIA ALA PUENT DE ARLA%ON
        WORD # 463 OCCURS   1 TIMES.

AQUESSA            7430 5ELCID0953 EN ******* CORRIDA X DIAS OUIERON AMORAR.
        WORD # 464 OCCURS   1 TIMES.

AQUESTA            3490 5ELCID0440 VOS CON C DE ******* NUESTRA CONPA@A,
                   4736 5ELCID0600 DIOS, QUE BUENO ES EL GOZO POR ******* MA@ANA
                   6285 5ELCID0800 REFECHOS SON TODOS ESOS CHRISTIANOS CON ******* GANAN%IA.
                   6860 5ELCID0876 VEN%IO DOS REYES DE MOROS EN ******* BATALLA.
                   8742 5ELCID1111 CONPE%AREMOS ******* LID CAMPAL,
                  13472 5ELCID1707 HYO UOS CANTE LA MISSA POR ******* MA@ANA;
                  15970 5ELCID2025 DE ******* GUISA ALOS PIES LE CAYO.
                  18952 5ELCID2398 PLOGO A DIOS, ******* FUE EL ARRANCADA.
                  21388 5ELCID2719 NOS VENGAREMOS ******* POR LA DEL LEON.
                  22235 5ELCID2832 PAR ******* BARBA QUE NADI NON MESSO,
                  22385 5ELCID2852 POR ******* ONDRA QUE VOS DIESTES A ESTO QUE NOS CUNTIO;
                  24893 5ELCID3170 CON ******* FABLA TORNAFON ALA CORT:
                  25013 5ELCID3186 PAR ******* BARBA QUE NADI NON MESSO,
                  25363 5ELCID3229 NOS BIEN LA SABEMOS ******* RAZON,
                  25852 5ELCID3293 DEXASSEDES UOS, %ID, DE ******* RAZON;
        WORD # 465 OCCURS  15 TIMES.
           INDEX OF DIVERSIFICATION =  1596.29 WITH STANDARD DEVIATION OF  1328.71

AQUESTAS           2143 5ELCID0270 CON ******** MYS DUE@AS DE QUIEN SO YO SERUIDA.
                  10500 5ELCID1331 CON ******** TODAS DE VALEN%IA ES SE@OR,
                  14156 5ELCID1792 CON ******** RIQUEZAS TANTAS A VALEN%IA SON ENTRADOS.
                  20656 5ELCID2622 CON ******** NUEUAS VERNAS AL CAMPEADOR.
        WORD # 466 OCCURS   4 TIMES.

AQUESTE             947 5ELCID0121 QUE NON LAS CATEDES EN TODO ******* A@O.
                   1016 5ELCID0130 O QUE GANAN%IA NOS DARA POR TODO ******* A@O?
                   3826 5ELCID0484 CON ******* AUER TORNAN SE ESSA CONPA@A;
```

WORD C# PREFIX CONTEXT

AQUESTE (CON'T)

```
                 4016 5ELCID0510 MANDO PARTIR TOD ******* AUER,
                 8460 5ELCID1075 PAGADO UOS HE POR TODO ******* A@O;
                11408 5ELCID1444 ******* MONESTERIO NO LO QUIERA OLBIDAR,
                13246 5ELCID1679 BIEN FATA LAS TIENDAS DURA ******* ALCAZ,
                18284 5ELCID2314 ******* ERA EL REY BUCAR, SIL OUIESTES CONTAR.
                20141 5ELCID2557 CON ******* CONSSEIO AMOS TORNADOS SON,
                21927 5ELCID2789 LOS GANADOS FIEROS NON NOS COMAN EN ******* MONT
                23546 5ELCID2999 ******* CONSSEIO LOS YFANTES DE CARRION.
                23577 5ELCID3003 ******* FUE PADRE DEL BUEN ENPERADOR;
                23934 5ELCID3049 TERNE VIGILIA EN ******* SANTO LOGAR.
                24048 5ELCID3065 E PERO VERMUEZ & ******* MU@O GUSTIOZ
                24435 5ELCID3115 EN ******* ESCANO QUEMDIESTES UOS ENDON;
       WORD # 467 OCCURS  15 TIMES.
          INDEX OF DIVERSIFICATION =  1676.71 WITH STANDARD DEVIATION OF  1647.40

AQUESTO           6959 5ELCID0890 SOBRE ******* TODO, DEZIR UOS QUIERO, MINAYA:
                  8709 5ELCID1106 AMENOS DE LID NOS PARTIRA *******;
                  9897 5ELCID1255 AFEUOS TODO ******* PUESTO EN BUEN RECABDO.
                 10240 5ELCID1296 QUANDO LO OYO MYO %ID, DE ******* FUE PAGADO:
                 10373 5ELCID1314 ALEGRE FUE DE ******* MINAYA ALBARFANEZ,
                 10790 5ELCID1366 POR TAL FAGO ******* QUE SIRUAN ASO SE@OR.
                 16951 5ELCID2146 TOMAD *******, & BESO UUESTRAS MANOS.
                 17676 5ELCID2236 QUANDO OUIERON ******* FECHO, SALIERON DEL PALA%IO,
                 20496 5ELCID2602 EL FIZO *******, LA MADRE LO DOBLAUA;
       WORD # 468 OCCURS   9 TIMES.
          INDEX OF DIVERSIFICATION =  1691.13 WITH STANDARD DEVIATION OF  2011.14

AQUESTOL         28460 5ELCID3634 TRES DOBLES DE LORIGA TENIE FERNANDO, ******** PRESTO,
       WORD # 469 OCCURS   1 TIMES.

AQUESTOS          5167 5ELCID0654 CON ******** DOS REYES QUE DIZEN FFARIZ & GALUE;
                  9945 5ELCID1261 ******** MYOS VASSALOS QUE CURIAN A VALEN%IA & ANDAN AROBDANDO.
                 11141 5ELCID1410 DE ******** XV DIAS, SIDIOS NOS CURIARE DE MAL,
                 12347 5ELCID1568 AFEUOS TODOS ******** RE%IBEN A MINAYA
                 13935 5ELCID1765 QUIERO LAS CASAR CON DE ******** MYOS VASSALLOS;
                 15757 5ELCID2000 A ******** DOS MANDO EL CAMPEADOR QUE CURIEN A VALEN%IA
                 17878 5ELCID2262 HYAS YUAN PARTIENDO ******** OSPEDADOS,
                 17932 5ELCID2269 VENIDOS SON ACASTIELLA ******** OSPEDADOS,
                 19979 5ELCID2535 POR ******** GUEGOS QUE YUAN LEUANTANDO,
                 21381 5ELCID2718 HYRAN ******** MANDADOS AL %ID CAMPEADOR;
                 22189 5ELCID2826 VAN ******** MANDADOS A VALEN%IA LA MAYOR;
                 24323 5ELCID3101 CON ******** %IENTO QUE ADOBAR MANDO,
                 24468 5ELCID3119 ACA POSARE CON TODOS ******** MIOS.
                 29131 5ELCID3720 LOS PRIMEROS FUERON GRANDES, MAS ******** SON MIIORES;
       WORD # 470 OCCURS  14 TIMES.
          INDEX OF DIVERSIFICATION =  1842.38 WITH STANDARD DEVIATION OF  1443.65

AQUEXAN           9226 5ELCID1174 MAL SE ******* LOS DE VALEN%IA QUE NON SABENT QUES FAR,
       WORD # 471 OCCURS   1 TIMES.

AQUI              1947 5ELCID0247 PUES QUE **** UOS VEO, PRENDET DE MI OSPEDADO.
                  2002 5ELCID0253 EUADES **** PORA DO@A XIMENA DOUOS C MARCHOS.
                  3566 5ELCID0449 E YO CON LO C **** FINCARE EN LA %AGA,
                  4053 5ELCID0516 **** NON LO PUEDEN VENDER NIN DAR EN PRESENTAIA;
                  5576 5ELCID0702 QUEDAS SED, MENADAS, **** EN ESTE LOGAR,
                  6424 5ELCID0820 EUADES **** ORO & PLATA VNA VESA LE@A,
                  6524 5ELCID0832 ALA TORNADA, SI NOS FALLAREDES ****;
                  7734 5ELCID0990 PUES ADELLANT YRAN TRAS NOS, **** SEA LA BATALLA;
                  8288 5ELCID1055 **** FEREMOS LA MORADA, NO NOS PARTIREMOS AMOS.
                  8296 5ELCID1056 **** DIXO EL CONDE: DE VOLUNTAD & DE GRADO.
                  9918 5ELCID1258 DELOS QUE SON **** & COMIGO GANARON ALGO;
                 10532 5ELCID1335 FEUOS **** LAS SE@AS, VERDAD UOS DIGO YO:
                 10832 5ELCID1372 **** ENTRARON EN FABLA LOS YFFANTES DE CARRION:
                 11821 5ELCID1499 AFEUOS **** PERO VERMUEZ & MU@O GUSTIOZ QUE UOS QUIEREN
                                  SIN HART,
                 12586 5ELCID1597 AFE ME ****, SE@OR, YO UUESTRAS FIJAS & AMAS,
                 14798 5ELCID1870 AUOS, MINAYA ALBARFANEZ, & EA PERO VERMUEZ ****,
                 14817 5ELCID1872 E GUARNIR UOS DE TODAS ARMAS COMMO UOS DIXIEREDES ****,
                 14832 5ELCID1874 DOUOS IIJ CAUALLOS & PRENDED LOS ****.
                 16026 5ELCID2032 ASSI ESTANDO, DEDES ME UUESTRA AMOR, QUE LO OYAN QUANTOS
                                  **** SON.
                 16037 5ELCID2034 **** UOS PERDONO & DOUOS MY AMOR,
                 16396 5ELCID2079 DELLA & DELLA PARTE, QUANTOS QUE **** SON,
                 16476 5ELCID2089 DAD LAS **** QUISIEREDES UOS, CA YO PAGADO SO.
                 16767 5ELCID2123 EVAD **** UUESTROS FIJOS, QUANDO UUESTROS YERNOS SON;
                 16805 5ELCID2128 **** LO DIGO ANTE MYO SE@OR EL REY ALFONSSO:
                 16873 5ELCID2135 RESPONDIO EL REY: AFE **** ALBARFANEZ;
                 18654 5ELCID2361 **** LEGO MYNAYA ALBARFANEZ: OYD, YA %ID, CANPEADOR LEAL
                 19106 5ELCID2417 **** RESPUSO MYO %ID: ESTO NON SERA VERDAD.
                 19417 5ELCID2460 EUUESTROS YERNOS **** SON ENSAYADOS,
                 19813 5ELCID2512 **** ESTA CON MYO %ID EL OBISPO DO IHERONIMO,
                 19863 5ELCID2519 EUADES ****, YERNOS, LA MI MUGIER DE PRO,
                 20019 5ELCID2540 VAYAMOS PORA CARRION, **** MUCHO DETARDAMOS.
                 20175 5ELCID2561 EA MYNAYA ALBARFANEZ & A QUANTOS **** SON:
                 20366 5ELCID2584 **** RE%IBEN LAS FIJAS DEL CAMPEADOR;
```

WORD C# PREFIX CONTEXT

AQUI (CON'T)

21358 5ELCID2715 **** SEREDES ESCARNIDAS EN ESTOS FIEROS MONTES.
21969 5ELCID2795 SI DIOS NON NOS VALE, **** MORREMOS NOS.
22411 5ELCID2854 ASSI LO FFAGO YO QUE **** ESTO.
25183 5ELCID3207 **** VERIEDES QUEXAR SE YFANTES DE CARRION
25219 5ELCID3211 QUE AL NO NOS DEMANDASSE, QUE **** FINCO LA BOZ. . .
25344 5ELCID3227 QUE **** LO ENTERGEDES DENTRO EN LA CORT.
25592 5ELCID3259 O EN ALGUNA RAZON? **** LO MEIORARE A JUUIZYO DELA CORT.
26229 5ELCID3344 ESTOT LIDIARE **** ANTEL REY DON ALFONSSO
26287 5ELCID3352 DAQUESTOS AMOS **** QUEDO LA RAZON.
27223 5ELCID3480 **** LES PONGO PLAZO DE DENTRO EN MI CORT,
28023 5ELCID3577 **** TIENEN SU VANDO LOS YFANTES DE CARRION,
WORD # 472 OCCURS 44 TIMES.
INDEX OF DIVERSIFICATION = 605.42 WITH STANDARD DEVIATION OF 652.05

AQUIEN
13952 5ELCID1767 QUE LO SEPAN EN CASTIELLA, ****** SIRUIERON TANTO.
16704 5ELCID2115 CONPE%O MYO %ID ADAR ****** QUIERE PRENDER SO DON,
WORD # 473 OCCURS 2 TIMES.

AQUIM
21095 5ELCID2681 ***** PARTO DE UOS COMMO DE MALOS & DE TRAYDORES.
WORD # 474 OCCURS 1 TIMES.

AQUIS
8535 5ELCID1085 ***** CONPIE%A LA GESTA DE MYO %ID EL DE BIUAR.
16684 5ELCID2113 ***** METIO EN NUEUAS MYO %ID EL CAMPEADOR;
17990 5ELCID2276 LAS COPLAS DESTE CANTAR ***** VAN ACABANDO.
19193 5ELCID2428 ***** ONDRO MYO %ID & QUANTOS CONEL SON.
WORD # 475 OCCURS 4 TIMES.

ARABIA
2659 5ELCID0336 TRES REYES DE ****** TE VINIERON ADORAR,
WORD # 476 OCCURS 1 TIMES.

ARAGON
5850 5ELCID0740 GALIN GAR%IA, EL BUENO DE ******,
9333 5ELCID1187 POR ****** & POR NAUARRA PREGON MANDO ECHAR,
15732 5ELCID1996 GALIND GAR%IAZ, EL QUE FUE DE ******:
15755 5ELCID1999 ALUAR SALUADOREZ & GALIND GARCIAZ EL DE ******,
26603 5ELCID3396 E EL OTRO YFANTE DE ******;
26626 5ELCID3399 POR SER REYNAS DE NAUARRA & DE ******,
26668 5ELCID3405 QUANDO MELAS DEMANDAN DE NAUARRA & DE ******.
26782 5ELCID3420 PORA LOS YFANTES DE NAUARRA & DE ******,
26991 5ELCID3448 LOS YFANTES DE NAUARRA & DE ******;
29107 5ELCID3717 ANDIDIERON EN PLEYTOS LOS DE NAUARRA & DE ******,
29162 5ELCID3723 QUANDO SE@ORAS SON SUS FIJAS DE NAUARRA & DE ******.
WORD # 477 OCCURS 11 TIMES.
INDEX OF DIVERSIFICATION = 2330.20 WITH STANDARD DEVIATION OF 3665.95

ARANCADA
6389 5ELCID0814 DESTA BATALLA QUE AUEMOS ********;
9703 5ELCID1233 MAS MUCHO FUE PROUECHOSA, SABET, ESTA ********:
WORD # 478 OCCURS 2 TIMES.

ARANCADO
6059 5ELCID0769 ******** ES EL REY FARIZ & GALUE;
6227 5ELCID0793 QUANDO TAL BATALLA AUEMOS ********.
WORD # 479 OCCURS 2 TIMES.

ARANCAR
8971 5ELCID1142 ******* SE LAS ESTACAS & ACOSTAR SE ATODAS PARTES LOS TENDALES.
9001 5ELCID1145 MAGER LES PESA, OUIERON SE ADAR & A *******.
WORD # 480 OCCURS 2 TIMES.

ARBUXEDO
11775 5ELCID1493 POR EL VAL DE ******** PIENSSAN A DEPRUNAR.
WORD # 481 OCCURS 1 TIMES.

ARBUXUELO
12158 5ELCID1543 ********* ARRIBA PRIUADO AGUIJAUAN,
20910 5ELCID2656 TRO%IERON ********* & LEGARON A SALON,
WORD # 482 OCCURS 2 TIMES.

ARCAS
879 5ELCID0113 TIENE DOS ***** LENNAS DE ORO ESMERADO.
1418 5ELCID0181 SIUOS LA ADUXIER DALLA; SI NON, CONTALDA SOBRE LAS *****. . . .
1483 5ELCID0189 YA DON RACHEL & VIDAS, EN UUESTRAS MANOS SON LAS *****;
WORD # 483 OCCURS 3 TIMES.

ARCH
5472 5ELCID0690 COMMO SODES MUY BUENO, TENER LA EDES SIN ****;
WORD # 484 OCCURS 1 TIMES.

ARCHAS
675 5ELCID0085 CON UUESTRO CONSEGO BASTIR QUIERO DOS ******;
926 5ELCID0119 PRENDED LAS ****** & METED LAS EN UUESTRO SALUO;
988 5ELCID0127 ESTAS ****** PRENDAMOS LAS AMAS,
1119 5ELCID0144 POR ADUZIR LAS ****** & METER LAS EN UUESTRO SALUO,
1142 5ELCID0147 LAS ****** ADUCHAS, PRENDET SEYES %IENTOS MARCOS.
1251 5ELCID0161 QUE SOBRE AQUELAS ****** DAR LE YEN VJ %IENTOS MARCOS
1298 5ELCID0166 DIXO MARTIN ANTOLINEZ: CARGEN LAS ****** PRIUADO.
1329 5ELCID0170 ALCARGAR DELAS ****** VERIEDES GOZO TANTO:
WORD # 485 OCCURS 8 TIMES.
INDEX OF DIVERSIFICATION = 92.43 WITH STANDARD DEVIATION OF 80.09

ARDIDA
626 5ELCID0079 MARTIN ANTOLINEZ, SODES ****** LAN%A
WORD # 486 OCCURS 1 TIMES.

```
WORD                 C#  PREFIX                          CONTEXT

ARDIDO              26345 5ELCID3359 ******:
          WORD # 487 OCCURS    1 TIMES.

ARDIMENT             4315 5ELCID0549 NON LO SABEN LOS MOROS EL ******** QUE AN.
          WORD # 488 OCCURS    1 TIMES.

AREBATA              4420 5ELCID0562 QUE DE DIA NIN DE NOCH NON LES DIESSEN *******,
          WORD # 489 OCCURS    1 TIMES.

AREZEBIR            15156 5ELCID1917 APRIESSA CAUALGA, ******** LOS SALIO;
          WORD # 490 OCCURS    1 TIMES.

AREZIADO            10200 5ELCID1291 DE PIE & DE CAUALLO MUCHO ERA ********.
          WORD # 491 OCCURS    1 TIMES.

ARLAZON              2306 5ELCID0290 EN AQUES DIA ALA PUENT DE *******
          WORD # 492 OCCURS    1 TIMES.

ARLANZON              437 5ELCID0055 SALIO POR LA PUERTA & EN ******** POSAUA.
                     1571 5ELCID0201 EXIDO ES DE BURGOS & ******** A PASXADO,
          WORD # 493 OCCURS    2 TIMES.

ARMA                15674 5ELCID1988 TANTA BUENA **** & TANTO BUEN CAUALLO COREDOR,
          WORD # 494 OCCURS    1 TIMES.

ARMADO               5409 5ELCID0683 ****** ES MYO ZID CON QUANTOS QUE EL HA;
                    18716 5ELCID2368 AFEUOS EL OBISPO DON IHERONIMO MUY BIEN ******,
          WORD # 495 OCCURS    2 TIMES.

ARMADOS             13306 5ELCID1687 POR LA MANANA PRIETA TODOS ******* SEADES,
                    13500 5ELCID1711 SALIDOS SON TODOS ******* POR LAS TORRES DE VANZIA,
                    27984 5ELCID3571 TODOS TRES SON ******* LOS DEL CAMPEADOR,
          WORD # 496 OCCURS    3 TIMES.

ARMAN               27837 5ELCID3552 EN OTRO LOGAR SE ***** LOS YFANTES DE CARRION,
          WORD # 497 OCCURS    1 TIMES.

ARMAR                5520 5ELCID0695 QUE PRIESSA VA EN LOS MOROS, E TORNARON SE A *****;
                     5530 5ELCID0697 VERIEDES ***** SE MOROS, APRIESSA ENTRAR EN AZ.
                     8915 5ELCID1135 MA@ANA ERA & PIENSSAN SE DE *****,
          WORD # 498 OCCURS    3 TIMES.

ARMAS                5061 5ELCID0639 TRES MILL MOROS LEUEDES CON ***** DE LIDIAR;
                     5213 5ELCID0659 E DE NOCH EN BUELTOS ANDAN EN *****;
                     6242 5ELCID0795 DE ESCUDOS & DE ***** & DE OTROS AUERES LARGOS;
                     7703 5ELCID0986 APRIESSA UOS GUARNID & METEDOS EN LAS *****.
                     7744 5ELCID0991 APRETAD LOS CAUALLOS, & BISTADES LAS *****.
                     7822 5ELCID1001 LAS ***** AUIEN PRESAS & SEDIEN SOBRE LOS CAUALLOS.
                     8830 5ELCID1123 APAREIADOS ME SED A CAUALLOS & *****;
                     9638 5ELCID1224 VINO LOS VER CON XXX MILL DE *****.
                    11944 5ELCID1514 LUEGO TOMAN ***** & TOMANSE A DEPORTAR,
                    12200 5ELCID1548 E BUEN CAUALLO EN DIESTRO QUE UA ANTE SUS *****.
                    12435 5ELCID1577 DELANTE SU MUGIER & DE SUS FIJAS QUERIE TENER LAS *****.
                    12504 5ELCID1586 MYO ZID SALIO SOBREL, & ***** DE FUSTE TOMAUA,
                    12627 5ELCID1602 ***** TENIENDO & TABLADOS QUEBRANTANDO.
                    12815 5ELCID1626 CON L VEZES MILL DE *****, TODOS FUERON CONPLIDOS,
                    12928 5ELCID1640 ENTRARE EN LAS *****, NON LO PODRE DEXAR;
                    14005 5ELCID1774 ENTRE TIENDAS & ***** & VESTIDOS PREZIADOS
                    14229 5ELCID1800 TANTOS AUIEN DE AUERES, DE CAUALLOS & DE *****;
                    14813 5ELCID1872 E GUARNIR UOS DE TODAS ***** COMMO UOS DIXIEREDES AQUI,
                    17724 5ELCID2243 DIOS, QUE BIEN TOUIERON ***** EL ZID & SUS VASSALOS
                    18772 5ELCID2375 PENDON TRAYO A CORCAS & ***** DE SE@AL,
                    18900 5ELCID2391 DAUAN LE GRANDES COLPES, MAS NOL FALSSAN LAS *****.
                    20402 5ELCID2589 TODOS PRENDEN ***** & CAUALGAN A VIGOR,
                    20561 5ELCID2610 AGRANDES GUARNJMIENTOS, ACAUALLOS & *****.
                    20585 5ELCID2613 POR LA HUERTA DE VALENZIA TENIENDO SALIEN *****;
                    21029 5ELCID2673 ***** YUA TENIENDO, PAROS ANTE LOS YFANTES;
                    21151 5ELCID2687 TENIENDO YUAN ***** ALTROZIR DE SALON;
                    22654 5ELCID2887 ***** YUA TENIENDO & GRANT GOZO QUE FAZE;
                    22725 5ELCID2896 TENIENDO YUAN *****, ENTRARON SE ALA CIBDAD;
                    24126 5ELCID3076 E QUE NON PARESCAN LAS *****, BIEN PRESOS LOS CORDONES;
                    25941 5ELCID3305 SI YO RESPONDIER, TU NON ENTRARAS EN *****.
                    27143 5ELCID3469 ***** & CAUALLOS TIENEN LOS DEL CANPEADOR,
                    27771 5ELCID3544 DE NOCHE BELARON LAS ***** & ROGARON AL CRIADOR.
                    27819 5ELCID3550 HYAS METIEN EN ***** LOS DEL BUEN CAMPEADOR,
                    28920 5ELCID3694 LAS ***** QUE Y RASTARON EL SELAS TOMO.
          WORD # 499 OCCURS   34 TIMES.
             INDEX OF DIVERSIFICATION =    722.00 WITH STANDARD DEVIATION OF    736.50

ARMINAS             21626 5ELCID2749 LEUARON LES LOS MANTOS & LAS PIELES *******,
          WORD # 500 OCCURS    1 TIMES.

ARMINO              26446 5ELCID3374 MANTO ****** & VN BRIAL RASTRANDO,
          WORD # 501 OCCURS    1 TIMES.
```

```
WORD              C#  PREFIX                    CONTEXT

ARMINOS          24118 5ELCID3075 SOBRE LAS LORIGAS ******* & PELI%ONES,
        WORD # 502 OCCURS    1 TIMES.

AROBDANDO         9954 5ELCID1261 AQUESTOS MYOS VASSALOS CUE CURIAN A VALEN%IA & ANDAN *********.
        WORD # 503 OCCURS    1 TIMES.

AROBDAS           5199 5ELCID0658 LAS *******, QUE LOS MOROS SACAN, DE DIA
                  5217 5ELCID0660 MUCHAS SON LAS ******* & GRANDE ES EL ALMOFALLA.
                  5503 5ELCID0694 VIERON LO LAS ******* DELOS MOROS, AL ALMOFALLA SEUAN TORNAR.
        WORD # 504 OCCURS    3 TIMES.

ARRANCADA         4591 5ELCID0583 DEGUISA UA MYO %ID COMMO SIESCAPASSE DE *********.
                  4639 5ELCID0588 MYO %ID, QUANDO LOS VIO FUERA, COGIOS COMMO DE *********.
                  4812 5ELCID0609 LUEGO LEGAUAN LOS SOS, CA FECHA ES EL *********.
                  9105 5ELCID1158 QUE DIOS LE AIUDARA & FIZIERA ESTA *********.
                  9658 5ELCID1227 FATA DENTRO EN XATIUA DURO EL *********,
                 14381 5ELCID1819 DESTA LID QUE HA ********* CC CAUALLOS LE ENBIAUA ENPRESENTAIA,
                 18955 5ELCID2398 PLOGO A DIOS, AQUESTA FUE EL *********.
                 19330 5ELCID2448 DESTA ********* NOS YREMOS PAGADOS.
                 19486 5ELCID2469 DESTA *********, QUE LO TENIEN EN SO SALUO,
                 19785 5ELCID2508 DAQUESTA ********* QUE LIDIARON DE CORA%ON
        WORD # 505 OCCURS   10 TIMES.
           INDEX OF DIVERSIFICATION =  1687.22 WITH STANDARD DEVIATION OF  2138.91

ARRANCADO        13744 5ELCID1741 QUANDO AL REY DE MARUECOS ASSI LO AN *********,
                 14622 5ELCID1849 POCOS DIAS HA, REY, QUE VNA LID A *********:
                 19317 5ELCID2446 COMMO AL REY BUCAR AVEMOS *********.
                 19615 5ELCID2485 DESTA BATALLA QUE HAN *********
                 28749 5ELCID3671 LOS DOS HAN *********: DJREUOS DE MUNO GUSTIOZ,
        WORD # 506 OCCURS    5 TIMES.
           INDEX OF DIVERSIFICATION =  3750.25 WITH STANDARD DEVIATION OF  4084.33

ARRANCAMOS       19403 5ELCID2458 MATASTES ABUCAR & ********** EL CANPO.
        WORD # 507 OCCURS    1 TIMES.

ARRANCAR         13065 5ELCID1656 CON DIOS A QUESTA LID YO LA HE DE ********.
                 13584 5ELCID1721 PLOGO AL CRIADOR & OUIERON LOS DE ********.
                 18462 5ELCID2337 ******** MELOS TREUO CON LA MER%ED DEL CRIADOR.
                 18969 5ELCID2400 VERIEDES QUEBRAR TANTAS CUERDAS & ******** SE LAS ESTACAS
                 26059 5ELCID3321 DELOS PRIMEROS COLPES OF LE DE ********;
                 27555 5ELCID3519 PORA ******** MOROS DEL CANPO & SER SEGUDADOR;
        WORD # 508 OCCURS    6 TIMES.
           INDEX OF DIVERSIFICATION =  2897.00 WITH STANDARD DEVIATION OF  2951.08

ARRANCO          10522 5ELCID1333 E FIZO %INCO LIDES CAMPALES & TODAS LAS *******.
                 19692 5ELCID2497 ******* LAS LIDES COMMO PLAZE AL CRIADOR,
        WORD # 509 OCCURS    2 TIMES.

ARRANCOLOS        9645 5ELCID1226 ********** MYO %ID EL DELA LUENGA BARBA.
                 14634 5ELCID1851 CON %INQUAENTA MILL ********** DEL CAMPO;
        WORD # 510 OCCURS    2 TIMES.

ARRAS            20202 5ELCID2565 QUE LES DIEMOS POR ***** & POR ONORES;
                 20248 5ELCID2570 VOS LES DIESTES VILLAS E TIERRAS POR ***** ENTIERRAS DE CARRION,
        WORD # 511 OCCURS    2 TIMES.

ARREADOS         19506 5ELCID2471 FUERON EN VALEN%IA MUY BIEN ********,
        WORD # 512 OCCURS    1 TIMES.

ARRENDO          21837 5ELCID2779 ******* EL CAUALLO, A ELLAS ADELINO;
        WORD # 513 OCCURS    1 TIMES.

ARRIADOS         14036 5ELCID1778 QUE ANDAN ******** & NON HA QUI TOMALOS,
        WORD # 514 OCCURS    1 TIMES.

ARRIAZES         24953 5ELCID3179 LAS MA%ANAS & LOS ******** TODOS DORO SON.
        WORD # 515 OCCURS    1 TIMES.

ARRIBA            2815 5ELCID0355 AL%OLAS ******, LEGOLAS ALA FAZ,
                  3781 5ELCID0478 E DESI ****** TORNAN SE CON LA GANAN%IA,
                  3788 5ELCID0479 FENARES ****** & POR GUADALFAIARA.
                  4258 5ELCID0542 VANSSE FENARES ****** QUANTO PUEDEN ANDAR,
                 12159 5ELCID1543 ARBUXUELO ****** PRIUADO AGUIJAUAN,
                 19140 5ELCID2421 ****** AL%O COLADA, VN GRANT COLPE DADOL HA,
                 19371 5ELCID2454 DE XX ****** HA MOROS MATADO;
        WORD # 516 OCCURS    7 TIMES.
           INDEX OF DIVERSIFICATION =  2758.33 WITH STANDARD DEVIATION OF  3651.96

ARRIBADO         12836 5ELCID1629 ******** AN LAS NAUES, FUERA ERAN EXIDOS,
        WORD # 517 OCCURS    1 TIMES.

ARRIBADOS        22091 5ELCID2811 ALAS AGUAS DE DUERO ELLOS ********* SON,
        WORD # 518 OCCURS    1 TIMES.
```

WORD C# PREFIX CONTEXT

```
ARRIBAN%A            4028 5ELCID0512 SOS CAUALLEROS YAN *********,
        WORD # 519 OCCURS   1 TIMES.

ARRICH              23839 5ELCID3037 E AL CONDE DON ****** & A QUANTOS QUE Y SON;
        WORD # 520 OCCURS   1 TIMES.

ART                  4523 5ELCID0575 EL FIZO VN *** & NON LO DETARDAUA:
                    21057 5ELCID2676 HYO SIRUIENDO UOS SIN ***, & UOS CONSSEIASTES PORA MI MUERT.
        WORD # 521 OCCURS   2 TIMES.

ARUEN%O              9668 5ELCID1229 MOROS EN ******* AMIDOS BEUER AGUA.
        WORD # 522 OCCURS   1 TIMES.

ARZON                5807 5ELCID0733 QUAL LIDIA BIEN SOBRE EXORADO *****
        WORD # 523 OCCURS   1 TIMES.

ARZONES              5691 5ELCID0717 ENCLINARON LAS CARAS DE SUSO DE LOS *******,
                     6413 5ELCID0818 SE@AS ESPADAS DELOS ******* COLGADAS.
                    28336 5ELCID3617 ENCLINAUAN LAS CARAS SOBRE LOS *******,
        WORD # 524 OCCURS   3 TIMES.

AS                  19045 5ELCID2410 VERTE ** CON EL %ID, EL DE LA BARBA GRANT,
        WORD # 525 OCCURS   1 TIMES.

ASABOR              17492 5ELCID2213 DE PIE & ******, DIOS, QUE QUEDOS ENTRARON
        WORD # 526 OCCURS   1 TIMES.

ASALUO              28194 5ELCID3599 HYO LOS ADUX ****** ATIERRAS DE CARRION;
        WORD # 527 OCCURS   1 TIMES.

ASANT               21216 5ELCID2696 ADIESTRO DEXAN ***** ESTEUAN, MAS CAE ALUEN;
        WORD # 528 OCCURS   1 TIMES.

ASANTESTEUAN        22336 5ELCID2845 ************ EL MANDADO LEGO
        WORD # 529 OCCURS   1 TIMES.

ASARAGO%A            7078 5ELCID0905 ********* SUS NUEUAS LEGAUAN,
                     7138 5ELCID0914 ********* METUDA LA EN PARIA.
        WORD # 530 OCCURS   2 TIMES.

ASCONDEN              230 5ELCID0030 ******** SE DE MYO %ID, CA NOL OSAN DEZIR NADA.
        WORD # 531 OCCURS   1 TIMES.

ASCUCHO             26638 5ELCID3401 AESTO CALLARON & ******* TODA LA CORT.
        WORD # 532 OCCURS   1 TIMES.

ASERUIR             27013 5ELCID3451 AVER LAS HEDES *******, MAL QUE UOS PESE AUOS.
        WORD # 533 OCCURS   1 TIMES.

ASI                  6610 5ELCID0844 *** LO AN ASMADO & METUDO EN CARTA:
                     7584 5ELCID0972 *** VIENE ES FOR%ADO QUE EL CONDE AMANOS SELE CUYDO TOMAR.
                    11583 5ELCID1468 *** COMMO A MY DIXIERON, HY LOS PODREDES FALAR;
                    15961 5ELCID2024 *** SABE DAR OMILDAN%A A ALFONSSO SO SE@OR.
                    16347 5ELCID2074 *** LO MANDE CHRISTUS QUE SEA ASO PRO.
                    16843 5ELCID2132 PUES QUE CASADES MYS FIJAS, *** COMMO AUOS PLAZ,
                    19079 5ELCID2414 *** COMMO SEMEIA, EN MI LA QUIERES ENSAYAR.
        WORD # 534 OCCURS   7 TIMES.
           INDEX OF DIVERSIFICATION =  2077.17 WITH STANDARD DEVIATION OF  1765.76

ASIL                 7060 5ELCID0902 EL POYO DE MYO %ID **** DIRAN POR CARTA.
                    27028 5ELCID3453 **** CRE%E LA ONDRA A MYO %ID EL CAMPEADOR
        WORD # 535 OCCURS   2 TIMES.

ASILOS               7447 5ELCID0955 QUE EL SALIDO DE CASTIELLA ****** TRAE TAN MAL.
        WORD # 536 OCCURS   1 TIMES.

ASIS                 2974 5ELCID0375 **** PARTEN VNOS DOTROS COMMO LA V@A DELA CARNE.
        WORD # 537 OCCURS   1 TIMES.

ASMADO               6613 5ELCID0844 ASI LO AN ****** & METUDO EN CARTA:
        WORD # 538 OCCURS   1 TIMES.

ASMARON              4095 5ELCID0521 ******* LOS MOROS IIJ MILL MARCOS DE PLATA.
        WORD # 539 OCCURS   1 TIMES.

ASMO                 4116 5ELCID0524 **** MYO %ID CON TODA SU CONPA@A
        WORD # 540 OCCURS   1 TIMES.

ASO                   548 5ELCID0069 PAGOS MYO %ID EL CAMPEADOR & TODOS LOS OTROS QUEUAN
                                     *** %ERUICIO
                     1844 5ELCID0234 CON ESTOS CAUALLEROS QUEL SIRUEN *** SABOR.
                    10793 5ELCID1366 POR TAL FAGO AQUESTO QUE SIRUAN *** SE@OR.
                    16353 5ELCID2074 ASI LO MANDE CHRISTUS QUE SEA *** PRO.
                    20783 5ELCID2639 DELO QUE OUIEREN HUEBOS SIRUAN LAS *** SABOR,
```

WORD C# PREFIX CONTEXT

ASO (CON'T)

```
                 23757 5ELCID3026 BILTAR SE QUIERE & ONDRAR *** SE@OS.
                 25027 5ELCID3188 *** SOBRINO POR NONBREL LAMO,
        WORD # 541 OCCURS   7 TIMES.
          INDEX OF DIVERSIFICATION =  4078.83 WITH STANDARD DEVIATION OF  2928.82

ASOMAR            7175 5ELCID0919 QUANDO VIO MYO %ID ****** A MINAYA,
        WORD # 542 OCCURS   1 TIMES.

ASONRRISAR        9996 5ELCID1266 ALEGRAS LE EL CORA%ON & TORNOS **********:
        WORD # 543 OCCURS   1 TIMES.

ASORRIENDA       28708 5ELCID3666 EL CAUALLO **********, & MESURANDOL DEL ESPADA,
        WORD # 544 OCCURS   1 TIMES.

ASOS              2473 5ELCID0312 **** CAUALLEROS MANDOLOS TODOS IUNTAR:
                  6287 5ELCID0801 **** CASTIELLOS ALOS MOROS DENTRO LOS AN TORNADOS,
                  7931 5ELCID1013 **** CREENDEROS MANDAR LO GUARDAUA.
                 26207 5ELCID3341 **** VASSALOS VIOLOS A DERREDOR;
        WORD # 545 OCCURS   4 TIMES.

ASSAN            11014 5ELCID1394 DE%IDO ES MYNAYA, ***** PERO VA ROGAR,
        WORD # 546 OCCURS   1 TIMES.

ASSENTO          22033 5ELCID2803 TANTO LAS ROGO FATA QUE LAS *******.
        WORD # 547 OCCURS   1 TIMES.

ASSE@OR          23002 5ELCID2930 CON EL DOS CAUALLEROS QUEL AGUARDAN CUM *******.
        WORD # 548 OCCURS   1 TIMES.

ASSER            13152 5ELCID1667 DESI AN ***** DEL OBISPO DON IHERONIMO,
        WORD # 549 OCCURS   1 TIMES.

ASSI               245 5ELCID0032 **** COMMO LEGO ALA PUERTA, FALOLA BIEN %ERRADA,
                   259 5ELCID0033 POR MIEDO DEL REY ALFONSSO, QUE **** LO AUIEN PARADO
                   478 5ELCID0061 **** POSO MYO %ID COMMO SI FUESSE EN MONTA@A.
                  1086 5ELCID0139 DIXO RACHEL & VIDAS:  NON SE FAZE **** EL MERCADO,
                  1113 5ELCID0143 E NOS UOS AIUDAREMOS, QUE **** ES AGUISADO,
                  1185 5ELCID0153 **** COMMO ENTRARON, AL %ID BESARON LE LAS MANOS.
                  1379 5ELCID0177 **** ES UUESTRA VENTURA GRANDES SON UUESTRAS GANAN%IAS,
                  1745 5ELCID0223 SI UOS **** LO FIZIEREDES & LA UENTURA ME FUERE COMPLIDA,
                  2056 5ELCID0259 BIEN LAS ABASTAD, YO **** UOS LO MANDO;
                  2549 5ELCID0322 CUEMO LO MANDO MYO %ID, **** LO AN TODOS HA FAR.
                  5018 5ELCID0635 **** FFERA LO DE SILOCA, QUE ES DEL OTRA PART.
                  7230 5ELCID0927 QUE MINAYA ALBARFANEZ **** ERA LEGADO,
                 10485 5ELCID1329 **** FIZO %EBOLLA & ADELANT CASTEION,
                 10629 5ELCID1347 QUANDO **** FAZE A SU GUISA EL %ID CAMPEADOR
                 10954 5ELCID1386 EN TODO SODES PRO, EN ESTO **** LO FAGADES:
                 11034 5ELCID1397 **** FFAGA A UUESTRAS FIJAS AMAS.
                 13100 5ELCID1661 **** FFAZIE ALAS DUE@AS & A SUS FIJAS AMAS ADOS:
                 13741 5ELCID1741 QUANDO AL REY DE MARUECOS **** LO AN ARRANCADO,
                 13765 5ELCID1745 **** ENTRO SOBRE BAUIECA, EL ESPADA EN LA MANO.
                 13986 5ELCID1771 COMMO LO DIXO EL %ID **** LO HAN ACABADO.
                 14324 5ELCID1812 POR QUE **** LAS ENBIO COND ELLAS SON PAGADAS,
                 14833 5ELCID1875 **** COMMO SEMEIA & LA VELUNTAD MELO DIZ.
                 16016 5ELCID2032 **** ESTANDO, DEDES ME UUESTRA AMOR, QUE LO OYAN QUANTOS AQUI SON.
                 16198 5ELCID2055 RESPUSO MIO %ID: **** LO MANDE EL CRIADOR
                 16303 5ELCID2068 AL OTRO DIA MA@ANA, **** COMMO SALIO EL SOL,
                 16883 5ELCID2137 **** COMMO YO LAS PRENDO DAQUENT, COMMO SI FOSSE DELANT,
                 17228 5ELCID2179 VOS CON ELLOS SED, QUE **** UOS LO MANDO YO.
                 17573 5ELCID2223 SABEDES QUE AL REY **** GELO HE MANDADO,
                 17848 5ELCID2258 LOS VASSALLOS DE MIO %ID, **** SON ACORDADOS,
                 18167 5ELCID2298 EL LEON QUANDO LO VIO, **** EN VERGON%O,
                 18229 5ELCID2306 QUANDO LOS FALLARON & ELLOS VINIERON, **** VINIERON SIN COLOR;
                 18485 5ELCID2340 **** LO OTORGA DON PERO CUEMO SE ALABA FERRANDO.
                 19628 5ELCID2488 **** LO FAZEN TODOS, CA ERAN ACORDADOS.
                 19856 5ELCID2518 **** COMMO LEGARON, PAGOS EL CAMPEADOR:
                 20124 5ELCID2555 **** LAS ESCARNIREMOS ALAS FIJAS DEL CAMPEADOR,
                 20238 5ELCID2569 EL %ID QUE NOS CURIAUA DE **** SER AFONTADO;
                 20472 5ELCID2599 **** UOS PEDIMOS MER%ED NOS AMAS ADOS,
                 20524 5ELCID2606 **** COMMO YO TENGO, BIEN UOS HE CASADAS.
                 20717 5ELCID2630 RESPONDIEN LOS YERNOS: **** LO MANDE DIOS
                 20735 5ELCID2633 **** FAZIAN LOS CAUALLEROS DEL CAMPEADOR.
                 21304 5ELCID2708 **** LO MANDARON LOS YFANTES DE CARRION,
                 22406 5ELCID2854 **** LO FFAGO YO QUE AQUI ESTO.
                 22976 5ELCID2927 **** COMMO DESCAUALGA AQUEL MU@O GUSTIOZ
                 23003 5ELCID2931 **** COMMO ENTRARON POR MEDIO DELA CORT,
                 23352 5ELCID2975 **** COMMO LO DIXO, SUYO ERA EL CUYDADO:
                 23421 5ELCID2983 POR TODAS SUS TIERRAS **** LO YUAN PENSSANDO,
                 23462 5ELCID2988 PRENDEN SO CONSSEIO **** PARIENTES COMMO SON,
                 23733 5ELCID3023 BUENAS CONPA@AS QUE **** AN TAL SE@OR.
                 24173 5ELCID3083 **** COMMO LO ADICHO, TODOS ADOBADOS SON.
                 24334 5ELCID3103 **** YUA MYO %ID ADOBADO ALLA CORT.
                 24870 5ELCID3167 DEMOS LE SUS ESPADAS, QUANDO **** FINCA LA BOZ,
                 25227 5ELCID3212 SI PLOGUIERE AL REY, **** DEZIMOS NOS: DIXO EL REY
```

```
WORD                C#  PREFIX                                CONTEXT

ASSI (CON'T)

                  25339 5ELCID3226 MAS EN NUESTRC IUUIZIC **** LC MANDAMOS NOS,
                  26571 5ELCID3392 **** CCMMO ACABAN ESTA RAZCN,
                  26824 5ELCID3426 QUE CUEMO ES CICHO **** SEA, CMEIOR.
                  27319 5ELCID3491 ESSORA RESPUSC EL REY: **** LC MANDE DIOS
                  27398 5ELCID3500 ATODOS LOS ROGAUA **** CCMMC HAN SABOR;
                  27436 5ELCID3505 QUANDO TODAS ESTAS NUEUAS **** PUESTAS SON,
                  28511 5ELCID3641 **** LO TENIEN LAS YENTES QUE MAL FERIDO ES DE MUERT.
                  29193 5ELCID3728 **** FFAGAMCS NCS TCDCS IUSTOS & PECCADORES
        WORD # 550 OCCURS  60 TIMES.
           INDEX OF DIVERSIFICATICN =   489.64 WITH STANDARD DEVIATION OF   636.82

ASSIL              1267 5ELCID0163 CA ***** DIERAN LA FE & GELO AUIEN IURADO,
                  25309 5ELCID3222 QUANDO DE NUESTRCS AUERES ***** PRENDE SABOR:
        WORD # 551 OCCURS   2 TIMES.

ASSILO            25245 5ELCID3214 DIXO EL BUEN REY: ****** OTORGO YO.
        WORD # 552 OCCURS   1 TIMES.

ASSINIESTRO       21180 5ELCID2691 *********** DEXAN ATINEZA, VNA PE@A MUY FUERT,
                  21201 5ELCID2694 *********** DEXAN AGRIZA QUE ALAMOS POBLO,
        WORD # 553 OCCURS   2 TIMES.

ASSIS             21722 5ELCID2762 LA DESCNDRA DEL LECN ***** YRA VENGANDO.
                  25019 5ELCID3187 ***** YRAN VENGANDC DCN ELUIRA & DONA SOL.
        WORD # 554 OCCURS   2 TIMES.

ASSO              25296 5ELCID3220 TORNAN CON EL CONSSEIC E FABLAUAN **** SABOR:
        WORD # 555 OCCURS   1 TIMES.

ASSOMAR           11010 5ELCID1393 TAN GRAND FUE EL GOZO QUANDOL VIERON *******.
        WORD # 556 OCCURS   1 TIMES.

ASSOMARON         17200 5ELCID2176 QUANDO A ELLA *********, LCS GOZOS SON MAYORES.
        WORD # 557 OCCURS   1 TIMES.

ASSOMAS           21660 5ELCID2753  QUAL VENTURA SERIE SI ******* ESSORA EL %ID CAMPEADOR
        WORD # 558 OCCURS   1 TIMES.

ASSOMASSE         21569 5ELCID2742 QUE ********* ESSORA EL %ID CAMPEADOR
        WORD # 559 OCCURS   1 TIMES.

ASSUR             28755 5ELCID3672 CON ***** GON%ALEZ CCMMC SE ADOBO.
                  28768 5ELCID3674 ***** GCN%ALEZ, FUR%UDC & DE VALOR,
        WORD # 560 OCCURS   2 TIMES.

ASSUREZ           23619 5ELCID3008 E ASUR GON%ALEZ & GCN%ALO *******,
                  28891 5ELCID3690 DIXO GON%ALC *******: NCL FIRGADES, POR DIOS
        WORD # 561 OCCURS   2 TIMES.

ASSUS             22299 5ELCID2840 ADUXIESSEN ***** FIJAS A VALEN%IA LA MAYOR.
        WORD # 562 OCCURS   1 TIMES.

ASTA              18918 5ELCID2393 EN BRA%O EL ESCUDO & ABAXO EL ****,
        WORD # 563 OCCURS   1 TIMES.

ASTAS             15540 5ELCID1969 TANTO BUEN PENDON METER EN BUENAS *****,
                  28084 5ELCID3585 EMANO PRENDEN LAS ***** DELOS FIERROS TAIADORES,
                  28267 5ELCID3609 MAS DE VJ ***** DE LAN%AS QUE NON LEGASSEN AL MOION.
        WORD # 564 OCCURS   3 TIMES.

ASTIL              2806 5ELCID0354 CORRIO LA SANGRE POR EL ***** AYUSO, LAS MANOS SE OUO DE VNTAR,
                  18861 5ELCID2387 EL ***** A QUEBRADO & METIC MANO AL ESPADA.
                  28867 5ELCID3687 VERMEIO SALIC EL *****, & LA LAN%A & EL PENDON.
        WORD # 565 OCCURS   3 TIMES.

ASTURIAS          22954 5ELCID2924 E DELAS ******** BIEN A SAN %ALUADOR,
        WORD # 566 OCCURS   1 TIMES.

ASU                 243 5ELCID0031 EL CAMPEADOR ADELINO *** POSADA;
                   4748 5ELCID0602 TIENEN BUENOS CAUALLCS, SABET, *** GUISA LES ANDAN;
                  10915 5ELCID1381 SI LEUAREDES LAS DUENAS, SIRUAN LAS *** SABOR,
                  14934 5ELCID1888 CASAR QUEREMOS CON ELLAS *** ONDRA & A NUESTRA PRO.
                  15814 5ELCID2005 E OTRAS DUE@AS QUE LAS SIRUEN *** SABOR;
        WORD # 567 OCCURS   5 TIMES.
           INDEX OF DIVERSIFICATION =  3891.75 WITH STANDARD DEVIATION OF  2209.05

ASUR              17163 5ELCID2172 EVAY **** GON%ALEZ, CUE ERA BULICOR,
                  23615 5ELCID3008 E **** GON%ALEZ & GCN%ALC ASSUREZ,
                  26439 5ELCID3373 **** GCN%ALEZ ENTRAUA PCR EL PALA%IO,
        WORD # 568 OCCURS   3 TIMES.

ASUS               2011 5ELCID0254 AELLA & **** FIJAS & ASUS DUENAS SIRUADES LAS EST A@O.
                   2014 5ELCID0254 AELLA & ASUS FIJAS & **** DUENAS SIRUADES LAS EST A@O.
                  17242 5ELCID2181 VERAN **** ESPCSAS, A DCN ELUIRA & A DONA SOL.
                  22017 5ELCID2801 COGIO DEL AGUA ENEL & **** PRIMAS DIO;
```

WORD C# PREFIX CONTEXT

ASUS (CON'T)

```
                      22664 5ELCID2888 MYO %ID **** FIJAS YUA LAS ABRA%AR,
          WORD # 569 OCCURS   5 TIMES.
             INDEX OF DIVERSIFICATION =  5162.25 WITH STANDARD DEVIATION OF  7035.02

ATAL                   2973 5ELCID0374 LORANDO DELOS OIOS, QUE NON VIESTES ****,
                      27546 5ELCID3518 MAS **** CAUALLO CUM EST PORA TAL COMMO VOS,
                      29021 5ELCID3707 **** LE CONTESCA O SI QUIER PEOR.
          WORD # 570 OCCURS   3 TIMES.

ATALAYA               13196 5ELCID1673 VIOLO EL ******* & TANXO EL ESQUILA;
          WORD # 571 OCCURS   1 TIMES.

ATALES                20706 5ELCID2629 ****** COSAS FED QUE EN PLAZER CAYA ANOS.
          WORD # 572 OCCURS   1 TIMES.

ATAMORES               5524 5ELCID0696 ANTE ROYDO DE ******** LA TIERRA QUERIE QUEBRAR;
                      13080 5ELCID1658 A VNA GRAND PRIESSA TANIEN LOS ********;
                      13141 5ELCID1666 AQUELOS ******** AUOS LOS PONDRAN DELANT & VEREDES QUANLES SON,
                      18535 5ELCID2345 EN LA VESTE DELOS MOROS LOS ******** SONANDO;
          WORD # 573 OCCURS   4 TIMES.

ATAN                   2998 5ELCID0378 **** GRAND SABOR FABLO MINAYA ALBARFANEZ:
                      10440 5ELCID1323 LOS PIES & LAS MANOS, COMMO **** BUEN SE@OR,
                      17396 5ELCID2201 **** FIRME MIENTRE & DE TODO CORA%ON
                      21478 5ELCID2731 **** MALOS ENSSIENPLOS NON FAGADES SOBRE NOS:
          WORD # 574 OCCURS   4 TIMES.

ATANTAS               15572 5ELCID1974 CON EL REY ******* BUENAS CONPA@AS.
          WORD # 575 OCCURS   1 TIMES.

ATANTO                 9751 5ELCID1239 DIXO MYO %ID DE LA SU BOCA ******:
                      14480 5ELCID1831 ALEGRE FUE EL REY, NON VIESTES ******,
                      22453 5ELCID2860 ****** UOS LO GRADIMOS COMMO SI VIESSEMOS AL CRAIDOR;
          WORD # 576 OCCURS   3 TIMES.

ATANTOS               13594 5ELCID1723 ******* MATA DE MOROS QUE NON FUERON CONTADOS;
          WORD # 577 OCCURS   1 TIMES.

ATECA                  4337 5ELCID0552 PASSO A BOUIERCA & ***** QUE ES ADELANT,
          WORD # 578 OCCURS   1 TIMES.

ATENDIERON            27710 5ELCID3537 DOS DIAS ********** A YFANTES DE CARRION.
          WORD # 579 OCCURS   1 TIMES.

ATERCER                4110 5ELCID0523 ******* DIA DADOS FUERON SJN FALLA.
          WORD # 580 OCCURS   1 TIMES.

ATI                      52 5ELCID0008 GRADO ***, SE@OR PADRE, QUE ESTAS EN ALTO
                       1688 5ELCID0217 *** LO GRADESCO, DIOS, QUE %IELO & TIERRA GUIAS;
                       2864 5ELCID0362 *** ADORO & CREO DE TODO VOLUNTAD,
                       8678 5ELCID1102 VIOLO MYO %ID, TOMOS AMARAUILLAR: GRADO ***, PADRE SPIRITAL
                      22775 5ELCID2902 EN BUEN ORA TE CRIE *** EN LA MI CORT
                      25930 5ELCID3304 AMI LO DIZEN, *** DAN LAS OREIADAS.
          WORD # 581 OCCURS   6 TIMES.
             INDEX OF DIVERSIFICATION =  5174.60 WITH STANDARD DEVIATION OF  5305.83
ATIERRA                 971 5ELCID0125 QUANDO ******* DE MOROS ENTRO, QUE GRANT AUER SACO;
                      23747 5ELCID3025 FIRIOS ******* MYO %ID EL CAMPEADOR;
          WORD # 582 OCCURS   2 TIMES.

ATIERRAS              19916 5ELCID2526 BUENOS MANDADOS YRAN ******** DE CARRION.
                      20046 5ELCID2544 DIGAMOS QUE LAS LEUAREMOS ******** DE CARRION,
                      20414 5ELCID2590 POR QUE ESCURREN SUS FIJAS DEL CAMPEADOR ******** DE CARRION.
                      20460 5ELCID2597 AGORA NOS ENVIADES ******** DE CARRION,
                      20695 5ELCID2627 HYR LAS HEMOS VER ******** DE CARRION.
                      27154 5ELCID3470 NOS ANTES ABREMOS AYR ******** DE CARRION.
                      28195 5ELCID3599 HYO LOS ADUX ASALUO ******** DE CARRION;
          WORD # 583 OCCURS   7 TIMES.
             INDEX OF DIVERSIFICATION =  1378.83 WITH STANDARD DEVIATION OF  2513.50

ATINEZA               21182 5ELCID2691 ASSINIESTRO DEXAN *******, VNA PE@A MUY FUERT,
          WORD # 584 OCCURS   1 TIMES.

ATIZON                28536 5ELCID3643 QUANDO LO VIO FERRANGO%ALEZ, CONUUO ******;
          WORD # 585 OCCURS   1 TIMES.

ATOD                   1434 5ELCID0184 **** EL PRIMER COLPE IIJ MARCOS DE PLATA ECHARON,
                      16489 5ELCID2090 GRA%IAS, DIXO EL REY, AUOS & **** ESTA CORT.
                      16896 5ELCID2138 SED PADRINO DELLOS **** EL VELAR;
                      26342 5ELCID3359 LO QUE LES FIZIEMOS SER LES HA RETRAYDO; ESTO LIDIARE **** EL MAS
          WORD # 586 OCCURS   4 TIMES.

ATODA                 22260 5ELCID2835 PESO A MYO %ID & ***** SU CORT, & ALBARFANEZ DALMA & DE CORA%ON.
          WORD # 587 OCCURS   1 TIMES.
```

WORD C# PREFIX CONTEXT

ATODAS 2823 5ELCID0356 ABRIO SOS OIOS, CATO ****** PARTES,
7455 5ELCID0956 LOS MANDADOS SON YDOS ****** PARTES;
8978 5ELCID1142 ARANCAR SE LAS ESTACAS & ACOSTAR SE ****** PARTES LOS TENDALES.
9418 5ELCID1197 ANDIDIERON LOS PREGONES, SABET, ****** PARTES,
9490 5ELCID1206 SONANDO VAN SUS NUEUAS TODAS ****** PARTES.
10754 5ELCID1362 ****** LAS ESCUELLAS QUE A EL DIZEN SE@OR
WORD # 588 OCCURS 6 TIMES.
INDEX OF DIVERSIFICATION = 1585.20 WITH STANDARD DEVIATION OF 1802.17

ATODO 1794 5ELCID0228 DIXO MARTIN ANTOLINEZ: VERE ALA MUGIER ***** MYO SOLAZ,
15372 5ELCID1946 ACORDAR UOS YEDES DESPUES ***** LO MEIOR.
20383 5ELCID2586 QUANDO SON PAGADOS ***** SO SABOR,
20869 5ELCID2650 DIOS, QUE BIEN LOS SIRUIO ***** SO SABOR
21333 5ELCID2711 DEPORTAR SE QUIEREN CON ELLAS ***** SU SABOR.
WORD # 589 OCCURS 5 TIMES.
INDEX OF DIVERSIFICATION = 4883.75 WITH STANDARD DEVIATION OF 6177.39

ATODOS 1462 5ELCID0187 %INCO ESCUDEROS TIENE DON MARTINO, ****** LOS CARGAUA.
1893 5ELCID0241 TU QUE ****** QUIAS, VALA MYO %ID EL CANPEADOR.
2992 5ELCID0377 ****** ESPERANDO, LA CABE%A TORNANDO UA.
3400 5ELCID0429 DIXOLES ****** COMMO QUERIE TRASNOCHAR;
4857 5ELCID0614 GRADO A DIOS DEL %IELO & ****** LOS SOS SANTOS,
7987 5ELCID1020 EL NON LO QUIERE COMER, ****** LOS SOSANAUA:
9704 5ELCID1234 ****** LOS MENORES CAYERON C MARCOS DE PLATA.
9808 5ELCID1246 ****** LES DIO EN VALEN%IA CASAS & HEREDADES
15906 5ELCID2017 ****** LOS SOS ESTAR LOS MANDO,
17099 5ELCID2164 ESTO PLOGO AL REY, & ****** LOS SOLTO;
18499 5ELCID2341 PLOGO A MYO %ID & ****** SOS VASSALLOS;
22359 5ELCID2848 RE%IBEN AMINAYA & ****** SUS VARONES,
23332 5ELCID2972 SALUDAD MELOS ******, ENTRELLOS AYA ESPA%IO;
27395 5ELCID3500 ****** LOS ROGAUA ASSI COMMO HAN SABOR;
28246 5ELCID3606 BIEN GELO DEMOSTRARON ****** VJ COMMO SON,
WORD # 590 OCCURS 15 TIMES.
INDEX OF DIVERSIFICATION = 1912.14 WITH STANDARD DEVIATION OF 1728.59

ATOLINEZ 552 5ELCID0070 FABLO MARTIN ********, COREDES LO QUE A DICHO:
799 5ELCID0102 LEGO MARTIN ******** AGUISA DEMENBRADO:
WORD # 591 OCCURS 2 TIMES.

ATORGADO 20358 5ELCID2583 ******** LO HAN ESTO LOS YFFANTES DE CARRION.
WORD # 592 OCCURS 1 TIMES.

ATORGAN 24802 5ELCID3169 ******* LOS ALCALDES: TOD ESTO ES RAZON.
WORD # 593 OCCURS 1 TIMES.

ATORGAR 1544 5ELCID0198 ******* NOS HEDES ESTO QUE AUEMOS PARADO.
26706 5ELCID3411 QUE PLEGA AUOS, & ******* LO HE YO,
WORD # 594 OCCURS 2 TIMES.

ATORGARON 28545 5ELCID3645 ********* GELO LOS FIELES, PERO VERMUEZ LE DEXO.
WORD # 595 OCCURS 1 TIMES.

ATORNAR 9944 5ELCID1260 QUE SI ALGUNOS FURTARE O MENOS LE FALLAREN, EL AUER ME AURA ******
WORD # 596 OCCURS 1 TIMES.

ATRAS 8483 5ELCID1078 TORNANDO UA LA CABE%A & CATANDOS *****;
WORD # 597 OCCURS 1 TIMES.

ATRAUESSAUAN 12167 5ELCID1544 EL CAMPO DE TORAN%IO LUEGOL ************,
WORD # 598 OCCURS 1 TIMES.

ATREGO 10778 5ELCID1365 ****** LES LOS CUERPOS DE MAL & DE OCASION,
WORD # 599 OCCURS 1 TIMES.

AUED 28198 5ELCID3600 **** UUESTRO DERECHO, TUERTO NON QUERADES VOS,
WORD # 600 OCCURS 1 TIMES.

AUEDES 1204 5ELCID0155 YA DON RACHEL & VIDAS, ****** ME OLBIDADO
3896 5ELCID0494 DA QUESTA QUINTA QUE ME ****** MANDO,
5623 5ELCID0708 LOS QUE EL DEBDO ****** VEREMOS COMMO LA ACORREDES.
8139 5ELCID1037 SI LO FIZIEREDES, %ID, LO QUE ****** FABLADO,
8167 5ELCID1041 MAS QUANTO ****** PERDIDO & YO GANE EN CANPO,
8184 5ELCID1043 MAS QUANTO ****** PERDIDO NON UOS LO DARE,
8415 5ELCID1069 EN GRADO UOS LO TENGO LO QUE ME ****** DEXADO.
11350 5ELCID1436 POR LO QUE ****** FECHO BUEN COSIMENT Y AURA.
12067 5ELCID1530 DESTO QUE ****** FECHO UOS NON PERDEREDES NADA.
12579 5ELCID1596 SACADA ME ****** DE MUCHAS VERGUEN%AS MALAS;
14612 5ELCID1848 MUCHO PRE%IA LA ONDRA EL %ID QUEL ****** DADO.
16963 5ELCID2147 DIXO EL REY DON ALFONSSO: MUCHO ME ****** ENBARGADO.
16970 5ELCID2148 RE%IBO ESTE DON QUE ME ****** MANDADO;
16994 5ELCID2151 MYO %ID RUY DIAZ, MUCHO ME ****** ONDRADO,
18675 5ELCID2363 EUOS TAN DINNO QUE CON EL ****** PART.
25964 5ELCID3309 DIREUOS, %ID, COSTUBRES ****** TALES,

```
WORD                C#  PREFIX                               CONTEXT

AUEDES (CON'T)

                 28732 5ELCID3669 POR QUANTO ****** FECHO VENZIDA AUEDES ESTA BATALLA.
                 28735 5ELCID3669 POR QUANTO AUEDES FECHO VENZIDA ****** ESTA BATALLA.
        WORD # 601 OCCURS  18 TIMES.
           INDEX OF DIVERSIFICATION =  1618.47 WITH STANDARD DEVIATION OF  1848.93

AUEGALUON        11555 5ELCID1464 TIENELA *********, MYO AMIGO ES DE PAZ,
                 11655 5ELCID1477 EL MORO *********, QUANDO SOPO EL MENSSAIE,
                 11726 5ELCID1487 DIXO *********: FER LO HE DE VELUNTAD.
                 11848 5ELCID1502 E EL ALCAYAZ ********* CON SUS FUERZAS QUE TRAHE,
                 11969 5ELCID1517 QUANDO LEGO *********, CONTA OIO HA,
                 12049 5ELCID1528 HY *********, AMIGOL SODES SIN FALLA.
                 12173 5ELCID1545 VINIERON A MOLINA, LA QUE ********* MANDAUA.
                 12219 5ELCID1551 EL MORO ********* BIEN LOS SIRUIE SIN FALLA,
        WORD # 602 OCCURS   8 TIMES.
           INDEX OF DIVERSIFICATION =    93.86 WITH STANDARD DEVIATION OF    30.20

AUELLAS           6938 5ELCID0887 HONORES & TIERRAS ******* CONDONADAS,
        WORD # 603 OCCURS   1 TIMES.

AUELLO            3910 5ELCID0496 YO UOS LA SUELTA & ****** QUITADO.
        WORD # 604 OCCURS   1 TIMES.

AUEMOS             957 5ELCID0123 NOS HUEBOS ****** EN TODO DE GANAR ALGO.
                  1073 5ELCID0138 HUEBOS ****** QUE NOS DEDES LOS MARCHOS.
                  1549 5ELCID0198 ATORGAR NOS HEDES ESTO QUE ****** PARADO.
                  2541 5ELCID0321 CA EL PLAZO VIENE A ZERCA, MUCHO ****** DE ANDAR.
                  2723 5ELCID0344 MOSTRANDO LOS MIRACLOS, POR EN ****** QUE FABLAR:
                  4879 5ELCID0617 EN ESTE CASTIELLO GRAND AUER ****** PRESO,
                  6226 5ELCID0793 QUANDO TAL BATALLA ****** ARANCADO.
                  6388 5ELCID0814 DESTA BATALLA QUE ****** ARANCADA;
                  6538 5ELCID0834 POR LANCAS & POR ESPADAS ****** DE GUARIR,
                 10016 5ELCID1269 AGORA ****** RIQUIZA, MAS AUREMOS ADELANT.
                 10037 5ELCID1271 ENBIAR UOS QUIERO A CASTIELLA, DO ****** HEREDADES,
                 10049 5ELCID1273 DESTAS MIS GANANZIAS, QUE ****** FECHAS ACA,
                 11070 5ELCID1401 POR LEUAROS A VALENZIA QUE ****** POR HEREDAD.
                 17546 5ELCID2220 PUES QUE AFAZER LO ******, POR QUE LO YMOS TARDANDO?
                 19942 5ELCID2530 POR UOS ****** ONDRA & AVEMOS LIDIADO.
                 20182 5ELCID2562 DAD NOS NUESTRAS MUGIERES QUE ****** ABENDIZIONES;
                 20211 5ELCID2566 VERAN UUESTRAS FIJAS LO QUE ****** NOS,
                 20949 5ELCID2661 HYA PUES QUE ADEXAR ****** FIJAS DEL CAMPEADOR,
                 27632 5ELCID3528 PRESO ****** EL DEBDO & A PASSAR ES POR NOS;
        WORD # 605 OCCURS  19 TIMES.
           INDEX OF DIVERSIFICATION =  1480.94 WITH STANDARD DEVIATION OF  2090.91

AUENGALUON       12081 5ELCID1532 DIXO **********: PLAZME DESTA PRESENTAIA,
                 22614 5ELCID2881 AL MORO ********** DE CORAZON LE PLAZ,
        WORD # 606 OCCURS   2 TIMES.

AUER               651 5ELCID0082 BIEN LO VEDES QUE YO NO TRAYO ****, & HUEBOS ME SERIE
                   720 5ELCID0091 NON PUEDO TRAER EL ****, CA MUCHO ES PESADO,
                   919 5ELCID0118 E PRESTALDE DE **** LO QUE SEA GUISADO.
                   977 5ELCID0125 QUANDO ATIERRA DE MOROS ENTRO, QUE GRANT **** SACO;
                   984 5ELCID0126 NON DUERME SIN SOSPECHA QUI **** TRAE MONEDADO.
                  1039 5ELCID0133 PEDIR UOS A POCO POR DEXAR SO **** EN SALUO.
                  2486 5ELCID0314 POCO **** TRAYO, DAR UOS QUIERO UUESTRA PART.
                  3827 5ELCID0484 CON AQUESTE **** TORNAN SE ESSA CONPA@A;
                  4017 5ELCID0510 MANDO PARTIR TOD AQUESTE ****,
                  4878 5ELCID0617 EN ESTE CASTIELLO GRAND **** AUEMOS PRESO,
                  5370 5ELCID0678 ONDRASTES UOS, MINAYA, CA **** UOS LO YEDES DE FAR.
                  9576 5ELCID1217 ENEL **** MONEDADO XXX MILL MARCOS LE CAEN,
                  9888 5ELCID1254 TOMASSEN LE EL **** & PUSIESSEN LE EN VN PALO.
                  9941 5ELCID1260 QUE SI ALGUNOS FURTARE O MENOS LE FALLAREN, EL **** ME AURA ATORNAR
                 14496 5ELCID1834 **** ESTOS MENSAIES DEL QUE EN BUEN ORA NASCO.
                 17860 5ELCID2260 QUI **** QUIERE PRENDER BIEN ERA ABASTADO;
                 19483 5ELCID2468 LOS YERNOS DE MYO ZID QUANDO ESTE **** TOMARON
                 19679 5ELCID2495 QUE HE **** & TIERRA & ORO & ONOR,
                 20962 5ELCID2663 QUANTA RIQUIZA TIENE **** LA YEMOS NOS.
                 24787 5ELCID3157 COMIGO NON QUISIERON **** NADA & PERDIERON MI AMOR;
                 26330 5ELCID3358 MIENTRA QUE BIUAN PUEDEN **** SOSPIROS:
                 27974 5ELCID3570 NOLO QUERRIEN **** FECHO POR QUANTO HA EN CARRION.
        WORD # 607 OCCURS  22 TIMES.
           INDEX OF DIVERSIFICATION =  1300.10 WITH STANDARD DEVIATION OF  1471.40

AUERES             209 5ELCID0027 QUE PERDERIE LOS ****** & MAS LOS OIOS DELA CARA,
                   360 5ELCID0045 SI NON, PERDERIEMOS LOS ****** & LAS CASAS,
                   792 5ELCID0101 EN CUENTA DE SUS ******, DELOS QUE AUIEN GANADOS.
                   858 5ELCID0110 GRANDES ****** PRISO & MUCHO SOBEIANOS,
                  1348 5ELCID0172 GRADAN SE RACHEL & VIDAS CON ****** MONEDADOS,
                  6246 5ELCID0795 DE ESCUDOS & DE ARMAS & DE OTROS ****** LARGOS;
                  6318 5ELCID0804 DIO APARTIR ESTOS DINEROS & ESTOS ****** LARGOS;
                  9585 5ELCID1218 ELOS OTROS ****** QUIEN LOS PODRIE CONTAR?
                 14224 5ELCID1800 TANTOS AUIEN DE ******, DE CAUALLOS & DE ARMAS;
                 15600 5ELCID1978 QUANTOS QUISIESSEN ****** DORO O DE PLATA.
                 17841 5ELCID2257 NON FUERON EN CUENTA LOS ****** MONEDADOS.
```

WORD C# PREFIX CONTEXT

AUERES (CON'T)

```
                    19935 5ELCID2529 TANTOS AVEMOS DE ****** QUE NO SON CONTADOS;
                    20023 5ELCID2541 LOS ****** QUE TENEMOS GRANDES SON & SOBEIANOS,
                    20089 5ELCID2550 ****** LEUAREMOS GRANDES QUE VALEN GRANT VALOR;
                    20102 5ELCID2552 DAQUESTOS ****** SIENPRE SEREMOS RICOS OMNES,
                    21289 5ELCID2705 MANDARON CARGAR LAS AZEMILAS CON GRANDES ******,
                    22859 5ELCID2912 MYOS ****** SE ME AN LEUADO, QUE SOBEIANOS SON;
                    25177 5ELCID3206 DEN ME MIS ******, QUANDO MYOS YERNOS NON SON.
                    25257 5ELCID3216 DESTOS ****** QUE UOS DI YO, SIMELOS DADES, O DEDES DELLO RA%ON.
                    25308 5ELCID3222 QUANDO DE NUESTROS ****** ASSIL PRENDE SABOR;
                    25414 5ELCID3236 FABLO FERRANGO%ALEZ: ****** MONEDADOS NON TENEMOS NOS.
                    25856 5ELCID3294 DE UUESTROS ****** DE TODOS PAGADOS SODES.
                    26926 5ELCID3440 GRANDES ****** LES DIO MYO %ID EL CAMPEADOR,
                    27382 5ELCID3498 QUE PRENDAN DE SUS ****** QUANTO OUIEREN SABOR.
          WORD # 608 OCCURS  24 TIMES.
             INDEX OF DIVERSIFICATION =  1180.43 WITH STANDARD DEVIATION OF  1456.46

AUES                 6732 5ELCID0859 AL EXIR DE SALON MUCHO OUO BUENAS ****.
                    21638 5ELCID2751 E ALAS **** DEL MONTE & ALAS BESTIAS DELA FIERA GUISA.
                    23123 5ELCID2946 ALAS BESTIAS FIERAS & ALAS **** DEL MONT.
                    25659 5ELCID3267 ALAS BESTIAS FIERAS & ALAS **** DEL MONT;
          WORD # 609 OCCURS   4 TIMES.

AUIA                18747 5ELCID2372 POR SABOR QUE **** DE ALGUN MORO MATAR;
                    19561 5ELCID2478 QUANDO VEO LO QUE **** SABOR,
          WORD # 610 OCCURS   2 TIMES.

AUIDA                5073 5ELCID0641 PRENDET MELO *****, ADUZID MELO DELAND;
          WORD # 611 OCCURS   1 TIMES.

AUIE                   41 5ELCID0006 SOSPIRO MYO %ID, CA MUCHO **** GRANDES CUYDADOS.
                      166 5ELCID0022 EL REY DON ALFONSSO TANTO **** LA GRAND SAaA,
                      406 5ELCID0050 YA LO VEE EL %ID QUE DEL REY NON **** GRA%IA.
                      529 5ELCID0067 NON LO CONPRA, CA EL SELO **** CONSIGO;
                     2072 5ELCID0261 OTORGADO GELO **** EL ABBAT DE GRADO.
                     4427 5ELCID0563 QUE SOPIESSEN QUE MYO %ID ALLI **** FINCAN%A.
                     4442 5ELCID0565 QUE EL CAMPEADOR MYO %ID ALLI **** POBLADO,
                     4696 5ELCID0595 VIO QUE ENTRELLOS & EL CASTIELLO MUCHO **** GRAND PLA%A;
                     5997 5ELCID0760 AL REY FARIZ IIJ COLPES LE **** DADO;
                     8260 5ELCID1051 CON LOS CAUALLEROS QUE EL %ID LE **** DADOS
                     9984 5ELCID1265 TRES MILL & SEYS %IENTOS **** MYO %ID EL DE BIUAR;
                    12394 5ELCID1573 E ADUXIESSEN LE ABAUIECA; POCO **** QUEL GANARA,
                    14153 5ELCID1791 QUE CROUIESSE SOS NUEUAS DE MYO %ID QUE **** ALGO.
                    15957 5ELCID2023 LORANDO DELOS OIOS, TANTO **** EL GOZO MAYOR;
                    16293 5ELCID2067 PASSADO **** IIJ AaOS NO COMIERAN MEIOR.
                    18326 5ELCID2318 CA VEYEN TANTAS TIENDAS DE MOROS DE QUE NON **** SABOR.
                    19352 5ELCID2451 DELOS COLPES DELA LAN%A NON **** RECABDO;
                    24507 5ELCID3124 ALA BARBA QUE **** LUENGA & PRESA CONEL CORDON;
          WORD # 612 OCCURS  18 TIMES.
             INDEX OF DIVERSIFICATION =  1438.18 WITH STANDARD DEVIATION OF  1291.42

AUIEDES             13920 5ELCID1763 HYA MUGIER DAaA XIMENA, NOM LO ******* ROGADO?
          WORD # 613 OCCURS   1 TIMES.

AUIEN                 226 5ELCID0029 GRANDE DUELO ***** LAS YENTES CHRISTIANAS;
                      261 5ELCID0033 POR MIEDO DEL REY ALFONSSO, QUE ASSI LO ***** PARADO
                      795 5ELCID0101 EN CUENTA DE SUS AUERES, DELOS QUE ***** GANADOS.
                     1273 5ELCID0163 CA ASSIL DIERAN LA FE & GELO ***** IURADO,
                     3688 5ELCID0465 MOROS & MORAS ***** LOS DE GANAN%IA,
                     7247 5ELCID0929 E DE SUS COMPAaAS, AQUELAS QUE ***** DEXADAS
                     7823 5ELCID1001 LAS ARMAS ***** PRESAS & SEDIEN SOBRE LOS CAUALLOS.
                     9848 5ELCID1249 VELLO MYO %ID CON LOS AVERES QUE ***** TOMADOS,
                    12613 5ELCID1600 DEL GOZO QUE ***** DE LOS SOS OIOS LORAUAN.
                    13249 5ELCID1680 MUCHO ***** FECHO, PIESSAN DE CAUALGAR.
                    14222 5ELCID1800 TANTOS ***** DE AUERES, DE CAUALLOS & DE ARMAS;
                    14529 5ELCID1838 ADIO LO ***** LOS DEL QUE EN BUEN ORA NASCO,
                    16096 5ELCID2041 TODOS LOS DEMAS DESTO ***** SABOR;
                    17857 5ELCID2259 CADA VNO POR SI SOS DONES ***** DADOS.
                    18268 5ELCID2311 ELLOS ENESTO ESTANDO, DON ***** GRANT PESAR,
                    18539 5ELCID2346 AMARAULLA LO ***** MUCHOS DESSOS CHRISTIANOS,
                    19360 5ELCID2452 AQUELOS QUE GELOS DIERAN NON GELO ***** LOGRADO.
                    27967 5ELCID3569 DELO QUE ***** FECHO MUCHO REPISOS SON;
          WORD # 614 OCCURS  18 TIMES.
             INDEX OF DIVERSIFICATION =  1630.82 WITH STANDARD DEVIATION OF  2058.85

AUIENDO              8486 5ELCID1079 MYEDO YUA ******* QUE MYO %ID SE REPINTRA,
                    14877 5ELCID1880 FABLANDO EN SU CONSSEIO, ******* SU PORIDAD:
          WORD # 615 OCCURS   2 TIMES.

AUIGOR              13186 5ELCID1671 LOS MOROS DE MARRUECOS CAUALGAN ******,
          WORD # 616 OCCURS   1 TIMES.

AUN                   217 5ELCID0028 E *** DEMAS LOS CUERPOS & LAS ALMAS.
                      595 5ELCID0076 *** %ERCA OTARDE EL REY QUERER ME HA POR AMIGO;
                     1598 5ELCID0205 *** VEA EL DIA QUE DEMI AYADES ALGO
                     2241 5ELCID0282 PLEGA ADIOS & A SANTA MARIA, QUE *** CON MIS MANOS CASE
                                     ESTAS MIS
```

```
WORD                C#  PREFIX                              CONTEXT

AUN (CON'T)

              6298 5ELCID0802 MANDO MYO %ID *** QUELES DIESSEN ALGO.
              6920 5ELCID0885 *** ME PLAZE DE MYO %ID QUE FIZO TAL GANAN%IA.
       WORD # 617 OCCURS   6 TIMES.
          INDEX OF DIVERSIFICATION =  1339.60 WITH STANDARD DEVIATION OF  1534.80

AUNTODOS      3024 5ELCID0381 ******** ESTOS DUELOS EN GOZO SE TORNARAN;
       WORD # 618 OCCURS   1 TIMES.

AUOROZES     20863 5ELCID2649 SALIOLOS RECE%IR CON GRANDES ********;
       WORD # 619 OCCURS   1 TIMES.

AUOS          1534 5ELCID0196 DAMOS UOS ENDON **** XXX MARCHOS;
              2033 5ELCID0256 AQUELLAS UOS ACOMIENDO ****, ABBAT DON SANCHO;
              6932 5ELCID0886 SOBRESTO TODO, **** QUITO, MINAYA,
              8110 5ELCID1035 **** & DOS FIJOS DALGO QUITAR UOS HE LOS CUERPOS & DARUOS
                              E DE MANO.
              8155 5ELCID1040 **** & A OTROS DOS DAR UOS HE DE MANO.
              8178 5ELCID1042 SABET, NON UOS DARE **** VN DINERO MALO;
              8858 5ELCID1128 CAMPEADOR, FAGAMOS LO QUE **** PLAZE.
             10022 5ELCID1273 SI **** PLOGUIERE, MINAYA, & NON UOS CAYA EN PESAR,
             10566 5ELCID1339 RAZONAS POR VUESTRO VASSALLO & **** TIENE POR SE@OR.
             13013 5ELCID1651 **** GRADO, %ID, & AL PADRE SPIRITAL.
             13142 5ELCID1666 AQUELOS ATAMORES **** LOS PONDRAN DELANT & VEREDES QUANLES SON,
             13457 5ELCID1706 ****, %ID DON RODIRGO, EN BUEN ORA %INXIESTES ESPADA,
             13791 5ELCID1748 **** ME OMILLO, DUE@AS, GRANT PREZ UOS HE GA@ADO:
             14265 5ELCID1805 DELO QUE **** CAYO VOS NON GRADE%EDES NADA;
             14791 5ELCID1870 ****, MINAYA ALBARFANEZ, & EA PERO VERMUEZ AQUI,
             15349 5ELCID1943 CON TODO ESTO, **** DIXO ALFONSSO
             16012 5ELCID2031  MER%ED UOS PIDO ****, MYO NATURAL SE@OR,
             16069 5ELCID2037 GRADESCOLO A DIOS DEL %IELO & DESPUES ****,
             16164 5ELCID2050 E CRAS FEREMOS LO QUE PLOGIERE ****.
             16487 5ELCID2090 GRA%IAS, DIXO EL REY, **** & ATOD ESTA CORT.
             16835 5ELCID2131 YO UOS PIDO MER%ED ****, REY NATURAL:
             16845 5ELCID2132 PUES QUE CASADES MYS FIJAS, ASI COMMO **** PLAZ,
             17330 5ELCID2192 GRADO AL CRIADOR & ****, %ID, BARBA VELIDA
             17363 5ELCID2197 **** DIGO, MIS FIJAS, DON ELUIRA & DO@A SOL:
             20168 5ELCID2560 QUE PLEGA A DO@A XIMENA & PRIMERO ****
             21490 5ELCID2732 SI NOS FUEREMOS MAIADAS, ABILTAREDES ****,
             23047 5ELCID2936 MER%ED, REY ALFONSSO, DE LARGOS REYNOS **** DIZEN SE@OR
             23792 5ELCID3031 DELO QUE **** PESA AMI DUELE EL CORA%ON;
             23830 5ELCID3036 OMILLOM **** & ALCONDE DO REMOND
             23852 5ELCID3038 DIOS SALUE A NUESTROS AMIGOS & **** MAS, SE@OR
             24775 5ELCID3155 QUES ONDRASSEN CON ELLAS & SIRUIESSEN ****;
             25126 5ELCID3200 GRADO AL CRIADOR & ****, REY SE@OR,
             25807 5ELCID3287 COMMO YO ****, CONDE, ENEL CASTIELLO DE CABRA;
             25818 5ELCID3288 QUANDO PRIS A CABRA, & **** POR LA BARBA,
             26704 5ELCID3411 QUE PLEGA ****, & ATORGAR LO HE YO,
             26737 5ELCID3415 QUANDO **** PLAZE, OTORGO LO YO, SE@OR,
             26753 5ELCID3417 ****, OIARRA, & AUOS, YENEGO XIMENEZ,
             26756 5ELCID3417 AUOS, OIARRA, & ****, YENEGO XIMENEZ,
             27018 5ELCID3451 AVER LAS HEDES ASERUIR, MAL QUE UOS PESE ****.
             27535 5ELCID3517 SI **** LE TOLLIES, EL CAUALLO NO HAURIE TAN BUEN SE@OR.
             27905 5ELCID3560 SI BUENAS LAS TENEDES, PRO ABRAN ****;
       WORD # 620 OCCURS  41 TIMES.
          INDEX OF DIVERSIFICATION =   658.27 WITH STANDARD DEVIATION OF   928.24

AURA          5086 5ELCID0642 POR QUE SEME ENTRO EN MI TIERRA DERECHO ME **** ADAR.
              8884 5ELCID1131 BIEN LOS FERREDES, QUE DUBDA NON Y ****,
              9943 5ELCID1260 QUE SI ALGUNOS FURTARE O MENOS LE FALLAREN, EL AUER ME
                              **** ATORNAR
             10907 5ELCID1380 LEUEDES VN PORTERO, TENGO QUE UOS **** PRO;
             11355 5ELCID1436 POR LO QUE AUEDES FECHO BUEN COSIMENT Y ****.
             16829 5ELCID2130 DAQUEND VAYA CONMIGO; CUEDO QUEL **** PRO.
             24885 5ELCID3169 HYA MAS NON **** DERECHO DE NOS EL %ID CANPEADOR.
             28218 5ELCID3602 ENTODO MYO REYNO NON **** BUENA SABOR.
       WORD # 621 OCCURS   8 TIMES.
          INDEX OF DIVERSIFICATION =  3303.57 WITH STANDARD DEVIATION OF  2775.12

AURAN        20219 5ELCID2567 LOS FIJOS QUE OUIEREMOS EN QUE ***** PARTI%ION.
       WORD # 622 OCCURS   1 TIMES.

AUREDES       1223 5ELCID0157 ALO QUEM SEMEIA, DE LO MIO ******* ALGO;
             16001 5ELCID2029 SIESTO NON FECHES, NON ******* MY AMOR.
             27942 5ELCID3565 SI DEL CAMPO BIEN SALIDES, GRAND ONDRA ******* VOS;
       WORD # 623 OCCURS   3 TIMES.

AUREMOS      10019 5ELCID1269 AGORA AUEMOS RIQUIZA, MAS ******* ADELANT.
             17299 5ELCID2188 HYERNOS UOS ADUGO DE QUE ******* ONDRAN%A;
       WORD # 624 OCCURS   2 TIMES.

AURIA        15316 5ELCID1939 DESTE CASAMIENTO NON ***** SABOR;
             23780 5ELCID3029 CAUALGAD, %ID; SI NON, NON ***** DED SABOR;
       WORD # 625 OCCURS   2 TIMES.

AURIE          667 5ELCID0084 FER LO HE AMIDOS, DE GRADO NON ***** NADA.
              4128 5ELCID0525 QUE ENEL CASTIELLO NON Y ***** MORADA,
```

WORD C# PREFIX CONTEXT

AURIE (CON'T)

9771 5ELCID1241 NIN ENTRARIE ENELA TIGERA, NI VN PELO NON ***** TAIADO,
11087 5ELCID1403 TODO SERIE ALEGRE, QUE NON ***** NINGUN PESAR.
20976 5ELCID2665 NUNQUA ***** DERECHO DE NOS EL %ID CAMPEADOR.
WORD # 626 OCCURS 5 TIMES.
INDEX OF DIVERSIFICATION = 5076.25 WITH STANDARD DEVIATION OF 3662.07

AUUEROS 20597 5ELCID2615 VIOLO EN LOS ******* EL QUE EN BUEN ORA %INXO ESPADA,
WORD # 627 OCCURS 1 TIMES.

AUYA 9478 5ELCID1204 BIEN LA %ERCA MYO %ID, QUE NON Y **** HART;
13717 5ELCID1738 LAS OTRAS GANAN%IAS NON **** RECABDO.
WORD # 628 OCCURS 2 TIMES.

AUYE 23432 5ELCID2984 QUE NON FALIESSEN DELO QUE EN REY **** MANDADO.
WORD # 629 OCCURS 1 TIMES.

AUYEN 134 5ELCID0018 PLORANDO DELOS OIOS, TANTO ***** EL DOLOR.
9298 5ELCID1182 CON EL DELOS MONTES CLAROS ***** GUERRA TAN GRAND,
WORD # 630 OCCURS 2 TIMES.

AUZE 12016 5ELCID1523 ONDRAR UOS HEMOS TODOS, CA TALES LA SU ****,
18701 5ELCID2366 VERLO HEMOS CONDIOS & CON LA UUESTRA ****.
18725 5ELCID2369 PARAUAS DELANT AL CAMPEADOR, SIEMPRE CON LA BUEN ****:
WORD # 631 OCCURS 3 TIMES.

AVALEN%IA 11106 5ELCID1406 ENVIOLOS A MYO %ID, ********* DO ESTA,
WORD # 632 OCCURS 1 TIMES.

AVARONES 23387 5ELCID2979 E ALOS DE CARRION & ******** CASTELLANOS,
WORD # 633 OCCURS 1 TIMES.

AVEDES 20515 5ELCID2604 DE MI & DE UUESTRO PADRE BIEN ****** NUESTRA GRA%IA.
25773 5ELCID3283 QUE ****** UOS, CONDE, POR RETRAER LA MI BARBA?
WORD # 634 OCCURS 2 TIMES.

AVEMOS 19316 5ELCID2446 COMMO AL REY BUCAR ****** ARRANCADO.
19933 5ELCID2529 TANTOS ****** DE AUERES QUE NO SON CONTADOS;
19945 5ELCID2530 POR UOS AUEMOS ONDRA & ****** LIDIADO.
WORD # 635 OCCURS 3 TIMES.

AVENGALUON 20759 5ELCID2636 SALUDAD A MYO AMIGO EL MORO **********:
20850 5ELCID2647 FELOS EN MOLINA CON EL MORO **********.
20958 5ELCID2662 SI PUDIESSEMOS MATAR EL MORO **********,
21000 5ELCID2668 NON TIENE PORIDAD, DIXOLO **********:
21018 5ELCID2671 EL MORO **********, MUCHO ERA BUEN BARRAGAN,
WORD # 636 OCCURS 5 TIMES.
INDEX OF DIVERSIFICATION = 63.75 WITH STANDARD DEVIATION OF 41.88

AVER 9265 5ELCID1178 MALA CUETA ES, SE@ORES, **** MINGUA DE PAN,
19582 5ELCID2481 COMMO SON ONDRADOS & **** VOS GRANT PRO.
26545 5ELCID3388 EN TU AMISTAD NON QUIERO **** RA%ION.
27010 5ELCID3451 **** LAS HEDES ASERUIR, MAL QUE UOS PESE AUOS.
WORD # 637 OCCURS 4 TIMES.

AVERES 9846 5ELCID1249 VELLO MYO %ID CON LOS ****** QUE AUIEN TOMADOS,
25620 5ELCID3262 CON MUY GRAND ONDRA & ****** A NOMBRE;
WORD # 638 OCCURS 2 TIMES.

AVIE 10319 5ELCID1306 QUE EN TIERRAS DE VALEN%IA SE@OR **** OBISPO
24288 5ELCID3097 LA BARBA **** LUENGA & PRISOLA CON EL CORDON,
26460 5ELCID3376 EN LO QUE FABLO **** POCO RECABDO:
WORD # 639 OCCURS 3 TIMES.

AVIEDES 26994 5ELCID3449 ANTES LAS ******* PAREIAS PORA EN BRA%OS LAS TENER,
WORD # 640 OCCURS 1 TIMES.

AVIEN 27796 5ELCID3547 POR VER ESTA LID, CA ***** ENDE SABOR;
WORD # 641 OCCURS 1 TIMES.

AVISTAS 15355 5ELCID1944 QUE UOS VERNIE ******* DO OUIESSEDES SABOR;
22877 5ELCID2914 ADUGA MELOS *******, O AIUNTAS, O A CORTES,
23145 5ELCID2949 QUE GELOS LEUEDES *******, O AIUNTAS, O A CORTES;
WORD # 642 OCCURS 3 TIMES.

AVN 3295 5ELCID0416 *** ERA DE DIA, NON ERA PUESTO EL SOL,
4088 5ELCID0520 *** DELO QUE DIESSEN OUIESSEN GRAND GANAN%IA.
5908 5ELCID0749 ACOSTOS *** AGUAZIL QUE TENIE BUEN CAUALLO,
5958 5ELCID0755 FIRME SON LOS MOROS, *** NOS VAN DEL CAMPO.
9119 5ELCID1161 *** MAS AYUSSO, ADEYNA LA CASA;
10360 5ELCID1312 FUERA EL REY A SAN FAGUNT *** POCO HA,
12232 5ELCID1553 *** LAS FERRADURAS QUITAR GELAS MANDAUA;
12397 5ELCID1574 *** NON SABIE MYO %ID, EL QUE EN BUEN ORA %INXO ESPADA,
14679 5ELCID1857 *** VEA ORA QUE DE MI SEA PAGADO.
16446 5ELCID2085 PERTENE%EN PORA MIS FIJAS & *** PORA MEIORES.

WORD C# PREFIX CONTEXT

AVN (CON'T)

17004 5ELCID2153 *** BIUO SEYENDO, DE MI AYADES ALGO
18470 5ELCID2338 *** VEA EL ORA QUE UOS MERESCA DOS TANTO.
18502 5ELCID2342 *** SI DIOS QUISIERE & EL PADRE QUE ESTA EN ALTO,
22519 5ELCID2868 *** VEAMOS EL DIA QUE VOS PODAMOS VENGAR
23340 5ELCID2973 DESTO QUE LES ABINO *** BIEN SERAN ONDRADOS.
23652 5ELCID3013 *** NON ERA LEGADO EL QUE ENBUEN ORA NA%IO,
24841 5ELCID3164 *** GRAND AMOR NOS FAZE EL %ID CAMPEADOR,
25834 5ELCID3290 LA QUE YO MESSE *** NON ES EGUADA.
26322 5ELCID3357 POR QUE DEXAMOS SUS FIJAS *** NO NOS REPENTIMOS,
WORD # 643 OCCURS 19 TIMES.
INDEX OF DIVERSIFICATION = 1278.28 WITH STANDARD DEVIATION OF 1081.57

AVNA 4626 5ELCID0587 SALIERON DE ALCO%ER **** PRIESSA MUCH ESTRANA.
WORD # 644 OCCURS 1 TIMES.

AXATIUA 9118 5ELCID1160 LEGAN A GUIERA & LEGAN *******,
WORD # 645 OCCURS 1 TIMES.

AXERICA 8599 5ELCID1092 MYO %ID GA@O ******* & A ONDA & ALMENAR,
8721 5ELCID1108 LOS VNOS ******* & LOS OTROS A ALUCAD,
WORD # 646 OCCURS 2 TIMES.

AXUUAR 13012 5ELCID1650 POR CASAR SON UUESTRAS FIJAS, ADUZEN UOS ******.
20256 5ELCID2571 HYO QUIERO LES DAR ****** IIJ MILL MARCOS DE PLATA;
WORD # 647 OCCURS 2 TIMES.

AY 5338 5ELCID0674 BIEN SOMOS NOS VI %IENTOS, ALGUNOS ** DE MAS;
17584 5ELCID2224 NOLO QUIERO FALIR POR NADA DE QUANTO ** PARADO;
25539 5ELCID3253 MER%ED, ** REY SE@OR, POR AMOR DE CARIDAD
27046 5ELCID3455 SI ** QUI RESPONDA ODIZE DE NO,
WORD # 648 OCCURS 4 TIMES.

AYA 1401 5ELCID0179 %ID, BESO UUESTRA MANO ENDON QUE LA YO ***.
6815 5ELCID0870 MYO %ID RUY DIAZ DE DIOS *** SU GRA%IA
13486 5ELCID1709 LAS FERIDAS PRIMERAS QUE LAS *** YO OTORGADAS.
22884 5ELCID2915 COMMO *** DERECHO DE YFANTES DE CARRION,
23168 5ELCID2952 QUE *** MYO %ID DERECHO DE YFANTES DE CARRION.
23292 5ELCID2967 E QUE NON *** RENCURA PODIENDO YO VEDALLO.
23334 5ELCID2972 SALUDAD MELOS ATODOS, ENTRELLOS *** ESPA%IO;
WORD # 649 OCCURS 7 TIMES.
INDEX OF DIVERSIFICATION = 3654.50 WITH STANDARD DEVIATION OF 4051.12

AYADES 1604 5ELCID0205 AUN VEA EL DIA QUE DEMI ****** ALGO
10444 5ELCID1324 QUEL ****** MER%ED, SIUOS VALA EL CRIADOR
12987 5ELCID1647 YA MUGIER ONDRADA, NON ****** PESAR
13032 5ELCID1653 NON ****** PAUOR POR QUE ME VEADES LIDIAR,
13126 5ELCID1664 NON ****** MIEDO, CATODO ES UUESTRA PRO;
15385 5ELCID1948 ESTAS VISTAS OLAS ****** UOS,
16576 5ELCID2100 AL CRIADOR PLEGA QUE ****** ENDE SABOR.
17009 5ELCID2153 AVN BIUO SEYENDO, DE MI ****** ALGO
20480 5ELCID2600 QUE ****** UUESTROS MENSSAIES EN TIERRAS DE CARRION.
22502 5ELCID2865 DON ELUIRA & DO@A SOL, CUYDADO NON ******,
WORD # 650 OCCURS 10 TIMES.
INDEX OF DIVERSIFICATION = 2321.00 WITH STANDARD DEVIATION OF 2714.40

AYAMOS 15432 5ELCID1955 ****** VISTAS QUANDO LO QUIERE MYO SE@OR.
18705 5ELCID2367 DIXO MYO %ID: ****** MAS DE VAGAR.
20015 5ELCID2539 DESTO QUE ELLOS FABLARON NOS PARTE NON ******:
WORD # 651 OCCURS 3 TIMES.

AYAN 18405 5ELCID2329 QUE SEAN EN PAS & NON **** Y RA%ION.
29086 5ELCID3715 AGORA LAS **** QUITAS HEREDADES DE CARRION.
WORD # 652 OCCURS 2 TIMES.

AYDES 6884 5ELCID0880 QUEL ***** MER%ED, SIEL CRIADOR UOS VALA.
WORD # 653 OCCURS 1 TIMES.

AYFANTES 24716 5ELCID3148 ESTO LES DEMANDO ******** DE CARRION:
WORD # 654 OCCURS 1 TIMES.

AYNA 1671 5ELCID0214 MYO %ID & SUS CONPA@AS CAUALGAN TAN ****.
13227 5ELCID1676 DOS FALLAN CON LOS MOROS COMETIEN LOS TAN ****.
WORD # 655 OCCURS 2 TIMES.

AYNAL 16235 5ELCID2059 CATANDOL SEDIE LA BARBA, QUE TAN ***** CRE%IERA.
WORD # 656 OCCURS 1 TIMES.

AYR 27153 5ELCID3470 NOS ANTES ABREMOS *** ATIERRAS DE CARRION.
WORD # 657 OCCURS 1 TIMES.

AYRADO 715 5ELCID0090 QUANDO EN BURGOS ME VEDARON COMPRA & EL REY ME A ******,
891 5ELCID0114 YA LO VEDES QUE EL REY LEA ******.
1216 5ELCID0156 YA ME EXCO DE TIERRA, CA DEL REY SO ******.
6396 5ELCID0815 AL REY ALFONSSSO QUE ME A ******

WORD C# PREFIX CONTEXT

AYRADO (CON'T)

```
                    6897 5ELCID0882 CMNE ******, QUE DE SE@CR NON HA GRA%IA,
        WORD # 658 CCCURS    5 TIMES.
           INDEX OF DIVERSIFICATION =  1544.50 WITH STANDARD DEVIATION OF  2426.64

AYROLO              4971 5ELCID0629 ****** EL REY ALFONSSO, DE TIERRA ECHADO LO HA,
        WORD # 659 CCCURS    1 TIMES.

AYUDA              16601 5ELCID2103 TREZIENTOS MARCOS DE PLATA EN ***** LES DO YO,
        WORD # 660 CCCURS    1 TIMES.

AYUSO               2807 5ELCID0354 CORRIO LA SANGRE POR EL ASTIL *****, LAS MANOS SE OUO DE VNTAR,
                    3381 5ELCID0426 E POR LA LOMA ***** PIENSSAN DE ANDAR.
                    3537 5ELCID0446 FITA ***** & POR GUADALFAIARA, FATA ALCALA LEGEN LAS ALGARAS,
                    3948 5ELCID0501 E POR EL COBDO ***** LA SANGRE SESTELANDO,
                    4286 5ELCID0546 POR ESSAS TIERRAS ***** QUANTO PUEDEN ANDAR.
                    4331 5ELCID0551 E PASSO AALFAMA, LA FOZ ***** UA,
                    4538 5ELCID0577 COIO SALON ***** LA SU SE@A ALZADA,
                    4642 5ELCID0589 COIOS SALON *****, CON LOS SOS ABUELTA NADI.
                    6011 5ELCID0762 POR LA LORIGA ***** LA SANGRE DESTELLADO;
                    6136 5ELCID0781 POR EL COBDO ***** LA SANGRE DESTELLANDO.
                    6721 5ELCID0858 PASO SALON *****, AGUIJO CABA DELANT,
                   13605 5ELCID1724 POR EL COBDO ***** LA SANGRE DESTELLANDO.
                   19365 5ELCID2453 POR EL COBDO ***** LA SANGRE DESTELLANDO;
        WORD # 661 OCCURS   13 TIMES.
           INDEX OF DIVERSIFICATION =  1378.83 WITH STANDARD DEVIATION OF  2348.01

AYUSSO              9121 5ELCID1161 AVN MAS ******, ADEYNA LA CASA;
        WORD # 662 CCCURS    1 TIMES.

AZ                  5536 5ELCID0697 VERIEDES ARMAR SE MOROS, APRIESSA ENTRAR EN **.
                    5618 5ELCID0707 VO METER LA UUESTRA SE@A EN AQUELA MAYOR **;
                    5649 5ELCID0711 ESPOLONO EL CAUALLO, E METIOL ENEL MAYOR **.
                    5727 5ELCID0722 TODOS FIEREN ENEL ** DO ESTA PERO VERMUEZ.
        WORD # 663 OCCURS    4 TIMES.

AZEMILAS           21286 5ELCID2705 MANDARON CARGAR LAS ******** CON GRANDES AUERES,
        WORD # 664 OCCURS    1 TIMES.

AZEMILLAS          19645 5ELCID2490 EOTRAS ********* & CAMELOS LARGOS
        WORD # 665 CCCURS    1 TIMES.

AZES                5548 5ELCID0699 E FIZIERON DOS **** DE PEONES MEZCLADOS, QUILOS PODRIE CONTAR?
                    5556 5ELCID0700 LAS **** DE LOS MOROS YAS MUEUEN ADELANT,
                   18937 5ELCID2396 EN LAS **** PRIMERAS EL CAMPEADOR ENTRAUA,
        WORD # 666 OCCURS    3 TIMES.

BA                  1362 5ELCID0174 RACHEL AMYO %ID LA MANOL ** BESAR:
        WORD # 667 OCCURS    1 TIMES.

BADO               22578 5ELCID2876 ODIZEN **** DE REY, ALLA YUAN POSAR,
        WORD # 668 CCCURS    1 TIMES.

BALTASAR            2667 5ELCID0337 MELCHIOR & GASPAR & ********, ORO & TUS & MIRRA
        WORD # 669 OCCURS    1 TIMES.

BAN                 2364 5ELCID0298 TORNOS A SONRISAR; LEGAN LE TODOS, LA MANOL *** BESAR.
                   16499 5ELCID2092 *** BESAR LAS MANOS ALQUE EN ORA BUENA NA%IO;
        WORD # 670 CCCURS    2 TIMES.

BANDAS             24250 5ELCID3092 SOBRESTO VNA PIEL VERMEIA, LAS ****** DORO SON,
        WORD # 671 OCCURS    1 TIMES.

BANDO               5953 5ELCID0754 OY EN ESTE DIA DE UOS ABRE GRAND *****;
                   23632 5ELCID3010 E CON ELLOS GRAND ***** QUE ADUXIERON A LA CORT:
                   24420 5ELCID3113 NIN TODOS LOS DEL ***** DE YFANTES DE CARRION.
        WORD # 672 OCCURS    3 TIMES.

BARATA              9665 5ELCID1228 ENEL PASSAR DE XUCAR Y VERIEDES ******,
        WORD # 673 OCCURS    1 TIMES.

BARBA               2126 5ELCID0268 MER%ED, YA %ID, ***** TAN COMPLIDA
                    2181 5ELCID0274 ENCLINO LAS MANOS EN LA SU ***** VELIDA,
                    7254 5ELCID0930  DIOS, COMMO ES ALEGRE LA ***** VELIDA,
                    7921 5ELCID1011 Y BEN%IO ESTA BATALLA PORO ONDRO SU *****,
                    9651 5ELCID1226 ARRANCOLOS MYO %ID EL DELA LUENGA *****.
                    9740 5ELCID1238 YAL CRE%E LA ***** & VALE ALLONGANDO;
                   12514 5ELCID1587 VISTIOS EL SOBREGONEL; LUENGA TRAHE LA *****;
                   13120 5ELCID1663 PRISOS ALA ***** EL BUEN %ID CAMPEADOR:
                   16232 5ELCID2059 CATANDOL SEDIE LA *****, QUE TAN AYNAL CRE%IERA.
                   17332 5ELCID2192 GRADO AL CRIADOR & AUOS, %ID, ***** VELIDA
                   19052 5ELCID2410 VERTE AS CON EL %ID, EL DE LA ***** GRANT,
                   19546 5ELCID2476 AL%O LA MANO, ALA ***** SE TOMO:
                   22214 5ELCID2829 AL%O LA SU MANO, ALA ***** SE TOMO;
                   22236 5ELCID2832 PAR AQUESTA ***** QUE NADI NON MESSO,
                   24287 5ELCID3097 LA ***** AVIE LUENGA & PRISOLA CON EL CORDON,
```

WORD C# PREFIX CONTEXT

BARBA (CON'T)

24505 5ELCID3124 ALA ***** QUE AUIE LUENGA & PRESA CONEL CORDON;
25C09 5ELCID3185 AL%AUA LA MANC, ALA ***** SE TCMO;
25014 5ELCID3186 PAR AQUESTA ***** QUE NADI NON MESSO,
25704 5ELCID3273 DEXOLA CRE%ER & LUENGA TRAE LA *****;
25756 5ELCID3280 ESSORA EL CAMPEADCR PRISOS ALA *****;
25780 5ELCID3283 QUE AVEDES UOS, CONDE, POR RETRAER LA MI *****?
25821 5ELCID3288 QUANDO PRIS A CABRA, & AUCS POR LA *****,
27344 5ELCID3494 E SOLTAUA LA ***** & SACCLA DEL CORCON.
29070 5ELCID3713 PRISOS ALA ***** RUY DIAZ SO SE@OR;
WORD # 674 CCCURS 24 TIMES.
INDEX OF DIVERSIFICATION = 1170.48 WITH STANDARD DEVIATION OF 1300.10

BARBADO 6200 5ELCID0789 LA COFIA FRONZIDA DIOS, COMMO ES BIEN *******
WORD # 675 OCCURS 1 TIMES.

BARCAS 12824 5ELCID1627 ENTRARON SOBRE MAR, EN LAS ****** SON METIDOS,
WORD # 676 OCCURS 1 TIMES.

BAR%ILONA 7462 5ELCID0957 LEGARON LAS NUEUAS ALCONDE DE *********,
25080 5ELCID3195 DEL CONDE DE REMONT VERENGEL DE ********* LA MAYOR.
WORD # 677 OCCURS 2 TIMES.

BARNAX 26091 5ELCID3325 QUE MATARAS EL MORO & QUE FIZIERAS ******;
WORD # 678 OCCURS 1 TIMES.

BARRAGAN 21022 5ELCID2671 EL MORO AVENGALUON, MUCHO ERA BUEN ********,
WORD # 679 OCCURS 1 TIMES.

BASTIDOS 537 5ELCID0068 DE TODO CONDUCHO BIEN LOS OUO ********.
WORD # 680 OCCURS 1 TIMES.

BASTIR 672 5ELCID0085 CON UUESTRO CONSEGO ****** QUIERO DOS ARCHAS;
WORD # 681 OCCURS 1 TIMES.

BATALLA 5239 5ELCID0662 MESNADAS DE MYO %ID EXIR QUERIEN ALA *******,
5452 5ELCID0688 SI VEN%IEREMOS LA *******, CRE%REMOS EN RICTAD.
6225 5ELCID0793 QUANDO TAL ******* AUEMOS ARANCADO.
6386 5ELCID0814 DESTA ******* QUE AUEMOS ARANCADA;
6861 5ELCID0876 VEN%IO DOS REYES DE MOROS EN AQUESTA *******.
7684 5ELCID0984 QUE A MENOS DE ******* NOS PUEDEN DEN QUITAR.
7712 5ELCID0987 EL CONDE DON REMONT DAR NOS HA GRANT *******,
7723 5ELCID0989 AMENOS DE ******* NON NOS DEXARIE POR NADA.
7737 5ELCID0990 PUES ADELLANT YRAN TRAS NOS, AQUI SEA LA *******;
7887 5ELCID1008 VEN%IDO A ESTA ******* EL QUE EN BUEN ORA NASCO;
7917 5ELCID1011 Y BEN%IO ESTA ******* PORO ONDRO SU BARBA,
8016 5ELCID1023 PUES QUE TALES MAL CAL%ADOS ME VEN%IERON DE *******.
9644 5ELCID1225 APRES DELA VERTA OUIERON LA *******,
18344 5ELCID2321 YA EN ESTA ******* A ENTRAR ABREMOS NOS;
18388 5ELCID2327 POR ENTRAR EN ******* DESEAN CARRION.
18664 5ELCID2362 ESTA ******* EL CRIADOR LA FERA,
19189 5ELCID2427 VEN%IO LA ******* MARAUILLOSA & GRANT.
19535 5ELCID2475 DESPUES QUE ESTA ******* VEN%IERON & AL REY BUCAR MATO;
19612 5ELCID2485 DESTA ******* QUE HAN ARRANCADO
27860 5ELCID3555 QUE NON FUESSEN EN LA ******* LAS ESPADAS TAIADORES
28737 5ELCID3669 POR QUANTO AUEDES FECHO VEN%IDA AUEDES ESTA *******.
WORD # 682 OCCURS 21 TIMES.
INDEX OF DIVERSIFICATION = 1173.90 WITH STANDARD DEVIATION OF 2530.00

BATIEN 28337 5ELCID3618 ****** LOS CAUALLOS CON LOS ESPOLONES,
WORD # 683 OCCURS 1 TIMES.

BAUIECA 12526 5ELCID1589 POR NOMBRE EL CAUALLO ******* CAUALGA.
12538 5ELCID1591 DES DIA SE PRE%IO ******* EN QUANT GRANT FUE ESPA@A.
13527 5ELCID1714 DIO SALTO MYO %ID EN ******* EL SO CAUALLO;
13768 5ELCID1745 ASSI ENTRO SOBRE *******, EL ESPADA EN LA MANO.
16800 5ELCID2127 SOBREL SO CAUALLO ******* MYO %ID SALTO DAUA;
18921 5ELCID2394 AGUIJO A *******, EL CAUALLO QUE BIEN ANDA,
19123 5ELCID2419 MAS ******* EL DE MIO %ID ALCAN%ANDO LO VA.
WORD # 684 OCCURS 7 TIMES.
INDEX OF DIVERSIFICATION = 1098.50 WITH STANDARD DEVIATION OF 1226.00

BESAR 17049 5ELCID2159 ***** LAS MANOS, ESPEDIR SE DE REY ALFONSSO:
WORD # 685 OCCURS 1 TIMES.

BEGAS 27237 5ELCID3481 ACABO DE TRES SEMANAS, EN ***** DE CARRION,
WORD # 686 OCCURS 1 TIMES.

BELARON 27769 5ELCID3544 DE NOCHE ******* LAS ARMAS & ROGARON AL CRIADOR.
WORD # 687 OCCURS 1 TIMES.

BELLEM 2643 5ELCID0334 EN ****** APARE%IST, COMMO FUE TU VELUNTAD;
WORD # 688 OCCURS 1 TIMES.

BELMEZ 28471 5ELCID3636 EL ****** CON LA CAMISA & CON LA GUARNIZON
WORD # 689 OCCURS 1 TIMES.

WORD C# PREFIX CONTEXT

BELTRAN 23591 5ELCID3004 EL CCNDE DON FRUELLA & EL CONDE DON *******.
WORD # 690 OCCURS 1 TIMES.

BEN%IO 7915 5ELCID1011 Y ****** ESTA BATALLA PCRO ONDRO SU BARBA,
WORD # 691 OCCURS 1 TIMES.

BENDICTIONES 17701 5ELCID2240 DIOLES ************, LA MISSA A CANTADO.
WORD # 692 OCCURS 1 TIMES.

BENDI%ION 26790 5ELCID3421 QUE UOS LAS DE ACNDRA & A *********.
26924 5ELCID3439 ELLOS LAS PRISIERCN A ONDRA & A *********;
WORD # 693 OCCURS 2 TIMES.

BENDI%IONES 17597 5ELCID2226 E PRENDAN *********** & VAYAMOS RECABDANDO.
WORD # 694 OCCURS 1 TIMES.

BENDIXIERON 20543 5ELCID2608 AMOS LAS *********** & DIERON LES SU GRA%IA.
WORD # 695 OCCURS 1 TIMES.

BENDIZIENDOL 4254 5ELCID0541 LOS MOROS & LAS MORAS ************ ESTAN.
WORD # 696 OCCURS 1 TIMES.

BERLANGA 22587 5ELCID2877 ALA CASA DE ******** POSADA PRESA HAN.
WORD # 697 OCCURS 1 TIMES.

BES 4578 5ELCID0582 LAS OTRAS A *** LIEUA, VNA TIENDA A DEXADA.
WORD # 698 OCCURS 1 TIMES.

BESA 6875 5ELCID0879 **** UOS LOS PIES & LAS MANOS AMAS,
10552 5ELCID1338 **** UOS LAS MANOS & QUE LOS PRENDADES UOS;
14657 5ELCID1854 E EMBIA UOS DOZIENTOS CAUALLOS, & **** UOS LAS MANOS.
22790 5ELCID2904 POR MI **** LE LA MANO DALMA & DE CORA%ON,
23056 5ELCID2937 LOS PIES & LAS MANOS VOS **** EL CAMPEADOR;
23135 5ELCID2948 POR ESTO UOS **** LAS MANOS, COMMO VASSALLO A SE@OR,
23863 5ELCID3040 **** UOS LAS MANOS, & MIS FIJAS AMAS ADOS,
WORD # 699 OCCURS 7 TIMES.
INDEX OF DIVERSIFICATION = 2830.33 WITH STANDARD DEVIATION OF 3131.31

BESABA 23034 5ELCID2935 ****** LE LOS PIES AQUEL MU@O GUSTIOZ;
WORD # 700 OCCURS 1 TIMES.

BESAD 11407 5ELCID1443 POR MI AL CAMPEADOR LAS MANOS LE *****
15990 5ELCID2028 ***** LAS MANOS, CA LOS PIES NO;
WORD # 701 OCCURS 2 TIMES.

BESALDE 10065 5ELCID1275 DESI POR MI ******* LA MANO EFIRME GELO ROGAD
WORD # 702 OCCURS 1 TIMES.

BESAMOS 14594 5ELCID1846 POR MYO %ID EL CAMPEADOR TODO ESTO VOS *******;
27999 5ELCID3574 ******* VOS LAS MANOS, COMMO A REY & A SE@OR,
WORD # 703 OCCURS 2 TIMES.

BESAN 14573 5ELCID1844 ***** LA TIERRA & LOS PIES AMOS:
26604 5ELCID3397 ***** LAS MANOS AL REY DON ALFONSSO,
WORD # 704 OCCURS 2 TIMES.

BESANDO 22669 5ELCID2889 ******* LAS AAMAS, TORNOS DE SONRRISAR:
WORD # 705 OCCURS 1 TIMES.

BESAR 1363 5ELCID0174 RACHEL AMYO %ID LA MANOL BA *****:
2106 5ELCID0265 LORAUA DELOS OIOS, QUISOL ***** LAS MANOS:
2365 5ELCID0298 TORNOS A SONRISAR; LEGAN LE TODOS, LA MANOL BAN *****.
2930 5ELCID0369 DO@A XIMENA AL %ID LA MANOL VA *****,
16500 5ELCID2092 BAN ***** LAS MANOS ALQUE EN ORA BUENA NA%IO;
17671 5ELCID2235 A MYO %ID & A SU MUGIER VAN ***** LA MANO.
27493 5ELCID3512 FUE ***** LA MANO A SO SE@OR ALFONSSO;
WORD # 706 OCCURS 7 TIMES.
INDEX OF DIVERSIFICATION = 4354.00 WITH STANDARD DEVIATION OF 5816.01

BESARAN 13856 5ELCID1755 ENTRAREDES EN PREZ, & ******* UUESTRAS MANOS.
WORD # 707 OCCURS 1 TIMES.

BESAREDES 27002 5ELCID3450 AGORA ********* SUS MANOS & LAMAR LAS HEDES SE@ORAS,
WORD # 708 OCCURS 1 TIMES.

BESARON 1190 5ELCID0153 ASSI COMMO ENTRARON, AL %ID ******* LE LAS MANOS.
1238 5ELCID0159 DON RACHEL & VIDAS A MYO %ID ******* LE LAS MANOS.
13968 5ELCID1769 LEUANTARON SE TODAS & ******* LE LAS MANOS,
14692 5ELCID1858 ESTO PLOGO A MUCHOS & ******* LE LAS MANOS.
14849 5ELCID1877 ******* LE LAS MANOS & ENTRARON A POSAR;
17310 5ELCID2190 ******* LE LAS MANOS LA MUGIER & LAS FIJAS AMAS,
22716 5ELCID2895 ******* LAS MANOS LAS FIJAS AL PADRE.

WORD C# PREFIX CONTEXT

BESARON (CON'T)

```
                26798 5ELCID3423 ******* LAS MANOS DEL REY DON ALFONSSO,
        WORD # 709 OCCURS    8 TIMES.
           INDEX OF DIVERSIFICATION =  3657.29 WITH STANDARD DEVIATION OF  4488.26

BESAS            9877 5ELCID1252 QUE NINGUN OMNE DELOS SOS QUES LE NON SPIDIES, ONOL ***** LA MANO,
        WORD # 710 OCCURS    1 TIMES.

BESASSE         23684 5ELCID3017 QUE ******* LAS MANOS AL REY SO SE@OR:
        WORD # 711 OCCURS    1 TIMES.

BESAUA          10412 5ELCID1320 ****** LE LAS MANOS & FABLO TAN APUESTO:
                10427 5ELCID1322 ****** UOS LAS MANOS MYO %ID LIDIADOR,
                14376 5ELCID1818 CON SALUDES DEL %ID QUE LAS MANOS LE ******:
        WORD # 712 OCCURS    3 TIMES.

BESAUAN         12676 5ELCID1608 MADRE & FIJAS LAS MANOS LE *******.
                20540 5ELCID2607 AL PADRE & ALA MADRE LAS MANOS LES *******;
        WORD # 713 OCCURS    2 TIMES.

BESO             1394 5ELCID0179 %ID, **** UUESTRA MANO ENDON QUE LA YO AYA.
                 5486 5ELCID0692 AL %ID **** LA MANO, LA SE@A UA TOMAR.
                 6990 5ELCID0894 **** LE LAS MANOS MINAYA ALBARFANEZ:
                 7185 5ELCID0921 **** LE LA BOCA & LOS OIOS DELA CARA.
                10800 5ELCID1367 MYNAYA ALBARFANEZ LAS MANOS LE ****.
                16083 5ELCID2039 HYNOIOS FITOS LAS MANOS LE ****,
                16165 5ELCID2051 **** LE LA MANO MYO CID, LO OTORGO.
                16645 5ELCID2108 MYO %ID GELOS RE%IBE, LAS MANOS LE ****:
                16953 5ELCID2146 TOMAD AQUESTO, & **** UUESTRAS MANOS.
                23815 5ELCID3034 **** LE LA MANO & DESPUES LE SALUDO;
                24687 5ELCID3145 MYO %ID LA MANO **** AL REY & EN PIE SE LEUANTO;
                24972 5ELCID3180 RE%IBIO LAS ESPADAS, LAS MANOS LE ****,
                25106 5ELCID3198 **** LE LA MANO, EL ESPADA TOMO & RE%IBIO.
                26735 5ELCID3414 LEUANTOS MYO %ID, AL REY LAS MANOS LE ****;
                27275 5ELCID3486 MYO %ID AL REY LAS MANOS LE **** & DIXO: PLAZME, SE@OR.
                27439 5ELCID3506 **** UUESTRAS MANOS CON UUESTRA GRA%IA, SE@OR,
        WORD # 714 OCCURS   16 TIMES.
           INDEX OF DIVERSIFICATION =  1735.33 WITH STANDARD DEVIATION OF  2172.07

BESTIAS          8345 5ELCID1061 MANDAD NOS DAR LAS ******* & CAUALGEREMOS PRIUADO;
                17823 5ELCID2255 EN ******* SINES AL C SON MANDADOS;
                21240 5ELCID2699 ELAS ******* FIERAS QUE ANDAN ADERREDOR.
                21643 5ELCID2751 E ALAS AUES DEL MONTE & ALAS ******* DELA FIERA GUISA.
                22123 5ELCID2816 PRISO ******* & VESTIDOS DE PRO,
                23119 5ELCID2946 ALAS ******* FIERAS & ALAS AUES DEL MONT.
                25655 5ELCID3267 ALAS ******* FIERAS & ALAS AUES DEL MONT;
        WORD # 715 OCCURS    7 TIMES.
           INDEX OF DIVERSIFICATION =  2884.00 WITH STANDARD DEVIATION OF  3446.31

BEUED            8030 5ELCID1025 COMED, CONDE, DESTE PAN & ***** DESTE VINO.
        WORD # 716 OCCURS    1 TIMES.

BEUEMOS          8689 5ELCID1104 ******* SO VINO & COMEMOS EL SO PAN.
        WORD # 717 OCCURS    1 TIMES.

BEUER            9670 5ELCID1229 MOROS EN ARUEN%O AMIDOS ***** AGUA.
        WORD # 718 OCCURS    1 TIMES.

BIBDAS          18356 5ELCID2323 ****** REMANDRAN FIJAS DEL CAMPEADOR.
        WORD # 719 OCCURS    1 TIMES.

BIEN               47 5ELCID0007 FFABLO MYO %ID **** & TAN MESURADO:
                  251 5ELCID0032 ASSI COMMO LEGO ALA PUERTA, FALOLA **** %ERRADA,
                  312 5ELCID0039 NON SE ABRE LA PUERTA, CA **** ERA %ERRADA.
                  534 5ELCID0068 DE TODO CONDUCHO **** LOS OUO BASTIDOS.
                  644 5ELCID0082 **** LO VEDES QUE YO NO TRAYO AUER, & HUEBOS ME SERIE
                  680 5ELCID0086 YNCAMOS LAS CARENA, CA **** SERAN PESADAS,
                  687 5ELCID0087 CUBIERTAS DE GUADALME%I E **** ENCLAUEADAS.
                  695 5ELCID0088 LOS GUADAME%IS UERMEIOS & LOS CLAUOS **** DORADOS.
                  963 5ELCID0124 **** LO SABEMOS QUE EL ALGO GA@O,
                 1259 5ELCID0162 E **** GELAS GUARDARIEN FASTA CABO DEL A@O;
                 1489 5ELCID0190 YO, QUE ESTO UOS GANE, **** MERE%IAS CAL%AS.
                 2052 5ELCID0259 **** LAS ABASTAD, YO ASSI UOS LO MANDO;
                 2393 5ELCID0302 EN ANTES QUE YO MUERA, ALGUN **** UOS PUEDA FAR:
                 3065 5ELCID0386 **** SEPA EL ABBAT QUE BUEN GALARDON DELLO PRENDRA.
                 3218 5ELCID0405 VN SUENOL PRISO DUL%E, TAN **** SE ADURMJO.
                 3245 5ELCID0409 MIENTRA QUE VISQUIEREDES **** SE FARA LO TO.
                 3547 5ELCID0447 E **** ACOIAN TODAS LAS GANAN%IAS,
                 3869 5ELCID0490 DO YO UOS ENBIAS **** ABRIA TAL ESPERAN%A.
                 4369 5ELCID0557 **** PUEBLA EL ETERO, FIRME PRENDE LAS POSADAS,
                 4399 5ELCID0560 DERREDOR DEL OTERO, **** %ERCA DEL AGUA,
                 5332 5ELCID0674 **** SOMOS NOS VI %IENTOS, ALGUNOS AY DE MAS;
                 5804 5ELCID0733 QUAL LIDIA **** SOBRE EXORADO ARZON
                 5879 5ELCID0745 **** LO ACORREN MESNADAS DE CHRISTIANOS.
                 6117 5ELCID0778 AMYNAYA ALBARFANEZ **** LANCA EL CAUALLO,
                 6199 5ELCID0789 LA COFIA FRONZIDA  DIOS, COMMO ES **** BARBADO
```

WORD C# PREFIX CONTEXT

BIEN (CON'T)

6331 5ELCID0806 DIOS, QUE **** PAGC A TODOS SUS VASSALLOS,
6343 5ELCID0808 **** LO AGUISA EL QUE EN BUEN ORA NASCO,
6408 5ELCID0817 TODOS CON SIELLAS & MUY **** ENFRENADOS,
6508 5ELCID0830 A NUESTRO AMIGOS **** LES PODEDES DEZIR:
6637 5ELCID0847 QUE **** PAGO A SUS VASSALOS MISMOS
7215 5ELCID0925 MIENTRA UOS VISQUIEREDES, **** ME YRA AMJ, MINAYA
7871 5ELCID1006 LOS PENDONES & LAS LANZAS TAN **** LAS UAN ENPLEANDO,
8280 5ELCID1054 SI **** NON COMEDES, CONDE, DON YO SEA PAGADO,
8328 5ELCID1059 POR QUE EL CONDE DON REMONT TAN **** BOLUIE LAS MANOS.
8373 5ELCID1064 DAN LE TRES PALAFRES MUY **** ENSELLADOS
8877 5ELCID1131 **** LOS FERREDES, QUE CUBDA NON Y AURA,
8920 5ELCID1136 QUIS CADA VNO DELLOS **** SABE LO QUE HA DE FAR.
9470 5ELCID1204 **** LA ZERCA MYO ZID, QUE NON Y AUYA HART;
10185 5ELCID1290 **** ENTENDIDO ES DE LETRAS & MUCHO ACORDADO,
10258 5ELCID1298 QUANDO DIOS PRESTAR NOS QUIERE, NOS **** GELO GRADESCAMOS:
10303 5ELCID1304 DIERON LE EN VALENZIA O **** PUEDE ESTAR RICO.
10464 5ELCID1326 MAGER EN TIERRA AGENA, EL **** FAZE LO SO;
10849 5ELCID1374 **** CASARIEMOS CON SUS FIJAS PORA HUEBOS DE PRO.
10976 5ELCID1389 EL ZID QUE **** NOS QUIERA NADA NON PERDERA.
11565 5ELCID1465 CON OTROS ZIENTO CAUALLEROS **** UOS CONSSIGRA;
11882 5ELCID1507 **** SALIERON DEN ZIENTO QUE NON PAREZEN MAL,
12220 5ELCID1551 EL MORO AUEGALUON **** LOS SIRUIE SIN FALLA,
12338 5ELCID1567 CA **** SABE QUE ALBARFANEZ TRAHE TODO RECABDO;
12607 5ELCID1599 ALA MADRE & ALAS FIJAS **** LAS ABRAZAUA,
12876 5ELCID1634 TODO EL **** QUE YO HE, TODO LO TENGO DELANT:
13241 5ELCID1679 **** FATA LAS TIENDAS DURA AQUESTE ALCAZ,
13512 5ELCID1712 MIO ZID ALOS SOS VASSALOS TAN **** LOS ACORDANDO.
13535 5ELCID1715 DE TODAS GUARNIZONES MUY **** ES ADOBADO.
14075 5ELCID1782 QUANDO A MYO ZID CAYERON TANTOS, LOS OTROS **** PUEDEN FINCAR PAGADOS.
14819 5ELCID1873 QUE **** PARESCADES ANTE RUY DIAZ MYO ZID:
14845 5ELCID1876 TODAS ESTAS NUEUAS A **** ABRAN DE VENIR.
14857 5ELCID1878 **** LOS MANDO SERUIR DE QUANTO HUEBOS HAN.
15163 5ELCID1918 SONRRISOS MYO ZID & **** LOS ABRAZO:
15441 5ELCID1956 ESCRIUIEN CARTAS, **** LAS SELLO,
15526 5ELCID1967 E TANTO PALAFRE QUE **** ANDA,
16941 5ELCID2144 TRAYO VOS XX PALAFRES, ESTOS **** ADOBADOS,
16948 5ELCID2145 E XXX CAUALLOS CORREDORES, ESTOS **** ENSSELLADOS;
16985 5ELCID2150 QUEM FECHES QUE **** SEA GALARDONADO.
16997 5ELCID2152 DEUOS **** SO SERUIDO, & TENGON POR PAGADO;
17046 5ELCID2158 VERIEDES CAUALLEROS, QUE **** ANDANTES SON,
17306 5ELCID2189 GRADID MELO, MIS FIJAS, CA **** UOS HE CASADAS
17354 5ELCID2195 QUANDO UOS NOS CASAREDES **** SEREMOS RICAS.
17379 5ELCID2199 MAS **** SABET VERDAD QUE NON LO LEUANTE YO:
17419 5ELCID2204 **** MELO CREADES, QUE EL UOS CASA, CA NON YO.
17441 5ELCID2206 POR EL SUELO & SUSO TAN **** ENCORTINADO,
17525 5ELCID2217 TODOS LOS DE MYO ZID TAN **** SON ACORDADOS,
17722 5ELCID2243 DIOS, QUE **** TOUIERON ARMAS EL ZID & SUS VASSALOS
17751 5ELCID2246 LOS YFANTES DE CARRION **** AN CAUALGADO.
17863 5ELCID2260 QUI AUER QUIERE PRENDER **** ERA ABASTADO;
17910 5ELCID2266 GRANT **** DIZEN DELLOS, CA SERA AGUISADO.
17947 5ELCID2271 HY MORAN LOS YFANTES **** CERCA DE DOS AÐOS,
18650 5ELCID2360 SI CUETA FUERE, **** ME PODREDES HUUIAR.
18715 5ELCID2368 AFEUOS EL OBISPO DON IHERONIMO MUY **** ARMADO,
18874 5ELCID2388 ENSAYAUAS EL OBISPO, DIOS, QUE **** LIDIAUA
18925 5ELCID2394 AGUIJO A BAUIECA, EL CAUALLO QUE **** ANDA,
19303 5ELCID2444 SEQUE DE LIDIAR **** SODES PAGADOS;
19442 5ELCID2464 POR **** LO DIXO EL ZID, MAS ELLOS LO TOUIERON AMAL.
19505 5ELCID2471 FUERON EN VALENZIA MUY **** ARREADOS,
19879 5ELCID2521 **** UOS ABRAZEN & SIRUAN UOS DE CORAZON.
20296 5ELCID2576 **** LO SABEDES UOS QUE LAS GANE AGUISA DE VARON;
20350 5ELCID2582 SI **** LAS SERUIDES, YO UOS RENDRE BUEN GALARDON.
20514 5ELCID2604 DE MI & DE UUESTRO PADRE **** AVEDES NUESTRA GRAZIA.
20528 5ELCID2606 ASSI COMMO YO TENGO, **** UOS HE CASADAS.
20866 5ELCID2650 DIOS, QUE **** LOS SIRUIO ATODO SO SABOR
20993 5ELCID2667 VN MORO LATINADO **** GELO ENTENDIO;
21350 5ELCID2714 **** LO CREADES, DON ELUIRA & DOÐA SOL,
21805 5ELCID2774 SABET **** QUE SI ELLOS LE VIESSEN, NON ESCAPARA DE MUERT.
22251 5ELCID2834 QUE AMIS FIJAS **** LAS CASARE YO
22955 5ELCID2924 E DELAS ASTURIAS **** A SAN ZALUADOR,
23022 5ELCID2933 LEUANTOS EL REY, TAN **** LOS REZIBIO.
23213 5ELCID2957 FIZ LO POR ****, QUE FFUESSE A SU PRO.
23341 5ELCID2973 DESTO QUE LES ABINO AVN **** SERAN ONDRADOS.
23691 5ELCID3018 **** LO SOPIESSE QUE Y SERIE ESSA NOCH.
23721 5ELCID3022 **** AGUISADO VIENE EL ZID CON TODOS LOS SOS,
24083 5ELCID3070 COMIGO YRA MAL ANDA, QUE ES **** SABIDOR.
24127 5ELCID3076 E QUE NON PARESCAN LAS ARMAS, **** PRESOS LOS CORDONES;
24163 5ELCID3081 DO TALES ZIENTO TOUIER, **** SERE SIN PAUOR.
24226 5ELCID3089 AL PUNO **** ESTAN, CA EL SELO MANDO;
24516 5ELCID3125 EN SOS AGUISAMIENTOS **** SEMEIA VARON.
24747 5ELCID3152 HYO **** LAS QUERIA DALMA & DE CORAZON,
24857 5ELCID3166 **** NOS ABENDREMOS CON EL REY DON ALFONSSO.
24995 5ELCID3183 NOS LE PUEDEN CAMEAR, CA EL ZID **** LAS CONNOSZE;
25090 5ELCID3196 POR ESSO UOS LA DO QUE LA **** CURIEDES UOS.
25360 5ELCID3229 NOS **** LA SABEMOS AQUESTA RAZON,

WORD C# PREFIX CONTEXT

BIEN (CON'T)

25974 5ELCID3311 **** LO SABEDES QUE YC NON PUECO MAS;
26864 5ELCID3432 **** UCS DI VAGAR EN TOCA ESTA CORT,
26965 5ELCID3445 MAS **** SABEMOS LAS MA@AS QUE ELLOS HAN,
27090 5ELCID3461 SI DIOS QUISIERE QUE CESTA **** SALGAMOS NOS,
27372 5ELCID3497 ABRA%OLOS TAN **** & RUEGA LOS DE CORA%ON
27595 5ELCID3523 EL CAMPEADOR ALOS QUE HAN LICIAR TAN **** LOS CASTIGO:
27717 5ELCID3538 MUCHO VIENEN **** ADOBACOS DE CAUALLOS & DE GUARNIZONES,
27938 5ELCID3565 SI DEL CAMPO **** SALIDES, GRAND ONDRA AUREDES VOS;
28078 5ELCID3584 LOS ESCUDOS ALOS CUELLOS QUE **** BLOCADOS SON;
28118 5ELCID3590 QUE CADA VNO DELLOS **** FOS FERIR EL SO.
28132 5ELCID3592 MUY **** ACONPA@ADOS, CA MUCHOS PARIENTES SON.
28243 5ELCID3606 **** GELO DEMCSTRARON ATODOS VJ COMMO SON,
28406 5ELCID3628 **** EN DOS LCGARES EL ESTIL LE QUEBRO.
28626 5ELCID3655 RAXOL LOS PELCS DELA CABE%A, **** ALA CARNE LEGAUA;
29257 5ELCID3735 ALA VNOS PE@OS, QUE **** VOS LC DARARAN SOBRELOS.
WORD # 720 OCCURS 124 TIMES.
INDEX OF DIVERSIFICATION = 236.48 WITH STANCARD DEVIATION OF 237.91

BIENES 19408 5ELCID2459 TODOS ESTOS ****** DEUCS SON & DE UUESTROS VASSALLOS.
WORD # 721 OCCURS 1 TIMES.

BILTADA 14734 5ELCID1863 POR TAN ******* MIENTRE VEN%ER REYES DEL CAMPO,
WORD # 722 OCCURS 1 TIMES.

BILTAN%A 29008 5ELCID3705 GRANT ES LA ******** DE YFANTES DE CARRION.
WORD # 723 OCCURS 1 TIMES.

BILTAR 23752 5ELCID3026 ****** SE QUIERE & ONDRAR ASO SE@OS.
WORD # 724 OCCURS 1 TIMES.

BISTADES 7742 5ELCIDC991 APRETAD LOS CAUALLOS, & ******** LAS ARMAS.
WORD # 725 OCCURS 1 TIMES.

BIUA 8144 5ELCID1038 TANTO QUANTO YO ****, SERE DENT MARAUILLADO.
13849 5ELCID1754 ROGAND AL CRIADOR QUE UCS **** ALGUNT A@O,
WORD # 726 OCCURS 2 TIMES.

BIUADES 7285 5ELCID0934 YA ALBARFANEZ, ******* MUCHOS DIAS . . .
13895 5ELCID1760 SOMOS EN UUESTRA MER%ED, & ******* MUCHOS A@OS
WORD # 727 OCCURS 2 TIMES.

BIUAN 26328 5ELCID3358 MIENTRA QUE ***** PUECEN AUER SOSPIROS:
WORD # 728 OCCURS 1 TIMES.

BIUAR 77 5ELCID0011 ALA EXIDA DE ***** OUIERON LA CORNEIA DIESTRA,
2343 5ELCIDC295 QUANDO LO SOPC MYO %ID EL DE *****,
4325 5ELCIDC550 OTRO DIA MCUICS MYO %ID EL DE *****,
4970 5ELCIDC628 QUE A VNO QUE DIZIEN MYC %ID RUY DIAZ DE *****
5723 5ELCIDC721 YO SO RUY DIAZ, EL %ID CAMPEACOR DE *****
6705 5ELCIDC855 QUANDO QUITO A ALCO%ER MYO %IC EL DE *****,
7499 5ELCID0961 GRANDES TUERTCS ME TIENE MYO %ID EL DE *****.
7566 5ELCIDC969 ADELINAN TRAS MYO %ID EL BUENO DE *****,
7679 5ELCID0983 ESSORA LO CCNNOS%E MIC %IC EL DE *****.
8518 5ELCID1C82 HYDO ES EL CONDE, TCRNOS EL DE *****,
8544 5ELCID1085 AQUIS CONPIE%A LA GESTA DE MYO %ID EL DE *****.
8963 5ELCID1140 CA YO SO RUYDIAZ, MYO %ID EL DE *****
9444 5ELCID1200 CRE%IENDO UA RIQUEZA A MYO %IC EL DE *****.
9989 5ELCID1265 TRES MILL & SEYS %IENTOS AUIE MYO %ID EL DE *****;
10014 5ELCID1268 CON MAS POCCS YXIEMOS DE LA CASA DE *****.
10870 5ELCID1376 MYO %ID ES DE ***** & NCS DELOS CONDES DE CARRION.
10964 5ELCID1387 SALUDAD NOS A MYC %ID EL DE *****,
11198 5ELCID1416 HYR SE QUIERE A VALEN%IA A MYO %ID EL DE *****.
11484 5ELCID1454 AL ORA QUE LO SCPC MYC %IC EL DE *****,
13638 5ELCID1728 MYO %ID EL DE ***** FASTA ALLI LEGO EN ALCAZ,
21072 5ELCID2677 SI NOLO DEXAS POR MYC %IC EL CE *****,
26479 5ELCID3378 QUIEN NOS DARIE NUEUAS DE MYC %IC EL DE *****
WORD # 729 OCCURS 22 TIMES.
INDEX OF DIVERSIFICATION = 1256.24 WITH STANDARD DEVIATION OF 1869.38

BIUAS 21655 5ELCID2752 POR MUERTAS LAS DEXARCN, SABEC, QUE NON POR *****.
22468 5ELCID2861 EUOS A EL LO GRADIC, QUANDC ***** SOMOS NOS.
22508 5ELCID2866 QUANDO UOS SODES SA@AS & ***** & SIN OTRO MAL.
WORD # 730 OCCURS 3 TIMES.

BIUE 6666 5ELCID0850 QUI A BUEN SE@OR SIRUE, SIEMPRE **** EN DELI%IO.
WORD # 731 OCCURS 1 TIMES.

BIUIR 6548 5ELCIDC835 SI NON, ENESTA TIERRA ANGOSTA NON PODRIEMOS *****.
WORD # 732 OCCURS 1 TIMES.

BIUO 630 5ELCIDC080 SI YO ****, DOBLAR UCS HE LA SOLDADA.
10626 5ELCID1346 SEMEIA QUE EN TIERRA DE MOROS NON A **** OMNE,
15492 5ELCID1963 SYO **** SO, ALI YRE SIN FALLA.
17005 5ELCID2153 AVN **** SEYENDO, DE MI AYADES ALGO
WORD # 733 OCCURS 4 TIMES.

WORD C# PREFIX CONTEXT

BIUOS 4886 5ELCID0618 LOS MOROS YAZEN MUERTOS, DE ***** POCOS VEO.
6166 5ELCID0785 TANTOS MOROS YAZEN MUERTOS QUE POCOS ***** A DEXADOS,
WORD # 734 OCCURS 2 TIMES.

BLANCA 1433 5ELCID0183 SOBRELLA VNA SAUANA DE RANZAL & MUY ******.
24211 5ELCID3087 VISTIO CAMISA DE RANZAL TAN ****** COMMO EL SOL,
27336 5ELCID3493 LA CONFIA DE RANZAL QUE ****** ERA COMMO EL SOL,
WORD # 735 OCCURS 3 TIMES.

BLANCAS 18438 5ELCID2333 EN BRAZOS TENEDES MIS FIJAS TAN ******* COMMO EL SOL
24111 5ELCID3074 DE SUSO LAS LORIGAS TAN ******* COMMO EL SOL;
WORD # 736 OCCURS 2 TIMES.

BLANCOS 5769 5ELCID0729 TANTOS PENDONES ******* SALIR VERMEIOS EN SANGRE,
WORD # 737 OCCURS 1 TIMES.

BLOCA 28814 5ELCID3680 POR MEIO DE LA ***** DEL ESCUDOL QUEBRANTO;
WORD # 738 OCCURS 1 TIMES.

BLOCADOS 28079 5ELCID3584 LOS ESCUDOS ALOS CUELLOS QUE BIEN ******** SON;
WORD # 739 OCCURS 1 TIMES.

BOCA 7188 5ELCID0921 BESO LE LA **** & LOS OIOS DELA CARA.
9750 5ELCID1239 DIXO MYO ZID DE LA SU **** ATANTO:
11502 5ELCID1456 DE LA SU **** CONPEZO DE FABLAR:
11976 5ELCID1518 SONRRISANDO SE DELA ****, HYUALO ABRAZAR,
12045 5ELCID1527 SORRISOS DELA **** MINAYA ALBARFANEZ:
18092 5ELCID2289 DIZIENDO DELA ****: NON VERE CARRION
26362 5ELCID3362 CALA, ALEUOSO, **** SIN VERDAD
26422 5ELCID3370 AL PARTIR DELA LID POR TU **** LO DIRAS,
28430 5ELCID3631 QUEBRANTO LA **** DEL ESCUDO, A PART GELA ECHO,
28489 5ELCID3638 POR LA **** AFUERA LA SANGREL SALIO;
WORD # 740 OCCURS 10 TIMES.
INDEX OF DIVERSIFICATION = 2365.78 WITH STANDARD DEVIATION OF 2925.03

BOCADO 7993 5ELCID1021 NON COMBRE VN ****** POR QUANTO HA EN TODA ESPA@A,
WORD # 741 OCCURS 1 TIMES.

BOCAL 16090 5ELCID2040 LEUOS EN PIE & EN LA ***** SALUDO.
WORD # 742 OCCURS 1 TIMES.

BOCAS 139 5ELCID0019 DELAS SUS ***** TODOS DIZIAN UNA RAZON:
WORD # 743 OCCURS 1 TIMES.

BOCLADOS 15542 5ELCID1970 ESCUDOS ******** CON ORO & CON PLATA,
WORD # 744 OCCURS 1 TIMES.

BODAS 16609 5ELCID2104 QUE METAN EN SUS ***** ODO QUISIEREDES UOS;
16819 5ELCID2129 QUI QUIERE YR CONMIGO ALAS *****, O REZEBIR MI DON,
17077 5ELCID2162 SEREMOS ALAS ***** DELOS YFANTES DE CARRION
17766 5ELCID2248 RICAS FUERON LAS ***** EN EL ALCAZAR ONDRADO,
17794 5ELCID2251 QUINZE DIAS CONPLIDOS DURARON EN LAS *****,
17873 5ELCID2261 RICOS TORNAN A CASTIELLA LOS QUE ALAS ***** LEGARON.
WORD # 745 OCCURS 6 TIMES.
INDEX OF DIVERSIFICATION = 251.80 WITH STANDARD DEVIATION OF 261.19

BOLUIE 8329 5ELCID1059 POR QUE EL CONDE DON REMONT TAN BIEN ****** LAS MANOS.
WORD # 746 OCCURS 1 TIMES.

BOLUIERE 24651 5ELCID3140 JURO PAR SANT ESIDRO, EL QUE ******** MY CORT
WORD # 747 OCCURS 1 TIMES.

BOLUIO 6015 5ELCID0763 ****** LA RIENDA POR YR SE LE DEL CAMPO.
28657 5ELCID3659 ****** LA RIENDA AL CAUALLO POR TORNASSE DE CARA;
WORD # 748 OCCURS 2 TIMES.

BORRIANA 8607 5ELCID1093 TIERRAS DE ******** TODAS CONQUISTAS LAS HA.
8737 5ELCID1110 LOS DE ******** LUEGO VENGAN ACA;
WORD # 749 OCCURS 2 TIMES.

BOS 14974 5ELCID1893 MAS PUES *** LO QUEREDES, ENTREMOS EN LA RAZON.
WORD # 750 OCCURS 1 TIMES.

BOUIERCA 4335 5ELCID0552 PASSO A ******** & ATECA QUE ES ADELANT,
WORD # 751 OCCURS 1 TIMES.

BOZ 24873 5ELCID3167 DEMOS LE SUS ESPADAS, QUANDO ASSI FINCA LA ***,
25222 5ELCID3211 QUE AL NO NOS DEMANDASSE, QUE AQUI FINCO LA ***. . .
WORD # 752 OCCURS 2 TIMES.

BRACAS 19137 5ELCID2420 ALCANZOLO EL ZID ABUCAR A TRES ****** DEL MAR,
WORD # 753 OCCURS 1 TIMES.

WORD C# PREFIX CONTEXT

BRA%A 28844 5ELCID3684 DELA OTRA PART VNA ***** GELA ECHO,
WORD # 754 OCCURS 1 TIMES.

BRA%O 5921 5ELCID0750 DIOL TAL ESPADADA CON EL SO DIESTRO *****,
5944 5ELCID0753 CAUALGAD, MYNAYA, UOS SODES EL MYO DIESTRO *****
6132 5ELCIDC780 ESPADA TAIADOR, SANGRIENTO TRAE EL *****,
6363 5ELCIDC810 OYD, MYNAYA, SODES MYO DIESTRO *****
9798 5ELCID1244 CON EL MYNAYA ALBARFFANEZ QUE NOS LE PARTE DE SO *****.
18912 5ELCID2393 EN ***** EL ESCUDO & ABAXO EL ASTA,
19001 5ELCID2404 TANTO ***** CON LORIGA VERIEDES CAER A PART,
24034 5ELCID3063 VOS, MYNAYA ALBARFANEZ, EL MYO ***** MEIOR,
25034 5ELCID3189 TENDIO EL *****, LA ESPADA TIZON LE DIO;
25056 5ELCID3192 TENDIO EL *****, EL ESPADA COLADAL DIO;
WORD # 755 OCCURS 10 TIMES.
INDEX OF DIVERSIFICATION = 2125.11 WITH STANDARD DEVIATION OF 3174.31

BRA%OS 1590 5ELCID0203 RE%IBIOLO EL %ID ABIERTOS AMOS LOS ******:
2029 5ELCID0255 DUES FIJAS DEXO NI@AS & PRENDET LAS EN LOS ******;
3855 5ELCID0488 LOS ****** ABIERTOS RE%IBE A MINAYA:
18433 5ELCID2333 EN ****** TENEDES MIS FIJAS TAN BLANCAS COMMO EL SOL
21272 5ELCID2703 CON SUS MUGIERES EN ****** DEMUESTRAN LES AMOR;
21717 5ELCID2761 PUES NUESTRAS PAREIAS NON ERAN PORA EN ******.
26998 5ELCID3449 ANTES LAS AVIEDES PAREIAS PORA EN ****** LAS TENER,
WORD # 756 OCCURS 7 TIMES.
INDEX OF DIVERSIFICATION = 4233.66 WITH STANDARD DEVIATION OF 5377.69

BRIAL 18108 5ELCID2291 EL MANTO & EL ***** TODO SUZIO LO SACO.
24234 5ELCID3090 SOBRELLA VN ***** PRIMO DE %ICLATON,
26393 5ELCID3366 MAS NON VESTID EL MANTO NIN EL *****.
26449 5ELCID3374 MANTO ARMINO & VN ***** RASTRANDO,
WORD # 757 OCCURS 4 TIMES.

BRIALES 21632 5ELCID2750 MAS DEXAN LAS MARIDAS EN ******* & EN CAMISAS,
WORD # 758 OCCURS 1 TIMES.

BUCAR 18288 5ELCID2314 AQUESTE ERA EL REY *****, SIL OUIESTES CONTAR.
18987 5ELCID2402 LOS DE MYO %ID ALOS DE ***** DELAS TIENDAS LOS SACAN.
19034 5ELCID2408 MYO %ID AL REY ***** CAYOL EN ALCAZ:
19040 5ELCID2409 ACA TORNA, ***** VENIST DALENT MAR,
19062 5ELCID2412 RESPUSO ***** AL %ID: CONFONDA DIOS TAL AMISTAD
19117 5ELCID2418 BUEN CAUALLO TIENE ***** & GRANDES SALTOS FAZ,
19172 5ELCID2425 MATO A *****, AL REY DE ALEN MAR,
19315 5ELCID2446 COMMO AL REY ***** AVEMOS ARRANCADO.
19540 5ELCID2475 DESPUES QUE ESTA BATALLA VEN%IERON & AL REY ***** MATO;
19895 5ELCID2523 AAQUEL REY *****, TRAYDOR PROUADO.
WORD # 759 OCCURS 10 TIMES.
INDEX OF DIVERSIFICATION = 177.56 WITH STANDARD DEVIATION OF 225.70

BUELTA 13899 5ELCID1761 EN ****** CON EL ENTRARON AL PALA%IO,
WORD # 760 OCCURS 1 TIMES.

BUELTO 62 5ELCID0009 ESTO ME AN ****** MYOS ENEMIGOS MALOS.
WORD # 761 OCCURS 1 TIMES.

BUELTOS 4721 5ELCID0599 ******* SON CON ELLOS POR MEDIO DELA LA@A.
5210 5ELCID0659 E DE NOCH EN ******* ANDAN EN ARMAS;
WORD # 762 OCCURS 2 TIMES.

BUEN 146 5ELCID0020 DIOS, QUE **** VASSALO, SI OUIESSE BUEN SE@OR
150 5ELCID0020 DIOS, QUE BUEN VASSALO, SI OUIESSE **** SE@OR
327 5ELCIDC041 YA CAMPEADOR, EN **** ORA %INXIESTES ESPADA
459 5ELCID0058 MYO %ID RUY DIAZ, EL QUE EN **** ORA %INXO ESPADA,
561 5ELCIDC071 YA CANPEADOR, EN **** ORA FUESTES NA%IDO
619 5ELCIDC078 FABLO MYO %ID, EL QUE EN **** ORA %INXO ESPADA:
1367 5ELCIDC175 YA CANPEADOR, EN **** ORA %INXIESTES ESPADA
1501 5ELCID0192 DEMOS LE **** DON, CA EL NO LO HA BUSCADO.
1519 5ELCID0194 VOS LO MERE%EDES, DARUOS QUEREMOS **** DADO,
1529 5ELCIDC195 DE QUE FAGADES CAL%AS & RICA PIEL & **** MANTO.
1581 5ELCID0202 VINO PORA LA TIENDA DEL QUE EN **** ORA NASCO;
1610 5ELCID0206 VENGO, CAMPEADOR, CON TODO **** RECABDO:
1860 5ELCID0236 QUANDO LEGO A SAN PERO EL **** CAMPEADOR;
1932 5ELCID0245 CON TAN GRANT GOZO RE%IBEN AL QUE EN **** ORA NASCO.
2270 5ELCID0285 GRAND IANTAR LE FAZEN AL **** CAMPEADOR.
2517 5ELCID0318 EN SAN PERO A MATINS TANDRA EL **** ABBAT,
3010 5ELCID0379 %ID, DO SON UUESTROS ESFUER%OS? EN **** ORA NASQUIESTES DE MADRE;
3070 5ELCID0386 BIEN SEPA EL ABBAT QUE **** GALARDON DELLO PRENDRA.
3232 5ELCID0407 CAUALGAD, %ID, EL **** CAMPEADOR, CA NUNQUA
3238 5ELCID0408 EN TAN **** PUNTO CAUALGO VARON;
3471 5ELCID0437 TODA LA NOCHE IAZE EN %ELADA EL QUE EN **** ORA NASCO,
3482 5ELCID0439 YA %ID, EN **** ORA %INXIESTES ESPADA
3928 5ELCODC498 FATA QUE YO ME PAGE SOBRE MIO **** CAUALLO,
3995 5ELCID0507 COMIDIOS MYO %ID, EL QUE EN **** ORA FUE NADO,
4389 5ELCID0559 EL **** CANPEADOR QUE EN BUEN ORA NASCO,
4393 5ELCID0559 EL BUEN CANPEADOR QUE EN **** ORA NASCO,

WORD C# PREFIX CONTEXT

BUEN (CON'T)

4847 5ELCID0613 FABLO MYO %ID RUY DIAZ, EL QUE EN **** ORA FUE NADO:
5243 5ELCID0663 EL QUE EN **** ORA NASCO FIRME GELO VEDAUA.
5705 5ELCID0719 A GRANDES VOZES LAMA EL QUE EN **** ORA NASCO:
5813 5ELCID0734 MIO %ID RUY DIAZ EL **** LIDIADOR;
5912 5ELCID0749 ACOSTOS AVN AGUAZIL QUE TENIE **** CAUALLO,
5988 5ELCID0759 MYO %ID RUY DIAZ, EL QUE EN **** ORA NASCO,
6067 5ELCID0770 TAN **** DIA POR LA CHRISTIANDAD,
6183 5ELCID0787 YAS TORNAN LOS DEL QUE EN **** ORA NASCO.
6191 5ELCID0788 ANDAUA MYO %ID SOBRE SO **** CAUALLO,
6349 5ELCID0808 BIEN LO AGUISA EL QUE EN **** ORA NASCO,
6662 5ELCID0850 QUI A **** SE@OR SIRUE, SIEMPRE BIUE EN DELI%IO.
6850 5ELCID0875 MYO %ID RUY DIAZ, QUE EN **** ORA CINXO ESPADA. . .
7033 5ELCID0899 QUIERO UOS DEZIR DEL QUE EN **** ORA NASCO & %INXO ESPADA:
7294 5ELCID0935 NON LO TARDO EL QUE EN **** ORA NASCO,
7853 5ELCID1004 MANDO LOS FERIR MYO %ID, EL QUE EN **** ORA NASCO;
7891 5ELCID1008 VEN%IDO A ESTA BATALLA EL QUE EN **** ORA NASCO;
8269 5ELCID1052 COMIENDO VA EL CONDE DIOS, QUE DE **** GRADO
8276 5ELCID1053 SOBREL SEDIE EL QUE EN **** ORA NASCO:
8358 5ELCID1062 DEL DIA QUE FUE CONDE NON IANTE TAN DE **** GRADO,
8762 5ELCID1114 EL QUE EN **** ORA NASCO COMPE%O DE FABLAR:
9402 5ELCID1195 ESTO DIXO MYO %ID EL QUE EN **** ORA NASCO.
9734 5ELCID1237 CON MYO %ID RUY DIAZ, EL QUE EN **** ORA NASCO.
9900 5ELCID1255 AFEUOS TODO AQUESTO PUESTO EN **** RECABDO.
10273 5ELCID1300 E DAR GELO A ESTE **** CHRISTIANO;
10441 5ELCID1323 LOS PIES & LAS MANOS, COMMO ATAN **** SE@OR,
10512 5ELCID1332 OBISPO FIZO DE SU MANO EL **** CAMPEADOR,
10691 5ELCID1354 E YRIEN PORA VALEN%IA AL **** CAMPEADOR.
11352 5ELCID1436 POR LO QUE AUEDES FECHO **** COSIMENT Y AURA.
11507 5ELCID1457 QUI **** MANDADERO ENBIA, TAL DEUE SPERAR.
11989 5ELCID1520 TAN **** DIA CON UUSCO, MINAYA ALBARFANEZ
12179 5ELCID1546 EL OBISPO DON IHERONIMO, **** CHRISTIANO SIN FALLA,
12192 5ELCID1548 E **** CAUALLO EN DIESTRO QUE UA ANTE SUS ARMAS.
12288 5ELCID1560 AMYO %ID, EL QUE EN **** ORA NASCO,
12405 5ELCID1574 AVN NON SABIE MYO %ID, EL QUE EN **** ORA %INXO ESPADA,
12487 5ELCID1584 EL QUE EN **** ORA NASCO NON LO DETARDAUA:
12573 5ELCID1595 MER%ED, CAMPEADOR, EN **** ORA CINXIESTES ESPADA
12639 5ELCID1603 OYD LO QUE DIXO EL QUE EN **** ORA NASCO:
13087 5ELCID1659 ALEGRAUAS MIO %ID & DIXO: TAN **** DIA ES OY
13122 5ELCID1663 PRISOS ALA BARBA EL **** %ID CAMPEADOR:
13462 5ELCID1706 AUOS, %ID DON RODRIGO, EN **** ORA %INXIESTES ESPADA,
13658 5ELCID1730 DESDALLI SE TORNO EL QUE EN **** ORA NASCO,
14202 5ELCID1797 MYO %ID DON RODRIGO, EL QUE EN **** ORA NASCO,
14502 5ELCID1834 AUER ESTOS MENSAIES DEL QUE EN **** ORA NASCO.
14534 5ELCID1838 ADIO LO AUIEN LOS DEL QUE EN **** ORA NASCO,
14953 5ELCID1890 HYO ECHE DE TIERRA AL **** CAMPEADOR,
15107 5ELCID1910 DEZID A RUY DIAZ, EL QUE EN **** ORA NASCO,
15152 5ELCID1916 QUANDO LO SOPO EL **** CAMPEADOR,
15253 5ELCID1931 QUANDO LO OYO MYO %ID EL **** CAMPEADOR,
15481 5ELCID1961 SALUDAD ME MAYO %ID, EL QUE EN **** ORA %INXO ESPADA;
15535 5ELCID1969 TANTO **** PENDON METER EN BUENAS ASTAS,
15677 5ELCID1988 TANTA BUENA ARMA & TANTO **** CAUALLO COREDOR,
15820 5ELCID2006 RECABDADO HA, COMMO TAN **** VARON,
15835 5ELCID2008 FATA QUES TORNE EL QUE EN **** ORA NASCO.
15886 5ELCID2014 QUANDO VIERON QUE VINIE EL **** CAMPEADOR,
15903 5ELCID2016 DON LO OUO A OIO EL QUE EN **** ORA NASCO,
15933 5ELCID2020 COMMO LO COMIDIA EL QUE EN **** ORA NA%IO,
16184 5ELCID2053 OMILLAMOS NOS, %ID, EN **** ORA NASQUIESTES UOS
16522 5ELCID2094 FABLO EL REY DON ALFONSSO COMMO TAN **** SE@OR:
16795 5ELCID2126 DIOS QUE ESTA EN %IELO DEM DENT **** GALARDON.
17026 5ELCID2155 AFE DIOS DEL %IELO, QUE LO PONGA EN **** LOGAR
17126 5ELCID2167 ADELINAN PORA VALEN%IA, LA QUE EN **** PUNTO GANO.
17533 5ELCID2218 ESTAN PARANDO MIENTES ALQUE EN **** ORA NASCO.
17736 5ELCID2244 TRES CAUALLOS CAMEO EL QUE EN **** ORA NASCO.
17812 5ELCID2253 MYO %ID DON RODRIGO, EL QUE EN **** ORA NASCO,
17887 5ELCID2263 ESPIDIENDOS DE RUY DIAZ, EL QUE EN **** ORA NASCO,
18119 5ELCID2292 EN ESTO DESPERTO EL QUE EN **** ORA NA%IO;
18573 5ELCID2350 OYD LO QUE FABLO EL QUE EN **** ORA NASCO:
18724 5ELCID2369 PARAUAS DELANT AL CAMPEADOR, SIEMPRE CON LA **** AUZE:
18904 5ELCID2392 EL QUE EN **** ORA NASCO LOS OIOS LE FINCAUA,
19114 5ELCID2418 **** CAUALLO TIENE BUCAR & GRANDES SALTOS FAZ,
19223 5ELCID2432 EL QUE EN **** ORA NASCO.
19396 5ELCID2457 EA UOS, %ID, QUE EN **** ORA FUESTES NADO
19608 5ELCID2484 MANDO MYO %ID, EL QUE EN **** ORA NASCO,
20356 5ELCID2582 SI BIEN LAS SERUIDES, YO UOS RENDRE **** GALARDON.
20601 5ELCID2615 VIOLO EN LOS AUUEROS EL QUE EN **** ORA %INXO ESPADA,
20802 5ELCID2641 DE QUANTO EL FIZIERE YOL DAR POR ELLO **** GALARDON.
20819 5ELCID2643 HYAS TORNO PORA VALEN%IA EL QUE EN **** ORA NAS%IO.
21021 5ELCID2671 EL MORO AVENGALUON, MUCHO ERA **** BARRAGAN,
21157 5ELCID2688 CUEMMO DE **** SESO A MOLINA SE TORNO.
22184 5ELCID2825 DE CUER PESO ESTO AL **** REY DON ALFONSSO.
22421 5ELCID2855 AFFE DIOS DELOS %IELOS QUE UOS DE DENT **** GALARDON
22513 5ELCID2867 **** CASAMIENTO PERDIESTES, MEIOR PODREDES GANAR.
22642 5ELCID2885 AL QUE EN **** ORA NASCO LEGAUA EL MENSSAIE;
22742 5ELCID2898 EL QUE EN **** ORA NASCO NON QUISO TARDAR,

WORD C# PREFIX CONTEXT

BUEN (CON'T)

22771 5ELCID2902 EN **** ORA TE CRIE ATI EN LA MI CORT
22820 5ELCID2907 QUEL PESE AL **** REY CALMA & DE CORA%ON.
23303 5ELCID2968 DIZID LE AL CAMPEADCR, CUE EN **** ORA NASCO,
23564 5ELCID3001 EN LOS PRIMEROS VA EL **** REY DON ALFONSSO,
23581 5ELCID3003 AQUESTE FUE PADRE DEL **** ENPERADOR;
23718 5ELCID3021 E YUA RE%EBIR ALQUE EN **** ORA NA%IO.
23742 5ELCID3024 QUANDO LOOVO A DIO EL **** REY DON ALFFONSSO,
24069 5ELCID3068 E MARTIN MUNOZ, QUE EN **** PUNTO NA%IO,
24187 5ELCID3084 NOS DETIENE POR NADA EL QUE EN **** ORA NA%IO:
24192 5ELCID3085 CAL%AS DE **** PA@O EN SUS CAMAS METIO,
24283 5ELCID3096 QUE NON LE CONTALASSEN LOS PELOS AL **** %ID CANPEADOR;
24371 5ELCID3107 QUANDO LO VIERON ENTRAR AL QUE EN **** ORA NA%IO,
24378 5ELCID3108 LEUANTOS EN PIE EL **** REY DON ALFONSSO
24406 5ELCID3111 AGRANT ONDRA LO RE%IBEN AL QUE EN **** ORA NA%IO.
24533 5ELCID3127 ESSORA SE LEUO EN PIE EL **** REY DON ALFONSSO;
24581 5ELCID3132 POR EL AMOR DE MYO %ID EL QUE EN **** ORA NA%IO,
25072 5ELCID3194 PRENDED A COLADA, GANELA DE **** SE@OR,
25243 5ELCID3214 DIXO EL **** REY: ASSILO OTORGO YO.
25400 5ELCID3234 ENTERGEN A MYO %ID, EL QUE EN **** ORA NA%IO;
25497 5ELCID3247 PAGARON LOS YFANTES AL QUE EN **** ORA NASCO;
26205 5ELCID3340 QUANDO SE TORNO EL **** CAMPEADOR,
26751 5ELCID3416 ESSORA DIXO EL REY: DIOS UOS DE DEN **** GALARDON
27209 5ELCID3478 HYO VOS LO SOBRELIEUO COMMO **** VASSALLO FAZE A SE@OR,
27483 5ELCID3510 QUE EN TODAS NUESTRAS TIERRAS NON HA TAN **** VARON.
27543 5ELCID3517 SI AUOS LE TOLLIES, EL CAUALLO NO HAURIE TAN **** SE@OR.
27655 5ELCID3530 ALEGRE FUE DAQUESTO EL QUE EN **** ORA NA%IO;
27822 5ELCID3550 HYAS METIEN EN ARMAS LOS DEL **** CAMPEADOR,
28915 5ELCID3693 MANDO LIBRAR EL CANPO EL **** REY DON ALFONSSO,
28933 5ELCID3695 POR ONDRADOS SE PARTEN LOS DEL **** CAMPEADOR;
29049 5ELCID3710 FABLEMOS NOS DAQUESTE QUE EN **** ORA NA%IO.
29150 5ELCID3722 VED QUAL ONDRA CRE%E AL QUE EN **** ORA NA%IO,
29178 5ELCID3725 A TODOS ALCAN%A ONDRA POR EL QUE EN **** ORA NA%IO.
WORD # 763 OCCURS 142 TIMES.
INDEX OF DIVERSIFICATION = 204.90 WITH STANDARD DEVIATION OF 201.06

BUENA
2113 5ELCID0266 MER%ED, CAMPEADOR, EN ORA ***** FUESTES NADO
3157 5ELCID0397 DE SINIESTRO SANT ESTEUAN, VNA ***** %IPDAD,
9434 5ELCID1199 GRANDES YENTES SE LE ACCIEN DELA ***** CHRISTIANDAD.
9688 5ELCID1232 ***** FUE LA DE VALEN%IA QUANDO GANARON LA CASA,
10122 5ELCID1282 ESSORA DIXO MINAYA: DE ***** VOLUNTAD.
12213 5ELCID1550 ENTRADOS SON A MOLINA, ***** & RICA CASA;
12414 5ELCID1575 SI SERIE CORREDOR OSSI ABRIE ***** PARADA;
12737 5ELCID1617 DESTA GANAN%IA COMME ES ***** & GRAND.
13399 5ELCID1698 ESSORA DIXO EL %ID: DE ***** VOLUNTAD.
15673 5ELCID1988 TANTA ***** ARMA & TANTO BUEN CAUALLO COREDOR,
15681 5ELCID1989 TANTA ***** CAPA & MANTOS & PELLI%ONES;
16210 5ELCID2056 MYO %ID RUY DIAZ, QUE EN ORA ***** NASCO,
16506 5ELCID2092 BAN BESAR LAS MANOS ALQUE EN ORA ***** NA%IO;
17275 5ELCID2185 VENIDES, CAMPEADOR, EN ***** ORA %INXIESTES ESPADA
17341 5ELCID2193 TODO LO QUE UOS FECHES ES DE ***** GUISA.
22623 5ELCID2882 SALIOLOS A RE%EBIR DE ***** VOLUNTAD,
24026 5ELCID3062 E SSU OFRENDA HAN FECHA MUY ***** & CONPLIDA.
25471 5ELCID3244 TANTA ***** ESPADA CONTODA GUARNIZON;
27392 5ELCID3499 AESSOS & ALOS OTROS QUE DE ***** PARTE SON,
28219 5ELCID3602 ENTODO MYO REYNO NON AURA ***** SABOR.
29014 5ELCID3706 QUI ***** DUENA ESCARNE%E & LA DEXA DESPUES,
WORD # 764 OCCURS 21 TIMES.
INDEX OF DIVERSIFICATION = 1344.05 WITH STANDARD DEVIATION OF 1664.05

BUENAS
1758 5ELCID0224 MANDO AL UUESTRO ALTAR ****** DONAS & RICAS;
6731 5ELCID0859 AL EXIR DE SALON MUCHO OUO ****** AUES.
8376 5ELCID1065 E ****** VESTIDURAS DE PELI%ONES & DE MANTOS.
11166 5ELCID1412 HYTODAS LAS DUE@AS CON ELLAS QUANTAS ****** ELLAS HAN.
12598 5ELCID1598 CON DIOS & CON UUSCO ****** SON & CRIADAS.
15539 5ELCID1969 TANTO BUEN PENDON METER EN ****** ASTAS,
15573 5ELCID1974 CON EL REY ATANTAS ****** CONPA@AS.
16710 5ELCID2116 TANTAS ****** VISTIDURAS QUE DALFAYA SON.
17483 5ELCID2212 CON ****** VESTIDURAS & FUERTE MIENTRE ADOBADOS;
19511 5ELCID2472 CON DUCHOS A SAZONES, ****** PIELES & BUENOS MANTOS.
23730 5ELCID3023 ****** CONPA@AS QUE ASSI AN TAL SE@OR.
27900 5ELCID3560 SI ****** LAS TENEDES, PRO ABRAN AUOS;
WORD # 765 OCCURS 12 TIMES.
INDEX OF DIVERSIFICATION = 2375.55 WITH STANDARD DEVIATION OF 1580.71

BUENO
4731 5ELCID0600 DIOS, QUE ***** ES EL GOZO POR AQUESTA MA@ANA
5176 5ELCID0655 AL ***** DE MYO %ID EN ALCO%ER LEUAN %ERCAR.
5467 5ELCID0690 COMMO SODES MUY *****, TENER LA EDES SIN ARCH;
5848 5ELCID0740 GALIN GAR%IA, EL ***** DE ARAGON,
7564 5ELCID0969 ADELINAN TRAS MYO %ID EL ***** DE BIUAR,
11270 5ELCID1426 EL ***** DE MINAYA PENSOLAS DE ADOBAR
11298 5ELCID1430 EL ***** DE MINAYA PENSSAR QUIERE DE CAUALGAR;
12481 5ELCID1583 RE%IBIR SALIEN LAS DUENAS & AL ***** DE MINAYA.
13296 5ELCID1686 OY ES DIA ***** & MEIOR SERA CRAS:
14248 5ELCID1803 EL ***** DE MYO %ID NON LO TARDO POR NADA:

```
WORD                C#  PREFIX                         CONTEXT

BUENO (CON'T)

             16530 5ELCID2095 GRADO & GRA%IAS, CID, CCMMO TAN *****, & PRIMERO AL CRIADOR,
             19823 5ELCID2513 EL ***** DE ALBARFANEZ, CAUALLERO LIDIADOR,
             24089 5ELCID3071 E GALIND GAR%IEZ, EL ***** DARAGON;
      WORD # 766 OCCURS  13 TIMES.
         INDEX OF DIVERSIFICATION =  1612.17 WITH STANDARD DEVIATION OF  1449.14

BUENOS        3406 5ELCID0430 VASSALLOS TAN ****** POR CCRA%ON LO AN,
              3523 5ELCID0444 LAN%A, CAUALLEROS ****** QUE ACONPANE@ A MINAYA.
              4745 5ELCID0602 TIENEN ****** CAUALLOS, SABET, ASU GUISA LES ANDAN;
              5775 5ELCID0730 TANOS ****** CAUALLCS SIN SOS DUENOS ANDAR.
              5896 5ELCID0747 MAGER DE PIE ****** COLPES VA DANDO.
              6149 5ELCID0783 QUE A CASTIELLA YRAN ****** MANDADOS,
             10281 5ELCID1301 VOS, QUANDO YDES A CASTIELLA, LEUAREDES ****** MANDADOS.
             11891 5ELCID1508 EN ****** CAUALLOS A PETRALES & A CASCAUELES,
             13650 5ELCID1729 CON OTROS QUEL CONSIGEN DE SUS ****** VASSALLOS.
             14058 5ELCID1781 DELOS ****** & OTORGADOS CAYERON LE MILL & D CAUALLOS;
             15052 5ELCID1903 SED ****** MENSSAGEROS, & RUEGO UOS LO YO
             15552 5ELCID1971 MANTOS & PIELLES E ****** %ENDALES DADRIA?
             18128 5ELCID2293 VIO CER%ADO EL ESCA@O DE SUS ****** VARONES:
             18517 5ELCID2343 AMOS LOS MYOS YERNOS ****** SERAN EN CAPO.
             19310 5ELCID2445 ACARRION DE UOS YRAN ****** MANDADOS,
             19437 5ELCID2463 QUANDO AGORA SON ******, ADELANT SERAN PRE%IADOS.
             19514 5ELCID2472 CON DUCHOS A SAZONES, BUENAS PIELES & ****** MANTOS.
             19573 5ELCID2480 MANDADOS ****** YRAN DELLOS A CARRION,
             19913 5ELCID2526 ****** MANDADOS YRAN ATIERRAS DE CARRION.
             20902 5ELCID2655 ****** SE@OS CAUALLOS ALOS YFANTES DE CARRION.
             23995 5ELCID3058 ENTRE MINAYA & LOS ****** QUE Y HA
             24096 5ELCID3072 CON ESTOS CUNPLANSSE %IENTO DELOS ****** QUE Y SON.
             24963 5ELCID3179 MARAUILLAN SE DELLAS TODAS LOS OMNES ****** DELA CORT.
             27615 5ELCID3526 ****** MANDADOS ME VAYAN A VALEN%IA DE VOS.
             27788 5ELCID3546 MUCHOS SE JUNTARON DE ****** RICOS OMNES
             28063 5ELCID3582 ADUZEN LES LOS CAUALLOS ****** & CORREDORES,
             28097 5ELCID3587 DERREDOR DELLOS MUCHOS ****** VARONES.
      WORD # 767 OCCURS  27 TIMES.
         INDEX OF DIVERSIFICATION =   948.65 WITH STANDARD DEVIATION OF  1083.81

BUE@A          476 5ELCID0060 DERREDOR DEL VNA ***** CONPA@A.
             11232 5ELCID1421 POR YR CON ESTAS DUENAS ***** CONPANA SE FAZE.
      WORD # 768 OCCURS   2 TIMES.

BUE@OS        6974 5ELCID0892 ****** & VALIENTES PORA MYO %ID HUYAR,
      WORD # 769 OCCURS   1 TIMES.

BUESTAS       5681 5ELCID0716 ABAXAN LAS LAN%AS A ******* DELOS PENDONES,
      WORD # 770 OCCURS   1 TIMES.

BULIDOR      17167 5ELCID2172 EVAY ASUR GON%ALEZ, QUE ERA *******,
      WORD # 771 OCCURS   1 TIMES.

BURGALES       510 5ELCID0065 MARTIN ANTOLINEZ, EL ******** CONPLIDO,
              1512 5ELCID0193 MARTIN ANTOLINEZ, UN ******** CONTADO,
              5823 5ELCID0736 MARTIN ANTOLINEZ, EL ******** DE PRO,
             11524 5ELCID1459 E MARTIN ANTOLINEZ, VN ******** LEAL,
             11836 5ELCID1500 E MARTIN ANTOLINEZ, EL ******** NATURAL,
             15706 5ELCID1992 MARTIN MUNOZ & MARTIN ANTOLINEZ, EL ******** DE PRO,
             24055 5ELCID3066 E MARTIN ANTOLINEZ, EL ******** DE PRO,
             25051 5ELCID3191 A MARTIN ANTOLINEZ, EL ******** DE PRO,
      WORD # 772 OCCURS   8 TIMES.
         INDEX OF DIVERSIFICATION =  3504.86 WITH STANDARD DEVIATION OF  2938.96

BURGESAS       125 5ELCID0017 BURGESES & ******** POR LAS FINIESTRAS SON,
      WORD # 773 OCCURS   1 TIMES.

BURGESES       123 5ELCID0017 ******** & BURGESAS POR LAS FINIESTRAS SON,
      WORD # 774 OCCURS   1 TIMES.

BURGLES      22278 5ELCID2837 E MARTIN ANTOLINEZ, EL ******* DE PRO,
      WORD # 775 OCCURS   1 TIMES.

BURGOS          85 5ELCID0012 E ENTRANDO A ****** OUIERON LA SINIESTRA.
               110 5ELCID0015 MYO %ID RUY DIAZ POR ****** ENTRAUA,
               174 5ELCID0023 ANTES DELA NOCHE EN ****** DEL ENTRO SU CARTA,
               412 5ELCID0051 PARTIOS DELA PUERTA, POR ****** AGUIJAUA,
               492 5ELCID0062 VEDADA LAN CONPRA DENTRO EN ****** LA CASA,
               706 5ELCID0090 QUANDO EN ****** ME VEDARON COMPRA & EL REY ME A AYRADO,
               771 5ELCID0098 PASSO POR ******, AL CASTIELLO ENTRAUA,
              1175 5ELCID0151 QUE GELO NON VENTANSSEN DE ****** OMNE NADO.
              1569 5ELCID0201 EXIDO ES DE ****** & ARLAN%ON A PASXADO,
              1825 5ELCID0232 TORNAUAS MARTIN ANTOLINEZ A ****** & MYO %ID AAGUIJAR
              6439 5ELCID0822 EN SANTA MARIA DE ****** QUITEDES MILL MISSAS;
             11281 5ELCID1427 DELOS MEIORES GUARIMIENTOS QUE EN ****** PUDO FALAR,
             11367 5ELCID1438 SI NON, DEXAREMOS ******, YR LO HEMOS BUSCAR.
             24558 5ELCID3130 LA VNA FUE EN ******, & LA OTRA EN CARRION,
      WORD # 776 OCCURS  14 TIMES.
         INDEX OF DIVERSIFICATION =  1881.54 WITH STANDARD DEVIATION OF  3798.84
```

WORD C# PREFIX CONTEXT

BUSCA 7535 5ELCID0966 MAS QUANDO EL MELO *****, YR GELO HE YO DEMANDAR.
WORD # 777 OCCURS 1 TIMES.

BUSCADO 1508 5ELCID0192 DEMOS LE BUEN DON, CA EL NO LO HA *******.
21962 5ELCID2794 AGRANT PRIESSA SERE ******* YO;
WORD # 778 OCCURS 2 TIMES.

BUSCAR 4146 5ELCID0528 ****** NOS YE EL REY ALFONSSO CON TODA SU MESNADA.
4182 5ELCID0532 %ERCA ES EL REY ALFONSSO & ****** NOS VERNA.
7025 5ELCID0898 SI NULLA DUBDA YO A MYO %ID ****** GANAN%IA.
8427 5ELCID1071 SI ME VINIEREDES ******, FALLAR ME PODREDES;
8435 5ELCID1072 E SI NON, MANDEDES ******; O ME DEXAREDES
8465 5ELCID1076 DE VENIR UOS ****** SOL NON SERA PENSSADO.
11371 5ELCID1438 SI NON, DEXAREMOS BURGOS, YR LO HEMOS ******.
11819 5ELCID1498 VIRTOS DEL CAMPEADOR ANCS VIENEN ******.
12828 5ELCID1628 VAN ****** A VALEN%IA A MYO %ID DON RODRIGO.
15403 5ELCID1951 FASTA DO LO FALLASSEMOS ****** LO YREMOS NOS,
18743 5ELCID2371 POR ESSO SALI DE MI TIERRA & VIN UOS ******,
19733 5ELCID2502 NO LOS YRE ******, EN VALEN%IA SERE YO,
WORD # 779 OCCURS 12 TIMES.
INDEX OF DIVERSIFICATION = 1416.00 WITH STANDARD DEVIATION OF 1280.38

BUSCARE 3364 5ELCID0424 DESPUES QUI NOS ******* FALLAR NOS PODRA.
WORD # 780 OCCURS 1 TIMES.

BUSCAREN 24155 5ELCID3080 SI DESOBRA ******** YFANTES DE CARRION,
WORD # 781 OCCURS 1 TIMES.

BUSCARIE 4007 5ELCID0509 QUEL ******** MAL CON TODAS SUS MESNADAS.
WORD # 782 OCCURS 1 TIMES.

BUSCASTES 27957 5ELCID3567 CA TODOS LO SABEN QUE LO ********* VOS.
WORD # 783 OCCURS 1 TIMES.

BUSCO 23544 5ELCID2998 ENEMIGO DE MIO SID, QUE SIEMPREL ***** MAL,
WORD # 784 OCCURS 1 TIMES.

C 2007 5ELCID0253 EUADES AQUI PORA DO@A XIMENA DOUOS * MARCHOS.
3488 5ELCID0440 VOS CON * DE AQUESTA NUESTRA CONPA@A,
3565 5ELCID0449 E YO CON LO * AQUI FINCARE EN LA %AGA,
4034 5ELCID0513 A CADA VNO DELLOS CAEN * MARCHOS DE PLATA,
6327 5ELCID0805 EN LA SU QUINTA AL %ID CAEN * CAUALLOS.
8863 5ELCID1129 A MI DEDES * CAUALLEROS, QUE NON UOS PIDO MAS,
9708 5ELCID1234 ATODOS LOS MENORES CAYERON * MARCOS DE PLATA.
10055 5ELCID1274 DAR LE QUIERO * CAUALLOS, & UOS YO GELOS LEUAR;
11223 5ELCID1420 E EL SE TENIE * QUE ACUXIERA CALLA;
13752 5ELCID1743 CON * CAUALLEROS A VALEN%IA ES ENTRADO,
17826 5ELCID2255 EN BESTIAS SINES AL * SON MANDADOS;
WORD # 785 OCCURS 11 TIMES.
INDEX OF DIVERSIFICATION = 1580.90 WITH STANDARD DEVIATION OF 1259.47

CA 39 5ELCID0006 SOSPIRO MYO %ID, ** MUCHO AUIE GRANDES CUYDADOS.
100 5ELCID0014 ALBRICIA, ALBARFFANEZ, ** ECHADOS SOMOS DE TIERRA
235 5ELCID0030 ASCONDEN SE DE MYO %ID, ** NOL OSAN DEZIR NADA.
311 5ELCID0039 NON SE ABRE LA PUERTA, ** BIEN ERA %ERRADA.
526 5ELCID0067 NON LO CONPRA, ** EL SELO AUIE CONSIGO;
573 5ELCID0073 ** ACUSADO SERE DELO QUE UOS HE SERUIDO,
679 5ELCID0086 YNCAMOS LAS DARENA, ** BIEN SERAN PESADAS,
721 5ELCID0091 NON PUEDO TRAER EL AUER, ** MUCHO ES PESADO,
1165 5ELCID0150 NON VIENE ALA PUEENT, ** POR EL AGUA APASSADO,
1212 5ELCID0156 YA ME EXCO DE TIERRA, ** DEL REY SO AYRADO.
1266 5ELCID0163 ** ASSIL DIERAN LA FE & GELO AUIEN IURADO,
1317 5ELCID0169 ** AMOUER A MYO %ID ANTE QUE CANTE EL GALLO.
1350 5ELCID0173 ** MIENTRA QUE VISQUIESSEN REFECHOS ERAN AMOS.
1503 5ELCID0192 DEMOS LE BUEN DON, ** EL NO LO HA BUSCADO.
1540 5ELCID0197 MERE%ER NOLO HEDES, ** ESTO ES AGUISADO:
1652 5ELCID0212 MUCHO ES HUEBOS, ** %ERCA VIENE EL PLAZO.
2192 5ELCID0276 LEGOLAS AL CORA%ON, ** MUCHO LAS QUERIA.
2534 5ELCID0321 ** EL PLAZO VIENE A %ERCA, MUCHO AUEMOS DE ANDAR.
2737 5ELCID0346 RESU%ITEST A LAZARO, ** FUE TU VOLUNTAD;
2770 5ELCID0350 EL VNO ES EN PARAYSO, ** EL OTRO NON ENTRO ALA;
3098 5ELCID0390 ** EN YERMO O EN POBLADO PODER NOS HAN ALCAN%AR.
3234 5ELCID0407 CAUALGAD, %ID, EL BUEN CAMPEADOR, ** NUNQUA
4141 5ELCID0527 MOROS EN PAZ, ** ESCRIPTA ES LA CARTA,
4808 5ELCID0609 LUEGO LEGAUAN LOS SOS, ** FECHA ES EL ARRANCADA.
4908 5ELCID0621 COIAMOS LOS DE DENTRO, ** EL SENORIO TENEMOS,
5194 5ELCID0657 CRECEN ESTOS VIRTOS, ** YENTES SON SOBEIANAS.
5369 5ELCID0678 ONDRASTES UOS, MINAYA, ** AUER UOS LO YEDES DE FAR.
6169 5ELCID0786 ** EN ALCAZ SJN DUBDA LES FUERON DANDO.
6746 5ELCID0861 PESO ALOS DE ALCO%ER, ** PROLES FAZIE GRANT.
7954 5ELCID1016 PLOGO A MYO %ID, ** GRANDES SON LAS GANAN%IAS.
8190 5ELCID1044 ** HUEBOS MELO HE & PORA ESTOS MYOS VASSALLOS

WORD C# PREFIX CONTEXT

CA (CON'T)

```
                    8506 5ELCID1081 VNA DES LEATANZA ** NON LA FIZO ALGUANDRE.
                    8955 5ELCID1140 ** YO SO RUYDIAZ, MYO %ID EL DE BIUAR
                    9408 5ELCID1196 TORNAUAS A MURUIEDRO, ** EL SE LA A GANADA.
                   11617 5ELCID1472 YO FFINCARE EN VALEN%IA, ** LA TENGO POR HEREDAD.
                   11798 5ELCID1496 ESTO NON DETARDO, ** DE CORA%ON LO HAN;
                   11983 5ELCID1519 ENEL OMBRO LO SALUDA, ** TAL ES SU HUSAIE:
                   12012 5ELCID1523 ONDRAR UOS HEMOS TODOS, ** TALES LA SU AUZE,
                   12075 5ELCID1531 VAYAMOS POSAR, ** LA %ENA ES ADOBADA.
                   12307 5ELCID1563 ** DELO QUE MAS AMAUA YAL VIENE EL MANDADO.
                   12337 5ELCID1567 ** BIEN SABE QUE ALBARFANEZ TRAHE TODO RECABDO;
                   13622 5ELCID1726 SALIOS LE DE SOL ESPADA, ** MUCHOL ANDIDO EL CAUALLO,
                   14542 5ELCID1839 CUEDAN SE QUE ES ALMOFALLA, ** NON VIENEN CON MANDADO;
                   15993 5ELCID2028 BESAD LAS MANOS, ** LOS PIES NO;
                   16423 5ELCID2083 ** NON HAN GRANT HEDAND E DE DIAS PEQUENAS SON.
                   16479 5ELCID2089 DAD LAS AQUI QUISIEREDES UOS, ** YO PAGADO SO.
                   16660 5ELCID2110 VOS CASADES MIS FIJAS, ** NON GELAS DO YO.
                   17305 5ELCID2189 GRADID MELO, MIS FIJAS, ** BIEN UOS HE CASADAS
                   17426 5ELCID2204 BIEN MELO CREADES, QUE EL UOS CASA, ** NON YO.
                   17913 5ELCID2266 GRANT BIEN DIZEN DELLOS, ** SERA AGUISADO.
                   18317 5ELCID2318 ** VEYEN TANTAS TIENDAS DE MOROS DE QUE NON AUIE SABOR.
                   18456 5ELCID2336 ** DAQUELOS MOROS YO SO SABIDOR;
                   18543 5ELCID2347 ** NUNQUA LO VIERAN, CA NUEUOS SON LEGADOS.
                   18547 5ELCID2347 CA NUNQUA LO VIERAN, ** NUEUOS SON LEGADOS.
                   18627 5ELCID2357 CURIELOS QUI QUIER, ** DELLOS POCO MINCAL.
                   19632 5ELCID2488 ASSI LO FAZEN TODOS, ** ERAN ACORDADOS.
                   19725 5ELCID2501 ELLOS LO TEMEN, ** NON LO PIESSO YO:
                   20116 5ELCID2554 ** DE NATURA SOMOS DE CONDES DE CARRION.
                   21004 5ELCID2669 ACAYAZ, CURIATE DESTOS, ** ERES MYO SE@OR:
                   22830 5ELCID2908 EL CASO MIS FIJAS, ** NON GELAS DI YO;
                   22890 5ELCID2916 ** TAN GRANT ES LA RENCURA DENTRO EN MI CORA%ON.
                   23201 5ELCID2956 ** YO CASE SUS FIJAS CON YFANTES DE CARRION;
                   23483 5ELCID2991 ** Y VERNA MYO %ID EL CAMPEADOR;
                   23492 5ELCID2992 DARLEDES DERECHO, ** RENCURA HA DE UOS.
                   24228 5ELCID3089 AL PUNO BIEN ESTAN, ** EL SELO MANDO;
                   24625 5ELCID3137 TODOS METED Y MIENTES, ** SODES CO@OS%EDORES,
                   24632 5ELCID3138 POR ESCOGER EL DERECHO, ** TUERTO NON MANDO YO.
                   24728 5ELCID3150 ** UOS LAS CASASTES, REY, SABREDES QUE FER OY;
                   24909 5ELCID3172 NOLO PODEMOS NEGAR, ** DOS ESPADAS NOS DIO;
                   24992 5ELCID3183 NOS LE PUEDEN CAMEAR, ** EL %ID BIEN LAS CONNOS%E;
                   25043 5ELCID3190 PRENDET LA, SOBRINO, ** MEIORA EN SE@OR.
                   25279 5ELCID3218 NON ACUERDAN EN CONSSEIO, ** LOS HAUERES GRANDES SON:
                   25389 5ELCID3233 TORNAR GELOS QUIERO, ** TODOS FECHOS SON,
                   25781 5ELCID3284 ** DE QUANDO NASCO ADELI%IO FUE CRIADA,
                   25788 5ELCID3285 ** NON ME PRISO AELLA FIJO DE MUGIER NADA,
                   25884 5ELCID3298 ** NON PERTENE%IEN FIJAS DE YFAN%ONES.
                   26453 5ELCID3375 VERMEIO VIENE, ** ERA ALMORZADO;
                   26673 5ELCID3406 VOS LAS CASASTES ANTES, ** YO NON,
                   26718 5ELCID3413 ** CRE%E UOS Y ONDRA & TIERRA & ONOR.
                   26899 5ELCID3437 ** GRAND RENCURA HE DE YFANTES DE CARRION.
                   27070 5ELCID3459 ** EN ESTA CORT AFARTO HA PORA VOS,
                   27138 5ELCID3468 DANDOS, REY, PLAZO, ** CRAS SER NON PUEDE.
                   27571 5ELCID3521 ** POR UOS & POREL CAUALLO ONDRADOS SOMO NOS.
                   27645 5ELCID3529 PODEDES OYR DE MUERTOS, ** DE VENCIDOS NO.
                   27758 5ELCID3543 ** GRAND MIEDO OUIERON A ALFONSSO EL DE LEON.
                   27795 5ELCID3547 POR VER ESTA LID, ** AVIEN ENDE SABOR;
                   27828 5ELCID3551 TODOS TRES SE ACUERDAN, ** SON DE VN SE@OR.
                   27951 5ELCID3567 ** TODOS LO SABEN QUE LO BUSCASTES VOS.
                   28134 5ELCID3592 MUY BIEN ACONPA@ADOS, ** MUCHOS PARIENTES SON.
                   28205 5ELCID3601 ** QUI TUERTO QUISIERE FAZER, MAL GELO VEDARE YO,
                   28792 5ELCID3677 EN VAZIO FUE LA LAN%A, ** EN CARNE NOL TOMO.
          WORD # 786 OCCURS   91 TIMES.
             INDEX OF DIVERSIFICATION =    318.48 WITH STANDARD DEVIATION OF    400.92

CABA                6723 5ELCID0858 PASO SALON AYUSO, AGUIJO **** DELANT,
                    6754 5ELCID0862 AGUIJO MYO %ID, YUAS **** DELANT,
          WORD # 787 OCCURS    2 TIMES.

CABADELANT         22569 5ELCID2874 E MINAYA CON LAS DUE@AS YUA **********.
          WORD # 788 OCCURS    1 TIMES.

CABDAL              9602 5ELCID1220 QUANDO SU SE@A ****** SEDIE EN SOMO DEL ALCA%AR.
                   11335 5ELCID1434 SOLTARIEMOS LA GANAN%IA, QUE NOS DIESSE EL ******.
                   15431 5ELCID1954 SOBRE TAIO, QUE ES UNA AGUA ******,
          WORD # 789 OCCURS    3 TIMES.

CABDALES            5544 5ELCID0698 DE PARTE DELOS MOROS DOS SE@AS HA ********,
                   18283 5ELCID2313 CINQUAENTA MILL TIENDAS FINCADAS HA DELAS ********;
          WORD # 790 OCCURS    2 TIMES.

CABE               22844 5ELCID2910 SI DESONDRA Y **** ALGUNA CONTRA NOS,
          WORD # 791 OCCURS    1 TIMES.

CABECAS            21458 5ELCID2728 CORTANDOS LAS *******, MARTIRES SEREMOS NOS:
          WORD # 792 OCCURS    1 TIMES.
```

WORD C# PREFIX CONTEXT

```
CABE%A              10 5ELCID0002 TORNAUA LA ****** & ESAUA LOS CATANDO.
                  2995 5ELCID0377 ATODOS ESPERANDO, LA ****** TORNANDO UA.
                  8480 5ELCID1078 TORNANDO UA LA ****** & CATANDOS ATRAS;
                 13672 5ELCID1732 ALI PRE%IO ABAUIECA DELA ****** FASTA ACABO.
                 18174 5ELCID2299 ANTE MYO %ID LA ****** PREMIO & EL ROSTRO FINCO:
                 26187 5ELCID3338 EL LEON PREMIO LA ******, A MYO %ID ESPERO,
                 28625 5ELCID3655 RAXOL LOS PELOS DELA ******, BIEN ALA CARNE LEGAUA;
        WORD # 793 OCCURS    7 TIMES.
           INDEX OF DIVERSIFICATION =  4768.16 WITH STANDARD DEVIATION OF  1995.13

CABE%AS          19009 5ELCID2405 TANTAS ******* CON YELMOS QUE POR EL CAMPO CAEN,
        WORD # 794 OCCURS    1 TIMES.

CABEL            28829 5ELCID3682 APART LE PRISO, QUE NON ***** CORA%ON;
        WORD # 795 OCCURS    1 TIMES.

CABO               439 5ELCID0056 **** ESSA VILLA EN LA GLERA POSAUA,
                  1263 5ELCID0162 E BIEN GELAS GUARDARIEN FASTA **** DEL A@O;
                  6907 5ELCID0883 POR ACOGELLO A **** DE TRES SEMMANAS.
                  7148 5ELCID0915 QUANDO ESTO FECHO OUO, A **** DE TRES SEMANAS,
                  8393 5ELCID1067 FATA **** DEL ALBERGADA ESCURRIOLOS EL CASTELANO:
                  9125 5ELCID1162 **** DEL MAR TIERRA DE MOROS FIRME LA QUEBRANTA,
                 10723 5ELCID1358 QUANDO EN **** DE MI TIERRA A QUESTAS DUE@AS FUEREN,
                 12545 5ELCID1592 EN **** DEL COSSO MYO %ID DESCALGAUA,
                 13555 5ELCID1717 QUATRO MILL MENOS XXX CON MYO %ID VAN A ****,
                 13576 5ELCID1720 ENTRARON LES DEL OTRO ****.
                 14105 5ELCID1785 LA TIENDA DEL REY DE MARRUECOS, QUE DELAS OTRAS ES ****,
                 18840 5ELCID2384 EYUA LOS FERIR A **** DEL ALBERGADA.
                 23398 5ELCID2981 A **** DE VIJ SEMANAS QUE Y FUESSEN IUNTADOS;
        WORD # 796 OCCURS   13 TIMES.
           INDEX OF DIVERSIFICATION =  1912.25 WITH STANDARD DEVIATION OF  1933.45

CABOSO            1775 5ELCID0226 SPIDIOS EL ****** DE CUER & DE VELUNTAD.
                  7100 5ELCID0908 QUANDO VIO EL ****** QUE SE TARDAUA MINAYA,
                  7375 5ELCID0946 SONRRISOS EL ******, QUE NON LO PUDO ENDURAR:
                  8497 5ELCID1080 LO QUE NON FERIE EL ****** POR QUANTO ENEL MUNDO HA,
                 14167 5ELCID1793 EL OBISPO DON IHERONIMO, ****** CORONADO,
                 14259 5ELCID1804 DO SODES, ******? VENID ACA, MYNAYA;
                 26700 5ELCID3410 RUEGO UOS, %ID, ****** CAMPEADOR,
        WORD # 797 OCCURS    7 TIMES.
           INDEX OF DIVERSIFICATION =  4153.16 WITH STANDARD DEVIATION OF  4755.70

CABRA            25812 5ELCID3287 COMMO YO AUOS, CONDE, ENEL CASTIELLO DE *****;
                 25816 5ELCID3288 QUANDO PRIS A *****, & AUOS POR LA BARBA,
        WORD # 798 OCCURS    2 TIMES.

CA%ADO           13667 5ELCID1731 MUCHO ERA ALEGRE DELO QUE AN ******.
        WORD # 799 OCCURS    1 TIMES.

CADA              4030 5ELCID0513 A **** VNO DELLOS CAEN C MARCHOS DE PLATA,
                  8917 5ELCID1136 QUIS **** VNO DELLOS BIEN SABE LO QUE HA DE FAR.
                  9214 5ELCID1173 EN **** VNO DESTOS A@OS MYO %ID LES TOLIO EL PAN.
                 16591 5ELCID2102 ELLOS VAYAN CON UUSCO, **** QUEN ME TORNO YO.
                 16679 5ELCID2112 QUANDO SALIE EL SOL, QUES TORNASSE **** VNO DON SALIDOS SON.
                 16715 5ELCID2117 **** VNO LO QUE PIDE, NADI NOL DIZE DE NO.
                 17851 5ELCID2259 **** VNO POR SI SOS DONES AUIEN DADOS.
                 18689 5ELCID2365 EL DEBDO QUE A **** VNO A CONPLIR SERA.
                 28115 5ELCID3590 QUE **** VNO DELLOS BIEN FOS FERIR EL SO.
                 28311 5ELCID3614 **** VNO DELLOS MIENTES TIENE AL SO.
                 28350 5ELCID3620 **** VNO DELLOS MIENTES TIENE ALSO;
        WORD # 800 OCCURS   11 TIMES.
           INDEX OF DIVERSIFICATION =  2431.00 WITH STANDARD DEVIATION OF  3498.19

CADEL            23511 5ELCID2994 QUITE MYO REYNO, ***** NON HE SABOR.
        WORD # 801 OCCURS    1 TIMES.

CADIELLA          9136 5ELCID1163 GANARON PENA ********, LAS EXIDAS & LAS ENTRADAS.
                  9148 5ELCID1164 QUANDO EL %ID CAMPEADOR OUO PE@A ********,
                 10493 5ELCID1330 E PE@A ********, QUE ES VNA PE@A FUERT;
        WORD # 802 OCCURS    3 TIMES.

CADRAN           28367 5ELCID3622 CUEDAN SE QUE ESSORA ****** MUERTOS LOS QUE ESTAN ADERREDOR.
        WORD # 803 OCCURS    1 TIMES.

CAE              18961 5ELCID2399 MYO %ID CON LOS SUYOS *** EN ALCAN%A;
                 21219 5ELCID2696 ADIESTRO DEXAN ASANT ESTEUAN, MAS *** ALUEN;
        WORD # 804 OCCURS    2 TIMES.

CAEN              4033 5ELCID0513 A CADA VNO DELLOS **** C MARCHOS DE PLATA,
                  6326 5ELCID0805 EN LA SU QUINTA AL %ID **** C CAUALLOS.
                  9582 5ELCID1217 ENEL AUER MONEDADO XXX MILL MARCOS LE ****,
                 11312 5ELCID1431 AFEUOS RACHEL & VIDAS ALOS PIES LE ****:
                 18996 5ELCID2403 SACAN LOS DELAS TIENDAS, **** LOS EN ALCAZ;
                 19016 5ELCID2405 TANTAS CABE%AS CON YELMOS QUE POR EL CAMPO ****,
```

WORD C# PREFIX CONTEXT

CAEN (CON'T)

WORD # 805 OCCURS 6 TIMES.
INDEX OF DIVERSIFICATION = 2995.60 WITH STANDARD DEVIATION OF 2872.21

CAER 19005 5ELCID2404 TANTO BRA%O CON LORIGA VERIEDES **** A PART,
WORD # 806 OCCURS 1 TIMES.

CAFUYEN 6072 5ELCID0771 ******* LOS MOROS DE LA PART
WORD # 807 OCCURS 1 TIMES.

CALA 26360 5ELCID3362 ****, ALEUOSO, BOCA SIN VERDAD
26508 5ELCID3383 ****, ALEUOSO, MALO & TRAYDOR
WORD # 808 OCCURS 2 TIMES.

CALATAUTH 4500 5ELCID0572 ALOS DE *********, SABET, MALES PESAUA.
WORD # 809 OCCURS 1 TIMES.

CALATAYUCH 6099 5ELCID0775 PARA ********** QUANTO PUEDE SE VA.
6111 5ELCID0777 FATA ********** DURO EL SEGUDAR.
WORD # 810 OCCURS 2 TIMES.

CALATAYUH 5151 5ELCID0651 VINIERON ESSA NOCHE EN ********* POSAR.
WORD # 811 OCCURS 1 TIMES.

CALATAYUT 6605 5ELCID0843 E LOS DE *********, QUE ES MAS ONDRADA,
6740 5ELCID0860 PLOGO ALOS DE TERER & ALOS DE ********* MAS,
WORD # 812 OCCURS 2 TIMES.

CALATAYUTH 4950 5ELCID0626 E ALOS DE ********** NON PLAZE.
5007 5ELCID0633 PERDERAS **********, QUE NON PUEDE ESCAPAR,
WORD # 813 OCCURS 2 TIMES.

CAL%ADA 3178 5ELCID0400 LA ******* DE QUINEA YUA LA TRASPASSAR,
WORD # 814 OCCURS 1 TIMES.

CAL%ADAS 21413 5ELCID2722 ESPUELAS TIENEN ******** LOS MALOS TRAYDORES,
WORD # 815 OCCURS 1 TIMES.

CAL%ADOS 8012 5ELCID1023 PUES QUE TALES MAL ******** ME VEN%IERON DE BATALLA.
WORD # 816 OCCURS 1 TIMES.

CAL%AS 1491 5ELCID0190 YO, QUE ESTO UOS GANE, BIEN MERE%IAS ******.
1524 5ELCID0195 DE QUE FAGADES ****** & RICA PIEL & BUEN MANTO.
7752 5ELCID0992 ELLOS VIENEN CUESTA YUSO, & TODOS TRAHEN ******,
7767 5ELCID0994 NOS CAUALGAREMOS SIELLAS GALLEGAS, & HUESAS SOBRE ******;
24190 5ELCID3085 ****** DE BUEN PA@O EN SUS CAMAS METIO,
WORD # 817 OCCURS 5 TIMES.
INDEX OF DIVERSIFICATION = 5673.75 WITH STANDARD DEVIATION OF 7739.36

CALLAR 20151 5ELCID2558 FABLO FERAN GON%ALEZ & FIZO ****** LA CORT;
26694 5ELCID3409 LEUANTOS EL REY, FIZO ****** LA CORT:
WORD # 818 OCCURS 2 TIMES.

CALLARON 26636 5ELCID3401 AESTO ******** & ASCUCHO TODA LA CORT.
WORD # 819 OCCURS 1 TIMES.

CALLAS 25918 5ELCID3302 FABLA, PERO MUDO, VARON QUE TANTO ******
WORD # 820 OCCURS 1 TIMES.

CALLE 26559 5ELCID3390 DIXO EL REY ALFONSSO: ***** YA ESTA RAZON.
WORD # 821 OCCURS 1 TIMES.

CALLO 23181 5ELCID2953 EL REY VNA GRAND ORA ***** & COMIDIO;
WORD # 822 OCCURS 1 TIMES.

CALO 23079 5ELCID2940 ALTO FUE EL CASAMIENO **** QUISIESTES UOS
WORD # 823 OCCURS 1 TIMES.

CALOS 18600 5ELCID2354 ***** MOROS, CON DIOS, NON FINCARAN EN CANPO.
WORD # 824 OCCURS 1 TIMES.

CALUARIE 2749 5ELCID0347 ALOS IUDIOS TE DEXESTE PRENDER; DO DIZEN MONTE ********
WORD # 825 OCCURS 1 TIMES.

CAMARA 18073 5ELCID2286 FERRAN GON%ALEZ NON VIO ALLI DOS AL%ASSE, NIN ****** ABIERTA NIN
WORD # 826 OCCURS 1 TIMES.

CAMAS 24196 5ELCID3085 CAL%AS DE BUEN PA@O EN SUS ***** METIO,
WORD # 827 OCCURS 1 TIMES.

CAMEAR 24991 5ELCID3183 NOS LE PUEDEN ******, CA EL %ID BIEN LAS CONNOS%E;
WORD # 828 OCCURS 1 TIMES.

CAMEARON 16508 5ELCID2093 ******** LAS ESPADAS ANTEL REY DON ALFONSSO.
WORD # 829 OCCURS 1 TIMES.

WORD C# PREFIX CONTEXT

```
CAMELOS          19647 5ELCID2490 EOTRAS AZEMILLAS & ******* LARGOS
        WORD # 830 OCCURS   1 TIMES.

CAMEO            17732 5ELCID2244 TRES CAUALLOS ***** EL QUE EN BUEN ORA NASCO.
        WORD # 831 OCCURS   1 TIMES.

CAMISA           24207 5ELCID3087 VISTIO ****** DE RAN%AL TAN BLANCA COMMO EL SOL,
                 28474 5ELCID3636 EL BELMEZ CON LA ****** & CON LA GUARNIZON
        WORD # 832 OCCURS   2 TIMES.

CAMISAS          21407 5ELCID2721 PARAN LAS EN CUERPOS & EN ******* & EN %ICLATONES.
                 21538 5ELCID2738 RONPIEN LAS ******* & LAS CARNES AELLAS AMAS ADOS;
                 21584 5ELCID2744 SANGRIENTAS EN LAS ******* & TODOS LOS CICLATONES.
                 21635 5ELCID2750 MAS DEXAN LAS MARIDAS EN BRIALES & EN *******,
        WORD # 833 OCCURS   4 TIMES.

CAMPAL            6157 5ELCID0784 QUE MYO %ID RUY DIAZ LID ****** A VEN%IDA.
                  8744 5ELCID1111 CONPE%AREMOS AQUESTA LID ******,
        WORD # 834 OCCURS   2 TIMES.

CAMPALES         10518 5ELCID1333 E FIZO %INCO LIDES ******** & TODAS LAS ARRANCO.
        WORD # 835 OCCURS   1 TIMES.

CAMPA@AS          2274 5ELCID0286 TANEN LAS ******** EN SAN PERO A CLAMOR.
        WORD # 836 OCCURS   1 TIMES.

CAMPEADOR          241 5ELCID0031 EL ********* ADELINO ASU POSADA;
                   325 5ELCID0041 YA *********, EN BUEN ORA %INXIESTES ESPADA
                   542 5ELCID0069 PAGOS MYO %ID EL ********* & TODOS LOS OTROS QUEUAN ASO %ERUICIO
                   851 5ELCID0109 EL ********* POR LAS PARIAS FUE ENTRADO,
                   909 5ELCID0117 EL ********* DEXAR LAS HA EN UUESTRA MANO,
                  1183 5ELCID0152 AFEUOS LOS ALA TIENDA DEL ********* CONTADO;
                  1607 5ELCID0206 VENGO, *********, CON TODO BUEN RECABDO:
                  1861 5ELCID0236 QUANDO LEGO A SAN PERO EL BUEN *********;
                  2095 5ELCID0264 ANTEL ********* DO@A XIMENA FINCO LOS YNOIOS AMOS,
                  2271 5ELCID0285 GRAND IANTAR LE FAZEN AL BUEN *********.
                  2319 5ELCID0292 TODOS DEMANDAN POR MIO %ID EL *********;
                  2604 5ELCID0329 QUE AMIO %ID EL ********* QUE DIOS LE CURIAS DE MAL:
                  2885 5ELCID0364 POR MYO %ID EL *********, QUE DIOS LE CURIE DE MAL.
                  3150 5ELCID0396 YXIENDOS UA DE TIERRA EL ********* LEAL,
                  3233 5ELCID0407 CAUALGAD, %ID, EL BUEN *********, CA NUNQUA
                  3311 5ELCID0417 MANDO UER SUS YENTES MYO %ID EL *********:
                  3676 5ELCID0464 EL ********* SALIO DE LA %ELADA, CORRIE ACASTEION SIN FALLA.
                  3837 5ELCID0485 FELLOS EN CASTEION, O EL ********* ESTAUA.
                  3846 5ELCID0486 EL CASTIELO DEXO EN SO PODER, EL ********* CAUALGA,
                  3889 5ELCID0493 MUCHO UOS LO GRADESCO, ********* CONTADO.
                  4438 5ELCID0565 QUE EL ********* MYO %ID ALLI AUIE POBLADO,
                  4684 5ELCID0594 ELBUEN ********* LA SU CARA TORNAUA,
                  5361 5ELCID0677 DIXO EL *********:  A MI GUISA FABLASTES;
                  5608 5ELCID0706 EL CRIADOR UOS VALA, %ID ********* LEAL
                  5630 5ELCID0709 DIXO EL *********:  NON SEA, POR CARIDAD
                  5667 5ELCID0714 DIXO EL *********:  VALELDE, POR CARIDAD
                  5721 5ELCID0721 YO SO RUY DIAZ, EL %ID ********* DE BIUAR
                  5856 5ELCID0741 FELEZ MUNOZ SO SOBRINO DEL *********
                  5871 5ELCID0743 ACORREN LA SE@A & A MYO %ID EL *********.
                  6105 5ELCID0776 EL ********* YUAL EN AL CAZ,
                  6557 5ELCID0837 E EL ********* CON SU MESNADA.
                  6716 5ELCID0857 AL%O SU SE@A, EL ********* SE UA,
                  6952 5ELCID0889 MAS DEL %ID ********* YO NON UOS DIGO NADA.
                  7202 5ELCID0923 EL ********* FERMOSO SONRRISAUA:
                  8854 5ELCID1128 *********, FAGAMOS LO QUE AUOS PLAZE.
                  8906 5ELCID1134 COMMO GELO A DICHO, AL ********* MUCHO PLAZE.
                  9145 5ELCID1164 QUANDO EL %ID ********* OUO PE@A CADIELLA,
                  9593 5ELCID1219 ALEGRE ERA EL ********* CON TODOS LOS QUE HA,
                 10513 5ELCID1332 OBISPO FIZO DE SU MANO EL BUEN *********,
                 10586 5ELCID1341 DE TAN FIERAS GANAN%IAS COMMO A FECHAS EL *********
                 10602 5ELCID1343 E PLAZEM DELAS NUEUAS QUE FAZE EL *********;
                 10636 5ELCID1347 QUANDO ASSI FAZE A SU GUISA EL %ID *********
                 10692 5ELCID1354 E YRIEN PORA VALEN%IA AL BUEN *********.
                 10738 5ELCID1359 CATAD COMMO LAS SIRUADES UOS & EL *********.
                 10753 5ELCID1361 NON QUIERO QUE NADA PIERDA EL *********;
                 10777 5ELCID1364 SIRUAN LE SUS HEREDADES DO FUERE EL *********,
                 10813 5ELCID1369 LOS QUE QUISIEREN YR SEUIR AL *********
                 10848 5ELCID1373 MUCHO CRE%EN LAS NUEUAS DE MYO %ID EL *********,
                 10931 5ELCID1383 DESI ADELANT PIENSSE DELLAS EL *********.
                 11403 5ELCID1443 POR MI AL ********* LAS MANOS LE BESAD
                 11816 5ELCID1498 VIRTOS DEL ********* ANOS VIENEN BUSCAR.
                 12571 5ELCID1595 MER%ED, *********, EN BUEN ORA CINXIESTES ESPADA
                 13124 5ELCID1663 PRISOS ALA BARBA EL BUEN %ID *********:
                 13172 5ELCID1669 VOCA%ION ES QUE FIZO EL %ID *********.
                 13491 5ELCID1710 DIXO EL *********: DESA QUI UOS SEAN MANDADAS.
                 13886 5ELCID1759 DELANT EL ********* LOS YNOIOS FINCARON:
                 14055 5ELCID1780 MAGER DE TODO ESTO, EL ********* CONTADO
                 14590 5ELCID1846 POR MYO %ID EL ********* TODO ESTO VOS BESAMOS;
```

WORD C# PREFIX CONTEXT

CAMPEADOR (CON'T)

14929 5ELCID1887 QUE NOS DEMANDEDES FIJAS DEL *********;
14954 5ELCID1890 HYO ECHE DE TIERRA AL BUEN *********,
15012 5ELCID1898 SIRUEM MYO %ID EL *********, EL LO MERE%E,
15063 5ELCID1904 QUE GELO DIGADES ALBUEN *********:
15153 5ELCID1916 QUANDO LO SOPO EL BUEN *********,
15254 5ELCID1931 QUANDO LO OYO MYO %ID EL BUEN *********,
15458 5ELCID1958 LO QUE EL REY QUISIERE, ESSO FERA EL *********.
15655 5ELCID1985 DENTRO EN VALLEN%IA MYO %ID EL *********
15740 5ELCID1997 ESTOS SE ADOBAN POR YR CON EL *********,
15761 5ELCID2000 A AQUESTOS DOS MANDO EL ********* QUE CURIEN A VALEN%IA
15887 5ELCID2014 QUANDO VIERON QUE VINIE EL BUEN *********,
15989 5ELCID2027 LEUANTADOS EN PIE, YA %ID *********,
16008 5ELCID2030 HYNOIOS FITOS SEDIE EL *********:
16157 5ELCID2049 MYO HUESPED SEREDES, %ID *********,
16263 5ELCID2063 EL ********* ALOS SOS LO MANDO
16283 5ELCID2065 DE TAL GUISA LOS PAGA MYO %ID EL *********,
16346 5ELCID2073 COMETER QUIERO VN RUEGO A MYO %ID EL *********;
16422 5ELCID2082 NON ABRIA FIJAS DE CASAR, RESPUSO EL *********,
16637 5ELCID2107 LO QUE UOS PLOGIERE, DELLOS FET, *********.
16691 5ELCID2113 AQUIS METIO EN NUEUAS MYO %ID EL *********;
16765 5ELCID2122 METIOLOS EN PODER DE MYO %ID EL *********:
16781 5ELCID2124 OY DE MAS SABED QUE FER DELLOS, *********.
17261 5ELCID2183 MYO %ID EL ********* AL ALCA%AR ENTRAUA;
17273 5ELCID2185 VENIDES, *********, EN BUENA ORA %INXIESTES ESPADA
17537 5ELCID2219 EL ********* EN PIE ES LEUANTADO:
18026 5ELCID2280 YAZIES EN VN ESCA@O, DURMIE EL *********,
18055 5ELCID2284 ENBRA%AN LOS MANTOS LOS DEL *********,
18247 5ELCID2308 MANDOLO VEDAR MYO %ID EL *********.
18360 5ELCID2323 BIBDAS REMANDRAN FIJAS DEL *********.
18720 5ELCID2369 PARAUAS DELANT AL *********, SIEMPRE CON LA BUEN AUZE:
18940 5ELCID2396 EN LAS AZES PRIMERAS EL ********* ENTRAUA,
19231 5ELCID2433 MYO %ID RUY DIAZ, EL ********* CONTADO,
19531 5ELCID2474 GRANT FUE EL DIA LA CORT DEL *********,
19834 5ELCID2514 E OTROS MUCHOS QUE CRIO EL *********.
19847 5ELCID2516 RE%IBIOLOS MINAYA POR MYO %ID EL *********:
19861 5ELCID2518 ASSI COMMO LEGARON, PAGOS EL *********:
20041 5ELCID2543 PIDAMOS NUESTRAS MUGIERES AL %ID *********,
20064 5ELCID2546 SACAR LAS HEMOS DE VALEN%IA, DE PODER DEL *********;
20130 5ELCID2555 ASSI LAS ESCARNIREMOS ALAS FIJAS DEL *********,
20160 5ELCID2559 SI UOS VALA EL CRIADOR, %ID *********
20223 5ELCID2568 DIXO EL *********: DARUOS HE MYS FIJAS & ALGO DELO MYO;
20371 5ELCID2584 AQUI RE%IBEN LAS FIJAS DEL *********;
20413 5ELCID2590 POR QUE ESCURREN SUS FIJAS DEL ********* ATIERRAS DE CARRION.
20435 5ELCID2593 FINCARON LOS YNOIOS ANTEL %ID *********:
20660 5ELCID2622 CON AQUESTAS NUEUAS VERNAS AL *********.
20740 5ELCID2633 ASSI FAZIAN LOS CAUALLEROS DEL *********.
20932 5ELCID2658 TOD ESTO LES FIZO EL MORO POR EL AMOR DEL %ID *********.
20952 5ELCID2661 HYA PUES QUE ADEXAR AUEMOS FIJAS DEL *********,
20982 5ELCID2665 NUNQUA AURIE DERECHO DE NOS EL %ID *********.
21087 5ELCID2679 ELUEGO LEUARIA SUS FIJAS AL ********* LEAL;
21139 5ELCID2685 DA QUESTE CASAMIENTO QUE GRADE EL *********.
21385 5ELCID2718 HYRAN AQUESTOS MANDADOS AL %ID *********;
21573 5ELCID2742 QUE ASSOMASSE ESSORA EL %ID *********
21664 5ELCID2753 QUAL VENTURA SERIE SI ASSOMAS ESSORA EL %ID *********
21742 5ELCID2765 SOBRINO ERA DEL %ID *********;
22202 5ELCID2827 QUANDO GELO DIZEN A MYO %ID EL *********,
23058 5ELCID2937 LOS PIES & LAS MANOS VOS BESA EL *********;
23104 5ELCID2943 MAL MAIARON SUS FIJAS DEL %ID *********;
23288 5ELCID2966 E COMMO DEN DERECHO A MYO %ID EL *********,
23300 5ELCID2968 DIZID LE AL *********, QUE EN BUEN ORA NASCO,
23458 5ELCID2987 MIEDO HAN QUE Y VERNA MYO %ID EL *********;
23489 5ELCID2991 CA Y VERNA MYO %ID EL *********;
23645 5ELCID3011 EBAYR LE CUYDAN A MYO %ID EL *********.
23678 5ELCID3015 AL QUINTO DIA VENIDO ES MYO %ID EL *********;
23751 5ELCID3025 FIRIOS ATIERRA MYO %ID EL *********;
23814 5ELCID3033 AMEN, DIXO MYO %ID EL *********;
24259 5ELCID3093 SIEMPRE LA VISTE MYO %ID EL *********;
24433 5ELCID3114 EL REY DIXO AL %ID: VENID ACA SER, *********,
24676 5ELCID3143 AGORA DEMANDE MYO %ID EL *********:
24848 5ELCID3164 AVN GRAND AMOR NOS FAZE EL %ID *********,
25121 5ELCID3199 LUEGO SE LEUANTO MYO %ID EL *********;
25212 5ELCID3210 POR ESSOL DIEMOS SUS ESPADAS AL%ID *********,
25255 5ELCID3215 DIXO ALBARFANEZ LEUANTADOS EN PIE EL %ID *********:
25370 5ELCID3230 QUE DERECHO DEMANDA EL %ID *********.
25448 5ELCID3240 PAGEN LE EN APRE%IADURA & PRENDALO EL *********.
25753 5ELCID3280 ESSORA EL ********* PRISOS ALA BARBA;
26000 5ELCID3314 POR EL ********* MUCHO VALIESTES MAS.
26152 5ELCID3333 METISTET TRAS EL ESCA@O DE MYO %ID EL *********
26206 5ELCID3340 QUANDO SE TORNO EL BUEN *********,
26618 5ELCID3398 PIDEN SUS FIJAS A MYO %ID EL *********
26648 5ELCID3402 LEUANTOS EN PIE MYO %ID EL *********;
26701 5ELCID3410 RUEGO UOS, %ID, CABOSO *********,
26811 5ELCID3424 E DESPUES DE MYO %ID EL *********;
26863 5ELCID3431 E QUE NON PESE ESTO AL %ID *********:

WORD C# PREFIX CONTEXT

CAMPEADOR (CON'T)

```
                   26932 5ELCID3440 GRANDES AUERES LES DIO MYO %ID EL *********,
                   27036 5ELCID3453 ASIL CRE%E LA ONDRA A MYO %ID EL *********
                   27161 5ELCID3471 FABLO EL REY CONTRAL *********:
                   27189 5ELCID3475 ENESSORA DIXO EL REY: ACSADAS, *********.
                   27330 5ELCID3492 ALLI SE TOLLIO EL CAPIELO EL %ID *********,
                   27589 5ELCID3523 EL ********* ALOS QUE HAN LIDIAR TAN BIEN LOS CASTIGO:
                   27688 5ELCID3534 FELOS AL PLAZO LOS DEL *********,
                   27738 5ELCID3540 QUE SI LOS PUDIESSEN APARTAR ALOS DEL *********,
                   27823 5ELCID3550 HYAS METIEN EN ARMAS LOS DEL BUEN *********,
                   27934 5ELCID3564 QUE NADA NON MANCARA POR LOS DEL *********.
                   27987 5ELCID3571 TODOS TRES SON ARMADOS LOS DEL *********,
                   27998 5ELCID3573 DIXIERON LOS DEL *********:
                   28113 5ELCID3589 TODOS TRES SON ACORDADOS LOS DEL *********,
                   28190 5ELCID3598 ESTOS TRES CAUALLEROS DE MYO %ID EL *********
                   28310 5ELCID3613 ELLOS YFANTES DE CARRION ALOS DE *********;
                   28934 5ELCID3695 POR ONDRADOS SE PARTEN LOS DEL BUEN *********;
                   28980 5ELCID3701 FELOS EN VALEN%IA CON MYO %ID EL *********:
                   29004 5ELCID3704 ALEGRE FFUE DAQUESTO MYO %ID EL *********.
         WORD # 837 OCCURS 160 TIMES.
            INDEX OF DIVERSIFICATION =   179.90 WITH STANDARD DEVIATION OF   208.27

CAMPO               3934 5ELCID0499 LIDIANDO CON MOROS ENEL *****,
                    4280 5ELCID0545 PASSARON LAS AGUAS, ENTRARON AL ***** DE TORAN%IO,
                    5444 5ELCID0687 SI NOS MURIEREMOS EN *****, EN CASTIELLO NOS ENTRARAN,
                    5930 5ELCID0751 CORTOL POR LA %INTURA, EL MEDIO ECHO EN *****.
                    5962 5ELCID0755 FIRME SON LOS MOROS, AVN NOS VAN DEL *****.
                    6023 5ELCID0763 BOLUIO LA RIENDA POR YR SE LE DEL *****.
                    8898 5ELCID1133 COMMO FIO POR DIOS, EL ***** NUESTRO SERA.
                    9051 5ELCID1152 ROBAUAN EL ***** EPIENSSAN SE DE TORNAR.
                   10216 5ELCID1293 SOSPIRANDO EL OBISPO QUES VIESSE CON MOROS ENEL *****:
                   12163 5ELCID1544 EL ***** DE TORAN%IO LUEGOL ATRAUESSAUAN,
                   13735 5ELCID1740 QUE DIOS LES OUO MER%ED QUE VEN%IERON EL *****.
                   13807 5ELCID1749 VOS TENIENDO VALEN%IA, & YO VEN%I EL *****;
                   13843 5ELCID1753 CON TAL CUM ESTO SE VEN%EN MOROS DEL *****.
                   13995 5ELCID1772 MYNAYA ALBARFANEZ FUERA ERA ENEL *****,
                   14636 5ELCID1851 CON %INQUAENTA MILL ARRANCOLOS DEL *****;
                   14739 5ELCID1863 POR TAN BILTADA MIENTRE VEN%ER REYES DEL *****,
                   15948 5ELCID2022 LAS YERBAS DEL ***** A DIENTES LAS TOMO,
                   19015 5ELCID2405 TANTAS CABE%AS CON YELMOS QUE POR EL ***** CAEN,
                   19213 5ELCID2430 SABET, TODOS DE FIRME ROBAUAN EL *****.
                   19426 5ELCID2461 FARTOS DE LIDIAR CON MOROS ENEL *****.
                   19567 5ELCID2479 QUE LIDIARAN COMIGO EN ***** MYOS YERNOS AMOS ADOS;
                   19890 5ELCID2522 VEN%IEMOS MOROS EN ***** & MATAMOS
                   27611 5ELCID3525 E MUNO GUSTIOZ, FIRMES SED EN ***** AGUISA DE VARONES;
                   27743 5ELCID3541 QUE LOS MATASSEN EN ***** POR DESONDRA DE SO SE@OR.
                   27937 5ELCID3565 SI DEL ***** BIEN SALIDES, GRAND ONDRA AUREDES VOS;
                   28102 5ELCID3588 HYA SALIERON AL ***** DO ERAN LOS MOIONES.
                   28161 5ELCID3595 DO SEDIEN ENEL ***** FABLO EL REY DON ALFONSSO:
                   28240 5ELCID3605 LIBRAUAN SE DEL ***** TODOS ADERREDOR.
                   28278 5ELCID3610 SORTEAUAN LES EL *****, YA LES PARTIEN EL SOL,
                   28579 5ELCID3649 RELUMBRA TOD EL *****, TANTO ER LINPIA & CLARA;
                   28634 5ELCID3656 LO VNO CAYO ENEL ***** & LO AL SUSO FINCAUA.
                   28720 5ELCID3667 SACOL DEL MOJON; MARTIN ANTOLJNEZ EN EL ***** FINCAUA.
                   28899 5ELCID3691 VEN%UDO ES EL *****, QUANDO ESTO SE ACABO
         WORD # 838 OCCURS  33 TIMES.
            INDEX OF DIVERSIFICATION =   779.16 WITH STANDARD DEVIATION OF  1497.48

CAN                 3129 5ELCID0393 VINO MYO %ID IAZER A SPINAZ DE ***.
         WORD # 839 OCCURS   1 TIMES.

CANAL               5138 5ELCID0649 YXIERON DE %ELFA LA QUE DIZEN DE *****,
                    6808 5ELCID0869 EN SU MANO TENIE A %ELFA LA DE *****.
                    9392 5ELCID1194 TRES DIAS LE SPERARE EN ***** DE %ELFA.
         WORD # 840 OCCURS   3 TIMES.

CANDELAS            1919 5ELCID0244 CON LUMBRES & CON ******** AL CORAL DIERON SALTO.
                   23973 5ELCID3055 MANDO FAZER ******** & PONER ENEL ALTAR;
         WORD # 841 OCCURS   2 TIMES.

CANES              25628 5ELCID3263 QUANDO LAS NON QUERIEDES, YA ***** TRAYDORES,
         WORD # 842 OCCURS   1 TIMES.

CANPEADOR            559 5ELCID0071 YA *********, EN BUEN ORA FUESTES NA%IDO
                    1365 5ELCID0175 YA *********, EN BUEN ORA %INXIESTES ESPADA
                    1899 5ELCID0241 TU QUE ATODOS QUIAS, VALA MYO %ID EL *********.
                    2110 5ELCID0266 MER%ED, *********, EN ORA BUENA FUESTES NADO
                    2293 5ELCID0288 COMMO SEUA DE TIERRA MYO %ID EL *********;
                    4390 5ELCID0559 EL BUEN ********* QUE EN BUEN ORA NASCO,
                   11111 5ELCID1407 DEZID AL *********, QUE DIOS LE CURIE DE MAL,
                   17119 5ELCID2166 GRANDES SON LAS YENTES QUE VAN CONEL *********.
                   18376 5ELCID2325 VINO CON ESTAS NUEUAS A MUO %ID RUYDIAZ EL *********:
                   18661 5ELCID2361 AQUI LEGO MYNAYA ALBARFANEZ: OYD, YA %ID, ********* LEAL
                   19662 5ELCID2492 TODAS ESTAS GANAN%IAS FIZO EL *********.
                   19765 5ELCID2505 GRANDES SON LOS GOZOS EN VALEN%IA CON MYO %ID EL *********
                   20100 5ELCID2551 ESCARNIREMOS LAS FIJAS DEL *********.
```

WORD C# PREFIX CONTEXT

CANPEADOR (CON'T)

21988 5ELCID2797 SI UOS LO MERESCA, MYO PRIMO, NUESTRO PADRE EL *********,
22405 5ELCID2853 MUCHO UOS LO GRADE%E, ALLA CO ESTA, MYO %ID EL *********,
24285 5ELCID3096 QUE NON LE CONTALASSEN LOS PELOS AL BUEN %ID *********;
24891 5ELCID3169 HYA MAS NON AURA DERECHO DE NOS EL %ID *********.
27149 5ELCID3469 ARMAS & CAUALLOS TIENEN LOS DEL *********,
27874 5ELCID3556 COLADA & TIZON, QUE NON LIDIASSEN CON ELLAS LOS DEL *********;
27911 5ELCID3561 OTRO SI FARAN ALOS DEL *********.
29067 5ELCID3712 POR QUE TAN ONDRADOS FUERON LOS DEL *********.
29208 5ELCID3729 ESTAS SON LAS NUEUAS DE MYO %ID EL *********,
WORD # 843 OCCURS 22 TIMES.
INDEX OF DIVERSIFICATION = 1363.24 WITH STANDARD DEVIATION OF 1802.80

CANPO 8173 5ELCID1041 MAS QUANTO AUEDES PERDIDO & YO GANE EN *****,
13704 5ELCID1736 MESNADAS DE MYO %ID ROBADO AN EL *****;
18607 5ELCID2354 CALOS MOROS, CON DIOS, NON FINCARAN EN *****.
19405 5ELCID2458 MATASTES ABUCAR & ARRANCAMOS EL *****.
27558 5ELCID3519 PORA ARRANCAR MOROS DEL ***** & SER SEGUDADOR;
28913 5ELCID3693 MANDO LIBRAR EL ***** EL BUEN REY DON ALFONSSO,
WORD # 844 OCCURS 6 TIMES.
INDEX OF DIVERSIFICATION = 4147.00 WITH STANDARD DEVIATION OF 3063.74

CANSSADOS 21589 5ELCID2745 ********* SON DE FERIR ELLOS AMOS ADOS,
WORD # 845 OCCURS 1 TIMES.

CANTADO 17705 5ELCID2240 DIOLES BENDICTIONES, LA MISSA A *******.
WORD # 846 OCCURS 1 TIMES.

CANTAN 1847 5ELCID0235 APRIESSA ****** LOS GALLOS & QUIEREN QUEBRAR ALBORES,
WORD # 847 OCCURS 1 TIMES.

CANTAR 1770 5ELCID0225 ESTO & YO EN DEBDO QUE FAGA Y ****** MILL MISSAS.
17989 5ELCID2276 LAS COPLAS DESTE ****** AQUIS VAN ACABANDO.
WORD # 848 OCCURS 2 TIMES.

CANTARAN 2504 5ELCID0316 ALA MA@ANA, QUANDO LOS GALLOS ********,
WORD # 849 OCCURS 1 TIMES.

CANTAUA 13431 5ELCID1702 EL OBISPO DON IHERONIMO LA MISSA LES *******;
WORD # 850 OCCURS 1 TIMES.

CANTE 1324 5ELCID0169 CA AMOUER A MYO %ID ANTE QUE ***** EL GALLO.
1633 5ELCID0209 EN SAN PERO DE CARDENA YNOS ***** EL GALLO;
13468 5ELCID1707 HYO UOS ***** LA MISSA POR AQUESTA MA@ANA;
WORD # 851 OCCURS 3 TIMES.

CANTO 16314 5ELCID2069 EL OBISPO DON IHERONIMO LA MISSA *****.
WORD # 852 OCCURS 1 TIMES.

CA@ADOS 21 5ELCID0003 VIO PUERTAS ABIERTAS & V%OS SIN *******,
WORD # 853 OCCURS 1 TIMES.

CA@OS 21209 5ELCID2695 ALLI SON ***** DO A ELPHA EN%ERRO;
WORD # 854 OCCURS 1 TIMES.

CAPA 15682 5ELCID1989 TANTA BUENA **** & MANTOS & PELLI%ONES;
WORD # 855 OCCURS 1 TIMES.

CAPIELLA 12456 5ELCID1580 Y DEXAUA EL CAUALLO, PORA LA ******** ADELINAUA;
WORD # 856 OCCURS 1 TIMES.

CAPIELO 27327 5ELCID3492 ALLI SE TOLLIO EL ******* EL %ID CAMPEADOR,
WORD # 857 OCCURS 1 TIMES.

CAPO 18520 5ELCID2343 AMOS LOS MYOS YERNOS BUENOS SERAN EN ****.
WORD # 858 OCCURS 1 TIMES.

CARA 215 5ELCID0027 QUE PERDERIE LOS AUERES & MAS LOS OIOS DELA ****,
1673 5ELCID0215 LA **** DEL CAUALLO TORNO A SANTA MARIA,
1685 5ELCID0216 AL%O SU MANO DIESTRA, LA **** SE SANTIGUA:
3255 5ELCID0410 QUANDO DESPERTO EL %ID, LA **** SE SANTIGO;
3260 5ELCID0411 SINAUA LA ****, A DIOS SE ACOMENDO,
4687 5ELCID0594 ELBUEN CAMPEADOR LA SU **** TORNAUA,
7193 5ELCID0921 BESO LE LA BOCA & LOS OIOS DELA ****.
13446 5ELCID1704 EL QUE A QUI MURIERE LIDIANDO DE ****,
13761 5ELCID1744 FRONZIDA TRAHE LA ****, QUE ERA DESARMADO,
19247 5ELCID2436 LA **** FRONZIDA & ALMOFAR SOLTADO,
27463 5ELCID3508 EL REY AL%O LA MANO, LA **** SE SANTIGO;
28290 5ELCID3611 SALIEN LOS FIELES DE MEDIO, ELLOS **** POR CARA SON;
28292 5ELCID3611 SALIEN LOS FIELES DE MEDIO, ELLOS CARA POR **** SON;
28382 5ELCID3624 CON FERRAGON%ALEZ DE **** SE JUNTO;
28665 5ELCID3659 BOLUIO LA RIENDA AL CAUALLO POR TORNASSE DE ****;
WORD # 859 OCCURS 15 TIMES.
INDEX OF DIVERSIFICATION = 2031.14 WITH STANDARD DEVIATION OF 2669.82

WORD C# PREFIX CONTEXT

CARAS 369 5ELCID0046 E DEMAS LOS OIOS DELAS *****.
5686 5ELCID0717 ENCLINARON LAS ***** DE SUSO DE LOS ARZONES,
17287 5ELCID2186 MUCHOS DIAS UOS VEAMOS CON LOS OIOS DELAS *****
28333 5ELCID3617 ENCLINAUAN LAS ***** SOBRE LOS ARZONES,
WORD # 860 OCCURS 4 TIMES.

CARBONCLAS 6039 5ELCID0766 LAS ********** DEL YELMO ECHO GELAS APARTE,
19149 5ELCID2422 LAS ********** DEL YELMO TOLLIDAS GELA HA,
WORD # 861 OCCURS 2 TIMES.

CARCAUA 4410 5ELCID0561 A TODOS SOS VARONES MANDO FAZER VNA *******,
WORD # 862 OCCURS 1 TIMES.

CAR%EL 2695 5ELCID0340 SALUEST A DANIEL CON LOS LEONES EN LA MALA ******,
WORD # 863 OCCURS 1 TIMES.

CARDENA 1631 5ELCID0209 EN SAN PERO DE ******* YNOS CANTE EL GALLO;
1834 5ELCID0233 PORA SAN PERO DE ******* QUANTO PUDO A ESPOLEAR,
WORD # 864 OCCURS 2 TIMES.

CARGAR 20388 5ELCID2587 HYA MANDAUAN ****** YFFANTES DE CARRION.
21284 5ELCID2705 MANDARON ****** LAS AZEMILAS CON GRANDES AUERES,
WORD # 865 OCCURS 2 TIMES.

CARGAUA 1464 5ELCID0187 %INCO ESCUDEROS TIENE DON MARTINO, ATODOS LOS *******.
WORD # 866 OCCURS 1 TIMES.

CARGEN 1296 5ELCID0166 DIXO MARTIN ANTOLINEZ: ****** LAS ARCHAS PRIUADO.
WORD # 867 OCCURS 1 TIMES.

CARIDAD 5634 5ELCID0709 DIXO EL CAMPEADOR: NON SEA, POR *******
5670 5ELCID0714 DIXO EL CAMPEADOR: VALELDE, POR *******
5714 5ELCID0720 FERID LOS, CAUALLEROS, POR AMOR DE *******
18614 5ELCID2355 HYO UOS DIGO, %ID, POR TODA *******,
25545 5ELCID3253 MER%ED, AY REY SE@OR, POR AMOR DE *******
WORD # 868 OCCURS 5 TIMES.
INDEX OF DIVERSIFICATION = 4976.75 WITH STANDARD DEVIATION OF 6200.54

CARNE 2982 5ELCID0375 ASIS PARTEN VNOS DOTROS COMMO LA V@A DELA *****.
6051 5ELCID0767 CORTOL EL YELMO, QUE LEGO ALA *****;
20808 5ELCID2642 CUEMO LA V@A DELA ***** ELLOS PARTIDOS SON;
28403 5ELCID3627 PRISOL EN VAZIO, EN ***** NOL TOMO,
28482 5ELCID3637 DEDENTRO EN LA ***** VNA MANO GELA METIO;
28628 5ELCID3655 RAXOL LOS PELOS DELA CABE%A, BIEN ALA ***** LEGAUA;
28794 5ELCID3677 EN VAZIO FUE LA LAN%A, CA EN ***** NOL TOMO.
28834 5ELCID3683 METIOL POR LA ***** ADENTRO LA LAN%A CONEL PENDON,
WORD # 869 OCCURS 8 TIMES.
INDEX OF DIVERSIFICATION = 3692.14 WITH STANDARD DEVIATION OF 5619.21

CARNES 21541 5ELCID2738 RONPIEN LAS CAMISAS & LAS ****** AELLAS AMAS ADOS;
WORD # 870 OCCURS 1 TIMES.

CARO 18582 5ELCID2351 ALA, PERO VERMUEZ, EL MYO SOBRINO ****
WORD # 871 OCCURS 1 TIMES.

CAROS 810 5ELCID0103 O SODES, RACHEL & VIDAS, LOS MYOS AMIGOS *****?
WORD # 872 OCCURS 1 TIMES.

CARRERA 10145 5ELCID1284 CIENTO OMNES LE DIO MYO %ID A ALBARFANEZ POR SERUIR LE
EN LA *******,
20068 5ELCID2547 DESPUES EN LA ******* FEREMOS NUESTRO SABOR,
21754 5ELCID2767 ENLA ******* DO YUA DOLIOL EL CORA%ON,
WORD # 873 OCCURS 3 TIMES.

CARRIO 15578 5ELCID1975 LOS YFFANTES DE ****** MUCHO ALEGRES ANDAN,
WORD # 874 OCCURS 1 TIMES.

CARRION 10365 5ELCID1313 TORNOS A *******, Y LO PODRIE FALLAR.
10839 5ELCID1372 AQUI ENTRARON EN FABLA LOS YFFANTES DE *******:
10876 5ELCID1376 MYO %ID ES DE BIUAR & NOS DELOS CONDES DE *******.
10941 5ELCID1385 LOS YFFANTES DE ******* DANDO YUAN CONPA@A A MINAYA ALBARFANEZ:
14508 5ELCID1835 LOS YFANTES DE *******, SABET, YS A%ERTARON,
14868 5ELCID1879 DELOS YFFANTES DE ******* YO UOS QUIERO CONTAR,
15041 5ELCID1901 DIEGO & FERRANDO, LOS YFFANTES DE *******,
15077 5ELCID1906 POR CONSSAGRAR CON LOS YFFANTES DE *******.
15231 5ELCID1928 DE DAR SUS FIJAS ALOS YFANTES DE *******,
15302 5ELCID1937 E PIDEN ME MIS FIJAS PORA LOS YFANTES DE *******.
15622 5ELCID1981 LOS YFANTES DE ******* LIEUAN GRANDES CONPA@AS.
16179 5ELCID2052 ESSORA SELE OMILLAN LOS YFFANTES DE *******:
16372 5ELCID2076 QUE LAS DEDES POR MUGIERES ALOS YFANTES DE *******.
16440 5ELCID2084 DE GRANDES NUEUAS SON LOS YFANTES DE *******,
16498 5ELCID2091 LUEGO SE LEUANTARON LOS YFFANTES DE *******,
16543 5ELCID2096 QUEM DADES UUESTRAS FIJAS PORA LOS YFANTES DE *******.
16562 5ELCID2098 E DOLAS POR VELADAS ALOS YFANTES DE *******.
16586 5ELCID2101 AFELLOS EN UUESTRAS MANOS LOS YFANTES DE *******,

WORD C# PREFIX CONTEXT

CARRION (CON'T)

17081 5ELCID2162 SEREMOS ALAS BODAS DELOS YFANTES DE *******
17161 5ELCID2171 QUE SOPIESSEN SOS MA@AS DE LOS YFANTES DE *******.
17188 5ELCID2174 GRANT ONDRA LES DAN ALOS YFANTES DE *******.
17222 5ELCID2178 DAD LES VN REYAL & ALOS YFANTES DE *******,
17472 5ELCID2210 POR LOS YFFANTES DE ******* ESSORA ENBIARON,
17589 5ELCID2225 ALOS YFANTES DE ******* DAD LAS CON UUESTRA MANO,
17619 5ELCID2229 ALOS YFANTES DE ******* MINAYA VA FABLANDO:
17750 5ELCID2246 LOS YFANTES DE ******* BIEN AN CAUALGADO.
18019 5ELCID2279 CON EL AMOS SUS YERNOS LOS YFANTES DE *******.
18095 5ELCID2289 DIZIENDO DELA BOCA: NON VERE *******
18255 5ELCID2309 MUCHOS TOUIERON POR ENBAYDOS LOS YFANTES DE *******,
18316 5ELCID2317 MAS, SABED, DE CUER LES PESA ALOS YFANTES DE *******;
18355 5ELCID2322 ESTO ES AGUISADO POR NON VER *******,
18390 5ELCID2327 POR ENTRAR EN BATALLA DESEAN *******.
18431 5ELCID2332 DIOS UOS SALUE, YERNOS, YFANTES DE *******,
18448 5ELCID2334 HYO DESSEO LIDES, & UOS A *******;
19577 5ELCID2480 MANDADOS BUENOS YRAN DELLOS A *******,
19691 5ELCID2496 ESON MYOS YERNOS YFANTES DE *******;
19805 5ELCID2510 MUCHOS TIENEN POR RICOS LOS YFANTES DE *******.
19840 5ELCID2515 QUANDO ENTRARON LOS YFANTES DE *******,
19918 5ELCID2526 BUENOS MANDADOS YRAN ATIERRAS DE *******.
20018 5ELCID2540 VAYAMOS PORA *******, AQUI MUCHO DETARDAMOS.
20048 5ELCID2544 DIGAMOS QUE LAS LEUAREMOS ATIERRAS DE *******,
20088 5ELCID2549 NOS DE NATURA SOMOS DE CONDES DE *******
20123 5ELCID2554 CA DE NATURA SOMOS DE CONDES DE *******.
20191 5ELCID2563 LEUAR LAS HEMOS A NUESTRAS TIERRAS DE *******,
20251 5ELCID2570 VOS LES DIESTES VILLAS E TIERRAS POR ARRAS ENTIERRAS DE *******,
20365 5ELCID2583 ATORGADO LO HAN ESTO LOS YFFANTES DE *******.
20391 5ELCID2587 HYA MANDAUAN CARGAR YFFANTES DE *******.
20416 5ELCID2590 POR QUE ESCURREN SUS FIJAS DEL CAMPEADOR ATIERRAS DE *******.
20462 5ELCID2597 AGORA NOS ENVIADES ATIERRAS DE *******,
20486 5ELCID2600 QUE AYADES UUESTROS MENSSAIES EN TIERRAS DE *******.
20520 5ELCID2605 HYD A ******* DO SODES HEREDADAS,
20645 5ELCID2620 MANDOT QUE VAYAS CON ELLAS FATA DENTRO EN *******,
20697 5ELCID2627 HYR LAS HEMOS VER ATIERRAS DE *******.
20776 5ELCID2638 DIL QUE ENBIO MIS FIJAS A TIERRAS DE *******,
20829 5ELCID2644 PIENSSAN SE DE YR LOS YFANTES DE *******;
20843 5ELCID2646 AGUIJAN QUANTO PUEDEN YFANTES DE *******;
20908 5ELCID2655 BUENOS SE@OS CAUALLOS ALOS YFANTES DE *******.
20974 5ELCID2664 TAN EN SALUO LO ABREMOS COMMO LO DE *******;
20989 5ELCID2666 QUANDO ESTA FALSSEDAD DIZEN LOS DE *******,
21015 5ELCID2670 TU MUERT OY COSSEIAR ALOS YFANTES DE *******.
21052 5ELCID2675 DEZID ME, QUE UOS FIZ, YFANTES DE *******
21092 5ELCID2680 VOS NUQUA EN ******* ENTRARIEDES IAMAS.
21120 5ELCID2683 POCO PRE%IO LAS NUEUAS DELOS DE *******.
21170 5ELCID2689 YA MOUIERON DEL ANSSARERA LOS YFANTES DE *******,
21258 5ELCID2701 MANDAN FINCAR LA TIENDA YFANTES DE *******,
21310 5ELCID2708 ASSI LO MANDARON LOS YFANTES DE *******,
21349 5ELCID2713 TANTO MAL COMIDIERON LOS YFANTES DE *******;
21379 5ELCID2717 NON ABREDES PART EN TIERRAS DE *******.
21517 5ELCID2735 ESSORA LES CONPIE%AN ADAR LOS YFANTES DE *******;
21668 5ELCID2754 LOS YFANTES DE ******* ENEL ROBREDO DE CORPES
21730 5ELCID2763 ALABANDOS YUAN LOS YFANTES DE *******.
21790 5ELCID2771 O QUE AN FECHO LOS YFANTES DE *******.
21859 5ELCID2781 MAL SE ENSAYARON LOS YFANTES DE *******
21958 5ELCID2793 DE QUE NON ME FALLAREN LOS YFANTES DE *******,
22178 5ELCID2824 ALLABANDOS SEYAN LOS YFANTES DE *******.
22233 5ELCID2831 QUANDO TAL ONDRA MEAN DADA LOS YFANTES DE *******;
22247 5ELCID2833 NON LA LOGRARAN LOS YFANTES DE *******;
22711 5ELCID2894 DE MYOS YERNOS DE ******* DIOS ME FAGA VENGAR
22816 5ELCID2906 DESTA DESONDRA QUE MEAN FECHA LOS YFANTES DE *******
22889 5ELCID2915 COMMO AYA DERECHO DE YFANTES DE *******,
23074 5ELCID2939 CASASTES SUS FIJAS CON YFANTES DE *******,
23097 5ELCID2942 CUEMO NOS HAN ABILTADOS YFANTES DE *******:
23175 5ELCID2952 QUE AYA MYO %ID DERECHO DE YFANTES DE *******.
23209 5ELCID2956 CA YO CASE SUS FIJAS CON YFANTES DE *******;
23279 5ELCID2965 MANDARE COMMO Y VAYAN YFANTES DE *******,
23385 5ELCID2979 E ALOS DE ******* & AVARONES CASTELLANOS,
23441 5ELCID2985 HYA LES VA PESANDO ALSO YFANTES DE *******,
23524 5ELCID2995 HYA LO VIERON QUE ES AFER LOS YFANTES DE *******,
23551 5ELCID2999 AQUESTE CONSSEIO LOS YFANTES DE *******.
23613 5ELCID3007 EL CONDE DON GAR%IA CON YFANTES DE *******,
24158 5ELCID3080 SI DESOBRA BUSCAREN YFANTES DE *******,
24424 5ELCID3113 NIN TODOS LOS DEL BANCO DE YFANTES DE *******.
24526 5ELCID3126 NOL PUEDEN CATAR DE VERGUEN%A YFANTES DE *******.
24563 5ELCID3130 LA VNA FUE EN BURGOS, & LA OTRA EN *******,
24590 5ELCID3133 QUE RE%IBA DERECHO DE YFANTES DE *******.
24682 5ELCID3144 SABREMOS QUE RESPONDEN YFANTES DE *******.
24718 5ELCID3148 ESTO LES DEMANDO AYFANTES DE *******:
24822 5ELCID3161 ESSORA SALIEN APARTE YFFANTES DE *******,
25146 5ELCID3202 OTRA RENCURA HE DE YFANTES DE *******:
25189 5ELCID3207 AQUI VERIEDES QUEXAR SE YFANTES DE *******
25205 5ELCID3209 ESSORA RESPONDEN YFANTES DE *******:
25274 5ELCID3217 ESSORA SALIEN A PARTE YFANTES DE *******;

WORD C# PREFIX CONTEXT

CARRION (CON'T)

```
                25289 5ELCID3219 ESPESOS LOS HAN YFANTES DE *******.
                25319 5ELCID3223 PAGAR LE HEMCS DE HEREDADES ENTIERRAS DE *******.
                25385 5ELCID3232 ENTRAMOS MELOS DIERCN LCS YFANTES DE *******.
                25457 5ELCID3241 HYA VIERON QUE ES AFER LOS YFANTES DE *******.
                25566 5ELCID3256 DELOS YFANTES DE ******* QUEM DESONDRARON TAN MAL,
                25716 5ELCID3275 LOS DE ******* SCN DE NATURA TAL,
                25874 5ELCID3296 DE NATURA SCMCS DE CONDES DE *******:
                26499 5ELCID3381  QUIL DARIE CCN LCS DE ******* ACASAR?
                26840 5ELCID3428 MAS NON PLAZE ALOS YFANTES DE *******.
                26906 5ELCID3437 CA GRAND RENCURA HE DE YFANTES DE *******.
                27134 5ELCID3467 LUEGO FABLARON YFANTES DE *******:
                27156 5ELCID3470 NOS ANTES ABREMOS AYR ATIERRAS DE *******.
                27183 5ELCID3474 MAS QUIERO A VALEN%IA QUE TIERRAS DE *******.
                27239 5ELCID3481 ACABO DE TRES SEMANAS, EN BEGAS DE *******,
                27267 5ELCID3485 PRISIERON EL JUIZIO YFANTES DE *******.
                27674 5ELCID3532 MYO %ID PORA VALEN%IA, & EL REY PORA *******.
                27714 5ELCID3537 DOS DIAS ATENDIERCN A YFANTES DE *******.
                27841 5ELCID3552 EN OTRO LOGAR SE ARMAN LOS YFANTES DE *******,
                27918 5ELCID3562 LEUAD & SALID ALCAMPO, YFANTES DE *******,
                27964 5ELCID3568 HYA SEUAN REPINTIENDC YFANTES DE *******,
                27980 5ELCID3570 NOLO QUERRIEN AUER FECHC POR QUANTO HA EN *******.
                28030 5ELCID3577 AQUI TIENEN SU VANDO LCS YFANTES DE *******,
                28130 5ELCID3591 FEUOS DELA OTRA PART LCS YFANTES DE *******,
                28173 5ELCID3596 OYD QUE UOS DIGO, YFANTES DE *******:
                28197 5ELCID3599 HYO LOS ADUX ASALUO ATIERRAS DE *******;
                28228 5ELCID3603 HYA LES VA PESANDO ALCS YFANTES DE *******.
                28303 5ELCID3612 DESI VINIEN LOS DE MYC %ID ALOS YFANTES DE *******,
                28307 5ELCID3613 ELLOS YFANTES DE ******* ALOS DE CAMPEADOR;
                28948 5ELCID3697 GRANDES SON LOS PESARES POR TIERRAS DE *******.
                28988 5ELCID3702 POR MALOS LOS DEXARON ALOS YFANTES DE *******,
                29012 5ELCID3705 GRANT ES LA BILTAN%A DE YFANTES DE *******.
                29035 5ELCID3708 DEXEMOS NOS DE PLEYTCS DE YFANTES DE *******,
                29090 5ELCID3715 AGORA LAS AYAN QUITAS HEREDADES DE *******.
        WORD # 875 OCCURS 135 TIMES.
           INDEX OF DIVERSIFICATION =   138.74 WITH STANDARD DEVIATION OF   336.41

CARTA             178 5ELCID0023 ANTES DELA NOCHE EN BURGOS DEL ENTRO SU *****,
                  340 5ELCID0042 EL REY LO HA UEDADO, ANOCH DEL ETRO SU *****,
                 4024 5ELCID0511 SOS QUI@CNEROS QUE GELOS DIESSEN POR *****.
                 4145 5ELCID0527 MOROS EN PAZ, CA ESCRIPTA ES LA *****,
                 6617 5ELCID0844 ASI LO AN ASMADC & METUDO EN *****:
                 7063 5ELCID0902 EL POYO DE MYO %ID ASIL DIRAN POR *****.
        WORD # 876 OCCURS   6 TIMES.
           INDEX OF DIVERSIFICATION =  1376.00 WITH STANDARD DEVIATION OF  1615.69

CARTAS          15440 5ELCID1956 ESCRIUIEN ******, BIEN LAS SELLO,
                15466 5ELCID1959 AL REY ONDRADC DELANT LE ECHARON LAS ******;
                23370 5ELCID2977 ENBIA SUS ****** PORA LEON & A SANTI YAGUO,
        WORD # 877 OCCURS   3 TIMES.

CASA              396 5ELCID0049 ESTO LA NI@A DIXO & TORNOS PORA SU ****.
                  472 5ELCID0059 POSO EN LA GLERA QUANDO NOL COGE NADI EN ****;
                  494 5ELCID0062 VEDADA LAN CONPRA DENTRO EN BURGOS LA ****,
                 4497 5ELCID0571 E LOS DE TECA & LCS DE TERUAL LA ****;
                 6601 5ELCID0842 ENTRE LOS DE TECHA & LOS DE TERUEL LA ****,
                 9124 5ELCID1161 AVN MAS AYUSSO, ADEYNA LA ****;
                 9696 5ELCID1232 BUENA FUE LA DE VALEN%IA QUANDO GANARON LA ****,
                10012 5ELCID1268 CON MAS POCCS YXIEMOS DE LA **** DE BIUAR.
                12216 5ELCID1550 ENTRADOS SON A MOLINA, BUENA & RICA ****:
                12369 5ELCID1570 MANDO MYO %ID ALOS QUE HA EN SU ****
                12661 5ELCID1606 ENTRAD CCMIGO EN VALEN%IA LA ****,
                17145 5ELCID2170 EN **** DE MYC %ID NON A DOS MEIORES,
                17425 5ELCID2204 BIEN MELO CREADES, QUE EL UOS ****, CA NON YO.
                22585 5ELCID2877 ALA **** DE BERLANGA POSADA PRESA HAN.
                29137 5ELCID3721 AMAYOR ONDRA LAS **** QUE LO QUE PRIMERO FUE.
        WORD # 878 OCCURS  15 TIMES.
           INDEX OF DIVERSIFICATION =  2051.93 WITH STANDARD DEVIATION OF  2200.55

CASADAS         14246 5ELCID1802 E TODAS LAS OTRAS DUENAS QUE TIENEN POR *******.
                17309 5ELCID2189 GRADID MELO, MIS FIJAS, CA BIEN UOS HE *******
                20531 5ELCID2606 ASSI COMMO YO TENGO, BIEN UOS HE *******.
                20617 5ELCID2617 NOS PUEDE REPENTIR, QUE ******* LAS HA AMAS.
                22703 5ELCID2893 QUE UOS VEA MEIOR ******* DAQUI EN ADELANT.
        WORD # 879 OCCURS   5 TIMES.
           INDEX OF DIVERSIFICATION =  2113.25 WITH STANDARD DEVIATION OF  1442.43

CASADES         16657 5ELCID2110 VOS ******* MIS FIJAS, CA NON GELAS DO YO.
                16840 5ELCID2132 PUES QUE ******* MYS FIJAS, ASI COMMO AUOS PLAZ,
        WORD # 880 OCCURS   2 TIMES.

CASAMIENO       23078 5ELCID2940 ALTO FUE EL ********* CALO QUISIESTES UOS
        WORD # 881 OCCURS   1 TIMES.
```

WORD C# PREFIX CONTEXT

```
CASAMIENTO          14966 5ELCID1892 DEL ********** NON SE SIS ABRA SABOR:
                    15314 5ELCID1939 DESTE ********** NON AURIA SABOR:
                    16375 5ELCID2077 SEMEIAM EL ********** CNDRADO & CON GRANT PRO,
                    17374 5ELCID2198 DESTE UUSTRO ********** CRE%REMOS EN ONOR;
                    17978 5ELCID2275 QUES PAGE DES ********** MYO %ID O EL QUE LO ALGO
                    21135 5ELCID2685 DA QUESTE ********** QUE GRADE EL CAMPEADOR.
                    22514 5ELCID2867 BUEN ********** PERDIESTES, MEIOR PODREDES GANAR.
                    22686 5ELCID2891 HYO TOME EL **********, MAS NON OSE DEZIR AL.
                    23222 5ELCID2958 SI QUIER EL ********** FECHO NCN FUESSE OY
                    26711 5ELCID3412 ESTE ********** CY SE OTORGE EN ESTA CORT,
                    26760 5ELCID3418 ESTE ********** OTORGO UOS LE YO
        WORD # 882 OCCURS  11 TIMES.
           INDEX OF DIVERSIFICATION =  1178.40 WITH STANDARD DEVIATION OF  1204.64

CASAMIENTOS         19909 5ELCID2525 DESTOS NUESTRCS *********** UOS ABREDES HONOR.
                    20607 5ELCID2616 QUE ESTOS *********** NCN SERIEN SIN ALGUNA TACHA.
                    21696 5ELCID2758 DE NUESTROS *********** AGORA SOMOS VENGADOS;
                    26306 5ELCID3355 ESTOS *********** NCN FUESSEN APARE%IDOS
                    29118 5ELCID3719 FIZIERON SUS *********** CON CON ELUIRA & CON DO@A SOL.
        WORD # 883 OCCURS   5 TIMES.
           INDEX OF DIVERSIFICATION =  2301.25 WITH STANDARD DEVIATION OF  1791.75

CASAR               13006 5ELCID1650 POR ***** SCN UUESTRAS FIJAS, ADUZEN UOS AXUUAR.
                    13932 5ELCID1765 QUIERO LAS ***** CON DE ACUESTOS MYOS VASSALLOS;
                    14893 5ELCID1882 DEMANDEMOS SUS FIJAS PORA CON ELLAS *****;
                    14930 5ELCID1888 ***** QUEREMOS CON ELLAS ASU ONDRA & A NUESTRA PRO.
                    15045 5ELCID1902 SABOR HAN DE ***** CCN SUS FIJAS AMAS ADOS.
                    16419 5ELCID2082 NON ABRIA FIJAS DE *****, RESPUSO EL CAMPEADOR,
                    20108 5ELCID2553 PODREMOS ***** CON FIJAS DE REYES O DE ENPERADORES,
                    25876 5ELCID3297 DEUIEMOS ***** CCN FIJAS DE REYES O DE ENPERADORES,
        WORD # 884 OCCURS   8 TIMES.
           INDEX OF DIVERSIFICATION =  1837.57 WITH STANDARD DEVIATION OF  2117.37

CASARE              22253 5ELCID2834 QUE AMIS FIJAS BIEN LAS ****** YO
                    29094 5ELCID3716 SIN VERGUEN%A LAS ****** CAQUI PESE OAQUI NON.
        WORD # 885 OCCURS   2 TIMES.

CASAREDES           17353 5ELCID2195 QUANDO UOS NOS ********* BIEN SEREMOS RICAS.
        WORD # 886 OCCURS   1 TIMES.

CASARIEMOS          10850 5ELCID1374 BIEN ********** CON SUS FIJAS PORA HUEBOS DE PRO.
        WORD # 887 OCCURS   1 TIMES.

CASAS                 363 5ELCID0045 SI NON, PERDERIEMOS LOS AUERES & LAS *****,
                      896 5ELCID0115 DEXADO HA HEREDADES & ***** & PALA%IOS.
                     2296 5ELCID0289 VNOS DEXAN ***** & CTROS ONORES.
                     2384 5ELCID0301 VOS, QUE POR MI DEXADES ***** & HEREDADES,
                     4915 5ELCID0622 POSAREMOS EN SUS ***** & DELLOS NOS SERUIREMOS.
                     9813 5ELCID1246 ATODOS LES DIC EN VALEN%IA ***** & HEREDADES
        WORD # 888 OCCURS   6 TIMES.
           INDEX OF DIVERSIFICATION =  1889.00 WITH STANDARD DEVIATION OF  1922.74

CASASTES            23068 5ELCID2939 ******** SUS FIJAS CON YFANTES DE CARRION,
                    24731 5ELCID3150 CA UOS LAS ********, REY, SABREDES QUE FER OY;
                    26671 5ELCID3406 VOS LAS ******** ANTES, CA YO NON,
        WORD # 889 OCCURS   3 TIMES.

CASCAUELES          11897 5ELCID1508 EN BUENOS CAUALLOS A PETRALES & A **********,
        WORD # 890 OCCURS   1 TIMES.

CASCO               28592 5ELCID3651 EL ***** DE SOMO APART GELO ECHAUA,
        WORD # 891 OCCURS   1 TIMES.

CASE                 2245 5ELCID0282 PLEGA ADIOS & A SANTA MARIA, QUE AUN CON MIS MANOS ****
                                     ESTAS MIS
                    23203 5ELCID2956 CA YO **** SUS FIJAS CON YFANTES DE CARRION;
        WORD # 892 OCCURS   2 TIMES.

CASI                 8096 5ELCID1033 DIXO MYO %ID: COMED, CONDE, ALGO, **** NON COMEDES, NON VEREDES
        WORD # 893 OCCURS   1 TIMES.

CASO                16565 5ELCID2099 HYO LAS **** A UUESTRAS FIJAS CON UUESTRO AMOR,
                    22827 5ELCID2908 EL **** MIS FIJAS, CA NCN GELAS DI YO;
        WORD # 894 OCCURS   2 TIMES.

CASTEION             3445 5ELCID0435 ODIZEN ********, EL QUE ES SOBRE FENARES,
                     3496 5ELCID0441 PUES QUE A ******** SACAREMOS A %ELADA,. . . .
                     3573 5ELCID0450 TERNE YO ******** DON ABREMOS GRAND EN PARA.
                     3632 5ELCID0458 EN ******** TODOS SE LEUANTAUAN,
                     3665 5ELCID0462 CON POCAS DE GENTES QUE EN ******** FINCARON.
                     3741 5ELCID0473 GA@O A ******** & EL ORO ELA PLATA.
                     3834 5ELCID0485 FELLOS EN ********, C EL CAMPEADOR ESTAUA.
                     4076 5ELCID0518 FABLO CON LOS DE ********, & ENVIO AFITA & AGUADELFAGARA,
                     4158 5ELCID0529 QUITAR QUIERO ********, OYD, ESCUELLAS & MINYAYA
                     4172 5ELCID0531 EN ******** NON PODRIEMOS FINCAR;
                    10490 5ELCID1329 ASSI FIZO %EBOLLA & ADELANT ********,
```

```
WORD                C#  PREFIX                          CONTEXT

CASTEION (CON'T)

          WORD # 895 OCCURS  11 TIMES.
             INDEX OF DIVERSIFICATION =    703.50 WITH STANDARD DEVIATION OF  1973.35

CASTELANO              5906 5ELCID0748 VIOLO MYO %ID RUY DIAZ EL *********,
                       8398 5ELCID1067 FATA CABO DEL ALBERGACA ESCURRIOLOS EL *********:
          WORD # 896 OCCURS   2 TIMES.

CASTELLANAS           15640 5ELCID1983 NCN SON EN CUENTA, SABET, LAS ***********.
          WORD # 897 OCCURS   1 TIMES.

CASTELLANO             3904 5ELCID0495 PAGAR SE YA DELLA ALFCNSSO EL **********.
                      14144 5ELCID1790 ENBIAR LA QUIERO ALFCNSSO EL **********,
                      23367 5ELCID2976 NON LO DETIENE POR NACA ALFCNSSO EL **********,
          WORD # 898 OCCURS   3 TIMES.

CASTELLANOS           23388 5ELCID2979 E ALOS DE CARRICN & AVAFONES ***********,
          WORD # 899 OCCURS   1 TIMES.

CASTIELLA              1372 5ELCID0176 DE ********* UOS YDES PORA LAS YENTES ESTRANAS.
                       1707 5ELCID0219 DA QUI QUITC *********, PUES QUE EL REY HE EN YRA;
                       2281 5ELCID0287 POR ********* CYENDC UAN LCS PREGONES,
                       3174 5ELCID0399 PASSO PAR ALCOBIELLA QUE DE ********* FINES YA;
                       5316 5ELCID0672 DE ********* LA GENTIL EXIDCS SOMOS ACA,
                       6147 5ELCID0783 QUE A ********* YRAN BUENOS MANDADOS,
                       6382 5ELCIDC813 ENBIAR UOS QUIERC A ********* CON MANDADO
                       6821 5ELCIDC871 YDO ES A ********* ALBARFANEZ MINAYA,
                       7012 5ELCID0897 HYD POR ********* & DEXEN UOS ANDAR, MINAYA,
                       7153 5ELCIDC916 DE ********* VENICO ES MINAYA,
                       7446 5ELCIDC955 QUE EL SALIDO DE ********* ASILOS TRAE TAN MAL.
                       9343 5ELCID1188 A TIERRAS DE ********* ENBIO SUS MENSSAIES:
                      10035 5ELCID1271 ENBIAR UOS QUIERO A *********, DO AUEMOS HEREDADES,
                      10279 5ELCID1301 VOS, QUANDC YCES A *********, LEUAREDES BUENOS MANDADOS.
                      10336 5ELCID1309 ADELINO PORA ********* MINAYA ALBARFANEZ.
                      11928 5ELCID1512 O CUEMO SALIERA DE ********* ALBARFANEZ CON ESTAS DUE@AS
                                       QUE TRAHE.
                      13951 5ELCID1767 QUE LO SEPAN EN *********, AQUIEN SIRUIERON TANTO.
                      15518 5ELCID1966  QUI ENVIO POR ********* TANTA MULA PRE%IADA,
                      17869 5ELCID2261 RICOS TORNAN A ********* LOS QUE ALAS BODAS LEGARON.
                      20329 5ELCID2579 QUE LO SEPAN EN GALLIZIA & EN ********* & EN LEON,
                      22759 5ELCID2900 AL REY ALFCNSSO DE ********* PENSSO DE ENBIAR;
                      22784 5ELCID2903 LIEUES EL MANDADC A ********* AL REY ALFONSSO;
                      22946 5ELCID2923 REY ES DE ********* & REY ES CE LEON
                      23602 5ELCID3006 DE TODA ********* TCDCS LOS MEIORES
          WORD # 900 OCCURS  24 TIMES.
             INDEX OF DIVERSIFICATICN =    965.52 WITH STANDARD DEVIATION OF   868.28

CASTIELLO               773 5ELCID0098 PASSO POR BURGOS, AL ********* ENTRAUA,
                       4125 5ELCIDC525 QUE ENEL ********* NCN Y AURIE MORACA,
                       4242 5ELCID0540 DEL ********* QUE PRISIERON TODOS RICOS SE PARTEN;
                       4470 5ELCID0569 EL ********* DE ALCO%ER EN PARIA UA ENTRANDO.
                       4694 5ELCIDC595 VIO QUE ENTRELLCS & EL ********* MUCHO AUIE GRAND PLA%A;
                       4755 5ELCID0603 ENTRELLCS & EL ********* ENESSORA ENTRAUAN.
                       4793 5ELCID0607 DEXANDO UAN LCS DELANT, POR EL ********* SE TORNAUAN,
                       4876 5ELCID0617 EN ESTE ********* GRAND AUER AUEMOS PRESO,
                       4993 5ELCID0631 SACOLOS A %ELADA, EL ********* GANADO A;
                       5446 5ELCID0687 SI NOS MURIEREMOS EN CAMPO, EN ********* NOS ENTRARAN,
                      13632 5ELCID1727 METIOS LE EN GUIERA, VN ********* PALA%IANO;
                      22327 5ELCID2843 VINIERCN A SANTESTEUAN DE GORMAZ, VN ********* TAN FUERT,
                      25810 5ELCID3287 COMMO YO AUOS, CONDE, ENEL ********* DE CABRA;
          WORD # 9C1 OCCURS  13 TIMES.
             INDEX OF DIVERSIFICATION =  2085.42 WITH STANDARD DEVIATION OF  3220.53

CASTIELLOS             6288 5ELCID0801 ASOS ********** ALCS MCROS CENTRO LOS AN TORNADOS,
          WORD # 9C2 OCCURS   1 TIMES.

CASTIELO               3840 5ELCID0486 EL ******** DEXC EN SC PODER, EL CAMPEADOR CAUALGA,
                       4187 5ELCID0533 MAS EL ******** NCN LC QUIERO HERMAR;
          WORD # 9C3 OCCURS   2 TIMES.

CASTIGANDO            27843 5ELCID3553 SEDIELOS ********** EL CONDE GAR%IORDONEZ.
          WORD # 9C4 OCCURS   1 TIMES.

CASTIGAR               1797 5ELCID0229 ******** LOS HE CCMMO ABRAN AFAR.
                       3046 5ELCID0383 AL ABBAT DCN SANCHO TCRNAN DE ********,
          WORD # 9C5 OCCURS   2 TIMES.

CASTIGO               27597 5ELCID3523 EL CAMPEADOR ALOS QUE HAN LIDIAR TAN BIEN LOS *******:
          WORD # 9C6 OCCURS   1 TIMES.

CASTIOLLO              6673 5ELCID0851 QUANDO MYO %IC EL ********* QUISO QUITAR,
          WORD # 9C7 OCCURS   1 TIMES.

CATA                  25911 5ELCID3301 MYO %ID RUY DIAZ A PERO VERMUEZ ****;
          WORD # 9C8 OCCURS   1 TIMES.
```

WORD C# PREFIX CONTEXT

```
CATAD             1C731 5ELCID1359 ***** CCMMO LAS SIRUACES UOS & EL CAMPEADOR.
         WORD # 9C9 OCCURS   1 TIMES.

CATAMOS           18334 5ELCID2320 ******* LA GANAN%IA & LA PERDICA NO,
         WORD # 910 OCCURS   1 TIMES.

CATAN             12701 5ELCID1612 OIOS VELIDOS ***** A TOCAS PARTES,
         WORD # 911 OCCURS   1 TIMES.

CATANDO              14 5ELCID0002 TORNAUA LA CABE%A & ESAUA LOS *******.
                  19273 5ELCID2439 AL%O SOS OICS, ESTEUA ACELANT *******,
                  24494 5ELCID3123 ******* ESTAN A MYO %ID QUANTOS HA EN LA CORT,
         WORD # 912 OCCURS   3 TIMES.

CATANDOL          16229 5ELCID2059 ******** SEDIE LA BARBA, QUE TAN AYNAL CRE%IERA.
         WORD # 913 OCCURS   1 TIMES.

CATANDOS           8482 5ELCID1078 TORNANDC UA LA CABE%A & ******** ATRAS;
         WORD # 914 OCCURS   1 TIMES.

CATAR             24521 5ELCID3126 NOL PUEDEN ***** DE VERGUEN%A YFANTES DE CARRION.
         WORD # 915 OCCURS   1 TIMES.

CATARLE           27352 5ELCID3495 NOS FARTAN DE ******* QUANTOS HA EN LA CORT.
         WORD # 916 OCCURS   1 TIMES.

CATASSEN           1279 5ELCID0164 QUE SI ANTES LAS ******** QUE FUESSEN PERIURADOS,
         WORD # 917 OCCURS   1 TIMES.

CATEDES             944 5ELCID0121 QUE NON LAS ******* EN TODO AQUESTE A@O.
         WORD # 918 OCCURS   1 TIMES.

CATIUAS            4065 5ELCID0517 NIN CATIUOS NIN ******* NON QUISO TRAER EN SU CONPA@A.
         WORD # 919 OCCURS   1 TIMES.

CATIUO             8040 5ELCID1026 SI LO QUE DIGC FIZIEREDES, SALCREDES DE ******;
         WORD # 920 OCCURS   1 TIMES.

CATIUOS            4063 5ELCID0517 NIN ******* NIN CATIUAS NON QUISO TRAER EN SU CONPA@A.
         WORD # 921 OCCURS   1 TIMES.

CATO               2822 5ELCID0356 ABRIO SCS OIOS, **** ATCDAS PARTES,
                  24987 5ELCID3182 EN LAS MANCS LAS TIENE & AMAS LAS ****;
         WORD # 922 OCCURS   2 TIMES.

CATODO            13128 5ELCID1664 NON AYACES MIEDO, ****** ES UUESTRA PRO;
         WORD # 923 OCCURS   1 TIMES.

CAUALGA            2352 5ELCID0297 APRIESSA *******, RE%EBIR LOS SALIE,
                   3847 5ELCID0486 EL CASTIELO DEXC EN SC PODER, EL CAMPEADOR *******,
                  12527 5ELCID1589 POR NOMBRE EL CAUALLC BAUIECA *******.
                  15155 5ELCID1917 APRIESSA *******, ARE%EBIR LOS SALIO;
                  22649 5ELCID2886 PRIUADC *******, A RE%EBIR LCS SALE;
                  24329 5ELCID3102 APRIESSA *******, DE SAN SERUAN SALIO;
         WORD # 924 OCCURS   6 TIMES.
            INDEX OF DIVERSIFICATION =  4394.40 WITH STANDARD DEVIATION OF  3423.C3

CAUALGAD           3229 5ELCID0407 ********, %ID, EL BUEN CAMPEACOR, CA NUNQUA
                   5937 5ELCID0753 ********, MYNAYA, UCS SCDES EL MYO DIESTRO BRA%O
                  23775 5ELCID3029 ********, %ID; SI NCN, NCN AURIA DEC SABOR;
         WORD # 925 OCCURS   3 TIMES.

CAUALGADO         17753 5ELCID2246 LOS YFANTES DE CARRION BIEN AN *********.
         WORD # 926 OCCURS   1 TIMES.

CAUALGAN           1669 5ELCID0214 MYO %ID & SUS CONPA@AS ******** TAN AYNA.
                   5091 5ELCID0643 TRES MILL MCROS ******** & PIENSSAN DE ANDAR,
                  13185 5ELCID1671 LOS MOROS DE MARRUECCS ******** AUIGOR,
                  17475 5ELCID2211 ******** LOS YFFANTES, ADELANT ADELINAUAN AL PALA%IO,
                  2C404 5ELCID2589 TODOS PRENDEN ARMAS & ******** A VIGOR,
                  22314 5ELCID2842 APIRESSA ********, LCS DIAS & LAS NOCHES ANDAN;
                  28070 5ELCID3583 SANTIGUARON LAS SIELAS & ******** A VIGOR;
         WORD # 927 CCCURS   7 TIMES.
            INDEX OF DIVERSIFICATICN =  4399.16 WITH STANDARD DEVIATION OF  2227.86

CAUALGAR           2533 5ELCIDC320 LA MISSA DICHA, PENSSEMCS DE ********,
                   2567 5ELCID0324 ALOS MEDIADOS GALLOS PIESSAN CE ********.
                   2914 5ELCID0367 SALIERON DELA EGLESIA, YA CUIEREN ********.
                   2991 5ELCIDC376 MYC %ID CON LCS SOS VASSALLOS PENSSO DE ********,
                   3135 5ELCID0394 OTRO DIA MA@ANA PIENSSA DE ********.
                   3278 5ELCIDC413 OTRO DIA MA@ANA PIENSSAN DE ********;
                   3424 5ELCIDC432 ANTE QUE ANOCHESCA PIENSSAN DE ********;
                   4223 5ELCIDC537 CRAS ALA MA@ANA PENSEMOS DE ********,
                   5108 5ELCID0645 OTRO DIA MA@ANA PIENSSAN DE ********,
                   7403 5ELCID0949 CRAS ALA MA@ANA PENSSEMCS DE ********,
```

```
WORD                    C#  PREFIX                                 CONTEXT

CAUALGAR (CON'T)

                      9363 5ELCID1190 VINIESSE A MYC %ID QUE A SABOR DE ********;
                     11304 5ELCID1430 EL BUENO DE MINAYA PENSSAR QUIERE DE ********;
                     11385 5ELCID1440 MUCHAS YENTES SELE ACOGEN, PENSSO DE ********,
                     11440 5ELCID1448 HYAS ESPIDEN & PIENSSAN DE ********,
                     11627 5ELCID1473 ESTO ERA DICHO, PIENSSAN DE ********,
                     11743 5ELCID1489 ALA MA@ANA PIENSSAN DE ********;
                     11873 5ELCID1505 ESSORA DIXO MYNAYA: VAYMOS ********.
                     13253 5ELCID1680 MUCHO AUIEN FECHO, PIESSAN DE ********.
                     13316 5ELCID1688 DEZIR NOS HA LA MISSA, & PENSSAD DE ********,
                     14482 5ELCID1832 MANDO ******** APRIESSA TOSDOS SOS FIJOS DALGO,
                     20419 5ELCID2591 HYA QUIEREN ********, EN ESPIDIMIENTO SON.
                     20555 5ELCID2609 MYO %ID & LOS OTROS DE ******** PENSSAUAN,
                     21028 5ELCID2672 CO DOZIENTOS QUE TIENE YUA ********;
                     22542 5ELCID2870 OTRO DIA MA@ANA PIENSSAN DE ********,
        WORD # 928 OCCURS  24 TIMES.
           INDEX OF DIVERSIFICATION =   868.96 WITH STANDARD DEVIATION OF  1317.81

CAUALGAREMOS          7761 5ELCID0994 NOS ************ SIELLAS GALLEGAS, & HUESAS SOBRE CAL%AS;
        WORD # 929 OCCURS   1 TIMES.

CAUALGARON           17710 5ELCID2241 AL SALIR DELA ECCLEGIA ********** TAN PRIUADO,
        WORD # 930 OCCURS   1 TIMES.

CAUALGAUA              430 5ELCID0054 LA ORA%ION FECHA LUEGO *********;
                     15611 5ELCID1979 EL REY DON ALFONSSO A PRIESSA *********,
        WORD # 931 OCCURS   2 TIMES.

CAUALGAUAN           12151 5ELCID1541 OYDA ES LA MISSA, & LUEGO **********;
                     12250 5ELCID1555 OTRO DIA MANA@A LUEGO **********,
                     14360 5ELCID1816 OTRO DIA MANANA PRIUADO **********,
        WORD # 932 OCCURS   3 TIMES.

CAUALGE               3342 5ELCID0421 EL QUI QUISIERE COMER; & QUI NO, *******.
        WORD # 933 OCCURS   1 TIMES.

CAUALGEDES           11533 5ELCID1461 ********** CON %IENTO GUISADOS PORA HUEBOS DE LIDIAR;
        WORD # 934 OCCURS   1 TIMES.

CAUALGEREMOS          8347 5ELCID1061 MANDAD NOS DAR LAS BESTIAS & ************ PRIUADO;
        WORD # 935 OCCURS   1 TIMES.

CAUALGO               1150 5ELCID0148 MARTIN ANTOLINEZ ******* PRIUADO
                      3240 5ELCID0408 EN TAN BUEN PUNTO ******* VARON;
                      5963 5ELCID0756 ******* MINAYA, EL ESPADA EN LA MANO,
                     20877 5ELCID2651 OTRO DIA MA@ANA CON ELLOS *******,
                     22051 5ELCID2806 E PRIUADO ENEL CAUALLO LAS *******;
                     22269 5ELCID2836 ******* MINAYA CON PERO VERMUEZ
                     22903 5ELCID2917 MU@O GUSTIOZ PRIUADO *******,
                     23712 5ELCID3020 CON GRANDES YENTES EL REY *******
        WORD # 936 OCCURS   8 TIMES.
           INDEX OF DIVERSIFICATION =  3222.14 WITH STANDARD DEVIATION OF  5227.68

CAUALLERO             5312 5ELCID0671 PRIMERO FABLO MINAYA, VN ********* DE PRESTAR:
                      9715 5ELCID1235 LAS NUEUAS DEL ********* YAVEDES DO LEGAUAN.
                     11315 5ELCID1432 MER%ED, MINAYA, ********* DE PRESTAR
                     15723 5ELCID1995 MU@O GUSTIOZ, EL ********* DE PRO.

                     19826 5ELCID2513 EL BUENO DE ALBARFANEZ, ********* LIDIADOR,
        WORD # 937 OCCURS   5 TIMES.
           INDEX OF DIVERSIFICATION =  3627.50 WITH STANDARD DEVIATION OF  1359.83

CAUALLEROS            1841 5ELCID0234 CON ESTOS ********** QUEL SIRUEN ASO SABOR.
                      2309 5ELCID0291 %IENTO QUINZE ********** TODOS IUNTADOS SON;
                      2474 5ELCID0312 ASOS ********** MANDOLOS TODOS IUNTAR:
                      3522 5ELCID0444 LAN%A, ********** BUENOS QUE ACONPANE@ A MINAYA.
                      3748 5ELCID0474 SOS ********** LEGAN CON LA GANAN%IA,
                      4026 5ELCID0512 SOS ********** YAN ARRIBAN%A,
                      4708 5ELCID0597 FIRID LOS, **********, TODOS SINES DUBDAN%A;
                      4873 5ELCID0616 OYD AMI, ALBARFANEZ & TODOS LOS **********
                      5302 5ELCID0670 DEZID ME, **********, COMMO UOS PLAZE DE FAR.
                      5710 5ELCID0720 FERID LOS, **********, POR AMOR DE CARIDAD
                      6644 5ELCID0848 A ********** & A PEONES FECHOS LOS HA RICOS,
                      7382 5ELCID0947 HYA **********, DEZIR UOS HE LA VERDAD:
                      7690 5ELCID0985 YA **********, A PART FAZED LA GANAN%IA;
                      7769 5ELCID0995 %IENTO ********** DEUEMOS VEN%ER A QUELAS MESNADAS.
                      8255 5ELCID1051 CON LOS ********** QUE EL %ID LE AUIE DADOS
                      8308 5ELCID1057 CON ESTOS DOS ********** A PRIESSA VA IANTANDO;
                      8864 5ELCID1129 A MI DEDES C **********, QUE NON UOS PIDO MAS,
                      8946 5ELCID1139 FERID LOS, **********, DAMOR & DE GRADO & DE GRAND VOLUNTAD,
                      9546 5ELCID1213 LOS QUE FUERON DE PIE ********** SE FAZEN;
                     11099 5ELCID1405 DIO TRES ********** MYNAYA ALBARFANEZ,
                     11172 5ELCID1413 HYDOS SON LOS ********** & DELLO PENSSARAN,
                     11183 5ELCID1415 VERIEDES ********** VENIR DE TODAS PARTES,
                     11215 5ELCID1419 AMINAYA LXV ********** A CRE%IDOL HAN,
                     11487 5ELCID1453 DIREUOS DELOS ********** QUE LEUARON EL MENSSAIE:
```

WORD C# PREFIX CONTEXT

CAUALLEROS (CON'T)

```
11564 5ELCID1465 CCN OTRCS %IENTC ********** BIEN UOS CONSSIGRA;
11698 5ELCID1483 CO %IENTO ********** QUE PRIUADOL ACORRADES;
11788 5ELCID1495 ENVIO DOS ********** MYNAYA ALBARFANEZ QUE SOPIESSE LA VERDAD;
12317 5ELCID1564 DOZITOS ********** MANDC EXIR PRIUADO,
13288 5ELCID1685 OYD ME, **********, NCN RASTARA POR AL;
13372 5ELCID1695 DAD ME CXXX ********** PORA HUEBOS DE LIDIAR;
13753 5ELCID1743 CON C ********** A VALEN%IA ES ENTRADO,
15446 5ELCID1957 CCN DOS ********** LUEGC LAS ENBIO:
15916 5ELCID2018 SI NCN A ESTOS ********** QUE QUERIE DE CORA%ON;
17044 5ELCID2158 VERIEDES **********, QUE BIEN ANDANTES SON,
17463 5ELCID2209 TODOS SUS ********** A PRIESSA SON IUNTADOS.
20738 5ELCID2633 ASSI FAZIAN LCS ********** DEL CAMPEADOR.
20880 5ELCID2652 CON DOZIENTCS ********** ESCURRIR LOS MANDO.
22283 5ELCID2838 CON CC **********, CUALES MYO %ID MANDO;
22907 5ELCID2918 CCN EL DOS ********** CUEL SIRUAN A SO SABOR,
22998 5ELCID2930 CON EL DOS ********** QUEL AGUARDAN CUM ASSE@OR.
26578 5ELCID3393 AFFE DOS ********** ENTRARCN POR LA CORT;
27193 5ELCID3476 DAD ME UUESTROS ********** CCN TODAS UUESTRAS GUARNIZONES,
27283 5ELCID3487 ESTOS MIS TRES ********** EN UUESTRA MANO SON,
28185 5ELCID3598 ESTOS TRES ********** DE MYC %ID EL CAMPEADOR
WORD # 938 OCCURS 44 TIMES.
INDEX OF DIVERSIFICATICN = 611.65 WITH STANDARD DEVIATION OF 758.62
```

CAUALLO

```
1675 5ELCID0215 LA CARA DEL ******* TORNO A SANTA MARIA,
3929 5ELCID0498 FATA QUE YO ME PAGE SCBRE MIO BUEN *******,
5644 5ELCID0711 ESPOLONO EL *******, E METIOL ENEL MAYOR AZ.
5878 5ELCID0744 A MYNAYA ALBARFANEZ MATARCN LE EL *******,
5913 5ELCID0749 ACOSTOS AVN AGUAZIL QUE TENIE BUEN *******,
5936 5ELCID0752 AMYNAYA ALBARFANEZ YUAL DAR EL *******:
6120 5ELCID0778 AMYNAYA ALBARFANEZ BIEN LANCA EL *******,
6192 5ELCID0788 ANDAUA MYO %ID SOBRE SO BUEN *******,
7179 5ELCID0920 EL ******* CORRIENDO, UALC ABRA%AR SIN FALLA,
9044 5ELCID1151 DE PIES DE ******* LCS QUES PUDIERON ESCAPAR.
10197 5ELCID1291 DE PIE & DE ******* MUCHO ERA AREZIADO.
12193 5ELCID1548 E BUEN ******* EN DIESTRO QUE UA ANTE SUS ARMAS.
12453 5ELCID1580 Y DEXAUA EL *******, PORA LA CAPIELLA ADELINAUA;
12525 5ELCID1589 POR NOMBRE EL ******* BAUIECA CAUALGA.
13530 5ELCID1714 DIO SALTO MYO %ID EN BAUIECA EL SO *******;
13626 5ELCID1726 SALIOS LE DE SOL ESPACA, CA MUCHOL ANDIDO EL *******,
13790 5ELCID1747 MYO %ID FINCO ANTELLAS, TOUO LA RYENDA AL *******:
13834 5ELCID1752 VEDES EL ESPADA SANGRIENTA & SUDIENTO EL *******:
13865 5ELCID1756 ESTO DIXO MYO %ID, DI%IENDO DEL *******.
15678 5ELCID1988 TANTA BUENA ARMA & TANTO BUEN ******* COREDOR,
16799 5ELCID2127 SOBREL SO ******* BAUIECA MYO %ID SALTO DAUA;
18923 5ELCID2394 AGUIJO A BAUIECA, EL ******* QUE BIEN ANDA,
19090 5ELCID2415 MAS SI EL ******* NON ESTROPIE%A O COMIGO NON CAYE,
19115 5ELCID2418 BUEN ******* TIENE BUCAR & GRANDES SALTOS FAZ,
21839 5ELCID2779 ARRENDO EL *******, A ELLAS ADELINO;
22049 5ELCID2806 E PRIUADO ENEL ******* LAS CAUALGO;
22061 5ELCID2808 EL ******* PRISO POR LA RIENDA & LUEGO DENT LAS PARTIO,
25461 5ELCID3242 VERIEDES ADUZIR TANTO ******* CORREDOR,
26062 5ELCID3322 DID EL *******, TCUEL DO EN PORIDAD:
27488 5ELCID3511 MYO %ID ENEL ******* ADELANT SE LEGO,
27539 5ELCID3517 SI AUOS LE TOLLIES, EL ******* NO HAURIE TAN BUEN SE@OR.
27547 5ELCID3518 MAS ATAL ******* CUM EST PORA TAL COMMO VOS,
27576 5ELCID3521 CA POR UOS & POREL ******* ONDRADOS SOMO NOS.
28506 5ELCID3640 POR LA COPLA DEL ******* EN TIERRA LO ECHO.
28661 5ELCID3659 BOLUIO LA RIENDA AL ******* PCR TORNASSE DE CARA;
28707 5ELCID3666 EL ******* ASCORRIENDA, & MESURANDOL DEL ESPADA,
WORD # 939 OCCURS 36 TIMES.
INDEX OF DIVERSIFICATICN = 771.34 WITH STANDARD DEVIATION OF 931.85
```

CAUALLOS

```
4746 5ELCID0602 TIENEN BUENOS ********, SABET, ASU GUISA LES ANDAN;
5776 5ELCID0730 TANOS BUENOS ******** SIN SOS DUENOS ANDAR.
6255 5ELCID0796 DELOS MORISCOS, QUANDO SON LEGADOS, FFALLARON DX ********.
6328 5ELCID0805 EN LA SU QUINTA AL %ID CAEN C ********.
6402 5ELCID0816 QUIEROL ENBIAR EN DCN XXX ********,
6825 5ELCID0872 TREYNTA ******** AL REY LOS ENPRESENTAUA;
7740 5ELCID0991 APRETAD LOS ********, & BISTADES LAS ARMAS.
7829 5ELCID1001 LAS ARMAS AUIEN PRESAS & SEDIEN SOBRE LOS ********.
8828 5ELCID1123 APAREIADOS ME SED A ******** & ARMAS;
10056 5ELCID1274 DAR LE QUIERO C ********, & UOS YC GELOS LEUAR;
10540 5ELCID1336 %IENT ******** GRUESSCS & CORREDORES,
10605 5ELCID1344 RE%IBO ESTOS ******** QUEM ENBIA DE DON.
11892 5ELCID1508 EN BUENOS ******** A PETRALES & A CASCAUELES,
14033 5ELCID1777 NON PUDIERON ELLOS SABER LA CUENTA DE TODOS LOS ********,
14066 5ELCID1781 DELOS BUENOS & OTORGADOS CAYERON LE MILL & D ********;
14226 5ELCID1800 TANTOS AUIEN DE AUERES, DE ******** & DE ARMAS;
14296 5ELCID1809 CON ******** DESTA QUINTA QUE YO HE GANADA,
14333 5ELCID1813 ESTOS DOZIENTOS ******** YRAN EN PRESENTAIAS,
14383 5ELCID1819 DESTA LID QUE HA ARRANCADA CC ******** LE ENBIAUA ENPRESENTAIA,
14655 5ELCID1854 E EMBIA UOS DOZIENTOS ********, & BESA UOS LAS MANOS.
14748 5ELCID1864 COMMO SI LOS FALASSE MUERTOS ADUZIR SE LOS ********,
14779 5ELCID1868 ESTOS DOZIENTOS ******** QUEM ENBIA MYO %ID.
```

WORD C# PREFIX CONTEXT

CAUALLOS (CON'T)

14828 5ELCID1874 DOUOS IIJ ******** & PRENDED LOS AQUI.
15528 5ELCID1968 ******** GRUESSOS & COREDORES SJN FALLA,
15845 5ELCID2010 TANTOS ******** EN DIESTRO, GRUESSOS & CORREDORES,
16728 5ELCID2118 MYO %ID DELOS ******** LX DIO EN DON.
16945 5ELCID2145 E XXX ******** CORREDORES, ESTOS BIEN ENSSELLADOS;
17731 5ELCID2244 TRES ******** CAMEO EL QUE EN BUEN ORA NASCO.
17821 5ELCID2254 ENTRE PALAFRES & MULAS & CORREDORES ********,
19017 5ELCID2406 ******** SIN DUENOS SALIR A TODAS PARTES.
19643 5ELCID2489 CAYERON LE EN QUINTA AL %ID SEYX %IENTOS ********,
20271 5ELCID2573 ******** PORA EN DIESTRO FUERTES & CORREDORES,
20904 5ELCID2655 BUENOS SE@OS ******** ALOS YFANTES DE CARRION.
27145 5ELCID3469 ARMAS & ******** TIENEN LOS DEL CANPEADOR,
27720 5ELCID3538 MUCHO VIENEN BIEN ADOBADOS DE ******** & DE GUARNIZONES,
28062 5ELCID3582 ADUZEN LES LOS ******** BUENOS & CORREDORES,
28339 5ELCID3618 BATIEN LOS ******** CON LOS ESPOLONES,
WORD # 940 OCCURS 37 TIMES.
INDEX OF DIVERSIFICATION = 654.36 WITH STANDARD DEVIATION OF 1070.44

CAUALOS 14566 5ELCID1842 FIRIERON SE A TIERRA, DE%ENDIERON DELOS *******,
WORD # 941 OCCURS 1 TIMES.

CAYA 2482 5ELCID0313 OYD, VARONES, NON UOS **** EN PESAR;
10028 5ELCID1273 SI AUOS PLOGUIERE, MINAYA, & NON UOS **** EN PESAR,
20712 5ELCID2629 ATALES COSAS FED QUE EN PLAZER **** ANOS.
WORD # 942 OCCURS 3 TIMES.

CAYE 14190 5ELCID1796 LO QUE **** AEL MUCHO ERA SOBEIANO;
19096 5ELCID2415 MAS SI EL CAUALLO NON ESTROPIE%A O COMIGO NON ****,
19470 5ELCID2467 QUE ALA RA%ION **** SEYS %IENTOS MARCOS DE PLATA.
WORD # 943 OCCURS 3 TIMES.

CAYEN 5790 5ELCID0732 ***** EN VN POCO DE LOGAR MOROS MUERTOS MILL & CCC YA.
WORD # 944 OCCURS 1 TIMES.

CAYERON 9707 5ELCID1234 ATODOS LOS MENORES ******* C MARCOS DE PLATA.
14061 5ELCID1781 DELOS BUENOS & OTORGADOS ******* LE MILL & D CAUALLOS;
14071 5ELCID1782 QUANDO A MYO %ID ******* TANTOS, LOS OTROS BIEN PUEDEN FINCAR PAGADOS.
19635 5ELCID2489 ******* LE EN QUINTA AL %ID SEYX %IENTOS CAUALLOS,
WORD # 945 OCCURS 4 TIMES.

CAYESSE 10666 5ELCID1351 MER%ED UOS PIDE EL %ID, SIUOS ******* EN SABOR,
WORD # 946 OCCURS 1 TIMES.

CAYO 2682 5ELCID0339 A IONAS, QUANDO **** EN LA MAR,
10408 5ELCID1319 ALOS PIES DEL REY ALFONSSO **** CON GRAND DUELO,
14266 5ELCID1805 DELO QUE AUOS **** VOS NON GRADE%EDES NADA;
15975 5ELCID2025 DE AQUESTA GUISA ALOS PIES LE ****.
28632 5ELCID3656 LO VNO **** ENEL CAMPO & LO AL SUSO FINCAUA.
WORD # 947 OCCURS 5 TIMES.
INDEX OF DIVERSIFICATION = 6486.50 WITH STANDARD DEVIATION OF 4807.80

CAYOL 19035 5ELCID2408 MYO %ID AL REY BUCAR ***** EN ALCAZ:
WORD # 948 OCCURS 1 TIMES.

CAZ 6109 5ELCID0776 EL CAMPEADOR YUAL EN AL ***,
WORD # 949 OCCURS 1 TIMES.

CC 3503 5ELCID0442 VOS CON LOS ** YD UOS EN ALGARA; ALA VAYA ALBARABAREZ,
13943 5ELCID1766 ACADA VNA DELLAS DO LES ** MARCOS DE PLATA,
14382 5ELCID1819 DESTA LID QUE HA ARRANCADA ** CAUALLOS LE ENBIAUA ENPRESENTAIA,
22282 5ELCID2838 CON ** CAUALLEROS, QUALES MYO %ID MANDO;
25376 5ELCID3231 DESTOS IIJ MILL MARCOS LOS ** TENGO YO;
27411 5ELCID3502 LOS ** MARCOS AL REY LOS SOLTO.
WORD # 950 OCCURS 6 TIMES.
INDEX OF DIVERSIFICATION = 4780.60 WITH STANDARD DEVIATION OF 4212.83

CCC 1452 5ELCID0186 LOS OTROS *** EN ORO GELOS PAGAUAN.
4775 5ELCID0605 EN VN ORA & VN POCO DE LOGAR *** MOROS MATAN.
5800 5ELCID0732 CAYEN EN VN POCO DE LOGAR MOROS MUERTOS MILL & *** YA.
WORD # 951 OCCURS 3 TIMES.

CCIIJ 3765 5ELCID0476 AFEUOS LOS ***** ENEL ALGARA,
WORD # 952 OCCURS 1 TIMES.

CCXLV 29237 5ELCID3733 EN ERA DE MILL & ***** A@OS. EN EL ROMANZ
WORD # 953 OCCURS 1 TIMES.

CENA 22631 5ELCID2883 POR AMOR DE MYO %ID RICA **** LES DA.
WORD # 954 OCCURS 1 TIMES.

CERCA 17948 5ELCID2271 HY MORAN LOS YFANTES BIEN ***** DE DOS A@OS,
WORD # 955 OCCURS 1 TIMES.

CER%ADO 18123 5ELCID2293 VIO ******* EL ESCA@O DE SUS BUENOS VARONES:
WORD # 956 OCCURS 1 TIMES.

WORD C# PREFIX CONTEXT

```
CER%ER              15593 5ELCID1977 COMMO ELLOS TENIEN, ****** LES YA LA GANA%IA,
         WORD # 957 OCCURS   1 TIMES.

CHICAS               2141 5ELCID0269 FEM ANTE UOS YO & UUESTRAS FFIJAS, YFFANTES SON & DE DIAS ******
         WORD # 958 OCCURS   1 TIMES.

CHICOS               4662 5ELCID0591 LOS GRANDES & LOS ****** FUERA SALTO DAN,
                    15687 5ELCID1990 ****** & GRANDES VESTIDOS SON DE COLORES.
         WORD # 959 OCCURS   2 TIMES.

CHISTIANOS            741 5ELCID0093 DE NOCHE LO LIEUEN, QUE NON LO VEAN **********.
                     6261 5ELCID0797 GRAND ALEGREYA VA ENTRE ESSOS **********,
         WORD # 960 OCCURS   2 TIMES.

CHRISTIANA           7054 5ELCID0901 MIENTRA QUE SEA EL PUEBLO DE MOROS & DELA YENTE **********,
                    25804 5ELCID3286 NIMBLA MESSO FIJO DE MORO NIN DE **********,
         WORD # 961 OCCURS   2 TIMES.

CHRISTIANAS           229 5ELCID0029 GRANDE DUELO AUIEN LAS YENTES ***********;
                    13208 5ELCID1674 PRESTAS SON LAS MESaDAS DE LAS YENTES ***********,
                    13416 5ELCID1700 NOS DETARDAN DE ADOBASSE ESSAS YENTES ***********.
                    14220 5ELCID1799 ALEGRES SON POR VALEN%IA LAS YENTES ***********,
         WORD # 962 OCCURS   4 TIMES.

CHRISTIANDAD         6071 5ELCID0770 TAN BUEN DIA POR LA ************,
                     8781 5ELCID1116 DESPUES QUE NOS PARTIEMOS DELA LINPIA ************,
                     9435 5ELCID1199 GRANDES YENTES SE LE ACOIEN DELA BUENA ************.

         WORD # 963 OCCURS   3 TIMES.

CHRISTIANISMO        8049 5ELCID1027 SI NON, EN TODOS UUESTROS DIAS NON VEREDES *************.
                    10312 5ELCID1305  DIOS, QUE ALEGRE ERA TODO *************,
         WORD # 964 OCCURS   2 TIMES.

CHRISTIANO           1866 5ELCID0237 EL ABBAT DON SANCHO, ********** DEL CRIADOR,
                    10274 5ELCID1300 E DAR GELO A ESTE BUEN **********;
                    12180 5ELCID1546 EL OBISPO DON IHERONIMO, BUEN ********** SIN FALLA,
                    14129 5ELCID1788 E NON LA TOLLIESSE DENT **********:
         WORD # 965 OCCURS   4 TIMES.

CHRISTIANOS           840 5ELCID0107 QUE NON ME DESCUBRADES A MOROS NIN A ***********;
                     1132 5ELCID0145 QUE NON LO SEPAN MOROS NON ***********.
                     4451 5ELCID0566 VENIDO ES A MOROS, EXIDO ES DE ***********;
                     5787 5ELCID0731 LOS MOROS LAMAN MAFOMAT & LOS *********** SANTI YAGUE.
                     5884 5ELCID0745 BIEN LO ACORREN MESNADAS DE ***********.
                     6283 5ELCID0800 REFECHOS SON TODOS ESOS *********** CON AQUESTA GANAN%IA.
                     7558 5ELCID0968 GENTES SE LE ALEGAN GRANDES ENTRE MOROS & ***********,
                     7717 5ELCID0988 DE MOROS & DE *********** GENTES TRAE SOBEIANAS,
                     8101 5ELCID1033 ***********;
                     9369 5ELCID1191 %ERCAR QUIERE A VALEN%IA PORA *********** LA DAR.
                     9725 5ELCID1236 GRAND ALEGRIA ES ENTRE TODOS ESSOS ***********
                     9779 5ELCID1242 E QUE FABLASSEN DESTO MOROS & ***********.
                    10233 5ELCID1295 ALOS DIAS DEL SIEGLO NON LE LORASSEN ***********.
                    18542 5ELCID2346 AMARAULLA LO AUIEN MUCHOS DESSOS ***********,
                    19701 5ELCID2498 MOROS & *********** DE MI HAN GRANT PAUOR;
                    21464 5ELCID2729 MOROS & *********** DEPARTIRAN DESTA RAZON,
                    27510 5ELCID3514 EN MOROS NI EN *********** OTRO TAL NON HA OY,
         WORD # 966 OCCURS  17 TIMES.
              INDEX OF DIVERSIFICATION =  1665.88 WITH STANDARD DEVIATION OF  2343.59

CHRISTO             12802 5ELCID1624 E EL NON GELO GRADE%E SI NON A IHESU *******.
         WORD # 967 OCCURS   1 TIMES.

CHRISTUS            15264 5ELCID1933 ESTO GRADESCO A ******** EL MYO SEaOR.
                    16350 5ELCID2074 ASI LO MANDE ******** QUE SEA ASO PRO.
                    19551 5ELCID2477 GRADO A ********, QUE DEL MUNDO ES SEaOR,
                    22219 5ELCID2830 GRADO A ********, QUE DEL MUNDO ES SEaOR,
                    29190 5ELCID3727 DE ******** HAYA PERDON
         WORD # 968 OCCURS   5 TIMES.
              INDEX OF DIVERSIFICATION =  3480.50 WITH STANDARD DEVIATION OF  2493.69

CIBDAD              22729 5ELCID2896 TENIENDO YUAN ARMAS, ENTRARON SE ALA ******;
         WORD # 969 OCCURS   1 TIMES.

CICLATONES          21588 5ELCID2744 SANGRIENTAS EN LAS CAMISAS & TODOS LOS **********.
         WORD # 970 OCCURS   1 TIMES.

CID                 16170 5ELCID2051 BESO LE LA MANO MYO ***, LO OTORGO.
                    16527 5ELCID2095 GRADO & GRA%IAS, ***, COMMO TAN BUENO, & PRIMERO AL CRIADOR,
         WORD # 971 OCCURS   2 TIMES.

CIENTO              10132 5ELCID1284 ****** OMNES LE DIO MYO %ID A ALBARFANEZ POR SERUIR LE
                                     EN LA CARRERA,
         WORD # 972 OCCURS   1 TIMES.
```

WORD C# PREFIX CONTEXT

```
CINQUAENTA          18277 5ELCID2313 ********** MILL TIENDAS FINCADAS HA DELAS CABDALES;
        WORD # 973 OCCURS   1 TIMES.

CINQUAESMA          29188 5ELCID3726 PASSADO ES DESTE SIEGLO EL DIA DE **********.
        WORD # 974 OCCURS   1 TIMES.

CINXIESTES          12575 5ELCID1595 MER%ED, CAMPEADOR, EN BUEN ORA ********** ESPADA
        WORD # 975 OCCURS   1 TIMES.

CINXO                6852 5ELCID0875 MYO %ID RUY DIAZ, QUE EN BUEN ORA ***** ESPADA. . .
        WORD # 976 OCCURS   1 TIMES.

CLAMOR               2279 5ELCID0286 TANEN LAS CAMPA@AS EN SAN PERO A ******.
        WORD # 977 OCCURS   1 TIMES.

CLARA               20569 5ELCID2611 HYA SALIEN LOS YFANTES DE VALEN%IA LA *****,
                    28584 5ELCID3649 RELUMBRA TOD EL CAMPO, TANTO ER LINPIA & *****;
        WORD # 978 OCCURS   2 TIMES.

CLARO               16258 5ELCID2062 OTRO DIA MA@ANA, ***** SALIE EL SOL,
        WORD # 979 OCCURS   1 TIMES.

CLAROS               9297 5ELCID1182 CON EL DELOS MONTES ****** AUYEN GUERRA TAN GRAND,
                    21197 5ELCID2693 POR LOS MONTES ****** AGUIJAN A ESPOLON;
        WORD # 980 OCCURS   2 TIMES.

CLAUOS                694 5ELCID0088 LOS GUADAME%IS UERMEIOS & LOS ****** BIEN DORADOS.
        WORD # 981 OCCURS   1 TIMES.

CO                  11696 5ELCID1483 ** %IENTO CAUALLEROS QUE PRIUADOL ACORRADES;
                    21023 5ELCID2672 ** DOZIENTOS QUE TIENE YUA CAUALGAR;
        WORD # 982 OCCURS   2 TIMES.

COBDO                3947 5ELCID0501 E POR EL ***** AYUSO LA SANGRE SESTELANDO,
                     6135 5ELCID0781 POR EL ***** AYUSO LA SANGRE DESTELLANDO.
                    13604 5ELCID1724 POR EL ***** AYUSO LA SANGRE DESTELLANDO.
                    18149 5ELCID2296 MYO %ID FINCO EL *****, EN PIE SE LEUANTO,
                    19364 5ELCID2453 POR EL ***** AYUSO LA SANGRE DESTELLANDO;
        WORD # 983 OCCURS   5 TIMES.
           INDEX OF DIVERSIFICATION =  3853.25 WITH STANDARD DEVIATION OF  2786.01

COBRAR               2403 5ELCID0303 LO QUE PERDEDES DOBLADO UOS LO ******.
        WORD # 984 OCCURS   1 TIMES.

CO%ERAS              7755 5ELCID0993 ELAS SIELLAS ******* & LAS %INCHAS AMOIADAS;
        WORD # 985 OCCURS   1 TIMES.

COFIA                6194 5ELCID0789 LA ***** FRONZIDA  DIOS, COMMO ES BIEN BARBADO
                    19252 5ELCID2437 ***** SOBRE LOS PELOS FRONZIDA DELLA YA QUANTO.
                    24261 5ELCID3094 VNA ***** SOBRE LOS PELOS DUN ESCARIN DE PRO,
                    28611 5ELCID3653 ALLA LEUO EL ALMOFAR, FATA LA ***** LEGAUA,
                    28614 5ELCID3654 LA ***** & EL ALMOFAR TODO GELO LEUAUA,
        WORD # 986 OCCURS   5 TIMES.
           INDEX OF DIVERSIFICATION =  5604.00 WITH STANDARD DEVIATION OF  5442.42

COGE                  469 5ELCID0059 POSO EN LA GLERA QUANDO NOL **** NACI EN CASA;

        WORD # 987 OCCURS   1 TIMES.

COGER                 353 5ELCID0044 NON UOS OSARIEMOS ABRIR NON ***** POR NADA;
                     1621 5ELCID0208 MANDAD ***** LA TIENDA & VAYAMOS PRIUADO,
        WORD # 988 OCCURS   2 TIMES.

COGIDA               1663 5ELCID0213 ESTAS PALABRAS DICHAS, LA TIENDA ES ******.
                    21290 5ELCID2706 ****** HAN LA TIENDA DO ALBERGARON DE NOCH,
        WORD # 989 OCCURS   2 TIMES.

COGIERON             6096 5ELCID0774 E AGALUE NOL ******** ALLA;
        WORD # 990 OCCURS   1 TIMES.

COGIO               22012 5ELCID2801 ***** DEL AGUA ENEL & ASUS PRIMAS DIO;
        WORD # 991 OCCURS   1 TIMES.

COGIOS               4636 5ELCID0588 MYO %ID, QUANDO LOS VIO FUERA, ****** COMMO DE ARRANCADA.
        WORD # 992 OCCURS   1 TIMES.

COIAMOS              4904 5ELCID0621 ******* LOS DE DENTRO, CA EL SENORIO TENEMOS,
        WORD # 993 OCCURS   1 TIMES.

COIAN               13345 5ELCID1691 MAS VALE QUE NOS LOS VEZCAMOS, QUE ELLOS ***** EL PAN.
        WORD # 994 OCCURS   1 TIMES.

COIO                 2324 5ELCID0293 MARTIN ANTOLINEZ CON ELLOS ****.
                     4536 5ELCID0577 **** SALON AYUSO LA SU SE@A AL%ADA,
        WORD # 995 OCCURS   2 TIMES.
```

WORD C# PREFIX CONTEXT

COIOS 4640 5ELCID0589 ***** SALON AYUSO, CON LOS SOS ABUELTA NADI.
WORD # 996 OCCURS 1 TIMES.

COLADA 7905 5ELCID1010 HY GA@O A ****** QUE MAS VALE DE MILL MARCOS DE PLATA.
19142 5ELCID2421 ARRIBA AL%O ******, VN GRANT COLPE DADOL HA,
20292 5ELCID2575 DAR UOS HE DOS ESPADAS, A ****** & A TIZON,
21451 5ELCID2727 AL VNA DIZEN ****** & AL OTRA TIZON,
24758 5ELCID3153 DILES DOS ESPADAS, A ****** & A TIZON,
25069 5ELCID3194 PRENDED A ******, GANELA DE BUEN SE@OR,
25136 5ELCID3201 HYA PAGADO SO DE MIS ESPADAS, DE ****** & DE TIZON.
27864 5ELCID3556 ****** & TIZON, QUE NON LIDIASSEN CON ELLAS LOS DEL CANPEADOR;
28645 5ELCID3657 QUANDO ESTE COLPE A FERIDO ****** LA PRE%IADA,
WORD # 997 OCCURS 9 TIMES.
INDEX OF DIVERSIFICATION = 2591.50 WITH STANDARD DEVIATION OF 3669.51

COLADAL 25059 5ELCID3192 TENDIO EL BRA%O, EL ESPADA ******* DIO;
WORD # 998 OCCURS 1 TIMES.

COLADO 24930 5ELCID3175 SACARON LAS ESPADAS ****** & TIZON,
WORD # 999 OCCURS 1 TIMES.

COLGADAS 6414 5ELCID0818 SE@AS ESPADAS DELOS ARZONES ********.
WORD #1000 OCCURS 1 TIMES.

COLGAR 13157 5ELCID1668 ****** LOS HAN EN SANTA MARIA MADRE DEL CRIADOR.
WORD #1001 OCCURS 1 TIMES.

COLOR 18232 5ELCID2306 QUANDO LOS FALLARON & ELLOS VINIERON, ASSI VINIERON SIN *****;
WORD #1002 OCCURS 1 TIMES.

COLORES 15693 5ELCID1990 CHICOS & GRANDES VESTIDOS SON DE *******.
WORD #1003 OCCURS 1 TIMES.

COLPE 1437 5ELCID0184 ATOD EL PRIMER ***** IIJ MARCOS DE PLATA ECHARON,
6026 5ELCID0764 POR AQUEL ***** RANCADO ES EL FONSSADO.
6034 5ELCID0765 MARTIN ANTOLINEZ VN ***** DIO A GALUE,
19145 5ELCID2421 ARRIBA AL%O COLADA, VN GRANT ***** DADOL HA,
28423 5ELCID3630 VN ***** RESIBIERA, MAS OTRO FIRIO:
28540 5ELCID3644 ANTES QUE EL ***** ESPERASSE DIXO: VEN%UDO SO.
28587 5ELCID3650 DIOL VN *****, DE TRAUIESSOL TOMAUA,
28642 5ELCID3657 QUANDO ESTE ***** A FERIDO COLADA LA PRE%IADA,
28798 5ELCID3678 ESTE ***** FECHO, OTRO DIO MUNO GUSTIOZ,
WORD #1004 OCCURS 9 TIMES.
INDEX OF DIVERSIFICATION = 3419.13 WITH STANDARD DEVIATION OF 5147.86

COLPEL 28674 5ELCID3661 VN ****** DIO DE LANO, CON LO AGUDO NOL TOMAUA.
WORD #1005 OCCURS 1 TIMES.

COLPES 5660 5ELCID0713 DAN LE GRANDES ******, MAS NOL PUEDEN FALSSAR.
5744 5ELCID0724 SE@OS MOROS MATARON, TODOS DE SE@OS ******;
5897 5ELCID0747 MAGER DE PIE BUENOS ****** VA DANDO.
5995 5ELCID0760 AL REY FARIZ IIJ ****** LE AUIE DADO;
9678 5ELCID1230 AQUEL REY DE MARRUECOS CON TRES ****** ESCAPA.
13613 5ELCID1725 AL REY YU%EF TRES ****** LE OUO DADOS,
18853 5ELCID2386 ALOS PRIMEROS ****** DOS MOROS MATAUA DE LA LAN%A.
18895 5ELCID2391 DAUAN LE GRANDES ******, MAS NOL FALSSAN LAS ARMAS.
19348 5ELCID2451 DELOS ****** DELA LAN%A NON AUIE RECABDO;
21601 5ELCID2746 ENSAYANDOS AMOS QUAL DARA MEIORES ******.
26055 5ELCID3321 DELOS PRIMEROS ****** OF LE DE ARRANCAR;
28565 5ELCID3647 TALES FUERON LOS ****** QUE LES QUEBRARON AMAS.
28767 5ELCID3673 FIRIENSSEN EN LOS ESCUDOS VNOS TAN GRANDES ******;
WORD #1006 OCCURS 13 TIMES.
INDEX OF DIVERSIFICATION = 1924.58 WITH STANDARD DEVIATION OF 1988.92

COMAN 21925 5ELCID2789 LOS GANADOS FIEROS NON NOS ***** EN AQUESTE MONT
WORD #1007 OCCURS 1 TIMES.

COMBRE 7991 5ELCID1021 NON ****** VN BOCADO POR QUANTO HA EN TODA ESPA@A,
WORD #1008 OCCURS 1 TIMES.

COMED 8025 5ELCID1025 *****, CONDE, DESTE PAN & BEUED DESTE VINO.
8093 5ELCID1033 DIXO MYO %ID: *****, CONDE, ALGO, CASI NON COMEDES, NON VEREDES
8149 5ELCID1039 PUES *****, CONDE, & QUANDO FUEREDES IANTADO,
WORD #1009 OCCURS 3 TIMES.

COMEDE 8055 5ELCID1028 DIXO EL CONDE DON REMONT: ******, DON RODRIGO, & PENSSEDES DE FOLGAR.
WORD #1010 OCCURS 1 TIMES.

COMEDES 8098 5ELCID1033 DIXO MYO %ID: COMED, CONDE, ALGO, CASI NON *******, NON VEREDES
8282 5ELCID1054 SI BIEN NON *******, CONDE, DON YO SEA PAGADO,
WORD #1011 OCCURS 2 TIMES.

COMEMOS 8693 5ELCID1104 BEUEMOS SO VINO & ******* EL SO PAN.
WORD #1012 OCCURS 1 TIMES.

WORD C# PREFIX CONTEXT

```
COMER              3338 5ELCID0421 EL QUI QUISIERE *****; & QUI NO, CAUALGE.
                   7986 5ELCID1020 EL NON LO CUIERE *****, ATODOS LOS SOSANAUA:
                   8070 5ELCID1029 QUE YO DEXAR ME MORIR, CUE NON QUIERO *****.
                   8085 5ELCID1032 NOL PUEDEN FAZER ***** VN MUESSO DE PAN.
                  17458 5ELCID2208 SABOR ABRIEDES DE SER & DE ***** ENEL PALA%IO.
         WORD #1013 OCCURS    5 TIMES.
            INDEX OF DIVERSIFICATION =  3529.00 WITH STANDARD DEVIATION OF  4457.98

COMERES            7978 5ELCID1019 ADUZEN LE LOS *******, DELANT GELOS PARAUAN;
         WORD #1014 OCCURS    1 TIMES.

COMETER           10862 5ELCID1375 NON LA OSARIEMOS A ******* NOS ESTA RAZON,
                  16338 5ELCID2073 ******* QUIERO VN RUEGO A MYO %ID EL CAMPEADOR;
                  27750 5ELCID3542 EL ******* FUE MALO, QUE LO AL NOS ENPE%O,
         WORD #1015 OCCURS    3 TIMES.

COMETIEN          13224 5ELCID1676 DOS FALLAN CON LOS MOROS ******** LOS TAN AYNA.
         WORD #1016 OCCURS    1 TIMES.

COMIDIA           15929 5ELCID2020 COMMO LO ******* EL QUE EN BUEN ORA NA%IO,
         WORD #1017 OCCURS    1 TIMES.

COMIDIERON        21345 5ELCID2713 TANTO MAL ********** LOS YFANTES DE CARRION;
         WORD #1018 OCCURS    1 TIMES.

COMIDIO           14947 5ELCID1889 VNA GRANT ORA EL REY PENSSO & *******;
                  15260 5ELCID1932 VNA GRAND ORA PENSSO & *******;
                  22208 5ELCID2828 VNA GRAND ORA PENSSO & *******;
                  23183 5ELCID2953 EL REY VNA GRAND ORA CALLO & *******;
         WORD #1019 OCCURS    4 TIMES.

COMIDIOS           3989 5ELCID0507 ******** MYO %ID, EL QUE EN BUEN ORA FUE NADO,
         WORD #1020 OCCURS    1 TIMES.

COMIDRAN          28034 5ELCID3578 NON SABEMOS QUES ******** ELLOS OQUE NON;
         WORD #1021 OCCURS    1 TIMES.

COMIEN            13266 5ELCID1682 TORNADOS SON A MYO %ID LOS QUE ****** SO PAN;
         WORD #1022 OCCURS    1 TIMES.

COMIENDO           8262 5ELCID1052 ******** VA EL CONDE  DIOS, QUE DE BUEN GRADO
         WORD #1023 OCCURS    1 TIMES.

COMIERAN          16297 5ELCID2067 PASSADO AUIE IIJ A@OS NO ******** MEIOR.
         WORD #1024 OCCURS    1 TIMES.

COMIEREDES         8105 5ELCID1034 E SI UOS **********, DON YO SEA PAGADO,
         WORD #1025 OCCURS    1 TIMES.

COMIGO             8200 5ELCID1045 QUE ****** ANDAN LAZRADOS, & NON UOS LO DARE.
                   9375 5ELCID1192 QUIEN QUIERE YR ****** %ERCAR A VALEN%IA,
                   9920 5ELCID1258 DELOS QUE SON AQUI & ****** GANARON ALGO;
                  12657 5ELCID1606 ENTRAD ****** EN VALEN%IA LA CASA,
                  16817 5ELCID2129 QUI QUIERE YR ****** ALAS BODAS, O RE%EBIR MI DON,
                  16826 5ELCID2130 DAQUEND VAYA ******; CUEDO QUEL AURA PRO.
                  16902 5ELCID2139 QUANDO UOS IUNTAREDES ******, QUEM DIGADES LA UERDAT.
                  19094 5ELCID2415 MAS SI EL CAUALLO NON ESTROPIE%A O ****** NON CAYE,
                  19100 5ELCID2416 NON TE IUNTARAS ****** FATA DENTRO EN LA MAR.
                  19565 5ELCID2479 QUE LIDIARAN ****** EN CAMPO MYOS YERNOS AMOS ADOS;
                  24038 5ELCID3064 VOS YREDES ****** & EL OBISPO DON IHERONIMO
                  24077 5ELCID3070 ****** YRA MAL ANDA, QUE ES BIEN SABIDOR.
                  24784 5ELCID3157 ****** NON QUISIERON AUER NADA & PERDIERON MI AMOR;
                  27199 5ELCID3477 VAYAN ******, YO SERE EL CURIADOR;
         WORD #1026 OCCURS   14 TIMES.
            INDEX OF DIVERSIFICATION =  1460.46 WITH STANDARD DEVIATION OF  1583.15

COMME             12735 5ELCID1617 DESTA GANAN%IA ***** ES BUENA & GRAND.
         WORD #1027 OCCURS    1 TIMES.

COMMO               246 5ELCID0032 ASSI ***** LEGO ALA PUERTA, FALOLA BIEN %ERRADA,
                    482 5ELCID0061 ASSI POSO MYO %ID ***** SI FUESSE EN MONTA@A.
                   1186 5ELCID0153 ASSI ***** ENTRARON, AL %ID BESARON LE LAS MANOS.
                   1800 5ELCID0229 CASTIGAR LOS HE ***** ABRAN AFAR.
                   2211 5ELCID0279 ***** ALA MI ALMA YO TANTO UOS QUERIA.
                   2286 5ELCID0288 ***** SEUA DE TIERRA MYO %ID EL CANPEADOR;
                   2495 5ELCID0315 SED MEMBRADOS ***** LO DEUEDES FAR.
                   2645 5ELCID0334 EN BELLEM APARE%IST, ***** FUE TU VELUNTAD;
                   2675 5ELCID0338 TE OFFRE%IERON, ***** FUE TU VELUNTAD;
                   2842 5ELCID0359 ***** FUE TU VOLUNTAD.
                   2978 5ELCID0375 ASIS PARTEN VNOS DOTROS ***** LA V@A DELA CARNE.
                   3047 5ELCID0384 ***** SIRUA ADO@A XIMENA & ALAS FIJAS QUE HA,
                   3401 5ELCID0429 DIXOLES ATODOS ***** QUERIE TRASNOCHAR;
                   3474 5ELCID0438 ***** LOS CONSEIAUA MINAYA ALBARFANEZ:
```

WORD C# PREFIX CONTEXT

COMMO (CON'T)

4563 5ELCID0580 VEYEN LC LCS DE ALCO%ER, DICS, ***** SE ALABAUAN
4588 5ELCID0583 DEGUISA UA MYC %ID ***** SIESCAPASSE DE ARRANCADA.
4637 5ELCID0588 MYC %ID, QUANDC LCS VIC FUERA, COGIOS ***** DE ARRANCADA.
5303 5ELCID0670 DEZID ME, CAUALLERCS, ***** UOS PLAZE DE FAR.
5421 5ELCID0684 FABLAUA MYO %ID ***** OCREDES CONTAR:
5464 5ELCID0690 ***** SCDES MUY BUENO, TENER LA ECES SIN ARCH;
5625 5ELCID0708 LOS QUE EL DEBDO AUEDES VEREMOS ***** LA ACORREDES.
6197 5ELCID0789 LA COFIA FRCNZICA DICS, ***** ES BIEN BARBADO
7000 5ELCID0895 GRADO & GRA%IAS, REY, ***** A SE@OR NATURAL;
7221 5ELCID0926 DIOS, ***** FUE ALEGRE TODO AQUEL FONSSADO,
7250 5ELCID0930 DIOS, ***** ES ALEGRE LA BAREA VELIDA,
7274 5ELCID0933 DIOS, ***** FUE EL %ID PAGADO & FIZO GRANT ALEGRIA
8225 5ELCID1048 ***** QUE YRA A DE REY & DE TIERRA ES ECHADO.
8836 5ELCID1125 ***** OMNES EXIDCS DE TIERRA ESTRA@A,
8893 5ELCID1133 ***** FIO POR CIOS, EL CAMPO NUESTRC SERA.
8901 5ELCID1134 ***** GELO A DICHO, AL CAMPEADOR MUCHO PLAZE.
10439 5ELCID1323 LOS PIES & LAS MANOS, ***** ATAN BUEN SE@OR,
10582 5ELCID1341 DE TAN FIERAS GANAN%IAS ***** A FECHAS EL CAMPEADOR
10732 5ELCID1359 CATAD ***** LAS SIRUADES UOS & EL CAMPEADOR.
11584 5ELCID1468 ASI ***** A MY DIXIERCN, HY LCS PODREDES FALAR;
12124 5ELCID1538 DE TAN GRAND CONDUCHO ***** EN MEDINAL SACARON;
12243 5ELCID1554 AMYNAYA & ALAS DUE@AS, CIOS ***** LAS ONDRAUA
12707 5ELCID1613 MIRAN VALEN%IA ***** IAZE LA %IBDAD,
12948 5ELCID1642 EN ESTAS TIERRAS AGENAS VERAN LAS MORACAS ***** SE FAZEN,
12956 5ELCID1643 AFARTO VERAN POR LOS CIOS ***** SE GANA EL PAN.
13981 5ELCID1771 ***** LO DIXO EL %ID ASSI LC HAN ACABADO.
14132 5ELCID1789 TAL TIENDA ***** ESTA, QUE DE MARUECOS ES PASSADA,
14740 5ELCID1864 ***** SI LCS FALASSE MUERTOS ADUZIR SE LOS CAUALLOS,
14814 5ELCID1872 E GUARNIR UOS DE TODAS ARMAS ***** UOS DIXIEREDES AQUI,
14834 5ELCID1875 ASSI ***** SEMEIA & LA VELUNTAC MELO DIZ.
14911 5ELCID1885 MER%ED UOS PIDIMOS ***** A REY & SE@OR NATURAL;
15179 5ELCID1921 ***** SON LAS SALUDES DE ALFONSSO MYO SENOR.
15412 5ELCID1952 POR DAR LE GRAND ONDRA ***** A REY DE TIERRA.
15590 5ELCID1977 ***** ELLOS TENIEN, CER%ER LES YA LA GANA%IA,
15818 5ELCID2006 RECABDADO HA, ***** TAN BUEN VARON,
15927 5ELCID2020 ***** LC CCMICIA EL QUE EN BUEN ORA NA%IO,
16304 5ELCID2068 AL OTRC DIA MA@ANA, ASSI ***** SALIO EL SOL,
16520 5ELCID2094 FABLO EL REY DON ALFCNSSO ***** TAN BUEN SE@OR:
16528 5ELCID2095 GRADO & GRA%IAS, CID, ***** TAN BUENO, & PRIMERO AL CRIADOR,
16650 5ELCID2109 MUCHO UOS LC GRADESCC, ***** A REY & A SE@OR
16844 5ELCID2132 PUES QUE CASADES MYS FIJAS, ASI ***** AUOS PLAZ,
16884 5ELCID2137 ASSI ***** YO LAS PRENDO DAQUENT, COMMO SI FOSSE DELANT,
16889 5ELCID2137 ASSI CCMMO YO LAS PRENDC CAQUENT, ***** SI FOSSE DELANT,
18237 5ELCID2307 NON VIESTES TAL GUEGO ***** YUA POR LA CORT;
18439 5ELCID2333 EN BRA%OS TENEDES MIS FIJAS TAN BLANCAS ***** EL SOL
18825 5ELCID2382 NOS DAQUENT VEREMOS ***** LIDIA EL ABBAT.
19080 5ELCID2414 ASI ***** SEMEIA, EN MI LA QUIERES ENSAYAR.
19312 5ELCID2446 ***** AL REY BUCAR AVEMCS ARRANCADO.
19318 5ELCID2447 ***** YO FIC POR DICS & EN TOCOS LOS SOS SANTOS,
19578 5ELCID2481 ***** SCN CNDRADCS & AVER VCS GRANT PRO.
19695 5ELCID2497 ARRANCO LAS LIDES ***** PLAZE AL CRIADOR,
19857 5ELCID2518 ASSI ***** LEGARON, PAGCS EL CAMPEADOR:
20525 5ELCID2606 ASSI ***** YO TENGC, BIEN UOS HE CASADAS.
20764 5ELCID2637 RE%IBA A MYOS YERNOS ***** EL PUDIER MEIOR;
20971 5ELCID2664 TAN EN SALUC LC ABREMCS ***** LO DE CARRION;
21099 5ELCID2681 AQUIM PARTO DE UOS ***** DE MALOS & DE TRAYDORES.
22457 5ELCID2860 ATANTO UCS LO GRADIMOS ***** SI VIESSEMOS AL CRAIDOR;
22883 5ELCID2915 ***** AYA DERECHO DE YFANTES DE CARRION,
22977 5ELCID2927 ASSI ***** DESCAUALGA AQUEL MU@O GUSTIOZ
23004 5ELCID2931 ASSI ***** ENTRARCN POR MEDIO DELA CORT,
23138 5ELCID2948 POR ESTC UOS BESA LAS MANOS, ***** VASSALLO A SE@OR,
23164 5ELCID2951 E QUE UOS PESE, REY ***** SOCES SABIDOR;
23274 5ELCID2965 MANDARE ***** Y VAYAN YFANTES DE CARRION,
23281 5ELCID2966 E ***** DEN DERECHO A MYO %ID EL CAMPEADOR,
23353 5ELCID2975 ASSI ***** LO DIXC, SUYC ERA EL CUYDADO:
23464 5ELCID2988 PRENDEN SO CONSSEIC ASSI PARIENTES ***** SON,
23528 5ELCID2996 PRENDEN CONSSEIO PARIENTES ***** SON;
24112 5ELCID3074 DE SUSO LAS LORIGAS TAN BLANCAS ***** EL SOL;
24174 5ELCID3083 ASSI ***** LO ADICHO, TCDCS ADOBADOS SON.
24212 5ELCID3087 VISTIO CAMISA DE RAN%AL TAN BLANCA ***** EL SOL,
24460 5ELCID3118 SED EN UUESTRC ESCA@C ***** REY A SE@OR;
24699 5ELCID3146 MUCHO UOS LO GRADESCO ***** A REY & A SE@OR,
25478 5ELCID3245 RECIBIOLO MYO %ID ***** APRE%IARON ENLA CORT.
25805 5ELCID3287 ***** YC AUCS, CONDE, ENEL CASTIELLO DE CABRA;
26490 5ELCID3380 E PRENDER MAQUILAS, ***** LO SUELE FAR
26572 5ELCID3392 ASSI ***** ACABAN ESTA RAZCN,
26850 5ELCID3430 MER%ED UOS PIDO ***** A REY & A SE@OR,
27208 5ELCID3478 HYO VOS LO SOBRELIEUO ***** BUEN VASSALLO FAZE A SE@OR,
27338 5ELCID3493 LA CONFIA DE RAN%AL CUE BLANCA ERA ***** EL SOL,
27399 5ELCID3500 ATODOS LCS ROGAUA ASSI ***** HAN SABOR;
27552 5ELCID3518 MAS ATAL CAUALLO CUM EST PORA TAL ***** VOS,
28003 5ELCID3574 BESAMOS VOS LAS MANOS, ***** A REY & A SE@OR,
28248 5ELCID3606 BIEN GELO DEMCSTRARCN ATODOS VJ ***** SON,

WORD C# PREFIX CONTEXT

COMMO (CON'T)

```
                 28757 5ELCID3672 CON ASSUR GCN%ALEZ ***** SE ACOBO.
         WORD #1028 OCCURS  98 TIMES.
            INDEX OF DIVERSIFICATION =   292.93 WITH STANDARD DEVIATION OF   321.00

COMMOS            6211 5ELCID0791 VIC LOS SOS ****** VAN ALEGANDO:
         WORD #1029 OCCURS   1 TIMES.

COMO             27292 5ELCID3488 DAQUI UCS LOS ACOMIENDO **** A REY & A SE@OR.
         WORD #1030 OCCURS   1 TIMES.

COMPANA            659 5ELCID0083 PORA TODA MI *******;
         WORD #1031 OCCURS   1 TIMES.

COMPANAS         12744 5ELCID1618 MYO %ID & SUS ******** TAN AGRAND SABOR ESTAN.
         WORD #1032 OCCURS   1 TIMES.

COMPA@A          12208 5ELCID1549 ENTRE EL & ALBARFANEZ HYUAN A VNA *******.
                 28729 5ELCID3668 ESSORA DIXC EL REY: VENID UOS AMI *******;
         WORD #1033 OCCURS   2 TIMES.

COMPA@AS          4005 5ELCID0508 AL REY ALFONSSO QUE LEGARIEN SUS ********,
                  7244 5ELCID0929 E DE SUS ********, AQUELAS QUE AUIEN DEXADAS
                  9097 5ELCID1157 ALEGRE ERA EL %ID & TODAS SUS ********,
                 20577 5ELCID2612 ESPIENDOS DELAS DUE@AS & DE TODAS SUS ********.
                 20593 5ELCID2614 ALEGRE VA MYO %ID CON TODAS SUS ********.
                 23927 5ELCID3048 LAS MIS ******** ESTA NOCHE LEGARAN;
         WORD #1034 OCCURS   6 TIMES.
            INDEX OF DIVERSIFICATION =  3983.40 WITH STANDARD DEVIATION OF  4400.39

COMPE%ARON        6709 5ELCID0856 MOROS & MORAS ********** DE LORAR.
         WORD #1035 OCCURS   1 TIMES.

COMPE%O           8765 5ELCID1114 EL QUE EN BUEN ORA NASCO ******* DE FABLAR:
         WORD #1036 OCCURS   1 TIMES.

COMPE%OS          9452 5ELCID1201 QUANDO VIO MYO %ID LAS GENTES IUNTADAS, ******** DE PAGAR.
         WORD #1037 OCCURS   1 TIMES.

COMPLIDA          1753 5ELCID0223 SI UOS ASSI LO FIZIEREDES & LA UENTURA ME FUERE ********,
                  2128 5ELCID0268 MER%ED, YA %ID, BARBA TAN ********
                  2210 5ELCID0278 YA DO@A XIMENA, LA MI MUGIER TAN ********,
         WORD #1038 OCCURS   3 TIMES.

COMPLIDAS         4508 5ELCID0573 ALI YOGO MYO %ID ********* XV SEMMANAS.
                  5253 5ELCID0664 TOUIERON GELA EN %ERCA ********* TRES SEMANAS.
                 27681 5ELCID3533 MAS TRES SEMANAS DE PLAZO TODAS ********* SON.
         WORD #1039 OCCURS   3 TIMES.

COMPLIDOS         9511 5ELCID1209 NUEUE MESES *********, SABET, SOBRELLA IAZ;
         WORD #1040 OCCURS   1 TIMES.

COMPRA             709 5ELCID0090 QUANDO EN BURGOS ME VEDARON ****** & EL REY ME A AYRADO,
         WORD #1041 OCCURS   1 TIMES.

CON                179 5ELCID0024 *** GRAND RECABDO & FUERTE MIENTRE SELLADA:
                   341 5ELCID0043 *** GRANT RECABDO & FUERTE MIENTRE SELLADA.
                   383 5ELCID0048 MAS EL CRIADOR UOS UALA *** TODAS SUS UERTUDES SANTAS.
                   590 5ELCID0075 SI *** UUSCO ESCAPO SANO OBIUO,
                   669 5ELCID0085 *** UUESTRO CONSEGO BASTIR QUIERO DOS ARCHAS;
                   745 5ELCID0094 VEALO EL CRIADOR *** TODOS LOS SOS SANTOS,
                   815 5ELCID0104 EN PORIDAD FLABLAR QUERRIA *** AMOS.
                   933 5ELCID0120 *** GRAND IURA METED Y LAS FES AMOS,
                  1106 5ELCID0142 AMOS TRED ALCAMPEADOR *** TADO,
                  1152 5ELCID0149 *** RACHEL & VIDAS, DE VOLUTAD & DE GRADO.
                  1311 5ELCID0168 YO YRE *** UUSO, QUE ADUGAMOS LOS MARCOS,
                  1347 5ELCID0172 GRADAN SE RACHEL & VIDAS *** AUERES MONEDADOS,
                  1608 5ELCID0206 VENGO, CAMPEADOR, *** TODO BUEN RECABDO:
                  1814 5ELCID0231 ANTES SERE *** UUSCO QUE EL SOL QUIERA RAYAR.
                  1839 5ELCID0234 *** ESTOS CAUALLEROS QUEL SIRUEN ASO SABOR.
                  1879 5ELCID0239 Y ESTAUA DO@A XIMENA *** %INCO DUENAS DE PRO,
                  1915 5ELCID0244 *** LUMBRES & CON CANDELAS AL CORAL DIERON SALTO.
                  1918 5ELCID0244 CON LUMBRES & *** CANDELAS AL CORAL DIERON SALTO.
                  1924 5ELCID0245 *** TAN GRANT GOZO RE%IBEN AL QUE EN BUEN ORA NASCO.
                  1966 5ELCID0249 YO ADOBARE *** DUCHO PORA MI & PORA MIS VASSALLOS;
                  2080 5ELCID0262 AFEUOS DO@A XIMENA *** SUS FIJAS DO UA LEGANDO;
                  2142 5ELCID0270 *** AQUESTAS MYS DUE@AS DE QUIEN SO YO SERUIDA.
                  2242 5ELCID0282 PLEGA ADIOS & A SANTA MARIA, QUE AUN *** MIS MANOS CASE ESTAS MIS
                  2322 5ELCID0293 MARTIN ANTOLINEZ *** ELLOS COIO.
                  2420 5ELCID0305 PLOGO ALOS OTROS OMNES TODOS QUANTOS *** EL ESTAN.
                  2689 5ELCID0340 SALUEST A DANIEL *** LOS LEONES EN LA MALA CAR%EL,
                  2792 5ELCID0353 DIOT *** LA LAN%A ENEL COSTADO, DONT YXIO LA SANGRE,
                  2985 5ELCID0376 MYO %ID *** LOS SOS VASSALLOS PENSSO DE CAUALGAR,
                  3062 5ELCID0385 E A TODAS SUS DUENAS QUE *** ELLAS ESTAN;
                  3457 5ELCID0436 MYO %ID SE ECHO EN %ELADA *** AQUELOS QUE EL TRAE.
```

WORD C# PREFIX CONTEXT

CON (CON'T)

3487 5ELCID0440 VOS *** C DE AQUESTA NUESTRA CONPA@A,
3501 5ELCID0442 VOS *** LOS CC YD UCS EN ALGARA; ALA VAYA ALBARABAREZ,
3563 5ELCIDC449 E YO *** LO C AQUI FINCARE EN LA %AGA,
3609 5ELCID0455 E LOS CUE *** MYO %IC FICARAN EN LA %AGA.
3659 5ELCID0462 *** POCAS DE GENTES QUE EN CASTEION FINCARON.
3750 5ELCID0474 SOS CAUALLERCS LEGAN *** LA GANAN%IA,
3784 5ELCID0478 E DESI ARRIBA TCRNAN SE *** LA GANAN%IA,
3825 5ELCID0484 *** AQUESTE AUER TORNAN SE ESSA CONPA@A;
3850 5ELCID0487 SALIOLOS RE%EBIR *** ESTA SU MESNADA,
3874 5ELCID0491 ESSO *** ESTO SEA AIUNTADO;
3931 5ELCID0499 LIDIANDO *** MOROS ENEL CAMPO,
4009 5ELCID0509 QUEL BUSCARIE MAL *** TCDAS SUS MESNADAS.
4073 5ELCIDC518 FABLO *** LCS DE CASTEICN, & ENVIO AFITA & AGUADELFAGARA,
4119 5ELCID0524 ASMO MYC %IC *** TODA SU CONPA@A
4152 5ELCIDC528 BUSCAR NOS YE EL REY ALFCNSSO *** TODA SU MESNADA.
4224 5ELCID0538 *** ALFONSSC MYO SE@OR NON QUERRIA LIDIAR.
4465 5ELCID0568 AGARDANDO SEUA MYO %IC *** TODOS SUS VASSALLOS;
4643 5ELCID0589 COIOS SALON AYUSC, *** LCS SOS ABUELTA NADI.
4712 5ELCID0598 *** LA MER%ED DEL CRIADCR NUESTRA ES LA GANAN%IA
4723 5ELCIDC599 BUELTOS SON *** ELLOS POR MEDIO DELA LA@A.
4922 5ELCID0623 MYO %ID *** ESTA GANAN%IA EN ALCO%ER ESTA;
4958 5ELCID0627 AL REY DE VALEN%IA ENBIARCN *** MENSAIE,
5060 5ELCID0639 TRES MILL MCRCS LEUEDES *** ARMAS DE LIDIAR;
5064 5ELCID0640 *** LOS DELA FRCNTERA QUE UCS AIUDARAN,
5166 5ELCID0654 *** AQUESTCS DOS REYES QUE DIZEN FFARIZ & GALUE;
5266 5ELCID0666 MYO %ID *** LCS SCS TORNOS A ACORDAR:
5297 5ELCID0669 GRANDES SON LCS PODERES POR *** ELLOS LIDIAR;
5323 5ELCID0673 SI *** MOROS NON LIDIAREMOS, NO NOS DARAN DEL PAN.
5413 5ELCID0683 ARMADO ES MYC %ID *** QUANTOS QUE EL HA;
5476 5ELCID0691 MAS NON AGUIJEDES *** ELLA, SI YO NON UOS LO MANDAR.
5917 5ELCID0750 DIOL TAL ESPADADA *** EL SO DIESTRO BRA%O,
6284 5ELCID0800 REFECHCS SON TODOS ESCS CHRISTIANOS *** AQUESTA GANAN%IA.
6308 5ELCID0803 GRANT A EL GOZO MYO %ID *** TODOS SOS VASSALOS.
6375 5ELCID0812 A UUESTRA GUISA PRENDED *** UUESTRA MANO.
6383 5ELCID0813 ENBIAR UOS QUIERO A CASTIELLA *** MANDADO
6404 5ELCID0817 TODOS *** SIELLAS & MUY BIEN ENFRENADOS,
6477 5ELCID0826 MYNAYA ALBARFANEZ DESTO ES PAGADO; POR YR *** EL OMNES SON CONTADOS.
6494 5ELCIDC828 MYO %ID RUY DIAZ *** LOS SCS SE ACORDAUA:
6558 5ELCID0837 E EL CAMPEADOR *** SU MESNADA.
6588 5ELCID0841 SANO EL REY FARIZ, *** EL SE CONSEIAUAN.
7105 5ELCID0909 *** TODAS SUS YENTES FIZO VNA TRASNOCHADA;
7158 5ELCIDC917 DOZIENTOS *** EL, QUE TODOS %INEN ESPADAS;
7352 5ELCID0943 *** ESTAS GANAN%IAS ALA POSADA TORNANDO SEUAN,
8253 5ELCID1051 *** LOS CAUALLERCS QUE EL %IC LE AUIE DADOS
8305 5ELCID1057 *** ESTOS DOS CAUALLERCS A PRIESSA VA IANTANDO;
8520 5ELCID1083 JUNTOS *** SUS MESNADAS, CONPE%OLAS DE LEGAR
8622 5ELCID1095 EL *** TODO ESTO PRISC A MURUIEDRO.
8871 5ELCID1130 VOS *** LOS OTROS FIRADES LOS DELANT.
8886 5ELCID1132 YO *** LOS %IENTO ENTRARE DEL OTRA PART,
8927 5ELCID1137 *** LOS ALUCRES MYO %ID FERIR LOS VA:
9059 5ELCID1153 ENTRAUAN A MURUIEDRO *** ESTAS GANAN%IAS QUE TRAEN GRANDES.
9159 5ELCID1166 NON ES *** RECABDO EL DOLOR DE VALEN%IA.
9200 5ELCID1171 NON OSAN FUERAS EXIR NIN *** EL SE AIUNTAR;
9293 5ELCID1182 *** EL DELOS MONTES CLAROS AUYEN GUERRA TAN GRAND,
9594 5ELCID1219 ALEGRE ERA EL CAMPEADOR *** TODOS LOS QUE HA,
9612 5ELCID1221 YA FOLGAUA MYO %ID *** TOCAS SUS CONPA@AS;
9634 5ELCID1224 VINO LOS VER *** XXX MILL DE ARMAS.
9676 5ELCID1230 AQUEL REY DE MARRUECOS *** TRES COLPES ESCAPA.
9684 5ELCID1231 TORNADO ES MYO %ID *** TODA ESTA GANAN%IA.
9726 5ELCID1237 *** MYO %ID RUY DIAZ, EL QUE EN BUEN ORA NASCO.
9788 5ELCID1244 *** EL MYNAYA ALBARFFANEZ QUE NOS LE PARTE DE SO BRA%O.
9832 5ELCID1248 LOS QUE FUERON *** EL, & LOS DE DESPUES, TODOS SON PAGADOS;
9844 5ELCID1249 VELLO MYO %ID *** LOS AVERES QUE AUIEN TOMADOS,
9902 5ELCID1256 *** MINAYA ALBARFANEZ EL SEUA CONSEGAR:
10006 5ELCID1268 *** MAS POCOS YXIEMOS DE LA CASA DE BIUAR.
10213 5ELCID1293 SOSPIRANDO EL OBISPO QUES VIESSE *** MOROS ENEL CAMPO:
10223 5ELCID1294 QUE SIS FARTAS LIDIANDO & FIRIENDO *** SUS MANOS,
10376 5ELCID1315 *** ESTA PRESENTEIA ADELINO PORA ALLA;
10409 5ELCID1319 ALOS PIES DEL REY ALFONSSO CAYO *** GRAND DUELO,
10499 5ELCID1331 *** AQUESTAS TODAS DE VALEN%IA ES SE@OR,
10851 5ELCID1374 BIEN CASARIEMOS *** SUS FIJAS PORA HUEBOS DE PRO.
11052 5ELCID1399 SANO LO DEXE & *** TAN GRAND RICTAD.
11163 5ELCID1412 HYTODAS LAS DUE@AS *** ELLAS QUANTAS BUENAS ELLAS HAN.
11229 5ELCID1421 POR YR *** ESTAS DUENAS BUE@A CONPANA SE FAZE.
11339 5ELCID1435 HYO LO VERE *** EL %ID, SI DIOS ME LIEUA ALA.
11443 5ELCID1449 EL PORTERO *** ELLOS QUE LOS HA DE AGUARDAR;
11534 5ELCID1461 CAUALGEDES *** %IENTO GUISADOS PORA HUEBOS DE LIDIAR;
11561 5ELCID1465 *** OTROS %IENTO CAUALLEROS BIEN UOS CONSSIGRA;
11580 5ELCID1467 MY MUGIER & MIS FIJAS *** MYNAYA ALBARFFANEZ,
11592 5ELCID1469 *** GRAND ONDRA ADUZIC MELAS DELANT.
11662 5ELCID1478 SALIOLOS RE%EBIR *** GRANT GOZO QUE FAZE:
11734 5ELCID1488 ESSA NOCH *** DUCHO LES DIO GRAND,
11748 5ELCID1490 %IENTOL PIDIERON, MAS EL *** DOZIENTOS VA.
11806 5ELCID1497 EL VNO FINCO *** ELLOS & EL OTRO TORNO A ALBARFANEZ:

WORD C# PREFIX CONTEXT

CON (CON'T)

11849 5ELCID1502 E EL ALCAYAZ AUEGALUON *** SUS FUER%AS QUE TRAHE,
11930 5ELCID1512 O CUEMO SALIERA DE CASTIELLA ALBARFANEZ *** ESTAS DUE@AS QUE TRAHE.
11991 5ELCID1520 TAN BUEN DIA *** UUSCO, MINAYA ALBARFANEZ
12062 5ELCID1529 SI DIOS ME LEGARE AL %ID ELO VEA *** EL ALMA,
12268 5ELCID1558 *** ESTAS ALEGRIAS & NUEUAS TAN ONDRADAS
12458 5ELCID1581 *** QUANTOS QUE EL PUEDE, QUE CON ORAS SE ACORDARON,
12464 5ELCID1581 CON QUANTOS QUE EL PUEDE, QUE *** ORAS SE ACORDARON,
12471 5ELCID1582 SOBREPELI%AS VESTIDAS & *** CRUZES DE PLATA
12593 5ELCID1598 *** DIOS & CON UUSCO BUENAS SON & CRIADAS.
12596 5ELCID1598 CON DIOS & *** UUSCO BUENAS SON & CRIADAS.
12688 5ELCID1610 ADELINC MYO %ID *** ELLAS AL ALCA%AR,
12810 5ELCID1626 *** L VEZES MILL DE ARMAS, TODOS FUERON CONPLIDOS,
12884 5ELCID1635 *** AFAN GANE A VALEN%IA, & ELA POR HEREDAD,
13039 5ELCID1654 *** LA MER%ED DE DIOS & DE SANTA MARIA MADRE
13056 5ELCID1656 *** DIOS A QUESTA LID YC LA FE DE ARRANCAR.
13221 5ELCID1676 DOS FALLAN *** LOS MOROS COMETIEN LOS TAN AYNA.
13272 5ELCID1683 EL SELO VIO *** LOS CIOS, CUENTAN GELO DELANT,
13550 5ELCID1717 QUATRO MILL MENOS XXX *** MYO %ID VAN A CABO,
13644 5ELCID1729 *** OTROS QUEL CONSIGEN DE SUS BUENOS VASSALLOS.
13751 5ELCID1743 *** C CAUALLEROS A VALEN%IA ES ENTRADO,
13813 5ELCID1750 ESTO DIOS SE LO QUISO *** TODOS LOS SOS SANTOS,
13835 5ELCID1753 *** TAL CUM ESTO SE VEN%EN MOROS DEL CAMPO.
13900 5ELCID1761 EN BUELTA *** EL ENTRARON AL PALA%IO,
13908 5ELCID1762 E YUAN POSAR *** EL EN VNOS PRE%IOSOS ESCA@OS;
13933 5ELCID1765 QUIERO LAS CASAR *** DE AQUESTOS MYOS VASSALLOS;
14091 5ELCID1784 QUE A GANADO MYO %ID *** TODOS SUS VASSALLOS
14110 5ELCID1786 DOS TENDALES LA SUFREN, *** ORO SON LABRADOS;
14155 5ELCID1792 *** AQUESTAS RIQUEZAS TANTAS A VALEN%IA SON ENTRADOS.
14174 5ELCID1794 QUANDO ES FARTO DE LIDIAR *** AMAS LAS SUS MANOS,
14295 5ELCID1809 *** CAUALLOS DESTA QUINTA QUE YO HE GANADA,
14303 5ELCID1810 *** SIELLAS & CON FRENOS & CON SE@AS ESPADAS;
14306 5ELCID1810 CON SIELLAS & *** FRENOS & CON SE@AS ESPADAS;
14309 5ELCID1810 CON SIELLAS & CON FRENOS & *** SE@AS ESPADAS;
14354 5ELCID1815 MANDO A PERO VERMUEZ QUE FUESSE *** MYNAYA.
14368 5ELCID1818 *** SALUDES DEL %ID QUE LAS MANOS LE BESAUA:
14545 5ELCID1839 CUEDAN SE QUE ES ALMOFALLA, CA NON VIENEN *** MANDADO;
14631 5ELCID1851 *** %INQUAENTA MILL ARRANCOLOS DEL CAMPO;
14705 5ELCID1860 *** X DE SUS PARIENTES A PARTE DAUAN SALTO:
14891 5ELCID1882 DEMANDEMOS SUS FIJAS PORA *** ELLAS CASAR;
14905 5ELCID1884 VINIEN AL REY ALFONSSO *** ESTA PORIDAD:
14917 5ELCID1886 *** UUESTRO CONSSEIO LO QUEREMOS FER NOS,
14932 5ELCID1888 CASAR QUEREMOS *** ELLAS ASU ONDRA & A NUESTRA PRO.
15046 5ELCID1902 SABOR HAN DE CASAR *** SUS FIJAS AMAS ADOS.
15073 5ELCID1906 POR CONSSAGRAR *** LOS YFFANTES DE CARRION.
15136 5ELCID1914 ESPIDIENSSE AL REY, *** ESTO TORNADOS SON,
15276 5ELCID1935 *** GRAND AFAN GANE LO QUE HE YO;
15346 5ELCID1943 *** TODO ESTO, AUOS DIXO ALFONSSO
15444 5ELCID1957 *** DOS CAUALLEROS LUEGO LAS ENBIO:
15543 5ELCID1970 ESCUDOS BOCLADOS *** ORO & CON PLATA,
15546 5ELCID1970 ESCUDOS BOCLADOS CON ORO & *** PLATA,
15569 5ELCID1974 *** EL REY ATANTAS BUENAS CONPA@AS.
15626 5ELCID1982 *** EL REY VAN LEONESES & MESNADAS GALIZIANAS,
15738 5ELCID1997 ESTOS SE ADOBAN POR YR *** EL CAMPEADOR,
15867 5ELCID2012 HYAS VA PORA LAS VISTAS QUE *** EL REY PARO.
15891 5ELCID2015 RE%EBIR LO SALEN *** TAN GRAND ONOR.
15921 5ELCID2009 *** VNOS XV A TIERRAS FIRIO,
16378 5ELCID2077 SEMEIAM EL CASAMIENTO ONDRADO & *** GRANT PRO,
16569 5ELCID2099 HYO LAS CASO A UUESTRAS FIJAS *** UUESTRO AMOR,
16589 5ELCID2102 ELLOS VAYAN *** UUSCO, CADA QUEN ME TORNO YO.
16861 5ELCID2134 NON GELAS DARE YO *** MI MANO, NIN DED NON SE ALABARAN.
16876 5ELCID2136 PRENDELLAS *** UUESTRAS MANOS & DALDAS ALOS YFANTES,
16975 5ELCID2149 PLEGA AL CRIADOR *** TODOS LOS SOS SANTOS, ESTE PLAZER
17224 5ELCID2179 VOS *** ELLOS SED, QUE ASSI UOS LO MANDO YO.
17283 5ELCID2186 MUCHOS DIAS UOS VEAMOS *** LOS OIOS DELAS CARAS
17482 5ELCID2212 *** BUENAS VESTIDURAS & FUERTE MIENTRE ADOBADOS;
17501 5ELCID2214 RE%IBIO LOS MYO %ID *** TODOS SUS VASALLOS;
17592 5ELCID2225 ALOS YFANTES DE CARRION DAD LAS *** UUESTRA MANO,
17756 5ELCID2247 TORNAN SE *** LAS DUE@AS, A VALEN%IA AN ENTRADO;
17997 5ELCID2277 EL CRIADOR UOS VALLA *** TODOS LOS SOS SANTOS.
18007 5ELCID2278 EN VALEN%IA SEY MYO %ID *** TODOS SUS VASSALLOS,
18011 5ELCID2279 *** EL AMOS SUS YERNOS LOS YFANTES DE CARRION.
18101 5ELCID2290 TRAS VNA VIGA LAGAR METIOS *** GRANT PAUOR;
18368 5ELCID2325 VINO *** ESTAS NUEUAS A MUO %ID RUYDIAZ EL CANPEADOR:
18409 5ELCID2330 NOS *** UUSCO LA VENCREMOS, & VALER NOS HA EL CRIADOR.
18465 5ELCID2337 ARRANCAR MELOS TREUO *** LA MER%ED DEL CRIADOR.
18602 5ELCID2354 CALOS MOROS, *** DIOS, NON FINCARAN EN CANPO.
18632 5ELCID2358 HYO *** LOS MYOS FERIR QUIERO DELANT,
18639 5ELCID2359 VOS *** LOS UUESTROS FIRME MIENTRE ALA %AGA TENGADES;
18673 5ELCID2363 EUOS TAN DINNO QUE *** EL AUEDES PART.
18698 5ELCID2366 VERLO HEMOS CONDIOS & *** LA UUESTRA AUZE.
18722 5ELCID2369 PARAUAS DELANT AL CAMPEADOR, SIEMPRE *** LA BUEN AUZE:
18878 5ELCID2389 DOS MATO *** LAN%A & V CON EL ESPADA.
18882 5ELCID2389 DOS MATO CON LAN%A & V *** EL ESPADA.
18958 5ELCID2399 MYO %ID *** LOS SUYOS CAE EN ALCAN%A;

WORD C# PREFIX CONTEXT

CON (CON'T)

18977 5ELCID2401 EACOSTAR SE LCS TENDALES, *** HUEBRAS ERAN TANTAS.
19002 5ELCID2404 TANTO BRAZO *** LORIGA VERIEDES CAER A PART,
19010 5ELCID2405 TANTAS CABEZAS *** YELMCS QUE POR EL CAMPO CAEN,
19046 5ELCID2410 VERTE AS *** EL %ID, EL DE LA BARBA GRANT,
19201 5ELCID2429 *** ESTAS GRANAN%IAS YAS YUAN TORNANDO;
19233 5ELCID2434 *** DOS ESPADAS QUE EL PRE%IAUA ALGO
19423 5ELCID2461 FARTOS DE LIDIAR *** MOROS ENEL CAMPO.
19463 5ELCID2466 ALEGRE ES MYO %ID *** TCDAS SUS CONPA@AS,
19507 5ELCID2472 *** DUCHOS A SAZONES, BUENAS PIELES & BUENOS MANTOS.
19742 5ELCID2503 ELLOS ME DARAN PARIAS *** AIUCA DEL CRIADOR,
19761 5ELCID2505 GRANDES SON LCS GOZOS EN VALEN%IA *** MYO %ID EL CANPEADOR
19807 5ELCID2511 ELLOS *** LOS OTROS VINIERON ALA CORT;
19815 5ELCID2512 AQUI ESTA *** MYO %ID EL OBISPO DO IHERONIMO,
20109 5ELCID2553 PODREMOS CASAR *** FIJAS DE REYES O DE ENPERADORES,
20140 5ELCID2557 *** AQUESTE CONSSEIO AMOS TORNADOS SON,
20333 5ELCID2580 *** QUE RIQUEZA ENBIO MIOS YERNOS AMOS ADOS.
20590 5ELCID2614 ALEGRE VA MYO %ID *** TCDAS SUS COMPA@AS.
20640 5ELCID2620 MANDOT QUE VAYAS *** ELLAS FATA DENTRO EN CARRION,
20655 5ELCID2622 *** AQUESTAS NUEUAS VERNAS AL CAMPEADOR.
20729 5ELCID2632 EL PADRE *** LAS FIJAS LORAN DE CORA%ON,
20847 5ELCID2647 FELOS EN MOLINA *** EL MORO AVENGALUON.
20861 5ELCID2649 SALIOLOS RECEBIR *** GRANDES AUOROZES;
20875 5ELCID2651 OTRO DIA MA@ANA *** ELLOS CAUALGO,
20878 5ELCID2652 *** DOZIENTOS CAUALLEROS ESCURRIR LOS MANDO.
21106 5ELCID2682 HYRE *** UUESTRA GRA%IA, DON ELUIRA & DO@A SOL;
21236 5ELCID2698 LOS MONTES SON ALTOS, LAS RAMAS PUIAN *** LAS NUES,
21248 5ELCID2700 FALARON VN VERGEL *** VNA LINPIA FUENT;
21259 5ELCID2702 *** QUANTOS QUE ELLOS TRAEN Y IAZEN ESSA NOCH,
21268 5ELCID2703 *** SUS MUGIERES EN BRA%OS DEMUESTRAN LES AMOR;
21287 5ELCID2705 MANDARON CARGAR LAS AZEMILAS *** GRANDES AUERES,
21331 5ELCID2711 DEPORTAR SE QUIEREN *** ELLAS ATODO SU SABOR.
21518 5ELCID2736 *** LAS %INCHAS CORREDIZAS MAIAN LAS TAN SIN SABOR;
21527 5ELCID2737 *** LAS ESPUELAS AGUDAS, DON ELLAS AN MAL SABOR,
21997 5ELCID2799 *** VN SONBRERO QUE TIENE FELEZ MUNOZ,
22052 5ELCID2807 *** EL SO MANTO A AMAS LAS CUBRIO,
22271 5ELCID2836 CAUALGO MINAYA *** PERO VERMUEZ
22281 5ELCID2838 *** CC CAUALLEROS, QUALES MYO %ID MANDO;
22565 5ELCID2874 E MINAYA *** LAS DUE@AS YUA CABADELANT.
22733 5ELCID2897 GRAND GOZO FIZO *** ELLAS DO@A XIMENA SU MADRE.
22749 5ELCID2899 FABLOS *** LOS SOS EN SU PORIDAD,
22871 5ELCID2913 ESSO ME PUEDE PESAR *** LA OTRA DESONOR.
22904 5ELCID2918 *** EL DOS CAUALLEROS QUEL SIRUAN A SO SABOR,
22914 5ELCID2919 E *** EL ESCUDEROS QUE SON DE CRIAZON.
22995 5ELCID2930 *** EL DOS CAUALLEROS QUEL AGUARDAN CUM ASSE@OR.
23071 5ELCID2939 CASASTES SUS FIJAS *** YFANTES DE CARRION,
23206 5ELCID2956 CA YO CASE SUS FIJAS *** YFANTES DE CARRION;
23311 5ELCID2969 QUE DESTAS VIJ SEMANAS ADOBES *** SUS VASSALLOS,
23610 5ELCID3007 EL CONDE DON GAR%IA *** YFANTES DE CARRION,
23629 5ELCID3010 E *** ELLOS GRAND BANDO QUE ADUXIERON A LA CORT:
23707 5ELCID3020 *** GRANDES YENTES EL REY CAUALGO
23726 5ELCID3022 BIEN AGUISADO VIENE EL %ID *** TODOS LOS SOS,
23918 5ELCID3047 E YO *** LOS MYOS POSARE A SAN SERUAN:
24091 5ELCID3072 *** ESTOS CUNPLANSSE %IENTO DELOS BUENOS QUE Y SON.
24215 5ELCID3088 *** ORO & CON PLATA TODAS LAS PRESAS SON,
24218 5ELCID3088 CON ORO & *** PLATA TODAS LAS PRESAS SON,
24240 5ELCID3091 OBRADO ES *** ORO, PARE%EN PORO SON,
24269 5ELCID3095 *** ORO ES OBRADA, FECHA POR RAZON,
24292 5ELCID3097 LA BARBA AVIE LUENGA & PRISOLA *** EL CORDON,
24322 5ELCID3101 *** AQUESTOS %IENTO QUE ADOBAR MANDO,
24353 5ELCID3105 CUERDA MIENTRA ENTRA MYO %ID *** TODOS LOS SOS:
24466 5ELCID3119 ACA POSARE *** TODOS AQUESTOS MIOS.
24661 5ELCID3142 *** EL QUE TOUIERE DERECHO YO DESSA PART ME SO.
24771 5ELCID3155 QUES ONDRASSEN *** ELLAS & SIRUIESSEN AUOS;
24823 5ELCID3162 *** TODOS SUS PARIENTES & EL VANDO QUE Y SON;
24860 5ELCID3166 BIEN NOS ABENDREMOS *** EL REY DON ALFONSSO.
24892 5ELCID3170 *** AQUESTA FABLA TORNARON ALA CORT:
25098 5ELCID3197 SE QUE SI UOS ACAE%IERE, *** ELLA GANAREDES GRAND PREZ & GRAND VALOR.
25291 5ELCID3220 TORNAN *** EL CONSSEIO E FABLAUAN ASSO SABOR:
25615 5ELCID3262 *** MUY GRAND ONDRA & AVERES A NOMBRE;
25877 5ELCID3297 DEUIEMOS CASAR *** FIJAS DE REYES O DE ENPERADORES,
26046 5ELCID3320 PASSE POR TI, *** EL MORO ME OFF DE AIUNTAR,
26141 5ELCID3332 E TU, FERRANDO, QUE FIZIST *** EL PAUOR?
26312 5ELCID3356 POR CONSAGRAR *** MYO %ID DON RODRIGO
26496 5ELCID3381 QUIL DARIE *** LOS DE CARRION ACASAR?
27194 5ELCID3476 DAD ME UUESTROS CAUALLEROS *** TODAS UUESTRAS GUARNIZONES,
27442 5ELCID3506 BESO UUESTRAS MANOS *** UUESTRA GRA%IA, SE@OR,
27452 5ELCID3507 E YR ME QUIERO PORA VALEN%IA, *** AFAN LA GANE YO.
27728 5ELCID3539 E TODOS SUS PARIENTES *** ELLOS SON;
27870 5ELCID3556 COLADA & TIZON, QUE NON LIDIASSEN *** ELLAS LOS DEL CANPEADOR;
28152 5ELCID3594 QUE NON VARAGEN *** ELLOS DESI O DE NON.
28328 5ELCID3616 ABAXAN LAS LAN%AS ABUELTAS *** LOS PENDONES,
28340 5ELCID3618 BATIEN LOS CAUALLOS *** LOS ESPOLONES,
28379 5ELCID3624 *** FERRAGON%ALEZ DE CARA SE JUNTO;
28472 5ELCID3636 EL BELMEZ *** LA CAMISA & CON LA GUARNIZON

WORD C# PREFIX CONTEXT

CON (CON'T)

```
                  28476 5ELCID3636 EL BELMEZ CCN LA CAMISA & *** LA GUARNIZON
                  28654 5ELCID3658 VIO DIEGO GONZALEZ CUE NO ESCAPARIE *** EL ALMA;
                  28670 5ELCID3660 ESSORA MARTIN ANTOLINEZ REZIBIOL *** EL ESPADA,
                  28678 5ELCID3661 VN COLPEL DIC DE LANO, *** LO AGUCO NOL TOMAUA.
                  28754 5ELCID3672 *** ASSUR GONZALEZ COMMO SE ACOBO.
                  28847 5ELCID3685 *** EL DIO VNA TUERTA, CELA SIELLA LO ENCAMO,
                  28976 5ELCID3701 FELOS EN VALENZIA *** MYO ZID EL CAMPEADOR:
                  29111 5ELCID3718 OUIERON SU AIUNTA *** ALFCNSSO EL DE LEON,
                  29119 5ELCID3719 FIZIERON SUS CASAMIENTOS *** CON ELUIRA & CON DO@A SOL.
                  29123 5ELCID3719 FIZIERCN SUS CASAMIENTCS CCN DON ELUIRA & *** DO@A SOL.
        WORD #1042 OCCURS 292 TIMES.
           INDEX OF DIVERSIFICATICN =    98.46 WITH STANCARD DEVIATION OF   110.02

CONBIDAR            152 5ELCIDC021 ******** LE YEN DE GRADC, MAS NINGUNO NON OSAUA:
        WORD #1043 CCCURS   1 TIMES.

CONDE              7483 5ELCID0960 EL ***** ES MUY FOLON & DIXO VNA VANIDAT:
                   7590 5ELCID0972 ASI VIENE ES FORZADO CUE EL ***** AMANOS SELE CUYDO TOMAR.
                   7612 5ELCIDC975 DEL ***** DON REMCNT VENICC LES MENSAIE:
                   7628 5ELCID0977 DIGADES AL ***** NON LO TENGA A MAL,
                   7645 5ELCIDC979 RESPUSO EL *****:  ESTO NCN SERA VERCAD
                   7705 5ELCIDC987 EL ***** DCN REMONT DAR NCS HA GRANT BATALLA,
                   7895 5ELCID1009 AL ***** DCN REMONT A PRESCN LEAN TOMADO;
                   7925 5ELCID1012 PRISO LC AL *****, PORA SU TIERRA LO LEUAUA;
                   7968 5ELCID1018 EL ***** DCN REMCNT NCN GELO PREZIA NADA,
                   8026 5ELCID1025 COMED, *****, DESTE PAN & BEUEC DESTE VINO.
                   8052 5ELCID1028 DIXO EL ***** DCN REMCNT:  COMEDE, DON RODRIGO, & PENSSEDES
                                   DE FOLGAR.
                   8094 5ELCID1033 DIXO MYO ZID: COMED, *****, ALGO, CASI NON COMEDES, NON VEREDES
                   8129 5ELCID1036 QUANDO ESTC OYO EL *****, YAS YUA ALEGRANDO:
                   8150 5ELCID1039 PUES COMED, *****, & CUANCO FUEREDES IANTADO,
                   8239 5ELCID1049 ALEGRE ES EL ***** & PICIO AGUA ALAS MANOS,
                   8265 5ELCID1052 COMIENDO VA EL *****  DIOS, QUE DE BUEN GRADO
                   8283 5ELCID1054 SI BIEN NCN CCMEDES, *****, CCN YO SEA PAGADO,
                   8299 5ELCID1056 AQUI DIXO EL *****: DE VOLUNTAC & DE GRADO.
                   8324 5ELCID1059 POR QUE EL ***** CON REMCNT TAN BIEN BOLUIE LAS MANOS.
                   8353 5ELCID1062 DEL DIA QUE FUE ***** NON IANTE TAN DE BUEN GRADO,
                   8384 5ELCID1066 EL ***** DCN REMCNT ENTRE LOS COS ES ENTRADO.
                   8402 5ELCID1068 HYA UOS YDES, *****, AGUISA DE MUY FRANCO,
                   8472 5ELCID1077 AGUIJAUA EL ***** E PENSSAUA CE ANDAR,
                   8514 5ELCID1082 HYDO ES EL *****, TORNOS EL DE BIUAR,
                  10642 5ELCID1348 DIXO EL REY REY AL *****: CEXAC ESSA RAZON,
                  14513 5ELCID1836 EL ***** DCN GARZIA, SC ENEMIGO MALO.
                  14698 5ELCID1859 PESO AL ***** DCN GARZIA, E MAL ERA YRADO;
                  17926 5ELCID2268 ESTOS FUERCN FIJOS DEL ***** CON GONZALO.
                  19285 5ELCID2441 AMOS SCN FIJOS DEL ***** CON GCZALO.
                  23531 5ELCID2997 EL ***** DCN GARZIA EN ESTAS NUEUAS FUE,
                  23569 5ELCID3002 EL ***** DCN ANRRICH & EL CCNCE DON REMOND;
                  23574 5ELCID3002 EL CONDE DCN ANRRICH & EL ***** DON REMOND;
                  23584 5ELCID3004 EL ***** DCN FRUELLA & EL CONCE DON BELTRAN.
                  23589 5ELCID3004 EL CONDE DCN FRUELLA & EL ***** DON BELTRAN.
                  23607 5ELCID3007 EL ***** DON GARZIA CCN YFANTES DE CARRION,
                  23837 5ELCID3037 E AL ***** DCN ARRICH & A QUANTOS QUE Y SON;
                  24384 5ELCID3109 E EL ***** DCN ANRRICH & EL CCNCE DON REMONT
                  24389 5ELCID3109 E EL CONDE DCN ANRRICH & EL ***** DON REMONT
                  24604 5ELCID3135 ALCALDES SEAN DESTO EL ***** CCN ANRRICH & EL CONDE DON REMCND
                  24609 5ELCID3135 ALCALDES SEAN DESTO EL CONDE DCN ANRRICH & EL ***** DON REMCND
                  24811 5ELCID3160 DIXO EL ***** DON GARZIA: AESTO NOS FABLEMOS.
                  25075 5ELCID3195 DEL ***** DE REMCNT VERENCEL CE BARZILONA LA MAYOR.
                  25192 5ELCID3208 DJZE EL ***** DCN REMCNC: CEZIC DE SSI O DE NO.
                  25422 5ELCID3237 LUEGO RESPCNDIO EL ***** DCN REMOND:
                  25677 5ELCID3270 EL ***** DCN GARZIA EN PIE SE LEUANTAUA;
                  25775 5ELCID3283 QUE AVEDES UOS, *****, FOR RETRAER LA MI BARBA?
                  25808 5ELCID3287 COMMO YC AUCS, *****, ENEL CASTIELLO DE CABRA;
                  27219 5ELCID3479 QUE NON PRENCAN FUERZA DE ***** NIN DE YFANZON.
                  27362 5ELCID3496 ADELINC A EL EL ***** DCN ANRICH & EL CONDE DON REMOND;
                  27367 5ELCID3496 ADELINO A EL EL CONDE DCN ANRICH & EL ***** DON REMOND;
                  27845 5ELCID3553 SEDIELCS CASTIGANDO EL ***** GARZIORDONEZ.
        WORD #1044 CCCURS  51 TIMES.
           INDEX OF DIVERSIFICATICN =   406.24 WITH STANCARD DEVIATION OF   953.24

CONDERECHO         8701 5ELCID1105 SI NOS ZERCAR VIENEN, ********** LO FAZEN.
        WORD #1045 CCCURS   1 TIMES.

CONDES            10874 5ELCID1376 MYO ZID ES DE BIUAR & NOS CELCS ****** DE CARRION.
                  20086 5ELCID2549 NOS DE NATURA SCMCS DE ****** CE CARRION
                  20121 5ELCID2554 CA DE NATURA SCMOS DE ****** CE CARRION.
                  22969 5ELCID2926 ELLOS ****** GALLIZANCS A EL TIENEN POR SE@OR.
                  24615 5ELCID3136 E ESTOS OTRCS ****** QUE DEL VANDO NON SODES.
                  25872 5ELCID3296 DE NATURA SCMOS DE ****** DE CARRION:
                  26302 5ELCID3354 DE NATURA SCMOS DE LOS ****** MAS LIPIOS,
                  26958 5ELCID3444 ONDE SALIEN ****** DE PREZ & CE VALOR;
        WORD #1046 OCCURS   8 TIMES.
           INDEX OF DIVERSIFICATICN =  2296.71 WITH STANCARD CEVIATION OF  3186.47
```

```
WORD                C#  PREFIX                          CONTEXT

CONDIOS            18696 5ELCID2366 VERLO HEMOS ******* & CCN LA UUESTRA AUZE.
         WORD #1047 CCCURS    1 TIMES.

CONDONADAS          6939 5ELCID0887 HONORES & TIERRAS AUELLAS **********,
         WORD #1048 OCCURS    1 TIMES.

CONDUCHO             533 5ELCID0068 DE TODO ******** BIEN LCS OUO EASTICOS.
                   10705 5ELCID1356 HYO LES MANCARE DAR ******** MIENTRA QUE POR MJ TIERRA FUEREN,
                   11136 5ELCID1409 MIENTRA QUE FUEREMOS PCR SUS TIERRAS ******** NOS MANDO DAR.
                   11456 5ELCID1450 POR LA TIERRA DEL REY MUCHO ******** LES DAN.
                   12123 5ELCID1538 DE TAN GRAND ******** CCMMO EN MEDINAL SACARON:
         WORD #1049 OCCURS    5 TIMES.
            INDEX OF DIVERSIFICATION =  2896.50 WITH STANDARD DEVIATION OF  4851.82

CONDUCHOS          15555 5ELCID1972 ********* LARGCS EL REY ENBIAR MANCAUA
         WORD #1050 OCCURS    1 TIMES.

CONEL              17118 5ELCID2166 GRANDES SON LAS YENTES QUE VAN ***** CANPEADOR.
                   19199 5ELCID2428 AQUIS CNDRC MYO %ID & QUANTOS ***** SON.
                   24511 5ELCID3124 ALA BARBA QUE AUIE LUENGA & PRESA ***** CORDON;
                   28838 5ELCID3683 METIOL POR LA CARNE ACENTRO LA LAN%A ***** PENDON,
         WORD #1051 OCCURS    4 TIMES.

CONES%E            12040 5ELCID1526 MUCHOL TENGC POR TORPE QUI NON ******* LA VERDAD.
         WORD #1052 CCCURS    1 TIMES.

CONFIA             27332 5ELCID3493 LA ****** DE RAN%AL QUE BLANCA ERA COMMO EL SOL,
         WORD #1053 OCCURS    1 TIMES.

CONFONDA           19065 5ELCID2412 RESPUSO BUCAR AL %ID: ******** DIOS TAL AMISTAD
         WORD #1054 OCCURS    1 TIMES.

CONLOYO            27891 5ELCID3558 DIXIERON GELO AL REY, MAS NON GELO *******;
         WORD #1055 CCCURS    1 TIMES.

CONNOS%E            7674 5ELCID0983 ESSORA LO ******** MIO %ID EL DE BIUAR.
                   24997 5ELCID3183 NOS LE PUEDEN CAMEAR, CA EL %ID BIEN LAS ********;
         WORD #1056 CCCURS    2 TIMES.

CONNOS%IE          15233 5ELCID1929 QUEL ********* Y CNCRA & CRE%IE EN ONOR,
         WORD #1057 OCCURS    1 TIMES.

CONNOS%IO          23014 5ELCID2932 VIOLOS EL REY & ********* A MU@O GUSTIOZ;
         WORD #1058 CCCURS    1 TIMES.

CONNUSCO            3086 5ELCID0388 SI VIEREDES YENTES VENIR POR ******** YR,
         WORD #1059 OCCURS    1 TIMES.

CONORTANDO         22035 5ELCID2804 VALAS ********** & METIENDO CORA%ON
         WORD #1060 OCCURS    1 TIMES.

CONORTAR           18393 5ELCID2328 HYD LOS ********, SI UOS VALA EL CRIADOR,
         WORD #1061 CCCURS    1 TIMES.

CONPANA            11233 5ELCID1421 POR YR CON ESTAS DUENAS BUE@A ******* SE FAZE.
         WORD #1062 CCCURS    1 TIMES.

CONPA@A              114 5ELCID0016 EN SU ******* LX PENDONES; EXIEN LO UER MUGIERES & UARONES,
                     477 5ELCID0060 DERREDOR DEL VNA BUE@A *******.
                    2346 5ELCID0296 QUEL CRE%E *******, POR QUE MAS VALDRA,
                    3492 5ELCID0440 VOS CON C DE AQUESTA NUESTRA *******,
                    3831 5ELCID0484 CCN AQUESTE AUER TORNAN SE ESSA *******;
                    4071 5ELCID0517 NIN CATIUOS NIN CATIUAS NON QUISO TRAER EN SU *******.
                    4122 5ELCID0524 ASMO MYO %ID CON TOCA SU *******
                   10944 5ELCID1385 LOS YFFANTES CE CARRICN CANCO YUAN ******* A MINAYA ALBARFANEZ:
                   14367 5ELCID1817 E DOZIENTOS CMNES LIEUAN EN SU *******,
                   14465 5ELCID1829 QUE MANDASSE RE%EBIR A ESTA *******:
                   17103 5ELCID2165 LA ******* DEL %IC CRE%E, & LA CEL REY MENGO,
                   18481 5ELCID2339 EN VNA ******* TORNADCS SCN AMOS.
         WORD #1063 OCCURS   12 TIMES.
            INDEX OF DIVERSIFICATION =  1668.73 WITH STANCARD DEVIATION OF  2038.86

CONPA@AS            1668 5ELCID0214 MYO %ID & SUS ******** CAUALGAN TAN AYNA.
                    9615 5ELCID1221 YA FOLGAUA MYC %ID CCN TOCAS SUS ********;
                   12360 5ELCID1569 E ALAS DUENAS & ALAS NI@AS & ALAS OTRAS ********.
                   15574 5ELCID1974 CON EL REY ATANTAS BUENAS ********.
                   15625 5ELCID1981 LOS YFANTES DE CARRION LIEUAN GRANDES ********.
                   19466 5ELCID2466 ALEGRE ES MYO %ID CCN TCDAS SUS ********,
                   19769 5ELCID2506 DE TODAS SUS ******** & DE TODOS SUS VASSALLOS;
                   23731 5ELCID3023 BUENAS ******** QUE ASSI AN TAL SE@OR.
         WORD #1064 CCCURS    8 TIMES.
            INDEX OF DIVERSIFICATION =  3150.86 WITH STANCARD DEVIATION OF  2646.55

CONPE%AREMOS        8741 5ELCID1111 ************ AQUESTA LIC CAMPAL,
         WORD #1065 CCCURS    1 TIMES.
```

WORD C# PREFIX CONTEXT

CONPE%O 5600 5ELCID0705 LA SE@A TIENE EN MANO, ******* DE ESPOLONAR;
8585 5ELCID1090 CONTRA LA MAR SALADA ******* DE GUERREAR;
11503 5ELCID1456 DE LA SU BOCA ******* DE FABLAR:
16330 5ELCID2071 NON LO TARDO EL REY, LA RAZON *******:
16700 5ELCID2115 ******* MYO %ID ACAR AQUIEN QUIERE PRENDER SO DON,
25944 5ELCID3306 PERO VERMUEZ ******* DE FABLAR;
WORD #1066 OCCURS 6 TIMES.
INDEX OF DIVERSIFICATION = 4067.80 WITH STANDARD DEVIATION OF 3299.15

CONPE%OLAS 8523 5ELCID1083 JUNTOS CON SUS MESNADAS, ********** DE LEGAR
WORD #1067 OCCURS 1 TIMES.

CONPIE%A 8536 5ELCID1085 AQUIS ******** LA GESTA DE MYO %ID EL DE BIUAR.
WORD #1068 OCCURS 1 TIMES.

CONPIE%AN 15214 5ELCID1926 ESTO DIZIENDO, ********* LA RAZON,
20372 5ELCID2585 ********* A RE%EBIR LO QUE EL %ID MANDO.
21512 5ELCID2735 ESSORA LES ********* ADAR LOS YFANTES DE CARRION;
WORD #1069 OCCURS 3 TIMES.

CONPLIDA 24028 5ELCID3062 E SSU OFRENDA HAN FECHA MUY BUENA & ********.
WORD #1070 OCCURS 1 TIMES.

CONPLIDAS 7094 5ELCID0907 ALI SOUO MIO %ID ********* XV SEMANAS;
WORD #1071 OCCURS 1 TIMES.

CONPLIDO 511 5ELCID0065 MARTIN ANTOLINEZ, EL BURGALES ********,
28989 5ELCID3703 ******** HAN EL DEBDO QUE LES MANDO SO SE@OR;
WORD #1072 OCCURS 2 TIMES.

CONPLIDOS 12818 5ELCID1626 CON L VEZES MILL DE ARMAS, TODOS FUERON *********,
13238 5ELCID1678 QUINIENTOS MATARON DELLOS ********* ENES DIA.
17790 5ELCID2251 QUINZE DIAS ********* DURARON EN LAS BODAS,
19026 5ELCID2407 VII MIGEROS ********* DURO EL SEGUDAR.
WORD #1073 OCCURS 4 TIMES.

CONPLIR 18692 5ELCID2365 EL DEBDO QUE A CADA VNO A ******* SERA.
WORD #1074 OCCURS 1 TIMES.

CONPRA 489 5ELCID0062 VEDADA LAN ****** DENTRO EN BURGOS LA CASA,
525 5ELCID0067 NON LO ******, CA EL SELO AUIE CONSIGO;
WORD #1075 OCCURS 2 TIMES.

CONPRADA 4087 5ELCID0519 ESTA QUINTA POR QUANTO SERIE ********,
WORD #1076 OCCURS 1 TIMES.

CONQUISTA 12851 5ELCID1630 LEGARON A VALEN%IA, LA QUE MYO %ID A *********,
WORD #1077 OCCURS 1 TIMES.

CONQUISTAS 8609 5ELCID1093 TIERRAS DE BORRIANA TODAS ********** LAS HA.
WORD #1078 OCCURS 1 TIMES.

CONSAGRAR 26311 5ELCID3356 POR ********* CON MYO %ID DON RODRIGO
WORD #1079 OCCURS 1 TIMES.

CONSEGAR 9907 5ELCID1256 CON MINAYA ALBARFANEZ EL SEUA ********:
WORD #1080 OCCURS 1 TIMES.

CONSEGO 671 5ELCID0085 CON UUESTRO ******* BASTIR QUIERO DOS ARCHAS;
WORD #1081 OCCURS 1 TIMES.

CONSEGUIR 6532 5ELCID0833 SI NON, DO SOPIEREDES QUE SOMOS, YNDOS *********.
WORD #1082 OCCURS 1 TIMES.

CONSEIA 15321 5ELCID1940 MAS PUES LO ******* EL QUE MAS VALE QUE NOS,
WORD #1083 OCCURS 1 TIMES.

CONSEIANDO 954 5ELCID0122 RACHEL & VIDAS SEYEN SE **********:
WORD #1084 OCCURS 1 TIMES.

CONSEIAUA 3476 5ELCID0438 COMMO LOS ********* MINAYA ALBARFANEZ:
WORD #1085 OCCURS 1 TIMES.

CONSEIAUAN 6591 5ELCID0841 SANO EL REY FARIZ, CON EL SE **********.
WORD #1086 OCCURS 1 TIMES.

CONSEIO 2169 5ELCID0273 DAND NOS ******* POR AMOR DE SANTA MARIA
3037 5ELCID0382 DIOS QUE NOS DIO LAS ALMAS, ******* NOS DARA.
4999 5ELCID0632 SI NON DAS *******, A TECA & A TERUEL PERDERAS,
8655 5ELCID1099 PRISIERON SO ******* QUEL VINIESSEN %ERCAR.
9958 5ELCID1262 ALI DIXO MINAYA: ******* ES AGUISADO.
WORD #1087 OCCURS 5 TIMES.
INDEX OF DIVERSIFICATION = 1946.25 WITH STANDARD DEVIATION OF 1224.73

WORD C# PREFIX CONTEXT

```
CONSENTIR           27813 5ELCID3549 POR QUERER EL DERECHC & NON ********* EL TUERTO.
        WORD #1C88 OCCURS   1 TIMES.

CONSIGEN            13647 5ELCID1729 CON OTROS CUEL ******** DE SUS BUENOS VASSALLOS.
        WORD #1C89 OCCURS   1 TIMES.

CONSIGO               530 5ELCID0067 NON LO CONPRA, CA EL SELO AUIE *******;
        WORD #1C90 OCCURS   1 TIMES.

CONSINTRAN           5291 5ELCID0668 QUE NOS QUERAMOS YR DE NOCH NO NOS LO **********;
        WORD #1C91 OCCURS   1 TIMES.

CONSOLAR             9260 5ELCID1177 NIN AMIGO A AMIGO NOS PUEDEN ********.
        WORD #1C92 OCCURS   1 TIMES.

CONSSAGRAR          15072 5ELCID1906 POR ********** CCN LOS YFFANTES DE CARRION.
        WORD #1093 OCCURS   1 TIMES.

CONSSEIADO           9866 5ELCID1251 ESTO MANDO MYO %ID, MINAYA LO OUO **********:
        WORD #1C94 OCCURS   1 TIMES.

CONSSEIARON         19996 5ELCID2537 TAN MAL SE *********** ESTOS YFFANTES AMOS.
                    20943 5ELCID2660 ENTRAMOS HERMANOS *********** TRA%ION:
        WORD #1095 OCCURS   2 TIMES.

CONSSEIASTES        21060 5ELCID2676 HYO SIRUIENDO UOS SIN ART, & UOS ************ PORA MI MUERT.
        WORD #1096 OCCURS   1 TIMES.

CONSSEIAUA          15242 5ELCID1930 QUE GELO ********** DALMA & DE CORA%ON.
        WORD #1C97 OCCURS   1 TIMES.

CONSSEIO            14876 5ELCID1880 FABLANDO EN SU ********, AUIENDO SU PORIDAD:
                    14919 5ELCID1886 CON UUESTRO ******** LO QUEREMOS FER NOS,
                    20142 5ELCID2557 CON AQUESTE ******** AMOS TORNADOS SON,
                    23461 5ELCID2988 PRENDEN SO ******** ASSI PARIENTES COMMO SON,
                    23526 5ELCID2996 PRENDEN ******** PARIENTES COMMO SON;
                    23547 5ELCID2999 AQUESTE ******** LOS YFANTES DE CARRION.
                    25278 5ELCID3218 NON ACUERDAN EN ********, CA LOS HAUERES GRANDES SON:
                    25293 5ELCID3220 TORNAN CON EL ******** E FABLAUAN ASSO SABOR:
        WORD #1C98 OCCURS   8 TIMES.
           INDEX OF DIVERSIFICATION =  1487.14 WITH STANDARD DEVIATION OF  2073.51

CONSSIGRA           11567 5ELCID1465 CON OTROS %IENTO CAUALLEROS BIEN UOS *********;
        WORD #1C99 OCCURS   1 TIMES.

CONTADAS            12282 5ELCID1559 APRES SON DE VALEN%IA A TRES LEGUAS ********.
        WORD #1100 OCCURS   1 TIMES.

CONTADO              1184 5ELCID0152 AFEUOS LOS ALA TIENDA DEL CAMPEADOR *******;
                     1513 5ELCID0193 MARTIN ANTOLINEZ, UN BURGALES *******,
                     3890 5ELCID0493 MUCHO UOS LO GRADESCO, CAMPEADOR *******.
                     3957 5ELCID0502 ANTE RUY DIAZ EL LIDIADOR *******,
                    14056 5ELCID1780 MAGER DE TODO ESTO, EL CAMPEADOR *******
                    19232 5ELCID2433 MYO %ID RUY DIAZ, EL CAMPEADOR *******,
                    19621 5ELCID2486 QUE TODOS PRISIESSEN SO DERECHO *******,
        WORD #1101 OCCURS   7 TIMES.
           INDEX OF DIVERSIFICATION =  3071.83 WITH STANDARD DEVIATION OF  3950.72

CONTADOS             6481 5ELCID0826 MYNAYA ALBARFANEZ DESTO ES PAGADO; POR YR CON EL OMNES SON ********
                     9931 5ELCID1259 METER LOS HE EN ESCRIPTO, & TODOS SEAN ********,
                    13601 5ELCID1723 ATANTOS MATA DE MOROS QUE NON FUERON ********;
                    19656 5ELCID2491 TANTOS SON DE MUCHOS QUE NON SERIEN ********.
                    19939 5ELCID2529 TANTOS AVEMOS DE AUERES QUE NO SON ********;
        WORD #1102 OCCURS   5 TIMES.
           INDEX OF DIVERSIFICATION =  3363.50 WITH STANDARD DEVIATION OF  2368.90

CONTALASSEN         24279 5ELCID3096 QUE NON LE *********** LOS PELOS AL BUEN %ID CANPEADOR;
        WORD #1103 OCCURS   1 TIMES.

CONTALDA             1415 5ELCID0181 SIUOS LA ADUXIER DALLA; SI NON, ******** SOBRE LAS ARCAS. . . .
        WORD #1104 OCCURS   1 TIMES.

CONTANDO            14001 5ELCID1773 CONTODAS ESTAS YENTES ESCRIUIENDO & ********;
        WORD #1105 OCCURS   1 TIMES.

CONTAR               5423 5ELCID0684 FABLAUA MYO %ID COMMO ODREDES ******:
                     5554 5ELCID0699 E FIZIERON DOS AZES DE PEONES MEZCLADOS, QUILOS PODRIE ******?
                     9559 5ELCID1214 EL ORO & LA PLATA QUI EN VOS LO PODRIE ******?
                     9589 5ELCID1218 ELOS OTROS AUERES QUIEN LOS PODRIE ******?
                    10346 5ELCID1310 DEXARE UOS LAS POSADAS, NON LAS QUIERO ******.
                    14872 5ELCID1879 DELOS YFFANTES DE CARRION YO UOS QUIERO ******,
                    18291 5ELCID2314 AQUESTE ERA EL REY BUCAR, SIL OUIESTES ******.
                    22480 5ELCID2862 EN LOS DIAS DE VAGAR TODA NUESTRA RENCURA SABREMOS ******.
                    26010 5ELCID3315 LAS TUS MA@AS YO TELAS SABRE ******:
```

```
WORD                C#  PREFIX                          CONTEXT

CONTAR (CON'T)

         WORD #11C6 CCCURS   9 TIMES.
            INDEX OF DIVERSIFICATICN =  2572.38 WITH STANCARD DEVIATION OF  1921.16

CONTESCA            29023 5ELCID3707 ATAL LE ******** C SI QUIER PEOR.
         WORD #1107 CCCURS   1 TIMES.

CONTIGO              2760 5ELCID0349 DOS LADRONES *******, ESTOS DE SE@AS PARTES
         WORD #11C8 CCCURS   1 TIMES.

CONTODA             25473 5ELCID3244 TANTA BUENA ESPADA ******* GUARNIZON;
         WORD #11C9 CCCURS   1 TIMES.

CONTODAS            13996 5ELCID1773 ******** ESTAS YENTES ESCRIUIENDO & CONTANDO;
         WORD #1110 CCCURS   1 TIMES.

CONTRA               4379 5ELCID0558 LOS VNOS ****** LA SIERRA & LCS OTROS CONTRA LA AGUA.
                     4385 5ELCID0558 LOS VNCS CCNTRA LA SIERRA & LCS OTROS ****** LA AGUA.
                     8581 5ELCID1090 ****** LA MAR SALADA CONPE%O CE GUERREAR;
                    22846 5ELCID2910 SI DESCNDRA Y CABE ALGUNA ****** NOS,
         WORD #1111 CCCURS   4 TIMES.

CONTRAL             27160 5ELCID3471 FABLO EL REY ******* CAMPEADOR:
         WORD #1112 CCCURS   1 TIMES.

CONUUO              28535 5ELCID3643 QUANDO LO VIO FERRANGO%ALEZ, ****** ATIZON;
         WORD #1113 CCCURS   1 TIMES.

CO@OS%EDORES        22383 5ELCID2851 GRA%IAS, VARONES CE SANTESTEUAN, QUE SODES ************,
                    24627 5ELCID3137 TODOS METEC Y MIENTES, CA SODES ************,
         WORD #1114 CCCURS   2 TIMES.

COPLA               28504 5ELCID3640 POR LA ***** DEL CAUALLO EN TIERRA LO ECHO.
         WORD #1115 CCCURS   1 TIMES.

COPLAS              17987 5ELCID2276 LAS ****** DESTE CANTAR AQUIS VAN ACABANDO.
         WORD #1116 CCCURS   1 TIMES.

CORACON             13051 5ELCID1655 CRE%EM EL ******* POR QUE ESTADES DELANT,
         WORD #1117 CCCURS   1 TIMES.

CORA%ON               424 5ELCID0053 FINCO LCS Y@OIOS, DE ******* ROGAUA.
                     3408 5ELCID0430 VASSALLOS TAN BUENOS POR ******* LO AN,
                     9314 5ELCID1184 SOPOLC MYO %ID, DE ******* LE PLAZ:
                     9993 5ELCID1266 ALEGRAS LE EL ******* & TCRNOS ASONRRISAR:
                    10594 5ELCID1342  SI ME VALA SANT ESIDRO  PLAZME DE *******,
                    1C700 5ELCID1355 ESSORA DIXO EL REY: PLAZ ME DE *******;
                    11494 5ELCID1455 PLOGOL DE ******* & TCRNOS A ALEGRAR,
                    11800 5ELCID1496 ESTO NCN DETARDO, CA DE ******* LO HAN;
                    12652 5ELCID1605 MY ******* & MI ALMA,
                    13099 5ELCID1660 MIEDO A SU MUGIER & QUIEREL QUEBRAR EL *******,
                    13212 5ELCID1675 ADOBAN SE DE ******* E CAN SALTO DE LA VILLA;
                    15199 5ELCID1923 DIXO MYNAYA. CALMA & CE *******
                    15246 5ELCID1930 QUE GELO CONSSEIAUA DALMA & DE *******.
                    15381 5ELCID1947 ESSORA DIXO EL %ID: PLAZME DE *******.
                    15471 5ELCID1960 QUANDO LAS VIC, CE ******* SE PAGA:
                    15769 5ELCID2001 DALMA & DE *******, & TCDCS LOS QUE EN PODER DESSOS FOSSEN;
                    15807 5ELCID2004 EN QUE TIENE SU ALMA & SU *******,
                    15920 5ELCID2018 SI NON A ESTCS CAUALLERCS QUE QUERIE DE *******;
                    16036 5ELCID2033 DIXO EL REY ESTC FERE CALMA & CE *******;
                    16228 5ELCID2058 NON SE PUEDE FARTAR DEL, TANTOL QUERIE DE *******;
                    17402 5ELCID2201 ATAN FIRME MIENTRE & CE TODO *******
                    18782 5ELCID2377 MYC ******* QUE PUDIESSE FOLGAR,
                    18931 5ELCID2395 HYUA LCS FERIR DE ******* & CE ALMA.
                    19789 5ELCID2508 DAQUESTA ARRANCADA QUE LIDIARON DE *******
                    19886 5ELCID2521 BIEN UOS ABRA%EN & SIRUAN UOS DE *******.
                    20321 5ELCID2578 ALLA ME LEUADES LAS TELAS DEL *******.
                    2C636 5ELCID2619 PRIMO ERES DE MIS FIJAS AMAS DALMA & DE *******
                    2C668 5ELCID2623 DIXO FELEZ MUNCZ: PLAZME CALMA & DE *******.
                    2C734 5ELCID2632 EL PADRE CCN LAS FIJAS LORAN CE *******,
                    20858 5ELCID2648 EL MORO QUANDC LO SOPO, PLOGOL DE *******;
                    21759 5ELCID2767 ENLA CARRERA DO YUA DCLIOL EL *******,
                    22038 5ELCID2804 VALAS CONORTANDO & METIENDO *******
                    22121 5ELCID2815 QUANDO EL LC CYC PESCL CE *******,
                    22158 5ELCID2821 QUANDO SABIEN ESTC, PESCLES DE *******;
                    22268 5ELCID2835 PESO A MYO %ID & ATODA SU CORT, & ALBARFANEZ DALMA & DE *******.
                    22616 5ELCID2881 AL MORC AUENGALUCN DE ******* LE PLAZ,
                    22797 5ELCID2904 POR MI BESA LE LA MANC CALMA & DE *******,
                    22825 5ELCID2907 QUEL PESE AL BUEN REY CALMA & CE *******.
                    22899 5ELCID2916 CA TAN GRANT ES LA RENCURA DENTRO EN MI *******.
                    23192 5ELCID2954 VERDAD TE CIGC YC, QUE ME PESA DE *******,
                    23235 5ELCID2959 ENTRE YO & MYO %ID PESA NOS DE *******.
                    23706 5ELCID3019 QUANDO LO CYC EL REY, PLOGCL CE *******;
                    23789 5ELCID3030 SALUDAR NOS HEMCS DALMA & DE *******.
                    23797 5ELCID3031 DELO QUE AUOS PESA AMI CUELE EL *******;
```

WORD C# PREFIX CONTEXT

CORA%ON (CON'T)

24479 5ELCID3120 LO QUE DIXO EL %ID AL REY PLOGO DE *******.
24753 5ELCID3152 HYO BIEN LAS QUERIA CALMA & DE *******,
25004 5ELCID3184 ALEGROS LE TODEL CUERPO, SONRRISOS DE *******,
25605 5ELCID3260 A QUEM DESCUBRIESTES LAS TELAS DEL *******?
26883 5ELCID3434 DIXO EL REY: PLAZME DE *******.
27377 5ELCID3497 ABRA%OLOS TAN BIEN & RUEGA LOS DE *******
28058 5ELCID3581 ESSORA DIXO EL REY: DALMA & DE *******.
28830 5ELCID3682 APART LE PRISO, QUE NON CABEL *******;
WORD #1118 OCCURS 52 TIMES.
INDEX OF DIVERSIFICATION = 555.98 WITH STANDARD DEVIATION OF 940.61

CORA%ONES 5676 5ELCID0715 ENBRA%AN LOS ESCUDOS DELANT LOS *********,
5697 5ELCID0718 YUAN LOS FERIR DE FUERTES *********.
21559 5ELCID2740 YA LO SIENTEN ELLAS EN LOS SOS *********.
21896 5ELCID2785 PARTIERON SE LE LAS TELLAS DE DENTRO DE LOS *********,
28323 5ELCID3615 ABRA%AN LOS ESCUDOS DELANT LOS *********,
WORD #1119 OCCURS 5 TIMES.
INDEX OF DIVERSIFICATION = 5660.75 WITH STANDARD DEVIATION OF 7411.74

CORAL 1921 5ELCID0244 CON LUMBRES & CON CANDELAS AL ***** DIERON SALTO.
26379 5ELCID3364 SALISTE POR LA PUERTA, METISTET AL *****,
WORD #1120 OCCURS 2 TIMES.

CORANADO 11843 5ELCID1501 E EL OBISPO DON JERONIMO, ******** LEAL,
15713 5ELCID1993 EL OBISPO DON IERONIMO, ******** MEIOR,
WORD #1121 OCCURS 2 TIMES.

CORCAS 18770 5ELCID2375 PENDON TRAYO A ****** & ARMAS DE SE@AL,
WORD #1122 OCCURS 1 TIMES.

CORDON 24294 5ELCID3097 LA BARBA AVIE LUENGA & PRISOLA CON EL ******,
24512 5ELCID3124 ALA BARBA QUE AUIE LUENGA & PRESA CONEL ******;
27348 5ELCID3494 E SOLTAUA LA BARBA & SACOLA DEL ******.
WORD #1123 OCCURS 3 TIMES.

CORDONES 24130 5ELCID3076 E QUE NON PARESCAN LAS ARMAS, BIEN PRESOS LOS ********;
WORD #1124 OCCURS 1 TIMES.

COREDOR 15679 5ELCID1988 TANTA BUENA ARMA & TANTO BUEN CAUALLO *******,
WORD #1125 OCCURS 1 TIMES.

COREDORES 15531 5ELCID1968 CAUALLOS GRUESSOS & ********* SJN FALLA,
16946 5ELCID2145 E XXX CAUALLOS *********, ESTOS BIEN ENSSELLADOS;
WORD #1126 OCCURS 2 TIMES.

CORITA 5818 5ELCID0735 MYNAYA ALBARFANEZ, QEU ****** MANDO,
WORD #1127 OCCURS 1 TIMES.

CORMANAS 25926 5ELCID3303 HYO LAS HE FIJAS, & TU PRIMAS ********;
WORD #1128 OCCURS 1 TIMES.

CORNEIA 80 5ELCID0011 ALA EXIDA DE BIUAR OUIERON LA ******* DIESTRA,
WORD #1129 OCCURS 1 TIMES.

CORONADO 10176 5ELCID1288 DE PARTE DE ORIENT VINO VN ********;
11530 5ELCID1460 EL OBISPO DON IERONIMO, ******** DE PRESTAR,
14168 5ELCID1793 EL OBISPO DON IHERONIMO, CABOSO ********,
WORD #1130 OCCURS 3 TIMES.

CORPES 21228 5ELCID2697 ENTRADOS SON LOS YFANTES AL ROBREDO DE ******,
21618 5ELCID2748 POR MUERTAS LAS DEXARON ENEL ROBREDRO DE ******.
21672 5ELCID2754 LOS YFANTES DE CARRION ENEL ROBREDO DE ******
22078 5ELCID2809 TODOS TRES SE@EROS POR LOS ROBREDOS DE ******,
23117 5ELCID2945 DESENPARADAS LAS DEXARON ENEL ROBREDO DE ******,
24783 5ELCID3156 QUANDO DEXARON MIS FIJAS ENEL ROBREDO DE ******,
25653 5ELCID3266 SOLAS LAS DEXASTES ENEL ROBREDO DE ******,
WORD #1131 OCCURS 7 TIMES.
INDEX OF DIVERSIFICATION = 736.50 WITH STANDARD DEVIATION OF 577.65

CORRE 4356 5ELCID0555 A%ERCA ***** SALON, AGUA NOL PUEDENT VEDAR.
7420 5ELCID0952 DENT ***** MYC %ID A HUESCA & A MONT ALUAN;
WORD #1132 OCCURS 2 TIMES.

CORRED 3529 5ELCID0445 AOSADAS ******, QUE POR MIEDO NON DEXEDES NADA.
WORD #1133 OCCURS 1 TIMES.

CORREDIZAS 21521 5ELCID2736 CON LAS %INCHAS ********** MAIAN LAS TAN SIN SABOR;
WORD #1134 OCCURS 1 TIMES.

CORREDOR 12411 5ELCID1575 SI SERIE ******** OSSI ABRIE BUENA PARADA;
25462 5ELCID3242 VERIEDES ADUZIR TANTO CAUALLO ********,
27505 5ELCID3513 MANDASTES ME MOUER ABAUIECA EL ********,
WORD #1135 OCCURS 3 TIMES.

WORD C# PREFIX CONTEXT

```
CORREDORES        9108 5ELCID1159 DAUAN SUS ********** & FAZIEN LAS TRASNOCHADAS,
                 10543 5ELCID1336 %IENT CAUALLOS GRUESSOS & **********,
                 15850 5ELCID2010 TANTOS CAUALLOS EN DIESTRO, GRUESSOS & **********,
                 17820 5ELCID2254 ENTRE PALAFRES & MULAS & ********** CAUALLOS,
                 20277 5ELCID2573 CAUALLOS PORA EN DIESTRO FUERTES & **********,
                 28065 5ELCID3582 ADUZEN LES LOS CAUALLOS BUENOS & **********,
        WORD #1136 OCCURS   6 TIMES.
           INDEX OF DIVERSIFICATION =  3790.40 WITH STANDARD DEVIATION OF  2688.89

CORREM            7517 5ELCID0964 AGORA ****** LAS TIERRAS QUE EN MI ENPARA ESTAN;
        WORD #1137 OCCURS   1 TIMES.

CORREN            3771 5ELCID0477 E SIN DUBDA ******; FASTA ALCALA LEGO LA SE@A DE MINAYA,
        WORD #1138 OCCURS   1 TIMES.

CORRIDA           7431 5ELCID0953 EN AQUESSA ******* X DIAS OUIERON AMORAR.
                 12517 5ELCID1588 FIZO VNA *******, ESTA FUE TAN ESTRA@A.
        WORD #1139 OCCURS   2 TIMES.

CORRIDO          12530 5ELCID1590 QUANDO OUO *******, TODOS SE MARAUILLAUAN;
        WORD #1140 OCCURS   1 TIMES.

CORRIE            3681 5ELCID0464 EL CAMPEADOR SALIO DE LA %ELADA, ****** ACASTEION SIN FALLA.
                  7469 5ELCID0958 QUE MYO %ID RUY DIAZ CUEL ****** LA TIERRA TODA;
        WORD #1141 OCCURS   2 TIMES.

CORRIENDO         7180 5ELCID0920 EL CAUALLO *********, UALO ABRA%AR SIN FALLA,
        WORD #1142 OCCURS   1 TIMES.

CORRIO            2801 5ELCID0354 ****** LA SANGRE POR EL ASTIL AYUSO, LAS MANOS SE OUO DE VNTAR,
        WORD #1143 OCCURS   1 TIMES.

CORRO             3595 5ELCID0453 DA QUESTE A ***** FABLARA TODA ESPA@A.
        WORD #1144 OCCURS   1 TIMES.

CORT              7503 5ELCID0962 DENTRO EN MI **** TUERTO ME TOUO GRAND:
                 10746 5ELCID1360 OYD ME, ESCUELLAS, & TODA LA MI ****.
                 10937 5ELCID1384 ESPIDIOS MYNAYA & VASSE DELA ****.
                 15034 5ELCID1900 OTROS MANDADOS HA EN ESTA MI ****:
                 15312 5ELCID1938 ELLOS SON MUCHO VRGULLOSOS & AN PART EN LA ****,
                 16491 5ELCID2090 GRA%IAS, DIXO EL REY, AUOS & ATOD ESTA ****.
                 18049 5ELCID2283 EN GRANT MIEDO SE VIERON POR MEDIO DELA ****;
                 18206 5ELCID2303 ETORNARON SEAL APALA%IO PORA LA ****.
                 18241 5ELCID2307 NON VIESTES TAL GUEGO COMMO YUA POR LA ****;
                 19529 5ELCID2474 GRANT FUE EL DIA LA **** DEL CAMPEADOR,
                 19812 5ELCID2511 ELLOS CON LOS OTROS VINIERON ALA ****;
                 20153 5ELCID2558 FABLO FERAN GON%ALEZ & FIZO CALLAR LA ****;
                 22262 5ELCID2835 PESO A MYO %ID & ATODA SU ****, & ALBARFANEZ DALMA & DE CORA%ON.
                 22779 5ELCID2902 EN BUEN ORA TE CRIE ATI EN LA MI ****
                 22994 5ELCID2929 ADELINO PORAL PALA%IO DO ESTAUA LA ****,
                 23009 5ELCID2931 ASSI COMMO ENTRARON POR MEDIO DELA ****,
                 23261 5ELCID2963 PREGONARAN MI **** PORA DENTRO EN TOLLEDO,
                 23327 5ELCID2971 POR AMOR DE MYO %ID ESTA **** YO FAGO.
                 23390 5ELCID2980 QUE **** FAZIE EN TOLLEDO AQUEL REY ONDRADO,
                 23410 5ELCID2982 QUI NON VINIESSE ALA **** NON SE TOUIESSE POR SU VASSALLO.
                 23447 5ELCID2986 POR QUE EL REY FAZIE **** EN TOLLEDO,
                 23473 5ELCID2989 RUEGAN AL REY QUE LOS QUITE DESTA ****.
                 23507 5ELCID2993 QUI LO FER NON QUISIESSE, O NO YR A MI ****,
                 23558 5ELCID3000 LEGAUA EL PLAZO, QUERIEN YR ALA ****;
                 23637 5ELCID3010 E CON ELLOS GRAND BANDO QUE ADUXIERON A LA ****:
                 23808 5ELCID3032 DIOS LO MANDE QUE POR UOS SE ONDRE OY LA ****
                 23945 5ELCID3051 E YRE ALA **** ENANTES DE IANTAR.
                 24143 5ELCID3078 DAQUESTA GUISA QUIERO YR ALA ****,
                 24340 5ELCID3103 ASSI YUA MYO %ID ADOBADO ALLA ****.
                 24503 5ELCID3123 CATANDO ESTAN A MYO %ID QUANTOS HA EN LA ****,
                 24653 5ELCID3140 JURO PAR SANT ESIDRO, EL QUE BOLUIERE MY ****
                 24708 5ELCID3147 POR QUANTO ESTA **** FIZIESTES POR MI AMOR.
                 24881 5ELCID3168 E QUANDO LAS TOUIERE, PARTIR SEA LA ****;
                 24897 5ELCID3170 CON AQUESTA FABLA TORNARON ALA ****:
                 24948 5ELCID3177 SACA LAS ESPADAS & RELUMBRA TODA LA ****,
                 24965 5ELCID3179 MARAUILLAN SE DELLAS TODAS LOS OMNES BUENOS DELA ****.
                 25350 5ELCID3227 QUE AQUI LO ENTERGEDES DENTRO EN LA ****.
                 25481 5ELCID3245 RECIBIOLO MYO %ID COMMO APRE%IARON ENLA ****.
                 25557 5ELCID3255 OYD ME TODA LA **** & PESEUOS DE MYO MAL;
                 25598 5ELCID3259 O EN ALGUNA RAZON? AQUI LO MEIORARE A JUUIZYO DELA ****.
                 25675 5ELCID3269 SI NON RECUDEDES, VEA LO ESTA ****.
                 26582 5ELCID3393 AFFE DOS CAUALLEROS ENTRARON POR LA ****;
                 26641 5ELCID3401 AESTO CALLARON & ASCUCHO TODA LA ****.
                 26696 5ELCID3409 LEUANTOS EL REY, FIZO CALLAR LA ****:
                 26717 5ELCID3412 ESTE CASAMIENTO OY SE OTORGE EN ESTA ****,
                 26833 5ELCID3427 A MUCHOS PLAZE DE TOD ESTA ****,
                 26871 5ELCID3432 BIEN UOS DI VAGAR EN TODA ESTA ****,
                 26898 5ELCID3436 HYO UOS RUEGO QUE ME OYADES TODA LA ****,
                 27073 5ELCID3459 CA EN ESTA **** AFARTO HA PORA VOS,
```

WORD C# PREFIX CONTEXT

CORT (CON'T)

27129 5ELCID3466 DESTOS IIJ POR TRES QUE REBTARCN EN LA ****.
27231 5ELCID3480 AQUI LES PCNGO PLAZC CE DENTRO EN MI ****,
27357 5ELCID3495 NOS FARTAN DE CATARLE QUANTOS HA EN LA ****.
27587 5ELCID3522 ESSORA SE ESPIDIERCN, & LUEGOS PARTIO LA ****.
27898 5ELCID3559 NON SACASTES NINGUNA QUANCO OUIEMOS LA ****.
WORD #1145 OCCURS 54 TIMES.
INDEX OF DIVERSIFICATION = 383.81 WITH STANDARD DEVIATION OF 779.C2

CORTANDOS 21456 5ELCID2728 ********* LAS CABECAS, MARTIRES SEREMOS NOS:
WORD #1146 OCCURS 1 TIMES.

CORTAUA 28604 5ELCID3652 LAS MONCLURAS DEL YELMO TOCAS GELAS *******,
WORD #1147 OCCURS 1 TIMES.

CORTES 21499 5ELCID2733 RETRAER UOS LO AN EN VISTAS O EN ******.
22882 5ELCID2914 ADUGA MELOS AVISTAS, O AIUNTAS, O A ******,
23150 5ELCID2949 QUE GELOS LEUEDES AVISTAS, O AIUNTAS, O A ******;
24553 5ELCID3129 HYO, DE QUE FU REY, NON FIZ MAS DE DOS ******:
25696 5ELCID3272 VEZOS MYO %ID ALLAS ****** PREGONADAS;
25969 5ELCID3310 SIEMPRE EN LAS ****** PERO MUDO ME LAMADES
WORD #1148 OCCURS 6 TIMES.
INDEX OF DIVERSIFICATION = 893.00 WITH STANDARD DEVIATION OF 578.30

CORTH 9965 5ELCID1263 MANDO LOS VENIR ALA ***** & A TODOS LOS IUNTAR,
WORD #1149 OCCURS 1 TIMES.

CORTOL 5922 5ELCID0751 ****** POR LA %INTURA, EL MEDIO ECHO EN CAMPO.
6045 5ELCID0767 ****** EL YELMO, QUE LEGO ALA CARNE;
19155 5ELCID2423 ****** EL YELMO &, LIBRADO TODO LO HAL,
WORD #1150 OCCURS 3 TIMES.

COSA 14014 5ELCID1775 TANTO FALLAN DESTO QUE ES **** SOBEIANO.
17406 5ELCID2202 QUE YO NULLA **** NOL SOPE DEZIR DE NO.
18257 5ELCID2310 FIERA **** LES PESA DESTO QUE LES CUNTIO.
18596 5ELCID2353 MYOS YERNOS AMOS ADOS, LA **** QUE MUCHO AMO,
21074 5ELCID2678 TAL **** UOS FARIA QUE POR EL MUNDO SONAS,
WORD #1151 OCCURS 5 TIMES.
INDEX OF DIVERSIFICATION = 1764.00 WITH STANDARD DEVIATION OF 1417.C8

COSAS 496 5ELCID0063 DETODAS ***** QUANTAS SON DE UIANDA
2C707 5ELCID2629 ATALES ***** FED QUE EN PLAZER CAYA ANOS.
WORD #1152 OCCURS 2 TIMES.

COSEIO 9305 5ELCID1183 NON LES DIXO ******, NIN LOS VINO HUUIAR.
WORD #1153 OCCURS 1 TIMES.

COSIMENT 11353 5ELCID1436 POR LO QUE AUEDES FECHO BUEN ******** Y AURA.
WORD #1154 OCCURS 1 TIMES.

COSIMENTE 21579 5ELCID2743 TANTO LAS MAIARON QUE SIN ********* SON;
WORD #1155 OCCURS 1 TIMES.

COSSEIAR 21011 5ELCID2670 TU MUERT OY ******** ALOS YFANTES DE CARRION.
WORD #1156 OCCURS 1 TIMES.

COSSEIO 9246 5ELCID1176 NIN DA ******* PADRE A FIJO, NON FIJO A PADRE,
WORD #1157 OCCURS 1 TIMES.

COSSO 12547 5ELCID1592 EN CABO DEL ***** MYO %ID DESCALGAUA,
WORD #1158 OCCURS 1 TIMES.

COSTADO 2796 5ELCID0353 DIOT CON LA LAN%A ENEL *******, DONT YXIO LA SANGRE,
WORD #1159 OCCURS 1 TIMES.

COSTADOM 11605 5ELCID1470 E YO FINCARE EN VALEN%IA, QUE MUCHO ******** HA;
WORD #1160 OCCURS 1 TIMES.

COSTUBRES 25963 5ELCID3309 DIREUOS, %ID, ********* AUEDES TALES,
WORD #1161 OCCURS 1 TIMES.

COZINA 16270 5ELCID2064 QUE ADOBASSEN ****** PORA QUANTOS QUE YSON;
WORD #1162 OCCURS 1 TIMES.

COZINAL 7965 5ELCID1017 A MYO %ID DON RODRIGO GRANT ******* ADOBAUAN;
WORD #1163 OCCURS 1 TIMES.

CRAIDOR 22461 5ELCID2860 ATANTO UOS LO GRADIMOS COMMO SI VIESSEMOS AL *******;
WORD #1164 OCCURS 1 TIMES.

CRAS 4218 5ELCID0537 **** ALA MA@ANA PENSEMOS DE CAUALGAR,
5358 5ELCID0676 VAYAMOS LOS FERIR EN AQUEL DIA DE ****.
7398 5ELCID0949 **** ALA MA@ANA PENSSEMOS DE CAUALGAR,
13300 5ELCID1686 OY ES DIA BUENO & MEIOR SERA ****:
14286 5ELCID1808 E **** HA LA MA@ANA YR UOS HEDES SIN FALLA

WORD C# PREFIX CONTEXT

CRAS (CON'T)

16159 5ELCID2050 E **** FEREMOS LO QUE PLOGIERE AUOS.
23937 5ELCID3050 **** MA@ANA ENTRARE ALA %IBDAD,
27113 5ELCID3465 **** SEA LA LID, QUANDO SALIERE EL SOL,
27139 5ELCID3468 DANDOS, REY, PLAZO, CA **** SER NON PUEDE.
WORD #1165 OCCURS 9 TIMES.
INDEX OF DIVERSIFICATION = 2864.13 WITH STANDARD DEVIATION OF 2664.27

CREADES 17421 5ELCID2204 BIEN MELO *******, QUE EL UOS CASA, CA NON YO.
21352 5ELCID2714 BIEN LO *******, CON ELUIRA & DO@A SOL,
WORD #1166 OCCURS 2 TIMES.

CRECEN 5191 5ELCID0657 ****** ESTOS VIRTOS, CA YENTES SON SOBEIANAS.
WORD #1167 OCCURS 1 TIMES.

CRE%E 2345 5ELCID0296 QUEL ***** CONPA@A, POR QUE MAS VALDRA,
9738 5ELCID1238 YAL ***** LA BARBA & VALE ALLONGANDO;
12994 5ELCID1648 RIQUEZA ES QUE NOS A ***** MARAUILLOSA & GRAND;
14721 5ELCID1861 MARAUILLA ES DEL %ID, QUE SU ONDRA ***** TANTO
17106 5ELCID2165 LA CONPA@A DEL %ID *****, & LA DEL REY MENGO,
18301 5ELCID2316 QUE LES ***** LA GANAN%IA, GRADO AL CRIADOR.
26719 5ELCID3413 CA ***** UOS Y ONDRA & TIERRA & ONOR.
27029 5ELCID3453 ASIL ***** LA ONDRA A MYO %ID EL CAMPEADOR
29146 5ELCID3722 VED QUAL ONDRA ***** AL QUE EN BUEN ORA NA%IO,
WORD #1168 OCCURS 9 TIMES.
INDEX OF DIVERSIFICATION = 3349.13 WITH STANDARD DEVIATION OF 2952.25

CRE%EM 13049 5ELCID1655 ****** EL CORACON POR QUE ESTADES DELANT,
WORD #1169 OCCURS 1 TIMES.

CRE%EN 10841 5ELCID1373 MUCHO ****** LAS NUEUAS DE MYO %ID EL CAMPEADOR,
WORD #1170 OCCURS 1 TIMES.

CRE%ER 25699 5ELCID3273 DEXOLA ****** & LUENGA TRAE LA BARBA;
WORD #1171 OCCURS 1 TIMES.

CRE%IDOL 11217 5ELCID1419 AMINAYA LXV CAUALLEROS A ******** HAN,
WORD #1172 OCCURS 1 TIMES.

CRE%IE 15237 5ELCID1929 QUEL CONNOS%IE Y ONDRA & ****** EN ONOR,
WORD #1173 OCCURS 1 TIMES.

CRE%IENDO 9436 5ELCID1200 ********* UA RIQUEZA A MYO %ID EL DE BIUAR.
WORD #1174 OCCURS 1 TIMES.

CRE%IERA 16236 5ELCID2059 CATANDOL SEDIE LA BARBA, QUE TAN AYNAL ********.
WORD #1175 OCCURS 1 TIMES.

CRE%IES 25862 5ELCID3295 NON ******* VARAIA ENTRE NOS & VOS.
WORD #1176 OCCURS 1 TIMES.

CRE%IO 2410 5ELCID0304 PLOGO A MIO %ID, POR QUE ****** EN LA IANTAR,
WORD #1177 OCCURS 1 TIMES.

CRE%RA 15068 5ELCID1905 ABRA Y ONDRA & ****** EN ONOR,
WORD #1178 OCCURS 1 TIMES.

CRE%REMOS 5453 5ELCID0688 SI VEN%IEREMOS LA BATALLA, ********* EN RICTAD.
14894 5ELCID1883 ********* EN NUESTRA ONDRA & YREMOS ADELANT.
17375 5ELCID2198 DESTE UUSTRO CASAMIENTO ********* EN ONOR;
WORD #1179 OCCURS 3 TIMES.

CREENDEROS 7932 5ELCID1013 ASOS ********** MANDAR LO GUARDAUA.
WORD #1180 OCCURS 1 TIMES.

CREO 2867 5ELCID0362 ATI ADORO & **** DE TODO VOLUNTAD,
WORD #1181 OCCURS 1 TIMES.

CRESPO 24413 5ELCID3112 NOS QUISO LEUANTAR EL ****** DE GRA@ON,
WORD #1182 OCCURS 1 TIMES.

CRIAADOR 17362 5ELCID2196 MUGIER DO@A XIMENA, GRADO AL ********.
WORD #1183 OCCURS 1 TIMES.

CRIADA 25771 5ELCID3282 POR ESSO ES LUEGA QUEADELI%IO FUE ******.
25787 5ELCID3284 CA DE QUANDO NASCO ADELI%IO FUE ******,
WORD #1184 OCCURS 2 TIMES.

CRIADAS 12601 5ELCID1598 CON DIOS & CON UUSCO BUENAS SON & *******.
WORD #1185 OCCURS 1 TIMES.

CRIADO 5831 5ELCID0737 MU@O GUSTIOZ, QUE FUE SO ******,
WORD #1186 OCCURS 1 TIMES.

WORD C# PREFIX CONTEXT

CRIADOR
380 5ELCID0048 MAS EL ******* UOS UALA CON TODAS SUS UERTUDES SANTAS.
744 5ELCID0094 VEALO EL ******* CON TODOS LOS SOS SANTOS,
1868 5ELCID0237 EL ABBAT DON SANCHO, CHRISTIANO DEL *******,
1890 5ELCID0240 ROGANDO A SAN PERO & AL *******:
2595 5ELCID0328 ROGANDO AL ******* QUANTO ELLA MEIOR SABE,
3332 5ELCID0420 TEMPRANO DAT %EUADA, SI EL ******* UOS SALUE
4716 5ELCID0598 CON LA MER%ED DEL ******* NUESTRA ES LA GANAN%IA
5345 5ELCID0675 EN EL NOBRE DEL *******, QUE NON PASE POR AL:
5604 5ELCID0706 EL ******* UOS VALA, %ID CAMPEADOR LEAL
6368 5ELCID0811 DAQUESTA RIQUEZA QUE EL ******* NOS ADADO
6887 5ELCID0880 QUEL AYDES MER%ED, SIEL ******* UOS VALA.
8614 5ELCID1094 AIUDOL EL *******, EL SE@NOR QUE ES EN %IELO.
8772 5ELCID1115 OYD, MESNADAS, SI EL ******* UOS SALUE
8938 5ELCID1138 ENEL NOMBRE DEL ******* & DEL APOSTOL SANTI YAGUE,
10426 5ELCID1321 MER%ED, SE@OR ALFONSSO, POR AMOR DEL *******
10449 5ELCID1324 QUEL AYADES MER%ED, SIUOS VALA EL *******
10530 5ELCID1334 GRANDES SON LAS GANAN%IAS QUEL DIO EL *******,
10823 5ELCID1370 DE MI SEAN QUITOS & VAYAN ALA GRA%IA DEL *******.
10900 5ELCID1379 HYA UOS YDES, MYNAYA?, YD ALA GRA%IA DEL *******
11094 5ELCID1404 DIXO DO@A XIMENA: EL ******* LO MANDE
11361 5ELCID1437 DIXO RACHEL & VIDAS: EL ******* LO MANDE
11397 5ELCID1442 SI UOS VALA EL *******, MINAYA ALBARFANEZ,
12869 5ELCID1633 GRADO AL ******* & A PADRE ESPIRITAL
12903 5ELCID1637 GRADO AL ******* & A SANTA MARIA MADRE,
12980 5ELCID1646 QUES ESTO, %ID, SI EL ******* UOS SALUE
13139 5ELCID1665 ANTES DESTOS XV DIAS, SI PLOGIERE A *******,
13165 5ELCID1668 COLGAR LOS HAN EN SANTA MARIA MADRE DEL *******.
13331 5ELCID1690 HYR LOS HEMOS FFERIR ENEL NOMBRE DEL ******* & DEL APOSTOL SANTI
13579 5ELCID1721 PLOGO AL ******* & QUIERON LOS DE ARRANCAR.
13846 5ELCID1754 ROGAND AL ******* QUE UOS BIUA ALGUNT A@O,
14768 5ELCID1867 GRADO AL ******* & AL SE@OR SANT ESIDRO EL DE LEON
15211 5ELCID1925 DIXO MYO %ID: GRADO AL *******
16114 5ELCID2043 FABLO MYO %ID & DIXO ESTA RAZON: ESTO GRADESCO AL *******,
16202 5ELCID2055 RESPUSO MIO %ID: ASSI LO MANDE EL *******
16414 5ELCID2081 DANDOS LAS, MYO %ID, SI UOS VALA EL *******
16534 5ELCID2095 GRADO & GRA%IAS, CID, COMMO TAN BUENO, & PRIMERO AL *******,
16573 5ELCID2100 AL ******* PLEGA QUE AYADES ENDE SABOR.
16974 5ELCID2149 PLEGA AL ******* CON TODOS LOS SOS SANTOS, ESTE PLAZER
17290 5ELCID2187 GRADO AL *******, VENGO, MUGIER ONDRADA
17328 5ELCID2192 GRADO AL ******* & AUOS, %ID, BARBA VELIDA
17994 5ELCID2277 EL ******* UOS VALLA CON TODOS LOS SOS SANTOS.
18306 5ELCID2316 QUE LES CRE%E LA GANAN%IA, GRADO AL *******.
18398 5ELCID2328 HYD LOS CONORTAR, SI UOS VALA EL *******,
18418 5ELCID2330 NOS CON UUSCO LA VENCREMOS, & VALER NOS HA EL *******.
18469 5ELCID2337 ARRANCAR MELOS TREUO CON LA MER%ED DEL *******.
18666 5ELCID2362 ESTA BATALLA EL ******* LA FERA,
19698 5ELCID2497 ARRANCO LAS LIDES COMMO PLAZE AL *******,
19745 5ELCID2503 ELLOS ME DARAN PARIAS CON AIUDA DEL *******,
19926 5ELCID2528 GRADO AL ******* & A UOS, %ID ONDRADO,
20158 5ELCID2559 SI UOS VALA EL *******, %ID CAMPEADOR
20443 5ELCID2594 MER%ED UOS PEDIMOS, PADRE, SIUOS VALA EL *******
20505 5ELCID2603 ANDAD, FIJAS, DAQUI EL ******* VOS VALA
20690 5ELCID2626 QUE SI ADIOS PLOGUIERE & AL PADRE *******,
21567 5ELCID2741 QUAL VENTURA SERIE ESTA, SI PLOGUIESSE AL *******,
21910 5ELCID2787 DESPERTEDES, PRIMAS, POR AMOR DEL *******
21949 5ELCID2792 ESFOR%AD UOS, PRIMAS, POR AMOR DEL *******
21996 5ELCID2798 DANDOS DEL AGUA, SI UOS VALA EL *******
22694 5ELCID2892 PLEGA AL *******, QUE EN %IELO ESTA,
23242 5ELCID2960 AIUDAR LE ADERECHO, SIN SALUE EL *******
23907 5ELCID3045 MER%ED, YA REY, SI EL ******* UOS SALUE
23985 5ELCID3057 AL ******* ROGANDO & FABLANDO EN PORIDAD.
24542 5ELCID3128 OYD, MESNADAS, SIUOS VALA EL *******
25124 5ELCID3200 GRADO AL ******* & AUOS, REY SE@OR,
26271 5ELCID3349 QUANDO FUERE LA LID, SI PLOGUIERE AL *******,
26539 5ELCID3387 FALSSO A TODOS & MAS AL *******.
26660 5ELCID3404 ESTO GRADESCO YO AL *******,
27314 5ELCID3490 ONDRADOS MELOS ENBIAD A VALEN%IA, POR AMOR DEL *******
27431 5ELCID3504 MER%ED UOS PIDO, REY, POR AMOR DEL *******
27570 5ELCID3520 QUIEN VOS LO TOLLER QUISIERE NOL VALA EL *******,
27775 5ELCID3544 DE NOCHE BELARON LAS ARMAS & ROGARON AL *******.
28050 5ELCID3580 TENENDOS ADERECHO, POR AMOR DEL *******
28940 5ELCID3696 VEN%IERON ESTA LID, GRADO AL *******.
WORD #1187 OCCURS 72 TIMES.
INDEX OF DIVERSIFICATION = 401.25 WITH STANDARD DEVIATION OF 407.12

CRIASTES
16454 5ELCID2086 HYO LAS ENGENDRE AMAS & ******** LAS UOS
WORD #1188 OCCURS 1 TIMES.

CRIAZON
21303 5ELCID2707 ADELANT ERAN YDOS LOS DE *******:
22920 5ELCID2919 E CON EL ESCUDEROS QUE SON DE *******.
WORD #1189 OCCURS 2 TIMES.

CRIE
22774 5ELCID2902 EN BUEN ORA TE **** ATI EN LA MI CORT
WORD #1190 OCCURS 1 TIMES.

```
WORD                C#  PREFIX                    CONTEXT


CRIMINAL             2710 5ELCID0342 SALUEST A SANTA SUSANNA DEL FALSO ********;
        WORD #1191 OCCURS   1 TIMES.

CRIO                19832 5ELCID2514 E OTROS MUCHOS QUE **** EL CAMPEADOR.
        WORD #1192 OCCURS   1 TIMES.

CROA%ON              2191 5ELCID0276 LEGOLAS AL *******, CA MUCHO LAS QUERIA.
        WORD #1193 OCCURS   1 TIMES.

CROUIERON           26092 5ELCID3326 ********* TELO TODOS, MAS NON SABEN LA VERDAD.
        WORD #1194 OCCURS   1 TIMES.

CROUIESSE           14146 5ELCID1791 QUE ********* SOS NUEUAS DE MYO %ID QUE AUIE ALGO.
        WORD #1195 OCCURS   1 TIMES.

CROUO                2827 5ELCID0357 EN TI ***** AL ORA, POR END ES SALUO DE MAL;
        WORD #1196 OCCURS   1 TIMES.

CRUZ                 2753 5ELCID0348 PUSIERON TE EN **** POR NUMBRE EN GOLGOTA;
                     2779 5ELCID0351 ESTANDO EN LA ****, VERTUD FEZIST MUY GRANT.
        WORD #1197 OCCURS   2 TIMES.

CRUZES              12472 5ELCID1582 SOBREPELI%AS VESTIDAS & CON ****** DE PLATA
        WORD #1198 OCCURS   1 TIMES.

CUBERTURAS          11900 5ELCID1509 E A ********** DE %ENDALES, & ESCUDOS ALOS CUELLOS,
                    12496 5ELCID1585 ENSIELLAN LE ABAUIECA, ********** LE ECHAUAN,
        WORD #1199 OCCURS   2 TIMES.

CUBIERTAS             683 5ELCID0087 ********* DE GUADALME%I E BIEN ENCLAUEADAS.
        WORD #1200 OCCURS   1 TIMES.

CUBRIO              22059 5ELCID2807 CON EL SO MANTO A AMAS LAS ******,
                    24306 5ELCID3099 DESUSO ****** VN MANTO QUE ES DE GRANT VALOR,
        WORD #1201 OCCURS   2 TIMES.

CUEDA                4367 5ELCID0556 MOI %ID DON RODRIGO ALCO%ER ***** GANAR.
        WORD #1202 OCCURS   1 TIMES.

CUEDAN              14537 5ELCID1839 ****** SE QUE ES ALMOFALLA, CA NON VIENEN CON MANDADO;
                    28363 5ELCID3622 ****** SE QUE ESSORA CADRAN MUERTOS LOS QUE ESTAN ADERREDOR.
                    28876 5ELCID3688 TODOS SE ****** QUE FERIDO ES DE MUERT.
        WORD #1203 OCCURS   3 TIMES.

CUEDO               16827 5ELCID2130 DAQUEND VAYA COMIGO; ***** QUEL AURA PRO.
        WORD #1204 OCCURS   1 TIMES.

CUELLO              19343 5ELCID2450 EL ESCUDO TRAE AL ****** & TODO ESPADO;
        WORD #1205 OCCURS   1 TIMES.

CUELLOS             11906 5ELCID1509 E A CUBERTURAS DE %ENDALES, & ESCUDOS ALOS *******,
                    28076 5ELCID3584 LOS ESCUDOS ALOS ******* QUE BIEN BLOCADOS SON;
        WORD #1206 OCCURS   2 TIMES.

CUEMMO              21155 5ELCID2688 ****** DE BUEN SESO A MOLINA SE TORNO.
        WORD #1207 OCCURS   1 TIMES.

CUEMO                2544 5ELCID0322 ***** LO MANDO MYO %ID, ASSI LO AN TODOS HA FAR.
                    11925 5ELCID1512 O ***** SALIERA DE CASTIELLA ALBARFANEZ CON ESTAS DUE@AS QUE TRAHE.
                    18490 5ELCID2340 ASSI LO OTORGA DON PERO ***** SE ALABA FERRANDO.
                    20804 5ELCID2642 ***** LA V@A DELA CARNE ELLOS PARTIDOS SON;
                    22798 5ELCID2905 ***** YO SO SU VASSALLO, & EL ES MYO SE@OR,
                    23091 5ELCID2942 ***** NOS HAN ABILTADOS YFANTES DE CARRION:
                    26109 5ELCID3328 LENGUA SIN MANOS, ***** OSAS FABLAR?
                    26821 5ELCID3426 QUE ***** ES DICHO ASSI SEA, OMEIOR.
        WORD #1208 OCCURS   8 TIMES.
           INDEX OF DIVERSIFICATION =  3467.14 WITH STANDARD DEVIATION OF  3315.07

CUENDES             15612 5ELCID1980 ******* & PODESTADES & MUY GRANDES MESNADAS.
                    16335 5ELCID2072 OYD ME, LAS ESCUELLAS, ******* & YFAN%ONES
                    23270 5ELCID2964 QUE ALLA ME VAYAN ******* & YFAN%ONES,
        WORD #1209 OCCURS   3 TIMES.

CUENTA                789 5ELCID0101 EN ****** DE SUS AUERES, DELOS QUE AUIEN GANADOS.
                     7167 5ELCID0918 NON SON EN ******, SABET, LAS PEONADAS.
                     9975 5ELCID1264 QUANDO LOS FALLO, POR ****** FIZO LOS NONBRAR:
                    13687 5ELCID1734 LOS L MILL POR ****** FUERO NOTADOS:
                    14029 5ELCID1777 NON PUDIERON ELLOS SABER LA ****** DE TODOS LOS CAUALLOS,
                    14182 5ELCID1795 NON TIENE EN ****** LOS MOROS QUE HA MATADOS;
                    15637 5ELCID1983 NON SON EN ******, SABET, LAS CASTELLANAS.
                    17839 5ELCID2257 NON FUERON EN ****** LOS AUERES MONEDADOS.
        WORD #1210 OCCURS   8 TIMES.
           INDEX OF DIVERSIFICATION =  2434.71 WITH STANDARD DEVIATION OF  2157.16
```

WORD C# PREFIX CONTEXT

CUENTAN 13275 5ELCID1683 EL SELC VIO CCN LCS CIOS, ******* GELO DELANT,
WORD #1211 OCCURS 1 TIMES.

CUER 1777 5ELCID0226 SPIDIOS EL CABOSO DE **** & DE VELUNTAD.
5035 5ELCID0636 QUANDO LO OYO EL REY TAMIN, POR **** LE PESO MAL:
18310 5ELCID2317 MAS, SABED, DE **** LES PESA ALOS YFANTES DE CARRION;
22180 5ELCID2825 DE **** PESO ESTO AL BUEN REY DON ALFONSSO.
WORD #1212 OCCURS 4 TIMES.

CUERDA 8965 5ELCID1141 TANTA ****** DE TIENDA Y VERIEDES QUEBRAR,
24348 5ELCID3105 ****** MIENTRA ENTRA MYO %ID CCN TODOS LOS SOS:
WORD #1213 OCCURS 2 TIMES.

CUERDAS 18967 5ELCID2400 VERIEDES QUEBRAR TANTAS ******* & ARRANCAR SE LAS ESTACAS
WORD #1214 OCCURS 1 TIMES.

CUERPO 8003 5ELCID1022 ANTES PERDERE EL ****** & DEXARE EL ALMA,
25001 5ELCID3184 ALEGROS LE TODEL ******, SONRRISOS DE CORA%ON,
26221 5ELCID3343 RIEBTOT EL ****** PCR MALO & POR TRAYDOR;
WORD #1215 OCCURS 3 TIMES.

CUERPOS 220 5ELCID0028 E AUN DEMAS LCS ******* & LAS ALMAS.
6984 5ELCID0893 SUELTO LES LOS ******* & QUITO LES LAS HEREDADES.
8119 5ELCID1035 AUOS & DOS FIJOS DALGO QUITAR UOS HE LOS ******* & DARUOS E DE MANO.
10781 5ELCID1365 ATREGO LES LOS ******* DE MAL & DE OCASION,
14802 5ELCID1871 MANDO UOS LOS ******* ONDRADA MIENTRE SERUIR & VESTIR
21404 5ELCID2721 PARAN LAS EN ******* & EN CAMISAS & EN %ICLATONES.
26944 5ELCID3442 RIEBTOS LES LCS ******* PCR MALOS & POR TRAYDORES.
WORD #1216 OCCURS 7 TIMES.
INDEX OF DIVERSIFICATION = 4453.00 WITH STANDARD DEVIATION OF 2260.26

CUESTA 7747 5ELCID0992 ELLOS VIENEN ****** YUSO, & TODOS TRAHEN CAL%AS,
7832 5ELCID1002 VIERON LA ****** YUSO LA FUER%A DELOS FRANCOS;
7840 5ELCID1003 ALFONDON DELA ******, %ERCA ES DE LA@O,
WORD #1217 OCCURS 3 TIMES.

CUETA 9262 5ELCID1178 MALA ***** ES, SE@ORES, AVER MINGUA DE PAN,
9350 5ELCID1189 QUIEN QUIERE PERDER ***** & VENIR A RRITAD,
18648 5ELCID2360 SI ***** FUERE, BIEN ME PODREDES HUUIAR.
WORD #1218 OCCURS 3 TIMES.

CUEUAS 4270 5ELCID0544 POR LAS ****** DANQUITA ELLOS PASSANDO UAN,
WORD #1219 OCCURS 1 TIMES.

CUM 13837 5ELCID1753 CON TAL *** ESTO SE VEN%EN MOROS DEL CAMPO.
23001 5ELCID2930 CON EL DOS CAUALLEROS QUEL AGUARDAN *** ASSE@OR.
27548 5ELCID3518 MAS ATAL CAUALLO *** EST PORA TAL COMMO VOS,
WORD #1220 OCCURS 3 TIMES.

CUMPLE 25507 5ELCID3248 ENPRESTAN LES DELO AGENO, QUE NON LES ****** LO SUYO.
WORD #1221 OCCURS 1 TIMES.

CUMPLLIR 27302 5ELCID3489 ELLOS SON ADOBADOS PORA ******** TODO LO SO;
WORD #1222 OCCURS 1 TIMES.

CUNADOS 19850 5ELCID2517 ACA VENID, *******, QUE MAS VALEMOS POR UOS.
WORD #1223 OCCURS 1 TIMES.

CUNPLANSSE 24093 5ELCID3072 CON ESTOS ********** %IENTO DELOS BUENOS QUE Y SON.
WORD #1224 OCCURS 1 TIMES.

CUNPLIERON 21278 5ELCID2704 MAL GELO ********** CUANDO SALIE EL SOL
WORD #1225 OCCURS 1 TIMES.

CUNPLIR 20467 5ELCID2598 DEBDO NOS ES A ******* LO QUE MANDAREDES VOS.
27689 5ELCID3535 ******* QUIEREN EL DEBDO QUE LES MANDO SO SE@OR,
WORD #1226 OCCURS 2 TIMES.

CUNTIDA 23089 5ELCID2941 HYA UOS SABEDES LA ONDRA QUE ES ******* ANOS,
WORD #1227 OCCURS 1 TIMES.

CUNTIO 18032 5ELCID2281 MALA SOBREUIENTA, SABED, QUE LES ******:
18263 5ELCID2310 FIERA COSA LES PESA DESTO QUE LES ******.
20078 5ELCID2548 ANTE QUE NOS RETRAYAN LO QUE ****** DEL LEON.
22394 5ELCID2852 POR AQUESTA ONDRA QUE VOS DIESTES A ESTO QUE NOS ******;
WORD #1228 OCCURS 4 TIMES.

CURIADOR 27203 5ELCID3477 VAYAN COMIGO, YO SERE EL ********;
WORD #1229 OCCURS 1 TIMES.

CURIALDAS 10717 5ELCID1357 DE FONTA & DE MAL ********* & DE DESONOR;
WORD #1230 OCCURS 1 TIMES.

CURIAM 28703 5ELCID3665 VALME, DIOS GLORIOSO, RE@OR, & ****** DESTE ESPADA
WORD #1231 OCCURS 1 TIMES.

WORD C# PREFIX CONTEXT

```
CURIAN          9949 5ELCID1261 AQUESTOS MYOS VASSALOS QUE ****** A VALEN%IA & ANDAN AROBDANDO.
        WORD #1232 OCCURS   1 TIMES.

CURIANDO       12334 5ELCID1566 EL SEDIE EN VALEN%IA ******** & GUARDANDO,
        WORD #1233 OCCURS   1 TIMES.

CURIAR         26164 5ELCID3335 NOS %ERCAMOS EL ESCA@O POR ****** NUESTRO SE@OR,
        WORD #1234 OCCURS   1 TIMES.

CURIARE        11146 5ELCID1410 DE AQUESTOS XV DIAS, SIDIOS NOS ******* DE MAL,
        WORD #1235 OCCURS   1 TIMES.

CURIAS          2608 5ELCID0329 QUE AMIO %ID EL CAMPEADOR QUE DIOS LE ****** DE MAL:
        WORD #1236 OCCURS   1 TIMES.

CURIATE        21002 5ELCID2669 ACAYAZ, ******* DESTOS, CA ERES MYO SE@OR:
        WORD #1237 OCCURS   1 TIMES.

CURIAUA        20236 5ELCID2569 EL %ID QUE NOS ******* DE ASSI SER AFONTADO;
        WORD #1238 OCCURS   1 TIMES.

CURIE           2889 5ELCID0364 POR MYO %ID EL CAMPEADOR, QUE DIOS LE ***** DE MAL.
               11031 5ELCID1396 OMILOM, DO@A XIMENA, DIOS VOS ***** DE MAL,
               11115 5ELCID1407 DEZID AL CANPEADOR, QUE DIOS LE ***** DE MAL,
               22680 5ELCID2890  VENIDES, MIS FIJAS? DIOS UOS ***** DE MAL
        WORD #1239 OCCURS   4 TIMES.

CURIEDES       25091 5ELCID3196 POR ESSO UOS LA DO QUE LA BIEN ******** UOS.
        WORD #1240 OCCURS   1 TIMES.

CURIELOS       18624 5ELCID2357 ******** QUI QUIER, CA DELLOS POCO MINCAL.
        WORD #1241 OCCURS   1 TIMES.

CURIEN         15763 5ELCID2000 A AQUESTOS DOS MANDO EL CAMPEADOR QUE ****** A VALEN%IA
        WORD #1242 OCCURS   1 TIMES.

CURIES         18583 5ELCID2352 ****** ME ADIEGO & CURIES ME ADON FERNANDO,
               18587 5ELCID2352 CURIES ME ADIEGO & ****** ME ADON FERNANDO,
        WORD #1243 OCCURS   2 TIMES.

CUYDADO        22500 5ELCID2865 DON ELUIRA & DO@A SOL, ******* NON AYADES,
               23359 5ELCID2975 ASSI COMMO LO DIXO, SUYO ERA EL *******:
        WORD #1244 OCCURS   2 TIMES.

CUYDADOS          43 5ELCID0006 SOSPIRO MYO %ID, CA MUCHO AUIE GRANDES ********.
        WORD #1245 OCCURS   1 TIMES.

CUYDAN         23640 5ELCID3011 EBAYR LE ****** A MYO %ID EL CAMPEADOR.
        WORD #1246 OCCURS   1 TIMES.

CUYDARON       19493 5ELCID2470 ******** QUE EN SUS DIAS NUNQUA SERIEN MINGUADOS.
        WORD #1247 OCCURS   1 TIMES.

CUYDAUA        23246 5ELCID2961 LO QUE NON ******* FER DE TODA ESTA SAZON,
        WORD #1248 OCCURS   1 TIMES.

CUYDO           7593 5ELCID0972 ASI VIENE ES FOR%ADO QUE EL CONDE AMANOS SELE ***** TOMAR.
        WORD #1249 OCCURS   1 TIMES.

CXXX           13371 5ELCID1695 DAD ME **** CAUALLEROS PORA HUEBOS DE LIDIAR;
        WORD #1250 OCCURS   1 TIMES.

%AGA            3570 5ELCID0449 E YO CON LO C AQUI FINCARE EN LA ****,
                3591 5ELCID0452 FAZED ME MANDADO MUY PRIUADO ALA ****;
                3615 5ELCID0455 E LOS QUE CON MYO %ID FICARAN EN LA ****.
                3824 5ELCID0483 NON OSA NINGUNO DAR SALTO ALA ****.
               18645 5ELCID2359 VOS CON LOS UUESTROS FIRME MIENTRE ALA **** TENGADES;
        WORD #1251 OCCURS   5 TIMES.
           INDEX OF DIVERSIFICATION =  3767.75 WITH STANDARD DEVIATION OF  7368.69

%ALUADOR       22958 5ELCID2924 E DELAS ASTURIAS BIEN A SAN ********,
        WORD #1252 OCCURS   1 TIMES.

%APATOS        24200 5ELCID3086 SOBRELLAS VNOS ******* QUE A GRANT HUEBRA SON;
        WORD #1253 OCCURS   1 TIMES.

%EBOLA          9034 5ELCID1150 PRISIERON ****** & QUANTO QUE ES Y ADELANT.
        WORD #1254 OCCURS   1 TIMES.

%EBOLLA        10487 5ELCID1329 ASSI FIZO ******* & ADELANT CASTEION,
        WORD #1255 OCCURS   1 TIMES.

%ELADA          3456 5ELCID0436 MYO %ID SE ECHO EN ****** CON AQUELOS QUE EL TRAE.
                3467 5ELCID0437 TODA LA NOCHE IAZE EN ****** EL QUE EN BUEN ORA NASCO,
```

```
WORD                  C#  PREFIX                                    CONTEXT

%ELADA (CON'T)

                    3499 5ELCID0441 PUES QUE A CASTEION SACAREMOS A ******,. . . .
                    3680 5ELCID0464 EL CAMPEADOR SALIO DE LA ******, CORRIE ACASTEION SIN FALLA.
                    4786 5ELCID0606 DANDO GRANDES ALARIDOS LOS QUE ESTAN EN LA ******,
                    4991 5ELCID0631 SACOLOS A ******, EL CASTIELLO GANADO A;
         WORD #1256 OCCURS   6 TIMES.
            INDEX OF DIVERSIFICATION =   306.00 WITH STANDARD DEVIATION OF   454.95

%ELFA               5114 5ELCID0646 VINIERON A LA NOCH A ***** POSAR.
                    5133 5ELCID0649 YXIERON DE ***** LA QUE DIZEN DE CANAL,
                    6805 5ELCID0869 EN SU MANO TENIE A ***** LA DE CANAL.
                    9394 5ELCID1194 TRES DIAS LE SPERARE EN CANAL DE *****.
         WORD #1257 OCCURS   4 TIMES.

%ENA               12077 5ELCID1531 VAYAMOS POSAR, CA LA **** ES ADOBADA.
         WORD #1258 OCCURS   1 TIMES.

%ENADO              3212 5ELCID0404 Y SE ECHAUA MYO %ID DESPUES QUE FUE ******,
         WORD #1259 OCCURS   1 TIMES.

%ENDALES           11902 5ELCID1509 E A CUBERTURAS DE ********, & ESCUDOS ALOS CUELLOS,
                   15553 5ELCID1971 MANTOS & PIELLES E BUENOS ******** DADRIA?
         WORD #1260 OCCURS   2 TIMES.

%EPADES             2435 5ELCID0307 TRES AN POR TRO%IR, ******* QUE NON MAS.
         WORD #1261 OCCURS   1 TIMES.

%ERCA                596 5ELCID0076 AUN ***** OTARDE EL REY QUERER ME HA POR AMIGO;
                    1653 5ELCID0212 MUCHO ES HUEBOS, CA ***** VIENE EL PLAZO.
                    2539 5ELCID0321 CA EL PLAZO VIENE A *****, MUCHO AUEMOS DE ANDAR.
                    3114 5ELCID0392 ***** VIENE EL PLAZO POR EL REYNO QUITAR.
                    4176 5ELCID0532 ***** ES EL REY ALFONSSO & BUSCAR NOS VERNA.
                    4400 5ELCID0560 DERREDOR DEL OTERO, BIEN ***** DEL AGUA,
                    5252 5ELCID0664 TOUIERON GELA EN ***** COMPLIDAS TRES SEMANAS.
                    7841 5ELCID1003 ALFONDON DELA CUESTA, ***** ES DE LA@O,
                    9472 5ELCID1204 BIEN LA ***** MYO %ID, QUE NON Y AUYA HART;
                   11950 5ELCID1515 POR ***** DE SALON TAN GRANDES GOZOS VAN.
                   17796 5ELCID2252 HYA ***** DELOS XV DIAS YAS VAN LOS FIJOS DALGO.
                   26014 5ELCID3316 MIEMBRAT QUANDO LIDIAMOS ***** VALEN%IA LA GRAND;
         WORD #1262 OCCURS  12 TIMES.
            INDEX OF DIVERSIFICATION =  2309.73 WITH STANDARD DEVIATION OF  2502.35

%ERCADOS            8802 5ELCID1119 LOS DE VALEN%IA ******** NOS HAN;
         WORD #1263 OCCURS   1 TIMES.

%ERCAMOS           26160 5ELCID3335 NOS ******** EL ESCA@O POR CURIAR NUESTRO SE@OR,
         WORD #1264 OCCURS   1 TIMES.

%ERCAN             18057 5ELCID2285 E ****** EL ESCA@O & FINCAN SOBRE SO SE@OR.
         WORD #1265 OCCURS   1 TIMES.

%ERCAR              5183 5ELCID0655 AL BUENO DE MYO %ID EN ALCO%ER LEUAN ******.
                    8658 5ELCID1099 PRISIERON SO CONSEIO QUEL VINIESSEN ******.
                    8699 5ELCID1105 SI NOS ****** VIENEN, CONDERECHO LO FAZEN.
                    9364 5ELCID1191 ****** QUIERE A VALEN%IA PORA CHRISTIANOS LA DAR.
                    9376 5ELCID1192 QUIEN QUIERE YR COMIGO ****** A VALEN%IA,
                   18276 5ELCID2312 FUER%AS DE MARRUECOS VALEN%IA VIENEN ******;
         WORD #1266 OCCURS   6 TIMES.
            INDEX OF DIVERSIFICATION =  2617.60 WITH STANDARD DEVIATION OF  3789.60

%ERCAUAN           18891 5ELCID2390 LOS MOROS SON MUCHOS, DERREDOR LE ********,
         WORD #1267 OCCURS   1 TIMES.

%ERRADA              252 5ELCID0032 ASSI COMMO LEGO ALA PUERTA, FALOLA BIEN *******,
                     314 5ELCID0039 NON SE ABRE LA PUERTA, CA BIEN ERA *******.
         WORD #1268 OCCURS   2 TIMES.

%ERUICIO             549 5ELCID0069 PAGOS MYO %ID EL CAMPEADOR & TODOS LOS OTROS QUEUAN ASO ********
         WORD #1269 OCCURS   1 TIMES.

%ERUI%IO           12102 5ELCID1535 TODOS FUERON ALEGRES DEL ******** QUE TOMARON,
         WORD #1270 OCCURS   1 TIMES.

%ETINA              4293 5ELCID0547 ENTRE FARIZA & ****** MYO %ID YUA ALBERGAR.
         WORD #1271 OCCURS   1 TIMES.

%EUADA              3329 5ELCID0420 TEMPRANO DAT ******, SI EL CRIADOR UOS SALUE
                    3397 5ELCID0428 FIZO MYO %ID POSAR & ****** DAR.
                    4574 5ELCID0581 FALIDO A AMYO %ID EL PAN & LA ******.
                    6484 5ELCID0827 AGORA DAUAN ******, YA LA NOCH ERA ENTRADA,
         WORD #1272 OCCURS   4 TIMES.

%IBDAD              9540 5ELCID1212 QUANDO MYO %ID GA@O A VALEN%IA & ENTRO ENLA ******.
                   12710 5ELCID1613 MIRAN VALEN%IA COMMO IAZE LA ******,
                   23915 5ELCID3046 PENSSAD, SE@OR, DE ENTRAR ALA ******,
```

WORD C# PREFIX CONTEXT

%IBDAD (CON'T)

23941 5ELCID3050 CRAS MA@ANA ENTRARE ALA ******,
WORD #1273 OCCURS 4 TIMES.

%ICLATON 24237 5ELCID3090 SOBRELLA VN BRIAL PRIMO DE ********,
WORD #1274 OCCURS 1 TIMES.

%ICLATONES 20285 5ELCID2574 E MUCHAS VESTIDURAS DE PA@OS & DE **********;
21410 5ELCID2721 PARAN LAS EN CUERPOS & EN CAMISAS & EN **********.
21551 5ELCID2739 LINPIA SALIE LA SANGRE SOBRE LOS **********.
WORD #1275 OCCURS 3 TIMES.

%ID 38 5ELCID0006 SOSPIRO MYO ***, CA MUCHO AUIE GRANDES CUYDADOS.
46 5ELCID0007 FFABLO MYO *** BIEN & TAN MESURADO:
91 5ELCID0013 ME%IO MYO *** LOS OMBROS & ENGRAMEO LA TIESTA:
106 5ELCID0015 MYO *** RUY DIAZ POR BURGOS ENTRAUA,
189 5ELCID0025 QUE A MYO *** RUY DIAZ, QUE NADI NOL DIESSEN POSADA,
234 5ELCID0030 ASCONDEN SE DE MYO ***, CA NOL OSAN DEZIR NADA.
278 5ELCID0035 LOS DE MYO *** A ALTAS UOZES LAMAN,
293 5ELCID0037 AGUIIO MYO ***, ALA PUERTA SE LEGAUA,
370 5ELCID0047 ***, ENEL NUESTRO MAL UOS NON GANADES NADA;
401 5ELCID0050 YA LO VEE EL *** QUE DEL REY NON AUIE GRA%IA.
453 5ELCID0058 MYO *** RUY DIAZ, EL QUE EN BUEN ORA %INXO ESPADA,
481 5ELCID0061 ASSI POSO MYO *** COMMO SI FUESSE EN MONTA@A.
513 5ELCID0066 AMYO *** & ALOS SUYOS ABASTALES DE PAN & DE UINO;
540 5ELCID0069 PAGOS MYO *** EL CAMPEADOR & TODOS LOS OTROS QUEUAN ASO %ERUICIO
615 5ELCID0078 FABLO MYO ***, EL QUE EN BUEN ORA %INXO ESPADA:
1004 5ELCID0129 MAS DEZID NOS DEL ***, DE QUE SERA PAGADO,
1026 5ELCID0132 MYO *** QUERRA LO QUE SSEA AGUISADO;
1069 5ELCID0137 YA VEDES QUE ENTRA LA NOCH, EL *** ES PRESURADO,
1189 5ELCID0153 ASSI COMMO ENTRARON, AL *** BESARON LE LAS MANOS.
1196 5ELCID0154 SONRRISOS MYO ***, ESTAUALOS FABLANDO:
1237 5ELCID0159 DON RACHEL & VIDAS A MYO *** BESARON LE LAS MANOS.
1287 5ELCID0165 NON LES DIESSE MYO *** DELA GANAN%IA UN DINERO MALO.
1321 5ELCID0169 CA AMOUER A MYO *** ANTE QUE CANTE EL GALLO.
1359 5ELCID0174 RACHEL AMYO *** LA MANOL BA BESAR:
1393 5ELCID0179 ***, BESO UUESTRA MANO ENDON QUE LA YO AYA.
1405 5ELCID0180 PLAZME, DIXO EL ***, DAQUI SEA ANDADA.
1586 5ELCID0203 RE%IBIOLO EL *** ABIERTOS AMOS LOS BRA%OS:
1665 5ELCID0214 MYO *** & SUS CONPA@AS CAUALGAN TAN AYNA.
1828 5ELCID0232 TORNAUAS MARTIN ANTOLINEZ A BURGOS & MYO *** AAGUIJAR
1897 5ELCID0241 TU QUE ATODOS GUIAS, VALA MYO *** EL CANPEADOR.
1939 5ELCID0246 GRADESCO LO ADIOS, MYO ***, DIXO EL ABBAT DON SANCHO;
1956 5ELCID0248 DIXO EL ***: GRA%IAS, DON ABBAT, & SO UUESTRO PAGADO;
2125 5ELCID0268 MER%ED, YA ***, BARBA TAN COMPLIDA
2291 5ELCID0288 COMMO SEUA DE TIERRA MYO *** EL CANPEADOR;
2317 5ELCID0292 TODOS DEMANDAN POR MIO *** EL CAMPEADOR;
2340 5ELCID0295 QUANDO LO SOPO MYO *** EL DE BIUAR,
2368 5ELCID0299 FABLO MYO *** DE TODA VOLUNTAD:
2407 5ELCID0304 PLOGO A MIO ***, POR QUE CRE%IO EN LA IANTAR,
2444 5ELCID0308 MANDO EL REY A MYO *** A AGUARDAR,
2548 5ELCID0322 CUEMO LO MANDO MYO ***, ASSI LO AN TODOS HA FAR.
2577 5ELCID0326 MYO *** & SU MUGIER A LA EGLESIA UAN.
2602 5ELCID0329 QUE AMIO *** EL CAMPEADOR QUE DIOS LE CURIAS DE MAL:
2883 5ELCID0364 POR MYO *** EL CAMPEADOR, QUE DIOS LE CURIE DE MAL.
2916 5ELCID0368 EL *** A DO@A XIMENA YUA LA ABRA%AR;
2926 5ELCID0369 DO@A XIMENA AL *** LA MANOL VA BESAR,
2984 5ELCID0376 MYO *** CON LOS SOS VASSALLOS PENSSO DE CAUALGAR,
3004 5ELCID0379 ***, DO SON UUESTROS ESFUER%OS? EN BUEN ORA NASQUIESTES DE MADRE;
3124 5ELCID0393 VINO MYO *** IAZER A SPINAZ DE CAN.
3195 5ELCID0402 ALA FIGERUELA MYO *** IUA POSAR.
3208 5ELCID0404 Y SE ECHAUA MYO *** DESPUES QUE FUE %ENADO,
3230 5ELCID0407 CAUALGAD, ***, EL BUEN CAMPEADOR, CA NUNQUA
3253 5ELCID0410 QUANDO DESPERTO EL ***, LA CARA SE SANTIGO;
3309 5ELCID0417 MANDO UER SUS YENTES MYO *** EL CAMPEADOR:
3394 5ELCID0428 FIZO MYO *** POSAR & %EUADA DAR.
3430 5ELCID0433 POR TAL LO FAZE MYO *** QUE NO IO VENTASSE NADI.
3452 5ELCID0436 MYO *** SE ECHO EN %ELADA CON AQUELOS QUE EL TRAE.
3480 5ELCID0439 YA ***, EN BUEN ORA %INXIESTES ESPADA
3611 5ELCID0455 E LOS QUE CON MYO *** FICARAN EN LA %AGA.
3700 5ELCID0467 MYO *** DON RODRIGO ALA PUERTA ADELI@AUA;
3720 5ELCID0470 MIO *** RUY DIAZ POR LAS PUERTAS ENTRAUA,
3757 5ELCID0475 DEXAN LA A MYO ***, TODO ESTO NON PRE%IA NADA.
3991 5ELCID0507 COMIDIOS MYO ***, EL QUE EN BUEN ORA FUE NADO,
4051 5ELCID0515 TODA LA QUINTA A MYO *** FINCAUA.
4106 5ELCID0522 PLOGO A MYO *** DA QUESTA PRESENTAIA.
4118 5ELCID0524 ASMO MYO *** CON TODA SU CONPA@A
4235 5ELCID0539 LO QUE DIXO EL *** A TODOS LOS OTROS PLAZ.
4295 5ELCID0547 ENTRE FARIZA & %ETINA MYO *** YUA ALBERGAR.
4322 5ELCID0550 OTRO DIA MOUIOS MYO *** EL DE BIUAR,
4345 5ELCID0553 E SOBRE ALCO%ER MYO *** YUA POSAR,
4363 5ELCID0556 MOI *** DON RODRIGO ALCO%ER CUEDA GANAR.
4425 5ELCID0563 QUE SOPIESSEN QUE MYO *** ALLI AUIE FINCAN%A.
4440 5ELCID0565 QUE EL CAMPEADOR MYO *** ALLI AUIE POBLADO,
4464 5ELCID0568 AGARDANDO SEUA MYO *** CON TODOS SUS VASSALLOS;

WORD C# PREFIX CONTEXT

%ID (CON'T)

```
4482 5ELCID0570 LOS DE ALCO%ER A MYO *** YAL DAN PARIAS DE GRADO
4507 5ELCID0573 ALI YOGO MYO *** COMPLICAS XV SEMMANAS.
4514 5ELCID0574 QUANDO VIO MYO *** QUE ALCO%ER NON SELE DAUA;
4569 5ELCID0581 FALIDO A AMYO *** EL PAN & LA %EUADA.
4587 5ELCID0583 DEGUISA UA MYO *** COMMO SIESCAPASSE DE ARRANCADA.
4631 5ELCID0588 MYO ***, QUANDO LOS VIO FUERA, COGIOS COMMO DE ARRANCADA.
4739 5ELCID0601 MYO *** & ALBARFANEZ ADELANT AGUIIAUAN;
4762 5ELCID0604 LOS VASSALLOS DE MYO *** SIN PIEDAD LES DAUAN,
4814 5ELCID0610 MYO *** GA@O A ALCO%ER, SABENT, POR ESTA MA@A.
4841 5ELCID0613 FABLO MYO *** RUY DIAZ, EL QUE EN BUEN ORA FUE NADO:
4921 5ELCID0623 MYO *** CON ESTA GANAN%IA EN ALCO%ER ESTA;
4966 5ELCID0628 QUE A VNO QUE DIZIEN MYO *** RUY DIAZ DE BIUAR
5179 5ELCID0655 AL BUENO DE MYO *** EN ALCO%ER LEUAN %ERCAR.
5226 5ELCID0661 ALOS DE MYO *** YA LES TUELLEN EL AGUA.
5235 5ELCID0662 MESNADAS DE MYO *** EXIR QUERIEN ALA BATALLA,
5265 5ELCID0666 MYO *** CON LOS SOS TORNOS A ACORDAR:
5412 5ELCID0683 ARMADO ES MYO *** CON QUANTOS QUE EL HA;
5420 5ELCID0684 FABLAUA MYO *** COMMO ODREDES CONTAR:
5485 5ELCID0692 AL *** BESO LA MANO, LA SE@A UA TOMAR.
5565 5ELCID0701 PORA MYO *** & ALOS SOS A MANOS LOS TOMAR.
5607 5ELCID0706 EL CRIADOR UOS VALA, *** CAMPEADOR LEAL
5720 5ELCID0721 YO SO RUY DIAZ, EL *** CAMPEADOR DE BIUAR
5809 5ELCID0734 MIO *** RUY DIAZ EL BUEN LIDIADOR;
5869 5ELCID0743 ACORREN LA SE@A & A MYO *** EL CAMPEADOR.
5902 5ELCID0748 VIOLO MYO *** RUY DIAZ EL CASTELANO,
5982 5ELCID0759 MYO *** RUY DIAZ, EL QUE EN BUEN ORA NASCO,
6081 5ELCID0772 LOS DE MYO *** FIRIENDO EN ALCAZ,
6153 5ELCID0784 QUE MYO *** RUY DIAZ LID CAMPAL A VEN%IDA.
6188 5ELCID0788 ANDAUA MYO *** SOBRE SO BUEN CAUALLO,
6233 5ELCID0794 ESTA ALBERGADA LOS DE MYO *** LUEGO LA AN ROBADA
6297 5ELCID0802 MANDO MYO *** AUN QUELES DIESSEN ALGO.
6307 5ELCID0803 GRANT A EL GOZO MYO *** CON TODOS SOS VASSALOS.
6325 5ELCID0805 EN LA SU QUINTA AL *** CAEN C CAUALLOS.
6491 5ELCID0828 MYO *** RUY DIAZ CON LOS SOS SE ACORDAUA:
6574 5ELCID0839 TODOS LOS DIAS A MYO *** AGUARDAUAN
6629 5ELCID0846 MYO *** RUY DIAZ A ALCOL%ER ES VENIDO;
6671 5ELCID0851 QUANDO MYO *** EL CASTIELLO QUISO QUITAR,
6685 5ELCID0853  VASTE, MYO ***; NUESTRAS ORA%IONES UAYANTE DELANTE
6702 5ELCID0855 QUANDO QUITO A ALCO%ER MYO *** EL DE BIUAR,
6752 5ELCID0862 AGUIJO MYO ***, YUAS CABA DELANT,
6810 5ELCID0870 MYO *** RUY DIAZ DE DIOS AYA SU GRA%IA
6845 5ELCID0875 MYO *** RUY DIAZ, QUE EN BUEN ORA CINXO ESPADA. . .
6925 5ELCID0885 AUN ME PLAZE DE MYO *** QUE FIZO TAL GANAN%IA.
6951 5ELCID0889 MAS DEL *** CAMPEADOR YO NON UOS DIGO NADA.
6979 5ELCID0892 BUE@OS & VALIENTES PORA MYO *** HUYAR,
7024 5ELCID0898 SI NULLA DUBDA YD A MYO *** BUSCAR GANAN%IA.
7059 5ELCID0902 EL POYO DE MYO *** ASIL DIRAN POR CARTA.
7093 5ELCID0907 ALI SOUO MIO *** CONPLIDAS XV SEMANAS;
7174 5ELCID0919 QUANDO VIO MYO *** ASOMAR A MINAYA,
7277 5ELCID0933  DIOS, COMMO FUE EL *** PAGADO & FIZO GRANT ALEGRIA
7344 5ELCID0942 DE MYO *** RUY DIAZ QUE NON TEMIEN NINGUNA FONTA.
7368 5ELCID0945 PLOGO A MYO ***, & MUCHO A ALBARFANEZ.
7414 5ELCID0951 ESTON%ES SE MUDO EL *** AL PUERTO DE ALCAT,
7422 5ELCID0952 DENT CORRE MYO *** A HUESCA & A MONT ALUAN;
7465 5ELCID0958 QUE MYO *** RUY DIAZ QUEL CORRIE LA TIERRA TODA;
7496 5ELCID0961 GRANDES TUERTOS ME TIENE MYO *** EL DE BIUAR.
7562 5ELCID0969 ADELINAN TRAS MYO *** EL BUENO DE BIUAR,
7578 5ELCID0971 ALCON%ARON A MYO *** EN TEUAR & EL PINAR;
7596 5ELCID0973 MYO *** DON RODRIGO TRAE GRAND GANAN%IA,
7619 5ELCID0976 MYO *** QUANDO LO OYO, ENBIO PORA ALLA:
7676 5ELCID0983 ESSORA LO CONNOS%E MIO *** EL DE BIUAR.
7817 5ELCID1000 TODOS SON ADOBADOS QUANDO MYO *** ESTO OUO FABLADO;
7849 5ELCID1004 MANDO LOS FERIR MYO ***, EL QUE EN BUEN ORA NASCO;
7953 5ELCID1016 PLOGO A MYO ***, CA GRANDES SON LAS GANAN%IAS.
7961 5ELCID1017 A MYO *** DON RODRIGO GRANT COZINAL ADOBAUAN;
8018 5ELCID1024 MYO *** RUY DIAZ ODREDES LO QUE DIXO:
8092 5ELCID1033 DIXO MYO ***: COMED, CONDE, ALGO, CASI NON COMEDES, NON VEREDES
8136 5ELCID1037 SI LO FIZIEREDES, ***, LO QUE AUEDES FABLADO,
8258 5ELCID1051 CON LOS CAUALLEROS QUE EL *** LE AUIE DADOS
8316 5ELCID1058 PAGADO ES MYO ***, QUE LO ESTA AGUARDANDO,
8336 5ELCID1060 SI UOS PLOGUIERE, MYO ***, DE YR SOMOS GUISADOS;
8450 5ELCID1074 FOLGEDES, YA MYO ***, SODES EN UUESTRO SALUO.
8489 5ELCID1079 MYEDO YUA AUIENDO QUE MYO *** SE REPINTRA,
8541 5ELCID1085 AQUIS CONPIE%A LA GESTA DE MYO *** EL DE BIUAR.
8559 5ELCID1087 POBLADO HA MYO *** EL PUERTO DE ALUCANT,
8597 5ELCID1092 MYO *** GA@O AXERICA & A ONDA & ALMENAR,
8631 5ELCID1096 YA VIE MYO *** QUE DIOS LE YUA VALIENDO.
8674 5ELCID1102 VIOLO MYO ***, TOMOS AMARAUILLAR: GRADO ATI, PADRE SPIRITAL
8931 5ELCID1137 CON LOS ALUORES MYO *** FERIR LOS VA:
8960 5ELCID1140 CA YO SO RUYDIAZ, MYO *** EL DE BIUAR
9030 5ELCID1149 GRANDES SON LAS GANAN%IAS QUE MIO *** FECHAS HA.
9069 5ELCID1154 LAS NUEUAS DE MYO ***, SABET, SONANDO VAN,
9093 5ELCID1157 ALEGRE ERA EL *** & TODAS SUS COMPA@AS,
9144 5ELCID1164 QUANDO EL *** CAMPEADOR OUO PE@A CADIELLA,
```

WORD	C#	PREFIX	CONTEXT
%ID (CON'T)			
	9185	5ELCID1169	EN GANAR AQUELAS VILLAS MYO *** DURO IIJ A@OS.
	9219	5ELCID1173	EN CADA VNO DESTOS A@OS MYO *** LES TOLIO EL PAN.
	9312	5ELCID1184	SOPOLO MYO ***, DE CORAZON LE PLAZ;
	9326	5ELCID1186	AMANEZIO AMYO *** EN TIERRAS DE MON REAL.
	9358	5ELCID1190	VINIESSE A MYO *** QUE A SABOR DE CAUALGAR;
	9398	5ELCID1195	ESTO DIXO MYO *** EL QUE EN BUEN ORA NASCO.
	9441	5ELCID1200	CREZIENDO UA RIQUEZA A MYO *** EL DE BIUAR.
	9448	5ELCID1201	QUANDO VIO MYO *** LAS GENTES IUNTADAS, COMPEZOS DE PAGAR.
	9456	5ELCID1202	MYO *** DON RODRIGO NON LO QUISO DETARDAR,
	9474	5ELCID1204	BIEN LA ZERCA MYO ***, QUE NON Y AUYA HART;
	9497	5ELCID1207	MAS LE VIENEN A MYO ***, SABET, QUE NOS LE VAN.
	9533	5ELCID1212	QUANDO MYO *** GA@O A VALENZIA & ENTRO ENLA ZIBDAD.
	9568	5ELCID1216	MYO *** DON RODRIGO LA QUINTA MANDO TOMAR,
	9611	5ELCID1221	YA FOLGAUA MYO *** CON TODAS SUS CONPA@AS;
	9647	5ELCID1226	ARRANCOLOS MYO *** EL DELA LUENGA BARBA.
	9683	5ELCID1231	TORNADO ES MYO *** CON TODA ESTA GANANZIA.
	9728	5ELCID1237	CON MYO *** RUY DIAZ, EL QUE EN BUEN ORA NASCO.
	9746	5ELCID1239	DIXO MYO *** DE LA SU BOCA ATANTO:
	9781	5ELCID1243	MYO *** DON RODRIGO EN VALENZIA ESTA FOLGANDO,
	9824	5ELCID1247	DE QUE SON PAGADOS; EL AMOR DE MY *** YA LO YUAN PROUANDO.
	9843	5ELCID1249	VELLO MYO *** CON LOS AVERES QUE AUIEN TOMADOS,
	9862	5ELCID1251	ESTO MANDO MYO ***, MINAYA LO OUO CONSSEIADO:
	9986	5ELCID1265	TRES MILL & SEYS ZIENTOS AUIE MYO *** EL DE BIUAR;
	10096	5ELCID1279	LA MUGIER DE MYO *** & SUS FIJAS LAS YFFANTES
	10137	5ELCID1284	CIENTO OMNES LE DIO MYO *** A ALBARFANEZ POR SERUIR LE EN LA CARRERA,
	10205	5ELCID1292	LAS PROUEZAS DE MYO *** ANDAUALAS DEMANDANDO,
	10238	5ELCID1296	QUANDO LO OYO MYO ***, DE AQUESTO FUE PAGADO:
	10432	5ELCID1322	BESAUA UOS LAS MANOS MYO *** LIDIADOR,
	10635	5ELCID1347	QUANDO ASSI FAZE A SU GUISA EL *** CAMPEADOR
	10664	5ELCID1351	MERZED UOS PIDE EL ***, SIUOS CAYESSE EN SABOR,
	10846	5ELCID1373	MUCHO CREZEN LAS NUEUAS DE MYO *** EL CAMPEADOR,
	10867	5ELCID1376	MYO *** ES DE BIUAR & NOS DELOS CONDES DE CARRION.
	10961	5ELCID1387	SALUDAD NOS A MYO *** EL DE BIUAR,
	10974	5ELCID1389	EL *** QUE BIEN NOS QUIERA NADA NON PERDERA.
	11043	5ELCID1398	SALUDA UOS MYO *** ALLA ONDDE ELLE ESTA;
	11077	5ELCID1402	SI UOS VIESSE EL *** SA@AS & SIN MAL,
	11105	5ELCID1406	ENVIOLOS A MYO ***, AVALENZIA DO ESTA,
	11195	5ELCID1416	HYR SE QUIERE A VALENZIA A MYO *** EL DE BIUAR.
	11322	5ELCID1433	DESFECHOS NOS HA EL ***, SABET, SI NO NOS VAL;
	11341	5ELCID1435	HYO LO VERE CON EL ***, SI DIOS ME LIEUA ALA.
	11424	5ELCID1446	EL *** SIEMPRE VALDRA MAS.
	11481	5ELCID1454	AL ORA QUE LO SOPO MYO *** EL DE BIUAR,
	11690	5ELCID1482	MYO *** UOS SALUDAUA, & MANDOLO RECABDAR,
	11858	5ELCID1503	POR SABOR DE MYO *** DE GRAND ONDRAL DAR;
	12003	5ELCID1522	MUGIER DEL *** LIDIADOR ESSUS FFIJAS NATURALES;
	12059	5ELCID1529	SI DIOS ME LEGARE AL *** ELO VEA CON EL ALMA,
	12115	5ELCID1537	ONDRADO ES MYO *** EN VALENZIA DO ESTAUA
	12284	5ELCID1560	AMYO ***, EL QUE EN BUEN ORA NASCO,
	12301	5ELCID1562	ALEGRE FUE MYO ***, QUE NUNQUA MAS NIN TANTO,
	12363	5ELCID1570	MANDO MYO *** ALOS QUE HA EN SU CASA
	12401	5ELCID1574	AVN NON SABIE MYO ***, EL QUE EN BUEN ORA ZINXO ESPADA,
	12500	5ELCID1586	MYO *** SALIO SOBREL, & ARMAS DE FUSTE TOMAUA,
	12549	5ELCID1592	EN CABO DEL COSSO MYO *** DESCALGAUA,
	12687	5ELCID1610	ADELINO MYO *** CON ELLAS AL ALCAZAR,
	12741	5ELCID1618	MYO *** & SUS COMPANAS TAN AGRAND SABOR ESTAN.
	12782	5ELCID1622	PESOL AL REY DE MARRUECOS DE MYO *** DON RODRIGO:
	12833	5ELCID1628	VAN BUSCAR A VALENZIA A MYO *** DON RODRIGO.
	12849	5ELCID1630	LEGARON A VALENZIA, LA QUE MYO *** A CONQUISTA,
	12864	5ELCID1632	ESTAS NUEUAS A MYO *** ERAN VENIDAS;
	12977	5ELCID1646	QUES ESTO, ***, SI EL CRIADOR UOS SALUE
	13015	5ELCID1651	AUOS GRADO, ***, & AL PADRE SPIRITAL.
	13083	5ELCID1659	ALEGRAUAS MIO *** & DIXO: TAN BUEN DIA ES OY
	13123	5ELCID1663	PRISOS ALA BARBA EL BUEN *** CAMPEADOR:
	13171	5ELCID1669	VOCAZION ES QUE FIZO EL *** CAMPEADOR.
	13263	5ELCID1682	TORNADOS SON A MYO *** LOS QUE COMIEN SO PAN;
	13281	5ELCID1684	ALEGRE ES MYO *** POR QUANTO FECHO HAN:
	13364	5ELCID1694	PUES ESSO QUEREDES, ***, A MI MANDADES AL;
	13397	5ELCID1698	ESSORA DIXO EL ***: DE BUENA VOLUNTAD.
	13458	5ELCID1706	AUOS, *** DON RODIRGO, EN BUEN ORA ZINXIESTES ESPADA,
	13507	5ELCID1712	MIO *** ALOS SOS VASSALOS TAN BIEN LOS ACORDANDO.
	13525	5ELCID1714	DIO SALTO MYO *** EN BAUIECA EL SO CAUALLO;
	13552	5ELCID1717	QUATRO MILL MENOS XXX CON MYO *** VAN A CABO,
	13586	5ELCID1722	MYO *** ENPLEO LA LANZA, AL ESPADA METIO MANO,
	13635	5ELCID1728	MYO *** EL DE BIUAR FASTA ALLI LEGO EN ALCAZ,
	13700	5ELCID1736	MESNADAS DE MYO *** ROBADO AN EL CANPO;
	13722	5ELCID1739	ALEGRE ERA MYO *** & TODOS SOS VASSALLOS,
	13783	5ELCID1747	MYO *** FINCO ANTELLAS, TOUO LA RYENDA AL CAUALLO:
	13862	5ELCID1756	ESTO DIXO MYO ***, DIZIENDO DEL CAUALLO.
	13985	5ELCID1771	COMMO LO DIXO EL *** ASSI LO HAN ACABADO.
	14070	5ELCID1782	QUANDO A MYO *** CAYERON TANTOS, LOS OTROS BIEN PUEDEN FINCAR PAGADOS.
	14090	5ELCID1784	QUE A GANADO MYO *** CON TODOS SUS VASSALLOS
	14116	5ELCID1787	MANDO MYO *** RUY DIAZ QUE FITA SOUIESSE LA TIENDA,
	14151	5ELCID1791	QUE CROUIESSE SOS NUEUAS DE MYO *** QUE AUIE ALGO.
	14196	5ELCID1797	MYO *** DON RODRIGO, EL QUE EN BUEN ORA NASCO,

WORD C# PREFIX CONTEXT

%ID (CON'T)

14251 5ELCID1803 EL BUENO DE MYO *** NCN LC TARDO POR NADA:
14371 5ELCID1818 CCN SALUDES DEL *** QUE LAS MANOS LE BESAUA:
14467 5ELCID1830 MYO *** EL DE VALENZIA ENBIA SU PRESENTAIA.
14588 5ELCID1846 POR MYO *** EL CAMPEACCR TODO ESTO VOS BESAMOS;
14610 5ELCID1848 MUCHO PREZIA LA ONDRA EL *** QUEL AUEDES DADO.
14672 5ELCID1856 GRADESCCLO A MYO *** QUE TAL CCN ME HA ENBIADO;
14717 5ELCID1861 MARAUILLA ES DEL ***, QUE SU ONDRA CREZE TANTO
14783 5ELCID1868 ESTOS DOZIENTCS CAUALLOS QUEM ENBIA MYO ***.
14825 5ELCID1873 QUE BIEN PARESCADES ANTE RUY DIAZ MYO ***;
14883 5ELCID1881 LAS NUEUAS DEL *** MUCHC VAN ADELANT,
15010 5ELCID1898 SIRUEM MYO *** EL CAMPEADOR, EL LO MEREZE,
15095 5ELCID1909 DESPUES FAGA EL *** LC QUE QUIERE SABOR.
15129 5ELCID1913 ANDAR LE QUIERO A MYC *** EN TODA PRO.
15161 5ELCID1918 SONRRISOS MYO *** & BIEN LOS ABRAZO:
15208 5ELCID1925 DIXO MYO ***: GRADO AL CRIADOR
15251 5ELCID1931 QUANDO LO OYO MYO *** EL BUEN CAMPEADOR,
15378 5ELCID1947 ESSORA DIXO EL ***: PLAZME DE CORAZON.
15477 5ELCID1961 SALUDAD ME MAYO ***, EL QUE EN BUEN ORA ZINXO ESPADA;
15503 5ELCID1964 NON LO DETARDAN, A MYO *** SE TORNAUAN.
15653 5ELCID1985 DENTRO EN VALLENZIA MYO *** EL CAMPEADOR
15852 5ELCID2011 MYO *** SELCS GA@ARA, QUE NCN GELOS DIERAN EN DON.
15988 5ELCID2027 LEUANTADOS EN PIE, YA *** CAMPEADOR,
16053 5ELCID2036 FABLC MYO *** & DIXO: MERZED; YOLO REZIBO, ALFONSSO MYO SE@OR;
16106 5ELCID2043 FABLO MYO *** & DIXO ESTA RAZON: ESTO GRADESCO AL CRIADOR,
16156 5ELCID2049 MYO HUESPED SEREDES, *** CAMPEADOR,
16182 5ELCID2053 OMILLAMOS NOS, ***, EN BUEN ORA NASQUIESTES UOS
16197 5ELCID2055 RESPUSC MIO ***: ASSI LC MANDE EL CRIADOR
16204 5ELCID2056 MYO *** RUY DIAZ, QUE EN ORA BUENA NASCO,
16241 5ELCID2060 MARAUILLAN SE DE MYO *** QUANTOS QUE Y SON.
16281 5ELCID2065 DE TAL GUISA LOS PAGA MYO *** EL CAMPEADOR,
16344 5ELCID2073 COMETER QUIERO VN RUEGO A MYO *** EL CAMPEADOR;
16409 5ELCID2081 DANDOS LAS, MYO ***, SI UOS VALA EL CRIADOR
16639 5ELCID2108 MYO *** GELOS REZIBE, LAS MANOS LE BESO:
16689 5ELCID2113 AQUIS METIO EN NUEUAS MYO *** EL CAMPEADOR;
16702 5ELCID2115 CONPEZC MYO *** ADAR AQUIEN QUIERE PRENDER SO DON,
16726 5ELCID2118 MYO *** DELOS CAUALLCS LX DIO EN DON.
16763 5ELCID2122 METIOLOS EN PODER DE MYC *** EL CAMPEADOR:
16802 5ELCID2127 SOBREL SO CAUALLO BAUIECA MYO *** SALTO DAUA;
16989 5ELCID2151 MYO *** RUY DIAZ, MUCHO ME AUEDES ONDRADO,
17031 5ELCID2156 HYAS ESPIDIO MYO *** DE SO SE@OR ALFONSSO,
17070 5ELCID2161 HYREMOS EN PODER DE MUO *** A VALENZIA LA MAYOR;
17087 5ELCID2163 HE DELAS FIJAS DE MYO ***, DE DON ELUIRA & DO@A SOL.
17105 5ELCID2165 LA CONPA@A DEL *** CREZE, & LA DEL REY MENGO,
17148 5ELCID2170 EN CASA DE MYC *** NON A DOS MEIORES,
17195 5ELCID2175 AFELOS EN VALENZIA, LA QUE MYO *** GA@O;
17207 5ELCID2177 DIXO MYO *** ADON PERO & A MU@O GUSTIOZ:
17259 5ELCID2183 MYC *** EL CAMPEADOR AL ALCAZAR ENTRAUA;
17331 5ELCID2192 GRADO AL CRIADOR & AUCS, ***, BARBA VELIDA
17500 5ELCID2214 REZIBIO LOS MYO *** CCN TODOS SUS VASALLOS;
17523 5ELCID2217 TODOS LOS DE MYO *** TAN BIEN SON ACORDADOS,
17665 5ELCID2235 A MYO *** & A SU MUGIER VAN BESAR LA MANO.
17726 5ELCID2243 DIOS, QUE BIEN TOUIERON ARMAS EL *** & SUS VASSALOS
17740 5ELCID2245 MYO *** DELO QUE VEYE MUCHO ERA PAGADO:
17777 5ELCID2249 E AL OTRO DIA FIZO MYC *** FINCAR VIJ TABLADOS:
17806 5ELCID2253 MYO *** DON RODRIGO, EL QUE EN BUEN ORA NASCO,
17847 5ELCID2258 LOS VASSALLOS DE MIO ***, ASSI SON ACORDADOS,
17904 5ELCID2265 POR PAGADOS SE PARTEN DE MYO *** & DE SUS VASSALLOS.
17935 5ELCID2270 EL *** & SOS HYERNOS EN VALENZIA SON RASTADOS.
17962 5ELCID2273 ALEGRE ERA EL *** & TODOS SUS VASSALLOS.
17980 5ELCID2275 QUES PAGE DES CASAMIENTO MYO *** O EL QUE LO ALGO
18006 5ELCID2278 EN VALENZIA SEY MYO *** CON TODOS SUS VASSALLOS,
18146 5ELCID2296 MYC *** FINCO EL COBDO, EN PIE SE LEUANTO,
18172 5ELCID2299 ANTE MYO *** LA CABEZA PREMIO & EL ROSTRO FINCO;
18181 5ELCID2300 MYC *** DON RODRIGO ALCUELLO LO TOMO,
18208 5ELCID2304 MYO *** POR SOS YERNOS DEMANDO & NOLOS FALLO;
18245 5ELCID2308 MANDOLO VEDAR MYO *** EL CAMPEADOR.
18294 5ELCID2315 ALEGRAUAS EL *** & TODOS SUS VARONES,
18373 5ELCID2325 VINO CON ESTAS NUEUAS A MUO *** RUYDIAZ EL CANPEADOR:
18420 5ELCID2331 MYO *** DON RODRIGO SONRRISANDO SALIO:
18497 5ELCID2341 PLOGO A MYO *** & ATODOS SOS VASSALLOS;
18611 5ELCID2355 HYC UOS DIGO, ***, POR TODA CARIDAD,
18660 5ELCID2361 AQUI LEGO MYNAYA ALBARFANEZ: OYD, YA ***, CANPEADOR LEAL
18704 5ELCID2367 DIXO MYO ***: AYAMOS MAS DE VAGAR.
18788 5ELCID2378 EUOS, MYO ***, DE MI MAS UOS PAGAR.
18807 5ELCID2380 ESSORA DIXO MYO ***: LO QUE UOS QUEREDES PLAZ ME.
18957 5ELCID2399 MYC *** CON LOS SUYOS CAE EN ALCANZA;
18984 5ELCID2402 LOS DE MYO *** ALOS DE BUCAR DELAS TIENDAS LOS SACAN.
19031 5ELCID2408 MYO *** AL REY BUCAR CAYOL EN ALCAZ:
19048 5ELCID2410 VERTE AS CON EL ***, EL DE LA BARBA GRANT,
19064 5ELCID2412 RESPUSO BUCAR AL ***: CONFONDA DIOS TAL AMISTAD
19109 5ELCID2417 AQUI RESPUSO MYO ***: ESTO NON SERA VERDAD.
19127 5ELCID2419 MAS BAUIECA EL DE MIO *** ALCANZANDO LO VA.
19133 5ELCID2420 ALCANZOLO EL *** ABUCAR A TRES BRACAS DEL MAR,
19196 5ELCID2428 AQUIS ONDRO MYO *** & QUANTOS CONEL SON.

WORD C# PREFIX CONTEXT

%ID (CON'T)

19227 5ELCID2433 MYO *** RUY DIAZ, EL CAMPEADOR CONTADO,
19263 5ELCID2438 ALGO VIE MYO *** DELO QUE ERA PAGADO,
19290 5ELCID2442 ALEGROS MYO *** FERMOSO SONRRISANDO:
19393 5ELCID2457 EA UOS, ***, QUE EN BUEN ORA FUESTES NADO
19429 5ELCID2462 DIXO MYO ***: YO DESTO SO PAGADO;
19446 5ELCID2464 POR BIEN LO DIXO EL ***, MAS ELLOS LO TOUIERON AMAL.
19462 5ELCID2466 ALEGRE ES MYO *** CON TODAS SUS CONPA@AS,
19480 5ELCID2468 LOS YERNOS DE MYO *** QUANDO ESTE AUER TOMARON
19520 5ELCID2473 MUCHOS SON ALEGRES MYO *** & SUS VASSALLOS,
19604 5ELCID2484 MANDO MYO ***, EL QUE EN BUEN ORA NASCO,
19640 5ELCID2489 CAYERON LE EN QUINTA AL *** SEYX %IENTOS CAUALLOS,
19763 5ELCID2505 GRANDES SON LOS GOZOS EN VALEN%IA CON MYO *** EL CANPEADOR
19817 5ELCID2512 AQUI ESTA CON MYO *** EL OBISPO DO IHERONIMO,
19845 5ELCID2516 RE%IBIOLOS MINAYA POR MYO *** EL CAMPEADOR:
19930 5ELCID2528 GRADO AL CRIADOR & A UOS, *** ONDRADO,
19960 5ELCID2532 VASSALLOS DE MYO *** SEYEN SE SONRRISANDO:
20040 5ELCID2543 PIDAMOS NUESTRAS MUGIERES AL *** CAMPEADOR,
20159 5ELCID2559 SI UOS VALA EL CRIADOR, *** CAMPEADOR
20233 5ELCID2569 EL *** QUE NOS CURIAUA DE ASSI SER AFONTADO;
20378 5ELCID2585 CONPIE%AN A RE%EBIR LO QUE EL *** MANDO.
20434 5ELCID2593 FINCARON LOS YNOIOS ANTEL *** CAMPEADOR:
20489 5ELCID2601 ABRA%OLAS MYO *** & SALUDOLAS AMAS ADOS.
20550 5ELCID2609 MYO *** & LOS OTROS DE CAUALGAR PENSSAUAN,
20589 5ELCID2614 ALEGRE VA MYO *** CON TODAS SUS COMPA@AS.
20673 5ELCID2624 MINAYA ALBARFANEZ ANTE MYO *** SE PARO:
20678 5ELCID2625 TORNEMOS NOS, ***, A VALEN%IA LA MAYOR;
20896 5ELCID2654 ALAS FIJAS DEL *** EL MORO SUS DO@AS DIO,
20931 5ELCID2658 TOD ESTO LES FIZO EL MORO POR EL AMOR DEL *** CAMPEADOR.
20981 5ELCID2665 NUNQUA AURIE DERECHO DE NOS EL *** CAMPEADOR.
21069 5ELCID2677 SI NOLO DEXAS POR MYO *** EL DE BIUAR,
21384 5ELCID2718 HYRAN AQUESTOS MANDADOS AL *** CAMPEADOR;
21572 5ELCID2742 QUE ASSOMASSE ESSORA EL *** CAMPEADOR
21663 5ELCID2753 QUAL VENTURA SERIE SI ASSOMAS ESSORA EL *** CAMPEADOR
21741 5ELCID2765 SOBRINO ERA DEL *** CAMPEADOR;
22162 5ELCID2822 ALLAS FIJAS DEL *** DAN LES ESFUER%O.
22200 5ELCID2827 QUANDO GELO DIZEN A MYO *** EL CAMPEADOR,
22258 5ELCID2835 PESO A MYO *** & ATODA SU CORT, & ALBARFANEZ DALMA & DE CORA%ON.
22286 5ELCID2838 CON CC CAUALLEROS, QUALES MYO *** MANDO;
22403 5ELCID2853 MUCHO UOS LO GRADE%E, ALLA DO ESTA, MYO *** EL CANPEADOR,
22629 5ELCID2883 POR AMOR DE MYO *** RICA CENA LES DA.
22663 5ELCID2888 MYO *** ASUS FIJAS YUA LAS ABRA%AR,
23103 5ELCID2943 MAL MAIARON SUS FIJAS DEL *** CAMPEADOR;
23170 5ELCID2952 QUE AYA MYO *** DERECHO DE YFANTES DE CARRION.
23231 5ELCID2959 ENTRE YO & MYO *** PESA NOS DE CORA%ON.
23286 5ELCID2966 E COMMO DEN DERECHO A MYO *** EL CAMPEADOR,
23325 5ELCID2971 POR AMOR DE MYO *** ESTA CORT YO FAGO.
23349 5ELCID2974 ESPIDIOS MU@O GUSTIOZ, A MYO *** ES TORNADO.
23456 5ELCID2987 MIEDO HAN QUE Y VERNA MYO *** EL CAMPEADOR;
23487 5ELCID2991 CA Y VERNA MYO *** EL CAMPEADOR;
23643 5ELCID3011 EBAYR LE CUYDAN A MYO *** EL CAMPEADOR.
23676 5ELCID3015 AL QUINTO DIA VENIDO ES MYO *** EL CAMPEADOR;
23725 5ELCID3022 BIEN AGUISADO VIENE EL *** CON TODOS LOS SOS,
23749 5ELCID3025 FIRIOS ATIERRA MYO *** EL CAMPEADOR;
23776 5ELCID3029 CAUALGAD, ***; SI NON, NON AURIA DED SABOR;
23812 5ELCID3033 AMEN, DIXO MYO *** EL CAMPEADOR;
23897 5ELCID3044 ESSA NOCH MYO *** TAIO NON QUISO PASSAR;
23964 5ELCID3054 MYO *** RUY DIAZ EN SAN SERUAN POSADO.
24257 5ELCID3093 SIEMPRE LA VISTE MYO *** EL CAMPEADOR;
24284 5ELCID3096 QUE NON LE CONTALASSEN LOS PELOS AL BUEN *** CANPEADOR;
24337 5ELCID3103 ASSI YUA MYO *** ADOBADO ALLA CORT.
24352 5ELCID3105 CUERDA MIENTRA ENTRA MYO *** CON TODOS LOS SOS:
24429 5ELCID3114 EL REY DIXO AL ***: VENJD ACA SER, CAMPEADOR,
24474 5ELCID3120 LO QUE DIXO EL *** AL REY PLOGO DE CORA%ON.
24486 5ELCID3121 EN VN ESCA@O TORNI@O ESSORA MYO *** POSO,
24498 5ELCID3123 CATANDO ESTAN A MYO *** QUANTOS HA EN LA CORT,
24577 5ELCID3132 POR EL AMOR DE MYO *** EL QUE EN BUEN ORA NA%IO,
24674 5ELCID3143 AGORA DEMANDE MYO *** EL CAMPEADOR:
24684 5ELCID3145 MYO *** LA MANO BESO AL REY & EN PIE SE LEUANTO;
24847 5ELCID3164 AVN GRAND AMOR NOS FAZE EL *** CAMPEADOR,
24890 5ELCID3169 HYA MAS NON AURA DERECHO DE NOS EL *** CANPEADOR.
24994 5ELCID3183 NOS LE PUEDEN CAMEAR, CA EL *** BIEN LAS CONNOS%E;
25119 5ELCID3199 LUEGO SE LEUANTO MYO *** EL CAMPEADOR;
25237 5ELCID3213 ALO QUE DEMANDA EL *** QUEL RECUDADES VOS.
25254 5ELCID3215 DIXO ALBARFANEZ LEUANTADOS EN PIE EL *** CAMPEADOR:
25330 5ELCID3225 SI ESSO PLOGIERE AL ***, NON GELO VEDAMOS NOS;
25369 5ELCID3230 QUE DERECHO DEMANDA EL *** CAMPEADOR.
25396 5ELCID3234 ENTERGEN A MYO ***, EL QUE EN BUEN ORA NA%IO;
25477 5ELCID3245 RECIBIOLO MYO *** COMMO APRE%IARON ENLA CORT.
25519 5ELCID3250 ESTAS APRE%IADURAS MYO *** PRESAS LAS HA,
25694 5ELCID3272 VEZOS MYO *** ALLAS CORTES PREGONADAS;
25850 5ELCID3293 DEXASSEDES UOS, ***, DE AQUESTA RAZON;
25905 5ELCID3301 MYO *** RUY DIAZ A PERO VERMUEZ CATA;
25962 5ELCID3309 DIREUOS, ***, COSTUBRES AUEDES TALES,
26076 5ELCID3324 DELANT MYO *** & DELANTE TODOS OVISTE TE DE ALABAR

WORD C# PREFIX CONTEXT

%ID (CON'T)

26130 5ELCID3331 QUANDO DURMIE MYO *** & EL LEON SE DESATO?
26150 5ELCID3333 METISTET TRAS EL ESCA@O DE MYO *** EL CAMPEADOR
26171 5ELCID3336 FASTA DO DESPERTO MYO ***, EL QUE VALEN%IA GA@O;
26190 5ELCID3338 EL LEON PREMIO LA CABE%A, A MYO *** ESPERO,
26237 5ELCID3345 POR FIJAS DEL ***, DON ELUIRA & DONA SOL:
26314 5ELCID3356 POR CONSAGRAR CON MYO *** DON RODRIGO
26402 5ELCID3368 FIJAS DEL ***, POR QUE LAS VOS DEXASTES,
26476 5ELCID3378 QUIEN NOS DARIE NUEUAS DE MYO *** EL DE BIUAR
26616 5ELCID3398 PIDEN SUS FIJAS A MYO *** EL CAMPEADOR
26646 5ELCID3402 LEUANTOS EN PIE MYO *** EL CAMPEADOR;
26699 5ELCID3410 RUEGO UOS, ***, CABOSO CAMPEADOR,
26729 5ELCID3414 LEUANTOS MYO ***, AL REY LAS MANOS LE BESO;
26769 5ELCID3419 DE FIJAS DE MYO ***, DON ELUIRA & DO@A SOL,
26809 5ELCID3424 E DESPUES DE MYO *** EL CAMPEADOR;
26862 5ELCID3431 E QUE NON PESE ESTO AL *** CAMPEADOR:
26930 5ELCID3440 GRANDES AUERES LES DIO MYO *** EL CAMPEADOR,
27034 5ELCID3453 ASIL CRE%E LA ONDRA A MYO *** EL CAMPEADOR
27269 5ELCID3486 MYO *** AL REY LAS MANOS LE BESO & DIXO: PLAZME, SE@OR.
27329 5ELCID3492 ALLI SE TOLLIO EL CAPIELO EL *** CAMPEADOR,
27486 5ELCID3511 MYO *** ENEL CAUALLO ADELANT SE LEGO,
27667 5ELCID3532 MYO *** PORA VALEN%IA, & EL REY PORA CARRION.
28188 5ELCID3598 ESTOS TRES CAUALLEROS DE MYO *** EL CAMPEADOR
28299 5ELCID3612 DESI VINIEN LOS DE MYO *** ALOS YFANTES DE CARRION,
28954 5ELCID3698 EL REY ALOS DE MYO *** DE NOCHE LOS ENBIO,
28978 5ELCID3701 FELOS EN VALEN%IA CON MYO *** EL CAMPEADOR:
29002 5ELCID3704 ALEGRE FFUE DAQUESTO MYO *** EL CAMPEADOR.
29206 5ELCID3729 ESTAS SON LAS NUEUAS DE MYO *** EL CANPEADOR,
WORD #1276 OCCURS 436 TIMES.
INDEX OF DIVERSIFICATION = 66.05 WITH STANDARD DEVIATION OF 69.21

%ID. 27171 5ELCID3473 ENESSORA DIXO MIO **** NO LO FARE, SENOR.
WORD #1277 OCCURS 1 TIMES.

%IEGO 2786 5ELCID0352 LONGINOS ERA *****, QUE NUQUAS VIO ALGUANDRE,
WORD #1278 OCCURS 1 TIMES.

%IELLO 15339 5ELCID1942 AFE DIOS DEL ****** QUE NOS ACUERDE EN LO MIIOR.
WORD #1279 OCCURS 1 TIMES.

%IELO 1693 5ELCID0217 ATI LO GRADESCO, DIOS, QUE ***** & TIERRA GUIAS;
2617 5ELCID0330 YA SE@OR GLORIOSO, PADRE QUE EN ***** ESTAS,
2620 5ELCID0331 FEZIST ***** & TIERRA, EL TER%ERO EL MAR;
4855 5ELCID0614 GRADO A DIOS DEL ***** & ATODOS LOS SOS SANTOS,
8620 5ELCID1094 AIUDOL EL CRIADOR, EL SE@NOR QUE ES EN *****.
16066 5ELCID2037 GRADESCOLO A DIOS DEL ***** & DESPUES AUOS,
16792 5ELCID2126 DIOS QUE ESTA EN ***** DEM DENT BUEN GALARDON.
17021 5ELCID2155 AFE DIOS DEL *****, QUE LO PONGA EN BUEN LOGAR
22697 5ELCID2892 PLEGA AL CRIADOR, QUE EN ***** ESTA,
25761 5ELCID3281 GRADO A DIOS QUE ***** & TIERRA MANDA
27022 5ELCID3452 GRADO ADIOS DEL ***** & AQUEL REY DON ALFONSSO,
29079 5ELCID3714 GRADO AL REY DEL *****, MIS FIJAS VENGADAS SON
WORD #1280 OCCURS 12 TIMES.
INDEX OF DIVERSIFICATION = 2488.64 WITH STANDARD DEVIATION OF 2351.42

%IELOS 22416 5ELCID2855 AFFE DIOS DELOS ****** QUE UOS DE DENT BUEN GALARDON
WORD #1281 OCCURS 1 TIMES.

%IENT 10539 5ELCID1336 ***** CAUALLOS GRUESSOS & CORREDORES,
WORD #1282 OCCURS 1 TIMES.

%IENTO 2307 5ELCID0291 ****** QUINZE CAUALLEROS TODOS IUNTADOS SON;
4192 5ELCID0534 ****** MOROS & %IENTO MORAS QUIERO LAS QUITAR,
4195 5ELCID0534 %IENTO MOROS & ****** MORAS QUIERO LAS QUITAR,
7768 5ELCID0995 ****** CAUALLEROS DEUEMOS VEN%ER A QUELAS MESNADAS.
8888 5ELCID1132 YO CON LOS ****** ENTRARE DEL OTRA PART,
11535 5ELCID1461 CAUALGEDES CON ****** GUISADOS PORA HUEBOS DE LIDIAR;
11563 5ELCID1465 CON OTROS ****** CAUALLEROS BIEN UOS CONSSIGRA;
11697 5ELCID1483 CO ****** CAUALLEROS QUE PRIUADOL ACORRADES;
11885 5ELCID1507 BIEN SALIERON DEN ****** QUE NON PARE%EN MAL,
13694 5ELCID1735 NON ESCAPARON MAS DE ****** & QUATRO.
24094 5ELCID3072 CON ESTOS CUNPLANSSE ****** DELOS BUENOS QUE Y SON.
24161 5ELCID3081 DO TALES ****** TOUIER, BIEN SERE SIN PAUOR.
24324 5ELCID3101 CON AQUESTOS ****** QUE ADOBAR MANDO,
24362 5ELCID3106 EL VA EN MEDIO, ELOS ****** ADERREDOR.
24489 5ELCID3122 LOS ****** QUEL AGUARDAN POSAN ADERREDOR.
WORD #1283 OCCURS 15 TIMES.
INDEX OF DIVERSIFICATION = 1583.43 WITH STANDARD DEVIATION OF 2786.92

%IENTOL 11744 5ELCID1490 ******* PIDIERON, MAS EL CON DOZIENTOS VA.
WORD #1284 OCCURS 1 TIMES.

%IENTOS 1052 5ELCID0135 A MENESTER SEYS ******* MARCOS.
1146 5ELCID0147 LAS ARCHAS ADUCHAS, PRENDET SEYES ******* MARCOS.
1256 5ELCID0161 QUE SOBRE AQUELAS ARCHAS DAR LE YEN VJ ******* MARCOS

```
WORD                 C#  PREFIX                          CONTEXT

%IENTOS (CON'T)
                    1614 5ELCID0207 VOS VJ ******* & YO XXX HE GANADOS.
                    5336 5ELCID0674 BIEN SOMOS NOS VI *******, ALGUNOS AY DE MAS;
                    9983 5ELCID1265 TRES MILL & SEYS ******* AUIE MYO %ID EL DE BIUAR;
                   19472 5ELCID2467 QUE ALA RA%ICN CAYE SEYS ******* MARCOS DE PLATA.
                   19642 5ELCID2489 CAYERON LE EN QUINTA AL %ID SEYX ******* CAUALLOS,
          WORD #1285 OCCURS   8 TIMES.
             INDEX OF DIVERSIFICATION =  2654.71 WITH STANDARD DEVIATION OF  3565.98

%INCHAS             7758 5ELCID0993 ELAS SIELLAS CO%ERAS & LAS ******* AMOIADAS;
                   21421 5ELCID2723 EN MANO PRENDEN LAS ******* FUERTES & DURADORES.
                   21520 5ELCID2736 CON LAS ******* CORREDIZAS MAIAN LAS TAN SIN SABOR;
                   25643 5ELCID3265 A QUE LAS FIRIESTES A ******* & A ESPOLONES?
                   28497 5ELCID3639 QUEBRARON LE LAS *******, NINGUNA NOL OUO PRO,
          WORD #1286 OCCURS   5 TIMES.
             INDEX OF DIVERSIFICATION =  5183.75 WITH STANDARD DEVIATION OF  5896.48

%INCO               1457 5ELCID0187 ***** ESCUDEROS TIENE DON MARTINO, ATODOS LOS CARGAUA.
                    1880 5ELCID0239 Y ESTAUA DO@A XIMENA CON ***** DUENAS DE PRO,
                   10516 5ELCID1333 E FIZO ***** LIDES CAMPALES & TODAS LAS ARRANCO.
                   19792 5ELCID2509 VALIA DE ***** MILL MARCOS GANARON AMOS ADOS;
          WORD #1287 OCCURS   4 TIMES.

%INEN               7162 5ELCID0917 DOZIENTOS CON EL, QUE TODOS ***** ESPADAS;
          WORD #1288 OCCURS   1 TIMES.

%INQUAENTA         13557 5ELCID1718 ALOS ********** MILL VAN LOS FERIR DE GRADO;
                   14632 5ELCID1851 CON ********** MILL ARRANCOLOS DEL CAMPO;
          WORD #1289 OCCURS   2 TIMES.

%INTAS              4547 5ELCID0578 LAS LORIGAS VESTIDAS & ****** LAS ESPADAS,
          WORD #1290 OCCURS   1 TIMES.

%INTURA             5925 5ELCID0751 CORTOL POR LA *******, EL MEDIO ECHO EN CAMPO.
                   19165 5ELCID2424 FATA LA ******* EL ESPADA LEGADO HA.
          WORD #1291 OCCURS   2 TIMES.

%INXIESTES           329 5ELCID0041 YA CAMPEADOR, EN BUEN ORA ********** ESPADA
                    1369 5ELCID0175 YA CANPEADOR, EN BUEN ORA ********** ESPADA
                    3484 5ELCID0439 YA %ID, EN BUEN ORA ********** ESPADA
                   13464 5ELCID1706 AUOS, %ID DON RODIRGO, EN BUEN ORA ********** ESPADA,
                   17277 5ELCID2185  VENIDES, CAMPEADOR, EN BUENA ORA ********** ESPADA
          WORD #1292 OCCURS   5 TIMES.
             INDEX OF DIVERSIFICATION =  4236.00 WITH STANDARD DEVIATION OF  3995.23

%INXO                461 5ELCID0058 MYO %ID RUY DIAZ, EL QUE EN BUEN ORA ***** ESPADA,
                     621 5ELCID0078 FABLO MYO %ID, EL QUE EN BUEN ORA ***** ESPADA:
                    7037 5ELCID0899 QUIERO UOS DEZIR DEL QUE EN BUEN ORA NASCO & ***** ESPADA:
                   12407 5ELCID1574 AVN NON SABIE MYO %ID, EL QUE EN BUEN ORA ***** ESPADA,
                   15483 5ELCID1961 SALUDAD ME MAYO %ID, EL QUE EN BUEN ORA ***** ESPADA;
                   20603 5ELCID2615 VIOLO EN LOS AUUEROS EL QUE EN BUEN ORA ***** ESPADA,
          WORD #1293 OCCURS   6 TIMES.
             INDEX OF DIVERSIFICATION =  4027.40 WITH STANDARD DEVIATION OF  2478.09

%IPDAD              3158 5ELCID0397 DE SINIESTRO SANT ESTEUAN, VNA BUENA ******,
          WORD #1294 OCCURS   1 TIMES.

D                  14065 5ELCID1781 DELOS BUENOS & OTORGADOS CAYERON LE MILL & * CAUALLOS;
          WORD #1295 OCCURS   1 TIMES.

DA                  1704 5ELCID0219 ** QUI QUITO CASTIELLA, PUES QUE EL REY HE EN YRA;
                    3592 5ELCID0453 ** QUESTE A CORRO FABLARA TODA ESPA@A.
                    3891 5ELCID0494 ** QUESTA QUINTA QUE ME AUEDES MANDO,
                    4107 5ELCID0522 PLOGO A MYO %ID ** QUESTA PRESENTAIA.
                    6121 5ELCID0779 ** QUESTOS MOROS MATO XXX IIIJ;
                    6943 5ELCID0888 HYD & VENIT, ** QUI UOS DO MI GRA%IA;
                    9245 5ELCID1176 NIN ** COSSEIO PADRE A FIJO, NON FIJO A PADRE,
                   21133 5ELCID2685 ** QUESTE CASAMIENTO QUE GRADE EL CAMPEADOR.
                   22633 5ELCID2883 POR AMOR DE MYO %ID RICA CENA LES **.
                   23893 5ELCID3043 PORA TOLLEDO EL REY TORNADA **,
                   25959 5ELCID3308 MAS QUANDO ENPIE%A, SABED, NOL ** VAGAR:
          WORD #1296 OCCURS  11 TIMES.
             INDEX OF DIVERSIFICATION =  2424.50 WITH STANDARD DEVIATION OF  3404.76

DAD                13369 5ELCID1695 *** ME CXXX CAUALLEROS PORA HUEBOS DE LIDIAR;
                   16474 5ELCID2089 *** LAS AQUI QUISIEREDES UOS, CA YO PAGADO SO.
                   16847 5ELCID2133 *** MANERO A QUI LAS DE, QUANDO UOS LAS TOMADES;
                   17214 5ELCID2178 *** LES VN REYAL & ALOS YFANTES DE CARRION,
                   17590 5ELCID2225 ALOS YFANTES DE CARRION *** LAS CON UUESTRA MANO,
                   20177 5ELCID2562 *** NOS NUESTRAS MUGIERES QUE AUEMOS ABENDI%IONES;
                   27190 5ELCID3476 *** ME UUESTROS CAUALLEROS CON TODAS UUESTRAS GUARNIZONES,
          WORD #1297 OCCURS   7 TIMES.
             INDEX OF DIVERSIFICATION =  2302.50 WITH STANDARD DEVIATION OF  2611.29
```

WORD C# PREFIX CONTEXT

```
DADA          13826 5ELCID1751 QUANDO EN VUESTRA VENIDA TAL GANANZIA NOS AN ****.
              22229 5ELCID2831 QUANDO TAL CNDRA MEAN **** LOS YFANTES DE CARRION;
        WORD #1298 OCCURS   2 TIMES.

DADAS         20653 5ELCID2621 VERAS LAS HEREDADES QUE A MIS FIJAS ***** SON;
              27882 5ELCID3557 MUCHO ERAN REPENTIDOS LOS YFANTES POR QUANTO ***** SON;
        WORD #1299 OCCURS   2 TIMES.

DADES         16536 5ELCID2096 QUEM ***** UUESTRAS FIJAS PORA LOS YFANTES DE CARRION.
              25263 5ELCID3216 DESTOS AUERES QUE UOS DI YO, SIMELOS *****, O DEDES DELLO RAZON.
        WORD #1300 OCCURS   2 TIMES.

DADO           1520 5ELCID0194 VOS LO MEREZEDES, DARUOS QUEREMOS BUEN ****,
               5998 5ELCID0760 AL REY FARIZ IIJ COLPES LE AUIE ****;
              14613 5ELCID1848 MUCHO PREZIA LA ONDRA EL ZID QUEL AUEDES ****.
        WORD #1301 OCCURS   3 TIMES.

DADOL         19146 5ELCID2421 ARRIBA ALZO COLADA, VN GRANT COLPE ***** HA,
        WORD #1302 OCCURS   1 TIMES.

DADOS          4112 5ELCID0523 ATERCER DIA ***** FUERON SJN FALLA.
               8261 5ELCID1051 CON LOS CAUALLEROS QUE EL ZID LE AUIE *****
              13616 5ELCID1725 AL REY YUZEF TRES COLPES LE OUO *****,
              17858 5ELCID2259 CADA VNO POR SI SOS DONES AUIEN *****.
              26818 5ELCID3425 METIERON LAS FES, & LOS OMENAIES ***** SON,
        WORD #1303 OCCURS   5 TIMES.
           INDEX OF DIVERSIFICATION =  5675.50 WITH STANDARD DEVIATION OF  2256.53

DADRIA        15554 5ELCID1971 MANTOS & PIELLES E BUENOS ZENDALES ******?
        WORD #1304 OCCURS   1 TIMES.

DAL           25537 5ELCID3252 MAS QUANDO ESTO OUO ACABADO, PENSSARON LUEGO ***.
        WORD #1305 OCCURS   1 TIMES.

DALCANZ        7298 5ELCID0936 TIERRAS ******* NEGRAS LAS VA PARANDO,
        WORD #1306 OCCURS   1 TIMES.

DALDAS        16880 5ELCID2136 PRENDELLAS CON UUESTRAS MANOS & ****** ALOS YFANTES,
        WORD #1307 OCCURS   1 TIMES.

DALDO          6446 5ELCID0823 LO QUE ROMANEZIERE ***** A MI MUGIER & A MIS FIJAS,
        WORD #1308 OCCURS   1 TIMES.

DALENT        12923 5ELCID1639 VENIDOM ES DELIZIO DE TIERRAS ****** MAR,
              19042 5ELCID2409 ACA TORNA, BUCAR  VENIST ****** MAR,
        WORD #1309 OCCURS   2 TIMES.

DALFAYA       16713 5ELCID2116 TANTAS BUENAS VISTIDURAS QUE ******* SON.
        WORD #1310 OCCURS   1 TIMES.

DALGO          1641 5ELCID0210 VEREMOS UUESTRA MUGIER, MENBRADA FIJA *****.
               3976 5ELCID0504 PUES QUE POR MI GANAREDES QUES QUIER QUE SEA *****,
               8114 5ELCID1035 AUOS & DOS FIJOS ***** QUITAR UOS HE LOS CUERPOS & DARUOS E
                               DE MANO.
              12329 5ELCID1565 QUE REZIBAN A MYANAYA & ALAS DUENAS FIJAS *****;
              14487 5ELCID1832 MANDO CAUALGAR APRIESSA TOSDOS SOS FIJOS *****,
              17645 5ELCID2232 DOUOS ESTAS DUE@AS, AMAS SON FIJAS *****,
              17804 5ELCID2252 HYA ZERCA DELOS XV DIAS YAS VAN LOS FIJOS *****.
              17897 5ELCID2264 EA TODAS LAS DUE@AS & ALOS FIJOS *****;
        WORD #1311 OCCURS   8 TIMES.
           INDEX OF DIVERSIFICATION =  2321.29 WITH STANDARD DEVIATION OF  1695.79

DALLA          1412 5ELCID0181 SIUOS LA ADUXIER *****; SI NON, CONTALDA SOBRE LAS ARCAS. . . .
              11226 5ELCID1420 E EL SE TENIE C QUE ADUXIERA *****;
        WORD #1312 OCCURS   2 TIMES.

DALLENT       22555 5ELCID2873 ******* SE ESPIDIERON DELLOS, PIENSSAN SE DE TORNAR,
        WORD #1313 OCCURS   1 TIMES.

DALMA         15196 5ELCID1923 DIXO MYNAYA. ***** & DE CORAZON
              15243 5ELCID1930 QUE GELO CONSSEIAUA ***** & DE CORAZON.
              15766 5ELCID2001 ***** & DE CORAZON, & TODOS LOS QUE EN PODER DESSOS FOSSEN;
              16033 5ELCID2033 DIXO EL REY ESTO FERE ***** & DE CORAZON;
              20633 5ELCID2619 PRIMO ERES DE MIS FIJAS AMAS ***** & DE CORAZON
              20665 5ELCID2623 DIXO FELEZ MUNOZ: PLAZME ***** & DE CORAZON.
              22265 5ELCID2835 PESO A MYO ZID & ATODA SU CORT, & ALBARFANEZ ***** & DE CORAZON.
              22794 5ELCID2904 POR MI BESA LE LA MANO ***** & DE CORAZON,
              22822 5ELCID2907 QUEL PESE AL BUEN REY ***** & DE CORAZON.
              23786 5ELCID3030 SALUDAR NOS HEMOS ***** & DE CORAZON.
              24750 5ELCID3152 HYO BIEN LAS QUERIA ***** & DE CORAZON,
              28055 5ELCID3581 ESSORA DIXO EL REY: ***** & DE CORAZON.
        WORD #1314 OCCURS  12 TIMES.
           INDEX OF DIVERSIFICATION =  1168.00 WITH STANDARD DEVIATION OF  1486.54

DALUA         20833 5ELCID2645 POR SANTA MARIA ***** RAZIN FAZIAN LA POSADA,
        WORD #1315 OCCURS   1 TIMES.
```

```
WORD                 C#  PREFIX                                 CONTEXT

DAMOR                 8947 5ELCID1139 FERID LOS, CAUALLEROS, ***** & DE GRADO & DE GRAND VOLUNTAD,
                     13351 5ELCID1692 ESSORA DIXIERCN TODOS: ***** & DE VOLUNTAD.
                     17659 5ELCID2234 AMOS LAS RE%IBEN ***** & DE GRADO,
                     22551 5ELCID2872 FATA RIO *****, DANDC LES SOLAZ;
         WORD #1316 OCCURS   4 TIMES.

DAMOS                 1531 5ELCID0196 ***** UOS ENDCN AUOS XXX MARCHOS;
                     25436 5ELCID3239 POR JUUIZIO LO ***** ANTEL REY DON ALFONSSO:
         WORD #1317 OCCURS   2 TIMES.

DAN                   3443 5ELCID0434 ANDIDIERON DE NOCH, QUE VAGAR NON SE ***.
                      4484 5ELCID0570 LOS DE ALCO%ER A MYO %ID YAL *** PARIAS DE GRADO
                      4665 5ELCID0591 LOS GRANDES & LOS CHICOS FUERA SALTO ***,
                      5146 5ELCID0650 ANDIDIERCN TODOL DIA, QUE VAGAR NON SE ***,
                      5159 5ELCID0652 POR TODAS ESSAS TIERRAS LOS PREGONES ***;
                      5499 5ELCID0693 ABRIERON LAS PUERTAS, FUERA VN SALTO ***;
                      5657 5ELCID0713 *** LE GRANDES COLPES, MAS NOL PUEDEN FALSSAR.
                      7336 5ELCID0941 POR QUE *** PARIAS PLAZE ALOS DE SARAGO%A,
                      8368 5ELCID1064 *** LE TRES PALAFRES MUY BIEN ENSELLADOS
                     11458 5ELCID1450 POR LA TIERRA DEL REY MUCHO CONDUCHO LES ***.
                     13214 5ELCID1675 ADOBAN SE DE CORA%ON E *** SALTO DE LA VILLA;
                     17184 5ELCID2174 GRANT ONDRA LES *** ALOS YFANTES DE CARRION.
                     22163 5ELCID2822 ALLAS FIJAS DEL %ID *** LES ESFUER%O.
                     22929 5ELCID2921 NOS *** VAGAR LOS DIAS & LAS NOCHES.
                     25931 5ELCID3304 AMI LO DIZEN, ATI *** LAS OREIADAS.
         WORD #1318 OCCURS  15 TIMES.
            INDEX OF DIVERSIFICATION =  1605.29 WITH STANDARD DEVIATION OF  1569.72

DAND                  2167 5ELCID0273 **** NOS CONSEIO POR AMOR DE SANTA MARIA
         WORD #1319 OCCURS   1 TIMES.

DANDO                 1095 5ELCID0140 SI NON PRIMERO PRENDIENDO & DESPUES *****.
                      4778 5ELCID0606 ***** GRANDES ALARIDOS LOS QUE ESTAN EN LA %ELADA,
                      5899 5ELCID0747 MAGER DE PIE BUENOS COLPES VA *****.
                      6176 5ELCID0786 CA EN ALCAZ SJN DUBDA LES FUERON *****.
                     10942 5ELCID1385 LOS YFFANTES DE CARRION ***** YUAN CONPA@A A MINAYA ALBARFANEZ:
                     22552 5ELCID2872 FATA RIO DAMOR, ***** LES SOLAZ;
         WORD #1320 OCCURS   6 TIMES.
            INDEX OF DIVERSIFICATION =  4290.40 WITH STANDARD DEVIATION OF  4481.19

DANDOS               16406 5ELCID2081 ****** LAS, MYO %ID, SI UOS VALA EL CRIADOR
                     21989 5ELCID2798 ****** DEL AGUA, SI UOS VALA EL CRIADOR
                     27135 5ELCID3468 ******, REY, PLAZO, CA CRAS SER NON PUEDE.
         WORD #1321 OCCURS   3 TIMES.

DANIEL                2688 5ELCID0340 SALUEST A ****** CON LOS LEONES EN LA MALA CAR%EL,
         WORD #1322 OCCURS   1 TIMES.

DANQUITA              4271 5ELCID0544 POR LAS CUEUAS ******** ELLOS PASSANDO UAN,
         WORD #1323 OCCURS   1 TIMES.

DA@A                 13916 5ELCID1763 HYA MUGIER **** XIMENA, NOM LO AUIEDES ROGADO?
         WORD #1324 OCCURS   1 TIMES.

DA@O                  2000 5ELCID0252 NON QUIERO FAZER ENEL MONESTERIO VN DINERO DE ****;
         WORD #1325 OCCURS   1 TIMES.

DAQUEL               21735 5ELCID2764 MAS YO UOS DIRE ****** FELEZ MUNOZ.
         WORD #1326 OCCURS   1 TIMES.

DAQUELOS             18457 5ELCID2336 CA ******** MOROS YO SO SABIDOR;
         WORD #1327 OCCURS   1 TIMES.

DAQUEND              16824 5ELCID2130 ******* VAYA COMIGO; CUEDO QUEL AURA PRO.
         WORD #1328 OCCURS   1 TIMES.

DAQUENT              16888 5ELCID2137 ASSI COMMO YO LAS PRENDO *******, COMMO SI FOSSE DELANT,
                     18823 5ELCID2382 NOS ******* VEREMOS COMMO LIDIA EL ABBAT.
         WORD #1329 OCCURS   2 TIMES.

DAQUESTA              6364 5ELCID0811 ******** RIQUEZA QUE EL CRIADOR NOS ADADO
                     19784 5ELCID2508 ******** ARRANCADA QUE LIDIARON DE CORA%ON
                     24138 5ELCID3078 ******** GUISA QUIERO YR ALA CORT,
         WORD #1330 OCCURS   3 TIMES.

DAQUESTE             29046 5ELCID3710 FABLEMOS NOS ******** QUE EN BUEN ORA NA%IO.
         WORD #1331 OCCURS   1 TIMES.

DAQUESTO             27651 5ELCID3530 ALEGRE FUE ******** EL QUE EN BUEN ORA NA%IO;
                     29000 5ELCID3704 ALEGRE FFUE ******** MYO %IC EL CAMPEADOR.
         WORD #1332 OCCURS   2 TIMES.

DAQUESTOS            20101 5ELCID2552 ********* AUERES SIENPRE SEREMOS RICOS OMNES,
                     26285 5ELCID3352 ********* AMOS AQUI QUEDO LA RAZON.
         WORD #1333 OCCURS   2 TIMES.
```

WORD C# PREFIX CONTEXT

DAQUI 1406 5ELCID0180 PLAZME, DIXO EL %ID, ***** SEA ANDADA.
16544 5ELCID2097 ***** LAS PRENDO POR MIS MANOS DON ELUIRA & DONA SOL,
20503 5ELCID2603 ANDAD, FIJAS, ***** EL CRIADOR VOS VALA
22704 5ELCID2893 QUE UOS VEA MEIOR CASADAS ***** EN ADELANT.
27288 5ELCID3488 ***** UOS LOS ACOMIENDO COMO A REY & A SE@OR.
WORD #1334 OCCURS 5 TIMES.
INDEX OF DIVERSIFICATION = 6469.50 WITH STANDARD DEVIATION OF 5865.74

DAR 1058 5ELCID0136 DIXO RACHEL & VIDAS: *** GELOS DE GRADO.
1252 5ELCID0161 QUE SOBRE AQUELAS ARCHAS *** LE YEN VJ %IENTOS MARCOS
2488 5ELCID0314 POCO AUER TRAYO, *** UOS QUIERO UUESTRA PART.
3398 5ELCID0428 FIZO MYO %ID POSAR & %EUADA ***.
3821 5ELCID0483 NON OSA NINGUNO *** SALTO ALA %AGA.
4059 5ELCID0516 AQUI NON LO PUEDEN VENDER NIN *** EN PRESENTAIA;
5934 5ELCID0752 AMYNAYA ALBARFANEZ YUAL *** EL CAUALLO:
7708 5ELCID0987 EL CONDE DON REMONT *** NOS HA GRANT BATALLA,
8160 5ELCID1040 AUOS & A OTROS DOS *** UOS HE DE MANO.
8343 5ELCID1061 MANDAD NOS *** LAS BESTIAS & CAUALGEREMOS PRIUADO;
9371 5ELCID1191 %ERCAR QUIERE A VALEN%IA PORA CHRISTIANOS LA ***.
10052 5ELCID1274 *** LE QUIERO C CAUALLOS, & UOS YD GELOS LEUAR;
10269 5ELCID1300 E *** GELO A ESTE BUEN CHRISTIANO;
10704 5ELCID1356 HYO LES MANDARE *** CONDUCHO MIENTRA QUE POR MJ TIERRA FUEREN,
11139 5ELCID1409 MIENTRA QUE FUEREMOS POR SUS TIERRAS CONDUCHO NOS MANDO ***.
11862 5ELCID1503 POR SABOR DE MYO %ID DE GRANO ONDRAL ***;
13004 5ELCID1649 APOCO QUE VINIESTES, PRESENO UOS QUIEREN ***:
15225 5ELCID1928 DE *** SUS FIJAS ALOS YFANTES DE CARRION,
15364 5ELCID1945 QUERER UOS YE VER & *** UOS SU AMOR,
15408 5ELCID1952 POR *** LE GRAND ONDRA COMMO A REY DE TIERRA.
15963 5ELCID2024 ASI SABE *** OMILDAN%A A ALFONSSO SO SE@OR.
20255 5ELCID2571 HYO QUIERO LES *** AXUUAR IIJ MILL MARCOS DE PLATA;
20286 5ELCID2575 *** UOS HE DOS ESPADAS, A COLADA & A TIZON,
20799 5ELCID2641 DE QUANTO EL FIZIERE YOL *** POR ELLO BUEN GALARDON.
24921 5ELCID3174 *** GELAS QUEREMOS DELLANT ESTANDO UOS.
WORD #1335 OCCURS 25 TIMES.
INDEX OF DIVERSIFICATION = 993.29 WITH STANDARD DEVIATION OF 1151.82

DARA 1013 5ELCID0130 O QUE GANAN%IA NOS **** POR TODO AQUESTE A@O?
3039 5ELCID0382 DIOS QUE NOS DIO LAS ALMAS, CONSEIO NOS ****.
13323 5ELCID1689 EL OBISPO DO IHERONIMO SOLTURA NOS ****,
21599 5ELCID2746 ENSAYANDOS AMOS QUAL **** MEIORES COLPES.
WORD #1336 OCCURS 4 TIMES.

DARAGON 24090 5ELCID3071 E GALIND GAR%IEZ, EL BUENO *******;
WORD #1337 OCCURS 1 TIMES.

DARAN 4610 5ELCID0585 ANTES QUEL PRENDAN LOS DE TERUEL, SI NON NON NOS ***** DENT NADA;
5329 5ELCID0673 SI CON MOROS NON LIDIAREMOS, NO NOS ***** DEL PAN.
19740 5ELCID2503 ELLOS ME ***** PARIAS CON AIUDA DEL CRIADOR,
WORD #1338 OCCURS 3 TIMES.

DARARAN 29260 5ELCID3735 ALA VNOS PE@OS, QUE BIEN VOS LO ******* SOBRELOS.
WORD #1339 OCCURS 1 TIMES.

DARE 2067 5ELCID0260 POR VN MARCHO QUE DESPENDADES AL MONESTERIO **** YO QUATRO.
8177 5ELCID1042 SABET, NON UOS **** AUOS VN DINERO MALO;
8189 5ELCID1043 MAS QUANTO AUEDES PERDIDO NON UOS LO ****,
8207 5ELCID1045 QUE COMIGO ANDAN LAZRADOS, & NON UOS LO ****.
12091 5ELCID1533 ANTES DESTE TE%ER DIA UOS LA **** DOBLADA.
16859 5ELCID2134 NON GELAS **** YO CON MI MANO, NIN DED NON SE ALABARAN.
WORD #1340 OCCURS 6 TIMES.
INDEX OF DIVERSIFICATION = 2957.40 WITH STANDARD DEVIATION OF 2801.39

DARENA 678 5ELCID0086 YNCAMOS LAS ******, CA BIEN SERAN PESADAS,
WORD #1341 OCCURS 1 TIMES.

DARIE 26472 5ELCID3378 QUIEN NOS ***** NUEUAS DE MYO %ID EL DE BIUAR
26495 5ELCID3381 QUIL ***** CON LOS DE CARRION ACASAR?
WORD #1342 OCCURS 2 TIMES.

DARLEDES 23490 5ELCID2992 ******** DERECHO, CA RENCURA HA DE UOS.
WORD #1343 OCCURS 1 TIMES.

DARUOS 1517 5ELCID0194 VOS LO MERE%EDES, ****** QUEREMOS BUEN DADO,
8121 5ELCID1035 AUOS & DOS FIJOS DALGO QUITAR UOS HE LOS CUERPOS & ****** E DE MANO.
20224 5ELCID2568 DIXO EL CAMPEADOR: ****** HE MYS FIJAS & ALGO DELO MYO;
20262 5ELCID2572 ****** E MULAS & PALAFRES, MUY GRUESSOS DE SAZON,
WORD #1344 OCCURS 4 TIMES.

DAS 4998 5ELCID0632 SI NON *** CONSEIO, A TECA & A TERUEL PERDERAS,
26521 5ELCID3385 ALOS QUE *** PAZ, FARTAS LOS ADERREDOR.
WORD #1345 OCCURS 2 TIMES.

WORD C# PREFIX CONTEXT

DAT
829 5ELCID0106 RACHEL & VICAS, AMOS ME *** LAS MANOS,
3328 5ELCID0420 TEMPRANO *** %EUADA, SI EL CRIADOR UOS SALUE
29244 5ELCID3734 ES LEYDO, *** NOS DEL VINO; SI NON TENEDES DINEROS, ECHAD
WORD #1346 OCCURS 3 TIMES.

DAUA
305 5ELCID0038 SACO EL PIE DEL ESTRIBERA, UNA FERICAL ****;
4519 5ELCID0574 QUANDO VIO MYC %ID QUE ALCO%ER NON SELE ****;
7942 5ELCID1014 DE FUERA DELA TIENDA VN SALTO ****,
13438 5ELCID1703 LA MISSA DICHA, GRANT SULTURA LES ****:
16804 5ELCID2127 SOBREL SO CAUALLO BAUIECA MYO %ID SALTO ****;
28697 5ELCID3664 ESORA EL YFANTE TAN GRANDES VOZES ****:
WORD #1347 OCCURS 6 TIMES.
INDEX OF DIVERSIFICATION = 5677.40 WITH STANDARD DEVIATION OF 3578.86

DAUAN
3642 5ELCID0459 ABREN LAS PUERTAS, DE FUERA SALTO *****,
4766 5ELCID0604 LOS VASSALLOS DE MYO %ID SIN PIEDAD LES *****,
6483 5ELCID0827 AGORA ***** %EUADA, YA LA NOCH ERA ENTRADA,
9106 5ELCID1159 ***** SUS CORREDORES & FAZIEN LAS TRASNOCHADAS,
14712 5ELCID1860 CON X DE SUS PARIENTES A PARTE ***** SALTO:
18892 5ELCID2391 ***** LE GRANDES COLPES, MAS NOL FALSSAN LAS ARMAS.
WORD #1348 OCCURS 6 TIMES.
INDEX OF DIVERSIFICATION = 3049.00 WITH STANDARD DEVIATION OF 1835.67

DAUOS
15203 5ELCID1924 ES PAGADO, & ***** SU AMOR.
WORD #1349 OCCURS 1 TIMES.

DE
68 5ELCID0010 ALLI PIENSSAN ** AGUIIAR, ALLI SUELTAN LAS RIENDAS.
76 5ELCID0011 ALA EXIDA ** BIUAR CUIERON LA CORNEIA DIESTRA,
103 5ELCID0014 ALBRICIA, ALBARFFANEZ, CA ECHADOS SOMOS ** TIERRA
155 5ELCID0021 CONBIDAR LE YEN ** GRADO, MAS NINGUNO NON OSAUA:
232 5ELCID0030 ASCONDEN SE ** MYO %ID, CA NOL OSAN DEZIR NADA.
276 5ELCID0035 LOS ** MYO %ID A ALTAS UOZES LAMAN,
284 5ELCID0036 LOS ** DENTRO NON LES QUERIEN TORNAR PALABRA.
317 5ELCID0040 VNA NI@A ** NUEF A@OS A OIO SE PARAUA:
423 5ELCID0053 FINCO LOS YG@IOS, ** CORA%ON ROGAUA.
499 5ELCID0063 DETODAS COSAS QUANTAS SON ** UIANDA
518 5ELCID0066 AMYO %ID & ALOS SUYOS ABASTALES ** PAN & DE UINO;
521 5ELCID0066 AMYO %ID & ALOS SUYOS ABASTALES DE PAN & ** UINO;
531 5ELCID0068 ** TODO CONDUCHO BIEN LOS OUO BASTIDOS.
664 5ELCID0084 FER LO HE AMIDOS, ** GRADO NON AURIE NADA.
684 5ELCID0087 CUBIERTAS ** GUADALME%I E BIEN ENCLAUEADAS.
733 5ELCID0093 ** NOCHE LO LIEUEN, QUE NON LO VEAN CHISTIANOS.
790 5ELCID0101 EN CUENTA ** SUS AUERES, DELOS QUE AUIEN GANADOS.
881 5ELCID0113 TIENE DOS ARCAS LENNAS ** ORO ESMERADO.
918 5ELCID0118 E PRESTALDE ** AUER LO QUE SEA GUISADO.
960 5ELCID0123 NOS HUEBOS AUEMOS EN TODO ** GANAR ALGO.
972 5ELCID0125 QUANDO ATIERRA ** MOROS ENTRO, QUE GRANT AUER SACO;
1005 5ELCID0129 MAS DEZID NOS DEL %ID, ** QUE SERA PAGADO,
1023 5ELCID0131 RESPUSO MARTIN ANTOLINEZ A GUISA ** MENBRADO:
1045 5ELCID0134 ACOGEN SELE OMNES ** TODAS PARTES MEGUADOS,
1060 5ELCID0136 DIXO RACHEL & VIDAS: DAR GELOS ** GRADO.
1156 5ELCID0149 CON RACHEL & VIDAS, ** VOLUTAD & DE GRADO.
1159 5ELCID0149 CON RACHEL & VIDAS, DE VOLUTAD & ** GRADO.
1174 5ELCID0151 QUE GELO NON VENTANSSEN ** BURGOS OMNE NADO.
1210 5ELCID0156 YA ME EXCO ** TIERRA, CA DEL REY SO AYRADO.
1220 5ELCID0157 ALO QUEM SEMEIA, ** LO MIO AUREDES ALGO;
1371 5ELCID0176 ** CASTIELLA UOS YDES PORA LAS YENTES ESTRANAS.
1429 5ELCID0183 SOBRELLA VNA SAUANA ** RAN%AL & MUY BLANCA.
1440 5ELCID0184 ATOD EL PRIMER COLPE IIJ MARCOS ** PLATA ECHARON,
1521 5ELCID0195 ** QUE FAGADES CAL%AS & RICA PIEL & BUEN MANTO.
1564 5ELCID0200 GRADO EXIR DELA POSADA & ESPIDIOS ** AMOS.
1568 5ELCID0201 EXIDO ES ** BURGOS & ARLAN%ON A PASXADO,
1630 5ELCID0209 EN SAN PERO ** CARDENA YNOS CANTE EL GALLO;
1738 5ELCID0222 EL ME ACORRA ** NOCH & DE DIA
1741 5ELCID0222 EL ME ACORRA DE NOCH & ** DIA
1776 5ELCID0226 SPIDIOS EL CABOSO ** CUER & DE VELUNTAD.
1779 5ELCID0226 SPIDIOS EL CABOSO DE CUER & ** VELUNTAD.
1786 5ELCID0227 SUELTAN LAS RIENDAS & PIENSSAN ** AGUIJAR.
1833 5ELCID0233 PORA SAN PERO ** CARDENA QUANTO PUDO A ESPOLEAR,
1882 5ELCID0239 Y ESTAUA DO@A XIMENA CON %INCO DUENAS ** PRO,
1951 5ELCID0247 PUES QUE AQUI UOS VEO, PRENDET ** MI OSPEDADO.
1979 5ELCID0250 MAS POR QUE ME VO ** TIERRA, DOUOS L MARCHOS,
1999 5ELCID0252 NON QUIERO FAZER ENEL MONESTERIO VN DINERO ** DA@O;
2039 5ELCID0257 DELLAS & ** MI MUGIER FAGADES TODO RECABDO.
2075 5ELCID0261 OTORGADO GELO AUIE EL ABBAT ** GRADO.
2119 5ELCID0267 POR MALOS MESTUREROS ** TIERRA SODES ECHADO.
2139 5ELCID0269 FEM ANTE UOS YO & UUESTRAS FFIJAS, YFFANTES SON & ** DIAS CHICAS,
2146 5ELCID0270 CON AQUESTAS MYS DUE@AS ** QUIEN SO YO SERUIDA.
2172 5ELCID0273 DAND NOS CONSEIO POR AMOR ** SANTA MARIA
2251 5ELCID0283 O QUE ** VENTURA & ALGUNOS DIAS VIDA,
2261 5ELCID0284 E UOS, MUGIER ONDRADA, ** MY SEADES SERUIDA
2288 5ELCID0288 COMMO SEUA ** TIERRA MYO %ID EL CANPEADOR;
2305 5ELCID0290 EN AQUES DIA ALA PUENT ** ARLA%ON
2342 5ELCID0295 QUANDO LO SOPO MYO %ID EL ** BIUAR,

WORD C# PREFIX CONTEXT

DE (CON'T)

2369 5ELCID0299 FABLO MYO %ID ** TODA VOLUNTAD:
2426 5ELCID0306 LOS VJ DIAS ** PLAZO PASSADOS LOS AN,
2525 5ELCID0319 LA MISSA NOS DIRA, ESTA SERA ** SANTA TRINIDAD;
2532 5ELCID0320 LA MISSA DICHA, PENSSEMOS ** CAUALGAR,
2542 5ELCID0321 CA EL PLAZO VIENE A %ERCA, MUCHO AUEMOS ** ANDAR.
2566 5ELCID0324 ALOS MEDIADOS GALLOS PIESSAN ** CAUALGAR.
2609 5ELCID0329 QUE AMIO %ID EL CAMPEADOR QUE DIOS LE CURIAS ** MAL:
2653 5ELCID0335 PASTORES TO GLOORIFFICARON, OUIERON ** A LAUDARE,
2658 5ELCID0336 TRES REYES ** ARABIA TE VINIERON ADORAR,
2762 5ELCID0349 DOS LADRONES CONTIGO, ESTOS ** SE@AS PARTES
2812 5ELCID0354 CORRIO LA SANGRE POR EL ASTIL AYUSO, LAS MANOS SE OUO ** VNTAR,
2834 5ELCID0357 EN TI CROUO AL ORA, POR END ES SALUO ** MAL;
2856 5ELCID0361 TUERES REY ** LOS REYES & DE TODEL MUNDO PADRE,
2860 5ELCID0361 TUERES REY DE LOS REYES & ** TODEL MUNDO PADRE,
2868 5ELCID0362 ATI ADORO & CREO ** TODO VOLUNTAD,
2890 5ELCID0364 POR MYO %ID EL CAMPEADOR, QUE DIOS LE CURIE ** MAL.
2932 5ELCID0370 LORANDO ** LOS OIOS, QUE NON SABE QUE SE FAR.
2990 5ELCID0376 MYO %ID CON LOS SOS VASSALLOS PENSSO ** CAUALGAR,
3013 5ELCID0379 %ID, DO SON UUESTROS ESFUER%OS? EN BUEN ORA NASQUIESTES ** MADRE;
3016 5ELCID0380 PENSEMOS ** YR NUESTRA VIA, ESTO SEA DE VAGAR.
3022 5ELCID0380 PENSEMOS DE YR NUESTRA VIA, ESTO SEA ** VAGAR.
3045 5ELCID0383 AL ABBAT DON SANCHO TORNAN ** CASTIGAR,
3096 5ELCID0389 ABBAT, DEZILDES QUE PRENDAN EL RASTRO & PIESSEN ** ANDAR,
3112 5ELCID0391 SOLTARON LAS RIENDAS, PIESSAN ** ANDAR;
3128 5ELCID0393 VINO MYO %ID IAZER A SPINAZ ** CAN.
3134 5ELCID0394 OTRO DIA MA@ANA PIENSSA ** CAUALGAR.
3142 5ELCID0395 GRANDES YENTES SELE ACOIEN ESSA NOCH ** TODAS PARTES.
3147 5ELCID0396 YXIENDOS UA ** TIERRA EL CAMPEADOR LEAL,
3152 5ELCID0397 ** SINIESTRO SANT ESTEUAN, VNA BUENA %IPDAD,
3159 5ELCID0398 ** DIESTRO A LILON LAS TORRES, QUE MOROS LAS HAN;
3173 5ELCID0399 PASSO PAR ALCOBIELLA QUE ** CASTIELLA FINES YA;
3179 5ELCID0400 LA CAL%ADA ** QUINEA YUA LA TRASPASSAR,
3186 5ELCID0401 SOBRE NAUAS ** PALOS EL DUERO UA PASAR,
3201 5ELCID0403 VANSSELE ACOGIENDO YENTES ** TODAS PARTES.
3277 5ELCID0413 OTRO DIA MA@ANA PIENSSAN ** CAUALGAR;
3282 5ELCID0414 ES DIA A ** PLAZO, SEPADES QUE NON MAS.
3290 5ELCID0415 ALA SIERRA ** MIEDES ELLOS YUAN POSAR.
3297 5ELCID0416 AVN ERA ** DIA, NON ERA PUESTO EL SOL,
3368 5ELCID0425 ** NOCH PASSAN LA SIERRA, VINIDA ES LA MAN,
3383 5ELCID0426 E POR LA LOMA AYUSO PIENSSAN ** ANDAR.
3412 5ELCID0431 MANDADO ** SO SE@OR TODO LO HAN AFAR.
3423 5ELCID0432 ANTE QUE ANOCHESCA PIENSSAN ** CAUALGAR;
3437 5ELCID0434 ANDIDIERON ** NOCH, QUE VAGAR NON SE DAN.
3489 5ELCID0440 VOS CON C ** AQUESTA NUESTRA CONPA@A,
3555 5ELCID0448 QUE POR MIEDO ** LOS MOROS NON DEXEN NADA.
3639 5ELCID0459 ABREN LAS PUERTAS, ** FUERA SALTO DAUAN,
3661 5ELCID0462 CON POCAS ** GENTES QUE EN CASTEION FINCARON.
3669 5ELCID0463 LAS YENTES ** FUERA TODAS SON DE RAMADAS.
3673 5ELCID0463 LAS YENTES DE FUERA TODAS SON ** RAMADAS.
3678 5ELCID0464 EL CAMPEADOR SALIO ** LA %ELADA, CORRIE ACASTEION SIN FALLA.
3690 5ELCID0465 MOROS & MORAS AUIEN LOS ** GANAN%IA,
3777 5ELCID0477 E SIN DUBDA CORREN; FASTA ALCALA LEGO LA SE@A ** MINAYA,
3799 5ELCID0481 ** OUEIAS & DE VACAS & DE ROPAS & DE OTRAS RIQUIZAS LARGAS.
3802 5ELCID0481 DE OUEIAS & ** VACAS & DE ROPAS & DE OTRAS RIQUIZAS LARGAS.
3805 5ELCID0481 DE OUEIAS & DE VACAS & ** ROPAS & DE OTRAS RIQUIZAS LARGAS.
3808 5ELCID0481 DE OUEIAS & DE VACAS & DE ROPAS & ** OTRAS RIQUIZAS LARGAS.
3816 5ELCID0482 DERECHA VIENE LA SE@A ** MINAYA;
3960 5ELCID0503 NON PRENDRE ** UOS QUANTO UALE VN DINERO MALO.
4036 5ELCID0513 A CADA VNO DELLOS CAEN C MARCHOS ** PLATA,
4075 5ELCID0518 FABLO CON LOS ** CASTEION, & ENVIO AFITA & AGUADELFAGARA,
4101 5ELCID0521 ASMARON LOS MOROS IIJ MILL MARCOS ** PLATA.
4206 5ELCID0535 POR QUE LO PRIS DELLOS QUE ** MI NON DIGAN MAL.
4222 5ELCID0537 CRAS ALA MA@ANA PENSEMOS ** CAUALGAR,
4281 5ELCID0545 PASSARON LAS AGUAS, ENTRARON AL CAMPO ** TORAN%IO,
4324 5ELCID0550 OTRO DIA MOUIOS MYO %ID EL ** BIUAR,
4412 5ELCID0562 QUE ** DIA NIN DE NOCH NON LES DIESSEN AREBATA,
4415 5ELCID0562 QUE DE DIA NIN ** NOCH NON LES DIESSEN AREBATA,
4450 5ELCID0566 VENIDO ES A MOROS, EXIDO ES ** CHRISTIANOS;
4471 5ELCID0569 EL CASTIELLO ** ALCO%ER EN PARIA UA ENTRANDO.
4478 5ELCID0570 LOS ** ALCO%ER A MYO %ID YAL DAN PARIAS DE GRADO
4486 5ELCID0570 LOS DE ALCO%ER A MYO %ID YAL DAN PARIAS ** GRADO
4490 5ELCID0571 E LOS ** TECA & LOS DE TERUAL LA CASA;
4494 5ELCID0571 E LOS DE TECA & LOS ** TERUAL LA CASA;
4499 5ELCID0572 ALOS ** CALATAUTH, SABET, MALES PESAUA.
4551 5ELCID0579 AGUISA ** MENBRADO, POR SACAR LOS A%ELADA.
4560 5ELCID0580 VEYEN LO LOS ** ALCO%ER, DIOS, COMMO SE ALABAUAN
4590 5ELCID0583 DEGUISA UA MYO %ID COMMO SIESCAPASSE ** ARRANCADA.
4604 5ELCID0585 ANTES QUEL PRENDAN LOS ** TERUEL, SI NON NON NOS DARAN DENT NADA;
4624 5ELCID0587 SALIERON ** ALCO%ER AVNA PRIESSA MUCH ESTRANA.
4638 5ELCID0588 MYO %ID, QUANDO LOS VIO FUERA, COGIOS COMMO ** ARRANCADA.
4650 5ELCID0590 DIZEN LOS ** ALCO%ER: YA SE NOS VA LA GANA%IA
4760 5ELCID0604 LOS VASSALLOS ** MYO %ID SIN PIEDAD LES DAUAN,
4773 5ELCID0605 EN VN ORA & VN POCO ** LOGAR CCC MOROS MATAN.
4885 5ELCID0618 LOS MOROS YAZEN MUERTOS, ** BIUOS POCOS VEO.
4906 5ELCID0621 COIAMOS LOS ** DENTRO, CA EL SENORIO TENEMOS,

WORD C# PREFIX CONTEXT

DE (CON'T)

4939 5ELCID0625 MUCHO PESA ALCS ** TECA & ALOS DE TERUAL NON PLAZE,
4943 5ELCID0625 MUCHO PESA ALCS DE TECA & ALOS ** TERUAL NON PLAZE,
4949 5ELCID0626 E ALOS ** CALATAYUTH NON PLAZE.
4955 5ELCID0627 AL REY ** VALEN%IA ENBIARON CON MENSAIE,
4969 5ELCID0628 QUE A VNO QUE DIZIEN MYO %ID RUY DIAZ ** BIUAR
4975 5ELCID0629 AYROLO EL REY ALFCNSSC, ** TIERRA ECHADO LO HA,
5013 5ELCID0634 RIBERA ** SALCN TODA YRA AMAL,
5021 5ELCID0635 ASSI FFERA LO ** SILOCA, QUE ES DEL OTRA PART.
5042 5ELCID0637 TRES REYES VEO ** MCRCS DERREDOR CE MI ESTAR,
5045 5ELCID0637 TRES REYES VEO DE MORCS DERREDOR ** MI ESTAR,
5062 5ELCID0639 TRES MILL MCROS LEUEDES CON ARMAS ** LIDIAR;
5094 5ELCID0643 TRES MILL MCROS CAUALGAN & PIENSSAN ** ANDAR,
5107 5ELCID0645 OTRO DIA MA@ANA PIENSSAN ** CAUALGAR,
5118 5ELCID0647 POR LOS ** LA FRONTERA PIENSSAN DE ENVIAR;
5122 5ELCID0647 POR LOS DE LA FRONTERA FIENSSAN ** ENVIAR;
5128 5ELCID0648 NON LO DETIENEN, VIENEN ** TODAS PARTES.
5132 5ELCID0649 YXIERON ** %ELFA LA QUE DIZEN DE CANAL,
5137 5ELCID0649 YXIERON DE %ELFA LA QUE DIZEN ** CANAL,
5164 5ELCID0653 GENTES SE AIUNTARCN SCBEIANAS ** GRANDES
5177 5ELCID0655 AL BUENO ** MYO %ID EN ALCO%ER LEUAN %ERCAR.
5204 5ELCID0658 LAS AROBDAS, QUE LCS MOROS SACAN, ** DIA
5207 5ELCID0659 E ** NOCH EN BUELTOS ANDAN EN ARMAS;
5224 5ELCID0661 ALOS ** MYO %ID YA LES TUELLEN EL AGUA.
5233 5ELCID0662 MESNADAS ** MYO %ID EXIR QUERIEN ALA BATALLA,
5257 5ELCID0665 ACABO ** TRES SEMANAS, LA QUARTA QUERIE ENTRAR,
5286 5ELCID0668 QUE NOS QUERAMOS YR ** NOCH NO NOS LO CONSINTRAN;
5306 5ELCID0670 DEZID ME, CAUALLEROS, CCMMO UOS PLAZE ** FAR.
5313 5ELCID0671 PRIMERO FABLO MINAYA, VN CAUALLERO ** PRESTAR:
5315 5ELCID0672 ** CASTIELLA LA GENTIL EXIDCS SOMOS ACA,
5339 5ELCID0674 BIEN SOMOS NOS VI %IENTOS, ALGUNOS AY ** MAS;
5357 5ELCID0676 VAYAMOS LOS FERIR EN AQUEL DIA ** CRAS.
5374 5ELCID0678 ONDRASTES UOS, MINAYA, CA AUER UOS LO YEDES ** FAR.
5382 5ELCID0679 TODOS LCS MOROS & LAS MCRAS ** FUERA LOS MANDA ECHAR,
5400 5ELCID0681 ELDIA & LA NCCHE PIENSSAN SE ** ADOBAR.
5523 5ELCID0696 ANTE ROYDO ** ATAMORES LA TIERRA QUERIE QUEBRAR;
5537 5ELCID0698 ** PARTE DELCS MOROS DOS SE@AS HA CABDALES,
5549 5ELCID0699 E FIZIERON DOS AZES ** PEONES MEZCLADOS, QUILOS PODRIE CONTAR?
5557 5ELCID0700 LAS AZES ** LCS MOROS YAS MUEUEN ADELANT,
5601 5ELCID0705 LA SE@A TIENE EN MANC, CONPE%O ** ESPOLONAR;
5687 5ELCID0717 ENCLINARON LAS CARAS ** SUSO CE LOS ARZONES,
5689 5ELCID0717 ENCLINARON LAS CARAS DE SUSO ** LOS ARZONES,
5695 5ELCID0718 YUAN LOS FERIR ** FUERTES CCRA%ONES.
5713 5ELCID0720 FERID LOS, CAUALLERCS, POR AMOR ** CARIDAD
5722 5ELCID0721 YO SO RUY DIAZ, EL %ID CAMPEADOR ** BIUAR
5742 5ELCID0724 SE@OS MOROS MATARON, TODOS ** SE@OS COLPES;
5794 5ELCID0732 CAYEN EN VN POCO ** LOGAR MOROS MUERTOS MILL & CCC YA.
5824 5ELCID0736 MARTIN ANTOLINEZ, EL BURGALES ** PRO,
5849 5ELCID0740 GALIN GAR%IA, EL BUENC ** ARAGON,
5883 5ELCID0745 BIEN LO ACORREN MESNADAS ** CHRISTIANOS.
5894 5ELCID0747 MAGER ** PIE BUENOS CCLPES VA DANDO.
5949 5ELCID0754 OY EN ESTE DIA ** UOS ABRE GRAND BANDO;
6075 5ELCID0771 CAFUYEN LOS MOROS ** LA PART
6079 5ELCID0772 LOS ** MYO %ID FIRIENDO EN ALCAZ,
6231 5ELCID0794 ESTA ALBERGADA LOS ** MYO %ID LUEGO LA AN ROBADA
6238 5ELCID0795 ** ESCUDOS & DE ARMAS & DE OTROS AUERES LARGOS;
6241 5ELCID0795 DE ESCUDOS & ** ARMAS & DE CTROS AUERES LARGOS;
6244 5ELCID0795 DE ESCUDOS & DE ARMAS & ** OTRCS AUERES LARGOS;
6263 5ELCID0798 MAS ** QUINZE DE LOS SOS MENOS NON FALLARON.
6265 5ELCID0798 MAS DE QUINZE ** LOS SOS MENOS NON FALLARON.
6421 5ELCID0819 DIXO MYNAYA ALBARFANEZ: ESTO FARE YO ** GRADO.
6438 5ELCID0822 EN SANTA MARIA ** BURGOS QUITEDES MILL MISSAS;
6539 5ELCID0834 POR LANCAS & POR ESPADAS AUEMOS ** GUARIR,
6567 5ELCID0838 LA TIERRA ES ANGOSTA & SOBEIANA ** MALA;
6577 5ELCID0840 MOROS ** LAS FRONTERAS & VNAS YENTES ESTRANAS;
6594 5ELCID0842 ENTRE LCS ** TECHA & LOS DE TERUEL LA CASA,
6598 5ELCID0842 ENTRE LCS DE TECHA & LOS ** TERUEL LA CASA,
6604 5ELCID0843 E LOS ** CALATAYUT, QUE ES MAS ONDRADA,
6626 5ELCID0845 VENDIDO LES A ALCO%ER PCR TRES MILL MARCHOS ** PLATA.
6704 5ELCID0855 QUANDO QUITO A ALCO%ER MYO %ID EL ** BIUAR,
6710 5ELCID0856 MOROS & MORAS CCMPE%ARCN ** LORAR.
6727 5ELCID0859 AL EXIR ** SALON MUCHO OUO BUENAS AUES.
6735 5ELCID0860 PLOGO ALOS ** TERER & ALCS DE CALATAYUT MAS,
6739 5ELCID0860 PLOGO ALOS DE TERER & ALCS ** CALATAYUT MAS,
6744 5ELCID0861 PESO ALCS ** ALCO%ER, CA PROLES FAZIE GRANT.
6807 5ELCID0869 EN SU MANO TENIE A %ELFA LA ** CANAL.
6813 5ELCID0870 MYO %ID RUY DIAZ ** DIOS AYA SU GRA%IA
6857 5ELCID0876 VEN%IO DOS REYES ** MCRCS EN AQUESTA BATALLA.
6899 5ELCID0882 OMNE AYRADO, QUE ** SE@OR NON HA GRA%IA,
6908 5ELCID0883 POR ACOGELLO A CABO ** TRES SEMMANAS.
6914 5ELCID0884 MAS DESPUES QUE ** MOROS FUE, PRENDO ESTA PRESENTAIA;
6923 5ELCID0885 AUN ME PLAZE ** MYO %ID QUE FIZO TAL GANAN%IA.
6965 5ELCID0891 ** TODO MYO REYNO LOS QUE LO QUISIEREN FAR,
7049 5ELCID0901 MIENTRA QUE SEA EL PUEBLO ** MOROS & DELA YENTE CHRISTIANA,
7057 5ELCID0902 EL POYO ** MYO %ID ASIL DIRAN POR CARTA.

WORD C# PREFIX CONTEXT

DE (CON'T)

7070 5ELCIDC904 EL ** RIO MARTIN TODO LO METIO EN PARIA.
7119 5ELCIDC911 ALEN ** TERUEL DON RODRIGO PASSAUA,
7126 5ELCID0912 ENEL PINAR ** TEUAR DON ROY DIAZ POSAUA;
7149 5ELCID0915 QUANDO ESTO FECHO OUO, A CABO ** TRES SEMANAS,
7152 5ELCIDC916 ** CASTIELLA VENIDO ES MINAYA,
7236 5ELCIDC928 DIZIENDO LES SALUDES ** PRIMOS & DE HERMANOS,
7239 5ELCID0928 DIZIENDO LES SALUDES DE PRIMOS & ** HERMANOS,
7242 5ELCID0929 E ** SUS COMPA@AS, AQUELAS QUE AUIEN DEXADAS
7266 5ELCID0932 E QUEL DIXO SALUDES ** SU MUGIER & DE SUS FIJAS
7270 5ELCID0932 E QUEL DIXO SALUDES DE SU MUGIER & ** SUS FIJAS
7328 5ELCIDC940 PESANDO VA ALOS ** MON%ON & ALOS DE HUESCA;
7332 5ELCID0940 PESANDO VA ALOS DE MON%ON & ALOS ** HUESCA;
7340 5ELCID0941 POR QUE DAN PARIAS PLAZE ALOS ** SARAGO%A,
7342 5ELCID0942 ** MYO %ID RUY DIAZ QUE NON TEMIEN NINGUNA FONTA.
7402 5ELCID0949 CRAS ALA MA@ANA PENSSEMOS ** CAUALGAR,
7417 5ELCID0951 ESTON%ES SE MUDO EL %ID AL PUERTO ** ALCAT,
7445 5ELCID0955 QUE EL SALIDO ** CASTIELLA ASILOS TRAE TAN MAL.
7461 5ELCID0957 LEGARON LAS NUEUAS ALCONDE ** BAR%ILONA,
7498 5ELCID0961 GRANDES TUERTOS ME TIENE MYO %ID EL ** BIUAR.
7565 5ELCID0969 ADELINAN TRAS MYO %ID EL BUENO ** BIUAR,
7573 5ELCID0970 TRES DIAS & DOS NOCHES PENSSARON ** ANDAR,
7603 5ELCIDC974 DI%E ** VNA SIERRA & LEGAUA A VN VAL.
7651 5ELCIDC980 LO ** ANTES & DE AGORA TODOM LO PECHARA;
7654 5ELCID0980 LO DE ANTES & ** AGORA TODOM LO PECHARA;
7678 5ELCID0983 ESSORA LO CONNOS%E MIO %ID EL ** BIUAR.
7683 5ELCID0984 QUE A MENOS ** BATALLA NOS PUEDEN DEN QUITAR.
7713 5ELCIDC988 ** MOROS & DE CHRISTIANOS GENTES TRAE SOBEIANAS,
7716 5ELCIDC988 DE MOROS & ** CHRISTIANOS GENTES TRAE SOBEIANAS,
7722 5ELCIDC989 AMENOS ** BATALLA NON NOS DEXARIE POR NADA.
7805 5ELCIDC999 OY EN ESTE PINAR ** TEUAR POR TOLER ME LA GANAN%IA.
7843 5ELCID1003 ALFONDON DELA CUESTA, %ERCA ES ** LA@O,
7860 5ELCID1005 ESTO FAZEN LOS SOS ** VOLUNTAD & DE GRADO;
7863 5ELCID1005 ESTO FAZEN LOS SOS DE VOLUNTAD & ** GRADO;
7882 5ELCID1007 ALOS VNOS FIRIENDO & A LOS OTROS ** ROCANDO.
7909 5ELCID1010 HY GA@O A COLADA QUE MAS VALE ** MILL MARCOS DE PLATA.
7912 5ELCID1010 HY GA@O A COLADA QUE MAS VALE DE MILL MARCOS ** PLATA.
7936 5ELCID1014 ** FUERA DELA TIENDA VN SALTO DAUA,
7943 5ELCID1015 ** TODAS PARTES LOS SOS SE AIUNTARON;
8015 5ELCID1023 PUES QUE TALES MAL CAL%ADOS ME VEN%IERON ** BATALLA.
8039 5ELCID1026 SI LO QUE DIGO FIZIEREDES, SALDREDES ** CATIUO;
8060 5ELCID1028 DIXO EL CONDE DON REMONT: COMEDE, DON RODRIGO, & PENSSEDES ** FOLGAR.
8088 5ELCID1032 NOL PUEDEN FAZER COMER VN MUESSO ** PAN.
8123 5ELCID1035 AUOS & DOS FIJOS DALGO QUITAR UOS HE LOS CUERPOS & DARUOS E ** MANO.
8163 5ELCID1040 AUOS & A OTROS DOS DAR UOS HE ** MANO.
8211 5ELCID1046 PRENDIENDO DEUOS & ** OTROS YR NOS HEMOS PAGANDO;
8229 5ELCID1048 COMMO QUE YRA A ** REY & DE TIERRA ES ECHADO.
8232 5ELCID1048 COMMO QUE YRA A DE REY & ** TIERRA ES ECHADO.
8268 5ELCID1052 COMIENDO VA EL CONDE DIOS, QUE ** BUEN GRADO
8300 5ELCID1056 AQUI DIXO EL CONDE: ** VOLUNTAD & DE GRADO.
8303 5ELCID1056 AQUI DIXO EL CONDE: DE VOLUNTAD & ** GRADO.
8337 5ELCID1060 SI UOS PLOGUIERE, MYO %ID, ** YR SOMOS GUISADOS;
8357 5ELCID1062 DEL DIA QUE FUE CONDE NON IANTE TAN ** BUEN GRADO,
8378 5ELCID1065 E BUENAS VESTIDURAS ** PELI%ONES & DE MANTOS.
8381 5ELCID1065 E BUENAS VESTIDURAS DE PELI%ONES & ** MANTOS.
8404 5ELCID1068 HYA UOS YDES, CONDE, AGUISA ** MUY FRANCO,
8439 5ELCID1073 ** LO UUESTRO, O DELO MYO LEUAREDES ALGO.
8462 5ELCID1076 ** VENIR UOS BUSCAR SOL NON SERA PENSSADO.
8475 5ELCID1077 AGUIJAUA EL CONDE E PENSSAUA ** ANDAR,
8517 5ELCID1082 HYDO ES EL CONDE, TORNOS EL ** BIUAR,
8524 5ELCID1083 JUNTOS CON SUS MESNADAS, CONPE%OLAS ** LEGAR
8526 5ELCID1084 ** LA GANAN%IA QUE AN FECHA MARAUILLOSA & GRAND.
8539 5ELCID1085 AQUIS CONPIE%A LA GESTA ** MYO %ID EL DE BIUAR.
8543 5ELCID1085 AQUIS CONPIE%A LA GESTA DE MYO %ID EL ** BIUAR.
8562 5ELCID1087 POBLADO HA MYO %ID EL PUERTO ** ALUCANT,
8578 5ELCID1089 E DEXADO A HUESCA & LAS TIERRAS ** MONT ALUAN.
8586 5ELCID1090 CONTRA LA MAR SALADA CONPE%O ** GUERREAR;
8606 5ELCID1093 TIERRAS ** BORRIANA TODAS CONQUISTAS LAS HA.
8647 5ELCID1098 PESA ALOS ** VALEN%IA, SABET, NON LES PLAZE;
8660 5ELCID1100 TRASNOCHARON ** NOCH, AL ALUA DELA MAN
8667 5ELCID1101 A%ERCA ** MURUIEDRO TORNAN TIENDAS AFINCAR.
8705 5ELCID1106 AMENOS ** LID NOS PARTIRA AQUESTO;
8736 5ELCID1110 LOS ** BORRIANA LUEGO VENGAN ACA;
8766 5ELCID1114 EL QUE EN BUEN ORA NASCO COMPE%O ** FABLAR:
8800 5ELCID1119 LOS ** VALEN%IA %ERCADOS NOS HAN;
8839 5ELCID1125 COMMO OMNES EXIDOS ** TIERRA ESTRA@A,
8914 5ELCID1135 MA@ANA ERA & PIENSSAN SE ** ARMAR,
8925 5ELCID1136 QUIS CADA VNO DELLOS BIEN SABE LO QUE HA ** FAR.
8949 5ELCID1139 FERID LOS, CAUALLEROS, DAMOR & ** GRADO & DE GRAND VOLUNTAD,
8952 5ELCID1139 FERID LOS, CAUALLEROS, DAMOR & DE GRADO & ** GRAND VOLUNTAD,
8962 5ELCID1140 CA YO SO RUYDIAZ, MYO %ID EL ** BIUAR
8966 5ELCID1141 TANTA CUERDA ** TIENDA Y VERIEDES QUEBRAR,
9013 5ELCID1147 DOS REYES ** MOROS MATARON EN ES ALCAZ,
9041 5ELCID1151 ** PIES DE CAUALLO LOS QUES PUDIERON ESCAPAR.
9043 5ELCID1151 DE PIES ** CAUALLO LOS QUES PUDIERON ESCAPAR.

WORD C# PREFIX CONTEXT

DE (CON'T)

```
 9054 5ELCID1152 ROBAUAN EL CAMPO EPIENSSAN SE ** TORNAR.
 9067 5ELCID1154 LAS NUEUAS ** MYO %ID, SABET, SONANDO VAN,
 9129 5ELCID1162 CABO DEL MAR TIERRA ** MOROS FIRME LA QUEBRANTA,
 9163 5ELCID1166 NON ES CON RECABDO EL DOLOR ** VALEN%IA.
 9167 5ELCID1167 EN TIERRA ** MOROS PRENDIENDO & GANANDO,
 9190 5ELCID1170 ALOS ** VALEN%IA ESCARMENTADOS LOS HAN,
 9228 5ELCID1174 MAL SE AQUEXAN LOS ** VALEN%IA QUE NON SABENT QUES FAR,
 9235 5ELCID1175 ** NINGUNA PART QUE SEA NON LES VINIE PAN;
 9267 5ELCID1178 MALA CUETA ES, SE@ORES, AVER MINGUA ** PAN,
 9275 5ELCID1149 FIJOS & MUGIERES VER LO MURIR ** FANBRE.
 9288 5ELCID1181 POR EL REY ** MARRUECOS OUIERON A ENBIAR;
 9313 5ELCID1184 SOPOLO MYO %ID, ** CORA%ON LE PLAZ;
 9318 5ELCID1185 SALIO ** MURUIEDRO VNA NOCH EN TRASNOCHADA,
 9329 5ELCID1186 AMANE%IO AMYO %ID EN TIERRAS ** MON REAL.
 9342 5ELCID1188 A TIERRAS ** CASTIELLA ENBIO SUS MENSSAIES:
 9362 5ELCID1190 VINIESSE A MYO %ID QUE A SABOR ** CAUALGAR;
 9381 5ELCID1193 TODOS VENGAN ** GRADO, NINGUNO NON HA PREMIA,
 9393 5ELCID1194 TRES DIAS LE SPERARE EN CANAL ** %ELFA.
 9443 5ELCID1200 CRE%IENDO UA RIQUEZA A MYO %ID EL ** BIUAR.
 9453 5ELCID1201 QUANDO VIO MYO %ID LAS GENTES IUNTADAS, COMPE%OS ** PAGAR.
 9544 5ELCID1213 LOS QUE FUERON ** PIE CAUALLEROS SE FAZEN;
 9618 5ELCID1222 AQUEL REY ** SEUILLA EL MANDADO LEGAUA,
 9637 5ELCID1224 VINO LOS VER CON XXX MILL ** ARMAS.
 9661 5ELCID1228 ENEL PASSAR ** XUCAR Y VERIEDES BARATA,
 9674 5ELCID1230 AQUEL REY ** MARRUECOS CON TRES COLPES ESCAPA.
 9691 5ELCID1232 BUENA FUE LA ** VALEN%IA QUANDO GANARON LA CASA,
 9710 5ELCID1234 ATODOS LOS MENORES CAYERON C MARCOS ** PLATA.
 9747 5ELCID1239 DIXO MYO %ID ** LA SU BOCA ATANTO:
 9754 5ELCID1240 POR AMOR ** REY ALFFONSSO, QUE DE TIERRA ME A ECHADO,
 9758 5ELCID1240 POR AMOR DE REY ALFFONSSO, QUE ** TIERRA ME A ECHADO,
 9796 5ELCID1244 CON EL MYNAYA ALBARFFANEZ QUE NOS LE PARTE ** SO BRA%O.
 9802 5ELCID1245 LOS QUE EXIERON ** TIERRA DE RITAD SON ABONDADOS,
 9804 5ELCID1245 LOS QUE EXIERON DE TIERRA ** RITAD SON ABONDADOS,
 9816 5ELCID1247 ** QUE SON PAGADOS; EL AMOR DE MY %ID YA LO YUAN PROUANDO.
 9822 5ELCID1247 DE QUE SON PAGADOS; EL AMOR ** MY %ID YA LO YUAN PROUANDO.
 9836 5ELCID1248 LOS QUE FUERON CON EL, & LOS ** DESPUES, TODOS SON PAGADOS;
 9857 5ELCID1250 QUE SIS PUDIESSEN YR, FER LO YEN ** GRADO.
 9988 5ELCID1265 TRES MILL & SEYS %IENTOS AUIE MYO %ID EL ** BIUAR;
10010 5ELCID1268 CON MAS POCOS YXIEMOS ** LA CASA DE BIUAR.
10013 5ELCID1268 CON MAS POCOS YXIEMOS DE LA CASA ** BIUAR.
10094 5ELCID1279 LA MUGIER ** MYO %ID & SUS FIJAS LAS YFFANTES
10102 5ELCID1280 ** GUISA YRAN POR ELLAS QUE AGRAND ONDRA VERNAN
10121 5ELCID1282 ESSORA DIXO MINAYA: ** BUENA VOLUNTAD.
10130 5ELCID1283 PUES ESTO AN FABLADO, PIENSSAN SE ** ADOBAR.
10150 5ELCID1285 E MANDO MILL MARCOS ** PLATA A SAN PERO LEUAR
10170 5ELCID1288 ** PARTE DE ORIENT VINO VN CORONADO;
10172 5ELCID1288 DE PARTE ** ORIENT VINO VN CORONADO;
10188 5ELCID1290 BIEN ENTENDIDO ES ** LETRAS & MUCHO ACORDADO,
10193 5ELCID1291 ** PIE & DE CAUALLO MUCHO ERA AREZIADO.
10196 5ELCID1291 DE PIE & ** CAUALLO MUCHO ERA AREZIADO.
10203 5ELCID1292 LAS PROUEZAS ** MYO %ID ANDAUALAS DEMANDANDO,
10239 5ELCID1296 QUANDO LO OYO MYO %ID, ** AQUESTO FUE PAGADO:
10263 5ELCID1299 EN TIERRAS ** VALEN%IA FER QUIERO OBISPADO,
10316 5ELCID1306 QUE EN TIERRAS ** VALEN%IA SE@OR AVIE OBISPO
10329 5ELCID1308 TIERRAS ** VALENCIA REMANIDAS EN PAZ,
10372 5ELCID1314 ALEGRE FUE ** AQUESTO MINAYA ALBARFANEZ,
10382 5ELCID1316 ** MISSA ERA EXIDO ESSORA EL REY ALFONSSO,
10452 5ELCID1325 ECHASTES LE ** TIERRA, NON HA LA UUESTRA AMOR;
10502 5ELCID1331 CON AQUESTAS TODAS ** VALEN%IA ES SE@OR,
10508 5ELCID1332 OBISPO FIZO ** SU MANO EL BUEN CAMPEADOR,
10544 5ELCID1337 ** SIELLAS & DE FRENOS TODOS GUARNIDOS SON,
10547 5ELCID1337 DE SIELLAS & ** FRENOS TODOS GUARNIDOS SON,
10578 5ELCID1341 ** TAN FIERAS GANAN%IAS COMMO A FECHAS EL CAMPEADOR
10593 5ELCID1342  SI ME VALA SANT ESIDRO  PLAZME ** CORA%ON,
10608 5ELCID1344 RE%IBO ESTOS CAUALLOS QUEM ENBIA ** DON.
10622 5ELCID1346 SEMEIA QUE EN TIERRA ** MOROS NON A BIUO OMNE,
10658 5ELCID1350 FABLAUA MINAYA Y AGUISA ** VARON:
10699 5ELCID1355 ESSORA DIXO EL REY: PLAZ ME ** CORA%ON;
10712 5ELCID1357 ** FONTA & DE MAL CURIALDAS & DE DESONOR;
10715 5ELCID1357 DE FONTA & ** MAL CURIALDAS & DE DESONOR;
10719 5ELCID1357 DE FONTA & DE MAL CURIALDAS & ** DESONOR;
10724 5ELCID1358 QUANDO EN CABO ** MI TIERRA A QUESTAS DUE@AS FUEREN,
10782 5ELCID1365 ATREGO LES LOS CUERPOS ** MAL & DE OCASION,
10785 5ELCID1365 ATREGO LES LOS CUERPOS DE MAL & ** OCASION,
10814 5ELCID1370 ** MI SEAN QUITOS & VAYAN ALA GRA%IA DEL CRIADOR.
10838 5ELCID1372 AQUI ENTRARON EN FABLA LOS YFFANTES ** CARRION:
10844 5ELCID1373 MUCHO CRE%EN LAS NUEUAS ** MYO %ID EL CAMPEADOR,
10856 5ELCID1374 BIEN CASARIEMOS CON SUS FIJAS PORA HUEBOS ** PRO.
10869 5ELCID1376 MYO %ID ES ** BIUAR & NOS DELOS CONDES DE CARRION.
10875 5ELCID1376 MYO %ID ES DE BIUAR & NOS DELOS CONDES ** CARRION.
10940 5ELCID1385 LOS YFFANTES ** CARRION DANDO YUAN CONPA@A A MINAYA ALBARFANEZ:
10963 5ELCID1387 SALUDAD NOS A MYO %ID EL ** BIUAR,
11032 5ELCID1396 OMILOM, DO@A XIMENA, DIOS VOS CURIE ** MAL,
11116 5ELCID1407 DEZID AL CANPEADOR, QUE DIOS LE CURIE ** MAL,
```

WORD C# PREFIX CONTEXT

DE (CON'T)

11140 5ELCID1410 ** AQUESTOS XV DIAS, SIDICS NOS CURIARE DE MAL,
11147 5ELCID1410 DE AQUESTOS XV DIAS, SIDICS NOS CURIARE ** MAL,
11185 5ELCID1415 VERIEDES CAUALLEROS VENIR ** TODAS PARTES,
11197 5ELCID1416 HYR SE QUIERE A VALENZIA A MYO ZID EL ** BIUAR.
11211 5ELCID1418 DIZIENDO ESTO MYANAYA: ESTO FERE ** VELUNTAD.
11271 5ELCID1426 EL BUENO ** MINAYA PENSCLAS DE ADOBAR
11274 5ELCID1426 EL BUENO DE MINAYA PENSCLAS ** ADOBAR
11299 5ELCID1430 EL BUENO ** MINAYA PENSSAR QUIERE DE CAUALGAR;
11303 5ELCID1430 EL BUENO DE MINAYA PENSSAR QUIERE ** CAUALGAR;
11316 5ELCID1432 MERZED, MINAYA, CAUALLERO ** PRESTAR
11384 5ELCID1440 MUCHAS YENTES SELE ACOGEN, PENSSO ** CAUALGAR,
11433 5ELCID1447 RESPUSO MINAYA: FER LO HE ** VELUNTAD.
11439 5ELCID1448 HYAS ESPIDEN & PIENSSAN ** CAUALGAR,
11448 5ELCID1449 EL PORTERO CON ELLOS QUE LOS HA ** AGUARDAR;
11459 5ELCID1451 ** SAN PERO FASTA MEDINA EN V DIAS VAN,
11483 5ELCID1454 AL ORA QUE LO SOPO MYO ZID EL ** BIUAR,
11493 5ELCID1455 PLOGOL ** CORAZON & TORNOS A ALEGRAR,
11499 5ELCID1456 ** LA SU BOCA CONPEZO DE FABLAR:
11504 5ELCID1456 DE LA SU BOCA CONPEZO ** FABLAR:
11531 5ELCID1460 EL OBISPO DON IERONIMO, CORONADO ** PRESTAR,
11539 5ELCID1461 CAUALGEDES CON ZIENTO GUISADOS PORA HUEBOS ** LIDIAR;
11559 5ELCID1464 TIENELA AUEGALUON, MYO AMIGO ES ** PAZ,
11626 5ELCID1473 ESTO ERA DICHO, PIENSSAN ** CAUALGAR,
11634 5ELCID1474 E QUANTO QUE PUEDEN NON FINCAN ** ANDAR.
11670 5ELCID1479 VENIDES, LOS VASSALLOS ** MYO AMIGO NATURAL?
11730 5ELCID1487 DIXO AUEGALUON: FER LO HE ** VELUNTAD.
11742 5ELCID1489 ALA MA@ANA PIENSSAN ** CAUALGAR;
11761 5ELCID1492 PASSARON MATA ** TORANZ DE TAL GUISA QUE NINGUN MIEDO NON HAN,
11763 5ELCID1492 PASSARON MATA DE TORANZ ** TAL GUISA QUE NINGUN MIEDO NON HAN,
11774 5ELCID1493 POR EL VAL ** ARBUXEDO PIENSSAN A DEPRUNAR.
11799 5ELCID1496 ESTO NON DETARDO, CA ** CORAZON LO HAN;
11856 5ELCID1503 POR SABOR ** MYO ZID DE GRAND ONDRAL DAR;
11859 5ELCID1503 POR SABOR DE MYO ZID ** GRAND ONDRAL DAR;
11901 5ELCID1509 E A CUBERTURAS ** ZENDALES, & ESCUDOS ALOS CUELLOS,
11919 5ELCID1511 QUE SOPIENSSEN LOS OTROS ** QUE SESO ERA ALBARFANEZ
11927 5ELCID1512 O CUEMO SALIERA ** CASTIELLA ALBARFANEZ CON ESTAS DUE@AS QUE TRAH
11951 5ELCID1515 POR ZERCA ** SALON TAN GRANDES GOZOS VAN.
12120 5ELCID1538 ** TAN GRAND CONDUCHO COMMO EN MEDINAL SACARON;
12153 5ELCID1542 SALIERON ** MEDINA, & SALON PASSAUAN,
12164 5ELCID1544 EL CAMPO ** TORANZIO LUEGOL ATRAUESSAUAN,
12225 5ELCID1552 ** QUANTO QUE QUISIERON NON OUIERON FALLA,
12277 5ELCID1559 APRES SON ** VALENZIA A TRES LEGUAS CONTADAS.
12418 5ELCID1576 ALA PUERTA ** VALENZIA, DO FUESSE EN SO SALUO,
12429 5ELCID1577 DELANTE SU MUGIER & ** SUS FIJAS QUERIE TENER LAS ARMAS.
12473 5ELCID1582 SOBREPELIZAS VESTIDAS & CON CRUZES ** PLATA
12482 5ELCID1583 REZIBIR SALIEN LAS DUENAS & AL BUENO ** MINAYA.
12505 5ELCID1586 MYO ZID SALIO SOBREL, & ARMAS ** FUSTE TOMAUA,
12580 5ELCID1596 SACADA ME AUEDES ** MUCHAS VERGUENZAS MALAS;
12614 5ELCID1600 DEL GOZO QUE AUIEN ** LOS SOS OIOS LORAUAN.
12762 5ELCID1620 DEZIR UOS QUIERO NUEUAS ** ALENT PARTES DEL MAR,
12767 5ELCID1621 ** AQUEL REY YUCEF QUE EN MARRUECOS ESTA.
12778 5ELCID1622 PESOL AL REY ** MARRUECOS DE MYO ZID DON RODRIGO:
12780 5ELCID1622 PESOL AL REY DE MARRUECOS ** MYO ZID DON RODRIGO:
12805 5ELCID1625 AQUEL REY ** MARRUECOS AIUNTAUA SUS VIRTOS;
12814 5ELCID1626 CON L VEZES MILL ** ARMAS, TODOS FUERON CONPLIDOS,
12895 5ELCID1636 A MENOS ** MUERT NO LA PUEDO DEXAR;
12921 5ELCID1639 VENIDOM ES DELIZIO ** TIERRAS DALENT MAR,
13042 5ELCID1654 CON LA MERZED ** DIOS & DE SANTA MARIA MADRE
13045 5ELCID1654 CON LA MERZED DE DIOS & ** SANTA MARIA MADRE
13064 5ELCID1656 CON DIOS A QUESTA LID YO LA HE ** ARRANCAR.
13183 5ELCID1671 LOS MOROS ** MARRUECOS CAUALGAN AUIGOR,
13205 5ELCID1674 PRESTAS SON LAS MES@ADAS ** LAS YENTES CHRISTIANAS,
13211 5ELCID1675 ADOBAN SE ** CORAZON E DAN SALTO DE LA VILLA;
13216 5ELCID1675 ADOBAN SE DE CORAZON E DAN SALTO ** LA VILLA;
13252 5ELCID1680 MUCHO AUIEN FECHO, PIESSAN ** CAUALGAR.
13315 5ELCID1688 DEZIR NOS HA LA MISSA, & PENSSAD ** CAUALGAR,
13353 5ELCID1692 ESSORA DIXIERON TODOS: DAMOR & ** VOLUNTAD.
13375 5ELCID1695 DAD ME CXXX CAUALLEROS PORA HUEBOS ** LIDIAR;
13398 5ELCID1698 ESSORA DIXO EL ZID: ** BUENA VOLUNTAD.
13412 5ELCID1700 NOS DETARDAN ** ABOBASSE ESSAS YENTES CHRISTIANAS.
13421 5ELCID1701 ALOS MEDIADOS GALLOS, ANTES ** LA MA@ANA,
13445 5ELCID1704 EL QUE A QUI MURIERE LIDIANDO ** CARA,
13504 5ELCID1711 SALIDOS SON TODOS ARMADOS POR LAS TORRES ** VANZIA,
13519 5ELCID1713 DEXAN ALAS PUERTAS OMNES ** GRANT RECABDO.
13531 5ELCID1715 ** TODAS GUARNIZONES MUY BIEN ES ADOBADO.
13542 5ELCID1716 LA SE@A SACAN FUERA, ** VALENZIA DIERON SALTO,
13562 5ELCID1718 ALOS ZINQUAENTA MILL VAN LOS FERIR ** GRADO;
13583 5ELCID1721 PLOGO AL CRIADOR & OUIERON LOS ** ARRANCAR.
13596 5ELCID1723 ATANTOS MATA ** MOROS QUE NON FUERON CONTADOS;
13619 5ELCID1726 SALIOS LE ** SOL ESPADA, CA MUCHOL ANDIDO EL CAUALLO,
13637 5ELCID1728 MYO ZID EL ** BIUAR FASTA ALLI LEGO EN ALCAZ,
13648 5ELCID1729 CON OTROS QUEL CONSIGEN ** SUS BUENOS VASSALLOS.
13693 5ELCID1735 NON ESCAPARON MAS ** ZIENTO & QUATRO.
13698 5ELCID1736 MESNADAS ** MYO ZID ROBADO AN EL CANPO;

WORD C# PREFIX CONTEXT

DE (CON'T)

13739 5ELCID1741 QUANDO AL REY ** MARUECOS ASSI LO AN ARRANCADO,
13868 5ELCID1757 QUANDOL VIERON ** PIE, CUE ERA DESCAUALGADO,
13934 5ELCID1765 QUIERO LAS CASAR CON ** AQUESTOS MYOS VASSALLOS;
13945 5ELCID1766 ACADA VNA DELLAS DO LES CC MARCOS ** PLATA,
13956 5ELCID1768 LO ** UUESTRAS FIJAS VENIR SEA MAS POR ESPA%IO.
14030 5ELCID1777 NON PUDIERON ELLOS SABER LA CUENTA ** TODOS LOS CAUALLOS,
14051 5ELCID1780 MAGER ** TODO ESTO, EL CAMPEADOR CONTADO
14099 5ELCID1785 LA TIENDA DEL REY ** MARRUECOS, QUE DELAS OTRAS ES CABO,
14135 5ELCID1789 TAL TIENDA COMMO ESTA, QUE ** MARUECOS ES PASSADA,
14149 5ELCID1791 QUE CROUIESSE SOS NUEUAS ** MYO %ID QUE AUIE ALGO.
14172 5ELCID1794 QUANDO ES FARTO ** LICIAR CON AMAS LAS SUS MANOS,
14205 5ELCID1798 ** TODA LA SU QUINTA EL DIEZMO LA MANDADO.
14223 5ELCID1800 TANTOS AUIEN ** AUERES, DE CAUALLOS & DE ARMAS;
14225 5ELCID1800 TANTOS AUIEN DE AUERES, ** CAUALLOS & DE ARMAS;
14228 5ELCID1800 TANTOS AUIEN DE AUERES, DE CAUALLOS & ** ARMAS;
14249 5ELCID1803 EL BUENO ** MYO %ID NON LO TARDO POR NADA:
14314 5ELCID1811 POR AMOR ** MI MUGIER & DE MIS FIJAS AMAS,
14318 5ELCID1811 POR AMOR DE MI MUGIER & ** MIS FIJAS AMAS,
14399 5ELCID1821 SALIDOS SON ** VALEN%IA EPIENSSAN DE ANDAR,
14402 5ELCID1821 SALIDOS SON DE VALEN%IA EPIENSSAN ** ANDAR,
14469 5ELCID1830 MYO %ID EL ** VALEN%IA ENBIA SU PRESENTAIA.
14507 5ELCID1835 LOS YFANTES ** CARRION, SABET, YS A%ERTARON,
14626 5ELCID1850 A AQUEL REY ** MARRUECOS, YUCEFF POR NOMBRADO,
14667 5ELCID1855 DIXO EL REY DON ALFONSSO: RE%IBOLOS ** GRADO.
14683 5ELCID1857 AVN VEA ORA QUE ** MI SEA PAGADO.
14707 5ELCID1860 CON X ** SUS PARIENTES A PARTE DAUAN SALTO:
14775 5ELCID1867 GRADO AL CRIADOR & AL SE@OR SANT ESIDRO EL ** LEON
14811 5ELCID1872 E GUARNIR UOS ** TODAS ARMAS COMMO UOS DIXIEREDES AQUI,
14847 5ELCID1876 TODAS ESTAS NUEUAS A BIEN ABRAN ** VENIR.
14861 5ELCID1878 BIEN LOS MANDO SERUIR ** QUANTO HUEBOS HAN.
14867 5ELCID1879 DELOS YFFANTES ** CARRION YO UOS QUIERO CONTAR,
14950 5ELCID1890 HYC ECHE ** TIERRA AL BUEN CAMPEADOR,
15017 5ELCID1899 E ** MI ABRA PERDON; VINIESSEM A VISTAS, SI OUIESSE DENT SABOR.
15040 5ELCID1901 DIEGO & FERRANDO, LOS YFFANTES ** CARRION,
15044 5ELCID1902 SABOR HAN ** CASAR CON SUS FIJAS AMAS ADOS.
15076 5ELCID1906 POR CONSSAGRAR CON LOS YFFANTES ** CARRION.
15183 5ELCID1921 COMMO SON LAS SALUDES ** ALFONSSO MYO SENOR.
15198 5ELCID1923 DIXO MYNAYA. DALMA & ** CORA%ON
15222 5ELCID1927 LO QUEL ROGAUA ALFONSSO EL ** LEON
15224 5ELCID1928 ** DAR SUS FIJAS ALOS YFANTES DE CARRION,
15230 5ELCID1928 DE DAR SUS FIJAS ALOS YFANTES ** CARRION,
15245 5ELCID1930 QUE GELO CONSSEIAUA DALMA & ** CORA%ON.
15270 5ELCID1934 ECHADO FU ** TIERRA & TOLLIDA LA ONOR,
15301 5ELCID1937 E PIDEN ME MIS FIJAS PORA LOS YFANTES ** CARRION.
15380 5ELCID1947 ESSORA DIXO EL %ID: PLAZME ** CORA%ON.
15415 5ELCID1952 POR DAR LE GRAND ONDRA COMMO A REY ** TIERRA.
15470 5ELCID1960 QUANDO LAS VIO, ** CORA%ON SE PAGA:
15563 5ELCID1973 ALAS AGUAS ** TAIO, OLAS UISTAS SON APAREIADAS.
15577 5ELCID1975 LOS YFFANTES ** CARRIO MUCHO ALEGRES ANDAN,
15603 5ELCID1978 QUANTOS QUISIESSEN AUERES DORO O ** PLATA.
15621 5ELCID1981 LOS YFANTES ** CARRION LIEUAN GRANDES CONPA@AS.
15670 5ELCID1987 TANTA GRUESSA MULA & TANTO PALAFRE ** SAZON,
15692 5ELCID1990 CHICOS & GRANDES VESTIDOS SON ** COLORES.
15707 5ELCID1992 MARTIN MUNOZ & MARTIN ANTOLINEZ, EL BURGALES ** PRO,
15724 5ELCID1995 MU@O GUSTIOZ, EL CAUALLERO ** PRO.
15731 5ELCID1996 GALIND GAR%IAZ, EL QUE FUE ** ARAGON:
15754 5ELCID1999 ALUAR SALUADOREZ & GALIND GARCIAZ EL ** ARAGON,
15768 5ELCID2001 DALMA & ** CORA%ON, & TODOS LOS QUE EN PODER DESSOS FOSSEN;
15786 5ELCID2002 LAS PUERTAS DEL ALCA%AR QUE NON SE ABRIESSEN ** DIA NIN DE NOCH,
15789 5ELCID2002 LAS PUERTAS DEL ALCA%AR QUE NON SE ABRIESSEN DE DIA NIN ** NOCH,
15839 5ELCID2009 SALIEN ** VALEN%IA, AGUIJAN & ESPOLONAUAN.
15871 5ELCID2013 ** VN DIA ES LEGADO ANTES EL REY DON ALFONSSO.
15919 5ELCID2018 SI NON A ESTOS CAUALLEROS QUE QUERIE ** CORA%ON;
15969 5ELCID2025 ** AQUESTA GUISA ALOS PIES LE CAYO.
16035 5ELCID2033 DIXO EL REY ESTO FERE DALMA & ** CORA%ON;
16119 5ELCID2044 QUANDO HE LA GRA%IA ** DON ALFONSSO MYO SE@OR;
16128 5ELCID2045 VALER ME A DIOS ** DIA & DE NOCH.
16131 5ELCID2045 VALER ME A DIOS DE DIA & ** NOCH.
16178 5ELCID2052 ESSORA SELE OMILLAN LOS YFFANTES ** CARRION:
16227 5ELCID2058 NON SE PUEDE FARTAR DEL, TANTOL QUERIE ** CORA%ON;
16239 5ELCID2060 MARAUILLAN SE ** MYO %ID QUANTOS QUE Y SON.
16275 5ELCID2065 ** TAL GUISA LOS PAGA MYO %ID EL CAMPEADOR,
16317 5ELCID2070 AL SALIR ** LA MISSA TODOS IUNTADOS SON,
16371 5ELCID2076 QUE LAS DEDES POR MUGIERES ALOS YFANTES ** CARRION.
16418 5ELCID2082 NON ABRIA FIJAS ** CASAR, RESPUSO EL CAMPEADOR,
16429 5ELCID2083 CA NON HAN GRANT HEDAND E ** DIAS PEQUENAS SON.
16433 5ELCID2084 ** GRANDES NUEUAS SON LOS YFANTES DE CARRION,
16439 5ELCID2084 DE GRANDES NUEUAS SON LOS YFANTES ** CARRION,
16497 5ELCID2091 LUEGO SE LEUANTARON LOS YFFANTES ** CARRION,
16542 5ELCID2096 QUEM DADES UUESTRAS FIJAS PORA LOS YFANTES ** CARRION.
16561 5ELCID2098 E DOLAS POR VELADAS ALOS YFANTES ** CARRION.
16585 5ELCID2101 AFELLOS EN UUESTRAS MANOS LOS YFANTES ** CARRION,
16598 5ELCID2103 TREZIENTOS MARCOS ** PLATA EN AYUDA LES DO YO,
16698 5ELCID2114 TANTA GRUESSA MULA & TANTO PALAFRE ** SAZON

WORD C# PREFIX CONTEXT

DE (CON'T)

16723 5ELCID2117 CADA VNO LO QUE PIDE, NADI NOL DIZE ** NO.
16761 5ELCID2122 METIOLOS EN PODER ** MYO %ID EL CAMPEADOR:
16775 5ELCID2124 OY ** MAS SABED QUE FER DELLOS, CAMPEADOR.
16852 5ELCID2133 DAD MANERO A QUI LAS **, QUANDO UOS LAS TOMADES;
17007 5ELCID2153 AVN BIUO SEYENDO, ** MI AYADES ALGO
17032 5ELCID2156 HYAS ESPIDIO MYO %ID ** SO SE@OR ALFONSSO,
17054 5ELCID2159 BEFAR LAS MANOS, ESPEDIR SE ** REY ALFONSSO:
17068 5ELCID2161 HYREMOS EN PODER ** MUO %ID A VALEN%IA LA MAYOR;
17080 5ELCID2162 SEREMOS ALAS BODAS DELOS YFANTES ** CARRION
17085 5ELCID2163 HE DELAS FIJAS ** MYO %ID, DE DON ELUIRA & DO@A SOL.
17088 5ELCID2163 HE DELAS FIJAS DE MYO %ID, ** DON ELUIRA & DO@A SOL.
17146 5ELCID2170 EN CASA ** MYO %ID NON A DOS MEIORES,
17157 5ELCID2171 QUE SOPIESSEN SOS MA@AS ** LOS YFANTES DE CARRION.
17160 5ELCID2171 QUE SOPIESSEN SOS MA@AS DE LOS YFANTES ** CARRION.
17171 5ELCID2173 QUE ES LARGO ** LENGUA, MAS EN LO AL NON ES TAN PRO.
17187 5ELCID2174 GRANT ONDRA LES DAN ALOS YFANTES ** CARRION.
17221 5ELCID2178 DAD LES VN REYAL & ALOS YFANTES ** CARRION,
17297 5ELCID2188 HYERNOS UOS ADUGO ** QUE AUREMOS ONDRAN%A;
17340 5ELCID2193 TODO LO QUE UOS FECHES ES ** BUENA GUISA.
17400 5ELCID2201 ATAN FIRME MIENTRE & ** TODO CORA%ON
17410 5ELCID2202 QUE YO NULLA COSA NOL SOPE DEZIR ** NO.
17430 5ELCID2205 PENSSARON ** ADOBAR ESSORA EL PALA%IO,
17454 5ELCID2208 SABOR ABRIEDES ** SER & DE COMER ENEL PALA%IO.
17457 5ELCID2208 SABOR ABRIEDES DE SER & ** COMER ENEL PALA%IO.
17471 5ELCID2210 POR LOS YFFANTES ** CARRION ESSORA ENBIARON,
17489 5ELCID2213 ** PIE & ASABOR, DIOS, QUE QUEDOS ENTRARON
17521 5ELCID2217 TODOS LOS ** MYO %ID TAN BIEN SON ACORDADOS,
17582 5ELCID2224 NOLO QUIERO FALIR POR NADA ** QUANTO AY PARADO;
17588 5ELCID2225 ALOS YFANTES ** CARRION DAD LAS CON UUESTRA MANO,
17607 5ELCID2227 ESTOZ DIXO MINAYA: ESTO FARE YO ** GRADO.
17618 5ELCID2229 ALOS YFANTES ** CARRION MINAYA VA FABLANDO:
17661 5ELCID2234 AMOS LAS RE%IBEN DAMOR & ** GRADO,
17715 5ELCID2242 ALA GLERA ** VALEN%IA FUERA DIERON SALTO;
17749 5ELCID2246 LOS YFANTES ** CARRION BIEN AN CAUALGADO.
17845 5ELCID2258 LOS VASSALLOS ** MIO %ID, ASSI SON ACORDADOS,
17881 5ELCID2263 ESPIDIENDOS ** RUY DIAZ, EL QUE EN BUEN ORA NASCO,
17902 5ELCID2265 POR PAGADOS SE PARTEN ** MYO %ID & DE SUS VASSALLOS.
17906 5ELCID2265 POR PAGADOS SE PARTEN DE MYO %ID & ** SUS VASSALLOS.
17949 5ELCID2271 HY MORAN LOS YFANTES BIEN CERCA ** DOS A@OS,
18018 5ELCID2279 CON EL AMOS SUS YERNOS LOS YFANTES ** CARRION.
18034 5ELCID2282 SALIOS ** LA RED & DESATOS EL LEON.
18126 5ELCID2293 VIO CER%ADO EL ESCA@O ** SUS BUENOS VARONES:
18254 5ELCID2309 MUCHOS TOUIERON POR ENBAYDOS LOS YFANTES ** CARRION,
18272 5ELCID2312 FUER%AS ** MARRUECOS VALEN%IA VIENEN %ERCAR;
18309 5ELCID2317 MAS, SABED, ** CUER LES PESA ALOS YFANTES DE CARRION;
18315 5ELCID2317 MAS, SABED, DE CUER LES PESA ALOS YFANTES ** CARRION;
18321 5ELCID2318 CA VEYEN TANTAS TIENDAS ** MOROS DE QUE NON AUIE SABOR.
18323 5ELCID2318 CA VEYEN TANTAS TIENDAS DE MOROS ** QUE NON AUIE SABOR.
18430 5ELCID2332 DIOS UOS SALUE, YERNOS, YFANTES ** CARRION,
18680 5ELCID2364 MANDAD NOLOS FERIR ** QUAL PART UOS SEMEIAR,
18707 5ELCID2367 DIXO MYO %ID: AYAMOS MAS ** VAGAR.
18731 5ELCID2370 OY UOS DIX LA MISSA ** SANTA TRINIDADE.
18737 5ELCID2371 POR ESSO SALI ** MI TIERRA & VIN UOS BUSCAR,
18748 5ELCID2372 POR SABOR QUE AUIA ** ALGUN MORO MATAR;
18773 5ELCID2375 PENDON TRAYO A CORCAS & ARMAS ** SE@AL,
18789 5ELCID2378 EUOS, MYO %ID, ** MI MAS UOS PAGAR.
18857 5ELCID2386 ALOS PRIMEROS COLPES DOS MOROS MATAUA ** LA LAN%A.
18930 5ELCID2395 HYUA LOS FERIR ** CORA%ON & DE ALMA.
18933 5ELCID2395 HYUA LOS FERIR DE CORA%ON & ** ALMA.
18982 5ELCID2402 LOS ** MYO %ID ALOS DE BUCAR DELAS TIENDAS LOS SACAN.
18986 5ELCID2402 LOS DE MYO %ID ALOS ** BUCAR DELAS TIENDAS LOS SACAN.
19050 5ELCID2410 VERTE AS CON EL %ID, EL ** LA BARBA GRANT,
19125 5ELCID2419 MAS BAUIECA EL ** MIO %ID ALCAN%ANDO LO VA.
19175 5ELCID2425 MATO A BUCAR, AL REY ** ALEN MAR,
19209 5ELCID2430 SABET, TODOS ** FIRME ROBAUAN EL CAMPO.
19301 5ELCID2444 SEQUE ** LIDIAR BIEN SODES PAGADOS;
19307 5ELCID2445 ACARRION ** UOS YRAN BUENOS MANDADOS,
19369 5ELCID2454 ** XX ARRIBA HA MOROS MATADO;
19375 5ELCID2455 ** TODAS PARTES SOS VASSALLOS VAN LEGANDO;
19412 5ELCID2459 TODOS ESTOS BIENES DEUOS SON & ** UUESTROS VASSALLOS.
19421 5ELCID2461 FARTOS ** LIDIAR CON MOROS ENEL CAMPO.
19474 5ELCID2467 QUE ALA RA%ION CAYE SEYS %IENTOS MARCOS ** PLATA.
19478 5ELCID2468 LOS YERNOS ** MYO %ID QUANDO ESTE AUER TOMARON
19651 5ELCID2491 TANTOS SON ** MUCHOS QUE NON SERIEN CONTADOS.
19690 5ELCID2496 ESON MYOS YERNOS YFANTES ** CARRION;
19702 5ELCID2498 MOROS & CHRISTIANOS ** MI HAN GRANT PAUOR;
19716 5ELCID2500 QUE ABRAM ** MI SALTO QUI%AB ALGUNA NOCH
19766 5ELCID2506 ** TODAS SUS CONPA@AS & DE TODOS SUS VASSALLOS;
19771 5ELCID2506 DE TODAS SUS CONPA@AS & ** TODOS SUS VASSALLOS;
19779 5ELCID2507 GRANDES SON LOS GOZOS ** SUS YERNOS AMOS ADOS:
19788 5ELCID2508 DAQUESTA ARRANCADA QUE LIDIARON ** CORA%ON
19791 5ELCID2509 VALIA ** %INCO MILL MARCOS GANARON AMOS ADOS;
19804 5ELCID2510 MUCHOS TIENEN POR RICOS LOS YFANTES ** CARRION.
19824 5ELCID2513 EL BUENO ** ALBARFANEZ, CAUALLERO LIDIADOR,

WORD C# PREFIX CONTEXT

DE (CON'T)

19839 5ELCID2515 QUANDO ENTRARON LOS YFANTES ** CARRION,
19868 5ELCID2519 EUADES AQUI, YERNOS, LA MI MUGIER ** PRO,
19885 5ELCID2521 BIEN UOS ABRAZEN & SIRUAN UOS ** CORA%ON.
19917 5ELCID2526 BUENOS MANDADOS YRAN ATIERRAS ** CARRION.
19934 5ELCID2529 TANTOS AVEMOS ** AUERES QUE NO SON CONTADOS;
19958 5ELCID2532 VASSALLOS ** MYO %ID SEYEN SE SONRRISANDO:
20047 5ELCID2544 DIGAMOS QUE LAS LEUAREMOS ATIERRAS ** CARRION,
20059 5ELCID2546 SACAR LAS HEMOS ** VALEN%IA, DE PODER DEL CAMPEADOR;
20061 5ELCID2546 SACAR LAS HEMOS DE VALEN%IA, ** PODER DEL CAMPEADOR;
20082 5ELCID2549 NOS ** NATURA SOMOS DE CONDES DE CARRION
20085 5ELCID2549 NOS DE NATURA SOMOS ** CONDES DE CARRION
20087 5ELCID2549 NOS DE NATURA SOMOS DE CONDES ** CARRION
20111 5ELCID2553 PODREMOS CASAR CON FIJAS ** REYES O DE ENPERADORES,
20114 5ELCID2553 PODREMOS CASAR CON FIJAS DE REYES O ** ENPERADORES,
20117 5ELCID2554 CA ** NATURA SOMOS DE CONDES DE CARRION.
20120 5ELCID2554 CA DE NATURA SOMOS ** CONDES DE CARRION.
20122 5ELCID2554 CA DE NATURA SOMOS DE CONDES ** CARRION.
20190 5ELCID2563 LEUAR LAS HEMOS A NUESTRAS TIERRAS ** CARRION,
20237 5ELCID2569 EL %ID QUE NOS CURIAUA ** ASSI SER AFONTADO;
20250 5ELCID2570 VOS LES DIESTES VILLAS E TIERRAS POR ARRAS ENTIERRAS ** CARRION,
20260 5ELCID2571 HYO QUIERO LES DAR AXUUAR IIJ MILL MARCOS ** PLATA;
20269 5ELCID2572 DARUOS E MULAS & PALAFRES, MUY GRUESSOS ** SAZON,
20281 5ELCID2574 E MUCHAS VESTIDURAS ** PA@OS & DE %ICLATONES;
20284 5ELCID2574 E MUCHAS VESTIDURAS DE PA@OS & ** %ICLATONES;
20304 5ELCID2576 BIEN LO SABEDES UOS QUE LAS GANE AGUISA ** VARON;
20364 5ELCID2583 ATORGADO LO HAN ESTO LOS YFFANTES ** CARRION.
20390 5ELCID2587 HYA MANDAUAN CARGAR YFFANTES ** CARRION.
20415 5ELCID2590 POR QUE ESCURREN SUS FIJAS DEL CAMPEADOR ATIERRAS ** CARRION.
20461 5ELCID2597 AGORA NOS ENVIADES ATIERRAS ** CARRION,
20485 5ELCID2600 QUE AYADES UUESTROS MENSSAIES EN TIERRAS ** CARRION.
20508 5ELCID2604 ** MI & DE UUESTRO PADRE BIEN AVEDES NUESTRA GRA%IA.
20511 5ELCID2604 DE MI & ** UUESTRO PADRE BIEN AVEDES NUESTRA GRA%IA.
20554 5ELCID2609 MYO %ID & LOS OTROS ** CAUALGAR PENSSAUAN,
20566 5ELCID2611 HYA SALIEN LOS YFANTES ** VALEN%IA LA CLARA,
20574 5ELCID2612 ESPIENDOS DELAS DUE@AS & ** TODAS SUS COMPA@AS.
20581 5ELCID2613 POR LA HUERTA ** VALEN%IA TENIENDO SALIEN ARMAS;
20629 5ELCID2619 PRIMO ERES ** MIS FIJAS AMAS DALMA & DE CORA%ON
20635 5ELCID2619 PRIMO ERES DE MIS FIJAS AMAS DALMA & ** CORA%ON
20667 5ELCID2623 DIXO FELEZ MUNOZ: PLAZME DALMA & ** CORA%ON.
20696 5ELCID2627 HYR LAS HEMOS VER ATIERRAS ** CARRION.
20733 5ELCID2632 EL PADRE CON LAS FIJAS LORAN ** CORA%ON,
20775 5ELCID2638 DIL QUE ENBIO MIS FIJAS A TIERRAS ** CARRION,
20794 5ELCID2641 ** QUANTO EL FIZIERE YOL DAR POR ELLO BUEN GALARDON.
20824 5ELCID2644 PIENSSAN SE ** YR LOS YFANTES DE CARRION;
20828 5ELCID2644 PIENSSAN SE DE YR LOS YFANTES ** CARRION;
20842 5ELCID2646 AGUIJAN QUANTO PUEDEN YFANTES ** CARRION;
20857 5ELCID2648 EL MORO QUANDO LO SOPO, PLOGOL ** CORA%ON;
20891 5ELCID2653 HYUAN TRO%IR LOS MONTES, LOS QUE DIZEN ** LUZON.
20907 5ELCID2655 BUENOS SE@OS CAUALLOS ALOS YFANTES ** CARRION.
20973 5ELCID2664 TAN EN SALUO LO ABREMOS COMMO LO ** CARRION;
20978 5ELCID2665 NUÑQUA AURIE DERECHO ** NOS EL %ID CAMPEADOR.
20988 5ELCID2666 QUANDO ESTA FALSSEDAD DIZEN LOS ** CARRION,
21014 5ELCID2670 TU MUERT OY COSSEIAR ALOS YFANTES ** CARRION.
21051 5ELCID2675 DEZID ME, QUE UOS FIZ, YFANTES ** CARRION
21071 5ELCID2677 SI NOLO DEXAS POR MYO %ID EL ** BIUAR,
21097 5ELCID2681 AQUIM PARTO ** UOS COMMO DE MALOS & DE TRAYDORES.
21100 5ELCID2681 AQUIM PARTO DE UOS COMMO ** MALOS & DE TRAYDORES.
21103 5ELCID2681 AQUIM PARTO DE UOS COMMO DE MALOS & ** TRAYDORES.
21119 5ELCID2683 POCO PRE%IO LAS NUEUAS DELOS ** CARRION.
21128 5ELCID2684 DIOS LO QUIERA & LO MANDE, QUE ** TODEL MUNDO ES SE@OR,
21153 5ELCID2687 TENIENDO YUAN ARMAS ALTRO%IR ** SALON;
21156 5ELCID2688 CUEMMO ** BUEN SESO A MOLINA SE TORNO.
21169 5ELCID2689 YA MOUIERON DEL ANSSARERA LOS YFANTES ** CARRION,
21175 5ELCID2690 ACOIEN SE A ANDAR ** DIA & DE NOCH;
21178 5ELCID2690 ACOIEN SE A ANDAR DE DIA & ** NOCH;
21189 5ELCID2692 LA SIERRA ** MIEDES PASSARON LA ESTOZ,
21227 5ELCID2697 ENTRADOS SON LOS YFANTES AL ROBREDO ** CORPES,
21257 5ELCID2701 MANDAN FINCAR LA TIENDA YFANTES ** CARRION,
21296 5ELCID2706 COGIDA HAN LA TIENDA DO ALBERGARON ** NOCH,
21302 5ELCID2707 ADELANT ERAN YDOS LOS ** CRIAZON:
21309 5ELCID2708 ASSI LO MANDARON LOS YFANTES ** CARRION,
21348 5ELCID2713 TANTO MAL COMIDIERON LOS YFANTES ** CARRION;
21371 5ELCID2716 OY NOS PARTIREMOS, & DEXADAS SEREDES ** NOS;
21378 5ELCID2717 NON ABREDES PART EN TIERRAS ** CARRION.
21516 5ELCID2735 ESSORA LES CONPIE%AN ADAR LOS YFANTES ** CARRION;
21591 5ELCID2745 CANSSADOS SON ** FERIR ELLOS AMOS ADOS,
21617 5ELCID2748 POR MUERTAS LAS DEXARON ENEL ROBREDRO ** CORPES.
21667 5ELCID2754 LOS YFANTES ** CARRION ENEL ROBREDO DE CORPES
21671 5ELCID2754 LOS YFANTES DE CARRION ENEL ROBREDO ** CORPES
21694 5ELCID2758 ** NUESTROS CASAMIENTOS AGORA SOMOS VENGADOS;
21729 5ELCID2763 ALABANDOS YUAN LOS YFANTES ** CARRION.
21748 5ELCID2766 MANDARON LE YR ADELANTE, MAS ** SU GRADO NON FUE.
21760 5ELCID2768 ** TODOS LOS OTROS APARTE SE SALIO,
21789 5ELCID2771 O QUE AN FECHO LOS YFANTES ** CARRION.

WORD C# PREFIX CONTEXT

DE (CON'T)

21813 5ELCID2774 SABET BIEN QUE SI ELLOS LE VIESSEN, NON ESCAPARA ** MUERT.
21858 5ELCID2781 MAL SE ENSAYARON LOS YFANTES ** CARRION
21880 5ELCID2784 TANTO SON ** TRASPUESTAS QUE NON PUEDEN DEZIR NADA.
21892 5ELCID2785 PARTIERON SE LE LAS TELLAS ** DENTRO DE LOS CORA%ONES,
21894 5ELCID2785 PARTIERON SE LE LAS TELLAS DE DENTRO ** LOS CORA%ONES,
21950 5ELCID2793 ** QUE NON ME FALLAREN LOS YFANTES DE CARRION,
21957 5ELCID2793 DE QUE NON ME FALLAREN LOS YFANTES ** CARRION,
22009 5ELCID2800 NUEUO ERA & FRESCO, QUE ** VALEN%IAL SACO,
22077 5ELCID2809 TODOS TRES SE@EROS POR LOS ROBREDOS ** CORPES,
22088 5ELCID2811 ALAS AGUAS ** DUERO ELLOS ARRIBADOS SON,
22095 5ELCID2812 ALA TORRE ** DON VRRACA ELLE LAS DEXO.
22112 5ELCID2814 FALLO A DIEGO TELLEZ EL QUE ** ALBARFANEZ FUE;
22120 5ELCID2815 QUANDO EL LO OYO PESOL ** CORA%ON,
22126 5ELCID2816 PRISO BESTIAS & VESTIDOS ** PRO,
22148 5ELCID2820 LOS ** SANTESTEUAN, SIEMPRE MESURADOS SON,
22157 5ELCID2821 QUANDO SABIEN ESTO, PESOLES ** CORA%ON;
22177 5ELCID2824 ALLABANDOS SEYAN LOS YFANTES ** CARRION.
22179 5ELCID2825 ** CUER PESO ESTO AL BUEN REY DON ALFONSSO.
22232 5ELCID2831 QUANDO TAL ONDRA MEAN DADA LOS YFANTES ** CARRION;
22246 5ELCID2833 NON LA LOGRARAN LOS YFANTES ** CARRION;
22267 5ELCID2835 PESO A MYO %ID & ATODA SU CORT, & ALBARFANEZ DALMA & ** CORA%ON.
22279 5ELCID2837 E MARTIN ANTOLINEZ, EL BURGLES ** PRO,
22293 5ELCID2839 DIXOLES FUERTE MIENTRE QUE ANDIDIESSEN ** DIA & DE NOCH,
22296 5ELCID2839 DIXOLES FUERTE MIENTRE QUE ANDIDIESSEN DE DIA & ** NOCH,
22310 5ELCID2841 NON LO DETARDAN EL MANDADO ** SU SE@OR,
22324 5ELCID2843 VINIERON A SANTESTEUAN ** GORMAZ, VN CASTIELLO TAN FUERT,
22349 5ELCID2847 VARONES ** SANTESTEUAN, A GUISA DE MUY PROS,
22353 5ELCID2847 VARONES DE SANTESTEUAN, A GUISA ** MUY PROS,
22379 5ELCID2851 GRA%IAS, VARONES ** SANTESTEUAN, QUE SODES CO@OS%EDORES,
22419 5ELCID2855 AFFE DIOS DELOS %IELOS QUE UOS ** DENT BUEN GALARDON
22474 5ELCID2862 EN LOS DIAS ** VAGAR TODA NUESTRA RENCURA SABREMOS CONTAR.
22541 5ELCID2870 OTRO DIA MA@ANA PIENSSAN ** CAUALGAR,
22544 5ELCID2871 LOS ** SANTESTEUAN ESCURRIENDO LOS VAN
22561 5ELCID2873 DALLENT SE ESPIDIERON DELLOS, PIENSSAN SE ** TORNAR,
22573 5ELCID2875 TRO%IERON ALCO%EUA, ADIESTRO ** SANTESTEUAN DE GORMAZ,
22575 5ELCID2875 TRO%IERON ALCO%EUA, ADIESTRO DE SANTESTEUAN ** GORMAZ,
22579 5ELCID2876 ODIZEN BADO ** REY, ALLA YUAN POSAR,
22586 5ELCID2877 ALA CASA ** BERLANGA POSADA PRESA HAN.
22604 5ELCID2880 E ** MEDINA A MOLINA EN OTRO DIA VAN;
22615 5ELCID2881 AL MORO AUENGALUON ** CORA%ON LE PLAZ,
22622 5ELCID2882 SALIOLOS A RE%EBIR ** BUENA VOLUNTAD,
22627 5ELCID2883 POR AMOR ** MYO %ID RICA CENA LES DA.
22673 5ELCID2889 BESANDO LAS AAMAS, TORNOS ** SONRRISAR:
22681 5ELCID2890 VENIDES, MIS FIJAS? DIOS UOS CURIE ** MAL
22707 5ELCID2894 ** MYOS YERNOS DE CARRION DIOS ME FAGA VENGAR
22710 5ELCID2894 DE MYOS YERNOS ** CARRION DIOS ME FAGA VENGAR
22758 5ELCID2900 AL REY ALFONSSO ** CASTIELLA PENSSO DE ENBIAR;
22761 5ELCID2900 AL REY ALFONSSO DE CASTIELLA PENSSO ** ENBIAR;
22768 5ELCID2901 OERES, MU@O GUSTIOZ, MYO VASSALLO ** PRO,
22796 5ELCID2904 POR MI BESA LE LA MANO DALMA & ** CORA%ON,
22815 5ELCID2906 DESTA DESONDRA QUE MEAN FECHA LOS YFANTES ** CARRION
22824 5ELCID2907 QUEL PESE AL BUEN REY DALMA & ** CORA%ON.
22855 5ELCID2911 LA POCA & LA GRANT TODA ES ** MYO SE@OR.
22886 5ELCID2915 COMMO AYA DERECHO ** YFANTES DE CARRION,
22888 5ELCID2915 COMMO AYA DERECHO DE YFANTES ** CARRION,
22919 5ELCID2919 E CON EL ESCUDEROS QUE SON ** CRIAZON.
22922 5ELCID2920 SALIEN ** VALEN%IA & ANDAN QUANTO PUEDEN,
22945 5ELCID2923 REY ES ** CASTIELLA & REY ES DE LEON
22950 5ELCID2923 REY ES DE CASTIELLA & REY ES ** LEON
22964 5ELCID2925 FASTA DENTRO EN SANTI YAGUO ** TODO ES SE@OR,
23044 5ELCID2936 MER%ED, REY ALFONSSO, ** LARGOS REYNOS AUOS DIZEN SE@OR
23073 5ELCID2939 CASASTES SUS FIJAS CON YFANTES ** CARRION,
23096 5ELCID2942 CUEMO NOS HAN ABILTADOS YFANTES ** CARRION:
23116 5ELCID2945 DESENPARADAS LAS DEXARON ENEL ROBREDO ** CORPES,
23172 5ELCID2952 QUE AYA MYO %ID DERECHO ** YFANTES DE CARRION.
23174 5ELCID2952 QUE AYA MYO %ID DERECHO DE YFANTES ** CARRION.
23191 5ELCID2954 VERDAD TE DIGO YO, QUE ME PESA ** CORA%ON,
23208 5ELCID2956 CA YO CASE SUS FIJAS CON YFANTES ** CARRION;
23234 5ELCID2959 ENTRE YO & MYO %ID PESA NOS ** CORA%ON.
23248 5ELCID2961 LO QUE NON CUYDAUA FER ** TODA ESTA SAZON,
23278 5ELCID2965 MANDARE COMMO Y VAYAN YFANTES ** CARRION,
23319 5ELCID2970 VENGAM A TOLLEDO, ESTOL DO ** PLAZO.
23323 5ELCID2971 POR AMOR ** MYO %ID ESTA CORT YO FAGO.
23384 5ELCID2979 E ALOS ** CARRION & AVARONES CASTELLANOS,
23399 5ELCID2981 A CABO ** VIJ SEMANAS QUE Y FUESSEN IUNTADOS;
23440 5ELCID2985 HYA LES VA PESANDO ALSO YFANTES ** CARRION,
23495 5ELCID2992 DARLEDES DERECHO, CA RENCURA HA ** UOS.
23523 5ELCID2995 HYA LO VIERON QUE ES AFER LOS YFANTES ** CARRION,
23539 5ELCID2998 ENEMIGO ** MIO SID, QUE SIEMPREL BUSCO MAL,
23550 5ELCID2999 AQUESTE CONSSEIO LOS YFANTES ** CARRION.
23594 5ELCID3005 FUERON Y ** SU REYNO OTROS MUCHOS SABIDORES,
23600 5ELCID3006 ** TODA CASTIELLA TODOS LOS MEIORES
23612 5ELCID3007 EL CONDE DON GAR%IA CON YFANTES ** CARRION,
23646 5ELCID3012 ** TODAS PARTES ALLI IUNTADOS SON.

WORD C# PREFIX CONTEXT

DE (CON'T)

23705 5ELCID3019 QUANDO LO OYO EL REY, PLOGOL ** CORA%ON;
23788 5ELCID3030 SALUDAR NOS HEMOS DALMA & ** CCRA%ON.
23861 5ELCID3039 MI MUGIER DCNA XIMENA, CUE@A ES ** PRO,
23912 5ELCID3046 PENSSAD, SE@OR, ** ENTRAR ALA %IBDAD,
23947 5ELCID3051 E YRE ALA CORT ENANTES ** IANTAR.
23953 5ELCID3052 DIXO EL REY: PLAZME ** VELUNTAD.
23980 5ELCID3056 SABOR A ** VELAR ENESSA SANTIDAD,
24056 5ELCID3066 E MARTIN ANTOLINEZ, EL BURGALES ** PRO,
24106 5ELCID3074 ** SUSO LAS LORIGAS TAN BLANCAS COMMO EL SOL;
24145 5ELCID3079 POR ** MANDAR MYOS DERECHOS & DEZIR MI RAZON:
24157 5ELCID3080 SI DESOBRA BUSCAREN YFANTES ** CARRION,
24191 5ELCID3085 CAL%AS ** BUEN PA@O EN SUS CAMAS METIO,
24208 5ELCID3087 VISTIO CAMISA ** RAN%AL TAN BLANCA COMMO EL SOL,
24236 5ELCID3090 SOBRELLA VN BRIAL PRIMO ** %ICLATON,
24267 5ELCID3094 VNA COFIA SOBRE LOS PELOS DUN ESCARIN ** PRO,
24311 5ELCID3099 DESUSO CUBRIO VN MANTO QUE ES ** GRANT VALOR,
24330 5ELCID3102 APRIESSA CAUALGA, ** SAN SERUAN SALIO;
24343 5ELCID3104 ALA PUERTA ** FUERA DESCAUALGA A SABOR;
24414 5ELCID3112 NOS QUISO LEUANTAR EL CRESPO ** GRA@ON,
24421 5ELCID3113 NIN TODOS LOS DEL BANDO ** YFANTES DE CARRION.
24423 5ELCID3113 NIN TODOS LOS DEL BANCO DE YFANTES ** CARRION.
24478 5ELCID3120 LO QUE DIXO EL %ID AL REY PLOGO ** CORA%ON.
24522 5ELCID3126 NOL PUEDEN CATAR ** VERGUEN%A YFANTES DE CARRION.
24525 5ELCID3126 NOL PUEDEN CATAR DE VERGUEN%A YFANTES ** CARRION.
24544 5ELCID3129 HYC, ** QUE FU REY, NON FIZ MAS DE DOS CORTES:
24551 5ELCID3129 HYC, DE QUE FU REY, NCN FIZ MAS ** DOS CORTES:
24575 5ELCID3132 POR EL AMOR ** MYO %ID EL QUE EN BUEN ORA NA%IO,
24587 5ELCID3133 QUE RE%IBA DERECHO ** YFANTES DE CARRION.
24589 5ELCID3133 QUE RE%IBA DERECHO DE YFANTES ** CARRION.
24681 5ELCID3144 SABREMOS QUE RESPONDEN YFANTES ** CARRION.
24717 5ELCID3148 ESTO LES DEMANDO AYFANTES ** CARRION:
24742 5ELCID3151 MAS QUANDO SACARON MIS FIJAS ** VALEN%IA LA MAYOR,
24752 5ELCID3152 HYO BIEN LAS QUERIA DALMA & ** CORA%ON,
24767 5ELCID3154 ESTAS YO LAS GANE AGUISA ** VARON,
24782 5ELCID3156 QUANDO DEXARON MIS FIJAS ENEL ROBREDO ** CORPES,
24821 5ELCID3161 ESSORA SALIEN APARTE YFFANTES ** CARRION,
24887 5ELCID3169 HYA MAS NON AURA DERECHO ** NOS EL %ID CANPEADOR.
25003 5ELCID3184 ALEGROS LE TODEL CUERPO, SONRRISOS ** CORA%ON,
25052 5ELCID3191 A MARTIN ANTOLINEZ, EL BURGALES ** PRO,
25065 5ELCID3193 MARTIN ANTOLINEZ, MYO VASSALO ** PRO,
25071 5ELCID3194 PRENDED A COLADA, GANELA ** BUEN SE@OR,
25076 5ELCID3195 DEL CONDE ** REMONT VERENGEL DE BAR%ILONA LA MAYOR.
25079 5ELCID3195 DEL CONDE DE REMONT VERENGEL ** BAR%ILONA LA MAYOR.
25132 5ELCID3201 HYA PAGADO SO ** MIS ESPADAS, DE COLADA & DE TIZON.
25135 5ELCID3201 HYA PAGADO SO DE MIS ESPADAS, ** COLADA & DE TIZON.
25138 5ELCID3201 HYA PAGADO SO DE MIS ESPADAS, DE COLADA & ** TIZON.
25143 5ELCID3202 OTRA RENCURA HE ** YFANTES DE CARRION:
25145 5ELCID3202 OTRA RENCURA HE DE YFANTES ** CARRION:
25149 5ELCID3203 QUANDO SACARON ** VALEN%IA MIS FIJAS AMAS ADOS,
25163 5ELCID3204 EN ORO & EN PLATA TRES MILL MARCOS ** PLATA LES DIO;
25188 5ELCID3207 AQUI VERIEDES QUEXAR SE YFANTES ** CARRION
25196 5ELCID3208 DJZE EL CONDE DON REMOND: DEZID ** SSI O DE NO.
25199 5ELCID3208 DJZE EL CONDE DON REMOND: DEZID DE SSI O ** NO.
25204 5ELCID3209 ESSORA RESPONDEN YFANTES ** CARRION:
25273 5ELCID3217 ESSORA SALIEN A PARTE YFANTES ** CARRION;
25288 5ELCID3219 ESPESOS LOS HAN YFANTES ** CARRION.
25306 5ELCID3222 QUANDO ** NUESTROS AUERES ASSIL PRENDE SABOR;
25315 5ELCID3223 PAGAR LE HEMOS ** HEREDADES ENTIERRAS DE CARRION.
25318 5ELCID3223 PAGAR LE HEMOS DE HEREDADES ENTIERRAS ** CARRION.
25384 5ELCID3232 ENTRAMOS MELOS DIERON LOS YFANTES ** CARRION.
25456 5ELCID3241 HYA VIERON QUE ES AFER LOS YFANTES ** CARRION.
25468 5ELCID3243 TANTA GRUESSA MULA, TANTO PALAFRE ** SAZON,
25544 5ELCID3253 MER%ED, AY REY SE@OR, POR AMOR ** CARIDAD
25560 5ELCID3255 OYD ME TODA LA CORT & PESEUOS ** MYO MAL;
25565 5ELCID3256 DELOS YFANTES ** CARRION QUEM DESONDRARON TAN MAL,
25572 5ELCID3257 AMENOS ** RIEBTOS NO LOS PUEDO DEXAR.
25608 5ELCID3261 ALA SALIDA ** VALEN%IA MIS FIJAS VOS DI YO,
25634 5ELCID3264 POR QUE LAS SACAUADES ** VALEN%IA SUS HONORES?
25652 5ELCID3266 SOLAS LAS DEXASTES ENEL ROBREDO ** CORPES,
25689 5ELCID3271 MER%ED, YA REY, EL MEIOR ** TODA ESPA@A
25715 5ELCID3275 LOS ** CARRION SON DE NATURA TAL,
25718 5ELCID3275 LOS DE CARRION SON ** NATURA TAL,
25782 5ELCID3284 CA ** QUANDO NASCO ADELI%IO FUE CRIADA,
25794 5ELCID3285 CA NON ME PRISO AELLA FIJO ** MUGIER NADA,
25800 5ELCID3286 NIMBLA MESSO FIJO ** MORO NIN DE CHRISTIANA,
25803 5ELCID3286 NIMBLA MESSO FIJO DE MORO NIN ** CHRISTIANA,
25811 5ELCID3287 COMMO YO AUOS, CONDE, ENEL CASTIELLO ** CABRA;
25851 5ELCID3293 DEXASSEDES UOS, %ID, ** AQUESTA RAZON;
25854 5ELCID3294 ** UUESTROS AUERES DE TODOS PAGADOS SODES.
25857 5ELCID3294 DE UUESTROS AUERES ** TODOS PAGADOS SODES.
25868 5ELCID3296 ** NATURA SOMOS DE CONDES DE CARRION:
25871 5ELCID3296 DE NATURA SOMOS ** CONDES DE CARRION:
25873 5ELCID3296 DE NATURA SOMOS DE CONDES ** CARRION:
25879 5ELCID3297 DEUIEMOS CASAR CON FIJAS ** REYES O DE ENPERADORES,

WORD C# PREFIX CONTEXT

DE (CON'T)

```
25882 5ELCID3297 DEUIEMOS CASAR CCN FIJAS DE REYES O ** ENPERADORES,
25888 5ELCID3298 CA NON PERTENE%IEN FIJAS ** YFAN%ONES.
25945 5ELCID3306 PERO VERMUEZ CONPE%C ** FABLAR;
25994 5ELCID3313 MIENTES, FERRANDC, ** QUANTC DICHO HAS,
26051 5ELCID3320 PASSE POR TI, CCN EL MORO ME OFF ** AIUNTAR,
26058 5ELCID3321 DELOS PRIMEROS COLPES OF LE ** ARRANCAR;
26082 5ELCID3324 DELANT MYO %IC & DELANTE TODOS OVISTE TE ** ALABAR
26148 5ELCID3333 METISTET TRAS EL ESCA@C ** MYC %IC EL CAMPEADOR
26276 5ELCID3350 TULO OTORGARAS A GUISA ** TRAYDOR;
26278 5ELCID3351 ** QUANTO HE DICHO VERDADERO SERE YO.
26297 5ELCID3354 ** NATURA SOMOS DE LOS CONDES MAS LIPIOS,
26300 5ELCID3354 DE NATURA SOMOS ** LOS CONDES MAS LIPIOS,
26430 5ELCID3371 QUE ERES TRAYDOR & MINTIST ** QUANTO DICHO HAS.
26474 5ELCID3378  QUIEN NOS DARIE NUEUAS ** MYO %ID EL DE BIUAR
26478 5ELCID3378  QUIEN NOS DARIE NUEUAS DE MYO %ID EL ** BIUAR
26498 5ELCID3381  QUIL DARIE CON LOS ** CARRION ACASAR?
26596 5ELCID3395 EL VNO ES YFANTE ** NAUARRA
26602 5ELCID3396 E EL OTRO YFANTE ** ARAGON;
26622 5ELCID3399 POR SER REYNAS ** NAUARRA & DE ARAGON,
26625 5ELCID3399 POR SER REYNAS DE NAUARRA & ** ARAGON,
26664 5ELCID3405 QUANDO MELAS DEMANDAN ** NAUARRA & DE ARAGON.
26667 5ELCID3405 QUANDO MELAS DEMANDAN DE NAUARRA & ** ARAGON.
26749 5ELCID3416 ESSORA DIXO EL REY: DIOS UOS ** DEN BUEN GALARDON
26765 5ELCID3419 ** FIJAS DE MYO %ID, CON ELUIRA & DO@A SOL,
26767 5ELCID3419 DE FIJAS ** MYO %ID, CON ELUIRA & DO@A SOL,
26778 5ELCID3420 PORA LOS YFANTES ** NAUARRA & DE ARAGON,
26781 5ELCID3420 PORA LOS YFANTES DE NAUARRA & ** ARAGON,
26786 5ELCID3421 QUE UOS LAS ** ADNDRA & A BENDI%ION.
26807 5ELCID3424 E DESPUES ** MYO %ID EL CAMPEADOR;
26830 5ELCID3427 A MUCHOS PLAZE ** TOD ESTA CORT,
26839 5ELCID3428 MAS NON PLAZE ALOS YFANTES ** CARRION.
26882 5ELCID3434 DIXO EL REY: PLAZME ** CORA%ON.
26903 5ELCID3437 CA GRAND RENCURA HE ** YFANTES DE CARRION.
26905 5ELCID3437 CA GRAND RENCURA HE DE YFANTES ** CARRION.
26939 5ELCID3441 ELLOS LAS HAN DEXADAS A PESAR ** NOS.
26950 5ELCID3443 ** NATURA SODES DELOS DE VANIGOMEZ,
26954 5ELCID3443 DE NATURA SODES DELOS ** VANIGOMEZ,
26959 5ELCID3444 ONDE SALIEN CONDES ** PREZ & DE VALOR;
26962 5ELCID3444 ONDE SALIEN CONDES DE PREZ & ** VALOR;
26987 5ELCID3448 LOS YFANTES ** NAUARRA & DE ARAGON;
26990 5ELCID3448 LOS YFANTES DE NAUARRA & ** ARAGON;
27050 5ELCID3455 SI AY QUI RESPONDA ODIZE ** NO,
27133 5ELCID3467 LUEGO FABLARON YFANTES ** CARRION:
27155 5ELCID3470 NOS ANTES ABREMOS AYR ATIERRAS ** CARRION.
27182 5ELCID3474 MAS QUIERO A VALEN%IA QUE TIERRAS ** CARRION.
27218 5ELCID3479 QUE NON PRENDAN FUER%A ** CONDE NIN DE YFAN%ON.
27221 5ELCID3479 QUE NON PRENDAN FUER%A DE CONDE NIN ** YFAN%ON.
27227 5ELCID3480 AQUI LES PONGO PLAZO ** DENTRO EN MI CORT,
27233 5ELCID3481 ACABO ** TRES SEMANAS, EN BEGAS DE CARRION,
27238 5ELCID3481 ACABO DE TRES SEMANAS, EN BEGAS ** CARRION,
27266 5ELCID3485 PRISIERON EL JUIZIO YFANTES ** CARRION.
27333 5ELCID3493 LA CONFIA ** RAN%AL QUE BLANCA ERA COMMO EL SOL,
27351 5ELCID3495 NOS FARTAN ** CATARLE QUANTOS HA EN LA CORT.
27376 5ELCID3497 ABRA%OLOS TAN BIEN & RUEGA LOS ** CORA%ON
27380 5ELCID3498 QUE PRENDAN ** SUS AUERES QUANTO QUIEREN SABOR.
27391 5ELCID3499 AESSOS & ALOS OTROS QUE ** BUENA PARTE SON,
27473 5ELCID3509 HYO LO JURO PAR SANT ESIDRO EL ** LEON
27613 5ELCID3525 E MUNO GUSTIOZ, FIRMES SED EN CAMPO AGUISA ** VARONES;
27621 5ELCID3526 BUENOS MANDADOS ME VAYAN A VALEN%IA ** VOS.
27643 5ELCID3529 PODEDES OYR ** MUERTOS, CA DE VENCIDOS NO.
27646 5ELCID3529 PODEDES OYR DE MUERTOS, CA ** VENCIDOS NO.
27659 5ELCID3531 ESPIDIOS ** TODOS LOS QUE SOS AMIGOS SON.
27678 5ELCID3533 MAS TRES SEMANAS ** PLAZO TODAS COMPLIDAS SON.
27706 5ELCID3536 ELLOS SON ENPODER DEL REY DON ALFONSSO EL ** LEON;
27713 5ELCID3537 DOS DIAS ATENDIERON A YFANTES ** CARRION.
27719 5ELCID3538 MUCHO VIENEN BIEN ADOBADOS ** CAUALLOS & DE GUARNIZONES,
27722 5ELCID3538 MUCHO VIENEN BIEN ADOBADOS DE CAUALLOS & ** GUARNIZONES,
27746 5ELCID3541 QUE LOS MATASSEN EN CAMPO POR DESONDRA ** SO SE@OR.
27765 5ELCID3543 CA GRAND MIEDO OUIERON A ALFONSSO EL ** LEON.
27767 5ELCID3544 ** NOCHE BELARON LAS ARMAS & ROGARON AL CRIADOR.
27787 5ELCID3546 MUCHOS SE JUNTARON ** BUENOS RICOS OMNES
27830 5ELCID3551 TODOS TRES SE ACUERDAN, CA SON ** VN SE@OR.
27840 5ELCID3552 EN OTRO LOGAR SE ARMAN LOS YFANTES ** CARRION,
27917 5ELCID3562 LEUAD & SALID ALCAMPO, YFANTES ** CARRION,
27925 5ELCID3563 HUEBOS VOS ES QUE LIDIEDES AGUISA ** VARONES,
27963 5ELCID3568 HYA SEUAN REPINTIENDO YFANTES ** CARRION,
28015 5ELCID3575 QUE FIEL SEADES OY DELLOS & ** NOS;
28029 5ELCID3577 AQUI TIENEN SU VANDO LOS YFANTES ** CARRION,
28057 5ELCID3581 ESSORA DIXO EL REY: DALMA & ** CORA%ON.
28129 5ELCID3591 FEUOS DELA OTRA PART LOS YFANTES ** CARRION,
28156 5ELCID3594 QUE NON VARAGEN CON ELLOS DESI O ** NON.
28172 5ELCID3596 OYD QUE UOS DIGO, YFANTES ** CARRION:
28186 5ELCID3598 ESTOS TRES CAUALLEROS ** MYO %ID EL CAMPEADOR
28196 5ELCID3599 HYO LOS ADUX ASALUO ATIERRAS ** CARRION;
```

```
WORD                 C#  PREFIX                          CONTEXT

DE (CON'T)

                  28227 5ELCID3603 HYA LES VA PESANDO ALCS YFANTES ** CARRION.
                  28265 5ELCID3609 MAS ** VJ ASTAS DE LAN%AS QUE NON LEGASSEN AL MOION.
                  28268 5ELCID3609 MAS DE VJ ASTAS ** LAN%AS QUE NON LEGASSEN AL MOION.
                  28287 5ELCID3611 SALIEN LOS FIELES ** MEDIO, ELLOS CARA POR CARA SON;
                  28297 5ELCID3612 DESI VINIEN LOS ** MYO %ID ALOS YFANTES DE CARRION,
                  28302 5ELCID3612 DESI VINIEN LOS DE MYO %ID ALOS YFANTES ** CARRION,
                  28306 5ELCID3613 ELLOS YFANTES ** CARRION ALOS DE CAMPEADOR;
                  28309 5ELCID3613 ELLOS YFANTES DE CARRION ALOS ** CAMPEADOR;
                  28381 5ELCID3624 CON FERRAGON%ALEZ ** CARA SE JUNTO;
                  28456 5ELCID3634 TRES DOBLES ** LORIGA TENIE FERNANDO, AQUESTOL PRESTO,
                  28520 5ELCID3641 ASSI LO TENIEN LAS YENTES QUE MAL FERIDO ES ** MUERT.
                  28588 5ELCID3650 DIOL VN COLPE, ** TRAUIESSOL TOMAUA,
                  28593 5ELCID3651 EL CASCO ** SOMO APART GELO ECHAUA,
                  28664 5ELCID3659 BOLUIO LA RIENDA AL CAUALLO POR TORNASSE ** CARA;
                  28676 5ELCID3661 VN COLPEL DIO ** LANC, CON LO AGUDO NOL TOMAUA.
                  28751 5ELCID3671 LOS DOS HAN ARRANCADO: DJREUOS ** MUNO GUSTIOZ,
                  28772 5ELCID3674 ASSUR GON%ALEZ, FUR%UDO & ** VALOR,
                  28812 5ELCID3680 POR MEIO ** LA BLOCA DEL ESCUDOL QUEBRANTO;
                  28880 5ELCID3688 TODOS SE CUEDAN QUE FERIDO ES ** MUERT.
                  28947 5ELCID3697 GRANDES SON LOS PESARES POR TIERRAS ** CARRION.
                  28952 5ELCID3698 EL REY ALOS ** MYO %ID DE NOCHE LOS ENBIO,
                  28955 5ELCID3698 EL REY ALOS DE MYO %ID ** NOCHE LOS ENBIO,
                  28967 5ELCID3700 AGUISA ** MENBRADOS ANDAN DIAS & NOCHES,
                  28987 5ELCID3702 POR MALOS LOS DEXARON ALOS YFANTES ** CARRION,
                  29009 5ELCID3705 GRANT ES LA BILTAN%A ** YFANTES DE CARRION.
                  29011 5ELCID3705 GRANT ES LA BILTAN%A DE YFANTES ** CARRION.
                  29030 5ELCID3708 DEXEMOS NOS ** PLEYTOS DE YFANTES DE CARRION,
                  29032 5ELCID3708 DEXEMOS NOS DE PLEYTOS ** YFANTES DE CARRION,
                  29034 5ELCID3708 DEXEMOS NOS DE PLEYTOS DE YFANTES ** CARRION,
                  29089 5ELCID3715 AGORA LAS AYAN QUITAS HEREDADES ** CARRION.
                  29103 5ELCID3717 ANDIDIERON EN PLEYTOS LOS ** NAUARRA & DE ARAGON,
                  29106 5ELCID3717 ANDIDIERON EN PLEYTOS LOS DE NAUARRA & ** ARAGON,
                  29114 5ELCID3718 OUIERON SU AIUNTA CON ALFONSSO EL ** LEON,
                  29158 5ELCID3723 QUANDO SE@ORAS SON SUS FIJAS ** NAUARRA & DE ARAGON.
                  29161 5ELCID3723 QUANDO SE@ORAS SON SUS FIJAS DE NAUARRA & ** ARAGON.
                  29187 5ELCID3726 PASSADO ES DESTE SIEGLO EL DIA ** CINQUAESMA.
                  29189 5ELCID3727 ** CHRISTUS HAYA PERDON
                  29204 5ELCID3729 ESTAS SON LAS NUEUAS ** MYO %ID EL CANPEADOR,
                  29230 5ELCID3732 PER ABBAT LE ESCRIUIO ENEL MES ** MAYO,
                  29234 5ELCID3733 EN ERA ** MILL & CCXLV A@OS.  EN EL ROMANZ
         WORD #1350 OCCURS1023 TIMES.
            INDEX OF DIVERSIFICATION =    27.54 WITH STANDARD DEVIATION OF    29.52

DEBDAN            15585 5ELCID1976 LO VNO A ****** & LO OTRO PAGAUAN;
         WORD #1351 OCCURS   1 TIMES.

DEBDO              1766 5ELCID0225 ESTO & YO EN ***** QUE FAGA Y CANTAR MILL MISSAS.
                   5622 5ELCID0708 LOS QUE EL ***** AUEDES VEREMOS COMMO LA ACORREDES.
                  18686 5ELCID2365 EL ***** QUE A CADA VNO A CONPLIR SERA.
                  20463 5ELCID2598 ***** NOS ES A CUNPLIR LO QUE MANDAREDES VOS.
                  27634 5ELCID3528 PRESO AUEMOS EL ***** & A PASSAR ES POR NOS;
                  27692 5ELCID3535 CUNPLIR QUIEREN EL ***** QUE LES MANDO SO SE@OR,
                  28992 5ELCID3703 CONPLIDO HAN EL ***** QUE LES MANDO SO SE@OR;
         WORD #1352 OCCURS   7 TIMES.
            INDEX OF DIVERSIFICATION =  4536.66 WITH STANDARD DEVIATION OF  4863.51

DE%ENDIERON       14564 5ELCID1842 FIRIERON SE A TIERRA, *********** DELOS CAUALOS,
         WORD #1353 OCCURS   1 TIMES.

DE%IDO            11011 5ELCID1394 ****** ES MYNAYA, ASSAN PERO VA ROGAR,
         WORD #1354 OCCURS   1 TIMES.

DED                8363 5ELCID1063 EL SABOR QUE *** E NON SERA OLBIDADO.
                  16865 5ELCID2134 NON GELAS DARE YO CON MI MANO, NIN *** NON SE ALABARAN.
                  23781 5ELCID3029 CAUALGAD, %ID; SI NON, NON AURIA *** SABOR;
         WORD #1355 OCCURS   3 TIMES.

DEDENTRO          28479 5ELCID3637 ******** EN LA CARNE VNA MANO GELA METIO;
         WORD #1356 OCCURS   1 TIMES.

DEDES              1076 5ELCID0138 HUEBOS AUEMOS QUE NOS ***** LOS MARCHOS.
                   8862 5ELCID1129 A MI ***** C CAUALLEROS, QUE NON UOS PIDO MAS,
                  16018 5ELCID2032 ASSI ESTANDO, ***** ME UUESTRA AMOR, QUE LO OYAN QUANTOS
                                   AQUI SON.
                  16366 5ELCID2076 QUE LAS ***** POR MUGIERES ALOS YFANTES DE CARRION.
                  25265 5ELCID3216 DESTOS AUERES QUE UOS DI YO, SIMELOS DADES, O *****
                                   DELLO RA%ON.
         WORD #1357 OCCURS   5 TIMES.
            INDEX OF DIVERSIFICATION =  6046.25 WITH STANDARD DEVIATION OF  3867.23

DEGUISA            4584 5ELCID0583 ******* UA MYO %ID COMMO SIESCAPASSE DE ARRANCADA.
         WORD #1358 OCCURS   1 TIMES.

DEL                 175 5ELCID0023 ANTES DELA NOCHE EN BURGOS *** ENTRO SU CARTA,
                    255 5ELCID0033 POR MIEDO *** REY ALFONSSO, QUE ASSI LO AUIEN PARADO
                    301 5ELCID0038 SACO EL PIE *** ESTRIBERA, UNA FERIDAL DAUA;
```

WORD C# PREFIX CONTEXT

DEL (CON'T)

```
  337 5ELCID0042 EL REY LO HA UEDADO, ANCCH *** ETRO SU CARTA,
  403 5ELCID0050 YA LO VEE EL %ID QUE *** REY NON AUIE GRA%IA.
  474 5ELCID0060 DERREDCR *** VNA BUE@A CONPA@A.
  583 5ELCID0074 EN YRA *** RAY ALFFONSSC YC SERE METIDO.
 1003 5ELCID0129 MAS DEZID NOS *** %ID, DE QUE SERA PAGADO,
 1182 5ELCIDC152 AFEUOS LOS ALA TIENDA *** CAMPEADOR CONTADO;
 1213 5ELCID0156 YA ME EXCO DE TIERRA, CA *** REY SO AYRADO.
 1264 5ELCID0162 E BIEN GELAS GUARCARIEN FASTA CABO *** A@O;
 1421 5ELCID0182 EN MEDIC *** PALA%IC TENDIERON VN ALMOFALLA,
 1578 5ELCIDC202 VINO PORA LA TIENCA *** QUE EN BUEN ORA NASCO;
 1674 5ELCID0215 LA CARA *** CAUALLO TORNO A SANTA MARIA,
 1867 5ELCID0237 EL ABBAT DON SANCHC, CHRISTIANO *** CRIADOR,
 2450 5ELCIDC309 QUE, SI DESPUES *** PLAZC EN SU TIERRAL PUDIES TOMAR,
 2708 5ELCIDC342 SALUEST A SANTA SUSANNA *** FALSO CRIMINAL;
 2726 5ELCID0345 *** AGUA FEZIST VINC & CELA PIECRA PAN,
 3268 5ELCID0412 MUCHO ERA PAGADO *** SUE@O QUE A SO@ADO.
 3353 5ELCID0423 LA TIERRA *** REY ALFCNSSO ESTA NOCH LA PODEMOS QUITAR.
 4241 5ELCID0540 *** CASTIELLC QUE PRISIERCN TODOS RICOS SE PARTEN;
 4397 5ELCIDC560 DERREDOR *** CTERO, BIEN %ERCA DEL AGUA,
 4401 5ELCID0560 DERREDOR DEL CTERC, BIEN %ERCA *** AGUA,
 4667 5ELCID0592 ALSABOR *** PRENDER DELC AL NCN PIENSSAN NADA,
 4715 5ELCIDC598 CON LA MER%ED *** CRIADOR NUESTRA ES LA GANAN%IA
 4854 5ELCID0614 GRADO A DICS *** %IELC & ATODOS LOS SOS SANTOS,
 5025 5ELCID0635 ASSI FFERA LC DE SILOCA, CUE ES *** OTRA PART.
 5330 5ELCIDC673 SI CON MOROS NON LIDIAREMOS, NO NOS DARAN *** PAN.
 5344 5ELCID0675 EN EL NCBRE *** CRIADCR, QUE NON PASE POR AL:
 5855 5ELCIDC741 FELEZ MUNOZ SC SOBRINC *** CAMPEADOR
 5961 5ELCIDC755 FIRME SCN LCS MOROS, AVN NCS VAN *** CAMPO.
 6022 5ELCID0763 BOLUIO LA RIENDA POR YR SE LE *** CAMPO.
 6040 5ELCIDC766 LAS CARBONCLAS *** YELMC ECHO CELAS APARTE,
 6180 5ELCIDC787 YAS TORNAN LOS *** QUE EN BUEN ORA NASCO.
 6791 5ELCIDC867 DESI A MOLINA, QUE ES *** OTRA PART,
 6950 5ELCID0889 MAS *** %ID CAMPEADCR YC NON UOS DIGO NADA.
 7030 5ELCIDC899 QUIERO UOS DEZIR *** CUE EN BUEN ORA NASCO & %INXO ESPADA:
 7611 5ELCIDC975 *** CONDE DCN REMCNT VENICO LES MENSAIE;
 8349 5ELCID1062 *** DIA QUE FUE CONDE NCN IANTE TAN DE BUEN GRADO,
 8394 5ELCID1067 FATA CABO *** ALBERGADA ESCURRIOLOS EL CASTELANO:
 8890 5ELCID1132 YO CON LOS %IENTO ENTRARE *** OTRA PART,
 8937 5ELCID1138 ENEL NCMBRE *** CRIADCR & CEL APOSTOL SANTI YAGUE,
 8940 5ELCID1138 ENEL NOMBRE DEL CRIADCR & *** APOSTOL SANTI YAGUE,
 8988 5ELCID1144 *** OTRA PART ENTROLES ALBARFANEZ;
 9088 5ELCID1156 SCNANDO VAN SUS NUEUAS ALENT PARTE *** MAR.
 9126 5ELCID1162 CABO *** MAR TIERRA DE MOROS FIRME LA QUEBRANTA,
 9606 5ELCID1220 QUANDO SU SE@A CABDAL SEDIE EN SOMO *** ALCA%AR.
 9714 5ELCID1235 LAS NUEUAS *** CAUALLERC YAVEDES DO LEGAUAN.
10228 5ELCID1295 ALOS DIAS *** SIEGLO NON LE LORASSEN CHRISTIANOS.
10405 5ELCID1319 ALOS PIES *** REY ALFCNSSO CAYO CON GRAND DUELO,
10425 5ELCID1321 MER%ED, SE@OR ALFONSSC, POR AMOR *** CRIADOR
10680 5ELCID1353 SALDRIEN *** MONESTERIO DO ELLE LAS DEXO,
10822 5ELCID1370 DE MI SEAN QUITOS & VAYAN ALA GRA%IA *** CRIADOR.
10899 5ELCID1379 HYA UOS YDES, MYNAYA?, YD ALA GRA%IA *** CRIADOR
11391 5ELCID1441 GRAND DUELC ES AL PARTIR *** ABBAT:
11417 5ELCID1445 TODOS LOS DIAS *** SIEGLC EN LEUAR LO ADELANT
11453 5ELCID1450 POR LA TIERRA *** REY MUCHO CONDUCHO LES DAN.
11815 5ELCID1498 VIRTOS *** CAMPEADOR ANCS VIENEN BUSCAR.
12002 5ELCID1522 MUGIER *** %IC LIDIADCR ESSUS FFIJAS NATURALES;
12101 5ELCID1535 TODOS FUERCN ALEGRES *** %ERUI%IO QUE TOMARON,
12107 5ELCID1536 EL PORTERO *** REY QUITAR LO MANDAUA;
12546 5ELCID1592 EN CABO *** COSSO MYO %ID DESCALGAUA,
12610 5ELCID1600 *** GOZC QUE AUIEN DE LCS SCS OICS LORAUAN.
12712 5ELCID1614 E *** OTRA PARTE A CIO HAN EL MAR,
12765 5ELCID1620 DEZIR UCS QUIERO NUEUAS DE ALENT PARTES *** MAR,
13110 5ELCID1662 *** DIA QUE NASQUIERAN NCN VIERAN TAL TREMOR.
13153 5ELCID1667 DESI AN ASSER *** OBISPC DON IHERONIMO,
13164 5ELCID1668 COLGAR LOS HAN EN SANTA MARIA MADRE *** CRIADOR.
13330 5ELCID1690 HYR LOS HEMCS FFERIR ENEL NOMBRE *** CRIADOR & DEL APOSTOL SANTI
13333 5ELCID1690 HYR LOS HEMCS FFERIR ENEL NCMBRE DEL CRIADOR & *** APOSTOL SANTI
13384 5ELCID1696 QUANDO UOS LOS FUEREDES FERIR, ENTRARE YO *** OTRA PART;
13574 5ELCID1720 ENTRARON LES *** OTRC CABC.
13842 5ELCID1753 CON TAL CUM ESTO SE VEN%EN MOROS *** CAMPO.
13864 5ELCID1756 ESTO DIXC MYO %ID, DI%IENDO *** CAUALLO.
14097 5ELCID1785 LA TIENDA *** REY DE MARRUECOS, QUE DELAS OTRAS ES CABO,
14344 5ELCID1814 QUE NON DIGA MAL EL REY ALFONSSO *** QUE VALEN%IA MANDA.
14370 5ELCID1818 CCN SALUDES *** %ID QUE LAS MANOS LE BESAUA:
14499 5ELCID1834 AUER ESTOS MENSAIES *** QUE EN BUEN ORA NASCO.
14531 5ELCID1838 AOIO LO AUIEN LOS *** QUE EN BUEN ORA NASCO,
14635 5ELCID1851 CON %INQUAENTA MILL ARRANCOLOS *** CAMPO;
14716 5ELCID1861  MARAUILLA ES *** %ID, CUE SU ONDRA CRE%E TANTO
14738 5ELCID1863 POR TAN BILTACA MIENTRE VEN%ER REYES *** CAMPO,
14882 5ELCID1881 LAS NUEUAS *** %ID MUCHC VAN ACELANT,
14928 5ELCID1887 QUE NOS DEMANDEDES FIJAS *** CAMPEADOR;
14965 5ELCID1892 *** CASAMIENTC NON SE SIS ABRA SABOR;
15288 5ELCID1936 ADIOS LC GRADESCO QUE *** REY HE SU GRA%IA,
15338 5ELCID1942 AFE DICS *** %IELLO QUE NOS ACUERDE EN LO MIIOR.
```

WORD C# PREFIX CONTEXT

DEL (CON'T)

15780 5ELCID2002 LAS PUERTAS *** ALCAZAR QUE NON SE ABRIESSEN DE DIA NIN DE NOCH,
15823 5ELCID2007 QUE *** ALCAZAR VNA SALIR NON PUEDE,
15947 5ELCID2022 LAS YERBAS *** CAMPO A DIENTES LAS TOMO,
16065 5ELCID2037 GRADESCOLO A DIOS *** ZIELO & DESPUES AUOS,
16215 5ELCID2057 EN AQUEL DIA *** REY SO HUESPED FUE;
16224 5ELCID2058 NON SE PUEDE FARTAR ***, TANTOL QUERIE DE CORAZON;
17020 5ELCID2155 AFE DIOS *** ZIELO, QUE LO PONGA EN BUEN LOGAR
17104 5ELCID2165 LA CONPA@A *** ZID CREZE, & LA DEL REY MENGO,
17109 5ELCID2165 LA CONPA@A DEL ZID CREZE, & LA *** REY MENGO,
17631 5ELCID2231 POR MANO *** REY ALFONSSO, QUE AMI LO OUO MANDADO,
17679 5ELCID2236 QUANDO OUIERON AQUESTO FECHO, SALIERON *** PALAZIO,
17925 5ELCID2268 ESTOS FUERON FIJOS *** CONDE DON GONZALO.
18054 5ELCID2284 ENBRAZAN LOS MANTOS LOS *** CAMPEADOR,
18359 5ELCID2323 BIBDAS REMANDRAN FIJAS *** CAMPEADOR.
18468 5ELCID2337 ARRANCAR MELOS TREUO CON LA MERZED *** CRIADOR.
18841 5ELCID2384 EYUA LOS FERIR A CABO *** ALBERGADA.
19138 5ELCID2420 ALCANZOLO EL ZID ABUCAR A TRES BRACAS *** MAR,
19150 5ELCID2422 LAS CARBONCLAS *** YELMO TOLLICAS GELA HA,
19284 5ELCID2441 AMOS SON FIJOS *** CONDE DON GOZALO.
19530 5ELCID2474 GRANT FUE EL DIA LA CORT *** CAMPEADOR,
19553 5ELCID2477 GRADO A CHRISTUS, QUE *** MUNDO ES SE@OR,
19667 5ELCID2493 GRADO HA DIOS QUE *** MUNDO ES SE@OR
19744 5ELCID2503 ELLOS ME DARAN PARIAS CON AIUDA *** CRIADOR,
19903 5ELCID2524 GRADO A SANTA MARIA, MADRE *** NUESTRO SE@OR DIOS
20063 5ELCID2546 SACAR LAS HEMOS DE VALENZIA, DE PODER *** CAMPEADOR;
20079 5ELCID2548 ANTE QUE NOS RETRAYAN LO QUE CUNTIO *** LEON.
20099 5ELCID2551 ESCARNIREMOS LAS FIJAS *** CANPEADOR.
20129 5ELCID2555 ASSI LAS ESCARNIREMOS ALAS FIJAS *** CAMPEADOR,
20138 5ELCID2556 ANTES QUE NOS RETRAYAN LO QUE FUE *** LEON.
20320 5ELCID2578 ALLA ME LEUADES LAS TELAS *** CORAZON.
20370 5ELCID2584 AQUI REZIBEN LAS FIJAS *** CAMPEADOR;
20412 5ELCID2590 POR QUE ESCURREN SUS FIJAS *** CAMPEADOR ATIERRAS DE CARRION.
20739 5ELCID2633 ASSI FAZIAN LOS CAUALLEROS *** CAMPEADOR.
20895 5ELCID2654 ALAS FIJAS *** ZID EL MORO SUS DO@AS DIO,
20930 5ELCID2658 TOD ESTO LES FIZO EL MORO POR EL AMOR *** ZID CAMPEADOR.
20951 5ELCID2661 HYA PUES QUE ADEXAR AUEMOS FIJAS *** CAMPEADOR,
21165 5ELCID2689 YA MOUIERON *** ANSSARERA LOS YFANTES DE CARRION,
21391 5ELCID2719 NOS VENGAREMOS AQUESTA POR LA *** LEON.
21639 5ELCID2751 E ALAS AUES *** MONTE & ALAS BESTIAS DELA FIERA GUISA.
21720 5ELCID2762 LA DESONDRA *** LEON ASSIS YRA VENGANDO.
21740 5ELCID2765 SOBRINO ERA *** ZID CAMPEADOR;
21909 5ELCID2787 DESPERTEDES, PRIMAS, POR AMOR *** CRIADOR
21948 5ELCID2792 ESFORZAD UOS, PRIMAS, POR AMOR *** CRIADOR
21990 5ELCID2798 DANDOS *** AGUA, SI UOS VALA EL CRIADOR
22013 5ELCID2801 COGIO *** AGUA ENEL & ASUS PRIMAS DIO;
22161 5ELCID2822 ALLAS FIJAS *** ZID DAN LES ESFUERZO.
22221 5ELCID2830 GRADO A CHRISTUS, QUE *** MUNDO ES SE@OR,
23102 5ELCID2943 MAL MAIARON SUS FIJAS *** ZID CAMPEADOR;
23124 5ELCID2946 ALAS BESTIAS FIERAS & ALAS AUES *** MONT.
23580 5ELCID3003 AQUESTE FUE PADRE *** BUEN ENPERADOR;
24419 5ELCID3113 NIN TODOS LOS *** BANDO DE YFANTES DE CARRION.
24617 5ELCID3136 E ESTOS OTROS CONDES QUE *** VANDO NON SODES.
24937 5ELCID3176 PUSIERON LAS EN MANO *** REY SO SE@OR;
25074 5ELCID3195 *** CONDE DE REMONT VERENGEL DE BARZILONA LA MAYOR.
25604 5ELCID3260 A QUEM DESCUBRIESTES LAS TELAS *** CORAZON?
25660 5ELCID3267 ALAS BESTIAS FIERAS & ALAS AUES *** MONT;
26125 5ELCID3330 NON TE VIENE EN MIENTE EN VALENZIA LO *** LEON,
26177 5ELCID3337 LEUANTOS *** ESCA@O & FUES PORAL LEON;
26236 5ELCID3345 POR FIJAS *** ZID, DON ELUIRA & DONA SOL:
26366 5ELCID3363 LO *** LEON NON SE TE DEUE OLBIDAR;
26401 5ELCID3368 FIJAS *** ZID, POR QUE LAS VOS DEXASTES,
26801 5ELCID3423 BESARON LAS MANOS *** REY DON ALFONSSO,
26914 5ELCID3438 HYO LES DI MIS PRIMAS POR MANDADO *** REY ALFONSSO,
27021 5ELCID3452 GRADO ADIOS *** ZIELO & AQUEL REY DON ALFONSSO,
27148 5ELCID3469 ARMAS & CAUALLOS TIENEN LOS *** CANPEADOR,
27313 5ELCID3490 ONDRADOS MELOS ENBIAD A VALENZIA, POR AMOR *** CRIADOR
27347 5ELCID3494 E SOLTAUA LA BARBA & SACOLA *** CORDON.
27430 5ELCID3504 MERZED UOS PIDO, REY, POR AMOR *** CRIADOR
27557 5ELCID3519 PORA ARRANCAR MOROS *** CANPO & SER SEGUDADOR;
27687 5ELCID3534 FELOS AL PLAZO LOS *** CAMPEADOR,
27701 5ELCID3536 ELLOS SON ENPODER *** REY DON ALFONSSO EL DE LEON;
27737 5ELCID3540 QUE SI LOS PUDIESSEN APARTAR ALOS *** CAMPEADOR,
27821 5ELCID3550 HYAS METIEN EN ARMAS LOS *** BUEN CAMPEADOR,
27873 5ELCID3556 COLADA & TIZON, QUE NON LIDIASSEN CON ELLAS LOS *** CANPEADOR;
27910 5ELCID3561 OTRO SI FARAN ALOS *** CANPEADOR.
27933 5ELCID3564 QUE NADA NON MANCARA POR LOS *** CAMPEADOR.
27936 5ELCID3565 SI *** CAMPO BIEN SALIDES, GRAND ONDRA AUREDES VOS;
27986 5ELCID3571 TODOS TRES SON ARMADOS LOS *** CAMPEADOR,
27997 5ELCID3573 DIXIERON LOS *** CAMPEADOR:
28049 5ELCID3580 TENENDOS ADERECHO, POR AMOR *** CRIADOR
28112 5ELCID3589 TODOS TRES SON ACORDADOS LOS *** CAMPEADOR,
28239 5ELCID3605 LIBRAUAN SE *** CAMPO TODOS ADERREDOR.
28257 5ELCID3607 QUE POR Y SERIE VENZIDO QUI SALIESSE *** MOION.
28431 5ELCID3631 QUEBRANTO LA BOCA *** ESCUDO, A PART GELA ECHO,

WORD C# PREFIX CONTEXT

DEL (CON'T)

```
                    28505 5ELCID3640 POR LA COPLA *** CAUALLC EN TIERRA LO ECHO.
                    28600 5ELCID3652 LAS MONCLURAS *** YELMO TOCAS GELAS CORTAUA,
                    28711 5ELCID3666 EL CAUALLO ASORRIENDA, & MESURANDOL *** ESPADA,
                    28714 5ELCID3667 SACOL *** MOICN; MARTIN ANTOLJNEZ EN EL CAMPO FINCAUA.
                    28815 5ELCID3680 POR MEIO DE LA BLOCA *** ESCUDOL QUEBRANTO;
                    28932 5ELCID3695 POR ONDRADOS SE PARTEN LOS *** BUEN CAMPEADOR;
                    29066 5ELCID3712 POR QUE TAN ONDRADOS FUERON LOS *** CANPEADOR.
                    29078 5ELCID3714 GRADO AL REY *** %IELO, MIS FIJAS VENGADAS SON
                    29220 5ELCID3731 QUIEN ESCRIUIO ESTE LIBRO *** DIOS PARAYSO, AMEN
                    29246 5ELCID3734 ES LEYDO, DAT NOS *** VINO; SI NON TENEDES DINEROS, ECHAD
           WORD #1359 OCCURS 181 TIMES.
              INDEX OF DIVERSIFICATION =    160.51 WITH STANDARD DEVIATION OF    182.27

DELA                  171 5ELCID0023 ANTES **** NOCHE EN BURGOS DEL ENTRO SU CARTA,
                      214 5ELCID0027 QUE PERDERIE LOS AUERES & MAS LOS OIOS **** CARA,
                      409 5ELCID0051 PARTIOS **** PUERTA, POR BURGOS AGUIJAUA,
                     1288 5ELCID0165 NON LES DIESSE MYO %ID **** GANAN%IA UN DINERO MALO.
                     1560 5ELCID0200 GRADO EXIR **** POSADA & ESPIDIOS DE AMOS.
                     2731 5ELCID0345 DEL AGUA FEZIST VINO & **** PIEDRA PAN,
                     2910 5ELCID0367 SALIERON **** EGLESIA, YA QUIEREN CAUALGAR.
                     2981 5ELCID0375 ASIS PARTEN VNOS DOTROS COMMO LA V@A **** CARNE.
                     4727 5ELCID0599 BUELTOS SON CON ELLOS POR MEDIO **** LA@A.
                     5066 5ELCID0640 CON LOS **** FRONTERA QUE UOS AIUDARAN,
                     6694 5ELCID0854 NOS PAGADOS FINCADOS, SE@OR, **** TU PART.
                     7052 5ELCID0901 MIENTRA QUE SEA EL PUEBLO DE MOROS & **** YENTE CHRISTIANA,
                     7192 5ELCID0921 BESO LE LA BOCA & LOS OIOS **** CARA.
                     7839 5ELCID1003 ALFONDON **** CUESTA, %ERCA ES DE LA@O,
                     7938 5ELCID1014 DE FUERA **** TIENDA VN SALTO DAUA,
                     8664 5ELCID1100 TRASNOCHARON DE NOCH, AL ALUA **** MAN
                     8779 5ELCID1116 DESPUES QUE NOS PARTIEMOS **** LINPIA CHRISTIANDAD,
                     9422 5ELCID1198 AL SABOR **** GANAN%IA NON LO QUIERE DETARDAR,
                     9433 5ELCID1199 GRANDES YENTES SE LE ACOIEN **** BUENA CHRISTIANDAD.
                     9640 5ELCID1225 APRES **** VERTA OUIERON LA BATALLA,
                     9649 5ELCID1226 ARRANCOLOS MYO %ID EL **** LUENGA BARBA.
                    10936 5ELCID1384 ESPIDIOS MYNAYA & VASSE **** CORT.
                    11975 5ELCID1518 SONRRISANDO SE **** BOCA, HYUALO ABRA%AR,
                    12044 5ELCID1527 SORRISOS **** BOCA MINAYA ALBARFANEZ:
                    13671 5ELCID1732 ALI PRE%IO ABAUIECA **** CABE%A FASTA ACABO.
                    17696 5ELCID2239 ALA PUERTA **** ECLEGIA SEDIELLOS SPERANDO;
                    17708 5ELCID2241 AL SALIR **** ECCLEGIA CAUALGARON TAN PRIUADO,
                    18048 5ELCID2283 EN GRANT MIEDO SE VIERON POR MEDIO **** CORT;
                    18091 5ELCID2289 DIZIENDO **** BOCA: NON VERE CARRION
                    19349 5ELCID2451 DELOS COLPES **** LAN%A NON AUIE RECABDO;
                    20807 5ELCID2642 CUEMO LA V@A **** CARNE ELLOS PARTIDOS SON;
                    21644 5ELCID2751 E ALAS AUES DEL MONTE & ALAS BESTIAS **** FIERA GUISA.
                    23008 5ELCID2931 ASSI COMMO ENTRARON POR MEDIO **** CORT,
                    24964 5ELCID3179 MARAUILLAN SE DELLAS TODAS LOS OMNES BUENOS **** CORT.
                    25597 5ELCID3259 O EN ALGUNA RAZON? AQUI LO MEIORARE A JUUIZYO **** CORT.
                    26418 5ELCID3370 AL PARTIR **** LID POR TU BOCA LO DIRAS,
                    28124 5ELCID3591 FEUOS **** OTRA PART LOS YFANTES DE CARRION,
                    28624 5ELCID3655 RAXOL LOS PELOS **** CABE%A, BIEN ALA CARNE LEGAUA;
                    28840 5ELCID3684 **** OTRA PART VNA BRA%A GELA ECHO,
                    28852 5ELCID3685 CON EL DIO VNA TUERTA, **** SIELLA LO ENCAMO,
                    28858 5ELCID3686 AL TIRAR **** LAN%A EN TIERRA LO ECHO,
           WORD #1360 OCCURS  41 TIMES.
              INDEX OF DIVERSIFICATION =    716.17 WITH STANDARD DEVIATION OF    803.70

DELAND               5076 5ELCID0641 PRENDET MELO AUIDA, ADUZID MELO ******;
           WORD #1361 OCCURS   1 TIMES.

DELANT               4790 5ELCID0607 DEXANDO UAN LOS ******, POR EL CASTIELLO SE TORNAUAN,
                     5674 5ELCID0715 ENBRA%AN LOS ESCUDOS ****** LOS CORA%ONES,
                     6724 5ELCID0858 PASO SALON AYUSO, AGUIJO CABA ******,
                     6755 5ELCID0862 AGUIJO MYO %ID, YUAS CABA ******,
                     6799 5ELCID0868 LA TER%ERA TERUEL, QUE ESTAUA ******;
                     7979 5ELCID1019 ADUZEN LE LOS COMERES, ****** GELOS PARAUAN;
                     8248 5ELCID1050 E TIENEN GELO ****** & DIERON GELO PRIUADO.
                     8876 5ELCID1130 VOS CON LOS OTROS FIRADES LOS ******.
                    11268 5ELCID1425 E ALAS OTRAS DUE@AS QUE LAS SIRUEN ******,
                    11519 5ELCID1458 TU, MU@O GUSTIOZ & PERO VERMUEZ ******,
                    11597 5ELCID1469 CON GRAND ONDRA ADUZID MELAS ******.
                    11941 5ELCID1513 LOS QUE YUAN MESURANDO & LEGANDO ******
                    12883 5ELCID1634 TODO EL BIEN QUE YO HE, TODO LO TENGO ******:
                    13055 5ELCID1655 CRE%EM EL CORACON POR QUE ESTADES ******,
                    13145 5ELCID1666 AQUELOS ATAMORES AUOS LOS PONDRAN ****** & VEREDES QUANLES SON,
                    13277 5ELCID1683 EL SELO VIO CON LOS OIOS, CUENTAN GELO ******,
                    13884 5ELCID1759 ****** EL CAMPEADOR LOS YNOIOS FINCARON:
                    15462 5ELCID1959 AL REY ONDRADO ****** LE ECHARON LAS CARTAS;
                    16892 5ELCID2137 ASSI COMMO YO LAS PRENDO DAQUENT, COMMO SI FOSSE ******,
                    17509 5ELCID2215 AEL & EASSU MUGIER ****** SELE OMILLARON,
                    17624 5ELCID2230 AFEUOS ****** MINAYA, AMOS SODES HERMANOS.
                    18637 5ELCID2358 HYO CON LOS MYOS FERIR QUIERO ******,
                    18718 5ELCID2369 PARAUAS ****** AL CAMPEADOR, SIEMPRE CON LA BUEN AUZE:
                    18766 5ELCID2374 EA ESTAS FERIDAS YO QUIERO YR ******;
```

WORD C# PREFIX CONTEXT

DELANT (CON'T)

20451 5ELCID2596 ****** SODES AMOS, SE@ORA & SE@OR.
23025 5ELCID2934 ****** EL REY FINCO LOS YNOIOS AQUEL MU@O GUSTIOZ,
26074 5ELCID3324 ****** MYO %ID & DELANTE TODOS OVISTE TE DE ALABAR
27244 5ELCID3482 QUE FAGAN ESTA LID ****** ESTANDO YO;
28321 5ELCID3615 ABRA%AN LOS ESCUDOS ****** LOS CORA%ONES,
WORD #1362 OCCURS 29 TIMES.
INDEX OF DIVERSIFICATION = 839.39 WITH STANDARD DEVIATION OF 826.52

DELANTE
6689 5ELCID0853 VASTE, MYO %ID; NUESTRAS ORA%IONES UAYANTE *******
9277 5ELCID1180 ******* VEYEN SO DUELO, NON SE PUEDEN HUUIAR,
12425 5ELCID1577 ******* SU MUGIER & DE SUS FIJAS QUERIE TENER LAS ARMAS.
26078 5ELCID3324 DELANT MYO %ID & ******* TODOS OVISTE TE DE ALABAR
WORD #1363 OCCURS 4 TIMES.

DELANTEL
2591 5ELCID0327 ECHOS DO@A XIMENA EN LOS GRADOS ******** ALTAR,
WORD #1364 OCCURS 1 TIMES.

DELAS
137 5ELCID0019 ***** SUS BOCAS TODOS DIZIAN UNA RAZON:
368 5ELCID0046 E DEMAS LOS OIOS ***** CARAS.
1328 5ELCID0170 ALCARGAR ***** ARCHAS VERIEDES GOZO TANTO:
10597 5ELCID1343 E PLAZEM ***** NUEUAS QUE FAZE EL CAMPEADOR;
13230 5ELCID1677 SACAN LOS ***** HUERTAS MUCHO AFEA GUISA,
14044 5ELCID1779 LOS MOROS ***** TIERRAS GANADO SEAN Y ALGO;
14102 5ELCID1785 LA TIENDA DEL REY DE MARRUECOS, QUE ***** OTRAS ES CABO,
16736 5ELCID2119 TODOS SON PAGADOS ***** VISTAS QUANTOS QUE Y SON.
17083 5ELCID2163 HE ***** FIJAS DE MYO %ID, DE DON ELUIRA & DO@A SOL.
17286 5ELCID2186 MUCHOS DIAS UOS VEAMOS CON LOS OIOS ***** CARAS
18282 5ELCID2313 CINQUAENTA MILL TIENDAS FINCADAS HA ***** CABDALES;
18988 5ELCID2402 LOS DE MYO %ID ALOS DE BUCAR ***** TIENDAS LOS SACAN.
18994 5ELCID2403 SACAN LOS ***** TIENDAS, CAEN LOS EN ALCAZ;
20571 5ELCID2612 ESPIENDOS ***** DUE@AS & DE TODAS SUS COMPA@AS.
22953 5ELCID2924 E ***** ASTURIAS BIEN A SAN %ALUADOR,
28560 5ELCID3646 MARTIN ANTOLINEZ & DIEGO GONZALEZ FIRIERON SE ***** LAN%AS,
WORD #1365 OCCURS 16 TIMES.
INDEX OF DIVERSIFICATION = 1893.87 WITH STANDARD DEVIATION OF 2518.78

DELENT
12625 5ELCID1601 TODAS LAS SUS MESNADAS EN GRANT ****** ESTAUAN,
WORD #1366 OCCURS 1 TIMES.

DELIBRANDO
5980 5ELCID0758 ALOS QUE ALCAN%A VALOS **********.
WORD #1367 OCCURS 1 TIMES.

DELIBRAR
25953 5ELCID3307 DETIENES LE LA LENGUA, NON PUEDE ********,
WORD #1368 OCCURS 1 TIMES.

DELI%IO
6668 5ELCID0850 QUI A BUEN SE@OR SIRUE, SIEMPRE BIUE EN *******.
12920 5ELCID1639 VENIDOM ES ******* DE TIERRAS DALENT MAR,
WORD #1369 OCCURS 2 TIMES.

DELI@ADAS
15648 5ELCID1984 SUELTAN LAS RIENDAS, ALAS VISTAS SEUAN A *********.
WORD #1370 OCCURS 1 TIMES.

DELLA
3901 5ELCID0495 PAGAR SE YA ***** ALFONSSO EL CASTELLANO.
15506 5ELCID1965 ***** PART & DELLA PORA LAS VISTAS SE ADOBAUAN;
15509 5ELCID1965 DELLA PART & ***** PORA LAS VISTAS SE ADOBAUAN;
16390 5ELCID2079 ***** & DELLA PARTE, QUANTOS QUE AQUI SON,
16392 5ELCID2079 DELLA & ***** PARTE, QUANTOS QUE AQUI SON,
19257 5ELCID2437 COFIA SOBRE LOS PELOS FRONZIDA ***** YA QUANTO.
24637 5ELCID3139 ***** & DELLA PART EN PAZ SEAMOS OY.
24639 5ELCID3139 DELLA & ***** PART EN PAZ SEAMOS OY.
27109 5ELCID3464 NON DIGA NINGUNO ***** MAS VNA ENTEN%ION.
WORD #1371 OCCURS 9 TIMES.
INDEX OF DIVERSIFICATION = 2900.00 WITH STANDARD DEVIATION OF 3988.90

DELLANT
24924 5ELCID3174 DAR GELAS QUEREMOS ******* ESTANDO UOS.
WORD #1372 OCCURS 1 TIMES.

DELLAS
2037 5ELCID0257 ****** & DE MI MUGIER FAGADES TODO RECABDO.
10929 5ELCID1383 DESI ADELANT PIENSSE ****** EL CAMPEADOR.
11721 5ELCID1486 E FFATA EN VALEN%IA ****** NON UOS PARTADES.
13940 5ELCID1766 ACADA VNA ****** DO LES CC MARCOS DE PLATA,
24918 5ELCID3173 QUANDO LAS DEMANDA & ****** HA SABOR,
24959 5ELCID3179 MARAUILLAN SE ****** TODAS LOS OMNES BUENOS DELA CORT.
25528 5ELCID3251 SOS OMNES LAS TIENEN & ****** PENSSARAN.
WORD #1373 OCCURS 7 TIMES.
INDEX OF DIVERSIFICATION = 3914.17 WITH STANDARD DEVIATION OF 4764.23

DELLO
3072 5ELCID0386 BIEN SEPA EL ABBAT QUE BUEN GALARDON ***** PRENDRA.
11174 5ELCID1413 HYDOS SON LOS CAUALLEROS & ***** PENSSARAN,
25266 5ELCID3216 DESTOS AUERES QUE UOS DI YO, SIMELOS DADES, O DEDES ***** RA%ON.
WORD #1374 OCCURS 3 TIMES.

DELLOS
864 5ELCID0111 RETOUO ****** QUANTO QUE FUE ALGO;
4032 5ELCID0513 A CADA VNO ****** CAEN C MARCHOS DE PLATA,

WORD C# PREFIX CONTEXT

DELLOS (CON'T)

```
                4204 5ELCID0535 POR QUE LO PRIS ****** QUE DE MI NON DIGAN MAL.
                4917 5ELCID0622 POSAREMOS EN SUS CASAS & ****** NOS SERUIREMOS.
                8919 5ELCID1136 QUIS CADA VNO ****** BIEN SABE LO QUE HA DE FAR.
               13237 5ELCID1678 QUINIENTOS MATARON ****** CONPLIDOS ENES DIA.
               16635 5ELCID2107 LO QUE UOS PLOGIERE, ****** FET, CAMPEADOR.
               16780 5ELCID2124 OY DE MAS SABED QUE FER ******, CAMPEADOR.
               16895 5ELCID2138 SED PADRINO ****** ATOD EL VELAR;
               17912 5ELCID2266 GRANT BIEN DIZEN ******, CA SERA AGUISADO.
               18628 5ELCID2357 CURIELOS QUI QUIER, CA ****** POCO MINCAL.
               19575 5ELCID2480 MANDADOS BUENOS YRAN ****** A CARRION,
               22558 5ELCID2873 DALLENT SE ESPIDIERON ******, PIENSSAN SE DE TORNAR,
               28013 5ELCID3575 QUE FIEL SEADES OY ****** & DE NOS;
               28095 5ELCID3587 EDERREDOR ****** MUCHOS BUENOS VARONES.
               28117 5ELCID3590 QUE CADA VNO ****** BIEN FOS FERIR EL SO.
               28313 5ELCID3614 CADA VNO ****** MIENTES TIENE AL SO.
               28352 5ELCID3620 CADA VNO ****** MIENTES TIENE ALSO;
         WORD #1375 OCCURS  18 TIMES.
            INDEX OF DIVERSIFICATION =  1615.94 WITH STANDARD DEVIATION OF  1828.86

DELO             576 5ELCID0073 CA ACUSADO SERE **** QUE UOS HE SERUIDO,
                4089 5ELCID0520 AVN **** QUE DIESSEN CUIESSEN GRAND GANAN%IA.
                4669 5ELCID0592 ALSABOR DEL PRENDER **** AL NON PIENSSAN NADA,
                7634 5ELCID0978 **** SO NON LIEUO NADA, DEXEM YR EN PAZ.
                8443 5ELCID1073 DE LO UUESTRO, O **** MYO LEUAREDES ALGO.
               10286 5ELCID1302 PLOGO A ALBARFANEZ **** QUE DIXO DON RODRIGO.
               12031 5ELCID1525 EN PAZ O EN GERRA **** NUESTRO ABRA;
               12263 5ELCID1557 LOS SOS DESPENDIE EL MORO, QUE **** SO NON TOMAUA NADA.
               12308 5ELCID1563 CA **** QUE MAS AMAUA YAL VIENE EL MANDADO.
               13664 5ELCID1731 MUCHO ERA ALEGRE **** QUE AN CA%ADO.
               14263 5ELCID1805 **** QUE AUOS CAYO VOS NON GRADE%EDES NADA;
               17741 5ELCID2245 MYO %ID **** QUE VEYE MUCHO ERA PAGADO:
               19264 5ELCID2438 ALGO VIE MYO %ID **** QUE ERA PAGADO,
               19948 5ELCID2531 PENSAD **** OTRO, QUE LO NUESTRO TENEMOS LO EN SALUO.
               20230 5ELCID2568 DIXO EL CAMPEADOR: DARUOS HE MYS FIJAS & ALGO **** MYO;
               20777 5ELCID2639 **** QUE OUIEREN HUEBOS SIRUAN LAS ASO SABOR,
               21036 5ELCID2674 **** QUE EL MORO DIXO ALOS YFANTES NON PLAZE:
               23428 5ELCID2984 QUE NON FALIESSEN **** QUE EN REY AUYE MANDADO.
               23790 5ELCID3031 **** QUE AUOS PESA AMI DUELE EL CORA%ON;
               25502 5ELCID3248 ENPRESTAN LES **** AGENO, QUE NON LES CUMPLE LO SUYO.
               26876 5ELCID3433 DEZIR QUERRIA YA QUANTO **** MYO.
               27417 5ELCID3503 **** AL TANTO PRISO QUANT OUO SABOR.
               27965 5ELCID3569 **** QUE AUIEN FECHO MUCHO REPISOS SON;
               29036 5ELCID3709 **** QUE AN PRESO MUCHO AN MAL SABOR;
         WORD #1376 OCCURS  24 TIMES.
            INDEX OF DIVERSIFICATION =  1236.39 WITH STANDARD DEVIATION OF  1030.08

DELOS              1 5ELCID0001 ***** SOS OIOS TAN FUERTE MIENTRE LORANDO,
                 131 5ELCID0018 PLORANDO ***** OIOS, TANTO AUYEN EL DOLOR.
                 793 5ELCID0101 EN CUENTA DE SUS AUERES, ***** QUE AUIEN GANADOS.
                1873 5ELCID0238 REZAUA LOS MATINES ABUELTA ***** ALBORES.
                2103 5ELCID0265 LORAUA ***** OIOS, QUISOL BESAR LAS MANOS:
                2197 5ELCID0277 LORA ***** OIOS, TAN FUERTE MIENTRE SOSPIRA:
                2968 5ELCID0374 LORANDO ***** OIOS, QUE NON VIESTES ATAL,
                3736 5ELCID0472 QUINZE MOROS MATAUA ***** QUE ALCAN%AUA.
                5504 5ELCID0694 VIERON LO LAS AROBDAS ***** MOROS, AL ALMOFALLA SEUAN TORNAR.
                5539 5ELCID0698 DE PARTE ***** MOROS DOS SE@AS HA CABDALES,
                5682 5ELCID0716 ABAXAN LAS LAN%AS A BUESTAS ***** PENDONES,
                6248 5ELCID0796 ***** MORISCOS, QUANDO SON LEGADOS, FFALLARON DX CAUALLOS.
                6412 5ELCID0818 SE@AS ESPADAS ***** ARZONES COLGADAS.
                7836 5ELCID1002 VIERON LA CUESTA YUSO LA FUER%A ***** FRANCOS;
                9295 5ELCID1182 CON EL ***** MONTES CLAROS AUYEN GUERRA TAN GRAND,
                9870 5ELCID1252 QUE NINGUN OMNE ***** SOS QUES LE NON SPIDIES, ONDL BESAS
                                LA MANO,
                9915 5ELCID1258 ***** QUE SON AQUI & COMIGO GANARON ALGO;
               10873 5ELCID1376 MYO %ID ES DE BIUAR & NOS ***** CONDES DE CARRION.
               11243 5ELCID1423 ***** OTROS QUINIENTOS DEZIR UOS HE QUE FAZE:
               11276 5ELCID1427 ***** MEIORES GUARIMIENTOS QUE EN BURGOS PUDO FALAR,
               11486 5ELCID1453 DIREUOS ***** CAUALLEROS QUE LEUARON EL MENSSAIE:
               14057 5ELCID1781 ***** BUENOS & OTORGADOS CAYERON LE MILL & D CAUALLOS;
               14565 5ELCID1842 FIRIERON SE A TIERRA, DE%ENDIERON ***** CAUALOS,
               14865 5ELCID1879 ***** YFFANTES DE CARRION YO UOS QUIERO CONTAR,
               15954 5ELCID2023 LORANDO ***** OIOS, TANTO AUIE EL GOZO MAYOR;
               16727 5ELCID2118 MYO %ID ***** CAUALLOS LX DIO EN DON.
               17078 5ELCID2162 SEREMOS ALAS BODAS ***** YFANTES DE CARRION
               17797 5ELCID2252 HYA %ERCA ***** XV DIAS YAS VAN LOS FIJOS DALGO.
               18532 5ELCID2345 EN LA VESTE ***** MOROS LOS ATAMORES SONANDO;
               19347 5ELCID2451 ***** COLPES DELA LAN%A NON AUIE RECABDO;
               21118 5ELCID2683 POCO PRE%IO LAS NUEUAS ***** DE CARRION.
               22084 5ELCID2810 ENTRE NOCH & DIA SALIERON ***** MONTES;
               22415 5ELCID2855 AFFE DIOS ***** %IELOS QUE UOS DE DENT BUEN GALARDON
               22482 5ELCID2863 LORAUAN ***** OIOS LAS DUE@AS & ALBARFANEZ,
               24095 5ELCID3072 CON ESTOS CUNPLANSSE %IENTO ***** BUENOS QUE Y SON.
               25563 5ELCID3256 ***** YFANTES DE CARRION QUEM DESONDRARON TAN MAL,
               26053 5ELCID3321 ***** PRIMEROS COLPES OF LE DE ARRANCAR;
               26953 5ELCID3443 DE NATURA SODES ***** DE VANIGOMEZ,
```

WORD C# PREFIX CONTEXT

DELOS (CON'T)

28C85 5ELCID3585 EMANO PRENDEN LAS ASTAS ***** FIERROS TAIADORES,
WORD #1377 OCCURS 39 TIMES.
INDEX OF DIVERSIFICATION = 738.05 WITH STANDARD DEVIATION OF 593.97

DEM 16793 5ELCID2126 DIOS QUE ESTA EN %IELC *** DENT BUEN GALARDON.
WORD #1378 OCCURS 1 TIMES.

DEMANDA 24855 5ELCID3165 QUANDO DESONDRA DESUS FIJAS NO NOS ******* OY;
24916 5ELCID3173 QUANDO LAS ******* & DELLAS HA SABOR,
25235 5ELCID3213 ALO QUE ******* EL %ID CUEL RECUDADES VOS.
25367 5ELCID3230 QUE DERECHO ******* EL %ID CAMPEADOR.
WORD #1379 OCCURS 4 TIMES.

DEMANDAN 2314 5ELCID0292 TODOS ******** POR MIO %ID EL CAMPEADOR;
26663 5ELCID3405 QUANDO MELAS ******** DE NAUARRA & DE ARAGON.
WORD #1380 OCCURS 2 TIMES.

DEMANDANDO 10207 5ELCID1292 LAS PROUEZAS DE MYO %ID ANDAUALAS **********,
WORD #1381 OCCURS 1 TIMES.

DEMANDAR 7540 5ELCID0966 MAS QUANDO EL MELO BUSCA, YR GELO HE YO ********.
WORD #1382 OCCURS 1 TIMES.

DEMANDASSE 25217 5ELCID3211 QUE AL NO NOS **********, QUE AQUI FINCO LA BOZ. . .
WORD #1383 OCCURS 1 TIMES.

DEMANDAUA 768 5ELCID0097 POR RACHEL & VIDAS APRIESSA *********.
780 5ELCID0099 POR RACHEL & VIDAS APRIESSA *********.
WORD #1384 OCCURS 2 TIMES.

DEMANDE 24672 5ELCID3143 AGORA ******* MYO %ID EL CAMPEADOR:
WORD #1385 OCCURS 1 TIMES.

DEMANDEDES 14926 5ELCID1887 QUE NOS ********** FIJAS DEL CAMPEADOR;
WORD #1386 OCCURS 1 TIMES.

DEMANDEMOS 14887 5ELCID1882 ********** SUS FIJAS PORA CON ELLAS CASAR;
WORD #1387 OCCURS 1 TIMES.

DEMANDO 10347 5ELCID1311 ******* POR ALFONSSO, DE LO PODRIE FALLAR.
18212 5ELCID2304 MYO %ID POR SOS YERNOS ******* & NOLOS FALLO;
24715 5ELCID3148 ESTO LES ******* AYFANTES DE CARRION:
26212 5ELCID3342 ******* POR SUS YERNOS, NINGUNO NON FALLO
WORD #1388 OCCURS 4 TIMES.

DEMAS 218 5ELCID0028 E AUN ***** LOS CUERPOS & LAS ALMAS.
365 5ELCID0046 E ***** LOS OIOS DELAS CARAS.
16094 5ELCID2041 TODOS LOS ***** DESTO AUIEN SABOR;
27799 5ELCID3548 ***** SOBRE TODOS YES EL REY DON ALFONSSO,
WORD #1389 OCCURS 4 TIMES.

DEMENBRADO 801 5ELCID0102 LEGO MARTIN ATOLINEZ AGUISA **********:
WORD #1390 OCCURS 1 TIMES.

DEMI 1603 5ELCID0205 AUN VEA EL DIA QUE **** AYADES ALGO
WORD #1391 OCCURS 1 TIMES.

DEMOS 1499 5ELCID0192 ***** LE BUEN DON, CA EL NO LO HA BUSCADO.
4592 5ELCID0584 ***** SALTO A EL & FEREMOS GRANT GANA%IA,
24865 5ELCID3167 ***** LE SUS ESPADAS, QUANDO ASSI FINCA LA BOZ,
WORD #1392 OCCURS 3 TIMES.

DEMOSTRARON 28245 5ELCID3606 BIEN GELO *********** ATODOS VJ COMMO SON,
WORD #1393 OCCURS 1 TIMES.

DEMUESTRAN 21273 5ELCID2703 CON SUS MUGIERES EN BRA%OS ********** LES AMOR;
WORD #1394 OCCURS 1 TIMES.

DEMY 16933 5ELCID2143 DESTAS VISTAS QUE OUIEMOS, **** TOMEDES ALGO.
WORD #1395 OCCURS 1 TIMES.

DEN 7687 5ELCID0984 QUE A MENOS DE BATALLA NOS PUEDEN *** QUITAR.
11884 5ELCID1507 BIEN SALIERON *** %IENTO QUE NON PARE%EN MAL,
23282 5ELCID2966 E COMMO *** DERECHO A MYO %ID EL CAMPEADOR,
24793 5ELCID3158 *** ME MIS ESPADAS QUANDO MYOS YERNOS NON SON.
25174 5ELCID3206 *** ME MIS AUERES, QUANDO MYOS YERNOS NON SON.
26750 5ELCID3416 ESSORA DIXO EL REY: DIOS UOS DE *** BUEN GALARDON
WORD #1396 OCCURS 6 TIMES.
INDEX OF DIVERSIFICATION = 3811.60 WITH STANDARD DEVIATION OF 4465.47

DEND 21801 5ELCID2773 ELLOS NOL VIEN NI **** SABIEN RA%ION;
WORD #1397 OCCURS 1 TIMES.

DENLES 10921 5ELCID1382 FATA DENTRO EN MEDINA ****** QUANTO HUEBOS LES FUER,
WORD #1398 OCCURS 1 TIMES.

WORD C# PREFIX CONTEXT

DENT
4611 5ELCID0585 ANTES QUEL PRENDAN LOS DE TERUEL, SI NON NON NOS DARAN **** NADA;
7419 5ELCID0952 **** CORRE MYO %ID A HUESCA & A MONT ALUAN;
8146 5ELCID1038 TANTO QUANTO YO BIUA, SERE **** MARAUILLADO.
14128 5ELCID1788 E NON LA TOLLIESSE **** CHRISTIANO:
15026 5ELCID1899 E DE MI ABRA PERDON; VINIESSEM A VISTAS, SI OUIESSE **** SABOR.
16794 5ELCID2126 DIOS QUE ESTA EN %IELO DEM **** BUEN GALARDON.
21867 5ELCID2782 ADIOS PLEGA & A SANTA MARIA QUE **** PRENDAN ELLOS MAL GALARDON
22068 5ELCID2808 EL CAUALLO PRISO POR LA RIENDA & LUEGO **** LAS PARTIO,
22420 5ELCID2855 AFFE DIOS DELOS %IELOS QUE UOS DE **** BUEN GALARDON
22634 5ELCID2884 **** PORA VALEN%IA ADELINECHOS VAN.
WORD #1399 OCCURS 10 TIMES.
INDEX OF DIVERSIFICATION = 2001.56 WITH STANDARD DEVIATION OF 2178.97

DENTRO
285 5ELCID0036 LOS DE ****** NON LES QUERIEN TORNAR PALABRA.
490 5ELCID0062 VEDADA LAN CONPRA ****** EN BURGOS LA CASA,
2697 5ELCID0341 SALUEST ****** EN ROMA AL SE@OR SAN SABASTIAN,
4907 5ELCID0621 COIAMOS LOS DE ******, CA EL SENORIO TENEMOS,
6291 5ELCID0801 ASOS CASTIELLOS ALOS MOROS ****** LOS AN TORNADOS,
7500 5ELCID0962 ****** EN MI CORT TUERTO ME TOUO GRAND:
8637 5ELCID1097 ****** EN VALEN%IA NON ES POCO EL MIEDO.
9154 5ELCID1165 MALES PESA EN XATIUA & ****** EN GUIERA,
9653 5ELCID1227 FATA ****** EN XATIUA DURO EL ARRANCADA,
10918 5ELCID1382 FATA ****** EN MEDINA DENLES QUANTO HUEBOS LES FUER,
12291 5ELCID1561 ****** A VALEN%IA LIEUAN LE EL MANDADO.
15649 5ELCID1985 ****** EN VALLEN%IA MYO %ID EL CAMPEADOR
15791 5ELCID2003 ****** ES SU MUGIER & SUS FIJAS AMAS ADOS,
19102 5ELCID2416 NON TE IUNTARAS COMIGO FATA ****** EN LA MAR.
19708 5ELCID2499 ALA ****** EN MARRUECOS, OLAS MEZQUITAS SON,
20643 5ELCID2620 MANDOT QUE VAYAS CON ELLAS FATA ****** EN CARRION,
21893 5ELCID2785 PARTIERON SE LE LAS TELLAS DE ****** DE LOS CORA%ONES,
22137 5ELCID2818 EN SANTESTEUAN ****** LAS METIO,
22896 5ELCID2916 CA TAN GRANT ES LA RENCURA ****** EN MI CORA%ON.
22960 5ELCID2925 FASTA ****** EN SANTI YAGUO DE TODO ES SE@OR,
23263 5ELCID2963 PREGONARAN MI CORT PORA ****** EN TOLLEDO,
25347 5ELCID3227 QUE AQUI LO ENTERGEDES ****** EN LA CORT.
27228 5ELCID3480 AQUI LES PONGO PLAZO DE ****** EN MI CORT,
WORD #1400 OCCURS 23 TIMES.
INDEX OF DIVERSIFICATION = 1223.68 WITH STANDARD DEVIATION OF 954.88

DEPARTI%ION
20726 5ELCID2631 GRANDES FUERON LOS DUELOS ALA ************.
WORD #1401 OCCURS 1 TIMES.

DEPARTIRAN
21465 5ELCID2729 MOROS & CHRISTIANOS ********** DESTA RAZON,
WORD #1402 OCCURS 1 TIMES.

DEPORTAR
11948 5ELCID1514 LUEGO TOMAN ARMAS & TOMANSE A ********,
21328 5ELCID2711 ******** SE QUIEREN CON ELLAS ATODO SU SABOR.
WORD #1403 OCCURS 2 TIMES.

DEPRUNAR
11778 5ELCID1493 POR EL VAL DE ARBUXEDO PIENSSAN A ********.
WORD #1404 OCCURS 1 TIMES.

DERANCHE
5581 5ELCID0703 NON ******** NINGUNO FATA QUE YO LO MANDE.
WORD #1405 OCCURS 1 TIMES.

DERECHA
3812 5ELCID0482 ******* VIENE LA SE@A DE MINAYA;
WORD #1406 OCCURS 1 TIMES.

DERECHAS
17611 5ELCID2228 LEUANTAN SE ******** & METIOGELAS EN MANO.
WORD #1407 OCCURS 1 TIMES.

DERECHO
5084 5ELCID0642 POR QUE SEME ENTRO EN MI TIERRA ******* ME AURA ADAR.
19620 5ELCID2486 QUE TODOS PRISIESSEN SO ******* CONTADO,
20977 5ELCID2665 NUNQUA AURIE ******* DE NOS EL %ID CAMPEADOR.
22885 5ELCID2915 COMMO AYA ******* DE YFANTES DE CARRION,
23171 5ELCID2952 QUE AYA MYO %ID ******* DE YFANTES DE CARRION.
23283 5ELCID2966 E COMMO DEN ******* A MYO %ID EL CAMPEADOR,
23491 5ELCID2992 DARLEDES *******, CA RENCURA HA DE UOS.
24586 5ELCID3133 QUE RE%IBA ******* DE YFANTES DE CARRION.
24631 5ELCID3138 POR ESCOGER EL *******, CA TUERTO NON MANDO YO.
24665 5ELCID3142 CON EL QUE TOUIERE ******* YO DESSA PART ME SO.
24886 5ELCID3169 HYA MAS NON AURA ******* DE NOS EL %ID CANPEADOR.
25366 5ELCID3230 QUE ******* DEMANDA EL %ID CAMPEADOR.
25737 5ELCID3278 ******* FIZIERON POR QUE LAS HAN DEXADAS.
25894 5ELCID3299 POR QUE LAS DEXAMOS ******* FIZIEMOS NOS;
27810 5ELCID3549 POR QUERER EL ******* & NON CONSENTIR EL TUERTO.
28145 5ELCID3593 EL REY DIOLES FIELES POR DEZIR EL ******* & AL NON,
28200 5ELCID3600 AUED UUESTRO *******, TUERTO NON QUERADES VOS,
WORD #1408 OCCURS 17 TIMES.
INDEX OF DIVERSIFICATION = 1443.75 WITH STANDARD DEVIATION OF 3549.16

DERECHOS
24148 5ELCID3079 POR DE MANDAR MYOS ******** & DEZIR MI RAZON:
WORD #1409 OCCURS 1 TIMES.

WORD C# PREFIX CONTEXT

```
DERREDOR            473 5ELCID0060 ******** DEL VNA BUE@A CONPA@A.
                   3697 5ELCID0466 E ESSOS GA@ADOS QUANTOS EN ******** ANDAN.
                   4396 5ELCID0560 ******** DEL OTERO, BIEN %ERCA DEL AGUA,
                   5044 5ELCID0637 TRES REYES VEO DE MOROS ******** DE MI ESTAR,
                   7305 5ELCID0937 E A ******** TODO LO VA PREANDO.
                  16077 5ELCID2038 E A ESTAS MESNADAS QUE ESTAN A ********.
                  18889 5ELCID2390 LOS MOROS SON MUCHOS, ******** LE %ERCAUAN,
                  26211 5ELCID3341 ASOS VASSALOS VIOLOS A ********;
         WORD #1410 OCCURS    8 TIMES.
            INDEX OF DIVERSIFICATION =  3675.86 WITH STANDARD DEVIATION OF  3168.78

DES                8504 5ELCID1081 VNA *** LEATAN%A CA NON LA FIZO ALGUANDRE.
                  12534 5ELCID1591 *** DIA SE PRE%IO BAUIECA EN QUANT GRANT FUE ESPA@A.
                  17977 5ELCID2275 QUES PAGE *** CASAMIENTO MYO %ID O EL QUE LO ALGO
         WORD #1411 OCCURS    3 TIMES.

DESA              13492 5ELCID1710 DIXO EL CAMPEADOR: **** QUI UOS SEAN MANDADAS.
         WORD #1412 OCCURS    1 TIMES.

DESAFIE            7527 5ELCID0965 NON LO *******, NIL TORNE ENEMISTAD,
         WORD #1413 OCCURS    1 TIMES.

DESARMADO         13764 5ELCID1744 FRONZIDA TRAHE LA CARA, QUE ERA *********,
         WORD #1414 OCCURS    1 TIMES.

DESATO            26135 5ELCID3331 QUANDO DURMIE MYO %ID & EL LEON SE ******?
         WORD #1415 OCCURS    1 TIMES.

DESATOS           18038 5ELCID2282 SALIOS DE LA RED & ******* EL LEON.
         WORD #1416 OCCURS    1 TIMES.

DESCABE%EMOS       4900 5ELCID0620 QUE LOS ************ NADA NON GANAREMOS;
         WORD #1417 OCCURS    1 TIMES.

DESCALGAUA        12550 5ELCID1592 EN CABO DEL COSSO MYO %ID **********,
         WORD #1418 OCCURS    1 TIMES.

DESCAUALGA          419 5ELCID0052 LEGO A SANTA MARIA, LUEGO **********,
                  22978 5ELCID2927 ASSI COMMO ********** AQUEL MU@O GUSTIOZ
                  24345 5ELCID3104 ALA PUERTA DE FUERA ********** A SABOR;
         WORD #1419 OCCURS    3 TIMES.

DESCAUALGADO      13872 5ELCID1757 QUANDOL VIERON DE PIE, QUE ERA ************,
         WORD #1420 OCCURS    1 TIMES.

DESCAUALGAUA        451 5ELCID0057 FINCAUA LA TIENDA & LUEGO ************.
         WORD #1421 OCCURS    1 TIMES.

DESCAUALGO        21836 5ELCID2778 LAMANDO: PRIMAS, PRIMAS  LUEGO **********,
         WORD #1422 OCCURS    1 TIMES.

DESCREYDAS        12859 5ELCID1631 FINCARON LAS TIENDAS, & POSAN LAS YENTES **********.
         WORD #1423 OCCURS    1 TIMES.

DESCUBRADES         835 5ELCID0107 QUE NON ME *********** A MOROS NIN A CHRISTIANOS;
         WORD #1424 OCCURS    1 TIMES.

DESCUBRI          26071 5ELCID3323 FASTA ESTE DIA NOLO ******** A NADI;
         WORD #1425 OCCURS    1 TIMES.

DESCUBRIESTES     25601 5ELCID3260  A QUEM ************* LAS TELAS DEL CORA%ON?
         WORD #1426 OCCURS    1 TIMES.

DESDALLI          13652 5ELCID1730 ******** SE TORNO EL QUE EN BUEN ORA NASCO,
         WORD #1427 OCCURS    1 TIMES.

DESDE             16049 5ELCID2035 EN TODO MYO REYNO PARTE ***** OY.
         WORD #1428 OCCURS    1 TIMES.

DESEAN            18389 5ELCID2327 POR ENTRAR EN BATALLA ****** CARRION.
         WORD #1429 OCCURS    1 TIMES.

DESENPARADAS      23111 5ELCID2945 ************ LAS DEXARON ENEL ROBREDO DE CORPES,
         WORD #1430 OCCURS    1 TIMES.

DESENPARAS        11612 5ELCID1471 GRAND LOCURA SERIE SI LA **********;
         WORD #1431 OCCURS    1 TIMES.

DESENPARAUA        7117 5ELCID0910 DEXO EL POYO, TODO LO ***********,
         WORD #1432 OCCURS    1 TIMES.

DESEPARADA         3718 5ELCID0469 OUIERON MIEDO & FUE **********.
         WORD #1433 OCCURS    1 TIMES.

DESEREDE          10765 5ELCID1363 POR QUE LOS ********, TODO GELO SUELTO YO:
         WORD #1434 OCCURS    1 TIMES.
```

```
WORD                C#  PREFIX                                    CONTEXT

DESFECHOS          11318 5ELCID1433 ********* NOS HA EL %ID, SABET, SI NO NOS VAL;
        WORD #1435 OCCURS    1 TIMES.

DESI                3780 5ELCID0478 E **** ARRIBA TORNAN SE CON LA GANAN%IA,
                    5857 5ELCID0742 **** ADELANTE, QUANTOS QUE Y SON,
                    6786 5ELCID0867 **** A MOLINA, QUE ES DEL OTRA PART,
                    8727 5ELCID1119 **** A ONDA & LOS OTROS A ALMENAR,
                   10062 5ELCID1275 **** POR MI BESALDE LA MANO EFIRME GELO ROGAD
                   10926 5ELCID1383 **** ADELANT PIENSSE DELLAS EL CAMPEADOR.
                   13150 5ELCID1667 **** AN ASSER DEL OBISPO DON IHERONIMO,
                   20785 5ELCID2640 **** ESCURRA LAS FASTA MEDINA POR LA MI AMOR;
                   24393 5ELCID3110 E **** ADELANT, SABET, TODOS LOS OTROS:
                   27255 5ELCID3484 **** SEA VEN%IDO & ESCAPE POR TRAYDOR.
                   28154 5ELCID3594 QUE NON VARAGEN CON ELLOS **** O DE NON.
                   28294 5ELCID3612 **** VINIEN LOS DE MYO %ID ALOS YFANTES DE CARRION,
        WORD #1436 OCCURS   12 TIMES.
           INDEX OF DIVERSIFICATION =  2227.55 WITH STANDARD DEVIATION OF  2052.28

DESMANCHAN         28465 5ELCID3635 LAS DOS LE ********** & LA TER%ERA FINCO:
        WORD #1437 OCCURS    1 TIMES.

DESMANCHAR          5766 5ELCID0728 TANTA LORIGA FALSSA **********
        WORD #1438 OCCURS    1 TIMES.

DESNUDA             3730 5ELCID0471 EN MANO TRAE ******* EL ESPADA,
                   19072 5ELCID2413 EL ESPADA TIENES ******* EN LA MANO & VEOT AGUIJAR;
        WORD #1439 OCCURS    2 TIMES.

DESNUDAS            4798 5ELCID0608 LAS ESPADAS ********, A LA PUERTA SE PARAUAN.
                   23107 5ELCID2944 MAIADAS & ******** A GRANDE DESONOR,
        WORD #1440 OCCURS    2 TIMES.

DESOBRA            24154 5ELCID3080 SI ******* BUSCAREN YFANTES DE CARRION,
        WORD #1441 OCCURS    1 TIMES.

DESONDRA           21719 5ELCID2762 LA ******** DEL LEON ASSIS YRA VENGANDO.
                   22809 5ELCID2906 DESTA ******** QUE MEAN FECHA LOS YFANTES DE CARRION
                   22842 5ELCID2910 SI ******** Y CABE ALGUNA CONTRA NOS,
                   24850 5ELCID3165 QUANDO ******** DESUS FIJAS NO NOS DEMANDA OY;
                   27745 5ELCID3541 QUE LOS MATASSEN EN CAMPO POR ******** DE SO SE@OR.
        WORD #1442 OCCURS    5 TIMES.
           INDEX OF DIVERSIFICATION =  1505.50 WITH STANDARD DEVIATION OF  1228.02

DESONDRADO         23153 5ELCID2950 TIENES POR **********, MAS LA UUESTRA ES MAYOR,
        WORD #1443 OCCURS    1 TIMES.

DESONDRAR           7665 5ELCID0981 SABRA EL SALIDO A QUIEN VINO *********.
        WORD #1444 OCCURS    1 TIMES.

DESONDRARON        25568 5ELCID3256 DELOS YFANTES DE CARRION QUEM *********** TAN MAL,
        WORD #1445 OCCURS    1 TIMES.

DESONOR            10720 5ELCID1357 DE FONTA & DE MAL CURIALDAS & DE *******;
                   10831 5ELCID1371 MAS GANAREMOS EN ESTO QUE EN OTRA *******.
                   22840 5ELCID2909 QUANDO LAS HAN DEXADAS AGRANT *******,
                   22874 5ELCID2913 ESSO ME PUEDE PESAR CON LA OTRA *******.
                   23110 5ELCID2944 MAIADAS & DESNUDAS A GRANDE *******,
                   24727 5ELCID3149 POR MIS FIJAS QUEM DEXARON YO NON HE *******,
        WORD #1446 OCCURS    6 TIMES.
           INDEX OF DIVERSIFICATION =  2800.40 WITH STANDARD DEVIATION OF  5187.98

DESPA@A            29166 5ELCID3724 OY LOS REYES ******* SOS PARIENTES SON,
        WORD #1447 OCCURS    1 TIMES.

DESPENDADES         2064 5ELCID0260 POR VN MARCHO QUE *********** AL MONESTERIO DARE YO QUATRO.
        WORD #1448 OCCURS    1 TIMES.

DESPENDER          20033 5ELCID2542 MIENTRA QUE VISQUIEREMOS ********* NOLO PODREMOS.
        WORD #1449 OCCURS    1 TIMES.

DESPENDIE          12259 5ELCID1557 LOS SOS ********* EL MORO, QUE DELO SO NON TOMAUA NADA.
        WORD #1450 OCCURS    1 TIMES.

DESPENSSA           2046 5ELCID0258 SIESSA ********* UOS FALLE%IERE OUOS MENGUARE ALGO,
        WORD #1451 OCCURS    1 TIMES.

DESPERTEDES        21905 5ELCID2787 ***********, PRIMAS, POR AMOR DEL CRIADOR
        WORD #1452 OCCURS    1 TIMES.

DESPERTO            3251 5ELCID0410 QUANDO ******** EL %ID, LA CARA SE SANTIGO;
                   18115 5ELCID2292 EN ESTO ******** EL QUE EN BUEN ORA NA%IO;
                   26169 5ELCID3336 FASTA DO ******** MYO %ID, EL QUE VALEN%IA GA@O;
        WORD #1453 OCCURS    3 TIMES.
```

WORD C# PREFIX CONTEXT

DESPUES
1094 5ELCID0140 SI NON PRIMERO PRENDIENDO & ******* DANDO.
2449 5ELCID0309 QUE, SI ******* DEL PLAZO EN SU TIERRAL PUDIES TOMAR,
3209 5ELCID0404 Y SE ECHAUA MYO %ID ******* QUE FUE %ENADO,
3361 5ELCID0424 ******* QUI NOS BUSCARE FALLAR NOS PODRA.
6912 5ELCID0884 MAS ******* QUE DE MOROS FUE, PRENDO ESTA PRESENTAIA;
8775 5ELCID1116 ******* QUE NOS PARTIEMOS DELA LINPIA CHRISTIANDAD,
9837 5ELCID1248 LOS QUE FUERON CON EL, & LOS DE *******, TODOS SON PAGADOS;
15092 5ELCID1909 ******* FAGA EL %ID LO QUE QUIERE SABOR.
15371 5ELCID1946 ACORDAR UOS YEDES ******* ATODO LO MEIOR.
16068 5ELCID2037 GRADESCOLO A DIOS DEL %IELO & ******* AUOS,
19532 5ELCID2475 ******* QUE ESTA BATALLA VEN%IERON & AL REY BUCAR MATO;
20065 5ELCID2547 ******* EN LA CARRERA FEREMOS NUESTRO SABOR,
23820 5ELCID3034 BESO LE LA MANO & ******* LE SALUDO;
26806 5ELCID3424 E ******* DE MYO %ID EL CAMPEADOR;
27093 5ELCID3462 ******* VEREDES QUE DIXIESTES O QUE NO.
29020 5ELCID3706 QUI BUENA DUENA ESCARNE%E & LA DEXA *******,
WORD #1454 OCCURS 16 TIMES.
INDEX OF DIVERSIFICATION = 1860.73 WITH STANDARD DEVIATION OF 1579.51

DESSA
24667 5ELCID3142 CON EL QUE TOUIERE DERECHO YO ***** PART ME SO.
WORD #1455 OCCURS 1 TIMES.

DESSEO
18443 5ELCID2334 HYO ****** LIDES, & UOS A CARRION;
WORD #1456 OCCURS 1 TIMES.

DESSI
17041 5ELCID2157 NON QUIERE QUEL ESCURA, QUITOL ***** LUEGO.
WORD #1457 OCCURS 1 TIMES.

DESSO
1100 5ELCID0141 DIXO MARTIN ANTOLINEZ: YO ***** ME PAGO.
WORD #1458 OCCURS 1 TIMES.

DESSOS
15776 5ELCID2001 DALMA & DE CORA%ON, & TODOS LOS QUE EN PODER ****** FOSSEN;
18541 5ELCID2346 AMARAULLA LO AUIEN MUCHOS ****** CHRISTIANOS,
WORD #1459 OCCURS 2 TIMES.

DESTA
6385 5ELCID0814 ***** BATALLA QUE AUEMOS ARANCADA;
12083 5ELCID1532 DIXO AUENGALUON: PLAZME ***** PRESENTAIA,
12733 5ELCID1617 ***** GANAN%IA COMME ES BUENA & GRAND.
14271 5ELCID1806 ***** MI QUINTA, DIGO UOS SIN FALLA,
14297 5ELCID1809 CON CAUALLOS ***** QUINTA QUE YO HE GANADA,
14377 5ELCID1819 ***** LID QUE HA ARRANCADA CC CAUALLOS LE ENBIAUA ENPRESENTAIA,
19329 5ELCID2448 ***** ARRANCADA NOS YREMOS PAGADOS.
19485 5ELCID2469 ***** ARRANCADA, QUE LO TENIEN EN SO SALUO,
19611 5ELCID2485 ***** BATALLA QUE HAN ARRANCADO
21466 5ELCID2729 MOROS & CHRISTIANOS DEPARTIRAN ***** RAZON,
22808 5ELCID2906 ***** DESONDRA QUE MEAN FECHA LOS YFANTES DE CARRION
23472 5ELCID2989 RUEGAN AL REY QUE LOS QUITE ***** CORT.
25514 5ELCID3249 MAL ESCAPAN IOGADOS, SABED, ***** RAZON.
27089 5ELCID3461 SI DIOS QUISIERE QUE ***** BIEN SALGAMOS NOS,
WORD #1460 OCCURS 14 TIMES.
INDEX OF DIVERSIFICATION = 1591.62 WITH STANDARD DEVIATION OF 1807.03

DESTAS
10045 5ELCID1273 ****** MIS GANAN%IAS, QUE AUEMOS FECHAS ACA,
15488 5ELCID1962 SEAN LAS VISTAS ****** IIJ SEMANAS;
12065 5ELCID1530 ***** QUE AUEDES FECHO UOS NON PERDEREDES NADA.
14011 5ELCID1775 TANTO FALLAN ***** QUE ES COSA SOBEIANO.
16095 5ELCID2041 TODOS LOS DEMAS ***** AUIEN SABOR;
18260 5ELCID2310 FIERA COSA LES PESA ***** QUE LES CUNTIO.
19431 5ELCID2462 DIXO MYO %ID: YO ***** SO PAGADO;
20008 5ELCID2539 ***** QUE ELLOS FABLARON NOS PARTE NON AYAMOS:
23336 5ELCID2973 ***** QUE LES ABINO AVN BIEN SERAN ONDRADOS.
23872 5ELCID3041 ***** QUE NOS ABINO QUE UOS PESE, SE@OR.
24602 5ELCID3135 ALCALDES SEAN ***** EL CONDE DON ANRRICH & EL CONDE DON REMOND
27530 5ELCID3516 ESSORA DIXO EL REY: ***** NON HE SABOR;
WORD #1465 OCCURS 13 TIMES.
INDEX OF DIVERSIFICATION = 2198.33 WITH STANDARD DEVIATION OF 1399.77

DESTOS
9216 5ELCID1173 EN CADA VNO ****** A@OS MYO %ID LES TOLIO EL PAN.
13133 5ELCID1665 ANTES ****** XV DIAS, SI FLOGIERE A CRIADOR,
19907 5ELCID2525 ****** NUESTROS CASAMIENTOS UOS ABREDES HONOR.
21003 5ELCID2669 ACAYAZ, CURIATE ******, CA ERES MYO SE@OR:
25256 5ELCID3216 ****** AUERES QUE UOS DI YO, SIMELOS DADES, O DEDES DELLO RA%ON.
25371 5ELCID3231 ****** IIJ MILL MARCOS LOS CC TENGO YO;
26434 5ELCID3372 ****** AMOS LA RAZON FINCO.
27121 5ELCID3466 ****** IIJ POR TRES QUE REBTARON EN LA CORT.
WORD #1466 OCCURS 8 TIMES.
INDEX OF DIVERSIFICATION = 2556.86 WITH STANDARD DEVIATION OF 2460.89

DESUS
24851 5ELCID3165 QUANDO DESONDRA ***** FIJAS NO NOS DEMANDA OY;
WORD #1467 OCCURS 1 TIMES.

DESUSO
24305 5ELCID3099 ****** CUBRIO VN MANTO QUE ES DE GRANT VALOR,

WORD C# PREFIX CONTEXT

DESTO (CON'T)

16929 5ELCID2143 ****** VISTAS QUE QUIEMOS, CEMY TOMEDES ALGO.
17014 5ELCID2154 ADIOS UCS ACOMIENDO, ****** VISTAS ME PARTO.
23307 5ELCID2969 QUE ****** VIJ SEMANAS ADOBES CON SUS VASSALLOS,
WORD #1461 OCCURS 5 TIMES.
INDEX OF DIVERSIFICATION = 3314.50 WITH STANDARD DEVIATION OF 3018.92

DESTE 8027 5ELCID1025 COMED, CONDE, ***** PAN & BEUED DESTE VINO.
8031 5ELCID1025 COMED, CONDE, DESTE PAN & BEUED ***** VINO.
12086 5ELCID1533 ANTES ***** TE%ER DIA UCS LA CARE DOBLADA.
15313 5ELCID1939 ***** CASAMIENTO NON AURIA SABOR;
17372 5ELCID2198 ***** UUSTRO CASAMIENTO CRE%REMOS EN ONOR;
17988 5ELCID2276 LAS COPLAS ***** CANTAR AQUIS VAN ACABANDO.
28704 5ELCID3665 VALME, DIOS GLORIOSO, RE@OR, & CURIAM ***** ESPADA
29183 5ELCID3726 PASSADO ES ***** SIEGLO EL DIA DE CINQUAESMA.
WORD #1462 OCCURS 8 TIMES.
INDEX OF DIVERSIFICATION = 3021.29 WITH STANDARD DEVIATION OF 3710.30

DESTELLADO 6014 5ELCID0762 POR LA LORIGA AYUSO LA SANGRE **********;
WORD #1463 OCCURS 1 TIMES.

DESTELLANDO 6139 5ELCID0781 POR EL COBDO AYUSO LA SANGRE ***********.
13608 5ELCID1724 POR EL COBDO AYUSO LA SANGRE ***********.
19368 5ELCID2453 POR EL COBDO AYUSO LA SANGRE ***********;
WORD #1464 OCCURS 3 TIMES.

DESTO 1138 5ELCID0146 DIXO RACHEL & VIDAS: NOS ***** NOS PAGAMOS.
6472 5ELCID0826 MYNAYA ALBARFANEZ ***** ES PAGADO; POR YR CON EL OMNES SON CONTADOS.
9776 5ELCID1242 E QUE FABLASSEN ***** MOROS & CHRISTIANOS.
WORD #1468 OCCURS 1 TIMES.

DETARDA 15658 5ELCID1986 NON LO *******, PORA LAS VISTAS SE ADOBO;
WORD #1469 OCCURS 1 TIMES.

DETARDAMOS 20021 5ELCID2540 VAYAMOS PORA CARRION, AQUI MUCHO **********.
WORD #1470 OCCURS 1 TIMES.

DETARDAN 819 5ELCID0105 NON LO ********, TODOS TRES SE APARTARON.
13411 5ELCID1700 NOS ******** DE ADOBASSE ESSAS YENTES CHRISTIANAS.
15500 5ELCID1964 NON LO ********, A MYO %ID SE TORNAUAN.
22307 5ELCID2841 NON LO ******** EL MANDADO DE SU SE@OR,
WORD #1471 OCCURS 4 TIMES.

DETARDAR 9427 5ELCID1198 AL SABOR DELA GANAN%IA NON LO QUIERE ********,
9462 5ELCID1202 MYO %ID DON RODRIGO NON LO QUISO ********,
11881 5ELCID1506 ESSO FFUE APRIESSA FECHO, QUE NOS QUIEREN ********.
13360 5ELCID1693 FABLAUA MYNAYA, NON LO QUISO ********:
WORD #1472 OCCURS 4 TIMES.

DETARDAUA 4527 5ELCID0575 EL FIZO VN ART & NON LO *********:
12492 5ELCID1584 EL QUE EN BUEN ORA NASCO NON LO *********:
WORD #1473 OCCURS 2 TIMES.

DETARDEDES 5050 5ELCID0638 NON LO **********, LOS DOS YD PORA ALLA,
WORD #1474 OCCURS 1 TIMES.

DETARDO 11797 5ELCID1496 ESTO NON *******, CA DE CORA%ON LO HAN;
WORD #1475 OCCURS 1 TIMES.

DETARUA 762 5ELCID0096 MARTIN ANTOLINEZ NON LO *******,
WORD #1476 OCCURS 1 TIMES.

DETIENE 23362 5ELCID2976 NON LO ******* POR NADA ALFONSSO EL CASTELLANO,
24181 5ELCID3084 NOS ******* POR NADA EL QUE EN BUEN ORA NA%IO:
WORD #1477 OCCURS 2 TIMES.

DETIENEN 5126 5ELCID0648 NON LO ********, VIENEN DE TODAS PARTES.
WORD #1478 OCCURS 1 TIMES.

DETIENES 25947 5ELCID3307 ******** LE LA LENGUA, NON PUEDE DELIBRAR,
WORD #1479 OCCURS 1 TIMES.

DETODAS 495 5ELCID0063 ******* COSAS QUANTAS SON DE UIANDA
WORD #1480 OCCURS 1 TIMES.

DEUE 11511 5ELCID1457 QUI BUEN MANDADERO ENBIA, TAL **** SPERAR.
26371 5ELCID3363 LO DEL LEON NON SE TE **** OLBIDAR;
WORD #1481 OCCURS 2 TIMES.

DEUEDES 2497 5ELCID0315 SED MEMBRADOS COMMO LO ******* FAR.
WORD #1482 OCCURS 1 TIMES.

DEUEMOS 7770 5ELCID0995 %IENTO CAUALLEROS ******* VEN%ER A QUELAS MESNADAS.
WORD #1483 OCCURS 1 TIMES.

WORD C# PREFIX CONTEXT

DEUEN 8717 5ELCID1107 VAYAN LOS MANDADOS POR LOS QUE NOS ***** AIUDAR,
WORD #1484 OCCURS 1 TIMES.

DEUIEMOS 21702 5ELCID2759 NON LAS ******** TOMAR POR VARRAGANAS,
25875 5ELCID3297 ******** CASAR CON FIJAS DE REYES O DE ENPERADORES,
WORD #1485 OCCURS 2 TIMES.

DEUIEN 25723 5ELCID3276 NON GELAS ****** QUERER SUS FIJAS POR VARRAGANAS,
WORD #1486 OCCURS 1 TIMES.

DEUOS 2161 5ELCID0272 E NOS ***** PARTIR NOS HEMOS EN VIDA.
8209 5ELCID1046 PRENDIENDO ***** & DE OTROS YR NOS HEMOS PAGANDO;
16996 5ELCID2152 ***** BIEN SO SERUIDO, & TENGON POR PAGADO;
18800 5ELCID2379 SI ESTE AMOR NON FECHES, YO ***** ME QUIERO QUITAR.
19409 5ELCID2459 TODOS ESTOS BIENES ***** SON & DE UUESTROS VASSALLOS.
WORD #1487 OCCURS 5 TIMES.
INDEX OF DIVERSIFICATION = 4311.00 WITH STANDARD DEVIATION OF 3787.77

DEXA 4528 5ELCID0576 **** VNA TIENDA FITA & LAS OTRAS LEUAUA,
29019 5ELCID3706 QUI BUENA DUENA ESCARNE%E & LA **** DESPUES,
WORD #1488 OCCURS 2 TIMES.

DEXAD 10643 5ELCID1348 DIXO EL REY REY AL CONDE: ***** ESSA RAZON,
WORD #1489 OCCURS 1 TIMES.

DEXADA 4583 5ELCID0582 LAS OTRAS A BES LIEUA, VNA TIENDA A ******.
WORD #1490 OCCURS 1 TIMES.

DEXADAS 3656 5ELCID0461 TODOS SON EXIDOS, LAS PUERTAS ******* AN ABIERTAS
7248 5ELCID0929 E DE SUS COMPA@AS, AQUELAS QUE AUIEN *******
21369 5ELCID2716 OY NOS PARTIREMOS, & ******* SEREDES DE NOS;
22838 5ELCID2909 QUANDO LAS HAN ******* AGRANT DESONOR,
25743 5ELCID3278 DERECHO FIZIERON POR QUE LAS HAN *******.
26936 5ELCID3441 ELLOS LAS HAN ******* A PESAR DE NOS.
WORD #1491 OCCURS 6 TIMES.
INDEX OF DIVERSIFICATION = 4655.00 WITH STANDARD DEVIATION OF 5383.63

DEXADES 2383 5ELCID0301 VOS, QUE POR MI ******* CASAS & HEREDADES,
WORD #1492 OCCURS 1 TIMES.

DEXADO 892 5ELCID0115 ****** HA HEREDADES & CASAS & PALA%IOS.
8416 5ELCID1069 EN GRADO UOS LO TENGO LO QUE ME AUEDES ******.
8564 5ELCID1088 ****** A SARAGO%A & ALAS TIERRAS DUCA,
8572 5ELCID1089 E ****** A HUESCA & LAS TIERRAS DE MONT ALUAN.
WORD #1493 OCCURS 4 TIMES.

DEXADOS 6168 5ELCID0785 TANTOS MOROS YAZEN MUERTOS QUE POCOS BIUOS A *******,
WORD #1494 OCCURS 1 TIMES.

DEXAMOS 25893 5ELCID3299 POR QUE LAS ******* DERECHO FIZIEMOS NOS;
26319 5ELCID3357 POR QUE ******* SUS FIJAS AVN NO NOS REPENTIMOS,
26350 5ELCID3360 QUE POR QUE LAS ******* ONDRADOS SOMOS NOS.
WORD #1495 OCCURS 3 TIMES.

DEXAN 2295 5ELCID0289 VNOS ***** CASAS & OTROS ONORES.
3753 5ELCID0475 ***** LA A MYO %ID, TODO ESTO NON PRE%IA NADA.
4675 5ELCID0593 ABIERTAS ***** LAS PUERTAS QUE NINGUNO NON LAS GUARDA.
13515 5ELCID1713 ***** ALAS PUERTAS OMNES DE GRANT RECABDO.
21181 5ELCID2691 ASSINIESTRO ***** ATINEZA, VNA PE@A MUY FUERT,
21202 5ELCID2694 ASSINIESTRO ***** AGRIZA QUE ALAMOS POBLO,
21215 5ELCID2696 ADIESTRO ***** ASANT ESTEUAN, MAS CAE ALUEN;
21628 5ELCID2750 MAS ***** LAS MARIDAS EN BRIALES & EN CAMISAS,
WORD #1496 OCCURS 8 TIMES.
INDEX OF DIVERSIFICATION = 2760.86 WITH STANDARD DEVIATION OF 3800.55

DEXANDO 4787 5ELCID0607 ******* UAN LOS DELANT, POR EL CASTIELLO SE TORNAUAN,
WORD #1497 OCCURS 1 TIMES.

DEXAR 910 5ELCID0117 EL CAMPEADOR ***** LAS HA EN UUESTRA MANO,
1037 5ELCID0133 PEDIR UOS A POCO POR ***** SO AUER EN SALUO.
8064 5ELCID1029 QUE YO ***** ME MORIR, QUE NON QUIERO COMER.
12900 5ELCID1636 A MENOS DE MUERT NO LA PUEDO *****;
12932 5ELCID1640 ENTRARE EN LAS ARMAS, NON LO PODRE *****;
25577 5ELCID3257 AMENOS DE RIEBTOS NO LOS PUEDO *****.
WORD #1498 OCCURS 6 TIMES.
INDEX OF DIVERSIFICATION = 4932.40 WITH STANDARD DEVIATION OF 5267.51

DEXARA 4934 5ELCID0624 FIZO ENBIAR POR LA TIENDA QUE ****** ALLA.
WORD #1499 OCCURS 1 TIMES.

DEXARE 8005 5ELCID1022 ANTES PERDERE EL CUERPO & ****** EL ALMA,
10339 5ELCID1310 ****** UOS LAS POSADAS, NON LAS QUIERO CONTAR.
WORD #1500 OCCURS 2 TIMES.

```
WORD                  C#  PREFIX                    CONTEXT

DEXAREDES          8438 5ELCID1072 E SI NON, MANDEDES BUSCAR; O ME *********
        WORD #1501 OCCURS    1 TIMES.

DEXAREMOS         11366 5ELCID1438 SI NON, ********* BURGOS, YR LO HEMOS BUSCAR.
        WORD #1502 OCCURS    1 TIMES.

DEXARIE            7726 5ELCID0989 AMENOS DE BATALLA NON NOS ******* POR NADA.
        WORD #1503 OCCURS    1 TIMES.

DEXARON           21614 5ELCID2748 POR MUERTAS LAS ******* ENEL ROBREDRO DE CORPES.
                  21650 5ELCID2752 POR MUERTAS LAS *******, SABED, QUE NON POR BIUAS.
                  21676 5ELCID2755 POR MUERTAS LAS *******,
                  23113 5ELCID2945 DESENPARADAS LAS ******* ENEL ROBREDO DE CORPES,
                  24723 5ELCID3149 POR MIS FIJAS QUEM ******* YO NON HE DESONOR,
                  24777 5ELCID3156 QUANDO ******* MIS FIJAS ENEL ROBREDO DE CORPES,
                  28984 5ELCID3702 POR MALOS LOS ******* ALOS YFANTES DE CARRION,
        WORD #1504 OCCURS    7 TIMES.
           INDEX OF DIVERSIFICATION =  1227.33 WITH STANDARD DEVIATION OF  1631.44

DEXAS             21066 5ELCID2677 SI NOLO ***** POR MYO %ID EL DE BIUAR,
        WORD #1505 OCCURS    1 TIMES.

DEXASSEDES        25848 5ELCID3293 ********** UOS, %ID, DE AQUESTA RAZON;
        WORD #1506 OCCURS    1 TIMES.

DEXASTES          25649 5ELCID3266 SOLAS LAS ******** ENEL ROBREDO DE CORPES,
                  26246 5ELCID3346 POR QUANTO LAS ******** MENOS VALEDES VOS;
                  26407 5ELCID3368 FIJAS DEL %ID, POR QUE LAS VOS ********,
        WORD #1507 OCCURS    3 TIMES.

DEXAT              7404 5ELCID0950 ***** ESTAS POSADAS & YREMOS ADELANT.
        WORD #1508 OCCURS    1 TIMES.

DEXAUA            12451 5ELCID1580 Y ****** EL CAUALLO, PORA LA CAPIELLA ADELINAUA;
        WORD #1509 OCCURS    1 TIMES.

DEXE              10082 5ELCID1277 QUENLAS **** SACAR;
                  11050 5ELCID1399 SANO LO **** & CON TAN GRAND RICTAD.
        WORD #1510 OCCURS    2 TIMES.

DEXEDES            3534 5ELCID0445 AOSADAS CORRED, QUE POR MIEDO NON ******* NADA.
        WORD #1511 OCCURS    1 TIMES.

DEXEM              7639 5ELCID0978 DELO SO NON LIEUO NADA, ***** YR EN PAZ.
        WORD #1512 OCCURS    1 TIMES.

DEXEMOS           29028 5ELCID3708 ******* NOS DE PLEYTOS DE YFANTES DE CARRION,
        WORD #1513 OCCURS    1 TIMES.

DEXEN              3559 5ELCID0448 QUE POR MIEDO DE LOS MOROS NON ***** NADA.
                   7014 5ELCID0897 HYD POR CASTIELLA & ***** UOS ANDAR, MINAYA,
        WORD #1514 OCCURS    2 TIMES.

DEXESTE            2744 5ELCID0347 ALOS IUDIOS TE ******* PRENDER; DO DIZEN MONTE CALUARIE
        WORD #1515 OCCURS    1 TIMES.

DEXO                608 5ELCID0077 SI NON, QUANTO **** NOLO PRE%IO UN FIGO.
                   2022 5ELCID0255 DUES FIJAS **** NI@AS & PRENDET LAS EN LOS BRA%OS;
                   3841 5ELCID0486 EL CASTIELO **** EN SO PODER, EL CAMPEADOR CAUALGA,
                   7112 5ELCID0910 **** EL POYO, TODO LO DESENPARAUA,
                  10685 5ELCID1353 SALDRIEN DEL MONESTERIO DO ELLE LAS ****,
                  13745 5ELCID1742 **** ALBARFANEZ POR SABER TODO RECABDO.
                  22100 5ELCID2812 ALA TORRE DE DON VRRACA ELLE LAS ****.
                  28523 5ELCID3642 EL **** LA LAN%A & AL ESPADA METIO MANO,
                  28552 5ELCID3645 ATORGARON GELO LOS FIELES, PERO VERMUEZ LE ****.
        WORD #1516 OCCURS    9 TIMES.
           INDEX OF DIVERSIFICATION =  3492.00 WITH STANDARD DEVIATION OF  2714.80

DEXOLA            25698 5ELCID3273 ****** CRE%ER & LUENGA TRAE LA BARBA;
        WORD #1517 OCCURS    1 TIMES.

DEXOS             26192 5ELCID3339 ***** LE PRENDER ALCUELO, & ALA RED LE METIO.
        WORD #1518 OCCURS    1 TIMES.

DEZENO             9518 5ELCID1210 QUANDO VINO EL ******, CUIERON GELA ADAR.
        WORD #1519 OCCURS    1 TIMES.

DEZID              1001 5ELCID0129 MAS ***** NOS DEL %ID, DE QUE SERA PAGADO,
                   5300 5ELCID0670 ***** ME, CAUALLEROS, COMMO UOS PLAZE DE FAR.
                  11109 5ELCID1407 ***** AL CANPEADOR, QUE DIOS LE CURIE DE MAL,
                  15100 5ELCID1910 ***** A RUY DIAZ, EL QUE EN BUEN ORA NASCO,
                  21045 5ELCID2675  ***** ME, QUE UOS FIZ, YFANTES DE CARRION
                  25195 5ELCID3208 DIZE EL CONDE DON REMONO: ***** DE SSI O DE NO.
                  25578 5ELCID3258 *****  QUE UOS MERE%I, YFANTES, EN JUEGO O EN VERO
```

WORD C# PREFIX CONTEXT

DEZIO (CON'T)

```
               26884 5ELCID3435 *****, MYNAYA, LC CUF OUIERECES SABOR.
        WORD #1520 OCCURS   8 TIMES.
           INDEX OF DIVERSIFICATICN =  3696.57 WITH STANDARD DEVIATION OF  2116.11

DEZIDES        15090 5ELCID1908 ROGAR GELC EMCS LO QUE ******* UOS;
               27629 5ELCID3527 DIXO MARTIN ANTOLINEZ:  POR QUE LO *******, SE@OR
        WORD #1521 OCCURS   2 TIMES.

DEZILDES        3089 5ELCID0389 ABBAT, ******** QUE PRENDAN EL RASTRO & PIESSEN DE ANDAR,
        WORD #1522 OCCURS   1 TIMES.

DEZIMOS        25228 5ELCID3212 SI PLOGUIERE AL REY, ASSI ******* NOS: DIXO EL REY
        WORD #1523 OCCURS   1 TIMES.

DEZIR            238 5ELCID0030 ASCONDEN SE DE MYO %ID, CA NOL OSAN ***** NADA.
                6511 5ELCIDC830 A NUESTRO AMIGOS BIEN LES PODEDES *****:
                6961 5ELCIDC890 SOBRE AQUESTO TODO, ***** UOS QUIERO, MINAYA:
                7029 5ELCIDC899 QUIERO UOS ***** DEL QUE EN BUEN ORA NASCO & %INXO ESPADA:
                7383 5ELCIDC947 HYA CAUALLEROS, ***** UOS HE LA VERDAD:
               11246 5ELCID1423 DELOS OTROS QUINIENTOS ***** UOS HE QUE FAZE:
               12758 5ELCID1620 ***** UOS QUIERO NUEUAS DE ALENT PARTES DEL MAR,
               13308 5ELCID1688 ***** NOS HA LA MISSA, & PENSSAD DE CAUALGAR,
               14018 5ELCID1776 QUIERO UOS ***** LO QUE ES MAS GRANADO:
               17409 5ELCID2202 QUE YO NULLA COSA NOL SOPE ***** DE NO.
               21885 5ELCID2784 TANTO SON DE TRASPUESTAS QUE NON PUEDEN ***** NADA.
               22690 5ELCID2891 HYO TOME EL CASAMIENTO, MAS NON OSE ***** AL.
               24150 5ELCID3079 POR DE MANDAR MYOS DERECHOS & ***** MI RAZON:
               26549 5ELCID3389 FAZER TELO ***** QUE TALERES QUAL DIGO YO.
               26872 5ELCID3433 ***** QUERRIA YA QUANTO DELO MYO.
               28143 5ELCID3593 EL REY DIOLES FIELES POR ***** EL DERECHO & AL NON,
        WORD #1524 OCCURS  16 TIMES.
           INDEX OF DIVERSIFICATION =  1859.33 WITH STANDARD DEVIATION OF  1843.40

DI             22833 5ELCID2908 EL CASO MIS FIJAS, CA NON GELAS ** YO;
               25260 5ELCID3216 DESTOS AUERES QUE UOS ** YO, SIMELOS DADES, O DEDES DELLO RA%ON.
               25613 5ELCID3261 ALA SALIDA DE VALEN%IA MIS FIJAS VOS ** YO,
               26112 5ELCID3329 **, FERRANDO, OTORGA ESTA RAZON:
               26866 5ELCID3432 BIEN UOS ** VAGAR EN TODA ESTA CORT,
               26909 5ELCID3438 HYO LES ** MIS PRIMAS POR MANDADO DEL REY ALFONSSO,
        WORD #1525 OCCURS   6 TIMES.
           INDEX OF DIVERSIFICATION =   814.20 WITH STANDARD DEVIATION OF   936.96

DIA             1601 5ELCID0205 AUN VEA EL *** QUE DEMI AYADES ALGO
                1742 5ELCIDC222 EL ME ACORRA DE NOCH & DE ***
                1987 5ELCID0251 SI YO ALGUN *** VISQUIER, SERUOS HAN DOBLADOS.
                2302 5ELCIDC290 EN AQUES *** ALA PUENT DE ARLA%ON
                2466 5ELCIDC311 EL *** ES EXIDO, LA NOCH QUERIE ENTRAR,
                3131 5ELCIDC394 OTRO *** MA@ANA PIENSSA DE CAUALGAR.
                3274 5ELCID0413 OTRO *** MA@ANA PIENSSAN DE CAUALGAR;
                3280 5ELCID0414 ES *** A DE PLAZO, SEPADES QUE NON MAS.
                3298 5ELCIDC416 AVN ERA DE ***, NON ERA PUESTO EL SOL,
                4111 5ELCIDC523 ATERCER *** DADOS FUERON SJN FALLA.
                4319 5ELCIDC550 OTRO *** MOUIOS MYO %ID EL DE BIUAR,
                4413 5ELCID0562 QUE DE *** NIN DE NOCH NON LES DIESSEN AREBATA,
                5104 5ELCID0645 OTRO *** MA@ANA PIENSSAN DE CAUALGAR,
                5141 5ELCID0650 ANDIDIERON TODOL ***, QUE VAGAR NON SE DAN,
                5205 5ELCID0658 LAS AROBDAS, QUE LOS MOROS SACAN, DE ***
                5356 5ELCID0676 VAYAMOS LOS FERIR EN AQUEL *** DE CRAS.
                5403 5ELCIDC682 OTRO *** MA@ANA, EL SOL QUERIE APUNTAR,
                5948 5ELCIDC754 OY EN ESTE *** DE UOS ABRE GRAND BANDO;
                6068 5ELCIDC770 TAN BUEN *** POR LA CHRISTIANDAD,
                7311 5ELCID0938 ALTER%ER ***, DON YXO Y ES TORNADO.
                8073 5ELCID1030 FASTA TER%ER *** NOL PUEDEN ACORDAR.
                8350 5ELCID1062 DEL *** QUE FUE CONDE NON IANTE TAN DE BUEN GRADO,
                8755 5ELCID1113 ALTER%ER *** TODOS IUNTADOS SON,
               11648 5ELCID1476 E EL OTRO *** VINIERON A MOLINA POSAR.
               11990 5ELCID1520 TAN BUEN *** CON UUSCO, MINAYA ALBARFANEZ
               12088 5ELCID1533 ANTES DESTE TE%ER *** UOS LA DARE DOBLADA.
               12247 5ELCID1555 OTRO *** MANA@A LUEGO CAUALGAUAN,
               12535 5ELCID1591 DES *** SE PRE%IO BAUIECA EN QUANT GRANT FUE ESPA@A.
               13088 5ELCID1659 ALEGRAUAS MIO %ID & DIXO: TAN BUEN *** ES OY
               13111 5ELCID1662 DEL *** QUE NASQUIERAN NON VIERAN TAL TREMOR.
               13240 5ELCID1678 QUINIENTOS MATARON DELLOS CONPLIDOS ENES ***.
               13295 5ELCID1686 OY ES *** BUENO & MEIOR SERA CRAS:
               13402 5ELCID1699 ES *** ES SALIDO & LA NOCH ENTRADA ES,
               14357 5ELCID1816 OTRO *** MANANA PRIUADO CAUALGAUAN,
               15787 5ELCID2002 LAS PUERTAS DEL ALCA%AR QUE NON SE ABRIESSEN DE *** NIN DE NOCH,
               15873 5ELCID2013 DE VN *** ES LEGADO ANTES EL REY DON ALFONSSO.
               16129 5ELCID2045 VALER ME A DIOS DE *** & DE NOCH.
               16214 5ELCID2057 EN AQUEL *** DEL REY SO HUESPED FUE;
               16247 5ELCID2061 ES *** ES PASSADO, & ENTRADA ES LA NOCH;
               16256 5ELCID2062 OTRO *** MA@ANA, CLARO SALIE EL SOL,
               16301 5ELCID2068 AL OTRO *** MA@ANA, ASSI COMMO SALIO EL SOL,
               16671 5ELCID2111 LAS PALABRAS SON PUESTAS QUE OTRO *** MA@ANA
```

WORD C# PREFIX CONTEXT

DIA (CON'T)

```
                     17774 5ELCID2249 E AL OTRO *** FIZO MYO %ID FINCAR VIJ TABLADOS:
                     19527 5ELCID2474 GRANT FUE EL *** LA CCRT CEL CAMPEADOR,
                     20873 5ELCID2651 OTRO *** MA@ANA CON ELLCS CAUALGO,
                     21176 5ELCID2690 ACOIEN SE A ANDAR DE *** & DE NOCH:
                     21914 5ELCID2788 MIENTRA ES EL ***, ANTE QUE ENTRE LA NOCH,
                     22082 5ELCID2810 ENTRE NOCH & *** SALIERCN DELOS MONTES:
                     22294 5ELCID2839 DIXOLES FUERTE MIENTRE QUE ANDIDIESSEN DE *** & DE NOCH,
                     22522 5ELCID2868 AVN VEAMOS EL *** QUE VCS PODAMOS VENGAR
                     22538 5ELCID2870 OTRO *** MA@ANA PIENSSAN DE CAUALGAR,
                     22592 5ELCID2878 OTRO *** MA@ANA METEN SE A ANDAR,
                     22610 5ELCID2880 E DE MEDINA A MOLINA EN OTRO *** VAN:
                     23672 5ELCID3015 AL QUINTO *** VENIDC ES MYO %ID EL CAMPEADOR:
                     26069 5ELCID3323 FASTA ESTE *** NOLO DESCUBRI A NACI:
                     29186 5ELCID3726 PASSADO ES DESTE SIEGLO EL *** DE CINQUAESMA.
          WORD #1526 OCCURS  56 TIMES.
             INDEX OF DIVERSIFICATION =   500.55 WITH STANDARD DEVIATION OF   697.98

DIAGON%ALEZ          28683 5ELCID3662 *********** ESPADA TIENE EN MANO, MAS NOLA
          WORD #1527 OCCURS   1 TIMES.

DIAS                  1723 5ELCID0220 NON SE SIENTRARE Y MAS ENTODOS LOS MYOS ****.
                      2140 5ELCID0269 FEM ANTE UOS YO & UUESTRAS FFIJAS, YFFANTES SON & DE **** CHICAS,
                      2255 5ELCID0283 O QUE DE VENTURA & ALGUNOS **** VIDA,
                      2425 5ELCID0306 LOS VJ **** DE PLAZO PASSADOS LOS AN,
                      6462 5ELCID0824 QUE RUEGEN POR MI LAS NOCHES & LOS ****:
                      6571 5ELCID0839 TODOS LOS **** A MYO %ID AGUARDAUAN
                      7287 5ELCID0934 YA ALBARFANEZ, BIUADES MUCHOS ****   . . .
                      7433 5ELCID0953 EN AQUESSA CORRIDA X **** OUIERON AMORAR.
                      7568 5ELCID0970 TRES **** & DOS NOCHES PENSSARON DE ANDAR,
                      8046 5ELCID1027 SI NON, EN TODOS UUESTROS **** NON VEREDES CHRISTIANISMO.
                      9175 5ELCID1168 E DURMIENDO LOS **** & LAS NOCHES TRANOCHANDO,
                      9388 5ELCID1194 TRES **** LE SPERARE EN CANAL DE %ELFA.
                     10227 5ELCID1295 ALOS **** DEL SIEGLO NON LE LORASSEN CHRISTIANOS.
                     11143 5ELCID1410 DE AQUESTOS XV ****, SIDIOS NOS CURIARE DE MAL,
                     11416 5ELCID1445 TODOS LOS **** DEL SIEGLO EN LEUAR LO ADELANT
                     11466 5ELCID1451 DE SAN PERO FASTA MEDINA EN V **** VAN,
                     12187 5ELCID1547 LAS NOCHES & LOS **** LAS DUENAS AGUARDANDO.
                     13135 5ELCID1665 ANTES DESTOS XV ****, SI PLOGIERE A CRIADOR,
                     14413 5ELCID1823 ANDAN LOS **** & LAS NOCHES, & PASSADA HAN LA SIERRA,
                     14615 5ELCID1849 POCOS **** HA, REY, QUE VNA LID A ARRANCADO:
                     16430 5ELCID2083 CA NON HAN GRANT HEDAND E DE **** PEQUENAS SON.
                     17280 5ELCID2186 MUCHOS **** UOS VEAMOS CON LOS OIOS DELAS CARAS
                     17349 5ELCID2194 NON SERAN MENGUADAS EN TODOS UUESTROS ****
                     17789 5ELCID2251 QUINZE **** CONPLIDOS DURARON EN LAS BODAS,
                     17799 5ELCID2252 HYA %ERCA DELOS XV **** YAS VAN LOS FIJOS DALGO.
                     19497 5ELCID2470 CUYDARON QUE EN SUS **** NUNCUA SERIEN MINGUADOS.
                     19988 5ELCID2536 ELAS NOCHES & LOS **** TAN MAL LOS ESCARMENTANDO,
                     22316 5ELCID2842 APIRESSA CAUALGAN, LOS **** & LAS NOCHES ANDAN:
                     22473 5ELCID2862 EN LOS **** DE VAGAR TOCA NUESTRA RENCURA SABREMOS CONTAR.
                     22932 5ELCID2921 NOS DAN VAGAR LOS **** & LAS NOCHES.
                     27709 5ELCID3537 DOS **** ATENDIERON A YFANTES DE CARRION.
                     28970 5ELCID3700 AGUISA DE MENBRADOS ANDAN **** & NOCHES,
          WORD #1528 OCCURS  32 TIMES.
             INDEX OF DIVERSIFICATION =   877.94 WITH STANDARD DEVIATION OF  1107.47

DIAZ                   108 5ELCID0015 MYO %ID RUY **** POR BURGOS ENTRAUA,
                       191 5ELCID0025 QUE A MYO %ID RUY ****, QUE NADI NOL DIESSEN POSADA,
                       455 5ELCID0058 MYO %ID RUY ****, EL QUE EN BUEN ORA %INXO ESPADA,
                      3722 5ELCID0470 MIO %ID RUY **** POR LAS PUERTAS ENTRAUA,
                      3954 5ELCID0502 ANTE RUY **** EL LIDIADOR CONTADO,
                      4843 5ELCID0613 FABLO MYO %ID RUY ****, EL QUE EN BUEN ORA FUE NADO:
                      4968 5ELCID0628 QUE A VNO QUE DIZIEN MYO %ID RUY **** DE BIUAR
                      5718 5ELCID0721 YO SO RUY ****, EL %ID CAMPEADOR DE BIUAR
                      5811 5ELCID0734 MIO %ID RUY **** EL BUEN LIDIADOR:
                      5904 5ELCID0748 VIOLO MYO %ID RUY **** EL CASTELANO,
                      5984 5ELCID0759 MYO %ID RUY ****, EL QUE EN BUEN ORA NASCO,
                      6155 5ELCID0784 QUE MYO %ID RUY **** LID CAMPAL A VEN%IDA.
                      6493 5ELCID0828 MYO %ID RUY **** CON LOS SOS SE ACORDAUA:
                      6631 5ELCID0846 MYO %ID RUY **** A ALCOL%ER ES VENIDO:
                      6812 5ELCID0870 MYO %ID RUY **** DE DIOS AYA SU GRA%IA
                      6847 5ELCID0875 MYO %ID RUY ****, QUE EN BUEN ORA CINXO ESPADA. . .
                      7130 5ELCID0912 ENEL PINAR DE TEUAR DON ROY **** POSAUA:
                      7346 5ELCID0942 DE MYO %ID RUY **** QUE NON TEMIEN NINGUNA FONTA.
                      7467 5ELCID0958 QUE MYO %ID RUY **** QUEL CORRIE LA TIERRA TODA:
                      8020 5ELCID1024 MYO %ID RUY **** ODREDES LO QUE DIXO:
                      9730 5ELCID1237 CON MYO %ID RUY ****, EL QUE EN BUEN ORA NASCO.
                     14118 5ELCID1787 MANDO MYO %ID RUY **** QUE FITA SOUIESSE LA TIENDA,
                     14823 5ELCID1873 QUE BIEN PARESCADES ANTE RUY **** MYO %ID:
                     15103 5ELCID1910 DEZID A RUY ****, EL QUE EN BUEN ORA NASCO,
                     16206 5ELCID2056 MYO %ID RUY ****, QUE EN ORA BUENA NASCO,
                     16991 5ELCID2151 MYO %ID RUY ****, MUCHO ME AUEDES ONDRADO,
                     17883 5ELCID2263 ESPIDIENDOS DE RUY ****, EL QUE EN BUEN ORA NASCO,
                     19229 5ELCID2433 MYO %ID RUY ****, EL CAMPEADOR CONTADO,
                     23966 5ELCID3054 MYO %ID RUY **** EN SAN SERUAN POSADO.
```

```
WORD                C#  PREFIX                                     CONTEXT

DIAZ (CON'T)

               25907 5ELCID3301 MYO %ID RUY **** A PERO VERMUEZ CATA;
               29072 5ELCID3713 PRISOS ALA BARBA RUY **** SO SE@OR;
        WORD #1529 OCCURS  31 TIMES.
           INDEX OF DIVERSIFICATION =   964.47 WITH STANDARD DEVIATION OF  1290.47

DICHA           2530 5ELCID0320 LA MISSA *****, PENSSEMOS DE CAUALGAR,
               13434 5ELCID1703 LA MISSA *****, GRANT SULTURA LES DAUA:
        WORD #1530 OCCURS   2 TIMES.

DICHAS          1659 5ELCID0213 ESTAS PALABRAS ******, LA TIENDA ES COGIDA.
        WORD #1531 OCCURS   1 TIMES.

DICHO            557 5ELCID0070 FABLO MARTIN ATOLINEZ, ODREDES LO QUE A *****:
                8904 5ELCID1134 COMMO GELO A *****, AL CAMPEADOR MUCHO PLAZE.
               11624 5ELCID1473 ESTO ERA *****, PIENSSAN DE CAUALGAR,
               21143 5ELCID2686 ESTO LES HA *****, & EL MORO SE TORNO;
               25996 5ELCID3313 MIENTES, FERRANDO, DE QUANTO ***** HAS,
               26281 5ELCID3351 DE QUANTO HE ***** VERDADERO SERE YO.
               26432 5ELCID3371 QUE ERES TRAYDOR & MINTIST DE QUANTO ***** HAS.
               26823 5ELCID3426 QUE CUEMO ES ***** ASSI SEA, OMEIOR.
        WORD #1532 OCCURS   8 TIMES.
           INDEX OF DIVERSIFICATION =  3751.29 WITH STANDARD DEVIATION OF  3935.59

DI%E            7602 5ELCID0974 **** DE VNA SIERRA & LEGAUA A VN VAL.
        WORD #1533 OCCURS   1 TIMES.

DI%IENDO       13863 5ELCID1756 ESTO DIXO MYO %ID, ******** DEL CAUALLO.
        WORD #1534 OCCURS   1 TIMES.

DID            26060 5ELCID3322 *** EL CAUALLO, TOUEL DO EN PORIDAD:
        WORD #1535 OCCURS   1 TIMES.

DIEGO          15035 5ELCID1901 ***** & FERRANDO, LOS YFFANTES DE CARRION,
               17135 5ELCID2168 EA DON FERNANDO & A DON ***** AGUARDAR LOS MANDO
               17919 5ELCID2267 MUCHO ERAN ALEGRES ***** & FERRANDO;
               18084 5ELCID2288 ***** GON%ALEZ POR LA PUERTA SALIO,
               18555 5ELCID2348 MAS SE MARAUILLAN ENTRE ***** & FERRANDO,
               21438 5ELCID2725 POR DIOS UOS ROGAMOS, DON ***** & DON FERANDO
               22108 5ELCID2814 FALLO A ***** TELLEZ EL QUE DE ALBARFANEZ FUE;
               23621 5ELCID3009 E ***** & FERRANDO Y SON AMOS ADOS,
               26291 5ELCID3353 ***** GON%ALEZ ODREDES LO QUE DIXO:
               28556 5ELCID3646 MARTIN ANTOLINEZ & ***** GON%ALEZ FIRIERON SE DELAS LAN%AS,
               28649 5ELCID3658 VIO ***** GON%ALEZ QUE NO ESCAPARIE CON EL ALMA;
        WORD #1536 OCCURS  11 TIMES.
           INDEX OF DIVERSIFICATION =  1360.40 WITH STANDARD DEVIATION OF  1057.10

DIEMOS         20200 5ELCID2565 QUE LES ****** POR ARRAS & POR ONORES;
               25208 5ELCID3210 POR ESSOL ****** SUS ESPADAS AL%ID CAMPEADOR,
        WORD #1537 OCCURS   2 TIMES.

DIENTES        15950 5ELCID2022 LAS YERBAS DEL CAMPO A ******* LAS TOMO,
        WORD #1538 OCCURS   1 TIMES.

DIERA          25732 5ELCID3277 O QUIEN GELAS ***** POR PAREIAS OPOR VELADAS?
        WORD #1539 OCCURS   1 TIMES.

DIERAN          1268 5ELCID0163 CA ASSIL ****** LA FE & GELO AUIEN IURADO,
               15858 5ELCID2011 MYO %ID SELOS GA@ARA, QUE NON GELOS ****** EN DON.
               19357 5ELCID2452 AQUELOS QUE GELOS ****** NON GELO AUIEN LOGRADO.
        WORD #1540 OCCURS   3 TIMES.

DIERON          1922 5ELCID0244 CON LUMBRES & CON CANDELAS AL CORAL ****** SALTO.
                8250 5ELCID1050 E TIENEN GELO DELANT & ****** GELO PRIUADO.
               10298 5ELCID1304 ****** LE EN VALEN%IA O BIEN PUEDE ESTAR RICO.
               13544 5ELCID1716 LA SE@A SACAN FUERA, DE VALEN%IA ****** SALTO,
               17718 5ELCID2242 ALA GLERA DE VALEN%IA FUERA ****** SALTO;
               20545 5ELCID2608 AMOS LAS BENDIXIERON & ****** LES SU GRA%IA.
               25381 5ELCID3232 ENTRAMOS MELOS ****** LOS YFANTES DE CARRION.
        WORD #1541 OCCURS   7 TIMES.
           INDEX OF DIVERSIFICATION =  3908.83 WITH STANDARD DEVIATION OF  1539.79

DIESSE           202 5ELCID0026 E A QUEL QUE GELA ****** SOPIESSE UERA PALABRA,
                1285 5ELCID0165 NON LES ****** MYO %ID DELA GANAN%IA UN DINERO MALO.
               10159 5ELCID1286 E QUE LOS ****** AL ABBAT DON SANCHO.
               11333 5ELCID1434 SOLTARIEMOS LA GANAN%IA, QUE NOS ****** EL CABDAL.
        WORD #1542 OCCURS   4 TIMES.

DIESSEN          195 5ELCID0025 QUE A MYO %ID RUY DIAZ, QUE NADI NOL ******* POSADA,
                4022 5ELCID0511 SOS QUI@ONEROS QUE GELOS ******* POR CARTA.
                4091 5ELCID0520 AVN DELO QUE ******* CUIESSEN GRAND GANAN%IA.
                4419 5ELCID0562 QUE DE DIA NIN DE NOCH NON LES ******* AREBATA,
                6300 5ELCID0802 MANDO MYO %ID AUN QUELES ******* ALGO.
               26630 5ELCID3400 E QUE GELAS ******* A ONDRA & ABENDI%ION,
               28961 5ELCID3699 QUE NOLES ******* SALTO NIN OUIESSEN PAUOR.
```

WORD C# PREFIX CONTEXT

DIESSEN (CON'T)

WORD #1543 OCCURS 7 TIMES.
INDEX OF DIVERSIFICATION = 4793.33 WITH STANDARD DEVIATION OF 7734.66

DIESTES 20243 5ELCID2570 VOS LES ******* VILLAS E TIERRAS POR ARRAS ENTIERRAS DE CARRION,
22389 5ELCID2852 POR AQUESTA ONDRA QUE VOS ******* A ESTO QUE NOS CUNTIO;
WORD #1544 OCCURS 2 TIMES.

DIESTRA 81 5ELCID0011 ALA EXIDA DE BIUAR OUIERON LA CORNEIA *******,
1683 5ELCID0216 AL%O SU MANO *******, LA CARA SE SANTIGUA:
10573 5ELCID1340 AL%O LA MANO *******, EL REY SE SANTIGO:
WORD #1545 OCCURS 3 TIMES.

DIESTRO 3160 5ELCID0398 DE ******* A LILON LAS TORRES, QUE MOROS LAS HAN;
5920 5ELCID0750 DIOL TAL ESPADADA CON EL SO ******* BRA%O,
5943 5ELCID0753 CAUALGAD, MYNAYA, UOS SODES EL MYO ******* BRA%O
6362 5ELCID0810 OYD, MYNAYA, SODES MYO ******* BRA%O
12195 5ELCID1548 E BUEN CAUALLO EN ******* QUE UA ANTE SUS ARMAS.
15847 5ELCID2010 TANTOS CAUALLOS EN *******, GRUESSOS & CORREDORES,
20274 5ELCID2573 CAUALLOS PORA EN ******* FUERTES & CORREDORES,
WORD #1546 OCCURS 7 TIMES.
INDEX OF DIVERSIFICATION = 2851.33 WITH STANDARD DEVIATION OF 2277.64

DIEZMO 14211 5ELCID1798 DE TODA LA SU QUINTA EL ****** LA MANDADO.
WORD #1547 OCCURS 1 TIMES.

DIGA 14339 5ELCID1814 QUE NON **** MAL EL REY ALFONSSO DEL QUE VALEN%IA MANDA.
27107 5ELCID3464 NON **** NINGUNO DELLA MAS VNA ENTEN%ION.
WORD #1548 OCCURS 2 TIMES.

DIGADES 7626 5ELCID0977 ******* AL CONDE NON LO TENGA A MAL,
15061 5ELCID1904 QUE GELO ******* ALBUEN CAMPEADOR:
16904 5ELCID2139 QUANDO UOS IUNTAREDES COMIGO, QUEM ******* LA UERDAT.
WORD #1549 OCCURS 3 TIMES.

DIGAMOS 20042 5ELCID2544 ******* QUE LAS LEUAREMOS ATIERRAS DE CARRION,
WORD #1550 OCCURS 1 TIMES.

DIGAN 4209 5ELCID0535 POR QUE LO PRIS DELLOS QUE DE MI NON ***** MAL.
WORD #1551 OCCURS 1 TIMES.

DIGO 6956 5ELCID0889 MAS DEL %ID CAMPEADOR YO NON UOS **** NADA.
8036 5ELCID1026 SI LO QUE **** FIZIEREDES, SALDREDES DE CATIUO;
10537 5ELCID1335 FEUOS AQUI LAS SE@AS, VERDAD UOS **** YO:
14274 5ELCID1806 DESTA MI QUINTA, **** UOS SIN FALLA,
16807 5ELCID2128 AQUI LO **** ANTE MYO SE@OR EL REY ALFONSSO:
17364 5ELCID2197 AUOS ****, MIS FIJAS, DON ELUIRA & DO@A SOL:
18610 5ELCID2355 HYO UOS ****, %ID, POR TODA CARIDAD,
23186 5ELCID2954 VERDAD TE **** YO, QUE ME PESA DE CORA%ON,
26553 5ELCID3389 FAZER TELO DEZIR QUE TALERES QUAL **** YO.
27043 5ELCID3454 EN TODAS GUISAS TALES SODES QUALES **** YO;
28170 5ELCID3596 OYD QUE UOS ****, YFANTES DE CARRION:
WORD #1552 OCCURS 11 TIMES.
INDEX OF DIVERSIFICATION = 2120.40 WITH STANDARD DEVIATION OF 1431.73

DIL 20768 5ELCID2638 *** QUE ENBIO MIS FIJAS A TIERRAS DE CARRION,
WORD #1553 OCCURS 1 TIMES.

DILES 24754 5ELCID3153 ***** DOS ESPADAS, A COLADA & A TIZON,
WORD #1554 OCCURS 1 TIMES.

DINARADA 506 5ELCID0064 NON LE OSARIEN UENDER ALMENOS ********.
WORD #1555 OCCURS 1 TIMES.

DINERO 1291 5ELCID0165 NON LES DIESSE MYO %ID DELA GANAN%IA UN ****** MALO.
1998 5ELCID0252 NON QUIERO FAZER ENEL MONESTERIO VN ****** DE DA@O;
3965 5ELCID0503 NON PRENDRE DE UOS QUANTO UALE VN ****** MALO.
8180 5ELCID1042 SABET, NON UOS DARE AUOS VN ****** MALO;
WORD #1556 OCCURS 4 TIMES.

DINEROS 6315 5ELCID0804 DIO APARTIR ESTOS ******* & ESTOS AUERES LARGOS;
29251 5ELCID3734 ES LEYDO, DAT NOS DEL VINO; SI NON TENEDES *******, ECHAD
WORD #1557 OCCURS 2 TIMES.

DINNO 18671 5ELCID2363 EUOS TAN ***** QUE CON EL AUEDES PART.
WORD #1558 OCCURS 1 TIMES.

DIO 3034 5ELCID0382 DIOS QUE NOS *** LAS ALMAS, CONSEIO NOS DARA.
6035 5ELCID0765 MARTIN ANTOLINEZ VN COLPE *** A GALUE,
6312 5ELCID0804 *** APARTIR ESTOS DINEROS & ESTOS AUERES LARGOS;
6837 5ELCID0874 QUIN LOS *** ESTOS, SI UOS VALA DIOS, MYNAYA
9810 5ELCID1246 ATODOS LES *** EN VALEN%IA CASAS & HEREDADES
10135 5ELCID1284 CIENTO OMNES LE *** MYO %ID A ALBARFANEZ POR SERUIR LE EN LA CARRERA,
10528 5ELCID1334 GRANDES SON LAS GANAN%IAS QUEL *** EL CRIADOR,
11097 5ELCID1405 *** TRES CAUALLEROS MYNAYA ALBARFANEZ,
11239 5ELCID1422 LOS QUINIENTOS MARCOS *** MINAYA AL ABBAT,

WORD C# PREFIX CONTEXT

DIO (CON'T)

```
                    11737 5ELCID1488 ESSA NOCH CON DUCHO LES *** GRAND,
                    13522 5ELCID1714 *** SALTO MYO %ID EN BAUIECA EL SO CAUALLO;
                    14494 5ELCID1833 HYEN LCS PRIMEROS EL REY FUERA *** SALTO,
                    16730 5ELCID2118 MYO %ID DELOS CAUALLOS LX *** EN DON.
                    18142 5ELCID2295 HYA SE@OR CNDRADC, REBATA NOS *** EL LEON.
                    20901 5ELCID2654 ALAS FIJAS DEL %ID EL MORO SUS DO@AS ***,
                    22019 5ELCID2801 COGIO DEL AGUA ENEL & ASUS PRIMAS ***;
                    24913 5ELCID3172 NCLO PODEMOS NEGAR, CA DOS ESPADAS NOS ***;
                    25039 5ELCID3189 TENDIO EL BRA%O, LA ESPADA TIZON LE ***;
                    25060 5ELCID3192 TENDIO EL BRA%O, EL ESPADA COLADAL ***;
                    25166 5ELCID3204 EN ORO & EN PLATA TRES MILL MARCOS DE PLATA LES ***;
                    26928 5ELCID3440 GRANDES AUERES LES *** MYO %ID EL CAMPEADOR,
                    28675 5ELCID3661 VN COLPEL *** DE LANC, CON LO AGUDO NOL TOMAUA.
                    28801 5ELCID3678 ESTE COLPE FECHO, OTRC *** MUNO GUSTIOZ,
                    28849 5ELCID3685 CON EL *** VNA TUERTA, DELA SIELLA LO ENCAMO,
          WORD #1559 OCCURS  24 TIMES.
             INDEX OF DIVERSIFICATION =  1121.39 WITH STANDARD DEVIATION OF  1058.27

DIOL                 5914 5ELCID0750 **** TAL ESPADADA CCN EL SO DIESTRO BRA%O,
                    26585 5ELCID3650 **** VN COLPE, DE TRAUIESSOL TOMAUA,
          WORD #1560 OCCURS   2 TIMES.

DIOLES              17700 5ELCID2240 ****** BENDICTIONES, LA MISSA A CANTADO.
                    28140 5ELCID3593 EL REY ****** FIELES POR DEZIR EL DERECHO & AL NON,
          WORD #1561 OCCURS   2 TIMES.

DIOS                  144 5ELCID0020 ****, QUE BUEN VASSALO, SI OUIESSE BUEN SE@OR
                     1691 5ELCID0217 ATI LO GRADESCO, ****, QUE %IELO & TIERRA GUIAS;
                     1907 5ELCID0243 ****, QUE ALEGRE FUE EL ABBAT DON SANCHO
                     2606 5ELCID0329 QUE AMIO %ID EL CAMPEADOR QUE **** LE CURIAS DE MAL:
                     2887 5ELCID0364 POR MYO %ID EL CAMPEADOR, QUE **** LE CURIE DE MAL.
                     2963 5ELCID0373 AGORA NOS PARTIMOS, **** SABE EL AIUNTAR.
                     3031 5ELCID0382 **** QUE NOS DIO LAS ALMAS, CONSEIO NOS DARA.
                     3262 5ELCID0411 SINAUA LA CARA, A **** SE ACOMENDO,
                     3627 5ELCID0457 YXIE EL SOL, ****, QUE FERMOSO APUNTAUA
                     4562 5ELCID0580 VEYEN LO LOS DE ALCO%ER, ****, COMMO SE ALABAUAN
                     4729 5ELCID0600 ****, QUE BUENO ES EL GOZO POR AQUESTA MA@ANA
                     4853 5ELCID0614 GRADO A **** DEL %IELO & ATODOS LOS SOS SANTOS,
                     6196 5ELCID0789 LA COFIA FRONZIDA ****, COMMO ES BIEN BARBADO
                     6216 5ELCID0792 GRADO A ****, A QUEL QUE ESTA EN ALTO,
                     6329 5ELCID0806  ****, QUE BIEN PAGO A TODOS SUS VASSALLOS,
                     6512 5ELCID0831 **** NOS VALIO & VEN%IEMOS LA LIDIT.
                     6814 5ELCID0870 MYO %ID RUY DIAZ DE **** AYA SU GRA%IA
                     6842 5ELCID0874  QUIN LOS DIO ESTOS, SI UOS VALA ****, MYNAYA
                     7220 5ELCID0926  ****, COMMO FUE ALEGRE TODO AQUEL FONSSADO,
                     7249 5ELCID0930  ****, COMMO ES ALEGRE LA BARBA VELIDA,
                     7273 5ELCID0933  ****, COMMO FUE EL %ID PAGADO & FIZO GRANT ALEGRIA
                     8266 5ELCID1052 COMIENDO VA EL CONDE  ****, QUE DE BUEN GRADO
                     8633 5ELCID1096 YA VIE MYO %ID QUE **** LE YUA VALIENDO.
                     8748 5ELCID1112 YO FIO POR **** QUE EN NUESTRO PRO ENADRAN.
                     8794 5ELCID1118 GRADO A ****, LO NUESTRO FUE ADELANT.
                     8896 5ELCID1133 COMMO FIO POR ****, EL CAMPO NUESTRO SERA.
                     9099 5ELCID1158 QUE **** LE AIUDARA & FIZIERA ESTA ARRANCADA.
                     9999 5ELCID1267 GRADO A ****, MYNAYA, & A SANTA MARIA MADRE
                    10253 5ELCID1298 QUANDO **** PRESTAR NOS QUIERE, NOS BIEN GELO GRADESCAMOS:
                    10307 5ELCID1305  ****, QUE ALEGRE ERA TODA CHRISTIANISMO,
                    11029 5ELCID1396 OMILOM, DO@A XIMENA, **** VOS CURIE DE MAL,
                    11113 5ELCID1407 DEZID AL CANPEADOR, QUE **** LE CURIE DE MAL,
                    11343 5ELCID1435 HYO LO VERE CON EL %ID, SI **** ME LIEUA ALA.
                    12055 5ELCID1529 SI **** ME LEGARE AL %ID ELO VEA CON EL ALMA,
                    12242 5ELCID1554 AMYNAYA & ALAS DUE@AS, **** COMMO LAS ONDRAUA
                    12594 5ELCID1598 CON **** & CON UUSCO BUENAS SON & CRIADAS.
                    12731 5ELCID1616 AL%AN LAS MANOS PORA **** ROGAR,
                    13043 5ELCID1654 CON LA MER%ED DE **** & DE SANTA MARIA MADRE
                    13057 5ELCID1656 CON **** A QUESTA LID YO LA HE DE ARRANCAR.
                    13391 5ELCID1697 ODE AMAS ODEL VNA **** NOS VALDRA.
                    13452 5ELCID1705 PRENDOL YO LOS PECADOS, & **** LE ABRA EL ALMA.
                    13728 5ELCID1740 QUE **** LES OUO MER%ED QUE VEN%IERON EL CAMPO.
                    13809 5ELCID1750 ESTO **** SE LO QUISO CON TODOS LOS SOS SANTOS,
                    15337 5ELCID1942 AFE **** DEL %IELLO QUE NOS ACUERDE EN LO MIIOR.
                    16064 5ELCID2037 GRADESCOLO A **** DEL %IELO & DESPUES AUOS,
                    16127 5ELCID2045 VALER ME A **** DE DIA & DE NOCH.
                    16788 5ELCID2126 **** QUE ESTA EN %IELO DEM DENT BUEN GALARDON.
                    17019 5ELCID2155 AFE **** DEL %IELO, QUE LO PONGA EN BUEN LOGAR
                    17493 5ELCID2213 DE PIE & ASABOR, ****, QUE QUEDOS ENTRARON
                    17720 5ELCID2243 ****, QUE BIEN TOUIERON ARMAS EL %ID & SUS VASSALOS
                    18425 5ELCID2332 **** UOS SALUE, YERNOS, YFANTES DE CARRION,
                    18504 5ELCID2342 AVN SI **** QUISIERE & EL PADRE QUE ESTA EN ALTO,
                    18603 5ELCID2354 CALOS MOROS, CON ****, NON FINCARAN EN CANPO.
                    18848 5ELCID2385 POR LA SU VENTURA & **** QUEL AMAUA
                    18872 5ELCID2388 ENSAYAUAS EL OBISPO, ****, QUE BIEN LIDIAUA
                    18951 5ELCID2398 PLOGO A ****, AQUESTA FUE EL ARRANCADA.
                    19066 5ELCID2412 RESPUSO BUCAR AL %ID: CONFONDA **** TAL AMISTAD
                    19322 5ELCID2447 COMMO YO FIO POR **** & EN TODOS LOS SOS SANTOS,
```

WORD C# PREFIX CONTEXT

DIOS (CON'T)

19665 5ELCID2493 GRADO HA **** QUE DEL MUNDO ES SEÑOR
19906 5ELCID2524 GRADO A SANTA MARIA, MADRE DEL NUESTRO SEÑOR ****
20720 5ELCID2630 RESPONDIEN LOS YERNOS: ASSI LO MANDE ****
20864 5ELCID2650 ****, QUE BIEN LOS SIRUIO ATODO SO SABOR
21121 5ELCID2684 **** LO QUIERA & LO MANDE, QUE DE TODEL MUNDO ES SEÑOR,
21434 5ELCID2725 POR **** UOS ROGAMOS, DON DIEGO & DON FERANDO
21965 5ELCID2795 SI **** NON NOS VALE, AQUI MORREMOS NOS.
22414 5ELCID2855 AFFE **** DELOS %IELOS QUE UOS DE DENT BUEN GALARDON
22678 5ELCID2890 VENIDES, MIS FIJAS? **** UOS CURIE DE MAL
22712 5ELCID2894 DE MYOS YERNOS DE CARRION **** ME FAGA VENGAR
23482 5ELCID2990 DIXO EL REY: NO LO FERE, SIN SALUE ****
23798 5ELCID3032 **** LO MANDE QUE POR UOS SE ONDRE OY LA CORT
23846 5ELCID3038 **** SALUE A NUESTROS AMIGOS & AUOS MAS, SEÑOR
23887 5ELCID3042 RESPONDIO EL REY: SI FAGO, SIN SALUE ****
25759 5ELCID3281 GRADO A **** QUE %IELO & TIERRA MANDA
26570 5ELCID3391 LOS QUE AN REBTADO LIDIARAN, SIN SALUE ****
26747 5ELCID3416 ESSORA DIXO EL REY: **** UOS DE DEN BUEN GALARDON
27086 5ELCID3461 SI **** QUISIERE QUE DESTA BIEN SALGAMOS NOS,
27322 5ELCID3491 ESSORA RESPUSO EL REY: ASSI LO MANDE ****
28699 5ELCID3665 VALME, **** GLORIOSO, SEÑOR, & CURIAM DESTE ESPADA
28895 5ELCID3690 DIXO GON%ALO ASSUREZ: NOL FIRGADES, POR ****
29221 5ELCID3731 QUIEN ESCRIUIO ESTE LIBRO DEL **** PARAYSO, AMEN
WORD #1562 OCCURS 80 TIMES.
INDEX OF DIVERSIFICATION = 367.06 WITH STANDARD DEVIATION OF 393.93

DIOT 2791 5ELCID0353 **** CON LA LAN%A ENEL COSTADO, DONT YXIO LA SANGRE,
WORD #1563 OCCURS 1 TIMES.

DIRA 2522 5ELCID0319 LA MISSA NOS ****, ESTA SERA DE SANTA TRINIDAD;
WORD #1564 OCCURS 1 TIMES.

DIRAN 7061 5ELCID0902 EL POYO DE MYO %ID ASIL ***** POR CARTA.
WORD #1565 OCCURS 1 TIMES.

DIRAS 26424 5ELCID3370 AL PARTIR DELA LID POR TU BOCA LO *****,
WORD #1566 OCCURS 1 TIMES.

DIRE 21734 5ELCID2764 MAS YO UOS **** DAQUEL FELEZ MUNOZ.
WORD #1567 OCCURS 1 TIMES.

DIREUOS 11485 5ELCID1453 ******* DELOS CAUALLEROS QUE LEUARON EL MENSSAIE:
25961 5ELCID3309 *******, %ID, COSTUBRES AUEDES TALES,
WORD #1568 OCCURS 2 TIMES.

DIX 18728 5ELCID2370 OY UOS *** LA MISSA DE SANTA TRINIDADE.
WORD #1569 OCCURS 1 TIMES.

DIXIER 4166 5ELCID0530 LO QUE YO ****** NON LO TENGADES AMAL:
WORD #1570 OCCURS 1 TIMES.

DIXIERE 15119 5ELCID1912 DO EL *******, Y SEA EL MOION.
WORD #1571 OCCURS 1 TIMES.

DIXIEREDES 14816 5ELCID1872 E GUARNIR UOS DE TODAS ARMAS COMMO UOS ********** AQUI,
WORD #1572 OCCURS 1 TIMES.

DIXIERON 11587 5ELCID1468 ASI COMMO A MY ********, HY LOS PODREDES FALAR;
13349 5ELCID1692 ESSORA ******** TODOS: DAMOR & DE VOLUNTAD.
24008 5ELCID3060 MATINES & PRIMA ******** FAZAL ALBA,
25320 5ELCID3224 ******** LOS ALCALDES QUANDO MANFESTADOS SON:
27850 5ELCID3554 ANDIDIERON EN PLEYTO, ******** LO AL REY ALFONSSO,
27884 5ELCID3558 ******** GELO AL REY, MAS NON GELO CONLOYO;
27995 5ELCID3573 ******** LOS DEL CAMPEADOR:
28904 5ELCID3692 ******** LOS FIELES: ESTO OYMOS NOS.
WORD #1573 OCCURS 8 TIMES.
INDEX OF DIVERSIFICATION = 2472.86 WITH STANDARD DEVIATION OF 3715.76

DIXIESTES 27096 5ELCID3462 DESPUES VEREDES QUE ********* O QUE NO.
WORD #1574 OCCURS 1 TIMES.

DIXO 391 5ELCID0049 ESTO LA NIÑA **** & TORNOS PORA SU CASA.
1054 5ELCID0136 **** RACHEL & VIDAS: DAR GELOS DE GRADO.
1079 5ELCID0139 **** RACHEL & VIDAS: NON SE FAZE ASSI EL MERCADO,
1096 5ELCID0141 **** MARTIN ANTOLINEZ: YO DESSO ME PAGO.
1133 5ELCID0146 **** RACHEL & VIDAS: NOS DESTO NOS PAGAMOS.
1293 5ELCID0166 **** MARTIN ANTOLINEZ: CARGEN LAS ARCHAS PRIUADO.
1403 5ELCID0180 PLAZME, **** EL %ID, DAQUI SEA ANDADA.
1788 5ELCID0228 **** MARTIN ANTOLINEZ: VERE ALA MUGIER ATODO MYO SOLAZ,
1940 5ELCID0246 GRADESCO LO ADIOS, MYO %ID, **** EL ABBAT DON SANCHO;
1954 5ELCID0248 **** EL %ID: GRA%IAS, DON ABBAT, & SO UUESTRO PAGADO;
4233 5ELCID0539 LO QUE **** EL %ID A TODOS LOS OTROS PLAZ.
5359 5ELCID0677 **** EL CAMPEADOR: A MI GUISA FABLASTES;
5628 5ELCID0709 **** EL CAMPEADOR: NON SEA, POR CARIDAD
5665 5ELCID0714 **** EL CAMPEADOR: VALELDE, POR CARIDAD

WORD C# PREFIX CONTEXT

DIXO (CON'T)

```
 6415 5ELCID0819 **** MYNAYA ALBARFANEZ:  ESTO FARE YO DE GRADO.
 6890 5ELCID0881 **** EL REY:  MUCHO ES MAÐANA,
 7264 5ELCID0932 E QUEL **** SALUDES DE SU MUGIER & DE SUS FIJAS
 7488 5ELCID0960 EL CONDE ES MUY FOLON & **** VNA VANIDAT:
 8024 5ELCID1024 MYO %ID RUY DIAZ COREDES LO QUE ****:
 8050 5ELCID1028 **** EL CONDE DON REMONT:  COMEDE, DON RODRIGO, & PENSSEDES
                 DE FOLGAR.
 8090 5ELCID1033 **** MYO %ID: COMED, CONDE, ALGO, CASI NON COMEDES, NON VEREDES
 8297 5ELCID1056 AQUI **** EL CONDE: DE VOLUNTAD & DE GRADO.
 8851 5ELCID1127 OYD QUE **** MINAYA ALBARFANEZ:
 9304 5ELCID1183 NON LES **** COSEIO, NIN LOS VINO HUUIAR.
 9396 5ELCID1195 ESTO **** MYO %ID EL QUE EN BUEN ORA NASCO.
 9744 5ELCID1239 **** MYO %ID DE LA SU BOCA ATANTO:
 9956 5ELCID1262 ALI **** MINAYA: CONSEIO ES AGUISADO.
10119 5ELCID1282 ESSORA **** MINAYA: DE BUENA VOLUNTAD.
10288 5ELCID1302 PLOGO A ALBARFANEZ DELO QUE **** DON RODRIGO.
10637 5ELCID1348 **** EL REY REY AL CONDE: DEXAD ESSA RAZON,
10694 5ELCID1355 ESSORA **** EL REY: PLAZ ME DE CORA%ON;
11090 5ELCID1404 **** DOÐA XIMENA: EL CRIADOR LO MANDE
11356 5ELCID1437 **** RACHEL & VIDAS: EL CRIADOR LO MANDE
11725 5ELCID1487 **** AUEGALUON: FER LO HE DE VELUNTAD.
11870 5ELCID1505 ESSORA **** MYNAYA: VAYMOS CAUALGAR.
12080 5ELCID1532 **** AUENGALUON: PLAZME DESTA PRESENTAIA,
12635 5ELCID1603 OYD LO QUE **** EL QUE EN BUEN ORA NASCO:
13085 5ELCID1659 ALEGRAUAS MIO %ID & ****: TAN BUEN DIA ES OY
13395 5ELCID1698 ESSORA **** EL %ID: DE BUENA VOLUNTAD.
13489 5ELCID1710 **** EL CAMPEADOR: DESA QUI UOS SEAN MANDADAS.
13860 5ELCID1756 ESTO **** MYO %ID, DI%IENDO DEL CAUALLO.
13983 5ELCID1771 COMMO LO **** EL %ID ASSI LO HAN ACABADO.
14661 5ELCID1855 **** EL REY DON ALFONSSO: RE%IBOLOS DE GRADO.
14763 5ELCID1866 FABLO EL REY DON ALFONSSO & **** ESTA RAZON:
15194 5ELCID1923 **** MYNAYA. DALMA & DE CORA%ON
15206 5ELCID1925 **** MYO %ID: GRADO AL CRIADOR
15350 5ELCID1943 CON TODO ESTO, AUOS **** ALFONSSO
15376 5ELCID1947 ESSORA **** EL %ID: PLAZME DE CORA%ON.
15387 5ELCID1949 **** MINAYA, UOS SED SABIDOR.
16028 5ELCID2033 **** EL REY ESTO FERE DALMA & DE CORA%ON;
16055 5ELCID2036 FABLO MYO %ID & ****: MER%ED; YOLO RE%IBO, ALFONSSO MYO SEÐOR;
16108 5ELCID2043 FABLO MYO %ID & **** ESTA RAZON: ESTO GRADESCO AL CRIADOR,
16139 5ELCID2047 **** EL REY: NON ES AGUISADO OY:
16484 5ELCID2090 GRA%IAS, **** EL REY, AUOS & ATOD ESTA CORT.
16907 5ELCID2140 **** ALBARFANEZ: SEÐOR, AFE QUE ME PLAZ.
16956 5ELCID2147 **** EL REY DON ALFONSSO: MUCHO ME AUEDES ENBARGADO.
17205 5ELCID2177 **** MYO %ID ADON PERO & A MUÐO GUSTIOZ:
17602 5ELCID2227 ESTOZ **** MINAYA: ESTO FARE YO DE GRADO.
18702 5ELCID2367 **** MYO %ID: AYAMOS MAS DE VAGAR.
18805 5ELCID2380 ESSORA **** MYO %ID: LO QUE UOS QUEREDES PLAZ ME.
19427 5ELCID2462 **** MYO %ID: YO DESTO SO PAGADO;
19444 5ELCID2464 POR BIEN LO **** EL %ID, MAS ELLOS LO TOUIERON AMAL.
20221 5ELCID2568 **** EL CAMPEADOR: DARUOS HE MYS FIJAS & ALGO DELO MYO;
20661 5ELCID2623 **** FELEZ MUNOZ: PLAZME DALMA & DE CORA%ON.
21040 5ELCID2674 DELO QUE EL MORO **** ALOS YFANTES NON PLAZE:
23355 5ELCID2975 ASSI COMMO LO ****, SUYO ERA EL CUYDADO:
23474 5ELCID2990 **** EL REY: NO LO FERE, SIN SALUE DIOS
23810 5ELCID3033 AMEN, **** MYO %ID EL CAMPEADOR;
23949 5ELCID3052 **** EL REY: PLAZME DE VELUNTAD.
24427 5ELCID3114 EL REY **** AL %ID: VENJD ACA SER, CAMPEADOR,
24449 5ELCID3117 ESSORA **** MUCHAS MER%EDES EL QUE VALEN%IA GAÐO:
24472 5ELCID3120 LO QUE **** EL %ID AL REY PLOGO DE CORA%ON.
24809 5ELCID3160 **** EL CONDE DON GAR%IA: AESTO NOS FABLEMOS.
25230 5ELCID3212 SI PLOGUIERE AL REY, ASSI DEZIMOS NOS: **** EL REY
25241 5ELCID3214 **** EL BUEN REY: ASSILO OTORGO YO.
25248 5ELCID3215 **** ALBARFANEZ LEUANTADOS EN PIE EL %ID CAMPEADOR:
26296 5ELCID3353 DIEGO GON%ALEZ ODREDES LO QUE ****:
26555 5ELCID3390 **** EL REY ALFONSSO: CALLE YA ESTA RAZON.
26744 5ELCID3416 ESSORA **** EL REY: DIOS UOS DE DEN BUEN GALARDON
26878 5ELCID3434 **** EL REY: PLAZME DE CORA%ON.
27100 5ELCID3463 **** EL REY: FINE ESTA RAZON:
27169 5ELCID3473 ENESSORA **** MIO %ID. NO LO FARE, SENOR.
27185 5ELCID3475 ENESSORA **** EL REY: ACSADAS, CAMPEADOR.
27277 5ELCID3486 MYO %ID AL REY LAS MANOS LE BESO & ****: PLAZME, SEÐOR.
27527 5ELCID3516 ESSORA **** EL REY: DESTO NON HE SABOR;
27623 5ELCID3527 **** MARTIN ANTOLINEZ:  POR QUE LO DEZIDES, SEÐOR
28052 5ELCID3581 ESSORA **** EL REY: DALMA & DE CORA%ON.
28542 5ELCID3644 ANTES QUE EL COLPE ESPERASSE ****: VEN%UDO SO.
28723 5ELCID3668 ESSORA **** EL REY: VENID UOS AMI COMPAÐA;
28889 5ELCID3690 **** GON%ALO ASSUREZ: NOL FIRGADES, POR DIOS
```

WORD #1575 OCCURS 90 TIMES.
INDEX OF DIVERSIFICATION = 319.20 WITH STANDARD DEVIATION OF 391.12

DIXOLES

```
 3399 5ELCID0429 ******* ATODOS COMMO QUERIE TRASNOCHAR;
22288 5ELCID2839 ******* FUERTE MIENTRE QUE ANDIDIESSEN DE DIA & DE NOCH,
```

WORD #1576 OCCURS 2 TIMES.

DIXOLO

```
20999 5ELCID2668 NON TIENE PORIDAD, ****** AVENGALUON:
```

WORD #1577 OCCURS 1 TIMES.

WORD C# PREFIX CONTEXT

```
DIZ              14840 5ELCID1875 ASSI COMMO SEMEIA & LA VELUNTAD MELO ***.
        WORD #1578 OCCURS   1 TIMES.

DIZE              6140 5ELCID0782 **** MYNAYA:  AGORA SO PAGADO,
                  7196 5ELCID0922 TODO GELO ****, QUE NOL ENCUBRE NADA.
                 16722 5ELCID2117 CADA VNO LO QUE PIDE, NADI NOL **** DE NO.
                 25746 5ELCID3279 QUANTO EL **** NON GELO PREZIAMOS NADA.
                 28743 5ELCID3670 OTORGAN GELO LOS FIELES QUE **** VERDADERA PALABRA.
        WORD #1579 OCCURS   5 TIMES.
           INDEX OF DIVERSIFICATION =  5649.75 WITH STANDARD DEVIATION OF  4264.21

DIZEN             2747 5ELCID0347 ALOS IUDIOS TE DEXESTE PRENDER; DO ***** MONTE CALUARIE
                  4648 5ELCID0590 ***** LOS DE ALCOZER:  YA SE NOS VA LA GANAZIA
                  5136 5ELCID0649 YXIERON DE ZELFA LA QUE ***** DE CANAL,
                  5171 5ELCID0654 CON AQUESTOS DOS REYES QUE ***** FFARIZ & GALUE;
                 10760 5ELCID1362 ATODAS LAS ESCUELLAS QUE A EL ***** SE@OR
                 10879 5ELCID1377 NON LO ***** A NADI, & FINCO ESTA RAZON.
                 17911 5ELCID2266 GRANT BIEN ***** DELLOS, CA SERA AGUISADO.
                 20890 5ELCID2653 HYUAN TROZIR LOS MONTES, LOS QUE ***** DE LUZON.
                 20986 5ELCID2666 QUANDO ESTA FALSSEDAD ***** LOS DE CARRION,
                 21450 5ELCID2727 AL VNA ***** COLADA & AL OTRA TIZON,
                 22197 5ELCID2827 QUANDO GELO ***** A MYO ZID EL CAMPEADOR,
                 22599 5ELCID2879 AQUAL ***** MEDINA YUAN ALBERGAR,
                 23048 5ELCID2936 MERZED, REY ALFONSSO, DE LARGOS REYNOS AUOS ***** SE@OR
                 25929 5ELCID3304 AMI LO *****, ATI DAN LAS OREIADAS.
                 26585 5ELCID3394 AL VNO ***** OIARRA & AL OTRO YENEGO SIMENEZ,
        WORD #1580 OCCURS  15 TIMES.
           INDEX OF DIVERSIFICATION =  1701.71 WITH STANDARD DEVIATION OF  2196.41

DIZES            23195 5ELCID2955 E VERDAD ***** EN ESTO, TU, MU@O GUSTIOZ,
                 26527 5ELCID3386 NON ***** VERDAD AMIGO NI HA SE@OR,
        WORD #1581 OCCURS   2 TIMES.

DIZIAN             141 5ELCID0019 DELAS SUS BOCAS TODOS ****** UNA RAZON:
        WORD #1582 OCCURS   1 TIMES.

DIZID            23297 5ELCID2968 ***** LE AL CAMPEADOR, QUE EN BUEN ORA NASCO,
        WORD #1583 OCCURS   1 TIMES.

DIZIEN            4964 5ELCID0628 QUE A VNO QUE ****** MYO ZID RUY DIAZ DE BIUAR
        WORD #1584 OCCURS   1 TIMES.

DIZIENDO          7233 5ELCID0928 ******** LES SALUDES DE PRIMOS & DE HERMANOS,
                 11206 5ELCID1418 ******** ESTO MYANAYA: ESTO FERE DE VELUNTAD.
                 15213 5ELCID1926 ESTO ********, CONPIEZAN LA RAZON,
                 18090 5ELCID2289 ******** DELA BOCA: NON VERE CARRION
                 18523 5ELCID2344 ESTO VAN ******** & LAS YENTES SE ALEGANDO,
        WORD #1585 OCCURS   5 TIMES.
           INDEX OF DIVERSIFICATION =  2821.50 WITH STANDARD DEVIATION OF  1677.24

DJREUOS          28750 5ELCID3671 LOS DOS HAN ARRANCADO: ******* DE MUNO GUSTIOZ,
        WORD #1586 OCCURS   1 TIMES.

DJZE             25190 5ELCID3208 **** EL CONDE DON REMONO: DEZID DE SSI O DE NO.
        WORD #1587 OCCURS   1 TIMES.

DO                2083 5ELCID0262 AFEUOS DO@A XIMENA CON SUS FIJAS ** UA LEGANDO;
                  2329 5ELCID0294 VANSSE PORA SAN PERO ** ESTA EL QUE ENBUEN PUNTO NAZIO.
                  2746 5ELCID0347 ALOS IUDIOS TE DEXESTE PRENDER; ** DIZEN MONTE CALUARIE
                  3005 5ELCID0379 ZID, ** SON UUESTROS ESFUERZOS? EN BUEN ORA NASQUIESTES DE MADRE;
                  3865 5ELCID0490 ** YO UOS ENBIAS BIEN ABRIA TAL ESPERANZA.
                  4307 5ELCID0548 GRANDES SON LAS GANANZIAS QUE PRISO POR LA TIERRA ** UA.
                  5728 5ELCID0722 TODOS FIEREN ENEL AZ ** ESTA PERO VERMUEZ.
                  6527 5ELCID0833 SI NON, ** SOPIEREDES QUE SOMOS, YNDOS CONSEGUIR.
                  6946 5ELCID0888 HYD & VENIT, DA QUI UOS ** MI GRAZIA;
                  9717 5ELCID1235 LAS NUEUAS DEL CAUALLERO YAVEDES ** LEGAUAN.
                 10036 5ELCID1271 ENBIAR UOS QUIERO A CASTIELLA, ** AUEMOS HEREDADES,
                 10350 5ELCID1311 DEMANDO POR ALFONSSO, ** LO PODRIE FALLAR.
                 10393 5ELCID1317 AFE MINAYA LABARFANEZ ** LEGA TAN APUESTO;
                 10682 5ELCID1353 SALDRIEN DEL MONESTERIO ** ELLE LAS DEXO,
                 10774 5ELCID1364 SIRUAN LE SUS HEREDADES ** FUERE EL CAMPEADOR,
                 11107 5ELCID1406 ENVIOLOS A MYO ZID, AVALENZIA ** ESTA,
                 12118 5ELCID1537 ONDRADO ES MYO ZID EN VALENZIA ** ESTAUA
                 12420 5ELCID1576 ALA PUERTA DE VALENZIA, ** FUESSE EN SO SALUO,
                 13319 5ELCID1689 EL OBISPO ** IHERONIMO SOLTURA NOS DARA,
                 13941 5ELCID1766 ACADA VNA DELLAS ** LES CC MARCOS DE PLATA,
                 14257 5ELCID1804 ** SODES, CABOSO? VENID ACA, MYNAYA;
                 14448 5ELCID1827 LEGAN A VALADOLID, ** EL REY ALFONSSO ESTAUA;
                 15114 5ELCID1911 QUEL YRE A VISTAS ** FUERE AGUISADO;
                 15117 5ELCID1912 ** EL DIXIERE, Y SEA EL MOION.
                 15356 5ELCID1944 QUE UOS VERNIE AVISTAS ** OUIESSEDES SABOR;
                 15400 5ELCID1951 FASTA ** LO FALLASSEMOS BUSCAR LO YREMOS NOS,
```

WORD C# PREFIX CONTEXT

DO (CON'T)

```
          16603 5ELCID2103 TREZIENTOS MARCOS DE PLATA EN AYUDA LES ** YO,
          16663 5ELCID2110 VOS CASADES MIS FIJAS, CA NON GELAS ** YO.
          19218 5ELCID2431 ALAS TIENDAS ERAN LEGADOS, ** ESTAUA
          19820 5ELCID2512 AQUI ESTA CON MYO %ID EL OBISPO ** IHERONIMO,
          20052 5ELCID2545 ENSE@AR LAS HEMOS ** LAS HEREDADES SON.
          20314 5ELCID2577 MIOS FIJOS SODES AMOS, QUANDO MIS FIJAS VOS **;
          20521 5ELCID2605 HYD A CARRION ** SODES HEREDADAS,
          21210 5ELCID2695 ALLI SON CA@OS ** A ELPHA EN%ERRO;
          21294 5ELCID2706 COGIDA HAN LA TIENDA ** ALBERGARON DE NOCH,
          21688 5ELCID2757 POR LOS MONTES ** YUAN, ELLOS YUAN SE ALABANDO:
          21755 5ELCID2767 ENLA CARRERA ** YUA DOLIOL EL CORA%ON,
          22400 5ELCID2853 MUCHO UOS LO GRADE%E, ALLA ** ESTA, MYO %ID EL CANPEADOR,
          22442 5ELCID2858 MINAYA VA UER SUS PRIMAS ** SON,
          22991 5ELCID2929 ADELINO PORAL PALA%IO ** ESTAUA LA CORT,
          23318 5ELCID2970 VENGAM A TOLLEDO, ESTOL ** DE PLAZO.
          23833 5ELCID3036 OMILLOM AUOS & ALCONDE ** REMOND
          24159 5ELCID3081 ** TALES %IENTO TOUIER, BIEN SERE SIN PAUOR.
          25087 5ELCID3196 POR ESSO UOS LA ** QUE LA BIEN CURIEDES UOS.
          26064 5ELCID3322 DID EL CAUALLO, TOUEL ** EN PORIDAD:
          26168 5ELCID3336 FASTA ** DESPERTO MYO %ID, EL QUE VALEN%IA GA@O;
          27519 5ELCID3515 HY UOS LE ** EN DON, MANDEDES LE TOMAR, SE@OR.
          28103 5ELCID3588 HYA SALIERON AL CAMPO ** ERAN LOS MOIONES.
          28158 5ELCID3595 ** SEDIEN ENEL CAMPO FABLO EL REY DON ALFONSSO:
     WORD #1588 OCCURS  49 TIMES.
        INDEX OF DIVERSIFICATION =   542.23 WITH STANDARD DEVIATION OF   570.13

DOBLADA    4622 5ELCID0586 LA PARIA QUEL A PRESA TORNAR NOS LA HA *******.
          12092 5ELCID1533 ANTES DESTE TE%ER DIA UOS LA DARE *******.
     WORD #1589 OCCURS   2 TIMES.

DOBLADO    2400 5ELCID0303 LO QUE PERDEDES ******* UOS LO COBRAR.
     WORD #1590 OCCURS   1 TIMES.

DOBLADOS   1991 5ELCID0251 SI YO ALGUN DIA VISQUIER, SERUOS HAN ********.
     WORD #1591 OCCURS   1 TIMES.

DOBLAR      631 5ELCID0080 SI YO BIUO, ****** UOS HE LA SOLDADA.
     WORD #1592 OCCURS   1 TIMES.

DOBLAUA   20500 5ELCID2602 EL FIZO AQUESTO, LA MADRE LO *******;
     WORD #1593 OCCURS   1 TIMES.

DOBLES    28455 5ELCID3634 TRES ****** DE LORIGA TENIE FERNANDO, AQUESTOL PRESTO,
     WORD #1594 OCCURS   1 TIMES.

DOD       28347 5ELCID3619 TEMBRAR QUERIE LA TIERRA *** ERAN MOUEDORES.
     WORD #1595 OCCURS   1 TIMES.

DOLAS     16556 5ELCID2098 E ***** POR VELADAS ALOS YFANTES DE CARRION.
     WORD #1596 OCCURS   1 TIMES.

DOLIOL    21757 5ELCID2767 ENLA CARRERA DO YUA ****** EL CORA%ON,
     WORD #1597 OCCURS   1 TIMES.

DOLOR       136 5ELCID0018 PLORANDO DELOS OIOS, TANTO AUYEN EL *****.
           9162 5ELCID1166 NON ES CON RECABDO EL ***** DE VALEN%IA.
     WORD #1598 OCCURS   2 TIMES.

DON         163 5ELCID0022 EL REY *** ALFONSSO TANTO AUIE LA GRAND SA@A,
           1200 5ELCID0155 YA *** RACHEL & VIDAS, AUEDES ME OLBIDADO
           1231 5ELCID0159 *** RACHEL & VIDAS A MYO %ID BESARON LE LAS MANOS.
           1444 5ELCID0185 NOTOLOS *** MARTINO, SIN PESO LOS TOMAUA;
           1460 5ELCID0187 %INCO ESCUDEROS TIENE *** MARTINO, ATODOS LOS CARGAUA.
           1474 5ELCID0189 YA *** RACHEL & VIDAS, EN UUESTRAS MANOS SON LAS ARCAS;
           1502 5ELCID0192 DEMOS LE BUEN ***, CA EL NO LO HA BUSCADO.
           1552 5ELCID0199 GRADE%IOLO *** MARTINO & RECIBIO LOS MARCHOS;
           1864 5ELCID0237 EL ABBAT *** SANCHO, CHRISTIANO DEL CRIADOR,
           1913 5ELCID0243 DIOS, QUE ALEGRE FUE EL ABBAT *** SANCHO
           1943 5ELCID0246 GRADESCO LO ADIOS, MYO %ID, DIXO EL ABBAT *** SANCHO;
           1958 5ELCID0248 DIXO EL %ID: GRA%IAS, *** ABBAT, & SO UUESTRO PAGADO;
           2035 5ELCID0256 AQUELLAS UOS ACOMIENDO AUOS, ABBAT *** SANCHO;
           3042 5ELCID0383 AL ABBAT *** SANCHO TORNAN DE CASTIGAR,
           3076 5ELCID0387 TORNADO ES *** SANCHO, & FABLO ALBARFANEZ:
           3574 5ELCID0450 TERNE YO CASTEION *** ABREMOS GRAND EN PARA.
           3701 5ELCID0467 MYO %ID *** RODRIGO ALA PUERTA ADELI@AUA;
           4364 5ELCID0556 MOI %ID *** RODRIGO ALCO%ER CUEDA GANAR.
           6400 5ELCID0816 QUIEROL ENBIAR EN *** XXX CAUALLOS,
           7121 5ELCID0911 ALEN DE TERUEL *** RODRIGO PASSAUA,
           7128 5ELCID0912 ENEL PINAR DE TEUAR *** ROY DIAZ POSAUA;
           7312 5ELCID0938 ALTER%ER DIA, *** YXO Y ES TORNADO.
           7597 5ELCID0973 MYO %ID *** RODRIGO TRAE GRAND GANAN%IA,
           7613 5ELCID0975 DEL CONDE *** REMONT VENIDO LES MENSAIE;
           7706 5ELCID0987 EL CONDE *** REMONT DAR NOS HA GRANT BATALLA,
           7896 5ELCID1009 AL CONDE *** REMONT A PRESON LEAN TOMADO;
```

WORD C# PREFIX CONTEXT

DON (CON'T)

7962 5ELCID1017 A MYO %ID *** RODRIGO GRANT COZINAL ADOBAUAN;
7969 5ELCID1018 EL CONDE *** REMONT NON GELO PRE%IA NADA,
8053 5ELCID1028 DIXO EL CONDE *** REMONT: COMEDE, DON RODRIGO, & PENSSEDES DE FOLGAR.
8056 5ELCID1028 DIXO EL CONDE DON REMONT: COMEDE, *** RODRIGO, & PENSSEDES DE FOLGAR.
8106 5ELCID1034 E SI UOS COMIEREDES, *** YO SEA PAGADO,
8284 5ELCID1054 SI BIEN NON COMEDES, CONDE, *** YO SEA PAGADO,
8325 5ELCID1059 POR QUE EL CONDE *** REMONT TAN BIEN BOLUIE LAS MANOS.
8385 5ELCID1066 EL CONDE *** REMONT ENTRE LOS DOS ES ENTRADO.
9457 5ELCID1202 MYO %ID *** RODRIGO NON LO QUISO DETARDAR,
9569 5ELCID1216 MYO %ID *** RODRIGO LA QUINTA MANDO TOMAR,
9782 5ELCID1243 MYO %ID *** RODRIGO EN VALEN%IA ESTA FOLGANDO,
10162 5ELCID1286 E QUE LOS DIESSE AL ABBAT *** SANCHO.
10179 5ELCID1289 EL OBISPO *** IERONIMO SO NOMBRE ES LAMADO.
10289 5ELCID1302 PLOGO A ALBARFANEZ DELO QUE DIXO *** RODRIGO.
10292 5ELCID1303 AESTE *** IERONIMO YAL OTORGAN POR OBISPO;
10609 5ELCID1344 RE%IBO ESTOS CAUALLOS QUEM ENBIA DE ***.
11528 5ELCID1460 EL OBISPO *** IERONIMO, CORONADO DE PRESTAR,
11841 5ELCID1501 E EL OBISPO *** JERONIMO, CORANADO LEAL,
11957 5ELCID1516 *** LEGAN LOS OTROS, A MINAYA ALBARFANEZ SE UAN HOMILAR.
12177 5ELCID1546 EL OBISPO *** IHERONIMO, BUEN CHRISTIANO SIN FALLA,
12445 5ELCID1579 EL OBISPO *** IHERONIMO ADELANT SE ENTRAUA,
12783 5ELCID1622 PESOL AL REY DE MARRUECOS DE MYO %ID *** RODRIGO:
12834 5ELCID1628 VAN BUSCAR A VALEN%IA A MYO %ID *** RODRIGO.
13155 5ELCID1667 DESI AN ASSER DEL OBISPO *** IHERONIMO,
13426 5ELCID1702 EL OBISPO *** IHERONIMO LA MISSA LES CANTAUA;
13459 5ELCID1706 AUOS, %ID *** RODIRGO, EN BUEN ORA %INXIESTES ESPADA,
13477 5ELCID1708 PIDO UOS VN *** & SEAM PRESENTADO.
14165 5ELCID1793 EL OBISPO *** IHERONIMO, CABOSO CORONADO,
14197 5ELCID1797 MYO %ID *** RODRIGO, EL QUE EN BUEN ORA NASCO,
14430 5ELCID1825 POR EL REY *** ALFONSSO TOMAN SSE APREGUNTAR.
14514 5ELCID1836 EL CONDE *** GAR%IA, SO ENEMIGO MALO.
14549 5ELCID1840 EL REY *** ALFONSSO SEYSE SANTIGUANDO.
14664 5ELCID1855 DIXO EL REY *** ALFONSSO: RE%IBOLOS DE GRADO.
14675 5ELCID1856 GRADESCOLO A MYO %ID QUE TAL *** ME HA ENBIADO;
14699 5ELCID1859 PESO AL CONDE *** GAR%IA, E MAL ERA YRADO;
14760 5ELCID1866 FABLO EL REY *** ALFONSSO & DIXO ESTA RAZON:
14990 5ELCID1895 EL REY *** ALFONSSO ESSORA LOS LAMO,
15193 5ELCID1922 SI ES PAGADO O RE%IBIO EL ***?
15607 5ELCID1979 EL REY *** ALFONSSO A PRIESSA CAUALGAUA,
15711 5ELCID1993 EL OBISPO *** IERONIMO, CORANADO MEIOR,
15860 5ELCID2011 MYO %ID SELOS GA@ARA, QUE NON GELOS DIERAN EN ***.
15879 5ELCID2013 DE VN DIA ES LEGADO ANTES EL REY *** ALFONSSO.
15895 5ELCID2016 *** LO OUO A OIO EL QUE EN BUEN ORA NASCO,
15982 5ELCID2026 TAN GRAND PESAR OUO EL REY *** ALFONSSO:
16120 5ELCID2044 QUANDO HE LA GRA%IA DE *** ALFONSSO MYO SE@OR;
16310 5ELCID2069 EL OBISPO *** IHERONIMO LA MISSA CANTO.
16359 5ELCID2075 VUESTRAS FIJAS UOS PIDO, *** ELUIRA & DO@A SOL,
16469 5ELCID2088 AFELLAS EN UUESTRA MANO *** ELUIRA & DO@A SOL,
16513 5ELCID2093 CAMEARON LAS ESPADAS ANTEL REY *** ALFONSSO.
16518 5ELCID2094 FABLO EL REY *** ALFONSSO COMMO TAN BUEN SE@OR:
16550 5ELCID2097 DAQUI LAS PRENDO POR MIS MANOS *** ELUIRA & DONA SOL,
16681 5ELCID2112 QUANDO SALIE EL SOL, QUES TORNASSE CADA VNO *** SALIDOS SON.
16708 5ELCID2115 CONPE%O MYO %ID ADAR AQUIEN QUIERE PRENDER SO ***,
16732 5ELCID2118 MYO %ID DELOS CAUALLOS LX DIO EN ***.
16787 5ELCID2125 GRADESCOLO, REY, & PRENDO UUESTRO ***,
16823 5ELCID2129 QUI QUIERE YR COMIGO ALAS BODAS, O RE%EBIR MI ***,
16924 5ELCID2142 HYA REY *** ALFONSSO, SE@OR TAN ONDRADO,
16959 5ELCID2147 DIXO EL REY *** ALFONSSO: MUCHO ME AUEDES ENBARGADO.
16967 5ELCID2148 RE%IBO ESTE *** QUE ME AUEDES MANDADO;
17089 5ELCID2163 HE DELAS FIJAS DE MYO %ID, DE *** ELUIRA & DO@A SOL.
17130 5ELCID2168 EA *** FERNANDO & A DON DIEGO AGUARDAR LOS MANDO
17134 5ELCID2168 EA DON FERNANDO & A *** DIEGO AGUARDAR LOS MANDO
17245 5ELCID2181 VERAN ASUS ESPOSAS, A *** ELUIRA & A DONA SOL.
17367 5ELCID2197 AUOS DIGO, MIS FIJAS, *** ELUIRA & DO@A SOL:
17689 5ELCID2238 EL OBISPO *** IHERONIMO VISTIOS TAN PRIUADO,
17807 5ELCID2253 MYO %ID *** RODRIGO, EL QUE EN BUEN ORA NASCO,
17927 5ELCID2268 ESTOS FUERON FIJOS DEL CONDE *** GON%ALO.
18182 5ELCID2300 MYO %ID *** RODRIGO ALCUELLO LO TOMO,
18267 5ELCID2311 ELLOS ENESTO ESTANDO, *** AUIEN GRANT PESAR,
18421 5ELCID2331 MYO %ID *** RODRIGO SONRRISANDO SALIO:
18488 5ELCID2340 ASSI LO OTORGA *** PERO CUEMO SE ALABA FERRANDO.
18712 5ELCID2368 AFEUOS EL OBISPO *** IHERONIMO MUY BIEN ARMADO,
18831 5ELCID2383 EL OBISPO *** IHERONIMO PRISO A ESPOLONADA
19286 5ELCID2441 AMOS SON FIJOS DEL CONDE *** GO%ALO.
19874 5ELCID2520 EAMAS LA MYS FIJAS, *** ELUIRA & DO@A SOL;
20425 5ELCID2592 AMAS HERMANAS, *** ELUIRA & DO@A SOL,
20701 5ELCID2628 ADIOS LOS HACOMENDAMOS, *** ELUIRA & DO@A SOL,
21109 5ELCID2682 HYRE CON UUESTRA GRA%IA, *** ELUIRA & DO@A SOL;
21353 5ELCID2714 BIEN LO CREADES, *** ELUIRA & DO@A SOL,
21437 5ELCID2725 POR DIOS UOS ROGAMOS, *** DIEGO & DON FERANDO
21440 5ELCID2725 POR DIOS UOS ROGAMOS, DON DIEGO & *** FERANDO
21531 5ELCID2737 CON LAS ESPUELAS AGUDAS, *** ELLAS AN MAL SABOR,
21606 5ELCID2747 HYA NON PUEDEN FABLAR *** ELUIRA & DONA SOL;
21848 5ELCID2780 YA PRIMAS, LAS MIS PRIMAS, *** ELUIRA & DO@A SOL,

WORD C# PREFIX CONTEXT

DON (CON'T)

```
                 21900 5ELCID2786 LAMANDO: PRIMAS, PRIMAS, *** ELUIRA & DON SOL
                 21903 5ELCID2786 LAMANDO: PRIMAS, PRIMAS, DON ELUIRA & *** SOL
                 21931 5ELCID2790 VAN RECORDANDO *** ELUIRA & DO@A SOL,
                 22096 5ELCID2812 ALA TORRE DE *** VRRACA ELLE LAS DEXO.
                 22186 5ELCID2825 DE CUER PESO ESTO AL BUEN REY *** ALFONSSO.
                 22448 5ELCID2859 ENEL FINCAN LOS OIOS *** ELUIRA & DO@A SOL:
                 22495 5ELCID2865 *** ELUIRA & DO@A SOL, CUYDADO NON AYADES,
                 23532 5ELCID2997 EL CONDE *** GAR%IA EN ESTAS NUEUAS FUE,
                 23566 5ELCID3001 EN LOS PRIMEROS VA EL BUEN REY *** ALFONSSO,
                 23570 5ELCID3002 EL CONDE *** ANRRICH & EL CONDE DON REMOND;
                 23575 5ELCID3002 EL CONDE DON ANRRICH & EL CONDE *** REMOND;
                 23585 5ELCID3004 EL CONDE *** FRUELLA & EL CONDE DON BELTRAN.
                 23590 5ELCID3004 EL CONDE DON FRUELLA & EL CONDE *** BELTRAN.
                 23608 5ELCID3007 EL CONDE *** GAR%IA CON YFANTES DE CARRION,
                 23744 5ELCID3024 QUANDO LOOVO A DIO EL BUEN REY *** ALFFONSSO,
                 23838 5ELCID3037 E AL CONDE *** ARRICH & A QUANTOS QUE Y SON;
                 23957 5ELCID3053 EL REY *** ALFONSSO A TOLLEDO ES ENTRADO,
                 24042 5ELCID3064 VOS YREDES COMIGO & EL OBISPO *** IHERONIMO
                 24380 5ELCID3108 LEUANTOS EN PIE EL BUEN REY *** ALFONSSO
                 24385 5ELCID3109 E EL CONDE *** ANRRICH & EL CONDE DON REMONT
                 24390 5ELCID3109 E EL CONDE DON ANRRICH & EL CONDE *** REMONT
                 24535 5ELCID3127 ESSORA SE LEUO EN PIE EL BUEN REY *** ALFONSSO;
                 24605 5ELCID3135 ALCALDES SEAN DESTO EL CONDE *** ANRRICH & EL CONDE DON REMOND
                 24610 5ELCID3135 ALCALDES SEAN DESTO EL CONDE DON ANRRICH & EL CONDE *** REMOND
                 24812 5ELCID3160 DIXO EL CONDE *** GAR%IA: AESTO NOS FABLEMOS.
                 24863 5ELCID3166 BIEN NOS ABENDREMOS CON EL REY *** ALFONSSO.
                 24901 5ELCID3171 MER%ED, YA REY *** ALFONSSO, SODES NUESTRO SE@OR
                 24976 5ELCID3181 TORNOS AL ESCA@O *** SE LEUANTO;
                 25022 5ELCID3187 ASSIS YRAN VENGANDO *** ELUIRA & DONA SOL.
                 25193 5ELCID3208 DJZE EL CONDE *** REMOND: DEZID DE SSI O DE NO.
                 25357 5ELCID3228 A ESTAS PALABRAS FABLO EL REY *** ALFONSSO:
                 25423 5ELCID3237 LUEGO RESPONDIO EL CONDE *** REMOND:
                 25439 5ELCID3239 POR JUUIZIO LO DAMOS ANTEL REY *** ALFONSSO:
                 25678 5ELCID3270 EL CONDE *** GAR%IA EN PIE SE LEUANTAUA;
                 26232 5ELCID3344 ESTOT LIDIARE AQUI ANTEL REY *** ALFONSSO
                 26238 5ELCID3345 POR FIJAS DEL %ID, *** ELUIRA & DONA SOL:
                 26315 5ELCID3356 POR CONSAGRAR CON MYO %ID *** RODRIGO
                 26609 5ELCID3397 BESAN LAS MANOS AL REY *** ALFONSSO,
                 26770 5ELCID3419 DE FIJAS DE MYO %ID, *** ELUIRA & DO@A SOL,
                 26803 5ELCID3423 BESARON LAS MANOS DEL REY *** ALFONSSO,
                 26980 5ELCID3447 QUANDO PIDEN MIS PRIMAS, *** ELUIRA & DO@A SOL,
                 27026 5ELCID3452 GRADO ADIOS DEL %IELO & AQUEL REY *** ALFONSSO,
                 27363 5ELCID3496 ADELINO A EL EL CONDE *** ANRICH & EL CONDE DON REMOND;
                 27368 5ELCID3496 ADELINO A EL EL CONDE DON ANRICH & EL CONDE *** REMOND;
                 27521 5ELCID3515 HY UOS LE DO EN ***, MANDEDES LE TOMAR, SE@OR.
                 27703 5ELCID3536 ELLOS SON ENPOER DEL REY *** ALFONSSO EL DE LEON;
                 27805 5ELCID3548 DEMAS SOBRE TODOS YES EL REY *** ALFONSSO,
                 27993 5ELCID3572 HYUA LOS VER EL REY *** ALFONSSO;
                 28165 5ELCID3595 DO SEDIEN ENEL CAMPO FABLO EL REY *** ALFONSSO:
                 28778 5ELCID3675 FIRIO ENEL ESCUDO A *** MUNO GUSTIOZ,
                 28917 5ELCID3693 MANDO LIBRAR EL CANPO EL BUEN REY *** ALFONSSO,
                 29120 5ELCID3719 FIZIERON SUS CASAMIENTOS CON *** ELUIRA & CON DO@A SOL.
         WORD #1599 OCCURS 162 TIMES.
            INDEX OF DIVERSIFICATION =   178.86 WITH STANDARD DEVIATION OF   258.47

DONA             16553 5ELCID2097 DAQUI LAS PRENDO POR MIS MANOS DON ELUIRA & **** SOL,
                 17249 5ELCID2181 VERAN ASUS ESPOSAS, A DON ELUIRA & A **** SOL.
                 21609 5ELCID2747 HYA NON PUEDEN FABLAR DON ELUIRA & **** SOL;
                 23857 5ELCID3039 MI MUGIER **** XIMENA, DUE@A ES DE PRO,
                 25025 5ELCID3187 ASSIS YRAN VENGANDO DON ELUIRA & **** SOL.
                 26241 5ELCID3345 POR FIJAS DEL %ID, DON ELUIRA & **** SOL:
         WORD #1600 OCCURS   6 TIMES.
            INDEX OF DIVERSIFICATION =  1936.60 WITH STANDARD DEVIATION OF  1467.90

DONAS             1759 5ELCID0224 MANDO AL UUESTRO ALTAR BUENAS ***** & RICAS;
         WORD #1601 OCCURS   1 TIMES.

DOND             14327 5ELCID1812 POR QUE ASSI LAS ENBIO **** ELLAS SON PAGADAS,
         WORD #1602 OCCURS   1 TIMES.

DONES            17856 5ELCID2259 CADA UNO POR SI SOS ***** AUIEN DADOS.
         WORD #1603 OCCURS   1 TIMES.

DONT              2797 5ELCID0353 DIOT CON LA LAN%A ENEL COSTADO, **** YXIO LA SANGRE,
         WORD #1604 OCCURS   1 TIMES.

DONTA            11970 5ELCID1517 QUANDO LEGO AUEGALUON, ***** DIO HA,
         WORD #1605 OCCURS   1 TIMES.

DO@A              1877 5ELCID0239 Y ESTAUA **** XIMENA CON %INCO DUENAS DE PRO,
                  2004 5ELCID0253 EUADES AQUI PORA **** XIMENA DOUOS C MARCHOS.
                  2078 5ELCID0262 AFEUOS **** XIMENA CON SUS FIJAS DO UA LEGANDO;
                  2096 5ELCID0264 ANTEL CAMPEADOR **** XIMENA FINCO LOS YNOIOS AMOS,
                  2204 5ELCID0278 YA **** XIMENA, LA MI MUGIER TAN COMPLIDA,
```

WORD C# PREFIX CONTEXT

DO@A (CON'T)

```
2586 5ELCID0327 ECHOS **** XIMENA EN LOS GRADOS DELANTEL ALTAR,
2918 5ELCID0368 EL %ID A **** XIMENA YUA LA ABRA%AR;
2923 5ELCID0369 **** XIMENA AL %ID LA MANOL VA BESAR,
10672 5ELCID1352 POR SU MUGIER **** XIMENA & SUS FIJAS AMAS ADOS:
11027 5ELCID1396 CMILCM, **** XIMENA, DICS VCS CURIE DE MAL,
11091 5ELCID1404 DIXO **** XIMENA: EL CRIADOR LO MANDE
11253 5ELCID1424 MINAYA A **** XIMINA & A SUS FIJAS QUE HA,
12563 5ELCID1594 QUANDO LO VIO **** XIMENA, A PIES SE LE ECHAUA:
14232 5ELCID1801 ALEGRE ES **** XIMENA & SUS FIJAS AMAS,
16362 5ELCID2075 VUESTRAS FIJAS UCS PIDO, DON ELUIRA & **** SOL,
16472 5ELCID2088 AFELLAS EN UUESTRA MANO DON ELUIRA & **** SOL,
17092 5ELCID2163 HE DELAS FIJAS DE MYO %ID, DE DON ELUIRA & **** SOL.
17266 5ELCID2184 RE%IBIOLO **** XIMENA & SUS FIJAS AMAS:
17358 5ELCID2196 MUGIER **** XIMENA, GRADO AL CRIAADOR.
17370 5ELCID2197 AUOS DIGO, MIS FIJAS, DON ELUIRA & **** SOL:
19877 5ELCID2520 EAMAS LA MYS FIJAS, DON ELUIRA & **** SOL;
20164 5ELCID2560 QUE PLEGA A **** XIMENA & PRIMERO AUOS
20428 5ELCID2592 AMAS HERMANAS, DON ELUIRA & **** SOL,
20704 5ELCID2628 ADIOS UOS HACOMENDAMOS, DON ELUIRA & **** SOL,
21112 5ELCID2682 HYRE CON UUESTRA GRA%IA, DON ELUIRA & **** SOL;
21323 5ELCID2710 SI NON AMAS SUS MUGIERES **** ELUIRA & DO@A SOL:
21326 5ELCID2710 SI NON AMAS SUS MUGIERES DO@A ELUIRA & **** SOL:
21356 5ELCID2714 BIEN LO CREADES, DON ELUIRA & **** SOL,
21431 5ELCID2724 QUANDO ESTO VIERON LAS DUE@AS, FABLAUA **** SOL:
21851 5ELCID2780 YA PRIMAS, LAS MIS PRIMAS, DON ELUIRA & **** SOL,
21934 5ELCID2790 VAN RECORDANDO DON ELUIRA & **** SOL,
21977 5ELCID2796 TAN A GRANT DUELO FABLAUA **** SOL:
22451 5ELCID2859 ENEL FINCAN LOS OIOS DON ELUIRA & **** SOL:
22498 5ELCID2865 DON ELUIRA & **** SOL, CUYDADO NON AYADES,
22735 5ELCID2897 GRAND GOZO FIZO CON ELLAS **** XIMENA SU MADRE.
26773 5ELCID3419 DE FIJAS DE MYO %ID, DON ELUIRA & **** SOL,
26983 5ELCID3447 QUANDO PIDEN MIS PRIMAS, DON ELUIRA & **** SOL,
29124 5ELCID3719 FIZIERON SUS CASAMIENTOS CON DON ELUIRA & CON **** SOL.
WORD #1606 OCCURS 38 TIMES.
INDEX OF DIVERSIFICATION = 735.41 WITH STANDARD DEVIATION OF 1472.29

DO@AS 20900 5ELCID2654 ALAS FIJAS DEL %ID EL MORO SUS ***** DIO,
WORD #1607 OCCURS 1 TIMES.

DORADOS 696 5ELCID0088 LOS GUADAME%IS UERMEIOS & LOS CLAUOS BIEN *******.
WORD #1608 OCCURS 1 TIMES.

DORO 15601 5ELCID1978 QUANTOS QUISIESSEN AUERES **** O DE PLATA.
19185 5ELCID2426 E GANO A TIZON QUE MILL MARCOS **** VAL.
24251 5ELCID3092 SOBRESTO VNA PIEL VERMEIA, LAS BANDAS **** SON,
24955 5ELCID3179 LAS MA%ANAS & LOS ARRIAZES TODOS **** SON.
WORD #1609 OCCURS 4 TIMES.

DOS 674 5ELCID0085 CON UUESTRO CONSEGO BASTIR QUIERO *** ARCHAS;
878 5ELCID0113 TIENE *** ARCAS LENNAS DE ORO ESMERADO.
2758 5ELCID0349 *** LADRONES CONTIGO, ESTOS DE SE@AS PARTES
5052 5ELCID0638 NON LO DETARDEDES, LOS *** YD PORA ALLA,
5168 5ELCID0654 CON AQUESTOS *** REYES QUE DIZEN FFARIZ & GALUE;
5433 5ELCID0686 SI NON *** PEONES SOLOS POR LA PUERTA GUARDAR;
5541 5ELCID0698 DE PARTE DELOS MOROS *** SE@AS HA CABDALES,
5547 5ELCID0699 E FIZIERON *** AZES DE PEONES MEZCLADOS, QUILOS PODRIE CONTAR?
6000 5ELCID0761 LOS *** LE FALLEN, & EL VNOL HA TOMADO,
6855 5ELCID0876 VEN%IO *** REYES DE MOROS EN AQUESTA BATALLA.
7570 5ELCID0970 TRES DIAS & *** NOCHES PENSSARON DE ANDAR,
8112 5ELCID1035 AUOS & *** FIJOS DALGO QUITAR UOS HE LOS CUERPOS & DARUOS E
                DE MANO.
8159 5ELCID1040 AUOS & A OTROS *** DAR UOS HE DE MANO.
8307 5ELCID1057 CON ESTOS *** CAUALLEROS A PRIESSA VA IANTANDO;
8389 5ELCID1066 EL CONDE DON REMONT ENTRE LOS *** ES ENTRADO.
9011 5ELCID1147 *** REYES DE MOROS MATARON EN ES ALCAZ,
11787 5ELCID1495 ENVIO *** CAUALLEROS MYNAYA ALBARFANEZ QUE SOPIESSE LA VERDAD;
13219 5ELCID1676 *** FALLAN CON LOS MOROS COMETIEN LOS TAN AYNA.
14106 5ELCID1786 *** TENDALES LA SUFREN, CON ORO SON LABRADOS;
15177 5ELCID1920 EN POCAS TIERRAS A TALES *** VARONES.
15445 5ELCID1957 CON *** CAUALLEROS LUEGO LAS ENBIO:
15758 5ELCID2000 A AQUESTOS *** MANDO EL CAMPEADOR QUE CURIEN A VALEN%IA
17151 5ELCID2170 EN CASA DE MYO %ID NON A *** MEIORES,
17950 5ELCID2271 HY MORAN LOS YFANTES BIEN CERCA DE *** A@OS,
18070 5ELCID2286 FERRAN GON%ALEZ NON VIO ALLI *** AL%ASSE, NIN CAMARA ABIERTA NIN
18477 5ELCID2338 AVN VEA EL ORA QUE UOS MERESCA *** TANTO.
18854 5ELCID2386 ALOS PRIMEROS COLPES *** MOROS MATAUA DE LA LAN%A.
18876 5ELCID2389 *** MATO CON LAN%A & V CON EL ESPADA.
19234 5ELCID2434 CON *** ESPADAS QUE EL PRE%IAUA ALGO
20289 5ELCID2575 DAR UOS HE *** ESPADAS, A COLADA & A TIZON,
21442 5ELCID2726 *** ESPADAS TENEDES FUERTES & TAIADORES,
22906 5ELCID2918 CON EL *** CAUALLEROS QUEL SIRUAN A SO SABOR,
22997 5ELCID2930 CON EL *** CAUALLEROS QUEL AGUARDAN CUM ASSE@OR.
24552 5ELCID3129 HYO, DE QUE FU REY, NON FIZ MAS DE *** CORTES:
24755 5ELCID3153 DILES *** ESPADAS, A COLADA & A TIZON,
24910 5ELCID3172 NOLO PODEMOS NEGAR, CA *** ESPADAS NOS DIO:
```

WORD C# PREFIX CONTEXT

DOS (CON'T)

```
                26577 5ELCID3393 AFFE *** CAUALLEROS ENTRARON POR LA CORT;
                27708 5ELCID3537 *** DIAS ATENDIERCN A YFANTES DE CARRION.
                28408 5ELCID3628 BIEN EN *** LCGARES EL ESTIL LE QUEBRO.
                28463 5ELCID3635 LAS *** LE DESMANCHAN & LA TER%ERA FINCO:
                28747 5ELCID3671 LOS *** HAN ARRANCADO: CJREUCS DE MUNO GUSTIOZ,
         WORD #1610 CCCURS  41 TIMES.
            INDEX OF DIVERSIFICATICN =   700.82 WITH STANCARD DEVIATION OF   679.17

DOSON           23131 5ELCID2947 AFELAS SUS FIJAS EN VALENCIA *****.
         WORD #1611 CCCURS   1 TIMES.

DOTROS           2977 5ELCID0375 ASIS PARTEN VNOS ****** CCMMO LA V@A DELA CARNE.
         WORD #1612 OCCURS   1 TIMES.

DOUIRNA         26483 5ELCID3379 FUESSE A RIO ******* LOS MOLINOS PICAR
         WORD #1613 OCCURS   1 TIMES.

DOUOS            1981 5ELCID0250 MAS POR QUE ME VO DE TIERRA, ***** L MARCHOS,
                 2006 5ELCID0253 EUADES AQUI PORA DO@A XIMENA ***** C MARCHOS.
                 3878 5ELCID0492 ***** LA QUINTA, SI LA QUISIEREDES, MINAYA.
                14826 5ELCID1874 ***** IIJ CAUALLOS & PRENDED LOS AQUI.
                16041 5ELCID2034 AQUI UOS PERDONO & ***** MY AMOR,
                17639 5ELCID2232 ***** ESTAS DUE@AS, AMAS SCN FIJAS DALGO,
         WORD #1614 CCCURS   6 TIMES.
            INDEX OF DIVERSIFICATICN =  3130.60 WITH STANCARD DEVIATION OF  4426.03

DOZIENTOS        7157 5ELCID0917 ********* CCN EL, QUE TODOS %INEN ESPADAS;
                11749 5ELCID1490 %IENTOL PIDIERON, MAS EL CCN ********* VA.
                14332 5ELCID1813 ESTOS ********* CAUALLOS YRAN EN PRESENTAIAS,
                14362 5ELCID1817 E ********* OMNES LIEUAN EN SU CONPA@A,
                14654 5ELCID1854 E EMBIA UOS ********* CAUALLOS, & BESA UOS LAS MANOS.
                14778 5ELCID1868 ESTOS ********* CAUALLOS QUEM ENBIA MYO %ID.
                20879 5ELCID2652 CON ********* CAUALLEROS ESCURRIR LOS MANDO.
                21024 5ELCID2672 CO ********* QUE TIENE YUA CAUALGAR;
                25484 5ELCID3246 SOBRE LOS ********* MARCOS QUE TENIE EL REY ALFONSSO
         WORD #1615 OCCURS   9 TIMES.
            INDEX OF DIVERSIFICATICN =  2289.88 WITH STANDARD DEVIATION OF  2478.76

DOZITOS         12316 5ELCID1564 ******* CAUALLEROS MANDO EXIR PRIUADO,
         WORD #1616 OCCURS   1 TIMES.

DUBDA            3770 5ELCID0477 E SIN ***** CORREN; FASTA ALCALA LEGO LA SE@A DE MINAYA,
                 6173 5ELCID0786 CA EN ALCAZ SJN ***** LES FUERON DANDO.
                 7020 5ELCID0898 SI NULLA ***** YD A MYO %ID BUSCAR GANAN%IA.
                 8881 5ELCID1131 BIEN LOS FERREDES, QUE ***** NCN Y AURA,
         WORD #1617 OCCURS   4 TIMES.

DUBDAN%A         4711 5ELCID0597 FIRID LOS, CAUALLEROS, TODOS SINES ********;
         WORD #1618 CCCURS   1 TIMES.

DUCA             8570 5ELCID1088 DEXADO A SARAGO%A & ALAS TIERRAS ****,
         WORD #1619 CCCURS   1 TIMES.

DUCHO            1967 5ELCID0249 YO ADOBARE CON ***** PORA MI & PORA MIS VASSALLOS;
                11735 5ELCID1488 ESSA NOCH CON ***** LES DIO GRAND,
         WORD #1620 OCCURS   2 TIMES.

DUCHOS          19508 5ELCID2472 CON ****** A SAZONES, BUENAS PIELES & BUENOS MANTOS.
         WORD #1621 OCCURS   1 TIMES.

DUELE           23795 5ELCID3031 DELO QUE AUOS PESA AMI ***** EL CORA%ON;
         WORD #1622 CCCURS   1 TIMES.

DUELO             225 5ELCID0029 GRANDE ***** AUIEN LAS YENTES CHRISTIANAS;
                 9280 5ELCID1180 DELANTE VEYEN SO *****, NCN SE PUEDEN HUUIAR,
                10411 5ELCID1319 ALOS PIES DEL REY ALFONSSO CAYO CON GRAND *****,
                11387 5ELCID1441 GRAND ***** ES AL PARTIR DEL ABBAT:
                21975 5ELCID2796 TAN A GRANT ***** FABLAUA CO@A SOL:
         WORD #1623 CCCURS   5 TIMES.
            INDEX OF DIVERSIFICATICN =  5436.50 WITH STANDARD DEVIATION OF  5101.14

DUELOS           3026 5ELCID0381 AUNTODOS ESTOS ****** EN GOZO SE TORNARAN;
                20724 5ELCID2631 GRANDES FUERON LOS ****** ALA DEPARTI%ION.
         WORD #1624 OCCURS   2 TIMES.

DUENA           29015 5ELCID3706 QUI BUENA ***** ESCARNE%E & LA DEXA DESPUES,
         WORD #1625 OCCURS   1 TIMES.

DUENAS           1881 5ELCID0239 Y ESTAUA DO@A XIMENA CON %INCO ****** DE PRO,
                 2015 5ELCID0254 AELLA & ASUS FIJAS & ASUS ****** SIRUADES LAS EST A@O.
                 3060 5ELCID0385 E A TODAS SUS ****** QUE CON ELLAS ESTAN;
                 6468 5ELCID0825 SI LES YO VISCUIER, SERAN ****** RICAS.
                10912 5ELCID1381 SI LEUAREDES LAS ******, SIRUAN LAS ASU SABOR,
                11231 5ELCID1421 POR YR CCN ESTAS ****** BUE@A CONPANA SE FAZE.
                11472 5ELCID1452 FELOS EN MEDINA LAS ****** & ALBARFANEZ.
```

WORD C# PREFIX CONTEXT

DUENAS (CON'T)

```
                  12241 5ELCID1554 AMYNAYA & ALAS ******, DIOS COMMO LAS ONDRAUA
                  13103 5ELCID1661 ASSI FFAZIE ALAS ****** & A SUS FIJAS AMAS ADOS:
                  13777 5ELCID1746 RE%IBIEN LO LAS ****** QUE LO ESTAN ESPERANDO.
                  13794 5ELCID1748 AUOS ME OMILLO, ******, GRANT PREZ UOS HE GA@ADO:
                  13874 5ELCID1758 LAS ****** & LAS FIJAS & LA MUGIER QUE VALE ALGO
                  13923 5ELCID1764 ESTAS ****** QUE ADUXIESTES, QUE UOS SIRUEN TANTO,
                  15810 5ELCID2005 E OTRAS ****** QUE LAS SIRUEN ASU SABOR;
                  17322 5ELCID2191 ETODAS LAS ****** QUE LAS SIRUEN:
                  17641 5ELCID2232 DOUOS ESTAS ******, AMAS SON FIJAS DALGO,
                  17758 5ELCID2247 TORNAN SE CON LAS ******, A VALEN%IA AN ENTRADO;
                  17893 5ELCID2264 EA TODAS LAS ****** & ALOS FIJOS DALGO;
                  20572 5ELCID2612 ESPIENDOS DELAS ****** & DE TODAS SUS COMPA@AS.
                  21429 5ELCID2724 QUANDO ESTO VIERON LAS ******, FABLAUA DO@A SOL:
                  22485 5ELCID2863 LORAUAN DELOS OIOS LAS ****** & ALBARFANEZ,
                  22567 5ELCID2874 E MINAYA CON LAS ****** YUA CABADELANT.
          WORD #1629 OCCURS  25 TIMES.
             INDEX OF DIVERSIFICATION =   852.33 WITH STANDARD DEVIATION OF  1781.66

DUERME              980 5ELCID0126 NON ****** SIN SOSPECHA QUI AUER TRAE MONEDADO.
          WORD #1630 OCCURS   1 TIMES.

DUERO              3189 5ELCID0401 SOBRE NAUAS DE PALOS EL ***** UA PASAR,
                  22089 5ELCID2811 ALAS AGUAS DE ***** ELLOS ARRIBADOS SON,
          WORD #1631 OCCURS   2 TIMES.

DUES               2020 5ELCID0255 **** FIJAS DEXO NI@AS & PRENDET LAS EN LOS BRA%OS;
          WORD #1632 OCCURS   1 TIMES.

DUL%E              3216 5ELCID0405 VN SUENOL PRISO *****, TAN BIEN SE ADURMJO.
          WORD #1633 OCCURS   1 TIMES.

DUL%ES            24135 5ELCID3077 SOLOS MANTOS LAS ESPADAS ****** & TAIADORES;
          WORD #1634 OCCURS   1 TIMES.

DUN               24265 5ELCID3094 VNA COFIA SOBRE LOS PELOS *** ESCARIN DE PRO,
          WORD #1635 OCCURS   1 TIMES.

DUNA               3387 5ELCID0427 EN MEDIO **** MONTANA MARAUILLOSA & GRAND
          WORD #1636 OCCURS   1 TIMES.

DURA              13245 5ELCID1679 BIEN FATA LAS TIENDAS **** AQUESTE ALCAZ,
          WORD #1637 OCCURS   1 TIMES.

DURADORES         21424 5ELCID2723 EN MANO PRENDEN LAS %INCHAS FUERTES & *********.
          WORD #1638 OCCURS   1 TIMES.

DURAR              8810 5ELCID1120 SI EN ESTAS TIERRAS QUISIEREMOS *****,
          WORD #1639 OCCURS   1 TIMES.

DURARON           17791 5ELCID2251 QUINZE DIAS CONPLIDOS ******* EN LAS BODAS,
          WORD #1640 OCCURS   1 TIMES.

DURMIE            18024 5ELCID2280 YAZIES EN VN ESCA@O, ****** EL CAMPEADOR,
                  26128 5ELCID3331 QUANDO ****** MYO %ID & EL LEON SE DESATO?
          WORD #1641 OCCURS   2 TIMES.

                  12189 5ELCID1547 LAS NOCHES & LOS DIAS LAS ****** AGUARDANDO.
                  12327 5ELCID1565 QUE RE%IBAN A MYANAYA & ALAS ****** FIJAS DALGO;
                  12353 5ELCID1569 E ALAS ****** & ALAS NI@AS & ALAS OTRAS CONPA@AS.
                  12438 5ELCID1578 RE%EBIDAS LAS ****** A VNA GRANT ONDRAN%A,
                  12478 5ELCID1583 RE%IBIR SALIEN LAS ****** & AL BUENO DE MINAYA.
                  13176 5ELCID1670 ALEGRE SON LAS ******, PERDIENDO VAN EL PAUOR.
                  14242 5ELCID1802 E TODAS LAS OTRAS ****** QUE TIENEN POR CASADAS.
                  21504 5ELCID2734 LO QUE RUEGAN LAS ****** NON LES HA NINGUN PRO.
          WORD #1626 OCCURS  15 TIMES.
             INDEX OF DIVERSIFICATION =  1400.64 WITH STANDARD DEVIATION OF  2148.91

DUENOS             5779 5ELCID0730 TANOS BUENOS CAUALLOS SIN SOS ****** ANDAR.
                  19019 5ELCID2406 CAUALLOS SIN ****** SALIR A TODAS PARTES.
          WORD #1627 OCCURS   2 TIMES.

DUE@A             23859 5ELCID3039 MI MUGIER DONA XIMENA, ***** ES DE PRO,
          WORD #1628 OCCURS   1 TIMES.

DUE@AS             2087 5ELCID0263 SE@AS ****** LAS TRAEN & ADUZEN LAS ADELANT.
                   2145 5ELCID0270 CON AQUESTAS MYS ****** DE QUIEN SO YO SERUIDA.
                  10729 5ELCID1358 QUANDO EN CABO DE MI TIERRA A QUESTAS ****** FUEREN,
                  11001 5ELCID1392 ADELINO PORA SAN PERO, OLAS ****** ESTAN,
                  11023 5ELCID1395 QUANDO ACABO LA ORA%ION, ALAS ****** SE TORNO:
                  11162 5ELCID1412 HYTODAS LAS ****** CON ELLAS QUANTAS BUENAS ELLAS HAN.
                  11264 5ELCID1425 E ALAS OTRAS ****** QUE LAS SIRUEN DELANT,
                  11293 5ELCID1429 QUANDO ESTAS ****** ADOBADAS LAS HAN,
                  11932 5ELCID1512 O CUEMO SALIERA DE CASTIELLA ALBARFANEZ CON ESTAS ******
                                   QUE TRAHE.
                  11997 5ELCID1521 TRAEDES ESTAS ****** PORO VALDREMOS MAS,
```

WORD C# PREFIX CONTEXT

```
DURMIENDO          9173 5ELCID1168 E ********* LCS DIAS & LAS NOCFES TRANOCHANDO,
          WORD #1642 OCCURS    1 TIMES.

DURO               6112 5ELCIDC777 FATA CALATAYUCH **** EL SEGUDAR.
                   9021 5ELCID1148 FATA VALENZIA **** EL SEGUCAR.
                   9186 5ELCID1169 EN GANAR AQUELAS VILLAS MYO %ID **** IIJ A@OS.
                   9656 5ELCID1227 FATA DENTRC EN XATIUA **** EL ARRANCADA,
                  19027 5ELCID2407 VII MIGEROS CONPLIDOS **** EL SEGUDAR.
          WORD #1643 OCCURS    5 TIMES.
             INDEX OF DIVERSIFICATION =  3227.75 WITH STANDARD DEVIATION OF  4274.99

DX                 6254 5ELCID0796 DELOS MORISCOS, QUANDC SCN LEGADOS, FFALLARON ** CAUALLOS.
          WORD #1644 OCCURS    1 TIMES.

E                    29 5ELCID0005 * SIN FALCONES & SIN ADTORES MUDADOS.
                     82 5ELCID0012 * ENTRANDO A BURGOS OUIERON LA SINIESTRA.
                    197 5ELCIDC026 * A QUEL QUE GELA DIESSE SOPIESSE UERA PALABRA,
                    216 5ELCID0028 * AUN DEMAS LCS CUERPCS & LAS ALMAS.
                    364 5ELCID0046 * DEMAS LOS CIOS DELAS CARAS.
                    637 5ELCID0081 ESPESO * EL CRO & TOCA LA PLATA,
                    686 5ELCID0087 CUBIERTAS DE GUADALMEZI * BIEN ENCLAUEADAS.
                    916 5ELCIDC118 * PRESTALDE DE AUER LO QUE SEA GUISADO.
                   1108 5ELCIDC143 * NOS UCS AIUDAREMOS, QUE ASSI ES AGUISADO,
                   1258 5ELCID0162 * BIEN GELAS GUARDARIEN FASTA CABO DEL A@O;
                   2159 5ELCIDC272 * NOS DEUOS PARTIR NCS FEMOS EN VIDA.
                   2257 5ELCIDC284 * UOS, MUGIER ONDRADA, DE MY SEADES SERUIDA
                   2871 5ELCIDC363 * RUEGC A SAN PEYDRC QUE ME AIUDE A ROGAR
                   2941 5ELCID0371 * EL ALAS NI@AS TORNO LAS ACATAR:
                   3056 5ELCIDC385 * A TODAS SUS DUENAS CUE CON ELLAS ESTAN;
                   3377 5ELCID0426 * POR LA LCMA AYUSO PIENSSAN DE ANDAR.
                   3511 5ELCID0443 * ALBAR SALUADOREZ SIN FALLA, & GALIN GARZIA, VNA FARDIDA
                   3546 5ELCIDC447 * BIEN ACOIAN TODAS LAS GANANZIAS,
                   3561 5ELCID0449 * YO CCN LO C AQUI FINCARE EN LA %AGA,
                   3606 5ELCID0455 * LOS QUE CON MYO %ID FICARAN EN LA %AGA.
                   3692 5ELCID0466 * ESSOS GA@ADOS QUANTCS EN DERREDOR ANDAN.
                   3768 5ELCID0477 * SIN DUBDA CORREN; FASTA ALCALA LEGO LA SE@A DE MINAYA,
                   3779 5ELCID0478 * DESI ARRIBA TORNAN SE CON LA GANANZIA,
                   3944 5ELCID0501 * POR EL COBDC AYUSC LA SANGRE SESTELANDO,
                   4038 5ELCID0514 * A LOS PEONES LA MEATAD SIN FALLA;
                   4130 5ELCIDC526 * QUE SERIE RETENEDOR, MAS NON YAURIE AGUA.
                   4326 5ELCID0551 * PASSO AALFAMA, LA FOZ AYUSO UA,
                   4341 5ELCID0553 * SOBRE ALCCZER MYC %ID YUA POSAR,
                   4488 5ELCIDC571 * LOS DE TECA & LCS DE TERUAL LA CASA;
                   4947 5ELCID0626 * ALOS DE CALATAYUTH NON PLAZE.
                   5206 5ELCIDC659 * DE NOCH EN BUELTOS ANDAN EN ARMAS;
                   5456 5ELCIDC689 * VOS, PERO VERMUEZ, LA MI SE@A TOMAD;
                   5516 5ELCIDC695 QUE PRIESSA VA EN LOS MCROS, * TORNARON SE A ARMAR;
                   5545 5ELCIDC699 * FIZIERCN DOS AZES DE PEONES MEZCLADOS, QUILOS PODRIE CONTAR?
                   5645 5ELCID0711 ESPOLONO EL CAUALLO, * METIOL ENEL MAYOR AZ.
                   6093 5ELCIDC774 * AGALUE NCL CCGIERON ALLA;
                   6555 5ELCID0837 * EL CAMPEADOR CON SU MESNADA.
                   6602 5ELCID0843 * LOS DE CALATAYUT, QUE ES MAS ONDRADA,
                   7241 5ELCID0929 * DE SUS CCMPA@AS, AQUELAS QUE AUIEN DEXADAS
                   7262 5ELCIDC932 * QUEL DIXC SALUDES DE SU MUGIER & DE SUS FIJAS
                   7303 5ELCIDC937 * A DERREDOR TODO LO VA PREANDO.
                   8102 5ELCID1034 * SI UCS COMIEREDES, DON YO SEA PAGADO,
                   8122 5ELCID1035 AUOS & DOS FIJOS DALGO QUITAR UOS HE LOS CUERPOS & DARUOS *
                                   DE MANO.
                   8245 5ELCID1050 * TIENEN GELO DELANT & DIERON GELO PRIUADO.
                   8364 5ELCID1063 EL SABOR QUE DED * NCN SERA OLBIDADO.
                   8375 5ELCID1065 * BUENAS VESTIDURAS DE PELIZONES & DE MANTOS.
                   8431 5ELCID1C72 * SI NCN, MANDEDES BUSCAR; O ME DEXAREDES
                   8473 5ELCID1C77 AGUIJAUA EL CONDE * PENSSAUA DE ANDAR,
                   8571 5ELCID1089 * DEXADO A HUESCA & LAS TIERRAS DE MONT ALUAN.
                   8592 5ELCID1091 AORIENT EXE EL SCL, * TORNOS AESSA PART.
                   9172 5ELCID1168 * DURMIENDC LCS DIAS & LAS NOCFES TRANOCHANDO,
                   9773 5ELCID1242 * QUE FABLASSEN DESTO MCROS & CHRISTIANOS.
                  10146 5ELCID1285 * MANDO MILL MARCOS DE PLATA A SAN PERO LEUAR
                  10156 5ELCID1286 * QUE LOS DIESSE AL ABBAT DON SANCHO.
                  10268 5ELCID1300 * DAR GELO A ESTE BUEN CHRISTIANO;
                  10491 5ELCID1330 * PE@A CADIELLA, QUE ES VNA PE@A FUERT;
                  10514 5ELCID1333 * FIZO ZINCO LIDES CAMPALES & TODAS LAS ARRANCO.
                  10595 5ELCID1343 * PLAZEM DELAS NUEUAS QUE FAZE EL CAMPEADOR;
                  10686 5ELCID1354 * YRIEN PORA VALENZIA AL BUEN CAMPEADOR.
                  11219 5ELCID1420 * EL SE TENIE C QUE ACUXIERA DALLA;
                  11261 5ELCID1425 * ALAS OTRAS DUE@AS QUE LAS SIRUEN DELANT,
                  11520 5ELCID1459 * MARTIN ANTOLINEZ, VN BURGALES LEAL,
                  11598 5ELCID1470 * YO FINCARE EN VALENZIA, QUE MUCHO COSTADOM HA;
                  11628 5ELCID1474 * QUANTC QUE PUEDEN NCN FINCAN DE ANDAR.
                  11645 5ELCID1476 * EL OTRO DIA VINIERON A MOLINA POSAR.
                  11717 5ELCID1486 * FFATA EN VALENZIA DELLAS NON UOS PARTADES.
                  11779 5ELCID1494 * EN MEDINA TODO EL RECABDO ESTA;
                  11832 5ELCID1500 * MARTIN ANTOLINEZ, EL BURGALES NATURAL,
                  11838 5ELCID1501 * EL OBISPO DON JERONIMC, CORANADO LEAL,
                  11845 5ELCID1502 * EL ALCAYAZ AUEGALUCN CON SUS FUERZAS QUE TRAHE,
```

WORD C# PREFIX CONTEXT

E (CON'T)

```
11898 5ELCID1509 * A CUBERTURAS DE %ENCALES, & ESCUDOS ALOS CUELLOS,
11907 5ELCID1510 * EN LAS MANCS LAN%AS QUE PENCONES TRAEN,
12191 5ELCID1548 * BUEN CAUALLC EN DIESTRC QUE UA ANTE SUS ARMAS.
12351 5ELCID1569 * ALAS DUENAS & ALAS NI@AS & ALAS OTRAS CONPA@AS.
12379 5ELCID1572 * TODAS LAS PUERTAS & LAS EXICAS & LAS ENTRADAS,
12389 5ELCID1573 * ADUXIESSEN LE ABAUIECA; POCC AUIE QUEL GANARA,
12711 5ELCID1614 * DEL OTRA PARTE A OIC HAN EL MAR,
12793 5ELCID1624 * EL NCN GELC GRADE%E SI NON A IHESU CHRISTO.
13213 5ELCID1675 ADCBAN SE DE CORA%CN * CAN SALTO DE LA VILLA;
13905 5ELCID1762 * YUAN PCSAR CON EL EN VNOS PRE%IOSOS ESCA@OS;
14124 5ELCID1788 * NON LA TCLLIESSE DENT CHRISTIANO:
14238 5ELCID1802 * TODAS LAS OTRAS DUENAS CUE TIENEN POR CASADAS.
14285 5ELCID1808 * CRAS HA LA MA@ANA YR UOS HECES SIN FALLA
14361 5ELCID1817 * COZIENTOS CMNES LIEUAN EN SU CONPA@A,
14387 5ELCID1820 * SERUIR LO HE SIENPRE MIENTRA QUE OUISSE EL ALMA.
14651 5ELCID1854 * EMBIA UOS DOZIENTOS CAUALLOS, & BESA UOS LAS MANOS.
14701 5ELCID1859 PESO AL CONCE DON GAR%IA, * MAL ERA YRADO;
14808 5ELCID1872 * GUARNIR UOS DE TOCAS ARMAS CCMMO UOS DIXIEREDES AQUI,
15016 5ELCID1899 * DE MI ABRA PERDON; VINIESSEM A VISTAS, SI OUIESSE DENT SABOR.
15293 5ELCID1937 * PIDEN ME MIS FIJAS PORA LCS YFANTES DE CARRION.
15522 5ELCID1967 * TANTO PALAFRE QUE BIEN ANCA,
15551 5ELCID1971 MANTOS & PIELLES * BUENCS %ENCALES CACRIA?
15741 5ELCID1998 * TODOS LOS CTRCS QUE Y SCN.
15808 5ELCID2005 * OTRAS DUE@AS QUE LAS SIRUEN ASU SABOR;
16070 5ELCID2038 * A ESTAS MESNADAS QUE ESTAN A DERREDOR.
16158 5ELCID2050 * CRAS FEREMOS LO QUE PLOGIERE AUOS.
16428 5ELCID2083 CA NCN HAN GRANT HEDAND * DE CIAS PEQUENAS SON.
16555 5ELCID2098 * DOLAS POR VELADAS ALOS YFANTES CE CARRION.
16943 5ELCID2145 * XXX CAUALLCS CCREDCRES, ESTOS BIEN ENSSELLADOS;
17512 5ELCID2216 * YUAN POSAR EN VN PRE%IOSO ESCA@O.
17595 5ELCID2226 * PRENDAN BENDI%ICNES & VAYAMCS RECABDANDO.
17771 5ELCID2249 * AL OTRO DIA FIZO MYC %ID FINCAR VIJ TABLADOS:
18056 5ELCID2285 * %ERCAN EL ESCA@O & FINCAN SOBRE SO SE@OR.
18187 5ELCID2301 * LIEUA LO ADESTRANDO, ENLA REC LE METIO.
19178 5ELCID2426 * GANO A TIZON QUE MILL MARCOS DORO VAL.
19274 5ELCID2440 * VIO VENIR ADIEGO & A FERNANDO;
19828 5ELCID2514 * OTROS MUCHOS QUE CRIO EL CAMPEADOR.
20245 5ELCID2570 VOS LES DIESTES VILLAS * TIERRAS POR ARRAS ENTIERRAS DE CARRION
20263 5ELCID2572 DARUOS * MULAS & PALAFRES, MUY GRUESSOS DE SAZON,
20278 5ELCID2574 * MUCHAS VESTIDURAS DE PA@OS & DE %ICLATONES;
21636 5ELCID2751 * ALAS AUES DEL MCNTE & ALAS BESTIAS DELA FIERA GUISA.
22046 5ELCID2806 * PRIUADO ENEL CAUALLC LAS CAUALGO;
22274 5ELCID2837 * MARTIN ANTOLINEZ, EL BURGCES DE PRO,
22488 5ELCID2864 * PERO VERMUEZ OTRO TANTO LAS HA;
22563 5ELCID2874 * MINAYA CCN LAS DUE@AS YUA CABADELANT.
22603 5ELCID2880 * DE MEDINA A MOLINA EN OTRO CIA VAN;
22913 5ELCID2919 * CON EL ESCUDEROS QUE SCN CE CRIAZON.
22952 5ELCID2924 * DELAS ASTURIAS BIEN A SAN %ALUADOR,
23159 5ELCID2951 * QUE UCS PESE, REY CCMMO SCDES SABIDOR;
23193 5ELCID2955 * VERDAD DIZES EN ESTC, TU, MU@O GUSTIOZ,
23280 5ELCID2966 * COMMC DEN DERECHO A MYO %ID EL CAMPEADOR,
23289 5ELCID2967 * QUE NCN AYA RENCURA PCDIENDO YO VECALLO.
23382 5ELCID2979 * ALOS DE CARRICN & AVARONES CASTELLANOS,
23614 5ELCID3008 * ASUR GON%ALEZ & GON%ALO ASSUREZ,
23620 5ELCID3009 * DIEGO & FERRANDO Y SON AMOS ADOS,
23628 5ELCID3010 * CON ELLOS GRAND BANDO QUE ADUXIERON A LA CORT:
23713 5ELCID3021 * YUA RE%EBIR ALQUE EN BUEN ORA NA%IO.
23835 5ELCID3037 * AL CCNDE DON ARRICH & A QUANTOS QUE Y SON;
23916 5ELCID3047 * YO CCN LCS MYOS POSARE A SAN SERUAN:
23942 5ELCID3051 * YRE ALA CORT ENANTES CE IANTAR.
24020 5ELCID3062 * SSU OFRENDA HAN FECHA MUY BUENA & CONPLIDA.
24044 5ELCID3065 * PERO VERMUEZ & AQUESTE MU@O GUSTIOZ
24051 5ELCID3066 * MARTIN ANTOLINEZ, EL BURGALES DE PRO,
24058 5ELCID3067 * ALBAR ALBAREZ & ALBAR SALUADOREZ
24064 5ELCID3068 * MARTIN MUNOZ, QUE EN BUEN PUNTO NA%IO,
24072 5ELCID3069 * MYO SOBRINO FELEZ MUNOZ;
24085 5ELCID3071 * GALIND GAR%IEZ, EL BUENO CARAGON;
24121 5ELCID3076 * QUE NON PARESCAN LAS ARMAS, BIEN PRESOS LOS CORDONES;
24382 5ELCID3109 * EL CCNDE DON ANRRICH & EL CONDE DON REMONT
24392 5ELCID3110 * DESI ADELANT, SABET, TODCS LCS OTROS:
24612 5ELCID3136 * ESTOS OTRCS CCNDES QUE DEL VANDO NON SODES.
24874 5ELCID3168 * QUANDO LAS TOUIERE, PARTIR SEA LA CORT;
25294 5ELCID3220 TORNAN CON EL CONSSEIO * FABLAUAN ASSO SABOR:
26100 5ELCID3327 * ERES FERMOSC, MAS MAL VARRAGAN
26136 5ELCID3332 * TU, FERRANDO, QUE FIZIST CCN EL PAUOR?
26487 5ELCID3380 * PRENDER MAQUILAS, CCMMO LO SUELE FAR
26598 5ELCID3396 * EL OTRO YFANTE DE ARAGCN;
26627 5ELCID3400 * QUE GELAS DIESSEN A ONDRA & ABENDI%ION,
26805 5ELCID3424 * DESPUES DE MYO %ID EL CAMPEADOR;
26856 5ELCID3431 * QUE NCN PESE ESTO AL %IC CAMPEADOR:
27078 5ELCID3460 * QUI AL QUISIESSE SERIE SU OCASION.
27341 5ELCID3494 * SOLTAUA LA BARBA & SACOLA CEL CORDON.
27446 5ELCID3507 * YR ME QUIERC PORA VALEN%IA, CON AFAN LA GANE YO.
27605 5ELCID3525 * MUNO GUSTICZ, FIRMES SEC EN CAMPO AGUISA DE VARONES;
```

WORD C# PREFIX CONTEXT

E (CON'T)

```
                27724 5ELCID3539 * TODOS SUS PARIENTES CCN ELLOS SON;
        WORD #1645 OCCURS 155 TIMES.
           INDEX OF DIVERSIFICATION =   178.84 WITH STANDARD DEVIATION OF   214.93

EA              14795 5ELCID1870 AUOS, MINAYA ALBARFANEZ, & ** PERO VERMUEZ AQUI,
                17129 5ELCID2168 ** DON FERNANDO & A CCN DIEGO AGUARDAR LOS MANDO
                17890 5ELCID2264 ** TODAS LAS DUE@AS & ALOS FIJOS DALGO:
                18760 5ELCID2374 ** ESTAS FERIDAS YO CUIERO YR DELANT;
                19391 5ELCID2457 ** UOS, %ID, QUE EN BUEN CRA FUESTES NADO
                20169 5ELCID2561 ** MYNAYA ALBARFANEZ & A CUANTOS AQUI SON:
        WORD #1646 OCCURS   6 TIMES.
           INDEX OF DIVERSIFICATION =  1073.80 WITH STANDARD DEVIATION OF   709.06

EACOSTAR        18973 5ELCID2401 ******** SE LCS TENDALES, CON HUEBRAS ERAN TANTAS.
        WORD #1647 OCCURS   1 TIMES.

EAMAS           19870 5ELCID2520 ***** LA MYS FIJAS, CON ELUIRA & DO@A SOL;
        WORD #1648 OCCURS   1 TIMES.

EASSU           17507 5ELCID2215 AEL & ***** MUGIER DELANT SELE OMILLARON,
        WORD #1649 OCCURS   1 TIMES.

EBAYR           23638 5ELCID3011 ***** LE CUYDAN A MYO %ID EL CAMPEADOR.
        WORD #1650 OCCURS   1 TIMES.

ECCLEGIA        17709 5ELCID2241 AL SALIR DELA ******** CAUALGARON TAN PRIUADO,
        WORD #1651 OCCURS   1 TIMES.

ECHAD           29252 5ELCID3734 ES LEYDC, DAT NOS DEL VINO; SI NON TENEDES DINEROS, *****
        WORD #1652 OCCURS   1 TIMES.

ECHADO           2122 5ELCID0267 POR MALOS MESTUREROS DE TIERRA SODES ******.
                 4977 5ELCID0629 AYROLO EL REY ALFONSSO, DE TIERRA ****** LO HA,
                 8235 5ELCID1048 COMMO QUE YRA A DE REY & DE TIERRA ES ******.
                 9762 5ELCID1240 POR AMOR DE REY ALFFONSSO, QUE DE TIERRA ME A ******,
                15268 5ELCID1934 ****** FU DE TIERRA & TOLLICA LA ONOR,
        WORD #1653 OCCURS   5 TIMES.
           INDEX OF DIVERSIFICATION =  3285.50 WITH STANDARD DEVIATION OF  1654.19

ECHADOS           101 5ELCID0014 ALBRICIA, ALBARFFANEZ, CA ******* SOMOS DE TIERRA
        WORD #1654 OCCURS   1 TIMES.

ECHAR            5386 5ELCID0679 TODOS LOS MOROS & LAS MORAS DE FUERA LOS MANDA *****,
                 9339 5ELCID1187 POR ARAGON & POR NAUARRA PREGON MANDO *****,
                 9469 5ELCID1203 ADELINO PORA VALEN%IA & SOBRELLAS VA *****,
        WORD #1655 OCCURS   3 TIMES.

ECHARON          1442 5ELCID0184 ATOD EL PRIMER COLPE IIJ MARCOS DE PLATA *******,
                15464 5ELCID1959 AL REY ONDRADO DELANT LE ******* LAS CARTAS;
        WORD #1656 OCCURS   2 TIMES.

ECHASTES        10450 5ELCID1325 ******** LE DE TIERRA, NON HA LA UUESTRA AMOR;
        WORD #1657 OCCURS   1 TIMES.

ECHAUA           3206 5ELCID0404 Y SE ****** MYO %ID DESPUES QUE FUE %ENADO,
                12569 5ELCID1594 QUANDO LO VIO DO@A XIMENA, A PIES SE LE ******:
                28597 5ELCID3651 EL CASCO DE SOMO APART GELO ******,
        WORD #1658 OCCURS   3 TIMES.

ECHAUAN         12498 5ELCID1585 ENSIELLAN LE ABAUIECA, CUBERTURAS LE *******,
        WORD #1659 OCCURS   1 TIMES.

ECHE            14949 5ELCID1890 HYO **** DE TIERRA AL BUEN CAMPEADOR,
        WORD #1660 OCCURS   1 TIMES.

ECHO             3454 5ELCID0436 MYO %ID SE **** EN %ELACA CON AQUELOS QUE EL TRAE.
                 5928 5ELCID0751 CORTOL POR LA %INTURA, EL MEDIO **** EN CAMPO.
                 6042 5ELCID0766 LAS CARBONCLAS DEL YELMO **** GELAS APARTE,
                28436 5ELCID3631 QUEBRANTO LA BOCA DEL ESCUDO, A PART GELA ****,
                28510 5ELCID3640 POR LA COPLA DEL CAUALLO EN TIERRA LO ****.
                28846 5ELCID3684 DELA OTRA PART VNA BRA%A GELA ****,
                28863 5ELCID3686 AL TIRAR DELA LAN%A EN TIERRA LO ****,
        WORD #1661 OCCURS   7 TIMES.
           INDEX OF DIVERSIFICATION =  4233.83 WITH STANDARD DEVIATION OF  8945.84

ECHOS            2585 5ELCID0327 ***** DO@A XIMENA EN LOS GRADOS DELANTEL ALTAR,
        WORD #1662 OCCURS   1 TIMES.

ECLEGIA         17697 5ELCID2239 ALA PUERTA DELA ******* SEDIELLOS SPERANDO;
        WORD #1663 OCCURS   1 TIMES.

EDERREDOR       28094 5ELCID3587 ********* DELLOS MUCHOS BUENOS VARONES.
        WORD #1664 OCCURS   1 TIMES.
```

WORD C# PREFIX CONTEXT

EDES 5470 5ELCID0690 COMMO SCDES MUY BUENO, TENER LA **** SIN ARCH;
WORD #1665 OCCURS 1 TIMES.

EFAZIENDO 14955 5ELCID1891 ********* YO HA EL MAL, & EL AMI GRAND PRO,
WORD #1666 OCCURS 1 TIMES.

EFIRME 10068 5ELCID1275 DESI POR MI BESALDE LA MANO ****** GELO ROGAD
WORD #1667 OCCURS 1 TIMES.

EGLESIA 2583 5ELCID0326 MYO %ID & SU MUGIER A LA ******* UAN.
2911 5ELCID0367 SALIERCN DELA *******, YA QUIEREN CAUALGAR.
WORD #1668 OCCURS 2 TIMES.

EGUADA 25837 5ELCID3290 LA QUE YO MESSE AVN NCN ES ******.
WORD #1669 OCCURS 1 TIMES.

EL
135 5ELCID0018 PLORANDC DELOS OICS, TANTO AUYEN ** DOLOR.
161 5ELCID0022 ** REY DON ALFONSSO TANTO AUIE LA GRAND SA@A,
240 5ELCID0031 ** CAMPEADCR ADELINO ASU POSADA;
299 5ELCID0038 SACO ** PIE DEL ESTRIBERA, UNA FERICAL DAUA;
331 5ELCID0042 ** REY LO HA UEDADO, ANOCH DEL ETRO SU CARTA,
379 5ELCID0048 MAS ** CRIADCR UOS UALA CCN TCDAS SUS UERTUDES SANTAS.
400 5ELCID0050 YA LO VEE ** %ID QUE DEL REY NON AUIE GRA%IA.
456 5ELCID0058 MYO %ID RUY DIAZ, ** CUE EN BUEN ORA %INXO ESPADA,
509 5ELCID0065 MARTIN ANTOLINEZ, ** BURGALES CONPLIDO,
527 5ELCID0067 NON LO CONPRA, CA ** SELO AUIE CONSIGO;
541 5ELCID0069 PAGOS MYO %ID ** CAMPEADOR & TODOS LOS OTROS QUEUAN ASO %ERUICIO
598 5ELCID0076 AUN %ERCA CTARDE ** REY CUERER ME HA POR AMIGO;
616 5ELCID0078 FABLO MYO %ID, ** QUE EN BUEN ORA %INXO ESPADA:
638 5ELCID0081 ESPESO E ** ORO & TCCA LA PLATA,
711 5ELCID0090 QUANDO EN BURGCS ME VEDARON CCMPRA & ** REY ME A AYRADO,
719 5ELCID0091 NON PUEDO TRAER ** AUER, CA MUCHO ES PESADO,
743 5ELCID0094 VEALO ** CRIADCR CCN TODOS LOS SOS SANTOS,
850 5ELCID0109 ** CAMPEADCR POR LAS PARIAS FUE ENTRADO,
888 5ELCID0114 YA LO VEDES QUE ** REY LEA AYRADO.
908 5ELCID0117 ** CAMPEADCR DEXAR LAS HA EN UUESTRA MANO,
967 5ELCID0124 BIEN LO SABEMCS QUE ** ALGO GA@O,
1068 5ELCID0137 YA VEDES QUE ENTRA LA NCCH, ** %ID ES PRESURADO,
1087 5ELCID0139 DIXO RACHEL & VIDAS: NCN SE FAZE ASSI ** MERCADO,
1167 5ELCID0150 NON VIENE ALA PUEENT, CA POR ** AGUA APASSADO,
1244 5ELCID0160 MARTIN ANTOLINEZ ** PLEYTO A PARADO,
1325 5ELCID0169 CA AMOUER A MYO %ID ANTE QUE CANTE ** GALLO.
1404 5ELCID0180 PLAZME, DIXO ** %ID, CAQUI SEA ANDADA.
1435 5ELCID0184 ATOD ** PRIMER COLPE IIJ MARCOS DE PLATA ECHARON,
1504 5ELCID0192 DEMOS LE BUEN DON, CA ** NO LO HA BUSCADO.
1585 5ELCID0203 RE%IBIOLO ** %ID ABIERTCS AMOS LOS BRA%OS:
1594 5ELCID0204 VENIDES, MARTIN ANTOLINEZ, ** MIO FIEL VASSALO
1600 5ELCID0205 AUN VEA ** DIA QUE DEMI AYADES ALGO
1634 5ELCID0209 EN SAN PERC DE CARDENA YNOS CANTE ** GALLO;
1647 5ELCID0211 MESURAREMOS LA POSADA & QUITAREMOS ** REYNADO;
1655 5ELCID0212 MUCHO ES HUEBCS, CA %ERCA VIENE ** PLAZO.
1710 5ELCID0219 DA QUI QUITO CASTIELLA, PUES QUE ** REY HE EN YRA;
1735 5ELCID0222 ** ME ACORRA DE NOCH & DE DIA
1774 5ELCID0226 SPIDIOS ** CABOSC DE CUER & DE VELUNTAD.
1804 5ELCID0230 SI ** REY MELO QUISIERE TOMAR AMI NON MINCHAL.
1817 5ELCID0231 ANTES SERE CON UUSCO QUE ** SOL QUIERA RAYAR.
1859 5ELCID0236 QUANDO LEGO A SAN PERO ** BUEN CAMPEADOR;
1862 5ELCID0237 ** ABBAT DON SANCHO, CHRISTIANO DEL CRIADOR,
1898 5ELCID0241 TU QUE ATODOS QUIAS, VALA MYO %ID ** CANPEADOR.
1905 5ELCID0242 LAMAUAN ALA PUERTA, Y SCPIERON ** MANDADO;
1911 5ELCID0243 DIOS, QUE ALEGRE FUE ** ABBAT DON SANCHO
1941 5ELCID0246 GRADESCO LO ADIOS, MYO %ID, DIXO ** ABBAT DON SANCHO;
1955 5ELCID0248 DIXO ** %ID: GRA%IAS, DON ABBAT, & SO UUESTRO PAGADO;
2073 5ELCID0261 OTORGADO GELO AUIE ** ABBAT DE GRADO.
2292 5ELCID0288 COMMO SEUA DE TIERRA MYO %ID ** CANPEADOR;
2318 5ELCID0292 TODOS DEMANDAN POR MIO %ID ** CAMPEADOR;
2331 5ELCID0294 VANSSE PORA SAN PERO DO ESTA ** QUE ENBUEN PUNTO NA%IO.
2341 5ELCID0295 QUANDO LO SOPO MYO %ID ** DE BIUAR,
2421 5ELCID0305 PLOGO ALOS OTROS OMNES TODOS QUANTOS CON ** ESTAN.
2440 5ELCID0308 MANDO ** REY A MYO %ID A AGUARDAR,
2465 5ELCID0311 ** DIA ES EXIDO, LA NOCH QUERIE ENTRAR,
2516 5ELCID0318 EN SAN PERO A MATINS TANDRA ** BUEN ABBAT,
2535 5ELCID0321 CA ** PLAZO VIENE A %ERCA, MUCHO AUEMOS DE ANDAR.
2603 5ELCID0329 QUE AMIO %ID ** CAMPEADOR QUE DIOS LE CURIAS DE MAL:
2623 5ELCID0331 FEZIST %IELO & TIERRA, ** TER%ERO EL MAR;
2625 5ELCID0331 FEZIST %IELO & TIERRA, EL TER%ERO ** MAR;
2632 5ELCID0332 FEZIST ESTRELAS & LUNA & ** SOL PORA ESCALENTAR;
2765 5ELCID0350 ** VNO ES EN PARAYSO, CA EL OTRO NON ENTRO ALA;
2771 5ELCID0350 EL VNO ES EN PARAYSO, CA ** OTRO NON ENTRO ALA;
2805 5ELCID0354 CORRIO LA SANGRE POR ** ASTIL AYUSO, LAS MANOS SE OUO DE VNTAR,
2884 5ELCID0364 POR MYO %ID ** CAMPEADOR, QUE DIOS LE CURIE DE MAL.
2915 5ELCID0368 ** %ID A DO@A XIMENA YUA LA ABRA%AR;
2942 5ELCID0371 E ** ALAS NI@AS TORNO LAS ACATAR:
2965 5ELCID0373 AGORA NOS PARTIMOS, DIOS SABE ** AIUNTAR.

WORD	C#	PREFIX	CONTEXT
EL (CON'T)			
	3067	5ELCID0386	BIEN SEPA ** ABBAT QUE BUEN GALARDON DELLO PRENDRA.
	3092	5ELCID0389	ABBAT, DEZILDES QUE PRENDAN ** RASTRO & PIESSEN DE ANDAR,
	3116	5ELCID0392	%ERCA VIENE ** PLAZO POR EL REYNO QUITAR.
	3119	5ELCID0392	%ERCA VIENE EL PLAZO POR ** REYNO QUITAR.
	3149	5ELCID0396	YXIENDOS UA DE TIERRA ** CAMPEADOR LEAL,
	3188	5ELCID0401	SOBRE NAUAS DE PALOS ** DUERO UA PASAR,
	3221	5ELCID0406	** ANGEL GABRIEL A EL VINO EN SUE@O:
	3225	5ELCID0406	EL ANGEL GABRIEL A ** VINO EN SUE@O:
	3231	5ELCID0407	CAUALGAD, %ID, ** BUEN CAMPEADOR, CA NUNQUA
	3252	5ELCID0410	QUANDO DESPERTO ** %ID, LA CARA SE SANTIGO;
	3302	5ELCID0416	AVN ERA DE DIA, NON ERA PUESTO ** SOL,
	3310	5ELCID0417	MANDO UER SUS YENTES MYO %ID ** CAMPEADOR:
	3331	5ELCID0420	TEMPRANO DAT %EUADA, SI ** CRIADOR UOS SALUE
	3335	5ELCID0421	** QUI QUISIERE COMER; & QUI NO, CAUALGE.
	3446	5ELCID0435	ODIZEN CASTEION, ** QUE ES SOBRE FENARES,
	3460	5ELCID0436	MYO %ID SE ECHO EN %ELADA CON AQUELOS QUE ** TRAE.
	3468	5ELCID0437	TODA LA NOCHE IAZE EN %ELADA ** QUE EN BUEN ORA NASCO,
	3625	5ELCID0457	YXIE ** SOL, DIOS, QUE FERMOSO APUNTAUA
	3675	5ELCID0464	** CAMPEADOR SALIO DE LA %ELADA, CORRIE ACASTEION SIN FALLA.
	3731	5ELCID0471	EN MANO TRAE DESNUDA ** ESPADA,
	3743	5ELCID0473	GA@O A CASTEION & ** ORO ELA PLATA.
	3836	5ELCID0485	FELLOS EN CASTEION, O ** CAMPEADOR ESTAUA.
	3839	5ELCID0486	** CASTIELO DEXO EN SO PODER, EL CAMPEADOR CAUALGA,
	3845	5ELCID0486	EL CASTIELO DEXO EN SO PODER, ** CAMPEADOR CAUALGA,
	3903	5ELCID0495	PAGAR SE YA DELLA ALFONSSO ** CASTELLANO.
	3946	5ELCID0501	E POR ** COBDO AYUSO LA SANGRE SESTELANDO,
	3955	5ELCID0502	ANTE RUY DIAZ ** LIDIADOR CONTADO,
	3992	5ELCID0507	COMIDIOS MYO %ID, ** QUE EN BUEN ORA FUE NADO,
	4149	5ELCID0528	BUSCAR NOS YE ** REY ALFONSSO CON TODA SU MESNADA.
	4178	5ELCID0532	%ERCA ES ** REY ALFONSSO & BUSCAR NOS VERNA.
	4186	5ELCID0533	MAS ** CASTIELO NON LO QUIERO HERMAR;
	4234	5ELCID0539	LO QUE DIXO ** %ID A TODOS LOS OTROS PLAZ.
	4314	5ELCID0549	NON LO SABEN LOS MOROS ** ARDIMENT QUE AN.
	4323	5ELCID0550	OTRO DIA MOUIOS MYO %ID ** DE BIUAR,
	4371	5ELCID0557	BIEN PUEBLA ** ETERO, FIRME PRENDE LAS POSADAS,
	4388	5ELCID0559	** BUEN CANPEADOR QUE EN BUEN ORA NASCO,
	4437	5ELCID0565	QUE ** CAMPEADOR MYO %ID ALLI AUIE POBLADO,
	4469	5ELCID0569	** CASTIELLO DE ALCO%ER EN PARIA UA ENTRANDO.
	4520	5ELCID0575	** FIZO VN ART & NON LO DETARDAUA:
	4570	5ELCID0581	FALIDO A AMYO %ID ** PAN & LA %EUADA.
	4595	5ELCID0584	DEMOS SALTO A ** & FEREMOS GRANT GANA%IA,
	4693	5ELCID0595	VIO QUE ENTRELLOS & ** CASTIELLO MUCHO AUIE GRAND PLA%A:
	4733	5ELCID0600	DIOS, QUE BUENO ES ** GOZO POR AQUESTA MA@ANA
	4754	5ELCID0603	ENTRELLOS & ** CASTIELLO ENESSORA ENTRAUAN.
	4792	5ELCID0607	DEXANDO UAN LOS DELANT, POR ** CASTIELLO SE TORNAUAN,
	4811	5ELCID0609	LUEGO LEGAUAN LOS SOS, CA FECHA ES ** ARRANCADA.
	4844	5ELCID0613	FABLO MYO %ID RUY DIAZ, ** QUE EN BUEN ORA FUE NADO:
	4909	5ELCID0621	COIAMOS LOS DE DENTRO, CA ** SENORIO TENEMOS,
	4972	5ELCID0629	AYROLO ** REY ALFONSSO, DE TIERRA ECHADO LO HA,
	4992	5ELCID0631	SACOLOS A %ELADA, ** CASTIELLO GANADO A;
	5031	5ELCID0636	QUANDO LO OYO ** REY TAMIN, POR CUER LE PESO MAL:
	5221	5ELCID0660	MUCHAS SON LAS AROBDAS & GRANDE ES ** ALMOFALLA.
	5230	5ELCID0661	ALOS DE MYO %ID YA LES TUELLEN ** AGUA.
	5240	5ELCID0663	** QUE EN BUEN ORA NASCO FIRME GELO VEDAUA.
	5272	5ELCID0667	** AGUA NOS AN VEDADA, EXIR NOS HA EL PAN,
	5280	5ELCID0667	EL AGUA NOS AN VEDADA, EXIR NOS HA ** PAN,
	5342	5ELCID0675	EN ** NOBRE DEL CRIADOR, QUE NON PASE POR AL:
	5360	5ELCID0677	DIXO ** CAMPEADOR: A MI GUISA FABLASTES;
	5405	5ELCID0682	OTRO DIA MA@ANA, ** SOL QUERIE APUNTAR,
	5416	5ELCID0683	ARMADO ES MYO %ID CON QUANTOS QUE ** HA;
	5603	5ELCID0706	** CRIADOR UOS VALA, %ID CAMPEADOR LEAL
	5621	5ELCID0708	LOS QUE ** DEBDO AUEDES VEREMOS COMMO LA ACORREDES.
	5629	5ELCID0709	DIXO ** CAMPEADOR: NON SEA, POR CARIDAD
	5643	5ELCID0711	ESPOLONO ** CAUALLO, E METIOL ENEL MAYOR AZ.
	5666	5ELCID0714	DIXO ** CAMPEADOR: VALELDE, POR CARIDAD
	5702	5ELCID0719	A GRANDES VOZES LAMA ** QUE EN BUEN ORA NASCO:
	5719	5ELCID0721	YO SO RUY DIAZ, ** %ID CAMPEADOR DE BIUAR
	5812	5ELCID0734	MIO %ID RUY DIAZ ** BUEN LIDIADOR;
	5822	5ELCID0736	MARTIN ANTOLINEZ, ** BURGALES DE PRO,
	5834	5ELCID0738	MARTIN MU@OZ, ** QUE MANDO A MONT MAYOR,
	5847	5ELCID0740	GALIN GAR%IA, ** BUENO DE ARAGON,
	5870	5ELCID0743	ACORREN LA SE@A & A MYO %ID ** CAMPEADOR.
	5877	5ELCID0744	A MYNAYA ALBARFANEZ MATARON LE ** CAUALLO,
	5905	5ELCID0748	VIOLO MYO %ID RUY DIAZ ** CASTELANO,
	5918	5ELCID0750	DIOL TAL ESPADADA CON ** SO DIESTRO BRA%O,
	5926	5ELCID0751	CORTOL POR LA %INTURA, ** MEDIO ECHO EN CAMPO.
	5935	5ELCID0752	AMYNAYA ALBARFANEZ YUAL DAR ** CAUALLO:
	5941	5ELCID0753	CAUALGAD, MYNAYA, UOS SODES ** MYO DIESTRO BRA%O
	5965	5ELCID0756	CAUALGO MINAYA, ** ESPADA EN LA MANO,
	5985	5ELCID0759	MYO %ID RUY DIAZ, ** QUE EN BUEN ORA NASCO,
	6004	5ELCID0761	LOS DOS LE FALLEN, & ** VNOL HA TOMADO,
	6029	5ELCID0764	POR AQUEL COLPE RANCADO ES ** FONSSADO.
	6046	5ELCID0767	CORTOL ** YELMO, QUE LEGO ALA CARNE;
	6053	5ELCID0768	SABET, ** OTRO NON GEL OSO ESPERAR.

WORD C# PREFIX CONTEXT

EL (CON'T)

6061 5ELCID0769 ARANCADO ES ** REY FARIZ & GALUE:
6085 5ELCID0773 ** REY FARIZ EN TERUEL SE FUE ENTRAR,
6104 5ELCID0776 ** CAMPEADOR YUAL EN AL CAZ,
6113 5ELCID0777 FATA CALATAYUCH DURO ** SEGUDAR.
6119 5ELCID0778 AMYNAYA ALBARFANEZ BIEN LANCA ** CAUALLO,
6131 5ELCID0780 ESPADA TAIADOR, SANGRIENTO TRAE ** BRAZO,
6134 5ELCID0781 POR ** COBDO AYUSO LA SANGRE DESTELLANDO.
6304 5ELCID0803 GRANT A ** GOZO MYO %ID CON TODOS SOS VASSALOS.
6346 5ELCID0808 BIEN LO AGUISA ** QUE EN BUEN ORA NASCO,
6353 5ELCID0809 QUANTOS ** TRAE TODOS SON PAGADOS.
6367 5ELCID0811 DAQUESTA RIQUEZA QUE ** CRIADOR NOS ADADO
6478 5ELCID0826 MYNAYA ALBARFANEZ DESTO ES PAGADO; POR YR CON ** OMNES SON CONTADOS.
6556 5ELCID0837 E ** CAMPEADOR CON SU MESNADA.
6585 5ELCID0841 SANO ** REY FARIZ, CON EL SE CONSEIAUAN.
6589 5ELCID0841 SANO EL REY FARIZ, CON ** SE CONSEIAUAN.
6672 5ELCID0851 QUANDO MYO %ID ** CASTIELLO QUISO QUITAR,
6703 5ELCID0855 QUANDO QUITO A ALCO%ER MYO %ID ** DE BIUAR,
6715 5ELCID0857 AL%O SU SE@A, ** CAMPEADOR SE UA,
6768 5ELCID0864 ALTO ES ** POYO, MARAUILLOSO & GRANT;
6831 5ELCID0873 VIOLOS ** REY, FERMOSO SONRRISAUA:
6891 5ELCID0881 DIXO ** REY: MUCHO ES MA@ANA,
7047 5ELCID0901 MIENTRA QUE SEA ** PUEBLO DE MOROS & DELA YENTE CHRISTIANA,
7055 5ELCID0902 ** POYO DE MYO %ID ASIL DIRAN POR CARTA.
7069 5ELCID0904 ** DE RIO MARTIN TODO LO METIO EN PARIA.
7099 5ELCID0908 QUANDO VIO ** CABOSO QUE SE TARDAUA MINAYA,
7113 5ELCID0910 DEXO ** POYO, TODO LO DESENPARAUA,
7159 5ELCID0917 DOZIENTOS CON **, QUE TODOS %INEN ESPADAS;
7178 5ELCID0920 ** CAUALLO CORRIENDO, UALO ABRA%AR SIN FALLA,
7201 5ELCID0923 ** CAMPEADOR FERMOSO SONRRISAUA:
7276 5ELCID0933 DIOS, COMMO FUE ** %ID PAGADO & FIZO GRANT ALEGRIA
7291 5ELCID0935 NON LO TARDO ** QUE EN BUEN ORA NASCO,
7319 5ELCID0939 HYA VA ** MANDADO POR LAS TIERRAS TODAS,
7374 5ELCID0946 SONRRISOS ** CABOSO, QUE NON LO PUDO ENDURAR:
7413 5ELCID0951 ESTON%ES SE MUDO ** %ID AL PUERTO DE ALCAT,
7443 5ELCID0955 QUE ** SALIDO DE CASTIELLA ASILOS TRAE TAN MAL.
7482 5ELCID0960 ** CONDE ES MUY FOLON & DIXO VNA VANIDAT:
7497 5ELCID0961 GRANDES TUERTOS ME TIENE MYO %ID ** DE BIUAR.
7509 5ELCID0963 FIRIOM ** SOBRINO & NON LO ENMENDO MAS;
7533 5ELCID0966 MAS QUANDO ** MELO BUSCA, YR GELO HE YO DEMANDAR.
7563 5ELCID0969 ADELINAN TRAS MYO %ID ** BUENO DE BIUAR,
7582 5ELCID0971 ALCON%ARON A MYO %ID EN TEUAR & ** PINAR;
7589 5ELCID0972 ASI VIENE ES FOR%ADO QUE ** CONDE AMANOS SELE CUYDO TOMAR.
7644 5ELCID0979 RESPUSO ** CONDE: ESTO NON SERA VERDAD
7660 5ELCID0981 SABRA ** SALIDO A QUIEN VINO DESONDRAR.
7667 5ELCID0982 TORNOS ** MANDADERO QUANTO PUDO MAS;
7677 5ELCID0983 ESSORA LO CONNOS%E MIO %ID ** DE BIUAR.
7704 5ELCID0987 ** CONDE DON REMONT DAR NOS HA GRANT BATALLA,
7850 5ELCID1004 MANDO LOS FERIR MYO %ID, ** QUE EN BUEN ORA NASCO;
7888 5ELCID1008 VEN%IDO A ESTA BATALLA ** QUE EN BUEN ORA NASCO;
7967 5ELCID1018 ** CONDE DON REMONT NON GELO PRE%IA NADA,
7982 5ELCID1020 ** NON LO QUIERE COMER, ATODOS LOS SOSANAUA:
8002 5ELCID1022 ANTES PERDERE ** CUERPO & DEXARE EL ALMA,
8006 5ELCID1022 ANTES PERDERE EL CUERPO & DEXARE ** ALMA,
8051 5ELCID1028 DIXO ** CONDE DON REMONT: COMEDE, DON RODRIGO, & PENSSEDES DE FOLGAR.
8128 5ELCID1036 QUANDO ESTO OYO ** CONDE, YAS YUA ALEGRANDO:
8238 5ELCID1049 ALEGRE ES ** CONDE & PIDIO AGUA ALAS MANOS,
8257 5ELCID1051 CON LOS CAUALLEROS QUE ** %ID LE AUIE DADOS
8264 5ELCID1052 COMIENDO VA ** CONDE DIOS, QUE DE BUEN GRADO
8273 5ELCID1053 SOBREL SEDIE ** QUE EN BUEN ORA NASCO:
8298 5ELCID1056 AQUI DIXO ** CONDE: DE VOLUNTAD & DE GRADO.
8323 5ELCID1059 POR QUE ** CONDE DON REMONT TAN BIEN BOLUIE LAS MANOS.
8360 5ELCID1063 ** SABOR QUE DED E NON SERA OLBIDADO.
8383 5ELCID1066 ** CONDE DON REMONT ENTRE LOS DOS ES ENTRADO.
8397 5ELCID1067 FATA CABO DEL ALBERGADA ESCURRIOLOS ** CASTELANO:
8471 5ELCID1077 AGUIJAUA ** CONDE E PENSSAUA DE ANDAR,
8496 5ELCID1080 LO QUE NON FERIE ** CABOSO POR QUANTO ENEL MUNDO HA,
8513 5ELCID1082 HYDO ES ** CONDE, TORNOS EL DE BIUAR,
8516 5ELCID1082 HYDO ES EL CONDE, TORNOS ** DE BIUAR,
8542 5ELCID1085 AQUIS CONPIE%A LA GESTA DE MYO %ID ** DE BIUAR.
8560 5ELCID1087 POBLADO HA MYO %ID ** PUERTO DE ALUCANT,
8590 5ELCID1091 AORIENT EXE ** SOL, E TORNOS AESSA PART.
8613 5ELCID1094 AIUDOL ** CRIADOR, EL SE@NOR QUE ES EN %IELO.
8615 5ELCID1094 AIUDOL EL CRIADOR, ** SE@NOR QUE ES EN %IELO.
8621 5ELCID1095 ** CON TODO ESTO PRISO A MURUIEDRO.
8643 5ELCID1097 DENTRO EN VALEN%IA NON ES POCO ** MIEDO.
8694 5ELCID1104 BEUEMOS SO VINO & COMEMOS ** SO PAN.
8759 5ELCID1114 ** QUE EN BUEN ORA NASCO COMPE%O DE FABLAR:
8771 5ELCID1115 OYD, MESNADAS, SI ** CRIADOR UOS SALUE
8844 5ELCID1126 ALI PARE%RA ** QUE MERE%E LA SOLDADA.
8897 5ELCID1133 COMMO FIO POR DIOS, ** CAMPO NUESTRO SERA.
8961 5ELCID1140 CA YO SO RUYDIAZ, MYO %ID ** DE BIUAR
9004 5ELCID1146 GRAND ES ** GOZO QUE VA POR ES LOGAR.
9022 5ELCID1148 FATA VALEN%IA DURO ** SEGUDAR.
9050 5ELCID1152 ROBAUAN ** CAMPO EPIENSSAN SE DE TORNAR.

WORD C# PREFIX CONTEXT

EL (CON'T)

9092 5ELCID1157 ALEGRE ERA ** %ID & TODAS SUS COMPA@AS,
9143 5ELCID1164 QUANDO ** %ID CAMPEADOR OUO PE@A CADIELLA,
9161 5ELCID1166 NON ES CON RECABDO ** DOLOR DE VALEN%IA.
9201 5ELCID1171 NON OSAN FUERAS EXIR NIN CON ** SE AIUNTAR;
9222 5ELCID1173 EN CADA VNO DESTOS A@OS MYO %ID LES TOLIO ** PAN.
9286 5ELCID1181 POR ** REY DE MARRUECOS OUIERON A ENBIAR;
9294 5ELCID1182 CON ** DELOS MONTES CLAROS AUYEN GUERRA TAN GRAND,
9399 5ELCID1195 ESTO DIXO MYO %ID ** QUE EN BUEN ORA NASCO.
9409 5ELCID1196 TORNAUAS A MURUIEDRO, CA ** SE LA A GANADA.
9442 5ELCID1200 CRE%IENDO UA RIQUEZA A MYO %ID ** DE BIUAR.
9517 5ELCID1210 QUANDO VINO ** DEZENO, OUIERON GELA ADAR.
9549 5ELCID1214 ** ORO & LA PLATA QUI EN VOS LO PODRIE CONTAR?
9592 5ELCID1219 ALEGRE ERA ** CAMPEADOR CON TODOS LOS QUE HA,
9620 5ELCID1222 AQUEL REY DE SEUILLA ** MANDADO LEGAUA,
9648 5ELCID1226 ARRANCOLOS MYO %ID ** DELA LUENGA BARBA.
9657 5ELCID1227 FATA DENTRO EN XATIUA DURO ** ARRANCADA,
9731 5ELCID1237 CON MYO %ID RUY DIAZ, ** QUE EN BUEN ORA NASCO.
9789 5ELCID1244 CON ** MYNAYA ALBARFFANEZ QUE NOS LE PARTE DE SO BRA%O.
9820 5ELCID1247 DE QUE SON PAGADOS; ** AMOR DE MY %ID YA LO YUAN PROUANDO.
9833 5ELCID1248 LOS QUE FUERON CON **, & LOS DE DESPUES, TODOS SON PAGADOS;
9887 5ELCID1254 TOMASSEN LE ** AUER & PUSIESSEN LE EN VN PALO.
9905 5ELCID1256 CON MINAYA ALBARFANEZ ** SEUA CONSEGAR:
9940 5ELCID1260 QUE SI ALGUNOS FURTARE O MENOS LE FALLAREN, ** AUER ME AURA ATORNAR
9987 5ELCID1265 TRES MILL & SEYS %IENTOS AUIE MYO %ID ** DE BIUAR;
9992 5ELCID1266 ALEGRAS LE ** CORA%ON & TORNOS ASONRRISAR:
10090 5ELCID1278 ENBIARE POR ELLAS, & UOS SABED ** MENSAGE:
10177 5ELCID1289 ** OBISPO DON IERONIMO SO NOMBRE ES LAMADO.
10209 5ELCID1293 SOSPIRANDO ** OBISPO QUES VIESSE CON MOROS ENEL CAMPO:
10355 5ELCID1312 FUERA ** REY A SAN FAGUNT AVN POCO HA,
10387 5ELCID1316 DE MISSA ERA EXIDO ESSORA ** REY ALFONSSO,
10448 5ELCID1324 QUEL AYADES MER%ED, SIUOS VALA ** CRIADOR
10463 5ELCID1326 MAGER EN TIERRA AGENA, ** BIEN FAZE LO SO;
10511 5ELCID1332 OBISPO FIZO DE SU MANO ** BUEN CAMPEADOR,
10529 5ELCID1334 GRANDES SON LAS GANAN%IAS QUEL DIO ** CRIADOR,
10574 5ELCID1340 AL%O LA MANO DIESTRA, ** REY SE SANTIGO:
10585 5ELCID1341 DE TAN FIERAS GANAN%IAS COMMO A FECHAS ** CAMPEADOR
10601 5ELCID1343 E PLAZEM DELAS NUEUAS QUE FAZE ** CAMPEADOR;
10634 5ELCID1347 QUANDO ASSI FAZE A SU GUISA ** %ID CAMPEADOR
10638 5ELCID1348 DIXO ** REY REY AL CONDE: DEXAD ESSA RAZON,
10663 5ELCID1351 MER%ED UOS PIDE ** %ID, SIUOS CAYESSE EN SABOR,
10695 5ELCID1355 ESSORA DIXO ** REY: PLAZ ME DE CORA%ON;
10737 5ELCID1359 CATAD COMMO LAS SIRUADES UOS & ** CAMPEADOR.
10752 5ELCID1361 NON QUIERO QUE NADA PIERDA ** CAMPEADOR;
10759 5ELCID1362 ATODAS LAS ESCUELLAS QUE A ** DIZEN SE@OR
10776 5ELCID1364 SIRUAN LE SUS HEREDADES DO FUERE ** CAMPEADOR,
10802 5ELCID1368 SONRRISOS ** REY, TAN VELIDO FABLO:
10847 5ELCID1373 MUCHO CRE%EN LAS NUEUAS DE MYO %ID ** CAMPEADOR,
10930 5ELCID1383 DESI ADELANT PIENSSE DELLAS ** CAMPEADOR.
10962 5ELCID1387 SALUDAD NOS A MYO %ID ** DE BIUAR,
10973 5ELCID1389 ** %ID QUE BIEN NOS QUIERA NADA NON PERDERA.
11006 5ELCID1393 TAN GRAND FUE ** GOZO QUANDOL VIERON ASSOMAR.
11056 5ELCID1400 ** REY POR SU MER%ED SUELTAS ME UOS HA,
11076 5ELCID1402 SI UOS VIESSE ** %ID SA@AS & SIN MAL,
11093 5ELCID1404 DIXO DO@A XIMENA: ** CRIADOR LO MANDE
11124 5ELCID1408 QUE SU MUGIER & SUS FIJAS ** REY SUELTAS ME LAS HA,
11158 5ELCID1411 SEREMOS YO & SU MUGIER & SUS FIJAS QUE ** A
11196 5ELCID1416 HYR SE QUIERE A VALEN%IA A MYO %ID ** DE BIUAR.
11220 5ELCID1420 E ** SE TENIE O QUE ADUXIERA DALLA;
11269 5ELCID1426 ** BUENO DE MINAYA PENSOLAS DE ADOBAR
11297 5ELCID1430 ** BUENO DE MINAYA PENSSAR QUIERE DE CAUALGAR;
11321 5ELCID1433 DESFECHOS NOS HA ** %ID, SABET, SI NO NOS VAL;
11334 5ELCID1434 SOLTARIEMOS LA GANAN%IA, QUE NOS DIESSE ** CABDAL.
11340 5ELCID1435 HYO LO VERE CON ** %ID, SI DIOS ME LIEUA ALA.
11360 5ELCID1437 DIXO RACHEL & VIDAS: ** CRIADOR LO MANDE
11396 5ELCID1442 SI UOS VALA ** CRIADOR, MINAYA ALBARFANEZ,
11423 5ELCID1446 ** %ID SIEMPRE VALDRA MAS.
11441 5ELCID1449 ** PORTERO CON ELLOS QUE LOS HA DE AGUARDAR;
11482 5ELCID1454 AL ORA QUE LO SOPO MYO %ID ** DE BIUAR,
11490 5ELCID1453 DIREUOS DELOS CAUALLEROS QUE LEUARON **. MENSSAIE:
11526 5ELCID1460 ** OBISPO DON IERONIMO, CORONADO DE PRESTAR,
11646 5ELCID1476 E ** OTRO DIA VINIERON A MOLINA POSAR.
11653 5ELCID1477 ** MORO AUEGALUON, QUANDO SOPO EL MENSSAIE,
11658 5ELCID1477 EL MORO AUEGALUON, QUANDO SOPO ** MENSSAIE,
11747 5ELCID1490 %IENTOL PIDIERON, MAS ** CON DOZIENTOS VA.
11772 5ELCID1493 POR ** VAL DE ARBUXEDO PIENSSAN A DEPRUNAR.
11783 5ELCID1494 E EN MEDINA TODO ** RECABDO ESTA;
11803 5ELCID1497 ** VNO FINCO CON ELLOS & EL OTRO TORNO A ALBARFANEZ:
11809 5ELCID1497 EL VNO FINCO CON ELLOS & ** OTRO TORNO A ALBARFANEZ:
11835 5ELCID1500 E MARTIN ANTOLINEZ, ** BURGALES NATURAL,
11839 5ELCID1501 E ** OBISPO DON JERONIMO, CORANADO LEAL,
11846 5ELCID1502 E ** ALCAYAZ AUEGALUON CON SUS FUER%AS QUE TRAHE,
12063 5ELCID1529 SI DIOS ME LEGARE AL %ID ELO VEA CON ** ALMA,
12105 5ELCID1536 ** PORTERO DEL REY QUITAR LO MANDAUA;
12128 5ELCID1539 ** REY LO PAGO TODO, & QUITO SEUA MINAYA.

WORD C# PREFIX CONTEXT

EL (CON'T)

12162 5ELCID1544 ** CAMPO DE TORANZIO LUEGOL ATRAUESSAUAN,
12175 5ELCID1546 ** OBISPO DON IHERONIMO, BUEN CHRISTIANO SIN FALLA,
12202 5ELCID1549 ENTRE ** & ALBARFANEZ HYUAN A VNA COMPAÑA.
12217 5ELCID1551 ** MORO AUEGALUON BIEN LOS SIRUIE SIN FALLA,
12260 5ELCID1557 LOS SOS DESPENDIE ** MORO, QUE DELO SO NON TOMAUA NADA.
12285 5ELCID1560 AMYO %ID, ** QUE EN BUEN ORA NASCO,
12296 5ELCID1561 DENTRO A VALEN%IA LIEUAN LE ** MANDADO.
12314 5ELCID1563 CA DELO QUE MAS AMAUA YAL VIENE ** MANDADO.
12330 5ELCID1566 ** SEDIE EN VALEN%IA CURIANDO & GUARDANDO,
12372 5ELCID1571 QUE GUARDASSEN ** ALCA%AR & LAS OTRAS TORRES ALTAS
12402 5ELCID1574 AVN NON SABIE MYO %ID, ** QUE EN BUEN ORA %INXO ESPADA,
12443 5ELCID1579 ** OBISPO DON IHERONIMO ADELANT SE ENTRAUA,
12452 5ELCID1580 Y DEXAUA ** CAUALLO, PORA LA CAPIELLA ADELINAUA;
12461 5ELCID1581 CON QUANTOS QUE ** PUEDE, QUE CON ORAS SE ACORDARON,
12484 5ELCID1584 ** QUE EN BUEN ORA NASCO NON LO DETARDAUA:
12509 5ELCID1587 VISTIOS ** SOBREGONEL; LUENGA TRAHE LA BARBA;
12524 5ELCID1589 POR NOMBRE ** CAUALLO BAUIECA CAUALGA.
12636 5ELCID1603 OYD LO QUE DIXO ** QUE EN BUEN ORA NASCO:
12718 5ELCID1614 E DEL OTRA PARTE A OIO HAN ** MAR,
12749 5ELCID1619 ** YUIERNO ES EXIDO, QUE EL MAR%O QUIERE ENTRAR.
12754 5ELCID1619 EL YUIERNO ES EXIDO, QUE ** MAR%O QUIERE ENTRAR.
12794 5ELCID1624 E ** NON GELO GRADE%E SI NON A IHESU CHRISTO.
12875 5ELCID1634 TODO ** BIEN QUE YO HE, TODO LO TENGO DELANT:
12959 5ELCID1643 AFARTO VERAN POR LOS OIOS COMMO SE GANA ** PAN.
12979 5ELCID1646 QUES ESTO, %ID, SI ** CRIADOR UOS SALUE
13029 5ELCID1652 MUGIER, SED EN ESTE PALA%IO, & SI QUISIEREDES EN ** ALCA%AR;
13050 5ELCID1655 CRE%EM ** CORACON POR QUE ESTADES DELANT,
13098 5ELCID1660 MIEDO A SU MUGIER & QUIEREL QUEBRAR ** CORA%ON,
13121 5ELCID1663 PRISOS ALA BARBA ** BUEN %ID CAMPEADOR:
13170 5ELCID1669 VOCA%ION ES QUE FIZO ** %ID CAMPEADOR.
13179 5ELCID1670 ALEGRE SON LAS DUENAS, PERDIENDO VAN ** PAUOR.
13195 5ELCID1673 VIOLO ** ATALAYA & TANXO EL ESQUILA;
13199 5ELCID1673 VIOLO EL ATALAYA & TANXO ** ESQUILA;
13269 5ELCID1683 ** SELO VIO CON LOS OIOS, CUENTAN GELO DELANT,
13317 5ELCID1689 ** OBISPO DO IHERONIMO SOLTURA NOS DARA,
13346 5ELCID1691 MAS VALE QUE NOS LOS VEZCAMOS, QUE ELLOS COIAN ** PAN.
13396 5ELCID1698 ESSORA DIXO ** %ID: DE BUENA VOLUNTAD.
13424 5ELCID1702 ** OBISPO DON IHERONIMO LA MISSA LES CANTAUA;
13439 5ELCID1704 ** QUE A QUI MURIERE LIDIANDO DE CARA,
13455 5ELCID1705 PRENDOL YO LOS PECADOS, & DIOS LE ABRA ** ALMA.
13490 5ELCID1710 DIXO ** CAMPEADOR: DESA QUI UOS SEAN MANDADAS.
13528 5ELCID1714 DIO SALTO MYO %ID EN BAUIECA ** SO CAUALLO;
13603 5ELCID1724 POR ** COBDO AYUSO LA SANGRE DESTELLANDO.
13625 5ELCID1726 SALIOS LE DE SOL ESPADA, CA MUCHOL ANDIDO ** CAUALLO,
13636 5ELCID1728 MYO %ID ** DE BIUAR FASTA ALLI LEGO EN ALCAZ,
13655 5ELCID1730 DESDALLI SE TORNO ** QUE EN BUEN ORA NASCO,
13703 5ELCID1736 MESNADAS DE MYO %ID ROBADO AN ** CANPO;
13734 5ELCID1740 QUE DIOS LES OUO MER%ED QUE VEN%IERON ** CAMPO.
13769 5ELCID1745 ASSI ENTRO SOBRE BAUIECA, ** ESPADA EN LA MANO.
13806 5ELCID1749 VOS TENIENDO VALEN%IA, & YO VEN%I ** CAMPO;
13828 5ELCID1752 VEDES ** ESPADA SANGRIENTA & SUDIENTO EL CAUALLO:
13833 5ELCID1752 VEDES EL ESPADA SANGRIENTA & SUDIENTO ** CAUALLO:
13885 5ELCID1759 DELANT ** CAMPEADOR LOS YNOIOS FINCARON:
13901 5ELCID1761 EN BUELTA CON ** ENTRARON AL PALA%IO,
13909 5ELCID1762 E YUAN POSAR CON ** EN VNOS PRE%IOSOS ESCAÑOS:
13974 5ELCID1770 GRANT FUE ** ALEGRIA QUE FUE POR EL PALA%IO;
13979 5ELCID1770 GRANT FUE EL ALEGRIA QUE FUE POR ** PALA%IO;
13984 5ELCID1771 COMMO LO DIXO ** %ID ASSI LO HAN ACABADO.
14054 5ELCID1780 MAGER DE TODO ESTO, ** CAMPEADOR CONTADO
14143 5ELCID1790 ENBIAR LA QUIERO ALFONSSO ** CASTELLANO,
14163 5ELCID1793 ** OBISPO DON IHERONIMO, CABOSO CORONADO,
14199 5ELCID1797 MYO %ID DON RODRIGO, ** QUE EN BUEN ORA NASCO,
14210 5ELCID1798 DE TODA LA SU QUINTA ** DIEZMO LA MANDADO.
14247 5ELCID1803 ** BUENO DE MYO %ID NON LO TARDO POR NADA:
14341 5ELCID1814 QUE NON DIGA MAL ** REY ALFONSSO DEL QUE VALEN%IA MANDA.
14395 5ELCID1820 E SERUIR LO HE SIENPRE MIENTRA QUE OUISSE ** ALMA.
14428 5ELCID1825 POR ** REY DON ALFONSSO TOMAN SSE APREGUNTAR.
14449 5ELCID1827 LEGAN A VALADOLID, DO ** REY ALFONSSO ESTAUA;
14468 5ELCID1830 MYO %ID ** DE VALEN%IA ENBIA SU PRESENTAIA.
14476 5ELCID1831 ALEGRE FUE ** REY, NON VIESTES ATANTO,
14491 5ELCID1833 HYEN LOS PRIMEROS ** REY FUERA DIO SALTO,
14512 5ELCID1836 ** CONDE DON GAR%IA, SO ENEMIGO MALO.
14547 5ELCID1840 ** REY DON ALFONSSO SEYSE SANTIGUANDO.
14589 5ELCID1846 POR MYO %ID ** CAMPEADOR TODO ESTO VOS BESAMOS;
14609 5ELCID1848 MUCHO PRE%IA LA ONDRA ** %ID QUEL AUEDES DADO.
14662 5ELCID1855 DIXO ** REY DON ALFONSSO: RE%IBOLOS DE GRADO.
14727 5ELCID1862 EN LA ONDRA QUE ** HA NOS SEREMOS ABILTADOS;
14752 5ELCID1865 POR ESTO QUE ** FAZE NOS ABREMOS ENBARGO.
14758 5ELCID1866 FABLO ** REY DON ALFONSSO & DIXO ESTA RAZON:
14774 5ELCID1867 GRADO AL CRIADOR & AL SEÑOR SANT ESIDRO ** DE LEON
14943 5ELCID1889 VNA GRANT ORA ** REY PENSSO & COMIDIO;
14958 5ELCID1891 EFAZIENDO YO HA ** MAL, & EL AMI GRAND PRO,
14961 5ELCID1891 EFAZIENDO YO HA EL MAL, & ** AMI GRAND PRO,
14988 5ELCID1895 ** REY DON ALFONSSO ESSORA LOS LAMO,

WORD C# PREFIX CONTEXT

EL (CON'T)

15011 5ELCID1898 SIRUEM MYC %ID ** CAMPEADOR, EL LO MERE%E,
15013 5ELCID1898 SIRUEM MYO %ID EL CAMPEADCR, ** LO MERE%E,
15094 5ELCID1909 DESPUES FAGA ** %ID LC CUE CUIERE SABOR.
15104 5ELCID1910 DEZID A RUY DIAZ, ** CUE EN BUEN ORA NASCO,
15118 5ELCID1912 DO ** DIXIERE, Y SEA EL MOION.
15122 5ELCID1912 DO EL DIXIERE, Y SEA ** MOION.
15151 5ELCID1916 QUANDO LO SCPC ** BUEN CAMPEADOR,
15192 5ELCID1922 SI ES PAGADC C RE%IBIC ** DON?
15221 5ELCID1927 LO QUEL ROGAUA ALFCNSSO ** CE LEON
15252 5ELCID1931 QUANDO LO CYO MYO %ID ** BUEN CAMPEADOR,
15265 5ELCID1933 ESTC GRADESCC A CHRISTUS ** MYO SE@OR.
15322 5ELCID1940 MAS PUES LC CCNSEIA ** CUE MAS VALE QUE NOS,
15377 5ELCID1947 ESSORA DIXO ** %ID: PLAZME DE CORA%ON.
15396 5ELCID1950 NCN ERA MARAUILLA SICUISIESSE ** REY ALFONSSO,
15420 5ELCID1953 MAS LO QUE ** QUISIERE, ESSO QUERAMOS NOS.
15452 5ELCID1958 LO QUE ** REY QUISIERE, ESSO FERA EL CAMPEADOR.
15457 5ELCID1958 LO QUE EL REY CUISIERE, ESSO FERA ** CAMPEADOR.
15478 5ELCID1961 SALUDAD ME MAYO %ID, ** QUE EN BUEN ORA %INXO ESPADA;
15557 5ELCID1972 CONDUCHOS LARGCS ** REY ENBIAR MANDAUA
15570 5ELCID1974 CON ** REY ATANTAS BUENAS CONPA@AS.
15605 5ELCID1979 ** REY DON ALFCNSSO A PRIESSA CAUALGAUA,
15627 5ELCID1982 CON ** REY VAN LECNESES & MESNACAS GALIZIANAS,
15654 5ELCID1985 DENTRO EN VALLEN%IA MYO %ID ** CAMPEADOR
15705 5ELCID1992 MARTIN MUNCZ & MARTIN ANTCLINEZ, ** BURGALES DE PRO,
15709 5ELCID1993 ** OBISPO DCN IERCNIMC, CORANACO MEIOR,
15722 5ELCID1995 MU@O GUSTICZ, ** CAUALLERC CE PRO.
15728 5ELCID1996 GALIND GAR%IAZ, ** CUE FUE CE ARAGON:
15739 5ELCID1997 ESTOS SE ADOBAN POR YR CCN ** CAMPEADOR,
15753 5ELCID1999 ALUAR SALUACOREZ & GALINC GARCIAZ ** DE ARAGON,
15760 5ELCID2000 A AQUESTOS DOS MANDO ** CAMPEADOR QUE CURIEN A VALEN%IA
15832 5ELCID2008 FATA QUES TCRNE ** QUE EN BUEN ORA NASCO.
15868 5ELCID2012 HYAS VA PORA LAS VISTAS QUE CON ** REY PARO.
15877 5ELCID2013 DE VN DIA ES LEGADO ANTES ** REY DON ALFONSSO.
15885 5ELCID2014 QUANDO VIERCN QUE VINIE ** BUEN CAMPEADOR,
15900 5ELCID2016 DON LO CUO A CIO ** QUE EN BUEN ORA NASCO,
15930 5ELCID2020 CCMMO LC CCMIDIA ** CUE EN BUEN ORA NA%IO,
15958 5ELCID2023 LORANDO DELCS CICS, TANTC AUIE ** GOZO MAYOR;
15980 5ELCID2026 TAN GRAND PESAR OUO ** REY DCN ALFONSSO:
16007 5ELCID2030 HYNOIOS FITCS SECIE ** CAMPEACOR:
16029 5ELCID2033 DIXO ** REY ESTC FERE CALMA & DE CORA%ON;
16140 5ELCID2047 DIXO ** REY: NON ES AGUISACO OY:
16201 5ELCID2055 RESPUSC MIC %ID: ASSI LC MANDE ** CRIACOR
16260 5ELCID2062 OTRO DIA MA@ANA, CLARC SALIE ** SOL,
16262 5ELCID2063 ** CAMPEADCR ALOS SOS LC MANDO
16282 5ELCID2065 DE TAL GUISA LOS PAGA MYC %ID ** CAMPEADOR,
16306 5ELCID2068 AL OTRC DIA MA@ANA, ASSI CCMMC SALIO ** SOL,
16308 5ELCID2069 ** OBISPO DCN IHERONIMO LA MISSA CANTO.
16326 5ELCID2071 NON LO TARDO ** REY, LA RAZCN CONPE%O:
16345 5ELCID2073 COMETER QUIERO VN RUEGO A MYO %ID ** CAMPEADOR;
16374 5ELCID2077 SEMEIAM ** CASAMIENTC CNDRADO & CON GRANT PRO,
16413 5ELCID2081 DANDOS LAS, MYO %ID, SI UCS VALA ** CRIADOR
16421 5ELCID2082 NCN ABRIA FIJAS DE CASAR, RESPUSO ** CAMPEADOR,
16485 5ELCID2090 GRA%IAS, DIXO ** REY, AUOS & ATOD ESTA CORT.
16516 5ELCID2094 FABLO ** REY DCN ALFCNSSC CCMMO TAN BUEN SE@OR:
16675 5ELCID2112 QUANDO SALIE ** SCL, CUES TORNASSE CACA VNO DON SALIDOS SON.
16690 5ELCID2113 AQUIS METIO EN NUEUAS MYO %ID ** CAMPEADOR;
16750 5ELCID2121 ** REY ALOS YFANTES ALAS MANOS LES TOMO,
16764 5ELCID2122 METIOLCS EN PCDER DE MYC %ID ** CAMPEADOR:
16811 5ELCID2128 AQUI LC DIGC ANTE MYC SE@OR ** REY ALFONSSO:
16870 5ELCID2135 RESPONDIC ** REY: AFE AQUI ALBARFANEZ;
16897 5ELCID2138 SED PADRINC DELLOS ATCD ** VELAR;
16957 5ELCID2147 DIXO ** REY DON ALFCNSSO: MUCHO ME AUEDES ENBARGADO.
17239 5ELCID2180 QUANDO VINIERE LA MA@ANA, CUE APUNTARE ** SOL,
17260 5ELCID2183 MYO %ID ** CAMPEACOR AL ALCA%AR ENTRAUA;
17392 5ELCID2200 PEDIDAS UCS HA & RCGACAS ** MYO SE@OR ALFONSSO,
17423 5ELCID2204 BIEN MELO CREADES, QUE ** UOS CASA, CA NON YO.
17433 5ELCID2205 PENSSARCN DE ACOBAR ESSCRA ** PALA%IO,
17436 5ELCID2206 POR ** SUELO & SUSO TAN BIEN ENCORTINADO,
17536 5ELCID2219 ** CAMPEADOR EN PIE ES LEUANTADO:
17555 5ELCID2221 VENIT ACA, ALBARFANEZ, ** QUE YO QUIERO & AMO
17687 5ELCID2238 ** OBISPO DCN IHERCNIMO VISTICS TAN PRIUADO,
17725 5ELCID2243 DIOS, QUE BIEN TCUIERCN ARMAS ** %ID & SUS VASSALOS
17733 5ELCID2244 TRES CAUALLCS CAMEO ** CUE EN BUEN ORA NASCO.
17768 5ELCID2248 RICAS FUERCN LAS BODAS EN ** ALCA%AR ONDRADO,
17809 5ELCID2253 MYO %ID DON RCDRIGC, ** QUE EN BUEN ORA NASCO,
17884 5ELCID2263 ESPIDIENDOS DE RUY DIAZ, ** QUE EN BUEN ORA NASCO,
17934 5ELCID2270 ** %ID & SCS HYERNOS EN VALEN%IA SON RASTADOS.
17961 5ELCID2273 ALEGRE ERA ** %ID & TCDCS SUS VASSALLOS.
17982 5ELCID2275 QUES PAGE DES CASAMIENTC MYO %ID O ** QUE LO ALGO
17993 5ELCID2277 ** CRIACOR UOS VALLA CCN TODCS LOS SOS SANTOS.
18012 5ELCID2279 CON ** AMOS SUS YERNOS LOS YFANTES DE CARRION.
18025 5ELCID2280 YAZIES EN VN ESCA@O, DURMIE ** CAMPEADOR,
18039 5ELCID2282 SALIOS DE LA RED & DESATCS ** LEON.
18058 5ELCID2285 E %ERCAN ** ESCA@O & FINCAN SOBRE SO SE@OR.

WORD C# PREFIX CONTEXT

EL (CON'T)

```
18082 5ELCID2287 METIOS SOL ESCA@O, TANTO CUO ** PAUOR.
18104 5ELCID2291 ** MANTO & EL BRIAL TODO SUZIO LO SACO.
18107 5ELCID2291 EL MANTO & ** BRIAL TODO SUZIO LO SACO.
18116 5ELCID2292 EN ESTO DESPERTO ** QUE EN BUEN ORA NA%IO;
18124 5ELCID2293 VIO CER%ADO ** ESCA@O DE SUS BUENOS VARONES:
18143 5ELCID2295 HYA SE@OR ONDRADO, REBATA NOS DIO ** LEON.
18148 5ELCID2296 MYO %ID FINCO ** COBDO, EN PIE SE LEUANTO,
18154 5ELCID2297 ** MANTO TRAE ALCUELLO, & ADELINO PORA LEON;
18162 5ELCID2298 ** LEON QUANDO LO VIO, ASSI EN VERGON%O,
18177 5ELCID2299 ANTE MYO %ID LA CABE%A PREMIO & ** ROSTRO FINCO;
18246 5ELCID2308 MANDOLO VEDAR MYO %ID ** CAMPEADOR.
18286 5ELCID2314 AQUESTE ERA ** REY BUCAR, SIL OUIESTES CONTAR.
18293 5ELCID2315 ALEGRAUAS ** %ID & TODOS SUS VARONES,
18375 5ELCID2325 VINO CON ESTAS NUEUAS A MYO %ID RUYDIAZ ** CANPEADOR:
18397 5ELCID2328 HYD LOS CONORTAR, SI UOS VALA ** CRIADOR,
18417 5ELCID2330 NOS CON UUSCO LA VENCREMOS, & VALER NOS HA ** CRIADOR.
18440 5ELCID2333 EN BRA%OS TENEDES MIS FIJAS TAN BLANCAS COMMO ** SOL
18472 5ELCID2338 AVN VEA ** ORA QUE UOS MERESCA DOS TANTO.
18507 5ELCID2342 AVN SI DIOS QUISIERE & ** PADRE QUE ESTA EN ALTO,
18570 5ELCID2350 OYD LO QUE FABLO ** QUE EN BUEN ORA NASCO:
18579 5ELCID2351 ALA, PERO VERMUEZ, ** MYO SOBRINO CARO
18665 5ELCID2362 ESTA BATALLA ** CRIADOR LA FERA,
18674 5ELCID2363 EUOS TAN DINNO QUE CON ** AUEDES PART.
18685 5ELCID2365 ** DEBDO QUE A CADA VNO A CONPLIR SERA.
18710 5ELCID2368 AFEUOS ** OBISPO DON IHERONIMO MUY BIEN ARMADO,
18827 5ELCID2382 NOS DAQUENT VEREMOS COMMO LIDIA ** ABBAT.
18829 5ELCID2383 ** OBISPO DON IHERONIMO PRISO A ESPOLONADA
18860 5ELCID2387 ** ASTIL A QUEBRADO & METIO MANO AL ESPADA.
18870 5ELCID2388 ENSAYAUAS ** OBISPO, DIOS, QUE BIEN LIDIAUA
18883 5ELCID2389 DOS MATO CON LAN%A & V CON ** ESPADA.
18901 5ELCID2392 ** QUE EN BUEN ORA NASCO LOS OIOS LE FINCAUA,
18913 5ELCID2393 EN BRA%O ** ESCUDO & ABAXO EL ASTA,
18917 5ELCID2393 EN BRA%O EL ESCUDO & ABAXO ** ASTA,
18922 5ELCID2394 AGUIJO A BAUIECA, ** CAUALLO QUE BIEN ANDA,
18939 5ELCID2396 EN LAS AZES PRIMERAS ** CAMPEADOR ENTRAUA,
18954 5ELCID2398 PLOGO A DIOS, AQUESTA FUE ** ARRANCADA.
19014 5ELCID2405 TANTAS CABE%AS CON YELMOS QUE POR ** CAMPO CAEN,
19028 5ELCID2407 VII MIGEROS CONPLIDOS DURO ** SEGUDAR.
19047 5ELCID2410 VERTE AS CON ** %ID, EL DE LA BARBA GRANT,
19049 5ELCID2410 VERTE AS CON EL %ID, ** DE LA BARBA GRANT,
19069 5ELCID2413 ** ESPADA TIENES DESNUDA EN LA MANO & VEOT AGUIJAR;
19089 5ELCID2415 MAS SI ** CAUALLO NON ESTROPIE%A O COMIGO NON CAYE,
19124 5ELCID2419 MAS BAUIECA ** DE MIO %ID ALCAN%ANDO LO VA.
19132 5ELCID2420 ALCAN%OLO ** %ID ABUCAR A TRES BRACAS DEL MAR,
19156 5ELCID2423 CORTOL ** YELMO &, LIBRADO TODO LO HAL,
19166 5ELCID2424 FATA LA %INTURA ** ESPADA LEGADO HA.
19212 5ELCID2430 SABET, TODOS DE FIRME ROBAUAN ** CAMPO.
19220 5ELCID2432 ** QUE EN BUEN ORA NASCO.
19230 5ELCID2433 MYO %ID RUY DIAZ, ** CAMPEADOR CONTADO,
19237 5ELCID2434 CON DOS ESPADAS QUE ** PRE%IAUA ALGO
19339 5ELCID2450 ** ESCUDO TRAE AL CUELLO & TODO ESPADO;
19363 5ELCID2453 POR ** COBDO AYUSO LA SANGRE DESTELLANDO;
19404 5ELCID2458 MATASTES ABUCAR & ARRANCAMOS ** CANPO.
19445 5ELCID2464 POR BIEN LO DIXO ** %ID, MAS ELLOS LO TOUIERON AMAL.
19526 5ELCID2474 GRANT FUE ** DIA LA CORT DEL CAMPEADOR,
19605 5ELCID2484 MANDO MYO %ID, ** QUE EN BUEN ORA NASCO,
19661 5ELCID2492 TODAS ESTAS GANAN%IAS FIZO ** CANPEADOR.
19764 5ELCID2505 GRANDES SON LOS GOZOS EN VALEN%IA CON MYO %ID ** CANPEADOR
19818 5ELCID2512 AQUI ESTA CON MYO %ID ** OBISPO DO IHERONIMO,
19822 5ELCID2513 ** BUENO DE ALBARFANEZ, CAUALLERO LIDIADOR,
19833 5ELCID2514 E OTROS MUCHOS QUE CRIO ** CAMPEADOR.
19846 5ELCID2516 RE%IBIOLOS MINAYA POR MYO %ID ** CAMPEADOR:
19860 5ELCID2518 ASSI COMMO LEGARON, PAGOS ** CAMPEADOR:
20157 5ELCID2559 SI UOS VALA ** CRIADOR, %ID CAMPEADOR
20222 5ELCID2568 DIXO ** CAMPEADOR: DARUOS HE MYS FIJAS & ALGO DELO MYO;
20232 5ELCID2569 ** %ID QUE NOS CURIAUA DE ASSI SER AFONTADO;
20377 5ELCID2585 CONPIE%AN A RE%EBIR LO QUE ** %ID MANDO.
20442 5ELCID2594 MER%ED UOS PEDIMOS, PADRE, SIUOS VALA ** CRIADOR
20494 5ELCID2602 ** FIZO AQUESTO, LA MADRE LO DOBLAUA;
20504 5ELCID2603 ANDAD, FIJAS, DAQUI ** CRIADOR VOS VALA
20598 5ELCID2615 VIOLO EN LOS AUUEROS ** QUE EN BUEN ORA %INXO ESPADA,
20727 5ELCID2632 ** PADRE CON LAS FIJAS LORAN DE CORA%ON,
20757 5ELCID2636 SALUDAD A MYO AMIGO ** MORO AVENGALUON:
20765 5ELCID2637 RE%IBA A MYOS YERNOS COMMO ** PUDIER MEIOR;
20796 5ELCID2641 DE QUANTO ** FIZIERE YOL DAR POR ELLO BUEN GALARDON.
20816 5ELCID2643 HYAS TORNO PORA VALEN%IA ** QUE EN BUEN ORA NAS%IO.
20848 5ELCID2647 FELOS EN MOLINA CON ** MORO AVENGALUON.
20851 5ELCID2648 ** MORO QUANDO LO SOPO, PLOGOL DE CORA%ON;
20897 5ELCID2654 ALAS FIJAS DEL %ID ** MORO SUS DO@AS DIO,
20916 5ELCID2657 ODIZEN ** ANSSARERA ELLOS POSADOS SON.
20925 5ELCID2658 TOD ESTO LES FIZO ** MORO POR EL AMOR DEL %ID CAMPEADOR.
20928 5ELCID2658 TOD ESTO LES FIZO EL MORO POR ** AMOR DEL %ID CAMPEADOR.
20938 5ELCID2659 ELLOS VEYEN LA RIQUEZA QUE ** MORO SACO,
20956 5ELCID2662 SI PUDIESSEMOS MATAR ** MORO AVENGALUON,
```

WORD C# PREFIX CONTEXT

EL (CON'T)

20980 5ELCID2665 NUNQUA AURIE DERECHO DE NOS ** %ID CAMPEADOR.
21016 5ELCID2671 ** MORO AVENGALUON, MUCHO ERA BUEN BARRAGAN,
21038 5ELCID2674 DELO QUE ** MORO DIXO ALOS YFANTES NON PLAZE:
21070 5ELCID2677 SI NOLO DEXAS POR MYO %ID ** DE BIUAR,
21079 5ELCID2678 TAL COSA UOS FARIA QUE POR ** MUNDO SONAS,
21138 5ELCID2685 DA QUESTE CASAMIENTO QUE GRADE ** CAMPEADOR.
21145 5ELCID2686 ESTO LES HA DICHO, & ** MORO SE TORNO;
21281 5ELCID2704 MAL GELO CUNPLIERON CUANDO SALIE ** SOL
21571 5ELCID2742 QUE ASSOMASSE ESSORA ** %ID CAMPEADOR
21662 5ELCID2753 QUAL VENTURA SERIE SI ASSOMAS ESSORA ** %ID CAMPEADOR
21678 5ELCID2756 QUE ** VNA AL OTRA NOL TORNA RECABDO.
21758 5ELCID2767 ENLA CARRERA DO YUA DOLIOL ** CORA%ON,
21821 5ELCID2776 POR ** RASTRO TORNOS FELEZ MUNOZ,
21838 5ELCID2779 ARRENDO ** CAUALLO, A ELLAS ADELINO;
21913 5ELCID2788 MIENTRA ES ** DIA, ANTE QUE ENTRE LA NOCH,
21987 5ELCID2797 SI UOS LO MERESCA, MYO PRIMO, NUESTRO PADRE ** CANPEADOR,
21995 5ELCID2798 DANDOS DEL AGUA, SI UOS VALA ** CRIADOR
22053 5ELCID2807 CON ** SO MANTO A AMAS LAS CUBRIO,
22060 5ELCID2808 ** CAUALLO PRISO POR LA RIENDA & LUEGO DENT LAS PARTIO,
22110 5ELCID2814 FALLO A DIEGO TELLEZ ** QUE DE ALBARFANEZ FUE;
22116 5ELCID2815 QUANDO ** LO OYO PESOL DE CORA%ON,
22141 5ELCID2819 QUANTO ** MEIOR PUEDE ALLI LAS ONDRO.
22201 5ELCID2827 QUANDO GELO DIZEN A MYO %ID ** CAMPEADOR,
22277 5ELCID2837 E MARTIN ANTOLINEZ, ** BURGLES DE PRO,
22308 5ELCID2841 NON LO DETARDAN ** MANDADO DE SU SE@OR,
22337 5ELCID2845 ASANTESTEUAN ** MANDADO LEGO
22404 5ELCID2853 MUCHO UOS LO GRADE%E, ALLA DO ESTA, MYO %ID ** CANPEADOR,
22464 5ELCID2861 EUOS A ** LO GRADID, QUANDO BIUAS SOMOS NOS.
22521 5ELCID2868 AVN VEAMOS ** DIA QUE VOS PODAMOS VENGAR
22646 5ELCID2885 AL QUE EN BUEN ORA NASCO LEGAUA ** MENSSAIE;
22685 5ELCID2891 HYO TOME ** CASAMIENTO, MAS NON OSE DEZIR AL.
22739 5ELCID2898 ** QUE EN BUEN ORA NASCO NON QUISO TARDAR,
22781 5ELCID2903 LIEUES ** MANDADO A CASTIELLA AL REY ALFONSSO;
22804 5ELCID2905 CUEMO YO SO SU VASSALLO, & ** ES MYO SE@OR,
22826 5ELCID2908 ** CASO MIS FIJAS, CA NON GELAS DI YO;
22905 5ELCID2918 CON ** DOS CAUALLEROS QUEL SIRUAN A SO SABOR,
22915 5ELCID2919 E CON ** ESCUDEROS QUE SON DE CRIAZON.
22972 5ELCID2926 ELLOS CONDES GALLIZANOS A ** TIENEN POR SE@OR.
22996 5ELCID2930 CON ** DOS CAUALLEROS QUEL AGUARDAN CUM ASSE@OR.
23011 5ELCID2932 VIOLOS ** REY & CONNOS%IO A MU@O GUSTIOZ;
23019 5ELCID2933 LEUANTOS ** REY, TAN BIEN LOS RE%IBIO.
23026 5ELCID2934 DELANT ** REY FINCO LOS YNOIOS AQUEL MU@O GUSTIOZ,
23057 5ELCID2937 LOS PIES & LAS MANOS VOS BESA ** CAMPEADOR;
23077 5ELCID2940 ALTO FUE ** CASAMIENO CALO QUISIESTES UOS
23176 5ELCID2953 ** REY VNA GRAND ORA CALLO & COMIDIO;
23221 5ELCID2958 SI QUIER ** CASAMIENTO FECHO NON FUESSE OY
23241 5ELCID2960 AIUDAR LE ADERECHO, SIN SALUE ** CRIADOR
23287 5ELCID2966 E COMMO DEN DERECHO A MYO %ID ** CAMPEADOR,
23358 5ELCID2975 ASSI COMMO LO DIXO, SUYO ERA ** CUYDADO:
23366 5ELCID2976 NON LO DETIENE POR NADA ALFONSSO ** CASTELLANO,
23444 5ELCID2986 POR QUE ** REY FAZIE CORT EN TOLLEDO,
23457 5ELCID2987 MIEDO HAN QUE Y VERNA MYO %ID ** CAMPEADOR;
23475 5ELCID2990 DIXO ** REY: NO LO FERE, SIN SALUE DIOS
23488 5ELCID2991 CA Y VERNA MYO %ID ** CAMPEADOR;
23530 5ELCID2997 ** CONDE DON GAR%IA EN ESTAS NUEUAS FUE,
23553 5ELCID3000 LEGAUA ** PLAZO, QUERIEN YR ALA CORT;
23563 5ELCID3001 EN LOS PRIMEROS VA ** BUEN REY DON ALFONSSO,
23568 5ELCID3002 ** CONDE DON ANRRICH & EL CONDE DON REMOND;
23573 5ELCID3002 EL CONDE DON ANRRICH & ** CONDE DON REMOND;
23583 5ELCID3004 ** CONDE DON FRUELLA & EL CONDE DON BELTRAN.
23588 5ELCID3004 EL CONDE DON FRUELLA & ** CONDE DON BELTRAN.
23606 5ELCID3007 ** CONDE DON GAR%IA CON YFANTES DE CARRION,
23644 5ELCID3011 EBAYR LE CUYDAN A MYO %ID ** CAMPEADOR.
23656 5ELCID3013 AVN NON ERA LEGADO ** QUE ENBUEN ORA NA%IO,
23665 5ELCID3014 POR QUE SE TARDA ** REY NON HA SABOR.
23677 5ELCID3015 AL QUINTO DIA VENIDO ES MYO %ID ** CAMPEADOR;
23702 5ELCID3019 QUANDO LO OYO ** REY, PLOGOL DE CORA%ON;
23710 5ELCID3020 CON GRANDES YENTES ** REY CAUALGO
23724 5ELCID3022 BIEN AGUISADO VIENE ** %ID CON TODOS LOS SOS,
23741 5ELCID3024 QUANDO LOOVO A OIO ** BUEN REY DON ALFFONSSO,
23750 5ELCID3025 FIRIOS ATIERRA MYO %ID ** CAMPEADOR;
23762 5ELCID3027 QUANDO LO OYO ** REY, POR NADA NON TARDO;
23796 5ELCID3031 DELO QUE AUOS PESA AMI DUELE ** CORA%ON;
23813 5ELCID3033 AMEN, DIXO MYO %ID ** CAMPEADOR;
23881 5ELCID3042 RESPONDIO ** REY: SI FAGO, SIN SALUE DIOS
23890 5ELCID3043 PORA TOLLEDO ** REY TORNADA DA,
23906 5ELCID3045 MER%ED, YA REY, SI ** CRIADOR UOS SALUE
23950 5ELCID3052 DIXO ** REY: PLAZME DE VELUNTAD.
23955 5ELCID3053 ** REY DON ALFONSSO A TOLLEDO ES ENTRADO,
24018 5ELCID3061 SUELTA FUE LA MISSA ANTES QUE SALIESSE ** SOL,
24032 5ELCID3063 VOS, MYNAYA ALBARFANEZ, ** MYO BRA%O MEIOR,
24040 5ELCID3064 VOS YREDES COMIGO & ** OBISPO DON IHERONIMO
24054 5ELCID3066 E MARTIN ANTOLINEZ, ** BURGALES DE PRO,
24088 5ELCID3071 E GALINDO GAR%IEZ, ** BUENO DARAGON;

WORD C# PREFIX CONTEXT

EL (CON'T)

24113 5ELCID3074 DE SUSC LAS LCRIGAS TAN BLANCAS COMMO ** SOL;
24184 5ELCID3084 NOS DETIENE PCR NADA ** QUE EN BUEN ORA NA%IO:
24213 5ELCID3087 VISTIO CAMISA DE RAN%AL TAN BLANCA COMMO ** SOL,
24229 5ELCID3089 AL PUNO BIEN ESTAN, CA ** SELC MANDO:
24258 5ELCID3093 SIEMPRE LA VISTE MYO %ID ** CAMPEADOR;
24293 5ELCID3097 LA BARBA AVIE LUENGA & PRISOLA CCN ** CORDON,
24357 5ELCID3106 ** VA EN MEDIC, ELCS %IENTO ACERREDOR.
24377 5ELCID3108 LEUANTOS EN PIE ** BUEN REY DCN ALFONSSO
24383 5ELCID3109 E ** CCNDE DON ANRRICH & EL CCNDE DON REMONT
24388 5ELCID3109 E EL CCNDE DON ANRRICH & ** CCNDE DON REMONT
24412 5ELCID3112 NOS QUISO LEUANTAR ** CRESPC DE GRA@ON,
24425 5ELCID3114 ** REY DIXO AL %ID: VENJD ACA SER, CAMPEADOR,
24452 5ELCID3117 ESSORA DIXO MUCHAS MER%EDES ** QUE VALEN%IA GA@O:
24473 5ELCID3120 LO QUE DIXC ** %ID AL REY PLOGO DE CORA%ON.
24532 5ELCID3127 ESSORA SE LEUC EN PIE ** BUEN REY DON ALFONSSO;
24541 5ELCID3128 OYD, MESNACAS, SIUOS VALA ** CRIADOR
24573 5ELCID3132 POR ** AMOR DE MYC %ID EL QUE EN BUEN ORA NA%IO,
24578 5ELCID3132 POR EL AMOR DE MYC %ID ** QUE EN BUEN ORA NA%IO,
24603 5ELCID3135 ALCALDES SEAN DESTO ** CCNDE DON ANRRICH & EL CONDE DON REMOND
24608 5ELCID3135 ALCALDES SEAN DESTO EL CONDE DON ANRRICH & ** CONDE DON REMOND
24630 5ELCID3138 POR ESCOGER ** DERECHC, CA TUERTO NON MANDO YO.
24649 5ELCID3140 JURO PAR SANT ESIDRC, ** QUE BOLUIERE MY CORT
24657 5ELCID3141 QUITAR ME A ** REYNC, PERDERA MIAMOR.
24662 5ELCID3142 CON ** QUE TCUIERE DERECHO YO DESSA PART ME SO.
24675 5ELCID3143 AGCRA DEMANDE MYO %ID ** CAMPEADOR:
24810 5ELCID3160 DIXO ** CONDE DON GAR%IA: AESTC NOS FABLEMOS.
24828 5ELCID3162 CON TODCS SUS PARIENTES & ** VANDO QUE Y SON;
24846 5ELCID3164 AVN GRAND AMCR NOS FAZE ** %ID CAMPEADOR,
24861 5ELCID3166 BIEN NCS ABENDREMOS CCN ** REY DON ALFONSSO.
24889 5ELCID3169 HYA MAS NON AURA DERECHC DE NOS ** %ID CANPEADOR.
24993 5ELCID3183 NOS LE PUEDEN CAMEAR, CA ** %ID BIEN LAS CONNOS%E;
25033 5ELCID3189 TENDIO ** BRA%O, LA ESPACA TIZON LE DIO;
25050 5ELCID3191 A MARTIN ANTCLINEZ, ** BURGALES DE PRO,
25055 5ELCID3192 TENDIO ** BRA%O, EL ESPADA COLACAL DIO;
25057 5ELCID3192 TENDIO EL BRA%O, ** ESPADA COLACAL DIO;
25110 5ELCID3198 BESO LE LA MANO, ** ESPACA TOMO & RE%IBIO.
25120 5ELCID3199 LUEGO SE LEUANTO MYO %ID ** CAMPEADOR;
25191 5ELCID3208 DJZE ** CONDE DCN REMCND: DEZID DE SSI O DE NO.
25231 5ELCID3212 SI PLOGUIERE AL REY, ASSI DEZIMOS NOS: DIXO ** REY
25236 5ELCID3213 ALC QUE DEMANDA ** %ID QUEL RECUDADES VOS.
25242 5ELCID3214 DIXO ** BUEN REY: ASSILC CTORGO YO.
25253 5ELCID3215 DIXO ALBARFANEZ LEUANTADCS EN PIE ** %ID CAMPEADOR:
25292 5ELCID3220 TORNAN CON ** CONSSEJO E FABLAUAN ASSO SABOR:
25301 5ELCID3221 MUCHO NCS AFINCA ** QUE VALEN%IA GA@O,
25355 5ELCID3228 A ESTAS PALABRAS FABLC ** REY DON ALFONSSO:
25368 5ELCID3230 QUE DERECHO DEMANDA ** %ID CAMPEADOR.
25397 5ELCID3234 ENTERGEN A MYC %ID, ** QUE EN BUEN ORA NA%IO;
25421 5ELCID3237 LUEGO RESPCNDIO ** CCNDE DCN REMOND:
25425 5ELCID3238 ** ORO & LA PLATA ESPENDIESTES LO VOS;
25447 5ELCID3240 PAGEN LE EN APRE%IADURA & PRENDALO ** CAMPEADOR.
25488 5ELCID3246 SOBRE LOS DOZIENTOS MARCOS QUE TENIE ** REY ALFONSSO
25676 5ELCID3270 ** CONDE DCN GAR%IA EN PIE SE LEUANTAUA;
25687 5ELCID3271 MER%ED, YA REY, ** MEJOR DE TODA ESPA@A
25745 5ELCID3279 QUANTO ** DIZE NCN GELO PRE%IAMOS NADA.
25752 5ELCID3280 ESSORA ** CAMPEADOR PRISOS ALA BARBA;
25999 5ELCID3314 POR ** CAMPEADOR MUCHC VALIESTES MAS.
26038 5ELCID3319 SI YO NCN VUJAS, ** MORC TE JUGARA MAL;
26047 5ELCID3320 PASSE PCR TI, CON ** MORO ME OFF DE AIUNTAR,
26061 5ELCID3322 DID ** CAUALLC, TOUEL DC EN PORIDAD:
26086 5ELCID3325 QUE MATARAS ** MORC & QUE FIZIERAS BARNAX;
26132 5ELCID3331 QUANDO DURMIE MYO %ID & ** LEON SE DESATO?
26142 5ELCID3332 E TU, FERRANDO, QUE FIZIST CON ** PAUOR?
26146 5ELCID3333 METISTET TRAS ** ESCA@O DE MYO %ID EL CAMPEADOR
26151 5ELCID3333 METISTET TRAS EL ESCA@C DE MYC %ID ** CAMPEADOR
26161 5ELCID3335 NOS %ERCAMOS ** ESCA@C PCR CURIAR NUESTRO SE@OR,
26172 5ELCID3336 FASTA DO DESPERTC MYO %ID, ** QUE VALEN%IA GA@O;
26183 5ELCID3338 ** LEON PREMIC LA CABE%A, A MYC %ID ESPERO,
26204 5ELCID3340 QUANDO SE TCRNO ** BUEN CAMPEADOR,
26220 5ELCID3343 RIEBTOT ** CUERPC PCR MALO & POR TRAYDOR;
26343 5ELCID3359 LO QUE LES FIZIEMOS SER LES HA RETRAYDO; ESTO LIDIARE ATOD ** MAS
26389 5ELCID3366 MAS NON VESTID ** MANTO NIN EL BRIAL.
26392 5ELCID3366 MAS NON VESTIC EL MANTO NIN ** BRIAL.
26443 5ELCID3373 ASUR GCN%ALEZ ENTRAUA PCR ** PALA%IO,
26477 5ELCID3378 QUIEN NOS DARIE NUEUAS DE MYO %ID ** DE BIUAR
26556 5ELCID3390 DIXO ** REY ALFONSSC: CALLE YA ESTA RAZON.
26592 5ELCID3395 ** VNO ES YFANTE DE NAUARRA
26599 5ELCID3396 E ** OTRO YFANTE DE ARAGON;
26617 5ELCID3398 PIDEN SUS FIJAS A MYO %ID ** CAMPEADOR
26647 5ELCID3402 LEUANTOS EN PIE MYC %ID ** CAMPEADOR;
26691 5ELCID3409 LEUANTOS ** REY, FIZC CALLAR LA CORT:
26745 5ELCID3416 ESSORA DIXO ** REY: DIOS UOS DE DEN BUEN GALARDON
26810 5ELCID3424 E DESPUES DE MYO %ID ** CAMPEADOR;
26879 5ELCID3434 DIXO ** REY: PLAZME DE CORA%CN.
26931 5ELCID3440 GRANDES AUERES LES DIC MYO %ID ** CAMPEADOR,

WORD C# PREFIX CONTEXT

EL (CON'T)

```
27035 5ELCID3453 ASIL CREZE LA CNDRA A MYO %IC ** CAMPEADOR
27101 5ELCID3463 DIXO ** REY: FINE ESTA RAZON;
27119 5ELCID3465 CRAS SEA LA LID, QUANDO SALIERE ** SOL,
27158 5ELCID3471 FABLO ** REY CONTRAL CAMPEADOR:
27186 5ELCID3475 ENESSORA DIXO ** REY: ACSACAS, CAMPEACOR.
27202 5ELCID3477 VAYAN CCMIGO, YC SERE ** CURIACOR;
27263 5ELCID3485 PRISIERON ** JUIZIO YFANTES DE CARRION.
27317 5ELCID3491 ESSORA RESPUSC ** REY: ASSI LC MANDE DIOS
27326 5ELCID3492 ALLI SE TOLLIC ** CAPIELO EL %ID CAMPEADOR,
27328 5ELCID3492 ALLI SE TOLLIC EL CAPIELO ** %IC CAMPEADOR,
27339 5ELCID3493 LA CONFIA DE RAN%AL QUE BLANCA ERA COMMO ** SOL,
27360 5ELCID3496 ADELINO A ** EL CONDE DCN ANRICH & EL CONDE DON REMOND;
27361 5ELCID3496 ADELINO A EL ** CCNDE DCN ANRICH & EL CONDE DON REMOND;
27366 5ELCID3496 ADELINO A EL EL CCNDE DCN ANRICH & ** CONDE DON REMOND;
27457 5ELCID3508 ** REY AL%O LA MANO, LA CARA SE SANTIGO;
27472 5ELCID3509 HYO LO JURO PAR SANT ESIDRC ** DE LEON
27504 5ELCID3513 MANDASTES ME MOUER ABAUIECA ** CORREDOR,
27528 5ELCID3516 ESSORA DIXO ** REY: CESTO NON HE SABOR;
27538 5ELCID3517 SI AUOS LE TOLLIES, ** CAUALLC NO HAURIE TAN BUEN SE@OR.
27569 5ELCID3520 QUIEN VCS LO TCLLER QUISIERE NOL VALA ** CRIADOR,
27588 5ELCID3523 ** CAMPEADOR ALOS QUE HAN LIDIAR TAN BIEN LOS CASTIGO:
27633 5ELCID3528 PRESO AUEMOS ** DEBDC & A PASSAR ES POR NOS;
27652 5ELCID3530 ALEGRE FUE CAQUESTO ** QUE EN BUEN ORA NA%IO;
27671 5ELCID3532 MYO %ID PORA VALEN%IA, & ** REY PORA CARRION.
27691 5ELCID3535 CUNPLIR QUIEREN ** DEBDC QUE LES MANDO SO SE@OR,
27705 5ELCID3536 ELLOS SCN ENPCER DEL REY DCN ALFONSSO ** DE LEON;
27749 5ELCID3542 ** CCMETER FUE MALC, QUE LO AL NOS ENPE%O,
27764 5ELCID3543 CA GRAND MIEDC OUIERCN A ALFCNSSO ** DE LEON.
27803 5ELCID3548 DEMAS SOBRE TCDOS YES ** REY DCN ALFONSSO,
27809 5ELCID3549 POR QUERER ** DERECHO & NCN CONSENTIR EL TUERTO.
27814 5ELCID3549 POR QUERER EL DERECHC & NCN CONSENTIR ** TUERTO.
27844 5ELCID3553 SEDIELOS CASTIGANDO ** CONDE GAR%IORDONEZ.
27991 5ELCID3572 HYUA LCS VER ** REY DCN ALFCNSSO;
28053 5ELCID3581 ESSORA DIXO ** REY: CALMA & DE CORA%ON.
28121 5ELCID3590 QUE CADA VNO DELLOS BIEN FCS FERIR ** SO.
28138 5ELCID3593 ** REY DIOLES FIELES POR CEZIR EL DERECHO & AL NON,
28144 5ELCID3593 EL REY DIOLES FIELES POR CEZIR ** DERECHO & AL NON,
28163 5ELCID3595 DO SEDIEN ENEL CAMPO FABLO ** REY DON ALFONSSO:
28189 5ELCID3598 ESTOS TRES CAUALLERCS DE MYO %ID ** CAMPEADOR
28232 5ELCID3604 LOS FIELES & ** REY ENSE@ARCN LOS MOIONES,
28277 5ELCID3610 SORTEAUAN LES ** CAMPC, YA LES PARTIEN EL SOL,
28282 5ELCID3610 SORTEAUAN LES EL CAMPC, YA LES PARTIEN ** SOL,
28375 5ELCID3623 PERO VERMUEZ, ** QUE ANTES REBTO,
28396 5ELCID3626 FERRANGC%ALEZ A PERC VERMUEZ ** ESCUDOL PASSO,
28410 5ELCID3628 BIEN EN DOS LCGARES ** ESTIL LE QUEBRO.
28470 5ELCID3636 ** BELMEZ CCN LA CAMISA & CCN LA GUARNIZON
28522 5ELCID3642 ** DEXO LA LAN%A & AL ESPACA METIO MANO,
28539 5ELCID3644 ANTES QUE ** CCLPE ESPERASSE CIXO: VEN%UDO SO.
28578 5ELCID3649 RELUMBRA TCD ** CAMPO, TANTO ER LINPIA & CLARA;
28591 5ELCID3651 ** CASCO DE SCMC APART CELO ECHAUA,
28607 5ELCID3653 ALLA LEUO ** ALMOFAR, FATA LA COFIA LEGAUA,
28616 5ELCID3654 LA COFIA & ** ALMCFAR TCDO GELC LEUAUA,
28655 5ELCID3658 VIO DIEGO GCN%ALEZ QUE NO ESCAPARIE CON ** ALMA;
28671 5ELCID3660 ESSORA MARTIN ANTOLINEZ RE%IBICL CON ** ESPADA,
28692 5ELCID3664 ESCRA ** YFANTE TAN GRANDES VCZES CAUA:
28706 5ELCID3666 ** CAUALLO ASCRRIENCA, & MESURANDOL CEL ESPADA,
28719 5ELCID3667 SACOL DEL MCICN; MARTIN ANTOLJNEZ EN ** CAMPO FINCAUA.
28724 5ELCID3668 ESSORA DIXO ** REY: VENID UCS AMI COMPA@A;
28782 5ELCID3676 TRAS ** ESCUDC FALSSO GELA GUARNIZON;
28805 5ELCID3679 TRAS ** ESCUDC FALSSO GELA GUARNIZON,
28848 5ELCID3685 CON ** DIO VNA TUERTA, DELA SIELLA LO ENCAMO,
28866 5ELCID3687 VERMEIO SALIO ** ASTIL, & LA LAN%A & EL PENDON.
28872 5ELCID3687 VERMEIO SALIO EL ASTIL, & LA LAN%A & ** PENDON.
28898 5ELCID3691 VEN%UDO ES ** CAMPO, QUANDO ESTO SE ACABO
28912 5ELCID3693 MANDO LIBRAR ** CANPO EL BUEN REY DON ALFONSSO,
28914 5ELCID3693 MANDO LIBRAR EL CANPO ** BUEN REY DON ALFONSSO,
28924 5ELCID3694 LAS ARMAS QUE Y RASTARON ** SELAS TOMO.
28949 5ELCID3698 ** REY ALOS DE MYO %ID DE NOCHE LOS ENBIO,
28979 5ELCID3701 FELOS EN VALEN%IA CCN MYO %ID ** CAMPEADOR:
28991 5ELCID3703 CONPLIDO HAN ** DEBDC QUE LES MANDO SO SE@OR;
29003 5ELCID3704 ALEGRE FFUE CAQUESTC MYC %IC ** CAMPEADOR.
29113 5ELCID3718 OUIERON SU AIUNTA CCN ALFCNSSC ** DE LEON,
29175 5ELCID3725 A TODOS ALCAN%A CNDRA PCR ** QUE EN BUEN ORA NA%IO.
29185 5ELCID3726 PASSADO ES CESTE SIEGLC ** CIA DE CINQUAESMA.
29207 5ELCID3729 ESTAS SCN LAS NUEUAS DE MYO %ID ** CANPEADOR,
29240 5ELCID3733 EN ERA DE MILL & CCXLV A@CS. EN ** ROMANZ
WORD #1670 OCCURS 816 TIMES.
INDEX OF DIVERSIFICATION = 34.71 WITH STANDARD DEVIATION OF 36.67
```

```
ELA 3745 5ELCID0473 GA@O A CASTEJCN & EL ORC *** PLATA.
12890 5ELCID1635 CON AFAN GANE A VALEN%IA, & *** POR HEREDAD,
19622 5ELCID2487 *** SU QUINTA NCN FUESSE CLBIDADO.
WORD #1671 OCCURS 3 TIMES.
```

WORD C# PREFIX CONTEXT

ELAS 7753 5ELCID0993 **** SIELLAS COZERAS & LAS ZINCHAS AMOIADAS;
19984 5ELCID2536 **** NOCHES & LOS DIAS TAN MAL LOS ESCARMENTANDO,
21239 5ELCID2699 **** BESTIAS FIERAS QUE ANDAN ADERREDOR.
WORD #1672 OCCURS 3 TIMES.

ELBUEN 4683 5ELCID0594 ****** CAMPEADOR LA SU CARA TORNAUA,
WORD #1673 OCCURS 1 TIMES.

ELDIA 5394 5ELCID0681 ***** & LA NOCHE PIENSSAN SE DE ADOBAR.
WORD #1674 OCCURS 1 TIMES.

ELE 14998 5ELCID1896 A VNA CUADRA *** LOS APARTO:
23059 5ELCID2938 *** ES VUESTRO VASSALLO & UOS SODES SO SE@OS.
WORD #1675 OCCURS 2 TIMES.

ELLA 2597 5ELCID0328 ROGANDO AL CRIADOR QUANTO **** MEIOR SABE,
5477 5ELCID0691 MAS NON AGUIJEDES CON ****, SI YO NON UOS LO MANDAR.
17199 5ELCID2176 QUANDO A **** ASSOMAREN, LOS GOZOS SON MAYORES.
25099 5ELCID3197 SE QUE SI UOS ACAEZIERE, CON **** GANAREDES GRAND PREZ & GRAND VALOR.
WORD #1676 OCCURS 4 TIMES.

ELLAS 3063 5ELCID0385 E A TODAS SUS DUENAS QUE CON ***** ESTAN;
10086 5ELCID1278 ENBIARE POR *****, & UOS SABED EL MENSAGE:
10106 5ELCID1280 DE GUISA YRAN POR ***** QUE AGRAND ONDRA VERNAN
11164 5ELCID1412 HYTODAS LAS DUE@AS CON ***** QUANTAS BUENAS ELLAS HAN.
11167 5ELCID1412 HYTODAS LAS DUE@AS CON ELLAS QUANTAS BUENAS ***** HAN.
11713 5ELCID1485 QUE VAYADES POR *****, ADUGADES GELAS ACA,
12681 5ELCID1609 A TAN GRAND ONDRA ***** A VALENZIA ENTRAUAN.
12689 5ELCID1610 ADELINO MYO ZID CON ***** AL ALCAZAR,
14328 5ELCID1812 POR QUE ASSI LAS ENBIO DOND ***** SON PAGADAS,
14892 5ELCID1882 DEMANDEMOS SUS FIJAS PORA CON ***** CASAR;
14933 5ELCID1888 CASAR QUEREMOS CON ***** ASU ONDRA & A NUESTRA PRO.
20641 5ELCID2620 MANDOT QUE VAYAS CON ***** FATA DENTRO EN CARRION,
21332 5ELCID2711 DEPORTAR SE QUIEREN CON ***** ATODO SU SABOR.
21532 5ELCID2737 CON LAS ESPUELAS AGUDAS, DON ***** AN MAL SABOR,
21555 5ELCID2740 YA LO SIENTEN ***** EN LOS SOS CORAZONES.
21841 5ELCID2779 ARRENDO EL CAUALLO, A ***** ADELINO;
21875 5ELCID2783 VALAS TORNANDO A ***** AMAS ADOS;
22168 5ELCID2823 ALLI SOUIERON ***** FATA QUE SA@AS SON.
22734 5ELCID2897 GRAND GOZO FIZO CON ***** DO@A XIMENA SU MADRE.
24772 5ELCID3155 QUES ONDRASSEN CON ***** & SIRUIESSEN AUOS;
26250 5ELCID3347 ***** SON MUGIERES & VOS SODES VARONES,
27871 5ELCID3556 COLADA & TIZON, QUE NON LIDIASSEN CON ***** LOS DEL CANPEADOR;
WORD #1677 OCCURS 22 TIMES.
INDEX OF DIVERSIFICATION = 1180.33 WITH STANDARD DEVIATION OF 1842.97

ELLE 10683 5ELCID1353 SALDRIEN DEL MONESTERIO DO **** LAS DEXO,
11046 5ELCID1398 SALUDA UOS MYO ZID ALLA ONDDE **** ESTA;
22098 5ELCID2812 ALA TORRE DE DON VRRACA **** LAS DEXO.
WORD #1678 OCCURS 3 TIMES.

ELLO 15330 5ELCID1941 FABLEMOS EN ****, EN LA PORIDAD SEAMOS NOS.
20801 5ELCID2641 DE QUANTO EL FIZIERE YOL DAR POR **** BUEN GALARDON.
WORD #1679 OCCURS 2 TIMES.

ELLOS 2323 5ELCID0293 MARTIN ANTOLINEZ CON ***** COIO.
3292 5ELCID0415 ALA SIERRA DE MIEDES ***** YUAN POSAR.
4272 5ELCID0544 POR LAS CUEUAS DANQUITA ***** PASSANDO UAN,
4724 5ELCID0599 BUELTOS SON CON ***** POR MEDIO DELA LA@A.
5096 5ELCID0644 ***** VINIERON ALA NOCH EN SOGORUE POSAR.
5298 5ELCID0669 GRANDES SON LOS PODERES POR CON ***** LIDIAR;
7745 5ELCID0992 ***** VIENEN CUESTA YUSO, & TODOS TRAHEN CALZAS,
7777 5ELCID0996 ANTES QUE ***** LEGEN A LA@O, PRESENTEMOS LES LAS LANZAS;
8077 5ELCID1031 ***** PARTIENDO ESTAS GANANZIAS GRANDES,
11444 5ELCID1449 EL PORTERO CON ***** QUE LOS HA DE AGUARDAR;
11807 5ELCID1497 EL VNO FINCO CON ***** & EL OTRO TORNO A ALBARFANEZ:
13344 5ELCID1691 MAS VALE QUE NOS LOS VEZCAMOS, QUE ***** COIAN EL PAN.
14026 5ELCID1777 NON PUDIERON ***** SABER LA CUENTA DE TODOS LOS CAUALLOS,
15143 5ELCID1915 VAN PORA VALENZIA ***** & TODOS LOS SOS.
15303 5ELCID1938 ***** SON MUCHO VRGULLOSOS & AN PART EN LA CORT,
15591 5ELCID1977 COMMO ***** TENIEN, CERZER LES YA LA GANAZIA,
16381 5ELCID2078 ***** UOS LAS PIDEN & MANDO UOS LO YO.
16587 5ELCID2102 ***** VAYAN CON UUSCO, CADA QUEN ME TORNO YO.
17225 5ELCID2179 VOS CON ***** SED, QUE ASSI UOS LO MANDO YO.
18227 5ELCID2306 QUANDO LOS FALLARON & ***** VINIERON, ASSI VINIERON SIN COLOR;
18264 5ELCID2311 ***** ENESTO ESTANDO, DON AUIEN GRANT PESAR,
19448 5ELCID2464 POR BIEN LO DIXO EL ZID, MAS ***** LO TOUIERON AMAL.
19722 5ELCID2501 ***** LO TEMEN, CA NON LO PIESSO YO:
19738 5ELCID2503 ***** ME DARAN PARIAS CON AIUDA DEL CRIADOR,
19806 5ELCID2511 ***** CON LOS OTROS VINIERON ALA CORT;
20010 5ELCID2539 DESTO QUE ***** FABLARON NOS PARTE NON AYAMOS:
20809 5ELCID2642 CUEMO LA V@A DELA CARNE ***** PARTIDOS SON;
20876 5ELCID2651 OTRO DIA MA@ANA CON ***** CAUALGO,
20918 5ELCID2657 ODIZEN EL ANSSARERA ***** POSADOS SON.

```
WORD                C#  PREFIX                                CONTEXT

ELLOS (CON'T)

                  20933 5ELCID2659 ***** VEYEN LA RIQUEZA QUE EL MORO SACO,
                  21262 5ELCID2702 CON QUANTOS QUE ***** TRAEN Y IAZEN ESSA NOCH,
                  21339 5ELCID2712 TODOS ERAN YDOS, ***** IIIJ SOLOS SON,
                  21593 5ELCID2745 CANSSADOS SON DE FERIR ***** AMOS ADOS,
                  21690 5ELCID2757 POR LOS MONTES DO YUAN, ***** YUAN SE ALABANDO:
                  21797 5ELCID2773 ***** NOL VIEN NI DENC SABIEN RA%ION;
                  21808 5ELCID2774 SABET BIEN QUE SI ***** LE VIESSEN, NON ESCAPARA DE MUERT.
                  21869 5ELCID2782 ADIOS PLEGA & A SANTA MARIA QUE DENT PRENDAN ***** MAL GALARDON
                  22090 5ELCID2811 ALAS AGUAS DE DUERO ***** ARRIBADOS SON,
                  22968 5ELCID2926 ***** CONDES GALLIZANOS A EL TIENEN POR SE@OR.
                  23630 5ELCID3010 E CON ***** GRAND BANDO QUE ADUXIERON A LA CORT:
                  25170 5ELCID3205 HYO FAZIENDO ESTO, ***** ACABARON LO SO;
                  25404 5ELCID3235 QUANDO ***** LOS AN APECHAR, NON GELOS QUIERO YO.
                  26917 5ELCID3439 ***** LAS PRISIERON A ONDRA & A BENDI%ION;
                  26933 5ELCID3441 ***** LAS HAN DEXADAS A PESAR DE NOS.
                  26970 5ELCID3445 MAS BIEN SABEMOS LAS MA@AS QUE ***** HAN,
                  27298 5ELCID3489 ***** SON ADOBADOS PORA CUMPLLIR TODO LO SO;
                  27698 5ELCID3536 ***** SON ENPOER DEL REY DON ALFONSSO EL DE LEON;
                  27729 5ELCID3539 E TODOS SUS PARIENTES CON ***** SON;
                  28035 5ELCID3578 NON SABEMOS QUES COMIDRAN ***** OQUE NON;
                  28153 5ELCID3594 QUE NON VARAGEN CON ***** DESI O DE NON.
                  28289 5ELCID3611 SALIEN LOS FIELES DE MEDIO, ***** CARA POR CARA SON;
                  28304 5ELCID3613 ***** YFANTES DE CARRION ALOS DE CAMPEADOR;
        WORD #1680 OCCURS  52 TIMES.
           INDEX OF DIVERSIFICATION =   508.43 WITH STANDARD DEVIATION OF    657.25

ELO               12060 5ELCID1529 SI DIOS ME LEGARE AL %ID *** VEA CON EL ALMA,
        WORD #1681 OCCURS   1 TIMES.

ELOS               9583 5ELCID1218 **** OTROS AUERES QUIEN LOS PODRIE CONTAR?
                  24361 5ELCID3106 EL VA EN MEDIO, **** %IENTO ADERREDOR.
        WORD #1682 OCCURS   2 TIMES.

ELPHA             21212 5ELCID2695 ALLI SON CA@OS DO A ***** EN%ERRO;
        WORD #1683 OCCURS   1 TIMES.

ELUEGO            21082 5ELCID2679 ****** LEUARIA SUS FIJAS AL CAMPEADOR LEAL;
        WORD #1684 OCCURS   1 TIMES.

ELUIRA            16360 5ELCID2075 VUESTRAS FIJAS UOS PIDO, DON ****** & DO@A SOL,
                  16470 5ELCID2088 AFELLAS EN UUESTRA MANO DON ****** & DO@A SOL,
                  16551 5ELCID2097 DAQUI LAS PRENDO POR MIS MANOS DON ****** & DONA SOL,
                  17090 5ELCID2163 HE DELAS FIJAS DE MYO %ID, DE DON ****** & DO@A SOL.
                  17246 5ELCID2181 VERAN ASUS ESPOSAS, A DON ****** & A DONA SOL.
                  17368 5ELCID2197 AUOS DIGO, MIS FIJAS, DON ****** & DO@A SOL:
                  19875 5ELCID2520 EAMAS LA MYS FIJAS, DON ****** & DO@A SOL;
                  20426 5ELCID2592 AMAS HERMANAS, DON ****** & DO@A SOL,
                  20702 5ELCID2628 ADIOS UOS HACOMENDAMOS, DON ****** & DO@A SOL,
                  21110 5ELCID2682 HYRE CON UUESTRA GRA%IA, DON ****** & DO@A SOL;
                  21324 5ELCID2710 SI NON AMAS SUS MUGIERES DO@A ****** & DO@A SOL:
                  21354 5ELCID2714 BIEN LO CREADES, DON ****** & DO@A SOL,
                  21607 5ELCID2747 HYA NON PUEDEN FABLAR DON ****** & DONA SOL;
                  21849 5ELCID2780 YA PRIMAS, LAS MIS PRIMAS, DON ****** & DO@A SOL,
                  21901 5ELCID2786 LAMANDO: PRIMAS, PRIMAS, DON ****** & DON SOL
                  21932 5ELCID2790 VAN RECORDANDO DON ****** & DO@A SOL,
                  22131 5ELCID2817 HYUA RE%EBIR ADON ****** & ADONA@A SOL;
                  22449 5ELCID2859 ENEL FINCAN LOS OIOS DON ****** & DO@A SOL:
                  22496 5ELCID2865 DON ****** & DO@A SOL, CUYDADO NON AYADES,
                  25023 5ELCID3187 ASSIS YRAN VENGANDO DON ****** & DONA SOL.
                  26239 5ELCID3345 POR FIJAS DEL %ID, DON ****** & DONA SOL:
                  26771 5ELCID3419 DE FIJAS DE MYO %ID, DON ****** & DO@A SOL,
                  26981 5ELCID3447 QUANDO PIDEN MIS PRIMAS, DON ****** & DO@A SOL,
                  29121 5ELCID3719 FIZIERON SUS CASAMIENTOS CON DON ****** & CON DO@A SOL.
        WORD #1685 OCCURS  24 TIMES.
           INDEX OF DIVERSIFICATION =   553.83 WITH STANDARD DEVIATION OF    774.20

EMANO             28081 5ELCID3585 ***** PRENDEN LAS ASTAS DELOS FIERROS TAIADORES,
        WORD #1686 OCCURS   1 TIMES.

EMBIA             14652 5ELCID1854 E ***** UOS DOZIENTOS CAUALLOS, & BESA UOS LAS MANOS.
        WORD #1687 OCCURS   1 TIMES.

EMIENTE            8420 5ELCID1070 SI UOS VINIERE ******* QUE QUISIEREDES VENGALO,
        WORD #1688 OCCURS   1 TIMES.

EMOS               2225 5ELCID0280 YA LO VEDES QUE PARTIR NOS **** EN VIDA,
                  15087 5ELCID1908 ROGAR GELO **** LO QUE DEZIDES UOS;
        WORD #1689 OCCURS   2 TIMES.

EN                   57 5ELCID0008 GRADO ATI, SE@OR PADRE, QUE ESTAS ** ALTO
                    112 5ELCID0016 ** SU CONPA@A LX PENDONES; EXIEN LO UER MUGIERES & UARONES,
                    173 5ELCID0023 ANTES DELA NOCHE ** BURGOS DEL ENTRO SU CARTA,
                    326 5ELCID0041 YA CAMPEADOR, ** BUEN ORA %INXIESTES ESPADA
                    436 5ELCID0055 SALIO POR LA PUERTA & ** ARLAN%ON POSAUA.
```

WORD C# PREFIX CONTEXT

EN (CON'T)

442 5ELCID0056 CABO ESSA VILLA ** LA GLERA POSAUA,
458 5ELCID0058 MYO %ID RUY DIAZ, EL QUE ** BUEN ORA %INXO ESPADA,
464 5ELCID0059 POSO ** LA GLERA QUANDO NOL COGE NADI EN CASA;
471 5ELCID0059 POSO EN LA GLERA QUANDO NOL COGE NADI ** CASA;
485 5ELCID0061 ASSI POSO MYO %ID COMMO SI FUESSE ** MONTA@A.
491 5ELCID0062 VEDADA LAN CONPRA DENTRO ** BURGOS LA CASA,
560 5ELCID0071 YA CANPEADOR, ** BUEN ORA FUESTES NA%IDO
581 5ELCID0074 ** YRA DEL RAY ALFFONSSO YO SERE METIDO.
618 5ELCID0078 FABLO MYO %ID, EL QUE ** BUEN ORA %INXO ESPADA:
705 5ELCID0090 QUANDO ** BURGOS ME VEDARON COMPRA & EL REY ME A AYRADO,
784 5ELCID0100 RACHEL & VIDAS ** VNO ESTAUAN AMOS,
788 5ELCID0101 ** CUENTA DE SUS AUERES, DELOS QUE AUIEN GANADOS.
811 5ELCID0104 ** PORIDAD FLABLAR QUERRIA CON AMOS.
870 5ELCID0112 POR ** VINO AAQUESTO POR QUE FUE ACUSADO.
913 5ELCID0117 EL CAMPEADOR DEXAR LAS HA ** UUESTRA MANO,
930 5ELCID0119 PRENDED LAS ARCHAS & METED LAS ** UUESTRO SALUO;
945 5ELCID0121 QUE NON LAS CATEDES ** TODO AQUESTE A@O.
958 5ELCID0123 NOS HUEBOS AUEMOS ** TODO DE GANAR ALGO.
992 5ELCID0128 ** LOGAR LAS METAMOS QUE NON SEAN VENTADAS.
1040 5ELCID0133 PEDIR UOS A POCO POR DEXAR SO AUER ** SALUO.
1123 5ELCID0144 POR ADUZIR LAS ARCHAS & METER LAS ** UUESTRO SALUO,
1306 5ELCID0167 LEUALDAS, RACHEL & VIDAS, PONED LAS ** UUESTRO SALUO;
1337 5ELCID0171 NON LAS PODIEN PONER ** SOMO MAGER ERAU ESFOR%ADOS.
1366 5ELCID0175 YA CANPEADOR, ** BUEN ORA %INXIESTES ESPADA
1419 5ELCID0182 ** MEDIO DEL PALA%IO TENDIERON VN ALMOFALLA,
1453 5ELCID0186 LOS OTROS CCC ** ORO GELOS PAGAUAN.
1478 5ELCID0189 YA DON RACHEL & VIDAS, ** UUESTRAS MANOS SON LAS ARCAS;
1580 5ELCID0202 VINO PORA LA TIENDA DEL QUE ** BUEN ORA NASCO;
1627 5ELCID0209 ** SAN PERO DE CARDENA YNOS CANTE EL GALLO;
1713 5ELCID0219 DA QUI QUITO CASTIELLA, PUES QUE EL REY HE ** YRA;
1729 5ELCID0221 VUESTRA UERTUD ME UALA, GLORIOSA, ** MY EXIDA & ME AIUDE,
1765 5ELCID0225 ESTO & YO ** DEBDO QUE FAGA Y CANTAR MILL MISSAS.
1931 5ELCID0245 CON TAN GRANT GOZO RE%IBEN AL QUE ** BUEN ORA NASCO.
2027 5ELCID0255 DUES FIJAS DEXO NI@AS & PRENDET LAS ** LOS BRA%OS;
2111 5ELCID0266 MER%ED, CANPEADOR, ** ORA BUENA FUESTES NADO
2157 5ELCID0271 YO LO VEO QUE ESTADES UOS ** YDA
2165 5ELCID0272 E NOS DEUOS PARTIR NOS HEMOS ** VIDA.
2178 5ELCID0274 ENCLINO LAS MANOS ** LA SU BARBA VELIDA,
2226 5ELCID0280 YA LO VEDES QUE PARTIR NOS EMOS ** VIDA,
2275 5ELCID0286 TANEN LAS CAMPA@AS ** SAN PERO A CLAMOR.
2300 5ELCID0290 ** AQUES DIA ALA PUENT DE ARLA%ON
2387 5ELCID0302 ** ANTES QUE YO MUERA, ALGUN BIEN UOS PUEDA FAR:
2411 5ELCID0304 PLOGO A MIO %ID, POR QUE CRE%IO ** LA IANTAR,
2452 5ELCID0309 QUE, SI DESPUES DEL PLAZO ** SU TIERRAL PUDIES TOMAR,
2483 5ELCID0313 OYD, VARONES, NON UOS CAYA ** PESAR;
2510 5ELCID0318 ** SAN PERO A MATINS TANDRA EL BUEN ABBAT,
2588 5ELCID0327 ECHOS DO@A XIMENA ** LOS GRADOS DELANTEL ALTAR,
2616 5ELCID0330 YA SE@OR GLORIOSO, PADRE QUE ** %IELO ESTAS,
2638 5ELCID0333 PRISIST ENCARNA%ION ** SANTA MARIA MADRE,
2642 5ELCID0334 ** BELLEM APARE%IST, COMMO FUE TU VELUNTAD;
2683 5ELCID0339 A IONAS, QUANDO CAYO ** LA MAR,
2692 5ELCID0340 SALUEST A DANIEL CON LOS LEONES ** LA MALA CAR%EL,
2698 5ELCID0341 SALUEST DENTRO ** ROMA AL SE@OR SAN SABASTIAN,
2722 5ELCID0344 MOSTRANDO LOS MIRACLOS, POR ** AUEMOS QUE FABLAR:
2752 5ELCID0348 PUSIERON TE ** CRUZ POR NUMBRE EN GOLGOTA;
2756 5ELCID0348 PUSIERON TE EN CRUZ POR NUMBRE ** GOLGOTA;
2768 5ELCID0350 EL VNO ES ** PARAYSO, CA EL OTRO NON ENTRO ALA;
2777 5ELCID0351 ESTANDO ** LA CRUZ, VERTUD FEZIST MUY GRANT.
2825 5ELCID0357 ** TI CROUO AL ORA, POR END ES SALUO DE MAL;
2896 5ELCID0365 QUANDO OY NOS PARTIMOS, ** VIDA NOS FAZ IUNTAR.
3009 5ELCID0379 %ID, DO SON UUESTROS ESFUER%OS? ** BUEN ORA NASQUIESTES DE MADRE;
3027 5ELCID0381 AUNTODOS ESTOS DUELOS ** GOZO SE TORNARAN;
3099 5ELCID0390 CA ** YERMO O EN POBLADO PODER NOS HAN ALCAN%AR.
3102 5ELCID0390 CA EN YERMO O ** POBLADO PODER NOS HAN ALCAN%AR.
3227 5ELCID0406 EL ANGEL GABRIEL A EL VINO ** SUE@O:
3236 5ELCID0408 ** TAN BUEN PUNTO CAUALGO VARON;
3385 5ELCID0427 ** MEDIO DUNA MONTANA MARAUILLOSA & GRAND
3455 5ELCID0436 MYO %ID SE ECHO ** %ELADA CON AQUELOS QUE EL TRAE.
3466 5ELCID0437 TODA LA NOCHE IAZE ** %ELADA EL QUE EN BUEN ORA NASCO,
3470 5ELCID0437 TODA LA NOCHE IAZE EN %ELADA EL QUE ** BUEN ORA NASCO,
3481 5ELCID0439 YA %ID, ** BUEN ORA %INXIESTES ESPADA
3506 5ELCID0442 VOS CON LOS CC YD UOS ** ALGARA; ALA VAYA ALBARABAREZ,
3568 5ELCID0449 E YO CON LO C AQUI FINCARE ** LA %AGA,
3577 5ELCID0450 TERNE YO CASTEION CON ABREMOS GRAND ** PARA.
3613 5ELCID0455 E LOS QUE CON MYO %ID FICARAN ** LA %AGA.
3631 5ELCID0458 ** CASTEION TODOS SE LEUANTAUAN,
3664 5ELCID0462 CON POCAS DE GENTES QUE ** CASTEION FINCARON.
3696 5ELCID0466 E ESSOS GA@ADOS QUANTOS ** DERREDOR ANDAN.
3727 5ELCID0471 ** MANO TRAE DESNUDA EL ESPADA,
3833 5ELCID0485 FELLOS ** CASTEION, O EL CAMPEADOR ESTAUA.
3842 5ELCID0486 EL CASTIELO DEXO ** SO PODER, EL CAMPEADOR CAUALGA,
3919 5ELCID0497 ADIOS LO PROMETO, A AQUEL QUE ESTA ** ALTO:
3981 5ELCID0505 TODO LO OTRO AFELO ** UUESTRA MANO.
3994 5ELCID0507 COMIDIOS MYO %ID, EL QUE ** BUEN ORA FUE NADO,

WORD C# PREFIX CONTEXT

EN (CON'T)

4060 5ELCID0516 AQUI NCN LO PUEDEN VENDER NIN CAR ** PRESENTAIA;
4069 5ELCID0517 NIN CATIUOS NIN CATIUAS NON QUISO TRAER ** SU CONPA@A.
4139 5ELCID0527 MOROS ** PAZ, CA ESCRIPTA ES LA CARTA,
4171 5ELCID0531 ** CASTEICN NCN PCDRIEMCS FINCAR;
4348 5ELCID0554 ** VN CTERO REDCNDO, FUERTE & GRAND;
4392 5ELCID0559 EL BUEN CANPEADOR QUE ** BUEN ORA NASCO,
4452 5ELCID0567 ** LA SU VEZINDAD NON SE TREUEN GANAR TANTO.
4473 5ELCID0569 EL CASTIELLC CE ALCC%ER ** PARIA UA ENTRANDO.
4767 5ELCID0605 ** VN ORA & VN POCO DE LCGAR CCC MOROS MATAN.
4784 5ELCID0606 DANDO GRANDES ALARIDCS LOS QUE ESTAN ** LA %ELADA,
4829 5ELCID0611 VINO PERO VERMUEZ, QUE LA SE@A TEINE ** MANO,
4832 5ELCID0612 METIOLA ** SCMO EN TODO LO MAS ALTO.
4834 5ELCID0612 METIOLA EN SCMO ** TODO LO MAS ALTO.
4846 5ELCID0613 FABLO MYO %ID RUY DIAZ, EL QUE ** BUEN ORA FUE NADO:
4874 5ELCID0617 ** ESTE CASTIELLC GRANC AUER AUEMOS PRESO,
4913 5ELCID0622 POSAREMCS ** SUS CASAS & DELLOS NOS SERUIREMOS.
4925 5ELCID0623 MYO %ID CON ESTA GANAN%IA ** ALCO%ER ESTA;
4984 5ELCID0630 VINO PCSAR SOBRE ALCO%ER, ** VN TAN FUERTE LOGAR;
5081 5ELCID0642 POR QUE SEME ENTRO ** MI TIERRA DERECHO ME AURA ADAR.
5100 5ELCID0644 ELLOS VINIERON ALA NOCH ** SOGORUE POSAR.
5150 5ELCID0651 VINIERCN ESSA NOCHE ** CALATAYUH POSAR.
5180 5ELCID0655 AL BUENC DE MYO %ID ** ALCO%ER LEUAN %ERCAR.
5209 5ELCID0659 E DE NOCH ** BUELTOS ANDAN EN ARMAS;
5212 5ELCID0659 E DE NOCH EN BUELTOS ANDAN ** ARMAS;
5242 5ELCID0663 EL QUE ** BUEN ORA NASCC FIRME GELO VEDAUA.
5251 5ELCID0664 TOUIERON GELA ** %ERCA COMPLICAS TRES SEMANAS.
5341 5ELCID0675 ** EL NCBRE CEL CRIACCR, QUE NCN PASE POR AL:
5354 5ELCID0676 VAYAMOS LCS FERIR ** AQUEL DIA CE CRAS.
5443 5ELCID0687 SI NOS MURIEREMOS ** CAMPO, EN CASTIELLO NOS ENTRARAN,
5445 5ELCID0687 SI NOS MURIEREMOS EN CAMPO, ** CASTIELLO NOS ENTRARAN,
5454 5ELCID0688 SI VEN%IEREMOS LA BATALLA, CRE%REMOS ** RICTAD.
5513 5ELCID0695 QUE PRIESSA VA ** LCS MOROS, E TORNARON SE A ARMAR;
5535 5ELCID0697 VERIEDES ARMAR SE MORCS, APRIESSA ENTRAR ** AZ.
5577 5ELCID0702 QUEDAS SED, MENADAS, AQUI ** ESTE LOGAR,
5598 5ELCID0705 LA SE@A TIENE ** MANO, CONPE%O DE ESPOLONAR;
5615 5ELCID0707 VO METER LA UUESTRA SE@A ** AQUELA MAYOR AZ;
5704 5ELCID0719 A GRANDES VOZES LAMA EL QUE ** BUEN ORA NASCO:
5772 5ELCID0729 TANTOS PENDCNES BLANCCS SALIR VERMEIOS ** SANGRE,
5791 5ELCID0732 CAYEN ** VN POCO DE LCGAR MOROS MUERTOS MILL & CCC YA.
5929 5ELCID0751 CORTOL POR LA %INTURA, EL MEDIO ECHO ** CAMPO.
5946 5ELCID0754 OY ** ESTE DIA DE UOS ABRE GRAND BANDO;
5967 5ELCID0756 CAUALGO MINAYA, EL ESPADA ** LA MANO,
5987 5ELCID0759 MYO %ID RUY DIAZ, EL QUE ** BUEN ORA NASCO,
6083 5ELCID0772 LOS DE MYO %ID FIRIENDO ** ALCAZ,
6088 5ELCID0773 EL REY FARIZ ** TERUEL SE FUE ENTRAR,
6107 5ELCID0776 EL CAMPEADOR YUAL ** AL CAZ,
6170 5ELCID0786 CA ** ALCAZ SJN DUBDA LES FUERCN DANDO.
6182 5ELCID0787 YAS TORNAN LOS DEL QUE ** BUEN ORA NASCO.
6205 5ELCID0790 ALMOFAR ACUESTAS, LA ESPADA ** LA MANO.
6221 5ELCID0792 GRADO A DIOS, A QUEL QUE ESTA ** ALTO,
6320 5ELCID0805 ** LA SU QUINTA AL %ID CAEN C CAUALLOS.
6348 5ELCID0808 BIEN LO AGUISA EL QUE ** BUEN ORA NASCO,
6399 5ELCID0816 QUIEROL ENBIAR ** DON XXX CAUALLOS,
6435 5ELCID0822 ** SANTA MARIA DE BURGOS QUITEDES MILL MISSAS;
6616 5ELCID0844 ASI LO AN ASMADO & METUDO ** CARTA:
6652 5ELCID0849 ** TODOS LOS SOS NON FALLARIEDES VN MESQUINO.
6667 5ELCID0850 QUI A BUEN SE@OR SIRUE, SIEMPRE BIUE ** DELI%IO.
6758 5ELCID0863 Y FFINCO ** VN POYO QUE ES SOBRE MONT REAL;
6781 5ELCID0866 METIO ** PARIA ADOROCA EN ANTES,
6784 5ELCID0866 METIO EN PARIA ADOROCA ** ANTES,
6800 5ELCID0869 ** SU MANO TENIE A %ELFA LA DE CANAL.
6849 5ELCID0875 MYO %ID RUY DIAZ, QUE ** BUEN ORA CINXO ESPADA. . .
6859 5ELCID0876 VEN%IO DOS REYES DE MOROS ** AQUESTA BATALLA.
7032 5ELCID0899 QUIERO UOS DEZIR DEL QUE ** BUEN ORA NASCO & %INXO ESPADA:
7076 5ELCID0904 EL DE RIO MARTIN TODO LO METIO ** PARIA.
7141 5ELCID0914 ASARAGO%A METUDA LA ** PARIA.
7166 5ELCID0918 NON SON ** CUENTA, SABET, LAS PEONADAS.
7293 5ELCID0935 NON LO TARDO EL QUE ** BUEN ORA NASCO,
7389 5ELCID0948 QUI ** VN LOGAR MORA SIEMPRE, LO SO PUEDE MANGUAR;
7429 5ELCID0953 ** AQUESSA CORRIDA X DIAS OUIERON AMORAR.
7501 5ELCID0962 DENTRO ** MI CORT TUERTO ME TOUO GRAND:
7521 5ELCID0964 AGORA CORREM LAS TIERRAS QUE ** MI ENPARA ESTAN;
7579 5ELCID0971 ALCON%ARON A MYO %ID ** TEUAR & EL PINAR;
7641 5ELCID0978 DELO SO NON LIEUO NADA, DEXEM YR ** PAZ.
7701 5ELCID0986 APRIESSA UOS GUARNID & METEDOS ** LAS ARMAS.
7799 5ELCID0998 VERA REMONT VERENGEL TRAS QUIEN VINO ** ALCAN%A
7802 5ELCID0999 OY ** ESTE PINAR DE TEUAR POR TOLER ME LA GANAN%IA.
7852 5ELCID1004 MANDO LOS FERIR MYO %ID, EL QUE ** BUEN ORA NASCO;
7890 5ELCID1008 VEN%IDO A ESTA BATALLA EL QUE ** BUEN ORA NASCO;
7997 5ELCID1021 NON COMBRE VN BOCADO POR QUANTO HA ** TODA ESPA@A,
8043 5ELCID1027 SI NON, ** TODOS UUESTROS DIAS NON VEREDES CHRISTIANISMO.
8172 5ELCID1041 MAS QUANTO AUEDES PERDIDO & YO GANE ** CANPO,
8275 5ELCID1053 SOBREL SEDIE EL QUE ** BUEN ORA NASCO:
8407 5ELCID1069 ** GRADO UOS LO TENGO LO QUE ME AUEDES DEXADO.

WORD C# PREFIX CONTEXT

EN (CON'T)

8452 5ELCID1074 FOLGEDES, YA MYO %ID, SODES ** UUESTRO SALUO.
8619 5ELCID1094 AIUDOL EL CRIADOR, EL SE@NOR QUE ES ** %IELO.
8638 5ELCID1097 DENTRO ** VALEN%IA NON ES POCO EL MIEDO.
8681 5ELCID1103 ** SUS TIERRAS SOMOS & FEMOS LES TODOMAL,
8750 5ELCID1112 YO FIO POR DIOS QUE ** NUESTRO PRO ENADRAN.
8761 5ELCID1114 EL QUE ** BUEN ORA NASCO COMPE%O DE FABLAR:
8806 5ELCID1120 SI ** ESTAS TIERRAS QUISIEREMOS DURAR,
9016 5ELCID1147 DOS REYES DE MOROS MATARON ** ES ALCAZ,
9075 5ELCID1155 MIEDO AN ** VALEN%IA QUE NON SABEN QUESE FAR.
9151 5ELCID1165 MALES PESA ** XATIUA & DENTRO EN GUIERA,
9155 5ELCID1165 MALES PESA EN XATIUA & DENTRO ** GUIERA,
9165 5ELCID1167 ** TIERRA DE MOROS PRENDIENDO & GANANDO,
9180 5ELCID1169 ** GANAR AQUELAS VILLAS MYO %ID DURO IIJ A@OS.
9213 5ELCID1173 ** CADA VNO DESTOS A@OS MYO %ID LES TOLIO EL PAN.
9322 5ELCID1185 SALIO DE MURUIEDRO VNA NOCH ** TRASNOCHADA,
9327 5ELCID1186 AMANE%IO AMYO %ID ** TIERRAS DE MON REAL.
9391 5ELCID1194 TRES DIAS LE SPERARE ** CANAL DE %ELFA.
9401 5ELCID1195 ESTO DIXO MYO %ID EL QUE ** BUEN ORA NASCO.
9504 5ELCID1208 METIOLA ** PLAZO, SILES VINIESSEN HUUYAR.
9555 5ELCID1214 EL ORO & LA PLATA QUI ** VOS LO PODRIE CONTAR?
9604 5ELCID1220 QUANDO SU SE@A CABDAL SEDIE ** SOMO DEL ALCA%AR.
9654 5ELCID1227 FATA DENTRO ** XATIUA DURO EL ARRANCADA,
9667 5ELCID1229 MOROS ** ARUEN%O AMIDOS BEUER AGUA.
9733 5ELCID1237 CON MYO %ID RUY DIAZ, EL QUE ** BUEN ORA NASCO.
9784 5ELCID1243 MYO %ID DON RODRIGO ** VALEN%IA ESTA FOLGANDO,
9811 5ELCID1246 ATODOS LES DIO ** VALEN%IA CASAS & HEREDADES
9892 5ELCID1254 TOMASSEN LE EL AUER & PUSIESSEN LE ** VN PALO.
9899 5ELCID1255 AFEUOS TODO AQUESTO PUESTO ** BUEN RECABDO.
9926 5ELCID1259 METER LOS HE ** ESCRIPTO, & TODOS SEAN CONTADOS,
10029 5ELCID1273 SI AUOS PLOGUIERE, MINAYA, & NON UOS CAYA ** PESAR,
10143 5ELCID1284 CIENTO OMNES LE DIO MYO %ID A ALBARFANEZ POR SERUIR LE ** LA CARRERA,
10164 5ELCID1287 ** ESTAS NUEUAS TODOS SEA ALEGRANDO,
10250 5ELCID1297 OYD, MINAYA ALBARFANEZ, POR AQUEL QUE ESTA ** ALTO,
10261 5ELCID1299 ** TIERRAS DE VALEN%IA FER QUIERO OBISPADO,
10300 5ELCID1304 DIERON LE ** VALEN%IA O BIEN PUEDE ESTAR RICO.
10314 5ELCID1306 QUE ** TIERRAS DE VALEN%IA SE@OR AVIE OBISPO
10332 5ELCID1308 TIERRAS DE VALENCIA REMANIDAS ** PAZ,
10460 5ELCID1326 MAGER ** TIERRA AGENA, EL BIEN FAZE LO SO;
10620 5ELCID1346 SEMEIA QUE ** TIERRA DE MOROS NON A BIUO OMNE,
10667 5ELCID1351 MER%ED UOS PIDE EL %ID, SIUOS CAYESSE ** SABOR,
10722 5ELCID1358 QUANDO ** CABO DE MI TIERRA A QUESTAS DUE@AS FUEREN,
10826 5ELCID1371 MAS GANAREMOS ** ESTO QUE EN OTRA DESONOR.
10829 5ELCID1371 MAS GANAREMOS EN ESTO QUE ** OTRA DESONOR.
10834 5ELCID1372 AQUI ENTRARON ** FABLA LOS YFFANTES DE CARRION:
10919 5ELCID1382 FATA DENTRO ** MEDINA DENLES QUANTO HUEBOS LES FUER,
10948 5ELCID1386 ** TODO SODES PRO, EN ESTO ASSI LO FAGADES:
10952 5ELCID1386 EN TODO SODES PRO, ** ESTO ASSI LO FAGADES:
10966 5ELCID1388 SOMOS ** SO PRO QUANTO LO PODEMOS FAR;
11177 5ELCID1414 REMANE%IO ** SAN PERO MINAYA ALBARFANEZ.
11280 5ELCID1427 DELOS MEIORES GUARIMIENTOS QUE ** BURGOS PUDO FALAR,
11419 5ELCID1445 TODOS LOS DIAS DEL SIEGLO ** LEUAR LO ADELANT
11464 5ELCID1451 DE SAN PERO FASTA MEDINA ** V DIAS VAN,
11469 5ELCID1452 FELOS ** MEDINA LAS DUENAS & ALBARFANEZ.
11601 5ELCID1470 E YO FINCARE ** VALEN%IA, QUE MUCHO COSTADOM HA;
11615 5ELCID1472 YO FFINCARE ** VALEN%IA, CA LA TENGO POR HEREDAD.
11707 5ELCID1484 SU MUGIER & SUS FIJAS ** MEDINA ESTAN;
11719 5ELCID1486 E FFATA ** VALEN%IA DELLAS NON UOS PARTADES.
11780 5ELCID1494 E ** MEDINA TODO EL RECABDO ESTA;
11865 5ELCID1504 TODOS VIENEN ** VNO, AGORA LEGARAN.
11890 5ELCID1508 ** BUENOS CAUALLOS A PETRALES & A CASCAUELES,
11908 5ELCID1510 E ** LAS MANOS LAN%AS QUE PENDONES TRAEN,
12026 5ELCID1525 ** PAZ O EN GERRA DELO NUESTRO ABRA;
12029 5ELCID1525 EN PAZ O ** GERRA DELO NUESTRO ABRA;
12094 5ELCID1534 ENTRARON ** MEDINA, SIRUIALOS MINAYA,
12116 5ELCID1537 ONDRADO ES MYO %ID ** VALEN%IA DO ESTAUA
12125 5ELCID1538 DE TAN GRAND CONDUCHO COMMO ** MEDINAL SACARON;
12194 5ELCID1548 E BUEN CAUALLO ** DIESTRO QUE UA ANTE SUS ARMAS.
12252 5ELCID1556 FATA ** VALEN%IA SIRUIALOS SIN FALLA;
12287 5ELCID1560 AMYO %ID, EL QUE ** BUEN ORA NASCO,
12332 5ELCID1566 EL SEDIE ** VALEN%IA CURIANDO & GUARDANDO,
12367 5ELCID1570 MANDO MYO %ID ALOS QUE HA ** SU CASA
12404 5ELCID1574 AVN NON SABIE MYO %ID, EL QUE ** BUEN ORA %INXO ESPADA,
12422 5ELCID1576 ALA PUERTA DE VALEN%IA, DO FUESSE ** SO SALUO,
12486 5ELCID1584 EL QUE ** BUEN ORA NASCO NON LO DETARDAUA:
12539 5ELCID1591 DES DIA SE PRE%IO BAUIECA ** QUANT GRANT FUE ESPA@A.
12544 5ELCID1592 ** CABO DEL COSSO MYO %ID DESCALGAUA,
12572 5ELCID1595 MER%ED, CAMPEADOR, ** BUEN ORA CINXIESTES ESPADA
12623 5ELCID1601 TODAS LAS SUS MESNADAS ** GRANT DELENT ESTAUAN,
12638 5ELCID1603 OYD LO QUE DIXO EL QUE ** BUEN ORA NASCO:
12658 5ELCID1606 ENTRAD COMIGO ** VALEN%IA LA CASA,
12662 5ELCID1607 ** ESTA HEREDAD QUE UOS YO HE GANADA.
12772 5ELCID1621 DE AQUEL REY YUCEF QUE ** MARRUECOS ESTA.
12786 5ELCID1623 QUE ** MIS HEREDADES FUERTE MIETRE ES MIETDO,
12822 5ELCID1627 ENTRARON SOBRE MAR, ** LAS BARCAS SON METIDOS.

WORD C# PREFIX CONTEXT

EN (CON'T)

12926 5ELCID1640 ENTRARE ** LAS ARMAS, NCN LO PODRE DEXAR;
12941 5ELCID1642 ** ESTAS TIERRAS AGENAS VERAN LAS MORADAS COMMO SE FAZEN,
13022 5ELCID1652 MUGIER, SED ** ESTE PALA%IO, & SI QUISIEREDES EN EL ALCA%AR;
13028 5ELCID1652 MUGIER, SED EN ESTE PALA%IC, & SI QUISIEREDES ** EL ALCA%AR;
13160 5ELCID1668 COLGAR LOS HAN ** SANTA MARIA MADRE DEL CRIADOR.
13461 5ELCID1706 AUCS, %ID DCN RODIRGC, ** BUEN ORA %INXIESTES ESPADA,
13526 5ELCID1714 DIO SALTO MYO %ID ** BAUIECA EL SO CAUALLO;
13629 5ELCID1727 METIOS LE ** GUIERA, VN CASTIELLO PALA%IANO;
13642 5ELCID1728 MYO %ID EL DE BIUAR FASTA ALLI LEGO ** ALCAZ,
13657 5ELCID1730 DESDALLI SE TORNO EL QUE ** BUEN ORA NASCO,
13678 5ELCID1733 TODA ESTA GANAN%IA ** SU MANO A RASTADO.
13771 5ELCID1745 ASSI ENTRO SOBRE BAUIECA, EL ESPADA ** LA MANO.
13819 5ELCID1751 QUANDO ** VUESTRA VENIDA TAL GANAN%IA NOS AN DADA.
13853 5ELCID1755 ENTRAREDES ** PREZ, & BESARAN UUESTRAS MANOS.
13891 5ELCID1760 SOMOS ** UUESTRA MER%ED, & BIUADES MUCHOS A@OS
13898 5ELCID1761 ** BUELTA CON EL ENTRARCN AL PALA%IO,
13910 5ELCID1762 E YUAN POSAR CON EL ** VNOS PRE%IOSOS ESCA@OS;
13950 5ELCID1767 QUE LO SEPAN ** CASTIELLA, AQUIEN SIRUIERON TANTO.
14181 5ELCID1795 NCN TIENE ** CUENTA LOS MOROS QUE HA MATADOS;
14201 5ELCID1797 MYO %ID DON RODRIGO, EL QUE ** BUEN ORA NASCO,
14335 5ELCID1813 ESTOS DOZIENTOS CAUALLOS YRAN ** PRESENTAIAS,
14365 5ELCID1817 E DOZIENTOS OMNES LIEUAN ** SU CONPA@A,
14501 5ELCID1834 AUER ESTOS MENSAIES DEL QUE ** BUEN ORA NASCO.
14533 5ELCID1838 ADIO LO AUIEN LOS DEL QUE ** BUEN ORA NASCO,
14723 5ELCID1862 ** LA ONDRA QUE EL HA NOS SEREMOS ABILTADOS;
14874 5ELCID1880 FABLANDO ** SU CONSSEIO, AUIENDO SU PORIDAD:
14895 5ELCID1883 CRE%REMOS ** NUESTRA ONDRA & YREMOS ADELANT.
14978 5ELCID1893 MAS PUES BOS LO QUERECES, ENTREMOS ** LA RAZON.
15031 5ELCID1900 OTROS MANDADOS HA ** ESTA MI CORT:
15069 5ELCID1905 ABRA Y ONDRA & CRE%RA ** ONOR,
15106 5ELCID1910 DEZID A RUY DIAZ, EL QUE ** BUEN ORA NASCO,
15130 5ELCID1913 ANDAR LE QUIERO A MYO %ID ** TODA PRO.
15172 5ELCID1920 ** POCAS TIERRAS A TALES DOS VARONES.
15238 5ELCID1929 QUEL CONNOS%IE Y ONDRA & CRE%IE ** ONOR,
15310 5ELCID1938 ELLOS SON MUCHO VRGULLOSOS & AN PART ** LA CORT,
15329 5ELCID1941 FLABLEMOS ** ELLO, EN LA PORIDAD SEAMOS NOS.
15331 5ELCID1941 FLABLEMOS EN ELLO, ** LA PORIDAD SEAMOS NOS.
15343 5ELCID1942 AFE DIOS DEL %IELLO QUE NOS ACUERDE ** LO MIIOR.
15480 5ELCID1961 SALUDAD ME MAYO %ID, EL QUE ** BUEN ORA %INXO ESPADA;
15538 5ELCID1969 TANTO BUEN PENDON METER ** BUENAS ASTAS,
15636 5ELCID1983 NON SON ** CUENTA, SABET, LAS CASTELLANAS.
15650 5ELCID1985 DENTRO ** VALLEN%IA MYO %ID EL CAMPEADOR
15774 5ELCID2001 DALMA & DE CORA%ON, & TODOS LOS QUE ** PODER DESSOS FOSSEN;
15800 5ELCID2004 ** QUE TIENE SU ALMA & SU CORA%ON,
15834 5ELCID2008 FATA QUES TORNE EL QUE ** BUEN ORA NASCO.
15846 5ELCID2010 TANTOS CAUALLOS ** DIESTRO, GRUESSOS & CORREDORES,
15859 5ELCID2011 MYO %ID SELOS GA@ARA, QUE NON GELOS DIERAN ** DON.
15902 5ELCID2016 DON LO OUO A OIO EL QUE ** BUEN ORA NASCO,
15932 5ELCID2020 COMMO LO COMIDIA EL QUE ** BUEN ORA NA%IO,
15941 5ELCID2021 LOS YNOIOS & LAS MANOS ** TIERRA LOS FINCO,
15985 5ELCID2027 LEUANTADOS ** PIE, YA %ID CAMPEADOR,
16044 5ELCID2035 ** TODO MYO REYNO PARTE DESDE OY.
16085 5ELCID2040 LEUOS ** PIE & EN LA BOCAL SALUDO.
16088 5ELCID2040 LEUOS EN PIE & ** LA BOCAL SALUDO.
16183 5ELCID2053 OMILLAMOS NOS, %ID, ** BUEN ORA NASQUIESTES UOS
16188 5ELCID2054 ** QUANTO PODEMOS ANDAMOS EN UUESTRO PRO.
16192 5ELCID2054 EN QUANTO PODEMOS ANDAMOS ** UUESTRO PRO.
16208 5ELCID2056 MYO %ID RUY DIAZ, QUE ** ORA BUENA NASCO,
16212 5ELCID2057 ** AQUEL DIA DEL REY SO HUESPED FUE;
16289 5ELCID2066 TODOS ERAN ALEGRES & ACUERDAN ** VNA RAZON:
16460 5ELCID2087 ENTRE YO YELLAS ** UUESTRA MER%ED SOMOS NOS,
16466 5ELCID2088 AFELLAS ** UUESTRA MANO DON ELUIRA & DO@A SOL,
16504 5ELCID2092 BAN BESAR LAS MANOS ALQUE ** ORA BUENA NA%IO;
16580 5ELCID2101 AFELLOS ** UUESTRAS MANOS LOS YFANTES DE CARRION,
16600 5ELCID2103 TREZIENTOS MARCOS DE PLATA ** AYUDA LES DO YO,
16607 5ELCID2104 QUE METAN ** SUS BODAS ODO QUISIEREDES UOS;
16615 5ELCID2105 PUES FUEREN ** UUESTRO PODER EN VALEN%IA LA MAYOR,
16618 5ELCID2105 PUES FUEREN EN UUESTRO PODER ** VALEN%IA LA MAYOR,
16686 5ELCID2113 AQUIS METIO ** NUEUAS MYO %ID EL CAMPEADOR;
16731 5ELCID2118 MYO %ID DELOS CAUALLOS LX DIO ** DON.
16759 5ELCID2122 METIOLOS ** PODER DE MYO %ID EL CAMPEADOR:
16791 5ELCID2126 DIOS QUE ESTA ** %IELO DEM DENT BUEN GALARDON.
16919 5ELCID2141 TOD ESTO ES PUESTO, SABED, ** GRANT RECABDO.
17025 5ELCID2155 AFE DIOS DEL %IELO, QUE LO PONGA ** BUEN LOGAR
17066 5ELCID2161 HYREMOS ** PODER DE MYO %ID A VALEN%IA LA MAYOR;
17125 5ELCID2167 ADELINAN PORA VALEN%IA, LA QUE ** BUEN PUNTO GANO.
17144 5ELCID2170 ** CASA DE MYO %ID NON A DOS MEIORES,
17174 5ELCID2173 QUE ES LARGO DE LENGUA, MAS ** LO AL NON ES TAN PRO.
17190 5ELCID2175 AFELOS ** VALEN%IA, LA QUE MYO %ID GA@O;
17274 5ELCID2185 VENIDES, CAMPEADOR, ** BUENA ORA %INXIESTES ESPADA
17346 5ELCID2194 NON SERAN MENGUADAS ** TODOS UUESTROS DIAS
17376 5ELCID2198 DESTE UUSTRO CASAMIENTO CRE%REMOS ** ONOR;
17413 5ELCID2203 METIUOS ** SUS MANOS, FIJAS, AMAS ADOS;
17515 5ELCID2216 E YUAN POSAR ** VN PRE%IOSO ESCA@O.

WORD C# PREFIX CONTEXT

EN (CON'T)

17532 5ELCID2218 ESTAN PARANCO MIENTES ALQUE ** BUEN ORA NASCO.
17538 5ELCID2219 EL CAMPEADOR ** PIE ES LEUANTADO:
17566 5ELCID2222 AFFE AMAS MIS FIJAS, METOLAS ** UUESTRA MANO;
17614 5ELCID2228 LEUANTAN SE DERECHAS & METICGELAS ** MANO.
17735 5ELCID2244 TRES CAUALLOS CAMEC EL QUE ** BUEN ORA NASCO.
17767 5ELCID2248 RICAS FUERON LAS BODAS ** EL ALCAZAR ONDRADO,
17792 5ELCID2251 QUINZE DIAS CONPLIDOS DURARON ** LAS BODAS,
17811 5ELCID2253 MYO %ID DON RODRIGO, EL QUE ** BUEN ORA NASCO,
17822 5ELCID2255 ** BESTIAS SINES AL C SON MANDADOS;
17838 5ELCID2257 NON FUERON ** CUENTA LOS AUERES MONEDADOS.
17886 5ELCID2263 ESPIDIENDOS DE RUY DIAZ, EL QUE ** BUEN ORA NASCO,
17939 5ELCID2270 EL %ID & SOS HYERNOS ** VALEN%IA SON RASTADOS.
18002 5ELCID2278 ** VALEN%IA SEY MYO %ID CON TODOS SUS VASSALLOS,
18021 5ELCID2280 YAZIES ** VN ESCA@O, DURMIE EL CAMPEADOR,
18041 5ELCID2283 ** GRANT MIEDO SE VIERON POR MEDIO DELA CORT;
18113 5ELCID2292 ** ESTO DESPERTO EL QUE EN BUEN ORA NA%IO;
18118 5ELCID2292 EN ESTO DESPERTO EL QUE ** BUEN ORA NA%IO;
18150 5ELCID2296 MYO %ID FINCO EL COBDO, ** PIE SE LEUANTO,
18168 5ELCID2298 EL LEON QUANDO LO VIO, ASSI ** VERGON%O,
18342 5ELCID2321 YA ** ESTA BATALLA A ENTRAR ABREMOS NOS;
18387 5ELCID2327 POR ENTRAR ** BATALLA DESEAN CARRION.
18401 5ELCID2329 QUE SEAN ** PAS & NON AYAN Y RA%ION.
18432 5ELCID2333 ** BRA%OS TENEDES MIS FIJAS TAN BLANCAS COMMO EL SOL
18449 5ELCID2335 ** VALEN%IA FOLGAD A TODO UUESTRO SABOR,
18479 5ELCID2339 ** VNA CONPA@A TORNADOS SON AMOS.
18511 5ELCID2342 AVN SI DIOS QUISIERE & EL PADRE QUE ESTA ** ALTO,
18519 5ELCID2343 AMOS LOS MYOS YERNOS BUENOS SERAN ** CAPO.
18529 5ELCID2345 ** LA VESTE DELOS MOROS LOS ATAMORES SONANDO;
18572 5ELCID2350 OYD LO QUE FABLO EL QUE ** BUEN ORA NASCO:
18606 5ELCID2354 CALOS MOROS, CON DIOS, NON FINCARAN ** CANPO.
18903 5ELCID2392 EL QUE ** BUEN ORA NASCO LOS OIOS LE FINCAUA,
18911 5ELCID2393 ** BRA%O EL ESCUDO & ABAXO EL ASTA,
18935 5ELCID2396 ** LAS AZES PRIMERAS EL CAMPEADOR ENTRAUA,
18962 5ELCID2399 MYO %ID CON LOS SUYOS CAE ** ALCAN%A;
18998 5ELCID2403 SACAN LOS DELAS TIENDAS, CAEN LOS ** ALCAZ;
19036 5ELCID2408 MYO %ID AL REY BUCAR CAYOL ** ALCAZ:
19073 5ELCID2413 EL ESPADA TIENES DESNUDA ** LA MANO & VEOT AGUIJAR;
19082 5ELCID2414 ASI COMMO SEMEIA, ** MI LA QUIERES ENSAYAR.
19103 5ELCID2416 NON TE IUNTARAS CCMIGO FATA DENTRO ** LA MAR.
19222 5ELCID2432 EL QUE ** BUEN ORA NASCO.
19324 5ELCID2447 COMMO YO FIO POR DIOS & ** TODOS LOS SOS SANTOS,
19389 5ELCID2456 GRADO ADIOS & AL PADRE QUE ESTA ** ALTO,
19395 5ELCID2457 EA UOS, %ID, QUE ** BUEN ORA FUESTES NADO
19490 5ELCID2469 DESTA ARRANCADA, QUE LO TENIEN ** SO SALUO,
19495 5ELCID2470 CUYDARON QUE ** SUS DIAS NUNQUA SERIEN MINGUADOS.
19502 5ELCID2471 FUERON ** VALEN%IA MUY BIEN ARREADOS,
19566 5ELCID2479 QUE LIDIARAN COMIGO ** CAMPO MYOS YERNOS AMOS ADOS;
19600 5ELCID2483 LO VNO ES NUESTRO, LO OTRO HAN ** SALUO.
19607 5ELCID2484 MANDO MYO %ID, EL QUE ** BUEN ORA NASCO,
19637 5ELCID2489 CAYERON LE ** QUINTA AL %ID SEYX %IENTOS CAUALLOS,
19709 5ELCID2499 ALA DENTRO ** MARRUECOS, OLAS MEZQUITAS SON,
19734 5ELCID2502 NO LOS YRE BUSCAR, ** VALEN%IA SERE YO,
19759 5ELCID2505 GRANDES SON LOS GOZOS ** VALEN%IA CON MYO %ID EL CANPEADOR
19889 5ELCID2522 VEN%IEMOS MOROS ** CAMPO & MATAMOS
19955 5ELCID2531 PENSAD DELO OTRO, QUE LO NUESTRO TENEMOS LO ** SALUO.
19969 5ELCID2533 QUIEN LIDIARA MEIOR OQUIEN FUERA ** ALCAN%O;
20066 5ELCID2547 DESPUES ** LA CARRERA FEREMOS NUESTRO SABOR,
20195 5ELCID2564 METER LAS HEMOS ** LAS VILLAS
20217 5ELCID2567 LOS FIJOS QUE OUIEREMOS ** QUE AURAN PARTI%ION.
20273 5ELCID2573 CAUALLOS PORA ** DIESTRO FUERTES & CORREDORES,
20325 5ELCID2579 QUE LO SEPAN ** GALLIZIA & EN CASTIELLA & EN LEON,
20328 5ELCID2579 QUE LO SEPAN EN GALLIZIA & ** CASTIELLA & EN LEON,
20331 5ELCID2579 QUE LO SEPAN EN GALLIZIA & EN CASTIELLA & ** LEON,
20420 5ELCID2591 HYA QUIEREN CAUALGAR, ** ESPIDIMIENTO SON.
20483 5ELCID2600 QUE AYADES UUESTROS MENSSAIES ** TIERRAS DE CARRION.
20595 5ELCID2615 VIOLO ** LOS AUUEROS EL QUE EN BUEN ORA %INXO ESPADA,
20600 5ELCID2615 VIOLO EN LOS AUUEROS EL QUE ** BUEN ORA %INXO ESPADA,
20644 5ELCID2620 MANDOT QUE VAYAS CON ELLAS FATA DENTRO ** CARRION,
20710 5ELCID2629 ATALES COSAS FED QUE ** PLAZER CAYA ANOS.
20818 5ELCID2643 HYAS TORNO PORA VALEN%IA EL QUE ** BUEN ORA NAS%IO.
20845 5ELCID2647 FELOS ** MOLINA CON EL MORO AVENGALUON.
20967 5ELCID2664 TAN ** SALUO LO ABREMOS COMMO LO DE CARRION;
21091 5ELCID2680 VOS NUQUA ** CARRION ENTRARIEDES IAMAS.
21271 5ELCID2703 CON SUS MUGIERES ** BRA%OS DEMUESTRAN LES AMOR;
21361 5ELCID2715 AQUI SEREDES ESCARNIDAS ** ESTOS FIEROS MONTES.
21376 5ELCID2717 NON ABREDES PART ** TIERRAS DE CARRION.
21403 5ELCID2721 PARAN LAS ** CUERPOS & EN CAMISAS & EN %ICLATONES.
21406 5ELCID2721 PARAN LAS EN CUERPOS & ** CAMISAS & EN %ICLATONES.
21409 5ELCID2721 PARAN LAS EN CUERPOS & EN CAMISAS & ** %ICLATONES.
21417 5ELCID2723 ** MANO PRENDEN LAS %INCHAS FUERTES & DURADORES.
21495 5ELCID2733 RETRAER UOS LO AN ** VISTAS O EN CORTES.
21498 5ELCID2733 RETRAER UOS LO AN EN VISTAS O ** CORTES.
21556 5ELCID2740 YA LO SIENTEN ELLAS ** LOS SOS CORA%ONES.
21582 5ELCID2744 SANGRIENTAS ** LAS CAMISAS & TODOS LOS CICLATONES.

WORD C# PREFIX CONTEXT

EN (CON'T)

```
21631 5ELCID2750 MAS DEXAN LAS MARIDAS ** BRIALES & EN CAMISAS,
21634 5ELCID2750 MAS DEXAN LAS MARIDAS EN BRIALES & ** CAMISAS,
21716 5ELCID2761 PUES NUESTRAS PAREIAS NCN ERAN PORA ** BRA%OS.
21767 5ELCID2769 ** VN MONTE ESPESSO FELEZ MUNCZ SE METIO,
21926 5ELCID2789 LOS GANADOS FIEROS NCN NOS COMAN ** AQUESTE MONT
22135 5ELCID2818 ** SANTESTEUAN DENTRO LAS METIC,
22471 5ELCID2862 ** LOS DIAS DE VAGAR TOCA NUESTRA RENCURA SABREMOS CONTAR.
22608 5ELCID2880 E DE MEDINA A MOLINA ** CTRO DIA VAN;
22641 5ELCID2885 AL QUE ** BUEN CRA NASCC LEGAUA EL MENSSAIE;
22696 5ELCID2892 PLEGA AL CRIADOR, QUE ** %IELO ESTA,
22705 5ELCID2893 QUE UOS VEA MEIOR CASADAS DAQUI ** ADELANT.
22741 5ELCID2898 EL QUE ** BUEN CRA NASCC NON QUISO TARDAR,
22752 5ELCID2899 FABLOS CON LOS SOS ** SU PORIDAD,
22770 5ELCID2902 ** BUEN ORA TE CRIE ATI EN LA MI CORT
22776 5ELCID2902 EN BUEN ORA TE CRIE ATI ** LA MI CORT
22897 5ELCID2916 CA TAN GRANT ES LA RENCURA DENTRO ** MI CORA%ON.
22938 5ELCID2922 AL REY ** SAN FAGUNT LC FALLC.
22961 5ELCID2925 FASTA DENTRO ** SANTI YAGUO DE TODO ES SE@OR,
23129 5ELCID2947 AFELAS SUS FIJAS ** VALENCIA COSON.
23196 5ELCID2955 E VERDAD DIZES ** ESTC, TU, MU@O GUSTIOZ,
23264 5ELCID2963 PREGONARAN MI CORT PORA DENTRO ** TOLLEDO,
23302 5ELCID2968 DIZID LE AL CAMPEADOR, QUE ** BUEN ORA NASCO,
23392 5ELCID2980 QUE CORT FAZIE ** TOLLEDO AQUEL REY ONDRADO,
23430 5ELCID2984 QUE NON FALIESSEN DELO QUE ** REY AUYE MANDADO.
23448 5ELCID2986 POR QUE EL REY FAZIE CORT ** TOLLEDO,
23534 5ELCID2997 EL CONDE DON GAR%IA ** ESTAS NUEUAS FUE,
23559 5ELCID3001 ** LOS PRIMEROS VA EL BUEN REY DON ALFONSSO,
23717 5ELCID3021 E YUA RE%EBIR ALQUE ** BUEN ORA NA%IO.
23933 5ELCID3049 TERNE VIGILIA ** AQUESTE SANTO LOGAR.
23967 5ELCID3054 MYO %ID RUY DIAZ ** SAN SERUAN POSADO.
23989 5ELCID3057 AL CRIADOR ROGANDC & FABLANDO ** PORIDAD.
24068 5ELCID3068 E MARTIN MUNOZ, QUE ** BUEN PUNTO NA%IO,
24186 5ELCID3084 NOS DETIENE POR NADA EL QUE ** BUEN ORA NA%IO:
24194 5ELCID3085 CAL%AS DE BUEN PA@O ** SUS CAMAS METIO,
24359 5ELCID3106 EL VA ** MEDIO, ELOS %IENTO ADERREDOR.
24370 5ELCID3107 QUANDO LO VIERON ENTRAR AL QUE ** BUEN ORA NA%IO,
24375 5ELCID3108 LEUANTOS ** PIE EL BUEN REY DON ALFONSSO
24405 5ELCID3111 AGRANT ONDRA LO RE%IBEN AL QUE ** BUEN ORA NA%IO.
24434 5ELCID3115 ** AQUESTE ESCANO QUEMDIESTES UOS ENDON;
24457 5ELCID3118 SED ** UUESTRC ESCA@O COMMO REY A SE@OR;
24480 5ELCID3121 ** VN ESCA@C TORNI@O ESSORA MYO %ID POSO,
24501 5ELCID3123 CATANDO ESTAN A MYO %ID QUANTOS HA ** LA CORT,
24513 5ELCID3125 ** SOS AGUISAMIENTOS BIEN SEMEIA VARON.
24530 5ELCID3127 ESSORA SE LEUO ** PIE EL BUEN REY DON ALFONSSO;
24557 5ELCID3130 LA VNA FUE ** BURGOS, & LA OTRA EN CARRION,
24562 5ELCID3130 LA VNA FUE EN BURGOS, & LA OTRA ** CARRION,
24580 5ELCID3132 POR EL AMOR DE MYO %ID EL QUE ** BUEN ORA NA%IO,
24641 5ELCID3139 DELLA & DELLA PART ** PAZ SEAMOS OY.
24691 5ELCID3145 MYO %ID LA MANO BESO AL REY & ** PIE SE LEUANTO;
24935 5ELCID3176 PUSIERON LAS ** MANO DEL REY SO SE@OR;
24979 5ELCID3182 ** LAS MANOS LAS TIENE & AMAS LAS CATO:
25045 5ELCID3190 PRENDET LA, SOBRINO, CA MEIORA ** SE@OR.
25155 5ELCID3204 ** ORO & EN PLATA TRES MILL MARCOS DE PLATA LES DIO;
25158 5ELCID3204 EN ORO & ** PLATA TRES MILL MARCOS DE PLATA LES DIO;
25251 5ELCID3215 DIXO ALBARFANEZ LEUANTADOS ** PIE EL %ID CAMPEADOR:
25277 5ELCID3218 NON ACUERDAN ** CONSSEIO, CA LOS HAUERES GRANDES SON:
25336 5ELCID3226 MAS ** NUESTRO IUUIZIO ASSI LO MANDAMOS NOS,
25348 5ELCID3227 QUE AQUI LO ENTERGEDES DENTRO ** LA CORT.
25399 5ELCID3234 ENTERGEN A MYO %ID, EL QUE ** BUEN ORA NA%IO;
25443 5ELCID3240 PAGEN LE ** APRE%IADURA & PRENDALO EL CAMPEADOR.
25496 5ELCID3247 PAGARON LOS YFANTES AL QUE ** BUEN ORA NASCO;
25583 5ELCID3258 DEZID  QUE UOS MERE%I, YFANTES, ** JUEGO O EN VERO
25586 5ELCID3258 DEZID  QUE UOS MERE%I, YFANTES, EN JUEGO O ** VERO
25589 5ELCID3259 O ** ALGUNA RAZON? AQUI LO MEIORARE A JUUIZYO DELA CORT.
25680 5ELCID3270 EL CONDE DON GAR%IA ** PIE SE LEUANTAUA;
25839 5ELCID3291 FERRANGO%ALEZ ** PIE SE LEUNATO,
25940 5ELCID3305 SI YO RESPONDIER, TU NON ENTRARAS ** ARMAS.
25967 5ELCID3310 SIEMPRE ** LAS CORTES PERO MUDO ME LAMADES
26065 5ELCID3322 DID EL CAUALLO, TOUEL DO ** PORIDAD:
26120 5ELCID3330  NON TE VIENE ** MIENTE EN VALEN%IA LO DEL LEON,
26122 5ELCID3330  NON TE VIENE EN MIENTE ** VALEN%IA LO DEL LEON,
26257 5ELCID3348 ** TODAS GUISAS MAS VALEN QUE VOS.
26356 5ELCID3361 MARTIN ANTOLINEZ ** PIE SE LEUANTAUA;
26456 5ELCID3376 ** LO QUE FABLO AVIE POCO RECABDO:
26504 5ELCID3382 ESSORA MUNO GUSTIOZ ** PIE SE LEUANTO;
26540 5ELCID3388 ** TU AMISTAD NON QUIERO AVER RA%ION.
26643 5ELCID3402 LEUANTOS ** PIE MYO %ID EL CAMPEADOR;
26679 5ELCID3407 AFE MIS FIJAS, ** UUESTRAS MANOS SON:
26715 5ELCID3412 ESTE CASAMIENTO OY SE OTORGE ** ESTA CORT,
26792 5ELCID3422 LEUANTOS ** PIE OIARRA & YNEGO XIMENEZ,
26843 5ELCID3429 MYNAYA ALBAFANEZ ** PIE SE LEUANTO;
26868 5ELCID3432 BIEN UOS DI VAGAR ** TODA ESTA CORT,
26997 5ELCID3449 ANTES LAS AVIEDES PAREIAS PORA ** BRA%OS LAS TENER,
27037 5ELCID3454 ** TODAS GUISAS TALES SODES QUALES DIGO YO;
```

WORD C# PREFIX CONTEXT

EN (CON'T)

```
                 27060 5ELCID3457 GOMEZ PELAYET ** PIE SE LEUANTO;
                 27071 5ELCID3459 CA ** ESTA CORT AFARTC HA PORA VOS,
                 27127 5ELCID3466 DESTOS IIJ POR TRES QUE REBTARON ** LA CORT.
                 27229 5ELCID3480 AQUI LES PONGC PLAZC DE DENTRC ** MI CORT,
                 27236 5ELCID3481 ACABO DE TRES SEMANAS, ** BEGAS DE CARRION,
                 27284 5ELCID3487 ESTOS MIS TRES CAUALLERCS ** UUESTRA MANO SON,
                 27355 5ELCID3495 NOS FARTAN DE CATARLE QUANTOS HA ** LA CORT.
                 27476 5ELCID3510 QUE ** TODAS NUESTRAS TIERRAS NON HA TAN BUEN VARON.
                 27506 5ELCID3514 ** MOROS NI EN CHRISTIANOS OTRO TAL NON HA OY,
                 27509 5ELCID3514 EN MOROS NI ** CHRISTIANOS OTRO TAL NON HA OY,
                 27520 5ELCID3515 HY UOS LE DO ** DON, MANDEDES LE TOMAR, SE@OR.
                 27610 5ELCID3525 E MUNO GUSTIOZ, FIRMES SED ** CAMPO AGUISA DE VARONES;
                 27654 5ELCID3530 ALEGRE FUE DAQUESTO EL QUE ** BUEN ORA NA%IO;
                 27742 5ELCID3541 QUE LOS MATASSEN ** CAMPO POR DESONDRA DE SO SE@OR.
                 27818 5ELCID3550 HYAS METIEN ** ARMAS LOS DEL BUEN CAMPEADOR,
                 27833 5ELCID3552 ** OTRO LOGAR SE ARMAN LOS YFANTES DE CARRION,
                 27848 5ELCID3554 ANDIDIERON ** PLEYTC, DIXIERCN LO AL REY ALFONSSO,
                 27858 5ELCID3555 QUE NON FUESSEN ** LA BATALLA LAS ESPADAS TAIADORES
                 27979 5ELCID3570 NOLO QUERRIEN AUER FECHC POR QUANTO HA ** CARRION.
                 28038 5ELCID3579 ** UUESTRA MANO NOS METIC NUESTRO SE@OR;
                 28176 5ELCID3597 ESTA LID ** TOLEDO LAFIZIERADES, MAS NON QUISIESTES VOS.
                 28386 5ELCID3625 FIRIENSSE ** LOS ESCUDOS SIN TODO PAUOR.
                 28400 5ELCID3627 PRISOL ** VAZIO, EN CARNE NOL TOMO,
                 28402 5ELCID3627 PRISOL EN VAZIO, ** CARNE NOL TOMO,
                 28407 5ELCID3628 BIEN ** DOS LOGARES EL ESTIL LE QUEBRO.
                 28480 5ELCID3637 DEDENTRO ** LA CARNE VNA MANO GELA METIO;
                 28507 5ELCID3640 POR LA COPLA DEL CAUALLO ** TIERRA LO ECHO.
                 28686 5ELCID3662 DIAGON%ALEZ ESPADA TIENE ** MANO, MAS NOLA
                 28718 5ELCID3667 SACOL DEL MOION; MARTIN ANTOLJNEZ ** EL CAMPO FINCAUA.
                 28761 5ELCID3673 FIRIENSSEN ** LOS ESCUDOS VNOS TAN GRANDES COLPES;
                 28787 5ELCID3677 ** VAZIO FUE LA LAN%A, CA EN CARNE NOL TOMO.
                 28793 5ELCID3677 EN VAZIO FUE LA LAN%A, CA ** CARNE NOL TOMO.
                 28860 5ELCID3686 AL TIRAR DELA LAN%A ** TIERRA LO ECHO,
                 28974 5ELCID3701 FELOS ** VALEN%IA CON MYO %ID EL CAMPEADOR:
                 29048 5ELCID3710 FABLEMOS NOS DAQUESTE QUE ** BUEN ORA NA%IO.
                 29056 5ELCID3711 GRANDES SON LOS GOZOS ** VALEN%IA LA MAYOR,
                 29100 5ELCID3717 ANDIDIERON ** PLEYTOS LOS DE NAUARRA & DE ARAGON,
                 29149 5ELCID3722 VED QUAL ONDRA CRE%E AL QUE ** BUEN ORA NA%IO,
                 29177 5ELCID3725 A TODOS ALCAN%A ONDRA POR EL QUE ** BUEN ORA NA%IO.
                 29209 5ELCID3730 ** ESTE LOGAR SE ACABA ESTA RAZON.
                 29232 5ELCID3733 ** ERA DE MILL & CCXLV A@OS.  EN EL ROMANZ
                 29239 5ELCID3733 EN ERA DE MILL & CCXLV A@OS.  ** EL ROMANZ
        WORD #1690 OCCURS 551 TIMES.
           INDEX OF DIVERSIFICATION =    52.06 WITH STANDARD DEVIATION OF    50.80

ENADRAN           8753 5ELCID1112 YO FIO POR DIOS QUE EN NUESTRO PRO *******.
        WORD #1691 OCCURS   1 TIMES.

ENANTES          23946 5ELCID3051 E YRE ALA CORT ******* DE IANTAR.
        WORD #1692 OCCURS   1 TIMES.

ENBARGADO        16964 5ELCID2147 DIXO EL REY DON ALFONSSO: MUCHO ME AUEDES *********.
        WORD #1693 OCCURS   1 TIMES.

ENBARGO          14756 5ELCID1865 POR ESTO QUE EL FAZE NOS ABREMOS *******.
        WORD #1694 OCCURS   1 TIMES.

ENBAYDOS         18251 5ELCID2309 MUCHOS TOUIERON POR ******** LOS YFANTES DE CARRION,
        WORD #1695 OCCURS   1 TIMES.

ENBIA             6872 5ELCID0878 A UOS, REY ONDRADO, ***** ESTA PRESENTAIA;
                 10607 5ELCID1344 RE%IBO ESTOS CAUALLOS QUEM ***** DE DON.
                 11509 5ELCID1457 QUI BUEN MANDADERO *****, TAL DEUE SPERAR.
                 14471 5ELCID1830 MYO %ID EL DE VALEN%IA ***** SU PRESENTAIA.
                 14781 5ELCID1868 ESTOS DOZIENTOS CAUALLOS QUEM ***** MYO %ID.
                 23368 5ELCID2977 ***** SUS CARTAS PORA LEON & A SANTI YAGUO,
        WORD #1696 OCCURS   6 TIMES.
           INDEX OF DIVERSIFICATION =  3298.20 WITH STANDARD DEVIATION OF  3276.67

ENBIAD           27308 5ELCID3490 ONDRADOS MELOS ****** A VALEN%IA, POR AMOR DEL CRIADOR
        WORD #1697 OCCURS   1 TIMES.

ENBIADO          14678 5ELCID1856 GRADESCOLO A MYO %ID QUE TAL DON ME HA *******;
        WORD #1698 OCCURS   1 TIMES.

ENBIAR            4929 5ELCID0624 FIZO ****** POR LA TIENDA QUE DEXARA ALLA.
                  6378 5ELCID0813 ****** UOS QUIERO A CASTIELLA CON MANDADO
                  6398 5ELCID0816 QUIEROL ****** EN DON XXX CAUALLOS,
                  9292 5ELCID1181 POR EL REY DE MARRUECOS OUIERON A ******;
                 10031 5ELCID1271 ****** UOS QUIERO A CASTIELLA, DO AUEMOS HEREDADES,
                 14139 5ELCID1790 ****** LA QUIERO ALFONSSO EL CASTELLANO,
                 15559 5ELCID1972 CONDUCHOS LARGOS EL REY ****** MANDAUA
                 22762 5ELCID2900 AL REY ALFONSSO DE CASTIELLA PENSSO DE ******;
        WORD #1699 OCCURS   8 TIMES.
           INDEX OF DIVERSIFICATION =  2546.57 WITH STANDARD DEVIATION OF  2461.90
```

WORD C# PREFIX CONTEXT

ENBIARE 10084 5ELCID1278 ******* POR ELLAS, & UOS SABED EL MENSAGE:
WORD #1700 OCCURS 1 TIMES.

ENBIARON 4957 5ELCID0627 AL REY DE VALEN%IA ******** CON MENSAIE,
17474 5ELCID2210 POR LOS YFFANTES DE CARRION ESSORA ********,
WORD #1701 OCCURS 2 TIMES.

ENBIAS 3868 5ELCID0490 DO YO UOS ****** BIEN ABRIA TAL ESPERAN%A.
WORD #1702 OCCURS 1 TIMES.

ENBIAUA 14385 5ELCID1819 DESTA LID QUE HA ARRANCADA CC CAUALLOS LE ******* ENPRESENTAIA,
WORD #1703 OCCURS 1 TIMES.

ENBIO 7623 5ELCID0976 MYO %ID QUANDO LO OYO, ***** PORA ALLA:
9344 5ELCID1188 A TIERRAS DE CASTIELLA ***** SUS MENSSAIES:
14326 5ELCID1812 POR QUE ASSI LAS ***** COMO ELLAS SON PAGADAS,
15449 5ELCID1957 CON DOS CAUALLEROS LUEGO LAS *****:
20336 5ELCID2580 CON QUE RIQUEZA ***** MIOS YERNOS AMOS ADOS.
20770 5ELCID2638 DIL QUE ***** MIS FIJAS A TIERRAS DE CARRION,
23682 5ELCID3016 ALUAR FANEZ ADELANTEL *****,
28958 5ELCID3698 EL REY ALOS DE MYO %ID DE NOCHE LOS *****,
WORD #1704 OCCURS 8 TIMES.
INDEX OF DIVERSIFICATION = 3046.86 WITH STANDARD DEVIATION OF 2016.77

ENBRA%AN 5671 5ELCID0715 ******** LOS ESCUDOS DELANT LOS CORA%ONES,
18050 5ELCID2284 ******** LOS MANTOS LOS DEL CAMPEADOR,
WORD #1705 OCCURS 2 TIMES.

ENBRA%O 2186 5ELCID0275 ALAS SUS FIJAS ******* LAS PRENDIA,
WORD #1706 OCCURS 1 TIMES.

ENBUEN 2333 5ELCID0294 VANSSE PORA SAN PERO DO ESTA EL QUE ****** PUNTO NA%IO.
23658 5ELCID3013 AVN NON ERA LEGADO EL QUE ****** ORA NA%IO,
WORD #1707 OCCURS 2 TIMES.

ENCAMO 28421 5ELCID3629 FIRME ESTIDO PERO VERMUEZ, POR ESSO NOS ******;
28855 5ELCID3685 CON EL DIO VNA TUERTA, DELA SIELLA LO ******,
WORD #1708 OCCURS 2 TIMES.

ENCARNA%ION 2637 5ELCID0333 PRISIST *********** EN SANTA MARIA MADRE,
WORD #1709 OCCURS 1 TIMES.

ENCLINO 2175 5ELCID0274 ******* LAS MANOS EN LA SU BARBA VELIDA,
WORD #1714 OCCURS 1 TIMES.

ENCORTINADO 17442 5ELCID2206 POR EL SUELO & SUSO TAN BIEN ***********,
WORD #1715 OCCURS 1 TIMES.

ENCUBRE 7199 5ELCID0922 TODO GELO DIZE, QUE NOL ******* NADA.
WORD #1716 OCCURS 1 TIMES.

EN%ERRO 21213 5ELCID2695 ALLI SON CA%OS DO A ELPHA *******;
WORD #1717 OCCURS 1 TIMES.

END 2831 5ELCID0357 EN TI CROUO AL ORA, POR *** ES SALUO DE MAL;
WORD #1718 OCCURS 1 TIMES.

ENDE 16577 5ELCID2100 AL CRIADOR PLEGA QUE AYADES **** SABOR.
27797 5ELCID3547 POR VER ESTA LID, CA AVIEN **** SABOR;
WORD #1719 OCCURS 2 TIMES.

ENDON 1397 5ELCID0179 %ID, BESO UUESTRA MANO ***** QUE LA YO AYA.
1533 5ELCID0196 DAMOS UOS ***** AUOS XXX MARCHOS;
24439 5ELCID3115 EN AQUESTE ESCANO QUEMDIESTES UOS *****;
WORD #1720 OCCURS 3 TIMES.

ENDURAR 5594 5ELCID0704 AQUEL PERO VERMUEZ NON LO PUDO *******,
7380 5ELCID0946 SONRRISOS EL CABOSO, QUE NON LO PUDO *******:
WORD #1721 OCCURS 2 TIMES.

```
WORD                C#  PREFIX                              CONTEXT

ENEL                   371 5ELCID0047 %ID, **** NUESTRO MAL UCS NON GANADES NADA;
                      1995 5ELCID0252 NON QUIERO FAZER **** MCNESTERIO VN DINERO DE DA@O;
                      2795 5ELCID0353 DIOT CON LA LAN%A **** COSTADC, DONT YXIO LA SANGRE,
                      2836 5ELCID0358 **** MONUMENTC RESU%ITEST, FUST ALOS YNFIERNOS,
                      3604 5ELCID0454 NONBRADCS SCN LOS QUE YRAN **** ALGARA,
                      3766 5ELCID0476 AFEUOS LOS CCIIJ **** ALGARA,
                      3933 5ELCID0499 LIDIANDO CON MOROS **** CAMPO,
                      4124 5ELCID0525 QUE **** CASTIELLO NCN Y AURIE MORADA,
                      5647 5ELCID0711 ESPOLONO EL CAUALLO, E METIOL **** MAYOR AZ.
                      5726 5ELCID0722 TODOS FIEREN **** AZ DO ESTA PERO VERMUEZ.
                      7041 5ELCID0900 AQUEL POYO **** PRISO POSADA;
                      7124 5ELCID0912 **** PINAR DE TEUAR DCN RCY DIAZ POSAUA;
                      8500 5ELCID1080 LO QUE NON FERIE EL CABOSC POR QUANTO **** MUNDO HA,
                      8935 5ELCID1138 **** NOMBRE DEL CRIADOR & DEL APOSTOL SANTI YAGUE,
                      9575 5ELCID1217 **** AUER MONEDADO XXX MILL MARCOS LE CAEN,
                      9659 5ELCID1228 **** PASSAR DE XUCAR Y VERIEDES BARATA,
                     10215 5ELCID1293 SOSPIRANDO EL OBISPO QUES VIESSE CON MOROS **** CAMPO:
                     11979 5ELCID1519 **** OMBRO LO SALUDA, CA TAL ES SU HUSAIE:
                     12695 5ELCID1611 ALA LAS SUBIE **** MAS ALTO LOGAR;
                     13328 5ELCID1690 HYR LOS HEMOS FFERIR **** NOMBRE DEL CRIADOR & DEL APOSTOL SANTI
                     13994 5ELCID1772 MYNAYA ALBARFANEZ FUERA ERA **** CAMPO,
                     17459 5ELCID2208 SABOR ABRIEDES DE SER & DE COMER **** PALA%IO.
                     19425 5ELCID2461 FARTOS DE LIDIAR CON MOROS **** CAMPO.
                     21615 5ELCID2748 POR MUERTAS LAS DEXARON **** ROBREDRO DE CORPES.
                     21669 5ELCID2754 LOS YFANTES DE CARRION **** ROBREDO DE CORPES
                     22015 5ELCID2801 COGIO DEL AGUA **** & ASUS PRIMAS DIO;
                     22048 5ELCID2806 E PRIUADO **** CAUALLC LAS CAUALGO;
                     22444 5ELCID2859 **** FINCAN LOS CIOS DON ELUIRA & DO@A SOL:
                     23114 5ELCID2945 DESENPARADAS LAS DEXARON **** ROBREDO DE CORPES,
                     23976 5ELCID3055 MANDO FAZER CANDELAS & PONER **** ALTAR;
                     24314 5ELCID3100 **** ABRIEN QUE VER QUANTOS QUE Y SON.
                     24780 5ELCID3156 QUANDO DEXARON MIS FIJAS **** ROBREDO DE CORPES,
                     25650 5ELCID3266 SOLAS LAS DEXASTES **** ROBREDO DE CORPES,
                     25809 5ELCID3287 COMMO YO AUOS, CONDE, **** CASTIELLO DE CABRA;
                     27487 5ELCID3511 MYO %ID **** CAUALLO ADELANT SE LEGO,
                     28160 5ELCID3595 DO SEDIEN **** CAMPO FABLO EL REY DON ALFONSSO:
                     28633 5ELCID3656 LO VNO CAYO **** CAMPO & LO AL SUSO FINCAUA.
                     28775 5ELCID3675 FIRIO **** ESCUDO A DON MUNO GUSTIOZ,
                     29228 5ELCID3732 PER ABBAT LE ESCRIUIO **** MES DE MAYO,
          WORD #1722 OCCURS  39 TIMES.
             INDEX OF DIVERSIFICATION =    758.39 WITH STANDARD DEVIATION OF    741.72

ENELA                 9765 5ELCID1241 NIN ENTRARIE ***** TIGERA, NI VN PELO NON AURIE TAIADO,
          WORD #1723 OCCURS   1 TIMES.

ENEMIGO              14517 5ELCID1836 EL CONDE DON GAR%IA, SO ******* MALO.
                     23538 5ELCID2998 ******* DE MIO SID, QUE SIEMPREL BUSCO MAL,
          WORD #1724 OCCURS   2 TIMES.

ENEMIGOS                64 5ELCID0009 ESTO ME AN BUELTO MYOS ******** MALOS.
          WORD #1725 OCCURS   1 TIMES.

ENEMISTAD             7530 5ELCID0965 NON LO DESAFIE, NIL TORNE *********,
          WORD #1726 OCCURS   1 TIMES.

ENES                 13239 5ELCID1678 QUINIENTOS MATARON DELLOS CONPLIDOS **** DIA.
          WORD #1727 OCCURS   1 TIMES.

ENESSA               23982 5ELCID3056 SABOR A DE VELAR ****** SANTIDAD,
          WORD #1728 OCCURS   1 TIMES.

ENESSORA              4756 5ELCID0603 ENTRELLOS & EL CASTIELLO ******** ENTRAUAN.
                     27168 5ELCID3473 ******** DIXO MIO %ID. NO LO FARE, SENOR.
                     27184 5ELCID3475 ******** DIXO EL REY: ACSADAS, CAMPEADOR.
          WORD #1729 OCCURS   3 TIMES.

ENESTA                6543 5ELCID0835 SI NON, ****** TIERRA ANGOSTA NON PODRIEMOS BIUIR.
          WORD #1730 OCCURS   1 TIMES.

ENESTO               18265 5ELCID2311 ELLOS ****** ESTANDO, DON AUIEN GRANT PESAR,
          WORD #1731 OCCURS   1 TIMES.

ENFFUR%ION           22368 5ELCID2849 PRESENTAN A MINAYA ESSA NOCH GRANT **********;
          WORD #1732 OCCURS   1 TIMES.

ENFRENADOS            6409 5ELCID0817 TODOS CON SIELLAS & MUY BIEN **********,
          WORD #1733 OCCURS   1 TIMES.

ENGENDRASTES         20446 5ELCID2595 VOS NOS ************, NUESTRA MADRE NOS PARIO;
          WORD #1734 OCCURS   1 TIMES.

ENGENDRE             16451 5ELCID2086 HYO LAS ******** AMAS & CRIASTES LAS UOS
          WORD #1735 OCCURS   1 TIMES.
```

WORD C# PREFIX CONTEXT

```
ENGRAMEO            95 5ELCID0013 ME%IO MYO %ID LOS OMBROS & ******** LA TIESTA:
        WORD #1736 OCCURS    1 TIMES.

ENLA              9539 5ELCID1212 QUANDO MYO %ID GA@O A VALEN%IA & ENTRO **** %IBDAD.
                 18191 5ELCID2301 E LIEUA LO ADESTRANDO, **** RED LE METIO.
                 21753 5ELCID2767 **** CARRERA DO YUA DOLIOL EL CORA%ON,
                 25480 5ELCID3245 RECIBIOLO MYO %ID COMMO APRE%IARON **** CORT.
        WORD #1737 OCCURS    4 TIMES.

ENMENDO           7514 5ELCID0963 FIRIOM EL SOBRINO & NON LO ******* MAS;
        WORD #1738 OCCURS    1 TIMES.

ENPARA            7523 5ELCID0964 AGORA CORREM LAS TIERRAS QUE EN MI ****** ESTAN;
        WORD #1739 OCCURS    1 TIMES.

ENPARAN           9630 5ELCID1223 QUE PRESA ES VALEN%IA, QUE NON GELA *******;
        WORD #1740 OCCURS    1 TIMES.

ENPDER           27700 5ELCID3536 ELLOS SON ****** DEL REY DON ALFONSSO EL DE LEON;
        WORD #1741 OCCURS    1 TIMES.

ENPE%O           27757 5ELCID3542 EL COMETER FUE MALO, QUE LO AL NOS ******,
        WORD #1742 OCCURS    1 TIMES.

ENPE@AR            725 5ELCID0092 ******* GELO HE POR LO QUE FUERE GUISADO;
        WORD #1743 OCCURS    1 TIMES.

ENPERADOR        23582 5ELCID3003 AQUESTE FUE PADRE DEL BUEN *********;
        WORD #1744 OCCURS    1 TIMES.

ENPERADORES      20115 5ELCID2553 PODREMOS CASAR CON FIJAS DE REYES O DE ***********,
                 25883 5ELCID3297 DEUIEMOS CASAR CON FIJAS DE REYES O DE ***********,
        WORD #1745 OCCURS    2 TIMES.

ENPIE%A          25956 5ELCID3308 MAS QUANDO *******, SABED, NOL DA VAGAR:
        WORD #1746 OCCURS    1 TIMES.

ENPLEANDO         7874 5ELCID1006 LOS PENDONES & LAS LAN%AS TAN BIEN LAS UAN *********,
        WORD #1747 OCCURS    1 TIMES.

ENPLEO           13587 5ELCID1722 MYO %ID ****** LA LAN%A, AL ESPADA METIO MANO,
        WORD #1748 OCCURS    1 TIMES.

ENPLEYE           3936 5ELCID0500 QUE ******* LA LAN%A & AL ESPADA META MANO,
        WORD #1749 OCCURS    1 TIMES.

ENPRESENTAIA     14386 5ELCID1819 DESTA LID QUE HA ARRANCADA CC CAUALLOS LE ENBIAUA ************,
        WORD #1750 OCCURS    1 TIMES.

ENPRESENTAUA      6829 5ELCID0872 TREYNTA CAUALLOS AL REY LOS ************;
        WORD #1751 OCCURS    1 TIMES.

ENPRESTAN        25500 5ELCID3248 ********* LES DELO AGENO, QUE NON LES CUMPLE LO SUYO.
        WORD #1752 OCCURS    1 TIMES.

ENSAYADOS        19419 5ELCID2460 EUUESTROS YERNOS AQUI SON *********,
        WORD #1753 OCCURS    1 TIMES.

ENSAYANDOS       21596 5ELCID2746 ********** AMOS QUAL DARA MEIORES COLPES.
        WORD #1754 OCCURS    1 TIMES.

ENSAYAR          18780 5ELCID2376 SI PLOGIESSE ADIOS QUERRIA LAS *******,
                 18821 5ELCID2381 AFE LOS MOROS A OIO, YD LOS *******.
                 19086 5ELCID2414 ASI COMMO SEMEIA, EN MI LA QUIERES *******.
                 26028 5ELCID3318 VIST VN MORO, FUSTEL *******; ANTES FUXISTE QUE ALTE ALEGASSES.
        WORD #1755 OCCURS    4 TIMES.

ENSAYARON        21855 5ELCID2781 MAL SE ********* LOS YFANTES DE CARRION.
        WORD #1756 OCCURS    1 TIMES.

ENSAYAUA         28690 5ELCID3663 ********,
        WORD #1757 OCCURS    1 TIMES.

ENSAYAUAS        18869 5ELCID2388 ********* EL OBISPO, DIOS, QUE BIEN LIDIAUA
        WORD #1758 OCCURS    1 TIMES.

ENSELLADOS        8374 5ELCID1064 DAN LE TRES PALAFRES MUY BIEN **********
        WORD #1759 OCCURS    1 TIMES.

ENSELLAR          2509 5ELCID0317 NON UOS TARDEDES, MANDEDES ********;
        WORD #1760 OCCURS    1 TIMES.

ENSE@AR          20049 5ELCID2545 ******* LAS HEMOS DO LAS HEREDADES SON.
        WORD #1761 OCCURS    1 TIMES.
```

WORD C# PREFIX CONTEXT

```
ENSE@ARON          28234 5ELCID3604 LOS FIELES & EL REY ********* LOS MOIONES,
        WORD #1762 OCCURS   1 TIMES.

ENSIELLAN          12493 5ELCID1585 ********* LE ABAUIECA, CUBERTURAS LE ECHAUAN,
        WORD #1763 OCCURS   1 TIMES.

ENSSELLADOS        16949 5ELCID2145 E XXX CAUALLOS COREDORES, ESTOS BIEN ***********;
        WORD #1764 OCCURS   1 TIMES.

ENSSIENPLOS        21480 5ELCID2731 ATAN MALOS *********** NON FAGADES SOBRE NOS:
        WORD #1765 OCCURS   1 TIMES.

ENTEN%ION          27112 5ELCID3464 NON DIGA NINGUNO DELLA MAS VNA *********.
        WORD #1766 OCCURS   1 TIMES.

ENTENDIDO          10186 5ELCID1290 BIEN ********* ES DE LETRAS & MUCHO ACORDADO,
        WORD #1767 OCCURS   1 TIMES.

ENTENDIO           20995 5ELCID2667 VN MORO LATINADO BIEN GELO ********;
        WORD #1768 OCCURS   1 TIMES.

ENTERGEDES         25346 5ELCID3227 QUE AQUI LO ********** DENTRO EN LA CORT.
        WORD #1769 OCCURS   1 TIMES.

ENTERGEN           25393 5ELCID3234 ******** A MYO %ID, EL QUE EN BUEN ORA NA%IO;
        WORD #1770 OCCURS   1 TIMES.

ENTIERRAS          20249 5ELCID2570 VOS LES DIESTES VILLAS E TIERRAS POR ARRAS ********* DE CARRION,
                   25317 5ELCID3223 PAGAR LE HEMOS DE HEREDADES ********* DE CARRION.
        WORD #1771 OCCURS   2 TIMES.

ENTODAS            10647 5ELCID1349 QUE ******* GUISAS MIIOR ME SIRUE QUE UOS.
                   26408 5ELCID3369 ******* GUISAS, SABED, QUE MAS VALEN QUE VOS.
        WORD #1772 OCCURS   2 TIMES.

ENTODO             28214 5ELCID3602 ****** MYO REYNO NON AURA BUENA SABOR.
        WORD #1773 OCCURS   1 TIMES.

ENTODOS             1720 5ELCID0220 NON SE SIENTRARE Y MAS ******* LOS MYOS DIAS.
        WORD #1774 OCCURS   1 TIMES.

ENTRA               1065 5ELCID0137 YA VEDES QUE ***** LA NOCH, EL %ID ES PRESURADO,
                   24350 5ELCID3105 CUERDA MIENTRA ***** MYO %ID CON TODOS LOS SOS:
        WORD #1775 OCCURS   2 TIMES.

ENTRAD             12656 5ELCID1606 ****** COMIGO EN VALEN%IA LA CASA,
        WORD #1776 OCCURS   1 TIMES.

ENTRADA             6489 5ELCID0827 AGORA DAUAN %EUADA, YA LA NOCH ERA *******,
                   13408 5ELCID1699 ES DIA ES SALIDO & LA NOCH ******* ES,
                   16251 5ELCID2061 ES DIA ES PASSADO, & ******* ES LA NOCH;
                   16746 5ELCID2120 PARTIR SE QUIEREN, QUE ******* ERA LA NOCH.
        WORD #1777 OCCURS   4 TIMES.

ENTRADAS            9141 5ELCID1163 GANARON PENA CADIELLA, LAS EXIDAS & LAS ********.
                   12388 5ELCID1572 E TODAS LAS PUERTAS & LAS EXIDAS & LAS ********,
        WORD #1778 OCCURS   2 TIMES.

ENTRADO              856 5ELCID0109 EL CAMPEADOR POR LAS PARIAS FUE *******,
                    8391 5ELCID1066 EL CONDE DON REMONT ENTRE LOS DOS ES *******.
                   13757 5ELCID1743 CON C CAUALLEROS A VALEN%IA ES *******,
                   17762 5ELCID2247 TORNAN SE CON LAS DUE@AS, A VALEN%IA AN *******;
                   23962 5ELCID3053 EL REY DON ALFONSSO A TOLLEDO ES *******,
        WORD #1779 OCCURS   5 TIMES.
           INDEX OF DIVERSIFICATION =  5775.50 WITH STANDARD DEVIATION OF  1480.81

ENTRADOS           12209 5ELCID1550 ******** SON A MOLINA, BUENA & RICA CASA;
                   14162 5ELCID1792 CON AQUESTAS RIQUEZAS TANTAS A VALEN%IA SON ********.
                   21221 5ELCID2697 ******** SON LOS YFANTES AL ROBREDO DE CORPES,
        WORD #1780 OCCURS   3 TIMES.

ENTRAMOS           20941 5ELCID2660 ******** HERMANOS CONSSEIARON TRA%ION:
                   25379 5ELCID3232 ******** MELOS DIERON LOS YFANTES DE CARRION.
        WORD #1781 OCCURS   2 TIMES.

ENTRANDO              83 5ELCID0012 E ******** A BURGOS OUIERON LA SINIESTRA.
                    4476 5ELCID0569 EL CASTIELLO DE ALCO%ER EN PARIA UA ********.
        WORD #1782 OCCURS   2 TIMES.

ENTRAR              2472 5ELCID0311 EL DIA ES EXIDO, LA NOCH QUERIE ******,
                    5263 5ELCID0665 ACABO DE TRES SEMANAS, LA QUARTA QUERIE ******,
                    5534 5ELCID0697 VERIEDES ARMAR SE MOROS, APRIESSA ****** EN AZ.
                    6092 5ELCID0773 EL REY FARIZ EN TERUEL SE FUE ******,
```

```
WORD                C#  PREFIX                                CONTEXT

ENTRAR (CON'T)

                  9484 5ELCID1205 VIEDALES EXIR & VIEDALES ******.
                 12757 5ELCID1619 EL YUIERNO ES EXIDO, QUE EL MAR%O QUIERE ******.
                 18346 5ELCID2321 YA EN ESTA BATALLA A ****** ABREMOS NOS;
                 18386 5ELCID2327 POR ****** EN BATALLA DESEAN CARRION.
                 23913 5ELCID3046 PENSSAD, SE@OR, DE ****** ALA %IBDAD,
                 24367 5ELCID3107 QUANDO LO VIERON ****** AL QUE EN BUEN ORA NA%IO,
          WORD #1783 OCCURS  10 TIMES.
             INDEX OF DIVERSIFICATION =  2431.78 WITH STANDARD DEVIATION OF  2211.32

ENTRARAN          5448 5ELCID0687 SI NOS MURIEREMOS EN CAMPO, EN CASTIELLO NOS ********,
          WORD #1784 OCCURS   1 TIMES.

ENTRARAS         25939 5ELCID3305 SI YO RESPONDIER, TU NON ******** EN ARMAS.
          WORD #1785 OCCURS   1 TIMES.

ENTRARE           8889 5ELCID1132 YO CON LOS %IENTO ******* DEL OTRA PART,
                 12925 5ELCID1640 ******* EN LAS ARMAS, NON LO PODRE DEXAR;
                 13382 5ELCID1696 QUANDO UOS LOS FUEREDES FERIR, ******* YO DEL OTRA PART;
                 23939 5ELCID3050 CRAS MA@ANA ******* ALA %IBDAD,
          WORD #1786 OCCURS   4 TIMES.

ENTRAREDES       13852 5ELCID1755 ********** EN PREZ, & BESARAN UUESTRAS MANOS.
          WORD #1787 OCCURS   1 TIMES.

ENTRARIE          9764 5ELCID1241 NIN ******** ENELA TIGERA, NI VN PELO NON AURIE TAIADO,
          WORD #1788 OCCURS   1 TIMES.

ENTRARIEDES      21093 5ELCID2680 VOS NUQUA EN CARRION *********** IAMAS.
          WORD #1789 OCCURS   1 TIMES.

ENTRARON          1187 5ELCID0153 ASSI COMMO ********, AL %ID BESARON LE LAS MANOS.
                  4278 5ELCID0545 PASSARON LAS AGUAS, ******** AL CAMPO DE TORAN%IO,
                 10833 5ELCID1372 AQUI ******** EN FABLA LOS YFFANTES DE CARRION:
                 12093 5ELCID1534 ******** EN MEDINA, SIRUIALOS MINAYA,
                 12819 5ELCID1627 ******** SOBRE MAR, EN LAS BARCAS SON METIDOS,
                 13572 5ELCID1720 ******** LES DEL OTRO CABO.
                 13902 5ELCID1761 EN BUELTA CON EL ******** AL PALA%IO,
                 14854 5ELCID1877 BESARON LE LAS MANOS & ******** A POSAR;
                 17496 5ELCID2213 DE PIE & ASABOR, DIOS, QUE QUEDOS ********
                 19836 5ELCID2515 QUANDO ******** LOS YFANTES DE CARRION,
                 22726 5ELCID2896 TENIENDO YUAN ARMAS, ******** SE ALA CIBDAD;
                 23005 5ELCID2931 ASSI COMMO ******** POR MEDIO DELA CORT,
                 26579 5ELCID3393 AFFE DOS CAUALLEROS ******** POR LA CORT;
          WORD #1790 OCCURS  13 TIMES.
             INDEX OF DIVERSIFICATION =  2115.00 WITH STANDARD DEVIATION OF  1812.80

ENTRASSEN        17783 5ELCID2250 ANTES QUE ********* AIANTAR TODOS LOS QUEBRANTARON.
          WORD #1791 OCCURS   1 TIMES.

ENTRAUA            111 5ELCID0015 MYO %ID RUY DIAZ POR BURGOS *******,
                   774 5ELCID0098 PASSO POR BURGOS, AL CASTIELLO *******,
                  3726 5ELCID0470 MIO %ID RUY DIAZ POR LAS PUERTAS *******,
                 12449 5ELCID1579 EL OBISPO DON IHERONIMO ADELANT SE *******,
                 17264 5ELCID2183 MYO %ID EL CAMPEADOR AL ALCA%AR *******;
                 18941 5ELCID2396 EN LAS AZES PRIMERAS EL CAMPEADOR *******,
                 26441 5ELCID3373 ASUR GON%ALEZ ******* POR EL PALA%IO,
          WORD #1792 OCCURS   7 TIMES.
             INDEX OF DIVERSIFICATION =  4387.33 WITH STANDARD DEVIATION OF  3223.24

ENTRAUAN          4757 5ELCID0603 ENTRELLOS & EL CASTIELLO ENESSORA ********.
                  9056 5ELCID1153 ******** A MURUIEDRO CON ESTAS GANAN%IAS QUE TRAEN GRANDES.
                 12684 5ELCID1609 A TAN GRAND ONDRA ELLAS A VALEN%IA ********.
          WORD #1793 OCCURS   3 TIMES.

ENTRE             1492 5ELCID0191 ***** RACHEL & VIDAS APARTE YXIERON AMOS:
                  4290 5ELCID0547 ***** FARIZA & %ETINA MYO %ID YUA ALBERGAR.
                  6259 5ELCID0797 GRAND ALEGREYA VA ***** ESSOS CHISTIANOS,
                  6592 5ELCID0842 ***** LOS DE TECHA & LOS DE TERUEL LA CASA,
                  7555 5ELCID0968 GENTES SE LE ALEGAN GRANDES ***** MOROS & CHRISTIANOS,
                  8387 5ELCID1066 EL CONDE DON REMONT ***** LOS DOS ES ENTRADO.
                  9722 5ELCID1236 GRAND ALEGRIA ES ***** TODOS ESSOS CHRISTIANOS
                 12201 5ELCID1549 ***** EL & ALBARFANEZ HYUAN A VNA COMPA@A.
                 13705 5ELCID1737 ***** ORO & PLATA FALLARON TRES MILL MARCOS,
                 14002 5ELCID1774 ***** TIENDAS & ARMAS & VESTIDOS PRE%IADOS
                 16457 5ELCID2087 ***** YO YELLAS EN UUESTRA MER%ED SOMOS NOS,
                 17815 5ELCID2254 ***** PALAFRES & MULAS & CORREDORES CAUALLOS,
                 18554 5ELCID2348 MAS SE MARAUILLAN ***** DIEGO & FERRANDO,
                 21917 5ELCID2788 MIENTRA ES EL DIA, ANTE QUE ***** LA NOCH,
                 22079 5ELCID2810 ***** NOCH & DIA SALIERON DELOS MONTES;
                 23227 5ELCID2959 ***** YO & MYO %ID PESA NOS DE CORA%ON.
                 23991 5ELCID3058 ***** MINAYA & LOS BUENOS QUE Y HA
                 25864 5ELCID3295 NON CRE%IES VARAIA ***** NOS & VOS.
          WORD #1794 OCCURS  18 TIMES.
             INDEX OF DIVERSIFICATION =  1432.65 WITH STANDARD DEVIATION OF   933.28
```

WORD C# PREFIX CONTEXT

ENTRELLOS 4691 5ELCID0595 VIO QUE ********* & EL CASTIELLO MUCHO AUIE GRAND PLA%A;
4752 5ELCID0603 ********* & EL CASTIELLC ENESSORA ENTRAUAN.
23333 5ELCID2972 SALUDAD MELOS ATODOS, ********* AYA ESPA%IO;
WORD #1795 OCCURS 3 TIMES.

ENTREMOS 14977 5ELCID1893 MAS PUES BOS LO QUERECES, ******** EN LA RAZON.
WORD #1796 OCCURS 1 TIMES.

ENTRO 176 5ELCID0023 ANTES DELA NOCHE EN BURGOS DEL ***** SU CARTA,
974 5ELCID0125 QUANDO ATIERRA DE MOROS *****, QUE GRANT AUER SACO;
2774 5ELCID0350 EL VNO ES EN PARAYSO, CA EL OTRO NON ***** ALA;
5080 5ELCID0642 POR QUE SEME ***** EN MI TIERRA DERECHO ME AURA ADAR.
9538 5ELCID1212 QUANDO MYO %ID GA@O A VALEN%IA & ***** ENLA %IBDAD.
13766 5ELCID1745 ASSI ***** SOBRE BAUIECA, EL ESPADA EN LA MANO.
WORD #1797 OCCURS 6 TIMES.
INDEX OF DIVERSIFICATION = 2717.00 WITH STANDARD DEVIATION OF 1581.66

ENTROLES 8991 5ELCID1144 DEL OTRA PART ******** ALBARFANEZ;
WORD #1798 OCCURS 1 TIMES.

ENVIADES 20459 5ELCID2597 AGORA NOS ******** ATIERRAS DE CARRION,
WORD #1799 OCCURS 1 TIMES.

ENVIAR 5123 5ELCID0647 POR LOS DE LA FRONTERA PIENSSAN DE ******;
WORD #1800 OCCURS 1 TIMES.

ENVIAUA 14453 5ELCID1828 ******* LE MANDADO PERO VERMUEZ & MYNAYA,
WORD #1801 OCCURS 1 TIMES.

ENVIO 4078 5ELCID0518 FABLO CON LOS DE CASTEION, & ***** AFITA & AGUADELFAGARA,
11786 5ELCID1495 ***** DOS CAUALLEROS MYNAYA ALBARFANEZ QUE SOPIESSE LA VERDAD;
15516 5ELCID1966 QUI ***** POR CASTIELLA TANTA MULA PRE%IADA,
WORD #1802 OCCURS 3 TIMES.

ENVIOLOS 11102 5ELCID1406 ******** A MYO %ID, AVALEN%IA DO ESTA,
WORD #1803 OCCURS 1 TIMES.

EOTRAS 19644 5ELCID2490 ****** AZEMILLAS & CAMELOS LARGOS
WORD #1804 OCCURS 1 TIMES.

EPIENSSAN 9052 5ELCID1152 ROBAUAN EL CAMPO ********* SE DE TORNAR.
14401 5ELCID1821 SALIDOS SON DE VALEN%IA ********* DE ANDAR,
WORD #1805 OCCURS 2 TIMES.

ER 28581 5ELCID3649 RELUMBRA TOD EL CAMPO, TANTO ** LINPIA & CLARA;
WORD #1806 OCCURS 1 TIMES.

ERA 313 5ELCID0039 NON SE ABRE LA PUERTA, CA BIEN *** %ERRADA.
2785 5ELCID0352 LONGINOS *** %IEGO, QUE NUQUAS VIO ALGUANDRE,
3266 5ELCID0412 MUCHO *** PAGADO DEL SUE@O QUE A SO@ADO.
3296 5ELCID0416 AVN *** DE DIA, NON ERA PUESTO EL SOL,
3300 5ELCID0416 AVN ERA DE DIA, NON *** PUESTO EL SOL,
6488 5ELCID0827 AGORA DAUAN %EUADA, YA LA NOCH *** ENTRADA,
7231 5ELCID0927 QUE MINAYA ALBARFANEZ ASSI *** LEGADO,
8910 5ELCID1135 MA@ANA *** & PIENSSAN SE DE ARMAR,
9091 5ELCID1157 ALEGRE *** EL %ID & TODAS SUS COMPA@AS,
9591 5ELCID1219 ALEGRE *** EL CAMPEADOR CON TODOS LOS QUE HA,
10199 5ELCID1291 DE PIE & DE CAUALLO MUCHO *** AREZIADO.
10310 5ELCID1305 DIOS, QUE ALEGRE *** TODO CHRISTIANISMO,
10384 5ELCID1316 DE MISSA *** EXIDO ESSORA EL REY ALFONSSO,
11623 5ELCID1473 ESTO *** DICHO, PIENSSAN DE CAUALGAR,
11922 5ELCID1511 QUE SOPIENSSEN LES OTROS DE QUE SESO *** ALBARFANEZ
13662 5ELCID1731 MUCHO *** ALEGRE DELO QUE AN CA%ADO.
13720 5ELCID1739 ALEGRE *** MYO %ID & TODOS SOS VASSALLOS,
13763 5ELCID1744 FRONZIDA TRAHE LA CARA, QUE *** DESARMADO,
13871 5ELCID1757 QUANDOL VIERON DE PIE, QUE *** DESCAUALGADO,
13993 5ELCID1772 MYNAYA ALBARFANEZ FUERA *** ENEL CAMPO,
14193 5ELCID1796 LO QUE CAYE AEL MUCHO *** SOBEIANO;
14703 5ELCID1859 PESO AL CONDE DON GAR%IA, E MAL *** YRADO;
15393 5ELCID1950 NON *** MARAUILLA SIQUISIESSE EL REY ALFONSSO,
16747 5ELCID2120 PARTIR SE QUIEREN, QUE ENTRADA *** LA NOCH.
17166 5ELCID2172 EVAY ASUR GON%ALEZ, QUE *** BULIDOR,
17745 5ELCID2245 MYO %ID DELO QUE VEYE MUCHO *** PAGADO:
17864 5ELCID2260 QUI AUER QUIERE PRENDER BIEN *** ABASTADO;
17960 5ELCID2273 ALEGRE *** EL %ID & TODOS SUS VASSALLOS.
18285 5ELCID2314 AQUESTE *** EL REY BUCAR, SIL OUIESTES CONTAR.
19266 5ELCID2438 ALGO VIE MYO %ID DELO QUE *** PAGADO,
21020 5ELCID2671 EL MORO AVENGALUON, MUCHO *** BUEN BARRAGAN,
21739 5ELCID2765 SOBRINO *** DEL %ID CAMPEADOR;
22005 5ELCID2800 NUEUO *** & FRESCO, QUE DE VALEN%IAL SACO,
23357 5ELCID2975 ASSI COMMO LO DIXO, SUYO *** EL CUYDADO:
23654 5ELCID3013 AVN NON *** LEGADO EL QUE ENBUEN ORA NA%IO,
26454 5ELCID3375 VERMEIO VIENE, CA *** ALMORZADO;

WORD C# PREFIX CONTEXT

ERA (CON'T)

```
             27337 5ELCID3493 LA CONFIA DE RAN%AL QUE BLANCA *** COMMO EL SOL,
             29233 5ELCID3733 EN *** DE MILL & CCXLV A@OS.  EN EL ROMANZ
      WORD #1807 OCCURS  38 TIMES.
         INDEX OF DIVERSIFICATION =    780.62 WITH STANDARD DEVIATION OF    827.20

ERAN          1355 5ELCID0173 CA MIENTRA QUE VISQUIESSEN REFECHOS **** AMOS.
              3987 5ELCID0506 ESTAS GANAN%IAS ALLI **** IUNTADAS.
              9561 5ELCID1215 TODOS **** RICOS QUANTOS QUE ALLI HA.
             12841 5ELCID1629 ARRIBADO AN LAS NAUES, FUERA **** EXIDOS,
             12865 5ELCID1632 ESTAS NUEUAS A MYO %ID **** VENIDAS;
             16285 5ELCID2066 TODOS **** ALEGRES & ACUERDAN EN VNA RAZON:
             17917 5ELCID2267 MUCHO **** ALEGRES DIEGO & FERRANDO;
             17957 5ELCID2272 LOS AMORES QUELES FAZEN MUCHO **** SOBEIANOS.
             18979 5ELCID2401 EACOSTAR SE LOS TENDALES, CON HUEBRAS **** TANTAS.
             19216 5ELCID2431 ALAS TIENDAS **** LEGADOS, DO ESTAUA
             19633 5ELCID2488 ASSI LO FAZEN TODOS, CA **** ACORDADOS.
             21299 5ELCID2707 ADELANT **** YDOS LOS DE CRIAZON:
             21337 5ELCID2712 TODOS **** YDOS, ELLOS IIIJ SOLOS SON,
             21714 5ELCID2761 PUES NUESTRAS PAREIAS NON **** PORA EN BRA%OS.
             27876 5ELCID3557 MUCHO **** REPENTIDOS LOS YFANTES POR QUANTO DADAS SON;
             28104 5ELCID3588 HYA SALIERON AL CAMPO DO **** LOS MOIONES.
             28348 5ELCID3619 TEMBRAR QUERIE LA TIERRA DOD **** MOUEDORES.
      WORD #1808 OCCURS  17 TIMES.
         INDEX OF DIVERSIFICATION =  1686.06 WITH STANDARD DEVIATION OF  1997.56

ERAU          1340 5ELCID0171 NON LAS PODIEN PONER EN SOMO MAGER **** ESFOR%ADOS.
      WORD #1809 OCCURS   1 TIMES.

ERES         20628 5ELCID2619 PRIMO **** DE MIS FIJAS AMAS DALMA & DE CORA%ON
             21005 5ELCID2669 ACAYAZ, CURIATE DESTOS, CA **** MYO SE@OR:
             26101 5ELCID3327 E **** FERMOSO, MAS MAL VARRAGAN
             26426 5ELCID3371 QUE **** TRAYDOR & MINTIST DE QUANTO DICHO HAS.
      WORD #1810 OCCURS   4 TIMES.

ES             723 5ELCID0091 NON PUEDO TRAER EL AUER, CA MUCHO ** PESADO,
              1070 5ELCID0137 YA VEDES QUE ENTRA LA NOCH, EL %ID ** PRESURADO,
              1114 5ELCID0143 E NOS UOS AIUDAREMOS, QUE ASSI ** AGUISADO,
              1380 5ELCID0177 ASSI ** UUESTRA VENTURA GRANDES SON UUESTRAS GANAN%IAS,
              1542 5ELCID0197 MERE%ER NOLO FEDES, CA ESTO ** AGUISADO:
              1567 5ELCID0201 EXIDO ** DE BURGOS & ARLAN%ON A PASXADO,
              1650 5ELCID0212 MUCHO ** HUEBOS, CA %ERCA VIENE EL PLAZO.
              1662 5ELCID0213 ESTAS PALABRAS DICHAS, LA TIENDA ** COGIDA.
              2467 5ELCID0311 EL DIA ** EXIDO, LA NOCH QUERIE ENTRAR,
              2767 5ELCID0350 EL VNO ** EN PARAYSO, CA EL OTRO NON ENTRO ALA;
              2832 5ELCID0357 EN TI CROUO AL ORA, POR END ** SALUO DE MAL;
              3075 5ELCID0387 TORNADO ** DON SANCHO, & FABLO ALBARFANEZ:
              3279 5ELCID0414 ** DIA A DE PLAZO, SEPADES QUE NON MAS.
              3348 5ELCID0422 PASSAREMOS LA SIERRA QUE FIERA ** & GRAND,
              3374 5ELCID0425 DE NOCH PASSAN LA SIERRA, VINIDA ** LA MAN,
              3448 5ELCID0435 ODIZEN CASTEION, EL QUE ** SOBRE FENARES,
              4143 5ELCID0527 MOROS EN PAZ, CA ESCRIPTA ** LA CARTA,
              4177 5ELCID0532 %ERCA ** EL REY ALFONSSO & BUSCAR NOS VERNA.
              4339 5ELCID0552 PASSO A BOUIERCA & ATECA QUE ** ADELANT,
              4445 5ELCID0566 VENIDO ** A MOROS, EXIDO ES DE CHRISTIANOS;
              4449 5ELCID0566 VENIDO ES A MOROS, EXIDO ** DE CHRISTIANOS;
              4718 5ELCID0598 CON LA MER%ED DEL CRIADOR NUESTRA ** LA GANAN%IA
              4732 5ELCID0600 DIOS, QUE BUENO ** EL GOZO POR AQUESTA MA@ANA
              4810 5ELCID0609 LUEGO LEGAUAN LOS SOS, CA FECHA ** EL ARRANCADA.
              5024 5ELCID0635 ASSI FFERA LO DE SILOCA, QUE ** DEL OTRA PART.
              5220 5ELCID0660 MUCHAS SON LAS AROBDAS & GRANDE ** EL ALMOFALLA.
              5410 5ELCID0683 ARMADO ** MYO %ID CON QUANTOS QUE EL HA;
              6028 5ELCID0764 POR AQUEL COLPE RANCADO ** EL FONSSADO.
              6060 5ELCID0769 ARANCADO ** EL REY FARIZ & GALUE;
              6198 5ELCID0789 LA COFIA FRONZIDA  DIOS, COMMO ** BIEN BARBADO
              6473 5ELCID0826 MYNAYA ALBARFANEZ DESTO ** PAGADO; POR YR CON EL OMNES
                              SON CONTADOS.
              6550 5ELCID0836 YA ** AGUISADO, MA@ANAS FUE MINAYA,
              6563 5ELCID0838 LA TIERRA ** ANGOSTA & SOBEIANA DE MALA;
              6607 5ELCID0843 E LOS DE CALATAYUT, QUE ** MAS ONDRADA,
              6634 5ELCID0846 MYO %ID RUY DIAZ A ALCOL%ER ** VENIDO;
              6762 5ELCID0863 Y FFINCO EN VN POYO QUE ** SOBRE MONT REAL;
              6767 5ELCID0864 ALTO ** EL POYO, MARAUILLOSO & GRANT;
              6790 5ELCID0867 DESI A MOLINA, QUE ** DEL OTRA PART,
              6819 5ELCID0871 YDO ** A CASTIELLA ALBARFANEZ MINAYA,
              6863 5ELCID0877 SOBEIANA **, SE@OR, LA SU GANA%IA.
              6894 5ELCID0881 DIXO EL REY:  MUCHO ** MA@ANA,
              7155 5ELCID0916 DE CASTIELLA VENIDO ** MINAYA,
              7251 5ELCID0930  DIOS, COMMO ** ALEGRE LA BARBA VELIDA,
              7315 5ELCID0938 ALTER%ER DIA, DON YXO Y ** TORNADO.
              7484 5ELCID0960 EL CONDE ** MUY FOLON & DIXO VNA VANIDAT:
              7586 5ELCID0972 ASI VIENE ** FOR%ADO QUE EL CONDE AMANOS SELE CUYDO TOMAR.
              7842 5ELCID1003 ALFONDON DELA CUESTA, %ERCA ** DE LA@O,
              8234 5ELCID1048 COMMO QUE YRA A DE REY & DE TIERRA ** ECHADO.
              8237 5ELCID1049 ALEGRE ** EL CONDE & PIDIO AGUA ALAS MANOS,
              8314 5ELCID1058 PAGADO ** MYO %ID, QUE LO ESTA AGUARDANDO,
```

WORD C# PREFIX CONTEXT

ES (CON'T)

```
 8390 5ELCID1066 EL CONDE DCN REMONT ENTRE LCS DOS ** ENTRADO.
 8512 5ELCID1082 HYDO ** EL CONDE, TCRNOS EL DE BIUAR,
 8618 5ELCID1094 AIUDOL EL CRIADOR, EL SE@NOR QUE ** EN %IELO.
 8641 5ELCID1097 DENTRO EN VALEN%IA NON ** POCO EL MIEDO.
 9003 5ELCID1146 GRAND ** EL GOZO QUE VA POR ES LOGAR.
 9009 5ELCID1146 GRAND ES EL GOZO QUE VA POR ** LOGAR.
 9017 5ELCID1147 DOS REYES DE MOROS MATARON EN ** ALCAZ,
 9038 5ELCID1150 PRISIERON %EBCLA & QUANTO QUE ** Y ADELANT.
 9158 5ELCID1166 NON ** CCN RECABDO EL DOLOR DE VALEN%IA.
 9263 5ELCID1178 MALA CUETA **, SE@ORES, AVER MINGUA DE PAN,
 9529 5ELCID1211 GRANDES SON LOS GOZOS QUE VAN POR ** LOGAR,
 9625 5ELCID1223 QUE PRESA ** VALEN%IA, QUE NCN GELA ENPARAN;
 9681 5ELCID1231 TORNADO ** MYO %ID CON TODA ESTA GANAN%IA.
 9721 5ELCID1236 GRAND ALEGRIA ** ENTRE TODOS ESSOS CHRISTIANOS
 9959 5ELCID1262 ALI DIXO MINAYA: CONSEIO ** AGUISADO.
10183 5ELCID1289 EL OBISPO DON IERONIMO SO NOMBRE ** LAMADO.
10187 5ELCID1290 BIEN ENTENDIDO ** DE LETRAS & MUCHO ACORDADO,
10483 5ELCID1328 PRISO A ALMENAR & A MURUIEDRO QUE ** MIYOR,
10495 5ELCID1330 E PE@A CADIELLA, QUE ** VNA PE@A FUERT;
10504 5ELCID1331 CON AQUESTAS TODAS DE VALEN%IA ** SE@OR,
10868 5ELCID1376 MYO %ID ** DE BIUAR & NOS DELOS CONDES DE CARRION.
10991 5ELCID1391 HYDO ** MYNAYA, TORNANSSE LOS YFFANTES.
11012 5ELCID1394 DE%IDO ** MYNAYA, ASSAN PERO VA ROGAR,
11373 5ELCID1439 HYDO ** PORA SAN PERO MINAYA ALBARFANEZ,
11388 5ELCID1441 GRAND DUELO ** AL PARTIR DEL ABBAT:
11558 5ELCID1464 TIENELA AUEGALUON, MYO AMIGO ** DE PAZ,
11985 5ELCID1519 ENEL OMBRO LO SALUDA, CA TAL ** SU HUSAIE:
12078 5ELCID1531 VAYAMOS POSAR, CA LA %ENA ** ACOBADA.
12113 5ELCID1537 ONDRADO ** MYO %ID EN VALEN%IA DO ESTAUA
12138 5ELCID1540 PASSADA ** LA NOCHE, VENIDA ES LA MA@ANA,
12142 5ELCID1540 PASSADA ES LA NOCHE, VENIDA ** LA MA@ANA,
12146 5ELCID1541 OYDA ** LA MISSA, & LUEGO CAUALGAUAN;
12724 5ELCID1615 MIRAN LA HUERTA, ESPESSA ** & GRAND;
12736 5ELCID1617 DESTA GANAN%IA COMME ** BUENA & GRAND.
12751 5ELCID1619 EL YUIERNO ** EXIDO, QUE EL MAR%O QUIERE ENTRAR.
12791 5ELCID1623 QUE EN MIS HEREDADES FUERTE MIETRE ** MIETDO,
12919 5ELCID1639 VENIDOM ** DELI%IO DE TIERRAS DALENT MAR,
12990 5ELCID1648 RIQUEZA ** QUE NOS A CRE%E MARAUILLOSA & GRAND;
13089 5ELCID1659 ALEGRAUAS MIO %ID & DIXO: TAN BUEN DIA ** OY
13129 5ELCID1664 NON AYADES MIEDO, CATODO ** UUESTRA PRO;
13167 5ELCID1669 VOCA%ION ** QUE FIZO EL %ID CAMPEADOR.
13279 5ELCID1684 ALEGRE ** MYO %ID POR QUANTO FECHO HAN:
13294 5ELCID1686 OY ** DIA BUENO & MEIOR SERA CRAS:
13401 5ELCID1699 ** DIA ES SALIDO & LA NOCH ENTRADA ES,
13403 5ELCID1699 ES DIA ** SALIDO & LA NOCH ENTRADA ES,
13409 5ELCID1699 ES DIA ES SALIDO & LA NOCH ENTRADA **,
13536 5ELCID1715 DE TODAS GUARNIZONES MUY BIEN ** ADOBADO.
13756 5ELCID1743 CON C CAUALLEROS A VALEN%IA ** ENTRADO,
14013 5ELCID1775 TANTO FALLAN DESTO QUE ** COSA SOBEIANO.
14021 5ELCID1776 QUIERO UOS DEZIR LO QUE ** MAS GRANADO:
14104 5ELCID1785 LA TIENDA DEL REY DE MARRUECOS, QUE DELAS OTRAS ** CABO,
14137 5ELCID1789 TAL TIENDA COMMO ESTA, QUE DE MARUECOS ** PASSADA,
14170 5ELCID1794 QUANDO ** FARTO DE LIDIAR CON AMAS LAS SUS MANOS,
14231 5ELCID1801 ALEGRE ** DO@A XIMENA & SUS FIJAS AMAS,
14540 5ELCID1839 CUEDAN SE QUE ** ALMOFALLA, CA NON VIENEN CON MANDADO;
14715 5ELCID1861  MARAUILLA ** DEL %ID, QUE SU ONDRA CRE%E TANTO
15188 5ELCID1922 SI ** PAGADO O RE%IBIO EL DON?
15200 5ELCID1924 ** PAGADO, & DAUOS SU AMOR.
15428 5ELCID1954 SOBRE TAIO, QUE ** UNA AGUA CABDAL,
15792 5ELCID2003 DENTRO ** SU MUGIER & SUS FIJAS AMAS ADOS,
15874 5ELCID2013 DE VN DIA ** LEGADO ANTES EL REY DON ALFONSSO.
16143 5ELCID2047 DIXO EL REY: NON ** AGUISADO OY:
16246 5ELCID2061 ** DIA ES PASSADO, & ENTRADA ES LA NOCH;
16248 5ELCID2061 ES DIA ** PASSADO, & ENTRADA ES LA NOCH;
16252 5ELCID2061 ES DIA ES PASSADO, & ENTRADA ** LA NOCH;
16916 5ELCID2141 TOD ESTO ** PUESTO, SABED, EN GRANT RECABDO.
17169 5ELCID2173 QUE ** LARGO DE LENGUA, MAS EN LO AL NON ES TAN PRO.
17178 5ELCID2173 QUE ES LARGO DE LENGUA, MAS EN LO AL NON ** TAN PRO.
17339 5ELCID2193 TODO LO QUE UOS FECHES ** DE BUENA GUISA.
17540 5ELCID2219 EL CAMPEADOR EN PIE ** LEUANTADO:
18350 5ELCID2322 ESTO ** AGUISADO POR NON VER CARRION,
19337 5ELCID2449 MYNAYA ALBARFANEZ ESSORA ** LEGADO,
19460 5ELCID2466 ALEGRE ** MYO %ID CON TODAS SUS CONPA@AS,
19555 5ELCID2477 GRADO A CHRISTUS, QUE DEL MUNDO ** SE@OR,
19595 5ELCID2483 LO VNO ** NUESTRO, LO OTRO HAN EN SALUO.
19669 5ELCID2493 GRADO HA DIOS QUE DEL MUNDO ** SE@OR
20465 5ELCID2598 DEBDO NOS ** A CUNPLIR LO QUE MANDAREDES VOS.
21131 5ELCID2684 DIOS LO QUIERA & LO MANDE, QUE DE TODEL MUNDO ** SE@OR,
21912 5ELCID2788 MIENTRA ** EL DIA, ANTE QUE ENTRE LA NOCH,
22223 5ELCID2830 GRADO A CHRISTUS, QUE DEL MUNDO ** SE@OR,
22805 5ELCID2905 CUEMO YO SO SU VASSALLO, & EL ** MYO SE@OR,
22854 5ELCID2911 LA POCA & LA GRANT TODA ** DE MYO SE@OR.
22893 5ELCID2916 CA TAN GRANT ** LA RENCURA DENTRO EN MI CORA%ON.
22944 5ELCID2923 REY ** DE CASTIELLA & REY ES DE LEON
```

WORD C# PREFIX CONTEXT

ES (CON'T)

```
                    22949 5ELCID2923 REY ES DE CASTIELLA & REY ** DE LEON
                    22966 5ELCID2925 FASTA DENTRO EN SANTI YAGUO DE TODO ** SE@OR,
                    23060 5ELCID2938 ELE ** VUESTRO VASSALLO & UOS SODES SO SE@OS.
                    23088 5ELCID2941 HYA UOS SABEDES LA ONDRA QUE ** CUNTIDA ANOS,
                    23157 5ELCID2950 TIENES POR DESONDRADO, MAS LA UUESTRA ** MAYOR,
                    23350 5ELCID2974 ESPIDIOS MU@O GUSTIOZ, A MYO %ID ** TORNADO.
                    23519 5ELCID2995 HYA LO VIERON QUE ** AFER LOS YFANTES DE CARRION,
                    23674 5ELCID3015 AL QUINTO DIA VENIDO ** MYO %ID EL CAMPEADOR;
                    23860 5ELCID3039 MI MUGIER DONA XIMENA, DUE@A ** DE PRO,
                    23961 5ELCID3053 EL REY DON ALFONSSO A TOLLEDO ** ENTRADO,
                    24082 5ELCID3070 COMIGO YRA MAL ANDA, QUE ** BIEN SABIDOR.
                    24239 5ELCID3091 OBRADO ** CON ORO, PARE%EN PORO SON,
                    24271 5ELCID3095 CON ORO ** OBRADA, FECHA POR RAZON,
                    24310 5ELCID3099 DESUSO CUBRIO VN MANTO QUE ** DE GRANT VALOR,
                    24807 5ELCID3169 ATORGAN LOS ALCALDES: TOD ESTO ** RAZON.
                    25452 5ELCID3241 HYA VIERON QUE ** AFER LOS YFANTES DE CARRION.
                    25767 5ELCID3282 POR ESSO ** LUEGA QUEADELI%IO FUE CRIADA.
                    25836 5ELCID3290 LA QUE YO MESSE AVN NON ** EGUADA.
                    26594 5ELCID3395 EL VNO ** YFANTE DE NAUARRA
                    26822 5ELCID3426 QUE CUEMO ** DICHO ASSI SEA, OMEIOR.
                    27638 5ELCID3528 PRESO AUEMOS EL DEBDO & A PASSAR ** POR NOS;
                    27777 5ELCID3545 TROCIDA ** LA NOCHE, YA QUIEBRAN LOS ALBORES.
                    27921 5ELCID3563 HUEBOS VOS ** QUE LIDIEDES AGUISA DE VARONES,
                    28519 5ELCID3641 ASSI LO TENIEN LAS YENTES QUE MAL FERIDO ** DE MUERT.
                    28879 5ELCID3688 TODOS SE CUEDAN QUE FERIDO ** DE MUERT.
                    28897 5ELCID3691 VEN%UDO ** EL CAMPO, QUANDO ESTO SE ACABO
                    29006 5ELCID3705 GRANT ** LA BILTAN%A DE YFANTES DE CARRION.
                    29182 5ELCID3726 PASSADO ** DESTE SIEGLO EL DIA DE CINQUAESMA.
                    29242 5ELCID3734 ** LEYDO, DAT NOS DEL VINO; SI NON TENEDES DINEROS, ECHAD
          WORD #1811 OCCURS 163 TIMES.
             INDEX OF DIVERSIFICATION =   175.04 WITH STANDARD DEVIATION OF   207.79

ESAUA                  12 5ELCID0002 TORNAUA LA CABE%A & ***** LOS CATANDO.
          WORD #1812 OCCURS   1 TIMES.

ESCALENTAR           2635 5ELCID0332 FEZIST ESTRELAS & LUNA & EL SOL PORA **********;
          WORD #1813 OCCURS   1 TIMES.

ESCANO              24436 5ELCID3115 EN AQUESTE ****** QUEMDIESTES UOS ENDON;
          WORD #1814 OCCURS   1 TIMES.

ESCA@O              17518 5ELCID2216 E YUAN POSAR EN VN PRE%IOSO ******.
                    18023 5ELCID2280 YAZIES EN VN ******, DURMIE EL CAMPEADOR,
                    18059 5ELCID2285 E %ERCAN EL ****** & FINCAN SOBRE SO SE@OR.
                    18079 5ELCID2287 METIOS SOL ******, TANTO OUO EL PAUOR.
                    18125 5ELCID2293 VIO CER%ADO EL ****** DE SUS BUENOS VARONES:
                    24459 5ELCID3118 SED EN UUESTRO ****** COMMO REY A SE@OR;
                    24482 5ELCID3121 EN VN ****** TORNI@O ESSORA MYO %ID POSO,
                    24975 5ELCID3181 TORNOS AL ****** DON SE LEUANTO;
                    26147 5ELCID3333 METISTET TRAS EL ****** DE MYO %ID EL CAMPEADOR
                    26162 5ELCID3335 NOS %ERCAMOS EL ****** POR CURIAR NUESTRO SE@OR,
                    26178 5ELCID3337 LEUANTOS DEL ****** & FUES PORAL LEON;
          WORD #1815 OCCURS  11 TIMES.
             INDEX OF DIVERSIFICATION =   865.00 WITH STANDARD DEVIATION OF  1957.79

ESCA@OS             13913 5ELCID1762 E YUAN POSAR CON EL EN VNOS PRE%IOSOS *******;
          WORD #1816 OCCURS   1 TIMES.

ESCAPA               9679 5ELCID1230 AQUEL REY DE MARRUECOS CON TRES COLPES ******.
          WORD #1817 OCCURS   1 TIMES.

ESCAPAN             25511 5ELCID3249 MAL ******* IOGADOS, SABED, DESTA RAZON.
          WORD #1818 OCCURS   1 TIMES.

ESCAPAR              2464 5ELCID0310 POR ORO NIN POR PLATA NON PODRIE *******.
                     5011 5ELCID0633 PERDERAS CALATAYUTH, QUE NON PUEDE *******,
                     9048 5ELCID1151 DE PIES DE CAUALLO LOS QUES PUDIERON *******.
          WORD #1819 OCCURS   3 TIMES.

ESCAPARA            21812 5ELCID2774 SABET BIEN QUE SI ELLOS LE VIESSEN, NON ******** DE MUERT.
          WORD #1820 OCCURS   1 TIMES.

ESCAPARIE           28653 5ELCID3658 VIO DIEGO GON%ALEZ QUE NO ********* CON EL ALMA;
          WORD #1821 OCCURS   1 TIMES.

ESCAPARON           13691 5ELCID1735 NON ********* MAS DE %IENTO & QUATRO.
          WORD #1822 OCCURS   1 TIMES.

ESCAPE              27259 5ELCID3484 DESI SEA VEN%IDO & ****** POR TRAYDOR.
          WORD #1823 OCCURS   1 TIMES.

ESCAPO                592 5ELCID0075 SI CON UUSCO ****** SANO OBIUO,
          WORD #1824 OCCURS   1 TIMES.
```

WORD C# PREFIX CONTEXT

ESCARIN 24266 5ELCID3094 VNA COFIA SOBRE LOS PELOS DUN ******* DE PRO,
WORD #1825 OCCURS 1 TIMES.

ESCARMENTADOS 9192 5ELCID1170 ALOS DE VALEN%IA ************* LOS HAN,
WORD #1826 OCCURS 1 TIMES.

ESCARMENTANDO 19992 5ELCID2536 ELAS NOCHES & LOS DIAS TAN MAL LOS *************,
WORD #1827 OCCURS 1 TIMES.

ESCARMENTAR 8816 5ELCID1121 FIRME MIENTRE SON ESTOS A ***********.
WORD #1828 OCCURS 1 TIMES.

ESCARNE%E 29016 5ELCID3706 QUI BUENA DUENA ********* & LA DEXA DESPUES,
WORD #1829 OCCURS 1 TIMES.

ESCARNIDAS 21360 5ELCID2715 AQUI SEREDES ********** EN ESTOS FIEROS MONTES.
WORD #1830 OCCURS 1 TIMES.

ESCARNIREMOS 20096 5ELCID2551 ************ LAS FIJAS DEL CANPEADOR.
20126 5ELCID2555 ASSI LAS ************ ALAS FIJAS DEL CAMPEADOR,
WORD #1831 OCCURS 2 TIMES.

ESCOGER 24629 5ELCID3138 POR ******* EL DERECHO, CA TUERTO NON MANDO YO.
WORD #1832 OCCURS 1 TIMES.

ESCONBRARON 28262 5ELCID3608 TODAS LAS YENTES *********** ADERREDOR,
WORD #1833 OCCURS 1 TIMES.

ESCRIPTA 4142 5ELCID0527 MOROS EN PAZ, CA ******** ES LA CARTA,
WORD #1834 OCCURS 1 TIMES.

ESCRIPTO 9927 5ELCID1259 METER LOS HE EN ********, & TODOS SEAN CONTADOS,
WORD #1835 OCCURS 1 TIMES.

ESCRIUIEN 15439 5ELCID1956 ********* CARTAS, BIEN LAS SELLO,
WORD #1836 OCCURS 1 TIMES.

ESCRIUIENDO 13999 5ELCID1773 CONTODAS ESTAS YENTES *********** & CONTANDO;
WORD #1837 OCCURS 1 TIMES.

ESCRIUIO 29217 5ELCID3731 QUIEN ******** ESTE LIBRO DEL DIOS PARAYSO, AMEN
29227 5ELCID3732 PER ABBAT LE ******** ENEL MES DE MAYO,
WORD #1838 OCCURS 2 TIMES.

ESCUDEROS 1458 5ELCID0187 %INCO ********* TIENE DON MARTINO, ATODOS LOS CARGAUA.
22916 5ELCID2919 E CON EL ********* QUE SON DE CRIAZON.
WORD #1839 OCCURS 2 TIMES.

ESCUDO 18914 5ELCID2393 EN BRA%O EL ****** & ABAXO EL ASTA,
19340 5ELCID2450 EL ****** TRAE AL CUELLO & TODO ESPADO;
28432 5ELCID3631 QUEBRANTO LA BOCA DEL ******, A PART GELA ECHO,
28776 5ELCID3675 FIRIO ENEL ****** A DON MUNO GUSTIOZ,
28783 5ELCID3676 TRAS EL ****** FALSSO GELA GUARNIZON;
28806 5ELCID3679 TRAS EL ****** FALSSO GELA GUARNIZON,
WORD #1840 OCCURS 6 TIMES.
INDEX OF DIVERSIFICATION = 1977.40 WITH STANDARD DEVIATION OF 3981.03

ESCUDOL 28397 5ELCID3626 FERRANGO%ALEZ A PERO VERMUEZ EL ******* PASSO,
28816 5ELCID3680 POR MEIO DE LA BLOCA DEL ******* QUEBRANTO;
WORD #1841 OCCURS 2 TIMES.

ESCUDOS 5673 5ELCID0715 ENBRA%AN LOS ******* DELANT LOS CORA%ONES,
6239 5ELCID0795 DE ******* & DE ARMAS & DE OTROS AUERES LARGOS;
11904 5ELCID1509 E A CUBERTURAS DE %ENDALES, & ******* ALOS CUELLOS,
15541 5ELCID1970 ******* BOCLADOS CON ORO & CON PLATA,
28074 5ELCID3584 LOS ******* ALOS CUELLOS QUE BIEN BLOCADOS SON;
28320 5ELCID3615 ABRA%AN LOS ******* DELANT LOS CORA%ONES,
28388 5ELCID3625 FIRIENSSE EN LOS ******* SIN TODO PAUOR.
28763 5ELCID3673 FIRIENSSEN EN LOS ******* VNOS TAN GRANDES COLPES;
WORD #1842 OCCURS 8 TIMES.
INDEX OF DIVERSIFICATION = 3297.57 WITH STANDARD DEVIATION OF 4596.34

ESCUELLAS 4160 5ELCID0529 QUITAR QUIERO CASTEJON, OYD, ********* & MINYAYA
10741 5ELCID1360 OYD ME, *********, & TODA LA MI CORT.
10756 5ELCID1362 ATODAS LAS ********* QUE A EL DIZEN SE@OR
16334 5ELCID2072 OYD ME, LAS *********, CUENDES & YFAN%ONES
WORD #1843 OCCURS 4 TIMES.

ESCURA 17039 5ELCID2157 NON QUIERE QUEL ******, QUITOL DESSI LUEGO.
WORD #1844 OCCURS 1 TIMES.

ESCURRA 20786 5ELCID2640 DESI ******* LAS FASTA MEDINA POR LA MI AMOR;
WORD #1845 OCCURS 1 TIMES.

WORD C# PREFIX CONTEXT

ESCURREN 20409 5ELCID2590 POR QUE ******** SUS FIJAS DEL CAMPEADOR ATIERRAS DE CARRION.
WORD #1846 OCCURS 1 TIMES.

ESCURRIENDO 22546 5ELCID2871 LOS DE SANTESTEUAN *********** LOS VAN
WORD #1847 OCCURS 1 TIMES.

ESCURRIOLOS 8396 5ELCID1067 FATA CABO DEL ALBERGADA *********** EL CASTELANO:
WORD #1848 OCCURS 1 TIMES.

ESCURRIR 20881 5ELCID2652 CON DOZIENTOS CAUALLEROS ******** LOS MANDO.
WORD #1849 OCCURS 1 TIMES.

ESFOR%AD 21943 5ELCID2792 ******** UOS, PRIMAS, POR AMOR DEL CRIADOR
WORD #1850 OCCURS 1 TIMES.

ESFOR%ADOS 1341 5ELCID0171 NON LAS PODIEN PONER EN SOMO MAGER ERAU **********.
WORD #1851 OCCURS 1 TIMES.

ESFUER%AN 22041 5ELCID2805 FATA QUE *********, & AMAS LAS TOMO
WORD #1852 OCCURS 1 TIMES.

ESFUER%O 22165 5ELCID2822 ALLAS FIJAS DEL %ID DAN LES ********.
WORD #1853 OCCURS 1 TIMES.

ESFUER%OS 3008 5ELCID0379 %ID, DO SON UUESTROS *********? EN BUEN ORA NASQUIESTES DE MADRE;
WORD #1854 OCCURS 1 TIMES.

ESIDRO 10591 5ELCID1342 SI ME VALA SANT ****** PLAZME DE CORA%ON,
14773 5ELCID1867 GRADO AL CRIADOR & AL SE@OR SANT ****** EL DE LEON
23770 5ELCID3028 PAR SANT ******, VERDAD NON SERA OY
24648 5ELCID3140 JURO PAR SANT ******, EL QUE BOLUIERE MY CORT
27471 5ELCID3509 HYO LO JURO PAR SANT ****** EL DE LEON
WORD #1855 OCCURS 5 TIMES.
INDEX OF DIVERSIFICATION = 4219.00 WITH STANDARD DEVIATION OF 3461.30

ESMERADO 883 5ELCID0113 TIENE DOS ARCAS LENNAS DE ORO ********.
WORD #1856 OCCURS 1 TIMES.

ESON 19686 5ELCID2496 **** MYOS YERNOS YFANTES DE CARRION;
WORD #1857 OCCURS 1 TIMES.

ESORA 28691 5ELCID3664 ***** EL YFANTE TAN GRANDES VOZES DAUA:
WORD #1858 OCCURS 1 TIMES.

ESOS 6282 5ELCID0800 REFECHOS SON TODOS **** CHRISTIANOS CON AQUESTA GANAN%IA.
WORD #1859 OCCURS 1 TIMES.

ESPA%IO 13963 5ELCID1768 LO DE UUESTRAS FIJAS VENIR SEA MAS POR *******.
23335 5ELCID2972 SALUDAD MELOS ATODOS, ENTRELLOS AYA *******;
WORD #1860 OCCURS 2 TIMES.

ESPADA 330 5ELCID0041 YA CAMPEADOR, EN BUEN ORA %INXIESTES ******
462 5ELCID0058 MYO %ID RUY DIAZ, EL QUE EN BUEN ORA %INXO ******,
622 5ELCID0078 FABLO MYO %ID, EL QUE EN BUEN ORA %INXO ******:
1370 5ELCID0175 YA CANPEADOR, EN BUEN ORA %INXIESTES ******
3485 5ELCID0439 YA %ID, EN BUEN ORA %INXIESTES ******
3732 5ELCID0471 EN MANO TRAE DESNUDA EL ******,
3941 5ELCID0500 QUE ENPLEYE LA LAN%A & AL ****** META MANO,
5890 5ELCID0746 LA LAN%A A QUEBRADA, AL ****** METIO MANO,
5966 5ELCID0756 CAUALGO MINAYA, EL ****** EN LA MANO,
6127 5ELCID0780 ****** TAIADOR, SANGRIENTO TRAE EL BRA%O,
6204 5ELCID0790 ALMOFAR ACUESTAS, LA ****** EN LA MANO.
6853 5ELCID0875 MYO %ID RUY DIAZ, QUE EN BUEN ORA CINXO ******. . .
7038 5ELCID0899 QUIERO UOS DEZIR DEL QUE EN BUEN ORA NASCO & %INXO ******:
12408 5ELCID1574 AVN NON SABIE MYO %ID, EL QUE EN BUEN ORA %INXO ******,
12576 5ELCID1595 MER%ED, CAMPEADOR, EN BUEN ORA CINXIESTES ******
13465 5ELCID1706 AUOS, %ID DON RODIRGO, EN BUEN ORA %INXIESTES ******,
13591 5ELCID1722 MYO %ID ENPLEO LA LAN%A, AL ****** METIO MANO,
13621 5ELCID1726 SALIOS LE DE SOL ******, CA MUCHOL ANDIDO EL CAUALLO,
13770 5ELCID1745 ASSI ENTRO SOBRE BAUIECA, EL ****** EN LA MANO.
13829 5ELCID1752 VEDES EL ****** SANGRIENTA & SUDIENTO EL CAUALLO:
15484 5ELCID1961 SALUDAD ME MAYO %ID, EL QUE EN BUEN ORA %INXO ******;
17278 5ELCID2185 VENIDES, CAMPEADOR, EN BUENA ORA %INXIESTES ******
18868 5ELCID2387 EL ASTIL A QUEBRADO & METIO MANO AL ******.
18884 5ELCID2389 DOS MATO CON LAN%A & V CON EL ******.
19070 5ELCID2413 EL ****** TIENES DESNUDA EN LA MANO & VEOT AGUIJAR;
19167 5ELCID2424 FATA LA %INTURA EL ****** LEGADO HA.
20604 5ELCID2615 VIOLO EN LOS AUUEROS EL QUE EN BUEN ORA %INXO ******,
25036 5ELCID3189 TENDIO EL BRA%O, LA ****** TIZON LE DIO;
25058 5ELCID3192 TENDIO EL BRA%O, EL ****** COLADAL DIO;
25111 5ELCID3198 BESO LE LA MANO, EL ****** TOMO & RE%IBIO.
25472 5ELCID3244 TANTA BUENA ****** CONTODA GUARNIZON;
28528 5ELCID3642 EL DEXO LA LAN%A & AL ****** METIO MANO,
28575 5ELCID3648 MARTIN ANTOLINEZ MANO METIO AL ******,

WORD C# PREFIX CONTEXT

ESPADA (CON'T)

28672 5ELCID3660 ESSORA MARTIN ANTOLINEZ RE%IBIOL CON EL ******,
28684 5ELCID3662 DIAGON%ALEZ ****** TIENE EN MANO, MAS NOLA
28705 5ELCID3665 VALME, DIOS GLORIOSO, RE@OR, & CURIAM DESTE ******
28712 5ELCID3666 EL CAUALLO ASORRIENDA, & MESURANDOL DEL ******,
WORD #1861 OCCURS 37 TIMES.
INDEX OF DIVERSIFICATION = 787.39 WITH STANDARD DEVIATION OF 1270.73

ESPADADA 5916 5ELCID0750 DIOL TAL ******** CON EL SO DIESTRO BRA%O,
WORD #1862 OCCURS 1 TIMES.

ESPADAS 4549 5ELCID0578 LAS LORIGAS VESTIDAS & %INTAS LAS *******,
4797 5ELCID0608 LAS ******* DESNUDAS, A LA PUERTA SE PARAUAN.
6411 5ELCID0818 SE@AS ******* DELOS ARZONES COLGADAS.
6537 5ELCID0834 POR LANCAS & POR ******* AUEMOS DE GUARIR,
7163 5ELCID0917 DOZIENTOS CON EL, QUE TODOS %INEN *******;
14311 5ELCID1810 CON SIELLAS & CON FRENOS & CON SE@AS *******;
16510 5ELCID2093 CAMEARON LAS ******* ANTEL REY DON ALFONSSO.
19235 5ELCID2434 CON DOS ******* QUE EL PRE%IAUA ALGO
20290 5ELCID2575 DAR UOS HE DOS *******, A COLADA & A TIZON,
21443 5ELCID2726 DOS ******* TENEDES FUERTES & TAIADORES,
24134 5ELCID3077 SOLOS MANTOS LAS ******* DUL%ES & TAIADORES;
24756 5ELCID3153 DILES DOS *******, A COLADA & A TIZON,
24796 5ELCID3158 DEN ME MIS ******* QUANDO MYOS YERNOS NON SON.
24868 5ELCID3167 DEMOS LE SUS *******, QUANDO ASSI FINCA LA BOZ,
24911 5ELCID3172 NOLO PODEMOS NEGAR, CA DOS ******* NOS DIO;
24929 5ELCID3175 SACARON LAS ******* COLADO & TIZON,
24943 5ELCID3177 SACA LAS ******* & RELUMBRA TODA LA CORT,
24968 5ELCID3180 RE%IBIO LAS *******, LAS MANOS LE BESO,
25134 5ELCID3201 HYA PAGADO SO DE MIS *******, DE COLADA & DE TIZON.
25210 5ELCID3210 POR ESSOL DIEMOS SUS ******* AL%ID CAMPEADOR,
27862 5ELCID3555 QUE NON FUESSEN EN LA BATALLA LAS ******* TAIADORES
WORD #1863 OCCURS 21 TIMES.
INDEX OF DIVERSIFICATION = 1164.65 WITH STANDARD DEVIATION OF 1722.93

ESPADO 19346 5ELCID2450 EL ESCUDO TRAE AL CUELLO & TODO ******;
WORD #1864 OCCURS 1 TIMES.

ESPANTA 25713 5ELCID3274 LOS VNOS LE HAN MIEDO & LOS OTROS *******.
WORD #1865 OCCURS 1 TIMES.

ESPA@A 3598 5ELCID0453 DA QUESTE A CORRO FABLARA TODA ******.
7999 5ELCID1021 NON COMBRE VN BOCADO POR QUANTO HA EN TODA ******,
12543 5ELCID1591 DES DIA SE PRE%IO BAUIECA EN QUANT GRANT FUE ******.
25691 5ELCID3271 MER%ED, YA REY, EL MEIOR DE TODA ******
WORD #1866 OCCURS 4 TIMES.

ESPEDIR 17052 5ELCID2159 BEFAR LAS MANOS, ******* SE DE REY ALFONSSO:
WORD #1867 OCCURS 1 TIMES.

ESPENDIESTES 25430 5ELCID3238 EL ORO & LA PLATA ************ LO VOS;
WORD #1868 OCCURS 1 TIMES.

ESPERAN%A 3872 5ELCID0490 DO YO UOS ENBIAS BIEN ABRIA TAL *********.
WORD #1869 OCCURS 1 TIMES.

ESPERANDO 2993 5ELCID0377 ATODOS *********, LA CABE%A TORNANDO UA.
13781 5ELCID1746 RE%IBIEN LO LAS DUE@AS QUE LO ESTAN *********.
WORD #1870 OCCURS 2 TIMES.

ESPERAR 6058 5ELCID0768 SABET, EL OTRO NON GEL OSO *******.
WORD #1871 OCCURS 1 TIMES.

ESPERASSE 28541 5ELCID3644 ANTES QUE EL COLPE ********* DIXO: VEN%UDO SO.
WORD #1872 OCCURS 1 TIMES.

ESPERO 26191 5ELCID3338 EL LEON PREMIO LA CABE%A, A MYO %ID ******,
WORD #1873 OCCURS 1 TIMES.

ESPESO 636 5ELCID0081 ****** E EL ORO & TODA LA PLATA,
WORD #1874 OCCURS 1 TIMES.

ESPESOS 25284 5ELCID3219 ******* LOS HAN YFANTES DE CARRION.
WORD #1875 OCCURS 1 TIMES.

ESPESSA 12723 5ELCID1615 MIRAN LA HUERTA, ******* ES & GRAND;
WORD #1876 OCCURS 1 TIMES.

ESPESSO 21770 5ELCID2769 EN VN MONTE ******* FELEZ MUNOZ SE METIO,
WORD #1877 OCCURS 1 TIMES.

ESPIDEN 11436 5ELCID1448 HYAS ******* & PIENSSAN DE CAUALGAR,
WORD #1878 OCCURS 1 TIMES.

ESPIDIENDOS 17880 5ELCID2263 *********** DE RUY DIAZ, EL QUE EN BUEN ORA NASCO,
WORD #1879 OCCURS 1 TIMES.

WORD C# PREFIX CONTEXT

```
ESPIDIENSSE         15133 5ELCID1914 *********** AL REY, CON ESTO TORNADOS SON,
          WORD #1880 OCCURS   1 TIMES.

ESPIDIERON          22557 5ELCID2873 CALLENT SE ********** DELLOS, PIENSSAN SE DE TORNAR,
                    27582 5ELCID3522 ESSORA SE **********, & LUEGOS PARTIO LA CORT.
          WORD #1881 OCCURS   2 TIMES.

ESPIDIMIENTO        20421 5ELCID2591 HYA QUIEREN CAUALGAR, EN ************ SON.
          WORD #1882 OCCURS   1 TIMES.

ESPIDIO             10891 5ELCID1378 MINAYA ALBARFANEZ ALBUEN REY SE *******.
                    17029 5ELCID2156 HYAS ******* MYO %ID DE SO SE@OR ALFONSSO,
          WORD #1883 OCCURS   2 TIMES.

ESPIDIOS             1563 5ELCID0200 GRADO EXIR DELA POSADA & ******** DE AMOS.
                    10932 5ELCID1384 ******** MYNAYA & VASSE DELA CORT.
                    23344 5ELCID2974 ******** MU@O GUSTIOZ, A MYO %ID ES TORNADO.
                    27658 5ELCID3531 ******** DE TODOS LOS QUE SOS AMIGOS SON.
          WORD #1884 OCCURS   4 TIMES.

ESPIENDOS           20570 5ELCID2612 ********* DELAS DUE@AS & DE TODAS SUS COMPA@AS.
          WORD #1885 OCCURS   1 TIMES.

ESPIRITAL           12873 5ELCID1633 GRADO AL CRIADOR & A PADRE *********
          WORD #1886 OCCURS   1 TIMES.

ESPOLEAR             1838 5ELCID0233 PORA SAN PERO DE CARDENA QUANTO PUDO A ********,
          WORD #1887 OCCURS   1 TIMES.

ESPOLON             21200 5ELCID2693 POR LOS MONTES CLAROS AGUIJAN A *******;
          WORD #1888 OCCURS   1 TIMES.

ESPOLONADA          18835 5ELCID2383 EL OBISPO DON IHERONIMO PRISO A **********
          WORD #1889 OCCURS   1 TIMES.

ESPOLONAR            5602 5ELCID0705 LA SE@A TIENE EN MANO, CONPE%O DE *********;
          WORD #1890 OCCURS   1 TIMES.

ESPOLONAUAN         15843 5ELCID2009 SALIEN DE VALEN%IA, AGUIJAN & ***********.
          WORD #1891 OCCURS   1 TIMES.

ESPOLONEAUAN         4705 5ELCID0596 MANDO TORNAR LA SE@A, A PRIESSA ************.
          WORD #1892 OCCURS   1 TIMES.

ESPOLONES           25646 5ELCID3265 A QUE LAS FIRIESTES A %INCHAS & A *********?
                    28342 5ELCID3618 BATIEN LOS CAUALLOS CON LOS *********,
          WORD #1893 OCCURS   2 TIMES.

ESPOLONO             5642 5ELCID0711 ******** EL CAUALLO, E METIOL ENEL MAYOR AZ.
          WORD #1894 OCCURS   1 TIMES.

ESPOSAS             17243 5ELCID2181 VERAN ASUS *******, A DON ELUIRA & A DONA SOL.
          WORD #1895 OCCURS   1 TIMES.

ESPUELAS            21411 5ELCID2722 ******** TIENEN CAL%ADAS LOS MALOS TRAYDORES,
                    21529 5ELCID2737 CON LAS ******** AGUDAS, CON ELLAS AN MAL SABOR,
          WORD #1896 OCCURS   2 TIMES.

ESQUILA             13200 5ELCID1673 VIOLO EL ATALAYA & TANXO EL *******;
          WORD #1897 OCCURS   1 TIMES.

ESSA                  440 5ELCID0056 CABO **** VILLA EN LA GLERA POSAUA,
                     3140 5ELCID0395 GRANDES YENTES SELE ACOJEN **** NOCH DE TODAS PARTES.
                     3830 5ELCID0484 CON AQUESTE AUER TORNAN SE **** CONPA@A;
                     5148 5ELCID0651 VINIERON **** NOCHE EN CALATAYUH POSAR.
                    10644 5ELCID1348 DIXO EL REY REY AL CONDE: DEXAD **** RAZON,
                    11732 5ELCID1488 **** NOCH CON DUCHO LES DIO GRAND,
                    17252 5ELCID2182 TODOS **** NOCH FUERON A SUS POSADAS,
                    21266 5ELCID2702 CON QUANTOS QUE ELLOS TRAEN Y IAZEN **** NOCH,
                    22365 5ELCID2849 PRESENTAN A MINAYA **** NOCH GRANT ENFFUR%ION;
                    22435 5ELCID2857 ADELINAN A POSAR PORA FOLGAR **** NOCH.
                    22529 5ELCID2869 HY IAZEN **** NOCHE, & TAN GRAND GOZO QUE FAZEN.
                    23697 5ELCID3018 BIEN LO SOPIESSE QUE Y SERIE **** NOCH.
                    23894 5ELCID3044 **** NOCH MYO %ID TAIO NON QUISO PASSAR;
                    27068 5ELCID3458 QUE VAL, MINAYA, TODA **** RAZON?
          WORD #1898 OCCURS  14 TIMES.
             INDEX OF DIVERSIFICATION =  2047.31 WITH STANDARD DEVIATION OF  1950.04

ESSAS                4284 5ELCID0546 POR ***** TIERRAS AYUSO QUANTO PUEDEN ANDAR.
                     4431 5ELCID0564 POR TODAS ***** TIERRAS YUAN LOS MANDADOS,
                     5155 5ELCID0652 POR TODAS ***** TIERRAS LOS PREGONES DAN;
                     7133 5ELCID0913 TODAS ***** TIERRAS TODAS LAS PREAUA,
```

WORD C# PREFIX CONTEXT

ESSAS (CON'T)

```
                13414 5ELCID1700 NOS DETARDAN DE ABOBASSE ***** YENTES CHRISTIANAS.
       WORD #1899 OCCURS    5 TIMES.
          INDEX OF DIVERSIFICATION =  2281.50 WITH STANDARD DEVIATION OF  2773.08

ESSI            27944 5ELCID3566 **** FUERES VENZIDOS, NON REBTEDES A NOS,
       WORD #1900 OCCURS    1 TIMES.

ESSO             3873 5ELCID0491 **** CON ESTO SEA AIUNTADO;
                11874 5ELCID1506 **** FFUE APRIESSA FECHO, QUE NOS QUIEREN DETARDAR.
                13362 5ELCID1694 PUES **** QUEREDES, %ID, A MI MANDADES AL;
                15422 5ELCID1953 MAS LO QUE EL QUISIERE, **** QUERAMOS NOS.
                15455 5ELCID1958 LO QUE EL REY QUISIERE, **** FERA EL CAMPEADOR.
                18735 5ELCID2371 POR **** SALI DE MI TIERRA & VIN UOS BUSCAR,
                22867 5ELCID2913 **** ME PUEDE PESAR CON LA OTRA DESONOR.
                24170 5ELCID3082 RESPONDIERON TODOS: NOS **** QUEREMOS, SE@OR.
                25084 5ELCID3196 POR **** UOS LA DO QUE LA BIEN CURIEDES UOS.
                25327 5ELCID3225 SI **** PLOGIERE AL %ID, NON GELO VEDAMOS NOS;
                25766 5ELCID3282 POR **** ES LUEGA QUEADELI%IO FUE CRIADA.
                28419 5ELCID3629 FIRME ESTIDO PERO VERMUEZ, POR **** NOS ENCAMO;
       WORD #1901 OCCURS   12 TIMES.
          INDEX OF DIVERSIFICATION =  2230.45 WITH STANDARD DEVIATION OF  2309.91

ESSOL           25207 5ELCID3210 POR ***** DIEMOS SUS ESPADAS AL%ID CAMPEADOR,
       WORD #1902 OCCURS    1 TIMES.

ESSORA           7672 5ELCID0983 ****** LO CONNOS%E MIO %ID EL DE BIUAR.
                10118 5ELCID1282 ****** DIXO MINAYA: DE BUENA VOLUNTAD.
                10386 5ELCID1316 DE MISSA ERA EXIDO ****** EL REY ALFONSSO,
                10693 5ELCID1355 ****** DIXO EL REY: PLAZ ME DE CORA%ON;
                11869 5ELCID1505 ****** DIXO MYNAYA: VAYMOS CAUALGAR.
                13348 5ELCID1692 ****** DIXIERON TODOS: DAMOR & DE VOLUNTAD.
                13394 5ELCID1698 ****** DIXO EL %ID: DE BUENA VOLUNTAD.
                14992 5ELCID1895 EL REY DON ALFONSSO ****** LOS LAMO,
                15375 5ELCID1947 ****** DIXO EL %ID: PLAZME DE CORA%ON.
                16173 5ELCID2052 ****** SELE OMILLAN LOS YFFANTES DE CARRION:
                17432 5ELCID2205 PENSSARON DE ADOBAR ****** EL PALA%IO,
                17473 5ELCID2210 POR LOS YFFANTES DE CARRION ****** ENBIARON,
                18804 5ELCID2380 ****** DIXO MYO %ID: LO QUE UOS QUEREDES PLAZ ME.
                19336 5ELCID2449 MYNAYA ALBARFANEZ ****** ES LEGADO,
                21510 5ELCID2735 ****** LES CONPIE%AN ADAR LOS YFANTES DE CARRION;
                21570 5ELCID2742 QUE ASSOMASSE ****** EL %ID CAMPEADOR
                21661 5ELCID2753  QUAL VENTURA SERIE SI ASSOMAS ****** EL %ID CAMPEADOR
                24448 5ELCID3117 ****** DIXO MUCHAS MER%EDES EL QUE VALEN%IA GA@O:
                24484 5ELCID3121 EN VN ESCA@O TORNI@O ****** MYO %ID POSO,
                24527 5ELCID3127 ****** SE LEUO EN PIE EL BUEN REY DON ALFONSSO;
                24817 5ELCID3161 ****** SALIEN APARTE YFFANTES DE CARRION,
                25201 5ELCID3209 ****** RESPONDEN YFANTES DE CARRION:
                25268 5ELCID3217 ****** SALIEN A PARTE YFANTES DE CARRION;
                25751 5ELCID3280 ****** EL CAMPEADOR PRISOS ALA BARBA;
                26501 5ELCID3382 ****** MUNO GUSTIOZ EN PIE SE LEUANTO;
                26743 5ELCID3416 ****** DIXO EL REY: DIOS UOS DE DEN BUEN GALARDON
                27315 5ELCID3491 ****** RESPUSO EL REY: ASSI LO MANDE DIOS
                27526 5ELCID3516 ****** DIXO EL REY: DESTO NON HE SABOR;
                27580 5ELCID3522 ****** SE ESPIDIERON, & LUEGOS PARTIO LA CORT.
                28051 5ELCID3581 ****** DIXO EL REY: DALMA & DE CORA%ON.
                28366 5ELCID3622 CUEDAN SE QUE ****** CADRAN MUERTOS LOS QUE ESTAN ADERREDOR.
                28666 5ELCID3660 ****** MARTIN ANTOLINEZ RE%IBIOL CON EL ESPADA,
                28722 5ELCID3668 ****** DIXO EL REY: VENID UOS AMI COMPA@A;
       WORD #1903 OCCURS   33 TIMES.
          INDEX OF DIVERSIFICATION =   656.81 WITH STANDARD DEVIATION OF   745.76

ESSOS            3693 5ELCID0466 E ***** GA@ADOS QUANTOS EN DERREDOR ANDAN.
                 6260 5ELCID0797 GRAND ALEGREYA VA ENTRE ***** CHISTIANOS,
                 9724 5ELCID1236 GRAND ALEGRIA ES ENTRE TODOS ***** CHRISTIANOS
       WORD #1904 OCCURS    3 TIMES.

ESSUS           12005 5ELCID1522 MUGIER DEL %ID LIDIADOR ***** FFIJAS NATURALES;
       WORD #1905 OCCURS    1 TIMES.

EST              2018 5ELCID0254 AELLA & ASUS FIJAS & ASUS DUENAS SIRUADES LAS *** A@O.
                27549 5ELCID3518 MAS ATAL CAUALLO CUM *** PORA TAL COMMO VOS,
       WORD #1906 OCCURS    2 TIMES.

ESTA              565 5ELCID0072 **** NOCH YGAMOS & UAYMOS NOS AL MATINO,
                 2330 5ELCID0294 VANSSE PORA SAN PERO DO **** EL QUE ENBUEN PUNTO NA%IO.
                 2523 5ELCID0319 LA MISSA NOS DIRA, **** SERA DE SANTA TRINIDAD;
                 3356 5ELCID0423 LA TIERRA DEL REY ALFONSSO **** NOCH LA PODEMOS QUITAR.
                 3851 5ELCID0487 SALIOLOS RE%EBIR CON **** SU MESNADA,
                 3918 5ELCID0497 ADIOS LO PROMETO, A AQUEL QUE **** EN ALTO:
                 4082 5ELCID0519 **** QUINTA POR QUANTO SERIE CONPRADA,
                 4820 5ELCID0610 MYO %ID GA@O A ALCO%ER, SABENT, POR **** MA@A.
                 4923 5ELCID0623 MYO %ID CON **** GANAN%IA EN ALCO%ER ESTA;
                 4927 5ELCID0623 MYO %ID CON ESTA GANAN%IA EN ALCO%ER ****;
                 5391 5ELCID0680 QUE NON SOPIESSE NINGUNO **** SU PORIDAD.
```

WORD C# PREFIX CONTEXT

ESTA (CON'T)

```
5729 5ELCID0722 TODOS FIEREN ENEL AZ DO **** PERO VERMUEZ.
6220 5ELCID0792 GRADO A DIOS, A QUEL QUE **** EN ALTO,
6228 5ELCID0794 **** ALBERGADA LOS DE MYO %ID LUEGO LA AN ROBADA
6873 5ELCID0878 A UOS, REY ONDRADO, ENBIA **** PRESENTAIA;
6918 5ELCID0884 MAS DESPUES QUE DE MOROS FUE, PRENDO **** PRESENTAIA;
7886 5ELCID1008 VEN%IDO A **** BATALLA EL QUE EN BUEN ORA NASCO;
7916 5ELCID1011 Y BEN%IO **** BATALLA PORO ONDRO SU BARBA,
8218 5ELCID1047 ABREMOS **** VIDA MIENTRA PLOGIERE AL PADRE SANTO,
8319 5ELCID1058 PAGADO ES MYO %ID, QUE LO **** AGUARDANDO,
9104 5ELCID1158 QUE DIOS LE AIUDARA & FIZIERA **** ARRANCADA.
9686 5ELCID1231 TORNADO ES MYO %ID CON TODA **** GANAN%IA.
9702 5ELCID1233 MAS MUCHO FUE PROUECHOSA, SABET, **** ARANCADA:
9786 5ELCID1243 MYO %ID DON RODRIGO EN VALEN%IA **** FOLGANDO,
10249 5ELCID1297 OYD, MINAYA ALBARFANEZ, POR AQUEL QUE **** EN ALTO,
10377 5ELCID1315 CON **** PRESENTEIA ADELINO PORA ALLA;
10864 5ELCID1375 NON LA OSARIEMOS A COMETER NOS **** RAZON,
10884 5ELCID1377 NON LO DIZEN A NADI, & FINCO **** RAZON.
11047 5ELCID1398 SALUDA UOS MYO %ID ALLA ONDDE ELLE ****;
11108 5ELCID1406 ENVIOLOS A MYO %ID, AVALEN%IA DO ****,
11785 5ELCID1494 E EN MEDINA TODO EL RECABDO ****;
12518 5ELCID1588 FIZO VNA CORRIDA, **** FUE TAN ESTRA@A.
12663 5ELCID1607 EN **** HEREDAD QUE UOS YO HE GANADA.
12774 5ELCID1621 DE AQUEL REY YUCEF QUE EN MARRUECOS ****.
13676 5ELCID1733 TODA **** GANAN%IA EN SU MANO A RASTADO.
14133 5ELCID1789 TAL TIENDA COMMO ****, QUE DE MARUECOS ES PASSADA,
14464 5ELCID1829 QUE MANDASSE RE%EBIR A **** CONPA@A:
14764 5ELCID1866 FABLO EL REY DON ALFONSSO & DIXO **** RAZON:
14906 5ELCID1884 VINIEN AL REY ALFONSSO CON **** PORIDAD:
15032 5ELCID1900 OTROS MANDADOS HA EN **** MI CORT:
16109 5ELCID2043 FABLO MYO %ID & DIXO **** RAZON: ESTO GRADESCO AL CRIADOR,
16490 5ELCID2090 GRA%IAS, DIXO EL REY, AUOS & ATOD **** CORT.
16790 5ELCID2126 DIOS QUE **** EN %IELO DEM DENT BUEN GALARDON.
18343 5ELCID2321 YA EN **** BATALLA A ENTRAR ABREMOS NOS;
18510 5ELCID2342 AVN SI DIOS QUISIERE & EL PADRE QUE **** EN ALTO,
18663 5ELCID2362 **** BATALLA EL CRIADOR LA FERA,
19388 5ELCID2456 GRADO ADIOS & AL PADRE QUE **** EN ALTO,
19534 5ELCID2475 DESPUES QUE **** BATALLA VEN%IERON & AL REY BUCAR MATO;
19814 5ELCID2512 AQUI **** CON MYO %ID EL OBISPO DO IHERONIMO,
20984 5ELCID2666 QUANDO **** FALSSEDAD DIZEN LOS DE CARRION,
21563 5ELCID2741  QUAL VENTURA SERIE ****, SI PLOGUIESSE AL CRIADOR,
22401 5ELCID2853 MUCHO UOS LO GRADE%E, ALLA DO ****, MYO %ID EL CANPEADOR,
22698 5ELCID2892 PLEGA AL CRIADOR, QUE EN %IELO ****,
23250 5ELCID2961 LO QUE NON CUYDAUA FER DE TODA **** SAZON,
23326 5ELCID2971 POR AMOR DE MYO %ID **** CORT YO FAGO.
23928 5ELCID3048 LAS MIS COMPA@AS **** NOCHE LEGARAN;
24564 5ELCID3131 **** TER%ERA A TOLLEDO LA VIN FER OY,
24707 5ELCID3147 POR QUANTO **** CORT FIZIESTES POR MI AMOR.
25674 5ELCID3269 SI NON RECUDEDES, VEA LO **** CORT.
26115 5ELCID3329 DI, FERRANDO, OTORGA **** RAZON:
26561 5ELCID3390 DIXO EL REY ALFONSSO: CALLE YA **** RAZON.
26574 5ELCID3392 ASSI COMMO ACABAN **** RAZON,
26716 5ELCID3412 ESTE CASAMIENTO OY SE OTORGE EN **** CORT,
26832 5ELCID3427 A MUCHOS PLAZE DE TOD **** CORT,
26870 5ELCID3432 BIEN UOS DI VAGAR EN TODA **** CORT,
27072 5ELCID3459 CA EN **** CORT AFARTO HA PORA VOS,
27104 5ELCID3463 DIXO EL REY: FINE **** RAZON;
27163 5ELCID3472 SEA **** LIS O MANDAREDES VOS.
27242 5ELCID3482 QUE FAGAN **** LID DELANT ESTANDO YO;
27793 5ELCID3547 POR VER **** LID, CA AVIEN ENDE SABOR;
28174 5ELCID3597 **** LID EN TOLEDO LAFIZIERADES, MAS NON QUISIESTES VOS.
28736 5ELCID3669 POR QUANTO AUEDES FECHO VEN%IDA AUEDES **** BATALLA.
28936 5ELCID3696 VEN%IERON **** LID, GRADO AL CRIADOR.
29214 5ELCID3730 EN ESTE LOGAR SE ACABA **** RAZON.
WORD #1907 OCCURS 74 TIMES.
   INDEX OF DIVERSIFICATION =   391.45 WITH STANDARD DEVIATION OF   364.84
```

ESTACAS

```
8974 5ELCID1142 ARANCAR SE LAS ******* & ACOSTAR SE ATODAS PARTES LOS TENDALES.
18972 5ELCID2400 VERIEDES QUEBRAR TANTAS CUERDAS & ARRANCAR SE LAS *******
WORD #1908 OCCURS 2 TIMES.
```

ESTADES

```
2155 5ELCID0271 YO LO VEO QUE ******* UOS EN YDA
13054 5ELCID1655 CRE%EM EL CORACON POR QUE ******* DELANT,
WORD #1909 OCCURS 2 TIMES.
```

ESTAN

```
2422 5ELCID0305 PLOGO ALOS OTROS OMNES TODOS QUANTOS CON EL *****.
3064 5ELCID0385 E A TODAS SUS DUENAS QUE CON ELLAS *****;
4255 5ELCID0541 LOS MOROS & LAS MORAS BENDIZIENDOL *****.
4783 5ELCID0606 DANDO GRANDES ALARIDOS LOS QUE ***** EN LA %ELADA,
7524 5ELCID0964 AGORA CORREM LAS TIERRAS QUE EN MI ENPARA *****;
11002 5ELCID1392 ADELINO PORA SAN PERO, OLAS DUE@AS *****,
11709 5ELCID1484 SU MUGIER & SUS FIJAS EN MEDINA *****;
12748 5ELCID1618 MYO %ID & SUS COMPANAS TAN AGRAND SABOR *****.
13191 5ELCID1672 POR LAS HUERTAS ADENTRO ***** SINES PAUOR.
13780 5ELCID1746 RE%IBIEN LO LAS DUE@AS QUE LO ***** ESPERANDO.
```

WORD C# PREFIX CONTEXT

ESTAN (CON'T)

16075 5ELCID2038 E A ESTAS MESNADAS QUE ***** A DERREDOR.
17528 5ELCID2218 ***** PARANDO MIENTES ALQUE EN BUEN ORA NASCO.
18218 5ELCID2305 MAGER LOS ***** LAMANDO, NINGUNO NON RESPONDE.
24227 5ELCID3089 AL PUNO BIEN *****, CA EL SELO MANDO;
24495 5ELCID3123 CATANDO ***** A MYO %ID QUANTOS HA EN LA CORT,
28371 5ELCID3622 CUEDAN SE QUE ESSORA CADRAN MUERTOS LOS QUE ***** ADERREDOR.
WORD #1910 OCCURS 16 TIMES.
INDEX OF DIVERSIFICATION = 1728.93 WITH STANDARD DEVIATION OF 1647.71

ESTANDO
2776 5ELCID0351 ******* EN LA CRUZ, VERTUD FEZIST MUY GRANT.
7064 5ELCID0903 ******* ALLI, MUCHA TIERRA PREAUA,
16017 5ELCID2032 ASSI *******, DEDES ME UUESTRA AMOR, QUE LO OYAN QUANTOS AQUI SON.
18266 5ELCID2311 ELLOS ENESTO *******, DON AUIEN GRANT PESAR,
24925 5ELCID3174 DAR GELAS QUEREMOS DELLANT ******* UOS.
27245 5ELCID3482 QUE FAGAN ESTA LID DELANT ******* YO;
WORD #1911 OCCURS 6 TIMES.
INDEX OF DIVERSIFICATION = 4892.80 WITH STANDARD DEVIATION OF 2897.39

ESTAR
5047 5ELCID0637 TRES REYES VEC DE MOROS DERREDOR DE MI *****,
10305 5ELCID1304 DIERON LE EN VALENZIA O BIEN PUEDE ***** RICO.
15909 5ELCID2017 ATODOS LOS SOS ***** LOS MANDO,
WORD #1912 OCCURS 3 TIMES.

ESTAS
56 5ELCID0008 GRADO ATI, SE@OR PADRE, QUE ***** EN ALTO
987 5ELCID0127 ***** ARCHAS PRENDAMOS LAS AMAS,
1657 5ELCID0213 ***** PALABRAS DICHAS, LA TIENDA ES COGIDA.
2246 5ELCID0282 PLEGA ADIOS & A SANTA MARIA, QUE AUN CON MIS MANOS CASE ***** MIS
2618 5ELCID0330 YA SE@OR GLORIOSO, PADRE QUE EN %IELO *****,
3984 5ELCID0506 ***** GANAN%IAS ALLI ERAN IUNTADAS.
5971 5ELCID0757 POR ***** FUER%AS FUERTE MIENTRE LIDIANDO,
7353 5ELCID0943 CON ***** GANAN%IAS ALA POSADA TORNANDO SEUAN,
7405 5ELCID0950 DEXAT ***** POSADAS & YREMOS ADELANT.
8079 5ELCID1031 ELLOS PARTIENDO ***** GANAN%IAS GRANDES,
8807 5ELCID1120 SI EN ***** TIERRAS QUISIEREMOS DURAR,
9060 5ELCID1153 ENTRAUAN A MURUIEDRO CON ***** GANAN%IAS QUE TRAEN GRANDES.
10165 5ELCID1287 EN ***** NUEUAS TODOS SEA ALEGRANDO,
11230 5ELCID1421 POR YR CON ***** DUENAS BUE@A CONPANA SE FAZE.
11292 5ELCID1429 QUANDO ***** DUE@AS ADOBADAS LAS HAN,
11931 5ELCID1512 O CUEMO SALIERA DE CASTIELLA ALBARFANEZ CON ***** DUE@AS QUE TRAHE.
11996 5ELCID1521 TRAEDES ***** DUE@AS PORO VALDREMOS MAS,
12269 5ELCID1558 CON ***** ALEGRIAS & NUEUAS TAN ONDRADAS
12860 5ELCID1632 ***** NUEUAS A MYO %ID ERAN VENIDAS;
12942 5ELCID1642 EN ***** TIERRAS AGENAS VERAN LAS MORADAS COMMO SE FAZEN,
13922 5ELCID1764 ***** DUE@AS QUE ADUXIESTES, QUE UOS SIRUEN TANTO,
13997 5ELCID1773 CONTODAS ***** YENTES ESCRIUIENDO & CONTANDO;
14842 5ELCID1876 TODAS ***** NUEUAS A BIEN ABRAN DE VENIR.
15382 5ELCID1948 ***** VISTAS OLAS AYADES UOS,
16072 5ELCID2038 E A ***** MESNADAS QUE ESTAN A DERREDOR.
17640 5ELCID2232 DOUOS ***** DUE@AS, AMAS SON FIJAS DALGO,
18369 5ELCID2325 VINO CON ***** NUEUAS A MUO %ID RUYDIAZ EL CANPEADOR:
18761 5ELCID2374 EA ***** FERIDAS YO QUIERO YR DELANT;
19202 5ELCID2429 CON ***** GRANAN%IAS YAS YUAN TORNANDO;
19658 5ELCID2492 TODAS ***** GANAN%IAS FIZO EL CANPEADOR.
23535 5ELCID2997 EL CONDE DON GAR%IA EN ***** NUEUAS FUE,
24762 5ELCID3154 ***** YO LAS GANE AGUISA DE VARON,
25352 5ELCID3228 A ***** PALABRAS FABLO EL REY DON ALFONSSO:
25516 5ELCID3250 ***** APRE%IADURAS MYO %ID PRESAS LAS HA,
27434 5ELCID3505 QUANDO TODAS ***** NUEUAS ASSI PUESTAS SON,
28088 5ELCID3586 ***** TRES LAN%AS TRAEN SENOS PENDONES;
29200 5ELCID3729 ***** SON LAS NUEUAS DE MYO %ID EL CANPEADOR,
WORD #1913 OCCURS 37 TIMES.
INDEX OF DIVERSIFICATION = 808.56 WITH STANDARD DEVIATION OF 725.71

ESTAUA
1876 5ELCID0239 Y ****** DO@A XIMENA CON %INCO DUENAS DE PRO,
3838 5ELCID0485 FELLOS EN CASTEION, O EL CAMPEADOR ******.
6798 5ELCID0868 LA TER%ERA TERUEL, QUE ****** DELANT;
12119 5ELCID1537 ONDRADO ES MYO %ID EN VALENZIA DO ******
14452 5ELCID1827 LEGAN A VALADOLID, DO EL REY ALFONSSO ******;
19219 5ELCID2431 ALAS TIENDAS ERAN LEGADOS, DO ******
22992 5ELCID2929 ADELINO PORAL PALA%IO DO ****** LA CORT,
WORD #1914 OCCURS 7 TIMES.
INDEX OF DIVERSIFICATION = 3518.33 WITH STANDARD DEVIATION OF 1342.58

ESTAUALOS
1197 5ELCID0154 SONRRISOS MYO %ID, ********* FABLANDO:
WORD #1915 OCCURS 1 TIMES.

ESTAUAN
786 5ELCID0100 RACHEL & VIDAS EN VNO ******* AMOS,
12626 5ELCID1601 TODAS LAS SUS MESNADAS EN GRANT DELENT *******,
WORD #1916 OCCURS 2 TIMES.

ESTE
4875 5ELCID0617 EN **** CASTIELLO GRAND AUER AUEMOS PRESO,
5578 5ELCID0702 QUEDAS SED, MENADAS, AQUI EN **** LOGAR,
5947 5ELCID0754 OY EN **** DIA DE UOS ABRE GRAND BANDO;
7803 5ELCID0999 OY EN **** PINAR DE TEUAR POR TOLER ME LA GANAN%IA.

WORD C# PREFIX CONTEXT

ESTE (CON'T)

```
                    10272 5ELCID1300 E DAR GELO A **** BUEN CHRISTIANO;
                    13023 5ELCID1652 MUGIER, SED EN **** PALAZIO, & SI QUISIEREDES EN EL ALCAZAR;
                    16966 5ELCID2148 REZIBO **** DON QUE ME AUEDES MANDADO;
                    16980 5ELCID2149 PLEGA AL CRIADOR CON TODOS LOS SOS SANTOS, **** PLAZER
                    17063 5ELCID2160 MERZED UOS SEA & FAZED NOS **** PERDON:
                    18795 5ELCID2379 SI **** AMOR NON FECHES, YO DEUOS ME QUIERO QUITAR.
                    19482 5ELCID2468 LOS YERNOS DE MYO ZID QUANDO **** AUER TOMARON
                    26068 5ELCID3323 FASTA **** DIA NOLO DESCUBRI A NACI;
                    26710 5ELCID3412 **** CASAMIENTO OY SE OTORGE EN ESTA CORT,
                    26759 5ELCID3418 **** CASAMIENTO OTORGO UOS LE YO
                    28641 5ELCID3657 QUANDO **** COLPE A FERIDO COLADA LA PREZIADA,
                    28797 5ELCID3678 **** COLPE FECHO, OTRO DIO MUNO GUSTIOZ,
                    29210 5ELCID3730 EN **** LOGAR SE ACABA ESTA RAZON.
                    29218 5ELCID3731 QUIEN ESCRIUIO **** LIBRO DEL DIOS PARAYSO, AMEN
         WORD #1917 OCCURS   18 TIMES.
            INDEX OF DIVERSIFICATION =  1430.94 WITH STANDARD DEVIATION OF  1757.74

ESTEUA              19271 5ELCID2439 ALZO SOS OIOS, ****** ADELANT CATANDO,
         WORD #1918 OCCURS    1 TIMES.

ESTEUAN              3155 5ELCID0397 DE SINIESTRO SANT *******, VNA BUENA ZIPDAD,
                    21217 5ELCID2696 ADIESTRO DEXAN ASANT *******, MAS CAE ALUEN;
         WORD #1919 OCCURS    2 TIMES.

ESTIDO              28415 5ELCID3629 FIRME ****** PERO VERMUEZ, POR ESSO NOS ENCAMO;
         WORD #1920 OCCURS    1 TIMES.

ESTIL               28411 5ELCID3628 BIEN EN DOS LOGARES EL ***** LE QUEBRO.
         WORD #1921 OCCURS    1 TIMES.

ESTO                   59 5ELCID0009 **** ME AN BUELTO MYOS ENEMIGOS MALOS.
                      388 5ELCID0049 **** LA NI@A DIXO & TORNOS PORA SU CASA.
                     1466 5ELCID0188 QUANDO **** OUO FECHO, ODREDES LO QUE FABLAUA:
                     1486 5ELCID0190 YO, QUE **** UOS GANE, BIEN MEREZIAS CALZAS.
                     1541 5ELCID0197 MEREZER NOLO HEDES, CA **** ES AGUISADO:
                     1547 5ELCID0198 ATORGAR NOS HEDES **** QUE AUEMOS PARADO.
                     1762 5ELCID0225 **** & YO EN DEBDO QUE FAGA Y CANTAR MILL MISSAS.
                     3020 5ELCID0380 PENSEMOS DE YR NUESTRA VIA, **** SEA DE VAGAR.
                     3759 5ELCID0475 DEXAN LA A MYO ZID, TODO **** NON PREZIA NADA.
                     3875 5ELCID0491 ESSO CON **** SEA AIUNTADO;
                     6418 5ELCID0819 DIXO MYNAYA ALBARFANEZ:  **** FARE YO DE GRADO.
                     7004 5ELCID0896 **** FECHES AGORA, AL FEREDES ADELANT.
                     7144 5ELCID0915 QUANDO **** FECHO OUO, A CABO DE TRES SEMANAS,
                     7646 5ELCID0979 RESPUSO EL CONDE:  **** NON SERA VERDAD
                     7818 5ELCID1000 TODOS SON ADOBADOS QUANDO MYO ZID **** OUO FABLADO;
                     7856 5ELCID1005 **** FAZEN LOS SOS DE VOLUNTAD & DE GRADO;
                     8126 5ELCID1036 QUANDO **** OYO EL CONDE, YAS YUA ALEGRANDO:
                     8624 5ELCID1095 EL CON TODO **** PRISO A MURUIEDRO.
                     9395 5ELCID1195 **** DIXO MYO ZID EL QUE EN BUEN ORA NASCO.
                     9859 5ELCID1251 **** MANDO MYO ZID, MINAYA LO OUO CONSSEIADO:
                    10125 5ELCID1283 PUES **** AN FABLADO, PIENSSAN SE DE ADOBAR.
                    10827 5ELCID1371 MAS GANAREMOS EN **** QUE EN OTRA DESONOR.
                    10953 5ELCID1386 EN TODO SODES PRO, EN **** ASSI LO FAGADES:
                    10984 5ELCID1390 RESPUSO MYNAYA: **** NON MEA POR QUE PESAR.
                    11207 5ELCID1418 DIZIENDO **** MYANAYA: ESTO FERE DE VELUNTAD.
                    11209 5ELCID1418 DIZIENDO ESTO MYANAYA: **** FERE DE VELUNTAD.
                    11622 5ELCID1473 **** ERA DICHO, PIENSSAN DE CAUALGAR,
                    11795 5ELCID1496 **** NON DETARDO, CA DE CORAZON LO HAN;
                    12976 5ELCID1646  QUES ****, ZID, SI EL CRIADOR UOS SALUE
                    13808 5ELCID1750 **** DIOS SE LO QUISO CON TODOS LOS SOS SANTOS,
                    13838 5ELCID1753 CON TAL CUM **** SE VENZEN MOROS DEL CAMPO.
                    13859 5ELCID1756 **** DIXO MYO ZID, DIZIENDO DEL CAUALLO.
                    14053 5ELCID1780 MAGER DE TODO ****, EL CAMPEADOR CONTADO
                    14592 5ELCID1846 POR MYO ZID EL CAMPEADOR TODO **** VOS BESAMOS;
                    14687 5ELCID1858 **** PLOGO A MUCHOS & BESARON LE LAS MANOS.
                    14750 5ELCID1865 POR **** QUE EL FAZE NOS ABREMOS ENBARGO.
                    15137 5ELCID1914 ESPIDIENSSE AL REY, CON **** TORNADOS SON,
                    15212 5ELCID1926 **** DIZIENDO, CONPIEZAN LA RAZON,
                    15261 5ELCID1933 **** GRADESCO A CHRISTUS EL MYO SE@OR.
                    15348 5ELCID1943 CON TODO ****, AUOS DIXO ALFONSSO
                    16031 5ELCID2033 DIXO EL REY **** FERE DALMA & DE CORAZON;
                    16111 5ELCID2043 FABLO MYO ZID & DIXO ESTA RAZON: **** GRADESCO AL CRIADOR,
                    16915 5ELCID2141 TOD **** ES PUESTO, SABED, EN GRANT RECABDO.
                    17094 5ELCID2164 **** PLOGO AL REY, & ATODOS LOS SOLTO;
                    17604 5ELCID2227 ESTOZ DIXO MINAYA: **** FARE YO DE GRADO.
                    18114 5ELCID2292 EN **** DESPERTO EL QUE EN BUEN ORA NAZIO;
                    18131 5ELCID2294 QUES ****, MESNADAS, O QUE QUEREDES UOS?
                    18349 5ELCID2322 **** ES AGUISADO POR NON VER CARRION,
                    18521 5ELCID2344 **** VAN DIZIENDO & LAS YENTES SE ALEGANDO,
                    19110 5ELCID2417 AQUI RESPUSO MYO ZID: **** NON SERA VERDAD.
                    20361 5ELCID2583 ATORGADO LO HAN **** LOS YFFANTES DE CARRION.
                    20922 5ELCID2658 TOD **** LES FIZO EL MORO POR EL AMOR DEL ZID CAMPEADOR.
                    21140 5ELCID2686 **** LES HA DICHO, & EL MORO SE TORNO;
                    21426 5ELCID2724 QUANDO **** VIERON LAS DUE@AS, FABLAUA DO@A SOL:
```

WORD C# PREFIX CONTEXT

ESTO (CON'T)

```
                22155 5ELCID2821 QUANDO SABIEN ****, PESCLES DE CORA%ON;
                22182 5ELCID2825 DE CUER PESO **** AL BUEN REY CON ALFONSSO.
                22391 5ELCID2852 POR AQUESTA ONDRA QUE VCS DIESTES A **** QUE NOS CUNTIO;
                22412 5ELCID2854 ASSI LO FFAGO YO QUE AQUI ****.
                23133 5ELCID2948 POR **** UOS BESA LAS MANOS, COMMO VASSALLO A SE@OR,
                23197 5ELCID2955 E VERDAD DIZES EN ****, TU, MU@O GUSTIOZ,
                24298 5ELCID3098 POR TALLO FAZE **** CUE RECABCAR QUIERE TODO LO SUYO;
                24713 5ELCID3148 **** LES DEMANDO AYFANTES DE CARRION:
                24806 5ELCID3169 ATCRGAN LOS ALCALDES: TCD **** ES RAZON.
                25169 5ELCID3205 HYO FAZIENDO ****, ELLCS ACABARON LO SO;
                25532 5ELCID3252 MAS QUANDO **** OUC ACABADO, PENSSARON LUEGO DAL.
                26340 5ELCID3359 LO QUE LES FIZIEMOS SER LES HA RETRAYDO; **** LIDIARE
                                 ATOD EL MAS
                26656 5ELCID3404 **** GRADESCC YO AL CRIADOR,
                26860 5ELCID3431 E QUE NON PESE **** AL %ID CAMPEADOR:
                26972 5ELCID3446 **** GRADESCC YC ALCRIADCR,
                28901 5ELCID3691 VEN%UDO ES EL CAMPO, QUANDO **** SE ACABO
                28907 5ELCID3692 DIXIERCN LCS FIELES: **** CYMOS NOS.
        WORD #1922 OCCURS  71 TIMES.
           INDEX OF DIVERSIFICATION =   411.11 WITH STANDARD DEVIATION OF   460.50

ESTOL           23317 5ELCID2970 VENGAM A TOLLEDC, ***** DO DE PLAZO.
        WORD #1923 OCCURS   1 TIMES.

ESTON%ES         7410 5ELCID0951 ******** SE MUDO EL %ID AL PUERTO DE ALCAT,
        WORD #1924 OCCURS   1 TIMES.

ESTOS            1840 5ELCID0234 CON ***** CAUALLEROS QUEL SIRUEN ASO SABOR.
                 2761 5ELCID0349 DOS LADRONES CONTIGO, ***** DE SE@AS PARTES
                 3025 5ELCID0381 AUNTODOS ***** DUELCS EN GOZO SE TORNARAN;
                 5192 5ELCID0657 CRECEN ***** VIRTCS, CA YENTES SON SOBEIANAS.
                 6314 5ELCID0804 DIO APARTIR ***** DINEROS & ESTOS AUERES LARGOS;
                 6317 5ELCID0804 DIO APARTIR ESTOS DINEROS & ***** AUERES LARGOS;
                 6838 5ELCID0874  QUIN LOS DIO *****, SI UOS VALA DIOS, MYNAYA
                 8196 5ELCID1044 CA HUEBOS MELO HE & PORA ***** MYOS VASSALLOS
                 8306 5ELCID1057 CON ***** DOS CAUALLEROS A PRIESSA VA IANTANDO;
                 8814 5ELCID1121 FIRME MIENTRE SON ***** A ESCARMENTAR.
                10604 5ELCID1344 RE%IBO ***** CAUALLOS QUEM ENBIA DE DON.
                14331 5ELCID1813 ***** DOZIENTOS CAUALLOS YRAN EN PRESENTAIAS,
                14497 5ELCID1834 AUER ***** MENSAIES DEL QUE EN BUEN ORA NASCO.
                14777 5ELCID1868 ***** DOZIENTOS CAUALLOS QUEM ENBIA MYO %ID.
                15733 5ELCID1997 ***** SE ADOBAN POR YR CON EL CAMPEADOR,
                15915 5ELCID2018 SI NON A ***** CAUALLEROS QUE QUERIE DE CORA%ON;
                16940 5ELCID2144 TRAYO VOS XX PALAFRES, ***** BIEN ADOBADOS,
                16947 5ELCID2145 E XXX CAUALLOS COREDORES, ***** BIEN ENSSELLADOS;
                17922 5ELCID2268 ***** FUERON FIJOS DEL CONDE DON GON%ALO.
                19407 5ELCID2459 TODOS ***** BIENES DEUOS SON & DE UUESTROS VASSALLOS.
                19997 5ELCID2537 TAN MAL SE CONSSEIARON ***** YFFANTES AMOS.
                20606 5ELCID2616 QUE ***** CASAMIENTOS NON SERIEN SIN ALGUNA TACHA.
                21362 5ELCID2715 AQUI SEREDES ESCARNIDAS EN ***** FIEROS MONTES.
                24092 5ELCID3072 CON ***** CUNPLANSSE %IENTO DELOS BUENOS QUE Y SON.
                24613 5ELCID3136 E ***** OTROS CONDES QUE DEL VANDO NON SODES.
                26305 5ELCID3355 ***** CASAMIENTOS NON FUESSEN APARE%IDOS
                27280 5ELCID3487 ***** MIS TRES CAUALLEROS EN UUESTRA MANO SON,
                28183 5ELCID3598 ***** TRES CAUALLEROS DE MYO %ID EL CAMPEADOR
        WORD #1925 OCCURS  28 TIMES.
           INDEX OF DIVERSIFICATION =   974.67 WITH STANDARD DEVIATION OF   867.23

ESTOT           26227 5ELCID3344 ***** LIDIARE AQUI ANTEL REY DON ALFONSSO
        WORD #1926 OCCURS   1 TIMES.

ESTOZ           17601 5ELCID2227 ***** DIXO MINAYA: ESTO FARE YO DE GRADO.
                21193 5ELCID2692 LA SIERRA DE MIEDES PASSARON LA *****,
        WORD #1927 OCCURS   2 TIMES.

ESTRANA          4629 5ELCID0587 SALIERON DE ALCO%ER AVNA PRIESSA MUCH *******.
        WORD #1928 OCCURS   1 TIMES.

ESTRANAS         1378 5ELCID0176 DE CASTIELLA UOS YDES PORA LAS YENTES ********.
                 6583 5ELCID0840 MOROS DE LAS FRONTERAS & VNAS YENTES ********;
                10113 5ELCID1281 AESTAS TIERRAS ******** QUE NOS PUDIEMOS GANAR.
        WORD #1929 OCCURS   3 TIMES.

ESTRA@A          8841 5ELCID1125 COMMO OMNES EXIDOS DE TIERRA *******,
                12521 5ELCID1588 FIZO VNA CORRIDA, ESTA FUE TAN *******.
        WORD #1930 OCCURS   2 TIMES.

ESTRELAS         2628 5ELCID0332 FEZIST ******** & LUNA & EL SOL PORA ESCALENTAR;
        WORD #1931 OCCURS   1 TIMES.

ESTRIBERA         302 5ELCID0038 SACO EL PIE DEL *********, UNA FERIDAL DAUA;
        WORD #1932 OCCURS   1 TIMES.

ESTROPIE%A      19092 5ELCID2415 MAS SI EL CAUALLO NON ********** O COMIGO NON CAYE,
        WORD #1933 OCCURS   1 TIMES.
```

```
WORD                C#  PREFIX                        CONTEXT

ETERO              4372 5ELCID0557 BIEN PUEBLA EL *****, FIRME PRENDE LAS POSADAS,
       WORD #1934 OCCURS   1 TIMES.

ETODAS            17320 5ELCID2191 ****** LAS DUE@AS QUE LAS SIRUEN:
       WORD #1935 OCCURS   1 TIMES.

ETORNARON         18201 5ELCID2303 ********* SEAL APALA%IO PORA LA CORT.
       WORD #1936 OCCURS   1 TIMES.

ETRO                338 5ELCID0042 EL REY LO HA UEDADO, ANOCH DEL **** SU CARTA,
       WORD #1937 OCCURS   1 TIMES.

EUADES             2001 5ELCID0253 ****** AQUI PORA DO@A XIMENA DOUOS C MARCHOS.
                   6423 5ELCID0820 ****** AQUI ORO & PLATA VNA UESA LE@A,
                  18377 5ELCID2326 ****** QUE PAUOR HAN UUESTROS YERNOS TAN OSADOS,
                  19862 5ELCID2519 ****** AQUI, YERNOS, LA MI MUGIER DE PRO,
       WORD #1938 OCCURS   4 TIMES.

EUOS              18669 5ELCID2363 **** TAN DINNO QUE CON EL AUEDES PART.
                  18786 5ELCID2378 ****, MYO %ID, DE MI MAS UOS PAGAR.
                  22462 5ELCID2861 **** A EL LO GRADID, QUANDO BIUAS SOMOS NOS.
       WORD #1939 OCCURS   3 TIMES.

EUUESTROS         19415 5ELCID2460 ********* YERNOS AQUI SON ENSAYADOS,
       WORD #1940 OCCURS   1 TIMES.

EVAD              16766 5ELCID2123 **** AQUI UUESTROS FIJOS, QUANDO UUESTROS YERNOS SON;
       WORD #1941 OCCURS   1 TIMES.

EVAY              17162 5ELCID2172 **** ASUR GON%ALEZ, QUE ERA BULIDOR,
       WORD #1942 OCCURS   1 TIMES.

EXCO               1209 5ELCID0156 YA ME **** DE TIERRA, CA DEL REY SO AYRADO.
       WORD #1943 OCCURS   1 TIMES.

EXE                8589 5ELCID1091 AORIENT *** EL SOL, E TORNOS AESSA PART.
       WORD #1944 OCCURS   1 TIMES.

EXIDA                75 5ELCID0011 ALA ***** DE BIUAR OUIERON LA CORNEIA DIESTRA,
                   1731 5ELCID0221 VUESTRA UERTUD ME UALA, GLORIOSA, EN MY ***** & ME AIUDE,
       WORD #1945 OCCURS   2 TIMES.

EXIDAS             9138 5ELCID1163 GANARON PENA CADIELLA, LAS ****** & LAS ENTRADAS.
                  12385 5ELCID1572 E TODAS LAS PUERTAS & LAS ****** & LAS ENTRADAS,
       WORD #1946 OCCURS   2 TIMES.

EXIDO              1566 5ELCID0201 ***** ES DE BURGOS & ARLAN%ON A PASXADO,
                   2468 5ELCID0311 EL DIA ES *****, LA NOCH QUERIE ENTRAR,
                   4448 5ELCID0566 VENIDO ES A MOROS, ***** ES DE CHRISTIANOS;
                  10385 5ELCID1316 DE MISSA ERA ***** ESSORA EL REY ALFONSSO,
                  12752 5ELCID1619 EL YUIERNO ES *****, QUE EL MAR%O QUIERE ENTRAR.
       WORD #1947 OCCURS   5 TIMES.
          INDEX OF DIVERSIFICATION =  2795.50 WITH STANDARD DEVIATION OF  2183.50

EXIDOS             3653 5ELCID0461 TODOS SON ******, LAS PUERTAS DEXADAS AN ABIERTAS
                   5319 5ELCID0672 DE CASTIELLA LA GENTIL ****** SOMOS ACA,
                   8838 5ELCID1125 COMMO OMNES ****** DE TIERRA ESTRA@A,
                  12842 5ELCID1629 ARRIBADO AN LAS NAUES, FUERA ERAN ******,
       WORD #1948 OCCURS   4 TIMES.

EXIEN               117 5ELCID0016 EN SU CONPA@A LX PENDONES; ***** LO UER MUGIERES & UARONES,
       WORD #1949 OCCURS   1 TIMES.

EXIERON            9801 5ELCID1245 LOS QUE ******* DE TIERRA DE RITAD SON ABONDADOS,
       WORD #1950 OCCURS   1 TIMES.

EXIR               1559 5ELCID0200 GRADO **** DELA POSADA & ESPIDIOS DE AMOS.
                   5236 5ELCID0662 MESNADAS DE MYO %ID **** QUERIEN ALA BATALLA,
                   5277 5ELCID0667 EL AGUA NOS AN VEDADA, **** NOS HA EL PAN,
                   6726 5ELCID0859 AL **** DE SALON MUCHO OUO BUENAS AUES.
                   9198 5ELCID1171 NON OSAN FUERAS **** NIN CON EL SE AIUNTAR;
                   9481 5ELCID1205 VIEDALES **** & VIEDALES ENTRAR.
                  12319 5ELCID1564 DOZITOS CAUALLEROS MANDO **** PRIUADO,
       WORD #1951 OCCURS   7 TIMES.
          INDEX OF DIVERSIFICATION =  1792.33 WITH STANDARD DEVIATION OF  1453.99

EXORADO            5806 5ELCID0733 QUAL LIDIA BIEN SOBRE ******* ARZON
       WORD #1952 OCCURS   1 TIMES.

EYUA              18836 5ELCID2384 **** LOS FERIR A CABO DEL ALBERGADA.
       WORD #1953 OCCURS   1 TIMES.

&                    11 5ELCID0002 TORNAUA LA CABE%A * ESAUA LOS CATANDO.
                     18 5ELCID0003 VIO PUERTAS ABIERTAS * V%OS SIN CA@ADOS,
```

WORD C# PREFIX CONTEXT

& (CON'T)

```
  26 5ELCID0004 ALCANDARAS UAZIAS SIN PIELLES * SIN MANTOS
  32 5ELCID0005 E SIN FALCONES * SIN ADTORES MUDADOS.
  48 5ELCID0007 FFABLO MYO %ID BIEN * TAN MESURADO:
  94 5ELCID0013 ME%IO MYO %ID LOS OMBROS * ENGRAMEO LA TIESTA:
 121 5ELCID0016 EN SU CONPA@A LX PENDONES; EXIEN LO UER MUGIERES * UARONES,
 124 5ELCID0017 BURGESES * BURGESAS POR LAS FINIESTRAS SON,
 182 5ELCID0024 CON GRAND RECABDO * FUERTE MIENTRE SELLADA:
 210 5ELCID0027 QUE PERDERIE LOS AUERES * MAS LOS OIOS DELA CARA,
 221 5ELCID0028 E AUN DEMAS LOS CUERPOS * LAS ALMAS.
 344 5ELCID0043 CON GRANT RECABDO * FUERTE MIENTRE SELLADA.
 361 5ELCID0045 SI NON, PERDERIEMOS LOS AUERES * LAS CASAS,
 392 5ELCID0049 ESTO LA NI@A DIXO * TORNOS PORA SU CASA.
 435 5ELCID0055 SALIO POR LA PUERTA * EN ARLAN%ON POSAUA.
 449 5ELCID0057 FINCAUA LA TIENDA * LUEGO DESCAUALGAUA.
 514 5ELCID0066 AMYO %ID * ALOS SUYOS ABASTALES DE PAN & DE UINO;
 520 5ELCID0066 AMYO %ID & ALOS SUYOS ABASTALES DE PAN * DE UINO;
 543 5ELCID0069 PAGOS MYO %ID EL CAMPEADOR * TODOS LOS OTROS QUEUAN ASO %ERUICIO
 568 5ELCID0072 ESTA NOCH YGAMOS * UAYMOS NOS AL MATINO,
 640 5ELCID0081 ESPESO E EL ORO * TODA LA PLATA,
 652 5ELCID0082 BIEN LO VEDES QUE YO NO TRAYO AUER, * HUEBOS ME SERIE
 692 5ELCID0088 LOS GUADAME%IS UERMEIOS * LOS CLAUOS BIEN DORADOS.
 699 5ELCID0089 POR RACHEL * VIDAS UAYADES ME PRIUADO:
 710 5ELCID0090 QUANDO EN BURGOS ME VEDARON COMPRA * EL REY ME A AYRADO,
 754 5ELCID0095 YO MAS NON PUEDO * AMYDOS LO FAGO.
 765 5ELCID0097 POR RACHEL * VIDAS APRIESSA DEMANDAUA.
 777 5ELCID0099 POR RACHEL * VIDAS APRIESSA DEMANDAUA.
 782 5ELCID0100 RACHEL * VIDAS EN VNO ESTAUAN AMOS,
 805 5ELCID0103 O SODES, RACHEL * VIDAS, LOS MYOS AMIGOS CAROS?
 825 5ELCID0106 RACHEL * VIDAS, AMOS ME DAT LAS MANOS,
 860 5ELCID0110 GRANDES AUERES PRISO * MUCHO SOBEIANOS,
 895 5ELCID0115 DEXADO HA HEREDADES * CASAS & PALA%IOS.
 897 5ELCID0115 DEXADO HA HEREDADES & CASAS * PALA%IOS.
 927 5ELCID0119 PRENDED LAS ARCHAS * METED LAS EN UUESTRO SALUO;
 950 5ELCID0122 RACHEL * VIDAS SEYEN SE CONSEIANDO:
1056 5ELCID0136 DIXO RACHEL * VIDAS:  DAR GELOS DE GRADO.
1081 5ELCID0139 DIXO RACHEL * VIDAS:  NON SE FAZE ASSI EL MERCADO,
1093 5ELCID0140 SI NON PRIMERO PRENDIENDO * DESPUES DANDO.
1120 5ELCID0144 POR ADUZIR LAS ARCHAS * METER LAS EN UUESTRO SALUO,
1135 5ELCID0146 DIXO RACHEL * VIDAS:  NOS DESTO NOS PAGAMOS.
1154 5ELCID0149 CON RACHEL * VIDAS, DE VOLUTAD & DE GRADO.
1158 5ELCID0149 CON RACHEL & VIDAS, DE VOLUTAD * DE GRADO.
1202 5ELCID0155 YA DON RACHEL * VIDAS, AUEDES ME OLBIDADO
1233 5ELCID0159 DON RACHEL * VIDAS A MYO %ID BESARON LE LAS MANOS.
1271 5ELCID0163 CA ASSIL DIERAN LA FE * GELO AUIEN IURADO,
1302 5ELCID0167 LEUALDAS, RACHEL * VIDAS, PONED LAS EN UUESTRO SALUO;
1345 5ELCID0172 GRADAN SE RACHEL * VIDAS CON AUERES MONEDADOS,
1391 5ELCID0178 VNA PIEL VERMEIA MORISCA * ONDRADA,
1431 5ELCID0183 SOBRELLA VNA SAUANA DE RAN%AL * MUY BLANCA.
1476 5ELCID0189 YA DON RACHEL * VIDAS, EN UUESTRAS MANOS SON LAS ARCAS;
1494 5ELCID0191 ENTRE RACHEL * VIDAS APARTE YXIERON AMOS:
1525 5ELCID0195 DE QUE FAGADES CAL%AS * RICA PIEL & BUEN MANTO.
1528 5ELCID0195 DE QUE FAGADES CAL%AS & RICA PIEL * BUEN MANTO.
1554 5ELCID0199 GRADE%IOLO DON MARTINO * RECIBIO LOS MARCHOS;
1562 5ELCID0200 GRADO EXIR DELA POSADA * ESPIDIOS DE AMOS.
1570 5ELCID0201 EXIDO ES DE BURGOS * ARLAN%ON A PASXADO,
1615 5ELCID0207 VOS VJ %IENTOS * YO XXX HE GANADOS.
1624 5ELCID0208 MANDAD COGER LA TIENDA * VAYAMOS PRIUADO,
1645 5ELCID0211 MESURAREMOS LA POSADA * QUITAREMOS EL REYNADO;
1666 5ELCID0214 MYO %ID * SUS CONPA@AS CAUALGAN TAN AYNA.
1694 5ELCID0217 ATI LO GRADESCO, DIOS, QUE %IELO * TIERRA GUIAS;
1732 5ELCID0221 VUESTRA UERTUD ME UALA, GLORIOSA, EN MY EXIDA * ME AIUDE,
1740 5ELCID0222 EL ME ACORRA DE NOCH * DE DIA
1748 5ELCID0223 SI UOS ASSI LO FIZIEREDES * LA UENTURA ME FUERE COMPLIDA,
1760 5ELCID0224 MANDO AL UUESTRO ALTAR BUENAS DONAS * RICAS;
1763 5ELCID0225 ESTO * YO EN DEBDO QUE FAGA Y CANTAR MILL MISSAS.
1778 5ELCID0226 SPIDIOS EL CABOSO DE CUER * DE VELUNTAD.
1784 5ELCID0227 SUELTAN LAS RIENDAS * PIENSSAN DE AGUIJAR.
1826 5ELCID0232 TORNAUAS MARTIN ANTOLINEZ A BURGOS * MYO %ID AAGUIJAR
1850 5ELCID0235 APRIESSA CANTAN LOS GALLOS * QUIEREN QUEBRAR ALBORES,
1888 5ELCID0240 ROGANDO A SAN PERO * AL CRIADOR:
1917 5ELCID0244 CON LUMBRES * CON CANDELAS AL CORAL DIERON SALTO.
1960 5ELCID0248 DIXO EL %ID:  GRA%IAS, DON ABBAT, * SO UUESTRO PAGADO;
1970 5ELCID0249 YO ADOBARE CON DUCHO PORA MI * PORA MIS VASSALLOS;
2010 5ELCID0254 AELLA * ASUS FIJAS & ASUS DUENAS SIRUADES LAS EST A@O.
2013 5ELCID0254 AELLA & ASUS FIJAS * ASUS DUENAS SIRUADES LAS EST A@O.
2024 5ELCID0255 DUES FIJAS DEXO NI@AS * PRENDET LAS EN LOS BRA%OS;
2038 5ELCID0257 DELLAS * DE MI MUGIER FAGADES TODO RECABDO.
2090 5ELCID0263 SE@AS DUE@AS LAS TRAEN * ADUZEN LAS ADELANT.
2133 5ELCID0269 FEM ANTE UOS YO * UUESTRAS FFIJAS, YFFANTES SON & DE
                DIAS CHICAS,
2138 5ELCID0269 FEM ANTE UOS YO & UUESTRAS FFIJAS, YFFANTES SON * DE
                DIAS CHICAS,
2230 5ELCID0281 YO YRE * UOS FINCAREDES REMANIDA.
2236 5ELCID0282 PLEGA ADIOS * A SANTA MARIA, QUE AUN CON MIS MANOS CASE
                ESTAS MIS
2253 5ELCID0283 O QUE DE VENTURA * ALGUNOS DIAS VIDA,
2297 5ELCID0289 VNOS DEXAN CASAS * OTROS ONORES.
```

WORD C# PREFIX CONTEXT

& (CON'T)

2375 5ELCID0300 YO RUEGO ADIOS * AL PADRE SPIRITAL,
2385 5ELCID0301 VOS, QUE POR MI DEXADES CASAS * HEREDADES,
2578 5ELCID0326 MYO %ID * SU MUGIER A LA EGLESIA UAN.
2621 5ELCID0331 FEZIST %IELO * TIERRA, EL TER%ERO EL MAR;
2629 5ELCID0332 FEZIST ESTRELAS * LUNA & EL SOL PORA ESCALENTAR;
2631 5ELCID0332 FEZIST ESTRELAS & LUNA * EL SOL PORA ESCALENTAR;
2664 5ELCID0337 MELCHIOR * GASPAR & BALTASAR, ORO & TUS & MIRRA
2666 5ELCID0337 MELCHIOR & GASPAR * BALTASAR, ORO & TUS & MIRRA
2669 5ELCID0337 MELCHIOR & GASPAR & BALTASAR, ORO * TUS & MIRRA
2671 5ELCID0337 MELCHIOR & GASPAR & BALTASAR, ORO & TUS * MIRRA
2730 5ELCID0345 DEL AGUA FEZIST VINO * DELA PIEDRA PAN,
2849 5ELCID0360 QUEBRANTESTE LAS PUERTAS * SAQUESTE LOS PADRES SANTOS.
2859 5ELCID0361 TUERES REY DE LOS REYES * DE TODEL MUNDO PADRE,
2866 5ELCID0362 ATI ADORO * CREO DE TODO VOLUNTAD,
2952 5ELCID0372 ADIOS UOS ACOMIENDO, FIJAS, * A LA MUGIER & AL PADRE SPIRITAL;
2956 5ELCID0372 ADIOS UOS ACOMIENDO, FIJAS, & A LA MUGIER * AL PADRE SPIRITAL;
3051 5ELCID0384 COMMO SIRUA ADO@A XIMENA * ALAS FIJAS QUE HA,
3078 5ELCID0387 TORNADO ES DON SANCHO, * FABLO ALBARFANEZ:
3094 5ELCID0389 ABBAT, DEZILDES QUE PRENDAN EL RASTRO * PIESSEN DE ANDAR,
3315 5ELCID0418 SIN LAS PEONADAS * OMNES VALIENTES QUE SON,
3339 5ELCID0421 EL QUI QUISIERE COMER; * QUI NO, CAUALGE.
3349 5ELCID0422 PASSAREMOS LA SIERRA QUE FIERA ES * GRAND,
3390 5ELCID0427 EN MEDIO DUNA MONTANA MARAUILLOSA * GRAND
3396 5ELCID0428 FIZO MYO %ID POSAR * %EUADA DAR.
3516 5ELCID0443 E ALBAR SALUADOREZ SIN FALLA, * GALIN GAR%IA, VNA FARDIDA
3538 5ELCID0446 FITA AYUSO * POR GUADALFAIARA, FATA ALCALA LEGEN LAS ALGARAS,
3620 5ELCID0456 YA QUIEBRAN LOS ALBORES * VINIE LA MA@ANA,
3647 5ELCID0460 POR VER SUS LAUORES * TODAS SUS HEREDADES.
3686 5ELCID0465 MOROS * MORAS AUIEN LOS DE GANAN%IA,
3716 5ELCID0469 OUIERON MIEDO * FUE DESEPARADA.
3742 5ELCID0473 GA@O A CASTEION * EL ORO ELA PLATA.
3789 5ELCID0479 FENARES ARRIBA * POR GUADALFAIARA.
3801 5ELCID0481 DE OUEIAS * DE VACAS & DE ROPAS & DE OTRAS RIQUIZAS LARGAS.
3804 5ELCID0481 DE OUEIAS & DE VACAS * DE ROPAS & DE OTRAS RIQUIZAS LARGAS.
3807 5ELCID0481 DE OUEIAS & DE VACAS & DE ROPAS * DE OTRAS RIQUIZAS LARGAS.
3909 5ELCID0496 YO UOS LA SUELTA * AUELLO QUITADO.
3939 5ELCID0500 QUE ENPLEYE LA LAN%A * AL ESPADA META MANO,
4077 5ELCID0518 FABLO CON LOS DE CASTEION, * ENVIO AFITA & AGUADELFAGARA,
4080 5ELCID0518 FABLO CON LOS DE CASTEION, & ENVIO AFITA * AGUADELFAGARA,
4161 5ELCID0529 QUITAR QUIERO CASTEION, OYD, ESCUELLAS * MINYAYA
4181 5ELCID0532 %ERCA ES EL REY ALFONSSO * BUSCAR NOS VERNA.
4194 5ELCID0534 %IENTO MOROS * %IENTO MORAS QUIERO LAS QUITAR,
4214 5ELCID0536 TODOS SODES PAGADOS * NINGUNO POR PAGAR.
4251 5ELCID0541 LOS MOROS * LAS MORAS BENDIZIENDOL ESTAN.
4265 5ELCID0543 TRO%EN LAS ALCARIAS * YUAN ADELANT,
4292 5ELCID0547 ENTRE FARIZA * %ETINA MYO %ID YUA ALBERGAR.
4336 5ELCID0552 PASSO A BOUIERCA * ATECA QUE ES ADELANT,
4353 5ELCID0554 EN VN OTERO REDONDO, FUERTE * GRAND;
4382 5ELCID0558 LOS VNOS CONTRA LA SIERRA * LOS OTROS CONTRA LA AGUA.
4492 5ELCID0571 E LOS DE TECA * LOS DE TERUAL LA CASA;
4524 5ELCID0575 EL FIZO VN ART * NON LO DETARDAUA:
4532 5ELCID0576 DEXA VNA TIENDA FITA * LAS OTRAS LEUAUA,
4546 5ELCID0578 LAS LORIGAS VESTIDAS * %INTAS LAS ESPADAS,
4572 5ELCID0581 FALIDO A MYO %ID EL PAN * LA %EUADA.
4596 5ELCID0584 DEMOS SALTO A EL * FEREMOS GRANT GANA%IA,
4660 5ELCID0591 LOS GRANDES * LOS CHICOS FUERA SALTO DAN,
4692 5ELCID0595 VIO QUE ENTRELLOS * EL CASTIELLO MUCHO AUIE GRAND PLA%A;
4740 5ELCID0601 MYO %ID * ALBARFANEZ ADELANT AGUIIAUAN;
4753 5ELCID0603 ENTRELLOS * EL CASTIELLO ENESSORA ENTRAUAN.
4770 5ELCID0605 EN VN ORA * VN POCO DE LOGAR CCC MOROS MATAN.
4856 5ELCID0614 GRADO A DIOS DEL %IELO * ATODOS LOS SOS SANTOS,
4865 5ELCID0615 YA MEIORAREMOS POSADAS ADUENOS * ACAUALLOS.
4870 5ELCID0616 OYD AMI, ALBARFANEZ * TODOS LOS CAUALLEROS
4891 5ELCID0619 LOS MOROS * LAS MORAS VENDER NON LOS PODREMOS,
4916 5ELCID0622 POSAREMOS EN SUS CASAS * DELLOS NOS SERUIREMOS.
4941 5ELCID0625 MUCHO PESA ALOS DE TECA * ALOS DE TERUAL NON PLAZE,
5002 5ELCID0632 SI NON DAS CONSEIO, A TECA * A TERUEL PERDERAS,
5092 5ELCID0643 TRES MILL MOROS CAUALGAN * PIENSSAN DE ANDAR,
5173 5ELCID0654 CON AQUESTOS DOS REYES QUE DIZEN FFARIZ * GALUE;
5187 5ELCID0656 FINCARON LAS TIENDAS * PRENDEND LAS POSADAS,
5218 5ELCID0660 MUCHAS SON LAS AROBDAS * GRANDE ES EL ALMOFALLA.
5379 5ELCID0679 TODOS LOS MOROS * LAS MORAS DE FUERA LOS MANDA ECHAR,
5395 5ELCID0681 ELDIA * LA NOCHE PIENSSAN SE DE ADOBAR.
5566 5ELCID0701 PORA MYO %ID * ALOS SOS A MANOS LOS TOMAR.
5756 5ELCID0726 VERIEDES TANTAS LAN%AS PREMER * AL%AR,
5761 5ELCID0727 TANTA ADAGARA FORADAR * PASSAR,
5785 5ELCID0731 LOS MOROS LAMAN MAFOMAT * LOS CHRISTIANOS SANTI YAGUE.
5799 5ELCID0732 CAYEN EN VN POCO DE LOGAR MOROS MUERTOS MILL * CCC YA.
5842 5ELCID0739 ALBAR ALBAREZ * ALBAR SALUADOREZ,
5866 5ELCID0743 ACORREN LA SE@A * A MYO %ID EL CAMPEADOR.
6003 5ELCID0761 LOS DOS LE FALLEN, * EL VNOL HA TOMADO,
6064 5ELCID0769 ARANCADO ES EL REY FARIZ * GALUE;
6240 5ELCID0795 DE ESCUDOS * DE ARMAS & DE OTROS AUERES LARGOS;
6243 5ELCID0795 DE ESCUDOS & DE ARMAS * DE OTROS AUERES LARGOS;

WORD	C#	PREFIX	CONTEXT
& (CON'T)			
	6273	5ELCIDC799	TRAEN ORO * PLATA QUE NCN SABEN RECABDO;
	6316	5ELCIDC804	DIO APARTIR ESTOS DINEROS * ESTOS AUERES LARGOS;
	6339	5ELCIDC807	ALOS PEONES * A LOS ENCAUALGADOS
	6406	5ELCIDC817	TODOS CCN SIELLAS * MUY BIEN ENFRENADOS,
	6426	5ELCIDC820	EUADES AQUI ORO * PLATA VNA VESA LE@A,
	6450	5ELCIDC823	LO QUE ROMANE%IERE DALDC A MI MUGIER * A MIS FIJAS,
	6460	5ELCIDC824	CUE RUEGEN POR MI LAS NOCHES * LOS DIAS;
	6515	5ELCIDC831	DIOS NOS VALIO * VEN%IEMOS LA LIDIT.
	6535	5ELCIDC834	POR LANCAS * POR ESPADAS AUEMCS DE GUARIR,
	6565	5ELCIDC838	LA TIERRA ES ANGOSTA * SOBEIANA DE MALA;
	6580	5ELCIDC840	MOROS DE LAS FRONTERAS * VNAS YENTES ESTRANAS;
	6596	5ELCIDC842	ENTRE LOS DE TECHA * LOS DE TERUEL LA CASA,
	6614	5ELCIDC844	ASI LO AN ASMADC * METUDO EN CARTA:
	6645	5ELCIDC848	A CAUALLEROS * A PEONES FECHOS LOS HA RICOS,
	6677	5ELCIDC852	MOROS * MORAS TOMARON SE A QUEXAR:
	6707	5ELCIDC856	MOROS * MORAS COMPE%ARON DE LORAR.
	6737	5ELCIDC860	PLOGO ALOS DE TERER * ALOS DE CALATAYUT MAS,
	6771	5ELCIDC864	ALTO ES EL POYO, MARAUILLOSO * GRANT;
	6879	5ELCIDC879	BESA UOS LOS PIES * LAS MANOS AMAS,
	6936	5ELCIDC887	HONORES * TIERRAS AUELLAS CONDONADAS,
	6941	5ELCIDC888	HYD * VENIT, DA QUI UOS DO MI GRA%IA;
	6975	5ELCIDC892	BUE@OS * VALIENTES PORA MYO %ID HUYAR,
	6985	5ELCIDC893	SUELTO LES LOS CUERPOS * QUITO LES LAS HEREDADES.
	6997	5ELCIDC895	GRADO * GRA%IAS, REY, COMMO A SE@OR NATURAL;
	7013	5ELCIDC897	HYD POR CASTIELLA * DEXEN UOS ANDAR, MINAYA,
	7036	5ELCIDC899	QUIERO UOS DEZIR DEL QUE EN BUEN ORA NASCO * %INXO ESPADA:
	7051	5ELCIDC901	MIENTRA QUE SEA EL PUEBLC DE MOROS * DELA YENTE CHRISTIANA,
	7189	5ELCIDC921	BESO LE LA BOCA * LOS OIOS DELA CARA.
	7207	5ELCIDC924	GRADO ADIOS * ALAS SUS VERTUDES SANTAS;
	7238	5ELCIDC928	DIZIENDC LES SALUDES DE PRIMOS * DE HERMANOS,
	7269	5ELCIDC932	E QUEL DIXO SALUDES DE SU MUGIER * DE SUS FIJAS
	7279	5ELCIDC933	DIOS, COMMO FUE EL %ID PAGADO * FIZO GRANT ALEGRIA
	7330	5ELCIDC940	PESANDO VA ALOS DE MON%ON * ALOS DE HUESCA;
	7369	5ELCIDC945	PLOGO A MYO %ID, * MUCHO A ALBARFANEZ.
	7407	5ELCIDC950	DEXAT ESTAS POSADAS * YREMOS ADELANT.
	7425	5ELCIDC952	DENT CORRE MYO %ID A HUESCA * A MONT ALUAN;
	7476	5ELCIDC959	OUO GRAND PESAR * TOUOS LO A GRAND FONTA.
	7487	5ELCIDC960	EL CONDE ES MUY FOLON * DIXO VNA VANIDAT:
	7511	5ELCIDC963	FIRIOM EL SOBRINO * NON LO ENMENDO MAS;
	7545	5ELCIDC967	GRANDES SON LOS PODERES * A PRIESSA SEUAN LEGANDO,
	7557	5ELCIDC968	GENTES SE LE ALEGAN GRANDES ENTRE MOROS * CHRISTIANOS,
	7569	5ELCIDC970	TRES DIAS * DOS NOCHES PENSSARON DE ANDAR,
	7581	5ELCIDC971	ALCON%ARON A MYO %ID EN TEUAR * EL PINAR;
	7606	5ELCIDC974	DI%E DE VNA SIERRA * LEGAUA A VN VAL.
	7653	5ELCIDC980	LO DE ANTES * DE AGORA TODOM LO PECHARA;
	7699	5ELCIDC986	APRIESSA UOS GUARNID * METEDOS EN LAS ARMAS.
	7715	5ELCIDC988	DE MOROS * DE CHRISTIANOS GENTES TRAE SOBEIANAS,
	7741	5ELCIDC991	APRETAD LOS CAUALLOS, * BISTADES LAS ARMAS.
	7749	5ELCIDC992	ELLOS VIENEN CUESTA YUSO, * TODOS TRAHEN CAL%AS,
	7756	5ELCIDC993	ELAS SIELLAS CO%ERAS * LAS %INCHAS AMOIADAS;
	7764	5ELCIDC994	NOS CAUALGAREMOS SIELLAS GALLEGAS, * HUESAS SOBRE CAL%AS;
	7825	5ELCID1001	LAS ARMAS AUIEN PRESAS * SEDIEN SOBRE LOS CAUALLOS.
	7862	5ELCID1005	ESTO FAZEN LOS SOS DE VOLUNTAD * DE GRADO;
	7867	5ELCID1006	LOS PENDONES * LAS LAN%AS TAN BIEN LAS UAN ENPLEANDO,
	7878	5ELCID1007	ALOS VNOS FIRIENDO * A LOS OTROS DE ROCANDO.
	8004	5ELCID1022	ANTES PERDERE EL CUERPO * DEXARE EL ALMA,
	8029	5ELCID1025	COMED, CONDE, DESTE PAN * BEUED DESTE VINO.
	8058	5ELCID1028	DIXO EL CONDE DON REMONT: COMEDE, DON RODRIGO, * PENSSEDES DE FOLGAR.
	8111	5ELCID1035	AUOS * DOS FIJOS DALGO QUITAR UOS HE LOS CUERPOS & DARUOS E DE MANO.
	8120	5ELCID1035	AUOS & DOS FIJOS DALGO QUITAR UOS HE LOS CUERPOS * DARUOS E DE MANO.
	8151	5ELCID1039	PUES COMED, CONDE, * QUANDO FUEREDES IANTADO,
	8156	5ELCID1040	AUOS * A OTROS DOS DAR UOS HE DE MANO.
	8169	5ELCID1041	MAS QUANTO AUEDES PERDIDO * YO GANE EN CANPO,
	8194	5ELCID1044	CA HUEBOS MELO HE * PORA ESTOS MYOS VASSALLOS
	8203	5ELCID1045	QUE COMIGO ANDAN LAZRADOS, * NON UOS LO DARE.
	8210	5ELCID1046	PRENDIENDO DEUOS * DE OTROS YR NOS HEMOS PAGANDO;
	8231	5ELCID1048	COMMO QUE YRA A DE REY * DE TIERRA ES ECHADO.
	8240	5ELCID1049	ALEGRE ES EL CONDE * PIDIO AGUA ALAS MANOS,
	8249	5ELCID1050	E TIENEN GELO DELANT * DIERON GELO PRIUADO.
	8302	5ELCID1056	AQUI DIXO EL CONDE: DE VOLUNTAD * DE GRADO.
	8346	5ELCID1061	MANDAD NOS DAR LAS BESTIAS * CAUALGEREMOS PRIUADO;
	8380	5ELCID1065	E BUENAS VESTIDURAS DE PELI%ONES * DE MANTOS.
	8481	5ELCID1078	TORNANDO UA LA CABE%A * CATANDOS ATRAS;
	8533	5ELCID1084	DE LA GANAN%IA QUE AN FECHA MARAUILLOSA * GRAND.
	8567	5ELCID1088	DEXADO A SARAGO%A * ALAS TIERRAS DUCA,
	8575	5ELCID1089	E DEXADO A HUESCA * LAS TIERRAS DE MONT ALUAN.
	8600	5ELCID1092	MYO %ID GA@O AXERICA * A ONDA & ALMENAR,
	8603	5ELCID1092	MYO %ID GA@O AXERICA & A ONDA * ALMENAR,
	8685	5ELCID1103	EN SUS TIERRAS SOMOS * FEMOS LES TODOMAL,
	8692	5ELCID1104	BEUEMOS SO VINO * COMEMOS EL SO PAN.
	8722	5ELCID1108	LOS VNOS AXERICA * LOS OTROS A ALUCAD,
	8730	5ELCID1119	DESI A ONDA * LOS OTROS A ALMENAR,
	8820	5ELCID1122	PASSE LA NOCHE * VENGA LA MA@ANA,
	8829	5ELCID1123	APAREIADOS ME SED A CAUALLOS * ARMAS;

WORD C# PREFIX CONTEXT

& (CON'T)

8911 5ELCID1135 MA@ANA ERA * PIENSSAN SE DE ARMAR,
8939 5ELCID1138 ENEL NCMBRE DEL CRIADOR * DEL APOSTOL SANTI YAGUE,
8948 5ELCID1139 FERID LCS, CAUALLERCS, DAMOR * DE GRADO & DE GRAND VOLUNTAD,
8951 5ELCID1139 FERID LCS, CAUALLERCS, DAMOR & DE GRADO * DE GRAND VOLUNTAD,
8975 5ELCID1142 ARANCAR SE LAS ESTACAS * ACOSTAR SE ATODAS PARTES LOS TENDALES.
8999 5ELCID1145 MAGER LES PESA, CUIERCN SE ADAR * A ARANCAR.
9035 5ELCID1150 PRISIERON %EBCLA * QUANTC CUE ES Y ADELANT.
9C94 5ELCID1157 ALEGRE ERA EL %ID * TCDAS SUS CCMPA@AS,
9102 5ELCID1158 QUE DIOS LE AIUDARA * FIZIERA ESTA ARRANCADA.
9109 5ELCID1159 DAUAN SUS CORREDORES * FAZIEN LAS TRASNOCHADAS,
9116 5ELCID1160 LEGAN A GUIERA * LEGAN AXATIUA,
9139 5ELCID1163 GANARON PENA CADIELLA, LAS EXIDAS * LAS ENTRADAS.
9153 5ELCID1165 MALES PESA EN XATIUA * DENTRO EN GUIERA,
9170 5ELCID1167 EN TIERRA DE MOROS PRENDIENDO * GANANDO,
9176 5ELCID1168 E DURMIENDC LOS DIAS * LAS NOCHES TRANOCHANDO,
9208 5ELCID1172 TAIAUA LES LAS HUERTAS * FAZIA LES GRAND MAL,
9270 5ELCID1149 FIJOS * MUGIERES VER LO MURIR DE FANBRE.
9334 5ELCID1187 POR ARAGCN * POR NAUARRA PREGCN MANDO ECHAR,
9351 5ELCID1189 QUIEN CUIERE PERDER CUETA * VENIR A RRITAD,
9466 5ELCID1203 ADELINO PORA VALEN%IA * SOBRELLAS VA ECHAR,
9482 5ELCID1205 VIEDALES EXIR * VIEDALES ENTRAR.
9537 5ELCID1212 QUANDO MYO %ID GA@O A VALEN%IA * ENTRO ENLA %IBDAD.
9551 5ELCID1214 EL ORO * LA PLATA QUI EN VCS LO PODRIE CONTAR?
9741 5ELCID1238 YAL CRE%E LA BARBA * VALE ALLONGANDO;
9778 5ELCID1242 E QUE FABLASSEN DESTC MOROS * CHRISTIANOS.
9814 5ELCID1246 ATODOS LES DIO EN VALEN%IA CASAS * HEREDADES
9834 5ELCID1248 LOS QUE FUERCN CON EL, * LCS DE DESPUES, TODOS SON PAGADOS;
9889 5ELCID1254 TOMASSEN LE EL AUER * PUSIESSEN LE EN VN PALO.
9919 5ELCID1258 DELOS QUE SCN ACUI * CCMIGO GANARON ALGO;
9928 5ELCID1259 METER LCS HE EN ESCRIPTC, * TCDOS SEAN CONTADOS,
9952 5ELCID1261 AQUESTOS MYOS VASSALOS QUE CURIAN A VALEN%IA * ANDAN AROBDANDO.
9966 5ELCID1263 MANDO LCS VENIR ALA CCRTH * A TODOS LOS IUNTAR,
9981 5ELCID1265 TRES MILL * SEYS %IENTOS AUIE MYO %ID EL DE BIUAR;
9994 5ELCID1266 ALEGRAS LE EL CORA%ON * TORNOS ASONRRISAR:
10001 5ELCID1267 GRADO A DICS, MYNAYA, * A SANTA MARIA MADRE
10025 5ELCID1273 SI AUOS PLOGUIERE, MINAYA, * NON UOS CAYA EN PESAR,
10057 5ELCID1274 DAR LE QUIERO C CAUALLOS, * UOS YO GELOS LEUAR;
10074 5ELCID1276 POR MI MUGIER * MIS FIJAS, SI FUERE SU MER%ED,
10087 5ELCID1278 ENBIARE POR ELLAS, * UCS SABED EL MENSAGE:
10097 5ELCID1279 LA MUGIER DE MYC %ID * SUS FIJAS LAS YFFANTES
10190 5ELCID1290 BIEN ENTENDIDC ES DE LETRAS * MUCHO ACORDADO,
10195 5ELCID1291 DE PIE * DE CAUALLO MUCHO ERA AREZIADO.
10221 5ELCID1294 QUE SIS FARTAS LIDIANDO * FIRIENDO CON SUS MANOS,
10324 5ELCID1307 ALEGRE FUE MINAYA * SPIDIOS & VINOS.
10326 5ELCID1307 ALEGRE FUE MINAYA & SPIDIOS * VINOS.
10416 5ELCID1320 BESAUA LE LAS MANOS * FABLO TAN APUESTO:
10436 5ELCID1323 LOS PIES * LAS MANOS, COMMO ATAN BUEN SE@OR,
10471 5ELCID1327 GANADA A XERICA * A CNDA POR NCMBRE,
10479 5ELCID1328 PRISO A ALMENAR * A MURUIEDRO QUE ES MIYOR,
10488 5ELCID1329 ASSI FIZO %EBOLLA * ADELANT CASTEION,
10519 5ELCID1333 E FIZO %INCC LIDES CAMPALES * TODAS LAS ARRANCO.
10542 5ELCID1336 %IENT CAUALLCS GRUESSCS * CORREDORES,
10546 5ELCID1337 DE SIELLAS * DE FRENCS TODOS GUARNIDOS SON,
10556 5ELCID1338 BESA UOS LAS MANOS * CUE LOS PRENDADES UOS;
10565 5ELCID1339 RAZONAS POR VUESTRO VASSALLC * AUOS TIENE POR SE@OR.
10674 5ELCID1352 POR SU MUGIER DO@A XIMENA * SUS FIJAS AMAS ADOS:
10714 5ELCID1357 DE FONTA * DE MAL CURIALDAS & DE DESONOR;
10718 5ELCID1357 DE FONTA & DE MAL CURIALDAS * DE DESONOR;
10736 5ELCID1359 CATAD CCMMC LAS SIRUADES UOS * EL CAMPEADOR.
10742 5ELCID1360 OYD ME, ESCUELLAS, * TOCA LA MI CORT.
10784 5ELCID1365 ATREGO LES LCS CUERPOS DE MAL * DE OCASION,
10818 5ELCID1370 DE MI SEAN QUITOS * VAYAN ALA GRA%IA DEL CRIADOR.
10871 5ELCID1376 MYC %ID ES DE BIUAR * NCS DELOS CONDES DE CARRION.
10882 5ELCID1377 NON LO DIZEN A NADI, * FINCC ESTA RAZON.
10934 5ELCID1384 ESPIDIOS MYNAYA * VASSE DELA CORT.
11051 5ELCID1399 SANO LO DEXE * CON TAN GRAND RICTAD.
11079 5ELCID1402 SI UOS VIESSE EL %ID SA@AS * SIN MAL,
11121 5ELCID1408 QUE SU MUGIER * SUS FIJAS EL REY SUELTAS ME LAS HA,
11151 5ELCID1411 SEREMOS YO * SU MUGIER & SUS FIJAS QUE EL A
11154 5ELCID1411 SEREMOS YO & SU MUGIER * SUS FIJAS QUE EL A
11173 5ELCID1413 HYDOS SON LCS CAUALLEROS * DELLO PENSSARAN,
11255 5ELCID1424 MINAYA A DO@A XIMINA * A SUS FIJAS QUE HA,
11285 5ELCID1428 PALAFRES * MULAS, QUE NCN PARESCAN MAL.
11307 5ELCID1431 AFEUOS RACHEL * VIDAS ALOS PIES LE CAEN:
11358 5ELCID1437 DIXO RACHEL * VIDAS: EL CRIADOR LO MANDE
11437 5ELCID1448 HYAS ESPIDEN * PIENSSAN DE CAUALGAR,
11473 5ELCID1452 FELOS EN MEDINA LAS DUENAS * ALBARFANEZ.
11495 5ELCID1455 PLOGOL DE CORA%CN * TORNOS A ALEGRAR,
11516 5ELCID1458 TU, MU@C GUSTIOZ * PERC VERMUEZ DELANT,
11577 5ELCID1467 MY MUGIER * MIS FIJAS CCN MYNAYA ALBARFFANEZ,
11640 5ELCID1475 TRO%IERON A SANTA MARIA * VINIERON ALBERGAR A FRONTAEL,
11693 5ELCID1482 MYO %ID UOS SALUDAUA, * MANDOLO RECABDAR,
11704 5ELCID1484 SU MUGIER * SUS FIJAS EN MEDINA ESTAN:
11757 5ELCID1491 PASSAN LAS MONTANAS, QUE SCN FIERAS * GRANDES,

WORD C# PREFIX CONTEXT

& (CON'T)

11808 5ELCID1497 EL VNO FINCO CON ELLOS * EL OTRO TORNO A ALBARFANEZ:
11824 5ELCID1499 AFEUOS AQUI PERO VERMUEZ * MU@O GUSTIOZ QUE UOS QUIEREN SIN HAR
11895 5ELCID1508 EN BUENOS CAUALLOS A PETRALES * A CASCAUELES,
11903 5ELCID1509 E A CUBERTURAS DE %ENDALES, * ESCUDOS ALOS CUELLOS,
11939 5ELCID1513 LOS QUE YUAN MESURANDO * LEGANDO DELANT
11945 5ELCID1514 LUEGO TOMAN ARMAS * TOMANSE A DEPORTAR,
12133 5ELCID1539 EL REY LO PAGO TODO, * QUITO SEUA MINAYA.
12149 5ELCID1541 OYDA ES LA MISSA, * LUEGO CAUALGAUAN;
12155 5ELCID1542 SALIERON DE MEDINA, * SALON PASSAUAN,
12185 5ELCID1547 LAS NOCHES * LOS DIAS LAS DUENAS AGUARDANDO.
12203 5ELCID1549 ENTRE EL * ALBARFANEZ HYUAN A VNA COMPA@A.
12214 5ELCID1550 ENTRADOS SON A MOLINA, BUENA * RICA CASA;
12239 5ELCID1554 AMYNAYA * ALAS DUE@AS, DIOS COMMO LAS ONDRAUA
12271 5ELCID1558 CON ESTAS ALEGRIAS * NUEUAS TAN ONDRADAS
12325 5ELCID1565 QUE RE%IBAN A MYANAYA * ALAS DUENAS FIJAS DALGO;
12335 5ELCID1566 EL SEDIE EN VALEN%IA CURIANDO * GUARDANDO,
12354 5ELCID1569 E ALAS DUENAS * ALAS NI@AS & ALAS OTRAS CONPA@AS.
12357 5ELCID1569 E ALAS DUENAS & ALAS NI@AS * ALAS OTRAS CONPA@AS.
12374 5ELCID1571 QUE GUARDASSEN EL ALCA%AR * LAS OTRAS TORRES ALTAS
12383 5ELCID1572 E TODAS LAS PUERTAS * LAS EXIDAS & LAS ENTRADAS,
12386 5ELCID1572 E TODAS LAS PUERTAS & LAS EXIDAS * LAS ENTRADAS,
12428 5ELCID1577 DELANTE SU MUGIER * DE SUS FIJAS QUERIE TENER LAS ARMAS.
12470 5ELCID1582 SOBREPELI%AS VESTIDAS * CON CRUZES DE PLATA
12479 5ELCID1583 RE%IBIR SALIEN LAS DUENAS * AL BUENO DE MINAYA.
12503 5ELCID1586 MYO %ID SALIO SOBREL, * ARMAS DE FUSTE TOMAUA,
12555 5ELCID1593 ADELINO A SU MUGIER * A SUS FIJAS AMAS;
12591 5ELCID1597 AFE ME AQUI, SE@OR, YO UUESTRAS FIJAS * AMAS,
12595 5ELCID1598 CON DIOS * CON UUSCO BUENAS SON & CRIADAS.
12600 5ELCID1598 CON DIOS & CON UUSCO BUENAS SON * CRIADAS.
12604 5ELCID1599 ALA MADRE * ALAS FIJAS BIEN LAS ABRA%AUA,
12629 5ELCID1602 ARMAS TENIENDO * TABLADOS QUEBRANTANDO.
12644 5ELCID1604 VOS, QUERIDA * ONDRADA MUGIER, & AMAS MIS FIJAS,
12647 5ELCID1604 VOS, QUERIDA & ONDRADA MUGIER, * AMAS MIS FIJAS,
12653 5ELCID1605 MY CORA%ON * MI ALMA,
12671 5ELCID1608 MADRE * FIJAS LAS MANOS LE BESAUAN.
12725 5ELCID1615 MIRAN LA HUERTA, ESPESSA ES * GRAND;
12738 5ELCID1617 DESTA GANAN%IA COMME ES BUENA * GRAND.
12742 5ELCID1618 MYO %ID * SUS COMPANAS TAN AGRAND SABOR ESTAN.
12855 5ELCID1631 FINCARON LAS TIENDAS, * POSAN LAS YENTES DESCREYDAS.
12870 5ELCID1633 GRADO AL CRIADOR * A PADRE ESPIRITAL
12889 5ELCID1635 CON AFAN GANE A VALEN%IA, * ELA POR HEREDAD,
12904 5ELCID1637 GRADO AL CRIADOR * A SANTA MARIA MADRE,
12911 5ELCID1638 MIS FIJAS * MI MUGIER QUE LAS TENGO ACA;
12935 5ELCID1641 MIS FIJAS * MI MUGIER VERME AN LIDIAR,
12963 5ELCID1644 SU MUGIER * SUS FIJAS SUBIOLAS AL ALCA%AR,
12996 5ELCID1648 RIQUEZA ES QUE NOS A CRE%E MARAUILLOSA * GRAND;
13016 5ELCID1651 AUOS GRADO, %ID, * AL PADRE SPIRITAL.
13025 5ELCID1652 MUGIER, SED EN ESTE PALA%IO, * SI QUISIEREDES EN EL ALCA%AR;
13044 5ELCID1654 CON LA MER%ED DE DIOS * DE SANTA MARIA MADRE
13070 5ELCID1657 FINCADAS SON LAS TIENDAS * PARE%EN LOS ALUORES,
13084 5ELCID1659 ALEGRAUAS MIO %ID * DIXO: TAN BUEN DIA ES OY
13095 5ELCID1660 MIEDO A SU MUGIER * QUIEREL QUEBRAR EL CORA%ON,
13104 5ELCID1661 ASSI FFAZIE ALAS DUE@AS * A SUS FIJAS AMAS ADOS:
13146 5ELCID1666 AQUELOS ATAMORES AUOS LOS PONDRAN DELANT * VEREDES QUANLES SON,
13197 5ELCID1673 VIOLO EL ATALAYA * TANXO EL ESQUILA;
13297 5ELCID1686 OY ES DIA BUENO * MEIOR SERA CRAS:
13313 5ELCID1688 DEZIR NOS HA LA MISSA, * PENSSAD DE CAUALGAR,
13332 5ELCID1690 HYR LOS HEMOS FFERIR ENEL NOMBRE DEL CRIADOR * DEL APOSTOL SANTI
13352 5ELCID1692 ESSORA DIXIERON TODOS: DAMOR * DE VOLUNTAD.
13405 5ELCID1699 ES DIA ES SALIDO * LA NOCH ENTRADA ES,
13451 5ELCID1705 PRENDOL YO LOS PECADOS, * DIOS LE ABRA EL ALMA.
13478 5ELCID1708 PIDO UOS VN DON * SEAM PRESENTADO.
13566 5ELCID1719 ALUAR ALUAREZ * ALUAR SALUADOREZ & MINAYA ALBARFANEZ
13569 5ELCID1719 ALUAR ALUAREZ & ALUAR SALUADOREZ * MINAYA ALBARFANEZ
13580 5ELCID1721 PLOGO AL CRIADOR * OUIERON LOS DE ARRANCAR.
13695 5ELCID1735 NON ESCAPARON MAS DE %IENTO * QUATRO.
13707 5ELCID1737 ENTRE ORO * PLATA FALLARON TRES MILL MARCOS,
13723 5ELCID1739 ALEGRE ERA MYO %ID * TODOS SOS VASSALLOS,
13803 5ELCID1749 VOS TENIENDO VALEN%IA, * YO VEN%I EL CAMPO;
13831 5ELCID1752 VEDES EL ESPADA SANGRIENTA * SUDIENTO EL CAUALLO:
13855 5ELCID1755 ENTRAREDES EN PREZ, * BESARAN UUESTRAS MANOS.
13875 5ELCID1758 LAS DUE@AS * LAS FIJAS & LA MUGIER QUE VALE ALGO
13878 5ELCID1758 LAS DUE@AS & LAS FIJAS * LA MUGIER QUE VALE ALGO
13894 5ELCID1760 SOMOS EN UUESTRA MER%ED, * BIUADES MUCHOS A@OS
13967 5ELCID1769 LEUANTARON SE TODAS * BESARON LE LAS MANOS,
14000 5ELCID1773 CONTODAS ESTAS YENTES ESCRIUIENDO * CONTANDO;
14004 5ELCID1774 ENTRE TIENDAS * ARMAS & VESTIDOS PRE%IADOS
14006 5ELCID1774 ENTRE TIENDAS & ARMAS * VESTIDOS PRE%IADOS
14037 5ELCID1778 QUE ANDAN ARRIADOS * NON HA QUI TOMALOS,
14059 5ELCID1781 DELOS BUENOS * OTORGADOS CAYERON LE MILL & D CAUALLOS;
14064 5ELCID1781 DELOS BUENOS & OTORGADOS CAYERON LE MILL * D CAUALLOS;
14082 5ELCID1783 TANTA TIENDA PRE%IADA * TANTO TENDAL OBRADO
14227 5ELCID1800 TANTOS AUIEN DE AUERES, DE CAUALLOS * DE ARMAS;
14234 5ELCID1801 ALEGRE ES DO@A XIMENA * SUS FIJAS AMAS,

WORD C# PREFIX CONTEXT

& (CON'T)

14305 5ELCID1810 CON SIELLAS * CON FRENOS & CON SE@AS ESPADAS;
14308 5ELCID1810 CON SIELLAS & CON FRENOS * CON SE@AS ESPADAS;
14317 5ELCID1811 POR AMOR DE MI MUGIER * DE MIS FIJAS AMAS,
14414 5ELCID1823 ANDAN LOS DIAS * LAS NOCHES, & PASSADA HAN LA SIERRA,
14417 5ELCID1823 ANDAN LOS DIAS & LAS NOCHES, * PASSADA HAN LA SIERRA,
14439 5ELCID1826 PASSANDO VAN LAS SIERRAS * LOS MONTES & LAS AGUAS,
14442 5ELCID1826 PASSANDO VAN LAS SIERRAS & LOS MONTES * LAS AGUAS,
14458 5ELCID1828 ENVIAUA LE MANDADO PERO VERMUEZ * MYNAYA,
14522 5ELCID1837 ALOS VNOS PLAZE * ALOS OTROS VA PESANDO.
14554 5ELCID1841 MYNAYA * PER VERMUEZ ADELANT SON LEGADOS,
14576 5ELCID1844 BESAN LA TIERRA * LOS PIES AMOS:
14600 5ELCID1847 A UOS LAMA POR SE@OR, * TIENES POR UUESTRO VASSALLO,
14656 5ELCID1854 E EMBIA UOS DOZIENTOS CAUALLOS, * BESA UOS LAS MANOS.
14691 5ELCID1858 ESTO PLOGO A MUCHOS * BESARON LE LAS MANOS.
14762 5ELCID1866 FABLO EL REY DON ALFONSSO * DIXO ESTA RAZON:
14769 5ELCID1867 GRADO AL CRIADOR * AL SE@OR SANT ESIDRO EL DE LEON
14794 5ELCID1870 AUOS, MINAYA ALBARFANEZ, * EA PERO VERMUEZ AQUI,
14806 5ELCID1871 MANDO UOS LOS CUERPOS ONDRADA MIENTRE SERUIR * VESTIR
14829 5ELCID1874 DOUOS IIJ CAUALLOS * PRENDED LOS AQUI.
14836 5ELCID1875 ASSI COMMO SEMEIA * LA VELUNTAD MELO DIZ.
14853 5ELCID1877 BESARON LE LAS MANOS * ENTRARON A POSAR;
14898 5ELCID1883 CRE%REMOS EN NUESTRA ONDRA * YREMOS ADELANT.
14914 5ELCID1885 MER%ED UOS PIDIMOS COMMO A REY * SE@OR NATURAL;
14936 5ELCID1888 CASAR QUEREMOS CON ELLAS ASU ONDRA * A NUESTRA PRO.
14946 5ELCID1889 VNA GRANT ORA EL REY PENSSO * COMIDIO;
14960 5ELCID1891 EFAZIENDO YO HA EL MAL, * EL AMI GRAND PRO,
14984 5ELCID1894 A MYNAYA ALBARFANEZ * A PERO VERMUEZ
15004 5ELCID1897 OYD ME, MYNAYA, * VOS, PER VERMUEZ:
15036 5ELCID1901 DIEGO * FERRANDO, LOS YFFANTES DE CARRION,
15054 5ELCID1903 SED BUENOS MENSSAGEROS, * RUEGO UOS LO YO
15067 5ELCID1905 ABRA Y ONDRA * CRE%RA EN ONOR,
15080 5ELCID1907 FABLO MYNAYA * PLOGO A PER VERMUEZ:
15144 5ELCID1915 VAN PORA VALEN%IA ELLOS * TODOS LOS SOS.
15162 5ELCID1918 SONRRISOS MYO %ID * BIEN LOS ABRA%O:
15168 5ELCID1919 VENIDES, MYNAYA, * VOS, PERO VERMUEZ
15197 5ELCID1923 DIXO MYNAYA. DALMA * DE CORA%ON
15202 5ELCID1924 ES PAGADO, * DAUOS SU AMOR.
15236 5ELCID1929 QUEL CONNOS%IE Y ONDRA * CRE%IE EN ONOR,
15244 5ELCID1930 QUE GELO CONSSEIAUA DALMA * DE CORA%ON.
15259 5ELCID1932 VNA GRAND ORA PENSSO * COMIDIO;
15272 5ELCID1934 ECHADO FU DE TIERRA * TOLLIDA LA ONOR,
15307 5ELCID1938 ELLOS SON MUCHO VRGULLOSOS * AN PART EN LA CORT,
15363 5ELCID1945 QUERER UOS YE VER * DAR UOS SU AMOR,
15508 5ELCID1965 DELLA PART * DELLA PORA LAS VISTAS SE ADOBAUAN;
15530 5ELCID1968 CAUALLOS GRUESSOS * COREDORES SJN FALLA,
15545 5ELCID1970 ESCUDOS BOCLADOS CON ORO * CON PLATA,
15549 5ELCID1971 MANTOS * PIELLES E BUENOS %ENDALES CADRIA?
15586 5ELCID1976 LO VNO A DEBDAN * LO OTRO PAGAUAN;
15613 5ELCID1980 CUENDES * PODESTADES & MUY GRANDES MESNADAS.
15615 5ELCID1980 CUENDES & PODESTADES * MUY GRANDES MESNADAS.
15631 5ELCID1982 CON EL REY VAN LEONESES * MESNADAS GALIZIANAS,
15667 5ELCID1987 TANTA GRUESSA MULA * TANTO PALAFRE DE SAZON,
15675 5ELCID1988 TANTA BUENA ARMA * TANTO BUEN CAUALLO COREDOR,
15683 5ELCID1989 TANTA BUENA CAPA * MANTOS & PELLI%ONES;
15685 5ELCID1989 TANTA BUENA CAPA & MANTOS * PELLI%ONES;
15688 5ELCID1990 CHICOS * GRANDES VESTIDOS SON DE COLORES.
15696 5ELCID1991 MYNAYA ALBARFANEZ * AQUEL PERO VERMUEZ,
15702 5ELCID1992 MARTIN MUNOZ * MARTIN ANTOLINEZ, EL BURGALES DE PRO,
15717 5ELCID1994 ALUAR ALUAREZ * ALUAR SAUADOREZ,
15750 5ELCID1999 ALUAR SALUADOREZ * GALIND GARCIAZ EL DE ARAGON,
15767 5ELCID2001 DALMA * DE CORA%ON, & TODOS LOS QUE EN PODER DESSOS FOSSEN;
15770 5ELCID2001 DALMA & DE CORA%ON, * TODOS LOS QUE EN PODER DESSOS FOSSEN;
15795 5ELCID2003 DENTRO ES SU MUGIER * SUS FIJAS AMAS ADOS,
15805 5ELCID2004 EN QUE TIENE SU ALMA * SU CORA%ON,
15842 5ELCID2009 SALIEN DE VALEN%IA, AGUIJAN * ESPOLONAUAN.
15849 5ELCID2010 TANTOS CAUALLOS EN DIESTRO, GRUESSOS * CORREDORES,
15938 5ELCID2021 LOS YNOIOS * LAS MANOS EN TIERRA LOS FINCO,
16034 5ELCID2033 DIXO EL REY ESTO FERE DALMA * DE CORA%ON;
16040 5ELCID2034 AQUI UOS PERDONO * DOUOS MY AMOR,
16054 5ELCID2036 FABLO MYO %ID * DIXO: MER%ED; YOLO RE%IBO, ALFONSSO MYO SE@OR;
16067 5ELCID2037 GRADESCOLO A DIOS DEL %IELO * DESPUES AUOS,
16087 5ELCID2040 LEUOS EN PIE * EN LA BOCAL SALUDO.
16101 5ELCID2042 PESO A ALBARDIAZ * A GARCIORDONEZ.
16107 5ELCID2043 FABLO MYO %ID * DIXO ESTA RAZON: ESTO GRADESCO AL CRIADOR,
16130 5ELCID2045 VALER ME A DIOS DE DIA * DE NOCH.
16149 5ELCID2048 VOS AGORA LEGASTES, * NOS VINJEMOS ANOCH;
16250 5ELCID2061 ES DIA ES PASSADO, * ENTRADA ES LA NOCH;
16287 5ELCID2066 TODOS ERAN ALEGRES * ACUERDAN EN VNA RAZON:
16336 5ELCID2072 OYD ME, LAS ESCUELLAS, CUENDES * YFAN%ONES
16361 5ELCID2075 VUESTRAS FIJAS UOS PIDO, DON ELUIRA * DO@A SOL,
16377 5ELCID2077 SEMEIAM EL CASAMIENTO ONDRADO * CON GRANT PRO,
16385 5ELCID2078 ELLOS UOS LAS PIDEN * MANDO UOS LO YO.
16391 5ELCID2079 DELLA * DELLA PARTE, CUANTOS QUE AQUI SON,
16400 5ELCID2080 LOS MIOS * LOS UUESTROS QUE SEAN ROGADORES;

WORD C# PREFIX CONTEXT

& (CON'T)

16445 5ELCID2085 PERTENE%EN PCRA MIS FIJAS * AVN PORA MEIORES.
16453 5ELCID2086 HYO LAS ENGENDRE AMAS * CRIASTES LAS UOS
16471 5ELCID2088 AFELLAS EN UUESTRA MANO DCN ELUIRA * DO@A SOL,
16488 5ELCID2090 GRA%IAS, DIXO EL REY, AUOS * ATOD ESTA CORT.
16525 5ELCID2095 GRADO * GRA%IAS, CID, CCMMO TAN BUENO, & PRIMERO AL CRIADOR,
16531 5ELCID2095 GRADO & GRA%IAS, CID, CCMMO TAN BUENO, * PRIMERO AL CRIADOR,
16552 5ELCID2097 DAQUI LAS PRENDO POR MIS MANOS DON ELUIRA * DONA SOL,
16624 5ELCID2106 LOS YERNOS * LAS FIJAS TODOS UUESTROS FIJOS SON:
16653 5ELCID2109 MUCHO UCS LO GRADESCO, CCMMO A REY * A SE@OR
16695 5ELCID2114 TANTA GRUESSA MULA * TANTO PALAFRE DE SAZON
16784 5ELCID2125 GRADESCOLO, REY, * PRENDO UUESTRO DON,
16879 5ELCID2136 PRENDELLAS CCN UUESTRAS MANOS * DALDAS ALOS YFANTES,
16952 5ELCID2146 TOMAD AQUESTO, * BESO UUESTRAS MANOS.
17000 5ELCID2152 DEUOS BIEN SO SERUIDO, * TENGON POR PAGADO;
17060 5ELCID2160 MER%ED UOS SEA * FAZED NOS ESTE PERDON:
17091 5ELCID2163 HE DELAS FIJAS DE MYO %ID, DE DON ELUIRA * DO@A SOL.
17098 5ELCID2164 ESTO PLOGO AL REY, * ATODOS LOS SOLTO;
17107 5ELCID2165 LA CONPA@A DEL %ID CRE%E, * LA DEL REY MENGO,
17132 5ELCID2168 EA DON FERNANDO * A DON DIEGO AGUARDAR LOS MANDO
17141 5ELCID2169 APERO VERMUEZ * MUNO GUSTIOZ,
17210 5ELCID2177 DIXO MYO %ID ADON PERO * A MU@O GUSTIOZ:
17218 5ELCID2178 DAD LES VN REYAL * ALOS YFANTES DE CARRION,
17247 5ELCID2181 VERAN ASUS ESPOSAS, A DON ELUIRA * A DONA SOL.
17268 5ELCID2184 RE%IBIOLO DO@A XIMENA * SUS FIJAS AMAS:
17316 5ELCID2190 BESARON LE LAS MANOS LA MUGIER * LAS FIJAS AMAS,
17329 5ELCID2192 GRADO AL CRIADOR * AUOS, %ID, BARBA VELIDA
17369 5ELCID2197 AUOS DIGO, MIS FIJAS, DON ELUIRA * DO@A SOL:
17390 5ELCID2200 PEDIDAS UOS HA * ROGADAS EL MYO SE@OR ALFONSSO,
17399 5ELCID2201 ATAN FIRME MIENTRE * DE TODO CORA%ON
17438 5ELCID2206 POR EL SUELO * SUSO TAN BIEN ENCORTINADO,
17445 5ELCID2207 TANTA PORPOLA * TANTO XAMED & TANTO PA@O PRECIADO.
17448 5ELCID2207 TANTA PORPOLA & TANTO XAMED * TANTO PA@O PRECIADO.
17456 5ELCID2208 SABOR ABRIEDES DE SER * DE COMER ENEL PALA%IO.
17485 5ELCID2212 CON BUENAS VESTIDURAS * FUERTE MIENTRE ADOBADOS;
17491 5ELCID2213 DE PIE * ASABOR, DIOS, QUE QUEDOS ENTRARON
17506 5ELCID2215 AEL * EASSU MUGIER DELANT SELE OMILLARON,
17559 5ELCID2221 VENIT ACA, ALBARFANEZ, EL QUE YO QUIERO * AMO
17598 5ELCID2226 E PRENDAN BENDI%IONES * VAYAMOS RECABDANDO.
17612 5ELCID2228 LEUANTAN SE DERECHAS * METIOGELAS EN MANO.
17653 5ELCID2233 QUE LAS TOMASSEDES POR MUGIERES A ONDRA * A RECABDO.
17660 5ELCID2234 AMOS LAS RE%IBEN DAMOR * DE GRADO,
17666 5ELCID2235 A MYO %ID * A SU MUGIER VAN BESAR LA MANO.
17727 5ELCID2243 DIOS, QUE BIEN TOUIERON ARMAS EL %ID * SUS VASSALOS
17817 5ELCID2254 ENTRE PALAFRES * MULAS & CORREDORES CAUALLOS,
17819 5ELCID2254 ENTRE PALAFRES & MULAS * CORREDORES CAUALLOS,
17830 5ELCID2256 MANTOS * PELLI%ONES & OTROS VESTIDOS LARGOS;
17832 5ELCID2256 MANTOS & PELLI%ONES * OTROS VESTIDOS LARGOS;
17894 5ELCID2264 EA TODAS LAS DUE@AS * ALOS FIJOS DALGO;
17905 5ELCID2265 POR PAGADOS SE PARTEN DE MYO %ID * DE SUS VASSALLOS.
17920 5ELCID2267 MUCHO ERAN ALEGRES DIEGO * FERRANDO;
17936 5ELCID2270 EL %ID * SOS HYERNOS EN VALEN%IA SON RASTADOS.
17963 5ELCID2273 ALEGRE ERA EL %ID * TODOS SUS VASSALLOS.
17971 5ELCID2274 PLEGA A SANTA MARIA * AL PADRE SANTO
18037 5ELCID2282 SALIOS DE LA RED * DESATOS EL LEON.
18060 5ELCID2285 E %ERCAN EL ESCA@O * FINCAN SOBRE SO SE@OR.
18106 5ELCID2291 EL MANTO * EL BRIAL TODO SUZIO LO SACO.
18158 5ELCID2297 EL MANTO TRAE ALCUELLO, * ADELINO PORA LEON;
18176 5ELCID2299 ANTE MYO %ID LA CABE%A PREMIO * EL ROSTRO FINCO;
18213 5ELCID2304 MYO %ID POR SOS YERNOS DEMANDO * NOLOS FALLO;
18226 5ELCID2306 QUANDO LOS FALLARON * ELLOS VINIERON, ASSI VINIERON SIN COLOR;
18295 5ELCID2315 ALEGRAUAS EL %ID * TODOS SUS VARONES,
18337 5ELCID2320 CATAMOS LA GANAN%IA * LA PERDIDA NO,
18403 5ELCID2329 QUE SEAN EN PAS * NON AYAN Y RA%ION.
18413 5ELCID2330 NOS CON UUSCO LA VENCREMOS, * VALER NOS HA EL CRIADOR.
18445 5ELCID2334 HYO DESSEO LIDES, * UOS A CARRION;
18498 5ELCID2341 PLOGO A MYO %ID * ATODOS SOS VASSALLOS;
18506 5ELCID2342 AVN SI DIOS QUISIERE * EL PADRE QUE ESTA EN ALTO,
18524 5ELCID2344 ESTO VAN DIZIENDO * LAS YENTES SE ALEGANDO,
18556 5ELCID2348 MAS SE MARAUILLAN ENTRE DIEGO * FERRANDO,
18586 5ELCID2352 CURIES ME ADIEGO * CURIES ME ADON FERNANDO,
18697 5ELCID2366 VERLO HEMOS CONDIOS * CON LA UUESTRA AUZE.
18740 5ELCID2371 POR ESSO SALI DE MI TIERRA * VIN UOS BUSCAR,
18754 5ELCID2373 MI ORDEN * MIS MANOS QUERRIA LAS ONDRAR,
18771 5ELCID2375 PENDON TRAYO A CORCAS * ARMAS DE SE@AL,
18847 5ELCID2385 POR LA SU VENTURA * DIOS QUEL AMAUA
18864 5ELCID2387 EL ASTIL A QUEBRADO * METIO MANO AL ESPADA.
18880 5ELCID2389 DOS MATO CON LAN%A * V CON EL ESPADA.
18915 5ELCID2393 EN BRA%O EL ESCUDO * ABAXO EL ASTA,
18932 5ELCID2395 HYUA LOS FERIR DE CORA%ON * DE ALMA.
18945 5ELCID2397 ABATIO A VIJ * A IIIJ MATAUA.
18968 5ELCID2400 VERIEDES QUEBRAR TANTAS CUERDAS * ARRANCAR SE LAS ESTACAS
19058 5ELCID2411 SALUDAR NOS HEMOS AMOS, * TAIAREMOS AMISTAS.
19076 5ELCID2413 EL ESPADA TIENES DESNUDA EN LA MANO * VEOT AGUIJAR;
19118 5ELCID2418 BUEN CAUALLO TIENE BUCAR * GRANDES SALTOS FAZ,

WORD C# PREFIX CONTEXT

& (CON'T)

19158 5ELCID2423 CORTOL EL YELMO *, LIBRADO TODO LO MAL,
19191 5ELCID2427 VENZIO LA BATALLA MARAUILLOSA * GRANT.
19197 5ELCID2428 AQUIS ONDRO MYO %ID * QUANTOS CONEL SON.
19249 5ELCID2436 LA CARA FRONZIDA * ALMOFAR SOLTADO,
19278 5ELCID2440 E VIO VENIR ADIEGO * A FERNANDO;
19323 5ELCID2447 COMMO YO FIO POR DIOS * EN TODOS LOS SOS SANTOS,
19344 5ELCID2450 EL ESCUDO TRAE AL CUELLO * TODO ESPADO;
19384 5ELCID2456 GRADO ADIOS * AL PADRE QUE ESTA EN ALTO,
19402 5ELCID2458 MATASTES ABUCAR * ARRANCAMOS EL CANPO.
19411 5ELCID2459 TODOS ESTOS BIENES DEUOS SON * DE UUESTROS VASSALLOS.
19513 5ELCID2472 CON DUCHOS A SAZONES, BUENAS PIELES * BUENOS MANTOS.
19521 5ELCID2473 MUCHOS SON ALEGRES MYO %ID * SUS VASSALLOS,
19537 5ELCID2475 DESPUES QUE ESTA BATALLA VENZIERON * AL REY BUCAR MATO;
19581 5ELCID2481 COMMO SON ONDRADOS * AVER VOS GRANT PRO.
19646 5ELCID2490 EOTRAS AZEMILLAS * CAMELOS LARGOS
19680 5ELCID2495 QUE HE AUER * TIERRA & ORO & ONOR,
19682 5ELCID2495 QUE HE AUER & TIERRA * ORO & ONOR,
19684 5ELCID2495 QUE HE AUER & TIERRA & ORO * ONOR,
19700 5ELCID2498 MOROS * CHRISTIANOS DE MI HAN GRANT PAUOR;
19770 5ELCID2506 DE TODAS SUS CONPA@AS * DE TODOS SUS VASSALLOS;
19876 5ELCID2520 EAMAS LA MYS FIJAS, DON ELUIRA * DO@A SOL;
19882 5ELCID2521 BIEN UOS ABRAZEN * SIRUAN UOS DE CORAZON.
19891 5ELCID2522 VENZIEMOS MOROS EN CAMPO * MATAMOS
19927 5ELCID2528 GRADO AL CRIADOR * A UOS, %ID ONDRADO,
19944 5ELCID2530 POR UOS AUEMOS ONDRA * AVEMOS LIDIADO.
19986 5ELCID2536 ELAS NOCHES * LOS DIAS TAN MAL LOS ESCARMENTANDO,
20028 5ELCID2541 LOS AUERES QUE TENEMOS GRANDES SON * SOBEIANOS,
20149 5ELCID2558 FABLO FERAN GONZALEZ * FIZO CALLAR LA CORT;
20166 5ELCID2560 QUE PLEGA A DO@A XIMENA * PRIMERO AUOS
20172 5ELCID2561 EA MYNAYA ALBARFANEZ * A QUANTOS AQUI SON:
20203 5ELCID2565 QUE LES DIEMOS POR ARRAS * POR ONORES;
20228 5ELCID2568 DIXO EL CAMPEADOR: DARUOS HE MYS FIJAS * ALGO DELO MYO;
20265 5ELCID2572 DARUOS E MULAS * PALAFRES, MUY GRUESSOS DE SAZON,
20276 5ELCID2573 CAUALLOS PORA EN DIESTRO FUERTES * CORREDORES,
20283 5ELCID2574 E MUCHAS VESTIDURAS DE PA@OS * DE %ICLATONES;
20293 5ELCID2575 DAR UOS HE DOS ESPADAS, A COLADA * A TIZON,
20327 5ELCID2579 QUE LO SEPAN EN GALLIZIA * EN CASTIELLA & EN LEON,
20330 5ELCID2579 QUE LO SEPAN EN GALLIZIA & EN CASTIELLA * EN LEON,
20403 5ELCID2589 TODOS PRENDEN ARMAS * CAUALGAN A VIGOR,
20427 5ELCID2592 AMAS HERMANAS, DON ELUIRA * DO@A SOL,
20455 5ELCID2596 DELANT SODES AMOS, SE@ORA * SE@OR.
20490 5ELCID2601 ABRAZOLAS MYO %ID * SALUDOLAS AMAS ADOS.
20510 5ELCID2604 DE MI * DE UUESTRO PADRE BIEN AVEDES NUESTRA GRA%IA.
20534 5ELCID2607 AL PADRE * ALA MADRE LAS MANOS LES BESAUAN;
20544 5ELCID2608 AMOS LAS BENDIXIERON * DIERON LES SU GRA%IA.
20551 5ELCID2609 MYO %ID * LOS OTROS DE CAUALGAR PENSSAUAN,
20560 5ELCID2610 AGRANDES GUARNJMIENTOS, ACAUALLOS * ARMAS.
20573 5ELCID2612 ESPIENDOS DELAS DUE@AS * DE TODAS SUS COMPA@AS.
20634 5ELCID2619 PRIMO ERES DE MIS FIJAS AMAS DALMA * DE CORAZON
20666 5ELCID2623 DIXO FELEZ MUNOZ: PLAZME DALMA * DE CORAZON.
20687 5ELCID2626 QUE SI ADIOS PLOGUIERE * AL PADRE CRIADOR,
20703 5ELCID2628 ADIOS UOS HACOMENDAMOS, DON ELUIRA * DO@A SOL,
20911 5ELCID2656 TROZIERON ARBUXUELO * LEGARON A SALON,
21058 5ELCID2676 HYO SIRUIENDO UOS SIN ART, * UOS CONSSEIASTES PORA MI MUERT.
21102 5ELCID2681 AQUIM PARTO DE UOS COMMO DE MALOS * DE TRAYDORES.
21111 5ELCID2682 HYRE CON UUESTRA GRA%IA, DON ELUIRA * DO@A SOL;
21124 5ELCID2684 DIOS LO QUIERA * LO MANDE, QUE DE TODEL MUNDO ES SE@OR,
21144 5ELCID2686 ESTO LES HA DICHO, * EL MORO SE TORNO;
21177 5ELCID2690 ACOIEN SE A ANDAR DE DIA * DE NOCH;
21325 5ELCID2710 SI NON AMAS SUS MUGIERES DO@A ELUIRA * DO@A SOL:
21355 5ELCID2714 BIEN LO CREADES, DON ELUIRA * DO@A SOL,
21368 5ELCID2716 OY NOS PARTIREMOS, * DEXADAS SEREDES DE NOS;
21398 5ELCID2720 ALLI LES TUELLEN LOS MANTOS * LOS PELLIZONES,
21405 5ELCID2721 PARAN LAS EN CUERPOS * EN CAMISAS & EN %ICLATONES.
21408 5ELCID2721 PARAN LAS EN CUERPOS & EN CAMISAS * EN %ICLATONES.
21423 5ELCID2723 EN MANO PRENDEN LAS %INCHAS FUERTES * DURADORES.
21439 5ELCID2725 POR DIOS UOS ROGAMOS, DON DIEGO * DON FERANDO
21446 5ELCID2726 DOS ESPADAS TENEDES FUERTES * TAIADORES,
21452 5ELCID2727 AL VNA DIZEN COLADA * AL OTRA TIZON,
21463 5ELCID2729 MOROS * CHRISTIANOS DEPARTIRAN DESTA RAZON,
21539 5ELCID2738 RONPIEN LAS CAMISAS * LAS CARNES AELLAS AMAS ADOS;
21585 5ELCID2744 SANGRIENTAS EN LAS CAMISAS * TODOS LOS CICLATONES.
21608 5ELCID2747 HYA NON PUEDEN FABLAR DON ELUIRA * DONA SOL;
21623 5ELCID2749 LEUARON LES LOS MANTOS * LAS PIELES ARMINAS,
21633 5ELCID2750 MAS DEXAN LAS MARIDAS EN BRIALES * EN CAMISAS,
21641 5ELCID2751 E ALAS AUES DEL MONTE * ALAS BESTIAS DELA FIERA GUISA.
21793 5ELCID2772 VIOLOS VENIR * OYO VNA RAZON,
21850 5ELCID2780 YA PRIMAS, LAS MIS PRIMAS, DON ELUIRA * DO@A SOL,
21862 5ELCID2782 ADIOS PLEGA * A SANTA MARIA QUE DENT PRENDAN ELLOS MAL GALARDON
21902 5ELCID2786 LAMANDO: PRIMAS, PRIMAS, DON ELUIRA * DON SOL
21933 5ELCID2790 VAN RECORDANDO DON ELUIRA * DO@A SOL,
21939 5ELCID2791 ABRIERON LOS OIOS * VIERON AFELEZ MUNOZ.
22006 5ELCID2800 NUEUO ERA * FRESCO, QUE DE VALEN%IAL SACO,
22016 5ELCID2801 COGIO DEL AGUA ENEL * ASUS PRIMAS DIO;

WORD C# PREFIX CONTEXT

& (CON'T)

```
22023 5ELCID2802 MUCHO SON LAZRADAS * AMAS LAS FARTO.
22036 5ELCID2804 VALAS CONORTANDO * METIENDO CORAZON
22042 5ELCID2805 FATA QUE ESFUERZAN, * AMAS LAS TOMO
22066 5ELCID2808 EL CAUALLO PRISO POR LA RIENDA * LUEGO DENT LAS PARTIO,
22081 5ELCID2810 ENTRE NOCH * DIA SALIERON DELOS MONTES;
22124 5ELCID2816 PRISO BESTIAS * VESTIDOS DE PRO,
22132 5ELCID2817 HYUA REZEBIR ADON ELUIRA * ADONaA SOL;
22207 5ELCID2828 VNA GRAND ORA PENSSO * COMIDIO;
22259 5ELCID2835 PESO A MYO ZID * ATODA SU CORT, & ALBARFANEZ DALMA & DE CORAZON
22263 5ELCID2835 PESO A MYO ZID & ATODA SU CORT, * ALBARFANEZ DALMA & DE CORAZON
22266 5ELCID2835 PESO A MYO ZID & ATODA SU CORT, & ALBARFANEZ DALMA * DE CORAZON.
22295 5ELCID2839 DIXOLES FUERTE MIENTRE QUE ANDICIESSEN DE DIA * DE NOCH,
22317 5ELCID2842 APIRESSA CAUALGAN, LOS DIAS * LAS NOCHES ANDAN;
22358 5ELCID2848 REZIBEN AMINAYA * ATODOS SUS VARONES,
22426 5ELCID2856 TODOS GELO GRADEZEN * SOS PAGADOS SON,
22450 5ELCID2859 ENEL FINCAN LOS OIOS DON ELUIRA * DOaA SOL:
22486 5ELCID2863 LORAUAN DELOS OIOS LAS DUEaAS * ALBARFANEZ,
22497 5ELCID2865 DON ELUIRA * DOaA SOL, CUYDADO NON AYADES,
22507 5ELCID2866 QUANDO UOS SODES SAaAS * BIUAS & SIN OTRO MAL.
22509 5ELCID2866 QUANDO UOS SODES SAaAS & BIUAS * SIN OTRO MAL.
22531 5ELCID2869 HY IAZEN ESSA NOCHE, * TAN GRAND GOZO QUE FAZEN.
22657 5ELCID2887 ARMAS YUA TENIENDO * GRANT GOZO QUE FAZE;
22795 5ELCID2904 POR MI BESA LE LA MANO DALMA * DE CORAZON,
22803 5ELCID2905 CUEMO YO SO SU VASSALLO, * EL ES MYO SEaOR,
22823 5ELCID2907 QUEL PESE AL BUEN REY DALMA * DE CORAZON.
22850 5ELCID2911 LA POCA * LA GRANT TODA ES DE MYO SEaOR.
22924 5ELCID2920 SALIEN DE VALENZIA * ANDAN QUANTO PUEDEN,
22933 5ELCID2921 NOS DAN VAGAR LOS DIAS * LAS NOCHES.
22947 5ELCID2923 REY ES DE CASTIELLA * REY ES DE LEON
22985 5ELCID2928 OMILLOS ALOS SANTOS * ROGO ACRIADOR;
23013 5ELCID2932 VIOLOS EL REY * CONNOSZIO A MUaO GUSTIOZ;
23052 5ELCID2937 LOS PIES * LAS MANOS VOS BESA EL CAMPEADOR;
23063 5ELCID2938 ELE ES VUESTRO VASSALLO * UOS SODES SO SEaOS.
23106 5ELCID2944 MAIADAS * DESNUDAS A GRANDE DESONOR,
23121 5ELCID2946 ALAS BESTIAS FIERAS * ALAS AUES DEL MONT.
23182 5ELCID2953 EL REY VNA GRAND ORA CALLO * COMIDIO;
23229 5ELCID2959 ENTRE YO * MYO ZID PESA NOS DE CORAZON.
23271 5ELCID2964 QUE ALLA ME VAYAN CUENDES * YFANZONES,
23373 5ELCID2977 ENBIA SUS CARTAS PORA LEON * A SANTI YAGUO,
23379 5ELCID2978 ALOS PORTOGALESES * A GALIZIANOS,
23386 5ELCID2979 E ALOS DE CARRION * AVARONES CASTELLANOS,
23572 5ELCID3002 EL CONDE DON ANRRICH * EL CONDE DON REMOND;
23587 5ELCID3004 EL CONDE DON FRUELLA * EL CONDE DON BELTRAN.
23617 5ELCID3008 E ASUR GONZALEZ * GONZALO ASSUREZ,
23622 5ELCID3009 E DIEGO * FERRANDO Y SON AMOS ADOS,
23755 5ELCID3026 BILTAR SE QUIERE * ONDRAR ASO SEaOS.
23787 5ELCID3030 SALUDAR NOS HEMOS DALMA * DE CORAZON.
23819 5ELCID3034 BESO LE LA MANO * DESPUES LE SALUDO;
23831 5ELCID3036 OMILLOM AUOS * ALCONDE DO REMOND
23840 5ELCID3037 E AL CONDE DON ARRICH * A QUANTOS QUE Y SON;
23851 5ELCID3038 DIOS SALUE A NUESTROS AMIGOS * AUOS MAS, SEaOR
23867 5ELCID3040 BESA UOS LAS MANOS, * MIS FIJAS AMAS ADOS,
23974 5ELCID3055 MANDO FAZER CANDELAS * PONER ENEL ALTAR;
23987 5ELCID3057 AL CRIADOR ROGANDO * FABLANDO EN PORIDAD.
23993 5ELCID3058 ENTRE MINAYA * LOS BUENOS QUE Y HA
24006 5ELCID3060 MATINES * PRIMA DIXIERON FAZAL ALBA,
24027 5ELCID3062 E SSU OFRENDA HAN FECHA MUY BUENA * CONPLIDA.
24039 5ELCID3064 VOS YREDES COMIGO * EL OBISPO DON IHERONIMO
24047 5ELCID3065 E PERO VERMUEZ * AQUESTE MUaO GUSTIOZ
24061 5ELCID3067 E ALBAR ALBAREZ * ALBAR SALUADOREZ
24119 5ELCID3075 SOBRE LAS LORIGAS ARMINOS * PELIZONES,
24136 5ELCID3077 SOLOS MANTOS LAS ESPADAS DULZES * TAIADORES;
24149 5ELCID3079 POR DE MANDAR MYOS DERECHOS * DEZIR MI RAZON:
24217 5ELCID3088 CON ORO * CON PLATA TODAS LAS PRESAS SON,
24290 5ELCID3097 LA BARBA AVIE LUENGA * PRISOLA CON EL CORDON,
24387 5ELCID3109 E EL CONDE DON ANRRICH * EL CONDE DON REMONT
24509 5ELCID3124 ALA BARBA QUE AUIE LUENGA * PRESA CONEL CORDON;
24559 5ELCID3130 LA VNA FUE EN BURGOS, * LA OTRA EN CARRION,
24607 5ELCID3135 ALCALDES SEAN DESTO EL CONDE DON ANRRICH * EL CONDE DON REMOND
24638 5ELCID3139 DELLA * DELLA PART EN PAZ SEAMOS OY.
24690 5ELCID3145 MYO ZID LA MANO BESO AL REY * EN PIE SE LEUANTO;
24702 5ELCID3146 MUCHO UOS LO GRADESCO COMMO A REY * A SEaOR,
24751 5ELCID3152 HYO BIEN LAS QUERIA DALMA * DE CORAZON,
24759 5ELCID3153 DILES DOS ESPADAS, A COLADA * A TIZON,
24773 5ELCID3155 QUES ONDRASSEN CON ELLAS * SIRUIESSEN AUOS;
24789 5ELCID3157 COMIGO NON QUISIERON AUER NADA * PERDIERON MI AMOR;
24827 5ELCID3162 CON TODOS SUS PARIENTES * EL VANDO QUE Y SON;
24837 5ELCID3163 APRIESSA LO YUAN TRAYENDO * ACUERDAN LA RAZON:
24917 5ELCID3173 QUANDO LAS DEMANDA * DELLAS HA SABOR,
24931 5ELCID3175 SACARON LAS ESPADAS COLADO * TIZON,
24944 5ELCID3177 SACA LAS ESPADAS * RELUMBRA TODA LA CORT,
24951 5ELCID3179 LAS MAZANAS * LOS ARRIAZES TODOS DORO SON.
24984 5ELCID3182 EN LAS MANOS LAS TIENE * AMAS LAS DATO;
25024 5ELCID3187 ASSIS YRAN VENGANDO DON ELUIRA * DONA SOL.
```

WORD C# PREFIX CONTEXT

& (CON'T)

25103 5ELCID3197 SE QUE SI UOS ACAE%IERE, CON ELLA GANAREDES GRAND PREZ * GRAND VALOR.
25113 5ELCID3198 BESO LE LA MANO, EL ESPADA TOMO * RE%IBIO.
25125 5ELCID3200 GRADO AL CRIADOR * AUOS, REY SE@OR,
25137 5ELCID3201 HYA PAGADO SO DE MIS ESPADAS, DE COLADA * DE TIZON.
25157 5ELCID3204 EN ORO * EN PLATA TRES MILL MARCOS DE PLATA LES DIO;
25427 5ELCID3238 EL ORO * LA PLATA ESPENDIESTES LO VOS;
25445 5ELCID3240 PAGEN LE EN APRE%IADURA * PRENDALO EL CAMPEADOR.
25527 5ELCID3251 SOS OMNES LAS TIENEN * DELLAS PENSSARAN.
25558 5ELCID3255 OYD ME TODA LA CORT * PESEUOS DE MYO MAL;
25619 5ELCID3262 CON MUY GRAND ONDRA * AVERES A NOMBRE;
25644 5ELCID3265 A QUE LAS FIRIESTES A %INCHAS * A ESPOLONES?
25657 5ELCID3267 ALAS BESTIAS FIERAS * ALAS AUES DEL MONT;
25700 5ELCID3273 DEXOLA CRE%ER * LUENGA TRAE LA BARBA;
25710 5ELCID3274 LOS VNOS LE HAN MIEDO * LOS OTROS ESPANTA.
25762 5ELCID3281 GRADO A DIOS QUE %IELO * TIERRA MANDA
25817 5ELCID3288 QUANDO PRIS A CABRA, * AUOS POR LA BARBA,
25866 5ELCID3295 NON CRE%IES VARAIA ENTRE NOS * VOS.
25923 5ELCID3303 HYO LAS HE FIJAS, * TU PRIMAS CORMANAS;
26077 5ELCID3324 DELANT MYO %ID * DELANTE TODOS OVISTE TE DE ALABAR
26088 5ELCID3325 QUE MATARAS EL MORO * QUE FIZIERAS BARNAX;
26131 5ELCID3331 QUANDO DURMIE MYO %ID * EL LEON SE DESATO?
26179 5ELCID3337 LEUANTOS DEL ESCA@O * FUES PORAL LEON;
26196 5ELCID3339 DEXOS LE PRENDER ALCUELO, * ALA RED LE METIO.
26224 5ELCID3343 RIEBTOT EL CUERPO POR MALO * POR TRAYDOR;
26240 5ELCID3345 POR FIJAS DEL %ID, DON ELUIRA * DONA SOL:
26253 5ELCID3347 ELLAS SON MUGIERES * VOS SODES VARONES,
26428 5ELCID3371 QUE ERES TRAYDOR * MINTIST DE QUANTO DICHO HAS.
26447 5ELCID3374 MANTO ARMINO * VN BRIAL RASTRANDO,
26511 5ELCID3383 CALA, ALEUOSO, MALO * TRAYDOR
26536 5ELCID3387 FALSSO A TODOS * MAS AL CRIADOR.
26587 5ELCID3394 AL VNO DIZEN OIARRA * AL OTRO YENEGO SIMENEZ,
26624 5ELCID3399 POR SER REYNAS DE NAUARRA * DE ARAGON,
26633 5ELCID3400 E QUE GELAS DIESSEN A ONDRA * ABENDI%ION,
26637 5ELCID3401 AESTO CALLARON * ASCUCHO TODA LA CORT.
26666 5ELCID3405 QUANDO MELAS DEMANDAN DE NAUARRA * DE ARAGON.
26705 5ELCID3411 QUE PLEGA AUOS, * ATORGAR LO HE YO,
26723 5ELCID3413 CA CRE%E UOS Y ONDRA * TIERRA & ONOR.
26725 5ELCID3413 CA CRE%E UOS Y ONDRA & TIERRA * ONOR.
26755 5ELCID3417 AUOS, OIARRA, * AUOS, YENEGO XIMENEZ,
26772 5ELCID3419 DE FIJAS DE MYO %ID, DON ELUIRA * DO@A SOL,
26780 5ELCID3420 PORA LOS YFANTES DE NAUARRA * DE ARAGON,
26788 5ELCID3421 QUE UOS LAS DE AONDRA * A BENDI%ION.
26795 5ELCID3422 LEUANTOS EN PIE OIARRA * YNEGO XIMENEZ,
26815 5ELCID3425 METIERON LAS FES, * LOS OMENAIES DADOS SON,
26853 5ELCID3430 MER%ED UOS PIDO COMMO A REY * A SE@OR,
26922 5ELCID3439 ELLOS LAS PRISIERON A ONDRA * A BENDI%ION;
26947 5ELCID3442 RIEBTOS LES LOS CUERPOS POR MALOS * POR TRAYDORES.
26961 5ELCID3444 ONDE SALIEN CONDES DE PREZ * DE VALOR;
26982 5ELCID3447 QUANDO PIDEN MIS PRIMAS, DON ELUIRA * DO@A SOL,
26989 5ELCID3448 LOS YFANTES DE NAUARRA * DE ARAGON;
27005 5ELCID3450 AGORA BESAREDES SUS MANOS * LAMAR LAS HEDES SE@ORAS,
27023 5ELCID3452 GRADO ADIOS DEL %IELO * AQUEL REY DON ALFONSSO,
27144 5ELCID3469 ARMAS * CAUALLOS TIENEN LOS DEL CANPEADOR,
27258 5ELCID3484 DESI SEA VEN%IDO * ESCAPE POR TRAYDOR.
27276 5ELCID3486 MYO %ID AL REY LAS MANOS LE BESO * DIXO: PLAZME, SE@OR.
27295 5ELCID3488 DAQUI UOS LOS ACOMIENDO COMO A REY * A SE@OR.
27345 5ELCID3494 E SOLTAUA LA BARBA * SACOLA DEL CORDON.
27365 5ELCID3496 ADELINO A EL EL CONDE DON ANRICH * EL CONDE DON REMOND;
27373 5ELCID3497 ABRA%OLOS TAN BIEN * RUEGA LOS DE CORA%ON
27387 5ELCID3499 AESSOS * ALOS OTROS QUE DE BUENA PARTE SON,
27559 5ELCID3519 PORA ARRANCAR MOROS DEL CANPO * SER SEGUDADOR;
27574 5ELCID3521 CA POR UOS * POREL CAUALLO ONDRADOS SOMO NOS.
27583 5ELCID3522 ESSORA SE ESPIDIERON, * LUEGOS PARTIO LA CORT.
27601 5ELCID3524 HYA MARTIN ANTOLINEZ, * VOS, PERO VERMUEZ,
27635 5ELCID3528 PRESO AUEMOS EL DEBDO * A PASSAR ES POR NOS;
27670 5ELCID3532 MYO %ID PORA VALEN%IA, * EL REY PORA CARRION.
27721 5ELCID3538 MUCHO VIENEN BIEN ADOBADOS DE CAUALLOS * DE GUARNIZONES,
27772 5ELCID3544 DE NOCHE BELARON LAS ARMAS * ROGARON AL CRIADOR.
27811 5ELCID3549 POR QUERER EL DERECHO * NON CONSENTIR EL TUERTO.
27865 5ELCID3556 COLADA * TIZON, QUE NON LIDIASSEN CON ELLAS LOS DEL CANPEADOR;
27913 5ELCID3562 LEUAD * SALID ALCAMPO, YFANTES DE CARRION,
28006 5ELCID3574 BESAMOS VOS LAS MANOS, COMMO A REY * A SE@OR,
28014 5ELCID3575 QUE FIEL SEADES OY DELLOS * DE NOS;
28056 5ELCID3581 ESSORA DIXO EL REY: DALMA * DE CORA%ON.
28064 5ELCID3582 ADUZEN LES LOS CAUALLOS BUENOS * CORREDORES,
28069 5ELCID3583 SANTIGUARON LAS SIELAS * CAUALGAN A VIGOR;
28146 5ELCID3593 EL REY DIOLES FIELES POR DEZIR EL DERECHO * AL NON,
28231 5ELCID3604 LOS FIELES * EL REY ENSE@ARON LOS MOIONES,
28466 5ELCID3635 LAS DOS LE DESMANCHAN * LA TER%ERA FINCO:
28475 5ELCID3636 EL BELMEZ CON LA CAMISA * CON LA GUARNIZON
28526 5ELCID3642 EL DEXO LA LAN%A * AL ESPADA METIO MANO,
28555 5ELCID3646 MARTIN ANTOLINEZ * DIEGO GON%ALEZ FIRIERON SE DELAS LAN%AS,
28583 5ELCID3649 RELUMBRA TOD EL CAMPO, TANTO ER LINPIA * CLARA;
28615 5ELCID3654 LA COFIA * EL ALMOFAR TODO GELO LEUAUA,

WORD C# PREFIX CONTEXT

& (CON'T)

28635 5ELCID3656 LO VNO CAYO ENEL CAMPO * LO AL SUSO FINCAUA.
28702 5ELCID3665 VALME, DIOS GLORIOSO, REaOR, * CURIAM DESTE ESPADA
28709 5ELCID3666 EL CAUALLO ASORRIENDA, * MESURANDOL DEL ESPADA,
28771 5ELCID3674 ASSUR GON%ALEZ, FUR%UDO * DE VALOR,
28868 5ELCID3687 VERMEIO SALIO EL ASTIL, * LA LAN%A & EL PENDON.
28871 5ELCID3687 VERMEIO SALIO EL ASTIL, & LA LAN%A * EL PENDON.
28885 5ELCID3689 LA LAN%A RECOMBRO * SOBREL SE PARO;
28971 5ELCID3700 AGUISA DE MENBRADOS ANDAN DIAS * NOCHES,
29017 5ELCID3706 QUI BUENA DUENA ESCARNE%E * LA DEXA DESPUES,
29105 5ELCID3717 ANDIDIERON EN PLEYTOS LOS DE NAUARRA * DE ARAGON,
29122 5ELCID3719 FIZIERON SUS CASAMIENTOS CON DON ELUIRA * CON DOaA SOL.
29160 5ELCID3723 QUANDO SEaORAS SON SUS FIJAS DE NAUARRA * DE ARAGON.
29198 5ELCID3728 ASSI FFAGAMOS NOS TODOS IUSTOS * PECCADORES
29236 5ELCID3733 EN ERA DE MILL * CCXLV AaOS. EN EL ROMANZ
WORD #1954 OCCURS 856 TIMES.
INDEX OF DIVERSIFICATION = 33.18 WITH STANDARD DEVIATION OF 35.57

FABLA 10835 5ELCID1372 AQUI ENTRARON EN ***** LOS YFFANTES DE CARRION:
24894 5ELCID3170 CON AQUESTA ***** TORNARON ALA CORT:
25912 5ELCID3302 *****, PERO MUDO, VARON QUE TANTO CALLAS
WORD #1955 OCCURS 3 TIMES.

FABLADO 7820 5ELCID1000 TODOS SON ADOBADOS QUANDO MYO %ID ESTO OUO *******;
8140 5ELCID1037 SI LO FIZIEREDES, %ID, LO QUE AUEDES *******,
10127 5ELCID1283 PUES ESTO AN *******, PIENSSAN SE DE ADOBAR.
WORD #1956 OCCURS 3 TIMES.

FABLANDO 1198 5ELCID0154 SONRRISOS MYO %ID, ESTAUALOS ********:
14873 5ELCID1880 ******** EN SU CONSSEIO, AUIENDO SU PORIDAD:
17622 5ELCID2229 ALOS YFANTES DE CARRION MINAYA VA ********:
23988 5ELCID3057 AL CRIADOR ROGANDO & ******** EN PORIDAD.
WORD #1957 OCCURS 4 TIMES.

FABLAR 2725 5ELCID0344 MOSTRANDO LOS MIRACLOS, POR EN AUEMOS QUE ******:
8767 5ELCID1114 EL QUE EN BUEN ORA NASCO COMPE%O DE ******:
11505 5ELCID1456 DE LA SU BOCA CONPE%O DE ******:
21605 5ELCID2747 HYA NON PUEDEN ****** DON ELUIRA & DONA SOL;
25946 5ELCID3306 PERO VERMUEZ CONPE%O DE ******;
26111 5ELCID3328 LENGUA SIN MANOS, CUEMO OSAS ******?
WORD #1958 OCCURS 6 TIMES.
INDEX OF DIVERSIFICATION = 4676.20 WITH STANDARD DEVIATION OF 3725.01

FABLARA 3596 5ELCID0453 DA QUESTE A CORRO ******* TODA ESPAaA.
WORD #1959 OCCURS 1 TIMES.

FABLARON 20011 5ELCID2539 DESTO QUE ELLOS ******** NOS PARTE NON AYAMOS:
27131 5ELCID3467 LUEGO ******** YFANTES DE CARRION:
WORD #1960 OCCURS 2 TIMES.

FABLASSEN 9775 5ELCID1242 E QUE ********* DESTO MOROS & CHRISTIANOS.
WORD #1961 OCCURS 1 TIMES.

FABLASTES 5365 5ELCID0677 DIXO EL CAMPEADOR: A MI GUISA *********;
WORD #1962 OCCURS 1 TIMES.

FABLAUA 1472 5ELCID0188 QUANDO ESTO OUO FECHO, ODREDES LO QUE *******:
5418 5ELCID0684 ******* MYO %ID COMMO ODREDES CONTAR:
10654 5ELCID1350 ******* MINAYA Y AGUISA DE VARON:
13355 5ELCID1693 ******* MYNAYA, NON LO QUISO DETARDAR:
21430 5ELCID2724 QUANDO ESTO VIERON LAS DUEaAS, ******* DOaA SOL:
21976 5ELCID2796 TAN A GRANT DUELO ******* DOaA SOL:
WORD #1963 OCCURS 6 TIMES.
INDEX OF DIVERSIFICATION = 4099.80 WITH STANDARD DEVIATION OF 2815.27

FABLAUAN 25295 5ELCID3220 TORNAN CON EL CONSSEIO E ******** ASSO SABOR:
WORD #1964 OCCURS 1 TIMES.

FABLEMOS 24816 5ELCID3160 DIXO EL CONDE DON GAR%IA: AESTO NOS ********.
29044 5ELCID3710 ******** NOS DAQUESTE QUE EN BUEN ORA NA%IO.
WORD #1965 OCCURS 2 TIMES.

FABLO 550 5ELCID0070 ***** MARTIN ATOLINEZ, ODREDES LO QUE A DICHO:
613 5ELCID0078 ***** MYO %ID, EL QUE EN BUEN ORA %INXO ESPADA:
2366 5ELCID0299 ***** MYO %ID DE TODA VOLUNTAD:
3001 5ELCID0378 ATAN GRAND SABOR ***** MINAYA ALBARFANEZ:
3079 5ELCID0387 TORNADO ES DON SANCHO, & ***** ALBARFANEZ:
4072 5ELCID0518 ***** CON LOS DE CASTEION, & ENVIO AFITA & AGUADELFAGARA,
4839 5ELCID0613 ***** MYO %ID RUY DIAZ, EL QUE EN BUEN ORA FUE NADO:
5309 5ELCID0671 PRIMERO ***** MINAYA, VN CAUALLERO DE PRESTAR:
10417 5ELCID1320 BESAUA LE LAS MANOS & ***** TAN APUESTO:
10806 5ELCID1368 SONRRISOS EL REY, TAN VELIDO *****:
11682 5ELCID1481 ***** MUaO GUSTIOZ, NON SPERO A NADI:
14757 5ELCID1866 ***** EL REY DON ALFONSSO & DIXO ESTA RAZON:
15078 5ELCID1907 ***** MYNAYA & PLOGO A PER VERMUEZ:

WORD C# PREFIX CONTEXT

FABLO (CON'T)

```
                16051 5ELCID2036 ***** MYO %ID & DIXO: MER%ED; YOLO RE%IBO, ALFONSSO MYO SE@OR;
                16104 5ELCID2043 ***** MYO %ID & DIXC ESTA RAZON: ESTO GRADESCO AL CRIADOR,
                16515 5ELCID2094 ***** EL REY DON ALFCNSSO CCMMO TAN BUEN SE@OR:
                18569 5ELCID2350 OYD LO QUE ***** EL QUE EN BUEN ORA NASCO:
                19921 5ELCID2527 AESTAS PALABRAS ***** FERAN GCN%ALEZ:
                20146 5ELCID2558 ***** FERAN GCN%ALEZ & FIZO CALLAR LA CORT;
                25354 5ELCID3228 A ESTAS PALABRAS ***** EL REY CON ALFONSSO:
                25412 5ELCID3236 ***** FERRANGO%ALEZ: AUERES MCNEDADOS NON TENEMOS NOS.
                25847 5ELCID3292 AALTAS VOZES CNDREDES QUE *****:
                26459 5ELCID3376 EN LO QUE ***** AVIE PCCO RECABDO:
                27157 5ELCID3471 ***** EL REY CONTRAL CAMPEADOR:
                28162 5ELCID3595 DO SEDIEN ENEL CAMPO ***** EL REY DON ALFONSSO:
        WORD #1966 OCCURS  25 TIMES.
           INDEX OF DIVERSIFICATICN =  1149.50 WITH STANDARD DEVIATION OF  1421.67

FABLOS          22748 5ELCID2899 ****** CON LOS SOS EN SU PORIDAD,
        WORD #1967 OCCURS   1 TIMES.

FAGA             1768 5ELCID0225 ESTO & YO EN DEBDO QUE **** Y CANTAR MILL MISSAS.
                15093 5ELCID1909 DESPUES **** EL %ID LC QUE QUIERE SABOR.
                22714 5ELCID2894 DE MYOS YERNOS DE CARRICN DIOS ME **** VENGAR
        WORD #1968 OCCURS   3 TIMES.

FAGADES          1523 5ELCID0195 DE QUE ******* CAL%AS & RICA PIEL & BUEN MANTO.
                 2042 5ELCID0257 DELLAS & DE MI MUGIER ******* TODO RECABDO.
                10956 5ELCID1386 EN TODO SODES PRO, EN ESTO ASSI LO *******:
                21482 5ELCID2731 ATAN MALOS ENSSIENPLOS NON ******* SOBRE NOS:
        WORD #1969 OCCURS   4 TIMES.

FAGAMOS          8855 5ELCID1128 CAMPEADOR, ******* LO QUE AUOS PLAZE.
        WORD #1970 OCCURS   1 TIMES.

FAGAN           27241 5ELCID3482 QUE ***** ESTA LID DELANT ESTANDO YO;
        WORD #1971 OCCURS   1 TIMES.

FAGO              757 5ELCID0095 YO MAS NON PUEDO & AMYDOS LO ****.
                10789 5ELCID1366 POR TAL **** AQUESTO QUE SIRUAN ASO SE@OR.
                23329 5ELCID2971 POR AMOR DE MYO %ID ESTA CORT YO ****.
                23884 5ELCID3042 RESPONDIO EL REY: SI ****, SIN SALUE DIOS
        WORD #1972 OCCURS   4 TIMES.

FAGUNT          10359 5ELCID1312 FUERA EL REY A SAN ****** AVN POCO HA,
                22940 5ELCID2922 AL REY EN SAN ****** LO FALLO.
        WORD #1973 OCCURS   2 TIMES.

FALAR           11283 5ELCID1427 DELOS MEIORES GUARIMIENTOS QUE EN BURGOS PUDO *****,
                11591 5ELCID1468 ASI COMMO A MY DIXIERON, HY LOS PODREDES *****:
        WORD #1974 OCCURS   2 TIMES.

FALARON         21245 5ELCID2700 ******* VN VERGEL CON VNA LINPIA FUENT;
        WORD #1975 OCCURS   1 TIMES.

FALASSE         14743 5ELCID1864 COMMO SI LOS ******* MUERTOS ADUZIR SE LOS CAUALLOS,
        WORD #1976 OCCURS   1 TIMES.

FALCONES           31 5ELCID0005 E SIN ******** & SIN ADTORES MUDADOS.
        WORD #1977 OCCURS   1 TIMES.

FALIDO           4566 5ELCID0581 ****** A AMYO %ID EL PAN & LA %EUADA.
        WORD #1978 OCCURS   1 TIMES.

FALIESSEN       23427 5ELCID2984 QUE NON ********* DELO QUE EN REY AUYE MANDADO.
        WORD #1979 OCCURS   1 TIMES.

FALIR           17579 5ELCID2224 NOLO QUIERO ***** POR NADA DE QUANTO AY PARADO;
        WORD #1980 OCCURS   1 TIMES.

FALLA            3515 5ELCID0443 E ALBAR SALUADOREZ SIN *****, & GALIN GAR%IA, VNA FARDIDA
                 3684 5ELCID0464 EL CAMPEADOR SALIO DE LA %ELADA, CORRIE ACASTEION SIN *****.
                 4045 5ELCID0514 E A LOS PEONES LA MEATAD SIN *****;
                 4115 5ELCID0523 ATERCER DIA DADOS FUERON SJN *****.
                 7184 5ELCID0920 EL CAUALLO CORRIENDO, UALO ABRA%AR SIN *****,
                12053 5ELCID1528 HY AUEGALUON, AMIGOL SODES SIN *****.
                12182 5ELCID1546 EL OBISPO DON IHERONIMO, BUEN CHRISTIANO SIN *****,
                12224 5ELCID1551 EL MORO AUEGALUON BIEN LOS SIRUIE SIN *****,
                12231 5ELCID1552 DE QUANTO QUE QUISIERON NON OUIERON *****,
                12256 5ELCID1556 FATA EN VALEN%IA SIRUIALOS SIN *****;
                14277 5ELCID1806 DESTA MI QUINTA, DIGO UOS SIN *****,
                14294 5ELCID1808 E CRAS HA LA MA@ANA YR UOS HEDES SIN *****
                15497 5ELCID1963 SYO BIUU SO, ALI YRE SIN *****.
                15533 5ELCID1968 CAUALLOS GRUESSOS & CCREDORES SJN *****,
        WORD #1981 OCCURS  14 TIMES.
           INDEX OF DIVERSIFICATICN =   923.46 WITH STANDARD DEVIATION OF  1520.19
```

WORD C# PREFIX CONTEXT

```
FALLAN             13220 5ELCID1676 DOS ****** CON LOS MOROS COMETIEN LOS TAN AYNA.
                   14010 5ELCID1775 TANTO ****** DESTO QUE ES COSA SOBEIANO.
        WORD #1982 OCCURS   2 TIMES.

FALLAR              3365 5ELCID0424 DESPUES QUI NOS BUSCARE ****** NOS PODRA.
                    8428 5ELCID1071 SI ME VINIEREDES BUSCAR, ****** ME PODREDES;
                   10353 5ELCID1311 DEMANDO POR ALFONSSO, DO LO PODRIE ******.
                   10369 5ELCID1313 TORNOS A CARRION, Y LO PODRIE ******.
        WORD #1983 OCCURS   4 TIMES.

FALLAREDES          6523 5ELCID0832 ALA TORNADA, SI NOS ********** AQUI;
        WORD #1984 OCCURS   1 TIMES.

FALLAREN            9939 5ELCID1260 QUE SI ALGUNOS FURTARE O MENOS LE ********, EL AUER ME
                                    AURA ATORNAR
                   21954 5ELCID2793 DE QUE NON ME ******** LOS YFANTES DE CARRION,
        WORD #1985 OCCURS   2 TIMES.

FALLARIEDES         6657 5ELCID0849 EN TODOS LOS SOS NON *********** VN MESQUINO.
        WORD #1986 OCCURS   1 TIMES.

FALLARON            6270 5ELCID0798 MAS DE QUINZE DE LOS SOS MENOS NON ********.
                   13709 5ELCID1737 ENTRE ORO & PLATA ******** TRES MILL MARCOS,
                   18225 5ELCID2306 QUANDO LOS ******** & ELLOS VINIERON, ASSI VINIERON SIN COLOR;
        WORD #1987 OCCURS   3 TIMES.

FALLASSEMOS        15402 5ELCID1951 FASTA DO LO *********** BUSCAR LO YREMOS NOS,
        WORD #1988 OCCURS   1 TIMES.

FALLAUAN           19973 5ELCID2534 MAS NON ******** Y ADIEGO NI AFERRANDO.
        WORD #1989 OCCURS   1 TIMES.

FALLE%IERE          2048 5ELCID0258 SIESSA DESPENSSA UOS ********** OUOS MENGUARE ALGO,
        WORD #1990 OCCURS   1 TIMES.

FALLEN              6002 5ELCID0761 LOS DOS LE ******, & EL VNOL HA TOMADO,
        WORD #1991 OCCURS   1 TIMES.

FALLO               9973 5ELCID1264 QUANDO LOS *****, POR CUENTA FIZO LOS NONBRAR:
                   18215 5ELCID2304 MYO %ID POR SOS YERNOS DEMANDO & NOLOS *****;
                   21826 5ELCID2777 ***** SUS PRIMAS AMORTE%IDAS AMAS ADOS.
                   22106 5ELCID2814 ***** A DIEGO TELLEZ EL QUE DE ALBARFANEZ FUE;
                   22942 5ELCID2922 AL REY EN SAN FAGUNT LO *****.
                   26218 5ELCID3342 DEMANDO POR SUS YERNOS, NINGUNO NON *****
        WORD #1992 OCCURS   6 TIMES.
           INDEX OF DIVERSIFICATION =  3248.00 WITH STANDARD DEVIATION OF  3150.37

FALOLA               250 5ELCID0032 ASSI COMMO LEGO ALA PUERTA, ****** BIEN %ERRADA,
        WORD #1993 OCCURS   1 TIMES.

FALSO               2709 5ELCID0342 SALUEST A SANTA SUSANNA DEL ***** CRIMINAL;
        WORD #1994 OCCURS   1 TIMES.

FALSSA              5765 5ELCID0728 TANTA LORIGA ****** DESMANCHAR
        WORD #1995 OCCURS   1 TIMES.

FALSSAN            18898 5ELCID2391 DAUAN LE GRANDES COLPES, MAS NOL ******* LAS ARMAS.
        WORD #1996 OCCURS   1 TIMES.

FALSSAR             5664 5ELCID0713 DAN LE GRANDES COLPES, MAS NOL PUEDEN *******.
        WORD #1997 OCCURS   1 TIMES.

FALSSEDAD          20985 5ELCID2666 QUANDO ESTA ********* DIZEN LOS DE CARRION,
        WORD #1998 OCCURS   1 TIMES.

FALSSO             26533 5ELCID3387 ****** A TODOS & MAS AL CRIADOR.
                   28784 5ELCID3676 TRAS EL ESCUDO ****** GELA GUARNIZON;
                   28807 5ELCID3679 TRAS EL ESCUDO ****** GELA GUARNIZON,
                   28821 5ELCID3681 NOL PUDO GUARIR, ****** GELA GUARNIZON,
        WORD #1999 OCCURS   4 TIMES.

FANBRE              9276 5ELCID1149 FIJOS & MUGIERES VER LO MURIR DE ******.
        WORD #2000 OCCURS   1 TIMES.

FANEZ              23680 5ELCID3016 ALUAR ***** ADELANTEL ENBIO,
        WORD #2001 OCCURS   1 TIMES.

FAR                 2396 5ELCID0302 EN ANTES QUE YO MUERA, ALGUN BIEN UOS PUEDA ***:
                    2498 5ELCID0315 SED MEMBRADOS COMMO LO DEUEDES ***.
                    2554 5ELCID0322 CUEMO LO MANDO MYO %ID, ASSI LO AN TODOS HA ***.
                    2940 5ELCID0370 LORANDO DE LOS OIOS, QUE NON SABE QUE SE ***.
                    5307 5ELCID0670 DEZID ME, CAUALLEROS, COMMO UOS PLAZE DE ***.
                    5375 5ELCID0678 ONDRASTES UOS, MINAYA, CA AUER UOS LO YEDES DE ***.
                    6973 5ELCID0891 DE TODO MYO REYNO LOS QUE LO QUISIEREN ***,
                    8926 5ELCID1136 QUIS CADA VNO DELLOS BIEN SABE LO QUE HA DE ***.
```

WORD C# PREFIX CONTEXT

FAR (CON'T)

```
                 9081 5ELCID1155 MIEDO AN EN VALENZIA QUE NON SABEN QUESE ***.
                 9234 5ELCID1174 MAL SE AQUEXAN LOS DE VALENZIA QUE NON SABENT QUES ***,
                10972 5ELCID1388 SOMOS EN SO PRO QUANTO LO PODEMOS ***;
                11574 5ELCID1466 HYD PORA MEDINA QUANTO LO PUDIEREDES ***,
                26493 5ELCID3380 E PRENDER MAQUILAS, COMMO LO SUELE ***
        WORD #2002 OCCURS  13 TIMES.
           INDEX OF DIVERSIFICATION =  2007.08 WITH STANDARD DEVIATION OF  4153.38

FARA             3247 5ELCID0409 MIENTRA QUE VISQUIEREDES BIEN SE **** LO TO.
        WORD #2003 OCCURS   1 TIMES.

FARAN           27908 5ELCID3561 OTRO SI ***** ALOS DEL CANPEADOR.
        WORD #2004 OCCURS   1 TIMES.

FARDIDA          3520 5ELCID0443 E ALBAR SALUADOREZ SIN FALLA, & GALIN GARZIA, VNA *******
                 3863 5ELCID0489  VENIDES, ALBARFANEZ, UNA ******* LANZA
        WORD #2005 OCCURS   2 TIMES.

FARE              844 5ELCID0108 POR SIEMPRE UOS **** RICOS, QUE NON SEADES MENGUADOS.
                 6419 5ELCID0819 DIXO MYNAYA ALBARFANEZ:  ESTO **** YO DE GRADO.
                17605 5ELCID2227 ESTOZ DIXO MINAYA: ESTO **** YO DE GRADO.
                27174 5ELCID3473 ENESSORA DIXO MIO ZID. NO LO ****, SENOR.
        WORD #2006 OCCURS   4 TIMES.

FARIA           21076 5ELCID2678 TAL COSA UOS ***** QUE POR EL MUNDO SONAS,
        WORD #2007 OCCURS   1 TIMES.

FARIZ            5993 5ELCID0760 AL REY ***** IIJ COLPES LE AUIE DADO;
                 6063 5ELCID0769 ARANCADO ES EL REY ***** & GALUE;
                 6087 5ELCID0773 EL REY ***** EN TERUEL SE FUE ENTRAR,
                 6587 5ELCID0841 SANO EL REY *****, CON EL SE CONSEIAUAN.
        WORD #2008 OCCURS   4 TIMES.

FARIZA           4291 5ELCID0547 ENTRE ****** & ZETINA MYO ZID YUA ALBERGAR.
        WORD #2009 OCCURS   1 TIMES.

FARTAN          27350 5ELCID3495 NOS ****** DE CATARLE QUANTOS HA EN LA CORT.
        WORD #2010 OCCURS   1 TIMES.

FARTAR          16223 5ELCID2058 NON SE PUEDE ****** DEL, TANTOL QUERIE DE CORAZON;
        WORD #2011 OCCURS   1 TIMES.

FARTAS          10219 5ELCID1294 QUE SIS ****** LIDIANDO & FIRIENDO CON SUS MANOS,
                26523 5ELCID3385 ALOS QUE DAS PAZ, ****** LOS ADERREDOR.
        WORD #2012 OCCURS   2 TIMES.

FARTO           14171 5ELCID1794 QUANDO ES ***** DE LIDIAR CON AMAS LAS SUS MANOS,
                22026 5ELCID2802 MUCHO SON LAZRADAS & AMAS LAS *****.
        WORD #2013 OCCURS   2 TIMES.

FARTOS          19420 5ELCID2461 ****** DE LIDIAR CON MOROS ENEL CAMPO.
        WORD #2014 OCCURS   1 TIMES.

FASTA            1262 5ELCID0162 E BIEN GELAS GUARDARIEN ***** CABO DEL A@O;
                 3772 5ELCID0477 E SIN DUBDA CORREN; ***** ALCALA LEGO LA SE@A DE MINAYA,
                 8071 5ELCID1030 ***** TERZER DIA NOL PUEDEN ACORDAR.
                11462 5ELCID1451 DE SAN PERO ***** MEDINA EN V DIAS VAN,
                13639 5ELCID1728 MYO ZID EL DE BIUAR ***** ALLI LEGO EN ALCAZ,
                13673 5ELCID1732 ALI PREZIO ABAUIECA DELA CABEZA ***** ACABO.
                15399 5ELCID1951 ***** DO LO FALLASSEMOS BUSCAR LO YREMOS NOS,
                20788 5ELCID2640 DESI ESCURRA LAS ***** MEDINA POR LA MI AMOR;
                21775 5ELCID2770 ***** QUE VIESSE VENIR SUS PRIMAS AMAS ADOS
                22959 5ELCID2925 ***** DENTRO EN SANTI YAGUO DE TODO ES SE@OR,
                26067 5ELCID3323 ***** ESTE DIA NOLO DESCUBRI A NACI;
                26167 5ELCID3336 ***** DO DESPERTO MYO ZID, EL QUE VALENZIA GA@O;
        WORD #2015 OCCURS  12 TIMES.
           INDEX OF DIVERSIFICATION =  2263.09 WITH STANDARD DEVIATION OF  1694.10

FATA             3541 5ELCID0446 FITA AYUSO & POR GUADALFAIARA, **** ALCALA LEGEN LAS ALGARAS,
                 3921 5ELCID0498 **** QUE YO ME PAGE SOBRE MIO BUEN CAUALLO,
                 5583 5ELCID0703 NON DERANCHE NINGUNO **** QUE YO LO MANDE.
                 6110 5ELCID0777 **** CALATAYUCH DURO EL SEGUDAR.
                 8392 5ELCID1067 **** CABO DEL ALBERGADA ESCURRIOLOS EL CASTELANO:
                 9019 5ELCID1148 **** VALENZIA DURO EL SEGUDAR.
                 9652 5ELCID1227 **** DENTRO EN XATIUA DURO EL ARRANCADA,
                10917 5ELCID1382 **** DENTRO EN MEDINA DENLES QUANTO HUEBOS LES FUER,
                12251 5ELCID1556 **** EN VALENZIA SIRUIALOS SIN FALLA;
                13242 5ELCID1679 BIEN **** LAS TIENDAS DURA AQUESTE ALCAZ,
                15829 5ELCID2008 **** QUES TORNE EL QUE EN BUEN ORA NASCO.
                19101 5ELCID2416 NON TE IUNTARAS COMIGO **** DENTRO EN LA MAR.
                19163 5ELCID2424 **** LA ZINTURA EL ESPADA LEGADO HA.
                20642 5ELCID2620 MANDOT QUE VAYAS CON ELLAS **** DENTRO EN CARRION,
                22030 5ELCID2803 TANTO LAS ROGO **** QUE LAS ASSENTO.
                22039 5ELCID2805 **** QUE ESFUERZAN, & AMAS LAS TOMO
```

WORD C# PREFIX CONTEXT

FATA (CON'T)

```
                    22169 5ELCID2823 ALLI SOUIERON ELLAS **** QUE SA@AS SON.
                    22549 5ELCID2872 **** RIO DAMOR, DANDO LES SOLAZ;
                    28609 5ELCID3653 ALLA LEUO EL ALMOFAR, **** LA COFIA LEGAUA,
         WORD #2016 OCCURS  19 TIMES.
            INDEX OF DIVERSIFICATION =  1391.67 WITH STANDARD DEVIATION OF  1476.03

FAZ                  2818 5ELCID0355 AL%OLAS ARRIBA, LEGOLAS ALA ***,
                     2899 5ELCID0365 QUANDO OY NOS PARTIMOS, EN VIDA NOS *** IUNTAR.
                    19121 5ELCID2418 BUEN CAUALLO TIENE BUCAR & GRANDES SALTOS ***,
         WORD #2017 OCCURS   3 TIMES.

FAZAL               24009 5ELCID3060 MATINES & PRIMA DIXIERON ***** ALBA,
         WORD #2018 OCCURS   1 TIMES.

FAZE                 1085 5ELCID0139 DIXO RACHEL & VIDAS:  NON SE **** ASSI EL MERCADO,
                     3428 5ELCID0433 POR TAL LO **** MYO %ID QUE NO IO VENTASSE NADI.
                    10465 5ELCID1326 MAGER EN TIERRA AGENA, EL BIEN **** LO SO;
                    10600 5ELCID1343 E PLAZEM DELAS NUEUAS QUE **** EL CAMPEADOR;
                    10630 5ELCID1347 QUANDO ASSI **** A SU GUISA EL %ID CAMPEADOR
                    11235 5ELCID1421 POR YR CON ESTAS DUENAS BUE@A CONPANA SE ****.
                    11250 5ELCID1423 DELOS OTROS QUINIENTOS DEZIR UOS HE QUE ****:
                    11666 5ELCID1478 SALIOLOS RE%EBIR CON GRANT GOZO QUE ****:
                    14753 5ELCID1865 POR ESTO QUE EL **** NOS ABREMOS ENBARGO.
                    22661 5ELCID2887 ARMAS YUA TENIENDO & GRANT GOZO QUE ****;
                    24297 5ELCID3098 POR TALLO **** ESTO QUE RECABDAR QUIERE TODO LO SUYO;
                    24845 5ELCID3164 AVN GRAND AMOR NOS **** EL %ID CAMPEADOR,
                    27211 5ELCID3478 HYC VOS LO SOBRELIEUO COMMO BUEN VASSALLO **** A SE@OR,
         WORD #2019 OCCURS  13 TIMES.
            INDEX OF DIVERSIFICATION =  2176.17 WITH STANDARD DEVIATION OF  2685.44

FAZED                3585 5ELCID0452 ***** ME MANDADO MUY PRIUADO ALA %AGA;
                     7693 5ELCID0985 YA CAUALLEROS, A PART ***** LA GANAN%IA:
                    17061 5ELCID2160 MER%ED UOS SEA & ***** NOS ESTE PERDON:
         WORD #2020 OCCURS   3 TIMES.

FAZEN                2268 5ELCID0285 GRAND IANTAR LE ***** AL BUEN CAMPEADOR.
                     5748 5ELCID0725 ALA TORNADA QUE ***** OTROS TANTOS SON.
                     7857 5ELCID1005 ESTO ***** LOS SOS DE VOLUNTAD & DE GRADO;
                     8703 5ELCID1105 SI NOS %ERCAR VIENEN, CONDERECHO LO *****.
                     9548 5ELCID1213 LOS QUE FUERON DE PIE CAUALLEROS SE *****;
                    12950 5ELCID1642 EN ESTAS TIERRAS AGENAS VERAN LAS MORADAS COMMO SE *****,
                    17955 5ELCID2272 LOS AMORES QUELES ***** MUCHO ERAN SOBEIANOS.
                    19630 5ELCID2488 ASSI LO ***** TODOS, CA ERAN ACORDADOS.
                    22536 5ELCID2869 HY IAZEN ESSA NOCHE, & TAN GRAND GOZO QUE *****.
         WORD #2021 OCCURS   9 TIMES.
            INDEX OF DIVERSIFICATION =  2532.50 WITH STANDARD DEVIATION OF  1439.90

FAZER                1994 5ELCID0252 NON QUIERO ***** ENEL MONESTERIO VN DINERO DE DA@O;
                     4408 5ELCID0561 A TODOS SOS VARONES MANDO ***** VNA CARCAUA,
                     8084 5ELCID1032 NOL PUEDEN ***** COMER VN MUESSO DE PAN.
                    23972 5ELCID3055 MANDO ***** CANDELAS & PONER ENEL ALTAR;
                    26547 5ELCID3389 ***** TELO DEZIR QUE TALERES QUAL DIGO YO.
                    28209 5ELCID3601 CA QUI TUERTO QUISIERE *****, MAL GELO VEDARE YO,
         WORD #2022 OCCURS   6 TIMES.
            INDEX OF DIVERSIFICATION =  5242.00 WITH STANDARD DEVIATION OF  5994.08

FAZIA                9209 5ELCID1172 TAIAUA LES LAS HUERTAS & ***** LES GRAND MAL,
         WORD #2023 OCCURS   1 TIMES.

FAZIAN              20736 5ELCID2633 ASSI ****** LOS CAUALLEROS DEL CAMPEADOR.
                    20835 5ELCID2645 POR SANTA MARIA DALUA RAZIN ****** LA POSADA,
         WORD #2024 OCCURS   2 TIMES.

FAZIE                6748 5ELCID0861 PESO ALOS DE ALCO%ER, CA PROLES ***** GRANT.
                    23391 5ELCID2980 QUE CORT ***** EN TOLLEDO AQUEL REY ONDRADO,
                    23446 5ELCID2986 POR QUE EL REY ***** CORT EN TOLLEDO,
         WORD #2025 OCCURS   3 TIMES.

FAZIEN               9110 5ELCID1159 DAUAN SUS CORREDORES & ****** LAS TRASNOCHADAS,
         WORD #2026 OCCURS   1 TIMES.

FAZIENDO            25168 5ELCID3205 HYO ******** ESTO, ELLOS ACABARON LO SO;
         WORD #2027 OCCURS   1 TIMES.

FE                   1270 5ELCID0163 CA ASSIL DIERAN LA ** & GELO AUIEN IURADO,
         WORD #2028 OCCURS   1 TIMES.

FECHA                 428 5ELCID0054 LA ORA%ION ***** LUEGO CAUALGAUA;
                     2903 5ELCID0366 LA ORA%ION *****, LA MISSA ACABADA LA AN,
                     4809 5ELCID0609 LUEGO LEGAUAN LOS SOS, CA ***** ES EL ARRANCADA.
                     8531 5ELCID1084 DE LA GANAN%IA QUE AN ***** MARAUILLOSA & GRAND.
                    22812 5ELCID2906 DESTA DESONDRA QUE MEAN ***** LOS YFANTES DE CARRION
                    24024 5ELCID3062 E SSU OFRENDA HAN ***** MUY BUENA & CONPLIDA.
                    24273 5ELCID3095 CON ORO ES OBRADA, ***** POR RAZON,
```

WORD C# PREFIX CONTEXT

FECHA (CON'T)

WORD #2029 OCCURS 7 TIMES.
INDEX OF DIVERSIFICATION = 3973.17 WITH STANDARD DEVIATION OF 5183.16

FECHAS 9031 5ELCID1149 GRANDES SON LAS GANANZIAS QUE MIO ZID ****** HA.
10050 5ELCID1273 DESTAS MIS GANANZIAS, QUE AUEMOS ****** ACA,
10584 5ELCID1341 DE TAN FIERAS GANANZIAS COMMO A ****** EL CAMPEADOR
WORD #2030 OCCURS 3 TIMES.

FECHES 7005 5ELCID0896 ESTO ****** AGORA, AL FEREDES ADELANT.
15999 5ELCID2029 SIESTO NON ******, NON AUREDES MY AMOR.
16983 5ELCID2150 QUEM ****** QUE BIEN SEA GALARDONADO.
17338 5ELCID2193 TODO LO QUE UOS ****** ES DE BUENA GUISA.
18798 5ELCID2379 SI ESTE AMOR NON ******, YO DEUOS ME QUIERO QUITAR.
WORD #2031 OCCURS 5 TIMES.
INDEX OF DIVERSIFICATION = 2947.25 WITH STANDARD DEVIATION OF 4055.83

FECHO 1468 5ELCID0188 QUANDO ESTO OUO *****, ODREDES LO QUE FABLAUA:
7145 5ELCID0915 QUANDO ESTO ***** OUO, A CABO DE TRES SEMANAS,
11351 5ELCID1436 POR LO QUE AUEDES ***** BUEN COSIMENT Y AURA.
11877 5ELCID1506 ESSO FFUE APRIESSA *****, QUE NOS QUIEREN DETARDAR.
12068 5ELCID1530 DESTO QUE AUEDES ***** UOS NON PERDEREDES NADA.
13250 5ELCID1680 MUCHO AUIEN *****, PIESSAN DE CAUALGAR.
13284 5ELCID1684 ALEGRE ES MYO ZID POR QUANTO ***** HAN:
17677 5ELCID2236 QUANDO OUIERON AQUESTO *****, SALIERON DEL PALAZIO,
21786 5ELCID2771 O QUE AN ***** LOS YFANTES DE CARRION.
23223 5ELCID2958 SI QUIER EL CASAMIENTO ***** NON FUESSE OY
27968 5ELCID3569 DELO QUE AUIEN ***** MUCHO REPISOS SON:
27975 5ELCID3570 NOLO QUERRIEN AUER ***** POR QUANTO HA EN CARRION.
28733 5ELCID3669 POR QUANTO AUEDES ***** VENZICA AUEDES ESTA BATALLA.
28799 5ELCID3678 ESTE COLPE *****, OTRO DIO MUNO GUSTIOZ,
WORD #2032 OCCURS 14 TIMES.
INDEX OF DIVERSIFICATION = 2101.38 WITH STANDARD DEVIATION OF 2150.80

FECHOS 6648 5ELCID0848 A CAUALLEROS & A PEONES ****** LOS HA RICOS,
25391 5ELCID3233 TORNAR GELOS QUIERO, CA TODOS ****** SON,
WORD #2033 OCCURS 2 TIMES.

FED 20708 5ELCID2629 ATALES COSAS *** QUE EN PLAZER CAYA ANOS.
WORD #2034 OCCURS 1 TIMES.

FELEZ 5851 5ELCID0741 ***** MUNOZ SO SOBRINO DEL CAMPEADOR
20625 5ELCID2618 OHERES, MYO SOBRINO, TU, ***** MUNOZ,
20662 5ELCID2623 DIXO ***** MUNOZ: PLAZME DALMA & DE CORAZON.
20744 5ELCID2634 OYAS, SOBRINO, TU, ***** MUNOZ
21736 5ELCID2764 MAS YO UOS DIRE DAQUEL ***** MUNOZ.
21771 5ELCID2769 EN VN MONTE ESPESSO ***** MUNOZ SE METIO,
21824 5ELCID2776 POR EL RASTRO TORNOS ***** MUNOZ,
22002 5ELCID2799 CON VN SONBRERO QUE TIENE ***** MUNOZ,
22104 5ELCID2813 A SANTESTEUAN VINO ***** MUNOZ,
24075 5ELCID3069 E MYO SOBRINO ***** MUNOZ;
WORD #2035 OCCURS 10 TIMES.
INDEX OF DIVERSIFICATION = 2023.89 WITH STANDARD DEVIATION OF 4825.62

FELLOS 3832 5ELCID0485 ****** EN CASTEION, O EL CAMPEADOR ESTAUA.
WORD #2036 OCCURS 1 TIMES.

FELOS 11468 5ELCID1452 ***** EN MEDINA LAS DUENAS & ALBARFANEZ.
20844 5ELCID2647 ***** EN MOLINA CON EL MORO AVENGALUON.
27683 5ELCID3534 ***** AL PLAZO LOS DEL CAMPEADOR,
28973 5ELCID3701 ***** EN VALENZIA CON MYO ZID EL CAMPEADOR:
WORD #2037 OCCURS 4 TIMES.

FEM 2129 5ELCID0269 *** ANTE UOS YO & UUESTRAS FFIJAS, YFFANTES SON & DE DIAS CHICAS,
WORD #2038 OCCURS 1 TIMES.

FEMOS 8686 5ELCID1103 EN SUS TIERRAS SOMOS & ***** LES TODOMAL,
WORD #2039 OCCURS 1 TIMES.

FENARES 3450 5ELCID0435 ODIZEN CASTEION, EL QUE ES SOBRE *******,
3787 5ELCID0479 ******* ARRIBA & POR GUADALFAIARA.
4257 5ELCID0542 VANSSE ******* ARRIBA QUANTO PUEDEN ANDAR,
WORD #2040 OCCURS 3 TIMES.

FER 660 5ELCID0084 *** LO HE AMIGOS, DE GRADO NON AURIE NADA.
9854 5ELCID1250 QUE SIS PUDIESSEN YR, *** LO YEN DE GRADO.
10265 5ELCID1299 EN TIERRAS DE VALENZIA *** QUIERO OBISPADO,
11430 5ELCID1447 RESPUSO MINAYA: *** LO HE DE VELUNTAD.
11727 5ELCID1487 DIXO AUEGALUON: *** LO HE DE VELUNTAD.
12025 5ELCID1524 MAGER QUE MAL LE QUERAMOS, NON GELO PODREMOS ***,
14922 5ELCID1886 CON UUESTRO CONSSEIO LO QUEREMOS *** NOS,
16779 5ELCID2124 OY DE MAS SABED QUE *** DELLOS, CAMPEADOR.
23247 5ELCID2961 LO QUE NON CUYDAUA *** DE TODA ESTA SAZON,
23499 5ELCID2993 QUI LO *** NON QUISIESSE, O NO YR A MI CORT,
24570 5ELCID3131 ESTA TERZERA A TOLLEDO LA VIN *** OY,

WORD C# PREFIX CONTEXT

FER (CON'T)

```
                    24735 5ELCID3150 CA UOS LAS CASASTES, REY, SABREDES QUE *** OY;
          WORD #2041 OCCURS  12 TIMES.
             INDEX OF DIVERSIFICATION =  2187.64 WITH STANDARD DEVIATION OF  2974.14

FERA                15456 5ELCID1958 LO QUE EL REY QUISIERE, ESSO **** EL CAMPEADOR.
                    18668 5ELCID2362 ESTA BATALLA EL CRIADOR LA ****,
          WORD #2042 OCCURS   2 TIMES.

FERAN               19922 5ELCID2527 AESTAS PALABRAS FABLO ***** GON%ALEZ:
                    20147 5ELCID2558 FABLO ***** GON%ALEZ & FIZO CALLAR LA CORT;
          WORD #2043 OCCURS   2 TIMES.

FERANDO             21441 5ELCID2725 POR DIOS UOS ROGAMOS, DON DIEGO & DON *******
          WORD #2044 OCCURS   1 TIMES.

FERE                11210 5ELCID1418 DIZIENDO ESTO MYANAYA: ESTO **** DE VELUNTAD.
                    16032 5ELCID2033 DIXO EL REY ESTO **** DALMA & DE CORA%ON;
                    23479 5ELCID2990 DIXO EL REY: NO LO ****, SIN SALUE DIOS
                    26688 5ELCID3408 SIN UUESTRO MANDADO NADA NON **** YO.
          WORD #2045 OCCURS   4 TIMES.

FEREDES              7008 5ELCID0896 ESTO FECHES AGORA, AL ******* ADELANT.
          WORD #2046 OCCURS   1 TIMES.

FEREMOS              4597 5ELCID0584 DEMOS SALTO A EL & ******* GRANT GANA%IA,
                     8289 5ELCID1055 AQUI ******* LA MORADA, NO NOS PARTIREMOS AMOS.
                    16160 5ELCID2050 E CRAS ******* LO QUE PLOGIERE AUOS.
                    20069 5ELCID2547 DESPUES EN LA CARRERA ******* NUESTRO SABOR,
          WORD #2047 OCCURS   4 TIMES.

FERID                5708 5ELCID0720 ***** LOS, CAUALLEROS, POR AMOR DE CARIDAD
                     8944 5ELCID1139 ***** LOS, CAUALLEROS, DAMOR & DE GRADO & DE GRAND VOLUNTAD,
          WORD #2048 OCCURS   2 TIMES.

FERIDAL               304 5ELCID0038 SACO EL PIE DEL ESTRIBERA, UNA ******* DAUA;
          WORD #2049 OCCURS   1 TIMES.

FERIDAS             13482 5ELCID1709 LAS ******* PRIMERAS QUE LAS AYA YO OTORGADAS.
                    18762 5ELCID2374 EA ESTAS ******* YO QUIERO YR DELANT;
                    26020 5ELCID3317 PEDIST LAS ******* PRIMERAS ALCANPEADOR LEAL,
          WORD #2050 OCCURS   3 TIMES.

FERIDO              28518 5ELCID3641 ASSI LO TENIEN LAS YENTES QUE MAL ****** ES DE MUERT.
                    28644 5ELCID3657 QUANDO ESTE COLPE A ****** COLADA LA PRE%IADA,
                    28878 5ELCID3688 TODOS SE CUEDAN QUE ****** ES DE MUERT.
          WORD #2051 OCCURS   3 TIMES.

FERIE                8495 5ELCID1080 LO QUE NON ***** EL CABOSO POR QUANTO ENEL MUNDO HA,
          WORD #2052 OCCURS   1 TIMES.

FERIR                5353 5ELCID0676 VAYAMOS LOS ***** EN AQUEL DIA DE CRAS.
                     5694 5ELCID0718 YUAN LOS ***** DE FUERTES CORA%ONES.
                     7847 5ELCID1004 MANDO LOS ***** MYO %ID, EL QUE EN BUEN ORA NASCO;
                     8932 5ELCID1137 CON LOS ALUORES MYO %ID ***** LOS VA:
                    13381 5ELCID1696 QUANDO UOS LOS FUEREDES *****, ENTRARE YO DEL OTRA PART;
                    13561 5ELCID1718 ALOS %INQUAENTA MILL VAN LOS ***** DE GRADO;
                    18635 5ELCID2358 HYO CON LOS MYOS ***** QUIERO DELANT,
                    18679 5ELCID2364 MANDAD NOLOS ***** DE QUAL PART UOS SEMEIAR,
                    18838 5ELCID2384 EYUA LOS ***** A CABO DEL ALBERGADA.
                    18929 5ELCID2395 HYUA LOS ***** DE CORA%ON & DE ALMA.
                    21592 5ELCID2745 CANSSADOS SON DE ***** ELLOS AMOS ADOS,
                    28120 5ELCID3590 QUE CADA VNO DELLOS BIEN FOS ***** EL SO.
          WORD #2053 OCCURS  12 TIMES.
             INDEX OF DIVERSIFICATION =  2068.73 WITH STANDARD DEVIATION OF  2326.39

FERMOSO              3629 5ELCID0457 YXIE EL SOL, DIOS, QUE ******* APUNTAUA
                     6833 5ELCID0873 VIOLOS EL REY, ******* SONRRISAUA:
                     7203 5ELCID0923 EL CAMPEADOR ******* SONRRISAUA:
                    19291 5ELCID2442 ALEGROS MYO %ID ******* SONRRISANDO:
                    26102 5ELCID3327 E ERES *******, MAS MAL VARRAGAN
          WORD #2054 OCCURS   5 TIMES.
             INDEX OF DIVERSIFICATION =  5617.25 WITH STANDARD DEVIATION OF  5054.80

FERNANDO            17131 5ELCID2168 EA DON ******** & A DON DIEGO AGUARDAR LOS MANDO
                    18590 5ELCID2352 CURIES ME ADIEGO & CURIES ME ADON ********,
                    19280 5ELCID2440 E VIO VENIR ADIEGO & A ********;
                    28459 5ELCID3634 TRES DOBLES DE LORIGA TENIE ********, AQUESTOL PRESTO,
          WORD #2055 OCCURS   4 TIMES.

FERRADURAS          12234 5ELCID1553 AVN LAS ********** QUITAR GELAS MANDAUA;
          WORD #2056 OCCURS   1 TIMES.

FERRAGON%ALEZ       28380 5ELCID3624 CON ************* DE CARA SE JUNTO;
          WORD #2057 OCCURS   1 TIMES.
```

WORD C# PREFIX CONTEXT

```
FERRAN              18065 5ELCID2286 ****** GON%ALEZ NCN VIO ALLI COS AL%ASSE, NIN CAMARA ABIERTA NIN
        WORD #2C58 CCCURS   1 TIMES.

FERRANDO            15037 5ELCID1901 DIEGO & ********, LOS YFFANTES DE CARRION,
                    17921 5ELCID2267 MUCHO ERAN ALEGRES DIEGO & ********;
                    18493 5ELCID2340 ASSI LC OTCRGA DON PERO CUEMO SE ALABA ********.
                    18557 5ELCID2348 MAS SE MARAUILLAN ENTRE DIEGO & ********,
                    23623 5ELCID3009 E DIEGO & ******** Y SCN AMOS ADOS,
                    25993 5ELCID3313 MIENTES, ********, DE QUANTO DICHO HAS,
                    26113 5ELCID3329 DI, ********, OTCRGA ESTA RAZCN:
                    26138 5ELCID3332 E TU, ********, QUE FIZIST CCN EL PAUOR?
                    26154 5ELCID3334 METISTET, ********, PCRC MENOS VALES OY.
        WORD #2059 OCCURS   9 TIMES.
           INDEX OF DIVERSIFICATION =  1388.63 WITH STANCARD DEVIATION OF  1870.71

FERRANGO%ALEZ       25413 5ELCID3236 FABLO *************: AUERES MONEDADOS NON TENEMOS NOS.
                    25838 5ELCID3291 ************* EN PIE SE LEUNATC,
                    28392 5ELCID3626 ************* A PERO VERMUEZ EL ESCUDOL PASSO,
                    28534 5ELCID3643 QUANDO LC VIO *************, CCNUUO ATIZON:
        WORD #206C CCCURS   4 TIMES.

FERREDES             8879 5ELCID1131 BIEN LOS ********, QUE DUBCA NON Y AURA,
        WORD #2061 CCCURS   1 TIMES.

FES                   939 5ELCID0120 CON GRAND IURA METED Y LAS *** AMOS,
                    26814 5ELCID3425 METIERCN LAS ***, & LCS CMENAIES CADOS SON,
        WORD #2062 CCCURS   2 TIMES.

FET                 16636 5ELCID2107 LO QUE UOS PLCGIERE, DELLOS ***, CAMPEADOR.
        WORD #2063 OCCURS   1 TIMES.

FEUOS               10531 5ELCID1335 ***** AQUI LAS SE@AS, VERCAC UOS DIGO YO:
                    28123 5ELCID3591 ***** DELA CTRA PART LOS YFANTES DE CARRION,
        WORD #2064 OCCURS   2 TIMES.

FEZIST               2619 5ELCID0331 ****** %IELC & TIERRA, EL TER%ERO EL MAR;
                     2627 5ELCID0332 ****** ESTRELAS & LUNA & EL SOL PORA ESCALENTAR;
                     2728 5ELCID0345 DEL AGUA ****** VINO & CELA PIECRA PAN,
                     2781 5ELCID0351 ESTANDO EN LA CRUZ, VERTUD ****** MUY GRANT.
        WORD #2065 OCCURS   4 TIMES.

FFABLO                 44 5ELCID0007 ****** MYO %IC BIEN & TAN MESURADO:
        WORD #2066 OCCURS   1 TIMES.

FFAGA               11035 5ELCID1397 ASSI ***** A UUESTRAS FIJAS AMAS.
        WORD #2067 OCCURS   1 TIMES.

FFAGAMOS            29194 5ELCID3728 ASSI ******** NCS TODOS IUSTOS & PECCADORES
        WORD #2068 OCCURS   1 TIMES.

FFAGO               22408 5ELCID2854 ASSI LC ***** YO QUE ACUI ESTC.
        WORD #2C69 OCCURS   1 TIMES.

FFALLARON            6253 5ELCID0796 DELOS MORISCOS, QUANDC SON LEGADOS, ********* DX CAUALLOS.
        WORD #2070 OCCURS   1 TIMES.

FFARIZ               5172 5ELCIDC654 CON AQUESTOS COS REYES CUE DIZEN ****** & GALUE;
        WORD #2C71 CCCURS   1 TIMES.

FFATA               11718 5ELCID1486 E ***** EN VALEN%IA CELLAS NCN UOS PARTADES.
        WORD #2072 CCCURS   1 TIMES.

FFAZIE              13101 5ELCID1661 ASSI ****** ALAS DUE@AS & A SUS FIJAS AMAS ADOS:
        WORD #2073 OCCURS   1 TIMES.

FFERA                5019 5ELCID0635 ASSI ***** LC DE SILOCA, QUE ES DEL OTRA PART.
        WORD #2074 OCCURS   1 TIMES.

FFERIR              13327 5ELCID1690 HYR LOS HEMOS ****** ENEL NOMBRE DEL CRIADOR & DEL APOSTOL SANTI
        WORD #2075 OCCURS   1 TIMES.

FFIJAS               2135 5ELCID0269 FEM ANTE UOS YO & UUESTRAS ******, YFFANTES SON & DE DIAS CHICAS,
                    12006 5ELCID1522 MUGIER DEL %IC LIDIADCR ESSUS ****** NATURALES;
        WORD #2076 OCCURS   2 TIMES.

FFINCARE            11614 5ELCID1472 YO ******** EN VALEN%IA, CA LA TENGO POR HEREDAD.
        WORD #2077 CCCURS   1 TIMES.

FFINCO               6757 5ELCID0863 Y ****** EN VN POYO QUE ES SOBRE MONT REAL;
        WORD #2078 CCCURS   1 TIMES.

FFUE                11875 5ELCID1506 ESSO **** APRIESSA FECHC, QUE NOS QUIEREN DETARDAR.
                    28999 5ELCID3704 ALEGRE **** DAQUESTC MYC %IC EL CAMPEADOR.
        WORD #2C79 CCCURS   2 TIMES.
```

```
WORD                 C#  PREFIX                          CONTEXT

FFUESSE            23215 5ELCID2957 FIZ LO POR BIEN, QUE ******* A SU PRO.
           WORD #2080 OCCURS   1 TIMES.

FICARAN             3612 5ELCID0455 E LOS QUE CON MYO %ID ******* EN LA %AGA.
           WORD #2081 OCCURS   1 TIMES.

FIEL                1596 5ELCID0204  VENIDES, MARTIN ANTOLINEZ, EL MIO **** VASSALO
                   28010 5ELCID3575 QUE **** SEADES OY DELLOS & DE NOS;
           WORD #2082 OCCURS   2 TIMES.

FIELES             28141 5ELCID3593 EL REY DIOLES ****** POR DEZIR EL DERECHO & AL NON,
                   28230 5ELCID3604 LOS ****** & EL REY ENSE@ARON LOS MOIONES,
                   28286 5ELCID3611 SALIEN LOS ****** DE MEDIO, ELLOS CARA POR CARA SON;
                   28548 5ELCID3645 ATORGARON GELO LOS ******, PERO VERMUEZ LE DEXO.
                   28741 5ELCID3670 OTORGAN GELO LOS ****** QUE DIZE VERDADERA PALABRA.
                   28906 5ELCID3692 DIXIERON LOS ******: ESTO OYMOS NOS.
           WORD #2083 OCCURS   6 TIMES.
              INDEX OF DIVERSIFICATION =   152.00 WITH STANDARD DEVIATION OF     82.36

FIERA               3347 5ELCID0422 PASSAREMOS LA SIERRA QUE ***** ES & GRAND,
                   18256 5ELCID2310 ***** COSA LES PESA DESTO QUE LES CUNTIO.
                   21645 5ELCID2751 E ALAS AUES DEL MONTE & ALAS BESTIAS DELA ***** GUISA.
           WORD #2084 OCCURS   3 TIMES.

FIERAS             10580 5ELCID1341 DE TAN ****** GANAN%IAS COMMO A FECHAS EL CAMPEADOR
                   11756 5ELCID1491 PASSAN LAS MONTANAS, QUE SON ****** & GRANDES,
                   21241 5ELCID2699 ELAS BESTIAS ****** QUE ANDAN ADERREDOR.
                   23120 5ELCID2946 ALAS BESTIAS ****** & ALAS AUES DEL MONT.
                   25656 5ELCID3267 ALAS BESTIAS ****** & ALAS AUES DEL MONT;
           WORD #2085 OCCURS   5 TIMES.
              INDEX OF DIVERSIFICATION =  3768.00 WITH STANDARD DEVIATION OF  3850.92

FIEREN              5725 5ELCID0722 TODOS ****** ENEL AZ DO ESTA PERO VERMUEZ.
           WORD #2086 OCCURS   1 TIMES.

FIEROS             21363 5ELCID2715 AQUI SEREDES ESCARNIDAS EN ESTOS ****** MONTES.
                   21922 5ELCID2789 LOS GANADOS ****** NON NOS COMAN EN AQUESTE MONT
           WORD #2087 OCCURS   2 TIMES.

FIERROS            28086 5ELCID3585 EMANO PRENDEN LAS ASTAS DELOS ******* TAIADORES,
           WORD #2088 OCCURS   1 TIMES.

FIGERUELA           3193 5ELCID0402 ALA ********* MYO %ID IUA POSAR.
           WORD #2089 OCCURS   1 TIMES.

FIGO                 612 5ELCID0077 SI NON, QUANTO DEXO NOLO PRE%IO UN ****.
           WORD #2090 OCCURS   1 TIMES.

FIJA                1640 5ELCID0210 VEREMOS UUESTRA MUGIER, MENBRADA **** DALGO.
           WORD #2091 OCCURS   1 TIMES.

FIJAS               2012 5ELCID0254 AELLA & ASUS ***** & ASUS DUENAS SIRUADES LAS EST A@O.
                    2021 5ELCID0255 DUES ***** DEXO NI@AS & PRENDET LAS EN LOS BRA%OS;
                    2082 5ELCID0262 AFEUOS DO@A XIMENA CON SUS ***** DO UA LEGANDO;
                    2185 5ELCID0275 ALAS SUS ***** ENBRA%O LAS PRENDIA,
                    2248 5ELCID0282 *****,
                    2951 5ELCID0372 ADIOS UOS ACOMIENDO, *****, & A LA MUGIER & AL PADRE SPIRITAL;
                    3053 5ELCID0384 COMMO SIRUA ADO@A XIMENA & ALAS ***** QUE HA,
                    6453 5ELCID0823 LO QUE ROMANE%IERE DALDO A MI MUGIER & A MIS *****,
                    7272 5ELCID0932 E QUEL DIXO SALUDES DE SU MUGIER & DE SUS *****
                   10076 5ELCID1276 POR MI MUGIER & MIS *****, SI FUERE SU MER%ED,
                   10099 5ELCID1279 LA MUGIER DE MYO %ID & SUS ***** LAS YFFANTES
                   10676 5ELCID1352 POR SU MUGIER DO@A XIMENA & SUS ***** AMAS ADOS:
                   10853 5ELCID1374 BIEN CASARIEMOS CON SUS ***** PORA HUEBOS DE PRO.
                   11038 5ELCID1397 ASSI FFAGA A UUESTRAS ***** AMAS.
                   11123 5ELCID1408 QUE SU MUGIER & SUS ***** EL REY SUELTAS ME LAS HA,
                   11156 5ELCID1411 SEREMOS YO & SU MUGIER & SUS ***** QUE EL A
                   11258 5ELCID1424 MINAYA A DO@A XIMINA & A SUS ***** QUE HA,
                   11579 5ELCID1467 MY MUGIER & MIS ***** CON MYNAYA ALBARFFANEZ,
                   11706 5ELCID1484 SU MUGIER & SUS ***** EN MEDINA ESTAN;
                   12328 5ELCID1565 QUE RE%IBAN A MYANAYA & ALAS DUENAS ***** DALGO;
                   12431 5ELCID1577 DELANTE SU MUGIER & DE SUS ***** QUERIE TENER LAS ARMAS.
                   12558 5ELCID1593 ADELINO A SU MUGIER & A SUS ***** AMAS;
                   12590 5ELCID1597 AFE ME AQUI, SE@OR, YO UUESTRAS ***** & AMAS,
                   12606 5ELCID1599 ALA MADRE & ALAS ***** BIEN LAS ABRA%AUA,
                   12650 5ELCID1604 VOS, QUERIDA & ONDRADA MUGIER, & AMAS MIS *****,
                   12672 5ELCID1608 MADRE & ***** LAS MANOS LE BESAUAN.
                   12910 5ELCID1638 MIS ***** & MI MUGIER QUE LAS TENGO ACA;
                   12934 5ELCID1641 MIS ***** & MI MUGIER VERME AN LIDIAR,
                   12965 5ELCID1644 SU MUGIER & SUS ***** SUBIOLAS AL ALCA%AR,
                   13009 5ELCID1650 POR CASAR SON UUESTRAS *****, ADUZEN UOS AXUUAR.
                   13107 5ELCID1661 ASSI FFAZIE ALAS DUE@AS & A SUS ***** AMAS ADOS:
                   13877 5ELCID1758 LAS DUE@AS & LAS ***** & LA MUGIER QUE VALE ALGO
```

WORD C# PREFIX CONTEXT

FIJAS (CON'T)

```
13958 5ELCID1768 LO DE UUESTRAS ***** VENIR SEA MAS POR ESPA%IO.
14236 5ELCID1801 ALEGRE ES DO@A XIMENA & SUS ***** AMAS,
14320 5ELCID1811 POR AMOR DE MI MUGIER & DE MIS ***** AMAS,
14889 5ELCID1882 DEMANDEMOS SUS ***** PORA CON ELLAS CASAR;
14927 5ELCID1887 QUE NOS DEMANDEDES ***** DEL CAMPEADOR;
15048 5ELCID1902 SABOR HAN DE CASAR CON SUS ***** AMAS ADOS.
15227 5ELCID1928 DE DAR SUS ***** ALOS YFANTES DE CARRION,
15297 5ELCID1937 E PIDEN ME MIS ***** PORA LOS YFANTES DE CARRION.
15797 5ELCID2003 DENTRO ES SU MUGIER & SUS ***** AMAS ADOS,
16356 5ELCID2075 VUESTRAS ***** UOS PIDO, DON ELUIRA & DO@A SOL,
16417 5ELCID2082 NON ABRIA ***** DE CASAR, RESPUSO EL CAMPEADOR,
16444 5ELCID2085 PERTENE%EN PORA MIS ***** & AVN PORA MEIORES.
16538 5ELCID2096 QUEM DADES UUESTRAS ***** PORA LOS YFANTES DE CARRION.
16568 5ELCID2099 HYO LAS CASO A UUESTRAS ***** CON UUESTRO AMOR,
16626 5ELCID2106 LOS YERNOS & LAS ***** TODOS UUESTROS FIJOS SON:
16659 5ELCID2110 VOS CASADES MIS *****, CA NON GELAS DO YO.
16842 5ELCID2132 PUES QUE CASADES MYS *****, ASI COMMO AUOS PLAZ,
17084 5ELCID2163 HE DELAS ***** DE MYO %ID, DE DON ELUIRA & DO@A SOL.
17270 5ELCID2184 RE%IBIOLO DO@A XIMENA & SUS ***** AMAS:
17304 5ELCID2189 GRADID MELO, MIS *****, CA BIEN UOS HE CASADAS
17318 5ELCID2190 BESARON LE LAS MANOS LA MUGIER & LAS ***** AMAS,
17366 5ELCID2197 AUOS DIGO, MIS *****, DON ELUIRA & DO@A SOL:
17416 5ELCID2203 METIUOS EN SUS MANOS, *****, AMAS ADOS;
17564 5ELCID2222 AFFE AMAS MIS *****, METOLAS EN UUESTRA MANO;
17644 5ELCID2232 DOUOS ESTAS DUE@AS, AMAS SON ***** DALGO,
18358 5ELCID2323 BIBDAS REMANDRAN ***** DEL CAMPEADOR.
18436 5ELCID2333 EN BRA%OS TENEDES MIS ***** TAN BLANCAS COMMO EL SOL
19873 5ELCID2520 EAMAS LA MYS *****, DON ELUIRA & DO@A SOL;
20098 5ELCID2551 ESCARNIREMOS LAS ***** DEL CANPEADOR.
20110 5ELCID2553 PODREMOS CASAR CON ***** DE REYES O DE ENPERADORES,
20128 5ELCID2555 ASSI LAS ESCARNIREMOS ALAS ***** DEL CAMPEADOR,
20208 5ELCID2566 VERAN UUESTRAS ***** LO QUE AUEMOS NOS,
20227 5ELCID2568 DIXO EL CAMPEADOR: DARUOS HE MYS ***** & ALGO DELO MYO;
20312 5ELCID2577 MIOS FIJOS SODES AMOS, QUANDO MIS ***** VOS DO;
20343 5ELCID2581 A MIS ***** SIRUADES, QUE UUESTRAS MUGIERES SON;
20369 5ELCID2584 AQUI RE%IBEN LAS ***** DEL CAMPEADOR;
20411 5ELCID2590 POR QUE ESCURREN SUS ***** DEL CAMPEADOR ATIERRAS DE CARRION.
20502 5ELCID2603 ANDAD, *****, DAQUI EL CRIADOR VOS VALA
20631 5ELCID2619 PRIMO ERES DE MIS ***** AMAS DALMA & DE CORA%ON
20652 5ELCID2621 VERAS LAS HEREDADES QUE A MIS ***** DADAS SON;
20731 5ELCID2632 EL PADRE CON LAS ***** LORAN DE CORA%ON,
20772 5ELCID2638 DIL QUE ENBIO MIS ***** A TIERRAS DE CARRION,
20894 5ELCID2654 ALAS ***** DEL %ID EL MORO SUS DO@AS DIO,
20950 5ELCID2661 HYA PUES QUE ADEXAR AUEMOS ***** DEL CAMPEADOR,
21085 5ELCID2679 ELUEGO LEUARIA SUS ***** AL CAMPEADOR LEAL;
22160 5ELCID2822 ALLAS ***** DEL %ID DAN LES ESFUER%O.
22250 5ELCID2834 QUE AMIS ***** BIEN LAS CASARE YO
22300 5ELCID2840 ADUXIESSEN ASSUS ***** A VALEN%IA LA MAYOR.
22665 5ELCID2888 MYO %ID ASUS ***** YUA LAS ABRA%AR,
22677 5ELCID2890  VENIDES, MIS *****? DIOS UOS CURIE DE MAL
22720 5ELCID2895 BESARON LAS MANOS LAS ***** AL PADRE.
22829 5ELCID2908 EL CASO MIS *****, CA NON GELAS DI YO;
23070 5ELCID2939 CASASTES SUS ***** CON YFANTES DE CARRION,
23101 5ELCID2943 MAL MAIARON SUS ***** DEL %ID CAMPEADOR;
23128 5ELCID2947 AFELAS SUS ***** EN VALENCIA DOSON.
23205 5ELCID2956 CA YO CASE SUS ***** CON YFANTES DE CARRION;
23869 5ELCID3040 BESA UOS LAS MANOS, & MIS ***** AMAS ADOS,
24721 5ELCID3149 POR MIS ***** QUEM DEXARON YO NON HE DESONOR,
24741 5ELCID3151 MAS QUANDO SACARON MIS ***** DE VALEN%IA LA MAYOR,
24779 5ELCID3156 QUANDO DEXARON MIS ***** ENEL ROBREDO DE CORPES,
24852 5ELCID3165 QUANDO DESONDRA DESUS ***** NO NOS DEMANDA OY;
25152 5ELCID3203 QUANDO SACARON DE VALEN%IA MIS ***** AMAS ADOS,
25611 5ELCID3261 ALA SALIDA DE VALEN%IA MIS ***** VOS DI YO,
25726 5ELCID3276 NON GELAS DEUIEN QUERER SUS ***** POR VARRAGANAS,
25878 5ELCID3297 DEUIEMOS CASAR CON ***** DE REYES O DE ENPERADORES,
25887 5ELCID3298 CA NON PERTENE%IEN ***** DE YFAN%ONES.
25922 5ELCID3303 HYO LAS HE *****, & TU PRIMAS CORMANAS;
26235 5ELCID3345 POR ***** DEL %ID, DON ELUIRA & DONA SOL:
26321 5ELCID3357 POR QUE DEXAMOS SUS ***** AVN NO NOS REPENTIMOS,
26400 5ELCID3368 ***** DEL %ID, POR QUE LAS VOS DEXASTES,
26613 5ELCID3398 PIDEN SUS ***** A MYO %ID EL CAMPEADOR
26678 5ELCID3407 AFE MIS *****, EN UUESTRAS MANOS SON:
26766 5ELCID3419 DE ***** DE MYO %ID, DON ELUIRA & DO@A SOL,
29081 5ELCID3714 GRADO AL REY DEL %IELO, MIS ***** VENGADAS SON
29157 5ELCID3723 QUANDO SE@ORAS SON SUS ***** DE NAUARRA & DE ARAGON.
WORD #2092 OCCURS 107 TIMES.
   INDEX OF DIVERSIFICATION =    255.08 WITH STANDARD DEVIATION OF    513.02
```

FIJO

```
 9249 5ELCID1176 NIN DA COSSEIO PADRE A ****, NON FIJO A PADRE,
 9251 5ELCID1176 NIN DA COSSEIO PADRE A FIJO, NON **** A PADRE,
25793 5ELCID3285 CA NON ME PRISO AELLA **** DE MUGIER NADA,
25799 5ELCID3286 NIMBLA MESSO **** DE MORO NIN DE CHRISTIANA,
WORD #2093 OCCURS    4 TIMES.
```

WORD C# PREFIX CONTEXT

```
FIJOS             8113 5ELCID1035 AUOS & DOS ***** DALGC QUITAR UOS HE LOS CUERPOS & DARUOS E
                                  DE MANO.
                  9269 5ELCID1149 ***** & MUGIERES VER LO MURIR CE FANBRE.
                 14486 5ELCID1832 MANDO CAUALGAR APRIESSA TOSCOS SOS ***** DALGO,
                 16629 5ELCID2106 LOS YERNOS & LAS FIJAS TODOS UUESTROS ***** SON:
                 16769 5ELCID2123 EVAD AQUI UUESTROS *****, QUANCO UUESTROS YERNOS SON;
                 17803 5ELCID2252 HYA %ERCA DELCS XV DIAS YAS VAN LOS ***** DALGO.
                 17896 5ELCID2264 EA TODAS LAS DUE@AS & ALOS ***** CALGO;
                 17924 5ELCID2268 ESTOS FUERCN ***** DEL CCNDE CCN GON%ALO.
                 19283 5ELCID2441 AMCS SON ***** DEL CONDE CON GO%ALO.
                 19297 5ELCID2443  VENIDES, MYCS YERNCS, MYOS ***** SODES AMOS
                 20214 5ELCID2567 LOS ***** QUE QUIEREMCS EN QUE AURAN PARTI%ION.
                 20307 5ELCID2577 MIOS ***** SOCES AMCS, CUANCO MIS FIJAS VOS DO;
         WORD #2094 OCCURS  12 TIMES.
            INDEX OF DIVERSIFICATION =  1107.55 WITH STANDARD CEVIATION OF  1530.46

FINCA            24871 5ELCID3167 DEMOS LE SUS ESPACAS, QUANCC ASSI ***** LA BOZ,
         WORD #2095 OCCURS   1 TIMES.

FINCADAS         12974 5ELCID1645 AL%AUAN LOS OJOS, TIENDAS VIERCN ********:
                 13066 5ELCID1657 ******** SCN LAS TIENCAS & PARE%EN LOS ALUORES,
                 18280 5ELCID2313 CINQUAENTA MILL TIENDAS ******** HA DELAS CABDALES;
         WORD #2096 OCCURS   3 TIMES.

FINCADOS          6692 5ELCID0854 NOS PAGADOS ********, SE@CR, CELA TU PART.
                 14572 5ELCID1843 ANTEL REY ALFONSSO LOS YNOIOS ********,
         WORD #2097 OCCURS   2 TIMES.

FINCAN           11633 5ELCID1474 E QUANTO QUE PUEDEN NCN ****** DE ANCAR.
                 18061 5ELCID2285 E %ERCAN EL ESCA@O & ****** SOBRE SO SE@OR.
                 22445 5ELCID2859 ENEL ****** LCS OIOS DON ELUIRA & DO@A SOL:
         WORD #2098 OCCURS   3 TIMES.

FINCAN%A          4428 5ELCID0563 QUE SOPIESSEN QUE MYO %ID ALLI AUIE ********.
         WORD #2099 OCCURS   1 TIMES.

FINCAR            4175 5ELCID0531 EN CASTEJON NCN PODRIEMCS ******;
                 14077 5ELCID1782 QUANDO A MYO %ID CAYERCN TANTOS, LOS OTROS BIEN PUEDEN
                                  ****** PAGADOS.
                 17778 5ELCID2249 E AL OTRO DIA FIZC MYC %ID ****** VIJ TABLADOS:
                 21253 5ELCID2701 MANDAN ****** LA TIENCA YFANTES DE CARRION,
         WORD #2100 OCCURS   4 TIMES.

FINCARAN         18605 5ELCID2354 CALOS MOROS, CCN DICS, NCN ******** EN CANPO.
         WORD #2101 OCCURS   1 TIMES.

FINCARE           3567 5ELCID0449 E YO CCN LO C AQUI ******* EN LA %AGA,
                 11600 5ELCID1470 E YO ******* EN VALEN%IA, QUE MUCHO COSTADOM HA;
         WORD #2102 OCCURS   2 TIMES.

FINCAREDES        2232 5ELCID0281 YO YRE & UOS ********** REMANIDA.
         WORD #2103 OCCURS   1 TIMES.

FINCARON          3666 5ELCID0462 CON POCAS DE GENTES QUE EN CASTEJON ********.
                  5184 5ELCID0656 ******** LAS TIENCAS & PRENDENC LAS POSADAS,
                 12852 5ELCID1631 ******** LAS TIENDAS, & POSAN LAS YENTES DESCREYDAS.
                 13889 5ELCID1759 DELANT EL CAMPEADOR LCS YNOJOS ********:
                 20430 5ELCID2593 ******** LCS YNOIOS ANTEL %IC CAMPEADOR:
         WORD #2104 OCCURS   5 TIMES.
            INDEX OF DIVERSIFICATION =  4190.00 WITH STANCARD DEVIATION OF  3401.21

FINCAUA            446 5ELCID0057 ******* LA TIENDA & LUEGO DESCAUALGAUA.
                  4052 5ELCID0515 TODA LA QUINTA A MYC %ID *******.
                 18910 5ELCID2392 EL QUE EN BUEN CRA NASCC LOS OJOS LE *******,
                 28639 5ELCID3656 LO VNO CAYO ENEL CAMPO & LO AL SUSO *******.
                 28721 5ELCID3667 SACOL DEL MOJON; MARTIN ANTOLJNEZ EN EL CAMPO *******.
         WORD #2105 OCCURS   5 TIMES.
            INDEX OF DIVERSIFICATION =  7067.75 WITH STANCARD DEVIATION OF  6546.11

FINCO              420 5ELCID0053 ***** LCS Y@OIOS, DE CORA%ON ROGAUA.
                  2098 5ELCID0264 ANTEL CAMPEADCR DO@A XIMENA ***** LOS YNOJOS AMOS,
                 10397 5ELCID1318 ***** SOS YNOJOS ANTE TCDEL PUEBLO,
                 10883 5ELCID1377 NCN LO DIZEN A NADI, & ***** ESTA RAZON.
                 11805 5ELCID1497 EL VNO ***** CON ELLCS & EL OTRO TORNO A ALBARFANEZ:
                 13257 5ELCID1681 ALBAR SALUADCREZ PRESC ***** ALLA.
                 13784 5ELCID1747 MYO %ID ***** ANTELLAS, TOUO LA RYENDA AL CAUALLO:
                 15944 5ELCID2021 LOS YNOJOS & LAS MANCS EN TIERRA LOS *****,
                 18147 5ELCID2296 MYO %ID ***** EL COBDC, EN PIE SE LEUANTO,
                 18179 5ELCID2299 ANTE MYO %ID LA CABE%A PREMIO & EL ROSTRO *****;
                 23028 5ELCID2934 DELANT EL REY ***** LCS YNOJOS AQUEL MU@O GUSTIOZ,
                 25220 5ELCID3211 QUE AL NO NOS DEMANDASSE, QUE AQUI ***** LA BCZ. . .
                 26438 5ELCID3372 DESTOS AMOS LA RAZCN *****.
                 28469 5ELCID3635 LAS DOS LE DESMANCHAN & LA TER%ERA *****:
         WORD #2106 OCCURS  14 TIMES.
            INDEX OF DIVERSIFICATION =  2156.62 WITH STANCARD DEVIATION OF  2200.16
```

```
WORD                C#  PREFIX                          CONTEXT

FINE              27103 5ELCID3463 DIXO EL REY: **** ESTA RAZON;
        WORD #2107 OCCURS   1 TIMES.

FINES              3175 5ELCID0399 PASSO PAR ALCOBIELLA QUE DE CASTIELLA ***** YA;
        WORD #2108 OCCURS   1 TIMES.

FINIESTRAS          128 5ELCID0017 BURGESES & BURGESAS POR LAS ********** SON,
        WORD #2109 OCCURS   1 TIMES.

FIO                8746 5ELCID1112 YO *** POR DIOS QUE EN NUESTRO PRO ENADRAN.
                   8894 5ELCID1133 COMMO *** POR DIOS, EL CAMPO NUESTRO SERA.
                  19320 5ELCID2447 COMMO YO *** POR DIOS & EN TODOS LOS SOS SANTOS,
        WORD #2110 OCCURS   3 TIMES.

FIRADES            8874 5ELCID1130 VOS CON LOS OTROS ******* LOS DELANT.
        WORD #2111 OCCURS   1 TIMES.

FIRGADES           7788 5ELCID0997 POR VNO QUE ********, TRES SIELLAS YRAN VAZIAS.
                  28893 5ELCID3690 DIXO GONZALO ASSUREZ: NOL ********, POR DIOS
        WORD #2112 OCCURS   2 TIMES.

FIRID              4706 5ELCID0597 ***** LOS, CAUALLEROS, TODOS SINES DUBDANZA;
        WORD #2113 OCCURS   1 TIMES.

FIRIENDO           6082 5ELCID0772 LOS DE MYO %ID ******** EN ALCAZ,
                   7877 5ELCID1007 ALOS VNOS ******** & A LOS OTROS DE ROCANDO.
                  10222 5ELCID1294 QUE SIS FARTAS LIDIANDO & ******** CON SUS MANOS,
        WORD #2114 OCCURS   3 TIMES.

FIRIENSSE         28385 5ELCID3625 ********* EN LOS ESCUDOS SIN TODO PAUOR.
        WORD #2115 OCCURS   1 TIMES.

FIRIENSSEN        28760 5ELCID3673 ********** EN LOS ESCUDOS VNOS TAN GRANDES COLPES;
        WORD #2116 OCCURS   1 TIMES.

FIRIERON          14560 5ELCID1842 ******** SE A TIERRA, DE%ENDIERON DELOS CAUALOS,
                  28558 5ELCID3646 MARTIN ANTOLINEZ & DIEGO GONZALEZ ******** SE DELAS LANZAS,
        WORD #2117 OCCURS   2 TIMES.

FIRIESTES         25641 5ELCID3265 A QUE LAS ********* A %INCHAS & A ESPOLONES?
        WORD #2118 OCCURS   1 TIMES.

FIRIO             15926 5ELCID2009 CON VNOS XV A TIERRAS *****,
                  28427 5ELCID3630 VN COLPE RESIBIERA, MAS OTRO *****:
                  28774 5ELCID3675 ***** ENEL ESCUDO A DON MUNO GUSTIOZ,
        WORD #2119 OCCURS   3 TIMES.

FIRIOM             7508 5ELCID0963 ****** EL SOBRINO & NON LO ENMENDO MAS;
        WORD #2120 OCCURS   1 TIMES.

FIRIOS            23746 5ELCID3025 ****** ATIERRA MYO %ID EL CAMPEADOR;
        WORD #2121 OCCURS   1 TIMES.

FIRME              4373 5ELCID0557 BIEN PUEBLA EL ETERO, ***** PRENDE LAS POSADAS,
                   5246 5ELCID0663 EL QUE EN BUEN ORA NASCO ***** GELO VEDAUA.
                   5954 5ELCID0755 ***** SON LOS MOROS, AVN NOS VAN DEL CAMPO.
                   7086 5ELCID0906 NON PLAZE ALOS MOROS, ***** MIENTRE LES PESAUA.
                   8811 5ELCID1121 ***** MIENTRE SON ESTOS A ESCARMENTAR.
                   9131 5ELCID1162 CABO DEL MAR TIERRA DE MOROS ***** LA QUEBRANTA,
                  17397 5ELCID2201 ATAN ***** MIENTRE & DE TODO CORAZON
                  18642 5ELCID2359 VOS CON LOS UUESTROS ***** MIENTRE ALA %AGA TENGADES;
                  19210 5ELCID2430 SABET, TODOS DE ***** ROBAUAN EL CAMPO.
                  28414 5ELCID3629 ***** ESTIDO PERO VERMUEZ, POR ESSO NOS ENCAMO;
        WORD #2122 OCCURS  10 TIMES.
           INDEX OF DIVERSIFICATION =  2670.22 WITH STANDARD DEVIATION OF  3469.82

FIRMES            27608 5ELCID3525 E MUNO GUSTIOZ, ****** SED EN CAMPO AGUISA DE VARONES;
        WORD #2123 OCCURS   1 TIMES.

FITA               3536 5ELCID0446 **** AYUSO & POR GUADALFAIARA, FATA ALCALA LEGEN LAS ALGARAS,
                   4531 5ELCID0576 DEXA VNA TIENDA **** & LAS OTRAS LEUAUA,
                  14120 5ELCID1787 MANDO MYO %ID RUY DIAZ QUE **** SOUIESSE LA TIENDA,
        WORD #2124 OCCURS   3 TIMES.

FITOS             16005 5ELCID2030 HYNOIOS ***** SEDIE EL CAMPEADOR:
                  16079 5ELCID2039 HYNOIOS ***** LAS MANOS LE BESO,
        WORD #2125 OCCURS   2 TIMES.

FIZ               21049 5ELCID2675  DEZID ME, QUE UOS ***, YFANTES DE CARRION
                  23210 5ELCID2957 *** LO POR BIEN, QUE FFUESSE A SU PRO.
                  24549 5ELCID3129 HYO, DE QUE FU REY, NON *** MAS DE DOS CORTES:
        WORD #2126 OCCURS   3 TIMES.
```

```
WORD                    C#  PREFIX                                CONTEXT

FIZIEMOS           25895 5ELCID3299 POR QUE LAS DEXAMOS DERECHO ********* NOS;
                   26335 5ELCID3359 LO QUE LES ********* SER LES HA RETRAYDO; ESTO LIDIARE
                                    ATOD EL MAS
        WORD #2127 OCCURS   2 TIMES.

FIZIERA             9103 5ELCID1158 QUE DIOS LE AIUDARA & ******* ESTA ARRANCADA.
        WORD #2128 OCCURS   1 TIMES.

FIZIERAS           26090 5ELCID3325 QUE MATARAS EL MORO & QUE ******** BARNAX;
        WORD #2129 OCCURS   1 TIMES.

FIZIERE            20797 5ELCID2641 DE QUANTO EL ******* YOL DAR POR ELLO BUEN GALARDON.
        WORD #2130 OCCURS   1 TIMES.

FIZIEREDES          1747 5ELCID0223 SI UOS ASSI LO ********** & LA UENTURA ME FUERE COMPLIDA,
                    8037 5ELCID1026 SI LO QUE DIGO **********, SALDREDES DE CATIUO;
                    8135 5ELCID1037 SI LO **********, %ID, LO QUE AUEDES FABLADO,
        WORD #2131 OCCURS   3 TIMES.

FIZIERON            5546 5ELCID0699 E ******** DOS AZES DE PEONES MEZCLADOS, QUILOS PODRIE CONTAR?
                   25738 5ELCID3278 DERECHO ******** POR QUE LAS HAN DEXADAS.
                   29116 5ELCID3719 ******** SUS CASAMIENTOS CON DON ELUIRA & CON DO@A SOL.
        WORD #2132 OCCURS   3 TIMES.

FIZIESTES          24709 5ELCID3147 POR QUANTO ESTA CORT ********* POR MI AMOR.
                   25665 5ELCID3268 POR QUANTO LES ********* MENOS VALEDES VOS.
        WORD #2133 OCCURS   2 TIMES.

FIZIST             26140 5ELCID3332 E TU, FERRANDO, QUE ****** CON EL PAUOR?
        WORD #2134 OCCURS   1 TIMES.

FIZO                3392 5ELCID0428 **** MYO %ID POSAR & %EUADA DAR.
                    4521 5ELCID0575 EL **** VN ART & NON LO DETARDAUA:
                    4928 5ELCID0624 **** ENBIAR POR LA TIENDA QUE DEXARA ALLA.
                    6927 5ELCID0885 AUN ME PLAZE DE MYO %ID QUE **** TAL GANAN%IA.
                    7109 5ELCID0909 CON TODAS SUS YENTES **** VNA TRASNOCHADA;
                    7280 5ELCID0933  DIOS, COMMO FUE EL %ID PAGADO & **** GRANT ALEGRIA
                    8509 5ELCID1081 VNA DES LEATAN%A CA NON LA **** ALGUANDRE.
                    9976 5ELCID1264 QUANDO LOS FALLO, POR CUENTA **** LOS NONBRAR:
                   10486 5ELCID1329 ASSI **** %EBOLLA & ADELANT CASTEION,
                   10507 5ELCID1332 OBISPO **** DE SU MANO EL BUEN CAMPEADOR,
                   10515 5ELCID1333 E **** %INCO LIDES CAMPALES & TODAS LAS ARRANCO.
                   12515 5ELCID1588 **** VNA CORRIDA, ESTA FUE TAN ESTRA@A.
                   13169 5ELCID1669 VOCA%ION ES QUE **** EL %ID CAMPEADOR.
                   14640 5ELCID1852 LAS GANAN%IAS QUE **** MUCHO SON SOBEIANAS,
                   17775 5ELCID2249 E AL OTRO DIA **** MYO %ID FINCAR VIJ TABLADOS:
                   19660 5ELCID2492 TODAS ESTAS GANAN%IAS **** EL CANPEADOR.
                   20150 5ELCID2558 FABLO FERAN GON%ALEZ & **** CALLAR LA CORT;
                   20495 5ELCID2602 EL **** AQUESTO, LA MADRE LO DOBLAUA;
                   20924 5ELCID2658 TOD ESTO LES **** EL MORO POR EL AMOR DEL %ID CAMPEADOR.
                   22732 5ELCID2897 GRAND GOZO **** CON ELLAS DO@A XIMENA SU MADRE.
                   26693 5ELCID3409 LEUANTOS EL REY, **** CALLAR LA CORT:
        WORD #2135 OCCURS  21 TIMES.
           INDEX OF DIVERSIFICATION =  1164.05 WITH STANDARD DEVIATION OF  1069.91

FLABLAR              813 5ELCID0104 EN PORIDAD ******* QUERRIA CON AMOS.
        WORD #2136 OCCURS   1 TIMES.

FLABLEMOS          15328 5ELCID1941 ********* EN ELLO, EN LA PORIDAD SEAMOS NOS.
        WORD #2137 OCCURS   1 TIMES.

FOLGAD             18451 5ELCID2335 EN VALEN%IA ****** A TODO UUESTRO SABOR,
        WORD #2138 OCCURS   1 TIMES.

FOLGANDO            9787 5ELCID1243 MYO %ID DON RODRIGO EN VALEN%IA ESTA ********,
        WORD #2139 OCCURS   1 TIMES.

FOLGAR              8061 5ELCID1028 DIXO EL CONDE DON REMONT:  COMEDE, DON RODRIGO, &
                                    PENSSEDES DE ******.
                   18785 5ELCID2377 MYO CORA%ON QUE PUDIESSE ******,
                   22434 5ELCID2857 ADELINAN A POSAR PORA ****** ESSA NOCH.
        WORD #2140 OCCURS   3 TIMES.

FOLGAUA             9609 5ELCID1221 YA ******* MYO %ID CON TODAS SUS CONPA@AS;
        WORD #2141 OCCURS   1 TIMES.

FOLGEDES            8447 5ELCID1074 ********, YA MYO %ID, SODES EN UUESTRO SALUO.
        WORD #2142 OCCURS   1 TIMES.

FOLON               7486 5ELCID0960 EL CONDE ES MUY ***** & DIXO VNA VANIDAT:
        WORD #2143 OCCURS   1 TIMES.

FONSSADO            6030 5ELCID0764 POR AQUEL COLPE RANCADO ES EL ********.
                    7226 5ELCID0926  DIOS, COMMO FUE ALEGRE TODO AQUEL ********,
        WORD #2144 OCCURS   2 TIMES.

FONTA               7351 5ELCID0942 DE MYO %ID RUY DIAZ QUE NON TEMIEN NINGUNA *****.
                    7481 5ELCID0959 OUO GRAND PESAR & TOUOS LO A GRAND *****.
```

WORD C# PREFIX CONTEXT

10713 5ELCID1357 DE ***** & DE MAL CURIALCAS & DE DESONOR;
WORD #2145 OCCURS 3 TIMES.

FORADAR 5760 5ELCID0727 TANTA ADAGARA ******* & PASSAR,
WORD #2146 OCCURS 1 TIMES.

FOR%ADO 7587 5ELCID0972 ASI VIENE ES ******* QUE EL CONDE AMANOS SELE CUYDO TOMAR.
WORD #2147 OCCURS 1 TIMES.

FOS 28119 5ELCID3590 QUE CADA VNO DELLOS BIEN *** FERIR EL SO.
WORD #2148 OCCURS 1 TIMES.

FOSSE 16891 5ELCID2137 ASSI COMMO YO LAS PRENDO DAQUENT, COMMO SI ***** DELANT,
WORD #2149 OCCURS 1 TIMES.

FOSSEN 15777 5ELCID2001 DALMA & DE CORA%ON, & TODOS LOS QUE EN PODER DESSOS ******;
WORD #2150 OCCURS 1 TIMES.

FOZ 4330 5ELCID0551 E PASSO AALFAMA, LA *** AYUSO UA,
WORD #2151 OCCURS 1 TIMES.

FRANCO 8406 5ELCID1068 HYA UOS YDES, CONDE, AGUISA DE MUY ******,
WORD #2152 OCCURS 1 TIMES.

FRANCOS 7837 5ELCID1002 VIERON LA CUESTA YUSO LA FUER%A DELOS *******;
WORD #2153 OCCURS 1 TIMES.

FRENOS 10548 5ELCID1337 DE SIELLAS & DE ****** TODOS GUARNIDOS SON,
14307 5ELCID1810 CON SIELLAS & CON ****** & CON SE@AS ESPADAS;
WORD #2154 OCCURS 2 TIMES.

FRESCO 22007 5ELCID2800 NUEUO ERA & ******, QUE DE VALEN%IAL SACO,
WORD #2155 OCCURS 1 TIMES.

FRONTAEL 11644 5ELCID1475 TRO%IERON A SANTA MARIA & VINIERON ALBERGAR A ********,
WORD #2156 OCCURS 1 TIMES.

FRONTERA 5067 5ELCID0640 CON LOS DELA ******** QUE UOS AIUDARAN,
5120 5ELCID0647 POR LOS DE LA ******** PIENSSAN DE ENVIAR;
WORD #2157 OCCURS 2 TIMES.

FRONTERAS 6579 5ELCID0840 MOROS DE LAS ********* & VNAS YENTES ESTRANAS;
WORD #2158 OCCURS 1 TIMES.

FRONZIDA 6195 5ELCID0789 LA COFIA ******** DIOS, COMMO ES BIEN BARBADO
13758 5ELCID1744 ******** TRAHE LA CARA, QUE ERA DESARMADO,
19248 5ELCID2436 LA CARA ******** & ALMOFAR SOLTADO,
19256 5ELCID2437 COFIA SOBRE LOS PELOS ******** DELLA YA QUANTO.
WORD #2159 OCCURS 4 TIMES.

FRUELLA 23586 5ELCID3004 EL CONDE DON ******* & EL CONDE DON BELTRAN.
WORD #2160 OCCURS 1 TIMES.

FU 15269 5ELCID1934 ECHADO ** DE TIERRA & TOLLIDA LA ONOR,
19672 5ELCID2494 ANTES ** MINGUADO, AGORA RICO SO,
WORD #2161 OCCURS 3 TIMES.

FUE 855 5ELCID0109 EL CAMPEADOR POR LAS PARIAS *** ENTRADO,
867 5ELCID0111 RETOUO DELLOS QUANTO QUE *** ALGO;
875 5ELCID0112 POR EN VINO AAQUESTO POR QUE *** ACUSADO.
1910 5ELCID0243 DIOS, QUE ALEGRE *** EL ABBAT DON SANCHO
2646 5ELCID0334 EN BELLEM APARE%IST, COMMO *** TU VELUNTAD;
2676 5ELCID0338 TE OFFRE%IERON, COMMO *** TU VELUNTAD;
2738 5ELCID0346 RESU%ITEST A LAZARO, CA *** TU VOLUNTAD;
2843 5ELCID0359 COMMO *** TU VOLUNTAD.
3211 5ELCID0404 Y SE ECHAUA MYO %ID DESPUES QUE *** %ENADO,
3717 5ELCID0469 QUIERON MIEDO & *** DESEPARADA.
3997 5ELCID0507 COMIDIOS MYO %ID, EL QUE EN BUEN ORA *** NADO,
4849 5ELCID0613 FABLO MYO %ID RUY DIAZ, EL QUE EN BUEN ORA *** NADO:
5829 5ELCID0737 MU@O GUSTIOZ, QUE *** SO CRIADO,
6091 5ELCID0773 EL REY FARIZ EN TERUEL SE *** ENTRAR,
6553 5ELCID0836 YA ES AGUISADO, MA@ANAS *** MINAYA,
6916 5ELCID0884 MAS DESPUES QUE DE MOROS ***, PRENDO ESTA PRESENTAIA;
7222 5ELCID0926 DIOS, COMMO *** ALEGRE TODO AQUEL FONSSADO,
7275 5ELCID0933 DIOS, COMMO *** EL %ID PAGADO & FIZO GRANT ALEGRIA
8352 5ELCID1062 DEL DIA QUE *** CONDE NON IANTE TAN DE BUEN GRADO,
8783 5ELCID1117 NON *** A NUESTRO GRADO NI NOS NON PUDIEMOS MAS,
8797 5ELCID1118 GRADO A DIOS, LO NUESTRO *** ADELANT.
9689 5ELCID1232 BUENA *** LA DE VALEN%IA QUANDO GANARON LA CASA,
9699 5ELCID1233 MAS MUCHO *** PROUECHOSA, SABET, ESTA ARANCADA:
10241 5ELCID1296 QUANDO LO OYO MYO %ID, DE AQUESTO *** PAGADO:
10322 5ELCID1307 ALEGRE *** MINAYA & SPICIOS & VINOS.
10371 5ELCID1314 ALEGRE *** DE AQUESTO MINAYA ALBARFANEZ,

WORD C# PREFIX CONTEXT

FUE (CON'T)

```
                11005 5ELCID1393 TAN GRAND *** EL GOZO QUANDOL VIERON ASSOMAR.
                12299 5ELCID1562 ALEGRE *** MYO %ID, QUE NUNQUA MAS NIN TANTO,
                12519 5ELCID1588 FIZO VNA CORRIDA, ESTA *** TAN ESTRA@A.
                12542 5ELCID1591 DES DIA SE PRE%IO BAUIECA EN QUANT GRANT *** ESPA@A.
                13973 5ELCID1770 GRANT *** EL ALEGRIA QUE FUE POR EL PALA%IO;
                13977 5ELCID1770 GRANT FUE EL ALEGRIA QUE *** POR EL PALA%IO;
                14475 5ELCID1831 ALEGRE *** EL REY, NON VIESTES ATANTO,
                15730 5ELCID1996 GALIND GAR%IAZ, EL QUE *** DE ARAGON:
                16219 5ELCID2057 EN AQUEL DIA DEL REY SO HUESPED ***;
                18953 5ELCID2398 PLOGO A DIOS, AQUESTA *** EL ARRANCADA.
                19525 5ELCID2474 GRANT *** EL DIA LA CORT DEL CAMPEADOR,
                20137 5ELCID2556 ANTES QUE NOS RETRAYAN LO QUE *** DEL LEON.
                21752 5ELCID2766 MANDARON LE YR ADELANTE, MAS DE SU GRADO NON ***.
                22114 5ELCID2814 FALLO A DIEGO TELLEZ EL QUE DE ALBARFANEZ ***;
                23076 5ELCID2940 ALTO *** EL CASAMIENO CALO QUISIESTES UOS
                23537 5ELCID2997 EL CONDE DON GAR%IA EN ESTAS NUEUAS ***,
                23578 5ELCID3003 AQUESTE *** PADRE DEL BUEN ENPERADOR;
                24012 5ELCID3061 SUELTA *** LA MISSA ANTES QUE SALIESSE EL SOL,
                24556 5ELCID3130 LA VNA *** EN BURGOS, & LA OTRA EN CARRION,
                25770 5ELCID3282 POR ESSO ES LUEGA QUEADELI%IO *** CRIADA.
                25786 5ELCID3284 CA DE QUANDO NASCO ADELI%IO *** CRIADA,
                27492 5ELCID3512 *** BESAR LA MANO A SO SE@OR ALFONSSO;
                27650 5ELCID3530 ALEGRE *** DAQUESTO EL QUE EN BUEN ORA NA%IO;
                27751 5ELCID3542 EL COMETER *** MALO, QUE LO AL NOS ENPE%O,
                28789 5ELCID3677 EN VAZIO *** LA LAN%A, CA EN CARNE NOL TOMO.
                29142 5ELCID3721 AMAYOR ONDRA LAS CASA QUE LO QUE PRIMERO ***.
         WORD #2162 OCCURS  52 TIMES.
            INDEX OF DIVERSIFICATION =   553.65 WITH STANDARD DEVIATION OF   555.82

FUENT           21251 5ELCID2700 FALARON VN VERGEL CON VNA LINPIA *****;
         WORD #2163 OCCURS   1 TIMES.

FUER            10925 5ELCID1382 FATA DENTRO EN MEDINA DENLES QUANTO HUEBOS LES ****,
         WORD #2164 OCCURS   1 TIMES.

FUERA            3640 5ELCID0459 ABREN LAS PUERTAS, DE ***** SALTO DAUAN,
                 3670 5ELCID0463 LAS YENTES DE ***** TODAS SON DE RAMADAS.
                 4635 5ELCID0588 MYO %ID, QUANDO LOS VIO *****, COGIOS COMMO DE ARRANCADA.
                 4663 5ELCID0591 LOS GRANDES & LOS CHICOS ***** SALTO DAN,
                 5383 5ELCID0679 TODOS LOS MOROS & LAS MORAS DE ***** LOS MANDA ECHAR,
                 5426 5ELCID0685 TODOS YSCAMOS *****, QUE NADI NON RASTE,
                 5496 5ELCID0693 ABRIERON LAS PUERTAS, ***** VN SALTO DAN;
                 7937 5ELCID1014 DE ***** DELA TIENDA VN SALTO DAUA,
                10354 5ELCID1312 ***** EL REY A SAN FAGUNT AVN POCO HA,
                12840 5ELCID1629 ARRIBADO AN LAS NAUES, ***** ERAN EXIDOS,
                13541 5ELCID1716 LA SE@A SACAN *****, DE VALEN%IA DIFRON SALTO,
                13992 5ELCID1772 MYNAYA ALBARFANEZ ***** ERA ENEL CAMPO,
                14493 5ELCID1833 HYEN LOS PRIMEROS EL REY ***** DIO SALTO,
                17717 5ELCID2242 ALA GLERA DE VALEN%IA ***** DIERON SALTO;
                19968 5ELCID2533 QUIEN LIDIARA MEIOR OQUIEN ***** EN ALCAN%O;
                24344 5ELCID3104 ALA PUERTA DE ***** DESCAUALGA A SABOR;
         WORD #2165 OCCURS  16 TIMES.
            INDEX OF DIVERSIFICATION =  1379.27 WITH STANDARD DEVIATION OF  1373.68

FUERAS           9197 5ELCID1171 NON OSAN ****** EXIR NIN CON EL SE AIUNTAR;
         WORD #2166 OCCURS   1 TIMES.

FUERCA            269 5ELCID0034 QUE SI NON LA QUEBRANTAS POR ******, QUE NON GELA ABRIESE NADI.
         WORD #2167 OCCURS   1 TIMES.

FUER%A           7835 5ELCID1002 VIERON LA CUESTA YUSO LA ****** DELOS FRANCOS;
                27217 5ELCID3479 QUE NON PRENDAN ****** DE CONDE NIN DE YFAN%ON.
         WORD #2168 OCCURS   2 TIMES.

FUER%AS          5972 5ELCID0757 POR ESTAS ******* FUERTE MIENTRE LIDIANDO,
                11851 5ELCID1502 E EL ALCAYAZ AUEGALUON CON SUS ******* QUE TRAHE,
                18271 5ELCID2312 ******* DE MARRUECOS VALEN%IA VIENEN %ERCAR;
         WORD #2169 OCCURS   3 TIMES.

FUERE             731 5ELCID0092 ENPE@AR GELO HE POR LO QUE ***** GUISADO;
                 1752 5ELCID0223 SI UOS ASSI LO FIZIEREDES & LA UENTURA ME ***** COMPLIDA,
                 3581 5ELCID0451 SICUETA UOS ***** ALGUNA AL ALGARA,
                10078 5ELCID1276 POR MI MUGIER & MIS FIJAS, SI ***** SU MER%ED,
                10775 5ELCID1364 SIRUAN LE SUS HEREDADES DO ***** EL CAMPEADOR,
                15115 5ELCID1911 QUEL YRE A VISTAS DO ***** AGUISADO;
                18649 5ELCID2360 SI CUETA *****, BIEN ME PODREDES HUUIAR.
                26265 5ELCID3349 QUANDO ***** LA LID, SI PLOGUIERE AL CRIADOR,
         WORD #2170 OCCURS   8 TIMES.
            INDEX OF DIVERSIFICATION =  3646.71 WITH STANDARD DEVIATION OF  2685.52

FUEREDES         8153 5ELCID1039 PUES COMED, CONDE, & QUANDO ******** IANTADO,
                13380 5ELCID1696 QUANDO UOS LOS ******** FERIR, ENTRARE YO DEL OTRA PART;
         WORD #2171 OCCURS   2 TIMES.

FUEREMOS        11132 5ELCID1409 MIENTRA QUE ******** POR SUS TIERRAS CONDUCHO NOS MANDO DAR.
```

WORD C# PREFIX CONTEXT

FUEREMOS (CON'T)

21487 5ELCID2732 SI NOS ******** MAIADAS, ABILTAREDES AUOS,
WORD #2172 OCCURS 2 TIMES.

FUEREN 10711 5ELCID1356 HYO LES MANDARE DAR CONDUCHO MIENTRA QUE POR MJ TIERRA ******,
10730 5ELCID1358 QUANDO EN CABO DE MI TIERRA A QUESTAS DUE@AS ******,
16614 5ELCID2105 PUES ****** EN UUESTRO PODER EN VALEN%IA LA MAYOR,
WORD #2173 OCCURS 3 TIMES.

FUERES 27945 5ELCID3566 ESSI ****** VEN%IDOS, NON REBTEDES A NOS,
WORD #2174 OCCURS 1 TIMES.

FUERO 13688 5ELCID1734 LOS L MILL POR CUENTA ***** NOTADOS:
WORD #2175 OCCURS 1 TIMES.

FUERON 4113 5ELCID0523 ATERCER DIA DADOS ****** SJN FALLA.
6175 5ELCID0786 CA EN ALCAZ SJN DUBDA LES ****** DANDO.
7436 5ELCID0954 ****** LOS MANDADOS A TODAS PARTES,
9543 5ELCID1213 LOS QUE ****** DE PIE CAUALLEROS SE FAZEN;
9831 5ELCID1248 LOS QUE ****** CON EL, & LOS DE DESPUES, TODOS SON PAGADOS;
12099 5ELCID1535 TODOS ****** ALEGRES DEL %ERUI%IO QUE TOMARON,
12817 5ELCID1626 CON L VEZES MILL DE ARMAS, TODOS ****** CONPLIDOS,
13600 5ELCID1723 ATANTOS MATA DE MOROS QUE NON ****** CONTADOS;
17254 5ELCID2182 TODOS ESSA NOCH ****** A SUS POSADAS,
17764 5ELCID2248 RICAS ****** LAS BODAS EN EL ALCA%AR ONDRADO,
17837 5ELCID2257 NON ****** EN CUENTA LOS AUERES MONEDADOS.
17923 5ELCID2268 ESTOS ****** FIJOS DEL CONDE DON GON%ALO.
19501 5ELCID2471 ****** EN VALEN%IA MUY BIEN ARREADOS,
20722 5ELCID2631 GRANDES ****** LOS DUELOS ALA DEPARTI%ION.
23592 5ELCID3005 ****** Y DE SU REYNO OTROS MUCHOS SABIDORES,
24000 5ELCID3059 ACORDADOS ******, QUANDO VINO LA MAN.
28563 5ELCID3647 TALES ****** LOS COLPES QUE LES QUEBRARON AMAS.
29064 5ELCID3712 POR QUE TAN ONDRADOS ****** LOS DEL CANPEADOR.
29128 5ELCID3720 LOS PRIMEROS ****** GRANDES, MAS AQUESTOS SON MIIORES;
WORD #2176 OCCURS 19 TIMES.
INDEX OF DIVERSIFICATION = 1388.72 WITH STANDARD DEVIATION OF 1305.14

FUERT 10498 5ELCID1330 E PE@A CADIELLA, QUE ES VNA PE@A *****;
21186 5ELCID2691 ASSINIESTRO DEXAN ATINEZA, VNA PE@A MUY *****,
22329 5ELCID2843 VINIERON A SANTESTEUAN DE GORMAZ, VN CASTIELLO TAN *****,
WORD #2177 OCCURS 3 TIMES.

FUERTE 5 5ELCID0001 DELOS SOS OIOS TAN ****** MIENTRE LORANDO,
183 5ELCID0024 CON GRAND RECABDO & ****** MIENTRE SELLADA:
345 5ELCID0043 CON GRANT RECABDO & ****** MIENTRE SELLADA.
2200 5ELCID0277 LORA DELOS OIOS, TAN ****** MIENTRE SOSPIRA:
4352 5ELCID0554 EN VN OTERO REDONDO, ****** & GRAND;
4987 5ELCID0630 VINO POSAR SOBRE ALCO%ER, EN VN TAN ****** LOGAR;
5973 5ELCID0757 POR ESTAS FUER%AS ****** MIENTRE LIDIANDO,
12789 5ELCID1623 QUE EN MIS HEREDADES ****** MIETRE ES MIETDO,
17486 5ELCID2212 CON BUENAS VESTIDURAS & ****** MIENTRE ADOBADOS;
22289 5ELCID2839 DIXOLES ****** MIENTRE QUE ANDIDIESSEN DE DIA & DE NOCH,
WORD #2178 OCCURS 10 TIMES.
INDEX OF DIVERSIFICATION = 2475.00 WITH STANDARD DEVIATION OF 2395.80

FUERTES 5696 5ELCID0718 YUAN LOS FERIR DE ******* CORA%ONES.
20275 5ELCID2573 CAUALLOS PORA EN DIESTRO ******* & CORREDORES,
21422 5ELCID2723 EN MANO PRENDEN LAS %INCHAS ******* & DURADORES.
21445 5ELCID2726 DOS ESPADAS TENEDES ******* & TAIADORES,
WORD #2179 OCCURS 4 TIMES.

FUES 26180 5ELCID3337 LEUANTOS DEL ESCA@O & **** PORAL LEON;
WORD #2180 OCCURS 1 TIMES.

FUESSE 484 5ELCID0061 ASSI POSO MYO %ID COMMO SI ****** EN MONTA@A.
12421 5ELCID1576 ALA PUERTA DE VALEN%IA, DO ****** EN SO SALUO,
14353 5ELCID1815 MANDO A PERO VERMUEZ QUE ****** CON MYNAYA.
19626 5ELCID2487 ELA SU QUINTA NON ****** OLBIDADO.
23225 5ELCID2958 SI QUIER EL CASAMIENTO FECHO NON ****** OY
26480 5ELCID3379 ****** A RIO DOUIRNA LOS MOLINOS PICAR
WORD #2181 OCCURS 6 TIMES.
INDEX OF DIVERSIFICATION = 5198.20 WITH STANDARD DEVIATION OF 3950.27

FUESSEDES 16133 5ELCID2046 ********* MY HUESPED, SIUOS PLOGIESSE, SE@OR.
WORD #2182 OCCURS 1 TIMES.

FUESSEMOS 21708 5ELCID2760 SI NON ********* ROGADOS,
WORD #2183 OCCURS 1 TIMES.

FUESSEN 1281 5ELCID0164 QUE SI ANTES LAS CATASSEN QUE ******* PERIURADOS,
23404 5ELCID2981 A CABO DE VIJ SEMANAS QUE Y ******* IUNTADOS;
26308 5ELCID3355 ESTOS CASAMIENTOS NON ******* APARE%IDOS
27857 5ELCID3555 QUE NON ******* EN LA BATALLA LAS ESPADAS TAIADORES
WORD #2184 OCCURS 4 TIMES.

```
WORD                    C#   PREFIX                              CONTEXT

FUESTES              563 5ELCID0071 YA CANPEADOR, EN BUEN ORA ******* NA%IDO
                    2114 5ELCID0266 MER%ED, CANPEADOR, EN ORA BUENA ******* NADO
                   19398 5ELCID2457 EA UOS, %ID, QUE EN BUEN ORA ******* NADO
         WORD #2185 OCCURS    3 TIMES.

FUR%UDO            28770 5ELCID3674 ASSUR GON%ALEZ, ******* & DE VALOR,
         WORD #2186 OCCURS    1 TIMES.

FURTARE             9935 5ELCID1260 QUE SI ALGUNOS ******* O MENOS LE FALLAREN, EL AUER ME
                                    AURA ATORNAR
         WORD #2187 OCCURS    1 TIMES.

FUST                2839 5ELCID0358 ENEL MONUMENTO RESU%ITEST, **** ALOS YNFIERNOS,
         WORD #2188 OCCURS    1 TIMES.

FUSTE              12506 5ELCID1586 MYO %ID SALIO SOBREL, & ARMAS DE ***** TOMAUA,
         WORD #2189 OCCURS    1 TIMES.

FUSTED             26380 5ELCID3365 ****** METER TRAS LA VIGA LAGAR,
         WORD #2190 OCCURS    1 TIMES.

FUSTEL             26027 5ELCID3318 VIST VN MORO, ****** ENSAYAR; ANTES FUXISTE QUE ALTE ALEGASSES.
         WORD #2191 OCCURS    1 TIMES.

FUXISTE            26030 5ELCID3318 VIST VN MORO, FUSTEL ENSAYAR; ANTES ******* QUE ALTE ALEGASSES.
         WORD #2192 OCCURS    1 TIMES.

GABRIEL             3223 5ELCID0406 EL ANGEL ******* A EL VINO EN SUE@O:
         WORD #2193 OCCURS    1 TIMES.

GALARDON            3071 5ELCID0386 BIEN SEPA EL ABBAT QUE BUEN ******** DELLO PRENDRA.
                   16796 5ELCID2126 DIOS QUE ESTA EN %IELO DEM DENT BUEN ********.
                   20357 5ELCID2582 SI BIEN LAS SERUIDES, YO UOS RENDRE BUEN ********.
                   20803 5ELCID2641 DE QUANTO EL FIZIERE YOL DAR POR ELLO BUEN ********.
                   21871 5ELCID2782 ADIOS PLEGA & A SANTA MARIA QUE DENT PRENDAN ELLOS MAL ********
                   22422 5ELCID2855 AFFE DIOS DELOS %IELOS QUE UOS DE DENT BUEN ********
                   26752 5ELCID3416 ESSORA DIXO EL REY: DIOS UOS DE DEN BUEN ********
         WORD #2194 OCCURS    7 TIMES.
            INDEX OF DIVERSIFICATION =  3945.83 WITH STANDARD DEVIATION OF  5059.32

GALARDONADO        16987 5ELCID2150 QUEM FECHES QUE BIEN SEA ***********.
         WORD #2195 OCCURS    1 TIMES.

GALIN               3517 5ELCID0443 E ALBAR SALUADOREZ SIN FALLA, & ***** GAR%IA, VNA FARDIDA
                    5845 5ELCID0740 ***** GAR%IA, EL BUENO DE ARAGON,
         WORD #2196 OCCURS    2 TIMES.

GALIND             15726 5ELCID1996 ****** GAR%IAZ, EL QUE FUE DE ARAGON:
                   15751 5ELCID1999 ALUAR SALUADOREZ & ****** GARCIAZ EL DE ARAGON,
                   24086 5ELCID3071 E ****** GAR%IEZ, EL BUENO DARAGON;
         WORD #2197 OCCURS    3 TIMES.

GALIZIANAS         15633 5ELCID1982 CON EL REY VAN LEONESES & MESNADAS **********,
         WORD #2198 OCCURS    1 TIMES.

GALIZIANOS         23381 5ELCID2978 ALOS PORTOGALESES & A **********,
         WORD #2199 OCCURS    1 TIMES.

GALLEGAS            7763 5ELCID0994 NOS CAUALGAREMOS SIELLAS ********, & HUESAS SOBRE CAL%AS;
         WORD #2200 OCCURS    1 TIMES.

GALLIZANOS         22970 5ELCID2926 ELLOS CONDES ********** A EL TIENEN POR SE@OR.
         WORD #2201 OCCURS    1 TIMES.

GALLIZIA           20326 5ELCID2579 QUE LO SEPAN EN ******** & EN CASTIELLA & EN LEON,
         WORD #2202 OCCURS    1 TIMES.

GALLO               1326 5ELCID0169 CA AMOUER A MYO %ID ANTE QUE CANTE EL *****.
                    1635 5ELCID0209 EN SAN PERO DE CARDENA YNOS CANTE EL *****;
         WORD #2203 OCCURS    2 TIMES.

GALLOS              1849 5ELCID0235 APRIESSA CANTAN LOS ****** & QUIEREN QUEBRAR ALBORES,
                    2503 5ELCID0316 ALA MA@ANA, QUANDO LOS ****** CANTARAN,
                    2564 5ELCID0324 ALOS MEDIADOS ****** PIESSAN DE CAUALGAR.
                   13419 5ELCID1701 ALOS MEDIADOS ******, ANTES DE LA MA@ANA,
         WORD #2204 OCCURS    4 TIMES.

GALUE               5174 5ELCID0654 CON AQUESTOS DOS REYES QUE DIZEN FFARIZ & *****;
                    6037 5ELCID0765 MARTIN ANTOLINEZ VN COLPE DIO A *****,
                    6065 5ELCID0769 ARANCADO ES EL REY FARIZ & *****;
         WORD #2205 OCCURS    3 TIMES.

GANA               12958 5ELCID1643 AFARTO VERAN POR LOS OIOS COMMO SE **** EL PAN.
         WORD #2206 OCCURS    1 TIMES.

GANA%IA             4599 5ELCID0584 DEMOS SALTO A EL & FEREMOS GRANT *******,
```

WORD C# PREFIX CONTEXT

GANA%IA (CON'T)

```
                  4657 5ELCID0590 DIZEN LOS DE ALCO%ER:  YA SE NOS VA LA *******
                  6867 5ELCID0877 SOBEIANA ES, SE@OR, LA SU *******.
                 15597 5ELCID1977 COMMO ELLOS TENIEN, CER%ER LES YA LA *******,
        WORD #2207 OCCURS   4 TIMES.

GANA%IAS          3796 5ELCID0480 TANTO TRAEN LAS GRANDES ********, MUCHOS GA@ADOS.
        WORD #2208 OCCURS   1 TIMES.

GANADA            9413 5ELCID1196 TORNAUAS A MURUIEDRO, CA EL SE LA A ******.
                 10468 5ELCID1327 ****** A XERICA & A ONDA POR NOMBRE,
                 12669 5ELCID1607 EN ESTA HEREDAD QUE UOS YO HE ******.
                 14302 5ELCID1809 CON CAUALLOS DESTA QUINTA QUE YO HE ******,
        WORD #2209 OCCURS   4 TIMES.

GANADAS          19592 5ELCID2482 SOBEIANAS SON LAS GANAN%IAS QUETODOS AN *******;
        WORD #2210 OCCURS   1 TIMES.

GANADES            376 5ELCID0047 %ID, ENEL NUESTRO MAL UOS NON ******* NADA;
        WORD #2211 OCCURS   1 TIMES.

GANADO            4994 5ELCID0631 SACOLOS A %ELADA, EL CASTIELLO ****** A;
                 14046 5ELCID1779 LOS MOROS DELAS TIERRAS ****** SEAN Y ALGO;
                 14088 5ELCID1784 QUE A ****** MYO %ID CON TODOS SUS VASSALLOS
        WORD #2212 OCCURS   3 TIMES.

GANADOS            796 5ELCID0101 EN CUENTA DE SUS AUERES, DELOS QUE AUIEN *******.
                  1619 5ELCID0207 VOS VJ %IENTOS & YO XXX HE *******.
                 21921 5ELCID2789 LOS ******* FIEROS NON NOS COMAN EN AQUESTE MONT
        WORD #2213 OCCURS   3 TIMES.

GANAN%IA          1011 5ELCID0130 O QUE ******** NOS DARA POR TODO AQUESTE A@O?
                  1289 5ELCID0165 NON LES DIESSE MYO %ID DELA ******** UN DINERO MALO.
                  3691 5ELCID0465 MOROS & MORAS AUIEN LOS DE ********,
                  3752 5ELCID0474 SOS CAUALLEROS LEGAN CON LA ********,
                  3786 5ELCID0478 E DESI ARRIBA TORNAN SE CON LA ********,
                  4094 5ELCID0520 AVN DELO QUE DIESSEN OUIESSEN GRAND ********.
                  4720 5ELCID0598 CON LA MER%ED DEL CRIADOR NUESTRA ES LA ********
                  4924 5ELCID0623 MYO %ID CON ESTA ******** EN ALCO%ER ESTA;
                  6286 5ELCID0800 REFECHOS SON TODOS ESOS CHRISTIANOS CON AQUESTA ********.
                  6929 5ELCID0885 AUN ME PLAZE DE MYO %ID QUE FIZO TAL ********.
                  7026 5ELCID0898 SI NULLA DUBDA YO A MYO %ID BUSCAR ********.
                  7601 5ELCID0973 MYO %ID DON RODRIGO TRAE GRAND ********,
                  7695 5ELCID0985 YA CAUALLEROS, A PART FAZED LA ********;
                  7811 5ELCID0999 OY EN ESTE PINAR DE TEUAR POR TOLER ME LA ********.
                  8528 5ELCID1084 DE LA ******** QUE AN FECHA MARAUILLOSA & GRAND.
                  9423 5ELCID1198 AL SABOR DELA ******** NON LO QUIERE DETARDAR,
                  9687 5ELCID1231 TORNADO ES MYO %ID CON TODA ESTA ********.
                 11330 5ELCID1434 SOLTARIEMOS LA ********, QUE NOS DIESSE EL CABDAL.
                 12734 5ELCID1617 DESTA ******** COMME ES BUENA & GRAND.
                 13677 5ELCID1733 TODA ESTA ******** EN SU MANO A RASTADO.
                 13823 5ELCID1751 QUANDO EN VUESTRA VENIDA TAL ******** NOS AN DADA.
                 18303 5ELCID2316 QUE LES CRE%E LA ********, GRADO AL CRIADOR.
                 18336 5ELCID2320 CATAMOS LA ******** & LA PERDIDA NO,
        WORD #2214 OCCURS  23 TIMES.
           INDEX OF DIVERSIFICATION =   786.50 WITH STANDARD DEVIATION OF  1032.91

GANAN%IAS         1386 5ELCID0177 ASSI ES UUESTRA VENTURA GRANDES SON UUESTRAS *********,
                  3551 5ELCID0447 E BIEN ACOIAN TODAS LAS *********,
                  3985 5ELCID0506 ESTAS ********* ALLI ERAN IUNTADAS.
                  4301 5ELCID0548 GRANDES SON LAS ********* QUE PRISO POR LA TIERRA DO UA.
                  7354 5ELCID0943 CON ESTAS ********* ALA POSADA TORNANDO SEUAN,
                  7362 5ELCID0944 TODOS SON ALEGRES, ********* TRAEN GRANDES.
                  7958 5ELCID1016 PLOGO A MYO %ID, CA GRANDES SON LAS *********.
                  8080 5ELCID1031 ELLOS PARTIENDO ESTAS ********* GRANDES,
                  9027 5ELCID1149 GRANDES SON LAS ********* QUE MIO %ID FECHAS HA.
                  9061 5ELCID1153 ENTRAUAN A MURUIEDRO CON ESTAS ********* QUE TRAEN GRANDES.
                 10047 5ELCID1273 DESTAS MIS *********, QUE AUEMOS FECHAS ACA,
                 10526 5ELCID1334 GRANDES SON LAS ********* QUEL DIO EL CRIADOR,
                 10581 5ELCID1341 DE TAN FIERAS ********* COMMO A FECHAS EL CAMPEADOR
                 13715 5ELCID1738 LAS OTRAS ********* NON AUYA RECABDO.
                 14405 5ELCID1822 TALLES ********* TRAEN QUE SON A AGUARDAR.
                 14638 5ELCID1852 LAS ********* QUE FIZO MUCHO SON SOBEIANAS,
                 19454 5ELCID2465 TODAS LAS ********* A VALEN%IA SON LEGADAS;
                 19589 5ELCID2482 SOBEIANAS SON LAS ********* QUETODOS AN GANADAS;
                 19659 5ELCID2492 TODAS ESTAS ********* FIZO EL CANPEADOR.
        WORD #2215 OCCURS  19 TIMES.
           INDEX OF DIVERSIFICATION =  1014.17 WITH STANDARD DEVIATION OF  1367.44

GANANDO           9171 5ELCID1167 EN TIERRA DE MOROS PRENDIENDO & *******,
        WORD #2216 OCCURS   1 TIMES.

GANAR              961 5ELCID0123 NOS HUEBOS AUEMOS EN TODO DE ***** ALGO.
                  4368 5ELCID0556 MOI %ID DON RODRIGO ALCO%ER CUEDA *****.
                  4459 5ELCID0567 EN LA SU VEZINDAD NON SE TREUEN ***** TANTO.
```

WORD C# PREFIX CONTEXT

GANAR (CON'T)

```
                 5656 5ELCID0712 MOROS LE RE%IBEN POR LA SE@A *****,
                 9181 5ELCID1169 EN ***** AQUELAS VILLAS MYO %ID DURO IIJ A@OS.
                10117 5ELCID1281 AESTAS TIERRAS ESTRANAS QUE NOS PUDIEMOS *****.
                22518 5ELCID2867 BUEN CASAMIENTO PERDIESTES, MEIOR PODREDES *****.
        WORD #2217 OCCURS   7 TIMES.
           INDEX OF DIVERSIFICATION =  3591.83 WITH STANDARD DEVIATION OF  4531.77

GANARA          12396 5ELCID1573 E ADUXIESSEN LE ABAUIECA; POCO AUIE QUEL ******,
        WORD #2218 OCCURS   1 TIMES.

GANAREDES        3971 5ELCID0504 PUES QUE POR MI ********* QUES QUIER QUE SEA DALGO,
                25100 5ELCID3197 SE QUE SI UOS ACAE%IERE, CON ELLA ********* GRAND PREZ &
                                 GRAND VALOR.
        WORD #2219 OCCURS   2 TIMES.

GANAREMOS        4903 5ELCID0620 QUE LOS DESCABE%EMOS NADA NON *********;
                10825 5ELCID1371 MAS ********* EN ESTO QUE EN OTRA DESONOR.
        WORD #2220 OCCURS   2 TIMES.

GANARON          9134 5ELCID1163 ******* PENA CADIELLA, LAS EXIDAS & LAS ENTRADAS.
                 9694 5ELCID1232 BUENA FUE LA DE VALEN%IA QUANDO ******* LA CASA,
                 9921 5ELCID1258 DELOS QUE SON AQUI & COMIGO ******* ALGO;
                19795 5ELCID2509 VALIA DE %INCO MILL MARCOS ******* AMOS ADOS;
        WORD #2221 OCCURS   4 TIMES.

GANE             1488 5ELCID0190 YO, QUE ESTO UOS ****, BIEN MERE%IAS CAL%AS.
                 8171 5ELCID1041 MAS QUANTO AUEDES PERDIDO & YO **** EN CANPO,
                12886 5ELCID1635 CON AFAN **** A VALEN%IA, & ELA POR HEREDAD,
                15279 5ELCID1935 CON GRAND AFAN **** LO QUE HE YO;
                20302 5ELCID2576 BIEN LO SABEDES UOS QUE LAS **** AGUISA DE VARON;
                24765 5ELCID3154 ESTAS YO LAS **** AGUISA DE VARON,
                27455 5ELCID3507 E YR ME QUIERO PORA VALEN%IA, CON AFAN LA **** YO.
        WORD #2222 OCCURS   7 TIMES.
           INDEX OF DIVERSIFICATION =  4326.83 WITH STANDARD DEVIATION OF  1588.98

GANELA          25070 5ELCID3194 PRENDED A COLADA, ****** DE BUEN SE@OR,
        WORD #2223 OCCURS   1 TIMES.

GANO            17128 5ELCID2167 ADELINAN PORA VALEN%IA, LA QUE EN BUEN PUNTO ****.
                19179 5ELCID2426 E **** A TIZON QUE MILL MARCOS DORO VAL.
        WORD #2224 OCCURS   2 TIMES.

GA@ADO          13799 5ELCID1748 AUOS ME OMILLO, DUE@AS, GRANT PREZ UOS HE ******:
        WORD #2225 OCCURS   1 TIMES.

GA@ADOS          3694 5ELCID0466 E ESSOS ******* QUANTOS EN DERREDOR ANDAN.
                 3798 5ELCID0480 TANTO TRAEN LAS GRANDES GANA%IAS, MUCHOS *******.
        WORD #2226 OCCURS   2 TIMES.

GA@ARA          15854 5ELCID2011 MYO %ID SELOS ******, QUE NON GELOS DIERAN EN DON.
        WORD #2227 OCCURS   1 TIMES.

GA@O              969 5ELCID0124 BIEN LO SABEMOS QUE EL ALGO ****,
                 3739 5ELCID0473 **** A CASTEION & EL ORO ELA PLATA.
                 4815 5ELCID0610 MYO %ID **** A ALCO%ER, SABENT, POR ESTA MA@A.
                 7903 5ELCID1010 HY **** A COLADA QUE MAS VALE DE MILL MARCOS DE PLATA.
                 8598 5ELCID1092 MYO %ID **** AXERICA & A ONDA & ALMENAR,
                 9534 5ELCID1212 QUANDO MYO %ID **** A VALEN%IA & ENTRO ENLA %IBDAD.
                17196 5ELCID2175 AFELOS EN VALEN%IA, LA QUE MYO %ID ****;
                24455 5ELCID3117 ESSORA DIXO MUCHAS MER%EDES EL QUE VALEN%IA ****:
                25304 5ELCID3221 MUCHO NOS AFINCA EL QUE VALEN%IA ****,
                26175 5ELCID3336 FASTA DO DESPERTO MYO %ID, EL QUE VALEN%IA ****;
        WORD #2228 OCCURS  10 TIMES.
           INDEX OF DIVERSIFICATION =  2799.67 WITH STANDARD DEVIATION OF  2784.12

GARCIAZ         15752 5ELCID1999 ALUAR SALUADOREZ & GALIND ******* EL DE ARAGON,
        WORD #2229 OCCURS   1 TIMES.

GARCIORDONEZ    16103 5ELCID2042 PESO A ALBARDIAZ & A ************.
        WORD #2230 OCCURS   1 TIMES.

GAR%IA           3518 5ELCID0443 E ALBAR SALUADOREZ SIN FALLA, & GALIN ******, VNA FARDIDA
                 5846 5ELCID0740 GALIN ******, EL BUENO DE ARAGON,
                14515 5ELCID1836 EL CONDE DON ******, SO ENEMIGO MALO.
                14700 5ELCID1859 PESO AL CONDE DON ******, E MAL ERA YRADO;
                23533 5ELCID2997 EL CONDE DON ****** EN ESTAS NUEUAS FUE,
                23609 5ELCID3007 EL CONDE DON ****** CON YFANTES DE CARRION,
                24813 5ELCID3160 DIXO EL CONDE DON ******: AESTO NOS FABLEMOS.
                25679 5ELCID3270 EL CONDE DON ****** EN PIE SE LEUANTAUA;
        WORD #2231 OCCURS   8 TIMES.
           INDEX OF DIVERSIFICATION =  3164.86 WITH STANDARD DEVIATION OF  3887.46

GAR%IAZ         15727 5ELCID1996 GALIND *******, EL QUE FUE DE ARAGON:
        WORD #2232 OCCURS   1 TIMES.
```

```
WORD                    C#  PREFIX                              CONTEXT

GAR%IEZ             24087 5ELCID3071 E GALIND *******, EL BUENO CARAGON;
        WORD #2233 OCCURS   1 TIMES.

GAR%IORDONEZ        10617 5ELCID1345 MAGER PLOGO AL REY, MUCHO PESO A ************:
                    27846 5ELCID3553 SEDIELOS CASTIGANDO EL CONDE ************.
        WORD #2234 OCCURS   2 TIMES.

GASPAR               2665 5ELCID0337 MELCHIOR & ****** & BALTASAR, ORO & TUS & MIRRA
        WORD #2235 OCCURS   1 TIMES.

GEL                  6056 5ELCID0768 SABET, EL OTRO NON *** OSO ESPERAR.
        WORD #2236 OCCURS   1 TIMES.

GELA                  201 5ELCID0026 E A QUEL QUE **** DIESSE SOPIESSE UERA PALABRA,
                      272 5ELCID0034 QUE SI NON LA QUEBRANTAS POR FUERCA, QUE NON **** ABRIESE NADI.
                     5250 5ELCID0664 TOUIERON **** EN %ERCA COMPLIDAS TRES SEMANAS.
                     9520 5ELCID1210 QUANDO VINO EL DEZENO, OUIERON **** ADAR.
                     9629 5ELCID1223 QUE PRESA ES VALEN%IA, QUE NON **** ENPARAN;
                    19153 5ELCID2422 LAS CARBONCLAS DEL YELMO TOLLIDAS **** HA,
                    28435 5ELCID3631 QUEBRANTO LA BOCA DEL ESCUDO, A PART **** ECHO,
                    28485 5ELCID3637 DEDENTRO EN LA CARNE VNA MANO **** METIO;
                    28785 5ELCID3676 TRAS EL ESCUDO FALSSO **** GUARNIZON;
                    28808 5ELCID3679 TRAS EL ESCUDO FALSSO **** GUARNIZON,
                    28822 5ELCID3681 NOL PUDO GUARIR, FALSSO **** GUARNIZON,
                    28845 5ELCID3684 DELA OTRA PART VNA BRA%A **** ECHO,
        WORD #2237 OCCURS  12 TIMES.
           INDEX OF DIVERSIFICATION =  2603.00 WITH STANDARD DEVIATION OF  3813.10

GELAS                1260 5ELCID0162 E BIEN ***** GUARDARIEN FASTA CABO DEL A@O;
                     6043 5ELCID0766 LAS CARBONCLAS DEL YELMO ECHO ***** APARTE,
                    11715 5ELCID1485 QUE VAYADES POR ELLAS, ADUGADES ***** ACA,
                    12236 5ELCID1553 AVN LAS FERRADURAS QUITAR ***** MANDAUA;
                    16662 5ELCID2110 VOS CASADES MIS FIJAS, CA NON ***** DO YO.
                    16858 5ELCID2134 NON ***** DARE YO CON MI MANO, NIN DED NON SE ALABARAN.
                    22832 5ELCID2908 EL CASO MIS FIJAS, CA NON ***** DI YO;
                    24922 5ELCID3174 DAR ***** QUEREMOS DELLANT ESTANDO UOS.
                    25722 5ELCID3276 NON ***** DEUIEN QUERER SUS FIJAS POR VARRAGANAS,
                    25731 5ELCID3277 O QUIEN ***** DIERA POR PAREIAS OPOR VELADAS?
                    26629 5ELCID3400 E QUE ***** DIESSEN A ONDRA & ABENDI%ION,
                    28603 5ELCID3652 LAS MONCLURAS DEL YELMO TODAS ***** CORTAUA,
        WORD #2238 OCCURS  12 TIMES.
           INDEX OF DIVERSIFICATION =  2484.73 WITH STANDARD DEVIATION OF  2288.68

GELO                  726 5ELCID0092 ENPE@AR **** HE POR LO QUE FUERE GUISADO;
                     1171 5ELCID0151 QUE **** NON VENTANSSEN DE BURGOS OMNE NADO.
                     1272 5ELCID0163 CA ASSIL DIERAN LA FE & **** AUIEN IURADO,
                     2071 5ELCID0261 OTORGADO **** AUIE EL ABBAT DE GRADO.
                     5247 5ELCID0663 EL QUE EN BUEN ORA NASCO FIRME **** VEDAUA.
                     7195 5ELCID0922 TODO **** DIZE, QUE NOL ENCUBRE NADA.
                     7537 5ELCID0966 MAS QUANDO EL MELO BUSCA, YR **** HE YO DEMANDAR.
                     7972 5ELCID1018 EL CONDE DON REMONT NON **** PRE%IA NADA,
                     8247 5ELCID1050 E TIENEN **** DELANT & DIERON GELO PRIUADO.
                     8251 5ELCID1050 E TIENEN GELO DELANT & DIERON **** PRIUADO.
                     8902 5ELCID1134 COMMO **** A DICHO, AL CAMPEADOR MUCHO PLAZE.
                    10069 5ELCID1275 DESI POR MI BESALDE LA MANO EFIRME **** ROGAD
                    10259 5ELCID1298 QUANDO DIOS PRESTAR NOS QUIERE, NOS BIEN **** GRADESCAMOS:
                    10270 5ELCID1300 E DAR **** A ESTE BUEN CHRISTIANO;
                    10767 5ELCID1363 POR QUE LOS DESEREDE, TODO **** SUELTO YO;
                    12023 5ELCID1524 MAGER QUE MAL LE QUERAMOS, NON **** PODREMOS FER,
                    12796 5ELCID1624 E EL NON **** GRADE%E SI NON A IHESU CHRISTO.
                    13276 5ELCID1683 EL SELO VIO CON LOS OIOS, CUENTAN **** DELANT,
                    15060 5ELCID1904 QUE **** DIGADES ALBUEN CAMPEADOR:
                    15086 5ELCID1908 ROGAR **** EMOS LO QUE DEZIDES UOS;
                    15241 5ELCID1930 QUE **** CONSSEIAUA DALMA & DE CORA%ON.
                    17574 5ELCID2223 SABEDES QUE AL REY ASSI **** HE MANDADO,
                    19359 5ELCID2452 AQUELOS QUE GELOS DIERAN NON **** AUIEN LOGRADO.
                    20994 5ELCID2667 VN MORO LATINADO BIEN **** ENTENDIO;
                    21277 5ELCID2704 MAL **** CUNPLIERON QUANDO SALIE EL SOL
                    22196 5ELCID2827 QUANDO **** DIZEN A MYO %ID EL CAMPEADOR,
                    22370 5ELCID2850 NON **** QUISO TOMAR, MAS MUCHO GELO GRADIO:
                    22375 5ELCID2850 NON GELO QUISO TOMAR, MAS MUCHO **** GRADIO:
                    22424 5ELCID2856 TODOS **** GRADE%EN & SOS PAGADOS SON,
                    25332 5ELCID3225 SI ESSO PLOGIERE AL %ID, NON **** VEDAMOS NOS;
                    25748 5ELCID3279 QUANTO EL DIZE NON **** PRE%IAMOS NADA.
                    27885 5ELCID3558 DIXIERON **** AL REY, MAS NON GELO CONLOYO;
                    27890 5ELCID3558 DIXIERON GELO AL REY, MAS NON **** CONLOYO;
                    28211 5ELCID3601 CA QUI TUERTO QUISIERE FAZER, MAL **** VEDARE YO,
                    28244 5ELCID3606 BIEN **** DEMOSTRARON ATODOS VJ COMMO SON,
                    28438 5ELCID3632 PASSO **** TODO, QUE NADA NOL VALIO,
                    28546 5ELCID3645 ATORGARON **** LOS FIELES, PERO VERMUEZ LE DEXO.
                    28596 5ELCID3651 EL CASCO DE SOMO APART **** ECHAUA,
                    28619 5ELCID3654 LA COFIA & EL ALMOFAR TODO **** LEUAUA,
                    28739 5ELCID3670 OTORGAN **** LOS FIELES QUE DIZE VERDADERA PALABRA.
        WORD #2239 OCCURS  40 TIMES.
           INDEX OF DIVERSIFICATION =   717.28 WITH STANDARD DEVIATION OF   862.94
```

WORD C# PREFIX CONTEXT

GELOS
1059 5ELCID0136 DIXO RACHEL & VIDAS: CAR ***** DE GRADO.
1455 5ELCID0186 LOS OTROS CCC EN ORO ***** PAGAUAN.
4021 5ELCID0511 SOS QUI@ONEROS QUE ***** DIESSEN POR CARTA.
7980 5ELCID1019 ADUZEN LE LOS COMERES, DELANT ***** PARAUAN;
10060 5ELCID1274 DAR LE QUIERO C CAUALLOS, & UOS YD ***** LEUAR;
15857 5ELCID2011 MYO %ID SELOS GA@ARA, QUE NON ***** DIERAN EN DON.
16640 5ELCID2108 MYO %ID ***** RE%IBE, LAS MANOS LE BESO:
19356 5ELCID2452 AQUELOS QUE ***** DIERAN NON GELO AUIEN LOGRADO.
23143 5ELCID2949 QUE ***** LEUEDES AVISTAS, O AIUNTAS, O A CORTES;
25387 5ELCID3233 TORNAR ***** QUIERO, CA TODOS FECHOS SON,
25409 5ELCID3235 QUANDO ELLOS LOS AN APECHAR, NON ***** QUIERO YO.
WORD #2240 OCCURS 11 TIMES.
INDEX OF DIVERSIFICATION = 2434.00 WITH STANDARD DEVIATION OF 1777.06

GENTES
3662 5ELCID0462 CON POCAS DE ****** QUE EN CASTEION FINCARON.
5160 5ELCID0653 ****** SE AIUNTARON SOBEIANAS DE GRANDES
7550 5ELCID0968 ****** SE LE ALEGAN GRANDES ENTRE MOROS & CHRISTIANOS,
7718 5ELCID0988 DE MOROS & DE CHRISTIANOS ****** TRAE SOBEIANAS,
9450 5ELCID1201 QUANDO VIO MYO %ID LAS ****** IUNTADAS, COMPE%OS DE PAGAR.
WORD #2241 OCCURS 5 TIMES.
INDEX OF DIVERSIFICATION = 1446.00 WITH STANDARD DEVIATION OF 932.54

GENTIL
5318 5ELCID0672 DE CASTIELLA LA ****** EXIDOS SOMOS ACA,
6504 5ELCID0829 HYDES UOS, MYNAYA, ACASTIELLA LA ******?
WORD #2242 OCCURS 2 TIMES.

GERRA
6775 5ELCID0865 NON TEME *****, SABET, A NULLA PART.
12030 5ELCID1525 EN PAZ O EN ***** DELO NUESTRO ABRA;
WORD #2243 OCCURS 2 TIMES.

GESTA
8538 5ELCID1085 AQUIS CONPIE%A LA ***** DE MYO %ID EL DE BIUAR.
WORD #2244 OCCURS 1 TIMES.

GLERA
444 5ELCID0056 CABO ESSA VILLA EN LA ***** POSAUA,
466 5ELCID0059 POSO EN LA ***** QUANDO NOL COGE NADI EN CASA;
17714 5ELCID2242 ALA ***** DE VALEN%IA FUERA DIERON SALTO;
WORD #2245 OCCURS 3 TIMES.

GLOORIFFICARON
2651 5ELCID0335 PASTORES TO **************, QUIERON DE A LAUDARE,
WORD #2246 OCCURS 1 TIMES.

GLORIOSA
1701 5ELCID0218 VALAN ME TUS VERTUDES, ******** SANTA MARIA
1728 5ELCID0221 VUESTRA UERTUD ME UALA, ********, EN MY EXIDA & ME AIUDE,
WORD #2247 OCCURS 2 TIMES.

GLORIOSO
2613 5ELCID0330 YA SE@OR ********, PADRE QUE EN %IELO ESTAS,
28700 5ELCID3665 VALME, DIOS ********, RE@OR, & CURIAM DESTE ESPADA
WORD #2248 OCCURS 2 TIMES.

GO%ALO
19287 5ELCID2441 AMOS SON FIJOS DEL CONDE DON ******.
WORD #2249 OCCURS 1 TIMES.

GOLGOTA
2757 5ELCID0348 PUSIERON TE EN CRUZ POR NUMBRE EN *******;
WORD #2250 OCCURS 1 TIMES.

GOMEZ
27058 5ELCID3457 ***** PELAYET EN PIE SE LEUANTO;
WORD #2251 OCCURS 1 TIMES.

GON%ALEZ
17164 5ELCID2172 EVAY ASUR ********, QUE ERA BULIDOR,
18066 5ELCID2286 FERRAN ******** NON VIO ALLI DOS AL%ASSE, NIN CAMARA ABIERTA NIN
18085 5ELCID2288 DIEGO ******** POR LA PUERTA SALIO,
19923 5ELCID2527 AESTAS PALABRAS FABLO FERAN ********:
20148 5ELCID2558 FABLO FERAN ******** & FIZO CALLAR LA CORT;
23616 5ELCID3008 E ASUR ******** & GON%ALO ASSUREZ,
26292 5ELCID3353 DIEGO ******** ODREDES LO QUE DIXO:
26440 5ELCID3373 ASUR ******** ENTRAUA POR EL PALA%IO,
28557 5ELCID3646 MARTIN ANTOLINEZ & DIEGO ******** FIRIERON SE DELAS LAN%AS,
28650 5ELCID3658 VIO DIEGO ******** QUE NO ESCAPARIE CON EL ALMA;
28756 5ELCID3672 CON ASSUR ******** COMMO SE ADOBO.
28769 5ELCID3674 ASSUR ********, FUR%UDO & DE VALOR,
WORD #2252 OCCURS 12 TIMES.
INDEX OF DIVERSIFICATION = 1054.00 WITH STANDARD DEVIATION OF 1253.44

GON%ALO
17928 5ELCID2268 ESTOS FUERON FIJOS DEL CONDE DON *******.
23618 5ELCID3008 E ASUR GON%ALEZ & ******* ASSUREZ,
28890 5ELCID3690 DIXO ******* ASSUREZ: NOL FIRGADES, POR DIOS
WORD #2253 OCCURS 3 TIMES.

GORMAZ
22325 5ELCID2843 VINIERON A SANTESTEUAN DE ******, VN CASTIELLO TAN FUERT,
22576 5ELCID2875 TRO%IERON ALCO%EUA, ADIESTRO DE SANTESTEUAN DE ******,
WORD #2254 OCCURS 2 TIMES.

WORD C# PREFIX CONTEXT

GOZO
1331 5ELCID0170 ALCARGAR DELAS ARCHAS VERIECES **** TANTO:
1927 5ELCID0245 CON TAN GRANT **** RE%IBEN AL QUE EN BUEN ORA NASCO.
3028 5ELCID0381 AUNTODOS ESTOS DUELOS EN **** SE TORNARAN;
4734 5ELCID0600 DIOS, QUE BUENO ES EL **** POR AQUESTA MA@ANA
6305 5ELCID0803 GRANT A EL **** MYO %ID CON TODOS SOS VASSALOS.
9005 5ELCID1146 GRAND ES EL **** QUE VA POR ES LOGAR.
11007 5ELCID1393 TAN GRAND FUE EL **** QUANDOL VIERON ASSOMAR.
11664 5ELCID1478 SALIOLOS RE%EBIR CON GRANT **** QUE FAZE:
12611 5ELCID1600 DEL **** QUE AUIEN DE LOS SOS OIOS LORAUAN.
15959 5ELCID2023 LORANDO DELOS OIOS, TANTO AUIE EL **** MAYOR;
22534 5ELCID2869 HY IAZEN ESSA NOCHE, & TAN GRAND **** QUE FAZEN.
22659 5ELCID2887 ARMAS YUA TENIENDO & GRANT **** QUE FAZE;
22731 5ELCID2897 GRAND **** FIZO CON ELLAS DO@A XIMENA SU MADRE.
WORD #2255 OCCURS 13 TIMES.
INDEX OF DIVERSIFICATION = 1782.33 WITH STANDARD DEVIATION OF 1805.79

GOZOS
9525 5ELCID1211 GRANDES SON LOS ***** QUE VAN POR ES LOGAR,
11955 5ELCID1515 POR %ERCA DE SALON TAN GRANDES ***** VAN.
17202 5ELCID2176 QUANDO A ELLA ASSOMARON, LOS ***** SON MAYORES.
19758 5ELCID2505 GRANDES SON LOS ***** EN VALEN%IA CON MYO %ID EL CANPEADOR
19778 5ELCID2507 GRANDES SON LOS ***** DE SUS YERNOS AMOS ADOS:
29055 5ELCID3711 GRANDES SON LOS ***** EN VALEN%IA LA MAYOR,
WORD #2256 OCCURS 6 TIMES.
INDEX OF DIVERSIFICATION = 3905.00 WITH STANDARD DEVIATION OF 3526.61

GRA%IA
407 5ELCID0050 YA LO VEE EL %ID QUE DEL REY NON AUIE ******.
6817 5ELCID0870 MYO %ID RUY DIAZ DE DIOS AYA SU ******
6903 5ELCID0882 OMNE AYRADO, QUE DE SE@OR NON HA ******,
6948 5ELCID0888 HYD & VENIT, DA QUI UOS DO MI ******;
10821 5ELCID1370 DE MI SEAN QUITOS & VAYAN ALA ****** DEL CRIADOR.
10898 5ELCID1379 HYA UOS YDES, MYNAYA?, YD ALA ****** DEL CRIADOR
15292 5ELCID1936 ADIOS LO GRADESCO QUE DEL REY HE SU ******,
16118 5ELCID2044 QUANDO HE LA ****** DE DON ALFONSSO MYO SE@OR;
20517 5ELCID2604 DE MI & DE UUESTRO PADRE BIEN AVEDES NUESTRA ******.
20548 5ELCID2608 AMOS LAS BENDIXIERON & DIERON LES SU ******.
21108 5ELCID2682 HYRE CON UUESTRA ******, DON ELUIRA & DO@A SOL;
27444 5ELCID3506 BESO UUESTRAS MANOS CON UUESTRA ******, SE@OR,
WORD #2257 OCCURS 12 TIMES.
INDEX OF DIVERSIFICATION = 2456.91 WITH STANDARD DEVIATION OF 2635.32

GRA%IAS
1957 5ELCID0248 DIXO EL %ID: *******, DON ABBAT, & SO UUESTRO PAGADO;
6998 5ELCID0895 GRADO & *******, REY, COMMO A SE@OR NATURAL;
16483 5ELCID2090 *******, DIXO EL REY, AUOS & ATOD ESTA CORT.
16526 5ELCID2095 GRADO & *******, CID, COMMO TAN BUENO, & PRIMERO AL CRIADOR,
22377 5ELCID2851 *******, VARONES DE SANTESTEUAN, QUE SODES CO@OS%EDORES,
WORD #2258 OCCURS 5 TIMES.
INDEX OF DIVERSIFICATION = 5104.00 WITH STANDARD DEVIATION OF 3888.82

GRADAN
1342 5ELCID0172 ****** SE RACHEL & VIDAS CON AUERES MONEDADOS,
WORD #2259 OCCURS 1 TIMES.

GRADE
21137 5ELCID2685 DA QUESTE CASAMIENTO QUE ***** EL CAMPEADOR.
WORD #2260 OCCURS 1 TIMES.

GRADE%E
12797 5ELCID1624 E EL NON GELO ******* SI NON A IHESU CHRISTO.
22398 5ELCID2853 MUCHO UOS LO *******, ALLA DO ESTA, MYO %ID EL CANPEADOR,
WORD #2261 OCCURS 2 TIMES.

GRADE%EDES
14269 5ELCID1805 DELO QUE AUOS CAYO VOS NON ********** NADA;
WORD #2262 OCCURS 1 TIMES.

GRADE%EN
22425 5ELCID2856 TODOS GELO ******** & SOS PAGADOS SON,
WORD #2263 OCCURS 1 TIMES.

GRADE%IOLO
1551 5ELCID0199 ********** DON MARTINO & RECIBIO LOS MARCHOS;
WORD #2264 OCCURS 1 TIMES.

GRADESCAMOS
10260 5ELCID1298 QUANDO DIOS PRESTAR NOS QUIERE, NOS BIEN GELO ***********:
WORD #2265 OCCURS 1 TIMES.

GRADESCO
1690 5ELCID0217 ATI LO ********, DIOS, QUE %IELO & TIERRA GUIAS;
1935 5ELCID0246 ******** LO ADIOS, MYO %ID, DIXO EL ABBAT DON SANCHO;
3888 5ELCID0493 MUCHO UOS LO ********, CAMPEADOR CONTADO.
15262 5ELCID1933 ESTO ******** A CHRISTUS EL MYO SE@OR.
15286 5ELCID1936 ADIOS LO ******** QUE DEL REY HE SU GRA%IA,
16112 5ELCID2043 FABLO MYO %ID & DIXO ESTA RAZON: ESTO ******** AL CRIADOR,
16649 5ELCID2109 MUCHO UOS LO ********, COMMO A REY & A SE@OR
24698 5ELCID3146 MUCHO UOS LO ******** COMMO A REY & A SE@OR,
26657 5ELCID3404 ESTO ******** YO AL CRIADOR,
26973 5ELCID3446 ESTO ******** YO ALCRIADOR,
WORD #2266 OCCURS 10 TIMES.
INDEX OF DIVERSIFICATION = 2808.22 WITH STANDARD DEVIATION OF 4060.66

WORD C# PREFIX CONTEXT

GRADESCOLO 14669 5ELCID1856 ********** A MYO %ID QUE TAL DON ME HA ENBIADO;
16062 5ELCID2037 ********** A DIOS DEL %IELO & DESPUES AUOS,
16782 5ELCID2125 **********, REY, & PRENDO UUESTRO DON,
WORD #2267 OCCURS 3 TIMES.

GRADID 17301 5ELCID2189 ****** MELO, MIS FIJAS, CA BIEN UOS HE CASADAS
22466 5ELCID2861 EUOS A EL LO ******, QUANDO BIUAS SOMOS NOS.
WORD #2268 OCCURS 2 TIMES.

GRADIMOS 22456 5ELCID2860 ATANTO UOS LO ******** COMMO SI VIESSEMOS AL CRAIDOR;
WORD #2269 OCCURS 1 TIMES.

GRADIO 22376 5ELCID2850 NON GELO QUISO TOMAR, MAS MUCHO GELO ******:
WORD #2270 OCCURS 1 TIMES.

GRADO 51 5ELCID0008 ***** ATI, SE@OR PADRE, QUE ESTAS EN ALTO
156 5ELCID0021 CONBIDAR LE YEN DE *****, MAS NINGUNO NON OSAUA:
665 5ELCID0084 FER LO HE AMIDOS, DE ***** NON AURIE NADA.
1061 5ELCID0136 DIXO RACHEL & VIDAS: DAR GELOS DE *****.
1160 5ELCID0149 CON RACHEL & VIDAS, DE VOLUTAD & DE *****.
1558 5ELCID0200 ***** EXIR DELA POSADA & ESPIDIOS DE AMOS.
2076 5ELCID0261 OTORGADO GELO AUIE EL ABBAT DE *****.
4487 5ELCID0570 LOS DE ALCO%ER A MYO %ID YAL DAN PARIAS DE *****
4851 5ELCID0614 ***** A DIOS DEL %IELO & ATODOS LOS SOS SANTOS,
6214 5ELCID0792 ***** A DIOS, A QUEL QUE ESTA EN ALTO,
6422 5ELCID0819 DIXO MYNAYA ALBARFANEZ: ESTO FARE YO DE *****.
6996 5ELCID0895 ***** & GRA%IAS, REY, COMMO A SE@OR NATURAL;
7205 5ELCID0924 ***** ADIOS & ALAS SUS VERTUDES SANTAS;
7864 5ELCID1005 ESTO FAZEN LOS SOS DE VOLUNTAD & DE *****;
8270 5ELCID1052 COMIENDO VA EL CONDE DIOS, QUE DE BUEN *****
8304 5ELCID1056 AQUI DIXO EL CONDE: DE VOLUNTAD & DE *****.
8359 5ELCID1062 DEL DIA QUE FUE CONDE NON IANTE TAN DE BUEN *****,
8408 5ELCID1069 EN ***** UOS LO TENGO LO QUE ME AUEDES DEXADO.
8677 5ELCID1102 VIOLO MYO %ID, TOMOS AMARAUILLAR: ***** ATI, PADRE SPIRITAL
8786 5ELCID1117 NON FUE A NUESTRO ***** NI NOS NON PUDIEMOS MAS,
8792 5ELCID1118 ***** A DIOS, LO NUESTRO FUE ADELANT.
8950 5ELCID1139 FERID LOS, CAUALLEROS, DAMOR & DE ***** & DE GRAND VOLUNTAD,
9382 5ELCID1193 TODOS VENGAN DE *****, NINGUNO NON HA PREMIA,
9858 5ELCID1250 QUE SIS PUDIESSEN YR, FER LO YEN DE *****.
9997 5ELCID1267 ***** A DIOS, MYNAYA, & A SANTA MARIA MADRE
12867 5ELCID1633 ***** AL CRIADOR & A PADRE ESPIRITAL
12901 5ELCID1637 ***** AL CRIADOR & A SANTA MARIA MADRE,
13014 5ELCID1651 AUOS *****, %ID, & AL PADRE SPIRITAL.
13563 5ELCID1718 ALOS %INQUAENTA MILL VAN LOS FERIR DE *****;
14668 5ELCID1855 DIXO EL REY DON ALFONSSO: RE%IBOLOS DE *****.
14766 5ELCID1867 ***** AL CRIADOR & AL SE@OR SANT ESIDRO EL DE LEON
15209 5ELCID1925 DIXO MYO %ID: ***** AL CRIADOR
16524 5ELCID2095 ***** & GRA%IAS, CID, COMMO TAN BUENO, & PRIMERO AL CRIADOR,
17288 5ELCID2187 ***** AL CRIADOR, VENGO, MUGIER ONDRADA
17326 5ELCID2192 ***** AL CRIADOR & AUOS, %ID, BARBA VELIDA
17360 5ELCID2196 MUGIER DO@A XIMENA, ***** AL CRIAADOR.
17608 5ELCID2227 ESTOZ DIXO MINAYA: ESTO FARE YO DE *****.
17662 5ELCID2234 AMOS LAS RE%IBEN DAMOR & DE *****,
18304 5ELCID2316 QUE LES CRE%E LA GANAN%IA, ***** AL CRIADOR.
19382 5ELCID2456 ***** ADIOS & AL PADRE QUE ESTA EN ALTO,
19549 5ELCID2477 ***** A CHRISTUS, QUE DEL MUNDO ES SE@OR,
19663 5ELCID2493 ***** HA DIOS QUE DEL MUNDO ES SE@OR
19898 5ELCID2524 ***** A SANTA MARIA, MADRE DEL NUESTRO SE@OR DIOS
19924 5ELCID2528 ***** AL CRIADOR & A UOS, %ID ONDRADO,
21750 5ELCID2766 MANDARON LE YR ADELANTE, MAS DE SU ***** NON FUE.
22217 5ELCID2830 ***** A CHRISTUS, QUE DEL MUNDO ES SE@OR,
23823 5ELCID3035 ***** ADIOS, QUANDO UOS VEO, SE@OR.
25122 5ELCID3200 ***** AL CRIADOR & AUOS, REY SE@OR,
25757 5ELCID3281 ***** A DIOS QUE %IELO & TIERRA MANDA
27019 5ELCID3452 ***** ADIOS DEL %IELO & AQUEL REY DON ALFONSSO,
28938 5ELCID3696 VEN%IERON ESTA LID, ***** AL CRIADOR.
29075 5ELCID3714 ***** AL REY DEL %IELO, MIS FIJAS VENGADAS SON
WORD #2271 OCCURS 52 TIMES.
INDEX OF DIVERSIFICATION = 568.10 WITH STANDARD DEVIATION OF 652.06

GRADOS 2590 5ELCID0327 ECHOS DO@A XIMENA EN LOS ****** DELANTEL ALTAR,
WORD #2272 OCCURS 1 TIMES.

GRANADO 14023 5ELCID1776 QUIERO UOS DEZIR LO QUE ES MAS *******:
WORD #2273 OCCURS 1 TIMES.

GRANAN%IAS 19203 5ELCID2429 CON ESTAS ********** YAS YUAN TORNANDO;
WORD #2274 OCCURS 1 TIMES.

GRAND 168 5ELCID0022 EL REY DON ALFONSSO TANTO AUIE LA ***** SA@A,
180 5ELCID0024 CON ***** RECABDO & FUERTE MIENTRE SELLADA:
934 5ELCID0120 CON ***** IURA METED Y LAS FES AMOS,
2265 5ELCID0285 ***** IANTAR LE FAZEN AL BUEN CAMPEADOR.
2575 5ELCID0325 TANEN A MATINES A VNA PRIESSA TAN *****;
2999 5ELCID0378 ATAN ***** SABOR FABLO MINAYA ALBARFANEZ:

WORD C# PREFIX CONTEXT

GRAND (CON'T)

3350 5ELCID0422 PASSAREMOS LA SIERRA QUE FIERA ES & *****,
3391 5ELCID0427 EN MEDIO DUNA MONTANA MARAUILLOSA & *****
3576 5ELCID0450 TERNE YO CASTEION DON ABREMOS ***** EN PARA.
4093 5ELCID0520 AVN DELO QUE DIESSEN CUIESSEN ***** GANAN%IA.
4354 5ELCID0554 EN VN OTERO REDONDO, FUERTE & *****;
4697 5ELCID0595 VIO QUE ENTRELLOS & EL CASTIELLO MUCHO AUIE ***** PLA%A;
4877 5ELCID0617 EN ESTE CASTIELLO ***** AUER AUEMOS PRESO,
5952 5ELCID0754 OY EN ESTE DIA DE UOS AERE ***** BANDO;
6256 5ELCID0797 ***** ALEGREYA VA ENTRE ESSOS CHISTIANOS,
7474 5ELCID0959 OUO ***** PESAR & TOUOS LO A GRAND FONTA.
7480 5ELCID0959 OUO GRAND PESAR & TOUOS LO A ***** FONTA.
7507 5ELCID0962 DENTRO EN MI CORT TUERTO ME TOUO *****:
7600 5ELCID0973 MYO %ID DON RODRIGO TRAE ***** GANAN%IA,
8534 5ELCID1084 DE LA GANAN%IA QUE AN FECHA MARAUILLOSA & *****.
8953 5ELCID1139 FERID LOS, CAUALLEROS, DAMOR & DE GRADO & DE ***** VOLUNTAD,
9002 5ELCID1146 ***** ES EL GOZO QUE VA POR ES LOGAR.
9211 5ELCID1172 TAIAUA LES LAS HUERTAS & FAZIA LES ***** MAL,
9301 5ELCID1182 CON EL DELOS MONTES CLAROS AUYEN GUERRA TAN *****,
9719 5ELCID1236 ***** ALEGRIA ES ENTRE TODOS ESSOS CHRISTIANOS
10410 5ELCID1319 ALOS PIES DEL REY ALFONSSO CAYO CON ***** DUELO,
11004 5ELCID1393 TAN ***** FUE EL GOZO QUANDOL VIERON ASSOMAR.
11054 5ELCID1399 SANO LO DEXE & CON TAN ***** RICTAD.
11386 5ELCID1441 ***** DUELO ES AL PARTIR DEL ABBAT:
11593 5ELCID1469 CON ***** ONDRA ADUZID MELAS DELANT.
11607 5ELCID1471 ***** LOCURA SERIE SI LA DESENPARAS;
11738 5ELCID1488 ESSA NOCH CON DUCHO LES DIO *****,
11860 5ELCID1503 POR SABOR DE MYO %ID DE ***** ONDRAL DAR;
12122 5ELCID1538 DE TAN ***** CONDUCHO COMMO EN MEDINAL SACARON;
12679 5ELCID1609 A TAN ***** ONDRA ELLAS A VALEN%IA ENTRAUAN.
12726 5ELCID1615 MIRAN LA HUERTA, ESPESSA ES & *****;
12739 5ELCID1617 DESTA GANAN%IA COMME ES BUENA & *****.
12997 5ELCID1648 RIQUEZA ES QUE NOS A CRE%E MARAUILLOSA & *****;
13076 5ELCID1658 A VNA ***** PRIESSA TANIEN LOS ATAMORES;
14963 5ELCID1891 EFAZIENDO YO HA EL MAL, & EL AMI ***** PRO,
15256 5ELCID1932 VNA ***** ORA PENSSO & COMIDIO;
15277 5ELCID1935 CON ***** AFAN GANE LO QUE HE YO;
15410 5ELCID1952 POR DAR LE ***** ONDRA COMMO A REY DE TIERRA.
15893 5ELCID2015 RE%EBIR LO SALEN CON TAN ***** ONOR.
15977 5ELCID2026 TAN ***** PESAR OUO EL REY DON ALFONSSO:
22204 5ELCID2828 VNA ***** ORA PENSSO & COMIDIO;
22533 5ELCID2869 HY IAZEN ESSA NOCHE, & TAN ***** GOZO QUE FAZEN.
22730 5ELCID2897 ***** GOZO FIZO CON ELLAS DO@A XIMENA SU MADRE.
23179 5ELCID2953 EL REY VNA ***** ORA CALLO & COMIDIO;
23631 5ELCID3010 E CON ELLOS ***** BANDO QUE ADUXIERON A LA CORT:
24842 5ELCID3164 AVN ***** AMOR NOS FAZE EL %ID CAMPEADOR,
25101 5ELCID3197 SE QUE SI UOS ACAE%IERE, CON ELLA GANAREDES ***** PREZ
& GRAND VALOR.
25104 5ELCID3197 SE QUE SI UOS ACAE%IERE, CON ELLA GANAREDES GRAND PREZ &
***** VALOR.
25617 5ELCID3262 CON MUY ***** ONDRA & AVERES A NOMBRE;
26017 5ELCID3316 MIEMBRAT QUANDO LIDIAMOS %ERCA VALEN%IA LA *****;
26900 5ELCID3437 CA ***** RENCURA HE DE YFANTES DE CARRION.
27759 5ELCID3543 CA ***** MIEDO OUIERON A ALFONSSO EL DE LEON.
27940 5ELCID3565 SI DEL CAMPO BIEN SALIDES, ***** ONDRA AUREDES VOS;
WORD #2275 OCCURS 58 TIMES.
INDEX OF DIVERSIFICATION = 486.23 WITH STANDARD DEVIATION OF 865.61

GRANDE
224 5ELCID0029 ****** DUELO AUIEN LAS YENTES CHRISTIANAS;
5219 5ELCID0660 MUCHAS SON LAS AROBDAS & ****** ES EL ALMOFALLA.
23109 5ELCID2944 MAIADAS & DESNUDAS A ****** DESONOR,
24591 5ELCID3134 ****** TUERTO LE HAN TENIDO, SABEMOS LO TODOS NOS;
WORD #2276 OCCURS 4 TIMES.

GRANDES
42 5ELCID0006 SOSPIRO MYO %ID, CA MUCHO AUIE ******* CUYDADOS.
857 5ELCID0110 ******* AUERES PRISO & MUCHO SOBEIANOS,
1383 5ELCID0177 ASSI ES UUESTRA VENTURA ******* SON UUESTRAS GANAN%IAS,
3136 5ELCID0395 ******* YENTES SELE ACCIEN ESSA NOCH DE TODAS PARTES.
3795 5ELCID0480 TANTO TRAEN LAS ******* GANA%IAS, MUCHOS GA@ADOS.
4298 5ELCID0548 ******* SON LAS GANAN%IAS QUE PRISO POR LA TIERRA DO UA.
4659 5ELCID0591 LOS ******* & LOS CHICOS FUERA SALTO DAN,
4779 5ELCID0606 DANDO ******* ALARIDOS LOS QUE ESTAN EN LA %ELADA,
5165 5ELCID0653 GENTES SE AIUNTARON SOBEIANAS DE *******
5292 5ELCID0669 ******* SON LOS PODERES POR CON ELLOS LIDIAR;
5659 5ELCID0713 DAN LE ******* COLPES, MAS NOL PUEDEN FALSSAR.
5699 5ELCID0719 A ******* VOZES LAMA EL QUE EN BUEN ORA NASCO:
7364 5ELCID0944 TODOS SON ALEGRES, GANAN%IAS TRAEN *******.
7491 5ELCID0961 ******* TUERTOS ME TIENE MYO %ID EL DE BIUAR.
7541 5ELCID0967 ******* SON LOS PODERES & A PRIESSA SEUAN LEGANDO,
7554 5ELCID0968 GENTES SE LE ALEGAN ******* ENTRE MOROS & CHRISTIANOS,
7955 5ELCID1016 PLOGO A MYO %ID, CA ******* SON LAS GANAN%IAS.
8081 5ELCID1031 ELLOS PARTIENDO ESTAS GANAN%IAS *******,
9024 5ELCID1149 ******* SON LAS GANAN%IAS QUE MIO %ID FECHAS HA.
9064 5ELCID1153 ENTRAUAN A MURUIEDRO CON ESTAS GANAN%IAS QUE TRAEN *******.
9428 5ELCID1199 ******* YENTES SE LE ACCIEN DELA BUENA CHRISTIANDAD.
9522 5ELCID1211 ******* SON LOS GOZOS QUE VAN POR ES LOGAR,
10523 5ELCID1334 ******* SON LAS GANAN%IAS QUEL DIO EL CRIADOR,

WORD C# PREFIX CONTEXT

GRANDES (CON'T)

11758 5ELCID1491 PASSAN LAS MONTANAS, QUE SON FIERAS & *******,
11954 5ELCID1515 POR %ERCA DE SALON TAN ******* GOZOS VAN.
15617 5ELCID1980 CUENDES & PODESTADES & MUY ******* MESNADAS.
15624 5ELCID1981 LOS YFANTES DE CARRION LIEUAN ******* CONPA@AS.
15689 5ELCID1990 CHICOS & ******* VESTIDOS SON DE COLORES.
16434 5ELCID2084 DE ******* NUEUAS SON LOS YFANTES DE CARRION,
17112 5ELCID2166 ******* SON LAS YENTES QUE VAN CONEL CANPEADOR.
18894 5ELCID2391 DAUAN LE ******* COLPES, MAS NOL FALSSAN LAS ARMAS.
19119 5ELCID2418 BUEN CAUALLO TIENE BUCAR & ******* SALTOS FAZ,
19755 5ELCID2505 ******* SON LOS GOZOS EN VALEN%IA CON MYO %ID EL CANPEADOR
19775 5ELCID2507 ******* SON LOS GOZOS DE SUS YERNOS AMOS ADOS:
20026 5ELCID2541 LOS AUERES QUE TENEMOS ******* SON & SOBEIANOS,
20091 5ELCID2550 AUERES LEUAREMOS ******* QUE VALEN GRANT VALOR;
20392 5ELCID2588 ******* SON LAS NUEUAS POR VALEN%IA LA MAYOR,
20721 5ELCID2631 ******* FUERON LOS DUELOS ALA DEPARTI%ION.
20862 5ELCID2649 SALIOLOS RECEBIR CON ******* AUOROZES;
21288 5ELCID2705 MANDARON CARGAR LAS AZEMILAS CON ******* AUERES,
23708 5ELCID3020 CON ******* YENTES EL REY CAUALGO
25282 5ELCID3218 NON ACUERDAN EN CONSSEIO, CA LOS HAUERES ******* SON:
26925 5ELCID3440 ******* AUERES LES DIO MYO %ID EL CAMPEADOR,
28695 5ELCID3664 ESORA EL YFANTE TAN ******* VOZES DAUA:
28766 5ELCID3673 FIRIENSSEN EN LOS ESCUDOS VNOS TAN ******* COLPES;
28941 5ELCID3697 ******* SON LOS PESARES POR TIERRAS DE CARRION.
29052 5ELCID3711 ******* SON LOS GOZOS EN VALEN%IA LA MAYOR,
29129 5ELCID3720 LOS PRIMEROS FUERON *******, MAS AQUESTOS SON MIIORES;

WORD #2277 OCCURS 48 TIMES.
INDEX OF DIVERSIFICATION = 617.87 WITH STANDARD DEVIATION OF 758.53

GRANT

342 5ELCID0043 CON ***** RECABDO & FUERTE MIENTRE SELLADA.
976 5ELCID0125 QUANDO ATIERRA DE MOROS ENTRO, QUE ***** AUER SACO;
1926 5ELCID0245 CON TAN ***** GOZO RE%IBEN AL QUE EN BUEN ORA NASCO.
2783 5ELCID0351 ESTANDO EN LA CRUZ, VERTUD FEZIST MUY *****.
4598 5ELCID0584 DEMOS SALTO A EL & FEREMOS ***** GANA%IA,
6302 5ELCID0803 ***** A EL GOZO MYO %ID CON TODOS SOS VASSALOS.
6749 5ELCID0861 PESO ALOS DE ALCO%ER, CA PROLES FAZIE *****.
6772 5ELCID0864 ALTO ES EL POYO, MARAUILLOSO & *****;
7281 5ELCID0933 DIOS, COMMO FUE EL %ID PAGADO & FIZO ***** ALEGRIA
7711 5ELCID0987 EL CONDE DON REMONT DAR NOS HA ***** BATALLA,
7964 5ELCID1017 A MYO %ID DON RODRIGO ***** COZINAL ADOBAUAN;
11663 5ELCID1478 SALIOLOS RE%EBIR CON ***** GOZO QUE FAZE:
12441 5ELCID1578 RE%EBIDAS LAS DUENAS A VNA ***** ONDRAN%A,
12541 5ELCID1591 DES DIA SE PRE%IO BAUIECA EN QUANT ***** FUE ESPA@A.
12624 5ELCID1601 TODAS LAS SUS MESNADAS EN ***** DELENT ESTAUAN,
13435 5ELCID1703 LA MISSA DICHA, ***** SULTURA LES DAUA:
13520 5ELCID1713 DEXAN ALAS PUERTAS OMNES DE ***** RECABDO.
13795 5ELCID1748 AUOS ME OMILLO, DUE@AS, ***** PREZ UOS HE GA@ADO:
13972 5ELCID1770 ***** FUE EL ALEGRIA QUE FUE POR EL PALA%IO;
14941 5ELCID1889 VNA ***** ORA EL REY PENSSO & COMIDIO;
16379 5ELCID2077 SEMEIAM EL CASAMIENTO ONDRADO & CON ***** PRO,
16426 5ELCID2083 CA NON HAN ***** HEDAND E DE DIAS PEQUENAS SON.
16920 5ELCID2141 TOD ESTO ES PUESTO, SABED, EN ***** RECABDO.
17181 5ELCID2174 ***** ONDRA LES DAN ALOS YFANTES DE CARRION.
17909 5ELCID2266 ***** BIEN DIZEN DELLOS, CA SERA AGUISADO.
18042 5ELCID2283 EN ***** MIEDO SE VIERON POR MEDIO DELA CORT;
18102 5ELCID2290 TRAS VNA VIGA LAGAR METIOS CON ***** PAUOR;
18269 5ELCID2311 ELLOS ENESTO ESTANDO, DON AUIEN ***** PESAR,
19053 5ELCID2410 VERTE AS CON EL %ID, EL DE LA BARBA *****,
19144 5ELCID2421 ARRIBA AL%O COLADA, VN ***** COLPE DADOL HA,
19192 5ELCID2427 VEN%IO LA BATALLA MARAUILLOSA & *****.
19524 5ELCID2474 ***** FUE EL DIA LA CORT DEL CAMPEADOR,
19584 5ELCID2481 COMMO SON ONDRADOS & AVER VOS ***** PRO.
19705 5ELCID2498 MOROS & CHRISTIANOS DE MI HAN ***** PAUOR;
20094 5ELCID2550 AUERES LEUAREMOS GRANDES QUE VALEN ***** VALOR;
21974 5ELCID2796 TAN A ***** DUELO FABLAUA DO@A SOL:
22367 5ELCID2849 PRESENTAN A MINAYA ESSA NOCH ***** ENFFUR%ION;
22658 5ELCID2887 ARMAS YUA TENIENDO & ***** GOZO QUE FAZE;
22852 5ELCID2911 LA POCA & LA ***** TODA ES DE MYO SE@OR.
22892 5ELCID2916 CA TAN ***** ES LA RENCURA DENTRO EN MI CORA%ON.
24203 5ELCID3086 SOBRELLAS VNOS %APATOS QUE A ***** HUEBRA SON;
24312 5ELCID3099 DESUSO CUBRIO VN MANTO QUE ES DE ***** VALOR,
29005 5ELCID3705 ***** ES LA BILTAN%A DE YFANTES DE CARRION.

WORD #2278 OCCURS 43 TIMES.
INDEX OF DIVERSIFICATION = 681.45 WITH STANDARD DEVIATION OF 947.83

GRA@ON

24415 5ELCID3112 NOS QUISO LEUANTAR EL CRESPO DE ******,

WORD #2279 OCCURS 1 TIMES.

GRUESSA

15665 5ELCID1987 TANTA ******* MULA & TANTO PALAFRE DE SAZON,
16693 5ELCID2114 TANTA ******* MULA & TANTO PALAFRE DE SAZON
25464 5ELCID3243 TANTA ******* MULA, TANTO PALAFRE DE SAZON,

WORD #2280 OCCURS 3 TIMES.

GRUESSOS

10541 5ELCID1336 %IENT CAUALLOS ******** & CORREDORES,
15529 5ELCID1968 CAUALLOS ******** & CCREDORES SIN FALLA,

WORD C# PREFIX CONTEXT

GRUESSOS (CON'T)

15848 5ELCID2010 TANTOS CAUALLCS EN DIESTRO, ******** & CORREDORES,
20268 5ELCID2572 DARUOS E MULAS & PALAFRES, MUY ******** DE SAZON,
WORD #2281 OCCURS 4 TIMES.

GUADALFAIARA 3540 5ELCID0446 FITA AYUSO & POR ************, FATA ALCALA LEGEN LAS ALGARAS,
3791 5ELCID0479 FENARES ARRIBA & POR ************.
WORD #2282 OCCURS 2 TIMES.

GUADALME%I 685 5ELCID0087 CUBIERTAS DE ********** E BIEN ENCLAUEADAS.
WORD #2283 OCCURS 1 TIMES.

GUADAME%IS 690 5ELCID0088 LOS ********** UERMEIOS & LOS CLAUOS BIEN DORADOS.
WORD #2284 OCCURS 1 TIMES.

GUARDA 4682 5ELCID0593 ABIERTAS DEXAN LAS PUERTAS QUE NINGUNO NON LAS ******.
WORD #2285 OCCURS 1 TIMES.

GUARDANDO 12336 5ELCID1566 EL SEDIE EN VALEN%IA CURIANDO & *********,
WORD #2286 OCCURS 1 TIMES.

GUARDAR 5439 5ELCID0686 SI NON DOS PEONES SOLOS POR LA PUERTA *******;
WORD #2287 OCCURS 1 TIMES.

GUARDARIEN 1261 5ELCID0162 E BIEN GELAS ********** FASTA CABO DEL A@O;
WORD #2288 OCCURS 1 TIMES.

GUARDASSEN 12371 5ELCID1571 QUE ********** EL ALCA%AR & LAS OTRAS TORRES ALTAS
WORD #2289 OCCURS 1 TIMES.

GUARDAUA 7935 5ELCID1013 ASOS CREENDEROS MANDAR LO ********.
WORD #2290 OCCURS 1 TIMES.

GUARIMIENTOS 11278 5ELCID1427 DELOS MEIORES ************ QUE EN BURGOS PUDO FALAR,
WORD #2291 OCCURS 1 TIMES.

GUARIR 6540 5ELCID0834 POR LANCAS & POR ESPADAS AUEMOS DE ******,
28820 5ELCID3681 NOL PUDO ******, FALSSO GELA GUARNIZON,
WORD #2292 OCCURS 2 TIMES.

GUARNID 7698 5ELCID0986 APRIESSA UOS ******* & METEDOS EN LAS ARMAS.
WORD #2293 OCCURS 1 TIMES.

GUARNIDOS 10550 5ELCID1337 DE SIELLAS & DE FRENOS TODOS ********* SON,
WORD #2294 OCCURS 1 TIMES.

GUARNIR 14809 5ELCID1872 E ******* UOS DE TODAS ARMAS COMMO UOS DIXIEREDES AQUI,
WORD #2295 OCCURS 1 TIMES.

GUARNIZON 25474 5ELCID3244 TANTA BUENA ESPADA CONTODA *********;
28478 5ELCID3636 EL BELMEZ CON LA CAMISA & CON LA *********
28786 5ELCID3676 TRAS EL ESCUDO FALSSO GELA *********;
28809 5ELCID3679 TRAS EL ESCUDO FALSSO GELA *********,
28823 5ELCID3681 NOL PUDO GUARIR, FALSSO GELA *********,
WORD #2296 OCCURS 5 TIMES.
INDEX OF DIVERSIFICATION = 836.25 WITH STANDARD DEVIATION OF 1450.94

GUARNIZONES 13533 5ELCID1715 DE TODAS *********** MUY BIEN ES ACOBADO.
24105 5ELCID3073 VELMEZES VESTIDOS POR SUFRIR LAS ***********,
27197 5ELCID3476 DAD ME UUESTROS CAUALLEROS CON TODAS UUESTRAS ***********,
27723 5ELCID3538 MUCHO VIENEN BIEN ADOBADOS DE CAUALLOS & DE ***********,
WORD #2297 OCCURS 4 TIMES.

GUARNJMIENTOS 20558 5ELCID2610 AGRANDES *************, ACAUALLOS & ARMAS.
WORD #2298 OCCURS 1 TIMES.

GUEGO 18236 5ELCID2307 NON VIESTES TAL ***** COMMO YUA POR LA CORT;
WORD #2299 OCCURS 1 TIMES.

GUEGOS 19980 5ELCID2535 POR AQUESTOS ****** QUE YUAN LEUANTANDO,
WORD #2300 OCCURS 1 TIMES.

GUERRA 9299 5ELCID1182 CON EL DELOS MONTES CLAROS AUYEN ****** TAN GRAND,
WORD #2301 OCCURS 1 TIMES.

GUERREAR 8587 5ELCID1090 CONTRA LA MAR SALADA CONPE%O DE ********;
WORD #2302 OCCURS 1 TIMES.

GUIAS 1696 5ELCID0217 ATI LO GRADESCO, DIOS, QUE %IELO & TIERRA *****;
WORD #2303 OCCURS 1 TIMES.

GUIERA 9115 5ELCID1160 LEGAN A ****** & LEGAN AXATIUA,
9156 5ELCID1165 MALES PESA EN XATIUA & DENTRO EN ******,
13630 5ELCID1727 METIOS LE EN ******, VN CASTIELLO PALA%IANO;
WORD #2304 OCCURS 3 TIMES.

WORD C# PREFIX CONTEXT

GUIERE 9426 5ELCID1198 AL SABOR DELA GANAN%IA NCN LO ****** DETARDAR,
WORD #2305 OCCURS 1 TIMES.

GUISA 1022 5ELCID0131 RESPUSC MARTIN ANTOLINEZ A ***** DE MENBRADO:
4749 5ELCID0602 TIENEN BUENOS CAUALLCS, SABET, ASU ***** LES ANDAN;
5364 5ELCID0677 DIXO EL CAMPEADOR: A MI ***** FABLASTES;
6373 5ELCID0812 A UUESTRA ***** PRENDED CCN UUESTRA MANO.
10103 5ELCID1280 DE ***** YRAN POR ELLAS QUE AGRAND ONDRA VERNAN
10633 5ELCID1347 QUANDO ASSI FAZE A SU ***** EL %ID CAMPEADOR
11765 5ELCID1492 PASSARON MATA DE TCRANZ DE TAL ***** QUE NINGUN MIEDO NON HAN,
13234 5ELCID1677 SACAN LOS DELAS HUERTAS MUCHO AFEA *****,
15971 5ELCID2025 DE AQUESTA ***** ALCS PIES LE CAYO.
16277 5ELCID2065 DE TAL ***** LOS PAGA MYO %ID EL CAMPEADOR,
17342 5ELCID2193 TODO LO QUE UCS FECHES ES DE BUENA *****.
21646 5ELCID2751 E ALAS AUES DEL MONTE & ALAS BESTIAS DELA FIERA *****.
22352 5ELCID2847 VARONES DE SANTESTEUAN, A ***** DE MUY PROS,
24139 5ELCID3078 DAQUESTA ***** QUIERO YR ALA CORT,
26275 5ELCID3350 TULO OTORGARAS A ***** DE TRAYCOR;
WORD #2306 OCCURS 15 TIMES.
INDEX OF DIVERSIFICATION = 1802.79 WITH STANDARD DEVIATION OF 1326.27

GUISADO 732 5ELCID0092 ENPE@AR GELO HE PCR LC QUE FUERE *******;
923 5ELCID0118 E PRESTALDE DE AUER LO QUE SEA *******.
WORD #2307 OCCURS 2 TIMES.

GUISADOS 8340 5ELCID1060 SI UOS PLOGUIERE, MYO %ID, DE YR SOMOS ********;
11536 5ELCID1461 CAUALGEDES CCN %IENTO ******** PORA HUEBOS DE LIDIAR;
WORD #2308 OCCURS 2 TIMES.

GUISAS 10648 5ELCID1349 QUE ENTODAS ****** MIIOR ME SIRUE QUE UOS.
26259 5ELCID3348 EN TODAS ****** MAS VALEN QUE VOS.
26409 5ELCID3369 ENTODAS ******, SABED, QUE MAS VALEN QUE VOS.
27039 5ELCID3454 EN TODAS ****** TALES SCDES QUALES DIGO YO;
WORD #2309 OCCURS 4 TIMES.

GUSTIOZ 5827 5ELCID0737 MU@O *******, QUE FUE SO CRIADO,
11515 5ELCID1458 TU, MU@O ******* & PERO VERMUEZ DELANT,
11684 5ELCID1481 FABLO MU@O *******, NCN SPERO A NADI:
11826 5ELCID1499 AFEUOS AQUI PERO VERMUEZ & MU@O ******* QUE UOS QUIEREN SIN HART,
15721 5ELCID1995 MU@O *******, EL CAUALLERO DE PRO.
17143 5ELCID2169 APERO VERMUEZ & MUNO *******,
17213 5ELCID2177 DIXO MYO %ID ADON PERO & A MU@O *******:
18366 5ELCID2324 OYO LA PORIDAD AQUEL MU@O *******,
22765 5ELCID2901 OERES, MU@O *******, MYO VASSALLO DE PRO,
22901 5ELCID2917 MU@O ******* PRIUADO CAUALGO,
22981 5ELCID2927 ASSI COMMO DESCAUALGA AQUEL MU@O *******
23017 5ELCID2932 VIOLOS EL REY & CONNOS%IO A MU@O *******;
23033 5ELCID2934 DELANT EL REY FINCO LOS YNOIOS AQUEL MU@O *******,
23040 5ELCID2935 BESABA LE LOS PIES AQUEL MU@O *******;
23200 5ELCID2955 E VERDAD DIZES EN ESTO, TU, MU@O *******,
23346 5ELCID2974 ESPIDIOS MU@O *******, A MYO %ID ES TORNADO.
24050 5ELCID3065 E PERO VERMUEZ & AQUESTE MU@O *******
26503 5ELCID3382 ESSORA MUNO ******* EN PIE SE LEUANTO;
27607 5ELCID3525 E MUNO *******, FIRMES SED EN CAMPO AGUISA DE VARONES;
28753 5ELCID3671 LOS DOS HAN ARRANCADO: DJREUOS DE MUNO *******,
28780 5ELCID3675 FIRIO ENEL ESCUDO A DCN MUNO *******,
28803 5ELCID3678 ESTE COLPE FECHO, OTRO DIO MUNO *******,
WORD #2310 OCCURS 22 TIMES.
INDEX OF DIVERSIFICATION = 1093.10 WITH STANDARD DEVIATION OF 1647.15

HA 334 5ELCID0042 EL REY LO ** UEDADO, ANOCH DEL ETRO SU CARTA,
602 5ELCID0076 AUN %ERCA OTARDE EL REY QUERER ME ** POR AMIGO;
893 5ELCID0115 DEXADO ** HEREDADES & CASAS & PALA%IOS.
912 5ELCID0117 EL CAMPEADOR DEXAR LAS ** EN UUESTRA MANO,
1507 5ELCID0192 DEMOS LE BUEN DON, CA EL NO LO ** BUSCADO.
2553 5ELCID0322 CUEMO LO MANDO MYO %ID, ASSI LO AN TODOS ** FAR.
3055 5ELCID0384 COMMO SIRUA ADO@A XIMENA & ALAS FIJAS QUE **,
4621 5ELCID0586 LA PARIA QUEL A PRESA TCRNAR NOS LA ** DOBLADA.
4979 5ELCID0629 AYROLO EL REY ALFCNSSC, DE TIERRA ECHADO LO **,
5279 5ELCID0667 EL AGUA NOS AN VEDADA, EXIR NOS ** EL PAN,
5417 5ELCID0683 ARMADO ES MYO %ID CON QUANTOS QUE EL **;
5543 5ELCID0698 DE PARTE DELOS MOROS DOS SE@AS ** CABDALES,
6006 5ELCID0761 LOS DOS LE FALLEN, & EL VNOL ** TOMADO,
6650 5ELCID0848 A CAUALLEROS & A PEONES FECHOS LOS ** RICOS,
6902 5ELCID0882 OMNE AYRADO, QUE DE SE@OR NON ** GRA%IA,
7710 5ELCID0987 EL CONDE DON REMONT DAR NOS ** GRANT BATALLA,
7996 5ELCID1021 NON COMBRE VN BOCADO POR QUANTO ** EN TODA ESPA@A,
8502 5ELCID1080 LO QUE NON FERIE EL CABOSO POR QUANTO ENEL MUNDO **,
8557 5ELCID1087 POBLADO ** MYO %ID EL PUERTO DE ALUCANT,
8611 5ELCID1093 TIERRAS DE BORRIANA TODAS CONQUISTAS LAS **.
8924 5ELCID1136 QUIS CADA VNO DELLOS BIEN SABE LO QUE ** DE FAR.
9032 5ELCID1149 GRANDES SON LAS GANAN%IAS QUE MIO %ID FECHAS **.
9385 5ELCID1193 TODOS VENGAN DE GRADO, NINGUNO NON ** PREMIA,

WORD C# PREFIX CONTEXT

HA (CON'T)

9566 5ELCID1215 TODOS ERAN RICOS QUANTOS QUE ALLI **.
9598 5ELCID1219 ALEGRE ERA EL CAMPEADOR CON TODOS LOS QUE **,
10362 5ELCID1312 FUERA EL REY A SAN FAGUNT AVN POCO **,
10455 5ELCID1325 ECHASTES LE DE TIERRA, NON ** LA UUESTRA AMOR;
11064 5ELCID1400 EL REY POR SU MER%ED SUELTAS ME UOS **,
11129 5ELCID1408 QUE SU MUGIER & SUS FIJAS EL REY SUELTAS ME LAS **,
11260 5ELCID1424 MINAYA A DO@A XIMINA & A SUS FIJAS QUE **,
11320 5ELCID1433 DESFECHOS NOS ** EL %ID, SABET, SI NO NOS VAL;
11447 5ELCID1449 EL PORTERO CON ELLOS QUE LOS ** DE AGUARDAR;
11606 5ELCID1470 E YO FINCARE EN VALEN%IA, QUE MUCHO COSTADOM **;
11972 5ELCID1517 QUANDO LEGO AUEGALUON, DONTA OIO **,
12366 5ELCID1570 MANDO MYO %ID ALOS QUE ** EN SU CASA
13310 5ELCID1688 DEZIR NOS ** LA MISSA, & PENSSAD DE CAUALGAR,
14039 5ELCID1778 QUE ANDAN ARRIADOS & NON ** QUI TOMALOS,
14186 5ELCID1795 NON TIENE EN CUENTA LOS MOROS QUE ** MATADOS;
14287 5ELCID1808 E CRAS ** LA MA@ANA YR UOS HECES SIN FALLA
14380 5ELCID1819 DESTA LID QUE ** ARRANCADA CC CAUALLOS LE ENBIAUA ENPRESENTAIA,
14616 5ELCID1849 POCOS DIAS **, REY, QUE VNA LID A ARRANCADO:
14677 5ELCID1856 GRADESCOLO A MYO %ID QUE TAL DON ME ** ENBIADO;
14728 5ELCID1862 EN LA ONDRA QUE EL ** NOS SEREMOS ABILTADOS;
14957 5ELCID1891 EFAZIENDO YO ** EL MAL, & EL AMI GRANO PRO,
15030 5ELCID1900 OTROS MANDADOS ** EN ESTA MI CORT:
15817 5ELCID2006 RECABDADO **, COMMO TAN BUEN VARON,
17389 5ELCID2200 PEDIDAS UOS ** & ROGADAS EL MYO SE@OR ALFONSSO,
18281 5ELCID2313 CINQUAENTA MILL TIENDAS FINCADAS ** DELAS CABDALES;
18416 5ELCID2330 NOS CON UUSCO LA VENCREMOS, & VALER NOS ** EL CRIADOR.
19147 5ELCID2421 ARRIBA AL%O COLADA, VN GRANT COLPE DADOL **,
19154 5ELCID2422 LAS CARBONCLAS DEL YELMO TOLLIDAS GELA **,
19169 5ELCID2424 FATA LA %INTURA EL ESPADA LEGADO **.
19372 5ELCID2454 DE XX ARRIBA ** MOROS MATADO;
19664 5ELCID2493 GRADO ** DIOS QUE DEL MUNDO ES SE@OR
20619 5ELCID2617 NOS PUEDE REPENTIR, QUE CASADAS LAS ** AMAS.
21142 5ELCID2686 ESTO LES ** DICHO, & EL MORO SE TORNO;
21507 5ELCID2734 LO QUE RUEGAN LAS DUENAS NON LES ** NINGUN PRO.
22494 5ELCID2864 E PERO VERMUEZ OTRO TANTO LAS **;
23494 5ELCID2992 DARLEDES DERECHO, CA RENCURA ** DE UOS.
23668 5ELCID3014 POR QUE SE TARDA EL REY NON ** SABOR.
23998 5ELCID3058 ENTRE MINAYA & LOS BUENOS QUE Y **
24500 5ELCID3123 CATANDO ESTAN A MYO %ID QUANTOS ** EN LA CORT,
24919 5ELCID3173 QUANDO LAS DEMANDA & DELLAS ** SABOR,
25522 5ELCID3250 ESTAS APRE%IADURAS MYO %ID PRESAS LAS **,
26338 5ELCID3359 LO QUE LES FIZIEMOS SER LES ** RETRAYDO; ESTO LIDIARE ATOD EL MAS
26531 5ELCID3386 NON DIZES VERDAD AMIGO NI ** SE@OR,
27075 5ELCID3459 CA EN ESTA CORT AFARTO ** PORA VOS,
27354 5ELCID3495 NOS FARTAN DE CATARLE QUANTOS ** EN LA CORT.
27481 5ELCID3510 QUE EN TODAS NUESTRAS TIERRAS NON ** TAN BUEN VARON.
27514 5ELCID3514 EN MOROS NI EN CHRISTIANOS OTRO TAL NON ** OY,
27978 5ELCID3570 NOLO QUERRIEN AUER FECHO POR QUANTO ** EN CARRION.

WORD #2311 OCCURS 71 TIMES.
INDEX OF DIVERSIFICATION = 393.91 WITH STANDARD DEVIATION OF 353.09

HACOMENDAMOS 20700 5ELCID2628 ADIOS UOS ************, DON ELUIRA & DO@A SOL,
WORD #2312 OCCURS 1 TIMES.

HAL 19162 5ELCID2423 CORTOL EL YELMO &, LIBRADO TODO LO ***,
WORD #2313 OCCURS 1 TIMES.

HAN

1990 5ELCID0251 SI YO ALGUN DIA VISGUIER, SERUOS *** DOBLADOS.
3106 5ELCID0390 CA EN YERMO O EN POBLADO PODER NOS *** ALCAN%AR.
3168 5ELCID0398 DE DIESTRO A LILON LAS TORRES, QUE MOROS LAS ***;
3417 5ELCID0431 MANDADO DE SO SE@OR TODO LO *** AFAR.
8804 5ELCID1119 LOS DE VALEN%IA %ERCADOS NOS ***;
9194 5ELCID1170 ALOS DE VALEN%IA ESCARMENTADOS LOS ***,
11168 5ELCID1412 HYTODAS LAS DUE@AS CON ELLAS QUANTAS BUENAS ELLAS ***.
11218 5ELCID1419 AMINAYA LXV CAUALLEROS A CRE%IDOL ***,
11296 5ELCID1429 QUANDO ESTAS DUE@AS ADOBADAS LAS ***,
11770 5ELCID1492 PASSARON MATA DE TORANZ DE TAL GUISA QUE NINGUN MIEDO NON ***,
11802 5ELCID1496 ESTO NON DETARDO, CA DE CORA%ON LO ***;
12717 5ELCID1614 E DEL OTRA PARTE A OIO *** EL MAR,
13159 5ELCID1668 COLGAR LOS *** EN SANTA MARIA MADRE DEL CRIADOR.
13285 5ELCID1684 ALEGRE ES MYO %ID POR QUANTO FECHO ***:
13988 5ELCID1771 COMMO LO DIXO EL %ID ASSI LO *** ACABADO.
14419 5ELCID1823 ANDAN LOS DIAS & LAS NOCHES, & PASSADA *** LA SIERRA,
14864 5ELCID1878 BIEN LOS MANDO SERUIR DE QUANTO HUEBOS ***.
15043 5ELCID1902 SABOR *** DE CASAR CON SUS FIJAS AMAS ADOS.
16425 5ELCID2083 CA NON *** GRANT HEDAND E DE DIAS PEQUENAS SON.
18197 5ELCID2302 AMARAUILLA LO *** QUANTOS QUE YSON,
18380 5ELCID2326 EUADES QUE PAUOR *** UUESTROS YERNOS TAN OSADOS,
19599 5ELCID2483 LO VNO ES NUESTRO, LO OTRO *** EN SALUO.
19614 5ELCID2485 DESTA BATALLA QUE *** ARRANCADO
19704 5ELCID2498 MOROS & CHRISTIANOS DE MI *** GRANT PAUOR;
20360 5ELCID2583 ATORGADO LO *** ESTO LOS YFANTES DE CARRION.
21291 5ELCID2706 COGIDA *** LA TIENDA DO ALBERGARON DE NOCH,
22590 5ELCID2877 ALA CASA DE BERLANGA POSADA PRESA ***.
22837 5ELCID2909 QUANDO LAS *** DEXADAS AGRANT DESONOR,

WORD C# PREFIX CONTEXT

HAN (CON'T)

```
                 23093 5ELCID2942 CUEMO NOS *** ABILTADOS YFANTES DE CARRION:
                 23451 5ELCID2987 MIEDO *** QUE Y VERNA MYO %ID EL CAMPEADOR;
                 24023 5ELCID3062 E SSU OFRENDA *** FECHA MUY BUENA & CONPLIDA.
                 24594 5ELCID3134 GRANDE TUERTO LE *** TENIDO, SABEMOS LO TODOS NOS;
                 25286 5ELCID3219 ESPESOS LOS *** YFANTES DE CARRION.
                 25708 5ELCID3274 LOS VNOS LE *** MIEDO & LOS OTROS ESPANTA.
                 25742 5ELCID3278 DERECHO FIZIERON POR QUE LAS *** DEXADAS.
                 26935 5ELCID3441 ELLOS LAS *** DEXADAS A PESAR DE NOS.
                 26971 5ELCID3445 MAS BIEN SABEMOS LAS MA@AS QUE ELLOS ***,
                 27400 5ELCID3500 ATODOS LOS ROGAUA ASSI COMMO *** SABOR;
                 27592 5ELCID3523 EL CAMPEADOR ALOS QUE *** LIDIAR TAN BIEN LOS CASTIGO:
                 28748 5ELCID3671 LOS DOS *** ARRANCADO: DIREUOS DE MUNO GUSTIOZ,
                 28990 5ELCID3703 CONPLIDO *** EL DEBDO QUE LES MANDO SO SE@OR;
       WORD #2314 OCCURS  41 TIMES.
          INDEX OF DIVERSIFICATION =   674.00 WITH STANDARD DEVIATION OF   913.10

HART              9479 5ELCID1204 BIEN LA %ERCA MYO %ID, QUE NON Y AUYA ****;
                 11831 5ELCID1499 AFEUOS AQUI PERO VERMUEZ & MU@O GUSTIOZ QUE UOS
                                  QUIEREN SIN ****,
       WORD #2315 OCCURS   2 TIMES.

HAS              25997 5ELCID3313 MIENTES, FERRANDO, DE QUANTO DICHO ***,
                 26433 5ELCID3371 QUE ERES TRAYDOR & MINTIST DE QUANTO DICHO ***.
       WORD #2316 OCCURS   2 TIMES.

HAUERES          25281 5ELCID3218 NON ACUERDAN EN CONSSEIO, CA LOS ******* GRANDES SON:
       WORD #2317 OCCURS   1 TIMES.

HAURIE           27541 5ELCID3517 SI AUOS LE TOLLIES, EL CAUALLO NO ****** TAN BUEN SE@OR.
       WORD #2318 OCCURS   1 TIMES.

HAYA             29191 5ELCID3727 DE CHRISTUS **** PERDON
       WORD #2319 OCCURS   1 TIMES.

HE                 579 5ELCID0073 CA ACUSADO SERE DELO QUE UOS ** SERUIDO,
                   633 5ELCID0080 SI YO BIUO, DOBLAR UOS ** LA SOLDADA.
                   662 5ELCID0084 FER LO ** AMIDOS, DE GRADO NON AURIE NADA.
                   727 5ELCID0092 ENPE@AR GELO ** POR LO QUE FUERE GUISADO;
                  1618 5ELCID0207 VOS VJ %IENTOS & YO XXX ** GANADOS.
                  1712 5ELCID0219 DA QUI QUITO CASTIELLA, PUES QUE EL REY ** EN YRA;
                  1799 5ELCID0229 CASTIGAR LOS ** COMMO ABRAN AFAR.
                  7385 5ELCID0947 HYA CAUALLEROS, DEZIR UOS ** LA VERDAD:
                  7538 5ELCID0966 MAS QUANDO EL MELO BUSCA, YR GELO ** YO DEMANDAR.
                  8117 5ELCID1035 AUOS & DOS FIJOS DALGO QUITAR UOS ** LOS CUERPOS & DARUOS
                                  E DE MANO.
                  8162 5ELCID1040 AUOS & A OTROS DOS DAR UOS ** DE MANO.
                  8193 5ELCID1044 CA HUEBOS MELO ** & PORA ESTOS MYOS VASSALLOS
                  8457 5ELCID1075 PAGADO UOS ** POR TODO AQUESTE A@O;
                  9925 5ELCID1259 METER LOS ** EN ESCRIPTO, & TODOS SEAN CONTADOS,
                 11248 5ELCID1423 DELOS OTROS QUINIENTOS DEZIR UOS ** QUE FAZE:
                 11432 5ELCID1447 RESPUSO MINAYA: FER LO ** DE VELUNTAD.
                 11729 5ELCID1487 DIXO AUEGALUON: FER LO ** DE VELUNTAD.
                 12668 5ELCID1607 EN ESTA HEREDAD QUE UOS YO ** GANADA.
                 12879 5ELCID1634 TODO EL BIEN QUE YO **, TODO LO TENGO DELANT:
                 13063 5ELCID1656 CON DIOS A QUESTA LID YO LA ** DE ARRANCAR.
                 13798 5ELCID1748 AUOS ME OMILLO, DUE@AS, GRANT PREZ UOS ** GA@ADO:
                 14301 5ELCID1809 CON CAUALLOS DESTA QUINTA QUE YO ** GANADA,
                 14390 5ELCID1820 E SERUIR LO ** SIENPRE MIENTRA QUE OUISSE EL ALMA.
                 15282 5ELCID1935 CON GRAND AFAN GANE LO QUE ** YO;
                 15290 5ELCID1936 ADIOS LO GRADESCO QUE DEL REY ** SU GRA%IA,
                 16116 5ELCID2044 QUANDO ** LA GRA%IA DE DON ALFONSSO MYO SE@OR;
                 17082 5ELCID2163 ** DELAS FIJAS DE MYO %ID, DE DON ELUIRA & DO@A SOL.
                 17308 5ELCID2189 GRADID MELO, MIS FIJAS, CA BIEN UOS ** CASADAS
                 17575 5ELCID2223 SABEDES QUE AL REY ASSI GELO ** MANDADO,
                 19678 5ELCID2495 QUE ** AUER & TIERRA & ORO & ONOR,
                 20225 5ELCID2568 DIXO EL CAMPEADOR: DARUOS ** MYS FIJAS & ALGO DELO MYO;
                 20288 5ELCID2575 DAR UOS ** DOS ESPADAS, A COLADA & A TIZON,
                 20530 5ELCID2606 ASSI COMMO YO TENGO, BIEN UOS ** CASADAS.
                 23513 5ELCID2994 QUITE MYO REYNO, DADEL NON ** SABOR.
                 24726 5ELCID3149 POR MIS FIJAS QUEM DEXARON YO NON ** DESONOR,
                 25142 5ELCID3202 OTRA RENCURA ** DE YFANTES DE CARRION:
                 25921 5ELCID3303 HYO LAS ** FIJAS, & TU PRIMAS CORMANAS;
                 26280 5ELCID3351 DE QUANTO ** DICHO VERDADERO SERE YO.
                 26708 5ELCID3411 QUE PLEGA AUOS, & ATORGAR LO ** YO,
                 26902 5ELCID3437 CA GRAND RENCURA ** DE YFANTES DE CARRION.
                 27532 5ELCID3516 ESSORA DIXO EL REY: DESTO NON ** SABOR;
       WORD #2320 OCCURS  41 TIMES.
          INDEX OF DIVERSIFICATION =   672.82 WITH STANDARD DEVIATION OF  1003.76

HEDAND           16427 5ELCID2083 CA NON HAN GRANT ****** E DE DIAS PEQUENAS SON.
       WORD #2321 OCCURS   1 TIMES.

HEDES             1539 5ELCID0197 MERE%ER NOLO *****, CA ESTO ES AGUISADO:
                  1546 5ELCID0198 ATORGAR NOS ***** ESTO QUE AUEMOS PARADO.
                 14292 5ELCID1808 E CRAS HA LA MA@ANA YR UOS ***** SIN FALLA
                 27008 5ELCID3450 AGORA BESAREDES SUS MANOS & LAMAR LAS ***** SE@ORAS,
```

WORD C# PREFIX CONTEXT

HEDES (CON'T)

```
                     27012 5ELCID3451 AVER LAS ***** ASERUIR, MAL QUE UOS PESE AUOS.
        WORD #2322 OCCURS    5 TIMES.
           INDEX OF DIVERSIFICATION =  6367.25 WITH STANDARD DEVIATION OF  7347.08

HEMOS                 2164 5ELCID0272 E NOS DEUOS PARTIR NOS ***** EN VIDA.
                      8215 5ELCID1046 PRENDIENDO DEUOS & DE OTROS YR NOS ***** PAGANDO;
                     11370 5ELCID1438 SI NON, DEXAREMOS BURGOS, YR LO ***** BUSCAR.
                     12010 5ELCID1523 ONDRAR UOS ***** TODOS, CA TALES LA SU AUZE,
                     13326 5ELCID1690 HYR LOS ***** FFERIR ENEL NOMBRE DEL CRIADOR & DEL APOSTOL SANTI
                     18695 5ELCID2366 VERLO ***** CONDIOS & CON LA UUESTRA AUZE.
                     19056 5ELCID2411 SALUDAR NOS ***** AMOS, & TAIAREMOS AMISTAS.
                     20051 5ELCID2545 ENSE@AR LAS ***** DO LAS HEREDADES SON.
                     20058 5ELCID2546 SACAR LAS ***** DE VALENZIA, DE PODER DEL CAMPEADOR;
                     20186 5ELCID2563 LEUAR LAS ***** A NUESTRAS TIERRAS DE CARRION,
                     20194 5ELCID2564 METER LAS ***** EN LAS VILLAS
                     20693 5ELCID2627 HYR LAS ***** VER ATIERRAS DE CARRION.
                     23785 5ELCID3030 SALUDAR NOS ***** DALMA & DE CORAZON.
                     25314 5ELCID3223 PAGAR LE ***** DE HEREDADES ENTIERRAS DE CARRION.
        WORD #2323 OCCURS   14 TIMES.
           INDEX OF DIVERSIFICATION =  1779.77 WITH STANDARD DEVIATION OF  2032.97

HERDADES             10773 5ELCID1364 SIRUAN LE SUS ******** DO FUERE EL CAMPEADOR,
        WORD #2324 OCCURS    1 TIMES.

HEREDAD              11072 5ELCID1401 POR LEUAROS A VALENZIA QUE AUEMOS POR *******.
                     11621 5ELCID1472 YO FFINCARE EN VALENZIA, CA LA TENGO POR *******.
                     12664 5ELCID1607 EN ESTA ******* QUE UOS YO HE GANADA.
                     12892 5ELCID1635 CON AFAN GANE A VALENZIA, & ELA POR *******,
        WORD #2325 OCCURS    4 TIMES.

HEREDADAS            20523 5ELCID2605 HYD A CARRION DO SODES *********,
        WORD #2326 OCCURS    1 TIMES.

HEREDADES              894 5ELCID0115 DEXADO HA ********* & CASAS & PALAZIOS.
                      2386 5ELCID0301 VOS, QUE POR MI DEXADES CASAS & *********,
                      3650 5ELCID0460 POR VER SUS LAUORES & TODAS SUS *********.
                      6989 5ELCID0893 SUELTO LES LOS CUERPOS & QUITO LES LAS *********.
                      9815 5ELCID1246 ATODOS LES DIO EN VALENZIA CASAS & *********
                     10038 5ELCID1271 ENBIAR UOS QUIERO A CASTIELLA, DO AUEMOS *********,
                     12788 5ELCID1623 QUE EN MIS ********* FUERTE MIETRE ES MIETDO,
                     20054 5ELCID2545 ENSE@AR LAS HEMOS DO LAS ********* SON.
                     20648 5ELCID2621 VERAS LAS ********* QUE A MIS FIJAS DADAS SON;
                     25316 5ELCID3223 PAGAR LE HEMOS DE ********* ENTIERRAS DE CARRION.
                     29088 5ELCID3715 AGORA LAS AYAN QUITAS ********* DE CARRION.
        WORD #2327 OCCURS   11 TIMES.
           INDEX OF DIVERSIFICATION =  2818.40 WITH STANDARD DEVIATION OF  2114.68

HERMANAS             20424 5ELCID2592 AMAS ********, DON ELUIRA & DO@A SOL,
        WORD #2328 OCCURS    1 TIMES.

HERMANOS              7240 5ELCID0928 DIZIENDO LES SALUDES DE PRIMOS & DE ********,
                     17628 5ELCID2230 AFEUOS DELANT MINAYA, AMOS SODES ********.
                     18329 5ELCID2319 AMOS ******** A PART SALIDOS SON:
                     20007 5ELCID2538 AMOS SALIERON A PART, VERA MIENTRE SON ********;
                     20942 5ELCID2660 ENTRAMOS ******** CONSSEIARON TRAZION:
        WORD #2329 OCCURS    5 TIMES.
           INDEX OF DIVERSIFICATION =  3424.50 WITH STANDARD DEVIATION OF  4660.32

HERMAR                4191 5ELCID0533 MAS EL CASTIELO NON LO QUIERO ******;
        WORD #2330 OCCURS    1 TIMES.

HOMILAR              11966 5ELCID1516 DON LEGAN LOS OTROS, A MINAYA ALBARFANEZ SE UAN *******.
        WORD #2331 OCCURS    1 TIMES.

HONOR                19912 5ELCID2525 DESTOS NUESTROS CASAMIENTOS UOS ABREDES *****.
        WORD #2332 OCCURS    1 TIMES.

HONORES               6935 5ELCID0887 ******* & TIERRAS AUELLAS CONDONADAS,
                     25637 5ELCID3264 POR QUE LAS SACAUADES DE VALENZIA SUS *******?
        WORD #2333 OCCURS    2 TIMES.

HUEBOS                 653 5ELCID0082 BIEN LO VEDES QUE YO NO TRAYO AUER, & ****** ME SERIE
                       956 5ELCID0123 NOS ****** AUEMOS EN TODO DE GANAR ALGO.
                      1072 5ELCID0138 ****** AUEMOS QUE NOS DEDES LOS MARCHOS.
                      1651 5ELCID0212 MUCHO ES ******, CA ZERCA VIENE EL PLAZO.
                      8191 5ELCID1044 CA ****** MELO HE & PORA ESTOS MYOS VASSALLOS
                     10855 5ELCID1374 BIEN CASARIEMOS CON SUS FIJAS PORA ****** DE PRO.
                     10923 5ELCID1382 FATA DENTRO EN MEDINA DENLES QUANTO ****** LES FUER,
                     11538 5ELCID1461 CAUALGEDES CON ZIENTO GUISADOS PORA ****** DE LIDIAR;
                     13374 5ELCID1695 DAD ME CXXX CAUALLEROS PORA ****** DE LIDIAR;
                     14863 5ELCID1878 BIEN LOS MANDO SERUIR DE QUANTO ****** HAN.
                     20780 5ELCID2639 DELO QUE OUIEREN ****** SIRUAN LAS ASO SABOR,
                     27919 5ELCID3563 ****** VOS ES QUE LIDIEDES AGUISA DE VARONES,
        WORD #2334 OCCURS   12 TIMES.
           INDEX OF DIVERSIFICATION =  2477.73 WITH STANDARD DEVIATION OF  2732.60
```

WORD C# PREFIX CONTEXT

```
HUEBRA          24204 5ELCID3086 SOBRELLAS VNOS %APATOS QUE A GRANT ****** SON;
        WORD #2335 OCCURS   1 TIMES.

HUEBRAS         18978 5ELCID2401 EACOSTAR SE LOS TENDALES, CON ******* ERAN TANTAS.
        WORD #2336 OCCURS   1 TIMES.

HUERTA          12722 5ELCID1615 MIRAN LA ******, ESPESSA ES & GRAND;
                20580 5ELCID2613 POR LA ****** DE VALEN%IA TENIENDO SALIEN ARMAS;
        WORD #2337 OCCURS   2 TIMES.

HUERTAS          9207 5ELCID1172 TAIAUA LES LAS ******* & FAZIA LES GRAND MAL,
                13189 5ELCID1672 POR LAS ******* ADENTRO ESTAN SINES PAUOR.
                13231 5ELCID1677 SACAN LOS DELAS ******* MUCHO AFEA GUISA,
        WORD #2338 OCCURS   3 TIMES.

HUESAS           7765 5ELCID0994 NOS CAUALGAREMOS SIELLAS GALLEGAS, & ****** SOBRE CAL%AS;
        WORD #2339 OCCURS   1 TIMES.

HUESCA           7333 5ELCID0940 PESANDO VA ALOS DE MON%ON & ALOS DE ******;
                 7424 5ELCID0952 DENT CORRE MYO %ID A ****** & A MONT ALUAN;
                 8574 5ELCID1089 E DEXADO A ****** & LAS TIERRAS DE MONT ALUAN.
        WORD #2340 OCCURS   3 TIMES.

HUESPED         16135 5ELCID2046 FUESSEDES MY *******, SIUOS PLOGIESSE, SE@OR.
                16154 5ELCID2049 MYO ******* SEREDES, %ID CAMPEADOR,
                16218 5ELCID2057 EN AQUEL DIA DEL REY SO ******* FUE;
        WORD #2341 OCCURS   3 TIMES.

HUSAIE          11987 5ELCID1519 ENEL OMBRO LO SALUDA, CA TAL ES SU ******:
        WORD #2342 OCCURS   1 TIMES.

HUUIAR           9284 5ELCID1180 DELANTE VEYEN SO DUELO, NON SE PUEDEN ******,
                 9309 5ELCID1183 NON LES DIXO COSEIO, NIN LOS VINO ******.
                18653 5ELCID2360 SI CUETA FUERE, BIEN ME PODREDES ******.
        WORD #2343 OCCURS   3 TIMES.

HUUYAR           9508 5ELCID1208 METIOLA EN PLAZO, SILES VINIESSEN ******.
        WORD #2344 OCCURS   1 TIMES.

HUYAR            6980 5ELCID0892 BUE@OS & VALIENTES PORA MYO %ID *****,
        WORD #2345 OCCURS   1 TIMES.

HY               7902 5ELCID1010 ** GA@O A COLADA QUE MAS VALE DE MILL MARCOS DE PLATA.
                11588 5ELCID1468 ASI COMMO A MY DIXIERON, ** LOS PODREDES FALAR;
                12048 5ELCID1528 ** AUEGALUON, AMIGOL SODES SIN FALLA.
                17943 5ELCID2271 ** MORAN LOS YFANTES BIEN CERCA DE DOS A@OS,
                22330 5ELCID2844 ** ALBERGARON POR VERDAD VNA NOCH.
                22527 5ELCID2869 ** IAZEN ESSA NOCHE, & TAN GRAND GOZO QUE FAZEN.
                27516 5ELCID3515 ** UOS LE DO EN DON, MANDEDES LE TOMAR, SE@OR.
        WORD #2346 OCCURS   7 TIMES.
           INDEX OF DIVERSIFICATION =  3268.00 WITH STANDARD DEVIATION OF  2391.89

HYA              7317 5ELCID0939 *** VA EL MANDADO POR LAS TIERRAS TODAS,
                 7381 5ELCID0947 *** CAUALLEROS, DEZIR UOS HE LA VERDAD:
                 8399 5ELCID1068 *** UOS YDES, CONDE, AGUISA DE MUY FRANCO,
                10892 5ELCID1379 *** UOS YDES, MYNAYA?, YD ALA GRA%IA DEL CRIADOR
                13914 5ELCID1763 *** MUGIER DA@A XIMENA, NOM LO AUIEDES ROGADO?
                16922 5ELCID2142 *** REY DON ALFONSSO, SE@OR TAN ONDRADO,
                17795 5ELCID2252 *** %ERCA DELOS XV DIAS YAS VAN LOS FIJOS DALGO.
                18137 5ELCID2295 *** SE@OR ONDRADO, REBATA NOS DIO EL LEON.
                20386 5ELCID2587 *** MANDAUAN CARGAR YFFANTES DE CARRION.
                20417 5ELCID2591 *** QUIEREN CAUALGAR, EN ESPIDIMIENTO SON.
                20562 5ELCID2611 *** SALIEN LOS YFANTES DE VALEN%IA LA CLARA,
                20945 5ELCID2661 *** PUES QUE ADEXAR AUEMOS FIJAS DEL CAMPEADOR,
                21602 5ELCID2747 *** NON PUEDEN FABLAR DON ELUIRA & DONA SOL;
                23082 5ELCID2941 *** UOS SABEDES LA ONDRA QUE ES CUNTIDA ANOS,
                23434 5ELCID2985 *** LES VA PESANDO ALSO YFANTES DE CARRION,
                23515 5ELCID2995 *** LO VIERON QUE ES AFER LOS YFANTES DE CARRION,
                24882 5ELCID3169 *** MAS NON AURA DERECHO DE NOS EL %ID CANPEADOR.
                25129 5ELCID3201 *** PAGADO SO DE MIS ESPADAS, DE COLADA & DE TIZON.
                25449 5ELCID3241 *** VIERON QUE ES AFER LOS YFANTES DE CARRION.
                26463 5ELCID3377 *** VARONES, QUIEN VIO NUNCA TAL MAL?
                27598 5ELCID3524 *** MARTIN ANTOLINEZ, & VOS, PERO VERMUEZ,
                27959 5ELCID3568 *** SEUAN REPINTIENDO YFANTES DE CARRION,
                28099 5ELCID3588 *** SALIERON AL CAMPO DO ERAN LOS MOIONES.
                28221 5ELCID3603 *** LES VA PESANDO ALOS YFANTES DE CARRION.
        WORD #2347 OCCURS  24 TIMES.
           INDEX OF DIVERSIFICATION =   907.87 WITH STANDARD DEVIATION OF   948.89

HYAS            11435 5ELCID1448 **** ESPIDEN & PIENSSAN DE CAUALGAR,
                15861 5ELCID2012 **** VA PORA LAS VISTAS QUE CON EL REY PARO.
                17028 5ELCID2156 **** ESPIDIO MYO %ID DE SO SE@OR ALFONSSO,
```

WORD C# PREFIX CONTEXT

HYAS (CON'T)

```
                17875 5ELCID2262 **** YUAN PARTIENDO ACUESTOS OSPEDADOS,
                20812 5ELCID2643 **** TORNO PORA VALENZIA EL QUE EN BUEN ORA NASZIO.
                27816 5ELCID3550 **** METIEN EN ARMAS LOS DEL BUEN CAMPEADOR,
        WORD #2348 OCCURS    6 TIMES.
           INDEX OF DIVERSIFICATION =  3275.20 WITH STANDARD DEVIATION OF  2533.94

HYD              6940 5ELCID0888 *** & VENIT, DA QUI UOS DO MI GRAZIA;
                 7010 5ELCID0897 *** POR CASTIELLA & DEXEN UOS ANDAR, MINAYA,
                11568 5ELCID1466 *** PORA MEDINA QUANTO LO PUDIEREDES FAR,
                18391 5ELCID2328 *** LOS CONORTAR, SI UOS VALA EL CRIADOR,
                20518 5ELCID2605 *** A CARRION DO SODES HEREDADAS,
        WORD #2349 OCCURS    5 TIMES.
           INDEX OF DIVERSIFICATION =  3393.50 WITH STANDARD DEVIATION OF  2930.71

HYDES            6499 5ELCID0829  ***** UOS, MYNAYA, ACASTIELLA LA GENTIL?
        WORD #2350 OCCURS    1 TIMES.

HYDO             8511 5ELCID1082 **** ES EL CONDE, TORNOS EL DE BIUAR,
                10990 5ELCID1391 **** ES MYNAYA, TORNANSSE LOS YFFANTES.
                11372 5ELCID1439 **** ES PORA SAN PERO MINAYA ALBARFANEZ,
        WORD #2351 OCCURS    3 TIMES.

HYDOS           11169 5ELCID1413 ***** SON LOS CAUALLEROS & DELLO PENSSARAN,
        WORD #2352 OCCURS    1 TIMES.

HYEN            14488 5ELCID1833 **** LOS PRIMEROS EL REY FUERA DIO SALTO,
        WORD #2353 OCCURS    1 TIMES.

HYERNOS         17294 5ELCID2188 ******* UOS ADUGO DE QUE AUREMOS ONDRANZA;
                17938 5ELCID2270 EL ZID & SOS ******* EN VALENZIA SON RASTADOS.
        WORD #2354 OCCURS    2 TIMES.

HYNOIOS         16004 5ELCID2030 ******* FITOS SEDIE EL CAMPEADOR:
                16078 5ELCID2039 ******* FITOS LAS MANOS LE BESO,
        WORD #2355 OCCURS    2 TIMES.

HYO             10701 5ELCID1356 *** LES MANDARE DAR CONDUCHO MIENTRA QUE POR MJ TIERRA FUEREN,
                11336 5ELCID1435 *** LO VERE CON EL ZID, SI DIOS ME LIEUA ALA.
                13466 5ELCID1707 *** UOS CANTE LA MISSA POR AQUESTA MA@ANA;
                14948 5ELCID1890 *** ECHE DE TIERRA AL BUEN CAMPEADOR,
                16449 5ELCID2086 *** LAS ENGENDRE AMAS & CRIASTES LAS UOS
                16563 5ELCID2099 *** LAS CASO A UUESTRAS FIJAS CON UUESTRO AMOR,
                18442 5ELCID2334 *** DESSEO LIDES, & UOS A CARRION;
                18608 5ELCID2355 *** UOS DIGO, ZID, POR TODA CARIDAD,
                18631 5ELCID2358 *** CON LOS MYOS FERIR QUIERO DELANT,
                20252 5ELCID2571 *** QUIERO LES DAR AXUUAR IIJ MILL MARCOS DE PLATA;
                21053 5ELCID2676 *** SIRUIENDO UOS SIN ART, & UOS CONSSEIASTES PORA MI MUERT.
                22683 5ELCID2891 *** TOME EL CASAMIENTO, MAS NON OSE DEZIR AL.
                24543 5ELCID3129 ***, DE QUE FU REY, NON FIZ MAS DE DOS CORTES:
                24746 5ELCID3152 *** BIEN LAS QUERIA DALMA & DE CORAZON,
                25167 5ELCID3205 *** FAZIENDO ESTO, ELLOS ACABARON LO SO;
                25919 5ELCID3303 *** LAS HE FIJAS, & TU PRIMAS CORMANAS;
                26890 5ELCID3436 *** UOS RUEGO QUE ME OYADES TODA LA CORT,
                26907 5ELCID3438 *** LES DI MIS PRIMAS POR MANDADO DEL REY ALFONSSO,
                27052 5ELCID3456 *** SO ALBARFANEZ PORA TODEL MEIOR.
                27204 5ELCID3478 *** VOS LO SOBRELIEUO COMMO BUEN VASSALLO FAZE A SE@OR,
                27466 5ELCID3509 *** LO JURO PAR SANT ESIDRO EL DE LEON
                28191 5ELCID3599 *** LOS ADUX ASALUO ATIERRAS DE CARRION;
        WORD #2356 OCCURS   22 TIMES.
           INDEX OF DIVERSIFICATION =   831.86 WITH STANDARD DEVIATION OF   712.24

HYOLLO          26394 5ELCID3367 ****** LIDIARE, NON PASSARA POR AL:
        WORD #2357 OCCURS    1 TIMES.

HYR             11188 5ELCID1416 *** SE QUIERE A VALENZIA A MYO ZID EL DE BIUAR.
                13324 5ELCID1690 *** LOS HEMOS FFERIR ENEL NOMBRE DEL CRIADOR & DEL APOSTOL SANTI
                20691 5ELCID2627 *** LAS HEMOS VER ATIERRAS DE CARRION.
        WORD #2358 OCCURS    3 TIMES.

HYRAN           21380 5ELCID2718 ***** AQUESTOS MANDADOS AL ZID CAMPEADOR;
        WORD #2359 OCCURS    1 TIMES.

HYRE            21105 5ELCID2682 **** CON UUESTRA GRAZIA, DON ELUIRA & DO@A SOL;
        WORD #2360 OCCURS    1 TIMES.

HYREMOS          8831 5ELCID1124 ******* VER AQUELA SU ALMOFALLA,
                17065 5ELCID2161 ******* EN PODER DE MUO ZID A VALENZIA LA MAYOR;
        WORD #2361 OCCURS    2 TIMES.

HYTODAS         11160 5ELCID1412 ******* LAS DUE@AS CON ELLAS QUANTAS BUENAS ELLAS HAN.
        WORD #2362 OCCURS    1 TIMES.

HYUA            18927 5ELCID2395 **** LOS FERIR DE CORAZON & DE ALMA.
                22128 5ELCID2817 **** REZEBIR ADON ELUIRA & ADON@A SOL;
```

WORD C# PREFIX CONTEXT

HYUA (CON'T)

```
                    27988 5ELCID3572 **** LOS VER EL REY DCN ALFCNSSO;
         WORD #2363 OCCURS    3 TIMES.

HYUALO              11977 5ELCID1518 SONRRISANDO SE DELA BOCA, ****** ABRAZAR,
         WORD #2364 OCCURS    1 TIMES.

HYUAN               12205 5ELCID1549 ENTRE EL & ALBARFANEZ ***** A VNA COMPA@A.
                    20884 5ELCID2653 ***** TROZIR LOS MONTES, LOS QUE DIZEN DE LUZON.
         WORD #2365 OCCURS    2 TIMES.

IAMAS               21094 5ELCID2680 VOS NUQUA EN CARRICN ENTRARIEDES *****.
         WORD #2366 OCCURS    1 TIMES.

IANTADO              8154 5ELCID1039 PUES COMED, CONDE, & QUANDO FUEREDES *******,
         WORD #2367 OCCURS    1 TIMES.

IANTANDO             8312 5ELCID1057 CON ESTOS DOS CAUALLEROS A PRIESSA VA ********;
         WORD #2368 OCCURS    1 TIMES.

IANTAR               2266 5ELCID0285 GRAND ****** LE FAZEN AL BUEN CAMPEADOR.
                     2413 5ELCID0304 PLOGO A MIC %ID, POR QUE CREZIO EN LA ******,
                    23948 5ELCID3051 E YRE ALA CCRT ENANTES DE ******.
         WORD #2369 OCCURS    3 TIMES.

IANTE                8355 5ELCID1062 DEL DIA QUE FUE CONDE NCN ***** TAN DE BUEN GRADO,
         WORD #2370 OCCURS    1 TIMES.

IAZ                  9514 5ELCID1209 NUEUE MESES COMPLIDOS, SABET, SOBRELLA ***;
         WORD #2371 OCCURS    1 TIMES.

IAZE                 3465 5ELCID0437 TODA LA NOCHE **** EN %ELADA EL QUE EN BUEN ORA NASCO,
                    11551 5ELCID1463 VAYADES A MOLINA, QUE **** MAS ADELANT,
                    12708 5ELCID1613 MIRAN VALENZIA COMMO **** LA %IBDAD,
         WORD #2372 OCCURS    3 TIMES.

IAZEN               21265 5ELCID2702 CON QUANTOS QUE ELLOS TRAEN Y ***** ESSA NOCH,
                    22528 5ELCID2869 HY ***** ESSA NOCHE, & TAN GRAND GOZO QUE FAZEN.
         WORD #2373 OCCURS    2 TIMES.

IAZER                3125 5ELCID0393 VINO MYO %ID ***** A SPINAZ DE CAN.
         WORD #2374 OCCURS    1 TIMES.

IAZREDES            20752 5ELCID2635 POR MOLINA YREDES, VNA NOCH Y ********;
         WORD #2375 OCCURS    1 TIMES.

IERONIMO            10180 5ELCID1289 EL OBISPO DCN ******** SO NOMBRE ES LAMADO.
                    10293 5ELCID1303 AESTE DON ******** YAL CTCRGAN POR OBISPO;
                    11529 5ELCID1460 EL OBISPO DCN ********, CCRCNADO DE PRESTAR,
                    15712 5ELCID1993 EL OBISPO DON ********, CORANADO MEIOR,
         WORD #2376 OCCURS    4 TIMES.

IHERONIMO           12178 5ELCID1546 EL OBISPO DCN *********, BUEN CHRISTIANO SIN FALLA,
                    12446 5ELCID1579 EL OBISPO DCN ********* ADELANT SE ENTRAUA,
                    13156 5ELCID1667 DESI AN ASSER DEL OBISPC DCN *********,
                    13320 5ELCID1689 EL OBISPO DC ********* SCLTURA NOS DARA,
                    13427 5ELCID1702 EL OBISPO DON ********* LA MISSA LES CANTAUA;
                    14166 5ELCID1793 EL OBISPO DCN *********, CABOSO CORONADO,
                    16311 5ELCID2069 EL OBISPO DON ********* LA MISSA CANTO.
                    17690 5ELCID2238 EL OBISPO DCN ********* VISTICS TAN PRIUADO,
                    18713 5ELCID2368 AFEUOS EL CBISPO DCN ********* MUY BIEN ARMADO,
                    18832 5ELCID2383 EL OBISPO DCN ********* PRISO A ESPOLONADA
                    19821 5ELCID2512 AQUI ESTA CCN MYO %ID EL CBISPO DO *********,
                    24043 5ELCID3064 VOS YREDES CCMIGC & EL CBISPO DON *********
         WORD #2377 OCCURS   12 TIMES.
            INDEX OF DIVERSIFICATICN =  1077.64 WITH STANCARD DEVIATION OF  1213.64

IHESU               12801 5ELCID1624 E EL NON GELC GRADEZE SI NON A ***** CHRISTO.
         WORD #2378 OCCURS    1 TIMES.

IIIJ                 6126 5ELCID0779 DA QUESTOS MCROS MATO XXX ****;
                    18947 5ELCID2397 ABATIO A VIJ & A **** MATAUA.
                    21340 5ELCID2712 TODOS ERAN YDCS, ELLOS **** SOLOS SON,
         WORD #2379 OCCURS    3 TIMES.

IIJ                  1438 5ELCID0184 ATOD EL PRIMER COLPE *** MARCOS DE PLATA ECHARON,
                     4098 5ELCID0521 ASMARON LOS MCROS *** MILL MARCOS DE PLATA.
                     5994 5ELCID0760 AL REY FARIZ *** COLPES LE AUIE DADO;
                     9187 5ELCID1169 EN GANAR AQUELAS VILLAS MYO %ID DURO *** A@OS.
                    14827 5ELCID1874 DOUOS *** CAUALLOS & PRENDED LOS AQUI.
                    15489 5ELCID1962 SEAN LAS VISTAS DESTAS *** SEMANAS;
                    16294 5ELCID2067 PASSADO AUIE *** A@OS NC CCMIERAN MEIOR.
                    20257 5ELCID2571 HYO QUIERO LES DAR AXUUAR *** MILL MARCOS DE PLATA;
                    25372 5ELCID3231 DESTOS *** MILL MARCOS LOS CC TENGO YO;
                    27122 5ELCID3466 DESTOS *** POR TRES QUE REBTARON EN LA CORT.
```

WORD C# PREFIX CONTEXT

IIJ (CON'T)

```
          WORD #2380 OCCURS  10 TIMES.
             INDEX OF DIVERSIFICATION =  2852.78 WITH STANDARD DEVIATION OF  1781.72

IO                   3433 5ELCID0433 POR TAL LO FAZE MYO %ID QUE NO ** VENTASSE NADI.
          WORD #2381 OCCURS   1 TIMES.

IOGADOS             25512 5ELCID3249 MAL ESCAPAN *******, SABED, DESTA RAZON.
          WORD #2382 OCCURS   1 TIMES.

IONAS                2680 5ELCID0339 A *****, QUANDO CAYO EN LA MAR,
          WORD #2383 OCCURS   1 TIMES.

IUA                  3196 5ELCID0402 ALA FIGERUELA MYO %ID *** POSAR.
          WORD #2384 OCCURS   1 TIMES.

IUDIOS               2742 5ELCID0347 ALOS ****** TE DEXESTE PRENDER; DO DIZEN MONTE CALUARIE
          WORD #2385 OCCURS   1 TIMES.

IUNTADAS             3988 5ELCID0506 ESTAS GANAN%IAS ALLI ERAN ********.
                     9451 5ELCID1201 QUANDO VIO MYO %ID LAS GENTES ********, COMPE%OS DE PAGAR.
          WORD #2386 OCCURS   2 TIMES.

IUNTADOS             2311 5ELCID0291 %IENTO QUINZE CAUALLEROS TODOS ******** SON;
                     8757 5ELCID1113 ALTER%ER DIA TODOS ******** SON,
                    16321 5ELCID2070 AL SALIR DE LA MISSA TODOS ******** SON,
                    17467 5ELCID2209 TODOS SUS CAUALLEROS A PRIESSA SON ********.
                    23405 5ELCID2981 A CABO DE VIJ SEMANAS QUE Y FUESSEN ********;
                    23650 5ELCID3012 DE TODAS PARTES ALLI ******** SON.
          WORD #2387 OCCURS   6 TIMES.
             INDEX OF DIVERSIFICATION =  4266.80 WITH STANDARD DEVIATION OF  3328.95

IUNTAR               2477 5ELCID0312 ASOS CAUALLEROS MANDOLOS TODOS ******:
                     2900 5ELCID0365 QUANDO OY NOS PARTIMOS, EN VIDA NOS FAZ ******.
                     9970 5ELCID1263 MANDO LOS VENIR ALA CORTH & A TODOS LOS ******,
          WORD #2388 OCCURS   3 TIMES.

IUNTARAS            19099 5ELCID2416 NON TE ******** COMIGO FATA DENTRO EN LA MAR.
          WORD #2389 OCCURS   1 TIMES.

IUNTAREDES          16901 5ELCID2139 QUANDO UOS ********** COMIGO, QUEM DIGADES LA UERDAT.
          WORD #2390 OCCURS   1 TIMES.

IURA                  935 5ELCID0120 CON GRAND **** METED Y LAS FES AMOS,
          WORD #2391 OCCURS   1 TIMES.

IURADO               1274 5ELCID0163 CA ASSIL DIERAN LA FE & GELO AUIEN ******,
          WORD #2392 OCCURS   1 TIMES.

IUSTOS              29197 5ELCID3728 ASSI FFAGAMOS NOS TODOS ****** & PECCADORES
          WORD #2393 OCCURS   1 TIMES.

IUUIZIO             25338 5ELCID3226 MAS EN NUESTRO ******* ASSI LO MANDAMOS NOS,
          WORD #2394 OCCURS   1 TIMES.

JERONIMO            11842 5ELCID1501 E EL OBISPO DON ********, CORANADO LEAL,
          WORD #2395 OCCURS   1 TIMES.

JUEGO               25584 5ELCID3258 DEZID  QUE UOS MERE%I, YFANTES, EN ***** O EN VERO
          WORD #2396 OCCURS   1 TIMES.

JUGARA              26041 5ELCID3319 SI YO NON VUJAS, EL MORO TE ****** MAL;
          WORD #2397 OCCURS   1 TIMES.

JUIZIO              27264 5ELCID3485 PRISIERON EL ****** YFANTES DE CARRION.
          WORD #2398 OCCURS   1 TIMES.

JUNTADOS            28361 5ELCID3621 TODOS TRES POR TRES YA ******** SON:
          WORD #2399 OCCURS   1 TIMES.

JUNTARON            27786 5ELCID3546 MUCHOS SE ******** DE BUENOS RICOS OMNES
          WORD #2400 OCCURS   1 TIMES.

JUNTO               28384 5ELCID3624 CON FERRAGON%ALEZ DE CARA SE *****;
          WORD #2401 OCCURS   1 TIMES.

JUNTOS               8519 5ELCID1083 ****** CON SUS MESNADAS, CONPE%OLAS DE LEGAR
          WORD #2402 OCCURS   1 TIMES.

JURO                24645 5ELCID3140 **** PAR SANT ESIDRO, EL QUE BOLUIERE MY CORT
                    27468 5ELCID3509 HYO LO **** PAR SANT ESIDRO EL DE LEON
          WORD #2403 OCCURS   2 TIMES.

JUUIZIO             25434 5ELCID3239 POR ******* LO DAMOS ANTEL REY DON ALFONSSO:
          WORD #2404 OCCURS   1 TIMES.
```

WORD C# PREFIX CONTEXT

```
JUUIZYO          25596 5ELCID3259 O EN ALGUNA RAZON? AQUI LO MEIORARE A ******* DELA CORT.
        WORD #2405 OCCURS   1 TIMES.

L                 1982 5ELCID0250 MAS POR QUE ME VC DE TIERRA, DOUOS * MARCHOS,
                 12811 5ELCID1626 CON * VEZES MILL DE ARMAS, TODOS FUERON CONPLIDOS,
                 13684 5ELCID1734 LOS * MILL PCR CUENTA FUERO NOTADOS:
        WORD #2406 OCCURS   3 TIMES.

LA                   9 5ELCID0002 TORNAUA ** CABE%A & ESAUA LOS CATANDO.
                    79 5ELCID0011 ALA EXIDA DE BIUAR CUIERON ** CORNEIA DIESTRA,
                    87 5ELCID0012 E ENTRANDO A BURGOS OUIERON ** SINIESTRA.
                    96 5ELCID0013 ME%IO MYO %ID LOS OMBROS & ENGRAMEO ** TIESTA:
                   167 5ELCID0022 EL REY DON ALFONSSO TANTO AUIE ** GRAND SA@A,
                   266 5ELCID0034 QUE SI NON ** QUEBRANTAS POR FUERCA, QUE NON GELA ABRIESE NADI.
                   309 5ELCID0039 NON SE ABRE ** PUERTA, CA BIEN ERA %ERRADA.
                   389 5ELCID0049 ESTO ** NI@A DIXO & TORNOS PORA SU CASA.
                   426 5ELCID0054 ** ORA%ION FECHA LUEGO CAUALGAUA;
                   433 5ELCID0055 SALIO POR ** PUERTA & EN ARLAN%ON POSAUA.
                   443 5ELCID0056 CABO ESSA VILLA EN ** GLERA POSAUA,
                   447 5ELCID0057 FINCAUA ** TIENDA & LUEGO DESCAUALGAUA.
                   465 5ELCID0059 POSO EN ** GLERA QUANDO NOL COGE NADI EN CASA;
                   493 5ELCID0062 VEDADA LAN CONPRA DENTRO EN BURGOS ** CASA,
                   634 5ELCID0080 SI YO BIUO, DOBLAR UOS HE ** SOLDADA.
                   642 5ELCID0081 ESPESO E EL ORO & TODA ** PLATA,
                  1066 5ELCID0137 YA VEDES QUE ENTRA ** NOCH, EL %ID ES PRESURADO,
                  1269 5ELCID0163 CA ASSIL DIERAN ** FE & GELO AUIEN IURADO,
                  1360 5ELCID0174 RACHEL AMYO %ID ** MANOL BA BESAR:
                  1399 5ELCID0179 %ID, BESO UUESTRA MANO ENDON QUE ** YO AYA.
                  1410 5ELCID0181 SIUOS ** ADUXIER CALLA; SI NON, CONTALDA SOBRE LAS ARCAS. . . .
                  1576 5ELCID0202 VINO PORA ** TIENDA DEL QUE EN BUEN ORA NASCO;
                  1622 5ELCID0208 MANDAD COGER ** TIENDA & VAYAMOS PRIUADO,
                  1643 5ELCID0211 MESURAREMOS ** POSADA & QUITAREMOS EL REYNADO;
                  1660 5ELCID0213 ESTAS PALABRAS DICHAS, ** TIENDA ES COGIDA.
                  1672 5ELCID0215 ** CARA DEL CAUALLO TORNO A SANTA MARIA,
                  1684 5ELCID0216 AL%O SU MANO DIESTRA, ** CARA SE SANTIGUA:
                  1749 5ELCID0223 SI UOS ASSI LO FIZIEREDES & ** UENTURA ME FUERE COMPLIDA,
                  2179 5ELCID0274 ENCLINO LAS MANOS EN ** SU BARBA VELIDA,
                  2206 5ELCID0278 YA DO@A XIMENA, ** MI MUGIER TAN COMPLIDA,
                  2362 5ELCID0298 TORNOS A SONRISAR; LEGAN LE TODOS, ** MANOL BAN BESAR.
                  2412 5ELCID0304 PLOGO A MIO %ID, POR QUE CRE%IO EN ** IANTAR,
                  2469 5ELCID0311 EL DIA ES EXIDO, ** NOCH QUERIE ENTRAR,
                  2519 5ELCID0319 ** MISSA NOS DIRA, ESTA SERA DE SANTA TRINIDAD;
                  2528 5ELCID0320 ** MISSA DICHA, PENSSEMOS DE CAUALGAR,
                  2557 5ELCID0323 PASSANDO UA ** NOCH, VINIENDO LA MAN;
                  2560 5ELCID0323 PASSANDO UA LA NOCH, VINIENDO ** MAN;
                  2582 5ELCID0326 MYO %ID & SU MUGIER A ** EGLESIA UAN.
                  2684 5ELCID0339 A IONAS, QUANDO CAYO EN ** MAR,
                  2693 5ELCID0340 SALUEST A DANIEL CON LOS LEONES EN ** MALA CAR%EL,
                  2778 5ELCID0351 ESTANDO EN ** CRUZ, VERTUD FEZIST MUY GRANT.
                  2793 5ELCID0353 DIOT CON ** LAN%A ENEL COSTADO, DONT YXIO LA SANGRE,
                  2799 5ELCID0353 DIOT CON LA LAN%A ENEL COSTADO, DONT YXIO ** SANGRE,
                  2802 5ELCID0354 CORRIO ** SANGRE POR EL ASTIL AYUSO, LAS MANOS SE OUO DE VNTAR,
                  2901 5ELCID0366 ** ORA%ION FECHA, LA MISSA ACABADA LA AN,
                  2904 5ELCID0366 LA ORA%ION FECHA, ** MISSA ACABADA LA AN,
                  2907 5ELCID0366 LA ORA%ION FECHA, LA MISSA ACABADA ** AN,
                  2921 5ELCID0368 EL %ID A DO@A XIMENA YUA ** ABRA%AR:
                  2927 5ELCID0369 DO@A XIMENA AL %ID ** MANOL VA BESAR,
                  2954 5ELCID0372 ADIOS UOS ACOMIENDO, FIJAS, & A ** MUGIER & AL PADRE SPIRITAL;
                  2979 5ELCID0375 ASIS PARTEN VNOS DOTROS COMMO ** V@A DELA CARNE.
                  2994 5ELCID0377 ATODOS ESPERANDO, ** CABE%A TORNANDO UA.
                  3177 5ELCID0400 ** CAL%ADA DE QUINEA YUA LA TRASPASSAR,
                  3182 5ELCID0400 LA CAL%ADA DE QUINEA YUA ** TRASPASSAR,
                  3254 5ELCID0410 QUANDO DESPERTO EL %ID, ** CARA SE SANTIGO;
                  3259 5ELCID0411 SINAUA ** CARA, A DIOS SE ACOMENDO,
                  3344 5ELCID0422 PASSAREMOS ** SIERRA QUE FIERA ES & GRAND,
                  3351 5ELCID0423 ** TIERRA DEL REY ALFONSSO ESTA NOCH LA PODEMOS QUITAR.
                  3358 5ELCID0423 LA TIERRA DEL REY ALFONSSO ESTA NOCH ** PODEMOS QUITAR.
                  3371 5ELCID0425 DE NOCH PASSAN ** SIERRA, VINIDA ES LA MAN,
                  3375 5ELCID0425 DE NOCH PASSAN LA SIERRA, VINIDA ES ** MAN,
                  3379 5ELCID0426 E POR ** LOMA AYUSO PIENSSAN DE ANDAR.
                  3463 5ELCID0437 TODA ** NOCHE IAZE EN %ELADA EL QUE EN BUEN ORA NASCO,
                  3569 5ELCID0449 E YO CON LO C AQUI FINCARE EN ** %AGA,
                  3614 5ELCID0455 E LOS QUE CON MYO %ID FICARAN EN ** %AGA.
                  3622 5ELCID0456 YA QUIEBRAN LOS ALBORES & VINIE ** MA@ANA,
                  3679 5ELCID0464 EL CAMPEADOR SALIO DE ** %ELADA, CORRIE ACASTEION SIN FALLA.
                  3708 5ELCID0468 LOS QUE ** TIENEN, QUANDO VIERON LA REBATA,
                  3712 5ELCID0468 LOS QUE LA TIENEN, QUANDO VIERON ** REBATA,
                  3751 5ELCID0474 SOS CAUALLEROS LEGAN CON ** GANAN%IA,
                  3754 5ELCID0475 DEXAN ** A MYO %ID, TODO ESTO NON PRE%IA NADA.
                  3775 5ELCID0477 E SIN DUBDA CORREN; FASTA ALCALA LEGO ** SE@A DE MINAYA,
                  3785 5ELCID0478 E DESI ARRIBA TORNAN SE CON ** GANAN%IA,
                  3814 5ELCID0482 DERECHA VIENE ** SE@A DE MINAYA;
                  3879 5ELCID0492 DOUOS ** QUINTA, SI LA QUISIEREDES, MINAYA.
                  3882 5ELCID0492 DOUOS LA QUINTA, SI ** QUISIEREDES, MINAYA.
```

WORD C# PREFIX CONTEXT

LA (CON'T)

```
3907 5ELCID0496 YO UOS ** SUELTA & AUELLO QUITADO.
3937 5ELCID0500 QUE ENPLEYE ** LANZA & AL ESPACA META MANO,
3949 5ELCID0501 E POR EL COBDO AYUSO ** SANGRE SESTELANDO,
4042 5ELCID0514 E A LOS PEONES ** MEATAD SIN FALLA;
4047 5ELCID0515 TODA ** QUINTA A MYO ZID FINCAUA.
4144 5ELCID0527 MOROS EN PAZ, CA ESCRIPTA ES ** CARTA,
4305 5ELCID0548 GRANDES SON LAS GANANZIAS QUE PRISO POR ** TIERRA DO UA.
4329 5ELCID0551 E PASSO AALFAMA, ** FOZ AYUSO UA,
4380 5ELCID0558 LOS VNOS CONTRA ** SIERRA & LOS OTROS CONTRA LA AGUA.
4386 5ELCID0558 LOS VNOS CONTRA LA SIERRA & LOS OTROS CONTRA ** AGUA.
4453 5ELCID0567 EN ** SU VEZINDAD NON SE TREUEN GANAR TANTO.
4496 5ELCID0571 E LOS DE TECA & LOS DE TERUAL ** CASA;
4539 5ELCID0577 COIO SALON AYUSO ** SU SE@A ALZADA,
4573 5ELCID0581 FALIDO A AMYO ZID EL PAN & ** ZEUADA.
4613 5ELCID0586 ** PARIA QUEL A PRESA TORNAR NOS LA HA DOBLADA.
4620 5ELCID0586 LA PARIA QUEL A PRESA TORNAR NOS ** HA DOBLADA.
4656 5ELCID0590 DIZEN LOS DE ALCOZER:  YA SE NOS VA ** GANAZIA
4685 5ELCID0594 ELBUEN CAMPEADOR ** SU CARA TORNAUA,
4701 5ELCID0596 MANDO TORNAR ** SE@A, A PRIESSA ESPOLONEAUAN.
4713 5ELCID0598 CON ** MERZED DEL CRIADOR NUESTRA ES LA GANANZIA
4719 5ELCID0598 CON LA MERZED DEL CRIADOR NUESTRA ES ** GANANZIA
4785 5ELCID0606 DANDO GRANDES ALARIDOS LOS QUE ESTAN EN ** ZELADA,
4800 5ELCID0608 LAS ESPADAS DESNUDAS, A ** PUERTA SE PARAUAN.
4826 5ELCID0611 VINO PERO VERMUEZ, QUE ** SE@A TEINE EN MANO,
4931 5ELCID0624 FIZO ENBIAR POR ** TIENDA QUE DEXARA ALLA.
5111 5ELCID0646 VINIERON A ** NOCH A ZELFA POSAR.
5119 5ELCID0647 POR LOS DE ** FRONTERA PIENSSAN DE ENVIAR;
5134 5ELCID0649 YXIERON DE ZELFA ** QUE DIZEN DE CANAL,
5260 5ELCID0665 ACABO DE TRES SEMANAS, ** QUARTA QUERIE ENTRAR,
5317 5ELCID0672 DE CASTIELLA ** GENTIL EXIDOS SOMOS ACA,
5396 5ELCID0681 ELDIA & ** NOCHE PIENSSAN SE DE ADOBAR.
5437 5ELCID0686 SI NON DOS PEONES SOLOS POR ** PUERTA GUARDAR;
5451 5ELCID0688 SI VENZIEREMOS ** BATALLA, CREZREMOS EN RICTAD.
5460 5ELCID0689 E VOS, PERO VERMUEZ, ** MI SE@A TOMAD;
5469 5ELCID0690 COMMO SODES MUY BUENO, TENER ** EDES SIN ARCH;
5487 5ELCID0692 AL ZID BESO ** MANO, LA SE@A UA TOMAR.
5489 5ELCID0692 AL ZID BESO LA MANO, ** SE@A UA TOMAR.
5525 5ELCID0696 ANTE ROYDO DE ATAMORES ** TIERRA QUERIE QUEBRAR;
5595 5ELCID0705 ** SE@A TIENE EN MANO, CONPEZO DE ESPOLONAR;
5612 5ELCID0707 VO METER ** UUESTRA SE@A EN AQUELA MAYOR AZ;
5626 5ELCID0708 LOS QUE EL DEBDO AUEDES VEREMOS COMMO ** ACORREDES.
5654 5ELCID0712 MOROS LE REZIBEN POR ** SE@A GANAR,
5864 5ELCID0743 ACORREN ** SE@A & A MYO ZID EL CAMPEADOR.
5885 5ELCID0746 ** LANZA A QUEBRADA, AL ESPADA METIO MANO,
5924 5ELCID0751 CORTOL POR ** ZINTURA, EL MEDIO ECHO EN CAMPO.
5968 5ELCID0756 CAUALGO MINAYA, EL ESPADA EN ** MANO,
6009 5ELCID0762 POR ** LORIGA AYUSO LA SANGRE DESTELLADO;
6012 5ELCID0762 POR LA LORIGA AYUSO ** SANGRE DESTELLADO;
6016 5ELCID0763 BOLUIO ** RIENDA POR YR SE LE DEL CAMPO.
6070 5ELCID0770 TAN BUEN DIA POR ** CHRISTIANDAD,
6076 5ELCID0771 CAFUYEN LOS MOROS DE ** PART
6137 5ELCID0781 POR EL COBDO AYUSO ** SANGRE DESTELLANDO.
6193 5ELCID0789 ** COFIA FRONZIDA  DIOS, COMMO ES BIEN BARBADO
6203 5ELCID0790 ALMOFAR ACUESTAS, ** ESPADA EN LA MANO.
6206 5ELCID0790 ALMOFAR ACUESTAS, LA ESPADA EN ** MANO.
6235 5ELCID0794 ESTA ALBERGADA LOS DE MYO ZID LUEGO ** AN ROBADA
6321 5ELCID0805 EN ** SU QUINTA AL ZID CAEN C CAUALLOS.
6486 5ELCID0827 AGORA DAUAN ZEUADA, YA ** NOCH ERA ENTRADA,
6503 5ELCID0829  HYDES UOS, MYNAYA, ACASTIELLA ** GENTIL?
6517 5ELCID0831 DIOS NOS VALIO & VENZIEMOS ** LIDIT.
6561 5ELCID0838 ** TIERRA ES ANGOSTA & SOBEIANA DE MALA;
6600 5ELCID0842 ENTRE LOS DE TECHA & LOS DE TERUEL ** CASA,
6794 5ELCID0868 ** TERZERA TERUEL, QUE ESTAUA DELANT;
6806 5ELCID0869 EN SU MANO TENIE A ZELFA ** DE CANAL.
6865 5ELCID0877 SOBEIANA ES, SE@OR, ** SU GANAZIA.
7140 5ELCID0914 ASARAGOZA METUDA ** EN PARIA.
7187 5ELCID0921 BESO LE ** BOCA & LOS OIOS DELA CARA.
7253 5ELCID0930  DIOS, COMMO ES ALEGRE ** BARBA VELIDA,
7386 5ELCID0947 HYA CAUALLEROS, DEZIR UOS HE ** VERDAD:
7470 5ELCID0958 QUE MYO ZID RUY DIAZ QUEL CORRIE ** TIERRA TODA;
7694 5ELCID0985 YA CAUALLEROS, A PART FAZED ** GANANZIA;
7736 5ELCID0990 PUES ADELLANT YRAN TRAS NOS, AQUI SEA ** BATALLA;
7810 5ELCID0999 OY EN ESTE PINAR DE TEUAR POR TOLER ME ** GANANZIA.
7831 5ELCID1002 VIERON ** CUESTA YUSO LA FUERZA DELOS FRANCOS;
7834 5ELCID1002 VIERON LA CUESTA YUSO ** FUERZA DELOS FRANCOS;
8290 5ELCID1055 AQUI FEREMOS ** MORADA, NO NOS PARTIREMOS AMOS.
8479 5ELCID1078 TORNANDO UA ** CABEZA & CATANDOS ATRAS;
8508 5ELCID1081 VNA DES LEATANZA CA NON ** FIZO ALGUANDRE.
8527 5ELCID1084 DE ** GANANZIA QUE AN FECHA MARAUILLOSA & GRAND.
8537 5ELCID1085 AQUIS CONPIEZA ** GESTA DE MYO ZID EL DE BIUAR.
8582 5ELCID1090 CONTRA ** MAR SALADA CONPEZO DE GUERREAR;
8818 5ELCID1122 PASSE ** NOCHE & VENGA LA MA@ANA,
8822 5ELCID1122 PASSE LA NOCHE & VENGA ** MA@ANA,
8847 5ELCID1126 ALI PAREZRA EL QUE MEREZE ** SOLDADA.
```

WORD C# PREFIX CONTEXT

LA (CON'T)

9123 5ELCID1161 AVN MAS AYUSSC, ADEYNA ** CASA;
9132 5ELCID1162 CABO DEL MAR TIERRA DE MOROS FIRME ** QUEBRANTA,
9370 5ELCID1191 %ERCAR QUIERE A VALEN%IA PORA CHRISTIANOS ** DAR.
9411 5ELCID1196 TORNAUAS A MURUIEDRC, CA EL SE ** A GANADA.
9471 5ELCID1204 BIEN ** %ERCA MYO %ID, QUE NCN Y AUYA HART;
9552 5ELCID1214 EL ORO & ** PLATA QUI EN VCS LO PODRIE CONTAR?
9571 5ELCID1216 MYO %ID DCN RODRIGO ** QUINTA MANDO TOMAR,
9643 5ELCID1225 APRES DELA VERTA CUIERON ** BATALLA,
9690 5ELCID1232 BUENA FUE ** DE VALEN%IA QUANDO GANARON LA CASA,
9695 5ELCID1232 BUENA FUE LA DE VALEN%IA QUANDO GANARON ** CASA,
9739 5ELCID1238 YAL CRE%E ** BARBA & VALE ALLONGANDO;
9748 5ELCID1239 DIXO MYO %ID DE ** SU BCCA ATANTO:
9878 5ELCID1252 QUE NINGUN CMNE DELOS SCS QUES LE NON SPIDIES, ONOL BESAS ** MANO,
10011 5ELCID1268 CON MAS POCCS YXIEMOS DE ** CASA DE BIUAR.
10066 5ELCID1275 DESI POR MI BESALDE ** MANO EFIRME GELO ROGAD
10092 5ELCID1279 ** MUGIER DE MYO %ID & SUS FIJAS LAS YFFANTES
10144 5ELCID1284 CIENTO CMNES LE DIO MYO %ID A ALBARFANEZ POR SERUIR LE EN ** CARRERA,
10456 5ELCID1325 ECHASTES LE DE TIERRA, NON HA ** UUESTRA AMOR;
10571 5ELCID1340 AL%O ** MANC DIESTRA, EL REY SE SANTIGO:
10744 5ELCID1360 OYD ME, ESCUELLAS, & TODA ** MI CORT.
10859 5ELCID1375 NON ** OSARIEMOS A COMETER NOS ESTA RAZON,
11020 5ELCID1395 QUANDO ACABO ** ORA%ICN, ALAS DUE@AS SE TORNO:
11329 5ELCID1434 SOLTARIEMOS ** GANAN%IA, QUE NOS DIESSE EL CABDAL.
11451 5ELCID1450 POR ** TIERRA DEL REY MUCHO CONDUCHO LES DAN.
11500 5ELCID1456 DE ** SU BOCA CONPE%O DE FABLAR:
11611 5ELCID1471 GRAND LOCURA SERIE SI ** DESENPARAS;
11618 5ELCID1472 YO FFINCARE EN VALEN%IA, CA ** TENGO POR HEREDAD.
11793 5ELCID1495 ENVIO DOS CAUALLEROS MYNAYA ALBARFANEZ QUE SOPIESSE ** VERDAD;
12014 5ELCID1523 ONDRAR UOS HEMOS TODOS, CA TALES ** SU AUZE,
12041 5ELCID1526 MUCHOL TENGO POR TORPE QUI NON CONES%E ** VERDAD.
12076 5ELCID1531 VAYAMOS POSAR, CA ** %ENA ES ADOBADA.
12090 5ELCID1533 ANTES DESTE TE%ER DIA UCS ** DARE DOBLADA.
12139 5ELCID1540 PASSADA ES ** NOCHE, VENIDA ES LA MA@ANA,
12143 5ELCID1540 PASSADA ES LA NOCHE, VENIDA ES ** MA@ANA,
12147 5ELCID1541 OYDA ES ** MISSA, & LUEGO CAUALGAUAN;
12171 5ELCID1545 VINIERCN A MOLINA, ** QUE AUEGALUON MANDAUA.
12455 5ELCID1580 Y DEXAUA EL CAUALLO, PORA ** CAPIELLA ADELINAUA;
12513 5ELCID1587 VISTIOS EL SOBREGONEL; LUENGA TRAHE ** BARBA;
12660 5ELCID1606 ENTRAD COMIGO EN VALEN%IA ** CASA,
12709 5ELCID1613 MIRAN VALEN%IA COMMO IAZE ** %IBDAD,
12721 5ELCID1615 MIRAN ** HUERTA, ESPESSA ES & GRAND;
12846 5ELCID1630 LEGARON A VALEN%IA, ** QUE MYO %ID A CONQUISTA,
12898 5ELCID1636 A MENOS DE MUERT NO ** PUEDC DEXAR;
13040 5ELCID1654 CON ** MER%ED DE DIOS & DE SANTA MARIA MADRE
13062 5ELCID1656 CON DIOS A CUESTA LID YO ** HE DE ARRANCAR.
13217 5ELCID1675 ADOBAN SE DE CORA%ON E DAN SALTO DE ** VILLA;
13302 5ELCID1687 POR ** MANANA PRIETA TODOS ARMADOS SEADES,
13311 5ELCID1688 DEZIR NOS HA ** MISSA, & PENSSAD DE CAUALGAR,
13406 5ELCID1699 ES DIA ES SALIDO & ** NOCH ENTRADA ES,
13422 5ELCID1701 ALOS MEDIADOS GALLOS, ANTES DE ** MA@ANA,
13428 5ELCID1702 EL OBISPO DON IHERONIMO ** MISSA LES CANTAUA;
13432 5ELCID1703 ** MISSA DICHA, GRANT SULTURA LES DAUA:
13469 5ELCID1707 HYO UOS CANTE ** MISSA POR AQUESTA MA@ANA;
13538 5ELCID1716 ** SE@A SACAN FUERA, DE VALEN%IA DIERON SALTO,
13588 5ELCID1722 MYO %ID ENPLEO ** LAN%A, AL ESPADA METIO MANO,
13606 5ELCID1724 POR EL COBDC AYUSO ** SANGRE DESTELLANDO.
13760 5ELCID1744 FRONZIDA TRAHE ** CARA, QUE ERA DESARMADO,
13772 5ELCID1745 ASSI ENTRO SOBRE BAUIECA, EL ESPADA EN ** MANO.
13787 5ELCID1747 MYO %ID FINCO ANTELLAS, TOUO ** RYENDA AL CAUALLO:
13879 5ELCID1758 LAS DUE@AS & LAS FIJAS & ** MUGIER QUE VALE ALGO
14028 5ELCID1777 NON PUDIERON ELLOS SABER ** CUENTA DE TODOS LOS CAUALLOS,
14095 5ELCID1785 ** TIENDA DEL REY DE MARRUECOS, QUE DELAS OTRAS ES CABO,
14108 5ELCID1786 DOS TENDALES ** SUFREN, CON ORO SON LABRADOS;
14122 5ELCID1787 MANDO MYO %ID RUY DIAZ QUE FITA SOUIESSE ** TIENDA,
14126 5ELCID1788 E NON ** TOLLIESSE DENT CHRISTIANO:
14140 5ELCID1790 ENBIAR ** QUIERO ALFONSSO EL CASTELLANO,
14207 5ELCID1798 DE TODA ** SU QUINTA EL DIEZMO LA MANDADO.
14212 5ELCID1798 DE TODA LA SU QUINTA EL DIEZMO ** MANDADO.
14288 5ELCID1808 E CRAS HA ** MA@ANA YR UOS HEDES SIN FALLA
14420 5ELCID1823 ANDAN LOS DIAS & LAS NOCHES, & PASSADA HAN ** SIERRA,
14574 5ELCID1844 BESAN ** TIERRA & LOS PIES AMOS:
14607 5ELCID1848 MUCHO PRE%IA ** ONDRA EL %ID QUEL AUEDES DADO.
14724 5ELCID1862 EN ** ONDRA QUE EL HA NOS SEREMOS ABILTADOS;
14837 5ELCID1875 ASSI COMMO SEMEIA & ** VELUNTAD MELO DIZ.
14979 5ELCID1893 MAS PUES BOS LO QUEREDES, ENTREMOS EN ** RAZON.
15215 5ELCID1926 ESTO DIZIENDC, CONPIE%AN ** RAZON,
15274 5ELCID1934 ECHADO FU DE TIERRA & TOLLIDA ** ONOR,
15311 5ELCID1938 ELLOS SON MUCHO VRGULLOSOS & AN PART EN ** CORT,
15332 5ELCID1941 FLABLEMOS EN ELLO, EN ** PORIDAD SEAMOS NOS.
15596 5ELCID1977 COMMO ELLOS TENIEN, CER%ER LES YA ** GANA%IA,
16089 5ELCID2040 LEUOS EN PIE & EN ** BOCAL SALUDO.
16117 5ELCID2044 QUANDO HE ** GRA%IA DE DON ALFONSSO MYO SE@OR;
16167 5ELCID2051 BESO LE ** MANO MYO CID, LO OTORGO.
16231 5ELCID2059 CATANDOL SEDIE ** BARBA, QUE TAN AYNAL CRE%IERA.

WORD C# PREFIX CONTEXT

LA (CON'T)

16253 5ELCID2061 ES DIA ES PASSADO, & ENTRADA ES ** NOCH;
16312 5ELCID2069 EL OBISPO DON IHERONIMO ** MISSA CANTO.
16318 5ELCID2070 AL SALIR DE ** MISSA TODOS IUNTADOS SON,
16328 5ELCID2071 NON LO TARDO EL REY, ** RAZON CONPE%O:
16620 5ELCID2105 PUES FUEREN EN UUESTRO PODER EN VALEN%IA ** MAYOR,
16748 5ELCID2120 PARTIR SE QUIEREN, QUE ENTRADA ERA ** NOCH.
16905 5ELCID2139 QUANDO UOS IUNTAREDES COMIGO, QUEM DIGADES ** UERDAT.
17073 5ELCID2161 HYREMOS EN PODER DE MUO %ID A VALEN%IA ** MAYOR;
17102 5ELCID2165 ** CONPA@A DEL %ID CRE%E, & LA DEL REY MENGO,
17108 5ELCID2165 LA CONPA@A DEL %ID CRE%E, & ** DEL REY MENGO,
17123 5ELCID2167 ADELINAN PORA VALEN%IA, ** QUE EN BUEN PUNTO GANO.
17192 5ELCID2175 AFELOS EN VALEN%IA, ** QUE MYO %ID GA@O;
17235 5ELCID2180 QUANDO VINIERE ** MA@ANA, QUE APUNTARE EL SOL,
17314 5ELCID2190 BESARON LE LAS MANOS ** MUGIER & LAS FIJAS AMAS,
17672 5ELCID2235 A MYO %ID & A SU MUGIER VAN BESAR ** MANO.
17702 5ELCID2240 DIOLES BENDICTIONES, ** MISSA A CANTADO.
18035 5ELCID2282 SALIOS DE ** RED & DESATOS EL LEON.
18087 5ELCID2288 DIEGO GON%ALEZ POR ** PUERTA SALIO,
18173 5ELCID2299 ANTE MYO %ID ** CABE%A PREMIO & EL ROSTRO FINCO;
18205 5ELCID2303 ETORNARON SEAL APALA%IO PORA ** CORT.
18240 5ELCID2307 NON VIESTES TAL GUEGO COMMO YUA POR ** CORT;
18302 5ELCID2316 QUE LES CRE%E ** GANAN%IA, GRADO AL CRIADOR.
18335 5ELCID2320 CATAMOS ** GANAN%IA & LA PERDIDA NO,
18338 5ELCID2320 CATAMOS LA GANAN%IA & ** PERDIDA NO,
18362 5ELCID2324 OYO ** PORIDAD AQUEL MU@O GUSTIOZ,
18411 5ELCID2330 NOS CON UUSCO ** VENCREMOS, & VALER NOS HA EL CRIADOR.
18466 5ELCID2337 ARRANCAR MELOS TREUO CON ** MER%ED DEL CRIADOR.
18530 5ELCID2345 EN ** VESTE DELOS MOROS LOS ATAMORES SONANDO;
18559 5ELCID2349 POR ** SU VOLUNTAD NON SERIEN ALLI LEGADOS.
18595 5ELCID2353 MYOS YERNOS AMOS ADOS, ** COSA QUE MUCHO AMO,
18667 5ELCID2362 ESTA BATALLA EL CRIADOR ** FERA,
18699 5ELCID2366 VERLO HEMOS CONDIOS & CON ** UUESTRA AUZE.
18723 5ELCID2369 PARAUAS DELANT AL CAMPEADOR, SIEMPRE CON ** BUEN AUZE:
18729 5ELCID2370 OY UOS DIX ** MISSA DE SANTA TRINIDADE.
18844 5ELCID2385 POR ** SU VENTURA & DIOS QUEL AMAUA
18858 5ELCID2386 ALOS PRIMEROS COLPES DOS MOROS MATAUA DE ** LAN%A.
19051 5ELCID2410 VERTE AS CON EL %ID, EL DE ** BARBA GRANT,
19074 5ELCID2413 EL ESPADA TIENES DESNUDA EN ** MANO & VEOT AGUIJAR;
19084 5ELCID2414 ASI COMMO SEMEIA, EN MI ** QUIERES ENSAYAR.
19104 5ELCID2416 NON TE IUNTARAS COMIGO FATA DENTRO EN ** MAR.
19164 5ELCID2424 FATA ** %INTURA EL ESPADA LEGADO HA.
19188 5ELCID2427 VEN%IO ** BATALLA MARAUILLOSA & GRANT.
19241 5ELCID2435 POR ** MATAN%A VINIA TAN PRIUADO,
19246 5ELCID2436 ** CARA FRONZIDA & ALMOFAR SOLTADO,
19366 5ELCID2453 POR EL COBDO AYUSO ** SANGRE DESTELLANDO;
19528 5ELCID2474 GRANT FUE EL DIA ** CORT DEL CAMPEADOR,
19543 5ELCID2476 AL%O ** MANO, ALA BARBA SE TOMO:
19865 5ELCID2519 EUADES AQUI, YERNOS, ** MI MUGIER DE PRO,
19871 5ELCID2520 EAMAS ** MYS FIJAS, DON ELUIRA & DO@A SOL;
20067 5ELCID2547 DESPUES EN ** CARRERA FEREMOS NUESTRO SABOR,
20152 5ELCID2558 FABLO FERAN GON%ALEZ & FIZO CALLAR ** CORT;
20398 5ELCID2588 GRANDES SON LAS NUEUAS POR VALEN%IA ** MAYOR,
20497 5ELCID2602 EL FIZO AQUESTO, ** MADRE LO DOBLAUA;
20568 5ELCID2611 HYA SALIEN LOS YFANTES DE VALEN%IA ** CLARA,
20579 5ELCID2613 POR ** HUERTA DE VALEN%IA TENIENDO SALIEN ARMAS;
20681 5ELCID2625 TORNEMOS NOS, %ID, A VALEN%IA ** MAYOR;
20791 5ELCID2640 DESI ESCURRA LAS FASTA MEDINA POR ** MI AMOR;
20805 5ELCID2642 CUEMO ** V@A DELA CARNE ELLOS PARTIDOS SON;
20836 5ELCID2645 POR SANTA MARIA DALUA RAZIN FAZIAN ** POSADA,
20935 5ELCID2659 ELLOS VEYEN ** RIQUEZA QUE EL MORO SACO,
20963 5ELCID2663 QUANTA RIQUIZA TIENE AUER ** YEMOS NOS.
21187 5ELCID2692 ** SIERRA DE MIEDES PASSARON LA ESTOZ,
21192 5ELCID2692 LA SIERRA DE MIEDES PASSARON ** ESTOZ,
21254 5ELCID2701 MANDAN FINCAR ** TIENDA YFANTES DE CARRION,
21292 5ELCID2706 COGIDA HAN ** TIENDA DO ALBERGARON DE NOCH,
21390 5ELCID2719 NOS VENGAREMOS AQUESTA POR ** DEL LEON.
21547 5ELCID2739 LINPIA SALIE ** SANGRE SOBRE LOS %ICLATONES.
21718 5ELCID2762 ** DESONDRA DEL LEON ASSIS YRA VENGANDO.
21918 5ELCID2788 MIENTRA ES EL DIA, ANTE QUE ENTRE ** NOCH,
22064 5ELCID2808 EL CAUALLO PRISO POR ** RIENDA & LUEGO DENT LAS PARTIO,
22193 5ELCID2826 VAN AQUESTOS MANDADOS A VALEN%IA ** MAYOR;
22210 5ELCID2829 AL%O ** SU MANO, ALA BARBA SE TOMO;
22242 5ELCID2833 NON ** LOGRARAN LOS YFANTES DE CARRION;
22303 5ELCID2840 ADUXIESSEN ASSUS FIJAS A VALEN%IA ** MAYOR.
22777 5ELCID2902 EN BUEN ORA TE CRIE ATI EN ** MI CORT
22792 5ELCID2904 POR MI BESA LE ** MANO CALMA & DE CORA%ON,
22848 5ELCID2911 ** POCA & LA GRANT TODA ES DE MYO SE@OR.
22851 5ELCID2911 LA POCA & ** GRANT TODA ES DE MYO SE@OR.
22872 5ELCID2913 ESSO ME PUEDE PESAR CON ** OTRA DESONOR.
22894 5ELCID2916 CA TAN GRANT ES ** RENCURA DENTRO EN MI CORA%ON.
22993 5ELCID2929 ADELINO PORAL PALA%IO DO ESTAUA ** CORT,
23085 5ELCID2941 HYA UOS SABEDES ** ONDRA QUE ES CUNTIDA ANOS,
23155 5ELCID2950 TIENES POR DESONDRADO, MAS ** UUESTRA ES MAYOR,
23636 5ELCID3010 E CON ELLOS GRAND BANDO QUE ADUXIERON A ** CORT:

WORD C# PREFIX CONTEXT

LA (CON'T)

23807 5ELCID3032 DIOS LO MANDE QUE POR UOS SE ONDRE OY ** CORT
23817 5ELCID3034 BESO LE ** MANO & DESPUES LE SALUDO;
24003 5ELCID3059 ACORDADOS FUERON, QUANDO VINO ** MAN.
24013 5ELCID3061 SUELTA FUE ** MISSA ANTES QUE SALIESSE EL SOL,
24254 5ELCID3093 SIEMPRE ** VISTE MYO %IC EL CAMPEADOR;
24286 5ELCID3097 ** BARBA AVIE LUENGA & PRISOLA CON EL CORDON,
24502 5ELCID3123 CATANDO ESTAN A MYO %ID QUANTOS HA EN ** CORT,
24554 5ELCID3130 ** VNA FUE EN BURGOS, & LA OTRA EN CARRION,
24560 5ELCID3130 LA VNA FUE EN BURGOS, & ** OTRA EN CARRION,
24568 5ELCID3131 ESTA TER%ERA A TOLLEDO ** VIN FER OY,
24685 5ELCID3145 MYO %ID ** MANO BESO AL REY & EN PIE SE LEUANTO;
24744 5ELCID3151 MAS QUANDO SACARON MIS FIJAS DE VALEN%IA ** MAYOR,
24839 5ELCID3163 APRIESSA LO YUAN TRAYENDO & ACUERDAN ** RAZON:
24872 5ELCID3167 DEMOS LE SUS ESPADAS, QUANDO ASSI FINCA ** BOZ,
24880 5ELCID3168 E QUANDO LAS TOUIERE, PARTIR SEA ** CORT;
24947 5ELCID3177 SACA LAS ESPADAS & RELUMBRA TODA ** CORT,
25006 5ELCID3185 AL%AUA ** MANO, ALA BARBA SE TOMO;
25035 5ELCID3189 TENDIO EL BRA%O, ** ESPADA TIZON LE DIO;
25041 5ELCID3190 PRENDET **, SOBRINO, CA MEIORA EN SE@OR.
25081 5ELCID3195 DEL CONDE DE REMONT VERENGEL DE BAR%ILONA ** MAYOR.
25086 5ELCID3196 POR ESSO UOS ** DO QUE LA BIEN CURIEDES UOS.
25089 5ELCID3196 POR ESSO UOS LA DO QUE ** BIEN CURIEDES UOS.
25108 5ELCID3198 BESO LE ** MANO, EL ESPADA TOMO & RE%IBIO.
25221 5ELCID3211 QUE AL NO NOS DEMANDASSE, QUE AQUI FINCO ** BOZ. . .
25349 5ELCID3227 QUE AQUI LO ENTERGEDES DENTRO EN ** CORT.
25361 5ELCID3229 NOS BIEN ** SABEMOS AQUESTA RAZON,
25428 5ELCID3238 EL ORO & ** PLATA ESPENDIESTES LO VOS;
25546 5ELCID3254 ** RENCURA MAYOR NON SEME PUEDE OLBIDAR.
25556 5ELCID3255 OYD ME TODA ** CORT & PESEUOS DE MYO MAL;
25703 5ELCID3273 DEXOLA CRE%ER & LUENGA TRAE ** BARBA;
25778 5ELCID3283 QUE AVEDES UOS, CONDE, POR RETRAER ** MI BARBA?
25820 5ELCID3288 QUANDO PRIS A CABRA, & AUOS POR ** BARBA,
25830 5ELCID3290 ** QUE YO MESSE AVN NON ES EGUADA.
25949 5ELCID3307 DETIENES LE ** LENGUA, NON PUEDE DELIBRAR,
26016 5ELCID3316 MIEMBRAT QUANDO LIDIAMOS %ERCA VALEN%IA ** GRAND;
26098 5ELCID3326 CROUIERON TELO TODOS, MAS NON SABEN ** VERDAD.
26186 5ELCID3338 EL LEON PREMIO ** CABE%A, A MYO %ID ESPERO,
26266 5ELCID3349 QUANDO FUERE ** LID, SI PLOGUIERE AL CRIADOR,
26289 5ELCID3352 DAQUESTOS AMOS AQUI QUEDO ** RAZON.
26375 5ELCID3364 SALISTE POR ** PUERTA, METISTET AL CORAL,
26383 5ELCID3365 FUSTED METER TRAS ** VIGA LAGAR,
26436 5ELCID3372 DESTOS AMOS ** RAZON FINCO.
26581 5ELCID3393 AFFE DOS CAUALLEROS ENTRARON POR ** CORT;
26640 5ELCID3401 AESTO CALLARON & ASCUCHO TODA ** CORT.
26695 5ELCID3409 LEUANTOS EL REY, FIZO CALLAR ** CORT:
26897 5ELCID3436 HYO UOS RUEGO QUE ME OYADES TODA ** CORT,
27030 5ELCID3453 ASIL CRE%E ** ONDRA A MYO %ID EL CAMPEADOR
27115 5ELCID3465 CRAS SEA ** LID, QUANDO SALIERE EL SOL,
27128 5ELCID3466 DESTOS IIJ POR TRES QUE REBTARON EN ** CORT.
27253 5ELCID3483 QUEN NON VINIERE AL PLAZO PIERDA ** RAZON,
27331 5ELCID3493 ** CONFIA DE RAN%AL QUE BLANCA ERA COMMO EL SOL,
27343 5ELCID3494 E SOLTAUA ** BARBA & SACOLA DEL CORDON.
27356 5ELCID3495 NOS FARTAN DE CATARLE QUANTOS HA EN ** CORT.
27454 5ELCID3507 E YR ME QUIERO PORA VALEN%IA, CON AFAN ** GANE YO.
27460 5ELCID3508 EL REY AL%O ** MANO, LA CARA SE SANTIGO;
27462 5ELCID3508 EL REY AL%O LA MANO, ** CARA SE SANTIGO;
27494 5ELCID3512 FUE BESAR ** MANO A SO SE@OR ALFONSSO;
27586 5ELCID3522 ESSORA SE ESPIDIERON, & LUEGOS PARTIO ** CORT.
27778 5ELCID3545 TROCIDA ES ** NOCHE, YA QUIEBRAN LOS ALBORES.
27859 5ELCID3555 QUE NON FUESSEN EN ** BATALLA LAS ESPADAS TAIADORES
27897 5ELCID3559 NON SACASTES NINGUNA QUANDO OUIEMOS ** CORT.
28345 5ELCID3619 TEMBRAR QUERIE ** TIERRA DOD ERAN MOUEDORES.
28429 5ELCID3631 QUEBRANTO ** BOCA DEL ESCUDO, A PART GELA ECHO,
28445 5ELCID3633 METIOL ** LAN%A POR LOS PECHOS, QUE NADA NOL VALIO;
28467 5ELCID3635 LAS DOS LE DESMANCHAN & ** TER%ERA FINCO:
28473 5ELCID3636 EL BELMEZ CON ** CAMISA & CON LA GUARNIZON
28477 5ELCID3636 EL BELMEZ CON LA CAMISA & CON ** GUARNIZON
28481 5ELCID3637 DEDENTRO EN ** CARNE VNA MANO GELA METIO;
28488 5ELCID3638 POR ** BOCA AFUERA LA SANGREL SALIO;
28491 5ELCID3638 POR LA BOCA AFUERA ** SANGREL SALIO;
28503 5ELCID3640 POR ** COPLA DEL CAUALLO EN TIERRA LO ECHO.
28524 5ELCID3642 EL DEXO ** LAN%A & AL ESPADA METIO MANO,
28610 5ELCID3653 ALLA LEUO EL ALMOFAR, FATA ** COFIA LEGAUA,
28613 5ELCID3654 ** COFIA & EL ALMOFAR TODO GELO LEUAUA,
28646 5ELCID3657 QUANDO ESTE COLPE A FERIDO COLADA ** PRE%IADA,
28658 5ELCID3659 BOLUIO ** RIENDA AL CAUALLO POR TORNASSE DE CARA;
28790 5ELCID3677 EN VAZIO FUE ** LAN%A, CA EN CARNE NOL TOMO.
28813 5ELCID3680 POR MEIO DE ** BLOCA DEL ESCUDOL QUEBRANTO;
28833 5ELCID3683 METIOL POR ** CARNE ADENTRO LA LAN%A CONEL PENDON,
28836 5ELCID3683 METIOL POR LA CARNE ADENTRO ** LAN%A CONEL PENDON,
28869 5ELCID3687 VERMEIO SALIO EL ASTIL, & ** LAN%A & EL PENDON.
28882 5ELCID3689 ** LAN%A RECOMBRO & SOBREL SE PARO;
29007 5ELCID3705 GRANT ES ** BILTAN%A DE YFANTES DE CARRION.
29018 5ELCID3706 QUI BUENA DUENA ESCARNE%E & ** DEXA DESPUES,

WORD C# PREFIX CONTEXT

LA (CON'T)

29058 5ELCID3711 GRANDES SON LOS GOZOS EN VALEN%IA ** MAYOR,
WORD #2407 OCCURS 413 TIMES.
INDEX OF DIVERSIFICATION = 69.51 WITH STANDARD DEVIATION OF 84.54

LABARFANEZ 10392 5ELCID1317 AFE MINAYA ********** DO LEGA TAN APUESTO;
WORD #2408 OCCURS 1 TIMES.

LABRADOS 14113 5ELCID1786 DOS TENDALES LA SUFREN, CON ORO SON ********;
WORD #2409 OCCURS 1 TIMES.

LADRONES 2759 5ELCID0349 DOS ******** CONTIGO, ESTOS DE SE@AS PARTES
WORD #2410 OCCURS 1 TIMES.

LAFIZIERADES 28178 5ELCID3597 ESTA LID EN TOLEDO ************, MAS NON QUISIESTES VOS.
WORD #2411 OCCURS 1 TIMES.

LAGAR 18099 5ELCID2290 TRAS VNA VIGA ***** METIOS CON GRANT PAUOR;
26385 5ELCID3365 FUSTED METER TRAS LA VIGA *****,
WORD #2412 OCCURS 2 TIMES.

LAMA 5701 5ELCID0719 A GRANDES VOZES **** EL QUE EN BUEN ORA NASCO:
14597 5ELCID1847 A UOS **** POR SE@OR, & TIENES POR UUESTRO VASSALLO,
WORD #2413 OCCURS 2 TIMES.

LAMADES 25973 5ELCID3310 SIEMPRE EN LAS CORTES PERO MUDO ME *******
WORD #2414 OCCURS 1 TIMES.

LAMADO 10184 5ELCID1289 EL OBISPO DON IERONIMO SO NOMBRE ES ******.
WORD #2415 OCCURS 1 TIMES.

LAMAN 282 5ELCID0035 LOS DE MYO %ID A ALTAS UOZES *****,
5783 5ELCID0731 LOS MOROS ***** MAFOMAT & LOS CHRISTIANOS SANTI YAGUE.
WORD #2416 OCCURS 2 TIMES.

LAMANDO 18219 5ELCID2305 MAGER LOS ESTAN *******, NINGUNO NON RESPONDE.
21832 5ELCID2778 *******: PRIMAS, PRIMAS LUEGO DESCAUALGO,
21897 5ELCID2786 *******: PRIMAS, PRIMAS, DON ELUIRA & DON SOL
WORD #2417 OCCURS 3 TIMES.

LAMAR 27006 5ELCID3450 AGORA BESAREDES SUS MANOS & ***** LAS HEDES SE@ORAS,
WORD #2418 OCCURS 1 TIMES.

LAMAUAN 1900 5ELCID0242 ******* ALA PUERTA, Y SOPIERON EL MANDADO;
WORD #2419 OCCURS 1 TIMES.

LAMO 14994 5ELCID1895 EL REY DON ALFONSSO ESSORA LOS ****,
25031 5ELCID3188 ASO SOBRINO POR NONBREL ****,
WORD #2420 OCCURS 2 TIMES.

LAN 488 5ELCID0062 VEDADA *** CONPRA DENTRO EN BURGOS LA CASA,
WORD #2421 OCCURS 1 TIMES.

LANCAS 6534 5ELCID0834 POR ****** & POR ESPADAS AUEMOS DE GUARIR,
WORD #2422 OCCURS 1 TIMES.

LAN%A 627 5ELCID0079 MARTIN ANTOLINEZ, SODES ARDIDA *****
2794 5ELCID0353 DIOT CON LA ***** ENEL COSTADO, DONT YXIO LA SANGRE,
3521 5ELCID0444 *****, CAUALLEROS BUENOS QUE ACONPANE@ A MINAYA.
3864 5ELCID0489 VENIDES, ALBARFANEZ, UNA FARDIDA *****
3938 5ELCID0500 QUE ENPLEYE LA ***** & AL ESPADA META MANO,
5886 5ELCID0746 LA ***** A QUEBRADA, AL ESPADA METIO MANO,
13589 5ELCID1722 MYO %ID ENPLEO LA *****, AL ESPADA METIO MANO,
18859 5ELCID2386 ALOS PRIMEROS COLPES DOS MOROS MATAUA DE LA *****.
18879 5ELCID2389 DOS MATO CON ***** & V CON EL ESPADA.
19350 5ELCID2451 DELOS COLPES DELA ***** NON AUIE RECABDO;
28446 5ELCID3633 METIOL LA ***** POR LOS PECHOS, QUE NADA NOL VALIO;
28525 5ELCID3642 EL DEXO LA ***** & AL ESPADA METIO MANO,
28791 5ELCID3677 EN VAZIO FUE LA *****, CA EN CARNE NOL TOMO.
28837 5ELCID3683 METIOL POR LA CARNE ADENTRO LA ***** CONEL PENDON,
28859 5ELCID3686 AL TIRAR DELA ***** EN TIERRA LO ECHO,
28870 5ELCID3687 VERMEIO SALIO EL ASTIL, & LA ***** & EL PENDON.
28883 5ELCID3689 LA ***** RECOMBRO & SOBREL SE PARO;
WORD #2423 OCCURS 17 TIMES.
INDEX OF DIVERSIFICATION = 1765.00 WITH STANDARD DEVIATION OF 2937.01

LAN%AS 3322 5ELCID0419 NOTO TREZIENTAS ****** QUE TODAS TIENEN PENDONES.
5679 5ELCID0716 ABAXAN LAS ****** A BUESTAS DELOS PENDONES,
5733 5ELCID0723 TREZIENTAS ****** SON, TODAS TIENEN PENDONES;
5754 5ELCID0726 VERIEDES TANTAS ****** PREMER & AL%AR,
7784 5ELCID0996 ANTES QUE ELLOS LEGEN A LA@O, PRESENTEMOS LES LAS ******;
7869 5ELCID1006 LOS PENDONES & LAS ****** TAN BIEN LAS UAN ENPLEANDO,
11911 5ELCID1510 E EN LAS MANOS ****** QUE PENDONES TRAEN,
28090 5ELCID3586 ESTAS TRES ****** TRAEN SENOS PENDONES;
28269 5ELCID3609 MAS DE VJ ASTAS DE ****** QUE NON LEGASSEN AL MOION.

WORD C# PREFIX CONTEXT

LAN%AS (CON'T)

```
                28326 5ELCID3616 ABAXAN LAS ****** ABUELTAS CON LOS PENDONES,
                28561 5ELCID3646 MARTIN ANTOLINEZ & DIEGO GON%ALEZ FIRIERON SE DELAS ******,
      WORD #2424 OCCURS  11 TIMES.
         INDEX OF DIVERSIFICATION =  2522.90 WITH STANDARD DEVIATION OF  4990.81

LANDA            6118 5ELCID0778 AMYNAYA ALBARFANEZ BIEN ***** EL CAUALLO,
      WORD #2425 OCCURS   1 TIMES.

LANO            28677 5ELCID3661 VN COLPEL DIO DE ****, CON LO AGUDO NOL TOMAUA.
      WORD #2426 OCCURS   1 TIMES.

LA@A             4728 5ELCID0599 BUELTOS SON CON ELLOS POR MEDIO DELA ****.
      WORD #2427 OCCURS   1 TIMES.

LA@O             7780 5ELCID0996 ANTES QUE ELLOS LEGEN A ****, PRESENTEMOS LES LAS LAN%AS;
                 7844 5ELCID1003 ALFONDON DELA CUESTA, %ERCA ES DE ****,
      WORD #2428 OCCURS   2 TIMES.

LARGAS           3811 5ELCID0481 DE OUEIAS & DE VACAS & DE ROPAS & DE OTRAS RIQUIZAS ******.
      WORD #2429 OCCURS   1 TIMES.

LARGO           17170 5ELCID2173 QUE ES ***** DE LENGUA, MAS EN LO AL NON ES TAN PRO.
      WORD #2430 OCCURS   1 TIMES.

LARGOS           6247 5ELCID0795 DE ESCUDOS & DE ARMAS & DE OTROS AUERES ******;
                 6319 5ELCID0804 DIO APARTIR ESTOS DINEROS & ESTOS AUERES ******;
                15556 5ELCID1972 CONDUCHOS ****** EL REY ENBIAR MANDAUA
                17835 5ELCID2256 MANTOS & PELLI%ONES & OTROS VESTIDOS ******;
                19648 5ELCID2490 EOTRAS AZEMILLAS & CAMELOS ******
                23045 5ELCID2936 MER%ED, REY ALFONSSO, DE ****** REYNOS AUOS DIZEN SE@OR
      WORD #2431 OCCURS   6 TIMES.
         INDEX OF DIVERSIFICATION =  3358.60 WITH STANDARD DEVIATION OF  3496.90

LAS                72 5ELCID0010 ALLI PIENSSAN DE AGUIIAR, ALLI SUELTAN *** RIENDAS.
                  127 5ELCID0017 BURGESES & BURGESAS POR *** FINIESTRAS SON,
                  222 5ELCID0028 E AUN DEMAS LOS CUERPOS & *** ALMAS.
                  227 5ELCID0029 GRANDE DUELO AUIEN *** YENTES CHRISTIANAS;
                  362 5ELCID0045 SI NON, PERDERIEMOS LOS AUERES & *** CASAS,
                  677 5ELCID0086 YNCAMOS *** DARENA, CA BIEN SERAN PESADAS,
                  830 5ELCID0106 RACHEL & VIDAS, AMOS ME DAT *** MANOS,
                  853 5ELCID0109 EL CAMPEADOR POR *** PARIAS FUE ENTRADO,
                  901 5ELCID0116 AQUELAS NON *** PUEDE LEUAR, SINON, SER YEN VENTADAS;
                  911 5ELCID0117 EL CAMPEADOR DEXAR *** HA EN UUESTRA MANO,
                  925 5ELCID0119 PRENDED *** ARCHAS & METED LAS EN UUESTRO SALUO;
                  929 5ELCID0119 PRENDED LAS ARCHAS & METED *** EN UUESTRO SALUO;
                  938 5ELCID0120 CON GRAND IURA METED Y *** FES AMOS,
                  943 5ELCID0121 QUE NON *** CATEDES EN TODO AQUESTE A@O.
                  990 5ELCID0127 ESTAS ARCHAS PRENDAMOS *** AMAS,
                  994 5ELCID0128 EN LOGAR *** METAMOS QUE NON SEAN VENTADAS.
                 1118 5ELCID0144 POR ADUZIR *** ARCHAS & METER LAS EN UUESTRO SALUO,
                 1122 5ELCID0144 POR ADUZIR LAS ARCHAS & METER *** EN UUESTRO SALUO,
                 1141 5ELCID0147 *** ARCHAS ADUCHAS, PRENDET SEYES %IENTOS MARCOS.
                 1192 5ELCID0153 ASSI COMMO ENTRARON, AL %ID BESARON LE *** MANOS.
                 1240 5ELCID0159 DON RACHEL & VIDAS A MYO %ID BESARON LE *** MANOS.
                 1278 5ELCID0164 QUE SI ANTES *** CATASSEN QUE FUESSEN PERIURADOS,
                 1297 5ELCID0166 DIXO MARTIN ANTOLINEZ:  CARGEN *** ARCHAS PRIUADO.
                 1305 5ELCID0167 LEUALDAS, RACHEL & VIDAS, PONED *** EN UUESTRO SALUO;
                 1334 5ELCID0171 NON *** PODIEN PONER EN SOMO MAGER ERAU ESFOR%ADOS.
                 1376 5ELCID0176 DE CASTIELLA UOS YDES PORA *** YENTES ESTRANAS.
                 1417 5ELCID0181 SIUOS LA ADUXIER DALLA; SI NON, CONTALDA SOBRE *** ARCAS. . . .
                 1482 5ELCID0189 YA DON RACHEL & VIDAS, EN UUESTRAS MANOS SON *** ARCAS;
                 1782 5ELCID0227 SUELTAN *** RIENDAS & PIENSSAN DE AGUIJAR.
                 2017 5ELCID0254 AELLA & ASUS FIJAS & ASUS DUENAS SIRUADES *** EST A@O.
                 2026 5ELCID0255 DUES FIJAS DEXO NI@AS & PRENDET *** EN LOS BRA%OS;
                 2053 5ELCID0259 BIEN *** ABASTAD, YO ASSI UOS LO MANDO;
                 2088 5ELCID0263 SE@AS DUE@AS *** TRAEN & ADUZEN LAS ADELANT.
                 2092 5ELCID0263 SE@AS DUE@AS LAS TRAEN & ADUZEN *** ADELANT.
                 2107 5ELCID0265 LORAUA DELOS OIOS, QUISOL BESAR *** MANOS:
                 2176 5ELCID0274 ENCLINO *** MANOS EN LA SU BARBA VELIDA,
                 2187 5ELCID0275 ALAS SUS FIJAS ENBRA%O *** PRENDIA,
                 2194 5ELCID0276 LEGOLAS AL CORA%ON, CA MUCHO *** QUERIA.
                 2273 5ELCID0286 TANEN *** CAMPA@AS EN SAN PERO A CLAMOR.
                 2808 5ELCID0354 CORRIO LA SANGRE POR EL ASTIL AYUSO, *** MANOS SE OUO DE VNTAR,
                 2847 5ELCID0360 QUEBRANTESTE *** PUERTAS & SAQUESTE LOS PADRES SANTOS.
                 2946 5ELCID0371 E EL ALAS NI@AS TORNO *** ACATAR:
                 3035 5ELCID0382 DIOS QUE NOS DIO *** ALMAS, CONSEIO NOS DARA.
                 3109 5ELCID0391 SOLTARON *** RIENDAS, PIESSAN DE ANDAR;
                 3163 5ELCID0398 DE DIESTRO A LILON *** TORRES, QUE MOROS LAS HAN;
                 3167 5ELCID0398 DE DIESTRO A LILON LAS TORRES, QUE MOROS *** HAN;
                 3313 5ELCID0418 SIN *** PEONADAS & OMNES VALIENTES QUE SON,
                 3544 5ELCID0446 FITA AYUSO & POR GUADALFAIARA, FATA ALCALA LEGEN *** ALGARAS,
                 3550 5ELCID0447 E BIEN ACOIAN TODAS *** GANAN%IAS,
                 3637 5ELCID0459 ABREN *** PUERTAS, DE FUERA SALTO DAUAN,
                 3654 5ELCID0461 TODOS SON EXIDOS, *** PUERTAS DEXADAS AN ABIERTAS
```

WORD C# PREFIX CONTEXT

LAS (CON'T)

3667 5ELCID0463 *** YENTES DE FUERA TODAS SON DE RAMADAS.
3724 5ELCID0470 MIO %ID RUY DIAZ POR *** PUERTAS ENTRAUA,
3794 5ELCID0480 TANTO TRAEN *** GRANDES GANA%IAS, MUCHOS GA@ADOS.
4198 5ELCID0534 %IENTO MOROS & %IENTO MORAS QUIERO *** QUITAR,
4252 5ELCID0541 LOS MOROS & *** MORAS BENDIZIENDOL ESTAN.
4263 5ELCID0543 TRO%EN *** ALCARIAS & YUAN ADELANT,
4269 5ELCID0544 POR *** CUEUAS DANQUITA ELLOS PASSANDO UAN,
4276 5ELCID0545 PASSARON *** AGUAS, ENTRARON AL CAMPO DE TORAN%IO,
4300 5ELCID0548 GRANDES SON *** GANAN%IAS QUE PRISO POR LA TIERRA DO UA.
4375 5ELCID0557 BIEN PUEBLA EL OTERO, FIRME PRENDE *** POSADAS,
4533 5ELCID0576 DEXA VNA TIENDA FITA & *** OTRAS LEUAUA,
4543 5ELCID0578 *** LORIGAS VESTIDAS & %INTAS LAS ESPADAS,
4548 5ELCID0578 LAS LORIGAS VESTIDAS & %INTAS *** ESPADAS,
4575 5ELCID0582 *** OTRAS A BES LIEUA, VNA TIENDA A DEXADA.
4676 5ELCID0593 ABIERTAS DEXAN *** PUERTAS QUE NINGUNO NON LAS GUARDA.
4681 5ELCID0593 ABIERTAS DEXAN LAS PUERTAS QUE NINGUNO NON *** GUARDA.
4796 5ELCID0608 *** ESPADAS DESNUDAS, A LA PUERTA SE PARAUAN.
4892 5ELCID0619 LOS MOROS & *** MORAS VENDER NON LOS PODREMOS,
5185 5ELCID0656 FINCARON *** TIENDAS & PRENDEND LAS POSADAS,
5189 5ELCID0656 FINCARON LAS TIENDAS & PRENDEND *** POSADAS,
5198 5ELCID0658 *** AROBDAS, QUE LOS MOROS SACAN, DE DIA
5216 5ELCID0660 MUCHAS SON *** AROBDAS & GRANDE ES EL ALMOFALLA.
5380 5ELCID0679 TODOS LOS MOROS & *** MORAS DE FUERA LOS MANDA ECHAR,
5494 5ELCID0693 ABRIERON *** PUERTAS, FUERA VN SALTO DAN;
5502 5ELCID0694 VIERON LO *** AROBDAS DELOS MOROS, AL ALMOFALLA SEUAN TORNAR.
5555 5ELCID0700 *** AZES DE LOS MOROS YAS MUEUEN ADELANT,
5678 5ELCID0716 ABAXAN *** LAN%AS A BUESTAS DELOS PENDONES,
5685 5ELCID0717 ENCLINARON *** CARAS DE SUSO DE LOS ARZONES,
6038 5ELCID0766 *** CARBONCLAS DEL YELMO ECHO GELAS APARTE,
6458 5ELCID0824 QUE RUEGEN POR MI *** NOCHES & LOS DIAS;
6578 5ELCID0840 MOROS DE *** FRONTERAS & VNAS YENTES ESTRANAS;
6880 5ELCID0879 BESA UOS LOS PIES & *** MANOS AMAS,
6988 5ELCID0893 SUELTO LES LOS CUERPOS & QUITO LES *** HEREDADES.
6992 5ELCID0894 BESO LE *** MANOS MINAYA ALBARFANEZ:
7136 5ELCID0913 TODAS ESSAS TIERRAS TODAS *** PREAUA,
7169 5ELCID0918 NON SON EN CUENTA, SABET, *** PEONADAS.
7259 5ELCID0931 QUE ALBARFANEZ PAGO *** MILL MISSAS,
7300 5ELCID0936 TIERRAS DALCANZ NEGRAS *** VA PARANDO,
7322 5ELCID0939 HYA VA EL MANDADO POR *** TIERRAS TODAS,
7458 5ELCID0957 LEGARON *** NUEUAS ALCONDE DE BAR%ILONA,
7518 5ELCID0964 AGORA CORREM *** TIERRAS QUE EN MI ENPARA ESTAN;
7702 5ELCID0986 APRIESSA UOS GUARNID & METEDOS EN *** ARMAS.
7743 5ELCID0991 APRETAD LOS CAUALLOS, & BISTADES *** ARMAS.
7757 5ELCID0993 ELAS SIELLAS CO%ERAS & *** %INCHAS AMOIADAS;
7783 5ELCID0996 ANTES QUE ELLOS LEGEN A LA@O, PRESENTEMOS LES *** LAN%AS;
7821 5ELCID1001 *** ARMAS AUIEN PRESAS & SEDIEN SOBRE LOS CAUALLOS.
7868 5ELCID1006 LOS PENDONES & *** LAN%AS TAN BIEN LAS UAN ENPLEANDO,
7872 5ELCID1006 LOS PENDONES & LAS LAN%AS TAN BIEN *** UAN ENPLEANDO,
7957 5ELCID1016 PLOGO A MYO %ID, CA GRANDES SON *** GANAN%IAS.
8330 5ELCID1059 POR QUE EL CONDE DON REMONT TAN BIEN BOLUIE *** MANOS.
8344 5ELCID1061 MANDAD NOS DAR *** BESTIAS & CAUALGEREMOS PRIUADO;
8576 5ELCID1089 E DEXADO A HUESCA & *** TIERRAS DE MONT ALUAN.
8610 5ELCID1093 TIERRAS DE BORRIANA TODAS CONQUISTAS *** HA.
8973 5ELCID1142 ARANCAR SE *** ESTACAS & ACOSTAR SE ATODAS PARTES LOS TENDALES.
9026 5ELCID1149 GRANDES SON *** GANAN%IAS QUE MIO %ID FECHAS HA.
9065 5ELCID1154 *** NUEUAS DE MYO %ID, SABET, SONANDO VAN,
9111 5ELCID1159 DAUAN SUS CORREDORES & FAZIEN *** TRASNOCHADAS,
9137 5ELCID1163 GANARON PENA CADIELLA, *** EXIDAS & LAS ENTRADAS.
9140 5ELCID1163 GANARON PENA CADIELLA, LAS EXIDAS & *** ENTRADAS.
9177 5ELCID1168 E DURMIENDO LOS DIAS & *** NOCHES TRANOCHANDO,
9206 5ELCID1172 TAIAUA LES *** HUERTAS & FAZIA LES GRAND MAL,
9449 5ELCID1201 QUANDO VIO MYO %ID *** GENTES IUNTADAS, COMPE%OS DE PAGAR.
9712 5ELCID1235 *** NUEUAS DEL CAUALLERO YAVEDES DO LEGAUAN.
10100 5ELCID1279 LA MUGIER DE MYO %ID & SUS FIJAS *** YFFANTES
10201 5ELCID1292 *** PROUEZAS DE MYO %ID ANDAUALAS DEMANDANDO,
10341 5ELCID1310 DEXARE UOS *** POSADAS, NON LAS QUIERO CONTAR.
10344 5ELCID1310 DEXARE UOS LAS POSADAS, NON *** QUIERO CONTAR.
10414 5ELCID1320 BESAUA LE *** MANOS & FABLO TAN APUESTO:
10429 5ELCID1322 BESAUA UOS *** MANOS MYO %ID LIDIADOR,
10437 5ELCID1323 LOS PIES & *** MANOS, COMMO ATAN BUEN SE@OR,
10521 5ELCID1333 E FIZO %INCO LIDES CAMPALES & TODAS *** ARRANCO.
10525 5ELCID1334 GRANDES SON *** GANAN%IAS QUEL DIO EL CRIADOR,
10533 5ELCID1335 FEUOS AQUI *** SE@AS, VERDAD UOS DIGO YO:
10554 5ELCID1338 BESA UOS *** MANOS & QUE LOS PRENDADES UOS;
10684 5ELCID1353 SALDRIEN DEL MONESTERIO DO ELLE *** DEXO,
10733 5ELCID1359 CATAD COMMO *** SIRUADES UOS & EL CAMPEADOR.
10755 5ELCID1362 ATODAS *** ESCUELLAS QUE A EL DIZEN SE@OR
10797 5ELCID1367 MYNAYA ALBARFANEZ *** MANOS LE BESO.
10842 5ELCID1373 MUCHO CRE%EN *** NUEUAS DE MYO %ID EL CAMPEADOR,
10911 5ELCID1381 SI LEUAREDES *** DUENAS, SIRUAN LAS ASU SABOR,
10914 5ELCID1381 SI LEUAREDES LAS DUENAS, SIRUAN *** ASU SABOR,
11128 5ELCID1408 QUE SU MUGIER & SUS FIJAS EL REY SUELTAS ME *** HA,
11161 5ELCID1412 HYTODAS *** DUE@AS CON ELLAS QUANTAS BUENAS ELLAS HAN.
11266 5ELCID1425 E ALAS OTRAS DUE@AS QUE *** SIRUEN DELANT,

WORD C# PREFIX CONTEXT

LAS (CON'T)

```
11295 5ELCID1429 QUANDO ESTAS DUE@AS ADOBADAS *** HAN,
11404 5ELCID1443 POR MI AL CAMPEADOR *** MANOS LE BESAD
11471 5ELCID1452 FELOS EN MEDINA *** DUENAS & ALBARFANEZ.
11752 5ELCID1491 PASSAN *** MONTANAS, QUE SON FIERAS & GRANDES,
11909 5ELCID1510 E EN *** MANOS LANZAS QUE PENDONES TRAEN,
12183 5ELCID1547 *** NOCHES & LOS DIAS LAS DUENAS AGUARDANDO.
12188 5ELCID1547 LAS NOCHES & LOS DIAS *** DUENAS AGUARDANDO.
12233 5ELCID1553 AVN *** FERRADURAS QUITAR GELAS MANDAUA;
12244 5ELCID1554 AMYNAYA & ALAS DUE@AS, DIOS COMMO *** ONDRAUA
12375 5ELCID1571 QUE GUARDASSEN EL ALCAZAR & *** OTRAS TORRES ALTAS
12381 5ELCID1572 E TODAS *** PUERTAS & LAS EXIDAS & LAS ENTRADAS,
12384 5ELCID1572 E TODAS LAS PUERTAS & *** EXIDAS & LAS ENTRADAS,
12387 5ELCID1572 E TODAS LAS PUERTAS & LAS EXIDAS & *** ENTRADAS,
12434 5ELCID1577 DELANTE SU MUGIER & DE SUS FIJAS QUERIE TENER *** ARMAS.
12437 5ELCID1578 REZEBIDAS *** DUENAS A VNA GRANT ONDRANZA,
12477 5ELCID1583 REZIBIR SALIEN *** DUENAS & AL BUENO DE MINAYA.
12608 5ELCID1599 ALA MADRE & ALAS FIJAS BIEN *** ABRAZAUA,
12620 5ELCID1601 TODAS *** SUS MESNADAS EN GRANT DELENT ESTAUAN,
12673 5ELCID1608 MADRE & FIJAS *** MANOS LE BESAUAN.
12693 5ELCID1611 ALA *** SUBIE ENEL MAS ALTO LOGAR;
12728 5ELCID1616 ALZAN *** MANOS PORA DIOS ROGAR,
12823 5ELCID1627 ENTRARON SOBRE MAR, EN *** BARCAS SON METIDOS,
12838 5ELCID1629 ARRIBADO AN *** NAUES, FUERA ERAN EXIDOS,
12853 5ELCID1631 FINCARON *** TIENDAS, & POSAN LAS YENTES DESCREYDAS.
12857 5ELCID1631 FINCARON LAS TIENDAS, & POSAN *** YENTES DESCREYDAS.
12915 5ELCID1638 MIS FIJAS & MI MUGIER QUE *** TENGO ACA;
12927 5ELCID1640 ENTRARE EN *** ARMAS, NON LO PODRE DEXAR;
12946 5ELCID1642 EN ESTAS TIERRAS AGENAS VERAN *** MORADAS COMMO SE FAZEN,
13068 5ELCID1657 FINCADAS SON *** TIENDAS & PAREZEN LOS ALUORES,
13175 5ELCID1670 ALEGRE SON *** DUENAS, PERDIENDO VAN EL PAUOR.
13188 5ELCID1672 POR *** HUERTAS ADENTRO ESTAN SINES PAUOR.
13203 5ELCID1674 PRESTAS SON *** MES@ADAS DE LAS YENTES CHRISTIANAS,
13206 5ELCID1674 PRESTAS SON LAS MES@ADAS DE *** YENTES CHRISTIANAS,
13243 5ELCID1679 BIEN FATA *** TIENDAS DURA AQUESTE ALCAZ,
13481 5ELCID1709 *** FERIDAS PRIMERAS QUE LAS AYA YO OTORGADAS.
13485 5ELCID1709 LAS FERIDAS PRIMERAS QUE *** AYA YO OTORGADAS.
13502 5ELCID1711 SALIDOS SON TODOS ARMADOS POR *** TORRES DE VANZIA,
13713 5ELCID1738 *** OTRAS GANANZIAS NON AUYA RECABDO.
13776 5ELCID1746 REZIBIEN LO *** DUE@AS QUE LO ESTAN ESPERANDO.
13873 5ELCID1758 *** DUE@AS & LAS FIJAS & LA MUGIER QUE VALE ALGO
13876 5ELCID1758 LAS DUE@AS & *** FIJAS & LA MUGIER QUE VALE ALGO
13931 5ELCID1765 QUIERO *** CASAR CON DE AQUESTOS MYOS VASSALLOS;
13970 5ELCID1769 LEUANTARON SE TODAS & BESARON LE *** MANOS,
14176 5ELCID1794 QUANDO ES FARTO DE LIDIAR CON AMAS *** SUS MANOS,
14218 5ELCID1799 ALEGRES SON POR VALENZIA *** YENTES CHRISTIANAS,
14240 5ELCID1802 E TODAS *** OTRAS DUENAS QUE TIENEN POR CASADAS.
14325 5ELCID1812 POR QUE ASSI *** ENBIO DOND ELLAS SON PAGADAS,
14373 5ELCID1818 CON SALUDES DEL ZID QUE *** MANOS LE BESAUA:
14415 5ELCID1823 ANDAN LOS DIAS & *** NOCHES, & PASSADA HAN LA SIERRA,
14423 5ELCID1824 QUE *** OTRAS TIERRAS PARTE.
14437 5ELCID1826 PASSANDO VAN *** SIERRAS & LOS MONTES & LAS AGUAS,
14443 5ELCID1826 PASSANDO VAN LAS SIERRAS & LOS MONTES & *** AGUAS,
14637 5ELCID1852 *** GANANZIAS QUE FIZO MUCHO SON SOBEIANAS,
14659 5ELCID1854 E EMBIA UOS DOZIENTOS CAUALLOS, & BESA UOS *** MANOS.
14694 5ELCID1858 ESTO PLOGO A MUCHOS & BESARON LE *** MANOS.
14851 5ELCID1877 BESARON LE *** MANOS & ENTRARON A POSAR;
14880 5ELCID1881 *** NUEUAS DEL ZID MUCHO VAN ADELANT,
15181 5ELCID1921 COMMO SON *** SALUDES DE ALFONSSO MYO SENOR.
15442 5ELCID1956 ESCRIUIEN CARTAS, BIEN *** SELLO,
15448 5ELCID1957 CON DOS CAUALLEROS LUEGO *** ENBIO:
15465 5ELCID1959 AL REY ONDRADO DELANT LE ECHARON *** CARTAS;
15468 5ELCID1960 QUANDO *** VIO, DE CORAZON SE PAGA:
15486 5ELCID1962 SEAN *** VISTAS DESTAS IIJ SEMANAS;
15511 5ELCID1965 DELLA PART & DELLA PORA *** VISTAS SE ADOBAUAN;
15639 5ELCID1983 NON SON EN CUENTA, SABET, *** CASTELLANAS.
15642 5ELCID1984 SUELTAN *** RIENDAS, ALAS VISTAS SEUAN A DELI@ADAS.
15660 5ELCID1986 NON LO DETARDA, PORA *** VISTAS SE ADOBO;
15778 5ELCID2002 *** PUERTAS DEL ALCAZAR QUE NON SE ABRIESSEN DE DIA NIN DE NOCH,
15812 5ELCID2005 E OTRAS DUE@AS QUE *** SIRUEN ASU SABOR;
15864 5ELCID2012 HYAS VA PORA *** VISTAS QUE CON EL REY PARO.
15939 5ELCID2021 LOS YNOIOS & *** MANOS EN TIERRA LOS FINCO,
15945 5ELCID2022 *** YERBAS DEL CAMPO A DIENTES LAS TOMO,
15951 5ELCID2022 LAS YERBAS DEL CAMPO A DIENTES *** TOMO,
15991 5ELCID2028 BESAD *** MANOS, CA LOS PIES NO;
16080 5ELCID2039 HYNOIOS FITOS *** MANOS LE BESO,
16333 5ELCID2072 OYD ME, *** ESCUELLAS, CUENDES & YFANZONES
16365 5ELCID2076 QUE *** DEDES POR MUGIERES ALOS YFANTES DE CARRION.
16383 5ELCID2078 ELLOS UOS *** PIDEN & MANDO UOS LO YO.
16407 5ELCID2081 DANDOS ***, MYO ZID, SI UOS VALA EL CRIADOR
16450 5ELCID2086 HYO *** ENGENDRE AMAS & CRIASTES LAS UOS
16455 5ELCID2086 HYO LAS ENGENDRE AMAS & CRIASTES *** UOS
16475 5ELCID2089 DAD *** AQUI QUISIEREDES UOS, CA YO PAGADO SO.
16501 5ELCID2092 BAN BESAR *** MANOS ALQUE EN ORA BUENA NAZIO;
16509 5ELCID2093 CAMEARON *** ESPADAS ANTEL REY DON ALFONSSO.
```

WORD C# PREFIX CONTEXT

LAS (CON'T)

```
16545 5ELCID2097 DAQUI *** PRENDO POR MIS MANOS DON ELUIRA & DONA SOL,
16564 5ELCID2099 HYO *** CASO A UUESTRAS FIJAS CON UUESTRO AMOR,
16625 5ELCID2106 LOS YERNOS & *** FIJAS TODOS UUESTROS FIJOS SON:
16642 5ELCID2108 MYO %ID GELOS RE%IBE, *** MANOS LE BESO:
16665 5ELCID2111 *** PALABRAS SON PUESTAS QUE OTRO DIA MA@ANA
16851 5ELCID2133 DAD MANERO A QUI *** DE, QUANDO UOS LAS TOMADES;
16855 5ELCID2133 DAD MANERO A QUI LAS DE, QUANDO UOS *** TOMADES;
16886 5ELCID2137 ASSI COMMO YO *** PRENDO DAQUENT, COMMO SI FOSSE DELANT,
17050 5ELCID2159 BESAR *** MANOS, ESPEDIR SE DE REY ALFONSSO:
17114 5ELCID2166 GRANDES SON *** YENTES QUE VAN CONEL CANPEADOR.
17312 5ELCID2190 BESARON LE *** MANOS LA MUGIER & LAS FIJAS AMAS,
17317 5ELCID2190 BESARON LE LAS MANOS LA MUGIER & *** FIJAS AMAS,
17321 5ELCID2191 ETODAS *** DUE@AS QUE LAS SIRUEN:
17324 5ELCID2191 ETODAS LAS DUE@AS QUE *** SIRUEN:
17591 5ELCID2225 ALOS YFANTES DE CARRION DAD *** CON UUESTRA MANO,
17647 5ELCID2233 QUE *** TOMASSEDES POR MUGIERES A ONDRA & A RECABDO.
17657 5ELCID2234 AMOS *** RE%IBEN DAMOR & DE GRADO,
17757 5ELCID2247 TORNAN SE CON *** DUE@AS, A VALEN%IA AN ENTRADO;
17765 5ELCID2248 RICAS FUERON *** BODAS EN EL ALCA%AR ONDRADO,
17793 5ELCID2251 QUINZE DIAS CONPLIDOS DURARON EN *** BODAS,
17892 5ELCID2264 EA TODAS *** DUE@AS & ALOS FIJOS DALGO;
17986 5ELCID2276 *** COPLAS DESTE CANTAR AQUIS VAN ACABANDO.
18525 5ELCID2344 ESTO VAN DIZIENDO & *** YENTES SE ALEGANDO,
18758 5ELCID2373 MI ORDEN & MIS MANOS QUERRIA *** ONDRAR,
18779 5ELCID2376 SI PLOGIESSE ADIOS QUERRIA *** ENSAYAR,
18899 5ELCID2391 DAUAN LE GRANDES COLPES, MAS NOL FALSSAN *** ARMAS.
18936 5ELCID2396 EN *** AZES PRIMERAS EL CAMPEADOR ENTRAUA,
18971 5ELCID2400 VERIEDES QUEBRAR TANTAS CUERDAS & ARRANCAR SE *** ESTACAS
19148 5ELCID2422 *** CARBONCLAS DEL YELMO TOLLIDAS GELA HA,
19453 5ELCID2465 TODAS *** GANAN%IAS A VALEN%IA SON LEGADAS;
19588 5ELCID2482 SOBEIANAS SON *** GANAN%IAS QUETODOS AN GANADAS;
19693 5ELCID2497 ARRANCO *** LIDES COMMO PLAZE AL CRIADOR,
20044 5ELCID2544 DIGAMOS QUE *** LEUAREMOS ATIERRAS DE CARRION,
20050 5ELCID2545 ENSE@AR *** HEMOS DO LAS HEREDADES SON.
20053 5ELCID2545 ENSE@AR LAS HEMOS DO *** HEREDADES SON.
20057 5ELCID2546 SACAR *** HEMOS DE VALEN%IA, DE PODER DEL CAMPEADOR;
20097 5ELCID2551 ESCARNIREMOS *** FIJAS DEL CANPEADOR.
20125 5ELCID2555 ASSI *** ESCARNIREMOS ALAS FIJAS DEL CAMPEADOR,
20185 5ELCID2563 LEUAR *** HEMOS A NUESTRAS TIERRAS DE CARRION,
20193 5ELCID2564 METER *** HEMOS EN LAS VILLAS
20196 5ELCID2564 METER LAS HEMOS EN *** VILLAS
20301 5ELCID2576 BIEN LO SABEDES UOS QUE *** GANE AGUISA DE VARON;
20318 5ELCID2578 ALLA ME LEUADES *** TELAS DEL CORA%ON.
20351 5ELCID2582 SI BIEN *** SERUIDES, YO UOS RENDRE BUEN GALARDON.
20368 5ELCID2584 AQUI RE%IBEN *** FIJAS DEL CAMPEADOR;
20394 5ELCID2588 GRANDES SON *** NUEUAS POR VALEN%IA LA MAYOR,
20537 5ELCID2607 AL PADRE & ALA MADRE *** MANOS LES BESAUAN;
20542 5ELCID2608 AMOS *** BENDIXIERON & DIERON LES SU GRA%IA.
20618 5ELCID2617 NOS PUEDE REPENTIR, QUE CASADAS *** HA AMAS.
20647 5ELCID2621 VERAS *** HEREDADES QUE A MIS FIJAS DADAS SON;
20692 5ELCID2627 HYR *** HEMOS VER ATIERRAS DE CARRION.
20730 5ELCID2632 EL PADRE CON *** FIJAS LORAN DE CORA%ON,
20782 5ELCID2639 DELO QUE OUIEREN HUEBOS SIRUAN *** ASO SABOR,
20787 5ELCID2640 DESI ESCURRA *** FASTA MEDINA POR LA MI AMOR;
21116 5ELCID2683 POCO PRE%IO *** NUEUAS DELOS DE CARRION.
21233 5ELCID2698 LOS MONTES SON ALTOS, *** RAMAS PUIAN CON LAS NUES,
21237 5ELCID2698 LOS MONTES SON ALTOS, LAS RAMAS PUIAN CON *** NUES,
21285 5ELCID2705 MANDARON CARGAR *** AZEMILAS CON GRANDES AUERES,
21402 5ELCID2721 PARAN *** EN CUERPOS & EN CAMISAS & EN %ICLATONES.
21420 5ELCID2723 EN MANO PRENDEN *** %INCHAS FUERTES & DURADORES.
21428 5ELCID2724 QUANDO ESTO VIERON *** DUE@AS, FABLAUA DO@A SOL:
21457 5ELCID2728 CORTANDOS *** CABECAS, MARTIRES SEREMOS NOS:
21503 5ELCID2734 LO QUE RUEGAN *** DUENAS NON LES HA NINGUN PRO.
21519 5ELCID2736 CON *** %INCHAS CORREDIZAS MAIAN LAS TAN SIN SABOR;
21523 5ELCID2736 CON LAS %INCHAS CORREDIZAS MAIAN *** TAN SIN SABOR;
21528 5ELCID2737 CON *** ESPUELAS AGUDAS, DON ELLAS AN MAL SABOR,
21537 5ELCID2738 RONPIEN *** CAMISAS & LAS CARNES AELLAS AMAS ADOS;
21540 5ELCID2738 RONPIEN LAS CAMISAS & *** CARNES AELLAS AMAS ADOS;
21575 5ELCID2743 TANTO *** MAIARON QUE SIN COSIMENTE SON;
21583 5ELCID2744 SANGRIENTAS EN *** CAMISAS & TODOS LOS CICLATONES.
21613 5ELCID2748 POR MUERTAS *** DEXARON ENEL ROBREDRO DE CORPES.
21624 5ELCID2749 LEUARON LES LOS MANTOS & *** PIELES ARMINAS,
21629 5ELCID2750 MAS DEXAN *** MARIDAS EN BRIALES & EN CAMISAS,
21649 5ELCID2752 POR MUERTAS *** DEXARON, SABED, QUE NON POR BIUAS.
21675 5ELCID2755 POR MUERTAS *** DEXARON,
21701 5ELCID2759 NON *** DEUIEMOS TOMAR POR VARRAGANAS,
21845 5ELCID2780 YA PRIMAS, *** MIS PRIMAS, DON ELUIRA & DO@A SOL,
21890 5ELCID2785 PARTIERON SE LE *** TELLAS DE DENTRO DE LOS CORA%ONES,
22025 5ELCID2802 MUCHO SON LAZRADAS & AMAS *** FARTO.
22028 5ELCID2803 TANTO *** ROGO FATA QUE LAS ASSENTO.
22032 5ELCID2803 TANTO LAS ROGO FATA QUE *** ASSENTO.
22044 5ELCID2805 FATA QUE ESFUER%AN, & AMAS *** TOMO
22050 5ELCID2806 E PRIUADO ENEL CAUALLO *** CAUALGO;
22058 5ELCID2807 CON EL SO MANTO A AMAS *** CUBRIO,
```

WORD C# PREFIX CONTEXT

LAS (CON'T)

```
22069 5ELCID2808 EL CAUALLO PRISO POR LA RIENDA & LUEGO DENT *** PARTIO,
22099 5ELCID2812 ALA TORRE DE DON VRRACA ELLE *** DEXO.
22138 5ELCID2818 EN SANTESTEUAN DENTRO *** METIO,
22145 5ELCID2819 QUANTO EL MEIOR PUEDE ALLI *** ONDRO.
22252 5ELCID2834 QUE AMIS FIJAS BIEN *** CASARE YO
22318 5ELCID2842 APIRESSA CAUALGAN, LOS DIAS & *** NOCHES ANDAN;
22484 5ELCID2863 LORAUAN DELOS OIOS *** DUE@AS & ALBARFANEZ,
22493 5ELCID2864 E PERO VERMUEZ OTRO TANTO *** HA;
22566 5ELCID2874 E MINAYA CON *** DUE@AS YUA CABADELANT.
22667 5ELCID2888 MYO %ID ASUS FIJAS YUA *** ABRA%AR,
22670 5ELCID2889 BESANDO *** AAMAS, TORNOS DE SONRRISAR:
22717 5ELCID2895 BESARON *** MANOS LAS FIJAS AL PADRE.
22719 5ELCID2895 BESARON LAS MANOS *** FIJAS AL PADRE.
22836 5ELCID2909 QUANDO *** HAN DEXADAS AGRANT DESONOR,
22934 5ELCID2921 NOS DAN VAGAR LOS DIAS & *** NOCHES.
23053 5ELCID2937 LOS PIES & *** MANOS VOS BESA EL CAMPEADOR;
23112 5ELCID2945 DESENPARADAS *** DEXARON ENEL ROBREDO DE CORPES,
23136 5ELCID2948 POR ESTO UOS BESA *** MANOS, COMMO VASSALLO A SE@OR,
23685 5ELCID3017 QUE BESASSE *** MANOS AL REY SO SE@OR:
23865 5ELCID3040 BESA UOS *** MANOS, & MIS FIJAS AMAS ADOS,
23925 5ELCID3048 *** MIS COMPA@AS ESTA NOCHE LEGARAN;
24104 5ELCID3073 VELMEZES VESTIDOS POR SUFRIR *** GUARNIZONES,
24108 5ELCID3074 DE SUSO *** LORIGAS TAN BLANCAS COMMO EL SOL;
24116 5ELCID3075 SOBRE *** LORIGAS ARMINOS & PELI%ONES,
24125 5ELCID3076 E QUE NON PARESCAN *** ARMAS, BIEN PRESOS LOS CORDONES;
24133 5ELCID3077 SOLOS MANTOS *** ESPADAS DUL%ES & TAIADORES;
24221 5ELCID3088 CON ORO & CON PLATA TODAS *** PRESAS SON,
24249 5ELCID3092 SOBRESTO VNA PIEL VERMEIA, *** BANCAS DORO SON,
24730 5ELCID3150 CA UOS *** CASASTES, REY, SABREDES QUE FER OY;
24748 5ELCID3152 HYO BIEN *** QUERIA DALMA & DE CORA%ON,
24764 5ELCID3154 ESTAS YO *** GANE AGUISA DE VARON,
24876 5ELCID3168 E QUANDO *** TOUIERE, PARTIR SEA LA CORT;
24915 5ELCID3173 QUANDO *** DEMANDA & DELLAS HA SABOR,
24928 5ELCID3175 SACARON *** ESPADAS COLADO & TIZON,
24934 5ELCID3176 PUSIERON *** EN MANO DEL REY SO SE@OR;
24942 5ELCID3177 SACA *** ESPADAS & RELUMBRA TODA LA CORT,
24949 5ELCID3179 *** MA%ANAS & LOS ARRIAZES TODOS DORO SON.
24967 5ELCID3180 RE%IBIO *** ESPADAS, LAS MANOS LE BESO,
24969 5ELCID3180 RE%IBIO LAS ESPADAS, *** MANOS LE BESO,
24980 5ELCID3182 EN *** MANOS LAS TIENE & AMAS LAS CATO;
24982 5ELCID3182 EN LAS MANOS *** TIENE & AMAS LAS CATO;
24986 5ELCID3182 EN LAS MANOS LAS TIENE & AMAS *** CATO;
24996 5ELCID3183 NOS LE PUEDEN CAMEAR, CA EL %ID BIEN *** CONNOS%E;
25521 5ELCID3250 ESTAS APRE%IADURAS MYO %ID PRESAS *** HA,
25525 5ELCID3251 SOS OMNES *** TIENEN & DELLAS PENSSARAN.
25602 5ELCID3260  A QUEM DESCUBRIESTES *** TELAS DEL CORA%ON?
25624 5ELCID3263 QUANDO *** NON QUERIEDES, YA CANES TRAYDORES,
25632 5ELCID3264 POR QUE *** SACAUADES DE VALEN%IA SUS HONORES?
25640 5ELCID3265 A QUE *** FIRIESTES A %INCHAS & A ESPOLONES?
25648 5ELCID3266 SOLAS *** DEXASTES ENEL ROBREDO DE CORPES,
25741 5ELCID3278 DERECHO FIZIERON POR QUE *** HAN DEXADAS.
25892 5ELCID3299 POR QUE *** DEXAMOS DERECHO FIZIEMOS NOS;
25920 5ELCID3303 HYO *** HE FIJAS, & TU PRIMAS CORMANAS;
25932 5ELCID3304 AMI LO DIZEN, ATI DAN *** OREIADAS.
25968 5ELCID3310 SIEMPRE EN *** CORTES PERO MUDO ME LAMADES
26004 5ELCID3315 *** TUS MA@AS YO TELAS SABRE CONTAR:
26019 5ELCID3317 PEDIST *** FERIDAS PRIMERAS ALCANPEADOR LEAL,
26245 5ELCID3346 POR QUANTO *** DEXASTES MENOS VALEDES VOS;
26349 5ELCID3360 QUE POR QUE *** DEXAMOS ONDRADOS SOMOS NOS.
26405 5ELCID3368 FIJAS DEL %ID, POR QUE *** VOS DEXASTES,
26605 5ELCID3397 BESAN *** MANOS AL REY DON ALFONSSO,
26670 5ELCID3406 VOS *** CASASTES ANTES, CA YO NON,
26732 5ELCID3414 LEUANTOS MYO %ID, AL REY *** MANOS LE BESO;
26785 5ELCID3421 QUE UOS *** DE AONDRA & A BENDI%ION.
26799 5ELCID3423 BESARON *** MANOS DEL REY DON ALFONSSO,
26813 5ELCID3425 METIERON *** FES, & LOS OMENAIES DADOS SON,
26918 5ELCID3439 ELLOS *** PRISIERON A ONDRA & A BENDI%ION;
26934 5ELCID3441 ELLOS *** HAN DEXADAS A PESAR DE NOS.
26967 5ELCID3445 MAS BIEN SABEMOS *** MA@AS QUE ELLOS HAN,
26993 5ELCID3449 ANTES *** AVIEDES PAREIAS PORA EN BRA%OS LAS TENER,
26999 5ELCID3449 ANTES LAS AVIEDES PAREIAS PORA EN BRA%OS *** TENER,
27007 5ELCID3450 AGORA BESAREDES SUS MANOS & LAMAR *** HEDES SE@ORAS,
27011 5ELCID3451 AVER *** HEDES ASERUIR, MAL QUE UOS PESE AUOS.
27272 5ELCID3486 MYO %ID AL REY *** MANOS LE BESO & DIXO: PLAZME, SE@OR.
27770 5ELCID3544 DE NOCHE BELARON *** ARMAS & ROGARON AL CRIADOR.
27861 5ELCID3555 QUE NON FUESSEN EN LA BATALLA *** ESPADAS TAIADORES
27901 5ELCID3560 SI BUENAS *** TENEDES, PRO ABRAN AUOS;
28001 5ELCID3574 BESAMOS VOS *** MANOS, COMMO A REY & A SE@OR,
28067 5ELCID3583 SANTIGUARON *** SIELAS & CAUALGAN A VIGOR;
28083 5ELCID3585 EMANO PRENDEN *** ASTAS DELOS FIERROS TAIADORES,
28260 5ELCID3608 TODAS *** YENTES ESCONBRARON ADERREDOR,
28325 5ELCID3616 ABAXAN *** LAN%AS ABUELTAS CON LOS PENDONES,
28332 5ELCID3617 ENCLINAUAN *** CARAS SOBRE LOS ARZONES,
28462 5ELCID3635 *** DOS LE DESMANCHAN & LA TER%ERA FINCO:
```

WORD C# PREFIX CONTEXT

LAS (CON'T)

```
                 28496 5ELCID3639 QUEBRARON LE *** %INCHAS, NINGUNA NOL OUO PRO,
                 28514 5ELCID3641 ASSI LO TENIEN *** YENTES QUE MAL FERIDO ES DE MUERT.
                 28598 5ELCID3652 *** MONCLURAS DEL YELMO TODAS GELAS CORTAUA,
                 28919 5ELCID3694 *** ARMAS QUE Y RASTARON EL SELAS TOMO.
                 29085 5ELCID3715 AGORA *** AYAN QUITAS HEREDADES DE CARRION.
                 29093 5ELCID3716 SIN VERGUEN%A *** CASARE OAQUI PESE OAQUI NON.
                 29136 5ELCID3721 AMAYOR ONDRA *** CASA QUE LO QUE PRIMERO FUE.
                 29202 5ELCID3729 ESTAS SON *** NUEUAS DE MYO %ID EL CANPEADOR,
         WORD #2432 OCCURS 395 TIMES.
            INDEX OF DIVERSIFICATION =     72.93 WITH STANDARD DEVIATION OF     98.97

LATINADO         20992 5ELCID2667 VN MORO ******** BIEN GELO ENTENDIO;
         WORD #2433 OCCURS   1 TIMES.

LAUDARE           2655 5ELCID0335 PASTORES TO GLOORIFFICARON, OUIERON DE A *******,
         WORD #2434 OCCURS   1 TIMES.

LAUORES           3646 5ELCID0460 POR VER SUS ******* & TODAS SUS HEREDADES.
         WORD #2435 OCCURS   1 TIMES.

LAZARO            2736 5ELCID0346 RESU%ITEST A ******, CA FUE TU VOLUNTAD;
         WORD #2436 OCCURS   1 TIMES.

LAZRADAS         22022 5ELCID2802 MUCHO SON ******** & AMAS LAS FARTO.
         WORD #2437 OCCURS   1 TIMES.

LAZRADOS          8202 5ELCID1045 QUE COMIGO ANDAN ********, & NON UOS LO DARE.
         WORD #2438 OCCURS   1 TIMES.

LE                 153 5ELCID0021 CONBIDAR ** YEN DE GRADO, MAS NINGUNO NON OSAUA:
                   502 5ELCID0064 NON ** OSARIEN UENDER ALMENOS DINARADA.
                  1191 5ELCID0153 ASSI COMMO ENTRARON, AL %ID BESARON ** LAS MANOS.
                  1239 5ELCID0159 DON RACHEL & VIDAS A MYO %ID BESARON ** LAS MANOS.
                  1253 5ELCID0161 QUE SOBRE AQUELAS ARCHAS DAR ** YEN VJ %IENTOS MARCOS
                  1500 5ELCID0192 DEMOS ** BUEN DON, CA EL NO LO HA BUSCADO.
                  2267 5ELCID0285 GRAND IANTAR ** FAZEN AL BUEN CAMPEADOR.
                  2360 5ELCID0298 TORNOS A SONRISAR; LEGAN ** TODOS, LA MANOL BAN BESAR.
                  2607 5ELCID0329 QUE AMIO %ID EL CAMPEADOR QUE DIOS ** CURIAS DE MAL:
                  2888 5ELCID0364 POR MYO %ID EL CAMPEADOR, QUE DIOS ** CURIE DE MAL.
                  5036 5ELCID0636 QUANDO LO OYO EL REY TAMIN, POR CUER ** PESO MAL:
                  5651 5ELCID0712 MOROS ** RE%IBEN POR LA SE@A GANAR,
                  5658 5ELCID0713 DAN ** GRANDES COLPES, MAS NOL PUEDEN FALSSAR.
                  5876 5ELCID0744 A MYNAYA ALBARFANEZ MATARON ** EL CAUALLO,
                  5996 5ELCID0760 AL REY FARIZ IIJ COLPES ** AUIE DADO;
                  6001 5ELCID0761 LOS DOS ** FALLEN, & EL VNOL HA TOMADO,
                  6021 5ELCID0763 BOLUIO LA RIENDA POR YR SE ** DEL CAMPO.
                  6991 5ELCID0894 BESO ** LAS MANOS MINAYA ALBARFANEZ:
                  7186 5ELCID0921 BESO ** LA BOCA & LOS OIOS DELA CARA.
                  7552 5ELCID0968 GENTES SE ** ALEGAN GRANDES ENTRE MOROS & CHRISTIANOS,
                  7976 5ELCID1019 ADUZEN ** LOS COMERES, DELANT GELOS PARAUAN;
                  8259 5ELCID1051 CON LOS CAUALLEROS QUE EL %ID ** AUIE DADOS
                  8369 5ELCID1064 DAN ** TRES PALAFRES MUY BIEN ENSELLADOS
                  8634 5ELCID1096 YA VIE MYO %ID QUE DIOS ** YUA VALIENDO.
                  9100 5ELCID1158 QUE DIOS ** AIUDARA & FIZIERA ESTA ARRANCADA.
                  9315 5ELCID1184 SOPOLO MYO %ID, DE CORA%ON ** PLAZ;
                  9389 5ELCID1194 TRES DIAS ** SPERARE EN CANAL DE %ELFA.
                  9431 5ELCID1199 GRANDES YENTES SE ** ACOIEN DELA BUENA CHRISTIANDAD.
                  9493 5ELCID1207 MAS ** VIENEN A MYO %ID, SABET, QUE NOS LE VAN.
                  9501 5ELCID1207 MAS LE VIENEN A MYO %ID, SABET, QUE NOS ** VAN.
                  9581 5ELCID1217 ENEL AUER MONEDADO XXX MILL MARCOS ** CAEN,
                  9794 5ELCID1244 CON EL MYNAYA ALBARFFANEZ QUE NOS ** PARTE DE SO BRA%O.
                  9873 5ELCID1252 QUE NINGUN OMNE DELOS SOS QUES ** NON SPIDIES, ONOL BESAS LA MANO,
                  9886 5ELCID1254 TOMASSEN ** EL AUER & PUSIESSEN LE EN VN PALO.
                  9891 5ELCID1254 TOMASSEN LE EL AUER & PUSIESSEN ** EN VN PALO.
                  9938 5ELCID1260 QUE SI ALGUNOS FURTARE O MENOS ** FALLAREN, EL AUER ME
                                  AURA ATORNAR
                  9991 5ELCID1266 ALEGRAS ** EL CORA%ON & TORNOS ASONRRISAR:
                 10053 5ELCID1274 DAR ** QUIERO C CAUALLOS, & UOS YD GELOS LEUAR;
                 10134 5ELCID1284 CIENTO OMNES ** DIO MYO %ID A ALBARFANEZ POR SERUIR LE EN
                                  LA CARRERA,
                 10142 5ELCID1284 CIENTO OMNES LE DIO MYO %ID A ALBARFANEZ POR SERUIR ** EN
                                  LA CARRERA,
                 10231 5ELCID1295 ALOS DIAS DEL SIEGLO NON ** LORASSEN CHRISTIANOS.
                 10299 5ELCID1304 DIERON ** EN VALEN%IA O BIEN PUEDE ESTAR RICO.
                 10413 5ELCID1320 BESAUA ** LAS MANOS & FABLO TAN APUESTO:
                 10451 5ELCID1325 ECHASTES ** DE TIERRA, NON HA LA UUESTRA AMOR;
                 10771 5ELCID1364 SIRUAN ** SUS HERDADES DO FUERE EL CAMPEADOR,
                 10799 5ELCID1367 MYNAYA ALBARFANEZ LAS MANOS ** BESO.
                 11114 5ELCID1407 DEZID AL CANPEADOR, QUE DIOS ** CURIE DE MAL,
                 11311 5ELCID1431 AFEUOS RACHEL & VIDAS ALOS PIES ** CAEN:
                 11406 5ELCID1443 POR MI AL CAMPEADOR LAS MANOS ** BESAD
                 12020 5ELCID1524 MAGER QUE MAL ** QUERAMOS, NON GELO PODREMOS FER,
                 12295 5ELCID1561 DENTRO A VALEN%IA LIEUAN ** EL MANDADO.
                 12391 5ELCID1573 E ADUXIESSEN ** ABAUIECA; POCO AUIE QUEL GANARA,
                 12494 5ELCID1585 ENSIELLAN ** ABAUIECA, CUBERTURAS LE ECHAUAN,
                 12497 5ELCID1585 ENSIELLAN LE ABAUIECA, CUBERTURAS ** ECHAUAN,
                 12568 5ELCID1594 QUANDO LO VIO DO@A XIMENA, A PIES SE ** ECHAUA:
```

```
WORD                    C#  PREFIX                          CONTEXT

LE (CON'T)

                  12675 5ELCID1608 MADRE & FIJAS LAS MANCS ** BESAUAN.
                  13453 5ELCID1705 PRENDOL YO LOS PECADCS, & DIOS ** ABRA EL ALMA.
                  13614 5ELCID1725 AL REY YU%EF TRES CCLPES ** OUO DADOS,
                  13618 5ELCID1726 SALIOS ** DE SOL ESPACA, CA MUCHOL ANDIDO EL CAUALLO,
                  13628 5ELCID1727 METIOS ** EN GUIERA, VN CASTIELLO PALA%IANO;
                  13969 5ELCID1769 LEUANTARON SE TODAS & BESARON ** LAS MANOS,
                  14062 5ELCID1781 DELOS BUENOS & OTORGADOS CAYERON ** MILL & D CAUALLOS;
                  14375 5ELCID1818 CON SALUDES DEL %ID QUE LAS MANOS ** BESAUA:
                  14384 5ELCID1819 DESTA LID QUE HA ARRANCADA CC CAUALLOS ** ENBIAUA ENPRESENTAIA,
                  14454 5ELCID1828 ENVIAUA ** MANDADO PERO VERMUEZ & MYNAYA,
                  14693 5ELCID1858 ESTO PLOGO A MUCHOS & BESARON ** LAS MANOS.
                  14850 5ELCID1877 BESARON ** LAS MANOS & ENTRARON A POSAR;
                  15125 5ELCID1913 ANDAR ** QUIERO A MYO %ID EN TODA PRO.
                  15409 5ELCID1952 POR DAR ** GRAND ONDRA COMMO A REY DE TIERRA.
                  15463 5ELCID1959 AL REY ONDRADO DELANT ** ECHARON LAS CARTAS;
                  15974 5ELCID2025 DE AQUESTA GUISA ALOS PIES ** CAYO.
                  16082 5ELCID2039 HYNOIOS FITOS LAS MANOS ** BESO,
                  16166 5ELCID2051 BESO ** LA MANO MYO CID, LO OTORGO.
                  16644 5ELCID2108 MYO %ID GELOS RE%IBE, LAS MANOS ** BESO:
                  17311 5ELCID2190 BESARON ** LAS MANOS LA MUGIER & LAS FIJAS AMAS,
                  18193 5ELCID2301 E LIEUA LO ADESTRANDO, ENLA RED ** METIO.
                  18890 5ELCID2390 LOS MOROS SON MUCHOS, DERREDOR ** %ERCAUAN,
                  18893 5ELCID2391 DAUAN ** GRANDES COLPES, MAS NOL FALSSAN LAS ARMAS.
                  18909 5ELCID2392 EL QUE EN BUEN ORA NASCO LOS OIOS ** FINCAUA,
                  19636 5ELCID2489 CAYERON ** EN QUINTA AL %ID SEYX %IENTOS CAUALLOS,
                  21744 5ELCID2766 MANDARON ** YR ADELANTE, MAS DE SU GRADO NON FUE.
                  21809 5ELCID2774 SABET BIEN QUE SI ELLOS ** VIESSEN, NON ESCAPARA DE MUERT.
                  21889 5ELCID2785 PARTIERON SE ** LAS TELLAS DE DENTRO DE LOS CORA%ONES,
                  22617 5ELCID2881 AL MORO AUENGALUON DE CORA%ON ** PLAZ,
                  22791 5ELCID2904 POR MI BESA ** LA MANO DALMA & DE CORA%ON,
                  23035 5ELCID2935 BESABA ** LOS PIES AQUEL MU@O GUSTIOZ;
                  23237 5ELCID2960 AIUDAR ** ADERECHO, SIN SALUE EL CRIADOR
                  23298 5ELCID2968 DIZID ** AL CAMPEADOR, QUE EN BUEN ORA NASCO,
                  23639 5ELCID3011 EBAYR ** CUYDAN A MYO %ID EL CAMPEADOR.
                  23816 5ELCID3034 BESO ** LA MANO & DESPUES LE SALUDO;
                  23821 5ELCID3034 BESO LE LA MANO & DESPUES ** SALUDO;
                  24278 5ELCID3096 QUE NON ** CONTALASSEN LOS PELOS AL BUEN %ID CANPEADOR;
                  24593 5ELCID3134 GRANDE TUERTO ** HAN TENIDO, SABEMOS LO TODOS NOS;
                  24866 5ELCID3167 DEMOS ** SUS ESPADAS, QUANDO ASSI FINCA LA BOZ,
                  24971 5ELCID3180 RE%IBIO LAS ESPADAS, LAS MANOS ** BESO,
                  24989 5ELCID3183 NOS ** PUEDEN CAMEAR, CA EL %ID BIEN LAS CONNOS%E;
                  24999 5ELCID3184 ALEGROS ** TODEL CUERPO, SONRRISOS DE CORA%ON,
                  25038 5ELCID3189 TENDIO EL BRA%O, LA ESPADA TIZON ** DIO;
                  25107 5ELCID3198 BESO ** LA MANO, EL ESPADA TOMO & RE%IBIO.
                  25313 5ELCID3223 PAGAR ** HEMOS DE HEREDADES ENTIERRAS DE CARRION.
                  25442 5ELCID3240 PAGEN ** EN APRE%IADURA & PRENDALO EL CAMPEADOR.
                  25707 5ELCID3274 LOS VNOS ** HAN MIEDO & LOS OTROS ESPANTA.
                  25948 5ELCID3307 DETIENES ** LA LENGUA, NON PUEDE DELIBRAR,
                  26057 5ELCID3321 DELOS PRIMEROS COLPES OF ** DE ARRANCAR;
                  26193 5ELCID3339 DEXOS ** PRENDER ALCUELO, & ALA RED LE METIO.
                  26199 5ELCID3339 DEXOS LE PRENDER ALCUELO, & ALA RED ** METIO.
                  26734 5ELCID3414 LEUANTOS MYO %ID, AL REY LAS MANOS ** BESO;
                  26763 5ELCID3418 ESTE CASAMIENTO OTORGO UOS ** YO
                  27274 5ELCID3486 MYO %ID AL REY LAS MANOS ** BESO & DIXO: PLAZME, SE@OR.
                  27518 5ELCID3515 HY UOS ** DO EN DON, MANDEDES LE TOMAR, SE@OR.
                  27523 5ELCID3515 HY UOS LE DO EN DON, MANDEDES ** TOMAR, SE@OR.
                  27536 5ELCID3517 SI AUOS ** TOLLIES, EL CAUALLO NO HAURIE TAN BUEN SE@OR.
                  28412 5ELCID3628 BIEN EN DOS LOGARES EL ESTIL ** QUEBRO.
                  28464 5ELCID3635 LAS DOS ** DESMANCHAN & LA TER%ERA FINCO:
                  28495 5ELCID3639 QUEBRARON ** LAS %INCHAS, NINGUNA NOL OUO PRO,
                  28551 5ELCID3645 ATORGARON GELO LOS FIELES, PERO VERMUEZ ** DEXO.
                  28825 5ELCID3682 APART ** PRISO, QUE NON CABEL CORA%ON;
                  29022 5ELCID3707 ATAL ** CONTESCA O SI QUIER PEOR.
                  29226 5ELCID3732 PER ABBAT ** ESCRIUIO ENEL MES DE MAYO,
           WORD #2439 OCCURS 119 TIMES.
              INDEX OF DIVERSIFICATION =   245.38 WITH STANDARD DEVIATION OF   334.94

LEA                 890 5ELCID0114 YA LO VEDES QUE EL REY *** AYRADO.
           WORD #2440 OCCURS   1 TIMES.

LEAL               3151 5ELCID0396 YXIENDOS UA DE TIERRA EL CAMPEADOR ****,
                   5609 5ELCID0706 EL CRIADOR UOS VALA, %ID CAMPEADOR ****
                  11525 5ELCID1459 E MARTIN ANTOLINEZ, VN BURGALES ****,
                  11844 5ELCID1501 E EL OBISPO DON JERONIMO, CORANADO ****,
                  18662 5ELCID2361 AQUI LEGO MYNAYA ALBARFANEZ: OYD, YA %ID, CANPEADOR ****
                  21088 5ELCID2679 ELUEGO LEUARIA SUS FIJAS AL CAMPEADOR ****;
                  26023 5ELCID3317 PEDIST LAS FERIDAS PRIMERAS ALCANPEADOR ****,
           WORD #2441 OCCURS   7 TIMES.
              INDEX OF DIVERSIFICATION =  3811.00 WITH STANDARD DEVIATION OF  2477.07

LEAN               7900 5ELCID1009 AL CONDE DON REMONT A PRESON **** TOMADO;
           WORD #2442 OCCURS   1 TIMES.

LEATAN%A           8505 5ELCID1081 VNA DES ******** CA NON LA FIZO ALGUANDRE.
           WORD #2443 OCCURS   1 TIMES.
```

WORD C# PREFIX CONTEXT

LEGA 10394 5ELCID1317 AFE MINAYA LABARFANEZ DO **** TAN APUESTO;
WORD #2444 OCCURS 1 TIMES.

LEGADAS 19458 5ELCID2465 TODAS LAS GANANZIAS A VALENZIA SON *******;
WORD #2445 OCCURS 1 TIMES.

LEGADO 7232 5ELCID0927 QUE MINAYA ALBARFANEZ ASSI ERA ******,
15875 5ELCID2013 DE VN DIA ES ****** ANTES EL REY DON ALFONSSO.
19168 5ELCID2424 FATA LA ZINTURA EL ESPADA ****** HA.
19338 5ELCID2449 MYNAYA ALBARFANEZ ESSORA ES ******,
23655 5ELCID3013 AVN NON ERA ****** EL QUE ENBUEN ORA NAZIO,
WORD #2446 OCCURS 5 TIMES.
INDEX OF DIVERSIFICATION = 4104.75 WITH STANDARD DEVIATION OF 3501.52

LEGADOS 6252 5ELCID0796 DELOS MORISCOS, QUANDO SON *******, FFALLARON DX CAUALLOS.
14559 5ELCID1841 MYNAYA & PER VERMUEZ ADELANT SON *******,
18550 5ELCID2347 CA NUNQUA LO VIERAN, CA NUEUOS SON *******.
18565 5ELCID2349 POR LA SU VOLUNTAD NON SERIEN ALLI *******.
19217 5ELCID2431 ALAS TIENDAS ERAN *******, DO ESTAUA
WORD #2447 OCCURS 5 TIMES.
INDEX OF DIVERSIFICATION = 3240.25 WITH STANDARD DEVIATION OF 3800.74

LEGAN 2359 5ELCID0298 TORNOS A SONRISAR; ***** LE TODOS, LA MANOL BAN BESAR.
3749 5ELCID0474 SOS CAUALLEROS ***** CON LA GANANZIA,
9113 5ELCID1160 ***** A GUIERA & LEGAN AXATIUA,
9117 5ELCID1160 LEGAN A GUIERA & ***** AXATIUA,
11958 5ELCID1516 DON ***** LOS OTROS, A MINAYA ALBARFANEZ SE UAN HOMILAR.
14445 5ELCID1827 ***** A VALADOLID, DO EL REY ALFONSSO ESTAUA;
WORD #2448 OCCURS 6 TIMES.
INDEX OF DIVERSIFICATION = 2416.20 WITH STANDARD DEVIATION OF 1984.11

LEGANDO 2085 5ELCID0262 AFEUOS DO@A XIMENA CON SUS FIJAS DO UA *******;
7549 5ELCID0967 GRANDES SON LOS PODERES & A PRIESSA SEUAN *******,
11940 5ELCID1513 LOS QUE YUAN MESURANDO & ******* DELANT
19381 5ELCID2455 DE TODAS PARTES SOS VASSALLOS VAN *******;
WORD #2449 OCCURS 4 TIMES.

LEGAR 8525 5ELCID1083 JUNTOS CON SUS MESNADAS, CONPEZOLAS DE *****
WORD #2450 OCCURS 1 TIMES.

LEGARAN 11868 5ELCID1504 TODOS VIENEN EN VNO, AGORA *******.
23930 5ELCID3048 LAS MIS COMPA@AS ESTA NOCHE *******;
WORD #2451 OCCURS 2 TIMES.

LEGARE 12057 5ELCID1529 SI DIOS ME ****** AL ZID ELO VEA CON EL ALMA,
WORD #2452 OCCURS 1 TIMES.

LEGARIEN 4003 5ELCID0508 AL REY ALFONSSO QUE ******** SUS COMPA@AS,
WORD #2453 OCCURS 1 TIMES.

LEGARON 7457 5ELCID0957 ******* LAS NUEUAS ALCONDE DE BARZILONA,
12843 5ELCID1630 ******* A VALENZIA, LA QUE MYO ZID A CONQUISTA,
17874 5ELCID2261 RICOS TORNAN A CASTIELLA LOS QUE ALAS BODAS *******.
19858 5ELCID2518 ASSI COMMO *******, PAGOS EL CAMPEADOR:
20912 5ELCID2656 TROZIERON ARBUXUELO & ******* A SALON,
WORD #2454 OCCURS 5 TIMES.
INDEX OF DIVERSIFICATION = 3362.75 WITH STANDARD DEVIATION OF 2168.55

LEGASSEN 28272 5ELCID3609 MAS DE VJ ASTAS DE LANZAS QUE NON ******** AL MOION.
WORD #2455 OCCURS 1 TIMES.

LEGASTES 16148 5ELCID2048 VOS AGORA ********, & NOS VINJEMOS ANOCH;
WORD #2456 OCCURS 1 TIMES.

LEGAUA 297 5ELCID0037 AGUIIO MYO ZID, ALA PUERTA SE ******,
7607 5ELCID0974 DIZE DE VNA SIERRA & ****** A VN VAL.
9622 5ELCID1222 AQUEL REY DE SEUILLA EL MANDADO ******,
22645 5ELCID2885 AL QUE EN BUEN ORA NASCO ****** EL MENSSAIE;
23552 5ELCID3000 ****** EL PLAZO, QUERIEN YR ALA CORT;
28612 5ELCID3653 ALLA LEUO EL ALMOFAR, FATA LA COFIA ******,
28629 5ELCID3655 RAXOL LOS PELOS DELA CABEZA, BIEN ALA CARNE ******;
WORD #2457 OCCURS 7 TIMES.
INDEX OF DIVERSIFICATION = 4721.00 WITH STANDARD DEVIATION OF 4893.62

LEGAUAN 4805 5ELCID0609 LUEGO ******* LOS SOS, CA FECHA ES EL ARRANCADA.
7081 5ELCID0905 ASARAGOZA SUS NUEUAS *******,
9718 5ELCID1235 LAS NUEUAS DEL CAUALLERO YAVEDES DO *******.
WORD #2458 OCCURS 3 TIMES.

LEGEN 3543 5ELCID0446 FITA AYUSO & POR GUADALFAIARA, FATA ALCALA ***** LAS ALGARAS,
7778 5ELCID0996 ANTES QUE ELLOS ***** A LA@O, PRESENTEMOS LES LAS LANZAS;
WORD #2459 OCCURS 2 TIMES.

WORD C# PREFIX CONTEXT

LEGO 247 5ELCID0032 ASSI COMMO **** ALA PUERTA, FALOLA BIEN %ERRADA,
414 5ELCID0052 **** A SANTA MARIA, LUEGO DESCAUALGA,
797 5ELCID0102 **** MARTIN ATOLINEZ AGUISA DEMENBRADO:
1855 5ELCID0236 QUANDO **** A SAN PERO EL BUEN CAMPEADOR;
3774 5ELCID0477 E SIN DUBDA CORREN; FASTA ALCALA **** LA SE@A DE MINAYA,
6049 5ELCID0767 CORTOL EL YELMO, QUE **** ALA CARNE;
11968 5ELCID1517 QUANDO **** AUEGALUON, DONTA OIO HA,
13641 5ELCID1728 MYO %ID EL DE BIUAR FASTA ALLI **** EN ALCAZ,
18655 5ELCID2361 AQUI **** MYNAYA ALBARFANEZ: OYD, YA %ID, CANPEADOR LEAL
22339 5ELCID2845 ASANTESTEUAN EL MANDADO ****
27491 5ELCID3511 MYO %ID ENEL CAUALLO ADELANT SE ****,
WORD #2460 OCCURS 11 TIMES.
INDEX OF DIVERSIFICATION = 2723.40 WITH STANDARD DEVIATION OF 2082.13

LEGOLAS 2189 5ELCID0276 ******* AL CRCA%ON, CA MUCHO LAS QUERIA.
2816 5ELCID0355 AL%OLAS ARRIBA, ******* ALA FAZ,
WORD #2461 OCCURS 2 TIMES.

LEGUAS 12281 5ELCID1559 APRES SON DE VALEN%IA A TRES ****** CONTADAS.
WORD #2462 OCCURS 1 TIMES.

LENGUA 17172 5ELCID2173 QUE ES LARGO DE ******, MAS EN LO AL NON ES TAN PRO.
25950 5ELCID3307 DETIENES LE LA ******, NON PUEDE DELIBRAR,
26106 5ELCID3328 ****** SIN MANOS, CUEMO OSAS FABLAR?
WORD #2463 OCCURS 3 TIMES.

LENNAS 880 5ELCID0113 TIENE DOS ARCAS ****** DE ORO ESMERADO.
WORD #2464 OCCURS 1 TIMES.

LE@A 6430 5ELCID0820 EUADES AQUI ORO & PLATA VNA VESA ****,
WORD #2465 OCCURS 1 TIMES.

LEON 14776 5ELCID1867 GRADO AL CRIADOR & AL SE@OR SANT ESIDRO EL DE ****
15223 5ELCID1927 LO QUEL ROGAUA ALFONSSO EL DE ****
18040 5ELCID2282 SALIOS DE LA RED & DESATOS EL ****.
18144 5ELCID2295 HYA SE@OR ONDRADO, REBATA NOS DIO EL ****.
18161 5ELCID2297 EL MANTO TRAE ALCUELLO, & ADELINO PORA ****;
18163 5ELCID2298 EL **** QUANDO LO VIO, ASSI EN VERGON%O,
20080 5ELCID2548 ANTE QUE NOS RETRAYAN LO QUE CUNTIO DEL ****.
20139 5ELCID2556 ANTES QUE NOS RETRAYAN LO QUE FUE DEL ****.
20332 5ELCID2579 QUE LO SEPAN EN GALLIZIA & EN CASTIELLA & EN ****,
21392 5ELCID2719 NOS VENGAREMOS AQUESTA POR LA DEL ****.
21721 5ELCID2762 LA DESONDRA DEL **** ASSIS YRA VENGANDO.
22951 5ELCID2923 REY ES DE CASTIELLA & REY ES DE ****
23372 5ELCID2977 ENBIA SUS CARTAS PORA **** & A SANTI YAGUO,
26126 5ELCID3330 NON TE VIENE EN MIENTE EN VALEN%IA LO DEL ****,
26133 5ELCID3331 QUANDO DURMIE MYO %ID & EL **** SE DESATO?
26182 5ELCID3337 LEUANTOS DEL ESCA@O & FUES PORAL ****;
26184 5ELCID3338 EL **** PREMIO LA CABE%A, A MYO %ID ESPERO,
26367 5ELCID3363 LO DEL **** NON SE TE DEUE OLBIDAR;
27474 5ELCID3509 HYO LO JURO PAR SANT ESIDRO EL DE ****
27707 5ELCID3536 ELLOS SON ENPODER DEL REY DON ALFONSSO EL DE ****;
27766 5ELCID3543 CA GRAND MIEDO OUIERON A ALFONSSO EL DE ****.
29115 5ELCID3718 OUIERON SU AIUNTA CON ALFONSSO EL DE ****,
WORD #2466 OCCURS 22 TIMES.
INDEX OF DIVERSIFICATION = 681.81 WITH STANDARD DEVIATION OF 886.47

LEONES 2691 5ELCID0340 SALUEST A DANIEL CON LOS ****** EN LA MALA CAR%EL,
WORD #2467 OCCURS 1 TIMES.

LEONESES 15630 5ELCID1982 CON EL REY VAN ******** & MESNADAS GALIZIANAS,
WORD #2468 OCCURS 1 TIMES.

LES 287 5ELCID0036 LOS DE DENTRO NON *** QUERIEN TORNAR PALABRA.
1284 5ELCID0165 NON *** DIESSE MYO %ID DELA GANAN%IA UN DINERO MALO.
4418 5ELCID0562 QUE DE DIA NIN DE NOCH NON *** DIESSEN AREBATA,
4750 5ELCID0602 TIENEN BUENOS CAUALLOS, SABET, ASU GUISA *** ANDAN;
4765 5ELCID0604 LOS VASSALLOS DE MYO %ID SIN PIEDAD *** DAUAN,
5228 5ELCID0661 ALOS DE MYO %ID YA *** TUELLEN EL AGUA.
6174 5ELCID0786 CA EN ALCAZ SJN DUBDA *** FUERON DANDO.
6464 5ELCID0825 SI *** YO VISQUIER, SERAN DUENAS RICAS.
6509 5ELCID0830 A NUESTRO AMIGOS BIEN *** PODEDES DEZIR:
6619 5ELCID0845 VENDIDO *** A ALCO%ER POR TRES MILL MARCHOS DE PLATA.
6982 5ELCID0893 SUELTO *** LOS CUERPOS & QUITO LES LAS HEREDADES.
6987 5ELCID0893 SUELTO LES LOS CUERPOS & QUITO *** LAS HEREDADES.
7088 5ELCID0906 NON PLAZE ALOS MOROS, FIRME MIENTRE *** PESAUA.
7234 5ELCID0928 DIZIENDO *** SALUDES DE PRIMOS & DE HERMANOS,
7616 5ELCID0975 DEL CONDE DON REMONT VENIDO *** MENSAIE;
7782 5ELCID0996 ANTES QUE ELLOS LEGEN A LA@O, PRESENTEMOS *** LAS LAN%AS;
8651 5ELCID1098 PESA ALOS DE VALEN%IA, SABET, NON *** PLAZE;
8687 5ELCID1103 EN SUS TIERRAS SOMOS & FEMOS *** TODOMAL,
8994 5ELCID1145 MAGER *** PESA, OUIERON SE ADAR & A ARANCAR.
9205 5ELCID1172 TAIAUA *** LAS HUERTAS & FAZIA LES GRAND MAL,

WORD C# PREFIX CONTEXT

LES (CON'T)

```
 9210 5ELCID1172 TAIAUA LES LAS HUERTAS & FAZIA *** GRAND MAL,
 9220 5ELCID1173 EN CADA VNO DESTOS A@OS MYO %ID *** TOLIO EL PAN.
 9241 5ELCID1175 DE NINGUNA PART QUE SEA NON *** VINIE PAN;
 9303 5ELCID1183 NON *** DIXO COSEIO, NIN LOS VINO HUUIAR.
 9809 5ELCID1246 ATODOS *** DIO EN VALEN%IA CASAS & HEREDADES
10702 5ELCID1356 HYO *** MANDARE DAR CONDUCHO MIENTRA QUE POR MJ TIERRA FUEREN,
10779 5ELCID1365 ATREGO *** LOS CUERPOS DE MAL & DE OCASION,
10924 5ELCID1382 FATA DENTRO EN MEDINA DENLES QUANTO HUEBOS *** FUER,
11200 5ELCID1417 QUE *** TOUIESSE PRO ROGAUAN A ALBARFANEZ;
11457 5ELCID1450 POR LA TIERRA DEL REY MUCHO CONDUCHO *** DAN.
11736 5ELCID1488 ESSA NOCH CON DUCHO *** DIO GRAND,
11917 5ELCID1511 QUE SOPIENSSEN *** OTROS DE QUE SESO ERA ALBARFANEZ
13430 5ELCID1702 EL OBISPO DON IHERONIMO LA MISSA *** CANTAUA;
13437 5ELCID1703 LA MISSA DICHA, GRANT SULTURA *** DAUA:
13573 5ELCID1720 ENTRARON *** DEL OTRO CABO.
13729 5ELCID1740 QUE DIOS *** OUO MER%ED QUE VEN%IERON EL CAMPO.
13942 5ELCID1766 ACADA VNA DELLAS DO *** CC MARCOS DE PLATA,
15594 5ELCID1977 COMMO ELLOS TENIEN, CER%ER *** YA LA GANA%IA,
16602 5ELCID2103 TREZIENTOS MARCOS DE PLATA EN AYUDA *** DO YO,
16756 5ELCID2121 EL REY ALOS YFANTES ALAS MANOS *** TOMO,
17183 5ELCID2174 GRANT ONDRA *** DAN ALOS YFANTES DE CARRION.
17215 5ELCID2178 DAD *** VN REYAL & ALOS YFANTES DE CARRION,
18031 5ELCID2281 MALA SOBREUIENTA, SABED, QUE *** CUNTIO:
18258 5ELCID2310 FIERA COSA *** PESA DESTO QUE LES CUNTIO.
18262 5ELCID2310 FIERA COSA LES PESA DESTO QUE *** CUNTIO.
18300 5ELCID2316 QUE *** CRE%E LA GANAN%IA, GRADO AL CRIADOR.
18311 5ELCID2317 MAS, SABED, DE CUER *** PESA ALOS YFANTES DE CARRION;
20199 5ELCID2565 QUE *** DIEMOS POR ARRAS & POR ONORES;
20242 5ELCID2570 VOS *** DIESTES VILLAS E TIERRAS POR ARRAS ENTIERRAS DE CARRION,
20254 5ELCID2571 HYO QUIERO *** DAR AXUUAR IIJ MILL MARCOS DE PLATA;
20539 5ELCID2607 AL PADRE & ALA MADRE LAS MANOS *** BESAUAN;
20546 5ELCID2608 AMOS LAS BENDIXIERON & DIERON *** SU GRA%IA.
20923 5ELCID2658 TOD ESTO *** FIZO EL MORO POR EL AMOR DEL %ID CAMPEADOR.
21141 5ELCID2686 ESTO *** HA DICHO, & EL MORO SE TORNO;
21274 5ELCID2703 CON SUS MUGIERES EN BRA%OS DEMUESTRAN *** AMOR;
21394 5ELCID2720 ALLI *** TUELLEN LOS MANTOS & LOS PELLI%ONES,
21506 5ELCID2734 LO QUE RUEGAN LAS DUENAS NON *** HA NINGUN PRO.
21511 5ELCID2735 ESSORA *** CONPIE%AN ADAR LOS YFANTES DE CARRION;
21620 5ELCID2749 LEUARON *** LOS MANTOS & LAS PIELES ARMINAS,
22164 5ELCID2822 ALLAS FIJAS DEL %ID DAN *** ESFUER%O.
22553 5ELCID2872 FATA RIO DAMOR, DANDO *** SOLAZ;
22632 5ELCID2883 POR AMOR DE MYO %ID RICA CENA *** DA.
23338 5ELCID2973 DESTO QUE *** ABINO AVN BIEN SERAN ONDRADOS.
23435 5ELCID2985 HYA *** VA PESANDO ALSO YFANTES DE CARRION,
24714 5ELCID3148 ESTO *** DEMANDO AYFANTES DE CARRION:
25165 5ELCID3204 EN ORO & EN PLATA TRES MILL MARCOS DE PLATA *** DIO;
25501 5ELCID3248 ENPRESTAN *** DELO AGENO, QUE NON LES CUMPLE LO SUYO.
25506 5ELCID3248 ENPRESTAN LES DELO AGENO, QUE NON *** CUMPLE LO SUYO.
25664 5ELCID3268 POR QUANTO *** FIZIESTES MENOS VALEDES VOS.
26334 5ELCID3359 LO QUE *** FIZIEMOS SER LES HA RETRAYDO; ESTO LIDIARE ATOD
                 EL MAS
26337 5ELCID3359 LO QUE LES FIZIEMOS SER *** HA RETRAYDO; ESTO LIDIARE ATOD
                 EL MAS
26908 5ELCID3438 HYO *** DI MIS PRIMAS POR MANDADO DEL REY ALFONSSO,
26927 5ELCID3440 GRANDES AUERES *** DIO MYO %ID EL CAMPEADOR,
26942 5ELCID3442 RIEBTOS *** LOS CUERPOS POR MALOS & POR TRAYDORES.
27224 5ELCID3480 AQUI *** PONGO PLAZO DE DENTRO EN MI CORT,
27694 5ELCID3535 CUNPLIR QUIEREN EL DEBDO QUE *** MANDO SO SE@OR,
28060 5ELCID3582 ADUZEN *** LOS CAUALLOS BUENOS & CORREDORES,
28222 5ELCID3603 HYA *** VA PESANDO ALOS YFANTES DE CARRION.
28276 5ELCID3610 SORTEAUAN *** EL CAMPO, YA LES PARTIEN EL SOL,
28280 5ELCID3610 SORTEAUAN LES EL CAMPO, YA *** PARTIEN EL SOL,
28567 5ELCID3647 TALES FUERON LOS COLPES QUE *** QUEBRARON AMAS.
28994 5ELCID3703 CONPLIDO HAN EL DEBDO QUE *** MANDO SO SE@OR;
WORD #2469 OCCURS 82 TIMES.
   INDEX OF DIVERSIFICATION = 353.41 WITH STANDARD DEVIATION OF 498.93

LETRAS      10189 5ELCID1290 BIEN ENTENDIDO ES DE ****** & MUCHO ACORDADO,
WORD #2470 OCCURS 1 TIMES.

LEUAD       27912 5ELCID3562 ***** & SALID ALCAMPO, YFANTES DE CARRION,
WORD #2471 OCCURS 1 TIMES.

LEUADES     20317 5ELCID2578 ALLA ME ******* LAS TELAS DEL CORA%ON.
WORD #2472 OCCURS 1 TIMES.

LEUADO      22863 5ELCID2912 MYOS AUERES SE ME AN ******, QUE SOBEIANOS SON;
WORD #2473 OCCURS 1 TIMES.

LEUALDAS     1300 5ELCID0167 ********, RACHEL & VIDAS, PONED LAS EN UUESTRO SALUO;
WORD #2474 OCCURS 1 TIMES.

LEUAN        5182 5ELCID0655 AL BUENO DE MYO %ID EN ALCO%ER ***** %ERCAR.
WORD #2475 OCCURS 1 TIMES.

LEUANTADO   17541 5ELCID2219 EL CAMPEADOR EN PIE ES *********:
WORD #2476 OCCURS 1 TIMES.
```

WORD C# PREFIX CONTEXT

```
LEUANTADOS          15984 5ELCID2027 ********** EN PIE, YA %ID CAMPEADOR,
                    25250 5ELCID3215 DIXO ALBARFANEZ ********** EN PIE EL %ID CAMPEADOR:
        WORD #2477 OCCURS   2 TIMES.

LEUANTAN            17609 5ELCID2228 ******** SE DERECHAS & METIOGELAS EN MANO.
        WORD #2478 OCCURS   1 TIMES.

LEUANTANDO          19983 5ELCID2535 POR AQUESTOS GUEGOS QUE YUAN **********,
        WORD #2479 OCCURS   1 TIMES.

LEUANTAR            24411 5ELCID3112 NOS QUISO ******** EL CRESPO DE GRA@ON,
        WORD #2480 OCCURS   1 TIMES.

LEUANTARON          13964 5ELCID1769 ********** SE TODAS & BESARON LE LAS MANOS,
                    16494 5ELCID2091 LUEGO SE ********** LOS YFFANTES DE CARRION,
        WORD #2481 OCCURS   2 TIMES.

LEUANTAUA           25683 5ELCID3270 EL CONDE DON GAR%IA EN PIE SE *********;
                    26359 5ELCID3361 MARTIN ANTOLINEZ EN PIE SE *********;
        WORD #2482 OCCURS   2 TIMES.

LEUANTAUAN           3635 5ELCID0458 EN CASTEION TODOS SE **********,
        WORD #2483 OCCURS   1 TIMES.

LEUANTE             17385 5ELCID2199 MAS BIEN SABET VERDAD QUE NON LO ******* YO:
        WORD #2484 OCCURS   1 TIMES.

LEUANTO             18153 5ELCID2296 MYO %ID FINCO EL COBDO, EN PIE SE *******,
                    24694 5ELCID3145 MYO %ID LA MANO BESO AL REY & EN PIE SE *******;
                    24978 5ELCID3181 TORNOS AL ESCA@O DON SE *******;
                    25117 5ELCID3199 LUEGO SE ******* MYO %ID EL CAMPEADOR:
                    26507 5ELCID3382 ESSORA MUNO GUSTIOZ EN PIE SE *******;
                    26846 5ELCID3429 MYNAYA ALBAFANEZ EN PIE SE *******;
                    27063 5ELCID3457 GOMEZ PELAYET EN PIE SE *******;
        WORD #2485 OCCURS   7 TIMES.
           INDEX OF DIVERSIFICATION =  1484.00 WITH STANDARD DEVIATION OF  2519.82

LEUANTOS            23018 5ELCID2933 ******** EL REY, TAN BIEN LOS RE%IBIO.
                    24374 5ELCID3108 ******** EN PIE EL BUEN REY DON ALFONSSO
                    26176 5ELCID3337 ******** DEL ESCA@O & FUES PORAL LEON;
                    26642 5ELCID3402 ******** EN PIE MYO %ID EL CAMPEADOR;
                    26690 5ELCID3409 ******** EL REY, FIZO CALLAR LA CORT:
                    26727 5ELCID3414 ******** MYO %ID, AL REY LAS MANOS LE BESO:
                    26791 5ELCID3422 ******** EN PIE OIARRA & YNEGO XIMENEZ,
        WORD #2486 OCCURS   7 TIMES.
           INDEX OF DIVERSIFICATION =   627.83 WITH STANDARD DEVIATION OF   766.59

LEUAR                 903 5ELCID0116 AQUELAS NON LAS PUEDE *****, SINON, SER YEN VENTADAS;
                    10061 5ELCID1274 DAR LE QUIERO C CAUALLOS, & UOS YD GELOS *****;
                    10155 5ELCID1285 E MANDO MILL MARCOS DE PLATA A SAN PERO *****
                    11420 5ELCID1445 TODOS LOS DIAS DEL SIEGLO EN ***** LO ADELANT
                    20184 5ELCID2563 ***** LAS HEMOS A NUESTRAS TIERRAS DE CARRION,
        WORD #2487 OCCURS   5 TIMES.
           INDEX OF DIVERSIFICATION =  4819.25 WITH STANDARD DEVIATION OF  4807.86

LEUAREDES            8445 5ELCID1073 DE LO UUESTRO, O DELO MYO ********* ALGO.
                    10280 5ELCID1301 VOS, QUANDO YDES A CASTIELLA, ********* BUENOS MANDADOS.
                    10910 5ELCID1381 SI ********* LAS DUENAS, SIRUAN LAS ASU SABOR,
        WORD #2488 OCCURS   3 TIMES.

LEUAREMOS           20045 5ELCID2544 DIGAMOS QUE LAS ********* ATIERRAS DE CARRION,
                    20090 5ELCID2550 AUERES ********* GRANDES QUE VALEN GRANT VALOR;
        WORD #2489 OCCURS   2 TIMES.

LEUARIA             21083 5ELCID2679 ELUEGO ******* SUS FIJAS AL CAMPEADOR LEAL;
        WORD #2490 OCCURS   1 TIMES.

LEUARON             11489 5ELCID1453 DIREUOS DELOS CAUALLEROS QUE ******* EL MENSSAIE:
                    21619 5ELCID2749 ******* LES LOS MANTOS & LAS PIELES ARMINAS,
        WORD #2491 OCCURS   2 TIMES.

LEUAROS             11066 5ELCID1401 POR ******* A VALEN%IA QUE AUEMOS POR HEREDAD.
        WORD #2492 OCCURS   1 TIMES.

LEUAUA               4535 5ELCID0576 DEXA VNA TIENDA FITA & LAS OTRAS ******,
                     7930 5ELCID1012 PRISO LO AL CONDE, PORA SU TIERRA LO ******;
                    28620 5ELCID3654 LA COFIA & EL ALMOFAR TODO GELO ******,
        WORD #2493 OCCURS   3 TIMES.

LEUEDES              5059 5ELCID0639 TRES MILL MOROS ******* CON ARMAS DE LIDIAR;
                    10901 5ELCID1380 ******* VN PORTERO, TENGO QUE UOS AURA PRO;
                    23144 5ELCID2949 QUE GELOS ******* AVISTAS, O AIUNTAS, O A CORTES;
        WORD #2494 OCCURS   3 TIMES.
```

WORD C# PREFIX CONTEXT

LEUNATO 25842 5ELCID3291 FERRANGO%ALEZ EN PIE SE *******,
WORD #2495 OCCURS 1 TIMES.

LEUO 24529 5ELCID3127 ESSORA SE **** EN PIE EL BUEN REY DON ALFONSSO;
28606 5ELCID3653 ALLA **** EL ALMOFAR, FATA LA COFIA LEGAUA,
WORD #2496 OCCURS 2 TIMES.

LEUOS 16084 5ELCID2040 ***** EN PIE & EN LA BOCAL SALUDO.
WORD #2497 OCCURS 1 TIMES.

LEYDO 29243 5ELCID3734 ES *****, DAT NOS DEL VINO; SI NON TENEDES DINEROS, ECHAD
WORD #2498 OCCURS 1 TIMES.

LIBRADO 19159 5ELCID2423 CORTOL EL YELMO &, ******* TODO LO HAL,
WORD #2499 OCCURS 1 TIMES.

LIBRAR 28911 5ELCID3693 MANDO ****** EL CANPO EL BUEN REY DON ALFONSSO,
WORD #2500 OCCURS 1 TIMES.

LIBRAUAN 28237 5ELCID3605 ******** SE DEL CAMPO TODOS ADERREDOR.
WORD #2501 OCCURS 1 TIMES.

LIBRO 29219 5ELCID3731 QUIEN ESCRIUIO ESTE ***** DEL DIOS PARAYSO, AMEN
WORD #2502 OCCURS 1 TIMES.

LID 6156 5ELCID0784 QUE MYO %ID RUY DIAZ *** CAMPAL A VEN%IDA.
8706 5ELCID1106 AMENOS DE *** NOS PARTIRA AQUESTO;
8743 5ELCID1111 CONPE%AREMOS AQUESTA *** CAMPAL,
13060 5ELCID1656 CON DIOS A QUESTA *** YO LA HE DE ARRANCAR.
14378 5ELCID1819 DESTA *** QUE HA ARRANCADA CC CAUALLOS LE ENBIAUA ENPRESENTAIA,
14620 5ELCID1849 POCOS DIAS HA, REY, QUE VNA *** A ARRANCADO:
26267 5ELCID3349 QUANDO FUERE LA ***, SI PLOGUIERE AL CRIADOR,
26419 5ELCID3370 AL PARTIR DELA *** POR TU BOCA LO DIRAS,
27116 5ELCID3465 CRAS SEA LA ***, QUANDO SALIERE EL SOL,
27243 5ELCID3482 QUE FAGAN ESTA *** DELANT ESTANDO YO;
27794 5ELCID3547 POR VER ESTA ***, CA AVIEN ENDE SABOR;
28175 5ELCID3597 ESTA *** EN TOLEDO LAFIZIERADES, MAS NON QUISIESTES VOS.
28937 5ELCID3696 VEN%IERON ESTA ***, GRADO AL CRIADOR.
WORD #2503 OCCURS 13 TIMES.
INDEX OF DIVERSIFICATION = 1897.42 WITH STANDARD DEVIATION OF 3315.19

LIDES 10517 5ELCID1333 E FIZO %INCO ***** CAMPALES & TODAS LAS ARRANCO.
18444 5ELCID2334 HYO DESSEO *****, & UOS A CARRION;
19694 5ELCID2497 ARRANCO LAS ***** COMMO PLAZE AL CRIADOR,
WORD #2504 OCCURS 3 TIMES.

LIDIA 5803 5ELCID0733 QUAL ***** BIEN SOBRE EXORADO ARZON
18826 5ELCID2382 NOS DAQUENT VEREMOS COMMO ***** EL ABBAT.
WORD #2505 OCCURS 2 TIMES.

LIDIADO 19946 5ELCID2530 POR UOS AUEMOS ONDRA & AVEMOS *******.
WORD #2506 OCCURS 1 TIMES.

LIDIADOR 3956 5ELCID0502 ANTE RUY DIAZ EL ******** CONTADO,
5814 5ELCID0734 MIO %ID RUY DIAZ EL BUEN ********;
10433 5ELCID1322 BESAUA UOS LAS MANOS MYO %ID ********,
12004 5ELCID1522 MUGIER DEL %ID ******** ESSUS FFIJAS NATURALES;
19827 5ELCID2513 EL BUENO DE ALBARFANEZ, CAUALLERO ********,
WORD #2507 OCCURS 5 TIMES.
INDEX OF DIVERSIFICATION = 3966.75 WITH STANDARD DEVIATION OF 2914.48

LIDIAMOS 26013 5ELCID3316 MIEMBRAT QUANDO ******** %ERCA VALEN%IA LA GRAND;
WORD #2508 OCCURS 1 TIMES.

LIDIANDO 3930 5ELCID0499 ******** CON MOROS ENEL CAMPO,
5975 5ELCID0757 POR ESTAS FUER%AS FUERTE MIENTRE ********,
10220 5ELCID1294 QUE SIS FARTAS ******** & FIRIENDO CON SUS MANOS,
13444 5ELCID1704 EL QUE A QUI MURIERE ******** DE CARA,
WORD #2509 OCCURS 4 TIMES.

LIDIAR 4230 5ELCID0538 CON ALFONSSO MYO SE@OR NON QUERRIA ******.
5063 5ELCID0639 TRES MILL MOROS LEUEDES CON ARMAS DE ******;
5299 5ELCID0669 GRANDES SON LOS PODERES POR CON ELLOS ******;
11540 5ELCID1461 CAUALGEDES CON %IENTO GUISADOS PORA HUEBOS DE ******;
12940 5ELCID1641 MIS FIJAS & MI MUGIER VERME AN ******,
13038 5ELCID1653 NON AYADES PAUOR POR QUE ME VEADES ******,
13376 5ELCID1695 DAD ME CXXX CAUALLEROS PORA HUEBOS DE ******;
14173 5ELCID1794 QUANDO ES FARTO DE ****** CON AMAS LAS SUS MANOS,
19302 5ELCID2444 SEQUE DE ****** BIEN SODES PAGADOS;
19422 5ELCID2461 FARTOS DE ****** CON MOROS ENEL CAMPO.
27593 5ELCID3523 EL CAMPEADOR ALOS QUE HAN ****** TAN BIEN LOS CASTIGO:
WORD #2510 OCCURS 11 TIMES.
INDEX OF DIVERSIFICATION = 2335.30 WITH STANDARD DEVIATION OF 2998.56

WORD C# PREFIX CONTEXT

LIDIARA 19965 5ELCID2533 QUIEN ******* MEIOR OQUIEN FUERA EN ALCAN%O;
WORD #2511 OCCURS 1 TIMES.

LIDIARAN 19564 5ELCID2479 QUE ******** COMIGO EN CAMPO MYOS YERNOS AMOS ADOS;
26567 5ELCID3391 LOS QUE AN REBTADO ********, SIN SALUE DIOS
WORD #2512 OCCURS 2 TIMES.

LIDIARE 26228 5ELCID3344 ESTOT ******* AQUI ANTEL REY DON ALFONSSO
26341 5ELCID3359 LO QUE LES FIZIEMOS SER LES HA RETRAYDO; ESTO ******* ATOD EL MAS
26395 5ELCID3367 HYOLLO *******, NON PASSARA POR AL:
WORD #2513 OCCURS 3 TIMES.

LIDIAREMOS 5326 5ELCID0673 SI CON MOROS NON **********, NO NOS DARAN DEL PAN.
WORD #2514 OCCURS 1 TIMES.

LIDIARON 19787 5ELCID2508 DAQUESTA ARRANCADA QUE ******** DE CORA%ON
WORD #2515 OCCURS 1 TIMES.

LIDIASSEN 27869 5ELCID3556 COLADA & TIZON, QUE NON ********* CON ELLAS LOS DEL CANPEADOR;
WORD #2516 OCCURS 1 TIMES.

LIDIAUA 18875 5ELCID2388 ENSAYAUAS EL OBISPO, DIOS, QUE BIEN *******
WORD #2517 OCCURS 1 TIMES.

LIDIEDES 27923 5ELCID3563 HUEBOS VOS ES QUE ******** AGUISA DE VARONES,
WORD #2518 OCCURS 1 TIMES.

LIDIT 6518 5ELCID0831 DIOS NOS VALIO & VEN%IEMOS LA *****.
WORD #2519 OCCURS 1 TIMES.

LIEUA 4579 5ELCID0582 LAS OTRAS A BES *****, VNA TIENDA A DEXADA.
11345 5ELCID1435 HYO LO VERE CON EL %ID, SI DIOS ME ***** ALA.
18188 5ELCID2301 E ***** LO ADESTRANDO, ENLA RED LE METIO.
WORD #2520 OCCURS 3 TIMES.

LIEUAN 12294 5ELCID1561 DENTRO A VALEN%IA ****** LE EL MANDADO.
14364 5ELCID1817 E DOZIENTOS OMNES ****** EN SU CONPA@A,
15623 5ELCID1981 LOS YFANTES DE CARRION ****** GRANDES CONPA@AS.
WORD #2521 OCCURS 3 TIMES.

LIEUEN 736 5ELCID0093 DE NOCHE LO ******, QUE NON LO VEAN CHISTIANOS.
WORD #2522 OCCURS 1 TIMES.

LIEUES 22780 5ELCID2903 ****** EL MANDADO A CASTIELLA AL REY ALFONSSO;
WORD #2523 OCCURS 1 TIMES.

LIEUO 7637 5ELCID0978 DELO SO NON ***** NADA, DEXEM YR EN PAZ.
WORD #2524 OCCURS 1 TIMES.

LILON 3162 5ELCID0398 DE DIESTRO A ***** LAS TORRES, QUE MOROS LAS HAN;
WORD #2525 OCCURS 1 TIMES.

LINPIA 8780 5ELCID1116 DESPUES QUE NOS PARTIEMOS DELA ****** CHRISTIANDAD,
21250 5ELCID2700 FALARON VN VERGEL CON VNA ****** FUENT;
21545 5ELCID2739 ****** SALIE LA SANGRE SOBRE LOS %ICLATONES.
28582 5ELCID3649 RELUMBRA TOD EL CAMPO, TANTO ER ****** & CLARA;
WORD #2526 OCCURS 4 TIMES.

LIPIOS 26304 5ELCID3354 DE NATURA SOMOS DE LOS CONDES MAS ******,
WORD #2527 OCCURS 1 TIMES.

LIS 27164 5ELCID3472 SEA ESTA *** O MANDAREDES VOS.
WORD #2528 OCCURS 1 TIMES.

LO 118 5ELCID0016 EN SU CONPA@A LX PENDONES; EXIEN ** UER MUGIERES & UARONES,
260 5ELCID0033 POR MIEDO DEL REY ALFONSSO, QUE ASSI ** AUIEN PARADO
333 5ELCID0042 EL REY ** HA UEDADO, ANOCH DEL ETRO SU CARTA,
398 5ELCID0050 YA ** VEE EL %ID QUE DEL REY NON AUIE GRA%IA.
524 5ELCID0067 NON ** CONPRA, CA EL SELO AUIE CONSIGO;
554 5ELCID0070 FABLO MARTIN ATOLINEZ, ODREDES ** QUE A DICHO:
645 5ELCID0082 BIEN ** VEDES QUE YO NO TRAYO AUER, & HUEBOS ME SERIE
661 5ELCID0084 FER ** HE AMIDOS, DE GRADO NON AURIE NADA.
729 5ELCID0092 ENPE@AR GELO HE POR ** QUE FUERE GUISADO;
735 5ELCID0093 DE NOCHE ** LIEUEN, QUE NON LO VEAN CHISTIANOS.
739 5ELCID0093 DE NOCHE LO LIEUEN, QUE NON ** VEAN CHISTIANOS.
756 5ELCID0095 YO MAS NON PUEDO & AMYDOS ** FAGO.
761 5ELCID0096 MARTIN ANTOLINEZ NON ** DETARUA,
818 5ELCID0105 NON ** DETARDAN, TODOS TRES SE APARTARON.
885 5ELCID0114 YA ** VEDES QUE EL REY LEA AYRADO.
920 5ELCID0118 E PRESTALDE DE AUER ** QUE SEA GUISADO.
964 5ELCID0124 BIEN ** SABEMOS QUE EL ALGO GA@O,
1028 5ELCID0132 MYO %ID QUERRA ** QUE SSEA AGUISADO;
1128 5ELCID0145 QUE NON ** SEPAN MOROS NON CHRISTIANOS.
1221 5ELCID0157 ALO QUEM SEMEIA, DE ** MIO AUREDES ALGO;

WORD C# PREFIX CONTEXT

LO (CON'T)

1470 5ELCID0188 QUANDO ESTO CUO FECHO, ODREDES ** QUE FABLAUA:
1506 5ELCID0192 DEMOS LE BUEN DON, CA EL NO ** HA BUSCADO.
1515 5ELCID0194 VOS ** MERE%EDES, DARUOS QUEREMOS BUEN DADO,
1689 5ELCID0217 ATI ** GRADESCO, DIOS, QUE %IELO & TIERRA GUIAS:
1746 5ELCID0223 SI UOS ASSI ** FIZIEREDES & LA UENTURA ME FUERE COMPLIDA,
1936 5ELCID0246 GRADESCO ** ADIOS, MYO %ID, DIXO EL ABBAT DON SANCHO;
2058 5ELCID0259 BIEN LAS ABASTAD, YO ASSI UOS ** MANDO;
2152 5ELCID0271 YO ** VEO QUE ESTADES UOS EN YDA
2220 5ELCID0280 YA ** VEDES QUE PARTIR NOS EMOS EN VIDA,
2337 5ELCID0295 QUANDO ** SOPO MYO %ID EL DE BIUAR,
2397 5ELCID0303 ** QUE PERDEDES DOBLADO UOS LO COBRAR.
2402 5ELCID0303 LO QUE PERDEDES DOBLADO UOS ** COBRAR.
2496 5ELCID0315 SED MEMBRADOS COMMO ** DEUEDES FAR.
2545 5ELCID0322 CUEMO ** MANDO MYO %ID, ASSI LO AN TODOS HA FAR.
2550 5ELCID0322 CUEMO LO MANDO MYO %ID, ASSI ** AN TODOS HA FAR.
3248 5ELCID0409 MIENTRA QUE VISQUIEREDES BIEN SE FARA ** TO.
3409 5ELCID0430 VASSALLOS TAN BUENOS POR CORA%ON ** AN,
3416 5ELCID0431 MANDADO DE SO SE@OR TODO ** HAN AFAR.
3427 5ELCID0433 POR TAL ** FAZE MYO %ID QUE NO IO VENTASSE NADI.
3564 5ELCID0449 E YO CON ** C AQUI FINCARE EN LA %AGA,
3887 5ELCID0493 MUCHO UOS ** GRADESCO, CAMPEADOR CONTADO.
3913 5ELCID0497 ADIOS ** PROMETO, A AQUEL QUE ESTA EN ALTO:
3978 5ELCID0505 TODO ** OTRO AFELO EN UUESTRA MANO.
4055 5ELCID0516 AQUI NON ** PUEDEN VENDER NIN DAR EN PRESENTAIA;
4163 5ELCID0530 ** QUE YO DIXIER NON LO TENGADES AMAL:
4168 5ELCID0530 LO QUE YO DIXIER NON ** TENGADES AMAL:
4189 5ELCID0533 MAS EL CASTIELO NON ** QUIERO HERMAR:
4202 5ELCID0535 POR QUE ** PRIS DELLOS QUE DE MI NON DIGAN MAL.
4231 5ELCID0539 ** QUE DIXO EL %ID A TODOS LOS OTROS PLAZ.
4310 5ELCID0549 NON ** SABEN LOS MOROS EL ARDIMENT QUE AN.
4526 5ELCID0575 EL FIZO VN ART & NON ** DETARDAUA:
4558 5ELCID0580 VEYEN ** LOS DE ALCO%ER, DIOS, COMMO SE ALABAUAN
4836 5ELCID0612 METIOLA EN SOMO EN TODO ** MAS ALTO.
4978 5ELCID0629 AYROLO EL REY ALFONSSO, DE TIERRA ECHADO ** HA,
5020 5ELCID0635 ASSI FFERA ** DE SILOCA, QUE ES DEL OTRA PART.
5029 5ELCID0636 QUANDO ** OYO EL REY TAMIN, POR CUER LE PESO MAL:
5049 5ELCID0638 NON ** DETARDEDES, LOS DOS YD PORA ALLA,
5125 5ELCID0648 NON ** DETIENEN, VIENEN DE TODAS PARTES.
5290 5ELCID0668 QUE NOS QUERAMOS YR DE NOCH NO NOS ** CONSINTRAN;
5372 5ELCID0678 ONDRASTES UOS, MINAYA, CA AUER UOS ** YEDES DE FAR.
5482 5ELCID0691 MAS NON AGUIJEDES CON ELLA, SI YO NON UOS ** MANDAR.
5501 5ELCID0694 VIERON ** LAS AROBDAS DELOS MOROS, AL ALMOFALLA SEUAN TORNAR.
5586 5ELCID0703 NON DERANCHE NINGUNO FATA QUE YO ** MANDE.
5592 5ELCID0704 AQUEL PERO VERMUEZ NON ** PUDO ENDURAR,
5890 5ELCID0745 BIEN ** ACORREN MESNADAS DE CHRISTIANOS.
6344 5ELCID0808 BIEN ** AGUISA EL QUE EN BUEN ORA NASCO,
6443 5ELCID0823 ** QUE ROMANE%IERE DALDO A MI MUGIER & A MIS FIJAS,
6611 5ELCID0844 ASI ** AN ASMADO & METUDO EN CARTA:
6971 5ELCID0891 DE TODO MYO REYNO LOS QUE ** QUISIEREN FAR,
7074 5ELCID0904 EL DE RIO MARTIN TODO ** METIO EN PARIA.
7116 5ELCID0910 DEXO EL POYO, TODO ** DESENPARAUA,
7289 5ELCID0935 NON ** TARDO EL QUE EN BUEN ORA NASCO,
7307 5ELCID0937 E A DERREDOR TODO ** VA PREANDO.
7378 5ELCID0946 SONRRISOS EL CABOSO, QUE NON ** PUDO ENDURAR:
7394 5ELCID0948 QUI EN VN LOGAR MORA SIEMPRE, ** SO PUEDE MANGUAR;
7478 5ELCID0959 OUO GRAND PESAR & TOUOS ** A GRAND FONTA.
7513 5ELCID0963 FIRIOM EL SOBRINO & NON ** ENMENDO MAS;
7526 5ELCID0965 NON ** DESAFIE, NIL TORNE ENEMISTAD,
7621 5ELCID0976 MYO %ID QUANDO ** OYO, ENBIO PORA ALLA:
7630 5ELCID0977 DIGADES AL CONDE NON ** TENGA A MAL,
7650 5ELCID0980 ** DE ANTES & DE AGORA TODOM LO PECHARA;
7657 5ELCID0980 LO DE ANTES & DE AGORA TODOM ** PECHARA;
7673 5ELCID0983 ESSORA ** CONNOS%E MIO %ID EL DE BIUAR.
7923 5ELCID1012 PRISO ** AL CONDE, PORA SU TIERRA LO LEUAUA;
7929 5ELCID1012 PRISO LO AL CONDE, PORA SU TIERRA ** LEUAUA;
7934 5ELCID1013 ASOS CREENDEROS MANDAR ** GUARDAUA.
7984 5ELCID1020 EL NON ** QUIERE COMER, ATODOS LOS SOSANAUA:
8022 5ELCID1024 MYO %ID RUY DIAZ ODREDES ** QUE DIXO:
8034 5ELCID1026 SI ** QUE DIGO FIZIEREDES, SALDREDES DE CATIUO;
8134 5ELCID1037 SI ** FIZIEREDES, %ID, LO QUE AUEDES FABLADO,
8137 5ELCID1037 SI LO FIZIEREDES, %ID, ** QUE AUEDES FABLADO,
8188 5ELCID1043 MAS QUANTO AUEDES PERDIDO NON UOS ** DARE,
8206 5ELCID1045 QUE COMIGO ANDAN LAZRADOS, & NON UOS ** DARE.
8318 5ELCID1058 PAGADO ES MYO %ID, QUE ** ESTA AGUARDANDO,
8410 5ELCID1069 EN GRADO UOS ** TENGO LO QUE ME AUEDES DEXADO.
8412 5ELCID1069 EN GRADO UOS LO TENGO ** QUE ME AUEDES DEXADO.
8440 5ELCID1073 DE ** UUESTRO, O DELO MYO LEUAREDES ALGO.
8492 5ELCID1080 ** QUE NON FERIE EL CABOSO POR QUANTO ENEL MUNDO HA,
8702 5ELCID1105 SI NOS %ERCAR VIENEN, CONDERECHO ** FAZEN.
8795 5ELCID1118 GRADO A DIOS, ** NUESTRO FUE ADELANT.
8856 5ELCID1128 CAMPEADOR, FAGAMOS ** QUE AUOS PLAZE.
8922 5ELCID1136 QUIS CADA VNO DELLOS BIEN SABE ** QUE HA DE FAR.
9273 5ELCID1149 FIJOS & MUGIERES VER ** MURIR DE FANBRE.
9425 5ELCID1198 AL SABOR DELA GANAN%IA NON ** QUIERE DETARDAR,

WORD C# PREFIX CONTEXT

LO (CON'T)

9460 5ELCID1202 MYO %ID DON RODRIGO NON ** QUISO DETARDAR,
9557 5ELCID1214 EL ORO & LA PLATA QUI EN VOS ** PODRIE CONTAR?
9826 5ELCID1247 DE QUE SON PAGADOS; EL AMOR DE MY %ID YA ** YUAN PROUANDO.
9855 5ELCID1250 QUE SIS PUDIESSEN YR, FER ** YEN DE GRADO.
9864 5ELCID1251 ESTO MANDO MYO %ID, MINAYA ** OUO CONSSEIADO:
10235 5ELCID1296 QUANDO ** OYO MYO %ID, DE AQUESTO FUE PAGADO:
10351 5ELCID1311 DEMANDO POR ALFONSSO, DO ** PODRIE FALLAR.
10367 5ELCID1313 TORNOS A CARRION, Y ** PODRIE FALLAR.
10466 5ELCID1326 MAGER EN TIERRA AGENA, EL BIEN FAZE ** SO;
10878 5ELCID1377 NON ** DIZEN A NADI, & FINCO ESTA RAZON.
10955 5ELCID1386 EN TODO SODES PRO, EN ESTO ASSI ** FAGADES:
10970 5ELCID1388 SOMOS EN SO PRO QUANTO ** PODEMOS FAR;
11049 5ELCID1399 SANO ** DEXE & CON TAN GRAND RICTAD.
11095 5ELCID1404 DIXO DO@A XIMENA: EL CRIADOR ** MANDE
11337 5ELCID1435 HYO ** VERE CON EL %ID, SI DIOS ME LIEUA ALA.
11348 5ELCID1436 POR ** QUE AUEDES FECHO BUEN COSIMENT Y AURA.
11362 5ELCID1437 DIXO RACHEL & VIDAS: EL CRIADOR ** MANDE
11369 5ELCID1438 SI NON, DEXAREMOS BURGOS, YR ** HEMOS BUSCAR.
11411 5ELCID1444 AQUESTE MONESTERIO NO ** QUIERA OLBIDAR,
11421 5ELCID1445 TODOS LOS DIAS DEL SIEGLO EN LEUAR ** ADELANT
11431 5ELCID1447 RESPUSO MINAYA: FER ** HE DE VELUNTAD.
11478 5ELCID1454 AL ORA QUE ** SOPO MYO %ID EL DE BIUAR,
11572 5ELCID1466 HYD PORA MEDINA QUANTO ** PUDIEREDES FAR,
11728 5ELCID1487 DIXO AUEGALUON: FER ** HE DE VELUNTAD.
11801 5ELCID1496 ESTO NON DETARDO, CA DE CORA%ON ** HAN;
11981 5ELCID1519 ENEL OMBRO ** SALUDA, CA TAL ES SU HUSAIE:
12110 5ELCID1536 EL PORTERO DEL REY QUITAR ** MANDAUA;
12130 5ELCID1539 EL REY ** PAGO TODO, & QUITO SEUA MINAYA.
12491 5ELCID1584 EL QUE EN BUEN ORA NASCO NON ** DETARDAUA:
12561 5ELCID1594 QUANDO ** VIO DO@A XIMENA, A PIES SE LE ECHAUA:
12633 5ELCID1603 OYD ** QUE DIXO EL QUE EN BUEN ORA NASCO:
12881 5ELCID1634 TODO EL BIEN QUE YO HE, TODO ** TENGO DELANT:
12930 5ELCID1640 ENTRARE EN LAS ARMAS, NON ** PODRE DEXAR;
13358 5ELCID1693 FABLAUA MYNAYA, NON ** QUISO DETARDAR:
13742 5ELCID1741 QUANDO AL REY DE MARUECOS ASSI ** AN ARRANCADO,
13775 5ELCID1746 RE%IBIEN ** LAS DUE@AS QUE LO ESTAN ESPERANDO.
13779 5ELCID1746 RE%IBIEN LO LAS DUE@AS QUE ** ESTAN ESPERANDO.
13811 5ELCID1750 ESTO DIOS SE ** QUISO CON TODOS LOS SOS SANTOS,
13919 5ELCID1763 HYA MUGIER DA@A XIMENA, NOM ** AUIEDES ROGADO?
13948 5ELCID1767 QUE ** SEPAN EN CASTIELLA, AQUIEN SIRUIERON TANTO.
13955 5ELCID1768 ** DE UUESTRAS FIJAS VENIR SEA MAS POR ESPA%IO.
13982 5ELCID1771 COMMO ** DIXO EL %ID ASSI LO HAN ACABADO.
13987 5ELCID1771 COMMO LO DIXO EL %ID ASSI ** HAN ACABADO.
14019 5ELCID1776 QUIERO UOS DEZIR ** QUE ES MAS GRANADO:
14188 5ELCID1796 ** QUE CAYE AEL MUCHO ERA SOBEIANO;
14253 5ELCID1803 EL BUENO DE MYO %ID NON ** TARDO POR NADA:
14279 5ELCID1807 PRENDED ** QUE QUISIEREDES, LO OTRO REMANGA.
14282 5ELCID1807 PRENDED LO QUE QUISIEREDES, ** OTRO REMANGA.
14389 5ELCID1820 E SERUIR ** HE SIENPRE MIENTRA QUE OUISSE EL ALMA.
14528 5ELCID1838 ADIO ** AUIEN LOS DEL QUE EN BUEN ORA NASCO,
14920 5ELCID1886 CON UUESTRO CONSSEIO ** QUEREMOS FER NOS,
14975 5ELCID1893 MAS PUES BOS ** QUEREDES, ENTREMOS EN LA RAZON.
15014 5ELCID1898 SIRUEM MYO %ID EL CAMPEADOR, EL ** MERE%E,
15057 5ELCID1903 SED BUENOS MENSSAGEROS, & RUEGO UOS ** YO
15088 5ELCID1908 ROGAR GELO EMOS ** QUE DEZIDES UOS;
15096 5ELCID1909 DESPUES FAGA EL %ID ** QUE OUIERE SABOR.
15149 5ELCID1916 QUANDO ** SOPO EL BUEN CAMPEADOR,
15217 5ELCID1927 ** QUEL ROGAUA ALFONSSO EL DE LEON
15248 5ELCID1931 QUANDO ** OYO MYO %ID EL BUEN CAMPEADOR,
15280 5ELCID1935 CON GRAND AFAN GANE ** QUE HE YO;
15285 5ELCID1936 ADIOS ** GRADESCO QUE DEL REY HE SU GRA%IA,
15320 5ELCID1940 MAS PUES ** CONSEIA EL QUE MAS VALE QUE NOS,
15344 5ELCID1942 AFE DIOS DEL %IELLO QUE NOS ACUERDE EN ** MIIOR.
15373 5ELCID1946 ACORDAR UOS YEDES DESPUES ATODO ** MEIOR.
15401 5ELCID1951 FASTA DO ** FALLASSEMOS BUSCAR LO YREMOS NOS,
15404 5ELCID1951 FASTA DO LO FALLASSEMOS BUSCAR ** YREMOS NOS,
15418 5ELCID1953 MAS ** QUE EL QUISIERE, ESSO QUERAMOS NOS.
15435 5ELCID1955 AYAMOS VISTAS QUANDO ** QUIERE MYO SE@OR.
15450 5ELCID1958 ** QUE EL REY QUISIERE, ESSO FERA EL CAMPEADOR.
15499 5ELCID1964 NON ** DETARDAN, A MYO %ID SE TORNAUAN.
15582 5ELCID1976 ** VNO A DEBDAN & LO OTRO PAGAUAN;
15587 5ELCID1976 LO VNO A DEBDAN & ** OTRO PAGAUAN;
15657 5ELCID1986 NON ** DETARDA, PORA LAS VISTAS SE ADOBO;
15889 5ELCID2015 RE%EBIR ** SALEN CON TAN GRAND ONOR.
15896 5ELCID2016 DON ** OUO A CIO EL QUE EN BUEN ORA NASCO,
15928 5ELCID2020 COMMO ** COMIDIA EL QUE EN BUEN ORA NA%IO,
16023 5ELCID2032 ASSI ESTANDO, DEDES ME UUESTRA AMOR, QUE ** OYAN QUANTOS AQUI SON.
16161 5ELCID2050 E CRAS FEREMOS ** QUE PLOGIERE AUOS.
16171 5ELCID2051 BESO LE LA MANO MYO CID, ** OTORGO.
16199 5ELCID2055 RESPUSO MIO %ID: ASSI ** MANDE EL CRIADOR
16266 5ELCID2063 EL CAMPEADOR ALOS SOS ** MANDO
16324 5ELCID2071 NON ** TARDO EL REY, LA RAZON CONPE%O:
16348 5ELCID2074 ASI ** MANDE CHRISTUS QUE SEA ASO PRO.
16388 5ELCID2078 ELLOS UOS LAS PIDEN & MANDO UOS ** YO.

WORD C# PREFIX CONTEXT

LO (CON'T)

16631 5ELCID2107 ** QUE UOS PLOGIERE, DELLOS FET, CAMPEADOR.
16648 5ELCID2109 MUCHO UOS ** GRADESCO, COMMO A REY & A SE@OR
16717 5ELCID2117 CADA VNO ** QUE PIDE, NADI NOL DIZE DE NO.
16806 5ELCID2128 AQUI ** DIGO ANTE MYO SE@OR EL REY ALFONSSO:
17023 5ELCID2155 AFE DIOS DEL %IELO, QUE ** PONGA EN BUEN LOGAR
17175 5ELCID2173 QUE ES LARGO DE LENGUA, MAS EN ** AL NON ES TAN PRO.
17230 5ELCID2179 VOS CON ELLOS SED, QUE ASSI UOS ** MANDO YO.
17335 5ELCID2193 TODO ** QUE UOS FECHES ES DE BUENA GUISA.
17384 5ELCID2199 MAS BIEN SABET VERDAD QUE NON ** LEUANTE YO:
17545 5ELCID2220 PUES QUE AFAZER ** AUEMOS, POR QUE LO YMOS TARDANDO?
17549 5ELCID2220 PUES QUE AFAZER LO AUEMOS, POR QUE ** YMOS TARDANDO?
17636 5ELCID2231 POR MANO DEL REY ALFONSSO, QUE AMI ** OUO MANDADO,
17984 5ELCID2275 QUES PAGE DES CASAMIENTO MYO %ID O EL QUE ** ALGO
18111 5ELCID2291 EL MANTO & EL BRIAL TODO SUZIO ** SACO.
18165 5ELCID2298 EL LEON QUANDO ** VIO, ASSI EN VERGON%O,
18185 5ELCID2300 MYO %ID DON RODRIGO ALCUELLO ** TOMO,
18189 5ELCID2301 E LIEUA ** ADESTRANDO, ENLA RED LE METIO.
18196 5ELCID2302 AMARAUILLA ** HAN QUANTOS QUE YSON,
18486 5ELCID2340 ASSI ** OTORGA DON PERO CUEMO SE ALABA FERRANDO.
18538 5ELCID2346 AMARAULLA ** AUIEN MUCHOS DESSOS CHRISTIANOS,
18545 5ELCID2347 CA NUNQUA ** VIERAN, CA NUEUOS SON LEGADOS.
18567 5ELCID2350 OYD ** QUE FABLO EL QUE EN BUEN ORA NASCO:
18808 5ELCID2380 ESSORA DIXO MYO %ID: ** QUE UOS QUEREDES PLAZ ME.
19129 5ELCID2419 MAS BAUIECA EL DE MIO %ID ALCAN%ANDO ** VA.
19161 5ELCID2423 CORTOL EL YELMO &, LIBRADO TODO ** HAL,
19443 5ELCID2464 POR BIEN ** DIXO EL %ID, MAS ELLOS LO TOUIERON AMAL.
19449 5ELCID2464 POR BIEN LO DIXO EL %ID, MAS ELLOS ** TOUIERON AMAL.
19488 5ELCID2469 DESTA ARRANCADA, QUE ** TENIEN EN SO SALUO,
19559 5ELCID2478 QUANDO VEO ** QUE AUIA SABOR,
19593 5ELCID2483 ** VNO ES NUESTRO, LO OTRO HAN EN SALUO.
19597 5ELCID2483 LO VNO ES NUESTRO, ** OTRO HAN EN SALUO.
19629 5ELCID2488 ASSI ** FAZEN TODOS, CA ERAN ACORDADOS.
19723 5ELCID2501 ELLOS ** TEMEN, CA NON LO PIESSO YO:
19727 5ELCID2501 ELLOS LO TEMEN, CA NON ** PIESSO YO:
19951 5ELCID2531 PENSAD DELO OTRO, QUE ** NUESTRO TENEMOS LO EN SALUO.
19954 5ELCID2531 PENSAD DELO OTRO, QUE LO NUESTRO TENEMOS ** EN SALUO.
20076 5ELCID2548 ANTE QUE NOS RETRAYAN ** QUE CUNTIO DEL LEON.
20135 5ELCID2556 ANTES QUE NOS RETRAYAN ** QUE FUE DEL LEON.
20209 5ELCID2566 VERAN UUESTRAS FIJAS ** QUE AUEMOS NOS,
20297 5ELCID2576 BIEN ** SABEDES UOS QUE LAS GANE AGUISA DE VARON;
20323 5ELCID2579 QUE ** SEPAN EN GALLIZIA & EN CASTIELLA & EN LEON,
20359 5ELCID2583 ATORGADO ** HAN ESTO LOS YFFANTES DE CARRION.
20375 5ELCID2585 CONPIE%AN A RE%EBIR ** QUE EL %ID MANDO.
20468 5ELCID2598 DEBDO NOS ES A CUNPLIR ** QUE MANDAREDES VOS.
20499 5ELCID2602 EL FIZO AQUESTO, LA MADRE ** DOBLAUA;
20718 5ELCID2630 RESPONDIEN LOS YERNOS: ASSI ** MANDE DIOS
20854 5ELCID2648 EL MORO QUANDO ** SOPO, PLOGOL DE CORA%ON;
20969 5ELCID2664 TAN EN SALUO ** ABREMOS COMMO LO DE CARRION;
20972 5ELCID2664 TAN EN SALUO LO ABREMOS COMMO ** DE CARRION;
21122 5ELCID2684 DIOS ** QUIERA & LO MANDE, QUE DE TODEL MUNDO ES SE@OR,
21125 5ELCID2684 DIOS LO QUIERA & ** MANDE, QUE DE TODEL MUNDO ES SE@OR,
21305 5ELCID2708 ASSI ** MANDARON LOS YFANTES DE CARRION,
21351 5ELCID2714 BIEN ** CREADES, DON ELUIRA & DO@A SOL,
21470 5ELCID2730 QUE POR ** QUE NOS MERE%EMOS NO LO PRENDEMOS NOS;
21475 5ELCID2730 QUE POR LO QUE NOS MERE%EMOS NO ** PRENDEMOS NOS;
21493 5ELCID2733 RETRAER UOS ** AN EN VISTAS O EN CORTES.
21500 5ELCID2734 ** QUE RUEGAN LAS DUENAS NON LES HA NINGUN PRO.
21553 5ELCID2740 YA ** SIENTEN ELLAS EN LOS SOS CORA%ONES.
21981 5ELCID2797 SI UOS ** MERESCA, MYO PRIMO, NUESTRO PADRE EL CANPEADOR,
22117 5ELCID2815 QUANDO EL ** OYO PESOL DE CORA%ON,
22306 5ELCID2841 NON ** DETARDAN EL MANDADO DE SU SE@OR,
22397 5ELCID2853 MUCHO UOS ** GRADE%E, ALLA DO ESTA, MYO %ID EL CANPEADOR,
22407 5ELCID2854 ASSI ** FFAGO YO QUE AQUI ESTO.
22455 5ELCID2860 ATANTO UOS ** GRADIMOS COMMO SI VIESSEMOS AL CRAIDOR;
22465 5ELCID2861 EUOS A EL ** GRADID, QUANDO BIUAS SOMOS NOS.
22941 5ELCID2922 AL REY EN SAN FAGUNT ** FALLO.
23211 5ELCID2957 FIZ ** POR BIEN, QUE FFUESSE A SU PRO.
23243 5ELCID2961 ** QUE NON CUYDAUA FER DE TODA ESTA SAZON,
23354 5ELCID2975 ASSI COMMO ** DIXO, SUYO ERA EL CUYDADO:
23361 5ELCID2976 NON ** DETIENE POR NADA ALFONSSO EL CASTELLANO,
23422 5ELCID2983 POR TODAS SUS TIERRAS ASSI ** YUAN PENSSANDO,
23478 5ELCID2990 DIXO EL REY: NO ** FERE, SIN SALUE DIOS
23498 5ELCID2993 QUI ** FER NON QUISIESSE, O NO YR A MI CORT,
23516 5ELCID2995 HYA ** VIERON QUE ES AFER LOS YFANTES DE CARRION,
23692 5ELCID3018 BIEN ** SOPIESSE QUE Y SERIE ESSA NOCH.
23700 5ELCID3019 QUANDO ** OYO EL REY, PLOGOL DE CORA%ON;
23760 5ELCID3027 QUANDO ** OYO EL REY, POR NADA NON TARDO;
23799 5ELCID3032 DIOS ** MANDE QUE POR UOS SE ONDRE OY LA CORT
24175 5ELCID3083 ASSI COMMO ** ADICHO, TODOS ADOBADOS SON.
24303 5ELCID3098 POR TALLO FAZE ESTO QUE RECABDAR QUIERE TODO ** SUYO;
24365 5ELCID3107 QUANDO ** VIERON ENTRAR AL QUE EN BUEN ORA NA%IO,
24401 5ELCID3111 AGRANT ONDRA ** RE%IBEN AL QUE EN BUEN ORA NA%IO.
24470 5ELCID3120 ** QUE DIXO EL %ID AL REY PLOGO DE CORA%ON.
24597 5ELCID3134 GRANDE TUERTO LE HAN TENIDO, SABEMOS ** TODOS NOS;

WORD C# PREFIX CONTEXT

LO (CON'T)

24697 5ELCID3146 MUCHO UOS ** GRADESCO CCMMO A REY & A SE@OR,
24834 5ELCID3163 APRIESSA ** YUAN TRAYENDO & ACUERDAN LA RAZON:
25172 5ELCID3205 HYO FAZIENDO ESTO, ELLOS ACABARON ** SO;
25340 5ELCID3226 MAS EN NUESTRO IUUIZIO ASSI ** MANDAMOS NOS,
25345 5ELCID3227 QUE AQUI ** ENTERGEDES DENTRO EN LA CORT.
25431 5ELCID3238 EL ORO & LA PLATA ESPENDIESTES ** VOS;
25435 5ELCID3239 POR JUUIZIO ** DAMOS ANTEL REY DON ALFONSSO:
25508 5ELCID3248 ENPRESTAN LES DELO AGENO, QUE NON LES CUMPLE ** SUYO.
25593 5ELCID3259 O EN ALGUNA RAZON? AQUI ** MEIORARE A JUUIZYO DELA CORT.
25673 5ELCID3269 SI NON RECUDEDES, VEA ** ESTA CORT.
25928 5ELCID3304 AMI ** DIZEN, ATI DAN LAS OREIADAS.
25975 5ELCID3311 BIEN ** SABEDES QUE YO NON PUEDO MAS;
25983 5ELCID3312 POR ** QUE YO CUIER AFER POR MI NON MANCARA.
26124 5ELCID3330 NON TE VIENE EN MIENTE EN VALEN%IA ** DEL LEON,
26294 5ELCID3353 DIEGO GON%ALEZ ODREDES ** QUE DIXO:
26332 5ELCID3359 ** QUE LES FIZIEMOS SER LES HA RETRAYDO; ESTO LIDIARE ATOD EL MAS
26365 5ELCID3363 ** DEL LEON NON SE TE DEUE OLBIDAR;
26423 5ELCID3370 AL PARTIR DELA LID POR TU BOCA ** DIRAS,
26457 5ELCID3376 EN ** QUE FABLO AVIE POCO RECABDO:
26491 5ELCID3380 E PRENDER MAQUILAS, COMMO ** SUELE FAR
26707 5ELCID3411 QUE PLEGA AUOS, & ATORGAR ** HE YO,
26740 5ELCID3415 QUANDO AUOS PLAZE, OTORGO ** YO, SE@OR,
26886 5ELCID3435 DEZID, MYNAYA, ** QUE OUIEREDES SABOR.
27173 5ELCID3473 ENESSORA DIXO MIO %ID. NO ** FARE, SENOR.
27206 5ELCID3478 HYO VOS ** SOBRELIEUO COMMO BUEN VASSALLO FAZE A SE@OR,
27304 5ELCID3489 ELLOS SON ADOBADOS PORA CUMPLLIR TODO ** SO;
27320 5ELCID3491 ESSORA RESPUSO EL REY: ASSI ** MANDE DIOS
27467 5ELCID3509 HYO ** JURO PAR SANT ESIDRO EL DE LEON
27564 5ELCID3520 QUIEN VOS ** TOLLER QUISIERE NOL VALA EL CRIADOR,
27628 5ELCID3527 DIXO MARTIN ANTOLINEZ: POR QUE ** DEZIDES, SE@OR
27754 5ELCID3542 EL COMETER FUE MALO, QUE ** AL NOS ENPE%O,
27851 5ELCID3554 ANDIDIERON EN PLEYTO, DIXIERON ** AL REY ALFONSSO,
27953 5ELCID3567 CA TODOS ** SABEN QUE LO BUSCASTES VOS.
27956 5ELCID3567 CA TODOS LO SABEN QUE ** BUSCASTES VOS.
28509 5ELCID3640 POR LA COPLA DEL CAUALLO EN TIERRA ** ECHO.
28512 5ELCID3641 ASSI ** TENIEN LAS YENTES QUE MAL FERIDO ES DE MUERT.
28532 5ELCID3643 QUANDO ** VIO FERRANGO%ALEZ, CONUUO ATIZON;
28630 5ELCID3656 ** VNO CAYO ENEL CAMPO & LO AL SUSO FINCAUA.
28636 5ELCID3656 LO VNO CAYO ENEL CAMPO & ** AL SUSO FINCAUA.
28679 5ELCID3661 VN COLPEL DIO DE LANO, CON ** AGUDO NOL TOMAUA.
28854 5ELCID3685 CON EL DIO VNA TUERTA, DELA SIELLA ** ENCAMO,
28862 5ELCID3686 AL TIRAR DELA LAN%A EN TIERRA ** ECHO,
29139 5ELCID3721 AMAYOR ONDRA LAS CASA QUE ** QUE PRIMERO FUE.
29259 5ELCID3735 ALA VNOS PE@OS, QUE BIEN VOS ** DARARAN SOBRELOS.
WORD #2529 OCCURS 316 TIMES.
INDEX OF DIVERSIFICATION = 91.51 WITH STANDARD DEVIATION OF 105.48

LOCURA 11608 5ELCID1471 GRAND ****** SERIE SI LA DESENPARAS;
WORD #2530 OCCURS 1 TIMES.

LOGAR 993 5ELCID0128 EN ***** LAS METAMOS QUE NON SEAN VENTADAS.
4774 5ELCID0605 EN VN ORA & VN POCO DE ***** CCC MOROS MATAN.
4988 5ELCID0630 VINO POSAR SOBRE ALCO%ER, EN VN TAN FUERTE *****;
5579 5ELCID0702 QUEDAS SED, MENADAS, AQUI EN ESTE *****,
5795 5ELCID0732 CAYEN EN VN POCO DE ***** MOROS MUERTOS MILL & CCC YA.
7391 5ELCID0948 QUI EN VN ***** MORA SIEMPRE, LO SO PUEDE MANGUAR;
9010 5ELCID1146 GRAND'ES EL GOZO QUE VA POR ES *****.
9530 5ELCID1211 GRANDES SON LOS GOZOS QUE VAN POR ES *****,
12698 5ELCID1611 ALA LAS SUBIE ENEL MAS ALTO *****;
17027 5ELCID2155 AFE DIOS DEL %IELO, QUE LO PONGA EN BUEN *****
23936 5ELCID3049 TERNE VIGILIA EN AQUESTE SANTO *****.
27835 5ELCID3552 EN OTRO ***** SE ARMAN LOS YFANTES DE CARRION,
29211 5ELCID3730 EN ESTE ***** SE ACABA ESTA RAZON.
WORD #2531 OCCURS 13 TIMES.
INDEX OF DIVERSIFICATION = 2350.50 WITH STANDARD DEVIATION OF 2076.45

LOGARES 28409 5ELCID3628 BIEN EN DOS ******* EL ESTIL LE QUEBRO.
WORD #2532 OCCURS 1 TIMES.

LOGRADO 19361 5ELCID2452 AQUELOS QUE GELOS DIERAN NON GELO AUIEN *******.
WORD #2533 OCCURS 1 TIMES.

LOGRARAN 22243 5ELCID2833 NON LA ******** LOS YFANTES DE CARRION;
WORD #2534 OCCURS 1 TIMES.

LOMA 3380 5ELCID0426 E POR LA **** AYUSO PIENSSAN DE ANDAR.
WORD #2535 OCCURS 1 TIMES.

LONGINOS 2784 5ELCID0352 ******** ERA %IEGO, QUE NUQUAS VIO ALGUANDRE,
WORD #2536 OCCURS 1 TIMES.

LOOVO 23738 5ELCID3024 QUANDO ***** A OIO EL BUEN REY DON ALFFONSSO,
WORD #2537 OCCURS 1 TIMES.

WORD C# PREFIX CONTEXT

LORA 2196 5ELCID0277 **** DELOS OICS, TAN FUERTE MIENTRE SOSPIRA:
WORD #2538 OCCURS 1 TIMES.

LORAN 20732 5ELCID2632 EL PADRE CCN LAS FIJAS ***** DE CORA%ON,
WORD #2539 OCCURS 1 TIMES.

LORANDO 7 5ELCID0001 DELOS SCS OIOS TAN FUERTE MIENTRE *******,
2931 5ELCID0370 ******* DE LCS OIOS, QUE NON SABE QUE SE FAR.
2967 5ELCID0374 ******* DELOS OIOS, CUE NCN VIESTES ATAL,
15953 5ELCID2023 ******* DELCS OIOS, TANTO AUIE EL GOZO MAYOR;
WORD #2540 OCCURS 4 TIMES.

LORAR 6711 5ELCID0856 MOROS & MORAS COMPE%ARON DE *****.
WORD #2541 OCCURS 1 TIMES.

LORASSEN 10232 5ELCID1295 ALOS DIAS DEL SIEGLO NCN LE ******** CHRISTIANOS.
WORD #2542 OCCURS 1 TIMES.

LORAUA 2102 5ELCID0265 ****** DELOS OIOS, QUISCL BESAR LAS MANOS:
WORD #2543 OCCURS 1 TIMES.

LORAUAN 12618 5ELCID1600 DEL GOZO QUE AUIEN DE LCS SOS OIOS *******.
22481 5ELCID2863 ******* DELCS OIOS LAS DUE@AS & ALBARFANEZ,
WORD #2544 OCCURS 2 TIMES.

LORIGA 5764 5ELCID0728 TANTA ****** FALSSA DESMANCHAR
6010 5ELCID0762 POR LA ****** AYUSO LA SANGRE DESTELLADO;
19003 5ELCID2404 TANTO BRA%C CON ****** VERIEDES CAER A PART,
28457 5ELCID3634 TRES DCBLES DE ****** TENIE FERNANDO, AQUESTOL PRESTO,
WORD #2545 OCCURS 4 TIMES.

LORIGAS 4544 5ELCID0578 LAS ******* VESTICAS & %INTAS LAS ESPADAS,
24109 5ELCID3074 DE SUSO LAS ******* TAN BLANCAS COMMO EL SOL;
24117 5ELCID3075 SOBRE LAS ******* ARMINCS & PELI%ONES,
WORD #2546 OCCURS 3 TIMES.

LOS 13 5ELCID0002 TORNAUA LA CABE%A & ESAUA *** CATANDO.
92 5ELCID0013 ME%IO MYO %ID *** CMBROS & ENGRAMEO LA TIESTA:
208 5ELCID0027 QUE PERDERIE *** AUERES & MAS LOS OIOS DELA CARA,
212 5ELCID0027 QUE PERDERIE LOS AUERES & MAS *** OIOS DELA CARA,
219 5ELCID0028 E AUN DEMAS *** CUERPCS & LAS ALMAS.
275 5ELCID0035 *** DE MYO %ID A ALTAS UOZES LAMAN,
283 5ELCID0036 *** DE DENTRO NON LES QUERIEN TORNAR PALABRA.
359 5ELCID0045 SI NON, PERDERIEMOS *** AUERES & LAS CASAS,
366 5ELCID0046 E DEMAS *** OIOS DELAS CARAS.
421 5ELCID0053 FINCO *** Y@OICS, DE CORA%CN ROGAUA.
535 5ELCID0068 DE TODO CONDUCHO BIEN *** OUO BASTIDOS.
545 5ELCID0069 PAGOS MYO %ID EL CAMPEADOR & TODOS *** OTROS QUEUAN ASO %ERUICIO
689 5ELCID0088 *** GUADAME%IS UERMEICS & LCS CLAUOS BIEN DORADOS.
693 5ELCID0088 LOS GUADAME%IS UERMEICS & *** CLAUOS BIEN DORADOS.
747 5ELCID0094 VEALO EL CRIADOR CCN TODOS *** SOS SANTOS,
807 5ELCID0103 O SODES, RACHEL & VIDAS, *** MYOS AMIGOS CAROS?
1077 5ELCID0138 HUEBOS AUEMCS QUE NOS DEDES *** MARCHOS.
1179 5ELCID0152 AFEUOS *** ALA TIENDA DEL CAMPEADOR CONTADO;
1315 5ELCID0168 YO YRE CON UUSO, QUE ADUGAMOS *** MARCOS,
1448 5ELCID0185 NOTOLOS DON MARTINO, SIN PESO *** TOMAUA;
1450 5ELCID0186 *** OTROS CCC EN ORO GELOS PAGAUAN.
1463 5ELCID0187 %INCO ESCUDEROS TIENE DCN MARTINO, ATODOS *** CARGAUA.
1556 5ELCID0199 GRADE%IOLO DON MARTINO & RECIBIO *** MARCHOS;
1589 5ELCID0203 RE%IBIOLO EL %ID ABIERTCS AMOS *** BRA%OS:
1721 5ELCID0220 NON SE SIENTRARE Y MAS ENTODOS *** MYOS DIAS.
1798 5ELCID0229 CASTIGAR *** HE CCMMO ABRAN AFAR.
1848 5ELCID0235 APRIESSA CANTAN *** GALLOS & QUIEREN QUEBRAR ALBORES,
1870 5ELCID0238 REZAUA *** MATINES ABUELTA DELOS ALBORES.
2028 5ELCID0255 DUES FIJAS DEXO NI@AS & PRENDET LAS EN *** BRA%OS;
2099 5ELCID0264 ANTEL CAMPEADCR DO@A XIMENA FINCO *** YNOIOS AMOS,
2284 5ELCID0287 POR CASTIELLA OYENDO UAN *** PREGONES,
2354 5ELCID0297 APRIESSA CAUALGA, RE%EBIR *** SALIE,
2423 5ELCID0306 *** VJ DIAS DE PLAZO PASSADOS LOS AN,
2429 5ELCID0306 LOS VJ DIAS DE PLAZO PASSADOS *** AN,
2502 5ELCID0316 ALA MA@ANA, QUANDO *** GALLOS CANTARAN,
2589 5ELCID0327 ECHOS DO@A XIMENA EN *** GRADOS DELANTEL ALTAR,
2690 5ELCID0340 SALUEST A DANIEL CON *** LEONES EN LA MALA CAR%EL,
2719 5ELCID0344 MOSTRANDO *** MIRACLCS, POR EN AUEMOS QUE FABLAR:
2851 5ELCID0360 QUEBRANTESTE LAS PUERTAS & SAQUESTE *** PADRES SANTOS.
2857 5ELCID0361 TUERES REY DE *** REYES & DE TODEL MUNDO PADRE,
2933 5ELCID0370 LORANDO DE *** OIOS, QUE NON SABE QUE SE FAR.
2986 5ELCID0376 MYO %ID CON *** SCS VASSALLOS PENSSO DE CAUALGAR,
3475 5ELCID0438 COMMO *** CONSEIAUA MINAYA ALBARFANEZ:
3502 5ELCID0442 VOS CON *** CC YD UOS EN ALGARA; ALA VAYA ALBARABAREZ,
3556 5ELCID0448 QUE POR MIEDO DE *** MOROS NON DEXEN NADA.
3601 5ELCID0454 NONBRADOS SON *** QUE YRAN ENEL ALGARA,
3607 5ELCID0455 E *** QUE CCN MYO %ID FICARAN EN LA %AGA.
3618 5ELCID0456 YA QUIEBRAN *** ALBORES & VINIE LA MA@ANA,

WORD C# PREFIX CONTEXT

LOS (CON'T)

```
3689 5ELCID0465 MOROS & MORAS AUIEN *** DE GANANZIA,
3706 5ELCID0468 *** QUE LA TIENEN, QUANDO VIERON LA REBATA,
3764 5ELCID0476 AFEUOS *** CCIIJ ENEL ALGARA,
3854 5ELCID0488 *** BRAZOS ABIERTOS REZIBE A MINAYA:
4040 5ELCID0514 E A *** PEONES LA MEATAD SIN FALLA;
4074 5ELCID0518 FABLO CON *** DE CASTEION, & ENVIO AFITA & AGUADELFAGARA,
4096 5ELCID0521 ASMARON *** MOROS IIJ MILL MARCOS DE PLATA.
4238 5ELCID0539 LO QUE DIXO EL ZID A TODOS *** OTROS PLAZ.
4249 5ELCID0541 *** MOROS & LAS MORAS BENDIZIENDOL ESTAN.
4312 5ELCID0549 NON LO SABEN *** MOROS EL ARDIMENT QUE AN.
4377 5ELCID0558 *** VNOS CONTRA LA SIERRA & LOS OTROS CONTRA LA AGUA.
4383 5ELCID0558 LOS VNOS CONTRA LA SIERRA & *** OTROS CONTRA LA AGUA.
4434 5ELCID0564 POR TODAS ESSAS TIERRAS YUAN *** MANDADOS,
4477 5ELCID0570 *** DE ALCOZER A MYO ZID YAL DAN PARIAS DE GRADO
4489 5ELCID0571 E *** DE TECA & LOS DE TERUAL LA CASA;
4493 5ELCID0571 E LOS DE TECA & *** DE TERUAL LA CASA;
4555 5ELCID0579 AGUISA DE MENBRADO, POR SACAR *** AZELADA.
4559 5ELCID0580 VEYEN LO *** DE ALCOZER, DIOS, COMMO SE ALABAUAN
4603 5ELCID0585 ANTES QUEL PRENDAN *** DE TERUEL, SI NON NON NOS DARAN
                DENT NADA;
4633 5ELCID0588 MYO ZID, QUANDO *** VIO FUERA, COGIOS COMMO DE ARRANCADA.
4644 5ELCID0589 COIOS SALON AYUSO, CON *** SOS ABUELTA NADI.
4649 5ELCID0590 DIZEN *** DE ALCOZER: YA SE NOS VA LA GANAZIA
4658 5ELCID0591 *** GRANDES & LOS CHICOS FUERA SALTO DAN,
4661 5ELCID0591 LOS GRANDES & *** CHICOS FUERA SALTO DAN,
4707 5ELCID0597 FIRID ***, CAUALLEROS, TODOS SINES DUBDANZA;
4758 5ELCID0604 *** VASSALLOS DE MYO ZID SIN PIEDAD LES DAUAN,
4781 5ELCID0606 DANDO GRANDES ALARIDOS *** QUE ESTAN EN LA ZELADA,
4789 5ELCID0607 DEXANDO UAN *** DELANT, POR EL CASTIELLO SE TORNAUAN,
4806 5ELCID0609 LUEGO LEGAUAN *** SOS, CA FECHA ES EL ARRANCADA.
4858 5ELCID0614 GRADO A DIOS DEL ZIELO & ATODOS *** SOS SANTOS,
4872 5ELCID0616 OYD AMI, ALBARFANEZ & TODOS *** CAUALLEROS
4881 5ELCID0618 *** MOROS YAZEN MUERTOS, DE BIUOS POCOS VEO.
4889 5ELCID0619 *** MOROS & LAS MORAS VENDER NON LOS PODREMOS,
4896 5ELCID0619 LOS MOROS & LAS MORAS VENDER NON *** PODREMOS,
4899 5ELCID0620 QUE *** DESCABEZEMOS NADA NON GANAREMOS;
4905 5ELCID0621 COIAMOS *** DE DENTRO, CA EL SENORIO TENEMOS,
5051 5ELCID0638 NON LO DETARDEDES, *** DOS YD PORA ALLA,
5065 5ELCID0640 CON *** DELA FRONTERA QUE UOS AIUDARAN,
5117 5ELCID0647 POR *** DE LA FRONTERA PIENSSAN DE ENVIAR;
5157 5ELCID0652 POR TODAS ESSAS TIERRAS *** PREGONES DAN;
5201 5ELCID0658 LAS AROBDAS, QUE *** MOROS SACAN, DE DIA
5267 5ELCID0666 MYO ZID CON *** SOS TORNOS A ACORDAR:
5294 5ELCID0669 GRANDES SON *** PODERES POR CON ELLOS LIDIAR;
5352 5ELCID0676 VAYAMOS *** FERIR EN AQUEL DIA DE CRAS.
5377 5ELCID0679 TODOS *** MOROS & LAS MORAS DE FUERA LOS MANDA ECHAR,
5384 5ELCID0679 TODOS LOS MOROS & LAS MORAS DE FUERA *** MANDA ECHAR,
5514 5ELCID0695 QUE PRIESSA VA EN *** MOROS, E TORNARON SE A ARMAR;
5558 5ELCID0700 LAS AZES DE *** MOROS YAS MUEUEN ADELANT,
5571 5ELCID0701 PORA MYO ZID & ALOS SOS A MANOS *** TOMAR.
5619 5ELCID0708 *** QUE EL DEBDO AUEDES VEREMOS COMMO LA ACORREDES.
5672 5ELCID0715 ENBRAZAN *** ESCUDOS DELANT LOS CORAZONES,
5675 5ELCID0715 ENBRAZAN LOS ESCUDOS DELANT *** CORAZONES,
5690 5ELCID0717 ENCLINARON LAS CARAS DE SUSO DE *** ARZONES,
5693 5ELCID0718 YUAN *** FERIR DE FUERTES CORAZONES.
5709 5ELCID0720 FERID ***, CAUALLEROS, POR AMOR DE CARIDAD
5781 5ELCID0731 *** MOROS LAMAN MAFOMAT & LOS CHRISTIANOS SANTI YAGUE.
5786 5ELCID0731 LOS MOROS LAMAN MAFOMAT & *** CHRISTIANOS SANTI YAGUE.
5956 5ELCID0755 FIRME SON *** MOROS, AVN NOS VAN DEL CAMPO.
5999 5ELCID0761 *** DOS LE FALLEN, & EL VNOL HA TOMADO,
6073 5ELCID0771 CAFUYEN *** MOROS DE LA PART
6078 5ELCID0772 *** DE MYO ZID FIRIENDO EN ALCAZ,
6179 5ELCID0787 YAS TORNAN *** DEL QUE EN BUEN ORA NASCO.
6209 5ELCID0791 VIO *** SOS COMMOS VAN ALEGANDO:
6230 5ELCID0794 ESTA ALBERGADA *** DE MYO ZID LUEGO LA AN ROBADA
6266 5ELCID0798 MAS DE QUINZE DE *** SOS MENOS NON FALLARON.
6292 5ELCID0801 ASOS CASTIELLOS ALOS MOROS DENTRO *** AN TORNADOS,
6341 5ELCID0807 ALOS PEONES & A *** ENCAUALGADOS
6461 5ELCID0824 QUE RUEGEN POR MI LAS NOCHES & *** DIAS;
6495 5ELCID0828 MYO ZID RUY DIAZ CON *** SOS SE ACORDAUA:
6570 5ELCID0839 TODOS *** DIAS A MYO ZID AGUARDAUAN
6593 5ELCID0842 ENTRE *** DE TECHA & LOS DE TERUEL LA CASA,
6597 5ELCID0842 ENTRE LOS DE TECHA & *** DE TERUEL LA CASA,
6603 5ELCID0843 E *** DE CALATAYUT, QUE ES MAS ONDRADA,
6649 5ELCID0848 A CAUALLEROS & A PEONES FECHOS *** HA RICOS,
6654 5ELCID0849 EN TODOS *** SOS NON FALLARIEDES VN MESQUINO.
6828 5ELCID0872 TREYNTA CAUALLOS AL REY *** ENPRESENTAUA;
6836 5ELCID0874  QUIN *** DIO ESTOS, SI UOS VALA DIOS, MYNAYA
6877 5ELCID0879 BESA UOS *** PIES & LAS MANOS AMAS,
6969 5ELCID0891 DE TODO MYO REYNO *** QUE LO QUISIEREN FAR,
6983 5ELCID0893 SUELTO LES *** CUERPOS & QUITO LES LAS HEREDADES.
7190 5ELCID0921 BESO LE LA BOCA & *** OIOS DELA CARA.
7437 5ELCID0954 FUERON *** MANDADOS A TODAS PARTES,
7451 5ELCID0956 *** MANDADOS SON YDOS ATODAS PARTES;
7543 5ELCID0967 GRANDES SON *** PODERES & A PRIESSA SEUAN LEGANDO,
```

WORD C# PREFIX CONTEXT

LOS (CON'T)

7739 5ELCID0991 APRETAD *** CAUALLOS, & BISTADES LAS ARMAS.
7828 5ELCID1001 LAS ARMAS AUIEN PRESAS & SEDIEN SOBRE *** CAUALLOS.
7846 5ELCID1004 MANDO *** FERIR MYO %ID, EL QUE EN BUEN ORA NASCO;
7858 5ELCID1005 ESTO FAZEN *** SOS DE VOLUNTAD & DE GRADO;
7865 5ELCID1006 *** PENDONES & LAS LAN%AS TAN BIEN LAS UAN ENPLEANDO,
7880 5ELCID1007 ALOS VNOS FIRIENDO & A *** OTROS DE ROCANDO.
7946 5ELCID1015 DE TODAS PARTES *** SOS SE AIUNTARON;
7977 5ELCID1019 ADUZEN LE *** COMERES, DELANT GELOS PARAUAN;
7988 5ELCID1020 EL NON LO QUIERE COMER, ATODOS *** SOSANAUA:
8118 5ELCID1035 AUOS & DOS FIJOS DALGO QUITAR UOS HE *** CUERPOS & DARUOS E DE MANO.
8254 5ELCID1051 CON *** CAUALLEROS QUE EL %ID LE AUIE DADOS
8388 5ELCID1066 EL CONDE DON REMONT ENTRE *** DOS ES ENTRADO.
8548 5ELCID1086 TAN RICOS SON *** SOS QUE NON SABEN QUE SE AN.
8711 5ELCID1107 VAYAN *** MANDADOS POR LOS QUE NOS DEUEN AIUDAR,
8714 5ELCID1107 VAYAN LOS MANDADOS POR *** QUE NOS DEUEN AIUDAR,
8719 5ELCID1108 *** VNOS AXERICA & LOS OTROS A ALUCAD,
8723 5ELCID1108 LOS VNOS AXERICA & *** OTROS A ALUCAD,
8731 5ELCID1119 DESI A ONDA & *** OTROS A ALMENAR,
8735 5ELCID1110 *** DE BORRIANA LUEGO VENGAN ACA;
8799 5ELCID1119 *** DE VALEN%IA %ERCADOS NOS HAN;
8872 5ELCID1130 VOS CON *** OTROS FIRADES LOS DELANT.
8875 5ELCID1130 VOS CON LOS OTROS FIRADES *** DELANT.
8878 5ELCID1131 BIEN *** FERREDES, QUE DUBDA NON Y AURA,
8887 5ELCID1132 YO CON *** %IENTO ENTRARE DEL OTRA PART,
8928 5ELCID1137 CON *** ALUORES MYO %ID FERIR LOS VA:
8933 5ELCID1137 CON LOS ALUORES MYO %ID FERIR *** VA:
8945 5ELCID1139 FERID ***, CAUALLEROS, DAMOR & DE GRADO & DE GRAND VOLUNTAD,
8980 5ELCID1142 ARANCAR SE LAS ESTACAS & ACOSTAR SE ATODAS PARTES *** TENDALES.
9045 5ELCID1151 DE PIES DE CAUALLO *** QUES PUDIERON ESCAPAR.
9174 5ELCID1168 E DURMIENDO *** DIAS & LAS NOCHES TRANOCHANDO,
9193 5ELCID1170 ALOS DE VALEN%IA ESCARMENTADOS *** HAN,
9227 5ELCID1174 MAL SE AQUEXAN *** DE VALEN%IA QUE NON SABENT QUES FAR,
9307 5ELCID1183 NON LES DIXO COSEIO, NIN *** VINO HUUIAR.
9415 5ELCID1197 ANDIDIERON *** PREGONES, SABET, ATODAS PARTES,
9524 5ELCID1211 GRANDES SON *** GOZOS QUE VAN POR ES LOGAR,
9541 5ELCID1213 *** QUE FUERON DE PIE CAUALLEROS SE FAZEN;
9587 5ELCID1218 ELOS OTROS AUERES QUIEN *** PODRIE CONTAR?
9596 5ELCID1219 ALEGRE ERA EL CAMPEADOR CON TODOS *** QUE HA,
9632 5ELCID1224 VINO *** VER CON XXX MILL DE ARMAS.
9705 5ELCID1234 ATODOS *** MENORES CAYERON C MARCOS DE PLATA.
9799 5ELCID1245 *** QUE EXIERON DE TIERRA DE RITAD SON ABONDADOS,
9829 5ELCID1248 *** QUE FUERON CON EL, & LOS DE DESPUES, TODOS SON PAGADOS;
9835 5ELCID1248 LOS QUE FUERON CON EL, & *** DE DESPUES, TODOS SON PAGADOS;
9845 5ELCID1249 VELLO MYO %ID CON *** AVERES QUE AUIEN TOMADOS,
9924 5ELCID1259 METER *** HE EN ESCRIPTO, & TODOS SEAN CONTADOS,
9962 5ELCID1263 MANDO *** VENIR ALA CORTH & A TODOS LOS IUNTAR,
9969 5ELCID1263 MANDO LOS VENIR ALA CORTH & A TODOS *** IUNTAR,
9972 5ELCID1264 QUANDO *** FALLO, POR CUENTA FIZO LOS NONBRAR:
9977 5ELCID1264 QUANDO LOS FALLO, POR CUENTA FIZO *** NONBRAR:
10158 5ELCID1286 E QUE *** DIESSE AL ABBAT DON SANCHO.
10434 5ELCID1323 *** PIES & LAS MANOS, COMMO ATAN BUEN SE@OR,
10558 5ELCID1338 BESA UOS LAS MANOS & QUE *** PRENDADES UOS;
10764 5ELCID1363 POR QUE *** DESEREDE, TODO GELO SUELTO YO;
10780 5ELCID1365 ATREGO LES *** CUERPOS DE MAL & DE OCASION,
10807 5ELCID1369 *** QUE QUISIEREN YR SEUIR AL CAMPEADOR
10836 5ELCID1372 AQUI ENTRARON EN FABLA *** YFFANTES DE CARRION:
10938 5ELCID1385 *** YFFANTES DE CARRION DANDO YUAN CONPA@A A MINAYA ALBARFANEZ:
10994 5ELCID1391 HYDO ES MYNAYA, TORNANSSE *** YFFANTES.
11171 5ELCID1413 HYDOS SON *** CAUALLEROS & DELLO PENSSARAN,
11236 5ELCID1422 *** QUINIENTOS MARCOS DIO MINAYA AL ABBAT,
11415 5ELCID1445 TODOS *** DIAS DEL SIEGLO EN LEUAR LO ADELANT
11446 5ELCID1449 EL PORTERO CON ELLOS QUE *** HA DE AGUARDAR;
11589 5ELCID1468 ASI COMMO A MY DIXIERON, HY *** PODREDES FALAR;
11668 5ELCID1479 VENIDES, *** VASSALLOS DE MYO AMIGO NATURAL?
11935 5ELCID1513 *** QUE YUAN MESURANDO & LEGANDO DELANT
11959 5ELCID1516 DON LEGAN *** OTROS, A MINAYA ALBARFANEZ SE UAN HOMILAR.
12186 5ELCID1547 LAS NOCHES & *** DIAS LAS DUENAS AGUARDANDO.
12221 5ELCID1551 EL MORO AUEGALUON BIEN *** SIRUIE SIN FALLA,
12257 5ELCID1557 *** SOS DESPENDIE EL MORO, QUE DELO SO NON TOMAUA NADA.
12615 5ELCID1600 DEL GOZO QUE AUIEN DE *** SOS OIOS LORAUAN.
12954 5ELCID1643 AFARTO VERAN POR *** OIOS COMMO SE GANA EL PAN.
12970 5ELCID1645 AL%AUAN *** OIOS, TIENDAS VIERON FINCADAS:
13072 5ELCID1657 FINCADAS SON LAS TIENDAS & PARE%EN *** ALUORES,
13079 5ELCID1658 A VNA GRAND PRIESSA TANIEN *** ATAMORES;
13143 5ELCID1666 AQUELOS ATAMORES AUOS *** PONDRAN DELANT & VEREDES QUANLES SON,
13158 5ELCID1668 COLGAR *** HAN EN SANTA MARIA MADRE DEL CRIADOR.
13181 5ELCID1671 *** MOROS DE MARRUECOS CAUALGAN AUIGOR,
13222 5ELCID1676 DOS FALLAN CON *** MOROS COMETIEN LOS TAN AYNA.
13225 5ELCID1676 DOS FALLAN CON LOS MOROS COMETIEN *** TAN AYNA.
13229 5ELCID1677 SACAN *** DELAS HUERTAS MUCHO AFEA GUISA,
13264 5ELCID1682 TORNADOS SON A MYO %ID *** QUE COMIEN SO PAN;
13273 5ELCID1683 EL SELO VIO CON *** OIOS, CUENTAN GELO DELANT,
13325 5ELCID1690 HYR *** HEMOS FFERIR ENEL NOMBRE DEL CRIADOR & DEL APOSTOL SANTI
13341 5ELCID1691 MAS VALE QUE NOS *** VEZCAMOS, QUE ELLOS COIAN EL PAN.

WORD C# PREFIX CONTEXT

LOS (CON'T)

13379 5ELCID1696 QUANDO UOS *** FUEREDES FERIR, ENTRARE YO DEL OTRA PART;
13449 5ELCID1705 PRENDOL YO *** PECADOS, & DIOS LE ABRA EL ALMA.
13513 5ELCID1712 MIO %ID ALOS SOS VASSALOS TAN BIEN *** ACORDANDO.
13560 5ELCID1718 ALOS %INQUAENTA MILL VAN *** FERIR DE GRADO;
13582 5ELCID1721 PLOGO AL CRIADOR & OUIERON *** DE ARRANCAR.
13683 5ELCID1734 *** L MILL POR CUENTA FUERO NOTADOS:
13815 5ELCID1750 ESTO DIOS SE LO QUISO CON TODOS *** SOS SANTOS,
13887 5ELCID1759 DELANT EL CAMPEADOR *** YNOIOS FINCARON:
14032 5ELCID1777 NON PUDIERON ELLOS SABER LA CUENTA DE TODOS *** CAUALLOS,
14042 5ELCID1779 *** MOROS DELAS TIERRAS GANADO SEAN Y ALGO;
14073 5ELCID1782 QUANDO A MYO %ID CAYERON TANTOS, *** OTROS BIEN PUEDEN FINCAR PAGADOS
14183 5ELCID1795 NON TIENE EN CUENTA *** MOROS QUE HA MATADOS;
14412 5ELCID1823 ANDAN *** DIAS & LAS NOCHES, & PASSADA HAN LA SIERRA,
14440 5ELCID1826 PASSANDO VAN LAS SIERRAS & *** MONTES & LAS AGUAS,
14489 5ELCID1833 HYEN *** PRIMEROS EL REY FUERA DIO SALTO,
14505 5ELCID1835 *** YFANTES DE CARRION, SABET, YS A%ERTARON,
14530 5ELCID1838 ADIO LO AUIEN *** DEL QUE EN BUEN ORA NASCO,
14570 5ELCID1843 ANTEL REY ALFONSSO *** YNOIOS FINCADOS,
14577 5ELCID1844 BESAN LA TIERRA & *** PIES AMOS:
14648 5ELCID1853 RICOS SON VENIDOS TODOS *** SOS VASSALLOS,
14742 5ELCID1864 COMMO SI *** FALASSE MUERTOS ADUZIR SE LOS CAUALLOS,
14747 5ELCID1864 COMMO SI LOS FALASSE MUERTOS ADUZIR SE *** CAUALLOS,
14801 5ELCID1871 MANDO UOS *** CUERPOS ONDRADA MIENTRE SERUIR & VESTIR
14831 5ELCID1874 DOUOS IIJ CAUALLOS & PRENDED *** AQUI.
14858 5ELCID1878 BIEN *** MANDO SERUIR DE QUANTO HUEBOS HAN.
14993 5ELCID1895 EL REY DON ALFONSSO ESSORA *** LAMO,
14999 5ELCID1896 A VNA QUADRA ELE *** APARTO:
15038 5ELCID1901 DIEGO & FERRANDO, *** YFFANTES DE CARRION,
15074 5ELCID1906 POR CONSSAGRAR CON *** YFFANTES DE CARRION.
15146 5ELCID1915 VAN PORA VALEN%IA ELLOS & TODOS *** SOS.
15157 5ELCID1917 APRIESSA CAUALGA, ARE%EBIR *** SALIO:
15164 5ELCID1918 SONRRISOS MYO %ID & BIEN *** ABRA%O:
15299 5ELCID1937 E PIDEN ME MIS FIJAS PORA *** YFANTES DE CARRION.
15575 5ELCID1975 *** YFFANTES DE CARRIO MUCHO ALEGRES ANDAN,
15619 5ELCID1981 *** YFANTES DE CARRION LIEUAN GRANDES CONPA@AS.
15743 5ELCID1998 E TODOS *** OTROS QUE Y SON.
15772 5ELCID2001 DALMA & DE CORA%ON, & TODOS *** QUE EN PODER DESSOS FOSSEN;
15907 5ELCID2017 ATODOS *** SOS ESTAR LOS MANDO,
15910 5ELCID2017 ATODOS LOS SOS ESTAR *** MANDO,
15936 5ELCID2021 *** YNOIOS & LAS MANOS EN TIERRA LOS FINCO,
15943 5ELCID2021 LOS YNOIOS & LAS MANOS EN TIERRA *** FINCO,
15994 5ELCID2028 BESAD LAS MANOS, CA *** PIES NO;
16093 5ELCID2041 TODOS *** DEMAS DESTO AUIEN SABOR;
16176 5ELCID2052 ESSORA SELE OMILLAN *** YFFANTES DE CARRION:
16278 5ELCID2065 DE TAL GUISA *** PAGA MYO %ID EL CAMPEADOR,
16398 5ELCID2080 *** MIOS & LOS UUESTROS QUE SEAN ROGADORES;
16401 5ELCID2080 LOS MIOS & *** UUESTROS QUE SEAN ROGADORES;
16437 5ELCID2084 DE GRANDES NUEUAS SON *** YFANTES DE CARRION,
16495 5ELCID2091 LUEGO SE LEUANTARON *** YFFANTES DE CARRION,
16540 5ELCID2096 QUEM DADES UUESTRAS FIJAS PORA *** YFANTES DE CARRION.
16583 5ELCID2101 AFELLOS EN UUESTRAS MANOS *** YFANTES DE CARRION,
16622 5ELCID2106 *** YERNOS & LAS FIJAS TODOS UUESTROS FIJOS SON:
16977 5ELCID2149 PLEGA AL CRIADOR CON TODOS *** SOS SANTOS, ESTE PLAZER
17100 5ELCID2164 ESTO PLOGO AL REY, & ATODOS *** SOLTO;
17137 5ELCID2168 EA DON FERNANDO & A DON DIEGO AGUARDAR *** MANDO
17158 5ELCID2171 QUE SOPIESSEN SOS MA@AS DE *** YFANTES DE CARRION.
17201 5ELCID2176 QUANDO A ELLA ASSOMARON, *** GOZOS SON MAYORES.
17284 5ELCID2186 MUCHOS DIAS UOS VEAMOS CON *** OIOS DELAS CARAS
17469 5ELCID2210 POR *** YFFANTES DE CARRION ESSORA ENBIARON,
17476 5ELCID2211 CAUALGAN *** YFFANTES, ADELANT ADELINAUAN AL PALA%IO,
17498 5ELCID2214 RE%IBIO *** MYO %ID CON TODOS SUS VASALLOS;
17520 5ELCID2217 TODOS *** DE MYO %ID TAN BIEN SON ACORDADOS,
17747 5ELCID2246 *** YFANTES DE CARRION BIEN AN CAUALGADO.
17786 5ELCID2250 ANTES QUE ENTRASSEN AIANTAR TODOS *** QUEBRANTARON.
17802 5ELCID2252 HYA %ERCA DELOS XV DIAS YAS VAN *** FIJOS DALGO.
17840 5ELCID2257 NON FUERON EN CUENTA *** AUERES MONEDADOS.
17843 5ELCID2258 *** VASSALLOS DE MIO %ID, ASSI SON ACORDADOS,
17870 5ELCID2261 RICOS TORNAN A CASTIELLA *** QUE ALAS BODAS LEGARON.
17945 5ELCID2271 HY MORAN *** YFANTES BIEN CERCA DE DOS A@OS,
17952 5ELCID2272 *** AMORES QUELES FAZEN MUCHO ERAN SOBEIANOS.
17999 5ELCID2277 EL CRIADOR UOS VALLA CON TODOS *** SOS SANTOS.
18016 5ELCID2279 CON EL AMOS SUS YERNOS *** YFANTES DE CARRION.
18051 5ELCID2284 ENBRA%AN *** MANTOS LOS DEL CAMPEADOR,
18053 5ELCID2284 ENBRA%AN LOS MANTOS *** DEL CAMPEADOR,
18217 5ELCID2305 MAGER *** ESTAN LAMANDO, NINGUNO NON RESPONDE.
18224 5ELCID2306 QUANDO *** FALLARON & ELLOS VINIERON, ASSI VINIERON SIN COLOR;
18252 5ELCID2309 MUCHOS TOUIERON POR ENBAYDOS *** YFANTES DE CARRION,
18392 5ELCID2328 HYD *** CONORTAR, SI UOS VALA EL CRIADOR,
18514 5ELCID2343 AMOS *** MYOS YERNOS BUENOS SERAN EN CAPO.
18534 5ELCID2345 EN LA VESTE DELOS MOROS *** ATAMORES SONANDO;
18617 5ELCID2356 QUE OY *** YFANTES AMI POR AMO NON ABRAN;
18633 5ELCID2358 HYO CON *** MYOS FERIR QUIERO DELANT,
18640 5ELCID2359 VOS CON *** UUESTROS FIRME MIENTRE ALA %AGA TENGADES;
18815 5ELCID2381 AFE *** MOROS A OIO, YO LOS ENSAYAR.

WORD C# PREFIX CONTEXT

LOS (CON'T)

18820 5ELCID2381 AFE LOS MOROS A OIO, YO *** ENSAYAR.
18837 5ELCID2384 EYUA *** FERIR A CABO DEL ALBERGADA.
18885 5ELCID2390 *** MOROS SON MUCHOS, DERREDOR LE %ERCAUAN,
18907 5ELCID2392 EL QUE EN BUEN ORA NASCO *** OIOS LE FINCAUA,
18928 5ELCID2395 HYUA *** FERIR DE CORA%ON & DE ALMA.
18959 5ELCID2399 MYO %ID CON *** SUYOS CAE EN ALCAN%A;
18975 5ELCID2401 EACOSTAR SE *** TENDALES, CON HUEBRAS ERAN TANTAS.
18981 5ELCID2402 *** DE MYO %ID ALOS DE BUCAR DELAS TIENDAS LOS SACAN.
18990 5ELCID2402 LOS DE MYO %ID ALOS DE BUCAR DELAS TIENDAS *** SACAN.
18993 5ELCID2403 SACAN *** DELAS TIENDAS, CAEN LOS EN ALCAZ;
18997 5ELCID2403 SACAN LOS DELAS TIENDAS, CAEN *** EN ALCAZ;
19254 5ELCID2437 COFIA SOBRE *** PELOS FRONZIDA DELLA YA QUANTO.
19326 5ELCID2447 COMMO YO FIO POR DIOS & EN TODOS *** SOS SANTOS,
19476 5ELCID2468 *** YERNOS DE MYO %ID QUANDO ESTE AUER TOMARON
19731 5ELCID2502 NO *** YRE BUSCAR, EN VALEN%IA SERE YO,
19757 5ELCID2505 GRANDES SON *** GOZOS EN VALEN%IA CON MYO %ID EL CANPEADOR
19777 5ELCID2507 GRANDES SON *** GOZOS DE SUS YERNOS AMOS ADOS:
19802 5ELCID2510 MUCHOS TIENEN POR RICOS *** YFANTES DE CARRION.
19808 5ELCID2511 ELLOS CON *** OTROS VINIERON ALA CORT;
19837 5ELCID2515 QUANDO ENTRARON *** YFANTES DE CARRION,
19987 5ELCID2536 ELAS NOCHES & *** DIAS TAN MAL LOS ESCARMENTANDO,
19991 5ELCID2536 ELAS NOCHES & LOS DIAS TAN MAL *** ESCARMENTANDO,
20022 5ELCID2541 *** AUERES QUE TENEMOS GRANDES SON & SOBEIANOS,
20213 5ELCID2567 *** FIJOS QUE OUIEREMOS EN QUE AURAN PARTI%ION.
20362 5ELCID2583 ATORGADO LO HAN ESTO *** YFFANTES DE CARRION.
20431 5ELCID2593 FINCARON *** YNOIOS ANTEL %ID CAMPEADOR:
20552 5ELCID2609 MYO %ID & *** OTROS DE CAUALGAR PENSSAUAN,
20564 5ELCID2611 HYA SALIEN *** YFANTES DE VALEN%IA LA CLARA,
20596 5ELCID2615 VIOLO EN *** AUUEROS EL QUE EN BUEN ORA %INXO ESPADA,
20715 5ELCID2630 RESPONDIEN *** YERNOS: ASSI LO MANDE DIOS
20723 5ELCID2631 GRANDES FUERON *** DUELOS ALA DEPARTI%ION.
20737 5ELCID2633 ASSI FAZIAN *** CAUALLEROS DEL CAMPEADOR.
20826 5ELCID2644 PIENSSAN SE DE YR *** YFANTES DE CARRION;
20867 5ELCID2650 DIOS, QUE BIEN *** SIRUIO ATODO SO SABOR
20882 5ELCID2652 CON DOZIENTOS CAUALLEROS ESCURRIR *** MANDO.
20886 5ELCID2653 HYUAN TRO%IR *** MONTES, LOS QUE DIZEN DE LUZON.
20888 5ELCID2653 HYUAN TRO%IR LOS MONTES, *** QUE DIZEN DE LUZON.
20987 5ELCID2666 QUANDO ESTA FALSSEDAD DIZEN *** DE CARRION,
21034 5ELCID2673 ARMAS YUA TENIENDO, PAROS ANTE *** YFANTES;
21167 5ELCID2689 YA MOUIERON DEL ANSSARERA *** YFANTES DE CARRION,
21195 5ELCID2693 POR *** MONTES CLAROS AGUIJAN A ESPOLON;
21223 5ELCID2697 ENTRADOS SON *** YFANTES AL ROBREDO DE CORPES,
21229 5ELCID2698 *** MONTES SON ALTOS, LAS RAMAS PUIAN CON LAS NUES,
21301 5ELCID2707 ADELANT ERAN YDOS *** DE CRIAZON:
21307 5ELCID2708 ASSI LO MANDARON *** YFANTES DE CARRION,
21346 5ELCID2713 TANTO MAL COMIDIERON *** YFANTES DE CARRION;
21396 5ELCID2720 ALLI LES TUELLEN *** MANTOS & LOS PELLI%ONES,
21399 5ELCID2720 ALLI LES TUELLEN LOS MANTOS & *** PELLI%ONES,
21414 5ELCID2722 ESPUELAS TIENEN CAL%ADAS *** MALOS TRAYDORES,
21514 5ELCID2735 ESSORA LES CONPIE%AN ADAR *** YFANTES DE CARRION;
21550 5ELCID2739 LINPIA SALIE LA SANGRE SOBRE *** %ICLATONES.
21557 5ELCID2740 YA LO SIENTEN ELLAS EN *** SOS CORA%ONES.
21587 5ELCID2744 SANGRIENTAS EN LAS CAMISAS & TODOS *** CICLATONES.
21621 5ELCID2749 LEUARON LES *** MANTOS & LAS PIELES ARMINAS,
21665 5ELCID2754 *** YFANTES DE CARRION ENEL ROBREDO DE CORPES
21686 5ELCID2757 POR *** MONTES DO YUAN, ELLOS YUAN SE ALABANDO:
21727 5ELCID2763 ALABANDOS YUAN *** YFANTES DE CARRION.
21762 5ELCID2768 DE TODOS *** OTROS APARTE SE SALIO,
21787 5ELCID2771 O QUE AN FECHO *** YFANTES DE CARRION.
21816 5ELCID2775 VANSSE *** YFANTES, AGUIJAN AESPOLON.
21856 5ELCID2781 MAL SE ENSAYARON *** YFANTES DE CARRION
21895 5ELCID2785 PARTIERON SE LE LAS TELLAS DE DENTRO DE *** CORA%ONES,
21920 5ELCID2789 *** GANADOS FIEROS NON NOS COMAN EN AQUESTE MONT
21937 5ELCID2791 ABRIERON *** OIOS & VIERON AFELEZ MUNOZ.
21955 5ELCID2793 DE QUE NON ME FALLAREN *** YFANTES DE CARRION,
22075 5ELCID2809 TODOS TRES SE@EROS POR *** ROBREDOS DE CORPES,
22147 5ELCID2820 *** DE SANTESTEUAN, SIEMPRE MESURADOS SON,
22175 5ELCID2824 ALLABANDOS SEYAN *** YFANTES DE CARRION.
22230 5ELCID2831 QUANDO TAL ONDRA MEAN DADA *** YFANTES DE CARRION;
22244 5ELCID2833 NON LA LOGRARAN *** YFANTES DE CARRION;
22315 5ELCID2842 APIRESSA CAUALGAN, *** DIAS & LAS NOCHES ANDAN;
22446 5ELCID2859 ENEL FINCAN *** OIOS DON ELUIRA & DO@A SOL:
22472 5ELCID2862 EN *** DIAS DE VAGAR TODA NUESTRA RENCURA SABREMOS CONTAR.
22543 5ELCID2871 *** DE SANTESTEUAN ESCURRIENDO LOS VAN
22547 5ELCID2871 LOS DE SANTESTEUAN ESCURRIENDO *** VAN
22652 5ELCID2886 PRIUADO CAUALGA, A RE%EBIR *** SALE;
22750 5ELCID2899 FABLOS CON *** SOS EN SU PORIDAD,
22813 5ELCID2906 DESTA DESONDRA QUE MEAN FECHA *** YFANTES DE CARRION
22931 5ELCID2921 NOS DAN VAGAR *** DIAS & LAS NOCHES.
23023 5ELCID2933 LEUANTOS EL REY, TAN BIEN *** RE%IBIO.
23029 5ELCID2934 DELANT EL REY FINCO *** YNOIOS AQUEL MU@O GUSTIOZ,
23036 5ELCID2935 BESABA LE *** PIES AQUEL MU@O GUSTIOZ;
23050 5ELCID2937 *** PIES & LAS MANOS VOS BESA EL CAMPEADOR;
23470 5ELCID2989 RUEGAN AL REY QUE *** QUITE DESTA CORT.

WORD C# PREFIX CONTEXT

LOS (CON'T)

23521 5ELCID2995 HYA LO VIERON QUE ES AFER *** YFANTES DE CARRION,
23548 5ELCID2999 AQUESTE CONSSEIO *** YFANTES DE CARRION.
23560 5ELCID3001 EN *** PRIMEROS VA EL BUEN REY DON ALFONSSO,
23604 5ELCID3006 DE TODA CASTIELLA TODOS *** MEIORES
23728 5ELCID3022 BIEN AGUISADO VIENE EL %ID CON TODOS *** SOS,
23919 5ELCID3047 E YO CON *** MYOS POSARE A SAN SERUAN:
23994 5ELCID3058 ENTRE MINAYA & *** BUENOS QUE Y HA
24129 5ELCID3076 E QUE NON PARESCAN LAS ARMAS, BIEN PRESOS *** CORDONES;
24263 5ELCID3094 VNA COFIA SOBRE *** PELOS DUN ESCARIN DE PRO,
24280 5ELCID3096 QUE NON LE CONTALASSEN *** PELOS AL BUEN %ID CANPEADOR;
24355 5ELCID3105 CUERDA MIENTRA ENTRA MYO %ID CON TODOS *** SOS:
24397 5ELCID3110 E DESI ADELANT, SABET, TODOS *** OTROS:
24418 5ELCID3113 NIN TODOS *** DEL BANDO DE YFANTES DE CARRION.
24488 5ELCID3122 *** %IENTO QUEL AGUARDAN POSAN ADERREDOR.
24803 5ELCID3169 ATORGAN *** ALCALDES: TOD ESTO ES RAZON.
24952 5ELCID3179 LAS MA%ANAS & *** ARRIAZES TODOS DORO SON.
24961 5ELCID3179 MARAUILLAN SE DELLAS TODAS *** OMNES BUENOS DELA CORT.
25280 5ELCID3218 NON ACUERDAN EN CONSSEIO, CA *** HAUERES GRANDES SON:
25285 5ELCID3219 ESPESOS *** HAN YFANTES DE CARRION.
25321 5ELCID3224 DIXIERON *** ALCALDES QUANDO MANFESTADOS SON:
25375 5ELCID3231 DESTOS IIJ MILL MARCOS *** CC TENGO YO;
25382 5ELCID3232 ENTRAMOS MELOS DIERON *** YFANTES DE CARRION.
25405 5ELCID3235 QUANDO ELLOS *** AN APECHAR, NON GELOS QUIERO YO.
25454 5ELCID3241 HYA VIERON QUE ES AFER *** YFANTES DE CARRION.
25483 5ELCID3246 SOBRE *** DOZIENTOS MARCOS QUE TENIE EL REY ALFONSSO
25492 5ELCID3247 PAGARON *** YFANTES AL QUE EN BUEN ORA NASCO;
25575 5ELCID3257 AMENOS DE RIEBTOS NO *** PUEDO DEXAR.
25705 5ELCID3274 *** VNOS LE HAN MIEDO & LOS OTROS ESPANTA.
25711 5ELCID3274 LOS VNOS LE HAN MIEDO & *** OTROS ESPANTA.
25714 5ELCID3275 *** DE CARRION SON DE NATURA TAL,
26301 5ELCID3354 DE NATURA SOMOS DE *** CONDES MAS LIPIOS,
26484 5ELCID3379 FUESSE A RIO DOUIRNA *** MOLINOS PICAR
26497 5ELCID3381 QUIL DARIE CON *** DE CARRION ACASAR?
26524 5ELCID3385 ALOS QUE DAS PAZ, FARTAS *** ADERREDOR.
26563 5ELCID3391 *** QUE AN REBTADO LIDIARAN, SIN SALUE DIOS
26776 5ELCID3420 PORA *** YFANTES DE NAUARRA & DE ARAGON,
26816 5ELCID3425 METIERON LAS FES, & *** OMENAIES DADOS SON,
26943 5ELCID3442 RIEBTOS LES *** CUERPOS POR MALOS & POR TRAYDORES.
26985 5ELCID3448 *** YFANTES DE NAUARRA & DE ARAGON;
27147 5ELCID3469 ARMAS & CAUALLOS TIENEN *** DEL CANPEADOR,
27290 5ELCID3488 DAQUI UOS *** ACOMIENDO COMO A REY & A SE@OR.
27375 5ELCID3497 ABRA%OLOS TAN BIEN & RUEGA *** DE CORA%ON
27396 5ELCID3500 ATODOS *** ROGAUA ASSI COMMO HAN SABOR;
27410 5ELCID3502 *** CC MARCOS AL REY LOS SOLTO.
27415 5ELCID3502 LOS CC MARCOS AL REY *** SOLTO.
27596 5ELCID3523 EL CAMPEADOR ALOS QUE HAN LIDIAR TAN BIEN *** CASTIGO:
27661 5ELCID3531 ESPIDIOS DE TODOS *** QUE SOS AMIGOS SON.
27686 5ELCID3534 FELOS AL PLAZO *** DEL CAMPEADOR,
27733 5ELCID3540 QUE SI *** PUDIESSEN APARTAR ALOS DEL CAMPEADOR,
27740 5ELCID3541 QUE *** MATASSEN EN CAMPO POR DESONDRA DE SO SE@OR.
27782 5ELCID3545 TROCIDA ES LA NOCHE, YA QUIEBRAN *** ALBORES.
27820 5ELCID3550 HYAS METIEN EN ARMAS *** DEL BUEN CAMPEADOR,
27838 5ELCID3552 EN OTRO LOGAR SE ARMAN *** YFANTES DE CARRION,
27872 5ELCID3556 COLADA & TIZON, QUE NON LIDIASSEN CON ELLAS *** DEL CANPEADOR;
27878 5ELCID3557 MUCHO ERAN REPENTIDOS *** YFANTES POR QUANTO DADAS SON;
27932 5ELCID3564 QUE NADA NON MANCARA POR *** DEL CAMPEADOR.
27985 5ELCID3571 TODOS TRES SON ARMADOS *** DEL CAMPEADOR,
27989 5ELCID3572 HYUA *** VER EL REY DON ALFONSSO;
27996 5ELCID3573 DIXIERON *** DEL CAMPEADOR:
28027 5ELCID3577 AQUI TIENEN SU VANDO *** YFANTES DE CARRION,
28061 5ELCID3582 ADUZEN LES *** CAUALLOS BUENOS & CORREDORES,
28073 5ELCID3584 *** ESCUDOS ALOS CUELLOS QUE BIEN BLOCADOS SON;
28105 5ELCID3588 HYA SALIERON AL CAMPO DO ERAN *** MOIONES.
28111 5ELCID3589 TODOS TRES SON ACORDADOS *** DEL CAMPEADOR,
28127 5ELCID3591 FEUOS DELA OTRA PART *** YFANTES DE CARRION,
28192 5ELCID3599 HYO *** ADUX ASALUO ATIERRAS DE CARRION;
28229 5ELCID3604 *** FIELES & EL REY ENSE@ARON LOS MOIONES,
28235 5ELCID3604 LOS FIELES & EL REY ENSE@ARON *** MOIONES,
28285 5ELCID3611 SALIEN *** FIELES DE MEDIO, ELLOS CARA POR CARA SON;
28296 5ELCID3612 DESI VINIEN *** DE MYO %ID ALOS YFANTES DE CARRION,
28319 5ELCID3615 ABRA%AN *** ESCUDOS DELANT LOS CORA%ONES,
28322 5ELCID3615 ABRA%AN LOS ESCUDOS DELANT *** CORA%ONES,
28329 5ELCID3616 ABAXAN LAS LAN%AS ABUELTAS CON *** PENDONES,
28335 5ELCID3617 ENCLINAUAN LAS CARAS SOBRE *** ARZONES,
28338 5ELCID3618 BATIEN *** CAUALLOS CON LOS ESPOLONES,
28341 5ELCID3618 BATIEN LOS CAUALLOS CON *** ESPOLONES,
28369 5ELCID3622 CUEDAN SE QUE ESSORA CADRAN MUERTOS *** QUE ESTAN ADERREDOR.
28387 5ELCID3625 FIRIENSSE EN *** ESCUDOS SIN TODO PAUOR.
28448 5ELCID3633 METIOL LA LAN%A POR *** PECHOS, QUE NADA NOL VALIO;
28547 5ELCID3645 ATORGARON GELO *** FIELES, PERO VERMUEZ LE DEXO.
28564 5ELCID3647 TALES FUERON *** COLPES QUE LES QUEBRARON AMAS.
28622 5ELCID3655 RAXOL *** PELOS DELA CABE%A, BIEN ALA CARNE LEGAUA;
28740 5ELCID3670 OTORGAN GELO *** FIELES QUE DIZE VERDADERA PALABRA.
28746 5ELCID3671 *** DOS HAN ARRANCADO: DJREUOS DE MUNO GUSTIOZ,

WORD C# PREFIX CONTEXT

LOS (CON'T)

```
                  28762 5ELCID3673 FIRIENSSEN EN *** ESCUDOS VNOS TAN GRANDES COLPES:
                  28905 5ELCID3692 DIXIERON *** FIELES: ESTO OYMOS NOS.
                  28931 5ELCID3695 POR ONDRADOS SE PARTEN *** DEL BUEN CAMPEADOR;
                  28943 5ELCID3697 GRANDES SON *** PESARES POR TIERRAS DE CARRION.
                  28957 5ELCID3698 EL REY ALOS DE MYO %ID DE NOCHE *** ENBIO,
                  28983 5ELCID3702 POR MALOS *** DEXARON ALOS YFANTES DE CARRION,
                  29054 5ELCID3711 GRANDES SON *** GOZOS EN VALEN%IA LA MAYOR,
                  29065 5ELCID3712 POR QUE TAN ONDRADOS FUERON *** DEL CANPEADOR.
                  29102 5ELCID3717 ANDIDIERON EN PLEYTOS *** DE NAUARRA & DE ARAGON,
                  29126 5ELCID3720 *** PRIMEROS FUERON GRANDES, MAS AQUESTOS SON MIIORES;
                  29164 5ELCID3724 OY *** REYES DESPA@A SOS PARIENTES SON,
        WORD #2547 OCCURS 479 TIMES.
           INDEX OF DIVERSIFICATION =    59.99 WITH STANDARD DEVIATION OF    72.14

LUEGA             25768 5ELCID3282 POR ESSO ES ***** QUEADELI%IO FUE CRIADA.
        WORD #2548 OCCURS   1 TIMES.

LUEGO               418 5ELCID0052 LEGO A SANTA MARIA, ***** DESCAUALGA,
                    429 5ELCID0054 LA ORA%ION FECHA ***** CAUALGAUA;
                    450 5ELCID0057 FINCAUA LA TIENDA & ***** DESCAUALGAUA.
                   4804 5ELCID0609 ***** LEGAUAN LOS SOS, CA FECHA ES EL ARRANCADA.
                   6234 5ELCID0794 ESTA ALBERGADA LOS DE MYO %ID ***** LA AN ROBADA
                   8738 5ELCID1110 LOS DE BORRIANA ***** VENGAN ACA;
                  11942 5ELCID1514 ***** TOMAN ARMAS & TOMANSE A DEPORTAR,
                  12150 5ELCID1541 OYDA ES LA MISSA, & ***** CAUALGAUAN;
                  12249 5ELCID1555 OTRO DIA MANA@A ***** CAUALGAUAN,
                  15447 5ELCID1957 CON DOS CAUALLEROS ***** LAS ENBIO:
                  16492 5ELCID2091 ***** SE LEUANTARON LOS YFFANTES DE CARRION,
                  17042 5ELCID2157 NON QUIERE QUEL ESCURA, QUITOL DESSI *****.
                  21835 5ELCID2778 LAMANDO: PRIMAS, PRIMAS  ***** DESCAUALGO,
                  22067 5ELCID2808 EL CAUALLO PRISO POR LA RIENDA & ***** DENT LAS PARTIO,
                  25115 5ELCID3199 ***** SE LEUANTO MYO %ID EL CAMPEADOR;
                  25419 5ELCID3237 ***** RESPONDIO EL CONDE DON REMOND:
                  25536 5ELCID3252 MAS QUANDO ESTO OUO ACABADO, PENSSARON ***** DAL.
                  27130 5ELCID3467 ***** FABLARON YFANTES DE CARRION:
        WORD #2549 OCCURS  18 TIMES.
           INDEX OF DIVERSIFICATION =  1570.29 WITH STANDARD DEVIATION OF  1624.13

LUEGOL            12166 5ELCID1544 EL CAMPO DE TORAN%IO ****** ATRAUESSAUAN,
        WORD #2550 OCCURS   1 TIMES.

LUEGOS            27584 5ELCID3522 ESSORA SE ESPIDIERON, & ****** PARTIO LA CORT.
        WORD #2551 OCCURS   1 TIMES.

LUENGA             9650 5ELCID1226 ARRANCOLOS MYO %ID EL DELA ****** BARBA.
                  12511 5ELCID1587 VISTIOS EL SOBREGONEL; ****** TRAHE LA BARBA;
                  24289 5ELCID3097 LA BARBA AVIE ****** & PRISOLA CON EL CORDON,
                  24508 5ELCID3124 ALA BARBA QUE AUIE ****** & PRESA CONEL CORDON;
                  25701 5ELCID3273 DEXOLA CRE%ER & ****** TRAE LA BARBA;
        WORD #2552 OCCURS   5 TIMES.
           INDEX OF DIVERSIFICATION =  4011.75 WITH STANDARD DEVIATION OF  5290.53

LUMBRES            1916 5ELCID0244 CON ******* & CON CANDELAS AL CORAL DIERON SALTO.
        WORD #2553 OCCURS   1 TIMES.

LUNA               2630 5ELCID0332 FEZIST ESTRELAS & **** & EL SOL PORA ESCALENTAR;
        WORD #2554 OCCURS   1 TIMES.

LUZON             20892 5ELCID2653 HYUAN TRO%IR LOS MONTES, LOS QUE DIZEN DE *****.
        WORD #2555 OCCURS   1 TIMES.

LX                  115 5ELCID0016 EN SU CONPA@A ** PENDONES: EXIEN LO UER MUGIERES & UARONES,
                  16729 5ELCID2118 MYO %ID DELOS CAUALLOS ** DIO EN DON.
        WORD #2556 OCCURS   2 TIMES.

LXV               11214 5ELCID1419 AMINAYA *** CAUALLEROS A CRE%IDOL HAN,
        WORD #2557 OCCURS   1 TIMES.

MA%ANAS           24950 5ELCID3179 LAS ******* & LOS ARRIAZES TODOS DORO SON.
        WORD #2558 OCCURS   1 TIMES.

MADRE              2641 5ELCID0333 PRISIST ENCARNA%ION EN SANTA MARIA *****,
                   3014 5ELCID0379 %ID, DO SON UUESTROS ESFUER%OS? EN BUEN ORA NASQUIESTES DE *****;
                  10005 5ELCID1267 GRADO A DIOS, MYNAYA, & A SANTA MARIA *****
                  12603 5ELCID1599 ALA ***** & ALAS FIJAS BIEN LAS ABRA%AUA,
                  12670 5ELCID1608 ***** & FIJAS LAS MANOS LE BESAUAN.
                  12908 5ELCID1637 GRADO AL CRIADOR & A SANTA MARIA *****,
                  13048 5ELCID1654 CON LA MER%ED DE DIOS & DE SANTA MARIA *****
                  13163 5ELCID1668 COLGAR LOS HAN EN SANTA MARIA ***** DEL CRIADOR.
                  19902 5ELCID2524 GRADO A SANTA MARIA, ***** DEL NUESTRO SE@OR DIOS
                  20448 5ELCID2595 VOS NOS ENGENDRASTES, NUESTRA ***** NOS PARIO;
                  20498 5ELCID2602 EL FIZO AQUESTO, LA ***** LO DOBLAUA;
                  20536 5ELCID2607 AL PADRE & ALA ***** LAS MANOS LES BESAUAN;
```

WORD C# PREFIX CONTEXT

MADRE (CON'T)

22738 5ELCID2897 GRAND GOZO FIZO CON ELLAS DO@A XIMENA SU *****.
WORD #2559 OCCURS 13 TIMES.
INDEX OF DIVERSIFICATION = 1673.75 WITH STANDARD DEVIATION OF 2571.95

MAFOMAT 5784 5ELCID0731 LOS MOROS LAMAN ******* & LOS CHRISTIANOS SANTI YAGUE.
WORD #2560 OCCURS 1 TIMES.

MAGER 1339 5ELCID0171 NON LAS PODIEN PONER EN SOMO ***** ERAU ESFOR%ADOS.
5893 5ELCID0747 ***** DE PIE BUENOS COLPES VA DANDO.
8993 5ELCID1145 ***** LES PESA, OUIERON SE ADAR & A ARANCAR.
10459 5ELCID1326 ***** EN TIERRA AGENA, EL BIEN FAZE LO SO;
10610 5ELCID1345 ***** PLOGO AL REY, MUCHO PESO A GAR%IORDONEZ:
12017 5ELCID1524 ***** QUE MAL LE QUERAMOS, NON GELO PODREMOS FER,
14050 5ELCID1780 ***** DE TODO ESTO, EL CAMPEADOR CONTADO
18216 5ELCID2305 ***** LOS ESTAN LAMANDO, NINGUNO NON RESPONDE.
24440 5ELCID3116 ***** QUE ALGUNOS PESA, MEIOR SODES QUE NOS.
WORD #2561 OCCURS 9 TIMES.
INDEX OF DIVERSIFICATION = 2886.63 WITH STANDARD DEVIATION OF 2000.73

MAIADAS 21488 5ELCID2732 SI NOS FUEREMOS *******, ABILTAREDES AUOS,
23105 5ELCID2944 ******* & DESNUDAS A GRANDE DESONOR,
WORD #2562 OCCURS 2 TIMES.

MAIAN 21522 5ELCID2736 CON LAS %INCHAS CORREDIZAS ***** LAS TAN SIN SABOR;
WORD #2563 OCCURS 1 TIMES.

MAIARON 21576 5ELCID2743 TANTO LAS ******* QUE SIN COSIMENTE SON;
23099 5ELCID2943 MAL ******* SUS FIJAS DEL %ID CAMPEADOR;
WORD #2564 OCCURS 2 TIMES.

MAL 373 5ELCID0047 %ID, ENEL NUESTRO *** UOS NON GANADES NADA;
2610 5ELCID0329 QUE AMIO %ID EL CAMPEADOR QUE DIOS LE CURIAS DE ***:
2835 5ELCID0357 EN TI CROUO AL ORA, POR END ES SALUO DE ***;
2891 5ELCID0364 POR MYO %ID EL CAMPEADOR, QUE DIOS LE CURIE DE ***.
4C08 5ELCID0509 QUEL BUSCARIE *** CON TODAS SUS MESNADAS.
4210 5ELCID0535 POR QUE LO PRIS DELLOS QUE DE MI NON DIGAN ***.
5038 5ELCID0636 QUANDO LO OYO EL REY TAMIN, POR CUER LE PESO ***:
7450 5ELCID0955 QUE EL SALIDO DE CASTIELLA ASILOS TRAE TAN ***.
7633 5ELCID0977 DIGADES AL CONDE NON LO TENGA A ***,
8011 5ELCID1023 PUES QUE TALES *** CAL%ADOS ME VEN%IERON DE BATALLA.
9212 5ELCID1172 TAIAUA LES LAS HUERTAS & FAZIA LES GRAND ***,
9224 5ELCID1174 *** SE AQUEXAN LOS DE VALEN%IA QUE NON SABENT QUES FAR,
10716 5ELCID1357 DE FONTA & DE *** CURIALDAS & DE DESONOR;
10783 5ELCID1365 ATREGO LES LOS CUERPOS DE *** & DE OCASION,
11033 5ELCID1396 OMILOM, DO@A XIMENA, DIOS VOS CURIE DE ***,
11081 5ELCID1402 SI UOS VIESSE EL %ID SA@AS & SIN ***,
11117 5ELCID1407 DEZID AL CANPEADOR, QUE DIOS LE CURIE DE ***,
11148 5ELCID1410 DE AQUESTOS XV DIAS, SIDIOS NOS CURIARE DE ***,
11290 5ELCID1428 PALAFRES & MULAS, QUE NON PARESCAN ***.
11889 5ELCID1507 BIEN SALIERON DEN %IENTO QUE NON PARE%EN ***,
12019 5ELCID1524 MAGER QUE *** LE QUERAMOS, NON GELO PODREMOS FER,
14340 5ELCID1814 QUE NON DIGA *** EL REY ALFONSSO DEL QUE VALEN%IA MANDA.
14702 5ELCID1859 PESO AL CONDE DON GAR%IA, E *** ERA YRADO;
14959 5ELCID1891 EFAZIENDO YO HA EL ***, & EL AMI GRAND PRO,
19990 5ELCID2536 ELAS NOCHES & LOS DIAS TAN *** LOS ESCARMENTANDO,
19994 5ELCID2537 TAN *** SE CONSSEIARON ESTOS YFFANTES AMOS.
21276 5ELCID2704 *** GELO CUNPLIERON QUANDO SALIE EL SOL
21344 5ELCID2713 TANTO *** COMIDIERON LOS YFANTES DE CARRION;
21534 5ELCID2737 CON LAS ESPUELAS AGUDAS, CON ELLAS AN *** SABOR,
21853 5ELCID2781 *** SE ENSAYARON LOS YFANTES DE CARRION
21870 5ELCID2782 ADIOS PLEGA & A SANTA MARIA QUE DENT PRENDAN ELLOS *** GALARDON
22512 5ELCID2866 QUANDO UOS SODES SA@AS & BIUAS & SIN OTRO ***.
22682 5ELCID2890 VENIDES, MIS FIJAS? DIOS UOS CURIE DE ***
23098 5ELCID2943 *** MAIARON SUS FIJAS DEL %ID CAMPEADOR;
23545 5ELCID2998 ENEMIGO DE MIO SID, QUE SIEMPREL BUSCO ***,
24079 5ELCID3070 COMIGO YRA *** ANDA, QUE ES BIEN SABIDOR.
25510 5ELCID3249 *** ESCAPAN IOGADOS, SABED, DESTA RAZON.
25562 5ELCID3255 OYD ME TODA LA CORT & PESEUOS DE MYO ***;
25570 5ELCID3256 DELOS YFANTES DE CARRION QUEM DESONDRARON TAN ***,
26042 5ELCID3319 SI YO NON VUJAS, EL MORO TE JUGARA ***;
26104 5ELCID3327 E ERES FERMOSO, MAS *** VARRAGAN
26469 5ELCID3377 HYA VARONES, QUIEN VIO NUNCA TAL ***?
27014 5ELCID3451 AVER LAS HEDES ASERUIR, *** QUE UOS PESE AUOS.
28210 5ELCID3601 CA QUI TUERTO QUISIERE FAZER, *** GELO VEDARE YO,
28517 5ELCID3641 ASSI LO TENIEN LAS YENTES QUE *** FERIDO ES DE MUERT.
29042 5ELCID3709 DELO QUE AN PRESO MUCHO AN *** SABOR;
WORD #2565 OCCURS 46 TIMES.
INDEX OF DIVERSIFICATION = 636.09 WITH STANDARD DEVIATION OF 919.31

MALA 2694 5ELCID0340 SALUEST A DANIEL CON LOS LEONES EN LA **** CAR%EL,
6568 5ELCID0838 LA TIERRA ES ANGOSTA & SOBEIANA DE ****;
9261 5ELCID1178 **** CUETA ES, SE@ORES, AVER MINGUA DE PAN,
18027 5ELCID2281 **** SOBREUIENTA, SABED, QUE LES CUNTIO:
WORD #2566 OCCURS 4 TIMES.

MALAS 12583 5ELCID1596 SACADA ME AUEDES DE MUCHAS VERGUEN%AS *****;
WORD #2567 OCCURS 1 TIMES.

WORD C# PREFIX CONTEXT

```
MALES          4502 5ELCID0572 ALCS DE CALATAUTH, SABET, ***** PESAUA.
               9149 5ELCID1165 ***** PESA EN XATIUA & CENTRO EN GUIERA,
      WORD #2568 OCCURS   2 TIMES.

MALO           1292 5ELCID0165 NON LES DIESSE MYO %ID DELA GANAN%IA UN DINERO ****.
               3966 5ELCID0503 NCN PRENDRE DE UOS QUANTO UALE VN DINERO ****.
               8181 5ELCID1042 SABET, NCN UOS DARE AUOS VN DINERO ****;
              14518 5ELCID1836 EL CCNDE DON GAR%IA, SO ENEMIGO ****.
              26223 5ELCID3343 RIEBTOT EL CUERPC PCR **** & PCR TRAYCOR;
              26510 5ELCID3383 CALA, ALEUCSC, **** & TRAYCOR
              27752 5ELCID3542 EL CCMETER FUE ****, CUE LO AL NOS ENPE%O,
      WORD #2569 OCCURS   7 TIMES.
         INDEX OF DIVERSIFICATION =  4409.00 WITH STANDARD DEVIATION OF  4171.75

MALOS            65 5ELCID0009 ESTO ME AN BUELTO MYOS ENEMIGOS *****.
               2117 5ELCID0267 POR ***** MESTUREROS DE TIERRA SODES ECHADO.
              21101 5ELCID2681 AQUIM PARTC DE UCS COMMO DE ***** & DE TRAYDORES.
              21415 5ELCID2722 ESPUELAS TIENEN CAL%ADAS LOS ***** TRAYDORES,
              21479 5ELCID2731 ATAN ***** ENSSIENPLCS NON FAGADES SOBRE NOS:
              26946 5ELCID3442 RIEBTOS LES LCS CUERPCS POR ***** & POR TRAYDORES.
              28982 5ELCID3702 POR ***** LOS DEXARON ALCS YFANTES DE CARRION,
      WORD #2570 OCCURS   7 TIMES.
         INDEX OF DIVERSIFICATION =  4818.50 WITH STANDARD DEVIATION OF  7202.40

MAN            2561 5ELCID0323 PASSANDO UA LA NOCH, VINIENDO LA ***;
               3376 5ELCID0425 DE NOCH PASSAN LA SIERRA, VINICA ES LA ***,
               8665 5ELCID1100 TRASNOCHARON DE NOCH, AL ALUA DELA ***
              24004 5ELCID3059 ACORDADOS FUERON, QUANDC VINO LA ***.
      WORD #2571 OCCURS   4 TIMES.

MANANA        13303 5ELCID1687 POR LA ****** PRIETA TODOS ARMADOS SEADES,
              14358 5ELCID1816 OTRO DIA ****** PRIUADO CAUALGAUAN,
      WORD #2572 OCCURS   2 TIMES.

MANA@A        12248 5ELCID1555 OTRO DIA ****** LUEGO CAUALGAUAN,
      WORD #2573 OCCURS   1 TIMES.

MANCARA       25991 5ELCID3312 POR LO QUE YO CUIER AFER POR MI NON *******.
              27930 5ELCID3564 QUE NADA NCN ******* PCR LOS DEL CAMPEADOR.
      WORD #2574 OCCURS   2 TIMES.

MANDA          5385 5ELCID0679 TODOS LCS MOROS & LAS MORAS DE FUERA LOS ***** ECHAR,
              14347 5ELCID1814 QUE NON DIGA MAL EL REY ALFONSSO DEL QUE VALEN%IA *****.
              25764 5ELCID3281 GRADO A DICS QUE %IELC & TIERRA *****
      WORD #2575 OCCURS   3 TIMES.

MANDAD         1620 5ELCID0208 ****** COGER LA TIENDA & VAYAMCS PRIUADO,
               8341 5ELCID1061 ****** NOS CAR LAS BESTIAS & CAUALGEREMOS PRIUADO;
              18677 5ELCID2364 ****** NOLCS FERIR DE QUAL PART UOS SEMEIAR,
      WORD #2576 OCCURS   3 TIMES.

MANDADAS      13496 5ELCID1710 DIXO EL CAMPEADOR: DESA QUI UOS SEAN ********.
      WORD #2577 OCCURS   1 TIMES.

MANDADERO      7668 5ELCID0982 TORNCS EL ********* QUANTO PUCO MAS;
              11508 5ELCID1457 QUI BUEN ********* ENBIA, TAL DEUE SPERAR.
      WORD #2578 OCCURS   2 TIMES.

MANDADES      13367 5ELCID1694 PUES ESSO QUEREDES, %ID, A MI ******** AL;
      WORD #2579 OCCURS   1 TIMES.

MANDADO        1906 5ELCID0242 LAMAUAN ALA PUERTA, Y SCPIERON EL *******;
               3411 5ELCID0431 ******* DE SO SE@OR TCDC LC HAN AFAR.
               3587 5ELCID0452 FAZED ME ******* MUY PRIUADO ALA %AGA;
               6384 5ELCID0813 ENBIAR UOS CUIERO A CASTIELLA CON *******
               7320 5ELCID0939 HYA VA EL ******* PCR LAS TIERRAS TODAS,
               9621 5ELCID1222 AQUEL REY DE SEUILLA EL ******* LEGAUA,
              12297 5ELCID1561 DENTRO A VALEN%IA LIEUAN LE EL *******.
              12315 5ELCID1563 CA DELC QUE MAS AMAUA YAL VIENE EL *******.
              14213 5ELCID1798 DE TODA LA SU QUINTA EL DIEZMO LA *******.
              14455 5ELCID1828 ENVIAUA LE ******* PERC VERMUEZ & MYNAYA,
              14546 5ELCID1839 CUEDAN SE QUE ES ALMOFALLA, CA NON VIENEN CON *******;
              16971 5ELCID2148 RE%IBO ESTE DCN QUE ME AUEDES *******;
              17576 5ELCID2223 SABEDES QUE AL REY ASSI GELO HE *******,
              17638 5ELCID2231 POR MANO DEL REY ALFONSSO, QUE AMI LO OUO *******,
              22309 5ELCID2841 NON LO DETARDAN EL ******* CE SU SE@OR,
              22338 5ELCID2845 ASANTESTEUAN EL ******* LEGO
              22782 5ELCID2903 LIEUES EL ******* A CASTIELLA AL REY ALFONSSO;
              23433 5ELCID2984 QUE NON FALIESSEN DELC CUE EN REY AUYE *******.
              26685 5ELCID3408 SIN UUESTRO ******* NADA NCN FERE YO.
              26913 5ELCID3438 HYO LES DI MIS PRIMAS PCR ******* DEL REY ALFONSSO,
      WORD #2580 OCCURS  20 TIMES.
         INDEX OF DIVERSIFICATION =  1315.16 WITH STANDARD DEVIATION OF  1364.74
```

WORD C# PREFIX CONTEXT

```
MANDADOS            4435 5ELCID0564 POR TODAS ESSAS TIERRAS YUAN LOS ********,
                    6150 5ELCID0783 QUE A CASTIELLA YRAN BUENOS ********,
                    7438 5ELCID0954 FUERON LOS ******** A TODAS PARTES,
                    7452 5ELCID0956 LOS ******** SON YDCS ATODAS PARTES;
                    8712 5ELCID1107 VAYAN LOS ******** POR LCS QUE NOS DEUEN AIUDAR,
                   10282 5ELCID1301 VOS, QUANDO YDES A CASTIELLA, LEUAREDES BUENOS ********.
                   15029 5ELCID1900 OTROS ******** HA EN ESTA MI CORT:
                   17828 5ELCID2255 EN BESTIAS SINES AL C SCN ********;
                   19311 5ELCID2445 ACARRION DE UCS YRAN BUENOS ********,
                   19572 5ELCID2480 ******** BUENCS YRAN DELLOS A CARRION,
                   19914 5ELCID2526 BUENOS ******** YRAN ATIERRAS DE CARRION.
                   21382 5ELCID2718 HYRAN AQUESTOS ******** AL %ID CAMPEADOR;
                   22190 5ELCID2826 VAN AQUESTOS ******** A VALEN%IA LA MAYOR;
                   27616 5ELCID3526 BUENOS ******** ME VAYAN A VALEN%IA DE VOS.
         WORD #2581 OCCURS  14 TIMES.
            INDEX OF DIVERSIFICATION =  1782.15 WITH STANDARD DEVIATION OF  1641.13

MANDAMOS           25341 5ELCID3226 MAS EN NUESTRO IUUIZIO ASSI LO ******** NOS,
         WORD #2582 OCCURS   1 TIMES.

MANDAN             21252 5ELCID2701 ****** FINCAR LA TIENDA YFANTES DE CARRION,
         WORD #2583 OCCURS   1 TIMES.

MANDAR              5483 5ELCID0691 MAS NON AGUIJEDES CON ELLA, SI YO NON UOS LO ******.
                    7933 5ELCID1013 ASOS CREENDERCS ****** LO GUARDAUA.
                   24146 5ELCID3079 POR DE ****** MYOS DERECHOS & DEZIR MI RAZON:
         WORD #2584 OCCURS   3 TIMES.

MANDARE            10703 5ELCID1356 HYO LES ******* DAR CONDUCHO MIENTRA QUE POR MJ TIERRA FUEREN,
                   23273 5ELCID2965 ******* COMMO Y VAYAN YFANTES DE CARRION,
         WORD #2585 OCCURS   2 TIMES.

MANDAREDES         20470 5ELCID2598 DEBDO NOS ES A CUNPLIR LO QUE ********** VOS.
                   27166 5ELCID3472 SEA ESTA LIS O ********** VOS.
         WORD #2586 OCCURS   2 TIMES.

MANDARON           21283 5ELCID2705 ******** CARGAR LAS AZEMILAS CON GRANDES AUERES,
                   21306 5ELCID2708 ASSI LO ******** LOS YFANTES DE CARRION,
                   21743 5ELCID2766 ******** LE YR ADELANTE, MAS DE SU GRADO NON FUE.
         WORD #2587 OCCURS   3 TIMES.

MANDASSE           14461 5ELCID1829 QUE ******** RE%EBIR A ESTA CONPA@A:
         WORD #2588 OCCURS   1 TIMES.

MANDASTES          27500 5ELCID3513 ********* ME MOUER ABAUIECA EL CORREDOR,
         WORD #2589 OCCURS   1 TIMES.

MANDAUA            12111 5ELCID1536 EL PORTERO DEL REY QUITAR LO *******;
                   12174 5ELCID1545 VINIERON A MOLINA, LA QUE AUEGALUON *******.
                   12237 5ELCID1553 AVN LAS FERRADURAS QUITAR GELAS *******;
                   15560 5ELCID1972 CONDUCHOS LARGOS EL REY ENBIAR *******
         WORD #2590 OCCURS   4 TIMES.

MANDAUAN           20387 5ELCID2587 HYA ******** CARGAR YFFANTES DE CARRION.
         WORD #2591 OCCURS   1 TIMES.

MANDE               5587 5ELCID0703 NON DERANCHE NINGUNO FATA QUE YO LO *****.
                   11096 5ELCID1404 DIXO DO@A XIMENA: EL CRIADOR LO *****
                   11363 5ELCID1437 DIXO RACHEL & VIDAS: EL CRIADOR LO *****
                   16200 5ELCID2055 RESPUSO MIO %ID: ASSI LO ***** EL CRIADOR
                   16349 5ELCID2074 ASI LO ***** CHRISTUS QUE SEA ASO PRO.
                   20719 5ELCID2630 RESPONDIEN LOS YERNOS: ASSI LO ***** DIOS
                   21126 5ELCID2684 DIOS LO QUIERA & LO *****, QUE DE TODEL MUNDO ES SE@OR,
                   23800 5ELCID3032 DIOS LO ***** QUE POR UOS SE ONDRE OY LA CORT
                   27321 5ELCID3491 ESSORA RESPUSO EL REY: ASSI LO ***** DIOS
         WORD #2592 OCCURS   9 TIMES.
            INDEX OF DIVERSIFICATION =  2715.75 WITH STANDARD DEVIATION OF  2191.01

MANDEDES            2508 5ELCID0317 NON UOS TARDEDES, ******** ENSELLAR;
                    8434 5ELCID1072 E SI NON, ******** BUSCAR; O ME DEXAREDES
                   27522 5ELCID3515 HY UOS LE DO EN DON, ******** LE TOMAR, SE@OR.
         WORD #2593 OCCURS   3 TIMES.

MANDO               1754 5ELCID0224 ***** AL UUESTRO ALTAR BUENAS DONAS & RICAS;
                    2059 5ELCID0259 BIEN LAS ABASTAD, YO ASSI UOS LO *****;
                    2439 5ELCID0308 ***** EL REY A MYO %ID A AGUARDAR,
                    2546 5ELCID0322 CUEMO LO ***** MYO %ID, ASSI LO AN TODOS HA FAR.
                    3304 5ELCID0417 ***** UER SUS YENTES MYO %ID EL CAMPEADOR:
                    3897 5ELCID0494 DA QUESTA QUINTA QUE ME AUEDES *****,
                    4013 5ELCID0510 ***** PARTIR TOD AQUESTE AUER,
                    4407 5ELCID0561 A TODOS SOS VARONES ***** FAZER VNA CARCAUA,
                    4699 5ELCID0596 ***** TORNAR LA SE@A, A PRIESSA ESPOLONEAUAN.
```

WORD C# PREFIX CONTEXT

MANDO (CON'T)

5819 5ELCID0735 MYNAYA ALBARFANEZ, QEU CORITA *****,
5836 5ELCID0738 MARTIN MU@OZ, EL QUE ***** A MONT MAYOR,
6295 5ELCID0802 ***** MYO %ID AUN QUELES DIESSEN ALGO.
7845 5ELCID1004 ***** LOS FERIR MYO %ID, EL QUE EN BUEN ORA NASCO;
9338 5ELCID1187 POR ARAGON & POR NAUARRA PREGON ***** ECHAR,
9573 5ELCID1216 MYO %ID DON RODRIGO LA QUINTA ***** TOMAR,
9860 5ELCID1251 ESTO ***** MYO %ID, MINAYA LO OUO CONSSEIADO:
9961 5ELCID1263 ***** LOS VENIR ALA CORTH & A TODOS LOS IUNTAR,
10147 5ELCID1285 E ***** MILL MARCOS DE PLATA A SAN PERO LEUAR
11138 5ELCID1409 MIENTRA QUE FUEREMOS POR SUS TIERRAS CONDUCHO NOS ***** DAR.
12318 5ELCID1564 DOZITOS CAUALLEROS ***** EXIR PRIUADO,
12361 5ELCID1570 ***** MYO %ID ALOS QUE HA EN SU CASA
14114 5ELCID1787 ***** MYO %ID RUY DIAZ QUE FITA SOUIESSE LA TIENDA,
14348 5ELCID1815 ***** A PERO VERMUEZ QUE FUESSE CON MYNAYA.
14481 5ELCID1832 ***** CAUALGAR APRIESSA TOSDOS SOS FIJOS DALGO,
14799 5ELCID1871 ***** UOS LOS CUERPOS ONDRADA MIENTRE SERUIR & VESTIR
14859 5ELCID1878 BIEN LOS ***** SERUIR DE QUANTO HUEBOS HAN.
15759 5ELCID2000 A AQUESTOS DOS ***** EL CAMPEADOR QUE CURIEN A VALEN%IA
15911 5ELCID2017 ATODOS LOS SOS ESTAR LOS *****,
16267 5ELCID2063 EL CAMPEADOR ALOS SOS LO *****
16386 5ELCID2078 ELLOS UOS LAS PIDEN & ***** UOS LO YO.
17138 5ELCID2168 EA DON FERNANDO & A CON DIEGO AGUARDAR LOS *****
17231 5ELCID2179 VOS CON ELLOS SED, QUE ASSI UOS LO ***** YO.
19602 5ELCID2484 ***** MYO %ID, EL QUE EN BUEN ORA NASCO,
20379 5ELCID2585 CONPIE%AN A RE%EBIR LO QUE EL %ID *****.
20883 5ELCID2652 CON DOZIENTOS CAUALLEROS ESCURRIR LOS *****.
22287 5ELCID2838 CON CC CAUALLEROS, QUALES MYO %ID *****;
23971 5ELCID3055 ***** FAZER CANDELAS & PONER ENEL ALTAR;
24231 5ELCID3089 AL PUNO BIEN ESTAN, CA EL SELO *****;
24327 5ELCID3101 CON AQUESTOS %IENTO QUE ADOBAR *****,
24635 5ELCID3138 POR ESCOGER EL DERECHO, CA TUERTO NON ***** YO.
27695 5ELCID3535 CUNPLIR QUIEREN EL DEBDO QUE LES ***** SO SE@OR,
28910 5ELCID3693 ***** LIBRAR EL CANPO EL BUEN REY DON ALFONSSO,
28995 5ELCID3703 CONPLIDO HAN EL DEBDO QUE LES ***** SO SE@OR;
WORD #2594 OCCURS 43 TIMES.
INDEX OF DIVERSIFICATION = 647.60 WITH STANDARD DEVIATION OF 689.99

MANDOLO 11694 5ELCID1482 MYO %ID UOS SALUDAUA, & ******* RECABDAR,
18242 5ELCID2308 ******* VEDAR MYO %ID EL CAMPEADOR.
WORD #2595 OCCURS 2 TIMES.

MANDOLOS 2475 5ELCID0312 ASOS CAUALLEROS ******** TODOS IUNTAR:
WORD #2596 OCCURS 1 TIMES.

MANDOT 20637 5ELCID2620 ****** QUE VAYAS CON ELLAS FATA DENTRO EN CARRION,
WORD #2597 OCCURS 1 TIMES.

MANERO 16848 5ELCID2133 DAD ****** A QUI LAS DE, QUANDO UOS LAS TOMADES;
WORD #2598 OCCURS 1 TIMES.

MANFESTADOS 25324 5ELCID3224 DIXIERON LOS ALCALDES QUANDO *********** SON:
WORD #2599 OCCURS 1 TIMES.

MANGUAR 7397 5ELCID0948 QUI EN VN LOGAR MORA SIEMPRE, LO SO PUEDE *******;
WORD #2600 OCCURS 1 TIMES.

MANO 915 5ELCID0117 EL CAMPEADOR DEXAR LAS HA EN UUESTRA ****,
1396 5ELCID0179 %ID, BESO UUESTRA **** ENDON QUE LA YO AYA.
1682 5ELCID0216 AL%O SU **** DIESTRA, LA CARA SE SANTIGUA:
3728 5ELCID0471 EN **** TRAE DESNUDA EL ESPADA,
3943 5ELCID0500 QUE ENPLEYE LA LAN%A & AL ESPADA META ****,
3983 5ELCID0505 TODO LO OTRO AFELO EN UUESTRA ****.
4830 5ELCID0611 VINO PERO VERMUEZ, QUE LA SE@A TEINE EN ****,
5488 5ELCID0692 AL %ID BESO LA ****, LA SE@A UA TOMAR.
5599 5ELCID0705 LA SE@A TIENE EN ****, CONPE%O DE ESPOLONAR;
5892 5ELCID0746 LA LAN%A A QUEBRADA, AL ESPADA METIO ****,
5969 5ELCID0756 CAUALGO MINAYA, EL ESPADA EN LA ****,
6207 5ELCID0790 ALMOFAR ACUESTAS, LA ESPADA EN LA ****.
6377 5ELCID0812 A UUESTRA GUISA PRENDED CON UUESTRA ****.
6802 5ELCID0869 EN SU **** TENIE A %ELFA LA DE CANAL.
8124 5ELCID1035 AUOS & DOS FIJOS DALGO QUITAR UOS HE LOS CUERPOS & DARUOS E DE ****.
8164 5ELCID1040 AUOS & A OTROS DOS DAR UOS HE DE ****.
9879 5ELCID1252 QUE NINGUN OMNE DELOS SOS QUES LE NON SPIDIES, ONOL BESAS LA ****,
10067 5ELCID1275 DESI POR MI BESALDE LA **** EFIRME GELO ROGAD
10510 5ELCID1332 OBISPO FIZO DE SU **** EL BUEN CAMPEADOR,
10572 5ELCID1340 AL%O LA **** DIESTRA, EL REY SE SANTIGO:
13593 5ELCID1722 MYO %ID ENPLEO LA LAN%A, AL ESPADA METIO ****,
13680 5ELCID1733 TODA ESTA GANAN%IA EN SU **** A RASTADO.
13773 5ELCID1745 ASSI ENTRO SOBRE BAUIECA, EL ESPADA EN LA ****.
16168 5ELCID2051 BESO LE LA **** MYO CID, LO OTORGO.
16468 5ELCID2088 AFELLAS EN UUESTRA **** DON ELUIRA & DO@A SOL,
16863 5ELCID2134 NON GELAS DARE YO CON MI ****, NIN DED NON SE ALABARAN.
17568 5ELCID2222 AFFE AMAS MIS FIJAS, METOLAS EN UUESTRA ****;
17594 5ELCID2225 ALOS YFANTES DE CARRION DAD LAS CON UUESTRA ****,

WORD C# PREFIX CONTEXT

MANO (CON'T)

```
17615 5ELCID2228 LEUANTAN SE DERECHAS & METIOGELAS EN ****.
17630 5ELCID2231 POR **** DEL REY ALFONSSO, QUE AMI LO OUO MANDADO,
17673 5ELCID2235 A MYO %ID & A SU MUGIER VAN BESAR LA ****.
18866 5ELCID2387 EL ASTIL A QUEBRADO & METIO **** AL ESPADA.
19075 5ELCID2413 EL ESPADA TIENES DESNUDA EN LA **** & VEOT AGUIJAR;
19544 5ELCID2476 AL%O LA ****, ALA BARBA SE TOMO:
21418 5ELCID2723 EN **** PRENDEN LAS %INCHAS FUERTES & DURADORES.
22212 5ELCID2829 AL%O LA SU ****, ALA BARBA SE TOMO;
22793 5ELCID2904 POR MI BESA LE LA **** DALMA & DE CORA%ON,
23818 5ELCID3034 BESO LE LA **** & DESPUES LE SALUDO;
24686 5ELCID3145 MYO %ID LA **** BESO AL REY & EN PIE SE LEUANTO;
24936 5ELCID3176 PUSIERON LAS EN **** DEL REY SO SE@OR;
25007 5ELCID3185 AL%AUA LA ****, ALA BARBA SE TOMO;
25109 5ELCID3198 BESO LE LA ****, EL ESPADA TOMO & RE%IBIO.
27286 5ELCID3487 ESTOS MIS TRES CAUALLEROS EN UUESTRA **** SON,
27461 5ELCID3508 EL REY AL%O LA ****, LA CARA SE SANTIGO;
27495 5ELCID3512 FUE BESAR LA **** A SO SE@OR ALFONSSO;
28040 5ELCID3579 EN UUESTRA **** NOS METIO NUESTRO SE@OR;
28484 5ELCID3637 DEDENTRO EN LA CARNE VNA **** GELA METIO;
28530 5ELCID3642 EL DEXO LA LAN%A & AL ESPADA METIO ****,
28572 5ELCID3648 MARTIN ANTOLINEZ **** METIO AL ESPADA,
28687 5ELCID3662 DIAGON%ALEZ ESPADA TIENE EN ****, MAS NOLA
WORD #2601 OCCURS 50 TIMES.
   INDEX OF DIVERSIFICATION =   565.78 WITH STANDARD DEVIATION OF   710.16

MANOL
 1361 5ELCID0174 RACHEL AMYO %ID LA ***** BA BESAR:
 2363 5ELCID0298 TORNOS A SONRISAR; LEGAN LE TODOS, LA ***** BAN BESAR.
 2928 5ELCID0369 DO@A XIMENA AL %ID LA ***** VA BESAR.
WORD #2602 OCCURS  3 TIMES.

MANOS
  831 5ELCID0106 RACHEL & VIDAS, AMOS ME DAT LAS *****,
 1193 5ELCID0153 ASSI COMMO ENTRARON, AL %ID BESARON LE LAS *****.
 1241 5ELCID0159 DON RACHEL & VIDAS A MYO %ID BESARON LE LAS *****.
 1480 5ELCID0189 YA DON RACHEL & VIDAS, EN UUESTRAS ***** SON LAS ARCAS;
 2108 5ELCID0265 LORAUA DELOS OIOS, QUISOL BESAR LAS *****:
 2177 5ELCID0274 ENCLINO LAS ***** EN LA SU BARBA VELIDA,
 2244 5ELCID0282 PLEGA ADIOS & A SANTA MARIA, QUE AUN CON MIS ***** CASE ESTAS MI
 2809 5ELCID0354 CORRIO LA SANGRE POR EL ASTIL AYUSO, LAS ***** SE OUO DE VNTAR,
 5570 5ELCID0701 PORA MYO %ID & ALOS SOS A ***** LOS TOMAR.
 6881 5ELCID0879 BESA UOS LOS PIES & LAS ***** AMAS,
 6993 5ELCID0894 BESO LE LAS ***** MINAYA ALBARFANEZ:
 8244 5ELCID1049 ALEGRE ES EL CONDE & PIDIO AGUA ALAS *****,
 8331 5ELCID1059 POR QUE EL CONDE DON REMONT TAN BIEN BOLUIE LAS *****.
10225 5ELCID1294 QUE SIS FARTAS LIDIANDO & FIRIENDO CON SUS *****,
10415 5ELCID1320 BESAUA LE LAS ***** & FABLO TAN APUESTO:
10430 5ELCID1322 BESAUA UOS LAS ***** MYO %ID LIDIADOR,
10438 5ELCID1323 LOS PIES & LAS *****, COMMO ATAN BUEN SE@OR,
10555 5ELCID1338 BESA UOS LAS ***** & QUE LOS PRENDADES UOS;
10798 5ELCID1367 MYNAYA ALBARFANEZ LAS ***** LE BESO.
11405 5ELCID1443 POR MI AL CAMPEADOR LAS ***** LE BESAD
11910 5ELCID1510 E EN LAS ***** LAN%AS QUE PENDONES TRAEN,
12674 5ELCID1608 MADRE & FIJAS LAS ***** LE BESAUAN.
12729 5ELCID1616 AL%AN LAS ***** PORA DIOS ROGAR,
13858 5ELCID1755 ENTRAREDES EN PREZ, & BESARAN UUESTRAS *****.
13971 5ELCID1769 LEUANTARON SE TODAS & BESARON LE LAS *****,
14178 5ELCID1794 QUANDO ES FARTO DE LIDIAR CON AMAS LAS SUS *****,
14374 5ELCID1818 CON SALUDES DEL %ID QUE LAS ***** LE BESAUA:
14660 5ELCID1854 E EMBIA UOS DOZIENTOS CAUALLOS, & BESA UOS LAS *****.
14695 5ELCID1858 ESTO PLOGO A MUCHOS & BESARON LE LAS *****.
14852 5ELCID1877 BESARON LE LAS ***** & ENTRARON A POSAR;
15940 5ELCID2021 LOS YNOIOS & LAS ***** EN TIERRA LOS FINCO,
15992 5ELCID2028 BESAD LAS *****, CA LOS PIES NO;
16081 5ELCID2039 HYNOIOS FITOS LAS ***** LE BESO,
16502 5ELCID2092 BAN BESAR LAS ***** ALQUE EN ORA BUENA NA%IO;
16549 5ELCID2097 DAQUI LAS PRENDO POR MIS ***** DON ELUIRA & DONA SOL,
16582 5ELCID2101 AFELLOS EN UUESTRAS ***** LOS YFANTES DE CARRION,
16643 5ELCID2108 MYO %ID GELOS RE%IBE, LAS ***** LE BESO:
16755 5ELCID2121 EL REY ALOS YFANTES ALAS ***** LES TOMO,
16878 5ELCID2136 PRENDELLAS CON UUESTRAS ***** & DALDAS ALOS YFANTES,
16955 5ELCID2146 TOMAD AQUESTO, & BESO UUESTRAS *****.
17051 5ELCID2159 BEFAR LAS *****, ESPEDIR SE DE REY ALFONSSO:
17313 5ELCID2190 BESARON LE LAS ***** LA MUGIER & LAS FIJAS AMAS,
17415 5ELCID2203 METIUOS EN SUS *****, FIJAS, AMAS ADOS;
18756 5ELCID2373 MI ORDEN & MIS ***** QUERRIA LAS ONDRAR,
20538 5ELCID2607 AL PADRE & ALA MADRE LAS ***** LES BESAUAN;
22718 5ELCID2895 BESARON LAS ***** LAS FIJAS AL PADRE.
23054 5ELCID2937 LOS PIES & LAS ***** VOS BESA EL CAMPEADOR;
23137 5ELCID2948 POR ESTO UOS BESA LAS *****, COMMO VASSALLO A SE@OR,
23686 5ELCID3017 QUE BESASSE LAS ***** AL REY SO SE@OR:
23866 5ELCID3040 BESA UOS LAS *****, & MIS FIJAS AMAS ADOS,
24970 5ELCID3180 RE%IBIO LAS ESPADAS, LAS ***** LE BESO,
24981 5ELCID3182 EN LAS ***** LAS TIENE & AMAS LAS CATO;
26108 5ELCID3328 LENGUA SIN *****, CUEMO OSAS FABLAR?
26606 5ELCID3397 BESAN LAS ***** AL REY DON ALFONSSO,
```

WORD C# PREFIX CONTEXT

MANOS (CON'T)

```
                    26681 5ELCID3407 AFE MIS FIJAS, EN UUESTRAS ***** SON:
                    26733 5ELCID3414 LEUANTOS MYO %ID, AL REY LAS ***** LE BESO;
                    26800 5ELCID3423 BESARON LAS ***** DEL REY DON ALFONSSO,
                    27004 5ELCID3450 AGORA BESAREDES SUS ***** & LAMAR LAS HEDES SE@ORAS,
                    27273 5ELCID3486 MYO %ID AL REY LAS ***** LE BESO & DIXO: PLAZME, SE@OR.
                    27441 5ELCID3506 BESO UUESTRAS ***** CON UUESTRA GRA%IA, SE@OR,
                    28002 5ELCID3574 BESAMOS VOS LAS *****, COMMO A REY & A SE@OR,
           WORD #2603 OCCURS  61 TIMES.
              INDEX OF DIVERSIFICATION =   451.85 WITH STANDARD DEVIATION OF   593.83

MANTO                1530 5ELCID0195 DE QUE FAGADES CAL%AS & RICA PIEL & BUEN *****.
                    18105 5ELCID2291 EL ***** & EL BRIAL TODO SUZIO LO SACO.
                    18155 5ELCID2297 EL ***** TRAE ALCUELLO, & ADELINO PORA LEON;
                    22055 5ELCID2807 CON EL SO ***** A AMAS LAS CUBRIO,
                    24308 5ELCID3099 DESUSO CUBRIO VN ***** QUE ES DE GRANT VALOR,
                    26390 5ELCID3366 MAS NON VESTID EL ***** NIN EL BRIAL.
                    26445 5ELCID3374 ***** ARMINO & VN BRIAL RASTRANDO,
           WORD #2604 OCCURS   7 TIMES.
              INDEX OF DIVERSIFICATION =  4151.50 WITH STANDARD DEVIATION OF  6259.34

MANTOS                 28 5ELCID0004 ALCANDARAS UAZIAS SIN PIELLES & SIN ******
                     8382 5ELCID1065 E BUENAS VESTIDURAS DE PELI%ONES & DE ******.
                    15548 5ELCID1971 ****** & PIELLES E BUENOS %ENDALES DADRIA?
                    15684 5ELCID1989 TANTA BUENA CAPA & ****** & PELLI%ONES;
                    17829 5ELCID2256 ****** & PELLI%ONES & OTROS VESTIDOS LARGOS;
                    18052 5ELCID2284 ENBRA%AN LOS ****** LOS DEL CAMPEADOR,
                    19515 5ELCID2472 CON DUCHOS A SAZONES, BUENAS PIELES & BUENOS ******.
                    21397 5ELCID2720 ALLI LES TUELLEN LOS ****** & LOS PELLI%ONES,
                    21622 5ELCID2749 LEUARON LES LOS ****** & LAS PIELES ARMINAS,
                    24132 5ELCID3077 SOLOS ****** LAS ESPADAS DUL%ES & TAIADORES;
           WORD #2605 OCCURS  10 TIMES.
              INDEX OF DIVERSIFICATION =  2677.22 WITH STANDARD DEVIATION OF  3026.70

MA@A                 4821 5ELCID0610 MYO %ID GA@O A ALCO%ER, SABENT, POR ESTA ****.
           WORD #2606 OCCURS   1 TIMES.

MA@ANA               2500 5ELCID0316 ALA ******, QUANDO LOS GALLOS CANTARAN,
                     3132 5ELCID0394 OTRO DIA ****** PIENSSA DE CAUALGAR.
                     3275 5ELCID0413 OTRO DIA ****** PIENSSAN DE CAUALGAR;
                     3623 5ELCID0456 YA QUIEBRAN LOS ALBORES & VINIE LA ******,
                     4220 5ELCID0537 CRAS ALA ****** PENSEMOS DE CAUALGAR,
                     4737 5ELCID0600 DIOS, QUE BUENO ES EL GOZO POR AQUESTA ******
                     5105 5ELCID0645 OTRO DIA ****** PIENSSAN DE CAUALGAR,
                     5404 5ELCID0682 OTRO DIA ******, EL SOL QUERIE APUNTAR,
                     6895 5ELCID0881 DIXO EL REY:  MUCHO ES ******,
                     7400 5ELCID0949 CRAS ALA ****** PENSSEMOS DE CAUALGAR,
                     8823 5ELCID1122 PASSE LA NOCHE & VENGA LA ******,
                     8909 5ELCID1135 ****** ERA & PIENSSAN SE DE ARMAR,
                    11740 5ELCID1489 ALA ****** PIENSSAN DE CAUALGAR;
                    12144 5ELCID1540 PASSADA ES LA NOCHE, VENIDA ES LA ******,
                    13423 5ELCID1701 ALOS MEDIADOS GALLOS, ANTES DE LA ******,
                    13473 5ELCID1707 HYO UOS CANTE LA MISSA POR AQUESTA ******;
                    14289 5ELCID1808 E CRAS HA LA ****** YR UOS HEDES SIN FALLA
                    16257 5ELCID2062 OTRO DIA ******, CLARO SALIE EL SOL,
                    16302 5ELCID2068 AL OTRO DIA ******, ASSI COMMO SALIO EL SOL,
                    16672 5ELCID2111 LAS PALABRAS SON PUESTAS QUE OTRO DIA ******
                    17236 5ELCID2180 QUANDO VINIERE LA ******, QUE APUNTARE EL SOL,
                    20874 5ELCID2651 OTRO DIA ****** CON ELLOS CAUALGO,
                    22539 5ELCID2870 OTRO DIA ****** PIENSSAN DE CAUALGAR,
                    22593 5ELCID2878 OTRO DIA ****** METEN SE A ANDAR,
                    23938 5ELCID3050 CRAS ****** ENTRARE ALA %IBDAD,
           WORD #2607 OCCURS  25 TIMES.
              INDEX OF DIVERSIFICATION =   892.25 WITH STANDARD DEVIATION OF   917.98

MA@ANAS              6552 5ELCID0836 YA ES AGUISADO, ******* FUE MINAYA,
           WORD #2608 OCCURS   1 TIMES.

MA@AS               17156 5ELCID2171 QUE SOPIESSEN SOS ***** DE LOS YFANTES DE CARRION.
                    26006 5ELCID3315 LAS TUS ***** YO TELAS SABRE CONTAR:
                    26968 5ELCID3445 MAS BIEN SABEMOS LAS ***** QUE ELLOS HAN,
           WORD #2609 OCCURS   3 TIMES.

MAQUILAS            26489 5ELCID3380 E PRENDER ********, COMMO LO SUELE FAR
           WORD #2610 OCCURS   1 TIMES.

MAR                  2626 5ELCID0331 FEZIST %IELO & TIERRA, EL TER%ERO EL ***;
                     2685 5ELCID0339 A IONAS, QUANDO CAYO EN LA ***,
                     8583 5ELCID1090 CONTRA LA *** SALADA CONPE%O DE GUERREAR;
                     9089 5ELCID1156 SONANDO VAN SUS NUEUAS ALENT PARTE DEL ***.
                     9127 5ELCID1162 CABO DEL *** TIERRA DE MOROS FIRME LA QUEBRANTA,
                    12719 5ELCID1614 E DEL OTRA PARTE A OIO HAN EL ***,
                    12766 5ELCID1620 DEZIR UOS QUIERO NUEUAS DE ALENT PARTES DEL ***,
                    12821 5ELCID1627 ENTRARON SOBRE ***, EN LAS BARCAS SON METIDOS,
                    12924 5ELCID1639 VENIDOM ES DELI%IO DE TIERRAS DALENT ***,
```

WORD C# PREFIX CONTEXT

MAR (CON'T)

19043 5ELCID2409 ACA TORNA, BUCAR VENIST CALENT ***,
19105 5ELCID2416 NCN TE IUNTARAS CCMIGC FATA CENTRO EN LA ***.
19139 5ELCID2420 ALCAN%OLO EL %ID ABUCAR A TRES BRACAS DEL ***,
19177 5ELCID2425 MATO A BUCAR, AL REY CF ALEN ***,
WORD #2611 OCCURS 13 TIMES.
INDEX OF DIVERSIFICATICN = 1378.25 WITH STANCARD CEVIATION OF 2385.30

MARAUILLA 14714 5ELCID1861 ********* ES DEL %ID, QUE SU ONDRA CRE%E TANTO
15394 5ELCID1950 NCN ERA ********* SIQUISIESSE EL REY ALFONSSO,
WORD #2612 OCCURS 2 TIMES.

MARAUILLADO 8147 5ELCID1038 TANTO QUANTC YO BIUA, SERE CENT ***********.
WORD #2613 OCCURS 1 TIMES.

MARAUILLAN 16237 5ELCID2060 ********** SE DE MYO %IC QUANTOS QUE Y SON.
18553 5ELCID2348 MAS SE ********** ENTRE DIEGO & FERRANDO,
24957 5ELCID3179 ********** SE DELLAS TOCAS LOS CMNES BUENOS DELA CORT.
WORD #2614 OCCURS 3 TIMES.

MARAUILLAUAN 12533 5ELCID1590 QUANDO CUO CORRIDO, TOCCS SE ************;
WORD #2615 OCCURS 1 TIMES.

MARAUILLOSA 3389 5ELCID0427 EN MEDIO DUNA MONTANA *********** & GRAND
8532 5ELCID1084 DE LA GANAN%IA QUE AN FECHA *********** & GRAND.
12995 5ELCID1648 RIQUEZA ES QUE NOS A CRE%E *********** & GRAND;
19190 5ELCID2427 VEN%IO LA BATALLA *********** & GRANT.
WORD #2616 OCCURS 4 TIMES.

MARAUILLOSO 6770 5ELCID0864 ALTO ES EL PCYO, *********** & GRANT;
WORD #2617 OCCURS 1 TIMES.

MARCHO 2062 5ELCID0260 POR VN ****** QUE DESPENDADES AL MONESTERIO DARE YO QUATRO.
WORD #2618 OCCURS 1 TIMES.

MARCHOS 1078 5ELCID0138 HUEBOS AUEMCS QUE NOS CEDES LOS *******.
1536 5ELCID0196 DAMOS UCS ENDON AUOS XXX *******;
1557 5ELCID0199 GRADE%IOLO DCN MARTINC & RECIBIO LOS *******;
1983 5ELCID0250 MAS POR QUE ME VC DE TIERRA, CQUOS L *******,
2008 5ELCID0253 EUADES AQUI PORA DO@A XIMENA CQUOS C *******.
4035 5ELCID0513 A CADA VNO DELLOS CAEN C ******* DE PLATA,
6625 5ELCID0845 VENDIDO LES A ALCO%ER PCR TRES MILL ******* DE PLATA.
WORD #2619 OCCURS 7 TIMES.
INDEX OF DIVERSIFICATICN = 923.50 WITH STANCARD DEVIATION OF 1102.81

MARCOS 1053 5ELCID0135 A MENESTER SEYS %IENTCS ******.
1147 5ELCID0147 LAS ARCHAS ADUCHAS, PRENDET SEYES %IENTOS ******.
1257 5ELCID0161 QUE SOBRE AQUELAS ARCHAS DAR LE YEN VJ %IENTOS ******
1316 5ELCID0168 YO YRE CON UUSO, QUE ADUGAMOS LOS ******,
1439 5ELCID0184 ATOD EL PRIMER COLPE IIJ ****** DE PLATA ECHARON,
4100 5ELCID0521 ASMARON LOS MOROS IIJ MILL ****** DE PLATA.
7911 5ELCID1010 HY GA@O A CCLADA QUE MAS VALE CE MILL ****** DE PLATA.
9580 5ELCID1217 ENEL AUER MONECADO XXX MILL ****** LE CAEN,
9709 5ELCID1234 ATODOS LOS MENORES CAYERON C ****** DE PLATA.
10149 5ELCID1285 E MANDO MILL ****** DE PLATA A SAN PERO LEUAR
11238 5ELCID1422 LOS QUINIENTOS ****** DIO MINAYA AL ABBAT,
13712 5ELCID1737 ENTRE ORO & PLATA FALLARCN TRES MILL ******,
13944 5ELCID1766 ACADA VNA DELLAS DO LES CC ****** DE PLATA,
16597 5ELCID2103 TREZIENTOS ****** DE PLATA EN AYUDA LES DO YO,
19184 5ELCID2426 E GANO A TIZON QUE MILL ****** DORO VAL.
19473 5ELCID2467 QUE ALA RA%ION CAYE SEYS %IENTOS ****** DE PLATA.
19794 5ELCID2509 VALIA DE %INCC MILL ****** GANARON AMOS ADOS;
20259 5ELCID2571 HYO QUIERO LES CAR AXUUAR IIJ MILL ****** DE PLATA;
25162 5ELCID3204 EN ORO & EN PLATA TRES MILL ****** DE PLATA LES DIO;
25374 5ELCID3231 DESTOS IIJ MILL ****** LOS CC TENGO YO;
25485 5ELCID3246 SOBRE LCS DOZIENTCS ****** QUE TENIE EL REY ALFONSSO
27412 5ELCID3502 LOS CC ****** AL REY LOS SOLTO.
WORD #2620 OCCURS 22 TIMES.
INDEX OF DIVERSIFICATION = 1254.19 WITH STANCARD DEVIATION OF 1429.31

MAR%O 12755 5ELCID1619 EL YUIERNO ES EXICO, QUE EL ***** QUIERE ENTRAR.
WORD #2621 OCCURS 1 TIMES.

MARIA 417 5ELCID0052 LEGO A SANTA *****, LUEGO DESCAUALGA,
1679 5ELCID0215 LA CARA DEL CAUALLC TORNO A SANTA *****,
1703 5ELCID0218 VALAN ME TUS VERTUDES, GLORIOSA SANTA *****
2174 5ELCID0273 DAND NCS CONSEIC POR AMOR DE SANTA *****
2239 5ELCID0282 PLEGA ADIOS & A SANTA *****, QUE AUN CON MIS MANOS CASE ESTAS MIS
2640 5ELCID0333 PRISIST ENCARNA%ICN EN SANTA ***** MADRE,
6437 5ELCID0822 EN SANTA ***** DE BURGOS QUITEDES MILL MISSAS;
10004 5ELCID1267 GRADO A DICS, MYNAYA, & A SANTA ***** MADRE
11543 5ELCID1462 POR SANTA ***** UCS VAYADES PASSAR,
11639 5ELCID1475 TRO%IERON A SANTA ***** & VINIERON ALBERGAR A FRONTAEL,
12907 5ELCID1637 GRADO AL CRIADOR & A SANTA ***** MADRE,
13047 5ELCID1654 CON LA MER%ED DE DIOS & DE SANTA ***** MADRE

WORD C# PREFIX CONTEXT

MARIA (CON'T)

13162 5ELCID1668 COLGAR LOS HAN EN SANTA ***** MADRE DEL CRIADOR.
17683 5ELCID2237 PORA SANTA ***** A PRIESSA ADELINNANDO;
17970 5ELCID2274 PLEGA A SANTA ***** & AL PADRE SANTO
19901 5ELCID2524 GRADO A SANTA *****, MADRE DEL NUESTRO SE@OR DIOS
20832 5ELCID2645 POR SANTA ***** DALUA RAZIN FAZIAN LA POSADA,
21865 5ELCID2782 ADIOS PLEGA & A SANTA ***** QUE DENT PRENDAN ELLOS MAL GALARDON
WORD #2622 OCCURS 18 TIMES.
INDEX OF DIVERSIFICATION = 1260.65 WITH STANDARD DEVIATION OF 1420.03

MARIDAS 21630 5ELCID2750 MAS DEXAN LAS ******* EN BRIALES & EN CAMISAS,
WORD #2623 OCCURS 1 TIMES.

MARRUECOS 9289 5ELCID1181 POR EL REY DE ********* OUIERON A ENBIAR;
9675 5ELCID1230 AQUEL REY DE ********* CON TRES COLPES ESCAPA.
12773 5ELCID1621 DE AQUEL REY YUCEF QUE EN ********* ESTA.
12779 5ELCID1622 PESOL AL REY DE ********* DE MYO %ID CON RODRIGO:
12806 5ELCID1625 AQUEL REY DE ********* AIUNTAUA SUS VIRTOS;
13184 5ELCID1671 LOS MOROS DE ********* CAUALGAN AUIGOR,
14100 5ELCID1785 LA TIENDA DEL REY DE *********, QUE DELAS OTRAS ES CABO,
14627 5ELCID1850 A AQUEL REY DE *********, YUCEFF POR NOMBRADO,
18273 5ELCID2312 FUER%AS DE ********* VALEN%IA VIENEN %ERCAR;
19710 5ELCID2499 ALA DENTRO EN *********, OLAS MEZQUITAS SON,
WORD #2624 OCCURS 10 TIMES.
INDEX OF DIVERSIFICATION = 1156.89 WITH STANDARD DEVIATION OF 1336.93

MARTIN 507 5ELCID0065 ****** ANTOLINEZ, EL BURGALES CONPLIDO,
551 5ELCID0070 FABLO ****** ATOLINEZ, ODREDES LO QUE A DICHO:
623 5ELCID0079 ****** ANTOLINEZ, SODES ARDIDA LAN%A
758 5ELCID0096 ****** ANTOLINEZ NON LO DETARUA,
798 5ELCID0102 LEGO ****** ATOLINEZ AGUISA DEMENBRADO:
1019 5ELCID0131 RESPUSO ****** ANTOLINEZ A GUISA DE MENBRADO:
1097 5ELCID0141 DIXO ****** ANTOLINEZ: YO DESSO ME PAGO.
1148 5ELCID0148 ****** ANTOLINEZ CAUALGO PRIUADO
1242 5ELCID0160 ****** ANTOLINEZ EL PLEYTO A PARADO,
1294 5ELCID0166 DIXO ****** ANTOLINEZ: CARGEN LAS ARCHAS PRIUADO.
1509 5ELCID0193 ****** ANTOLINEZ, UN BURGALES CONTADO,
1592 5ELCID0204 VENIDES, ****** ANTOLINEZ, EL MIO FIEL VASSALO
1789 5ELCID0228 DIXO ****** ANTOLINEZ: VERE ALA MUGIER ATODO MYO SOLAZ,
1822 5ELCID0232 TORNAUAS ****** ANTOLINEZ A BURGOS & MYO %ID AAGUIJAR
2320 5ELCID0293 ****** ANTOLINEZ CON ELLOS COIO.
5820 5ELCID0736 ****** ANTOLINEZ, EL BURGALES DE PRO,
5832 5ELCID0738 ****** MU@OZ, EL QUE MANDO A MONT MAYOR,
6031 5ELCID0765 ****** ANTOLINEZ VN COLPE DIO A GALUE,
7072 5ELCID0904 EL DE RIO ****** TODO LO METIO EN PARIA.
11521 5ELCID1459 E ****** ANTOLINEZ, VN BURGALES LEAL,
11833 5ELCID1500 E ****** ANTOLINEZ, EL BURGALES NATURAL,
15700 5ELCID1992 ****** MUNOZ & MARTIN ANTOLINEZ, EL BURGALES DE PRO,
15703 5ELCID1992 MARTIN MUNOZ & ****** ANTOLINEZ, EL BURGALES DE PRO,
22275 5ELCID2837 E ****** ANTOLINEZ, EL BURGLES DE PRO,
24052 5ELCID3066 E ****** ANTOLINEZ, EL BURGALES DE PRO,
24065 5ELCID3068 E ****** MUNOZ, QUE EN BUEN PUNTO NA%IO,
25048 5ELCID3191 A ****** ANTOLINEZ, EL BURGALES DE PRO,
25061 5ELCID3193 ****** ANTOLINEZ, MYO VASSALO DE PRO,
26354 5ELCID3361 ****** ANTOLINEZ EN PIE SE LEUANTAUA;
27599 5ELCID3524 HYA ****** ANTOLINEZ, & VOS, PERO VERMUEZ,
27624 5ELCID3527 DIXO ****** ANTOLINEZ: POR QUE LO DEZIDES, SE@OR
28553 5ELCID3646 ****** ANTOLINEZ & DIEGO GON%ALEZ FIRIERON SE DELAS LAN%AS,
28570 5ELCID3648 ****** ANTOLINEZ MANO METIO AL ESPADA,
28667 5ELCID3660 ESSORA ****** ANTOLINEZ RE%IBIOL CON EL ESPADA,
28716 5ELCID3667 SACOL DEL MOJON; ****** ANTOLJNEZ EN EL CAMPO FINCAUA.
WORD #2625 OCCURS 35 TIMES.
INDEX OF DIVERSIFICATION = 828.68 WITH STANDARD DEVIATION OF 1524.19

MARTINO 1445 5ELCID0185 NOTOLOS DON *******, SIN PESO LOS TOMAUA;
1461 5ELCID0187 %INCO ESCUDEROS TIENE DON *******, ATODOS LOS CARGAUA.
1553 5ELCID0199 GRADE%IOLO DON ******* & RECIBIO LOS MARCHOS;
WORD #2626 OCCURS 3 TIMES.

MARTIRES 21459 5ELCID2728 CORTANDOS LAS CABECAS, ******** SEREMOS NOS:
WORD #2627 OCCURS 1 TIMES.

MARUECOS 13740 5ELCID1741 QUANDO AL REY DE ******** ASSI LO AN ARRANCADO,
14136 5ELCID1789 TAL TIENDA COMMO ESTA, QUE DE ******** ES PASSADA,
WORD #2628 OCCURS 2 TIMES.

MAS 157 5ELCID0021 CONBIDAR LE YEN DE GRADO, *** NINGUNO NON OSAUA:
211 5ELCID0027 QUE PERDERIE LOS AUERES & *** LOS OIOS DELA CARA,
378 5ELCID0048 *** EL CRIADOR UOS UALA CON TODAS SUS UERTUDES SANTAS.
751 5ELCID0095 YO *** NON PUEDO & AMYDOS LO FAGO.
1000 5ELCID0129 *** DEZID NOS DEL %ID, DE QUE SERA PAGADO,
1719 5ELCID0220 NON SE SIENTRARE Y *** ENTODOS LOS MYOS DIAS.
1974 5ELCID0250 *** POR QUE ME VO DE TIERRA, DOUOS L MARCHOS,
2349 5ELCID0296 QUEL CRE%E CONPA@A, POR QUE *** VALDRA,
2438 5ELCID0307 TRES AN POR TRO%IR, %EPADES QUE NON ***.

WORD C# PREFIX CONTEXT

MAS (CON'T)

3287 5ELCID0414 ES DIA A DE PLAZC, SEPACES QUE NON ***.
4134 5ELCID0526 E QUE SERIE RETENEDOR, *** NON YAURIE AGUA.
4185 5ELCID0533 *** EL CASTIELO NCN LC CUIERO HERMAR;
4837 5ELCID0612 METIOLA EN SOMO EN TODO LO *** ALTO.
5340 5ELCID0674 BIEN SOMOS NOS VI %IENTOS, ALGUNOS AY DE ***;
5473 5ELCID0691 *** NON AGUIJEDES CON ELLA, SI YO NON UOS LO MANDAR.
5661 5ELCID0713 DAN LE GRANDES COLPES, *** NOL PUEDEN FALSSAR.
6262 5ELCID0798 *** DE QUINZE DE LCS SOS MENOS NON FALLARON.
6608 5ELCID0843 E LOS DE CALATAYUT, QUE ES *** ONDRADA,
6741 5ELCID0860 PLOGO ALOS DE TERER & ALOS DE CALATAYUT ***,
6911 5ELCID0884 *** DESPUES QUE DE MOROS FUE, PRENDO ESTA PRESENTAIA;
6949 5ELCID0889 *** DEL %ID CAMPEADCR YO NON UOS DIGO NADA.
7515 5ELCID0963 FIRIOM EL SOBRINO & NCN LC ENMENDO ***;
7531 5ELCID0966 *** QUANDO EL MELO BUSCA, YR GELO HE YO DEMANDAR.
7671 5ELCID0982 TORNOS EL MANDADERO QUANTO PUDO ***:
7907 5ELCID1010 HY GA@O A COLADA QUE *** VALE DE MILL MARCOS DE PLATA.
8165 5ELCID1041 *** QUANTO AUEDES PERDIDO & YO GANE EN CANPO,
8182 5ELCID1043 *** QUANTO AUEDES PERDIDO NCN UOS LO DARE,
8791 5ELCID1117 NON FUE A NUESTRO GRADO NI NOS NON PUDIEMOS ***,
8869 5ELCID1129 A MI DEDES C CAUALLERCS, QUE NCN UOS PIDO ***,
9120 5ELCID1161 AVN *** AYUSSC, ADEYNA LA CASA;
9492 5ELCID1207 *** LE VIENEN A MYO %ID, SABET, QUE NOS LE VAN.
9697 5ELCID1233 *** MUCHO FUE PROUECHCSA, SABET, ESTA ARANCADA:
10007 5ELCID1268 CON *** POCCS YXIEMOS DE LA CASA DE BIUAR.
10018 5ELCID1269 AGORA AUEMOS RIQUIZA, *** AUREMOS ADELANT.
10824 5ELCID1371 *** GANAREMOS EN ESTO QUE EN OTRA DESONOR.
11427 5ELCID1446 EL %ID SIEMPRE VALDRA ***.
11552 5ELCID1463 VAYADES A MOLINA, QUE IAZE *** ADELANT,
11746 5ELCID1490 %IENTOL PIDIERON, *** EL CON DOZIENTOS VA.
12000 5ELCID1521 TRAEDES ESTAS DUE@AS PORO VALDREMOS ***,
12304 5ELCID1562 ALEGRE FUE MYO %ID, QUE NUNQUA *** NIN TANTO,
12310 5ELCID1563 CA DELO QUE *** AMAUA YAL VIENE EL MANDADO.
12696 5ELCID1611 ALA LAS SUBIE ENEL *** ALTO LOGAR;
13337 5ELCID1691 *** VALE QUE NOS LOS VEZCAMOS, QUE ELLOS COIAN EL PAN.
13692 5ELCID1735 NON ESCAPARON *** DE %IENTO & QUATRO.
13961 5ELCID1768 LO DE UUESTRAS FIJAS VENIR SEA *** POR ESPA%IO.
14022 5ELCID1776 QUIERO UOS DEZIR LO QUE ES *** GRANADO:
14972 5ELCID1893 *** PUES BCS LO QUEREDES, ENTREMOS EN LA RAZON.
15318 5ELCID1940 *** PUES LC CONSEIA EL QUE MAS VALE QUE NOS,
15324 5ELCID1940 MAS PUES LC CCNSEIA EL QUE *** VALE QUE NOS,
15417 5ELCID1953 *** LO QUE EL QUISIERE, ESSO QUERAMOS NOS.
16776 5ELCID2124 OY DE *** SABED QUE FER DELLOS, CAMPEADOR.
17173 5ELCID2173 QUE ES LARGO DE LENGUA, *** EN LO AL NON ES TAN PRO.
17378 5ELCID2199 *** BIEN SABET VERDAD QUE NON LC LEUANTE YO:
18307 5ELCID2317 ***, SABED, DE CUER LES PESA ALOS YFANTES DE CARRION;
18551 5ELCID2348 *** SE MARAUILLAN ENTRE DIEGO & FERRANDO,
18706 5ELCID2367 DIXO MYO %ID: AYAMOS *** DE VAGAR.
18791 5ELCID2378 EUCS, MYO %ID, DE MI *** UOS PAGAR.
18896 5ELCID2391 DAUAN LE GRANDES COLPES, *** NOL FALSSAN LAS ARMAS.
19087 5ELCID2415 *** SI EL CAUALLO NON ESTROPIE%A O COMIGO NON CAYE,
19122 5ELCID2419 *** BAUIECA EL DE MIO %ID ALCAN%ANDO LO VA.
19447 5ELCID2464 POR BIEN LC DIXO EL %ID, *** ELLOS LO TOUIERON AMAL.
19852 5ELCID2517 ACA VENID, CUNADOS, QUE *** VALEMOS POR UOS.
19971 5ELCID2534 *** NON FALLAUAN Y ADIEGO NI AFERRANDO.
21218 5ELCID2696 ADIESTRO DEXAN ASANT ESTEUAN, *** CAE ALUEN;
21627 5ELCID2750 *** DEXAN LAS MARICAS EN BRIALES & EN CAMISAS,
21731 5ELCID2764 *** YO UCS DIRE DAQUEL FELEZ MUNOZ.
21747 5ELCID2766 MANDARON LE YR ADELANTE, *** DE SU GRADO NON FUE.
22373 5ELCID2850 NON GELO QUISC TOMAR, *** MUCHO GELO GRADIO:
22687 5ELCID2891 HYO TOME EL CASAMIENTC, *** NON OSE DEZIR AL.
23154 5ELCID2950 TIENES POR DESONDRADO, *** LA UUESTRA ES MAYOR,
23853 5ELCID3038 DIOS SALUE A NUESTROS AMIGOS & AUOS ***, SE@OR
24550 5ELCID3129 HYO, DE QUE FU REY, NCN FIZ *** DE DOS CORTES:
24737 5ELCID3151 *** QUANDO SACARON MIS FIJAS DE VALEN%IA LA MAYOR,
24883 5ELCID3169 HYA *** NON AURA DERECHO DE NOS EL %ID CANPEADOR.
25335 5ELCID3226 *** EN NUESTRO IUUIZIO ASSI LO MANDAMOS NOS,
25530 5ELCID3252 *** QUANDO ESTO OUO ACABADO, PENSSARON LUEGO DAL.
25897 5ELCID3300 *** NOS PRE%IAMOS, SABET, QUE MENOS NO.
25954 5ELCID3308 *** QUANDO ENPIE%A, SABED, NOL CA VAGAR:
25981 5ELCID3311 BIEN LO SABEDES QUE YO NON PUEDO ***;
26003 5ELCID3314 POR EL CAMPEADOR MUCHO VALIESTES ***.
26095 5ELCID3326 CROUIERON TELO TODOS, *** NON SABEN LA VERDAD.
26103 5ELCID3327 E ERES FERMOSO, *** MAL VARRAGAN
26260 5ELCID3348 EN TODAS GUISAS *** VALEN QUE VOS.
26303 5ELCID3354 DE NATURA SOMOS DE LOS CONDES *** LIPIOS,
26344 5ELCID3359 LO QUE LES FIZIEMOS SER LES HA RETRAYDO; ESTO LIDIARE ATOD EL ***
26386 5ELCID3366 *** NON VESTIO EL MANTO NIN EL BRIAL.
26412 5ELCID3369 ENTODAS GUISAS, SABED, QUE *** VALEN QUE VOS.
26537 5ELCID3387 FALSSO A TODOS & *** AL CRIADOR.
26834 5ELCID3428 *** NON PLAZE ALOS YFANTES DE CARRION.
26964 5ELCID3445 *** BIEN SABEMOS LAS MA@AS QUE ELLOS HAN,
27110 5ELCID3464 NCN DIGA NINGUNO DELLA *** VNA ENTEN%ION.
27176 5ELCID3474 *** QUIERO A VALEN%IA QUE TIERRAS DE CARRION.
27545 5ELCID3518 *** ATAL CAUALLO CUM EST PORA TAL COMMO VOS,

WORD C# PREFIX CONTEXT

MAS (CON'T)

27675 5ELCID3533 *** TRES SEMANAS DE PLAZO TODAS COMPLIDAS SON.
27888 5ELCID3558 DIXIERCN GELO AL REY, *** NON GELO CONLOYO;
28179 5ELCID3597 ESTA LIC EN TOLEDO LAFIZIERADES, *** NON QUISIESTES VOS.
28264 5ELCID3609 *** DE VJ ASTAS DE LAN%AS QUE NON LEGASSEN AL MOION.
28425 5ELCID3630 VN COLPE RESIBIERA, *** CTRO FIRIO:
28688 5ELCID3662 DIAGONZALEZ ESPADA TIENE EN MANO, *** NOLA
29130 5ELCID3720 LOS PRIMEROS FUERON GRANDES, *** AQUESTOS SON MIIORES;
WORD #2629 OCCURS 100 TIMES.
INDEX OF DIVERSIFICATION = 291.66 WITH STANDARD DEVIATION OF 273.55

MATA
11760 5ELCID1492 PASSARON **** DE TORANZ DE TAL GUISA QUE NINGUN MIEDO NON HAN,
13595 5ELCID1723 ATANTOS **** DE MOROS QUE NON FUERON CONTADOS;
WORD #2630 OCCURS 2 TIMES.

MATADO
19374 5ELCID2454 DE XX ARRIBA HA MOROS ******;
WORD #2631 OCCURS 1 TIMES.

MATADOS
14187 5ELCID1795 NON TIENE EN CUENTA LOS MOROS QUE HA *******;
WORD #2632 OCCURS 1 TIMES.

MATAMOS
19892 5ELCID2522 VEN%IEMOS MOROS EN CAMPO & *******
WORD #2633 OCCURS 1 TIMES.

MATAN
4777 5ELCID0605 EN VN ORA & VN POCO DE LOGAR CCC MOROS *****.
WORD #2634 OCCURS 1 TIMES.

MATAN%A
19242 5ELCID2435 POR LA ******* VINIA TAN PRIUADO,
WORD #2635 OCCURS 1 TIMES.

MATAR
18751 5ELCID2372 POR SABOR QUE AUIA DE ALGUN MORO *****;
20955 5ELCID2662 SI PUDIESSEMOS ***** EL MORO AVENGALUON,
WORD #2636 OCCURS 2 TIMES.

MATARAS
26085 5ELCID3325 QUE ******* EL MORO & QUE FIZIERAS BARNAX;
WORD #2637 OCCURS 1 TIMES.

MATARON
5740 5ELCID0724 SE@OS MOROS *******, TODOS DE SE@OS COLPES;
5875 5ELCID0744 A MYNAYA ALBARFANEZ ******* LE EL CAUALLO,
9015 5ELCID1147 DOS REYES DE MOROS ******* EN ES ALCAZ,
13236 5ELCID1678 QUINIENTOS ******* DELLOS CONPLIDOS ENES DIA.
WORD #2638 OCCURS 4 TIMES.

MATASSEN
27741 5ELCID3541 QUE LOS ******** EN CAMPO POR DESONDRA DE SO SE@OR.
WORD #2639 OCCURS 1 TIMES.

MATASTES
19400 5ELCID2458 ******** ABUCAR & ARRANCAMOS EL CANPO.
WORD #2640 OCCURS 1 TIMES.

MATAUA
3735 5ELCID0472 QUINZE MOROS ****** DELOS QUE ALCAN%AUA.
18856 5ELCID2386 ALOS PRIMEROS COLPES DOS MOROS ****** DE LA LAN%A.
18948 5ELCID2397 ABATIO A VIJ & A IIIJ ******.
WORD #2641 OCCURS 3 TIMES.

MATINES
1871 5ELCID0238 REZAUA LOS ******* ABUELTA DELOS ALBORES.
2570 5ELCID0325 TANEN A ******* A VNA PRIESSA TAN GRAND;
24005 5ELCID3060 ******* & PRIMA DIXIERON FAZAL ALBA,
WORD #2642 OCCURS 3 TIMES.

MATINO
572 5ELCID0072 ESTA NOCH YGAMOS & UAYMOS NOS AL ******,
WORD #2643 OCCURS 1 TIMES.

MATINS
2514 5ELCID0318 EN SAN PERO A ****** TANDRA EL BUEN ABBAT,
WORD #2644 OCCURS 1 TIMES.

MATO
6124 5ELCID0779 DA QUESTOS MOROS **** XXX IIIJ;
18877 5ELCID2389 DOS **** CON LAN%A & V CON EL ESPADA.
19170 5ELCID2425 **** A BUCAR, AL REY DE ALEN MAR,
19541 5ELCID2475 DESPUES QUE ESTA BATALLA VEN%IERON & AL REY BUCAR ****;
WORD #2645 OCCURS 4 TIMES.

MAYO
15476 5ELCID1961 SALUDAD ME **** %ID, EL QUE EN BUEN ORA %INXO ESPADA;
29231 5ELCID3732 PER ABBAT LE ESCRIUIO ENEL MES DE ****,
WORD #2646 OCCURS 2 TIMES.

MAYOR
5617 5ELCID0707 VO METER LA UUESTRA SE@A EN AQUELA ***** AZ;
5648 5ELCID0711 ESPOLONO EL CAUALLO, E METIOL ENEL ***** AZ.
5839 5ELCID0738 MARTIN MU@OZ, EL QUE MANDO A MONT *****,
15960 5ELCID2023 LORANDO DELOS OIOS, TANTO AUIE EL GOZO *****;
16621 5ELCID2105 PUES FUEREN EN UUESTRO PODER EN VALEN%IA LA *****,
17074 5ELCID2161 HYREMOS EN PODER DE MUO %ID A VALEN%IA LA *****;
20399 5ELCID2588 GRANDES SON LAS NUEUAS POR VALEN%IA LA *****,
20682 5ELCID2625 TORNEMOS NOS, %ID, A VALEN%IA LA *****;
22194 5ELCID2826 VAN AQUESTOS MANDADOS A VALEN%IA LA *****;
22304 5ELCID2840 ADUXIESSEN ASSUS FIJAS A VALEN%IA LA *****.

WORD C# PREFIX CONTEXT

MAYOR (CON'T)

23158 5ELCID2950 TIENES POR DESONDRADC, MAS LA UUESTRA ES *****,
24745 5ELCID3151 MAS QUANDO SACARON MIS FIJAS DE VALENZIA LA *****,
25082 5ELCID3195 DEL CONDE DE REMONT VERENGEL DE BARZILONA LA *****.
25548 5ELCID3254 LA RENCURA ***** NON SEME PUEDE OLBIDAR.
29059 5ELCID3711 GRANDES SON LOS GOZOS EN VALENZIA LA *****,
WORD #2647 OCCURS 15 TIMES.
INDEX OF DIVERSIFICATION = 1673.43 WITH STANDARD DEVIATION OF 2677.57

MAYORES 17204 5ELCID2176 QUANDO A ELLA ASSOMARON, LOS GOZOS SON *******.
WORD #2648 OCCURS 1 TIMES.

ME
60 5ELCID0009 ESTO ** AN BUELTO MYOS ENEMIGOS MALOS.
601 5ELCID0076 AUN ZERCA OTARDE EL REY QUERER ** HA POR AMIGO;
654 5ELCID0082 BIEN LO VEDES QUE YO NO TRAYO AUER, & HUEBOS ** SERIE
702 5ELCID0089 POR RACHEL & VIDAS UAYADES ** PRIUADO:
707 5ELCID0090 QUANDO EN BURGOS ** VEDARON COMPRA & EL REY ME A AYRADO,
713 5ELCID0090 QUANDO EN BURGOS ME VEDARON COMPRA & EL REY ** A AYRADO,
828 5ELCID0106 RACHEL & VIDAS, AMOS ** DAT LAS MANOS,
834 5ELCID0107 QUE NON ** DESCUBRADES A MOROS NIN A CHRISTIANOS;
1101 5ELCID0141 DIXO MARTIN ANTOLINEZ: YO DESSO ** PAGO.
1205 5ELCID0155 YA DON RACHEL & VIDAS, AUEDES ** OLBIDADO
1208 5ELCID0156 YA ** EXCO DE TIERRA, CA DEL REY SO AYRADO.
1698 5ELCID0218 VALAN ** TUS VERTUDES, GLORIOSA SANTA MARIA
1726 5ELCID0221 VUESTRA UERTUD ** UALA, GLORIOSA, EN MY EXIDA & ME AIUDE,
1733 5ELCID0221 VUESTRA UERTUD ME UALA, GLORIOSA, EN MY EXIDA & ** AIUDE,
1736 5ELCID0222 EL ** ACORRA DE NOCH & DE DIA
1751 5ELCID0223 SI UOS ASSI LO FIZIEREDES & LA UENTURA ** FUERE COMPLIDA,
1977 5ELCID0250 MAS POR QUE ** VO DE TIERRA, DOUOS L MARCHOS,
2877 5ELCID0363 E RUEGO A SAN PEYDRO QUE ** AIUDE A ROGAR
3586 5ELCID0452 FAZED ** MANDADO MUY PRIUADO ALA ZAGA;
3895 5ELCID0494 DA QUESTA QUINTA QUE ** AUEDES MANDO,
3924 5ELCOD0498 FATA QUE YO ** PAGE SOBRE MIO BUEN CAUALLO,
5085 5ELCID0642 POR QUE SEME ENTRO EN MI TIERRA DERECHO ** AURA ADAR.
5301 5ELCID0670 DEZID **, CAUALLEROS, COMMO UOS PLAZE DE FAR.
6394 5ELCID0815 AL REY ALFONSSSO QUE ** A AYRADO
6921 5ELCID0885 AUN ** PLAZE DE MYO ZID QUE FIZO TAL GANANZIA.
7216 5ELCID0925 MIENTRA UOS VISQUIEREDES, BIEN ** YRA AMJ, MINAYA
7493 5ELCID0961 GRANDES TUERTOS ** TIENE MYO ZID EL DE BIUAR.
7505 5ELCID0962 DENTRO EN MI CORT TUERTO ** TOUO GRAND:
7809 5ELCID0999 OY EN ESTE PINAR DE TEUAR POR TOLER ** LA GANANZIA.
8013 5ELCID1023 PUES QUE TALES MAL CALZADOS ** VENZIERON DE BATALLA.
8065 5ELCID1029 QUE YO DEXAR ** MORIR, QUE NON QUIERO COMER.
8414 5ELCID1069 EN GRADO UOS LO TENGO LO QUE ** AUEDES DEXADO.
8425 5ELCID1071 SI ** VINIEREDES BUSCAR, FALLAR ME PODREDES;
8429 5ELCID1071 SI ME VINIEREDES BUSCAR, FALLAR ** PODREDES;
8437 5ELCID1072 E SI NON, MANDEDES BUSCAR; O ** DEXAREDES
8825 5ELCID1123 APAREIADOS ** SED A CAUALLOS & ARMAS;
9760 5ELCID1240 POR AMOR DE REY ALFFONSSO, QUE DE TIERRA ** A ECHADO,
9942 5ELCID1260 QUE SI ALGUNOS FURTARE O MENOS LE FALLAREN, EL AUER ** AURA ATORNAR
10588 5ELCID1342 SI ** VALA SANT ESIDRO PLAZME DE CORAZON,
10650 5ELCID1349 QUE ENTODAS GUISAS MIIOR ** SIRUE QUE UOS.
10698 5ELCID1355 ESSORA DIXO EL REY: PLAZ ** DE CORAZON;
10740 5ELCID1360 OYD **, ESCUELLAS, & TODA LA MI CORT.
11062 5ELCID1400 EL REY POR SU MERZED SUELTAS ** UOS HA,
11127 5ELCID1408 QUE SU MUGIER & SUS FIJAS EL REY SUELTAS ** LAS HA,
11344 5ELCID1435 HYO LO VERE CON EL ZID, SI DIOS ** LIEUA ALA.
11676 5ELCID1480 AMY NON ** PESA, SABET, MUCHO ME PLAZE
11680 5ELCID1480 AMY NON ME PESA, SABET, MUCHO ** PLAZE
12056 5ELCID1529 SI DIOS ** LEGARE AL ZID ELO VEA CON EL ALMA,
12578 5ELCID1596 SACADA ** AUEDES DE MUCHAS VERGUENZAS MALAS;
12585 5ELCID1597 AFE ** AQUI, SEaOR, YO UUESTRAS FIJAS & AMAS,
13036 5ELCID1653 NON AYADES PAUOR POR QUE ** VEADES LIDIAR,
13287 5ELCID1685 OYD **, CAUALLEROS, NON RASTARA POR AL;
13370 5ELCID1695 DAD ** CXXX CAUALLEROS FORA HUEBOS DE LIDIAR;
13792 5ELCID1748 AUOS ** OMILLO, DUEaAS, GRANT PREZ UOS HE GAaADO:
14676 5ELCID1856 GRADESCOLO A MYO ZID QUE TAL DON ** HA ENBIADO;
14788 5ELCID1869 MYO REYNO ADELANT MEIOR ** PODRA SERUIR.
15002 5ELCID1897 OYD **, MYNAYA, & VOS, PER VERMUEZ:
15295 5ELCID1937 E PIDEN ** MIS FIJAS PORA LOS YFANTES DE CARRION.
15475 5ELCID1961 SALUDAD ** MAYO ZID, EL QUE EN BUEN ORA ZINXO ESPADA;
16019 5ELCID2032 ASSI ESTANDO, DEDES ** UUESTRA AMOR, QUE LO OYAN QUANTOS AQUI SON.
16125 5ELCID2045 VALER ** A DIOS DE DIA & DE NOCH.
16332 5ELCID2072 OYD **, LAS ESCUELLAS, CUENDES & YFANZONES
16593 5ELCID2102 ELLOS VAYAN CON UUSCO, CADA QUEN ** TORNO YO.
16912 5ELCID2140 DIXO ALBARFANEZ: SEaOR, AFE QUE ** PLAZ.
16962 5ELCID2147 DIXO EL REY DON ALFONSSO: MUCHO ** AUEDES ENBARGADO.
16969 5ELCID2148 REZIBO ESTE DON QUE ** AUEDES MANDADO;
16993 5ELCID2151 MYO ZID RUY DIAZ, MUCHO ** AUEDES ONDRADO,
17016 5ELCID2154 ADIOS UOS ACOMIENDO, DESTAS VISTAS ** PARTO.
18584 5ELCID2352 CURIES ** ADIEGO & CURIES ME ADON FERNANDO,
18588 5ELCID2352 CURIES ME ADIEGO & CURIES ** ADON FERNANDO,
18651 5ELCID2360 SI CUETA FUERE, BIEN ** PODREDES HUUIAR.
18801 5ELCID2379 SI ESTE AMOR NON FECHES, YO DEUOS ** QUIERO QUITAR.
18813 5ELCID2380 ESSORA DIXO MYO ZID: LO QUE UOS QUEREDES PLAZ **.

WORD C# PREFIX CONTEXT

ME (CON'T)

```
                19739 5ELCID2503 ELLOS ** DARAN PARIAS CON AIUDA DEL CRIADOR,
                20316 5ELCID2578 ALLA ** LEUADES LAS TELAS DEL CORA%ON.
                21046 5ELCID2675  DEZID **, QUE UOS FIZ, YFANTES DE CARRION
                21953 5ELCID2793 DE QUE NON ** FALLAREN LOS YFANTES DE CARRION,
                22713 5ELCID2894 DE MYOS YERNOS DE CARRION DIOS ** FAGA VENGAR
                22861 5ELCID2912 MYOS AUERES SE ** AN LEUADO, QUE SOBEIANOS SON;
                22868 5ELCID2913 ESSO ** PUEDE PESAR CON LA OTRA DESONOR.
                23189 5ELCID2954 VERDAD TE DIGO YO, QUE ** PESA DE CORA%ON,
                23268 5ELCID2964 QUE ALLA ** VAYAN CUENDES & YFAN%ONES,
                24655 5ELCID3141 QUITAR ** A EL REYNO, PERDERA MIAMOR.
                24669 5ELCID3142 CON EL QUE TOUIERE DERECHO YO DESSA PART ** SO.
                24794 5ELCID3158 DEN ** MIS ESPADAS QUANDO MYOS YERNOS NON SON.
                25175 5ELCID3206 DEN ** MIS AUERES, QUANDO MYOS YERNOS NON SON.
                25554 5ELCID3255 OYD ** TODA LA CORT & PESEUOS DE MYO MAL;
                25790 5ELCID3285 CA NON ** PRISO AELLA FIJO DE MUGIER NADA,
                25972 5ELCID3310 SIEMPRE EN LAS CORTES PERO MUDO ** LAMADES
                26049 5ELCID3320 PASSE POR TI, CON EL MORO ** OFF DE AIUNTAR,
                26894 5ELCID3436 HYO UOS RUEGO QUE ** OYADES TODA LA CORT,
                27191 5ELCID3476 DAD ** UUESTROS CAUALLEROS CON TODAS UUESTRAS GUARNIZONES,
                27448 5ELCID3507 E YR ** QUIERO PORA VALEN%IA, CON AFAN LA GANE YO.
                27501 5ELCID3513 MANDASTES ** MOUER ABAUIECA EL CORREDOR,
                27617 5ELCID3526 BUENOS MANDADOS ** VAYAN A VALEN%IA DE VOS.
       WORD #2649 OCCURS  95 TIMES.
          INDEX OF DIVERSIFICATION =   292.16 WITH STANDARD DEVIATION OF   333.58

MEA             10986 5ELCID1390 RESPUSO MYNAYA: ESTO NON *** POR QUE PESAR.
       WORD #2650 OCCURS   1 TIMES.

MEAN            22228 5ELCID2831 QUANDO TAL ONDRA **** DADA LOS YFANTES DE CARRION;
                22811 5ELCID2906 DESTA DESONDRA QUE **** FECHA LOS YFANTES DE CARRION
       WORD #2651 OCCURS   2 TIMES.

MEATAD           4043 5ELCID0514 E A LOS PEONES LA ****** SIN FALLA;
       WORD #2652 OCCURS   1 TIMES.

ME%IO              89 5ELCID0013 ***** MYO %ID LOS OMBROS & ENGRAMEO LA TIESTA:
       WORD #2653 OCCURS   1 TIMES.

MEDIADOS         2563 5ELCID0324 ALOS ******** GALLOS PIESSAN DE CAUALGAR.
                13418 5ELCID1701 ALOS ******** GALLOS, ANTES DE LA MA@ANA,
       WORD #2654 OCCURS   2 TIMES.

MEDINA          10920 5ELCID1382 FATA DENTRO EN ****** DENLES QUANTO HUEBOS LES FUER,
                11463 5ELCID1451 DE SAN PERO FASTA ****** EN V DIAS VAN,
                11470 5ELCID1452 FELOS EN ****** LAS DUENAS & ALBARFANEZ.
                11570 5ELCID1466 HYD PORA ****** QUANTO LO PUDIEREDES FAR,
                11708 5ELCID1484 SU MUGIER & SUS FIJAS EN ****** ESTAN;
                11781 5ELCID1494 E EN ****** TODO EL RECABDO ESTA;
                12095 5ELCID1534 ENTRARON EN ******, SIRUIALOS MINAYA,
                12154 5ELCID1542 SALIERON DE ******, & SALON PASSAUAN,
                20789 5ELCID2640 DESI ESCURRA LAS FASTA ****** POR LA MI AMOR;
                22600 5ELCID2879 AQUAL DIZEN ****** YUAN ALBERGAR,
                22605 5ELCID2880 E DE ****** A MOLINA EN OTRO DIA VAN;
       WORD #2655 OCCURS  11 TIMES.
          INDEX OF DIVERSIFICATION =  1167.50 WITH STANDARD DEVIATION OF  2679.56

MEDINAL         12126 5ELCID1538 DE TAN GRAND CONDUCHO COMMO EN ******* SACARON;
       WORD #2656 OCCURS   1 TIMES.

MEDIO            1420 5ELCID0182 EN ***** DEL PALA%IO TENDIERON VN ALMOFALLA,
                 3386 5ELCID0427 EN ***** DUNA MONTANA MARAUILLOSA & GRAND
                 4726 5ELCID0599 BUELTOS SON CON ELLOS POR ***** DELA LA@A.
                 5927 5ELCID0751 CORTOL POR LA %INTURA, EL ***** ECHO EN CAMPO.
                18047 5ELCID2283 EN GRANT MIEDO SE VIERON POR ***** DELA CORT;
                23007 5ELCID2931 ASSI COMMO ENTRARON POR ***** DELA CORT,
                24360 5ELCID3106 EL VA EN *****, ELOS %IENTO ADERREDOR.
                28288 5ELCID3611 SALIEN LOS FIELES DE *****, ELLOS CARA POR CARA SON;
       WORD #2657 OCCURS   8 TIMES.
          INDEX OF DIVERSIFICATION =  3837.29 WITH STANDARD DEVIATION OF  3931.33

MEGUADOS         1048 5ELCID0134 ACOGEN SELE OMNES DE TODAS PARTES ********,
       WORD #2658 OCCURS   1 TIMES.

MEIO            28811 5ELCID3680 POR **** DE LA BLOCA DEL ESCUDOL QUEBRANTO;
       WORD #2659 OCCURS   1 TIMES.

MEIOR            2598 5ELCID0328 ROGANDO AL CRIADOR QUANTO ELLA ***** SABE,
                13298 5ELCID1686 OY ES DIA BUENO & ***** SERA CRAS:
                14787 5ELCID1869 MYO REYNO ADELANT ***** ME PODRA SERUIR.
                15374 5ELCID1946 ACORDAR UOS YEDES DESPUES ATODO LO *****.
                15714 5ELCID1993 EL OBISPO DON IERONIMO, CORANADO *****,
                16298 5ELCID2067 PASSADO AUIE IIJ A@OS NO COMIERAN *****.
                19966 5ELCID2533 QUIEN LIDIARA ***** OQUIEN FUERA EN ALCAN%O;
                20767 5ELCID2637 RE%IBA A MYOS YERNOS COMMO EL PUDIER *****;
```

WORD C# PREFIX CONTEXT

MEIOR (CON'T)

22142 5ELCID2819 QUANTO EL ***** PUEDE ALLI LAS ONDRO.
22516 5ELCID2867 BUEN CASAMIENTO PERDIESTES, ***** PODREDES GANAR.
22702 5ELCID2893 QUE UOS VEA ***** CASADAS DAQUI EN ADELANT.
24035 5ELCID3063 VOS, MYNAYA ALBARFANEZ, EL MYO BRAZO *****,
24444 5ELCID3116 MAGER QUE ALGUNOS PESA, ***** SODES QUE NOS.
25688 5ELCID3271 MERZED, YA REY, EL ***** DE TODA ESPA@A
27057 5ELCID3456 HYO SO ALBARFANEZ PORA TODEL *****.
WORD #2660 OCCURS 15 TIMES.
INDEX OF DIVERSIFICATION = 1746.07 WITH STANDARD DEVIATION OF 2721.76

MEIORA 25044 5ELCID3190 PRENDET LA, SOBRINO, CA ****** EN SE@OR.
WORD #2661 OCCURS 1 TIMES.

MEIORARE 25594 5ELCID3259 O EN ALGUNA RAZON? AQUI LO ******** A JUUIZYO DELA CORT.
WORD #2662 OCCURS 1 TIMES.

MEIORAREMOS 4862 5ELCID0615 YA *********** POSADAS ADUENOS & ACAUALLOS.
WORD #2663 OCCURS 1 TIMES.

MEIORES 11277 5ELCID1427 DELOS ******* GUARIMIENTOS QUE EN BURGOS PUDO FALAR,
16448 5ELCID2085 PERTENEZEN PORA MIS FIJAS & AVN PORA *******.
17152 5ELCID2170 EN CASA DE MYO ZID NON A DOS *******,
21600 5ELCID2746 ENSAYANDOS AMOS QUAL DARA ******* COLPES.
23605 5ELCID3006 DE TODA CASTIELLA TODOS LOS *******
WORD #2664 OCCURS 5 TIMES.
INDEX OF DIVERSIFICATION = 3081.00 WITH STANDARD DEVIATION OF 2085.24

MELAS 11596 5ELCID1469 CON GRAND ONDRA ADUZID ***** DELANT.
26662 5ELCID3405 QUANDO ***** DEMANDAN DE NAUARRA & DE ARAGON.
WORD #2665 OCCURS 2 TIMES.

MELCHIOR 2663 5ELCID0337 ******** & GASPAR & BALTASAR, ORO & TUS & MIRRA
WORD #2666 OCCURS 1 TIMES.

MELO 1806 5ELCID0230 SI EL REY **** QUISIERE TOMAR AMI NON MINCHAL.
5072 5ELCID0641 PRENDET **** AUIDA, ADUZID MELO DELAND;
5075 5ELCID0641 PRENDET MELO AUIDA, ADUZID **** DELAND;
7534 5ELCID0966 MAS QUANDO EL **** BUSCA, YR GELO HE YO DEMANDAR.
8192 5ELCID1044 CA HUEBOS **** HE & PORA ESTOS MYOS VASSALLOS
14839 5ELCID1875 ASSI COMMO SEMEIA & LA VELUNTAD **** DIZ.
17302 5ELCID2189 GRADID ****, MIS FIJAS, CA BIEN UOS HE CASADAS
17420 5ELCID2204 BIEN **** CREADES, QUE EL UOS CASA, CA NON YO.
WORD #2667 OCCURS 8 TIMES.
INDEX OF DIVERSIFICATION = 2229.57 WITH STANDARD DEVIATION OF 2330.28

MELOS 18463 5ELCID2337 ARRANCAR ***** TREUO CON LA MERZED DEL CRIADOR.
22876 5ELCID2914 ADUGA ***** AVISTAS, O AIUNTAS, O A CORTES,
23331 5ELCID2972 SALUDAD ***** ATODOS, ENTRELLOS AYA ESPAZIO;
25380 5ELCID3232 ENTRAMOS ***** DIERON LOS YFANTES DE CARRION.
27307 5ELCID3490 ONDRADOS ***** ENBIAD A VALENZIA, POR AMOR DEL CRIADOR
WORD #2668 OCCURS 5 TIMES.
INDEX OF DIVERSIFICATION = 2210.00 WITH STANDARD DEVIATION OF 1636.99

MEMBRADOS 2494 5ELCID0315 SED ********* COMMO LO DEUEDES FAR.
WORD #2669 OCCURS 1 TIMES.

MENADAS 5575 5ELCID0702 QUEDAS SED, *******, AQUI EN ESTE LOGAR,
WORD #2670 OCCURS 1 TIMES.

MENBRADA 1639 5ELCID0210 VEREMOS UUESTRA MUGIER, ******** FIJA DALGO.
WORD #2671 OCCURS 1 TIMES.

MENBRADO 1024 5ELCID0131 RESPUSO MARTIN ANTOLINEZ A GUISA DE ********:
4552 5ELCID0579 AGUISA DE ********, POR SACAR LOS AZELADA.
WORD #2672 OCCURS 2 TIMES.

MENBRADOS 28968 5ELCID3700 AGUISA DE ********* ANDAN DIAS & NOCHES,
WORD #2673 OCCURS 1 TIMES.

MENESTER 1050 5ELCID0135 A ******** SEYS ZIENTOS MARCOS.
WORD #2674 OCCURS 1 TIMES.

MENGO 17111 5ELCID2165 LA CONPA@A DEL ZID CREZE, & LA DEL REY *****,
WORD #2675 OCCURS 1 TIMES.

MENGUADAS 17345 5ELCID2194 NON SERAN ********* EN TODOS UUESTROS DIAS
WORD #2676 OCCURS 1 TIMES.

MENGUADOS 849 5ELCID0108 POR SIEMPRE UOS FARE RICOS, QUE NON SEADES *********.
1230 5ELCID0158 MIENTRA QUE VIVADES NON SEREDES *********.
WORD #2677 OCCURS 2 TIMES.

MENGUARE 2050 5ELCID0258 SIESSA DESPENSSA UOS FALLEZIERE OUOS ******** ALGO,
WORD #2678 OCCURS 1 TIMES.

```
WORD                C#  PREFIX                              CONTEXT

MENORES              9706 5ELCID1234 ATODOS LOS ******* CAYERON C MARCOS DE PLATA.
        WORD #2679 OCCURS   1 TIMES.

MENOS                6268 5ELCID0798 MAS DE QUINZE DE LOS SOS ***** NON FALLARON.
                     7682 5ELCID0984 QUE A ***** DE BATALLA NOS PUEDEN DEN QUITAR.
                     9937 5ELCID1260 QUE SI ALGUNOS FURTARE O ***** LE FALLAREN, EL AUER ME AURA
                                     ATORNAR
                    12894 5ELCID1636 A ***** DE MUERT NO LA PUEDO DEXAR;
                    13548 5ELCID1717 QUATRO MILL ***** XXX CON MYO %ID VAN A CABO,
                    25666 5ELCID3268 POR QUANTO LES FIZIESTES ***** VALEDES VOS.
                    25902 5ELCID3300 MAS NOS PRE%IAMOS, SABET, QUE ***** NO.
                    26156 5ELCID3334 METISTET, FERRANDO, PORO ***** VALES OY.
                    26247 5ELCID3346 POR QUANTO LAS DEXASTES ***** VALEDES VOS;
        WORD #2680 OCCURS   9 TIMES.
           INDEX OF DIVERSIFICATION =  2496.38 WITH STANDARD DEVIATION OF  4023.77

MENSAGE             10091 5ELCID1278 ENBIARE POR ELLAS, & UOS SABED EL *******:
        WORD #2681 OCCURS   1 TIMES.

MENSAIE              4959 5ELCID0627 AL REY DE VALEN%IA ENBIARON CON *******,
                     7617 5ELCID0975 DEL CONDE DON REMONT VENIDO LES *******;
        WORD #2682 OCCURS   2 TIMES.

MENSAIES            14498 5ELCID1834 AUER ESTOS ******** DEL QUE EN BUEN ORA NASCO.
        WORD #2683 OCCURS   1 TIMES.

MENSSAGEROS         15053 5ELCID1903 SED BUENOS ***********, & RUEGO UOS LO YO
        WORD #2684 OCCURS   1 TIMES.

MENSSAIE            11491 5ELCID1453 DIREUOS DELOS CAUALLEROS QUE LEUARON EL ********:
                    11659 5ELCID1477 EL MORO AUEGALUON, QUANDO SOPO EL ********,
                    22647 5ELCID2885 AL QUE EN BUEN ORA NASCO LEGAUA EL ********;
        WORD #2685 OCCURS   3 TIMES.

MENSSAIES            9346 5ELCID1188 A TIERRAS DE CASTIELLA ENBIO SUS *********:
                    20482 5ELCID2600 QUE AYADES UUESTROS ********* EN TIERRAS DE CARRION.
        WORD #2686 OCCURS   2 TIMES.

MERCADO              1088 5ELCID0139 DIXO RACHEL & VIDAS:  NON SE FAZE ASSI EL *******,
        WORD #2687 OCCURS   1 TIMES.

MER%ED               2109 5ELCID0266 ******, CANPEADOR, EN ORA BUENA FUESTES NADO
                     2123 5ELCID0268 ******, YA %ID, BARBA TAN COMPLIDA
                     4714 5ELCID0598 CON LA ****** DEL CRIADOR NUESTRA ES LA GANAN%IA
                     6885 5ELCID0880 QUEL AYDES ******, SIEL CRIADOR UOS VALA.
                    10080 5ELCID1276 POR MI MUGIER & MIS FIJAS, SI FUERE SU ******,
                    10420 5ELCID1321 ******, SE@OR ALFONSSO, POR AMOR DEL CRIADOR
                    10445 5ELCID1324 QUEL AYADES ******, SIUOS VALA EL CRIADOR
                    10660 5ELCID1351 ****** UOS PIDE EL %ID, SIUOS CAYESSE EN SABOR,
                    11060 5ELCID1400 EL REY POR SU ****** SUELTAS ME UOS HA,
                    11313 5ELCID1432 ******, MINAYA, CAUALLERO DE PRESTAR
                    12570 5ELCID1595 ******, CAMPEADOR, EN BUEN ORA CINXIESTES ESPADA
                    13041 5ELCID1654 CON LA ****** DE DIOS & DE SANTA MARIA MADRE
                    13731 5ELCID1740 QUE DIOS LES OUO ****** QUE VEN%IERON EL CAMPO.
                    13893 5ELCID1760 SOMOS EN UUESTRA ******, & BIUADES MUCHOS A@OS
                    14580 5ELCID1845 ******, REY ALFONSSO, SODES TAN ONDRADO
                    14908 5ELCID1885 ****** UOS PIDIMOS COMMO A REY & SE@OR NATURAL;
                    16009 5ELCID2031  ****** UOS PIDO AUOS, MYO NATURAL SE@OR,
                    16056 5ELCID2036 FABLO MYO %ID & DIXO: ******; YOLO RE%IBO, ALFONSSO MYO SE@OR;
                    16462 5ELCID2087 ENTRE YO YELLAS EN UUESTRA ****** SOMOS NOS,
                    16834 5ELCID2131 YO UOS PIDO ****** AUOS, REY NATURAL:
                    17057 5ELCID2160 ****** UOS SEA & FAZED NOS ESTE PERDON:
                    18467 5ELCID2337 ARRANCAR MELOS TREUO CON LA ****** DEL CRIADOR.
                    20436 5ELCID2594 ****** UOS PEDIMOS, PADRE, SIUOS VALA EL CRIADOR
                    20475 5ELCID2599 ASSI UOS PEDIMOS ****** NOS AMAS ADOS,
                    23041 5ELCID2936 ******, REY ALFONSSO, DE LARGOS REYNOS AUOS DIZEN SE@OR
                    23902 5ELCID3045 ******, YA REY, SI EL CRIADOR UOS SALUE
                    24898 5ELCID3171 ******, YA REY DON ALFONSSO, SODES NUESTRO SE@OR
                    25538 5ELCID3253 ******, AY REY SE@OR, POR AMOR DE CARIDAD
                    25684 5ELCID3271 ******, YA REY, EL MEIOR DE TODA ESPA@A
                    26649 5ELCID3403 ******, REY ALFONSSO, VOS SODES MYO SE@OR
                    26847 5ELCID3430 ****** UOS PIDO COMMO A REY & A SE@OR,
                    27424 5ELCID3504 ****** UOS PIDO, REY, POR AMOR DEL CRIADOR
        WORD #2688 OCCURS  32 TIMES.
           INDEX OF DIVERSIFICATION =   815.61 WITH STANDARD DEVIATION OF   850.85

MER%EDES            24451 5ELCID3117 ESSORA DIXO MUCHAS ******** EL QUE VALEN%IA GA@O:
        WORD #2689 OCCURS   1 TIMES.

MERE%E               8846 5ELCID1126 ALI PARE%RA EL QUE ****** LA SOLDADA.
                    15015 5ELCID1898 SIRUEM MYO %ID EL CAMPEADOR, EL LO ******,
        WORD #2690 OCCURS   2 TIMES.

MERE%EDES            1516 5ELCID0194 VOS LO *********, DARUOS QUEREMOS BUEN DADO,
        WORD #2691 OCCURS   1 TIMES.
```

WORD C# PREFIX CONTEXT

MERE%EMOS 21473 5ELCID2730 QUE POR LO QUE NOS ********* NO LO PRENDEMOS NOS;
WORD #2692 OCCURS 1 TIMES.

MERE%ER 1537 5ELCID0197 ******* NOLO HEDES, CA ESTO ES AGUISADO:
WORD #2693 OCCURS 1 TIMES.

MERE%I 25581 5ELCID3258 DEZID QUE UOS ******, YFANTES, EN JUEGO O EN VERO
WORD #2694 OCCURS 1 TIMES.

MERE%IAS 1490 5ELCID0190 YO, QUE ESTO UOS GANE, BIEN ******** CAL%AS.
WORD #2695 OCCURS 1 TIMES.

MERESCA 18476 5ELCID2338 AVN VEA EL ORA QUE UOS ******* DOS TANTO.
21982 5ELCID2797 SI UOS LO *******, MYO PRIMO, NUESTRO PADRE EL CANPEADOR,
WORD #2696 OCCURS 2 TIMES.

MES 29229 5ELCID3732 PER ABBAT LE ESCRIUIO ENEL *** DE MAYO,
WORD #2697 OCCURS 1 TIMES.

MESES 9510 5ELCID1209 NUEUE ***** COMPLIDOS, SABET, SOBRELLA IAZ;
WORD #2698 OCCURS 1 TIMES.

MESNADA 3853 5ELCID0487 SALIOLOS RE%EBIR CON ESTA SU *******,
4155 5ELCID0528 BUSCAR NOS YE EL REY ALFONSSO CON TODA SU *******.
6560 5ELCID0837 E EL CAMPEADOR CON SU *******.
WORD #2699 OCCURS 3 TIMES.

MESNADAS 4012 5ELCID0509 QUEL BUSCARIE MAL CON TODAS SUS ********.
5232 5ELCID0662 ******** DE MYO %ID EXIR QUERIEN ALA BATALLA,
5882 5ELCID0745 BIEN LO ACORREN ******** DE CHRISTIANOS.
7774 5ELCID0995 %IENTO CAUALLEROS DEUEMOS VEN%ER A QUELAS ********.
8522 5ELCID1083 JUNTOS CON SUS ********, CONPE%OLAS DE LEGAR
8769 5ELCID1115 OYD, ********, SI EL CRIADOR UOS SALUE
12622 5ELCID1601 TODAS LAS SUS ******** EN GRANT DELENT ESTAUAN,
13697 5ELCID1736 ******** DE MYO %ID ROBADO AN EL CANPO;
15618 5ELCID1980 CUENDES & PODESTADES & MUY GRANDES ********.
15632 5ELCID1982 CON EL REY VAN LEONESES & ******** GALIZIANAS,
16073 5ELCID2038 E A ESTAS ******** QUE ESTAN A DERREDOR.
18132 5ELCID2294 QUES ESTO, ********, O QUE QUEREDES UOS?
24538 5ELCID3128 OYD, ********, SIUOS VALA EL CRIADOR
WORD #2700 OCCURS 13 TIMES.
INDEX OF DIVERSIFICATION = 1709.50 WITH STANDARD DEVIATION OF 1813.18

MES@ADAS 13204 5ELCID1674 PRESTAS SON LAS ******** DE LAS YENTES CHRISTIANAS,
WORD #2701 OCCURS 1 TIMES.

MESQUINO 6659 5ELCID0849 EN TODOS LOS SOS NON FALLARIEDES VN ********.
WORD #2702 OCCURS 1 TIMES.

MESSE 25833 5ELCID3290 LA QUE YO ***** AVN NON ES EGUADA.
WORD #2703 OCCURS 1 TIMES.

MESSO 22240 5ELCID2832 PAR AQUESTA BARBA QUE NADI NON *****,
25018 5ELCID3186 PAR AQUESTA BARBA QUE NADI NON *****,
25798 5ELCID3286 NIMBLA ***** FIJO DE MORO NIN DE CHRISTIANA,
25827 5ELCID3289 NON YOUO RAPAZ QUE NON ***** SU PULGADA;
WORD #2704 OCCURS 4 TIMES.

MESTUREROS 2118 5ELCID0267 POR MALOS ********** DE TIERRA SODES ECHADO.
WORD #2705 OCCURS 1 TIMES.

MESURADO 50 5ELCID0007 FFABLO MYO %ID BIEN & TAN ********:
WORD #2706 OCCURS 1 TIMES.

MESURADOS 22151 5ELCID2820 LOS DE SANTESTEUAN, SIEMPRE ********* SON,
WORD #2707 OCCURS 1 TIMES.

MESURANDO 11938 5ELCID1513 LOS QUE YUAN ********* & LEGANDO DELANT
WORD #2708 OCCURS 1 TIMES.

MESURANDOL 28710 5ELCID3666 EL CAUALLO ASORRIENDA, & ********** DEL ESPADA,
WORD #2709 OCCURS 1 TIMES.

MESURAREMOS 1642 5ELCID0211 *********** LA POSADA & QUITAREMOS EL REYNADO;
WORD #2710 OCCURS 1 TIMES.

META 3942 5ELCID0500 QUE ENPLEYE LA LAN%A & AL ESPADA **** MANO,
WORD #2711 OCCURS 1 TIMES.

METAMOS 995 5ELCID0128 EN LOGAR LAS ******* QUE NON SEAN VENTADAS.
WORD #2712 OCCURS 1 TIMES.

METAN 16606 5ELCID2104 QUE ***** EN SUS BODAS ODO QUISIEREDES UOS;

WORD #2713 OCCURS 1 TIMES.

WORD C# PREFIX CONTEXT

```
METED                928 5ELCID0119 PRENDED LAS ARCHAS & ***** LAS EN UUESTRO SALUO;
                     936 5ELCID0120 CON GRAND IURA ***** Y LAS FES AMOS,
                   24622 5ELCID3137 TODOS ***** Y MIENTES, CA SODES CO@OS%EDORES,
          WORD #2714 OCCURS   3 TIMES.

METEDOS             7700 5ELCID0986 APRIESSA UOS GUARNID & ******* EN LAS ARMAS.
          WORD #2715 OCCURS   1 TIMES.

METEN              22594 5ELCID2878 OTRO DIA MA@ANA ***** SE A ANDAR,
          WORD #2716 OCCURS   1 TIMES.

METER               1121 5ELCID0144 POR ADUZIR LAS ARCHAS & ***** LAS EN UUESTRO SALUO,
                    5611 5ELCID0707 VO ***** LA UUESTRA SE@A EN AQUELA MAYOR AZ;
                    9923 5ELCID1259 ***** LOS HE EN ESCRIPTO, & TODOS SEAN CONTADOS,
                   15537 5ELCID1969 TANTO BUEN PENDON ***** EN BUENAS ASTAS,
                   20192 5ELCID2564 ***** LAS HEMOS EN LAS VILLAS
                   26381 5ELCID3365 FUSTED ***** TRAS LA VIGA LAGAR,
          WORD #2717 OCCURS   6 TIMES.
             INDEX OF DIVERSIFICATION =  5051.00 WITH STANDARD DEVIATION OF   810.82

METIDO               588 5ELCID0074 EN YRA DEL RAY ALFFONSSO YO SERE ******.
          WORD #2718 OCCURS   1 TIMES.

METIDOS            12826 5ELCID1627 ENTRARON SOBRE MAR, EN LAS BARCAS SON *******,
          WORD #2719 OCCURS   1 TIMES.

METIEN             27817 5ELCID3550 HYAS ****** EN ARMAS LOS DEL BUEN CAMPEADOR,
          WORD #2720 OCCURS   1 TIMES.

METIENDO           22037 5ELCID2804 VALAS CONORTANDO & ******** CORA%ON
          WORD #2721 OCCURS   1 TIMES.

METIERON           26812 5ELCID3425 ******** LAS FES, & LOS OMENAIES DADOS SON,
          WORD #2722 OCCURS   1 TIMES.

METIO               5891 5ELCID0746 LA LAN%A A QUEBRADA, AL ESPADA ***** MANO,
                    6780 5ELCID0866 ***** EN PARIA ADORCCA EN ANTES,
                    7075 5ELCID0904 EL DE RIO MARTIN TODO LO ***** EN PARIA.
                   13592 5ELCID1722 MYO %ID ENPLEO LA LAN%A, AL ESPADA ***** MANO,
                   16685 5ELCID2113 AQUIS ***** EN NUEUAS MYO %ID EL CAMPEADOR;
                   18194 5ELCID2301 E LIEUA LO ADESTRANDO, ENLA RED LE *****.
                   18865 5ELCID2387 EL ASTIL A QUEBRADO & ***** MANO AL ESPADA.
                   21774 5ELCID2769 EN VN MONTE ESPESSO FELEZ MUNOZ SE *****,
                   22139 5ELCID2818 EN SANTESTEUAN DENTRO LAS *****,
                   24197 5ELCID3085 CAL%AS DE BUEN PA@O EN SUS CAMAS *****,
                   26200 5ELCID3339 DEXOS LE PRENDER ALCUELO, & ALA RED LE *****.
                   28042 5ELCID3579 EN UUESTRA MANO NOS ***** NUESTRO SE@OR;
                   28486 5ELCID3637 DEDENTRO EN LA CARNE VNA MANO GELA *****;
                   28529 5ELCID3642 EL DEXO LA LAN%A & AL ESPADA ***** MANO,
                   28573 5ELCID3648 MARTIN ANTOLINEZ MANO ***** AL ESPADA,
          WORD #2723 OCCURS  15 TIMES.
             INDEX OF DIVERSIFICATION =  1619.14 WITH STANDARD DEVIATION OF  1739.39

METIOGELAS         17613 5ELCID2228 LEUANTAN SE DERECHAS & ********** EN MANO.
          WORD #2724 OCCURS   1 TIMES.

METIOL              5646 5ELCID0711 ESPOLONO EL CAUALLO, E ****** ENEL MAYOR AZ.
                   28444 5ELCID3633 ****** LA LAN%A POR LOS PECHOS, QUE NADA NOL VALIO;
                   28831 5ELCID3683 ****** POR LA CARNE ADENTRO LA LAN%A CONEL PENDON,
          WORD #2725 OCCURS   3 TIMES.

METIOLA             4831 5ELCID0612 ******* EN SOMO EN TODO LO MAS ALTO.
                    9503 5ELCID1208 ******* EN PLAZO, SILES VINIESSEN HUUYAR.
          WORD #2726 OCCURS   2 TIMES.

METIOLOS           16758 5ELCID2122 ******** EN PODER DE MYO %ID EL CAMPEADOR:
          WORD #2727 OCCURS   1 TIMES.

METIOS             13627 5ELCID1727 ****** LE EN GUIERA, VN CASTIELLO PALA%IANO;
                   18077 5ELCID2287 ****** SOL ESCA@O, TANTO OUO EL PAUOR.
                   18100 5ELCID2290 TRAS VNA VIGA LAGAR ****** CON GRANT PAUOR;
          WORD #2728 OCCURS   3 TIMES.

METISTET           26144 5ELCID3333 ******** TRAS EL ESCA@O DE MYO %ID EL CAMPEADOR
                   26153 5ELCID3334 ********, FERRANDO, PORO MENOS VALES OY.
                   26377 5ELCID3364 SALISTE POR LA PUERTA, ******** AL CORAL,
          WORD #2729 OCCURS   3 TIMES.

METIUOS            17412 5ELCID2203 ******* EN SUS MANOS, FIJAS, AMAS ADOS;
          WORD #2730 OCCURS   1 TIMES.

METOLAS            17565 5ELCID2222 AFFE AMAS MIS FIJAS, ******* EN UUESTRA MANO;
          WORD #2731 OCCURS   1 TIMES.
```

WORD C# PREFIX CONTEXT

```
METUDA            7139 5ELCID0914 ASARAGO%A ****** LA EN PARIA.
         WORD #2732 OCCURS    1 TIMES.

METUDO            6615 5ELCID0844 ASI LO AN ASMADO & ****** EN CARTA:
         WORD #2733 OCCURS    1 TIMES.

MEZCLADOS         5551 5ELCID0699 E FIZIERON DOS AZES DE PEONES *********, QUILOS PODRIE CONTAR?
         WORD #2734 OCCURS    1 TIMES.

MEZQUITAS        19712 5ELCID2499 ALA DENTRO EN MARRUECOS, OLAS ********* SON,
         WORD #2735 OCCURS    1 TIMES.

MI                 658 5ELCID0083 PORA TODA ** COMPANA;
                  1952 5ELCID0247 PUES QUE AQUI UOS VEO, PRENDET DE ** OSPEDADO.
                  1969 5ELCID0249 YO ADOBARE CON DUCHO PORA ** & PORA MIS VASSALLOS;
                  2040 5ELCID0257 DELLAS & DE ** MUGIER FAGADES TODO RECABDO.
                  2207 5ELCID0278 YA DO@A XIMENA, LA ** MUGIER TAN COMPLIDA,
                  2213 5ELCID0279 COMMO ALA ** ALMA YO TANTO UOS QUERIA.
                  2382 5ELCID0301 VOS, QUE POR ** DEXADES CASAS & HEREDADES,
                  3970 5ELCID0504 PUES QUE POR ** GANAREDES QUES QUIER QUE SEA DALGO,
                  4207 5ELCID0535 POR QUE LO PRIS DELLOS QUE DE ** NON DIGAN MAL.
                  5046 5ELCID0637 TRES REYES VEO DE MOROS DERREDOR DE ** ESTAR,
                  5082 5ELCID0642 POR QUE SEME ENTRO EN ** TIERRA DERECHO ME AURA ADAR.
                  5363 5ELCID0677 DIXO EL CAMPEADOR:  A ** GUISA FABLASTES;
                  5461 5ELCID0689 E VOS, PERO VERMUEZ, LA ** SE@A TOMAD;
                  6448 5ELCID0823 LO QUE ROMANE%IERE DALDO A ** MUGIER & A MIS FIJAS,
                  6457 5ELCID0824 QUE RUEGEN POR ** LAS NOCHES & LOS DIAS;
                  6947 5ELCID0888 HYD & VENIT, DA QUI UOS DO ** GRA%IA;
                  7502 5ELCID0962 DENTRO EN ** CORT TUERTO ME TOUO GRAND:
                  7522 5ELCID0964 AGORA CORREM LAS TIERRAS QUE EN ** ENPARA ESTAN;
                  8861 5ELCID1129 A ** DEDES C CAUALLEROS, QUE NON UOS PIDO MAS,
                 10064 5ELCID1275 DESI POR ** BESALDE LA MANO EFIRME GELO ROGAD
                 10072 5ELCID1276 POR ** MUGIER & MIS FIJAS, SI FUERE SU MER%ED,
                 10725 5ELCID1358 QUANDO EN CABO DE ** TIERRA A QUESTAS DUE@AS FUEREN,
                 10745 5ELCID1360 OYD ME, ESCUELLAS, & TODA LA ** CORT.
                 10815 5ELCID1370 DE ** SEAN QUITOS & VAYAN ALA GRA%IA DEL CRIADOR.
                 11401 5ELCID1443 POR ** AL CAMPEADOR LAS MANOS LE BESAD
                 12654 5ELCID1605 MY CORA%ON & ** ALMA,
                 12912 5ELCID1638 MIS FIJAS & ** MUGIER QUE LAS TENGO ACA;
                 12936 5ELCID1641 MIS FIJAS & ** MUGIER VERME AN LIDIAR,
                 13366 5ELCID1694 PUES ESSO QUEREDES, %ID, A ** MANDADES AL;
                 14272 5ELCID1806 DESTA ** QUINTA, DIGO UOS SIN FALLA,
                 14315 5ELCID1811 POR AMOR DE ** MUGIER & DE MIS FIJAS AMAS,
                 14684 5ELCID1857 AVN VEA ORA QUE DE ** SEA PAGADO.
                 15018 5ELCID1899 E DE ** ABRA PERDON; VINIESSEM A VISTAS, SI OUIESSE DENT SABOR.
                 15033 5ELCID1900 OTROS MANDADOS HA EN ESTA ** CORT:
                 16822 5ELCID2129 QUI QUIERE YR COMIGO ALAS BODAS, O RE%EBIR ** DON,
                 16862 5ELCID2134 NON GELAS DARE YO CON ** MANO, NIN DED NON SE ALABARAN.
                 17008 5ELCID2153 AVN BIUO SEYENDO, DE ** AYADES ALGO
                 18738 5ELCID2371 POR ESSO SALI DE ** TIERRA & VIN UOS BUSCAR,
                 18752 5ELCID2373 ** ORDEN & MIS MANOS QUERRIA LAS ONDRAR,
                 18790 5ELCID2378 EUOS, MYO %ID, DE ** MAS UOS PAGAR.
                 19083 5ELCID2414 ASI COMMO SEMEIA, EN ** LA QUIERES ENSAYAR.
                 19703 5ELCID2498 MOROS & CHRISTIANOS DE ** HAN GRANT PAUOR;
                 19717 5ELCID2500 QUE ABRAM DE ** SALTO QUI%AB ALGUNA NOCH
                 19866 5ELCID2519 EUADES AQUI, YERNOS, LA ** MUGIER DE PRO,
                 20509 5ELCID2604 DE ** & DE UUESTRO PADRE BIEN AVEDES NUESTRA GRA%IA.
                 20792 5ELCID2640 DESI ESCURRA LAS FASTA MEDINA POR LA ** AMOR;
                 21062 5ELCID2676 HYO SIRUIENDO UOS SIN ART, & UOS CONSSEIASTES PORA ** MUERT.
                 22778 5ELCID2902 EN BUEN ORA TE CRIE ATI EN LA ** CORT
                 22789 5ELCID2904 POR ** BESA LE LA MANO DALMA & DE CORA%ON,
                 22898 5ELCID2916 CA TAN GRANT ES LA RENCURA DENTRO EN ** CORA%ON.
                 23260 5ELCID2963 PREGONARAN ** CORT PORA DENTRO EN TOLLEDO,
                 23506 5ELCID2993 QUI LO FER NON QUISIESSE, O NO YR A ** CORT,
                 23855 5ELCID3039 ** MUGIER DONA XIMENA, DUE@A ES DE PRO,
                 24151 5ELCID3079 POR DE MANDAR MYOS DERECHOS & DEZIR ** RAZON:
                 24711 5ELCID3147 POR QUANTO ESTA CORT FIZIESTES POR ** AMOR.
                 24791 5ELCID3157 COMIGO NON QUISIERON AUER NADA & PERDIERON ** AMOR;
                 25779 5ELCID3283 QUE AVEDES UOS, CONDE, POR RETRAER LA ** BARBA?
                 25989 5ELCID3312 POR LO QUE YO QUIER AFER POR ** NON MANCARA.
                 27230 5ELCID3480 AQUI LES PONGO PLAZO DE DENTRO EN ** CORT,
         WORD #2736 OCCURS   59 TIMES.
            INDEX OF DIVERSIFICATION =    457.14 WITH STANDARD DEVIATION OF    510.93

MIAMOR           24660 5ELCID3141 QUITAR ME A EL REYNO, PERDERA ******.
         WORD #2737 OCCURS    1 TIMES.

MIEDES            3291 5ELCID0415 ALA SIERRA DE ****** ELLOS YUAN POSAR.
                 21190 5ELCID2692 LA SIERRA DE ****** PASSARON LA ESTOZ,
         WORD #2738 OCCURS    2 TIMES.
```

WORD C# PREFIX CONTEXT

MIEDO 254 5ELCID0033 POR ***** DEL REY ALFONSSO, QUE ASSI LO AUIEN PARADO
3532 5ELCID0445 AOSADAS CORRED, QUE POR ***** NON DEXEDES NADA.
3554 5ELCID0448 QUE POR ***** DE LOS MOROS NON DEXEN NADA.
3715 5ELCID0469 OUIERON ***** & FUE DESEPARADA.
8644 5ELCID1097 DENTRO EN VALEN%IA NON ES POCO EL *****.
9073 5ELCID1155 ***** AN EN VALEN%IA QUE NON SABEN QUESE FAR.
11768 5ELCID1492 PASSARON MATA DE TORANZ DE TAL GUISA QUE NINGUN ***** NON HAN,
13091 5ELCID1660 ***** A SU MUGIER & QUIEREL QUEBRAR EL CORA%ON,
13127 5ELCID1664 NON AYADES *****, CATODO ES UUESTRA PRO;
18043 5ELCID2283 EN GRANT ***** SE VIERON POR MEDIO DELA CORT;
23450 5ELCID2987 ***** HAN QUE Y VERNA MYO %ID EL CAMPEADOR;
25709 5ELCID3274 LOS VNOS LE HAN ***** & LOS OTROS ESPANTA.
27760 5ELCID3543 CA GRAND ***** OUIERON A ALFONSSO EL DE LEON.
WORD #2739 OCCURS 13 TIMES.
INDEX OF DIVERSIFICATION = 2291.17 WITH STANDARD DEVIATION OF 1998.40

MIEMBRAT 26011 5ELCID3316 ******** QUANDO LIDIAMOS %ERCA VALEN%IA LA GRAND;
WORD #2740 OCCURS 1 TIMES.

MIENTE 26121 5ELCID3330 NON TE VIENE EN ****** EN VALEN%IA LO DEL LEON,
WORD #2741 OCCURS 1 TIMES.

MIENTES 17530 5ELCID2218 ESTAN PARANDO ******* ALQUE EN BUEN ORA NASCO.
24624 5ELCID3137 TODOS METED Y *******, CA SODES CO@OS%EDORES,
25992 5ELCID3313 *******, FERRANDO, DE QUANTO DICHO HAS,
28314 5ELCID3614 CADA VNO DELLOS ******* TIENE AL SO.
28353 5ELCID3620 CADA VNO DELLOS ******* TIENE ALSO;
WORD #2742 OCCURS 5 TIMES.
INDEX OF DIVERSIFICATION = 2704.75 WITH STANDARD DEVIATION OF 3071.65

MIENTRA 1225 5ELCID0158 ******* QUE VIVADES NON SEREDES MENGUADOS.
1351 5ELCID0173 CA ******* QUE VISQUIESSEN REFECHOS ERAN AMOS.
3242 5ELCID0409 ******* QUE VISQUIEREDES BIEN SE FARA LO TO.
7044 5ELCID0901 ******* QUE SEA EL PUEBLO DE MOROS & DELA YENTE CHRISTIANA,
7212 5ELCID0925 ******* UOS VISQUIEREDES, BIEN ME YRA AMJ, MINAYA
8220 5ELCID1047 ABREMOS ESTA VIDA ******* PLOGIERE AL PADRE SANTO,
10706 5ELCID1356 HYO LES MANDARE DAR CONDUCHO ******* QUE POR MJ TIERRA FUEREN,
11130 5ELCID1409 ******* QUE FUEREMOS POR SUS TIERRAS CONDUCHO NOS MANDO DAR.
14392 5ELCID1820 E SERUIR LO HE SIENPRE ******* QUE OUISSE EL ALMA.
20030 5ELCID2542 ******* QUE VISQUIEREMOS DESPENDER NOLO PODREMOS.
21911 5ELCID2788 ******* ES EL DIA, ANTE QUE ENTRE LA NOCH,
24349 5ELCID3105 CUERDA ******* ENTRA MYO %ID CON TODOS LOS SOS:
26326 5ELCID3358 ******* QUE BIUAN PUEDEN AUER SOSPIROS:
WORD #2743 OCCURS 13 TIMES.
INDEX OF DIVERSIFICATION = 2090.75 WITH STANDARD DEVIATION OF 1617.08

MIENTRE 6 5ELCID0001 DELOS SOS OIOS TAN FUERTE ******* LORANDO,
184 5ELCID0024 CON GRAND RECABDO & FUERTE ******* SELLADA:
346 5ELCID0043 CON GRANT RECABDO & FUERTE ******* SELLADA.
2201 5ELCID0277 LORA DELOS OIOS, TAN FUERTE ******* SOSPIRA:
5974 5ELCID0757 POR ESTAS FUER%AS FUERTE ******* LIDIANDO,
7087 5ELCID0906 NON PLAZE ALOS MOROS, FIRME ******* LES PESAUA.
8812 5ELCID1121 FIRME ******* SON ESTOS A ESCARMENTAR.
14735 5ELCID1863 POR TAN BILTADA ******* VEN%ER REYES DEL CAMPO,
14804 5ELCID1871 MANDO UOS LOS CUERPOS ONDRADA ******* SERUIR & VESTIR
17398 5ELCID2201 ATAN FIRME ******* & DE TODO CORA%ON
17487 5ELCID2212 CON BUENAS VESTIDURAS & FUERTE ******* ADOBADOS;
18643 5ELCID2359 VOS CON LOS UUESTROS FIRME ******* ALA %AGA TENGADES;
20005 5ELCID2538 AMOS SALIERON A PART, VERA ******* SON HERMANOS;
22290 5ELCID2839 DIXOLES FUERTE ******* QUE ANDIDIESSEN DE DIA & DE NOCH,
WORD #2744 OCCURS 14 TIMES.
INDEX OF DIVERSIFICATION = 1713.15 WITH STANDARD DEVIATION OF 1682.92

MIETDO 12792 5ELCID1623 QUE EN MIS HEREDADES FUERTE MIETRE ES ******,
WORD #2745 OCCURS 1 TIMES.

MIETRE 12790 5ELCID1623 QUE EN MIS HEREDADES FUERTE ****** ES MIETDO,
WORD #2746 OCCURS 1 TIMES.

MIGEROS 19025 5ELCID2407 VII ******* CONPLIDOS DURO EL SEGUDAR.
WORD #2747 OCCURS 1 TIMES.

MIIOR 10649 5ELCID1349 QUE ENTODAS GUISAS ***** ME SIRUE QUE UOS.
15345 5ELCID1942 AFE DIOS DEL %IELLO QUE NOS ACUERDE EN LO *****.
WORD #2748 OCCURS 2 TIMES.

MIIORES 29133 5ELCID3720 LOS PRIMEROS FUERON GRANDES, MAS AQUESTOS SON *******;
WORD #2749 OCCURS 1 TIMES.

MILL 1771 5ELCID0225 ESTO & YO EN DEBDO QUE FAGA Y CANTAR **** MISSAS.
4099 5ELCID0521 ASMARON LOS MOROS IIJ **** MARCOS DE PLATA.
5057 5ELCID0639 TRES **** MOROS LEUEDES CON ARMAS DE LIDIAR;
5089 5ELCID0643 TRES **** MOROS CAUALGAN & PIENSSAN DE ANDAR,
5798 5ELCID0732 CAYEN EN VN POCO DE LOGAR MOROS MUERTOS **** & CCC YA.
6441 5ELCID0822 EN SANTA MARIA DE BURGOS QUITEDES **** MISSAS;

WORD C# PREFIX CONTEXT

MILL (CON'T)

6624 5ELCID0845 VENDIDO LES A ALCO%ER POR TRES **** MARCHOS DE PLATA.
7260 5ELCID0931 QUE ALBARFANEZ PAGO LAS **** MISSAS,
7910 5ELCID1010 HY GA@O A COLADA QUE MAS VALE DE **** MARCOS DE PLATA.
9579 5ELCID1217 ENEL AUER MONEDADO XXX **** MARCOS LE CAEN,
9636 5ELCID1224 VINO LOS VER CON XXX **** DE ARMAS.
9980 5ELCID1265 TRES **** & SEYS %IENTOS AUIE MYO %ID EL DE BIUAR;
10148 5ELCID1285 E MANDO **** MARCOS DE PLATA A SAN PERO LEUAR
12813 5ELCID1626 CON L VEZES **** DE ARMAS, TODOS FUERON CONPLIDOS,
13547 5ELCID1717 CUATRO **** MENOS XXX CON MYO %ID VAN A CABO,
13558 5ELCID1718 ALOS %INQUAENTA **** VAN LOS FERIR DE GRADO;
13685 5ELCID1734 LOS L **** POR CUENTA FUERO NOTADOS:
13711 5ELCID1737 ENTRE ORO & PLATA FALLARON TRES **** MARCOS,
14063 5ELCID1781 DELOS BUENOS & OTORGADOS CAYERON LE **** & D CAUALLOS;
14633 5ELCID1851 CON %INQUAENTA **** ARRANCOLOS DEL CAMPO;
18278 5ELCID2313 CINQUAENTA **** TIENDAS FINCADAS HA DELAS CABDALES;
19183 5ELCID2426 E GANO A TIZON QUE **** MARCOS DORO VAL.
19793 5ELCID2509 VALIA DE %INCO **** MARCOS GANARON AMOS ADOS;
20258 5ELCID2571 HYO QUIERO LES DAR AXUUAR IIJ **** MARCOS DE PLATA;
25161 5ELCID3204 EN ORO & EN PLATA TRES **** MARCOS DE PLATA LES DIO;
25373 5ELCID3231 DESTOS IIJ **** MARCOS LOS CC TENGO YO;
29235 5ELCID3733 EN ERA DE **** & CCXLV A@OS. EN EL ROMANZ

WORD #2750 OCCURS 27 TIMES.
INDEX OF DIVERSIFICATION = 1055.31 WITH STANDARD DEVIATION OF 1324.23

MINAYA
3002 5ELCID0378 ATAN GRAND SABOR FABLO ****** ALBARFANEZ:
3477 5ELCID0438 COMMO LOS CONSEIAUA ****** ALBARFANEZ:
3527 5ELCID0444 LAN%A, CAUALLEROS BUENOS QUE ACONPANE@ A ******.
3778 5ELCID0477 E SIN DUBDA CORREN; FASTA ALCALA LEGO LA SE@A DE ******,
3817 5ELCID0482 DERECHA VIENE LA SE@A DE ******;
3859 5ELCID0488 LOS BRA%OS ABIERTOS RE%IBE A ******:
3884 5ELCID0492 DOUOS LA QUINTA, SI LA QUISIEREDES, ******.
5310 5ELCID0671 PRIMERO FABLO ******, VN CAUALLERO DE PRESTAR:
5368 5ELCID0678 ONDRASTES UOS, ******, CA AUER UOS LO YEDES DE FAR.
5964 5ELCID0756 CAUALGO ******, EL ESPADA EN LA MANO,
6554 5ELCID0836 YA ES AGUISADO, MA@ANAS FUE ******,
6823 5ELCID0871 YDO ES A CASTIELLA ALBARFANEZ ******,
6934 5ELCID0886 SOBRESTO TODO, AUOS QUITO, ******,
6964 5ELCID0890 SOBRE AQUESTO TODO, DEZIR UOS QUIERO, ******:
6994 5ELCID0894 BESO LE LAS MANOS ****** ALBARFANEZ:
7017 5ELCID0897 HYD POR CASTIELLA & DEXEN UOS ANDAR, ******,
7104 5ELCID0908 QUANDO VIO EL CABOSO QUE SE TARDAUA ******,
7156 5ELCID0916 DE CASTIELLA VENIDO ES ******,
7177 5ELCID0919 QUANDO VIO MYO %ID ASOMAR A ******,
7219 5ELCID0925 MIENTRA UOS VISQUIEREDES, BIEN ME YRA AMJ, ******
7228 5ELCID0927 QUE ****** ALBARFANEZ ASSI ERA LEGADO,
8852 5ELCID1127 OYD QUE DIXO ****** ALBARFANEZ:
9863 5ELCID1251 ESTO MANDO MYO %ID, ****** LO OUO CONSSEIADO:
9903 5ELCID1256 CON ****** ALBARFANEZ EL SEUA CONSEGAR:
9911 5ELCID1257 SI UOS QUISIEREDES, ******, QUIERO SABER RECABDO
9957 5ELCID1262 ALI DIXO ******: CONSEIO ES AGUISADO.
10024 5ELCID1273 SI AUOS PLOGUIERE, ******, & NON UOS CAYA EN PESAR,
10120 5ELCID1282 ESSORA DIXO ******: DE BUENA VOLUNTAD.
10244 5ELCID1297 OYD, ****** ALBARFANEZ, POR AQUEL QUE ESTA EN ALTO,
10323 5ELCID1307 ALEGRE FUE ****** & SPIDIOS & VINOS.
10337 5ELCID1309 ADELINO PORA CASTIELLA ****** ALBARFANEZ.
10374 5ELCID1314 ALEGRE FUE DE AQUESTO ****** ALBARFANEZ,
10391 5ELCID1317 AFE ****** LABARFANEZ DO LEGA TAN APUESTO;
10655 5ELCID1350 FABLAUA ****** Y AGUISA DE VARON:
10886 5ELCID1378 ****** ALBARFANEZ ALBUEN REY SE ESPIDIO.
10946 5ELCID1385 LOS YFFANTES DE CARRION DANDO YUAN CONPA@A A ****** ALBARFANEZ:
11180 5ELCID1414 REMANE%IO EN SAN PERO ****** ALBARFANEZ.
11240 5ELCID1422 LOS QUINIENTOS MARCOS DIO ****** AL ABBAT,
11251 5ELCID1424 ****** A DO@A XIMINA & A SUS FIJAS QUE HA,
11272 5ELCID1426 EL BUENO DE ****** PENSOLAS DE ADOBAR
11300 5ELCID1430 EL BUENO DE ****** PENSSAR QUIERE DE CAUALGAR;
11314 5ELCID1432 MER%ED, ******, CAUALLERO DE PRESTAR
11377 5ELCID1439 HYDO ES PORA SAN PERO ****** ALBARFANEZ,
11398 5ELCID1442 SI UOS VALA EL CRIADOR, ****** ALBARFANEZ,
11429 5ELCID1447 RESPUSO ******: FER LO HE DE VELUNTAD.
11962 5ELCID1516 DON LEGAN LOS OTROS, A ****** ALBARFANEZ SE UAN HOMILAR.
11993 5ELCID1520 TAN BUEN DIA CON UUSCO, ****** ALBARFANEZ
12046 5ELCID1527 SORRISOS DELA BOCA ****** ALBARFANEZ:
12097 5ELCID1534 ENTRARON EN MEDINA, SIRUIALOS ******,
12136 5ELCID1539 EL REY LO PAGO TODO, & QUITO SEUA ******.
12350 5ELCID1568 AFEUOS TODOS AQUESTOS RE%IBEN A ******
12483 5ELCID1583 RE%IBIR SALIEN LAS DUENAS & AL BUENO DE ******.
13570 5ELCID1719 ALUAR ALUAREZ & ALUAR SALUADOREZ & ****** ALBARFANEZ
14792 5ELCID1870 AUOS, ****** ALBARFANEZ, & EA PERO VERMUEZ AQUI,
15388 5ELCID1949 DIXO ******, UOS SED SABIDOR.
17603 5ELCID2227 ESTOZ DIXO ******: ESTO FARE YO DE GRADO.
17620 5ELCID2229 ALOS YFANTES DE CARRION ****** VA FABLANDO:
17625 5ELCID2230 AFEUOS DELANT ******, AMOS SODES HERMANOS.
19842 5ELCID2516 RE%IBIOLOS ****** POR MYO %ID EL CAMPEADOR:
20669 5ELCID2624 ****** ALBARFANEZ ANTE MYO %ID SE PARO:

WORD C# PREFIX CONTEXT

MINAYA (CON'T)

```
                 22270 5ELCID2836 CAUALGO ****** CON PERO VERMUEZ
                 22364 5ELCID2849 PRESENTAN A ****** ESSA NOCH GRANT ENFFURXION;
                 22437 5ELCID2858 ****** VA UER SUS PRIMAS DO SON,
                 22564 5ELCID2874 E ****** CON LAS DUE@AS YUA CABADELANT.
                 23992 5ELCID3058 ENTRE ****** & LOS BUENOS QUE Y HA
                 27066 5ELCID3458 QUE VAL, ******, TODA ESSA RAZON?
         WORD #2751 OCCURS  66 TIMES.
            INDEX OF DIVERSIFICATION =   369.22 WITH STANDARD DEVIATION OF   638.50

MINCAL           18630 5ELCID2357 CURIELCS QUI QUIER, CA DELLCS POCO ******.
         WORD #2752 OCCURS   1 TIMES.

MINCHAL           1811 5ELCID0230 SI EL REY MELO QUISIERE TOMAR AMI NON *******.
         WORD #2753 OCCURS   1 TIMES.

MINGUA            9266 5ELCID1178 MALA CUETA ES, SE@ORES, AVER ****** DE PAN,
         WORD #2754 OCCURS   1 TIMES.

MINGUADO         19673 5ELCID2494 ANTES FU ********, AGORA RICO SO,
         WORD #2755 OCCURS   1 TIMES.

MINGUADOS        19500 5ELCID2470 CUYDARON QUE EN SUS DIAS NUNQUA SERIEN *********.
         WORD #2756 OCCURS   1 TIMES.

MINGUAUA          6434 5ELCID0821 QUE NADA NOL ********;
         WORD #2757 OCCURS   1 TIMES.

MINTIST          26429 5ELCID3371 QUE ERES TRAYDOR & ******* DE QUANTO DICHO HAS.
         WORD #2758 OCCURS   1 TIMES.

MINYAYA           4162 5ELCID0529 QUITAR QUIERO CASTEJON, OYD, ESCUELLAS & *******
         WORD #2759 OCCURS   1 TIMES.

MIO               1222 5ELCID0157 ALO QUEM SEMEIA, DE LO *** AUREDES ALGO;
                  1595 5ELCID0204  VENIDES, MARTIN ANTOLINEZ, EL *** FIEL VASSALO
                  2316 5ELCID0292 TODOS DEMANDAN POR *** XID EL CAMPEADOR;
                  2406 5ELCID0304 PLOGO A *** XID, POR QUE CREXIO EN LA IANTAR,
                  3719 5ELCID0470 *** XID RUY DIAZ POR LAS PUERTAS ENTRAUA,
                  3927 5ELCOD0498 FATA QUE YO ME PAGE SOBRE *** BUEN CAUALLO,
                  5808 5ELCID0734 *** XID RUY DIAZ EL BUEN LIDIADOR;
                  7092 5ELCID0907 ALI SOUO *** XID CONPLIDAS XV SEMANAS;
                  7675 5ELCID0983 ESSORA LO CONNOSXE *** XID EL DE BIUAR.
                  9029 5ELCID1149 GRANDES SON LAS GANANXIAS QUE *** XID FECHAS HA.
                 13082 5ELCID1659 ALEGRAUAS *** XID & DIXO: TAN BUEN DIA ES OY
                 13506 5ELCID1712 *** XID ALOS SOS VASSALOS TAN BIEN LOS ACORDANDO.
                 16196 5ELCID2055 RESPUSO *** XID: ASSI LO MANDE EL CRIADOR
                 17846 5ELCID2258 LOS VASSALLOS DE *** XID, ASSI SON ACORDADOS,
                 19126 5ELCID2419 MAS BAUIECA EL DE *** XID ALCANXANDO LO VA.
                 23540 5ELCID2998 ENEMIGO DE *** SID, QUE SIEMPREL BUSCO MAL,
                 27170 5ELCID3473 ENESSORA DIXO *** XID. NO LO FARE, SENOR.
         WORD #2760 OCCURS  17 TIMES.
            INDEX OF DIVERSIFICATION =  1620.75 WITH STANDARD DEVIATION OF  1380.27

MIOS             16399 5ELCID2080 LOS **** & LOS UUESTROS QUE SEAN ROGADORES;
                 20306 5ELCID2577 **** FIJOS SODES AMOS, CUANDO MIS FIJAS VOS DO;
                 20337 5ELCID2580 CON QUE RIQUEZA ENBIO **** YERNOS AMOS ADOS.
                 24469 5ELCID3119 ACA POSARE CON TODOS AQUESTOS ****.
         WORD #2761 OCCURS   4 TIMES.

MIRACLOS          2720 5ELCID0344 MOSTRANDO LOS ********, POR EN AUEMOS QUE FABLAR:
         WORD #2762 OCCURS   1 TIMES.

MIRAN            12705 5ELCID1613 ***** VALENXIA COMMO IAZE LA XIBDAD,
                 12720 5ELCID1615 ***** LA HUERTA, ESPESSA ES & GRAND;
         WORD #2763 OCCURS   2 TIMES.

MIRRA             2672 5ELCID0337 MELCHIOR & GASPAR & BALTASAR, ORO & TUS & *****
         WORD #2764 OCCURS   1 TIMES.

MIS               1972 5ELCID0249 YO ADOBARE CON DUCHO PORA MI & PORA *** VASSALLOS;
                  2243 5ELCID0282 PLEGA ADIOS & A SANTA MARIA, QUE AUN CON *** MANOS CASE
                                  ESTAS MIS
                  2247 5ELCID0282 PLEGA ADIOS & A SANTA MARIA, QUE AUN CON MIS MANOS CASE
                                  ESTAS ***
                  6452 5ELCID0823 LO QUE ROMANEXIERE DALDO A MI MUGIER & A *** FIJAS,
                 10046 5ELCID1273 DESTAS *** GANANXIAS, QUE AUEMOS FECHAS ACA,
                 10075 5ELCID1276 POR MI MUGIER & *** FIJAS, SI FUERE SU MERXED,
                 11578 5ELCID1467 MY MUGIER & *** FIJAS CON MYNAYA ALBARFFANEZ,
                 12649 5ELCID1604 VOS, QUERIDA & ONDRADA MUGIER, & AMAS *** FIJAS,
                 12787 5ELCID1623 QUE EN *** HEREDADES FUERTE MIETRE ES MIETDO,
                 12909 5ELCID1638 *** FIJAS & MI MUGIER QUE LAS TENGO ACA;
                 12933 5ELCID1641 *** FIJAS & MI MUGIER VERME AN LIDIAR,
                 14319 5ELCID1811 POR AMOR DE MI MUGIER & DE *** FIJAS AMAS,
                 15296 5ELCID1937 E PIDEN ME *** FIJAS PORA LOS YFANTES DE CARRION.
                 16443 5ELCID2085 PERTENEXEN PORA *** FIJAS & AVN PORA MEIORES.
                 16548 5ELCID2097 DAQUI LAS PRENDO POR *** MANOS DON ELUIRA & DONA SOL,
```

```
WORD                  C#  PREFIX                       CONTEXT

MIS (CON'T)

                  16658 5ELCID2110 VOS CASADES *** FIJAS, CA NON GELAS DO YO.
                  17303 5ELCID2189 GRADID MELO, *** FIJAS, CA BIEN UOS HE CASADAS
                  17365 5ELCID2197 AUOS DIGO, *** FIJAS, DON ELUIRA & DO@A SOL:
                  17563 5ELCID2222 AFFE AMAS *** FIJAS, METOLAS EN UUESTRA MANO;
                  18435 5ELCID2333 EN BRA%OS TENEDES *** FIJAS TAN BLANCAS COMMO EL SOL
                  18755 5ELCID2373 MI ORDEN & *** MANOS QUERRIA LAS ONDRAR,
                  20311 5ELCID2577 MIOS FIJOS SODES AMOS, QUANDO *** FIJAS VOS DO;
                  20342 5ELCID2581 A *** FIJAS SIRUADES, QUE UUESTRAS MUGIERES SON;
                  20630 5ELCID2619 PRIMO ERES DE *** FIJAS AMAS DALMA & DE CORA%ON
                  20651 5ELCID2621 VERAS LAS HEREDADES QUE A *** FIJAS DADAS SON;
                  20771 5ELCID2638 DIL QUE ENBIO *** FIJAS A TIERRAS DE CARRION,
                  21846 5ELCID2780 YA PRIMAS, LAS *** PRIMAS, DON ELUIRA & DO@A SOL,
                  22676 5ELCID2890  VENIDES, *** FIJAS? DICS UOS CURIE DE MAL
                  22828 5ELCID2908 EL CASO *** FIJAS, CA NON GELAS DI YO;
                  23868 5ELCID3040 BESA UOS LAS MANOS, & *** FIJAS AMAS ADOS,
                  23926 5ELCID3048 LAS *** COMPA@AS ESTA NOCHE LEGARAN;
                  24720 5ELCID3149 POR *** FIJAS QUEM DEXARON YO NON HE DESONOR,
                  24740 5ELCID3151 MAS QUANDO SACARON *** FIJAS DE VALEN%IA LA MAYOR,
                  24778 5ELCID3156 QUANDO DEXARON *** FIJAS ENEL ROBREDO DE CORPES,
                  24795 5ELCID3158 DEN ME *** ESPADAS QUANDO MYOS YERNOS NON SON.
                  25133 5ELCID3201 HYA PAGADO SO DE *** ESPADAS, DE COLADA & DE TIZON.
                  25151 5ELCID3203 QUANDO SACARON DE VALEN%IA *** FIJAS AMAS ADOS,
                  25176 5ELCID3206 DEN ME *** AUERES, QUANDO MYOS YERNOS NON SON.
                  25610 5ELCID3261 ALA SALIDA DE VALEN%IA *** FIJAS VOS DI YO,
                  26677 5ELCID3407 AFE *** FIJAS, EN UUESTRAS MANOS SON:
                  26910 5ELCID3438 HYO LES DI *** PRIMAS POR MANDADO DEL REY ALFONSSO,
                  26978 5ELCID3447 QUANDO PIDEN *** PRIMAS, DON ELUIRA & DO@A SOL,
                  27281 5ELCID3487 ESTOS *** TRES CAUALLEROS EN UUESTRA MANO SON,
                  29080 5ELCID3714 GRADO AL REY DEL %IELO, *** FIJAS VENGADAS SON
        WORD #2765 OCCURS  44 TIMES.
           INDEX OF DIVERSIFICATION =   629.42 WITH STANDARD DEVIATION OF   893.02

MISMOS             6642 5ELCID0847 QUE BIEN PAGO A SUS VASSALOS ******
        WORD #2766 OCCURS   1 TIMES.

MISSA              2520 5ELCID0319 LA ***** NOS DIRA, ESTA SERA DE SANTA TRINIDAD;
                   2529 5ELCID0320 LA ***** DICHA, PENSSEMOS DE CAUALGAR,
                   2905 5ELCID0366 LA ORA%ION FECHA, LA ***** ACABADA LA AN,
                  10383 5ELCID1316 DE ***** ERA EXIDO ESSORA EL REY ALFONSSO,
                  12148 5ELCID1541 OYDA ES LA *****, & LUEGO CAUALGAUAN;
                  13312 5ELCID1688 DEZIR NOS HA LA *****, & PENSSAD DE CAUALGAR,
                  13429 5ELCID1702 EL OBISPO DON IHERONIMO LA ***** LES CANTAUA;
                  13433 5ELCID1703 LA ***** DICHA, GRANT SULTURA LES DAUA:
                  13470 5ELCID1707 HYO UOS CANTE LA ***** POR ACUESTA MA@ANA;
                  16313 5ELCID2069 EL OBISPO DON IHERONIMO LA ***** CANTO.
                  16319 5ELCID2070 AL SALIR DE LA ***** TODOS IUNTADOS SON,
                  17703 5ELCID2240 DIOLES BENDICTIONES, LA ***** A CANTADO.
                  18730 5ELCID2370 OY UOS DIX LA ***** DE SANTA TRINIDADE.
                  24014 5ELCID3061 SUELTA FUE LA ***** ANTES QUE SALIESSE EL SOL,
        WORD #2767 OCCURS  14 TIMES.
           INDEX OF DIVERSIFICATION =  1652.38 WITH STANDARD DEVIATION OF  2309.09

MISSAS             1772 5ELCID0225 ESTO & YO EN DEBDO QUE FAGA Y CANTAR MILL ******.
                   6442 5ELCID0822 EN SANTA MARIA DE BURGOS QUITEDES MILL ******;
                   7261 5ELCID0931 QUE ALBARFANEZ PAGO LAS MILL ******,
        WORD #2768 OCCURS   3 TIMES.

MIYOR             10484 5ELCID1328 PRISO A ALMENAR & A MURUIEDRO QUE ES *****,
        WORD #2769 OCCURS   1 TIMES.

MJ                10709 5ELCID1356 HYO LES MANDARE DAR CONDUCHO MIENTRA QUE POR ** TIERRA FUEREN,
        WORD #2770 OCCURS   1 TIMES.

MOI                4362 5ELCID0556 *** %ID DON RODRIGO ALCO%ER CUEDA GANAR.
        WORD #2771 OCCURS   1 TIMES.

MOION             15123 5ELCID1912 DO EL DIXIERE, Y SEA EL *****.
                  28258 5ELCID3607 QUE POR Y SERIE VEN%IDO QUI SALIESSE DEL *****.
                  28274 5ELCID3609 MAS DE VJ ASTAS DE LAN%AS QUE NON LEGASSEN AL *****.
                  28715 5ELCID3667 SACOL DEL *****; MARTIN ANTOLJNEZ EN EL CAMPO FINCAUA.
        WORD #2772 OCCURS   4 TIMES.

MOIONES           28106 5ELCID3588 HYA SALIERON AL CAMPO DO ERAN LOS *******.
                  28236 5ELCID3604 LOS FIELES & EL REY ENSE@ARON LOS *******,
        WORD #2773 OCCURS   2 TIMES.

MOLINA             6788 5ELCID0867 DESI A ******, QUE ES DEL OTRA PART,
                  11549 5ELCID1463 VAYADES A ******, QUE IAZE MAS ADELANT,
                  11651 5ELCID1476 E EL OTRO DIA VINIERON A ****** POSAR.
                  12170 5ELCID1545 VINIERON A ******, LA QUE AUEGALUON MANDAUA.
                  12212 5ELCID1550 ENTRADOS SON A ******, BUENA & RICA CASA;
                  20747 5ELCID2635 POR ****** YREDES, VNA NOCH Y IAZREDES;
                  20846 5ELCID2647 FELOS EN ****** CON EL MORO AVENGALUON.
                  21160 5ELCID2688 CUEMMO DE BUEN SESO A ****** SE TORNO.
```

WORD C# PREFIX CONTEXT

MOLINA (CON'T)

```
                    22607 5ELCID2880 E DE MEDINA A ****** EN OTRO DIA VAN;
          WORD #2774 OCCURS   9 TIMES.
             INDEX OF DIVERSIFICATION =  1976.38 WITH STANDARD DEVIATION OF  3087.23

MOLINOS             26485 5ELCID3379 FUESSE A RIO DOUIRNA LOS ******* PICAR
          WORD #2775 OCCURS   1 TIMES.

MON                  9330 5ELCID1186 AMANE%IO AMYO %ID EN TIERRAS DE *** REAL.
          WORD #2776 OCCURS   1 TIMES.

MONCLURAS           28599 5ELCID3652 LAS ********* DEL YELMO TODAS GELAS CORTAUA,
          WORD #2777 OCCURS   1 TIMES.

MON%ON               7329 5ELCID0940 PESANDO VA ALOS DE ****** & ALOS DE HUESCA;
          WORD #2778 OCCURS   1 TIMES.

MONEDADO              986 5ELCID0126 NON DUERME SIN SOSPECHA QUI AUER TRAE ********.
                     9577 5ELCID1217 ENEL AUER ******** XXX MILL MARCOS LE CAEN,
          WORD #2779 OCCURS   2 TIMES.

MONEDADOS            1349 5ELCID0172 GRADAN SE RACHEL & VIDAS CON AUERES *********,
                    17842 5ELCID2257 NON FUERON EN CUENTA LOS AUERES *********.
                    25415 5ELCID3236 FABLO FERRANGO%ALEZ: AUERES ********* NON TENEMOS NOS.
          WORD #2780 OCCURS   3 TIMES.

MONESTERIO           1996 5ELCID0252 NON QUIERO FAZER ENEL ********** VN DINERO DE DA@O;
                     2066 5ELCID0260 POR VN MARCHO QUE DESPENDADES AL ********** DARE YO QUATRO.
                    10681 5ELCID1353 SALDRIEN DEL ********** DO ELLE LAS DEXO,
                    11409 5ELCID1444 AQUESTE ********** NO LO QUIERA OLBIDAR,
          WORD #2781 OCCURS   4 TIMES.

MONT                 5838 5ELCID0738 MARTIN MU@OZ, EL QUE MANDO A **** MAYOR,
                     6764 5ELCID0863 Y FFINCO EN VN POYO QUE ES SOBRE **** REAL;
                     7427 5ELCID0952 DENT CORRE MYO %ID A HUESCA & A **** ALUAN;
                     8579 5ELCID1089 E DEXADO A HUESCA & LAS TIERRAS DE **** ALUAN.
                    21928 5ELCID2789 LOS GANADOS FIEROS NON NOS COMAN EN AQUESTE ****
                    23125 5ELCID2946 ALAS BESTIAS FIERAS & ALAS AUES DEL ****.
                    25661 5ELCID3267 ALAS BESTIAS FIERAS & ALAS AUES DEL ****;
          WORD #2782 OCCURS   7 TIMES.
             INDEX OF DIVERSIFICATION =  3302.83 WITH STANDARD DEVIATION OF  4963.71

MONTANA              3388 5ELCID0427 EN MEDIO DUNA ******* MARAUILLOSA & GRAND
          WORD #2783 OCCURS   1 TIMES.

MONTANAS            11753 5ELCID1491 PASSAN LAS ********, QUE SON FIERAS & GRANDES,
          WORD #2784 OCCURS   1 TIMES.

MONTA@A               486 5ELCID0061 ASSI POSO MYO %ID COMMO SI FUESSE EN *******.
          WORD #2785 OCCURS   1 TIMES.

MONTE                2748 5ELCID0347 ALOS IUDIOS TE DEXESTE PRENDER; DO DIZEN ***** CALUARIE
                    21640 5ELCID2751 E ALAS AUES DEL ***** & ALAS BESTIAS DELA FIERA GUISA.
                    21769 5ELCID2769 EN VN ***** ESPESSO FELEZ MUNOZ SE METIO,
          WORD #2786 OCCURS   3 TIMES.

MONTES               9296 5ELCID1182 CON EL DELOS ****** CLAROS AUYEN GUERRA TAN GRAND,
                    14441 5ELCID1826 PASSANDO VAN LAS SIERRAS & LOS ****** & LAS AGUAS,
                    20887 5ELCID2653 HYUAN TRO%IR LOS ******, LOS QUE DIZEN DE LUZON.
                    21196 5ELCID2693 POR LOS ****** CLAROS AGUIJAN A ESPOLON;
                    21230 5ELCID2698 LOS ****** SON ALTOS, LAS RAMAS PUIAN CON LAS NUES,
                    21364 5ELCID2715 AQUI SEREDES ESCARNIDAS EN ESTOS FIEROS ******.
                    21687 5ELCID2757 POR LOS ****** DO YUAN, ELLOS YUAN SE ALABANDO:
                    22085 5ELCID2810 ENTRE NOCH & DIA SALIERON DELOS ******;
          WORD #2787 OCCURS   8 TIMES.
             INDEX OF DIVERSIFICATION =  1826.00 WITH STANDARD DEVIATION OF  2739.64

MONUMENTO            2837 5ELCID0358 ENEL ********* RESU%ITEST, FUST ALOS YNFIERNOS,
          WORD #2788 OCCURS   1 TIMES.

MORA                 7392 5ELCID0948 QUI EN VN LOGAR **** SIEMPRE, LO SO PUEDE MANGUAR;
          WORD #2789 OCCURS   1 TIMES.

MORADA               4129 5ELCID0525 QUE ENEL CASTIELLO NON Y AURIE ******,
                     8291 5ELCID1055 AQUI FEREMOS LA ******, NO NOS PARTIREMOS AMOS.
          WORD #2790 OCCURS   2 TIMES.

MORADAS             12947 5ELCID1642 EN ESTAS TIERRAS AGENAS VERAN LAS ******* COMMO SE FAZEN,
          WORD #2791 OCCURS   1 TIMES.

MORAN               17944 5ELCID2271 HY ***** LOS YFANTES BIEN CERCA DE DOS A@OS,
          WORD #2792 OCCURS   1 TIMES.

MORAS                3687 5ELCID0465 MOROS & ***** AUIEN LOS DE GANAN%IA,
                     4196 5ELCID0534 %IENTO MOROS & %IENTO ***** QUIERO LAS QUITAR,
```

WORD C# PREFIX CONTEXT

MORAS (CON'T)

4253 5ELCID0541 LOS MOROS & LAS ***** BENDIZIENDOL ESTAN.
4893 5ELCID0619 LOS MOROS & LAS ***** VENDER NON LOS PODREMOS,
5381 5ELCID0679 TODOS LOS MOROS & LAS ***** DE FUERA LOS MANDA ECHAR,
6678 5ELCID0852 MOROS & ***** TOMARON SE A QUEXAR:
6708 5ELCID0856 MOROS & ***** COMPEZARON DE LORAR.
WORD #2793 OCCURS 7 TIMES.
INDEX OF DIVERSIFICATION = 502.50 WITH STANDARD DEVIATION OF 463.06

MORIR
8066 5ELCID1029 QUE YO DEXAR ME *****, QUE NON QUIERO COMER.
WORD #2794 OCCURS 1 TIMES.

MORISCA
1390 5ELCID0178 VNA PIEL VERMEIA ******* & ONDRADA,
WORD #2795 OCCURS 1 TIMES.

MORISCOS
6249 5ELCID0796 DELOS ********, QUANDO SON LEGADOS, FFALLARON DX CAUALLOS.
WORD #2796 OCCURS 1 TIMES.

MORO
11654 5ELCID1477 EL **** AUEGALUON, QUANDO SOPO EL MENSSAIE,
12218 5ELCID1551 EL **** AUEGALUON BIEN LOS SIRUIE SIN FALLA,
12261 5ELCID1557 LOS SOS DESPENDIE EL ****, QUE DELO SO NON TOMAUA NADA.
18750 5ELCID2372 POR SABOR QUE AUIA DE ALGUN **** MATAR;
20758 5ELCID2636 SALUDAD A MYO AMIGO EL **** AVENGALUON:
20849 5ELCID2647 FELOS EN MOLINA CON EL **** AVENGALUON.
20852 5ELCID2648 EL **** QUANDO LO SOPO, PLOGOL DE CORAZON;
20898 5ELCID2654 ALAS FIJAS DEL %ID EL **** SUS DO@AS DIO,
20926 5ELCID2658 TOD ESTO LES FIZO EL **** POR EL AMOR DEL %ID CAMPEADOR.
20939 5ELCID2659 ELLOS VEYEN LA RIQUEZA QUE EL **** SACO,
20957 5ELCID2662 SI PUDIESSEMOS MATAR EL **** AVENGALUON,
20991 5ELCID2667 VN **** LATINADO BIEN GELO ENTENDIO;
21017 5ELCID2671 EL **** AVENGALUON, MUCHO ERA BUEN BARRAGAN,
21039 5ELCID2674 DELO QUE EL **** DIXO ALOS YFANTES NON PLAZE:
21146 5ELCID2686 ESTO LES HA DICHO, & EL **** SE TORNO;
22613 5ELCID2881 AL **** AUENGALUON DE CORAZON LE PLAZ,
25801 5ELCID3286 NIMBLA MESSO FIJO DE **** NIN DE CHRISTIANA,
26026 5ELCID3318 VIST VN ****, FUSTEL ENSAYAR; ANTES FUXISTE QUE ALTE ALEGASSES.
26039 5ELCID3319 SI YO NON VUJAS, EL **** TE JUGARA MAL;
26048 5ELCID3320 PASSE POR TI, CON EL **** ME OFF DE AIUNTAR,
26087 5ELCID3325 QUE MATARAS EL **** & QUE FIZIERAS BARNAX;
WORD #2797 OCCURS 21 TIMES.
INDEX OF DIVERSIFICATION = 720.65 WITH STANDARD DEVIATION OF 1596.65

MOROS
837 5ELCID0107 QUE NON ME DESCUBRADES A ***** NIN A CHRISTIANOS;
973 5ELCID0125 QUANDO ATIERRA DE ***** ENTRO, QUE GRANT AUER SACO;
1130 5ELCID0145 QUE NON LO SEPAN ***** NON CHRISTIANOS.
3166 5ELCID0398 DE DIESTRO A LILON LAS TORRES, QUE ***** LAS HAN;
3557 5ELCID0448 QUE POR MIEDO DE LOS ***** NON DEXEN NADA.
3685 5ELCID0465 ***** & MORAS AUIEN LOS DE GANANZIA,
3734 5ELCID0472 QUINZE ***** MATAUA DELOS QUE ALCANZAUA.
3932 5ELCID0499 LIDIANDO CON ***** ENEL CAMPO,
4097 5ELCID0521 ASMARON LOS ***** IIJ MILL MARCOS DE PLATA.
4138 5ELCID0527 ***** EN PAZ, CA ESCRIPTA ES LA CARTA,
4193 5ELCID0534 %IENTO ***** & %IENTO MORAS QUIERO LAS QUITAR,
4250 5ELCID0541 LOS ***** & LAS MORAS BENDIZIENDOL ESTAN.
4313 5ELCID0549 NON LO SABEN LOS ***** EL ARDIMENT QUE AN.
4447 5ELCID0566 VENIDO ES A *****, EXIDO ES DE CHRISTIANOS;
4776 5ELCID0605 EN VN ORA & VN POCO DE LOGAR CCC ***** MATAN.
4882 5ELCID0618 LOS ***** YAZEN MUERTOS, DE BIUOS POCOS VEO.
4890 5ELCID0619 LOS ***** & LAS MORAS VENDER NON LOS PODREMOS,
5043 5ELCID0637 TRES REYES VEO DE ***** DERREDOR DE MI ESTAR,
5058 5ELCID0639 TRES MILL ***** LEUEDES CON ARMAS DE LIDIAR;
5090 5ELCID0643 TRES MILL ***** CAUALGAN & PIENSSAN DE ANDAR,
5202 5ELCID0658 LAS AROBDAS, QUE LOS ***** SACAN, DE DIA
5324 5ELCID0673 SI CON ***** NON LIDIAREMOS, NO NOS DARAN DEL PAN.
5378 5ELCID0679 TODOS LOS ***** & LAS MORAS DE FUERA LOS MANDA ECHAR,
5505 5ELCID0694 VIERON LO LAS AROBDAS DELOS *****, AL ALMOFALLA SEUAN TORNAR.
5515 5ELCID0695 QUE PRIESSA VA EN LOS *****, E TORNARON SE A ARMAR;
5532 5ELCID0697 VERIEDES ARMAR SE *****, APRIESSA ENTRAR EN AZ.
5540 5ELCID0698 DE PARTE DELOS ***** DOS SE@AS HA CABDALES,
5559 5ELCID0700 LAS AZES DE LOS ***** YAS MUEUEN ADELANT,
5650 5ELCID0712 ***** LE REZIBEN POR LA SE@A GANAR,
5739 5ELCID0724 SE@OS ***** MATARON, TODOS DE SE@OS COLPES;
5782 5ELCID0731 LOS ***** LAMAN MAFOMAT & LOS CHRISTIANOS SANTI YAGUE.
5796 5ELCID0732 CAYEN EN VN POCO DE LOGAR ***** MUERTOS MILL & CCC YA.
5957 5ELCID0755 FIRME SON LOS *****, AVN NOS VAN DEL CAMPO.
6074 5ELCID0771 CAFUYEN LOS ***** DE LA PART
6123 5ELCID0779 DA QUESTOS ***** MATO XXX IIIJ;
6161 5ELCID0785 TANTOS ***** YAZEN MUERTOS QUE POCOS BIUOS A DEXADOS,
6290 5ELCID0801 ASOS CASTIELLOS ALOS ***** DENTRO LOS AN TORNADOS,
6576 5ELCID0840 ***** DE LAS FRONTERAS & VNAS YENTES ESTRANAS;
6676 5ELCID0852 ***** & MORAS TOMARON SE A QUEXAR:
6706 5ELCID0856 ***** & MORAS COMPEZARON DE LORAR.
6858 5ELCID0876 VENZIO DOS REYES DE ***** EN AQUESTA BATALLA.
6915 5ELCID0884 MAS DESPUES QUE DE ***** FUE, PRENDO ESTA PRESENTAIA;
7050 5ELCID0901 MIENTRA QUE SEA EL PUEBLO DE ***** & DELA YENTE CHRISTIANA,

WORD C# PREFIX CONTEXT

MOROS (CON'T)

7085 5ELCID0906 NON PLAZE ALCS *****, FIRME MIENTRE LES PESAUA.
7556 5ELCID0968 GENTES SE LE ALEGAN GRANDES ENTRE ***** & CHRISTIANOS,
7714 5ELCID0988 DE ***** & DE CHRISTIANOS GENTES TRAE SOBEIANAS,
8982 5ELCID1143 ***** SON MUCHCS, YA QUIEREN RECONBRAR.
9014 5ELCID1147 DOS REYES DE ***** MATARON EN ES ALCAZ,
9130 5ELCID1162 CABO DEL MAR TIERRA DE ***** FIRME LA QUEBRANTA,
9168 5ELCID1167 EN TIERRA DE ***** PRENDIENDO & GANANDO,
9666 5ELCID1229 ***** EN ARUENZO AMIDCS BEUER AGUA.
9777 5ELCID1242 E QUE FABLASSEN DESTC ***** & CHRISTIANOS.
10214 5ELCID1293 SOSPIRANDO EL OBISPO QUES VIESSE CON ***** ENEL CAMPO:
10623 5ELCID1346 SEMEIA QUE EN TIERRA DE ***** NON A BIUO OMNE,
13182 5ELCID1671 LOS ***** DE MARRUECCS CAUALGAN AUIGOR,
13223 5ELCID1676 DOS FALLAN CON LOS ***** COMETIEN LOS TAN AYNA.
13597 5ELCID1723 ATANTOS MATA DE ***** QUE NCN FUERON CONTADOS;
13841 5ELCID1753 CON TAL CUM ESTO SE VENZEN ***** DEL CAMPO.
14043 5ELCID1779 LOS ***** DELAS TIERRAS GANADO SEAN Y ALGO;
14184 5ELCID1795 NON TIENE EN CUENTA LCS ***** QUE HA MATADOS;
18322 5ELCID2318 CA VEYEN TANTAS TIENDAS DE ***** DE QUE NON AUIE SABOR.
18458 5ELCID2336 CA DAQUELOS ***** YO SO SABIDOR;
18533 5ELCID2345 EN LA VESTE DELOS ***** LOS ATAMORES SONANDO;
18601 5ELCID2354 CALOS *****, CON DIOS, NON FINCARAN EN CANPO.
18816 5ELCID2381 AFE LOS ***** A OIO, YO LOS ENSAYAR.
18855 5ELCID2386 ALOS PRIMEROS COLPES DOS ***** MATAUA DE LA LANZA.
18886 5ELCID2390 LOS ***** SCN MUCHOS, DERREDOR LE ZERCAUAN,
19373 5ELCID2454 DE XX ARRIBA HA ***** MATADO;
19424 5ELCID2461 FARTOS DE LIDIAR CON ***** ENEL CAMPO.
19699 5ELCID2498 ***** & CHRISTIANOS DE MI HAN GRANT PAUOR;
19888 5ELCID2522 VENZIEMOS ***** EN CAMPC & MATAMOS
21462 5ELCID2729 ***** & CHRISTIANCS DEPARTIRAN DESTA RAZON,
27507 5ELCID3514 EN ***** NI EN CHRISTIANOS OTRO TAL NON HA OY,
27556 5ELCID3519 PORA ARRANCAR ***** DEL CANPO & SER SEGUDADOR;
WORD #2798 OCCURS 74 TIMES.
INDEX OF DIVERSIFICATION = 365.01 WITH STANDARD DEVIATION OF 920.13

MORREMOS 21970 5ELCID2795 SI DIOS NON NOS VALE, AQUI ******** NOS.
WORD #2799 OCCURS 1 TIMES.

MOSTRANDO 2718 5ELCID0344 ********* LOS MIRACLOS, POR EN AUEMOS QUE FABLAR:
WORD #2800 OCCURS 1 TIMES.

MOUEDORES 28349 5ELCID3619 TEMBRAR QUERIE LA TIERRA DOD ERAN *********.
WORD #2801 OCCURS 1 TIMES.

MOUER 27502 5ELCID3513 MANDASTES ME ***** ABAUIECA EL CORREDOR,
WORD #2802 OCCURS 1 TIMES.

MOUIERON 21164 5ELCID2689 YA ******** DEL ANSSARERA LOS YFANTES DE CARRION,
WORD #2803 OCCURS 1 TIMES.

MOUIOS 4320 5ELCID0550 OTRO DIA ****** MYO ZID EL DE BIUAR,
WORD #2804 OCCURS 1 TIMES.

MUCH 4628 5ELCID0587 SALIERON DE ALCOZER AVNA PRIESSA **** ESTRANA.
WORD #2805 OCCURS 1 TIMES.

MUCHA 7066 5ELCID0903 ESTANDO ALLI, ***** TIERRA PREAUA,
WORD #2806 OCCURS 1 TIMES.

MUCHAS 5214 5ELCID0660 ****** SON LAS ARCBDAS & GRANDE ES EL ALMOFALLA.
11379 5ELCID1440 ****** YENTES SELE ACOGEN, PENSSO DE CAUALGAR,
12581 5ELCID1596 SACADA ME AUEDES DE ****** VERGUENZAS MALAS;
20279 5ELCID2574 E ****** VESTIDURAS DE PA@OS & DE ZICLATONES;
24450 5ELCID3117 ESSORA DIXO ****** MERZEDES EL QUE VALENZIA GA@O:
WORD #2807 OCCURS 5 TIMES.
INDEX OF DIVERSIFICATION = 4808.00 WITH STANDARD DEVIATION OF 2804.91

MUCHO 40 5ELCID0006 SOSPIRO MYO ZID, CA ***** AUIE GRANDES CUYDADOS.
722 5ELCID0091 NON PUEDO TRAER EL AUER, CA ***** ES PESADO,
861 5ELCID0110 GRANDES AUERES PRISO & ***** SOBEIANOS,
1649 5ELCID0212 ***** ES HUEBOS, CA ZERCA VIENE EL PLAZO.
2193 5ELCID0276 LEGOLAS AL CORAZON, CA ***** LAS QUERIA.
2540 5ELCID0321 CA EL PLAZO VIENE A ZERCA, ***** AUEMOS DE ANDAR.
3265 5ELCID0412 ***** ERA PAGADO DEL SUE@O QUE A SO@ADO.
3885 5ELCID0493 ***** UOS LO GRADESCO, CAMPEADOR CONTADO.
4695 5ELCID0595 VIO QUE ENTRELLOS & EL CASTIELLO ***** AUIE GRAND PLAZA;
4936 5ELCID0625 ***** PESA ALOS DE TECA & ALOS DE TERUAL NON PLAZE,
6729 5ELCID0859 AL EXIR DE SALON ***** OUO BUENAS AUES.
6893 5ELCID0881 DIXO EL REY: ***** ES MA@ANA,
7370 5ELCID0945 PLOGO A MYO ZID, & ***** A ALBARFANEZ.
8907 5ELCID1134 COMMO GELO A DICHO, AL CAMPEADOR ***** PLAZE.
9698 5ELCID1233 MAS ***** FUE PROUECHOSA, SABET, ESTA ARANCADA:
10191 5ELCID1290 BIEN ENTENDIDO ES DE LETRAS & ***** ACORDADO,
10198 5ELCID1291 DE PIE & DE CAUALLO ***** ERA AREZIADO.
10614 5ELCID1345 MAGER PLOGO AL REY, ***** PESO A GARZIORDONEZ:

WORD C# PREFIX CONTEXT

MUCHO (CON'T)

```
10840 5ELCID1373 ***** CREZEN LAS NUEUAS DE MYO %ID EL CAMPEADOR,
11455 5ELCID1450 POR LA TIERRA DEL REY ***** CONDUCHO LES DAN.
11604 5ELCID1470 E YO FINCARE EN VALEN%IA, QUE ***** COSTADOM HA;
11679 5ELCID1480 AMY NON ME PESA, SABET, ***** ME PLAZE
13232 5ELCID1677 SACAN LOS DELAS HUERTAS ***** AFEA GUISA,
13248 5ELCID1680 ***** AUIEN FECHO, PIESSAN DE CAUALGAR.
13661 5ELCID1731 ***** ERA ALEGRE DELO QUE AN CA%ADO.
14192 5ELCID1796 LO QUE CAYE AEL ***** ERA SOBEIANO;
14605 5ELCID1848 ***** PRE%IA LA ONDRA EL %ID QUEL AUEDES DADO.
14641 5ELCID1852 LAS GANAN%IAS QUE FIZO ***** SON SOBEIANAS,
14884 5ELCID1881 LAS NUEUAS DEL %ID ***** VAN ADELANT,
15305 5ELCID1938 ELLOS SON ***** VRGULLOSOS & AN PART EN LA CORT,
15579 5ELCID1975 LOS YFFANTES DE CARRIO ***** ALEGRES ANDAN,
16646 5ELCID2109 ***** UOS LO GRADESCO, COMMO A REY & A SE@OR
16961 5ELCID2147 DIXO EL REY DON ALFONSSO: ***** ME AUEDES ENBARGADO.
16992 5ELCID2151 MYO %ID RUY DIAZ, ***** ME AUEDES ONDRADO,
17744 5ELCID2245 MYO %ID DELO QUE VEYE ***** ERA PAGADO:
17916 5ELCID2267 ***** ERAN ALEGRES DIEGO & FERRANDO;
17956 5ELCID2272 LOS AMORES QUELES FAZEN ***** ERAN SOBEIANOS.
18598 5ELCID2353 MYOS YERNOS AMOS ADOS, LA COSA QUE ***** AMO,
20020 5ELCID2540 VAYAMOS PORA CARRION, AQUI ***** DETARDAMOS.
21019 5ELCID2671 EL MORO AVENGALUON, ***** ERA BUEN BARRAGAN,
22020 5ELCID2802 ***** SON LAZRADAS & AMAS LAS FARTO.
22374 5ELCID2850 NON GELO QUISO TOMAR, MAS ***** GELO GRADIO:
22395 5ELCID2853 ***** UOS LO GRADE%E, ALLA DO ESTA, MYO %ID EL CANPEADOR,
24695 5ELCID3146 ***** UOS LO GRADESCO COMMO A REY & A SE@OR,
25298 5ELCID3221 ***** NOS AFINCA EL QUE VALEN%IA GA@O,
26001 5ELCID3314 POR EL CAMPEADOR ***** VALIESTES MAS.
27715 5ELCID3538 ***** VIENEN BIEN ADOBADOS DE CAUALLOS & DE GUARNIZONES,
27875 5ELCID3557 ***** ERAN REPENTIDOS LOS YFANTES POR QUANTO DADAS SON;
27969 5ELCID3569 DELO QUE AUIEN FECHO ***** REPISOS SON;
29040 5ELCID3709 DELO QUE AN PRESO ***** AN MAL SABOR;
WORD #2808 OCCURS 50 TIMES.
INDEX OF DIVERSIFICATION = 590.84 WITH STANDARD DEVIATION OF 526.85

MUCHOL
12034 5ELCID1526 ****** TENGO POR TORPE QUI NON CONES%E LA VERDAD.
13623 5ELCID1726 SALIOS LE DE SOL ESPADA, CA ****** ANDIDO EL CAUALLO,
WORD #2809 OCCURS 2 TIMES.

MUCHOS
3797 5ELCID0480 TANTO TRAEN LAS GRANDES GANA%IAS, ****** GA@ADOS.
7286 5ELCID0934 YA ALBARFANEZ, BIUADES ****** DIAS . . .
8984 5ELCID1143 MOROS SON ******, YA QUIEREN RECONBRAR.
13896 5ELCID1760 SOMOS EN UUESTRA MER%ED, & BIUADES ****** A@OS
14690 5ELCID1858 ESTO PLOGO A ****** & BESARON LE LAS MANOS.
17279 5ELCID2186 ****** DIAS UOS VEAMOS CON LOS OIOS DELAS CARAS
18248 5ELCID2309 ****** TOUIERON POR ENBAYDOS LOS YFANTES DE CARRION,
18540 5ELCID2346 AMARAULLA LO AUIEN ****** DESSOS CHRISTIANOS,
18888 5ELCID2390 LOS MOROS SON ******, DERREDOR LE %ERCAUAN,
19516 5ELCID2473 ****** SON ALEGRES MYO %ID & SUS VASSALLOS,
19652 5ELCID2491 TANTOS SON DE ****** QUE NON SERIEN CONTADOS.
19798 5ELCID2510 ****** TIENEN POR RICOS LOS YFANTES DE CARRION.
19830 5ELCID2514 E OTROS ****** QUE CRIO EL CAMPEADOR.
23598 5ELCID3005 FUERON Y DE SU REYNO OTROS ****** SABIDORES,
26828 5ELCID3427 A ****** PLAZE DE TOD ESTA CORT,
27784 5ELCID3546 ****** SE JUNTARON DE BUENOS RICOS OMNES
28096 5ELCID3587 EDERREDOR DELLOS ****** BUENOS VARONES.
28135 5ELCID3592 MUY BIEN ACONPA@ADOS, CA ****** PARIENTES SON.
WORD #2810 OCCURS 18 TIMES.
INDEX OF DIVERSIFICATION = 1430.65 WITH STANDARD DEVIATION OF 1559.21

MUDADOS
35 5ELCID0005 E SIN FALCONES & SIN ADTORES *******.
WORD #2811 OCCURS 1 TIMES.

MUDO
7412 5ELCID0951 ESTON%ES SE **** EL %ID AL PUERTO DE ALCAT,
25914 5ELCID3302 FABLA, PERO ****, VARON QUE TANTO CALLAS
25971 5ELCID3310 SIEMPRE EN LAS CORTES PERO **** ME LAMADES
WORD #2812 OCCURS 3 TIMES.

MUERA
2391 5ELCID0302 EN ANTES QUE YO *****, ALGUN BIEN UOS PUEDA FAR:
WORD #2813 OCCURS 1 TIMES.

MUERT
12896 5ELCID1636 A MENOS DE ***** NO LA PUEDO DEXAR;
21009 5ELCID2670 TU ***** OY COSSEIAR ALOS YFANTES DE CARRION.
21063 5ELCID2676 HYO SIRUIENDO UOS SIN ART, & UOS CONSSEIASTES PORA MI *****.
21814 5ELCID2774 SABET BIEN QUE SI ELLOS LE VIESSEN, NON ESCAPARA DE *****.
28521 5ELCID3641 ASSI LO TENIEN LAS YENTES QUE MAL FERIDO ES DE *****.
28881 5ELCID3688 TODOS SE CUEDAN QUE FERIDO ES DE *****.
WORD #2814 OCCURS 6 TIMES.
INDEX OF DIVERSIFICATION = 3196.00 WITH STANDARD DEVIATION OF 3885.78

MUERTAS
21612 5ELCID2748 POR ******* LAS DEXARON ENEL ROBREDRO DE CORPES.
21648 5ELCID2752 POR ******* LAS DEXARON, SABED, QUE NON POR BIUAS.
21674 5ELCID2755 POR ******* LAS DEXARON,
WORD #2815 OCCURS 3 TIMES.
```

WORD C# PREFIX CONTEXT

MUERTOS 4884 5ELCID0618 LOS MOROS YAZEN *******, DE BIUOS POCOS VEO.
5797 5ELCID0732 CAYEN EN VN PCCC DE LCGAR MOROS ******* MILL & CCC YA.
6163 5ELCIDC785 TANTOS MORCS YAZEN ******* QUE POCOS BIUOS A DEXADOS,
14744 5ELCID1864 COMMO SI LCS FALASSE ******* ACUZIR SE LOS CAUALLOS,
27644 5ELCID3529 PODEDES OYR DE *******, CA DE VENCIDOS NO.
28368 5ELCID3622 CUEDAN SE QUE ESSORA CACRAN ******* LOS QUE ESTAN ADERREDOR.
WORD #2816 CCCURS 6 TIMES.
INDEX OF DIVERSIFICATICN = 4695.80 WITH STANCARD DEVIATION OF 5727.91

MUESSO 8087 5ELCID1032 NOL PUEDEN FAZER CCMER VN ****** DE PAN.
WORD #2817 OCCURS 1 TIMES.

MUEUEN 5561 5ELCID0700 LAS AZES DE LCS MORCS YAS ****** ADELANT,
WORD #2818 OCCURS 1 TIMES.

MUGIER 1638 5ELCID0210 VEREMOS UUESTRA ******, MENBRACA FIJA DALGO.
1793 5ELCIDC228 DIXO MARTIN ANTOLINEZ: VERE ALA ****** ATODO MYO SOLAZ,
2041 5ELCID0257 DELLAS & DE MI ****** FAGADES TODO RECABDO.
2208 5ELCID0278 YA DO@A XIMENA, LA MI ****** TAN COMPLIDA,
2259 5ELCID0284 E UOS, ****** ONDRACA, DE MY SEADES SERUIDA
2580 5ELCIDC326 MYO %ID & SU ****** A LA EGLESIA UAN.
2955 5ELCID0372 ADIOS UOS ACOMIENDC, FIJAS, & A LA ****** & AL PADRE SPIRITAL;
6449 5ELCID0823 LO QUE ROMANE%IERE DALDC A MI ****** & A MIS FIJAS,
7268 5ELCID0932 E QUEL DIXO SALUDES DE SU ****** & DE SUS FIJAS
10073 5ELCID1276 POR MI ****** & MIS FIJAS, SI FUERE SU MER%ED,
10093 5ELCID1279 LA ****** DE MYC %ID & SUS FIJAS LAS YFFANTES
10671 5ELCID1352 POR SU ****** DO@A XIMENA & SUS FIJAS AMAS ADOS:
11120 5ELCID1408 QUE SU ****** & SUS FIJAS EL REY SUELTAS ME LAS HA,
11153 5ELCID1411 SEREMOS YO & SU ****** & SUS FIJAS QUE EL A
11576 5ELCID1467 MY ****** & MIS FIJAS CON MYNAYA ALBARFFANEZ,
11703 5ELCID1484 SU ****** & SUS FIJAS EN MEDINA ESTAN;
12001 5ELCID1522 ****** DEL %ID LIDIADOR ESSUS FFIJAS NATURALES;
12427 5ELCID1577 DELANTE SU ****** & DE SUS FIJAS QUERIE TENER LAS ARMAS.
12554 5ELCID1593 ADELINO A SU ****** & A SUS FIJAS AMAS;
12646 5ELCID1604 VOS, QUERIDA & ONDRADA ******, & AMAS MIS FIJAS,
12913 5ELCID1638 MIS FIJAS & MI ****** QUE LAS TENGO ACA;
12937 5ELCID1641 MIS FIJAS & MI ****** VERME AN LIDIAR,
12962 5ELCID1644 SU ****** & SUS FIJAS SUBIOLAS AL ALCA%AR,
12984 5ELCID1647 YA ****** ONDRADA, NON AYADES PESAR
13020 5ELCID1652 ******, SED EN ESTE PALA%IO, & SI QUISIEREDES EN EL ALCA%AR;
13094 5ELCID1660 MIEDO A SU ****** & QUIEREL QUEBRAR EL CORA%ON,
13880 5ELCID1758 LAS DUE@AS & LAS FIJAS & LA ****** QUE VALE ALGO
13915 5ELCID1763 HYA ****** DA@A XIMENA, NOM LO AUIEDES ROGADO?
14316 5ELCID1811 POR AMOR DE MI ****** & DE MIS FIJAS AMAS,
15794 5ELCID2003 DENTRO ES SU ****** & SUS FIJAS AMAS ADOS,
17292 5ELCID2187 GRADO AL CRIADOR, VENGO, ****** ONDRADA
17315 5ELCID2190 BESARON LE LAS MANOS LA ****** & LAS FIJAS AMAS,
17357 5ELCID2196 ****** DO@A XIMENA, GRADO AL CRIAADOR.
17508 5ELCID2215 AEL & EASSU ****** DELANT SELE OMILLARON,
17669 5ELCID2235 A MYO %ID & A SU ****** VAN BESAR LA MANO.
19867 5ELCID2519 EUADES AQUI, YERNOS, LA MI ****** DE PRO,
21315 5ELCID2709 QUE NON YFINCAS NINGUNO, ****** NIN VARON,
23856 5ELCID3039 MI ****** DONA XIMENA, DUE@A ES DE PRO,
25795 5ELCID3285 CA NON ME PRISO AELLA FIJO DE ****** NADA,
WORD #2819 OCCURS 39 TIMES.
INDEX OF DIVERSIFICATION = 634.71 WITH STANCARD DEVIATION OF 889.28

MUGIERES 120 5ELCID0016 EN SU CONPA@A LX PENDONES; EXIEN LO UER ******** & UARONES,
9271 5ELCID1149 FIJOS & ******** VER LO MURIR DE FANBRE.
16368 5ELCID2076 QUE LAS DEDES POR ******** ALOS YFANTES DE CARRION.
17650 5ELCID2233 QUE LAS TOMASSEDES POR ******** A ONDRA & A RECABDO.
20038 5ELCID2543 PIDAMOS NUESTRAS ******** AL %ID CAMPEADOR,
20180 5ELCID2562 DAD NOS NUESTRAS ******** QUE AUEMOS ABENDI%IONES;
20347 5ELCID2581 A MIS FIJAS SIRUADES, QUE UUESTRAS ******** SON;
21270 5ELCID2703 CON SUS ******** EN BRA%OS DEMUESTRAN LES AMOR;
21322 5ELCID2710 SI NON AMAS SUS ******** DO@A ELUIRA & DO@A SOL:
26252 5ELCID3347 ELLAS SON ******** & VOS SODES VARONES,
WORD #2820 OCCURS 10 TIMES.
INDEX OF DIVERSIFICATION = 2902.56 WITH STANDARD DEVIATION OF 3368.72

MULA 15520 5ELCID1966 QUI ENVIO POR CASTIELLA TANTA **** PRE%IADA,
15666 5ELCID1987 TANTA GRUESSA **** & TANTO PALAFRE DE SAZON,
16694 5ELCID2114 TANTA GRUESSA **** & TANTO PALAFRE DE SAZON
25465 5ELCID3243 TANTA GRUESSA ****, TANTO PALAFRE DE SAZON,
WORD #2821 OCCURS 4 TIMES.

MULAS 11286 5ELCID1428 PALAFRES & *****, QUE NON PARESCAN MAL.
17818 5ELCID2254 ENTRE PALAFRES & ***** & CORREDORES CAUALLOS,
20264 5ELCID2572 DARUOS E ***** & PALAFRES, MUY GRUESSOS DE SAZON,
WORD #2822 OCCURS 3 TIMES.

MUNDO 2862 5ELCIDC361 TUERES REY DE LOS REYES & DE TODEL ***** PADRE,
8501 5ELCID1080 LO QUE NON FERIE EL CABOSO POR QUANTO ENEL ***** HA,
19554 5ELCID2477 GRADO A CHRISTUS, QUE DEL ***** ES SE@OR,
19668 5ELCID2493 GRADO HA DIOS QUE DEL ***** ES SE@OR

WORD C# PREFIX CONTEXT

MUNDO (CON'T)

```
                     21080 5ELCID2678 TAL COSA UOS FARIA QUE POR EL ***** SONAS,
                     21130 5ELCID2684 DIOS LO QUIERA & LO MANDE, QUE DE TODEL ***** ES SE@OR,
                     22222 5ELCID2830 GRADO A CHRISTUS, QUE DEL ***** ES SE@OR,
           WORD #2823 OCCURS   7 TIMES.
              INDEX OF DIVERSIFICATION =  3225.67 WITH STANDARD DEVIATION OF  4352.02

MUNO                 17142 5ELCID2169 APERO VERMUEZ & **** GUSTIOZ,
                     26502 5ELCID3382 ESSORA **** GUSTIOZ EN PIE SE LEUANTO:
                     27606 5ELCID3525 E **** GUSTIOZ, FIRMES SED EN CAMPO AGUISA DE VARONES;
                     28752 5ELCID3671 LOS DOS HAN ARRANCADO: DIREUOS DE **** GUSTIOZ,
                     28779 5ELCID3675 FIRIO ENEL ESCUDO A DON **** GUSTIOZ,
                     28802 5ELCID3678 ESTE COLPE FECHO, OTRO DIO **** GUSTIOZ,
           WORD #2824 OCCURS   6 TIMES.
              INDEX OF DIVERSIFICATION =  2331.00 WITH STANDARD DEVIATION OF  3967.11

MUNOZ                 5852 5ELCID0741 FELEZ ***** SO SOBRINO DEL CAMPEADOR
                     15701 5ELCID1992 MARTIN ***** & MARTIN ANTOLINEZ, EL BURGALES DE PRO,
                     20626 5ELCID2618  OHERES, MYO SOBRINO, TU, FELEZ *****,
                     20663 5ELCID2623 DIXO FELEZ *****: PLAZME DALMA & DE CORA%ON.
                     20745 5ELCID2634 OYAS, SOBRINO, TU, FELEZ *****
                     21737 5ELCID2764 MAS YO UOS DIRE DAQUEL FELEZ *****.
                     21772 5ELCID2769 EN VN MONTE ESPESSO FELEZ ***** SE METIO,
                     21825 5ELCID2776 POR EL RASTRO TORNOS FELEZ *****,
                     21942 5ELCID2791 ABRIERON LOS OIOS & VIERON AFELEZ *****.
                     22003 5ELCID2799 CON VN SONBRERO QUE TIENE FELEZ *****,
                     22105 5ELCID2813 A SANTESTEUAN VINO FELEZ *****,
                     24066 5ELCID3068 E MARTIN *****, QUE EN BUEN PUNTO NA%IO,
                     24076 5ELCID3069 E MYO SOBRINO FELEZ *****;
           WORD #2825 OCCURS  13 TIMES.
              INDEX OF DIVERSIFICATION =  1517.67 WITH STANDARD DEVIATION OF  2991.68

MU@O                  5826 5ELCID0737 **** GUSTIOZ, QUE FUE SO CRIADO,
                     11514 5ELCID1458 TU, **** GUSTIOZ & PERO VERMUEZ DELANT,
                     11683 5ELCID1481 FABLO **** GUSTIOZ, NON SPERO A NADI:
                     11825 5ELCID1499 AFEUOS AQUI PERO VERMUEZ & **** GUSTIOZ QUE UOS QUIEREN SIN HART,
                     15720 5ELCID1995 **** GUSTIOZ, EL CAUALLERO DE PRO.
                     17212 5ELCID2177 DIXO MYO %ID ADON PERO & A **** GUSTIOZ:
                     18365 5ELCID2324 OYO LA PORIDAD AQUEL **** GUSTIOZ,
                     22764 5ELCID2901 OERES, **** GUSTIOZ, MYO VASSALLO DE PRO,
                     22900 5ELCID2917 **** GUSTIOZ PRIUADO CAUALGO,
                     22980 5ELCID2927 ASSI COMMO DESCAUALGA AQUEL **** GUSTIOZ
                     23016 5ELCID2932 VIOLOS EL REY & CONNOS%IO A **** GUSTIOZ;
                     23032 5ELCID2934 DELANT EL REY FINCO LOS YNOIOS AQUEL **** GUSTIOZ,
                     23039 5ELCID2935 BESABA LE LOS PIES AQUEL **** GUSTIOZ;
                     23199 5ELCID2955 E VERDAD DIZES EN ESTO, TU, **** GUSTIOZ,
                     23345 5ELCID2974 ESPIDIOS **** GUSTIOZ, A MYO %ID ES TORNADO.
                     24049 5ELCID3065 E PERO VERMUEZ & AQUESTE **** GUSTIOZ
           WORD #2826 OCCURS  16 TIMES.
              INDEX OF DIVERSIFICATION =  1213.87 WITH STANDARD DEVIATION OF  1869.11

MU@OZ                 5833 5ELCID0738 MARTIN *****, EL QUE MANDO A MONT MAYOR,
           WORD #2827 OCCURS   1 TIMES.

MUO                  17069 5ELCID2161 HYREMOS EN PODER DE *** %ID A VALEN%IA LA MAYOR;
                     18372 5ELCID2325 VINO CON ESTAS NUEUAS A *** %ID RUYDIAZ EL CANPEADOR:
           WORD #2828 OCCURS   2 TIMES.

MURIERE              13443 5ELCID1704 EL QUE A QUI ******* LIDIANDO DE CARA,
           WORD #2829 OCCURS   1 TIMES.

MURIEREMOS            5442 5ELCID0687 SI NOS ********** EN CAMPO, EN CASTIELLO NOS ENTRARAN,
           WORD #2830 OCCURS   1 TIMES.

MURIR                 9274 5ELCID1149 FIJOS & MUGIERES VER LO ***** DE FANBRE.
           WORD #2831 OCCURS   1 TIMES.

MURUIEDRO             8627 5ELCID1095 EL CON TODO ESTO PRISO A *********.
                      8668 5ELCID1101 A%ERCA DE ********* TORNAN TIENDAS AFINCAR.
                      9058 5ELCID1153 ENTRAUAN A ********* CON ESTAS GANAN%IAS QUE TRAEN GRANDES.
                      9319 5ELCID1185 SALIO DE ********* VNA NOCH EN TRASNOCHADA,
                      9407 5ELCID1196 TORNAUAS A *********, CA EL SE LA A GANADA.
                     10481 5ELCID1328 PRISO A ALMENAR & A ********* QUE ES MIYOR,
           WORD #2832 OCCURS   6 TIMES.
              INDEX OF DIVERSIFICATION =   369.80 WITH STANDARD DEVIATION OF   417.03

MUY                   1432 5ELCID0183 SOBRELLA VNA SAUANA DE RAN%AL & *** BLANCA.
                      2782 5ELCID0351 ESTANDO EN LA CRUZ, VERTUD FEZIST *** GRANT.
                      3588 5ELCID0452 FAZED ME MANDADO *** PRIUADO ALA %AGA;
                      5466 5ELCID0690 COMMO SODES *** BUENO, TENER LA EDES SIN ARCH;
                      6407 5ELCID0817 TODOS CON SIELLAS & *** BIEN ENFRENADOS,
                      7485 5ELCID0960 EL CONDE ES *** FOLON & DIXO VNA VANIDAT:
                      8372 5ELCID1064 DAN LE TRES PALAFRES *** BIEN ENSELLADOS
                      8405 5ELCID1068 HYA UOS YDES, CONDE, AGUISA DE *** FRANCO,
                     13534 5ELCID1715 DE TODAS GUARNIZONES *** BIEN ES ADOBADO.
```

WORD C# PREFIX CONTEXT

MUY (CON'T)

15616 5ELCID1980 CUENDES & PODESTADES & *** GRANDES MESNADAS.
18714 5ELCID2368 AFEUOS EL OBISPO DON IHERONIMO *** BIEN ARMADO,
19504 5ELCID2471 FUERON EN VALENZIA *** BIEN ARREADOS,
20267 5ELCID2572 DARUOS E MULAS & PALAFRES, *** GRUESSOS DE SAZON,
21185 5ELCID2691 ASSINIESTRO DEXAN ATINEZA, VNA PE@A *** FUERT,
22354 5ELCID2847 VARONES DE SANTESTEUAN, A GUISA DE *** PROS,
24025 5ELCID3062 E SSU OFRENDA HAN FECHA *** BUENA & CONPLIDA.
25616 5ELCID3262 CON *** GRAND ONDRA & AVERES A NOMBRE;
28131 5ELCID3592 *** BIEN ACONPA@ADOS, CA MUCHOS PARIENTES SON.
WORD #2833 OCCURS 18 TIMES.
INDEX OF DIVERSIFICATION = 1569.53 WITH STANDARD DEVIATION OF 1178.08

MY
1730 5ELCID0221 VUESTRA UERTUD ME UALA, GLORIOSA, EN ** EXIDA & ME AIUDE,
2262 5ELCID0284 E UOS, MUGIER ONDRADA, DE ** SEADES SERUIDA
9823 5ELCID1247 DE QUE SON PAGADOS; EL AMOR DE ** %ID YA LO YUAN PROUANDO.
11575 5ELCID1467 ** MUGIER & MIS FIJAS CON MYNAYA ALBARFFANEZ,
11586 5ELCID1468 ASI COMMO A ** DIXIERON, HY LOS PODREDES FALAR;
12651 5ELCID1605 ** CORA%ON & MI ALMA,
16002 5ELCID2029 SIESTO NON FECHES, NON AUREDES ** AMOR.
16042 5ELCID2034 AQUI UOS PERDONO & DOUOS ** AMOR,
16134 5ELCID2046 FUESSEDES ** HUESPED, SIUOS PLOGIESSE, SE@OR.
24652 5ELCID3140 JURO PAR SANT ESIDRO, EL QUE BOLUIERE ** CORT
WORD #2834 OCCURS 10 TIMES.
INDEX OF DIVERSIFICATION = 2545.89 WITH STANDARD DEVIATION OF 3299.08

MYANAYA
11208 5ELCID1418 DIZIENDO ESTO *******: ESTO FERE DE VELUNTAD.
12324 5ELCID1565 QUE RE%IBAN A ******* & ALAS DUENAS FIJAS DALGO;
WORD #2835 OCCURS 2 TIMES.

MYEDO
8484 5ELCID1079 ***** YUA AUIENDO QUE MYO %ID SE REPINTRA,
WORD #2836 OCCURS 1 TIMES.

MYNAYA
5815 5ELCID0735 ****** ALBARFANEZ, QEU CORITA MANDO,
5873 5ELCID0744 A ****** ALBARFANEZ MATARON LE EL CAUALLO,
5938 5ELCID0753 CAUALGAD, ******, UOS SODES EL MYO DIESTRO BRA%O
6141 5ELCID0782 DIZE ******: AGORA SO PAGADO,
6359 5ELCID0810 OYD, ******, SODES MYO DIESTRO BRA%O
6416 5ELCID0819 DIXO ****** ALBARFANEZ: ESTO FARE YO DE GRADO.
6470 5ELCID0826 ****** ALBARFANEZ DESTO ES PAGADO; POR YR CON EL OMNES SON CONTADOS.
6501 5ELCID0829 HYDES UOS, ******, ACASTIELLA LA GENTIL?
6843 5ELCID0874 QUIN LOS DIO ESTOS, SI UOS VALA DIOS, ******
9790 5ELCID1244 CON EL ****** ALBARFFANEZ QUE NOS LE PARTE DE SO BRA%O.
10000 5ELCID1267 GRADO A DIOS, ******, & A SANTA MARIA MADRE
10795 5ELCID1367 ****** ALBARFANEZ LAS MANOS LE BESO.
10895 5ELCID1379 HYA UOS YDES, ******?, YD ALA GRA%IA DEL CRIADOR
10933 5ELCID1384 ESPIDIOS ****** & VASSE DELA CORT.
10983 5ELCID1390 RESPUSO ******: ESTO NON MEA POR QUE PESAR.
10992 5ELCID1391 HYDO ES ******, TORNANSSE LOS YFFANTES.
11013 5ELCID1394 DE%IDO ES ******, ASSAN PERO VA ROGAR,
11100 5ELCID1405 DIO TRES CAUALLEROS ****** ALBARFANEZ,
11581 5ELCID1467 MY MUGIER & MIS FIJAS CON ****** ALBARFFANEZ,
11789 5ELCID1495 ENVIO DOS CAUALLEROS ****** ALBARFANEZ QUE SOPIESSE LA VERDAD;
11871 5ELCID1505 ESSORA DIXO ******: VAYMOS CAUALGAR.
13356 5ELCID1693 FABLAUA ******, NON LO QUISO DETARDAR:
13990 5ELCID1772 ****** ALBARFANEZ FUERA ERA ENEL CAMPO,
14262 5ELCID1804 DO SODES, CABOSO? VENID ACA, ******;
14355 5ELCID1815 MANDO A PERO VERMUEZ QUE FUESSE CON ******.
14459 5ELCID1828 ENVIAUA LE MANDADO PERO VERMUEZ & ******,
14553 5ELCID1841 ****** & PER VERMUEZ ADELANT SON LEGADOS,
14982 5ELCID1894 A ****** ALBARFANEZ & A PERO VERMUEZ
15003 5ELCID1897 OYD ME, ******, & VOS, PER VERMUEZ:
15079 5ELCID1907 FABLO ****** & PLOGO A PER VERMUEZ:
15167 5ELCID1919 VENIDES, ******, & VOS, PERO VERMUEZ
15694 5ELCID1991 ****** ALBARFANEZ & AQUEL PERO VERMUEZ,
18656 5ELCID2361 AQUI LEGO ****** ALBARFANEZ: OYD, YA %ID, CANPEADOR LEAL
19334 5ELCID2449 ****** ALBARFANEZ ESSORA ES LEGADO,
20170 5ELCID2561 EA ****** ALBARFANEZ & A QUANTOS AQUI SON:
22342 5ELCID2846 QUE VINIE ****** POR SUS PRIMAS AMAS ADOS.
24030 5ELCID3063 VOS, ****** ALBARFANEZ, EL MYO BRA%O MEIOR,
26841 5ELCID3429 ****** ALBAFANEZ EN PIE SE LEUANTO:
26885 5ELCID3435 DEZID, ******, LO QUE OUIEREDES SABOR.
WORD #2837 OCCURS 39 TIMES.
INDEX OF DIVERSIFICATION = 553.47 WITH STANDARD DEVIATION OF 850.91

MYNAYA.
15195 5ELCID1923 DIXO ******* CALMA & DE CORA%ON
WORD #2838 OCCURS 1 TIMES.

MYO
37 5ELCID0006 SOSPIRO *** %ID, CA MUCHO AUIE GRANDES CUYDADOS.
45 5ELCID0007 FFABLO *** %ID BIEN & TAN MESURADO:
90 5ELCID0013 ME%IO *** %ID LOS OMBROS & ENGRAMEO LA TIESTA:
105 5ELCID0015 *** %ID RUY DIAZ POR BURGOS ENTRAUA,
188 5ELCID0025 QUE A *** %ID RUY DIAZ, QUE NADI NOL DIESSEN POSADA,
233 5ELCID0030 ASCONDEN SE DE *** %ID, CA NOL OSAN DEZIR NADA.
277 5ELCID0035 LOS DE *** %ID A ALTAS UOZES LAMAN,

WORD C# PREFIX CONTEXT

MYO (CON'T)

292 5ELCID0037 AGUIIO *** %ID, ALA PUERTA SE LEGAUA,
452 5ELCID0058 *** %ID RUY DIAZ, EL QUE EN BUEN ORA %INXO ESPADA,
480 5ELCID0061 ASSI POSO *** %ID CCMMO SI FUESSE EN MONTA@A.
539 5ELCID0069 PAGOS *** %ID EL CAMPEADOR & TODOS LOS OTROS QUEUAN ASO %ERUICIO
614 5ELCID0078 FABLO *** %ID, EL QUE EN BUEN ORA %INXO ESPADA:
1025 5ELCID0132 *** %ID QUERRA LO QUE SSEA AGUISADO;
1195 5ELCID0154 SONRRISOS *** %ID, ESTAUALOS FABLANDO:
1236 5ELCID0159 DON RACHEL & VIDAS A *** %ID BESARON LE LAS MANOS.
1286 5ELCID0165 NON LES DIESSE *** %ID DELA GANAN%IA UN DINERO MALO.
1320 5ELCID0169 CA AMOUER A *** %ID ANTE QUE CANTE EL GALLO.
1664 5ELCID0214 *** %ID & SUS CONPA@AS CAUALGAN TAN AYNA.
1795 5ELCID0228 DIXO MARTIN ANTOLINEZ: VERE ALA MUGIER ATODO *** SOLAZ,
1827 5ELCID0232 TORNAUAS MARTIN ANTOLINEZ A BURGOS & *** %ID AAGUIJAR
1896 5ELCID0241 TU QUE ATODOS QUIAS, VALA *** %ID EL CANPEADOR.
1938 5ELCID0246 GRADESCO LO ADIOS, *** %ID, DIXO EL ABBAT DON SANCHO;
2290 5ELCID0288 COMMO SEUA DE TIERRA *** %ID EL CANPEADOR;
2339 5ELCID0295 QUANDO LO SOPO *** %ID EL DE BIUAR,
2367 5ELCID0299 FABLO *** %ID DE TODA VOLUNTAD:
2443 5ELCID0308 MANDO EL REY A *** %ID A AGUARDAR,
2547 5ELCID0322 CUEMO LO MANDO *** %ID, ASSI LO AN TODOS HA FAR.
2576 5ELCID0326 *** %ID & SU MUGIER A LA EGLESIA UAN.
2882 5ELCID0364 POR *** %ID EL CAMPEADOR, QUE DIOS LE CURIE DE MAL.
2983 5ELCID0376 *** %ID CON LOS SOS VASSALLOS PENSSO DE CAUALGAR,
3123 5ELCID0393 VINO *** %ID IAZER A SPINAZ DE CAN.
3194 5ELCID0402 ALA FIGERUELA *** %ID IUA POSAR.
3207 5ELCID0404 Y SE ECHAUA *** %ID DESPUES QUE FUE %ENADO,
3308 5ELCID0417 MANDO UER SUS YENTES *** %ID EL CAMPEADOR:
3393 5ELCID0428 FIZO *** %ID POSAR & %EUADA DAR.
3429 5ELCID0433 POR TAL LO FAZE *** %ID QUE NO IO VENTASSE NADI.
3451 5ELCID0436 *** %ID SE ECHO EN %ELADA CON AQUELOS QUE EL TRAE.
3610 5ELCID0455 E LOS QUE CON *** %ID FICARAN EN LA %AGA.
3699 5ELCID0467 *** %ID DON RODRIGO ALA PUERTA ADELI@AUA;
3756 5ELCID0475 DEXAN LA A *** %ID, TODO ESTO NON PRE%IA NADA.
3990 5ELCID0507 COMIDIOS *** %ID, EL QUE EN BUEN ORA FUE NADO,
4050 5ELCID0515 TODA LA QUINTA A *** %ID FINCAUA.
4105 5ELCID0522 PLOGO A *** %ID DA QUESTA PRESENTAIA.
4117 5ELCID0524 ASMO *** %ID CON TODA SU CONPA@A
4226 5ELCID0538 CON ALFONSSO *** SE@OR NON QUERRIA LIDIAR.
4294 5ELCID0547 ENTRE FARIZA & %ETINA *** %ID YUA ALBERGAR.
4321 5ELCID0550 OTRO DIA MOUIOS *** %ID EL DE BIUAR,
4344 5ELCID0553 E SOBRE ALCO%ER *** %ID YUA POSAR,
4424 5ELCID0563 QUE SOPIESSEN QUE *** %ID ALLI AUIE FINCAN%A.
4439 5ELCID0565 QUE EL CAMPEADOR *** %ID ALLI AUIE POBLADO,
4463 5ELCID0568 AGARDANDO SEUA *** %ID CON TODOS SUS VASSALLOS;
4481 5ELCID0570 LOS DE ALCO%ER A *** %ID YAL DAN PARIAS DE GRADO
4506 5ELCID0573 ALI YOGO *** %ID COMPLIDAS XV SEMMANAS.
4513 5ELCID0574 QUANDO VIO *** %ID QUE ALCO%ER NON SELE DAUA;
4586 5ELCID0583 DEGUISA UA *** %ID COMMO SIESCAPASSE DE ARRANCADA.
4630 5ELCID0588 *** %ID, QUANDO LOS VIO FUERA, COGIOS COMMO DE ARRANCADA.
4738 5ELCID0601 *** %ID & ALBARFANEZ ADELANT AGUIIAUAN;
4761 5ELCID0604 LOS VASSALLOS DE *** %ID SIN PIEDAD LES DAUAN,
4813 5ELCID0610 *** %ID GA@O A ALCO%ER, SABENT, POR ESTA MA@A.
4840 5ELCID0613 FABLO *** %ID RUY DIAZ, EL QUE EN BUEN ORA FUE NADO:
4920 5ELCID0623 *** %ID CON ESTA GANAN%IA EN ALCO%ER ESTA;
4965 5ELCID0628 QUE A VNO QUE DIZIEN *** %ID RUY DIAZ DE BIUAR
5178 5ELCID0655 AL BUENO DE *** %ID EN ALCO%ER LEUAN %ERCAR.
5225 5ELCID0661 ALOS DE *** %ID YA LES TUELLEN EL AGUA.
5234 5ELCID0662 MESNADAS DE *** %ID EXIR QUERIEN ALA BATALLA,
5264 5ELCID0666 *** %ID CON LOS SOS TORNOS A ACORDAR:
5411 5ELCID0683 ARMADO ES *** %ID CON QUANTOS QUE EL HA;
5419 5ELCID0684 FABLAUA *** %ID COMMO ODREDES CONTAR:
5564 5ELCID0701 PORA *** %ID & ALOS SOS A MANOS LOS TOMAR.
5868 5ELCID0743 ACORREN LA SE@A & A *** %ID EL CAMPEADOR.
5901 5ELCID0748 VIOLO *** %ID RUY DIAZ EL CASTELANO,
5942 5ELCID0753 CAUALGAD, MYNAYA, UOS SODES EL *** DIESTRO BRA%O
5981 5ELCID0759 *** %ID RUY DIAZ, EL QUE EN BUEN ORA NASCO,
6080 5ELCID0772 LOS DE *** %ID FIRIENDO EN ALCAZ,
6152 5ELCID0784 QUE *** %ID RUY DIAZ LID CAMPAL A VEN%IDA.
6187 5ELCID0788 ANDAUA *** %ID SOBRE SO BUEN CAUALLO,
6232 5ELCID0794 ESTA ALBERGADA LOS DE *** %ID LUEGO LA AN ROBADA
6296 5ELCID0802 MANDO *** %ID AUN QUELES DIESSEN ALGO.
6306 5ELCID0803 GRANT A EL GOZO *** %ID CON TODOS SOS VASSALOS.
6361 5ELCID0810 OYD, MYNAYA, SODES *** DIESTRO BRA%O
6490 5ELCID0828 *** %ID RUY DIAZ CON LOS SOS SE ACORDAUA:
6573 5ELCID0839 TODOS LOS DIAS A *** %ID AGUARDAUAN
6628 5ELCID0846 *** %ID RUY DIAZ A ALCOL%ER ES VENIDO;
6670 5ELCID0851 QUANDO *** %ID EL CASTIELLO QUISO QUITAR,
6684 5ELCID0853 VASTE, *** %ID; NUESTRAS ORA%IONES UAYANTE DELANTE
6701 5ELCID0855 QUANDO QUITO A ALCO%ER *** %ID EL DE BIUAR,
6751 5ELCID0862 AGUIJO *** %ID, YUAS CAEA DELANT,
6809 5ELCID0870 *** %ID RUY DIAZ DE DIOS AYA SU GRA%IA
6844 5ELCID0875 *** %ID RUY DIAZ, QUE EN BUEN ORA CINXO ESPADA. . .
6924 5ELCID0885 AUN ME PLAZE DE *** %ID QUE FIZO TAL GANAN%IA.
6967 5ELCID0891 DE TODO *** REYNO LOS QUE LO QUISIEREN FAR,

WORD C# PREFIX CONTEXT

MYO (CON'T)

6978 5ELCID0892 BUE@OS & VALIENTES PORA *** %ID HUYAR,
7023 5ELCID0898 SI NULLA DUBDA YD A *** %ID BUSCAR GANAN%IA.
7058 5ELCID0902 EL POYO DE *** %ID ASIL DIRAN POR CARTA.
7173 5ELCID0919 QUANDO VIO *** %ID ASOMAR A MINAYA,
7343 5ELCID0942 DE *** %ID RUY DIAZ QUE NON TEMIEN NINGUNA FONTA.
7367 5ELCID0945 PLOGO A *** %ID, & MUCHO A ALBARFANEZ.
7421 5ELCID0952 DENT CORRE *** %ID A HUESCA & A MONT ALUAN;
7464 5ELCID0958 QUE *** %ID RUY DIAZ QUEL CORRIE LA TIERRA TODA;
7495 5ELCID0961 GRANDES TUERTOS ME TIENE *** %ID EL DE BIUAR.
7561 5ELCID0969 ADELINAN TRAS *** %ID EL BUENO DE BIUAR,
7577 5ELCID0971 ALCON%ARON A *** %ID EN TEUAR & EL PINAR;
7595 5ELCID0973 *** %ID DON RODRIGO TRAE GRAND GANAN%IA,
7618 5ELCID0976 *** %ID QUANDO LO OYO, ENBIO PORA ALLA:
7816 5ELCID1000 TODOS SON ADOBADOS QUANDO *** %ID ESTO OUO FABLADO;
7848 5ELCID1004 MANDO LOS FERIR *** %ID, EL QUE EN BUEN ORA NASCO;
7952 5ELCID1016 PLOGO A *** %ID, CA GRANDES SON LAS GANAN%IAS.
7960 5ELCID1017 A *** %ID DON RODRIGO GRANT COZINAL ADOBAUAN;
8017 5ELCID1024 *** %ID RUY DIAZ ODREDES LO QUE DIXO:
8091 5ELCID1033 DIXO *** %ID: COMED, CONDE, ALGO, CASI NON COMEDES, NON VEREDES
8315 5ELCID1058 PAGADO ES *** %ID, QUE LO ESTA AGUARDANDO,
8335 5ELCID1060 SI UOS PLOGUIERE, *** %ID, DE YR SOMOS GUISADOS;
8444 5ELCID1073 DE LO UUESTRO, O DELO *** LEUAREDES ALGO.
8449 5ELCID1074 FOLGEDES, YA *** %ID, SODES EN UUESTRO SALUO.
8488 5ELCID1079 MYEDO YUA AUIENDO QUE *** %ID SE REPINTRA,
8540 5ELCID1085 AQUIS CONPIE%A LA GESTA DE *** %ID EL DE BIUAR.
8558 5ELCID1087 POBLADO HA *** %ID EL PUERTO DE ALUCANT,
8596 5ELCID1092 *** %ID GA@O AXERICA & A ONDA & ALMENAR,
8630 5ELCID1096 YA VIE *** %ID QUE DIOS LE YUA VALIENDO.
8673 5ELCID1102 VIOLO *** %ID, TOMOS AMARAUILLAR: GRADO ATI, PADRE SPIRITAL
8930 5ELCID1137 CON LOS ALUORES *** %ID FERIR LOS VA:
8959 5ELCID1140 CA YO SO RUYDIAZ, *** %ID EL DE BIUAR
9068 5ELCID1154 LAS NUEUAS DE *** %ID, SABET, SONANDO VAN,
9184 5ELCID1169 EN GANAR AQUELAS VILLAS *** %ID DURO IIJ A@OS.
9218 5ELCID1173 EN CADA VNO DESTOS A@OS *** %ID LES TOLIO EL PAN.
9311 5ELCID1184 SOPOLO *** %ID, DE CORA%ON LE PLAZ;
9357 5ELCID1190 VINIESSE A *** %ID QUE A SABOR DE CAUALGAR;
9397 5ELCID1195 ESTO DIXO *** %ID EL QUE EN BUEN ORA NASCO.
9440 5ELCID1200 CRE%IENDO UA RIQUEZA A *** %ID EL DE BIUAR.
9447 5ELCID1201 QUANDO VIO *** %ID LAS GENTES IUNTADAS, COMPE%OS DE PAGAR.
9455 5ELCID1202 *** %ID DON RODRIGO NON LO QUISO DETARDAR,
9473 5ELCID1204 BIEN LA %ERCA *** %ID, QUE NON Y AUYA HART;
9496 5ELCID1207 MAS LE VIENEN A *** %ID, SABET, QUE NOS LE VAN.
9532 5ELCID1212 QUANDO *** %ID GA@O A VALEN%IA & ENTRO ENLA %IBDAD.
9567 5ELCID1216 *** %ID DON RODRIGO LA QUINTA MANDO TOMAR,
9610 5ELCID1221 YA FOLGAUA *** %ID CON TODAS SUS CONPA@AS;
9646 5ELCID1226 ARRANCOLOS *** %ID EL DELA LUENGA BARBA.
9682 5ELCID1231 TORNADO ES *** %ID CON TODA ESTA GANAN%IA.
9727 5ELCID1237 CON *** %ID RUY DIAZ, EL QUE EN BUEN ORA NASCO.
9745 5ELCID1239 DIXO *** %ID DE LA SU BOCA ATANTO:
9780 5ELCID1243 *** %ID DON RODRIGO EN VALEN%IA ESTA FOLGANDO,
9842 5ELCID1249 VELLO *** %ID CON LOS AVERES QUE AUIEN TOMADOS,
9861 5ELCID1251 ESTO MANDO *** %ID, MINAYA LO OUO CONSSEIADO:
9985 5ELCID1265 TRES MILL & SEYS %IENTOS AUIE *** %ID EL DE BIUAR;
10042 5ELCID1272 AL REY ALFONSSO *** SE@OR NATURAL;
10095 5ELCID1279 LA MUGIER DE *** %ID & SUS FIJAS LAS YFFANTES
10136 5ELCID1284 CIENTO OMNES LE DIO *** %ID A ALBARFANEZ POR SERUIR LE EN
LA CARRERA,
10204 5ELCID1292 LAS PROUEZAS DE *** %ID ANDAUALAS DEMANDANDO,
10237 5ELCID1296 QUANDO LO OYO *** %ID, DE AQUESTO FUE PAGADO:
10431 5ELCID1322 BESAUA UOS LAS MANOS *** %ID LIDIADOR,
10845 5ELCID1373 MUCHO CRE%EN LAS NUEUAS DE *** %ID EL CAMPEADOR,
10866 5ELCID1376 *** %ID ES DE BIUAR & NOS DELOS CONDES DE CARRION.
10960 5ELCID1387 SALUDAD NOS A *** %ID EL DE BIUAR,
11042 5ELCID1398 SALUDA UOS *** %ID ALLA ONDE ELLE ESTA;
11104 5ELCID1406 ENVIOLOS A *** %ID, AVALEN%IA DO ESTA,
11194 5ELCID1416 HYR SE QUIERE A VALEN%IA A *** %ID EL DE BIUAR.
11480 5ELCID1454 AL ORA QUE LO SOPO *** %ID EL DE BIUAR,
11556 5ELCID1464 TIENELA AUEGALUON, *** AMIGO ES DE PAZ,
11671 5ELCID1479 VENIDES, LOS VASSALLOS DE *** AMIGO NATURAL?
11689 5ELCID1482 *** %ID UOS SALUDAUA, & MANDOLO RECABDAR,
11857 5ELCID1503 POR SABOR DE *** %ID DE GRAND ONDRAL DAR;
12114 5ELCID1537 ONDRADO ES *** %ID EN VALEN%IA DO ESTAUA
12300 5ELCID1562 ALEGRE FUE *** %ID, QUE NUNQUA MAS NIN TANTO,
12362 5ELCID1570 MANDO *** %ID ALOS QUE HA EN SU CASA
12400 5ELCID1574 AVN NON SABIE *** %ID, EL QUE EN BUEN ORA %INXO ESPADA,
12499 5ELCID1586 *** %ID SALIO SOBREL, & ARMAS DE FUSTE TOMAUA,
12548 5ELCID1592 EN CABO DEL COSSO *** %ID DESCALGAUA,
12686 5ELCID1610 ADELINO *** %ID CON ELLAS AL ALCA%AR,
12740 5ELCID1618 *** %ID & SUS CONPANAS TAN AGRAND SABOR ESTAN.
12781 5ELCID1622 PESOL AL REY DE MARRUECOS DE *** %ID DON RODRIGO:
12832 5ELCID1628 VAN BUSCAR A VALEN%IA A *** %ID DON RODRIGO.
12848 5ELCID1630 LEGARON A VALEN%IA, LA QUE *** %ID A CONQUISTA,
12863 5ELCID1632 ESTAS NUEUAS A *** %ID ERAN VENIDAS;
13262 5ELCID1682 TORNADOS SON A *** %ID LOS QUE COMIEN SO PAN;
13280 5ELCID1684 ALEGRE ES *** %ID POR QUANTO FECHO HAN:

WORD C# PREFIX CONTEXT

MYO (CON'T)

13524 5ELCID1714 DIO SALTO *** %ID EN BAUIECA EL SO CAUALLO;
13551 5ELCID1717 QUATRO MILL MENOS XXX CON *** %ID VAN A CABO,
13585 5ELCID1722 *** %ID ENPLEO LA LANZA, AL ESPADA METIO MANO,
13634 5ELCID1728 *** %ID EL DE BIUAR FASTA ALLI LEGO EN ALCAZ,
13699 5ELCID1736 MESNADAS DE *** %ID ROBADO AN EL CANPO;
13721 5ELCID1739 ALEGRE ERA *** %ID & TODOS SOS VASSALLOS,
13782 5ELCID1747 *** %ID FINCO ANTELLAS, TOUO LA RYENDA AL CAUALLO:
13861 5ELCID1756 ESTO DIXO *** %ID, DI%IENDO DEL CAUALLO.
14069 5ELCID1782 QUANDO A *** %ID CAYERON TANTOS, LOS OTROS BIEN PUEDEN
FINCAR PAGADOS.
14089 5ELCID1784 QUE A GANADO *** %ID CON TODOS SUS VASSALLOS
14115 5ELCID1787 MANDO *** %ID RUY DIAZ QUE FITA SOUIESSE LA TIENDA,
14150 5ELCID1791 QUE CROUIESSE SOS NUEUAS DE *** %ID QUE AUIE ALGO.
14195 5ELCID1797 *** %ID DON RODRIGO, EL QUE EN BUEN ORA NASCO,
14250 5ELCID1803 EL BUENO DE *** %ID NON LO TARDO POR NADA:
14466 5ELCID1830 *** %ID EL DE VALEN%IA ENBIA SU PRESENTAIA.
14587 5ELCID1846 POR *** %ID EL CAMPEADOR TODO ESTO VOS BESAMOS;
14671 5ELCID1856 GRADESCOLO A *** %ID QUE TAL DON ME HA ENBIADO;
14782 5ELCID1868 ESTOS DOZIENTOS CAUALLOS QUEM ENBIA *** %ID.
14784 5ELCID1869 *** REYNO ADELANT MEIOR ME PODRA SERUIR.
14824 5ELCID1873 QUE BIEN PARESCADES ANTE RUY DIAZ *** %ID;
15009 5ELCID1898 SIRUEM *** %ID EL CAMPEADOR, EL LO MERE%E,
15128 5ELCID1913 ANDAR LE QUIERO A *** %ID EN TODA PRO.
15160 5ELCID1918 SONRRISOS *** %ID & BIEN LOS ABRA%O:
15185 5ELCID1921 COMMO SON LAS SALUDES DE ALFONSSO *** SENOR.
15207 5ELCID1925 DIXO *** %ID: GRADO AL CRIADOR
15250 5ELCID1931 QUANDO LO OYO *** %ID EL BUEN CAMPEADOR,
15266 5ELCID1933 ESTO GRADESCO A CHRISTUS EL *** SE@OR.
15437 5ELCID1955 AYAMOS VISTAS QUANDO LO QUIERE *** SE@OR.
15502 5ELCID1964 NON LO DETARDAN, A *** %ID SE TORNAUAN.
15652 5ELCID1985 DENTRO EN VALLEN%IA *** %ID EL CAMPEADOR
15851 5ELCID2011 *** %ID SELOS GA@ARA, QUE NON GELOS DIERAN EN DON.
16013 5ELCID2031 MER%ED UOS PIDO AUOS, *** NATURAL SE@OR,
16046 5ELCID2035 EN TODO *** REYNO PARTE DESDE OY.
16052 5ELCID2036 FABLO *** %ID & DIXO: MER%ED; YOLO RE%IBO, ALFONSSO MYO SE@OR;
16060 5ELCID2036 FABLO MYO %ID & DIXO: MER%ED; YOLO RE%IBO, ALFONSSO *** SE@OR;
16105 5ELCID2043 FABLO *** %ID & DIXO ESTA RAZON: ESTO GRADESCO AL CRIADOR,
16122 5ELCID2044 QUANDO HE LA GRA%IA DE DON ALFONSSO *** SE@OR;
16153 5ELCID2049 *** HUESPED SEREDES, %ID CAMPEADOR,
16169 5ELCID2051 BESO LE LA MANO *** CID, LO OTORGO.
16203 5ELCID2056 *** %ID RUY DIAZ, QUE EN ORA BUENA NASCO,
16240 5ELCID2060 MARAUILLAN SE DE *** %ID QUANTOS QUE Y SON.
16280 5ELCID2065 DE TAL GUISA LOS PAGA *** %ID EL CAMPEADOR,
16343 5ELCID2073 COMETER QUIERO VN RUEGO A *** %ID EL CAMPEADOR;
16408 5ELCID2081 DANDOS LAS, *** %ID, SI UOS VALA EL CRIADOR
16638 5ELCID2108 *** %ID GELOS RE%IBE, LAS MANOS LE BESO:
16688 5ELCID2113 AQUIS METIO EN NUEUAS *** %ID EL CAMPEADOR;
16701 5ELCID2115 CONPE%O *** %ID ADAR AQUIEN QUIERE PRENDER SO DON,
16725 5ELCID2118 *** %ID DELOS CAUALLOS LX DIO EN DON.
16762 5ELCID2122 METIOLOS EN PODER DE *** %ID EL CAMPEADOR:
16801 5ELCID2127 SOBREL SO CAUALLO BAUIECA *** %ID SALTO DAUA;
16809 5ELCID2128 AQUI LO DIGO ANTE *** SE@OR EL REY ALFONSSO:
16988 5ELCID2151 *** %ID RUY DIAZ, MUCHO ME AUEDES ONDRADO,
17030 5ELCID2156 HYAS ESPIDIO *** %ID DE SO SE@OR ALFONSSO,
17086 5ELCID2163 HE DELAS FIJAS DE *** %ID, DE DON ELUIRA & DO@A SOL.
17147 5ELCID2170 EN CASA DE *** %ID NON A DOS MEIORES,
17194 5ELCID2175 AFELOS EN VALEN%IA, LA QUE *** %ID GA@O;
17206 5ELCID2177 DIXO *** %ID ADON PERO & A MU@O GUSTIOZ:
17258 5ELCID2183 *** %ID EL CAMPEADOR AL ALCA%AR ENTRAUA;
17393 5ELCID2200 PEDIDAS UOS HA & ROGADAS EL *** SE@OR ALFONSSO,
17499 5ELCID2214 RE%IBIO LOS *** %ID CON TODOS SUS VASALLOS;
17522 5ELCID2217 TODOS LOS DE *** %ID TAN BIEN SON ACORDADOS,
17664 5ELCID2235 A *** %ID & A SU MUGIER VAN BESAR LA MANO.
17739 5ELCID2245 *** %ID DELO QUE VEYE MUCHO ERA PAGADO:
17776 5ELCID2249 E AL OTRO DIA FIZO *** %ID FINCAR VIJ TABLADOS:
17805 5ELCID2253 *** %ID DON RODRIGO, EL QUE EN BUEN ORA NASCO,
17903 5ELCID2265 POR PAGADOS SE PARTEN DE *** %ID & DE SUS VASSALLOS.
17979 5ELCID2275 QUES PAGE DES CASAMIENTO *** %ID O EL QUE LO ALGO
18005 5ELCID2278 EN VALEN%IA SEY *** %ID CON TODOS SUS VASSALLOS,
18145 5ELCID2296 *** %ID FINCO EL CODDO, EN PIE SE LEUANTO,
18171 5ELCID2299 ANTE *** %ID LA CABE%A PREMIO & EL ROSTRO FINCO;
18180 5ELCID2300 *** %ID DON RODRIGO ALCUELLO LO TOMO,
18207 5ELCID2304 *** %ID POR SOS YERNOS DEMANDO & NOLOS FALLO;
18244 5ELCID2308 MANDOLO VEDAR *** %ID EL CAMPEADOR.
18419 5ELCID2331 *** %ID DON RODRIGO SONRRISANDO SALIO:
18496 5ELCID2341 PLOGO A *** %ID & ATODOS SOS VASSALLOS;
18580 5ELCID2351 ALA, PERO VERMUEZ, EL *** SOBRINO CARO
18703 5ELCID2367 DIXO *** %ID: AYAMOS MAS DE VAGAR.
18781 5ELCID2377 *** CORA%ON QUE PUDIESSE FOLGAR,
18787 5ELCID2378 EUOS, *** %ID, DE MI MAS UOS PAGAR.
18806 5ELCID2380 ESSORA DIXO *** %ID: LO QUE UOS QUEREDES PLAZ ME.
18956 5ELCID2399 *** %ID CON LOS SUYOS CAE EN ALCAN%A;
18983 5ELCID2402 LOS DE *** %ID ALOS DE BUCAR DELAS TIENDAS LOS SACAN.
19030 5ELCID2408 *** %ID AL REY BUCAR CAYOL EN ALCAZ:
19108 5ELCID2417 AQUI RESPUSO *** %ID: ESTO NON SERA VERDAD.

WORD C# PREFIX CONTEXT

MYO (CON'T)

19195 5ELCID2428 AQUIS CNDRO *** %ID & QUANTOS CONEL SON.
19226 5ELCID2433 *** %ID RUY DIAZ, EL CAMPEADOR CONTADO,
19262 5ELCID2438 ALGO VIE *** %ID DELO QUE ERA PAGADO,
19289 5ELCID2442 ALEGROS *** %ID FERMOSO SONRRISANDO:
19428 5ELCID2462 DIXO *** %ID: YO DESTO SO PAGADO;
19461 5ELCID2466 ALEGRE ES *** %ID CON TODAS SUS CONPA@AS,
19479 5ELCID2468 LOS YERNOS DE *** %ID QUANDO ESTE AUER TOMARON
19519 5ELCID2473 MUCHOS SON ALEGRES *** %ID & SUS VASSALLOS,
19603 5ELCID2484 MANDO *** %ID, EL QUE EN BUEN ORA NASCO,
19762 5ELCID2505 GRANDES SON LOS GOZOS EN VALEN%IA CON *** %ID EL CANPEADOR
19816 5ELCID2512 AQUI ESTA CON *** %ID EL OBISPO DO IHERONIMO,
19844 5ELCID2516 RE%IBIOLOS MINAYA POR *** %ID EL CAMPEADOR:
19959 5ELCID2532 VASSALLOS DE *** %ID SEYEN SE SONRRISANDO:
20231 5ELCID2568 DIXO EL CAMPEADOR: CARUCS FE MYS FIJAS & ALGO DELO ***;
20488 5ELCID2601 ABRA%OLAS *** %ID & SALUDOLAS AMAS ADOS.
20549 5ELCID2609 *** %ID & LOS OTROS DE CAUALGAR PENSSAUAN,
20588 5ELCID2614 ALEGRE VA *** %ID CON TODAS SUS COMPA@AS.
20622 5ELCID2618 OHERES, *** SOBRINO, TU, FELEZ MUNOZ,
20672 5ELCID2624 MINAYA ALBARFANEZ ANTE *** %ID SE PARO:
20755 5ELCID2636 SALUDAD A *** AMIGO EL MORO AVENGALUON:
21006 5ELCID2669 ACAYAZ, CURIATE DESTOS, CA ERES *** SE@OR:
21068 5ELCID2677 SI NOLO DEXAS POR *** %ID EL DE BIUAR,
21983 5ELCID2797 SI UOS LO MERESCA, *** PRIMO, NUESTRO PADRE EL CANPEADOR,
22199 5ELCID2827 QUANDO GELO DIZEN A *** %ID EL CAMPEADOR,
22257 5ELCID2835 PESO A *** %ID & ATODA SU CORT, & ALBARFANEZ DALMA & DE CORA%ON.
22285 5ELCID2838 CON CC CAUALLEROS, QUALES *** %ID MANDO;
22402 5ELCID2853 MUCHO UOS LO GRADE%E, ALLA DO ESTA, *** %ID EL CANPEADOR,
22628 5ELCID2883 POR AMOR DE *** %ID RICA CENA LES DA.
22662 5ELCID2888 *** %ID ASUS FIJAS YUA LAS ABRA%AR,
22766 5ELCID2901 OERES, MU@O GUSTIOZ, *** VASSALLO DE PRO,
22806 5ELCID2905 CUEMO YO SO SU VASSALLO, & EL ES *** SE@OR,
22856 5ELCID2911 LA POCA & LA GRANT TODA ES DE *** SE@OR.
23169 5ELCID2952 QUE AYA *** %ID DERECHO DE YFANTES DE CARRION.
23230 5ELCID2959 ENTRE YO & *** %ID PESA NOS DE CORA%ON.
23257 5ELCID2962 ANDARAN MYOS PORTEROS POR TODO *** REYNO,
23285 5ELCID2966 E COMMO DEN DERECHO A *** %ID EL CAMPEADOR,
23324 5ELCID2971 POR AMOR DE *** %ID ESTA CORT YO FAGO.
23348 5ELCID2974 ESPIDIOS MU@O GUSTIOZ, A *** %ID ES TORNADO.
23455 5ELCID2987 MIEDO HAN QUE Y VERNA *** %ID EL CAMPEADOR;
23486 5ELCID2991 CA Y VERNA *** %ID EL CAMPEADOR;
23509 5ELCID2994 QUITE *** REYNO, CADEL NON HE SABOR.
23642 5ELCID3011 EBAYR LE CUYDAN A *** %ID EL CAMPEADOR.
23675 5ELCID3015 AL QUINTO DIA VENIDO ES *** %ID EL CAMPEADOR;
23748 5ELCID3025 FIRIOS ATIERRA *** %ID EL CAMPEADOR;
23811 5ELCID3033 AMEN, DIXO *** %ID EL CAMPEADOR;
23896 5ELCID3044 ESSA NOCH *** %ID TAIO NON QUISO PASSAR;
23963 5ELCID3054 *** %ID RUY DIAZ EN SAN SERUAN POSADO.
24033 5ELCID3063 VOS, MYNAYA ALBARFANEZ, EL *** BRA%O MEIOR,
24073 5ELCID3069 E *** SOBRINO FELEZ MUNOZ;
24256 5ELCID3093 SIEMPRE LA VISTE *** %ID EL CAMPEADOR;
24336 5ELCID3103 ASSI YUA *** %ID ADOBADO ALLA CORT.
24351 5ELCID3105 CUERDA MIENTRA ENTRA *** %ID CON TODOS LOS SOS:
24485 5ELCID3121 EN VN ESCA@O TORNI@O ESSORA *** %ID POSO,
24497 5ELCID3123 CATANDO ESTAN A *** %ID QUANTOS HA EN LA CORT,
24576 5ELCID3132 POR EL AMOR DE *** %ID EL QUE EN BUEN ORA NA%IO,
24673 5ELCID3143 AGORA DEMANDE *** %ID EL CAMPEADOR:
24683 5ELCID3145 *** %ID LA MANO BESO AL REY & EN PIE SE LEUANTO;
25063 5ELCID3193 MARTIN ANTOLINEZ, *** VASSALO DE PRO,
25118 5ELCID3199 LUEGO SE LEUANTO *** %ID EL CAMPEADOR;
25395 5ELCID3234 ENTERGEN A *** %ID, EL QUE EN BUEN ORA NA%IO;
25476 5ELCID3245 RECIBIOLO *** %ID COMMO APRE%IARON ENLA CORT.
25518 5ELCID3250 ESTAS APRE%IADURAS *** %ID PRESAS LAS HA,
25561 5ELCID3255 OYD ME TODA LA CORT & PESEUOS DE *** MAL:
25693 5ELCID3272 VEZOS *** %ID ALLAS CORTES PREGONADAS;
25904 5ELCID3301 *** %ID RUY DIAZ A PERO VERMUEZ CATA;
26075 5ELCID3324 DELANT *** %ID & DELANTE TODOS OVISTE TE DE ALABAR
26129 5ELCID3331 QUANDO DURMIE *** %ID & EL LEON SE DESATO?
26149 5ELCID3333 METISTET TRAS EL ESCA@O DE *** %ID EL CAMPEADOR
26170 5ELCID3336 FASTA DO DESPERTO *** %ID, EL QUE VALEN%IA GA@O;
26189 5ELCID3338 EL LEON PREMIO LA CABE%A, A *** %ID ESPERO,
26313 5ELCID3356 POR CONSAGRAR CON *** %ID DON RODRIGO
26475 5ELCID3378 QUIEN NOS DARIE NUEUAS DE *** %ID EL DE BIUAR
26615 5ELCID3398 PIDEN SUS FIJAS A *** %ID EL CAMPEADOR
26645 5ELCID3402 LEUANTOS EN PIE *** %ID EL CAMPEADOR;
26654 5ELCID3403 MER%ED, REY ALFONSSO, VOS SODES *** SE@OR
26728 5ELCID3414 LEUANTOS *** %ID, AL REY LAS MANOS LE BESO;
26768 5ELCID3419 DE FIJAS DE *** %ID, DON ELUIRA & DO@A SOL,
26808 5ELCID3424 E DESPUES DE *** %ID EL CAMPEADOR;
26877 5ELCID3433 DEZIR QUERRIA YA QUANTO DELO ***.
26929 5ELCID3440 GRANDES AUERES LES DIO *** %ID EL CAMPEADOR,
27033 5ELCID3453 ASIL CRE%E LA ONDRA A *** %ID EL CAMPEADOR
27268 5ELCID3486 *** %ID AL REY LAS MANOS LE BESO & DIXO: PLAZME, SE@OR.
27485 5ELCID3511 *** %ID ENEL CAUALLO ADELANT SE LEGO,
27666 5ELCID3532 *** %ID PORA VALEN%IA, & EL REY PORA CARRION.

WORD C# PREFIX CONTEXT

MYO (CON'T)

```
                 28187 5ELCID3598 ESTOS TRES CAUALLERCS DE *** %IC EL CAMPEADOR
                 28215 5ELCID3602 ENTODO *** REYNC NCN AURA BUENA SABOR.
                 28298 5ELCID3612 DESI VINIEN LCS DE *** %ID ALOS YFANTES DE CARRION,
                 28953 5ELCID3698 EL REY ALOS DE *** %IC DE NCCHE LOS ENBIO,
                 28977 5ELCID3701 FELOS EN VALENZIA CCN *** %ID EL CAMPEADOR:
                 29001 5ELCID3704 ALEGRE FFUE CAQUESTO *** %IC EL CAMPEADCR.
                 29205 5ELCID3729 ESTAS SCN LAS NUEUAS CE *** %IC EL CANPEADOR,
         WORD #2839 CCCURS 35C TIMES.
            INDEX OF DIVERSIFICATICN =    82.58 WITH STANCARD DEVIATION OF    95.77

MYOS                63 5ELCID0009 ESTO ME AN BUELTO **** ENEMIGOS MALOS.
                   808 5ELCID0103 O SODES, RACHEL & VIDAS, LOS **** AMIGOS CAROS?
                  1722 5ELCID0220 NCN SE SIENTRARE Y MAS ENTODOS LOS **** DIAS.
                  8197 5ELCID1044 CA HUEBOS MELC HE & PCRA ESTOS **** VASSALLOS
                  9946 5ELCID1261 AQUESTOS **** VASSALCS CUE CURIAN A VALENZIA & ANDAN AROBDANDO.
                 13936 5ELCID1765 QUIERO LAS CASAR CCN DE AQUESTOS **** VASSALLOS;
                 18515 5ELCID2343 AMOS LCS **** YERNOS BUENOS SERAN EN CAPO.
                 18591 5ELCID2353 **** YERNOS AMCS ADOS, LA COSA QUE MUCHO AMO,
                 18634 5ELCID2358 HYO CON LOS **** FERIR CUIERO CELANT,
                 19294 5ELCID2443  VENIDES, **** YERNCS, MYCS FIJOS SODES AMOS
                 19296 5ELCID2443  VENIDES, MYCS YERNOS, **** FIJOS SODES AMOS
                 19568 5ELCID2479 QUE LIDIARAN CCMIGO EN CAMPC **** YERNOS AMOS ADOS;
                 19687 5ELCID2496 ESON **** YERNOS YFANTES DE CARRION;
                 20762 5ELCID2637 REZIBA A **** YERNCS COMMO EL PUDIER MEIOR;
                 22708 5ELCID2894 DE **** YERNOS DE CARRICN DIOS ME FAGA VENGAR
                 22858 5ELCID2912 **** AUERES SE ME AN LEUADO, QUE SOBEIANOS SON;
                 23253 5ELCID2962 ANDARAN **** PCRTERCS PCR TCDC MYO REYNO,
                 23920 5ELCID3047 E YO CCN LCS **** PCSARE A SAN SERUAN:
                 24147 5ELCID3079 POR DE MANCAR **** CERECHOS & CEZIR MI RAZON:
                 24798 5ELCID3158 DEN ME MIS ESPADAS CUANDC **** YERNOS NON SON.
                 25179 5ELCID3206 DEN ME MIS AUERES, CUANDO **** YERNOS NON SON.
         WORD #2840 CCCURS  21 TIMES.
            INDEX OF DIVERSIFICATICN =  1254.80 WITH STANCARD CEVIATION OF  1753.78

MYS               2144 5ELCID0270 CON AQUESTAS *** DUE@AS DE QUIEN SO YO SERUIDA.
                 16841 5ELCID2132 PUES QUE CASADES *** FIJAS, ASI COMMO AUOS PLAZ,
                 19872 5ELCID2520 EAMAS LA *** FIJAS, CCN ELUIRA & DO@A SOL;
                 20226 5ELCID2568 DIXO EL CAMPEADOR: DARUCS HE *** FIJAS & ALGO DELO MYO;
         WORD #2841 CCCURS   4 TIMES.

NA%IDO             564 5ELCID0071 YA CANPEADOR, EN BUEN ORA FUESTES ******
         WORD #2842 OCCURS   1 TIMES.

NA%IO             2335 5ELCID0294 VANSSE PORA SAN PERC DO ESTA EL QUE ENBUEN PUNTO *****.
                 15935 5ELCID2020 CCMMO LC CCMICIA EL QUE EN BUEN ORA *****,
                 16507 5ELCID2092 BAN BESAR LAS MANCS ALQUE EN CRA BUENA *****:
                 18121 5ELCID2292 EN ESTO DESPERTO EL QUE EN BUEN ORA *****;
                 23660 5ELCID3013 AVN NCN ERA LEGADC EL QUE ENBUEN ORA *****,
                 23720 5ELCID3021 E YUA REZEBIR ALQUE EN BUEN ORA *****.
                 24071 5ELCID3068 E MARTIN MUNOZ, QUE EN BUEN PUNTO *****,
                 24189 5ELCID3084 NOS DETIENE PCR NADA EL QUE EN BUEN ORA *****:
                 24373 5ELCID3107 QUANDO LO VIERON ENTRAR AL QUE EN BUEN ORA *****,
                 24408 5ELCID3111 AGRANT ONDRA LO REZIBEN AL QUE EN BUEN ORA *****.
                 24583 5ELCID3132 POR EL AMOR DE MYO %IC EL QUE EN BUEN ORA *****,
                 25402 5ELCID3234 ENTERGEN A MYC %ID, EL CUE EN BUEN ORA *****;
                 27657 5ELCID3530 ALEGRE FUE DAQUESTC EL CUE EN BUEN ORA *****;
                 29051 5ELCID3710 FABLEMCS NOS DAQUESTE QUE EN BUEN ORA *****.
                 29152 5ELCID3722 VED QUAL ONDRA CREZE AL QUE EN BUEN ORA *****,
                 29180 5ELCID3725 A TODOS ALCANZA CNDRA PCR EL CUE EN BUEN ORA *****.
         WORD #2843 CCCURS  16 TIMES.
            INDEX OF DIVERSIFICATICN =  1788.67 WITH STANCARD DEVIATION OF  3570.17

NADA               239 5ELCID0030 ASCONDEN SE DE MYO %IC, CA NOL OSAN DEZIR ****.
                   355 5ELCID0044 NCN UOS OSARIEMCS ABRIR NCN COGER POR ****;
                   377 5ELCID0047 %ID, ENEL NUESTRO MAL UCS NON GANADES ****;
                   668 5ELCID0084 FER LO HE AMICOS, DE GRADC NON AURIE ****.
                  3535 5ELCID0445 AOSADAS CORRED, QUE PCR MIEDO NON DEXEDES ****.
                  3560 5ELCID0448 QUE POR MIEDC DE LCS MCRCS NCN CEXEN ****.
                  3762 5ELCID0475 DEXAN LA A MYC %ID, TCCC ESTO NON PREZIA ****.
                  4612 5ELCIDC585 ANTES QUEL PRENDAN LCS CE TERUEL, SI NON NON NOS DARAN DENT ****;
                  4673 5ELCIDC592 ALSABOR DEL PRENDER DELC AL NON PIENSSAN ****,
                  4901 5ELCID0620 QUE LOS DESCABEZEMOS **** NCN GANAREMOS;
                  6432 5ELCIDC821 QUE **** NOL MINGUAUA;
                  6957 5ELCIDC889 MAS DEL %ID CAMPEADCR YC NCN UOS DIGO ****.
                  7200 5ELCID0922 TODO GELC DIZE, QUE NCL ENCUBRE ****.
                  7638 5ELCIDC978 DELO SO NON LIEUC ****, DEXEM YR EN PAZ.
                  7728 5ELCID0989 AMENOS DE BATALLA NCN NOS DEXARIE POR ****.
                  7974 5ELCID1018 EL CONDE DON REMCNT NCN GELO PREZIA ****,
                 1C750 5ELCID1361 NON QUIERO QUE **** PIERCA EL CAMPEADOR;
                 1C979 5ELCID1389 EL %ID QUE BIEN NOS CUIERA **** NON PERDERA.
                 12072 5ELCID1530 DESTO QUE AUEDES FECHC UCS NCN PERDEREDES ****.
                 12267 5ELCID1557 LOS SOS DESPENDIE EL MORO, QUE DELO SO NON TOMAUA ****.
                 14256 5ELCID1803 EL BUENC DE MYO %ID NCN LO TARCO POR ****:
                 1427C 5ELCID1805 DELO QUE AUCS CAYO VCS NCN GRACEZEDES ****;
```

WORD C# PREFIX CONTEXT

NADA (CON'T)

```
                     17581 5ELCID2224 NOLO QUIERO FALIR POR **** DE QUANTO AY PARADO;
                     21886 5ELCID2784 TANTO SCN DE TRASPUESTAS QUE NON PUEDEN DEZIR ****.
                     23364 5ELCID2976 NON LO DETIENE POR **** ALFONSSO EL CASTELLANO,
                     23765 5ELCID3027 QUANDO LO CYO EL REY, PCR **** NON TARDO;
                     24183 5ELCID3084 NOS DETIENE POR **** EL QUE EN BUEN ORA NA%IO:
                     24788 5ELCID3157 CCMIGO NON CUISIERCN AUER **** & PERDIERON MI AMOR;
                     25750 5ELCID3279 QUANTO EL DIZE NCN GELO PRE%IAMOS ****.
                     25796 5ELCID3285 CA NON ME PRISO AELLA FIJO DE MUGIER ****,
                     26686 5ELCID3408 SIN UUESTRO MANDADO **** NCN FERE YO.
                     27928 5ELCID3564 QUE **** NCN MANCARA POR LOS DEL CAMPEADOR.
                     28441 5ELCID3632 PASSO GELO TCDO, QUE **** NOL VALIO,
                     28451 5ELCID3633 METIOL LA LAN%A POR LCS PECHOS, QUE **** NOL VALIO;
         WORD #2844 OCCURS  34 TIMES.
            INDEX OF DIVERSIFICATION =   853.91 WITH STANDARD DEVIATION OF  1072.57

NADI                   193 5ELCID0025 QUE A MYO %ID RUY DIAZ, QUE **** NOL DIESSEN POSADA,
                       274 5ELCID0034 QUE SI NON LA QUEBRANTAS POR FUERCA, QUE NON GELA ABRIESE ****.
                       470 5ELCID0059 POSO EN LA GLERA QUANDO NOL COGE **** EN CASA;
                      3435 5ELCID0433 POR TAL LO FAZE MYO %ID QUE NO IO VENTASSE ****.
                      4647 5ELCID0589 COIOS SALON AYUSO, CCN LCS SOS ABUELTA ****.
                      5428 5ELCID0685 TODOS YSCAMOS FUERA, QUE **** NON RASTE,
                     1C881 5ELCID1377 NCN LO DIZEN A ****, & FINCO ESTA RAZON.
                     11688 5ELCID1481 FABLO MU@O GUSTIOZ, NCN SPERO A ****:
                     16720 5ELCID2117 CADA VNO LO QUE PIDE, **** NOL DIZE DE NO.
                     22238 5ELCID2832 PAR AQUESTA BARBA QUE **** NCN MESSO,
                     25016 5ELCID3186 PAR AQUESTA BARBA QUE **** NCN MESSO,
                     26073 5ELCID3323 FASTA ESTE DIA NOLO DESCUBRI A ****;
         WORD #2845 OCCURS  12 TIMES.
            INDEX OF DIVERSIFICATION =  2351.73 WITH STANDARD DEVIATION OF  2121.72

NADO                  1177 5ELCID0151 QUE GELO NON VENTANSSEN DE BURGOS OMNE ****.
                      2115 5ELCID0266 MER%ED, CANPEADOR, EN ORA BUENA FUESTES ****
                      3998 5ELCID0507 COMIDIOS MYO %ID, EL QUE EN BUEN ORA FUE ****,
                      4850 5ELCID0613 FABLO MYO %ID RUY DIAZ, EL QUE EN BUEN ORA FUE ****:
                     19399 5ELCID2457 EA UOS, %ID, QUE EN BUEN ORA FUESTES ****
         WORD #2846 OCCURS   5 TIMES.
            INDEX OF DIVERSIFICATION =  4554.50 WITH STANDARD DEVIATION OF  6678.69

NASCO                 1583 5ELCID0202 VINO PORA LA TIENDA DEL QUE EN BUEN ORA *****;
                      1934 5ELCID0245 CON TAN GRANT GOZO RE%IBEN AL QUE EN BUEN ORA *****.
                      3473 5ELCID0437 TODA LA NOCHE IAZE EN %ELADA EL QUE EN BUEN ORA *****,
                      4395 5ELCID0559 EL BUEN CANPEADOR QUE EN BUEN ORA *****,
                      5245 5ELCID0663 EL QUE EN BUEN ORA ***** FIRME GELO VEDAUA.
                      5707 5ELCID0719 A GRANDES VOZES LAMA EL QUE EN BUEN ORA *****:
                      5990 5ELCID0759 MYO %ID RUY DIAZ, EL QUE EN BUEN ORA *****,
                      6185 5ELCID0787 YAS TORNAN LOS DEL QUE EN BUEN ORA *****.
                      6351 5ELCID0808 BIEN LO AGUISA EL QUE EN BUEN ORA *****,
                      7035 5ELCID0899 QUIERO UOS DEZIR DEL QUE EN BUEN ORA ***** & %INXO ESPADA:
                      7296 5ELCID0935 NON LO TARDO EL QUE EN BUEN ORA *****,
                      7855 5ELCID1004 MANDO LOS FERIR MYO %ID, EL QUE EN BUEN ORA *****;
                      7893 5ELCID1008 VEN%IDO A ESTA BATALLA EL QUE EN BUEN ORA *****;
                      8278 5ELCID1053 SOBREL SEDIE EL QUE EN BUEN ORA *****:
                      8764 5ELCID1114 EL QUE EN BUEN ORA ***** COMPE%O DE FABLAR:
                      9404 5ELCID1195 ESTO DIXO MYO %ID EL QUE EN BUEN ORA *****.
                      9736 5ELCID1237 CON MYO %ID RUY DIAZ, EL QUE EN BUEN ORA *****.
                     12290 5ELCID1560 AMYO %ID, EL QUE EN BUEN ORA *****,
                     12489 5ELCID1584 EL QUE EN BUEN ORA ***** NON LO DETARDAUA:
                     12641 5ELCID1603 OYD LO QUE DIXO EL QUE EN BUEN ORA *****:
                     13660 5ELCID1730 DESDALLI SE TORNO EL QUE EN BUEN ORA *****,
                     14204 5ELCID1797 MYO %ID DON RODRIGO, EL QUE EN BUEN ORA *****,
                     14504 5ELCID1834 AUER ESTOS MENSAIES DEL QUE EN BUEN ORA *****.
                     14536 5ELCID1838 AOIO LO AUIEN LOS DEL QUE EN BUEN ORA *****,
                     15109 5ELCID1910 DEZID A RUY DIAZ, EL QUE EN BUEN ORA *****,
                     15837 5ELCID2008 FATA QUES TORNE EL QUE EN BUEN ORA *****.
                     15905 5ELCID2016 DON LO CUO A OIO EL QUE EN BUEN ORA *****,
                     16211 5ELCID2056 MYO %ID RUY DIAZ, QUE EN ORA BUENA *****,
                     17535 5ELCID2218 ESTAN PARANDO MIENTES ALQUE EN BUEN ORA *****.
                     17738 5ELCID2244 TRES CAUALLOS CAMEO EL QUE EN BUEN ORA *****.
                     17814 5ELCID2253 MYO %ID DON RODRIGO, EL QUE EN BUEN ORA *****,
                     17889 5ELCID2263 ESPIDIENDOS DE RUY DIAZ, EL QUE EN BUEN ORA *****,
                     18575 5ELCID2350 OYD LO QUE FABLO EL QUE EN BUEN ORA *****:
                     18906 5ELCID2392 EL QUE EN BUEN ORA ***** LOS OIOS LE FINCAUA,
                     19225 5ELCID2432 EL QUE EN BUEN ORA *****.
                     19610 5ELCID2484 MANDO MYO %ID, EL QUE EN BUEN ORA *****,
                     22644 5ELCID2885 AL QUE EN BUEN ORA ***** LEGAUA EL MENSSAIE;
                     22744 5ELCID2898 EL QUE EN BUEN ORA ***** NON QUISO TARDAR,
                     23305 5ELCID2968 DIZID LE AL CAMPEADOR, QUE EN BUEN ORA *****,
                     25499 5ELCID3247 PAGARON LOS YFANTES AL QUE EN BUEN ORA *****;
                     25784 5ELCID3284 CA DE QUANDO ***** ADELI%IO FUE CRIADA,
         WORD #2847 OCCURS  41 TIMES.
            INDEX OF DIVERSIFICATION =   604.02 WITH STANDARD DEVIATION OF   671.07

NAS%IO               20821 5ELCID2643 HYAS TORNO PORA VALEN%IA EL QUE EN BUEN ORA ******.
         WORD #2848 OCCURS   1 TIMES.
```

WORD C# PREFIX CONTEXT

NASQUIERAN 13113 5ELCID1662 DEL DIA QUE ********** NON VIERAN TAL TREMOR.
WORD #2849 CCCURS 1 TIMES.

NASQUIESTES 3012 5ELCID0379 %ID, DO SON UUESTROS ESFUER%OS? EN BUEN ORA *********** DE MADRE;
16186 5ELCID2053 OMILLAMOS NOS, %ID, EN BUEN ORA *********** UOS
WORD #2850 OCCURS 2 TIMES.

NATURA 20083 5ELCID2549 NOS DE ****** SCMOS DE CONDES DE CARRION
20118 5ELCID2554 CA DE ****** SOMOS DE CCNDES DE CARRION.
25719 5ELCID3275 LOS DE CARRICN SON DE ****** TAL,
25869 5ELCID3296 DE ****** SCMCS DE CCNDES DE CARRION:
26298 5ELCID3354 DE ****** SCMCS DE LCS CONDES MAS LIPIOS,
26951 5ELCID3443 DE ****** SODES DELOS DE VANIGCMEZ,
WORD #2851 CCCURS 6 TIMES.
INDEX OF DIVERSIFICATION = 1372.60 WITH STANDARD DEVIATION OF 2375.47

NATURAL 7003 5ELCID0895 GRADO & GRA%IAS, REY, CCMMO A SE@OR *******;
10044 5ELCID1272 AL REY ALFCNSSO MYO SE@OR *******;
11673 5ELCID1479 VENIDES, LOS VASSALLCS DE MYC AMIGO *******?
11837 5ELCID1500 E MARTIN ANTOLINEZ, EL BURGALES *******,
14916 5ELCID1885 MER%ED UCS PIDIMOS CCMMC A REY & SE@OR *******;
16014 5ELCID2031 MER%ED UOS PIDO AUOS, MYO ******* SE@OR,
16837 5ELCID2131 YO UOS PIDO MER%ED AUCS, REY *******:
WORD #2852 OCCURS 7 TIMES.
INDEX OF DIVERSIFICATION = 1638.00 WITH STANDARD DEVIATION OF 1197.79

NATURALES 12007 5ELCID1522 MUGIER DEL %ID LIDIADOR ESSUS FFIJAS *********;
WORD #2853 OCCURS 1 TIMES.

NAUARRA 9336 5ELCID1187 POR ARAGON & POR ******* PREGON MANDO ECHAR,
26597 5ELCID3395 EL VNO ES YFANTE DE *******
26623 5ELCID3399 POR SER REYNAS DE ******* & DE ARAGON,
26665 5ELCID3405 QUANDO MELAS DEMANDAN DE ******* & DE ARAGON.
26779 5ELCID3420 PORA LCS YFANTES DE ******* & DE ARAGON,
26988 5ELCID3448 LOS YFANTES DE ******* & DE ARAGON;
29104 5ELCID3717 ANDIDIERON EN PLEYTCS LCS DE ******* & DE ARAGON,
29159 5ELCID3723 QUANDO SE@ORAS SCN SUS FIJAS DE ******* & DE ARAGON.
WORD #2854 CCCURS 8 TIMES.
INDEX OF DIVERSIFICATION = 2830.86 WITH STANDARD DEVIATION OF 6407.61

NAUAS 3185 5ELCID0401 SOBRE ***** DE PALOS EL DUERO UA PASAR,
WORD #2855 CCCURS 1 TIMES.

NAUES 12839 5ELCID1629 ARRIBADO AN LAS *****, FUERA ERAN EXIDOS,
WORD #2856 CCCURS 1 TIMES.

NEGAR 24908 5ELCID3172 NOLO PODEMOS *****, CA DOS ESPADAS NOS DIO;
WORD #2857 CCCURS 1 TIMES.

NEGRAS 7299 5ELCID0936 TIERRAS DALCANZ ****** LAS VA PARANDO,
WORD #2858 CCCURS 1 TIMES.

NI 8787 5ELCID1117 NON FUE A NUESTRO GRADO ** NOS NON PUDIEMOS MAS,
9767 5ELCID1241 NIN ENTRARIE ENELA TIGERA, ** VN PELO NON AURIE TAIADO,
19976 5ELCID2534 MAS NON FALLAUAN Y ADIEGO ** AFERRANDO.
21800 5ELCID2773 ELLOS NOL VIEN ** DEND SABIEN RA%ION;
26530 5ELCID3386 NON DIZES VERDAD AMIGO ** HA SE@OR,
27508 5ELCID3514 EN MOROS ** EN CHRISTIANOS CTRO TAL NON HA OY,
WORD #2859 OCCURS 6 TIMES.
INDEX OF DIVERSIFICATION = 3743.20 WITH STANDARD DEVIATION OF 3928.91

NIL 7528 5ELCID0965 NCN LO DESAFIE, *** TORNE ENEMISTAD,
WORD #2860 CCCURS 1 TIMES.

NIMBLA 25797 5ELCID3286 ****** MESSO FIJO DE MORO NIN DE CHRISTIANA,
WORD #2861 OCCURS 1 TIMES.

NIN 838 5ELCID0107 QUE NON ME DESCUBRADES A MOROS *** A CHRISTIANOS;
2459 5ELCID0310 POR ORO *** PCR PLATA NCN PODRIE ESCAPAR.
4058 5ELCID0516 AQUI NCN LO PUEDEN VENDER *** DAR EN PRESENTAIA;
4062 5ELCID0517 *** CATIUOS NIN CATIUAS NON QUISO TRAER EN SU CONPA@A.
4064 5ELCID0517 NIN CATIUOS *** CATIUAS NON QUISO TRAER EN SU CONPA@A.
4414 5ELCID0562 QUE DE DIA *** DE NOCH NON LES DIESSEN AREBATA,
9199 5ELCID1171 NON OSAN FUERAS EXIR *** CCN EL SE AIUNTAR;
9244 5ELCID1176 *** DA COSSEIO PADRE A FIJO, NCN FIJO A PADRE,
9254 5ELCID1177 *** AMIGO A AMIGO NCS PUEDEN CONSOLAR.
9306 5ELCID1183 NON LES DIXO CCSEIO, *** LCS VINO HUUIAR.
9763 5ELCID1241 *** ENTRARIE ENELA TIGERA, NI VN PELO NON AURIE TAIADO,
12305 5ELCID1562 ALEGRE FUE MYC %ID, QUE NUNQUA MAS *** TANTO,
15788 5ELCID2002 LAS PUERTAS DEL ALCA%AR QUE NCN SE ABRIESSEN DE DIA *** DE NOCH,
16864 5ELCID2134 NON GELAS DARE YO CON MI MANO, *** DED NON SE ALABARAN.
[illegible] 5ELCID2286 FERRAN GON%ALEZ NCN VIO ALLI DCS AL%ASSE, *** CAMARA

WORD C# PREFIX CONTEXT

NIN (CON'T)

```
                 21316 5ELCID2709 QUE NON YFINCAS NINGUNO, MUGIER *** VARON,
                 24416 5ELCID3113 *** TODOS LOS DEL BANDO DE YFANTES DE CARRION.
                 25802 5ELCID3286 NIMBLA MESSO FIJO DE MORO *** DE CHRISTIANA,
                 26391 5ELCID3366 MAS NON VESTID EL MANTO *** EL BRIAL.
                 27220 5ELCID3479 QUE NON PRENDAN FUER%A DE CONDE *** DE YFAN%ON.
                 28963 5ELCID3699 QUE NOLES DIESSEN SALTO *** QUIESSEN PAUOR.
        WORD #2862 OCCURS  22 TIMES.
           INDEX OF DIVERSIFICATION =  1338.29 WITH STANDARD DEVIATION OF  1379.62

NINGUN            9868 5ELCID1252 QUE ****** OMNE DELOS SOS QUES LE NON SPIDIES, ONOL BESAS LA MANO,
                 11088 5ELCID1403 TODO SERIE ALEGRE, QUE NON AURIE ****** PESAR.
                 11767 5ELCID1492 PASSARON MATA DE TORANZ DE TAL GUISA QUE ****** MIEDO NON HAN,
                 21508 5ELCID2734 LO QUE RUEGAN LAS DUENAS NON LES HA ****** PRO.
        WORD #2863 OCCURS   4 TIMES.

NINGUNA           7350 5ELCID0942 DE MYO %ID RUY DIAZ QUE NON TEMIEN ******* FONTA.
                  9236 5ELCID1175 DE ******* PART QUE SEA NON LES VINIE PAN;
                 27894 5ELCID3559 NON SACASTES ******* QUANDO OUIEMOS LA CORT.
                 28498 5ELCID3639 QUEBRARON LE LAS %INCHAS, ******* NOL OUO PRO,
        WORD #2864 OCCURS   4 TIMES.

NINGUNO            158 5ELCID0021 CONBIDAR LE YEN DE GRADO, MAS ******* NON OSAUA:
                  3820 5ELCID0483 NON OSA ******* DAR SALTO ALA %AGA.
                  4215 5ELCID0536 TODOS SODES PAGADOS & ******* POR PAGAR.
                  4679 5ELCID0593 ABIERTAS DEXAN LAS PUERTAS QUE ******* NON LAS GUARDA.
                  5390 5ELCID0680 QUE NON SOPIESSE ******* ESTA SU PORIDAD.
                  5582 5ELCID0703 NON DERANCHE ******* FATA QUE YO LO MANDE.
                  9383 5ELCID1193 TODOS VENGAN DE GRADO, ******* NON HA PREMIA,
                 18220 5ELCID2305 MAGER LOS ESTAN LAMANDO, ******* NON RESPONDE.
                 21314 5ELCID2709 QUE NON YFINCAS *******, MUGIER NIN VARON,
                 26216 5ELCID3342 DEMANDO POR SUS YERNOS, ******* NON FALLO
                 27108 5ELCID3464 NON DIGA ******* DELLA MAS VNA ENTEN%ION.
        WORD #2865 OCCURS  11 TIMES.
           INDEX OF DIVERSIFICATION =  2694.00 WITH STANDARD DEVIATION OF  2761.48

NI@A               316 5ELCID0040 VNA **** DE NUEF A@OS A OIO SE PARAUA:
                   390 5ELCID0049 ESTO LA **** DIXO & TORNOS PORA SU CASA.
        WORD #2866 OCCURS   2 TIMES.

NI@AS             2023 5ELCID0255 DUES FIJAS DEXO ***** & PRENDET LAS EN LOS BRA%OS;
                  2944 5ELCID0371 E EL ALAS ***** TORNO LAS ACATAR:
                 12356 5ELCID1569 E ALAS DUENAS & ALAS ***** & ALAS OTRAS CONPA@AS.
        WORD #2867 OCCURS   3 TIMES.

NO                 649 5ELCID0082 BIEN LO VEDES QUE YO ** TRAYO AUER, & HUEBOS ME SERIE
                  1505 5ELCID0192 DEMOS LE BUEN DON, CA EL ** LO HA BUSCADO.
                  3341 5ELCID0421 EL QUI QUISIERE COMER; & QUI **, CAUALGE.
                  3432 5ELCID0433 POR TAL LO FAZE MYO %ID QUE ** IO VENTASSE NADI.
                  5288 5ELCID0668 QUE NOS QUERAMOS YR DE NOCH ** NOS LO CONSINTRAN;
                  5327 5ELCID0673 SI CON MOROS NON LIDIAREMOS, ** NOS DARAN DEL PAN.
                  8292 5ELCID1055 AQUI FEREMOS LA MORADA, ** NOS PARTIREMOS AMOS.
                 11325 5ELCID1433 DESFECHOS NOS HA EL %ID, SABET, SI ** NOS VAL;
                 11410 5ELCID1444 AQUESTE MONESTERIO ** LO QUIERA OLBIDAR,
                 12897 5ELCID1636 A MENOS DE MUERT ** LA PUEDO DEXAR;
                 15996 5ELCID2028 BESAD LAS MANOS, CA LOS PIES **;
                 16296 5ELCID2067 PASSADO AUIE IIJ A@OS ** COMIERAN MEIOR.
                 16724 5ELCID2117 CADA VNO LO QUE PIDE, NADI NOL DIZE DE **.
                 17411 5ELCID2202 QUE YO NULLA COSA NOL SOPE DEZIR DE **.
                 18340 5ELCID2320 CATAMOS LA GANAN%IA & LA PERDIDA **,
                 19730 5ELCID2502 ** LOS YRE BUSCAR, EN VALEN%IA SERE YO,
                 19937 5ELCID2529 TANTOS AVEMOS DE AUERES QUE ** SON CONTADOS;
                 21474 5ELCID2730 QUE POR LO QUE NOS MERE%EMOS ** LO PRENDEMOS NOS;
                 23477 5ELCID2990 DIXO EL REY: ** LO FERE, SIN SALUE DIOS
                 23503 5ELCID2993 QUI LO FER NON QUISIESSE, O ** YR A MI CORT,
                 24853 5ELCID3165 QUANDO DESONDRA DESUS FIJAS ** NOS DEMANDA OY;
                 25200 5ELCID3208 DJZE EL CONDE DON REMONC: DEZID DE SSI O DE **.
                 25215 5ELCID3211 QUE AL ** NOS DEMANDASSE, QUE AQUI FINCO LA BOZ. . .
                 25574 5ELCID3257 AMENOS DE RIEBTOS ** LOS PUEDO DEXAR.
                 25903 5ELCID3300 MAS NOS PRE%IAMOS, SABET, QUE MENOS **.
                 26323 5ELCID3357 POR QUE DEXAMOS SUS FIJAS AVN ** NOS REPENTIMOS,
                 27051 5ELCID3455 SI AY QUI RESPONDA ODIZE DE **,
                 27099 5ELCID3462 DESPUES VEREDES QUE DIXIESTES O QUE **.
                 27172 5ELCID3473 ENESSORA DIXO MIO %ID. ** LO FARE, SENOR.
                 27540 5ELCID3517 SI AUOS LE TOLLIES, EL CAUALLO ** HAURIE TAN BUEN SE@OR.
                 27648 5ELCID3529 PODEDES OYR DE MUERTOS, CA DE VENCIDOS **.
                 28022 5ELCID3576 ADERECHO NOS VALED, ANINGUN TUERTO **.
                 28652 5ELCID3658 VIO DIEGO GON%ALEZ QUE ** ESCAPARIE CON EL ALMA;
        WORD #2868 OCCURS  33 TIMES.
           INDEX OF DIVERSIFICATION =   874.09 WITH STANDARD DEVIATION OF   922.86

NOBRE             5343 5ELCID0675 EN EL ***** DEL CRIADOR, QUE NON PASE POR AL:
        WORD #2869 OCCURS   1 TIMES.
```

WORD C# PREFIX CONTEXT

NOCH
566 5ELCID0072 ESTA **** YGAMOS & UAYMOS NOS AL MATINO,
1067 5ELCID0137 YA VEDES QUE ENTRA LA ****, EL %ID ES PRESURADO,
1739 5ELCID0222 EL ME ACORRA DE **** & DE DIA
2470 5ELCID0311 EL DIA ES EXIDO, LA **** CUERIE ENTRAR,
2558 5ELCID0323 PASSANDO UA LA ****, VINIENDO LA MAN;
3141 5ELCID0395 GRANDES YENTES SELE ACOIEN ESSA **** DE TODAS PARTES.
3357 5ELCID0423 LA TIERRA DEL REY ALFONSSO ESTA **** LA PODEMOS QUITAR.
3369 5ELCID0425 DE **** PASSAN LA SIERRA, VINIDA ES LA MAN,
3438 5ELCID0434 ANDIDIERON DE ****, QUE VAGAR NON SE DAN.
4416 5ELCID0562 QUE DE DIA NIN DE **** NON LES DIESSEN AREBATA,
5099 5ELCID0644 ELLOS VINIERON ALA **** EN SOGORUE POSAR.
5112 5ELCID0646 VINIERON A LA **** A %ELFA POSAR.
5208 5ELCID0659 E DE **** EN BUELTOS ANDAN EN ARMAS;
5287 5ELCID0668 QUE NOS QUERAMOS YR DE **** NO NOS LO CONSINTRAN;
6487 5ELCID0827 AGORA DAUAN %EUADA, YA LA **** ERA ENTRADA,
8661 5ELCID1100 TRASNOCHARON DE ****, AL ALUA DELA MAN
9321 5ELCID1185 SALIO DE MURUIEDRO VNA **** EN TRASNOCHADA,
11733 5ELCID1488 ESSA **** CON DUCHO LES DIO GRAND,
13407 5ELCID1699 ES DIA ES SALIDO & LA **** ENTRADA ES,
15790 5ELCID2002 LAS PUERTAS DEL ALCA%AR QUE NON SE ABRIESSEN DE DIA NIN DE ****
16132 5ELCID2045 VALER ME A DIOS DE DIA & DE ****.
16254 5ELCID2061 ES DIA ES PASSADO, & ENTRADA ES LA ****;
16749 5ELCID2120 PARTIR SE QUIEREN, QUE ENTRADA ERA LA ****.
17253 5ELCID2182 TODOS ESSA **** FUERON A SUS POSADAS,
19721 5ELCID2500 QUE ABRAM DE MI SALTO QUI%AB ALGUNA ****
20750 5ELCID2635 POR MOLINA YREDES, VNA **** Y IAZREDES;
21179 5ELCID2690 ACOIEN SE A ANDAR DE DIA & DE ****;
21267 5ELCID2702 CON QUANTOS QUE ELLOS TRAEN Y IAZEN ESSA ****,
21297 5ELCID2706 COGIDA HAN LA TIENDA DO ALBERGARON DE ****,
21919 5ELCID2788 MIENTRA ES EL DIA, ANTE QUE ENTRE LA ****,
22080 5ELCID2810 ENTRE **** & DIA SALIERON DELOS MONTES;
22297 5ELCID2839 DIXOLES FUERTE MIENTRE QUE ANDIDIESSEN DE DIA & DE ****,
22335 5ELCID2844 HY ALBERGARON POR VERDAD VNA ****.
22366 5ELCID2849 PRESENTAN A MINAYA ESSA **** GRANT ENFFUR%ION;
22436 5ELCID2857 ADELINAN A POSAR PORA FOLGAR ESSA ****.
23698 5ELCID3018 BIEN LO SOPIESSE QUE Y SERIE ESSA ****.
23895 5ELCID3044 ESSA **** MYO %ID TAIO NON QUISO PASSAR;
WORD #2870 OCCURS 37 TIMES.
INDEX OF DIVERSIFICATION = 647.03 WITH STANDARD DEVIATION OF 735.42

NOCHE
172 5ELCID0023 ANTES DELA ***** EN BURGOS DEL ENTRO SU CARTA,
734 5ELCID0093 DE ***** LO LIEUEN, QUE NON LO VEAN CHISTIANOS.
3464 5ELCID0437 TODA LA ***** IAZE EN %ELADA EL QUE EN BUEN ORA NASCO,
5149 5ELCID0651 VINIERON ESSA ***** EN CALATAYUH POSAR.
5397 5ELCID0681 ELDIA & LA ***** PIENSSAN SE DE ADOBAR.
8819 5ELCID1122 PASSE LA ***** & VENGA LA MA@ANA,
12140 5ELCID1540 PASSADA ES LA *****, VENIDA ES LA MA@ANA,
22530 5ELCID2869 HY IAZEN ESSA *****, & TAN GRAND GOZO QUE FAZEN.
23929 5ELCID3048 LAS MIS COMPA@AS ESTA ***** LEGARAN;
27768 5ELCID3544 DE ***** BELARON LAS ARMAS & ROGARON AL CRIADOR.
27779 5ELCID3545 TROCIDA ES LA *****, YA QUIEBRAN LOS ALBORES.
28956 5ELCID3698 EL REY ALOS DE MYO %ID DE ***** LOS ENBIO,
WORD #2871 OCCURS 12 TIMES.
INDEX OF DIVERSIFICATION = 2615.73 WITH STANDARD DEVIATION OF 2900.37

NOCHES
6459 5ELCID0824 QUE RUEGEN POR MI LAS ****** & LOS DIAS;
7571 5ELCID0970 TRES DIAS & DOS ****** PENSSARON DE ANDAR,
9178 5ELCID1168 E DURMIENDO LOS DIAS & LAS ****** TRANOCHANDO,
12184 5ELCID1547 LAS ****** & LOS DIAS LAS DUENAS AGUARDANDO.
14416 5ELCID1823 ANDAN LOS DIAS & LAS ******, & PASSADA HAN LA SIERRA,
19985 5ELCID2536 ELAS ****** & LOS DIAS TAN MAL LOS ESCARMENTANDO,
22319 5ELCID2842 APRESSA CAUALGAN, LOS DIAS & LAS ****** ANDAN;
22935 5ELCID2921 NOS DAN VAGAR LOS DIAS & LAS ******.
28972 5ELCID3700 AGUISA DE MENBRADOS ANDAN DIAS & ******,
WORD #2872 OCCURS 9 TIMES.
INDEX OF DIVERSIFICATION = 2813.13 WITH STANDARD DEVIATION OF 1991.72

NOL
194 5ELCID0025 QUE A MYO %ID RUY DIAZ, QUE NADI *** DIESSEN POSADA,
236 5ELCID0030 ASCONDEN SE DE MYO %ID, CA *** OSAN DEZIR NADA.
468 5ELCID0059 POSO EN LA GLERA QUANDO *** COGE NACI EN CASA;
4359 5ELCID0555 A%ERCA CORRE SALON, AGUA *** PUEDENT VEDAR.
5662 5ELCID0713 DAN LE GRANDES COLPES, MAS *** PUEDEN FALSSAR.
6095 5ELCID0774 E AGALUE *** COGIERON ALLA;
6433 5ELCID0821 QUE NADA *** MINGUAUA;
7198 5ELCID0922 TODO GELO DIZE, QUE *** ENCUBRE NADA.
8074 5ELCID1030 FASTA TER%ER DIA *** PUEDEN ACORDAR.
8082 5ELCID1032 *** PUEDEN FAZER COMER VN MUESSO DE PAN.
16721 5ELCID2117 CADA VNO LO QUE PIDE, NADI *** DIZE DE NO.
17407 5ELCID2202 QUE YO NULLA COSA *** SOPE DEZIR DE NO.
18897 5ELCID2391 DAUAN LE GRANDES COLPES, MAS *** FALSSAN LAS ARMAS.
21682 5ELCID2756 QUE EL VNA AL OTRA *** TORNA RECABDO.
21798 5ELCID2773 ELLOS *** VIEN NI DENO SABIEN RA%ION;
24519 5ELCID3126 *** PUEDEN CATAR DE VERGUEN%A YFANTES DE CARRION.
25958 5ELCID3308 MAS QUANDO ENPIE%A, SABED, *** DA VAGAR:
27567 5ELCID3520 QUIEN VOS LO TOLLER QUISIERE *** VALA EL CRIADOR,

WORD C# PREFIX CONTEXT

NOL (CON'T)

```
                28404 5ELCID3627 PRISOL EN VAZIC, EN CARNE *** TOMO,
                28442 5ELCID3632 PASSO GELO TODO, QUE NADA *** VALIO,
                28452 5ELCID3633 METIOL LA LANZA POR LOS PECHOS, QUE NADA *** VALIO;
                28499 5ELCID3639 QUEBRARON LE LAS %INCHAS, NINGUNA *** OUO PRO,
                28681 5ELCID3661 VN COLPEL DIO DE LANC, CON LO AGUDO *** TOMAUA.
                28795 5ELCID3677 EN VAZIO FUE LA LANZA, CA EN CARNE *** TOMO.
                28818 5ELCID3681 *** PUDO GUARIR, FALSSO GELA GUARNIZON,
                28892 5ELCID3690 DIXO GONZALO ASSUREZ: *** FIRGADES, POR DIOS
         WORD #2873 OCCURS  26 TIMES.
            INDEX OF DIVERSIFICATION =  1146.92 WITH STANDARD DEVIATION OF  1865.44

NOLA            28689 5ELCID3662 DIAGONZALEZ ESPADA TIENE EN MANO, MAS ****
         WORD #2874 OCCURS   1 TIMES.

NOLES           28960 5ELCID3699 QUE ***** DIESSEN SALTO NIN OUIESSEN PAUOR.
         WORD #2875 OCCURS   1 TIMES.

NOLO              609 5ELCID0077 SI NON, QUANTO DEXO **** PRE%IO UN FIGO.
                 1538 5ELCID0197 MERE%ER **** HEDES, CA ESTO ES AGUISADO:
                17577 5ELCID2224 **** QUIERO FALIR POR NADA DE QUANTO AY PARADO;
                20034 5ELCID2542 MIENTRA QUE VISQUIEREMOS DESPENDER **** PODREMOS.
                21065 5ELCID2677 SI **** DEXAS POR MYO %ID EL DE BIUAR,
                24906 5ELCID3172 **** PODEMOS NEGAR, CA DOS ESPADAS NOS DIO;
                26070 5ELCID3323 FASTA ESTE DIA **** DESCUBRI A NADI;
                27972 5ELCID3570 **** QUERRIEN AUER FECHO POR QUANTO HA EN CARRION.
         WORD #2876 OCCURS   8 TIMES.
            INDEX OF DIVERSIFICATION =  3908.00 WITH STANDARD DEVIATION OF  5446.34

NOLOS           18214 5ELCID2304 MYO %ID POR SOS YERNOS DEMANDO & ***** FALLO;
                18678 5ELCID2364 MANDAD ***** FERIR DE QUAL PART UOS SEMEIAR,
         WORD #2877 OCCURS   2 TIMES.

NOM             13918 5ELCID1763 HYA MUGIER DA@A XIMENA, *** LO AUIEDES ROGADO?
         WORD #2878 OCCURS   1 TIMES.

NOMBRADO        14630 5ELCID1850 A AQUEL REY DE MARRUECOS, YUCEFF POR ********,
         WORD #2879 OCCURS   1 TIMES.

NOMBRE           8936 5ELCID1138 ENEL ****** DEL CRIADOR & DEL APOSTOL SANTI YAGUE,
                10182 5ELCID1289 EL OBISPO DON IERONIMO SO ****** ES LAMADO.
                10475 5ELCID1327 GANADA A XERICA & A ONDA POR ******,
                12523 5ELCID1589 POR ****** EL CAUALLO BAUIECA CAUALGA.
                13329 5ELCID1690 HYR LOS HEMOS FFERIR ENEL ****** DEL CRIADOR & DEL APOSTOL SANTI
                25622 5ELCID3262 CON MUY GRAND ONDRA & AVERES A ******;
         WORD #2880 OCCURS   6 TIMES.
            INDEX OF DIVERSIFICATION =  3336.20 WITH STANDARD DEVIATION OF  5047.66

NON               159 5ELCID0021 CONBIDAR LE YEN DE GRADO, MAS NINGUNO *** OSAUA:
                  265 5ELCID0034 QUE SI *** LA QUEBRANTAS POR FUERCA, QUE NON GELA ABRIESE NADI.
                  271 5ELCID0034 QUE SI NON LA QUEBRANTAS POR FUERCA, QUE *** GELA ABRIESE NADI.
                  286 5ELCID0036 LOS DE DENTRO *** LES QUERIEN TORNAR PALABRA.
                  306 5ELCID0039 *** SE ABRE LA PUERTA, CA BIEN ERA %ERRADA.
                  348 5ELCID0044 *** UOS OSARIEMOS ABRIR NON COGER POR NADA;
                  352 5ELCID0044 NON UOS OSARIEMOS ABRIR *** COGER POR NADA;
                  357 5ELCID0045 SI ***, PERDERIEMOS LOS AUERES & LAS CASAS,
                  375 5ELCID0047 %ID, ENEL NUESTRO MAL UOS *** GANADES NADA;
                  405 5ELCID0050 YA LO VEE EL %ID QUE DEL REY *** AUIE GRA%IA.
                  501 5ELCID0064 *** LE OSARIEN UENDER ALMENOS DINARADA.
                  523 5ELCID0067 *** LO CONPRA, CA EL SELO AUIE CONSIGO;
                  606 5ELCID0077 SI ***, QUANTO DEXO NOLO PRE%IO UN FIGO.
                  666 5ELCID0084 FER LO HE AMIDOS, DE GRADO *** AURIE NADA.
                  716 5ELCID0091 *** PUEDO TRAER EL AUER, CA MUCHO ES PESADO,
                  738 5ELCID0093 DE NOCHE LO LIEUEN, QUE *** LO VEAN CHISTIANOS.
                  752 5ELCID0095 YO MAS *** PUEDO & AMYDOS LO FAGO.
                  760 5ELCID0096 MARTIN ANTOLINEZ *** LO DETARDA,
                  817 5ELCID0105 *** LO DETARDAN, TODOS TRES SE APARTARON.
                  833 5ELCID0107 QUE *** ME DESCUBRADES A MOROS NIN A CHRISTIANOS;
                  847 5ELCID0108 POR SIEMPRE UOS FARE RICOS, QUE *** SEADES MENGUADOS.
                  900 5ELCID0116 AQUELAS *** LAS PUEDE LEUAR, SINON, SER YEN VENTADAS;
                  942 5ELCID0121 QUE *** LAS CATEDES EN TODO AQUESTE A@O.
                  979 5ELCID0126 *** DUERME SIN SOSPECHA QUI AUER TRAE MONEDADO.
                  997 5ELCID0128 EN LOGAR LAS METAMOS QUE *** SEAN VENTADAS.
                 1083 5ELCID0139 DIXO RACHEL & VIDAS:  *** SE FAZE ASSI EL MERCADO,
                 1090 5ELCID0140 SI *** PRIMERO PRENDIENDO & DESPUES DANDO.
                 1127 5ELCID0145 QUE *** LO SEPAN MOROS NON CHRISTIANOS.
                 1131 5ELCID0145 QUE NON LO SEPAN MOROS *** CHRISTIANOS.
                 1161 5ELCID0150 *** VIENE ALA PUEENT, CA POR EL AGUA APASSADO,
                 1172 5ELCID0151 QUE GELO *** VENTANSSEN DE BURGOS OMNE NADO.
                 1228 5ELCID0158 MIENTRA QUE VIVADES *** SEREDES MENGUADOS.
                 1283 5ELCID0165 *** LES DIESSE MYO %ID DELA GANAN%IA UN DINERO MALO.
                 1333 5ELCID0171 *** LAS PODIEN PONER EN SOMO MAGER ERAU ESFOR%ADOS.
                 1414 5ELCID0181 SIUOS LA ADUXIER DALLA; SI ***, CONTALDA SOBRE LAS ARCAS. . . .
                 1715 5ELCID0220 *** SE SIENTRARE Y MAS ENTODOS LOS MYOS DIAS.
                 1810 5ELCID0230 SI EL REY MELO QUISIERE TOMAR AMI *** MINCHAL.
```

WORD C# PREFIX CONTEXT

NON (CON'T)

```
1992 5ELCID0252 *** QUIERO FAZER ENEL MCNESTERIO VN CINERO DE DA@O;
2437 5ELCID0307 TRES AN POR TRO%IR, %EPADES QUE *** MAS.
2462 5ELCID0310 POR ORC NIN PCR PLATA *** PCDRIE ESCAPAR.
2480 5ELCID0313 OYD, VARONES, *** UCS CAYA EN PESAR;
2505 5ELCID0317 *** UOS TARDEDES, MANDEDES ENSELLAR;
2773 5ELCID0350 EL VNO ES EN PARAYSC, CA EL OTRO *** ENTRO ALA;
2936 5ELCID0370 LORANDO DE LOS OICS, QUE *** SABE QUE SE FAR.
2971 5ELCID0374 LORANDO DELOS OIOS, CUE *** VIESTES ATAL,
3286 5ELCID0414 ES DIA A DE PLAZC, SEPADES QUE *** MAS.
3299 5ELCID0416 AVN ERA DE DIA, *** ERA PUESTC EL SOL,
3441 5ELCID0434 ANDIDIERON DE NOCH, QUE VAGAR *** SE DAN.
3533 5ELCID0445 AOSADAS CORREC, QUE POR MIEDO *** DEXEDES NADA.
3558 5ELCID0448 QUE POR MIEDC DE LOS MOROS *** DEXEN NADA.
3760 5ELCID0475 DEXAN LA A MYC %ID, TCDC ESTO *** PRE%IA NADA.
3818 5ELCID0483 *** OSA NINGUNC CAR SALTC ALA %AGA.
3958 5ELCID0503 *** PRENDRE DE UOS QUANTO UALE VN DINERO MALO.
4054 5ELCID0516 AQUI *** LO PUEDEN VENDER NIN CAR EN PRESENTAIA;
4066 5ELCID0517 NIN CATIUOS NIN CATIUAS *** QUISO TRAER EN SU CONPA@A.
4126 5ELCID0525 QUE ENEL CASTIELLO *** Y AURIE MORADA,
4135 5ELCID0526 E QUE SERIE RETENEDCR, MAS *** YAURIE AGUA.
4167 5ELCID0530 LO QUE YO DIXIER *** LO TENGADES AMAL:
4173 5ELCID0531 EN CASTEION *** PCDRIEMCS FINCAR;
4188 5ELCID0533 MAS EL CASTIELO *** LO CUIERO HERMAR;
4208 5ELCID0535 POR QUE LO PRIS DELLCS QUE DE MI *** DIGAN MAL.
4228 5ELCID0538 CON ALFONSSO MYO SE@OR *** QUERRIA LIDIAR.
4309 5ELCID0549 *** LO SABEN LOS MOROS EL ARDIMENT QUE AN.
4417 5ELCID0562 QUE DE DIA NIN DE NOCH *** LES DIESSEN AREBATA,
4456 5ELCID0567 EN LA SU VEZINDAD *** SE TREUEN GANAR TANTO.
4517 5ELCID0574 QUANDO VIO MYC %ID CUE ALCO%ER *** SELE DAUA;
4525 5ELCID0575 EL FIZO VN ART & *** LO DETARDAUA:
4607 5ELCID0585 ANTES CUEL PRENDAN LCS DE TERUEL, SI *** NON NOS DARAN
                DENT NADA;
4608 5ELCID0585 ANTES CUEL PRENDAN LCS DE TERUEL, SI NON *** NOS DARAN
                DENT NADA;
4671 5ELCID0592 ALSABOR DEL PRENDER DELC AL *** PIENSSAN NADA,
4680 5ELCID0593 ABIERTAS DEXAN LAS PUERTAS QUE NINGUNO *** LAS GUARDA.
4895 5ELCID0619 LOS MOROS & LAS MORAS VENDER *** LOS PODREMOS,
4902 5ELCID0620 QUE LOS DESCABE%EMOS NADA *** GANAREMOS;
4945 5ELCID0625 MUCHO PESA ALCS DE TECA & ALOS DE TERUAL *** PLAZE,
4951 5ELCID0626 E ALOS DE CALATAYUTH *** PLAZE.
4997 5ELCID0632 SI *** DAS CONSEIO, A TECA & A TERUEL PERDERAS,
5009 5ELCID0633 PERDERAS CALATAYUTH, CUE *** PUEDE ESCAPAR,
5048 5ELCID0638 *** LO DETARDEDES, LOS DOS YD PORA ALLA,
5124 5ELCID0648 *** LO DETIENEN, VIENEN DE TODAS PARTES.
5144 5ELCID0650 ANDIDIERON TODOL DIA, QUE VAGAR *** SE DAN,
5325 5ELCID0673 SI CON MOROS *** LIDIAREMOS, NO NOS DARAN DEL PAN.
5347 5ELCID0675 EN EL NOBRE DEL CRIADOR, QUE *** PASE POR AL:
5388 5ELCID0680 QUE *** SOPIESSE NINGUNC ESTA SU PORIDAD.
5429 5ELCID0685 TODOS YSCAMOS FUERA, QUE NADI *** RASTE,
5432 5ELCID0686 SI *** DOS PEONES SOLCS POR LA PUERTA GUARDAR;
5474 5ELCID0691 MAS *** AGUIJEDES CON ELLA, SI YO NON UOS LO MANDAR.
5480 5ELCID0691 MAS NON AGUIJEDES CON ELLA, SI YO *** UOS LO MANDAR.
5580 5ELCID0703 *** DERANCHE NINGUNC FATA QUE YO LO MANDE.
5591 5ELCID0704 AQUEL PERO VERMUEZ *** LO PUDC ENDURAR,
5631 5ELCID0709 DIXO EL CAMPEADOR:  *** SEA, POR CARIDAD
5638 5ELCID0710 RESPUSO PERO VERMUEZ:  *** RASTARA POR AL.
6055 5ELCID0768 SABET, EL OTRO *** GEL OSO ESPERAR.
6269 5ELCID0798 MAS DE QUINZE DE LOS SOS MENOS *** FALLARON.
6276 5ELCID0799 TRAEN ORO & PLATA QUE *** SABEN RECABDO;
6526 5ELCID0833 SI ***, DO SOPIEREDES QUE SOMOS, YNDOS CONSEGUIR.
6542 5ELCID0835 SI ***, ENESTA TIERRA ANGOSTA NON PODRIEMOS BIUIR.
6546 5ELCID0835 SI NON, ENESTA TIERRA ANGOSTA *** PODRIEMOS BIUIR.
6656 5ELCID0849 EN TODOS LOS SOS *** FALLARIEDES VN MESQUINO.
6773 5ELCID0865 *** TEME GERRA, SABET, A NULLA PART.
6901 5ELCID0882 OMNE AYRADC, QUE DE SE@OR *** HA GRA%IA,
6954 5ELCID0889 MAS DEL %ID CAMPEADOR YC *** UOS DIGO NADA.
7082 5ELCID0906 *** PLAZE ALOS MOROS, FIRME MIENTRE LES PESAUA.
7164 5ELCID0918 *** SON EN CUENTA, SABET, LAS PEONADAS.
7288 5ELCID0935 *** LO TARDO EL QUE EN BUEN ORA NASCO,
7348 5ELCID0942 DE MYO %ID RUY DIAZ QUE *** TEMIEN NINGUNA FONTA.
7377 5ELCID0946 SONRRISOS EL CABOSO, QUE *** LO PUDO ENDURAR:
7512 5ELCID0963 FIRIOM EL SOBRINO & *** LO ENMENDO MAS;
7525 5ELCID0965 *** LO DESAFIE, NIL TORNE ENEMISTAD,
7629 5ELCID0977 DIGADES AL CONDE *** LO TENGA A MAL,
7636 5ELCID0978 DELO SO *** LIEUC NADA, DEXEM YR EN PAZ.
7647 5ELCID0979 RESPUSO EL CONDE:  ESTO *** SERA VERDAD
7724 5ELCID0989 AMENOS DE BATALLA *** NOS DEXARIE POR NADA.
7971 5ELCID1018 EL CONDE DON REMONT *** GELO PRE%IA NADA,
7983 5ELCID1020 EL *** LO QUIERE COMER, ATODOS LOS SOSANAUA:
7990 5ELCID1021 *** COMBRE VN BOCADO POR QUANTO HA EN TODA ESPA@A,
8042 5ELCID1027 SI ***, EN TODOS UUESTROS DIAS NON VEREDES CHRISTIANISMO.
8047 5ELCID1027 SI NON, EN TODOS UUESTROS DIAS *** VEREDES CHRISTIANISMO.
8068 5ELCID1029 QUE YO DEXAR ME MORIR, QUE *** QUIERO COMER.
8097 5ELCID1033 DIXO MYO %ID: COMED, CONDE, ALGO, CASI *** COMEDES, NON VEREDES
8099 5ELCID1033 DIXO MYO %ID: COMED, CONDE, ALGO, CASI NON COMEDES, *** VEREDES
8175 5ELCID1042 SABET, *** UOS DARE AUOS VN DINERO MALO;
```

WORD C# PREFIX CONTEXT

NON (CON'T)

8186 5ELCID1043 MAS QUANTO AUEDES PERDICO *** UOS LO DARE,
8204 5ELCID1045 QUE COMIGO ANDAN LAZRADOS, & *** UOS LO DARE.
8281 5ELCID1054 SI BIEN *** COMEDES, CONDE, DON YO SEA PAGADO,
8354 5ELCID1062 DEL DIA QUE FUE CONDE *** IANTE TAN DE BUEN GRADO,
8365 5ELCID1063 EL SABOR QUE DED E *** SERA OLBIDADO.
8433 5ELCID1072 E SI ***, MANDEDES BUSCAR; O ME DEXAREDES
8467 5ELCID1076 DE VENIR UOS BUSCAR SOL *** SERA PENSSADO.
8494 5ELCID1080 LO QUE *** FERIE EL CABOSO POR QUANTO ENEL MUNDO HA,
8507 5ELCID1081 VNA DES LEATANZA CA *** LA FIZO ALGUANDRE.
8551 5ELCID1086 TAN RICOS SON LOS SOS QUE *** SABEN QUE SE AN.
8640 5ELCID1097 DENTRO EN VALENZIA *** ES POCO EL MIEDO.
8650 5ELCID1098 PESA ALOS DE VALENZIA, SABET, *** LES PLAZE;
8782 5ELCID1117 *** FUE A NUESTRO GRADO NI NOS NON PUDIEMOS MAS,
8789 5ELCID1117 NON FUE A NUESTRO GRADO NI NOS *** PUDIEMOS MAS,
8866 5ELCID1129 A MI DEDES C CAUALLEROS, QUE *** UOS PIDO MAS,
8882 5ELCID1131 BIEN LOS FERREDES, QUE DUBDA *** Y AURA,
9078 5ELCID1155 MIEDO AN EN VALENZIA QUE *** SABEN QUESE FAR.
9157 5ELCID1166 *** ES CON RECABDO EL DOLOR DE VALENZIA.
9195 5ELCID1171 *** OSAN FUERAS EXIR NIN CON EL SE AIUNTAR;
9231 5ELCID1174 MAL SE AQUEXAN LOS DE VALENZIA QUE *** SABENT QUES FAR,
9240 5ELCID1175 DE NINGUNA PART QUE SEA *** LES VINIE PAN;
9250 5ELCID1176 NIN DA COSSEIO PADRE A FIJO, *** FIJO A PADRE,
9281 5ELCID1180 DELANTE VEYEN SO DUELO, *** SE PUEDEN HUUIAR,
9302 5ELCID1183 *** LES DIXO COSEIO, NIN LOS VINO HUUIAR.
9384 5ELCID1193 TODOS VENGAN DE GRADO, NINGUNO *** HA PREMIA,
9424 5ELCID1198 AL SABOR DELA GANANZIA *** LO QUIERE DETARDAR,
9459 5ELCID1202 MYO ZID DON RODRIGO *** LO QUISO DETARDAR,
9476 5ELCID1204 BIEN LA ZERCA MYO ZID, QUE *** Y AUYA HART;
9628 5ELCID1223 QUE PRESA ES VALENZIA, QUE *** GELA ENPARAN;
9770 5ELCID1241 NIN ENTRARIE ENELA TIGERA, NI VN PELO *** AURIE TAIADO,
9874 5ELCID1252 QUE NINGUN OMNE DELOS SOS QUES LE *** SPIDIES, ONOL BESAS LA MANO,
10026 5ELCID1273 SI AUOS PLOGUIERE, MINAYA, & *** UOS CAYA EN PESAR,
10230 5ELCID1295 ALOS DIAS DEL SIEGLO *** LE LORASSEN CHRISTIANOS.
10343 5ELCID1310 DEXARE UOS LAS POSADAS, *** LAS QUIERO CONTAR.
10454 5ELCID1325 ECHASTES LE DE TIERRA, *** HA LA UUESTRA AMOR;
10624 5ELCID1346 SEMEIA QUE EN TIERRA DE MOROS *** A BIUO OMNE,
10747 5ELCID1361 *** QUIERO QUE NADA PIERDA EL CAMPEADOR;
10858 5ELCID1375 *** LA OSARIEMOS A COMETER NOS ESTA RAZON,
10877 5ELCID1377 *** LO DIZEN A NADI, & FINCO ESTA RAZON.
10980 5ELCID1389 EL ZID QUE BIEN NOS QUIERA NADA *** PERDERA.
10985 5ELCID1390 RESPUSO MYNAYA: ESTO *** MEA POR QUE PESAR.
11086 5ELCID1403 TODO SERIE ALEGRE, QUE *** AURIE NINGUN PESAR.
11288 5ELCID1428 PALAFRES & MULAS, QUE *** PARESCAN MAL.
11365 5ELCID1438 SI ***, DEXAREMOS BURGOS, YR LO HEMOS BUSCAR.
11632 5ELCID1474 E QUANTO QUE PUEDEN *** FINCAN DE ANDAR.
11675 5ELCID1480 AMY *** ME PESA, SABET, MUCHO ME PLAZE
11685 5ELCID1481 FABLO MUÑO GUSTIOZ, *** SPERO A NADI:
11722 5ELCID1486 E FFATA EN VALENZIA DELLAS *** UOS PARTADES.
11769 5ELCID1492 PASSARON MATA DE TORANZ DE TAL GUISA QUE NINGUN MIEDO *** HAN,
11796 5ELCID1496 ESTO *** DETARDO, CA DE CORAZON LO HAN;
11887 5ELCID1507 BIEN SALIERON DEN ZIENTO QUE *** PAREZEN MAL,
12022 5ELCID1524 MAGER QUE MAL LE QUERAMOS, *** GELO PODREMOS FER,
12039 5ELCID1526 MUCHOL TENGO POR TORPE QUI *** CONESZE LA VERDAD.
12070 5ELCID1530 DESTO QUE AUEDES FECHO UOS *** PERDEREDES NADA.
12229 5ELCID1552 DE QUANTO QUE QUISIERON *** OUIERON FALLA,
12265 5ELCID1557 LOS SOS DESPENDIE EL MORO, QUE DELO SO *** TOMAUA NADA.
12398 5ELCID1574 AVN *** SABIE MYO ZID, EL QUE EN BUEN ORA ZINXO ESPADA,
12490 5ELCID1584 EL QUE EN BUEN ORA NASCO *** LO DETARDAUA:
12795 5ELCID1624 E EL *** GELO GRADEZE SI NON A IHESU CHRISTO.
12799 5ELCID1624 E EL NON GELO GRADEZE SI *** A IHESU CHRISTO.
12929 5ELCID1640 ENTRARE EN LAS ARMAS, *** LO PODRE DEXAR;
12986 5ELCID1647 YA MUGIER ONDRADA, *** AYADES PESAR
13031 5ELCID1653 *** AYADES PAUOR POR QUE ME VEADES LIDIAR,
13114 5ELCID1662 DEL DIA QUE NASQUIERAN *** VIERAN TAL TREMOR.
13125 5ELCID1664 *** AYADES MIEDO, CATODO ES UUESTRA PRO;
13289 5ELCID1685 OYD ME, CAUALLEROS, *** RASTARA POR AL;
13357 5ELCID1693 FABLAUA MYNAYA, *** LO QUISO DETARDAR:
13599 5ELCID1723 ATANTOS MATA DE MOROS QUE *** FUERON CONTADOS;
13690 5ELCID1735 *** ESCAPARON MAS DE ZIENTO & QUATRO.
13716 5ELCID1738 LAS OTRAS GANANZIAS *** AUYA RECABDO.
14024 5ELCID1777 *** PUDIERON ELLOS SABER LA CUENTA DE TODOS LOS CAUALLOS,
14038 5ELCID1778 QUE ANDAN ARRIADOS & *** HA QUI TOMALOS,
14125 5ELCID1788 E *** LA TOLLIESSE DENT CHRISTIANO:
14179 5ELCID1795 *** TIENE EN CUENTA LOS MOROS QUE HA MATADOS;
14252 5ELCID1803 EL BUENO DE MYO ZID *** LO TARDO POR NADA:
14268 5ELCID1805 DELO QUE AUOS CAYO VOS *** GRADEZEDES NADA;
14338 5ELCID1814 QUE *** DIGA MAL EL REY ALFONSSO DEL QUE VALENZIA MANDA.
14478 5ELCID1831 ALEGRE FUE EL REY, *** VIESTES ATANTO,
14543 5ELCID1839 CUEDAN SE QUE ES ALMOFALLA, CA *** VIENEN CON MANDADO;
14967 5ELCID1892 DEL CASAMIENTO *** SE SIS ABRA SABOR;
15315 5ELCID1939 DESTE CASAMIENTO *** AURIA SABOR;
15392 5ELCID1950 *** ERA MARAUILLA SIQUISIESSE EL REY ALFONSSO,
15498 5ELCID1964 *** LO DETARDAN, A MYO ZID SE TORNAUAN.
15634 5ELCID1983 *** SON EN CUENTA, SABET, LAS CASTELLANAS.

WORD C# PREFIX CONTEXT

NON (CON'T)

15656 5ELCID1986 *** LO DETARDA, PORA LAS VISTAS SE ADOBO;
15783 5ELCID2002 LAS PUERTAS DEL ALCA%AR QUE *** SE ABRIESSEN DE DIA NIN DE NOCH,
15827 5ELCID2007 QUE DEL ALCA%AR VNA SALIR *** PUECE,
15856 5ELCID2011 MYO %ID SELOS GA@ARA, QUE *** GELOS DIERAN EN DON.
15913 5ELCID2018 SI *** A ESTOS CAUALLEROS QUE QUERIE DE CORA%ON;
15998 5ELCID2029 SIESTO *** FECHES, NON AUREDES MY AMOR.
16000 5ELCID2029 SIESTO NON FECHES, *** AUREDES MY AMOR.
16142 5ELCID2047 DIXO EL REY: *** ES AGUISADO OY:
16220 5ELCID2058 *** SE PUEDE FARTAR DEL, TANTOL QUERIE DE CORA%ON;
16323 5ELCID2071 *** LO TARDO EL REY, LA RAZON CONPE%O:
16415 5ELCID2082 *** ABRIA FIJAS DE CASAR, RESPUSO EL CAMPEADOR,
16424 5ELCID2083 CA *** HAN GRANT HEDAND E DE DIAS PEQUENAS SON.
16661 5ELCID2110 VOS CASADES MIS FIJAS, CA *** GELAS DO YO.
16857 5ELCID2134 *** GELAS DARE YO CON MI MANO, NIN DED NON SE ALABARAN.
16866 5ELCID2134 NON GELAS DARE YO CON MI MANO, NIN DED *** SE ALABARAN.
17036 5ELCID2157 *** QUIERE QUEL ESCURA, QUITOL DESSI LUEGO.
17149 5ELCID2170 EN CASA DE MYO %ID *** A DOS MEIORES,
17177 5ELCID2173 QUE ES LARGO DE LENGUA, MAS EN LO AL *** ES TAN PRO.
17343 5ELCID2194 *** SERAN MENGUADAS EN TODOS UUESTROS DIAS
17383 5ELCID2199 MAS BIEN SABET VERDAD QUE *** LO LEUANTE YO:
17427 5ELCID2204 BIEN MELO CREADES, QUE EL UOS CASA, CA *** YO.
17836 5ELCID2257 *** FUERON EN CUENTA LOS AUERES MONEDADOS.
18067 5ELCID2286 FERRAN GON%ALEZ *** VIO ALLI DOS AL%ASSE, NIN CAMARA ABIERTA NIN
18093 5ELCID2289 DIZIENDO DELA BOCA: *** VERE CARRION
18221 5ELCID2305 MAGER LOS ESTAN LAMANDO, NINGUNO *** RESPONDE.
18233 5ELCID2307 *** VIESTES TAL GUEGO COMMO YUA POR LA CORT;
18325 5ELCID2318 CA VEYEN TANTAS TIENDAS DE MOROS DE QUE *** AUIE SABOR.
18353 5ELCID2322 ESTO ES AGUISADO POR *** VER CARRION,
18404 5ELCID2329 QUE SEAN EN PAS & *** AYAN Y RA%ION.
18562 5ELCID2349 POR LA SU VOLUNTAD *** SERIEN ALLI LEGADOS.
18604 5ELCID2354 CALOS MOROS, CON DIOS, *** FINCARAN EN CANPO.
18622 5ELCID2356 QUE OY LOS YFANTES AMI POR AMO *** ABRAN;
18797 5ELCID2379 SI ESTE AMOR *** FECHES, YO DEUOS ME QUIERO QUITAR.
19091 5ELCID2415 MAS SI EL CAUALLO *** ESTROPIE%A O COMIGO NON CAYE,
19095 5ELCID2415 MAS SI EL CAUALLO NON ESTROPIE%A O COMIGO *** CAYE,
19097 5ELCID2416 *** TE IUNTARAS COMIGO FATA DENTRO EN LA MAR.
19111 5ELCID2417 AQUI RESPUSO MYO %ID: ESTO *** SERA VERDAD.
19351 5ELCID2451 DELOS COLPES DELA LAN%A *** AUIE RECABDO;
19358 5ELCID2452 AQUELOS QUE GELOS DIERAN *** GELO AUIEN LOGRADO.
19625 5ELCID2487 ELA SU QUINTA *** FUESSE OLBIDADO.
19654 5ELCID2491 TANTOS SON DE MUCHOS QUE *** SERIEN CONTADOS.
19726 5ELCID2501 ELLOS LO TEMEN, CA *** LO PIESSO YO:
19972 5ELCID2534 MAS *** FALLAUAN Y ADIEGO NI AFERRANDO.
20014 5ELCID2539 DESTO QUE ELLOS FABLARON NOS PARTE *** AYAMOS:
20608 5ELCID2616 QUE ESTOS CASAMIENTOS *** SERIEN SIN ALGUNA TACHA.
20996 5ELCID2668 *** TIENE PORIDAD, DIXOLO AVENGALUON:
21043 5ELCID2674 DELO QUE EL MORO DIXO ALOS YFANTES *** PLAZE:
21312 5ELCID2709 QUE *** YFINCAS NINGUNO, MUGIER NIN VARON,
21319 5ELCID2710 SI *** AMAS SUS MUGIERES DO@A ELUIRA & DO@A SOL:
21373 5ELCID2717 *** ABREDES PART EN TIERRAS DE CARRION.
21481 5ELCID2731 ATAN MALOS ENSSIENPLOS *** FAGADES SOBRE NOS:
21505 5ELCID2734 LO QUE RUEGAN LAS DUENAS *** LES HA NINGUN PRO.
21603 5ELCID2747 HYA *** PUEDEN FABLAR DON ELUIRA & DONA SOL;
21653 5ELCID2752 POR MUERTAS LAS DEXARON, SABED, QUE *** POR BIUAS.
21700 5ELCID2759 *** LAS DEUIEMOS TOMAR POR VARRAGANAS,
21707 5ELCID2760 SI *** FUESSEMOS ROGADOS,
21713 5ELCID2761 PUES NUESTRAS PAREIAS *** ERAN PORA EN BRA%OS.
21751 5ELCID2766 MANDARON LE YR ADELANTE, MAS DE SU GRADO *** FUE.
21811 5ELCID2774 SABET BIEN QUE SI ELLOS LE VIESSEN, *** ESCAPARA DE MUERT.
21883 5ELCID2784 TANTO SON DE TRASPUESTAS QUE *** PUEDEN DEZIR NADA.
21923 5ELCID2789 LOS GANADOS FIEROS *** NOS COMAN EN AQUESTE MONT
21952 5ELCID2793 DE QUE *** ME FALLAREN LOS YFANTES DE CARRION,
21966 5ELCID2795 SI DIOS *** NOS VALE, AQUI MORREMOS NOS.
22239 5ELCID2832 PAR AQUESTA BARBA QUE NADI *** MESSO,
22241 5ELCID2833 *** LA LOGRARAN LOS YFANTES DE CARRION;
22305 5ELCID2841 *** LO DETARDAN EL MANDADO DE SU SE@OR,
22369 5ELCID2850 *** GELO QUISO TOMAR, MAS MUCHO GELO GRADIO:
22501 5ELCID2865 DON ELUIRA & DO@A SOL, CUYDADO *** AYADES,
22688 5ELCID2891 HYO TOME EL CASAMIENTO, MAS *** OSE DEZIR AL.
22745 5ELCID2898 EL QUE EN BUEN ORA NASCO *** QUISO TARDAR,
22831 5ELCID2908 EL CASO MIS FIJAS, CA *** GELAS DI YO:
23224 5ELCID2958 SI QUIER EL CASAMIENTO FECHO *** FUESSE OY
23245 5ELCID2961 LO QUE *** CUYDAUA FER DE TODA ESTA SAZON,
23291 5ELCID2967 E QUE *** AYA RENCURA PODIENDO YO VEDALLO.
23360 5ELCID2976 *** LO DETIENE POR NADA ALFONSSO EL CASTELLANO,
23407 5ELCID2982 QUI *** VINIESSE ALA CORT NON SE TOUIESSE POR SU VASSALLO.
23411 5ELCID2982 QUI NON VINIESSE ALA CORT *** SE TOUIESSE POR SU VASSALLO.
23426 5ELCID2984 QUE *** FALIESSEN DELO QUE EN REY AUYE MANDADO.
23500 5ELCID2993 QUI LO FER *** QUISIESSE, O NO YR A MI CORT,
23512 5ELCID2994 QUITE MYO REYNO, CADEL *** HE SABOR.
23653 5ELCID3013 AVN *** ERA LEGADO EL QUE ENBUEN ORA NA%IO,
23667 5ELCID3014 POR QUE SE TARDA EL REY *** HA SABOR.
23766 5ELCID3027 QUANDO LO OYO EL REY, POR NADA *** TARDO;
23772 5ELCID3028 PAR SANT ESIDRO, VERDAD *** SERA OY

WORD C# PREFIX CONTEXT

NON (CON'T)

23778 5ELCID3029 CAUALGAD, %ID; SI ***, NCN AURIA DEC SABOR;
23779 5ELCID3029 CAUALGAD, %ID; SI NON, *** AURIA DEC SABOR;
23899 5ELCID3044 ESSA NOCH MYC %ID TAIC *** CUISO PASSAR;
24123 5ELCID3076 E QUE *** PARESCAN LAS ARMAS, BIEN PRESOS LOS CORDONES;
24277 5ELCID3096 QUE *** LE CCNTALASSEN LOS PELOS AL BUEN %ID CANPEADOR;
24548 5ELCID3129 HYO, DE QUE FU REY, *** FIZ MAS DE DOS CORTES:
24619 5ELCID3136 E ESTOS OTROS CONDES QUE DEL VANDO *** SODES.
24634 5ELCID3138 POR ESCOGER EL DERECHC, CA TUERTO *** MANDO YO.
24725 5ELCID3149 POR MIS FIJAS QUEM DEXARON YO *** HE DESONOR,
24785 5ELCID3157 CCMIGO *** QUISIERCN AUER NADA & PERDIERON MI AMOR;
24800 5ELCID3158 DEN ME MIS ESPADAS QUANCC MYOS YERNOS *** SON.
24884 5ELCID3169 HYA MAS *** AURA DERECHO DE NOS EL %ID CANPEADOR.
25017 5ELCID3186 PAR AQUESTA BARBA QUE NACI *** MESSO,
25181 5ELCID3206 DEN ME MIS AUERES, QUANDC MYOS YERNOS *** SON.
25275 5ELCID3218 *** ACUERDAN EN CCNSSEIC, CA LOS HAUERES GRANDES SON:
25331 5ELCID3225 SI ESSC PLCGIERE AL %ID, *** GELO VECAMOS NOS;
25408 5ELCID3235 QUANDO ELLCS LCS AN APECHAR, *** GELOS QUIERO YO.
25416 5ELCID3236 FABLO FERRANGO%ALEZ: AUERES MCNEDADOS *** TENEMOS NOS.
25505 5ELCID3248 ENPRESTAN LES DELO AGENC, QUE *** LES CUMPLE LO SUYO.
25549 5ELCID3254 LA RENCURA MAYOR *** SEME PUEDE OLBICAR.
25625 5ELCID3263 QUANDO LAS *** QUERIEDES, YA CANES TRAYDORES,
25670 5ELCID3269 SI *** RECUDEDES, VEA LO ESTA CORT.
25721 5ELCID3276 *** GELAS DEUIEN QUERER SUS FIJAS POR VARRAGANAS,
25747 5ELCID3279 QUANTO EL DIZE *** GELO PRE%IAMOS NADA.
25789 5ELCID3285 CA *** ME PRISC AELLA FIJO DE MUGIER NADA,
25822 5ELCID3289 *** YOUO RAPAZ QUE NON MESSO SU PULGADA;
25826 5ELCID3289 NCN YOUO RAPAZ QUE *** MESSO SU PULGADA;
25835 5ELCID3290 LA QUE YO MESSE AVN *** ES EGUADA.
25861 5ELCID3295 *** CRE%IES VARAIA ENTRE NOS & VOS.
25885 5ELCID3298 CA *** PERTENE%IEN FIJAS DE YFAN%ONES.
25938 5ELCID3305 SI YO RESPONDIER, TU *** ENTRARAS EN ARMAS.
25951 5ELCID3307 DETIENES LE LA LENGUA, *** PUEDE DELIBRAR,
25979 5ELCID3311 BIEN LO SABEDES QUE YO *** PUEDO MAS;
25990 5ELCID3312 POR LO QUE YO CUIER AFER POR MI *** MANCARA.
26036 5ELCID3319 SI YO *** VUJAS, EL MORC TE JUGARA MAL;
26096 5ELCID3326 CROUIERCN TELC TCDOS, MAS *** SABEN LA VERDAD.
26117 5ELCID3330 *** TE VIENE EN MIENTE EN VALEN%IA LO DEL LEON,
26217 5ELCID3342 DEMANDO POR SUS YERNOS, NINGUNO *** FALLO
26307 5ELCID3355 ESTOS CASAMIENTOS *** FUESSEN APARE%IDOS
26368 5ELCID3363 LO DEL LEON *** SE TE DEUE OLBICAR;
26387 5ELCID3366 MAS *** VESTID EL MANTO NIN EL BRIAL.
26396 5ELCID3367 HYOLLO LIDIARE, *** PASSARA POR AL:
26526 5ELCID3386 *** DIZES VERDAD AMIGC NI HA SE@OR,
26543 5ELCID3388 EN TU AMISTAD *** QUIERO AVER RA%ION.
26675 5ELCID3406 VOS LAS CASASTES ANTES, CA YO ***,
26687 5ELCID3408 SIN UUESTRO MANDADC NADA *** FERE YO.
26835 5ELCID3428 MAS *** PLAZE ALOS YFANTES DE CARRION.
26858 5ELCID3431 E QUE *** PESE ESTO AL %ID CAMPEADOR:
27106 5ELCID3464 *** DIGA NINGUNO DELLA MAS VNA ENTEN%ION.
27141 5ELCID3468 DANDOS, REY, PLAZO, CA CRAS SER *** PUEDE.
27215 5ELCID3479 QUE *** PRENDAN FUER%A DE CONDE NIN DE YFAN%ON.
27248 5ELCID3483 QUEN *** VINIERE AL PLAZO PIERDA LA RAZON,
27409 5ELCID3501 TALES YA QUE PRENDEN, TALES YA QUE ***.
27480 5ELCID3510 QUE EN TODAS NUESTRAS TIERRAS *** HA TAN BUEN VARON.
27513 5ELCID3514 EN MOROS NI EN CHRISTIANOS OTRO TAL *** HA OY,
27531 5ELCID3516 ESSORA DIXO EL REY: DESTO *** HE SABOR;
27812 5ELCID3549 POR QUERER EL DERECHO & *** CONSENTIR EL TUERTO.
27856 5ELCID3555 QUE *** FUESSEN EN LA BATALLA LAS ESPADAS TAIADORES
27868 5ELCID3556 COLADA & TIZON, QUE *** LIDIASSEN CON ELLAS LOS DEL CANPEADOR;
27889 5ELCID3558 DIXIERCN GELO AL REY, MAS *** GELO CONLOYO;
27892 5ELCID3559 *** SACASTES NINGUNA QUANDO OUIEMOS LA CORT.
27929 5ELCID3564 QUE NADA *** MANCARA POR LOS DEL CAMPEADOR.
27947 5ELCID3566 ESSI FUERES VEN%IDOS, *** REBTEDES A NOS,
28031 5ELCID3578 *** SABEMOS QUES CCMIDRAN ELLOS OQUE NON;
28037 5ELCID3578 NON SABEMOS QUES CCMIDRAN ELLOS OQUE ***;
28148 5ELCID3593 EL REY DIOLES FIELES POR DEZIR EL DERECHO & AL ***,
28150 5ELCID3594 QUE *** VARAGEN CON ELLOS DESI O DE NON.
28157 5ELCID3594 QUE NON VARAGEN CON ELLCS DESI O DE ***.
28180 5ELCID3597 ESTA LID EN TOLEDO LAFIZIERADES, MAS *** QUISIESTES VOS.
28202 5ELCID3600 AUED UUESTRO DERECHO, TUERTO *** QUERADES VOS,
28217 5ELCID3602 ENTODO MYO REYNO *** AURA BUENA SABOR.
28271 5ELCID3609 MAS DE VJ ASTAS DE LAN%AS QUE *** LEGASSEN AL MOION.
28828 5ELCID3682 APART LE PRISO, QUE *** CABEL CORA%ON;
29098 5ELCID3716 SIN VERGUEN%A LAS CASARE OAQUI PESE OAQUI ***.
29249 5ELCID3734 ES LEYDO, DAT NOS DEL VINO; SI *** TENEDES DINEROS, ECHAD
WORD #2881 OCCURS 364 TIMES.
INDEX OF DIVERSIFICATION = 79.14 WITH STANDARD DEVIATION OF 91.25

NONBRADOS 3599 5ELCID0454 ********* SON LOS QUE YRAN ENEL ALGARA,
WORD #2882 OCCURS 1 TIMES.

NONBRAR 9978 5ELCID1264 QUANDO LOS FALLO, POR CUENTA FIZO LOS *******:
WORD #2883 OCCURS 1 TIMES.

WORD C# PREFIX CONTEXT

```
NONBREL             25030 5ELCID3188 ASO SOBRINC POR ******* LAMC,
        WORD #2884 CCCURS   1 TIMES.

NOS                   570 5ELCID0072 ESTA NOCH YGAMOS & UAYMCS *** AL MATINO,
                      955 5ELCID0123 *** HUEBOS AUEMOS EN TODO DE GANAR ALGO.
                     1002 5ELCID0129 MAS DEZID *** DEL %ID, CE CUE SERA PAGADO,
                     1012 5ELCIDC130 O QUE GANAN%IA *** DARA PCR TODO AQUESTE A@O?
                     1075 5ELCIDC138 HUEBOS AUEMOS QUE *** DEDES LOS MARCHOS.
                     1109 5ELCID0143 E *** UCS AIUDAREMOS, QUE ASSI ES AGUISADO,
                     1137 5ELCID0146 DIXO RACHEL & VIDAS:  *** DESTC NOS PAGAMOS.
                     1139 5ELCIDC146 DIXO RACHEL & VIDAS:  NCS DESTO *** PAGAMOS.
                     1545 5ELCID0198 ATORGAR *** HEDES ESTC CUE AUEMOS PARADO.
                     2160 5ELCIDC272 E *** DEUOS PARTIR NOS HEMOS EN VIDA.
                     2163 5ELCIDC272 E NOS DEUOS PARTIR *** HEMOS EN VIDA.
                     2168 5ELCID0273 DAND *** CCNSEIC PCR AMCR CE SANTA MARIA
                     2224 5ELCID0280 YA LO VEDES QUE PARTIR *** EMCS EN VICA,
                     2521 5ELCID0319 LA MISSA *** DIRA, ESTA SERA CE SANTA TRINIDAD;
                     2894 5ELCID0365 QUANDO OY *** PARTIMOS, EN VICA NOS FAZ IUNTAR.
                     2898 5ELCID0365 QUANDO OY NOS PARTIMOS, EN VICA *** FAZ IUNTAR.
                     2961 5ELCIDC373 AGCRA *** PARTIMCS, CICS SABE EL AIUNTAR.
                     3033 5ELCID0382 DIOS QUE *** DIO LAS ALMAS, CONSEIO NOS DARA.
                     3038 5ELCID0382 DIOS QUE NOS DIO LAS ALMAS, CONSEIO *** DARA.
                     3105 5ELCIDC390 CA EN YERMC C EN POBLADC PCDER *** HAN ALCAN%AR.
                     3363 5ELCIDC424 DESPUES QUI *** BUSCARE FALLAR NOS PODRA.
                     3366 5ELCID0424 DESPUES QUI NCS BUSCARE FALLAR *** PODRA.
                     4147 5ELCID0528 BUSCAR *** YE EL REY ALFCNSSO CON TOCA SU MESNACA.
                     4183 5ELCIDC532 %ERCA ES EL REY ALFCNSSC & BUSCAR *** VERNA.
                     4609 5ELCID0585 ANTES QUEL PRENCAN LCS CE TERUEL, SI NON NON *** DARAN DENT NADA;
                     4619 5ELCID0586 LA PARIA QUEL A PRESA TCRNAR *** LA HA DOBLADA.
                     4654 5ELCID0590 DIZEN LCS DE ALCO%ER:  YA SE *** VA LA GANA%IA
                     4918 5ELCIDC622 POSAREMOS EN SUS CASAS & DELLCS *** SERUIREMOS.
                     5274 5ELCID0667 EL AGUA *** AN VECACA, EXIR NCS HA EL PAN,
                     5278 5ELCID0667 EL AGUA NOS AN VECACA, EXIR *** HA EL PAN,
                     5283 5ELCID0668 QUE *** QUERAMOS YR DE NOCH NO NOS LO CONSINTRAN;
                     5289 5ELCID0668 QUE NOS QUERAMCS YR DE NOCH NO *** LO CONSINTRAN;
                     5328 5ELCID0673 SI CON MOROS NON LIDIAREMOS, NC *** DARAN DEL PAN.
                     5334 5ELCID0674 BIEN SCMOS *** VI %IENTOS, ALGUNOS AY DE MAS;
                     5441 5ELCIDC687 SI *** MURIEREMOS EN CAMPC, EN CASTIELLO NOS ENTRARAN,
                     5447 5ELCID0687 SI NOS MURIEREMOS EN CAMPO, EN CASTIELLO *** ENTRARAN,
                     5959 5ELCIDC755 FIRME SCN LCS MCRCS, AVN *** VAN CEL CAMPO.
                     6369 5ELCID0811 DAQUESTA RIQUEZA QUE EL CRIADOR *** ADADO
                     6513 5ELCIDC831 DIOS *** VALIC & VEN%IEMCS LA LIDIT.
                     6522 5ELCIDC832 ALA TORNADA, SI *** FALLAREDES AQUI;
                     6690 5ELCIDC854 *** PAGADOS FINCADCS, SE@OR, CELA TU PART.
                     7685 5ELCIDC984 QUE A MENOS DE BATALLA *** PUECEN DEN QUITAR.
                     7709 5ELCID0987 EL CCNDE DCN REMCNT CAR *** HA GRANT BATALLA,
                     7725 5ELCIDC989 AMENOS DE BATALLA NCN *** DEXARIE POR NADA.
                     7733 5ELCID0990 PUES ADELLANT YRAN TRAS ***, AQUI SEA LA BATALLA;
                     7760 5ELCID0994 *** CAUALGAREMOS SIELLAS GALLEGAS, & HUESAS SOBRE CAL%AS;
                     8214 5ELCID1046 PRENDIENDO DEUOS & DE OTRCS YR *** HEMOS PAGANDO;
                     8293 5ELCID1055 AQUI FEREMCS LA MORADA, NC *** PARTIREMOS AMOS.
                     8342 5ELCID1061 MANDAD *** CAR LAS BESTIAS & CAUALGEREMOS PRIUADO;
                     8698 5ELCID1105 SI *** %ERCAR VIENEN, CCNDERECHO LO FAZEN.
                     8707 5ELCID1106 AMENOS DE LIC *** PARTIRA AQUESTO;
                     8716 5ELCID1107 VAYAN LOS MANDADOS POR LCS QUE *** DEUEN AIUDAR,
                     8777 5ELCID1116 DESPUES QUE *** PARTIEMCS DELA LINPIA CHRISTIANDAD,
                     8788 5ELCID1117 NON FUE A NUESTRO GRADO NI *** NON PUDIEMOS MAS,
                     8803 5ELCID1119 LOS DE VALEN%IA %ERCADOS *** HAN;
                     9258 5ELCID1177 NIN AMIGO A AMIGO *** PUEDEN CONSOLAR.
                     9500 5ELCID1207 MAS LE VIENEN A MYO %ID, SABET, QUE *** LE VAN.
                     9793 5ELCID1244 CON EL MYNAYA ALBARFFANEZ QUE *** LE PARTE DE SO BRA%O.
                    10115 5ELCID1281 AESTAS TIERRAS ESTRANAS QUE *** PUDIEMOS GANAR.
                    10255 5ELCID1298 QUANDO DIOS PRESTAR *** QUIERE, NOS BIEN GELO GRADESCAMOS:
                    10257 5ELCID1298 QUANDO DIOS PRESTAR NCS QUIERE, *** BIEN GELO GRADESCAMOS:
                    10863 5ELCID1375 NON LA OSARIEMOS A CCMETER *** ESTA RAZON,
                    10872 5ELCID1376 MYO %ID ES DE BIUAR & *** DELCS CONDES DE CARRION.
                    10958 5ELCID1387 SALUDAD *** A MYC %ID EL DE BIUAR,
                    10977 5ELCID1389 EL %ID QUE BIEN *** QUIERA NACA NON PERDERA.
                    11137 5ELCID1409 MIENTRA QUE FUEREMOS POR SUS TIERRAS CONDUCHO *** MANDO DAR.
                    11145 5ELCID1410 DE AQUESTOS XV DIAS, SICIOS *** CURIARE DE MAL,
                    11319 5ELCID1433 DESFECHOS *** HA EL %ID, SABET, SI NO NOS VAL;
                    11326 5ELCID1433 DESFECHOS NOS HA EL %ID, SABET, SI NO *** VAL;
                    11332 5ELCID1434 SOLTARIEMOS LA GANAN%IA, QUE *** DIESSE EL CABDAL.
                    11879 5ELCID1506 ESSO FFUE APRIESSA FECHC, QUE *** QUIEREN DETARDAR.
                    12992 5ELCID1648 RIQUEZA ES QUE *** A CRE%E MARAUILLOSA & GRAND;
                    13309 5ELCID1688 DEZIR *** HA LA MISSA, & PENSSAD DE CAUALGAR,
                    13322 5ELCID1689 EL OBISPO DC IHERCNIMC SCLTURA *** DARA,
                    13340 5ELCID1691 MAS VALE QUE *** LCS VEZCAMOS, QUE ELLOS COIAN EL PAN.
                    13392 5ELCID1697 ODE AMAS ODEL VNA DIOS *** VALDRA.
                    13410 5ELCID1700 *** DETARDAN CE ABOBASSE ESSAS YENTES CHRISTIANAS.
                    13824 5ELCID1751 QUANDO EN VUESTRA VENICA TAL GANAN%IA *** AN DADA.
                    14729 5ELCID1862 EN LA ONDRA QUE EL HA *** SEREMOS ABILTADOS;
                    14754 5ELCID1865 POR ESTO QUE EL FAZE *** ABREMOS ENBARGO.
                    14923 5ELCID1886 CON UUESTRC CCNSSEIC LO QUEREMCS FER ***,
```

WORD C# PREFIX CONTEXT

NOS (CON'T)

14925 5ELCID1887 QUE *** DEMANDEDES FIJAS DEL CAMPEADOR;
15327 5ELCID1940 MAS PUES LO CONSEIA EL QUE MAS VALE QUE ***,
15335 5ELCID1941 FABLEMOS EN ELLO, EN LA PORIDAD SEAMOS ***.
15341 5ELCID1942 AFE DIOS DEL %IELLO QUE *** ACUERDE EN LO MIIOR.
15406 5ELCID1951 FASTA DO LO FALLASSEMOS BUSCAR LO YREMOS ***,
15424 5ELCID1953 MAS LO QUE EL QUISIERE, ESSO QUERAMOS ***.
16150 5ELCID2048 VOS AGORA LEGASTES, & *** VINJEMOS ANOCH;
16181 5ELCID2053 OMILLAMOS ***, %ID, EN BUEN ORA NASQUIESTES UOS
16464 5ELCID2087 ENTRE YO YELLAS EN UUESTRA MER%ED SOMOS ***,
17062 5ELCID2160 MER%ED UOS SEA & FAZED *** ESTE PERDON:
17352 5ELCID2195 QUANDO UOS *** CASAREDES BIEN SEREMOS RICAS.
18141 5ELCID2295 HYA SE@OR ONDRADO, REBATA *** DIO EL LEON.
18348 5ELCID2321 YA EN ESTA BATALLA A ENTRAR ABREMOS ***;
18408 5ELCID2330 *** CON UUSCO LA VENCREMOS, & VALER NOS HA EL CRIADOR.
18415 5ELCID2330 NOS CON UUSCO LA VENCREMOS, & VALER *** HA EL CRIADOR.
18822 5ELCID2382 *** DAQUENT VEREMOS COMMO LIDIA EL ABBAT.
19055 5ELCID2411 SALUDAR *** HEMOS AMOS, & TAIAREMOS AMISTAS.
19331 5ELCID2448 DESTA ARRANCADA *** YREMOS PAGADOS.
20012 5ELCID2539 DESTO QUE ELLOS FABLARON *** PARTE NON AYAMOS:
20074 5ELCID2548 ANTE QUE *** RETRAYAN LO QUE CUNTIO DEL LEON.
20081 5ELCID2549 *** DE NATURA SOMOS DE CONDES DE CARRION
20133 5ELCID2556 ANTES QUE *** RETRAYAN LO QUE FUE DEL LEON.
20178 5ELCID2562 DAD *** NUESTRAS MUGIERES QUE AUEMOS ABENDI%IONES;
20212 5ELCID2566 VERAN UUESTRAS FIJAS LO QUE AUEMOS ***,
20235 5ELCID2569 EL %ID QUE *** CURIAUA DE ASSI SER AFONTADO;
20445 5ELCID2595 VOS *** ENGENDRASTES, NUESTRA MADRE NOS PARIO;
20449 5ELCID2595 VOS NOS ENGENDRASTES, NUESTRA MADRE *** PARIO;
20458 5ELCID2597 AGORA *** ENVIADES ATIERRAS DE CARRION,
20464 5ELCID2598 DEBDO *** ES A CUNPLIR LO QUE MANDAREDES VOS.
20476 5ELCID2599 ASSI UOS PEDIMOS MER%ED *** AMAS ADOS,
20613 5ELCID2617 *** PUEDE REPENTIR, QUE CASADAS LAS HA AMAS.
20677 5ELCID2625 TORNEMOS ***, %ID, A VALEN%IA LA MAYOR;
20965 5ELCID2663 QUANTA RIQUIZA TIENE AUER LA YEMOS ***.
20979 5ELCID2665 NUNQUA AURIE DERECHO DE *** EL %ID CAMPEADOR.
21366 5ELCID2716 OY *** PARTIREMOS, & DEXADAS SEREDES DE NOS;
21372 5ELCID2716 OY NOS PARTIREMOS, & DEXADAS SEREDES DE ***;
21386 5ELCID2719 *** VENGAREMOS AQUESTA POR LA DEL LEON.
21461 5ELCID2728 CORTANDOS LAS CABECAS, MARTIRES SEREMOS ***:
21472 5ELCID2730 QUE POR LO QUE *** MERE%EMOS NO LO PRENDEMOS NOS;
21477 5ELCID2730 QUE POR LO QUE NOS MERE%EMOS NO LO PRENDEMOS ***;
21484 5ELCID2731 ATAN MALOS ENSSIENPLOS NON FAGADES SOBRE ***:
21486 5ELCID2732 SI *** FUEREMOS MAIADAS, ABILTAREDES AUOS,
21924 5ELCID2789 LOS GANADOS FIEROS NON *** COMAN EN AQUESTE MONT
21967 5ELCID2795 SI DIOS NON *** VALE, AQUI MORREMOS NOS.
21971 5ELCID2795 SI DIOS NON NOS VALE, AQUI MORREMOS ***.
22393 5ELCID2852 POR AQUESTA ONDRA QUE VOS DIESTES A ESTO QUE *** CUNTIO;
22470 5ELCID2861 EUOS A EL LO GRADID, QUANDO BIUAS SOMOS ***.
22847 5ELCID2910 SI DESONDRA Y CABE ALGUNA CONTRA ***,
22928 5ELCID2921 *** DAN VAGAR LOS DIAS & LAS NOCHES.
23092 5ELCID2942 CUEMO *** HAN ABILTADOS YFANTES DE CARRION:
23233 5ELCID2959 ENTRE YO & MYO %ID PESA *** DE CORA%ON.
23784 5ELCID3030 SALUDAR *** HEMOS DALMA & DE CORA%ON.
23874 5ELCID3041 DESTO QUE *** ABINO QUE UOS PESE, SE@OR.
24169 5ELCID3082 RESPONDIERON TODOS: *** ESSO QUEREMOS, SE@OR.
24180 5ELCID3084 *** DETIENE POR NADA EL QUE EN BUEN ORA NA%IO:
24409 5ELCID3112 *** QUISO LEUANTAR EL CRESPO DE GRA@ON,
24447 5ELCID3116 MAGER QUE ALGUNOS PESA, MEIOR SODES QUE ***.
24599 5ELCID3134 GRANDE TUERTO LE HAN TENIDO, SABEMOS LO TODOS ***;
24815 5ELCID3160 DIXO EL CONDE DON GAR%IA: AESTO *** FABLEMOS.
24844 5ELCID3164 AVN GRAND AMOR *** FAZE EL %ID CAMPEADOR,
24854 5ELCID3165 QUANDO DESONDRA DESUS FIJAS NO *** DEMANDA OY;
24858 5ELCID3166 BIEN *** ABENDREMOS CON EL REY DON ALFONSSO.
24888 5ELCID3169 HYA MAS NON AURA DERECHO DE *** EL %ID CANPEADOR.
24912 5ELCID3172 NOLO PODEMOS NEGAR, CA DOS ESPADAS *** DIO;
24988 5ELCID3183 *** LE PUEDEN CAMEAR, CA EL %ID BIEN LAS CONNOS%E;
25216 5ELCID3211 QUE AL NO *** DEMANDASSE, QUE AQUI FINCO LA BOZ. . .
25229 5ELCID3212 SI PLOGUIERE AL REY, ASSI DEZIMOS ***: DIXO EL REY
25299 5ELCID3221 MUCHO *** AFINCA EL QUE VALEN%IA GA@O,
25334 5ELCID3225 SI ESSO PLOGIERE AL %ID, NON GELO VEDAMOS ***;
25342 5ELCID3226 MAS EN NUESTRO IUUIZIO ASSI LO MANDAMOS ***,
25359 5ELCID3229 *** BIEN LA SABEMOS AQUESTA RAZON,
25418 5ELCID3236 FABLO FERRANGO%ALEZ: AUERES MONEDADOS NON TENEMOS ***.
25865 5ELCID3295 NON CRE%IES VARAIA ENTRE *** & VOS.
25896 5ELCID3299 POR QUE LAS DEXAMOS DERECHO FIZIEMOS ***;
25898 5ELCID3300 MAS *** PRE%IAMOS, SABET, QUE MENOS NO.
26159 5ELCID3335 *** %ERCAMOS EL ESCA@O POR CURIAR NUESTRO SE@OR,
26324 5ELCID3357 POR QUE DEXAMOS SUS FIJAS AVN NO *** REPENTIMOS,
26353 5ELCID3360 QUE POR QUE LAS DEXAMOS ONDRADOS SOMOS ***.
26471 5ELCID3378 QUIEN *** DARIE NUEUAS DE MYO %ID EL DE BIUAR
26940 5ELCID3441 ELLOS LAS HAN DEXADAS A PESAR DE ***.
27092 5ELCID3461 SI DIOS QUISIERE QUE DESTA BIEN SALGAMOS ***,
27150 5ELCID3470 *** ANTES ABREMOS AYR ATIERRAS DE CARRION.
27349 5ELCID3495 *** FARTAN DE CATARLE QUANTOS HA EN LA CORT.
27579 5ELCID3521 CA POR UOS & POREL CAUALLO ONDRADOS SOMO ***.

WORD C# PREFIX CONTEXT

NOS (CON'T)

```
                  27640 5ELCID3528 PRESO AUEMCS EL DEBDO & A PASSAR ES POR ***;
                  27756 5ELCID3542 EL COMETER FUE MALO, CUE LO AL *** ENPE%O,
                  27950 5ELCID3566 ESSI FUERES VEN%IDOS, NCN REBTEDES A ***,
                  28016 5ELCID3575 QUE FIEL SEADES OY DELLCS & DE ***;
                  28018 5ELCID3576 ADERECHO *** VALED, ANINGUN TUERTO NO.
                  28041 5ELCID3579 EN UUESTRA MANO *** METIC NUESTRO SE@OR;
                  28420 5ELCID3629 FIRME ESTIDO PERO VERMUEZ, POR ESSO *** ENCAMO;
                  28909 5ELCID3692 DIXIERCN LCS FIELES: ESTO OYMOS ***.
                  29029 5ELCID3708 DEXEMOS *** DE PLEYTCS DE YFANTES DE CARRION,
                  29045 5ELCID3710 FABLEMOS *** DAQUESTE CUE EN BUEN ORA NA%IO.
                  29195 5ELCID3728 ASSI FFAGAMCS *** TODCS IUSTOS & PECCADORES
                  29245 5ELCID3734 ES LEYDC, DAT *** DEL VINO; SI NON TENEDES DINEROS, ECHAD
         WORD #2885 OCCURS 177 TIMES.
            INDEX OF DIVERSIFICATICN =   161.93 WITH STANCARD DEVIATION OF   213.61

NOTADOS           13689 5ELCID1734 LOS L MILL PCR CUENTA FUERO *******:
         WORD #2886 OCCURS   1 TIMES.

NOTO               3320 5ELCID0419 **** TREZIENTAS LAN%AS CUE TOCAS TIENEN PENDONES.
         WORD #2887 OCCURS   1 TIMES.

NOTOLOS            1443 5ELCID0185 ******* DON MARTINO, SIN PESO LOS TOMAUA;
         WORD #2888 OCCURS   1 TIMES.

NUEF                318 5ELCID0040 VNA NI@A DE **** A@OS A OIO SE PARAUA:
         WORD #2889 OCCURS   1 TIMES.

NUES              21238 5ELCID2698 LOS MONTES SON ALTOS, LAS RAMAS PUIAN CON LAS ****,
         WORD #2890 OCCURS   1 TIMES.

NUESTRA            3018 5ELCID0380 PENSEMOS DE YR ******* VIA, ESTO SEA DE VAGAR.
                   3491 5ELCID0440 VOS CON C DE AQUESTA ******* CCNPA@A,
                   4717 5ELCID0598 CON LA MER%ED DEL CRIADOR ******* ES LA GANAN%IA
                  14896 5ELCID1883 CRE%REMOS EN ******* ONDRA & YREMOS ADELANT.
                  14938 5ELCID1888 CASAR QUEREMCS CON ELLAS ASU ONDRA & A ******* PRO.
                  20447 5ELCID2595 VOS NOS ENGENDRASTES, ******* MADRE NOS PARIO;
                  20516 5ELCID2604 DE MI & DE UUESTRO PACRE BIEN AVEDES ******* GRA%IA.
                  22477 5ELCID2862 EN LOS DIAS DE VAGAR TOCA ******* RENCURA SABREMOS CONTAR.
         WORD #2891 OCCURS   8 TIMES.
            INDEX OF DIVERSIFICATION =  2778.86 WITH STANDARD DEVIATION OF  3773.74

NUESTRAS           6686 5ELCID0853  VASTE, MYO %ID; ******** ORA%IONES UAYANTE DELANTE
                  20037 5ELCID2543 PIDAMOS ******** MUGIERES AL %ID CAMPEADOR,
                  20179 5ELCID2562 DAD NOS ******** MUGIERES CUE AUEMOS ABENDI%IONES;
                  20188 5ELCID2563 LEUAR LAS HEMOS A ******** TIERRAS DE CARRION,
                  21711 5ELCID2761 PUES ******** PAREIAS NCN ERAN PORA EN BRA%OS.
                  27478 5ELCID3510 QUE EN TODAS ******** TIERRAS NON HA TAN BUEN VARON.
         WORD #2892 OCCURS   6 TIMES.
            INDEX OF DIVERSIFICATION =  4157.40 WITH STANDARD DEVIATION OF  5643.27

NUESTRO             372 5ELCID0047 %ID, ENEL ******* MAL UOS NON GANADES NADA;
                   6506 5ELCID0830 A ******* AMIGOS BIEN LES PODEDES DEZIR:
                   8751 5ELCID1112 YO FIO POR DIOS QUE EN ******* PRO ENADRAN.
                   8785 5ELCID1117 NON FUE A ******* GRADO NI NOS NON PUDIEMOS MAS,
                   8796 5ELCID1118 GRADO A DIOS, LO ******* FUE ADELANT.
                   8899 5ELCID1133 COMMO FIO POR DIOS, EL CAMPO ******* SERA.
                  12032 5ELCID1525 EN PAZ O EN GERRA DELO ******* ABRA;
                  19596 5ELCID2483 LO VNO ES *******, LO OTRO HAN EN SALUO.
                  19904 5ELCID2524 GRADO A SANTA MARIA, MADRE DEL ******* SE@OR DIOS
                  19952 5ELCID2531 PENSAD DELO OTRO, QUE LO ******* TENEMOS LO EN SALUO.
                  20070 5ELCID2547 DESPUES EN LA CARRERA FEREMOS ******* SABOR,
                  21985 5ELCID2797 SI UOS LO MERESCA, MYO PRIMO, ******* PADRE EL CANPEADOR,
                  24904 5ELCID3171 MER%ED, YA REY DON ALFONSSO, SODES ******* SE@OR
                  25337 5ELCID3226 MAS EN ******* IUUIZIO ASSI LO MANDAMOS NOS,
                  26165 5ELCID3335 NOS %ERCAMOS EL ESCA@O POR CURIAR ******* SE@OR,
                  28043 5ELCID3579 EN UUESTRA MANO NOS METIO ******* SE@OR;
         WORD #2893 OCCURS  16 TIMES.
            INDEX OF DIVERSIFICATION =  1843.73 WITH STANDARD DEVIATION OF  2320.11

NUESTROS          19908 5ELCID2525 DESTOS ******** CASAMIENTOS UOS ABREDES HONOR.
                  21695 5ELCID2758 DE ******** CASAMIENTOS AGORA SOMOS VENGADOS;
                  23849 5ELCID3038 DIOS SALUE A ******** AMIGOS & AUOS MAS, SE@OR
                  25307 5ELCID3222 QUANDO DE ******** AUERES ASSIL PRENDE SABOR;
         WORD #2894 OCCURS   4 TIMES.

NUEUAS             7080 5ELCID0905 ASARAGO%A SUS ****** LEGAUAN,
                   7459 5ELCID0957 LEGARON LAS ****** ALCONDE DE BAR%ILONA,
                   9066 5ELCID1154 LAS ****** DE MYO %ID, SABET, SONANDO VAN,
                   9085 5ELCID1156 SONANDO VAN SUS ****** ALENT PARTE DEL MAR.
                   9488 5ELCID1206 SONANDO VAN SUS ****** TODAS ATODAS PARTES.
                   9713 5ELCID1235 LAS ****** DEL CAUALLERO YAVEDES DO LEGAUAN.
                  10166 5ELCID1287 EN ESTAS ****** TODOS SEA ALEGRANDO,
                  10598 5ELCID1343 E PLAZEM DELAS ****** QUE FAZE EL CAMPEADOR;
                  10843 5ELCID1373 MUCHO CRE%EN LAS ****** DE MYO %ID EL CAMPEADOR,
```

WORD C# PREFIX CONTEXT

NUEUAS (CON'T)

```
                 12272 5ELCID1558 CCN ESTAS ALEGRIAS & ****** TAN ONDRADAS
                 12761 5ELCID1620 DEZIR UOS QUIERO ****** DE ALENT PARTES DEL MAR,
                 12861 5ELCID1632 ESTAS ****** A MYC %ID ERAN VENIDAS;
                 14148 5ELCID1791 QUE CRCUIESSE SOS ****** DE MYC %ID QUE AUIE ALGO.
                 14843 5ELCID1876 TODAS ESTAS ****** A BIEN ABRAN DE VENIR.
                 14881 5ELCID1881 LAS ****** DEL %ID MUCHC VAN ADELANT,
                 16435 5ELCID2084 DE GRANDES ****** SCN LCS YFANTES DE CARRION,
                 16687 5ELCID2113 AQUIS METIO EN ****** MYO %ID EL CAMPEADOR;
                 18370 5ELCID2325 VINO CCN ESTAS ****** A MUO %ID RUYDIAZ EL CANPEADOR:
                 20395 5ELCID2588 GRANDES SON LAS ****** PCR VALEN%IA LA MAYOR,
                 20657 5ELCID2622 CON AQUESTAS ****** VERNAS AL CAMPEADOR.
                 21117 5ELCID2683 POCO PRE%IC LAS ****** CELOS CE CARRION.
                 23536 5ELCID2997 EL CONDE DCN GAR%IA EN ESTAS ****** FUE,
                 26473 5ELCID3378  QUIEN NOS DARIE ****** DE MYC %ID EL DE BIUAR
                 27435 5ELCID3505 QUANDO TODAS ESTAS ****** ASSI PUESTAS SON,
                 29203 5ELCID3729 ESTAS SON LAS ****** CE MYO %ID EL CANPEADOR,
          WORD #2895 OCCURS  25 TIMES.
             INDEX OF DIVERSIFICATION =   920.79 WITH STANDARD DEVIATION OF   824.91

NUEUE             9509 5ELCID1209 ***** MESES COMPLIDOS, SABET, SOBRELLA IAZ;
          WORD #2896 OCCURS   1 TIMES.

NUEUO            22004 5ELCID2800 ***** ERA & FRESCO, QUE DE VALEN%IAL SACO,
          WORD #2897 OCCURS   1 TIMES.

NUEUOS           18548 5ELCID2347 CA NUNCUA LO VIERAN, CA ****** SON LEGADOS.
          WORD #2898 OCCURS   1 TIMES.

NULLA             6778 5ELCID0865 NON TEME GERRA, SABET, A ***** PART.
                  7019 5ELCID0898 SI ***** DUBCA YD A MYO %IC BUSCAR GANAN%IA.
                 17405 5ELCID2202 QUE YO ***** COSA NCL SCPE CEZIR CE NO.
          WORD #2899 OCCURS   3 TIMES.

NUMBRE            2755 5ELCID0348 PUSIERCN TE EN CRUZ PCR ****** EN GOLGOTA;
          WORD #2900 OCCURS   1 TIMES.

NUNCA            26467 5ELCID3377 HYA VARCNES, CUIEN VIC ***** TAL MAL?
          WORD #2901 OCCURS   1 TIMES.

NUNQUA            3235 5ELCID0407 CAUALGAC, %ID, EL BUEN CAMPEADCR, CA ******
                 12303 5ELCID1562 ALEGRE FUE MYC %IC, QUE ****** MAS NIN TANTO,
                 18544 5ELCID2347 CA ****** LC VIERAN, CA NUEUCS SON LEGADOS.
                 19498 5ELCID2470 CUYDARCN QUE EN SUS CIAS ****** SERIEN MINGUADOS.
                 20975 5ELCID2665 ****** AURIE DERECHO DE NOS EL %ID CAMPEADOR.
          WORD #2902 OCCURS   5 TIMES.
             INDEX OF DIVERSIFICATION =  4434.00 WITH STANDARD DEVIATION OF  3898.44

NUQUA            21090 5ELCID2680 VOS ***** EN CARRICN ENTRARIECES IAMAS.
          WORD #2903 OCCURS   1 TIMES.

NUQUAS            2788 5ELCID0352 LONGINCS ERA %IEGC, QUE ****** VIO ALGUANDRE,
          WORD #2904 OCCURS   1 TIMES.

O                  802 5ELCID0103 * SODES, RACHEL & VIDAS, LOS MYOS AMIGOS CAROS?
                  1009 5ELCID0130 * QUE GANAN%IA NOS DARA POR TODO AQUESTE A@O?
                  2249 5ELCID0283 * CUE DE VENTURA & ALGUNOS CIAS VIDA,
                  3101 5ELCID0390 CA EN YERMC * EN POBLACC PODER NOS HAN ALCAN%AR.
                  3835 5ELCID0485 FELLOS EN CASTEICN, * EL CAMPEACOR ESTAUA.
                  8436 5ELCID1072 E SI NON, MANDEDES BUSCAR; * ME CEXAREDES
                  8442 5ELCID1073 DE LO UUESTRO, * DELO MYO LEUAREDES ALGO.
                  9936 5ELCID1260 QUE SI ALGUNOS FURTARE * MENOS LE FALLAREN, EL AUER ME
                                  AURA ATORNAR
                 10302 5ELCID1304 DIERCN LE EN VALEN%IA * BIEN PUEDE ESTAR RICO.
                 11924 5ELCID1512 * CUEMO SALIERA DE CASTIELLA ALBARFANEZ CON ESTAS DUE@AS
                                  QUE TRAHE.
                 12028 5ELCID1525 EN PAZ * EN GERRA DELO NUESTRO ABRA;
                 15190 5ELCID1922 SI ES PAGADO * RE%IBIO EL DCN?
                 15602 5ELCID1978 QUANTOS QUISIESSEN AUERES DORO * CE PLATA.
                 16820 5ELCID2129 QUI QUIERE YR COMIGO ALAS BODAS, * RE%EBIR MI DON,
                 17981 5ELCID2275 QUES PAGE CES CASAMIENTO MYC %ID * EL QUE LO ALGO
                 18133 5ELCID2294 QUES ESTC, MESNADAS, * CUE CUEREDES UOS?
                 19093 5ELCID2415 MAS SI EL CAUALLC NON ESTROPIE%A * COMIGO NON CAYE,
                 19749 5ELCID2504 QUE PAGUEN AMI * A QUI YO CUIER SABOR.
                 20113 5ELCID2553 PODREMCS CASAR CON FIJAS DE REYES * DE ENPERADORES,
                 21497 5ELCID2733 RETRAER UOS LO AN EN VISTAS * EN CORTES.
                 21783 5ELCID2771 * QUE AN FECHC LOS YFANTES DE CARRION.
                 22878 5ELCID2914 ADUGA MELOS AVISTAS, * AIUNTAS, O A CORTES,
                 22880 5ELCID2914 ADUGA MELOS AVISTAS, C AIUNTAS, * A CORTES,
                 23146 5ELCID2949 QUE GELCS LEUEDES AVISTAS, * AIUNTAS, O A CORTES;
                 23148 5ELCID2949 QUE GELCS LEUEDES AVISTAS, O AIUNTAS, * A CORTES;
                 23502 5ELCID2993 QUI LO FER NCN QUISIESSE, * NO YR A MI CORT,
                 25198 5ELCID3208 DJZE EL CONDE DCN REMCNC: CEZIC DE SSI * DE NO.
                 25264 5ELCID3216 DESTOS AUERES QUE UOS DI YC, SIMELOS CADES, * DEDES
                                  DELLO RA%CN.
                 25585 5ELCID3258 DEZID  QUE UOS MERE%I, YFANTES, EN JUEGO * EN VERO
                 25588 5ELCID3259 * EN ALGUNA RAZON? ACUI LO MEIORARE A JUUIZYO DELA CORT.
                 25729 5ELCID3277 * QUIEN GELAS DIERA PCR PAREIAS OPOR VELADAS?
```

WORD C# PREFIX CONTEXT

O (CON'T)

```
                    25881 5ELCID3297 DEUIEMCS CASAR CON FIJAS CE REYES * DE ENPERADORES,
                    27097 5ELCID3462 DESPUES VEREDES QUE DIXIESTES * QUE NO.
                    27165 5ELCID3472 SEA ESTA LIS * MANCAREDES VCS.
                    28155 5ELCID3594 QUE NON VARAGEN CON ELLOS DESI * DE NON.
                    29024 5ELCID3707 ATAL LE CONTESCA * SI CUIER PECR.
         WORD #2905 OCCURS  36 TIMES.
            INDEX OF DIVERSIFICATION =   805.34 WITH STANCARD DEVIATION OF   945.73

OAQUI               29095 5ELCID3716 SIN VERGUEN%A LAS CASARE ***** PESE OAQUI NON.
                    29097 5ELCID3716 SIN VERGUEN%A LAS CASARE OAQUI PESE ***** NON.
         WORD #2906 OCCURS   2 TIMES.

OBISPADO            10267 5ELCID1299 EN TIERRAS DE VALEN%IA FER CUIERO ********,
         WORD #2907 OCCURS   1 TIMES.

OBISPO              10178 5ELCID1289 EL ****** DCN IERONIMO SO NOMBRE ES LAMADO.
                    10210 5ELCID1293 SOSPIRANDO EL ****** QUES VIESSE CON MOROS ENEL CAMPO:
                    10297 5ELCID1303 AESTE DON IERCNIMO YAL CTORGAN POR ******;
                    10320 5ELCID1306 QUE EN TIERRAS DE VALEN%IA SE@OR AVIE ******
                    10506 5ELCID1332 ****** FIZO DE SU MANC EL BUEN CAMPEADOR,
                    11527 5ELCID1460 EL ****** DON IERONIMO, CORONACO DE PRESTAR,
                    11840 5ELCID1501 E EL ****** DCN JERCNIMC, CORANADO LEAL,
                    12176 5ELCID1546 EL ****** DCN IHERCNIMC, BUEN CHRISTIANO SIN FALLA,
                    12444 5ELCID1579 EL ****** DON IHERONIMO ADELANT SE ENTRAUA,
                    13154 5ELCID1667 DESI AN ASSER DEL ****** DCN IHERONIMO,
                    13318 5ELCID1689 EL ****** DO IHERCNIMC SCLTURA NOS CARA,
                    13425 5ELCID1702 EL ****** DCN IHERCNIMO LA MISSA LES CANTAUA;
                    14164 5ELCID1793 EL ****** DCN IHERCNIMO, CABOSO CORONADO,
                    15710 5ELCID1993 EL ****** DCN IERCNIMC, CCRANACO MEIOR,
                    16309 5ELCID2069 EL ****** DON IHERCNIMO LA MISSA CANTO.
                    17688 5ELCID2238 EL ****** CON IHERCNIMC VISTICS TAN PRIUADO,
                    18711 5ELCID2368 AFEUOS EL ****** DCN IHERCNIMO MUY BIEN ARMADO,
                    18830 5ELCID2383 EL ****** DCN IHERCNIMC PRISO A ESPOLONADA
                    18871 5ELCID2388 ENSAYAUAS EL ******, DICS, CUE BIEN LIDIAUA
                    19819 5ELCID2512 AQUI ESTA CCN MYO %ID EL ****** DO IHERONIMO,
                    24041 5ELCID3064 VOS YREDES CCMIGC & EL ****** DON IHERONIMO
         WORD #2908 OCCURS  21 TIMES.
            INDEX OF DIVERSIFICATICN =   692.15 WITH STANCARD CEVIATION OF   953.81

OBIUO                 594 5ELCID0075 SI CON UUSCO ESCAPO SANO *****,
         WORD #2909 OCCURS   1 TIMES.

OBRADA              24272 5ELCID3095 CON ORO ES ******, FECHA POR RAZON,
         WORD #2910 OCCURS   1 TIMES.

OBRADO              14085 5ELCID1783 TANTA TIENDA PRE%IADA & TANTO TENDAL ******
                    24238 5ELCID3091 ****** ES CCN ORO, PARE%EN PORC SON,
         WORD #2911 OCCURS   2 TIMES.

OCASION             10786 5ELCID1365 ATREGO LES LCS CUERPCS CF MAL & DE *******,
                    27084 5ELCID3460 E QUI AL QUISIESSE SERIE SU *******.
         WORD #2912 OCCURS   2 TIMES.

ODE                 13387 5ELCID1697 *** AMAS ODEL VNA DICS NOS VALCRA.
         WORD #2913 OCCURS   1 TIMES.

ODEL                13389 5ELCID1697 ODE AMAS **** VNA DICS NOS VALCRA.
         WORD #2914 OCCURS   1 TIMES.

ODIZE               27049 5ELCID3455 SI AY QUI RESPCNDA ***** DE NO,
         WORD #2915 OCCURS   1 TIMES.

ODIZEN               3444 5ELCID0435 ****** CASTEION, EL QUE ES SOBRE FENARES,
                    20915 5ELCID2657 ****** EL ANSSARERA ELLCS PCSADOS SON.
                    22577 5ELCID2876 ****** BADO CE REY, ALLA YUAN POSAR,
         WORD #2916 OCCURS   3 TIMES.

ODO                 16610 5ELCID2104 QUE METAN EN SUS BODAS *** CUISIEREDES UOS;
         WORD #2917 OCCURS   1 TIMES.

ODREDES               553 5ELCID0070 FABLO MARTIN ATCLINEZ, ******* LO QUE A DICHO:
                     1469 5ELCID0188 QUANDO ESTC CUO FECHC, ******* LO QUE FABLAUA:
                     5422 5ELCID0684 FABLAUA MYO %ID CCMMO ******* CCNTAR:
                     8021 5ELCID1024 MYO %ID RUY CIAZ ******* LC CUE DIXO:
                    26293 5ELCID3353 DIEGO GCN%ALEZ ******* LC QUE CIXO:
         WORD #2918 OCCURS   5 TIMES.
            INDEX OF DIVERSIFICATION =  6434.00 WITH STANCARD CEVIATION OF  7988.52

OERES               22763 5ELCID2901 *****, MU@O GUSTIOZ, MYC VASSALLO DE PRO,
         WORD #2919 OCCURS   1 TIMES.

OF                  26056 5ELCID3321 DELOS PRIMEROS CCLPES ** LE DE ARRANCAR;
         WORD #2920 OCCURS   1 TIMES.
```

WORD C# PREFIX CONTEXT

```
OFF              26050 5ELCID3320 PASSE POR TI, CCN EL MORO ME *** DE AIUNTAR,
          WORD #2921 OCCURS   1 TIMES.

OFFRE%IERON       2674 5ELCID0338 TE ***********, CCMMO FUE TU VELUNTAD;
          WORD #2922 OCCURS   1 TIMES.

OFRENDA          24022 5ELCID3062 E SSU ******* HAN FECHA MUY BUENA & CONPLIDA.
          WORD #2923 OCCURS   1 TIMES.

OFUESSE           9883 5ELCID1253 SIL PUDIESSEN PRENDER ******* ALCAN%ADO,
          WORD #2924 OCCURS   1 TIMES.

OHERES           20621 5ELCID2618  ******, MYO SOBRINO, TU, FELEZ MUNOZ,
          WORD #2925 OCCURS   1 TIMES.

OIARRA           26586 5ELCID3394 AL VNO DIZEN ****** & AL OTRO YENEGO SIMENEZ,
                 26754 5ELCID3417 AUOS, ******, & AUOS, YENEGO XIMENEZ,
                 26794 5ELCID3422 LEUANTOS EN PIE ****** & YNEGO XIMENEZ,
          WORD #2926 OCCURS   3 TIMES.

OIO                321 5ELCID0040 VNA NI@A DE NUEF A@OS A *** SE PARAUA:
                 11971 5ELCID1517 QUANDO LEGO AUEGALUON, DONTA *** HA,
                 12716 5ELCID1614 E DEL OTRA PARTE A *** HAN EL MAR,
                 15899 5ELCID2016 DON LO OUO A *** EL QUE EN BUEN ORA NASCO,
                 18818 5ELCID2381 AFE LOS MOROS A ***, YO LOS ENSAYAR.
                 23740 5ELCID3024 QUANDO LOOVO A *** EL BUEN REY DON ALFFONSSO,
          WORD #2927 OCCURS   6 TIMES.
             INDEX OF DIVERSIFICATION =  4682.80 WITH STANDARD DEVIATION OF  4167.30

OIOS                 3 5ELCID0001 DELOS SOS **** TAN FUERTE MIENTRE LORANDO,
                   132 5ELCID0018 PLORANDO DELOS ****, TANTO AUYEN EL DOLOR.
                   213 5ELCID0027 QUE PERDERIE LOS AUERES & MAS LOS **** DELA CARA,
                   367 5ELCID0046 E DEMAS LOS **** DELAS CARAS.
                  2104 5ELCID0265 LORAUA DELOS ****, QUISOL BESAR LAS MANOS:
                  2198 5ELCID0277 LORA DELOS ****, TAN FUERTE MIENTRE SOSPIRA:
                  2821 5ELCID0356 ABRIO SOS ****, CATO ATODAS PARTES,
                  2934 5ELCID0370 LORANDO DE LOS ****, QUE NON SABE QUE SE FAR.
                  2969 5ELCID0374 LORANDO DELOS ****, QUE NON VIESTES ATAL,
                  7191 5ELCID0921 BESO LE LA BOCA & LOS **** DELA CARA.
                 12617 5ELCID1600 DEL GOZO QUE AUIEN DE LOS SOS **** LORAUAN.
                 12699 5ELCID1612 **** VELIDOS CATAN A TODAS PARTES,
                 12955 5ELCID1643 AFARTO VERAN POR LOS **** COMMO SE GANA EL PAN.
                 12971 5ELCID1645 AL%AUAN LOS ****, TIENDAS VIERON FINCADAS:
                 13274 5ELCID1683 EL SELO VIO CON LOS ****, CUENTAN GELO DELANT,
                 15955 5ELCID2023 LORANDO DELOS ****, TANTO AUIE EL GOZO MAYOR:
                 17285 5ELCID2186 MUCHOS DIAS UOS VEAMOS CON LOS **** DELAS CARAS
                 18908 5ELCID2392 EL QUE EN BUEN ORA NASCO LOS **** LE FINCAUA,
                 19270 5ELCID2439 AL%O SOS ****, ESTEUA ADELANT CATANDO,
                 21938 5ELCID2791 ABRIERON LOS **** & VIERON AFELEZ MUNOZ.
                 22447 5ELCID2859 ENEL FINCAN LOS **** CON ELUIRA & DO@A SOL:
                 22483 5ELCID2863 LORAUAN DELOS **** LAS DUE@AS & ALBARFANEZ,
          WORD #2928 OCCURS  22 TIMES.
             INDEX OF DIVERSIFICATION =  1069.48 WITH STANDARD DEVIATION OF  1515.62

OLAS             11000 5ELCID1392 ADELINO PORA SAN PERO, **** DUE@AS ESTAN,
                 15384 5ELCID1948 ESTAS VISTAS **** AYADES UOS,
                 15565 5ELCID1973 ALAS AGUAS DE TAIO, **** UISTAS SON APAREIADAS.
                 19711 5ELCID2499 ALA DENTRO EN MARRUECOS, **** MEZQUITAS SON,
          WORD #2929 OCCURS   4 TIMES.

OLBIDADO          1206 5ELCID0155 YA DON RACHEL & VIDAS, AUEDES ME ********
                  8367 5ELCID1063 EL SABOR QUE DED E NON SERA ********.
                 19627 5ELCID2487 ELA SU QUINTA NON FUESSE ********.
          WORD #2930 OCCURS   3 TIMES.

OLBIDAR          11413 5ELCID1444 AQUESTE MONESTERIO NO LO QUIERA *******,
                 25552 5ELCID3254 LA RENCURA MAYOR NON SEME PUEDE *******.
                 26372 5ELCID3363 LO DEL LEON NON SE TE DEUE *******;
          WORD #2931 OCCURS   3 TIMES.

OMBRO            11980 5ELCID1519 ENEL ***** LO SALUDA, CA TAL ES SU HUSAIE:
          WORD #2932 OCCURS   1 TIMES.

OMBROS              93 5ELCID0013 ME%IO MYO %ID LOS ****** & ENGRAMEO LA TIESTA:
          WORD #2933 OCCURS   1 TIMES.

OMEIOR           26826 5ELCID3426 QUE CUEMO ES DICHO ASSI SEA, ******.
          WORD #2934 OCCURS   1 TIMES.

OMENAIES         26817 5ELCID3425 METIERON LAS FES, & LOS ******** DADOS SON,
          WORD #2935 OCCURS   1 TIMES.

OMILDAN%A        15964 5ELCID2024 ASI SABE DAR ********* A ALFONSSO SO SE@OR.
          WORD #2936 OCCURS   1 TIMES.
```

```
WORD                C#  PREFIX                      CONTEXT

OMILLAMOS          16180 5ELCID2053 ********* NCS, %ID, EN BUEN CRA NASQUIESTES UOS
      WORD #2937 OCCURS    1 TIMES.

OMILLAN            16175 5ELCID2052 ESSORA SELE ******* LCS YFFANTES DE CARRION:
      WORD #2938 OCCURS    1 TIMES.

OMILLARON          17511 5ELCID2215 AEL & EASSU MUGIER DELANT SELE *********,
      WORD #2939 OCCURS    1 TIMES.

OMILLO             13793 5ELCID1748 AUOS ME ******, DUE@AS, GRANT PREZ UOS HE GA@ADO:
      WORD #2940 OCCURS    1 TIMES.

OMILLOM            23829 5ELCID3036 ******* AUCS & ALCONDE DO REMCND
      WORD #2941 OCCURS    1 TIMES.

OMILLOS            22982 5ELCID2928 ******* ALOS SANTOS & RCGO ACRIADOR;
      WORD #2942 OCCURS    1 TIMES.

OMILOM             11026 5ELCID1396 ******, DO@A XIMENA, DICS VOS CURIE DE MAL,
      WORD #2943 OCCURS    1 TIMES.

OMNE                1176 5ELCID0151 QUE GELO NCN VENTANSSEN DE BURGOS **** NADO.
                    6896 5ELCID0882 **** AYRADC, CUE DE SE@CR NCN HA GRA%IA,
                    9869 5ELCID1252 QUE NINGUN **** DELCS SCS QUES LE NON SPIDIES, ONOL
                                    BESAS LA MANO,
                   10627 5ELCID1346 SEMEIA QUE EN TIERRA DE MORCS NON A BIUO ****,
      WORD #2944 OCCURS    4 TIMES.

OMNES               1044 5ELCID0134 ACOGEN SELE ***** DE TCDAS PARTES MEGUADOS,
                    2417 5ELCID0305 PLOGO ALOS OTROS ***** TODOS QUANTOS CON EL ESTAN.
                    3316 5ELCID0418 SIN LAS PEONADAS & ***** VALIENTES QUE SON,
                    6479 5ELCID0826 MYNAYA ALBARFANEZ DESTO ES PAGADO; POR YR CON EL *****
                                    SON CONTADOS.
                    8837 5ELCID1125 COMMO ***** EXIDOS DE TIERRA ESTRA@A,
                   10133 5ELCID1284 CIENTO ***** LE DIO MYO %ID A ALBARFANEZ POR SERUIR LE EN
                                    LA CARRERA,
                   13518 5ELCID1713 DEXAN ALAS PUERTAS ***** DE GRANT RECABDO.
                   14363 5ELCID1817 E DOZIENTOS ***** LIEUAN EN SU CONPA@A,
                   20106 5ELCID2552 DAQUESTOS AUERES SIENPRE SEREMOS RICOS *****,
                   24962 5ELCID3179 MARAUILLAN SE DELLAS TODAS LOS ***** BUENOS DELA CORT.
                   25524 5ELCID3251 SOS ***** LAS TIENEN & DELLAS PENSSARAN.
                   27790 5ELCID3546 MUCHOS SE JUNTARON DE BUENOS RICOS *****
      WORD #2945 OCCURS   12 TIMES.
         INDEX OF DIVERSIFICATION =  2430.45 WITH STANDARD DEVIATION OF  1705.63

ONDA                8602 5ELCID1092 MYO %ID GA@O AXERICA & A **** & ALMENAR,
                    8729 5ELCID1119 DESI A **** & LCS OTROS A ALMENAR,
                   10473 5ELCID1327 GANADA A XERICA & A **** PCR NOMBRE,
      WORD #2946 OCCURS    3 TIMES.

ONDDE              11045 5ELCID1398 SALUDA UOS MYO %ID ALLA ***** ELLE ESTA;
      WORD #2947 OCCURS    1 TIMES.

ONDE               26956 5ELCID3444 **** SALIEN CONDES DE PREZ & DE VALOR;
      WORD #2948 OCCURS    1 TIMES.

ONDRA              10109 5ELCID1280 DE GUISA YRAN POR ELLAS QUE AGRAND ***** VERNAN
                   11594 5ELCID1469 CON GRAND ***** ADUZID MELAS DELANT.
                   12680 5ELCID1609 A TAN GRAND ***** ELLAS A VALEN%IA ENTRAUAN.
                   14608 5ELCID1848 MUCHO PRE%IA LA ***** EL %ID QUEL AUEDES DADO.
                   14720 5ELCID1861  MARAUILLA ES DEL %ID, QUE SU ***** CRE%E TANTO
                   14725 5ELCID1862 EN LA ***** QUE EL HA NOS SEREMOS ABILTADOS;
                   14897 5ELCID1883 CRE%REMOS EN NUESTRA ***** & YREMOS ADELANT.
                   14935 5ELCID1888 CASAR QUEREMOS CON ELLAS ASU ***** & A NUESTRA PRO.
                   15066 5ELCID1905 ABRA Y ***** & CRE%RA EN ONOR,
                   15235 5ELCID1929 QUEL CONNOS%IE Y ***** & CRE%IE EN ONOR,
                   15411 5ELCID1952 POR DAR LE GRAND ***** COMMO A REY DE TIERRA.
                   17182 5ELCID2174 GRANT ***** LES DAN ALOS YFANTES DE CARRION.
                   17652 5ELCID2233 QUE LAS TOMASSEDES POR MUGIERES A ***** & A RECABDO.
                   19943 5ELCID2530 POR UOS AUEMOS ***** & AVEMOS LIDIADO.
                   22227 5ELCID2831 QUANDO TAL ***** MEAN DADA LOS YFANTES DE CARRION;
                   22386 5ELCID2852 POR AQUESTA ***** QUE VOS DIESTES A ESTO QUE NOS CUNTIO;
                   23086 5ELCID2941 HYA UOS SABEDES LA ***** QUE ES CUNTIDA ANOS,
                   24400 5ELCID3111 AGRANT ***** LO RE%IBEN AL QUE EN BUEN ORA NA%IO.
                   25618 5ELCID3262 CON MUY GRAND ***** & AVERES A NOMBRE;
                   26632 5ELCID3400 E QUE GELAS DIESSEN A ***** & ABENDI%ION,
                   26722 5ELCID3413 CA CRE%E UOS Y ***** & TIERRA & ONOR.
                   26921 5ELCID3439 ELLOS LAS PRISIERON A ***** & A BENDI%ION;
                   27031 5ELCID3453 ASIL CRE%E LA ***** A MYO %ID EL CAMPEADOR
                   27941 5ELCID3565 SI DEL CAMPO BIEN SALIDES, GRAND ***** AUREDES VOS;
                   29135 5ELCID3721 AMAYOR ***** LAS CASA QUE LO QUE PRIMERO FUE.
                   29145 5ELCID3722 VED QUAL ***** CRE%E AL QUE EN BUEN ORA NA%IO,
                   29173 5ELCID3725 A TODOS ALCAN%A ***** POR EL QUE EN BUEN ORA NA%IO.
      WORD #2949 OCCURS   27 TIMES.
         INDEX OF DIVERSIFICATION =   732.23 WITH STANDARD DEVIATION OF   751.92
```

WORD C# PREFIX CONTEXT

ONDRADA 1392 5ELCID0178 VNA PIEL VERMEIA MORISCA & *******,
2260 5ELCID0284 E UOS, MUGIER *******, DE MY SEADES SERUIDA
6609 5ELCID0843 E LOS DE CALATAYUT, QUE ES MAS *******,
12645 5ELCID1604 VOS, QUERIDA & ******* MUGIER, & AMAS MIS FIJAS,
12985 5ELCID1647 YA MUGIER *******, NON AYADES PESAR
14803 5ELCID1871 MANDO UOS LOS CUERPOS ******* MIENTRE SERUIR & VESTIR
17293 5ELCID2187 GRADO AL CRIADOR, VENGO, MUGIER *******
WORD #2950 OCCURS 7 TIMES.
INDEX OF DIVERSIFICATION = 2649.17 WITH STANDARD DEVIATION OF 2171.68

ONDRADAS 12274 5ELCID1558 CON ESTAS ALEGRIAS & NUEUAS TAN ********
WORD #2951 OCCURS 1 TIMES.

ONDRADO 6871 5ELCID0878 A UOS, REY *******, ENBIA ESTA PRESENTAIA;
12112 5ELCID1537 ******* ES MYO %ID EN VALEN%IA DO ESTAUA
14585 5ELCID1845 MER%ED, REY ALFONSSO, SODES TAN *******
15461 5ELCID1959 AL REY ******* DELANT LE ECHARON LAS CARTAS;
16376 5ELCID2077 SEMEIAM EL CASAMIENTO ******* & CON GRANT PRO,
16928 5ELCID2142 HYA REY DON ALFONSSO, SE@OR TAN *******,
16995 5ELCID2151 MYO %ID RUY DIAZ, MUCHO ME AUEDES *******,
17770 5ELCID2248 RICAS FUERON LAS BODAS EN EL ALCA%AR *******,
18139 5ELCID2295 HYA SE@OR *******, REBATA NOS DIO EL LEON.
19931 5ELCID2528 GRADO AL CRIADOR & A UOS, %ID *******,
23396 5ELCID2980 QUE CORT FAZIE EN TOLLEDO AQUEL REY *******,
WORD #2952 OCCURS 11 TIMES.
INDEX OF DIVERSIFICATION = 1651.50 WITH STANDARD DEVIATION OF 1637.90

ONDRADOS 19580 5ELCID2481 COMMO SON ******** & AVER VOS GRANT PRO.
23343 5ELCID2973 DESTO QUE LES ABINO AVN BIEN SERAN ********.
26351 5ELCID3360 QUE POR QUE LAS DEXAMOS ******** SOMOS NOS.
27306 5ELCID3490 ******** MELOS ENBIAD A VALEN%IA, POR AMOR DEL CRIADOR
27577 5ELCID3521 CA POR UOS & POREL CAUALLO ******** SOMO NOS.
28928 5ELCID3695 POR ******** SE PARTEN LOS DEL BUEN CAMPEADOR;
29063 5ELCID3712 POR QUE TAN ******** FUERON LOS DEL CANPEADOR.
WORD #2953 OCCURS 7 TIMES.
INDEX OF DIVERSIFICATION = 1579.50 WITH STANDARD DEVIATION OF 1486.55

ONDRAL 11861 5ELCID1503 POR SABOR DE MYO %ID DE GRAND ****** DAR;
WORD #2954 OCCURS 1 TIMES.

ONDRAN%A 12442 5ELCID1578 RE%EBIDAS LAS DUENAS A VNA GRANT ********,
17300 5ELCID2188 HYERNOS UOS ADUGO DE QUE AUREMOS ********;
WORD #2955 OCCURS 2 TIMES.

ONDRAR 12008 5ELCID1523 ****** UOS HEMOS TODOS, CA TALES LA SU AUZE,
18759 5ELCID2373 MI ORDEN & MIS MANOS QUERRIA LAS ******,
23756 5ELCID3026 BILTAR SE QUIERE & ****** ASO SE@OS.
WORD #2956 OCCURS 3 TIMES.

ONDRASSEN 24770 5ELCID3155 QUES ********* CON ELLAS & SIRUIESSEN AUOS;
WORD #2957 OCCURS 1 TIMES.

ONDRASTES 5366 5ELCID0678 ********* UOS, MINAYA, CA AUER UOS LO YEDES DE FAR.
WORD #2958 OCCURS 1 TIMES.

ONDRAUA 12245 5ELCID1554 AMYNAYA & ALAS DUE@AS, DIOS COMMO LAS *******
WORD #2959 OCCURS 1 TIMES.

ONDRE 23805 5ELCID3032 DIOS LO MANDE QUE POR UOS SE ***** OY LA CORT
WORD #2960 OCCURS 1 TIMES.

ONDREDES 25845 5ELCID3292 AALTAS VOZES ******** QUE FABLO:
WORD #2961 OCCURS 1 TIMES.

ONDRO 7919 5ELCID1011 Y BEN%IO ESTA BATALLA PORO ***** SU BARBA,
19194 5ELCID2428 AQUIS ***** MYO %ID & QUANTOS CONEL SON.
22146 5ELCID2819 QUANTO EL MEIOR PUEDE ALLI LAS *****.
WORD #2962 OCCURS 3 TIMES.

ONOL 9876 5ELCID1252 QUE NINGUN OMNE DELOS SOS QUES LE NON SPIDIES, ****
BESAS LA MANO,
WORD #2963 OCCURS 1 TIMES.

ONOR 15070 5ELCID1905 ABRA Y ONDRA & CRE%RA EN ****,
15239 5ELCID1929 QUEL CONNOS%IE Y ONDRA & CRE%IE EN ****,
15275 5ELCID1934 ECHADO FU DE TIERRA & TOLLICA LA ****,
15894 5ELCID2015 RE%EBIR LO SALEN CON TAN GRANC ****.
17377 5ELCID2198 DESTE UUSTRO CASAMIENTO CRE%REMOS EN ****;
19685 5ELCID2495 QUE HE AUER & TIERRA & ORO & ****,
26726 5ELCID3413 CA CRE%E UOS Y ONDRA & TIERRA & ****.
WORD #2964 OCCURS 7 TIMES.
INDEX OF DIVERSIFICATION = 1941.67 WITH STANDARD DEVIATION OF 2640.88

ONORES 2299 5ELCID0289 VNOS DEXAN CASAS & OTROS ******.
20205 5ELCID2565 QUE LES DIEMOS POR ARRAS & POR ******;
WORD #2965 OCCURS 2 TIMES.

WORD C# PREFIX CONTEXT

```
OPOR             25735 5ELCID3277 O QUIEN GELAS DIERA POR PAREIAS **** VELADAS?
        WORD #2966 OCCURS    1 TIMES.

OQUE             28036 5ELCID3578 NON SABEMOS QUES CCMIDRAN ELLOS **** NON;
        WORD #2967 OCCURS    1 TIMES.

OQUIEN           19967 5ELCID2533 QUIEN LIDIARA MEIOR ****** FUERA EN ALCAN%O;
        WORD #2968 OCCURS    1 TIMES.

ORA                328 5ELCID0041 YA CAMPEADCR, EN BUEN *** %INXIESTES ESPADA
                   460 5ELCID0058 MYO %ID RUY DIAZ, EL CUE EN BUEN *** %INXO ESPADA,
                   562 5ELCID0071 YA CANPEADOR, EN BUEN *** FUESTES NA%IDO
                   620 5ELCID0078 FABLO MYO %ID, EL QUE EN BUEN *** %INXO ESPADA:
                  1368 5ELCID0175 YA CANPEADCR, EN BUEN *** %INXIESTES ESPADA
                  1582 5ELCID0202 VINO PORA LA TIENCA CEL CUE EN BUEN *** NASCO;
                  1933 5ELCID0245 CON TAN GRANT GCZO RE%IBEN AL QUE EN BUEN *** NASCO.
                  2112 5ELCID0266 MER%ED, CANPEADOR, EN *** BUENA FUESTES NADO
                  2829 5ELCID0357 EN TI CROUC AL ***, PCR END ES SALUO DE MAL;
                  3011 5ELCID0379 %ID, DO SON UUESTROS ESFUER%OS? EN BUEN *** NASQUIESTES DE MADRE;
                  3472 5ELCID0437 TODA LA NOCHE IAZE EN %ELADA EL QUE EN BUEN *** NASCO,
                  3483 5ELCID0439 YA %ID, EN BUEN *** %INXIESTES ESPADA
                  3996 5ELCID0507 COMIDIOS MYC %ID, EL CUE EN BUEN *** FUE NADO,
                  4394 5ELCID0559 EL BUEN CANPEADCR QUE EN BUEN *** NASCO,
                  4769 5ELCID0605 EN VN *** & VN POCO DE LOGAR CCC MOROS MATAN.
                  4848 5ELCID0613 FABLO MYO %ID RUY DIAZ, EL QUE EN BUEN *** FUE NADO:
                  5244 5ELCID0663 EL QUE EN BUEN *** NASCC FIRME GELO VEDAUA.
                  5706 5ELCID0719 A GRANDES VOZES LAMA EL QUE EN BUEN *** NASCO:
                  5989 5ELCID0759 MYO %ID RUY DIAZ, EL CUE EN BUEN *** NASCO,
                  6184 5ELCID0787 YAS TORNAN LOS DEL QUE EN BUEN *** NASCO.
                  6350 5ELCID0808 BIEN LC AGUISA EL QUE EN BUEN *** NASCO,
                  6851 5ELCID0875 MYC %ID RUY DIAZ, QUE EN BUEN *** CINXO ESPADA. . .
                  7034 5ELCID0899 QUIERO UOS DEZIR CEL QUE EN BUEN *** NASCO & %INXO ESPADA:
                  7295 5ELCID0935 NCN LC TARDC EL QUE EN BUEN *** NASCO,
                  7854 5ELCID1004 MANDO LOS FERIR MYO %ID, EL QUE EN BUEN *** NASCO;
                  7892 5ELCID1008 VEN%IDO A ESTA BATALLA EL QUE EN BUEN *** NASCO;
                  8277 5ELCID1053 SOBREL SEDIE EL QUE EN BUEN *** NASCO:
                  8763 5ELCID1114 EL QUE EN BUEN *** NASCC CCMPE%O DE FABLAR:
                  9403 5ELCID1195 ESTO DIXO MYC %ID EL CUE EN BUEN *** NASCO.
                  9735 5ELCID1237 CON MYO %ID RUY DIAZ, EL QUE EN BUEN *** NASCO.
                 11476 5ELCID1454 AL *** QUE LO SOPC MYC %IC EL DE BIUAR,
                 12289 5ELCID1560 AMYO %ID, EL QUE EN BUEN *** NASCO,
                 12406 5ELCID1574 AVN NON SABIE MYO %ID, EL CUE EN BUEN *** %INXO ESPADA,
                 12488 5ELCID1584 EL QUE EN BUEN *** NASCC NCN LO DETARDAUA:
                 12574 5ELCID1595 MER%ED, CAMPEADOR, EN BUEN *** CINXIESTES ESPADA
                 12640 5ELCID1603 OYD LO QUE DIXO EL QUE EN BUEN *** NASCO:
                 13463 5ELCID1706 AUCS, %ID DCN RODIRGC, EN BUEN *** %INXIESTES ESPADA,
                 13659 5ELCID1730 DESDALLI SE TCRNO EL CUE EN BUEN *** NASCO,
                 14203 5ELCID1797 MYC %ID DON RCDRIGC, EL CUE EN BUEN *** NASCO,
                 14503 5ELCID1834 AUER ESTOS MENSAIES CEL CUE EN BUEN *** NASCO.
                 14535 5ELCID1838 AOIO LO AUIEN LOS DEL QUE EN BUEN *** NASCO,
                 14681 5ELCID1857 AVN VEA *** QUE DE MI SEA PAGACO.
                 14942 5ELCID1889 VNA GRANT *** EL REY PENSSC & COMIDIO;
                 15108 5ELCID1910 DEZID A RUY DIAZ, EL QUE EN BUEN *** NASCO,
                 15257 5ELCID1932 VNA GRAND *** PENSSC & CCMIDIO:
                 15482 5ELCID1961 SALUDAD ME MAYO %ID, EL QUE EN BUEN *** %INXO ESPADA;
                 15836 5ELCID2008 FATA QUES TCRNE EL QUE EN BUEN *** NASCO.
                 15904 5ELCID2016 DON LO OUO A CIO EL QUE EN BUEN *** NASCO,
                 15934 5ELCID2020 CCMMO LC CCMICIA EL CUE EN BUEN *** NA%IO,
                 16185 5ELCID2053 CMILLAMCS NCS, %ID, EN BUEN *** NASQUIESTES UOS
                 16209 5ELCID2056 MYO %ID RUY DIAZ, QUE EN *** BUENA NASCO,
                 16505 5ELCID2092 BAN BESAR LAS MANCS ALCUE EN *** BUENA NA%IO;
                 17276 5ELCID2185  VENIDES, CAMPEADOR, EN BUENA *** %INXIESTES ESPADA
                 17534 5ELCID2218 ESTAN PARANDO MIENTES ALQUE EN BUEN *** NASCO.
                 17737 5ELCID2244 TRES CAUALLOS CAMEO EL QUE EN BUEN *** NASCO.
                 17813 5ELCID2253 MYO %ID DON RCDRIGO, EL QUE EN BUEN *** NASCO,
                 17888 5ELCID2263 ESPIDIENDOS DE RUY DIAZ, EL QUE EN BUEN *** NASCO,
                 18120 5ELCID2292 EN ESTO DESPERTO EL QUE EN BUEN *** NA%IO;
                 18473 5ELCID2338 AVN VEA EL *** QUE UOS MERESCA DOS TANTO.
                 18574 5ELCID2350 OYD LO QUE FABLO EL QUE EN BUEN *** NASCO:
                 18905 5ELCID2392 EL QUE EN BUEN *** NASCC LOS CIOS LE FINCAUA,
                 19224 5ELCID2432 EL QUE EN BUEN *** NASCO.
                 19397 5ELCID2457 EA UOS, %ID, QUE EN BUEN *** FUESTES NADO
                 19609 5ELCID2484 MANDO MYO %ID, EL QUE EN BUEN *** NASCO,
                 20602 5ELCID2615 VIOLO EN LOS AUUERCS EL QUE EN BUEN *** %INXO ESPADA,
                 20820 5ELCID2643 HYAS TCRNO PORA VALEN%IA EL QUE EN BUEN *** NAS%IO.
                 22205 5ELCID2828 VNA GRAND *** PENSSC & CCMIDIO;
                 22643 5ELCID2885 AL QUE EN BUEN *** NASCC LEGAUA EL MENSSAIE;
                 22743 5ELCID2898 EL QUE EN BUEN *** NASCC NCN QUISO TARDAR,
                 22772 5ELCID2902 EN BUEN *** TE CRIE ATI EN LA MI CORT
                 23180 5ELCID2953 EL REY VNA GRAND *** CALLC & COMIDIO;
                 23304 5ELCID2968 DIZID LE AL CAMPEADOR, QUE EN BUEN *** NASCO,
                 23659 5ELCID3013 AVN NON ERA LEGADO EL QUE ENBUEN *** NA%IO,
```

WORD C# PREFIX CONTEXT

ORA (CON'T)

23719 5ELCID3021 E YUA RE%EBIR ALQUE EN BUEN *** NA%IO.
24188 5ELCID3084 NOS DETIENE POR NADA EL QUE EN BUEN *** NA%IO:
24372 5ELCID3107 QUANDO LO VIERON ENTRAR AL QUE EN BUEN *** NA%IO,
24407 5ELCID3111 AGRANT ONDRA LO RE%IBEN AL QUE EN BUEN *** NA%IO.
24582 5ELCID3132 POR EL AMOR DE MYO %ID EL QUE EN BUEN *** NA%IO,
25401 5ELCID3234 ENTERGEN A MYO %ID, EL QUE EN BUEN *** NA%IO;
25498 5ELCID3247 PAGARON LOS YFANTES AL QUE EN BUEN *** NASCO;
27656 5ELCID3530 ALEGRE FUE DAQUESTO EL QUE EN BUEN *** NA%IO;
29050 5ELCID3710 FABLEMOS NOS DAQUESTE QUE EN BUEN *** NA%IO.
29151 5ELCID3722 VED QUAL ONDRA CRE%E AL QUE EN BUEN *** NA%IO,
29179 5ELCID3725 A TODOS ALCAN%A ONDRA POR EL QUE EN BUEN *** NA%IO.
WORD #2969 OCCURS 84 TIMES.
INDEX OF DIVERSIFICATION = 346.60 WITH STANDARD DEVIATION OF 377.87

ORA%ION
427 5ELCID0054 LA ******* FECHA LUEGO CAUALGAUA;
2902 5ELCID0366 LA ******* FECHA, LA MISSA ACABADA LA AN,
11021 5ELCID1395 QUANDO ACABO LA *******, ALAS DUE@AS SE TORNO:
26518 5ELCID3384 ANTES ALMUERZAS QUE VAYAS A *******,
WORD #2970 OCCURS 4 TIMES.

ORA%IONES
6687 5ELCID0853 VASTE, MYO %ID; NUESTRAS ********* UAYANTE DELANTE
WORD #2971 OCCURS 1 TIMES.

ORAS
12465 5ELCID1581 CON QUANTOS QUE EL PUEDE, QUE CON **** SE ACORDARON,
WORD #2972 OCCURS 1 TIMES.

ORDEN
18753 5ELCID2373 MI ***** & MIS MANOS QUERRIA LAS ONDRAR,
WORD #2973 OCCURS 1 TIMES.

OREIADAS
25933 5ELCID3304 AMI LO DIZEN, ATI DAN LAS ********.
WORD #2974 OCCURS 1 TIMES.

ORIENT
10173 5ELCID1288 DE PARTE DE ****** VINO VN CORONADO;
WORD #2975 OCCURS 1 TIMES.

ORO
639 5ELCID0081 ESPESO E EL *** & TODA LA PLATA,
882 5ELCID0113 TIENE DOS ARCAS LENNAS DE *** ESMERADO.
1454 5ELCID0186 LOS OTROS CCC EN *** GELOS PAGAUAN.
2458 5ELCID0310 POR *** NIN POR PLATA NON PODRIE ESCAPAR.
2668 5ELCID0337 MELCHIOR & GASPAR & BALTASAR, *** & TUS & MIRRA
3744 5ELCID0473 GA@O A CASTEION & EL *** ELA PLATA.
6272 5ELCID0799 TRAEN *** & PLATA QUE NON SABEN RECABDO;
6425 5ELCID0820 EUADES AQUI *** & PLATA VNA VESA LE@A,
9550 5ELCID1214 EL *** & LA PLATA QUI EN VOS LO PODRIE CONTAR?
13706 5ELCID1737 ENTRE *** & PLATA FALLARON TRES MILL MARCOS,
14111 5ELCID1786 DOS TENDALES LA SUFREN, CON *** SON LABRADOS;
15544 5ELCID1970 ESCUDOS BOCLADOS CON *** & CON PLATA,
19683 5ELCID2495 QUE HE AUER & TIERRA & *** & ONOR,
24216 5ELCID3088 CON *** & CON PLATA TODAS LAS PRESAS SON,
24241 5ELCID3091 OBRADO ES CON ***, PARE%EN PORO SON,
24270 5ELCID3095 CON *** ES OBRADA, FECHA POR RAZON,
25156 5ELCID3204 EN *** & EN PLATA TRES MILL MARCOS DE PLATA LES DIO;
25426 5ELCID3238 EL *** & LA PLATA ESPENDIESTES LO VOS;
WORD #2976 OCCURS 18 TIMES.
INDEX OF DIVERSIFICATION = 1457.06 WITH STANDARD DEVIATION OF 1594.20

OSA
3819 5ELCID0483 NON *** NINGUNO DAR SALTO ALA %AGA.
WORD #2977 OCCURS 1 TIMES.

OSADOS
18384 5ELCID2326 EUADES QUE PAUOR HAN UUESTROS YERNOS TAN ******,
WORD #2978 OCCURS 1 TIMES.

OSAN
237 5ELCID0030 ASCONDEN SE DE MYO %ID, CA NOL **** DEZIR NADA.
9196 5ELCID1171 NON **** FUERAS EXIR NIN CON EL SE AIUNTAR;
WORD #2979 OCCURS 2 TIMES.

OSARIEMOS
350 5ELCID0044 NON UOS ********* ABRIR NON COGER POR NADA;
10860 5ELCID1375 NON LA ********* A COMETER NOS ESTA RAZON,
WORD #2980 OCCURS 2 TIMES.

OSARIEN
503 5ELCID0064 NON LE ******* UENDER ALMENOS DINARADA.
WORD #2981 OCCURS 1 TIMES.

OSAS
26110 5ELCID3328 LENGUA SIN MANOS, CUEMO **** FABLAR?
WORD #2982 OCCURS 1 TIMES.

OSAUA
160 5ELCID0021 CONBIDAR LE YEN DE GRADO, MAS NINGUNO NON *****:
WORD #2983 OCCURS 1 TIMES.

OSE
22689 5ELCID2891 HYO TOME EL CASAMIENTO, MAS NON *** DEZIR AL.
WORD #2984 OCCURS 1 TIMES.

OSO
6057 5ELCID0768 SABET, EL OTRO NON GEL *** ESPERAR.
WORD #2985 OCCURS 1 TIMES.

WORD C# PREFIX CONTEXT

OSPEDADO 1953 5ELCID0247 PUES QUE AQUI UOS VEO, PRENDET DE MI ********.
WORD #2986 OCCURS 1 TIMES.

OSPEDADOS 17879 5ELCID2262 HYAS YUAN PARTIENDO AQUESTOS *********,
17933 5ELCID2269 VENIDOS SON ACASTIELLA AQUESTOS *********,
WORD #2987 OCCURS 2 TIMES.

OSSI 12412 5ELCID1575 SI SERIE CORREDOR **** ABRIE BUENA PARADA;
WORD #2988 OCCURS 1 TIMES.

OTARDE 597 5ELCID0076 AUN %ERCA ****** EL REY QUERER ME HA POR AMIGO;
WORD #2989 OCCURS 1 TIMES.

OTERO 4350 5ELCID0554 EN VN ***** REDONDO, FUERTE & GRAND;
4398 5ELCID0560 DERREDOR DEL *****, BIEN %ERCA DEL AGUA,
WORD #2990 OCCURS 2 TIMES.

OTORGA 18487 5ELCID2340 ASSI LO ****** DON PERO CUEMO SE ALABA FERRANDO.
26114 5ELCID3329 DI, FERRANDO, ****** ESTA RAZON:
WORD #2991 OCCURS 2 TIMES.

OTORGADAS 13488 5ELCID1709 LAS FERIDAS PRIMERAS QUE LAS AYA YO *********.
WORD #2992 OCCURS 1 TIMES.

OTORGADO 2070 5ELCID0261 ******** GELO AUIE EL ABBAT DE GRADO.
WORD #2993 OCCURS 1 TIMES.

OTORGADOS 14060 5ELCID1781 DELOS BUENOS & ********* CAYERON LE MILL & D CAUALLOS;
WORD #2994 OCCURS 1 TIMES.

OTORGAN 10295 5ELCID1303 AESTE DON IERONIMO YAL ******* POR OBISPO;
28738 5ELCID3670 ******* GELO LOS FIELES QUE DIZE VERDADERA PALABRA.
WORD #2995 OCCURS 2 TIMES.

OTORGARAS 26273 5ELCID3350 TULO ********* A GUISA DE TRAYDOR;
WORD #2996 OCCURS 1 TIMES.

OTORGE 26714 5ELCID3412 ESTE CASAMIENTO OY SE ****** EN ESTA CORT,
WORD #2997 OCCURS 1 TIMES.

OTORGO 16172 5ELCID2051 BESO LE LA MANO MYO CID, LO ******.
25246 5ELCID3214 DIXO EL BUEN REY: ASSILO ****** YO.
26739 5ELCID3415 QUANDO AUOS PLAZE, ****** LO YO, SE@OR,
26761 5ELCID3418 ESTE CASAMIENTO ****** UOS LE YO
WORD #2998 OCCURS 4 TIMES.

OTRA 5026 5ELCID0635 ASSI FFERA LO DE SILOCA, QUE ES DEL **** PART.
6792 5ELCID0867 DESI A MOLINA, QUE ES DEL **** PART,
8891 5ELCID1132 YO CON LOS %IENTO ENTRARE DEL **** PART,
8989 5ELCID1144 DEL **** PART ENTROLES ALBARFANEZ;
10830 5ELCID1371 MAS GANAREMOS EN ESTO QUE EN **** DESONOR.
12713 5ELCID1614 E DEL **** PARTE A OIO HAN EL MAR,
13385 5ELCID1696 QUANDO UOS LOS FUEREDES FERIR, ENTRARE YO DEL **** PART;
21454 5ELCID2727 AL VNA DIZEN COLADA & AL **** TIZON,
21681 5ELCID2756 QUE EL VNA AL **** NOL TORNA RECABDO.
22873 5ELCID2913 ESSO ME PUEDE PESAR CON LA **** DESONOR.
24561 5ELCID3130 LA VNA FUE EN BURGOS, & LA **** EN CARRION,
25140 5ELCID3202 **** RENCURA HE DE YFANTES DE CARRION:
28125 5ELCID3591 FEUOS DELA **** PART LOS YFANTES DE CARRION,
28841 5ELCID3684 DELA **** PART VNA BRA%A GELA ECHO,
WORD #2999 OCCURS 14 TIMES.
INDEX OF DIVERSIFICATION = 1830.92 WITH STANDARD DEVIATION OF 2051.06

OTRAS 3809 5ELCID0481 DE OUEIAS & DE VACAS & DE ROPAS & DE ***** RIQUIZAS LARGAS.
4534 5ELCID0576 DEXA VNA TIENDA FITA & LAS ***** LEUAUA,
4576 5ELCID0582 LAS ***** A BES LIEUA, VNA TIENDA A DEXADA.
11263 5ELCID1425 E ALAS ***** DUE@AS QUE LAS SIRUEN DELANT,
12359 5ELCID1569 E ALAS DUENAS & ALAS NI@AS & ALAS ***** CONPA@AS.
12376 5ELCID1571 QUE GUARDASSEN EL ALCA%AR & LAS ***** TORRES ALTAS
13714 5ELCID1738 LAS ***** GANAN%IAS NON AUYA RECABDO.
14103 5ELCID1785 LA TIENDA DEL REY DE MARRUECOS, QUE DELAS ***** ES CABO,
14241 5ELCID1802 E TODAS LAS ***** DUENAS QUE TIENEN POR CASADAS.
14424 5ELCID1824 QUE LAS ***** TIERRAS PARTE.
15809 5ELCID2005 E ***** DUE@AS QUE LAS SIRUEN ASU SABOR;
WORD #3000 OCCURS 11 TIMES.
INDEX OF DIVERSIFICATION = 1199.00 WITH STANDARD DEVIATION OF 1998.81

OTRO 2772 5ELCID0350 EL VNO ES EN PARAYSO, CA EL **** NON ENTRO ALA;
3130 5ELCID0394 **** DIA MA@ANA PIENSSA DE CAUALGAR.
3273 5ELCID0413 **** DIA MA@ANA PIENSSAN DE CAUALGAR;
3979 5ELCID0505 TODO LO **** AFELO EN UUESTRA MANO.
4318 5ELCID0550 **** DIA MOUIOS MYO %ID EL DE BIUAR,
5103 5ELCID0645 **** DIA MA@ANA PIENSSAN DE CAUALGAR,

WORD C# PREFIX CONTEXT

OTRO (CON'T)

```
                 5402 5ELCID0682 **** DIA MA@ANA, EL SOL QUFRIE APUNTAR,
                 6054 5ELCID0768 SABET, EL **** NON GEL CSO ESPERAR.
                11647 5ELCID1476 E EL **** DIA VINIERCN A MOLINA POSAR.
                11810 5ELCID1497 EL VNO FINCO CON ELLCS & EL **** TORNO A ALBARFANEZ:
                12246 5ELCID1555 **** DIA MANA@A LUEGC CAUALGAUAN,
                13575 5ELCID1720 ENTRARCN LES CFL **** CABC.
                14283 5ELCID1807 PRENDED LO QUE QUISIERECES, LO **** REMANGA.
                14356 5ELCID1816 **** DIA MANANA PRIUACO CAUALGAUAN,
                15588 5ELCID1976 LO VNO A DEBDAN & LO **** PAGAUAN;
                16255 5ELCID2062 **** DIA MA@ANA, CLARC SALIE EL SOL,
                16300 5ELCID2068 AL **** DIA MA@ANA, ASSI COMMC SALIO EL SOL,
                16670 5ELCID2111 LAS PALABRAS SON PUESTAS QUE **** DIA MA@ANA
                17773 5ELCID2249 E AL **** DIA FIZO MYO %ID FINCAR VIJ TABLADOS:
                19598 5ELCID2483 LO VNO ES NUESTRO, LC **** HAN EN SALUO.
                19949 5ELCID2531 PENSAD DELC ****, QUE LC NUESTRO TENEMOS LO EN SALUO.
                20872 5ELCID2651 **** DIA MA@ANA CON ELLCS CAUALGO,
                22491 5ELCID2864 E PERO VERMUEZ **** TANTO LAS HA;
                22511 5ELCID2866 QUANDO UOS SODES SA@AS & BIUAS & SIN **** MAL.
                22537 5ELCID2870 **** DIA MA@ANA PIENSSAN DE CAUALGAR,
                22591 5ELCID2878 **** DIA MA@ANA METEN SE A ANDAR,
                22609 5ELCID2880 E DE MEDINA A MOLINA EN **** DIA VAN;
                26589 5ELCID3394 AL VNO DIZEN CIARRA & AL **** YENEGO SIMENEZ,
                26600 5ELCID3396 E EL **** YFANTE DE ARAGCN;
                27511 5ELCID3514 EN MOROS NI EN CHRISTIANOS **** TAL NON HA OY,
                27834 5ELCID3552 EN **** LOGAR SE ARMAN LOS YFANTES DE CARRION,
                27906 5ELCID3561 **** SI FARAN ALOS DEL CANPEADOR.
                28426 5ELCID3630 VN COLPE RESIBIERA, MAS **** FIRIO:
                28800 5ELCID3678 ESTE CCLPE FECHC, **** DIC MUNO GUSTIOZ,
          WORD #3001 OCCURS  34 TIMES.
             INDEX OF DIVERSIFICATION =   787.73 WITH STANDARD DEVIATION OF  1153.45

OTROS              546 5ELCID0069 PAGOS MYO %ID EL CAMPEADOR & TODOS LOS ***** QUEUAN ASO
                                  %ERUICIO
                  1451 5ELCID0186 LOS ***** CCC EN ORO GELCS PAGAUAN.
                  2298 5ELCID0289 VNOS DEXAN CASAS & ***** ONORES.
                  2416 5ELCID0305 PLOGO ALOS ***** OMNES TODOS QUANTOS CON EL ESTAN.
                  4239 5ELCID0539 LO QUE DIXO EL %ID A TODOS LOS ***** PLAZ.
                  4384 5ELCID0558 LOS VNCS CONTRA LA SIERRA & LOS ***** CONTRA LA AGUA.
                  5749 5ELCID0725 ALA TORNADA QUE FAZEN ***** TANTOS SON.
                  6245 5ELCID0795 DE ESCUDOS & DE ARMAS & DE ***** AUERES LARGOS;
                  7881 5ELCID1007 ALOS VNOS FIRIENDO & A LOS ***** DE ROCANDO.
                  8158 5ELCID1040 AUOS & A ***** DOS DAR UOS HE DE MANO.
                  8212 5ELCID1046 PRENDIENDO DEUOS & DE ***** YR NOS HEMOS PAGANDO;
                  8724 5ELCID1108 LOS VNOS AXERICA & LOS ***** A ALUCAD,
                  8732 5ELCID1119 DESI A ONDA & LOS ***** A ALMENAR,
                  8873 5ELCID1130 VOS CON LOS ***** FIRADES LOS DELANT.
                  9584 5ELCID1218 ELOS ***** AUERES QUIEN LOS PODRIE CONTAR?
                 11244 5ELCID1423 DELOS ***** QUINIENTOS DEZIR UOS HE QUE FAZE:
                 11562 5ELCID1465 CON ***** %IENTO CAUALLEROS BIEN UOS CONSSIGRA;
                 11918 5ELCID1511 QUE SOPIENSSEN LES ***** DE QUE SESO ERA ALBARFANEZ
                 11960 5ELCID1516 DON LEGAN LOS *****, A MINAYA ALBARFANEZ SE UAN HOMILAR.
                 13645 5ELCID1729 CON ***** QUEL CONSIGEN DE SUS BUENOS VASSALLOS.
                 14074 5ELCID1782 QUANDO A MYO %ID CAYERON TANTOS, LOS ***** BIEN PUEDEN
                                  FINCAR PAGADOS.
                 14524 5ELCID1837 ALOS VNOS PLAZE & ALOS ***** VA PESANDO.
                 15028 5ELCID1900 ***** MANDADOS HA EN ESTA MI CORT:
                 15744 5ELCID1998 E TODOS LOS ***** QUE Y SON.
                 17833 5ELCID2256 MANTOS & PELLI%ONES & ***** VESTIDOS LARGOS;
                 19809 5ELCID2511 ELLOS CON LOS ***** VINIERON ALA CORT;
                 19829 5ELCID2514 E ***** MUCHOS QUE CRIO EL CAMPEADOR.
                 20553 5ELCID2609 MYO %ID & LOS ***** DE CAUALGAR PENSSAUAN,
                 21763 5ELCID2768 DE TODOS LOS ***** APARTE SE SALIO,
                 23597 5ELCID3005 FUERON Y DE SU REYNO ***** MUCHOS SABIDORES,
                 24398 5ELCID3110 E DESI ADELANT, SABET, TODOS LOS *****:
                 24614 5ELCID3136 E ESTOS ***** CONDES QUE DEL VANDO NON SODES.
                 25712 5ELCID3274 LOS VNOS LE HAN MIEDO & LOS ***** ESPANTA.
                 27389 5ELCID3499 AESSOS & ALOS ***** QUE DE BUENA PARTE SON,
          WORD #3002 OCCURS  34 TIMES.
             INDEX OF DIVERSIFICATION =   812.42 WITH STANDARD DEVIATION OF   661.85

OUEIAS            3800 5ELCID0481 DE ****** & DE VACAS & DE ROPAS & DE OTRAS RIQUIZAS LARGAS.
          WORD #3003 OCCURS   1 TIMES.

OUIEMOS          16932 5ELCID2143 DESTAS VISTAS QUE *******, DEMY TOMEDES ALGO.
                 27896 5ELCID3559 NON SACASTES NINGUNA QUANDO ******* LA CORT.
          WORD #3004 OCCURS   2 TIMES.

OUIER            19753 5ELCID2504 QUE PAGUEN AMI O A QUI YO ***** SABOR.
                 25986 5ELCID3312 POR LO QUE YO ***** AFER POR MI NON MANCARA.
          WORD #3005 OCCURS   2 TIMES.

OUIERE           15098 5ELCID1909 DESPUES FAGA EL %ID LO QUE ****** SABOR.
          WORD #3006 OCCURS   1 TIMES.

OUIEREDES        26888 5ELCID3435 DEZID, MYNAYA, LO QUE ********* SABOR.
          WORD #3007 OCCURS   1 TIMES.
```

WORD C# PREFIX CONTEXT

OUIEREMOS 20216 5ELCID2567 LOS FIJOS QUE ********* EN QUE AURAN PARTI%ION.
WORD #3008 OCCURS 1 TIMES.

OUIEREN 20779 5ELCID2639 DELO QUE ******* HUEBOS SIRUAN LAS ASO SABOR,
27384 5ELCID3498 QUE PRENDAN DE SUS AUERES QUANTO ******* SABOR.
WORD #3009 OCCURS 2 TIMES.

OUIERON 78 5ELCID0011 ALA EXIDA DE BIUAR ******* LA CORNEIA DIESTRA,
86 5ELCID0012 E ENTRANDO A BURGOS ******* LA SINIESTRA.
2652 5ELCID0335 PASTORES TC GLOORIFFICARON, ******* DE A LAUDARE,
3714 5ELCID0469 ******* MIEDO & FUE DESEPARADA.
7434 5ELCID0953 EN AQUESSA CORRIDA X DIAS ******* AMORAR.
8996 5ELCID1145 MAGER LES PESA, ******* SE ADAR & A ARANCAR.
9290 5ELCID1181 POR EL REY DE MARRUECOS ******* A ENBIAR;
9519 5ELCID1210 QUANDO VINO EL DEZENO, ******* GELA ADAR.
9642 5ELCID1225 APRES DELA VERTA ******* LA BATALLA,
12230 5ELCID1552 DE QUANTO QUE QUISIERON NON ******* FALLA,
13581 5ELCID1721 PLOGO AL CRIADOR & ******* LOS DE ARRANCAR.
17675 5ELCID2236 QUANDO ******* ACUESTO FECHO, SALIERON DEL PALA%IO,
27761 5ELCID3543 CA GRAND MIEDO ******* A ALFONSSO EL DE LEON.
29108 5ELCID3718 ******* SU AIUNTA CON ALFONSSO EL DE LEON,
WORD #3010 OCCURS 14 TIMES.
INDEX OF DIVERSIFICATION = 2232.08 WITH STANDARD DEVIATION OF 2710.23

OUIESSE 149 5ELCID0020 DIOS, QUE BUEN VASSALO, SI ******* BUEN SE@OR
15025 5ELCID1899 E DE MI ABRA PERDON; VINIESSEM A VISTAS, SI ******* DENT SABOR.
WORD #3011 OCCURS 2 TIMES.

OUIESSEDES 15357 5ELCID1944 QUE UOS VERNIE AVISTAS DO ********** SABOR;
WORD #3012 OCCURS 1 TIMES.

OUIESSEN 4092 5ELCID0520 AVN DELO QUE DIESSEN ******** GRAND GANAN%IA.
28964 5ELCID3699 QUE NOLES DIESSEN SALTO NIN ******** PAUOR.
WORD #3013 OCCURS 2 TIMES.

OUIESTES 18290 5ELCID2314 AQUESTE ERA EL REY BUCAR, SIL ******** CONTAR.
WORD #3014 OCCURS 1 TIMES.

OUISSE 14394 5ELCID1820 E SERUIR LO HE SIENPRE MIENTRA QUE ****** EL ALMA.
WORD #3015 OCCURS 1 TIMES.

OUO 536 5ELCID0068 DE TODO CONDUCHO BIEN LOS *** BASTIDOS.
1467 5ELCID0188 QUANDO ESTO *** FECHO, CODREDES LO QUE FABLAUA:
2811 5ELCID0354 CORRIO LA SANGRE POR EL ASTIL AYUSO, LAS MANOS SE *** DE VNTAR,
6730 5ELCID0859 AL EXIR DE SALON MUCHO *** BUENAS AUES.
7146 5ELCID0915 QUANDO ESTO FECHO ***, A CABO DE TRES SEMANAS,
7473 5ELCID0959 *** GRAND PESAR & TOUOS LO A GRAND FONTA.
7819 5ELCID1000 TODOS SON ADOBADOS QUANDO MYO %ID ESTO *** FABLADO;
9146 5ELCID1164 QUANDO EL %ID CAMPEADOR *** PE@A CADIELLA,
9865 5ELCID1251 ESTO MANDO MYO %ID, MINAYA LO *** CONSSEIADO:
12529 5ELCID1590 QUANDO *** CORRIDO, TODOS SE MARAUILLAUAN;
13615 5ELCID1725 AL REY YU%EF TRES COLPES LE *** DADOS,
13730 5ELCID1740 QUE DIOS LES *** MER%ED QUE VEN%IERON EL CAMPO.
15897 5ELCID2016 DON LO *** A OIO EL QUE EN BUEN ORA NASCO,
15979 5ELCID2026 TAN GRAND PESAR *** EL REY DON ALFONSSO:
17637 5ELCID2231 POR MANO DEL REY ALFONSSO, QUE AMI LO *** MANDADO,
18081 5ELCID2287 METIOS SOL ESCA@O, TANTO *** EL PAUOR.
25533 5ELCID3252 MAS QUANDO ESTO *** ACABADO, PENSSARON LUEGO DAL.
27422 5ELCID3503 DELO AL TANTO PRISO QUANT *** SABOR.
28500 5ELCID3639 QUEBRARON LE LAS %INCHAS, NINGUNA NOL *** PRO,
WORD #3016 OCCURS 19 TIMES.
INDEX OF DIVERSIFICATION = 1552.56 WITH STANDARD DEVIATION OF 1773.44

OUOS 2049 5ELCID0258 SIESSA DESPENSSA UOS FALLE%IERE **** MENGUARE ALGO,
WORD #3017 OCCURS 1 TIMES.

OVISTE 26080 5ELCID3324 DELANT MYO %ID & DELANTE TODOS ****** TE DE ALABAR
WORD #3018 OCCURS 1 TIMES.

OY 2893 5ELCID0365 QUANDO ** NOS PARTIMOS, EN VIDA NOS FAZ IUNTAR.
5945 5ELCID0754 ** EN ESTE DIA DE UOS ABRE GRAND BANDO;
7801 5ELCID0999 ** EN ESTE PINAR DE TEUAR POR TOLER ME LA GANAN%IA.
13090 5ELCID1659 ALEGRAUAS MIO %ID & DIXO: TAN BUEN DIA ES **
13293 5ELCID1686 ** ES DIA BUENO & MEIOR SERA CRAS:
16050 5ELCID2035 EN TODO MYO REYNO PARTE DESDE **.
16145 5ELCID2047 DIXO EL REY: NON ES AGUISADO **:
16774 5ELCID2124 ** DE MAS SABED QUE FER DELLOS, CAMPEADOR.
18616 5ELCID2356 QUE ** LOS YFANTES AMI POR AMO NON ABRAN;
18726 5ELCID2370 ** UOS DIX LA MISSA DE SANTA TRINIDADE.
21010 5ELCID2670 TU MUERT ** COSSEIAR ALOS YFANTES DE CARRION.
21365 5ELCID2716 ** NOS PARTIREMOS, & DEXADAS SEREDES DE NOS;
23226 5ELCID2958 SI QUIER EL CASAMIENTO FECHO NON FUESSE **
23774 5ELCID3028 PAR SANT ESIDRO, VERDAD NON SERA **
23806 5ELCID3032 DIOS LO MANDE QUE POR UOS SE ONDRE ** LA CORT

WORD C# PREFIX CONTEXT

OY (CON'T)

```
                24571 5ELCID3131 ESTA TER%ERA A TOLLEDC LA VIN FER **,
                24644 5ELCID3139 DELLA & DELLA PART EN PAZ SEAMOS **.
                24736 5ELCID3150 CA UOS LAS CASASTES, REY, SABREDES QUE FER **;
                24856 5ELCID3165 QUANDO DESONDRA DESUS FIJAS NC NOS DEMANDA **;
                26158 5ELCID3334 METISTET, FERRANDO, PORC MENOS VALES **.
                26712 5ELCID3412 ESTE CASAMIENTO ** SE OTORGE EN ESTA CORT,
                27515 5ELCID3514 EN MOROS NI EN CHRISTIANOS OTRO TAL NON HA **,
                28012 5ELCID3575 QUE FIEL SEADES ** DELLOS & DE NOS;
                29163 5ELCID3724 ** LOS REYES DESPA@A SOS PARIENTES SON,
        WORD #3019 OCCURS  24 TIMES.
           INDEX OF DIVERSIFICATION =  1141.17 WITH STANDARD DEVIATION OF  1281.32

OYADES          26895 5ELCID3436 HYO UOS RUEGO QUE ME ****** TODA LA CORT,
        WORD #3020 OCCURS   1 TIMES.

OYAN            16024 5ELCID2032 ASSI ESTANDO, DEDES ME UUESTRA AMOR, QUE LO **** QUANTOS
                                 AQUI SON.
        WORD #3021 OCCURS   1 TIMES.

OYAS            20741 5ELCID2634 ****, SOBRINO, TU, FELEZ MUNOZ
        WORD #3022 OCCURS   1 TIMES.

OYD              2478 5ELCID0313 ***, VARONES, NON UOS CAYA EN PESAR;
                 4159 5ELCID0529 QUITAR QUIERO CASTEION, ***, ESCUELLAS & MINYAYA
                 4867 5ELCID0616 *** AMI, ALBARFANEZ & TODOS LOS CAUALLEROS
                 6358 5ELCID0810 ***, MYNAYA, SODES MYO DIESTRO BRA%O
                 8768 5ELCID1115 ***, MESNADAS, SI EL CRIADOR UOS SALUE
                 8849 5ELCID1127 *** QUE DIXO MINAYA ALBARFANEZ:
                10243 5ELCID1297 ***, MINAYA ALBARFANEZ, POR AQUEL QUE ESTA EN ALTO,
                10739 5ELCID1360 *** ME, ESCUELLAS, & TODA LA MI CORT.
                12632 5ELCID1603 *** LO QUE DIXO EL QUE EN BUEN ORA NASCO:
                13286 5ELCID1685 *** ME, CAUALLEROS, NON RASTARA POR AL;
                15001 5ELCID1897 *** ME, MYNAYA, & VOS, FER VERMUEZ:
                16331 5ELCID2072 *** ME, LAS ESCUELLAS, CUENDES & YFAN%ONES
                18566 5ELCID2350 *** LO QUE FABLO EL QUE EN BUEN ORA NASCO:
                18658 5ELCID2361 AQUI LEGO MYNAYA ALBARFANEZ: ***, YA %ID, CANPEADOR LEAL
                24537 5ELCID3128 ***, MESNADAS, SIUOS VALA EL CRIADOR
                25553 5ELCID3255 *** ME TODA LA CORT & PESEUOS DE MYO MAL;
                28167 5ELCID3596 *** QUE UOS DIGO, YFANTES DE CARRION:
        WORD #3023 OCCURS  17 TIMES.
           INDEX OF DIVERSIFICATION =  1604.56 WITH STANDARD DEVIATION OF  1377.47

OYDA            12145 5ELCID1541 **** ES LA MISSA, & LUEGO CAUALGAUAN;
        WORD #3024 OCCURS   1 TIMES.

OYENDO           2282 5ELCID0287 POR CASTIELLA ****** UAN LOS PREGONES,
        WORD #3025 OCCURS   1 TIMES.

OYMOS           28908 5ELCID3692 DIXIERON LOS FIELES: ESTO ***** NOS.
        WORD #3026 OCCURS   1 TIMES.

OYO              5030 5ELCID0636 QUANDO LO *** EL REY TAMIN, POR CUER LE PESO MAL:
                 7622 5ELCID0976 MYO %ID QUANDO LO ***, ENBIO PORA ALLA:
                 8127 5ELCID1036 QUANDO ESTO *** EL CONDE, YAS YUA ALEGRANDO:
                10236 5ELCID1296 QUANDO LO *** MYO %ID, DE AQUESTO FUE PAGADO:
                15249 5ELCID1931 QUANDO LO *** MYO %ID EL BUEN CAMPEADOR,
                18361 5ELCID2324 *** LA PORIDAD AQUEL MU@O GUSTIOZ,
                21794 5ELCID2772 VIOLOS VENIR & *** VNA RAZON,
                22118 5ELCID2815 QUANDO EL LO *** PESOL DE CORA%ON,
                23701 5ELCID3019 QUANDO LO *** EL REY, PLOGOL DE CORA%ON;
                23761 5ELCID3027 QUANDO LO *** EL REY, POR NADA NON TARDO;
        WORD #3027 OCCURS  10 TIMES.
           INDEX OF DIVERSIFICATION =  2080.22 WITH STANDARD DEVIATION OF  1645.17

OYR             27642 5ELCID3529 PODEDES *** DE MUERTOS, CA DE VENCIDOS NO.
        WORD #3028 OCCURS   1 TIMES.

PADRE              54 5ELCID0008 GRADO ATI, SE@OR *****, QUE ESTAS EN ALTO
                 2377 5ELCID0300 YO RUEGO ADIOS & AL ***** SPIRITAL,
                 2614 5ELCID0330 YA SE@OR GLORIOSO, ***** QUE EN %IELO ESTAS,
                 2863 5ELCID0361 TUERES REY DE LOS REYES & DE TODEL MUNDO *****,
                 2958 5ELCID0372 ADIOS UOS ACOMIENDO, FIJAS, & A LA MUGIER & AL ***** SPIRITAL;
                 8223 5ELCID1047 ABREMOS ESTA VIDA MIENTRA PLOGIERE AL ***** SANTO,
                 8679 5ELCID1102 VIOLO MYO %ID, TOMOS AMARAUILLAR: GRADO ATI, ***** SPIRITAL
                 9247 5ELCID1176 NIN DA COSSEIO ***** A FIJO, NON FIJO A PADRE,
                 9253 5ELCID1176 NIN DA COSSEIO PADRE A FIJO, NON FIJO A *****,
                12872 5ELCID1633 GRADO AL CRIADOR & A ***** ESPIRITAL
                13018 5ELCID1651 AUOS GRADO, %ID, & AL ***** SPIRITAL.
                17973 5ELCID2274  PLEGA A SANTA MARIA & AL ***** SANTO
                18508 5ELCID2342 AVN SI DIOS QUISIERE & EL ***** QUE ESTA EN ALTO,
                19386 5ELCID2456 GRADO ADIOS & AL ***** QUE ESTA EN ALTO,
                20439 5ELCID2594 MER%ED UOS PEDIMOS, *****, SIUOS VALA EL CRIADOR
                20513 5ELCID2604 DE MI & DE UUESTRO ***** BIEN AVEDES NUESTRA GRA%IA.
                20533 5ELCID2607 AL ***** & ALA MADRE LAS MANOS LES BESAUAN;
                20689 5ELCID2626 QUE SI ADIOS PLOGUIERE & AL ***** CRIADOR,
```

WORD C# PREFIX CONTEXT

PADRE (CON'T)

```
                  20728 5ELCID2632 EL ***** CON LAS FIJAS LORAN DE CORA%ON,
                  21986 5ELCID2797 SI UOS LO MERESCA, MYO PRIMO, NUESTRO ***** EL CANPEADOR,
                  22722 5ELCID2895 BESARON LAS MANOS LAS FIJAS AL *****.
                  23579 5ELCID3003 AQUESTE FUE ***** DEL BUEN ENPERADOR;
         WORD #3029 OCCURS  22 TIMES.
            INDEX OF DIVERSIFICATION =  1119.24 WITH STANDARD DEVIATION OF  1583.47

PADRES             2852 5ELCID0360 QUEBRANTESTE LAS PUERTAS & SAQUESTE LOS ****** SANTOS.
         WORD #3030 OCCURS   1 TIMES.

PADRINO           16894 5ELCID2138 SED ******* DELLOS ATOD EL VELAR;
         WORD #3031 OCCURS   1 TIMES.

PAGA              15473 5ELCID1960 QUANDO LAS VIO, DE CORA%ON SE ****:
                  16279 5ELCID2065 DE TAL GUISA LOS **** MYO %ID EL CAMPEADOR,
         WORD #3032 OCCURS   2 TIMES.

PAGADAS           14330 5ELCID1812 POR QUE ASSI LAS ENBIO DOND ELLAS SON *******,
         WORD #3033 OCCURS   1 TIMES.

PAGADO             1008 5ELCID0129 MAS DEZID NOS DEL %ID, DE QUE SERA ******,
                   1963 5ELCID0248 DIXO EL %ID:  GRA%IAS, DON ABBAT, & SO UUESTRO ******;
                   3267 5ELCID0412 MUCHO ERA ****** DEL SUE@O QUE A SO@ADO.
                   6144 5ELCID0782 DIZE MYNAYA:  AGORA SO ******,
                   6474 5ELCID0826 MYNAYA ALBARFANEZ DESTO ES ******; POR YR CON EL OMNES
                                   SON CONTADOS.
                   7278 5ELCID0933  DIOS, COMMO FUE EL %ID ****** & FIZO GRANT ALEGRIA
                   8109 5ELCID1034 E SI UOS COMIEREDES, DON YO SEA ******,
                   8287 5ELCID1054 SI BIEN NON COMEDES, CONDE, DON YO SEA ******,
                   8313 5ELCID1058 ****** ES MYO %ID, QUE LO ESTA AGUARDANDO,
                   8455 5ELCID1075 ****** UOS HE POR TODO AQUESTE A@O;
                  10242 5ELCID1296 QUANDO LO OYO MYO %ID, DE AQUESTO FUE ******:
                  14686 5ELCID1857 AVN VEA ORA QUE DE MI SEA ******.
                  15189 5ELCID1922 SI ES ****** O RE%IBIO EL DON?
                  15201 5ELCID1924 ES ******, & DAUOS SU AMOR.
                  16481 5ELCID2089 DAD LAS AQUI QUISIEREDES UOS, CA YO ****** SO.
                  17003 5ELCID2152 DEUOS BIEN SO SERUIDO, & TENGON POR ******;
                  17746 5ELCID2245 MYO %ID DELO QUE VEYE MUCHO ERA ******:
                  19267 5ELCID2438 ALGO VIE MYO %ID DELO QUE ERA ******,
                  19433 5ELCID2462 DIXO MYO %ID: YO DESTO SO ******;
                  25130 5ELCID3201 HYA ****** SO DE MIS ESPADAS, DE COLADA & DE TIZON.
         WORD #3034 OCCURS  20 TIMES.
            INDEX OF DIVERSIFICATION =  1268.58 WITH STANDARD DEVIATION OF  1531.49

PAGADOS            4213 5ELCID0536 TODOS SODES ******* & NINGUNO POR PAGAR.
                   6357 5ELCID0809 QUANTOS EL TRAE TODOS SON *******.
                   6691 5ELCID0854 NOS ******* FINCADOS, SE@OR, DELA TU PART.
                   9819 5ELCID1247 DE QUE SON *******; EL AMOR DE MY %ID YA LO YUAN PROUANDO.
                   9840 5ELCID1248 LOS QUE FUERON CON EL, & LOS DE DESPUES, TODOS SON *******:
                  14078 5ELCID1782 QUANDO A MYO %ID CAYERON TANTOS, LOS OTROS BIEN PUEDEN
                                   FINCAR *******.
                  16735 5ELCID2119 TODOS SON ******* DELAS VISTAS QUANTOS QUE Y SON.
                  17899 5ELCID2265 POR ******* SE PARTEN DE MYO %ID & DE SUS VASSALLOS.
                  19305 5ELCID2444 SEQUE DE LIDIAR BIEN SODES *******;
                  19333 5ELCID2448 DESTA ARRANCADA NOS YREMOS *******.
                  20382 5ELCID2586 QUANDO SON ******* ATODO SO SABOR,
                  22428 5ELCID2856 TODOS GELO GRADE%EN & SOS ******* SON,
                  25859 5ELCID3294 DE UUESTROS AUERES DE TODOS ******* SODES.
         WORD #3035 OCCURS  13 TIMES.
            INDEX OF DIVERSIFICATION =  1802.83 WITH STANDARD DEVIATION OF  1377.03

PAGAMOS            1140 5ELCID0146 DIXO RACHEL & VIDAS:  NOS DESTO NOS *******.
         WORD #3036 OCCURS   1 TIMES.

PAGANDO            8216 5ELCID1046 PRENDIENDO DEUOS & DE OTROS YR NOS HEMOS *******;
         WORD #3037 OCCURS   1 TIMES.

PAGAR              3898 5ELCID0495 ***** SE YA DELLA ALFONSSO EL CASTELLANO.
                   4217 5ELCID0536 TODOS SODES PAGADOS & NINGUNO POR *****.
                   9454 5ELCID1201 QUANDO VIO MYO %ID LAS GENTES IUNTADAS, COMPE%OS DE *****.
                  18793 5ELCID2378 EUOS, MYO %ID, DE MI MAS UOS *****.
                  25312 5ELCID3223 ***** LE HEMOS DE HEREDADES ENTIERRAS DE CARRION.
         WORD #3038 OCCURS   5 TIMES.
            INDEX OF DIVERSIFICATION =  5352.50 WITH STANDARD DEVIATION OF  3768.39

PAGARON           25491 5ELCID3247 ******* LOS YFANTES AL QUE EN BUEN ORA NASCO:
         WORD #3039 OCCURS   1 TIMES.

PAGAUAN            1456 5ELCID0186 LOS OTROS CCC EN ORO GELOS *******.
                  15589 5ELCID1976 LO VNO A DEBDAN & LO OTRO *******;
         WORD #3040 OCCURS   2 TIMES.

PAGE               3925 5ELCCD0498 FATA QUE YO ME **** SOBRE MIO BUEN CAUALLO,
                  17976 5ELCID2275 QUES **** DES CASAMIENTO MYO %ID O EL QUE LO ALGO
         WORD #3041 OCCURS   2 TIMES.
```

WORD C# PREFIX CONTEXT

PAGEN 25441 5ELCID3240 ***** LE EN APRE%IADURA & PRENDALO EL CAMPEADOR.
WORD #3042 OCCURS 1 TIMES.

PAGO 1102 5ELCID0141 DIXO MARTIN ANTOLINEZ: YO DESSO ME ****.
6332 5ELCID0806 DIOS, QUE BIEN **** A TODOS SUS VASSALLOS,
6638 5ELCID0847 QUE BIEN **** A SUS VASSALOS MISMOS
7258 5ELCID0931 QUE ALBARFANEZ **** LAS MILL MISSAS,
12131 5ELCID1539 EL REY LO **** TODO, & QUITO SEUA MINAYA.
WORD #3043 OCCURS 5 TIMES.
INDEX OF DIVERSIFICATION = 2756.25 WITH STANDARD DEVIATION OF 2656.27

PAGOS 538 5ELCID0069 ***** MYO %ID EL CAMPEADOR & TODOS LOS OTROS QUEUAN ASO %ERUICIO
19859 5ELCID2518 ASSI COMMO LEGARON, ***** EL CAMPEADOR:
WORD #3044 OCCURS 2 TIMES.

PAGUEN 19747 5ELCID2504 QUE ****** AMI O A QUI YO QUIER SABOR.
WORD #3045 OCCURS 1 TIMES.

PALABRA 205 5ELCID0026 E A QUEL QUE GELA DIESSE SOPIESSE UERA *******,
290 5ELCID0036 LOS DE DENTRO NON LES QUERIEN TORNAR *******.
28745 5ELCID3670 OTORGAN GELO LOS FIELES QUE DIZE VERDADERA *******.
WORD #3046 OCCURS 3 TIMES.

PALABRAS 1658 5ELCID0213 ESTAS ******** DICHAS, LA TIENDA ES COGIDA.
16666 5ELCID2111 LAS ******** SON PUESTAS QUE OTRO DIA MA@ANA
19920 5ELCID2527 AESTAS ******** FABLO FERAN GON%ALEZ:
25353 5ELCID3228 A ESTAS ******** FABLO EL REY CON ALFONSSO:
WORD #3047 OCCURS 4 TIMES.

PALA%IANO 13633 5ELCID1727 METIOS LE EN GUIERA, VN CASTIELLO *********;
WORD #3048 OCCURS 1 TIMES.

PALA%IO 1422 5ELCID0182 EN MEDIO DEL ******* TENDIERON VN ALMOFALLA,
13024 5ELCID1652 MUGIER, SED EN ESTE *******, & SI QUISIEREDES EN EL ALCA%AR;
13904 5ELCID1761 EN BUELTA CON EL ENTRARON AL *******,
13980 5ELCID1770 GRANT FUE EL ALEGRIA QUE FUE POR EL *******;
17434 5ELCID2205 PENSSARON DE ADOBAR ESSORA EL *******,
17460 5ELCID2208 SABOR ABRIEDES DE SER & DE COMER ENEL *******.
17481 5ELCID2211 CAUALGAN LOS YFFANTES, ADELANT ADELINAUAN AL *******,
17680 5ELCID2236 QUANDO OUIERON AQUESTO FECHO, SALIERON DEL *******,
22990 5ELCID2929 ADELINO PORAL ******* DO ESTAUA LA CORT,
26444 5ELCID3373 ASUR GON%ALEZ ENTRAUA POR EL *******,
WORD #3049 OCCURS 10 TIMES.
INDEX OF DIVERSIFICATION = 2779.22 WITH STANDARD DEVIATION OF 3839.22

PALA%IOS 898 5ELCID0115 DEXADO HA HEREDADES & CASAS & ********.
WORD #3050 OCCURS 1 TIMES.

PALAFRE 15524 5ELCID1967 E TANTO ******* QUE BIEN ANDA,
15669 5ELCID1987 TANTA GRUESSA MULA & TANTO ******* DE SAZON,
16697 5ELCID2114 TANTA GRUESSA MULA & TANTO ******* DE SAZON
25467 5ELCID3243 TANTA GRUESSA MULA, TANTO ******* DE SAZON,
WORD #3051 OCCURS 4 TIMES.

PALAFRES 8371 5ELCID1064 DAN LE TRES ******** MUY BIEN ENSELLADOS
11284 5ELCID1428 ******** & MULAS, QUE NON PARESCAN MAL.
16939 5ELCID2144 TRAYO VOS XX ********, ESTOS BIEN ADOBADOS,
17816 5ELCID2254 ENTRE ******** & MULAS & CORREDORES CAUALLOS,
20266 5ELCID2572 DARUOS E MULAS & ********, MUY GRUESSOS DE SAZON,
WORD #3052 OCCURS 5 TIMES.
INDEX OF DIVERSIFICATION = 2972.75 WITH STANDARD DEVIATION OF 1988.59

PALO 9894 5ELCID1254 TOMASSEN LE EL AUER & PUSIESSEN LE EN VN ****.
WORD #3053 OCCURS 1 TIMES.

PALOS 3187 5ELCID0401 SOBRE NAUAS DE ***** EL DUERO UA PASAR,
WORD #3054 OCCURS 1 TIMES.

PAN 519 5ELCID0066 AMYO %ID & ALOS SUYOS ABASTALES DE *** & DE UINO;
2733 5ELCID0345 DEL AGUA FEZIST VINO & DELA PIEDRA ***,
4571 5ELCID0581 FALIDO A AMYO %ID EL *** & LA %EUADA.
5281 5ELCID0667 EL AGUA NOS AN VEDADA, EXIR NOS HA EL ***,
5331 5ELCID0673 SI CON MOROS NON LIDIAREMOS, NO NOS DARAN DEL ***.
8028 5ELCID1025 COMED, CONDE, DESTE *** & BEUED DESTE VINO.
8089 5ELCID1032 NOL PUEDEN FAZER COMER VN MUESSO DE ***.
8696 5ELCID1104 BEUEMOS SO VINO & COMEMOS EL SO ***.
9223 5ELCID1173 EN CADA VNO DESTOS A@OS MYO %ID LES TOLIO EL ***.
9243 5ELCID1175 DE NINGUNA PART QUE SEA NON LES VINIE ***;
9268 5ELCID1178 MALA CUETA ES, SE@ORES, AVER MINGUA DE ***,
12960 5ELCID1643 AFARTO VERAN POR LOS OIOS COMMO SE GANA EL ***.
13268 5ELCID1682 TORNADOS SON A MYO %ID LOS QUE COMIEN SO ***;
13347 5ELCID1691 MAS VALE QUE NOS LOS VEZCAMOS, QUE ELLOS COIAN EL ***.
WORD #3055 OCCURS 14 TIMES.
INDEX OF DIVERSIFICATION = 985.77 WITH STANDARD DEVIATION OF 1217.41

WORD C# PREFIX CONTEXT

```
PA@O              17450 5ELCID2207 TANTA PORPOLA & TANTO XAMED & TANTO **** PRECIADO.
                  24193 5ELCID3085 CAL%AS DE BUEN **** EN SUS CAMAS METIO,
         WORD #3056 OCCURS    2 TIMES.

PA@OS             20282 5ELCID2574 E MUCHAS VESTIDURAS DE ***** & DE %ICLATONES;
         WORD #3057 OCCURS    1 TIMES.

PAR                3170 5ELCID0399 PASSO *** ALCOBIELLA QUE DE CASTIELLA FINES YA;
                  22234 5ELCID2832 *** AQUESTA BARBA QUE NADI NON MESSO,
                  23768 5ELCID3028 *** SANT ESIDRO, VERDAD NON SERA OY
                  24646 5ELCID3140 JURO *** SANT ESIDRO, EL QUE BOLUIERE MY CORT
                  25012 5ELCID3186 *** AQUESTA BARBA QUE NADI NON MESSO,
                  27469 5ELCID3509 HYO LO JURO *** SANT ESIDRO EL DE LEON
         WORD #3058 OCCURS    6 TIMES.
            INDEX OF DIVERSIFICATION =  4858.80 WITH STANDARD DEVIATION OF  7978.76

PARA               3578 5ELCID0450 TERNE YO CASTEION DON ABREMOS GRAND EN ****.
                   6098 5ELCID0775 **** CALATAYUCH QUANTO PUEDE SE VA.
         WORD #3059 OCCURS    2 TIMES.

PARADA            12415 5ELCID1575 SI SERIE CORREDOR OSSI ABRIE BUENA ******;
         WORD #3060 OCCURS    1 TIMES.

PARADO              262 5ELCID0033 POR MIEDO DEL REY ALFONSSO, QUE ASSI LO AUIEN ******
                   1247 5ELCID0160 MARTIN ANTOLINEZ EL PLEYTO A ******,
                   1550 5ELCID0198 ATORGAR NOS HEDES ESTO QUE AUEMOS ******.
                  17585 5ELCID2224 NOLO QUIERO FALIR POR NADA DE QUANTO AY ******;
         WORD #3061 OCCURS    4 TIMES.

PARAN             21401 5ELCID2721 ***** LAS EN CUERPOS & EN CAMISAS & EN %ICLATONES.
         WORD #3062 OCCURS    1 TIMES.

PARANDO            7302 5ELCID0936 TIERRAS DALCANZ NEGRAS LAS VA *******,
                  17529 5ELCID2218 ESTAN ******* MIENTES ALQUE EN BUEN ORA NASCO.
         WORD #3063 OCCURS    2 TIMES.

PARAUA              323 5ELCID0040 VNA NI@A DE NUEF A@OS A OIO SE ******:
         WORD #3064 OCCURS    1 TIMES.

PARAUAN            4803 5ELCID0608 LAS ESPADAS DESNUDAS, A LA PUERTA SE *******.
                   7981 5ELCID1019 ADUZEN LE LOS COMERES, DELANT GELOS *******;
         WORD #3065 OCCURS    2 TIMES.

PARAUAS           18717 5ELCID2369 ******* DELANT AL CAMPEADOR, SIEMPRE CON LA BUEN AUZE:
         WORD #3066 OCCURS    1 TIMES.

PARAYSO            2769 5ELCID0350 EL VNO ES EN *******, CA EL OTRO NON ENTRO ALA;
                  29222 5ELCID3731 QUIEN ESCRIUIO ESTE LIBRO DEL DIOS *******, AMEN
         WORD #3067 OCCURS    2 TIMES.

PARE%EN           11888 5ELCID1507 BIEN SALIERON DEN %IENTO QUE NON ******* MAL,
                  13071 5ELCID1657 FINCADAS SON LAS TIENDAS & ******* LOS ALUORES,
                  24242 5ELCID3091 OBRADO ES CON ORO, ******* PORO SON,
         WORD #3068 OCCURS    3 TIMES.

PARE%RA            8843 5ELCID1126 ALI ******* EL QUE MERE%E LA SOLDADA.
         WORD #3069 OCCURS    1 TIMES.

PAREIAS           21712 5ELCID2761 PUES NUESTRAS ******* NON ERAN PORA EN BRA%OS.
                  25734 5ELCID3277 O QUIEN GELAS DIERA POR ******* OPOR VELADAS?
                  26995 5ELCID3449 ANTES LAS AVIEDES ******* PORA EN BRA%OS LAS TENER,
         WORD #3070 OCCURS    3 TIMES.

PARESCADES        14820 5ELCID1873 QUE BIEN ********** ANTE RUY DIAZ MYO %ID;
         WORD #3071 OCCURS    1 TIMES.

PARESCAN          11289 5ELCID1428 PALAFRES & MULAS, QUE NON ******** MAL.
                  24124 5ELCID3076 E QUE NON ******** LAS ARMAS, BIEN PRESOS LOS CORDONES;
         WORD #3072 OCCURS    2 TIMES.

PARIA              4474 5ELCID0569 EL CASTIELLO DE ALCO%ER EN ***** UA ENTRANDO.
                   4614 5ELCID0586 LA ***** QUEL A PRESA TORNAR NOS LA HA DOBLADA.
                   6782 5ELCID0866 METIO EN ***** ADOROCA EN ANTES,
                   7077 5ELCID0904 EL DE RIO MARTIN TODO LO METIO EN *****.
                   7142 5ELCID0914 ASARAGO%A METUDA LA EN *****.
         WORD #3073 OCCURS    5 TIMES.
            INDEX OF DIVERSIFICATION =   666.00 WITH STANDARD DEVIATION OF  1005.24

PARIAS              854 5ELCID0109 EL CAMPEADOR POR LAS ****** FUE ENTRADO,
                   4485 5ELCID0570 LOS DE ALCO%ER A MYO %ID YAL DAN ****** DE GRADO
                   7337 5ELCID0941 POR QUE DAN ****** PLAZE ALOS DE SARAGO%A,
                  19741 5ELCID2503 ELLOS ME DARAN ****** CON AIUDA DEL CRIADOR,
         WORD #3074 OCCURS    4 TIMES.
```

WORD C# PREFIX CONTEXT

```
PARIENTES       14709 5ELCID1860 CON X DE SUS ********* A PARTE DAUAN SALTO:
                23463 5ELCID2988 PRENDEN SO CONSSEIO ASSI ********* COMMO SON,
                23527 5ELCID2996 PRENDEN CONSSEIO ********* COMMO SON;
                24826 5ELCID3162 CON TODOS SUS ********* & EL VANDO QUE Y SON;
                27727 5ELCID3539 E TODOS SUS ********* CON ELLOS SON;
                28136 5ELCID3592 MUY BIEN ACONPA@ADOS, CA MUCHOS ********* SON.
                29168 5ELCID3724 OY LOS REYES DESPA@A SOS ********* SON,
          WORD #3075 OCCURS    7 TIMES.
             INDEX OF DIVERSIFICATION =  2408.83 WITH STANDARD DEVIATION OF  3259.70

PARIO           20450 5ELCID2595 VOS NOS ENGENDRASTES, NUESTRA MADRE NOS *****;
          WORD #3076 OCCURS    1 TIMES.

PARO            15870 5ELCID2012 HYAS VA PORA LAS VISTAS QUE CON EL REY ****.
                20675 5ELCID2624 MINAYA ALBARFANEZ ANTE MYO %ID SE ****:
                28888 5ELCID3689 LA LAN%A RECOMBRO & SOBREL SE ****;
          WORD #3077 OCCURS    3 TIMES.

PAROS           21032 5ELCID2673 ARMAS YUA TENIENDO, ***** ANTE LOS YFANTES;
          WORD #3078 OCCURS    1 TIMES.

PART             2492 5ELCID0314 POCO AUER TRAYO, DAR UOS QUIERO UUESTRA ****.
                 5027 5ELCID0635 ASSI FFERA LO DE SILOCA, QUE ES DEL OTRA ****.
                 6077 5ELCID0771 CAFUYEN LOS MOROS DE LA ****
                 6696 5ELCID0854 NOS PAGADOS FINCADOS, SE@OR, DELA TU ****.
                 6779 5ELCID0865 NON TEME GERRA, SABET, A NULLA ****.
                 6793 5ELCID0867 DESI A MOLINA, QUE ES DEL OTRA ****,
                 7692 5ELCID0985 YA CAUALLEROS, A **** FAZED LA GANAN%IA;
                 8595 5ELCID1091 AORIENT EXE EL SOL, E TORNOS AESSA ****.
                 8892 5ELCID1132 YO CON LOS %IENTO ENTRARE DEL OTRA ****,
                 8990 5ELCID1144 DEL OTRA **** ENTROLES ALBARFANEZ;
                 9237 5ELCID1175 DE NINGUNA **** QUE SEA NON LES VINIE PAN;
                13386 5ELCID1696 QUANDO UOS LOS FUEREDES FERIR, ENTRARE YO DEL OTRA ****;
                15309 5ELCID1938 ELLOS SON MUCHO VRGULLOSOS & AN **** EN LA CORT,
                15507 5ELCID1965 DELLA **** & DELLA PORA LAS VISTAS SE ADOBAUAN;
                18331 5ELCID2319 AMOS HERMANOS A **** SALIDOS SON:
                18676 5ELCID2363 EUOS TAN DINNO QUE CON EL AUEDES ****.
                18682 5ELCID2364 MANDAD NOLOS FERIR DE QUAL **** UOS SEMEIAR,
                19007 5ELCID2404 TANTO BRA%O CON LORIGA VERIEDES CAER A ****,
                20003 5ELCID2538 AMOS SALIERON A ****, VERA MIENTRE SON HERMANOS;
                21375 5ELCID2717 NON ABREDES **** EN TIERRAS DE CARRION.
                24640 5ELCID3139 DELLA & DELLA **** EN PAZ SEAMOS OY.
                24668 5ELCID3142 CON EL QUE TOUIERE DERECHO YO DESSA **** ME SO.
                28126 5ELCID3591 FEUOS DELA OTRA **** LOS YFANTES DE CARRION,
                28434 5ELCID3631 QUEBRANTO LA BOCA DEL ESCUDO, A **** GELA ECHO,
                28842 5ELCID3684 DELA OTRA **** VNA BRA%A GELA ECHO,
          WORD #3079 OCCURS   25 TIMES.
             INDEX OF DIVERSIFICATION =  1096.92 WITH STANDARD DEVIATION OF  1245.46

PARTADES        11724 5ELCID1486 E FFATA EN VALEN%IA DELLAS NON UOS ********.
          WORD #3080 OCCURS    1 TIMES.

PARTE            5538 5ELCID0698 DE ***** DELOS MOROS DOS SE@AS HA CABDALES,
                 9087 5ELCID1156 SONANDO VAN SUS NUEUAS ALENT ***** DEL MAR.
                 9795 5ELCID1244 CON EL MYNAYA ALBARFFANEZ QUE NOS LE ***** DE SO BRA%O.
                10171 5ELCID1288 DE ***** DE ORIENT VINO VN CORONADO;
                12714 5ELCID1614 E DEL OTRA ***** A OIO HAN EL MAR,
                14426 5ELCID1824 QUE LAS OTRAS TIERRAS *****.
                14711 5ELCID1860 CON X DE SUS PARIENTES A ***** DAUAN SALTO:
                16048 5ELCID2035 EN TODO MYO REYNO ***** DESDE OY.
                16393 5ELCID2079 DELLA & DELLA *****, QUANTOS QUE AQUI SON,
                20013 5ELCID2539 DESTO QUE ELLOS FABLARON NOS ***** NON AYAMOS:
                25271 5ELCID3217 ESSORA SALIEN A ***** YFANTES DE CARRION;
                27393 5ELCID3499 AESSOS & ALOS OTROS QUE DE BUENA ***** SON,
          WORD #3081 OCCURS   12 TIMES.
             INDEX OF DIVERSIFICATION =  1985.82 WITH STANDARD DEVIATION OF  1626.52

PARTEN           2975 5ELCID0375 ASIS ****** VNOS DOTROS COMMO LA V@A DELA CARNE.
                 4248 5ELCID0540 DEL CASTIELLO QUE PRISIERON TODOS RICOS SE ******;
                17901 5ELCID2265 POR PAGADOS SE ****** DE MYO %ID & DE SUS VASSALLOS.
                28930 5ELCID3695 POR ONDRADOS SE ****** LOS DEL BUEN CAMPEADOR;
          WORD #3082 OCCURS    4 TIMES.

PARTES           1047 5ELCID0134 ACOGEN SELE OMNES DE TODAS ****** MEGUADOS,
                 2764 5ELCID0349 DOS LADRONES CONTIGO, ESTOS DE SE@AS ******
                 2824 5ELCID0356 ABRIO SOS OIOS, CATO ATODAS ******,
                 3144 5ELCID0395 GRANDES YENTES SELE ACOIEN ESSA NOCH DE TODAS ******.
                 3203 5ELCID0403 VANSSELE ACOGIENDO YENTES DE TODAS ******.
                 5130 5ELCID0648 NON LO DETIENEN, VIENEN DE TODAS ******.
                 7441 5ELCID0954 FUERON LOS MANDADOS A TODAS ******,
                 7456 5ELCID0956 LOS MANDADOS SON YDOS ATODAS ******;
                 7945 5ELCID1015 DE TODAS ****** LOS SOS SE AIUNTARON;
                 8979 5ELCID1142 ARANCAR SE LAS ESTACAS & ACOSTAR SE ATODAS ****** LOS TENDALES.
                 9419 5ELCID1197 ANDIDIERON LOS PREGONES, SABET, ATODAS ******,
```

WORD C# PREFIX CONTEXT

PARTES (CON'T)

9491 5ELCID1206 SONANDO VAN SUS NUEUAS TODAS ATODAS ******.
11187 5ELCID1415 VERIEDES CAUALLEROS VENIR DE TODAS ******,
12704 5ELCID1612 DIOS VELIDOS CATAN A TODAS ******,
12764 5ELCID1620 DEZIR UOS QUIERO NUEUAS DE ALENT ****** DEL MAR,
19023 5ELCID2406 CAUALLOS SIN DUENOS SALIR A TODAS ******.
19377 5ELCID2455 DE TODAS ****** SOS VASSALLOS VAN LEGANDO;
23648 5ELCID3012 DE TODAS ****** ALLI IUNTADOS SON.
WORD #3083 OCCURS 18 TIMES.
INDEX OF DIVERSIFICATION = 1328.47 WITH STANDARD DEVIATION OF 1701.00

PARTIZION 20220 5ELCID2567 LOS FIJOS QUE OUIEREMOS EN QUE AURAN *********.
WORD #3084 OCCURS 1 TIMES.

PARTIDOS 20810 5ELCID2642 CUEMO LA VaA DELA CARNE ELLOS ******** SON;
WORD #3085 OCCURS 1 TIMES.

PARTIEMOS 8778 5ELCID1116 DESPUES QUE NOS ********* DELA LINPIA CHRISTIANDAD,
WORD #3086 OCCURS 1 TIMES.

PARTIEN 28281 5ELCID3610 SORTEAUAN LES EL CAMPO, YA LES ******* EL SOL,
WORD #3087 OCCURS 1 TIMES.

PARTIENDO 8078 5ELCID1031 ELLOS ********* ESTAS GANANZIAS GRANDES,
17877 5ELCID2262 HYAS YUAN ********* ACUESTOS OSPEDADOS,
WORD #3088 OCCURS 2 TIMES.

PARTIERON 21887 5ELCID2785 ********* SE LE LAS TELLAS DE DENTRO DE LOS CORAZONES,
WORD #3089 OCCURS 1 TIMES.

PARTIMOS 2895 5ELCID0365 QUANDO OY NOS ********, EN VIDA NOS FAZ IUNTAR.
2962 5ELCID0373 AGORA NOS ********, DIOS SABE EL AIUNTAR.
WORD #3090 OCCURS 2 TIMES.

PARTIO 22070 5ELCID2808 EL CAUALLO PRISO POR LA RIENDA & LUEGO DENT LAS ******,
27585 5ELCID3522 ESSORA SE ESPIDIERON, & LUEGOS ****** LA CORT.
WORD #3091 OCCURS 2 TIMES.

PARTIOS 408 5ELCID0051 ******* DELA PUERTA, POR BURGOS AGUIJAUA,
WORD #3092 OCCURS 1 TIMES.

PARTIR 2162 5ELCID0272 E NOS DEUOS ****** NOS HEMOS EN VIDA.
2223 5ELCID0280 YA LO VEDES QUE ****** NOS EMOS EN VIDA,
4014 5ELCID0510 MANDO ****** TOD AQUESTE AUER,
11390 5ELCID1441 GRAND DUELO ES AL ****** DEL ABBAT:
16742 5ELCID2120 ****** SE QUIEREN, QUE ENTRADA ERA LA NOCH.
24878 5ELCID3168 E QUANDO LAS TOUIERE, ****** SEA LA CORT;
26417 5ELCID3370 AL ****** DELA LID POR TU BOCA LO DIRAS,
WORD #3093 OCCURS 7 TIMES.
INDEX OF DIVERSIFICATION = 4041.50 WITH STANDARD DEVIATION OF 3369.66

PARTIRA 8708 5ELCID1106 AMENOS DE LID NOS ******* ACUESTO;
WORD #3094 OCCURS 1 TIMES.

PARTIREMOS 8294 5ELCID1055 AQUI FEREMOS LA MORADA, NO NOS ********** AMOS.
21367 5ELCID2716 OY NOS **********, & DEXADAS SEREDES DE NOS;
WORD #3095 OCCURS 2 TIMES.

PARTO 17017 5ELCID2154 ADIOS UOS ACOMIENDO, DESTAS VISTAS ME *****.
21096 5ELCID2681 AQUIM ***** DE UOS COMMO DE MALOS & DE TRAYDORES.
WORD #3096 OCCURS 2 TIMES.

PAS 18402 5ELCID2329 QUE SEAN EN *** & NON AYAN Y RAZION.
WORD #3097 OCCURS 1 TIMES.

PASAR 3191 5ELCID0401 SOBRE NAUAS DE PALOS EL DUERO UA *****,
WORD #3098 OCCURS 1 TIMES.

PASE 5348 5ELCID0675 EN EL NOBRE DEL CRIADOR, QUE NON **** POR AL:
WORD #3099 OCCURS 1 TIMES.

PASO 6719 5ELCID0858 **** SALON AYUSO, AGUIJO CABA DELANT,
WORD #3100 OCCURS 1 TIMES.

PASSADA 12137 5ELCID1540 ******* ES LA NOCHE, VENIDA ES LA MAaANA,
14138 5ELCID1789 TAL TIENDA COMMO ESTA, QUE DE MARUECOS ES *******,
14418 5ELCID1823 ANDAN LOS DIAS & LAS NOCHES, & ******* HAN LA SIERRA,
WORD #3101 OCCURS 3 TIMES.

PASSADO 16249 5ELCID2061 ES DIA ES *******, & ENTRADA ES LA NOCH;
16292 5ELCID2067 ******* AUIE IIJ AaOS NO COMIERAN MEIOR.
29181 5ELCID3726 ******* ES DESTE SIEGLO EL DIA DE CINQUAESMA.
WORD #3102 OCCURS 3 TIMES.

PASSADOS 2428 5ELCID0306 LOS VJ DIAS DE PLAZO ******** LOS AN,
WORD #3103 OCCURS 1 TIMES.

WORD C# PREFIX CONTEXT

PASSAN 3370 5ELCID0425 DE NOCH ****** LA SIERRA, VINIEA ES LA MAN,
11751 5ELCID1491 ****** LAS MONTANAS, QUE SON FIERAS & GRANDES,
WORD #3104 OCCURS 2 TIMES.

PASSANDO 2555 5ELCID0323 ******** UA LA NOCH, VINIENDO LA MAN;
4273 5ELCID0544 POR LAS CUEUAS DANQUITA ELLOS ******** UAN,
14435 5ELCID1826 ******** VAN LAS SIERRAS & LOS MONTES & LAS AGUAS,
WORD #3105 OCCURS 3 TIMES.

PASSAR 5762 5ELCID0727 TANTA ADAGARA FORADAR & ******,
9660 5ELCID1228 ENEL ****** DE XUCAR Y VERIEDES BARATA,
11546 5ELCID1462 POR SANTA MARIA UOS VAYADES ******,
23901 5ELCID3044 ESSA NOCH MYO %ID TAIO NON QUISO ******;
27637 5ELCID3528 PRESO AUEMOS EL DEBDO & A ****** ES POR NOS;
WORD #3106 OCCURS 5 TIMES.
INDEX OF DIVERSIFICATION = 5467.75 WITH STANDARD DEVIATION OF 4680.68

PASSARA 26397 5ELCID3367 HYELLO LIDIARE, NON ******* POR AL:
WORD #3107 OCCURS 1 TIMES.

PASSAREMOS 3343 5ELCID0422 ********** LA SIERRA QUE FIERA ES & GRAND,
WORD #3108 OCCURS 1 TIMES.

PASSARON 4275 5ELCID0545 ******** LAS AGUAS, ENTRARON AL CAMPO DE TORAN%IO,
11759 5ELCID1492 ******** MATA DE TORANZ DE TAL GUISA QUE NINGUN MIEDO NON HAN,
21191 5ELCID2692 LA SIERRA DE MIEDES ******** LA ESTOZ,
WORD #3109 OCCURS 3 TIMES.

PASSAUA 7123 5ELCID0911 ALEN DE TERUEL DON RODRIGO *******,
WORD #3110 OCCURS 1 TIMES.

PASSAUAN 12157 5ELCID1542 SALIERON DE MEDINA, & SALON ********,
WORD #3111 OCCURS 1 TIMES.

PASSE 8817 5ELCID1122 ***** LA NOCHE & VENGA LA MA@ANA,
26043 5ELCID3320 ***** POR TI, CON EL MORO ME OFF DE AIUNTAR,
WORD #3112 OCCURS 2 TIMES.

PASSO 769 5ELCID0098 ***** POR BURGOS, AL CASTIELLO ENTRAUA,
3169 5ELCID0399 ***** PAR ALCOBIELLA QUE DE CASTIELLA FINES YA;
4327 5ELCID0551 E ***** AALFAMA, LA FOZ AYUSO UA,
4333 5ELCID0552 ***** A BOUIERCA & ATECA QUE ES ADELANT,
28398 5ELCID3626 FERRANGO%ALEZ A PERO VERMUEZ EL ESCUDOL *****,
28437 5ELCID3632 ***** GELO TODO, QUE NADA NOL VALIO,
WORD #3113 OCCURS 6 TIMES.
INDEX OF DIVERSIFICATION = 5532.60 WITH STANDARD DEVIATION OF 10405.80

PASTORES 2649 5ELCID0335 ******** TE GLORIFFICARON, OUIERON DE A LAUDARE,
WORD #3114 OCCURS 1 TIMES.

PASXADO 1573 5ELCID0201 EXIDO ES DE BURGOS & ARLAN%ON A *******,
WORD #3115 OCCURS 1 TIMES.

PAUOR 13033 5ELCID1653 NON AYADES ***** POR QUE ME VEADES LIDIAR,
13180 5ELCID1670 ALEGRE SON LAS DUENAS, PERDIENDO VAN EL *****.
13193 5ELCID1672 POR LAS HUERTAS ADENTRO ESTAN SINES *****.
18083 5ELCID2287 METIOS SOL ESCA@O, TANTO OUO EL *****.
18103 5ELCID2290 TRAS VNA VIGA LAGAR METIOS CON GRANT *****;
18379 5ELCID2326 EUADES QUE ***** HAN UUESTROS YERNOS TAN OSADOS,
19706 5ELCID2498 MOROS & CHRISTIANOS DE MI HAN GRANT *****;
24166 5ELCID3081 DO TALES %IENTO TOUIER, BIEN SERE SIN *****.
26143 5ELCID3332 E TU, FERRANDO, QUE FIZIST CON EL *****?
28391 5ELCID3625 FIRIENSSE EN LOS ESCUDOS SIN TODO *****.
28965 5ELCID3699 QUE NOLES DIESSEN SALTO NIN OUIESSEN *****.
WORD #3116 OCCURS 11 TIMES.
INDEX OF DIVERSIFICATION = 1592.20 WITH STANDARD DEVIATION OF 1812.66

PAZ 4140 5ELCID0527 MOROS EN ***, CA ESCRIPTA ES LA CARTA,
7642 5ELCID0978 DELO SO NON LIEUO NADA, DEXEM YR EN ***.
10333 5ELCID1308 TIERRAS DE VALENCIA REMANIDAS EN ***,
11560 5ELCID1464 TIENELA AUEGALUON, MYO AMIGO ES DE ***,
12027 5ELCID1525 EN *** O EN GERRA DELO NUESTRO ABRA;
24642 5ELCID3139 DELLA & DELLA PART EN *** SEAMOS OY.
26522 5ELCID3385 ALOS QUE DAS ***, FARTAS LOS ADERREDOR.
WORD #3117 OCCURS 7 TIMES.
INDEX OF DIVERSIFICATION = 3729.33 WITH STANDARD DEVIATION OF 4481.28

PECADOS 13450 5ELCID1705 PRENDOL YO LOS *******, & DIOS LE ABRA EL ALMA.
WORD #3118 OCCURS 1 TIMES.

PECCADORES 29199 5ELCID3728 ASSI FFAGAMOS NOS TODOS IUSTOS & **********
WORD #3119 OCCURS 1 TIMES.

PECHARA 7658 5ELCID0980 LO DE ANTES & DE AGORA TODOM LO *******;
WORD #3120 OCCURS 1 TIMES.

```
WORD                     C#   PREFIX                                        CONTEXT


PECHOS              28449 5ELCID3633 METIOL LA LAN%A POR LCS ******, QUE NADA NOL VALIO;
         WORD #3121 OCCURS    1 TIMES.

PEDIDAS             17387 5ELCID2200 ******* UOS HA & ROGACAS EL MYC SE@OR ALFONSSO,
         WORD #3122 CCCURS    1 TIMES.

PEDIMOS             20438 5ELCID2594 MER%ED UOS *******, PACRE, SIUOS VALA EL CRIADOR
                    20474 5ELCID2599 ASSI UOS ******* MER%ED NOS AMAS ADOS,
         WORD #3123 CCCURS    2 TIMES.

PEDIR                1032 5ELCID0133 ***** UOS A PCCO POR DEXAR SO AUER EN SALUO.
         WORD #3124 CCCURS    1 TIMES.

PEDIST              26018 5ELCID3317 ****** LAS FERIDAS PRIMERAS ALCANPEADOR LEAL,
         WORD #3125 OCCURS    1 TIMES.

PELAYET             27059 5ELCID3457 GOMEZ ******* EN PIE SE LEUANTO;
         WORD #3126 OCCURS    1 TIMES.

PELI%ONES            8379 5ELCID1065 E BUENAS VESTIDURAS DE ********* & DE MANTOS.
                    24120 5ELCID3075 SOBRE LAS LCRIGAS ARMINOS & *********,
         WORD #3127 CCCURS    2 TIMES.

PELLI%ONES          15686 5ELCID1989 TANTA BUENA CAPA & MANTOS & **********;
                    17831 5ELCID2256 MANTOS & ********** & OTRCS VESTIDOS LARGOS;
                    21400 5ELCID2720 ALLI LES TUELLEN LOS MANTCS & LOS **********,
         WORD #3128 CCCURS    3 TIMES.

PELO                 9769 5ELCID1241 NIN ENTRARIE ENELA TIGERA, NI VN **** NON AURIE TAIADO,
         WORD #3129 CCCURS    1 TIMES.

PELOS               19255 5ELCID2437 COFIA SOBRE LCS ***** FRONZIDA DELLA YA QUANTO.
                    24264 5ELCID3094 VNA COFIA SOBRE LOS ***** DUN ESCARIN DE PRO,
                    24281 5ELCID3096 QUE NON LE CCNTALASSEN LCS ***** AL BUEN %ID CANPEADOR;
                    28623 5ELCID3655 RAXOL LCS ***** DELA CABE%A, BIEN ALA CARNE LEGAUA;
         WORD #3130 OCCURS    4 TIMES.

PENA                 9135 5ELCID1163 GANARON **** CADIELLA, LAS EXICAS & LAS ENTRADAS.
         WORD #3131 CCCURS    1 TIMES.

PENDON              15536 5ELCID1969 TANTO BUEN ****** METER EN BUENAS ASTAS,
                    18767 5ELCID2375 ****** TRAYC A CORCAS & ARMAS DE SE@AL,
                    28839 5ELCID3683 METIOL POR LA CARNE ACENTRO LA LAN%A CONEL ******,
                    28873 5ELCID3687 VERMEIO SALIC EL ASTIL, & LA LAN%A & EL ******.
         WORD #3132 OCCURS    4 TIMES.

PENDONES              116 5ELCID0016 EN SU CONPA@A LX ********; EXIEN LO UER MUGIERES & UARONES,
                     3326 5ELCID0419 NOTO TREZIENTAS LAN%AS CUE TOCAS TIENEN ********.
                     5683 5ELCID0716 ABAXAN LAS LAN%AS A BUESTAS CELOS ********,
                     5737 5ELCID0723 TREZIENTAS LAN%AS SCN, TCCAS TIENEN ********;
                     5768 5ELCID0729 TANTOS ******** BLANCCS SALIR VERMEIOS EN SANGRE,
                     7866 5ELCID1006 LOS ******** & LAS LAN%AS TAN BIEN LAS UAN ENPLEANDO,
                    11913 5ELCID1510 E EN LAS MANCS LAN%AS QUE ******** TRAEN,
                    28093 5ELCID3586 ESTAS TRES LAN%AS TRAEN SENCS ********;
                    28330 5ELCID3616 ABAXAN LAS LAN%AS ABUELTAS CON LOS ********,
         WORD #3133 OCCURS    9 TIMES.
            INDEX OF DIVERSIFICATION =  3525.75 WITH STANDARD DEVIATION OF  5331.68

PENSAD              19947 5ELCID2531 ****** DELC CTRO, QUE LC NUESTRO TENEMOS LO EN SALUO.
         WORD #3134 CCCURS    1 TIMES.

PENSEMOS             3015 5ELCID0380 ******** DE YR NUESTRA VIA, ESTO SEA DE VAGAR.
                     4221 5ELCID0537 CRAS ALA MA@ANA ******** DE CAUALGAR,
         WORD #3135 CCCURS    2 TIMES.

PENSOLAS            11273 5ELCID1426 EL BUENC DE MINAYA ******** DE ADOBAR
         WORD #3136 CCCURS    1 TIMES.

PENSSAD             13314 5ELCID1688 DEZIR NCS HA LA MISSA, & ******* DE CAUALGAR,
                    23910 5ELCID3046 *******, SE@OR, DE ENTRAR ALA %IBDAD,
         WORD #3137 OCCURS    2 TIMES.

PENSSADO             8469 5ELCID1076 DE VENIR UOS BUSCAR SCL NCN SERA ********.
         WORD #3138 OCCURS    1 TIMES.

PENSSANDO           23424 5ELCID2983 POR TODAS SUS TIERRAS ASSI LO YUAN *********,
         WORD #3139 OCCURS    1 TIMES.

PENSSAR             11301 5ELCID1430 EL BUENC DE MINAYA ******* CUIERE DE CAUALGAR;
         WORD #314C CCCURS    1 TIMES.

PENSSARAN           11175 5ELCID1413 HYDOS SCN LOS CAUALLEROS & CELLO *********,
                    25529 5ELCID3251 SOS CMNES LAS TIENEN & CELLAS *********.
         WORD #3141 OCCURS    2 TIMES.
```

WORD C# PREFIX CONTEXT

```
PENSSARON          7572 5ELCID0970 TRES DIAS & DCS NOCHES ********* DE ANDAR,
                  17429 5ELCID2205 ********* DE ADCBAR ESSCRA EL PALA%IO,
                  25535 5ELCID3252 MAS QUANDO ESTC CUC ACABACO, ********* LUEGO DAL.
        WORD #3142 OCCURS   3 TIMES.

PENSSAUA           8474 5ELCID1077 AGUIJAUA EL CCNDE E ******** DE ANDAR,
        WORD #3143 OCCURS   1 TIMES.

PENSSAUAN         20556 5ELCID2609 MYO %ID & LOS OTROS DE CAUALGAR *********,
        WORD #3144 OCCURS   1 TIMES.

PENSSEDES          8059 5ELCID1028 DIXO EL CONDE DCN REMCNT:  CCMEDE, DON RODRIGO, & *********
                                   DE FOLGAR.
        WORD #3145 OCCURS   1 TIMES.

PENSSEMOS          2531 5ELCID0320 LA MISSA DICHA, ********* DE CAUALGAR,
                   7401 5ELCID0949 CRAS ALA MAaANA ********* DE CAUALGAR,
        WORD #3146 OCCURS   2 TIMES.

PENSSO             2989 5ELCID0376 MYO %ID CON LCS SOS VASSALLOS ****** DE CAUALGAR,
                  11383 5ELCID1440 MUCHAS YENTES SELE ACOGEN, ****** DE CAUALGAR,
                  14945 5ELCID1889 VNA GRANT ORA EL REY ****** & COMIDIO;
                  15258 5ELCID1932 VNA GRAND ORA ****** & CCMIDIC;
                  22206 5ELCID2828 VNA GRAND ORA ****** & CCMIDIC;
                  22760 5ELCID2900 AL REY ALFONSSO DE CASTIELLA ****** DE ENBIAR;
        WORD #3147 OCCURS   6 TIMES.
           INDEX OF DIVERSIFICATION =  3953.20 WITH STANDARD DEVIATION OF  3662.25

PE@A               9147 5ELCID1164 QUANDO EL %ID CAMPEADOR OUO **** CADIELLA,
                  10492 5ELCID1330 E **** CADIELLA, QUE ES VNA PE@A FUERT;
                  10497 5ELCID1330 E PE@A CADIELLA, QUE ES VNA **** FUERT;
                  21184 5ELCID2691 ASSINIESTRO DEXAN ATINEZA, VNA **** MUY FUERT,
        WORD #3148 OCCURS   4 TIMES.

PE@OS             29255 5ELCID3735 ALA VNOS *****, QUE BIEN VOS LO DARARAN SOBRELOS.
        WORD #3149 OCCURS   1 TIMES.

PEONADAS           3314 5ELCID0418 SIN LAS ******** & OMNES VALIENTES QUE SON,
                   7170 5ELCID0918 NCN SON EN CUENTA, SABET, LAS ********.
        WORD #3150 OCCURS   2 TIMES.

PEONES             4041 5ELCID0514 E A LOS ****** LA MEATAC SIN FALLA;
                   5434 5ELCID0686 SI NON DOS ****** SOLOS POR LA PUERTA GUARDAR;
                   5550 5ELCID0699 E FIZIERON DOS AZES DE ****** MEZCLADOS, QUILOS PODRIE CONTAR?
                   6338 5ELCID0807 ALOS ****** & A LOS ENCAUALGADOS
                   6647 5ELCID0848 A CAUALLEROS & A ****** FECHOS LOS HA RICOS,
        WORD #3151 OCCURS   5 TIMES.
           INDEX OF DIVERSIFICATION =   650.50 WITH STANDARD DEVIATION OF   569.36

PEOR              29027 5ELCID3707 ATAL LE CONTESCA O SI QUIER ****.
        WORD #3152 OCCURS   1 TIMES.

PEQUENAS          16431 5ELCID2083 CA NON HAN GRANT HEDAND E DE DIAS ******** SON.
        WORD #3153 OCCURS   1 TIMES.

PER               14555 5ELCID1841 MYNAYA & *** VERMUEZ ADELANT SON LEGADOS,
                  15006 5ELCID1897 OYD ME, MYNAYA, & VOS, *** VERMUEZ:
                  15083 5ELCID1907 FABLO MYNAYA & PLOGO A *** VERMUEZ:
                  29224 5ELCID3732 *** ÀBBAT LE ESCRIUIO ENEL MES DE MAYO,
        WORD #3154 OCCURS   4 TIMES.

PERDEDES           2399 5ELCID0303 LO QUE ******** DOBLADO UOS LO COBRAR.
        WORD #3155 OCCURS   1 TIMES.

PERDER             9349 5ELCID1189 QUIEN QUIERE ****** CUETA & VENIR A RRITAD,
        WORD #3156 OCCURS   1 TIMES.

PERDERA           10981 5ELCID1389 EL %ID QUE BIEN NOS QUIERA NADA NON *******.
                  24659 5ELCID3141 QUITAR ME A EL REYNO, ******* MIAMOR.
        WORD #3157 OCCURS   2 TIMES.

PERDERAS           5005 5ELCID0632 SI NON DAS CONSEIO, A TECA & A TERUEL ********,
                   5006 5ELCID0633 ******** CALATAYUTH, QUE NON PUEDE ESCAPAR,
        WORD #3158 OCCURS   2 TIMES.

PERDERE            8001 5ELCID1022 ANTES ******* EL CUERPO & DEXARE EL ALMA,
        WORD #3159 OCCURS   1 TIMES.

PERDEREDES        12071 5ELCID1530 DESTO QUE AUEDES FECHO UOS NON ********** NADA.
        WORD #3160 OCCURS   1 TIMES.

PERDERIE            207 5ELCID0027 QUE ******** LOS AUERES & MAS LOS OIOS DELA CARA,
        WORD #3161 OCCURS   1 TIMES.
```

WORD C# PREFIX CONTEXT

PERDERIEMOS 358 5ELCID0045 SI NCN, *********** LCS AUERES & LAS CASAS,
WORD #3162 OCCURS 1 TIMES.

PERDIDA 18339 5ELCID2320 CATAMOS LA GANANZIA & LA ******* NO,
WORD #3163 OCCURS 1 TIMES.

PERDIDO 8168 5ELCID1041 MAS QUANTO AUEDES ******* & YO GANE EN CANPO,
8185 5ELCID1043 MAS QUANTO AUEDES ******* NCN UOS LO DARE,
WORD #3164 OCCURS 2 TIMES.

PERDIENDO 13177 5ELCID1670 ALEGRE SON LAS DUENAS, ********* VAN EL PAUOR.
WORD #3165 OCCURS 1 TIMES.

PERDIERON 24790 5ELCID3157 CCMIGO NON QUISIERCN AUER NACA & ********* MI AMOR;
WORD #3166 OCCURS 1 TIMES.

PERDIESTES 22515 5ELCID2867 BUEN CASAMIENTO **********, MEIOR PODREDES GANAR.
WORD #3167 OCCURS 1 TIMES.

PERDON 15020 5ELCID1899 E DE MI ABRA ******; VINIESSEM A VISTAS, SI OUIESSE DENT SABOR.
17064 5ELCID2160 MERZED UOS SEA & FAZED NOS ESTE ******:
29192 5ELCID3727 DE CHRISTUS HAYA ******
WORD #3168 OCCURS 3 TIMES.

PERDONO 16039 5ELCID2034 AQUI UOS ******* & DOUCS MY AMOR,
WORD #3169 OCCURS 1 TIMES.

PERIURADOS 1282 5ELCID0164 QUE SI ANTES LAS CATASSEN QUE FUESSEN **********,
WORD #3170 OCCURS 1 TIMES.

PERO 1629 5ELCID0209 EN SAN **** DE CARDENA YNOS CANTE EL GALLO;
1832 5ELCID0233 PORA SAN **** DE CARDENA QUANTO PUDO A ESPOLEAR,
1858 5ELCID0236 QUANDO LEGO A SAN **** EL BUEN CAMPEADOR;
1887 5ELCID0240 ROGANDO A SAN **** & AL CRIADOR:
2277 5ELCID0286 TANEN LAS CAMPA@AS EN SAN **** A CLAMOR.
2328 5ELCID0294 VANSSE PORA SAN **** DO ESTA EL QUE ENBUEN PUNTO NAZIO.
2512 5ELCID0318 EN SAN **** A MATINS TANDRA EL BUEN ABBAT,
4823 5ELCID0611 VINO **** VERMUEZ, QUE LA SE@A TEINE EN MANO,
5458 5ELCID0689 E VOS, **** VERMUEZ, LA MI SE@A TOMAD;
5589 5ELCID0704 AQUEL **** VERMUEZ NON LO PUDO ENCURAR,
5636 5ELCID0710 RESPUSO **** VERMUEZ: NON RASTARA POR AL.
5730 5ELCID0722 TODOS FIEREN ENEL AZ DO ESTA **** VERMUEZ.
10154 5ELCID1285 E MANDO MILL MARCOS DE PLATA A SAN **** LEUAR
10999 5ELCID1392 ADELINO PORA SAN ****, CLAS DUE@AS ESTAN,
11015 5ELCID1394 DEZIDO ES MYNAYA, ASSAN **** VA ROGAR,
11179 5ELCID1414 REMANEZIO EN SAN **** MINAYA ALBARFANEZ.
11376 5ELCID1439 HYDO ES PORA SAN **** MINAYA ALBARFANEZ,
11461 5ELCID1451 DE SAN **** FASTA MEDINA EN V DIAS VAN,
11517 5ELCID1458 TU, MU@O GUSTIOZ & **** VERMUEZ DELANT,
11822 5ELCID1499 AFEUOS AQUI **** VERMUEZ & MU@O GUSTIOZ QUE UOS QUIEREN SIN HAR
14350 5ELCID1815 MANDO A **** VERMUEZ QUE FUESSE CON MYNAYA.
14456 5ELCID1828 ENVIAUA LE MANDADO **** VERMUEZ & MYNAYA,
14796 5ELCID1870 AUOS, MINAYA ALBARFANEZ, & EA **** VERMUEZ AQUI,
14986 5ELCID1894 A MYNAYA ALBARFANEZ & A **** VERMUEZ
15170 5ELCID1919 VENIDES, MYNAYA, & VCS, **** VERMUEZ
15698 5ELCID1991 MYNAYA ALBARFANEZ & AQUEL **** VERMUEZ,
17209 5ELCID2177 DIXO MYO ZID ADON **** & A MU@O GUSTIOZ:
18489 5ELCID2340 ASSI LO OTORGA DON **** CUEMO SE ALABA FERRANDO.
18577 5ELCID2351 ALA, **** VERMUEZ, EL MYO SOBRINO CARO
22272 5ELCID2836 CAUALGO MINAYA CON **** VERMUEZ
22489 5ELCID2864 E **** VERMUEZ OTRO TANTO LAS HA;
24045 5ELCID3065 E **** VERMUEZ & AQUESTE MU@O GUSTIOZ
25909 5ELCID3301 MYO ZID RUY DIAZ A **** VERMUEZ CATA;
25913 5ELCID3302 FABLA, **** MUDO, VARCN QUE TANTO CALLAS
25942 5ELCID3306 **** VERMUEZ CONPEZO DE FABLAR;
25970 5ELCID3310 SIEMPRE EN LAS CORTES **** MUDO ME LAMADES
27603 5ELCID3524 HYA MARTIN ANTOLINEZ, & VOS, **** VERMUEZ,
28373 5ELCID3623 **** VERMUEZ, EL QUE ANTES REBTO,
28394 5ELCID3626 FERRANGOZALEZ A **** VERMUEZ EL ESCUDOL PASSO,
28416 5ELCID3629 FIRME ESTIDO **** VERMUEZ, POR ESSO NOS ENCAMO;
28549 5ELCID3645 ATORGARON GELO LOS FIELES, **** VERMUEZ LE DEXO.
WORD #3171 OCCURS 41 TIMES.
INDEX OF DIVERSIFICATION = 672.00 WITH STANDARD DEVIATION OF 1037.90

PERTENEZEN 16441 5ELCID2085 ********** PORA MIS FIJAS & AVN PORA MEIORES.
WORD #3172 OCCURS 1 TIMES.

PERTENEZIEN 25886 5ELCID3298 CA NON *********** FIJAS DE YFANZONES.
WORD #3173 OCCURS 1 TIMES.

PESA 4937 5ELCID0625 MUCHO **** ALOS DE TECA & ALOS DE TERUAL NON PLAZE,
8645 5ELCID1098 **** ALOS DE VALENZIA, SABET, NON LES PLAZE;
8995 5ELCID1145 MAGER LES ****, OUIERON SE ADAR & A ARANCAR.

WORD C# PREFIX CONTEXT

PESA (CON'T)

9150 5ELCID1165 MALES **** EN XATIUA & DENTRO EN GUIERA,
11677 5ELCID1480 AMY NON ME ****, SABET, MUCHO ME PLAZE
18259 5ELCID2310 FIERA COSA LES **** DESTO QUE LES CUNTIO.
18312 5ELCID2317 MAS, SABED, DE CUER LES **** ALOS YFANTES DE CARRION;
23190 5ELCID2954 VERDAD TE DIGO YO, QUE ME **** DE CORA%ON,
23232 5ELCID2959 ENTRE YO & MYO %ID **** NOS DE CORA%ON.
23793 5ELCID3031 DELO QUE AUOS **** AMI DUELE EL CORA%ON;
24443 5ELCID3116 MAGER QUE ALGUNOS ****, MEIOR SODES QUE NOS.
WORD #3174 OCCURS 11 TIMES.
INDEX OF DIVERSIFICATION = 1949.60 WITH STANDARD DEVIATION OF 2359.20

PESADAS 682 5ELCID0086 YNCAMOS LAS DARENA, CA BIEN SERAN *******,
WORD #3175 OCCURS 1 TIMES.

PESADO 724 5ELCID0091 NON PUEDO TRAER EL AUER, CA MUCHO ES ******,
WORD #3176 OCCURS 1 TIMES.

PESANDO 7325 5ELCID0940 ******* VA ALOS DE MON%ON & ALOS DE HUESCA;
14526 5ELCID1837 ALOS UNOS PLAZE & ALOS OTROS VA *******.
23437 5ELCID2985 HYA LES VA ******* ALSO YFANTES DE CARRION,
28224 5ELCID3603 HYA LES VA ******* ALOS YFANTES DE CARRION.
WORD #3177 OCCURS 4 TIMES.

PESAR 2484 5ELCID0313 OYD, VARONES, NON UOS CAYA EN *****;
7475 5ELCID0959 OUO GRAND ***** & TOUOS LO A GRAND FONTA.
10030 5ELCID1273 SI AUOS PLOGUIERE, MINAYA, & NON UOS CAYA EN *****,
10989 5ELCID1390 RESPUSO MYNAYA: ESTO NON MEA POR QUE *****.
11089 5ELCID1403 TODO SERIE ALEGRE, QUE NON AURIE NINGUN *****.
12988 5ELCID1647 YA MUGIER ONDRADA, NON AYADES *****
15978 5ELCID2026 TAN GRAND ***** OUO EL REY DON ALFONSSO:
18270 5ELCID2311 ELLOS ENESTO ESTANDO, DON AUIEN GRANT *****,
22870 5ELCID2913 ESSO ME PUEDE ***** CON LA OTRA DESONOR.
26938 5ELCID3441 ELLOS LAS HAN DEXADAS A ***** DE NOS.
WORD #3178 OCCURS 10 TIMES.
INDEX OF DIVERSIFICATION = 2716.11 WITH STANDARD DEVIATION OF 1636.75

PESARES 28944 5ELCID3697 GRANDES SON LOS ******* POR TIERRAS DE CARRION.
WORD #3179 OCCURS 1 TIMES.

PESAUA 4503 5ELCID0572 ALOS DE CALATAUTH, SABET, MALES ******.
7089 5ELCID0906 NON PLAZE ALOS MOROS, FIRME MIENTRE LES ******.
WORD #3180 OCCURS 2 TIMES.

PESE 22818 5ELCID2907 QUEL **** AL BUEN REY DALMA & DE CORA%ON.
23162 5ELCID2951 E QUE UOS ****, REY COMMO SODES SABIDOR;
23878 5ELCID3041 DESTO QUE NOS ABINO QUE UOS ****, SE@OR.
26859 5ELCID3431 E QUE NON **** ESTO AL %ID CAMPEADOR:
27017 5ELCID3451 AVER LAS HEDES ASERUIR, MAL QUE UOS **** AUOS.
29096 5ELCID3716 SIN VERGUEN%A LAS CASARE OAQUI **** OAQUI NON.
WORD #3181 OCCURS 6 TIMES.
INDEX OF DIVERSIFICATION = 1254.60 WITH STANDARD DEVIATION OF 1222.90

PESEUOS 25559 5ELCID3255 OYD ME TODA LA CORT & ******* DE MYO MAL;
WORD #3182 OCCURS 1 TIMES.

PESO 1447 5ELCID0185 NOTOLOS DON MARTINO, SIN **** LOS TOMAUA;
5037 5ELCID0636 QUANDO LO OYO EL REY TAMIN, POR CUER LE **** MAL:
6742 5ELCID0861 **** ALOS DE ALCO%ER, CA PROLES FAZIE GRANT.
10615 5ELCID1345 MAGER PLOGO AL REY, MUCHO **** A GAR%IORDONEZ:
14696 5ELCID1859 **** AL CONDE DON GAR%IA, E MAL ERA YRADO;
16098 5ELCID2042 **** A ALBARDIAZ & A GARCIORDONEZ.
22181 5ELCID2825 DE CUER **** ESTO AL BUEN REY DON ALFONSSO.
22255 5ELCID2835 **** A MYO %ID & ATODA SU CORT, & ALBARFANEZ DALMA & DE CORA%ON.
WORD #3183 OCCURS 8 TIMES.
INDEX OF DIVERSIFICATION = 2971.57 WITH STANDARD DEVIATION OF 2023.63

PESOL 12775 5ELCID1622 ***** AL REY DE MARRUECOS DE MYO %ID DON RODRIGO:
22119 5ELCID2815 QUANDO EL LO OYO ***** DE CORA%ON,
WORD #3184 OCCURS 2 TIMES.

PESOLES 22156 5ELCID2821 QUANDO SABIEN ESTO, ******* DE CORA%ON;
WORD #3185 OCCURS 1 TIMES.

PETRALES 11894 5ELCID1508 EN BUENOS CAUALLOS A ******** & A CASCAUELES,
WORD #3186 OCCURS 1 TIMES.

PEYDRO 2875 5ELCID0363 E RUEGO A SAN ****** QUE ME AIUDE A ROGAR
WORD #3187 OCCURS 1 TIMES.

PICAR 26486 5ELCID3379 FUESSE A RIO DOUIRNA LOS MOLINOS *****
WORD #3188 OCCURS 1 TIMES.

PIDAMOS 20036 5ELCID2543 ******* NUESTRAS MUGIERES AL %ID CAMPEADOR,
WORD #3189 OCCURS 1 TIMES.

```
WORD                C#  PREFIX                        CONTEXT

PIDE             10662 5ELCID1351 MER%ED UOS **** EL %ID, SIUOS CAYESSE EN SABOR,
                 16719 5ELCID2117 CADA VNO LO QUE ****, NADI NOL DIZE DE NO.
         WORD #3190 OCCURS    2 TIMES.

PIDEN            15294 5ELCID1937 E ***** ME MIS FIJAS PORA LOS YFANTES DE CARRION.
                 16384 5ELCID2078 ELLOS UOS LAS ***** & MANDO UOS LO YO.
                 26611 5ELCID3398 ***** SUS FIJAS A MYO %ID EL CAMPEADOR
                 26977 5ELCID3447 QUANDO ***** MIS PRIMAS, DON ELUIRA & DO@A SOL,
         WORD #3191 OCCURS    4 TIMES.

PIDIERON         11745 5ELCID1490 %IENTOL ********, MAS EL CON DOZIENTOS VA.
         WORD #3192 OCCURS    1 TIMES.

PIDIMOS          14910 5ELCID1885 MER%ED UOS ******* COMMO A REY & SE@OR NATURAL;
         WORD #3193 OCCURS    1 TIMES.

PIDIO             8241 5ELCID1049 ALEGRE ES EL CONDE & ***** AGUA ALAS MANOS,
         WORD #3194 OCCURS    1 TIMES.

PIDO              8868 5ELCID1129 A MI DEDES C CAUALLEROS, QUE NON UOS **** MAS,
                 13474 5ELCID1708 **** UOS VN DON & SEAM PRESENTADO.
                 16011 5ELCID2031  MER%ED UOS **** AUOS, MYO NATURAL SE@OR,
                 16358 5ELCID2075 VUESTRAS FIJAS UOS ****, DON ELUIRA & DO@A SOL,
                 16833 5ELCID2131 YO UOS **** MER%ED AUOS, REY NATURAL:
                 26849 5ELCID3430 MER%ED UOS **** COMMO A REY & A SE@OR,
                 27426 5ELCID3504 MER%ED UOS ****, REY, POR AMOR DEL CRIADOR
         WORD #3195 OCCURS    7 TIMES.
            INDEX OF DIVERSIFICATION =  3092.00 WITH STANDARD DEVIATION OF  3774.94

PIE                300 5ELCID0038 SACO EL *** DEL ESTRIBERA, UNA FERIDAL DAUA;
                  5895 5ELCID0747 MAGER DE *** BUENOS COLPES VA DANDO.
                  9545 5ELCID1213 LOS QUE FUERON DE *** CAUALLEROS SE FAZEN;
                 10194 5ELCID1291 DE *** & DE CAUALLO MUCHO ERA AREZIADO.
                 13869 5ELCID1757 QUANDOL VIERON DE ***, QUE ERA DESCAUALGADO,
                 15986 5ELCID2027 LEUANTADOS EN ***, YA %ID CAMPEADOR,
                 16086 5ELCID2040 LEUOS EN *** & EN LA BOCAL SALUDO.
                 17490 5ELCID2213 DE *** & ASABOR, DIOS, QUE QUEDOS ENTRARON
                 17539 5ELCID2219 EL CAMPEADOR EN *** ES LEUANTADO:
                 18151 5ELCID2296 MYO %ID FINCO EL COBDO, EN *** SE LEUANTO,
                 24376 5ELCID3108 LEUANTOS EN *** EL BUEN REY DON ALFONSSO
                 24531 5ELCID3127 ESSORA SE LEUO EN *** EL BUEN REY DON ALFONSSO;
                 24692 5ELCID3145 MYO %ID LA MANO BESO AL REY & EN *** SE LEUANTO;
                 25252 5ELCID3215 DIXO ALBARFANEZ LEUANTADOS EN *** EL %ID CAMPEADOR:
                 25681 5ELCID3270 EL CONDE DON GAR%IA EN *** SE LEUANTAUA;
                 25840 5ELCID3291 FERRANGO%ALEZ EN *** SE LEUNATO,
                 26357 5ELCID3361 MARTIN ANTOLINEZ EN *** SE LEUANTAUA;
                 26505 5ELCID3382 ESSORA MUNO GUSTIOZ EN *** SE LEUANTO;
                 26644 5ELCID3402 LEUANTOS EN *** MYO %ID EL CAMPEADOR;
                 26793 5ELCID3422 LEUANTOS EN *** OIARRA & YNEGO XIMENEZ,
                 26844 5ELCID3429 MYNAYA ALBAFANEZ EN *** SE LEUANTO;
                 27061 5ELCID3457 GOMEZ PELAYET EN *** SE LEUANTO;
         WORD #3196 OCCURS   22 TIMES.
            INDEX OF DIVERSIFICATION =  1273.33 WITH STANDARD DEVIATION OF  1884.07

PIEDAD            4764 5ELCID0604 LOS VASSALLOS DE MYO %ID SIN ****** LES DAUAN,
         WORD #3197 OCCURS    1 TIMES.

PIEDRA            2732 5ELCID0345 DEL AGUA FEZIST VINO & DELA ****** PAN,
         WORD #3198 OCCURS    1 TIMES.

PIEL              1388 5ELCID0178 VNA **** VERMEIA MORISCA & ONDRADA,
                  1527 5ELCID0195 DE QUE FAGADES CAL%AS & RICA **** & BUEN MANTO.
                 24247 5ELCID3092 SOBRESTO VNA **** VERMEIA, LAS BANDAS DORO SON,
         WORD #3199 OCCURS    3 TIMES.

PIELES           19512 5ELCID2472 CON DUCHOS A SAZONES, BUENAS ****** & BUENOS MANTOS.
                 21625 5ELCID2749 LEUARON LES LOS MANTOS & LAS ****** ARMINAS,
         WORD #3200 OCCURS    2 TIMES.

PIELLES             25 5ELCID0004 ALCANDARAS UAZIAS SIN ******* & SIN MANTOS
                 15550 5ELCID1971 MANTOS & ******* E BUENOS %ENCALES DADRIA?
         WORD #3201 OCCURS    2 TIMES.

PIENSSA           3133 5ELCID0394 OTRO DIA MA@ANA ******* DE CAUALGAR.
         WORD #3202 OCCURS    1 TIMES.

PIENSSAN            67 5ELCID0010 ALLI ******** DE AGUIIAR, ALLI SUELTAN LAS RIENDAS.
                  1785 5ELCID0227 SUELTAN LAS RIENDAS & ******** DE AGUIJAR.
                  3276 5ELCID0413 OTRO DIA MA@ANA ******** DE CAUALGAR;
                  3382 5ELCID0426 E POR LA LOMA AYUSO ******** DE ANDAR.
                  3422 5ELCID0432 ANTE QUE ANOCHESCA ******** DE CAUALGAR;
                  4672 5ELCID0592 ALSABOR DEL PRENDER DELO AL NON ******** NADA,
                  5093 5ELCID0643 TRES MILL MOROS CAUALGAN & ******** DE ANDAR,
```

WORD C# PREFIX CONTEXT

PIENSSAN (CON'T)

```
            5106 5ELCIDC645 OTRO DIA MA@ANA ******** DE CAUALGAR,
            5121 5ELCID0647 POR LOS DE LA FRONTERA ******** DE ENVIAR;
            5398 5ELCIDC681 ELDIA & LA NOCHE ******** SE DE ADOBAR.
            8912 5ELCID1135 MA@ANA ERA & ******** SE DE ARMAR,
           10128 5ELCID1283 PUES ESTO AN FABLADO, ******** SE DE ADOBAR.
           11438 5ELCID1448 HYAS ESPIDEN & ******** DE CAUALGAR,
           11625 5ELCID1473 ESTO ERA DICHO, ******** DE CAUALGAR,
           11741 5ELCID1489 ALA MA@ANA ******** DE CAUALGAR;
           11776 5ELCID1493 POR EL VAL DE ARBUXEDO ******** A DEPRUNAR.
           20822 5ELCID2644 ******** SE DE YR LOS YFANTES DE CARRION;
           22540 5ELCID2870 OTRO DIA MA@ANA ******** DE CAUALGAR,
           22559 5ELCID2873 DALLENT SE ESPIDIERON DELLOS, ******** SE DE TORNAR,
     WORD #3203 OCCURS  19 TIMES.
        INDEX OF DIVERSIFICATION =  1248.56 WITH STANDARD DEVIATION OF  2159.44

PIENSSE    10928 5ELCID1383 DESI ADELANT ******* DELLAS EL CAMPEADOR.
     WORD #3204 OCCURS   1 TIMES.

PIERDA     10751 5ELCID1361 NON QUIERO QUE NADA ****** EL CAMPEADOR;
           27252 5ELCID3483 QUEN NON VINIERE AL PLAZO ****** LA RAZON,
     WORD #3205 OCCURS   2 TIMES.

PIES        6878 5ELCID0879 BESA UOS LOS **** & LAS MANOS AMAS,
            9042 5ELCID1151 DE **** DE CAUALLO LOS QUES PUDIERON ESCAPAR.
           10404 5ELCID1319 ALOS **** DEL REY ALFONSSO CAYO CON GRAND DUELO,
           10435 5ELCID1323 LOS **** & LAS MANOS, COMMO ATAN BUEN SE@OR,
           11310 5ELCID1431 AFEUOS RACHEL & VIDAS ALOS **** LE CAEN:
           12566 5ELCID1594 QUANDO LO VIO DO@A XIMENA, A **** SE LE ECHAUA:
           14578 5ELCID1844 BESAN LA TIERRA & LOS **** AMOS:
           15973 5ELCID2025 DE AQUESTA GUISA ALOS **** LE CAYO.
           15995 5ELCID2028 BESAD LAS MANOS, CA LOS **** NO;
           23037 5ELCID2935 BESABA LE LOS **** AQUEL MU@O GUSTIOZ;
           23051 5ELCID2937 LOS **** & LAS MANOS VOS BESA EL CAMPEADOR;
     WORD #3206 OCCURS  11 TIMES.
        INDEX OF DIVERSIFICATION =  1616.30 WITH STANDARD DEVIATION OF  2063.17

PIESSAN     2565 5ELCID0324 ALOS MEDIADOS GALLOS ******* DE CAUALGAR.
            3111 5ELCID0391 SOLTARON LAS RIENDAS, ******* DE ANDAR;
           13251 5ELCID1680 MUCHO AUIEN FECHO, ******* DE CAUALGAR.
     WORD #3207 OCCURS   3 TIMES.

PIESSEN     3095 5ELCID0389 ABBAT, DEZILDES QUE PRENDAN EL RASTRO & ******* DE ANDAR,
     WORD #3208 OCCURS   1 TIMES.

PIESSO     19728 5ELCID2501 ELLOS LO TEMEN, CA NON LO ****** YO:
     WORD #3209 OCCURS   1 TIMES.

PINAR       7125 5ELCID0912 ENEL ***** DE TEUAR CON ROY DIAZ POSAUA;
            7583 5ELCID0971 ALCON%ARON A MYO %ID EN TEUAR & EL *****;
            7804 5ELCID0999 OY EN ESTE ***** DE TEUAR POR TOLER ME LA GANAN%IA.
     WORD #3210 OCCURS   3 TIMES.

PLA%A       4698 5ELCID0595 VIO QUE ENTRELLOS & EL CASTIELLO MUCHO AUIE GRAND *****;
     WORD #3211 OCCURS   1 TIMES.

PLATA        643 5ELCID0081 ESPESO E EL ORO & TODA LA *****,
            1441 5ELCID0184 ATOD EL PRIMER COLPE IIJ MARCOS DE ***** ECHARON,
            2461 5ELCID0310 POR ORO NIN POR ***** NON PODRIE ESCAPAR.
            3746 5ELCID0473 GA@O A CASTEJON & EL ORO ELA *****.
            4037 5ELCID0513 A CADA VNO DELLOS CAEN C MARCHOS DE *****,
            4102 5ELCID0521 ASMARON LOS MOROS IIJ MILL MARCOS DE *****.
            6274 5ELCID0799 TRAEN ORO & ***** QUE NON SABEN RECABDO;
            6427 5ELCID0820 EUADES AQUI ORO & ***** VNA VESA LE@A,
            6627 5ELCID0845 VENDIDO LES A ALCO%ER POR TRES MILL MARCHOS DE *****.
            7913 5ELCID1010 HY GA@O A COLADA QUE MAS VALE DE MILL MARCOS DE *****.
            9553 5ELCID1214 EL ORO & LA ***** QUI EN VOS LO PODRIE CONTAR?
            9711 5ELCID1234 ATODOS LOS MENORES CAYERON C MARCOS DE *****.
           10151 5ELCID1285 E MANDO MILL MARCOS DE ***** A SAN PERO LEUAR
           12474 5ELCID1582 SOBREPELI%AS VESTIDAS & CON CRUZES DE *****
           13708 5ELCID1737 ENTRE ORO & ***** FALLARON TRES MILL MARCOS,
           13946 5ELCID1766 ACADA VNA DELLAS DO LES CC MARCOS DE *****,
           15547 5ELCID1970 ESCUDOS BOCLADOS CON ORO & CON *****,
           15604 5ELCID1978 QUANTOS QUISIESSEN AUERES DORO O DE *****.
           16599 5ELCID2103 TREZIENTOS MARCOS DE ***** EN AYUDA LES DO YO,
           19475 5ELCID2467 QUE ALA RA%ION CAYE SEYS %IENTOS MARCOS DE *****.
           20261 5ELCID2571 HYO QUIERO LES DAR AXUUAR IIJ MILL MARCOS DE *****;
           24219 5ELCID3088 CON ORO & CON ***** TODAS LAS PRESAS SON,
           25159 5ELCID3204 EN ORO & EN ***** TRES MILL MARCOS DE PLATA LES DIO;
           25164 5ELCID3204 EN ORO & EN PLATA TRES MILL MARCOS DE ***** LES DIO;
           25429 5ELCID3238 EL ORO & LA ***** ESPENDIESTES LO VOS;
     WORD #3212 OCCURS  25 TIMES.
        INDEX OF DIVERSIFICATION =  1031.75 WITH STANDARD DEVIATION OF  1004.41
```

WORD C# PREFIX CONTEXT

PLAZ 4240 5ELCIDC539 LO QUE DIXO EL %ID A TODOS LOS OTROS ****.
9316 5ELCID1184 SOPOLO MYO %ID, DE CCRA%CN LE ****;
10697 5ELCID1355 ESSORA DIXC EL REY: **** ME DE CORA%ON;
16846 5ELCID2132 PUES QUE CASADES MYS FIJAS, ASI CCMMO AUOS ****,
16913 5ELCID2140 DIXO ALBARFANEZ: SE@CR, AFE QUE ME ****.
18812 5ELCID2380 ESSORA DIXC MYC %ID: LC CUF UCS QUEREDES **** ME.
22618 5ELCID2881 AL MORO AUENGALUCN DE CCRA%CN LE ****,
WORD #3213 CCCURS 7 TIMES.
INDEX OF DIVERSIFICATICN = 3062.00 WITH STANCARD DEVIATION OF 2336.13

PLAZE 4946 5ELCIDC625 MUCHO PESA ALCS DE TECA & ALOS DE TERUAL NON *****,
4952 5ELCIDC626 E ALOS DE CALATAYUTH NON *****.
5305 5ELCIDC670 DEZID ME, CAUALLERCS, CCMMO UOS ***** DE FAR.
6922 5ELCID0885 AUN ME ***** DE MYO %ID QUE FIZO TAL GANAN%IA.
7083 5ELCIDC906 NCN ***** ALCS MCRCS, FIRME MIENTRE LES PESAUA.
7338 5ELCID0941 POR QUE DAN PARIAS ***** ALOS DE SARAGO%A,
8652 5ELCID1098 PESA ALCS DE VALEN%IA, SABET, NON LES *****;
8859 5ELCID1128 CAMPFADOR, FAGAMCS LC QUE AUOS *****.
8908 5ELCID1134 CCMMO GELO A DICHO, AL CAMPEADCR MUCHO *****.
11681 5ELCID1480 AMY NON ME PESA, SABET, MUCHC ME *****
14521 5ELCID1837 ALCS VNOS ***** & ALCS CTRCS VA PESANDO.
19696 5ELCID2497 ARRANCO LAS LIDES CCMMO ***** AL CRIADOR,
21C44 5ELCID2674 DELO QUE EL MCRC DIXO ALOS YFANTES NON *****:
26738 5ELCID3415 QUANDO AUOS *****, OTCRGO LC YC, SE@OR,
26829 5ELCID3427 A MUCHOS ***** DE TCD ESTA CORT,
26836 5ELCID3428 MAS NON ***** ALOS YFANTES DE CARRION.
WORD #3214 CCCURS 16 TIMES.
INDEX OF DIVERSIFICATICN = 1458.33 WITH STANCARD DEVIATION OF 1879.21

PLAZEM 10596 5ELCID1343 E ****** DELAS NUEUAS QUE FAZE EL CAMPEADOR;
WORD #3215 CCCURS 1 TIMES.

PLAZER 16981 5ELCID2149 PLEGA AL CRIADOR CON TODOS LOS SOS SANTOS, ESTE ******
2C711 5ELCID2629 ATALES COSAS FED QUE EN ****** CAYA ANOS.
WORD #3216 OCCURS 2 TIMES.

PLAZME 1402 5ELCIDC180 ******, DIXC EL %ID, CACUI SEA ANDACA.
10592 5ELCID1342 SI ME VALA SANT ESIDRO ****** DE CORA%ON,
12082 5ELCID1532 DIXO AUENGALUCN: ****** DESTA PRESENTAIA,
15379 5ELCID1947 ESSORA DIXO EL %ID: ****** DE CORA%ON.
20664 5ELCID2623 DIXO FELEZ MUNOZ: ****** CALMA & DE CORA%ON.
23952 5ELCID3052 DIXO EL REY: ****** DE VELUNTAC.
26881 5ELCID3434 DIXO EL REY: ****** DE CCRA%CN.
27278 5ELCID3486 MYO %ID AL REY LAS MANCS LE BESO & DIXO: ******, SE@OR.
WORD #3217 OCCURS 8 TIMES.
INDEX OF DIVERSIFICATICN = 3695.57 WITH STANCARD DEVIATION OF 2868.59

PLAZO 1656 5ELCID0212 MUCHO ES HUEBOS, CA %ERCA VIENE EL *****.
2427 5ELCID0306 LOS VJ DIAS DE ***** PASSADCS LOS AN,
2451 5ELCID0309 QUE, SI DESPUES DEL ***** EN SU TIERRAL PUDIES TOMAR,
2536 5ELCIDC321 CA EL ***** VIENE A %ERCA, MUCHO AUEMOS DE ANDAR.
3117 5ELCIDC392 %ERCA VIENE EL ***** PCR EL REYNO QUITAR.
3283 5ELCID0414 ES DIA A DE *****, SEPADES CUE NON MAS.
9505 5ELCID1208 METIOLA EN *****, SILES VINIESSEN HUUYAR.
23320 5ELCID2970 VENGAM A TCLLEDC, ESTCL DO DE *****.
23554 5ELCID3000 LEGAUA EL *****, QUERIEN YR ALA CORT;
27137 5ELCID3468 DANDOS, REY, *****, CA CRAS SER NON PUEDE.
27226 5ELCID3480 AQUI LES PONGC ***** DE DENTRO EN MI CORT,
27251 5ELCID3483 QUEN NCN VINIERE AL ***** PIERCA LA RAZON,
27679 5ELCID3533 MAS TRES SEMANAS DE ***** TOCAS COMPLIDAS SON.
27685 5ELCID3534 FELOS AL ***** LCS DEL CAMPEACOR,
WORD #3218 CCCURS 14 TIMES.
INDEX OF DIVERSIFICATICN = 2001.23 WITH STANCARD DEVIATION OF 3994.82

PLEGA 2234 5ELCIDC282 ***** ADIOS & A SANTA MARIA, QUE AUN CON MIS MANOS CASE ESTAS MIS
16574 5ELCID2100 AL CRIADOR ***** QUE AYADES ENDE SABOR.
16972 5ELCID2149 ***** AL CRIACOR CON TODCS LCS SOS SANTOS, ESTE PLAZER
17967 5ELCID2274 ***** A SANTA MARIA & AL PADRE SANTO
20162 5ELCID2560 QUE ***** A DO@A XIMENA & PRIMERO AUOS
21861 5ELCID2782 ADIOS ***** & A SANTA MARIA QUE DENT PRENDAN ELLOS MAL GALARDCN
22692 5ELCID2892 ***** AL CRIADOR, CUE EN %IELC ESTA,
267C3 5ELCID3411 QUE ***** AUCS, & ATCRGAR LC HE YO,
WORD #3219 CCCURS 8 TIMES.
INDEX OF DIVERSIFICATICN = 3494.57 WITH STANCARD DEVIATION OF 4928.39

PLEYTO 1245 5ELCID0160 MARTIN ANTCLINEZ EL ****** A PARADO,
27849 5ELCID3554 ANDIDIERON EN ******, DIXIERCN LO AL REY ALFONSSO,
WORD #322C CCCURS 2 TIMES.

PLEYTOS 29031 5ELCID3708 DEXEMOS NOS DE ******* CE YFANTES DE CARRION,
29101 5ELCID3717 ANDIDIERON EN ******* LCS DE NAUARRA & DE ARAGON,
WORD #3221 CCCURS 2 TIMES.

PLOGIERE 8221 5ELCID1047 ABREMOS ESTA VICA MIENTRA ******** AL PADRE SANTO,
13137 5ELCID1665 ANTES DESTCS XV DIAS, SI ******** A CRIADOR,

WORD C# PREFIX CONTEXT

PLOGIERE (CON'T)

16163 5ELCID2050 E CRAS FEREMOS LO QUE ******** AUOS.
16634 5ELCID2107 LO QUE UOS ********, DELLOS FET, CAMPEADOR.
25328 5ELCID3225 SI ESSO ******** AL %ID, NON GELO VEDAMOS NOS;
WORD #3222 OCCURS 5 TIMES.
INDEX OF DIVERSIFICATION = 4275.75 WITH STANDARD DEVIATION OF 3462.60

PLOGIESSE
16137 5ELCID2046 FUESSEDES MY HUESPED, SIUOS *********, SE@OR.
18776 5ELCID2376 SI ********* ADIOS QUERRIA LAS ENSAYAR,
WORD #3223 OCCURS 2 TIMES.

PLOGO
2404 5ELCID0304 ***** A MIO %ID, POR QUE CRE%IO EN LA IANTAR,
2414 5ELCID0305 ***** ALOS OTROS OMNES TODOS QUANTOS CON EL ESTAN.
4103 5ELCID0522 ***** A MYO %ID DA QUESTA PRESENTAIA.
6733 5ELCID0860 ***** ALOS DE TERER & ALOS DE CALATAYUT MAS,
7365 5ELCID0945 ***** A MYO %ID, & MUCHO A ALBARFANEZ.
7950 5ELCID1016 ***** A MYO %ID, CA GRANDES SON LAS GANAN%IAS.
10283 5ELCID1302 ***** A ALBARFANEZ DELO QUE DIXO DON RODRIGO.
10611 5ELCID1345 MAGER ***** AL REY, MUCHO PESO A GAR%IORDONEZ:
13577 5ELCID1721 ***** AL CRIADOR & OUIERON LOS DE ARRANCAR.
14688 5ELCID1858 ESTO ***** A MUCHOS & BESARON LE LAS MANOS.
15081 5ELCID1907 FABLO MYNAYA & ***** A PER VERMUEZ:
17095 5ELCID2164 ESTO ***** AL REY, & ATODOS LOS SOLTO;
18494 5ELCID2341 ***** A MYO %ID & ATODOS SOS VASSALLOS;
18949 5ELCID2398 ***** A DIOS, AQUESTA FUE EL ARRANCADA.
24477 5ELCID3120 LO QUE DIXO EL %ID AL REY ***** DE CORA%ON.
WORD #3224 OCCURS 15 TIMES.
INDEX OF DIVERSIFICATION = 1575.64 WITH STANDARD DEVIATION OF 1473.50

PLOGOL
11492 5ELCID1455 ****** DE CORA%ON & TORNOS A ALEGRAR,
20856 5ELCID2648 EL MORO QUANDO LO SOPO, ****** DE CORA%ON;
23704 5ELCID3019 QUANDO LO OYO EL REY, ****** DE CORA%ON;
WORD #3225 OCCURS 3 TIMES.

PLOGUIERE
8334 5ELCID1060 SI UOS *********, MYO %ID, DE YR SOMOS GUISADOS;
10023 5ELCID1273 SI AUOS *********, MINAYA, & NON UOS CAYA EN PESAR,
20686 5ELCID2626 QUE SI ADIOS ********* & AL PADRE CRIADOR,
25224 5ELCID3212 SI ********* AL REY, ASSI DEZIMOS NOS: DIXO EL REY
26269 5ELCID3349 QUANDO FUERE LA LID, SI ********* AL CRIADOR,
WORD #3226 OCCURS 5 TIMES.
INDEX OF DIVERSIFICATION = 4482.75 WITH STANDARD DEVIATION OF 4390.21

PLOGUIESSE
21565 5ELCID2741 QUAL VENTURA SERIE ESTA, SI ********** AL CRIADOR,
WORD #3227 OCCURS 1 TIMES.

PLORANDO
130 5ELCID0018 ******** DELOS OIOS, TANTO AUYEN EL DOLOR.
WORD #3228 OCCURS 1 TIMES.

POBLADO
3103 5ELCID0390 CA EN YERMO O EN ******* PODER NOS HAN ALCAN%AR.
4443 5ELCID0565 QUE EL CAMPEADOR MYO %ID ALLI AUIE *******,
8556 5ELCID1087 ******* HA MYO %ID EL PUERTO DE ALUCANT,
WORD #3229 OCCURS 3 TIMES.

POBLO
21206 5ELCID2694 ASSINIESTRO DEXAN AGRIZA QUE ALAMOS *****,
WORD #3230 OCCURS 1 TIMES.

POCA
22849 5ELCID2911 LA **** & LA GRANT TOCA ES DE MYO SE@OR.
WORD #3231 OCCURS 1 TIMES.

POCAS
3660 5ELCID0462 CON ***** DE GENTES QUE EN CASTEION FINCARON.
15173 5ELCID1920 EN ***** TIERRAS A TALES DOS VARONES.
WORD #3232 OCCURS 2 TIMES.

POCO
1035 5ELCID0133 PEDIR UOS A **** POR DEXAR SO AUER EN SALUO.
2485 5ELCID0314 **** AUER TRAYO, DAR UOS QUIERO UUESTRA PART.
4772 5ELCID0605 EN VN ORA & VN **** DE LOGAR CCC MOROS MATAN.
5793 5ELCID0732 CAYEN EN VN **** DE LOGAR MOROS MUERTOS MILL & CCC YA.
8642 5ELCID1097 DENTRO EN VALEN%IA NON ES **** EL MIEDO.
10361 5ELCID1312 FUERA EL REY A SAN FAGUNT AVN **** HA,
12393 5ELCID1573 E ADUXIESSEN LE ABAUIECA; **** AUIE QUEL GANARA,
18629 5ELCID2357 CURIELOS QUI QUIER, CA DELLOS **** MINCAL.
21114 5ELCID2683 **** PRE%IO LAS NUEUAS DELOS DE CARRION.
26461 5ELCID3376 EN LO QUE FABLO AVIE **** RECABDO:
WORD #3233 OCCURS 10 TIMES.
INDEX OF DIVERSIFICATION = 2824.11 WITH STANDARD DEVIATION OF 1781.79

POCOS
4887 5ELCID0618 LOS MOROS YAZEN MUERTOS, DE BIUOS ***** VEO.
6165 5ELCID0785 TANTOS MOROS YAZEN MUERTOS QUE ***** BIUOS A DEXADOS,
10008 5ELCID1268 CON MAS ***** YXIEMOS DE LA CASA DE BIUAR.
14614 5ELCID1849 ***** DIAS HA, REY, QUE VNA LID A ARRANCADO:
WORD #3234 OCCURS 4 TIMES.

PODAMOS
22525 5ELCID2868 AVN VEAMOS EL DIA QUE VOS ******* VENGAR
WORD #3235 OCCURS 1 TIMES.

WORD C# PREFIX CONTEXT

PODEDES 6510 5ELCID0830 A NUESTRO AMIGOS BIEN LES ******* DEZIR:
27641 5ELCID3529 ******* OYR DE MUERTOS, CA DE VENCIDOS NO.
WORD #3236 OCCURS 2 TIMES.

PODEMOS 3359 5ELCID0423 LA TIERRA DEL REY ALFONSSO ESTA NOCH LA ******* QUITAR.
10971 5ELCID1388 SOMOS EN SO PRO QUANTO LO ******* FAR;
16190 5ELCID2054 EN QUANTO ******* ANDAMOS EN UUESTRO PRO.
24907 5ELCID3172 NOLO ******* NEGAR, CA DOS ESPADAS NOS DIO;
WORD #3237 OCCURS 4 TIMES.

PODER 3104 5ELCID0390 CA EN YERMO O EN POBLADO ***** NOS HAN ALCANZAR.
3844 5ELCID0486 EL CASTIELO DEXO EN SO *****, EL CAMPEADOR CAUALGA,
15775 5ELCID2001 DALMA & DE CORAZON, & TODOS LOS QUE EN ***** DESSOS FOSSEN;
16617 5ELCID2105 PUES FUEREN EN UUESTRO ***** EN VALENZIA LA MAYOR,
16760 5ELCID2122 METIOLOS EN ***** DE MYO ZID EL CAMPEADOR:
17067 5ELCID2161 HYREMOS EN ***** DE MIO ZID A VALENZIA LA MAYOR;
20062 5ELCID2546 SACAR LAS HEMOS DE VALENZIA, DE ***** DEL CAMPEADOR;
WORD #3238 OCCURS 7 TIMES.
INDEX OF DIVERSIFICATION = 2825.33 WITH STANDARD DEVIATION OF 4577.36

PODERES 5295 5ELCID0669 GRANDES SON LOS ******* POR CON ELLOS LIDIAR;
7544 5ELCID0967 GRANDES SON LOS ******* & A PRIESSA SEUAN LEGANDO,
WORD #3239 OCCURS 2 TIMES.

PODESTADES 15614 5ELCID1980 CUENDES & ********** & MUY GRANDES MESNADAS.
WORD #3240 OCCURS 1 TIMES.

PODIEN 1335 5ELCID0171 NON LAS ****** PONER EN SOMO MAGER ERAU ESFORZADOS.
WORD #3241 OCCURS 1 TIMES.

PODIENDO 23294 5ELCID2967 E QUE NON AYA RENCURA ******** YO VEDALLO.
WORD #3242 OCCURS 1 TIMES.

PODRA 3367 5ELCID0424 DESPUES QUI NOS BUSCARE FALLAR NOS *****.
14789 5ELCID1869 MYO REYNO ADELANT MEIOR ME ***** SERUIR.
WORD #3243 OCCURS 2 TIMES.

PODRE 12931 5ELCID1640 ENTRARE EN LAS ARMAS, NON LO ***** DEXAR;
WORD #3244 OCCURS 1 TIMES.

PODREDES 8430 5ELCID1071 SI ME VINIEREDES BUSCAR, FALLAR ME ********;
11590 5ELCID1468 ASI COMMO A MY DIXIERON, HY LOS ******** FALAR;
18652 5ELCID2360 SI CUETA FUERE, BIEN ME ******** HUUIAR.
22517 5ELCID2867 BUEN CASAMIENTO PERDIESTES, MEIOR ******** GANAR.
WORD #3245 OCCURS 4 TIMES.

PODREMOS 4897 5ELCID0619 LOS MOROS & LAS MORAS VENDER NON LOS ********,
12024 5ELCID1524 MAGER QUE MAL LE QUERAMOS, NON GELO ******** FER,
20035 5ELCID2542 MIENTRA QUE VISQUIEREMOS DESPENDER NOLO ********.
20107 5ELCID2553 ******** CASAR CON FIJAS DE REYES O DE ENPERADORES,
WORD #3246 OCCURS 4 TIMES.

PODRIE 2463 5ELCID0310 POR ORO NIN POR PLATA NON ****** ESCAPAR.
5553 5ELCID0699 E FIZIERON DOS AZES DE PEONES MEZCLADOS, QUILOS ****** CONTAR?
9558 5ELCID1214 EL ORO & LA PLATA QUI EN VOS LO ****** CONTAR?
9588 5ELCID1218 ELOS OTROS AUERES QUIEN LOS ****** CONTAR?
10352 5ELCID1311 DEMANDO POR ALFONSSO, DO LO ****** FALLAR.
10368 5ELCID1313 TORNOS A CARRION, Y LO ****** FALLAR.
WORD #3247 OCCURS 6 TIMES.
INDEX OF DIVERSIFICATION = 1580.00 WITH STANDARD DEVIATION OF 1849.00

PODRIEMOS 4174 5ELCID0531 EN CASTEION NON ********* FINCAR;
6547 5ELCID0835 SI NON, ENESTA TIERRA ANGOSTA NON ********* BIUIR.
WORD #3248 OCCURS 2 TIMES.

PONDRAN 13144 5ELCID1666 AQUELOS ATAMORES AUOS LOS ******* DELANT & VEREDES QUANLES SON,
WORD #3249 OCCURS 1 TIMES.

PONED 1304 5ELCID0167 LEUALDAS, RACHEL & VIDAS, ***** LAS EN UUESTRO SALUO;
WORD #3250 OCCURS 1 TIMES.

PONER 1336 5ELCID0171 NON LAS PODIEN ***** EN SOMO MAGER ERAU ESFORZADOS.
23975 5ELCID3055 MANDO FAZER CANDELAS & ***** ENEL ALTAR;
WORD #3251 OCCURS 2 TIMES.

PONGA 17024 5ELCID2155 AFE DIOS DEL ZIELO, QUE LO ***** EN BUEN LOGAR
WORD #3252 OCCURS 1 TIMES.

PONGO 27225 5ELCID3480 AQUI LES ***** PLAZO DE DENTRO EN MI CORT,
WORD #3253 OCCURS 1 TIMES.

POR 109 5ELCID0015 MYO ZID RUY DIAZ *** BURGOS ENTRAUA,
126 5ELCID0017 BURGESES & BURGESAS *** LAS FINIESTRAS SON,
253 5ELCID0033 *** MIEDO DEL REY ALFONSSO, QUE ASSI LO AUIEN PARADO

WORD C# PREFIX CONTEXT

POR (CON'T)

```
 268 5ELCID0034 QUE SI NON LA QUEBRANTAS *** FUERCA, QUE NON GELA ABRIESE NADI.
 354 5ELCID0044 NCN UOS OSARIEMOS ABRIR NON COGER *** NADA;
 411 5ELCID0051 PARTIOS DELA PUERTA, *** BURGOS AGUIJAUA,
 432 5ELCID0055 SALIO *** LA PUERTA & EN ARLANZON POSAUA.
 603 5ELCID0076 AUN %ERCA CTARDE EL REY QUERER ME HA *** AMIGO;
 697 5ELCID0089 *** RACHEL & VIDAS UAYADES ME PRIUADO:
 728 5ELCID0092 ENPE@AR GELC FE *** LC QUE FUERE GUISADO;
 763 5ELCID0097 *** RACHEL & VIDAS APRIESSA DEMANDAUA.
 770 5ELCID0098 PASSO *** BURGOS, AL CASTIELLO ENTRAUA,
 775 5ELCID0099 *** RACHEL & VIDAS APRIESSA DEMANDAUA.
 841 5ELCID0108 *** SIEMPRE UCS FARE RICOS, QUE NON SEADES MENGUADOS.
 852 5ELCID0109 EL CAMPEADOR *** LAS PARIAS FUE ENTRADO,
 869 5ELCID0112 *** EN VINO AAQUESTC POR QUE FUE ACUSADO.
 873 5ELCID0112 POR EN VINO AAQUESTO *** QUE FUE ACUSADO.
1014 5ELCID0130 O QUE GANAN%IA NCS DARA *** TODO AQUESTE A@O?
1036 5ELCID0133 PEDIR UCS A POCO *** DEXAR SO AUER EN SALUO.
1116 5ELCID0144 *** ADUZIR LAS ARCHAS & METER LAS EN UUESTRO SALUO,
1166 5ELCID0150 NCN VIENE ALA PUEENT, CA *** EL AGUA APASSADO,
1975 5ELCID0250 MAS *** QUE ME VC DE TIERRA, DOUOS L MARCHOS,
2060 5ELCID0260 *** VN MARCHO QUE DESPENDADES AL MONESTERIO DARE YO QUATRO.
2116 5ELCID0267 *** MALCS MESTUREROS DE TIERRA SODES ECHADO.
2170 5ELCID0273 DAND NCS CCNSEIO *** AMCR DE SANTA MARIA
2280 5ELCID0287 *** CASTIELLA OYENDO UAN LCS PREGONES,
2315 5ELCID0292 TODOS DEMANDAN *** MIO %ID EL CAMPEADOR;
2347 5ELCID0296 QUEL CRE%E CONPA@A, *** QUE MAS VALDRA,
2381 5ELCID0301 VCS, QUE *** MI DEXADES CASAS & HEREDADES,
2408 5ELCID0304 PLOGO A MIO %ID, *** QUE CRE%IO EN LA IANTAR,
2433 5ELCID0307 TRES AN *** TRO%IR, %EPADES QUE NON MAS.
2457 5ELCID0310 *** ORC NIN PCR PLATA NCN PODRIE ESCAPAR.
2460 5ELCID0310 POR ORO NIN *** PLATA NCN PODRIE ESCAPAR.
2711 5ELCID0343 *** TIERRA ANDICISTE XXXIJ A@OS, SE@OR SPIRITAL,
2721 5ELCID0344 MOSTRANDO LCS MIRACLOS, *** EN AUEMOS QUE FABLAR:
2754 5ELCID0348 PUSIERON TE EN CRUZ *** NUMBRE EN GOLGOTA;
2804 5ELCID0354 CORRIO LA SANGRE *** EL ASTIL AYUSO, LAS MANOS SE OUO DE VNTAR,
2830 5ELCID0357 EN TI CROUO AL ORA, *** END ES SALUO DE MAL;
2881 5ELCID0364 *** MYO %ID EL CAMPEADOR, QUE DIOS LE CURIE DE MAL.
3085 5ELCID0388 SI VIEREDES YENTES VENIR *** CCNNUSCO YR,
3118 5ELCID0392 %ERCA VIENE EL PLAZO *** EL REYNO QUITAR.
3378 5ELCID0426 E *** LA LOMA AYUSO PIENSSAN DE ANDAR.
3407 5ELCID0430 VASSALLOS TAN BUENOS *** CORA%CN LO AN,
3425 5ELCID0433 *** TAL LO FAZE MYO %ID QUE NO IO VENTASSE NADI.
3531 5ELCID0445 AOSADAS CORRED, QUE *** MIEDO NON DEXEDES NADA.
3539 5ELCID0446 FITA AYUSO & *** GUADALFAIARA, FATA ALCALA LEGEN LAS ALGARAS,
3553 5ELCID0448 QUE *** MIEDO DE LOS MOROS NCN DEXEN NADA.
3643 5ELCID0460 *** VER SUS LAUORES & TODAS SUS HEREDADES.
3723 5ELCID0470 MIO %ID RUY DIAZ *** LAS PUERTAS ENTRAUA,
3790 5ELCID0479 FENARES ARRIBA & *** GUADALFAIARA.
3945 5ELCID0501 E *** EL COBDO AYUSO LA SANGRE SESTELANDO,
3969 5ELCID0504 PUES QUE *** MI GANAREDES QUES QUIER QUE SEA DALGO,
4023 5ELCID0511 SOS QUI@ONEROS QUE GELOS DIESSEN *** CARTA.
4084 5ELCID0519 ESTA QUINTA *** QUANTC SERIE CONPRADA,
4200 5ELCID0535 *** QUE LO PRIS DELLOS QUE DE MI NON DIGAN MAL.
4216 5ELCID0536 TODOS SODES PAGADOS & NINGUNO *** PAGAR.
4268 5ELCID0544 *** LAS CUEUAS DANQUITA ELLOS PASSANDO UAN,
4283 5ELCID0546 *** ESSAS TIERRAS AYUSO QUANTO PUEDEN ANDAR.
4304 5ELCID0548 GRANDES SON LAS GANAN%IAS QUE PRISO *** LA TIERRA DO UA.
4429 5ELCID0564 *** TODAS ESSAS TIERRAS YUAN LCS MANDADOS,
4553 5ELCID0579 AGUISA DE MENBRADO, *** SACAR LOS A%ELADA.
4725 5ELCID0599 BUELTOS SON CON ELLOS *** MEDIO DELA LA@A.
4735 5ELCID0600 DIOS, QUE BUENO ES EL GOZO *** AQUESTA MA@ANA
4791 5ELCID0607 DEXANDO UAN LCS DELANT, *** EL CASTIELLO SE TORNAUAN,
4819 5ELCID0610 MYO %ID GA@O A ALCO%ER, SABENT, *** ESTA MA@A.
4930 5ELCID0624 FIZO ENBIAR *** LA TIENDA QUE DEXARA ALLA.
5034 5ELCID0636 QUANDO LO OYO EL REY TAMIN, *** CUER LE PESO MAL:
5077 5ELCID0642 *** QUE SEME ENTRO EN MI TIERRA DERECHO ME AURA ADAR.
5116 5ELCID0647 *** LOS DE LA FRONTERA PIENSSAN DE ENVIAR;
5153 5ELCID0652 *** TODAS ESSAS TIERRAS LCS PREGONES DAN;
5296 5ELCID0669 GRANDES SON LCS PODERES *** CCN ELLOS LIDIAR;
5349 5ELCID0675 EN EL NOBRE DEL CRIADOR, QUE NON PASE *** AL:
5436 5ELCID0686 SI NON DOS PEONES SOLOS *** LA PUERTA GUARDAR;
5633 5ELCID0709 DIXO EL CAMPEADOR:  NCN SEA, *** CARIDAD
5640 5ELCID0710 RESPUSO PERO VERMUEZ:  NCN RASTARA *** AL.
5653 5ELCID0712 MOROS LE RE%IBEN *** LA SE@A GANAR,
5669 5ELCID0714 DIXO EL CAMPEADOR:  VALELDE, *** CARIDAD
5711 5ELCID0720 FERID LOS, CAUALLEROS, *** AMOR DE CARIDAD
5923 5ELCID0751 CORTOL *** LA %INTURA, EL MEDIO ECHO EN CAMPO.
5970 5ELCID0757 *** ESTAS FUER%AS FUERTE MIENTRE LIDIANDO,
6008 5ELCID0762 *** LA LORIGA AYUSO LA SANGRE DESTELLADO;
6018 5ELCID0763 BOLUIO LA RIENDA *** YR SE LE DEL CAMPO.
6024 5ELCID0764 *** AQUEL COLPE RANCADO ES EL FONSSADO.
6069 5ELCID0770 TAN BUEN DIA *** LA CHRISTIANDAD,
6133 5ELCID0781 *** EL COBDO AYUSO LA SANGRE DESTELLANDO.
6456 5ELCID0824 QUE RUEGEN *** MI LAS NOCHES & LOS DIAS;
6475 5ELCID0826 MYNAYA ALBARFANEZ DESTO ES PAGADO; *** YR CON EL OMNES
                SON CONTADOS.
```

WORD C# PREFIX CONTEXT

POR (CON'T)

6533 5ELCIDC834 *** LANCAS & POR ESPACAS AUEMOS DE GUARIR,
6536 5ELCIDC834 POR LANCAS & *** ESPACAS AUEMOS DE GUARIR,
6622 5ELCIDC845 VENDIDO LES A ALCO%ER *** TRES MILL MARCHOS DE PLATA.
6904 5ELCIDC883 *** ACOGELLO A CABO DE TRES SEMMANAS.
7011 5ELCIDC897 HYD *** CASTIELLA & DEXEN UOS ANDAR, MINAYA,
7062 5ELCIDC902 EL POYO DE MYO %ID ASIL DIRAN *** CARTA.
7321 5ELCID0939 HYA VA EL MANDADO *** LAS TIERRAS TODAS,
7334 5ELCID0941 *** QUE DAN PARIAS PLAZE ALOS DE SARAGO%A,
7727 5ELCIDC989 AMENOS DE BATALLA NON NOS DEXARIE *** NADA.
7785 5ELCIDC997 *** VNO QUE FIRGADES, TRES SIELLAS YRAN VAZIAS.
7807 5ELCIDC999 OY EN ESTE PINAR DE TEUAR *** TOLER ME LA GANAN%IA.
7994 5ELCID1021 NON COMBRE VN BOCADO *** QUANTO HA EN TODA ESPA@A,
8321 5ELCID1059 *** QUE EL CONDE DON REMONT TAN BIEN BOLUIE LAS MANOS.
8458 5ELCID1075 PAGADO UOS HE *** TODO AQUESTE A@O;
8498 5ELCID1080 LO QUE NON FERIE EL CABOSO *** QUANTO ENEL MUNDO HA,
8713 5ELCID1107 VAYAN LOS MANDADOS *** LOS QUE NOS DEUEN AIUDAR,
8747 5ELCID1112 YO FIO *** DIOS QUE EN NUESTRO PRO ENADRAN.
8895 5ELCID1133 COMMO FIO *** DIOS, EL CAMPO NUESTRO SERA.
9008 5ELCID1146 GRAND ES EL GOZO QUE VA *** ES LOGAR.
9285 5ELCID1181 *** EL REY DE MARRUECOS OUIERON A ENBIAR;
9332 5ELCID1187 *** ARAGON & POR NAUARRA PREGON MANDO ECHAR,
9335 5ELCID1187 POR ARAGON & *** NAUARRA PREGON MANDO ECHAR,
9528 5ELCID1211 GRANDES SON LOS GOZOS QUE VAN *** ES LOGAR,
9752 5ELCID1240 *** AMOR DE REY ALFFONSSO, QUE DE TIERRA ME A ECHADO,
9974 5ELCID1264 QUANDO LOS FALLO, *** CUENTA FIZO LOS NONBRAR:
10063 5ELCID1275 DESI *** MI BESALDE LA MANO EFIRME GELO ROGAD
10071 5ELCID1276 *** MI MUGIER & MIS FIJAS, SI FUERE SU MER%ED,
10085 5ELCID1278 ENBIARE *** ELLAS, & UOS SABED EL MENSAGE:
10105 5ELCID1280 DE GUISA YRAN *** ELLAS QUE AGRAND ONDRA VERNAN
10140 5ELCID1284 CIENTO OMNES LE DIO MYO %ID A ALBARFANEZ *** SERUIR LE EN LA CARRERA,
10246 5ELCID1297 OYD, MINAYA ALBARFANEZ, *** AQUEL QUE ESTA EN ALTO,
10296 5ELCID1303 AESTE DON IERONIMO YAL OTORGAN *** OBISPO;
10348 5ELCID1311 DEMANDO *** ALFONSSO, DO LO PODRIE FALLAR.
10423 5ELCID1321 MER%ED, SE@OR ALFONSSO, *** AMOR DEL CRIADOR
10474 5ELCID1327 GANADA A XERICA & A ONDA *** NOMBRE,
10562 5ELCID1339 RAZONAS *** VUESTRO VASSALLO & AUOS TIENE POR SE@OR.
10568 5ELCID1339 RAZONAS POR VUESTRO VASSALLO & AUOS TIENE *** SE@OR.
10669 5ELCID1352 *** SU MUGIER DO@A XIMENA & SUS FIJAS AMAS ADOS:
10708 5ELCID1356 HYO LES MANDARE DAR CONDUCHO MIENTRA QUE *** MJ TIERRA FUEREN,
10762 5ELCID1363 *** QUE LOS DESEREDE, TODO GELO SUELTO YO;
10787 5ELCID1366 *** TAL FAGO AQUESTO QUE SIRUAN ASO SE@OR.
10987 5ELCID1390 RESPUSO MYNAYA: ESTO NON MEA *** QUE PESAR.
11058 5ELCID1400 EL REY *** SU MER%ED SUELTAS ME UOS HA,
11065 5ELCID1401 *** LEUAROS A VALEN%IA QUE AUEMOS POR HEREDAD.
11071 5ELCID1401 POR LEUAROS A VALEN%IA QUE AUEMOS *** HEREDAD.
11133 5ELCID1409 MIENTRA QUE FUEREMOS *** SUS TIERRAS CONDUCHO NOS MANDO DAR.
11227 5ELCID1421 *** YR CON ESTAS DUENAS BUE@A CONPANA SE FAZE.
11347 5ELCID1436 *** LO QUE AUEDES FECHO BUEN COSIMENT Y AURA.
11400 5ELCID1443 *** MI AL CAMPEADOR LAS MANOS LE BESAD
11450 5ELCID1450 *** LA TIERRA DEL REY MUCHO CONDUCHO LES DAN.
11541 5ELCID1462 *** SANTA MARIA UOS VAYADES PASSAR,
11620 5ELCID1472 YO FFINCARE EN VALEN%IA, CA LA TENGO *** HEREDAD.
11712 5ELCID1485 QUE VAYADES *** ELLAS, ADUGADES GELAS ACA,
11771 5ELCID1493 *** EL VAL DE ARBUXEDO PIENSSAN A DEPRUNAR.
11854 5ELCID1503 *** SABOR DE MYO %ID DE GRAND ONDRAL DAR;
11949 5ELCID1515 *** %ERCA DE SALON TAN GRANDES GOZOS VAN.
12036 5ELCID1526 MUCHOL TENGO *** TORPE QUI NON CONES%E LA VERDAD.
12522 5ELCID1589 *** NOMBRE EL CAUALLO BAUIECA CAUALGA.
12891 5ELCID1635 CON AFAN GANE A VALEN%IA, & ELA *** HEREDAD,
12953 5ELCID1643 AFARTO VERAN *** LOS OIOS COMMO SE GANA EL PAN.
13005 5ELCID1650 *** CASAR SON UUESTRAS FIJAS, ADUZEN UOS AXUUAR.
13034 5ELCID1653 NON AYADES PAUOR *** QUE ME VEADES LIDIAR,
13052 5ELCID1655 CRE%EM EL CORACON *** QUE ESTADES DELANT,
13187 5ELCID1672 *** LAS HUERTAS ADENTRO ESTAN SINES PAUOR.
13282 5ELCID1684 ALEGRE ES MYO %ID *** QUANTO FECHO HAN:
13291 5ELCID1685 OYD ME, CAUALLEROS, NON RASTARA *** AL;
13301 5ELCID1687 *** LA MANANA PRIETA TODOS ARMADOS SEADES,
13471 5ELCID1707 HYO UOS CANTE LA MISSA *** AQUESTA MA@ANA;
13501 5ELCID1711 SALIDOS SON TODOS ARMADOS *** LAS TORRES DE VAN%IA,
13602 5ELCID1724 *** EL COBDO AYUSO LA SANGRE DESTELLANDO.
13686 5ELCID1734 LOS L MILL *** CUENTA FUERO NOTADOS:
13747 5ELCID1742 DEXO ALBARFANEZ *** SABER TODO RECABDO.
13962 5ELCID1768 LO DE UUESTRAS FIJAS VENIR SEA MAS *** ESPA%IO.
13978 5ELCID1770 GRANT FUE EL ALEGRIA QUE FUE *** EL PALA%IO;
14216 5ELCID1799 ALEGRES SON *** VALEN%IA LAS YENTES CHRISTIANAS,
14245 5ELCID1802 E TODAS LAS OTRAS DUENAS QUE TIENEN *** CASADAS.
14255 5ELCID1803 EL BUENO DE MYO %ID NON LO TARDO *** NADA:
14312 5ELCID1811 *** AMOR DE MI MUGIER & DE MIS FIJAS AMAS,
14322 5ELCID1812 *** QUE ASSI LAS ENBIO DOND ELLAS SON PAGADAS,
14427 5ELCID1825 *** EL REY DON ALFONSSO TOMAN SSE APREGUNTAR.
14586 5ELCID1846 *** MYO %ID EL CAMPEADOR TODO ESTO VOS BESAMOS;
14598 5ELCID1847 A UOS LAMA *** SE@OR, & TIENES POR UUESTRO VASSALLO,
14602 5ELCID1847 A UOS LAMA POR SE@OR, & TIENES *** UUESTRO VASSALLO,
14629 5ELCID1850 A AQUEL REY DE MARRUECOS, YUCEFF *** NOMBRADO,

WORD C# PREFIX CONTEXT

POR (CON'T)

```
14732 5ELCID1863 *** TAN BILTADA MIENTRE VENZER REYES DEL CAMPO,
14749 5ELCID1865 *** ESTO QUE EL FAZE NOS ABREMOS ENBARGO.
15071 5ELCID1906 *** CONSSAGRAR CON LOS YFFANTES DE CARRION.
15407 5ELCID1952 *** DAR LE GRAND ONDRA COMMO A REY DE TIERRA.
15517 5ELCID1966  QUI ENVIO *** CASTIELLA TANTA MULA PREZIADA,
15736 5ELCID1997 ESTOS SE ACOBAN *** YR CON EL CAMPEADOR,
16367 5ELCID2076 QUE LAS DEDES *** MUGIERES ALOS YFANTES DE CARRION.
16547 5ELCID2097 DAQUI LAS PRENDO *** MIS MANOS DON ELUIRA & DONA SOL,
16557 5ELCID2098 E DOLAS *** VELADAS ALOS YFANTES DE CARRION.
17002 5ELCID2152 DEUOS BIEN SO SERUIDO, & TENGON *** PAGADO;
17435 5ELCID2206 *** EL SUELO & SUSO TAN BIEN ENCORTINADO,
17468 5ELCID2210 *** LOS YFFANTES DE CARRION ESSORA ENBIARON,
17547 5ELCID2220 PUES QUE AFAZER LO AUEMOS, *** QUE LO YMOS TARDANDO?
17580 5ELCID2224 NOLO QUIERO FALIR *** NADA DE QUANTO AY PARADO;
17629 5ELCID2231 *** MANO DEL REY ALFONSSO, QUE AMI LO OUO MANDADO,
17649 5ELCID2233 QUE LAS TOMASSEDES *** MUGIERES A ONDRA & A RECABDO.
17853 5ELCID2259 CADA VNO *** SI SOS DONES AUIEN DADOS.
17898 5ELCID2265 *** PAGADOS SE PARTEN DE MYO ZID & DE SUS VASSALLOS.
18046 5ELCID2283 EN GRANT MIEDO SE VIERON *** MEDIO DELA CORT;
18086 5ELCID2288 DIEGO GONZALEZ *** LA PUERTA SALIO,
18209 5ELCID2304 MYO ZID *** SOS YERNOS DEMANDO & NOLOS FALLO;
18239 5ELCID2307 NON VIESTES TAL GUEGO COMMO YUA *** LA CORT;
18250 5ELCID2309 MUCHOS TOUIERON *** ENBAYDOS LOS YFANTES DE CARRION,
18352 5ELCID2322 ESTO ES AGUISADO *** NON VER CARRION,
18385 5ELCID2327 *** ENTRAR EN BATALLA DESEAN CARRION.
18558 5ELCID2349 *** LA SU VOLUNTAD NON SERIEN ALLI LEGADOS.
18612 5ELCID2355 HYO UOS DIGO, ZID, *** TODA CARIDAD,
18620 5ELCID2356 QUE OY LOS YFANTES AMI *** AMO NON ABRAN;
18734 5ELCID2371 *** ESSO SALI DE MI TIERRA & VIN UOS BUSCAR,
18744 5ELCID2372 *** SABOR QUE AUIA DE ALGUN MORO MATAR;
18843 5ELCID2385 *** LA SU VENTURA & DIOS QUEL AMAUA
19013 5ELCID2405 TANTAS CABEZAS CON YELMOS QUE *** EL CAMPO CAEN,
19240 5ELCID2435 *** LA MATANZA VINIA TAN PRIUADO,
19321 5ELCID2447 COMMO YO FIO *** DIOS & EN TODOS LOS SOS SANTOS,
19362 5ELCID2453 *** EL COBDO AYUSO LA SANGRE DESTELLANDO;
19441 5ELCID2464 *** BIEN LO DIXO EL ZID, MAS ELLOS LO TOUIERON AMAL.
19800 5ELCID2510 MUCHOS TIENEN *** RICOS LOS YFANTES DE CARRION.
19843 5ELCID2516 REZIBIOLOS MINAYA *** MYO ZID EL CAMPEADOR:
19854 5ELCID2517 ACA VENID, CUNADOS, QUE MAS VALEMOS *** UOS.
19940 5ELCID2530 *** UOS AUEMOS ONDRA & AVEMOS LIDIADO.
19978 5ELCID2535 *** AQUESTOS GUEGOS QUE YUAN LEUANTANDO,
20201 5ELCID2565 QUE LES DIEMOS *** ARRAS & POR ONORES;
20204 5ELCID2565 QUE LES DIEMOS POR ARRAS & *** ONORES;
20247 5ELCID2570 VOS LES DIESTES VILLAS E TIERRAS *** ARRAS ENTIERRAS DE CARRION,
20396 5ELCID2588 GRANDES SON LAS NUEUAS *** VALENZIA LA MAYOR,
20407 5ELCID2590 *** QUE ESCURREN SUS FIJAS DEL CAMPEADOR ATIERRAS DE CARRION.
20578 5ELCID2613 *** LA HUERTA DE VALENZIA TENIENDO SALIEN ARMAS;
20746 5ELCID2635 *** MOLINA YREDES, VNA NOCH Y IAZREDES;
20790 5ELCID2640 DESI ESCURRA LAS FASTA MEDINA *** LA MI AMOR;
20800 5ELCID2641 DE QUANTO EL FIZIERE YOL DAR *** ELLO BUEN GALARDON.
20830 5ELCID2645 *** SANTA MARIA DALUA RAZIN FAZIAN LA POSADA,
20927 5ELCID2658 TOD ESTO LES FIZO EL MORO *** EL AMOR DEL ZID CAMPEADOR.
21067 5ELCID2677 SI NOLO DEXAS *** MYO ZID EL DE BIUAR,
21078 5ELCID2678 TAL COSA UOS FARIA QUE *** EL MUNDO SONAS,
21194 5ELCID2693 *** LOS MONTES CLAROS AGUIJAN A ESPOLON;
21389 5ELCID2719 NOS VENGAREMOS AQUESTA *** LA DEL LEON.
21433 5ELCID2725 *** DIOS UOS ROGAMOS, DON DIEGO & DON FERANDO
21469 5ELCID2730 QUE *** LO QUE NOS MEREZEMOS NO LO PRENDEMOS NOS;
21611 5ELCID2748 *** MUERTAS LAS DEXARON ENEL ROBREDRO DE CORPES.
21647 5ELCID2752 *** MUERTAS LAS DEXARON, SABED, QUE NON POR BIUAS.
21654 5ELCID2752 POR MUERTAS LAS DEXARON, SABED, QUE NON *** BIUAS.
21673 5ELCID2755 *** MUERTAS LAS DEXARON,
21685 5ELCID2757 *** LOS MONTES DO YUAN, ELLOS YUAN SE ALABANDO:
21704 5ELCID2759 NON LAS DEUIEMOS TOMAR *** VARRAGANAS,
21820 5ELCID2776 *** EL RASTRO TORNOS FELEZ MUNOZ,
21907 5ELCID2787 DESPERTEDES, PRIMAS, *** AMOR DEL CRIADOR
21946 5ELCID2792 ESFORZAD UOS, PRIMAS, *** AMOR DEL CRIADOR
22063 5ELCID2808 EL CAUALLO PRISO *** LA RIENDA & LUEGO DENT LAS PARTIO,
22074 5ELCID2809 TODOS TRES SEñEROS *** LOS ROBREDOS DE CORPES,
22332 5ELCID2844 HY ALBERGARON *** VERDAD VNA NOCH.
22343 5ELCID2846 QUE VINIE MYNAYA *** SUS PRIMAS AMAS ADOS.
22384 5ELCID2852 *** AQUESTA ONDRA QUE VOS DIESTES A ESTO QUE NOS CUNTIO;
22625 5ELCID2883 *** AMOR DE MYO ZID RICA CENA LES DA.
22788 5ELCID2904 *** MI BESA LE LA MANO DALMA & DE CORAZON,
22974 5ELCID2926 ELLOS CONDES GALLIZANOS A EL TIENEN *** SEñOR.
23006 5ELCID2931 ASSI COMMO ENTRARON *** MEDIO DELA CORT,
23132 5ELCID2948 *** ESTO UOS BESA LAS MANOS, COMMO VASSALLO A SEñOR,
23152 5ELCID2950 TIENES *** DESONDRADO, MAS LA UUESTRA ES MAYOR,
23212 5ELCID2957 FIZ LO *** BIEN, QUE FFUESSE A SU PRO.
23255 5ELCID2962 ANDARAN MYOS PORTEROS *** TODO MYO REYNO,
23321 5ELCID2971 *** AMOR DE MYO ZID ESTA CORT YO FAGO.
23363 5ELCID2976 NON LO DETIENE *** NADA ALFONSSO EL CASTELLANO,
23414 5ELCID2982 QUI NON VINIESSE ALA CORT NON SE TOUIESSE *** SU VASSALLO.
23417 5ELCID2983 *** TODAS SUS TIERRAS ASSI LO YUAN PENSSANDO,
```

WORD C# PREFIX CONTEXT

POR (CON'T)

```
23442 5ELCID2986 *** QUE EL REY FAZIE CORT EN TOLLEDO,
23661 5ELCID3014 *** QUE SE TARDA EL REY NON HA SABOR.
23764 5ELCID3027 QUANDO LO OYO EL REY, *** NADA NON TARDO;
23802 5ELCID3032 DIOS LO MANDE QUE *** UOS SE ONDRE OY LA CORT
24102 5ELCID3073 VELMEZES VESTIDOS *** SUFRIR LAS GUARNIZONES,
24144 5ELCID3079 *** DE MANDAR MYOS DERECHOS & DEZIR MI RAZON:
24182 5ELCID3084 NOS DETIENE *** NADA EL QUE EN BUEN ORA NA%IO:
24274 5ELCID3095 CON ORO ES OBRADA, FECHA *** RAZON,
24295 5ELCID3098 *** TALLO FAZE ESTO QUE RECABDAR QUIERE TODO LO SUYO;
24572 5ELCID3132 *** EL AMOR DE MYO %ID EL QUE EN BUEN ORA NA%IO,
24628 5ELCID3138 *** ESCOGER EL DERECHO, CA TUERTO NON MANDO YO.
24705 5ELCID3147 *** QUANTO ESTA CORT FIZIESTES POR MI AMOR.
24710 5ELCID3147 POR QUANTO ESTA CORT FIZIESTES *** MI AMOR.
24719 5ELCID3149 *** MIS FIJAS QUEM DEXARON YO NON HE DESONOR,
25029 5ELCID3188 ASO SOBRINO *** NONBREL LAMO,
25083 5ELCID3196 *** ESSO UOS LA DO QUE LA BIEN CURIEDES UOS.
25206 5ELCID3210 *** ESSOL DIEMOS SUS ESPADAS AL%ID CAMPEADOR,
25433 5ELCID3239 *** JUUIZIO LO DAMOS ANTEL REY DON ALFONSSO:
25542 5ELCID3253 MER%ED, AY REY SE@OR, *** AMOR DE CARIDAD
25630 5ELCID3264 *** QUE LAS SACAUADES DE VALEN%IA SUS HONORES?
25662 5ELCID3268 *** QUANTO LES FIZIESTES MENOS VALEDES VOS.
25727 5ELCID3276 NON GELAS DEUIEN QUERER SUS FIJAS *** VARRAGANAS,
25733 5ELCID3277 O QUIEN GELAS DIERA *** PAREIAS OPOR VELADAS?
25739 5ELCID3278 DERECHO FIZIERON *** QUE LAS HAN DEXADAS.
25765 5ELCID3282 *** ESSO ES LUEGA QUEADELI%IO FUE CRIADA.
25776 5ELCID3283 QUE AVEDES UOS, CONDE, *** RETRAER LA MI BARBA?
25819 5ELCID3288 QUANDO PRIS A CABRA, & AUOS *** LA BARBA,
25890 5ELCID3299 *** QUE LAS DEXAMOS DERECHO FIZIEMOS NOS;
25982 5ELCID3312 *** LO QUE YO OUIER AFER POR MI NON MANCARA.
25988 5ELCID3312 POR LO QUE YO OUIER AFER *** MI NON MANCARA.
25998 5ELCID3314 *** EL CAMPEADOR MUCHO VALIESTES MAS.
26044 5ELCID3320 PASSE *** TI, CON EL MORO ME OFF DE AIUNTAR,
26163 5ELCID3335 NOS %ERCAMOS EL ESCA@O *** CURIAR NUESTRO SE@OR,
26213 5ELCID3342 DEMANDO *** SUS YERNOS, NINGUNO NON FALLO
26222 5ELCID3343 RIEBTOT EL CUERPO *** MALO & POR TRAYDOR;
26225 5ELCID3343 RIEBTOT EL CUERPO POR MALO & *** TRAYDOR;
26234 5ELCID3345 *** FIJAS DEL %ID, DON ELUIRA & DONA SOL:
26243 5ELCID3346 *** QUANTO LAS DEXASTES MENOS VALEDES VOS;
26310 5ELCID3356 *** CONSAGRAR CON MYO %ID DON RODRIGO
26317 5ELCID3357 *** QUE DEXAMOS SUS FIJAS AVN NO NOS REPENTIMOS,
26347 5ELCID3360 QUE *** QUE LAS DEXAMOS ONDRADOS SOMOS NOS.
26374 5ELCID3364 SALISTE *** LA PUERTA, METISTET AL CORAL,
26398 5ELCID3367 HYOLLO LIDIARE, NON PASSARA *** AL:
26403 5ELCID3368 FIJAS DEL %ID, *** QUE LAS VOS DEXASTES,
26420 5ELCID3370 AL PARTIR DELA LID *** TU BOCA LO DIRAS,
26442 5ELCID3373 ASUR GON%ALEZ ENTRAUA *** EL PALA%IO,
26580 5ELCID3393 AFFE DOS CAUALLEROS ENTRARON *** LA CORT;
26619 5ELCID3399 *** SER REYNAS DE NAUARRA & DE ARAGON,
26912 5ELCID3438 HYO LES DI MIS PRIMAS *** MANDADO DEL REY ALFONSSO,
26945 5ELCID3442 RIEBTOS LES LOS CUERPOS *** MALOS & POR TRAYDORES.
26948 5ELCID3442 RIEBTOS LES LOS CUERPOS POR MALOS & *** TRAYDORES.
27123 5ELCID3466 DESTOS IIJ *** TRES QUE REBTARON EN LA CORT.
27260 5ELCID3484 DESI SEA VEN%IDO & ESCAPE *** TRAYDOR.
27311 5ELCID3490 ONDRADOS MELOS ENBIAD A VALEN%IA, *** AMOR DEL CRIADOR
27428 5ELCID3504 MER%ED UOS PIDO, REY, *** AMOR DEL CRIADOR
27572 5ELCID3521 CA *** UOS & POREL CAUALLO ONDRADOS SOMO NOS.
27626 5ELCID3527 DIXO MARTIN ANTOLINEZ:  *** QUE LO DEZIDES, SE@OR
27639 5ELCID3528 PRESO AUEMOS EL DEBDO & A PASSAR ES *** NOS;
27744 5ELCID3541 QUE LOS MATASSEN EN CAMPO *** DESONDRA DE SO SE@OR.
27791 5ELCID3547 *** VER ESTA LID, CA AVIEN ENDE SABOR;
27807 5ELCID3549 *** QUERER EL DERECHO & NON CONSENTIR EL TUERTO.
27880 5ELCID3557 MUCHO ERAN REPENTIDOS LOS YFANTES *** QUANTO DADAS SON;
27931 5ELCID3564 QUE NADA NON MANCARA *** LOS DEL CAMPEADOR.
27976 5ELCID3570 NOLO QUERRIEN AUER FECHO *** QUANTO HA EN CARRION.
28047 5ELCID3580 TENENDOS ADERECHO, *** AMOR DEL CRIADOR
28142 5ELCID3593 EL REY DIOLES FIELES *** DEZIR EL DERECHO & AL NON,
28251 5ELCID3607 QUE *** Y SERIE VEN%IDO QUI SALIESSE DEL MOION.
28291 5ELCID3611 SALIEN LOS FIELES DE MEDIO, ELLOS CARA *** CARA SON;
28358 5ELCID3621 TODOS TRES *** TRES YA JUNTADOS SON:
28418 5ELCID3629 FIRME ESTIDO PERO VERMUEZ, *** ESSO NOS ENCAMO;
28447 5ELCID3633 METIOL LA LAN%A *** LOS PECHOS, QUE NADA NOL VALIO;
28487 5ELCID3638 *** LA BOCA AFUERA LA SANGREL SALIO;
28502 5ELCID3640 *** LA COPLA DEL CAUALLO EN TIERRA LO ECHO.
28662 5ELCID3659 BOLUIO LA RIENDA AL CAUALLO *** TORNASSE DE CARA;
28730 5ELCID3669 *** QUANTO AUEDES FECHO VEN%IDA AUEDES ESTA BATALLA.
28810 5ELCID3680 *** MEIO DE LA BLOCA DEL ESCUDOL QUEBRANTO;
28832 5ELCID3683 METIOL *** LA CARNE ADENTRO LA LAN%A CONEL PENDON,
28894 5ELCID3690 DIXO GON%ALO ASSUREZ: NOL FIRGADES, *** DIOS
28927 5ELCID3695 *** ONDRADOS SE PARTEN LOS DEL BUEN CAMPEADOR;
28945 5ELCID3697 GRANDES SON LOS PESARES *** TIERRAS DE CARRION.
28981 5ELCID3702 *** MALOS LOS DEXARON ALOS YFANTES DE CARRION,
29060 5ELCID3712 *** QUE TAN ONDRADOS FUERON LOS DEL CANPEADOR.
29174 5ELCID3725 A TODOS ALCAN%A ONDRA *** EL QUE EN BUEN ORA NA%IO.
WORD #3254 OCCURS 338 TIMES.
   INDEX OF DIVERSIFICATION =     85.25 WITH STANDARD DEVIATION OF     98.23
```

WORD C# PREFIX CONTEXT

PORA
394 5ELCID0049 ESTO LA NI@A DIXO & TORNOS **** SU CASA.
656 5ELCID0083 **** TODA MI COMPANA;
1375 5ELCID0176 DE CASTIELLA UOS YDES **** LAS YENTES ESTRANAS.
1575 5ELCID0202 VINO **** LA TIENDA DEL QUE EN BUEN ORA NASCO;
1830 5ELCID0233 **** SAN PERO DE CARDENA QUANTO PUDO A ESPOLEAR,
1968 5ELCID0249 YO ADOBARE CON DUCHO **** MI & PORA MIS VASSALLOS;
1971 5ELCID0249 YO ADOBARE CON DUCHO PORA MI & **** MIS VASSALLOS;
2003 5ELCID0253 EUADES AQUI **** DO@A XIMENA DOUOS C MARCHOS.
2326 5ELCID0294 VANSSE **** SAN PERO DO ESTA EL QUE ENBUEN PUNTO NA%IO.
2634 5ELCID0332 FEZIST ESTRELAS & LUNA & EL SOL **** ESCALENTAR;
5054 5ELCID0638 NON LO DETARDEDES, LOS DOS YD **** ALLA,
5563 5ELCID0701 **** MYO %ID & ALOS SOS A MANOS LOS TOMAR.
6977 5ELCID0892 BUE@OS & VALIENTES **** MYO %ID HUYAR,
7624 5ELCID0976 MYO %ID QUANDO LO OYO, ENBIO **** ALLA:
7926 5ELCID1012 PRISO LO AL CONDE, **** SU TIERRA LO LEUAUA;
8195 5ELCID1044 CA HUEBOS MELO HE & **** ESTOS MYOS VASSALLOS
9368 5ELCID1191 %ERCAR QUIERE A VALEN%IA **** CHRISTIANOS LA DAR.
9464 5ELCID1203 ADELINO **** VALEN%IA & SOBRELLAS VA ECHAR,
10335 5ELCID1309 ADELINO **** CASTIELLA MINAYA ALBARFANEZ.
10380 5ELCID1315 CON ESTA PRESENTEIA ADELINO **** ALLA;
10688 5ELCID1354 E YRIEN **** VALEN%IA AL BUEN CAMPEADOR.
10854 5ELCID1374 BIEN CASARIEMOS CON SUS FIJAS **** HUEBOS DE PRO.
10997 5ELCID1392 ADELINO **** SAN PERO, OLAS DUE@AS ESTAN,
11374 5ELCID1439 HYDO ES **** SAN PERO MINAYA ALBARFANEZ,
11537 5ELCID1461 CAUALGEDES CON %IENTO GUISADOS **** HUEBOS DE LIDIAR;
11569 5ELCID1466 HYD **** MEDINA QUANTO LO PUDIEREDES FAR,
12454 5ELCID1580 Y DEXAUA EL CAUALLO, **** LA CAPIELLA ADELINAUA;
12730 5ELCID1616 AL%AN LAS MANOS **** DIOS ROGAR,
13373 5ELCID1695 DAD ME CXXX CAUALLEROS **** HUEBOS DE LIDIAR;
14890 5ELCID1882 DEMANDEMOS SUS FIJAS **** CON ELLAS CASAR;
15141 5ELCID1915 VAN **** VALEN%IA ELLOS & TODOS LOS SOS.
15298 5ELCID1937 E PIDEN ME MIS FIJAS **** LOS YFANTES DE CARRION.
15510 5ELCID1965 DELLA PART & DELLA **** LAS VISTAS SE ADOBAUAN;
15659 5ELCID1986 NON LO DETARDA, **** LAS VISTAS SE ADOBO;
15863 5ELCID2012 HYAS VA **** LAS VISTAS QUE CON EL REY PARO.
16271 5ELCID2064 QUE ADOBASSEN COZINA **** QUANTOS QUE YSON;
16442 5ELCID2085 PERTENE%EN **** MIS FIJAS & AVN PORA MEIORES.
16447 5ELCID2085 PERTENE%EN PORA MIS FIJAS & AVN **** MEIORES.
16539 5ELCID2096 QUEM DADES UUESTRAS FIJAS **** LOS YFANTES DE CARRION.
17121 5ELCID2167 ADELINAN **** VALEN%IA, LA QUE EN BUEN PUNTO GANO.
17681 5ELCID2237 **** SANTA MARIA A PRIESSA ADELINNANDO;
18160 5ELCID2297 EL MANTO TRAE ALCUELLO, & ADELINO **** LEON;
18204 5ELCID2303 ETORNARON SEAL APALA%IO **** LA CORT.
20017 5ELCID2540 VAYAMOS **** CARRION, AQUI MUCHO DETARDAMOS.
20272 5ELCID2573 CAUALLOS **** EN DIESTRO FUERTES & CORREDORES,
20814 5ELCID2643 HYAS TORNO **** VALEN%IA EL QUE EN BUEN ORA NAS%IO.
21061 5ELCID2676 HYO SIRUIENDO UOS SIN ART, & UOS CONSSEIASTES **** MI MUERT.
21715 5ELCID2761 PUES NUESTRAS PAREIAS NON ERAN **** EN BRA%OS.
22433 5ELCID2857 ADELINAN A POSAR **** FOLGAR ESSA NOCH.
22635 5ELCID2884 DENT **** VALEN%IA ADELINECHOS VAN.
23262 5ELCID2963 PREGONARAN MI CORT **** DENTRO EN TOLLEDO,
23371 5ELCID2977 ENBIA SUS CARTAS **** LEON & A SANTI YAGUO,
23888 5ELCID3043 **** TOLLEDO EL REY TORNADA DA,
26775 5ELCID3420 **** LOS YFANTES DE NAUARRA & DE ARAGON,
26996 5ELCID3449 ANTES LAS AVIEDES PAREIAS **** EN BRA%OS LAS TENER,
27055 5ELCID3456 HYO SO ALBARFANEZ **** TODEL MEIOR.
27076 5ELCID3459 CA EN ESTA CORT AFARTO HA **** VOS,
27301 5ELCID3489 ELLOS SON ADOBADOS **** CUMPLLIR TODO LO SO;
27450 5ELCID3507 E YR ME QUIERO **** VALEN%IA, CON AFAN LA GANE YO.
27550 5ELCID3518 MAS ATAL CAUALLO CUM EST **** TAL COMMO VOS,
27554 5ELCID3519 **** ARRANCAR MOROS DEL CANPO & SER SEGUDADOR;
27668 5ELCID3532 MYO %ID **** VALEN%IA, & EL REY PORA CARRION.
27673 5ELCID3532 MYO %ID PORA VALEN%IA, & EL REY **** CARRION.
WORD #3255 OCCURS 63 TIMES.
INDEX OF DIVERSIFICATION = 438.98 WITH STANDARD DEVIATION OF 554.68

PORAL
22989 5ELCID2929 ADELINO ***** PALA%IO DO ESTAUA LA CORT,
26181 5ELCID3337 LEUANTOS DEL ESCA@O & FUES ***** LEON;
WORD #3256 OCCURS 2 TIMES.

POREL
27575 5ELCID3521 CA POR UOS & ***** CAUALLO ONDRADOS SOMO NOS.
WORD #3257 OCCURS 1 TIMES.

PORIDAD
812 5ELCID0104 EN ******* FLABLAR QUERRIA CON AMOS.
5393 5ELCID0680 QUE NON SOPIESSE NINGUNO ESTA SU *******.
14879 5ELCID1880 FABLANDO EN SU CONSSEIO, AUIENDO SU *******:
14907 5ELCID1884 VINIEN AL REY ALFONSSO CON ESTA *******:
15333 5ELCID1941 FLABLEMOS EN ELLO, EN LA ******* SEAMOS NOS.
18363 5ELCID2324 OYO LA ******* AQUEL MU@O GUSTIOZ,
20998 5ELCID2668 NON TIENE *******, DIXOLO AVENGALUON:
22754 5ELCID2899 FABLOS CON LOS SOS EN SU *******,
23990 5ELCID3057 AL CRIADOR ROGANDO & FABLANDO EN *******.

```
WORD                C#  PREFIX                          CONTEXT

PORIDAD (CON'T)

              26066 5ELCID3322 DID EL CAUALLC, TOUEL DC EN *******:
       WORD #3258 OCCURS  10 TIMES.
          INDEX OF DIVERSIFICATICN =  2805.00 WITH STANDARD DEVIATICN OF  2857.76

PORO           7918 5ELCID1011 Y BEN%IO ESTA BATALLA **** ONDRO SU BARBA,
              11998 5ELCID1521 TRAEDES ESTAS DUE@AS **** VALDREMOS MAS,
              24243 5ELCID3091 OBRADO ES CCN ORO, PARE%EN **** SON,
              26155 5ELCID3334 METISTET, FERRANDC, **** MENOS VALES OY.
       WORD #3259 OCCURS   4 TIMES.

PORPOLA       17444 5ELCID2207 TANTA ******* & TANTO XAMED & TANTO PA@O PRECIADO.
       WORD #3260 OCCURS   1 TIMES.

PORTERO       10903 5ELCID1380 LEUEDES VN *******, TENGO QUE UOS AURA PRO;
              11442 5ELCID1449 EL ******* CCN ELLOS CUE LOS HA DE AGUARDAR;
              12106 5ELCID1536 EL ******* DEL REY QUITAR LO MANDAUA;
       WORD #3261 OCCURS   3 TIMES.

PORTEROS      23254 5ELCID2962 ANDARAN MYOS ******** PCR TODO MYO REYNO,
       WORD #3262 OCCURS   1 TIMES.

PORTOGALESES  23378 5ELCID2978 ALOS ************ & A GALIZIANOS,
       WORD #3263 OCCURS   1 TIMES.

POSADA          196 5ELCID0025 QUE A MYO %ID RUY DIAZ, QUE NADI NOL DIESSEN ******,
                244 5ELCID0031 EL CAMPEADOR ADELINO ASU ******;
               1561 5ELCID0200 GRADO EXIR DELA ****** & ESPIDIOS DE AMOS.
               1644 5ELCID0211 MESURAREMOS LA ****** & QUITAREMOS EL REYNADO;
               7043 5ELCID0900 AQUEL POYO ENEL PRISO ******;
               7356 5ELCID0943 CON ESTAS GANAN%IAS ALA ****** TORNANDO SEUAN,
              20837 5ELCID2645 POR SANTA MARIA DALUA RAZIN FAZIAN LA ******,
              22588 5ELCID2877 ALA CASA DE BERLANGA ****** PRESA HAN.
       WORD #3264 OCCURS   8 TIMES.
          INDEX OF DIVERSIFICATION =  3197.86 WITH STANDARD DEVIATION OF  4901.79

POSADAS        4376 5ELCID0557 BIEN PUEBLA EL OTERO, FIRME PRENDE LAS *******,
               4863 5ELCID0615 YA MEIORAREMOS ******* ADUENOS & ACAUALLOS.
               5190 5ELCID0656 FINCARON LAS TIENDAS & PRENDEND LAS *******,
               7406 5ELCID0950 DEXAT ESTAS ******* & YREMOS ADELANT.
              10342 5ELCID1310 DEXARE UOS LAS *******, NON LAS QUIERO CONTAR.
              17257 5ELCID2182 TODOS ESSA NOCH FUERON A SUS *******,
       WORD #3265 OCCURS   6 TIMES.
          INDEX OF DIVERSIFICATION =  2575.20 WITH STANDARD DEVIATION OF  2669.65

POSADO        23970 5ELCID3054 MYO %ID RUY DIAZ EN SAN SERUAN ******.
       WORD #3266 OCCURS   1 TIMES.

POSADOS       20919 5ELCID2657 ODIZEN EL ANSSARERA ELLOS ******* SON.
       WORD #3267 OCCURS   1 TIMES.

POSAN         12856 5ELCID1631 FINCARON LAS TIENDAS, & ***** LAS YENTES DESCREYDAS.
              24492 5ELCID3122 LOS %IENTO QUEL AGUARDAN ***** ADERREDOR.
       WORD #3268 OCCURS   2 TIMES.

POSAR          3197 5ELCID0402 ALA FIGERUELA MYO %ID IUA *****.
               3294 5ELCID0415 ALA SIERRA DE MIEDES ELLOS YUAN *****.
               3395 5ELCID0428 FIZO MYO %ID ***** & %EUADA DAR.
               4347 5ELCID0553 E SOBRE ALCO%ER MYO %ID YUA *****,
               4981 5ELCID0630 VINO ***** SOBRE ALCO%ER, EN VN TAN FUERTE LOGAR;
               5102 5ELCID0644 ELLOS VINIERON ALA NOCH EN SOGORUE *****.
               5115 5ELCID0646 VINIERON A LA NOCH A %ELFA *****.
               5152 5ELCID0651 VINIERON ESSA NOCHE EN CALATAYUH *****.
              11652 5ELCID1476 E EL OTRO DIA VINIERON A MOLINA *****.
              12074 5ELCID1531 VAYAMOS *****, CA LA %ENA ES ADOBADA.
              13907 5ELCID1762 E YUAN ***** CON EL EN VNOS PRE%IOSOS ESCA@OS;
              14856 5ELCID1877 BESARON LE LAS MANOS & ENTRARON A *****;
              17514 5ELCID2216 E YUAN ***** EN VN PRE%IOSO ESCA@O.
              22432 5ELCID2857 ADELINAN A ***** PORA FOLGAR ESSA NOCH.
              22583 5ELCID2876 ODIZEN BADO DE REY, ALLA YUAN *****,
       WORD #3269 OCCURS  15 TIMES.
          INDEX OF DIVERSIFICATION =  1383.71 WITH STANDARD DEVIATION OF  2008.88

POSARE        23921 5ELCID3047 E YO CCN LOS MYOS ****** A SAN SERUAN:
              24465 5ELCID3119 ACA ****** CCN TODOS AQUESTOS MIOS.
       WORD #3270 OCCURS   2 TIMES.

POSAREMOS      4912 5ELCID0622 ********* EN SUS CASAS & DELLOS NOS SERUIREMOS.
       WORD #3271 OCCURS   1 TIMES.

POSAUA          438 5ELCID0055 SALIO POR LA PUERTA & EN ARLAN%ON ******.
                445 5ELCID0056 CABO ESSA VILLA EN LA GLERA ******,
               7131 5ELCID0912 ENEL PINAR DE TEUAR DON ROY DIAZ ******;
       WORD #3272 OCCURS   3 TIMES.
```

WORD C# PREFIX CONTEXT

POSO 463 5ELCID0059 **** EN LA GLERA QUANDO NOL COGE NADI EN CASA;
479 5ELCID0061 ASSI **** MYO %ID COMMO SI FUESSE EN MONTAaA.
24487 5ELCID3121 EN VN ESCAaO TORNIaO ESSORA MYO %ID ****,
WORD #3273 OCCURS 3 TIMES.

POYO 6760 5ELCID0863 Y FFINCO EN VN **** QUE ES SOBRE MONT REAL;
6769 5ELCID0864 ALTO ES EL ****, MARAUILLOSO & GRANT;
7040 5ELCID0900 AQUEL **** ENEL PRISO POSADA;
7056 5ELCID0902 EL **** DE MYO %ID ASIL DIRAN POR CARTA.
7114 5ELCID0910 DEXO EL ****, TODO LO DESENPARAUA,
WORD #3274 OCCURS 5 TIMES.
INDEX OF DIVERSIFICATION = 87.50 WITH STANDARD DEVIATION OF 123.58

PREANDO 7309 5ELCID0937 E A DERREDOR TODO LO VA *******.
WORD #3275 OCCURS 1 TIMES.

PREAUA 7068 5ELCID0903 ESTANDO ALLI, MUCHA TIERRA ******,
7137 5ELCID0913 TODAS ESSAS TIERRAS TODAS LAS ******,
WORD #3276 OCCURS 2 TIMES.

PRECIADO 17451 5ELCID2207 TANTA PORPOLA & TANTO XAMED & TANTO PAaO ********.
WORD #3277 OCCURS 1 TIMES.

PRE%IA 3761 5ELCID0475 DEXAN LA A MYO %ID, TODO ESTO NON ****** NADA.
7973 5ELCID1018 EL CONDE DON REMONT NON GELO ****** NADA,
14606 5ELCID1848 MUCHO ****** LA ONDRA EL %ID QUEL AUEDES DADO.
WORD #3278 OCCURS 3 TIMES.

PRE%IADA 14081 5ELCID1783 TANTA TIENDA ******** & TANTO TENDAL OBRADO
15521 5ELCID1966 QUI ENVIO POR CASTIELLA TANTA MULA ********,
28647 5ELCID3657 QUANDO ESTE COLPE A FERIDO COLADA LA ********,
WORD #3279 OCCURS 3 TIMES.

PRE%IADOS 14008 5ELCID1774 ENTRE TIENDAS & ARMAS & VESTIDOS *********
19440 5ELCID2463 QUANDO AGORA SON BUENOS, ADELANT SERAN *********.
WORD #3280 OCCURS 2 TIMES.

PRE%IAMOS 25749 5ELCID3279 QUANTO EL DIZE NON GELO ********* NADA.
25899 5ELCID3300 MAS NOS *********, SABET, QUE MENOS NO.
WORD #3281 OCCURS 2 TIMES.

PRE%IAUA 19238 5ELCID2434 CON DOS ESPADAS QUE EL ******** ALGO
WORD #3282 OCCURS 1 TIMES.

PRE%IO 610 5ELCID0077 SI NON, QUANTO DEXO NOLO ****** UN FIGO.
12537 5ELCID1591 DES DIA SE ****** BAUIECA EN QUANT GRANT FUE ESPAaA.
13669 5ELCID1732 ALI ****** ABAUIECA DELA CABE%A FASTA ACABO.
21115 5ELCID2683 POCO ****** LAS NUEUAS DELOS DE CARRION.
WORD #3283 OCCURS 4 TIMES.

PRE%IOSO 17517 5ELCID2216 E YUAN POSAR EN VN ******** ESCAaO.
WORD #3284 OCCURS 1 TIMES.

PRE%IOSOS 13912 5ELCID1762 E YUAN POSAR CON EL EN VNOS ********* ESCAaOS;
WORD #3285 OCCURS 1 TIMES.

PREGON 9337 5ELCID1187 POR ARAGON & POR NAUARRA ****** MANDO ECHAR,
WORD #3286 OCCURS 1 TIMES.

PREGONADAS 25697 5ELCID3272 VEZOS MYO %ID ALLAS CORTES **********;
WORD #3287 OCCURS 1 TIMES.

PREGONARAN 23259 5ELCID2963 ********** MI CORT PORA DENTRO EN TOLLEDO,
WORD #3288 OCCURS 1 TIMES.

PREGONES 2285 5ELCID0287 POR CASTIELLA OYENDO UAN LOS ********,
5158 5ELCID0652 POR TODAS ESSAS TIERRAS LOS ******** DAN;
9416 5ELCID1197 ANDIDIERON LOS ********, SABET, ATODAS PARTES,
WORD #3289 OCCURS 3 TIMES.

PREMER 5755 5ELCID0726 VERIEDES TANTAS LAN%AS ****** & AL%AR,
WORD #3290 OCCURS 1 TIMES.

PREMIA 9386 5ELCID1193 TODOS VENGAN DE GRADO, NINGUNO NON HA ******,
WORD #3291 OCCURS 1 TIMES.

PREMIO 18175 5ELCID2299 ANTE MYO %ID LA CABE%A ****** & EL ROSTRO FINCO;
26185 5ELCID3338 EL LEON ****** LA CABE%A, A MYO %ID ESPERO,
WORD #3292 OCCURS 2 TIMES.

PRENDADES 10559 5ELCID1338 BESA UOS LAS MANOS & QUE LOS ********* UOS;
WORD #3293 OCCURS 1 TIMES.

WORD C# PREFIX CONTEXT

```
PRENDALO            25446 5ELCID3240 PAGEN LE EN APRE%IADURA & ******** EL CAMPEADOR.
        WORD #3294 OCCURS    1 TIMES.

PRENDAMOS             989 5ELCID0127 ESTAS ARCHAS ********* LAS AMAS,
        WORD #3295 OCCURS    1 TIMES.

PRENDAN              3091 5ELCID0389 ABBAT, DEZILDES QUE ******* EL RASTRO & PIESSEN DE ANDAR,
                     4602 5ELCID0585 ANTES QUEL ******* LCS DE TERUEL, SI NON NON NOS DARAN DENT NADA;
                    17596 5ELCID2226 E ******* BENDI%ICNES & VAYAMOS RECABCANDO.
                    21868 5ELCID2782 ADIOS PLEGA & A SANTA MARIA QUE DENT ******* ELLOS MAL GALARDCN
                    27216 5ELCID3479 QUE NON ******* FUER%A CE CCNCE NIN DE YFAN%ON.
                    27379 5ELCID3498 QUE ******* DE SUS AUERES CUANTO OUIEREN SABOR.
        WORD #3296 OCCURS    6 TIMES.
           INDEX OF DIVERSIFICATION =  4856.60 WITH STANCARD DEVIATION OF  5000.59

PRENDE               4374 5ELCID0557 BIEN PUEBLA EL ETERC, FIRME ****** LAS POSADAS,
                    25310 5ELCID3222 QUANDO DE NUESTRCS AUERES ASSIL ****** SABOR;
        WORD #3297 OCCURS    2 TIMES.

PRENDED               924 5ELCID0119 ******* LAS ARCHAS & METED LAS EN UUESTRO SALUO;
                     6374 5ELCIDC812 A UUESTRA GUISA ******* CCN UUESTRA MANO.
                    14278 5ELCID1807 ******* LO CUE QUISIEREDES, LC OTRO REMANGA.
                    14830 5ELCID1874 DOUOS IIJ CAUALLCS & ******* LCS AQUI.
                    25067 5ELCID3194 ******* A CCLADA, GANELA DE BUEN SE@OR,
        WORD #3298 OCCURS    5 TIMES.
           INDEX OF DIVERSIFICATION =  6034.75 WITH STANCARD CEVIATION OF  4145.50

PRENDELLAS          16875 5ELCID2136 ********** CCN UUESTRAS MANCS & DALCAS ALOS YFANTES,
        WORD #3299 OCCURS    1 TIMES.

PRENDEMOS           21476 5ELCID2730 QUE POR LO QUE NCS MERE%EMCS NO LO ********* NOS;
        WORD #3300 OCCURS    1 TIMES.

PRENDEN             20401 5ELCID2589 TODOS ******* ARMAS & CAUALGAN A VIGOR,
                    21419 5ELCID2723 EN MANO ******* LAS %INCHAS FUERTES & DURADORES.
                    23459 5ELCID2988 ******* SO CCNSSEIO ASSI PARIENTES COMMO SON,
                    23525 5ELCID2996 ******* CCNSSEIO PARIENTES CCMMO SON;
                    27405 5ELCID3501 TALES YA QUE *******, TALES YA QUE NON.
                    28082 5ELCID3585 EMANO ******* LAS ASTAS DELOS FIERROS TAIADORES,
        WORD #3301 OCCURS    6 TIMES.
           INDEX OF DIVERSIFICATION =  1535.20 WITH STANDARD DEVIATION OF  1492.94

PRENDEND             5188 5ELCIDC656 FINCARCN LAS TIENCAS & ******** LAS POSADAS,
        WORD #3302 OCCURS    1 TIMES.

PRENDER              2745 5ELCID0347 ALOS IUDIOS TE DEXESTE *******; DO DIZEN MONTE CALUARIE
                     4668 5ELCIDC592 ALSABOR DEL ******* DELC AL NCN PIENSSAN NADA,
                     9882 5ELCID1253 SIL PUDIESSEN ******* OFUESSE ALCAN%ADO,
                    16706 5ELCID2115 CONPE%C MYC %ID ACAR AQUIEN QUIERE ******* SO DCN,
                    17862 5ELCID2260 QUI AUER QUIERE ******* BIEN ERA ABASTADO;
                    26194 5ELCID3339 DEXOS LE ******* ALCUELC, & ALA REC LE METIO.
                    26488 5ELCID3380 E ******* MAQUILAS, CCMMC LC SUELE FAR
        WORD #3303 OCCURS    7 TIMES.
           INDEX OF DIVERSIFICATION =  3956.17 WITH STANCARD CEVIATION OF  3296.69

PRENDET              1144 5ELCID0147 LAS ARCHAS ACUCHAS, ******* SEYES %IENTOS MARCOS.
                     1950 5ELCID0247 PUES QUE AQUI UCS VEC, ******* DE MI OSPEDADO.
                     2025 5ELCID0255 DUES FIJAS DEXC NI@AS & ******* LAS EN LOS BRA%OS;
                     5071 5ELCIDC641 ******* MELO AUIDA, ACUZIC MELO DELAND;
                    25040 5ELCID3190 ******* LA, SCBRINC, CA MEIORA EN SE@OR.
        WORD #3304 OCCURS    5 TIMES.
           INDEX OF DIVERSIFICATION =  5973.00 WITH STANCARD CEVIATION OF  9415.23

PRENDIA              2188 5ELCID0275 ALAS SUS FIJAS ENBRA%C LAS *******,
        WORD #3305 OCCURS    1 TIMES.

PRENDIENDO           1092 5ELCID0140 SI NON PRIMERC ********** & DESPUES DANDO.
                     8208 5ELCID1046 ********** DEUOS & DE OTRCS YR NOS HEMOS PAGANDO;
                     9169 5ELCID1167 EN TIERRA DE MOROS ********** & GANANDO,
        WORD #3306 OCCURS    3 TIMES.

PRENDO               6917 5ELCID0884 MAS DESPUES QUE DE MOROS FUE, ****** ESTA PRESENTAIA;
                    16546 5ELCID2097 DAQUI LAS ****** PCR MIS MANOS CON ELUIRA & DONA SOL,
                    16785 5ELCID2125 GRADESCOLO, REY, & ****** UUESTRO DON,
                    16887 5ELCID2137 ASSI COMMO YO LAS ****** CAQUENT, COMMO SI FOSSE DELANT,
        WORD #3307 OCCURS    4 TIMES.

PRENDOL             13447 5ELCID1705 ******* YO LOS PECADOS, & DIOS LE ABRA EL ALMA.
        WORD #3308 OCCURS    1 TIMES.

PRENDRA              3073 5ELCID0386 BIEN SEPA EL ABBAT QUE BUEN GALARDON DELLO *******.
        WORD #3309 OCCURS    1 TIMES.

PRENDRE              3959 5ELCID0503 NON ******* CE UOS QUANTO UALE VN DINERO MALO.
        WORD #3310 OCCURS    1 TIMES.
```

WORD C# PREFIX CONTEXT

```
PRESA             4617 5ELCID0586 LA PARIA QUEL A ***** TCRNAR NOS LA HA DOBLADA.
                  9624 5ELCID1223 QUE ***** ES VALENZIA, QUE NON CELA ENPARAN;
                 22589 5ELCID2877 ALA CASA DE BERLANGA POSADA ***** HAN.
                 24510 5ELCID3124 ALA BARBA QUE AUIE LUENGA & ***** CONEL CORDON;
        WORD #3311 OCCURS   4 TIMES.

PRESAS            7824 5ELCID1001 LAS ARMAS AUIEN ****** & SEDIEN SOBRE LOS CAUALLOS.
                 24222 5ELCID3088 CCN ORO & CCN PLATA TODAS LAS ****** SON,
                 25520 5ELCID3250 ESTAS APREZIADURAS MYC %ID ****** LAS HA,
        WORD #3312 OCCURS   3 TIMES.

PRESEND          13001 5ELCID1649 APOCO QUE VINIESTES, ******* UOS QUIEREN DAR:
        WORD #3313 OCCURS   1 TIMES.

PRESENTADO       13480 5ELCID1708 PIDO UOS VN DON & SEAM **********.
        WORD #3314 OCCURS   1 TIMES.

PRESENTAIA        4061 5ELCID0516 AQUI NON LO PUEDEN VENDER NIN DAR EN **********;
                  4109 5ELCID0522 PLOGO A MYO %ID DA QUESTA **********.
                  6874 5ELCID0878 A UOS, REY ONDRADO, ENBIA ESTA **********;
                  6919 5ELCID0884 MAS DESPUES QUE DE MOROS FUE, PRENDO ESTA **********;
                 12084 5ELCID1532 DIXO AUENGALUON: PLAZME DESTA **********,
                 14473 5ELCID1830 MYO %ID EL DE VALEN%IA ENBIA SU **********.
        WORD #3315 OCCURS   6 TIMES.
             INDEX OF DIVERSIFICATION =  2081.40 WITH STANDARD DEVIATION OF  2141.97

PRESENTAIAS      14336 5ELCID1813 ESTOS DOZIENTOS CAUALLOS YRAN EN ***********,
        WORD #3316 OCCURS   1 TIMES.

PRESENTAN        22362 5ELCID2849 ********* A MINAYA ESSA NOCH GRANT ENFFUR%ION;
        WORD #3317 OCCURS   1 TIMES.

PRESENTEIA       10378 5ELCID1315 CON ESTA ********** ADELINO PORA ALLA;
        WORD #3318 OCCURS   1 TIMES.

PRESENTEMOS       7781 5ELCID0996 ANTES QUE ELLOS LEGEN A LA@O, *********** LES LAS LAN%AS;
        WORD #3319 OCCURS   1 TIMES.

PRESO             4880 5ELCID0617 EN ESTE CASTIELLO GRAND AUER AUEMOS *****,
                 13256 5ELCID1681 ALBAR SALUADOREZ ***** FINCO ALLA.
                 27631 5ELCID3528 ***** AUEMOS EL DEBDO & A PASSAR ES POR NOS;
                 29039 5ELCID3709 DELO QUE AN ***** MUCHO AN MAL SABOR;
        WORD #3320 OCCURS   4 TIMES.

PRESON            7899 5ELCID1009 AL CONDE DON REMONT A ****** LEAN TOMADO;
        WORD #3321 OCCURS   1 TIMES.

PRESOS           24128 5ELCID3076 E QUE NON PARESCAN LAS ARMAS, BIEN ****** LOS CORDONES;
        WORD #3322 OCCURS   1 TIMES.

PRESTALDE          917 5ELCID0118 E ********* DE AUER LO QUE SEA GUISADO.
        WORD #3323 OCCURS   1 TIMES.

PRESTAR           5314 5ELCID0671 PRIMERO FABLO MINAYA, VN CAUALLERO DE *******:
                 10254 5ELCID1298 QUANDO DIOS ******* NOS QUIERE, NOS BIEN GELO GRADESCAMOS:
                 11317 5ELCID1432 MER%ED, MINAYA, CAUALLERO DE *******
                 11532 5ELCID1460 EL OBISPO DON IERONIMO, CORONADO DE *******,
        WORD #3324 OCCURS   4 TIMES.

PRESTAS          13201 5ELCID1674 ******* SON LAS MES@ADAS DE LAS YENTES CHRISTIANAS,
        WORD #3325 OCCURS   1 TIMES.

PRESTO           28461 5ELCID3634 TRES DOBLES DE LORIGA TENIE FERNANDO, AQUESTOL ******,
        WORD #3326 OCCURS   1 TIMES.

PRESURADO         1071 5ELCID0137 YA VEDES QUE ENTRA LA NOCH, EL %ID ES *********,
        WORD #3327 OCCURS   1 TIMES.

PREZ             13796 5ELCID1748 AUOS ME OMILLO, DUE@AS, GRANT **** UOS HE GA@ADO:
                 13854 5ELCID1755 ENTRAREDES EN ****, & BESARAN UUESTRAS MANOS.
                 25102 5ELCID3197 SE QUE SI UOS ACAE%IERE, CON ELLA GANAREDES GRAND ****
                                  & GRAND VALOR.
                 26960 5ELCID3444 ONDE SALIEN CONDES DE **** & DE VALOR;
        WORD #3328 OCCURS   4 TIMES.

PRIESSA           2573 5ELCID0325 TANEN A MATINES A VNA ******* TAN GRAND;
                  4627 5ELCID0587 SALIERON DE ALCO%ER AVNA ******* MUCH ESTRANA.
                  4704 5ELCID0596 MANDO TORNAR LA SE@A, A ******* ESPOLONEAUAN.
                  5511 5ELCID0695 QUE ******* VA EN LOS MOROS, E TORNARON SE A ARMAR;
                  7547 5ELCID0967 GRANDES SON LOS PODERES & A ******* SEUAN LEGANDO,
                  8310 5ELCID1057 CON ESTOS DOS CAUALLEROS A ******* VA IANTANDO;
                 13077 5ELCID1658 A VNA GRAND ******* TANIEN LOS ATAMORES;
                 15610 5ELCID1979 EL REY DON ALFONSSO A ******* CAUALGAUA,
                 17465 5ELCID2209 TODOS SUS CAUALLEROS A ******* SON IUNTADOS.
                 17685 5ELCID2237 PORA SANTA MARIA A ******* ADELINNANDO;
```

```
WORD                C#  PREFIX                                    CONTEXT

PRIESSA (CON'T)

                 21960 5ELCID2794 AGRANT ******* SERE BUSCADO YO;
        WORD #3329 OCCURS  11 TIMES.
           INDEX OF DIVERSIFICATION =  1937.70 WITH STANDARD DEVIATION OF  1595.95

PRIETA           13304 5ELCID1687 POR LA MANANA ****** TODOS ARMADOS SEADES,
        WORD #3330 OCCURS   1 TIMES.

PRIMA            24007 5ELCID3060 MATINES & ***** DIXIERON FAZAL ALBA,
        WORD #3331 OCCURS   1 TIMES.

PRIMAS           21780 5ELCID2770 FASTA QUE VIESSE VENIR SUS ****** AMAS ADOS
                 21828 5ELCID2777 FALLO SUS ****** AMORTE%IDAS AMAS ADOS.
                 21833 5ELCID2778 LAMANDO: ******, PRIMAS  LUEGO DESCAUALGO,
                 21834 5ELCID2778 LAMANDO: PRIMAS, ******  LUEGO DESCAUALGO,
                 21844 5ELCID2780 YA ******, LAS MIS PRIMAS, DON ELUIRA & DO@A SOL,
                 21847 5ELCID2780 YA PRIMAS, LAS MIS ******, DON ELUIRA & DO@A SOL,
                 21898 5ELCID2786 LAMANDO: ******, PRIMAS, DON ELUIRA & DON SOL
                 21899 5ELCID2786 LAMANDO: PRIMAS, ******, DON ELUIRA & DON SOL
                 21906 5ELCID2787 DESPERTEDES, ******, POR AMOR DEL CRIADOR
                 21945 5ELCID2792 ESFOR%AD UOS, ******, POR AMOR DEL CRIADOR
                 22018 5ELCID2801 COGIO DEL AGUA ENEL & ASUS ****** DIO;
                 22345 5ELCID2846 QUE VINIE MYNAYA POR SUS ****** AMAS ADOS.
                 22441 5ELCID2858 MINAYA VA UER SUS ****** DO SON,
                 25925 5ELCID3303 HYO LAS HE FIJAS, & TU ****** CORMANAS;
                 26911 5ELCID3438 HYO LES DI MIS ****** POR MANDADO DEL REY ALFONSSO,
                 26979 5ELCID3447 QUANDO PIDEN MIS ******, DON ELUIRA & DO@A SOL,
        WORD #3332 OCCURS  16 TIMES.
           INDEX OF DIVERSIFICATION =   345.60 WITH STANDARD DEVIATION OF   904.01

PRIMER            1436 5ELCID0184 ATOD EL ****** COLPE IIJ MARCOS DE PLATA ECHARON,
        WORD #3333 OCCURS   1 TIMES.

PRIMERAS         13483 5ELCID1709 LAS FERIDAS ******** QUE LAS AYA YO OTORGADAS.
                 18938 5ELCID2396 EN LAS AZES ******** EL CAMPEADOR ENTRAUA,
                 26021 5ELCID3317 PEDIST LAS FERIDAS ******** ALCANPEADOR LEAL,
        WORD #3334 OCCURS   3 TIMES.

PRIMERO           1091 5ELCID0140 SI NON ******* PRENDIENDO & DESPUES DANDO.
                  5308 5ELCID0671 ******* FABLO MINAYA, VN CAUALLERO DE PRESTAR:
                 16532 5ELCID2095 GRADO & GRA%IAS, CID, COMMO TAN BUENO, & ******* AL CRIADOR,
                 20167 5ELCID2560 QUE PLEGA A DO@A XIMENA & ******* AUOS
                 29141 5ELCID3721 AMAYOR ONDRA LAS CASA QUE LO QUE ******* FUE.
        WORD #3335 OCCURS   5 TIMES.
           INDEX OF DIVERSIFICATION =  7011.50 WITH STANDARD DEVIATION OF  3688.11

PRIMEROS         14490 5ELCID1833 HYEN LOS ******** EL REY FUERA DIO SALTO,
                 18852 5ELCID2386 ALOS ******** COLPES DOS MOROS MATAUA DE LA LAN%A.
                 23561 5ELCID3001 EN LOS ******** VA EL BUEN REY DON ALFONSSO,
                 26054 5ELCID3321 DELOS ******** COLPES OF LE DE ARRANCAR;
                 29127 5ELCID3720 LOS ******** FUERON GRANDES, MAS AQUESTOS SON MIIORES;
        WORD #3336 OCCURS   5 TIMES.
           INDEX OF DIVERSIFICATION =  3658.25 WITH STANDARD DEVIATION OF  1048.76

PRIMO            20627 5ELCID2619 ***** ERES DE MIS FIJAS AMAS DALMA & DE CORA%ON
                 21984 5ELCID2797 SI UOS LO MERESCA, MYO *****, NUESTRO PADRE EL CANPEADOR,
                 24235 5ELCID3090 SOBRELLA VN BRIAL ***** DE %ICLATON,
        WORD #3337 OCCURS   3 TIMES.

PRIMOS            7237 5ELCID0928 DIZIENDO LES SALUDES DE ****** & DE HERMANOS,
        WORD #3338 OCCURS   1 TIMES.

PRIS              4203 5ELCID0535 POR QUE LO **** DELLOS QUE DE MI NON DIGAN MAL.
                 25814 5ELCID3288 QUANDO **** A CABRA, & AUOS POR LA BARBA,
        WORD #3339 OCCURS   2 TIMES.

PRISIERON         4244 5ELCID0540 DEL CASTIELLO QUE ********* TODOS RICOS SE PARTEN;
                  8653 5ELCID1099 ********* SO CONSEIO QUEL VINIESSEN %ERCAR.
                  9033 5ELCID1150 ********* %EBOLA & QUANTO QUE ES Y ADELANT.
                 26919 5ELCID3439 ELLOS LAS ********* A ONDRA & A BENDI%ION;
                 27262 5ELCID3485 ********* EL JUIZIO YFANTES DE CARRION.
        WORD #3340 OCCURS   5 TIMES.
           INDEX OF DIVERSIFICATION =  5753.50 WITH STANDARD DEVIATION OF  8309.70

PRISIESSEN       19618 5ELCID2486 QUE TODOS ********** SO DERECHO CONTADO,
        WORD #3341 OCCURS   1 TIMES.

PRISIST           2636 5ELCID0333 ******* ENCARNA%ION EN SANTA MARIA MADRE,
        WORD #3342 OCCURS   1 TIMES.

PRISO              859 5ELCID0110 GRANDES AUERES ***** & MUCHO SOBEIANOS,
                  3215 5ELCID0405 VN SUENOL ***** DUL%E, TAN BIEN SE ADURMJO.
                  4303 5ELCID0548 GRANDES SON LAS GANAN%IAS QUE ***** POR LA TIERRA DO UA.
                  7042 5ELCID0900 AQUEL POYO ENEL ***** POSADA;
                  7922 5ELCID1012 ***** LO AL CONDE, PORA SU TIERRA LO LEUAUA;
                  8625 5ELCID1095 EL CON TODO ESTO ***** A MURUIEDRO.
```

```
WORD                C#  PREFIX                                   CONTEXT

PRISO (CON'T)

              10476 5ELCID1328 ***** A ALMENAR & A MURUIEDRO QUE ES MIYOR,
              18833 5ELCID2383 EL OBISPO DON IHERONIMO ***** A ESPOLONADA
              22062 5ELCID2808 EL CAUALLO ***** POR LA RIENDA & LUEGO DENT LAS PARTIO,
              22122 5ELCID2816 ***** BESTIAS & VESTIDOS DE PRO,
              25791 5ELCID3285 CA NON ME ***** AELLA FIJO DE MUGIER NADA,
              27420 5ELCID3503 DELO AL TANTO ***** QUANT CUO SABOR.
              28826 5ELCID3682 APART LE *****, QUE NON CABEL CORA%ON;
        WORD #3343 OCCURS  13 TIMES.
           INDEX OF DIVERSIFICATION =  2329.58 WITH STANDARD DEVIATION OF  2176.60

PRISOL        28399 5ELCID3627 ****** EN VAZIO, EN CARNE NOL TOMO,
        WORD #3344 OCCURS   1 TIMES.

PRISOLA       24291 5ELCID3097 LA BARBA AVIE LUENGA & ******* CON EL CORDON,
        WORD #3345 OCCURS   1 TIMES.

PRISOS        13118 5ELCID1663 ****** ALA BARBA EL BUEN %ID CAMPEADOR:
              25754 5ELCID3280 ESSORA EL CAMPEADOR ****** ALA BARBA;
              29068 5ELCID3713 ****** ALA BARBA RUY DIAZ SO SE@OR;
        WORD #3346 OCCURS   3 TIMES.

PRIUADO         703 5ELCID0089 POR RACHEL & VIDAS UAYADES ME *******:
               1151 5ELCID0148 MARTIN ANTOLINEZ CAUALGO *******
               1299 5ELCID0166 DIXO MARTIN ANTOLINEZ:  CARGEN LAS ARCHAS *******.
               1626 5ELCID0208 MANDAD COGER LA TIENDA & VAYAMOS *******,
               3589 5ELCID0452 FAZED ME MANDADO MUY ******* ALA %AGA;
               8252 5ELCID1050 E TIENEN GELO DELANT & DIERON GELO *******.
               8348 5ELCID1061 MANDAD NOS DAR LAS BESTIAS & CAUALGEREMOS *******;
              12160 5ELCID1543 ARBUXUELO ARRIBA ******* AGUIJAUAN,
              12320 5ELCID1564 DOZITOS CAUALLEROS MANDO EXIR *******,
              14359 5ELCID1816 OTRO DIA MANANA ******* CAUALGAUAN,
              17693 5ELCID2238 EL OBISPO DON IHERONIMO VISTIOS TAN *******,
              17712 5ELCID2241 AL SALIR DELA ECCLEGIA CAUALGARON TAN *******,
              19245 5ELCID2435 POR LA MATAN%A VINIA TAN *******,
              22047 5ELCID2806 E ******* ENEL CAUALLO LAS CAUALGO;
              22648 5ELCID2886 ******* CAUALGA, A RE%EBIR LOS SALE;
              22902 5ELCID2917 MU@O GUSTIOZ ******* CAUALGO,
        WORD #3347 OCCURS  16 TIMES.
           INDEX OF DIVERSIFICATION =  1478.93 WITH STANDARD DEVIATION OF  1547.81

PRIUADOL      11700 5ELCID1483 CO %IENTO CAUALLEROS QUE ******** ACORRADES;
        WORD #3348 OCCURS   1 TIMES.

PRO            1883 5ELCID0239 Y ESTAUA DO@A XIMENA CON %INCO DUENAS DE ***,
               5825 5ELCID0736 MARTIN ANTOLINEZ, EL BURGALES DE ***,
               8752 5ELCID1112 YO FIO POR DIOS QUE EN NUESTRO *** ENADRAN.
              10857 5ELCID1374 BIEN CASARIEMOS CON SUS FIJAS PORA HUEBOS DE ***.
              10908 5ELCID1380 LEUEDES VN PORTERO, TENGO QUE UOS AURA ***;
              10951 5ELCID1386 EN TODO SODES ***, EN ESTO ASSI LO FAGADES:
              10968 5ELCID1388 SOMOS EN SO *** QUANTO LO PODEMOS FAR;
              11202 5ELCID1417 QUE LES TOUIESSE *** ROGAUAN A ALBARFANEZ;
              13131 5ELCID1664 NON AYADES MIEDO, CATODO ES UUESTRA ***;
              14939 5ELCID1888 CASAR QUEREMOS CON ELLAS ASU ONDRA & A NUESTRA ***.
              14964 5ELCID1891 EFAZIENDO YO HA EL MAL, & EL AMI GRAND ***,
              15132 5ELCID1913 ANDAR LE QUIERO A MYO %ID EN TODA ***.
              15708 5ELCID1992 MARTIN MUNOZ & MARTIN ANTOLINEZ, EL BURGALES DE ***,
              15725 5ELCID1995 MU@O GUSTIOZ, EL CAUALLERO DE ***.
              16194 5ELCID2054 EN QUANTO PODEMOS ANDAMOS EN UUESTRO ***.
              16354 5ELCID2074 ASI LO MANDE CHRISTUS QUE SEA ASO ***.
              16380 5ELCID2077 SEMEIAM EL CASAMIENTO ONDRADO & CON GRANT ***,
              16830 5ELCID2130 DAQUEND VAYA COMIGO; CUEDO QUEL AURA ***.
              17180 5ELCID2173 QUE ES LARGO DE LENGUA, MAS EN LO AL NON ES TAN ***.
              19585 5ELCID2481 COMMO SON ONDRADOS & AVER VOS GRANT ***.
              19869 5ELCID2519 EUADES AQUI, YERNOS, LA MI MUGIER DE ***,
              21509 5ELCID2734 LO QUE RUEGAN LAS DUENAS NON LES HA NINGUN ***.
              22127 5ELCID2816 PRISO BESTIAS & VESTIDOS DE ***,
              22280 5ELCID2837 E MARTIN ANTOLINEZ, EL BURGLES DE ***,
              22769 5ELCID2901 DERES, MU@O GUSTIOZ, MYO VASSALLO DE ***,
              23218 5ELCID2957 FIZ LO POR BIEN, QUE FFUESSE A SU ***.
              23862 5ELCID3039 MI MUGIER DONA XIMENA, DUE@A ES DE ***,
              24057 5ELCID3066 E MARTIN ANTOLINEZ, EL BURGALES DE ***,
              24268 5ELCID3094 VNA COFIA SOBRE LOS PELOS DUN ESCARIN DE ***,
              25053 5ELCID3191 A MARTIN ANTOLINEZ, EL BURGALES DE ***,
              25066 5ELCID3193 MARTIN ANTOLINEZ, MYO VASSALO DE ***,
              27903 5ELCID3560 SI BUENAS LAS TENEDES, *** ABRAN AUOS;
              28501 5ELCID3639 QUEBRARON LE LAS %INCHAS, NINGUNA NOL OUO ***,
        WORD #3349 OCCURS  33 TIMES.
           INDEX OF DIVERSIFICATION =   830.81 WITH STANDARD DEVIATION OF  1036.40

PROLES         6747 5ELCID0861 PESO ALOS DE ALCO%ER, CA ****** FAZIE GRANT.
        WORD #3350 OCCURS   1 TIMES.

PROMETO        3914 5ELCID0497 ADIOS LO *******, A AQUEL QUE ESTA EN ALTO:
        WORD #3351 OCCURS   1 TIMES.
```

WORD C# PREFIX CONTEXT

PROS 22355 5ELCID2847 VARONES DE SANTESTEUAN, A GUISA DE MUY ****,
WORD #3352 OCCURS 1 TIMES.

PROUADO 19897 5ELCID2523 AAQUEL REY BUCAR, TRAYDOR *******.
WORD #3353 OCCURS 1 TIMES.

PROUANDO 9828 5ELCID1247 DE QUE SON PAGADOS; EL AMOR DE MY %ID YA LO YUAN ********.
WORD #3354 OCCURS 1 TIMES.

PROUECHOSA 9700 5ELCID1233 MAS MUCHO FUE **********, SABET, ESTA ARANCADA:
WORD #3355 OCCURS 1 TIMES.

PROUEZAS 10202 5ELCID1292 LAS ******** DE MYO %ID ANDAUALAS DEMANDANDO,
WORD #3356 OCCURS 1 TIMES.

PUDIEMOS 8790 5ELCID1117 NON FUE A NUESTRO GRADO NI NOS NON ******** MAS,
10116 5ELCID1281 AESTAS TIERRAS ESTRANAS QUE NOS ******** GANAR.
WORD #3357 OCCURS 2 TIMES.

PUDIER 20766 5ELCID2637 RE%IBA A MYOS YERNOS COMMO EL ****** MEIOR;
WORD #3358 OCCURS 1 TIMES.

PUDIEREDES 11573 5ELCID1466 HYD PORA MEDINA QUANTO LO ********** FAR,
WORD #3359 OCCURS 1 TIMES.

PUDIERON 9047 5ELCID1151 DE PIES DE CAUALLO LOS QUES ******** ESCAPAR.
14025 5ELCID1777 NON ******** ELLOS SABER LA CUENTA DE TODOS LOS CAUALLOS,
WORD #3360 OCCURS 2 TIMES.

PUDIES 2455 5ELCID0309 QUE, SI DESPUES DEL PLAZO EN SU TIERRAL ****** TOMAR,
WORD #3361 OCCURS 1 TIMES.

PUDIESSE 18784 5ELCID2377 MYO CORA%ON QUE ******** FOLGAR,
WORD #3362 OCCURS 1 TIMES.

PUDIESSEMOS 20954 5ELCID2662 SI *********** MATAR EL MORO AVENGALUON,
WORD #3363 OCCURS 1 TIMES.

PUDIESSEN 9852 5ELCID1250 QUE SIS ********* YR, FER LO YEN DE GRADO.
9881 5ELCID1253 SIL ********* PRENDER OFUESSE ALCAN%ADO,
27734 5ELCID3540 QUE SI LOS ********* APARTAR ALOS DEL CAMPEADOR,
WORD #3364 OCCURS 3 TIMES.

PUDO 1836 5ELCID0233 PORA SAN PERO DE CARDENA QUANTO **** A ESPOLEAR,
5593 5ELCID0704 AQUEL PERO VERMUEZ NON LO **** ENDURAR,
7379 5ELCID0946 SONRRISOS EL CABOSO, QUE NON LO **** ENDURAR:
7670 5ELCID0982 TORNOS EL MANDADERO QUANTO **** MAS;
11282 5ELCID1427 DELOS MEIORES GUARIMIENTOS QUE EN BURGOS **** FALAR,
28819 5ELCID3681 NOL **** GUARIR, FALSSO GELA GUARNIZON,
WORD #3365 OCCURS 6 TIMES.
INDEX OF DIVERSIFICATION = 5395.60 WITH STANDARD DEVIATION OF 6934.80

PUEBLA 4370 5ELCID0557 BIEN ****** EL ETERO, FIRME PRENDE LAS POSADAS,
WORD #3366 OCCURS 1 TIMES.

PUEBLO 7048 5ELCID0901 MIENTRA QUE SEA EL ****** DE MOROS & DELA YENTE CHRISTIANA,
10402 5ELCID1318 FINCO SOS YNOIOS ANTE TODEL ******,
WORD #3367 OCCURS 2 TIMES.

PUEDA 2395 5ELCID0302 EN ANTES QUE YO MUERA, ALGUN BIEN UOS ***** FAR:
WORD #3368 OCCURS 1 TIMES.

PUEDE 902 5ELCID0116 AQUELAS NON LAS ***** LEUAR, SINON, SER YEN VENTADAS;
5010 5ELCID0633 PERDERAS CALATAYUTH, QUE NON ***** ESCAPAR,
6101 5ELCID0775 PARA CALATAYUCH QUANTO ***** SE VA.
7396 5ELCID0948 QUI EN VN LOGAR MORA SIEMPRE, LO SO ***** MANGUAR;
10304 5ELCID1304 DIERON LE EN VALEN%IA O BIEN ***** ESTAR RICO.
12462 5ELCID1581 CON QUANTOS QUE EL *****, QUE CON ORAS SE ACORDARON,
15828 5ELCID2007 QUE DEL ALCA%AR VNA SALIR NON *****,
16222 5ELCID2058 NON SE ***** FARTAR DEL, TANTOL QUERIE DE CORA%ON;
20614 5ELCID2617 NOS ***** REPENTIR, QUE CASADAS LAS HA AMAS.
22143 5ELCID2819 QUANTO EL MEIOR ***** ALLI LAS ONDRO.
22869 5ELCID2913 ESSO ME ***** PESAR CON LA OTRA DESONOR.
25551 5ELCID3254 LA RENCURA MAYOR NON SEME ***** OLBIDAR.
25952 5ELCID3307 DETIENES LE LA LENGUA, NON ***** DELIBRAR,
27142 5ELCID3468 DANDOS, REY, PLAZO, CA CRAS SER NON *****.
WORD #3369 OCCURS 14 TIMES.
INDEX OF DIVERSIFICATION = 2017.46 WITH STANDARD DEVIATION OF 1363.26

PUEDEN 4056 5ELCID0516 AQUI NON LO ****** VENDER NIN DAR EN PRESENTAIA;
4260 5ELCID0542 VANSSE FENARES ARRIBA QUANTO ****** ANDAR,
4288 5ELCID0546 POR ESSAS TIERRAS AYUSO QUANTO ****** ANDAR.
5663 5ELCID0713 DAN LE GRANDES COLPES, MAS NOL ****** FALSSAR.

WORD C# PREFIX CONTEXT

PUEDEN (CON'T)

```
                 7686 5ELCID0984 QUE A MENOS DE BATALLA NOS ****** DEN QUITAR.
                 8075 5ELCID1030 FASTA TER%ER DIA NOL ****** ACORDAR.
                 8083 5ELCID1032 NOL ****** FAZER COMER VN MUESSO DE PAN.
                 9259 5ELCID1177 NIN AMIGO A AMIGO NOS ****** CONSOLAR.
                 9283 5ELCID1180 DELANTE VEYEN SO DUELO, NON SE ****** HUUIAR,
                11631 5ELCID1474 E QUANTO QUE ****** NON FINCAN DE ANDAR.
                14076 5ELCID1782 QUANDO A MYO %ID CAYERON TANTOS, LOS OTROS BIEN ******
                                 FINCAR PAGADOS.
                20840 5ELCID2646 AGUIJAN QUANTO ****** YFANTES DE CARRION;
                21604 5ELCID2747 HYA NON ****** FABLAR DON ELUIRA & DONA SOL;
                21884 5ELCID2784 TANTO SON DE TRASPUESTAS QUE NON ****** DEZIR NADA.
                22927 5ELCID2920 SALIEN DE VALEN%IA & ANDAN QUANTO ******,
                24520 5ELCID3126 NOL ****** CATAR DE VERGUEN%A YFANTES DE CARRION.
                24990 5ELCID3183 NOS LE ****** CAMBAR, CA EL %ID BIEN LAS CONNOS%E;
                26329 5ELCID3358 MIENTRA QUE BIUAN ****** AUER SOSPIROS:
        WORD #3370 OCCURS 18 TIMES.
           INDEX OF DIVERSIFICATION = 1309.18 WITH STANDARD DEVIATION OF 1618.70

PUEDENT          4360 5ELCID0555 A%ERCA CORRE SALON, AGUA NOL ******* VEDAR.
        WORD #3371 OCCURS  1 TIMES.

PUEDO             717 5ELCID0091 NON ***** TRAER EL AUER, CA MUCHO ES PESADO,
                  753 5ELCID0095 YO MAS NON ***** & AMYDOS LO FAGO.
                12899 5ELCID1636 A MENOS DE MUERT NO LA ***** DEXAR;
                25576 5ELCID3257 AMENOS DE RIEBTOS NO LOS ***** DEXAR.
                25980 5ELCID3311 BIEN LO SABEDES QUE YO NON ***** MAS;
        WORD #3372 OCCURS  5 TIMES.
           INDEX OF DIVERSIFICATION = 6314.75 WITH STANDARD DEVIATION OF 7043.70

PUEENT           1164 5ELCID0150 NON VIENE ALA ******, CA POR EL AGUA APASSADO,
        WORD #3373 OCCURS  1 TIMES.

PUENT            2304 5ELCID0290 EN AQUES DIA ALA ***** DE ARLA%ON
        WORD #3374 OCCURS  1 TIMES.

PUERTA            249 5ELCID0032 ASSI COMMO LEGO ALA ******, FALOLA BIEN %ERRADA,
                  295 5ELCID0037 AGUIIO MYO %ID, ALA ****** SE LEGAUA,
                  310 5ELCID0039 NON SE ABRE LA ******, CA BIEN ERA %ERRADA.
                  410 5ELCID0051 PARTIOS DELA ******, POR BURGOS AGUIJAUA,
                  434 5ELCID0055 SALIO POR LA ****** & EN ARLAN%ON POSAUA.
                 1902 5ELCID0242 LAMAUAN ALA ******, Y SOPIERON EL MANDADO;
                 3704 5ELCID0467 MYO %ID DON RODRIGO ALA ****** ADELI@AUA;
                 4801 5ELCID0608 LAS ESPADAS DESNUDAS, A LA ****** SE PARAUAN.
                 5438 5ELCID0686 SI NON DOS PEONES SOLOS POR LA ****** GUARDAR;
                12417 5ELCID1576 ALA ****** DE VALEN%IA, DO FUESSE EN SO SALUO,
                17695 5ELCID2239 ALA ****** DELA ECLEGIA SEDIELLOS SPERANDO;
                18088 5ELCID2288 DIEGO GON%ALEZ POR LA ****** SALIO,
                24342 5ELCID3104 ALA ****** DE FUERA DESCAUALGA A SABOR;
                26376 5ELCID3364 SALISTE POR LA ******, METISTET AL CORAL,
        WORD #3375 OCCURS 14 TIMES.
           INDEX OF DIVERSIFICATION = 2008.77 WITH STANDARD DEVIATION OF 2491.37

PUERTAS            16 5ELCID0003 VIO ******* ABIERTAS & V%OS SIN CA@ADOS,
                 2848 5ELCID0360 QUEBRANTESTE LAS ******* & SACUESTE LOS PADRES SANTOS.
                 3638 5ELCID0459 ABREN LAS *******, DE FUERA SALTO DAUAN,
                 3655 5ELCID0461 TODOS SON EXIDOS, LAS ******* DEXADAS AN ABIERTAS
                 3725 5ELCID0470 MIO %ID RUY DIAZ POR LAS ******* ENTRAUA,
                 4677 5ELCID0593 ABIERTAS DEXAN LAS ******* QUE NINGUNO NON LAS GUARDA.
                 5495 5ELCID0693 ABRIERON LAS *******, FUERA VN SALTO DAN;
                12382 5ELCID1572 E TODAS LAS ******* & LAS EXIDAS & LAS ENTRADAS,
                13517 5ELCID1713 DEXAN ALAS ******* OMNES DE GRANT RECABDO.
                15779 5ELCID2002 LAS ******* DEL ALCA%AR QUE NON SE ABRIESSEN DE DIA
                                 NIN DE NOCH,
        WORD #3376 OCCURS 10 TIMES.
           INDEX OF DIVERSIFICATION = 1750.44 WITH STANDARD DEVIATION OF 2134.61

PUERTO           7416 5ELCID0951 ESTON%ES SE MUDO EL %ID AL ****** DE ALCAT,
                 8561 5ELCID1087 POBLADO HA MYO %ID EL ****** DE ALUCANT,
        WORD #3377 OCCURS  2 TIMES.

PUES             1708 5ELCID0219 DA QUI QUITO CASTIELLA, **** QUE EL REY HE EN YRA;
                 1945 5ELCID0247 **** QUE AQUI UOS VEO, PRENDET DE MI OSPEDADO.
                 3493 5ELCID0441 **** QUE A CASTEION SACAREMOS A %ELADA,. . . .
                 3967 5ELCID0504 **** QUE POR MI GANAREDES QUES QUIER QUE SEA DALGO,
                 7729 5ELCID0990 **** ADELLANT YRAN TRAS NOS, AQUI SEA LA BATALLA;
                 8008 5ELCID1023 **** QUE TALES MAL CAL%ADOS ME VEN%IERON DE BATALLA.
                 8148 5ELCID1039 **** COMED, CONDE, & QUANDO FUEREDES IANTADO,
                10124 5ELCID1283 **** ESTO AN FABLADO, PIENSSAN SE DE ADOBAR.
                13361 5ELCID1694 **** ESSO QUEREDES, %ID, A MI MANDADES AL;
                14973 5ELCID1893 MAS **** BOS LO QUEREDES, ENTREMOS EN LA RAZON.
                15319 5ELCID1940 MAS **** LO CONSEIA EL QUE MAS VALE QUE NOS,
                16613 5ELCID2105 **** FUEREN EN UUESTRO PODER EN VALEN%IA LA MAYOR,
                16838 5ELCID2132 **** QUE CASADES MYS FIJAS, ASI COMMO AUOS PLAZ,
                17542 5ELCID2220 **** QUE AFAZER LO AUEMOS, POR QUE LO YMOS TARDANDO?
                20946 5ELCID2661 HYA **** QUE ADEXAR AUEMOS FIJAS DEL CAMPEADOR,
```

```
WORD                C#  PREFIX                          CONTEXT

PUES (CON'T)

              21710 5ELCID2761 **** NUESTRAS PAREIAS NCN ERAN PORA EN BRA%OS.
        WORD #3378 OCCURS  16 TIMES.
          INDEX OF DIVERSIFICATICN =  1332.47 WITH STANCARD DEVIATION OF  1246.36

PUESTAS       16668 5ELCID2111 LAS PALABRAS SON ******* QUE OTRO DIA MA@ANA
              27437 5ELCID3505 QUANDO TODAS ESTAS NUEUAS ASSI ******* SON,
        WORD #3379 OCCURS   2 TIMES.

PUESTO         3301 5ELCID0416 AVN ERA DE DIA, NCN ERA ****** EL SOL,
               9898 5ELCID1255 AFEUOS TODC AQUESTO ****** EN BUEN RECABDO.
              16917 5ELCID2141 TOD ESTO ES ******, SABED, EN GRANT RECABDO.
        WORD #3380 OCCURS   3 TIMES.

PUIAN         21235 5ELCID2698 LOS MONTES SCN ALTOS, LAS RAMAS ***** CON LAS NUES,
        WORD #3381 OCCURS   1 TIMES.

PULGADA       25829 5ELCID3289 NCN YOUO RAPAZ QUE NON MESSO SU *******;
        WORD #3382 OCCURS   1 TIMES.

PUNO          24225 5ELCID3089 AL **** BIEN ESTAN, CA EL SELC MANDO;
        WORD #3383 OCCURS   1 TIMES.

PUNTO          2334 5ELCID0294 VANSSE PORA SAN PERO DO ESTA EL QUE ENBUEN ***** NA%IO.
               3239 5ELCID0408 EN TAN BUEN ***** CAUALGO VARON;
              17127 5ELCID2167 ADELINAN PORA VALEN%IA, LA CUE EN BUEN ***** GANO.
              24070 5ELCID3068 E MARTIN MUNCZ, QUE EN BUEN ***** NA%IO,
        WORD #3384 OCCURS   4 TIMES.

PUSIERON       2750 5ELCID0348 ******** TE EN CRUZ POR NUMBRE EN GOLGOTA;
              24933 5ELCID3176 ******** LAS EN MANO DEL REY SO SE@OR;
        WORD #3385 OCCURS   2 TIMES.

PUSIESSEN      9890 5ELCID1254 TOMASSEN LE EL AUER & ********* LE EN VN PALO.
        WORD #3386 OCCURS   1 TIMES.

QEU            5817 5ELCID0735 MYNAYA ALBARFANEZ, *** CORITA MANDO,
        WORD #3387 OCCURS   1 TIMES.

QUADRA        14997 5ELCID1896 A VNA ****** ELE LOS APARTO:
        WORD #3388 OCCURS   1 TIMES.

QUAL           5802 5ELCID0733 **** LIDIA BIEN SOBRE EXORADO ARZON
              18681 5ELCID2364 MANDAD NOLOS FERIR DE **** PART UOS SEMEIAR,
              21560 5ELCID2741  **** VENTURA SERIE ESTA, SI PLOGUIESSE AL CRIADOR,
              21598 5ELCID2746 ENSAYANDOS AMOS **** CARA MEIORES COLPES.
              21656 5ELCID2753  **** VENTURA SERIE SI ASSOMAS ESSORA EL %ID CAMPEADOR
              26552 5ELCID3389 FAZER TELO DEZIR QUE TALERES **** DIGO YO.
              29144 5ELCID3722 VED **** ONDRA CRE%E AL QUE EN BUEN ORA NA%IO,
        WORD #3389 OCCURS   7 TIMES.
          INDEX OF DIVERSIFICATION =  3889.33 WITH STANDARD DEVIATION OF  4775.84

QUALES        22284 5ELCID2838 CON CC CAUALLERCS, ****** MYO %ID MANDO;
              27042 5ELCID3454 EN TODAS GUISAS TALES SODES ****** DIGO YO;
        WORD #3390 OCCURS   2 TIMES.

QUANDO          467 5ELCID0059 POSO EN LA GLERA ****** NOL COGE NADI EN CASA;
                704 5ELCID0090 ****** EN BURGOS ME VEDARCN COMPRA & EL REY ME A AYRADO,
                970 5ELCID0125 ****** ATIERRA DE MOROS ENTRO, QUE GRANT AUER SACO;
               1465 5ELCID0188 ****** ESTO OUO FECHO, ODREDES LO QUE FABLAUA:
               1854 5ELCID0236 ****** LEGO A SAN PERO EL BUEN CAMPEADOR;
               2336 5ELCID0295 ****** LO SOPO MYO %ID EL DE BIUAR,
               2501 5ELCID0316 ALA MA@ANA, ****** LOS GALLOS CANTARAN,
               2681 5ELCID0339 A IONAS, ****** CAYO EN LA MAR,
               2892 5ELCID0365 ****** OY NOS PARTIMOS, EN VIDA NOS FAZ IUNTAR.
               3250 5ELCID0410 ****** DESPERTO EL %ID, LA CARA SE SANTIGO;
               3710 5ELCID0468 LOS QUE LA TIENEN, ****** VIERCN LA REBATA,
               4511 5ELCID0574 ****** VIO MYO %ID QUE ALCO%ER NON SELE DAUA;
               4632 5ELCID0588 MYO %ID, ****** LOS VIO FUERA, COGIOS COMMO DE ARRANCADA.
               5028 5ELCID0636 ****** LO OYO EL REY TAMIN, POR CUER LE PESO MAL:
               6223 5ELCID0793 ****** TAL BATALLA AUEMOS ARANCADO.
               6250 5ELCID0796 DELOS MORISCOS, ****** SON LEGADOS, FFALLARON DX CAUALLOS.
               6669 5ELCID0851 ****** MYO %ID EL CASTIELLO QUISO QUITAR,
               6697 5ELCID0855 ****** QUITO A ALCO%ER MYO %ID EL DE BIUAR,
               7097 5ELCID0908 ****** VIO EL CABOSO QUE SE TARDAUA MINAYA,
               7143 5ELCID0915 ****** ESTO FECHO OUO, A CABO DE TRES SEMANAS,
               7171 5ELCID0919 ****** VIO MYO %ID ASOMAR A MINAYA,
               7532 5ELCID0966 MAS ****** EL MELO BUSCA, YR GELO HE YO DEMANDAR.
               7620 5ELCID0976 MYO %ID ****** LO OYO, ENBIO PORA ALLA:
               7815 5ELCID1000 TODOS SON ADOBADOS ****** MYO %ID ESTO OUO FABLADO;
               8125 5ELCID1036 ****** ESTO OYO EL CONDE, YAS YUA ALEGRANDO:
               8152 5ELCID1039 PUES COMED, CONDE, & ****** FUEREDES IANTADO,
               9142 5ELCID1164 ****** EL %ID CAMPEADOR OUO PE@A CADIELLA,
               9445 5ELCID1201 ****** VIO MYO %ID LAS GENTES IUNTADAS, COMPE%OS DE PAGAR.
               9515 5ELCID1210 ****** VINO EL DEZENO, OUIERON GELA ADAR.
               9531 5ELCID1212 ****** MYO %ID GA@O A VALEN%IA & ENTRO ENLA %IBDAD.
```

WORD C# PREFIX CONTEXT

QUANDO (CON'T)

9599 5ELCID1220 ****** SU SE@A CABDAL SEDIE EN SOMO DEL ALCA%AR.
9693 5ELCID1232 BUENA FUE LA DE VALEN%IA ****** GANARON LA CASA,
9971 5ELCID1264 ****** LOS FALLO, POR CUENTA FIZO LOS NONBRAR:
10234 5ELCID1296 ****** LO OYO MYO %ID, DE AQUESTO FUE PAGADO:
10252 5ELCID1298 ****** DIOS PRESTAR NOS QUIERE, NOS BIEN GELO GRADESCAMOS:
10276 5ELCID1301 VOS, ****** YDES A CASTIELLA, LEUAREDES BUENOS MANDADOS.
10628 5ELCID1347 ****** ASSI FAZE A SU GUISA EL %ID CAMPEADOR
10721 5ELCID1358 ****** EN CABO DE MI TIERRA A QUESTAS DUE@AS FUEREN,
11018 5ELCID1395 ****** ACABO LA ORA%ION, ALAS DUE@AS SE TORNO:
11291 5ELCID1429 ****** ESTAS DUE@AS ADOBADAS LAS HAN,
11656 5ELCID1477 EL MORO AUEGALUON, ****** SOPO EL MENSSAIE,
11967 5ELCID1517 ****** LEGO AUEGALUON, DONTA OIO HA,
12528 5ELCID1590 ****** OUO CORRIDO, TODOS SE MARAUILLAUAN;
12560 5ELCID1594 ****** LO VIO DO@A XIMENA, A PIES SE LE ECHAUA:
13377 5ELCID1696 ****** UOS LOS FUEREDES FERIR, ENTRARE YO DEL OTRA PART;
13736 5ELCID1741 ****** AL REY DE MARUECOS ASSI LO AN ARRANCADO,
13818 5ELCID1751 ****** EN VUESTRA VENIDA TAL GANAN%IA NOS AN DADA.
14067 5ELCID1782 ****** A MYO %ID CAYERON TANTOS, LOS OTROS BIEN PUEDEN FINCAR PAGADOS.
14169 5ELCID1794 ****** ES FARTO DE LIDIAR CON AMAS LAS SUS MANOS,
15148 5ELCID1916 ****** LO SOPO EL BUEN CAMPEADOR,
15247 5ELCID1931 ****** LO OYO MYO %ID EL BUEN CAMPEADOR,
15434 5ELCID1955 AYAMOS VISTAS ****** LO QUIERE MYO SE@OR.
15467 5ELCID1960 ****** LAS VIO, DE CORA%ON SE PAGA:
15881 5ELCID2014 ****** VIERON QUE VINIE EL BUEN CAMPEADOR,
16115 5ELCID2044 ****** HE LA GRA%IA DE DON ALFONSSO MYO SE@OR;
16673 5ELCID2112 ****** SALIE EL SOL, QUES TORNASSE CADA VNO DON SALIDOS SON.
16770 5ELCID2123 EVAD AQUI UUESTROS FIJOS, ****** UUESTROS YERNOS SON;
16853 5ELCID2133 DAD MANERO A QUI LAS DE, ****** UOS LAS TOMADES;
16899 5ELCID2139 ****** UOS IUNTAREDES COMIGO, QUEM DIGADES LA UERDAT.
17197 5ELCID2176 ****** A ELLA ASSOMARON, LOS GOZOS SON MAYORES.
17233 5ELCID2180 ****** VINIERE LA MA@ANA, QUE APUNTARE EL SOL,
17350 5ELCID2195 ****** UOS NOS CASAREDES BIEN SEREMOS RICAS.
17674 5ELCID2236 ****** OUIERON AQUESTO FECHO, SALIERON DEL PALA%IO,
18164 5ELCID2298 EL LEON ****** LO VIO, ASSI EN VERGON%O,
18223 5ELCID2306 ****** LOS FALLARON & ELLOS VINIERON, ASSI VINIERON SIN COLOR;
19434 5ELCID2463 ****** AGORA SON BUENOS, ADELANT SERAN PRE%IADOS.
19481 5ELCID2468 LOS YERNOS DE MYO %ID ****** ESTE AUER TOMARON
19557 5ELCID2478 ****** VEO LO QUE AUIA SABOR,
19835 5ELCID2515 ****** ENTRARON LOS YFANTES DE CARRION,
20310 5ELCID2577 MIOS FIJOS SODES AMOS, ****** MIS FIJAS VOS DO;
20380 5ELCID2586 ****** SON PAGADOS ATODO SO SABOR,
20853 5ELCID2648 EL MORO ****** LO SOPO, PLOGOL DE CORA%ON;
20983 5ELCID2666 ****** ESTA FALSSEDAD DIZEN LOS DE CARRION,
21279 5ELCID2704 MAL GELO CUNPLIERON ****** SALIE EL SOL
21425 5ELCID2724 ****** ESTO VIERON LAS DUE@AS, FABLAUA DO@A SOL:
22115 5ELCID2815 ****** EL LO OYO PESOL DE CORA%ON,
22153 5ELCID2821 ****** SABIEN ESTO, PESOLES DE CORA%ON;
22195 5ELCID2827 ****** GELO DIZEN A MYO %ID EL CAMPEADOR,
22225 5ELCID2831 ****** TAL ONDRA MEAN DADA LOS YFANTES DE CARRION;
22467 5ELCID2861 EUOS A EL LO GRADID, ****** BIUAS SOMOS NOS.
22503 5ELCID2866 ****** UOS SODES SA@AS & BIUAS & SIN OTRO MAL.
22835 5ELCID2909 ****** LAS HAN DEXADAS AGRANT DESONOR,
23699 5ELCID3019 ****** LO OYO EL REY, PLOGOL DE CORA%ON;
23737 5ELCID3024 ****** LOOVO A DIO EL BUEN REY DON ALFFONSSO,
23759 5ELCID3027 ****** LO OYO EL REY, POR NADA NON TARDO;
23825 5ELCID3035 GRADO ADIOS, ****** UOS VEO, SE@OR.
24001 5ELCID3059 ACORDADOS FUERON, ****** VINO LA MAN.
24364 5ELCID3107 ****** LO VIERON ENTRAR AL QUE EN BUEN ORA NA%IO,
24738 5ELCID3151 MAS ****** SACARON MIS FIJAS DE VALEN%IA LA MAYOR,
24776 5ELCID3156 ****** DEXARON MIS FIJAS ENEL ROBREDO DE CORPES,
24797 5ELCID3158 DEN ME MIS ESPADAS ****** MYOS YERNOS NON SON.
24849 5ELCID3165 ****** DESONDRA DESUS FIJAS NO NOS DEMANDA OY;
24869 5ELCID3167 DEMOS LE SUS ESPADAS, ****** ASSI FINCA LA BOZ,
24875 5ELCID3168 E ****** LAS TOUIERE, PARTIR SEA LA CORT;
24914 5ELCID3173 ****** LAS DEMANDA & DELLAS HA SABOR,
25147 5ELCID3203 ****** SACARON DE VALEN%IA MIS FIJAS AMAS ADOS,
25178 5ELCID3206 DEN ME MIS AUERES, ****** MYOS YERNOS NON SON.
25305 5ELCID3222 ****** DE NUESTROS AUERES ASSIL PRENDE SABOR;
25323 5ELCID3224 DIXIERON LOS ALCALDES ****** MANFESTADOS SON:
25403 5ELCID3235 ****** ELLOS LOS AN APECHAR, NON GELOS QUIERO YO.
25531 5ELCID3252 MAS ****** ESTO OUO ACABADO, PENSSARON LUEGO DAL.
25623 5ELCID3263 ****** LAS NON QUERIEDES, YA CANES TRAYDORES,
25783 5ELCID3284 CA DE ****** NASCO ADELI%IO FUE CRIADA,
25813 5ELCID3288 ****** PRIS A CABRA, & AUOS POR LA BARBA,
25955 5ELCID3308 MAS ****** ENPIE%A, SABED, NOL DA VAGAR:
26012 5ELCID3316 MIEMBRAT ****** LIDIAMOS %ERCA VALEN%IA LA GRAND;
26127 5ELCID3331 ****** DURMIE MYO %ID & EL LEON SE DESATO?
26201 5ELCID3340 ****** SE TORNO EL BUEN CAMPEADOR,
26264 5ELCID3349 ****** FUERE LA LID, SI PLOGUIERE AL CRIADOR,
26661 5ELCID3405 ****** MELAS DEMANDAN DE NAUARRA & DE ARAGON.
26736 5ELCID3415 ****** AUOS PLAZE, OTORGO LO YO, SE@OR,
26976 5ELCID3447 ****** PIDEN MIS PRIMAS, DON ELUIRA & DO@A SOL,
27117 5ELCID3465 CRAS SEA LA LID, ****** SALIERE EL SOL,
27432 5ELCID3505 ****** TODAS ESTAS NUEUAS ASSI PUESTAS SON,

```
WORD                C#  PREFIX                          CONTEXT

QUANDO (CON'T)

                 27895 5ELCID3559 NON SACASTES NINGUNA ****** CUIEMOS LA CORT.
                 28531 5ELCID3643 ****** LO VIC FERRANGO%ALEZ, CONUUO ATIZON;
                 28640 5ELCID3657 ****** ESTE CCLPE A FERIDO COLACA LA PRE%IADA,
                 28900 5ELCID3691 VEN%UDC ES EL CAMPO, ****** ESTC SE ACABO
                 29153 5ELCID3723 ****** SE@CRAS SON SUS FIJAS DE NAUARRA & DE ARAGON.
        WORD #3391 OCCURS 119 TIMES.
          INDEX OF DIVERSIFICATION =   242.10 WITH STANDARD DEVIATION OF   247.53

QUANDOL          11008 5ELCID1393 TAN GRAND FUE EL GOZO ******* VIERON ASSOMAR.
                 13866 5ELCID1757 ******* VIERCN DE PIE, CUE ERA DESCAUALGADO,
        WORD #3392 OCCURS   2 TIMES.

QUANLES          13148 5ELCID1666 AQUELOS ATAMORES AUOS LCS PONCRAN DELANT & VEREDES ******* SON,
        WORD #3393 OCCURS   1 TIMES.

QUANT            12540 5ELCID1591 DES DIA SE PRE%IO BAUIECA EN ***** GRANT FUE ESPA@A.
                 27421 5ELCID3503 DELO AL TANTC PRISO ***** OUO SABOR.
        WORD #3394 OCCURS   2 TIMES.

QUANTA           20959 5ELCID2663 ****** RIQUIZA TIENE AUER LA YEMOS NOS.
        WORD #3395 OCCURS   1 TIMES.

QUANTAS            497 5ELCID0063 DETODAS COSAS ******* SCN DE UIANDA
                 11165 5ELCID1412 HYTODAS LAS DUE@AS CCN ELLAS ******* BUENAS ELLAS HAN.
        WORD #3396 OCCURS   2 TIMES.

QUANTO             607 5ELCID0077 SI NCN, ****** DEXO NCLO PRE%IO UN FIGO.
                   865 5ELCID0111 RETOUO DELLCS ****** CUE FUE ALGO;
                  1835 5ELCID0233 PORA SAN PERO DE CARDENA ****** PUDO A ESPOLEAR,
                  2596 5ELCID0328 ROGANDC AL CRIADOR ****** ELLA MEIOR SABE,
                  3962 5ELCID0503 NCN PRENDRE DE UOS ****** UALE VN DINERO MALO.
                  4085 5ELCID0519 ESTA QUINTA PCR ****** SERIE CONPRACA,
                  4259 5ELCID0542 VANSSE FENARES ARRIBA ****** PUEDEN ANDAR,
                  4287 5ELCID0546 POR ESSAS TIERRAS AYUSO ****** PUEDEN ANDAR.
                  6100 5ELCID0775 PARA CALATAYUCH ****** PUEDE SE VA.
                  7669 5ELCID0982 TORNOS EL MANCADERO ****** PUDO MAS;
                  7995 5ELCID1021 NCN COMBRE VN BOCADO POR ****** HA EN TODA ESPA@A,
                  8142 5ELCID1038 TANTO ****** YO BIUA, SERE DENT MARAUILLADO.
                  8166 5ELCID1041 MAS ****** AUEDES PERCICO & YO GANE EN CANPO,
                  8183 5ELCID1043 MAS ****** AUEDES PERCICO NCN UCS LO CARE,
                  8499 5ELCID1080 LO QUE NCN FERIE EL CABCSO POR ****** ENEL MUNDO HA,
                  9036 5ELCID1150 PRISIERCN %EBOLA & ****** CUE ES Y ADELANT.
                 10922 5ELCID1382 FATA DENTRC EN MEDINA DENLES ****** HUEBOS LES FUER,
                 10969 5ELCID1388 SOMOS EN SO PRO ****** LO PODEMOS FAR;
                 11571 5ELCID1466 HYD PORA MEDINA ****** LO PUDIEREDES FAR,
                 11629 5ELCID1474 E ****** QUE PUEDEN NCN FINCAN DE ANDAR.
                 12226 5ELCID1552 DE ****** QUE QUISIERCN NON CUIERON FALLA,
                 13283 5ELCID1684 ALEGRE ES MYO %ID PCR ****** FECHO HAN:
                 14862 5ELCID1878 BIEN LOS MANDC SERUIR DE ****** HUEBOS HAN.
                 16189 5ELCID2054 EN ****** PCDEMCS ANDAMCS EN UUESTRO PRO.
                 17583 5ELCID2224 NOLO QUIERO FALIR PCR NADA DE ****** AY PARADO;
                 19259 5ELCID2437 COFIA SOBRE LCS PELCS FRONZIDA DELLA YA ******.
                 20795 5ELCID2641 DE ****** EL FIZIERE YOL DAR POR ELLO BUEN GALARDON.
                 20839 5ELCID2646 AGUIJAN ****** PUEDEN YFANTES DE CARRION;
                 22140 5ELCID2819 ****** EL MEIOR PUEDE ALLI LAS ONDRO.
                 22926 5ELCID2920 SALIEN DE VALEN%IA & ANDAN ****** PUEDEN,
                 24706 5ELCID3147 POR ****** ESTA CORT FIZIESTES POR MI AMOR.
                 25663 5ELCID3268 POR ****** LES FIZIESTES MENOS VALEDES VOS.
                 25744 5ELCID3279 ****** EL DIZE NCN GELO PRE%IAMOS NADA.
                 25995 5ELCID3313 MIENTES, FERRANDO, DE ****** DICHO HAS,
                 26244 5ELCID3346 POR ****** LAS DEXASTES MENOS VALEDES VOS;
                 26279 5ELCID3351 DE ****** HE DICHO VERDADERO SERE YO.
                 26431 5ELCID3371 QUE ERES TRAYDOR & MINTIST DE ****** DICHO HAS.
                 26875 5ELCID3433 DEZIR QUERRIA YA ****** DELC MYO.
                 27383 5ELCID3498 QUE PRENDAN DE SUS AUERES ****** OUIEREN SABOR.
                 27881 5ELCID3557 MUCHO ERAN REPENTIDOS LOS YFANTES POR ****** DADAS SON;
                 27977 5ELCID3570 NOLO QUERRIEN AUER FECHO POR ****** HA EN CARRION.
                 28731 5ELCID3669 POR ****** AUEDES FECHO VEN%IDA AUEDES ESTA BATALLA.
        WORD #3397 OCCURS  42 TIMES.
          INDEX OF DIVERSIFICATION =   684.95 WITH STANDARD DEVIATION OF   613.81

QUANTOS           2419 5ELCID0305 PLOGO ALOS OTROS OMNES TODOS ******* CON EL ESTAN.
                  3695 5ELCID0466 E ESSOS GA@ADOS ******* EN DERREDOR ANDAN.
                  5414 5ELCID0683 ARMADO ES MYO %ID CON ******* QUE EL HA;
                  5859 5ELCID0742 DESI ADELANTE, ******* CUE Y SCN,
                  6352 5ELCID0809 ******* EL TRAE TODCS SCN PAGADOS.
                  9563 5ELCID1215 TODOS ERAN RICOS ******* QUE ALLI HA.
                 12459 5ELCID1581 CON ******* QUE EL PUEDE, QUE CON ORAS SE ACORDARON,
                 15598 5ELCID1978 ******* QUISIESSEN AUERES DORO O DE PLATA.
                 16025 5ELCID2032 ASSI ESTANDO, DEDES ME UUESTRA AMOR, QUE LO OYAN *******
                                  AQUI SON.
                 16242 5ELCID2060 MARAUILLAN SE DE MYO %ID ******* QUE Y SON.
                 16272 5ELCID2064 QUE ADOBASSEN COZINA PORA ******* QUE YSON;
                 16394 5ELCID2079 DELLA & DELLA PARTE, ******* QUE AQUI SON,
                 16738 5ELCID2119 TODOS SON PAGADOS DELAS VISTAS ******* QUE Y SON.
```

WORD C# PREFIX CONTEXT

QUANTOS (CON'T)

18198 5ELCID2302 AMARAUILLA LO HAN ******* QUE YSON,
19198 5ELCID2428 AQUIS CNDRO MYO %ID & ******* CONEL SON.
20174 5ELCID2561 EA MYNAYA ALBARFANEZ & A ******* AQUI SON:
21260 5ELCID2702 CON ******* QUE ELLOS TRAEN Y IAZEN ESSA NOCH,
23842 5ELCID3037 E AL CCNDE DCN ARRICH & A ******* QUE Y SON;
24318 5ELCID3100 ENEL ABRIEN QUE VER ******* QUE Y SON.
24499 5ELCID3123 CATANDO ESTAN A MYO %ID ******* HA EN LA CORT,
27353 5ELCID3495 NOS FARTAN DE CATARLE ******* HA EN LA CORT.
WORD #3398 OCCURS 21 TIMES.
INDEX OF DIVERSIFICATION = 1245.70 WITH STANDARD DEVIATION OF 1104.73

QUARTA 5261 5ELCID0665 ACABO DE TRES SEMANAS, LA ****** QUERIE ENTRAR,
WORD #3399 OCCURS 1 TIMES.

QUATRO 2069 5ELCID0260 POR VN MARCHO QUE DESPENDADES AL MONESTERIO DARE YO ******.
13546 5ELCID1717 ****** MILL MENOS XXX CON MYO %ID VAN A CABO,
13696 5ELCID1735 NON ESCAPARON MAS DE %IENTO & ******.
WORD #3400 OCCURS 3 TIMES.

QUE 55 5ELCID0008 GRADO ATI, SE@OR PADRE, *** ESTAS EN ALTO
145 5ELCID0020 DIOS, *** BUEN VASSALO, SI OUIESSE BUEN SE@OR
186 5ELCID0025 *** A MYO %ID RUY DIAZ, QUE NADI NOL DIESSEN POSADA,
192 5ELCID0025 QUE A MYO %ID RUY DIAZ, *** NADI NOL DIESSEN POSADA,
200 5ELCID0026 E A QUEL *** GELA DIESSE SOPIESSE UERA PALABRA,
206 5ELCID0027 *** PERDERIE LOS AUERES & MAS LOS OIOS DELA CARA,
258 5ELCID0033 POR MIEDO DEL REY ALFONSSO, *** ASSI LO AUIEN PARADO
263 5ELCID0034 *** SI NON LA QUEBRANTAS POR FUERCA, QUE NON GELA ABRIESE NADI.
270 5ELCID0034 QUE SI NON LA QUEBRANTAS POR FUERCA, *** NON GELA ABRIESE NADI.
402 5ELCID0050 YA LO VEE EL %ID *** DEL REY NON AUIE GRA%IA.
457 5ELCID0058 MYO %ID RUY DIAZ, EL *** EN BUEN ORA %INXO ESPADA,
555 5ELCID0070 FABLO MARTIN ATOLINEZ, ODREDES LO *** A DICHO:
577 5ELCID0073 CA ACUSADO SERE DELO *** UOS HE SERUIDO,
617 5ELCID0078 FABLO MYO %ID, EL *** EN BUEN ORA %INXO ESPADA:
647 5ELCID0082 BIEN LO VEDES *** YO NO TRAYO AUER, & HUEBOS ME SERIE
730 5ELCID0092 ENPE@AR GELO HE POR LO *** FUERE GUISADO;
737 5ELCID0093 DE NOCHE LO LIEUEN, *** NON LO VEAN CHISTIANOS.
794 5ELCID0101 EN CUENTA DE SUS AUERES, DELOS *** AUIEN GANADOS.
832 5ELCID0107 *** NON ME DESCUBRADES A MOROS NIN A CHRISTIANOS;
846 5ELCID0108 POR SIEMPRE UOS FARE RICOS, *** NON SEADES MENGUADOS.
866 5ELCID0111 RETOUO DELLOS QUANTO *** FUE ALGO;
874 5ELCID0112 POR EN VINO AAQUESTO POR *** FUE ACUSADO.
887 5ELCID0114 YA LO VEDES *** EL REY LEA AYRADO.
921 5ELCID0118 E PRESTALDE DE AUER LO *** SEA GUISADO.
941 5ELCID0121 *** NON LAS CATEDES EN TODO AQUESTE A@O.
966 5ELCID0124 BIEN LO SABEMOS *** EL ALGO GA@O,
975 5ELCID0125 QUANDO ATIERRA DE MOROS ENTRO, *** GRANT AUER SACO;
996 5ELCID0128 EN LOGAR LAS METAMOS *** NON SEAN VENTADAS.
1006 5ELCID0129 MAS DEZID NOS DEL %ID, DE *** SERA PAGADO,
1010 5ELCID0130 O *** GANAN%IA NOS DARA POR TODO AQUESTE A@O?
1029 5ELCID0132 MYO %ID QUERRA LO *** SSEA AGUISADO;
1064 5ELCID0137 YA VEDES *** ENTRA LA NOCH, EL %ID ES PRESURADO,
1074 5ELCID0138 HUEBOS AUEMOS *** NOS DEDES LOS MARCHOS.
1112 5ELCID0143 E NOS UOS AIUDAREMOS, *** ASSI ES AGUISADO,
1126 5ELCID0145 *** NON LO SEPAN MOROS NON CHRISTIANOS.
1170 5ELCID0151 *** GELO NON VENTANSSEN DE BURGOS OMNE NADO.
1226 5ELCID0158 MIENTRA *** VIVADES NON SEREDES MENGUADOS.
1248 5ELCID0161 *** SOBRE AQUELAS ARCHAS DAR LE YEN VJ %IENTOS MARCOS
1275 5ELCID0164 *** SI ANTES LAS CATASSEN QUE FUESSEN PERIURADOS,
1280 5ELCID0164 QUE SI ANTES LAS CATASSEN *** FUESSEN PERIURADOS,
1313 5ELCID0168 YO YRE CON UUSO, *** ADUGAMOS LOS MARCOS,
1323 5ELCID0169 CA AMOUER A MYO %ID ANTE *** CANTE EL GALLO.
1352 5ELCID0173 CA MIENTRA *** VISQUIESSEN REFECHOS ERAN AMOS.
1398 5ELCID0179 %ID, BESO UUESTRA MANO ENDON *** LA YO AYA.
1471 5ELCID0188 QUANDO ESTO OUO FECHO, ODREDES LO *** FABLAUA:
1485 5ELCID0190 YO, *** ESTO UOS GANE, BIEN MERE%IAS CAL%AS.
1522 5ELCID0195 DE *** FAGADES CAL%AS & RICA PIEL & BUEN MANTO.
1548 5ELCID0198 ATORGAR NOS HEDES ESTO *** AUEMOS PARADO.
1579 5ELCID0202 VINO PORA LA TIENDA DEL *** EN BUEN ORA NASCO;
1602 5ELCID0205 AUN VEA EL DIA *** DEMI AYADES ALGO
1692 5ELCID0217 ATI LO GRADESCO, DIOS, *** %IELO & TIERRA GUIAS;
1709 5ELCID0219 DA QUI QUITO CASTIELLA, PUES *** EL REY HE EN YRA;
1767 5ELCID0225 ESTO & YO EN DEBDO *** FAGA Y CANTAR MILL MISSAS.
1816 5ELCID0231 ANTES SERE CON UUSCO *** EL SOL QUIERA RAYAR.
1892 5ELCID0241 TU *** ATODOS GUIAS, VALA MYO %ID EL CANPEADOR.
1908 5ELCID0243 DIOS, *** ALEGRE FUE EL ABBAT DON SANCHO
1930 5ELCID0245 CON TAN GRANT GOZO RE%IBEN AL *** EN BUEN ORA NASCO.
1946 5ELCID0247 PUES *** AQUI UOS VEO, PRENDET DE MI OSPEDADO.
1976 5ELCID0250 MAS POR *** ME VO DE TIERRA, DOUOS L MARCHOS,
2063 5ELCID0260 POR VN MARCHO *** DESPENDADES AL MONESTERIO DARE YO QUATRO.
2154 5ELCID0271 YO LO VEO *** ESTADES UOS EN YDA
2222 5ELCID0280 YA LO VEDES *** PARTIR NOS EMOS EN VIDA,
2240 5ELCID0282 PLEGA ADIOS & A SANTA MARIA, *** AUN CON MIS MANOS CASE
ESTAS MIS
2250 5ELCID0283 O *** DE VENTURA & ALGUNOS DIAS VIDA,
2332 5ELCID0294 VANSSE PORA SAN PERO DO ESTA EL *** ENBUEN PUNTO NA%IO.

WORD C# PREFIX CONTEXT

QUE (CON'T)

2348 5ELCID0296 QUEL CRE%E CCNPA@A, PCR *** MAS VALDRA,
2380 5ELCID0301 VOS, *** POR MI DEXADES CASAS & HEREDADES,
2389 5ELCID0302 EN ANTES *** YO MUERA, ALGUN BIEN UOS PUEDA FAR:
2398 5ELCID0303 LO *** PERDEDES DCBLADO UOS LO COBRAR.
2409 5ELCID0304 PLOGO A MIO %ID, POR *** CRE%IO EN LA IANTAR,
2436 5ELCID0307 TRES AN POR TRO%IR, %EPADES *** NON MAS.
2447 5ELCID0309 ***, SI DESPUES DEL PLAZO EN SU TIERRAL PUDIES TOMAR,
2600 5ELCID0329 *** AMIO %ID EL CAMPEADOR QUE DIOS LE CURIAS DE MAL:
2605 5ELCID0329 QUE AMIO %ID EL CAMPEADOR *** DIOS LE CURIAS DE MAL:
2615 5ELCID0330 YA SE@OR GLORIOSO, PADRE *** EN %IELO ESTAS,
2724 5ELCID0344 MOSTRANDO LOS MIRACLOS, POR EN AUEMOS *** FABLAR:
2787 5ELCID0352 LONGINOS ERA %IEGO, *** NUQUAS VIO ALGUANDRE,
2876 5ELCID0363 E RUEGO A SAN PEYDRO *** ME AIUDE A ROGAR
2886 5ELCID0364 POR MYO %ID EL CAMPEADOR, *** DIOS LE CURIE DE MAL.
2935 5ELCID0370 LORANDO DE LOS OIOS, *** NON SABE QUE SE FAR.
2938 5ELCID0370 LORANDO DE LOS OIOS, QUE NON SABE *** SE FAR.
2970 5ELCID0374 LORANDO DELOS OIOS, *** NON VIESTES ATAL,
3032 5ELCID0382 DIOS *** NOS DIO LAS ALMAS, CONSEIO NOS DARA.
3054 5ELCID0384 COMMO SIRUA ADO@A XIMENA & ALAS FIJAS *** HA,
3061 5ELCID0385 E A TODAS SUS DUENAS *** CON ELLAS ESTAN;
3069 5ELCID0386 BIEN SEPA EL ABBAT *** BUEN GALARDON DELLO PRENDRA.
3090 5ELCID0389 ABBAT, DEZILDES *** PRENDAN EL RASTRO & PIESSEN DE ANDAR,
3165 5ELCID0398 DE DIESTRO A LILON LAS TORRES, *** MOROS LAS HAN;
3172 5ELCID0399 PASSO PAR ALCOBIELLA *** DE CASTIELLA FINES YA;
3210 5ELCID0404 Y SE ECHAUA MYO %ID DESPUES *** FUE %ENADO,
3243 5ELCID0409 MIENTRA *** VISQUIEREDES BIEN SE FARA LO TO.
3270 5ELCID0412 MUCHO ERA PAGADO DEL SUE@O *** A SO@ADO.
3285 5ELCID0414 ES DIA A DE PLAZO, SEPADES *** NON MAS.
3318 5ELCID0418 SIN LAS PEONADAS & OMNES VALIENTES *** SON,
3323 5ELCID0419 NOTO TREZIENTAS LAN%AS *** TODAS TIENEN PENDONES.
3346 5ELCID0422 PASSAREMOS LA SIERRA *** FIERA ES & GRAND,
3420 5ELCID0432 ANTE *** ANOCHESCA PIENSSAN DE CAUALGAR;
3431 5ELCID0433 POR TAL LO FAZE MYO %ID *** NO IO VENTASSE NADI.
3439 5ELCID0434 ANDIDIERON DE NOCH, *** VAGAR NON SE DAN.
3447 5ELCID0435 ODIZEN CASTEION, EL *** ES SOBRE FENARES,
3459 5ELCID0436 MYO %ID SE ECHO EN %ELADA CON AQUELOS *** EL TRAE.
3469 5ELCID0437 TODA LA NOCHE IAZE EN %ELADA EL *** EN BUEN ORA NASCO,
3494 5ELCID0441 PUES *** A CASTEION SACAREMOS A %ELADA,. . . .
3524 5ELCID0444 LAN%A, CAUALLEROS BUENOS *** ACONPANE@ A MINAYA.
3530 5ELCID0445 AOSADAS CORRED, *** POR MIEDO NON DEXEDES NADA.
3552 5ELCID0448 *** POR MIEDO DE LOS MOROS NON DEXEN NADA.
3602 5ELCID0454 NONBRADOS SON LOS *** YRAN ENEL ALGARA,
3608 5ELCID0455 E LOS *** CON MYO %ID FICARAN EN LA %AGA.
3628 5ELCID0457 YXIE EL SOL, DIOS, *** FERMOSO APUNTAUA
3663 5ELCID0462 CON POCAS DE GENTES *** EN CASTEION FINCARON.
3707 5ELCID0468 LOS *** LA TIENEN, QUANDO VIERON LA REBATA,
3737 5ELCID0472 QUINZE MOROS MATAUA DELOS *** ALCAN%AUA.
3894 5ELCID0494 DA QUESTA QUINTA *** ME AUEDES MANDO,
3917 5ELCID0497 ADIOS LO PROMETO, A AQUEL *** ESTA EN ALTO:
3922 5ELCID0498 FATA *** YO ME PAGE SOBRE MIO BUEN CAUALLO,
3935 5ELCID0500 *** ENPLEYE LA LAN%A & AL ESPADA META MANO,
3968 5ELCID0504 PUES *** POR MI GANAREDES QUES QUIER QUE SEA DALGO,
3974 5ELCID0504 PUES QUE POR MI GANAREDES QUES QUIER *** SEA DALGO,
3993 5ELCID0507 COMIDIOS MYO %ID, EL *** EN BUEN ORA FUE NADO,
4002 5ELCID0508 AL REY ALFONSSO *** LEGARIEN SUS COMPA@AS,
4020 5ELCID0511 SOS QUI@ONEROS *** GELOS DIESSEN POR CARTA.
4090 5ELCID0520 AVN DELO *** DIESSEN OUIESSEN GRAND GANAN%IA.
4123 5ELCID0525 *** ENEL CASTIELLO NON Y AURIE MORADA,
4131 5ELCID0526 E *** SERIE RETENEDOR, MAS NON YAURIE AGUA.
4164 5ELCID0530 LO *** YO DIXIER NON LO TENGADES AMAL:
4201 5ELCID0535 POR *** LO PRIS DELLOS QUE DE MI NON DIGAN MAL.
4205 5ELCID0535 POR QUE LO PRIS DELLOS *** DE MI NON DIGAN MAL.
4232 5ELCID0539 LO *** DIXO EL %ID A TODOS LOS OTROS PLAZ.
4243 5ELCID0540 DEL CASTIELLO *** PRISIERON TODOS RICOS SE PARTEN;
4302 5ELCID0548 GRANDES SON LAS GANAN%IAS *** PRISO POR LA TIERRA DO UA.
4316 5ELCID0549 NON LO SABEN LOS MOROS EL ARDIMENT *** AN.
4338 5ELCID0552 PASSO A BOUIERCA & ATECA *** ES ADELANT,
4391 5ELCID0559 EL BUEN CANPEADOR *** EN BUEN ORA NASCO,
4411 5ELCID0562 *** DE DIA NIN DE NOCH NON LES DIESSEN AREBATA,
4421 5ELCID0563 *** SOPIESSEN QUE MYO %ID ALLI AUIE FINCAN%A.
4423 5ELCID0563 QUE SOPIESSEN *** MYO %ID ALLI AUIE FINCAN%A.
4436 5ELCID0565 *** EL CAMPEADOR MYO %ID ALLI AUIE POBLADO,
4515 5ELCID0574 QUANDO VIO MYO %ID *** ALCO%ER NON SELE DAUA;
4678 5ELCID0593 ABIERTAS DEXAN LAS PUERTAS *** NINGUNO NON LAS GUARDA.
4690 5ELCID0595 VIO *** ENTRELLOS & EL CASTIELLO MUCHO AUIE GRAND PLA%A;
4730 5ELCID0600 DIOS, *** BUENO ES EL GOZO POR AQUESTA MA@ANA
4782 5ELCID0606 DANDO GRANDES ALARIDOS LOS *** ESTAN EN LA %ELADA,
4825 5ELCID0611 VINO PERO VERMUEZ, *** LA SE@A TEINE EN MANO,
4845 5ELCID0613 FABLO MYO %ID RUY DIAZ, EL *** EN BUEN ORA FUE NADO:
4898 5ELCID0620 *** LOS DESCABE%EMOS NADA NON GANAREMOS;
4933 5ELCID0624 FIZO ENBIAR POR LA TIENDA *** DEXARA ALLA.
4960 5ELCID0628 *** A VNO QUE DIZIEN MYO %ID RUY DIAZ DE BIUAR
4963 5ELCID0628 QUE A VNO *** DIZIEN MYO %ID RUY DIAZ DE BIUAR
5008 5ELCID0633 PERDERAS CALATAYUTH, *** NON PUEDE ESCAPAR,

WORD C# PREFIX CONTEXT

QUE (CON'T)

5023 5ELCID0635 ASSI FFERA LO DE SILOCA, *** ES DEL OTRA PART.
5068 5ELCID0640 CON LOS DELA FRONTERA *** UOS AIUDARAN,
5078 5ELCID0642 POR *** SEME ENTRO EN MI TIERRA DERECHO ME AURA ADAR.
5135 5ELCID0649 YXIERON DE %ELFA LA *** DIZEN DE CANAL,
5142 5ELCID0650 ANDIDIERON TODOL DIA, *** VAGAR NON SE DAN,
5170 5ELCID0654 CON AQUESTOS DOS REYES *** DIZEN FFARIZ & GALUE;
5200 5ELCID0658 LAS AROBDAS, *** LOS MOROS SACAN, DE DIA
5241 5ELCID0663 EL *** EN BUEN ORA NASCO FIRME GELO VEDAUA.
5282 5ELCID0668 *** NOS QUERAMOS YR DE NOCH NO NOS LO CONSINTRAN;
5346 5ELCID0675 EN EL NOBRE DEL CRIADOR, *** NON PASE POR AL:
5387 5ELCID0680 *** NON SOPIESSE NINGUNO ESTA SU PORIDAD.
5415 5ELCID0683 ARMADO ES MYO %ID CON QUANTOS *** EL HA;
5427 5ELCID0685 TODOS YSCAMOS FUERA, *** NADI NON RASTE,
5510 5ELCID0695 *** PRIESSA VA EN LOS MOROS, E TORNARON SE A ARMAR;
5584 5ELCID0703 NON DERANCHE NINGUNO FATA *** YO LO MANDE.
5620 5ELCID0708 LOS *** EL DEBDO AUEDES VEREMOS COMMO LA ACORREDES.
5703 5ELCID0719 A GRANDES VOZES LAMA EL *** EN BUEN ORA NASCO:
5747 5ELCID0725 ALA TORNADA *** FAZEN OTROS TANTOS SON.
5828 5ELCID0737 MU@O GUSTIOZ, *** FUE SO CRIADO,
5835 5ELCID0738 MARTIN MU@OZ, EL *** MANDO A MONT MAYOR,
5860 5ELCID0742 DESI ADELANTE, QUANTOS *** Y SON,
5910 5ELCID0749 ACOSTOS AVN AGUAZIL *** TENIE BUEN CAUALLO,
5977 5ELCID0758 ALOS *** ALCAN%A VALOS DELIBRANDO.
5986 5ELCID0759 MYO %ID RUY DIAZ, EL *** EN BUEN ORA NASCO,
6048 5ELCID0767 CORTOL EL YELMO, *** LEGO ALA CARNE;
6145 5ELCID0783 *** A CASTIELLA YRAN BUENOS MANDADOS,
6151 5ELCID0784 *** MYO %ID RUY DIAZ LIO CAMPAL A VEN%IDA.
6164 5ELCID0785 TANTOS MOROS YAZEN MUERTOS *** POCOS BIUOS A DEXADOS,
6181 5ELCID0787 YAS TORNAN LOS DEL *** EN BUEN ORA NASCO.
6219 5ELCID0792 GRADO A DIOS, A QUEL *** ESTA EN ALTO,
6275 5ELCID0799 TRAEN ORO & PLATA *** NON SABEN RECABDO;
6330 5ELCID0806 DIOS, *** BIEN PAGO A TODOS SUS VASSALLOS,
6347 5ELCID0808 BIEN LO AGUISA EL *** EN BUEN ORA NASCO,
6366 5ELCID0811 DAQUESTA RIQUEZA *** EL CRIADOR NOS ADADO
6387 5ELCID0814 DESTA BATALLA *** AUEMOS ARANCADA;
6393 5ELCID0815 AL REY ALFONSSSO *** ME A AYRADO
6431 5ELCID0821 *** NADA NOL MINGUAUA;
6444 5ELCID0823 LO *** ROMANE%IERE DALDO A MI MUGIER & A MIS FIJAS,
6454 5ELCID0824 *** RUEGEN POR MI LAS NOCHES & LOS DIAS;
6529 5ELCID0833 SI NON, DO SOPIEREDES *** SOMOS, YNDOS CONSEGUIR.
6606 5ELCID0843 E LOS DE CALATAYUT, *** ES MAS ONDRADA,
6636 5ELCID0847 *** BIEN PAGO A SUS VASSALOS MISMOS
6761 5ELCID0863 Y FFINCO EN VN POYO *** ES SOBRE MONT REAL;
6789 5ELCID0867 DESI A MOLINA, *** ES DEL OTRA PART,
6797 5ELCID0868 LA TER%ERA TERUEL, *** ESTAUA DELANT;
6848 5ELCID0875 MYO %ID RUY DIAZ, *** EN BUEN ORA CINXO ESPADA. . .
6898 5ELCID0882 OMNE AYRADO, *** DE SE@OR NON HA GRA%IA,
6913 5ELCID0884 MAS DESPUES *** DE MOROS FUE, PRENDO ESTA PRESENTAIA;
6926 5ELCID0885 AUN ME PLAZE DE MYO %ID *** FIZO TAL GANAN%IA.
6970 5ELCID0891 DE TODO MYO REYNO LOS *** LO QUISIEREN FAR,
7031 5ELCID0899 QUIERO UOS DEZIR DEL *** EN BUEN ORA NASCO & %INXO ESPADA:
7045 5ELCID0901 MIENTRA *** SEA EL PUEBLO DE MOROS & DELA YENTE CHRISTIANA,
7101 5ELCID0908 QUANDO VIO EL CABOSO *** SE TARDAUA MINAYA,
7160 5ELCID0917 DOZIENTOS CON EL, *** TODOS %INEN ESPADAS;
7197 5ELCID0922 TODO GELO DIZE, *** NOL ENCUBRE NADA.
7227 5ELCID0927 *** MINAYA ALBARFANEZ ASSI ERA LEGADO,
7246 5ELCID0929 E DE SUS COMPA@AS, AQUELAS *** AUIEN DEXADAS
7256 5ELCID0931 *** ALBARFANEZ PAGO LAS MILL MISSAS,
7292 5ELCID0935 NON LO TARDO EL *** EN BUEN ORA NASCO,
7335 5ELCID0941 POR *** DAN PARIAS PLAZE ALOS DE SARAGO%A,
7347 5ELCID0942 DE MYO %ID RUY DIAZ *** NON TEMIEN NINGUNA FONTA.
7376 5ELCID0946 SONRRISOS EL CABOSO, *** NON LO PUDO ENDURAR:
7442 5ELCID0955 *** EL SALIDO DE CASTIELLA ASILOS TRAE TAN MAL.
7463 5ELCID0958 *** MYO %ID RUY DIAZ QUEL CORRIE LA TIERRA TODA;
7520 5ELCID0964 AGORA CORREM LAS TIERRAS *** EN MI ENPARA ESTAN;
7588 5ELCID0972 ASI VIENE ES FOR%ADO *** EL CONDE AMANOS SELE CUYDO TOMAR.
7680 5ELCID0984 *** A MENOS DE BATALLA NOS PUEDEN DEN QUITAR.
7776 5ELCID0996 ANTES *** ELLOS LEGEN A LA@O, PRESENTEMOS LES LAS LAN%AS;
7787 5ELCID0997 POR VNO *** FIRGADES, TRES SIELLAS YRAN VAZIAS.
7851 5ELCID1004 MANDO LOS FERIR MYO %ID, EL *** EN BUEN ORA NASCO;
7889 5ELCID1008 VEN%IDO A ESTA BATALLA EL *** EN BUEN ORA NASCO,
7906 5ELCID1010 HY GA@O A COLADA *** MAS VALE DE MILL MARCOS DE PLATA.
8009 5ELCID1023 PUES *** TALES MAL CAL%ADOS ME VEN%IERON DE BATALLA.
8023 5ELCID1024 MYO %ID RUY DIAZ ODREDES LO *** DIXO:
8035 5ELCID1026 SI LO *** DIGO FIZIEREDES, SALDREDES DE CATIUO;
8062 5ELCID1029 *** YO DEXAR ME MORIR, QUE NON QUIERO COMER.
8067 5ELCID1029 QUE YO DEXAR ME MORIR, *** NON QUIERO COMER.
8138 5ELCID1037 SI LO FIZIEREDES, %ID, LO *** AUEDES FABLADO,
8199 5ELCID1045 *** COMIGO ANDAN LAZRADOS, & NON UOS LO DARE.
8226 5ELCID1048 COMMO *** YRA A DE REY & DE TIERRA ES ECHADO.
8256 5ELCID1051 CON LOS CAUALLEROS *** EL %ID LE AUIE DADOS
8267 5ELCID1052 COMIENDO VA EL CONDE DIOS, *** DE BUEN GRADO
8274 5ELCID1053 SOBREL SEDIE EL *** EN BUEN ORA NASCO:
8317 5ELCID1058 PAGADO ES MYO %ID, *** LO ESTA AGUARDANDO,

WORD C# PREFIX CONTEXT

QUE (CON'T)

```
8322 5ELCID1059 POR *** EL CONDE DON REMONT TAN BIEN BOLUIE LAS MANOS.
8351 5ELCID1062 DEL DIA *** FUE CONDE NON IANTE TAN DE BUEN GRADO,
8362 5ELCID1063 EL SABOR *** DED E NON SERA OLBIDADO.
8413 5ELCID1069 EN GRADO UOS LO TENGO LO *** ME AUEDES DEXADO.
8421 5ELCID1070 SI UOS VINIERE EMIENTE *** QUISIEREDES VENGALO,
8487 5ELCID1079 MYEDO YUA AUIENDO *** MYO %ID SE REPINTRA,
8493 5ELCID1080 LO *** NON FERIE EL CABOSO POR QUANTO ENEL MUNDO HA,
8529 5ELCID1084 DE LA GANAN%IA *** AN FECHA MARAUILLOSA & GRAND.
8550 5ELCID1086 TAN RICOS SON LOS SOS *** NON SABEN QUE SE AN.
8553 5ELCID1086 TAN RICOS SON LOS SOS QUE NON SABEN *** SE AN.
8617 5ELCID1094 AIUDOL EL CRIADOR, EL SE@NOR *** ES EN %IELO.
8632 5ELCID1096 YA VIE MYO %ID *** DIOS LE YUA VALIENDO.
8715 5ELCID1107 VAYAN LOS MANDADOS POR LOS *** NOS DEUEN AIUDAR,
8749 5ELCID1112 YO FIO POR DIOS *** EN NUESTRO PRO ENADRAN.
8760 5ELCID1114 EL *** EN BUEN ORA NASCO COMPE%O DE FABLAR:
8776 5ELCID1116 DESPUES *** NOS PARTIEMOS DELA LINPIA CHRISTIANDAD,
8845 5ELCID1126 ALI PARE%RA EL *** MERE%E LA SOLDADA.
8850 5ELCID1127 OYD *** DIXO MINAYA ALBARFANEZ:
8857 5ELCID1128 CAMPEADOR, FAGAMOS LO *** AUOS PLAZE.
8865 5ELCID1129 A MI DEDES C CAUALLEROS, *** NON UOS PIDO MAS,
8880 5ELCID1131 BIEN LOS FERREDES, *** DUBDA NON Y AURA,
8923 5ELCID1136 QUIS CADA VNO DELLOS BIEN SABE LO *** HA DE FAR.
9006 5ELCID1146 GRAND ES EL GOZO *** VA POR ES LOGAR.
9028 5ELCID1149 GRANDES SON LAS GANAN%IAS *** MIO %ID FECHAS HA.
9037 5ELCID1150 PRISIERON %EBOLA & QUANTO *** ES Y ADELANT.
9062 5ELCID1153 ENTRAUAN A MURUIEDRO CON ESTAS GANAN%IAS *** TRAEN GRANDES.
9077 5ELCID1155 MIEDO AN EN VALEN%IA *** NON SABEN QUESE FAR.
9098 5ELCID1158 *** DIOS LE AIUDARA & FIZIERA ESTA ARRANCADA.
9230 5ELCID1174 MAL SE AQUEXAN LOS DE VALEN%IA *** NON SABENT QUES FAR,
9238 5ELCID1175 DE NINGUNA PART *** SEA NON LES VINIE PAN;
9359 5ELCID1190 VINIESSE A MYO %ID *** A SABOR DE CAUALGAR;
9400 5ELCID1195 ESTO DIXO MYO %ID EL *** EN BUEN ORA NASCO.
9475 5ELCID1204 BIEN LA %ERCA MYO %ID, *** NON Y AUYA HART;
9499 5ELCID1207 MAS LE VIENEN A MYO %ID, SABET, *** NOS LE VAN.
9526 5ELCID1211 GRANDES SON LOS GOZOS *** VAN POR ES LOGAR,
9542 5ELCID1213 LOS *** FUERON DE PIE CAUALLEROS SE FAZEN;
9564 5ELCID1215 TODOS ERAN RICOS QUANTOS *** ALLI HA.
9597 5ELCID1219 ALEGRE ERA EL CAMPEADOR CON TODOS LOS *** HA,
9623 5ELCID1223 *** PRESA ES VALEN%IA, QUE NON GELA ENPARAN;
9627 5ELCID1223 QUE PRESA ES VALEN%IA, *** NON GELA ENPARAN;
9732 5ELCID1237 CON MYO %ID RUY DIAZ, EL *** EN BUEN ORA NASCO.
9757 5ELCID1240 POR AMOR DE REY ALFFONSSO, *** DE TIERRA ME A ECHADO,
9774 5ELCID1242 E *** FABLASSEN DESTO MOROS & CHRISTIANOS.
9792 5ELCID1244 CON EL MYNAYA ALBARFFANEZ *** NOS LE PARTE DE SO BRA%O.
9800 5ELCID1245 LOS *** EXIERON DE TIERRA DE RITAD SON ABONDADOS,
9817 5ELCID1247 DE *** SON PAGADOS; EL AMOR DE MY %ID YA LO YUAN PROUANDO.
9830 5ELCID1248 LOS *** FUERON CON EL, & LOS DE DESPUES, TODOS SON PAGADOS;
9847 5ELCID1249 VELLO MYO %ID CON LOS AVERES *** AUIEN TOMADOS,
9850 5ELCID1250 *** SIS PUDIESSEN YR, FER LO YEN DE GRADO.
9867 5ELCID1252 *** NINGUN OMNE DELOS SOS QUES LE NON SPIDIES, ONOL BESAS
                LA MANO,
9916 5ELCID1258 DELOS *** SON AQUI & COMIGO GANARON ALGO;
9932 5ELCID1260 *** SI ALGUNOS FURTARE O MENOS LE FALLAREN, EL AUER ME
                AURA ATORNAR
9948 5ELCID1261 AQUESTOS MYOS VASSALOS *** CURIAN A VALEN%IA & ANDAN AROBDANDO.
10048 5ELCID1273 DESTAS MIS GANAN%IAS, *** AUEMOS FECHAS ACA,
10107 5ELCID1280 DE GUISA YRAN POR ELLAS *** AGRAND ONDRA VERNAN
10114 5ELCID1281 AESTAS TIERRAS ESTRANAS *** NOS PUDIEMOS GANAR.
10157 5ELCID1286 E *** LOS DIESSE AL ABBAT DON SANCHO.
10217 5ELCID1294 *** SIS FARTAS LIDIANDO & FIRIENDO CON SUS MANOS,
10248 5ELCID1297 OYD, MINAYA ALBARFANEZ, POR AQUEL *** ESTA EN ALTO,
10287 5ELCID1302 PLOGO A ALBARFANEZ DELO *** DIXO DON RODRIGO.
10308 5ELCID1305  DIOS, *** ALEGRE ERA TODA CHRISTIANISMO,
10313 5ELCID1306 *** EN TIERRAS DE VALEN%IA SE@OR AVIE OBISPO
10482 5ELCID1328 PRISO A ALMENAR & A MURUIEDRO *** ES MIYOR,
10494 5ELCID1330 E PE@A CADIELLA, *** ES VNA PE@A FUERT;
10557 5ELCID1338 BESA UOS LAS MANOS & *** LOS PRENDADES UOS;
10599 5ELCID1343 E PLAZEM DELAS NUEUAS *** FAZE EL CAMPEADOR;
10619 5ELCID1346 SEMEIA *** EN TIERRA DE MOROS NON A BIUO OMNE,
10646 5ELCID1349 *** ENTODAS GUISAS MIIOR ME SIRUE QUE UOS.
10652 5ELCID1349 QUE ENTODAS GUISAS MIIOR ME SIRUE *** UOS.
10707 5ELCID1356 HYO LES MANDARE DAR CONDUCHO MIENTRA *** POR MJ TIERRA FUEREN,
10749 5ELCID1361 NON QUIERO *** NADA PIERDA EL CAMPEADOR;
10757 5ELCID1362 ATODAS LAS ESCUELLAS *** A EL DIZEN SE@OR
10763 5ELCID1363 POR *** LOS DESEREDE, TODO GELO SUELTO YO;
10791 5ELCID1366 POR TAL FAGO AQUESTO *** SIRUAN ASO SE@OR.
10808 5ELCID1369 LOS *** QUISIEREN YR SEUIR AL CAMPEADOR
10828 5ELCID1371 MAS GANAREMOS EN ESTO *** EN OTRA DESONOR.
10905 5ELCID1380 LEUEDES VN PORTERO, TENGO *** UOS AURA PRO;
10975 5ELCID1389 EL %ID *** BIEN NOS QUIERA NADA NON PERDERA.
10988 5ELCID1390 RESPUSO MYNAYA: ESTO NON MEA POR *** PESAR.
11069 5ELCID1401 POR LEUAROS A VALEN%IA *** AUEMOS POR HEREDAD.
11085 5ELCID1403 TODO SERIE ALEGRE, *** NON AURIE NINGUN PESAR.
11112 5ELCID1407 DEZID AL CANPEADOR, *** DIOS LE CURIE DE MAL,
11118 5ELCID1408 *** SU MUGIER & SUS FIJAS EL REY SUELTAS ME LAS HA,
11131 5ELCID1409 MIENTRA *** FUEREMOS POR SUS TIERRAS CONDUCHO NOS MANDO DAR.
```

WORD C# PREFIX CONTEXT

QUE (CON'T)

11157 5ELCID1411 SEREMOS YO & SU MUGIER & SUS FIJAS *** EL A
11199 5ELCID1417 *** LES TOUIESSE PRO ROGAUAN A ALBARFANEZ;
11224 5ELCID1420 E EL SE TENIE C *** ADUXIERA DALLA;
11249 5ELCID1423 DELOS OTROS QUINIENTOS DEZIR UOS HE *** FAZE:
11259 5ELCID1424 MINAYA A DO@A XIMINA & A SUS FIJAS *** HA,
11265 5ELCID1425 E ALAS OTRAS DUE@AS *** LAS SIRUEN DELANT,
11279 5ELCID1427 DELOS MEIORES GUARIMIENTOS *** EN BURGOS PUDO FALAR,
11287 5ELCID1428 PALAFRES & MULAS, *** NON PARESCAN MAL.
11331 5ELCID1434 SOLTARIEMOS LA GANAN%IA, *** NOS DIESSE EL CABDAL.
11349 5ELCID1436 POR LO *** AUEDES FECHO BUEN COSIMENT Y AURA.
11445 5ELCID1449 EL PORTERO CON ELLOS *** LOS HA DE AGUARDAR;
11477 5ELCID1454 AL ORA *** LO SOPO MYO %ID EL DE BIUAR,
11488 5ELCID1453 DIREUOS DELOS CAUALLEROS *** LEUARON EL MENSSAIE:
11550 5ELCID1463 VAYADES A MOLINA, *** IAZE MAS ADELANT,
11603 5ELCID1470 E YO FINCARE EN VALEN%IA, *** MUCHO COSTADOM HA;
11630 5ELCID1474 E QUANTO *** PUEDEN NON FINCAN DE ANDAR.
11665 5ELCID1478 SALIOLOS RE%EBIR CON GRANT GOZO *** FAZE:
11699 5ELCID1483 CO %IENTO CAUALLEROS *** PRIUADOL ACORRADES;
11710 5ELCID1485 *** VAYADES POR ELLAS, ADUGADES GELAS ACA,
11754 5ELCID1491 PASSAN LAS MONTANAS, *** SON FIERAS & GRANDES,
11766 5ELCID1492 PASSARON MATA DE TORANZ DE TAL GUISA *** NINGUN MIEDO NON HAN,
11791 5ELCID1495 ENVIO DOS CAUALLEROS MYNAYA ALBARFANEZ *** SOPIESSE LA VERDAD;
11827 5ELCID1499 AFEUOS AQUI PERO VERMUEZ & MU@O GUSTIOZ *** UOS QUIEREN SIN HART,
11852 5ELCID1502 E EL ALCAYAZ AUEGALUON CON SUS FUER%AS *** TRAHE,
11878 5ELCID1506 ESSO FFUE APRIESSA FECHO, *** NOS QUIEREN DETARDAR.
11886 5ELCID1507 BIEN SALIERON DEN %IENTO *** NON PARE%EN MAL,
11912 5ELCID1510 E EN LAS MANOS LAN%AS *** PENDONES TRAEN,
11915 5ELCID1511 *** SOPIENSSEN LES OTROS DE QUE SESO ERA ALBARFANEZ
11920 5ELCID1511 QUE SOPIENSSEN LES OTROS DE *** SESO ERA ALBARFANEZ
11933 5ELCID1512 O CUEMO SALIERA DE CASTIELLA ALBARFANEZ CON ESTAS DUE@AS *** TRAHE.
11936 5ELCID1513 LOS *** YUAN MESURANDO & LEGANDO DELANT
12018 5ELCID1524 MAGER *** MAL LE QUERAMOS, NON GELO PODREMOS FER,
12066 5ELCID1530 DESTO *** AUEDES FECHO UOS NON PERDEREDES NADA.
12103 5ELCID1535 TODOS FUERON ALEGRES DEL %ERUI%IO *** TOMARON,
12172 5ELCID1545 VINIERON A MOLINA, LA *** AUEGALUON MANDAUA.
12196 5ELCID1548 E BUEN CAUALLO EN DIESTRO *** UA ANTE SUS ARMAS.
12227 5ELCID1552 DE QUANTO *** QUISIERON NON OUIERON FALLA,
12262 5ELCID1557 LOS SOS DESPENDIE EL MORO, *** DELO SO NON TOMAUA NADA.
12286 5ELCID1560 AMYO %ID, EL *** EN BUEN ORA NASCO,
12302 5ELCID1562 ALEGRE FUE MYO %ID, *** NUNCUA MAS NIN TANTO,
12309 5ELCID1563 CA DELO *** MAS AMAUA YAL VIENE EL MANDADO.
12321 5ELCID1565 *** RE%IBAN A MYANAYA & ALAS DUENAS FIJAS DALGO;
12340 5ELCID1567 CA BIEN SABE *** ALBARFANEZ TRAHE TODO RECABDO;
12365 5ELCID1570 MANDO MYO %ID ALOS *** HA EN SU CASA
12370 5ELCID1571 *** GUARDASSEN EL ALCA%AR & LAS OTRAS TORRES ALTAS
12403 5ELCID1574 AVN NON SABIE MYO %ID, EL *** EN BUEN ORA %INXO ESPADA,
12460 5ELCID1581 CON QUANTOS *** EL PUEDE, QUE CON ORAS SE ACORDARON,
12463 5ELCID1581 CON QUANTOS QUE EL PUEDE, *** CON ORAS SE ACORDARON,
12485 5ELCID1584 EL *** EN BUEN ORA NASCO NON LO DETARDAUA:
12612 5ELCID1600 DEL GOZO *** AUIEN DE LOS SOS OIOS LORAUAN.
12634 5ELCID1603 OYD LO *** DIXO EL QUE EN BUEN ORA NASCO:
12637 5ELCID1603 OYD LO QUE DIXO EL *** EN BUEN ORA NASCO:
12665 5ELCID1607 EN ESTA HEREDAD *** UOS YO HE GANADA.
12753 5ELCID1619 EL YUIERNO ES EXIDO, *** EL MAR%O QUIERE ENTRAR.
12771 5ELCID1621 DE AQUEL REY YUCEF *** EN MARRUECOS ESTA.
12785 5ELCID1623 *** EN MIS HEREDADES FUERTE MIETRE ES MIETDO,
12847 5ELCID1630 LEGARON A VALEN%IA, LA *** MYO %ID A CONQUISTA,
12877 5ELCID1634 TODO EL BIEN *** YO HE, TODO LO TENGO DELANT:
12914 5ELCID1638 MIS FIJAS & MI MUGIER *** LAS TENGO ACA;
12991 5ELCID1648 RIQUEZA ES *** NOS A CRE%E MARAUILLOSA & GRAND;
12999 5ELCID1649 APOCO *** VINIESTES, PRESEND UOS QUIEREN DAR:
13035 5ELCID1653 NON AYADES PAUOR POR *** ME VEADES LIDIAR,
13053 5ELCID1655 CRE%EM EL CORACON POR *** ESTADES DELANT,
13112 5ELCID1662 DEL DIA *** NASQUIERAN NON VIERAN TAL TREMOR.
13168 5ELCID1669 VOCA%ION ES *** FIZO EL %ID CAMPEADOR.
13265 5ELCID1682 TORNADOS SON A MYO %ID LOS *** COMIEN SO PAN;
13339 5ELCID1691 MAS VALE *** NOS LOS VEZCAMOS, QUE ELLOS COIAN EL PAN.
13343 5ELCID1691 MAS VALE QUE NOS LOS VEZCAMOS, *** ELLOS COIAN EL PAN.
13440 5ELCID1704 EL *** A QUI MURIERE LIDIANDO DE CARA,
13484 5ELCID1709 LAS FERIDAS PRIMERAS *** LAS AYA YO OTORGADAS.
13598 5ELCID1723 ATANTOS MATA DE MOROS *** NON FUERON CONTADOS;
13656 5ELCID1730 DESDALLI SE TORNO EL *** EN BUEN ORA NASCO,
13665 5ELCID1731 MUCHO ERA ALEGRE DELO *** AN CA%ADO.
13727 5ELCID1740 *** DIOS LES OUO MER%ED QUE VEN%IERON EL CAMPO.
13732 5ELCID1740 QUE DIOS LES OUO MER%ED *** VEN%IERON EL CAMPO.
13762 5ELCID1744 FRONZIDA TRAHE LA CARA, *** ERA DESARMADO,
13778 5ELCID1746 RE%IBIEN LO LAS DUE@AS *** LO ESTAN ESPERANDO.
13847 5ELCID1754 ROGAND AL CRIADOR *** UOS BIUA ALGUNT A@O,
13870 5ELCID1757 QUANDOL VIERON DE PIE, *** ERA DESCAUALGADO,
13881 5ELCID1758 LAS DUE@AS & LAS FIJAS & LA MUGIER *** VALE ALGO
13924 5ELCID1764 ESTAS DUE@AS *** ADUXIESTES, QUE UOS SIRUEN TANTO,
13926 5ELCID1764 ESTAS DUE@AS QUE ADUXIESTES, *** UOS SIRUEN TANTO,
13947 5ELCID1767 *** LO SEPAN EN CASTIELLA, AQUIEN SIRUIERON TANTO.
13976 5ELCID1770 GRANT FUE EL ALEGRIA *** FUE POR EL PALA%IO;

WORD C# PREFIX CONTEXT

QUE (CON'T)

14012 5ELCID1775 TANTO FALLAN DESTO *** ES COSA SOBEIANO.
14020 5ELCID1776 QUIERO UOS DEZIR LO *** ES MAS GRANADO:
14034 5ELCID1778 *** ANDAN ARRIADOS & NON HA QUI TOMALOS,
14086 5ELCID1784 *** A GANADO MYO %ID CON TODOS SUS VASSALLOS
14101 5ELCID1785 LA TIENDA DEL REY DE MARRUECOS, *** DELAS OTRAS ES CABO,
14119 5ELCID1787 MANDO MYO %ID RUY DIAZ *** FITA SOUIESSE LA TIENDA,
14134 5ELCID1789 TAL TIENDA COMMO ESTA, *** DE MARUECOS ES PASSADA,
14145 5ELCID1791 *** CROUIESSE SOS NUEUAS DE MYO %ID QUE AUIE ALGO.
14152 5ELCID1791 QUE CRCUIESSE SOS NUEUAS DE MYO %ID *** AUIE ALGO.
14185 5ELCID1795 NON TIENE EN CUENTA LOS MOROS *** HA MATADOS;
14189 5ELCID1796 LO *** CAYE AEL MUCHO ERA SOBEIANO:
14200 5ELCID1797 MYO %ID DON RODRIGO, EL *** EN BUEN ORA NASCO,
14243 5ELCID1802 E TODAS LAS OTRAS DUENAS *** TIENEN POR CASADAS.
14264 5ELCID1805 DELO *** AUOS CAYO VOS NON GRADE%EDES NADA;
14280 5ELCID1807 PRENDED LO *** QUISIEREDES, LO OTRO REMANGA.
14299 5ELCID1809 CON CAUALLOS DESTA QUINTA *** YO HE GANADA,
14323 5ELCID1812 POR *** ASSI LAS ENBIO DOND ELLAS SON PAGADAS,
14337 5ELCID1814 *** NON DIGA MAL EL REY ALFONSSO DEL QUE VALEN%IA MANDA.
14345 5ELCID1814 QUE NON DIGA MAL EL REY ALFONSSO DEL *** VALEN%IA MANDA.
14352 5ELCID1815 MANDO A PERO VERMUEZ *** FUESSE CON MYNAYA.
14372 5ELCID1818 CON SALUDES DEL %ID *** LAS MANOS LE BESAUA:
14379 5ELCID1819 DESTA LID *** HA ARRANCADA CC CAUALLOS LE ENBIAUA ENPRESENTAIA,
14393 5ELCID1820 E SERUIR LO HE SIENPRE MIENTRA *** OUISSE EL ALMA.
14407 5ELCID1822 TALLES GANAN%IAS TRAEN *** SON A AGUARDAR.
14422 5ELCID1824 *** LAS OTRAS TIERRAS PARTE.
14460 5ELCID1829 *** MANDASSE RE%EBIR A ESTA CONPA@A:
14500 5ELCID1834 AUER ESTOS MENSAIES DEL *** EN BUEN ORA NASCO.
14532 5ELCID1838 ADIO LO AUIEN LOS DEL *** EN BUEN ORA NASCO,
14539 5ELCID1839 CUEDAN SE *** ES ALMOFALLA, CA NON VIENEN CON MANDADO;
14618 5ELCID1849 POCOS DIAS HA, REY, *** VNA LID A ARRANCADO:
14639 5ELCID1852 LAS GANAN%IAS *** FIZO MUCHO SON SOBEIANAS,
14673 5ELCID1856 GRADESCOLO A MYO %ID *** TAL DON ME HA ENBIADO;
14682 5ELCID1857 AVN VEA ORA *** DE MI SEA PAGADO.
14718 5ELCID1861 MARAUILLA ES DEL %ID, *** SU ONDRA CRE%E TANTO
14726 5ELCID1862 EN LA ONDRA *** EL HA NOS SEREMOS ABILTADOS;
14751 5ELCID1865 POR ESTO *** EL FAZE NOS ABREMOS ENBARGO.
14818 5ELCID1873 *** BIEN PARESCADES ANTE RUY DIAZ MYO %ID;
14924 5ELCID1887 *** NOS DEMANDEDES FIJAS DEL CAMPEADOR;
15059 5ELCID1904 *** GELO DIGADES ALBUEN CAMPEADOR:
15089 5ELCID1908 ROGAR GELO EMOS LO *** DEZIDES UOS;
15097 5ELCID1909 DESPUES FAGA EL %ID LO *** OUIERE SABOR.
15105 5ELCID1910 DEZID A RUY DIAZ, EL *** EN BUEN ORA NASCO,
15240 5ELCID1930 *** GELO CONSSEIAUA DALMA & DE CORA%ON.
15281 5ELCID1935 CON GRAND AFAN GANE LO *** HE YO;
15287 5ELCID1936 ADIOS LO GRADESCO *** DEL REY HE SU GRA%IA,
15323 5ELCID1940 MAS PUES LO CONSEIA EL *** MAS VALE QUE NOS,
15326 5ELCID1940 MAS PUES LO CONSEIA EL QUE MAS VALE *** NOS,
15340 5ELCID1942 AFE DIOS DEL %IELLO *** NOS ACUERDE EN LO MIIOR.
15352 5ELCID1944 *** UOS VERNIE AVISTAS DO OUIESSEDES SABOR;
15419 5ELCID1953 MAS LO *** EL QUISIERE, ESSO QUERAMOS NOS.
15427 5ELCID1954 SOBRE TAIO, *** ES UNA AGUA CABDAL,
15451 5ELCID1958 LO *** EL REY QUISIERE, ESSO FERA EL CAMPEADOR.
15479 5ELCID1961 SALUDAD ME MAYO %ID, EL *** EN BUEN ORA %INXO ESPADA;
15525 5ELCID1967 E TANTO PALAFRE *** BIEN ANDA,
15729 5ELCID1996 GALIND GAR%IAZ, EL *** FUE DE ARAGON:
15745 5ELCID1998 E TODOS LOS OTROS *** Y SON.
15762 5ELCID2000 A AQUESTOS DOS MANDO EL CAMPEADOR *** CURIEN A VALEN%IA
15773 5ELCID2001 DALMA & DE CORA%ON, & TODOS LOS *** EN PODER DESSOS FOSSEN;
15782 5ELCID2002 LAS PUERTAS DEL ALCA%AR *** NON SE ABRIESSEN DE DIA NIN DE NOCH,
15801 5ELCID2004 EN *** TIENE SU ALMA & SU CORA%ON,
15811 5ELCID2005 E OTRAS DUE@AS *** LAS SIRUEN ASU SABOR;
15822 5ELCID2007 *** DEL ALCA%AR VNA SALIR NON PUEDE,
15833 5ELCID2008 FATA QUES TORNE EL *** EN BUEN ORA NASCO.
15855 5ELCID2011 MYO %ID SELOS GA@ARA, *** NON GELOS DIERAN EN DON.
15866 5ELCID2012 HYAS VA PORA LAS VISTAS *** CON EL REY PARO.
15883 5ELCID2014 QUANDO VIERON *** VINIE EL BUEN CAMPEADOR,
15901 5ELCID2016 DON LO OUO A OIO EL *** EN BUEN ORA NASCO,
15917 5ELCID2018 SI NON A ESTOS CAUALLEROS *** QUERIE DE CORA%ON;
15931 5ELCID2020 COMMO LO COMIDIA EL *** EN BUEN ORA NA%IO,
16022 5ELCID2032 ASSI ESTANDO, DEDES ME UUESTRA AMOR, *** LO OYAN QUANTOS
AQUI SON.
16074 5ELCID2038 E A ESTAS MESNADAS *** ESTAN A DERREDOR.
16162 5ELCID2050 E CRAS FEREMOS LO *** PLOGIERE AUOS.
16207 5ELCID2056 MYO %ID RUY DIAZ, *** EN ORA BUENA NASCO,
16233 5ELCID2059 CATANDOL SEDIE LA BARBA, *** TAN AYNAL CRE%IERA.
16243 5ELCID2060 MARAUILLAN SE DE MYO %ID QUANTOS *** Y SON.
16268 5ELCID2064 *** ADOBASSEN COZINA PORA QUANTOS QUE YSON;
16273 5ELCID2064 QUE ADOBASSEN COZINA PORA QUANTOS *** YSON;
16351 5ELCID2074 ASI LO MANDE CHRISTUS *** SEA ASO PRO.
16364 5ELCID2076 *** LAS DEDES POR MUGIERES ALOS YFANTES DE CARRION.
16395 5ELCID2079 DELLA & DELLA PARTE, QUANTOS *** AQUI SON,
16403 5ELCID2080 LOS MIOS & LOS UUESTROS *** SEAN ROGADORES;
16575 5ELCID2100 AL CRIADOR PLEGA *** AYADES ENDE SABOR.
16605 5ELCID2104 *** METAN EN SUS BODAS DO QUISIEREDES UOS;
16632 5ELCID2107 LO *** UOS PLOGIERE, DELLOS FET, CAMPEADOR.

WORD C# PREFIX CONTEXT

QUE (CON'T)

16669 5ELCID2111 LAS PALABRAS SON PUESTAS *** OTRO DIA MA@ANA
16712 5ELCID2116 TANTAS BUENAS VISTIDURAS *** CALFAYA SON.
16718 5ELCID2117 CADA VNO LO *** PIDE, NADI NOL DIZE DE NO.
16739 5ELCID2119 TODOS SON PAGADOS DELAS VISTAS QUANTOS *** Y SON.
16745 5ELCID2120 PARTIR SE CUIEREN, *** ENTRADA ERA LA NOCH.
16778 5ELCID2124 OY DE MAS SABED *** FER DELLOS, CAMPEADOR.
16789 5ELCID2126 DIOS *** ESTA EN %IELO CEM CENT BUEN GALARDON.
16839 5ELCID2132 PUES *** CASADES MYS FIJAS, ASI COMMO AUOS PLAZ,
16911 5ELCID2140 DIXO ALBARFANEZ: SE@OR, AFE *** ME PLAZ.
16931 5ELCID2143 DESTAS VISTAS *** OUIEMOS, DEMY TOMEDES ALGO.
16968 5ELCID2148 RE%IBO ESTE DON *** ME AUEDES MANDADO;
16984 5ELCID2150 QUEM FECHES *** BIEN SEA GALARDONADO.
17022 5ELCID2155 AFE DIOS DEL %IELO, *** LO PONGA EN BUEN LOGAR
17045 5ELCID2158 VERIEDES CAUALLEROS, *** BIEN ANDANTES SON,
17116 5ELCID2166 GRANDES SON LAS YENTES *** VAN CONEL CANPEADOR.
17124 5ELCID2167 ADELINAN PORA VALEN%IA, LA *** EN BUEN PUNTO GANO.
17153 5ELCID2171 *** SOPIESSEN SOS MA@AS DE LOS YFANTES DE CARRION.
17165 5ELCID2172 EVAY ASUR GON%ALEZ, *** ERA BULIDOR,
17168 5ELCID2173 *** ES LARGO DE LENGUA, MAS EN LO AL NON ES TAN PRO.
17193 5ELCID2175 AFELOS EN VALEN%IA, LA *** MYO %ID GA@O;
17227 5ELCID2179 VOS CON ELLOS SED, *** ASSI UOS LO MANDO YO.
17237 5ELCID2180 QUANDO VINIERE LA MA@ANA, *** APUNTARE EL SOL,
17298 5ELCID2188 HYERNOS UOS ADUGO DE *** AUREMOS ONDRAN%A;
17323 5ELCID2191 ETODAS LAS DUE@AS *** LAS SIRUEN:
17336 5ELCID2193 TODO LO *** UOS FECHES ES DE BUENA GUISA.
17382 5ELCID2199 MAS BIEN SABET VERDAD *** NON LO LEUANTE YO:
17403 5ELCID2202 *** YO NULLA COSA NOL SOPE DEZIR DE NO.
17422 5ELCID2204 BIEN MELO CREADES, *** EL UOS CASA, CA NON YO.
17494 5ELCID2213 DE PIE & ASABOR, DIOS, *** QUEDOS ENTRARON
17543 5ELCID2220 PUES *** AFAZER LO AUEMOS, POR QUE LO YMOS TARDANDO?
17548 5ELCID2220 PUES QUE AFAZER LO AUEMOS, POR *** LO YMOS TARDANDO?
17556 5ELCID2221 VENIT ACA, ALBARFANEZ, EL *** YO QUIERO & AMO
17570 5ELCID2223 SABEDES *** AL REY ASSI GELO HE MANDADO,
17634 5ELCID2231 POR MANO DEL REY ALFONSSO, *** AMI LO OUO MANDADO,
17646 5ELCID2233 *** LAS TOMASSEDES POR MUGIERES A ONDRA & A RECABDO.
17721 5ELCID2243 DIOS, *** BIEN TOUIERON ARMAS EL %ID & SUS VASSALOS
17734 5ELCID2244 TRES CAUALLOS CAMEO EL *** EN BUEN ORA NASCO.
17742 5ELCID2245 MYO %ID DELO *** VEYE MUCHO ERA PAGADO:
17782 5ELCID2250 ANTES *** ENTRASSEN AIANTAR TODOS LOS QUEBRANTARON.
17810 5ELCID2253 MYO %ID DON RODRIGO, EL *** EN BUEN ORA NASCO,
17871 5ELCID2261 RICOS TORNAN A CASTIELLA LOS *** ALAS BODAS LEGARON.
17885 5ELCID2263 ESPIDIENDOS DE RUY DIAZ, EL *** EN BUEN ORA NASCO,
17983 5ELCID2275 QUES PAGE DES CASAMIENTO MYO %ID O EL *** LO ALGO
18030 5ELCID2281 MALA SOBREUIENTA, SABED, *** LES CUNTIO:
18117 5ELCID2292 EN ESTO DESPERTO EL *** EN BUEN ORA NA%IO;
18134 5ELCID2294 QUES ESTO, MESNADAS, O *** QUEREDES UOS?
18199 5ELCID2302 AMARAUILLA LO HAN QUANTOS *** YSON,
18261 5ELCID2310 FIERA COSA LES PESA DESTO *** LES CUNTIO.
18299 5ELCID2316 *** LES CRE%E LA GANAN%IA, GRADO AL CRIADOR.
18324 5ELCID2318 CA VEYEN TANTAS TIENDAS DE MOROS DE *** NON AUIE SABOR.
18378 5ELCID2326 EUADES *** PAUOR HAN UUESTROS YERNOS TAN OSADOS,
18399 5ELCID2329 *** SEAN EN PAS & NON AYAN Y RA%ION.
18474 5ELCID2338 AVN VEA EL ORA *** UOS MERESCA DOS TANTO.
18509 5ELCID2342 AVN SI DIOS QUISIERE & EL PADRE *** ESTA EN ALTO,
18568 5ELCID2350 OYD LO *** FABLO EL QUE EN BUEN ORA NASCO:
18571 5ELCID2350 OYD LO QUE FABLO EL *** EN BUEN ORA NASCO:
18597 5ELCID2353 MYOS YERNOS AMOS ADOS, LA COSA *** MUCHO AMO,
18615 5ELCID2356 *** OY LOS YFANTES AMI POR AMO NON ABRAN;
18672 5ELCID2363 EUOS TAN DINNO *** CON EL AUEDES PART.
18687 5ELCID2365 EL DEBDO *** A CADA VNO A CONPLIR SERA.
18746 5ELCID2372 POR SABOR *** AUIA DE ALGUN MORO MATAR;
18783 5ELCID2377 MYO CORA%ON *** PUDIESSE FOLGAR,
18809 5ELCID2380 ESSORA DIXO MYO %ID: LO *** UOS QUEREDES PLAZ ME.
18873 5ELCID2388 ENSAYAUAS EL OBISPO, DIOS, *** BIEN LIDIAUA
18902 5ELCID2392 EL *** EN BUEN ORA NASCO LOS OIOS LE FINCAUA,
18924 5ELCID2394 AGUIJO A BAUIECA, EL CAUALLO *** BIEN ANDA,
19012 5ELCID2405 TANTAS CABE%AS CON YELMOS *** POR EL CAMPO CAEN,
19182 5ELCID2426 E GANO A TIZON *** MILL MARCOS DORO VAL.
19221 5ELCID2432 EL *** EN BUEN ORA NASCO.
19236 5ELCID2434 CON DOS ESPADAS *** EL PRE%IAUA ALGO
19265 5ELCID2438 ALGO VIE MYO %ID DELO *** ERA PAGADO,
19355 5ELCID2452 AQUELOS *** GELOS DIERAN NON GELO AUIEN LOGRADO.
19387 5ELCID2456 GRADO ADIOS & AL PADRE *** ESTA EN ALTO,
19394 5ELCID2457 EA UOS, %ID, *** EN BUEN ORA FUESTES NADO
19467 5ELCID2467 *** ALA RA%ION CAYE SEYS %IENTOS MARCOS DE PLATA.
19487 5ELCID2469 DESTA ARRANCADA, *** LO TENIEN EN SO SALUO,
19494 5ELCID2470 CUYDARON *** EN SUS DIAS NUNQUA SERIEN MINGUADOS.
19533 5ELCID2475 DESPUES *** ESTA BATALLA VEN%IERON & AL REY BUCAR MATO;
19552 5ELCID2477 GRADO A CHRISTUS, *** DEL MUNDO ES SE@OR,
19560 5ELCID2478 QUANDO VEO LO *** AUIA SABOR,
19563 5ELCID2479 *** LIDIARAN COMIGO EN CAMPO MYOS YERNOS AMOS ADOS;
19606 5ELCID2484 MANDO MYO %ID, EL *** EN BUEN ORA NASCO,
19613 5ELCID2485 DESTA BATALLA *** HAN ARRANCADO
19616 5ELCID2486 *** TODOS PRISIESSEN SO DERECHO CONTADO,

WORD C# PREFIX CONTEXT

QUE (CON'T)

```
19653 5ELCID2491 TANTOS SON DE MUCHOS *** NON SERIEN CONTADOS.
19666 5ELCID2493 GRADO HA DIOS *** DEL MUNDO ES SE@OR
19677 5ELCID2495 *** HE AUER & TIERRA & ORO & ONOR,
19714 5ELCID2500 *** ABRAM DE MI SALTO QUI%AB ALGUNA NOCH
19746 5ELCID2504 *** PAGUEN AMI O A QUI YO QUIER SABOR.
19786 5ELCID2508 DAQUESTA ARRANCADA *** LIDIARON DE CORA%ON
19831 5ELCID2514 E OTROS MUCHOS *** CRIO EL CAMPEADOR.
19851 5ELCID2517 ACA VENID, CUNADOS, *** MAS VALEMOS POR UOS.
19936 5ELCID2529 TANTOS AVEMOS DE AUERES *** NO SON CONTADOS;
19950 5ELCID2531 PENSAD DELO OTRO, *** LO NUESTRO TENEMOS LO EN SALUO.
19981 5ELCID2535 POR AQUESTOS GUEGOS *** YUAN LEUANTANDO,
20009 5ELCID2539 DESTO *** ELLOS FABLARON NOS PARTE NON AYAMOS:
20024 5ELCID2541 LOS AUERES *** TENEMOS GRANDES SON & SOBEIANOS,
20031 5ELCID2542 MIENTRA *** VISQUIEREMOS DESPENDER NOLO PODREMOS.
20043 5ELCID2544 DIGAMOS *** LAS LEUAREMOS ATIERRAS DE CARRION,
20073 5ELCID2548 ANTE *** NOS RETRAYAN LO QUE CUNTIO DEL LEON.
20077 5ELCID2548 ANTE QUE NOS RETRAYAN LO *** CUNTIO DEL LEON.
20092 5ELCID2550 AUERES LEUAREMOS GRANDES *** VALEN GRANT VALOR;
20132 5ELCID2556 ANTES *** NOS RETRAYAN LO QUE FUE DEL LEON.
20136 5ELCID2556 ANTES QUE NOS RETRAYAN LO *** FUE DEL LEON.
20161 5ELCID2560 *** PLEGA A DO@A XIMENA & PRIMERO AUOS
20181 5ELCID2562 DAD NOS NUESTRAS MUGIERES *** AUEMOS ABENDI%IONES;
20198 5ELCID2565 *** LES DIEMOS POR ARRAS & POR ONORES;
20210 5ELCID2566 VERAN UUESTRAS FIJAS LO *** AUEMOS NOS,
20215 5ELCID2567 LOS FIJOS *** QUIEREMOS EN QUE AURAN PARTI%ION.
20218 5ELCID2567 LOS FIJOS QUE QUIEREMOS EN *** AURAN PARTI%ION.
20234 5ELCID2569 EL %ID *** NOS CURIAUA DE ASSI SER AFONTADO;
20300 5ELCID2576 BIEN LO SABEDES UOS *** LAS GANE AGUISA DE VARON;
20322 5ELCID2579 *** LO SEPAN EN GALLIZIA & EN CASTIELLA & EN LEON,
20334 5ELCID2580 CON *** RIQUEZA ENBIO MIOS YERNOS AMOS ADOS.
20345 5ELCID2581 A MIS FIJAS SIRUADES, *** UUESTRAS MUGIERES SON;
20376 5ELCID2585 CONPIE%AN A RE%EBIR LO *** EL %ID MANDO.
20408 5ELCID2590 POR *** ESCURREN SUS FIJAS DEL CAMPEADOR ATIERRAS DE CARRION.
20469 5ELCID2598 DEBDO NOS ES A CUNPLIR LO *** MANDAREDES VOS.
20479 5ELCID2600 *** AYADES UUESTROS MENSSAIES EN TIERRAS DE CARRION.
20599 5ELCID2615 VIOLO EN LOS AUUEROS EL *** EN BUEN ORA %INXO ESPADA,
20605 5ELCID2616 *** ESTOS CASAMIENTOS NON SERIEN SIN ALGUNA TACHA.
20616 5ELCID2617 NOS PUEDE REPENTIR, *** CASADAS LAS HA AMAS.
20638 5ELCID2620 MANDOT *** VAYAS CON ELLAS FATA DENTRO EN CARRION,
20649 5ELCID2621 VERAS LAS HEREDADES *** A MIS FIJAS DADAS SON;
20683 5ELCID2626 *** SI ADIOS PLOGUIERE & AL PADRE CRIADOR,
20709 5ELCID2629 ATALES COSAS FED *** EN PLAZER CAYA ANOS.
20769 5ELCID2638 DIL *** ENBIO MIS FIJAS A TIERRAS DE CARRION,
20778 5ELCID2639 DELO *** OUIEREN HUEBOS SIRUAN LAS ASO SABOR,
20817 5ELCID2643 HYAS TORNO PORA VALEN%IA EL *** EN BUEN ORA NAS%IO.
20865 5ELCID2650 DIOS, *** BIEN LOS SIRUIO ATODO SO SABOR
20889 5ELCID2653 HYUAN TRO%IR LOS MONTES, LOS *** DIZEN DE LUZON.
20937 5ELCID2659 ELLOS VEYEN LA RIQUEZA *** EL MORO SACO,
20947 5ELCID2661 HYA PUES *** ADEXAR AUEMOS FIJAS DEL CAMPEADOR,
21025 5ELCID2672 CO DOZIENTOS *** TIENE YUA CAUALGAR;
21037 5ELCID2674 DELO *** EL MORO DIXO ALOS YFANTES NON PLAZE:
21047 5ELCID2675  DEZID ME, *** UOS FIZ, YFANTES DE CARRION
21077 5ELCID2678 TAL COSA UOS FARIA *** POR EL MUNDO SONAS,
21127 5ELCID2684 DIOS LO QUIERA & LO MANDE, *** DE TODEL MUNDO ES SE@OR,
21136 5ELCID2685 DA QUESTE CASAMIENTO *** GRADE EL CAMPEADOR.
21204 5ELCID2694 ASSINIESTRO DEXAN AGRIZA *** ALAMOS POBLO,
21242 5ELCID2699 ELAS BESTIAS FIERAS *** ANDAN ADERREDOR.
21261 5ELCID2702 CON QUANTOS *** ELLOS TRAEN Y IAZEN ESSA NOCH,
21311 5ELCID2709 *** NON YFINCAS NINGUNO, MUGIER NIN VARON,
21468 5ELCID2730 *** POR LO QUE NOS MERE%EMOS NO LO PRENDEMOS NOS;
21471 5ELCID2730 QUE POR LO *** NOS MERE%EMOS NO LO PRENDEMOS NOS;
21501 5ELCID2734 LO *** RUEGAN LAS DUENAS NON LES HA NINGUN PRO.
21568 5ELCID2742 *** ASSOMASSE ESSORA EL %ID CAMPEADOR
21577 5ELCID2743 TANTO LAS MAIARON *** SIN COSIMENTE SON;
21652 5ELCID2752 POR MUERTAS LAS DEXARON, SABED, *** NON POR BIUAS.
21677 5ELCID2756 *** EL VNA AL OTRA NOL TORNA RECABDO.
21776 5ELCID2770 FASTA *** VIESSE VENIR SUS PRIMAS AMAS ADOS
21784 5ELCID2771 O *** AN FECHO LOS YFANTES DE CARRION.
21806 5ELCID2774 SABET BIEN *** SI ELLOS LE VIESSEN, NON ESCAPARA DE MUERT.
21866 5ELCID2782 ADIOS PLEGA & A SANTA MARIA *** DENT PRENDAN ELLOS MAL GALARDON
21882 5ELCID2784 TANTO SON DE TRASPUESTAS *** NON PUEDEN DEZIR NADA.
21916 5ELCID2788 MIENTRA ES EL DIA, ANTE *** ENTRE LA NOCH,
21951 5ELCID2793 DE *** NON ME FALLAREN LOS YFANTES DE CARRION,
22000 5ELCID2799 CON VN SONBRERO *** TIENE FELEZ MUNOZ,
22008 5ELCID2800 NUEUO ERA & FRESCO, *** DE VALEN%IAL SACO,
22031 5ELCID2803 TANTO LAS ROGO FATA *** LAS ASSENTO.
22040 5ELCID2805 FATA *** ESFUER%AN, & AMAS LAS TOMO
22111 5ELCID2814 FALLO A DIEGO TELLEZ EL *** DE ALBARFANEZ FUE;
22170 5ELCID2823 ALLI SOUIERON ELLAS FATA *** SA@AS SON.
22220 5ELCID2830 GRADO A CHRISTUS, *** DEL MUNDO ES SE@OR,
22237 5ELCID2832 PAR AQUESTA BARBA *** NADI NON MESSO,
22248 5ELCID2834 *** AMIS FIJAS BIEN LAS CASARE YO
22291 5ELCID2839 DIXOLES FUERTE MIENTRE *** ANDIDIESSEN DE DIA & DE NOCH,
22340 5ELCID2846 *** VINIE MYNAYA POR SUS PRIMAS AMAS ADOS.
```

WORD C# PREFIX CONTEXT

QUE (CON'T)

22381 5ELCID2851 GRA%IAS, VARCNES DE SANTESTEUAN, *** SODES CO@OS%EDORES,
22387 5ELCID2852 POR AQUESTA ONDRA *** VOS DIESTES A ESTO QUE NOS CUNTIO;
22392 5ELCID2852 POR AQUESTA ONDRA QUE VCS DIESTES A ESTO *** NOS CUNTIO;
22410 5ELCID2854 ASSI LC FFAGC YC *** AQUI ESTO.
22417 5ELCID2855 AFFE DIOS DELOS %IELOS *** UOS DE DENT BUEN GALARDON
22523 5ELCID2868 AVN VEAMOS EL DIA *** VCS PCDAMOS VENGAR
22535 5ELCID2869 HY IAZEN ESSA NOCHE, & TAN GRAND GOZO *** FAZEN.
22640 5ELCID2885 AL *** EN BUEN CRA NASCC LEGAUA EL MENSSAIE;
22660 5ELCID2887 ARMAS YUA TENIENDC & GRANT GOZC *** FAZE;
22695 5ELCID2892 PLEGA AL CRIADOR, *** EN %IELO ESTA,
22699 5ELCID2893 *** UOS VEA MEICR CASADAS DAQUI EN ACELANT.
22740 5ELCID2898 EL *** EN BUEN ORA NASCC NON CUISO TARDAR,
22810 5ELCID2906 DESTA DESONDRA *** MEAN FECHA LOS YFANTES DE CARRION
22864 5ELCID2912 MYCS AUERES SE ME AN LEUADO, *** SOBEIANOS SON;
22917 5ELCID2919 E CON EL ESCUDEROS *** SCN DE CRIAZON.
23087 5ELCID2941 HYA UOS SABEDES LA ONDRA *** ES CUNTIDA ANOS,
23142 5ELCID2949 *** GELCS LEUEDES AVISTAS, O AIUNTAS, O A CORTES;
23160 5ELCID2951 E *** UOS PESE, REY CCMMO SODES SABIDOR;
23167 5ELCID2952 *** AYA MYO %ID DERECHO DE YFANTES DE CARRION.
23188 5ELCID2954 VERDAD TE DIGO YO, *** ME PESA DE CORA%ON,
23214 5ELCID2957 FIZ LO POR BIEN, *** FFUESSE A SU PRO.
23244 5ELCID2961 LO *** NON CUYDAUA FER DE TODA ESTA SAZON,
23266 5ELCID2964 *** ALLA ME VAYAN CUENDES & YFAN%ONES,
23290 5ELCID2967 E *** NCN AYA RENCURA PCDIENDC YO VEDALLO.
23301 5ELCID2968 DIZID LE AL CAMPEADCR, *** EN BUEN ORA NASCO,
23306 5ELCID2969 *** DESTAS VIJ SEMANAS ADOBES CON SUS VASSALLOS,
23337 5ELCID2973 DESTO *** LES ABINO AVN BIEN SERAN ONDRADOS.
23389 5ELCID2980 *** CORT FAZIE EN TOLLEDO AQUEL REY ONDRADO,
23402 5ELCID2981 A CABO DE VIJ SEMANAS *** Y FUESSEN IUNTADOS;
23425 5ELCID2984 *** NON FALIESSEN DELC CUE EN REY AUYE MANDADO.
23429 5ELCID2984 QUE NON FALIESSEN DELO *** EN REY AUYE MANDADO.
23443 5ELCID2986 POR *** EL REY FAZIE CORT EN TOLLEDO,
23452 5ELCID2987 MIEDO HAN *** Y VERNA MYO %ID EL CAMPEADOR;
23469 5ELCID2989 RUEGAN AL REY *** LOS QUITE DESTA CORT.
23518 5ELCID2995 HYA LO VIERON *** ES AFER LOS YFANTES DE CARRION,
23542 5ELCID2998 ENEMIGO DE MIO SID, *** SIEMPREL BUSCO MAL,
23633 5ELCID3010 E CON ELLOS GRAND BANDO *** ACUXIERON A LA CORT:
23657 5ELCID3013 AVN NON ERA LEGADO EL *** ENBUEN ORA NA%IO,
23662 5ELCID3014 POR *** SE TARDA EL REY NON HA SABOR.
23683 5ELCID3017 *** BESASSE LAS MANOS AL REY SO SE@OR:
23694 5ELCID3018 BIEN LC SOPIESSE *** Y SERIE ESSA NOCH.
23732 5ELCID3023 BUENAS CONPA@AS *** ASSI AN TAL SE@OR.
23791 5ELCID3031 DELO *** AUOS PESA AMI DUELE EL CORA%ON;
23801 5ELCID3032 DIOS LO MANDE *** POR UCS SE ONDRE OY LA CORT
23843 5ELCID3037 E AL CONDE DON ARRICH & A CUANTOS *** Y SON;
23873 5ELCID3041 DESTO *** NOS ABINO QUE UOS PESE, SE@OR.
23876 5ELCID3041 DESTO QUE NOS ABINO *** UOS PESE, SE@OR.
23996 5ELCID3058 ENTRE MINAYA & LOS BUENOS *** Y HA
24016 5ELCID3061 SUELTA FUE LA MISSA ANTES *** SALIESSE EL SOL,
24067 5ELCID3068 E MARTIN MUNOZ, *** EN BUEN PUNTO NA%IO,
24081 5ELCID3070 CCMIGO YRA MAL ANCA, *** ES BIEN SABIDOR.
24097 5ELCID3072 CON ESTOS CUNPLANSSE %IENTO DELOS BUENOS *** Y SON.
24122 5ELCID3C76 E *** NCN PARESCAN LAS ARMAS, BIEN PRESOS LOS CORDONES;
24185 5ELCID3084 NOS DETIENE POR NADA EL *** EN BUEN ORA NA%IO:
24201 5ELCID3086 SOBRELLAS VNOS %APATOS *** A GRANT HUEBRA SON;
24276 5ELCID3096 *** NON LE CONTALASSEN LOS PELOS AL BUEN %ID CANPEADOR;
24299 5ELCID3098 POR TALLO FAZE ESTO *** RECABDAR QUIERE TODO LO SUYO;
24309 5ELCID3099 DESUSO CUBRIO VN MANTC *** ES DE GRANT VALOR,
24316 5ELCID3100 ENEL ABRIEN *** VER QUANTOS QUE Y SON.
24319 5ELCID3100 ENEL ABRIEN QUE VER QUANTOS *** Y SON.
24325 5ELCID3101 CON AQUESTOS %IENTO *** ADOBAR MANDO,
24369 5ELCID3107 QUANDO LO VIERON ENTRAR AL *** EN BUEN ORA NA%IO,
24404 5ELCID3111 AGRANT ONDRA LO RE%IBEN AL *** EN BUEN ORA NA%IO.
24441 5ELCID3116 MAGER *** ALGUNCS PESA, MEIOR SODES QUE NOS.
24446 5ELCID3116 MAGER QUE ALGUNOS PESA, MEIOR SODES *** NOS.
24453 5ELCID3117 ESSORA DIXO MUCHAS MER%EDES EL *** VALEN%IA GA@O:
24471 5ELCID3120 LO *** DIXC EL %ID AL REY PLOGO DE CORA%ON.
24506 5ELCID3124 ALA BARBA *** AUIE LUENGA & PRESA CONEL CORDON;
24545 5ELCID3129 HYO, DE *** FU REY, NCN FIZ MAS DE DOS CORTES:
24579 5ELCID3132 POR EL AMOR DE MYO %ID EL *** EN BUEN ORA NA%IO,
24584 5ELCID3133 *** RE%IBA DERECHO DE YFANTES DE CARRION.
24616 5ELCID3136 E ESTOS OTROS CONDES *** DEL VANDO NON SODES.
24650 5ELCID3140 JURO PAR SANT ESIDRO, EL *** BOLUIERE MY CORT
24663 5ELCID3142 CON EL *** TOUIERE DERECHO YO DESSA PART ME SO.
24678 5ELCID3144 SABREMOS *** RESPONDEN YFANTES DE CARRION.
24734 5ELCID3150 CA UOS LAS CASASTES, REY, SABREDES *** FER OY;
24830 5ELCID3162 CON TODOS SUS PARIENTES & EL VANDO *** Y SON;
25015 5ELCID3186 PAR AQUESTA BARBA *** NADI NON MESSO,
25088 5ELCID3196 POR ESSO UOS LA DO *** LA BIEN CURIEDES UOS.
25094 5ELCID3197 SE *** SI UOS ACAE%IERE, CON ELLA GANAREDES GRAND PREZ & GRAND VALOR.
25213 5ELCID3211 *** AL NO NOS DEMANDASSE, QUE AQUI FINCO LA BOZ. . .
25218 5ELCID3211 QUE AL NO NOS DEMANDASSE, *** AQUI FINCO LA BOZ. . .
25234 5ELCID3213 ALO *** DEMANDA EL %ID QUEL RECUDADES VOS.
25258 5ELCID3216 DESTOS AUERES *** UOS DI YO, SIMELOS DADES, O DEDES DELLO RA%ON.

WORD C# PREFIX CONTEXT

QUE (CON'T)

25302 5ELCID3221 MUCHO NOS AFINCA EL *** VALEN%IA GA@O,
25343 5ELCID3227 *** AQUI LO ENTERGEDES DENTRO EN LA CORT.
25365 5ELCID3230 *** DERECHO DEMANDA EL %ID CAMPEADOR.
25398 5ELCID3234 ENTERGEN A MYO %ID, EL *** EN BUEN ORA NA%IO;
25451 5ELCID3241 HYA VIERON *** ES AFER LOS YFANTES DE CARRION.
25486 5ELCID3246 SOBRE LOS DOZIENTOS MARCOS *** TENIE EL REY ALFONSSO
25495 5ELCID3247 PAGARON LOS YFANTES AL *** EN BUEN ORA NASCO;
25504 5ELCID3248 ENPRESTAN LES DELO AGENO, *** NON LES CUMPLE LO SUYO.
25579 5ELCID3258 DEZID *** UOS MERE%I, YFANTES, EN JUEGO O EN VERO
25631 5ELCID3264 POR *** LAS SACAUADES DE VALEN%IA SUS HONORES?
25639 5ELCID3265 A *** LAS FIRIESTES A %INCHAS & A ESPOLONES?
25740 5ELCID3278 DERECHO FIZIERON POR *** LAS HAN DEXADAS.
25760 5ELCID3281 GRADO A DIOS *** %IELO & TIERRA MANDA
25772 5ELCID3283 *** AVEDES UOS, CONDE, POR RETRAER LA MI BARBA?
25825 5ELCID3289 NON YOUO RAPAZ *** NON MESSO SU PULGADA;
25831 5ELCID3290 LA *** YO MESSE AVN NON ES EGUADA.
25846 5ELCID3292 AALTAS VOZES ONDREDES *** FABLO:
25891 5ELCID3299 POR *** LAS DEXAMOS DERECHO FIZIEMOS NOS;
25901 5ELCID3300 MAS NOS PRE%IAMOS, SABET, *** MENOS NO.
25916 5ELCID3302 FABLA, PERO MUDO, VARON *** TANTO CALLAS
25977 5ELCID3311 BIEN LO SABEDES *** YO NON PUEDO MAS;
25984 5ELCID3312 POR LO *** YO QUIER AFER POR MI NON MANCARA.
26031 5ELCID3318 VIST VN MORO, FUSTEL ENSAYAR; ANTES FUXISTE *** ALTE ALEGASSES.
26084 5ELCID3325 *** MATARAS EL MORO & QUE FIZIERAS BARNAX;
26089 5ELCID3325 QUE MATARAS EL MORO & *** FIZIERAS BARNAX;
26139 5ELCID3332 E TU, FERRANDO, *** FIZIST CON EL PAUOR?
26173 5ELCID3336 FASTA DO DESPERTO MYO %ID, EL *** VALEN%IA GA@O;
26262 5ELCID3348 EN TODAS GUISAS MAS VALEN *** VOS.
26295 5ELCID3353 DIEGO GON%ALEZ ODREDES LO *** DIXO:
26318 5ELCID3357 POR *** DEXAMOS SUS FIJAS AVN NO NOS REPENTIMOS,
26327 5ELCID3358 MIENTRA *** BIUAN PUEDEN AUER SOSPIROS:
26333 5ELCID3359 LO *** LES FIZIEMOS SER LES HA RETRAYDO; ESTO LIDIARE ATOD EL MAS
26346 5ELCID3360 *** POR QUE LAS DEXAMOS ONDRADOS SOMOS NOS.
26348 5ELCID3360 QUE POR *** LAS DEXAMOS ONDRADOS SOMOS NOS.
26404 5ELCID3368 FIJAS DEL %ID, POR *** LAS VOS DEXASTES,
26411 5ELCID3369 ENTODAS GUISAS, SABED, *** MAS VALEN QUE VOS.
26414 5ELCID3369 ENTODAS GUISAS, SABED, QUE MAS VALEN *** VOS.
26425 5ELCID3371 *** ERES TRAYDOR & MINTIST DE QUANTO DICHO HAS.
26458 5ELCID3376 EN LO *** FABLO AVIE POCO RECABDO:
26515 5ELCID3384 ANTES ALMUERZAS *** VAYAS A ORA%ION,
26520 5ELCID3385 ALOS *** DAS PAZ, FARTAS LOS ADERREDOR.
26550 5ELCID3389 FAZER TELO DEZIR *** TALERES QUAL DIGO YO.
26564 5ELCID3391 LOS *** AN REBTADO LIDIARAN, SIN SALUE DIOS
26628 5ELCID3400 E *** GELAS DIESSEN A ONDRA & ABENDI%ION,
26702 5ELCID3411 *** PLEGA AUOS, & ATORGAR LO HE YO,
26783 5ELCID3421 *** UOS LAS DE AONDRA & A BENDI%ION.
26820 5ELCID3426 *** CUEMO ES DICHO ASSI SEA, OMEIOR.
26857 5ELCID3431 E *** NON PESE ESTO AL %ID CAMPEADOR:
26887 5ELCID3435 DEZID, MYNAYA, LO *** OUIEREDES SABOR.
26893 5ELCID3436 HYO UOS RUEGO *** ME OYADES TODA LA CORT,
26969 5ELCID3445 MAS BIEN SABEMOS LAS MA@AS *** ELLOS HAN,
27015 5ELCID3451 AVER LAS HEDES ASERUIR, MAL *** UOS PESE AUOS.
27064 5ELCID3458 *** VAL, MINAYA, TODA ESSA RAZON?
27088 5ELCID3461 SI DIOS QUISIERE *** DESTA BIEN SALGAMOS NOS,
27095 5ELCID3462 DESPUES VEREDES *** DIXIESTES O QUE NO.
27098 5ELCID3462 DESPUES VEREDES QUE DIXIESTES O *** NO.
27125 5ELCID3466 DESTOS IIJ POR TRES *** REBTARON EN LA CORT.
27180 5ELCID3474 MAS QUIERO A VALEN%IA *** TIERRAS DE CARRION.
27214 5ELCID3479 *** NON PRENDAN FUER%A DE CONDE NIN DE YFAN%ON.
27240 5ELCID3482 *** FAGAN ESTA LID DELANT ESTANDO YO;
27335 5ELCID3493 LA CONFIA DE RAN%AL *** BLANCA ERA COMMO EL SOL,
27378 5ELCID3498 *** PRENDAN DE SUS AUERES QUANTO OUIEREN SABOR.
27390 5ELCID3499 AESSOS & ALOS OTROS *** DE BUENA PARTE SON,
27404 5ELCID3501 TALES YA *** PRENDEN, TALES YA QUE NON.
27408 5ELCID3501 TALES YA QUE PRENDEN, TALES YA *** NON.
27475 5ELCID3510 *** EN TODAS NUESTRAS TIERRAS NON HA TAN BUEN VARON.
27591 5ELCID3523 EL CAMPEADOR ALOS *** HAN LIDIAR TAN BIEN LOS CASTIGO:
27627 5ELCID3527 DIXO MARTIN ANTOLINEZ: POR *** LO DEZIDES, SE@OR
27653 5ELCID3530 ALEGRE FUE DAQUESTO EL *** EN BUEN ORA NA%IO;
27662 5ELCID3531 ESPIDIOS DE TODOS LOS *** SOS AMIGOS SON.
27693 5ELCID3535 CUNPLIR QUIEREN EL DEBDO *** LES MANDO SO SE@OR,
27731 5ELCID3540 *** SI LOS PUDIESSEN APARTAR ALOS DEL CAMPEADOR,
27739 5ELCID3541 *** LOS MATASSEN EN CAMPO POR DESONORA DE SO SE@OR.
27753 5ELCID3542 EL COMETER FUE MALO, *** LO AL NOS ENPE%O,
27855 5ELCID3555 *** NON FUESSEN EN LA BATALLA LAS ESPADAS TAIADORES
27867 5ELCID3556 COLADA & TIZON, *** NON LIDIASSEN CON ELLAS LOS DEL CANPEADOR;
27922 5ELCID3563 HUEBOS VOS ES *** LIDIEDES AGUISA DE VARONES,
27927 5ELCID3564 *** NADA NON MANCARA POR LOS DEL CAMPEADOR.
27955 5ELCID3567 CA TODOS LO SABEN *** LO BUSCASTES VOS.
27966 5ELCID3569 DELO *** AUIEN FECHO MUCHO REPISOS SON;
28009 5ELCID3575 *** FIEL SEADES OY DELLOS & DE NOS;
28077 5ELCID3584 LOS ESCUDOS ALOS CUELLOS *** BIEN BLOCADOS SON;
28114 5ELCID3590 *** CADA VNO DELLOS BIEN FOS FERIR EL SO.
28149 5ELCID3594 *** NON VARAGEN CON ELLOS DESI O DE NON.

WORD C# PREFIX CONTEXT

QUE (CON'T)

28168 5ELCID3596 OYD *** UOS DIGO, YFANTES DE CARRION:
28250 5ELCID3607 *** POR Y SERIE VEN%IDO QUI SALIESSE DEL MOION.
28270 5ELCID3609 MAS DE VJ ASTAS DE LAN%AS *** NON LEGASSEN AL MOION.
28365 5ELCID3622 CUEDAN SE *** ESSORA CAdRAN MUERTOS LOS QUE ESTAN ADERREDOR.
28370 5ELCID3622 CUEDAN SE QUE ESSORA CAdRAN MUERTOS LOS *** ESTAN ADERREDOR.
28376 5ELCID3623 PERO VERMUEZ, EL *** ANTES REBTO,
28440 5ELCID3632 PASSO GELO TODO, *** NADA NOL VALIO,
28450 5ELCID3633 METIOL LA LAN%A POR LOS PECHOS, *** NADA NOL VALIO;
28516 5ELCID3641 ASSI LO TENIEN LAS YENTES *** MAL FERIDO ES DE MUERT.
28538 5ELCID3644 ANTES *** EL COLPE ESPERASSE DIXO: VEN%UDO SO.
28566 5ELCID3647 TALES FUERON LOS COLPES *** LES QUEBRARON AMAS.
28651 5ELCID3658 VIO DIEGO GON%ALEZ *** NO ESCAPARIE CON EL ALMA;
28742 5ELCID3670 OTORGAN GELO LOS FIELES *** DIZE VERDADERA PALABRA.
28827 5ELCID3682 APART LE PRISO, *** NON CABEL CORA%ON;
28877 5ELCID3688 TODOS SE CUEDAN *** FERIDO ES DE MUERT.
28921 5ELCID3694 LAS ARMAS *** Y RASTARON EL SELAS TOMO.
28959 5ELCID3699 *** NOLES DIESSEN SALTO NIN DUIESSEN PAUOR.
28993 5ELCID3703 CONPLIDO HAN EL DEBDO *** LES MANDO SO SE@OR;
29037 5ELCID3709 DELO *** AN PRESO MUCHO AN MAL SABOR;
29047 5ELCID3710 FABLEMOS NOS DAQUESTE *** EN BUEN ORA NA%IO.
29061 5ELCID3712 POR *** TAN ONDRADOS FUERON LOS DEL CANPEADOR.
29138 5ELCID3721 AMAYOR ONDRA LAS CASA *** LO QUE PRIMERO FUE.
29140 5ELCID3721 AMAYOR ONDRA LAS CASA QUE LO *** PRIMERO FUE.
29148 5ELCID3722 VED QUAL ONDRA CRE%E AL *** EN BUEN ORA NA%IO,
29176 5ELCID3725 A TODOS ALCAN%A ONDRA POR EL *** EN BUEN ORA NA%IO.
29256 5ELCID3735 ALA VNOS PE@OS, *** BIEN VOS LO DARARAN SOBRELOS.
WORD #3401 OCCURS 847 TIMES.
INDEX OF DIVERSIFICATION = 33.52 WITH STANDARD DEVIATION OF 30.56

QUEADELI%IO 25769 5ELCID3282 POR ESSO ES LUEGA *********** FUE CRIADA.
WORD #3402 OCCURS 1 TIMES.

QUEBRADA 5888 5ELCID0746 LA LAN%A A ********, AL ESPADA METIO MANO,
WORD #3403 OCCURS 1 TIMES.

QUEBRADO 18863 5ELCID2387 EL ASTIL A ******** & METIO MANO AL ESPADA.
WORD #3404 OCCURS 1 TIMES.

QUEBRANTA 9133 5ELCID1162 CABO DEL MAR TIERRA DE MOROS FIRME LA *********,
WORD #3405 OCCURS 1 TIMES.

QUEBRANTANDO 12631 5ELCID1602 ARMAS TENIENDO & TABLADOS ************.
WORD #3406 OCCURS 1 TIMES.

QUEBRANTARON 17787 5ELCID2250 ANTES QUE ENTRASSEN AIANTAR TODOS LOS ************.
WORD #3407 OCCURS 1 TIMES.

QUEBRANTAS 267 5ELCID0034 QUE SI NON LA ********** POR FUERCA, QUE NON GELA ABRIESE NADI.
WORD #3408 OCCURS 1 TIMES.

QUEBRANTESTE 2846 5ELCID0360 ************ LAS PUERTAS & SAQUESTE LOS PADRES SANTOS.
WORD #3409 OCCURS 1 TIMES.

QUEBRANTO 28428 5ELCID3631 ********* LA BOCA DEL ESCUDO, A PART GELA ECHO,
28817 5ELCID3680 POR MEIO DE LA BLOCA DEL ESCUDOL *********;
WORD #3410 OCCURS 2 TIMES.

QUEBRAR 1852 5ELCID0235 APRIESSA CANTAN LOS GALLOS & QUIEREN ******* ALBORES,
5528 5ELCID0696 ANTE ROYDO DE ATAMORES LA TIERRA QUERIE *******;
8970 5ELCID1141 TANTA CUERDA DE TIENDA Y VERIEDES *******,
13097 5ELCID1660 MIEDO A SU MUGIER & QUIEREL ******* EL CORA%ON,
18965 5ELCID2400 VERIEDES ******* TANTAS CUERDAS & ARRANCAR SE LAS ESTACAS
WORD #3411 OCCURS 5 TIMES.
INDEX OF DIVERSIFICATION = 4277.25 WITH STANDARD DEVIATION OF 1097.30

QUEBRARON 28494 5ELCID3639 ********* LE LAS %INCHAS, NINGUNA NOL OUO PRO,
28568 5ELCID3647 TALES FUERON LOS COLPES QUE LES ********* AMAS.
WORD #3412 OCCURS 2 TIMES.

QUEBRO 28413 5ELCID3628 BIEN EN DOS LOGARES EL ESTIL LE ******.
WORD #3413 OCCURS 1 TIMES.

QUEDAS 5573 5ELCID0702 ****** SED, MENADAS, AQUI EN ESTE LOGAR,
WORD #3414 OCCURS 1 TIMES.

QUEDO 26288 5ELCID3352 DAQUESTOS AMOS AQUI ***** LA RAZON.
WORD #3415 OCCURS 1 TIMES.

QUEDOS 17495 5ELCID2213 DE PIE & ASABOR, DIOS, QUE ****** ENTRARON
WORD #3416 OCCURS 1 TIMES.

QUEL 199 5ELCID0026 E A **** QUE GELA DIESSE SOPIESSE UERA PALABRA,
1842 5ELCID0234 CON ESTOS CAUALLEROS **** SIRUEN ASO SABOR.
2344 5ELCID0296 **** CRE%E CONPA@A, POR QUE MAS VALDRA,
4006 5ELCID0509 **** BUSCARIE MAL CON TODAS SUS MESNADAS.

WORD C# PREFIX CONTEXT

QUEL (CON'T)

```
                    4601 5ELCID0585 ANTES **** PRENDAN LOS DE TERUEL, SI NON NON NOS DARAN
                                    DENT NADA;
                    4615 5ELCID0586 LA PARIA **** A PRESA TORNAR NOS LA HA DOBLADA.
                    6218 5ELCID0792 GRADO A DIOS, A **** QUE ESTA EN ALTO,
                    6883 5ELCID0880 **** AYDES MER%ED, SIEL CRIADOR UOS VALA.
                    7263 5ELCID0932 E **** DIXO SALUDES DE SU MUGIER & DE SUS FIJAS
                    7468 5ELCID0958 QUE MYO %ID RUY DIAZ **** CORRIE LA TIERRA TODA;
                    8656 5ELCID1099 PRISIERON SO CONSEIO **** VINIESSEN %ERCAR.
                   10443 5ELCID1324 **** AYADES MER%ED, SIUOS VALA EL CRIADOR
                   10527 5ELCID1334 GRANDES SON LAS GANAN%IAS **** DIO EL CRIADOR,
                   12395 5ELCID1573 E ADUXIESSEN LE ABAUIECA; POCO AUIE **** GANARA,
                   13646 5ELCID1729 CON OTROS **** CONSIGEN DE SUS BUENOS VASSALLOS.
                   14611 5ELCID1848 MUCHO PRE%IA LA ONDRA EL %ID **** AUEDES DADO.
                   15110 5ELCID1911 **** YRE A VISTAS DO FUERE AGUISADO;
                   15218 5ELCID1927 LO **** ROGAUA ALFONSSO EL DE LEON
                   15232 5ELCID1929 **** CONNOS%IE Y ONDRA & CRE%IE EN ONOR,
                   16828 5ELCID2130 DAQUEND VAYA COMIGO; CUEDO **** AURA PRO.
                   17038 5ELCID2157 NON QUIERE **** ESCURA, QUITOL DESSI LUEGO.
                   18849 5ELCID2385 POR LA SU VENTURA & DIOS **** AMAUA
                   22817 5ELCID2907 **** PESE AL BUEN REY DALMA & DE CORA%ON.
                   22908 5ELCID2918 CON EL DOS CAUALLEROS **** SIRUAN A SO SABOR,
                   22999 5ELCID2930 CON EL DOS CAUALLEROS **** AGUARDAN CUM ASSE@OR.
                   24490 5ELCID3122 LOS %IENTO **** AGUARDAN POSAN ADERREDOR.
                   25238 5ELCID3213 ALO QUE DEMANDA EL %ID **** RECUDADES VOS.
         WORD #3417 OCCURS  27 TIMES.
            INDEX OF DIVERSIFICATION =    962.04 WITH STANDARD DEVIATION OF    903.90

QUELAS              7773 5ELCID0995 %IENTO CAUALLEROS DEUEMOS VEN%ER A ****** MESNADAS.
         WORD #3418 OCCURS   1 TIMES.

QUELES              6299 5ELCID0802 MANDO MYO %ID AUN ****** DIESSEN ALGO.
                   17954 5ELCID2272 LOS AMORES ****** FAZEN MUCHO ERAN SOBEIANOS.
         WORD #3419 OCCURS   2 TIMES.

QUEM                1218 5ELCID0157 ALO **** SEMEIA, DE LO MIO AUREDES ALGO;
                   10606 5ELCID1344 RE%IBO ESTOS CAUALLOS **** ENBIA DE DON.
                   14780 5ELCID1868 ESTOS DOZIENTOS CAUALLOS **** ENBIA MYO %ID.
                   16535 5ELCID2096 **** DADES UUESTRAS FIJAS PORA LOS YFANTES DE CARRION.
                   16903 5ELCID2139 QUANDO UOS IUNTAREDES COMIGO, **** DIGADES LA UERDAT.
                   16982 5ELCID2150 **** FECHES QUE BIEN SEA GALARDONADO.
                   24722 5ELCID3149 POR MIS FIJAS **** DEXARON YO NON HE DESONOR,
                   25567 5ELCID3256 DELOS YFANTES DE CARRION **** DESONDRARON TAN MAL,
                   25600 5ELCID3260  A **** DESCUBRIESTES LAS TELAS DEL CORA%ON?
         WORD #3420 OCCURS   9 TIMES.
            INDEX OF DIVERSIFICATION =  3046.75 WITH STANDARD DEVIATION OF  3685.71

QUEMDIESTES        24437 5ELCID3115 EN AQUESTE ESCANO *********** UOS ENDON;
         WORD #3421 OCCURS   1 TIMES.

QUEN               16592 5ELCID2102 ELLOS VAYAN CON UUSCO, CADA **** ME TORNO YO.
                   27247 5ELCID3483 **** NON VINIERE AL PLAZO PIERDA LA RAZON,
         WORD #3422 OCCURS   2 TIMES.

QUENLAS            10081 5ELCID1277 ******* DEXE SACAR;
         WORD #3423 OCCURS   1 TIMES.

QUERADES           28203 5ELCID3600 AUED UUESTRO DERECHO, TUERTO NON ******** VOS,
         WORD #3424 OCCURS   1 TIMES.

QUERAMOS            5284 5ELCID0668 QUE NOS ******** YR DE NOCH NO NOS LO CONSINTRAN;
                   12021 5ELCID1524 MAGER QUE MAL LE ********, NON GELO PODREMOS FER,
                   15423 5ELCID1953 MAS LO QUE EL QUISIERE, ESSO ******** NOS.
         WORD #3425 OCCURS   3 TIMES.

QUEREDES           13363 5ELCID1694 PUES ESSO ********, %ID, A MI MANDADES AL;
                   14976 5ELCID1893 MAS PUES BOS LO ********, ENTREMOS EN LA RAZON.
                   18135 5ELCID2294 QUES ESTO, MESNADAS, O QUE ******** UOS?
                   18811 5ELCID2380 ESSORA DIXO MYO %ID: LO QUE UOS ******** PLAZ ME.
         WORD #3426 OCCURS   4 TIMES.

QUEREMOS            1518 5ELCID0194 VOS LO MERE%EDES, DARUOS ******** BUEN DADO,
                   14921 5ELCID1886 CON UUESTRO CONSSEIO LO ******** FER NOS,
                   14931 5ELCID1888 CASAR ******** CON ELLAS ASU ONDRA & A NUESTRA PRO.
                   24171 5ELCID3082 RESPONDIERON TODOS: NOS ESSO ********, SE@OR.
                   24923 5ELCID3174 DAR GELAS ******** DELLANT ESTANDO UOS.
         WORD #3427 OCCURS   5 TIMES.
            INDEX OF DIVERSIFICATION =  5850.25 WITH STANDARD DEVIATION OF  6548.16

QUERER               600 5ELCID0076 AUN %ERCA OTARDE EL REY ****** ME HA POR AMIGO;
                   15359 5ELCID1945 ****** UOS YE VER & DAR UOS SU AMOR,
                   25724 5ELCID3276 NON GELAS DEUIEN ****** SUS FIJAS POR VARRAGANAS,
                   27808 5ELCID3549 POR ****** EL DERECHO & NON CONSENTIR EL TUERTO.
         WORD #3428 OCCURS   4 TIMES.

QUERIA              2195 5ELCID0276 LEGOLAS AL CORA%ON, CA MUCHO LAS ******.
                    2218 5ELCID0279 COMMO ALA MI ALMA YO TANTO UOS ******.
```

```
WORD                C#  PREFIX                          CONTEXT

QUERIA (CON'T)

                24749 5ELCID3152 HYO BIEN LAS ****** DALMA & DE CORA%ON,
        WORD #3429 OCCURS   3 TIMES.

QUERIDA         12643 5ELCID1604 VOS, ******* & ONDRADA MUGIER, & AMAS MIS FIJAS,
        WORD #3430 OCCURS   1 TIMES.

QUERIE           2471 5ELCID0311 EL DIA ES EXIDO, LA NOCH ****** ENTRAR,
                 3402 5ELCID0429 DIXOLES ATODOS COMMO ****** TRASNOCHAR;
                 5262 5ELCID0665 ACABO DE TRES SEMANAS, LA QUARTA ****** ENTRAR,
                 5407 5ELCID0682 OTRO DIA MA@ANA, EL SOL ****** APUNTAR,
                 5527 5ELCID0696 ANTE ROYDO DE ATAMORES LA TIERRA ****** QUEBRAR;
                12432 5ELCID1577 DELANTE SU MUGIER & DE SUS FIJAS ****** TENER LAS ARMAS.
                15918 5ELCID2018 SI NON A ESTOS CAUALLEROS QUE ****** DE CORA%ON;
                16226 5ELCID2058 NON SE PUEDE FARTAR DEL, TANTOL ****** DE CORA%ON;
                28344 5ELCID3619 TEMBRAR ****** LA TIERRA DOD ERAN MOUEDORES.
        WORD #3431 OCCURS   9 TIMES.
           INDEX OF DIVERSIFICATION =  3233.13 WITH STANDARD DEVIATION OF  4267.11

QUERIEDES       25626 5ELCID3263 QUANDO LAS NON *********, YA CANES TRAYDORES,
        WORD #3432 OCCURS   1 TIMES.

QUERIEN           288 5ELCID0036 LOS DE DENTRO NON LES ******* TORNAR PALABRA.
                 5237 5ELCID0662 MESNADAS DE MYO %ID EXIR ******* ALA BATALLA,
                23555 5ELCID3000 LEGAUA EL PLAZO, ******* YR ALA CORT;
        WORD #3433 OCCURS   3 TIMES.

QUERRA           1027 5ELCID0132 MYO %ID ****** LO QUE SSEA AGUISADO;
        WORD #3434 OCCURS   1 TIMES.

QUERRIA           814 5ELCID0104 EN PORIDAD FLABLAR ******* CON AMOS.
                 4229 5ELCID0538 CON ALFONSSO MYO SE@OR NON ******* LIDIAR.
                18757 5ELCID2373 MI ORDEN & MIS MANOS ******* LAS ONDRAR,
                18778 5ELCID2376 SI PLOGIESSE ADIOS ******* LAS ENSAYAR,
                26873 5ELCID3433 DEZIR ******* YA QUANTO DELO MYO.
        WORD #3435 OCCURS   5 TIMES.
           INDEX OF DIVERSIFICATION =  6513.75 WITH STANDARD DEVIATION OF  6284.55

QUERRIEN        27973 5ELCID3570 NOLO ******** AUER FECHO POR QUANTO HA EN CARRION.
        WORD #3436 OCCURS   1 TIMES.

QUES             3972 5ELCID0504 PUES QUE POR MI GANAREDES **** QUIER QUE SEA DALGO,
                 9046 5ELCID1151 DE PIES DE CAUALLO LOS **** PUDIERON ESCAPAR.
                 9233 5ELCID1174 MAL SE AQUEXAN LOS DE VALEN%IA QUE NON SABENT **** FAR,
                 9872 5ELCID1252 QUE NINGUN OMNE DELOS SOS **** LE NON SPIDIES, ONOL BESAS LA MANO,
                10211 5ELCID1293 SOSPIRANDO EL OBISPO **** VIESSE CON MOROS ENEL CAMPO:
                12975 5ELCID1646  **** ESTO, %ID, SI EL CRIADOR UOS SALUE
                15830 5ELCID2008 FATA **** TORNE EL QUE EN BUEN ORA NASCO.
                16677 5ELCID2112 QUANDO SALIE EL SOL, **** TORNASSE CADA VNO DON SALIDOS SON.
                17975 5ELCID2275 **** PAGE DES CASAMIENTO MYO %ID O EL QUE LO ALGO
                18130 5ELCID2294 **** ESTO, MESNADAS, O QUE QUEREDES UOS?
                24769 5ELCID3155 **** ONDRASSEN CON ELLAS & SIRUIESSEN AUOS;
                28033 5ELCID3578 NON SABEMOS **** COMIDRAN ELLOS OQUE NON;
        WORD #3437 OCCURS  12 TIMES.
           INDEX OF DIVERSIFICATION =  2186.36 WITH STANDARD DEVIATION OF  2159.18

QUESE            9080 5ELCID1155 MIEDO AN EN VALEN%IA QUE NON SABEN ***** FAR.
        WORD #3438 OCCURS   1 TIMES.

QUESTA           3892 5ELCID0494 DA ****** QUINTA QUE ME AUEDES MANDO,
                 4108 5ELCID0522 PLOGO A MYO %ID DA ****** PRESENTAIA.
                13059 5ELCID1656 CON DIOS A ****** LID YO LA HE DE ARRANCAR.
        WORD #3439 OCCURS   3 TIMES.

QUESTAS         10728 5ELCID1358 QUANDO EN CABO DE MI TIERRA A ******* DUE@AS FUEREN,
        WORD #3440 OCCURS   1 TIMES.

QUESTE           3593 5ELCID0453 DA ****** A CORRO FABLARA TODA ESPA@A.
                21134 5ELCID2685 DA ****** CASAMIENTO QUE GRADE EL CAMPEADOR.
        WORD #3441 OCCURS   2 TIMES.

QUESTOS          6122 5ELCID0779 DA ******* MOROS MATO XXX IIIJ;
        WORD #3442 OCCURS   1 TIMES.

QUETODOS        19590 5ELCID2482 SOBEIANAS SON LAS GANAN%IAS ******** AN GANADAS;
        WORD #3443 OCCURS   1 TIMES.

QUEUAN            547 5ELCID0069 PAGOS MYO %ID EL CAMPEADOR & TODOS LOS OTROS ****** ASO %ERUICIO
        WORD #3444 OCCURS   1 TIMES.

QUEXAR           6682 5ELCID0852 MOROS & MORAS TOMARON SE A ******:
                25185 5ELCID3207 AQUI VERIEDES ****** SE YFANTES DE CARRION
        WORD #3445 OCCURS   2 TIMES.
```

WORD C# PREFIX CONTEXT

QUI

983 5ELCID0126 NON DUERME SIN SOSPECHA *** AUER TRAE MONEDADO.
1705 5ELCID0219 DA *** QUITO CASTIELLA, PUES QUE EL REY HE EN YRA;
3336 5ELCID0421 EL *** QUISIERE COMER; & QUI NO, CAUALGE.
3340 5ELCID0421 EL QUI QUISIERE COMER; & *** NO, CAUALGE.
3362 5ELCID0424 DESPUES *** NOS BUSCARE FALLAR NOS PODRA.
6660 5ELCID0850 *** A BUEN SE@OR SIRUE, SIEMPRE BIUE EN DELI%IO.
6944 5ELCID0888 HYD & VENIT, DA *** UOS DO MI GRA%IA;
7388 5ELCID0948 *** EN VN LOGAR MORA SIEMPRE, LO SO PUEDE MANGUAR;
9554 5ELCID1214 EL ORO & LA PLATA *** EN VOS LO PODRIE CONTAR?
11506 5ELCID1457 *** BUEN MANDADERO ENBIA, TAL DEUE SPERAR.
12038 5ELCID1526 MUCHOL TENGO POR TORPE *** NON CONES%E LA VERDAD.
13442 5ELCID1704 EL QUE A *** MURIERE LIDIANDO DE CARA,
13493 5ELCID1710 DIXO EL CAMPEADOR: DESA *** UOS SEAN MANDADAS.
14040 5ELCID1778 QUE ANDAN ARRIADOS & NON HA *** TOMALOS,
15515 5ELCID1966 *** ENVIO POR CASTIELLA TANTA MULA PRE%IADA,
16814 5ELCID2129 *** QUIERE YR COMIGO ALAS BODAS, O RE%EBIR MI DON,
16850 5ELCID2133 DAD MANERO A *** LAS DE, QUANDO UOS LAS TOMADES;
17859 5ELCID2260 *** AUER QUIERE PRENDER BIEN ERA ABASTADO;
18625 5ELCID2357 CURIELOS *** QUIER, CA DELLOS POCO MINCAL.
19751 5ELCID2504 QUE PAGUEN AMI O A *** YO OUIER SABOR.
23406 5ELCID2982 *** NON VINIESSE ALA CORT NON SE TOUIESSE POR SU VASSALLO.
23497 5ELCID2993 *** LO FER NON QUISIESSE, O NO YR A MI CORT,
27047 5ELCID3455 SI AY *** RESPONDA ODIZE DE NO,
27079 5ELCID3460 E *** AL QUISIESSE SERIE SU OCASION.
28206 5ELCID3601 CA *** TUERTO QUISIERE FAZER, MAL GELO VEDARE YO,
28255 5ELCID3607 QUE POR Y SERIE VEN%IDO *** SALIESSE DEL MOION.
29013 5ELCID3706 *** BUENA DUENA ESCARNE%E & LA DEXA DESPUES,
WORD #3446 OCCURS 27 TIMES.
INDEX OF DIVERSIFICATION = 1077.08 WITH STANDARD DEVIATION OF 1090.52

QUIAS

1894 5ELCID0241 TU QUE ATODOS *****, VALA MYO %ID EL CANPEADOR.
WORD #3447 OCCURS 1 TIMES.

QUI%AB

19719 5ELCID2500 QUE ABRAM DE MI SALTO ****** ALGUNA NOCH
WORD #3448 OCCURS 1 TIMES.

QUIEBRAN

3617 5ELCID0456 YA ******** LOS ALBORES & VINIE LA MA@ANA,
27781 5ELCID3545 TROCIDA ES LA NOCHE, YA ******** LOS ALBORES.
WORD #3449 OCCURS 2 TIMES.

QUIEN

2147 5ELCID0270 CON AQUESTAS MYS DUE@AS DE ***** SO YO SERUIDA.
7663 5ELCID0981 SABRA EL SALIDO A ***** VINO DESONDRAR.
7797 5ELCID0998 VERA REMONT VERENGEL TRAS ***** VINO EN ALCAN%A
9347 5ELCID1189 ***** QUIERE PERDER CUETA & VENIR A RRITAD,
9372 5ELCID1192 ***** QUIERE YR COMIGO %ERCAR A VALEN%IA,
9586 5ELCID1218 ELOS OTROS AUERES ***** LOS PODRIE CONTAR?
19964 5ELCID2533 ***** LIDIARA MEIOR OQUIEN FUERA EN ALCAN%O;
25730 5ELCID3277 O ***** GELAS DIERA POR PAREIAS OPOR VELADAS?
26465 5ELCID3377 HYA VARONES, ***** VIO NUNCA TAL MAL?
26470 5ELCID3378 ***** NOS DARIE NUEUAS DE MYO %ID EL DE BIUAR
27562 5ELCID3520 ***** VOS LO TOLLER QUISIERE NOL VALA EL CRIADOR,
29216 5ELCID3731 ***** ESCRIUIO ESTE LIBRO DEL DIOS PARAYSO, AMEN
WORD #3450 OCCURS 12 TIMES.
INDEX OF DIVERSIFICATION = 2459.82 WITH STANDARD DEVIATION OF 3342.14

QUIER

3973 5ELCID0504 PUES QUE POR MI GANAREDES QUES ***** QUE SEA DALGO,
18626 5ELCID2357 CURIELOS QUI *****, CA DELLOS POCO MINCAL.
23220 5ELCID2958 SI ***** EL CASAMIENTO FECHO NON FUESSE OY
29026 5ELCID3707 ATAL LE CONTESCA O SI ***** PEOR.
WORD #3451 OCCURS 4 TIMES.

QUIERA

1819 5ELCID0231 ANTES SERE CON UUSCO QUE EL SOL ****** RAYAR.
10978 5ELCID1389 EL %ID QUE BIEN NOS ****** NADA NON PERDERA.
11412 5ELCID1444 AQUESTE MONESTERIO NO LO ****** OLBIDAR,
21123 5ELCID2684 DIOS LO ****** & LO MANDE, QUE DE TODEL MUNDO ES SE@OR,
WORD #3452 OCCURS 4 TIMES.

QUIERE

7985 5ELCID1020 EL NON LO ****** COMER, ATODOS LOS SOSANAUA:
9348 5ELCID1189 QUIEN ****** PERDER CUETA & VENIR A RRITAD,
9365 5ELCID1191 %ERCAR ****** A VALEN%IA PORA CHRISTIANOS LA DAR.
9373 5ELCID1192 QUIEN ****** YR COMIGO %ERCAR A VALEN%IA,
10256 5ELCID1298 QUANDO DIOS PRESTAR NOS ******, NOS BIEN GELO GRADESCAMOS:
11190 5ELCID1416 HYR SE ****** A VALEN%IA A MYO %ID EL DE BIUAR.
11302 5ELCID1430 EL BUENO DE MINAYA PENSSAR ****** DE CAUALGAR;
12756 5ELCID1619 EL YUIERNO ES EXIDO, QUE EL MAR%O ****** ENTRAR.
15436 5ELCID1955 AYAMOS VISTAS QUANDO LO ****** MYO SE@OR.
16705 5ELCID2115 CONPE%O MYO %ID ADAR AQUIEN ****** PRENDER SO DON,
16815 5ELCID2129 QUI ****** YR COMIGO ALAS BODAS, O RE%EBIR MI DON,
17037 5ELCID2157 NON ****** QUEL ESCURA, QUITOL DESSI LUEGO.
17861 5ELCID2260 QUI AUER ****** PRENDER BIEN ERA ABASTADO;
23754 5ELCID3026 BILTAR SE ****** & ONDRAR ASO SE@OS.
24301 5ELCID3098 POR TALLO FAZE ESTO QUE RECABDAR ****** TODO LO SUYO;
WORD #3453 OCCURS 15 TIMES.
INDEX OF DIVERSIFICATION = 1164.43 WITH STANDARD DEVIATION OF 1548.73

```
WORD                C#  PREFIX                                  CONTEXT

QUIEREL            13096 5ELCID1660 MIEDO A SU MUGIER & ******* QUEBRAR EL CORA%ON,
        WORD #3454 OCCURS    1 TIMES.

QUIEREN             1851 5ELCID0235 APRIESSA CANTAN LOS GALLOS & ******* QUEBRAR ALBORES,
                    2913 5ELCID0367 SALIERON DELA EGLESIA, YA ******* CAUALGAR.
                    8986 5ELCID1143 MOROS SON MUCHOS, YA ******* RECONBRAR.
                   11829 5ELCID1499 AFEUOS AQUI PERO VERMUEZ & MU@O GUSTIOZ QUE UOS ******* SIN HART,
                   11880 5ELCID1506 ESSO FFUE APRIESSA FECHO, QUE NOS ******* DETARDAR.
                   13003 5ELCID1649 APOCO QUE VINIESTES, PRESEND UOS ******* DAR:
                   16744 5ELCID2120 PARTIR SE *******, QUE ENTRADA ERA LA NOCH.
                   20418 5ELCID2591 HYA ******* CAUALGAR, EN ESPIDIMIENTO SON.
                   21330 5ELCID2711 DEPORTAR SE ******* CON ELLAS ATODO SU SABOR.
                   27690 5ELCID3535 CUNPLIR ******* EL DEBDO QUE LES MANDO SO SE@OR,
        WORD #3455 OCCURS   10 TIMES.
           INDEX OF DIVERSIFICATION =  2870.00 WITH STANDARD DEVIATION OF  2289.83

QUIERES            19085 5ELCID2414 ASI COMMO SEMEIA, EN MI LA ******* ENSAYAR.
        WORD #3456 OCCURS    1 TIMES.

QUIERO               673 5ELCID0085 CON UUESTRO CONSEGO BASTIR ****** DOS ARCHAS;
                    1993 5ELCID0252 NON ****** FAZER ENEL MONESTERIO VN DINERO DE DA@O;
                    2490 5ELCID0314 POCO AUER TRAYO, DAR UOS ****** UUESTRA PART.
                    4157 5ELCID0529 QUITAR ****** CASTEION, OYD, ESCUELLAS & MINYAYA
                    4190 5ELCID0533 MAS EL CASTIELO NON LO ****** HERMAR;
                    4197 5ELCID0534 %IENTO MOROS & %IENTO MORAS ****** LAS QUITAR,
                    6380 5ELCID0813 ENBIAR UOS ****** A CASTIELLA CON MANDADO
                    6963 5ELCID0890 SOBRE AQUESTO TODO, DEZIR UOS ******, MINAYA:
                    7027 5ELCID0899 ****** UOS DEZIR DEL QUE EN BUEN ORA NASCO & %INXO ESPADA:
                    8069 5ELCID1029 QUE YO DEXAR ME MORIR, QUE NON ****** COMER.
                    9912 5ELCID1257 SI UOS QUISIEREDES, MINAYA, ****** SABER RECABDO
                   10033 5ELCID1271 ENBIAR UOS ****** A CASTIELLA, DO AUEMOS HEREDADES,
                   10054 5ELCID1274 DAR LE ****** C CAUALLOS, & UOS YD GELOS LEUAR;
                   10266 5ELCID1299 EN TIERRAS DE VALEN%IA FER ****** OBISPADO,
                   10345 5ELCID1310 DEXARE UOS LAS POSADAS, NON LAS ****** CONTAR.
                   10748 5ELCID1361 NON ****** QUE NADA PIERDA EL CAMPEADOR;
                   12760 5ELCID1620 DEZIR UOS ****** NUEUAS DE ALENT PARTES DEL MAR,
                   13930 5ELCID1765 ****** LAS CASAR CON DE AQUESTOS MYOS VASSALLOS;
                   14016 5ELCID1776 ****** UOS DEZIR LO QUE ES MAS GRANADO:
                   14141 5ELCID1790 ENBIAR LA ****** ALFONSSO EL CASTELLANO,
                   14871 5ELCID1879 DELOS YFFANTES DE CARRION YO UOS ****** CONTAR,
                   15126 5ELCID1913 ANDAR LE ****** A MYO %ID EN TODA PRO.
                   16339 5ELCID2073 COMETER ****** VN RUEGO A MYO %ID EL CAMPEADOR;
                   17558 5ELCID2221 VENIT ACA, ALBARFANEZ, EL QUE YO ****** & AMO
                   17578 5ELCID2224 NOLO ****** FALIR POR NADA DE QUANTO AY PARADO;
                   18636 5ELCID2358 HYO CON LOS MYOS FERIR ****** DELANT,
                   18764 5ELCID2374 EA ESTAS FERIDAS YO ****** YR DELANT;
                   18802 5ELCID2379 SI ESTE AMOR NON FECHES, YO DEUOS ME ****** QUITAR.
                   20253 5ELCID2571 HYO ****** LES DAR AXUUAR IIJ MILL MARCOS DE PLATA;
                   24140 5ELCID3078 DAQUESTA GUISA ****** YR ALA CORT,
                   25388 5ELCID3233 TORNAR GELOS ******, CA TODOS FECHOS SON,
                   25410 5ELCID3235 QUANDO ELLOS LOS AN APECHAR, NON GELOS ****** YO.
                   26544 5ELCID3388 EN TU AMISTAD NON ****** AVER RA%ION.
                   27177 5ELCID3474 MAS ****** A VALEN%IA QUE TIERRAS DE CARRION.
                   27449 5ELCID3507 E YR ME ****** PORA VALEN%IA, CON AFAN LA GANE YO.
        WORD #3457 OCCURS   35 TIMES.
           INDEX OF DIVERSIFICATION =   786.53 WITH STANDARD DEVIATION OF   855.80

QUIEROL             6397 5ELCID0816 ******* ENBIAR EN DON XXX CAUALLOS,
        WORD #3458 OCCURS    1 TIMES.

QUIL               26494 5ELCID3381  **** DARIE CON LOS DE CARRION ACASAR?
        WORD #3459 OCCURS    1 TIMES.

QUILOS              5552 5ELCID0699 E FIZIERON DOS AZES DE PEONES MEZCLADOS, ****** PODRIE CONTAR?
        WORD #3460 OCCURS    1 TIMES.

QUIN                6835 5ELCID0874  **** LOS DIO ESTOS, SI UOS VALA DIOS, MYNAYA
        WORD #3461 OCCURS    1 TIMES.

QUINEA              3180 5ELCID0400 LA CAL%ADA DE ****** YUA LA TRASPASSAR,
        WORD #3462 OCCURS    1 TIMES.

QUINIENTOS         11237 5ELCID1422 LOS ********** MARCOS DIO MINAYA AL ABBAT,
                   11245 5ELCID1423 DELOS OTROS ********** DEZIR UOS HE QUE FAZE:
                   13235 5ELCID1678 ********** MATARON DELLOS CONPLIDOS ENES DIA.
        WORD #3463 OCCURS    3 TIMES.

QUINTA              3880 5ELCID0492 DOUOS LA ******, SI LA QUISIEREDES, MINAYA.
                    3893 5ELCID0494 DA QUESTA ****** QUE ME AUEDES MANDO,
                    4048 5ELCID0515 TODA LA ****** A MYO %ID FINCAUA.
                    4083 5ELCID0519 ESTA ****** POR QUANTO SERIE CONPRADA,
                    6323 5ELCID0805 EN LA SU ****** AL %ID CAEN C CAUALLOS.
                    9572 5ELCID1216 MYO %ID DON RODRIGO LA ****** MANDO TOMAR,
                   14209 5ELCID1798 DE TODA LA SU ****** EL DIEZMO LA MANDADO.
```

WORD C# PREFIX CONTEXT

QUINTA (CON'T)

14273 5ELCID1806 DESTA MI ******, DIGC UCS SIN FALLA,
14298 5ELCID1809 CON CAUALLCS DESTA ****** QUE YO HE GANADA,
19624 5ELCID2487 ELA SU ****** NON FUESSE OLBIDADO.
19638 5ELCID2489 CAYERON LE EN ****** AL %ID SEYX %IENTOS CAUALLOS,
WORD #3464 OCCURS 11 TIMES.
INDEX OF DIVERSIFICATION = 1574.80 WITH STANDARD DEVIATION OF 2125.00

QUINTO 23671 5ELCID3015 AL ****** DIA VENIDO ES MYO %ID EL CAMPEADOR;
WORD #3465 OCCURS 1 TIMES.

QUINZE 2308 5ELCID0291 %IENTO ****** CAUALLERCS TODOS IUNTADOS SON;
3733 5ELCID0472 ****** MORCS MATAUA DELOS QUE ALCAN%AUA.
6264 5ELCID0798 MAS DE ****** DE LCS SOS MENOS NON FALLARON.
17788 5ELCID2251 ****** DIAS CONPLIDOS DURARON EN LAS BODAS,
WORD #3466 OCCURS 4 TIMES.

QUI@ONEROS 4019 5ELCID0511 SOS ********** QUE GELOS DIESSEN POR CARTA.
WORD #3467 OCCURS 1 TIMES.

QUIS 8916 5ELCID1136 **** CADA VNO DELLOS BIEN SABE LO QUE HA DE FAR.
WORD #3468 OCCURS 1 TIMES.

QUISIERE 1807 5ELCID0230 SI EL REY MELO ******** TOMAR AMI NON MINCHAL.
3337 5ELCID0421 EL QUI ******** COMER; & QUI NO, CAUALGE.
15421 5ELCID1953 MAS LO QUE EL ********, ESSO QUERAMOS NOS.
15454 5ELCID1958 LO QUE EL REY ********, ESSO FERA EL CAMPEADOR.
18505 5ELCID2342 AVN SI DIOS ******** & EL PADRE QUE ESTA EN ALTO,
27087 5ELCID3461 SI DIOS ******** QUE DESTA BIEN SALGAMOS NOS,
27566 5ELCID3520 QUIEN VOS LO TOLLER ******** NOL VALA EL CRIADOR,
28208 5ELCID3601 CA QUI TUERTO ******** FAZER, MAL GELO VEDARE YO,
WORD #3469 OCCURS 8 TIMES.
INDEX OF DIVERSIFICATION = 3770.57 WITH STANDARD DEVIATION OF 4697.39

QUISIEREDES 3883 5ELCID0492 DOUOS LA QUINTA, SI LA ***********, MINAYA.
8422 5ELCID1070 SI UOS VINIERE EMIENTE QUE *********** VENGALO,
9910 5ELCID1257 SI UOS ***********, MINAYA, QUIERO SABER RECABDO
13027 5ELCID1652 MUGIER, SED EN ESTE PALA%IO, & SI *********** EN EL ALCA%AR;
14281 5ELCID1807 PRENDED LO QUE ***********, LO OTRO REMANGA.
16477 5ELCID2089 DAD LAS AQUI *********** UOS, CA YO PAGADO SO.
16611 5ELCID2104 QUE METAN EN SUS BODAS DOO *********** UOS;
WORD #3470 OCCURS 7 TIMES.
INDEX OF DIVERSIFICATION = 2120.33 WITH STANDARD DEVIATION OF 1545.63

QUISIEREMOS 8809 5ELCID1120 SI EN ESTAS TIERRAS *********** CURAR,
WORD #3471 OCCURS 1 TIMES.

QUISIEREN 6972 5ELCID0891 DE TODO MYO REYNO LOS QUE LO ********* FAR,
10809 5ELCID1369 LOS QUE ********* YR SEUIR AL CAMPEADOR
WORD #3472 OCCURS 2 TIMES.

QUISIERON 12228 5ELCID1552 DE QUANTO QUE ********* NON OUIERON FALLA,
24786 5ELCID3157 CCMIGO NON ********* AUER NADA & PERDIERON MI AMOR;
WORD #3473 OCCURS 2 TIMES.

QUISIESSE 23501 5ELCID2993 QUI LO FER NON *********, O NO YR A MI CORT,
27081 5ELCID3460 E QUI AL ********* SERIE SU OCASION.
WORD #3474 OCCURS 2 TIMES.

QUISIESSEN 15599 5ELCID1978 QUANTOS ********** AUERES DORO O DE PLATA.
WORD #3475 OCCURS 1 TIMES.

QUISIESTES 23080 5ELCID2940 ALTO FUE EL CASAMIENO CALO ********** UOS
28181 5ELCID3597 ESTA LID EN TOLEDO LAFIZIERADES, MAS NON ********** VOS.
WORD #3476 OCCURS 2 TIMES.

QUISO 4067 5ELCID0517 NIN CATIUOS NIN CATIUAS NON ***** TRAER EN SU CONPA@A.
6674 5ELCID0851 QUANDO MYO %ID EL CASTIELLO ***** QUITAR,
9461 5ELCID1202 MYO %ID DON RODRIGO NON LO ***** DETARDAR,
13359 5ELCID1693 FABLAUA MYNAYA, NON LO ***** DETARDAR:
13812 5ELCID1750 ESTO DIOS SE LO ***** CON TODOS LOS SOS SANTOS,
22371 5ELCID2850 NON GELO ***** TOMAR, MAS MUCHO GELO GRADIO:
22746 5ELCID2898 EL QUE EN BUEN ORA NASCO NON ***** TARDAR,
23900 5ELCID3044 ESSA NOCH MYO %ID TAIO NON ***** PASSAR;
24410 5ELCID3112 NOS ***** LEUANTAR EL CRESPO DE GRA@ON,
WORD #3477 OCCURS 9 TIMES.
INDEX OF DIVERSIFICATION = 2541.88 WITH STANDARD DEVIATION OF 2757.40

QUISOL 2105 5ELCID0265 LORAUA DELOS OIOS, ****** BESAR LAS MANOS:
WORD #3478 OCCURS 1 TIMES.

QUITADO 3911 5ELCID0496 YO UOS LA SUELTA & AUELLO *******.
WORD #3479 OCCURS 1 TIMES.

QUITAR 3121 5ELCID0392 %ERCA VIENE EL PLAZO POR EL REYNO ******.
3360 5ELCID0423 LA TIERRA DEL REY ALFONSSO ESTA NOCH LA PODEMOS ******.

WORD C# PREFIX CONTEXT

QUITAR (CON'T)

4156 5ELCID0529 ****** QUIERO CASTEION, OYD, ESCUELLAS & MINYAYA
4199 5ELCID0534 %IENTO MOROS & %IENTO MORAS QUIERO LAS ******,
6675 5ELCID0851 QUANDO MYO %ID EL CASTIELLO QUISO ******,
7688 5ELCID0984 QUE A MENOS DE BATALLA NOS PUEDEN DEN ******.
8115 5ELCID1035 AUOS & DOS FIJOS DALGO ****** UOS HE LOS CUERPOS & DARUOS E DE MANO.
12109 5ELCID1536 EL PORTERO DEL REY ****** LO MANDAUA;
12235 5ELCID1553 AVN LAS FERRADURAS ****** GELAS MANDAUA;
18803 5ELCID2379 SI ESTE AMOR NON FECHES, YO DEUOS ME QUIERO ******.
24654 5ELCID3141 ****** ME A EL REYNO, PERDERA MIAMOR.
WORD #3480 OCCURS 11 TIMES.
INDEX OF DIVERSIFICATION = 2152.30 WITH STANDARD DEVIATION OF 2472.19

QUITAREMOS 1646 5ELCID0211 MESURAREMOS LA POSADA & ********** EL REYNADO;
WORD #3481 OCCURS 1 TIMES.

QUITAS 29087 5ELCID3715 AGORA LAS AYAN ****** HEREDADES DE CARRION.
WORD #3482 OCCURS 1 TIMES.

QUITE 23471 5ELCID2989 RUEGAN AL REY QUE LOS ***** DESTA CORT.
23508 5ELCID2994 ***** MYO REYNO, CADEL NON HE SABOR.
WORD #3483 OCCURS 2 TIMES.

QUITEDES 6440 5ELCID0822 EN SANTA MARIA DE BURGOS ******** MILL MISSAS;
WORD #3484 OCCURS 1 TIMES.

QUITO 1706 5ELCID0219 DA QUI ***** CASTIELLA, PUES QUE EL REY HE EN YRA;
6698 5ELCID0855 QUANDO ***** A ALCO%ER MYO %ID EL DE BIUAR,
6933 5ELCID0886 SOBRESTO TODO, AUOS *****, MINAYA,
6986 5ELCID0893 SUELTO LES LOS CUERPOS & ***** LES LAS HEREDADES.
12134 5ELCID1539 EL REY LO PAGO TODO, & ***** SEUA MINAYA.
WORD #3485 OCCURS 5 TIMES.
INDEX OF DIVERSIFICATION = 2606.00 WITH STANDARD DEVIATION OF 2845.71

QUITOL 17040 5ELCID2157 NON QUIERE QUEL ESCURA, ****** DESSI LUEGO.
WORD #3486 OCCURS 1 TIMES.

QUITOS 10817 5ELCID1370 DE MI SEAN ****** & VAYAN ALA GRA%IA DEL CRIADOR.
WORD #3487 OCCURS 1 TIMES.

RACHEL 698 5ELCID0089 POR ****** & VIDAS UAYADES ME PRIUADO:
764 5ELCID0097 POR ****** & VIDAS APRIESSA DEMANDAUA.
776 5ELCID0099 POR ****** & VIDAS APRIESSA DEMANDAUA.
781 5ELCID0100 ****** & VIDAS EN VNO ESTAUAN AMOS,
804 5ELCID0103 O SODES, ****** & VIDAS, LOS MYOS AMIGOS CAROS?
824 5ELCID0106 ****** & VIDAS, AMOS ME DAT LAS MANOS,
949 5ELCID0122 ****** & VIDAS SEYEN SE CONSEIANDO:
1055 5ELCID0136 DIXO ****** & VIDAS: DAR GELOS DE GRADO.
1080 5ELCID0139 DIXO ****** & VIDAS: NON SE FAZE ASSI EL MERCADO,
1134 5ELCID0146 DIXO ****** & VIDAS: NOS DESTO NOS PAGAMOS.
1153 5ELCID0149 CON ****** & VIDAS, DE VOLUTAD & DE GRADO.
1201 5ELCID0155 YA DON ****** & VIDAS, AUEDES ME OLBIDADO
1232 5ELCID0159 DON ****** & VIDAS A MYO %ID BESARON LE LAS MANOS.
1301 5ELCID0167 LEUALDAS, ****** & VIDAS, PONED LAS EN UUESTRO SALUO;
1344 5ELCID0172 GRADAN SE ****** & VIDAS CON AUERES MONEDADOS,
1357 5ELCID0174 ****** AMYO %ID LA MANOL BA BESAR:
1475 5ELCID0189 YA DON ****** & VIDAS, EN UUESTRAS MANOS SON LAS ARCAS;
1493 5ELCID0191 ENTRE ****** & VIDAS APARTE YXIERON AMOS:
11306 5ELCID1431 AFEUOS ****** & VIDAS ALOS PIES LE CAEN:
11357 5ELCID1437 DIXO ****** & VIDAS: EL CRIADOR LO MANDE
WORD #3488 OCCURS 20 TIMES.
INDEX OF DIVERSIFICATION = 560.00 WITH STANDARD DEVIATION OF 2240.76

RA%ION 18407 5ELCID2329 QUE SEAN EN PAS & NON AYAN Y ******.
19469 5ELCID2467 QUE ALA ****** CAYE SEYS %IENTOS MARCOS DE PLATA.
21803 5ELCID2773 ELLOS NOL VIEN NI DEND SABIEN ******;
26546 5ELCID3388 EN TU AMISTAD NON QUIERO AVER ******.
WORD #3489 OCCURS 4 TIMES.

RA%ON 25267 5ELCID3216 DESTOS AUERES QUE UOS DI YO, SIMELOS DADES, O DEDES DELLO *****.
WORD #3490 OCCURS 1 TIMES.

RAMADAS 3674 5ELCID0463 LAS YENTES DE FUERA TODAS SON DE *******.
WORD #3491 OCCURS 1 TIMES.

RAMAS 21234 5ELCID2698 LOS MONTES SON ALTOS, LAS ***** PUIAN CON LAS NUES,
WORD #3492 OCCURS 1 TIMES.

RANCADO 6027 5ELCID0764 POR AQUEL COLPE ******* ES EL FONSSADO.
WORD #3493 OCCURS 1 TIMES.

RAN%AL 1430 5ELCID0183 SOBRELLA VNA SAUANA DE ****** & MUY BLANCA.
24209 5ELCID3087 VISTIO CAMISA DE ****** TAN BLANCA COMMO EL SOL,
27334 5ELCID3493 LA CONFIA DE ****** QUE BLANCA ERA COMMO EL SOL,
WORD #3494 OCCURS 3 TIMES.

WORD C# PREFIX CONTEXT

```
RAPAZ             25824 5ELCID3289 NON YOUC ***** QUE NON MESSC SU PULGADA;
         WORD #3495 OCCURS   1 TIMES.

RASTADO           13682 5ELCID1733 TODA ESTA GANAN%IA EN SU MANO A *******.
         WORD #3496 OCCURS   1 TIMES.

RASTADOS          17942 5ELCID2270 EL %ID & SOS HYERNOS EN VALEN%IA SON ********.
         WORD #3497 OCCURS   1 TIMES.

RASTARA            5639 5ELCID0710 RESPUSC PERO VERMUEZ:  NON ******* POR AL.
                  13290 5ELCID1685 OYD ME, CAUALLERCS, NCN ******* POR AL;
         WORD #3498 OCCURS   2 TIMES.

RASTARON          28923 5ELCID3694 LAS ARMAS CUE Y ******** EL SELAS TOMO.
         WORD #3499 OCCURS   1 TIMES.

RASTE              5430 5ELCID0685 TODOS YSCAMOS FUERA, QUE NADI NON *****,
         WORD #3500 OCCURS   1 TIMES.

RASTRANDO         26450 5ELCID3374 MANTO ARMINO & VN BRIAL *********,
         WORD #3501 OCCURS   1 TIMES.

RASTRO             3093 5ELCID0389 ABBAT, DEZILDES QUE PRENDAN EL ****** & PIESSEN DE ANDAR,
                  21822 5ELCID2776 POR EL ****** TORNOS FELEZ MUNOZ,
         WORD #3502 OCCURS   2 TIMES.

RAXOL             28621 5ELCID3655 ***** LOS PELOS DELA CABE%A, BIEN ALA CARNE LEGAUA;
         WORD #3503 OCCURS   1 TIMES.

RAY                 584 5ELCID0074 EN YRA DEL *** ALFFONSSC YO SERE METIDO.
         WORD #3504 OCCURS   1 TIMES.

RAYAR              1820 5ELCID0231 ANTES SERE CON UUSCO QUE EL SOL QUIERA *****.
         WORD #3505 OCCURS   1 TIMES.

RAZIN             20834 5ELCID2645 POR SANTA MARIA DALUA ***** FAZIAN LA POSADA,
         WORD #3506 OCCURS   1 TIMES.

RAZON               143 5ELCID0019 DELAS SUS BOCAS TODOS DIZIAN UNA *****:
                  10645 5ELCID1348 DIXO EL REY REY AL CONDE: CEXAC ESSA *****,
                  10865 5ELCID1375 NON LA OSARIEMOS A COMETER NOS ESTA *****,
                  10885 5ELCID1377 NON LO DIZEN A NACI, & FINCO ESTA *****.
                  14765 5ELCID1866 FABLO EL REY DON ALFONSSO & DIXO ESTA *****:
                  14980 5ELCID1893 MAS PUES BOS LO QUEREDES, ENTREMOS EN LA *****.
                  15216 5ELCID1926 ESTO DIZIENDO, CONPIE%AN LA *****,
                  16110 5ELCID2043 FABLO MYO %ID & DIXO ESTA *****: ESTO GRADESCO AL CRIADOR,
                  16291 5ELCID2066 TODOS ERAN ALEGRES & ACUERDAN EN VNA *****:
                  16329 5ELCID2071 NCN LO TARDO EL REY, LA ***** CONPE%O:
                  21467 5ELCID2729 MOROS & CHRISTIANCS DEPARTIRAN DESTA *****,
                  21796 5ELCID2772 VIOLOS VENIR & OYO VNA *****,
                  24152 5ELCID3079 POR DE MANDAR MYOS DERECHOS & DEZIR MI *****:
                  24275 5ELCID3095 CON ORO ES OBRADA, FECHA POR *****,
                  24808 5ELCID3169 ATORGAN LOS ALCALDES: TOD ESTO ES *****.
                  24840 5ELCID3163 APRIESSA LO YUAN TRAYENDO & ACUERDAN LA *****:
                  25364 5ELCID3229 NOS BIEN LA SABEMOS ACUESTA *****,
                  25515 5ELCID3249 MAL ESCAPAN IOGADOS, SABED, DESTA *****.
                  25591 5ELCID3259 O EN ALGUNA *****? ACUI LO MEIORARE A JUUIZYO DELA CORT.
                  25853 5ELCID3293 DEXASSEDES UOS, %ID, DE AQUESTA *****;
                  26116 5ELCID3329 DI, FERRANDO, OTORGA ESTA *****:
                  26290 5ELCID3352 DAQUESTOS AMOS ACUI QUEDO LA *****.
                  26437 5ELCID3372 DESTOS AMOS LA ***** FINCO.
                  26562 5ELCID3390 DIXO EL REY ALFONSSO: CALLE YA ESTA *****.
                  26575 5ELCID3392 ASSI COMMO ACABAN ESTA *****,
                  27069 5ELCID3458 QUE VAL, MINAYA, TODA ESSA *****?
                  27105 5ELCID3463 DIXO EL REY: FINE ESTA *****;
                  27254 5ELCID3483 QUEN NCN VINIERE AL PLAZO PIERDA LA *****,
                  29215 5ELCID3730 EN ESTE LOGAR SE ACABA ESTA *****.
         WORD #3507 OCCURS  29 TIMES.
            INDEX OF DIVERSIFICATION =  1037.29 WITH STANDARD DEVIATION OF  2220.49

RAZONAS           10561 5ELCID1339 ******* POR VUESTRO VASSALLO & AUOS TIENE POR SE@OR.
         WORD #3508 OCCURS   1 TIMES.

REAL               6765 5ELCID0863 Y FFINCO EN VN POYO QUE ES SOBRE MONT ****;
                   9331 5ELCID1186 AMANE%IO AMYO %ID EN TIERRAS DE MON ****.
         WORD #3509 OCCURS   2 TIMES.

REBATA             3713 5ELCID0468 LOS QUE LA TIENEN, QUANDO VIERON LA ******,
                  18140 5ELCID2295 HYA SE@OR CNDRADO, ****** NOS DIO EL LEON.
         WORD #3510 OCCURS   2 TIMES.

REBTADO           26566 5ELCID3391 LOS QUE AN ******* LIDIARAN, SIN SALUE DIOS
         WORD #3511 OCCURS   1 TIMES.
```

WORD C# PREFIX CONTEXT

```
REBTARON            27126 5ELCID3466 DESTOS IIJ PCR TRES QUE ******** EN LA CORT.
        WORD #3512 OCCURS   1 TIMES.

REBTEDES            27948 5ELCID3566 ESSI FUERES VEN%IDOS, NON ******** A NOS,
        WORD #3513 OCCURS   1 TIMES.

REBTO               28378 5ELCID3623 PERO VERMUEZ, EL QUE ANTES *****,
        WORD #3514 OCCURS   1 TIMES.

RECABDADO           15816 5ELCID2006 ********* HA, COMMO TAN BUEN VARON,
        WORD #3515 OCCURS   1 TIMES.

RECABDANDO          17600 5ELCID2226 E PRENDAN BENDI%IONES & VAYAMOS **********.
        WORD #3516 OCCURS   1 TIMES.

RECABDAR            11695 5ELCID1482 MYO %ID UOS SALUDAUA, & MANDOLO ********,
                    24300 5ELCID3098 POR TALLC FAZE ESTC CUE ******** QUIERE TODO LO SUYO;
        WORD #3517 OCCURS   2 TIMES.

RECABDO               181 5ELCID0024 CCN GRAND ******* & FUERTE MIENTRE SELLADA:
                      343 5ELCID0043 CCN GRANT ******* & FUERTE MIENTRE SELLADA.
                     1611 5ELCID0206 VENGO, CAMPEADOR, CCN TCDO BUEN *******:
                     2044 5ELCID0257 DELLAS & DE MI MUGIER FAGADES TODO *******.
                     6278 5ELCID0799 TRAEN CRO & PLATA QUE NCN SABEN *******;
                     9160 5ELCID1166 NON ES CON ******* EL DCLCR DE VALEN%IA.
                     9901 5ELCID1255 AFEUOS TODC AQUESTC PUESTC EN BUEN *******.
                     9914 5ELCID1257 SI UOS QUISIEREDES, MINAYA, CUIERO SABER *******
                    11784 5ELCID1494 E EN MEDINA TCDC EL ******* ESTA;
                    12344 5ELCID1567 CA BIEN SABE QUE ALBARFANEZ TRAHE TODO *******;
                    13521 5ELCID1713 DEXAN ALAS PUERTAS CMNES CE GRANT *******.
                    13718 5ELCID1738 LAS OTRAS GANAN%IAS NCN AUYA *******.
                    13750 5ELCID1742 DEXO ALBARFANEZ POR SABER TODO *******.
                    16921 5ELCID2141 TOD ESTC ES PUESTO, SABED, EN GRANT *******.
                    17655 5ELCID2233 QUE LAS TOMASSEDES PCR MUGIERES A ONDRA & A *******.
                    19353 5ELCID2451 DELOS COLPES DELA LAN%A NON AUIE *******;
                    21684 5ELCID2756 QUE EL VNA AL OTRA NCL TORNA *******.
                    26462 5ELCID3376 EN LO QUE FABLO AVIE POCO *******:
        WORD #3518 OCCURS  18 TIMES.
           INDEX OF DIVERSIFICATION =  1544.94 WITH STANDARD DEVIATION OF  1477.97

RECEBIR             20860 5ELCID2649 SALIOLOS ******* CON GRANDES AUOROZES;
        WORD #3519 OCCURS   1 TIMES.

RECIBIO              1555 5ELCID0199 GRADE%IOLO DON MARTINO & ******* LOS MARCHOS;
        WORD #3520 OCCURS   1 TIMES.

RECIBIOLO           25475 5ELCID3245 ********* MYO %ID COMMC APRE%IARON ENLA CORT.
        WORD #3521 OCCURS   1 TIMES.

RECOMBRO            28884 5ELCID3689 LA LAN%A ******** & SOBREL SE PARO;
        WORD #3522 OCCURS   1 TIMES.

RECONBRAR            8987 5ELCID1143 MOROS SON MUCHOS, YA CUIEREN *********.
        WORD #3523 OCCURS   1 TIMES.

RECORDANDO          21930 5ELCID2790 VAN ********** CON ELUIRA & DO@A SOL,
        WORD #3524 OCCURS   1 TIMES.

RECUDADES           25239 5ELCID3213 ALC QUE DEMANDA EL %ID QUEL ********* VOS.
        WORD #3525 OCCURS   1 TIMES.

RECUDEDES           25671 5ELCID3269 SI NON *********, VEA LC ESTA CORT.
        WORD #3526 OCCURS   1 TIMES.

RE%EBIDAS           12436 5ELCID1578 ********* LAS DUENAS A VNA GRANT ONDRAN%A,
        WORD #3527 OCCURS   1 TIMES.

RE%EBIR              2353 5ELCID0297 APRIESSA CAUALGA, ******* LOS SALIE,
                     3849 5ELCID0487 SALIOLOS ******* CON ESTA SU MESNADA,
                    11661 5ELCID1478 SALIOLOS ******* CCN GRANT GOZO QUE FAZE:
                    14462 5ELCID1829 QUE MANDASSE ******* A ESTA CONPA@A:
                    15888 5ELCID2015 ******* LO SALEN CCN TAN GRAND ONOR.
                    16821 5ELCID2129 QUI QUIERE YR CCMIGC ALAS BODAS, O ******* MI DON,
                    20374 5ELCID2585 CONPIE%AN A ******* LC CUE EL %ID MANDO.
                    22129 5ELCID2817 HYUA ******* ADCN ELUIRA & ADON@A SOL;
                    22621 5ELCID2882 SALIOLOS A ******* DE BUENA VOLUNTAD,
                    22651 5ELCID2886 PRIUADC CAUALGA, A ******* LOS SALE;
                    23715 5ELCID3021 E YUA ******* ALQUE EN BUEN ORA NA%IO.
        WORD #3528 OCCURS  11 TIMES.
           INDEX OF DIVERSIFICATION =  2135.20 WITH STANDARD DEVIATION OF  2247.47

RE%IBA              20760 5ELCID2637 ****** A MYOS YERNOS COMMO EL PUDIER MEIOR;
                    24585 5ELCID3133 QUE ****** DERECHO DE YFANTES DE CARRION.
        WORD #3529 OCCURS   2 TIMES.
```

WORD C# PREFIX CONTEXT

```
RE%IBAN          12322 5ELCID1565 QUE ******* A MYANAYA & ALAS DUENAS FIJAS DALGO;
         WORD #3530 OCCURS    1 TIMES.

RE%IBE            3857 5ELCID0488 LOS BRA%OS ABIERTOS ****** A MINAYA:
                 16641 5ELCID2108 MYO %ID GELOS ******, LAS MANOS LE BESO:
         WORD #3531 OCCURS    2 TIMES.

RE%IBEN           1928 5ELCID0245 CON TAN GRANT GOZO ******* AL QUE EN BUEN ORA NASCO.
                  5652 5ELCID0712 MOROS LE ******* POR LA SE@A GANAR,
                 12348 5ELCID1568 AFEUOS TODOS AQUESTOS ******* A MINAYA
                 17658 5ELCID2234 AMOS LAS ******* DAMOR & DE GRADO,
                 20367 5ELCID2584 AQUI ******* LAS FIJAS DEL CAMPEADOR;
                 22356 5ELCID2848 ******* AMINAYA & ATODOS SUS VARONES,
                 24402 5ELCID3111 AGRANT ONDRA LO ******* AL QUE EN BUEN ORA NA%IO.
         WORD #3532 OCCURS    7 TIMES.
            INDEX OF DIVERSIFICATION =  3744.67 WITH STANDARD DEVIATION OF  1907.96

RE%IBIEN         13774 5ELCID1746 ******** LO LAS DUE@AS QUE LO ESTAN ESPERANDO.
         WORD #3533 OCCURS    1 TIMES.

RE%IBIO          15191 5ELCID1922 SI ES PAGADO O ******* EL DON?
                 17497 5ELCID2214 ******* LOS MYO %ID CON TODOS SUS VASALLOS;
                 23024 5ELCID2933 LEUANTOS EL REY, TAN BIEN LOS *******.
                 24966 5ELCID3180 ******* LAS ESPADAS, LAS MANOS LE BESO,
                 25114 5ELCID3198 BESO LE LA MANO, EL ESPADA TOMO & *******.
         WORD #3534 OCCURS    5 TIMES.
            INDEX OF DIVERSIFICATION =  2479.75 WITH STANDARD DEVIATION OF  2239.21

RE%IBIOL         28669 5ELCID3660 ESSORA MARTIN ANTOLINEZ ******** CON EL ESPADA,
         WORD #3535 OCCURS    1 TIMES.

RE%IBIOLO         1584 5ELCID0203 ********* EL %ID ABIERTOS AMOS LOS BRA%OS:
                 17265 5ELCID2184 ********* DO@A XIMENA & SUS FIJAS AMAS:
         WORD #3536 OCCURS    2 TIMES.

RE%IBIOLOS       19841 5ELCID2516 ********** MINAYA POR MYO %ID EL CAMPEADOR:
         WORD #3537 OCCURS    1 TIMES.

RE%IBIR          12475 5ELCID1583 ******* SALIEN LAS DUENAS & AL BUENO DE MINAYA.
         WORD #3538 OCCURS    1 TIMES.

RE%IBO           10603 5ELCID1344 ****** ESTOS CAUALLOS QUEM ENBIA DE DON.
                 16058 5ELCID2036 FABLO MYO %ID & DIXO: MER%ED; YOLO ******, ALFONSSO MYO SE@OR;
                 16965 5ELCID2148 ****** ESTE DON QUE ME AUEDES MANDADO;
         WORD #3539 OCCURS    3 TIMES.

RE%IBOLOS        14666 5ELCID1855 DIXO EL REY DON ALFONSSO: ********* DE GRADO.
         WORD #3540 OCCURS    1 TIMES.

RED              18036 5ELCID2282 SALIOS DE LA *** & DESATOS EL LEON.
                 18192 5ELCID2301 E LIEUA LO ADESTRANDO, ENLA *** LE METIO.
                 26198 5ELCID3339 DEXOS LE PRENDER ALCUELO, & ALA *** LE METIO.
         WORD #3541 OCCURS    3 TIMES.

REDONDO           4351 5ELCID0554 EN VN OTERO *******, FUERTE & GRAND;
         WORD #3542 OCCURS    1 TIMES.

REFECHOS          1354 5ELCID0173 CA MIENTRA QUE VISQUIESSEN ******** ERAN AMOS.
                  6279 5ELCID0800 ******** SON TODOS ESOS CHRISTIANOS CON AQUESTA GANAN%IA.
         WORD #3543 OCCURS    2 TIMES.

RELUMBRA         24945 5ELCID3177 SACA LAS ESPADAS & ******** TODA LA CORT,
                 28576 5ELCID3649 ******** TOD EL CAMPO, TANTO ER LINPIA & CLARA;
         WORD #3544 OCCURS    2 TIMES.

REMANDRAN        18357 5ELCID2323 BIBDAS ********* FIJAS DEL CAMPEADOR.
         WORD #3545 OCCURS    1 TIMES.

REMANE%IO        11176 5ELCID1414 ********* EN SAN PERO MINAYA ALBARFANEZ.
         WORD #3546 OCCURS    1 TIMES.

REMANGA          14284 5ELCID1807 PRENDED LO QUE QUISIEREDES, LO OTRO *******.
         WORD #3547 OCCURS    1 TIMES.

REMANIDA          2233 5ELCID0281 YO YRE & UOS FINCAREDES ********.
         WORD #3548 OCCURS    1 TIMES.

REMANIDAS        10331 5ELCID1308 TIERRAS DE VALENCIA ********* EN PAZ,
         WORD #3549 OCCURS    1 TIMES.

REMOND           23576 5ELCID3002 EL CONDE DON ANRRICH & EL CONDE DON ******;
                 23834 5ELCID3036 OMILLOM AUOS & ALCONDE DO ******
                 24611 5ELCID3135 ALCALDES SEAN DESTO EL CONDE DON ANRRICH & EL CONDE DON ******
                 25194 5ELCID3208 DIZE EL CONDE DON ******: DEZID DE SSI O DE NO.
```

WORD C# PREFIX CONTEXT

REMOND (CON'T)

25424 5ELCID3237 LUEGO RESPONDIO EL CONDE DON ******:
27369 5ELCID3496 ADELINO A EL EL CONDE DON ANRICH & EL CONDE DON ******;
WORD #3550 OCCURS 6 TIMES.
INDEX OF DIVERSIFICATION = 757.60 WITH STANDARD DEVIATION OF 701.56

REMONT
7614 5ELCID0975 DEL CONDE DON ****** VENIDO LES MENSAIE;
7707 5ELCID0987 EL CONDE DON ****** DAR NOS HA GRANT BATALLA,
7794 5ELCID0998 VERA ****** VERENGEL TRAS QUIEN VINO EN ALCANZA
7897 5ELCID1009 AL CONDE DON ****** A PRESON LEAN TOMADO;
7970 5ELCID1018 EL CONDE DON ****** NON GELO PREZIA NADA,
8054 5ELCID1028 DIXO EL CONDE DON ******: COMEDE, DON RODRIGO, & PENSSEDES DE FOLGAR.
8326 5ELCID1059 POR QUE EL CONDE DON ****** TAN BIEN BOLUIE LAS MANOS.
8386 5ELCID1066 EL CONDE DON ****** ENTRE LOS DOS ES ENTRADO.
24391 5ELCID3109 E EL CONDE DON ANRRICH & EL CONDE DON ******
25077 5ELCID3195 DEL CONDE DE ****** VERENGEL DE BARZILONA LA MAYOR.
WORD #3551 OCCURS 10 TIMES.
INDEX OF DIVERSIFICATION = 1939.33 WITH STANDARD DEVIATION OF 5278.06

RENCURA
22478 5ELCID2862 EN LOS DIAS DE VAGAR TODA NUESTRA ******* SABREMOS CONTAR.
22895 5ELCID2916 CA TAN GRANT ES LA ******* DENTRO EN MI CORAZON.
23293 5ELCID2967 E QUE NON AYA ******* PODIENDO YO VEDALLO.
23493 5ELCID2992 DARLEDES DERECHO, CA ******* HA DE UOS.
25141 5ELCID3202 OTRA ******* HE DE YFANTES DE CARRION:
25547 5ELCID3254 LA ******* MAYOR NON SEME PUEDE OLBIDAR.
26901 5ELCID3437 CA GRAND ******* HE DE YFANTES DE CARRION.
WORD #3552 OCCURS 7 TIMES.
INDEX OF DIVERSIFICATION = 736.17 WITH STANDARD DEVIATION OF 604.29

RENDRE
20355 5ELCID2582 SI BIEN LAS SERUIDES, YO UOS ****** BUEN GALARDON.
WORD #3553 OCCURS 1 TIMES.

REaOR
28701 5ELCID3665 VALME, DIOS GLORIOSO, *****, & CURIAM DESTE ESPADA
WORD #3554 OCCURS 1 TIMES.

REPENTIDOS
27877 5ELCID3557 MUCHO ERAN ********** LOS YFANTES POR QUANTO DADAS SON;
WORD #3555 OCCURS 1 TIMES.

REPENTIMOS
26325 5ELCID3357 POR QUE DEXAMOS SUS FIJAS AVN NO NOS **********,
WORD #3556 OCCURS 1 TIMES.

REPENTIR
20615 5ELCID2617 NOS PUEDE ********, QUE CASADAS LAS HA AMAS.
WORD #3557 OCCURS 1 TIMES.

REPINTIENDO
27961 5ELCID3568 HYA SEUAN *********** YFANTES DE CARRION,
WORD #3558 OCCURS 1 TIMES.

REPINTRA
8491 5ELCID1079 MYEDO YUA AUIENDO QUE MYO ZID SE ********,
WORD #3559 OCCURS 1 TIMES.

REPISOS
27970 5ELCID3569 DELO QUE AUIEN FECHO MUCHO ******* SON;
WORD #3560 OCCURS 1 TIMES.

RESIBIERA
28424 5ELCID3630 VN COLPE *********, MAS OTRO FIRIO:
WORD #3561 OCCURS 1 TIMES.

RESPONDA
27048 5ELCID3455 SI AY QUI ******** ODIZE DE NO,
WORD #3562 OCCURS 1 TIMES.

RESPONDE
18222 5ELCID2305 MAGER LOS ESTAN LAMANDO, NINGUNO NON ********.
WORD #3563 OCCURS 1 TIMES.

RESPONDEN
24679 5ELCID3144 SABREMOS QUE ********* YFANTES DE CARRION.
25202 5ELCID3209 ESSORA ********* YFANTES DE CARRION:
WORD #3564 OCCURS 2 TIMES.

RESPONDIEN
20714 5ELCID2630 ********** LOS YERNOS: ASSI LO MANDE DIOS
WORD #3565 OCCURS 1 TIMES.

RESPONDIER
25936 5ELCID3305 SI YO **********, TU NON ENTRARAS EN ARMAS.
WORD #3566 OCCURS 1 TIMES.

RESPONDIERON
24167 5ELCID3082 ************ TODOS: NOS ESSO QUEREMOS, SEaOR.
WORD #3567 OCCURS 1 TIMES.

RESPONDIO
16869 5ELCID2135 ********* EL REY: AFE AQUI ALBARFANEZ;
23880 5ELCID3042 ********* EL REY: SI FAGO, SIN SALUE DIOS
25420 5ELCID3237 LUEGO ********* EL CONDE DON REMOND:
WORD #3568 OCCURS 3 TIMES.

RESPUSO
1018 5ELCID0131 ******* MARTIN ANTOLINEZ A GUISA DE MENBRADO:
5635 5ELCID0710 ******* PERO VERMUEZ: NON RASTARA POR AL.
7643 5ELCID0979 ******* EL CONDE: ESTO NON SERA VERDAD
10982 5ELCID1390 ******* MYNAYA: ESTO NON MEA POR QUE PESAR.
11428 5ELCID1447 ******* MINAYA: FER LO HE DE VELUNTAD.

```
WORD                C#  PREFIX                              CONTEXT

RESPUSO (CON'T)

                 16195 5ELCID2055 ******* MIO %ID: ASSI LC MANDE EL CRIADOR
                 16420 5ELCID2C82 NON ABRIA FIJAS DE CASAR, ******* EL CAMPEADOR,
                 19061 5ELCID2412 ******* BUCAR AL %ID: CONFONDA DIOS TAL AMISTAD
                 19107 5ELCID2417 AQUI ******* MYO %ID: ESTC NON SERA VERDAD.
                 27316 5ELCID3491 ESSORA ******* EL REY: ASSI LC MANDE DIOS
         WORD #3569 OCCURS  10 TIMES.
            INDEX OF DIVERSIFICATION =  2921.00 WITH STANDARD DEVIATION OF  2669.12

RESU%ITEST        2734 5ELCID0346 ********** A LAZARC, CA FUE TU VOLUNTAD;
                  2838 5ELCID0358 ENEL MONUMENTO **********, FUST ALOS YNFIERNOS,
         WORD #3570 OCCURS   2 TIMES.

RETENEDOR         4133 5ELCID0526 E QUE SERIE *********, MAS NON YAURIE AGUA.
         WORD #3571 OCCURS   1 TIMES.

RETOUO             863 5ELCID0111 ****** DELLOS QUANTO QUE FUE ALGO;
         WORD #3572 OCCURS   1 TIMES.

RETRAER          21491 5ELCID2733 ******* UOS LO AN EN VISTAS O EN CORTES.
                 25777 5ELCID3283 QUE AVEDES UOS, CCNDE, POR ******* LA MI BARBA?
         WORD #3573 OCCURS   2 TIMES.

RETRAYAN         20075 5ELCID2548 ANTE QUE NOS ******** LO QUE CUNTIO DEL LEON.
                 20134 5ELCID2556 ANTES QUE NOS ******** LO QUE FUE DEL LEON.
         WORD #3574 OCCURS   2 TIMES.

RETRAYDO         26339 5ELCID3359 LO QUE LES FIZIEMOS SER LES HA ********; ESTO LIDIARE
                                  ATOD EL MAS
         WORD #3575 OCCURS   1 TIMES.

REY                162 5ELCID0022 EL *** DON ALFCNSSO TANTO AUIE LA GRAND SA@A,
                   256 5ELCID0033 POR MIEDO DEL *** ALFCNSSO, QUE ASSI LO AUIEN PARADO
                   332 5ELCID0042 EL *** LO HA UEDADO, ANOCH DEL ETRO SU CARTA,
                   404 5ELCID0050 YA LO VEE EL %ID QUE DEL *** NON AUIE GRA%IA.
                   599 5ELCID0076 AUN %ERCA OTARDE EL *** QUERER ME HA POR AMIGO;
                   712 5ELCIDC090 QUANDO EN BURGOS ME VEDARCN COMPRA & EL *** ME A AYRADO,
                   889 5ELCID0114 YA LO VEDES QUE EL *** LEA AYRADO.
                  1214 5ELCID0156 YA ME EXCO DE TIERRA, CA DEL *** SO AYRADO.
                  1711 5ELCID0219 DA QUI QUITO CASTIELLA, PUES QUE EL *** HE EN YRA;
                  1805 5ELCID0230 SI EL *** MELC QUISIERE TOMAR AMI NON MINCHAL.
                  2441 5ELCID0308 MANDO EL *** A MYO %ID A AGUARDAR,
                  2855 5ELCID0361 TUERES *** DE LCS REYES & DE TODEL MUNDO PADRE,
                  3354 5ELCID0423 LA TIERRA DEL *** ALFCNSSO ESTA NOCH LA PODEMOS QUITAR.
                  4000 5ELCID0508 AL *** ALFCNSSO QUE LEGARIEN SUS COMPA@AS,
                  4150 5ELCID0528 BUSCAR NOS YE EL *** ALFCNSSO CON TODA SU MESNADA.
                  4179 5ELCIDC532 %ERCA ES EL *** ALFCNSSC & BUSCAR NOS VERNA.
                  4954 5ELCID0627 AL *** DE VALEN%IA ENBIARCN CON MENSAIE,
                  4973 5ELCID0629 AYROLO EL *** ALFCNSSO, DE TIERRA ECHADO LO HA,
                  5032 5ELCIDC636 QUANDO LO CYO EL *** TAMIN, POR CUER LE PESO MAL:
                  5992 5ELCIDC760 AL *** FARIZ IIJ COLPES LE AUIE DADO;
                  6062 5ELCIDC769 ARANCADO ES EL *** FARIZ & GALUE;
                  6086 5ELCID0773 EL *** FARIZ EN TERUEL SE FUE ENTRAR,
                  6391 5ELCID0815 AL *** ALFCNSSSO QUE ME A AYRADO
                  6586 5ELCID0841 SANO EL *** FARIZ, CCN EL SE CONSEIAUAN.
                  6827 5ELCID0872 TREYNTA CAUALLOS AL *** LOS ENPRESENTAUA;
                  6832 5ELCIDC873 VIOLOS EL ***, FERMCSC SONRRISAUA:
                  6870 5ELCIDC878 A UOS, *** CNDRADO, ENBIA ESTA PRESENTAIA;
                  6892 5ELCID0881 DIXO EL ***:  MUCHO ES MA@ANA,
                  6999 5ELCIDC895 GRADO & GRA%IAS, ***, CCMMO A SE@OR NATURAL;
                  8230 5ELCID1048 CCMMO QUE YRA A CE *** & DE TIERRA ES ECHADO.
                  9287 5ELCID1181 POR EL *** DE MARRUECCS OUIERON A ENBIAR;
                  9617 5ELCID1222 AQUEL *** DE SEUILLA EL MANCADO LEGAUA,
                  9673 5ELCID1230 AQUEL *** DE MARRUECOS CON TRES COLPES ESCAPA.
                  9755 5ELCID1240 POR AMOR DE *** ALFFCNSSO, QUE DE TIERRA ME A ECHADO,
                 10040 5ELCID1272 AL *** ALFONSSC MYO SE@CR NATURAL;
                 10356 5ELCID1312 FUERA EL *** A SAN FAGUNT AVN POCO HA,
                 10388 5ELCID1316 DE MISSA ERA EXIDO ESSORA EL *** ALFONSSO,
                 10406 5ELCID1319 ALCS PIES DEL *** ALFCNSSO CAYO CON GRAND DUELO,
                 10575 5ELCID1340 AL%O LA MANO DIESTRA, EL *** SE SANTIGO:
                 10613 5ELCID1345 MAGER PLOGO AL ***, MUCHC PESC A GAR%IORDONEZ:
                 10639 5ELCID1348 DIXO EL *** REY AL CCNDE: DEXAC ESSA RAZON,
                 10640 5ELCID1348 DIXO EL REY *** AL CCNDE: DEXAC ESSA RAZON,
                 10696 5ELCID1355 ESSORA DIXO EL ***: PLAZ ME DE CORA%ON;
                 10803 5ELCID1368 SONRRISOS EL ***, TAN VELIDO FABLO:
                 10889 5ELCID1378 MINAYA ALBARFANEZ ALBUEN *** SE ESPIDIO.
                 11057 5ELCID1400 EL *** POR SU MER%ED SUELTAS ME UOS HA,
                 11125 5ELCID1408 QUE SU MUGIER & SUS FIJAS EL *** SUELTAS ME LAS HA,
                 11454 5ELCID1450 POR LA TIERRA DEL *** MUCHO CONDUCHO LES DAN.
                 12108 5ELCID1536 EL PORTERO DEL *** QUITAR LO MANDAUA;
                 12129 5ELCID1539 EL *** LO PAGC TODO, & CUITC SEUA MINAYA.
                 12769 5ELCID1621 DE AQUEL *** YUCEF QUE EN MARRUECOS ESTA.
                 12777 5ELCID1622 PESOL AL *** DE MARRUECCS DE MYO %ID DON RODRIGO:
                 12804 5ELCID1625 AQUEL *** DE MARRUECCS AIUNTAUA SUS VIRTOS;
                 13610 5ELCID1725 AL *** YU%EF TRES COLPES LE OUO DADOS,
                 13738 5ELCID1741 QUANDO AL *** DE MARUECCS ASSI LO AN ARRANCADO,
                 14098 5ELCID1785 LA TIENDA DEL *** DE MARRUECOS, QUE DELAS OTRAS ES CABO,
```

WORD C# PREFIX CONTEXT

REY (CON'T)

```
14342 5ELCID1814 QUE NON DIGA MAL EL *** ALFONSSO DEL QUE VALEN%IA MANDA.
14429 5ELCID1825 POR EL *** DON ALFONSSO TOMAN SSE APREGUNTAR.
14450 5ELCID1827 LEGAN A VALADOLID, DO EL *** ALFONSSO ESTAUA;
14477 5ELCID1831 ALEGRE FUE EL ***, NON VIESTES ATANTO,
14492 5ELCID1833 HYEN LOS PRIMEROS EL *** FUERA DIO SALTO,
14548 5ELCID1840 EL *** DON ALFONSSO SEYSE SANTIGUANDO.
14568 5ELCID1843 ANTEL *** ALFONSSO LOS YNOIOS FINCADOS,
14581 5ELCID1845 MER%ED, *** ALFONSSO, SODES TAN ONDRADO
14617 5ELCID1849 POCOS DIAS HA, ***, QUE VNA LID A ARRANCADO:
14625 5ELCID1850 A AQUEL *** DE MARRUECOS, YUCEFF POR NOMBRADO,
14663 5ELCID1855 DIXO EL *** DON ALFONSSO: RE%IBOLOS DE GRADO.
14759 5ELCID1866 FABLO EL *** DON ALFONSSO & DIXO ESTA RAZON:
14903 5ELCID1884 VINIEN AL *** ALFONSSO CON ESTA PORIDAD:
14913 5ELCID1885 MER%ED UOS PIDIMOS COMMO A *** & SE@OR NATURAL;
14944 5ELCID1889 VNA GRANT ORA EL *** PENSSO & COMIDIO;
14989 5ELCID1895 EL *** DON ALFONSSO ESSORA LOS LAMO,
15135 5ELCID1914 ESPIDIENSSE AL ***, CON ESTO TORNADOS SON,
15289 5ELCID1936 ADIOS LO GRADESCO QUE DEL *** HE SU GRA%IA,
15397 5ELCID1950 NON ERA MARAUILLA SIQUISIESSE EL *** ALFONSSO,
15414 5ELCID1952 POR DAR LE GRAND ONDRA COMMO A *** DE TIERRA.
15453 5ELCID1958 LO QUE EL *** QUISIERE, ESSO FERA EL CAMPEADOR.
15460 5ELCID1959 AL *** ONDRADO DELANT LE ECHARON LAS CARTAS;
15558 5ELCID1972 CONDUCHOS LARGOS EL *** ENBIAR MANDAUA
15571 5ELCID1974 CON EL *** ATANTAS BUENAS CONPA@AS.
15606 5ELCID1979 EL *** DON ALFONSSO A PRIESSA CAUALGAUA,
15628 5ELCID1982 CON EL *** VAN LEONESES & MESNADAS GALIZIANAS,
15869 5ELCID2012 HYAS VA PORA LAS VISTAS QUE CON EL *** PARO.
15878 5ELCID2013 DE VN DIA ES LEGADO ANTES EL *** DON ALFONSSO.
15981 5ELCID2026 TAN GRAND PESAR OUO EL *** DON ALFONSSO:
16030 5ELCID2033 DIXO EL *** ESTO FERE DALMA & DE CORA%ON;
16141 5ELCID2047 DIXO EL ***: NON ES AGUISADO OY:
16216 5ELCID2057 EN AQUEL DIA DEL *** SO HUESPED FUE;
16327 5ELCID2071 NON LO TARDO EL ***, LA RAZON CONPE%O:
16486 5ELCID2090 GRA%IAS, DIXO EL ***, AUOS & ATOD ESTA CORT.
16512 5ELCID2093 CAMEARON LAS ESPADAS ANTEL *** DON ALFONSSO.
16517 5ELCID2094 FABLO EL *** DON ALFONSSO COMMO TAN BUEN SE@OR:
16652 5ELCID2109 MUCHO UOS LO GRADESCO, COMMO A *** & A SE@OR
16751 5ELCID2121 EL *** ALOS YFANTES ALAS MANOS LES TOMO,
16783 5ELCID2125 GRADESCOLO, ***, & PRENDO UUESTRO DON,
16812 5ELCID2128 AQUI LO DIGO ANTE MYO SE@OR EL *** ALFONSSO:
16836 5ELCID2131 YO UOS PIDO MER%ED AUOS, *** NATURAL:
16871 5ELCID2135 RESPONDIO EL ***: AFE AQUI ALBARFANEZ;
16923 5ELCID2142 HYA *** DON ALFONSSO, SE@OR TAN ONDRADO,
16958 5ELCID2147 DIXO EL *** DON ALFONSSO: MUCHO ME AUEDES ENBARGADO.
17055 5ELCID2159 BEFAR LAS MANOS, ESPEDIR SE DE *** ALFONSSO:
17097 5ELCID2164 ESTO PLOGO AL ***, & ATODOS LOS SOLTO;
17110 5ELCID2165 LA CONPA@A DEL %ID CRE%E, & LA DEL *** MENGO,
17572 5ELCID2223 SABEDES QUE AL *** ASSI GELO HE MANDADO,
17632 5ELCID2231 POR MANO DEL *** ALFONSSO, QUE AMI LO OUO MANDADO,
18287 5ELCID2314 AQUESTE ERA EL *** BUCAR, SIL OUIESTES CONTAR.
19033 5ELCID2408 MYO %ID AL *** BUCAR CAYOL EN ALCAZ:
19174 5ELCID2425 MATO A BUCAR, AL *** DE ALEN MAR,
19314 5ELCID2446 COMMO AL *** BUCAR AVEMOS ARRANCADO.
19539 5ELCID2475 DESPUES QUE ESTA BATALLA VEN%IERON & AL *** BUCAR MATO;
19894 5ELCID2523 AAQUEL *** BUCAR, TRAYDOR PROUADO.
22185 5ELCID2825 DE CUER PESO ESTO AL BUEN *** DON ALFONSSO.
22580 5ELCID2876 ODIZEN BADO DE ***, ALLA YUAN POSAR,
22756 5ELCID2900 AL *** ALFONSSO DE CASTIELLA PENSSO DE ENBIAR;
22786 5ELCID2903 LIEUES EL MANDADO A CASTIELLA AL *** ALFONSSO;
22821 5ELCID2907 QUEL PESE AL BUEN *** DALMA & DE CORA%ON.
22937 5ELCID2922 AL *** EN SAN FAGUNT LO FALLO.
22943 5ELCID2923 *** ES DE CASTIELLA & REY ES DE LEON
22948 5ELCID2923 REY ES DE CASTIELLA & *** ES DE LEON
23012 5ELCID2932 VIOLOS EL *** & CONNOS%IO A MU@O GUSTIOZ;
23020 5ELCID2933 LEUANTOS EL ***, TAN BIEN LOS RE%IBIO.
23027 5ELCID2934 DELANT EL *** FINCO LOS YNOIOS AQUEL MU@O GUSTIOZ,
23042 5ELCID2936 MER%ED, *** ALFONSSO, DE LARGOS REYNOS AUOS DIZEN SE@OR
23163 5ELCID2951 E QUE UOS PESE, *** COMMO SODES SABIDOR;
23177 5ELCID2953 EL *** VNA GRAND ORA CALLO & COMIDIO;
23395 5ELCID2980 QUE CORT FAZIE EN TOLLEDO AQUEL *** ONDRADO,
23431 5ELCID2984 QUE NON FALIESSEN DELO QUE EN *** AUYE MANDADO.
23445 5ELCID2986 POR QUE EL *** FAZIE CORT EN TOLLEDO,
23468 5ELCID2989 RUEGAN AL *** QUE LOS QUITE DESTA CORT.
23476 5ELCID2990 DIXO EL ***: NO LO FERE, SIN SALUE DIOS
23565 5ELCID3001 EN LOS PRIMEROS VA EL BUEN *** DON ALFONSSO,
23666 5ELCID3014 POR QUE SE TARDA EL *** NON HA SABOR.
23688 5ELCID3017 QUE BESASSE LAS MANOS AL *** SO SE@OR:
23703 5ELCID3019 QUANDO LO OYO EL ***, PLOGOL DE CORA%ON;
23711 5ELCID3020 CON GRANDES YENTES EL *** CAUALGO
23743 5ELCID3024 QUANDO LOOVO A OIO EL BUEN *** DON ALFFONSSO,
23763 5ELCID3027 QUANDO LO OYO EL ***, POR NADA NON TARDO;
23882 5ELCID3042 RESPONDIO EL ***: SI FAGO, SIN SALUE DIOS
23891 5ELCID3043 PORA TOLLEDO EL *** TORNADA DA,
23904 5ELCID3045 MER%ED, YA ***, SI EL CRIADOR UOS SALUE
```

WORD C# PREFIX CONTEXT

REY (CON'T)

23951 5ELCID3052 DIXO EL ***: PLAZME DE VELUNTAC.
23956 5ELCID3053 EL *** DON ALFONSSO A TOLLEDO ES ENTRADO,
24379 5ELCID3108 LEUANTOS EN PIE EL BUEN *** DON ALFONSSO
24426 5ELCID3114 EL *** DIXO AL %ID: VENJD ACA SER, CAMPEADOR,
24461 5ELCID3118 SED EN UUESTRO ESCA@O COMMO *** A SE@OR;
24476 5ELCID3120 LO QUE DIXO EL %ID AL *** PLOGO DE CORA%ON.
24534 5ELCID3127 ESSORA SE LEUO EN PIE EL BUEN *** DON ALFONSSO;
24547 5ELCID3129 HYO, DE QUE FU ***, NON FIZ MAS DE DOS CORTES:
24689 5ELCID3145 MYO %ID LA MANO BESO AL *** & EN PIE SE LEUANTO;
24701 5ELCID3146 MUCHO UOS LO GRADESCO COMMO A *** & A SE@OR,
24732 5ELCID3150 CA UOS LAS CASASTES, ***, SABREDES QUE FER OY;
24862 5ELCID3166 BIEN NOS ABENDREMOS CON EL *** DON ALFONSSO.
24900 5ELCID3171 MER%ED, YA *** DON ALFONSSO, SODES NUESTRO SE@OR
24938 5ELCID3176 PUSIERON LAS EN MANO DEL *** SO SE@OR;
25127 5ELCID3200 GRADO AL CRIADOR & AUOS, *** SE@OR,
25226 5ELCID3212 SI PLOGUIERE AL ***, ASSI DEZIMOS NOS: DIXO EL REY
25232 5ELCID3212 SI PLOGUIERE AL REY, ASSI DEZIMOS NOS: DIXO EL ***
25244 5ELCID3214 DIXO EL BUEN ***: ASSILO OTORGO YO.
25356 5ELCID3228 A ESTAS PALABRAS FABLO EL *** DON ALFONSSO:
25438 5ELCID3239 POR JUUIZIO LO DAMOS ANTEL *** DON ALFONSSO:
25489 5ELCID3246 SOBRE LOS DOZIENTOS MARCOS QUE TENIE EL *** ALFONSSO
25540 5ELCID3253 MER%ED, AY *** SE@OR, POR AMOR DE CARIDAD
25686 5ELCID3271 MER%ED, YA ***, EL MEIOR DE TODA ESPA@A
26231 5ELCID3344 ESTOT LIDIARE AQUI ANTEL *** DON ALFONSSO
26557 5ELCID3390 DIXO EL *** ALFONSSO: CALLE YA ESTA RAZON.
26608 5ELCID3397 BESAN LAS MANOS AL *** DON ALFONSSO,
26650 5ELCID3403 MER%ED, *** ALFONSSO, VOS SODES MYO SE@OR
26692 5ELCID3409 LEUANTOS EL ***, FIZO CALLAR LA CORT:
26731 5ELCID3414 LEUANTOS MYO %ID, AL *** LAS MANOS LE BESO;
26746 5ELCID3416 ESSORA DIXO EL ***: DIOS UOS DE DEN BUEN GALARDON
26802 5ELCID3423 BESARON LAS MANOS DEL *** DON ALFONSSO,
26852 5ELCID3430 MER%ED UOS PIDO COMMO A *** & A SE@OR,
26880 5ELCID3434 DIXO EL ***: PLAZME DE CORA%ON.
26915 5ELCID3438 HYO LES DI MIS PRIMAS POR MANDADO DEL *** ALFONSSO,
27025 5ELCID3452 GRADO ADIOS DEL %IELO & AQUEL *** DON ALFONSSO,
27102 5ELCID3463 DIXO EL ***: FINE ESTA RAZON;
27136 5ELCID3468 DANDOS, ***, PLAZO, CA CRAS SER NON PUEDE.
27159 5ELCID3471 FABLO EL *** CONTRAL CAMPEADOR:
27187 5ELCID3475 ENESSORA DIXO EL ***: AOSADAS, CAMPEADOR.
27271 5ELCID3486 MYO %ID AL *** LAS MANOS LE BESO & DIXO: PLAZME, SE@OR.
27294 5ELCID3488 DAQUI UOS LOS ACOMIENDO COMO A *** & A SE@OR.
27318 5ELCID3491 ESSORA RESPUSO EL ***: ASSI LO MANDE DIOS
27414 5ELCID3502 LOS CC MARCOS AL *** LOS SOLTO.
27427 5ELCID3504 MER%ED UOS PIDO, ***, POR AMOR DEL CRIADOR
27458 5ELCID3508 EL *** AL%O LA MANO, LA CARA SE SANTIGO;
27529 5ELCID3516 ESSORA DIXO EL ***: DESTO NON HE SABOR;
27672 5ELCID3532 MYO %ID PORA VALEN%IA, & EL *** PORA CARRION.
27702 5ELCID3536 ELLOS SON ENPOER DEL *** DON ALFONSSO EL DE LEON;
27804 5ELCID3548 DEMAS SOBRE TODOS YES EL *** DON ALFONSSO,
27853 5ELCID3554 ANDIDIERON EN PLEYTO, DIXIERON LO AL *** ALFONSSO,
27887 5ELCID3558 DIXIERON GELO AL ***, MAS NON GELO CONLOYO;
27992 5ELCID3572 HYUA LOS VER EL *** DON ALFONSSO;
28005 5ELCID3574 BESAMOS VOS LAS MANOS, COMMO A *** & A SE@OR,
28054 5ELCID3581 ESSORA DIXO EL ***: DALMA & DE CORA%ON.
28139 5ELCID3593 EL *** DIOLES FIELES POR DEZIR EL DERECHO & AL NON,
28164 5ELCID3595 DO SEDIEN ENEL CAMPO FABLO EL *** DON ALFONSSO:
28233 5ELCID3604 LOS FIELES & EL *** ENSE@ARON LOS MOIONES,
28725 5ELCID3668 ESSORA DIXO EL ***: VENID UOS AMI COMPA@A;
28916 5ELCID3693 MANDO LIBRAR EL CANPO EL BUEN *** DON ALFONSSO,
28950 5ELCID3698 EL *** ALOS DE MYO %ID DE NOCHE LOS ENBIO,
29077 5ELCID3714 GRADO AL *** DEL %IELO, MIS FIJAS VENGADAS SON
WORD #3576 OCCURS 201 TIMES.
INDEX OF DIVERSIFICATION = 143.57 WITH STANDARD DEVIATION OF 250.74

REYAL 17217 5ELCID2178 DAD LES VN ***** & ALOS YFANTES DE CARRION,
WORD #3577 OCCURS 1 TIMES.

REYES 2657 5ELCID0336 TRES ***** DE ARABIA TE VINIERON ADORAR,
2858 5ELCID0361 TUERES REY DE LOS ***** & DE TODEL MUNDO PADRE,
5040 5ELCID0637 TRES ***** VEC DE MOROS DERREDOR DE MI ESTAR,
5169 5ELCID0654 CON AQUESTOS DOS ***** QUE DIZEN FFARIZ & GALUE;
6856 5ELCID0876 VEN%IO DOS ***** DE MOROS EN AQUESTA BATALLA.
9012 5ELCID1147 DOS ***** DE MOROS MATARON EN ES ALCAZ,
14737 5ELCID1863 POR TAN BILTADA MIENTRE VEN%ER ***** DEL CAMPO,
20112 5ELCID2553 PODREMOS CASAR CON FIJAS DE ***** O DE ENPERADORES,
25880 5ELCID3297 DEUIEMOS CASAR CON FIJAS DE ***** O DE ENPERADORES,
29165 5ELCID3724 OY LOS ***** DESPA@A SOS PARIENTES SON,
WORD #3578 OCCURS 10 TIMES.
INDEX OF DIVERSIFICATION = 2944.23 WITH STANDARD DEVIATION OF 2235.09

REYNADO 1648 5ELCID0211 MESURAREMOS LA POSADA & QUITAREMOS EL *******;
WORD #3579 OCCURS 1 TIMES.

REYNAS 26621 5ELCID3399 POR SER ****** DE NAUARRA & DE ARAGON,
WORD #3580 OCCURS 1 TIMES.

WORD C# PREFIX CONTEXT

REYNO
3120 5ELCID0392 %ERCA VIENE EL PLAZO POR EL ***** QUITAR.
6968 5ELCID0891 DE TODO MYO ***** LOS QUE LO QUISIEREN FAR,
14785 5ELCID1869 MYO ***** ADELANT MEIOR ME PODRA SERUIR.
16047 5ELCID2035 EN TODO MYO ***** PARTE DESDE OY.
23258 5ELCID2962 ANDARAN MYOS PORTEROS POR TODO MYO *****,
23510 5ELCID2994 QUITE MYO *****, CADEL NON HE SABOR.
23596 5ELCID3005 FUERON Y DE SU ***** OTROS MUCHOS SABIDORES,
24658 5ELCID3141 QUITAR ME A EL *****, PERDERA MIAMOR.
28216 5ELCID3602 ENTODO MYO ***** NON AURA BUENA SABOR.
WORD #3581 OCCURS 9 TIMES.
INDEX OF DIVERSIFICATION = 3136.00 WITH STANDARD DEVIATION OF 3038.69

REYNOS
23046 5ELCID2936 MER%ED, REY ALFONSSO, DE LARGOS ****** AUOS DIZEN SE@OR
WORD #3582 OCCURS 1 TIMES.

REZAUA
1869 5ELCID0238 ****** LOS MATINES ABUELTA DELOS ALBORES.
WORD #3583 OCCURS 1 TIMES.

RIBERA
5012 5ELCID0634 ****** DE SALON TODA YRA AMAL,
WORD #3584 OCCURS 1 TIMES.

RICA
1526 5ELCID0195 DE QUE FAGADES CAL%AS & **** PIEL & BUEN MANTO.
12215 5ELCID1550 ENTRADOS SON A MOLINA, BUENA & **** CASA;
22630 5ELCID2883 POR AMOR DE MYO %ID **** CENA LES DA.
WORD #3585 OCCURS 3 TIMES.

RICAS
1761 5ELCID0224 MANDO AL UUESTRO ALTAR BUENAS DONAS & *****;
6469 5ELCID0825 SI LES YO VISQUIER, SERAN DUENAS *****.
17356 5ELCID2195 QUANDO UOS NOS CASAREDES BIEN SEREMOS *****.
17763 5ELCID2248 ***** FUERON LAS BODAS EN EL ALCA%AR ONDRADO,
WORD #3586 OCCURS 4 TIMES.

RICO
10306 5ELCID1304 DIERON LE EN VALEN%IA O BIEN PUEDE ESTAR ****.
19675 5ELCID2494 ANTES FU MINGUADO, AGORA **** SO,
WORD #3587 OCCURS 2 TIMES.

RICOS
845 5ELCID0108 POR SIEMPRE UOS FARE *****, QUE NON SEADES MENGUADOS.
4246 5ELCID0540 DEL CASTIELLO QUE PRISIERON TODOS ***** SE PARTEN;
6651 5ELCID0848 A CAUALLEROS & A PEONES FECHOS LOS HA *****,
8546 5ELCID1086 TAN ***** SON LOS SOS QUE NON SABEN QUE SE AN.
9562 5ELCID1215 TODOS ERAN ***** QUANTOS QUE ALLI HA.
14644 5ELCID1853 ***** SON VENIDOS TODOS LOS SOS VASSALLOS,
17866 5ELCID2261 ***** TORNAN A CASTIELLA LOS QUE ALAS BODAS LEGARON.
19801 5ELCID2510 MUCHOS TIENEN POR ***** LOS YFANTES DE CARRION.
20105 5ELCID2552 DAQUESTOS AUERES SIENPRE SEREMOS ***** OMNES,
27789 5ELCID3546 MUCHOS SE JUNTARON DE BUENOS ***** OMNES
WORD #3588 OCCURS 10 TIMES.
INDEX OF DIVERSIFICATION = 2992.78 WITH STANDARD DEVIATION OF 2247.17

RICTAD
5455 5ELCID0688 SI VEN%IEREMOS LA BATALLA, CRE%REMOS EN ******.
11055 5ELCID1399 SANO LO DEXE & CON TAN GRAND ******.
WORD #3589 OCCURS 2 TIMES.

RIEBTOS
25573 5ELCID3257 AMENOS DE ******* NO LOS PUEDO DEXAR.
26941 5ELCID3442 ******* LES LOS CUERPOS POR MALOS & POR TRAYDORES.
WORD #3590 OCCURS 2 TIMES.

RIEBTOT
26219 5ELCID3343 ******* EL CUERPO POR MALO & POR TRAYDOR;
WORD #3591 OCCURS 1 TIMES.

RIENDA
6017 5ELCID0763 BOLUIO LA ****** POR YR SE LE DEL CAMPO.
22065 5ELCID2808 EL CAUALLO PRISO POR LA ****** & LUEGO DENT LAS PARTIO,
28659 5ELCID3659 BOLUIO LA ****** AL CAUALLO POR TORNASSE DE CARA;
WORD #3592 OCCURS 3 TIMES.

RIENDAS
73 5ELCID0010 ALLI PIENSSAN DE AGUIIAR, ALLI SUELTAN LAS *******.
1783 5ELCID0227 SUELTAN LAS ******* & PIENSSAN DE AGUIJAR.
3110 5ELCID0391 SOLTARON LAS *******, PIESSAN DE ANDAR;
15643 5ELCID1984 SUELTAN LAS *******, ALAS VISTAS SEUAN A DELI@ADAS.
WORD #3593 OCCURS 4 TIMES.

RIO
7071 5ELCID0904 EL DE *** MARTIN TODO LO METIO EN PARIA.
22550 5ELCID2872 FATA *** DAMOR, DANDO LES SOLAZ;
26482 5ELCID3379 FUESSE A *** DOUIRNA LOS MOLINOS PICAR
WORD #3594 OCCURS 3 TIMES.

RIQUEZA
6365 5ELCID0811 DAQUESTA ******* QUE EL CRIADOR NOS ADADO
9438 5ELCID1200 CRE%IENDO UA ******* A MYO %ID EL DE BIUAR.
12989 5ELCID1648 ******* ES QUE NOS A CRE%E MARAUILLOSA & GRAND;
20335 5ELCID2580 CON QUE ******* ENBIO MIOS YERNOS AMOS ADOS.
20936 5ELCID2659 ELLOS VEYEN LA ******* QUE EL MORO SACO,
WORD #3595 OCCURS 5 TIMES.
INDEX OF DIVERSIFICATION = 3641.75 WITH STANDARD DEVIATION OF 2786.83

WORD C# PREFIX CONTEXT

RIQUEZAS 14157 5ELCID1792 CON AQUESTAS ******** TANTAS A VALEN%IA SON ENTRADOS.
WORD #3596 OCCURS 1 TIMES.

RIQUIZA 10017 5ELCID1269 AGORA AUEMOS *******, MAS AUREMOS ADELANT.
20960 5ELCID2663 QUANTA ******* TIENE AUER LA YEMOS NOS.
WORD #3597 OCCURS 2 TIMES.

RIQUIZAS 3810 5ELCID0481 DE OUEIAS & DE VACAS & DE ROPAS & DE OTRAS ******** LARGAS.
WORD #3598 OCCURS 1 TIMES.

RITAD 9805 5ELCID1245 LOS QUE EXIERON DE TIERRA DE ***** SON ABONDADOS,
WORD #3599 OCCURS 1 TIMES.

ROBADA 6237 5ELCID0794 ESTA ALBERGADA LOS DE MYO %ID LUEGO LA AN ******
WORD #3600 OCCURS 1 TIMES.

ROBADO 13701 5ELCID1736 MESNADAS DE MYO %ID ****** AN EL CANPO;
WORD #3601 OCCURS 1 TIMES.

ROBAUAN 9049 5ELCID1152 ******* EL CAMPO EPIENSSAN SE DE TORNAR.
19211 5ELCID2430 SABET, TODOS DE FIRME ******* EL CAMPO.
WORD #3602 OCCURS 2 TIMES.

ROBREDO 21226 5ELCID2697 ENTRADOS SON LOS YFANTES AL ******* DE CORPES,
21670 5ELCID2754 LOS YFANTES DE CARRION ENEL ******* DE CORPES
23115 5ELCID2945 DESENPARADAS LAS DEXARON ENEL ******* DE CORPES,
24781 5ELCID3156 QUANDO DEXARON MIS FIJAS ENEL ******* DE CORPES,
25651 5ELCID3266 SOLAS LAS DEXASTES ENEL ******* DE CORPES,
WORD #3603 OCCURS 5 TIMES.
INDEX OF DIVERSIFICATION = 1105.25 WITH STANDARD DEVIATION OF 554.52

ROBREDOS 22076 5ELCID2809 TODOS TRES SE@EROS POR LOS ******** DE CORPES,
WORD #3604 OCCURS 1 TIMES.

ROBREDRO 21616 5ELCID2748 POR MUERTAS LAS DEXARON ENEL ******** DE CORPES.
WORD #3605 OCCURS 1 TIMES.

ROCANDO 7883 5ELCID1007 ALOS VNOS FIRIENDO & A LOS OTROS DE *******.
WORD #3606 OCCURS 1 TIMES.

RODIRGO 13460 5ELCID1706 AUOS, %ID DON *******, EN BUEN ORA %INXIESTES ESPADA,
WORD #3607 OCCURS 1 TIMES.

RODRIGO 3702 5ELCID0467 MYO %ID DON ******* ALA PUERTA ADELI@AUA;
4365 5ELCID0556 MOI %ID DON ******* ALCO%ER CUEDA GANAR.
7122 5ELCID0911 ALEN DE TERUEL DON ******* PASSAUA,
7598 5ELCID0973 MYO %ID DON ******* TRAE GRAND GANAN%IA,
7963 5ELCID1017 A MYO %ID DON ******* GRANT COZINAL ADOBAUAN;
8057 5ELCID1028 DIXO EL CONDE DON REMONT: COMEDE, DON *******, & PENSSEDES DE FOLGAR.
9458 5ELCID1202 MYO %ID DON ******* NON LO QUISO DETARDAR,
9570 5ELCID1216 MYO %ID DON ******* LA QUINTA MANDO TOMAR,
9783 5ELCID1243 MYO %ID DON ******* EN VALEN%IA ESTA FOLGANDO,
10290 5ELCID1302 PLOGO A ALBARFANEZ DELO QUE DIXO DON *******.
12784 5ELCID1622 PESOL AL REY DE MARRUECOS DE MYO %ID DON *******:
12835 5ELCID1628 VAN BUSCAR A VALEN%IA A MYO %ID DON *******.
14198 5ELCID1797 MYO %ID DON *******, EL QUE EN BUEN ORA NASCO,
17808 5ELCID2253 MYO %ID DON *******, EL QUE EN BUEN ORA NASCO,
18183 5ELCID2300 MYO %ID DON ******* ALCUELLO LO TOMO,
18422 5ELCID2331 MYO %ID DON ******* SONRRISANDO SALIO:
26316 5ELCID3356 POR CONSAGRAR CON MYO %ID DON *******
WORD #3608 OCCURS 17 TIMES.
INDEX OF DIVERSIFICATION = 1412.38 WITH STANDARD DEVIATION OF 2038.80

ROGAD 10070 5ELCID1275 DESI POR MI BESALDE LA MANO EFIRME GELO *****
WORD #3609 OCCURS 1 TIMES.

ROGADAS 17391 5ELCID2200 PEDIDAS UOS HA & ******* EL MYO SE@OR ALFONSSO,
WORD #3610 OCCURS 1 TIMES.

ROGADO 13921 5ELCID1763 HYA MUGIER DA@A XIMENA, NOM LO AUIEDES ******?
WORD #3611 OCCURS 1 TIMES.

ROGADORES 16405 5ELCID2080 LOS MIOS & LOS UUESTROS QUE SEAN *********;
WORD #3612 OCCURS 1 TIMES.

ROGADOS 21709 5ELCID2760 SI NON FUESSEMOS *******,
WORD #3613 OCCURS 1 TIMES.

ROGAMOS 21436 5ELCID2725 POR DIOS UOS *******, DON DIEGO & DON FERANDO
WORD #3614 OCCURS 1 TIMES.

ROGAND 13844 5ELCID1754 ****** AL CRIADOR QUE UOS BIUA ALGUNT A@O,
WORD #3615 OCCURS 1 TIMES.

WORD C# PREFIX CONTEXT

```
ROGANDO          1884 5ELCID0240 ******* A SAN PERO & AL CRIADOR:
                 2593 5ELCID0328 ******* AL CRIADOR QUANTO ELLA MEIOR SABE,
                23986 5ELCID3057 AL CRIADOR ******* & FABLANDO EN PORIDAD.
        WORD #3616 OCCURS   3 TIMES.

ROGAR            2880 5ELCID0363 E RUEGO A SAN PEYDRO QUE ME AIUDE A *****
                11017 5ELCID1394 DE%IDO ES MYNAYA, ASSAN PERO VA *****,
                12732 5ELCID1616 AL%AN LAS MANOS PORA DIOS *****,
                15085 5ELCID1908 ***** GELO EMOS LO QUE DEZIDES UOS;
        WORD #3617 OCCURS   4 TIMES.

ROGARON         27773 5ELCID3544 DE NOCHE BELARON LAS ARMAS & ******* AL CRIADOR.
        WORD #3618 OCCURS   1 TIMES.

ROGAUA            425 5ELCID0053 FINCO LOS Y@OIOS, DE CORA%ON ******.
                15219 5ELCID1927 LO QUEL ****** ALFONSSO EL DE LEON
                27397 5ELCID3500 ATODOS LOS ****** ASSI COMMO HAN SABOR;
        WORD #3619 OCCURS   3 TIMES.

ROGAUAN         11203 5ELCID1417 QUE LES TOUIESSE PRO ******* A ALBARFANEZ;
        WORD #3620 OCCURS   1 TIMES.

ROGO            22029 5ELCID2803 TANTO LAS **** FATA QUE LAS ASSENTO.
                22986 5ELCID2928 OMILLOS ALOS SANTOS & **** ACRIADOR;
        WORD #3621 OCCURS   2 TIMES.

ROMA             2699 5ELCID0341  SALUEST DENTRO EN **** AL SE@OR SAN SABASTIAN,
        WORD #3622 OCCURS   1 TIMES.

ROMANE%IERE     6445 5ELCID0823 LO QUE *********** DALDO A MI MUGIER & A MIS FIJAS,
        WORD #3623 OCCURS   1 TIMES.

ROMANZ          29241 5ELCID3733 EN ERA DE MILL & CCXLV A@OS.  EN EL ******
        WORD #3624 OCCURS   1 TIMES.

RONPIEN         21536 5ELCID2738 ******* LAS CAMISAS & LAS CARNES AELLAS AMAS ADOS;
        WORD #3625 OCCURS   1 TIMES.

ROPAS            3806 5ELCID0481 DE OUEIAS & DE VACAS & DE ***** & DE OTRAS RIQUIZAS LARGAS.
        WORD #3626 OCCURS   1 TIMES.

ROSTRO          18178 5ELCID2299 ANTE MYO %ID LA CABE%A PREMIO & EL ****** FINCO;
        WORD #3627 OCCURS   1 TIMES.

ROY              7129 5ELCID0912 ENEL PINAR DE TEUAR DON *** DIAZ POSAUA;
        WORD #3628 OCCURS   1 TIMES.

ROYDO            5522 5ELCID0696 ANTE ***** DE ATAMORES LA TIERRA QUERIE QUEBRAR;
        WORD #3629 OCCURS   1 TIMES.

RRITAD           9354 5ELCID1189 QUIEN QUIERE PERDER CUETA & VENIR A ******,
        WORD #3630 OCCURS   1 TIMES.

RUEGA           27374 5ELCID3497 ABRA%OLOS TAN BIEN & ***** LOS DE CORA%ON
        WORD #3631 OCCURS   1 TIMES.

RUEGAN          21502 5ELCID2734 LO QUE ****** LAS DUENAS NON LES HA NINGUN PRO.
                23466 5ELCID2989 ****** AL REY QUE LOS QUITE DESTA CORT.
        WORD #3632 OCCURS   2 TIMES.

RUEGEN           6455 5ELCID0824 QUE ****** POR MI LAS NOCHES & LOS DIAS;
        WORD #3633 OCCURS   1 TIMES.

RUEGO            2373 5ELCID0300 YO ***** ADIOS & AL PADRE SPIRITAL,
                 2872 5ELCID0363 E ***** A SAN PEYDRO QUE ME AIUDE A ROGAR
                15055 5ELCID1903 SED BUENOS MENSSAGEROS, & ***** UOS LO YO
                16341 5ELCID2073 COMETER QUIERO VN ***** A MYO %ID EL CAMPEADOR;
                26697 5ELCID3410 ***** UOS, %ID, CABOSO CAMPEADOR,
                26892 5ELCID3436 HYO UOS ***** QUE ME CYADES TODA LA CORT,
        WORD #3634 OCCURS   6 TIMES.
          INDEX OF DIVERSIFICATION =  4902.80 WITH STANDARD DEVIATION OF  5860.39

RUY               107 5ELCID0015 MYO %ID *** DIAZ POR BURGOS ENTRAUA,
                  190 5ELCID0025 QUE A MYO %ID *** DIAZ, QUE NADI NOL DIESSEN POSADA,
                  454 5ELCID0058 MYO %ID *** DIAZ, EL QUE EN BUEN ORA %INXO ESPADA,
                 3721 5ELCID0470 MIO %ID *** DIAZ POR LAS PUERTAS ENTRAUA,
                 3953 5ELCID0502 ANTE *** DIAZ EL LIDIADOR CONTADO,
                 4842 5ELCID0613 FABLO MYO %ID *** DIAZ, EL QUE EN BUEN ORA FUE NADO:
                 4967 5ELCID0628 QUE A VNO QUE DIZIEN MYO %ID *** DIAZ DE BIUAR
                 5717 5ELCID0721 YO SO *** DIAZ, EL %ID CAMPEADOR DE BIUAR
                 5810 5ELCID0734 MIO %ID *** DIAZ EL BUEN LIDIADOR;
                 5903 5ELCID0748 VIOLO MYO %ID *** DIAZ EL CASTELANO,
```

WORD C# PREFIX CONTEXT

RUY (CON'T)

```
                    5983 5ELCID0759 MYO %ID *** DIAZ, EL CUE EN BUEN ORA NASCO,
                    6154 5ELCID0784 QUE MYO %ID *** DIAZ LID CAMPAL A VEN%IDA.
                    6492 5ELCID0828 MYO %ID *** DIAZ CON LOS SOS SE ACORDAUA:
                    6630 5ELCID0846 MYO %ID *** DIAZ A ALCOL%ER ES VENIDO;
                    6811 5ELCID0870 MYO %ID *** DIAZ DE DIOS AYA SU GRA%IA
                    6846 5ELCID0875 MYO %ID *** DIAZ, QUE EN BUEN ORA CINXO ESPADA. . .
                    7345 5ELCID0942 DE MYO %ID *** DIAZ QUE NON TEMIEN NINGUNA FONTA.
                    7466 5ELCID0958 QUE MYO %ID *** DIAZ CUEL CORRIE LA TIERRA TODA;
                    8019 5ELCID1024 MYO %ID *** DIAZ ODREDES LO QUE DIXO:
                    9729 5ELCID1237 CON MYO %ID *** DIAZ, EL QUE EN BUEN ORA NASCO.
                   14117 5ELCID1787 MANDO MYO %ID *** DIAZ QUE FITA SOUIESSE LA TIENDA,
                   14822 5ELCID1873 QUE BIEN PARESCADES ANTE *** DIAZ MYO %ID;
                   15102 5ELCID1910 DEZID A *** DIAZ, EL QUE EN BUEN ORA NASCO,
                   16205 5ELCID2056 MYO %ID *** DIAZ, QUE EN ORA BUENA NASCO,
                   16990 5ELCID2151 MYO %ID *** DIAZ, MUCHO ME AUEDES ONDRADO,
                   17882 5ELCID2263 ESPIDIENDOS DE *** DIAZ, EL QUE EN BUEN ORA NASCO,
                   19228 5ELCID2433 MYO %ID *** DIAZ, EL CAMPEADOR CONTADO,
                   23965 5ELCID3054 MYO %ID *** DIAZ EN SAN SERUAN POSADO.
                   25906 5ELCID3301 MYO %ID *** DIAZ A PERO VERMUEZ CATA;
                   29071 5ELCID3713 PRISOS ALA BARBA *** DIAZ SO SE@OR;
        WORD #3635 OCCURS  30 TIMES.
           INDEX OF DIVERSIFICATION =   997.76 WITH STANDARD DEVIATION OF  1301.81

RUYDIAZ             8958 5ELCID1140 CA YO SO *******, MYO %ID EL DE BIUAR
                   18374 5ELCID2325 VINO CON ESTAS NUEUAS A MUO %ID ******* EL CANPEADOR:
        WORD #3636 OCCURS   2 TIMES.

RYENDA             13788 5ELCID1747 MYO %ID FINCO ANTELLAS, TOUO LA ****** AL CAUALLO:
        WORD #3637 OCCURS   1 TIMES.

SABASTIAN           2703 5ELCID0341  SALUEST DENTRO EN ROMA AL SE@OR SAN *********,
        WORD #3638 OCCURS   1 TIMES.

SABE                2599 5ELCID0328 ROGANDO AL CRIADOR QUANTO ELLA MEIOR ****,
                    2937 5ELCID0370 LORANDO DE LOS OIOS, QUE NON **** QUE SE FAR.
                    2964 5ELCID0373 AGORA NOS PARTIMOS, DIOS **** EL AIUNTAR.
                    8921 5ELCID1136 QUIS CADA VNO DELLOS BIEN **** LO QUE HA DE FAR.
                   12339 5ELCID1567 CA BIEN **** QUE ALBARFANEZ TRAHE TODO RECABDO;
                   15962 5ELCID2024 ASI **** DAR OMILDAN%A A ALFONSSO SO SE@OR.
        WORD #3639 OCCURS   6 TIMES.
           INDEX OF DIVERSIFICATION =  2671.60 WITH STANDARD DEVIATION OF  2484.74

SABED              10089 5ELCID1278 ENBIARE POR ELLAS, & UOS ***** EL MENSAGE:
                   16777 5ELCID2124 OY DE MAS ***** QUE FER DELLOS, CAMPEADOR.
                   16918 5ELCID2141 TOD ESTO ES PUESTO, *****, EN GRANT RECABDO.
                   18029 5ELCID2281 MALA SOBREUIENTA, *****, QUE LES CUNTIO:
                   18308 5ELCID2317 MAS, *****, DE CUER LES PESA ALOS YFANTES DE CARRION;
                   21651 5ELCID2752 POR MUERTAS LAS DEXARON, *****, QUE NON POR BIUAS.
                   25513 5ELCID3249 MAL ESCAPAN IOGADOS, *****, DESTA RAZON.
                   25957 5ELCID3308 MAS QUANDO ENPIE%A, *****, NOL CA VAGAR:
                   26410 5ELCID3369 ENTODAS GUISAS, *****, QUE MAS VALEN QUE VOS.
        WORD #3640 OCCURS   9 TIMES.
           INDEX OF DIVERSIFICATION =  2039.13 WITH STANDARD DEVIATION OF  2368.17

SABEDES            17569 5ELCID2223 ******* QUE AL REY ASSI GELO HE MANDADO,
                   20298 5ELCID2576 BIEN LO ******* UOS QUE LAS GANE AGUISA DE VARON;
                   23084 5ELCID2941 HYA UOS ******* LA ONDRA QUE ES CUNTIDA ANOS,
                   25976 5ELCID3311 BIEN LO ******* QUE YO NON PUEDO MAS;
        WORD #3641 OCCURS   4 TIMES.

SABEMOS              965 5ELCID0124 BIEN LO ******* QUE EL ALGO GA@O,
                   24596 5ELCID3134 GRANDE TUERTO LE HAN TENIDO, ******* LO TODOS NOS;
                   25362 5ELCID3229 NOS BIEN LA ******* ACUESTA RAZON,
                   26966 5ELCID3445 MAS BIEN ******* LAS MA@AS QUE ELLOS HAN,
                   28032 5ELCID3578 NON ******* QUES COMIDRAN ELLOS OQUE NON;
        WORD #3642 OCCURS   5 TIMES.
           INDEX OF DIVERSIFICATION =  6765.75 WITH STANDARD DEVIATION OF 11248.17

SABEN               4311 5ELCID0549 NON LO ***** LOS MOROS EL ARDIMENT QUE AN.
                    6277 5ELCID0799 TRAEN ORO & PLATA QUE NON ***** RECABDO;
                    8552 5ELCID1086 TAN RICOS SON LOS SOS QUE NON ***** QUE SE AN.
                    9079 5ELCID1155 MIEDO AN EN VALEN%IA QUE NON ***** QUESE FAR.
                   26097 5ELCID3326 CROUIERON TELO TODOS, MAS NON ***** LA VERDAD.
                   27954 5ELCID3567 CA TODOS LO ***** QUE LO BUSCASTES VOS.
        WORD #3643 OCCURS   6 TIMES.
           INDEX OF DIVERSIFICATION =  4727.60 WITH STANDARD DEVIATION OF  6902.55

SABENT              4818 5ELCID0610 MYO %ID GA@O A ALCO%ER, ******, POR ESTA MA@A.
                    9232 5ELCID1174 MAL SE AQUEXAN LOS DE VALEN%IA QUE NON ****** QUES FAR,
        WORD #3644 OCCURS   2 TIMES.

SABER               9913 5ELCID1257 SI UOS QUISIEREDES, MINAYA, QUIERO ***** RECABDO
                   13748 5ELCID1742 DEXO ALBARFANEZ POR ***** TODO RECABDO.
                   14027 5ELCID1777 NON PUDIERON ELLOS ***** LA CUENTA DE TODOS LOS CAUALLOS,
        WORD #3645 OCCURS   3 TIMES.
```

WORD C# PREFIX CONTEXT

```
SABET          4501 5ELCID0572 ALOS DE CALATAUTH, *****, MALES PESAUA.
               4747 5ELCID0602 TIENEN BUENOS CAUALLOS, *****, ASU GUISA LES ANDAN;
               6052 5ELCID0768 *****, EL OTRO NON GEL OSO ESPERAR.
               6776 5ELCID0865 NON TEME GERRA, *****, A NULLA PART.
               7168 5ELCID0918 NON SON EN CUENTA, *****, LAS PEONADAS.
               8174 5ELCID1042 *****, NON UOS DARE AUOS VN DINERO MALO;
               8649 5ELCID1098 PESA ALOS DE VALEN%IA, *****, NON LES PLAZE;
               9070 5ELCID1154 LAS NUEUAS DE MYO %ID, *****, SONANDO VAN,
               9417 5ELCID1197 ANDIDIERON LOS PREGONES, *****, ATODAS PARTES,
               9498 5ELCID1207 MAS LE VIENEN A MYO %ID, *****, QUE NOS LE VAN.
               9512 5ELCID1209 NUEUE MESES COMPLIDOS, *****, SOBRELLA IAZ;
               9701 5ELCID1233 MAS MUCHO FUE PROUECHOSA, *****, ESTA ARANCADA:
              11323 5ELCID1433 DESFECHOS NOS HA EL %ID, *****, SI NO NOS VAL;
              11678 5ELCID1480 AMY NON ME PESA, *****, MUCHO ME PLAZE
              14509 5ELCID1835 LOS YFANTES DE CARRION, *****, YS A%ERTARON,
              15638 5ELCID1983 NON SON EN CUENTA, *****, LAS CASTELLANAS.
              17380 5ELCID2199 MAS BIEN ***** VERDAD QUE NON LO LEUANTE YO:
              19207 5ELCID2430 *****, TODOS DE FIRME ROBAUAN EL CAMPO.
              21804 5ELCID2774 ***** BIEN QUE SI ELLOS LE VIESSEN, NON ESCAPARA DE MUERT.
              24395 5ELCID3110 E DESI ADELANT, *****, TODOS LOS OTROS:
              25900 5ELCID3300 MAS NOS PRE%IAMOS, *****, QUE MENOS NO.
       WORD #3646 OCCURS  21 TIMES.
          INDEX OF DIVERSIFICATION =  1068.95 WITH STANDARD DEVIATION OF   896.33

SABIDOR       15391 5ELCID1949 DIXO MINAYA, UOS SED *******.
              18461 5ELCID2336 CA DAQUELOS MOROS YO SO *******;
              23166 5ELCID2951 E QUE UOS PESE, REY COMMO SODES *******;
              24084 5ELCID3070 COMIGO YRA MAL ANDA, QUE ES BIEN *******.
       WORD #3647 OCCURS   4 TIMES.

SABIDORES     23599 5ELCID3005 FUERON Y DE SU REYNO OTROS MUCHOS *********,
       WORD #3648 OCCURS   1 TIMES.

SABIE         12399 5ELCID1574 AVN NON ***** MYO %ID, EL QUE EN BUEN ORA %INXO ESPADA,
       WORD #3649 OCCURS   1 TIMES.

SABIEN        21802 5ELCID2773 ELLOS NOL VIEN NI DEND ****** RA%ION;
              22154 5ELCID2821 QUANDO ****** ESTO, PESOLES DE CORA%ON;
       WORD #3650 OCCURS   2 TIMES.

SABOR          1845 5ELCID0234 CON ESTOS CAUALLEROS QUEL SIRUEN ASO *****.
               3000 5ELCID0378 ATAN GRAND ***** FABLO MINAYA ALBARFANEZ:
               8361 5ELCID1063 EL ***** QUE DED E NON SERA OLBIDADO.
               9361 5ELCID1190 VINIESSE A MYO %ID QUE A ***** DE CAUALGAR;
               9421 5ELCID1198 AL ***** DELA GANAN%IA NON LO QUIERE DETARDAR,
              10668 5ELCID1351 MER%ED UOS PIDE EL %ID, SIUOS CAYESSE EN *****,
              10916 5ELCID1381 SI LEUAREDES LAS DUENAS, SIRUAN LAS ASU *****,
              11855 5ELCID1503 POR ***** DE MYO %ID DE GRAND ONDRAL DAR;
              12747 5ELCID1618 MYO %ID & SUS COMPANAS TAN AGRAND ***** ESTAN.
              14971 5ELCID1892 DEL CASAMIENTO NON SE SIS ABRA *****;
              15027 5ELCID1899 E DE MI ABRA PERDON; VINIESSEM A VISTAS, SI OUIESSE DENT *****.
              15042 5ELCID1902 ***** HAN DE CASAR CON SUS FIJAS AMAS ADOS.
              15099 5ELCID1909 DESPUES FAGA EL %ID LO QUE QUIERE *****.
              15317 5ELCID1939 DESTE CASAMIENTO NON AURIA *****;
              15358 5ELCID1944 QUE UOS VERNIE AVISTAS DO OUIESSEDES *****;
              15815 5ELCID2005 E OTRAS DUE@AS QUE LAS SIRUEN ASU *****;
              16097 5ELCID2041 TODOS LOS DEMAS DESTO AUIEN *****;
              16578 5ELCID2100 AL CRIADOR PLEGA QUE AYADES ENDE *****.
              17452 5ELCID2208 ***** ABRIEDES DE SER & DE COMER ENEL PALA%IO.
              18327 5ELCID2318 CA VEYEN TANTAS TIENDAS DE MOROS DE QUE NON AUIE *****.
              18455 5ELCID2335 EN VALEN%IA FOLGAD A TODO UUESTRO *****,
              18745 5ELCID2372 POR ***** QUE AUIA DE ALGUN MORO MATAR;
              19562 5ELCID2478 QUANDO VEO LO QUE AUIA *****,
              19754 5ELCID2504 QUE PAGUEN AMI O A QUI YO OUIER *****.
              20071 5ELCID2547 DESPUES EN LA CARRERA FEREMOS NUESTRO *****,
              20385 5ELCID2586 QUANDO SON PAGADOS ATODO SO *****,
              20784 5ELCID2639 DELO QUE OUIEREN HUEBOS SIRUAN LAS ASO *****,
              20871 5ELCID2650 DIOS, QUE BIEN LOS SIRUIO ATODO SO *****
              21335 5ELCID2711 DEPORTAR SE QUIEREN CON ELLAS ATODO SU *****.
              21526 5ELCID2736 CON LAS %INCHAS CORREDIZAS MAIAN LAS TAN SIN *****;
              21535 5ELCID2737 CON LAS ESPUELAS AGUDAS, DON ELLAS AN MAL *****,
              22912 5ELCID2918 CON EL DOS CAUALLEROS QUEL SIRUAN A SO *****,
              23514 5ELCID2994 QUITE MYO REYNO, CADEL NON HE *****.
              23669 5ELCID3014 POR QUE SE TARDA EL REY NON HA *****.
              23782 5ELCID3029 CAUALGAD, %ID; SI NON, NON AURIA DED *****;
              23978 5ELCID3056 ***** A DE VELAR ENESSA SANTIDAD,
              24347 5ELCID3104 ALA PUERTA DE FUERA DESCAUALGA A *****;
              24920 5ELCID3173 QUANDO LAS DEMANDA & DELLAS HA *****,
              25297 5ELCID3220 TORNAN CON EL CONSSEIO E FABLAUAN ASSO *****:
              25311 5ELCID3222 QUANDO DE NUESTROS AUERES ASSIL PRENDE *****;
              26889 5ELCID3435 DEZID, MYNAYA, LO QUE OUIEREDES *****.
              27385 5ELCID3498 QUE PRENDAN DE SUS AUERES QUANTO OUIEREN *****.
```

WORD C# PREFIX CONTEXT

SABOR (CON'T)

```
                    27401 5ELCID3500 ATODOS LOS ROGAUA ASSI COMMO HAN *****;
                    27423 5ELCID3503 DELO AL TANTO PRISO QUANT OUO *****.
                    27533 5ELCID3516 ESSORA DIXO EL REY: DESTO NON HE *****;
                    27798 5ELCID3547 POR VER ESTA LID, CA AVIEN ENDE *****;
                    28220 5ELCID3602 ENTODO MYO REYNO NON AURA BUENA *****.
                    29043 5ELCID3709 DELO QUE AN PRESO MUCHO AN MAL *****;
         WORD #3651 OCCURS  48 TIMES.
            INDEX OF DIVERSIFICATION =   577.68 WITH STANDARD DEVIATION OF   856.20

SABRA                7659 5ELCID0981 ***** EL SALIDO A QUIEN VINO DESONDRAR.
         WORD #3652 OCCURS   1 TIMES.

SABRE               26009 5ELCID3315 LAS TUS MAaAS YO TELAS ***** CONTAR:
         WORD #3653 OCCURS   1 TIMES.

SABREDES            24733 5ELCID3150 CA UOS LAS CASASTES, REY, ******** QUE FER OY;
         WORD #3654 OCCURS   1 TIMES.

SABREMOS            22479 5ELCID2862 EN LOS DIAS DE VAGAR TODA NUESTRA RENCURA ******** CONTAR.
                    24677 5ELCID3144 ******** QUE RESPONDEN YFANTES DE CARRION.
         WORD #3655 OCCURS   2 TIMES.

SACA                24941 5ELCID3177 **** LAS ESPADAS & RELUMBRA TODA LA CORT,
         WORD #3656 OCCURS   1 TIMES.

SACADA              12577 5ELCID1596 ****** ME AUEDES DE MUCHAS VERGUENZAS MALAS;
         WORD #3657 OCCURS   1 TIMES.

SACAN                5203 5ELCID0658 LAS AROBDAS, QUE LOS MOROS *****, DE DIA
                    13228 5ELCID1677 ***** LOS DELAS HUERTAS MUCHO AFEA GUISA,
                    13540 5ELCID1716 LA SEaA ***** FUERA, DE VALENZIA DIERON SALTO,
                    18991 5ELCID2402 LOS DE MYO ZID ALOS DE BUCAR DELAS TIENDAS LOS *****.
                    18992 5ELCID2403 ***** LOS DELAS TIENDAS, CAEN LOS EN ALCAZ;
         WORD #3658 OCCURS   5 TIMES.
            INDEX OF DIVERSIFICATION =  3446.25 WITH STANDARD DEVIATION OF  3944.50

SACAR                4554 5ELCID0579 AGUISA DE MENBRADO, POR ***** LOS AZELADA.
                    10083 5ELCID1277 QUENLAS DEXE *****;
                    20056 5ELCID2546 ***** LAS HEMOS DE VALENZIA, DE PODER DEL CAMPEADOR;
         WORD #3659 OCCURS   3 TIMES.

SACAREMOS            3497 5ELCID0441 PUES QUE A CASTEION ********* A ZELADA,. . . .
         WORD #3660 OCCURS   1 TIMES.

SACARON             12127 5ELCID1538 DE TAN GRAND CONDUCHO COMMO EN MEDINAL *******;
                    24739 5ELCID3151 MAS QUANDO ******* MIS FIJAS DE VALENZIA LA MAYOR,
                    24927 5ELCID3175 ******* LAS ESPADAS COLADO & TIZON,
                    25148 5ELCID3203 QUANDO ******* DE VALENZIA MIS FIJAS AMAS ADOS,
         WORD #3661 OCCURS   4 TIMES.

SACASTES            27893 5ELCID3559 NON ******** NINGUNA QUANDO OUIEMOS LA CORT.
         WORD #3662 OCCURS   1 TIMES.

SACAUADES           25633 5ELCID3264 POR QUE LAS ********* DE VALENZIA SUS HONORES?
         WORD #3663 OCCURS   1 TIMES.

SACO                  298 5ELCID0038 **** EL PIE DEL ESTRIBERA, UNA FERIDAL DAUA;
                      978 5ELCID0125 QUANDO ATIERRA DE MOROS ENTRO, QUE GRANT AUER ****;
                    18112 5ELCID2291 EL MANTO & EL BRIAL TODO SUZIO LO ****.
                    20940 5ELCID2659 ELLOS VEYEN LA RIQUEZA QUE EL MORO ****,
                    22011 5ELCID2800 NUEUO ERA & FRESCO, QUE DE VALENZIAL ****,
         WORD #3664 OCCURS   5 TIMES.
            INDEX OF DIVERSIFICATION =  5427.25 WITH STANDARD DEVIATION OF  7859.54

SACOL               28713 5ELCID3667 ***** DEL MOION; MARTIN ANTOLJNEZ EN EL CAMPO FINCAUA.
         WORD #3665 OCCURS   1 TIMES.

SACOLA              27346 5ELCID3494 E SOLTAUA LA BARBA & ****** DEL CORDON.
         WORD #3666 OCCURS   1 TIMES.

SACOLOS              4989 5ELCID0631 ******* A ZELADA, EL CASTIELLO GANADO A;
         WORD #3667 OCCURS   1 TIMES.

SALADA               8584 5ELCID1090 CONTRA LA MAR ****** CONPEZO DE GUERREAR;
         WORD #3668 OCCURS   1 TIMES.

SALDREDES            8038 5ELCID1026 SI LO QUE DIGO FIZIEREDES, ********* DE CATIUO;
         WORD #3669 OCCURS   1 TIMES.

SALDRIEN            10679 5ELCID1353 ******** DEL MONESTERIO DO ELLE LAS DEXO,
         WORD #3670 OCCURS   1 TIMES.

SALE                22653 5ELCID2886 PRIUADO CAUALGA, A REZEBIR LOS ****;
         WORD #3671 OCCURS   1 TIMES.
```

WORD C# PREFIX CONTEXT

```
SALEN          15890 5ELCID2015 RE%EBIR LO ***** CON TAN GRANC ONOR.
         WORD #3672 OCCURS   1 TIMES.

SALGAMOS       27091 5ELCID3461 SI DIOS QUISIERE QUE DESTA BIEN ******** NOS,
         WORD #3673 OCCURS   1 TIMES.

SALI           18736 5ELCID2371 POR ESSO **** DE MI TIERRA & VIN UOS BUSCAR,
         WORD #3674 OCCURS   1 TIMES.

SALID          27914 5ELCID3562 LEUAD & ***** ALCAMPO, YFANTES DE CARRION,
         WORD #3675 OCCURS   1 TIMES.

SALIDA         25607 5ELCID3261 ALA ****** DE VALEN%IA MIS FIJAS VOS DI YO,
         WORD #3676 OCCURS   1 TIMES.

SALIDES        27939 5ELCID3565 SI DEL CAMPO BIEN *******, GRAND ONDRA AUREDES VOS;
         WORD #3677 OCCURS   1 TIMES.

SALIDO          7444 5ELCID0955 QUE EL ****** DE CASTIELLA ASILOS TRAE TAN MAL.
                7661 5ELCID0981 SABRA EL ****** A QUIEN VINO DESONDRAR.
               13404 5ELCID1699 ES DIA ES ****** & LA NOCH ENTRADA ES,
         WORD #3678 OCCURS   3 TIMES.

SALIDOS        13497 5ELCID1711 ******* SON TODOS ARMADOS POR LAS TORRES DE VAN%IA,
               14397 5ELCID1821 ******* SON DE VALEN%IA EPIENSSAN DE ANDAR,
               16682 5ELCID2112 QUANDO SALIE EL SOL, QUES TORNASSE CADA VNO DON ******* SON.
               18332 5ELCID2319 AMOS HERMANOS A PART ******* SON:
         WORD #3679 OCCURS   4 TIMES.

SALIE           2355 5ELCID0297 APRIESSA CAUALGA, RE%EBIR LOS *****,
               16259 5ELCID2062 OTRO DIA MA@ANA, CLARO ***** EL SOL,
               16674 5ELCID2112 QUANDO ***** EL SOL, QUES TORNASSE CADA VNO DON SALIDOS SON.
               21280 5ELCID2704  MAL GELO CUNPLIERON QUANDO ***** EL SOL
               21546 5ELCID2739 LINPIA ***** LA SANGRE SOBRE LOS %ICLATONES.
         WORD #3680 OCCURS   5 TIMES.
            INDEX OF DIVERSIFICATION =  4796.75 WITH STANDARD DEVIATION OF  6395.46

SALIEN         12476 5ELCID1583 RE%IBIR ****** LAS DUENAS & AL BUENO DE MINAYA.
               15838 5ELCID2009 ****** DE VALEN%IA, AGUIJAN & ESPOLONAUAN.
               20563 5ELCID2611 HYA ****** LOS YFANTES DE VALEN%IA LA CLARA,
               20584 5ELCID2613 POR LA HUERTA DE VALEN%IA TENIENDO ****** ARMAS;
               22921 5ELCID2920 ****** DE VALEN%IA & ANDAN QUANTO PUEDEN,
               24818 5ELCID3161 ESSORA ****** APARTE YFFANTES DE CARRION,
               25269 5ELCID3217 ESSORA ****** A PARTE YFANTES DE CARRION;
               26957 5ELCID3444 ONDE ****** CONDES DE PREZ & DE VALOR;
               28284 5ELCID3611 ****** LOS FIELES DE MEDIO, ELLOS CARA POR CARA SON;
         WORD #3681 OCCURS   9 TIMES.
            INDEX OF DIVERSIFICATION =  1975.00 WITH STANDARD DEVIATION OF  1524.39

SALIERA        11926 5ELCID1512 O CUEMO ******* DE CASTIELLA ALBARFANEZ CON ESTAS DUE@AS
                                    QUE TRAHE.
         WORD #3682 OCCURS   1 TIMES.

SALIERE        27118 5ELCID3465 CRAS SEA LA LID, QUANDO ******* EL SOL,
         WORD #3683 OCCURS   1 TIMES.

SALIERON        2909 5ELCID0367 ******** DELA EGLESIA, YA QUIEREN CAUALGAR.
                4623 5ELCID0587 ******** DE ALCO%ER AVNA PRIESSA MUCH ESTRANA.
               11883 5ELCID1507 BIEN ******** DEN %IENTO QUE NON PARE%EN MAL,
               12152 5ELCID1542 ******** DE MEDINA, & SALON PASSAUAN,
               17678 5ELCID2236 QUANDO OUIERON AQUESTO FECHO, ******** DEL PALA%IO,
               20001 5ELCID2538 AMOS ******** A PART, VERA MIENTRE SON HERMANOS;
               22083 5ELCID2810 ENTRE NOCH & DIA ******** DELOS MONTES;
               28100 5ELCID3588 HYA ******** AL CAMPO DO ERAN LOS MOIONES.
         WORD #3684 OCCURS   8 TIMES.
            INDEX OF DIVERSIFICATION =  3597.71 WITH STANDARD DEVIATION OF  2631.05

SALIESSE       24017 5ELCID3061 SUELTA FUE LA MISSA ANTES QUE ******** EL SOL,
               28256 5ELCID3607 QUE POR Y SERIE VEN%IDO QUI ******** DEL MOION.
         WORD #3685 OCCURS   2 TIMES.

SALIO            431 5ELCID0055 ***** POR LA PUERTA & EN ARLAN%ON POSAUA.
                3677 5ELCID0464 EL CAMPEADOR ***** DE LA %ELADA, CORRIE ACASTEION SIN FALLA.
                9317 5ELCID1185 ***** DE MURUIEDRO VNA NOCH EN TRASNOCHADA,
               12501 5ELCID1586 MYO %ID ***** SOBREL, & ARMAS DE FUSTE TOMAUA,
               15158 5ELCID1917 APRIESSA CAUALGA, ARE%EBIR LOS *****;
               16305 5ELCID2068 AL OTRO DIA MA@ANA, ASSI COMMO ***** EL SOL,
               18089 5ELCID2288 DIEGO GON%ALEZ POR LA PUERTA *****,
               18424 5ELCID2331 MYO %ID DON RODRIGO SONRRISANDO *****:
               21766 5ELCID2768 DE TODOS LOS OTROS APARTE SE *****,
               24333 5ELCID3102 APRIESSA CAUALGA, DE SAN SERUAN *****;
               28493 5ELCID3638 POR LA BOCA AFUERA LA SANGREL *****;
               28865 5ELCID3687 VERMEIO ***** EL ASTIL, & LA LAN%A & EL PENDON.
         WORD #3686 OCCURS  12 TIMES.
            INDEX OF DIVERSIFICATION =  2583.91 WITH STANDARD DEVIATION OF  1608.02
```

WORD C# PREFIX CONTEXT

SALIOLOS 3848 5ELCID0487 ******** REZEBIR CON ESTA SU MESNADA,
11660 5ELCID1478 ******** REZEBIR CON GRANT GOZO QUE FAZE:
20859 5ELCID2649 ******** RECEBIR CON GRANDES AUOROZES;
22619 5ELCID2882 ******** A REZEBIR DE BUENA VOLUNTAD,
WORD #3687 OCCURS 4 TIMES.

SALIOS 13617 5ELCID1726 ****** LE DE SOL ESPADA, CA MUCHOL ANDIDO EL CAUALLO,
18033 5ELCID2282 ****** DE LA RED & DESATOS EL LEON.
WORD #3688 OCCURS 2 TIMES.

SALIR 5770 5ELCID0729 TANTOS PENDONES BLANCOS ***** VERMEIOS EN SANGRE,
15826 5ELCID2007 QUE DEL ALCAZAR VNA ***** NON PUEDE,
16316 5ELCID2070 AL ***** DE LA MISSA TODOS IUNTADOS SON,
17707 5ELCID2241 AL ***** DELA ECCLEGIA CAUALGARON TAN PRIUADO,
19020 5ELCID2406 CAUALLOS SIN DUENOS ***** A TODAS PARTES.
WORD #3689 OCCURS 5 TIMES.
INDEX OF DIVERSIFICATION = 3311.50 WITH STANDARD DEVIATION OF 4514.11

SALISTE 26373 5ELCID3364 ******* POR LA PUERTA, METISTET AL CORAL,
WORD #3690 OCCURS 1 TIMES.

SALON 4357 5ELCID0555 AZERCA CORRE *****, AGUA NOL PUEDENT VEDAR.
4537 5ELCID0577 COIO ***** AYUSO LA SU SE@A ALZADA,
4641 5ELCID0589 COIOS ***** AYUSO, CON LOS SOS ABUELTA NADI.
5014 5ELCID0634 RIBERA DE ***** TODA YRA AMAL,
6720 5ELCID0858 PASO ***** AYUSO, AGUIJO CABA DELANT,
6728 5ELCID0859 AL EXIR DE ***** MUCHO OUO BUENAS AUES.
11952 5ELCID1515 POR ZERCA DE ***** TAN GRANDES GOZOS VAN.
12156 5ELCID1542 SALIERON DE MEDINA, & ***** PASSAUAN,
20914 5ELCID2656 TROZIERON ARBUXUELO & LEGARON A *****,
21154 5ELCID2687 TENIENDO YUAN ARMAS ALTROZIR DE *****;
WORD #3691 OCCURS 10 TIMES.
INDEX OF DIVERSIFICATION = 1865.33 WITH STANDARD DEVIATION OF 3078.88

SALTO 1923 5ELCID0244 CON LUMBRES & CON CANDELAS AL CORAL DIERON *****.
3641 5ELCID0459 ABREN LAS PUERTAS, DE FUERA ***** DAUAN,
3822 5ELCID0483 NON OSA NINGUNO DAR ***** ALA ZAGA.
4593 5ELCID0584 DEMOS ***** A EL & FEREMOS GRANT GANAZIA,
4664 5ELCID0591 LOS GRANDES & LOS CHICOS FUERA ***** DAN,
5498 5ELCID0693 ABRIERON LAS PUERTAS, FUERA VN ***** DAN;
7941 5ELCID1014 DE FUERA DELA TIENDA VN ***** DAUA,
13215 5ELCID1675 ADOBAN SE DE CORAZON E DAN ***** DE LA VILLA;
13523 5ELCID1714 DIO ***** MYO ZID EN BAUIECA EL SO CAUALLO;
13545 5ELCID1716 LA SE@A SACAN FUERA, DE VALENZIA DIERON *****,
14495 5ELCID1833 HYEN LOS PRIMEROS EL REY FUERA DIO *****,
14713 5ELCID1860 CON X DE SUS PARIENTES A PARTE DAUAN *****:
16803 5ELCID2127 SOBREL SO CAUALLO BAUIECA MYO ZID ***** DAUA;
17719 5ELCID2242 ALA GLERA DE VALENZIA FUERA DIERON *****;
19718 5ELCID2500 QUE ABRAM DE MI ***** QUIZAB ALGUNA NOCH
28962 5ELCID3699 QUE NOLES DIESSEN ***** NIN OUIESSEN PAUOR.
WORD #3692 OCCURS 16 TIMES.
INDEX OF DIVERSIFICATION = 1801.60 WITH STANDARD DEVIATION OF 2464.35

SALTOS 19120 5ELCID2418 BUEN CAUALLO TIENE BUCAR & GRANDES ****** FAZ,
WORD #3693 OCCURS 1 TIMES.

SALUADOREZ 3513 5ELCID0443 E ALBAR ********** SIN FALLA, & GALIN GARZIA, VNA FARDIDA
5844 5ELCID0739 ALBAR ALBAREZ & ALBAR **********,
13255 5ELCID1681 ALBAR ********** PRESO FINCO ALLA.
13568 5ELCID1719 ALUAR ALUAREZ & ALUAR ********** & MINAYA ALBARFANEZ
15749 5ELCID1999 ALUAR ********** & GALIND GARCIAZ EL DE ARAGON,
24063 5ELCID3067 E ALBAR ALBAREZ & ALBAR **********
WORD #3694 OCCURS 6 TIMES.
INDEX OF DIVERSIFICATION = 4109.00 WITH STANDARD DEVIATION OF 3531.05

SALUDA 11040 5ELCID1398 ****** UOS MYO ZID ALLA ONDDE ELLE ESTA;
11982 5ELCID1519 ENEL OMBRO LO ******, CA TAL ES SU HUSAIE:
WORD #3695 OCCURS 2 TIMES.

SALUDAD 10957 5ELCID1387 ******* NOS A MYO ZID EL DE BIUAR,
15474 5ELCID1961 ******* ME MAYO ZID, EL QUE EN BUEN ORA ZINXO ESPADA;
20753 5ELCID2636 ******* A MYO AMIGO EL MORO AVENGALUON:
23330 5ELCID2972 ******* MELOS ATODOS, ENTRELLOS AYA ESPAZIO;
WORD #3696 OCCURS 4 TIMES.

SALUDAR 19054 5ELCID2411 ******* NOS HEMOS AMOS, & TAIAREMOS AMISTAS.
23783 5ELCID3030 ******* NOS HEMOS DALMA & DE CORAZON.
WORD #3697 OCCURS 2 TIMES.

SALUDAUA 11692 5ELCID1482 MYO ZID UOS ********, & MANDOLO RECABDAR,
WORD #3698 OCCURS 1 TIMES.

WORD C# PREFIX CONTEXT

SALUDES 7235 5ELCID0928 DIZIENDO LES ******* DE PRIMOS & DE HERMANOS,
7265 5ELCID0932 E QUEL DIXO ******* DE SU MUGIER & DE SUS FIJAS
14369 5ELCID1818 CON ******* DEL %ID QUE LAS MANOS LE BESAUA:
15182 5ELCID1921 COMMO SON LAS ******* DE ALFONSSO MYO SENOR.
WORD #3699 OCCURS 4 TIMES.

SALUDO 16091 5ELCID2040 LEUOS EN PIE & EN LA BOCAL ******.
23822 5ELCID3034 BESO LE LA MANO & DESPUES LE ******;
WORD #3700 OCCURS 2 TIMES.

SALUDOLAS 20491 5ELCID2601 ABRA%OLAS MYO %ID & ********* AMAS ADOS.
WORD #3701 OCCURS 1 TIMES.

SALUE 3334 5ELCID0420 TEMPRANO DAT %EUADA, SI EL CRIADOR UOS *****
8774 5ELCID1115 OYD, MESNADAS, SI EL CRIADOR UOS *****
12982 5ELCID1646 QUES ESTO, %ID, SI EL CRIADOR UOS *****
18427 5ELCID2332 DIOS UOS *****, YERNOS, YFANTES DE CARRION,
23240 5ELCID2960 AIUDAR LE ADERECHO, SIN ***** EL CRIADOR
23481 5ELCID2990 DIXO EL REY: NO LO FERE, SIN ***** DIOS
23847 5ELCID3038 DIOS ***** A NUESTROS AMIGOS & AUOS MAS, SE@OR
23886 5ELCID3042 RESPONDIO EL REY: SI FAGO, SIN ***** DIOS
23909 5ELCID3045 MER%ED, YA REY, SI EL CRIADOR UOS *****
26569 5ELCID3391 LOS QUE AN REBTADO LICIARAN, SIN ***** DIOS
WORD #3702 OCCURS 10 TIMES.
INDEX OF DIVERSIFICATION = 2580.67 WITH STANDARD DEVIATION OF 2434.09

SALUEST 2686 5ELCID0340 ******* A DANIEL CON LOS LEONES EN LA MALA CAR%EL,
2696 5ELCID0341 ******* DENTRO EN ROMA AL SE@OR SAN SABASTIAN,
2704 5ELCID0342 ******* A SANTA SUSANNA DEL FALSO CRIMINAL;
WORD #3703 OCCURS 3 TIMES.

SALUO 932 5ELCID0119 PRENDED LAS ARCHAS & METED LAS EN UUESTRO *****;
1041 5ELCID0133 PEDIR UOS A POCO POR DEXAR SO AUER EN *****.
1125 5ELCID0144 POR ADUZIR LAS ARCHAS & METER LAS EN UUESTRO *****,
1308 5ELCID0167 LEUALDAS, RACHEL & VIDAS, PONED LAS EN UUESTRO *****;
2833 5ELCID0357 EN TI CROUO AL ORA, POR END ES ***** DE MAL;
8454 5ELCID1074 FOLGEDES, YA MYO %ID, SODES EN UUESTRO *****.
12424 5ELCID1576 ALA PUERTA DE VALEN%IA, DO FUESSE EN SO *****,
19492 5ELCID2469 DESTA ARRANCADA, QUE LO TENIEN EN SO *****,
19601 5ELCID2483 LO VNO ES NUESTRO, LO OTRO HAN EN *****.
19956 5ELCID2531 PENSAD DELO OTRO, QUE LO NUESTRO TENEMOS LO EN *****.
20968 5ELCID2664 TAN EN ***** LO ABREMOS COMMO LO DE CARRION;
WORD #3704 OCCURS 11 TIMES.
INDEX OF DIVERSIFICATION = 2002.60 WITH STANDARD DEVIATION OF 2597.20

SAN 1628 5ELCID0209 EN *** PERO DE CARDENA YNOS CANTE EL GALLO;
1831 5ELCID0233 PORA *** PERO DE CARDENA QUANTO PUDO A ESPOLEAR,
1857 5ELCID0236 QUANDO LEGO A *** PERO EL BUEN CAMPEADOR;
1886 5ELCID0240 ROGANDO A *** PERO & AL CRIADOR:
2276 5ELCID0286 TANEN LAS CAMPA@AS EN *** PERO A CLAMOR.
2327 5ELCID0294 VANSSE PORA *** PERO DO ESTA EL QUE ENBUEN PUNTO NA%IO.
2511 5ELCID0318 EN *** PERO A MATINS TANDRA EL BUEN ABBAT,
2702 5ELCID0341 SALUEST DENTRO EN ROMA AL SE@OR *** SABASTIAN,
2874 5ELCID0363 E RUEGO A *** PEYDRO QUE ME AIUDE A ROGAR
10153 5ELCID1285 E MANDO MILL MARCOS DE PLATA A *** PERO LEUAR
10358 5ELCID1312 FUERA EL REY A *** FAGUNT AVN POCO HA,
10998 5ELCID1392 ADELINO PORA *** PERO, OLAS DUE@AS ESTAN,
11178 5ELCID1414 REMANE%IO EN *** PERO MINAYA ALBARFANEZ.
11375 5ELCID1439 HYDO ES PORA *** PERO MINAYA ALBARFANEZ,
11460 5ELCID1451 DE *** PERO FASTA MEDINA EN V DIAS VAN,
22939 5ELCID2922 AL REY EN *** FAGUNT LO FALLO.
22957 5ELCID2924 E DELAS ASTURIAS BIEN A *** %ALUADOR,
23923 5ELCID3047 E YO CON LOS MYOS POSARE A *** SERUAN:
23968 5ELCID3054 MYO %ID RUY DIAZ EN *** SERUAN POSADO.
24331 5ELCID3102 APRIESSA CAUALGA, DE *** SERUAN SALIO;
WORD #3705 OCCURS 20 TIMES.
INDEX OF DIVERSIFICATION = 1193.89 WITH STANDARD DEVIATION OF 2976.93

SANCHO 1865 5ELCID0237 EL ABBAT DON ******, CHRISTIANO DEL CRIADOR,
1914 5ELCID0243 DIOS, QUE ALEGRE FUE EL ABBAT DON ******
1944 5ELCID0246 GRADESCO LO ADIOS, MYO %ID, DIXO EL ABBAT DON ******;
2036 5ELCID0256 AQUELLAS UOS ACOMIENDO AUOS, ABBAT DON ******;
3043 5ELCID0383 AL ABBAT DON ****** TORNAN DE CASTIGAR,
3077 5ELCID0387 TORNADO ES DON ******, & FABLO ALBARFANEZ:
10163 5ELCID1286 E QUE LOS DIESSE AL ABBAT DON ******.
WORD #3706 OCCURS 7 TIMES.
INDEX OF DIVERSIFICATION = 1382.00 WITH STANDARD DEVIATION OF 2820.01

SANGRE 2800 5ELCID0353 DIOT CON LA LAN%A ENEL COSTADO, DONT YXIO LA ******,
2803 5ELCID0354 CORRIO LA ****** POR EL ASTIL AYUSO, LAS MANOS SE OUO DE VNTAR,
3950 5ELCID0501 E POR EL COBDO AYUSO LA ****** SESTELANDO,
5773 5ELCID0729 TANTOS PENDONES BLANCOS SALIR VERMEIOS EN ******,
6013 5ELCID0762 POR LA LORIGA AYUSO LA ****** DESTELLADO;
6138 5ELCID0781 POR EL COBDO AYUSO LA ****** DESTELLANDO.
13607 5ELCID1724 POR EL COBDO AYUSO LA ****** DESTELLANDO.

```
WORD                C#  PREFIX                                    CONTEXT

SANGRE (CON'T)

                 19367 5ELCID2453 POR EL COBDC AYUSC LA ****** CESTELLANDO;
                 21548 5ELCID2739 LINPIA SALIE LA ****** SOBRE LOS %ICLATONES.
         WORD #37C7 OCCURS    9 TIMES.
            INDEX OF DIVERSIFICATICN =  2342.50 WITH STANCARD CEVIATION OF  279C.20

SANGREL          28492 5ELCID3638 POR LA BOCA AFUERA LA ******* SALIO;
         WORD #37C8 OCCURS    1 TIMES.

SANGRIENTA       13830 5ELCID1752  VEDES EL ESPADA ********** & SUDIENTO EL CAUALLO:
         WORD #37C9 OCCURS    1 TIMES.

SANGRIENTAS      21581 5ELCID2744 *********** EN LAS CAMISAS & TODOS LOS CICLATONES.
         WORD #371C OCCURS    1 TIMES.

SANGRIENTO        6129 5ELCIDC780 ESPADA TAIADOR, ********** TRAE EL BRA%O,
         WORD #3711 OCCURS    1 TIMES.

SANO               593 5ELCID0075 SI CON UUSCO ESCAPO **** OBIUC,
                  6584 5ELCID0841 **** EL REY FARIZ, CON EL SE CONSEIAUAN.
                 11048 5ELCID1399 **** LO DEXE & CCN TAN GRAND RICTAD.
         WORD #3712 CCCURS    3 TIMES.

SANT              3154 5ELCID0397 DE SINIESTRO **** ESTEUAN, VNA BUENA %IPDAD,
                 10590 5ELCID1342  SI ME VALA **** ESIDRO  PLAZME DE CORA%ON,
                 14772 5ELCID1867 GRADO AL CRIADOR & AL SE@OR **** ESIDRO EL DE LEON
                 23769 5ELCID3028 PAR **** ESIDRC, VERDAD NCN SERA OY
                 24647 5ELCID3140 JURO PAR **** ESIDRC, EL QUE BOLUIERE MY CORT
                 27470 5ELCID3509 HYO LO JURO PAR **** ESIDRO EL DE LEON
         WORD #3713 CCCURS    6 TIMES.
            INDEX OF DIVERSIFICATICN =  4862.20 WITH STANCARD DEVIATION OF  3324.75

SANTA              416 5ELCIDC052 LEGO A ***** MARIA, LUEGO DESCAUALGA,
                  1678 5ELCID0215 LA CARA DEL CAUALLC TORNO A ***** MARIA,
                  1702 5ELCID0218 VALAN ME TUS VERTUDES, GLORIOSA ***** MARIA
                  2173 5ELCID0273 DAND NCS CCNSEIC POR AMCR DE ***** MARIA
                  2238 5ELCIDC282 PLEGA ADIOS & A ***** MARIA, QUE AUN CON MIS MANOS CASE ESTAS MI
                  2526 5ELCIDC319 LA MISSA NCS DIRA, ESTA SERA DE ***** TRINIDAD;
                  2639 5ELCID0333 PRISIST ENCARNA%ICN EN ***** MARIA MADRE,
                  2706 5ELCIDC342 SALUEST A ***** SUSANNA DEL FALSO CRIMINAL;
                  6436 5ELCID0822 EN ***** MARIA DE BURGOS QUITEDES MILL MISSAS;
                 1C003 5ELCID1267 GRADO A DICS, MYNAYA, & A ***** MARIA MADRE
                 11542 5ELCID1462 POR ***** MARIA UOS VAYADES PASSAR,
                 11638 5ELCID1475 TRO%IERON A ***** MARIA & VINIERON ALBERGAR A FRONTAEL,
                 12906 5ELCID1637 GRADO AL CRIACOR & A ***** MARIA MACRE,
                 13C46 5ELCID1654 CON LA MER%ED DE DIOS & DE ***** MARIA MADRE
                 13161 5ELCID1668 COLGAR LOS HAN EN ***** MARIA MADRE DEL CRIADOR.
                 17682 5ELCID2237 PORA ***** MARIA A PRIESSA ACELINNANDO;
                 17969 5ELCID2274  PLEGA A ***** MARIA & AL PADRE SANTO
                 18732 5ELCID2370 OY UOS DIX LA MISSA DE ***** TRINIDADE.
                 19900 5ELCID2524 GRADO A ***** MARIA, MACRE DEL NUESTRO SE@OR DIOS
                 2C831 5ELCID2645 POR ***** MARIA CALUA RAZIN FAZIAN LA POSADA,
                 21864 5ELCID2782 ADIOS PLEGA & A ***** MARIA QUE DENT PRENDAN ELLOS MAL GALARDON
         WORD #3714 OCCURS   21 TIMES.
            INDEX OF DIVERSIFICATION =  1071.40 WITH STANDARD CEVIATION OF  1337.23

SANTAS             387 5ELCID0048 MAS EL CRIADOR UOS UALA CCN TOCAS SUS UERTUDES ******.
                  7211 5ELCIDC924 GRADO ADIOS & ALAS SUS VERTUDES ******;
         WORD #3715 OCCURS    2 TIMES.

SANTESTEUAN      22102 5ELCID2813 A *********** VINC FELEZ MUNOZ,
                 22136 5ELCID2818 EN *********** CENTRC LAS METIO,
                 22149 5ELCID2820 LOS DE ***********, SIEMPRE MESURADOS SON,
                 22323 5ELCID2843 VINIERON A *********** DE GORMAZ, VN CASTIELLO TAN FUERT,
                 22350 5ELCID2847 VARCNES DE ***********, A GUISA DE MUY PROS,
                 22380 5ELCID2851 GRA%IAS, VARCNES DE ***********, QUE SODES CO@OS%EDORES,
                 22545 5ELCID2871 LOS DE *********** ESCURRIENDO LOS VAN
                 22574 5ELCID2875 TRO%IERON ALCO%EUA, ACIESTRO DE *********** DE GORMAZ,
         WORD #3716 OCCURS    8 TIMES.
            INDEX OF DIVERSIFICATION =    66.43 WITH STANCARD CEVIATION OF    70.C8

SANTI             5788 5ELCID0731 LOS MOROS LAMAN MAFCMAT & LCS CHRISTIANOS ***** YAGUE.
                  8942 5ELCID1138 ENEL NCMBRE DEL CRIADCR & CEL APOSTOL ***** YAGUE,
                 13335 5ELCID1690 HYR LOS HEMCS FFERIR ENEL NOMBRE DEL CRIADOR & DEL APOSTOL *****
                 22962 5ELCID2925 FASTA DENTRC EN ***** YAGUO DE TODO ES SE@OR,
                 23375 5ELCID2977 ENBIA SUS CARTAS PORA LECN & A ***** YAGUO,
         WORD #3717 OCCURS    5 TIMES.
            INDEX OF DIVERSIFICATICN =  4395.75 WITH STANCARD CEVIATION OF  3863.C8

SANTIDAD         23983 5ELCID3056 SABOR A DE VELAR ENESSA ********,
         WORD #3718 OCCURS    1 TIMES.

SANTIGO           3257 5ELCID0410 QUANDO DESPERTO EL %ID, LA CARA SE *******;
                 1C577 5ELCID1340 AL%O LA MANO CIESTRA, EL REY SE *******:
                 27465 5ELCID3508 EL REY AL%C LA MANC, LA CARA SE *******;
         WORD #3719 OCCURS    3 TIMES.
```

WORD C# PREFIX CONTEXT

SANTIGUA 1687 5ELCID0216 AL%O SU MANO DIESTRA, LA CARA SE ********:
WORD #3720 OCCURS 1 TIMES.

SANTIGUANDO 14552 5ELCID1840 EL REY DON ALFONSSO SEYSE ***********.
WORD #3721 OCCURS 1 TIMES.

SANTIGUARON 28066 5ELCID3583 *********** LAS SIELAS & CAUALGAN A VIGOR;
WORD #3722 OCCURS 1 TIMES.

SANTO 8224 5ELCID1047 ABREMOS ESTA VIDA MIENTRA PLOGIERE AL PADRE *****,
17974 5ELCID2274 PLEGA A SANTA MARIA & AL PADRE *****
23935 5ELCID3049 TERNE VIGILIA EN AQUESTE ***** LOGAR.
WORD #3723 OCCURS 3 TIMES.

SANTOS 749 5ELCID0094 VEALO EL CRIADOR CON TODOS LOS SOS ******,
2853 5ELCID0360 QUEBRANTESTE LAS PUERTAS & SAQUESTE LOS PADRES ******.
4860 5ELCID0614 GRADO A DIOS DEL %IELO & ATODOS LOS SOS ******,
13817 5ELCID1750 ESTO DIOS SE LO QUISO CON TODOS LOS SOS ******,
16979 5ELCID2149 PLEGA AL CRIADOR CON TODOS LOS SOS ******, ESTE PLAZER
18001 5ELCID2277 EL CRIADOR UOS VALLA CON TODOS LOS SOS ******.
19328 5ELCID2447 COMMO YO FIO POR DIOS & EN TODOS LOS SOS ******,
22984 5ELCID2928 OMILLOS ALOS ****** & ROGO ACRIADOR;
WORD #3724 OCCURS 8 TIMES.
INDEX OF DIVERSIFICATION = 3175.43 WITH STANDARD DEVIATION OF 2714.92

SA@A 169 5ELCID0022 EL REY DON ALFONSSO TANTO AUIE LA GRAND ****,
WORD #3725 OCCURS 1 TIMES.

SA@AS 11078 5ELCID1402 SI UOS VIESSE EL %ID ***** & SIN MAL,
22171 5ELCID2823 ALLI SOUIERON ELLAS FATA QUE ***** SON.
22506 5ELCID2866 QUANDO UOS SODES ***** & BIUAS & SIN OTRO MAL.
WORD #3726 OCCURS 3 TIMES.

SAQUESTE 2850 5ELCID0360 QUEBRANTESTE LAS PUERTAS & ******** LOS PADRES SANTOS.
WORD #3727 OCCURS 1 TIMES.

SARAGO%A 7341 5ELCID0941 POR QUE DAN PARIAS PLAZE ALOS DE ********,
8566 5ELCID1088 DEXADO A ******** & ALAS TIERRAS DUCA,
WORD #3728 OCCURS 2 TIMES.

SAUADOREZ 15719 5ELCID1994 ALUAR ALUAREZ & ALUAR *********,
WORD #3729 OCCURS 1 TIMES.

SAUANA 1428 5ELCID0183 SOBRELLA VNA ****** DE RAN%AL & MUY BLANCA.
WORD #3730 OCCURS 1 TIMES.

SAZON 15671 5ELCID1987 TANTA GRUESSA MULA & TANTO PALAFRE DE *****,
16699 5ELCID2114 TANTA GRUESSA MULA & TANTO PALAFRE DE *****
20270 5ELCID2572 DARUOS E MULAS & PALAFRES, MUY GRUESSOS DE *****,
23251 5ELCID2961 LO QUE NON CUYDAUA FER DE TODA ESTA *****,
25469 5ELCID3243 TANTA GRUESSA MULA, TANTO PALAFRE DE *****,
WORD #3731 OCCURS 5 TIMES.
INDEX OF DIVERSIFICATION = 2448.50 WITH STANDARD DEVIATION OF 1097.65

SAZONES 19510 5ELCID2472 CON DUCHOS A *******, BUENAS PIELES & BUENOS MANTOS.
WORD #3732 OCCURS 1 TIMES.

SE 231 5ELCID0030 ASCONDEN ** DE MYO %ID, CA NOL OSAN DEZIR NADA.
296 5ELCID0037 AGUIIO MYO %ID, ALA PUERTA ** LEGAUA,
307 5ELCID0039 NON ** ABRE LA PUERTA, CA BIEN ERA %ERRÀDA.
322 5ELCID0040 VNA NI@A DE NUEF A@OS A OIO ** PARAUA:
822 5ELCID0105 NON LO DETARDAN, TODOS TRES ** APARTARON.
953 5ELCID0122 RACHEL & VIDAS SEYEN ** CONSEIANDO:
1084 5ELCID0139 DIXO RACHEL & VIDAS: NON ** FAZE ASSI EL MERCADO,
1343 5ELCID0172 GRADAN ** RACHEL & VIDAS CON AUERES MONEDADOS,
1686 5ELCID0216 AL%O SU MANO DIESTRA, LA CARA ** SANTIGUA:
1716 5ELCID0220 NON ** SIENTRARE Y MAS ENTODOS LOS MYOS DIAS.
2810 5ELCID0354 CORRIO LA SANGRE POR EL ASTIL AYUSO, LAS MANOS ** OUO DE VNTAR,
2939 5ELCID0370 LORANDO DE LOS OIOS, QUE NON SABE QUE ** FAR.
3029 5ELCID0381 AUNTODOS ESTOS DUELOS EN GOZO ** TORNARAN;
3205 5ELCID0404 Y ** ECHAUA MYO %ID DESPUES QUE FUE %ENADO,
3219 5ELCID0405 VN SUENOL PRISO DUL%E, TAN BIEN ** ADURMJO.
3246 5ELCID0409 MIENTRA QUE VISQUIEREDES BIEN ** FARA LO TO.
3256 5ELCID0410 QUANDO DESPERTO EL %ID, LA CARA ** SANTIGO;
3263 5ELCID0411 SINAUA LA CARA, A DIOS ** ACOMENDO,
3442 5ELCID0434 ANDIDIERON DE NOCH, QUE VAGAR NON ** DAN.
3453 5ELCID0436 MYO %ID ** ECHO EN %ELADA CON AQUELOS QUE EL TRAE.
3634 5ELCID0458 EN CASTEION TODOS ** LEUANTAUAN,
3783 5ELCID0478 E DESI ARRIBA TORNAN ** CON LA GANAN%IA,
3829 5ELCID0484 CON AQUESTE AUER TORNAN ** ESSA CONPA@A;
3899 5ELCID0495 PAGAR ** YA DELLA ALFONSSO EL CASTELLANO.
4247 5ELCID0540 DEL CASTIELLO QUE PRISIERON TODOS RICOS ** PARTEN;

WORD C# PREFIX CONTEXT

SE (CON'T)

4457 5ELCID0567 EN LA SU VEZINDAD NON ** TREUEN GANAR TANTO.
4564 5ELCID0580 VEYEN LO LOS DE ALCO%ER, DIOS, COMMO ** ALABAUAN
4653 5ELCID0590 DIZEN LOS DE ALCO%ER: YA ** NOS VA LA GANA%IA
4794 5ELCID0607 DEXANDO UAN LOS DELANT, POR EL CASTIELLO ** TORNAUAN,
4802 5ELCID0608 LAS ESPADAS DESNUDAS, A LA PUERTA ** PARAUAN.
5145 5ELCID0650 ANDIDIERON TODOL DIA, QUE VAGAR NON ** DAN,
5161 5ELCID0653 GENTES ** AIUNTARON SOBEIANAS DE GRANDES
5399 5ELCID0681 ELDIA & LA NOCHE PIENSSAN ** DE ADOBAR.
5518 5ELCID0695 QUE PRIESSA VA EN LOS MOROS, E TORNARON ** A ARMAR;
5531 5ELCID0697 VERIEDES ARMAR ** MOROS, APRIESSA ENTRAR EN AZ.
6020 5ELCID0763 BOLUIO LA RIENDA POR YR ** LE DEL CAMPO.
6090 5ELCID0773 EL REY FARIZ EN TERUEL ** FUE ENTRAR,
6102 5ELCID0775 PARA CALATAYUCH QUANTO PUEDE ** VA.
6497 5ELCID0828 MYO %ID RUY DIAZ CON LOS SOS ** ACORDAUA:
6590 5ELCID0841 SANO EL REY FARIZ, CON EL ** CONSEIAUAN.
6680 5ELCID0852 MOROS & MORAS TOMARON ** A QUEXAR:
6717 5ELCID0857 AL%O SU SE@A, EL CAMPEADOR ** UA,
7102 5ELCID0908 QUANDO VIO EL CABOSO QUE ** TARDAUA MINAYA,
7411 5ELCID0951 ESTON%ES ** MUDO EL %ID AL PUERTO DE ALCAT,
7551 5ELCID0968 GENTES ** LE ALEGAN GRANDES ENTRE MOROS & CHRISTIANOS,
7948 5ELCID1015 DE TODAS PARTES LOS SOS ** AIUNTARON;
8490 5ELCID1079 MYEDO YUA AUIENDO QUE MYO %ID ** REPINTRA,
8554 5ELCID1086 TAN RICOS SON LOS SOS QUE NON SABEN QUE ** AN.
8913 5ELCID1135 MA@ANA ERA & PIENSSAN ** DE ARMAR,
8972 5ELCID1142 ARANCAR ** LAS ESTACAS & ACOSTAR SE ATODAS PARTES LOS TENDALES.
8977 5ELCID1142 ARANCAR SE LAS ESTACAS & ACOSTAR ** ATODAS PARTES LOS TENDALES.
8997 5ELCID1145 MAGER LES PESA, OUIERON ** ADAR & A ARANCAR.
9053 5ELCID1152 ROBAUAN EL CAMPO EPIENSSAN ** DE TORNAR.
9202 5ELCID1171 NON OSAN FUERAS EXIR NIN CON EL ** AIUNTAR;
9225 5ELCID1174 MAL ** AQUEXAN LOS DE VALEN%IA QUE NON SABENT QUES FAR,
9282 5ELCID1180 DELANTE VEYEN SO DUELO, NON ** PUEDEN HUUIAR,
9410 5ELCID1196 TORNAUAS A MURUIEDRO, CA EL ** LA A GANADA.
9430 5ELCID1199 GRANDES YENTES ** LE ACOIEN DELA BUENA CHRISTIANDAD.
9547 5ELCID1213 LOS QUE FUERON DE PIE CAUALLEROS ** FAZEN;
10129 5ELCID1283 PUES ESTO AN FABLADO, PIENSSAN ** DE ADOBAR.
10576 5ELCID1340 AL%O LA MANO DIESTRA, EL REY ** SANTIGO:
10890 5ELCID1378 MINAYA ALBARFANEZ ALBUEN REY ** ESPIDIO.
11024 5ELCID1395 QUANDO ACABO LA ORA%ION, ALAS DUE@AS ** TORNO:
11189 5ELCID1416 HYR ** QUIERE A VALEN%IA A MYO %ID EL DE BIUAR.
11221 5ELCID1420 E EL ** TENIE O QUE ADUXIERA CALLA;
11234 5ELCID1421 POR YR CON ESTAS DUENAS BUE@A CONPANA ** FAZE.
11964 5ELCID1516 DON LEGAN LOS OTROS, A MINAYA ALBARFANEZ ** UAN HOMILAR.
11974 5ELCID1518 SONRRISANDO ** DELA BOCA, HYUALO ABRA%AR,
12448 5ELCID1579 EL OBISPO DON IHERONIMO ADELANT ** ENTRAUA,
12466 5ELCID1581 CON QUANTOS QUE EL PUEDE, QUE CON ORAS ** ACORDARON,
12532 5ELCID1590 QUANDO OUO CORRIDO, TODOS ** MARAUILLAUAN;
12536 5ELCID1591 DES DIA ** PRE%IO BAUIECA EN QUANT GRANT FUE ESPA@A.
12567 5ELCID1594 QUANDO LO VIO DO@A XIMENA, A PIES ** LE ECHAUA:
12949 5ELCID1642 EN ESTAS TIERRAS AGENAS VERAN LAS MORADAS COMMO ** FAZEN,
12957 5ELCID1643 AFARTO VERAN POR LOS OIOS COMMO ** GANA EL PAN.
13210 5ELCID1675 ADOBAN ** DE CORA%ON E DAN SALTO DE LA VILLA;
13653 5ELCID1730 DESDALLI ** TORNO EL QUE EN BUEN ORA NASCO,
13810 5ELCID1750 ESTO DIOS ** LO QUISO CON TODOS LOS SOS SANTOS,
13839 5ELCID1753 CON TAL CUM ESTO ** VEN%EN MOROS DEL CAMPO.
13965 5ELCID1769 LEUANTARON ** TODAS & BESARON LE LAS MANOS,
14538 5ELCID1839 CUEDAN ** QUE ES ALMOFALLA, CA NON VIENEN CON MANDADO;
14561 5ELCID1842 FIRIERON ** A TIERRA, DE%ENDIERON DELOS CAUALOS,
14746 5ELCID1864 COMMO SI LOS FALASSE MUERTOS ADUZIR ** LOS CAUALLOS,
14968 5ELCID1892 DEL CASAMIENTO NON ** SIS ABRA SABOR;
15472 5ELCID1960 QUANDO LAS VIO, DE CORA%ON ** PAGA:
15504 5ELCID1964 NON LO DETARDAN, A MYO %ID ** TORNAUAN.
15513 5ELCID1965 DELLA PART & DELLA PORA LAS VISTAS ** ADOBAUAN;
15662 5ELCID1986 NON LO DETARDA, PORA LAS VISTAS ** ADOBO;
15734 5ELCID1997 ESTOS ** ADOBAN POR YR CON EL CAMPEADOR,
15784 5ELCID2002 LAS PUERTAS DEL ALCA%AR QUE NON ** ABRIESSEN DE DIA NIN DE NOCH,
16221 5ELCID2058 NON ** PUEDE FARTAR DEL, TANTOL QUERIE DE CORA%ON;
16238 5ELCID2060 MARAUILLAN ** DE MYO %ID QUANTOS QUE Y SON.
16493 5ELCID2091 LUEGO ** LEUANTARON LOS YFFANTES DE CARRION,
16743 5ELCID2120 PARTIR ** QUIEREN, QUE ENTRADA ERA LA NOCH.
16867 5ELCID2134 NON GELAS DARE YO CON MI MANO, NIN DED NON ** ALABARAN.
17053 5ELCID2159 BESAR LAS MANOS, ESPEDIR ** DE REY ALFONSSO:
17610 5ELCID2228 LEUANTAN ** DERECHAS & METIOGELAS EN MANO.
17755 5ELCID2247 TORNAN ** CON LAS DUE@AS, A VALEN%IA AN ENTRADO;
17900 5ELCID2265 POR PAGADOS ** PARTEN DE MYO %ID & DE SUS VASSALLOS.
18044 5ELCID2283 EN GRANT MIEDO ** VIERON POR MEDIO DELA CORT;
18152 5ELCID2296 MYO %ID FINCO EL COBDO, EN PIE ** LEUANTO,
18491 5ELCID2340 ASSI LO OTORGA DON PERO CUEMO ** ALABA FERRANDO.
18527 5ELCID2344 ESTO VAN DIZIENDO & LAS YENTES ** ALEGANDO,
18552 5ELCID2348 MAS ** MARAUILLAN ENTRE DIEGO & FERRANDO,
18970 5ELCID2400 VERIEDES QUEBRAR TANTAS CUERDAS & ARRANCAR ** LAS ESTACAS
18974 5ELCID2401 EACOSTAR ** LOS TENDALES, CON HUEBRAS ERAN TANTAS.
19547 5ELCID2476 AL%O LA MANO, ALA BARBA ** TOMO:
19962 5ELCID2532 VASSALLOS DE MYO %ID SEYEN ** SONRRISANDO:
19995 5ELCID2537 TAN MAL ** CONSSEIARON ESTOS YFFANTES AMOS.

WORD C# PREFIX CONTEXT

SE (CON'T)

```
 20674 5ELCID2624 MINAYA ALBARFANEZ ANTE MYO %IC ** PARO:
 2C823 5ELCID2644 PIENSSAN ** DE YR LCS YFANTES DE CARRION;
 21147 5ELCID2686 ESTO LES HA DICHO, & EL MORC ** TORNO;
 21161 5ELCID2688 CUEMMO DE BUEN SESO A MCLINA ** TORNO.
 21172 5ELCID2690 ACOIEN ** A ANCAR DE CIA & DE NOCH;
 21329 5ELCID2711 DEPORTAR ** QUIEREN CCN ELLAS ATODO SU SABOR.
 21692 5ELCID2757 POR LOS MONTES DO YUAN, ELLOS YUAN ** ALABANDO:
 21765 5ELCID2768 DE TODCS LCS CTRCS APARTE ** SALIO,
 21773 5ELCID2769 EN VN MONTE ESPESSO FELEZ MUNOZ ** METIO,
 21854 5ELCID2781 MAL ** ENSAYARCN LOS YFANTES DE CARRION
 21888 5ELCID2785 PARTIERON ** LE LAS TELLAS CE CENTRO CE LOS CORA%ONES,
 22215 5ELCID2829 AL%O LA SU MANO, ALA BARBA ** TOMO;
 22556 5ELCID2873 DALLENT ** ESPIDIERCN DELLCS, PIENSSAN SE DE TORNAR,
 22560 5ELCID2873 DALLENT SE ESPIDIERCN DELLCS, PIENSSAN ** DE TORNAR,
 22595 5ELCID2878 OTRO DIA MA@ANA METEN ** A ANCAR,
 22727 5ELCID2896 TENIENDO YUAN ARMAS, ENTRARCN ** ALA CIBDAD;
 22860 5ELCID2912 MYCS AUERES ** ME AN LEUACO, QUE SOBEIANOS SON;
 23412 5ELCID2982 QUI NON VINIESSE ALA CORT NON ** TOUIESSE POR SU VASSALLO.
 23663 5ELCID3014 POR QUE ** TARCA EL REY NON HA SABOR.
 23753 5ELCID3026 BILTAR ** QUIERE & ONCRAR ASO SE@OS.
 23804 5ELCID3032 DICS LC MANDE QUE PCR UCS ** ONDRE OY LA CORT
 24528 5ELCID3127 ESSORA ** LEUO EN PIE EL BUEN REY DON ALFONSSO;
 24693 5ELCID3145 MYO %ID LA MANO BESO AL REY & EN PIE ** LEUANTO;
 24958 5ELCID3179 MARAUILLAN ** DELLAS TOCAS LOS OMNES BUENOS DELA CORT.
 24977 5ELCID3181 TORNOS AL ESCA@O DON ** LEUANTO;
 25010 5ELCID3185 AL%AUA LA MANO, ALA BARBA ** TOMO;
 25093 5ELCID3197 ** QUE SI UCS ACAE%IERE, CON ELLA GANAREDES GRAND PREZ &
                  GRAND VALOR.
 25116 5ELCID3199 LUEGO ** LEUANTC MYC %IC EL CAMPEADOR;
 25186 5ELCID3207 AQUI VERIEDES QUEXAR ** YFANTES DE CARRION
 25682 5ELCID3270 EL CONDE DON GAR%IA EN PIE ** LEUANTAUA;
 25841 5ELCID3291 FERRANGO%ALEZ EN PIE ** LEUNATO,
 26134 5ELCID3331 QUANDO DURMIE MYO %ID & EL LECN ** DESATO?
 26202 5ELCID3340 QUANDO ** TORNO EL BUEN CAMPEACOR,
 26358 5ELCID3361 MARTIN ANTOLINEZ EN PIE ** LEUANTAUA;
 26369 5ELCID3363 LO DEL LECN NCN ** TE DEUE OLBIDAR;
 26506 5ELCID3382 ESSORA MUNO GUSTICZ EN PIE ** LEUANTO;
 26713 5ELCID3412 ESTE CASAMIENTO OY ** OTORGE EN ESTA CORT,
 26845 5ELCID3429 MYNAYA ALBAFANEZ EN PIE ** LEUANTO;
 27062 5ELCID3457 GOMEZ PELAYET EN PIE ** LEUANTO;
 27324 5ELCID3492 ALLI ** TOLLIC EL CAPIELO EL %ID CAMPEADOR,
 27464 5ELCID3508 EL REY AL%O LA MANO, LA CARA ** SANTIGO;
 27490 5ELCID3511 MYO %ID ENEL CAUALLC ADELANT ** LEGO,
 27581 5ELCID3522 ESSORA ** ESPIDIERON, & LUEGOS PARTIO LA CORT.
 27785 5ELCID3546 MUCHOS ** JUNTARCN DE BUENOS RICOS OMNES
 27826 5ELCID3551 TODOS TRES ** ACUERDAN, CA SON DE VN SE@OR.
 27836 5ELCID3552 EN OTRO LOGAR ** ARMAN LOS YFANTES DE CARRION,
 28238 5ELCID3605 LIBRAUAN ** DEL CAMPO TCDOS ADERREDOR.
 28364 5ELCID3622 CUEDAN ** QUE ESSORA CACRAN MUERTOS LOS QUE ESTAN ADERREDOR.
 28383 5ELCID3624 CON FERRAGCN%ALEZ DE CARA ** JUNTO;
 28559 5ELCID3646 MARTIN ANTOLINEZ & DIEGC GON%ALEZ FIRIERON ** DELAS LAN%AS,
 28758 5ELCID3672 CON ASSUR GCN%ALEZ CCMMC ** ACOBO.
 28875 5ELCID3688 TODOS ** CUEDAN QUE FERIDO ES DE MUERT.
 28887 5ELCID3689 LA LAN%A RECOMBRO & SOBREL ** PARO;
 28902 5ELCID3691 VEN%UDO ES EL CAMPO, QUANDO ESTO ** ACABO
 28929 5ELCID3695 POR ONDRADOS ** PARTEN LOS CEL BUEN CAMPEADOR;
 29212 5ELCID3730 EN ESTE LOGAR ** ACABA ESTA RAZON.
WORD #3733 OCCURS 165 TIMES.
   INDEX OF DIVERSIFICATION =   175.71 WITH STANDARD DEVIATION OF   185.19

SEA     922 5ELCID0118 E PRESTALDE DE AUER LC QUE *** GUISADO.
       1407 5ELCID0180 PLAZME, DIXO EL %ID, CACUI ***  ANDADA.
       3021 5ELCID0380 PENSEMOS DE YR NUESTRA VIA, ESTO *** DE VAGAR.
       3876 5ELCID0491 ESSO CCN ESTO *** AIUNTADO;
       3975 5ELCID0504 PUES QUE POR MI GANAREDES QUES QUIER QUE *** DALGO,
       5632 5ELCID0709 DIXO EL CAMPEADOR:  NON ***, POR CARIDAD
       7046 5ELCID0901 MIENTRA QUE *** EL PUEBLO DE MOROS & DELA YENTE CHRISTIANA,
       7735 5ELCID0990 PUES ADELLANT YRAN TRAS NOS, AQUI *** LA BATALLA;
       8108 5ELCID1034 E SI UCS CCMIEREDES, DON YO *** PAGADO,
       8286 5ELCID1054 SI BIEN NON COMEDES, CONDE, DON YO *** PAGADO,
       9239 5ELCID1175 DE NINGUNA PART QUE *** NON LES VINIE PAN;
      10168 5ELCID1287 EN ESTAS NUEUAS TODOS *** ALEGRANDO,
      13960 5ELCID1768 LO DE UUESTRAS FIJAS VENIR *** MAS POR ESPA%IO.
      14685 5ELCID1857 AVN VEA ORA QUE DE MI *** PAGACO.
      15121 5ELCID1912 DO EL DIXIERE, Y *** EL MCION.
      16352 5ELCID2074 ASI LO MANDE CHRISTUS QUE *** ASO PRO.
      16986 5ELCID2150 QUEM FECHES QUE BIEN *** GALARDONADO.
      17059 5ELCID2160 MER%ED UOS *** & FAZED NOS ESTE PERDON:
      24879 5ELCID3168 E QUANDO LAS TCUIERE, PARTIR *** LA CORT;
      26825 5ELCID3426 QUE CUEMO ES DICHO ASSI ***, CMEIOR.
      27114 5ELCID3465 CRAS *** LA LID, QUANDO SALIERE EL SOL,
      27162 5ELCID3472 *** ESTA LIS C MANDAREDES VOS.
      27256 5ELCID3484 DESI *** VEN%IDC & ESCAPE PCR TRAYDOR.
WORD #3734 OCCURS  23 TIMES.
   INDEX OF DIVERSIFICATION =  1196.00 WITH STANDARD DEVIATION OF  1708.14
```

WORD C# PREFIX CONTEXT

SEADES 848 5ELCID0108 POR SIEMPRE UOS FARE RICOS, QUE NON ****** MENGUADOS.
2263 5ELCID0284 E UOS, MUGIER ONDRADA, DE MY ****** SERUIDA
13307 5ELCID1687 POR LA MANANA PRIETA TODOS ARMADOS ******,
28011 5ELCID3575 QUE FIEL ****** OY DELLOS & DE NOS;
WORD #3735 OCCURS 4 TIMES.

SEAL 18202 5ELCID2303 ETORNARON **** APALAZIO PORA LA CORT.
WORD #3736 OCCURS 1 TIMES.

SEAM 13479 5ELCID1708 PIDO UOS VN DON & **** PRESENTADO.
WORD #3737 OCCURS 1 TIMES.

SEAMOS 15334 5ELCID1941 FLABLEMOS EN ELLO, EN LA PORIDAD ****** NOS.
24643 5ELCID3139 DELLA & DELLA PART EN PAZ ****** OY.
WORD #3738 OCCURS 2 TIMES.

SEAN 998 5ELCID0128 EN LOGAR LAS METAMOS QUE NON **** VENTADAS.
9930 5ELCID1259 METER LOS HE EN ESCRIPTO, & TODOS **** CONTADOS,
10816 5ELCID1370 DE MI **** QUITOS & VAYAN ALA GRAZIA DEL CRIADOR.
13495 5ELCID1710 DIXO EL CAMPEADOR: DESA QUI UOS **** MANDADAS.
14047 5ELCID1779 LOS MOROS DELAS TIERRAS GANADO **** Y ALGO;
15485 5ELCID1962 **** LAS VISTAS DESTAS IIJ SEMANAS;
16404 5ELCID2080 LOS MIOS & LOS UUESTROS QUE **** ROGADORES;
18400 5ELCID2329 QUE **** EN PAS & NON AYAN Y RAZION.
24601 5ELCID3135 ALCALDES **** DESTO EL CONDE DON ANRRICH & EL CONDE DON REMOND
WORD #3739 OCCURS 9 TIMES.
INDEX OF DIVERSIFICATION = 2949.38 WITH STANDARD DEVIATION OF 3018.00

SED 2493 5ELCID0315 *** MEMBRADOS COMMO LO DEUEDES FAR.
5574 5ELCID0702 QUEDAS ***, MENADAS, AQUI EN ESTE LOGAR,
8826 5ELCID1123 APAREIADOS ME *** A CAUALLOS & ARMAS;
13021 5ELCID1652 MUGIER, *** EN ESTE PALAZIO, & SI QUISIEREDES EN EL ALCAZAR;
15051 5ELCID1903 *** BUENOS MENSSAGEROS, & RUEGO UOS LO YO
15390 5ELCID1949 DIXO MINAYA, UOS *** SABIDOR.
16893 5ELCID2138 *** PADRINO DELLOS ATOD EL VELAR;
17226 5ELCID2179 VOS CON ELLOS ***, QUE ASSI UOS LO MANDO YO.
24456 5ELCID3118 *** EN UUESTRO ESCA@O COMMO REY A SE@OR;
27609 5ELCID3525 E MUNO GUSTIOZ, FIRMES *** EN CAMPO AGUISA DE VARONES;
WORD #3740 OCCURS 10 TIMES.
INDEX OF DIVERSIFICATION = 2789.67 WITH STANDARD DEVIATION OF 2132.95

SEDIE 8272 5ELCID1053 SOBREL ***** EL QUE EN BUEN ORA NASCO:
9603 5ELCID1220 QUANDO SU SE@A CABDAL ***** EN SOMO DEL ALCAZAR.
12331 5ELCID1566 EL ***** EN VALENZIA CURIANDO & GUARDANDO,
16006 5ELCID2030 HYNOIOS FITOS ***** EL CAMPEADOR:
16230 5ELCID2059 CATANDOL ***** LA BARBA, QUE TAN AYNAL CREZIERA.
WORD #3741 OCCURS 5 TIMES.
INDEX OF DIVERSIFICATION = 1988.50 WITH STANDARD DEVIATION OF 1520.62

SEDIELLOS 17698 5ELCID2239 ALA PUERTA DELA ECLEGIA ********* SPERANDO;
WORD #3742 OCCURS 1 TIMES.

SEDIELOS 27842 5ELCID3553 ******** CASTIGANDO EL CONDE GARZIORDONEZ.
WORD #3743 OCCURS 1 TIMES.

SEDIEN 7826 5ELCID1001 LAS ARMAS AUIEN PRESAS & ****** SOBRE LOS CAUALLOS.
28159 5ELCID3595 DO ****** ENEL CAMPO FABLO EL REY DON ALFONSSO:
WORD #3744 OCCURS 2 TIMES.

SEGUDADOR 27561 5ELCID3519 PORA ARRANCAR MOROS DEL CANPO & SER *********;
WORD #3745 OCCURS 1 TIMES.

SEGUDAR 6114 5ELCID0777 FATA CALATAYUCH DURO EL *******.
9023 5ELCID1148 FATA VALENZIA DURO EL *******.
19029 5ELCID2407 VII MIGEROS CONPLIDOS DURO EL *******.
WORD #3746 OCCURS 3 TIMES.

SELAS 28925 5ELCID3694 LAS ARMAS QUE Y RASTARON EL ***** TOMO.
WORD #3747 OCCURS 1 TIMES.

SELE 1043 5ELCID0134 ACOGEN **** OMNES DE TODAS PARTES MEGUADOS,
3138 5ELCID0395 GRANDES YENTES **** ACOIEN ESSA NOCH DE TODAS PARTES.
4518 5ELCID0574 QUANDO VIO MYO ZID QUE ALCOZER NON **** DAUA;
7592 5ELCID0972 ASI VIENE ES FORZADO QUE EL CONDE AMANOS **** CUYDO TOMAR.
11381 5ELCID1440 MUCHAS YENTES **** ACOGEN, PENSSO DE CAUALGAR,
16174 5ELCID2052 ESSORA **** OMILLAN LOS YFFANTES DE CARRION:
17510 5ELCID2215 AEL & EASSU MUGIER DELANT **** OMILLARON,
WORD #3748 OCCURS 7 TIMES.
INDEX OF DIVERSIFICATION = 2743.50 WITH STANDARD DEVIATION OF 1390.21

SELLADA 185 5ELCID0024 CON GRAND RECABDO & FUERTE MIENTRE *******:
347 5ELCID0043 CON GRANT RECABDO & FUERTE MIENTRE *******.
WORD #3749 OCCURS 2 TIMES.

WORD C# PREFIX CONTEXT

```
SELLO        15443 5ELCID1956 ESCRIUIEN CARTAS, BIEN LAS *****,
      WORD #3750 OCCURS   1 TIMES.

SELO           528 5ELCID0067 NON LO CONPRA, CA EL **** AUIE CONSIGO;
             13270 5ELCID1683 EL **** VIO CCN LOS CIOS, CUENTAN GELO DELANT,
             24230 5ELCID3089 AL PUNO BIEN ESTAN, CA EL **** MANDO;
      WORD #3751 OCCURS   3 TIMES.

SELOS        15853 5ELCID2011 MYO %ID ***** GA@ARA, QUE NON GELOS DIERAN EN DON.
      WORD #3752 OCCURS   1 TIMES.

SEMANAS       5255 5ELCID0664 TOUIERON GELA EN %ERCA COMPLICAS TRES *******.
              5259 5ELCID0665 ACABO DE TRES *******, LA QUARTA QUERIE ENTRAR,
              7096 5ELCID0907 ALI SOUO MIO %ID CONPLICAS XV *******;
              7151 5ELCID0915 QUANDO ESTO FECHO OUO, A CABO DE TRES *******,
             15490 5ELCID1962 SEAN LAS VISTAS DESTAS IIJ *******;
             23309 5ELCID2969 QUE DESTAS VIJ ******* ADOBES CON SUS VASSALLOS,
             23401 5ELCID2981 A CABO DE VIJ ******* QUE Y FUESSEN IUNTADOS;
             27235 5ELCID3481 ACABO DE TRES *******, EN BEGAS DE CARRION,
             27677 5ELCID3533 MAS TRES ******* DE PLAZO TODAS COMPLIDAS SON.
      WORD #3753 OCCURS   9 TIMES.
         INDEX OF DIVERSIFICATION =  2801.75 WITH STANDARD DEVIATION OF  3507.41

SEME          5079 5ELCID0642 POR QUE **** ENTRO EN MI TIERRA DERECHO ME AURA ADAR.
             25550 5ELCID3254 LA RENCURA MAYOR NON **** PUEDE OLBIDAR.
      WORD #3754 OCCURS   2 TIMES.

SEMEIA        1219 5ELCID0157 ALO QUEM ******, DE LO MIO AUREDES ALGO;
             10618 5ELCID1346 ****** QUE EN TIERRA DE MOROS NON A BIUO OMNE,
             14835 5ELCID1875 ASSI COMMO ****** & LA VELUNTAD MELO DIZ.
             19081 5ELCID2414 ASI COMMO ******, EN MI LA QUIERES ENSAYAR.
             24517 5ELCID3125 EN SOS AGUISAMIENTOS BIEN ****** VARON.
      WORD #3755 OCCURS   5 TIMES.
         INDEX OF DIVERSIFICATION =  5823.50 WITH STANDARD DEVIATION OF  2449.74

SEMEIAM      16373 5ELCID2077 ******* EL CASAMIENTO ONDRADO & CON GRANT PRO,
      WORD #3756 OCCURS   1 TIMES.

SEMEIAR      18684 5ELCID2364 MANDAD NOLOS FERIR DE QUAL PART UOS *******,
      WORD #3757 OCCURS   1 TIMES.

SEMMANAS      4510 5ELCID0573 ALI YOGO MYO %ID COMPLIDAS XV ********.
              6910 5ELCID0883 POR ACOGELLO A CABO DE TRES ********.
      WORD #3758 OCCURS   2 TIMES.

SENOR        15186 5ELCID1921 COMMO SON LAS SALUDES DE ALFONSSO MYO *****.
             27175 5ELCID3473 ENESSORA DIXO MIO %ID. NO LO FARE, *****.
      WORD #3759 OCCURS   2 TIMES.

SENORIO       4910 5ELCID0621 COIAMOS LOS DE DENTRO, CA EL ******* TENEMOS,
      WORD #3760 OCCURS   1 TIMES.

SENOS        28092 5ELCID3586 ESTAS TRES LAN%AS TRAEN ***** PENDONES;
      WORD #3761 OCCURS   1 TIMES.

SE@A          3776 5ELCID0477 E SIN DUBDA CORREN; FASTA ALCALA LEGO LA **** DE MINAYA,
              3815 5ELCID0482 DERECHA VIENE LA **** DE MINAYA;
              4541 5ELCID0577 COIO SALON AYUSO LA SU **** ALZADA,
              4702 5ELCID0596 MANDO TORNAR LA ****, A PRIESSA ESPOLONEAUAN.
              4827 5ELCID0611 VINO PERO VERMUEZ, QUE LA **** TEINE EN MANO,
              5462 5ELCID0689 E VOS, PERO VERMUEZ, LA MI **** TOMAD;
              5490 5ELCID0692 AL %ID BESO LA MANO, LA **** UA TOMAR.
              5596 5ELCID0705 LA **** TIENE EN MANO, CONPE%O DE ESPOLONAR;
              5614 5ELCID0707 VO METER LA UUESTRA **** EN AQUELA MAYOR AZ;
              5655 5ELCID0712 MOROS LE RE%IBEN POR LA **** GANAR,
              5865 5ELCID0743 ACORREN LA **** & A MYO %ID EL CAMPEADOR.
              6714 5ELCID0857 AL%O SU ****, EL CAMPEADOR SE UA,
              9601 5ELCID1220 QUANDO SU **** CABDAL SEDIE EN SOMO DEL ALCA%AR.
             13539 5ELCID1716 LA **** SACAN FUERA, DE VALEN%IA DIERON SALTO,
      WORD #3762 OCCURS  14 TIMES.
         INDEX OF DIVERSIFICATION =   750.00 WITH STANDARD DEVIATION OF  1233.66

SE@AL        18774 5ELCID2375 PENDON TRAYO A CORCAS & ARMAS DE *****,
      WORD #3763 OCCURS   1 TIMES.

SE@AS         2086 5ELCID0263 ***** DUE@AS LAS TRAEN & ADUZEN LAS ADELANT.
              2763 5ELCID0349 DOS LADRONES CONTIGO, ESTOS DE ***** PARTES
              5542 5ELCID0698 DE PARTE DELOS MOROS DOS ***** HA CABDALES,
              6410 5ELCID0818 ***** ESPADAS DELOS ARZONES COLGADAS.
             10534 5ELCID1335 FEUOS AQUI LAS *****, VERDAD UOS DIGO YO:
             14310 5ELCID1810 CON SIELLAS & CON FRENOS & CON ***** ESPADAS;
      WORD #3764 OCCURS   6 TIMES.
         INDEX OF DIVERSIFICATION =  2443.80 WITH STANDARD DEVIATION OF  1605.84
```

WORD C# PREFIX CONTEXT

SE@EROS 22073 5ELCID2809 TODOS TRES ******* POR LOS ROBREDOS DE CORPES,
WORD #3765 OCCURS 1 TIMES.

SE@NOR 8616 5ELCID1094 AIUDOL EL CRIADOR, EL ****** QUE ES EN %IELO.
WORD #3766 OCCURS 1 TIMES.

SE@OR
53 5ELCID0008 GRADO ATI, ***** PADRE, QUE ESTAS EN ALTO
151 5ELCID0020 DIOS, QUE BUEN VASSALO, SI OUIESSE BUEN *****
2612 5ELCID0330 YA ***** GLORIOSO, PADRE QUE EN %IELO ESTAS,
2701 5ELCID0341 SALUEST DENTRO EN ROMA AL ***** SAN SABASTIAN,
2716 5ELCID0343 POR TIERRA ANDIDISTE XXXIJ A@OS, ***** SPIRITAL,
3414 5ELCID0431 MANDADO DE SO ***** TODO LO HAN AFAR.
4227 5ELCID0538 CON ALFONSSO MYO ***** NON QUERRIA LIDIAR.
6663 5ELCID0850 QUI A BUEN ***** SIRUE, SIEMPRE BIUE EN DELI%IO.
6693 5ELCID0854 NOS PAGADOS FINCADOS, *****, CELA TU PART.
6864 5ELCID0877 SOBEIANA ES, *****, LA SU GANA%IA.
6900 5ELCID0882 OMNE AYRADO, QUE DE ***** NON HA GRA%IA,
7002 5ELCID0895 GRADO & GRA%IAS, REY, COMMO A ***** NATURAL;
10043 5ELCID1272 AL REY ALFONSSO MYO ***** NATURAL;
10318 5ELCID1306 QUE EN TIERRAS DE VALEN%IA ***** AVIE OBISPO
10421 5ELCID1321 MER%ED, ***** ALFONSSO, POR AMOR DEL CRIADOR
10442 5ELCID1323 LOS PIES & LAS MANOS, COMMO ATAN BUEN *****,
10505 5ELCID1331 CON AQUESTAS TODAS DE VALEN%IA ES *****,
10569 5ELCID1339 RAZONAS POR VUESTRO VASSALLO & AUOS TIENE POR *****.
10761 5ELCID1362 ATODAS LAS ESCUELLAS QUE A EL DIZEN *****
10794 5ELCID1366 POR TAL FAGO AQUESTO QUE SIRUAN ASO *****.
12587 5ELCID1597 AFE ME AQUI, *****, YO UUESTRAS FIJAS & AMAS,
14599 5ELCID1847 A UOS LAMA POR *****, & TIENES POR UUESTRO VASSALLO,
14771 5ELCID1867 GRADO AL CRIADOR & AL ***** SANT ESIDRO EL DE LEON
14915 5ELCID1885 MER%ED UOS PIDIMOS COMMO A REY & ***** NATURAL;
15267 5ELCID1933 ESTO GRADESCO A CHRISTUS EL MYO *****.
15438 5ELCID1955 AYAMOS VISTAS QUANDO LO QUIERE MYO *****.
15968 5ELCID2024 ASI SABE DAR OMILDAN%A A ALFONSSO SO *****.
16015 5ELCID2031 MER%ED UOS PIDO AUOS, MYO NATURAL *****,
16061 5ELCID2036 FABLO MYO %ID & DIXO: MER%ED; YOLO RE%IBO, ALFONSSO MYO *****;
16123 5ELCID2044 QUANDO HE LA GRA%IA DE DON ALFONSSO MYO *****;
16138 5ELCID2046 FUESSEDES MY HUESPED, SIUOS PLOGIESSE, *****.
16523 5ELCID2094 FABLO EL REY CON ALFONSSO COMMO TAN BUEN *****:
16655 5ELCID2109 MUCHO UOS LO GRADESCO, COMMO A REY & A *****
16810 5ELCID2128 AQUI LO DIGO ANTE MYO ***** EL REY ALFONSSO:
16909 5ELCID2140 DIXO ALBARFANEZ: *****, AFE QUE ME PLAZ.
16926 5ELCID2142 HYA REY DON ALFONSSO, ***** TAN ONDRADO,
17034 5ELCID2156 HYAS ESPIDIO MYO %ID DE SO ***** ALFONSSO,
17394 5ELCID2200 PEDIDAS UOS HA & ROGADAS EL MYO ***** ALFONSSO,
18064 5ELCID2285 E %ERCAN EL ESCA@O & FINCAN SOBRE SO *****.
18138 5ELCID2295 HYA ***** ONDRADO, REBATA NOS DIO EL LEON.
19556 5ELCID2477 GRADO A CHRISTUS, QUE DEL MUNDO ES *****,
19670 5ELCID2493 GRADO HA DIOS QUE DEL MUNDO ES *****
19905 5ELCID2524 GRADO A SANTA MARIA, MADRE DEL NUESTRO ***** DIOS
20456 5ELCID2596 DELANT SODES AMOS, SE@ORA & *****.
21007 5ELCID2669 ACAYAZ, CURIATE DESTOS, CA ERES MYO *****:
21132 5ELCID2684 DIOS LO QUIERA & LO MANDE, QUE DE TODEL MUNDO ES *****,
22224 5ELCID2830 GRADO A CHRISTUS, QUE DEL MUNDO ES *****,
22312 5ELCID2841 NON LO DETARDAN EL MANDADO DE SU *****,
22807 5ELCID2905 CUEMO YO SO SU VASSALLO, & EL ES MYO *****,
22857 5ELCID2911 LA POCA & LA GRANT TODA ES DE MYO *****.
22967 5ELCID2925 FASTA DENTRO EN SANTI YAGUO DE TODO ES *****,
22975 5ELCID2926 ELLOS CONDES GALLIZANOS A EL TIENEN POR *****.
23049 5ELCID2936 MER%ED, REY ALFONSSO, DE LARGOS REYNOS AUOS DIZEN *****
23141 5ELCID2948 POR ESTO UOS BESA LAS MANOS, COMMO VASSALLO A *****,
23690 5ELCID3017 QUE BESASSE LAS MANOS AL REY SO *****:
23736 5ELCID3023 BUENAS CONPA@AS QUE ASSI AN TAL *****.
23828 5ELCID3035 GRADO ADIOS, QUANDO UOS VEO, *****.
23854 5ELCID3038 DIOS SALUE A NUESTROS AMIGOS & AUOS MAS, *****
23879 5ELCID3041 DESTO QUE NOS ABINO QUE UOS PESE, *****.
23911 5ELCID3046 PENSSAD, *****, DE ENTRAR ALA %IBDAD,
24172 5ELCID3082 RESPONDIERON TODOS: NOS ESSO QUEREMOS, *****.
24463 5ELCID3118 SED EN UUESTRO ESCA@O COMMO REY A *****;
24704 5ELCID3146 MUCHO UOS LO GRADESCO COMMO A REY & A *****,
24905 5ELCID3171 MER%ED, YA REY DON ALFONSSO, SODES NUESTRO *****
24940 5ELCID3176 PUSIERON LAS EN MANO DEL REY SO *****;
25046 5ELCID3190 PRENDET LA, SOBRINO, CA MEIORA EN *****.
25073 5ELCID3194 PRENDED A COLADA, GANELA DE BUEN *****,
25128 5ELCID3200 GRADO AL CRIADOR & AUOS, REY *****,
25541 5ELCID3253 MER%ED, AY REY *****, POR AMOR DE CARIDAD
26166 5ELCID3335 NOS %ERCAMOS EL ESCA@O POR CURIAR NUESTRO *****,
26532 5ELCID3386 NON DIZES VERDAD AMIGO NI HA *****,
26655 5ELCID3403 MER%ED, REY ALFONSSO, VOS SODES MYO *****
26742 5ELCID3415 QUANDO AUOS PLAZE, OTORGO LO YO, *****,
26855 5ELCID3430 MER%ED UOS PIDO COMMO A REY & A *****,
27213 5ELCID3478 HYO VOS LO SOBRELIEUO COMMO BUEN VASSALLO FAZE A *****,
27279 5ELCID3486 MYO %ID AL REY LAS MANOS LE BESO & DIXO: PLAZME, *****.
27297 5ELCID3488 DAQUI UOS LOS ACOMIENDO COMO A REY & A *****.
27445 5ELCID3506 BESO UUESTRAS MANOS CON UUESTRA GRA%IA, *****,

WORD C# PREFIX CONTEXT

SE@OR (CON'T)

```
                 27498 5ELCID3512 FUE BESAR LA MANO A SO ***** ALFONSSO;
                 27525 5ELCID3515 HY UOS LE DO EN DON, MANDEDES LE TOMAR, *****.
                 27544 5ELCID3517 SI AUOS LE TOLLIES, EL CAUALLO NO HAURIE TAN BUEN *****.
                 27630 5ELCID3527 DIXO MARTIN ANTOLINEZ:  POR QUE LO DEZIDES, *****
                 27697 5ELCID3535 CUNPLIR QUIEREN EL DEBDO QUE LES MANDO SO *****,
                 27748 5ELCID3541 QUE LOS MATASSEN EN CAMPO POR DESONDRA DE SO *****.
                 27832 5ELCID3551 TODOS TRES SE ACUERDAN, CA SON DE VN *****.
                 28008 5ELCID3574 BESAMOS VOS LAS MANOS, COMMO A REY & A *****,
                 28044 5ELCID3579 EN UUESTRA MANO NOS METIO NUESTRO *****;
                 28997 5ELCID3703 CONPLIDO HAN EL DEBDO QUE LES MANDO SO *****;
                 29074 5ELCID3713 PRISOS ALA BARBA RUY DIAZ SO *****;
        WORD #3767 OCCURS  89 TIMES.
           INDEX OF DIVERSIFICATION =   328.78 WITH STANDARD DEVIATION OF   569.06

SE@ORA           20454 5ELCID2596 DELANT SODES AMOS, ****** & SE@OR.
        WORD #3768 OCCURS   1 TIMES.

SE@ORAS          27009 5ELCID3450 AGORA BESAREDES SUS MANOS & LAMAR LAS HEDES *******,
                 29154 5ELCID3723 QUANDO ******* SON SUS FIJAS DE NAUARRA & DE ARAGON.
        WORD #3769 OCCURS   2 TIMES.

SE@ORES           9264 5ELCID1178 MALA CUETA ES, *******, AVER MINGUA DE PAN,
        WORD #3770 OCCURS   1 TIMES.

SE@OS             5738 5ELCID0724 ***** MOROS MATARON, TODOS DE SE@OS COLPES;
                  5743 5ELCID0724 SE@OS MOROS MATARON, TODOS DE ***** COLPES;
                 20903 5ELCID2655 BUENOS ***** CAUALLOS ALOS YFANTES DE CARRION.
                 23067 5ELCID2938 ELE ES VUESTRO VASSALLO & UOS SODES SO *****.
                 23758 5ELCID3026 BILTAR SE QUIERE & ONDRAR ASO *****.
        WORD #3771 OCCURS   5 TIMES.
           INDEX OF DIVERSIFICATION =  4504.00 WITH STANDARD DEVIATION OF  7160.21

SEPA              3066 5ELCID0386 BIEN **** EL ABBAT QUE BUEN GALARDON DELLO PRENDRA.
        WORD #3772 OCCURS   1 TIMES.

SEPADES           3284 5ELCID0414 ES DIA A DE PLAZO, ******* QUE NON MAS.
        WORD #3773 OCCURS   1 TIMES.

SEPAN             1129 5ELCID0145 QUE NON LO ***** MOROS NON CHRISTIANOS.
                 13949 5ELCID1767 QUE LO ***** EN CASTIELLA, AQUIEN SIRUIERON TANTO.
                 20324 5ELCID2579 QUE LO ***** EN GALLIZIA & EN CASTIELLA & EN LEON,
        WORD #3774 OCCURS   3 TIMES.

SEQUE            19300 5ELCID2444 ***** DE LIDIAR BIEN SODES PAGADOS;
        WORD #3775 OCCURS   1 TIMES.

SER                905 5ELCID0116 AQUELAS NON LAS PUEDE LEUAR, SINON, *** YEN VENTADAS;
                 17455 5ELCID2208 SABOR ABRIEDES DE *** & DE COMER ENEL PALA%IO.
                 20239 5ELCID2569 EL %ID QUE NOS CURIAUA DE ASSI *** AFONTADO;
                 24432 5ELCID3114 EL REY DIXO AL %ID: VENJD ACA ***, CAMPEADOR,
                 26336 5ELCID3359 LO QUE LES FIZIEMOS *** LES HA RETRAYDO; ESTO LIDIARE ATOD EL MAS
                 26620 5ELCID3399 POR *** REYNAS DE NAUARRA & DE ARAGON,
                 27140 5ELCID3468 DANDOS, REY, PLAZO, CA CRAS *** NON PUEDE.
                 27560 5ELCID3519 PORA ARRANCAR MOROS DEL CANPO & *** SEGUDADOR;
        WORD #3776 OCCURS   8 TIMES.
           INDEX OF DIVERSIFICATION =  3806.86 WITH STANDARD DEVIATION OF  5800.69

SERA              1007 5ELCID0129 MAS DEZID NOS DEL %ID, DE QUE **** PAGADO,
                  2524 5ELCID0319 LA MISSA NOS DIRA, ESTA **** DE SANTA TRINIDAD;
                  7648 5ELCID0979 RESPUSO EL CONDE:  ESTO NON **** VERDAD.
                  8366 5ELCID1063 EL SABOR QUE DED E NON **** OLBIDADO.
                  8468 5ELCID1076 DE VENIR UOS BUSCAR SOL NON **** PENSSADO.
                  8900 5ELCID1133 COMMO FIO POR DIOS, EL CAMPO NUESTRO ****.
                 13299 5ELCID1686 OY ES DIA BUENO & MEIOR **** CRAS:
                 17914 5ELCID2266 GRANT BIEN DIZEN DELLOS, CA **** AGUISADO.
                 18693 5ELCID2365 EL DEBDO QUE A CADA VNO A CONPLIR ****.
                 19112 5ELCID2417 AQUI RESPUSO MYO %ID: ESTO NON **** VERDAD.
                 23773 5ELCID3028 PAR SANT ESIDRO, VERDAD NON **** OY
        WORD #3777 OCCURS  11 TIMES.
           INDEX OF DIVERSIFICATION =  2275.60 WITH STANDARD DEVIATION OF  2123.85

SERAN              681 5ELCID0086 YNCAMOS LAS ARENA, CA BIEN ***** PESADAS,
                  6467 5ELCID0825 SI LES YO VISQUIER, ***** DUENAS RICAS.
                 17344 5ELCID2194 NON ***** MENGUADAS EN TODOS UUESTROS DIAS
                 18518 5ELCID2343 AMOS LOS MYOS YERNOS BUENOS ***** EN CAPO.
                 19439 5ELCID2463 QUANDO AGORA SON BUENOS, ADELANT ***** PRE%IADOS.
                 23342 5ELCID2973 DESTO QUE LES ABINO AVN BIEN ***** ONDRADOS.
        WORD #3778 OCCURS   6 TIMES.
           INDEX OF DIVERSIFICATION =  4531.20 WITH STANDARD DEVIATION OF  4078.68

SERE               575 5ELCID0073 CA ACUSADO **** DELO QUE UOS HE SERUIDO,
                   587 5ELCID0074 EN YRA DEL RAY ALFFONSSO YO **** METIDO.
                  1813 5ELCID0231 ANTES **** CON UUSCO QUE EL SOL QUIERA RAYAR.
                  8145 5ELCID1038 TANTO QUANTO YO BIUA, **** DENT MARAUILLADO.
                 19736 5ELCID2502 NO LOS YRE BUSCAR, EN VALEN%IA **** YO,
```

WORD C# PREFIX CONTEXT

SERE (CON'T)

21961 5ELCID2794 AGRANT PRIESSA **** BUSCADO YO;
24164 5ELCID3081 DO TALES %IENTO TOUIER, BIEN **** SIN PAUOR.
26283 5ELCID3351 DE QUANTO HE DICHO VERDADERO **** YO.
27201 5ELCID3477 VAYAN COMIGO, YO **** EL CURIADOR;
WORD #3779 OCCURS 9 TIMES.
INDEX OF DIVERSIFICATION = 3327.25 WITH STANDARD DEVIATION OF 3825.99

SEREDES
1229 5ELCID0158 MIENTRA QUE VIVADES NON ******* MENGUADOS.
16155 5ELCID2049 MYO HUESPED *******, %ID CAMPEADOR,
21359 5ELCID2715 AQUI ******* ESCARNIDAS EN ESTOS FIEROS MONTES.
21370 5ELCID2716 OY NOS PARTIREMOS, & DEXADAS ******* DE NOS;
WORD #3780 OCCURS 4 TIMES.

SEREMOS
11149 5ELCID1411 ******* YO & SU MUGIER & SUS FIJAS QUE EL A
14730 5ELCID1862 EN LA ONDRA QUE EL HA NOS ******* ABILTADOS;
17075 5ELCID2162 ******* ALAS BODAS DELOS YFANTES DE CARRION
17355 5ELCID2195 QUANDO UOS NOS CASAREDES BIEN ******* RICAS.
20104 5ELCID2552 DAQUESTOS AUERES SIENPRE ******* RICOS OMNES,
21460 5ELCID2728 CORTANDOS LAS CABECAS, MARTIRES ******* NOS:
WORD #3781 OCCURS 6 TIMES.
INDEX OF DIVERSIFICATION = 2061.20 WITH STANDARD DEVIATION OF 1278.02

SERIE
655 5ELCID0082 BIEN LO VEDES QUE YO NO TRAYO AUER, & HUEBOS ME *****
4086 5ELCID0519 ESTA QUINTA POR QUANTO ***** CONPRADA,
4132 5ELCID0526 E QUE ***** RETENEDOR, MAS NON YAURIE AGUA.
11083 5ELCID1403 TODO ***** ALEGRE, QUE NON AURIE NINGUN PESAR.
11609 5ELCID1471 GRAND LOCURA ***** SI LA DESENPARAS;
12410 5ELCID1575 SI ***** CORREDOR OSSI ABRIE BUENA PARADA;
21562 5ELCID2741 QUAL VENTURA ***** ESTA, SI PLOGUIESSE AL CRIADOR,
21658 5ELCID2753 QUAL VENTURA ***** SI ASSOMAS ESSORA EL %ID CAMPEADOR
23696 5ELCID3018 BIEN LO SOPIESSE QUE Y ***** ESSA NOCH.
27082 5ELCID3460 E QUI AL QUISIESSE ***** SU OCASION.
28253 5ELCID3607 QUE POR Y ***** VEN%IDO QUI SALIESSE DEL MOION.
WORD #3782 OCCURS 11 TIMES.
INDEX OF DIVERSIFICATION = 2758.80 WITH STANDARD DEVIATION OF 3084.04

SERIEN
18563 5ELCID2349 POR LA SU VOLUNTAD NON ****** ALLI LEGADOS.
19499 5ELCID2470 CUYDARON QUE EN SUS DIAS NUNQUA ****** MINGUADOS.
19655 5ELCID2491 TANTOS SON DE MUCHOS QUE NON ****** CONTADOS.
20609 5ELCID2616 QUE ESTOS CASAMIENTOS NON ****** SIN ALGUNA TACHA.
WORD #3783 OCCURS 4 TIMES.

SERUAN
23924 5ELCID3047 E YO CON LOS MYOS POSARE A SAN ******:
23969 5ELCID3054 MYO %ID RUY DIAZ EN SAN ****** POSADO.
24332 5ELCID3102 APRIESSA CAUALGA, DE SAN ****** SALIO;
WORD #3784 OCCURS 3 TIMES.

SERUIDA
2150 5ELCID0270 CON AQUESTAS MYS DUE@AS DE QUIEN SO YO *******.
2264 5ELCID0284 E UOS, MUGIER ONDRADA, DE MY SEADES *******
WORD #3785 OCCURS 2 TIMES.

SERUIDES
20352 5ELCID2582 SI BIEN LAS ********, YO UOS RENDRE BUEN GALARDON.
WORD #3786 OCCURS 1 TIMES.

SERUIDO
580 5ELCID0073 CA ACUSADO SERE DELO QUE UOS HE *******,
16999 5ELCID2152 DEUOS BIEN SO *******, & TENGON POR PAGADO;
WORD #3787 OCCURS 2 TIMES.

SERUIR
10141 5ELCID1284 CIENTO OMNES LE DIO MYO %ID A ALBARFANEZ POR ****** LE EN LA CARRERA,
14388 5ELCID1820 E ****** LO HE SIENPRE MIENTRA QUE OUISSE EL ALMA.
14790 5ELCID1869 MYO REYNO ADELANT MEIOR ME PODRA ******.
14805 5ELCID1871 MANDO UOS LOS CUERPOS ONDRADA MIENTRE ****** & VESTIR
14860 5ELCID1878 BIEN LOS MANDO ****** DE QUANTO HUEBOS HAN.
WORD #3788 OCCURS 5 TIMES.
INDEX OF DIVERSIFICATION = 1178.75 WITH STANDARD DEVIATION OF 2052.20

SERUIREMOS
4919 5ELCID0622 POSAREMOS EN SUS CASAS & DELLOS NOS **********.
WORD #3789 OCCURS 1 TIMES.

SERUOS
1989 5ELCID0251 SI YO ALGUN DIA VISGUIER, ****** HAN DOBLADOS.
WORD #3790 OCCURS 1 TIMES.

SESO
11921 5ELCID1511 QUE SOPIENSSEN LOS OTROS DE QUE **** ERA ALBARFANEZ
21158 5ELCID2688 CUEMMO DE BUEN **** A MOLINA SE TORNO.
WORD #3791 OCCURS 2 TIMES.

SESTELANDO
3951 5ELCID0501 E POR EL COBDO AYUSO LA SANGRE **********,
WORD #3792 OCCURS 1 TIMES.

SEUA
2287 5ELCID0288 COMMO **** DE TIERRA MYO %ID EL CANPEADOR;
4462 5ELCID0568 AGARDANDO **** MYO %ID CON TODOS SUS VASSALLOS;
9906 5ELCID1256 CON MINAYA ALBARFANEZ EL **** CONSEGAR:
12135 5ELCID1539 EL REY LO PAGO TODO, & QUITO **** MINAYA.
WORD #3793 OCCURS 4 TIMES.

```
WORD                 C#  PREFIX                              CONTEXT

SEUAN                     5508 5ELCID0694 VIERON LO LAS ARCBCAS DELOS MOROS, AL ALMOFALLA ***** TORNAR.
                          7358 5ELCID0943 CON ESTAS GANAN%IAS ALA PCSACA TORNANDO *****,
                          7548 5ELCID0967 GRANDES SON LOS PCDERES & A PRIESSA ***** LEGANDO,
                         15646 5ELCID1984 SUELTAN LAS RIENDAS, ALAS VISTAS ***** A DELI@ADAS.
                         27960 5ELCID3568 HYA ***** REPINTIENDO YFANTES DE CARRION,
             WORD #3794 OCCURS   5 TIMES.
                INDEX OF DIVERSIFICATION =  5612.00 WITH STANDARD DEVIATION OF  5616.87

SEUILLA                   9619 5ELCID1222 AQUEL REY DE ******* EL MANCACO LEGAUA,
             WORD #3795 OCCURS   1 TIMES.

SEUIR                    10811 5ELCID1369 LOS QUE QUISIEREN YR ***** AL CAMPEADOR
             WORD #3796 OCCURS   1 TIMES.

SEY                      18004 5ELCID2278 EN VALEN%IA *** MYO %ID CON TODOS SUS VASSALLOS,
             WORD #3797 OCCURS   1 TIMES.

SEYAN                    22174 5ELCID2824 ALLABANDOS ***** LOS YFANTES DE CARRION.
             WORD #3798 OCCURS   1 TIMES.

SEYEN                      952 5ELCID0122 RACHEL & VICAS ***** SE CONSEIANDO:
                         19961 5ELCID2532 VASSALLCS DE MYO %ID ***** SE SONRRISANDO:
             WORD #3799 OCCURS   2 TIMES.

SEYENDO                  17006 5ELCID2153 AVN BIUC *******, DE MI AYADES ALGO
             WORD #3800 OCCURS   1 TIMES.

SEYES                     1145 5ELCID0147 LAS ARCHAS ACUCHAS, PRENDET ***** %IENTOS MARCOS.
             WORD #3801 OCCURS   1 TIMES.

SEYS                      1051 5ELCID0135 A MENESTER **** %IENTCS MARCOS.
                          9982 5ELCID1265 TRES MILL & **** %IENTCS AUIE MYO %ID EL DE BIUAR;
                         19471 5ELCID2467 QUE ALA RA%ION CAYE **** %IENTOS MARCOS DE PLATA.
             WORD #3802 OCCURS   3 TIMES.

SEYSE                    14551 5ELCID1840 EL REY DON ALFONSSO ***** SANTIGUANDO.
             WORD #3803 OCCURS   1 TIMES.

SEYX                     19641 5ELCID2489 CAYERON LE EN QUINTA AL %ID **** %IENTOS CAUALLOS,
             WORD #3804 OCCURS   1 TIMES.

SI                         148 5ELCID0020 DIOS, QUE BUEN VASSALC, ** OUIESSE BUEN SE@OR
                           264 5ELCID0034 QUE ** NON LA QUEBRANTAS POR FUERCA, QUE NON GELA ABRIESE NADI.
                           356 5ELCID0045 ** NON, PERDERIEMOS LOS AUERES & LAS CASAS,
                           483 5ELCID0061 ASSI POSC MYC %ID COMMO ** FUESSE EN MONTA@A.
                           589 5ELCID0075 ** CON UUSCO ESCAPC SANC CBIUC,
                           605 5ELCID0077 ** NON, QUANTC DEXO NCLC PRE%IO UN FIGO.
                           628 5ELCID0080 ** YO BIUC, DCBLAR UOS HE LA SOLDADA.
                          1089 5ELCID0140 ** NON PRIMERC PRENDIENCO & DESPUES DANDO.
                          1276 5ELCID0164 QUE ** ANTES LAS CATASSEN QUE FUESSEN PERIURADOS,
                          1413 5ELCID0181 SIUOS LA ADUXIER CALLA; ** NON, CONTALDA SOBRE LAS ARCAS. . . .
                          1743 5ELCID0223 ** UOS ASSI LO FIZIEREDES & LA UENTURA ME FUERE COMPLIDA,
                          1803 5ELCID0230 ** EL REY MELC CUISIERE TCMAR AMI NON MINCHAL.
                          1984 5ELCID0251 ** YO ALGUN DIA VISGUIER, SERUOS HAN DOBLADOS.
                          2448 5ELCID0309 QUE, ** DESPUES DEL PLAZO EN SU TIERRAL PUDIES TOMAR,
                          3081 5ELCID0388 ** VIEREDES YENTES VENIR PCR CONNUSCO YR,
                          3330 5ELCID0420 TEMPRANO DAT %EUACA, ** EL CRIADOR UOS SALUE
                          3881 5ELCID0492 DOUOS LA QUINTA, ** LA CUISIEREDES, MINAYA.
                          4606 5ELCID0585 ANTES CUEL PRENDAN LOS DE TERUEL, ** NON NON NOS DARAN DENT NADA;
                          4996 5ELCID0632 ** NON CAS CCNSEIC, A TECA & A TERUEL PERDERAS,
                          5322 5ELCID0673 ** CON MORCS NON LIDIAREMCS, NO NOS DARAN DEL PAN.
                          5431 5ELCID0686 ** NCN DOS PECNES SOLCS POR LA PUERTA GUARDAR;
                          5440 5ELCID0687 ** NOS MURIEREMOS EN CAMPO, EN CASTIELLO NOS ENTRARAN,
                          5449 5ELCID0688 ** VEN%IEREMOS LA BATALLA, CRE%REMOS EN RICTAD.
                          5478 5ELCID0691 MAS NON AGUIJEDES CON ELLA, ** YO NON UOS LO MANDAR.
                          6463 5ELCID0825 ** LES YO VISCUIER, SERAN DUENAS RICAS.
                          6521 5ELCID0832 ALA TORNADA, ** NOS FALLAREDES AQUI;
                          6525 5ELCID0833 ** NON, DO SOPIEREDES QUE SOMOS, YNDOS CONSEGUIR.
                          6541 5ELCID0835 ** NON, ENESTA TIERRA ANGOSTA NON PODRIEMOS BIUIR.
                          6839 5ELCID0874  QUIN LOS DIO ESTOS, ** UOS VALA DIOS, MYNAYA
                          7018 5ELCID0898 ** NULLA DUBDA YD A MYO %ID BUSCAR GANAN%IA.
                          8033 5ELCID1026 ** LO CUE DIGC FIZIEREDES, SALCRECES DE CATIUO;
                          8041 5ELCID1027 ** NON, EN TODOS UUESTROS DIAS NON VEREDES CHRISTIANISMO.
                          8103 5ELCID1034 E ** UOS COMIEREDES, DON YO SEA PAGADO,
                          8133 5ELCID1037 ** LO FIZIEREDES, %ID, LO CUE AUEDES FABLADO,
                          8279 5ELCID1054 ** BIEN NON CCMEDES, CONDE, DON YO SEA PAGADO,
                          8332 5ELCID1060 ** UOS PLOGUIERE, MYO %ID, DE YR SOMOS GUISADOS;
                          8417 5ELCID1070 ** UOS VINIERE EMIENTE CUE QUISIEREDES VENGALO,
                          8424 5ELCID1071 ** ME VINIEREDES BUSCAR, FALLAR ME PODREDES;
                          8432 5ELCID1072 E ** NON, MANDEDES BUSCAR; O ME DEXAREDES
                          8697 5ELCID1105 ** NOS %ERCAR VIENEN, CONDERECHO LO FAZEN.
                          8770 5ELCID1115 OYD, MESNADAS, ** EL CRIADOR UOS SALUE
                          8805 5ELCID1120 ** EN ESTAS TIERRAS QUISIEREMOS DURAR,
                          9908 5ELCID1257 ** UOS QUISIEREDES, MINAYA, QUIERO SABER RECABDO
```

WORD C# PREFIX CONTEXT

SI (CON'T)

```
                 9933 5ELCID1260 QUE ** ALGUNCS FURTARE C MENOS LE FALLAREN, EL AUER ME AURA
                                 A TORNAR
                10021 5ELCID1273 ** AUOS PLCGUIERE, MINAYA, & NCN UOS CAYA EN PESAR,
                10077 5ELCID1276 POR MI MUGIER & MIS FIJAS, ** FUERE SU MER%ED,
                10587 5ELCID1342  ** ME VALA SANT ESIDRO  PLAZME DE CORA%ON,
                10909 5ELCID1381 ** LEUAREDES LAS DUENAS, SIRUAN LAS ASU SABOR,
                11073 5ELCID1402 ** UOS VIESSE EL %ID SA@AS & SIN MAL,
                11324 5ELCID1433 DESFECHOS NCS HA EL %ID, SABET, ** NO NOS VAL;
                11342 5ELCID1435 HYC LO VERE CCN EL %IC, ** CIOS ME LIEUA ALA.
                11364 5ELCID1438 ** NCN, DFXAREMCS BURGCS, YR LO HEMOS BUSCAR.
                11393 5ELCID1442  ** UOS VALA EL CRIADOR, MINAYA ALBARFANEZ,
                11610 5ELCID1471 GRAND LOCURA SERIE ** LA DESENPARAS;
                12054 5ELCID1529 ** DIOS ME LEGARE AL %IC ELC VEA CON EL ALMA,
                12409 5ELCID1575 ** SERIE CCRREDCR CSSI ABRIE BUENA PARADA;
                12798 5ELCID1624 E EL NCN GELO GRADE%E ** NON A IHESU CHRISTO.
                12978 5ELCID1646  QUES ESTO, %ID, ** EL CRIACOR UOS SALUE
                13026 5ELCID1652 MUGIER, SED EN ESTE PALA%IO, & ** QUISIEREDES EN EL ALCA%AR;
                13136 5ELCID1665 ANTES DESTCS XV DIAS, ** PLOGIERE A CRIADOR,
                14741 5ELCID1864 COMMO ** LCS FALASSE MUERTOS ACUZIR SE LOS CAUALLOS,
                15024 5ELCID1899 E DE MI ABRA PERDCN; VINIESSEM A VISTAS, ** OUIESSE DENT SABOR.
                15187 5ELCID1922 ** ES PAGADC O RE%IBIC EL CCN?
                15912 5ELCID2018 ** NON A ESTCS CAUALLERCS CUE QUERIE CE CORA%ON;
                16410 5ELCID2081 DANDOS LAS, MYO %ID, ** UCS VALA EL CRIADOR
                16890 5ELCID2137 ASSI CCMMO YC LAS PRENDC CAQUENT, COMMO ** FOSSE DELANT,
                17854 5ELCID2259 CADA VNO POR ** SCS DCNES AUIEN DADOS.
                18394 5ELCID2328 HYD LOS CONCRTAR, ** UOS VALA EL CRIADOR,
                18503 5ELCID2342 AVN ** DIOS QUISIERE & EL PACRE QUE ESTA EN ALTO,
                18647 5ELCID2360 ** CUETA FUERE, BIEN ME PODREDES HUUIAR.
                18775 5ELCID2376 ** PLOGIESSE ADICS CUERRIA LAS ENSAYAR,
                18794 5ELCID2379 ** ESTE AMCR NON FECHES, YO DEUOS ME QUIERO QUITAR.
                19088 5ELCID2415 MAS ** EL CAUALLC NON ESTROPIE%A O COMIGO NON CAYE,
                20154 5ELCID2559 ** UOS VALA EL CRIADOR, %ID CAMPEADOR
                20349 5ELCID2582 ** BIEN LAS SERUIDES, YC UOS RENDRE BUEN GALARDON.
                20684 5ELCID2626 QUE ** ADIOS PLOGUIERE & AL PADRE CRIADOR,
                20953 5ELCID2662 ** PUDIESSEMCS MATAR EL MORO AVENGALUON,
                21064 5ELCID2677 ** NOLO DEXAS POR MYC %IC EL CE BIUAR,
                21318 5ELCID2710 ** NON AMAS SUS MUGIERES DC@A ELUIRA & DO@A SOL:
                21485 5ELCID2732 ** NOS FUEREMCS MAIACAS, ABILTAREDES AUOS,
                21564 5ELCID2741  QUAL VENTURA SERIE ESTA, ** PLOGUIESSE AL CRIADOR,
                21659 5ELCID2753  QUAL VENTURA SERIE ** ASSOMAS ESSORA EL %ID CAMPEADOR
                21706 5ELCID2760 ** NON FUESSEMOS ROGACCS,
                21807 5ELCID2774 SABET BIEN QUE ** ELLOS LE VIESSEN, NON ESCAPARA DE MUERT.
                21964 5ELCID2795 ** DIOS NCN NCS VALE, ACUI MORREMOS NOS.
                21979 5ELCID2797 ** UOS LO MERESCA, MYC PRIMO, NUESTRO PADRE EL CANPEADOR,
                21992 5ELCID2798 DANDOS DEL AGUA, ** UCS VALA EL CRIADOR
                22458 5ELCID2860 ATANTO UOS LC GRADIMCS CCMMO ** VIESSEMOS AL CRAIDOR;
                22841 5ELCID2910 ** DESONDRA Y CABE ALGUNA CONTRA NOS,
                23219 5ELCID2958 ** QUIER EL CASAMIENTC FECHO NON FUESSE OY
                23777 5ELCID3029 CAUALGAD, %ID; ** NCN, NCN AURIA DEC SABOR;
                23883 5ELCID3042 RESPONDIO EL REY: ** FAGO, SIN SALUE DIOS
                23905 5ELCID3045 MER%ED, YA REY, ** EL CRIACCR UOS SALUE
                24153 5ELCID3C80 ** DESOBRA BUSCAREN YFANTES DE CARRION,
                25095 5ELCID3197 SE QUE ** UOS ACAE%IERE, CON ELLA GANAREDES GRAND PREZ &
                                 GRAND VALOR.
                25223 5ELCID3212 ** PLOGUIERE AL REY, ASSI CEZIMOS NOS: DIXO EL REY
                25326 5ELCID3225 ** ESSO PLCGIERE AL %ID, NON GELO VECAMOS NOS;
                25669 5ELCID3269 ** NON RECUDECES, VEA LC ESTA CORT.
                25934 5ELCID3305 ** YO RESPCNDIER, TU NCN ENTRARAS EN ARMAS.
                26034 5ELCID3319 ** YO NON VUJAS, EL MORC TE JUGARA MAL;
                26268 5ELCID3349 QUANDO FUERE LA LIC, ** PLOGUIERE AL CRIADOR,
                27045 5ELCID3455 ** AY QUI RESPONCA ODIZE DE NO,
                27085 5ELCID3461 ** DIOS QUISIERE CUE CESTA BIEN SALGAMOS NOS,
                27534 5ELCID3517 ** AUOS LE TOLLIES, EL CAUALLO NO HAURIE TAN BUEN SE@OR.
                27732 5ELCID3540 QUE ** LOS PUDIESSEN APARTAR ALOS DEL CAMPEADOR,
                27899 5ELCID3560 ** BUENAS LAS TENEDES, PRC ABRAN AUOS;
                27907 5ELCID3561 OTRO ** FARAN ALOS DEL CANPEACOR.
                27935 5ELCID3565 ** DEL CAMPO BIEN SALIDES, GRAND ONDRA AUREDES VOS;
                29025 5ELCID3707 ATAL LE CCNTESCA C ** QUIER PEOR.
                29248 5ELCID3734 ES LEYDO, DAT NOS DEL VINO; ** NON TENEDES DINEROS, ECHAD
        WORD #3805 OCCURS 110 TIMES.
           INDEX OF DIVERSIFICATION =   265.97 WITH STANCARD DEVIATION OF   299.56

SICUETA          3579 5ELCID0451 ******* UCS FUERE ALGUNA AL ALGARA,
        WORD #3806 OCCURS   1 TIMES.

SID             23541 5ELCID2998 ENEMIGO DE MIC ***, QUE SIEMPREL BUSCO MAL,
        WORD #3807 OCCURS   1 TIMES.

SIDIOS          11144 5ELCID1410 DE AQUESTOS XV CIAS, ****** NCS CURIARE DE MAL,
        WORD #3808 OCCURS   1 TIMES.

SIEGLO          10229 5ELCID1295 ALOS DIAS DEL ****** NCN LE LORASSEN CHRISTIANOS.
                11418 5ELCID1445 TODOS LCS CIAS DEL ****** EN LEUAR LO ADELANT
                29184 5ELCID3726 PASSADC ES DESTE ****** EL CIA DE CINQUAESMA.
        WORD #3809 OCCURS   3 TIMES.
```

WORD C# PREFIX CONTEXT

SIEL 6886 5ELCID0880 QUEL AYDES MER%ED, **** CRIADOR UOS VALA.
WORD #3810 OCCURS 1 TIMES.

SIELAS 28068 5ELCID3583 SANTIGUARON LAS ****** & CAUALGAN A VIGOR;
WORD #3811 OCCURS 1 TIMES.

SIELLA 28853 5ELCID3685 CON EL DIO VNA TUERTA, DELA ****** LO ENCAMO,
WORD #3812 OCCURS 1 TIMES.

SIELLAS 6405 5ELCID0817 TODOS CON ******* & MUY BIEN ENFRENADOS,
7754 5ELCID0993 ELAS ******* CO%ERAS & LAS %INCHAS AMOIADAS;
7762 5ELCID0994 NOS CAUALGAREMOS ******* GALLEGAS, & HUESAS SOBRE CAL%AS;
7790 5ELCID0997 POR VNO QUE FIRGADES, TRES ******* YRAN VAZIAS.
10545 5ELCID1337 DE ******* & DE FRENOS TODOS GUARNIDOS SON.
14304 5ELCID1810 CON ******* & CON FRENOS & CON SE@AS ESPADAS;
WORD #3813 OCCURS 6 TIMES.
INDEX OF DIVERSIFICATION = 1578.80 WITH STANDARD DEVIATION OF 1662.97

SIEMPRE 842 5ELCID0108 POR ******* UOS FARE RICOS, QUE NON SEADES MENGUADOS.
6665 5ELCID0850 QUI A BUEN SE@OR SIRUE, ******* BIUE EN DELI%IO.
7393 5ELCID0948 QUI EN VN LOGAR MORA *******, LO SO PUEDE MANGUAR;
11425 5ELCID1446 EL %ID ******* VALDRA MAS.
18721 5ELCID2369 PARAUAS DELANT AL CAMPEADOR, ******* CON LA BUEN AUZE:
22150 5ELCID2820 LOS DE SANTESTEUAN, ******* MESURADOS SON,
24253 5ELCID3093 ******* LA VISTE MYO %ID EL CAMPEADOR;
25966 5ELCID3310 ******* EN LAS CORTES PERO MUDO ME LAMADES
WORD #3814 OCCURS 8 TIMES.
INDEX OF DIVERSIFICATION = 3588.14 WITH STANDARD DEVIATION OF 2340.49

SIEMPREL 23543 5ELCID2998 ENEMIGO DE MIO SID, QUE ******** BUSCO MAL,
WORD #3815 OCCURS 1 TIMES.

SIENPRE 14391 5ELCID1820 E SERUIR LO HE ******* MIENTRA QUE OUISSE EL ALMA.
20103 5ELCID2552 DAQUESTOS AUERES ******* SEREMOS RICOS OMNES,
WORD #3816 OCCURS 2 TIMES.

SIENTEN 21554 5ELCID2740 YA LO ******* ELLAS EN LOS SOS CORA%ONES.
WORD #3817 OCCURS 1 TIMES.

SIENTRARE 1717 5ELCID0220 NON SE ********* Y MAS ENTODOS LOS MYOS DIAS.
WORD #3818 OCCURS 1 TIMES.

SIERRA 3289 5ELCID0415 ALA ****** DE MIEDES ELLOS YUAN POSAR.
3345 5ELCID0422 PASSAREMOS LA ****** QUE FIERA ES & GRAND,
3372 5ELCID0425 DE NOCH PASSAN LA ******, VINIDA ES LA MAN,
4381 5ELCID0558 LOS VNOS CONTRA LA ****** & LOS OTROS CONTRA LA AGUA.
7605 5ELCID0974 DI%E DE VNA ****** & LEGAUA A VN VAL.
14421 5ELCID1823 ANDAN LOS DIAS & LAS NOCHES, & PASSADA HAN LA ******,
21188 5ELCID2692 LA ****** DE MIEDES PASSARON LA ESTOZ,
WORD #3819 OCCURS 7 TIMES.
INDEX OF DIVERSIFICATION = 2982.17 WITH STANDARD DEVIATION OF 3170.82

SIERRAS 14438 5ELCID1826 PASSANDO VAN LAS ******* & LOS MONTES & LAS AGUAS,
WORD #3820 OCCURS 1 TIMES.

SIESCAPASSE 4589 5ELCID0583 DEGUISA UA MYO %ID COMMO *********** DE ARRANCADA.
WORD #3821 OCCURS 1 TIMES.

SIESSA 2045 5ELCID0258 ****** DESPENSSA UOS FALLE%IERE OUOS MENGUARE ALGO,
WORD #3822 OCCURS 1 TIMES.

SIESTO 15997 5ELCID2029 ****** NON FECHES, NON AUREDES MY AMOR.
WORD #3823 OCCURS 1 TIMES.

SIL 9880 5ELCID1253 *** PUDIESSEN PRENDER OFUESSE ALCAN%ADO,
18289 5ELCID2314 AQUESTE ERA EL REY BUCAR, *** OUIESTES CONTAR.
WORD #3824 OCCURS 2 TIMES.

SILES 9506 5ELCID1208 METIOLA EN PLAZO, ***** VINIESSEN HUUYAR.
WORD #3825 OCCURS 1 TIMES.

SILOCA 5022 5ELCID0635 ASSI FFERA LO DE ******, QUE ES DEL OTRA PART.
WORD #3826 OCCURS 1 TIMES.

SIMELOS 25262 5ELCID3216 DESTOS AUERES QUE UOS DI YO, ******* DADES, O DEDES DELLO RA%ON.
WORD #3827 OCCURS 1 TIMES.

SIMENEZ 26591 5ELCID3394 AL VNO DIZEN OIARRA & AL OTRO YENEGO *******,
WORD #3828 OCCURS 1 TIMES.

SIN 20 5ELCID0003 VIO PUERTAS ABIERTAS & V%OS *** CA@ADOS,
24 5ELCID0004 ALCANDARAS UAZIAS *** PIELLES & SIN MANTOS
27 5ELCID0004 ALCANDARAS UAZIAS SIN PIELLES & *** MANTOS
30 5ELCID0005 E *** FALCONES & SIN ADTORES MUDADOS.

WORD C# PREFIX CONTEXT

SIN (CON'T)

```
                 33 5ELCID0005 E SIN FALCONES & *** ADTORES MUDADOS.
                981 5ELCID0126 NON DUERME *** SOSPECHA QUI AUER TRAE MONEDADO.
               1446 5ELCID0185 NOTOLOS DON MARTINO, *** PESO LOS TOMAUA;
               3312 5ELCID0418 *** LAS PEONADAS & OMNES VALIENTES QUE SON,
               3514 5ELCID0443 E ALBAR SALUADOREZ *** FALLA, & GALIN GAR%IA, VNA FARDIDA
               3683 5ELCID0464 EL CAMPEADOR SALIO DE LA %ELADA, CORRIE ACASTEJON *** FALLA.
               3769 5ELCID0477 E *** DUBDA CORREN; FASTA ALCALA LEGO LA SE@A DE MINAYA,
               4044 5ELCID0514 E A LOS PEONES LA MEATAD *** FALLA;
               4763 5ELCID0604 LOS VASSALLOS DE MYO %ID *** PIEDAD LES DAUAN,
               5471 5ELCID0690 COMMO SODES MUY BUENO, TENER LA EDES *** ARCH;
               5777 5ELCID0730 TANOS BUENOS CAUALLOS *** SOS DUENOS ANDAR.
               7183 5ELCID0920 EL CAUALLO CORRIENDO, UALO ABRA%AR *** FALLA,
              11080 5ELCID1402 SI UOS VIESSE EL %ID SA@AS & *** MAL,
              11830 5ELCID1499 AFEUOS AQUI PERO VERMUEZ & MU@O GUSTIOZ QUE UOS QUIEREN *** HART
              12052 5ELCID1528 HY AUEGALUON, AMIGOL SODES *** FALLA.
              12181 5ELCID1546 EL OBISPO DON IHERONIMO, BUEN CHRISTIANO *** FALLA,
              12223 5ELCID1551 EL MORO AUEGALUON BIEN LOS SIRUIE *** FALLA,
              12255 5ELCID1556 FATA EN VALEN%IA SIRUIALOS *** FALLA;
              14276 5ELCID1806 DESTA MI QUINTA, DIGO UOS *** FALLA,
              14293 5ELCID1808 E CRAS HA LA MA@ANA YR UOS HEDES *** FALLA
              15496 5ELCID1963 SYO BIUO SO, ALI YRE *** FALLA.
              18231 5ELCID2306 QUANDO LOS FALLARON & ELLOS VINIERON, ASSI VINIERON *** COLOR;
              19018 5ELCID2406 CAUALLOS *** DUENOS SALIR A TODAS PARTES.
              20610 5ELCID2616 QUE ESTOS CASAMIENTOS NON SERIEN *** ALGUNA TACHA.
              21056 5ELCID2676 HYO SIRUIENDO UOS *** ART, & UOS CONSSEIASTES PORA MI MUERT.
              21525 5ELCID2736 CON LAS %INCHAS CORREDIZAS MAIAN LAS TAN *** SABOR;
              21578 5ELCID2743 TANTO LAS MAIARON QUE *** COSIMENTE SON;
              22510 5ELCID2866 QUANDO UOS SODES SA@AS & BIUAS & *** OTRO MAL.
              23239 5ELCID2960 AIUDAR LE ADERECHO, *** SALUE EL CRIADOR
              23480 5ELCID2990 DIXO EL REY: NO LO FERE, *** SALUE DIOS
              23885 5ELCID3042 RESPONDIO EL REY: SI FAGO, *** SALUE DIOS
              24165 5ELCID3081 DO TALES %IENTO TOUIER, BIEN SERE *** PAUOR.
              26107 5ELCID3328 LENGUA *** MANOS, CUEMO OSAS FABLAR?
              26363 5ELCID3362 CALA, ALEUOSO, BOCA *** VERDAD
              26568 5ELCID3391 LOS QUE AN REBTADO LIDIARAN, *** SALUE DIOS
              26683 5ELCID3408 *** UUESTRO MANDADO NADA NON FERE YO.
              28389 5ELCID3625 FIRIENSSE EN LOS ESCUDOS *** TODO PAUOR.
              29091 5ELCID3716 *** VERGUEN%A LAS CASARE OAQUI PESE OAQUI NON.
         WORD #3829 OCCURS  42 TIMES.
            INDEX OF DIVERSIFICATION =   708.05 WITH STANDARD DEVIATION OF    845.97

SINAUA         3258 5ELCID0411 ****** LA CARA, A DIOS SE ACOMENDO,
         WORD #3830 OCCURS   1 TIMES.

SINES          4710 5ELCID0597 FIRID LOS, CAUALLEROS, TODOS ***** DUBDAN%A;
              13192 5ELCID1672 POR LAS HUERTAS ADENTRO ESTAN ***** PAUOR.
              17824 5ELCID2255 EN BESTIAS ***** AL O SON MANDADOS;
         WORD #3831 OCCURS   3 TIMES.

SINIESTRA        88 5ELCID0012 E ENTRANDO A BURGOS OUIERON LA *********.
         WORD #3832 OCCURS   1 TIMES.

SINIESTRO      3153 5ELCID0397 DE ********* SANT ESTEUAN, VNA BUENA %IPDAD,
         WORD #3833 OCCURS   1 TIMES.

SINON           904 5ELCID0116 AQUELAS NON LAS PUEDE LEUAR, *****, SER YEN VENTADAS;
         WORD #3834 OCCURS   1 TIMES.

SIQUISIESSE   15395 5ELCID1950 NON ERA MARAUILLA *********** EL REY ALFONSSO,
         WORD #3835 OCCURS   1 TIMES.

SIRUA          3048 5ELCID0384 COMMO ***** ADO@A XIMENA & ALAS FIJAS QUE HA,
         WORD #3836 OCCURS   1 TIMES.

SIRUADES       2016 5ELCID0254 AELLA & ASUS FIJAS & ASUS DUENAS ******** LAS EST A@O.
              10734 5ELCID1359 CATAD COMMO LAS ******** UOS & EL CAMPEADOR.
              20344 5ELCID2581 A MIS FIJAS ********, QUE UUESTRAS MUGIERES SON;
         WORD #3837 OCCURS   3 TIMES.

SIRUAN        10770 5ELCID1364 ****** LE SUS HERDADES DO FUERE EL CAMPEADOR,
              10792 5ELCID1366 POR TAL FAGO AQUESTO QUE ****** ASO SE@OR.
              10913 5ELCID1381 SI LEUAREDES LAS DUENAS, ****** LAS ASU SABOR,
              19883 5ELCID2521 BIEN UOS ABRA%EN & ****** UOS DE CORA%ON.
              20781 5ELCID2639 DELO QUE OUIEREN HUEBOS ****** LAS ASO SABOR,
              22909 5ELCID2918 CON EL DOS CAUALLEROS QUEL ****** A SO SABOR,
         WORD #3838 OCCURS   6 TIMES.
            INDEX OF DIVERSIFICATION =  2426.80 WITH STANDARD DEVIATION OF  3752.99

SIRUE          6664 5ELCID0850 QUI A BUEN SE@OR *****, SIEMPRE BIUE EN DELI%IO.
              10651 5ELCID1349 QUE ENTODAS GUISAS MIIOR ME ***** QUE UOS.
         WORD #3839 OCCURS   2 TIMES.

SIRUEM        15008 5ELCID1898 ****** MYO %ID EL CAMPEADOR, EL LO MERE%E,
         WORD #3840 OCCURS   1 TIMES.
```

WORD C# PREFIX CONTEXT

SIRUEN 1843 5ELCID0234 CON ESTOS CAUALLEROS CUEL ****** ASO SABOR.
11267 5ELCID1425 E ALAS OTRAS DUE@AS QUE LAS ****** DELANT,
13928 5ELCID1764 ESTAS DUE@AS QUE ADUXIESTES, CUE UOS ****** TANTO,
15813 5ELCID2005 E OTRAS DUE@AS QUE LAS ****** ASU SABOR;
17325 5ELCID2191 ETODAS LAS DUE@AS QUE LAS ******:
WORD #3841 OCCURS 5 TIMES.
INDEX OF DIVERSIFICATION = 3869.50 WITH STANDARD DEVIATION OF 3733.14

SIRUIALOS 12096 5ELCID1534 ENTRARON EN MEDINA, ********* MINAYA,
12254 5ELCID1556 FATA EN VALEN%IA ********* SIN FALLA;
WORD #3842 OCCURS 2 TIMES.

SIRUIE 12222 5ELCID1551 EL MORO AUEGALUON BIEN LOS ****** SIN FALLA,
WORD #3843 OCCURS 1 TIMES.

SIRUIENDO 21054 5ELCID2676 HYO ********* UOS SIN ART, & UOS CONSSEIASTES PORA MI MUERT.
WORD #3844 OCCURS 1 TIMES.

SIRUIERON 13953 5ELCID1767 QUE LO SEPAN EN CASTIELLA, AQUIEN ********* TANTO.
WORD #3845 OCCURS 1 TIMES.

SIRUIESSEN 24774 5ELCID3155 QUES ONDRASSEN CON ELLAS & ********** AUOS;
WORD #3846 OCCURS 1 TIMES.

SIRUIO 20868 5ELCID2650 DIOS, QUE BIEN LOS ****** ATODO SO SABOR
WORD #3847 OCCURS 1 TIMES.

SIS 9851 5ELCID1250 QUE *** PUDIESSEN YR, FER LO YEN DE GRADO.
10218 5ELCID1294 QUE *** FARTAS LIDIANDO & FIRIENDO CON SUS MANOS,
14969 5ELCID1892 DEL CASAMIENTO NON SE *** ABRA SABOR;
WORD #3848 OCCURS 3 TIMES.

SIUOS 1409 5ELCID0181 ***** LA ADUXIER DALLA; SI NON, CONTALDA SOBRE LAS ARCAS. . . .
10446 5ELCID1324 QUEL AYADES MER%ED, ***** VALA EL CRIADOR
10665 5ELCID1351 MER%ED UOS PIDE EL %ID, ***** CAYESSE EN SABOR,
16136 5ELCID2046 FUESSEDES MY HUESPED, ***** PLOGIESSE, SE@OR.
20440 5ELCID2594 MER%ED UOS PEDIMOS, PADRE, ***** VALA EL CRIADOR
24539 5ELCID3128 OYD, MESNADAS, ***** VALA EL CRIADOR
WORD #3849 OCCURS 6 TIMES.
INDEX OF DIVERSIFICATION = 4625.00 WITH STANDARD DEVIATION OF 3161.25

SJN 4114 5ELCID0523 ATERCER DIA DADOS FUERON *** FALLA.
6172 5ELCID0786 CA EN ALCAZ *** DUBDA LES FUERON DANDO.
15532 5ELCID1968 CAUALLOS GRUESSOS & CORREDORES *** FALLA,
WORD #3850 OCCURS 3 TIMES.

SO 1038 5ELCID0133 PEDIR UOS A POCO POR DEXAR ** AUER EN SALUO.
1215 5ELCID0156 YA ME EXCO DE TIERRA, CA DEL REY ** AYRADO.
1961 5ELCID0248 DIXO EL %ID: GRA%IAS, DON ABBAT, & ** UUESTRO PAGADO;
2148 5ELCID0270 CON AQUESTAS MYS DUE@AS DE QUIEN ** YO SERUIDA.
3413 5ELCID0431 MANDADO DE ** SE@OR TODO LO HAN AFAR.
3843 5ELCID0486 EL CASTIELO DEXO EN ** PODER, EL CAMPEADOR CAUALGA,
5716 5ELCID0721 YO ** RUY DIAZ, EL %ID CAMPEADOR DE BIUAR
5830 5ELCID0737 MU@O GUSTIOZ, QUE FUE ** CRIADO,
5853 5ELCID0741 FELEZ MUNOZ ** SOBRINO DEL CAMPEADOR
5919 5ELCID0750 DIOL TAL ESPADADA CON EL ** DIESTRO BRA%O,
6143 5ELCID0782 DIZE MYNAYA: AGORA ** PAGADO,
6190 5ELCID0788 ANDAUA MYO %ID SOBRE ** BUEN CAUALLO,
7395 5ELCID0948 QUI EN VN LOGAR MORA SIEMPRE, LO ** PUEDE MANGUAR;
7635 5ELCID0978 DELO ** NON LIEUO NADA, DEXEM YR EN PAZ.
8654 5ELCID1099 PRISIERON ** CONSEIO QUEL VINIESSEN %ERCAR.
8690 5ELCID1104 BEUEMOS ** VINO & COMEMOS EL SO PAN.
8695 5ELCID1104 BEUEMOS SO VINO & COMEMOS EL ** PAN.
8957 5ELCID1140 CA YO ** RUYDIAZ, MYO %ID EL DE BIUAR
9279 5ELCID1180 DELANTE VEYEN ** DUELO, NON SE PUEDEN HUUIAR,
9797 5ELCID1244 CON EL MYNAYA ALBARFFANEZ QUE NOS LE PARTE DE ** BRA%O.
10181 5ELCID1289 EL OBISPO DON IERONIMO ** NOMBRE ES LAMADO.
10467 5ELCID1326 MAGER EN TIERRA AGENA, EL BIEN FAZE LO **;
10967 5ELCID1388 SOMOS EN ** PRO QUANTO LO PODEMOS FAR;
12264 5ELCID1557 LOS SOS DESPENDIE EL MORO, QUE DELO ** NON TOMAUA NADA.
12423 5ELCID1576 ALA PUERTA DE VALEN%IA, DO FUESSE EN ** SALUO,
13267 5ELCID1682 TORNADOS SON A MYO %ID LOS QUE COMIEN ** PAN;
13529 5ELCID1714 DIO SALTO MYO %ID EN BAUIECA EL ** CAUALLO;
14516 5ELCID1836 EL CONDE DON GAR%IA, ** ENEMIGO MALO.
15493 5ELCID1963 SYO BIUO **, ALI YRE SIN FALLA.
15967 5ELCID2024 ASI SABE DAR OMILDAN%A A ALFONSSO ** SE@OR.
16217 5ELCID2057 EN AQUEL DIA DEL REY ** HUESPED FUE;
16482 5ELCID2089 DAD LAS AQUI QUISIEREDES UOS, CA YO PAGADO **.
16707 5ELCID2115 CONPE%O MYO %ID ADAR AQUIEN QUIERE PRENDER ** DON,
16798 5ELCID2127 SOBREL ** CAUALLO BAUIECA MYO %ID SALTO DAUA;
16998 5ELCID2152 DEUOS BIEN ** SERUIDO, & TENGON POR PAGADO;
17033 5ELCID2156 HYAS ESPIDIO MYO %ID DE ** SE@OR ALFONSSO,
18063 5ELCID2285 E %ERCAN EL ESCA@O & FINCAN SOBRE ** SE@OR.
18460 5ELCID2336 CA DAQUELOS MOROS YO ** SABIDOR;

WORD C# PREFIX CONTEXT

SO (CON'T)

19432 5ELCID2462 DIXO MYO %ID: YO DESTO ** PAGADO;
19491 5ELCID2469 DESTA ARRANCADA, QUE LO TENIEN EN ** SALUO,
19619 5ELCID2486 QUE TODOS PRISIESSEN ** DERECHO CONTADO,
19676 5ELCID2494 ANTES FU MINGUADO, AGCRA RICO **,
20384 5ELCID2586 QUANDO SON PAGADOS ATODO ** SABOR,
20870 5ELCID2650 DIOS, QUE BIEN LOS SIRUIO ATODO ** SABOR
22054 5ELCID2807 CON EL ** MANTO A AMAS LAS CUBRIO,
22800 5ELCID2905 CUEMO YO ** SU VASSALLO, & EL ES MYO SE@OR,
22911 5ELCID2918 CON EL DOS CAUALLEROS QUEL SIRUAN A ** SABOR,
23066 5ELCID2938 ELE ES VUESTRO VASSALLO & UOS SODES ** SE@OS.
23460 5ELCID2988 PRENDEN ** CONSSEIO ASSI PARIENTES COMMO SON,
23689 5ELCID3017 QUE BESASSE LAS MANOS AL REY ** SE@OR:
24670 5ELCID3142 CON EL QUE TOUIERE DERECHO YO DESSA PART ME **.
24939 5ELCID3176 PUSIERON LAS EN MANO DEL REY ** SE@OR;
25131 5ELCID3201 HYA PAGADO ** DE MIS ESPADAS, DE COLADA & DE TIZON.
25173 5ELCID3205 HYO FAZIENDO ESTO, ELLOS ACABARON LO **;
27053 5ELCID3456 HYO ** ALBARFANEZ PORA TODEL MEIOR.
27305 5ELCID3489 ELLOS SON ADOBADOS PORA CUMPLLIR TODO LO **;
27497 5ELCID3512 FUE BESAR LA MANO A ** SE@OR ALFONSSO;
27696 5ELCID3535 CUNPLIR QUIEREN EL DEBDO QUE LES MANDO ** SE@OR,
27747 5ELCID3541 QUE LOS MATASSEN EN CAMPO POR DESONDRA DE ** SE@OR.
28122 5ELCID3590 QUE CADA VNO DELLOS BIEN FOS FERIR EL **.
28317 5ELCID3614 CADA VNO DELLOS MIENTES TIENE AL **.
28544 5ELCID3644 ANTES QUE EL COLPE ESPERASSE DIXO: VEN%UDO **.
28996 5ELCID3703 CONPLIDO HAN EL DEBDO QUE LES MANDO ** SE@OR;
29073 5ELCID3713 PRISOS ALA BARBA RUY DIAZ ** SE@OR;
WORD #3851 OCCURS 64 TIMES.
INDEX OF DIVERSIFICATION = 444.00 WITH STANDARD DEVIATION OF 443.08

SOBEIANA 6566 5ELCID0838 LA TIERRA ES ANGOSTA & ******** DE MALA;
6862 5ELCID0877 ******** ES, SE@OR, LA SU GANA%IA.
WORD #3852 OCCURS 2 TIMES.

SOBEIANAS 5163 5ELCID0653 GENTES SE AIUNTARON ********* DE GRANDES
5197 5ELCID0657 CRECEN ESTOS VIRTOS, CA YENTES SON *********.
7720 5ELCID0988 DE MOROS & DE CHRISTIANOS GENTES TRAE *********,
14643 5ELCID1852 LAS GANAN%IAS QUE FIZO MUCHO SON *********,
19586 5ELCID2482 ********* SON LAS GANAN%IAS QUETODOS AN GANADAS;
WORD #3853 OCCURS 5 TIMES.
INDEX OF DIVERSIFICATION = 3604.75 WITH STANDARD DEVIATION OF 2984.52

SOBEIANO 14015 5ELCID1775 TANTO FALLAN DESTO QUE ES COSA ********.
14194 5ELCID1796 LO QUE CAYE AEL MUCHO ERA ********;
WORD #3854 OCCURS 2 TIMES.

SOBEIANOS 862 5ELCID0110 GRANDES AUERES PRISO & MUCHO *********,
17958 5ELCID2272 LOS AMORES QUELES FAZEN MUCHO ERAN *********.
20029 5ELCID2541 LOS AUERES QUE TENEMOS GRANDES SON & *********,
22865 5ELCID2912 MYOS AUERES SE ME AN LEUADO, QUE ********* SON;
WORD #3855 OCCURS 4 TIMES.

SOBRE 1249 5ELCID0161 QUE ***** AQUELAS ARCHAS DAR LE YEN VJ %IENTOS MARCOS
1416 5ELCID0181 SIUOS LA ADUXIER DALLA; SI NON, CONTALDA ***** LAS ARCAS. . . .
3184 5ELCID0401 ***** NAUAS DE PALOS EL DUERO UA PASAR,
3449 5ELCID0435 ODIZEN CASTEION, EL QUE ES ***** FENARES,
3926 5ELCCD0498 FATA QUE YO ME PAGE ***** MIO BUEN CAUALLO,
4342 5ELCID0553 E ***** ALCO%ER MYO %ID YUA POSAR,
4982 5ELCID0630 VINO POSAR ***** ALCO%ER, EN VN TAN FUERTE LOGAR;
5805 5ELCID0733 QUAL LIDIA BIEN ***** EXORADO ARZON
6189 5ELCID0788 ANDAUA MYO %ID ***** SO BUEN CAUALLO,
6763 5ELCID0863 Y FFINCO EN VN POYO QUE ES ***** MONT REAL;
6958 5ELCID0890 ***** AQUESTO TODO, DEZIR UOS QUIERO, MINAYA:
7766 5ELCID0994 NOS CAUALGAREMOS SIELLAS GALLEGAS, & HUESAS ***** CAL%AS;
7827 5ELCID1001 LAS ARMAS AUIEN PRESAS & SEDIEN ***** LOS CAUALLOS.
12820 5ELCID1627 ENTRARON ***** MAR, EN LAS BARCAS SON METIDOS,
13767 5ELCID1745 ASSI ENTRO ***** BAUIECA, EL ESPADA EN LA MANO.
15425 5ELCID1954 ***** TAIO, QUE ES UNA AGUA CABDAL,
18062 5ELCID2285 E %ERCAN EL ESCA@O & FINCAN ***** SO SE@OR.
19253 5ELCID2437 COFIA ***** LOS PELOS FRONZIDA DELLA YA QUANTO.
21483 5ELCID2731 ATAN MALOS ENSSIENPLOS NON FAGADES ***** NOS:
21549 5ELCID2739 LINPIA SALIE LA SANGRE ***** LOS %ICLATONES.
24115 5ELCID3075 ***** LAS LORIGAS ARMINOS & PELI%ONES,
24262 5ELCID3094 VNA COFIA ***** LOS PELOS DUN ESCARIN DE PRO,
25482 5ELCID3246 ***** LOS DOZIENTOS MARCOS QUE TENIE EL REY ALFONSSO
27800 5ELCID3548 DEMAS ***** TODOS YES EL REY CON ALFONSSO,
28334 5ELCID3617 ENCLINAUAN LAS CARAS ***** LOS ARZONES,
WORD #3856 OCCURS 25 TIMES.
INDEX OF DIVERSIFICATION = 1127.54 WITH STANDARD DEVIATION OF 1160.85

SOBREGONEL 12510 5ELCID1587 VISTIOS EL **********; LUENGA TRAHE LA BARBA;
WORD #3857 OCCURS 1 TIMES.

SOBREL 8271 5ELCID1053 ****** SEDIE EL QUE EN BUEN ORA NASCO:
12502 5ELCID1586 MYO %ID SALIO ******, & ARMAS DE FUSTE TOMAUA,
16797 5ELCID2127 ****** SO CAUALLO BAUIECA MYO %ID SALTO DAUA;

```
WORD                  C#  PREFIX                                   CONTEXT

SOBREL (CON'T)

                    28886 5ELCID3689 LA LAN%A RECCMBRO & ****** SE PARO;
         WORD #3858 OCCURS   4 TIMES.

SOBRELIEUO          27207 5ELCID3478 HYO VOS LO ********** COMMO BUEN VASSALLO FAZE A SE@OR,
         WORD #3859 OCCURS   1 TIMES.

SOBRELLA             1426 5ELCID0183 ******** VNA SAUANA DE RAN%AL & MUY BLANCA.
                     9513 5ELCID1209 NUEUE MESES COMPLIDCS, SABET, ******** IAZ;
                    24232 5ELCID3090 ******** VN BRIAL PRIMO DE %ICLATON,
         WORD #3860 OCCURS   3 TIMES.

SOBRELLAS            9467 5ELCID1203 ADELINC PORA VALEN%IA & ********* VA ECHAR,
                    24198 5ELCID3086 ********* VNCS %APATCS QUE A GRANT HUEBRA SON;
         WORD #3861 OCCURS   2 TIMES.

SOBRELOS            29261 5ELCID3735 ALA VNOS PE@OS, QUE BIEN VOS LO DARARAN ********.
         WORD #3862 OCCURS   1 TIMES.

SOBREPELI%AS        12468 5ELCID1582 ************ VESTIDAS & CON CRUZES DE PLATA
         WORD #3863 OCCURS   1 TIMES.

SOBRESTO             6930 5ELCID0886 ******** TODO, AUOS QUITO, MINAYA,
                    24245 5ELCID3092 ******** VNA PIEL VERMEIA, LAS BANDAS DORO SON,
         WORD #3864 OCCURS   2 TIMES.

SOBREUIENTA         18028 5ELCID2281 MALA ***********, SABED, QUE LES CUNTIO:
         WORD #3865 OCCURS   1 TIMES.

SOBRINO              5854 5ELCID0741 FELEZ MUNOZ SO ******* DEL CAMPEADOR
                     7510 5ELCID0963 FIRIOM EL ******* & NCN LO ENMENDO MAS;
                    18581 5ELCID2351 ALA, PERO VERMUEZ, EL MYO ******* CARO
                    20623 5ELCID2618  OHERES, MYO *******, TU, FELEZ MUNOZ,
                    20742 5ELCID2634 OYAS, *******, TU, FELEZ MUNOZ
                    21738 5ELCID2765 ******* ERA DEL %ID CAMPEADOR;
                    24074 5ELCID3069 E MYO ******* FELEZ MUNOZ;
                    25028 5ELCID3188 ASO ******* PCR NONBREL LAMO,
                    25042 5ELCID3190 PRENDET LA, *******, CA MEIORA EN SE@OR.
         WORD #3866 OCCURS   9 TIMES.
            INDEX OF DIVERSIFICATION =  2397.50 WITH STANDARD DEVIATION OF  3602.18

SODES                 625 5ELCID0079 MARTIN ANTOLINEZ, ***** ARDIDA LAN%A
                      803 5ELCID0103 O *****, RACHEL & VIDAS, LOS MYOS AMIGOS CAROS?
                     2121 5ELCID0267 POR MALOS MESTUREROS DE TIERRA ***** ECHADO.
                     4212 5ELCID0536 TODOS ***** PAGADOS & NINGUNO POR PAGAR.
                     5465 5ELCID0690 COMMO ***** MUY BUENO, TENER LA EDES SIN ARCH;
                     5940 5ELCID0753 CAUALGAD, MYNAYA, UOS ***** EL MYO DIESTRO BRA%O
                     6360 5ELCID0810 OYD, MYNAYA, ***** MYO DIESTRO BRA%O
                     8451 5ELCID1074 FOLGEDES, YA MYO %ID, ***** EN UUESTRO SALUO.
                    10950 5ELCID1386 EN TODO ***** PRO, EN ESTO ASSI LO FAGADES:
                    12051 5ELCID1528 HY AUEGALUCN, AMIGOL ***** SIN FALLA.
                    14258 5ELCID1804 DO *****, CABOSO? VENID ACA, MYNAYA;
                    14583 5ELCID1845 MER%ED, REY ALFONSSO, ***** TAN ONDRADO
                    17627 5ELCID2230 AFEUOS DELANT MINAYA, AMOS ***** HERMANOS.
                    19298 5ELCID2443  VENIDES, MYOS YERNOS, MYOS FIJOS ***** AMOS
                    19304 5ELCID2444 SEQUE DE LIDIAR BIEN ***** PAGADOS;
                    20308 5ELCID2577 MIOS FIJOS ***** AMOS, QUANDO MIS FIJAS VOS DO;
                    20452 5ELCID2596 DELANT ***** AMOS, SE@ORA & SE@OR.
                    20522 5ELCID2605 HYD A CARRION DO ***** HEREDADAS,
                    22382 5ELCID2851 GRA%IAS, VARONES DE SANTESTEUAN, QUE ***** CO@OS%EDORES,
                    22505 5ELCID2866 QUANDO UOS ***** SA@AS & BIUAS & SIN OTRO MAL.
                    23065 5ELCID2938 ELE ES VUESTRO VASSALLO & UOS ***** SO SE@OS.
                    23165 5ELCID2951 E QUE UOS PESE, REY COMMO ***** SABIDOR;
                    24445 5ELCID3116 MAGER QUE ALGUNOS PESA, MEIOR ***** QUE NOS.
                    24620 5ELCID3136 E ESTOS OTROS CONDES QUE DEL VANDO NON *****.
                    24626 5ELCID3137 TODOS METED Y MIENTES, CA ***** CO@OS%EDORES,
                    24903 5ELCID3171 MER%ED, YA REY DON ALFONSSO, ***** NUESTRO SE@OR
                    25860 5ELCID3294 DE UUESTROS AUERES DE TODOS PAGADOS *****.
                    26255 5ELCID3347 ELLAS SON MUGIERES & VOS ***** VARONES,
                    26653 5ELCID3403 MER%ED, REY ALFONSSO, VOS ***** MYO SE@OR
                    26952 5ELCID3443 DE NATURA ***** DELOS DE VANIGOMEZ,
                    27041 5ELCID3454 EN TODAS GUISAS TALES ***** QUALES DIGO YO;
         WORD #3867 OCCURS  31 TIMES.
            INDEX OF DIVERSIFICATION =   879.53 WITH STANDARD DEVIATION OF   863.48

SOGORUE              5101 5ELCID0644 ELLOS VINIERON ALA NOCH EN ******* POSAR.
         WORD #3868 OCCURS   1 TIMES.

SOL                  1818 5ELCID0231 ANTES SERE CON UUSCO QUE EL *** QUIERA RAYAR.
                     2633 5ELCID0332 FEZIST ESTRELAS & LUNA & EL *** PORA ESCALENTAR;
                     3303 5ELCID0416 AVN ERA DE DIA, NON ERA PUESTO EL ***,
                     3626 5ELCID0457 YXIE EL ***, DIOS, QUE FERMOSO APUNTAUA
                     5406 5ELCID0682 OTRO DIA MA@ANA, EL *** QUERIE APUNTAR,
                     8466 5ELCID1076 DE VENIR UOS BUSCAR *** NON SERA PENSSADO.
                     8591 5ELCID1091 AORIENT EXE EL ***, E TORNOS AESSA PART.
```

WORD C# PREFIX CONTEXT

SOL (CON'T)

```
13620 5ELCID1726 SALIOS LE DE *** ESPADA, CA MUCHOL ANDIDO EL CAUALLO,
16261 5ELCID2062 OTRO DIA MA@ANA, CLARO SALIE EL ***,
16307 5ELCID2068 AL OTRO DIA MA@ANA, ASSI COMMO SALIO EL ***,
16363 5ELCID2075 VUESTRAS FIJAS UOS PIDO, DON ELUIRA & DO@A ***,
16473 5ELCID2088 AFELLAS EN UUESTRA MANO DON ELUIRA & DO@A ***,
16554 5ELCID2097 DAQUI LAS PRENDO POR MIS MANOS DON ELUIRA & DONA ***,
16676 5ELCID2112 QUANDO SALIE EL ***, QUES TORNASSE CADA VNO DON SALIDOS SON.
17093 5ELCID2163 HE DELAS FIJAS DE MYO %ID, DE DON ELUIRA & DO@A ***.
17240 5ELCID2180 QUANDO VINIERE LA MA@ANA, QUE APUNTARE EL ***,
17250 5ELCID2181 VERAN ASUS ESPOSAS, A DON ELUIRA & A DONA ***.
17371 5ELCID2197 AUOS DIGO, MIS FIJAS, DON ELUIRA & DO@A ***:
18078 5ELCID2287 METIOS *** ESCA@O, TANTO CUO EL PAUOR.
18441 5ELCID2333 EN BRA%OS TENEDES MIS FIJAS TAN BLANCAS COMMO EL ***
19878 5ELCID2520 EAMAS LA MYS FIJAS, DON ELUIRA & DO@A ***;
20429 5ELCID2592 AMAS HERMANAS, DON ELUIRA & DO@A ***,
20705 5ELCID2628 ADIOS UOS HACOMENDAMOS, DON ELUIRA & DO@A ***,
21113 5ELCID2682 HYRE CON UUESTRA GRA%IA, DON ELUIRA & DO@A ***;
21282 5ELCID2704  MAL GELO CUNPLIERON QUANDO SALIE EL ***
21327 5ELCID2710 SI NON AMAS SUS MUGIERES DO@A ELUIRA & DO@A ***:
21357 5ELCID2714 BIEN LO CREADES, DON ELUIRA & DO@A ***,
21432 5ELCID2724 QUANDO ESTO VIERON LAS DUE@AS, FABLAUA DO@A ***:
21610 5ELCID2747 HYA NON PUEDEN FABLAR DON ELUIRA & DONA ***;
21852 5ELCID2780 YA PRIMAS, LAS MIS PRIMAS, DON ELUIRA & DO@A ***,
21904 5ELCID2786 LAMANDO: PRIMAS, PRIMAS, DON ELUIRA & DON ***
21935 5ELCID2790 VAN RECORDANDO DON ELUIRA & DO@A ***,
21978 5ELCID2796 TAN A GRANT DUELO FABLAUA DO@A ***:
22134 5ELCID2817 HYUA RE%EBIR ADON ELUIRA & ADON@A ***;
22452 5ELCID2859 ENEL FINCAN LOS OIOS DON ELUIRA & DO@A ***:
22499 5ELCID2865 DON ELUIRA & DO@A ***, CUYDADO NON AYADES,
24019 5ELCID3061 SUELTA FUE LA MISSA ANTES QUE SALIESSE EL ***,
24114 5ELCID3074 DE SUSO LAS LORIGAS TAN BLANCAS COMMO EL ***;
24214 5ELCID3087 VISTIO CAMISA DE RAN%AL TAN BLANCA COMMO EL ***,
25026 5ELCID3187 ASSIS YRAN VENGANDO DON ELUIRA & DONA ***.
26242 5ELCID3345 POR FIJAS DEL %ID, DON ELUIRA & DONA ***:
26774 5ELCID3419 DE FIJAS DE MYO %ID, DON ELUIRA & DO@A ***,
26984 5ELCID3447 QUANDO PIDEN MIS PRIMAS, DON ELUIRA & DO@A ***,
27120 5ELCID3465 CRAS SEA LA LID, QUANDO SALIERE EL ***,
27340 5ELCID3493 LA CONFIA DE RAN%AL QUE BLANCA ERA COMMO EL ***,
28283 5ELCID3610 SORTEAUAN LES EL CAMPO, YA LES PARTIEN EL ***,
29125 5ELCID3719 FIZIERON SUS CASAMIENTOS CON DON ELUIRA & CON DO@A ***.
WORD #3869 OCCURS  47 TIMES.
   INDEX OF DIVERSIFICATION =   592.63 WITH STANDARD DEVIATION OF   943.19

SOLAS        25647 5ELCID3266 ***** LAS DEXASTES ENEL ROBREDO DE CORPES,
WORD #3870 OCCURS   1 TIMES.

SOLAZ         1796 5ELCID0228 DIXO MARTIN ANTOLINEZ:  VERE ALA MUGIER ATODO MYO *****,
             22554 5ELCID2872 FATA RIO DAMOR, DANDO LES *****;
WORD #3871 OCCURS   2 TIMES.

SOLDADA        635 5ELCID0080 SI YO BIUO, DOBLAR UOS HE LA *******.
              8848 5ELCID1126 ALI PARE%RA EL QUE MERE%E LA *******.
WORD #3872 OCCURS   2 TIMES.

SOLOS         5435 5ELCID0686 SI NON DOS PEONES ***** POR LA PUERTA GUARDAR;
             21341 5ELCID2712 TODOS ERAN YDOS, ELLOS IIIJ ***** SON,
             24131 5ELCID3077 ***** MANTOS LAS ESPADAS DUL%ES & TAIADORES;
WORD #3873 OCCURS   3 TIMES.

SOLTADO      19251 5ELCID2436 LA CARA FRONZIDA & ALMOFAR *******,
WORD #3874 OCCURS   1 TIMES.

SOLTARIEMOS  11328 5ELCID1434 *********** LA GANAN%IA, QUE NOS DIESSE EL CABDAL.
WORD #3875 OCCURS   1 TIMES.

SOLTARON      3108 5ELCID0391 ******** LAS RIENDAS, PIESSAN DE ANDAR;
WORD #3876 OCCURS   1 TIMES.

SOLTAUA      27342 5ELCID3494 E ******* LA BARBA & SACOLA DEL CORDON.
WORD #3877 OCCURS   1 TIMES.

SOLTO        17101 5ELCID2164 ESTO PLOGO AL REY, & ATODOS LOS *****;
             27416 5ELCID3502 LOS CC MARCOS AL REY LOS *****.
WORD #3878 OCCURS   2 TIMES.

SOLTURA      13321 5ELCID1689 EL OBISPO DO IHERONIMO ******* NOS DARA,
WORD #3879 OCCURS   1 TIMES.

SOMO          1338 5ELCID0171 NON LAS PODIEN PONER EN **** MAGER ERAU ESFOR%ADOS.
              4833 5ELCID0612 METIOLA EN **** EN TODO LO MAS ALTO.
              9605 5ELCID1220 QUANDO SU SE@A CABDAL SEDIE EN **** DEL ALCA%AR.
             27578 5ELCID3521 CA POR UOS & POREL CAUALLO ONDRADOS **** NOS.
             28594 5ELCID3651 EL CASCO DE **** APART GELO ECHAUA,
WORD #3880 OCCURS   5 TIMES.
   INDEX OF DIVERSIFICATION =  6813.00 WITH STANDARD DEVIATION OF  7600.99
```

WORD C# PREFIX CONTEXT

SOMOS

102 5ELCID0014 ALBRICIA, ALBARFFANEZ, CA ECHADOS ***** DE TIERRA
5320 5ELCIDC672 DE CASTIELLA LA GENTIL EXIDOS ***** ACA,
5333 5ELCIDC674 BIEN ***** NOS VI %IENTOS, ALGUNOS AY DE MAS;
6530 5ELCIDC833 SI NON, DO SOPIEREDES QUE *****, YNDOS CONSEGUIR.
8339 5ELCID1060 SI UOS PLOGUIERE, MYO %ID, DE YR ***** GUISADOS;
8684 5ELCID1103 EN SUS TIERRAS ***** & FEMOS LES TODOMAL,
10965 5ELCID1388 ***** EN SO PRO QUANTO LO PODEMOS FAR;
13890 5ELCID1760 ***** EN UUESTRA MER%ED, & BIUADES MUCHOS A@OS
16463 5ELCID2C87 ENTRE YO YELLAS EN UUESTRA MER%ED ***** NOS,
20084 5ELCID2549 NOS DE NATURA ***** DE CONDES DE CARRION
20119 5ELCID2554 CA DE NATURA ***** DE CONDES DE CARRION.
21698 5ELCID2758 DE NUESTROS CASAMIENTOS AGORA ***** VENGADOS;
22469 5ELCID2861 EUOS A EL LO GRADID, QUANDO BIUAS ***** NOS.
2587C 5ELCID3296 DE NATURA ***** DE CONDES DE CARRION:
26299 5ELCID3354 DE NATURA ***** DE LOS CONDES MAS LIPIOS,
26352 5ELCID3360 QUE POR QUE LAS DEXAMOS ONDRADOS ***** NOS.

WORD #3881 OCCURS 16 TIMES.
INDEX OF DIVERSIFICATION = 1749.00 WITH STANDARD DEVIATION OF 1568.61

SON

129 5ELCIDC017 BURGESES & BURGESAS POR LAS FINIESTRAS ***,
498 5ELCID0063 DETODAS COSAS QUANTAS *** DE UIANDA
1384 5ELCID0177 ASSI ES UUESTRA VENTURA GRANDES *** UUESTRAS GANAN%IAS,
1481 5ELCIDC189 YA DON RACHEL & VIDAS, EN UUESTRAS MANOS *** LAS ARCAS;
2137 5ELCID0269 FEM ANTE UOS YO & UUESTRAS FFIJAS, YFFANTES *** & DE DIAS CHICAS,
2312 5ELCIDC291 %IENTO QUINZE CAUALLEROS TODOS IUNTADOS ***;
3006 5ELCID0379 %ID, DO *** UUESTROS ESFUER%OS? EN BUEN ORA NASQUIESTES DE MADRE;
3319 5ELCID0418 SIN LAS PEONADAS & OMNES VALIENTES QUE ***,
3600 5ELCIDC454 NONBRADOS *** LOS QUE YRAN ENEL ALGARA,
3652 5ELCIDC461 TODOS *** EXIDOS, LAS PUERTAS DEXADAS AN ABIERTAS
3672 5ELCID0463 LAS YENTES DE FUERA TODAS *** DE RAMADAS.
4299 5ELCID0548 GRANDES *** LAS GANAN%IAS QUE PRISO POR LA TIERRA DO UA.
4722 5ELCIDC599 BUELTOS *** CON ELLOS POR MEDIO DELA LA@A.
5196 5ELCID0657 CRECEN ESTOS VIRTOS, CA YENTES *** SOBEIANAS.
5215 5ELCID0660 MUCHAS *** LAS AROBDAS & GRANDE ES EL ALMOFALLA.
5293 5ELCID0669 GRANDES *** LOS PODERES POR CON ELLOS LIDIAR;
5734 5ELCID0723 TREZIENTAS LAN%AS ***, TODAS TIENEN PENDONES;
5751 5ELCID0725 ALA TORNADA QUE FAZEN OTROS TANTOS ***.
5862 5ELCID0742 DESI ADELANTE, QUANTOS QUE Y ***,
5955 5ELCID0755 FIRME *** LOS MOROS, AVN NOS VAN DEL CAMPO.
6251 5ELCIDC796 DELOS MORISCOS, QUANDO *** LEGADOS, FFALLARON DX CAUALLOS.
6280 5ELCID0800 REFECHOS *** TODOS ESOS CHRISTIANOS CON AQUESTA GANAN%IA.
6356 5ELCIDC809 QUANTOS EL TRAE TODOS *** PAGADOS.
6480 5ELCIDC826 MYNAYA ALBARFANEZ DESTO ES PAGADO; POR YR CON EL OMNES ***
CONTADOS.
7165 5ELCID0918 NON *** EN CUENTA, SABET, LAS PEONADAS.
7360 5ELCID0944 TODOS *** ALEGRES, GANAN%IAS TRAEN GRANDES.
7453 5ELCID0956 LOS MANDADOS *** YDOS ATODAS PARTES;
7542 5ELCID0967 GRANDES *** LOS PODERES & A PRIESSA SEUAN LEGANDO,
7813 5ELCID1000 TODOS *** ADOBADOS QUANDO MYO %ID ESTO OUO FABLADO;
7956 5ELCID1016 PLOGO A MYO %ID, CA GRANDES *** LAS GANAN%IAS.
8547 5ELCID1086 TAN RICOS *** LOS SOS QUE NON SABEN QUE SE AN.
8758 5ELCID1113 ALTER%ER DIA TODOS IUNTADOS ***,
8813 5ELCID1121 FIRME MIENTRE *** ESTOS A ESCARMENTAR.
8983 5ELCID1143 MOROS *** MUCHOS, YA QUIEREN RECONBRAR.
9025 5ELCID1149 GRANDES *** LAS GANAN%IAS QUE MIO %ID FECHAS HA.
9523 5ELCID1211 GRANDES *** LOS GOZOS QUE VAN POR ES LOGAR,
9806 5ELCID1245 LOS QUE EXIERON DE TIERRA DE RITAD *** ABONDADOS,
9818 5ELCID1247 DE QUE *** PAGADOS; EL AMOR DE MY %ID YA LO YUAN PROUANDO.
9839 5ELCID1248 LOS QUE FUERON CON EL, & LOS DE DESPUES, TODOS *** PAGADOS;
9917 5ELCID1258 DELOS QUE *** AQUI & COMIGO GANARON ALGO;
10524 5ELCID1334 GRANDES *** LAS GANAN%IAS QUEL DIO EL CRIADOR,
10551 5ELCID1337 DE SIELLAS & DE FRENOS TODOS GUARNIDOS ***,
11170 5ELCID1413 HYDOS *** LOS CAUALLEROS & DELLO PENSSARAN,
11755 5ELCID1491 PASSAN LAS MONTANAS, QUE *** FIERAS & GRANDES,
12210 5ELCID1550 ENTRADOS *** A MOLINA, BUENA & RICA CASA;
12276 5ELCID1559 APRES *** DE VALEN%IA A TRES LEGUAS CONTADAS.
12599 5ELCID1598 CON DIOS & CON UUSCO BUENAS *** & CRIADAS.
12825 5ELCID1627 ENTRARON SOBRE MAR, EN LAS BARCAS *** METIDOS,
13007 5ELCID1650 POR CASAR *** UUESTRAS FIJAS, ADUZEN UOS AXUUAR.
13067 5ELCID1657 FINCADAS *** LAS TIENDAS & PARE%EN LOS ALUORES,
13149 5ELCID1666 AQUELOS ATAMORES AUOS LOS PONDRAN DELANT & VEREDES QUANLES ***,
13174 5ELCID1670 ALEGRE *** LAS DUENAS, PERDIENDO VAN EL PAUOR.
13202 5ELCID1674 PRESTAS *** LAS MES@ADAS DE LAS YENTES CHRISTIANAS,
13260 5ELCID1682 TORNADOS *** A MYO %ID LOS QUE COMIEN SO PAN;
13498 5ELCID1711 SALIDOS *** TODOS ARMADOS POR LAS TORRES DE VAN%IA,
14112 5ELCID1786 DOS TENDALES LA SUFREN, CON ORO *** LABRADOS;
14161 5ELCID1792 CON AQUESTAS RIQUEZAS TANTAS A VALEN%IA *** ENTRADOS.
14215 5ELCID1799 ALEGRES *** POR VALEN%IA LAS YENTES CHRISTIANAS,
14329 5ELCID1812 POR QUE ASSI LAS ENBIO CONO ELLAS *** PAGADAS,
14398 5ELCID1821 SALIDOS *** DE VALEN%IA EPIENSSAN DE ANDAR,
14408 5ELCID1822 TALLES GANAN%IAS TRAEN QUE *** A AGUARDAR.
14558 5ELCID1841 MYNAYA & PER VERMUEZ ADELANT *** LEGADOS,
14642 5ELCID1852 LAS GANAN%IAS QUE FIZO MUCHO *** SOBEIANAS,

WORD C# PREFIX CONTEXT

SON (CON'T)

14645 5ELCID1853 RICOS *** VENIDOS TODOS LOS SOS VASSALLOS,
15139 5ELCID1914 ESPIDIENSSE AL REY, CON ESTO TORNADOS ***,
15180 5ELCID1921 COMMO *** LAS SALUDES DE ALFONSSO MYO SENOR.
15304 5ELCID1938 ELLOS *** MUCHO VRGULLOSOS & AN PART EN LA CORT,
15567 5ELCID1973 ALAS AGUAS DE TAIO, OLAS UISTAS *** APAREIADAS.
15635 5ELCID1983 NON *** EN CUENTA, SABET, LAS CASTELLANAS.
15691 5ELCID1990 CHICOS & GRANDES VESTIDOS *** DE COLORES.
15747 5ELCID1998 E TODOS LOS OTROS QUE Y ***.
16027 5ELCID2032 ASSI ESTANDO, DEDES ME UUESTRA AMOR, QUE LO OYAN QUANTOS AQUI ***.
16245 5ELCID2060 MARAUILLAN SE DE MYO %ID QUANTOS QUE Y ***.
16322 5ELCID2070 AL SALIR DE LA MISSA TODOS IUNTADOS ***,
16397 5ELCID2079 DELLA & DELLA PARTE, QUANTOS QUE AQUI ***,
16432 5ELCID2083 CA NON HAN GRANT HEDAND E DE DIAS PEQUENAS ***.
16436 5ELCID2084 DE GRANDES NUEUAS *** LOS YFANTES DE CARRION,
16630 5ELCID2106 LOS YERNOS & LAS FIJAS TODOS UUESTROS FIJOS ***:
16667 5ELCID2111 LAS PALABRAS *** PUESTAS QUE OTRO DIA MA@ANA
16683 5ELCID2112 QUANDO SALIE EL SOL, QUES TORNASSE CADA VNO DON SALIDOS ***.
16714 5ELCID2116 TANTAS BUENAS VISTIDURAS QUE DALFAYA ***.
16734 5ELCID2119 TODOS *** PAGADOS DELAS VISTAS QUANTOS QUE Y SON.
16741 5ELCID2119 TODOS SON PAGADOS DELAS VISTAS QUANTOS QUE Y ***.
16773 5ELCID2123 EVAD AQUI UUESTROS FIJOS, QUANDO UUESTROS YERNOS ***;
17048 5ELCID2158 VERIEDES CAUALLEROS, QUE BIEN ANDANTES ***,
17113 5ELCID2166 GRANDES *** LAS YENTES QUE VAN CONEL CANPEADOR.
17203 5ELCID2176 QUANDO A ELLA ASSOMARON, LOS GOZOS *** MAYORES.
17466 5ELCID2209 TODOS SUS CAUALLEROS A PRIESSA *** IUNTADOS.
17526 5ELCID2217 TODOS LOS DE MYO %ID TAN BIEN *** ACORDADOS,
17643 5ELCID2232 DOUOS ESTAS DUE@AS, AMAS *** FIJAS DALGO,
17827 5ELCID2255 EN BESTIAS SINES AL C *** MANDADOS;
17849 5ELCID2258 LOS VASSALLOS DE MIO %ID, ASSI *** ACORDADOS,
17930 5ELCID2269 VENIDOS *** ACASTIELLA AQUESTOS OSPEDADOS,
17941 5ELCID2270 EL %ID & SOS HYERNOS EN VALEN%IA *** RASTADOS.
18333 5ELCID2319 AMOS HERMANOS A PART SALIDOS ***:
18483 5ELCID2339 EN VNA CONPA@A TORNADOS *** AMOS.
18549 5ELCID2347 CA NUNQUA LO VIERAN, CA NUEUOS *** LEGADOS.
18887 5ELCID2390 LOS MOROS *** MUCHOS, DERREDOR LE %ERCAUAN,
19200 5ELCID2428 AQUIS ONDRO MYO %ID & QUANTOS CONEL ***.
19282 5ELCID2441 AMOS *** FIJOS DEL CONDE DON GO%ALO.
19410 5ELCID2459 TODOS ESTOS BIENES DEUOS *** & DE UUESTROS VASSALLOS.
19418 5ELCID2460 EUUESTROS YERNOS AQUI *** ENSAYADOS,
19436 5ELCID2463 QUANDO AGORA *** BUENOS, ADELANT SERAN PRE%IADOS.
19457 5ELCID2465 TODAS LAS GANAN%IAS A VALEN%IA *** LEGADAS;
19517 5ELCID2473 MUCHOS *** ALEGRES MYO %ID & SUS VASSALLOS,
19579 5ELCID2481 COMMO *** ONDRADOS & AVER VOS GRANT PRO.
19587 5ELCID2482 SOBEIANAS *** LAS GANAN%IAS QUETODOS AN GANADAS;
19650 5ELCID2491 TANTOS *** DE MUCHOS QUE NON SERIEN CONTADOS.
19713 5ELCID2499 ALA DENTRO EN MARRUECOS, OLAS MEZQUITAS ***,
19756 5ELCID2505 GRANDES *** LOS GOZOS EN VALEN%IA CON MYO %ID EL CANPEADOR
19776 5ELCID2507 GRANDES *** LOS GOZOS DE SUS YERNOS AMOS ADOS:
19938 5ELCID2529 TANTOS AVEMOS DE AUERES QUE NO *** CONTADOS;
20006 5ELCID2538 AMOS SALIERON A PART, VERA MIENTRE *** HERMANOS;
20027 5ELCID2541 LOS AUERES QUE TENEMOS GRANDES *** & SOBEIANOS,
20055 5ELCID2545 ENSE@AR LAS HEMOS DO LAS HEREDADES ***.
20145 5ELCID2557 CON AQUESTE CONSSEIO AMOS TORNADOS ***,
20176 5ELCID2561 EA MYNAYA ALBARFANEZ & A QUANTOS AQUI ***:
20348 5ELCID2581 A MIS FIJAS SIRUADES, QUE UUESTRAS MUGIERES ***;
20381 5ELCID2586 QUANDO *** PAGADOS ATODO SO SABOR,
20393 5ELCID2588 GRANDES *** LAS NUEUAS POR VALEN%IA LA MAYOR,
20422 5ELCID2591 HYA QUIEREN CAUALGAR, EN ESPIDIMIENTO ***.
20654 5ELCID2621 VERAS LAS HEREDADES QUE A MIS FIJAS DADAS ***;
20811 5ELCID2642 CUEMO LA V@A DELA CARNE ELLOS PARTIDOS ***;
20920 5ELCID2657 ODIZEN EL ANSSARERA ELLOS POSADOS ***.
21208 5ELCID2695 ALLI *** CA@OS DO A ELPHA EN%ERRO;
21222 5ELCID2697 ENTRADOS *** LOS YFANTES AL ROBREDO DE CORPES,
21231 5ELCID2698 LOS MONTES *** ALTOS, LAS RAMAS PUIAN CON LAS NUES,
21342 5ELCID2712 TODOS ERAN YDOS, ELLOS IIIJ SOLOS ***,
21580 5ELCID2743 TANTO LAS MAIARON QUE SIN COSIMENTE ***;
21590 5ELCID2745 CANSSADOS *** DE FERIR ELLOS AMOS ADOS,
21879 5ELCID2784 TANTO *** DE TRASPUESTAS QUE NON PUEDEN DEZIR NADA.
22021 5ELCID2802 MUCHO *** LAZRADAS & AMAS LAS FARTO.
22092 5ELCID2811 ALAS AGUAS DE DUERO ELLOS ARRIBADOS ***,
22152 5ELCID2820 LOS DE SANTESTEUAN, SIEMPRE MESURADOS ***,
22172 5ELCID2823 ALLI SOUIERON ELLAS FATA QUE SA@AS ***.
22429 5ELCID2856 TODOS GELO GRADE%EN & SOS PAGADOS ***,
22443 5ELCID2858 MINAYA VA UER SUS PRIMAS DO ***,
22866 5ELCID2912 MYOS AUERES SE ME AN LEUADO, QUE SOBEIANOS ***;
22918 5ELCID2919 E CON EL ESCUDEROS QUE *** DE CRIAZON.
23465 5ELCID2988 PRENDEN SO CONSSEIO ASSI PARIENTES COMMO ***,
23529 5ELCID2996 PRENDEN CONSSEIO PARIENTES COMMO ***;
23625 5ELCID3009 E DIEGO & FERRANDO Y *** AMOS ADOS,
23651 5ELCID3012 DE TODAS PARTES ALLI IUNTADOS ***.
23845 5ELCID3037 E AL CONDE DON ARRICH & A QUANTOS QUE Y ***;
24099 5ELCID3072 CON ESTOS CUNPLANSSE %IENTO DELOS BUENOS QUE Y ***.
24179 5ELCID3083 ASSI COMMO LO ADICHO, TODOS ADOBADOS ***.
24205 5ELCID3086 SOBRELLAS VNOS %APATOS QUE A GRANT HUEBRA ***;

WORD C# PREFIX CONTEXT

SON (CON'T)

24223 5ELCID3088 CON ORO & CON PLATA TODAS LAS PRESAS ***,
24244 5ELCID3091 OBRADO ES CCN ORO, PARE%EN PORO ***,
24252 5ELCID3092 SOBRESTO VNA PIEL VERMEIA, LAS BANDAS DORO ***,
24321 5ELCID3100 ENEL ABRIEN QUE VER QUANTOS QUE Y ***.
24801 5ELCID3158 DEN ME MIS ESPADAS QUANDO MYOS YERNOS NON ***.
24832 5ELCID3162 CON TODOS SUS PARIENTES & EL VANDO QUE Y ***;
24956 5ELCID3179 LAS MA%ANAS & LOS ARRIAZES TODOS DORO ***.
25182 5ELCID3206 DEN ME MIS AUERES, QUANDO MYOS YERNOS NON ***.
25283 5ELCID3218 NON ACUERDAN EN CONSSEIO, CA LOS HAUERES GRANDES ***:
25325 5ELCID3224 DIXIERON LOS ALCALDES QUANDO MANFESTADOS ***:
25392 5ELCID3233 TORNAR GELOS QUIERO, CA TODOS FECHOS ***,
25717 5ELCID3275 LOS DE CARRION *** DE NATURA TAL,
26251 5ELCID3347 ELLAS *** MUGIERES & VOS SODES VARONES,
26682 5ELCID3407 AFE MIS FIJAS, EN UUESTRAS MANOS ***:
26819 5ELCID3425 METIERON LAS FES, & LOS OMENAIES DADOS ***,
27287 5ELCID3487 ESTOS MIS TRES CAUALLEROS EN UUESTRA MANO ***,
27299 5ELCID3489 ELLOS *** ADOBADOS PORA CUMPLLIR TODO LO SO;
27394 5ELCID3499 AESSOS & ALOS OTROS QUE DE BUENA PARTE ***,
27438 5ELCID3505 QUANDO TODAS ESTAS NUEUAS ASSI PUESTAS ***,
27665 5ELCID3531 ESPIDIOS DE TODOS LOS QUE SOS AMIGOS ***.
27682 5ELCID3533 MAS TRES SEMANAS DE PLAZO TODAS COMPLIDAS ***.
27699 5ELCID3536 ELLOS *** ENPOER DEL REY DON ALFONSSO EL DE LEON;
27730 5ELCID3539 E TODOS SUS PARIENTES CON ELLOS ***;
27829 5ELCID3551 TODOS TRES SE ACUERDAN, CA *** DE VN SE@OR.
27883 5ELCID3557 MUCHO ERAN REPENTIDOS LOS YFANTES POR QUANTO DADAS ***;
27971 5ELCID3569 DELO QUE AUIEN FECHO MUCHO REPISOS ***;
27983 5ELCID3571 TODOS TRES *** ARMADOS LOS DEL CAMPEADOR,
28080 5ELCID3584 LOS ESCUDOS ALOS CUELLOS QUE BIEN BLOCADOS ***;
28109 5ELCID3589 TODOS TRES *** ACORDADOS LOS DEL CAMPEADOR,
28137 5ELCID3592 MUY BIEN ACONPA@ADOS, CA MUCHOS PARIENTES ***.
28249 5ELCID3606 BIEN GELO DEMOSTRARON ATODOS VJ COMMO ***,
28293 5ELCID3611 SALIEN LOS FIELES DE MEDIO, ELLOS CARA POR CARA ***;
28362 5ELCID3621 TODOS TRES POR TRES YA JUNTADOS ***:
28942 5ELCID3697 GRANDES *** LOS PESARES POR TIERRAS DE CARRION.
29053 5ELCID3711 GRANDES *** LOS GOZOS EN VALEN%IA LA MAYOR,
29083 5ELCID3714 GRADO AL REY DEL %IELO, MIS FIJAS VENGADAS ***
29132 5ELCID3720 LOS PRIMEROS FUERON GRANDES, MAS AQUESTOS *** MIIORES;
29155 5ELCID3723 QUANDO SE@ORAS *** SUS FIJAS DE NAUARRA & DE ARAGON.
29169 5ELCID3724 OY LOS REYES DESPA@A SOS PARIENTES ***,
29201 5ELCID3729 ESTAS *** LAS NUEUAS DE MYO %ID EL CANPEADOR,
WORD #3882 OCCURS 187 TIMES.
INDEX OF DIVERSIFICATION = 155.30 WITH STANDARD DEVIATION OF 178.38

SONANDO 9071 5ELCID1154 LAS NUEUAS DE MYO %ID, SABET, ******* VAN,
9082 5ELCID1156 ******* VAN SUS NUEUAS ALENT PARTE DEL MAR.
9485 5ELCID1206 ******* VAN SUS NUEUAS TODAS ATODAS PARTES.
18536 5ELCID2345 EN LA VESTE DELOS MOROS LOS ATAMORES *******;
WORD #3883 OCCURS 4 TIMES.

SONAS 21081 5ELCID2678 TAL COSA UOS FARIA QUE POR EL MUNDO *****,
WORD #3884 OCCURS 1 TIMES.

SONBRERO 21999 5ELCID2799 CON VN ******** QUE TIENE FELEZ MUNOZ,
WORD #3885 OCCURS 1 TIMES.

SONRISAR 2358 5ELCID0298 TORNOS A ********; LEGAN LE TODOS, LA MANOL BAN BESAR.
WORD #3886 OCCURS 1 TIMES.

SONRRISANDO 11973 5ELCID1518 *********** SE DELA BOCA, HYUALO ABRA%AR,
18423 5ELCID2331 MYO %ID DON RODRIGO *********** SALIO:
19292 5ELCID2442 ALEGROS MYO %ID FERMOSO ***********:
19963 5ELCID2532 VASSALLOS DE MYO %ID SEYEN SE ***********:
WORD #3887 OCCURS 4 TIMES.

SONRRISAR 22674 5ELCID2889 BESANDO LAS AAMAS, TORNOS DE *********:
WORD #3888 OCCURS 1 TIMES.

SONRRISAUA 6834 5ELCID0873 VIOLOS EL REY, FERMOSO **********:
7204 5ELCID0923 EL CAMPEADOR FERMOSO **********:
WORD #3889 OCCURS 2 TIMES.

SONRRISOS 1194 5ELCID0154 ********* MYO %ID, ESTAUALOS FABLANDO:
7373 5ELCID0946 ********* EL CABOSO, QUE NON LO PUDO ENDURAR:
10801 5ELCID1368 ********* EL REY, TAN VELIDO FABLO:
15159 5ELCID1918 ********* MYO %ID & BIEN LOS ABRA%O:
25002 5ELCID3184 ALEGROS LE TODEL CUERPO, ********* DE CORA%ON,
WORD #3890 OCCURS 5 TIMES.
INDEX OF DIVERSIFICATION = 5951.00 WITH STANDARD DEVIATION OF 2834.48

SO@ADO 3272 5ELCID0412 MUCHO ERA PAGADO DEL SUE@O QUE A ******.
WORD #3891 OCCURS 1 TIMES.

SOPE 17408 5ELCID2202 QUE YO NULLA COSA NOL **** DEZIR DE NO.
WORD #3892 OCCURS 1 TIMES.

```
WORD                 C#  PREFIX                                   CONTEXT

SOPIENSSEN          11916 5ELCID1511 QUE ********** LES OTROS DE QUE SESO ERA ALBARFANEZ
          WORD #3893 OCCURS   1 TIMES.

SOPIEREDES           6528 5ELCID0833 SI NON, DO ********** QUE SOMOS, YNDOS CONSEGUIR.
          WORD #3894 OCCURS   1 TIMES.

SOPIERON             1904 5ELCID0242 LAMAUAN ALA PUERTA, Y ******** EL MANDADO;
          WORD #3895 OCCURS   1 TIMES.

SOPIESSE              203 5ELCID0026 E A QUEL QUE GELA DIESSE ******** UERA PALABRA,
                     5389 5ELCID0680 QUE NON ******** NINGUNC ESTA SU PORIDAD.
                    11792 5ELCID1495 ENVIO DOS CAUALLEROS MYNAYA ALBARFANEZ QUE ******** LA VERDAD;
                    23693 5ELCID3018 BIEN LO ******** QUE Y SERIE ESSA NOCH.
          WORD #3896 OCCURS   4 TIMES.

SOPIESSEN            4422 5ELCID0563 QUE ********* QUE MYO %ID ALLI AUIE FINCAN%A.
                    17154 5ELCID2171 QUE ********* SOS MA@AS DE LOS YFANTES DE CARRION.
          WORD #3897 OCCURS   2 TIMES.

SOPO                 2338 5ELCID0295 QUANDO LO **** MYO %ID EL DE BIUAR,
                    11479 5ELCID1454 AL ORA QUE LO **** MYO %ID EL DE BIUAR,
                    11657 5ELCID1477 EL MORO AUEGALUON, QUANDO **** EL MENSSAIE,
                    15150 5ELCID1916 QUANDO LO **** EL BUEN CAMPEADOR,
                    20855 5ELCID2648 EL MORO QUANDO LO ****, PLOGOL DE CORA%ON;
          WORD #3898 OCCURS   5 TIMES.
             INDEX OF DIVERSIFICATION =  4628.25 WITH STANDARD DEVIATION OF  3769.08

SOPOLO               9310 5ELCID1184 ****** MYO %ID, DE CORA%ON LE PLAZ;
          WORD #3899 OCCURS   1 TIMES.

SORRISOS            12043 5ELCID1527 ******** DELA BOCA MINAYA ALBARFANEZ:
          WORD #3900 OCCURS   1 TIMES.

SORTEAUAN           28275 5ELCID3610 ********* LES EL CAMPO, YA LES PARTIEN EL SOL,
          WORD #3901 OCCURS   1 TIMES.

SOS                     2 5ELCID0001 DELOS *** OIOS TAN FUERTE MIENTRE LORANDO,
                      748 5ELCID0094 VEALO EL CRIADOR CON TODOS LOS *** SANTOS,
                     2820 5ELCID0356 ABRIO *** OIOS, CATO ATODAS PARTES,
                     2987 5ELCID0376 MYO %ID CON LOS *** VASSALLOS PENSSO DE CAUALGAR,
                     3747 5ELCID0474 *** CAUALLEROS LEGAN CON LA GANAN%IA,
                     4018 5ELCID0511 *** QUI@ONEROS QUE GELOS DIESSEN POR CARTA.
                     4025 5ELCID0512 *** CAUALLEROS YAN ARRIBAN%A,
                     4405 5ELCID0561 A TODOS *** VARONES MANDO FAZER VNA CARCAUA,
                     4645 5ELCID0589 COIOS SALON AYUSO, CON LOS *** ABUELTA NADI.
                     4807 5ELCID0609 LUEGO LEGAUAN LOS ***, CA FECHA ES EL ARRANCADA.
                     4859 5ELCID0614 GRADO A DIOS DEL %IELO & ATODOS LOS *** SANTOS,
                     5268 5ELCID0666 MYO %ID CON LOS *** TORNOS A ACORDAR:
                     5568 5ELCID0701 PORA MYO %ID & ALOS *** A MANOS LOS TOMAR.
                     5778 5ELCID0730 TANOS BUENOS CAUALLOS SIN *** DUENOS ANDAR.
                     6210 5ELCID0791 VIO LOS *** COMMOS VAN ALEGANDO:
                     6267 5ELCID0798 MAS DE QUINZE DE LOS *** MENOS NON FALLARON.
                     6310 5ELCID0803 GRANT A EL GOZO MYO %ID CON TODOS *** VASSALOS.
                     6496 5ELCID0828 MYO %ID RUY DIAZ CON LOS *** SE ACORDAUA:
                     6655 5ELCID0849 EN TODOS LOS *** NON FALLARIEDES VN MESQUINO.
                     7859 5ELCID1005 ESTO FAZEN LOS *** DE VOLUNTAD & DE GRADO;
                     7947 5ELCID1015 DE TODAS PARTES LOS *** SE AIUNTARON;
                     8549 5ELCID1086 TAN RICOS SON LOS *** QUE NON SABEN QUE SE AN.
                     9871 5ELCID1252 QUE NINGUN OMNE DELOS *** QUES LE NON SPIDIES, ONOL BESAS
                                     LA MANO,
                    10398 5ELCID1318 FINCO *** YNOIOS ANTE TODEL PUEBLO,
                    12258 5ELCID1557 LOS *** DESPENDIE EL MORO, QUE DELO SO NON TOMAUA NADA.
                    12616 5ELCID1600 DEL GOZO QUE AUIEN DE LOS *** OIOS LORAUAN.
                    13509 5ELCID1712 MIO %ID ALOS *** VASSALOS TAN BIEN LOS ACORDANDO.
                    13725 5ELCID1739 ALEGRE ERA MYO %ID & TODOS *** VASSALLOS,
                    13816 5ELCID1750 ESTO DIOS SE LO QUISO CON TODOS LOS *** SANTOS,
                    14147 5ELCID1791 QUE CROUIESSE *** NUEUAS DE MYO %ID QUE AUIE ALGO.
                    14485 5ELCID1832 MANDO CAUALGAR APRIESSA TOSDOS *** FIJOS DALGO,
                    14649 5ELCID1853 RICOS SON VENIDOS TODOS LOS *** VASSALLOS,
                    15147 5ELCID1915 VAN PORA VALEN%IA ELLOS & TODOS LOS ***.
                    15908 5ELCID2017 ATODOS LOS *** ESTAR LOS MANDO,
                    16265 5ELCID2063 EL CAMPEADOR ALOS *** LO MANDO
                    16978 5ELCID2149 PLEGA AL CRIADOR CON TODOS LOS *** SANTOS, ESTE PLAZER
                    17155 5ELCID2171 QUE SOPIESSEN *** MA@AS DE LOS YFANTES DE CARRION.
                    17855 5ELCID2259 CADA VNO POR SI *** DONES AUIEN DADOS.
                    17937 5ELCID2270 EL %ID & *** HYERNOS EN VALEN%IA SON RASTADOS.
                    18000 5ELCID2277 EL CRIADOR UOS VALLA CON TODOS LOS *** SANTOS.
                    18210 5ELCID2304 MYO %ID POR *** YERNOS DEMANDO & NOLOS FALLO;
                    18500 5ELCID2341 PLOGO A MYO %ID & ATODOS *** VASSALLOS;
                    19269 5ELCID2439 AL%O *** OIOS, ESTEUA ADELANT CATANDO,
                    19327 5ELCID2447 COMMO YO FIO POR DIOS & EN TODOS LOS *** SANTOS,
                    19378 5ELCID2455 DE TODAS PARTES *** VASSALLOS VAN LEGANDO;
                    21558 5ELCID2740 YA LO SIENTEN ELLAS EN LOS *** CORA%ONES.
                    22427 5ELCID2856 TODOS GELO GRADE%EN & *** PAGADOS SON,
```

WORD C# PREFIX CONTEXT

SOS (CON'T)

```
                  22751 5ELCID2899 FABLCS CCN LCS *** EN SU PORICAD,
                  23729 5ELCID3022 BIEN AGUISADO VIENE EL %ID CON TODOS LOS ***,
                  24356 5ELCID3105 CUERDA MIENTRA ENTRA MYC %IC CCN TOCOS LOS ***:
                  24514 5ELCID3125 EN *** AGUISAMIENTOS BIEN SEMEIA VARON.
                  25523 5ELCID3251 *** CMNES LAS TIENEN & CELLAS PENSSARAN.
                  27663 5ELCID3531 ESPIDIOS DE TCDCS LCS QUE *** AMIGOS SON.
                  29167 5ELCID3724 OY LOS REYES CESPA@A *** PARIENTES SON,
         WORD #3902 OCCURS  54 TIMES.
            INDEX OF DIVERSIFICATION =   549.28 WITH STANCARD DEVIATION OF   561.02

SOSANAUA           7989 5ELCID1020 EL NON LO QUIERE CCMER, ATOCOS LOS ********:
         WORD #3903 OCCURS   1 TIMES.

SOSPECHA            982 5ELCID0126 NON DUERME SIN ******** QUI AUER TRAE MONEDADO.
         WORD #3904 OCCURS   1 TIMES.

SOSPIRA            2202 5ELCID0277 LORA DELOS CIOS, TAN FUERTE MIENTRE *******:
         WORD #3905 OCCURS   1 TIMES.

SOSPIRANDO        10208 5ELCID1293 ********** EL CBISPO QUES VIESSE CON MOROS ENEL CAMPO:
         WORD #3906 OCCURS   1 TIMES.

SOSPIRO              36 5ELCID0006 ******* MYO %ID, CA MUCHO AUIE GRANDES CUYDADOS.
         WORD #3907 OCCURS   1 TIMES.

SOSPIROS          26331 5ELCID3358 MIENTRA QUE BIUAN PUECEN AUER ********:
         WORD #3908 OCCURS   1 TIMES.

SOUIERON          22167 5ELCID2823 ALLI ******** ELLAS FATA QUE SA@AS SON.
         WORD #3909 OCCURS   1 TIMES.

SOUIESSE          14121 5ELCID1787 MANDO MYO %ID RUY DIAZ QUE FITA ******** LA TIENDA,
         WORD #3910 OCCURS   1 TIMES.

SOUO               7091 5ELCID0907 ALI **** MIO %ID CONPLICAS XV SEMANAS;
         WORD #3911 OCCURS   1 TIMES.

SPERANDO          17699 5ELCID2239 ALA PUERTA DELA ECLEGIA SECIELLOS ********;
         WORD #3912 OCCURS   1 TIMES.

SPERAR            11512 5ELCID1457 QUI BUEN MANCADERO ENBIA, TAL DEUE ******.
         WORD #3913 OCCURS   1 TIMES.

SPERARE            9390 5ELCID1194 TRES DIAS LE ******* EN CANAL DE %ELFA.
         WORD #3914 OCCURS   1 TIMES.

SPERO             11686 5ELCID1481 FABLO MU@O GUSTIOZ, NON ***** A NADI:
         WORD #3915 OCCURS   1 TIMES.

SPIDIES            9875 5ELCID1252 QUE NINGUN CMNE DELOS SCS QUES LE NON *******, ONOL BESAS
                                   LA MANO,
         WORD #3916 OCCURS   1 TIMES.

SPIDIOS            1773 5ELCID0226 ******* EL CABOSO DE CUER & DE VELUNTAD.
                  10325 5ELCID1307 ALEGRE FUE MINAYA & ******* & VINOS.
         WORD #3917 OCCURS   2 TIMES.

SPINAZ             3127 5ELCID0393 VINO MYO %ID IAZER A ****** DE CAN.
         WORD #3918 OCCURS   1 TIMES.

SPIRITAL           2378 5ELCID0300 YO RUEGO ADICS & AL PADRE ********,
                   2717 5ELCID0343 POR TIERRA ANCIDISTE XXXIJ A@CS, SE@OR ********,
                   2959 5ELCID0372 ADIOS UOS ACOMIENDO, FIJAS, & A LA MUGIER & AL PADRE ********;
                   8680 5ELCID1102 VIOLO MYO %ID, TCMOS AMARAUILLAR: GRACO ATI, PADRE ********
                  13019 5ELCID1651 AUOS GRADO, %ID, & AL PADRE ********.
         WORD #3919 OCCURS   5 TIMES.
            INDEX OF DIVERSIFICATION =  2659.25 WITH STANCARD DEVIATION OF  2794.19

SSE               14433 5ELCID1825 POR EL REY DON ALFCNSSO TCMAN *** APREGUNTAR.
         WORD #3920 OCCURS   1 TIMES.

SSEA               1030 5ELCID0132 MYO %ID QUERRA LO QUE **** AGUISACO;
         WORD #3921 OCCURS   1 TIMES.

SSI               25197 5ELCID3208 DJZE EL CONDE DON REMCNC: CEZIC DE *** O DE NO.
         WORD #3922 OCCURS   1 TIMES.

SSU               24021 5ELCID3062 E *** CFRENCA HAN FECHA MUY BUENA & CONPLIDA.
         WORD #3923 OCCURS   1 TIMES.

SU                  113 5ELCID0016 EN ** CONPA@A LX PENDONES; EXIEN LO UER MUGIERES & UARONES,
                    177 5ELCID0023 ANTES DELA NOCHE EN BURGCS CEL ENTRO ** CARTA,
                    339 5ELCID0042 EL REY LO HA UECADC, ANCCH DEL ETRO ** CARTA,
                    395 5ELCID0049 ESTO LA NI@A DIXO & TCRNOS PORA ** CASA.
                   1681 5ELCID0216 AL%O ** MANC DIESTRA, LA CARA SE SANTIGUA:
```

WORD C# PREFIX CONTEXT

SU (CON'T)

```
2180 5ELCID0274 ENCLINO LAS MANOS EN LA ** BARBA VELIDA,
2453 5ELCID0309 QUE, SI DESPUES DEL PLAZO EN ** TIERRAL PUDIES TOMAR,
2579 5ELCID0326 MYO %ID & ** MUGIER A LA EGLESIA UAN.
3852 5ELCID0487 SALIOLOS RE%EBIR CON ESTA ** MESNADA,
4070 5ELCID0517 NIN CATIUOS NIN CATIUAS NON QUISO TRAER EN ** CONPA@A.
4121 5ELCID0524 ASMO MYO %ID CON TODA ** CONPA@A
4154 5ELCID0528 BUSCAR NOS YE EL REY ALFONSSO CON TODA ** MESNADA.
4454 5ELCID0567 EN LA ** VEZINDAD NON SE TREUEN GANAR TANTO.
4540 5ELCID0577 COIO SALON AYUSO LA ** SE@A AL%ADA,
4686 5ELCID0594 ELBUEN CAMPEADOR LA ** CARA TORNAUA,
5392 5ELCID0680 QUE NON SOPIESSE NINGUNO ESTA ** PORIDAD.
6322 5ELCID0805 EN LA ** QUINTA AL %ID CAEN C CAUALLOS.
6559 5ELCID0837 E EL CAMPEADOR CON ** MESNADA.
6713 5ELCID0857 AL%O ** SE@A, EL CAMPEADOR SE UA,
6801 5ELCID0869 EN ** MANO TENIE A %ELFA LA DE CANAL.
6816 5ELCID0870 MYO %ID RUY DIAZ DE DIOS AYA ** GRA%IA
6866 5ELCID0877 SOBEIANA ES, SE@OR, LA ** GANA%IA.
7267 5ELCID0932 E QUEL DIXO SALUDES DE ** MUGIER & DE SUS FIJAS
7920 5ELCID1011 Y BEN%IO ESTA BATALLA PORO ONDRO ** BARBA,
7927 5ELCID1012 PRISO LO AL CONDE, PORA ** TIERRA LO LEUAUA;
8834 5ELCID1124 HYREMOS VER AQUELA ** ALMOFALLA,
9600 5ELCID1220 QUANDO ** SE@A CABDAL SEDIE EN SOMO DEL ALCA%AR.
9749 5ELCID1239 DIXO MYO %ID DE LA ** BOCA ATANTO:
10079 5ELCID1276 POR MI MUGIER & MIS FIJAS, SI FUERE ** MER%ED,
10509 5ELCID1332 OBISPO FIZO DE ** MANO EL BUEN CAMPEADOR,
10632 5ELCID1347 QUANDO ASSI FAZE A ** GUISA EL %ID CAMPEADOR
10670 5ELCID1352 POR ** MUGIER DO@A XIMENA & SUS FIJAS AMAS ADOS:
11059 5ELCID1400 EL REY POR ** MER%ED SUELTAS ME UOS HA,
11119 5ELCID1408 QUE ** MUGIER & SUS FIJAS EL REY SUELTAS ME LAS HA,
11152 5ELCID1411 SEREMOS YO & ** MUGIER & SUS FIJAS QUE EL A
11501 5ELCID1456 DE LA ** BOCA CONPE%O DE FABLAR:
11702 5ELCID1484 ** MUGIER & SUS FIJAS EN MEDINA ESTAN;
11986 5ELCID1519 ENEL OMBRO LO SALUDA, CA TAL ES ** HUSAIE:
12015 5ELCID1523 ONDRAR UOS HEMOS TODOS, CA TALES LA ** AUZE,
12368 5ELCID1570 MANDO MYO %ID ALOS QUE HA EN ** CASA
12426 5ELCID1577 DELANTE ** MUGIER & DE SUS FIJAS QUERIE TENER LAS ARMAS.
12553 5ELCID1593 ADELINO A ** MUGIER & A SUS FIJAS AMAS;
12961 5ELCID1644 ** MUGIER & SUS FIJAS SUBIOLAS AL ALCA%AR,
13093 5ELCID1660 MIEDO A ** MUGIER & QUIEREL QUEBRAR EL CORA%ON,
13679 5ELCID1733 TODA ESTA GANAN%IA EN ** MANO A RASTADO.
14208 5ELCID1798 DE TODA LA ** QUINTA EL DIEZMO LA MANDADO.
14366 5ELCID1817 E DOZIENTOS OMNES LIEUAN EN ** CONPA@A,
14472 5ELCID1830 MYO %ID EL DE VALEN%IA ENBIA ** PRESENTAIA.
14719 5ELCID1861  MARAUILLA ES DEL %ID, QUE ** ONDRA CRE%E TANTO
14875 5ELCID1880 FABLANDO EN ** CONSSEIO, AUIENDO SU PORIDAD:
14878 5ELCID1880 FABLANDO EN SU CONSSEIO, AUIENDO ** PORIDAD:
15204 5ELCID1924 ES PAGADO, & DAUOS ** AMOR.
15291 5ELCID1936 ADIOS LO GRADESCO QUE DEL REY HE ** GRA%IA,
15366 5ELCID1945 QUERER UOS YE VER & DAR UOS ** AMOR,
15793 5ELCID2003 DENTRO ES ** MUGIER & SUS FIJAS AMAS ADOS,
15803 5ELCID2004 EN QUE TIENE ** ALMA & SU CORA%ON,
15806 5ELCID2004 EN QUE TIENE SU ALMA & ** CORA%ON,
17668 5ELCID2235 A MYO %ID & A ** MUGIER VAN BESAR LA MANO.
18560 5ELCID2349 POR LA ** VOLUNTAD NON SERIEN ALLI LEGADOS.
18845 5ELCID2385 POR LA ** VENTURA & DIOS QUEL AMAUA
19623 5ELCID2487 ELA ** QUINTA NON FUESSE OLBIDADO.
20547 5ELCID2608 AMOS LAS BENDIXIERON & DIERON LES ** GRA%IA.
21334 5ELCID2711 DEPORTAR SE QUIEREN CON ELLAS ATODO ** SABOR.
21749 5ELCID2766 MANDARON LE YR ADELANTE, MAS DE ** GRADO NON FUE.
22211 5ELCID2829 AL%O LA ** MANO, ALA BARBA SE TOMO;
22261 5ELCID2835 PESO A MYO %ID & ATODA ** CORT, & ALBARFANEZ DALMA & DE CORA%ON.
22311 5ELCID2841 NON LO DETARDAN EL MANDADO DE ** SE@OR,
22737 5ELCID2897 GRAND GOZO FIZO CON ELLAS DO@A XIMENA ** MADRE.
22753 5ELCID2899 FABLOS CON LOS SOS EN ** PORIDAD,
22801 5ELCID2905 CUEMO YO SO ** VASSALLO, & EL ES MYO SE@OR,
23217 5ELCID2957 FIZ LO POR BIEN, QUE FFUESSE A ** PRO.
23415 5ELCID2982 QUI NON VINIESSE ALA CORT NON SE TOUIESSE POR ** VASSALLO.
23595 5ELCID3005 FUERON Y DE ** REYNO OTROS MUCHOS SABIDORES,
25828 5ELCID3289 NON YOUO RAPAZ QUE NON MESSO ** PULGADA;
27083 5ELCID3460 E QUI AL QUISIESSE SERIE ** OCASION.
28025 5ELCID3577 AQUI TIENEN ** VANDO LOS YFANTES DE CARRION,
29109 5ELCID3718 OUIERON ** AIUNTA CON ALFONSSO EL DE LEON,
WORD #3924 OCCURS 77 TIMES.
   INDEX OF DIVERSIFICATION =   380.53 WITH STANDARD DEVIATION OF   434.77

SUBIE       12694 5ELCID1611 ALA LAS ***** ENEL MAS ALTO LOGAR;
WORD #3925 OCCURS 1 TIMES.

SUBIOLAS    12966 5ELCID1644 SU MUGIER & SUS FIJAS ******** AL ALCA%AR,
WORD #3926 OCCURS 1 TIMES.

SUDIENTO    13832 5ELCID1752  VEDES EL ESPADA SANGRIENTA & ******** EL CAUALLO:
WORD #3927 OCCURS 1 TIMES.
```

WORD C# PREFIX CONTEXT

SUELE 26492 5ELCID3380 E PRENDER MAÇUILAS, CCMMO LO ***** FAR
WORD #3928 OCCURS 1 TIMES.

SUELO 17437 5ELCID2206 POR EL ***** & SUSO TAN BIEN ENCORTINADO,
WORD #3929 OCCURS 1 TIMES.

SUELTA 3908 5ELCID0496 YO UOS LA ****** & AUELLO QUITADO.
24011 5ELCID3061 ****** FUE LA MISSA ANTES QUE SALIESSE EL SOL,
WORD #3930 OCCURS 2 TIMES.

SUELTAN 71 5ELCID0010 ALLI PIENSSAN DE AGUIJAR, ALLI ******* LAS RIENDAS.
1781 5ELCID0227 ******* LAS RIENDAS & PIENSSAN DE AGUIJAR.
15641 5ELCID1984 ******* LAS RIENDAS, ALAS VISTAS SEUAN A DELI@ADAS.
WORD #3931 OCCURS 3 TIMES.

SUELTAS 11061 5ELCID1400 EL REY POR SU MER%ED ******* ME UOS HA,
11126 5ELCID1408 QUE SU MUGIER & SUS FIJAS EL REY ******* ME LAS HA,
WORD #3932 OCCURS 2 TIMES.

SUELTO 6981 5ELCID0893 ****** LES LOS CUERPOS & QUITO LES LAS HEREDADES.
10768 5ELCID1363 POR QUE LOS DESEREDE, TODO GELO ****** YO;
WORD #3933 OCCURS 2 TIMES.

SUENOL 3214 5ELCID0405 VN ****** PRISO DUL%E, TAN BIEN SE ADURMJO.
WORD #3934 OCCURS 1 TIMES.

SUE@O 3228 5ELCID0406 EL ANGEL GABRIEL A EL VINO EN *****:
3269 5ELCID0412 MUCHO ERA PAGADO DEL ***** QUE A SO@ADO.
WORD #3935 OCCURS 2 TIMES.

SUFREN 14109 5ELCID1786 DOS TENDALES LA ******, CON ORO SON LABRADOS;
WORD #3936 OCCURS 1 TIMES.

SUFRIR 24103 5ELCID3073 VELMEZES VESTIDOS POR ****** LAS GUARNIZONES,
WORD #3937 OCCURS 1 TIMES.

SULTURA 13436 5ELCID1703 LA MISSA DICHA, GRANT ******* LES DAUA:
WORD #3938 OCCURS 1 TIMES.

SUS 138 5ELCID0019 DELAS *** BOCAS TODOS DIZIAN UNA RAZON:
385 5ELCID0048 MAS EL CRIADOR UOS UALA CON TODAS *** UERTUDES SANTAS.
791 5ELCID0101 EN CUENTA DE *** AUERES, DELOS QUE AUIEN GANADOS.
1667 5ELCID0214 MYO %ID & *** CONPA@AS CAUALGAN TAN AYNA.
2081 5ELCID0262 AFEUOS DO@A XIMENA CON *** FIJAS DO UA LEGANDO;
2184 5ELCID0275 ALAS *** FIJAS ENBRA%O LAS PRENDIA,
3059 5ELCID0385 E A TODAS *** DUENAS QUE CON ELLAS ESTAN;
3306 5ELCID0417 MANDO UER *** YENTES MYO %ID EL CAMPEADOR:
3645 5ELCID0460 POR VER *** LAUORES & TODAS SUS HEREDADES.
3649 5ELCID0460 POR VER SUS LAUORES & TODAS *** HEREDADES.
4004 5ELCID0508 AL REY ALFONSSO QUE LEGARIEN *** COMPA@AS,
4011 5ELCID0509 QUEL BUSCARIE MAL CON TODAS *** MESNADAS.
4467 5ELCID0568 AGARDANDO SEUA MYO %ID CON TODOS *** VASSALLOS;
4914 5ELCID0622 POSAREMOS EN *** CASAS & DELLOS NOS SERUIREMOS.
6335 5ELCID0806 DIOS, QUE BIEN PAGO A TODOS *** VASSALLOS,
6640 5ELCID0847 QUE BIEN PAGO A *** VASSALOS MISMOS
7079 5ELCID0905 ASARAGO%A *** NUEUAS LEGAUAN,
7107 5ELCID0909 CON TODAS *** YENTES FIZO VNA TRASNOCHADA;
7209 5ELCID0924 GRADO ADIOS & ALAS *** VERTUDES SANTAS;
7243 5ELCID0929 E DE *** COMPA@AS, AQUELAS QUE AUIEN DEXADAS
7271 5ELCID0932 E QUEL DIXO SALUDES DE SU MUGIER & DE *** FIJAS
8521 5ELCID1083 JUNTOS CON *** MESNADAS, CONPE%OLAS DE LEGAR
8682 5ELCID1103 EN *** TIERRAS SOMOS & FEMOS LES TODOMAL,
9084 5ELCID1156 SONANDO VAN *** NUEUAS ALENT PARTE DEL MAR.
9096 5ELCID1157 ALEGRE ERA EL %ID & TODAS *** COMPA@AS,
9107 5ELCID1159 DAUAN *** CORREDORES & FAZIEN LAS TRASNOCHADAS,
9345 5ELCID1188 A TIERRAS DE CASTIELLA ENBIO *** MENSSAIES:
9487 5ELCID1206 SONANDO VAN *** NUEUAS TODAS ATODAS PARTES.
9614 5ELCID1221 YA FOLGAUA MYO %ID CON TODAS *** CONPA@AS;
10098 5ELCID1279 LA MUGIER DE MYO %ID & *** FIJAS LAS YFFANTES
10224 5ELCID1294 QUE SIS FARTAS LIDIANDO & FIRIENDO CON *** MANOS,
10675 5ELCID1352 POR SU MUGIER DO@A XIMENA & *** FIJAS AMAS ADOS:
10772 5ELCID1364 SIRUAN LE *** HEREDADES DO FUERE EL CAMPEADOR,
10852 5ELCID1374 BIEN CASARIEMOS CON *** FIJAS PORA HUEBOS DE PRO.
11122 5ELCID1408 QUE SU MUGIER & *** FIJAS EL REY SUELTAS ME LAS HA,
11134 5ELCID1409 MIENTRA QUE FUEREMOS POR *** TIERRAS CONDUCHO NOS MANDO DAR.
11155 5ELCID1411 SEREMOS YO & SU MUGIER & *** FIJAS QUE EL A
11257 5ELCID1424 MINAYA A DO@A XIMINA & A *** FIJAS QUE HA,
11705 5ELCID1484 SU MUGIER & *** FIJAS EN MEDINA ESTAN;
11850 5ELCID1502 E EL ALCAYAZ AUEGALUON CON *** FUER%AS QUE TRAHE,
12199 5ELCID1548 E BUEN CAUALLO EN DIESTRO QUE UA ANTE *** ARMAS.
12430 5ELCID1577 DELANTE SU MUGIER & DE *** FIJAS QUERIE TENER LAS ARMAS.
12557 5ELCID1593 ADELINO A SU MUGIER & A *** FIJAS AMAS;
12621 5ELCID1601 TODAS LAS *** MESNADAS EN GRANT DELENT ESTAUAN,
12743 5ELCID1618 MYO %ID & *** COMPANAS TAN AGRAND SABOR ESTAN.

WORD C# PREFIX CONTEXT

SUS (CON'T)

12808 5ELCID1625 AQUEL REY DE MARRUECCS AIUNTAUA *** VIRTOS;
12964 5ELCID1644 SU MUGIER & *** FIJAS SUBIOLAS AL ALCA%AR,
13106 5ELCID1661 ASSI FFAZIE ALAS DUE@AS & A *** FIJAS AMAS ADOS:
13649 5ELCID1729 CCN OTRCS QUEL CONSIGEN DE *** BUENOS VASSALLOS.
14093 5ELCID1784 QUE A GANADO MYO %ID CON TODOS *** VASSALLOS
14177 5ELCID1794 QUANDO ES FARTO DE LICIAR CON AMAS LAS *** MANOS,
14235 5ELCID1801 ALEGRE ES DO@A XIMENA & *** FIJAS AMAS,
14708 5ELCID1860 CON X DE *** PARIENTES A PARTE CAUAN SALTO:
14888 5ELCID1882 DEMANDEMOS *** FIJAS PORA CON ELLAS CASAR;
15047 5ELCID1902 SABOR HAN DE CASAR CON *** FIJAS AMAS ADOS.
15226 5ELCID1928 DE DAR *** FIJAS ALOS YFANTES DE CARRION,
15796 5ELCID2003 DENTRO ES SU MUGIER & *** FIJAS AMAS ADOS,
16608 5ELCID2104 QUE METAN EN *** BODAS ODO QUISIEREDES UOS;
17256 5ELCID2182 TODOS ESSA NOCH FUERON A *** POSADAS,
17269 5ELCID2184 RE%IBIOLO DO@A XIMENA & *** FIJAS AMAS:
17414 5ELCID2203 METIUOS EN *** MANOS, FIJAS, AMAS ADOS;
17462 5ELCID2209 TODOS *** CAUALLEROS A PRIESSA SON IUNTADOS.
17503 5ELCID2214 RE%IBIO LOS MYO %ID CON TODOS *** VASALLOS;
17728 5ELCID2243 DIOS, QUE BIEN TOUIERON ARMAS EL %ID & *** VASSALOS
17907 5ELCID2265 POR PAGADOS SE PARTEN DE MYO %ID & DE *** VASSALLOS.
17965 5ELCID2273 ALEGRE ERA EL %ID & TODOS *** VASSALLOS.
18009 5ELCID2278 EN VALEN%IA SEY MYO %ID CON TODOS *** VASSALLOS,
18014 5ELCID2279 CON EL AMOS *** YERNOS LOS YFANTES DE CARRION.
18127 5ELCID2293 VIO CER%ADO EL ESCA@O DE *** BUENOS VARONES:
18297 5ELCID2315 ALEGRAUAS EL %ID & TODOS *** VARONES,
19465 5ELCID2466 ALEGRE ES MYO %ID CON TODAS *** CONPA@AS,
19496 5ELCID2470 CUYDARON QUE EN *** DIAS NUNCUA SERIEN MINGUADOS.
19522 5ELCID2473 MUCHOS SON ALEGRES MYO %ID & *** VASSALLOS,
19768 5ELCID2506 DE TODAS *** CONPA@AS & DE TODOS SUS VASSALLOS;
19773 5ELCID2506 DE TODAS SUS CONPA@AS & DE TODOS *** VASSALLOS;
19780 5ELCID2507 GRANDES SON LOS GOZOS DE *** YERNOS AMOS ADOS:
20410 5ELCID2590 POR QUE ESCURREN *** FIJAS DEL CAMPEADOR ATIERRAS DE CARRION.
20576 5ELCID2612 ESPIENDOS DELAS DUE@AS & DE TODAS *** COMPA@AS.
20592 5ELCID2614 ALEGRE VA MYO %ID CON TODAS *** COMPA@AS.
20899 5ELCID2654 ALAS FIJAS DEL %ID EL MORO *** DO@AS DIO,
21084 5ELCID2679 ELUEGO LEUARIA *** FIJAS AL CAMPEADOR LEAL;
21269 5ELCID2703 CON *** MUGIERES EN BRA%OS DEMUESTRAN LES AMOR;
21321 5ELCID2710 SI NON AMAS *** MUGIERES DO@A ELUIRA & DO@A SOL:
21779 5ELCID2770 FASTA QUE VIESSE VENIR *** PRIMAS AMAS ADOS
21827 5ELCID2777 FALLO *** PRIMAS AMORTE%IDAS AMAS ADOS.
22344 5ELCID2846 QUE VINIE MYNAYA POR *** PRIMAS AMAS ADOS.
22360 5ELCID2848 RE%IBEN AMINAYA & ATODOS *** VARONES,
22440 5ELCID2858 MINAYA VA UER *** PRIMAS DO SON,
23069 5ELCID2939 CASASTES *** FIJAS CON YFANTES DE CARRION,
23100 5ELCID2943 MAL MAIARON *** FIJAS DEL %ID CAMPEADOR;
23127 5ELCID2947 AFELAS *** FIJAS EN VALENCIA DOSON.
23204 5ELCID2956 CA YO CASE *** FIJAS CON YFANTES DE CARRION;
23312 5ELCID2969 QUE DESTAS VIJ SEMANAS ADOBES CON *** VASSALLOS,
23369 5ELCID2977 ENBIA *** CARTAS PORA LEON & A SANTI YAGUO,
23419 5ELCID2983 POR TODAS *** TIERRAS ASSI LO YUAN PENSSANDO,
24195 5ELCID3085 CAL%AS DE BUEN PA@O EN *** CAMAS METIO,
24825 5ELCID3162 CON TODOS *** PARIENTES & EL VANDO QUE Y SON;
24867 5ELCID3167 DEMOS LE *** ESPADAS, QUANDO ASSI FINCA LA BOZ,
25209 5ELCID3210 POR ESSOL DIEMOS *** ESPADAS AL%ID CAMPEADOR,
25636 5ELCID3264 POR QUE LAS SACAUADES DE VALEN%IA *** HONORES?
25725 5ELCID3276 NON GELAS DEUIEN QUERER *** FIJAS POR VARRAGANAS,
26214 5ELCID3342 DEMANDO POR *** YERNOS, NINGUNO NON FALLO
26320 5ELCID3357 POR QUE DEXAMOS *** FIJAS AVN NO NOS REPENTIMOS,
26612 5ELCID3398 PIDEN *** FIJAS A MYO %ID EL CAMPEADOR
27003 5ELCID3450 AGORA BESAREDES *** MANOS & LAMAR LAS HEDES SE@ORAS,
27381 5ELCID3498 QUE PRENDAN DE *** AUERES QUANTO OUIEREN SABOR.
27726 5ELCID3539 E TODOS *** PARIENTES CON ELLOS SON;
29117 5ELCID3719 FIZIERON *** CASAMIENTOS CON DON ELUIRA & CON DO@A SOL.
29156 5ELCID3723 QUANDO SE@ORAS SON *** FIJAS DE NAUARRA & DE ARAGON.
WORD #3939 OCCURS 109 TIMES.
INDEX OF DIVERSIFICATION = 267.69 WITH STANDARD DEVIATION OF 295.48

SUSANNA 2707 5ELCID0342 SALUEST A SANTA ******* DEL FALSO CRIMINAL;
WORD #3940 OCCURS 1 TIMES.

SUSO 5688 5ELCID0717 ENCLINARON LAS CARAS DE **** DE LOS ARZONES,
17439 5ELCID2206 POR EL SUELO & **** TAN BIEN ENCORTINADO,
24107 5ELCID3074 DE **** LAS LORIGAS TAN BLANCAS COMMO EL SOL;
28638 5ELCID3656 LO VNO CAYO ENEL CAMPO & LO AL **** FINCAUA.
WORD #3941 OCCURS 4 TIMES.

SUYO 23356 5ELCID2975 ASSI COMMO LO DIXO, **** ERA EL CUYDADO:
24304 5ELCID3098 POR TALLO FAZE ESTO QUE RECABDAR QUIERE TODO LO ****;
25509 5ELCID3248 ENPRESTAN LES DELO AGENO, QUE NON LES CUMPLE LO ****.
WORD #3942 OCCURS 3 TIMES.

SUYOS 516 5ELCID0066 AMYO %ID & ALOS ***** ABASTALES DE PAN & DE UINO;
18960 5ELCID2399 MYO %ID CON LOS ***** CAE EN ALCAN%A;
WORD #3943 OCCURS 2 TIMES.

WORD C# PREFIX CONTEXT

```
SUZIO           18110 5ELCID2291 EL MANTC & EL BRIAL TODC ***** LO SACO.
        WORD #3944 OCCURS    1 TIMES.

SYO             15491 5ELCID1963 *** BIUC SC, ALI YRE SIN FALLA.
        WORD #3945 OCCURS    1 TIMES.

TABLADOS        12630 5ELCID1602 ARMAS TENIENDC & ******** QUEBRANTANDO.
                17780 5ELCID2249 E AL OTRO DIA FIZC MYO %ID FINCAR VIJ ********:
        WORD #3946 OCCURS    2 TIMES.

TACHA           20612 5ELCID2616 QUE ESTOS CASAMIENTOS NCN SERIEN SIN ALGUNA *****.
        WORD #3947 OCCURS    1 TIMES.

TADO             1107 5ELCID0142 AMOS TRED ALCAMPEADOR CCN ****,
        WORD #3948 OCCURS    1 TIMES.

TAIADO           9772 5ELCID1241 NIN ENTRARIE ENELA TIGERA, NI VN PELO NON AURIE ******,
        WORD #3949 OCCURS    1 TIMES.

TAIADOR          6128 5ELCID0780 ESPADA *******, SANGRIENTO TRAE EL BRA%O,
        WORD #3950 OCCURS    1 TIMES.

TAIADORES       21447 5ELCID2726 DOS ESPADAS TENEDES FUERTES & *********,
                24137 5ELCID3077 SOLOS MANTOS LAS ESPADAS DUL%ES & *********;
                27863 5ELCID3555 QUE NON FUESSEN EN LA BATALLA LAS ESPADAS *********
                28087 5ELCID3585 EMANO PRENDEN LAS ASTAS DELOS FIERROS *********,
        WORD #3951 OCCURS    4 TIMES.

TAIAREMOS       19059 5ELCID2411 SALUDAR NOS HEMOS AMOS, & ********* AMISTAS.
        WORD #3952 OCCURS    1 TIMES.

TAIAUA           9204 5ELCID1172 ****** LES LAS HUERTAS & FAZIA LES GRAND MAL,
        WORD #3953 OCCURS    1 TIMES.

TAIO            15426 5ELCID1954 SOBRE ****, QUE ES UNA AGUA CABDAL,
                15564 5ELCID1973 ALAS AGUAS DE ****, OLAS UISTAS SON APAREIADAS.
                23898 5ELCID3044 ESSA NCCH MYO %ID **** NON QUISO PASSAR;
        WORD #3954 OCCURS    3 TIMES.

TAL              3426 5ELCID0433 POR *** LO FAZE MYO %ID QUE NO IO VENTASSE NADI.
                 3871 5ELCID0490 DO YO UOS ENBIAS BIEN ABRIA *** ESPERAN%A.
                 5915 5ELCID0750 DIOL *** ESPADADA CCN EL SO DIESTRO BRA%O,
                 6224 5ELCID0793 QUANDO *** BATALLA AUEMOS ARANCADO.
                 6928 5ELCID0885 AUN ME PLAZE DE MYO %ID QUE FIZO *** GANAN%IA.
                10788 5ELCID1366 POR *** FAGO AQUESTC QUE SIRUAN ASO SE@OR.
                11510 5ELCID1457 QUI BUEN MANDADERO ENBIA, *** DEUE SPERAR.
                11764 5ELCID1492 PASSARON MATA DE TORANZ DE *** GUISA QUE NINGUN MIEDO NON HAN,
                11984 5ELCID1519 ENEL OMBRO LO SALUDA, CA *** ES SU HUSAIE:
                13116 5ELCID1662 DEL DIA QUE NASQUIERAN NON VIERAN *** TREMOR.
                13822 5ELCID1751 QUANDO EN VUESTRA VENIDA *** GANAN%IA NOS AN DADA.
                13836 5ELCID1753 CCN *** CUM ESTO SE VEN%EN MOROS DEL CAMPO.
                14130 5ELCID1789 *** TIENDA COMMO ESTA, QUE DE MARUECOS ES PASSADA,
                14674 5ELCID1856 GRADESCOLO A MYO %ID QUE *** DON ME HA ENBIADO;
                16276 5ELCID2065 DE *** GUISA LOS PAGA MYO %ID EL CAMPEADOR,
                18235 5ELCID2307 NON VIESTES *** GUEGO COMMO YUA POR LA CORT;
                19067 5ELCID2412 RESPUSO BUCAR AL %ID: CONFONDA DIOS *** AMISTAD
                21073 5ELCID2678 *** COSA UOS FARIA QUE POR EL MUNDO SONAS,
                22226 5ELCID2831 QUANDO *** ONDRA MEAN DADA LOS YFANTES DE CARRION;
                23735 5ELCID3023 BUENAS CONPA@AS QUE ASSI AN *** SE@OR.
                25720 5ELCID3275 LOS DE CARRION SON DE NATURA ***,
                26468 5ELCID3377 HYA VARONES, QUIEN VIO NUNCA *** MAL?
                27512 5ELCID3514 EN MOROS NI EN CHRISTIANOS OTRO *** NON HA OY,
                27551 5ELCID3518 MAS ATAL CAUALLO CUM EST PORA *** COMMO VOS,
        WORD #3955 OCCURS   24 TIMES.
           INDEX OF DIVERSIFICATION =  1047.91 WITH STANDARD DEVIATION OF    896.36

TALERES         26551 5ELCID3389 FAZER TELO DEZIR QUE ******* CUAL DIGO YO.
        WORD #3956 OCCURS    1 TIMES.

TALES            8010 5ELCID1023 PUES QUE ***** MAL CAL%ADOS ME VEN%IERON DE BATALLA.
                12013 5ELCID1523 ONDRAR UOS HEMOS TODOS, CA ***** LA SU AUZE,
                15176 5ELCID1920 EN POCAS TIERRAS A ***** DOS VARONES.
                24160 5ELCID3081 DO ***** %IENTO TOUIER, BIEN SERE SIN PAUOR.
                25965 5ELCID3309 DIREUOS, %ID, COSTUBRES AUEDES *****,
                27040 5ELCID3454 EN TODAS GUISAS ***** SODES QUALES DIGO YO;
                27402 5ELCID3501 ***** YA QUE PRENDEN, TALES YA QUE NON.
                27406 5ELCID3501 TALES YA QUE PRENDEN, ***** YA QUE NON.
                28562 5ELCID3647 ***** FUERON LOS COLPES QUE LES QUEBRARON AMAS.
        WORD #3957 OCCURS    9 TIMES.
           INDEX OF DIVERSIFICATION =  2568.00 WITH STANDARD DEVIATION OF   2923.40

TALLES          14404 5ELCID1822 ****** GANAN%IAS TRAEN QUE SON A AGUARDAR.
        WORD #3958 OCCURS    1 TIMES.
```

WORD C# PREFIX CONTEXT

TALLO 24296 5ELCID3098 POR ***** FAZE ESTO QUE RECABDAR QUIERE TODO LO SUYO;
WORD #3959 OCCURS 1 TIMES.

TAMIN 5033 5ELCID0636 QUANDO LO OYO EL REY *****, POR CUER LE PESO MAL:
WORD #3960 OCCURS 1 TIMES.

TAN 4 5ELCID0001 DELOS SOS OIOS *** FUERTE MIENTRE LORANDO,
49 5ELCID0007 FFABLO MYO %ID BIEN & *** MESURADO:
1670 5ELCID0214 MYO %ID & SUS CONPA@AS CAUALGAN *** AYNA.
1925 5ELCID0245 CON *** GRANT GOZO RE%IBEN AL QUE EN BUEN ORA NASCO.
2127 5ELCID0268 MER%ED, YA %ID, BARBA *** COMPLIDA
2199 5ELCID0277 LORA DELOS OIOS, *** FUERTE MIENTRE SOSPIRA:
2209 5ELCID0278 YA DO@A XIMENA, LA MI MUGIER *** COMPLIDA,
2574 5ELCID0325 TANEN A MATINES A VNA PRIESSA *** GRAND;
3217 5ELCID0405 VN SUENOL PRISO DUL%E, *** BIEN SE ADURMJO.
3237 5ELCID0408 EN *** BUEN PUNTO CAUALGO VARON;
3405 5ELCID0430 VASSALLOS *** BUENOS POR CORA%ON LO AN,
4986 5ELCID0630 VINO POSAR SOBRE ALCO%ER, EN VN *** FUERTE LOGAR;
6066 5ELCID0770 *** BUEN DIA POR LA CHRISTIANDAD,
7449 5ELCID0955 QUE EL SALIDO DE CASTIELLA ASILOS TRAE *** MAL.
7870 5ELCID1006 LOS PENDONES & LAS LAN%AS *** BIEN LAS UAN ENPLEANDO,
8327 5ELCID1059 POR QUE EL CONDE DON REMONT *** BIEN BOLUIE LAS MANOS.
8356 5ELCID1062 DEL DIA QUE FUE CONDE NON IANTE *** DE BUEN GRADO,
8545 5ELCID1086 *** RICOS SON LOS SOS QUE NON SABEN QUE SE AN.
9300 5ELCID1182 CON EL DELOS MONTES CLAROS AUYEN GUERRA *** GRAND,
10395 5ELCID1317 AFE MINAYA LABARFANEZ DO LEGA *** APUESTO;
10418 5ELCID1320 BESAUA LE LAS MANOS & FABLO *** APUESTO:
10579 5ELCID1341 DE *** FIERAS GANAN%IAS COMMO A FECHAS EL CAMPEADOR
10804 5ELCID1368 SONRRISOS EL REY, *** VELIDO FABLO:
11003 5ELCID1393 *** GRAND FUE EL GOZO QUANDOL VIERON ASSOMAR.
11053 5ELCID1399 SANO LO DEXE & CON *** GRAND RICTAD.
11953 5ELCID1515 POR %ERCA DE SALON *** GRANDES GOZOS VAN.
11988 5ELCID1520 *** BUEN DIA CON UUSCO, MINAYA ALBARFANEZ
12121 5ELCID1538 DE *** GRAND CONDUCHO COMMO EN MEDINAL SACARON;
12273 5ELCID1558 CON ESTAS ALEGRIAS & NUEUAS *** ONDRADAS
12520 5ELCID1588 FIZO VNA CORRIDA, ESTA FUE *** ESTRA@A.
12678 5ELCID1609 A *** GRAND ONDRA ELLAS A VALEN%IA ENTRAUAN.
12745 5ELCID1618 MYO %ID & SUS COMPANAS *** AGRAND SABOR ESTAN.
13086 5ELCID1659 ALEGRAUAS MIO %ID & DIXO: *** BUEN DIA ES OY
13226 5ELCID1676 DOS FALLAN CON LOS MOROS COMETIEN LOS *** AYNA.
13511 5ELCID1712 MIO %ID ALOS SOS VASSALOS *** BIEN LOS ACORDANDO.
14584 5ELCID1845 MER%ED, REY ALFONSSO, SODES *** ONDRADO
14733 5ELCID1863 POR *** BILTADA MIENTRE VEN%ER REYES DEL CAMPO,
15819 5ELCID2006 RECABDADO HA, COMMO *** BUEN VARON,
15892 5ELCID2015 RE%EBIR LO SALEN CON *** GRAND ONOR.
15976 5ELCID2026 *** GRAND PESAR OUO EL REY DON ALFONSSO:
16234 5ELCID2059 CATANDOL SEDIE LA BARBA, QUE *** AYNAL CRE%IERA.
16521 5ELCID2094 FABLO EL REY DON ALFONSSO COMMO *** BUEN SE@OR:
16529 5ELCID2095 GRADO & GRA%IAS, CID, COMMO *** BUENO, & PRIMERO AL CRIADOR,
16927 5ELCID2142 HYA REY DON ALFONSSO, SE@OR *** ONDRADO,
17179 5ELCID2173 QUE ES LARGO DE LENGUA, MAS EN LO AL NON ES *** PRO.
17440 5ELCID2206 POR EL SUELO & SUSO *** BIEN ENCORTINADO,
17524 5ELCID2217 TODOS LOS DE MYO %ID *** BIEN SON ACORDADOS,
17692 5ELCID2238 EL OBISPO DON IHERONIMO VISTIOS *** PRIUADO,
17711 5ELCID2241 AL SALIR DELA ECCLEGIA CAUALGARON *** PRIUADO,
18383 5ELCID2326 EUADES QUE PAUOR HAN UUESTROS YERNOS *** OSADOS,
18437 5ELCID2333 EN BRA%OS TENEDES MIS FIJAS *** BLANCAS COMMO EL SOL
18670 5ELCID2363 EUOS *** DINNO QUE CON EL AUECES PART.
19244 5ELCID2435 POR LA MATAN%A VINIA *** PRIUADO,
19989 5ELCID2536 ELAS NOCHES & LOS DIAS *** MAL LOS ESCARMENTANDO,
19993 5ELCID2537 *** MAL SE CONSSEIARON ESTOS YFFANTES AMOS.
20966 5ELCID2664 *** EN SALUD LO ABREMOS COMMO LO DE CARRION;
21524 5ELCID2736 CON LAS %INCHAS CORRECIZAS MAIAN LAS *** SIN SABOR;
21972 5ELCID2796 *** A GRANT DUELO FABLAUA DO@A SOL:
22328 5ELCID2843 VINIERON A SANTESTEUAN DE GORMAZ, VN CASTIELLO *** FUERT,
22532 5ELCID2869 HY IAZEN ESSA NOCHE, & *** GRAND GOZO QUE FAZEN.
22891 5ELCID2916 CA *** GRANT ES LA RENCURA DENTRO EN MI CORA%ON.
23021 5ELCID2933 LEUANTOS EL REY, *** BIEN LOS RE%IBIO.
24110 5ELCID3074 DE SUSO LAS LORIGAS *** BLANCAS COMMO EL SOL;
24210 5ELCID3087 VISTIO CAMISA DE RAN%AL *** BLANCA COMMO EL SOL,
25569 5ELCID3256 DELOS YFANTES DE CARRION QUEM DESONDRARON *** MAL,
27371 5ELCID3497 ABRA%OLOS *** BIEN & RUEGA LOS DE CORA%ON
27482 5ELCID3510 QUE EN TODAS NUESTRAS TIERRAS NON HA *** BUEN VARON.
27542 5ELCID3517 SI AUOS LE TOLLIES, EL CAUALLO NO HAURIE *** BUEN SE@OR.
27594 5ELCID3523 EL CAMPEADOR ALOS QUE HAN LIDIAR *** BIEN LOS CASTIGO:
28694 5ELCID3664 ESORA EL YFANTE *** GRANDES VOZES DAUA:
28765 5ELCID3673 FIRIENSSEN EN LOS ESCUDOS VNOS *** GRANDES COLPES;
29062 5ELCID3712 POR QUE *** ONDRADOS FUERON LOS DEL CANPEADOR.
WORD #3961 OCCURS 72 TIMES.
INDEX OF DIVERSIFICATION = 408.27 WITH STANDARD DEVIATION OF 448.66

TANDRA 2515 5ELCID0318 EN SAN PERO A MATINS ****** EL BUEN ABBAT,
WORD #3962 OCCURS 1 TIMES.

WORD C# PREFIX CONTEXT

TANEN 2272 5ELCID0286 ***** LAS CAMPA@AS EN SAN PERO A CLAMOR.
2568 5ELCID0325 ***** A MATINES A VNA PRIESSA TAN GRAND;
WORD #3963 OCCURS 2 TIMES.

TANIEN 13078 5ELCID1658 A VNA GRAND PRIESSA ****** LOS ATAMORES;
WORD #3964 OCCURS 1 TIMES.

TANOS 5774 5ELCID0730 ***** BUENOS CAUALLOS SIN SOS DUENOS ANDAR.
WORD #3965 OCCURS 1 TIMES.

TANTA 5758 5ELCID0727 ***** ADAGARA FORADAR & PASSAR,
5763 5ELCID0728 ***** LORIGA FALSSA DESMANCHAR
8964 5ELCID1141 ***** CUERDA DE TIENDA Y VERIEDES QUEBRAR,
14079 5ELCID1783 ***** TIENDA PRE%IADA & TANTO TENDAL OBRADO
15519 5ELCID1966 QUI ENVIO POR CASTIELLA ***** MULA PRE%IADA,
15664 5ELCID1987 ***** GRUESSA MULA & TANTO PALAFRE DE SAZON,
15672 5ELCID1988 ***** BUENA ARMA & TANTO BUEN CAUALLO COREDOR,
15680 5ELCID1989 ***** BUENA CAPA & MANTOS & PELLI%ONES;
16692 5ELCID2114 ***** GRUESSA MULA & TANTO PALAFRE DE SAZON
17443 5ELCID2207 ***** PORPOLA & TANTO XAMED & TANTO PA@O PRECIADO.
25463 5ELCID3243 ***** GRUESSA MULA, TANTO PALAFRE DE SAZON,
25470 5ELCID3244 ***** BUENA ESPADA CONTODA GUARNIZON;
WORD #3966 OCCURS 12 TIMES.
INDEX OF DIVERSIFICATION = 1791.00 WITH STANDARD DEVIATION OF 2628.48

TANTAS 5753 5ELCID0726 VERIEDES ****** LAN%AS PREMER & AL%AR,
14158 5ELCID1792 CON AQUESTAS RIQUEZAS ****** A VALEN%IA SON ENTRADOS.
16709 5ELCID2116 ****** BUENAS VISTIDURAS QUE DALFAYA SON.
18319 5ELCID2318 CA VEYEN ****** TIENDAS DE MOROS DE QUE NON AUIE SABOR.
18966 5ELCID2400 VERIEDES QUEBRAR ****** CUERDAS & ARRANCAR SE LAS ESTACAS
18980 5ELCID2401 EACOSTAR SE LOS TENDALES, CON HUEBRAS ERAN ******.
19008 5ELCID2405 ****** CABE%AS CON YELMOS QUE POR EL CAMPO CAEN,
WORD #3967 OCCURS 7 TIMES.
INDEX OF DIVERSIFICATION = 2208.17 WITH STANDARD DEVIATION OF 3190.01

TANTO 133 5ELCID0018 PLORANDO DELOS OIOS, ***** AUYEN EL DOLOR.
165 5ELCID0022 EL REY DON ALFONSSO ***** AUIE LA GRAND SA@A,
1332 5ELCID0170 ALCARGAR DELAS ARCHAS VERIEDES GOZO *****:
2216 5ELCID0279 COMMO ALA MI ALMA YO ***** UOS QUERIA.
3792 5ELCID0480 ***** TRAEN LAS GRANDES GANA%IAS, MUCHOS GA@ADOS.
4460 5ELCID0567 EN LA SU VEZINDAD NON SE TREUEN GANAR *****.
8141 5ELCID1038 ***** QUANTO YO BIUA, SERE DENT MARAUILLADO.
12306 5ELCID1562 ALEGRE FUE MYO %ID, QUE NUNQUA MAS NIN *****,
13929 5ELCID1764 ESTAS DUE@AS QUE ADUXIESTES, QUE UOS SIRUEN *****,
13954 5ELCID1767 QUE LO SEPAN EN CASTIELLA, AQUIEN SIRUIERON *****.
14009 5ELCID1775 ***** FALLAN DESTO QUE ES COSA SOBEIANO.
14083 5ELCID1783 TANTA TIENDA PRE%IADA & ***** TENDAL OBRADO
14722 5ELCID1861 MARAUILLA ES DEL %ID, QUE SU ONDRA CRE%E *****
15523 5ELCID1967 E ***** PALAFRE QUE BIEN ANDA,
15534 5ELCID1969 ***** BUEN PENDON METER EN BUENAS ASTAS,
15668 5ELCID1987 TANTA GRUESSA MULA & ***** PALAFRE DE SAZON,
15676 5ELCID1988 TANTA BUENA ARMA & ***** BUEN CAUALLO COREDOR,
15956 5ELCID2023 LORANDO DELOS OIOS, ***** AUIE EL GOZO MAYOR;
16696 5ELCID2114 TANTA GRUESSA MULA & ***** PALAFRE DE SAZON
17446 5ELCID2207 TANTA PORPOLA & ***** XAMED & TANTO PA@O PRECIADO.
17449 5ELCID2207 TANTA PORPOLA & TANTO XAMED & ***** PA@O PRECIADO.
18080 5ELCID2287 METIOS SOL ESCA@O, ***** OUO EL PAUOR.
18478 5ELCID2338 AVN VEA EL ORA QUE UOS MERESCA DOS *****.
19000 5ELCID2404 ***** BRA%O CON LORIGA VERIEDES CAER A PART,
21343 5ELCID2713 ***** MAL COMIDIERON LOS YFANTES DE CARRION;
21574 5ELCID2743 ***** LAS MAIARON QUE SIN COSIMENTE SON;
21878 5ELCID2784 ***** SON DE TRASPUESTAS QUE NON PUEDEN DEZIR NADA.
22027 5ELCID2803 ***** LAS ROGO FATA QUE LAS ASSENTO.
22492 5ELCID2864 E PERO VERMUEZ OTRO ***** LAS HA;
25460 5ELCID3242 VERIEDES ADUZIR ***** CAUALLO CORREDOR,
25466 5ELCID3243 TANTA GRUESSA MULA, ***** PALAFRE DE SAZON,
25917 5ELCID3302 FABLA, PERO MUDO, VARON QUE ***** CALLAS
27419 5ELCID3503 DELO AL ***** PRISO QUANT OUO SABOR.
28580 5ELCID3649 RELUMBRA TOD EL CAMPO, ***** ER LINPIA & CLARA;
WORD #3968 OCCURS 34 TIMES.
INDEX OF DIVERSIFICATION = 861.03 WITH STANDARD DEVIATION OF 1055.76

TANTOL 16225 5ELCID2058 NON SE PUEDE FARTAR DEL, ****** QUERIE DE CORA%ON;
WORD #3969 OCCURS 1 TIMES.

TANTOS 5750 5ELCID0725 ALA TORNADA QUE FAZEN OTROS ****** SON.
5767 5ELCID0729 ****** PENDONES BLANCOS SALIR VERMEIOS EN SANGRE,
6160 5ELCID0785 ****** MOROS YAZEN MUERTOS QUE POCOS BIUOS A DEXADOS,
14072 5ELCID1782 QUANDO A MYO %ID CAYERON ******, LOS OTROS BIEN PUEDEN FINCAR PAGADOS.
14221 5ELCID1800 ****** AUIEN DE AUERES, DE CAUALLOS & DE ARMAS;
15844 5ELCID2010 ****** CAUALLOS EN DIESTRO, GRUESSOS & CORREDORES,
19649 5ELCID2491 ****** SON DE MUCHOS QUE NON SERIEN CONTADOS.
19932 5ELCID2529 ****** AVEMOS DE AUERES QUE NO SON CONTADOS;
WORD #3970 OCCURS 8 TIMES.
INDEX OF DIVERSIFICATION = 2025.00 WITH STANDARD DEVIATION OF 2922.22

```
WORD                    C#  PREFIX                                  CONTEXT

TANXO              13198 5ELCID1673 VIOLO EL ATALAYA & ***** EL ESCUILA;
          WORD #3971 OCCURS   1 TIMES.

TARDA              23664 5ELCID3014 POR QUE SE ***** EL REY NON HA SABOR.
          WORD #3972 OCCURS   1 TIMES.

TARDANDO           17551 5ELCID2220 PUES QUE AFAZER LO AUEMOS, POR QUE LO YMOS ********?
          WORD #3973 OCCURS   1 TIMES.

TARDAR             22747 5ELCID2898 EL QUE EN BUEN ORA NASCO NON QUISO ******,
          WORD #3974 OCCURS   1 TIMES.

TARDAUA             7103 5ELCID0908 QUANDO VIO EL CABOSO QUE SE ******* MINAYA,
          WORD #3975 OCCURS   1 TIMES.

TARDEDES            2507 5ELCID0317 NON UOS ********, MANDEDES ENSELLAR;
          WORD #3976 OCCURS   1 TIMES.

TARDO               7290 5ELCID0935 NON LO ***** EL QUE EN BUEN ORA NASCO,
                   14254 5ELCID1803 EL BUENO DE MYO %ID NON LO ***** POR NADA:
                   16325 5ELCID2071 NON LO ***** EL REY, LA RAZON CONPE%O:
                   23767 5ELCID3027 QUANDO LO OYO EL REY, POR NADA NON *****;
          WORD #3977 OCCURS   4 TIMES.

TE                  2660 5ELCID0336 TRES REYES DE ARABIA ** VINIERON ADORAR,
                    2673 5ELCID0338 ** OFFRE%IERON, COMMO FUE TU VELUNTAD;
                    2743 5ELCID0347 ALOS IUDIOS ** DEXESTE PRENDER; DO DIZEN MONTE CALUARIE
                    2751 5ELCID0348 PUSIERON ** EN CRUZ POR NUMBRE EN GOLGOTA;
                   19098 5ELCID2416 NON ** IUNTARAS COMIGO FATA DENTRO EN LA MAR.
                   22773 5ELCID2902 EN BUEN ORA ** CRIE ATI EN LA MI CORT
                   23185 5ELCID2954 VERDAD ** DIGO YO, QUE ME PESA DE CORA%ON,
                   26040 5ELCID3319 SI YO NON VUJAS, EL MORO ** JUGARA MAL;
                   26081 5ELCID3324 DELANT MYO %ID & DELANTE TODOS OVISTE ** DE ALABAR
                   26118 5ELCID3330  NON ** VIENE EN MIENTE EN VALEN%IA LO DEL LEON,
                   26370 5ELCID3363 LO DEL LEON NON SE ** DEUE OLBIDAR;
          WORD #3978 OCCURS  11 TIMES.
             INDEX OF DIVERSIFICATION =  2370.00 WITH STANDARD DEVIATION OF  5087.08

TECA                4491 5ELCID0571 E LOS DE **** & LOS DE TERUAL LA CASA;
                    4940 5ELCID0625 MUCHO PESA ALOS DE **** & ALOS DE TERUAL NON PLAZE,
                    5001 5ELCID0632 SI NON DAS CONSEIO, A **** & A TERUEL PERDERAS,
          WORD #3979 OCCURS   3 TIMES.

TECHA               6595 5ELCID0842 ENTRE LOS DE ***** & LOS DE TERUEL LA CASA,
          WORD #3980 OCCURS   1 TIMES.

TE%ER              12087 5ELCID1533 ANTES DESTE ***** DIA UOS LA DARE DOBLADA.
          WORD #3981 OCCURS   1 TIMES.

TEINE               4828 5ELCID0611 VINO PERO VERMUEZ, QUE LA SE@A ***** EN MANO,
          WORD #3982 OCCURS   1 TIMES.

TELAS              20319 5ELCID2578 ALLA ME LEUADES LAS ***** DEL CORA%ON.
                   25603 5ELCID3260  A QUEM DESCUBRIESTES LAS ***** DEL CORA%ON?
                   26008 5ELCID3315 LAS TUS MA@AS YO ***** SABRE CONTAR:
          WORD #3983 OCCURS   3 TIMES.

TELLAS             21891 5ELCID2785 PARTIERON SE LE LAS ****** DE DENTRO DE LOS CORA%ONES,
          WORD #3984 OCCURS   1 TIMES.

TELLEZ             22109 5ELCID2814 FALLO A DIEGO ****** EL QUE DE ALBARFANEZ FUE;
          WORD #3985 OCCURS   1 TIMES.

TELO               26093 5ELCID3326 CROUIERON **** TODOS, MAS NON SABEN LA VERDAD.
                   26548 5ELCID3389 FAZER **** DEZIR QUE TALERES QUAL DIGO YO.
          WORD #3986 OCCURS   2 TIMES.

TEMBRAR            28343 5ELCID3619 ******* QUERIE LA TIERRA DOD ERAN MOUEDORES.
          WORD #3987 OCCURS   1 TIMES.

TEME                6774 5ELCID0865 NON **** GERRA, SABET, A NULLA PART.
          WORD #3988 OCCURS   1 TIMES.

TEMEN              19724 5ELCID2501 ELLOS LO *****, CA NON LO PIESSO YO:
          WORD #3989 OCCURS   1 TIMES.

TEMIEN              7349 5ELCID0942 DE MYO %ID RUY DIAZ QUE NON ****** NINGUNA FONTA.
          WORD #3990 OCCURS   1 TIMES.

TEMPRANO            3327 5ELCID0420 ******** DAT %EUADA, SI EL CRIADOR UOS SALUE
          WORD #3991 OCCURS   1 TIMES.
```

```
WORD                 C#  PREFIX                              CONTEXT

TENDAL             14084 5ELCID1783 TANTA TIENDA PRE%IADA & TANTO ****** OBRADO
        WORD #3992 OCCURS   1 TIMES.

TENDALES            8981 5ELCID1142 ARANCAR SE LAS ESTACAS & ACOSTAR SE ATODAS PARTES LOS ********.
                   14107 5ELCID1786 DOS ******** LA SUFREN, CON ORO SON LABRADOS;
                   18976 5ELCID2401 EACOSTAR SE LOS ********, CON HUEBRAS ERAN TANTAS.
        WORD #3993 OCCURS   3 TIMES.

TENDIERON           1423 5ELCID0182 EN MEDIO DEL PALA%IO ********* VN ALMOFALLA,
        WORD #3994 OCCURS   1 TIMES.

TENDIO             25032 5ELCID3189 ****** EL BRA%O, LA ESPADA TIZON LE DIO;
                   25054 5ELCID3192 ****** EL BRA%O, EL ESPADA COLADAL DIO;
        WORD #3995 OCCURS   2 TIMES.

TENEDES            18434 5ELCID2333 EN BRA%OS ******* MIS FIJAS TAN BLANCAS COMMO EL SOL
                   21444 5ELCID2726 DOS ESPADAS ******* FUERTES & TAIADORES,
                   27902 5ELCID3560 SI BUENAS LAS *******, PRO ABRAN AUOS;
                   29250 5ELCID3734 ES LEYDO, DAT NOS DEL VINO; SI NON ******* DINEROS, ECHAD
        WORD #3996 OCCURS   4 TIMES.

TENEMOS             4911 5ELCID0621 COIAMOS LOS DE DENTRO, CA EL SENORIO *******,
                   19953 5ELCID2531 PENSAD DELO OTRO, QUE LO NUESTRO ******* LO EN SALUO.
                   20025 5ELCID2541 LOS AUERES QUE ******* GRANDES SON & SOBEIANOS,
                   25417 5ELCID3236 FABLO FERRANGO%ALEZ: AUERES MONEDADOS NON ******* NOS.
        WORD #3997 OCCURS   4 TIMES.

TENENDOS           28045 5ELCID3580 ******** ADERECHO, POR AMOR DEL CRIADOR
        WORD #3998 OCCURS   1 TIMES.

TENER               5468 5ELCID0690 COMMO SODES MUY BUENO, ***** LA EDES SIN ARCH;
                   12433 5ELCID1577 DELANTE SU MUGIER & DE SUS FIJAS QUERIE ***** LAS ARMAS.
                   27000 5ELCID3449 ANTES LAS AVIEDES PAREIAS PORA EN BRA%OS LAS *****,
        WORD #3999 OCCURS   3 TIMES.

TENGA               7631 5ELCID0977 DIGADES AL CONDE NON LO ***** A MAL,
        WORD #4000 OCCURS   1 TIMES.

TENGADES            4169 5ELCID0530 LO QUE YO DIXIER NON LO ******** AMAL:
                   18646 5ELCID2359 VOS CON LOS UUESTROS FIRME MIENTRE ALA %AGA ********;
        WORD #4001 OCCURS   2 TIMES.

TENGO               8411 5ELCID1069 EN GRADO UOS LO ***** LO QUE ME AUEDES DEXADO.
                   10904 5ELCID1380 LEUEDES VN PORTERO, ***** QUE UOS AURA PRO;
                   11619 5ELCID1472 YO FFINCARE EN VALEN%IA, CA LA ***** POR HEREDAD.
                   12035 5ELCID1526 MUCHOL ***** POR TORPE QUI NON CONES%E LA VERDAD.
                   12882 5ELCID1634 TODO EL BIEN QUE YO HE, TODO LO ***** DELANT:
                   12916 5ELCID1638 MIS FIJAS & MI MUGIER QUE LAS ***** ACA;
                   20527 5ELCID2606 ASSI COMMO YO *****, BIEN UOS HE CASADAS.
                   25377 5ELCID3231 DESTOS IIJ MILL MARCOS LOS CC ***** YO;
        WORD #4002 OCCURS   8 TIMES.
           INDEX OF DIVERSIFICATION =  2422.71 WITH STANDARD DEVIATION OF  2826.86

TENGON             17001 5ELCID2152 DEUOS BIEN SO SERUIDO, & ****** POR PAGADO;
        WORD #4003 OCCURS   1 TIMES.

TENIDO             24595 5ELCID3134 GRANDE TUERTO LE HAN ******, SABEMOS LO TODOS NOS;
        WORD #4004 OCCURS   1 TIMES.

TENIE               5911 5ELCID0749 ACOSTOS AVN AGUAZIL QUE ***** BUEN CAUALLO,
                    6803 5ELCID0869 EN SU MANO ***** A %ELFA LA DE CANAL.
                   11222 5ELCID1420 E EL SE ***** C QUE ADUXIERA DALLA;
                   25487 5ELCID3246 SOBRE LOS DOZIENTOS MARCOS QUE ***** EL REY ALFONSSO
                   28458 5ELCID3634 TRES DOBLES DE LORIGA ***** FERNANDO, AQUESTOL PRESTO,
        WORD #4005 OCCURS   5 TIMES.
           INDEX OF DIVERSIFICATION =  5635.75 WITH STANDARD DEVIATION OF  5931.51

TENIEN             15592 5ELCID1977 COMMO ELLOS ******, CER%ER LES YA LA GANA%IA,
                   19489 5ELCID2469 DESTA ARRANCADA, QUE LO ****** EN SO SALUO,
                   28513 5ELCID3641 ASSI LO ****** LAS YENTES QUE MAL FERIDO ES DE MUERT.
        WORD #4006 OCCURS   3 TIMES.

TENIENDO           12628 5ELCID1602 ARMAS ******** & TABLADOS QUEBRANTANDO.
                   13801 5ELCID1749 VOS ******** VALEN%IA, & YO VEN%I EL CAMPO;
                   20583 5ELCID2613 POR LA HUERTA DE VALEN%IA ******** SALIEN ARMAS;
                   21031 5ELCID2673 ARMAS YUA ********, PAROS ANTE LOS YFANTES;
                   21149 5ELCID2687 ******** YUAN ARMAS ALTRO%IR DE SALON;
                   22656 5ELCID2887 ARMAS YUA ******** & GRANT GOZO QUE FAZE;
                   22723 5ELCID2896 ******** YUAN ARMAS, ENTRARON SE ALA CIBDAD;
        WORD #4007 OCCURS   7 TIMES.
           INDEX OF DIVERSIFICATION =  1681.50 WITH STANDARD DEVIATION OF  2564.25

TER%ER              8072 5ELCID1030 FASTA ****** DIA NOL PUEDEN ACORDAR.
        WORD #4008 OCCURS   1 TIMES.
```

WORD C# PREFIX CONTEXT

```
TER%ERA            6795 5ELCIDC868 LA ******* TERUEL, CUE ESTAUA CELANT;
                  24565 5ELCID3131 ESTA ******* A TCLLEDC LA VIN FER OY,
                  28468 5ELCID3635 LAS DOS LE DESMANCHAN & LA ******* FINCO:
         WORD #4CC9 CCCURS   3 TIMES.

TER%ERO            2624 5ELCID0331 FEZIST %IELC & TIERRA, EL ******* EL MAR;
         WORD #4C10 CCCURS   1 TIMES.

TERER              6736 5ELCID0860 PLCGO ALOS DE ***** & ALOS DE CALATAYUT MAS,
         WORD #4011 CCCURS   1 TIMES.

TERNE              3571 5ELCID0450 ***** YC CASTEICN DCN ABREMCS GRAND EN PARA.
                  23931 5ELCID3049 ***** VIGILIA EN AQUESTE SANTO LOGAR.
         WORD #4012 CCCURS   2 TIMES.

TERUAL             4495 5ELCID0571 E LOS DE TECA & LCS CE ****** LA CASA;
                   4944 5ELCID0625 MUCHO PESA ALCS CE TECA & ALOS DE ****** NON PLAZE,
         WORD #4013 CCCURS   2 TIMES.

TERUEL             4605 5ELCID0585 ANTES CUEL PRENDAN LCS CE ******, SI NON NON NOS DARAN
                                   DENT NADA;
                   5CO4 5ELCIDC632 SI NON CAS CCNSEIC, A TECA & A ****** PERDERAS,
                   6C89 5ELCIDC773 EL REY FARIZ EN ****** SE FUE ENTRAR,
                   6599 5ELCID0842 ENTRE LCS DE TECHA & LCS CE ****** LA CASA,
                   6796 5ELCIDC868 LA TER%ERA ******, CUE ESTAUA CELANT;
                   7120 5ELCIDC911 ALEN DE ****** DCN RCCRIGO PASSAUA,
         WORD #4014 CCCURS   6 TIMES.
            INDEX OF DIVERSIFICATION =   502.00 WITH STANCARD CEVIATION OF   344.70

TEUAR              7127 5ELCIDC912 ENEL PINAR CE ***** DCN RCY CIAZ POSAUA;
                   7580 5ELCID0971 ALCCN%ARCN A MYC %ID EN ***** & EL PINAR;
                   7806 5ELCIDC999 OY EN ESTE PINAR DE ***** PCR TOLER ME LA GANAN%IA.
         WORD #4C15 CCCURS   3 TIMES.

TI                 2826 5ELCID0357 EN ** CROUO AL CRA, POR END ES SALUO DE MAL;
                  26045 5ELCID3320 PASSE POR **, CCN EL MORO ME OFF DE AIUNTAR,
         WORD #4016 CCCURS   2 TIMES.

TIENDA              448 5ELCID0057 FINCAUA LA ****** & LUEGO DESCAUALGAUA.
                   1181 5ELCID0152 AFEUOS LOS ALA ****** DEL CAMPEADOR CONTADO;
                   1577 5ELCIDC202 VINC PCRA LA ****** CEL CUE EN BUEN ORA NASCO;
                   1623 5ELCID0208 MANDAD COGER LA ****** & VAYAMOS PRIUADO,
                   1661 5ELCID0213 ESTAS PALABRAS DICHAS, LA ****** ES COGIDA.
                   4530 5ELCID0576 DEXA VNA ****** FITA & LAS CTRAS LEUAUA,
                   4581 5ELCID0582 LAS OTRAS A BES LIEUA, VNA ****** A DEXADA.
                   4932 5ELCID0624 FIZO ENBIAR PCR LA ****** QUE CEXARA ALLA.
                   7939 5ELCID1014 DE FUERA DELA ****** VN SALTO CAUA,
                   8967 5ELCID1141 TANTA CUERCA CE ****** Y VERIECES QUEBRAR,
                  14C80 5ELCID1783 TANTA ****** PRE%IACA & TANTO TENCAL OBRADO
                  14096 5ELCID1785 LA ****** DEL REY DE MARRUECOS, QUE DELAS OTRAS ES CABO,
                  14123 5ELCID1787 MANDO MYO %ID RUY DIAZ QUE FITA SOUIESSE LA ******,
                  14131 5ELCID1789 TAL ****** CCMMC ESTA, QUE CE MARUECOS ES PASSADA,
                  21255 5ELCID2701 MANDAN FINCAR LA ****** YFANTES DE CARRION,
                  21293 5ELCID2706 COGICA HAN LA ****** CC ALBERGARON DE NOCH,
         WORD #4C17 CCCURS  16 TIMES.
            INDEX OF DIVERSIFICATION =  1388.67 WITH STANCARD CEVIATION OF  2188.97

TIENDAS            5186 5ELCID0656 FINCARCN LAS ******* & PRENDEND LAS POSADAS,
                   8670 5ELCID1101 A%ERCA DE MURUIEDRC TCRNAN ******* AFINCAR.
                  12854 5ELCID1631 FINCARCN LAS *******, & POSAN LAS YENTES DESCREYDAS.
                  12972 5ELCID1645 AL%AUAN LOS CICS, ******* VIERCN FINCADAS:
                  13C69 5ELCID1657 FINCADAS SCN LAS ******* & PARE%EN LOS ALUORES,
                  13244 5ELCID1679 BIEN FATA LAS ******* DURA AQUESTE ALCAZ,
                  14003 5ELCID1774 ENTRE ******* & ARMAS & VESTICOS PRE%IADOS
                  18279 5ELCID2313 CINQUAENTA MILL ******* FINCACAS HA DELAS CABDALES;
                  18320 5ELCID2318 CA VEYEN TANTAS ******* CE MOROS DE QUE NON AUIE SABOR.
                  18989 5ELCID2402 LOS DE MYO %ID ALOS DE BUCAR CELAS ******* LOS SACAN.
                  18995 5ELCID2403 SACAN LCS DELAS *******, CAEN LOS EN ALCAZ;
                  19215 5ELCID2431 ALAS ******* ERAN LEGADCS, DO ESTAUA
         WORD #4018 CCCURS  12 TIMES.
            INDEX OF DIVERSIFICATION =  1274.36 WITH STANCARD CEVIATION OF  1765.33

TIENE               877 5ELCID0113 ***** DCS ARCAS LENNAS CE ORO ESMERADO.
                   1459 5ELCID0187 %INCO ESCUDERCS ***** DCN MARTINO, ATODOS LOS CARGAUA.
                   5597 5ELCIDC7C5 LA SE@A ***** EN MANC, CCNPE%C CE ESPOLONAR;
                   7494 5ELCID0961 GRANDES TUERTCS ME ***** MYO %ID EL DE BIUAR.
                  10567 5ELCID1339 RAZCNAS POR VUESTRC VASSALLC & AUOS ***** POR SE@OR.
                  14180 5ELCID1795 NON ***** EN CUENTA LCS MOROS QUE HA MATADOS;
                  158C2 5ELCID2004 EN QUE ***** SU ALMA & SU CORA%ON,
                  19116 5ELCID2418 BUEN CAUALLC ***** BUCAR & GRANDES SALTOS FAZ,
                  2C961 5ELCID2663 QUANTA RIQUIZA ***** AUER LA YEMOS NOS.
                  2C997 5ELCID2668 NON ***** PCRIDAD, DIXOLO AVENGALUON:
                  21026 5ELCID2672 CO DOZIENTOS QUE ***** YUA CAUALGAR;
                  22001 5ELCID2799 CON VN SONBRERO QUE ***** FELEZ MUNOZ,
                  24983 5ELCID3182 EN LAS MANOS LAS ***** & AMAS LAS CATO;
```

WORD C# PREFIX CONTEXT

TIENE (CON'T)

```
                  28315 5ELCID3614 CADA VNO DELLCS MIENTES ***** AL SO.
                  28354 5ELCID3620 CADA VNO DELLOS MIENTES ***** ALSO;
                  28685 5ELCID3662 DIAGON%ALEZ ESPADA ***** EN MANO, MAS NOLA
         WORD #4019 OCCURS  16 TIMES.
            INDEX OF DIVERSIFICATION =  1852.87 WITH STANDARD DEVIATION OF  1465.82

TIENELA           11554 5ELCID1464 ******* AUEGALUON, MYO AMIGO ES DE PAZ,
         WORD #4020 OCCURS   1 TIMES.

TIENEN             3325 5ELCID0419 NOTO TREZIENTAS LAN%AS QUE TODAS ****** PENDONES.
                   3709 5ELCID0468 LOS QUE LA ******, QUANDO VIERON LA REBATA,
                   4744 5ELCID0602 ****** BUENOS CAUALLOS, SABET, ASU GUISA LES ANDAN;
                   5736 5ELCID0723 TREZIENTAS LAN%AS SON, TODAS ****** PENDONES;
                   8246 5ELCID1050 E ****** GELO DELANT & DIERON GELO PRIUADO.
                  14244 5ELCID1802 E TODAS LAS OTRAS DUENAS QUE ****** POR CASADAS.
                  19799 5ELCID2510 MUCHOS ****** POR RICOS LOS YFANTES DE CARRION.
                  21412 5ELCID2722 ESPUELAS ****** CAL%ADAS LOS MALOS TRAYDORES,
                  22973 5ELCID2926 ELLOS CONDES GALLIZANOS A EL ****** POR SE@OR.
                  25526 5ELCID3251 SOS OMNES LAS ****** & DELLAS PENSSARAN.
                  27146 5ELCID3469 ARMAS & CAUALLOS ****** LOS DEL CANPEADOR,
                  28024 5ELCID3577 AQUI ****** SU VANDO LOS YFANTES DE CARRION,
         WORD #4021 OCCURS  12 TIMES.
            INDEX OF DIVERSIFICATION =  2244.36 WITH STANDARD DEVIATION OF  1866.28

TIENES            14601 5ELCID1847 A UOS LAMA POR SE@OR, & ****** POR UUESTRO VASSALLO,
                  19071 5ELCID2413 EL ESPADA ****** DESNUDA EN LA MANO & VEOT AGUIJAR;
                  23151 5ELCID2950 ****** POR DESONDRADO, MAS LA UUESTRA ES MAYOR,
         WORD #4022 OCCURS   3 TIMES.

TIERRA              104 5ELCID0014 ALBRICIA, ALBARFFANEZ, CA ECHADOS SOMOS DE ******
                   1211 5ELCID0156 YA ME EXCO DE ******, CA DEL REY SO AYRADO.
                   1695 5ELCID0217 ATI LO GRADESCO, DIOS, QUE %IELO & ****** GUIAS;
                   1980 5ELCID0250 MAS POR QUE ME VO DE ******, DOUOS L MARCHOS,
                   2120 5ELCID0267 POR MALOS MESTUREROS DE ****** SODES ECHADO.
                   2289 5ELCID0288 COMMO SEUA DE ****** MYO %ID EL CANPEADOR;
                   2622 5ELCID0331 FEZIST %IELO & ******, EL TER%ERO EL MAR;
                   2712 5ELCID0343 POR ****** ANDICISTE XXXIJ A@OS, SE@OR SPIRITAL,
                   3148 5ELCID0396 YXIENDOS UA DE ****** EL CAMPEADOR LEAL,
                   3352 5ELCID0423 LA ****** DEL REY ALFONSSO ESTA NOCH LA PODEMOS QUITAR.
                   4306 5ELCID0548 GRANDES SON LAS GANAN%IAS QUE PRISO POR LA ****** DO UA.
                   4976 5ELCID0629 AYROLO EL REY ALFONSSO, DE ****** ECHADO LO HA,
                   5083 5ELCID0642 POR QUE SEME ENTRO EN MI ****** DERECHO ME AURA ADAR.
                   5526 5ELCID0696 ANTE ROYDO DE ATAMORES LA ****** QUERIE QUEBRAR;
                   6544 5ELCID0835 SI NON, ENESTA ****** ANGOSTA NON PODRIEMOS BIUIR.
                   6562 5ELCID0838 LA ****** ES ANGOSTA & SOBEIANA DE MALA;
                   7067 5ELCID0903 ESTANDO ALLI, MUCHA ****** PREAUA,
                   7471 5ELCID0958 QUE MYO %ID RUY DIAZ QUEL CORRIE LA ****** TODA;
                   7928 5ELCID1012 PRISO LO AL CONDE, PORA SU ****** LO LEUAUA;
                   8233 5ELCID1048 COMMO QUE YRA A DE REY & DE ****** ES ECHADO.
                   8840 5ELCID1125 COMMO OMNES EXIDOS DE ****** ESTRA@A,
                   9128 5ELCID1162 CABO DEL MAR ****** DE MOROS FIRME LA QUEBRANTA,
                   9166 5ELCID1167 EN ****** DE MOROS PRENDIENDO & GANANDO,
                   9759 5ELCID1240 POR AMOR DE REY ALFFONSSO, QUE DE ****** ME A ECHADO,
                   9803 5ELCID1245 LOS QUE EXIERON DE ****** DE RITAD SON ABONDADOS,
                  10453 5ELCID1325 ECHASTES LE DE ******, NON HA LA UUESTRA AMOR;
                  10461 5ELCID1326 MAGER EN ****** AGENA, EL BIEN FAZE LO SO;
                  10621 5ELCID1346 SEMEIA QUE EN ****** DE MOROS NON A BIUO OMNE,
                  10710 5ELCID1356 HYO LES MANDARE DAR CONDUCHO MIENTRA QUE POR MJ ****** FUEREN,
                  10726 5ELCID1358 QUANDO EN CABO DE MI ****** A QUESTAS DUE@AS FUEREN,
                  11452 5ELCID1450 POR LA ****** DEL REY MUCHO CONDUCHO LES DAN.
                  14563 5ELCID1842 FIRIERON SE A ******, DE%ENDIERON DELOS CAUALOS,
                  14575 5ELCID1844 BESAN LA ****** & LOS PIES AMOS:
                  14951 5ELCID1890 HYO ECHE DE ****** AL BUEN CAMPEADOR,
                  15271 5ELCID1934 ECHADO FU DE ****** & TOLLIDA LA ONOR,
                  15416 5ELCID1952 POR DAR LE GRAND ONDRA COMMO A REY DE ******.
                  15942 5ELCID2021 LOS YNOIOS & LAS MANOS EN ****** LOS FINCO,
                  18739 5ELCID2371 POR ESSO SALI DE MI ****** & VIN UOS BUSCAR,
                  19681 5ELCID2495 QUE HE AUER & ****** & ORO & ONOR,
                  25763 5ELCID3281 GRADO A DIOS QUE %IELO & ****** MANDA
                  26724 5ELCID3413 CA CRE%E UOS Y ONDRA & ****** & ONOR.
                  28346 5ELCID3619 TEMBRAR QUERIE LA ****** ODO ERAN MOUEDORES.
                  28508 5ELCID3640 POR LA COPLA DEL CAUALLO EN ****** LO ECHO.
                  28861 5ELCID3686 AL TIRAR DELA LAN%A EN ****** LO ECHO,
         WORD #4023 OCCURS  44 TIMES.
            INDEX OF DIVERSIFICATION =   667.77 WITH STANDARD DEVIATION OF  1062.88

TIERRAL            2454 5ELCID0309 QUE, SI DESPUES DEL PLAZO EN SU ******* PUDIES TOMAR,
         WORD #4024 OCCURS   1 TIMES.

TIERRAS            4285 5ELCID0546 POR ESSAS ******* AYUSO QUANTO PUEDEN ANDAR.
                   4432 5ELCID0564 POR TODAS ESSAS ******* YUAN LOS MANDADOS,
                   5156 5ELCID0652 POR TODAS ESSAS ******* LOS PREGONES DAN;
                   6937 5ELCID0887 HONORES & ******* AUELLAS CONDONADAS,
                   7134 5ELCID0913 TODAS ESSAS ******* TODAS LAS PREAUA,
```

WORD C# PREFIX CONTEXT

TIERRAS (CON'T)

```
7297 5ELCID0936 ******* CALCANZ NEGRAS LAS VA PARANDO,
7323 5ELCID0939 HYA VA EL MANDADO POR LAS ******* TODAS,
7519 5ELCID0964 AGORA CORREN LAS ******* QUE EN MI ENPARA ESTAN;
8569 5ELCID1088 DEXADO A SARAGOZA & ALAS ******* DUCA,
8577 5ELCID1089 E DEXADO A HUESCA & LAS ******* DE MONT ALUAN.
8605 5ELCID1093 ******* DE BORRIANA TODAS CONQUISTAS LAS HA.
8683 5ELCID1103 EN SUS ******* SOMOS & FEMOS LES TODOMAL,
8808 5ELCID1120 SI EN ESTAS ******* QUISIEREMOS DURAR,
9328 5ELCID1186 AMANEZIO AMYO ZID EN ******* DE MON REAL.
9341 5ELCID1188 A ******* DE CASTIELLA ENBIO SUS MENSSAIES:
10112 5ELCID1281 AESTAS ******* ESTRANAS QUE NOS PUDIEMOS GANAR.
10262 5ELCID1299 EN ******* DE VALENZIA FER QUIERO OBISPADO,
10315 5ELCID1306 QUE EN ******* DE VALENZIA SEaOR AVIE OBISPO
10328 5ELCID1308 ******* DE VALENCIA REMANIDAS EN PAZ,
11135 5ELCID1409 MIENTRA QUE FUEREMOS POR SUS ******* CONDUCHO NOS MANDO DAR.
12922 5ELCID1639 VENIDOM ES DELIZIO DE ******* DALENT MAR,
12943 5ELCID1642 EN ESTAS ******* AGENAS VERAN LAS MORADAS COMMO SE FAZEN,
14045 5ELCID1779 LOS MOROS DELAS ******* GANADO SEAN Y ALGO;
14425 5ELCID1824 QUE LAS OTRAS ******* PARTE.
15174 5ELCID1920 EN POCAS ******* A TALES DOS VARONES.
15925 5ELCID2009 CON VNOS XV A ******* FIRIC,
20189 5ELCID2563 LEUAR LAS HEMOS A NUESTRAS ******* DE CARRION,
20246 5ELCID2570 VOS LES DIESTES VILLAS E ******* POR ARRAS ENTIERRAS DE CARRION,
20484 5ELCID2600 QUE AYADES UUESTROS MENSSAIES EN ******* DE CARRION.
20774 5ELCID2638 DIL QUE ENBIO MIS FIJAS A ******* DE CARRION,
21377 5ELCID2717 NON ABREDES PART EN ******* DE CARRION.
23420 5ELCID2983 POR TODAS SUS ******* ASSI LO YUAN PENSSANDO,
27181 5ELCID3474 MAS QUIERO A VALENZIA QUE ******* DE CARRION.
27479 5ELCID3510 QUE EN TODAS NUESTRAS ******* NON HA TAN BUEN VARON.
28946 5ELCID3697 GRANDES SON LOS PESARES POR ******* DE CARRION.
WORD #4025 OCCURS 35 TIMES.
INDEX OF DIVERSIFICATION = 724.32 WITH STANDARD DEVIATION OF 1007.98

TIESTA 97 5ELCID0013 MEZIO MYO ZID LOS OMBROS & ENGRAMEO LA ******:
WORD #4026 OCCURS 1 TIMES.

TIGERA 9766 5ELCID1241 NIN ENTRARIE ENELA ******, NI VN PELO NON AURIE TAIADO,
WORD #4027 OCCURS 1 TIMES.

TIRAR 28857 5ELCID3686 AL ***** DELA LANZA EN TIERRA LO ECHO,
WORD #4028 OCCURS 1 TIMES.

TIZON 19181 5ELCID2426 E GANO A ***** QUE MILL MARCOS DORO VAL.
20295 5ELCID2575 DAR UOS HE DOS ESPADAS, A COLADA & A *****,
21455 5ELCID2727 AL VNA DIZEN COLADA & AL OTRA *****,
24761 5ELCID3153 DILES DOS ESPADAS, A COLADA & A *****,
24932 5ELCID3175 SACARON LAS ESPADAS COLADO & *****,
25037 5ELCID3189 TENDIO EL BRAZO, LA ESPADA ***** LE DIO;
25139 5ELCID3201 HYA PAGADO SO DE MIS ESPADAS, DE COLADA & DE *****.
27866 5ELCID3556 COLADA & *****, QUE NON LIDIASSEN CON ELLAS LOS DEL CANPEADOR;
WORD #4029 OCCURS 8 TIMES.
INDEX OF DIVERSIFICATION = 1239.71 WITH STANDARD DEVIATION OF 1305.62

TO 2650 5ELCID0335 PASTORES ** GLOORIFFICARON, QUIERON DE A LAUDARE,
3249 5ELCID0409 MIENTRA QUE VISQUIEREDES BIEN SE FARA LO **.
WORD #4030 OCCURS 2 TIMES.

TOD 4015 5ELCID0510 MANDO PARTIR *** AQUESTE AUER,
16914 5ELCID2141 *** ESTO ES PUESTO, SABED, EN GRANT RECABDO.
20921 5ELCID2658 *** ESTO LES FIZO EL MORO POR EL AMOR DEL ZID CAMPEADOR.
24805 5ELCID3169 ATORGAN LOS ALCALDES: *** ESTO ES RAZON.
26831 5ELCID3427 A MUCHOS PLAZE DE *** ESTA CORT,
28577 5ELCID3649 RELUMBRA *** EL CAMPO, TANTO ER LINPIA & CLARA;
WORD #4031 OCCURS 6 TIMES.
INDEX OF DIVERSIFICATION = 4911.40 WITH STANDARD DEVIATION OF 4583.14

TODA 641 5ELCID0081 ESPESO E EL ORO & **** LA PLATA,
657 5ELCID0083 PORA **** MI COMPANA;
2370 5ELCID0299 FABLO MYO ZID DE **** VOLUNTAD:
3462 5ELCID0437 **** LA NOCHE IAZE EN ZELADA EL QUE EN BUEN ORA NASCO,
3597 5ELCID0453 DA QUESTE A CORRO FABLARA **** ESPAaA.
4046 5ELCID0515 **** LA QUINTA A MYO ZID FINCAUA.
4120 5ELCID0524 ASMO MYO ZID CON **** SU CONPAaA
4153 5ELCID0528 BUSCAR NOS YE EL REY ALFONSSO CON **** SU MESNADA.
5015 5ELCID0634 RIBERA DE SALON **** YRA AMAL,
7472 5ELCID0958 QUE MYO ZID RUY DIAZ QUEL CORRIE LA TIERRA ****;
7998 5ELCID1021 NON COMBRE VN BOCADO POR QUANTO HA EN **** ESPAaA,
9685 5ELCID1231 TORNADO ES MYO ZID CON **** ESTA GANANZIA.
10311 5ELCID1305 DIOS, QUE ALEGRE ERA **** CHRISTIANISMO,
10743 5ELCID1360 OYD ME, ESCUELLAS, & **** LA MI CORT.
13675 5ELCID1733 **** ESTA GANANZIA EN SU MANO A RASTADO.
14206 5ELCID1798 DE **** LA SU QUINTA EL DIEZMO LA MANDADO.
15131 5ELCID1913 ANDAR LE QUIERO A MYO ZID EN **** PRO.
18613 5ELCID2355 HYO UOS DIGO, ZID, POR **** CARIDAD,
```

WORD C# PREFIX CONTEXT

TODA (CON'T)

22476 5ELCID2862 EN LOS DIAS DE VAGAR **** NUESTRA RENCURA SABREMOS CONTAR.
22853 5ELCID2911 LA POCA & LA GRANT **** ES DE MYO SE@OR.
23249 5ELCID2961 LO QUE NON CUYDAUA FER DE **** ESTA SAZON,
23601 5ELCID3006 DE **** CASTIELLA TODOS LOS MEIORES
24946 5ELCID3177 SACA LAS ESPADAS & RELUMBRA **** LA CORT,
25555 5ELCID3255 OYD ME **** LA CORT & PESEUOS DE MYO MAL;
25690 5ELCID3271 MER%ED, YA REY, EL MEIOR DE **** ESPA@A
26639 5ELCID3401 AESTO CALLARON & ASCUCHO **** LA CORT.
26869 5ELCID3432 BIEN UOS DI VAGAR EN **** ESTA CORT,
26896 5ELCID3436 HYO UOS RUEGO QUE ME OYADES **** LA CORT,
27067 5ELCID3458 QUE VAL, MINAYA, **** ESSA RAZON?
WORD #4032 OCCURS 29 TIMES.
INDEX OF DIVERSIFICATION = 942.79 WITH STANDARD DEVIATION OF 1059.00

TODAS
384 5ELCID0048 MAS EL CRIADOR UOS UALA CON ***** SUS UERTUDES SANTAS.
1046 5ELCID0134 ACOGEN SELE OMNES DE ***** PARTES MEGUADOS,
3058 5ELCID0385 E A ***** SUS DUENAS QUE CON ELLAS ESTAN;
3143 5ELCID0395 GRANDES YENTES SELE ACOIEN ESSA NOCH DE ***** PARTES.
3202 5ELCID0403 VANSSELE ACOGIENDO YENTES DE ***** PARTES.
3324 5ELCID0419 NOTO TREZIENTAS LAN%AS QUE ***** TIENEN PENDONES.
3549 5ELCID0447 E BIEN ACOIAN ***** LAS GANAN%IAS,
3648 5ELCID0460 POR VER SUS LAUORES & ***** SUS HEREDADES.
3671 5ELCID0463 LAS YENTES DE FUERA ***** SON DE RAMADAS.
4010 5ELCID0509 QUEL BUSCARIE MAL CON ***** SUS MESNADAS.
4430 5ELCID0564 POR ***** ESSAS TIERRAS YUAN LOS MANDADOS,
5129 5ELCID0648 NON LO DETIENEN, VIENEN DE ***** PARTES.
5154 5ELCID0652 POR ***** ESSAS TIERRAS LOS PREGONES DAN;
5735 5ELCID0723 TREZIENTAS LAN%AS SON, ***** TIENEN PENDONES;
7106 5ELCID0909 CON ***** SUS YENTES FIZO VNA TRASNOCHADA;
7132 5ELCID0913 ***** ESSAS TIERRAS TODAS LAS PREAUA,
7135 5ELCID0913 TODAS ESSAS TIERRAS ***** LAS PREAUA,
7324 5ELCID0939 HYA VA EL MANDADO POR LAS TIERRAS *****,
7440 5ELCID0954 FUERON LOS MANDADOS A ***** PARTES,
7944 5ELCID1015 DE ***** PARTES LOS SOS SE AIUNTARON;
8608 5ELCID1093 TIERRAS DE BORRIANA ***** CONQUISTAS LAS HA.
9095 5ELCID1157 ALEGRE ERA EL %ID & ***** SUS COMPA@AS,
9489 5ELCID1206 SONANDO VAN SUS NUEUAS ***** ATODAS PARTES.
9613 5ELCID1221 YA FOLGAUA MYO %ID CON ***** SUS CONPA@AS;
10501 5ELCID1331 CON AQUESTAS ***** DE VALEN%IA ES SE@OR,
10520 5ELCID1333 E FIZO %INCO LIDES CAMPALES & ***** LAS ARRANCO.
11186 5ELCID1415 VERIEDES CAUALLEROS VENIR DE ***** PARTES,
12380 5ELCID1572 E ***** LAS PUERTAS & LAS EXIDAS & LAS ENTRADAS,
12619 5ELCID1601 ***** LAS SUS MESNADAS EN GRANT DELENT ESTAUAN,
12703 5ELCID1612 OIOS VELIDOS CATAN A ***** PARTES,
13532 5ELCID1715 DE ***** GUARNIZONES MUY BIEN ES ADOBADO.
13966 5ELCID1769 LEUANTARON SE ***** & BESARON LE LAS MANOS,
14239 5ELCID1802 E ***** LAS OTRAS DUENAS QUE TIENEN POR CASADAS.
14812 5ELCID1872 E GUARNIR UOS DE ***** ARMAS COMMO UOS DIXIEREDES AQUI,
14841 5ELCID1876 ***** ESTAS NUEUAS A BIEN ABRAN DE VENIR.
17891 5ELCID2264 EA ***** LAS DUE@AS & ALOS FIJOS DALGO;
19022 5ELCID2406 CAUALLOS SIN DUENOS SALIR A ***** PARTES.
19376 5ELCID2455 DE ***** PARTES SOS VASSALLOS VAN LEGANDO;
19452 5ELCID2465 ***** LAS GANAN%IAS A VALEN%IA SON LEGADAS;
19464 5ELCID2466 ALEGRE ES MYO %ID CON ***** SUS CONPA@AS,
19657 5ELCID2492 ***** ESTAS GANAN%IAS FIZO EL CANPEADOR.
19767 5ELCID2506 DE ***** SUS CONPA@AS & DE TODOS SUS VASSALLOS;
20575 5ELCID2612 ESPIENDOS DELAS DUE@AS & DE ***** SUS COMPA@AS.
20591 5ELCID2614 ALEGRE VA MYO %ID CON ***** SUS COMPA@AS.
23418 5ELCID2983 POR ***** SUS TIERRAS ASSI LO YUAN PENSSANDO,
23647 5ELCID3012 DE ***** PARTES ALLI IUNTADOS SON.
24220 5ELCID3088 CON ORO & CON PLATA ***** LAS PRESAS SON,
24960 5ELCID3179 MARAUILLAN SE DELLAS ***** LOS OMNES BUENOS DELA CORT.
26258 5ELCID3348 EN ***** GUISAS MAS VALEN QUE VOS.
27038 5ELCID3454 EN ***** GUISAS TALES SODES QUALES DIGO YO;
27195 5ELCID3476 DAD ME UUESTROS CAUALLEROS CON ***** UUESTRAS GUARNIZONES,
27433 5ELCID3505 QUANDO ***** ESTAS NUEUAS ASSI PUESTAS SON,
27477 5ELCID3510 QUE EN ***** NUESTRAS TIERRAS NON HA TAN BUEN VARON.
27680 5ELCID3533 MAS TRES SEMANAS DE PLAZO ***** COMPLIDAS SON.
28259 5ELCID3608 ***** LAS YENTES ESCOMBRARON ADERREDOR,
28602 5ELCID3652 LAS MONCLURAS DEL YELMO ***** GELAS CORTAUA,
WORD #4033 OCCURS 56 TIMES.
INDEX OF DIVERSIFICATION = 512.05 WITH STANDARD DEVIATION OF 630.31

TODEL
2861 5ELCID0361 TUERES REY DE LOS REYES & DE ***** MUNDO PADRE,
10401 5ELCID1318 FINCO SOS YNOIOS ANTE ***** PUEBLO,
21129 5ELCID2684 DIOS LO QUIERA & LO MANDE, QUE DE ***** MUNDO ES SE@OR,
25000 5ELCID3184 ALEGROS LE ***** CUERPO, SONRRISOS DE CORA%ON,
27056 5ELCID3456 HYO SO ALBARFANEZ PORA ***** MEIOR.
WORD #4034 OCCURS 5 TIMES.
INDEX OF DIVERSIFICATION = 6047.75 WITH STANDARD DEVIATION OF 3864.53

TODO
532 5ELCID0068 DE **** CONDUCHO BIEN LOS OUO BASTIDOS.
946 5ELCID0121 QUE NON LAS CATEDES EN **** AQUESTE A@O.
959 5ELCID0123 NOS HUEBOS AUEMOS EN **** DE GANAR ALGO.

WORD C# PREFIX CONTEXT

TODO (CON'T)

```
                    1015 5ELCIDO130 O QUE GANAN%IA NOS CARA PCR **** AQUESTE A@O?
                    1609 5ELCIDO206 VENGO, CAMPEADOR, CON **** BUEN RECABDO:
                    2043 5ELCIDO257 DELLAS & DE MI MUGIER FAGADES **** RECABDO.
                    2869 5ELCIDO362 ATI ADORO & CREO DE **** VOLUNTAD,
                    3415 5ELCIDO431 MANDADO DE SO SE@OR **** LO HAN AFAR.
                    3758 5ELCIDO475 DEXAN LA A MYO %ID, **** ESTO NON PRE%IA NADA.
                    3977 5ELCIDO505 **** LO OTRO AFELO EN UUESTRA MANO.
                    4835 5ELCIDO612 METIOLA EN SOMO EN **** LO MAS ALTO.
                    6931 5ELCIDO886 SOBRESTO ****, AUOS QUITO, MINAYA,
                    6960 5ELCIDO890 SOBRE AQUESTO ****, DEZIR UOS QUIERO, MINAYA:
                    6966 5ELCIDO891 DE **** MYO REYNO LOS QUE LO QUISIEREN FAR,
                    7073 5ELCIDO904 EL DE RIO MARTIN **** LO METIO EN PARIA.
                    7115 5ELCIDO910 DEXO EL POYO, **** LO DESENPARAUA,
                    7194 5ELCIDO922 **** GELO DIZE, QUE NOL ENCUBRE NADA.
                    7224 5ELCIDO926  DIOS, COMMO FUE ALEGRE **** AQUEL FONSSADO,
                    7306 5ELCIDO937 E A DERREDOR **** LO VA PREANDO.
                    8459 5ELCID1075 PAGADO UOS HE POR **** AQUESTE A@O;
                    8623 5ELCID1095 EL CON **** ESTO PRISO A MURUIEDRO.
                    9896 5ELCID1255 AFEUOS **** AQUESTO PUESTO EN BUEN RECABDO.
                   10766 5ELCID1363 POR QUE LOS DESEREDE, **** GELO SUELTO YO;
                   10949 5ELCID1386 EN **** SODES PRO, EN ESTO ASSI LO FAGADES:
                   11082 5ELCID1403 **** SERIE ALEGRE, QUE NON AURIE NINGUN PESAR.
                   11782 5ELCID1494 E EN MEDINA **** EL RECABDO ESTA;
                   12132 5ELCID1539 EL REY LO PAGO ****, & QUITO SEUA MINAYA.
                   12343 5ELCID1567 CA BIEN SABE QUE ALBARFANEZ TRAHE **** RECABDO;
                   12874 5ELCID1634 **** EL BIEN QUE YO HE, TODO LO TENGO DELANT:
                   12880 5ELCID1634 TODO EL BIEN QUE YO HE, **** LO TENGO DELANT:
                   13749 5ELCID1742 DEXO ALBARFANEZ POR SABER **** RECABDO.
                   14052 5ELCID1780 MAGER DE **** ESTO, EL CAMPEADOR CONTADO
                   14591 5ELCID1846 POR MYO %ID EL CAMPEADOR **** ESTO VOS BESAMOS;
                   15347 5ELCID1943 CON **** ESTO, AUOS DIXO ALFONSSO
                   16045 5ELCID2035 EN **** MYO REYNO PARTE DESDE OY.
                   17334 5ELCID2193 **** LO QUE UOS FECHES ES DE BUENA GUISA.
                   17401 5ELCID2201 ATAN FIRME MIENTRE & DE **** CORA%ON
                   18109 5ELCID2291 EL MANTO & EL BRIAL **** SUZIO LO SACO.
                   18453 5ELCID2335 EN VALEN%IA FOLGAD A **** UUESTRO SABOR,
                   19160 5ELCID2423 CORTOL EL YELMO &, LIBRADO **** LO HAL,
                   19345 5ELCID2450 EL ESCUDO TRAE AL CUELLO & **** ESPADO;
                   22965 5ELCID2925 FASTA DENTRO EN SANTI YAGUO DE **** ES SE@OR,
                   23256 5ELCID2962 ANDARAN MYOS PORTEROS POR **** MYO REYNO,
                   24302 5ELCID3098 POR TALLO FAZE ESTO QUE RECABDAR QUIERE **** LO SUYO;
                   27303 5ELCID3489 ELLOS SON ADOBADOS PORA CUMPLLIR **** LO SO;
                   28390 5ELCID3625 FIRIENSSE EN LOS ESCUDOS SIN **** PAUOR.
                   28439 5ELCID3632 PASSO GELO ****, QUE NADA NOL VALIO,
                   28618 5ELCID3654 LA COFIA & EL ALMOFAR **** GELO LEUAUA,
         WORD #4035 OCCURS   48 TIMES.
            INDEX OF DIVERSIFICATION =    596.57 WITH STANDARD DEVIATION OF    729.51

TODOL               5140 5ELCIDO650 ANDIDIERON ***** DIA, QUE VAGAR NON SE DAN,
         WORD #4036 OCCURS    1 TIMES.

TODOM               7656 5ELCIDO980 LO DE ANTES & DE AGORA ***** LO PECHARA;
         WORD #4037 OCCURS    1 TIMES.

TODOMAL             8688 5ELCID1103 EN SUS TIERRAS SOMOS & FEMOS LES *******,
         WORD #4038 OCCURS    1 TIMES.

TODOS                140 5ELCIDO019 DELAS SUS BOCAS ***** DIZIAN UNA RAZON:
                     544 5ELCIDO069 PAGOS MYO %ID EL CAMPEADOR & ***** LOS OTROS QUEUAN
                                    ASO %ERUICIO
                     746 5ELCIDO094 VEALO EL CRIADOR CON ***** LOS SOS SANTOS,
                     820 5ELCIDO105 NON LO DETARDAN, ***** TRES SE APARTARON.
                    2310 5ELCIDO291 %IENTO QUINZE CAUALLEROS ***** IUNTADOS SON;
                    2313 5ELCIDO292 ***** DEMANDAN POR MIO %ID EL CAMPEADOR;
                    2361 5ELCIDO298 TORNOS A SONRISAR; LEGAN LE *****, LA MANOL BAN BESAR.
                    2418 5ELCIDO305 PLOGO ALOS OTROS OMNES ***** QUANTOS CON EL ESTAN.
                    2476 5ELCIDO312 ASOS CAUALLEROS MANDOLOS ***** IUNTAR:
                    2552 5ELCIDO322 CUEMO LO MANDO MYO %ID, ASSI LO AN ***** HA FAR.
                    3633 5ELCIDO458 EN CASTEION ***** SE LEUANTAUAN,
                    3651 5ELCIDO461 ***** SON EXIDOS, LAS PUERTAS DEXADAS AN ABIERTAS
                    4211 5ELCIDO536 ***** SODES PAGADOS & NINGUNO POR PAGAR.
                    4237 5ELCIDO539 LO QUE DIXO EL %ID A ***** LOS OTROS PLAZ.
                    4245 5ELCIDO540 DEL CASTIELLO QUE PRISIERON ***** RICOS SE PARTEN;
                    4404 5ELCIDO561 A ***** SOS VARONES MANDO FAZER VNA CARCAUA,
                    4466 5ELCIDO568 AGARDANDO SEUA MYO %ID CON ***** SUS VASSALLOS;
                    4709 5ELCIDO597 FIRID LOS, CAUALLEROS, ***** SINES DUBDAN%A;
                    4871 5ELCIDO616 OYD AMI, ALBARFANEZ & ***** LOS CAUALLEROS
                    5376 5ELCIDO679 ***** LOS MOROS & LAS MORAS DE FUERA LOS MANDA ECHAR,
                    5424 5ELCIDO685 ***** YSCAMOS FUERA, QUE NADI NON RASTE,
                    5724 5ELCIDO722 ***** FIEREN ENEL AZ DO ESTA PERO VERMUEZ.
                    5741 5ELCIDO724 SE@OS MOROS MATARON, ***** DE SE@OS COLPES;
                    6281 5ELCIDO800 REFECHOS SON ***** ESOS CHRISTIANOS CON AQUESTA GANAN%IA.
                    6309 5ELCIDO803 GRANT A EL GOZO MYO %ID CON ***** SOS VASSALOS.
                    6334 5ELCIDO806  DIOS, QUE BIEN PAGO A ***** SUS VASSALLOS,
                    6355 5ELCIDO809 QUANTOS EL TRAE ***** SON PAGADOS.
```

WORD C# PREFIX CONTEXT

TODOS (CON'T)

6403 5ELCID0817 ***** CON SIELLAS & MUY BIEN ENFRENADOS,
6569 5ELCID0839 ***** LOS DIAS A MYO %ID AGUARDAUAN
6653 5ELCID0849 EN ***** LOS SOS NON FALLARIEDES VN MESQUINO.
7161 5ELCID0917 DOZIENTOS CON EL, QUE ***** %INEN ESPADAS;
7359 5ELCID0944 ***** SON ALEGRES, GANAN%IAS TRAEN GRANDES.
7750 5ELCID0992 ELLOS VIENEN CUESTA YUSO, & ***** TRAHEN CAL%AS,
7812 5ELCID1000 ***** SON ACOBADOS QUANDO MYO %ID ESTO OUO FABLADO;
8044 5ELCID1027 SI NON, EN ***** UUESTROS DIAS NON VEREDES CHRISTIANISMO.
8756 5ELCID1113 ALTER%ER DIA ***** IUNTADOS SON,
9379 5ELCID1193 ***** VENGAN DE GRADO, NINGUNO NON HA PREMIA,
9560 5ELCID1215 ***** ERAN RICOS QUANTOS QUE ALLI HA.
9595 5ELCID1219 ALEGRE ERA EL CAMPEADOR CON ***** LOS QUE HA,
9723 5ELCID1236 GRAND ALEGRIA ES ENTRE ***** ESSOS CHRISTIANOS
9838 5ELCID1248 LOS QUE FUERON CON EL, & LOS DE DESPUES, ***** SON PAGADOS;
9929 5ELCID1259 METER LOS HE EN ESCRIPTO, & ***** SEAN CONTADOS,
9968 5ELCID1263 MANDO LOS VENIR ALA CORTH & A ***** LOS IUNTAR,
10167 5ELCID1287 EN ESTAS NUEUAS ***** SEA ALEGRANDO,
10549 5ELCID1337 DE SIELLAS & DE FRENOS ***** GUARNIDOS SON,
11414 5ELCID1445 ***** LOS DIAS DEL SIEGLO EN LEUAR LO ADELANT
11863 5ELCID1504 ***** VIENEN EN VNO, AGORA LEGARAN.
12011 5ELCID1523 ONDRAR UOS HEMOS *****, CA TALES LA SU AUZE,
12098 5ELCID1535 ***** FUERON ALEGRES DEL %ERUI%IO QUE TOMARON,
12346 5ELCID1568 AFEUOS ***** AQUESTOS RE%IBEN A MINAYA
12531 5ELCID1590 QUANDO OUO CORRIDO, ***** SE MARAUILLAUAN;
12816 5ELCID1626 CON L VEZES MILL DE ARMAS, ***** FUERON CONPLIDOS,
13305 5ELCID1687 POR LA MANANA PRIETA ***** ARMADOS SEADES,
13350 5ELCID1692 ESSORA DIXIERON *****: AMOR & DE VOLUNTAD.
13499 5ELCID1711 SALIDOS SON ***** ARMADOS POR LAS TORRES DE VAN%IA,
13724 5ELCID1739 ALEGRE ERA MYO %ID & ***** SOS VASSALLOS,
13814 5ELCID1750 ESTO DIOS SE LO QUISO CON ***** LOS SOS SANTOS,
14031 5ELCID1777 NON PUDIERON ELLOS SABER LA CUENTA DE ***** LOS CAUALLOS,
14092 5ELCID1784 QUE A GANADO MYO %ID CON ***** SUS VASSALLOS
14647 5ELCID1853 RICOS SON VENIDOS ***** LOS SOS VASSALLOS,
15145 5ELCID1915 VAN PORA VALEN%IA ELLOS & ***** LOS SOS.
15742 5ELCID1998 E ***** LOS OTROS QUE Y SON.
15771 5ELCID2001 DALMA & DE CORA%ON, & ***** LOS QUE EN PODER DESSOS FOSSEN;
16092 5ELCID2041 ***** LOS DEMAS DESTO AUIEN SABOR;
16284 5ELCID2066 ***** ERAN ALEGRES & ACUERDAN EN VNA RAZON:
16320 5ELCID2070 AL SALIR DE LA MISSA ***** IUNTADOS SON,
16627 5ELCID2106 LOS YERNOS & LAS FIJAS ***** UUESTROS FIJOS SON:
16733 5ELCID2119 ***** SON PAGADOS DELAS VISTAS QUANTOS QUE Y SON.
16976 5ELCID2149 PLEGA AL CRIADOR CON ***** LOS SOS SANTOS, ESTE PLAZER
17251 5ELCID2182 ***** ESSA NOCH FUERON A SUS POSADAS,
17347 5ELCID2194 NON SERAN MENGUADAS EN ***** UUESTROS DIAS
17461 5ELCID2209 ***** SUS CAUALLEROS A PRIESSA SON IUNTADOS.
17502 5ELCID2214 RE%IBIO LOS MYO %ID CON ***** SUS VASALLOS;
17519 5ELCID2217 ***** LOS DE MYO %ID TAN BIEN SON ACORDADOS,
17785 5ELCID2250 ANTES QUE ENTRASSEN AIANTAR ***** LOS QUEBRANTARON.
17964 5ELCID2273 ALEGRE ERA EL %ID & ***** SUS VASSALLOS.
17998 5ELCID2277 EL CRIADOR UOS VALLA CON ***** LOS SOS SANTOS.
18008 5ELCID2278 EN VALEN%IA SEY MYO %ID CON ***** SUS VASSALLOS,
18296 5ELCID2315 ALEGRAUAS EL %ID & ***** SUS VARONES,
19208 5ELCID2430 SABET, ***** DE FIRME ROBAUAN EL CAMPO.
19325 5ELCID2447 COMMO YO FIO POR DIOS & EN ***** LOS SOS SANTOS,
19406 5ELCID2459 ***** ESTOS BIENES DEUOS SON & DE UUESTROS VASSALLOS.
19617 5ELCID2486 QUE ***** PRISIESSEN SO DERECHO CONTADO,
19631 5ELCID2488 ASSI LO FAZEN *****, CA ERAN ACORDADOS.
19772 5ELCID2506 DE TODAS SUS CONPA@AS & DE ***** SUS VASSALLOS;
20400 5ELCID2589 ***** PRENDEN ARMAS & CAUALGAN A VIGOR,
21336 5ELCID2712 ***** ERAN YDOS, ELLOS IIIJ SOLOS SON,
21586 5ELCID2744 SANGRIENTAS EN LAS CAMISAS & ***** LOS CICLATONES.
21761 5ELCID2768 DE ***** LOS OTROS APARTE SE SALIO,
22071 5ELCID2809 ***** TRES SE@EROS POR LOS ROBREDOS DE CORPES,
22423 5ELCID2856 ***** GELO GRADE%EN & SOS PAGADOS SON,
23603 5ELCID3006 DE TODA CASTIELLA ***** LOS MEIORES
23727 5ELCID3022 BIEN AGUISADO VIENE EL %ID CON ***** LOS SOS,
24168 5ELCID3082 RESPONDIERON *****: NOS ESSO QUEREMOS, SE@OR.
24177 5ELCID3083 ASSI COMMO LO ADICHO, ***** ACOBADOS SON.
24354 5ELCID3105 CUERDA MIENTRA ENTRA MYO %ID CON ***** LOS SOS:
24396 5ELCID3110 E DESI ADELANT, SABET, ***** LOS OTROS:
24417 5ELCID3113 NIN ***** LOS DEL BANCO DE YFANTES DE CARRION.
24467 5ELCID3119 ACA POSARE CON ***** AQUESTOS MIOS.
24598 5ELCID3134 GRANDE TUERTO LE HAN TENIDO, SABEMOS LO ***** NOS;
24621 5ELCID3137 ***** METED Y MIENTES, CA SODES CO@OS%EDORES,
24824 5ELCID3162 CON ***** SUS PARIENTES & EL VANDO QUE Y SON;
24954 5ELCID3179 LAS MA%ANAS & LOS ARRIAZES ***** DORO SON.
25390 5ELCID3233 TORNAR GELOS QUIERO, CA ***** FECHOS SON,
25858 5ELCID3294 DE UUESTROS AUERES DE ***** PAGADOS SODES.
26079 5ELCID3324 DELANT MYO %ID & DELANTE ***** OVISTE TE DE ALABAR
26094 5ELCID3326 CROUIERON TELO *****, MAS NON SABEN LA VERDAD.
26535 5ELCID3387 FALSSO A ***** & MAS AL CRIADOR.
27660 5ELCID3531 ESPIDIOS DE ***** LOS QUE SOS AMIGOS SON.
27725 5ELCID3539 E ***** SUS PARIENTES CON ELLOS SON;
27801 5ELCID3548 DEMAS SOBRE ***** YES EL REY DON ALFONSSO,

WORD C# PREFIX CONTEXT

TODOS (CON'T)

27824 5ELCID3551 ***** TRES SE ACUERDAN, CA SON DE VN SEaOR.
27952 5ELCID3567 CA ***** LO SABEN QUE LC BUSCASTES VOS.
27981 5ELCID3571 ***** TRES SCN ARMADOS LOS DEL CAMPEADOR,
28107 5ELCID3589 ***** TRES SCN ACORDADOS LOS DEL CAMPEADOR,
28241 5ELCID3605 LIBRAUAN SE DEL CAMPO ***** ADERREDOR.
28356 5ELCID3621 ***** TRES POR TRES YA JUNTADOS SON:
28874 5ELCID3688 ***** SE CUEDAN QUE FERIDO ES DE MUERT.
29171 5ELCID3725 A ***** ALCANZA ONDRA POR EL QUE EN BUEN ORA NA%IO.
29196 5ELCID3728 ASSI FFAGAMOS NOS ***** IUSTOS & PECCADORES
WORD #4039 OCCURS 120 TIMES.
INDEX OF DIVERSIFICATION = 243.17 WITH STANDARD DEVIATION OF 274.43

TOLEDO 28177 5ELCID3597 ESTA LID EN ****** LAFIZIERADES, MAS NON QUISIESTES VOS.
WORD #4040 OCCURS 1 TIMES.

TOLER 7808 5ELCID0999 OY EN ESTE PINAR DE TEUAR POR ***** ME LA GANAN%IA.
WORD #4041 OCCURS 1 TIMES.

TOLIO 9221 5ELCID1173 EN CADA VNO DESTOS AaOS MYO %ID LES ***** EL PAN.
WORD #4042 OCCURS 1 TIMES.

TOLLEDO 23265 5ELCID2963 PREGONARAN MI CORT PORA DENTRO EN *******,
23316 5ELCID2970 VENGAM A *******, ESTOL DO DE PLAZO.
23393 5ELCID2980 QUE CORT FAZIE EN ******* AQUEL REY ONDRADO,
23449 5ELCID2986 POR QUE EL REY FAZIE CORT EN *******,
23889 5ELCID3043 PORA ******* EL REY TORNADA DA,
23960 5ELCID3053 EL REY DON ALFONSSO A ******* ES ENTRADO,
24567 5ELCID3131 ESTA TER%ERA A ******* LA VIN FER OY,
WORD #4043 OCCURS 7 TIMES.
INDEX OF DIVERSIFICATION = 216.00 WITH STANDARD DEVIATION OF 243.40

TOLLER 27565 5ELCID3520 QUIEN VOS LO ****** QUISIERE NOL VALA EL CRIADOR,
WORD #4044 OCCURS 1 TIMES.

TOLLIDA 15273 5ELCID1934 ECHADO FU DE TIERRA & ******* LA ONOR-
WORD #4045 OCCURS 1 TIMES.

TOLLIDAS 19152 5ELCID2422 LAS CARBONCLAS DEL YELMO ******** GELA HA,
WORD #4046 OCCURS 1 TIMES.

TOLLIES 27537 5ELCID3517 SI AUOS LE *******, EL CAUALLO NO HAURIE TAN BUEN SEaOR.
WORD #4047 OCCURS 1 TIMES.

TOLLIESSE 14127 5ELCID1788 E NON LA ********* DENT CHRISTIANO:
WORD #4048 OCCURS 1 TIMES.

TOLLIO 27325 5ELCID3492 ALLI SE ****** EL CAPIELO EL %ID CAMPEADOR,
WORD #4049 OCCURS 1 TIMES.

TOMAD 5463 5ELCID0689 E VOS, PERO VERMUEZ, LA MI SEaA *****;
16950 5ELCID2146 ***** AQUESTO, & BESO UUESTRAS MANOS.
WORD #4050 OCCURS 2 TIMES.

TOMADES 16856 5ELCID2133 DAD MANERO A QUI LAS DE, QUANDO UOS LAS *******;
WORD #4051 OCCURS 1 TIMES.

TOMADO 6007 5ELCID0761 LOS DOS LE FALLEN, & EL VNOL HA ******,
7901 5ELCID1009 AL CONDE DON REMONT A PRESON LEAN ******;
WORD #4052 OCCURS 2 TIMES.

TOMADOS 9849 5ELCID1249 VELLO MYO %ID CON LOS AVERES QUE AUIEN *******,
WORD #4053 OCCURS 1 TIMES.

TOMALOS 14041 5ELCID1778 QUE ANDAN ARRIADOS & NON HA QUI *******,
WORD #4054 OCCURS 1 TIMES.

TOMAN 11943 5ELCID1514 LUEGO ***** ARMAS & TOMANSE A DEPORTAR,
14432 5ELCID1825 POR EL REY DON ALFONSSO ***** SSE APREGUNTAR.
WORD #4055 OCCURS 2 TIMES.

TOMANSE 11946 5ELCID1514 LUEGO TOMAN ARMAS & ******* A DEPORTAR,
WORD #4056 OCCURS 1 TIMES.

TOMAR 1808 5ELCID0230 SI EL REY MELO QUISIERE ***** AMI NON MINCHAL.
2456 5ELCID0309 QUE, SI DESPUES DEL PLAZO EN SU TIERRAL PUDIES *****,
5492 5ELCID0692 AL %ID BESO LA MANO, LA SEaA UA *****.
5572 5ELCID0701 PORA MYO %ID & ALOS SOS A MANOS LOS *****.
7594 5ELCID0972 ASI VIENE ES FOR%ADO QUE EL CONDE AMANOS SELE CUYDO *****.
9574 5ELCID1216 MYO %ID DON RODRIGO LA QUINTA MANDO *****,
21703 5ELCID2759 NON LAS DEUIEMOS ***** FOR VARRAGANAS,
22372 5ELCID2850 NON GELO QUISO *****, MAS MUCHO GELO GRADIO:
27524 5ELCID3515 HY UOS LE DO EN DON, MANDEDES LE *****, SEaOR.
WORD #4057 OCCURS 9 TIMES.
INDEX OF DIVERSIFICATION = 3213.50 WITH STANDARD DEVIATION OF 3947.72

WORD C# PREFIX CONTEXT

TOMARON 6679 5ELCID0852 MOROS & MORAS ******* SE A QUEXAR:
12104 5ELCID1535 TODOS FUERON ALEGRES DEL %ERUI%IO QUE *******,
19484 5ELCID2468 LOS YERNOS DE MYO %ID QUANDO ESTE AUER *******
WORD #4058 OCCURS 3 TIMES.

TOMASSEDES 17648 5ELCID2233 QUE LAS ********** POR MUGIERES A ONDRA & A RECABDO.
WORD #4059 OCCURS 1 TIMES.

TOMASSEN 9885 5ELCID1254 ******** LE EL AUER & PUSIESSEN LE EN VN PALO.
WORD #4060 OCCURS 1 TIMES.

TOMAUA 1449 5ELCID0185 NOTOLOS DON MARTINO, SIN PESO LOS ******;
12266 5ELCID1557 LOS SOS DESPENDIE EL MORO, QUE DELO SO NON ****** NADA.
12507 5ELCID1586 MYO %ID SALIO SOBREL, & ARMAS DE FUSTE ******,
28590 5ELCID3650 DIOL VN COLPE, DE TRAUIESSOL ******,
28682 5ELCID3661 VN COLPEL DIO DE LANO, CON LO AGUDO NOL ******.
WORD #4061 OCCURS 5 TIMES.
INDEX OF DIVERSIFICATION = 6807.25 WITH STANDARD DEVIATION OF 7965.09

TOME 22684 5ELCID2891 HYO **** EL CASAMIENTO, MAS NON OSE DEZIR AL.
WORD #4062 OCCURS 1 TIMES.

TOMEDES 16934 5ELCID2143 DESTAS VISTAS QUE OUIEMOS, DEMY ******* ALGO.
WORD #4063 OCCURS 1 TIMES.

TOMO 15952 5ELCID2022 LAS YERBAS DEL CAMPO A DIENTES LAS ****,
16757 5ELCID2121 EL REY ALOS YFANTES ALAS MANOS LES ****,
18186 5ELCID2300 MYO %ID DON RODRIGO ALCUELLO LO ****,
19548 5ELCID2476 AL%O LA MANO, ALA BARBA SE ****:
22045 5ELCID2805 FATA QUE ESFUER%AN, & AMAS LAS ****
22216 5ELCID2829 AL%O LA SU MANO, ALA BARBA SE ****;
25011 5ELCID3185 AL%AUA LA MANO, ALA BARBA SE ****;
25112 5ELCID3198 BESO LE LA MANO, EL ESPADA **** & RE%IBIO.
28405 5ELCID3627 PRISOL EN VAZIO, EN CARNE NOL ****,
28796 5ELCID3677 EN VAZIO FUE LA LAN%A, CA EN CARNE NOL ****.
28926 5ELCID3694 LAS ARMAS QUE Y RASTARON EL SELAS ****.
WORD #4064 OCCURS 11 TIMES.
INDEX OF DIVERSIFICATION = 1296.40 WITH STANDARD DEVIATION OF 1193.16

TOMOS 8675 5ELCID1102 VIOLO MYO %ID, ***** AMARAUILLAR: GRADO ATI, PADRE SPIRITAL
WORD #4065 OCCURS 1 TIMES.

TORAN%IO 4282 5ELCID0545 PASSARON LAS AGUAS, ENTRARON AL CAMPO DE ********,
12165 5ELCID1544 EL CAMPO DE ******** LUEGOL ATRAUESSAUAN,
WORD #4066 OCCURS 2 TIMES.

TORANZ 11762 5ELCID1492 PASSARON MATA DE ****** DE TAL GUISA QUE NINGUN MIEDO NON HAN,
WORD #4067 OCCURS 1 TIMES.

TORNA 19039 5ELCID2409 ACA *****, BUCAR VENIST DALENT MAR,
21683 5ELCID2756 QUE EL VNA AL OTRA NOL ***** RECABDO.
WORD #4068 OCCURS 2 TIMES.

TORNADA 5746 5ELCID0725 ALA ******* QUE FAZEN OTROS TANTOS SON.
6520 5ELCID0832 ALA *******, SI NOS FALLAREDES AQUI;
23892 5ELCID3043 PORA TOLLEDO EL REY ******* DA,
WORD #4069 OCCURS 3 TIMES.

TORNADO 3074 5ELCID0387 ******* ES DON SANCHO, & FABLO ALBARFANEZ:
7316 5ELCID0938 ALTER%ER DIA, DON YXO Y ES *******.
9680 5ELCID1231 ******* ES MYO %ID CON TODA ESTA GANAN%IA.
23351 5ELCID2974 ESPIDIOS MU@O GUSTIOZ, A MYO %ID ES *******.
WORD #4070 OCCURS 4 TIMES.

TORNADOS 6294 5ELCID0801 ASOS CASTIELLOS ALOS MOROS DENTRO LOS AN ********,
13259 5ELCID1682 ******** SON A MYO %ID LOS QUE COMIEN SO PAN;
15138 5ELCID1914 ESPIDIENSSE AL REY, CON ESTO ******** SON,
18482 5ELCID2339 EN VNA CONPA@A ******** SON AMOS.
20144 5ELCID2557 CON AQUESTE CONSSEIO AMOS ******** SON,
WORD #4071 OCCURS 5 TIMES.
INDEX OF DIVERSIFICATION = 3461.50 WITH STANDARD DEVIATION OF 2451.59

TORNAN 3044 5ELCID0383 AL ABBAT DON SANCHO ****** DE CASTIGAR,
3782 5ELCID0478 E DESI ARRIBA ****** SE CON LA GANAN%IA,
3828 5ELCID0484 CON AQUESTE AUER ****** SE ESSA CONPA@A;
6178 5ELCID0787 YAS ****** LOS DEL QUE EN BUEN ORA NASCO.
8669 5ELCID1101 A%ERCA DE MURUIEDRO ****** TIENDAS AFINCAR.
17754 5ELCID2247 ****** SE CON LAS DUE@AS, A VALEN%IA AN ENTRADO;
17867 5ELCID2261 RICOS ****** A CASTIELLA LOS QUE ALAS BODAS LEGARON.
25290 5ELCID3220 ****** CON EL CONSSEIO E FABLAUAN ASSO SABOR:
WORD #4072 OCCURS 8 TIMES.
INDEX OF DIVERSIFICATION = 3177.00 WITH STANDARD DEVIATION OF 3633.81

```
WORD                C#  PREFIX                    CONTEXT

TORNANDO             2996 5ELCID0377 ATCDOS ESPERANDC, LA CABE%A ******** UA.
                     7357 5ELCIDC943 CON ESTAS GANANZIAS ALA PCSADA ******** SEUAN,
                     8477 5ELCID1078 ******** UA LA CABE%A & CATANCOS ATRAS;
                    19206 5ELCID2429 CON ESTAS GRANANZIAS YAS YUAN ********;
                    21873 5ELCID2783 VALAS ******** A ELLAS AMAS ACOS;
          WORD #4C73 OCCURS   5 TIMES.
             INDEX OF DIVERSIFICATICN =  4718.25 WITH STANCARD DEVIATION OF  4219.47

TORNANSSE           10993 5ELCID1391 HYDO ES MYNAYA, ********* LCS YFFANTES.
          WORD #4074 OCCURS   1 TIMES.

TORNAR                289 5ELCID0036 LOS DE DENTRO NCN LES QUERIEN ****** PALABRA.
                     4618 5ELCID0586 LA PARIA QUEL A PRESA ****** NCS LA HA DOBLADA.
                     4700 5ELCIDC596 MANDO ****** LA SE@A, A PRIESSA ESPOLONEAUAN.
                     5509 5ELCID0694 VIERON LO LAS ARCBCAS DELOS MOROS, AL ALMOFALLA SEUAN ******.
                     9C55 5ELCID1152 ROBAUAN EL CAMPC EPIENSSAN SE CE ******.
                    22562 5ELCID2873 DALLENT SE ESPIDIERCN DELLCS, PIENSSAN SE DE ******,
                    25386 5ELCID3233 ****** GELCS QUIERO, CA TOCOS FECHOS SON,
          WORD #4C75 OCCURS   7 TIMES.
             INDEX OF DIVERSIFICATICN =  4181.83 WITH STANCARD DEVIATION OF  4845.88

TORNARAN             3030 5ELCIDC381 AUNTODCS ESTOS DUELOS EN GOZO SE ********;
          WORD #4076 OCCURS   1 TIMES.

TORNARON             5517 5ELCIDC695 QUE PRIESSA VA EN LOS MOROS, E ******** SE A ARMAR;
                    24895 5ELCID3170 CON AQUESTA FABLA ******** ALA CORT:
          WORD #4077 OCCURS   2 TIMES.

TORNASSE            16678 5ELCID2112 QUANDO SALIE EL SCL, CUES ******** CADA VNO DON SALIDOS SON.
                    28663 5ELCID3659 BOLUIO LA RIENDA AL CAUALLC POR ******** DE CARA;
          WORD #4C78 OCCURS   2 TIMES.

TORNAUA                 8 5ELCID0002 ******* LA CABE%A & ESAUA LCS CATANCO.
                     4688 5ELCIDC594 ELBUEN CAMPEACCR LA SU CARA *******,
          WORD #4079 OCCURS   2 TIMES.

TORNAUAN             4795 5ELCID0607 DEXANDC UAN LCS DELANT, POR EL CASTIELLO SE ********,
                    15505 5ELCID1964 NON LO DETARCAN, A MYC %IC SE ********.
          WORD #4C8C OCCURS   2 TIMES.

TORNAUAS             1821 5ELCID0232 ******** MARTIN ANTOLINEZ A BURGOS & MYO %ID AAGUIJAR
                     9405 5ELCID1196 ******** A MURUIEDRC, CA EL SE LA A GANADA.
          WORD #4C81 OCCURS   2 TIMES.

TORNE                7529 5ELCID0965 NON LO DESAFIE, NIL ***** ENEMISTAD,
                    15831 5ELCID2008 FATA QUES ***** EL QUE EN BUEN ORA NASCO.
          WORD #4082 OCCURS   2 TIMES.

TORNEMOS            20676 5ELCID2625 ******** NCS, %ID, A VALENZIA LA MAYOR;
          WORD #4C83 OCCURS   1 TIMES.

TORNI@O             24483 5ELCID3121 EN VN ESCA@O ******* ESSORA MYO %ID POSO,
          WORD #4C84 OCCURS   1 TIMES.

TORNO                1676 5ELCID0215 LA CARA DEL CAUALLO ***** A SANTA MARIA,
                     2945 5ELCID0371 E EL ALAS NI@AS ***** LAS ACATAR:
                    11025 5ELCID1395 QUANDO ACABC LA ORAZICN, ALAS CUE@AS SE *****:
                    11811 5ELCID1497 EL VNO FINCO CCN ELLCS & EL CTRO ***** A ALBARFANEZ:
                    13654 5ELCID1730 DESDALLI SE ***** EL QUE EN BUEN ORA NASCO,
                    16594 5ELCID2102 ELLOS VAYAN CCN UUSCC, CACA QUEN ME ***** YO.
                    2C813 5ELCID2643 HYAS ***** PORA VALENZIA EL QUE EN BUEN ORA NASZIO.
                    21148 5ELCID2686 ESTO LES HA DICHC, & EL MORO SE *****;
                    21162 5ELCID2688 CUEMMO DE BUEN SESO A MCLINA SE *****.
                    26203 5ELCID3340 QUANDO SE ***** EL BUEN CAMPEACOR,
          WORD #4C85 OCCURS  10 TIMES.
             INDEX OF DIVERSIFICATICN =  2724.22 WITH STANCARD DEVIATION OF  2646.63

TORNOS                393 5ELCID0049 ESTO LA NI@A DIXO & ****** PORA SU CASA.
                     2356 5ELCIDC298 ****** A SONRISAR; LEGAN LE TCCOS, LA MANOL BAN BESAR.
                     5269 5ELCIDC666 MYO %ID CON LCS SOS ****** A ACCRDAR:
                     7666 5ELCID0982 ****** EL MANDADERC CUANTC PUCO MAS;
                     8515 5ELCID1C82 HYDO ES EL CONDE, ****** EL DE BIUAR,
                     8593 5ELCID1091 AORIENT EXE EL SOL, E ****** AESSA PART.
                     9995 5ELCID1266 ALEGRAS LE EL CORAZON & ****** ASONRRISAR:
                    10363 5ELCID1313 ****** A CARRICN, Y LC PCDRIE FALLAR.
                    11496 5ELCID1455 PLOGOL DE CCRAZCN & ****** A ALEGRAR,
                    21823 5ELCID2776 POR EL RASTRO ****** FELEZ MUNOZ,
                    22672 5ELCID2889 BESANDO LAS AAMAS, ****** DE SCNRRISAR:
                    24973 5ELCID3181 ****** AL ESCA@C CCN SE LEUANTO;
          WORD #4C86 OCCURS  12 TIMES.
             INDEX OF DIVERSIFICATICN =  2233.55 WITH STANCARD DEVIATION OF  2827.25

TORPE               12037 5ELCID1526 MUCHOL TENGO POR ***** CUI NCN CONESZE LA VERDAD.
          WORD #4C87 OCCURS   1 TIMES.
```

WORD C# PREFIX CONTEXT

TORRE 18076 5ELCID2286 *****;
22094 5ELCID2812 ALA ***** DE DCN VRRACA ELLE LAS DEXO.
WORD #4C88 CCCURS 2 TIMES.

TORRES 3164 5ELCID0398 DE DIESTRO A LILON LAS ******, QUE MOROS LAS HAN;
12377 5ELCID1571 QUE GUARDASSEN EL ALCA%AR & LAS OTRAS ****** ALTAS
13503 5ELCID1711 SALIDOS SON TODOS ARMADOS POR LAS ****** DE VAN%IA,
WORD #4C89 CCCURS 3 TIMES.

TOSDOS 14484 5ELCID1832 MANDO CAUALGAR APRIESSA ****** SOS FIJOS DALGO,
WORD #4090 CCCURS 1 TIMES.

TOUEL 26063 5ELCID3322 DID EL CAUALLO, ***** DO EN PORIDAD:
WORD #4091 CCCURS 1 TIMES.

TOUIER 24162 5ELCID3081 DO TALES %IENTO ******, BIEN SERE SIN PAUOR.
WORD #4C92 CCCURS 1 TIMES.

TOUIERE 24664 5ELCID3142 CON EL QUE ******* DERECHO YO DESSA PART ME SO.
24877 5ELCID3168 E QUANDO LAS *******, PARTIR SEA LA CORT;
WORD #4093 CCCURS 2 TIMES.

TOUIERON 5249 5ELCID0664 ******** GELA EN %ERCA COMPLIDAS TRES SEMANAS.
17723 5ELCID2243 DIOS, QUE BIEN ******** ARMAS EL %ID & SUS VASSALOS
18249 5ELCID2309 MUCHOS ******** POR ENBAYDOS LOS YFANTES DE CARRION,
19450 5ELCID2464 POR BIEN LO DIXO EL %ID, MAS ELLOS LO ******** AMAL.
WORD #4094 CCCURS 4 TIMES.

TOUIESSE 11201 5ELCID1417 QUE LES ******** PRO ROGAUAN A ALBARFANEZ;
23413 5ELCID2982 QUI NON VINIESSE ALA CORT NON SE ******** POR SU VASSALLO.
WORD #4095 CCCURS 2 TIMES.

TOUO 7506 5ELCID0962 DENTRO EN MI CORT TUERTO ME **** GRAND:
13786 5ELCID1747 MYO %ID FINCO ANTELLAS, **** LA RYENDA AL CAUALLO:
WORD #4096 CCCURS 2 TIMES.

TOUOS 7477 5ELCID0959 OUO GRAND PESAR & ***** LO A GRAND FONTA.
WORD #4C97 CCCURS 1 TIMES.

TRA%ION 20944 5ELCID2660 ENTRAMOS HERMANOS CONSSEIARON *******:
WORD #4C98 CCCURS 1 TIMES.

TRAE 985 5ELCID0126 NON DUERME SIN SOSPECHA QUI AUER **** MONEDADO.
3461 5ELCID0436 MYO %ID SE ECHO EN %ELADA CON AQUELOS QUE EL ****.
3729 5ELCID0471 EN MANO **** DESNUDA EL ESPADA,
6130 5ELCID0780 ESPADA TAIADOR, SANGRIENTO **** EL BRA%O,
6354 5ELCID0809 QUANTOS EL **** TODOS SON PAGADOS.
7448 5ELCID0955 QUE EL SALIDO DE CASTIELLA ASILOS **** TAN MAL.
7599 5ELCID0973 MYO %ID DON RODRIGO **** GRAND GANAN%IA,
7719 5ELCID0988 DE MOROS & DE CHRISTIANOS GENTES **** SOBEIANAS,
18156 5ELCID2297 EL MANTO **** ALCUELLO, & ADELINO PORA LEON;
19341 5ELCID2450 EL ESCUDO **** AL CUELLO & TODO ESPADO;
25702 5ELCID3273 DEXOLA CRE%ER & LUENGA **** LA BARBA;
WORD #4C99 CCCURS 11 TIMES.
INDEX OF DIVERSIFICATION = 2470.70 WITH STANDARD DEVIATION OF 3382.24

TRAEDES 11995 5ELCID1521 ******* ESTAS DUE@AS PORO VALDREMOS MAS,
WORD #4100 CCCURS 1 TIMES.

TRAEN 2089 5ELCID0263 SE@AS DUE@AS LAS ***** & ADUZEN LAS ADELANT.
3793 5ELCID0480 TANTO ***** LAS GRANDES GANA%IAS, MUCHOS GA@ADOS.
6271 5ELCID0799 ***** ORO & PLATA QUE NON SABEN RECABDO;
7363 5ELCID0944 TODOS SON ALEGRES, GANAN%IAS ***** GRANDES.
9063 5ELCID1153 ENTRAUAN A MURUIEDRO CON ESTAS GANAN%IAS QUE ***** GRANDES.
11914 5ELCID1510 E EN LAS MANOS LAN%AS QUE PENDONES *****,
14406 5ELCID1822 TALLES GANAN%IAS ***** QUE SON A AGUARDAR.
21263 5ELCID2702 CON QUANTOS QUE ELLOS ***** Y IAZEN ESSA NOCH,
28091 5ELCID3586 ESTAS TRES LAN%AS ***** SENOS PENDONES;
WORD #4101 CCCURS 9 TIMES.
INDEX OF DIVERSIFICATION = 3249.25 WITH STANDARD DEVIATION OF 2286.35

TRAER 718 5ELCID0091 NON PUEDO ***** EL AUER, CA MUCHO ES PESADO,
4068 5ELCID0517 NIN CATIUOS NIN CATIUAS NON QUISO ***** EN SU CONPA@A.
WORD #4102 CCCURS 2 TIMES.

TRAHE 11853 5ELCID1502 E EL ALCAYAZ AUEGALUON CON SUS FUER%AS QUE *****,
11934 5ELCID1512 O CUEMO SALIERA DE CASTIELLA ALBARFANEZ CON ESTAS DUE@AS QUE *****.
12342 5ELCID1567 CA BIEN SABE QUE ALBARFANEZ ***** TODO RECABDO;
12512 5ELCID1587 VISTIOS EL SOBREGONEL; LUENGA ***** LA BARBA;
13759 5ELCID1744 FRONZIDA ***** LA CARA, QUE ERA DESARMADO,
WORD #4103 CCCURS 5 TIMES.
INDEX OF DIVERSIFICATION = 475.50 WITH STANDARD DEVIATION OF 531.89

TRAHEN 7751 5ELCID0992 ELLOS VIENEN CUESTA YUSO, & TODOS ****** CA[illegible]
WORD #4104 CCCURS 1 TIMES.

WORD C# PREFIX CONTEXT

```
TRANOCHANDO          9179 5ELCID1168 E DURMIENDO LOS DIAS & LAS NOCHES ***********,
        WORD #4105 OCCURS    1 TIMES.

TRAS                 7560 5ELCID0969 ADELINAN **** MYO %ID EL BUENO DE BIUAR,
                     7732 5ELCID0990 PUES ADELLANT YRAN **** NOS, AQUI SEA LA BATALLA:
                     7796 5ELCID0998 VERA REMONT VERENGEL **** QUIEN VINO EN ALCAN%A
                    18096 5ELCID2290 **** VNA VIGA LAGAR METIOS CON GRANT PAUOR;
                    26145 5ELCID3333 METISTET **** EL ESCA@O DE MYO %ID EL CAMPEADOR
                    26382 5ELCID3365 FUSTED METER **** LA VIGA LAGAR,
                    28781 5ELCID3676 **** EL ESCUDO FALSSO GELA GUARNIZON;
                    28804 5ELCID3679 **** EL ESCUDO FALSSO GELA GUARNIZON,
        WORD #4106 OCCURS    8 TIMES.
           INDEX OF DIVERSIFICATION =  3033.86 WITH STANDARD DEVIATION OF  4325.30

TRASNOCHADA          7111 5ELCID0909 CON TODAS SUS YENTES FIZO VNA ***********;
                     9323 5ELCID1185 SALIO DE MURUIEDRO VNA NOCH EN ***********,
        WORD #4107 OCCURS    2 TIMES.

TRASNOCHADAS         9112 5ELCID1159 DAUAN SUS CORREDORES & FAZIEN LAS ************,
        WORD #4108 OCCURS    1 TIMES.

TRASNOCHAR           3403 5ELCID0429 DIXOLES ATODOS COMMO QUERIE **********;
        WORD #4109 OCCURS    1 TIMES.

TRASNOCHARON         8659 5ELCID1100 ************ DE NOCH, AL ALUA DELA MAN
        WORD #4110 OCCURS    1 TIMES.

TRASPASSAR           3183 5ELCID0400 LA CAL%ADA DE QUINEA YUA LA **********,
        WORD #4111 OCCURS    1 TIMES.

TRASPUESTAS         21881 5ELCID2784 TANTO SON DE *********** QUE NON PUEDEN DEZIR NADA.
        WORD #4112 OCCURS    1 TIMES.

TRAUIESSOL          28589 5ELCID3650 DIOL VN COLPE, DE ********** TOMAUA,
        WORD #4113 OCCURS    1 TIMES.

TRAYDOR             19896 5ELCID2523 AAQUEL REY BUCAR, ******* PROUADO.
                    26226 5ELCID3343 RIEBTOT EL CUERPO POR MALO & POR *******;
                    26277 5ELCID3350 TULO OTORGARAS A GUISA DE *******;
                    26427 5ELCID3371 QUE ERES ******* & MINTIST DE QUANTO DICHO HAS.
                    26512 5ELCID3383 CALA, ALEUOSO, MALO & *******
                    27261 5ELCID3484 DESI SEA VEN%IDO & ESCAPE POR *******.
        WORD #4114 OCCURS    6 TIMES.
           INDEX OF DIVERSIFICATION =  1472.00 WITH STANDARD DEVIATION OF  2730.09

TRAYDORES           21104 5ELCID2681 AQUIM PARTO DE UOS COMMO DE MALOS & DE *********.
                    21416 5ELCID2722 ESPUELAS TIENEN CAL%ADAS LOS MALOS *********,
                    25629 5ELCID3263 QUANDO LAS NON QUERIEDES, YA CANES *********,
                    26949 5ELCID3442 RIEBTOS LES LOS CUERPOS POR MALOS & POR *********.
        WORD #4115 OCCURS    4 TIMES.

TRAYENDO            24836 5ELCID3163 APRIESSA LO YUAN ******** & ACUERDAN LA RAZON:
        WORD #4116 OCCURS    1 TIMES.

TRAYO                 650 5ELCID0082 BIEN LO VEDES QUE YO NO ***** AUER, & HUEBOS ME SERIE
                     2487 5ELCID0314 POCO AUER *****, DAR UOS QUIERO UUESTRA PART.
                    16936 5ELCID2144 ***** VOS XX PALAFRES, ESTOS BIEN ADOBADOS,
                    18768 5ELCID2375 PENDON ***** A CORCAS & ARMAS DE SE@AL,
        WORD #4117 OCCURS    4 TIMES.

TRED                 1104 5ELCID0142 AMOS **** ALCAMPEADOR CON TADO,
        WORD #4118 OCCURS    1 TIMES.

TREMOR              13117 5ELCID1662 DEL DIA QUE NASQUIERAN NON VIERAN TAL ******.
        WORD #4119 OCCURS    1 TIMES.

TRES                  821 5ELCID0105 NON LO DETARDAN, TODOS **** SE APARTARON.
                     2431 5ELCID0307 **** AN POR TRO%IR, %EPADES QUE NON MAS.
                     2656 5ELCID0336 **** REYES DE ARABIA TE VINIERON ADORAR,
                     5039 5ELCID0637 **** REYES VEO DE MOROS DERREDOR DE MI ESTAR,
                     5056 5ELCID0639 **** MILL MOROS LEUEDES CON ARMAS DE LIDIAR;
                     5088 5ELCID0643 **** MILL MOROS CAUALGAN & PIENSSAN DE ANDAR,
                     5254 5ELCID0664 TOUIERON GELA EN %ERCA COMPLIDAS **** SEMANAS.
                     5258 5ELCID0665 ACABO DE **** SEMANAS, LA QUARTA QUERIE ENTRAR,
                     6623 5ELCID0845 VENDIDO LES A ALCO%ER POR **** MILL MARCHOS DE PLATA.
                     6909 5ELCID0883 POR ACOGELLO A CABO DE **** SEMMANAS.
                     7150 5ELCID0915 QUANDO ESTO FECHO OUO, A CABO DE **** SEMANAS,
                     7567 5ELCID0970 **** DIAS & DOS NOCHES PENSSARON DE ANDAR,
                     7789 5ELCID0997 POR VNO QUE FIRGADES, **** SIELLAS YRAN VAZIAS.
                     8370 5ELCID1064 DAN LE **** PALAFRES MUY BIEN ENSELLADOS
                     9387 5ELCID1194 **** DIAS LE SPERARE EN CANAL DE %ELFA.
                     9677 5ELCID1230 AQUEL REY DE MARRUECOS CON **** COLPES ESCAPA.
                     9979 5ELCID1265 **** MILL & SEYS %IENTOS AUIE MYO %ID EL DE BIUAR;
```

```
WORD                    C#   PREFIX                                    CONTEXT

TRES (CON'T)

                    11098 5ELCID1405 DIO **** CAUALLEROS MYNAYA ALBARFANEZ,
                    12280 5ELCID1559 APRES SCN DE VALENZIA A **** LEGUAS CONTADAS.
                    13612 5ELCID1725 AL REY YUZEF **** CCLPES LE OUO DADOS,
                    13710 5ELCID1737 ENTRE ORO & PLATA FALLARON **** MILL MARCOS,
                    17730 5ELCID2244 **** CAUALLOS CAMEO EL CUE EN BUEN ORA NASCO.
                    19136 5ELCID2420 ALCANZCLO EL ZID ABUCAR A **** BRACAS DEL MAR,
                    22C72 5ELCID2809 TODOS **** SE@ERCS PCR LCS ROBRECOS CE CORPES,
                    25160 5ELCID3204 EN ORO & EN PLATA **** MILL MARCOS DE PLATA LES DIO;
                    27124 5ELCID3466 DESTOS IIJ PCR **** QUE REBTARON EN LA CORT.
                    27234 5ELCID3481 ACABO DE **** SEMANAS, EN BEGAS DE CARRION,
                    27282 5ELCID3487 ESTOS MIS **** CAUALLERCS EN UUESTRA MANO SON,
                    27676 5ELCID3533 MAS **** SEMANAS DE PLAZO TODAS COMPLIDAS SON.
                    27825 5ELCID3551 TODOS **** SE ACUERCAN, CA SON DE VN SE@OR.
                    27982 5ELCID3571 TODOS **** SCN ARMADOS LOS DEL CAMPEADOR,
                    28C89 5ELCID3586 ESTAS **** LANZAS TRAEN SENOS PENDONES;
                    28108 5ELCID3589 TODOS **** SON ACORDADCS LOS DEL CAMPEADOR,
                    28184 5ELCID3598 ESTOS **** CAUALLERCS DE MYO ZID EL CAMPEADOR
                    28357 5ELCID3621 TODOS **** POR TRES YA JUNTADCS SON:
                    28359 5ELCID3621 TODOS TRES POR **** YA JUNTADOS SON:
                    28454 5ELCID3634 **** DOBLES DE LORIGA TENIE FERNANDO, AQUESTOL PRESTO,
         WORD #4120 OCCURS  37 TIMES.
            INDEX OF DIVERSIFICATION =    766.58 WITH STANDARD DEVIATION OF  1010.93

TREUEN               4458 5ELCID0567 EN LA SU VEZINDAD NCN SE ****** GANAR TANTO.
         WORD #4121 OCCURS   1 TIMES.

TREUO               18464 5ELCID2337 ARRANCAR MELOS ***** CON LA MERZED DEL CRIADOR.
         WORD #4122 OCCURS   1 TIMES.

TREYNTA              6824 5ELCID0872 ******* CAUALLOS AL REY LOS ENPRESENTAUA;
         WORD #4123 OCCURS   1 TIMES.

TREZIENTAS           3321 5ELCID0419 NOTO ********** LANZAS CUE TODAS TIENEN PENDONES.
                     5732 5ELCID0723 ********** LANZAS SCN, TODAS TIENEN PENDONES;
         WORD #4124 OCCURS   2 TIMES.

TREZIENTOS          16596 5ELCID2103 ********** MARCCS DE PLATA EN AYUDA LES DO YO,
         WORD #4125 OCCURS   1 TIMES.

TRINIDAD             2527 5ELCID0319 LA MISSA NOS CIRA, ESTA SERA DE SANTA ********;
         WORD #4126 OCCURS   1 TIMES.

TRINIDADE           18733 5ELCID2370 OY UOS DIX LA MISSA DE SANTA *********.
         WORD #4127 OCCURS   1 TIMES.

TROCIDA             27776 5ELCID3545 ******* ES LA NOCHE, YA QUIEBRAN LOS ALBORES.
         WORD #4128 OCCURS   1 TIMES.

TROZEN               4262 5ELCID0543 ****** LAS ALCARIAS & YUAN ADELANT,
         WORD #4129 OCCURS   1 TIMES.

TROZIERON           11636 5ELCID1475 ********* A SANTA MARIA & VINIERON ALBERGAR A FRONTAEL,
                    2C909 5ELCID2656 ********* ARBUXUELO & LEGARCN A SALON,
                    22570 5ELCID2875 ********* ALCOZEUA, ADIESTRO DE SANTESTEUAN DE GORMAZ,
         WORD #4130 OCCURS   3 TIMES.

TROZIR               2434 5ELCID0307 TRES AN POR ******, ZEPADES QUE NON MAS.
                    2C885 5ELCID2653 HYUAN ****** LOS MONTES, LOS CUE DIZEN DE LUZON.
         WORD #4131 OCCURS   2 TIMES.

TU                   1891 5ELCID0241 ** QUE ATODOS QUIAS, VALA MYO ZID EL CANPEADOR.
                     2647 5ELCID0334 EN BELLEM APAREZIST, COMMO FUE ** VELUNTAD;
                     2677 5ELCID0338 TE OFFREZIERON, COMMO FUE ** VELUNTAD;
                     2739 5ELCID0346 RESUZITEST A LAZARO, CA FUE ** VOLUNTAD;
                     2844 5ELCID0359 COMMO FUE ** VOLUNTAD.
                     6695 5ELCID0854 NOS PAGADOS FINCADOS, SE@OR, DELA ** PART.
                    11513 5ELCID1458 **, MU@O GUSTIOZ & PERO VERMUEZ DELANT,
                    20624 5ELCID2618  OHERES, MYO SOBRINO, **, FELEZ MUNOZ,
                    2C743 5ELCID2634 OYAS, SOBRINO, **, FELEZ MUNOZ
                    21008 5ELCID2670 ** MUERT OY COSSEIAR ALCS YFANTES DE CARRION.
                    23198 5ELCID2955 E VERDAD DIZES EN ESTO, **, MU@O GUSTIOZ,
                    25924 5ELCID3303 HYO LAS HE FIJAS, & ** PRIMAS CORMANAS;
                    25937 5ELCID3305 SI YO RESPONDIER, ** NON ENTRARAS EN ARMAS.
                    26137 5ELCID3332 E **, FERRANDO, QUE FIZIST CON EL PAUOR?
                    26421 5ELCID3370 AL PARTIR DELA LID POR ** BOCA LO DIRAS,
                    26541 5ELCID3388 EN ** AMISTAD NON QUIERO AVER RAZION.
         WORD #4132 OCCURS  16 TIMES.
            INDEX OF DIVERSIFICATION =  1642.33 WITH STANDARD DEVIATION OF  2585.39

TUELLEN              5229 5ELCID0661 ALOS DE MYO ZID YA LES ******* EL AGUA.
                    21395 5ELCID2720 ALLI LES ******* LOS MANTOS & LOS PELLIZONES,
         WORD #4133 OCCURS   2 TIMES.

TUERES               2854 5ELCID0361 ****** REY DE LOS REYES & DE TODEL MUNDO PADRE,
         WORD #4134 OCCURS   1 TIMES.
```

```
WORD                    C#  PREFIX                         CONTEXT

TUERTA          28851 5ELCID3685 CON EL DIO VNA ******, DELA SIELLA LO ENCAMO,
         WORD #4135 OCCURS   1 TIMES.

TUERTO           7504 5ELCID0962 DENTRO EN MI CORT ****** ME TOUO GRAND:
                24592 5ELCID3134 GRANDE ****** LE HAN TENIDO, SABEMOS LO TODOS NOS;
                24633 5ELCID3138 POR ESCOGER EL DERECHO, CA ****** NON MANDO YO.
                27815 5ELCID3549 POR QUERER EL DERECHO & NON CONSENTIR EL ******.
                28021 5ELCID3576 ADERECHO NOS VALED, ANINGUN ****** NO.
                28201 5ELCID3600 AUED UUESTRO DERECHO, ****** NON QUERADES VOS,
                28207 5ELCID3601 CA QUI ****** QUISIERE FAZER, MAL GELO VEDARE YO,
         WORD #4136 OCCURS   7 TIMES.
            INDEX OF DIVERSIFICATION =  3449.50 WITH STANDARD DEVIATION OF  6793.61

TUERTOS          7492 5ELCID0961 GRANDES ******* ME TIENE MYO %ID EL DE BIUAR.
         WORD #4137 OCCURS   1 TIMES.

TULO            26272 5ELCID3350 **** OTORGARAS A GUISA DE TRAYDOR;
         WORD #4138 OCCURS   1 TIMES.

TUS              1699 5ELCID0218 VALAN ME *** VERTUDES, GLORIOSA SANTA MARIA
                 2670 5ELCID0337 MELCHIOR & GASPAR & BALTASAR, ORO & *** & MIRRA
                26005 5ELCID3315 LAS *** MA@AS YO TELAS SABRE CONTAR:
         WORD #4139 OCCURS   3 TIMES.

UA               2084 5ELCID0262 AFEUOS DO@A XIMENA CON SUS FIJAS DO ** LEGANDO;
                 2556 5ELCID0323 PASSANDO ** LA NOCH, VINIENDO LA MAN;
                 2997 5ELCID0377 ATODOS ESPERANDO, LA CABE%A TORNANDO **.
                 3146 5ELCID0396 YXIENDOS ** DE TIERRA EL CAMPEADOR LEAL,
                 3190 5ELCID0401 SOBRE NAUAS DE PALOS EL DUERO ** PASAR,
                 4308 5ELCID0548 GRANDES SON LAS GANAN%IAS QUE PRISO POR LA TIERRA DO **.
                 4332 5ELCID0551 E PASSO AALFAMA, LA FOZ AYUSO **,
                 4475 5ELCID0569 EL CASTIELLO DE ALCO%ER EN PARIA ** ENTRANDO.
                 4585 5ELCID0583 DEGUISA ** MYO %ID COMMO SIESCAPASSE DE ARRANCADA.
                 5491 5ELCID0692 AL %ID BESO LA MANO, LA SE@A ** TOMAR.
                 6718 5ELCID0857 AL%O SU SE@A, EL CAMPEADOR SE **,
                 8478 5ELCID1078 TORNANDO ** LA CABE%A & CATANDOS ATRAS;
                 9437 5ELCID1200 CRE%IENDO ** RIQUEZA A MYO %ID EL DE BIUAR.
                12197 5ELCID1548 E BUEN CAUALLO EN DIESTRO QUE ** ANTE SUS ARMAS.
         WORD #4140 OCCURS  14 TIMES.
            INDEX OF DIVERSIFICATION =   776.92 WITH STANDARD DEVIATION OF   807.18

UALA              382 5ELCID0048 MAS EL CRIADOR UOS **** CON TODAS SUS UERTUDES SANTAS.
                 1727 5ELCID0221 VUESTRA UERTUD ME ****, GLORIOSA, EN MY EXIDA & ME AIUDE,
         WORD #4141 OCCURS   2 TIMES.

UALE             3963 5ELCID0503 NON PRENDRE DE UOS QUANTO **** VN DINERO MALO.
         WORD #4142 OCCURS   1 TIMES.

UALO             7181 5ELCID0920 EL CAUALLO CORRIENDO, **** ABRA%AR SIN FALLA,
         WORD #4143 OCCURS   1 TIMES.

UAN              2283 5ELCID0287 POR CASTIELLA OYENDO *** LOS PREGONES,
                 2584 5ELCID0326 MYO %ID & SU MUGIER A LA EGLESIA ***.
                 4274 5ELCID0544 POR LAS CUEUAS DANQUITA ELLOS PASSANDO ***,
                 4788 5ELCID0607 DEXANDO *** LOS DELANT, POR EL CASTIELLO SE TORNAUAN,
                 7873 5ELCID1006 LOS PENDONES & LAS LAN%AS TAN BIEN LAS *** ENPLEANDO,
                11965 5ELCID1516 DON LEGAN LOS OTROS, A MINAYA ALBARFANEZ SE *** HOMILAR.
         WORD #4144 OCCURS   6 TIMES.
            INDEX OF DIVERSIFICATION =  1935.40 WITH STANDARD DEVIATION OF  1637.40

UARONES           122 5ELCID0016 EN SU CONPA@A LX PENDONES; EXIEN LO UER MUGIERES & *******,
         WORD #4145 OCCURS   1 TIMES.

UAYADES           701 5ELCID0089 POR RACHEL & VIDAS ******* ME PRIUADO:
         WORD #4146 OCCURS   1 TIMES.

UAYANTE          6688 5ELCID0853  VASTE, MYO %ID; NUESTRAS ORA%IONES ******* DELANTE
         WORD #4147 OCCURS   1 TIMES.

UAYMOS            569 5ELCID0072 ESTA NOCH YGAMOS & ****** NOS AL MATINO,
         WORD #4148 OCCURS   1 TIMES.

UAZIAS             23 5ELCID0004 ALCANDARAS ****** SIN PIELLES & SIN MANTOS
         WORD #4149 OCCURS   1 TIMES.

UEDADO            335 5ELCID0042 EL REY LO HA ******, ANOCH DEL ETRO SU CARTA,
         WORD #4150 OCCURS   1 TIMES.

UENDER            504 5ELCID0064 NON LE OSARIEN ****** ALMENOS DINARADA.
         WORD #4151 OCCURS   1 TIMES.

UENTURA          1750 5ELCID0223 SI UOS ASSI LO FIZIEREDES & LA ******* ME FUERE COMPLIDA,
         WORD #4152 OCCURS   1 TIMES.
```

WORD C# PREFIX CONTEXT

UER 119 5ELCID0016 EN SU CONPAÑA LX PENDONES; EXIEN LO *** MUGIERES & UARONES,
3305 5ELCID0417 MANDO *** SUS YENTES MYO %ID EL CAMPEADOR:
22439 5ELCID2858 MINAYA VA *** SUS PRIMAS DO SON,
WORD #4153 OCCURS 3 TIMES.

UERA 204 5ELCID0026 E A QUEL QUE GELA DIESSE SOPIESSE **** PALABRA,
WORD #4154 OCCURS 1 TIMES.

UERDAT 16906 5ELCID2139 QUANDO UOS IUNTAREDES CCMIGO, QUEM DIGADES LA ******.
WORD #4155 OCCURS 1 TIMES.

UERMEIOS 691 5ELCID0088 LOS GUADAME%IS ******** & LOS CLAUOS BIEN DORADOS.
WORD #4156 OCCURS 1 TIMES.

UERTUD 1725 5ELCID0221 VUESTRA ****** ME UALA, GLORIOSA, EN MY EXIDA & ME AIUDE,
WORD #4157 OCCURS 1 TIMES.

UERTUDES 386 5ELCID0048 MAS EL CRIADOR UOS UALA CON TODAS SUS ******** SANTAS.
WORD #4158 OCCURS 1 TIMES.

UIANDA 500 5ELCID0063 DETODAS COSAS QUANTAS SON DE ******
WORD #4159 OCCURS 1 TIMES.

UINO 522 5ELCID0066 AMYO %ID & ALOS SUYOS ABASTALES DE PAN & DE ****;
WORD #4160 OCCURS 1 TIMES.

UISTAS 15566 5ELCID1973 ALAS AGUAS DE TAIO, OLAS ****** SON APAREIADAS.
WORD #4161 OCCURS 1 TIMES.

UN 611 5ELCID0077 SI NON, QUANTO DEXO NOLO PRE%IO ** FIGO.
1290 5ELCID0165 NON LES DIESSE MYO %ID DELA GANAN%IA ** DINERO MALO.
1511 5ELCID0193 MARTIN ANTOLINEZ, ** BURGALES CONTADO,
WORD #4162 OCCURS 3 TIMES.

UNA 142 5ELCID0019 DELAS SUS BOCAS TODOS DIZIAN *** RAZON:
303 5ELCID0038 SACO EL PIE DEL ESTRIBERA, *** FERIDAL DAUA;
3862 5ELCID0489 VENIDES, ALBARFANEZ, *** FARDIDA LAN%A
15429 5ELCID1954 SOBRE TAIO, QUE ES *** AGUA CABDAL,
WORD #4163 OCCURS 4 TIMES.

UOS 349 5ELCID0044 NON *** OSARIEMOS ABRIR NON COGER POR NADA;
374 5ELCID0047 %ID, ENEL NUESTRO MAL *** NON GANADES NADA;
381 5ELCID0048 MAS EL CRIADOR *** UALA CON TODAS SUS UERTUDES SANTAS.
578 5ELCID0073 CA ACUSADO SERE DELO QUE *** HE SERUIDO,
632 5ELCID0080 SI YO BIUO, DOBLAR *** HE LA SOLDADA.
843 5ELCID0108 POR SIEMPRE *** FARE RICOS, QUE NON SEADES MENGUADOS.
1033 5ELCID0133 PEDIR *** A POCO POR DEXAR SO AUER EN SALUO.
1110 5ELCID0143 E NOS *** AIUDAREMOS, QUE ASSI ES AGUISADO,
1373 5ELCID0176 DE CASTIELLA *** YDES PORA LAS YENTES ESTRANAS.
1487 5ELCID0190 YO, QUE ESTO *** GANE, BIEN MERE%IAS CAL%AS.
1532 5ELCID0196 DAMOS *** ENDON AUOS XXX MARCHOS;
1744 5ELCID0223 SI *** ASSI LO FIZIEREDES & LA UENTURA ME FUERE COMPLIDA,
1948 5ELCID0247 PUES QUE AQUI *** VEO, PRENDET DE MI OSPEDADO.
2031 5ELCID0256 AQUELLAS *** ACOMIENDO AUOS, ABBAT DON SANCHO;
2047 5ELCID0258 SIESSA DESPENSSA *** FALLE%IERE OUOS MENGUARE ALGO,
2057 5ELCID0259 BIEN LAS ABASTAD, YO ASSI *** LO MANDO;
2131 5ELCID0269 FEM ANTE *** YO & UUESTRAS FFIJAS, YFFANTES SON & DE DIAS CHICAS,
2156 5ELCID0271 YO LO VEO QUE ESTADES *** EN YDA
2217 5ELCID0279 COMMO ALA MI ALMA YO TANTO *** QUERIA.
2231 5ELCID0281 YO YRE & *** FINCAREDES REMANIDA.
2258 5ELCID0284 E ***, MUGIER ONDRADA, DE MY SEADES SERUIDA
2394 5ELCID0302 EN ANTES QUE YO MUERA, ALGUN BIEN *** PUEDA FAR:
2401 5ELCID0303 LO QUE PERDEDES DOBLADO *** LO COBRAR.
2481 5ELCID0313 OYD, VARONES, NON *** CAYA EN PESAR;
2489 5ELCID0314 POCO AUER TRAYO, DAR *** QUIERO UUESTRA PART.
2506 5ELCID0317 NON *** TARDEDES, MANDEDES ENSELLAR;
2949 5ELCID0372 ADIOS *** ACOMIENDO, FIJAS, & A LA MUGIER & AL PADRE SPIRITAL;
3333 5ELCID0420 TEMPRANO DAT %EUADA, SI EL CRIADOR *** SALUE
3505 5ELCID0442 VOS CON LOS CC YD *** EN ALGARA; ALA VAYA ALBARABAREZ,
3580 5ELCID0451 SICUETA *** FUERE ALGUNA AL ALGARA,
3867 5ELCID0490 DO YO *** ENBIAS BIEN ABRIA TAL ESPERAN%A.
3886 5ELCID0493 MUCHO *** LO GRADESCO, CAMPEADOR CONTADO.
3906 5ELCID0496 YO *** LA SUELTA & AUELLO QUITADO.
3961 5ELCID0503 NON PRENDRE DE *** QUANTO UALE VN DINERO MALO.
5069 5ELCID0640 CON LOS DELA FRONTERA QUE *** AIUDARAN,
5304 5ELCID0670 DEZID ME, CAUALLEROS, COMMO *** PLAZE DE FAR.
5367 5ELCID0678 ONDRASTES ***, MINAYA, CA AUER UOS LO YEDES DE FAR.
5371 5ELCID0678 ONDRASTES UOS, MINAYA, CA AUER *** LO YEDES DE FAR.
5481 5ELCID0691 MAS NON AGUIJEDES CON ELLA, SI YO NON *** LO MANDAR.
5605 5ELCID0706 EL CRIADOR *** VALA, %ID CAMPEADOR LEAL
5939 5ELCID0753 CAUALGAD, MYNAYA, *** SODES EL MYO DIESTRO BRA%O
5950 5ELCID0754 OY EN ESTE DIA DE *** ABRE GRAND BANDO;

WORD C# PREFIX CONTEXT

UOS (CON'T)

6379 5ELCID0813 ENBIAR *** QUIERO A CASTIELLA CON MANDADO
6500 5ELCID0829 HYDES ***, MYNAYA, ACASTIELLA LA GENTIL?
6840 5ELCID0874 QUIN LOS DIO ESTOS, SI *** VALA DIOS, MYNAYA
6869 5ELCID0878 A ***, REY ONDRADO, ENBIA ESTA PRESENTAIA;
6876 5ELCID0879 BESA *** LOS PIES & LAS MANOS AMAS,
6888 5ELCID0880 QUEL AYDES MER%ED, SIEL CRIADOR *** VALA.
6945 5ELCID0888 HYD & VENIT, DA QUI *** DO MI GRA%IA;
6955 5ELCID0889 MAS DEL %ID CAMPEADOR YO NON *** DIGO NADA.
6962 5ELCID0890 SOBRE AQUESTO TODO, DEZIR *** QUIERO, MINAYA:
7015 5ELCID0897 HYD POR CASTIELLA & DEXEN *** ANDAR, MINAYA,
7028 5ELCID0899 QUIERO *** DEZIR DEL QUE EN BUEN ORA NASCO & %INXO ESPADA:
7213 5ELCID0925 MIENTRA *** VISQUIEREDES, BIEN ME YRA AMJ, MINAYA
7384 5ELCID0947 HYA CAUALLEROS, DEZIR *** HE LA VERDAD:
7697 5ELCID0986 APRIESSA *** GUARNID & METEDOS EN LAS ARMAS.
8104 5ELCID1034 E SI *** COMIEREDES, DON YO SEA PAGADO,
8116 5ELCID1035 AUOS & DOS FIJOS DALGO QUITAR *** HE LOS CUERPOS & DARUOS E DE MANO.
8161 5ELCID1040 AUOS & A OTROS DOS DAR *** HE DE MANO.
8176 5ELCID1042 SABET, NON *** DARE AUOS VN DINERO MALO;
8187 5ELCID1043 MAS QUANTO AUEDES PERDIDO NON *** LO DARE,
8205 5ELCID1045 QUE COMIGO ANDAN LAZRADOS, & NON *** LO DARE.
8333 5ELCID1060 SI *** PLOGUIERE, MYO %ID, DE YR SOMOS GUISADOS;
8400 5ELCID1068 HYA *** YDES, CONDE, AGUISA DE MUY FRANCO,
8409 5ELCID1069 EN GRADO *** LO TENGO LO QUE ME AUEDES DEXADO.
8418 5ELCID1070 SI *** VINIERE EMIENTE QUE QUISIEREDES VENGALO,
8456 5ELCID1075 PAGADO *** HE POR TODO AQUESTE A@O;
8464 5ELCID1076 DE VENIR *** BUSCAR SOL NON SERA PENSSADO.
8773 5ELCID1115 OYD, MESNADAS, SI EL CRIADOR *** SALUE
8867 5ELCID1129 A MI DEDES C CAUALLEROS, QUE NON *** PIDO MAS,
9909 5ELCID1257 SI *** QUISIEREDES, MINAYA, QUIERO SABER RECABDO
10027 5ELCID1273 SI AUOS PLOGUIERE, MINAYA, & NON *** CAYA EN PESAR,
10032 5ELCID1271 ENBIAR *** QUIERO A CASTIELLA, DO AUEMOS HEREDADES,
10058 5ELCID1274 DAR LE QUIERO C CAUALLOS, & *** YD GELOS LEUAR;
10088 5ELCID1278 ENBIARE POR ELLAS, & *** SABED EL MENSAGE:
10340 5ELCID1310 DEXARE *** LAS POSADAS, NON LAS QUIERO CONTAR.
10428 5ELCID1322 BESAUA *** LAS MANOS MYO %ID LIDIADOR,
10536 5ELCID1335 FEUOS AQUI LAS SE@AS, VERDAD *** DIGO YO:
10553 5ELCID1338 BESA *** LAS MANOS & QUE LOS PRENDADES UOS;
10560 5ELCID1338 BESA UOS LAS MANOS & QUE LOS PRENDADES ***;
10653 5ELCID1349 QUE ENTODAS GUISAS MIIOR ME SIRUE QUE ***.
10661 5ELCID1351 MER%ED *** PIDE EL %ID, SIUOS CAYESSE EN SABOR,
10735 5ELCID1359 CATAD COMMO LAS SIRUADES *** & EL CAMPEADOR.
10893 5ELCID1379 HYA *** YDES, MYNAYA?, YD ALA GRA%IA DEL CRIADOR
10906 5ELCID1380 LEUEDES VN PORTERO, TENGO QUE *** AURA PRO;
11041 5ELCID1398 SALUDA *** MYO %ID ALLA ONDDE ELLE ESTA;
11063 5ELCID1400 EL REY POR SU MER%ED SUELTAS ME *** HA,
11074 5ELCID1402 SI *** VIESSE EL %ID SA@AS & SIN MAL,
11247 5ELCID1423 DELOS OTROS QUINIENTOS DEZIR *** HE QUE FAZE:
11394 5ELCID1442 SI *** VALA EL CRIADOR, MINAYA ALBARFANEZ,
11544 5ELCID1462 POR SANTA MARIA *** VAYADES PASSAR,
11566 5ELCID1465 CON OTROS %IENTO CAUALLEROS BIEN *** CONSSIGRA;
11691 5ELCID1482 MYO %ID *** SALUDAUA, & MANDOLO RECABDAR,
11723 5ELCID1486 E FFATA EN VALEN%IA DELLAS NON *** PARTADES.
11828 5ELCID1499 AFEUOS AQUI PERO VERMUEZ & MU@O GUSTIOZ QUE *** QUIEREN SIN HART,
12009 5ELCID1523 ONDRAR *** HEMOS TODOS, CA TALES LA SU AUZE,
12069 5ELCID1530 DESTO QUE AUEDES FECHO *** NON PERDEREDES NADA.
12089 5ELCID1533 ANTES DESTE TE%ER DIA *** LA DARE DOBLADA.
12666 5ELCID1607 EN ESTA HEREDAD QUE *** YO HE GANADA.
12759 5ELCID1620 DEZIR *** QUIERO NUEUAS DE ALENT PARTES DEL MAR,
12981 5ELCID1646 QUES ESTO, %ID, SI EL CRIADOR *** SALUE
13002 5ELCID1649 APOCO QUE VINIESTES, PRESEND *** QUIEREN DAR:
13011 5ELCID1650 POR CASAR SON UUESTRAS FIJAS, ADUZEN *** AXUUAR.
13378 5ELCID1696 QUANDO *** LOS FUEREDES FERIR, ENTRARE YO DEL OTRA PART;
13467 5ELCID1707 HYO *** CANTE LA MISSA POR AQUESTA MA@ANA;
13475 5ELCID1708 PIDO *** VN DON & SEAM PRESENTADO.
13494 5ELCID1710 DIXO EL CAMPEADOR: DESA QUI *** SEAN MANDADAS.
13797 5ELCID1748 AUOS ME OMILLO, DUE@AS, GRANT PREZ *** HE GA@ADO:
13848 5ELCID1754 ROGAND AL CRIADOR QUE *** BIUA ALGUNT A@O,
13927 5ELCID1764 ESTAS DUE@AS QUE ADUXIESTES, QUE *** SIRUEN TANTO,
14017 5ELCID1776 QUIERO *** DEZIR LO QUE ES MAS GRANADO:
14275 5ELCID1806 DESTA MI QUINTA, DIGO *** SIN FALLA,
14291 5ELCID1808 E CRAS HA LA MA@ANA YR *** HEDES SIN FALLA
14596 5ELCID1847 A *** LAMA POR SE@OR, & TIENES POR UUESTRO VASSALLO,
14653 5ELCID1854 E EMBIA *** DOZIENTOS CAUALLOS, & BESA UOS LAS MANOS.
14658 5ELCID1854 E EMBIA UOS DOZIENTOS CAUALLOS, & BESA *** LAS MANOS.
14800 5ELCID1871 MANDO *** LOS CUERPOS ONDRADA MIENTRE SERUIR & VESTIR
14810 5ELCID1872 E GUARNIR *** DE TODAS ARMAS COMMO UOS DIXIEREDES AQUI,
14815 5ELCID1872 E GUARNIR UOS DE TODAS ARMAS COMMO *** DIXIEREDES AQUI,
14870 5ELCID1879 DELOS YFFANTES DE CARRION YO *** QUIERO CONTAR,
14909 5ELCID1885 MER%ED *** PIDIMOS COMMO A REY & SE@OR NATURAL;
15056 5ELCID1903 SED BUENOS MENSSAGEROS, & RUEGO *** LO YO
15091 5ELCID1908 ROGAR GELO EMOS LO QUE DEZIDES ***;
15353 5ELCID1944 QUE *** VERNIE AVISTAS DO OUIESSEDES SABOR;
15360 5ELCID1945 QUERER *** YE VER & DAR UOS SU AMOR,
15365 5ELCID1945 QUERER UOS YE VER & DAR *** SU AMOR,

WORD C# PREFIX CONTEXT

UOS (CON'T)

15369 5ELCID1946 ACORDAR *** YEDES DESPUES ATODO LO MEIOR.
15386 5ELCID1948 ESTAS VISTAS CLAS AYADES ***,
15389 5ELCID1949 DIXO MINAYA, *** SED SABIDOR.
16010 5ELCID2031 MER%ED *** PIDO AUOS, MYO NATURAL SE@OR,
16038 5ELCID2034 AQUI *** PERDCNC & DOUOS MY AMOR,
16187 5ELCID2053 CMILLAMCS NOS, %ID, EN BUEN ORA NASQUIESTES ***
16357 5ELCID2075 VUESTRAS FIJAS *** PIDO, DCN ELUIRA & DO@A SOL,
16382 5ELCID2078 ELLOS *** LAS PIDEN & MANDO UOS LO YO.
16387 5ELCID2078 ELLOS UOS LAS PIDEN & MANDO *** LO YO.
16411 5ELCID2081 DANDOS LAS, MYC %ID, SI *** VALA EL CRIADOR
16456 5ELCID2086 HYO LAS ENGENDRE AMAS & CRIASTES LAS ***
16478 5ELCID2089 DAD LAS AQUI QUISIEREDES ***, CA YO PAGADO SO.
16612 5ELCID2104 QUE METAN EN SUS BODAS CDO QUISIEREDES ***;
16633 5ELCID2107 LO QUE *** PLOGIERE, DELLCS FET, CAMPEADOR.
16647 5ELCID2109 MUCHO *** LO GRADESCO, COMMC A REY & A SE@OR
16832 5ELCID2131 YO *** PIDC MER%ED AUCS, REY NATURAL:
16854 5ELCID2133 DAD MANERO A QUI LAS DE, QUANDO *** LAS TOMADES;
16900 5ELCID2139 QUANDO *** IUNTAREDES CCMIGO, QUEM DIGADES LA UERDAT.
17012 5ELCID2154 ADIOS *** ACOMIENDO, DESTAS VISTAS ME PARTO.
17058 5ELCID2160 MER%ED *** SEA & FAZED NOS ESTE PERDON:
17229 5ELCID2179 VOS CON ELLCS SED, QUE ASSI *** LO MANDO YO.
17281 5ELCID2186 MUCHOS DIAS *** VEAMOS CCN LCS OIOS DELAS CARAS
17295 5ELCID2188 HYERNOS *** ADUGO DE QUE AUREMOS ONDRAN%A;
17307 5ELCID2189 GRADID MELO, MIS FIJAS, CA BIEN *** HE CASADAS
17337 5ELCID2193 TODO LC QUE *** FECHES ES DE BUENA GUISA.
17351 5ELCID2195 QUANDO *** NOS CASAREDES BIEN SEREMOS RICAS.
17388 5ELCID2200 PEDIDAS *** HA & ROGADAS EL MYO SE@OR ALFONSSO,
17424 5ELCID2204 BIEN MELO CREADES, QUE EL *** CASA, CA NON YO.
17995 5ELCID2277 EL CRIADOR *** VALLA CCN TODOS LOS SOS SANTOS.
18136 5ELCID2294 QUES ESTO, MESNADAS, C QUE QUEREDES ***?
18395 5ELCID2328 HYD LOS CONORTAR, SI *** VALA EL CRIADOR,
18426 5ELCID2332 DIOS *** SALUE, YERNOS, YFANTES DE CARRION,
18446 5ELCID2334 HYO DESSEO LIDES, & *** A CARRION;
18475 5ELCID2338 AVN VEA EL ORA QUE *** MERESCA DOS TANTO.
18609 5ELCID2355 HYO *** DIGO, %ID, PCR TODA CARIDAD,
18683 5ELCID2364 MANDAD NOLOS FERIR DE QUAL PART *** SEMEIAR,
18727 5ELCID2370 OY *** DIX LA MISSA DE SANTA TRINIDADE.
18742 5ELCID2371 POR ESSO SALI DE MI TIERRA & VIN *** BUSCAR,
18792 5ELCID2378 EUOS, MYO %ID, DE MI MAS *** PAGAR.
18810 5ELCID2380 ESSORA DIXO MYO %ID: LO QUE *** QUEREDES PLAZ ME.
19308 5ELCID2445 ACARRION DE *** YRAN BUENOS MANDADOS,
19392 5ELCID2457 EA ***, %ID, QUE EN BUEN ORA FUESTES NADO
19855 5ELCID2517 ACA VENID, CUNADOS, QUE MAS VALEMOS POR ***.
19880 5ELCID2521 BIEN *** ABRA%EN & SIRUAN UOS DE CORA%ON.
19884 5ELCID2521 BIEN UOS ABRA%EN & SIRUAN *** DE CORA%ON.
19910 5ELCID2525 DESTOS NUESTROS CASAMIENTOS *** ABREDES HONOR.
19929 5ELCID2528 GRADO AL CRIADOR & A ***, %ID ONDRADO,
19941 5ELCID2530 POR *** AUEMOS ONDRA & AVEMOS LIDIADO.
20155 5ELCID2559 SI *** VALA EL CRIADOR, %ID CAMPEADOR
20287 5ELCID2575 DAR *** HE DOS ESPADAS, A COLADA & A TIZON,
20299 5ELCID2576 BIEN LO SABEDES *** QUE LAS GANE AGUISA DE VARON;
20354 5ELCID2582 SI BIEN LAS SERUIDES, YO *** RENDRE BUEN GALARDON.
20437 5ELCID2594 MER%ED *** PEDIMOS, PADRE, SIUOS VALA EL CRIADOR
20473 5ELCID2599 ASSI *** PEDIMOS MER%ED NOS AMAS ADOS,
20529 5ELCID2606 ASSI COMMO YO TENGO, BIEN *** HE CASADAS.
20699 5ELCID2628 ADIOS *** HACOMENDAMOS, DON ELUIRA & DO@A SOL,
21048 5ELCID2675 DEZID ME, QUE *** FIZ, YFANTES DE CARRION
21055 5ELCID2676 HYO SIRUIENDO *** SIN ART, & UOS CONSSEIASTES PORA MI MUERT.
21059 5ELCID2676 HYO SIRUIENDO UOS SIN ART, & *** CONSSEIASTES PORA MI MUERT.
21075 5ELCID2678 TAL COSA *** FARIA QUE POR EL MUNDO SONAS,
21098 5ELCID2681 AQUIM PARTO DE *** COMMO DE MALOS & DE TRAYDORES.
21435 5ELCID2725 POR DIOS *** ROGAMOS, DON DIEGO & DON FERANDO
21492 5ELCID2733 RETRAER *** LO AN EN VISTAS O EN CORTES.
21733 5ELCID2764 MAS YO *** DIRE DAQUEL FELEZ MUNOZ.
21944 5ELCID2792 ESFOR%AD ***, PRIMAS, PCR AMOR DEL CRIADOR
21980 5ELCID2797 SI *** LO MERESCA, MYO PRIMO, NUESTRO PADRE EL CANPEADOR,
21993 5ELCID2798 DANDOS DEL AGUA, SI *** VALA EL CRIADOR
22396 5ELCID2853 MUCHO *** LO GRADE%E, ALLA DO ESTA, MYO %ID EL CANPEADOR,
22418 5ELCID2855 AFFE DIOS DELOS %IELOS QUE *** DE DENT BUEN GALARDON
22454 5ELCID2860 ATANTO *** LO GRADIMOS COMMO SI VIESSEMOS AL CRAIDOR;
22504 5ELCID2866 QUANDO *** SODES SA@AS & BIUAS & SIN OTRO MAL.
22679 5ELCID2890 VENIDES, MIS FIJAS? DIOS *** CURIE DE MAL
22700 5ELCID2893 QUE *** VEA MEIOR CASADAS DAQUI EN ADELANT.
23064 5ELCID2938 ELE ES VUESTRO VASSALLO & *** SODES SO SE@OS.
23081 5ELCID2940 ALTO FUE EL CASAMIENO CALO QUISIESTES ***
23083 5ELCID2941 HYA *** SABEDES LA ONDRA QUE ES CUNTIDA ANOS,
23134 5ELCID2948 POR ESTO *** BESA LAS MANOS, COMMO VASSALLO A SE@OR,
23161 5ELCID2951 E QUE *** PESE, REY COMMO SODES SABIDOR;
23496 5ELCID2992 DARLEDES DERECHO, CA RENCURA HA DE ***.
23803 5ELCID3032 DIOS LO MANDE QUE POR *** SE ONDRE OY LA CORT
23826 5ELCID3035 GRADO ADIOS, QUANDO *** VEO, SE@OR.
23864 5ELCID3040 BESA *** LAS MANOS, & MIS FIJAS AMAS ADOS,
23877 5ELCID3041 DESTO QUE NOS ABINO QUE *** PESE, SE@OR.
23908 5ELCID3045 MER%ED, YA REY, SI EL CRIADOR *** SALUE

WORD C# PREFIX CONTEXT

UOS (CON'T)

```
            24438 5ELCID3115 EN AQUESTE ESCANO QUEMDIESTES *** ENDON;
            24696 5ELCID3146 MUCHO *** LC GRADESCO CCMMO A REY & A SEaOR,
            24729 5ELCID3150 CA *** LAS CASASTES, REY, SABREDES QUE FER OY;
            24926 5ELCID3174 DAR GELAS QUEREMOS DELLANT ESTANDO ***.
            25085 5ELCID3196 POR ESSO *** LA DC QUE LA BIEN CURIEDES UOS.
            25092 5ELCID3196 POR ESSO UOS LA DC QUE LA BIEN CURIEDES ***.
            25096 5ELCID3197 SE QUE SI *** ACAE%IERE, CON ELLA GANAREDES GRAND PREZ
                             & GRAND VALOR.
            25259 5ELCID3216 DESTOS AUERES QUE *** DI YC, SIMELOS DADES, O DEDES DELLO RA%ON.
            25580 5ELCID3258 DEZID  QUE *** MERE%I, YFANTES, EN JUEGO O EN VERO
            25774 5ELCID3283 QUE AVEDES ***, CCNDE, POR RETRAER LA MI BARBA?
            25849 5ELCID3293 DEXASSEDES ***, %ID, DE AQUESTA RAZON;
            26698 5ELCID3410 RUEGO ***, %ID, CABOSC CAMPEADOR,
            26720 5ELCID3413 CA CRE%E *** Y CNDRA & TIERRA & ONOR.
            26748 5ELCID3416 ESSORA DIXO EL REY: DIOS *** DE DEN BUEN GALARDON
            26762 5ELCID3418 ESTE CASAMIENTO OTORGO *** LE YO
            26784 5ELCID3421 QUE *** LAS DE ACNDRA & A BENDI%ION.
            26848 5ELCID3430 MER%ED *** PIDO CCMMC A REY & A SEaOR,
            26865 5ELCID3432 BIEN *** DI VAGAR EN TODA ESTA CORT,
            26891 5ELCID3436 HYO *** RUEGO QUE ME OYADES TODA LA CORT,
            27016 5ELCID3451 AVER LAS HEDES ASERUIR, MAL QUE *** PESE AUOS.
            27289 5ELCID3488 DAQUI *** LOS ACOMIENDO COMO A REY & A SEaOR.
            27425 5ELCID3504 MER%ED *** PIDO, REY, POR AMOR DEL CRIADOR
            27517 5ELCID3515 HY *** LE DO EN DON, MANDEDES LE TOMAR, SEaOR.
            27573 5ELCID3521 CA POR *** & POREL CAUALLO ONDRADOS SOMO NOS.
            28169 5ELCID3596 OYD QUE *** DIGC, YFANTES DE CARRION:
            28727 5ELCID3668 ESSORA DIXO EL REY: VENID *** AMI COMPAaA;
      WORD #4164 OCCURS 236 TIMES.
         INDEX OF DIVERSIFICATION =   119.76 WITH STANDARD DEVIATION OF   165.98

UOZES                 281 5ELCID0035 LOS DE MYO %ID A ALTAS ***** LAMAN,
      WORD #4165 OCCURS   1 TIMES.

UUESTRA               914 5ELCID0117 EL CAMPEADOR DEXAR LAS HA EN ******* MANO,
                     1381 5ELCID0177 ASSI ES ******* VENTURA GRANDES SON UUESTRAS GANAN%IAS,
                     1395 5ELCID0179 %ID, BESO ******* MANC ENDON QUE LA YO AYA.
                     1637 5ELCID0210 VEREMOS ******* MUGIER, MENBRADA FIJA DALGO.
                     2491 5ELCID0314 POCO AUER TRAYO, DAR UOS QUIERO ******* PART.
                     3982 5ELCID0505 TODO LC OTRO AFELO EN ******* MANO.
                     5613 5ELCID0707 VO METER LA ******* SEaA EN AQUELA MAYOR AZ;
                     6372 5ELCID0812 A ******* GUISA PRENDED CON UUESTRA MANO.
                     6376 5ELCID0812 A UUESTRA GUISA PRENDED CON ******* MANO.
                    10457 5ELCID1325 ECHASTES LE DE TIERRA, NON HA LA ******* AMOR;
                    13130 5ELCID1664 NON AYADES MIEDO, CATODO ES ******* PRO;
                    13892 5ELCID1760 SOMOS EN ******* MER%ED, & BIUADES MUCHOS AaOS
                    16020 5ELCID2032 ASSI ESTANDO, DEDES ME ******* AMOR, QUE LO OYAN QUANTOS
                                     AQUI SON.
                    16461 5ELCID2087 ENTRE YO YELLAS EN ******* MER%ED SOMOS NOS,
                    16467 5ELCID2088 AFELLAS EN ******* MANO CON ELUIRA & DOaA SOL,
                    17567 5ELCID2222 AFFE AMAS MIS FIJAS, METOLAS EN ******* MANO;
                    17593 5ELCID2225 ALOS YFANTES DE CARRION DAD LAS CON ******* MANO,
                    18700 5ELCID2366 VERLO HEMOS CONDIOS & CON LA ******* AUZE.
                    21107 5ELCID2682 HYRE CON ******* GRA%IA, CON ELUIRA & DOaA SOL;
                    23156 5ELCID2950 TIENES POR DESONDRADO, MAS LA ******* ES MAYOR,
                    27285 5ELCID3487 ESTOS MIS TRES CAUALLEROS EN ******* MANO SON,
                    27443 5ELCID3506 BESO UUESTRAS MANOS CON ******* GRA%IA, SEaOR,
                    28039 5ELCID3579 EN ******* MANO NOS METIO NUESTRO SEaOR;
      WORD #4166 OCCURS  23 TIMES.
         INDEX OF DIVERSIFICATION =  1231.95 WITH STANDARD DEVIATION OF  1234.07

UUESTRAS             1385 5ELCID0177 ASSI ES UUESTRA VENTURA GRANDES SON ******** GANAN%IAS,
                     1479 5ELCID0189 YA DON RACHEL & VIDAS, EN ******** MANOS SON LAS ARCAS;
                     2134 5ELCID0269 FEM ANTE UOS YO & ******** FFIJAS, YFFANTES SON & DE DIAS
                                     CHICAS,
                    11037 5ELCID1397 ASSI FFAGA A ******** FIJAS AMAS.
                    12589 5ELCID1597 AFE ME AQUI, SEaOR, YO ******** FIJAS & AMAS,
                    13008 5ELCID1650 POR CASAR SON ******** FIJAS, ADUZEN UOS AXUUAR.
                    13857 5ELCID1755 ENTRAREDES EN PREZ, & BESARAN ******** MANOS.
                    13957 5ELCID1768 LO DE ******** FIJAS VENIR SEA MAS POR ESPA%IO.
                    16537 5ELCID2096 QUEM DADES ******** FIJAS PORA LOS YFANTES DE CARRION.
                    16567 5ELCID2099 HYO LAS CASO A ******** FIJAS CON UUESTRO AMOR,
                    16581 5ELCID2101 AFELLOS EN ******** MANOS LOS YFANTES DE CARRION,
                    16877 5ELCID2136 PRENDELLAS CON ******** MANOS & DALDAS ALOS YFANTES,
                    16954 5ELCID2146 TOMAD AQUESTO, & BESO ******** MANOS.
                    20207 5ELCID2566 VERAN ******** FIJAS LO QUE AUEMOS NOS,
                    20346 5ELCID2581 A MIS FIJAS SIRUADES, QUE ******** MUGIERES SON;
                    26680 5ELCID3407 AFE MIS FIJAS, EN ******** MANOS SON:
                    27196 5ELCID3476 DAD ME UUESTROS CAUALLEROS CON TODAS ******** GUARNIZONES,
                    27440 5ELCID3506 BESO ******** MANOS CON UUESTRA GRA%IA, SEaOR,
      WORD #4167 OCCURS  18 TIMES.
         INDEX OF DIVERSIFICATION =  1531.65 WITH STANDARD DEVIATION OF  2510.99

UUESTRO               670 5ELCID0085 CON ******* CONSEGO BASTIR QUIERO DOS ARCHAS;
                      931 5ELCID0119 PRENDED LAS ARCHAS & METED LAS EN ******* SALUO;
                     1124 5ELCID0144 POR ADUZIR LAS ARCHAS & METER LAS EN ******* SALUO,
                     1307 5ELCID0167 LEUALDAS, RACHEL & VIDAS, PONED LAS EN ******* SALUO;
                     1756 5ELCID0224 MANDO AL ******* ALTAR BUENAS DONAS & RICAS;
                     1962 5ELCID0248 DIXO EL %ID:  GRA%IAS, DON ABBAT, & SO ******* PAGADO;
```

WORD C# PREFIX CONTEXT

UUESTRO (CON'T)

```
                    8441 5ELCID1073 DE LO *******, C DELC MYO LEUAREDES ALGO.
                    8453 5ELCID1074 FOLGEDES, YA MYO %ID, SCDES EN ******* SALUO.
                   14603 5ELCID1847 A UOS LAMA PCR SE@OR, & TIENES POR ******* VASSALLO,
                   14918 5ELCID1886 CON ******* CCNSSEIC LC QUEREMCS FER NOS,
                   16193 5ELCID2054 EN QUANTO PCDEMCS ANDAMCS EN ******* PRO.
                   1657C 5ELCID2C99 HYO LAS CASC A UUESTRAS FIJAS CON ******* AMOR,
                   16616 5ELCID2105 PUES FUEREN EN ******* PCDER EN VALEN%IA LA MAYOR,
                   16786 5ELCID2125 GRADESCOLO, REY, & PRENCC ******* DON,
                   18454 5ELCID2335 EN VALEN%IA FCLGAD A TOCO ******* SABOR,
                   2C512 5ELCID2604 DE MI & DE ******* PACRE BIEN AVEDES NUESTRA GRA%IA.
                   24458 5ELCID3118 SED EN ******* ESCA@O CCMMO REY A SE@OR;
                   26684 5ELCID3408 SIN ******* MANCADO NACA NON FERE YO.
                   28199 5ELCID3600 AUED ******* DERECHC, TUERTO NON QUERADES VOS,
         WORD #4168 OCCURS  19 TIMES.
            INDEX OF DIVERSIFICATION =  1528.39 WITH STANDARD DEVIATION OF  2026.55

UUESTROS            3C07 5ELCID0379 %ID, DO SON ******** ESFUER%OS? EN BUEN ORA NASQUIESTES DE MADRE;
                    8045 5ELCID1027 SI NON, EN TODOS ******** DIAS NON VEREDES CHRISTIANISMO.
                   16402 5ELCID2080 LOS MIOS & LOS ******** QUE SEAN ROGADORES;
                   16628 5ELCID2106 LOS YERNOS & LAS FIJAS TODOS ******** FIJOS SON:
                   16768 5ELCID2123 EVAD AQUI ******** FIJCS, CUANDO UUESTROS YERNOS SON;
                   16771 5ELCID2123 EVAD AQUI UUESTROS FIJOS, QUANDO ******** YERNOS SON;
                   17348 5ELCID2194 NON SERAN MENGUACAS EN TODOS ******** DIAS
                   18381 5ELCID2326 EUADES QUE PAUOR HAN ******** YERNOS TAN OSADOS,
                   18641 5ELCID2359 VOS CON LOS ******** FIRME MIENTRE ALA %AGA TENGADES;
                   19413 5ELCID2459 TODOS ESTOS BIENES DEUOS SON & DE ******** VASSALLOS.
                   20481 5ELCID2600 QUE AYACES ******** MENSSAIES EN TIERRAS DE CARRION.
                   25855 5ELCID3294 DE ******** AUERES DE TCDOS PAGADOS SODES.
                   27192 5ELCID3476 DAD ME ******** CAUALLEROS CCN TODAS UUESTRAS GUARNIZONES,
         WORD #4169 OCCURS  13 TIMES.
            INDEX OF DIVERSIFICATICN =  2014.42 WITH STANCARD DEVIATION OF  2703.88

UUSCO                591 5ELCID0075 SI CON ***** ESCAPO SANC OBIUO,
                    1815 5ELCID0231 ANTES SERE CON ***** QUE EL SOL QUIERA RAYAR.
                   11992 5ELCID1520 TAN BUEN DIA CON *****, MINAYA ALBARFANEZ
                   12597 5ELCID1598 CON DIOS & CON ***** BUENAS SON & CRIADAS.
                   16590 5ELCID2102 ELLOS VAYAN CCN *****, CACA QUEN ME TORNO YO.
                   18410 5ELCID2330 NOS CON ***** LA VENCREMOS, & VALER NOS HA EL CRIADOR.
         WORD #4170 OCCURS   6 TIMES.
            INDEX OF DIVERSIFICATICN =  3562.80 WITH STANCARD DEVIATION OF  3911.16

UUSO                1312 5ELCID0168 YO YRE CON ****, QUE ADUGAMCS LOS MARCOS,
         WORD #4171 OCCURS   1 TIMES.

UUSTRO             17373 5ELCID2198 DESTE ****** CASAMIENTO CRE%REMOS EN ONOR;
         WORD #4172 OCCURS   1 TIMES.

V                  11465 5ELCID1451 DE SAN PERO FASTA MEDINA EN * DIAS VAN,
                   18881 5ELCID2389 DOS MATO CON LAN%A & * CON EL ESPADA.
         WORD #4173 OCCURS   2 TIMES.

VA                  2929 5ELCID0369 DO@A XIMENA AL %ID LA MANOL ** BESAR,
                    4655 5ELCID0590 DIZEN LCS DE ALCO%ER:  YA SE NOS ** LA GANA%IA
                    5512 5ELCIDC695 QUE PRIESSA ** EN LCS MCROS, E TORNARON SE A ARMAR;
                    5898 5ELCIDC747 MAGER DE PIE BUENOS COLPES ** DANDO.
                    6103 5ELCID0775 PARA CALATAYUCH QUANTO PUEDE SE **.
                    6258 5ELCIDC797 GRAND ALEGREYA ** ENTRE ESSOS CHISTIANOS,
                    7301 5ELCID0936 TIERRAS DALCANZ NEGRAS LAS ** PARANDO,
                    7308 5ELCIDC937 E A DERREDOR TODO LC ** PREANDC.
                    7318 5ELCIDC939 HYA ** EL MANDADO POR LAS TIERRAS TODAS,
                    7326 5ELCID0940 PESANDO ** ALCS DE MCN%CN & ALOS DE HUESCA;
                    8263 5ELCID1052 COMIENDO ** EL CONDE  DIOS, QUE DE BUEN GRADO
                    8311 5ELCID1057 CON ESTOS DOS CAUALLERCS A PRIESSA ** IANTANDO;
                    8934 5ELCID1137 CCN LOS ALUCRES MYO %ID FERIR LOS **:
                    9C07 5ELCID1146 GRAND ES EL GCZO QUE ** PCR ES LOGAR.
                    9468 5ELCID1203 ADELINC PORA VALEN%IA & SOBRELLAS ** ECHAR,
                   11C16 5ELCID1394 DE%IDO ES MYNAYA, ASSAN PERC ** ROGAR,
                   11750 5ELCID1490 %IENTOL PIDIERON, MAS EL CON DOZIENTOS **.
                   14525 5ELCID1837 ALCS VNOS PLAZE & ALCS CTRCS ** PESANDO.
                   15862 5ELCID2012 HYAS ** PORA LAS VISTAS QUE CON EL REY PARO.
                   17621 5ELCID2229 ALOS YFANTES CE CARRICN MINAYA ** FABLANDO:
                   19130 5ELCID2419 MAS BAUIECA EL DE MIC %ID ALCAN%ANDO LO **.
                   20587 5ELCID2614 ALEGRE ** MYO %ID CCN TCCAS SUS COMPA@AS.
                   22438 5ELCID2858 MINAYA ** UER SUS PRIMAS CO SCN,
                   23436 5ELCID2985 HYA LES ** PESANDO ALSO YFANTES DE CARRION,
                   23562 5ELCID3001 EN LOS PRIMEROS ** EL BUEN REY CON ALFONSSO,
                   24358 5ELCID3106 EL ** EN MEDIC, ELCS %IENTO ACERREDOR.
                   28223 5ELCID3603 HYA LES ** PESANDC ALCS YFANTES DE CARRION.
         WORD #4174 OCCURS  27 TIMES.
            INDEX OF DIVERSIFICATICN =   971.85 WITH STANCARD DEVIATION OF   934.30

VACAS               3803 5ELCID0481 DE OUEIAS & DE ***** & DE ROPAS & DE OTRAS RIQUIZAS LARGAS.
         WORD #4175 OCCURS   1 TIMES.
```

WORD C# PREFIX CONTEXT

```
VAGAR             3023 5ELCID0380 PENSEMOS DE YR NUESTRA VIA, ESTO SEA DE *****.
                  3440 5ELCID0434 ANDIDIERON DE NOCH, QUE ***** NON SE DAN.
                  5143 5ELCID0650 ANDIDIERON TODOL DIA, QUE ***** NON SE DAN,
                 18708 5ELCID2367 DIXO MYO %ID: AYAMOS MAS DE *****.
                 22475 5ELCID2862 EN LOS DIAS DE ***** TODA NUESTRA RENCURA SABREMOS CONTAR.
                 22930 5ELCID2921 NOS DAN ***** LOS DIAS & LAS NOCHES.
                 25960 5ELCID3308 MAS QUANDO ENPIE%A, SABED, NOL DA *****:
                 26867 5ELCID3432 BIEN UOS DI ***** EN TODA ESTA CORT,
        WORD #4176 OCCURS    8 TIMES.
          INDEX OF DIVERSIFICATION =  3405.29 WITH STANDARD DEVIATION OF  4659.48

VAL               7610 5ELCID0974 DI%E DE VNA SIERRA & LEGAUA A VN ***.
                 11327 5ELCID1433 DESFECHOS NOS HA EL %ID, SABET, SI NO NOS ***;
                 11773 5ELCID1493 POR EL *** DE ARBUXEDO PIENSSAN A DEPRUNAR.
                 19186 5ELCID2426 E GANO A TIZON QUE MILL MARCOS DORO ***.
                 27065 5ELCID3458 QUE ***, MINAYA, TODA ESSA RAZON?
        WORD #4177 OCCURS    5 TIMES.
          INDEX OF DIVERSIFICATION =  4862.75 WITH STANDARD DEVIATION OF  3484.34

VALA              1895 5ELCID0241 TU QUE ATODOS QUIAS, **** MYO %ID EL CANPEADOR.
                  5606 5ELCID0706 EL CRIADOR UOS ****, %ID CAMPEADOR LEAL
                  6841 5ELCID0874  QUIN LOS DIO ESTOS, SI UOS **** DIOS, MYNAYA
                  6889 5ELCID0880 QUEL AYDES MER%ED, SIEL CRIADOR UOS ****.
                 10447 5ELCID1324 QUEL AYADES MER%ED, SIUOS **** EL CRIADOR
                 10589 5ELCID1342  SI ME **** SANT ESIDRO  PLAZME DE CORA%ON,
                 11395 5ELCID1442  SI UOS **** EL CRIADOR, MINAYA ALBARFANEZ,
                 16412 5ELCID2081 DANDOS LAS, MYO %ID, SI UOS **** EL CRIADOR
                 18396 5ELCID2328 HYD LOS CONCRTAR, SI UOS **** EL CRIADOR,
                 20156 5ELCID2559 SI UOS **** EL CRIADOR, %ID CAMPEADOR
                 20441 5ELCID2594 MER%ED UOS PEDIMOS, PADRE, SIUOS **** EL CRIADOR
                 20507 5ELCID2603 ANDAD, FIJAS, DAQUI EL CRIADOR VOS ****
                 21994 5ELCID2798 DANDOS DEL AGUA, SI UOS **** EL CRIADOR
                 24540 5ELCID3128 OYD, MESNADAS, SIUOS **** EL CRIADOR
                 27568 5ELCID3520 QUIEN VOS LO TOLLER QUISIERE NOL **** EL CRIADOR,
        WORD #4178 OCCURS   15 TIMES.
          INDEX OF DIVERSIFICATION =  1832.79 WITH STANDARD DEVIATION OF  1561.59

VALADOLID        14447 5ELCID1827 LEGAN A *********, DO EL REY ALFONSSO ESTAUA;
        WORD #4179 OCCURS    1 TIMES.

VALAN             1697 5ELCID0218 ***** ME TUS VERTUDES, GLORIOSA SANTA MARIA
        WORD #4180 OCCURS    1 TIMES.

VALAS            21872 5ELCID2783 ***** TORNANDO A ELLAS AMAS ADOS;
                 22034 5ELCID2804 ***** CONORTANDO & METIENDO CORA%ON
        WORD #4181 OCCURS    2 TIMES.

VALDRA            2350 5ELCID0296 QUEL CRE%E CONPA@A, POR QUE MAS ******,
                 11426 5ELCID1446 EL %ID SIEMPRE ****** MAS.
                 13393 5ELCID1697 ODE AMAS ODEL VNA DIOS NOS ******.
        WORD #4182 OCCURS    3 TIMES.

VALDREMOS        11999 5ELCID1521 TRAEDES ESTAS DUE@AS POro ********* MAS,
        WORD #4183 OCCURS    1 TIMES.

VALE              7908 5ELCID1010 HY GA@O A COLADA QUE MAS **** DE MILL MARCOS DE PLATA.
                  9742 5ELCID1238 YAL CRE%E LA BARBA & **** ALLONGANDO;
                 13338 5ELCID1691 MAS **** QUE NOS LOS VEZCAMOS, QUE ELLOS COIAN EL PAN.
                 13882 5ELCID1758 LAS DUE@AS & LAS FIJAS & LA MUGIER QUE **** ALGO
                 15325 5ELCID1940 MAS PUES LO CONSEIA EL QUE MAS **** QUE NOS,
                 21968 5ELCID2795 SI DIOS NON NOS ****, AQUI MORREMOS NOS.
        WORD #4184 OCCURS    6 TIMES.
          INDEX OF DIVERSIFICATION =  2811.00 WITH STANDARD DEVIATION OF  2411.73

VALED            28019 5ELCID3576 ADERECHO NOS *****, ANINGUN TUERTO NO.
        WORD #4185 OCCURS    1 TIMES.

VALEDES          25667 5ELCID3268 POR QUANTO LES FIZIESTES MENOS ******* VOS.
                 26248 5ELCID3346 POR QUANTO LAS DEXASTES MENOS ******* VOS;
        WORD #4186 OCCURS    2 TIMES.

VALELDE           5668 5ELCID0714 DIXO EL CAMPEADOR:  *******, POR CARIDAD
        WORD #4187 OCCURS    1 TIMES.

VALEMOS          19853 5ELCID2517 ACA VENID, CUNADOS, QUE MAS ******* POR UOS.
        WORD #4188 OCCURS    1 TIMES.

VALEN            20093 5ELCID2550 AUERES LEUAREMOS GRANDES QUE ***** GRANT VALOR;
                 26261 5ELCID3348 EN TODAS GUISAS MAS ***** QUE VOS.
                 26413 5ELCID3369 ENTODAS GUISAS, SABED, QUE MAS ***** QUE VOS.
        WORD #4189 OCCURS    3 TIMES.

VALENCIA         10330 5ELCID1308 TIERRAS DE ******** REMANIDAS EN PAZ,
                 23130 5ELCID2947 AFELAS SUS FIJAS EN ******** DOSON.
        WORD #4190 OCCURS    2 TIMES.
```

WORD C# PREFIX CONTEXT

VALEN%IA

4956 5ELCIDC627 AL REY DE ******** ENBIARON CON MENSAIE,
8639 5ELCID1097 DENTRO EN ******** NCN ES POCO EL MIEDO.
8648 5ELCID1C98 PESA ALOS DE ********, SABET, NON LES PLAZE;
8801 5ELCID1119 LCS DE ******** %ERCADOS NOS HAN;
9020 5ELCID1148 FATA ******** DURO EL SEGUDAR.
9076 5ELCID1155 MIEDO AN EN ******** QUE NON SABEN QUESE FAR.
9164 5ELCID1166 NCN ES CON RECABDC EL DCLOR DE ********.
9191 5ELCID1170 ALCS DE ******** ESCARMENTADOS LOS HAN,
9229 5ELCID1174 MAL SE AQUEXAN LOS DE ******** QUE NON SABENT QUES FAR,
9367 5ELCID1191 %ERCAR QUIERE A ******** PORA CHRISTIANOS LA DAR.
9378 5ELCID1192 QUIEN QUIERE YR CCMIGC %ERCAR A ********,
9465 5ELCID1203 ADELINC PORA ******** & SCBRELLAS VA ECHAR,
9536 5ELCID1212 QUANDO MYO %ID GA@O A ******** & ENTRO ENLA %IBDAD.
9626 5ELCID1223 QUE PRESA ES ********, QUE NON GELA ENPARAN;
9692 5ELCID1232 BUENA FUE LA DE ******** QUANDO GANARON LA CASA,
9785 5ELCID1243 MYO %ID DON RODRIGO EN ******** ESTA FOLGANDO,
9812 5ELCID1246 ATODOS LES DIC EN ******** CASAS & HEREDADES
9951 5ELCID1261 AQUESTOS MYOS VASSALOS QUE CURIAN A ******** & ANDAN AROBDANDO.
1C264 5ELCID1299 EN TIERRAS DE ******** FER QUIERO OBISPADO,
10301 5ELCID1304 DIERON LE EN ******** C BIEN PUEDE ESTAR RICO.
10317 5ELCID1306 QUE EN TIERRAS DE ******** SE@OR AVIE OBISPO
10503 5ELCID1331 CON AQUESTAS TODAS DE ******** ES SE@OR,
10689 5ELCID1354 E YRIEN PORA ******** AL BUEN CAMPEADOR.
11068 5ELCID1401 POR LEUAROS A ******** QUE AUEMOS POR HEREDAD.
11192 5ELCID1416 HYR SE QUIERE A ******** A MYO %ID EL DE BIUAR.
11602 5ELCID1470 E YO FINCARE EN ********, QUE MUCHO COSTADOM HA;
11616 5ELCID1472 YO FFINCARE EN ********, CA LA TENGO POR HEREDAD.
11720 5ELCID1486 E FFATA EN ******** DELLAS NON UOS PARTADES.
12117 5ELCID1537 ONDRADO ES MYO %ID EN ******** DO ESTAUA
12253 5ELCID1556 FATA EN ******** SIRUIALOS SIN FALLA;
12278 5ELCID1559 APRES SON DE ******** A TRES LEGUAS CONTADAS.
12293 5ELCID1561 DENTRO A ******** LIEUAN LE EL MANDADO.
12333 5ELCID1566 EL SEDIE EN ******** CURIANDO & GUARDANDO,
12419 5ELCID1576 ALA PUERTA DE ********, DO FUESSE EN SO SALUO,
12659 5ELCID1606 ENTRAD CCMIGO EN ******** LA CASA,
12683 5ELCID1609 A TAN GRAND ONDRA ELLAS A ******** ENTRAUAN.
12706 5ELCID1613 MIRAN ******** COMMO IAZE LA %IBDAD,
12830 5ELCID1628 VAN BUSCAR A ******** A MYO %ID DON RODRIGO.
12845 5ELCID1630 LEGARON A ********, LA QUE MYO %ID A CONQUISTA,
12888 5ELCID1635 CON AFAN GANE A ********, & ELA POR HEREDAD,
13543 5ELCID1716 LA SE@A SACAN FUERA, DE ******** DIERON SALTO,
13755 5ELCID1743 CON C CAUALLEROS A ******** ES ENTRADO,
13802 5ELCID1749 VOS TENIENDO ********, & YO VEN%I EL CAMPO;
14160 5ELCID1792 CON AQUESTAS RIQUEZAS TANTAS A ******** SON ENTRADOS.
14217 5ELCID1799 ALEGRES SON POR ******** LAS YENTES CHRISTIANAS,
14346 5ELCID1814 QUE NON DIGA MAL EL REY ALFONSSO DEL QUE ******** MANDA.
14400 5ELCID1821 SALIDOS SON DE ******** EPIENSSAN DE ANDAR,
14470 5ELCID1830 MYO %ID EL DE ******** ENBIA SU PRESENTAIA.
15142 5ELCID1915 VAN PORA ******** ELLOS & TODOS LOS SOS.
15765 5ELCID2000 A AQUESTOS DOS MANDO EL CAMPEADOR QUE CURIEN A ********
15840 5ELCID2009 SALIEN DE ********, AGUIJAN & ESPOLONAUAN.
16619 5ELCID2105 PUES FUEREN EN UUESTRO PODER EN ******** LA MAYOR,
17C72 5ELCID2161 HYREMOS EN PODER DE MUO %ID A ******** LA MAYOR;
17122 5ELCID2167 ADELINAN PORA ********, LA QUE EN BUEN PUNTO GANO.
17191 5ELCID2175 AFELOS EN ********, LA QUE MYO %ID GA@O;
17716 5ELCID2242 ALA GLERA DE ******** FUERA DIERON SALTO;
17760 5ELCID2247 TORNAN SE CON LAS DUE@AS, A ******** AN ENTRADO;
17940 5ELCID2270 EL %ID & SOS HYERNOS EN ******** SON RASTADOS.
18003 5ELCID2278 EN ******** SEY MYO %ID CON TODOS SUS VASSALLOS,
18274 5ELCID2312 FUER%AS DE MARRUECOS ******** VIENEN %ERÇAR;
18450 5ELCID2335 EN ******** FOLGAD A TODO UUESTRO SABOR,
19456 5ELCID2465 TODAS LAS GANAN%IAS A ******** SON LEGADAS;
19503 5ELCID2471 FUERON EN ******** MUY BIEN ARREADOS,
19735 5ELCID2502 NO LOS YRE BUSCAR, EN ******** SERE YO,
19760 5ELCID2505 GRANDES SON LOS GOZOS EN ******** CON MYO %ID EL CANPEADOR
20060 5ELCID2546 SACAR LAS HEMOS DE ********, DE PODER DEL CAMPEADOR;
20397 5ELCID2588 GRANDES SON LAS NUEUAS POR ******** LA MAYOR,
20567 5ELCID2611 HYA SALIEN LOS YFANTES DE ******** LA CLARA,
20582 5ELCID2613 POR LA HUERTA DE ******** TENIENDO SALIEN ARMAS;
20680 5ELCID2625 TORNEMOS NOS, %ID, A ******** LA MAYOR;
20815 5ELCID2643 HYAS TORNO PORA ******** EL QUE EN BUEN ORA NAS%IO.
22192 5ELCID2826 VAN AQUESTOS MANDADOS A ******** LA MAYOR;
22302 5ELCID2840 ADUXIESSEN ASSUS FIJAS A ******** LA MAYOR.
22636 5ELCID2884 DENT PORA ******** ADELINECHOS VAN.
22923 5ELCID2920 SALIEN DE ******** & ANDAN QUANTO PUEDEN,
24454 5ELCID3117 ESSORA DIXO MUCHAS MER%EDES EL QUE ******** GA@O:
24743 5ELCID3151 MAS QUANDO SACARON MIS FIJAS DE ******** LA MAYOR,
25150 5ELCID3203 QUANDO SACARON DE ******** MIS FIJAS AMAS ADOS,
25303 5ELCID3221 MUCHO NOS AFINCA EL QUE ******** GA@O,
25609 5ELCID3261 ALA SALIDA DE ******** MIS FIJAS VOS DI YO,
25635 5ELCID3264 POR QUE LAS SACAUADES DE ******** SUS HONORES?
26015 5ELCID3316 MIEMBRAT QUANDO LIDIAMOS %ERCA ******** LA GRAND;

WORD C# PREFIX CONTEXT

VALEN%IA (CON'T)

```
                  26123 5ELCID3330  NCN TE VIENE EN MIENTE EN ******** LO DEL LEON,
                  26174 5ELCID3336 FASTA DO DESPERTO MYO %ID, EL QUE ******** GA@O;
                  27179 5ELCID3474 MAS QUIERO A ******** QUE TIERRAS DE CARRION.
                  27310 5ELCID3490 ONDRADOS MELOS ENBIAD A ********, POR AMOR DEL CRIADOR
                  27451 5ELCID3507 E YR ME QUIERC PORA ********, CON AFAN LA GANE YO.
                  27620 5ELCID3526 BUENOS MANDADOS ME VAYAN A ******** DE VOS.
                  27669 5ELCID3532 MYO %ID PCRA ********, & EL REY PORA CARRION.
                  28975 5ELCID3701 FELOS EN ******** CCN MYO %ID EL CAMPEADOR:
                  29057 5ELCID3711 GRANDES SON LCS GOZOS EN ******** LA MAYOR,
          WORD #4191 OCCURS  91 TIMES.
             INDEX OF DIVERSIFICATION =   266.79 WITH STANDARD DEVIATION OF   472.18

VALEN%IAL         22010 5ELCID2800 NUEUO ERA & FRESCC, QUE DE ********* SACO,
          WORD #4192 OCCURS   1 TIMES.

VALER             16124 5ELCID2045 ***** ME A DIOS DE DIA & DE NOCH.
                  18414 5ELCID2330 NOS CON UUSCO LA VENCREMOS, & ***** NOS HA EL CRIADOR.
          WORD #4193 OCCURS   2 TIMES.

VALES             26157 5ELCID3334 METISTET, FERRANDO, PORO MENOS ***** OY.
          WORD #4194 OCCURS   1 TIMES.

VALIA             19790 5ELCID2509 ***** DE %INCO MILL MARCOS GANARON AMOS ADOS;
          WORD #4195 OCCURS   1 TIMES.

VALIENDO           8636 5ELCID1096 YA VIE MYO %ID QUE DIOS LE YUA ********.
          WORD #4196 OCCURS   1 TIMES.

VALIENTES          3317 5ELCID0418 SIN LAS PECNADAS & OMNES ********* QUE SON,
                   6976 5ELCID0892 BUE@OS & ********* PCRA MYO %ID HUYAR,
          WORD #4197 OCCURS   2 TIMES.

VALIESTES         26002 5ELCID3314 POR EL CAMPEADOR MUCHO ********* MAS.
          WORD #4198 OCCURS   1 TIMES.

VALIO              6514 5ELCID0831 DIOS NOS ***** & VEN%IEMOS LA LIDIT.
                  28443 5ELCID3632 PASSO GELO TODO, QUE NACA NOL *****,
                  28453 5ELCID3633 METIOL LA LAN%A POR LOS PECHOS, QUE NADA NOL *****;
          WORD #4199 OCCURS   3 TIMES.

VALLA             17996 5ELCID2277 EL CRIADOR UOS ***** CON TODOS LOS SOS SANTOS.
          WORD #4200 OCCURS   1 TIMES.

VALLEN%IA         15651 5ELCID1985 DENTRO EN ********* MYO %ID EL CAMPEADOR
          WORD #4201 OCCURS   1 TIMES.

VALME             28698 5ELCID3665 *****, DIOS GLORIOSO, RE@OR, & CURIAM DESTE ESPADA
          WORD #4202 OCCURS   1 TIMES.

VALOR             20095 5ELCID2550 AUERES LEUAREMOS GRANDES QUE VALEN GRANT *****;
                  24313 5ELCID3099 DESUSO CUBRIO VN MANTO QUE ES DE GRANT *****,
                  25105 5ELCID3197 SE QUE SI UOS ACAE%IERE, CON ELLA GANAREDES GRAND PREZ
                                   & GRAND *****.
                  26963 5ELCID3444 ONDE SALIEN CONDES DE PREZ & DE *****;
                  28773 5ELCID3674 ASSUR GON%ALEZ, FUR%UDO & DE *****,
          WORD #4203 OCCURS   5 TIMES.
             INDEX OF DIVERSIFICATION =  2168.50 WITH STANDARD DEVIATION OF  1451.45

VALOS              5979 5ELCID0758 ALOS QUE ALCAN%A ***** DELIBRANDO.
          WORD #4204 OCCURS   1 TIMES.

VAN                5960 5ELCID0755 FIRME SON LOS MOROS, AVN NOS *** DEL CAMPO.
                   6212 5ELCID0791 VIO LOS SOS COMMOS *** ALEGANDO:
                   9072 5ELCID1154 LAS NUEUAS DE MYO %ID, SABET, SONANDO ***,
                   9083 5ELCID1156 SONANDO *** SUS NUEUAS ALENT PARTE DEL MAR.
                   9486 5ELCID1206 SONANDO *** SUS NUEUAS TODAS ATODAS PARTES.
                   9502 5ELCID1207 MAS LE VIENEN A MYO %ID, SABET, QUE NOS LE ***.
                   9527 5ELCID1211 GRANDES SON LOS GOZOS QUE *** POR ES LOGAR,
                  11467 5ELCID1451 DE SAN PERO FASTA MEDINA EN V DIAS ***,
                  11956 5ELCID1515 POR %ERCA DE SALON TAN GRANDES GOZOS ***.
                  12827 5ELCID1628 *** BUSCAR A VALEN%IA A MYO %ID DON RODRIGO.
                  13178 5ELCID1670 ALEGRE SON LAS DUENAS, PERDIENDO *** EL PAUOR.
                  13553 5ELCID1717 QUATRO MILL MENOS XXX CON MYO %ID *** A CABO,
                  13559 5ELCID1718 ALOS %INQUAENTA MILL *** LOS FERIR DE GRADO;
                  14436 5ELCID1826 PASSANDO *** LAS SIERRAS & LOS MONTES & LAS AGUAS,
                  14885 5ELCID1881 LAS NUEUAS DEL %ID MUCHO *** ADELANT,
                  15140 5ELCID1915 *** PORA VALEN%IA ELLOS & TODOS LOS SOS.
                  15629 5ELCID1982 CON EL REY *** LEONESES & MESNADAS GALIZIANAS,
                  17117 5ELCID2166 GRANDES SON LAS YENTES QUE *** CONEL CANPEADOR.
                  17670 5ELCID2235 A MYO %ID & A SU MUGIER *** BESAR LA MANO.
                  17801 5ELCID2252 HYA %ERCA DELOS XV DIAS YAS *** LOS FIJOS DALGO.
                  17991 5ELCID2276 LAS COPLAS DESTE CANTAR AQUIS *** ACABANDO.
                  18522 5ELCID2344 ESTO *** DIZIENDO & LAS YENTES SE ALEGANDO,
                  19380 5ELCID2455 DE TODAS PARTES SOS VASSALLOS *** LEGANDO;
                  21929 5ELCID2790 *** RECORDANDO CON ELUIRA & DO@A SOL,
```

WORD C# PREFIX CONTEXT

VAN (CON'T)

22188 5ELCID2826 *** AQUESTCS MANDADOS A VALENZIA LA MAYOR;
22548 5ELCID2871 LCS DE SANTESTEUAN ESCURRIENDC LOS ***
22611 5ELCID2880 E DE MEDINA A MOLINA EN OTRC DIA ***;
22638 5ELCID2884 DENT PCRA VALENZIA ADELINECHOS ***.
WORD #4205 OCCURS 28 TIMES.
INDEX OF DIVERSIFICATION = 616.70 WITH STANDARD DEVIATION OF 751.78

VANZIA 13505 5ELCID1711 SALIDOS SCN TCDCS ARMADOS POR LAS TORRES DE ******,
WORD #4206 OCCURS 1 TIMES.

VANDO 24618 5ELCID3136 E ESTOS OTROS CONDES QUE DEL ***** NON SODES.
24829 5ELCID3162 CON TODOS SUS PARIENTES & EL ***** QUE Y SON;
28026 5ELCID3577 AQUI TIENEN SU ***** LCS YFANTES DE CARRION,
WORD #4207 OCCURS 3 TIMES.

VANIDAT 7490 5ELCID0960 EL CONDE ES MUY FOLON & DIXO VNA *******:
WORD #4208 OCCURS 1 TIMES.

VANIGOMEZ 26955 5ELCID3443 DE NATURA SCDES DELOS DE *********,
WORD #4209 OCCURS 1 TIMES.

VANSSE 2325 5ELCID0294 ****** PORA SAN PERO DO ESTA EL QUE ENBUEN PUNTO NAZIO.
4256 5ELCID0542 ****** FENARES ARRIBA QUANTO PUEDEN ANDAR,
21815 5ELCID2775 ****** LOS YFANTES, AGUIJAN AESPOLON.
WORD #4210 OCCURS 3 TIMES.

VANSSELE 3198 5ELCID0403 ******** ACCGIENDO YENTES DE TOCAS PARTES.
WORD #4211 OCCURS 1 TIMES.

VARAGEN 28151 5ELCID3594 QUE NON ******* CON ELLCS DESI O DE NON.
WORD #4212 OCCURS 1 TIMES.

VARAIA 25863 5ELCID3295 NON CREZIES ****** ENTRE NOS & VOS.
WORD #4213 OCCURS 1 TIMES.

VARON 3241 5ELCID0408 EN TAN BUEN PUNTO CAUALGO *****;
10659 5ELCID1350 FABLAUA MINAYA Y AGUISA DE *****:
15821 5ELCID2006 RECABDADO HA, CCMMC TAN BUEN *****,
20305 5ELCID2576 BIEN LO SABEDES UOS QUE LAS GANE AGUISA DE *****;
21317 5ELCID2709 QUE NON YFINCAS NINGUNO, MUGIER NIN *****,
24518 5ELCID3125 EN SOS AGUISAMIENTOS BIEN SEMEIA *****.
24768 5ELCID3154 ESTAS YO LAS GANE AGUISA DE *****,
25915 5ELCID3302 FABLA, PERO MUDO, ***** QUE TANTO CALLAS
27484 5ELCID3510 QUE EN TODAS NUESTRAS TIERRAS NON HA TAN BUEN *****.
WORD #4214 OCCURS 9 TIMES.
INDEX OF DIVERSIFICATION = 3029.38 WITH STANDARD DEVIATION OF 2490.68

VARONES 2479 5ELCID0313 OYD, *******, NCN UCS CAYA EN PESAR;
4406 5ELCID0561 A TODOS SOS ******* MANDO FAZER VNA CARCAUA,
15178 5ELCID1920 EN POCAS TIERRAS A TALES DOS *******.
18129 5ELCID2293 VIO CERZADO EL ESCA@C DE SUS BUENOS *******:
18298 5ELCID2315 ALEGRAUAS EL ZID & TODCS SUS *******,
22348 5ELCID2847 ******* DE SANTESTEUAN, A GUISA DE MUY PROS,
22361 5ELCID2848 REZIBEN AMINAYA & ATODOS SUS *******,
22378 5ELCID2851 GRAZIAS, ******* DE SANTESTEUAN, QUE SODES CO@OSZEDORES,
26256 5ELCID3347 ELLAS SCN MUGIERES & VOS SODES *******,
26464 5ELCID3377 HYA *******, QUIEN VIO NUNCA TAL MAL?
27614 5ELCID3525 E MUNO GUSTIOZ, FIRMES SED EN CAMPO AGUISA DE *******;
27926 5ELCID3563 HUEBOS VOS ES QUE LIDIECES AGUISA DE *******,
28098 5ELCID3587 EDERREDOR DELLOS MUCHOS BUENOS *******.
WORD #4215 OCCURS 13 TIMES.
INDEX OF DIVERSIFICATION = 2133.92 WITH STANDARD DEVIATION OF 3114.87

VARRAGAN 26105 5ELCID3327 E ERES FERMOSO, MAS MAL ********
WORD #4216 OCCURS 1 TIMES.

VARRAGANAS 21705 5ELCID2759 NON LAS DEUIEMOS TOMAR POR **********,
25728 5ELCID3276 NCN GELAS DEUIEN QUERER SUS FIJAS POR **********,
WORD #4217 OCCURS 2 TIMES.

VASALLOS 17504 5ELCID2214 REZIBIO LOS MYO ZID CON TODOS SUS ********;
WORD #4218 OCCURS 1 TIMES.

VASSALLO 10564 5ELCID1339 RAZONAS POR VUESTRO ******** & AUOS TIENE POR SE@OR.
14604 5ELCID1847 A UOS LAMA POR SE@OR, & TIENES POR UUESTRO ********,
22767 5ELCID2901 OERES, MU@O GUSTIOZ, MYO ******** DE PRO,
22802 5ELCID2905 CUEMO YO SO SU ********, & EL ES MYO SE@OR,
23062 5ELCID2938 ELE ES VUESTRO ******** & UOS SODES SO SE@OS.
23139 5ELCID2948 POR ESTO UOS BESA LAS MANOS, COMMO ******** A SE@OR,
23416 5ELCID2982 QUI NON VINIESSE ALA CORT NON SE TOUIESSE POR SU ********.
27210 5ELCID3478 HYO VOS LO SOBRELIEUO COMMO BUEN ******** FAZE A SE@OR,
WORD #4219 OCCURS 8 TIMES.
INDEX OF DIVERSIFICATION = 2377.00 WITH STANDARD DEVIATION OF 3106.92

```
WORD                C#  PREFIX                      CONTEXT

VASSALLOS           1973 5ELCIDC249 YO ADOBARE CON DUCHO PORA MI & PORA MIS *********;
                    2988 5ELCID0376 MYO %ID CON LOS SOS ********* PENSSO DE CAUALGAR,
                    3404 5ELCID0430 ********* TAN BUENOS POR CORA%ON LO AN,
                    4468 5ELCID0568 AGARDANDO SEUA MYO %ID CON TODOS SUS *********;
                    4759 5ELCID0604 LOS ********* DE MYO %ID SIN PIEDAD LES DAUAN,
                    6336 5ELCID0806  DIOS, QUE BIEN PAGO A TODOS SUS *********,
                    8198 5ELCID1044 CA HUEBOS MELO HE & PORA ESTOS MYOS *********
                   11669 5ELCID1479  VENIDES, LOS ********* DE MYO AMIGO NATURAL?
                   13651 5ELCID1729 CON OTROS QUEL CONSIGEN DE SUS BUENOS *********.
                   13726 5ELCID1739 ALEGRE ERA MYO %ID & TODOS SOS *********,
                   13937 5ELCID1765 QUIERO LAS CASAR CON DE AQUESTOS MYOS *********;
                   14094 5ELCID1784 QUE A GANADO MYO %ID CON TODOS SUS *********
                   14650 5ELCID1853 RICOS SON VENIDOS TODOS LOS SOS *********,
                   17844 5ELCID2258 LOS ********* DE MIO %ID, ASSI SON ACORDADOS,
                   17908 5ELCID2265 POR PAGADOS SE PARTEN DE MYO %ID & DE SUS *********.
                   17966 5ELCID2273 ALEGRE ERA EL %ID & TODOS SUS *********.
                   18010 5ELCID2278 EN VALEN%IA SEY MYO %ID CON TODOS SUS *********,
                   18501 5ELCID2341 PLOGO A MYO %ID & ATODOS SOS *********;
                   19379 5ELCID2455 DE TODAS PARTES SOS ********* VAN LEGANDO;
                   19414 5ELCID2459 TODOS ESTOS BIENES DEUOS SON & DE UUESTROS *********.
                   19523 5ELCID2473 MUCHOS SON ALEGRES MYO %ID & SUS *********,
                   19774 5ELCID2506 DE TODAS SUS CONPA@AS & DE TODOS SUS *********;
                   19957 5ELCID2532 ********* DE MYO %ID SEYEN SE SONRRISANDO:
                   23313 5ELCID2969 QUE DESTAS VIJ SEMANAS ADOBES CON SUS *********,
         WORD #4220 OCCURS  24 TIMES.
            INDEX OF DIVERSIFICATION =   926.83 WITH STANDARD DEVIATION OF  1118.63

VASSALO              147 5ELCID0020 DIOS, QUE BUEN *******, SI OUIESSE BUEN SE@OR
                    1597 5ELCID0204  VENIDES, MARTIN ANTOLINEZ, EL MIO FIEL *******
                   25064 5ELCID3193 MARTIN ANTOLINEZ, MYO ******* DE PRO,
         WORD #4221 OCCURS   3 TIMES.

VASSALOS            6311 5ELCID0803 GRANT A EL GOZO MYO %ID CON TODOS SOS ********.
                    6641 5ELCID0847 QUE BIEN PAGO A SUS ******** MISMOS
                    9947 5ELCID1261 AQUESTOS MYOS ******** QUE CURIAN A VALEN%IA & ANDAN AROBDANDO.
                   13510 5ELCID1712 MIO %ID ALOS SOS ******** TAN BIEN LOS ACORDANDO.
                   17729 5ELCID2243 DIOS, QUE BIEN TOUIERON ARMAS EL %ID & SUS ********
                   26208 5ELCID3341 ASOS ******** VIOLOS A CERREDOR;
         WORD #4222 OCCURS   6 TIMES.
            INDEX OF DIVERSIFICATION =  3978.40 WITH STANDARD DEVIATION OF  2926.12

VASSE              10935 5ELCID1384 ESPIDIOS MYNAYA & ***** DELA CORT.
         WORD #4223 OCCURS   1 TIMES.

VASTE               6683 5ELCID0853  *****, MYO %ID; NUESTRAS ORA%IONES UAYANTE DELANTE
         WORD #4224 OCCURS   1 TIMES.

VAYA                3509 5ELCID0442 VOS CON LOS CC YD UOS EN ALGARA; ALA **** ALBARABAREZ,
                   16825 5ELCID2130 DAQUEND **** COMIGO; CUEDO QUEL AURA PRO.
         WORD #4225 OCCURS   2 TIMES.

VAYADES            11545 5ELCID1462 POR SANTA MARIA UOS ******* PASSAR,
                   11547 5ELCID1463 ******* A MOLINA, QUE IAZE MAS ADELANT,
                   11711 5ELCID1485 QUE ******* POR ELLAS, ADUGADES GELAS ACA,
         WORD #4226 OCCURS   3 TIMES.

VAYAMOS             1625 5ELCID0208 MANDAD COGER LA TIENDA & ******* PRIUADO,
                    5351 5ELCID0676 ******* LOS FERIR EN AQUEL DIA DE CRAS.
                   12073 5ELCID1531 ******* POSAR, CA LA %ENA ES ADOBADA.
                   17599 5ELCID2226 E PRENDAN BENDI%IONES & ******* RECABDANDO.
                   20016 5ELCID2540 ******* PORA CARRION, AQUI MUCHO DETARDAMOS.
         WORD #4227 OCCURS   5 TIMES.
            INDEX OF DIVERSIFICATION =  4596.75 WITH STANDARD DEVIATION OF  1905.23

VAYAN               8710 5ELCID1107 ***** LOS MANDADOS POR LOS QUE NOS DEUEN AIUDAR,
                   10819 5ELCID1370 DE MI SEAN QUITOS & ***** ALA GRA%IA DEL CRIADOR.
                   16588 5ELCID2102 ELLOS ***** CON UUSCO, CADA QUEN ME TORNO YO.
                   23269 5ELCID2964 QUE ALLA ME ***** CUENDES & YFAN%ONES,
                   23276 5ELCID2965 MANDARE COMMO Y ***** YFANTES DE CARRION,
                   27198 5ELCID3477 ***** COMIGO, YO SERE EL CURIADOR;
                   27618 5ELCID3526 BUENOS MANDADOS ME ***** A VALEN%IA DE VOS.
         WORD #4228 OCCURS   7 TIMES.
            INDEX OF DIVERSIFICATION =  3150.33 WITH STANDARD DEVIATION OF  2769.05

VAYAS              20639 5ELCID2620 MANDOT QUE ***** CON ELLAS FATA DENTRO EN CARRION,
                   26516 5ELCID3384 ANTES ALMUERZAS QUE ***** A ORA%ION,
         WORD #4229 OCCURS   2 TIMES.

VAYMOS             11872 5ELCID1505 ESSORA DIXO MYNAYA: ****** CAUALGAR.
         WORD #4230 OCCURS   1 TIMES.

VAZIAS              7792 5ELCID0997 POR UNO QUE FIRGADES, TRES SIELLAS YRAN ******.
         WORD #4231 OCCURS   1 TIMES.
```

WORD C# PREFIX CONTEXT

VAZIO 28401 5ELCID3627 PRISOL EN *****, EN CARNE NOL TOMO,
28788 5ELCID3677 EN ***** FUE LA LANZA, CA EN CARNE NOL TOMO.
WORD #4232 OCCURS 2 TIMES.

VZOS 19 5ELCID0003 VIO PUERTAS ABIERTAS & **** SIN CAÑADOS,
WORD #4233 OCCURS 1 TIMES.

VEA 1599 5ELCID0205 AUN *** EL DIA QUE DEMI AYADES ALGO
12061 5ELCID1529 SI DIOS ME LEGARE AL ZID ELO *** CON EL ALMA,
14680 5ELCID1857 AVN *** ORA QUE DE MI SEA PAGADO.
18471 5ELCID2338 AVN *** EL ORA QUE UOS MERESCA DOS TANTO.
22701 5ELCID2893 QUE UOS *** MEIOR CASADAS DAQUI EN ADELANT.
25672 5ELCID3269 SI NON RECUDEDES, *** LO ESTA CORT.
WORD #4234 OCCURS 6 TIMES.
INDEX OF DIVERSIFICATION = 4813.60 WITH STANDARD DEVIATION OF 3221.11

VEADES 13037 5ELCID1653 NON AYADES PAUOR POR QUE ME ****** LIDIAR,
WORD #4235 OCCURS 1 TIMES.

VEALO 742 5ELCID0094 ***** EL CRIADOR CON TODOS LOS SOS SANTOS,
WORD #4236 OCCURS 1 TIMES.

VEAMOS 17282 5ELCID2186 MUCHOS DIAS UOS ****** CON LOS OIOS DELAS CARAS
22520 5ELCID2868 AVN ****** EL DIA QUE VOS PODAMOS VENGAR
WORD #4237 OCCURS 2 TIMES.

VEAN 740 5ELCID0093 DE NOCHE LO LIEUEN, QUE NON LO **** CHISTIANOS.
WORD #4238 OCCURS 1 TIMES.

VED 29143 5ELCID3722 *** QUAL ONDRA CREZE AL QUE EN BUEN ORA NAZIO,
WORD #4239 OCCURS 1 TIMES.

VEDADA 487 5ELCID0062 ****** LAN CONPRA DENTRO EN BURGOS LA CASA,
5276 5ELCID0667 EL AGUA NOS AN ******, EXIR NOS HA EL PAN,
WORD #4240 OCCURS 2 TIMES.

VEDALLO 23296 5ELCID2967 E QUE NON AYA RENCURA PODIENDO YO *******.
WORD #4241 OCCURS 1 TIMES.

VEDAMOS 25333 5ELCID3225 SI ESSO PLOGIERE AL ZID, NON GELO ******* NOS;
WORD #4242 OCCURS 1 TIMES.

VEDAR 4361 5ELCID0555 AZERCA CORRE SALON, AGUA NOL PUEDENT *****.
18243 5ELCID2308 MANDOLO ***** MYO ZID EL CAMPEADOR.
WORD #4243 OCCURS 2 TIMES.

VEDARE 28212 5ELCID3601 CA QUI TUERTO QUISIERE FAZER, MAL GELO ****** YO,
WORD #4244 OCCURS 1 TIMES.

VEDARON 708 5ELCID0090 QUANDO EN BURGOS ME ******* COMPRA & EL REY ME A AYRADO,
WORD #4245 OCCURS 1 TIMES.

VEDAUA 5248 5ELCID0663 EL QUE EN BUEN ORA NASCO FIRME GELO ******.
WORD #4246 OCCURS 1 TIMES.

VEDES 646 5ELCID0082 BIEN LO ***** QUE YO NO TRAYO AUER, & HUEBOS ME SERIE
886 5ELCID0114 YA LO ***** QUE EL REY LEA AYRADO.
1063 5ELCID0137 YA ***** QUE ENTRA LA NOCH, EL ZID ES PRESURADO,
2221 5ELCID0280 YA LO ***** QUE PARTIR NOS EMOS EN VIDA,
13827 5ELCID1752 ***** EL ESPADA SANGRIENTA & SUDIENTO EL CAUALLO:
WORD #4247 OCCURS 5 TIMES.
INDEX OF DIVERSIFICATION = 3294.25 WITH STANDARD DEVIATION OF 5558.61

VEE 399 5ELCID0050 YA LO *** EL ZID QUE DEL REY NON AUIE GRAZIA.
WORD #4248 OCCURS 1 TIMES.

VELADAS 16558 5ELCID2098 E DOLAS POR ******* ALOS YFANTES DE CARRION.
25736 5ELCID3277 O QUIEN GELAS DIERA POR PAREIAS OPOR *******?
WORD #4249 OCCURS 2 TIMES.

VELAR 16898 5ELCID2138 SED PADRINO DELLOS ATOD EL *****;
23981 5ELCID3056 SABOR A DE ***** ENESSA SANTIDAD,
WORD #4250 OCCURS 2 TIMES.

VELIDA 2182 5ELCID0274 ENCLINO LAS MANOS EN LA SU BARBA ******,
7255 5ELCID0930 DIOS, COMMO ES ALEGRE LA BARBA ******,
17333 5ELCID2192 GRADO AL CRIADOR & AUOS, ZID, BARBA ******
WORD #4251 OCCURS 3 TIMES.

VELIDO 10805 5ELCID1368 SONRRISOS EL REY, TAN ****** FABLO:
WORD #4252 OCCURS 1 TIMES.

VELIDOS 12700 5ELCID1612 OIOS ******* CATAN A TODAS PARTES,
WORD #4253 OCCURS 1 TIMES.

```
WORD                  C#  PREFIX                          CONTEXT

VELLO              9841 5ELCID1249 ***** MYO %ID CON LOS AVERES QUE AUIEN TOMADOS,
       WORD #4254 OCCURS    1 TIMES.

VELMEZES          24100 5ELCID3073 ******** VESTIDCS POR SUFRIR LAS GUARNIZONES,
       WORD #4255 OCCURS    1 TIMES.

VELUNTAD           1780 5ELCID0226 SPIDIOS EL CABOSC DE CUER & DE ********.
                   2648 5ELCIDC334 EN BELLEM APARE%IST, CCMMO FUE TU ********;
                   2678 5ELCID0338 TE OFFRE%IERON, CCMMO FUE TU ********;
                  11212 5ELCID1418 DIZIENDC ESTO MYANAYA: ESTO FERE DE ********.
                  11434 5ELCID1447 RESPUSC MINAYA: FER LC FE CE ********.
                  11731 5ELCID1487 DIXO AUEGALUON: FER LC FE CE ********.
                  14838 5ELCID1875 ASSI CCMMO SEMEIA & LA ******** MELO DIZ.
                  23954 5ELCID3052 DIXO EL REY: PLAZME DE ********.
       WORD #4256 OCCURS    8 TIMES.
          INDEX OF DIVERSIFICATION =  3166.71 WITH STANDARD DEVIATION OF  4004.89

VENCIDOS          27647 5ELCID3529 PODEDES OYR DE MUERTCS, CA DE ******** NO.
       WORD #4257 OCCURS    1 TIMES.

VENCREMOS         18412 5ELCID2330 NOS CON UUSCO LA *********, & VALER NOS HA EL CRIADOR.
       WORD #4258 OCCURS    1 TIMES.

VEN%EN            13840 5ELCID1753 CON TAL CUM ESTO SE ****** MOROS DEL CAMPO.
       WORD #4259 OCCURS    1 TIMES.

VEN%ER             7771 5ELCID0995 %IENTO CAUALLEROS DEUEMCS ****** A QUELAS MESNADAS.
                  14736 5ELCID1863 POR TAN BILTACA MIENTRE ****** REYES DEL CAMPO,
       WORD #4260 OCCURS    2 TIMES.

VEN%I             13805 5ELCID1749 VOS TENIENDO VALEN%IA, & YO ***** EL CAMPO;
       WORD #4261 OCCURS    1 TIMES.

VEN%IDA            6159 5ELCID0784 QUE MYO %ID RUY DIAZ LID CAMPAL A *******.
                  28734 5ELCID3669 POR QUANTO AUEDES FECHO ******* AUEDES ESTA BATALLA.
       WORD #4262 OCCURS    2 TIMES.

VEN%IDO            7884 5ELCID1008 ******* A ESTA BATALLA EL QUE EN BUEN ORA NASCO;
                  27257 5ELCID3484 DESI SEA ******* & ESCAPE PCR TRAYDOR.
                  28254 5ELCID3607 QUE POR Y SERIE ******* QUI SALIESSE DEL MOION.
       WORD #4263 OCCURS    3 TIMES.

VEN%IDOS          27946 5ELCID3566 ESSI FUERES ********, NCN REBTEDES A NOS,
       WORD #4264 OCCURS    1 TIMES.

VEN%IEMOS          6516 5ELCIDC831 DIOS NOS VALIC & ********* LA LIDIT.
                  19887 5ELCID2522 ********* MCRCS EN CAMPC & MATAMOS
       WORD #4265 OCCURS    2 TIMES.

VEN%IEREMOS        5450 5ELCID0688 SI *********** LA BATALLA, CRE%REMOS EN RICTAD.
       WORD #4266 OCCURS    1 TIMES.

VEN%IERON          8014 5ELCID1023 PUES QUE TALES MAL CAL%ADOS ME ********* DE BATALLA.
                  13733 5ELCID1740 QUE DICS LES CUC MER%ED QUE ********* EL CAMPO.
                  19536 5ELCID2475 DESPUES QUE ESTA BATALLA ********* & AL REY BUCAR MATO;
                  28935 5ELCID3696 ********* ESTA LID, GRACC AL CRIADOR.
       WORD #4267 OCCURS    4 TIMES.

VEN%IO             6854 5ELCIDC876 ****** DOS REYES DE MCROS EN AQUESTA BATALLA.
                  19187 5ELCID2427 ****** LA BATALLA MARAUILLOSA & GRANT.
       WORD #4268 OCCURS    2 TIMES.

VEN%UDO           28543 5ELCID3644 ANTES QUE EL COLPE ESPERASSE DIXO: ******* SO.
                  28896 5ELCID3691 ******* ES EL CAMPC, CUANDO ESTO SE ACABO
       WORD #4269 OCCURS    2 TIMES.

VENDER             4057 5ELCID0516 AQUI NCN LC PUEDEN ****** NIN DAR EN PRESENTAIA;
                   4894 5ELCIDC619 LOS MORCS & LAS MCRAS ****** NCN LCS PODREMOS,
       WORD #427C OCCURS    2 TIMES.

VENDIDO            6618 5ELCID0845 ******* LES A ALCO%ER PCR TRES MILL MARCHOS DE PLATA.
       WORD #4271 OCCURS    1 TIMES.

VENGA              8821 5ELCID1122 PASSE LA NOCHE & ***** LA MA@ANA,
       WORD #4272 OCCURS    1 TIMES.

VENGADAS          29082 5ELCID3714 GRADO AL REY DEL %IELC, MIS FIJAS ******** SON
       WORD #4273 OCCURS    1 TIMES.

VENGADOS          21699 5ELCID2758 DE NUESTROS CASAMIENTCS AGORA SOMOS ********;
       WORD #4274 OCCURS    1 TIMES.

VENGALO            8423 5ELCID1070 SI UOS VINIERE EMIENTE CUE CUISIEREDES *******,
       WORD #4275 OCCURS    1 TIMES.
```

WORD C# PREFIX CONTEXT

VENGAM 23314 5ELCID2970 ****** A TOLLEDO, ESTCL DO CE PLAZO.
WORD #4276 OCCURS 1 TIMES.

VENGAN 8739 5ELCID1110 LOS DE BORRIANA LUEGO ****** ACA;
9380 5ELCID1193 TODOS ****** DE GRADO, NINGUNC NON HA PREMIA,
WORD #4277 OCCURS 2 TIMES.

VENGANDO 21724 5ELCID2762 LA DESCNDRA DEL LEON ASSIS YRA ********.
25021 5ELCID3187 ASSIS YRAN ******** DCN ELUIRA & CONA SOL.
WORD #4278 OCCURS 2 TIMES.

VENGAR 22526 5ELCID2868 AVN VEAMOS EL DIA QUE VCS PODAMOS ******
22715 5ELCID2894 DE MYOS YERNCS DE CARRICN DIOS ME FAGA ******
WORD #4279 OCCURS 2 TIMES.

VENGAREMOS 21387 5ELCID2719 NOS ********** AQUESTA POR LA CEL LEON.
WORD #4280 OCCURS 1 TIMES.

VENGO 1606 5ELCID0206 *****, CAMPEADOR, CCN TODO BUEN RECABDO:
17291 5ELCID2187 GRADO AL CRIADOR, *****, MUGIER ONDRADA
WORD #4281 OCCURS 2 TIMES.

VENID 14260 5ELCID1804 DO SODES, CABCSO? ***** ACA, MYNAYA;
19849 5ELCID2517 ACA *****, CUNADOS, QUE MAS VALEMOS POR UOS.
28726 5ELCID3668 ESSORA DIXC EL REY: ***** UCS AMI COMPA@A;
WORD #4282 OCCURS 3 TIMES.

VENIDA 12141 5ELCID1540 PASSADA ES LA NOCHE, ****** ES LA MA@ANA,
13821 5ELCID1751 QUANDO EN VUESTRA ****** TAL GANAN%IA NOS AN DADA.
WORD #4283 OCCURS 2 TIMES.

VENIDAS 12866 5ELCID1632 ESTAS NUEUAS A MYO %ID ERAN *******;
WORD #4284 OCCURS 1 TIMES.

VENIDES 1591 5ELCID0204 *******, MARTIN ANTOLINEZ, EL MIO FIEL VASSALO
3860 5ELCID0489 *******, ALBARFANEZ, UNA FARDIDA LAN%A
11667 5ELCID1479 *******, LCS VASSALLCS DE MYO AMIGO NATURAL?
15166 5ELCID1919 *******, MYNAYA, & VOS, PERO VERMUEZ
17272 5ELCID2185 *******, CAMPEADOR, EN BUENA ORA %INXIESTES ESPADA
19293 5ELCID2443 *******, MYCS YERNCS, MYOS FIJOS SODES AMOS
22675 5ELCID2890 *******, MIS FIJAS? DIOS UOS CURIE DE MAL
WORD #4285 OCCURS 7 TIMES.
INDEX OF DIVERSIFICATION = 3513.00 WITH STANDARD DEVIATION OF 2200.41

VENIDO 4444 5ELCID0566 ****** ES A MCRCS, EXIDC ES DE CHRISTIANOS;
6635 5ELCID0846 MYO %ID RUY DIAZ A ALCOL%ER ES ******;
7154 5ELCID0916 DE CASTIELLA ****** ES MINAYA,
7615 5ELCID0975 DEL CONDE DCN REMONT ****** LES MENSAIE;
23673 5ELCID3015 AL QUINTO DIA ****** ES MYO %ID EL CAMPEADOR;
WORD #4286 OCCURS 5 TIMES.
INDEX OF DIVERSIFICATION = 4806.25 WITH STANDARD DEVIATION OF 7543.28

VENIDOM 12918 5ELCID1639 ******* ES DELI%IC DE TIERRAS CALENT MAR,
WORD #4287 OCCURS 1 TIMES.

VENIDOS 14646 5ELCID1853 RICOS SCN ******* TODCS LOS SOS VASSALLOS,
17929 5ELCID2269 ******* SON ACASTIELLA AQUESTCS OSPEDADOS,
WORD #4288 OCCURS 2 TIMES.

VENIR 3084 5ELCID0388 SI VIEREDES YENTES ***** POR CCNNUSCO YR,
8463 5ELCID1076 DE ***** UOS BUSCAR SCL NCN SERA PENSSADO.
9352 5ELCID1189 QUIEN QUIERE PERDER CUETA & ***** A RRITAD,
9963 5ELCID1263 MANDO LCS ***** ALA CORTH & A TODOS LOS IUNTAR,
11184 5ELCID1415 VERIEDES CAUALLERCS ***** DE TCDAS PARTES,
13959 5ELCID1768 LO DE UUESTRAS FIJAS ***** SEA MAS POR ESPA%IO.
14848 5ELCID1876 TODAS ESTAS NUEUAS A BIEN ABRAN DE *****.
19276 5ELCID2440 E VIO ***** ADIEGO & A FERNANDO;
21778 5ELCID2770 FASTA QUE VIESSE ***** SUS PRIMAS AMAS ADOS
21792 5ELCID2772 VIOLOS ***** & CYO VNA RAZON,
WORD #4289 OCCURS 10 TIMES.
INDEX OF DIVERSIFICATION = 2077.67 WITH STANDARD DEVIATION OF 1839.11

VENIST 19041 5ELCID2409 ACA TORNA, BUCAR ****** CALENT MAR,
WORD #4290 OCCURS 1 TIMES.

VENIT 6942 5ELCID0888 HYD & *****, DA QUI UCS DO MI GRA%IA;
17552 5ELCID2221 ***** ACA, ALBARFANEZ, EL QUE YO QUIERO & AMO
WORD #4291 OCCURS 2 TIMES.

VENJD 24430 5ELCID3114 EL REY DIXO AL %ID: ***** ACA SER, CAMPEADOR,
WORD #4292 OCCURS 1 TIMES.

WORD C# PREFIX CONTEXT

VENTADAS 907 5ELCID0116 AQUELAS NON LAS PUEDE LEUAR, SINON, SER YEN ********;
999 5ELCID0128 EN LOGAR LAS METAMOS QUE NON SEAN ********.
WORD #4293 OCCURS 2 TIMES.

VENTANSSEN 1173 5ELCID0151 QUE GELO NON ********** DE BURGOS OMNE NADO.
WORD #4294 OCCURS 1 TIMES.

VENTASSE 3434 5ELCID0433 POR TAL LO FAZE MYO %ID QUE NO IO ******** NADI.
WORD #4295 OCCURS 1 TIMES.

VENTURA 1382 5ELCID0177 ASSI ES UUESTRA ******* GRANDES SON UUESTRAS GANAN%IAS,
2252 5ELCID0283 O QUE DE ******* & ALGUNOS DIAS VIDA,
18846 5ELCID2385 POR LA SU ******* & DIOS QUEL AMAUA
21561 5ELCID2741 QUAL ******* SERIE ESTA, SI PLOGUIESSE AL CRIADOR,
21657 5ELCID2753 QUAL ******* SERIE SI ASSOMAS ESSORA EL %ID CAMPEADOR
WORD #4296 OCCURS 5 TIMES.
INDEX OF DIVERSIFICATION = 5067.75 WITH STANDARD DEVIATION OF 7761.64

VEO 1949 5ELCID0247 PUES QUE AQUI UOS ***, PRENDET DE MI OSPEDADO.
2153 5ELCID0271 YO LO *** QUE ESTADES UOS EN YDA
4888 5ELCID0618 LOS MOROS YAZEN MUERTOS, DE BIUOS POCOS ***.
5041 5ELCID0637 TRES REYES *** DE MOROS DERREDOR DE MI ESTAR,
19558 5ELCID2478 QUANDO *** LO QUE AUIA SABOR,
23827 5ELCID3035 GRADO ADIOS, QUANDO UOS ***, SE@OR.
WORD #4297 OCCURS 6 TIMES.
INDEX OF DIVERSIFICATION = 4374.60 WITH STANDARD DEVIATION OF 5932.61

VEOT 19077 5ELCID2413 EL ESPADA TIENES DESNUDA EN LA MANO & **** AGUIJAR;
WORD #4298 OCCURS 1 TIMES.

VER 3644 5ELCID0460 POR *** SUS LAUORES & TODAS SUS HEREDADES.
8832 5ELCID1124 HYREMOS *** AQUELA SU ALMOFALLA,
9272 5ELCID1149 FIJOS & MUGIERES *** LO MURIR DE FANBRE.
9633 5ELCID1224 VINO LOS *** CON XXX MILL DE ARMAS.
15362 5ELCID1945 QUERER UOS YE *** & DAR UOS SU AMOR,
18354 5ELCID2322 ESTO ES AGUISADO POR NON *** CARRION,
20694 5ELCID2627 HYR LAS HEMOS *** ATIERRAS DE CARRION.
24317 5ELCID3100 ENEL ABRIEN QUE *** QUANTOS QUE Y SON.
27792 5ELCID3547 POR *** ESTA LID, CA AVIEN ENDE SABOR;
27990 5ELCID3572 HYUA LOS *** EL REY DON ALFONSSO;
WORD #4299 OCCURS 10 TIMES.
INDEX OF DIVERSIFICATION = 2704.11 WITH STANDARD DEVIATION OF 2057.63

VERA 7793 5ELCID0998 **** REMONT VERENGEL TRAS QUIEN VINO EN ALCAN%A
20004 5ELCID2538 AMOS SALIERON A PART, **** MIENTRE SON HERMANOS;
WORD #4300 OCCURS 2 TIMES.

VERAN 12945 5ELCID1642 EN ESTAS TIERRAS AGENAS ***** LAS MORADAS COMMO SE FAZEN,
12952 5ELCID1643 AFARTO ***** POR LOS OIOS COMMO SE GANA EL PAN.
17241 5ELCID2181 ***** ASUS ESPOSAS, A DON ELUIRA & A DONA SOL.
20206 5ELCID2566 ***** UUESTRAS FIJAS LO QUE AUEMOS NOS,
WORD #4301 OCCURS 4 TIMES.

VERAS 20646 5ELCID2621 ***** LAS HEREDADES QUE A MIS FIJAS DADAS SON;
WORD #4302 OCCURS 1 TIMES.

VERDAD 7387 5ELCID0947 HYA CAUALLEROS, DEZIR UOS HE LA ******:
7649 5ELCID0979 RESPUSO EL CONDE: ESTO NON SERA ******
10535 5ELCID1335 FEUOS AQUI LAS SE@AS, ****** UOS DIGO YO:
11794 5ELCID1495 ENVIO DOS CAUALLEROS MYNAYA ALBARFANEZ QUE SOPIESSE LA ******;
12042 5ELCID1526 MUCHOL TENGO POR TORPE QUI NON CONES%E LA ******.
17381 5ELCID2199 MAS BIEN SABET ****** QUE NON LO LEUANTE YO:
19113 5ELCID2417 AQUI RESPUSO MYO %ID: ESTO NON SERA ******.
22333 5ELCID2844 HY ALBERGARON POR ****** VNA NOCH.
23184 5ELCID2954 ****** TE DIGO YO, QUE ME PESA DE CORA%ON,
23194 5ELCID2955 E ****** DIZES EN ESTO, TU, MU@O GUSTIOZ,
23771 5ELCID3028 PAR SANT ESIDRO, ****** NON SERA OY
26099 5ELCID3326 CROUIERON TELO TODOS, MAS NON SABEN LA ******.
26364 5ELCID3362 CALA, ALEUOSO, BOCA SIN ******
26528 5ELCID3386 NON DIZES ****** AMIGO NI HA SE@OR,
WORD #4303 OCCURS 14 TIMES.
INDEX OF DIVERSIFICATION = 1471.38 WITH STANDARD DEVIATION OF 1589.24

VERDADERA 28744 5ELCID3670 OTORGAN GELO LOS FIELES QUE DIZE ********* PALABRA.
WORD #4304 OCCURS 1 TIMES.

VERDADERO 26282 5ELCID3351 DE QUANTO HE DICHO ********* SERE YO.
WORD #4305 OCCURS 1 TIMES.

VERE 1791 5ELCID0228 DIXO MARTIN ANTOLINEZ: **** ALA MUGIER ATODO MYO SOLAZ,
11338 5ELCID1435 HYO LO **** CON EL %ID, SI DIOS ME LIEUA ALA.
18094 5ELCID2289 DIZIENDO DELA BOCA: NON **** CARRION
WORD #4306 OCCURS 3 TIMES.

VEREDES 8048 5ELCID1027 SI NON, EN TODOS UUESTROS DIAS NON ******* CHRISTIANISMO.
8100 5ELCID1033 DIXO MYO %ID: COMED, CONDE, ALGO, CASI NON COMEDES, NON *******

```
WORD                    C#  PREFIX                                      CONTEXT

VEREDES (CON'T)

                   13147 5ELCID1666 AQUELOS ATAMORES AUOS LOS PONDRAN DELANT & ******* QUANLES SON,
                   27094 5ELCID3462 DESPUES ******* QUE DIXIESTES O QUE NO.
        WORD #4307 OCCURS   4 TIMES.

VEREMOS             1636 5ELCID0210 ******* UUESTRA MUGIER, MENBRADA FIJA DALGO.
                    5624 5ELCID0708 LOS QUE EL DEBDO AUEDES ******* COMMO LA ACORREDES.
                   18824 5ELCID2382 NOS DAQUENT ******* COMMO LIDIA EL ABBAT.
        WORD #4308 OCCURS   3 TIMES.

VERENGEL            7795 5ELCID0998 VERA REMONT ******** TRAS QUIEN VINO EN ALCAN%A
                   25078 5ELCID3195 DEL CONDE DE REMONT ******** DE BAR%ILONA LA MAYOR.
        WORD #4309 OCCURS   2 TIMES.

VERGEL             21247 5ELCID2700 FALARON VN ****** CON VNA LINPIA FUENT;
        WORD #4310 OCCURS   1 TIMES.

VERGON%O           18169 5ELCID2298 EL LEON QUANDO LO VIO, ASSI EN ********,
        WORD #4311 OCCURS   1 TIMES.

VERGUEN%A          24523 5ELCID3126 NOL PUEDEN CATAR DE ********* YFANTES DE CARRION.
                   29092 5ELCID3716 SIN ********* LAS CASARE DAQUI PESE DAQUI NON.
        WORD #4312 OCCURS   2 TIMES.

VERGUEN%AS         12582 5ELCID1596 SACADA ME AUEDES DE MUCHAS ********** MALAS;
        WORD #4313 OCCURS   1 TIMES.

VERIEDES            1330 5ELCID0170 ALCARGAR DELAS ARCHAS ******** GOZO TANTO:
                    5529 5ELCID0697 ******** ARMAR SE MOROS, APRIESSA ENTRAR EN AZ.
                    5752 5ELCID0726 ******** TANTAS LAN%AS PREMER & AL%AR,
                    8969 5ELCID1141 TANTA CUERDA DE TIENDA Y ******** QUEBRAR,
                    9664 5ELCID1228 ENEL PASSAR DE XUCAR Y ******** BARATA,
                   11182 5ELCID1415 ******** CAUALLEROS VENIR DE TODAS PARTES,
                   17043 5ELCID2158 ******** CAUALLEROS, QUE BIEN ANDANTES SON,
                   18964 5ELCID2400 ******** QUEBRAR TANTAS CUERDAS & ARRANCAR SE LAS ESTACAS
                   19004 5ELCID2404 TANTO BRA%O CON LORIGA ******** CAER A PART,
                   25184 5ELCID3207 AQUI ******** QUEXAR SE YFANTES DE CARRION
                   25458 5ELCID3242 ******** ADUZIR TANTO CAUALLO CORREDOR,
        WORD #4314 OCCURS  11 TIMES.
           INDEX OF DIVERSIFICATION =  2411.80 WITH STANDARD DEVIATION OF  2331.25

VERLO              18694 5ELCID2366 ***** HEMOS CONDIDS & CON LA UUESTRA AUZE.
        WORD #4315 OCCURS   1 TIMES.

VERME              12938 5ELCID1641 MIS FIJAS & MI MUGIER ***** AN LIDIAR,
        WORD #4316 OCCURS   1 TIMES.

VERMEIA             1389 5ELCID0178 VNA PIEL ******* MORISCA & ONDRADA,
                   24248 5ELCID3092 SOBRESTO VNA PIEL *******, LAS BANDAS DORO SON,
        WORD #4317 OCCURS   2 TIMES.

VERMEIO            26451 5ELCID3375 ******* VIENE, CA ERA ALMORZADO;
                   28864 5ELCID3687 ******* SALIO EL ASTIL, & LA LAN%A & EL PENDON.
        WORD #4318 OCCURS   2 TIMES.

VERMEIOS            5771 5ELCID0729 TANTOS PENDONES BLANCOS SALIR ******** EN SANGRE,
        WORD #4319 OCCURS   1 TIMES.

VERMUEZ             4824 5ELCID0611 VINO PERO *******, QUE LA SE@A TEINE EN MANO,
                    5459 5ELCID0689 E VOS, PERO *******, LA MI SE@A TOMAD;
                    5590 5ELCID0704 AQUEL PERO ******* NON LO PUDO ENDURAR,
                    5637 5ELCID0710 RESPUSO PERO *******:  NON RASTARA POR AL.
                    5731 5ELCID0722 TODOS FIEREN ENEL AZ DO ESTA PERO *******.
                   11518 5ELCID1458 TU, MU@O GUSTIOZ & PERO ******* DELANT,
                   11823 5ELCID1499 AFEUOS AQUI PERO ******* & MU@O GUSTIOZ QUE UOS QUIEREN SIN HART,
                   14351 5ELCID1815 MANDO A PERO ******* QUE FUESSE CON MYNAYA.
                   14457 5ELCID1828 ENVIAUA LE MANDADO PERO ******* & MYNAYA,
                   14556 5ELCID1841 MYNAYA & PER ******* ADELANT SON LEGADOS,
                   14797 5ELCID1870 AUOS, MINAYA ALBARFANEZ, & EA PERO ******* AQUI,
                   14987 5ELCID1894 A MYNAYA ALBARFANEZ & A PERO *******
                   15007 5ELCID1897 OYD ME, MYNAYA, & VOS, PER *******:
                   15084 5ELCID1907 FABLO MYNAYA & PLOGO A PER *******:
                   15171 5ELCID1919  VENIDES, MYNAYA, & VOS, PERO *******
                   15699 5ELCID1991 MYNAYA ALBARFANEZ & AQUEL PERO *******,
                   17140 5ELCID2169 APERO ******* & MUNO GUSTIOZ,
                   18578 5ELCID2351 ALA, PERO *******, EL MYO SOBRINO CARO
                   22273 5ELCID2836 CAUALGO MINAYA CON PERO *******
                   22490 5ELCID2864 E PERO ******* OTRO TANTO LAS HA;
                   24046 5ELCID3065 E PERO ******* & AQUESTE MU@O GUSTIOZ
                   25910 5ELCID3301 MYO %ID RUY DIAZ A PERO ******* CATA;
                   25943 5ELCID3306 PERO ******* CONPE%O DE FABLAR;
                   27604 5ELCID3524 HYA MARTIN ANTOLINEZ, & VOS, PERO *******,
                   28374 5ELCID3623 PERO *******, EL QUE ANTES REBTO,
                   28395 5ELCID3626 FERRANGO%ALEZ A PERO ******* EL ESCUDOL PASSO,
                   28417 5ELCID3629 FIRME ESTIDO PERO *******, POR ESSO NOS ENCAMO;
                   28550 5ELCID3645 ATORGARON GELO LOS FIELES, PERO ******* LE DEXO.
        WORD #4320 OCCURS  28 TIMES.
           INDEX OF DIVERSIFICATION =   877.74 WITH STANDARD DEVIATION OF  1345.58
```

WORD C# PREFIX CONTEXT

```
VERNA            4184 5ELCID0532 %ERCA ES EL REY ALFCNSSC & BUSCAR NOS *****.
                23454 5ELCID2987 MIEDO HAN QUE Y ***** MYO %ID EL CAMPEADOR;
                23485 5ELCID2991 CA Y ***** MYC %ID EL CAMPEACOR;
        WORD #4321 CCCURS   3 TIMES.

VERNAN          10110 5ELCID1280 DE GUISA YRAN POR ELLAS QUE AGRANC ONDRA ******
        WORD #4322 OCCURS   1 TIMES.

VERNAS          20658 5ELCID2622 CON AQUESTAS NUEUAS ****** AL CAMPEADOR.
        WORD #4323 CCCURS   1 TIMES.

VERNIE          15354 5ELCID1944 QUE UOS ****** AVISTAS CO OUIESSEDES SABOR;
        WORD #4324 OCCURS   1 TIMES.

VERO            25587 5ELCID3258 DEZID  QUE UCS MERE%I, YFANTES, EN JUEGO O EN ****
        WORD #4325 OCCURS   1 TIMES.

VERTA            9641 5ELCID1225 APRES DELA ***** CUIERON LA BATALLA,
        WORD #4326 OCCURS   1 TIMES.

VERTE           19044 5ELCID2410 ***** AS CON EL %ID, EL DE LA BARBA GRANT,
        WORD #4327 CCCURS   1 TIMES.

VERTUD           2780 5ELCID0351 ESTANDO EN LA CRUZ, ****** FEZIST MUY GRANT.
        WORD #4328 OCCURS   1 TIMES.

VERTUDES         1700 5ELCID0218 VALAN ME TUS ********, GLORIOSA SANTA MARIA
                 7210 5ELCID0924 GRADO ADIOS & ALAS SUS ******** SANTAS;
        WORD #4329 OCCURS   2 TIMES.

VESA             6429 5ELCID0820 EUADES AQUI ORC & PLATA VNA **** LE@A,
        WORD #4330 CCCURS   1 TIMES.

VESTE           18531 5ELCID2345 EN LA ***** DELCS MOROS LOS ATAMORES SONANDO;
        WORD #4331 OCCURS   1 TIMES.

VESTID          26388 5ELCID3366 MAS NON ****** EL MANTO NIN EL BRIAL.
        WORD #4332 CCCURS   1 TIMES.

VESTIDAS         4545 5ELCID0578 LAS LORIGAS ******** & %INTAS LAS ESPADAS,
                12469 5ELCID1582 SCBREPELI%AS ******** & CCN CRUZES CE PLATA
        WORD #4333 OCCURS   2 TIMES.

VESTIDOS        14007 5ELCID1774 ENTRE TIENDAS & ARMAS & ******** PRE%IADOS
                15690 5ELCID1990 CHICOS & GRANDES ******** SCN CE COLORES.
                17834 5ELCID2256 MANTOS & PELLI%CNES & CTROS ******** LARGOS;
                22125 5ELCID2816 PRISO BESTIAS & ******** DE PRC,
                24101 5ELCID3073 VELMEZES ******** PCR SUFRIR LAS GUARNIZONES,
        WORD #4334 OCCURS   5 TIMES.
           INDEX OF DIVERSIFICATICN =  2522.50 WITH STANCARD CEVIATION OF  1193.63

VESTIDURAS       8377 5ELCID1065 E BUENAS ********** DE PELI%ONES & DE MANTOS.
                17484 5ELCID2212 CCN BUENAS ********** & FUERTE MIENTRE ADOBADOS;
                20280 5ELCID2574 E MUCHAS ********** DE PA@OS & DE %ICLATONES;
        WORD #4335 CCCURS   3 TIMES.

VESTIR          14807 5ELCID1871 MANDO UOS LCS CUERPCS ONDRACA MIENTRE SERUIR & ******
        WORD #4336 OCCURS   1 TIMES.

VEYE            17743 5ELCID2245 MYO %ID DELO QUE **** MUCHO ERA PAGADO:
        WORD #4337 CCCURS   1 TIMES.

VEYEN            4557 5ELCID0580 ***** LO LCS DE ALCO%ER, DIOS, COMMO SE ALABAUAN
                 9278 5ELCID1180 DELANTE ***** SO DUELC, NCN SE PUEDEN HUUIAR,
                18318 5ELCID2318 CA ***** TANTAS TIENDAS DE MOROS DE QUE NON AUIE SABOR.
                20934 5ELCID2659 ELLOS ***** LA RIQUEZA CUE EL MORO SACO,
        WORD #4338 OCCURS   4 TIMES.

VEZCAMOS        13342 5ELCID1691 MAS VALE QUE NOS LOS ********, QUE ELLOS COIAN EL PAN.
        WORD #4339 CCCURS   1 TIMES.

VEZES           12812 5ELCID1626 CON L ***** MILL DE ARMAS, TODOS FUERON CONPLIDOS,
        WORD #4340 CCCURS   1 TIMES.

VEZINDAD         4455 5ELCID0567 EN LA SU ******** NCN SE TREUEN GANAR TANTO.
        WORD #4341 OCCURS   1 TIMES.

VEZOS           25692 5ELCID3272 ***** MYO %ID ALLAS CORTES PREGONADAS;
        WORD #4342 OCCURS   1 TIMES.

VI               5335 5ELCID0674 BIEN SCMOS NOS ** %IENTOS, ALGUNOS AY DE MAS;
        WORD #4343 OCCURS   1 TIMES.
```

WORD C# PREFIX CONTEXT

VIA 3019 5ELCID0380 PENSEMOS DE YR NUESTRA ***, ESTO SEA DE VAGAR.
WORD #4344 OCCURS 1 TIMES.

VIDA 2166 5ELCID0272 E NOS DEUOS PARTIR NOS HEMOS EN ****.
2227 5ELCID0280 YA LO VEDES QUE PARTIR NOS EMOS EN ****,
2256 5ELCID0283 O QUE DE VENTURA & ALGUNOS DIAS ****,
2897 5ELCID0365 QUANDO OY NOS PARTIMOS, EN **** NOS FAZ IUNTAR.
8219 5ELCID1047 ABREMOS ESTA **** MIENTRA PLOGIERE AL PADRE SANTO,
WORD #4345 OCCURS 5 TIMES.
INDEX OF DIVERSIFICATION = 1512.25 WITH STANDARD DEVIATION OF 2554.70

VIDAS 700 5ELCID0089 POR RACHEL & ***** UAYADES ME PRIUADO:
766 5ELCID0097 POR RACHEL & ***** APRIESSA DEMANDAUA.
778 5ELCID0099 POR RACHEL & ***** APRIESSA DEMANDAUA.
783 5ELCID0100 RACHEL & ***** EN VNO ESTAUAN AMOS,
806 5ELCID0103 O SODES, RACHEL & *****, LOS MYOS AMIGOS CAROS?
826 5ELCID0106 RACHEL & *****, AMOS ME DAT LAS MANOS,
951 5ELCID0122 RACHEL & ***** SEYEN SE CONSEIANDO:
1057 5ELCID0136 DIXO RACHEL & *****: DAR GELOS DE GRADO.
1082 5ELCID0139 DIXO RACHEL & *****: NON SE FAZE ASSI EL MERCADO,
1136 5ELCID0146 DIXO RACHEL & *****: NOS DESTO NOS PAGAMOS.
1155 5ELCID0149 CON RACHEL & *****, DE VOLUTAD & DE GRADO.
1203 5ELCID0155 YA DON RACHEL & *****, AUEDES ME OLBIDADO
1234 5ELCID0159 DON RACHEL & ***** A MYO %ID BESARON LE LAS MANOS.
1303 5ELCID0167 LEUALDAS, RACHEL & *****, PONED LAS EN UUESTRO SALUO;
1346 5ELCID0172 GRADAN SE RACHEL & ***** CON AUERES MONEDADOS,
1477 5ELCID0189 YA DON RACHEL & *****, EN UUESTRAS MANOS SON LAS ARCAS;
1495 5ELCID0191 ENTRE RACHEL & ***** APARTE YXIERON AMOS:
11308 5ELCID1431 AFEUOS RACHEL & ***** ALOS PIES LE CAEN:
11359 5ELCID1437 DIXO RACHEL & *****: EL CRIADOR LO MANDE
WORD #4346 OCCURS 19 TIMES.
INDEX OF DIVERSIFICATION = 591.17 WITH STANDARD DEVIATION OF 2301.52

VIE 8629 5ELCID1096 YA *** MYO %ID QUE DIOS LE YUA VALIENDO.
19261 5ELCID2438 ALGO *** MYO %ID DELO QUE ERA PAGADO,
WORD #4347 OCCURS 2 TIMES.

VIEDALES 9480 5ELCID1205 ******** EXIR & VIEDALES ENTRAR.
9483 5ELCID1205 VIEDALES EXIR & ******** ENTRAR.
WORD #4348 OCCURS 2 TIMES.

VIEN 21799 5ELCID2773 ELLOS NOL **** NI DEND SABIEN RA%ION;
WORD #4349 OCCURS 1 TIMES.

VIENE 1162 5ELCID0150 NON ***** ALA PUEENT, CA POR EL AGUA APASSADO,
1654 5ELCID0212 MUCHO ES HUEBOS, CA %ERCA ***** EL PLAZO.
2537 5ELCID0321 CA EL PLAZO ***** A %ERCA, MUCHO AUEMOS DE ANDAR.
3115 5ELCID0392 %ERCA ***** EL PLAZO POR EL REYNO QUITAR.
3813 5ELCID0482 DERECHA ***** LA SE@A DE MINAYA;
7585 5ELCID0972 ASI ***** ES FOR%ADO QUE EL CONDE AMANOS SELE CUYDO TOMAR.
12313 5ELCID1563 CA DELO QUE MAS AMAUA YAL ***** EL MANDADO.
23723 5ELCID3022 BIEN AGUISADO ***** EL %ID CON TODOS LOS SOS,
26119 5ELCID3330 NON TE ***** EN MIENTE EN VALEN%IA LO DEL LEON,
26452 5ELCID3375 VERMEIO *****, CA ERA ALMORZADO;
WORD #4350 OCCURS 10 TIMES.
INDEX OF DIVERSIFICATION = 2809.00 WITH STANDARD DEVIATION OF 3595.13

VIENEN 5127 5ELCID0648 NON LO DETIENEN, ****** DE TODAS PARTES.
7746 5ELCID0992 ELLOS ****** CUESTA YUSO, & TODOS TRAHEN CAL%AS,
8700 5ELCID1105 SI NOS %ERCAR ******, CONDERECHO LO FAZEN.
9494 5ELCID1207 MAS LE ****** A MYO %ID, SABET, QUE NOS LE VAN.
11818 5ELCID1498 VIRTOS DEL CAMPEADOR ANOS ****** BUSCAR.
11864 5ELCID1504 TODOS ****** EN VNO, AGORA LEGARAN.
14544 5ELCID1839 CUEDAN SE QUE ES ALMOFALLA, CA NON ****** CON MANDADO;
18275 5ELCID2312 FUER%AS DE MARRUECOS VALEN%IA ****** %ERCAR;
27716 5ELCID3538 MUCHO ****** BIEN ADOBADOS DE CAUALLOS & DE GUARNIZONES,
WORD #4351 OCCURS 9 TIMES.
INDEX OF DIVERSIFICATION = 2822.63 WITH STANDARD DEVIATION OF 2933.92

VIERAN 13115 5ELCID1662 DEL DIA QUE NASQUIERAN NON ****** TAL TREMOR.
18546 5ELCID2347 CA NUNQUA LO ******, CA NUEUOS SON LEGADOS.
WORD #4352 OCCURS 2 TIMES.

VIEREDES 3082 5ELCID0388 SI ******** YENTES VENIR POR CONNUSCO YR,
WORD #4353 OCCURS 1 TIMES.

VIERON 3711 5ELCID0468 LOS QUE LA TIENEN, QUANDO ****** LA REBATA,
5500 5ELCID0694 ****** LO LAS AROBDAS DELOS MOROS, AL ALMOFALLA SEUAN TORNAR.
7830 5ELCID1002 ****** LA CUESTA YUSO LA FUER%A DELOS FRANCOS;
11009 5ELCID1393 TAN GRAND FUE EL GOZO QUANDOL ****** ASSOMAR.
12973 5ELCID1645 AL%AUAN LOS OIOS, TIENDAS ****** FINCADAS:
13867 5ELCID1757 QUANDOL ****** DE PIE, QUE ERA DESCAUALGADO,
15882 5ELCID2014 QUANDO ****** QUE VINIE EL BUEN CAMPEADOR,
18045 5ELCID2283 EN GRANT MIEDO SE ****** POR MEDIO DELA CORT;
21427 5ELCID2724 QUANDO ESTO ****** LAS DUE@AS, FABLAUA DO@A SOL:

WORD C# PREFIX CONTEXT

VIERON (CON'T)

21940 5ELCID2791 ABRIERCN LCS CICS & ****** AFELEZ MUNOZ.
23517 5ELCID2995 HYA LO ****** QUE ES AFER LCS YFANTES DE CARRION,
24366 5ELCID3107 QUANDO LO ****** ENTRAR AL QUE EN BUEN ORA NA%IO,
25450 5ELCID3241 HYA ****** QUE ES AFER LCS YFANTES CE CARRION.
WORD #4354 OCCURS 13 TIMES.
INDEX OF DIVERSIFICATICN = 1810.58 WITH STANCARD CEVIATION OF 896.C8

VIESSE 10212 5ELCID1293 SOSPIRANDO EL CBISPO QUES ****** CON MOROS ENEL CAMPO:
11075 5ELCID1402 SI UOS ****** EL %ID SA@AS & SIN MAL,
21777 5ELCID2770 FASTA QUE ****** VENIR SUS PRIMAS AMAS ADOS
WORD #4355 OCCURS 3 TIMES.

VIESSEMOS 22459 5ELCID2860 ATANTO UOS LO GRADIMOS CCMMO SI ********* AL CRAIDOR;
WORD #4356 OCCURS 1 TIMES.

VIESSEN 21810 5ELCID2774 SABET BIEN QUE SI ELLOS LE *******, NON ESCAPARA DE MUERT.
WORD #4357 OCCURS 1 TIMES.

VIESTES 2972 5ELCID0374 LORANDO DELCS OIOS, QUE NON ******* ATAL,
14479 5ELCID1831 ALEGRE FUE EL REY, NON ******* ATANTO,
18234 5ELCID2307 NON ******* TAL GUEGO CCMMO YUA POR LA CORT;
WORD #4358 OCCURS 3 TIMES.

VIGA 18098 5ELCID2290 TRAS VNA **** LAGAR METIOS CON GRANT PAUOR;
26384 5ELCID3365 FUSTED METER TRAS LA **** LAGAR,
WORD #4359 OCCURS 2 TIMES.

VIGILIA 23932 5ELCID3049 TERNE ******* EN AQUESTE SANTO LOGAR.
WORD #4360 OCCURS 1 TIMES.

VIGOR 20406 5ELCID2589 TODOS PRENDEN ARMAS & CAUALGAN A *****,
28072 5ELCID3583 SANTIGUARON LAS SIELAS & CAUALGAN A *****;
WORD #4361 OCCURS 2 TIMES.

VII 19024 5ELCID2407 *** MIGEROS CONPLIDOS DURO EL SEGUDAR.
WORD #4362 OCCURS 1 TIMES.

VIJ 17779 5ELCID2249 E AL OTRO DIA FIZO MYO %ID FINCAR *** TABLADOS:
18944 5ELCID2397 ABATIO A *** & A IIIJ MATAUA.
23308 5ELCID2969 QUE DESTAS *** SEMANAS ADOBES CON SUS VASSALLOS,
23400 5ELCID2981 A CABO DE *** SEMANAS QUE Y FUESSEN IUNTADOS;
WORD #4363 OCCURS 4 TIMES.

VILLA 441 5ELCID0056 CABO ESSA ***** EN LA GLERA POSAUA,
13218 5ELCID1675 ADOBAN SE DE CORA%CN E DAN SALTO DE LA *****;
WORD #4364 OCCURS 2 TIMES.

VILLAS 9183 5ELCID1169 EN GANAR AQUELAS ****** MYO %ID DURO IIJ A@OS.
20197 5ELCID2564 METER LAS HEMOS EN LAS ******
20244 5ELCID2570 VOS LES DIESTES ****** E TIERRAS POR ARRAS ENTIERRAS DE CARRICN,
WORD #4365 OCCURS 3 TIMES.

VIN 18741 5ELCID2371 POR ESSO SALI DE MI TIERRA & *** UOS BUSCAR,
24569 5ELCID3131 ESTA TER%ERA A TOLLEDO LA *** FER OY,
WORD #4366 OCCURS 2 TIMES.

VINIA 19243 5ELCID2435 POR LA MATAN%A ***** TAN PRIUADO,
WORD #4367 OCCURS 1 TIMES.

VINIDA 3373 5ELCID0425 DE NOCH PASSAN LA SIERRA, ****** ES LA MAN,
WORD #4368 OCCURS 1 TIMES.

VINIE 3621 5ELCID0456 YA QUIEBRAN LOS ALBORES & ***** LA MA@ANA,
9242 5ELCID1175 DE NINGUNA PART QUE SEA NON LES ***** PAN;
15884 5ELCID2014 QUANDO VIERCN QUE ***** EL BUEN CAMPEADOR,
22341 5ELCID2846 QUE ***** MYNAYA POR SUS PRIMAS AMAS ADOS.
WORD #4369 OCCURS 4 TIMES.

VINIEN 14901 5ELCID1884 ****** AL REY ALFONSSO CON ESTA PORIDAD:
28295 5ELCID3612 DESI ****** LCS DE MYC %ID ALCS YFANTES DE CARRION,
WORD #4370 OCCURS 2 TIMES.

VINIENDO 2559 5ELCID0323 PASSANDO UA LA NOCH, ******** LA MAN;
WORD #4371 OCCURS 1 TIMES.

VINIERE 8419 5ELCID1070 SI UOS ******* EMIENTE QUE QUISIEREDES VENGALO,
17234 5ELCID2180 QUANDO ******* LA MA@ANA, QUE APUNTARE EL SOL,
27249 5ELCID3483 QUEN NCN ******* AL PLAZO PIERDA LA RAZON,
WORD #4372 OCCURS 3 TIMES.

VINIEREDES 8426 5ELCID1071 SI ME ********** BUSCAR, FALLAR ME PODREDES;
WORD #4373 OCCURS 1 TIMES.

WORD C# PREFIX CONTEXT

VINIERON 2661 5ELCID0336 TRES REYES DE ARABIA TE ******** ADORAR,
5097 5ELCID0644 ELLOS ******** ALA NOCH EN SOGORUE POSAR.
5109 5ELCID0646 ******** A LA NOCH A %ELFA POSAR.
5147 5ELCID0651 ******** ESSA NOCHE EN CALATAYUH POSAR.
11641 5ELCID1475 TRO%IERON A SANTA MARIA & ******** ALBERGAR A FRONTAEL,
11649 5ELCID1476 E EL OTRO DIA ******** A MOLINA POSAR.
12168 5ELCID1545 ******** A MOLINA, LA QUE AUEGALUON MANDAUA.
18228 5ELCID2306 QUANDO LOS FALLARON & ELLOS ********, ASSI VINIERON SIN COLOR;
18230 5ELCID2306 QUANDO LOS FALLARON & ELLOS VINIERON, ASSI ******** SIN COLOR;
19810 5ELCID2511 ELLOS CON LOS OTROS ******** ALA CORT;
22321 5ELCID2843 ******** A SANTESTEUAN DE GORMAZ, VN CASTIELLO TAN FUERT,
WORD #4374 OCCURS 11 TIMES.
INDEX OF DIVERSIFICATION = 1965.00 WITH STANDARD DEVIATION OF 2477.69

VINIESSE 9355 5ELCID1190 ******** A MYO %ID QUE A SABOR DE CAUALGAR;
23408 5ELCID2982 QUI NON ******** ALA CORT NON SE TOUIESSE POR SU VASSALLO.
WORD #4375 OCCURS 2 TIMES.

VINIESSEM 15021 5ELCID1899 E DE MI ABRA PERDON; ********* A VISTAS, SI OUIESSE DENT SABOR.
WORD #4376 OCCURS 1 TIMES.

VINIESSEN 8657 5ELCID1099 PRISIERON SO CONSEIO QUEL ********* %ERCAR.
9507 5ELCID1208 METIOLA EN PLAZO, SILES ********* HUUYAR.
WORD #4377 OCCURS 2 TIMES.

VINIESTES 13000 5ELCID1649 APOCO QUE *********, PRESEND UOS QUIEREN DAR:
WORD #4378 OCCURS 1 TIMES.

VINJEMOS 16151 5ELCID2048 VOS AGORA LEGASTES, & NOS ******** ANOCH;
WORD #4379 OCCURS 1 TIMES.

VINO 871 5ELCID0112 POR EN **** AAQUESTO POR QUE FUE ACUSADO.
1574 5ELCID0202 **** PORA LA TIENDA DEL QUE EN BUEN ORA NASCO;
2729 5ELCID0345 DEL AGUA FEZIST **** & DELA PIEDRA PAN,
3122 5ELCID0393 **** MYO %ID IAZER A SPINAZ DE CAN.
3226 5ELCID0406 EL ANGEL GABRIEL A EL **** EN SUE@O:
4822 5ELCID0611 **** PERO VERMUEZ, QUE LA SE@A TEINE EN MANO,
4980 5ELCID0630 **** POSAR SOBRE ALCO%ER, EN VN TAN FUERTE LOGAR;
7664 5ELCID0981 SABRA EL SALIDO A QUIEN **** DESONDRAR.
7798 5ELCID0998 VERA REMONT VERENGEL TRAS QUIEN **** EN ALCAN%A
8032 5ELCID1025 COMED, CONDE, DESTE PAN & BEUED DESTE ****.
8691 5ELCID1104 BEUEMOS SO **** & COMEMOS EL SO PAN.
9308 5ELCID1183 NON LES DIXO COSEIO, NIN LOS **** HUUIAR.
9516 5ELCID1210 QUANDO **** EL DEZENO, OUIERON GELA ADAR.
9631 5ELCID1224 **** LOS VER CON XXX MILL DE ARMAS.
10174 5ELCID1288 DE PARTE DE ORIENT **** VN CORONADO;
18367 5ELCID2325 **** CON ESTAS NUEUAS A MUO %ID RUYDIAZ EL CANPEADOR:
22103 5ELCID2813 A SANTESTEUAN **** FELEZ MUNOZ,
24002 5ELCID3059 ACORDADOS FUERON, QUANDO **** LA MAN.
29247 5ELCID3734 ES LEYDO, DAT NOS DEL ****; SI NON TENEDES DINEROS, ECHAD
WORD #4380 OCCURS 19 TIMES.
INDEX OF DIVERSIFICATION = 1575.44 WITH STANDARD DEVIATION OF 2175.73

VINOS 10327 5ELCID1307 ALEGRE FUE MINAYA & SPIDIOS & *****.
WORD #4381 OCCURS 1 TIMES.

VIO 15 5ELCID0003 *** PUERTAS ABIERTAS & V%OS SIN CA@ADOS,
2789 5ELCID0352 LONGINOS ERA %IEGO, QUE NUQUAS *** ALGUANDRE,
4512 5ELCID0574 QUANDO *** MYO %ID QUE ALCO%ER NON SELE DAUA;
4634 5ELCID0588 MYO %ID, QUANDO LOS *** FUERA, COGIOS COMMO DE ARRANCADA.
4689 5ELCID0595 *** QUE ENTRELLOS & EL CASTIELLO MUCHO AUIE GRAND PLA%A;
6208 5ELCID0791 *** LOS SOS COMMOS VAN ALEGANDO:
7098 5ELCID0908 QUANDO *** EL CABOSO QUE SE TARDAUA MINAYA,
7172 5ELCID0919 QUANDO *** MYO %ID ASOMAR A MINAYA,
9446 5ELCID1201 QUANDO *** MYO %ID LAS GENTES IUNTADAS, COMPE%OS DE PAGAR.
12562 5ELCID1594 QUANDO LO *** DO@A XIMENA, A PIES SE LE ECHAUA:
13271 5ELCID1683 EL SELO *** CON LOS OIOS, CUENTAN GELO DELANT,
15469 5ELCID1960 QUANDO LAS ***, DE CORA%ON SE PAGA:
18068 5ELCID2286 FERRAN GON%ALEZ NON *** ALLI DOS AL%ASSE, NIN CAMARA ABIERTA NIN
18122 5ELCID2293 *** CER%ADO EL ESCA@O DE SUS BUENOS VARONES:
18166 5ELCID2298 EL LEON QUANDO LO ***, ASSI EN VERGON%O,
19275 5ELCID2440 E *** VENIR ADIEGO & A FERNANDO;
26466 5ELCID3377 HYA VARONES, QUIEN *** NUNCA TAL MAL?
28533 5ELCID3643 QUANDO LO *** FERRANGO%ALEZ, CONUUO ATIZON;
28648 5ELCID3658 *** DIEGO GON%ALEZ QUE NO ESCAPARIE CON EL ALMA;
WORD #4382 OCCURS 19 TIMES.
INDEX OF DIVERSIFICATION = 1589.72 WITH STANDARD DEVIATION OF 1756.33

VIOLO 5900 5ELCID0748 ***** MYO %ID RUY DIAZ EL CASTELANO,
8672 5ELCID1102 ***** MYO %ID, TOMOS AMARAUILLAR: GRADO ATI, PADRE SPIRITAL
13194 5ELCID1673 ***** EL ATALAYA & TANXO EL ESQUILA;
20594 5ELCID2615 ***** EN LOS AUUEROS EL QUE EN BUEN ORA %INXO ESPADA,
WORD #4383 OCCURS 4 TIMES.

WORD C# PREFIX CONTEXT

```
VIOLOS            6830 5ELCID0873 ****** EL REY, FERMOSO SONRRISAUA:
                 21791 5ELCID2772 ****** VENIR & OYO VNA RAZON,
                 23010 5ELCID2932 ****** EL REY & CONNOS%IO A MU@O GUSTIOZ;
                 26209 5ELCID3341 ASOS VASSALOS ****** A DERREDOR;
        WORD #4384 OCCURS    4 TIMES.

VIRTOS            5193 5ELCID0657 CRECEN ESTOS ******, CA YENTES SON SOBEIANAS.
                 11814 5ELCID1498 ****** DEL CAMPEADOR ANOS VIENEN BUSCAR.
                 12809 5ELCID1625 AQUEL REY DE MARRUECOS AIUNTAUA SUS ******;
        WORD #4385 OCCURS    3 TIMES.

VISGUIER          1988 5ELCID0251 SI YO ALGUN DIA ********, SERUOS HAN DOBLADOS.
        WORD #4386 OCCURS    1 TIMES.

VISQUIER          6466 5ELCID0825 SI LES YO ********, SERAN DUENAS RICAS.
        WORD #4387 OCCURS    1 TIMES.

VISQUIEREDES      3244 5ELCID0409 MIENTRA QUE ************ BIEN SE FARA LO TO.
                  7214 5ELCID0925 MIENTRA UOS ************, BIEN ME YRA AMJ, MINAYA
        WORD #4388 OCCURS    2 TIMES.

VISQUIEREMOS     20032 5ELCID2542 MIENTRA QUE ************ DESPENDER NOLO PODREMOS.
        WORD #4389 OCCURS    1 TIMES.

VISQUIESSEN       1353 5ELCID0173 CA MIENTRA QUE *********** REFECHOS ERAN AMOS.
        WORD #4390 OCCURS    1 TIMES.

VIST             26024 5ELCID3318 **** VN MORO, FUSTEL ENSAYAR; ANTES FUXISTE QUE ALTE ALEGASSES.
        WORD #4391 OCCURS    1 TIMES.

VISTAS           15023 5ELCID1899 E DE MI ABRA PERDON; VINIESSEM A ******, SI OUIESSE DENT SABOR.
                 15113 5ELCID1911 QUEL YRE A ****** DO FUERE AGUISADO;
                 15383 5ELCID1948 ESTAS ****** OLAS AYADES UOS,
                 15433 5ELCID1955 AYAMOS ****** QUANDO LO QUIERE MYO SE@OR.
                 15487 5ELCID1962 SEAN LAS ****** DESTAS IIJ SEMANAS;
                 15512 5ELCID1965 DELLA PART & DELLA PORA LAS ****** SE ADOBAUAN;
                 15645 5ELCID1984 SUELTAN LAS RIENDAS, ALAS ****** SEUAN A DELI@ADAS.
                 15661 5ELCID1986 NON LO DETARDA, PORA LAS ****** SE ADOBO;
                 15865 5ELCID2012 HYAS VA PORA LAS ****** QUE CON EL REY PARO.
                 16737 5ELCID2119 TODOS SON PAGADOS DELAS ****** QUANTOS QUE Y SON.
                 16930 5ELCID2143 DESTAS ****** QUE OUIEMOS, DEMY TOMEDES ALGO.
                 17015 5ELCID2154 ADIOS UOS ACOMIENDO, DESTAS ****** ME PARTO.
                 21496 5ELCID2733 RETRAER UOS LO AN EN ****** O EN CORTES.
        WORD #4392 OCCURS   13 TIMES.
           INDEX OF DIVERSIFICATION =    538.42 WITH STANDARD DEVIATION OF  1262.72

VISTE            24255 5ELCID3093 SIEMPRE LA ***** MYO %ID EL CAMPEADOR;
        WORD #4393 OCCURS    1 TIMES.

VISTIDURAS       16711 5ELCID2116 TANTAS BUENAS ********** QUE DALFAYA SON.
        WORD #4394 OCCURS    1 TIMES.

VISTIO           24206 5ELCID3087 ****** CAMISA DE RAN%AL TAN BLANCA COMMO EL SOL,
        WORD #4395 OCCURS    1 TIMES.

VISTIOS          12508 5ELCID1587 ******* EL SOBREGONEL; LUENGA TRAHE LA BARBA;
                 17691 5ELCID2238 EL OBISPO DON IHERONIMO ******* TAN PRIUADO,
        WORD #4396 OCCURS    2 TIMES.

VIVADES           1227 5ELCID0158 MIENTRA QUE ******* NON SEREDES MENGUADOS.
        WORD #4397 OCCURS    1 TIMES.

VJ                1255 5ELCID0161 QUE SOBRE AQUELAS ARCHAS DAR LE YEN ** %IENTOS MARCOS
                  1613 5ELCID0207 VOS ** %IENTOS & YO XXX HE GANADOS.
                  2424 5ELCID0306 LOS ** DIAS DE PLAZO PASSADOS LOS AN,
                 28247 5ELCID3606 BIEN GELO DEMOSTRARON ATODOS ** COMMO SON,
                 28266 5ELCID3609 MAS DE ** ASTAS DE LAN%AS QUE NON LEGASSEN AL MOION.
        WORD #4398 OCCURS    5 TIMES.
           INDEX OF DIVERSIFICATION =   6751.75 WITH STANDARD DEVIATION OF 12717.64

VN                1424 5ELCID0182 EN MEDIO DEL PALA%IO TENDIERON ** ALMOFALLA,
                  1997 5ELCID0252 NON QUIERO FAZER ENEL MONESTERIO ** DINERO DE DA@O;
                  2061 5ELCID0260 POR ** MARCHO QUE DESPENDADES AL MONESTERIO DARE YO QUATRO.
                  3213 5ELCID0405 ** SUENOL PRISO DUL%E, TAN BIEN SE ADURMJO.
                  3964 5ELCID0503 NON PRENDRE DE UOS QUANTO UALE ** DINERO MALO.
                  4349 5ELCID0554 EN ** OTERO REDONDO, FUERTE & GRAND;
                  4522 5ELCID0575 EL FIZO ** ART & NON LO DETARDAUA:
                  4768 5ELCID0605 EN ** ORA & VN POCO DE LOGAR CCC MOROS MATAN.
                  4771 5ELCID0605 EN VN ORA & ** POCO DE LOGAR CCC MOROS MATAN.
                  4985 5ELCID0630 VINO POSAR SOBRE ALCO%ER, EN ** TAN FUERTE LOGAR;
                  5311 5ELCID0671 PRIMERO FABLO MINAYA, ** CAUALLERO DE PRESTAR:
                  5497 5ELCID0693 ABRIERON LAS PUERTAS, FUERA ** SALTO DAN;
                  5792 5ELCID0732 CAYEN EN ** POCO DE LOGAR MOROS MUERTOS MILL & CCC YA.
                  6033 5ELCID0765 MARTIN ANTOLINEZ ** COLPE DIO A GALUE,
                  6658 5ELCID0849 EN TODOS LOS SOS NON FALLARIEDES ** MESQUINO.
                  6759 5ELCID0863 Y FFINCO EN ** POYO QUE ES SOBRE MONT REAL;
```

WORD C# PREFIX CONTEXT

VN (CON'T)

```
7390 5ELCID0948 QUI EN ** LCGAR MORA SIEMPRE, LO SO PUEDE MANGUAR;
7609 5ELCIDC974 DI%E DE VNA SIERRA & LEGAUA A ** VAL.
7940 5ELCID1014 DE FUERA DELA TIENDA ** SALTC CAUA,
7992 5ELCID1021 NON COMBRE ** BOCADO POR QUANTO HA EN TODA ESPA@A,
8C86 5ELCID1032 NOL PUEDEN FAZER CCMER ** MUESSO CE PAN.
8179 5ELCID1042 SABET, NCN UOS DARE AUOS ** CINERO MALO;
9768 5ELCID1241 NIN ENTRARIE ENELA TIGERA, NI ** PELO NON AURIE TAIADO,
9893 5ELCID1254 TOMASSEN LE EL AUER & PUSIESSEN LE EN ** PALO.
1C175 5ELCID1288 DE PARTE DE ORIENT VINC ** CORCNACO;
1C902 5ELCID1380 LEUEDES ** PCRTERO, TENCO QUE UOS AURA PRO;
11523 5ELCID1459 E MARTIN ANTOLINEZ, ** BURGALES LEAL,
13476 5ELCID1708 PIDO UOS ** DCN & SEAM PRESENTADO.
13631 5ELCID1727 METIOS LE EN GUIERA, ** CASTIELLO PALA%IANO;
15872 5ELCID2013 DE ** DIA ES LEGACO ANTES EL REY DON ALFONSSO.
16340 5ELCID2073 COMETER QUIERO ** RUEGO A MYO %ID EL CAMPEADOR;
17216 5ELCID2178 DAD LES ** REYAL & ALCS YFANTES DE CARRION,
17516 5ELCID2216 E YUAN POSAR EN ** PRE%IOSO ESCA@O.
18022 5ELCID2280 YAZIES EN ** ESCA@O, CURMIE EL CAMPEADOR,
19143 5ELCID2421 ARRIBA AL%C COLADA, ** GRANT CCLPE DADOL HA,
2C990 5ELCID2667 ** MORC LATINADC BIEN GELC ENTENDIO;
21246 5ELCID2700 FALARON ** VERGEL CON VNA LINPIA FUENT;
21768 5ELCID2769 EN ** MONTE ESPESSO FELEZ MUNOZ SE METIO,
21998 5ELCID2799 CON ** SONBRERC QUE TIENE FELEZ MUNOZ,
22326 5ELCID2843 VINIERCN A SANTESTEUAN DE GCRMAZ, ** CASTIELLO TAN FUERT,
24233 5ELCID3090 SOBRELLA ** BRIAL PRIMO DE %ICLATON,
24307 5ELCID3099 DESUSO CUBRIO ** MANTC QUE ES CE GRANT VALOR,
24481 5ELCID3121 EN ** ESCA@C TORNI@C ESSORA MYO %ID POSO,
26025 5ELCID3318 VIST ** MORC, FUSTEL ENSAYAR; ANTES FUXISTE QUE ALTE ALEGASSES.
26448 5ELCID3374 MANTO ARMINC & ** BRIAL RASTRANDO,
27831 5ELCID3551 TODOS TRES SE ACUERCAN, CA SON DE ** SE@OR.
28422 5ELCID3630 ** COLPE RESIBIERA, MAS CTRC FIRIO:
28586 5ELCID3650 DIOL ** COLPE, DE TRAUIESSOL TOMAUA,
28673 5ELCID3661 ** COLPEL DIO DE LANC, CCN LC AGUDO NOL TOMAUA.
WORD #4399 OCCURS 49 TIMES.
INDEX OF DIVERSIFICATICN = 566.69 WITH STANCARD DEVIATION OF 578.46
```

VNA

```
315 5ELCID0040 *** NI@A DE NUEF A@CS A OIO SE PARAUA:
475 5ELCID0060 DERREDCR DEL *** BUE@A CONPA@A.
1387 5ELCIDC178 *** PIEL VERMEIA MORISCA & CNCRADA,
1427 5ELCID0183 SOBRELLA *** SAUANA DE RAN%AL & MUY BLANCA.
2572 5ELCIDC325 TANEN A MATINES A *** PRIESSA TAN GRAND;
3156 5ELCID0397 DE SINIESTRO SANT ESTEUAN, *** BUENA %IPDAD,
3519 5ELCID0443 E ALBAR SALUADCREZ SIN FALLA, & GALIN GAR%IA, *** FARDIDA
4409 5ELCID0561 A TODOS SOS VARCNES MANCO FAZER *** CARCAUA,
4529 5ELCID0576 DEXA *** TIENDA FITA & LAS CTRAS LEUAUA,
4580 5ELCID0582 LAS OTRAS A BES LIEUA, *** TIENCA A DEXADA.
6428 5ELCIDC820 EUADES AQUI ORC & PLATA *** VESA LE@A,
7110 5ELCIDC909 CCN TODAS SUS YENTES FIZC *** TRASNOCHADA;
7489 5ELCID0960 EL CONDE ES MUY FCLCN & DIXO *** VANIDAT:
7604 5ELCID0974 DI%E DE *** SIERRA & LEGAUA A VN VAL.
8503 5ELCID1081 *** DES LEATAN%A CA NCN LA FIZO ALGUANDRE.
9320 5ELCID1185 SALIC DE MURUIEDRO *** NCCH EN TRASNOCHADA,
1C496 5ELCID1330 E PE@A CADIELLA, QUE ES *** PE@A FUERT;
12207 5ELCID1549 ENTRE EL & ALBARFANEZ HYUAN A *** COMPA@A.
12440 5ELCID1578 RE%EBIDAS LAS DUENAS A *** GRANT ONDRAN%A,
12516 5ELCID1588 FIZO *** CORRICA, ESTA FUE TAN ESTRA@A.
13C75 5ELCID1658 A *** GRAND PRIESSA TANIEN LOS ATAMORES;
13390 5ELCID1697 ODE AMAS CDEL *** DICS NOS VALDRA.
13939 5ELCID1766 ACADA *** DELLAS DO LES CC MARCOS DE PLATA,
14619 5ELCID1849 POCOS DIAS HA, REY, QUE *** LIC A ARRANCADO:
14940 5ELCID1889 *** GRANT CRA EL REY PENSSC & COMICIO;
14996 5ELCID1896 A *** QUADRA ELE LOS APARTO:
15255 5ELCID1932 *** GRAND CRA PENSSC & COMICIC;
15825 5ELCID2007 QUE DEL ALCA%AR *** SALIR NCN PUEDE,
16290 5ELCID2066 TODOS ERAN ALEGRES & ACUERCAN EN *** RAZON:
18097 5ELCID2290 TRAS *** VIGA LAGAR METICS CON GRANT PAUOR;
18480 5ELCID2339 EN *** CONPA@A TCRNADCS SON AMOS.
2C749 5ELCID2635 POR MOLINA YREDES, *** NOCH Y IAZREDES;
21183 5ELCID2691 ASSINIESTRO DEXAN ATINEZA, *** PE@A MUY FUERT,
21249 5ELCID27C0 FALARON VN VERGEL CON *** LINPIA FUENT;
21449 5ELCID2727 AL *** DIZEN CCLADA & AL OTRA TIZON,
21679 5ELCID2756 QUE EL *** AL OTRA NCL TORNA RECABDO.
21795 5ELCID2772 VIOLOS VENIR & CYC *** RAZON,
22203 5ELCID2828 *** GRAND ORA PENSSO & CCMICIC;
22334 5ELCID2844 HY ALBERGARCN POR VERCAD *** NOCH.
23178 5ELCID2953 EL REY *** GRAND CRA CALLO & COMICIO:
24246 5ELCID3092 SOBRESTO *** PIEL VERMEIA, LAS BANDAS DORO SON,
24260 5ELCID3094 *** COFIA SOBRE LCS PELOS DUN ESCARIN DE PRO,
24555 5ELCID3130 LA *** FUE EN BURGCS, & LA CTRA EN CARRION,
27111 5ELCID3464 NON DIGA NINGUNO DELLA MAS *** ENTEN%ION.
28483 5ELCID3637 DEDENTRC EN LA CARNE *** MANO GELA METIO;
28843 5ELCID3684 DELA OTRA PART *** BRA%A GELA ECHO,
28850 5ELCID3685 CON EL DIO *** TUERTA, CELA SIELLA LO ENCAMO,
WORD #44CC OCCURS 47 TIMES.
INDEX OF DIVERSIFICATICN = 619.33 WITH STANCARD DEVIATION OF 615.58
```

WORD C# PREFIX CONTEXT

VNAS 6581 5ELCID0840 MOROS DE LAS FRONTERAS & **** YENTES ESTRANAS;
WORD #4401 OCCURS 1 TIMES.

VNO 785 5ELCID0100 RACHEL & VIDAS EN *** ESTAUAN AMOS,
2766 5ELCID0350 EL *** ES EN PARAYSO, CA EL OTRO NON ENTRO ALA;
4031 5ELCID0513 A CADA *** DELLOS CAEN C MARCHOS DE PLATA,
4962 5ELCID0628 QUE A *** QUE DIZIEN MYO %ID RUY DIAZ DE BIUAR
7786 5ELCID0997 POR *** QUE FIRGADES, TRES SIELLAS YRAN VAZIAS.
8918 5ELCID1136 QUIS CADA *** DELLOS BIEN SABE LO QUE HA DE FAR.
9215 5ELCID1173 EN CADA *** DESTOS A@OS MYO %ID LES TOLIO EL PAN.
11804 5ELCID1497 EL *** FINCO CON ELLOS & EL OTRO TORNO A ALBARFANEZ:
11866 5ELCID1504 TODOS VIENEN EN ***, AGORA LEGARAN.
15583 5ELCID1976 LO *** A DEBDAN & LO OTRO PAGAUAN;
16680 5ELCID2112 QUANDO SALIE EL SOL, QUES TORNASSE CADA *** DON SALIDOS SON.
16716 5ELCID2117 CADA *** LO QUE PIDE, NADI NOL DIZE DE NO.
17852 5ELCID2259 CADA *** POR SI SOS DONES AUIEN DADOS.
18690 5ELCID2365 EL DEBDO QUE A CADA *** A CONPLIR SERA.
19594 5ELCID2483 LO *** ES NUESTRO, LO OTRO HAN EN SALUO.
26584 5ELCID3394 AL *** DIZEN OIARRA & AL OTRO YENEGO SIMENEZ,
26593 5ELCID3395 EL *** ES YFANTE DE NAUARRA
28116 5ELCID3590 QUE CADA *** DELLOS BIEN FOS FERIR EL SO.
28312 5ELCID3614 CADA *** DELLOS MIENTES TIENE AL SO.
28351 5ELCID3620 CADA *** DELLOS MIENTES TIENE ALSO;
28631 5ELCID3656 LO *** CAYO ENEL CAMPO & LO AL SUSO FINCAUA.
WORD #4402 OCCURS 21 TIMES.
INDEX OF DIVERSIFICATION = 1391.30 WITH STANDARD DEVIATION OF 1667.04

VNOL 6005 5ELCID0761 LOS DOS LE FALLEN, & EL **** HA TOMADO,
WORD #4403 OCCURS 1 TIMES.

VNOS 2294 5ELCID0289 **** DEXAN CASAS & OTROS ONORES.
2976 5ELCID0375 ASIS PARTEN **** DOTROS COMMO LA V@A DELA CARNE.
4378 5ELCID0558 LOS **** CONTRA LA SIERRA & LOS OTROS CONTRA LA AGUA.
7876 5ELCID1007 ALOS **** FIRIENDO & A LOS OTROS DE ROCANDO.
8720 5ELCID1108 LOS **** AXERICA & LOS OTROS A ALUCAD,
13911 5ELCID1762 E YUAN POSAR CON EL EN **** PRE%IOSOS ESCA@OS;
14520 5ELCID1837 ALOS **** PLAZE & ALOS OTROS VA PESANDO.
15922 5ELCID2009 CON **** XV A TIERRAS FIRIO,
24199 5ELCID3086 SOBRELLAS **** %APATOS QUE A GRANT HUEBRA SON;
25706 5ELCID3274 LOS **** LE HAN MIEDO & LOS OTROS ESPANTA.
28764 5ELCID3673 FIRIENSSEN EN LOS ESCUDOS **** TAN GRANDES COLPES;
29254 5ELCID3735 ALA **** PE@OS, QUE BIEN VOS LO DARARAN SOBRELOS.
WORD #4404 OCCURS 12 TIMES.
INDEX OF DIVERSIFICATION = 2449.91 WITH STANDARD DEVIATION OF 2428.10

VNTAR 2813 5ELCID0354 CORRIO LA SANGRE POR EL ASTIL AYUSO, LAS MANOS SE OUO DE *****,
WORD #4405 OCCURS 1 TIMES.

V@A 2980 5ELCID0375 ASIS PARTEN VNOS DOTROS COMMO LA *** DELA CARNE.
20806 5ELCID2642 CUEMO LA *** DELA CARNE ELLOS PARTIDOS SON;
WORD #4406 OCCURS 2 TIMES.

VO 1978 5ELCID0250 MAS POR QUE ME ** DE TIERRA, DOUOS L MARCHOS,
5610 5ELCID0707 ** METER LA UUESTRA SE@A EN AQUELA MAYOR AZ;
WORD #4407 OCCURS 2 TIMES.

VOCA%ION 13166 5ELCID1669 ******** ES QUE FIZO EL %ID CAMPEADOR.
WORD #4408 OCCURS 1 TIMES.

VOLUNTAD 2371 5ELCID0299 FABLO MYO %ID DE TODA ********:
2740 5ELCID0346 RESU%ITEST A LAZARO, CA FUE TU ********;
2845 5ELCID0359 COMMO FUE TU ********.
2870 5ELCID0362 ATI ADORO & CREO DE TODO ********,
7861 5ELCID1005 ESTO FAZEN LOS SOS DE ******** & DE GRADO;
8301 5ELCID1056 AQUI DIXO EL CONDE: DE ******** & DE GRADO.
8954 5ELCID1139 FERID LOS, CAUALLEROS, DAMOR & DE GRADO & DE GRAND ********,
10123 5ELCID1282 ESSORA DIXO MINAYA: DE BUENA ********.
13354 5ELCID1692 ESSORA DIXIERON TODOS: DAMOR & DE ********.
13400 5ELCID1698 ESSORA DIXO EL %ID: DE BUENA ********.
18561 5ELCID2349 POR LA SU ******** NON SERIEN ALLI LEGADOS.
22624 5ELCID2882 SALIOLOS A RE%EBIR DE BUENA ********,
WORD #4409 OCCURS 12 TIMES.
INDEX OF DIVERSIFICATION = 1840.18 WITH STANDARD DEVIATION OF 2081.83

VOLUTAD 1157 5ELCID0149 CON RACHEL & VIDAS, DE ******* & DE GRADO.
WORD #4410 OCCURS 1 TIMES.

VOS 1514 5ELCID0194 *** LO MERE%ECES, DARUOS QUEREMOS BUEN DADO,
1612 5ELCID0207 *** VJ %IENTOS & YO XXX HE GANADOS.
2379 5ELCID0301 ***, QUE POR MI DEXADES CASAS & HEREDADES,
3486 5ELCID0440 *** CON C DE AQUESTA NUESTRA CONPA@A,
3500 5ELCID0442 *** CON LOS CC YD UOS EN ALGARA; ALA VAYA ALBARABAREZ,
5457 5ELCID0689 E ***, PERO VERMUEZ, LA MI SE@A TOMAD;

WORD C# PREFIX CONTEXT

VOS (CON'T)

```
 8870 5ELCID1130 *** CON LOS CTROS FIRADES LOS DELANT.
 9556 5ELCID1214 EL ORO & LA PLATA QUI EN *** LO PODRIE CONTAR?
10275 5ELCID1301 ***, QUANDC YDES A CASTIELLA, LEUAREDES BUENOS MANDADOS.
11030 5ELCID1396 CMILOM, DO@A XIMENA, DICS *** CURIE DE MAL,
12642 5ELCID1604 ***, QUERIDA & ONDRADA MUGIER, & AMAS MIS FIJAS,
13800 5ELCID1749 *** TENIENDC VALEN%IA, & YO VEN%I EL CAMPO;
14267 5ELCID1805 DELO QUE AUOS CAYC *** NON GRADE%EDES NADA;
14593 5ELCID1846 POR MYO %ID EL CAMPEADOR TODO ESTO *** BESAMOS;
15005 5ELCID1897 CYD ME, MYNAYA, & ***, PER VERMUEZ:
15169 5ELCID1919  VENIDES, MYNAYA, & ***, PERO VERMUEZ
16146 5ELCID2048 *** AGORA LEGASTES, & NOS VINJEMOS ANOCH;
16656 5ELCID2110 *** CASADES MIS FIJAS, CA NON GELAS DO YO.
16937 5ELCID2144 TRAYO *** XX PALAFRES, ESTOS BIEN ADOBADOS,
17223 5ELCID2179 *** CON ELLOS SED, QUE ASSI UOS LO MANDO YO.
18638 5ELCID2359 *** CON LOS UUESTROS FIRME MIENTRE ALA %AGA TENGADES;
19583 5ELCID2481 COMMO SON ONDRADOS & AVER *** GRANT PRO.
20241 5ELCID2570 *** LES DIESTES VILLAS E TIERRAS POR ARRAS ENTIERRAS DE CARRION,
20313 5ELCID2577 MIOS FIJOS SODES AMOS, QUANDO MIS FIJAS *** DO;
20444 5ELCID2595 *** NOS ENGENDRASTES, NUESTRA MADRE NOS PARIO;
20471 5ELCID2598 DEBDO NOS ES A CUNPLIR LO QUE MANDAREDES ***.
20506 5ELCID2603 ANDAD, FIJAS, DAQUI EL CRIADOR *** VALA
21089 5ELCID2680 *** NUQUA EN CARRION ENTRARIEDES IAMAS.
22388 5ELCID2852 POR AQUESTA ONDRA QUE *** DIESTES A ESTO QUE NOS CUNTIO;
22524 5ELCID2868 AVN VEAMOS EL DIA QUE *** PODAMOS VENGAR
23055 5ELCID2937 LOS PIES & LAS MANOS *** BESA EL CAMPEADOR;
24029 5ELCID3063 ***, MYNAYA ALBARFANEZ, EL MYO BRA%O MEIOR,
24036 5ELCID3064 *** YREDES CONMIGO & EL OBISPO DON IHERONIMO
25240 5ELCID3213 ALO QUE DEMANDA EL %ID QUEL RECUDADES ***.
25432 5ELCID3238 EL ORO & LA PLATA ESPENDIESTES LO ***;
25612 5ELCID3261 ALA SALIDA DE VALEN%IA MIS FIJAS *** DI YO,
25668 5ELCID3268 POR QUANTO LES FIZIESTES MENOS VALEDES ***.
25867 5ELCID3295 NON CRE%IES VARAIA ENTRE NOS & ***.
26249 5ELCID3346 POR QUANTO LAS DEXASTES MENOS VALEDES ***;
26254 5ELCID3347 ELLAS SON MUGIERES & *** SODES VARONES,
26263 5ELCID3348 EN TODAS GUISAS MAS VALEN QUE ***.
26406 5ELCID3368 FIJAS DEL %ID, POR QUE LAS *** DEXASTES,
26415 5ELCID3369 ENTODAS GUISAS, SABED, QUE MAS VALEN QUE ***.
26652 5ELCID3403 MER%ED, REY ALFONSSO, *** SODES MYO SE@OR
26669 5ELCID3406 *** LAS CASASTES ANTES, CA YO NON,
27077 5ELCID3459 CA EN ESTA CORT AFARTO HA PORA ***,
27167 5ELCID3472 SEA ESTA LIS O MANDAREDES ***.
27205 5ELCID3478 HYO *** LO SOBRELIEUO COMMO BUEN VASSALLO FAZE A SE@OR,
27553 5ELCID3518 MAS ATAL CAUALLO CUM EST PORA TAL COMMO ***,
27563 5ELCID3520 QUIEN *** LO TOLLER QUISIERE NOL VALA EL CRIADOR,
27602 5ELCID3524 HYA MARTIN ANTOLINEZ, & ***, PERO VERMUEZ,
27622 5ELCID3526 BUENOS MANDADOS ME VAYAN A VALEN%IA DE ***.
27920 5ELCID3563 HUEBOS *** ES QUE LIDIEDES AGUISA DE VARONES,
27943 5ELCID3565 SI DEL CAMPO BIEN SALIDES, GRAND ONDRA AUREDES ***;
27958 5ELCID3567 CA TODOS LO SABEN QUE LO BUSCASTES ***.
28000 5ELCID3574 BESAMOS *** LAS MANOS, COMMO A REY & A SE@OR,
28182 5ELCID3597 ESTA LID EN TOLEDO LAFIZIERADES, MAS NON QUISIESTES ***.
28204 5ELCID3600 AUED UUESTRO DERECHO, TUERTO NON QUERADES ***,
29258 5ELCID3735 ALA VNOS PE@OS, QUE BIEN *** LO DARARAN SOBRELOS.
WORD #4411 OCCURS  59 TIMES.
   INDEX OF DIVERSIFICATION =   477.34 WITH STANDARD DEVIATION OF   612.34

VOZES        5700 5ELCID0719 A GRANDES ***** LAMA EL QUE EN BUEN ORA NASCO:
            25844 5ELCID3292 AALTAS ***** ONDREDES QUE FABLO:
            28696 5ELCID3664 ESCRA EL YFANTE TAN GRANDES ***** DAUA:
WORD #4412 OCCURS   3 TIMES.

VRGULLOSOS  15306 5ELCID1938 ELLOS SON MUCHO ********** & AN PART EN LA CORT,
WORD #4413 OCCURS   1 TIMES.

VRRACA      22097 5ELCID2812 ALA TORRE DE DON ****** ELLE LAS DEXO.
WORD #4414 OCCURS   1 TIMES.

VUESTRA      1724 5ELCID0221 ******* UERTUD ME UALA, GLORIOSA, EN MY EXIDA & ME AIUDE,
            13820 5ELCID1751 QUANDO EN ******* VENIDA TAL GANAN%IA NOS AN DADA.
WORD #4415 OCCURS   2 TIMES.

VUESTRAS    16355 5ELCID2075 ******** FIJAS UOS PIDO, DON ELUIRA & DO@A SOL,
WORD #4416 OCCURS   1 TIMES.

VUESTRO     10563 5ELCID1339 RAZONAS POR ******* VASSALLO & AUOS TIENE POR SE@OR.
            23061 5ELCID2938 ELE ES ******* VASSALLO & UOS SODES SO SE@OS.
WORD #4417 OCCURS   2 TIMES.

VUJAS       26037 5ELCID3319 SI YO NON *****, EL MORO TE JUGARA MAL;
WORD #4418 OCCURS   1 TIMES.

X            7432 5ELCID0953 EN AQUESSA CORRIDA * DIAS OUIERON AMORAR.
            14706 5ELCID1860 CON * DE SUS PARIENTES A PARTE DAUAN SALTO:
WORD #4419 OCCURS   2 TIMES.
```

WORD C# PREFIX CONTEXT

XAMED 17447 5ELCID2207 TANTA PCRPCLA & TANTO ***** & TANTO PA@O PRECIADO.
WORD #4420 CCCURS 1 TIMES.

XATIUA 9152 5ELCID1165 MALES PESA EN ****** & CENTRO EN GUIERA,
9655 5ELCID1227 FATA DENTRC EN ****** DURO EL ARRANCADA,
WORD #4421 CCCURS 2 TIMES.

XERICA 1C470 5ELCID1327 GANADA A ****** & A CNDA POR NCMBRE,
WORD #4422 OCCURS 1 TIMES.

XIMENA 1878 5ELCID0239 Y ESTAUA DC@A ****** CON %INCO DUENAS DE PRO,
2005 5ELCID0253 EUADES AQUI PCRA DO@A ****** CCUOS C MARCHOS.
2079 5ELCID0262 AFEUOS DO@A ****** CCN SUS FIJAS DO UA LEGANDO;
2097 5ELCID0264 ANTEL CAMPEADCR DC@A ****** FINCO LOS YNOIOS AMOS,
2205 5ELCID0278 YA DO@A ******, LA MI MUGIER TAN COMPLIDA,
2587 5ELCID0327 ECHOS DO@A ****** EN LCS GRACCS DELANTEL ALTAR,
2919 5ELCID0368 EL %ID A DC@A ****** YUA LA ABRA%AR;
2924 5ELCID0369 DO@A ****** AL %ID LA MANOL VA BESAR,
3050 5ELCID0384 COMMO SIRUA ADO@A ****** & ALAS FIJAS QUE HA,
1C673 5ELCID1352 POR SU MUGIER DO@A ****** & SUS FIJAS AMAS ADOS:
11028 5ELCID1396 CMILCM, DO@A ******, CICS VCS CURIE DE MAL,
11C92 5ELCID1404 DIXO DC@A ******: EL CRIADOR LO MANDE
12564 5ELCID1594 QUANDO LC VIO DC@A ******, A PIES SE LE ECHAUA:
13917 5ELCID1763 HYA MUGIER DA@A ******, NCM LC AUIECES ROGADO?
14233 5ELCID1801 ALEGRE ES DC@A ****** & SUS FIJAS AMAS,
17267 5ELCID2184 RE%IBIOLO DC@A ****** & SUS FIJAS AMAS:
17359 5ELCID2196 MUGIER DO@A ******, GRACO AL CRIAADOR.
2C165 5ELCID2560 QUE PLEGA A DC@A ****** & PRIMERO AUOS
22736 5ELCID2897 GRAND GOZO FIZO CCN ELLAS DO@A ****** SU MADRE.
23858 5ELCID3039 MI MUGIER DCNA ******, CUE@A ES DE PRO,
WORD #4423 CCCURS 20 TIMES.
INDEX OF DIVERSIFICATION = 1155.84 WITH STANDARD DEVIATION OF 1858.49

XIMENEZ 26758 5ELCID3417 AUCS, CIARRA, & AUCS, YENEGC *******,
26797 5ELCID3422 LEUANTOS EN PIE CIARRA & YNEGC *******,
WORD #4424 CCCURS 2 TIMES.

XIMINA 11254 5ELCID1424 MINAYA A DO@A ****** & A SUS FIJAS QUE HA,
WORD #4425 OCCURS 1 TIMES.

XUCAR 9662 5ELCID1228 ENEL PASSAR DE ***** Y VERIEDES BARATA,
WORD #4426 OCCURS 1 TIMES.

XV 4509 5ELCID0573 ALI YOGC MYO %ID CCMPLICAS ** SEMMANAS.
7C95 5ELCIDC907 ALI SOUO MIC %IC CCMPLICAS ** SEMANAS;
11142 5ELCID1410 DE AQUESTOS ** DIAS, SIDICS NCS CURIARE DE MAL,
13134 5ELCID1665 ANTES DESTCS ** DIAS, SI PLCGIERE A CRIADOR,
15923 5ELCID2009 CON VNOS ** A TIERRAS FIRIO,
17798 5ELCID2252 HYA %ERCA DELCS ** DIAS YAS VAN LOS FIJOS DALGO.
WORD #4427 OCCURS 6 TIMES.
INDEX OF DIVERSIFICATION = 2656.80 WITH STANDARD DEVIATION OF 867.22

XX 16938 5ELCID2144 TRAYO VOS ** PALAFRES, ESTOS BIEN ADOBADOS,
19370 5ELCID2454 DE ** ARRIBA HA MORCS MATADO;
WORD #4428 OCCURS 2 TIMES.

XXX 1535 5ELCIDC196 DAMOS UCS ENDON AUOS *** MARCHOS;
1617 5ELCIDC207 VOS VJ %IENTOS & YO *** HE GANADOS.
6125 5ELCIDC779 DA QUESTOS MORCS MATC *** IIIJ;
6401 5ELCID0816 QUIEROL ENBIAR EN DON *** CAUALLOS,
9578 5ELCID1217 ENEL AUER MONEDADO *** MILL MARCOS LE CAEN,
9635 5ELCID1224 VINO LCS VER CCN *** MILL DE ARMAS.
13549 5ELCID1717 QUATRO MILL MENOS *** CCN MYO %ID VAN A CABO,
16944 5ELCID2145 E *** CAUALLCS CCREDCRES, ESTCS BIEN ENSSELLADOS;
WORD #4429 OCCURS 8 TIMES.
INDEX OF DIVERSIFICATION = 2200.29 WITH STANDARD DEVIATION OF 1975.99

XXXIJ 2714 5ELCID0343 POR TIERRA ANCIDISTE ***** A@OS, SE@OR SPIRITAL,
WORD #4430 CCCURS 1 TIMES.

Y 937 5ELCID0120 CCN GRAND IURA METED * LAS FES AMOS,
1718 5ELCIDC220 NON SE SIENTRARE * MAS ENTCDOS LOS MYOS DIAS.
1769 5ELCIDC225 ESTO & YO EN DEBDC QUE FAGA * CANTAR MILL MISSAS.
1875 5ELCIDC239 * ESTAUA DC@A XIMENA CCN %INCC DUENAS DE PRO,
1903 5ELCIDC242 LAMAUAN ALA PUERTA, * SCPIERON EL MANDADO;
3204 5ELCID0404 * SE ECHAUA MYO %ID DESPUES QUE FUE %ENADO,
4127 5ELCIDC525 QUE ENEL CASTIELLC NCN * AURIE MORADA,
5861 5ELCID0742 DESI ADELANTE, QUANTCS QUE * SON,
6756 5ELCIDC863 * FFINCO EN VN POYC QUE ES SOBRE MONT REAL;
7314 5ELCIDC938 ALTER%ER DIA, DCN YXC * ES TCRNADO.
7914 5ELCID1011 * BEN%IC ESTA BATALLA PCRC CNDRO SU BARBA,
8883 5ELCID1131 BIEN LCS FERREDES, QUE DUBDA NCN * AURA,
8968 5ELCID1141 TANTA CUERDA DE TIENDA * VERIEDES QUEBRAR,

WORD C# PREFIX CONTEXT

Y (CON'T)

```
 9039 5ELCID1150 PRISIERCN %EBCLA & CUANTO QUE ES * ADELANT.
 9477 5ELCID1204 BIEN LA %ERCA MYC %ID, QUE NON * AUYA HART;
 9663 5ELCID1228 ENEL PASSAR DE XUCAR * VERIEDES BARATA,
10366 5ELCID1313 TORNOS A CARRION, * LC PODRIE FALLAR.
10656 5ELCID1350 FABLAUA MINAYA * AGUISA DE VARCN:
11354 5ELCID1436 POR LO QUE AUEDES FECHC BUEN COSIMENT * AURA.
12450 5ELCID1580 * DEXAUA EL CAUALLO, PORA LA CAPIELLA ADELINAUA;
14048 5ELCID1779 LOS MOROS DELAS TIERRAS GANADC SEAN * ALGO;
15065 5ELCID1905 ABRA * CNDRA & CRE%RA EN CNOR,
15120 5ELCID1912 DO EL DIXIERE, * SEA EL MOICN.
15234 5ELCID1929 QUEL CCNNOS%IE * ONDRA & CRE%IE EN ONOR,
15746 5ELCID1998 E TODOS LCS CTRCS QUE * SCN.
16244 5ELCID2060 MARAUILLAN SE DE MYO %ID CUANTOS QUE * SON.
16740 5ELCID2119 TODOS SCN PAGADCS DELAS VISTAS QUANTOS QUE * SON.
18406 5ELCID2329 QUE SEAN EN PAS & NON AYAN * RA%ION.
19974 5ELCID2534 MAS NON FALLAUAN * ACIEGC NI AFERRANDO.
20751 5ELCID2635 POR MOLINA YREDES, VNA NOCH * IAZREDES;
21264 5ELCID2702 CCN QUANTOS QUE ELLOS TRAEN * IAZEN ESSA NOCH,
22843 5ELCID2910 SI DESONDRA * CABE ALGUNA CONTRA NOS,
23275 5ELCID2965 MANDARE COMMO * VAYAN YFANTES CE CARRION,
23403 5ELCID2981 A CABO DE VIJ SEMANAS QUE * FUESSEN IUNTADOS;
23453 5ELCID2987 MIEDO HAN QUE * VERNA MYO %ID EL CAMPEADOR;
23484 5ELCID2991 CA * VERNA MYC %ID EL CAMPEADOR;
23593 5ELCID3005 FUERON * DE SU REYNC CTROS MUCHOS SABIDORES,
23624 5ELCID3009 E DIEGO & FERRANDC * SON AMCS ACOS,
23695 5ELCID3018 BIEN LC SOPIESSE QUE * SERIE ESSA NOCH.
23844 5ELCID3037 E AL CCNDE DCN ARRICH & A QUANTOS QUE * SON;
23997 5ELCID3058 ENTRE MINAYA & LCS BUENCS QUE * HA
24098 5ELCID3072 CON ESTOS CUNPLANSSE %IENTO DELOS BUENOS QUE * SON.
24320 5ELCID3100 ENEL ABRIEN QUE VER QUANTOS QUE * SON.
24623 5ELCID3137 TODOS METED * MIENTES, CA SCDES CO@OS%EDORES,
24831 5ELCID3162 CON TODCS SUS PARIENTES & EL VANDO QUE * SON;
26721 5ELCID3413 CA CRE%E UCS * ONDRA & TIERRA & ONOR.
28252 5ELCID3607 QUE POR * SERIE VEN%IDC QUI SALIESSE DEL MOION.
28922 5ELCID3694 LAS ARMAS QUE * RASTARCN EL SELAS TOMO.
WORD #4431 OCCURS 48 TIMES.
   INDEX OF DIVERSIFICATION =   594.43 WITH STANDARD DEVIATION OF   555.87

YA
  324 5ELCID0041 ** CAMPEADOR, EN BUEN CRA %INXIESTES ESPADA
  397 5ELCID0050 ** LO VEE EL %ID QUE DEL REY NON AUIE GRA%IA.
  558 5ELCID0071 ** CANPEADCR, EN BUEN ORA FUESTES NA%IDO
  884 5ELCID0114 ** LO VEDES QUE EL REY LEA AYRADO.
 1062 5ELCID0137 ** VEDES QUE ENTRA LA NCCH, EL %ID ES PRESURADO,
 1199 5ELCID0155 ** DCN RACHEL & VIDAS, AUEDES ME OLBIDADO
 1207 5ELCID0156 ** ME EXCC DE TIERRA, CA DEL REY SO AYRADO.
 1364 5ELCID0175 ** CANPEADCR, EN BUEN ORA %INXIESTES ESPADA
 1473 5ELCID0189 ** DCN RACHEL & VIDAS, EN UUESTRAS MANOS SON LAS ARCAS;
 2124 5ELCID0268 MER%ED, ** %ID, BARBA TAN COMPLIDA
 2203 5ELCID0278 ** DO@A XIMENA, LA MI MUGIER TAN COMPLIDA,
 2219 5ELCID0280 ** LO VEDES QUE PARTIR NOS EMOS EN VIDA,
 2611 5ELCID0330 ** SE@CR GLCRICSO, PADRE QUE EN %IELO ESTAS,
 2912 5ELCID0367 SALIERCN DELA EGLESIA, ** QUIEREN CAUALGAR.
 3176 5ELCID0399 PASSO PAR ALCOBIELLA QUE DE CASTIELLA FINES **;
 3479 5ELCID0439 ** %ID, EN BUEN ORA %INXIESTES ESPADA
 3616 5ELCID0456 ** QUIEBRAN LCS ALBCRES & VINIE LA MA@ANA,
 3900 5ELCID0495 PAGAR SE ** DELLA ALFCNSSO EL CASTELLANO.
 4652 5ELCID0590 DIZEN LCS DE ALCO%ER:  ** SE NOS VA LA GANA%IA
 4861 5ELCID0615 ** MEIORAREMOS PCSADAS ACUENOS & ACAUALLOS.
 5227 5ELCID0661 ALCS DE MYC %ID ** LES TUELLEN EL AGUA.
 5801 5ELCID0732 CAYEN EN VN PCCC DE LCGAR MOROS MUERTOS MILL & CCC **.
 6485 5ELCID0827 AGORA DAUAN %EUADA, ** LA NOCH ERA ENTRADA,
 6549 5ELCID0836 ** ES AGUISADO, MA@ANAS FUE MINAYA,
 7283 5ELCID0934 ** ALBARFANEZ, BIUADES MUCHOS DIAS  . . .
 7689 5ELCID0985 ** CAUALLERCS, A PART FAZED LA GANAN%IA;
 8448 5ELCID1074 FOLGEDES, ** MYO %ID, SCDES EN UUESTRO SALUO.
 8628 5ELCID1096 ** VIE MYO %ID QUE DICS LE YUA VALIENDO.
 8985 5ELCID1143 MOROS SCN MUCHOS, ** QUIEREN RECONBRAR.
 9608 5ELCID1221 ** FOLGAUA MYC %ID CON TOCAS SUS CONPA@AS;
 9825 5ELCID1247 DE QUE SCN PAGADOS; EL AMOR DE MY %ID ** LO YUAN PROUANDO.
12983 5ELCID1647 ** MUGIER ONDRADA, NCN AYADES PESAR
15595 5ELCID1977 COMMO ELLOS TENIEN, CER%ER LES ** LA GANA%IA,
15987 5ELCID2027 LEUANTACOS EN PIE, ** %ID CAMPEADOR,
18341 5ELCID2321 ** EN ESTA BATALLA A ENTRAR AEREMOS NOS;
18659 5ELCID2361 AQUI LEGO MYNAYA ALBARFANEZ: OYD, ** %ID, CANPEADOR LEAL
19258 5ELCID2437 COFIA SCBRE LCS PELCS FRCNZIDA DELLA ** QUANTO.
21163 5ELCID2689 ** MOUIERON DEL ANSSARERA LOS YFANTES DE CARRION,
21552 5ELCID2740 ** LO SIENTEN ELLAS EN LCS SOS CORA%ONES.
21843 5ELCID2780 ** PRIMAS, LAS MIS PRIMAS, DON ELUIRA & DO@A SOL,
23903 5ELCID3045 MER%ED, ** REY, SI EL CRIADOR UOS SALUE
24899 5ELCID3171 MER%ED, ** REY DCN ALFCNSSO, SCDES NUESTRO SE@OR
25627 5ELCID3263 QUANDO LAS NCN QUERIECES, ** CANES TRAYDORES,
25685 5ELCID3271 MER%ED, ** REY, EL MEIOR DE TOCA ESPA@A
26560 5ELCID3390 DIXO EL REY ALFCNSSC: CALLE ** ESTA RAZON.
26874 5ELCID3433 DEZIR CUERRIA ** QUANTC DELC MYO.
```

WORD C# PREFIX CONTEXT

YA (CON'T)

27403 5ELCID3501 TALES ** QUE PRENDEN, TALES YA QUE NON.
27407 5ELCID3501 TALES YA QUE PRENDEN, TALES ** QUE NON.
27780 5ELCID3545 TROCIDA ES LA NOCHE, ** QUIEBRAN LOS ALBORES.
28279 5ELCID3610 SORTEAUAN LES EL CAMPO, ** LES PARTIEN EL SOL,
28360 5ELCID3621 TODOS TRES POR TRES ** JUNTADOS SON:
WORD #4432 OCCURS 51 TIMES.
INDEX OF DIVERSIFICATION = 559.72 WITH STANDARD DEVIATION OF 684.85

YAGUE
5789 5ELCID0731 LOS MOROS LAMAN MAFOMAT & LOS CHRISTIANOS SANTI *****.
8943 5ELCID1138 ENEL NOMBRE DEL CRIADOR & DEL APOSTOL SANTI *****,
13336 5ELCID1690 *****;
WORD #4433 OCCURS 3 TIMES.

YAGUO
22963 5ELCID2925 FASTA DENTRO EN SANTI ***** DE TODO ES SE@OR,
23376 5ELCID2977 ENBIA SUS CARTAS PORA LEON & A SANTI *****,
WORD #4434 OCCURS 2 TIMES.

YAL
4483 5ELCID0570 LOS DE ALCO%ER A MYO %ID *** DAN PARIAS DE GRADO
9737 5ELCID1238 *** CRE%E LA BARBA & VALE ALLONGANDO:
10294 5ELCID1303 AESTE DON IERONIMO *** OTORGAN POR OBISPO;
12312 5ELCID1563 CA DELO QUE MAS AMAUA *** VIENE EL MANDADO.
WORD #4435 OCCURS 4 TIMES.

YAN
4027 5ELCID0512 SOS CAUALLEROS *** ARRIBAN%A,
WORD #4436 OCCURS 1 TIMES.

YAS
5560 5ELCID0700 LAS AZES DE LOS MOROS *** MUEUEN ADELANT,
6177 5ELCID0787 *** TORNAN LOS DEL QUE EN BUEN ORA NASCO.
8130 5ELCID1036 QUANDO ESTO OYO EL CONDE, *** YUA ALEGRANDO:
17800 5ELCID2252 HYA %ERCA DELOS XV DIAS *** VAN LOS FIJOS DALGO.
19204 5ELCID2429 CON ESTAS GANAN%IAS *** YUAN TORNANDO;
WORD #4437 OCCURS 5 TIMES.
INDEX OF DIVERSIFICATION = 3410.00 WITH STANDARD DEVIATION OF 4208.54

YAURIE
4136 5ELCID0526 E QUE SERIE RETENEDOR, MAS NON ****** AGUA.
WORD #4438 OCCURS 1 TIMES.

YAVEDES
9716 5ELCID1235 LAS NUEUAS DEL CAUALLERO ******* DO LEGAUAN.
WORD #4439 OCCURS 1 TIMES.

YAZEN
4883 5ELCID0618 LOS MOROS ***** MUERTOS, DE BIUOS POCOS VEO.
6162 5ELCID0785 TANTOS MOROS ***** MUERTOS QUE POCOS BIUOS A DEXADOS,
WORD #4440 OCCURS 2 TIMES.

YAZIES
18020 5ELCID2280 ****** EN VN ESCA@O, DURMIE EL CAMPEADOR,
WORD #4441 OCCURS 1 TIMES.

YD
3504 5ELCID0442 VOS CON LOS CC ** UOS EN ALGARA; ALA VAYA ALBARABAREZ,
5053 5ELCID0638 NON LO DETARDEDES, LOS DOS ** PORA ALLA,
7021 5ELCID0898 SI NULLA DUBDA ** A MYO %ID BUSCAR GANAN%IA.
10059 5ELCID1274 DAR LE QUIERO C CAUALLOS, & UOS ** GELOS LEUAR;
10896 5ELCID1379 HYA UOS YDES, MYNAYA?, ** ALA GRA%IA DEL CRIADOR
18819 5ELCID2381 AFE LOS MOROS A OIO, ** LOS ENSAYAR.
WORD #4442 OCCURS 6 TIMES.
INDEX OF DIVERSIFICATION = 3062.00 WITH STANDARD DEVIATION OF 2831.36

YDA
2158 5ELCID0271 YO LO VEO QUE ESTADES UOS EN ***
WORD #4443 OCCURS 1 TIMES.

YDES
1374 5ELCID0176 DE CASTIELLA UOS **** PORA LAS YENTES ESTRANAS.
8401 5ELCID1068 HYA UOS ****, CONDE, AGUISA DE MUY FRANCO,
10277 5ELCID1301 VOS, QUANDO **** A CASTIELLA, LEUAREDES BUENOS MANDADOS.
10894 5ELCID1379 HYA UOS ****, MYNAYA?, YD ALA GRA%IA DEL CRIADOR
WORD #4444 OCCURS 4 TIMES.

YDO
6818 5ELCID0871 *** ES A CASTIELLA ALBARFANEZ MINAYA,
WORD #4445 OCCURS 1 TIMES.

YDOS
7454 5ELCID0956 LOS MANDADOS SON **** ATODAS PARTES;
21300 5ELCID2707 ADELANT ERAN **** LOS DE CRIAZON:
21338 5ELCID2712 TODOS ERAN ****, ELLOS IIIJ SOLOS SON,
WORD #4446 OCCURS 3 TIMES.

YE
4148 5ELCID0528 BUSCAR NOS ** EL REY ALFONSSO CON TODA SU MESNADA.
15361 5ELCID1945 QUERER UOS ** VER & DAR UOS SU AMOR,
WORD #4447 OCCURS 2 TIMES.

YEDES
5373 5ELCID0678 ONDRASTES UOS, MINAYA, CA AUER UOS LO ***** DE FAR.
15370 5ELCID1946 ACORDAR UOS ***** DESPUES ATODO LO MEIOR.
WORD #4448 OCCURS 2 TIMES.

YELLAS
16459 5ELCID2087 ENTRE YO ****** EN UUESTRA MER%ED SOMOS NOS,
WORD #4449 OCCURS 1 TIMES.

WORD C# PREFIX CONTEXT

```
YELMO           6C41 5ELCID0766 LAS CARBONCLAS DEL ***** ECHO CELAS APARTE,
                6047 5ELCIDC767 CORTOL EL *****, QUE LEGO ALA CARNE;
               19151 5ELCID2422 LAS CARBONCLAS DEL ***** TOLLICAS GELA HA,
               19157 5ELCID2423 CORTOL EL ***** &, LIBRADO TODO LO HAL,
               28601 5ELCID3652 LAS MONCLURAS DEL ***** TOCAS CELAS CORTAUA,
        WORD #445C OCCURS   5 TIMES.
           INDEX OF DIVERSIFICATION =  5639.00 WITH STANDARD DEVIATION OF  6674.97

YELMOS         19011 5ELCID2405 TANTAS CABE%AS CON ****** QUE POR EL CAMPO CAEN,
        WORD #4451 OCCURS   1 TIMES.

YEMOS          2C964 5ELCID2663 QUANTA RIQUIZA TIENE AUER LA ***** NOS.
        WORD #4452 OCCURS   1 TIMES.

YEN              154 5ELCID0021 CONBIDAR LE *** DE GRADO, MAS NINGUNO NON OSAUA:
                 906 5ELCID0116 AQUELAS NON LAS PUEDE LEUAR, SINON, SER *** VENTADAS;
                1254 5ELCID0161 QUE SOBRE AQUELAS ARCHAS DAR LE *** VJ %IENTOS MARCOS
                9856 5ELCID1250 QUE SIS PUDIESSEN YR, FER LO *** DE GRADO.
        WORD #4453 OCCURS   4 TIMES.

YENEGO         26590 5ELCID3394 AL VNO DIZEN CIARRA & AL OTRO ****** SIMENEZ,
               26757 5ELCID3417 AUOS, CIARRA, & AUOS, ****** XIMENEZ,
        WORD #4454 OCCURS   2 TIMES.

YENTE           7053 5ELCIDC901 MIENTRA QUE SEA EL PUEBLO DE MOROS & DELA ***** CHRISTIANA,
        WORD #4455 OCCURS   1 TIMES.

YENTES           228 5ELCID0029 GRANDE DUELO AUIEN LAS ****** CHRISTIANAS;
                1377 5ELCIDC176 DE CASTIELLA UOS YDES PORA LAS ****** ESTRANAS.
                3083 5ELCID0388 SI VIEREDES ****** VENIR POR CONNUSCO YR,
                3137 5ELCIDC395 GRANDES ****** SELE ACOIEN ESSA NOCH DE TODAS PARTES.
                3200 5ELCID0403 VANSSELE ACOGIENDO ****** DE TODAS PARTES.
                3307 5ELCIDC417 MANDO UER SUS ****** MYO %ID EL CAMPEADOR:
                3668 5ELCID0463 LAS ****** DE FUERA TODAS SON DE RAMADAS.
                5195 5ELCID0657 CRECEN ESTOS VIRTOS, CA ****** SON SOBEIANAS.
                6582 5ELCIDC840 MOROS DE LAS FRONTERAS & VNAS ****** ESTRANAS;
                7108 5ELCIDC909 CON TODAS SUS ****** FIZO VNA TRASNOCHADA;
                9429 5ELCID1199 GRANDES ****** SE LE ACOIEN DELA BUENA CHRISTIANDAD.
               11380 5ELCID1440 MUCHAS ****** SELE ACOGEN, PENSSO DE CAUALGAR,
               12858 5ELCID1631 FINCARON LAS TIENDAS, & POSAN LAS ****** DESCREYDAS.
               13207 5ELCID1674 PRESTAS SON LAS MES@ADAS DE LAS ****** CHRISTIANAS,
               13415 5ELCID1700 NOS DETARDAN DE ADOBASSE ESSAS ****** CHRISTIANAS.
               13998 5ELCID1773 CONTODAS ESTAS ****** ESCRIUIENDO & CONTANDO;
               14219 5ELCID1799 ALEGRES SON POR VALEN%IA LAS ****** CHRISTIANAS,
               17115 5ELCID2166 GRANDES SON LAS ****** QUE VAN CONEL CANPEADOR.
               18526 5ELCID2344 ESTO VAN DIZIENDO & LAS ****** SE ALEGANDO,
               23709 5ELCID3020 CON GRANDES ****** EL REY CAUALGO
               28261 5ELCID3608 TODAS LAS ****** ESCONBRARON ADERREDOR,
               28515 5ELCID3641 ASSI LO TENIEN LAS ****** QUE MAL FERIDO ES DE MUERT.
        WORD #4456 OCCURS  22 TIMES.
           INDEX OF DIVERSIFICATION =  1346.00 WITH STANDARD DEVIATION OF  1427.71

YERBAS         15946 5ELCID2022 LAS ****** DEL CAMPO A DIENTES LAS TOMO,
        WORD #4457 OCCURS   1 TIMES.

YERMO           3100 5ELCID0390 CA EN ***** O EN POBLADO PODER NOS HAN ALCAN%AR.
        WORD #4458 OCCURS   1 TIMES.

YERNOS         16623 5ELCID2106 LOS ****** & LAS FIJAS TODOS UUESTROS FIJOS SON:
               16772 5ELCID2123 EVAD AQUI UUESTROS FIJOS, QUANDO UUESTROS ****** SON;
               18C15 5ELCID2279 CON EL AMOS SUS ****** LOS YFANTES DE CARRION.
               18211 5ELCID2304 MYO %ID POR SOS ****** DEMANDO & NOLOS FALLO;
               18382 5ELCID2326 EUADES QUE PAUOR HAN UUESTROS ****** TAN OSADOS,
               18428 5ELCID2332 DIOS UOS SALUE, ******, YFANTES DE CARRION,
               18516 5ELCID2343 AMOS LOS MYOS ****** BUENOS SERAN EN CAPO.
               18592 5ELCID2353 MYOS ****** AMOS ADOS, LA COSA QUE MUCHO AMO,
               19295 5ELCID2443  VENIDES, MYOS ******, MYOS FIJOS SODES AMOS
               19416 5ELCID2460 EUUESTROS ****** AQUI SON ENSAYADOS,
               19477 5ELCID2468 LOS ****** DE MYO %ID QUANDO ESTE AUER TOMARON
               19569 5ELCID2479 QUE LIDIARAN COMIGO EN CAMPO MYOS ****** AMOS ADOS;
               19688 5ELCID2496 ESON MYOS ****** YFANTES DE CARRION;
               19781 5ELCID2507 GRANDES SON LOS GOZOS DE SUS ****** AMOS ADOS:
               19864 5ELCID2519 EUADES AQUI, ******, LA MI MUGIER DE PRO,
               20338 5ELCID2580 CON QUE RIQUEZA ENBIO MIOS ****** AMOS ADOS.
               2C716 5ELCID2630 RESPONDIEN LOS ******: ASSI LO MANDE DIOS
               2C763 5ELCID2637 RE%IBA A MYOS ****** COMMO EL PUDIER MEIOR;
               22709 5ELCID2894 DE MYOS ****** DE CARRION DIOS ME FAGA VENGAR
               24799 5ELCID3158 DEN ME MIS ESPADAS QUANDO MYOS ****** NON SON.
               25180 5ELCID3206 DEN ME MIS AUERES, QUANDO MYOS ****** NON SON.
               26215 5ELCID3342 DEMANDO POR SUS ******, NINGUNO NON FALLO
        WORD #4459 OCCURS  22 TIMES.
           INDEX OF DIVERSIFICATION =   455.76 WITH STANDARD DEVIATION OF   614.87
```

```
WORD                    C#  PREFIX                              CONTEXT

YES                 27802 5ELCID3548 DEMAS SCBRE TCDOS *** EL REY CCN ALFONSSO,
          WORD #4460 OCCURS    1 TIMES.

YFAN%ON             27222 5ELCID3479 QUE NON PRENDAN FUER%A DE CONCE NIN DE *******.
          WORD #4461 OCCURS    1 TIMES.

YFAN%ONES           16337 5ELCID2072 OYD ME, LAS ESCUELLAS, CUENDES & *********
                    23272 5ELCID2964 QUE ALLA ME VAYAN CUENDES & *********,
                    25889 5ELCID3298 CA NON PERTENE%IEN FIJAS DE *********.
          WORD #4462 OCCURS    3 TIMES.

YFANTE              26595 5ELCID3395 EL VNO ES ****** DE NAUARRA
                    26601 5ELCID3396 E EL OTRO ****** DE ARAGON;
                    28693 5ELCID3664 ESORA EL ****** TAN GRANDES VCZES DAUA:
          WORD #4463 OCCURS    3 TIMES.

YFANTES             14506 5ELCID1835 LOS ******* DE CARRION, SABET, YS A%ERTARON,
                    15229 5ELCID1928 DE DAR SUS FIJAS ALCS ******* DE CARRION,
                    15300 5ELCID1937 E PIDEN ME MIS FIJAS PCRA LCS ******* DE CARRION.
                    15620 5ELCID1981 LOS ******* DE CARRION LIEUAN GRANDES CONPA@AS.
                    16370 5ELCID2076 QUE LAS DEDES POR MUGIERES ALOS ******* DE CARRION.
                    16438 5ELCID2084 DE GRANDES NUEUAS SON LCS ******* DE CARRION,
                    16541 5ELCID2096 QUEM DACES UUESTRAS FIJAS PORA LOS ******* DE CARRION.
                    16560 5ELCID2098 E DOLAS POR VELADAS ALOS ******* DE CARRION.
                    16584 5ELCID2101 AFELLOS EN UUESTRAS MANCS LOS ******* DE CARRION,
                    16753 5ELCID2121 EL REY ALOS ******* ALAS MANOS LES TOMO,
                    16882 5ELCID2136 PRENDELLAS CON UUESTRAS MANOS & DALDAS ALOS *******,
                    17079 5ELCID2162 SEREMOS ALAS BCDAS DELOS ******* DE CARRION
                    17159 5ELCID2171 QUE SOPIESSEN SCS MA@AS DE LOS ******* DE CARRION.
                    17186 5ELCID2174 GRANT CNDRA LES DAN ALOS ******* DE CARRION.
                    17220 5ELCID2178 DAD LES VN REYAL & ALCS ******* DE CARRION,
                    17587 5ELCID2225 ALCS ******* DE CARRICN DAC LAS CON UUESTRA MANO,
                    17617 5ELCID2229 ALCS ******* DE CARRION MINAYA VA FABLANDO:
                    17748 5ELCID2246 LOS ******* DE CARRION BIEN AN CAUALGADO.
                    17946 5ELCID2271 HY MORAN LOS ******* BIEN CERCA DE DOS A@OS,
                    18017 5ELCID2279 CON EL AMOS SUS YERNCS LCS ******* DE CARRION.
                    18253 5ELCID2309 MUCHOS TOUIERCN POR ENBAYDCS LOS ******* DE CARRION,
                    18314 5ELCID2317 MAS, SABED, DE CUER LES PESA ALOS ******* DE CARRION;
                    18429 5ELCID2332 DIOS UCS SALUE, YERNCS, ******* DE CARRION,
                    18618 5ELCID2356 QUE OY LOS ******* AMI PCR AMC NON ABRAN;
                    19689 5ELCID2496 ESCN MYCS YERNOS ******* DE CARRION;
                    19803 5ELCID2510 MUCHOS TIENEN POR RICCS LOS ******* DE CARRION.
                    19838 5ELCID2515 QUANDO ENTRARCN LCS ******* DE CARRION,
                    20565 5ELCID2611 HYA SALIEN LOS ******* DE VALEN%IA LA CLARA,
                    20827 5ELCID2644 PIENSSAN SE DE YR LOS ******* DE CARRION;
                    20841 5ELCID2646 AGUIJAN QUANTO PUEDEN ******* DE CARRION;
                    20906 5ELCID2655 BUENOS SE@OS CAUALLCS ALOS ******* DE CARRION.
                    21013 5ELCID2670 TU MUERT OY COSSEIAR ALOS ******* DE CARRION.
                    21035 5ELCID2673 ARMAS YUA TENIENDC, PARCS ANTE LOS *******;
                    21042 5ELCID2674 DELO QUE EL MORO DIXO ALOS ******* NON PLAZE:
                    21050 5ELCID2675  DEZID ME, QUE UCS FIZ, ******* DE CARRION
                    21168 5ELCID2689 YA MOUIERON DEL ANSSARERA LOS ******* DE CARRION,
                    21224 5ELCID2697 ENTRADCS SCN LOS ******* AL ROBREDO DE CORPES,
                    21256 5ELCID2701 MANDAN FINCAR LA TIENDA ******* DE CARRION,
                    21308 5ELCID2708 ASSI LO MANDARCN LOS ******* DE CARRION,
                    21347 5ELCID2713 TANTO MAL CCMIDIERON LOS ******* DE CARRION;
                    21515 5ELCID2735 ESSORA LES CONPIE%AN ADAR LCS ******* DE CARRION;
                    21666 5ELCID2754 LOS ******* DE CARRION ENEL RCBREDO DE CORPES
                    21728 5ELCID2763 ALABANDOS YUAN LOS ******* DE CARRICN.
                    21788 5ELCID2771 C CUE AN FECHO LCS ******* DE CARRION.
                    21817 5ELCID2775 VANSSE LOS *******, AGUIJAN AESPOLON.
                    21857 5ELCID2781 MAL SE ENSAYARCN LOS ******* DE CARRION
                    21956 5ELCID2793 DE QUE NCN ME FALLAREN LCS ******* DE CARRION,
                    22176 5ELCID2824 ALLABANDOS SEYAN LOS ******* DE CARRION.
                    22231 5ELCID2831 QUANDO TAL CNDRA MEAN DADA LOS ******* DE CARRION;
                    22245 5ELCID2833 NON LA LCGRARAN LCS ******* DE CARRION;
                    22814 5ELCID2906 DESTA DESONDRA QUE MEAN FECHA LOS ******* DE CARRION
                    22887 5ELCID2915 COMMO AYA DERECHO DE ******* DE CARRION,
                    23072 5ELCID2939 CASASTES SUS FIJAS CON ******* DE CARRION,
                    23095 5ELCID2942 CUEMO NCS HAN ABILTADCS ******* DE CARRION:
                    23173 5ELCID2952 QUE AYA MYC %ID DERECHO DE ******* DE CARRION.
                    23207 5ELCID2956 CA YO CASE SUS FIJAS CCN ******* DE CARRION;
                    23277 5ELCID2965 MANDARE COMMO Y VAYAN ******* DE CARRION,
                    23439 5ELCID2985 HYA LES VA PESANDO ALSO ******* DE CARRION,
                    23522 5ELCID2995 HYA LO VIERON QUE ES AFER LCS ******* DE CARRION,
                    23549 5ELCID2999 AQUESTE CONSSEIC LOS ******* DE CARRION.
                    23611 5ELCID3007 EL CONDE DCN GAR%IA CON ******* DE CARRION,
                    24156 5ELCID3080 SI DESOBRA BUSCAREN ******* DE CARRION,
                    24422 5ELCID3113 NIN TODOS LCS DEL BANDO DE ******* DE CARRION.
                    24524 5ELCID3126 NOL PUEDEN CATAR DE VERGUEN%A ******* DE CARRION.
                    24588 5ELCID3133 QUE RE%IBA DERECHC DE ******* DE CARRION.
                    24680 5ELCID3144 SABREMCS QUE RESPCNDEN ******* DE CARRION.
                    25144 5ELCID3202 OTRA RENCURA HE DE ******* DE CARRION:
                    25187 5ELCID3207 AQUI VERIEDES QUEXAR SE ******* DE CARRION
                    25203 5ELCID3209 ESSORA RESPCNDEN ******* DE CARRION:
```

WORD C# PREFIX CONTEXT

YES (CON'T)

25272 5ELCID3217 ESSORA SALIEN A PARTE ******* DE CARRION;
25287 5ELCID3219 ESPESOS LOS HAN ******* DE CARRION.
25383 5ELCID3232 ENTRAMOS MELOS DIERON LOS ******* DE CARRION.
25455 5ELCID3241 HYA VIERON QUE ES AFER LOS ******* DE CARRION.
25493 5ELCID3247 PAGARON LOS ******* AL QUE EN BUEN ORA NASCO;
25564 5ELCID3256 DELOS ******* DE CARRION QUEM DESONDRARON TAN MAL,
25582 5ELCID3258 DEZID QUE UOS MERE%I, *******, EN JUEGO O EN VERO
26777 5ELCID3420 PORA LOS ******* DE NAUARRA & DE ARAGON,
26838 5ELCID3428 MAS NON PLAZE ALOS ******* DE CARRION.
26904 5ELCID3437 CA GRAND RENCURA HE DE ******* DE CARRION.
26986 5ELCID3448 LOS ******* DE NAUARRA & DE ARAGON;
27132 5ELCID3467 LUEGO FABLARON ******* DE CARRION:
27265 5ELCID3485 PRISIERON EL JUIZIO ******* DE CARRION.
27712 5ELCID3537 DOS DIAS ATENDIERON A ******* DE CARRION.
27839 5ELCID3552 EN OTRO LOGAR SE ARMAN LOS ******* DE CARRION,
27879 5ELCID3557 MUCHO ERAN REPENTIDOS LOS ******* POR QUANTO DADAS SON;
27916 5ELCID3562 LEUAD & SALID ALCAMPO, ******* DE CARRION,
27962 5ELCID3568 HYA SEUAN REPINTIENDO ******* DE CARRION,
28028 5ELCID3577 AQUI TIENEN SU VANDO LOS ******* DE CARRION,
28128 5ELCID3591 FEUOS DELA OTRA PART LOS ******* DE CARRION,
28171 5ELCID3596 OYD QUE UOS DIGO, ******* DE CARRION:
28226 5ELCID3603 HYA LES VA PESANDO ALOS ******* DE CARRION.
28301 5ELCID3612 DESI VINIEN LOS DE MYO %ID ALOS ******* DE CARRION,
28305 5ELCID3613 ELLOS ******* DE CARRION ALOS DE CAMPEADOR;
28986 5ELCID3702 POR MALOS LOS DEXARON ALOS ******* DE CARRION,
29010 5ELCID3705 GRANT ES LA BILTAN%A DE ******* DE CARRION.
29033 5ELCID3708 DEXEMOS NOS DE PLEYTOS DE ******* DE CARRION,
WORD #4464 OCCURS 96 TIMES.
INDEX OF DIVERSIFICATION = 151.92 WITH STANDARD DEVIATION OF 219.89

YFFANTES
2136 5ELCID0269 FEM ANTE UOS YO & UUESTRAS FFIJAS, ******** SON & DE DIAS CHICAS,
10101 5ELCID1279 LA MUGIER DE MYO %ID & SUS FIJAS LAS ********
10837 5ELCID1372 AQUI ENTRARON EN FABLA LOS ******** DE CARRION:
10939 5ELCID1385 LOS ******** DE CARRION DANDO YUAN CONPA@A A MINAYA ALBARFANEZ:
10995 5ELCID1391 HYDO ES MYNAYA, TORNANSSE LOS ********.
14866 5ELCID1879 DELOS ******** DE CARRION YO UOS QUIERO CONTAR,
15039 5ELCID1901 DIEGO & FERRANDO, LOS ******** DE CARRION,
15075 5ELCID1906 POR CONSSAGRAR CON LOS ******** DE CARRION.
15576 5ELCID1975 LOS ******** DE CARRIO MUCHO ALEGRES ANDAN,
16177 5ELCID2052 ESSORA SELE OMILLAN LOS ******** DE CARRION:
16496 5ELCID2091 LUEGO SE LEUANTARON LOS ******** DE CARRION,
17470 5ELCID2210 POR LOS ******** DE CARRION ESSORA ENBIARON,
17477 5ELCID2211 CAUALGAN LOS ********, ADELANT ADELINAUAN AL PALA%IO,
19998 5ELCID2537 TAN MAL SE CONSSEIARON ESTOS ******** AMOS.
20363 5ELCID2583 ATORGADO LO HAN ESTO LOS ******** DE CARRION.
20389 5ELCID2587 HYA MANDAUAN CARGAR ******** DE CARRION.
24820 5ELCID3161 ESSORA SALIEN APARTE ******** DE CARRION,
WORD #4465 OCCURS 17 TIMES.
INDEX OF DIVERSIFICATION = 1416.75 WITH STANDARD DEVIATION OF 2230.66

YFINCAS
21313 5ELCID2709 QUE NON ******* NINGUNO, MUGIER NIN VARON,
WORD #4466 OCCURS 1 TIMES.

YGAMOS
567 5ELCID0072 ESTA NOCH ****** & UAYMOS NOS AL MATINO,
WORD #4467 OCCURS 1 TIMES.

YMOS
17550 5ELCID2220 PUES QUE AFAZER LO AUEMOS, POR QUE LO **** TARDANDO?
WORD #4468 OCCURS 1 TIMES.

YNCAMOS
676 5ELCID0086 ******* LAS DARENA, CA BIEN SERAN PESADAS,
WORD #4469 OCCURS 1 TIMES.

YNDOS
6531 5ELCID0833 SI NON, DO SOPIEREDES QUE SOMOS, ***** CONSEGUIR.
WORD #4470 OCCURS 1 TIMES.

YNEGO
26796 5ELCID3422 LEUANTOS EN PIE OIARRA & ***** XIMENEZ,
WORD #4471 OCCURS 1 TIMES.

YNFIERNOS
2841 5ELCID0358 ENEL MONUMENTO RESU%ITEST, FUST ALOS *********,
WORD #4472 OCCURS 1 TIMES.

YNOIOS
2100 5ELCID0264 ANTEL CAMPEADOR DO@A XIMENA FINCO LOS ****** AMOS,
10399 5ELCID1318 FINCO SOS ****** ANTE TODEL PUEBLO,
13888 5ELCID1759 DELANT EL CAMPEADOR LOS ****** FINCARON:
14571 5ELCID1843 ANTEL REY ALFONSSO LOS ****** FINCADOS,
15937 5ELCID2021 LOS ****** & LAS MANOS EN TIERRA LOS FINCO,
20432 5ELCID2593 FINCARON LOS ****** ANTEL %ID CAMPEADOR:
23030 5ELCID2934 DELANT EL REY FINCO LOS ****** AQUEL MU@O GUSTIOZ,
WORD #4473 OCCURS 7 TIMES.
INDEX OF DIVERSIFICATION = 3487.33 WITH STANDARD DEVIATION OF 2732.13

YNOS
1632 5ELCID0209 EN SAN PERO DE CARDENA **** CANTE EL GALLO;
WORD #4474 OCCURS 1 TIMES.

WORD C# PREFIX CONTEXT

Y@OIOS 422 5ELCID0053 FINCO LOS ******, DE CCRA%ON ROGAUA.
WORD #4475 CCCURS 1 TIMES.

YO
586 5ELCID0074 EN YRA DEL RAY ALFFCNSSO ** SERE METIDO.
629 5ELCID0080 SI ** BIUO, DCBLAR UOS HE LA SCLDADA.
648 5ELCID0082 BIEN LC VEDES QUE ** NC TRAYO AUER, & HUEBOS ME SERIE
750 5ELCID0095 ** MAS NON PUEDO & AMYDCS LO FAGO.
1C99 5ELCID0141 DIXO MARTIN ANTCLINEZ: ** CESSO ME PAGO.
1309 5ELCID0168 ** YRE CCN UUSC, QUE ADUGAMOS LOS MARCOS,
1400 5ELCID0179 %ID, BESO UUESTRA MANO ENDCN QUE LA ** AYA.
1484 5ELCID0190 **, QUE ESTC UCS GANE, BIEN MERE%IAS CAL%AS.
1616 5ELCID0207 VOS VJ %IENTOS & ** XXX HE GANADOS.
1764 5ELCID0225 ESTO & ** EN DEBDC QUE FAGA Y CANTAR MILL MISSAS.
1964 5ELCID0249 ** ADOBARE CON DUCHC PORA MI & PORA MIS VASSALLOS;
1985 5ELCID0251 SI ** ALGUN DIA VISGUIER, SERUOS HAN DOBLADOS.
2055 5ELCID0259 BIEN LAS ABASTAD, ** ASSI UCS LO MANDO;
2068 5ELCID0260 POR VN MARCHC QUE DESPENDADES AL MONESTERIO DARE ** QUATRO.
2132 5ELCID0269 FEM ANTE UCS ** & UUESTRAS FFIJAS, YFFANTES SON & DE DIAS CHICAS,
2149 5ELCID0270 CON AQUESTAS MYS DUE@AS DE QUIEN SO ** SERUIDA.
2151 5ELCID0271 ** LO VEO QUE ESTADES UCS EN YDA
2215 5ELCID0279 COMMO ALA MI ALMA ** TANTC UOS QUERIA.
2228 5ELCID0281 ** YRE & UCS FINCAREDES REMANIDA.
2372 5ELCID0300 ** RUEGC ADIOS & AL PADRE SPIRITAL,
2390 5ELCID0302 EN ANTES QUE ** MUERA, ALGUN BIEN UOS PUEDA FAR:
3562 5ELCID0449 E ** CCN LC C AQUI FINCARE EN LA %AGA,
3572 5ELCID0450 TERNE ** CASTEICN DON ABREMCS GRAND EN PARA.
3866 5ELCID0490 DO ** UCS ENBIAS BIEN AERIA TAL ESPERAN%A.
3905 5ELCID0496 ** UOS LA SUELTA & AUELLC CUITADO.
3923 5ELCID0498 FATA QUE ** ME PAGE SCBRE MIO BUEN CAUALLO,
4165 5ELCID0530 LO QUE ** DIXIER NCN LC TENGADES AMAL:
5479 5ELCID0691 MAS NON AGUIJEDES CCN ELLA, SI ** NON UOS LO MANDAR.
5585 5ELCID0703 NON DERANCHE NINGUNC FATA QUE ** LO MANDE.
5715 5ELCID0721 ** SO RUY DIAZ, EL %ID CAMPEADCR DE BIUAR
6420 5ELCID0819 DIXO MYNAYA ALBARFANEZ: ESTC FARE ** DE GRADO.
6465 5ELCID0825 SI LES ** VISQUIER, SERAN DUENAS RICAS.
6953 5ELCID0889 MAS DEL %ID CAMPEADOR ** NCN UOS DIGO NADA.
7539 5ELCID0966 MAS QUANDO EL MELO BUSCA, YR GELO HE ** DEMANDAR.
8063 5ELCID1029 QUE ** DEXAR ME MORIR, QUE NON QUIERO COMER.
8107 5ELCID1034 E SI UCS CCMIEREDES, DON ** SEA PAGADO,
8143 5ELCID1038 TANTO QUANTO ** BIUA, SERE DENT MARAUILLADO.
8170 5ELCID1041 MAS QUANTO AUEDES PERDIDO & ** GANE EN CANPO,
8285 5ELCID1054 SI BIEN NON CCMEDES, CCNDE, DON ** SEA PAGADO,
8745 5ELCID1112 ** FIO PCR DICS QUE EN NUESTRO PRO ENADRAN.
8885 5ELCID1132 ** CON LOS %IENTC ENTRARE DEL OTRA PART,
8956 5ELCID1140 CA ** SO RUYDIAZ, MYC %ID EL DE BIUAR
10538 5ELCID1335 FEUOS AQUI LAS SE@AS, VERDAD UOS DIGO **:
10769 5ELCID1363 POR QUE LOS DESEREDE, TODO GELO SUELTO **;
11150 5ELCID1411 SEREMOS ** & SU MUGIER & SUS FIJAS QUE EL A
11599 5ELCID1470 E ** FINCARE EN VALEN%IA, QUE MUCHO COSTADOM HA;
11613 5ELCID1472 ** FFINCARE EN VALEN%IA, CA LA TENGC POR HEREDAD.
12588 5ELCID1597 AFE ME AQUI, SE@CR, ** UUESTRAS FIJAS & AMAS,
12667 5ELCID1607 EN ESTA HEREDAD QUE UCS ** HE GANADA.
12878 5ELCID1634 TODO EL BIEN QUE ** HE, TODC LO TENGO DELANT:
13061 5ELCID1656 CON DIOS A QUESTA LID ** LA HE DE ARRANCAR.
13383 5ELCID1696 QUANDO UOS LOS FUEREDES FERIR, ENTRARE ** DEL OTRA PART;
13448 5ELCID1705 PRENDOL ** LOS PECADCS, & DIOS LE ABRA EL ALMA.
13487 5ELCID1709 LAS FERIDAS PRIMERAS QUE LAS AYA ** OTORGADAS.
13804 5ELCID1749 VOS TENIENDO VALEN%IA, & ** VEN%I EL CAMPO;
14300 5ELCID1809 CON CAUALLOS DESTA QUINTA QUE ** HE GANADA,
14869 5ELCID1879 DELOS YFFANTES DE CARRICN ** UOS QUIERO CONTAR,
14956 5ELCID1891 EFAZIENDO ** HA EL MAL, & EL AMI GRAND PRO,
15058 5ELCID1903 SED BUENOS MENSSAGERCS, & RUEGO UOS LO **
15283 5ELCID1935 CCN GRAND AFAN GANE LC QUE HE **;
16389 5ELCID2078 ELLOS UCS LAS PIDEN & MANDC UCS LO **.
16458 5ELCID2087 ENTRE ** YELLAS EN UUESTRA MER%ED SOMOS NOS,
16480 5ELCID2089 DAD LAS AQUI QUISIEREDES UCS, CA ** PAGADO SO.
16595 5ELCID2102 ELLOS VAYAN CON UUSCO, CADA QUEN ME TORNO **.
16604 5ELCID2103 TREZIENTOS MARCCS DE PLATA EN AYUDA LES DO **,
16664 5ELCID2110 VOS CASADES MIS FIJAS, CA NCN GELAS DO **.
16831 5ELCID2131 ** UOS PIDO MER%ED AUCS, REY NATURAL:
16860 5ELCID2134 NON GELAS DARE ** CCN MI MANO, NIN DED NON SE ALABARAN.
16885 5ELCID2137 ASSI COMMO ** LAS PRENDO DAQUENT, COMMO SI FOSSE DELANT,
17232 5ELCID2179 VOS CON ELLOS SED, QUE ASSI UCS LO MANDO **.
17386 5ELCID2199 MAS BIEN SABET VERDAD QUE NON LO LEUANTE **:
17404 5ELCID2202 QUE ** NULLA COSA NOL SCPE DEZIR DE NO.
17428 5ELCID2204 BIEN MELO CREADES, QUE EL UCS CASA, CA NON **.
17557 5ELCID2221 VENIT ACA, ALBARFANEZ, EL QUE ** QUIERO & AMO
17606 5ELCID2227 ESTOZ DIXO MINAYA: ESTC FARE ** DE GRADO.
18459 5ELCID2336 CA DAQUELOS MORCS ** SC SABIDOR;
18763 5ELCID2374 EA ESTAS FERIDAS ** QUIERO YR DELANT;
18799 5ELCID2379 SI ESTE AMOR NON FECHES, ** DEUOS ME QUIERO QUITAR.
19319 5ELCID2447 COMMO ** FIO POR DIOS & EN TODOS LOS SOS SANTOS,
19430 5ELCID2462 DIXO MYC %ID: ** DESTC SC PAGADO;
19729 5ELCID2501 ELLOS LC TEMEN, CA NCN LC PIESSO **:

WORD C# PREFIX CONTEXT

YO (CON'T)

```
                  19737 5ELCID2502 NO LOS YRE BUSCAR, EN VALEN%IA SERE **,
                  19752 5ELCID2504 QUE PAGUEN AMI O A CUI ** CUIER SABOR.
                  20353 5ELCID2582 SI BIEN LAS SERUIDES, ** UOS RENDRE BUEN GALARDON.
                  20526 5ELCID2606 ASSI COMMO ** TENGO, BIEN UOS HE CASADAS.
                  21732 5ELCID2764 MAS ** UOS DIRE DAQUEL FELEZ MUNOZ.
                  21963 5ELCID2794 AGRANT PRIESSA SERE BUSCADO **;
                  22254 5ELCID2834 QUE AMIS FIJAS BIEN LAS CASARE **
                  22409 5ELCID2854 ASSI LO FFAGO ** QUE AQUI ESTO.
                  22799 5ELCID2905 CUEMO ** SO SU VASSALLO, & EL ES MYO SE@OR,
                  22834 5ELCID2908 EL CASO MIS FIJAS, CA NON GELAS DI **;
                  23187 5ELCID2954 VERDAD TE DIGO **, QUE ME PESA DE CORA%ON,
                  23202 5ELCID2956 CA ** CASE SUS FIJAS CON YFANTES DE CARRION;
                  23228 5ELCID2959 ENTRE ** & MYO %ID PESA NOS DE CORA%ON.
                  23295 5ELCID2967 E QUE NON AYA RENCURA PODIENDO ** VEDALLO.
                  23328 5ELCID2971 POR AMOR DE MYO %ID ESTA CORT ** FAGO.
                  23917 5ELCID3047 E ** CON LOS MYOS POSARE A SAN SERUAN:
                  24636 5ELCID3138 POR ESCOGER EL DERECHO, CA TUERTO NON MANDO **.
                  24666 5ELCID3142 CON EL QUE TOUIERE DERECHO ** DESSA PART ME SO.
                  24724 5ELCID3149 POR MIS FIJAS QUEM DEXARON ** NON HE DESONOR,
                  24763 5ELCID3154 ESTAS ** LAS GANE AGUISA DE VARON,
                  25247 5ELCID3214 DIXO EL BUEN REY: ASSILO OTORGO **.
                  25261 5ELCID3216 DESTOS AUERES QUE UOS DI **, SIMELOS DADES, O DEDES DELLO RA%ON.
                  25378 5ELCID3231 DESTOS IIJ MILL MARCOS LOS CC TENGO **;
                  25411 5ELCID3235 QUANDO ELLOS LOS AN AFECHAR, NON GELOS QUIERO **.
                  25614 5ELCID3261 ALA SALIDA DE VALEN%IA MIS FIJAS VOS DI **,
                  25806 5ELCID3287 COMMO ** AUOS, CONDE, ENEL CASTIELLO DE CABRA;
                  25832 5ELCID3290 LA QUE ** MESSE AVN NON ES EGUADA.
                  25935 5ELCID3305 SI ** RESPONDIER, TU NON ENTRARAS EN ARMAS.
                  25978 5ELCID3311 BIEN LO SABEDES QUE ** NON PUEDO MAS;
                  25985 5ELCID3312 POR LO QUE ** CUIER AFER POR MI NON MANCARA.
                  26007 5ELCID3315 LAS TUS MA@AS ** TELAS SABRE CONTAR:
                  26035 5ELCID3319 SI ** NON VUJAS, EL MORO TE JUGARA MAL;
                  26284 5ELCID3351 DE QUANTO HE DICHO VERDADERO SERE **.
                  26554 5ELCID3389 FAZER TELO DEZIR QUE TALERES QUAL DIGO **.
                  26658 5ELCID3404 ESTO GRADESCO ** AL CRIADOR,
                  26674 5ELCID3406 VOS LAS CASASTES ANTES, CA ** NON,
                  26689 5ELCID3408 SIN UUESTRO MANDADO NADA NON FERE **.
                  26709 5ELCID3411 QUE PLEGA AUOS, & ATORGAR LO HE **,
                  26741 5ELCID3415 QUANDO AUOS PLAZE, OTORGO LO **, SE@OR,
                  26764 5ELCID3418 ESTE CASAMIENTO OTORGO UOS LE **
                  26974 5ELCID3446 ESTO GRADESCO ** ALCRIADOR,
                  27044 5ELCID3454 EN TODAS GUISAS TALES SODES QUALES DIGO **;
                  27200 5ELCID3477 VAYAN COMIGO, ** SERE EL CURIADOR;
                  27246 5ELCID3482 QUE FAGAN ESTA LID DELANT ESTANDO **;
                  27456 5ELCID3507 E YR ME QUIERO PORA VALEN%IA, CON AFAN LA GANE **.
                  28213 5ELCID3601 CA QUI TUERTO QUISIERE FAZER, MAL GELO VEDARE **,
          WORD #4476 OCCURS 127 TIMES.
             INDEX OF DIVERSIFICATION =   218.26 WITH STANDARD DEVIATION OF   295.26

YOGO               4505 5ELCID0573 ALI **** MYO %ID COMPLIDAS XV SEMMANAS.
          WORD #4477 OCCURS   1 TIMES.

YOL               20798 5ELCID2641 DE QUANTO EL FIZIERE *** DAR POR ELLO BUEN GALARDON.
          WORD #4478 OCCURS   1 TIMES.

YOLO              16057 5ELCID2036 FABLO MYO %ID & DIXO: MER%ED; **** RE%IBO, ALFONSSO MYO SE@OR;
          WORD #4479 OCCURS   1 TIMES.

YOUO              25823 5ELCID3289 NON **** RAPAZ QUE NON MESSO SU PULGADA;
          WORD #4480 OCCURS   1 TIMES.

YR                 3017 5ELCID0380 PENSEMOS DE ** NUESTRA VIA, ESTO SEA DE VAGAR.
                   3087 5ELCID0388 SI VIEREDES YENTES VENIR POR CONNUSCO **,
                   5285 5ELCID0668 QUE NOS QUERAMOS ** DE NOCH NO NOS LO CONSINTRAN;
                   6019 5ELCID0763 BOLUIO LA RIENDA POR ** SE LE DEL CAMPO.
                   6476 5ELCID0826 MYNAYA ALBARFANEZ DESTO ES PAGADO; POR ** CON EL OMNES
                                   SON CONTADOS.
                   7536 5ELCID0966 MAS QUANDO EL MELO BUSCA, ** GELO HE YO DEMANDAR.
                   7640 5ELCID0978 DELO SO NON LIEUO NADA, DEXEM ** EN PAZ.
                   8213 5ELCID1046 PRENDIENDO DEUOS & DE OTROS ** NOS HEMOS PAGANDO;
                   8338 5ELCID1060 SI UOS PLOGUIERE, MYO %ID, DE ** SOMOS GUISADOS;
                   9374 5ELCID1192 QUIEN QUIERE ** COMIGO %ERCAR A VALEN%IA,
                   9853 5ELCID1250 QUE SIS PUDIESSEN **, FER LO YEN DE GRADO.
                  10810 5ELCID1369 LOS QUE QUISIEREN ** SEUIR AL CAMPEADOR
                  11228 5ELCID1421 POR ** CON ESTAS DUENAS BUE@A CONPANA SE FAZE.
                  11368 5ELCID1438 SI NON, DEXAREMOS BURGOS, ** LO HEMOS BUSCAR.
                  14290 5ELCID1808 E CRAS HA LA MA@ANA ** UOS HEDES SIN FALLA
                  15737 5ELCID1997 ESTOS SE ADOBAN POR ** CON EL CAMPEADOR,
                  16816 5ELCID2129 QUI QUIERE ** COMIGO ALAS BODAS, O RE%EBIR MI DON,
                  18765 5ELCID2374 EA ESTAS FERIDAS YO QUIERO ** DELANT;
                  20825 5ELCID2644 PIENSSAN SE DE ** LOS YFANTES DE CARRION;
                  21745 5ELCID2766 MANDARON LE ** ADELANTE, MAS DE SU GRADO NON FUE.
                  23504 5ELCID2993 QUI LO FER NON QUISIESSE, O NO ** A MI CORT,
                  23556 5ELCID3000 LEGAUA EL PLAZO, QUERIEN ** ALA CORT;
                  24141 5ELCID3078 DAQUESTA GUISA QUIERO ** ALA CORT,
```

WORD C# PREFIX CONTEXT

YR (CON'T)

```
                27447 5ELCID3507 E ** ME QUIERO PORA VALEN%IA, CON AFAN LA GANE YO.
         WORD #4481 OCCURS  24 TIMES.
            INDEX OF DIVERSIFICATION =  1061.17 WITH STANDARD DEVIATION OF   918.98

YRA               582 5ELCID0074 EN *** DEL RAY ALFFONSSO YO SERE METIDO.
                 1714 5ELCID0219 DA QUI QUITO CASTIELLA, PUES QUE EL REY HE EN ***;
                 5016 5ELCID0634 RIBERA DE SALON TODA *** AMAL,
                 7217 5ELCID0925 MIENTRA UOS VISQUIEREDES, BIEN ME *** AMJ, MINAYA
                 8227 5ELCID1048 COMMO QUE *** A DE REY & DE TIERRA ES ECHADO.
                21723 5ELCID2762 LA DESONDRA DEL LEON ASSIS *** VENGANDO.
                24078 5ELCID3070 COMIGO *** MAL ANDA, QUE ES BIEN SABIDOR.
         WORD #4482 OCCURS   7 TIMES.
            INDEX OF DIVERSIFICATION =  3915.00 WITH STANDARD DEVIATION OF  4769.21

YRADO           14704 5ELCID1859 PESO AL CONDE DON GAR%IA, E MAL ERA *****;
         WORD #4483 OCCURS   1 TIMES.

YRAN             3603 5ELCID0454 NONBRADOS SON LOS QUE **** ENEL ALGARA,
                 6148 5ELCID0783 QUE A CASTIELLA **** BUENOS MANDADOS,
                 7731 5ELCID0990 PUES ADELLANT **** TRAS NOS, AQUI SEA LA BATALLA;
                 7791 5ELCID0997 POR UNO QUE FIRGADES, TRES SIELLAS **** VAZIAS.
                10104 5ELCID1280 DE GUISA **** POR ELLAS QUE AGRAND ONDRA VERNAN
                14334 5ELCID1813 ESTOS DOZIENTOS CAUALLOS **** EN PRESENTAIAS,
                19309 5ELCID2445 ACARRION DE UOS **** BUENOS MANDADOS,
                19574 5ELCID2480 MANDADOS BUENOS **** DELLOS A CARRION,
                19915 5ELCID2526 BUENOS MANDADOS **** ATIERRAS DE CARRION.
                25020 5ELCID3187 ASSIS **** VENGANDO DON ELUIRA & DONA SOL.
         WORD #4484 OCCURS  10 TIMES.
            INDEX OF DIVERSIFICATION =  2378.67 WITH STANDARD DEVIATION OF  2008.18

YRE              1310 5ELCID0168 YO *** CON UUSO, QUE ADUGAMOS LOS MARCOS,
                 2229 5ELCID0281 YO *** & UOS FINCAREDES REMANIDA.
                15111 5ELCID1911 QUEL *** A VISTAS DO FUERE AGUISADO;
                15495 5ELCID1963 SYO BIUO SO, ALI *** SIN FALLA.
                19732 5ELCID2502 NO LOS *** BUSCAR, EN VALEN%IA SERE YO,
                23943 5ELCID3051 E *** ALA CORT ENANTES DE IANTAR.
         WORD #4485 OCCURS   6 TIMES.
            INDEX OF DIVERSIFICATION =  4525.60 WITH STANDARD DEVIATION OF  5004.30

YREDES          20748 5ELCID2635 POR MOLINA ******, VNA NOCH Y IAZREDES;
                24037 5ELCID3064 VOS ****** COMIGO & EL OBISPO DON IHERONIMO
         WORD #4486 OCCURS   2 TIMES.

YREMOS           7408 5ELCID0950 DEXAT ESTAS POSADAS & ****** ADELANT.
                14899 5ELCID1883 CRE%REMOS EN NUESTRA ONDRA & ****** ADELANT.
                15405 5ELCID1951 FASTA DO LO FALLASSEMOS BUSCAR LO ****** NOS,
                19332 5ELCID2448 DESTA ARRANCADA NOS ****** PAGADOS.
         WORD #4487 OCCURS   4 TIMES.

YRIEN           10687 5ELCID1354 E ***** PORA VALEN%IA AL BUEN CAMPEADOR.
         WORD #4488 OCCURS   1 TIMES.

YS              14510 5ELCID1835 LOS YFANTES DE CARRION, SABET, ** A%ERTARON,
         WORD #4489 OCCURS   1 TIMES.

YSCAMOS          5425 5ELCID0685 TODOS ******* FUERA, QUE NADI NON RASTE,
         WORD #4490 OCCURS   1 TIMES.

YSON            16274 5ELCID2064 QUE ADOBASSEN COZINA PORA QUANTOS QUE ****;
                18200 5ELCID2302 AMARAUILLA LO HAN QUANTOS QUE ****,
         WORD #4491 OCCURS   2 TIMES.

YUA              2920 5ELCID0368 EL %ID A DO@A XIMENA *** LA ABRA%AR:
                 3181 5ELCID0400 LA CAL%ADA DE QUINEA *** LA TRASPASSAR,
                 4296 5ELCID0547 ENTRE FARIZA & %ETINA MYO %ID *** ALBERGAR.
                 4346 5ELCID0553 E SOBRE ALCO%ER MYO %ID *** POSAR,
                 8131 5ELCID1036 QUANDO ESTO OYO EL CONDE, YAS *** ALEGRANDO:
                 8485 5ELCID1079 MYEDO *** AUIENDO QUE MYO %ID SE REPINTRA,
                 8635 5ELCID1096 YA VIE MYO %ID QUE DIOS LE *** VALIENDO.
                18238 5ELCID2307 NON VIESTES TAL GUEGO COMMO *** POR LA CORT:
                21027 5ELCID2672 CO DOZIENTOS QUE TIENE *** CAUALGAR;
                21030 5ELCID2673 ARMAS *** TENIENDO, PAROS ANTE LOS YFANTES;
                21756 5ELCID2767 ENLA CARRERA DO *** DOLIOL EL CORA%ON,
                22568 5ELCID2874 E MINAYA CON LAS DUE@AS *** CABADELANT.
                22655 5ELCID2887 ARMAS *** TENIENDO & GRANT GOZO QUE FAZE;
                22666 5ELCID2888 MYO %ID ASUS FIJAS *** LAS ABRA%AR,
                23714 5ELCID3021 E *** RE%EBIR ALQUE EN BUEN ORA NA%IO.
                24335 5ELCID3103 ASSI *** MYO %ID ADOBADO ALLA CORT.
         WORD #4492 OCCURS  16 TIMES.
            INDEX OF DIVERSIFICATION =  1426.67 WITH STANDARD DEVIATION OF  2505.54

YUAL             5933 5ELCID0752 AMYNAYA ALBARFANEZ **** DAR EL CAUALLO:
                 6106 5ELCID0776 EL CAMPEADOR **** EN AL CAZ,
         WORD #4493 OCCURS   2 TIMES.
```

WORD C# PREFIX CONTEXT

```
YUAN        3293 5ELCID0415 ALA SIERRA DE MIEDES ELLOS **** POSAR.
            4266 5ELCID0543 TRO%EN LAS ALCARIAS & **** ADELANT,
            4433 5ELCID0564 POR TODAS ESSAS TIERRAS **** LOS MANDADOS,
            5692 5ELCID0718 **** LOS FERIR DE FUERTES CORA%ONES.
            9827 5ELCID1247 DE QUE SON PAGADOS; EL AMOR DE MY %ID YA LO **** PROUANDO.
           10943 5ELCID1385 LOS YFFANTES DE CARRION DANDO **** CONPA@A A MINAYA ALBARFANEZ:
           11937 5ELCID1513 LOS QUE **** MESURANDO & LEGANDO DELANT
           13906 5ELCID1762 E **** POSAR CON EL EN VNOS PRE%IOSOS ESCA@OS;
           17513 5ELCID2216 E **** POSAR EN VN PRE%IOSO ESCA@O.
           17876 5ELCID2262 HYAS **** PARTIENDO AQUESTOS OSPEDADOS,
           19205 5ELCID2429 CON ESTAS GRANAN%IAS YAS **** TORNANDO;
           19982 5ELCID2535 POR AQUESTOS GUEGOS QUE **** LEUANTANDO,
           21150 5ELCID2687 TENIENDO **** ARMAS ALTRO%IR DE SALON;
           21689 5ELCID2757 POR LOS MONTES DO ****, ELLOS YUAN SE ALABANDO:
           21691 5ELCID2757 POR LOS MONTES DO YUAN, ELLOS **** SE ALABANDO:
           21726 5ELCID2763 ALABANDOS **** LOS YFANTES DE CARRION.
           22582 5ELCID2876 ODIZEN BADO DE REY, ALLA **** POSAR,
           22601 5ELCID2879 AQUAL DIZEN MEDINA **** ALBERGAR,
           22724 5ELCID2896 TENIENDO **** ARMAS, ENTRARON SE ALA CIBDAD;
           23423 5ELCID2983 POR TODAS SUS TIERRAS ASSI LO **** PENSSANDO,
           24835 5ELCID3163 APRIESSA LO **** TRAYENDO & ACUERDAN LA RAZON:
      WORD #4494 OCCURS  21 TIMES.
         INDEX OF DIVERSIFICATION =  1076.10 WITH STANDARD DEVIATION OF  1099.38

YUAS        6753 5ELCID0862 AGUIJO MYO %ID, **** CAEA DELANT,
      WORD #4495 OCCURS   1 TIMES.

YUCEF      12770 5ELCID1621 DE AQUEL REY ***** QUE EN MARRUECOS ESTA.
      WORD #4496 OCCURS   1 TIMES.

YUCEFF     14628 5ELCID1850 A AQUEL REY DE MARRUECOS, ****** POR NOMBRADO,
      WORD #4497 OCCURS   1 TIMES.

YU%EF      13611 5ELCID1725 AL REY ***** TRES COLPES LE OUO DADOS,
      WORD #4498 OCCURS   1 TIMES.

YUIERNO    12750 5ELCID1619 EL ******* ES EXIDO, QUE EL MAR%O QUIERE ENTRAR.
      WORD #4499 OCCURS   1 TIMES.

YUSO        7748 5ELCID0992 ELLOS VIENEN CUESTA ****, & TODOS TRAHEN CAL%AS,
            7833 5ELCID1002 VIERON LA CUESTA **** LA FUER%A DELOS FRANCOS;
      WORD #4500 OCCURS   2 TIMES.

YXIE        3624 5ELCID0457 **** EL SOL, DIOS, QUE FERMOSO APUNTAUA
      WORD #4501 OCCURS   1 TIMES.

YXIEMOS    10009 5ELCID1268 CON MAS POCOS ******* DE LA CASA DE BIUAR.
      WORD #4502 OCCURS   1 TIMES.

YXIENDOS    3145 5ELCID0396 ******** UA DE TIERRA EL CAMPEADOR LEAL,
      WORD #4503 OCCURS   1 TIMES.

YXIERON     1497 5ELCID0191 ENTRE RACHEL & VIDAS APARTE ******* AMOS:
            5131 5ELCID0649 ******* DE %ELFA LA QUE DIZEN DE CANAL,
      WORD #4504 OCCURS   2 TIMES.

YXIO        2798 5ELCID0353 DIOT CON LA LAN%A ENEL COSTADO, DONT **** LA SANGRE,
      WORD #4505 OCCURS   1 TIMES.

YXO         7313 5ELCID0938 ALTER%ER DIA, DON *** Y ES TORNADO.
      WORD #4506 OCCURS   1 TIMES.
```